Tolley's Employment Handbook

Tolley's Employment Handbook

by

Dame Elizabeth Slade DBE

Former High Court Judge,
A Recorder of the Crown Court,
A Master of the Bench of the Inner Temple,
Honorary Vice-President of the
Employment Law Bar Association

Thirty fourth Edition
by

members of
11 KBW Chambers
and

Holly Stout

Employment Judge, Employment Tribunals (England and Wales)

Andrew Blake

Barrister, sole practitioner

Sarah Bradford

Director of Writetax Ltd

Prof Dominic Regan

City Law School London, Solicitor

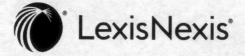

Members of the LexisNexis Group worldwide

United Kingdom	RELX (UK) Limited trading as LexisNexis, 1-3 Strand, London WC2N 5JR
Australia	LexisNexis, Chatswood, New South Wales
Austria	LexisNexis Verlag ARD Orac GmbH & Co KG, Vienna
Benelux	LexisNexis Benelux, Amsterdam
Canada	LexisNexis Canada, Markham, Ontario
China	LexisNexis China, Beijing and Shanghai
France	LexisNexis SA, Paris
Germany	LexisNexis GmbH, Dusseldorf
Hong Kong	LexisNexis Hong Kong, Hong Kong
India	LexisNexis India, New Delhi
Italy	GiuffrèEditore, Milan
Japan	LexisNexis Japan, Tokyo
Malaysia	Malayan Law Journal Sdn Bhd, Kuala Lumpur
New Zealand	LexisNexis NZ Ltd, Wellington
Singapore	LexisNexis Singapore, Singapore
South Africa	LexisNexis, Durban
USA	LexisNexis, Dayton, Ohio

© RELX (UK) Ltd 2020

Published by LexisNexis
This is a Tolley title

ISBN for this volume: 9780754556015

Visit LexisNexis at www.lexisnexis.co.uk

Preface

As I start typing this preface, the HMRC reports that 6.3 million UK workers are presently "furloughed". That would not have been a term that meant much to employment lawyers even 6 months ago. That was before the arrival of the Covid-19 virus. The country is presently in "lockdown". You cannot leave home without a "reasonable excuse". Going to work is not a reasonable excuse unless you cannot work from home. Almost all retail businesses are closed. Furloughed workers are employees who, by agreement with their employers, remain at home. The Government's "Coronavirus Job Retention Scheme" pays 80% of the employee's normal pay or £2500 per month whichever is the lower. Furloughed employees are not permitted to do any work or provide any service to their employer whilst on furlough. If an employer wants a grant under the scheme to meet wage costs, the furlough must last at least three weeks. The scheme has been introduced not by legislation but by means of a Treasury direction and often, apparently inconsistent, guidance from the HMRC. The guidance in particular has been poured over by rattled advisers and has a worrying tendency to evolve into a fresh version late on a Friday evening. It is presently in version 9. The intention has been that the Scheme should leave Employment Law undisturbed, but it has raised so many questions because of the myriad ways in which it interacts with that Law, that desperate lawyers have been pausing from over-analysis of thin material to chase after rumoured clarifications from individual HMRC officers. The Scheme is presently due to come to an end shortly after this edition is published and, for that reason (and because it is impossible to be sure that anything anyone says about the Scheme will still be true 72 hours later), we have not sought to cover it in detail. However, where the crisis has given rise to an actual change in the law (e.g. the *Working Time (Coronavirus) (Amendment) Regulations 2020, SI 2020/365* which allow for the carrying over of holiday entitlement for two years where the crisis means that it is not reasonably practicable to take some or all of the leave and the *Statutory Sick Pay (General) (Coronavirus Amendment) Regulations 2020, SI 2020/287*, which extend entitlement to Statutory Sick Pay to employees who isolate themselves to prevent infection or contamination with Covid-19 in accordance with Government guidance) that is, of course, covered.

The Government has begun to "actively encourage" those who cannot work from home to return to their workplaces. This has caused an sudden interest in *ss 44* and *100* of the *Employment Rights Act 1996* which protect employees from detriment and dismissal respectively where they absent themselves in circumstances of danger which they reasonably believe to be serious and imminent and which they cannot be reasonably expected avert. There is likely to be litigation on these previously little-regarded provisions but it will have take its place in the growing queue that has formed as a result of Employment Tribunals closing during lockdown.

When the Employment Tribunals start to hear substantive cases again, it will be under the gaze of the new ET President, Judge Barry Clarke. He is an exceptionally capable appointment and one of the few people with a realistic chance of matching the standard set by his predecessor, Judge Brian Doyle, who has faced a series of difficult sets of circumstances without ever departing from his characteristic qualities of good sense and kindness. We wish him every happiness in his retirement. One development that the new president may now face is an increase in the Employment Tribunal's jurisdiction. The Law Commission reported on 29 April 2020 with a series of sensible recommendations including allowing the Tribunal to consider breach of contract claims which arise whilst the employee is still employed. They have also proposed extending the standard time limit from 3 to 6 months and having a unified "just and equitable" test for extension of the time limit where a claim is not commenced in time.

In other parish news, the High Court bench has gained three excellent employment lawyers in Dame Jennifer Eady; Sir Thomas Linden; and Sir John Cavanagh. Dame

Jennifer made her mark as a circuit judge assigned to the EAT, just as she had in practice. Her patience, experience and insight make it certain that she will be every bit as prominent in her new role. Sir Thomas had a practice at the Employment Bar that was literally the envy of his contemporaries. The succinctness and clarity that characterised his advocacy will now be brought to bear from the bench. Sir John is a former Tolley's contributor, a former joint head of 11KBW Chambers and one of the finest people I know. Joy at his elevation is tempered by the loss of presence in Chambers.

Amongst the highlights for this new edition are two very significant Supreme Court cases. The first is *Royal Mail Group Ltd v Jhuti* [2019] UKSC 55 in which the Court considered who counts as the employer when determining what the employer's reason for dismissal is (see 55 UNFAIR DISMISSAL II). In *Jhuti* a line manager concocted capability concerns over an employee who had blown the whistle. The dismissing officer was deceived and genuinely believed that there were performance issues that merited dismissal. The Court held that a tribunal was entitled to look beyond the mind of the specific decision-maker in determining the reason (or principal reason) for a dismissal. The EAT have started the process of getting to grips with the implications of the decision in cases such as *Uddin v Ealing London Borough Council* UKEAT/0165/19 which looks at its relevance to the question of the reasonableness of a decision to dismiss.

The second Supreme Court case covered is *WM Morrisons Supermarkets plc v Various Claimants* [2020] UKSC 12 which dealt with vicarious liability in a case where a disaffected employee deliberately caused an enormous data breach. The court decided that the employer was not vicariously liable accepting arguments developed by Anya Proops QC who, by happy coincidence, contributes 57 VICARIOUS LIABILITY and who is better placed than anyone to explain the case and its significance.

The question of whether voluntary overtime income should be taken into account when calculating holiday pay rumbles on (see 30 HOLIDAYS). The Court of Appeal decided that it did in *East of England Ambulance Service NHS Trust v Flowers and Others* [2019] EWCA Civ 947 but the Supreme Court has given permission to appeal. This is just one area that is potentially affected by Brexit and Brexit-related amendments to domestic legislation have been added wherever that has been possible.

Thanks are due, as always, to the LexisNexis team who appear to have taken the Covid-crisis in their ultra-capable stride.

The law is stated as at 1 April 2020 with later developments included wherever possible. We would welcome your feedback, suggestions and corrections. I can be contacted at sean.jones@11kbw.com or via Twitter on @seanjonesqc.

Seán Jones QC

List of Contributors

Members of 11 King's Bench Walk Chambers

Edward Capewell, MA, MPhil, barrister - Employee Participation (17), Unfair Dismissal I, III (54), (56)

Leo Davidson, barrister - Financial Regulation in the UK (26)

Simon Forshaw, barrister - Restraint of Trade (42)

James Goudie QC, barrister - Education and Training (15), Service Lettings (44)

Paul Greatorex, barrister - Probationary Employees (37), Time Off Work (50)

Harini Iyengar MA (Oxon), BCL (Oxon), barrister - ACAS early conciliation (3), Insolvency (32)

Seán Jones QC, BA, BCL (Oxon), barrister - Discrimination and Equal Opportunities I (12), Discrimination and Equal Opportunities III (14), Maternity and Parental Rights (33)

Christopher Knight MA (Cantab), BCL (Oxon) barrister - Engagement of Employees (22)

Michael Lee MA (Cantab), barrister - Unfair Dismissal II (55)

Richard Leiper QC, LLB, MJuris, barrister - Financial penalties on employers (25), Transfer of Undertakings (53)

Peter Lockley, barrister - Data Protection (9)

Julian Milford MA, barrister - Continuous Employment (7), Data Protection (9), Redundancy I and II (39, 40)

Ben Mitchell, barrister - Equal Pay (24)

Thomas Ogg BA (Oxon), MSc (Oxon), barrister - Employee, Self-Employed or Worker? (16), References (41)

Christopher Parkin, barrister - Contract of Employment (8), Foreign Employees (27)

Marcus Pilgerstorfer QC, MA (Oxon), PhD, barrister - Part-Time Workers (34)

Nigel Porter MA (Cantab), LLM (Cantab), barrister - Introduction (1), Introduction to the Advisory, Conciliation and Arbitration Service (ACAS) (2), Codes of Practice (5), Disclosure of Information (11), Employees' Past Criminal Convictions (18), Human Rights (31), Pay I and II (35, 36), Temporary and Seasonal Employees (48)

Anya Proops QC, MA (Cantab), PhD, barrister - Vicarious Liability (57)

Zac Sammour, barrister - Children and Young Persons (4), Public Sector Employees (38)

Contents

x

Abbreviations and References

Abbreviations – General

ACAS	=	Advisory, Conciliation and Arbitration Service
ERRB	=	Enterprise and Regulatory Reform Bill
CA	=	Court of Appeal
CAC	=	Central Arbitration Committee
COET	=	Central Office of the Employment Tribunals
CRE	=	Commission for Racial Equality
DfEE	=	Department for Education and Employment
DRC	=	Disability Rights Commission
DSS	=	Department of Social Security
DTI	=	Department of Trade and Industry
EAT	=	Employment Appeal Tribunal
EEC	=	European Economic Community
EC	=	European Community
ECJ	=	European Court of Justice
EOC	=	Equal Opportunities Commission
HL	=	House of Lords
Pt	=	Part
Sch	=	Schedule
SI	=	Statutory Instrument
SR & O	=	Statutory Rules and Orders

Abbreviations – Statutes

DDA	=	Disability Discrimination Act 1995
DRCA	=	Disability Rights Commission Act 1999
EA	=	Employment Act (with date)
EPA	=	Employment Protection Act 1975
EPCA	=	Employment Protection (Consolidation) Act 1978
ETA	=	Employment Tribunals Act 1996
EqA	=	Equality Act 2010
EqPA	=	Equal Pay Act 1970
ERA 1996	=	Employment Rights Act 1996
ERA 1999	=	Employment Relations Act 1999
FA	=	Finance Act (with date)
HSWA	=	Health and Safety at Work etc. Act 1974
HRA	=	Human Rights Act 1998
ICTA	=	Income and Corporation Taxes Act 1988
OLA	=	Occupiers' Liability Act 1957
OSRPA	=	Offices, Shops and Railway Premises Act 1963
PIDA	=	Public Interest Disclosure Act 1998
RRA	=	Race Relations Act 1976
SBA	=	Supplementary Benefits Act 1976
SDA	=	Sex Discrimination Act 1975
SDA 1986	=	Sex Discrimination Act 1996
SSA	=	Social Security Act 1975
SSA 1986	=	Social Security Act 1986
SSAA	=	Social Security Administration Act 1992

Abbreviations and References

SSCBA	=	Social Security Contributions and Benefits Act 1992
SSHBA	=	Social Security and Housing Benefits Act 1982
SSPA	=	Social Security Pensions Act 1975
TUA	=	Trade Union Act 1984
TULRA	=	Trade Union and Labour Relations Act 1974
TULR(A)A	=	Trade Union and Labour Relations (Amendment) Act 1976
TULRCA	=	Trade Union and Labour Relations (Consolidation) Act 1992
TURERA	=	Trade Union Reform and Employment Rights Act 1993
UCTA	=	Unfair Contract Terms Act 1977
WA	=	Wages Act 1986

Law reports – Series referred to

AC	=	Law Reports, Appeal Cases
All ER	=	All England Law Reports
ATC	=	Annotated Tax Cases
BCLC	=	Butterworths Company Law Cases
Ch	=	Law Reports, Chancery Division
CMLR	=	Common Market Law Reports
Cr App Rep	=	Criminal Appeal Reports
FSR	=	Fleet Street Reports
ICR	=	Law Reports, Industrial Cases Reports
IDS	=	Incomes Data Services
IRLB	=	Industrial Relations Law Bulletin
IRLR	=	Industrial Relations Law Reports
ITR	=	Industrial Tribunal Reports
LJKB	=	Law Journal Reports, New Series, King's Bench (ended 1949)
Lloyd's Rep	=	Lloyd's List Law Reports
LS Gaz	=	Law Society's Gazette
PCC	=	Palmer's Company Cases
QB/KB	=	Law Reports, Queen's (King's) Bench Division
TLR	=	Times Law Reports (last year of publication 1952)
WLR	=	Weekly Law Reports

Table of Statutes

Table of Statutes

Table of Statutes

Table of Statutes

Table of Statutes

Table of Statutes

Table of Statutes

Table of Statutes

Table of Statutes

Table of Statutes

Table of Statutes

Table of Statutes

Table of Statutes

Table of Statutes

Table of EU Legislation

Table of EU Legislation

Table of EU Legislation

Regulations

Table of EU Legislation

Table of Statutory Instruments

Table of Statutory Instruments

Table of Statutory Instruments

D

E

Table of Statutory Instruments

Table of Statutory Instruments

Table of Statutory Instruments

Table of Statutory Instruments

Table of Statutory Instruments

Table of Statutory Instruments

Table of Statutory Instruments

Table of Statutory Instruments

Table of Statutory Instruments

Table of Statutory Instruments

Table of Cases

A

Table of Cases

Table of Cases

Table of Cases

Table of Cases

Table of Cases

Table of Cases

Table of Cases

Table of Cases

Table of Cases

Table of Cases

Table of Cases

Table of Cases

Table of Cases

C

Table of Cases

Table of Cases

Table of Cases

Table of Cases

Table of Cases

Table of Cases

D

Table of Cases

Table of Cases

Table of Cases

Table of Cases

E

Table of Cases

Table of Cases

Table of Cases

Table of Cases

G

Table of Cases

Table of Cases

Table of Cases

H

Table of Cases

Table of Cases

Table of Cases

Table of Cases

Table of Cases

Table of Cases

I

Table of Cases

Table of Cases

Table of Cases

Table of Cases

Table of Cases

Table of Cases

Table of Cases

Table of Cases

Table of Cases

Table of Cases

Table of Cases

Table of Cases

M

Table of Cases

Table of Cases

Table of Cases

Table of Cases

Table of Cases

Table of Cases

Table of Cases

Table of Cases

Table of Cases

Table of Cases

O

Table of Cases

Table of Cases

P

Table of Cases

Table of Cases

Table of Cases

Table of Cases

Q

R

Table of Cases

Table of Cases

Table of Cases

Table of Cases

Table of Cases

Table of Cases

Table of Cases

Table of Cases

Table of Cases

S

Table of Cases

Table of Cases

Table of Cases

Table of Cases

Table of Cases

Table of Cases

Table of Cases

Table of Cases

T

Table of Cases

Table of Cases

Table of Cases

U

Table of Cases

Table of Cases

W

Table of Cases

Table of Cases

Table of Cases

X

Y

Table of Cases

1   Introduction

1.1   SCOPE AND AIMS OF THIS BOOK ON EMPLOYMENT

Employment law is fully recognised today as a subject of the greatest importance. Legislation passed in recent years has transformed the law and created important new statutory rights and obligations. Employment law continues to develop at a rapid pace, with new domestic legislation creating or modifying statutory rights being enacted each year. Further, EC legislation and decisions of the European Court have had, and will continue to have, an important impact on certain areas of domestic employment law. Inevitably, a wealth of reported tribunal and court decisions on the meaning and effect of these new provisions has also built up.

This handbook seeks to explain the legislation in its context, along with the common law and the EC law on employment matters. It is intended as a reference guide for the employer, company secretary, manager or personnel officer involved daily in decisions concerning the rights of employees. It is also intended to serve as a comprehensive handbook on employment law for solicitors, employees, trade union officials, and all kinds of advisers and professional people.

The remainder of this chapter serves as an introduction to the subject by examining a number of fundamental aspects of current employment law. It concludes with a checklist of the areas of law relevant to the various stages of employment and a brief explanation of the standard scale of maximum fines which may be imposed upon conviction of an adult of a summary offence.

Employment law and trade union law. The main emphasis of this book is on the law affecting the individual employment relationship, ie directly applying to employers and their employees. It therefore provides detailed coverage of the law governing the contract of employment, termination of employment, redundancy, unfair dismissal, equal pay, the various forms of unlawful discrimination relevant to employment and numerous other individual employment rights. The importance of trade unions is nonetheless fully recognised, and the status, functions and liabilities of trade unions and the law relating to trade union membership are considered in appropriate chapters.

1.2   WHAT CONSTITUTES EMPLOYMENT?

One of the most fundamental questions asked is whether a particular worker is an employee or not. An employee is a person who agrees to work for another person pursuant to a *contract of employment* (or 'contract of service' to use the more traditional term). It is important to be able to distinguish a contract of employment from other types of agreement under which services are rendered. There are a number of characteristics which enable a contract of employment to be identified. One problem which can often arise is deciding whether a particular person doing work for another is working as an employee, ie under a contract of employment, or as an independent contractor (or 'self-employed' person) under a *contract for services*. These matters are discussed further in EMPLOYEE, SELF-EMPLOYED OR WORKER? **(16)**.

1.3   The contract of employment

The most important matters to be borne in mind are the following:

(a)   In general, the parties are free to agree whatever contractual terms they wish – this means, among other things, that they may agree that work is to be done either by an employee or by an independent contractor;

1.3 Introduction

(b) However, *all the terms* of the contract, and the way in which it is performed, will be looked at in deciding whether it is in substance a contract of employment or not, so it will not be sufficient merely to state that the contract is a contract for services and not a contract of employment;

(c) Whether or not the contract is a contract of employment, certain further terms may be implied, if not expressly agreed;

(d) If the contract *is* a contract of employment, all the statutory employment rights are capable of applying, if the relevant pre-conditions are satisfied, and (subject to limited exceptions) any term of the contract excluding these rights is usually *ineffective*;

(e) If the contract *is not* a contract of employment, the main statutory employment rights cannot apply, because they apply only for the benefit of people working under a contract of employment. However, there are some important statutory provisions which also apply to self-employed persons and/or 'workers' as defined in the relevant legislation.

For further details, see CONTRACT OF EMPLOYMENT (8) and EMPLOYEE, SELF-EMPLOYED OR WORKER? (16).

1.4 SOURCES OF EMPLOYMENT LAW

The legal rules governing employment law are derived from three principal sources:

(a) the common law, including the law of contract pursuant to which the contract of employment is enforced, and the law of torts (wrongful acts which cause damage or loss) which governs (for example) an employer's liability for acts of his employees, civil liability for industrial accidents and for strikes and other forms of industrial action;

(b) statute law, ie Acts of Parliament and Regulations, which operate outside the contract (eg the law on unfair dismissal); and

(c) Currently, European legislation and judgments of the European Court of Justice ('ECJ').

Some elements of these three sources are considered briefly below.

1.5 Terms of the contract of employment

Generally, the employer and employee are free to agree whatever terms they wish. Therefore, the most basic legal rules governing the employment relationship are those agreed by the parties themselves, for example, the type of work to be done, place of work, rate of pay, etc. In practice, the more detailed terms and conditions of the contract are often not discussed and agreed individually with each employee. Many employers have written standard terms and conditions of employment for all employees, sometimes drawn up and agreed in consultation with officials of recognised trade unions.

In cases where a disagreement arises, the main problem is often evidential. If an employer does not provide written particulars of the terms and conditions of employment, or if a particular matter was agreed orally but never put in writing, years later memories will have faded and there may be no reliable evidence of precisely what was agreed. This is one reason why employers are under a statutory obligation to provide a written summary of the main contractual terms to each employee within a short time after he begins his job. They must notify changes in the same way. (See 8.7 CONTRACT OF EMPLOYMENT.)

1.6   Domestic employment legislation

The main statutory employment rights are found in the *Employment Rights Act 1996*, as amended.

In relation to discrimination in employment, the protection afforded to employees and applicants for employment was, prior to 1 October 2010, found in a substantial body of anti-discrimination legislation, both primary and secondary. The main domestic statutory provisions prohibiting discrimination were:

(a)   *Equal Pay Act 1970*, as amended.

(b)   *Sex Discrimination Act 1975*, as amended.

(c)   *Race Relations Act 1976*, as amended.

(d)   *Disability Discrimination Act 1995*, as amended.

The Equality Act 2010

For all matters arising after 1 October 2011, the law in relation to all strands of discrimination is harmonised in the *Equality Act 2010*, which received Royal Assent on 8 April 2010. Under the *Equality Act 2010* the various grounds of discrimination are drawn together as "protected characteristics". The principal commencement order under the *Equality Act* (the *Equality Act 2010 (Commencement No 4, Savings, Consequential, Transitional, Transitory and Incidental Provisions and Revocation) Order 2010, SI 2010/2317*) brought into force the majority of the employment related provisions with effect from 1 October 2011.

The main Act governing trade unions and trade disputes is the *Trade Union and Labour Relations (Consolidation) Act 1992*, as amended.

The Act governing the presentation of complaints to an employment tribunal is the *Employment Tribunals Act 1996*.

In addition to the primary legislation, a substantial number of statutory instruments provide important and specific rights in relation to employment and are considered, where relevant, in the chapters of the book.

This book provides an account of the effect of all of these main legislative provisions, with references to the specific provisions and to decided cases. However, a reader who is called upon to consider the law in detail would probably be well advised to obtain copies of the Acts themselves in addition. The Acts are obtainable from the Stationery Office or through bookshops. The majority of relevant legislation, including Statutory Instruments, is available online from the legislation website (www.legislation.gov.uk). For those requiring a complete reprint of all the relevant legislation, compendia of employment legislation are published commercially by a number of law publishers. In a particular case of doubt or difficulty the reader should always consult a professional adviser.

1.7   European law (the current post-Brexit position)

With the passing of the *European Union (Withdrawal) Act 2018* there will be consequences for the application of European derived employment rights and legislation. Regulations have been drawn up including the *Employment Rights (Amendment) (EU Exit) Regulations 2019 (SI 2019/535)* which contain amendments to primary and secondary legislation to address failures of retained European Union Law to operate efficiently after the withdrawal of the United Kingdom from the European Union. It was anticipated that these *Regulations* would come into force shortly after exit day (31 January 2020). By the *European Union (Withdrawal Agreement) Act 2020, Sch 5, para 1* the amendments are not due, however, to come into effect until the "implementation period completion date" which is anticipated to be 31 December 2020. Accordingly, for the time being the relevant provisions of European Union Law remain, as before, and are summarised briefly below.

European legislative instruments. Where English domestic legislation has failed fully to implement EC Treaty obligations, individuals may rely in the English courts upon the EC Treaty, and, where the employer is the State, upon certain EC directives. (See EUROPEAN UNION LAW (24).)

In the employment context, this has been done in particular to establish claims for equal pay and equal treatment (see EQUAL PAY (23)).

EC legislation is also important where a business is transferred from one employer to another (see TRANSFER OF UNDERTAKINGS (52)). Other areas influenced by EC legislation include HEALTH AND SAFETY AT WORK – II (29), HOLIDAYS (30), the rules on written particulars of employment (see 8.4 CONTRACT OF EMPLOYMENT) and requirements for consultation in redundancy situations (see 40.2 REDUNDANCY – II).

Judgments of the European Court. Prior to the introduction of post-Brexit amendments, the ECJ remains the final arbiter in matters of interpretation of European legislation. Thus, its judgments are of importance in interpreting directly applicable European legislative instruments and also domestic legislation which implements European law obligations.

The *European Convention on Human Rights* is also relevant; the *Human Rights Act 1998* requires the court to interpret United Kingdom law in accordance with the Convention. This has clear implications in the employment context (see HUMAN RIGHTS (31)).

1.8   GEOGRAPHICAL SCOPE OF THIS BOOK

This book seeks to explain the law applying in England and Wales. Much of the relevant legislation applies, without significant differences, to *Scotland*. However, Scotland has a quite different legal system from that of England and Wales, and different legal traditions. It also has a separate system of courts and tribunals. This book should not be regarded as authoritative on the law applying in Scotland because specific matters of Scottish law have not been taken into consideration. For example, the explanation of attachment of earnings for payment of debts (PAY – II (36)) relates to England and Wales only; different procedures apply in Scotland.

The legal system and legal traditions of *Northern Ireland* are much more similar to those of England and Wales than are those of Scotland, but the legislation discussed in this book generally does not apply to Northern Ireland. It has a separate legislative code, although on employment law its provisions are co-ordinated with those of Great Britain. Northern Ireland also has a separate system of courts and tribunals. Therefore, while the law will often be similar, this book is not authoritative on Northern Ireland employment law and any reader in Northern Ireland is advised to consult the specific Northern Ireland legal sources on any particular issue.

This book does not contain an account of the laws relating to employment applying in the Channel Islands or the Isle of Man, nor of those foreign systems of law which may apply where an English employee is sent to work abroad. For the rules determining which system of law governs an employment relationship with international elements, see 27.9 FOREIGN EMPLOYEES.

1.9   STAGES OF EMPLOYMENT – CHECKLIST

The chapters of this book are arranged in alphabetical order to assist the reader in tracing all the areas of law that may relate to a particular problem. The following checklist sets out the chronological stages of employment, from selection for appointment to termination, and beyond, together with a list of chapters relevant to each stage.

All stages

General	CONTRACT OF EMPLOYMENT (8)
	EMPLOYEE, SELF-EMPLOYED OR WORKER? (16)
Discrimination	EQUAL PAY (23)
	DISCRIMINATION AND EQUAL OPPORTUNITIES– I (11), II (12), and III (13)
	EUROPEAN UNION LAW (24)
Statutory rights	CONTINUOUS EMPLOYMENT (7)
	PAY – I (35)
Chronological stages	
Selection for appointment	CHILDREN AND YOUNG PERSONS (4)
	EMPLOYEE'S PAST CRIMINAL CONVICTIONS (19)
	FOREIGN EMPLOYEES (27)
Terms of engagement	CONTRACT OF EMPLOYMENT (8)
	EMPLOYEE, SELF-EMPLOYED OR WORKER? (16)
	ENGAGEMENT OF EMPLOYEES (22)
	PROBATIONARY EMPLOYEES (37)
Duration of employment	CONTINUOUS EMPLOYMENT (7)
	TEMPORARY AND SEASONAL EMPLOYEES (48)
	TRANSFER OF UNDERTAKINGS (53)
Pay, etc	EQUAL PAY (23)
	PAY – I (35), and II (36)
	SICKNESS AND SICK PAY (45)
	TAXATION (47)
Terms and conditions (other than pay)	COLLECTIVE AGREEMENTS (6)
	CONTRACT OF EMPLOYMENT (8)
	DIRECTORS (9)
	EQUAL PAY (23)
	HOLIDAYS (30)
	PUBLIC SECTOR EMPLOYEES (38)
	RESTRAINT OF TRADE, CONFIDENTIALITY AND EMPLOYEE INTERVENTIONS (42)
	SERVICE LETTINGS (44)
	TRANSFER OF UNDERTAKINGS (53)
Safety and welfare	CHILDREN AND YOUNG PERSONS (4)
	EDUCATION AND TRAINING (14)
	HEALTH AND SAFETY AT WORK – I (28), and II (29)
	MATERNITY AND PARENTAL RIGHTS (33)
	PAY – I (35)
	SICKNESS AND SICK PAY (45)
	TIME OFF WORK (50)
	VICARIOUS LIABILITY (57)
	WORKING TIME (58)

1.9 Introduction

General management	ADVISORY, CONCILIATION AND ARBITRATION SERVICE (2)
	CODES OF PRACTICE (5)
	EMPLOYEE PARTICIPATION (17)
Trade unions	DISCLOSURE OF INFORMATION (10)
	HEALTH AND SAFETY AT WORK – II (29)
	TRADE UNIONS – I (51), and II (52)
Trade disputes	ADVISORY, CONCILIATION AND ARBITRATION SERVICE (2)
	CODES OF PRACTICE (5)
	STRIKES AND INDUSTRIAL ACTION (46)
Lay-offs	PAY – I (35)
	REDUNDANCY – I (39)
Discipline and breach of contract	TERMINATION OF EMPLOYMENT (49)
	UNFAIR DISMISSAL – II (55)
Termination of employment (generally)	TRADE UNIONS – I (51)
	MATERNITY AND PARENTAL RIGHTS (33)
	REFERENCES (41)
	RESTRAINT OF TRADE, CONFIDENTIALITY AND EMPLOYEE INTERVENTIONS (42)
	TERMINATION OF EMPLOYMENT (49)
	TRANSFER OF UNDERTAKINGS (53)
	UNFAIR DISMISSAL – I (54), II (55), and III (56)
	WRONGFUL DISMISSAL (59)
Redundancy	REDUNDANCY – I (39), and II (40)
	UNFAIR DISMISSAL – II (55)
Retirement	RETIREMENT (43)
Claims against employer – Dismissals	EMPLOYMENT TRIBUNALS: I (19), II (20), and III (21)
	REDUNDANCY – I (39), and II (40)
	UNFAIR DISMISSAL – I (54), II (55), and III (56)
	WRONGFUL DISMISSAL (59)
Insolvency of employer	INSOLVENCY OF EMPLOYER (32)

1.10 STANDARD SCALE OF FINES

At various points in the book, reference is made to the standard scale of maximum fines which may be imposed upon conviction of an adult of a summary offence (that is, one which falls to be tried by magistrates rather than by the Crown Court).

The standard scale of maximum fines is as follows.

Level on the scale	Amount of maximum fine (£)
1	200
2	500

6

3	1,000
4	2,500
5	Unlimited

(*Criminal Justice Act 1982, s 37(2)*, as substituted by *Criminal Justice Act 1991, s 17*. The previous limit of £5000 for level 5 on the standard scale of fines was removed in relation to certain offences committed after 12 March 2015 by *s 85* of the *Legal Aid, Sentencing and Punishment of Offenders Act 2012* which came into force on the same date. The *Legal Aid, Sentencing and Punishment of Offenders Act 2012 ss 86–87*, empowers the Secretary of State to increase the levels 1–4 of the standard scale fines to such sums considered appropriate. These provisions are, however, not yet in force).

It should be noted that the *Legal Aid, Sentencing and Punishment of Offenders Act 2012* makes provision in *s 85* for the removal of the £5000 maximum on the standard scale of fines and, by *ss 86–87*, empowers the Secretary of State to increase the levels 1–4 of the standard scale fines to such sums considered appropriate. No such increases have yet been made.

Where the Crown Court tries an offence and imposes a fine following a conviction, there is no maximum amount in the absence of some specific provision to the contrary (*Powers of Criminal Courts Act 1973, s 30; Criminal Law Act 1977, s 32(1)*).

Before a court (magistrates' court or Crown Court) fixes the amount of any fine, it must inquire into the financial circumstances of the offender. The amount must reflect the court's opinion of the seriousness of the offence, and the court must also take account of the circumstances of the case, including the financial circumstances of the offender. (*Criminal Justice Act 1991, s 19*, as substituted by *Criminal Justice Act 1993, s 65, Sch 3*.)

2   Introduction to the Advisory, Conciliation and Arbitration Service (ACAS)

2.1   The Advisory, Conciliation and Arbitration Service was established pursuant to powers conferred by the *Employment Protection Act 1975*. Its activities are now regulated by the *Trade Union and Labour Relations (Consolidation) Act 1992* (*'TULR(C)A 1992'*), as amended by the *Trade Union Reform and Employment Rights Act 1993* (*'TURERA 1993'*). ACAS continues in existence under *TULR(C)A 1992, s 247*. Its duties are to promote the improvement of industrial relations, in particular by exercising its functions in relation to the settlement of trade disputes (*TULR(C)A 1992, s 209* as amended by *TURERA 1993, s 43(1)*).

ACAS may charge fees for the exercise of its functions to persons who benefit from that exercise, and may be directed to do so by the Secretary of State (*TULR(C)A 1992, s 251A* as inserted by *TURERA 1993, s 44*). Fees are charged at present only for certain publications and seminars, and thus not for the key function of conciliation.

2.2   CONSTITUTION

The Secretary of State appoints the members of the Council of ACAS in accordance with the requirements laid down in *TULR(C)A 1992, s 248*. Those requirements ensure that both employers' organisations and workers' organisations are consulted before appointments are made and that a balance is maintained between employers' and workers' interests.

2.3   CONCILIATION

One function of ACAS is to conciliate in trade disputes. ACAS may appoint either an independent person or an officer of the Service to offer assistance to the parties to the dispute. During the course of conciliation the parties will be encouraged to use any existing agreed procedures to resolve the conflict (*TULR(C)A 1992, s 210*). Where ACAS exercises its functions under *s 210* with a view to bringing about a settlement of a recognition dispute, ACAS may be requested to hold a ballot of the workers involved in the dispute or ascertain the union membership of the workers involved in the dispute (*TULR(C)A 1992, s 210A(2)*). ACAS is not obliged to comply with such a request (*s 210A(9)*) but if a request is made under *s 210A(2)* and ACAS decides to act then it may require any party to the recognition dispute to supply ACAS with specified information concerning the workers involved in the dispute within a specified time (*s 210A(4)*). If there is non compliance ACAS will take no further steps to hold the ballot or ascertain the union membership of the workers involved in the dispute (*s 210A(8)*).

2.4   CONCILIATION IN EMPLOYMENT TRIBUNAL COMPLAINTS

ACAS appoints conciliation officers to conciliate on matters which are or could be the subject of proceedings before an employment tribunal (*TULR(C)A 1992, s 211*).

Conciliation officers may (and must if required to do so by a party to the complaint) take action to conciliate on most claims which can be brought before an employment tribunal, including claims of discrimination in employment, claims for equal pay and complaints against trade unions (*Employment Tribunals Act 1996* (*'ETA 1996'*), *s 18*). *Section 18* of the *ETA* has been amended as to the list of claims falling within the scope of ACAS conciliation by the *Employment Tribunals Act 1996 (Application of Conciliation Provisions) Order 2014 (SI*

2.4 Advisory, Conciliation and Arbitration Service (ACAS)

2014/431) as a consequence of the introduction of the now mandatory early conciliation procedure which is considered below. Either the person making the complaint or the person against whom the complaint or application is made may request the assistance of a conciliation officer. The power to conciliate also extends to redundancy payment cases (see **39.4** REDUNDANCY – I) and to issues relating to training (as introduced by the *Employment Relations Act 1999*; see *TULR(C)A 1992, s 70B*), detriment arising out of participation or involvement in a trade union recognition procedure pursuant to *TULR(C)A 1992, Sch A1 para 156* and complaints relating to failure to permit parental leave (see *ERA 1999, s 80*). A complete list of the employment tribunal jurisdictions to which the conciliation power applies is found in *subsections 18(1)(a)–(z4)* of the *ETA 1996* (as amended by, *inter alia*, the *Employment Tribunals Act 1996 (Application of Conciliation Provisions) Order 2014 (SI 2014/431))*.

Prior to May 2014, before a complaint was presented to an employment tribunal, the conciliation officer would only take action if requested to do so by either party to the potential complaint (*ETA 1996, s 18(3), (5)*, as amended with effect from 6 April 2009 by the *Employment Act 2008*). Upon receipt of such a request the conciliation officer would endeavour to promote a settlement between the parties without proceedings being instituted (*ETA 1996, s 18(3)*).

With effect from 6 May 2014 early conciliation of disputes is mandatory and failure to comply with the early conciliation process with result in a claim being rejected by the employment tribunal. The operation of the new early conciliation scheme is outlined in the next section.

2.5 ACAS EARLY CONCILIATION

The statutory framework introducing mandatory ACAS early conciliation in tribunal claims is contained in *ss 7* to *9* and *Schedules 1* and *2* of the *Enterprise and Regulatory Reform Act 2013*. These provisions came into force on 6 April 2014 by the *Enterprise and Regulatory Reform Act 2013 (Commencement No. 5, Transitional Provisions and Savings) Order 2014 (SI 2014/253)*. Transitional provisions covered the period between 6 April and 5 May 2014 during which early conciliation was available to prospective claimants but not compulsory. From 6 May 2014 early conciliation is mandatory for claims presented on or after 6 May 2014.

The Early Conciliation Rules of Procedure are set out in the *Schedule* to the *Employment Tribunals (Early Conciliation: Exemptions and Rules of Procedure) Regulations 2014 (SI 2014/254)* ("the *Regulations*") as amended by the *Employment Tribunals (Early Conciliation: Exemptions and Rules of Procedure) (Amendment) Regulations 2014 (SI 2014/847)*.

The *Regulations* set out a sequence of procedural steps that must be followed. Under the *Early Conciliation Rules of Procedure* ("the *Rules*") a potential claimant must make contact with ACAS by telephone (*Rule 3*) or by the submission of a form completed either online (available on the ACAS website) or by post (*Rule 2*) which must contain certain minimum information (i.e. the name and address of the prospective claimant and prospective respondent: *Rule 2(2)*. Failure to provide that information may result in the form being rejected (*Rule 2(3)*). Where there is more than one intended respondent a separate form must be completed for each (or each respondent identified by name in the telephone call to ACAS) (*Rule 4* as amended by the *Employment Tribunals (Early Conciliation: Exemptions and Rules of Procedure) (Amendment) Regulations 2014 (SI 2014/847)*). In *De Mota v ADR Network and the Co-operative Group* (UKEAT/0305/16) (13 September 2017) the EAT held that an application which named two respondents (and a subsequent ACAS certificate issued naming two respondents), although not strictly compliant with *Rule 4* and *Rule 8*, did not prevent the claimant's claim proceeding.

Upon submission of a valid form or telephone call, ACAS must make reasonable attempts to contact the prospective claimant (*Rule 5(1)*) and, if the prospective claimant consents, reasonable attempts to contact the prospective respondent(s) (*Rule 5(2)*). If ACAS is unable to contact the prospective claimant or respondent it must conclude that settlement is not possible (*Rule 5(3)*).

The period for early conciliation is one calendar month from receipt of the form under *Rule 2* or the telephone call under *Rule 3* (*Rule 6(1)*) during which period the conciliation officer must "endeavour to promote a settlement". The early conciliation period may be extended by the conciliation officer if the prospective claimant and prospective respondent consent and if the conciliation officer considers that there is a reasonable prospect of a settlement being achieved before the expiry of the extended period (*Rule 6(2)*). The extended period is a maximum of 14 days and no further extension is permitted (*Rule 6(3)*).

If during the conciliation period (or the extended period) the conciliation officer concludes that a settlement of all or part of a dispute is not possible ACAS must issue and an "early conciliation certificate" (*Rule 7(1)*). Similarly if the conciliation period (or the extended period if applicable) expires without settlement then the early conciliation certificate must be issued (*Rule 7(2)*). The early conciliation certificate must include the information listed in *Rule 8*, being the names and addresses of the prospective claimant and respondent, the date of receipt of the form under *Rule 2* or the telephone call under *Rule 3*, the date of issue of the certificate and the unique reference number (the "early conciliation number") given by ACAS to the early conciliation certificate. A certificate A copy of the early conciliation certificate must be provided by ACAS to the prospective claimant and, if ACAS has had contact with the prospective respondent during the conciliation period, to that party also (*Rule 9*). There is no provision in the legislation for the issue of a second certificate and so if further conciliation is entered into this is on a voluntary basis and the second period of conciliation does not have the effect of extending time limits (*Revenue and Customs Commissioners v Garau* UKEAT/O348/16 (24 March 2017).

The *Employment Tribunals (Constitution and Rules of Procedure) (Amendment) Regulations 2014 (SI 2014/271)* amends *Schedule 1* to the *Employment Tribunals (Constitution and Rules of Procedure) Regulations 2013* so as to require claimants either to provide to the employment tribunal as part of the claim the early conciliation number or to confirm that the claim does not involve "relevant proceedings" or to confirm that one of the exemptions from the early conciliation scheme applies (*Rule 10(1)(c)* as amended). Failure to comply with this obligation will mean the claim form is rejected (*Rule 10(2)* and *Rule 12* of *Sch 1* to the *2013 Regulations* as amended). A failure to name the correct respondent in the early conciliation process can result in a claim being subsequently dismissed under *Rule 12(1)(f)* of *Sch 1* to the *2013 Regulations* (*Giny v SNA Transport Ltd* UKEAT/0317/16 (22 May 2017)) although, if the error is considered a minor one, the employment tribunal has power under *Rule 12(2A)* to allow the claim to proceed.

The scheme applies to all "relevant proceedings" where ACAS is under a duty to promote a settlement. See *s 18* of the *Employment Tribunals Act 1996* ("*ETA*"). The *Employment Tribunals Act 1996 (Application of Conciliation Provisions) Order 2014 (SI 2014/431)* substitutes a new list of jurisdictions in *s 18* of the *ETA*. See *ETA, s 18(1)(a)–(z4)* (as amended). Subject to limited exceptions all claims which may be advanced by an individual claimant fall with the scope of mandatory early conciliation.

The exemptions from early conciliation are set out in *Reg 3* of the *Regulations*. There are five exemptions but the two most relevant are likely to be applications for interim relief and multiple claims where another claimant has already made contact with ACAS. The exemptions are as follows:

(a)   another person ("B") has complied with that requirement in relation to the same dispute and A wishes to institute proceedings on the same claim form as B;

2.5   Advisory, Conciliation and Arbitration Service (ACAS)

(b)   A institutes those relevant proceedings on the same claim form as proceedings which are not relevant proceedings;

(c)   A is able to show that the respondent has contacted ACAS in relation to a dispute, ACAS has not received information from A under s *18A(1)* of the *Employment Tribunals Act* in relation to that dispute, and the proceedings on the claim form relate to that dispute;

(d)   the proceedings are proceedings under *Part X* of the *Employment Rights Act 1996* (unfair dismissal) and the application to institute those proceedings is accompanied by an application under *s 128* of the *ERA* or *s 161* of the *Trade Union and Labour Relations (Consolidation) Act 1992* (interim relief cases);

(e)   A is instituting proceedings against the Security Service, the Secret Intelligence Service or the Government Communications Headquarters.

2.6   CONSEQUENTIAL AMENDMENTS TO TIME LIMITS FOR PRESENTATION OF CLAIMS

The tribunal time limits are extended to allow time for early conciliation. The time limit provisions in primary legislation have been amended by *Sch 2* to the *Enterprise and Regulatory Reform Act 2013*. The time limits in the various statutory instruments are amended by the *Enterprise and Regulatory Reform Act 2013 (Consequential Amendments) (Employment) Order 2014 (SI 2014/386)* and the *Employment Tribunals Act 1996 (Application of Conciliation Provisions) Order 2014 (SI 2014/431)* and, in the case of *TUPE*, the *Enterprise and Regulatory Reform Act 2013 (Consequential Amendments) (Employment) (No. 2) Order 2014 (SI 2014/853)*.

The statutory formula for the amendment of time limits is common to all the amending legislation and provides (using the example of the amendment to the time limits in the *ERA 1996* (see the new *s 207B*):

"207B   Extension of time limits to facilitate conciliation before institution of proceedings

(1)   This section applies where this Act provides for it to apply for the purposes of a provision of this Act (a "relevant provision").

But it does not apply to a dispute that is (or so much of a dispute as is) a relevant dispute for the purposes of section 207A.

(2)   In this section—

(a)   Day A is the day on which the complainant or applicant concerned complies with the requirement in subsection (1) of section 18A of the Employment Tribunals Act 1996 (requirement to contact ACAS before instituting proceedings) in relation to the matter in respect of which the proceedings are brought, and

(b)   Day B is the day on which the complainant or applicant concerned receives or, if earlier, is treated as receiving (by virtue of regulations made under subsection (11) of that section) the certificate issued under subsection (4) of that section.

(3)   In working out when a time limit set by a relevant provision expires the period beginning with the day after Day A and ending with Day B is not to be counted.

(4)   If a time limit set by a relevant provision would (if not extended by this subsection) expire during the period beginning with Day A and ending one month after Day B, the time limit expires instead at the end of that period.

(5)   Where an employment tribunal has power under this Act to extend a time
        limit set by a relevant provision, the power is exercisable in relation to the
        time limit as extended by this section."

Thus the period between initiation of contact with ACAS (Day A) and receipt (or deemed receipt) of the early conciliation certificate (Day B) does not count for limitation purposes (See, e.g., *ERA, s 207B(3)* above). If the certificate is sent by email, the day of receipt will be the same as the date of issue (*Rule 9(3)*). If posted, it will be the day it would have been delivered in the ordinary course of the post (*Rule 9(3)*). The certificate will state the date of issue and the method by which it is being sent (*Rule 8(e)*).

If the relevant time limit would, if not extended by *ERA s 207B(4)* expire "during the period beginning with Day A and ending one month after Day B" then the relevant time limit expires at the end of that period. (See, eg *ERA, s 207B(4)* above). The time limits in *ERA s 207B(3)* and *207B(4)* are to be applied sequentially. *Section 207B(3)* will apply in every case and *s 207B(4)* applies to the time limit as extended by *s 207B(3)* (*Luton Borough Council v Haque* (UKEAT/0180/17/JOJ) (12 April 2018).

The tribunal retains the familiar powers to extend time and those powers are "exercisable in relation to the time limit as extended by this section". Accordingly, a claim submitted after the extended limitation period may still be heard if it is just and equitable to do so (where that is the applicable statutory test) or if it was not reasonably practicable to present the claim in time (where that test applies).

In *DHL Supply Chain v Fazackerley* UKEAT/0019/18 (10 April 2018, unreported) reliance on advice provided by ACAS which contributed to a claim being presented out of time provided a basis for extension on the not reasonably practicable basis.

2.7   CONCILIATION AFTER PRESENTATION OF A COMPLAINT TO THE EMPLOYMENT TRIBUNAL

Once a complaint has been presented to an employment tribunal, a conciliation officer must conciliate whether or not he is requested to do so if he considers that he could conciliate with a reasonable prospect of success or when he is requested to do so by both parties (*ETA 1996, s 18C*).

Where the complaint is one of unfair dismissal, and the complainant has ceased to be employed by the employer against whom the complaint is made, the conciliation officer is required to seek the complainant's reinstatement or re-engagement (*ETA 1996, s 18C(2)(a)*). Where the complainant does not wish for either of these remedies, or where reinstatement or re-engagement is not practicable, the conciliation officer will attempt to obtain for him a sum by way of compensation (*ETA 1996, s 18C(2)(b)*). The same principles apply in relation to a potential complaint of unfair dismissal which has not been lodged in the employment tribunal at the time of conciliation (*ETA 1996, s 18(5)*). As a result of amendments made by the *Employment Act 2008* and the removal of the fixed periods for conciliation there is no limit upon the period during which a conciliation officer may seek to promote settlement by way of conciliation and this conciliation may in appropriate cases continue up to the point of an award of remedy by an employment tribunal.

Thus, if a complaint is presented to an employment tribunal, the respondent employer will often be contacted by a conciliation officer. The conciliation officer will usually outline the complainant's grievance and may convey the respondent's comments back to the complainant. If the respondent does not want his comments conveyed to the complainant he should make this clear to the conciliation officer. Nothing communicated to a conciliation officer in connection with the performance of his functions is admissible in evidence in any proceedings before an employment tribunal, except with the consent of the person who communicated it to the officer (*ETA 1996, s 18(7)*). It may also be of some comfort to those involved in the settlement of claims through ACAS to know that such communications attract absolute privilege for the purposes of any defamation proceedings as held in *Freer v Glover* [2005] EWHC 3341 (QB), [2006] IRLR 521 in which a solicitor acting for the employer involved in negotiations through ACAS was sued in defamation by the employee. Incidental publication of the alleged defamatory statement to ACAS staff was also protected by the privilege (*Lincoln v Daniels* [1962] 1 QB 237, [1961] 3 All ER 740, CA applied).

The important role of conciliation officers is emphasised by the fact that, subject to one important exception, an agreement to settle an employment tribunal complaint will only normally be binding on the parties if the agreement relates to a complaint or potential complaint where a conciliation officer has taken action in accordance with his statutory powers. The important exception concerns settlements reached after the employee has received advice from a relevant independent adviser (see EMPLOYMENT TRIBUNALS – I (19)). In other cases, an agreement to settle a claim or a potential claim is unenforceable, leaving the complainant free to pursue his claim before an employment tribunal (*ERA 1996, s 203(1), (2)*; *SDA 1975, s 77(4)(a)*; *RRA 1976, s 72(4)(a)*). In *Moore v Duport Furniture Products Ltd* [1982] ICR 84, [1982] IRLR 31, HL, a conciliation officer was considered to have taken such action in circumstances where the parties had already reached a settlement. In that case, the officer ascertained that they had truly reached agreement, which he then recorded in writing on a form designed for the purpose (Form COT 3). Where a conciliation officer assisted the parties in reaching an oral agreement, that agreement was held to be binding, notwithstanding that it had not been recorded in writing (*Gilbert v Kembridge Fibres Ltd* [1984] ICR 188, [1984] IRLR 52, EAT; see also *Hennessy v Craigmyle & Co Ltd* [1986] ICR 461, [1986] IRLR 300, CA). A conciliation officer is not under a duty to advise an employee on the relevant legislation, but an agreement reached with his assistance may be set aside if he acts partially or adopts unfair methods (*Slack v Greenham (Plant Hire) Ltd* [1983] ICR 617, [1983] IRLR 271, EAT). Nor will a tribunal be bound by a sham COT 3 designed to mislead a government department (*Trafford Carpets Ltd v Barker* IDS 440, p 16 (EAT/206/90)).

An attack upon the binding nature of a COT3 agreement on the basis that the conciliation officer had not advised the employees properly as to their rights was rejected by the EAT in *Clark v Redcar and Cleveland Borough Council* [2006] ICR 897, [2006] IRLR 324, EAT. As part of an overall settlement negotiated in equal pay claims the employees signed COT3 agreements limiting the amount of back pay to be paid. Subsequently they sought to set them aside on the basis of ACAS failing to provide advice that they could achieve considerably more in compensation by proceeding with the claims. The EAT reaffirmed that the function of ACAS was to promote settlement and not to advise upon the merits of a party's case and to do so might compromise the role of the conciliation officer. While best practice might sometimes suggest that the conciliation officer should caution the employee to take further advice, failure to do so would not provide grounds to set aside the COT3 which would only be set aside in cases of bad faith or impropriety by the conciliation officer.

In order to ensure that an agreement to settle a complaint or potential complaint is enforceable, parties should normally seek the assistance of a conciliation officer to promote a settlement and have him record the agreement on the appropriate form (COT3). This is not however mandatory for a settlement to be effective. The extent to which the conciliation officer must "take action" for the purposes of ousting the jurisdiction of the employment tribunal under *s 203* of the *ERA 1996* was considered by the EAT in *Alma Construction Ltd v Bonner* [2011] IRLR 204. The EAT held that the threshold for taking action was very low. The ACAS officer is not required to broker the settlement nor to record it, whether in a COT3 or otherwise. The duty is only to endeavour to promote settlement. So long as this has been done, the ACAS officer has taken action and, if a settlement was reached, it will be binding for the purposes of *ERA 1996, s 203* and the employment tribunal will have no jurisdiction subsequently to hear the claim. In that case the communication to the employer via the ACAS officer of the claimant's willingness to accept an offer of settlement was sufficient for the purposes of *ERA 1996, s 203.*

In *Livingstone v Hepworth Refractories Ltd* [1992] 3 CMLR 601, [1992] ICR 287, EAT, it was held that a COT3 made where the conciliation officer was acting under the *Employment Protection Consolidation Act 1978* (now *ERA 1996*) was only effective to settle discrimination or equal pay claims if it was expressly stated to include such claims, whether brought under domestic or European law.

2.8 Conciliation in complaints to Central Arbitration Committee

ACAS will seek to promote a settlement of complaints by recognised trade unions of failure to disclose information (*TULR(C)A 1992, s 183(2)*; see Trade Unions – I (51)).

2.9 ARBITRATION

Where a trade dispute exists or is apprehended, ACAS may, with the consent of all parties to the dispute, refer the matters in dispute for the arbitration of:

(a)   an independent arbitrator or arbitrators, not being an employee of ACAS; or

(b)   the Central Arbitration Committee.

(TULR(C)A 1992, s 212(1).)

However, ACAS will first consider the likelihood of the dispute being settled by conciliation and, in the absence of special reasons, a matter will not be referred to arbitration until any agreed disputes procedure has been exhausted (*TULR(C)A 1992, s 212(2), (3)*).

An award by an arbitrator may be published if ACAS so decides and all the parties concerned consent (*TULR(C)A 1992, s 212(4)(b)*).

The *Arbitration Act 1996, Part I* does not apply to such an arbitration (*TULR(C)A 1992, s 212(5)*).

2.10 THE EMPLOYMENT RIGHTS (DISPUTE RESOLUTION) ACT 1998

By *s 212A* of *TULR(C)A 1992* (introduced by *s 7* of the *Employment Rights (Dispute Resolution) Act 1998,* which came into force on 1 August 1998), ACAS was given the power to draw up a scheme for the voluntary (but binding) arbitration of unfair dismissal disputes subject to the approval of the Secretary of State. Following ACAS consultation on the scheme, which was expressed to be intended to be 'voluntary, speedy, informal, confidential and free from legal argument', the arbitration scheme came into effect in England and Wales on 21 May 2001. Guidance on the operation of the scheme is available on the ACAS website (www.acas.org.uk). The application of the scheme was, from 6 April 2004, extended to Scotland by the *ACAS Arbitration Scheme (Great Britain) Order 2004 (SI 2004/753).* The scheme may be summarised (in brief outline) as follows (for further detail see Employment Tribunals – I (19)).

First, it is important to note that the scheme is voluntary and is limited to unfair dismissal claims. If a claim for unfair dismissal is to be determined under the scheme, then any other claim (even if raised at the same time or on related facts) must go to the employment tribunal or be settled. If other related claims are to be heard in the employment tribunal, then the arbitration proceedings may be postponed pending the tribunal's determination.

2.10 Advisory, Conciliation and Arbitration Service (ACAS)

On submission of a claim to arbitration, both parties must waive in writing the right they would otherwise have in relation to an unfair dismissal claim. This includes waiver of the right to raise jurisdictional issues such as time limits, continuity of service and whether, in fact, the employee was dismissed.

The scheme provides for hearings to take place in private (unlike the normal tribunal procedure) and is intended to be speedy, non-legalistic and cost effective. The scheme is not intended for claims involving legal complexity or EC law; such claims, according to the Schedule, should remain the province of the employment tribunal. The arbitrators will be appointed by ACAS from the ACAS arbitration panel. In contrast to tribunal proceedings, the arbitration may take place anywhere, including the employee's place of work. There is no mechanism for compulsory attendance of witnesses or production of documents (although failure to produce/attend may be taken into account by the arbitrator in reaching his decision). Evidence will not be subject to the formality of tribunal procedure and will be given unsworn and without cross-examination. The arbitrator will, however, have the power to question witnesses or parties to determine the facts.

The arbitrator's decision will not take the form of detailed reasons. The arbitrator must, in reaching his decision, apply the recognised principles of fairness in the employment context (including ACAS Codes of Practice) and, additionally, must apply the *Human Rights Act 1998* and relevant EC law. The remedies available to a successful employee are the same as in the employment tribunal (reinstatement, re-engagement and compensation). The arbitrator's decision is final; there is no mechanism for appeal from the decision. The parties remain free to settle the matter at any time during the arbitration, however. To date the scheme has not proved to be very popular: the *ACAS Annual Report* 2006/07 revealed that in that year only three unfair dismissal cases were the subject of arbitration (down from 6 in 2005/06, 4 in 2004/05, 7 in 2003/04 and 23 in 2002/03). Data for subsequent years is not included in the relevant ACAS Reports.

The power of ACAS to arbitrate also extends to flexible working requests. See, on flexible working, *ERA 1996, ss 80F–80I* (as inserted by the *Employment Act 2002*). The ACAS flexible working arbitration scheme, introduced pursuant to *s 212A* of *TULR(C)A* (see the *ACAS (Flexible Working) Arbitration Scheme (England and Wales) Order 2003 (SI 2003/694)*) is similar in form and operation to the scheme relating to unfair dismissal. An arbitrator hears the claim and gives a final decision with limited rights of appeal or challenge available to the parties. If the parties have elected to go to arbitration, there is no right to go to the employment tribunal. The remedies and compensation which may be awarded by the arbitrator mirror those in the employment tribunal. As in the case of unfair dismissal arbitration, there is detailed guidance on the arbitration of flexible working disputes available on the ACAS website. Utilisation of this service is, however, infrequent. The *ACAS Annual Report* 2006–07 revealed that in that year no flexible working claims went to arbitration (the same as 2005/06; in 2004/05 one such claim went to arbitration). Data for subsequent years is not included in the relevant ACAS Reports.

2.11 ADVICE

ACAS is empowered, on request or on its own initiative, to give such advice as it thinks appropriate to employers, workers and their organisations on matters concerned with or affecting or likely to affect industrial relations. It may also publish general advice on matters connected with or affecting or likely to affect industrial relations (*TULR(C)A 1992, s 213* as substituted by *TURERA 1993, s 43(2)*). ACAS's helpline is extremely popular, with close to 1.5 million telephone and online queries received per year.

ACAS publishes a number of guides in relation to various employment law issues with a series of advisory booklets, leaflets and handbooks, the latter directed particularly to small firms. In addition, ACAS has a series of e-learning packages available on its website together with an online helpline. These publications are available from ACAS Public Enquiry Points and also from the ACAS website (www.acas.org.uk).

The ACAS telephone Helpline for all employment related questions is 0300 123 1100.

2.12   INQUIRY

ACAS may, if it thinks fit, inquire into any question relating to industrial relations generally or to industrial relations in any particular industry or in any particular undertaking or part of any undertaking (*TULR(C)A 1992, s 214(1)*).

The findings of such an inquiry, together with any advice given in connection with those findings, may be published by ACAS if it appears to it that publication is desirable for the improvement of industrial relations. Before deciding whether to publish, ACAS must send a draft of the findings to all the parties appearing to ACAS to be concerned, and take account of their views (*TULR(C)A 1992, s 214(2)*).

2.13   CODES OF PRACTICE

ACAS has a general power to issue new or revised Codes of Practice to give practical guidance for promoting the improvement of industrial relations (*TULR(C)A 1992, s 199*). It has issued five Codes of Practice so far:

No 1: Disciplinary and Grievance Procedures

No 2: Disclosure of Information

No 3: Time Off for Trade Union Duties

No.4: Code of Practice on Settlement Agreements (2013)

No 5: Handling in a Reasonable Manner Requests to Work Flexibly (2014)

The Codes have not remained static since their first issue in 1985 and have been the subject of a number of revisions.

A wholly new Code of Practice No 1 was issued with effect from 6 April 2009 to reflect the repeal by the *Employment Act 2008* of the statutory dispute resolution procedures in relation to matters of discipline and grievance (which had been introduced by *Part 3* of the *Employment Act 2002* (with effect from 1 October 2004) and the *Employment Act 2002 (Dispute Resolution) Regulations 2004 (SI 2004/752)*. Code of Practice No 1 was revised in minor respects in relation to accompaniment at disciplinary or grievance hearings and reissued on 11 March 2015. The relevant statutory instrument setting out the revised Code of Practice No 1 is (*SI 2015/649*).

The Code of Practice No 2 on Disclosure of Information (1998 edition, third revision 2003) deals with disclosure of information to trade unions for the purposes of collective bargaining pursuant to the obligations contained in *ss 181* and *182* of *TULR(C)A 1992*.

The Code of Practice No 3 on Time Off for Trade Union Duties was revised with effect from 1 January 2010 by order of the Secretary of State (*Employment Protection Code of Practice (Time Off for Trade Union Duties and Activities) Order 2009 (SI 2009/3223)*).

The fourth of the ACAS codes on Settlement Agreements was introduced as a consequence of *s 14* of the *Enterprise and Regulatory Reform Act 2013* and the introduction of protected conversations between employers and employees about terms of settlement for the termination of employment (see *s 111A* of the *ERA 1996*).

As in the case of the other Codes, it was made pursuant to *s 199* of *TULR(C)A 1992*, and was brought into force on 29 July 2013 by the *Employment Code of Practice (Settlements) Order 2013 (SI 2013/1665)*.

2.13 Advisory, Conciliation and Arbitration Service (ACAS)

The fifth of the ACAS Codes on flexible work requests was introduced with effect from 30 June 2014 following implementation of the changes made by the *Children and Families Act 2014* in relation to such requests. Again, it was made pursuant to *s 199 of TULR(C)A 1992*, and was brought into force by the *Code of Practice (Handling in a Reasonable Manner Requests to Work Flexibly) Order 2014 (SI 2014/1665)*.

For the legal effect of these Codes of Practice and the procedure to be followed in issuing them, see **5.3 CODES OF PRACTICE**.

2.14 CONTACTING ACAS

ACAS headquarters are at Euston Tower, 286 Euston Road, London NW1 3JJ. For information in relation to employment issues the ACAS Helpline (0300 123 1100) should be used. The majority of ACAS publications and guides may be downloaded from its website (
www.acas.org.uk).

ACAS regional offices

Acas East Midlands

Apex Court,
City Link,
Nottingham, NG2 4LA.

Acas East of England

Forest Heath District Council Offices,
College Heath Road,
Mildenhall,
Suffolk, IP28 7EY.

Acas London

Euston Tower,
286 Euston Road,
London, NW1 3DP

Acas North East

Newcastle Civic Centre,
Barras Bridge,
Newcastle upon Tyne, NE1 8QH.

Acas North West

3rd Floor,
Piccadilly Gate,
Store Street,
Manchester, M1 2WD

Acas North West

Redgrave Court,
Merton Road, Bootle,
Merseyside,
Liverpool, L20 7HS.

Acas South East

Civic Offices,
1st Floor,
Harlington Way,
Fleet,
Hampshire,   GU51 4AE.

Acas South West

Temple Quay House,
2 The Square,
Bristol, BS1 6DG.

Acas West Midlands

Victoria Square House,
Victoria Square,
Birmingham, B2 4AJ.

Acas Yorkshire and Humber

The Cube,
123 Albion Street,
Leeds, LS2 8ER.

Acas Scotland

151 West George Street,
Glasgow, G2 2JJ.

Acas Wales

Companies House,
Crown Way,
Cardiff, CF14 3UZ.

3   ACAS Conciliation

3.1   INTRODUCTION OF COMPULSORY EARLY CONCILIATION

A claimant will generally be required to prove that the dispute has been referred to ACAS for early conciliation before presenting a claim to the Employment Tribunal, by producing the early conciliation certificate, failing which the Employment Tribunal will not have jurisdiction over the claim (*Employment Tribunal Rules of Procedure, r 12*).

Following amendments which originated in the *Enterprise and Regulatory Reform Act 2013*, a new conciliation scheme run by the Advisory Conciliation and Arbitration Service (ACAS) came into operation on 6 April 2014 (*Enterprise and Regulatory Reform Act 2013 (Commencement No 5, Transitional Provisions and Savings) Order 2014, art 3 (SI 2014/253)*). Where a claimant had referred a dispute to ACAS between 6 April 2014 and 5 May 2014, and presented the claim form before 5 May 2014, the claim was treated as subject to a requirement of early conciliation, which was met on the day on which he or she referred the dispute to ACAS. The new regime came into force from 6 May 2014 (*SI 2014/253, art 4*).

Most employment tribunal proceedings are relevant proceedings for the purposes of early conciliation (*Employment Tribunals Act 1996, s 18(1)* as amended by the *ETA 1996 (Application of Conciliation Provisions) Order 2014 (SI 2014/431)*). Early conciliation is the process which applies to matters which could be the subject of relevant proceedings, *ie* to a potential claim, and conciliation is the process which applies to relevant proceedings themselves, *ie* to a claim which has been presented (*ETA 1996, s 18(1A)*). When proceeding under the provisions on early conciliation, the conciliation officer is, where appropriate, under a duty to have regard to the desirability of encouraging the use of other procedures available for the settlement of grievances (*ETA 1996, s 18(6)*). Anything communicated to a conciliation officer in connection with the performance of his conciliation functions will not be admissible in evidence in Employment Tribunal proceedings without the consent of the person who made the communication (*ETA 1996, s 18(7)*). Therefore, an employer has no right to know or rely on the content of the discussions which occurred between the employee and ACAS.

Before presenting an Employment Tribunal claim, the claimant must provide prescribed information to ACAS in the prescribed manner, about the matter (*ETA 1996, s 18A(1)*).

On receiving the prescribed information in the prescribed manner, ACAS must send a copy of it to a conciliation officer (*ETA 1996, s 18A(2)*), who will be under a duty during the early conciliation period to endeavour to promote a settlement between the would-be parties (*ETA 1996, s 18A(3)*).

If the conciliation officer concludes that a settlement is not possible or the early conciliation period expires without a settlement having been reached, then the conciliation officer will issue an early conciliation certificate to the employee (*ETA 1996, s 18A(4)*). Nevertheless, the conciliation officer may continue to endeavour to promote a settlement even after the early conciliation period has ended (*ETA 1996, s 18A(5)*).

3.2   EXEMPTIONS FROM EARLY CONCILIATION

Relevant proceedings may be commenced without the requirement for early conciliation in prescribed circumstances (*ETA 1996, s 18A(7)*). At present, exemptions from early conciliation exist in five cases: first, where the claimant institutes relevant proceedings to which the requirement for early conciliation would apply, however, another person has complied with the requirement for early conciliation in relation to the same dispute and the claimant wishes to institute proceedings on the same claim form; second, where the claimant institutes relevant proceedings on the same claim form as proceedings which are not relevant proceedings; third, where the claimant can prove that the respondent notified ACAS about a dispute, ACAS has not received information from the claimant under *ETA 1996, s 18A(1)* in relation to that dispute, and the proceedings on the claim form relate to that dispute; fourth, where the claim is for unfair dismissal and is accompanied by an application for interim relief under *ERA 1996, s 128* or *TULRCA 1992, s 161*; or, fifth, where the claimant is instituting proceedings against the Security Service, the Secret Intelligence Service or the Government Communications Headquarters (*Employment Tribunals (Early Conciliation: Exemptions and Rules of Procedure) Regulations 2014, art 3 (SI 2014/254)*).

3.3   THE EFFECTS OF THE REQUIREMENT FOR EARLY CONCILIATION

Where a claimant is subject to the requirement to contact ACAS before instituting Employment Tribunal proceedings, he or she may not present a claim without an early conciliation certificate (*ETA 1996, s 18A(8)*).

Where the proposed claim is of unfair dismissal, the conciliation officer is empowered to seek to promote the employee's reinstatement or re-engagement by the employer or its successor or an associated employer on terms which appear equitable to the conciliation officer, as an alternative to promoting agreement as to compensation (*ETA 1996, s 18A(9)*).

An employer may refer a workplace dispute to ACAS if he or she considers that it is likely to escalate into employment tribunal proceedings, where the employee has not already notified ACAS (*ETA 1996, s 18B(1)*), and an employee may refer a dispute to ACAS even though the case involves an exception to the requirement for early conciliation (*ETA 1996, s 18B(2)*). In both situations, the conciliation officer will still be under a duty to promote a settlement, however, the duration of that duty is open-ended, rather for the duration of the prescribed period (*ETA 1996, s 18B(3)* cf *ETA 1996, s 18A(3)*). Nevertheless, where the dispute is referred by the employer or by an employee whose potential claim is subject to an exception from the requirement for early conciliation, then the conciliation officer's duty to promote settlement comes to an end when either the conciliation officer concludes that a settlement is not possible, or the conciliation officer comes under a duty to promote settlement during the prescribed period under *section 18A(3)* of the *ETA 1996*, *ie* when the dispute is referred to ACAS by a prospective claimant in relevant proceedings. For disputes referred by the employer, or where there is an exception to the requirement for early conciliation, the conciliation officer is empowered in unfair dismissal cases to promote reinstatement, re-engagement, or agreed compensation (*ETA 1996, s 18B(6)*). It should be noted that where an employer refers the dispute to ACAS it will have no effect upon the limitation period, because the conciliation officer's duty is not linked to the prescribed period for early conciliation, nor to any obligation to issue a certificate of early conciliation. ACAS advises employers to telephone them if they would like to start early conciliation.

Where early conciliation fails and a claim is presented and a copy sent to ACAS, the existing system will continue, under which the conciliation officer will be under a duty to promote settlement where requested by both parties or where the officer considers that there would be a reasonable prospect of promoting a settlement (ETA 1996, s 18C(1)). The powers of the conciliation officer include promoting reinstatement, re-engagement and an agreed sum of compensation, where the claim is for unfair dismissal (*ETA 1996, s 18C(2)*).

3.4   THE EARLY CONCILIATION RULES OF PROCEDURE

The Early Conciliation Rules of Procedure (*Employment Tribunals (Early Conciliation: Exemption and Rules of Procedure) Regulations 2014, reg 5, Schedule*) prescribe the content of early conciliation.

Guidance is available at www.acas.org.uk/earlyconciliation, where the early conciliation notification form can also be found.

The form may be returned online or by post (*Early Conciliation Rules of Procedure, r 2(a)*).

Parties without internet access may telephone ACAS on 0300 123 11 22 (*Early Conciliation Rules of Procedure, r 1*). ACAS will then insert the prospective claimant's name and address and the prospective respondent's name and address to the early conciliation form (*Early Conciliation Rules of Procedure, r 3*).

On the notification form the employee is required to state his or her name and contact details and the employer's name and contact details (*Early Conciliation Rules of Procedure, r 2(2)*). The current ACAS form also requests the date on which employment started, the date on which employment ended if applicable, the job which the employee did, and the date on which the event about which the employee intends to complain took place.

If there is more than one respondent, the employee must present a separate early conciliation form for each respondent, or name each respondent by telephone (*Early Conciliation Rules of Procedure, r 4*). The correct name must be used for the respondent, otherwise the conciliation certificate will not match with the claim form and the employment tribunal will lack jurisdiction. The employee is not required to give any other details of the complaint in the notification form.

ACAS is required to make reasonable attempts to contact the prospective claimant and if he or she consents must make reasonable attempts to contact the prospective respondent (*Early Conciliation Rules of Procedure, r 5*).

3.5   Early conciliation through ACAS is voluntary for both the employer and the employee, although an employee who does not wish to use early conciliation is required to obtain a conciliation certificate before presenting an employment tribunal claim. No charge is made to either party to conciliation. Where ACAS is unable to make contact with either prospective party, then it must conclude that a settlement is not possible (*Early Conciliation Rules of Procedure, r 5*).

Given first that ACAS early conciliation is voluntary for claimants and second that discussions between employees and ACAS are confidential, it is not generally fruitful for an employer to try to raise complaints or jurisdictional arguments based on inconsistency between issues discussed at the early conciliation stage and the content of the claim form. Despite the existence of the early conciliation regime, employers may still be taken unawares by particular claims or allegations in the claim form, or by applications to amend claims.

In *Science Warehouse Limited v Mills* (2015) UKEAT/0224/15, [2016] IRLR 96 the Employment Appeal Tribunal ('the EAT') held that *s 18A* of the *ETA 1996* did not require that the early conciliation process was undertaken in respect of each claim, but used the broader terminology of 'matter', and also envisaged that the requirement to notify ACAS was one that fell on a prospective rather than on an existing claimant. Therefore, the EAT considered that where the claimant had previously lodged a valid employment tribunal claim, including her early conciliation reference, and was applying to amend to add a new but related claim, that was a matter for the employment tribunal's general case management powers and not subject to jurisdictional restrictions imposed by the early conciliation rules. Following the same principles, in *Mist v Derby Community Health Services NHS Trust* (2016) UKEAT/0170/15, [2016] All ER (D) 252 (Jan) the EAT held that an application to join a transferee in a transfer of undertakings claim as a second respondent fell to be considered as a possible amendment to an existing claim and did not require a further early conciliation certificate. Likewise, in *Compass Group UK & Ireland Ltd v Morgan* [2016] IRLR 924, the EAT held that an early conciliation certificate obtained by a prospective claimant could cover future events.

ACAS requests that potential claimants should notify ACAS themselves of their intention to claim, and that claimants' representatives should not do so. Once ACAS has checked the details and nature of the claim with the claimant, and a conciliator has made contact with the claimant and confirmed that the representative has been appointed, then ACAS will deal with the representative. ACAS has requested that representatives of groups of claimants should call ACAS to discuss how group conciliation works and the involvement of a specialist collective conciliator.

When ACAS first receives an early conciliation request, an acknowledgment will be sent online, by email or by post, depending upon the method of notification used by the party. ACAS will contact the notifier to check the information provided, find out what the claim is about and explain early conciliation. The next stage is for the claimant or the claimant's representative to call the ACAS conciliator so that the conciliator can understand the dispute and how the claimant would like it to be resolved. Once the conciliator and the claimant or the claimant's representative have spoken (unless there is a reason not to communicate by telephone) and the claimant has agreed to proceed with early conciliation, the conciliator will contact the employer to see if the employer is willing to take part in talks. If so, the conciliator will talk with both the claimant, or the claimant's representive, and the employer to see if they can reach agreement.

If the conciliator cannot contact the claimant over a reasonable period of time or the claimant indicates that he or she does not want to use early conciliation, then ACAS will close the case and issue an early conciliation certificate by email or post.

Most conciliation discussions will be by telephone. Under normal conditions, sometimes the conciliator will chair a meeting between the parties where it is considered helpful, however, given the rules on social distancing which have been imposed in response to the global coronavirus pandemic, the prospects of obtaining an in person ACAS conciliation meeting are much lower.

Any settlements which ACAS facilitates will be made on the COT3 form.

3.6   THE EFFECT ON THE LIMITATION PERIOD

The claimant must make a request for early conciliation during the limitation period. Once the request is made, time for presenting the claim stops running from the day after the employee refers the dispute to ACAS until the day after he or she receives the early conciliation certificate (see *art 2* of the *Employment and Regulatory Reform Act 2013 (Consequential Amendments) Order 2014 (SI 2014/386)*).

The conciliation officer will endeavour to promote a settlement for up to one month from receipt of the early notification form or the telephone call from the prospective claimant (*Early Conciliation Rules of Procedure, r 6(1)*).

If both parties agree that more time is needed for conciliation, the cessation can be extended only once for 14 days (*Early Conciliation Rules of Procedure, r 6(2) and (3)*).

After a maximum cessation of one month plus 14 days, if the matter is not resolved, the conciliator will end early conciliation and issue a conciliation certificate, as the conciliator will do if he or she concludes earlier that settlement is not possible (*Early Conciliation Rules of Procedure, r 7*).

The formal early conciliation certificate must contain the prospective claimant's name and address, the prospective respondent's name and address, the date of receipt by ACAS of the early conciliation form presented in accordance with Early Conciliation Rules, a unique reference number which the employee must provide when submitting his or her claim form to the employment tribunal, the date of issue of the certificate and the mode of transmission of the certificate (*Early Conciliation Rules of Procedure, r 8*). The conciliation certificate must be sent to the prospective claimant but will be copied to the employer only if the employer had been contacted by ACAS (*Early Conciliation Rules of Procedure, r 9(1)*). If ACAS has an email address for the recipient, the early conciliation certificate must be sent by email, otherwise it will be sent by post (*Early Conciliation Rules of Procedure, r 9(2)*). It will be deemed received the same day if emailed and received in the ordinary course of the post if posted *Early Conciliation Rules of Procedure, r 9*).

3.7   The limitation period will recommence after the early conciliation certificate has been received by the employee. The employee will have at least one month following receipt of the conciliation certificate in which to present his or her claim (*SI 2014/386*).

Thus, it can be seen that in most cases, involving a three-month limitation period, the maximum limitation period will, in strict theory, be one day short of five months and fourteen days, calculated as follows. If the employee contacts ACAS on the last day of the limitation period (which would be a risky strategy to adopt) then one day short of three months would have passed at the commencement of the early conciliation period. Time would then cease to run for a maximum of one month plus 14 days. Following the issue of the conciliation certificate, the employee would have a further month in which to present the claim.

On the other hand, where the employer refers the dispute to ACAS, the employee is not under a requirement to notify ACAS about the dispute before presenting his or her claim (*ETA 1996, ss 18A(7), 18B*)). In other words, one way in which an employer could try to encourage a claimant to present a claim within the normal limitation period would be notify ACAS about the dispute early during the limitation period, draw that fact to the employee's attention and point out that he or she was not required to contact ACAS. Nevertheless, it seems that it remains open to a prospective claimant to contact ACAS even where the employer has already done so (*ETA 1996, ss 18A(7)* and *18B(1)(b)*)).

The question whether a claim was presented in time or not will still be a matter for the Employment Tribunal and the ACAS conciliator will not be able to decide or advise on that issue, ACAS states. A claimant whose claim is out of time is still required to contact ACAS to obtain an early conciliation certificate (*ETA 1996, s 18A*). The prospective claimant and prospective respondent in such a situation would need to consider carefully the tactical advantages and disadvantages of engaging in a settlement discussion at that time, and of refusing to participate so that the certificate was issued straight away, since the involvement of ACAS after expiry of the limitation period would have no effect upon the limitation period.

4   Children and Young Persons

The employment of children and young persons is restricted by legislation, the most important of which is summarised below. In addition, a right for young persons in employment to take time off from work for study or training is outlined. Also summarised is the contractual capacity of children and young persons, insofar as it concerns contracts of employment.

Cross-reference. See EDUCATION AND TRAINING **(14)** for the 'Work Programme', apprenticeships and other training schemes.

4.1   DEFINITIONS CONCERNING CHILDREN AND YOUNG PERSONS

Child. For the purposes of the statutory provisions relating to the employment of children, a child is a person not over compulsory school age (at present, 16 years – see *Education Act 1996, s 8*) (*Education Act 1996, s 558*).

Young person. A person who has ceased to be a child and who is under the age of 18 years (*Education Act 1996, s 579(1)*). (However, note that there is a different definition in the *Management of Health and Safety at Work Regulations 1999* – see **4.5** below.)

Minor. A person who is under the age of 18 years (ie a child or young person) (*Family Law Reform Act 1969, s 1*).

4.2   RESTRICTIONS ON EMPLOYMENT OF CHILDREN

The *Children (Protection at Work) Regulations 1998 (SI 1998/276)* amended the *Children and Young Persons Acts 1933* and *1963* in order to implement the provisions of the *EC Young Workers Directive on the Protection of Young People at Work (94/33)* relating to the employment of children. The *Children (Protection at Work) Regulations 2000 (SI 2000/1333)* and the *Children (Protection at Work) (No 2) Regulations 2000 (SI 2000/2548)* made some additional minor amendments to the *Children and Young Persons Act 1933* so as to give further effect to the *EC Directive 94/33* referred to above.

The main provisions restricting the employment of children, as amended by the above-mentioned *Regulations*, are outlined below.

In general, no child may be employed whether paid or not:

(a)   if he is under the age of 14 years; or

(b)   to do any work other than light work; or

(c)   before the close of school hours on any day on which he is required to attend school; or

(d)   before seven o'clock in the morning or after seven o'clock in the evening on any day; or

(e)   for more than two hours on any day on which he is required to attend school; or

(f)   for more than 12 hours in any week in which he is required to attend school; or

(g)   for more than two hours on any Sunday; or

(h)   for more than eight hours or, if he is under the age of 15 years, for more than five hours on any day (other than Sunday) on which he is not required to attend school; or

4.2 Children and Young Persons

(i) for more than 35 hours or, if he is under the age of 15 years, for more than 25 hours in any week in which he is not required to attend school; or

(j) for more than four hours in any day without a rest break of at least one hour; or

(k) at any time in a year unless at that time, he has had (or could still have), during a school holiday, at least two consecutive weeks without employment.

'Light work' is defined by reference to the *EC Directive 94/33* referred to above, and means work which (on account of the inherent nature of the tasks which are involved and the particular conditions under which they are performed) is not likely to be harmful to a child's safety, health, development, attendance at school or participation in work experience.

(*Children and Young Persons Act 1933, s 18(1), (2A)* as amended; see also **4.3** below.)

In *Ashby v Addison (t/a Brayton News)* [2003] ICR 667, [2003] IRLR 211, the EAT held that a 15-year-old paper boy was not a 'worker' within the meaning of the *Working Time Regulations 1998*, and was therefore not entitled to four weeks' paid annual leave in accordance with *reg 13* (see **30.2** Holidays). The definition of 'young person' in those regulations (ie a person who is over compulsory school age and under 18 — see **4.6** below) was not intended to include a child. Children are provided for by separate legislation, namely the *Children and Young Persons Act 1933, s 18(1)* which had been amended to give effect to the *EC Young Workers Directive* and which provided, in relation to holidays, that during a school holiday a child must have two consecutive weeks without employment (see (k) above).

In *Bebbington v Palmer (t/a Sturry News)* (UKEAT/0371/09/DM) [2010] All ER (D) 47 (Sep) the EAT held that the reference in the *Children and Young Persons Act 1933, s 18* to the 'employment' of children does not mean that children who work are necessarily employed under a contract of service. The term 'employment' in *section 18* also includes children 'who are not employees in the strict sense of the word but are employed under contracts for services'. On the facts of that case, the claimant (a paper boy) was not an 'employee' and was therefore unable to claim unfair dismissal.

The *Education Act 1996, s 560* (replacing the *Education (Work Experience) Act 1973, s 1*) provides that, with certain exceptions, the enactments relating to the prohibition or regulation of the employment of a child in his last two years of compulsory schooling shall not apply where the employment is in pursuance of arrangements made or approved by the local authority, or by the governing body of a school on behalf of such an authority, with a view to providing him with work experience as a part of his education. However, the enactments regulating the employment of young persons apply to a child on a work experience programme (*Education Act 1996, s 560(4), (5)*). For the provisions relating to work experience for young persons, see **4.7** below.

4.3 Local authority powers

Local authorities are empowered under the *Children and Young Persons Acts 1933–1969* (as amended) to pass bye-laws restricting the employment of children. Among other matters, any such bye-laws may authorise:

(a) the employment on an occasional basis of children aged 13 years (notwithstanding anything in **4.2**(a) above) by their parents or guardians in light agricultural or horticultural work;

(b) the employment of children aged 13 years (notwithstanding anything in **4.2**(a) above) in categories of light work specified in the bye-law; and

(c) the employment of children for not more than one hour before the commencement of school hours on any day on which they are required to attend school (notwithstanding anything in **4.2**(c) above).

(*Children and Young Persons Act 1933, s 18(2), as amended.*)

An employer who breaches such a bye-law will be guilty of a criminal offence as will any person (other than the person employed) by whose act or default a contravention took place (*Children and Young Persons Act 1933, s 21*).

In *Portsea Island Mutual Co-operative Society Ltd v Leyland* [1978] IRLR 556, [1978] ICR 1195, the Divisional Court quashed the convictions recorded against the company under *CYPA 1934*, s 21. A milk roundsman, exceeding his authority and contrary to the company's instructions, had engaged a boy of 10 years of age to deliver milk on a Sunday before 9 am, contrary to the local authority's bye-laws. Talbot J held ([1978] IRLR 556 at 558) that an employer can be liable for such a contravention only if either he employed the child or if an agent of his who is engaged to take persons into his employment (eg a personnel manager) did so.

If it appears to a local authority that a child is being employed in such a manner as to be prejudicial to his health, or otherwise to render him unfit to obtain the full benefit of the education provided for him, the authority may serve a notice in writing on the employer: (a) prohibiting him from employing the child, or (b) imposing such restrictions upon his employment of the child as appear to be expedient in the child's interests (*Education Act 1996, s 559(1)*). A local authority may serve a notice in writing on the parent or employer of a child requiring the parent or employer to provide the authority, within such period as may be specified in the notice, with such information as appears to be necessary for enabling them to ascertain whether the child is being employed in such a manner as to render him unfit to obtain the full benefit of the education provided for him (*Education Act 1996, s 559(2)*). A person who (i) employs a child in contravention of any prohibition or restriction imposed under *s 559(1)*, or (ii) fails to comply with the requirements of a notice served under *s 559(2)*, is guilty of an offence and liable on summary conviction to a fine or imprisonment or both (*Education Act 1996, s 559(3), (4)*).

4.4   Other provisions

The other provisions are:

(a)   No child may be employed in any industrial undertaking unless the undertaking is one in which only members of the same family are employed (*Employment of Women, Young Persons and Children Act 1920, ss 1(1), 3(2)*).

(b)   No child may be employed in any sea-going United Kingdom ship (*Merchant Shipping Act 1995, s 55(1A)*, inserted by the *Merchant Shipping (Hours of Work) Regulations 2002 (SI 2002/2125)*).

(c)   Special provisions regulate the employment of children in entertainment (*Children and Young Persons Act 1933, ss 23–26* as amended by *EA 1989, Sch 3 Part III* and *SI 2000/1333*; A child shall not take part in a performance or otherwise take part in a sport, or work as a model for payment except under the authority of a licence granted by the local authority in whose area the child resides. (*Children and Young Persons Act 1963, ss 37, 39–42*). As from 13 May 2014 the power to grant licences was extended to children under 14. (*Children and Families Act 2014, s 90*)).

(d)   The *Management of Health and Safety at Work Regulations 1999 (SI 1999/3242)* also apply to the employment of children (see **4.5** below). In addition to its other obligations, every employer must, before employing a child, provide comprehensible and relevant information to the parents of (or those with parental responsibility for) the child on the outcome of the risk assessment detailed below, and on the control measures that the employer has introduced (*reg 10(2)*).

4.5 Children and Young Persons

4.5 EMPLOYMENT OF YOUNG PERSONS

Health and safety

In more recent years the emphasis on the regulation of the employment of young persons has shifted from restrictions on employment itself to ensuring adequate health and safety protection in employment (and regulating rest periods, breaks and night work — see **4.6** below). Thus the *Employment Act 1989, s 10(1)* repealed various enactments restricting the employment of young persons. In addition, the Secretary of State has power to repeal statutory provisions relating to the employment of persons or classes of persons who have not attained the age of 18 (or a specified lower age not less than 16); he may also amend such provisions so that they refer to school-leaving age rather than a specific age (*Employment Act 1989, s 10(3)(b), (c)*). But the exercise of those powers may not affect provisions relating to the employment of persons under school-leaving age (*Employment Act 1989, s 10(4)*). The powers given have so far been used to amend and revoke a number of statutory instruments (*Employment Act 1989 (Amendments and Revocations) Order 1989 (SI 1989/2311)*).

The *Health and Safety (Young Persons) Regulations 1997 (SI 1997/135)* ("the *1997 Regulations*") implemented the health and safety provisions of the *EC Directive on the Protection of Young People at Work (94/33)*. They were based on proposals set out in a consultative document published by the Health and Safety Commission in March 1996. The *1997 Regulations* amended the *Management of Health and Safety at Work Regulations 1992* ("the *1992 Regulations*"), extending the risk assessment and information requirements under the *1992 Regulations*, and removing outdated provisions relating to the health and safety of young persons.

Both the *1997 Regulations* and the *1992 Regulations* were then revoked and replaced by the *Management of Health and Safety at Work Regulations 1999 (SI 1999/3242)* ("the *1999 Regulations*"). The *1999 Regulations* incorporated the changes originally made by the *1997 Regulations*.

It is important to note that "young person" bears a different meaning in the *1999 Regulations* than under the *Education Act 1996*. Under the *1999 Regulations* 'young person' means any person under 18, so that it encompasses children and young persons as defined in the *Education Act 1996*.

The *1999 Regulations* do not apply to the master or crew of a ship (*reg 2*); for separate provisions governing the health and safety of young persons engaged as workers on United Kingdom ships, see the *Merchant Shipping and Fishing Vessels (Health and Safety at Work) (Employment of Young Persons) Regulations 1998 (SI 1998/2411)*. The last-named Regulations also prescribe rest periods for young persons so engaged: see **4.6** below.

Before young persons start work, the employer is required to assess the risks to their health and safety, taking particular account of:

(a)   their inexperience, their absence of awareness of existing or potential risks, and their immaturity;

(b)   the fitting-out and layout of the workplace and the workstation;

(c)   the nature, degree and duration of exposure to physical, biological and chemical agents;

(d)   the form, range and use of work equipment and the way in which it is handled;

(e)   the organisation of processes and activities;

(f)   the extent of the health and safety training provided or to be provided to young persons; and

(g)   risks from agents, processes and work listed in the Annex to *Directive 94/33* (referred to above).

(SI 1999/3242, Regulation 3(5))

In addition, every employer must ensure that young persons employed by him are protected at work from any risks to their health or safety which are a consequence of the factors referred to in (a) above *(reg 19(1))*. Furthermore, the employment of young persons is prohibited for work:

(i)   which is beyond their physical or psychological capacity;

(ii)   involving harmful exposure to agents which are toxic or carcinogenic, cause heritable genetic damage or harm to the unborn child, or which in any other way chronically affect human health;

(iii)   involving harmful exposure to radiation;

(iv)   involving the risk of accidents which it may reasonably be assumed cannot be recognised or avoided by young persons owing to their insufficient attention to safety or lack of experience or training; or

(v)   in which there is a risk to health from extreme cold or heat, noise or vibration.

In determining whether work will involve harm or risk for these purposes, the employer must have regard to the results of the assessment referred to above *(reg 19(2))*.

However, the prohibition in *reg 19(2)* does not apply in relation to a young person who is no longer a child where (1) the work is necessary for their training, (2) the young person will be supervised by a competent person, and (3) the risks are reduced to their lowest practicable level *(reg 19(3))*.

4.6   Rest periods, breaks and night work

Following the publication in February 1997 by the Department for Trade and Industry (DTI) of a consultation document to implement the provisions of *Directive 94/33* (see above) which cover night work, and entitlement to rest periods, for young persons, the DTI subsequently announced that it intended to implement those provisions by including them in the regulations for implementing the *EC Working Time Directive (93/104)*.

As detailed elsewhere in this work, *Directive 94/33* (see above) and the *EC Working Time Directive (93/104)* were implemented by the *Working Time Regulations 1998 (SI 1998/1833)*, which came into force on 1 October 1998. With regard to young persons (referred to in those *Regulations* as 'young workers'), *Directive 94/33* sets a limit on working time of eight hours per day and 40 hours per week, and prohibits night work altogether.

Certain provisions protecting young workers were added to existing special entitlements in the *1998 Regulations* which apply to young workers, are set out below:

(a)   a health and capacities assessment before being required to perform night work, and periodically thereafter *(reg 7(2))*;

(b)   a minimum daily continuous rest period of 12 hours *(reg 10(2))*;

(c)   two days off per week *(reg 11(3))*; and

(d)   a minimum 30-minute rest break where daily working time exceeds 4.5 hours *(reg 12(4))*.

Note that the protections and entitlements set out in (a) to (f) above are subject to the following exceptions.

Domestic servants. Regulations 5A, 6A, and *7(2)* do not apply in relation to a young worker employed as a domestic servant in a private household (*reg 19*, as amended).

Armed forces. Regulations 5A, 6A, 10(2) and *11(3)* do not apply in relation to a young worker serving as a member of the armed forces, although where such a young worker is accordingly required to work during the restricted period, or is not permitted the minimum rest period provided for in *reg 10(2)* or *11(3)*, he must be allowed an appropriate period of compensatory rest (*reg 25(2), (3)*, as amended).

Force majeure. Regulations 5A, 6A, 10(2) and *12(4)* do not apply in relation to a young worker where his employer requires him to undertake work which no adult worker is available to perform and which:

(i) is occasioned by either an occurrence due to unusual and unforeseeable circumstances, beyond the employer's control, or exceptional events, the consequences of which could not have been avoided despite the exercise of all due care by the employer;

(ii) is of a temporary nature; and

(iii) must be performed immediately.

Where the application of *regs 5A, 6A, 10(2)* or *12(4)* is excluded by virtue of (i) to (iii) above, and a young worker is accordingly required to work during a period which would otherwise be a rest period or rest break, his employer must allow him to take an equivalent period of compensatory rest within the following three weeks (*reg 27*, as amended).

Other restrictions applicable to young workers. Regulation 5A does not apply in relation to a young worker:

(1) where the young worker's employer requires him to undertake work which is necessary either to maintain continuity of service or production or to respond to a surge in demand for a service or product;

(2) where no adult worker is available to perform the work; and

(3) where performing the work would not adversely affect the young worker's education or training.

(*Regulation 27A(1)*, inserted by *SI 2002/3128*.)

In addition, in the circumstances referred to in (1) to (3) above:

(a) *reg 6A* does not apply in relation to a young worker employed:

(i) in a hospital or similar establishment; or

(ii) in connection with cultural, artistic, sporting or advertising activities; and

(b) *reg 6A* does not apply, except in so far as it prohibits work between midnight and 4am, in relation to a young worker employed in:

(i) agriculture;

(ii) retail trading;

(iii) postal or newspaper deliveries;

(iv) a catering business;

(v) a hotel, public house, restaurant, bar or similar establishment; or

(vi) a bakery.

(*Regulation 27A(2), (3)*, inserted by *SI 2002/3128*.)

Where the application of *reg 6A* is excluded by para (*a*) or (*b*) above, and a young worker is accordingly required to work during a period which would otherwise be a rest period or rest break:

(i)   he must be supervised by an adult worker where such supervision is necessary for the young worker's protection; and

(ii)   he must be allowed an equivalent period of compensatory rest.

(*Regulation 27A(4)*, inserted by *SI 2002/3128*.)

Remedies. Regulation 30 (as amended) provides that a young worker may complain to an employment tribunal where his employer has refused to permit him to exercise any right he has:

(1)   under *reg 10(2), 11(3)*, or *12(4)*; or

(2)   to compensatory rest under *reg 25(3), 27A(4)(b)* or *27(2)*.

The time limit for the presentation of such a complaint is three months beginning with the day on which it is alleged that the exercise of the right should have been permitted (or in the case of a rest period or leave extending over more than one day, the date on which it should have been permitted to begin). If the tribunal is satisfied that it was not reasonably practicable for the complaint to be presented within the period of three months (see **19.7** EMPLOYMENT TRIBUNALS – I), then this time may be extended.

Where the tribunal finds the complaint well-founded, it must make a declaration to that effect, and may make an award of compensation to be paid by the employer to the worker. The amount of the compensation will be such as the tribunal considers just and equitable in all the circumstances having regard to:

(a)   the employer's default in refusing to permit the worker to exercise his right; and

(b)   any loss sustained by the worker which is attributable to the matters complained of.

(For separate provisions governing rest periods for young persons engaged as workers on United Kingdom ships, see the *Merchant Shipping and Fishing Vessels (Health and Safety at Work) (Employment of Young Persons) Regulations 1998 (SI 1998/2411), reg 6*.)

4.7   WORK EXPERIENCE FOR YOUNG PERSONS AND OTHERS

The *Education Act 1996, s 560A* (as amended by the *Children and Families Act 2014*) provides that a local authority in England may secure the provision of work experience for persons in their area (a) who are over compulsory school age but under 19, or (b) who are aged 19 or over and for whom an Education and Health Care plan is maintained. A local authority in England must (i) encourage participation in work experience by persons in their area who are within (a) or (b) above and (ii) encourage employers to participate in the provision of work experience for such persons (*Education Act 1996, s 560A(2)*).

4.8 Children and Young Persons

4.8 TIME OFF FOR YOUNG PERSONS FOR STUDY OR TRAINING

England

Young persons in England have a duty to participate in education or training until the age of 18 (see *Education and Skills Act 2008 ("ESA 2008"), Part 1*, brought into force by the *Education and Skills Act 2008 (Commencement No 9 and Transitory Provision) Order 2013 (SI 2013/1204)*). This duty to participate in education or training applies to any person who is resident in England and who:

(a)   has ceased to be of compulsory school age;

(b)   has not reached the age of 18; and

(c)   has not attained a level 3 qualification.

   (*ESA 2008, section 1*).

Those in full-time occupation must participate in 'sufficient' relevant training or education. (*ESA 2008, s 2(1)*). A person is in full-time occupation if he works for at least 20 hours per week: (a) under a contract of employment; or (b) in any other way prescribed, otherwise than under a short-term contract or arrangement (*ESA 2008, s 5(1)*). The *Duty to Participate in Education or Training (Miscellaneous Provisions) Regulations 2013 (SI 2013/1205)* set out the definition of 'normal weekly working hours' and what is also to be treated as working for at least 20 hours. In addition, these regulations set out what constitutes: (i) a level 3 qualification, (ii) full time education (otherwise than at school) or training, (iii) the relevant period during which the duty applies, and (iv) further ways to calculate the requirement for 'sufficient' relevant training or education.

ESA 2008 also imposes corresponding duties on local education authorities and employers (from a date to be appointed) to enable and support participation in education and training. Enforcement provisions protecting employees from detriment or unfair dismissal for exercising (or proposing to exercise) a right to participate in education and training under *ESA 2008* are also yet to be appointed.

Scotland and Wales

The right for young persons in employment to take time off from work for study and training, by virtue of *ERA 1996, ss 63A–63C* (inserted by the *Teaching and Higher Education Act 1998, s 32*), which previously applied across Great Britain, now applies only to young persons in Scotland and Wales.

An employee in Scotland or Wales who:

(a)   is aged 16 or 17,

(b)   is not receiving full-time secondary or further education, and

(c)   has not attained the prescribed standard of achievement,

is entitled to be permitted by his employer to take time off during the employee's working hours in order to undertake study or training leading to a relevant qualification (*ERA 1996, s 63A(1)*). The study or training may be either on the premises of the employer (or principal – see below) or elsewhere (*ERA 1996, s 63A(7)*). For the 'prescribed standard of achievement', see the *Right to Time Off for Study or Training Regulations 2001 (SI 2001/2801)*, which revoked and replaced the *1999 Regulations (SI 1999/986)* with effect from 1 September 2001.

A 'relevant qualification' means an external qualification the attainment of which (i) would contribute to the attainment of the prescribed standard referred to in (c) above, or (ii) would be likely to enhance the employee's employment prospects, whether with his employer or otherwise (*ERA 1996, s 63A(2)(c)*). An 'external qualification' means an academic or vocational qualification awarded or authenticated by such person or body as may be specified in *Regulations* (as to which, see the *Schedule* to *SI 2001/2801* referred to above).

An employee who satisfies the requirements in (a) to (c) above, and is sub-contracted by his employer to another person ('the principal'), is entitled to be permitted by the principal to take time off for the purposes specified in *ERA 1996, s 63A(1 (ERA 1996, s 63A(3)*). An 18-year-old employee who is undertaking study or training leading to a relevant qualification which he began before attaining that age has a similar right to time off (*ERA 1996, s 63A(4)*).

The amount of time off that an employee is to be permitted to take, and the occasions on which and the conditions under which time off is to be taken, are those that are reasonable in the circumstances having regard, in particular, to (a) the requirements of the employee's study or training, and (b) the circumstances of the business of the employer (or the principal) and the effect of the employee's time off on the running of that business (*ERA 1996, s 63A(5)*).

An employee who is allowed time off is entitled to be paid for the time taken off at the 'appropriate hourly rate', ie one week's pay divided by the number of normal working hours in a week for that employee when employed under the contract of employment in force on the day when the time off is taken (*ERA 1996, s 63B(1), (2)*). (For the calculation of the normal hourly rate where the number of normal working hours differs from week to week or over a longer period, see *ERA 1996, s 63B(3), (4)*.)

Remedy for refusal of, or remuneration for, time off (Scotland and Wales)

If the employer (or principal) has unreasonably refused the employee time off or has refused to pay him, the employee may present a complaint to an employment tribunal (*ERA 1996, s 63C(1)*). The time limit for the presentation of such a complaint is three months beginning with the day on which it is alleged the time off should have been allowed (or, as the case may be, on which the time off was taken). If the tribunal is satisfied that it was not reasonably practicable for the complaint to be presented within the period of three months (see **19.7** EMPLOYMENT TRIBUNALS – I), then this time may be extended (*ERA 1996, s 63C(2)*).

If the employment tribunal finds the complaint well-founded, it will make a declaration to that effect (*ERA 1996, s 63C(3)*). If the complaint is of an unreasonable refusal to permit the employee to take time off, the tribunal will also order the employer or principal to pay the employee remuneration for the period during which the time off should have been allowed (*ERA 1996, s 63C(4)*). If the complaint is of a refusal to pay the employee for the time off, the tribunal will also order the employer or principal to pay the employee the amount due to him (*ERA 1996, s 63C(5)*).

4.9   Right not to suffer detriment

By virtue of *ERA 1996, s 47A* (inserted by the *Teaching and Higher Education Act 1998, s 44*), an employee who is entitled to (i) time off under *ERA 1996, s 63A(1)* or *63A(3)*, and (ii) remuneration under *ERA 1996, s 63B(1)* for that time off (see **4.8** above), has the right not to be subjected to a detriment (ie an action short of dismissal) by his employer or principal on the ground that the employee exercised (or proposed to exercise) that right or received (or sought to receive) such remuneration.

If the employee suffers such a detriment, the remedy is to complain to an employment tribunal pursuant to *ERA 1996, s 48*. (For details, see **29.10** HEALTH AND SAFETY AT WORK – II.)

Equivalent protection will be available to young persons in England when *s 47AA* comes into force. That provision will protect an employee with a right to be permitted to participate in education or training under *ss 27* or *28 ESA 2008* from suffering a detriment by reason of his or her attempt to exercise those rights.

4.10   Children and Young Persons

4.10   CONTRACTS OF EMPLOYMENT, AND MINORS

The general rule at common law is that a contract made by a minor is voidable by him at any point during his minority. One exception to that rule, which is significant for present purposes, is in respect of beneficial contracts of employment or apprenticeship. These contracts are binding on the minor.

A contract of service or apprenticeship which enables a minor to earn a living is likely to be upheld as binding on the minor on the basis that it is for his benefit (*Doyle v White City Stadium Ltd* [1935] 1 KB 110, 104 LJKB 140, CA); this principle was followed by analogy in *Chaplin v Leslie Frewin (Publishers) Ltd* [1966] Ch 71, [1965] 3 All ER 764, CA, which concerned a contract for the publication of a book; see also *Mills v Inland Revenue Commissioners* [1972] 3 All ER 977. *Doyle* and *Chaplin* were distinguished in *Proform Sports Management Ltd v Proactive Sports Management Ltd* [2006] EWHC 2812 (Ch), [2007] 1 All ER 542, which concerned a representation agreement with a professional footballer that had been entered into during his minority. Reference was also made to *Doyle* and *Chaplin* (albeit obiter) by Lady Hale in *Fisher v Brooker* [2009] UKHL 41, [2009] 4 All ER 789, in considering whether a minor can validly assign copyright by contract.

The effect of the entire contract must be considered; the contract will be upheld if on the whole it is for the minor's benefit (*Clements v London and North Western Rly Co* [1894] 2 QB 482, CA), but it will not be binding on the minor if it is not in his interests, or is clearly unreasonable or oppressive (*De Francesco v Barnum* (1890) 45 Ch D 430). Where a contract is, on the whole, for the minor's benefit, but it contains invalid covenants which are severable, such covenants may be struck out and the remainder of the contract upheld (see *Bromley v Smith* [1909] 2 KB 235, 78 LJKB 745).

The *Minors' Contracts Act 1987* made some limited amendments to the law relating to minors' contracts generally. In particular, it repealed the *Infants Relief Act 1874*, thereby enabling a minor, on or after reaching the age of majority, to ratify an otherwise unenforceable contract which he had entered into as a minor (*MCA 1987, s 1*).

5   Codes of Practice

Cross-references. See **10.4** DISCLOSURE OF INFORMATION for details of ACAS Code No 2 and **10.14** DISCLOSURE OF INFORMATION for the Codes of Practice in relation to Data Protection issued by the information Commissioner; **29.21** HEALTH AND SAFETY AT WORK – II for the HSC Code on Safety Representatives and Safety Committees; **50.2, 50.3** and **50.9** TIME OFF WORK for ACAS Code No 3 and the HSC Code on Time Off for Training of Safety Representatives.

5.1   The first Code of Practice (now revoked) was introduced under powers conferred by the *Industrial Relations Act 1971*. Since then a number of other Codes have been issued. Codes of Practice are written in clear terms for the layman in order to give practical guidance. Employers are advised to read the existing and any new Codes of Practice issued and to follow their provisions whenever applicable. Although following a Code of Practice does not guarantee success in any potential claim in an employment tribunal, the employer who can show that he has followed its provisions will be on firmer ground.

In broad terms, these Codes of Practice cannot be enforced by law. Nor does breach of a Code *of itself* give rise to any liability. However, Codes may be taken into account in legal proceedings. This chapter considers the powers which exist enabling specified bodies or people to issue Codes and the particular legal effect of the different Codes.

5.2   THE CODES OF PRACTICE ISSUED BY ACAS

Power to issue the Codes

ACAS is given statutory power to issue Codes of Practice, subject to approval by both Houses of Parliament. That power is now contained in the *Trade Union and Labour Relations (Consolidation) Act 1992* ('*TULR(C)A*'), *s 199*. Five such Codes (as amended) have been issued.

ACAS Code of Practice No 1 on Discipline and Grievance Procedures

The newest version of this Code was issued on 11 March 2015 by the *Code of Practice (Disciplinary and Grievance Procedures) Order 2015 (SI 2015/649)*. The revisions made to the previous version (which version came into force on 6 April 2009, replacing the previous 2004 revision of Code No 1) are, however, very limited and address only the EAT's decision in *Toal v GB Oils* [2013] IRLR 696 which had cast doubt on the previous version of the Code on the issue of whether an employer could reasonably object to the choice of a person to accompany an employee to a disciplinary or grievance hearing. The newest version of the Code continues to reflect the repeal of the statutory dispute resolution procedures by the *Employment Act 2008*. The Code, which comprises some 47 paragraphs, sets out practical guidance to employers, employees and representatives and lays down principles for the handling of disciplinary and grievance issues in the workplace. It should be noted that the Code does not apply to dismissals on grounds of redundancy. The excessive formalism of the statutory dispute resolution procedures is removed. A failure to follow the Code does not, of itself, give rise to automatic liability in any proceedings nor does it remove jurisdiction to hear the complaint from the employment tribunals. The employment tribunals are, however, obliged to take the Code into account and are empowered to adjust any award by up to 25% for an unreasonable failure to comply with any provision of the Code (see further **5.3** below).

In addition to the Code of Practice, ACAS has also published guidance dealing with disciplinary and grievance situations titled 'Discipline and Grievances at Work: The ACAS Guide'. Unlike the Code, employment tribunals are not expressly required to have regard to the ACAS guidance in reaching their decisions. In *McMillan v Airedale NHS Foundation Trust* [2014] EWCA Civ 1031, [2014] IRLR 803 the Court of Appeal observed, however, that whilst the guidance did not have the formal status of a code of practice, the guidance was "referred to in, and fills in the gaps in, the ACAS code of practice" and could, in that case, form part of the factual matrix for construing the relevant contractual disciplinary procedures.

ACAS Code of Practice No 2 on Disclosure of Information to Trade Unions for Collective Bargaining Purposes

This Code of Practice is in its third revision (2003) and sets out relatively short guidance in relation to the obligations to disclose information to trade unions for collective bargaining purposes pursuant to the provisions of *ss 181* and *182* of *TULR(C)A*. Under *TULR(C)A* information must be disclosed in accordance with good industrial relations practice and, in considering what is good industrial relations practice, regard is to be had to any relevant provisions of the Code. The provisions of the Code are to be taken into account in any proceedings before the Central Arbitration Committee (*TULR(C)A ss 181(2)(b)*, *181(4)* and *207(1)* and *(2)*). Paragraphs 4–12 of the Code provide guidance on the types of information to be disclosed and non-exhaustive examples of categories of information are set out in paragraph 11. Guidance on restrictions on the duty to disclose are provided in paragraphs 13–15 of the Code and the responsibilities of trade unions and employers are considered in paragraphs 16–21. Guidance on joint arrangements for disclosure of information are set out in paragraphs 22–23 of the Code.

ACAS Code of Practice No 3 on Time Off for Trade Union Duties and Activities. This Code of Practice has been revised with effect from 1 January 2010 by order of the Secretary of State (*Employment Protection Code of Practice (Time Off for Trade Union Duties and Activities) Order 2009 (SI 2009/3223)*). (See further TIME-OFF WORK **(50)**).

ACAS Code of Practice on Settlement Agreements (2013)

This, the fourth of the ACAS Codes, was introduced as a consequence of *s 14* of the *Enterprise and Regulatory Reform Act 2013* and the introduction of protected conversations between employers and employees about terms of settlement for the termination of employment (see *s 111A* of the *ERA 1996*). As in the case of the other Codes, it was made pursuant to *s 199* of *TULR(C)A 1992*, and was brought into force on 29 July 2013 by the *Employment Code of Practice (Settlements) Order 2013 (SI 2013/1665)*.

Acas Code of Practice on Handling in a Reasonable Manner Requests to Work Flexibly (2014)

This, the fifth and newest of the ACAS Codes was introduced with effect from 30 June 2014 following implementation of the changes made by the *Children and Families Act 2014* in relation to such requests. Again, it was made pursuant to *s 199* of *TULR(C)A 1992*, and was brought into force by the *Code of Practice (Handling in a Reasonable Manner Requests to Work Flexibly) Order 2014 (SI 2014/1665)*.

As each of the first three Codes has during their history been the subject of substantial revision, in all cases the most up-to-date versions of the Codes should always be consulted. Each of the ACAS Codes is available for download from the ACAS website (www.acas.org.uk).

Where ACAS proposes to issue a Code, or a revised Code, it must first publish a draft and consider any representations made to it. If ACAS decides to proceed, the draft (modified if need be) is transmitted to the Secretary of State, who may either approve it or publish his reasons for withholding approval. If the Secretary of State approves the draft, it is laid before Parliament (*TULR(C)A 1992, ss 200, 201*).

5.3   **Legal effect**

TULR(C)A 1992, s 207(1), (2) states that breach of the ACAS Codes does not render a person liable to proceedings. However, in any proceedings before an employment tribunal or the Central Arbitration Committee ('CAC'), any Code of Practice issued by ACAS is admissible in evidence and any provision of the Code which appears to the employment tribunal or the CAC to be relevant to any question arising in the proceedings must be taken into account in determining that question. It had long been established that non-compliance with a Code would not necessarily render a dismissal unfair, but 'a failure to follow a procedure prescribed in the Code may lead to the conclusion that a dismissal was unfair, which, if that procedure had been followed, would have been held to have been fair' (*W Devis & Sons Ltd v Atkins* [1977] AC 931 at 955). As a consequence of the amendments made by the *Employment Act 2008* (*s 3(1), (2)*) and the repeal of the statutory dispute resolution procedures, *s 207A* was added to TULR(C)A 1992 with effect from 6 April 2009 whereby an employment tribunal is empowered, in cases where it is satisfied that there was unreasonable failure to comply with the requirements of a relevant Code of Practice (that is to say Code of Practice No 1 as promulgated after 6 April 2009 and as revised from 11 March 2015), to reduce or increase the award by up to 25% (*TULR(C)A 1992, s 207A(2), (3)* and *(4)*). For s 207A to have application in a grievance procedures case the relevant grievance must be raised in writing (*Cadogan Hotel Partners v Ozog* (UKEAT/0001/14)).

5.4   **CODES ISSUED BY THE SECRETARY OF STATE RELATING TO INDUSTRIAL ACTION**

Power to issue the Codes

TULR(C)A 1992, ss 203 and *204* empower the Secretary of State to issue Codes of Practice, after consultation with ACAS, to be approved by both Houses of Parliament. Such Codes are to contain practical guidance for the purposes of promoting the improvement of industrial relations or promoting desirable practices in relation to the conduct by trade unions of ballots and elections. The Codes currently applicable are The Code on Picketing (2017 reissue), the Code of Practice on Industrial Action Ballots and Notice to Employers (2017 reissue) and the Code of Practice on Access and Unfair Practices During Recognition and Derecognition Ballots (2005). The Code on Picketing is a reissued and revised version of the previous Code (see *Employment Code of Practice (Picketing) Order 1992 (SI 1992/476)*). It came into force on 1 March 2017 and takes into account the amendments to relevant statutory provisions made by the Trade Union Act 2016. The revised Code was brought into effect by *The Code of Practice Picketing Order 2017 (SI 2017/237)*. The Code of Practice on Industrial Action Ballots and Notice to Employers also came into force on 1 March 2017 and similarly incorporates the relevant amendments made by the *Trade Union Act 2016*. That Code was brought into effect by *The Code of Practice (Industrial Action Ballots and Notice to Employers) Order 2017 (SI 2017/233)*. The other Code of Practice on Access and Unfair Practices During Recognition and Derecognition Ballots (2005) was laid before Parliament on 18 July 2005 and came into force on 1 October 2005. The 2005 Code incorporates changes made by the *Employment Relations Act 2004* (see Trade Unions – I, II (51, 52)) as well as updating and revising the earlier Codes but, to date, has not been revised in 2017.

The Department of Trade and Industry Codes may supersede any part of or all of a Code issued by ACAS or a previous DTI or Department of Employment Code (*TULR(C)A 1992, s 208(2)*) (see above).

5.5 Codes of Practice

5.5 Legal effect

Although a failure to comply with the Codes issued by the Secretary of State does not itself render a person liable to proceedings, the Codes are stated to be admissible in evidence and to be taken into account, if relevant, in any proceedings not only before an employment tribunal or the CAC but also, in the case of a DTI or Department for Education and Employment Code, in any court (*TULR(C)A 1992, s 207(1), (3)*). Thus, in *Thomas v National Union of Mineworkers (South Wales Area)* [1986] Ch 20, [1985] ICR 886, [1985] IRLR 136 at 920–921 Scott J granted an injunction, following violent picketing, to restrain the union from organising pickets in greater numbers than were suggested by the relevant Code.

5.6 CODES ISSUED BY THE BORDER AND IMMIGRATION AGENCY

The Border and Immigration Agency has issued two relevant Codes of Practice: the Border & Immigration Agency Code of Practice: Civil Penalties for Employers (2008) and the Border & Immigration Agency Code of Practice: Guidance for Employers for the Avoidance of Unlawful Discrimination in Employment Practice while Seeking to Prevent Illegal Working (2008). The Codes are made under the authority of *s 19* and *s 23* of the *Immigration, Asylum and Nationality Act 2006* and came into force on 29 February 2008.

The Civil Penalties Code gives guidance on the assessment of penalties in the event of employing illegal migrant workers and the factors taken into account in that assessment. The Code must be taken into account by the courts and may be used in legal proceedings.

The Guidance for Employers for the Avoidance of Unlawful Discrimination in Employment Practice while Seeking to Prevent Illegal Working Code provides guidance to employers on how to avoid a civil penalty for employing an illegal migrant worker in a way which does not result in unlawful race discrimination (paragraph 1). As a statutory code its provisions are admissible in evidence and must be taken into account in any relevant proceedings in the courts and in the employment tribunal. The Code seeks to summarise the relevant provisions prohibiting race discrimination and the responsibilities of an employer under *ss 15* and *21* of the *Immigration, Asylum and Nationality Act 2006* ("the *Act*") and provides short guidance in paragraphs 8.1–8.8 on avoiding race discrimination whilst complying with the responsibilities imposed by the Act.

5.7 THE POSITION PRIOR TO THE EQUALITY ACT 2010: (1) CODES RELATING TO RACIAL EQUALITY

History of the Codes

The *Race Relations Act 1976, s 47* empowered the Commission for Racial Equality to issue Codes of Practice containing practical guidance for either or both of the following purposes:

(a)   the elimination of discrimination in the field of employment; and

(b)   the promotion of equality of opportunity in that field between persons of different racial groups.

The first Code of Practice was issued in April 1984 by the Commission for Racial Equality ('CRE') and new Code of Practice on Racial Equality in Employment (2005) was issued in April 2006. This Code of Practice continues to apply to matters occurring before the coming into force of the relevant provisions of the *Equality Act 2010* on 1 October 2010.

The CRE had also published a Code of Practice on the Duty to Promote Racial Equality (in force from May 2002) as a consequence of the duty imposed by the *Race Relations (Amendment) Act 2000* on public bodies to promote racial equality (see DISCRIMINATION AND EQUAL OPPORTUNITIES – I (11), II(12), III (13)). This Code of Practice continues to apply to matters occurring before the coming into force of the relevant provisions of the *Equality Act 2010* on 1 October 2010.

5.8   Legal effect

The *Race Relations Act 1976, s 47(10)* (now repealed) provided that a failure to observe any provision in a Code of Practice shall not of itself render a person liable to proceedings. However, such Codes were admissible in evidence and, where relevant, were to be taken into account in any proceedings before an employment tribunal. See now, for matters occurring before 1 October 2010, *section 15(4)(b)* of the *Equality Act 2006* which maintains the admissibility of such Codes in evidence and provides that, where relevant, they be taken into account in determining any question arising in any such proceedings.

5.9   THE POSITION PRIOR TO THE EQUALITY ACT 2010: (2) CODES ISSUED BY THE EQUAL OPPORTUNITIES COMMISSION

History of the Codes relating to sex discrimination and equal pay

The *Sex Discrimination Act 1975, s 56A* empowered the Equal Opportunities Commission to issue Codes of Practice containing practical guidance for either or both of the following purposes:

(a)   the elimination of discrimination in the field of employment; and

(b)   the promotion of equality of opportunity in that field between men and women.

The Equal Opportunities Commission issued a Code of Practice which came into force on 30 April 1985. (See DISCRIMINATION AND EQUAL OPPORTUNITIES – I (11), II (12), III (13).)

A new Code of Practice on Equal Pay was introduced on 1 December 2003 by the *Code of Practice on Equal Pay Order 2003 (SI 2003/2865)*. This Code was admissible in evidence in any proceedings under the *SDA 1975* or the *Equal Pay Act 1970* (see **5.10** below) and included information on equal pay for pregnant women and those on maternity leave, the Equal Pay Questionnaire procedure and equal pay reviews and grievance procedures (see EQUAL PAY (23)). The Equal Opportunities Commission also issued the Gender Equality Duty Code of Practice (2007) in force from 6 April 2007 pursuant to *s 76E(1)* of the *SDA 1975*.

The Equal Opportunities Commission (along with the CRE and the Disability Rights Commission) was replaced with effect from 1 October 2007 by the Equality and Human Rights Commission established under the *Equality Act 2006*. The Codes of Practice relating to sex discrimination and equal pay continue to apply to matters occurring before the coming into force of the relevant provisions of the *Equality Act 2010* on 1 October 2010.

5.10   Legal effect

The *Sex Discrimination Act 1975, s 56A* (as amended by *TURERA 1993, Sch 7 para 15* and as modified by *SDA 1975, s 76E(3)*) provided that a failure to observe any provision in a Code of Practice shall not of itself render a person liable to proceedings. However, such Codes were admissible in evidence and, where relevant, were to be taken into account in any proceedings before an employment tribunal under that *Act* or the *Equal Pay Act 1970*.

5.10   Codes of Practice

See now, for matters occurring before 1 October 2010, *section 15(4)(b)* of the *Equality Act 2006* which maintains the admissibility of such Codes in evidence and provides that, where relevant, they be taken into account in determining any question arising in any such proceedings.

THE POSITION PRIOR TO THE EQUALITY ACT 2010: CODES RELATING TO DISABILITY

5.11   History of the Disability Codes

The *Disability Discrimination Act 1995, s 53* empowered the Secretary of State to issue Codes of Practice containing such practical guidance as he considers appropriate with a view to:

(a)   eliminating discrimination in the field of employment against disabled persons and persons who have had a disability; and

(b)   encouraging good practice in relation to the employment of disabled persons and persons who have had a disability.

The Disability Rights Commission Code of Practice on Employment and Occupation was promulgated under powers conferred by *s 53A* of the *Disability Discrimination Act 1995*.

The Disability Rights Commission (along with the CRE and the Equal Opportunities Commission) was replaced with effect from 1 October 2007 by the Equality and Human Rights Commission established under the *Equality Act 2006*. The Codes of Practice relating to disability continue to apply to matters occurring before the coming into force of the relevant provisions of the *Equality Act 2010* on 1 October 2010.

5.12   Legal effect

A failure on the part of any person to observe any provision of a Code of Practice did not of itself make that person liable to any proceedings. However, such a Code was admissible in evidence in any proceedings under the *DDA 1995* before an employment tribunal, a county court or a sheriff court and, where relevant, was to be taken into account in determining any question arising in any such proceedings (*DDA 1995, s 53A(8)* and *(8A)* (now repealed). For matters occurring before 1 October 2010, *s 15(4)(b)* of the *Equality Act 2006* applies, maintaining the admissibility of such Codes in evidence and provides that, where relevant, they be taken into account in determining any question arising in any such proceedings under the *DDA*.

5.13   GUIDANCE ON DISABILITY

In relation to the definition of disability, the Secretary of State, pursuant to *s 6(5)* of the *Equality Act 2010* and the *Equality Act 2010 (Guidance on the Definition of Disability) Appointed Day Order 2011 (SI 2011/1159)*, produced "Guidance On Matters to be Taken Into Account In Determining Questions Relating to the Definition of Disability (2011)" which came into force on 1 May 2011. The guidance does not impose legal obligations in itself but by *Schedule 1, Paragraph 12* to the *Equality Act 2010* the guidance must be taken into account by an adjudicating body on the issue whether a person is disabled.

5.14   THE EQUALITY ACT 2010: CODES OF PRACTICE ON EMPLOYMENT AND EQUAL PAY

The *Equality Act 2010* received Royal Assent (on 8 April 2010) and the major provisions relating to employment law were brought into force with effect from 1 October 2010. The Equality and Human Rights Commission consulted during 2010 on draft Codes of Practice, the purpose of which are to offer statutory guidance on the *Equality Act's* employment and equal pay implications.

With effect from 6 April 2011 the Codes of Practice under the previous legislation, considered in outline above, were revoked by *The Former Equality Commissions' Codes of Practice (Employment, Equal Pay, and Rights of Access for Disabled Persons) (Revocation) Order 2011 (SI 2011/776)* ("the *Revocation Order*"). By the *Revocation Order* each of the following Codes or Practice are revoked: the Code of Practice for the elimination of discrimination on the grounds of sex and marriage and the promotion of equality of opportunity in employment, issued by the former Equal Opportunities Commission under *section 56A* of the *Sex Discrimination Act 1975*, which came into effect on 30 April 1985 (*SI 1985/387*); the Code of Practice on Equal Pay, also issued by the former Equal Opportunities Commission under *section 56A* of the *Sex Discrimination Act 1975*, which came into effect on 1 December 2003 (*SI 2003/2865*); the Disability Discrimination Act 1995 Code of Practice on Employment and Occupation, issued by the former Disability Rights Commission under *section 53A* of the *Disability Discrimination Act 1995*, which came into effect on 1 October 2004 (*SI 2004/2302*); the revised Code of Practice on Racial Equality in Employment, issued by the former Commission for Racial Equality under *section 47* of the *Race Relations Act 1976*, which came into effect on 6 April 2006 (*SI 2006/630*); and the Disability Discrimination Act 1995 Code of Practice on Rights of Access: services to the public, public authority functions, private clubs and premises, issued by the former Disability Rights Commission under *section 53A* of the *Disability Discrimination Act 1995*, which came into effect on 4 December 2006 (*SI 2006/1967*).

The *Revocation Order* contains, in *art 3*, transitional provisions in relation to matters occurring, inter alia, prior to 1 October 2010. In any cases progressing through the employment tribunals relating to matters occurring prior to that date the previous various Codes of Practice considered above will remain relevant and applicable. In transitional cases the former Codes are to continue to have effect in relation to such proceedings for the purposes of *section 15(4)(b)* of the *Equality Act 2006*, which requires a court or tribunal to take a code into account in any case in which it appears to the court or tribunal to be relevant.

For matters occurring on or after 1 October 2010 the relevant Codes of Practice in the employment field will be the Equality Act 2010 Code of Practice on Employment and the Equality Act 2010 Code of Practice on Equal Pay. An additional new Code of Practice, the Equality Act 2010 Code of Practice on Services, Public Functions and Associations is outside the scope of this work. Each of the new codes are issued under *section 14(1)* of the *Equality Act 2006* (as amended by the *Equality Act 2010*) and are brought into force by the *Equality Act 2010 Codes of Practice (Services, Public Functions and Associations, Employment and Equal Pay) Order 2011 (SI 2011/857)*.

The Equality Act 2010 Code of Practice on Employment

The Code on Employment deals with all equalities issues in employment other than equal pay (see below). The Code is substantial, totalling over 300 pages. As previously, by *section 15(4)(b)* of the *Equality Act 2006*, the courts and employment tribunals are obliged to take the new Code into account in any relevant case.

The Code is divided into two parts. The scheme of Part One of the Code, which is divided into Chapters 2–15, is to summarise the law relating to the various protected characteristics (Chapter 2), and then direct and indirect discrimination (Chapters 3 and 4). Disability discrimination has two separate chapters (Chapters 5 and 6) and harassment, pregnancy and victimisation are also considered separately (Chapters 7, 8 and 9 respectively). The summary of the obligations under the Act is set out in Chapter 10 and work relationships other than employment are considered in Chapter 11. Positive action is addressed in Chapter 12. Thereafter occupational requirements (Chapter 13), pay and benefits (Chapter 14) and enforcement (Chapter 15) are summarised.

5.14 Codes of Practice

Part Two of the Code (beginning at page 218) provides guidance on avoiding discrimination in recruitment (Chapter 16) and in employment (Chapter 17). Guidance on the content of equalities policies is found in Chapter 18 and Chapter 19 deals with guidance on termination of employment. The Code concludes (beginning at page 294) with three appendices on the Meaning of Disability (Appendix 1), Monitoring (Appendix 2) and Making Reasonable Adjustments to Work Premises – Legal Considerations (Appendix 3). The Code may be found at https://www.equalityhumanrights.com/en/advice-and -guidance/equality-act codes-practice.

The Equality Act 2010 Code of Practice on Equal Pay

The Code of Practice on Equal Pay totals 62 pages. As previously the courts and employment tribunals are obliged to take the Code into account to the extent relevant in any equal pay case. (See paragraph 116 of the Code and *section 15(4)(b)* of the *Equality Act 2006*). The order of the Code is to, first, summarise the existing law relating to equal pay (paragraphs 22–91 of the Code). The provisions in relation to pregnancy, maternity and equal pay are summarised at paragraphs 92–101 with various examples. The new pay transparency provisions prohibiting secrecy are summarised at paragraphs 102-110. Thereafter the questionnaire procedure, burden of proof, employment tribunal procedure and awards are summarised (see paragraphs 111–157 of the Code). The second part of the Code (beginning at page 49) is a good practice guide headed "Good Equal Pay Practice" (see paragraphs 158–185 of the Code). The Code may be found at https ://www.equalityhumanrights.com/en/advice-and-guidance/equality-act-codes-practice.

5.15 CODES ISSUED BY THE HEALTH AND SAFETY EXECUTIVE

Power to issue the Codes

Regulations made under the *Health and Safety at Work, etc Act 1974 ('HSWA 1974')* are sometimes supplemented by Codes of Practice approved and/or issued by the Health and Safety Commission (for details of which see **28.28** HEALTH AND SAFETY AT WORK – I) (*HSWA 1974, s 16*). A full consideration of these codes is beyond the scope of this book. Two such codes are directly relevant to employment law: the HSE Code of Practice on Safety Representatives and Safety Committees and the HSE Code of Practice on Time Off for Training Safety Representatives. They both supplement the *Safety Representatives and Safety Committees Regulations 1977 (SI 1977/500)* as amended by *SI 1992/2051*, made under *HSWA 1974*.

5.16 Legal effect

Non-compliance with a relevant HSE Code does not of itself render a person liable to any civil or criminal proceedings. However, where in any criminal proceedings a person is alleged to have committed an offence by contravening a provision for which a code of practice was in force, if breach of the Code is established, the offence is proved unless the court is satisfied that the requirement or prohibition was complied with otherwise than by observance of the Code (*HSWA 1974, s 17*).

5.17 CODES ISSUED BY THE INFORMATION COMMISSIONER

The Information Commissioner issued the Employment Practices Data Protection Code in four parts: Part 1: Recruitment and Selection: March 2002; Part 2: Employment Records: August 2002; Part 3: Monitoring at Work: June 2003; Part 4: Information about Workers Health: December 2005. The Code in consolidated form (November 2011) may be obtained from https://ico.org.uk/media/for-organisations/documents/1064/the_employment _practices_code.pdf. The Code is issued pursuant to statutory authority conferred on the Information Commissioner by *s 51(3)(b)* of the *Data Protection Act 1998*. The Codes promulgated by the Information Commissioner do not have formal legal status or effect unlike the other codes of practice considered above. The Information Commissioner is, however, the enforcing authority for the purposes of the *Data Protection Act 1998* and the Code may reasonably be assumed to represent the views of the Information Commissioner in relation to the standards of practice to be expected of employers in relation to the subject matters covered by the Code. In addition to the Code, the Information Commissioner has also published guidance in relation to the Code: 'Employment Practices Code: Supplementary Guidance'. This too may be downloaded from the Information Commissioner's website (see https://ico.org.uk/media/for-organisations/documents/1066/employment_practice_code _supplementary_guidance.pdf).

The Information Commissioner has been seeking consultation responses on a new Code of Practice concerning the right of individuals to make a subject access request under *s 7* of the *Data Protection Act 1998*. This is likely to be significant to employers who are frequently faced with subject access requests prior to or contemporaneous with the commencement of litigation by employees. In summary the draft Code provide some practical guidance including best practice recommendations on staff training, having a subject access request policy and responding to subject access requests on a centralised basis. It is noteworthy that the code does not require data controllers to suspend routine data destruction policies (even after a subject access request is made) and recognises that staff may legitimately hold personal data on personal devices or email accounts and staff are not required under the code to search such data sources unless there is good reason to believe relevant personal data is held. If archived sources are known to differ from current sources of data then they should be searched but there is no obligation to search archives if there is evidence that the material is the same. Furthermore, data controllers are not to be required to use complicated methods of recovering deleted data if the data has been deleted in accordance with normal data retention and deletion policies.

5.18   REVISION AND REVOCATION OF CODES

Provision has been made for the revision by the appropriate authority of those codes which are issued under *TULR(C)A 1992, s 203* (ie the Secretary of State and BIS for the DTI Codes; see **5.4** above) or which are issued under *TULR(C)A 1992, s 199* (ie the ACAS Codes; see **5.2** above). ACAS may revise its codes under *TULR(C)A 1992, s 201* and the Secretary of State may revise the DTI (now BIS) codes under *TULR(C)A 1992, s 205*. Similar procedural provisions apply as in the case of making new codes. The Secretary of State may, with Parliamentary approval, revoke either an ACAS or a DTI/BIS Employment Code (*TULR(C)A 1992, ss 202, 206*). In the case of an ACAS Code, he may do so only at the request of ACAS.

6   Collective Agreements

6.1   INTRODUCTION TO COLLECTIVE AGREEMENTS

The practice of collective bargaining, by which wage rates and terms and conditions of employment of workers are determined by negotiations between employers and trade unions, leading to collective agreements, is still relatively common in traditional heavy industries and most of the public sector, although its importance in the economy as a whole has declined as the incidence of union recognition has fallen over the last 30 years. National bargaining between trade unions and employer representatives is still relatively widespread in the public sector, although there has for some years been considerable pressure from central Government to move to separate bargaining at regional level or for separate business units of large public sector employers. In some industries in the private sector also, negotiations between representatives of associations of employers and the recognised trade unions at national level lead to collective agreements which in practice set norms for the industry or sector concerned, although since the 1980s there has not been any statutory mechanism enabling workers within the sector to enforce the terms agreed collectively against a particular employer. This is in contrast to the practice which prevails widely in some other member states of the EU, and which is reflected in the provisions found in EU Directives permitting the domestic implementation of obligations introduced by the Directive by way of collective agreement as an alternative to legislation.

Under the British system, collective agreements are generally not legally enforceable between the collective parties (employers and unions); however, they may form the basis for the individual worker's contract of employment if it is agreed between the collective parties that they should do so. Whether a collective agreement, or a particular provision of the agreement, is in fact incorporated into the contract of a particular worker, however, is a matter of the construction and application of the express or implied terms of the contract between the worker and his or her employer, and not an automatic consequence of the stated intentions of the collective parties: see further **6.7** below.

6.2   DEFINITION

For the purposes of the *Trade Union and Labour Relations (Consolidation) Act 1992* ('*TULR(C)A 1992*'), a collective agreement is defined in *s 178* as 'any arrangement or agreement made by or on behalf of one or more trade unions and one or more employers or employers' associations' which relates to one or more of the following matters:

(*a*)   terms and conditions of employment, or the physical conditions in which any workers are required to work;

(*b*)   engagement or non–engagement, or termination or suspension of employment or the duties of employment, of one or more workers;

(*c*)   allocation of work or the duties of employment between workers or groups of workers;

(*d*)   matters of discipline;

(*e*)   a worker's membership or non-membership of a trade union;

(*f*)   facilities for officials of trade unions; and

(*g*)   facilities for negotiation or consultation, and other procedures, relating to any of the above matters, including the recognition by employers or employers' associations of the right of a trade union to represent workers in such negotiation or consultation or in the carrying out of such procedures.

This list of the possible subject matter for collective agreements does not mean that agreements must necessarily cover all of the listed areas. Employers are free (subject to the statutory procedure in *TULR(C)A 1992, Sch A1* for trade unions to obtain recognition) to agree to confer negotiating rights on a trade union to whatever more limited extent they may wish, as well as to define the categories of employees for whom the union is to be recognised, and similarly to make agreements covering only limited and specific aspects of the matters potentially within the scope of a collective agreement. This is a central feature of the voluntarist approach to the role of trade unions which has characterised British employment law for most of the post-war era. However, an employer may also seek to make a collective agreement covering a very limited range of issues with a union that is not independent of employer influence, in order to block an attempt by an independent union to obtain recognition; for the potential consequences of such a situation see *R (Boots Management Services Ltd) v Central Arbitration Committee* [2014] IRLR 887, EAT, and the subsequent litigation pursued by the Pharmacists' Defence Association Union unsuccessfully challenging the recognition of a non-independent union on human rights grounds: *Pharmacists' Defence Association Union v Boots Management Services Ltd* [2017] EWCA Civ 66, [2017] IRLR 355.

6.3   LEGAL STATUS

It was established in the landmark case of *Ford Motor Co v AUEW* [1969] 2 QB 303 that collective agreements are not, at common law, generally legally enforceable between the parties to them. The basis for this conclusion was that it was not the intention of the parties to create legal relations, a necessary ingredient of any contractually binding agreement. This has remained the position since, save for the period during which the *Industrial Relations Act 1971* was in force; this reversed the presumption established in the *Ford* case, replacing it with a presumption that any collective agreement was intended by the parties thereto to be legally enforceable, unless the contrary was stated. During the period the *Act* was in force (1 December 1971 to 16 September 1974) the practice of collective parties in the vast majority of cases was to insert a clause in any agreement stating 'this is not a legally enforceable agreement' (known as a 'TINALEA' clause).

6.4   Following the repeal of the *Industrial Relations Act 1971*, the position at common law was restored by statute (the *Trade Union and Labour Relations Act 1974, s 18*, now consolidated in *TULR(C)A 1992, s 179(3)*). By virtue of *s 179(3)*, any collective agreement made before 1 December 1971, or after 16 September 1974, will be conclusively presumed not to have been intended by the parties to the agreement to be a legally enforceable contract unless the agreement:

(a)   is in writing, and

(b)   contains a provision which (however expressed) states that the parties intend that the agreement shall be a legally enforceable contract,

in which event it is conclusively presumed to be intended to be legally enforceable. Despite including the phrase "however expressed", condition (*b*) may not be satisfied by a mere statement in the agreement that the parties are to be bound by it (*National Coal Board v National Union of Mineworkers* [1986] ICR 736, [1986] IRLR 439). It is possible for an agreement to state that the parties intend a particular part of it to be legally enforceable, in which case the presumption against enforceability would apply to the rest. The position for any agreement made during the currency of the *1971 Act* remains that there is a presumption that the parties intended the agreement to be legally enforceable, unless (as is usually the case for such agreements made during that period as remain in force) the contrary is stated within the agreement. It should be noted that the fact that the parties intend (or are presumed to intend) their agreement to be legally enforceable does not automatically mean that everything in it is enforceable; particular terms of an agreement may still not be enforceable, for instance for reasons of public policy, or because the language used is not sufficiently clear to be given effect.

Where an employer is required to recognise a trade union in accordance with the provisions of *TULR(C)A 1992, Sch A1* (see Trade Unions – I (51)), and the method of collective bargaining is specified by the Central Arbitration Committee under *paras 30* and *31* of *Sch A1*, any agreement reached through collective bargaining will have effect as a legally enforceable contract made between the parties; this will also be the case if the parties agree an alternative procedure for collective bargaining to that specified by the CAC. However, the only remedy for breach of any such agreement is an order for specific performance (*TULR(C)A 1992, Sch A1, para 31(6)*). It should be noted that the specified method that may be imposed under TULR(C)A Sch A1 covers only collective bargaining about pay, hours and holidays, not the wider range of issues within *s 178*: see *British Airline Pilots Association v Jet2.com Ltd* [2015] EWHC 1110 (QB), [2015] IRLR 543. However, the Court of Appeal, in an appeal by the union in that case, held that this was not limited to negotiations about proposals which if adopted would become part of the employees' contracts; it was sufficient that the proposals related to matters of pay, hours or holidays. Accordingly, the union, representing airline pilots, was entitled to negotiate on issues of rostering and crewing arrangements for the employer's flight crew: *British Airline Pilots Association v Jet2.com Ltd* [2017] EWCA Civ 20, [2017] IRLR 233.

6.5 INCORPORATION INTO INDIVIDUAL CONTRACTS OF EMPLOYMENT

Although the great majority of collective agreements are not legally enforceable by the union against the employer or vice versa, they may, and in most cases in practice do, have legally binding consequences as between the employer and the individual employee. Their terms may be incorporated into individual contracts of employment either because the contract expressly provides for such incorporation, or because incorporation is an implied term of the contract deriving from custom and practice in the industry. In either case, the collective agreement will be incorporated, notwithstanding that the particular employee may not approve of what the union has negotiated, or may even have ceased to belong to the relevant union (see, eg *Tocher v General Motors Scotland Ltd* [1981] IRLR 55, EAT). On the other hand, a collective agreement will not be incorporated into individual contracts of employment merely because the employer belongs to the association which negotiated that agreement (*Hamilton v Futura Floors Ltd* [1990] IRLR 478, Ct of Sess, OH).

It does not matter that the agreement is as between the parties to it not legally enforceable, since it is the terms as incorporated into the individual employee's contract that fall to be enforced, and the contract of employment will very rarely not be legally enforceable. Thus, for example, in *Marley v Forward Trust Group Ltd* [1986] ICR 891, [1986] IRLR 369, the Court of Appeal held that an employee could enforce the terms of a collective agreement on redundancy which was incorporated into his contract, even though the agreement itself was expressed to be 'binding in honour only'.

It may even be possible for the union concerned to rely on the *Contracts (Rights of Third Parties) Act 1999* to enforce the terms of a collective agreement not directly enforceable between it and the employer, but which has been incorporated into the individual contracts of the employees it represents. This was the case in *Cavanagh v Secretary of State for Work and Pensions* [2016] EWHC 1136 (QB), [2016] IRLR 591, [2016] ICR 826, where the issue was the check off (the deduction by the employer from employees' pay of trade union subscriptions, which are then paid over to the union). In this case the union was a third party to the individual contracts of employment into which (as the court held) the check off had been incorporated, but the term was clearly intended to benefit the union by ensuring the regular receipt of subscriptions. The equivalent legislation in Scotland is the *Contract (Third Party Rights) (Scotland) Act 2017*.

6.6 The basis for the incorporation of terms of a collective agreement into an individual contract of employment is usually that the contract of employment expressly states that this is to be the case, often in terms covering not only agreements current at the time of the making of the contract, but also future agreements. Incorporation by implication as a matter of custom and practice is most likely to be established by evidence in those industries and sectors of the economy where traditions of collective bargaining are most strongly established and there is a long practice of the benefits of collective agreements being observed by the employer; it is a matter of evidence in each case whether the practice of applying collectively agreed terms is sufficiently 'reasonable, certain and notorious' to be regarded as custom and practice, or whether the term relied on has been sufficiently consistently applied by the employer to be incorporated by implication. See further as to the application of custom and practice as a source of terms of the contract of employment [6.11] below.

A further, but in practice less common, way for collectively negotiated terms to be contractually enforceable by individual employees is where the union acts as agent for the employees in negotiating the terms, typically for a specific group of employees who have engaged the union to negotiate on their behalf. An example of this process is *Edwards v Skyways Ltd* [1964] 1 WLR 349.

6.7 Even where there is an express incorporation of collective agreements into individual contracts of employment, it does not follow that all provisions of the agreements between the employer and the relevant union or unions will be incorporated. Whether a particular provision will be held by the courts to be incorporated depends on whether it is considered 'apt' for incorporation. Terms specifying rates of pay, hours of work or entitlements to benefits will readily be held to be apt for incorporation, but at the other end of the scale terms setting out a procedure for the resolution of disputes between the union and the employer will equally readily be treated as not apt for incorporation as contractual terms enforceable by an individual employee.

The leading case on the correct approach to what is apt for incorporation is *Alexander v Standard Telephones and Cables plc* [1991] IRLR 286. Hobhouse J summarised the position, in terms which have since been regularly cited as authoritative, thus:

> 'The principles to be applied can therefore be summarised. The relevant contract is that between the individual employee and his employer; it is the contractual intention of those two parties which must be ascertained. In so far as that intention is to be found in a written document, that document must be construed on ordinary contractual principles. Insofar as there is no such document or that document is not complete or conclusive, their contractual intention has to be ascertained by inference from the other available material including collective agreements. The fact that another document is not itself contractual does not prevent it from being incorporated into the contract if that intention is shown as between the employer and the individual employee. Where a document is expressly incorporated by general words it is still be necessary to consider, in conjunction with the words of incorporation, whether any particular part of that document is apt to be a term of the contract; if it is inapt, the correct construction of the contract may be that it is not incorporated. Where it is not a case of express incorporation, but a matter of inferring the contractual intent, the character of the document and the relevant part of it, and whether it is apt to form part of the individual contract is central to the decision whether or not the inference should be drawn.' (para 31)

Provisions dealing with, for example, relations between an employer and a union operate at a collective level and are inappropriate for incorporation as terms of individual contracts. A number of cases illustrate the kind of provision which has been held not to be apt for incorporation into individual contracts. In *National Coal Board v National Union of Mineworkers* [1986] ICR 736, [1986] IRLR 439, the agreement set out the details of a conciliation scheme for the settlement of disputes. In the *Alexander* case itself, terms of a collective agreement specifying the procedure to be applied in a redundancy situation, and the criteria to be used for selection for redundancy, were held not to be apt for incorporation into the individual employees' contracts. Similarly in *Kaur v MG Rover Group Ltd* [2004] EWCA Civ 1507, [2005] IRLR 40 the Court of Appeal held that a provision in a collective agreement which stated that 'there will be no compulsory redundancy' did not have effect as a term of the individual contracts of employment between the employer and each employee.

In *Malone v British Airways plc* [2010] EWCA Civ 1225, [2011] IRLR 32, the Court of Appeal found that provisions of a collective agreement between the unions and the airline regarding minimum cabin crew complements for flights had not been incorporated into the contracts of employment. There was insufficient evidence of mutual intention to give the terms of the agreement enforceability by individual cabin crew members and the particular provisions were not apt for incorporation. The Court of Appeal focused in particular on what it saw as the disastrous consequences for the business if the provision were to be individually enforceable, such as flights having to be cancelled if not enough cabin crew members to fulfil the minimum manning levels were available, a consequence it concluded could not have been intended. See also *British Airline Pilots Association v Jet2.com Ltd* [2015] EWHC 1110 (QB), [2015] IRLR 543 (terms as to rostering arrangements for airline pilots not apt for incorporation, a point not in dispute in the subsequent successful appeal in this case: see **[6.4]** above).

A further example of a finding that a term was not appropriate for incorporation is the Court of Appeal's decision in *George v Ministry of Justice* [2013] EWCA Civ 324, [2013] All ER (D) 121 (Apr), a case relating to an agreement for time off in lieu for prison officers who had worked more than 39 hours in a week.

6.8   The kinds of terms most likely to be found to be apt for incorporation are those conferring specific benefits or imposing specific obligations on employees, such as rates of pay, provisions for specific future pay increases, changes in working hours, or conditions to be observed for the taking of leave; a good example of the incorporation of an agreement for future pay rises is *Cabinet Office v Beavan* [2014] IRLR 434. What is apt may also be affected by the history of how agreements between the collective parties have been incorporated into employees' contracts. In *Henry v London General Transport Services Ltd* [2002] EWCA Civ 488, [2002] IRLR 472, the employers entered into negotiations with a union, the TGWU, in preparation for a management buy-out. There had been a history of negotiations with the TGWU but there was no express incorporation of terms collectively agreed. The TGWU and the employers agreed a framework agreement which contained new and less advantageous terms and conditions, including reduced pay. The tribunal held that the terms of the framework agreement were so fundamental that the past practice of negotiations leading to the incorporation of terms collectively agreed was not such as to enable these changes to be incorporated into individual contracts. The Court of Appeal disagreed. The matters which were the subject of the framework agreement were apt for incorporation into individual contracts. Further, if the appropriate custom and practice was established, it could be expected to cover all contractual terms. The tribunal had been wrong to draw a distinction between fundamental and other terms without identifying a basis for that distinction.

In *Grainger v North East London NHS Foundation Trust* [2017] EWHC 2254 (QB), the High Court held that the provisions of a Job Evaluation Handbook which specified when changes in an employee's job would require a fresh job evaluation, were incorporated into the employees' contracts, but the employer's HR Handbook, which contained the procedure for carrying out a re-evaluation, was not.

Guidance has been given by the High Court as to when a collectively agreed disciplinary procedure will be regarded as incorporated into individual contracts: see *Hussain v Surrey and Sussex Healthcare NHS Trust* [2011] EWHC 1670 (QB), para 168, [2011] All ER (D) 91 (Jul). Relevant factors include the importance of the procedure, the level of detail prescribed, the certainty of the terms of the procedure, whether the terms would if contractual be workable and whether the provisions appear in the context of other provisions having contractual effect. See also *Cavanagh v Secretary of State for Work and Pensions*, discussed at [6.5] above.

In order for a term in a collective agreement to be incorporated into a contract of employment it may be necessary for an employee to have his attention drawn specifically to it. In *Worrall v Wilmott Dixon Partnerships Ltd* (UKEAT/0521/09) [2010] All ER (D) 107 (Jul), EAT, a council and its trade unions entered into a collective agreement regarding pay and redundancy and the terms were then inserted into a staff handbook. The handbook was generally available but not given to each employee. The EAT held that the term was not contractual as it had not been brought to the employee's attention and he could not therefore be said to have accepted the term. However, this analysis is open to question, since it was the employee who sought to rely on the agreement, as it conferred a substantial benefit on him in connection with his redundancy. Further, an express general incorporation of collective agreements into an individual's contract need not require that the individual has knowledge of each agreement; whether the incorporating provision does so require is a question of construction of the particular terms.

6.9 The principles applicable to the construction of collective agreements are the same as those which apply to other contracts: *Adams v British Airways plc* [1996] IRLR 574, CA. In particular, the Court of Appeal has confirmed that the principles for the construction of contracts set out by Lord Hoffmann in *Investors Compensation Scheme v West Bromwich Building Society* [1998] 1 All ER 98 apply: see *Bull v Nottinghamshire and City of Nottingham Fire Authority* [2007] EWCA Civ 240, [2007] ICR 1631. Where the terms of a collective agreement are truly ambiguous, it is permissible to look at a clearly established practice, which continues both before and after an agreement is made, as evidence of what the parties meant by the agreement (*Dunlop Tyres Ltd v Blows* [2001] EWCA Civ 1032, [2001] IRLR 629; see also CONTRACT OF EMPLOYMENT (8)). In both the *Bull* case and in *Briggs v Nottingham University Hospitals NHS Trust* [2010] EWCA Civ 264, [2010] IRLR 504, the Court of Appeal looked at the context of the agreement and whether the surrounding circumstances, purpose of the agreement and background to the negotiations lent support to a particular construction.

The construction of a collective agreement for a three year pay deal was considered by the Court of Appeal in *Anderson v London Fire and Emergency Planning Authority* [2013] EWCA Civ 321, [2013] IRLR 459. Reversing the EAT, the Court held that an agreement providing for two formulae for the third year's pay increase should be interpreted as requiring whichever formula produced the greater increase, since that gave effect to industrial common sense in the circumstances of the agreement. The court rejected the EAT's view (see [2012] IRLR 888) that the fact of two alternatives being stated gave the employer the right to choose which to implement as making no sense in the context of a negotiated pay agreement.

6.10 Like any contract, a collective agreement may have implied, as well as express, terms. The approach of the courts to whether a particular term should be implied into a collective agreement depends on the context as well as the term sought to be implied. In the case of *Ali v Christian Salvesen Food Services Ltd* [1997] ICR 25, [1997] IRLR 17, the Court of Appeal took a restrictive approach, acknowledging that such agreements are reached between the two sides of the industry and will inevitably involve compromises between their interests. The case concerned an 'annualised hours' contract, under which the employees were employed to work a notional 40-hour week but in fact were expected to work far more flexible hours based on an annual rota. There was no entitlement to overtime pay until the number of hours worked during a particular year exceeded a specified figure. The individual workers in the case had worked for more than 40 hours per week, but their contracts had been terminated before the number of hours worked in the year exceeded the specified figure. The question was whether they could claim overtime in respect of the number of hours which they had worked in excess of 40 per week. There was no express term which governed what should happen in this situation. The employees therefore based their case on an implied term. The Court of Appeal rejected the implication of a term to cover this situation. Waite LJ pointed out that this was one of several situations for which the collective agreement had not made provision. He refused to imply a term, stating that when a matter had not been covered in a collective agreement, the natural inference was that it had been intentionally omitted because it was either too controversial or too complicated to justify inclusion.

An example of a case where a term was held by the Court of Appeal to be implied into a collective agreement which was silent on the point is *Garratt v Mirror Group Newspapers Ltd* [2011] EWCA Civ 425, [2011] IRLR 591, [2011] ICR 880. The case concerned a collective agreement between the employer and a newly recognised trade union for enhanced redundancy terms. The employer had in practice for many years made enhanced payments but had always required employees to enter into compromise agreements as a condition of payment. This was (as the Court found) very well known, and had never been disputed. The agreement itself, which had been expressly incorporated into Mr Garratt's contract, was silent on the point of compromise agreements, but the Court readily upheld a finding in the County Court that the requirement for a compromise agreement was to be implied on the basis of the mutual understanding of the parties.

6.11   A related issue, which has arisen in a number of recent cases, usually in the context of claims for enhanced redundancy payments, is whether a policy or practice of the employer, such as making enhanced redundancy payments, has become a contractual entitlement by satisfying the requirements of a custom or practice. A custom or practice must be 'reasonable, certain and notorious', and its establishment in this type of context is likely to require evidence not just of a practice of payment over a period of time, but also that the payments were made in a manner indicative of a contractual entitlement of the affected employees to receive them. A full survey of recent cases on this point can be found in the judgment of Underhill LJ in *Park Cakes Ltd v Shumba* [2013] EWCA Civ 974, [2013] IRLR 800, where the Court also restates the principles applicable. The factors most likely to be relevant are listed at para 36 of Underhill LJ's judgment as the following:

–   On how many occasions and over how long a period the benefit in issue has been paid.

–   Whether the benefits have always been the same.

–   The extent to which the enhanced benefits in issue have been publicised, and in what terms.

–   How the terms concerned have been described by the employer (such as whether they have been labelled '*ex gratia*').

–   What (if anything) is said in the written contracts of the employees concerned.

–   Whether the employer's practice has been, viewed objectively, equivocal.

The Court also stressed that the burden of proof of a custom and practice is on the employees. Subsequent decisions applying, and illustrating the operation of, these principles are *CSC Computer Sciences Ltd v McAlinden* [2013] EWCA Civ 1435, [2013] All ER (D) 138 (Nov), *Peacock Stores v Peregrine* [2014] All ER (D) 22 (Apr) and *Migliacco v Samuel Smith (Southern) Ltd* (UKEAT/0267/14).

6.12   CHANGES TO COLLECTIVE AGREEMENTS

Once the terms of a collective agreement are incorporated into individual contracts, the relevant contractual terms are, as a matter of general principle, unaffected by the termination of the collective agreement (*Robertson v British Gas Corpn* [1983] ICR 351,

6.12   Collective Agreements

[1983] IRLR 302, CA; *Gibbons v Associated British Ports* [1985] IRLR 376; *Lee v GEC Plessey Telecommunications* [1993] IRLR 383). The question in each case is what the contract of employment provides, and the termination of a collective agreement is not determinative of that issue any more than its lack of legally binding status.

6.13   A related issue is the continuing effect of collective agreements following the transfer of employees under the *Transfer of Undertakings (Protection of Employment) Regulations 2006 (SI 2006/246) ('TUPE')* (see TRANSFER OF UNDERTAKINGS (53)). In *Whent v T Cartledge Ltd* [1997] IRLR 153, the employees had been employed by a local authority under contracts expressly incorporating collective agreements setting the rates of pay for local authority workers. They had transferred under *TUPE* to the respondent, which withdrew recognition from the trade union and pulled out of the collective agreement. The EAT nonetheless held that individuals retained the right under their individual contracts of employment to the benefits provided for by the collective agreement, including subsequent improvement in pay rates negotiated by the collective parties after the claimants' employment had transferred.

However, the Court of Appeal in *Alemo-Herron v Parkwood Leisure Ltd* [2010] EWCA Civ 24, [2010] IRLR 298 held, overruling *Whent*, that whilst the effect of *TUPE* was to preserve employees' contractual rights to the benefit of both current (at the time of the transfer) and later collective agreements and make them enforceable against the transferee, the judgment of the ECJ in *Werhof v Freeway Traffic Systems GmbH & Co KG*: C-499/04, [2005] ECR I-2397, [2006] IRLR 400 made clear that a static rather than dynamic interpretation of *Directive 2001/23/EC*, the parent Directive of *TUPE*, was required: the *Directive* did not require a transferee to be bound by a collective agreement other than the one in force at the time of the transfer. As *reg 4* of *TUPE* implemented *art 3(1)* of the *Directive*, a contractual term giving employees the right to pay increases negotiated from time to time by collective agreement was not protected on a transfer. The employees were not entitled to pay increases negotiated between the trade unions and local government employers after their transfer to a private sector employer.

Following a further appeal in *Alemo-Herron*, the Supreme Court held that the effect of *Werhof*, and in particular whether it required domestic legislation to go no further than the static approach adopted by the ECJ in *Werhof* itself, was unclear, and referred the case to the Court for clarification of this. The judgment of the Court (*Parkwood Leisure Ltd v Alemo-Herron*: C-426/11, [2013] IRLR 744) essentially confirms the approach of the Court of Appeal. The Court ruled that the Directive precludes national legislation which imposes on an employer to whom employees have transferred as part of a relevant transfer the terms of a subsequent collective agreement, if the transferee employer has not had the possibility of participating in the negotiating process leading to the adoption of the agreement. The principal reason given by the Court for this conclusion is that a 'dynamic' interpretation would undermine the right of transferee employers to conduct their business, a right safeguarded by the EU Charter of Fundamental Rights. The case was referred back to the Supreme Court for further consideration of the ECJ's judgment, but was settled before a further hearing could take place.

A subsequent case in the ECJ, *Asklepios Kliniken Langen-Seligstadt GmbH v Felja*: C-680/15, [2017] IRLR 653, has somewhat modified the position as set out in *Alemo-Herron*; the ECJ accepted that in some circumstances collective agreements could have what is termed a 'dynamic' effect following a transfer, provided that the employer's interests were sufficiently safeguarded.

As a separate point, the effect of subsequent statutory changes on collective agreements which have transferred under *TUPE* cannot be ignored. Thus in *Worrall v Wilmott Dixon Partnerships Ltd* (UKEAT/0521/09/DM), [2010] All ER (D) 107 (Jul), an agreement to confer additional pensionable service on employees taking voluntary redundancy was held no longer to be effective following a change in legislation making it unlawful to confer this category of benefit on employees.

6.14   CHANGING TERMS WITHOUT A COLLECTIVE AGREEMENT

Employers may wish to change the terms of employment of their employees which have been derived from a collective agreement, typically because of a wish to reduce costs.

The employer may seek, first, to try to reach agreement with the individual employees, in default of which they may determine to dismiss and re-engage the employees. In *Abrahall and others v Nottingham City Council and another* [2018] EWCA Civ 796, [2018] IRLR 628, [2018] ICR 1425 those who accepted the proposed new terms had an express entitlement to annual pay progression because, although the core contract offered did not make that clear the response form they signed made reference to an explanatory booklet that made it clear there was such an entitlement. Those dismissed and re-engaged received the same core contract but because they had not accepted the offer, had not completed a response form and therefore had not had the provision in the explanatory booklet incorporated by reference. The Court of Appeal held that they were nevertheless entitled to annual pay progression since they would reasonably have expected that the terms upon which they were being re-engaged were the same as those offered to their colleagues.

6.15   If no agreement can be reached either with the relevant trade union or the individual employees, the employer may seek to impose the changes unilaterally. Such cases are likely to raise the question whether there is a provision in the individuals' contracts of employment permitting the degree of unilateral variation of terms proposed. If not, and unless individual employees agree to a variation of contract, the employer cannot impose the new terms without taking the relatively drastic step of dismissing the employees and offering re-employment on the new terms. The question whether individual contracts contain provisions sufficiently wide to permit unilateral variation at the instance of the employer may therefore be of considerable importance.

The answer to this question will depend on the precise wording of the contract, as well as the particular changes proposed. The general approach of the courts to this question can be seen in two recent decisions, each rejecting the employer's attempt to apply a unilateral change following a failure of negotiations on the proposed change. In *Norman v National Audit Office* [2015] IRLR 634, EAT, the employees' standard contractual terms included a statement that conditions of service were 'subject to amendment', and that any changes would be notified to staff, either in general circulars for changes applying generally, or individually for changes directly affecting individuals. The employer sought to rely on this to validate reductions in the number of annual 'privilege day' holidays and the period for which sick pay would be paid. The EAT rejected this claim. The clause in issue went no further than to set out the mechanism by which amendments were to be notified: it did not clearly or unambiguously reserve the right of the employer to amend terms unilaterally without the employees' consent.

In *Sparks v Department for Transport* [2016] EWCA Civ 360, [2016] IRLR 519, [2016] ICR 695 the employees' contracts contained a statement that 'Your contract of employment cannot be changed detrimentally without your agreement. Consequently the Department will not change your terms and conditions of contract without your consent or that of a recognised trade union.' The Department wished to introduce a new absence management policy under which the number of days' absence before the 'trigger points' for disciplinary action were to be applied was to be reduced. The policy had previously been agreed with the relevant trade unions, but the change was not acceptable to the unions. The Department therefore proceeded to make the change unilaterally. The High Court, and on appeal the Court of Appeal, held that the original collectively agreed policy was apt for incorporation into individual contracts, and was therefore part of the employees' contracts, with the result that a detrimental change, such as that proposed, could not be made without a further collective agreement (which would be incorporated into individual contracts) or individual consent.

An example of a decision that an employer could make unilateral changes in the terms of its employees' contracts by relying on an express variation clause in the contract is *Bateman v Asda Stores Ltd* [2010] IRLR 370, [2010] All ER (D) 277 (Feb), EAT. In that case the employer's Colleague Handbook, which was incorporated into individual contracts, contained the statement that 'the Company reserves the right to review, revise, amend or replace the content of this handbook and introduce new policies from time to time'. This was held to be sufficient to permit the employer to impose changes in its pay structure, albeit with no individual employees suffering reductions in pay.

6.16 'NO STRIKE' CLAUSES

There are specific provisions restricting the incorporation into individual contracts of collective agreements which would restrict the right to take part in industrial action. Any provision of a collective agreement which prohibits or restricts the right of workers to engage in a strike or other industrial action, or has the effect of prohibiting or restricting that right, cannot be incorporated into the contract of employment of an individual worker unless the collective agreement:

(a)   is in writing; and

(b)   contains a provision stating that those terms shall or may be incorporated in such a contract; and

(c)   is reasonably accessible at his place of work to the worker to whom it applies and is available for him to consult during working hours; and

(d)   is one where each trade union which is a party to the agreement is an independent trade union (see **51.22** TRADE UNIONS – I); and

(e)   the individual contract with the worker expressly or impliedly incorporates those terms of the collective agreement relating to strikes.

(TULR(C)A 1992, s 180)

Despite the fact that a collective agreement and an individual's contract of employment may comply with all the requirements of *s 180*, a court cannot order specific performance of a contract of employment or grant an injunction restraining a breach, or threatened breach, of such a contract which would have the effect of compelling the employee to do any work or attend at any place for the doing of any work *(TULR(C)A 1992, s 236)*.

6.17 WORKFORCE AGREEMENTS

In a number of situations, statutory provisions giving effect in domestic law to EU Directives may be modified in their application by collective agreements. Examples are provisions in the *Working Time Regulations 1998* permitting the modification of some of the substantive rules in the *Regulations*, and the *Maternity and Parental Leave etc Regulations 1999* (allowing for the disapplication of the default rules for the taking of parental leave). Collective agreements may only be made where there is a recognised trade union with which the employer may negotiate. The disadvantages to employers and employees of the absence of any alternative facility for the modification of EU-derived statutory rights are met by provision in these *Regulations* for 'workforce agreements' negotiated between employers and elected representatives of the workforce. For details of the procedural requirements for a workforce agreement under the *Working Time Regulations 1998* (other provisions for workforce agreements are in essentially identical terms) see **58.4** WORKING TIME. Employee representatives elected to negotiate workforce agreements are afforded similar protection from retaliatory action to that afforded to trade union representatives.

6.18   DISCRIMINATORY AGREEMENTS

Under *section 145* of the *Equality Act 2010* terms in collective agreement, which discriminate against employees because of any protected characteristic are void. A qualifying person may apply to the Employment Tribunal for a declaration that the term is void (see *section 146*). A person qualifies under *section 146* if, but only if, he or she is, or seeks to be, an employee of the employer (or an employer) party to the collective agreement, and either is or may in the future be affected by the disputed term, or (if the term provides for particular treatment of individuals) may be subject in future to the treatment objected to. The remedy for a successful complainant is a declaration that the term is void.

Claims under *section 145* (as under the equivalent provisions in the various Acts and regulations replaced by the *Equality Act 2010*) are rare. An example of the use of the procedure (in an earlier formulation) is *Meade-Hill and National Union of Civil and Public Servants v British Council* [1996] 1 All ER 79, [1995] IRLR 478, CA, where a mobility clause was successfully challenged as indirectly discriminatory against female employees.

7   Continuous Employment

7.1   Many of the statutory employment protection rights such as the right to claim a redundancy payment and compensation for unfair dismissal are conferred only on those employees who have accrued sufficient continuous employment. Further, the calculation of a redundancy payment and of the basic award in unfair dismissal proceedings is based on the employee's length of continuous service. The length of an employee's period of continuous employment is calculated with a few exceptions according to provisions in *ERA 1996, ss 210–219*. The rules relating to continuity apply to employees, irrespective of whether they work full-time or part-time, and if part-time, irrespective of the number of hours worked per week.

The more important provisions relating to continuity of employment are set out in this chapter.

7.2   COMPUTATION OF PERIODS OF EMPLOYMENT

Questions arising as to whether an employee's employment is of a kind which counts towards a period of continuous employment, or whether periods are to be treated as forming a single period of continuous employment, are to be determined week by week, but the length of an employee's period of employment is to be computed in *calendar months* and *years of twelve months* (*ERA 1996, s 210(1), (2), (3)*).

7.3   Beginning and end of a period of continuous employment

Subject to the provisions of *ERA 1996, s 211(2), (3)* an employee's period of continuous employment for the purpose of calculating his entitlement to any right under *ERA 1996* begins with the day on which he actually starts work and ends with the day by reference to which the length of his period of continuous employment falls to be ascertained for the purposes of the employment right in question (*ERA 1996, s 211(1)*). It is important to note that the day on which an employee actually started work must be included in the reckoning under *ERA 1996, s 211*, so that if, for example, an employee starts work on 2 April, and is dismissed on 1 April the following year, he will have one year's continuous employment (see *Pacitti Jones v O'Brien* [2005] IRLR 888). In *General of the Salvation Army v Dewsbury* [1984] IRLR 222, [1984] ICR 498, the EAT held that 'starts work' in *EPCA 1978, s 151(3)* (the predecessor to *ERA 1996, s 211(1)*) was not intended to refer to the undertaking of the full-time duties of employment but was intended to refer to the beginning of the employee's employment under her contract of employment, which in that case was earlier than the former date.

7.4   EVENTS AFFECTING A PERIOD OF EMPLOYMENT

The rest of this chapter sets out the events which may affect the period of employment. The following matters are considered:

— weeks which count (see **7.6** below);

— change of employer (see **7.9** below);

— weeks, or part weeks, which do not count but which do not break continuity (see **7.10** below);

— events which break continuity (see **7.12** below).

7.5 Continuous Employment

7.5 PRELIMINARY POINTS

Presumption of continuity. A person's employment (by a particular employer) is presumed to have been continuous unless the contrary is shown (*ERA 1996, s 210(5)*). That presumption does not apply where the person's employer has changed: see *Jones v Schwarzenbach* (2015) UKEAT/0100/15, [2015] All ER (D) 145 (Sep). Except as provided in *ERA 1996, ss 215–217*, any week which does not count in computing a period of employment breaks the continuity of the period of employment (*ERA 1996, s 210(4)*).

Meaning of 'week'. For these purposes, a week runs from Sunday to Saturday (*ERA 1996, s 235*). So long as the employee is employed by the employer in two successive weeks, it does not matter that one job may have ended and another begun, nor how the first job ended (*Tipper v Roofdec Ltd* [1989] IRLR 419).

Statutory concept. The concept of continuity of employment is a statutory concept (see *Secretary of State for Employment v Globe Elastic Thread Co Ltd* [1979] IRLR 327, [1979] ICR 706). This means that parties cannot destroy it by means of a contractual agreement (see *Collison v BBC* [1998] IRLR 238). (See **7.7** below.)

7.6 WEEKS WHICH COUNT

The following weeks count towards a period of continuous employment.

(a) Any week during the whole or part of which the employee's relations with his employer are governed by a contract of employment (*ERA 1996, s 212(1)*).

In *Roach v CSB (Moulds) Ltd* [1991] IRLR 200, [1991] ICR 349, the EAT held that continuity had been broken where in two successive weeks the applicant had been employed first by the respondent, then by a third party, then by the respondent again in a different job. However, the EAT in Scotland held in *Sweeney v J & S Henderson (Concessions) Ltd* [1999] IRLR 306 that the long-criticised *Roach* decision was wrongly decided and that, so long as during the relevant weeks there is at least one day governed by a contract of employment with the relevant employer, it does not matter how the gap was created nor what the employee did during its currency (see also *Carrington v Harwich Dock Co Ltd* [1998] IRLR 567).

(b) Periods in which there is no contract of employment may count as periods of employment in certain circumstances. If in any week the employee is, for the whole or part of the week:

(i) incapable of work in consequence of illness or injury; or

(ii) absent from work on account of a temporary cessation of work; or

(iii) absent from work in circumstances such that, by arrangement or custom, he is regarded as continuing in the employment of his employer for all or any purposes,

that week will count as a period of employment (*ERA 1996, s 212(3)*).

Not more than 26 weeks count under (b)(i) above between any periods of employment which themselves count for continuity purposes (*ERA 1996, s 212(4)*). The problems arising from these provisions are considered in more detail in **7.7** below.

(c) An employee's contract of employment is deemed to continue during maternity leave with appropriate amendments so that there is no need for special provisions preserving continuity during the maternity period (*ss 71* and *73, ERA 1996* and *reg 9* of the *Maternity and Parental Leave Regulations 1999*). The same position applies in respect of continuity during any statutory adoption leave period (*ss 75A–B, ERA 1996* and *regs 19* and *21* of the *Paternity and Adoption Leave Regulations 2002 (SI 2002/2788)*); during parental leave (*ERA 1996 ss 76* and *77* and *reg 17* of the *Maternity and Parental Leave Regulations*); during paternity leave (*s 80C(1)*, *ERA 1996* and *reg 12* of the *Paternity and Adoption Leave Regulations*); and during shared parental leave (*s 75I*, *ERA 1996* and *reg 38* of the *Shared Parental Leave Regulations 2014 (SI 2014/3050)*.

(d)   Intervals in employment where employment is deemed to continue by virtue of the provisions of *ERA 1996, ss 92(7), 97(2), 138(1)* and *145(5)* respectively also count. *ERA 1996, ss 92(7)* and *145(5)* operate to treat an employee's employment as continuing until the expiry of the statutory minimum period of notice in circumstances where notice should have been given but was not, and the employee was thereby deprived of the minimum qualifying period of employment for claims for a written statement of reasons for dismissal, unfair dismissal and redundancy payments, respectively. *Section 138(1), ERA 1996* operates to preserve continuity where an employee dismissed for redundancy has his contract renewed or is re-engaged after an interval of not more than four weeks. If a dismissed employee is reinstated or re-engaged in consequence of the presentation of a 'relevant complaint of dismissal', or as a result of action taken by a conciliation officer under the *Employment Tribunals Act 1996, s 18*, or as a result of a relevant compromise contract (see **ACAS CONCILIATION (3)**), the employee's continuity of employment is preserved and the weeks in any intervening period count. Further, if the employee has been paid a redundancy payment and it is a term of his reinstatement or re-engagement that he repay that sum, the continuity of his employment for redundancy payments purposes is not broken (*Employment Protection (Continuity of Employment) Regulations 1996 (SI 1996/3147); ERA 1996, s 219*). The phrase 'relevant complaint of dismissal' in *reg 2* of *SI 1996/3147* is not defined, but it would certainly include a complaint of unfair dismissal, and arguably, other complaints (such as discrimination) in relation to dismissal: see *Lipinski v Ebbsfleet Autospray Centre Ltd* [2013] All ER (D) 123 (Sep).

7.7   Periods of 'no employment'

The true meaning of *ERA 1996, s 212(3)* (see **7.6**(b) above) has given rise to various difficulties of interpretation.

Generally. Section 212(3) applies only where there is no contract of employment in existence and not where there is a contract of employment in existence, but the employee is not required to perform any work under that contract (*Ford v Warwickshire County Council* [1986] IRLR 126, [1983] ICR 273; *Pearson v Kent County Council* [1993] IRLR 165). In *Pearson*, the Court of Appeal held that the critical question is why there is no contract during the week in question, and not why the previous contract of employment came to an end.

Illness and injury (s 212(3)(a)). This provision can apply so long as the employee is unfit for the work for which he was previously employed. Thus, continuity may be preserved even where the employee takes a temporary job with another employer until he is capable of returning to his former work (*Donnelly v Kelvin International Services* [1992] IRLR 496; see also *Pearson*, above).

Temporary cessation of work (s 212(3)(b)). In *Ford*, the House of Lords held that the continuity of employment of a teacher whose contract came to an end at the end of every summer term but who was re-engaged in the autumn term was preserved during the summer vacation by *EPCA 1978, Sch 13 para 9(1)(b)*, now *ERA 1996, s 212(3)(b)*. Lord Diplock at 285 said that 'temporary' meant lasting only for a relatively short time, and that it was necessary to ask whether the interval between the two contracts was short in relation to their combined duration. This has become known as the 'mathematical' approach.

7.7 Continuous Employment

The test for 'temporary cessation of work' under *s 212(3)(b)* does not require an examination of the expectation of parties of further work. What is required is to find the reason for the termination of the first contract of employment. If it has ended because of a temporary cessation of work, and the claimant is employed again, the case falls within *s 212(3)(b)*: *Hussain v Acorn Independent College* [2011] IRLR 463. So, in *Hussain*, a teacher who was employed as temporary cover in the summer term, and who was then employed permanently in the next college year when the teacher he was covering unexpectedly decided not to return to work, could aggregate both his temporary cover contract and his permanent contract for continuity purposes. It did not matter that he had no expectation of further work when his temporary cover contract expired.

In *Flack v Kodak Ltd* [1986] IRLR 255, [1986] ICR 775 the Court of Appeal had to consider whether six workers in the photo-finishing department of Kodak Ltd had sufficient continuous employment to pursue their employment protection rights. They had been employed intermittently over a number of years. Their period of employment depended on the extent of the department's work. The court decided that the correct approach in deciding whether a gap in an employee's employment, during which he is absent from work on account of a cessation of work, is a temporary cessation for the purposes of *EPCA 1978, Sch 13 para 9(1)(b)*, now *ERA 1996, s 212(3)(b)*, is to take into account all the relevant circumstances and in particular to consider the length of the period of absence in the context of the period of employment as a whole. Thus, the court did not apply a strictly 'mathematical' approach and held that the periods of absence did not break the continuity of employment (see also *Berwick Salmon Fisheries Co Ltd v Rutherford* [1991] IRLR 203).

However, in *Sillars v Charringtons Fuels Ltd* [1989] IRLR 152, [1989] ICR 475 the Court of Appeal held that it was still open to an employment tribunal, after considering the matter in the round, to conclude that the 'mathematical' approach should be applied in an appropriate case (for example, where there was a systematic pattern of events). That there was an intention to re-employ the applicant later did not necessarily mean that the cessation of work was temporary in the sense of being for a relatively short time.

The 'cessation of work' must involve a reduction in the employer's overall quantum of work, and not merely a decision to allocate work to some other employee (*Byrne v Birmingham City District Council* [1987] IRLR 191, [1987] ICR 519). *Byrne* was followed in *Letheby & Christopher Ltd v Bond* [1988] ICR 480.

Regarded as continuing in employment (s 212(3)(c)). This provision might apply to, for example, a period of unpaid leave. However, it was held in *Letheby* (see above) that an employee employed under single separate contracts, who went on holiday at a time convenient to her employers, was not absent from work in circumstances such that by arrangement or custom she was regarded as continuing in employment, where there was no prior agreement between the parties that after each holiday period there was to be some continuation of her employment.

The Court of Appeal in *Curr v Marks & Spencer plc* [2002] EWCA Civ 1852, [2003] ICR 443 stressed that *s 212(3)(c)* requires a mutual arrangement between employer and employee, and a 'meeting of minds' by the arrangement that both parties regard the ex-employee as continuing in employment for some purpose. The Court did not regard it as helpful to refer to the test of *s 212(3)(c)* as involving consideration of whether an employment relationship continues (regarded as the 'key question' by the EAT in *Letheby* and *Booth v United States of America* [1999] IRLR 16): this was not the statutory test. In *Curr*, an employee absent on a four-year maternity break scheme did not fall within *s 212(3)(c)*, although she was required to work for at least two weeks in each year of the break; was prohibited from accepting other paid employment without consulting her manager; and was in regular contact with the employer. This was because the other terms on which she took her maternity break clearly showed that employment was not regarded as continuing. On commencement of her break, she was required to resign, and was given her P45. At the end of the break, she had an option to be re-employed by the employer, but the scheme's emphasis on 're-employment' in fact showed that she was not regarded as continuing in employment during the break.

The EAT has reached conflicting decisions on whether an 'arrangement' under *s 212(3)(c)* can be made retrospectively. In *Murphy v A Birrell & Sons* [1978] IRLR 458 and *Morris v Walsh Western UK Ltd* [1997] IRLR 562, it held that a retrospective agreement to treat the period of an employee's absence as continuous was insufficient to preserve continuity of employment under *s 212(3)(c)* (because continuity of employment is a statutory concept – see *Secretary of State for Employment v Globe Elastic Thread Co Ltd* [1979] IRLR 327, [1979] ICR 706). On the other hand, in *Ingram v Foxon* [1985] IRLR 5, [1984] ICR 685 and *London Probation Board v Kirkpatrick* [2005] IRLR 443, the EAT held that there is no temporal qualification to the term "arrangement" in *s 212(3)(c)*, and that arrangements can be made retrospectively. The conflict in the authorities has been resolved by the EAT's decision in *Welton v Deluxe Retail Ltd* [2013] IRLR 166, [2013] ICR 428. Langstaff P stated that an "arrangement" within *s 212(3)(c)* was not able to bridge a gap in continuity of employment unless it was in existence before, or arose contemporaneously with, the relevant weeks of absence from work during which there was no contract. He reviewed the authorities in detail, and stated that *Kirkpatrick* should no longer be followed.

7.8   Part-timers

As mentioned in **7.1** above, there is no difference in the provisions for calculating periods of continuous employment, in relation to their application to part-time employees as against full-time employees.

7.9   CHANGE OF EMPLOYER

Normally, to be continuous, employment must be with one employer. Separate companies must normally be treated as quite distinct entities. The 'corporate veil' may only be pierced if it is a mere facade concealing the true facts (*National Dock Labour Board v Pinn & Wheeler Ltd* [1989] BCLC 647). However, note the following points.

(a)   *Associated employers.* If an employee of an employer is taken into the employment of another employer who, at the time when the employee enters his employment is an 'associated' employer of the former employer, that change will not break the continuity of the employee's employment (*ERA 1996, s 218(6)*).

For the purposes of *ERA 1996*, any two employers are to be treated as associated if one is a company of which the other (directly or indirectly) has control, or if both are companies of which a third person (directly or indirectly) has control (*ERA 1996, s 231*). The definition of 'control' in *s 231* has been problematic over the years. The EAT held in *Hair Colour Consultants Ltd v Mena* [1984] IRLR 386, [1984] ICR 671 that 'control' means voting control by a majority of shares, rather than de facto control (see also *South West Launderettes Ltd v Laidler* [1986] IRLR 305, [1986] ICR 455, *Secretary of State for Employment v Newbold* [1981] IRLR 305, *Umar v Pliastar Ltd* [1981] ICR 727 and *Washington Arts Association Ltd v Forster* [1983] ICR 346). However, the Court of Appeal in *Secretary of State for Employment v Chapman* [1989] ICR 771 held that whilst voting control is the usual and normal test for determining whether two employers are associated, that test is not conclusive. Further, the EAT held in *Tice v Cartwright* [1999] ICR 769 that the word 'control' in *s 231* dealt with practical rather than theoretical control so that two brothers in partnership controlled the company in which they each had a 50% shareholding. (*Tice v Cartwright* has been applied by the EAT in *Da Silva Junior v Composite Mouldings & Design Ltd* [2009] ICR 416. See also, *Hartford v Swiftrim Ltd* [1987]

7.9 Continuous Employment

IRLR 360, [1987] ICR 439; and *Zarb v British Brazilian Produce Co (Sales) Ltd* [1978] IRLR 78 cf *Strudick v IBL* [1988] IRLR 457, [1988] ICR 796; and *Russell v Elmdon Freight Terminal Ltd* [1989] ICR 629.)

The EAT has been willing to treat the term 'company' as including both a partnership of companies (*Pinkney v Sandpiper Drilling Ltd* [1989] IRLR 425) and a foreign entity equivalent to an English company (*Hancill v Marcon Engineering Ltd* [1990] IRLR 51, [1990] ICR 103). More recently, albeit in the context of the *Equal Pay Act 1970*, the Court of Session has observed in relation to identical words to *ERA 1996, s 218(6)*, contained in *Equal Pay Act 1970, s 1(6)*, that the meaning of "company" is a wide one, connoting "an association of persons for an economic purpose, usually entered into with legal advice and some degree of formality", and would include a LLP: see *Glasgow City Council v Fox Cross Claimants* [2014] CSIH 27, [2014] IRLR 532 at [42]-[45], citing *O'Neill v Phillips* [1999] 1 WLR 1092 at 1098 per Lord Hoffmann. However, not all bodies corporate (such as local authorities) are 'companies' within *ERA 1996, s 231* (see the ratio of the Court of Appeal in (*Gardiner v London Borough of Merton* [1980] IRLR 472). In *Hasley v Fair Employment Agency* [1989] IRLR 106, the Northern Ireland Court of Appeal pointed out that the section only requires the employer which is *controlled* to be a company; the *controlling* employer may be some other type of legal person.

(b) *Transfers of a business.* If a trade or business or an undertaking is transferred from one person to another, the period of employment of an employee in the trade or business or undertaking at the time of the transfer counts as a period of employment with the transferee and is regarded as unbroken (*ERA 1996, s 218(2)*).

ERA 1996, s 218(2) will generally apply in cases where there has been a transfer of an undertaking for the purposes of the *Transfer of Undertakings (Protection of Employment) Regulations 2006* ('*TUPE*'), in which case continuity of employment is in any event preserved under *TUPE* (see *TUPE, reg 4(1)*). However, the operation of *ERA 1996, s 218(2)* is not restricted to cases in which there has been a transfer under *TUPE*, and if for one reason or another *TUPE* does not apply, continuity of employment may nevertheless be preserved under the statute. See for example *Oakland v Wellswood (Yorkshire) Ltd* [2010] IRLR 82, [2010] ICR 902. In *Oakland*, the tribunal and EAT held that there had been no *TUPE* transfer, because the transferor was the subject of bankruptcy proceedings for the purposes of *reg 8(7)* of *TUPE*. Notwithstanding that, the Court of Appeal found that the employee's continuity of employment had been preserved by virtue of *ERA 1996, s 218(2)* (without needing to decide whether the tribunal's and EAT's conclusions on *reg 8(7)* of *TUPE* were correct). See further TRANSFER OF UNDERTAKINGS (53).

Case law on *ERA 1996, s 218(2)* has warned against artificial attempts to break continuity. In *Macer v Abafast Ltd* [1990] IRLR 137, [1990] ICR 234 and *Gibson v Motortune Ltd* [1990] ICR 740, the EAT stated that the machinery of *EPCA, Sch 13 para 17(2)*, the predecessor to *ERA 1996, s 218(2)*, could operate even where the machinery of transfer led to a gap of more than one week between periods of employment. This approach was adopted by the Court of Appeal in *Clark & Tokeley Ltd v Oakes* [1998] IRLR 577, on the basis that there will often not be a precise time of transfer, which can take place over an extended period; and that what had to be examined when considering whether an employee was employed 'at the time of transfer' was not the point when the legal formalities of transfer were completed, but the actual state of affairs as a matter of fact, which could cover a period of days or even weeks.

A similar result which preserves continuity may be obtained under *TUPE, reg 4(1)*, but on a different conceptual basis. Under *TUPE*, contrary to the position under *ERA 1996, s 218(2)*, a transfer takes place at a particular moment in time: see *Celtec Ltd v Astley* [2006] ICR 992, [2006] IRLR 635, HL. However, *TUPE* operates so as to preserve the continuity of employment of employees automatically unfairly dismissed prior to the transfer for reasons related to the transfer: see *TUPE, reg 4(3)* and *reg 7(1)* and *Litster v Forth Dry Dock and Engineering Co Ltd* [1989] IRLR 161, [1990] 1 AC 546; and see further TRANSFER OF UNDERTAKINGS **(53)**.

(c)   *Substitution of employer by statute.* If by or under an Act of Parliament, whether public or local, a contract of employment between any body corporate and an employee is modified and some other body corporate is substituted as the employer, the period of employment of the employee at the time when the modification takes effect counts as a period of employment with the second body corporate and is regarded as unbroken (*ERA 1996, s 218(3)*). For a case where, on the facts, the predecessor provision to *s 218(3)* was held not to apply, see *Gale v Northern General Hospital NHS Trust* [1994] IRLR 292.

(d)   *Employment in schools/the National Health Service.* If an employee of the governing body of a maintained school is taken into the employment of the local authority responsible for the school, or vice versa, continuity of employment is preserved (*ERA 1996, s 218(7)*). Similarly, in certain circumstances, continuity of employment is preserved when an employee's employment switches from one health service employer to another, if he is undergoing professional training which involves successive employment by a number of different health service employers (*ERA 1996, ss 218(8)–218(10)* and *Employment Protection (National Health Service) Order 1996 (SI 1996/638)*).

(e)   *Death of employer, partnerships, etc.* If, on the death of the employer, the employee passes into the employment of the personal representatives or trustees of the deceased, continuity is not broken. A change in partners, personal representatives or trustees does not break the continuity of an employee's employment (*ERA 1996, s 218(4), (5)*). The provision in *ERA 1996, s 218(5)* for preservation of continuity on a change in partners covers the situation where, after the change, there are no partners, but only a sole proprietor: see *Bower v Stevens* [2004] IRLR 957, [2004] ICR 1582 and *Jeetle v Elster* [1985] IRLR 227, [1985] ICR 389.

7.10   WEEKS WHICH DO NOT BREAK CONTINUITY

The following weeks do not count in the computation but do not break continuity. (This applies also where the events occur in only part of the week.)

(a)   Any week during which the employee takes part in a strike (*ERA 1996, s 216(1), (2)*).

(b)   Any week during which the employee is absent from work because of a lock-out (*ERA 1996, s 216(3)*).

(c)   For the purpose of calculating the qualifying period for pursuing a claim to a redundancy payment and for the purpose of calculating the amount of the payment, any week during which the employee (i) was employed outside Great Britain (*ERA 1996, s 215(2)(a)*), and (ii) was not an employed earner for the purposes of the *Social Security Contributions and Benefits Act 1992* in respect of whom a secondary Class 1 contribution was payable under that Act (whether or not the contribution was in fact paid) (*ERA 1996, s 215(2)(b)*). For all other purposes, continuity continues during periods in which the employee is engaged in work wholly or mainly outside Great Britain (*ERA 1996, s 215(1)(a)*).

7.11 Continuous Employment

(d) Where a person left employment because he was called into permanent service in the reserve or auxiliary armed forces, but has subsequently been re-employed by his former employer, his period of permanent service in the armed forces does not break continuity, provided that no more than 6 months have elapsed since the end of that permanent service: *ERA 1996, s 217* and the *Reserve Forces (Safeguard of Employment) Act 1985*.

7.11 'Postponement' of start of employment

If an employee's period of continuous employment includes one or more periods which do not count in computing the length of the period but do not break continuity, the beginning of the period is treated as *postponed* by the number of days falling within that intervening period, or, as the case may be, by the aggregate number of days falling within those periods (*ERA 1996, s 211(3)*).

7.12 EVENTS WHICH BREAK CONTINUITY

Except as is otherwise specifically provided in *ERA 1996, ss 215–217*, any week which does not count in the computation breaks the continuity of a period of employment (*ERA 1996, s 210(4)*).

The receipt of a redundancy payment breaks continuity for redundancy qualification and payment purposes (*ERA 1996, s 214*). However, *s 214* does not apply where an employee, having received a redundancy payment (or equivalent payment), is reinstated or re-engaged by his employer on terms which include a requirement to repay the amount of that payment, and that requirement is complied with (*Employment Protection (Continuity of Employment) Regulations 1996 (SI 1996/3147)* – see also **7.6**(d) above). *Section 214* also does not apply where a 'redundancy payment' paid by the employer is not a payment which he is statutorily obliged to make (*Rowan v Machinery Installations (South Wales) Ltd* [1981] IRLR 122, [1981] ICR 386; *Ross v Delrosa Caterers Ltd* [1981] ICR 393). Further, given that a 'redundancy payment' in this context means a statutory redundancy payment, and a right to such a payment depends on there having been a dismissal, it follows that where an employee's employment is transferred pursuant to *TUPE 1981*, there is no dismissal and therefore any payment received by the employee is not a statutory redundancy payment and will not break continuity under *s 214* (*Senior Heat Treatment v Bell* [1997] IRLR 614). However, this will not be the case where the Secretary of State has paid the equivalent of a statutory redundancy payment to an employee of an insolvent employer under *ERA 1996, s 167* (*Secretary of State for Trade and Industry v Lassman* [2000] IRLR 411).

7.13 TABLE OF QUALIFYING PERIODS FOR STATUTORY EMPLOYMENT PROTECTION RIGHTS

Employment right	Qualifying period
	NB Not all statutory employment protection rights require a qualifying period of continuous employment. For example, the general right to maternity leave does not depend upon 'continuous' employment as defined by *ERA 1996*.
Written statement of employment particulars	One month (see *ERA 1996, s 198*).
Guarantee payments/Payments during medical suspension	One month ending with the day before the period for which guarantee payment, etc is claimed (*ERA 1996, s 29(1)* and *s 65(1)*).

Employment right	Qualifying period
Minimum period of notice	One month (*ERA 1996, ss 86(1), 87(1)*).
	Any contract of a person who has been employed for three months which is a contract for a fixed term of one month or less is deemed for the purposes of *s 86* to have effect as if it were for an indefinite period and thus subject to the notice provisions (*ERA 1996, s 86(4)*).
Unfair dismissal Written reasons for dismissal	Two years (*ERA 1996, s 108(1)* and *s 92(3)*).
	If an employee is dismissed by reason of a medical suspension requirement or recommendation under an enactment or a Code of Practice providing for health and safety at work, the qualifying period is one month (*ERA 1996, s 108(2)*).
	In certain other cases of unfair dismissal, no qualifying period is necessary. These are where the reason or principal reason for the dismissal:
	(*a*) was a union-related reason (*TULRCA 1992, s 154*; and see **55.3**(a) UNFAIR DISMISSAL – **II**);
	(*b*) was the assertion of a statutory right (*ERA 1996, s 108(3)(g)*; and see **55.3**(c) UNFAIR DISMISSAL – **II**);
	(*c*) was a health and safety-related reason (*ERA 1996, s 108(3)(c)*; and see **55.3**(b) UNFAIR DISMISSAL – **II**);
	(*d*) was a reason related to pregnancy, childbirth or maternity; maternity leave; adoption leave; parental leave; paternity leave; shared parental leave; or time off for dependants under *ERA 1996, s 57* (*ERA 1996, s 108(3)(b)*; and see **33.9** MATERNITY AND PARENTAL RIGHTS);
	(*e*) was a reason connected with the performance by an employee who is a pension scheme trustee of his functions as such a trustee (*ERA 1996, s 108(3)(e)*; see **55.3**(e) UNFAIR DISMISSAL – **II**);
	(*f*) was a reason connected with the performance by an employee representative (see **40.4** REDUNDANCY – **II** and **53.18** TRANSFER OF UNDERTAKINGS), or a candidate in an election for such an employee representative, of his functions as such an employee representative or candidate (*ERA 1996, s 108(3)(f)*; see **55.3**(f) UNFAIR DISMISSAL – **II**);
	(*g*) was a reason connected with the refusal of Sunday work by a shop worker or betting worker (*ERA 1996, s 108(3)(d)*; see **55.3**(g) UNFAIR DISMISSAL – **II**);
	(*h*) was a reason related to working time (*ERA 1996, s 108(3)(dd)*; and see **55.3**(h) UNFAIR DISMISSAL – **II**);

Employment right		Qualifying period
	(*I*)	was a reason connected with the assertion of rights under the *National Minimum Wage Act 1998 (ERA 1996, s 108(3)(gg)*; see **55.3**(m) Unfair Dismissal – II);
	(*j*)	was a reason connected with the making of a protected disclosure under *ERA 1996, ss 43A–43L (ERA 1996, s 108(3)(ff)* and *s 103A*; see **55.3**(n) Unfair Dismissal – II);
	(*k*)	was a reason connected with the assertion of rights under the *Tax Credits Act 1999 (ERA 1996, s 108(3)(gh)*; see **55.3**(t) Unfair Dismissal – II);
	(*l*)	was a reason connected with the assertion of rights under the *Transnational Information and Consultation of Employees Regulations 1999 (ERA 1996, s 108(3)(hh)*; see **55.3**(u) Unfair Dismissal – II);
	(*m*)	was a reason connected with the assertion of rights under the *Part-time Workers (Prevention of Less Favourable Treatment) Regulations 2000 (SI 2000/1551) (ERA 1996, s 108(3)(i)*; see **55.3**(s) Unfair Dismissal – II);
	(*n*)	was a reason connected with the assertion of rights under the *Fixed-term Employees (Prevention of Less Favourable Treatment) Regulations 2002 (SI 2002/2034) (ERA 1996, s 108(3)(j)*; see **55.3**(v) Unfair Dismissal – II);
	(*o*)	was a reason connected with the assertion of flexible working rights under *ERA 1996, ss 80F–80G (ERA 1996, s 108(3)(gi)*; see **55.3** Unfair Dismissal – II);
	(*p*)	was a reason connected with trade union recognition or bargaining arrangements (*TULRCA 1992, Sch A1, paras 161–162* (see **55.3**(o) Unfair Dismissal – II);
	(*q*)	was that the employee exercised or sought to exercise the right, pursuant to *Employment Relations Act 1999, s 10*, to be accompanied to a disciplinary or grievance hearing or that the employee accompanied or sought to accompany another worker to such a hearing (*Employment Relations Act 1999, s 12(4)*. See **55.3**(p) Unfair Dismissal – II);
	(*r*)	was that the employee was dismissed for taking part in protected industrial action in the circumstances set out in *TULRCA 1992, s 238A*, introduced by the *Employment Relations Act 1999, s 16* and *Sch 5*. (See **55.3**(q) Unfair Dismissal – II; or
	(*s*)	was a reason connected with the exercise of various negotiation or consultation rights within a "European Company" as defined in the *European Public Limited-Liability Company Regulations 2004 (SI 2004/2326)*. (*ERA 1996, s 108(3)(k)*: see **55.3** Unfair Dismissal – II);

Employment right	Qualifying period
	(*t*) was a reason connected with the exercise of various negotiation or consultation rights under the *Information and Consultation of Employees Regulations 2004 (SI 2004/3426)*. *ERA 1996, s 108(3)(l)*: see **55.3** UNFAIR DISMISSAL – **II**);
	(*u*) was the fact that the employee has been summoned for jury service, or has been absent on jury service in the circumstances set out in *ERA 1996, s 98B*. (*ERA 1996, s 108(3)(aa)*: see **55.3** UNFAIR DISMISSAL – **II**);
	(*v*) was a selection for redundancy for a reason which would have been automatically unfair if it had been the reason for dismissal (*ERA 1996, s 108(3)(h), s 105*);
	(*w*) was a reason connected with an employee's performance of various functions or exercise of various entitlements under the *European Cooperative Society (Involvement of Employees) Regulations 2006 (SI 2006/2059)*: see *reg 31 of SI 2006/2059 and ERA 1996, s 108(3)(o)*. The *2006 Regulations* relate to the formation of, and employees' participation in, European Cooperative Societies;
	(*x*) was a reason connected with an employee's performance of various functions or exercise of various entitlements in respect of participation in a cross-border merger: see the *Companies (Cross-Border Mergers) Regulations 2007, regs 46–47* and *ERA 1996, s 108(3)(p)*. Note however that *ERA 1996, s 108(3)(p)* has been repealed with effect from 31 January 2020, so that this only applies to dismissals before that date;
	(*y*) was for a reason relating to a 'prohibited list' within *reg 3 of the Employment Relations Act 1999 (Blacklists) Regulations 2010*. This applies essentially when an employee has been dismissed because his name has been included on a 'blacklist' made or obtained by the employer, containing details of trade union membership or activities. See *ERA s 104F* and *s 108(3)(gl)*;

Employment right	Qualifying period
(z)	was that the employee made or proposed to make an application falling with *ERA 1996, s 63D* (statutory right to make request in relation to study or training); or exercised or sought to exercise various rights under the *Employee Study and Training (Procedural Requirements) Regulations 2010, SI 2010/155*; or exercised or proposed to exercise a right conferred on the employee under *ERA 1996, s 63F* (setting out the employer's duties in relation to an application under *ERA 1996, s 63D*); or brought proceedings against the employer under *ERA 1996, s 63I* (complaints to employment tribunals related to applications under *ERA 1996, s 63D*); or alleged the existence of any circumstance which would constitute a ground for bringing such proceedings. See *ERA 1996, s 104E* and *s 108(3)(gk)*, and the *Employee Study and Training (Procedural Requirements) Regulations 2010, SI 2010/155, reg 18*;
(za)	was a reason connected with an employee's performance or proposed performance of various functions or entitlements connected with negotiating rights in a European Public Limited-Liability Company. See *ERA 1996, s 108(3)(q)* and *reg 29(1)* of the *European Public Limited-Liability Company (Employee Involvement)(Great Britain) Regulations 2009 (SI 2009/2401)*;
(zb)	was a reason specified in *reg 17(3)* of the *Agency Workers Regulations 2010 (SI 2010/93)*, where the employee is an agency worker. See *ERA 1996, s 108(3)(r)* and *reg 17(1)* of the *Agency Workers Regulations 2010*.
(zc)	was a reason connected with the assertion of certain rights under the *Occupational and Personal Pension Schemes (Consultation by Employers and Miscellaneous Amendment) Regulations 2006, SI 2006/349* (see *ERA 1996, s 108(3)(m)*);
(zd)	was a reason specified in *ERA 1996, s 104D* (certain matters connected with the enrolment of employees in a pension scheme): see *ERA 1996, s 108(3)(gj)*;
(ze)	was that the employee refused to accept an offer by the employer for the employee to become an employee shareholder within the meaning of *ERA 1996, s 205A*. See *ERA 1996, s 104G* and *s 108(3)(gm)*.
(zf)	was a reason related to the employee's political opinions or affiliation. See *ERA 1996, s 108(4)*.

Employment right	Qualifying period
	(zg) was a reason connected to the employee's membership of a reserve force (as defined in *Armed Forces Act 2006, s 374*). See *ERA 1996, s 108(5)*.
	If the reason or principal reason for dismissal is the transfer of an undertaking, so that dismissal is automatically unfair by operation of reg *7(1)* of the *Transfer of Undertakings (Protection of Employment) Regulations 2006* ('*TUPE*'), the normal qualifying period applies (see *reg 7(6) TUPE*).
Redundancy payment	Two years (*ERA 1996, s 155*).
Consultation of appropriate representatives and notification of Secretary of State on redundancy	Three months, but only where the employment is under a fixed-term contract of three months or less or one made in contemplation of a specific task not expected to last for more than three months (*TULRCA 1992, s 282*).

8   Contract of Employment

Cross-references. See CHILDREN AND YOUNG PERSONS (4) for statutory restrictions on their employment; RESTRAINT OF TRADE, CONFIDENTIALITY AND EMPLOYEE INTERVENTIONS (42); and COLLECTIVE AGREEMENTS (6) for their respective effects on individual contracts; 23.5 EQUAL PAY for the statutory equality clause; 35.6 PAY – I for illegal deductions from wages; 46.16 STRIKES AND INDUSTRIAL ACTION for the effect of industrial action on contracts; and 56.2–56.5 UNFAIR DISMISSAL – III for reinstatement and re-engagement orders. See TERMINATION OF EMPLOYMENT (49) and WRONGFUL DISMISSAL (59) for termination of contract rules. For restrictions on contracting out of statutory provisions, see 23.14 EQUAL PAY, 39.14 REDUNDANCY – I and 54.19 UNFAIR DISMISSAL – I.

8.1   The contract of employment is dealt with in this chapter under the following heads:

(a)   Formation of the contract;

(b)   The statutory requirement for written particulars of contract;

(c)   Terms of the contract, including implied terms and unenforceable terms;

(d)   Changes to contractual terms; and

(e)   Remedies for breach of the employment contract.

This chapter does not deal with the question of whether a particular agreement under which a person works is a 'contract of *employment*' for the purposes of *ERA 1996 s 230(1)*. That question is considered in EMPLOYEE, SELF-EMPLOYED OR WORKER? (16).

8.2   FORMATION

Requirements

The usual requirements of contract law apply: offer, acceptance, consideration, intention to create legal relations and certainty. For examples of the application of these principles, see: *Moore v President of the Methodist Conference* [2011] EWCA Civ 1581, [2012] ICR 432, [2012] IRLR 229 and *Anar v Dresdner Kleinwort Ltd* [2011] EWCA Civ 229, [2011] All ER (D) 88 (Mar). The parties' agreement is to be construed objectively in the factual context prevailing at the time of the agreement. On the importance of certainty, see *Judge v Crown Leisure Ltd* [2005] EWCA Civ 571, [2005] IRLR 823, where it was held that statements made at a Christmas party and in vague terms (such as "in due course" and "eventually") did not amount to a contractually binding agreement to increase the employee's pay. Contrast this with *Anar*, where neither the informal nature of the employer's assurances nor the imprecise scope of those assurances automatically precluded their enforceability.

A contract of employment may also be implied from the parties' conduct where it is necessary to do so: *Franks v Reuters Ltd* [2003] EWCA Civ 417, [2003] IRLR 423; *Dacas v Brook Street Bureau (UK) Ltd* [2004] EWCA Civ 217, [2004] ICR 1437, [2004] IRLR 358 and *Cable & Wireless plc v Muscat* [2006] EWCA Civ 220, [2006] ICR 975, [2006] IRLR 354. The existence of a "factual substratum" suggestive of a contract of employment will not suffice to establish an implied contract (*Beattie v Leicester City Council* (UKEAT0386/09/SM) (20 January 2010, unreported)). Questions as to implied contracts of employment frequently arise in connection 'tripartite' relationships involving agency workers (see EMPLOYEE, SELF-EMPLOYED OR WORKER? (16)).

The fact that a contract of employment is void does not automatically mean that no "employment relationship" exists. For example, where a public authority's employment of an individual was *ultra vires*, there may nonetheless be a *de facto* employment relationship on the basis of which the individual may be treated as an employee for the purposes of *ERA s 230(1)* (*Eastbourne Borough Council v Foster* [2001] EWCA Civ 1091, [2001] LGR 529, [2002] ICR 234; *Lairikyengbam v Shrewsbury and Telford Hospital NHS Trust* [2010] ICR 66, [2009] All ER (D) 271 (Oct), EAT).

8.3   Form of the contract

A contract of employment may be either written or oral, or a mixture of the two. This means that – subject to the contractual principles summarised above – its form may range from a document drawn up by solicitors and signed by both parties, to a chat over a cup of tea in the canteen. One of the issues in *Cheltenham Borough Council v Laird* [2009] EWHC 1253 (QB), [2009] IRLR 621 (upheld on appeal: [2010] EWCA Civ 847) was whether the employment contract had been concluded by an oral agreement which predated the employee's completion of a medical questionnaire or by the consequent letter of appointment which post-dated that questionnaire. The court found the latter to be the case, observing that it would be reasonably expected practice for appointments at this senior managerial level to be concluded in writing.

As the court in *Laird* suggested, senior executives will usually be employed pursuant to written agreements drafted by solicitors. These agreements are often for a fixed term. A director's contract of employment whose guaranteed term is longer than two years must be approved by a resolution of the members of the company. A guaranteed period is the period for which the director's employment may continue other than at the instance of the company and within which the company may not terminate the employment (see **9.3** DIRECTORS and *Companies Act 2006, s 188*). In the event that the contract is not approved by the members, its provisions as to duration are void and there is instead substituted a term that the employment is terminable on reasonable notice (*s 189*). Such agreements frequently contain provisions dealing with the tenure by the employee of a directorship of the employing company. They may also contain restrictive covenants (see RESTRAINT OF TRADE, CONFIDENTIALITY AND EMPLOYEE INTERVENTIONS **(42)**).

Less senior employees may be asked to sign a standard form contract of employment. Alternatively, the contract may be contained in an exchange of letters, or terms may be agreed orally at an interview. Provided that the parties are in agreement over the essential terms of the contract, such as hours and wages, there will be a valid contract of employment enforceable by either party. However, an employer is under a duty to give his employees particulars in writing of certain important terms of their contracts (see **8.6** below).

8.4   Parties to the contract

Despite the rule that unincorporated associations can neither sue nor be sued in their own name, an employee can bring employment tribunal proceedings against the management committee of an unincorporated association: *Asim v Nazir* [2010] ICR 1225.

Occasionally, a question arises as to the identity of the employer where it is unclear which of a number of companies or other legal persons is the employer under the contract. In such cases, the employer is likely to be the person who has power to control the employee's activities (see *Clifford v Union of Democratic Mineworkers* [1991] IRLR 518; *Andrews v King (Inspector of Taxes)* [1991] STC 481, [1991] ICR 846). The question is resolved by considering all the circumstances (and documents) of the case (see for example the unreported Scottish case of *McVeigh v Livingstone* (UKEATS/0027/08/BI) (16 June 2009, unreported), where the tribunal scrutinised the claimant's wage slips, P60s and written particulars in resolving the question of whether the employer was the company or the individuals in control of that company).

See **27.8** FOREIGN EMPLOYEES for the rules as to which country's system of law governs the contract of employment.

See Temporary and Seasonal Employees (47) for a discussion of tripartite relationships involving agencies and service companies. See also *Heynike v 00222648 Limited* [2018] EWHC 303 (QB), [2018] All ER (D) 129 (Feb).

8.5   An employer may engage or refuse to engage any person who has legal capacity, subject only to the statutory provisions relating to Children and Young Persons (4), discrimination on grounds of race or sex or disability or age or religion or belief or sexual orientation or trade union membership or non-membership (see Discrimination and Equal Opportunities – I (11), II (12), and III (13), 51.2 Trade Unions – I) and the provisions relating to the employment of foreign nationals (see Foreign Employees (27)).

8.6   WRITTEN PARTICULARS OF CONTRACT

Although the law does not require the contract itself to be in writing, employers are required to give each employee a written statement of particulars of certain important terms of the contract (see *ERA 1996, s 1* and Continuous Employment (7)). This statement is not itself the contract of employment, but it offers (strong) persuasive (though not conclusive) evidence of the terms of the contract (*Robertson v British Gas Corpn* [1983] ICR 351, [1983] IRLR 302, CA; *System Floors (UK) Ltd v Daniel* [1982] ICR 54, [1981] IRLR 475; *Griffiths v Great Places Housing Group Ltd* (2017) UKEAT/0097/16/BA (unreported); *Born London Ltd v Spire Production Services Ltd* (2017) UKEAT/0255/16/LA (unreported)). Mandatory particulars (see *ERA 1996, s 1(4)*) can be seen as contractual in nature: *Eagland v British Telecommunications plc* [1993] ICR 644, CA.

This written statement of particulars must be given to the employee not later than two months after the beginning of the employment. If, during that period, the employee is to begin work outside the UK for more than a month, the statement must be given to him not later than the time he leaves the UK to begin work (*ERA 1996, s 2(5)*).

The statement may be given in instalments during the two-month period (*ERA 1996, s 1(1)*). However, certain of the particulars must be included in a single document. These are the names of the parties, the dates when employment and continuous employment began, the particulars of remuneration, hours and holidays, the job title or description, and the place of work (*ERA 1996, s 2(4)*).

Prior to the *Employment Rights (Employment Particulars and Paid Annual Leave) (Amendment) Regulations 2018* coming into force on 6 April 2020, an employee with more than one month's service was entitled to a statement of particulars even if the relationship ended in the second month of the two month period for giving a statement (*ERA 1996, s 198*): see *Stefanko v Maritime Hotel Ltd* [2019] IRLR 322. This is no longer the case.

Amendments to the *ERA 1996* introduced by the *Employment Act 2002* permit the use of documents as an alternative to a statement of particulars. If the employer gives the employee a contract of employment or an engagement letter which contains the information required by *ERA 1996, s 1* at the time when employment commences (*ERA 1996, s 7B*) or afterwards (*ERA 1996, s 7A(1)(c)*) that is sufficient to meet the obligations under *s 1*. If the document contains the material required by *s 3* (disciplinary procedure, etc) that is sufficient to comply with that section.

As a result of amendments enacted by the *Employment Rights (Employment Particulars and Paid Annual Leave) (Amendment) Regulations 2018* which came into force on 6 April 2020, statements must now be provided on the first day of employment, or in instalments within the first 2 months of employment with a requirement that the majority of particulars are provided on the first day of employment. The provisions (as amended) do not apply to employees who commence employment after 30 November 1993 and before 6 April 2020 (*ERA 1996 (as amended), Sch 2, para 7A*). However, the amendments will apply where such employees request a statement from the employer after 6 April 2020 (*ERA 1996 (as amended), Sch 2, para 7B*).

8.7　Contract of Employment

8.7　Particulars which must be given

Prior to 6 April 2020, particulars were only required to be given to employees. Following the amendment of *ERA 1996, s 1(3)* by the *Employment Rights (Miscellaneous Amendments) Regulations 2019*, that entitlement was extended to 'workers'.

The written statement must:

(a)　name the employer and the worker;

(b)　specify the date when the employment began; and

(c)　insofar as the statement is given to an 'employee', it must specify the date on which the employee's period of *continuous* employment began (taking into account any employment with a previous employer which counts towards that period).

(*ERA 1996, s 1(3)*.)

(For the day on which employment 'begins', see **7.3** Continuous Employment.)

It must also give the following particulars of terms of employment which are applicable as at a specified date not more than seven days before the date on which the statement, or instalment of a statement, is given:

(a) the scale or rate of remuneration, or the method of calculating remuneration;

(b) the intervals at which remuneration is paid (that is whether weekly, or monthly or at other specified intervals);

(c) any terms and conditions relating to hours of work (including any terms and conditions relating to normal working hours, the days of the week the worker is required to work, and whether or not such hours or days may be variable including how that variation is to be determined);

(d) any terms and conditions relating to:

    (i)　entitlement to holidays, including public holidays and holiday pay (the particulars being sufficient to enable the worker's entitlement, including any entitlement to accrued holiday pay on the termination of employment, to be precisely calculated);

    (ii)　incapacity for work due to sickness or injury, including any provisions for sick pay;

    (iii)　any other paid leave; and

    (iv)　pensions and pension schemes (unless the worker's pension rights depend on the terms of a pension scheme established under statute, and he is employed by a body or authority required under statute to give information concerning pension rights to new workers);

(da) any other benefits provided by the employer that do not fall within another paragraph of ERA 1996, s 1(4);

(e) the length of notice which the worker is obliged to give and entitled to receive to terminate his contract of employment or other worker's contract;

(f) the title of the job which the worker is employed to do or a brief description of the work for which the worker is employed;

(g) where the employment is not intended to be permanent, the period for which it is expected to continue or, if it is for a fixed term, the date when it is to end;

(ga) any probationary period, including any conditions and its duration (ie. a temporary period specified in the contract that commences at the beginning of employment and is intended to enable the employer to assess the worker's suitability for the employment);

(h) either the place of work or, where the worker is required or permitted to work at various places, an indication of that and of the employer's address;

(j) any collective agreements which directly affect the terms and conditions of the employment, including the persons by whom they were made where the employer is not a party;

(k) where the worker is required to work outside the UK for more than a month, certain further particulars concerning that period, the currency of remuneration, any additional remuneration and benefits, and any terms and conditions relating to return;

(l) any training entitlement provided by the employer;

(m) any part of that training entitlement which the employer requires the worker to complete; and

(n) any other training which the employer requires the worker to complete and which the employer will not bear the cost of.

(*ERA 1996, s 1(4), (5)* and *(6)*.)

Note that the particulars required were expanded on 6 April 2020 with the coming into force of the amendments in the *Employment Rights (Miscellaneous Amendments) Regulations 2019*. The list above is of the particulars required after that date. The amended provisions do not apply to employees who commence employment after 30 November 1993 and before 6 April 2020 (*ERA 1996* (as amended), *Sch 2, para 7A*). However, the amended provisions apply where such employees request a statement from the employer after 6 April 2020 (*ERA 1996* (as amended), *Sch 2, para 7B*).

Section 1(4)(a) does not require the employer to specify the nature of the payment as contractual or non-contractual. It is possible to state the "method of calculating the remuneration" without defining whether that payment has contractual effect: *Born London Limited v Spire Production Services Ltd* (2017) UKEAT/0255/16/LA (unreported). However, *section 1(4)(a)* is not satisfied only by providing the method of calculation (for example, hourly rate multiplied by the number of hours worked). Rather, the hourly rate must be specified: *Twenty-Four Seven Recruitment Services Ltd v Afonso* (2018) UKEAT/0311/17/LA (unreported).

Disciplinary and complaints procedures. The *ERA 1996* (as amended by *s 35, Employment Act 2002*) further requires that every statement given to an employee shall contain a note:

(A)   specifying any disciplinary rules applicable to the worker or referring to a document which is reasonably accessible to the worker and which specifies such rules. The employer must also specify any procedure applicable to the taking of disciplinary actions relating to the worker, or to a decision to dismiss the worker, or refer the worker to the provisions of another document which specifies such a procedure; and

(B)   specifying, by description or otherwise:

(i)   a person to whom the worker can apply if he is dissatisfied with any disciplinary decision relating to him or any decision to dismiss him; and

(ii)   a person to whom the worker can apply for the purpose of seeking redress of any grievance relating to his employment and the manner in which any such application should be made, and where there are further steps to be taken in any such application, explaining those steps or referring to a document which is reasonably accessible to the worker and which explains them (*ERA 1996, s 3(1)*).

The requirement to give a note of disciplinary and complaints procedures does not apply to rules, disciplinary decisions, decisions to dismiss, grievances or procedures relating to HEALTH AND SAFETY AT WORK – **II (29)** (*ERA 1996, s 3(2)*).

ERA 1996 docs not require there to be provisions in the contract on all these matters (see *Morley v Heritage plc* [1993] IRLR 400). It simply requires notice of such provisions that do exist to be given to the employee. Where there are no provisions relating to any of the matters listed above, that fact must be stated, eg where no contractual sick pay is provided (*ERA 1996, s 2(1)*).

8.8 Alternatives to inclusion of particulars in written statement

ERA 1996, s 2(2), (3) provides that the written statement of particulars:

(a) may refer the worker to the provisions of some other document which he has reasonable opportunities of reading in the course of his employment, or which is made reasonably accessible to him in some other way, for particulars of any of the matters specified in *ERA 1996, s 1(4)(d)(ii)* and *(iii)* and *(l)* (sickness, sick pay, pensions and training entitlement); and

(b) may refer the worker to the law or to a collective agreement which directly affects his terms and conditions for particulars of the matters specified in *s 1(4)(e), ERA 1996* (length of notice), provided that any such collective agreement is reasonably accessible to him.

8.9 Written particulars and changes in contract terms

Any changes in the contractual terms or in other matters of which written particulars must be given must be the subject of a written statement given to the worker at the earliest opportunity and in any event not later than one month after the change (or the time of leaving the UK to work for more than one month, if that is the cause of the change) (*ERA 1996, s 4(1), (3)*). Similar provisions concerning the documents in which particulars may be set out again apply.

A mere change of the employer's name, or a mere change in employer which does not break CONTINUOUS EMPLOYMENT (7), does not require a complete new statement under *ERA 1996, s 1*, but does require a statement of change under *s 4* (*ERA 1996, s 4(6), (8)*).

8.10 Exceptions

The requirement to give written particulars applies to all workers except:

(a) seamen of various kinds (*ERA 1996, s 199, s 5(1)*); and

(b) a person whose employment continues for less than one month (*ERA 1996, s 198*).

8.11 Workers' remedies for failure to give particulars

A worker who has not been provided with the necessary particulars may make a reference relating to the failure to an employment tribunal (*ERA 1996, s 11(1)*). Claims under *s 11* are a relatively speedy way of having contractual employment rights determined.

An application may be made by either the worker or the employer if a statement of particulars has purportedly been given, but a question arises as to the particulars which ought to have been included or referred to in it (*ERA 1996, s 11(2)*). Where no *express* term has been agreed, it may be that the tribunal is able to *imply* a term after considering all the facts and circumstances of the relationship between the employer and the employee concerned (*Mears v Safecar Security Ltd* [1982] ICR 626). However, if there has been no express or implied agreement upon a particular term, the tribunal has no power to invent a term for the parties (*Eagland v British Telecommunications plc* [1993] ICR 644; and see **8.14** below). Nor is *s 11* to be used as a means of clarifying or interpreting an ambiguous term (*Construction Industry Training Board v Leighton* [1978] IRLR 60). This was confirmed by the Court of Appeal in *Southern Cross Healthcare Co Ltd v Perkins* [2010] EWCA Civ 1442, [2011] ICR 285, [2011] IRLR 247, where Maurice Kay LJ held at para 29 that "the reference in *section 11(1)* of the *1996 Act* to a determination of 'what particulars ought to have been included', is not an invitation to judicial creativity, even under the rubric of "construction"".

An employer's failure to include a term in the statement of particulars does not mean that the employer is unable to enforce that term: *Lange v Georg Schüneman GmbH* [2001] IRLR 244, ECJ.

The tribunal will, if it finds such a reference under *s 11* well-founded, state the particulars which should have been given and the employer will be deemed to have given a statement including those particulars (*ERA 1996, s 12(1), (2)*). If the employer has been in breach of any of those terms, the worker may bring an action against him in the County Court or the High Court or, if the breach involves a deduction from pay, in the tribunal under *ERA 1996, ss 13–27* (the former *Wages Act 1986* provisions) (see **35.6 PAY – I**). The right to present a complaint for failure to provide written particulars may be exercised by an employee who has been employed for more than two months. If the employment has ceased, the application to the tribunal must be made before the end of the period of three months beginning with the date on which the employment ceased or within such further period as the tribunal considers reasonable where it was not reasonably practicable for the application to be made within three months (*ERA 1996, s 11(4)*). (See **20.91 EMPLOYMENT TRIBUNALS**.)

There is no right to claim damages for a breach of the statutory duty to give written particulars, although in certain special circumstances an employer may be under a contractual duty to take reasonable steps to publicise a term (*Scally v Southern Health and Social Services Board* [1991] ICR 771, HL).

In the event that an employee brings a claim of a type specified in *Sch 5* to the *Employment Act 2002* (a wide range of claims including, but not limited to, unfair dismissal, discrimination and breach of contract cases) against an employer which is resolved in favour of the employee and, at the time when the proceedings were commenced, the employer was in breach either of his duty to provide a statement of particulars under *ERA 1996, s 1* or to a statement of changes under *ERA 1996, s 4*, then the tribunal must award the employee two weeks' pay (and may award four weeks' pay) even if it makes no other award (*EmA 2002, s 38*). If the claim is unsuccessful or withdrawn, no award can be made: *Advanced Collection Limited v Gultekin* (UKEAT 10377114, 6 February 2015) If the tribunal does make an award in favour of the employee, it must increase that award by two weeks' pay (and may increase it by four weeks' pay). However, if there are exceptional circumstances that would make the award or the increase to the award unjust or inequitable, then the tribunal does not have to order the additional award.

8.12 TERMS OF THE CONTRACT

Freedom to agree

Agreement remains the pivotal issue in construing employment contracts. As the Supreme Court confirmed in *Autoclenz Ltd v Belcher* [2011] UKSC 41, [2011] 4 All ER 745 (in the context of whether or not individuals were 'workers'), the fundamental question is "what was the agreement between the parties?" If the evidence showed that the written contractual terms did not reflect the parties' true agreement, then it can to that extent be disregarded.

8.12   Contract of Employment

The parties are free to agree any terms they wish, subject to certain limitations set out below. In determining the terms of a contract, a tribunal will have to consider the provisions of a written contract (if any). However, even in the case where there is a written contract, it will not be correct to consider only its terms unless it is established that the parties intended that the document should contain all the terms of the contract. It is open to the parties to agree some terms in writing and others orally (see the discussion in *Carmichael v National Power plc* [1999] 4 All ER 897, [1999] 1 WLR 2042, para 19). If an employment tribunal is called upon to interpret the terms of a contract, it must apply the same principles as an ordinary court. This means, for example, the words used must be interpreted in the context which existed and was known to both parties at the time when the contract was made (*Investors Compensation Scheme Ltd v West Bromwich Building Society* [1998] 1 All ER 98, HL) but that the parties' subsequent conduct is not admissible in construing their original written agreement (*Hooper v British Railways Board* [1988] IRLR 517). Where the terms of a written contract are truly ambiguous, it may be permissible to construe what the parties meant by using evidence of a clearly established practice, which continued both before and after the contract was made (*Dunlop Tyres Ltd v Blows* [2001] IRLR 629, CA; see also COLLECTIVE AGREEMENTS (6)). This latter principle should, however, be approached with caution: courts and tribunals will be reluctant to draw inferences from later conduct (*Choudhry v Triesman* [2003] EWHC 1203 (Ch)). The nature of the relationship, and the power imbalance often inherent in the employment relationship, is a matter of context that the Court may consider: *Daniels v Lloyds Bank Plc* [2018] EWHC 660 (Comm), [2018] IRLR 813. The Tribunal may also consider whether a purported provision of a contract (or, indeed, the very basis of hiring an 'employee') is a 'sham' where neither party intended to create the legal rights and obligations which they set out (*Redrow Homes (Yorkshire) Ltd v Buckborough & Sewell* [2009] IRLR 34, EAT; *Protectacoat Firthglow Ltd v Szilagyi* [2009] EWCA Civ 98, [2009] ICR 835, [2009] IRLR 365; *Autoclenz*; see also EMPLOYEE, SELF-EMPLOYED OR WORKER? (16)).

8.13   Employer handbooks and policies

Employees will often be provided with a substantial volume of documentation on starting work. These documents may be presented under a variety of titles, such as employer policies and company handbooks. In practice, they are often more voluminous than the statement of written particulars or any document which is according to its own terms a contractual document. In many cases, it may be a matter of considerable practical importance to know whether or not these documents have contractual effect. This question may arise, for example, when the employer seeks to vary the provisions of a policy or of the company handbook. If the policy or handbook is contractual, it may not be unilaterally varied. The question may also arise when an employer is seeking to dismiss an employee. Where the handbook provides, for example, for a particular disciplinary procedure, and the employer proposes to dismiss in breach of that procedure, the employee may seek an injunction to restrain dismissal (see **8.42** below). Such an injunction can only be granted where the procedure relied upon has contractual effect. If the procedure does not have contractual force, there is no legal foundation for such an injunction.

The principles governing the incorporation of documents into contracts were summarised in *Hallett v Derby Hospitals NHS Foundation Trust* [2018] EWHC 796 (QB), [2018] 3 All ER 895. The overarching concern is what the parties intended on the basis of the words used and their context. The question is whether the parties have expressly or impliedly agreed that the document form part of the contract between them. If they have, the terms of the document must be "apt" to be incorporated. There is a distinction, in this respect, between "statements of entitlement ... intended to have contractual effect" and "quite distinct procedural, aspirational or discretionary matters" (see *Keeley v Fosroc International* [2006] IRLR 961, CA and *Sparks v Department for Transport* [2016] ICR 695, CA).

There is no single test for determining whether documents such as disciplinary procedures have contractual effect: factors to consider include the certainty, level of detail and workability of the relevant provision, its importance to the working relationship and its context (*Hussain v Surrey and Sussex Healthcare NHS Trust* [2011] EWHC 1670 (QB)).

A code or policy is only to be regarded as having contractual effect when it may be regarded as conferring rights on employees. If it only lays down standards of good practice which an employer would be expected to follow, it does not have contractual effect (*Wandsworth London Borough Council v D'Silva* [1998] IRLR 193, CA). In *D'Silva* the employer sought unilaterally to alter the terms of a sickness policy. The employee alleged that this would be in breach of contract. The Court of Appeal held that since the policy was not intended to confer rights but was only a statement of good practice, the employer could alter the terms without securing the agreement of the employees.

In contrast, in *Attrill & Other v Dresdner Kleinwort Limited & Anor* [2013] EWCA Civ 394, [2013] 3 All ER 607, the Court of Appeal held that the employer's announcement of a bonus pool (specifically aimed at retaining employees) during a 'Town Hall' meeting broadcast online was an offer capable of acceptance and of incorporation into the employees' contracts.

In *Keeley v Fosroc International Ltd* [2006] EWCA Civ 1277, [2006] IRLR 961, the Court of Appeal held that even where a handbook was expressly incorporated, that did not mean that the entire content of the handbook had contractual effect. It was particularly relevant to consider the importance of the provision for the employee. If it was clearly worded as conferring an entitlement on the employee, it was likely to have contractual effect. It was not determinative that the passage in the handbook was described as a policy.

Even where the policy is contractual, its effect will depend on the construction of the contract as a whole. Thus, the House of Lords held in *Taylor v Secretary of State for Scotland* [2000] IRLR 502 that the inclusion in the contract of an equal opportunities policy which undertook that there should be no discrimination on the grounds of age did not prevent the employer from dismissing an employee on the grounds that he had reached the minimum retirement age (see RETIREMENT (43)). See also *Bateman v Asda Stores Ltd* [2010] IRLR 370, [2010] All ER (D) 277 (Feb) where the handbook empowered the employer 'to review, revise, amend or replace' the contents of the handbook, including contractual matters such as pay. See also the *Attrill* case (above).

8.14   Express or implied terms

The terms of the contract may be express or implied or incorporated.

Express terms are those that the parties specifically by reference agree upon. The express terms of the contract may be found in a document described as the contract of employment or in an offer letter or in oral exchanges between the parties or in other documents. The provisions set out in a statement of written particulars will be evidence of the express terms, albeit that the statement of written particulars is not the contract itself. The parties may agree upon certain points by reference to a document such as a collective agreement which thereby becomes incorporated into the agreement between the parties (see 6.2 COLLECTIVE AGREEMENTS). See however, *Malone v British Airways* [2010] EWCA Civ 1225, [2011] ICR 125, [2011] IRLR 32, where the Court of Appeal upheld findings that provisions concerning staffing levels, set out in staff agreements and manuals, were not apt to be enforced by individual employees.

The core of a contract of employment is a contract whereby an employee agrees to work for an employer in return for pay. In the event that a contract of employment exists, this is the irreducible minimum. However, as set out below there are many other aspects to a contract of employment.

8.14   Contract of Employment

In *R v Hull University Visitor, ex p Page* [1992] ICR 67 at 80D–80F, Staughton LJ was of the view that a job advertisement should be read together with a letter of appointment (the case later went to the House of Lords: [1993] ICR 114). Implied and incorporated terms are dealt with below.

8.15   Common implied terms

Frequently, many terms of the contract will not be specifically set out or stated. There may be many rights and obligations on either side which are left unexpressed and unspecified. The general rule is that a term will be implied into a contract if it is so obvious that both parties would have regarded it as a term even though they had not expressly stated it as a term or if it is *necessary* to imply the term in order to give the contract business efficacy (*Liverpool City Council v Irwin* [1977] AC 239; *Scally v Southern Health and Social Services Board* [1991] ICR 771 at 781). Terms also may be implied if they are customary in the particular trade or calling, or form the usual practice of the particular employer, if it is sufficiently well known. Such a custom or practice must be 'reasonable, certain and notorious' (*Bond v CAV Ltd* [1983] IRLR 360; *Henry v London General Transport Services Ltd* [2002] ICR 910, [2002] IRLR 472). In order to become an implied term, a custom must be followed with regularity such that it becomes legitimate to infer that the parties follow the practice because they regard it as a legal obligation rather than that the practice is followed as a matter of policy: *Solectron Scotland Ltd v Roper* [2004] IRLR 4. In *Garratt v Mirror Group Newspapers Ltd* [2011] EWCA Civ 425, the Court of Appeal upheld an implied term that enhanced redundancy payments were available only to employees who signed compromise agreements. The Court of Appeal affirmed, and in some respects updated, these principles in *Park Cakes Ltd v Shuba* [2013] IRLR 800 and *CSC Computer Services Ltd v McAlinden* [2013] EWCA Civ 1435.

Terms commonly implied are the *employee's* duties of:

(a)   fidelity;

(b)   obedience;

(c)   working with due diligence and care;

(d)   not using or disclosing the employer's trade secrets or confidential information;

and the *employer's* duties:

(e)   to take care for the employee's health and safety;

(f)   to provide redress for grievances;

(g)   (in some cases) not merely to pay but to provide work;

and the duties of *both parties:*

(h)   not to destroy the relationship of trust and confidence (see below for more detail);

(i)   to give a reasonable period of notice of termination, when no specific notice period has been agreed.

The above list is not exhaustive: other duties can arise in various circumstances. Some of them are dealt with below.

Employee's duties

8.16   *Duty of fidelity—*

An employee has a duty to serve his employer faithfully and not to act against the interests of the employer's business.

A distinction must be drawn between the duty to serve the employer in good faith, which is owed by all employees, and fiduciary duties, which are not an incident of every employment relationship. When a person is a fiduciary (such as a trustee or a company director), he is obliged to pursue another's interests at the expense of his own. In the case of an employee, his obligation is to comply with the express and implied terms of his contract (for a discussion of the distinction, see *Nottingham University v Fishel* [2000] IRLR 471).

In *Sybron Corpn v Rochem Ltd* [1984] Ch 112, it was held that the terms and nature of a particular employment might be such that there was a contractual duty to disclose the misconduct of other employees (see also *Item Software (UK) Ltd v Fassihi* [2004] EWCA Civ 1244, [2005] ICR 450).

However, a mere employee is not under an implied obligation to reveal his own misconduct, but a fiduciary (such as a director) is under such an obligation (*Tesco Stores Ltd v Pook* [2004] IRLR 618; see also *Basildon Academies v Amadi* UKEAT 0343/14); *Item Software (UK) Ltd v Fassihi* [2004] EWCA Civ 1244, [2005] ICR 450, *GHLM Trading Ltd v Maroo* [2012] EWHC 61 (Ch)). Senior employees may owe fiduciary obligations by reason of their seniority even if they are not directors: *Shepherds Investments Ltd v Walters* [2006] EWHC 836 (Ch), [2007] IRLR 110.

As to the purely contractual duty of fidelity, the following summary of principles in *QBE Management Services v Dymoke* [2012] EWHC 80 (QB), [2012] IRLR 458 was cited in *EC Medica Group UK Ltd v Dearnsley Davidson* [2018] EWHC 1952 (Ch), [2018] All ER (D) 175 (Jul):

(1)   It is indisputable that an employee owes his employer a contractual duty of 'fidelity', but how far it extends will depend on the facts of each case (per Lord Green MR in *Hivac v Park Royal* [1946] Ch 169 at 174).

(2)   The more senior the staff the great the degree of loyalty, fidelity and diligence required (per Openshaw J in *UBS Wealth Management (UK) Ltd v Vestra Wealth LLP* [2008] IRLR 965 at paragraph [10]).

(3)   The first task of the court is to identify the nature of the employee's obligations of fidelity and then to decide whether the employee's activities are in breach (per Moses LJ in *Helmet Integrated Systems v Tunnard* [2007] IRLR 126 at paragraph [32]).

(4)   The mere fact that activities are described by an employee as 'preparatory' to competition does not mean that they are legitimate (per Moses LJ in *Helmet Integrated Systems v Tunnard* [2007] IRLR 126 at paragraph [28]).

(5)   It is a breach of the duty of fidelity for an employee to recruit or solicit another employee to act in competition (see *British Midland Tool v Midland International Tooling Ltd* [2003] 2 BCLC 523).

(6)   Attempts by senior employees to solicitor more junior staff constitutes particularly serious misconduct (*Sybron Corp v Rochem Ltd* [1984] Ch 112).

(7)   It is a breach of the duty of fidelity for an employee to misuse confidential information belonging to his employee (see *Faccenda Chicken Ltd v Fowler* [1987] Ch 117).

(8)   The court should ask whether the activities in which the employee is engaged affect his ability to serve his employer faithfully and honestly and to the best of his abilities (see *Shepherds Investments Ltd v Walters* [2007] IRLR 110 at paragraph [131])."

It would be in breach of an implied term of the contract of employment for the employee to set up a rival business to that of his employer during the period of his employment, unless he had been expressly permitted to do so, or to take more than preparatory steps towards doing so: *Balston Ltd v Headline Filters Ltd* [1990] FSR 385. However, mere preparations to set up a competing business after the termination of the employment are not necessarily a breach of contract (*Ixora Trading Inc v Jones* [1990] FSR 251).

The line between legitimate and illegitimate steps towards competing is difficult to draw. In *Helmet Integrated Systems Ltd v Tunnard* [2006] EWCA Civ 1735, [2007] IRLR 126 it was held that an employee did not act in breach of contract when he designed a product intended to compete with his employer's. The court reached this view partly on the basis that the contract of employment did not sufficiently restrict his ability to prepare for future competition. That analysis does not sit happily with the existence of the implied duty of fidelity. The court also noted that he was a salesman and not a technical designer. In principle, an employee crosses the line and acts unlawfully when his acts are inconsistent with his duty of fidelity (see *Shepherds Investments Ltd v Walters* [2006] EWHC 836 (Ch), [2007] IRLR 110, a case concerned primarily with directors; see also *Cobbetts LLP v Hodge* [2009] EWHC 786 (Ch), a case concerned with a solicitor negotiating for himself an equity share in a client company without obtaining the informed consent of his employer) and *Samsung Semiconductor Europe Ltd v Docherty* [2011] CSOH 32 (where the Court of Session stated that an employee's liability did not depend on his consciously assuming fiduciary duties). Another example (albeit that this was a case about a director's fiduciary duty) is *Foster Bryant Surveying Ltd v Bryant* [2007] EWCA Civ 200, [2007] IRLR 425. It is also a breach of contract for an employee to tender for future business from a customer of the employer in competition with the employer (*Adamson v B & L Cleaning Services Ltd* [1995] IRLR 193). For the implied obligation not to use or disclose the employer's trade secrets or confidential information, see **42.13 RESTRAINT OF TRADE, CONFIDENTIALITY AND EMPLOYEE INTERVENTIONS**.

8.17 *Duty to Obey Reasonable Employer Instructions—*

The employee is also obliged by the implied terms of his contract of employment to obey the reasonable instructions of his employer and to carry out his work conscientiously and honestly.

A work to rule or withdrawal of goodwill may amount to a breach of the implied obligation to serve the employer faithfully (*Secretary of State for Employment v Associated Society of Locomotive Engineers and Firemen (No 2)* [1972] 2 QB 455, [1972] ICR 19, CA; *British Telecommunications plc v Ticehurst* [1992] ICR 383).

The duties of obedience and fidelity are also owed to an employer to whom the employee is seconded (*Macmillan Inc v Bishopsgate Investment Trust plc* [1993] IRLR 393).

In *Cresswell v Inland Revenue Board* [1984] 2 All ER 713, [1984] ICR 508, it was held that an employee was expected to adapt to new methods and techniques in performing his duties, provided the employer arranged for him to receive the necessary training in the new skills and the nature of the work did not alter so radically that it was outside the contractual duties of the employee. If the employer has an express power to transfer the employee to other duties, he is not subject to an implied requirement to exercise that power reasonably, provided that he has some proper grounds for the exercise of the express power and he does not exercise it in such a way as to destroy trust and confidence between himself and the employee (*White v Reflecting Roadstuds Ltd* [1991] ICR 733). Similarly, an express right in the employer to require a particular number of hours per week to be worked must be construed as being subject to the employer's duty to safeguard the employee's health and safety (*Johnstone v Bloomsbury Health Authority* [1991] ICR 269).

8.18 *Duty to take due care in performance of duties—*

An employee owes a contractual duty of care to his employer, breach of which can support a claim for damages (*Janata Bank v Ahmed* [1981] ICR 791, [1981] IRLR 457 applying *Lister v Romford Ice and Cold Storage Co Ltd* [1957] AC 555).

Employer's duties

8.19   *Health and safety—*

It is an implied term of the contract of employment that the employer will take reasonable steps to ensure the employee's safety (see comments in *Dutton & Clark Ltd v Daly* [1985] IRLR 363, *Johnstone v Bloomsbury Health Authority* [1991] ICR 269 and HEALTH AND SAFETY AT WORK – I (28)). This includes providing a safe system of work. The duty to provide a safe system of work should not be limited to preventing physical injury. Employers also owe a duty to take reasonable care not to cause psychiatric harm to an employee by reason of the volume or character of work imposed on the employee. The standard of care depends on what is reasonable conduct for a person in the employer's position. What is reasonable depends on the nature of the relationship, the magnitude of the risk of injury that was reasonably foreseeable, the seriousness of the consequences for the employee if that injury should occur, and the cost and practicability of preventing the risk (*Walker v Northumberland County Council* [1995] IRLR 35).

In *Waltons & Morse v Dorrington* [1997] IRLR 488, it was held that a term was to be implied into every contract of employment that 'the employer will provide and monitor for employees, so far as is reasonably practicable, a working environment which is reasonably suitable for the performance by them of their contractual duties'. In that case, the employer acted in breach of the term by requiring a non-smoking secretary to work in a smoke-filled environment.

8.20   *Redress for grievances—*

In *W A Goold (Pearmak) Ltd v McConnell* [1995] IRLR 516, the EAT held that it was an implied term that the employer would 'reasonably and promptly afford a reasonable opportunity to their employees to obtain redress of any grievance they may have' (see also *Ministry of Defence v Guellard* [2009] All ER (D) 50 (Dec)). The basis for the implication of this term was the statutory obligation to include in the written statement of terms, a note specifying to whom and in what manner an employee might apply for the purpose of seeking redress of any grievance relating to employment (see **8.7** above).

8.21   *Duty to provide work—*

In some cases, it may be argued that the employer's only obligation is to pay and that there is no duty upon an employer to provide work. In other words, so long as the employee is fully remunerated, the employer can ask him to stay at home without being in breach of contract. A contract of employment may, however, be subject to an implied obligation to provide work where earnings vary according to the work done, where an individual such as an actor is dependent upon publicity, or where the employee has skills that may atrophy through lack of use: *Langston v Amalgamated Union of Engineering Workers* [1974] 1 All ER 980, [1974] ICR 180 and 510, CA; *Breach v Epsylon Industries Ltd* [1976] ICR 316; *Spencer v Marchington* [1988] IRLR 392; and cf *Warren v Mendy* [1989] ICR 525. See also *Christie v Carmichael* [2010] IRLR 1016, where the Scottish EAT found that the employer was entitled to place an employee on garden leave, notwithstanding the lack of an express contractual provision to that effect, partly on the basis that the employee's skills would not atrophy. The range of cases in which the court will imply an obligation to provide work has widened following the decision of the Court of Appeal in *William Hill Organisation Ltd v Tucker* [1999] ICR 291, [1998] IRLR 313. There it was held that the question of whether there was an obligation to provide work depended on the facts of each case. The question was whether the consideration moving from the employer extended to an obligation to permit the employee to do the work or whether it was confined to a duty to pay the agreed remuneration. See also *SG&R Valuation Service Co LLC v Boudrais* [2008] EWHC 1340 (QB), [2008] IRLR 770, where it was held that even where the employee's contract does confer on him a right to work, that right would be foregone if the employee demonstrated in a serious way that he was not ready or willing to work. This was approved in *Standard Life Health Care Ltd v Gorman* [2009] EWCA Civ 1292, [2010] IRLR 233.

8.22 Suspension only on reasonable grounds—

In *McClory v Post Office* [1992] ICR 758, the court was prepared to imply a term that the employer's express right to suspend the employee must only be exercised on reasonable grounds, although not to imply any term that the employer should when exercising that power observe the principles of natural justice. The case also contains a useful discussion of the circumstances in which an employee may have a contractual right to work overtime.

McClory was approved in *Watson v Durham University* [2008] EWCA Civ 1266, in the context of the employer making weak allegations of racism and then seeking to suspend the employee on that basis much later. An absence of reasonable or proper cause for a suspension may also amount to a breach of the implied term of trust and confidence (see 8.22D).

In *Marshall (Cambridge) Ltd v Hamblin* [1994] IRLR 260, the EAT held that an employee who has resigned has no right to work out his notice period (in the absence, of course, of any express term or custom and practice to the contrary). The employee's only right was to pay in lieu of notice, even though the majority of the employee's income was based on commission.

8.22a Employee's economic well-being—

In *Scally v Southern Health and Social Services Board* [1991] ICR 771, the House of Lords held that the employer was under an implied duty to take reasonable steps to bring to the employee's attention a right which he had (in that case, to purchase extra years' service for superannuation purposes) that would be lost unless he took certain action, given that the employee could not reasonably have been expected to be aware of the relevant contractual term without it being drawn to his attention.

However, there is no implied term that the employer will take reasonable care of his employees' economic well-being: *Crossley v Faithful & Gould Holdings* [2004] EWCA Civ 293, [2004] IRLR 377. See also *James-Bowen v Commissioner of Police of the Metropolis* [2018] UKSC 40, [2018] ICR 1353; see also *Don Benyatov v Credit Suisse Securities (Europe) Ltd* [2020] EWHC 85 (QB), [2020] IRLR 299.

8.22b Continuation of employment and ill health payments—

Where a contract of employment contains terms entitling the employee to benefits during a period of ill health and the continued receipt of such benefits is dependent on the individual remaining in the employer's employment, a term will be implied that the employer will not dismiss the employee while he remains incapacitated so as to deprive him of the continued receipt of those benefits (*Aspden v Webbs Poultry & Meat Group (Holdings) Ltd* [1996] IRLR 521). A similar approach was taken in Scotland in *Adin v Sedco Forex International Resources Ltd* [1997] IRLR 280 (and see *Brompton v AOC International Ltd* [1997] IRLR 639, para 38, CA).

The extent to which an employer may dismiss an employee who is in receipt of sick pay and/or who anticipates that, if his contract of employment continues in force, he will in due course be entitled to early retirement or to some other benefit was the issue in the Court of Session case of *Hill v General Accident Fire and Life Assurance Corpn plc* [1998] IRLR 641. The employee in that case was in receipt of sick pay. If he had remained employed and in receipt of sick pay for a further four months, he would have been entitled to an ill-health retirement pension or to sickness and accident benefit. The employer terminated his contract by reason of redundancy. Mr Hill sued alleging that the termination of his employment was in breach of the implied duty of trust and confidence and that, whilst he was absent sick and in receipt of sick pay or with an anticipation of early retirement or other benefits, his employment could be terminated only by reason of his own repudiatory breach of contract. The court held that a person in Mr Hill's position could not be dismissed by reason of his absence, or for a specious reason, or for no reason at all. The power to dismiss included, but was not limited to, the case where the employee acted in repudiatory breach of contract. Accordingly, a dismissal by reason of redundancy was not in breach of the implied term of trust and confidence. In *Villella v MFI Furniture Centres Ltd* [1999] IRLR 468, a case concerning Permanent Health Insurance, the High Court formulated an implied term that the employer would not terminate the contract of employment, save for cause other than ill health, in circumstances which would deprive the employee of his continuing entitlement to benefit.

It has also been held that where an employer provides a benefit such as PHI and the insurer fails to pay, there is an implied obligation on the employer to pursue the insurer for payment, including, if need be, by litigation: *Marlow v East Thames Housing Group Ltd* [2002] IRLR 798. The extent of the obligation would of course depend on the merits of the employee's argument.

The *Aspden* line of cases has been applied by analogy to the case where an employer proposes to dismiss for redundancy and employees have the benefit of a contractual redundancy package. In *Jenvey v Australian Broadcasting Corpn* [2002] EWHC 927 (QB), [2003] ICR 79 it was held that where the employer had proposed to dismiss for redundancy with the consequence that the employee would enjoy a contractual payment, it was an implied term that the employer would not then dismiss for any other reason (apart from cause) if to do so would defeat those contractual rights.

8.22c *Discretionary payments and benefits—*

Contracts of employment often contain provision for benefits that are dependent upon the exercise of discretion by the employer. By way of example, contracts providing an entitlement to bonus often confer a discretion on the employer in relation to the amount of the bonus (or, indeed, the decision to award a bonus at all: see *Small v Boots Company plc* [2009] IRLR 328). It is an implied term that such a discretion will be exercised in good faith, for a proper purpose and rationally: *Horkulak v Cantor Fitzgerald International* [2004] IRLR 942 (approving *Clark v Nomura International plc* [2000] IRLR 766) and *Brogden Bank plc v Investec Bank plc* [2014] IRLR 924. In *Horkulak*, damages for breach of contract by not making a bonus payment were assessed on the basis of what the employer would have paid had it exercised the discretion genuinely and rationally. The court stood in the shoes of the employer and decided what sums would have been awarded once it was established that the sum awarded by the employer was in breach of contract. See also *Small v Boots Co Plc* [2009] IRLR 328.

However, the Court of Appeal has subsequently stressed the limited role of the Court in such claims. It is no part of the Court's function to decide what bonus should have been awarded. The Court is concerned only to ensure that the employer complies with its legal obligation to exercise its discretion in good faith and rationally: see *Humphreys v Norilsk Nickel International (UK) Ltd* [2010] IRLR 976. The employer has a wide discretion and the burden of establishing that a bonus paid was irrational is 'a very high one': *Keen v Commerzbank AG* [2007] ICR 623, sub nom *Commerzbank AG v Keen* [2007] IRLR 132. However, the Court of Appeal has also held that once an employee makes out grounds that a decision is irrational the burden shifts to the employer to demonstrate that it has reached a reasonable decision, this may require evidence from the actual decision-maker: *Hills v Niksun Inc* [2016] EWCA Civ 115.

The Supreme Court's decision in *Braganza v BP Shipping Ltd* [2015] UKSC 17, [2015] ICR 449, [2015] IRLR 487 is authority for the proposition that contractual discretions (including discretions as to whether or not to pay a bonus) are reviewable by the courts on the public law Wednesbury standard: were the correct matters taken into account when making the decision and, even if the right matters were taken into account, is the result so unreasonable that no reasonable decision-maker could have made it. The antecedent step, however, is to identify the discretion and (as a matter of construction) to identify the purpose for which the discretion is to be exercised: *Daniels v Lloyds Bank plc* [2018] EWHC 660 (Comm), [2018] IRLR 813. However, where the reasons for exercising the discretion in a particular way are partly good and partly bad, if the decision (looked at overall) is good, the exercise of the discretion cannot be impugned. The question is not whether the reasons for the decision were reasonable, but whether the decision itself was: *No 1 West India Quay (Residential) Ltd v East Tower Apartments Ltd* [2018] EWCA Civ 250, [2018] 1 WLR 5682.

8.22d *Trust and confidence—*

It is now well established that employment contracts contain an implied term of mutual trust and confidence. This term is framed as follows: the parties to the contract will not, without reasonable and proper cause, conduct themselves in a manner calculated or likely to destroy or seriously damage the relationship of confidence and trust which should exist between employer and employee. This is a mutual duty, albeit that the overwhelming majority of the cases deal with breach of the term by the employer. This implied term has been approved by the House of Lords in the landmark decision of *Malik v BCCI SA (in liq)* [1998] AC 20, [1997] ICR 606. Although in *Malik* Lord Steyn said the term applied to conduct calculated **and** likely to have the requisite effects, the EAT has since confirmed that it is 'calculated **or** likely': *Baldwin v Brighton and Hove City Council* [2007] ICR 680, [2007] IRLR 232.

It has also been held that the test for determining whether the employer has acted in breach of this term is a severe one: the conduct of the employer must be such as to destroy or seriously damage the relationship (*Claridge v Daler Rowney Ltd* [2008] ICR 1267), and there must have been no reasonable and proper cause for the conduct (*Gogay v Hertfordshire County Council* [2000] IRLR 703, CA, paras 53–55; *Devon and Somerset Fire and Rescue Service v Tilke* (UKEAT/0303/09/RN) (25 January 2010, unreported)). This term is fundamental to the employment relationship and any breach of it is likely to be repudiatory: *Morrow v Safeway Stores plc* [2002] IRLR 9, EAT. However, it is important to bear in mind that both limbs of the term are important: conduct which destroys trust and confidence is not in breach of contract if there is a reasonable cause (*Hilton v Shiner Ltd Builders Merchants* [2001] IRLR 727). The Court of Appeal has deprecated the use of loose language in some cases which may appear to extend the scope of the implied term (into, for example, an obligation of 'fair dealing'). It is not a simple obligation to act fairly: *North West Anglia NHS Foundation Trust v Gregg* [2019] EWCA Civ 387, [2019] IRLR 570, para 115. The proper approach is to apply the language of the House of Lords in *Malik*: see *O'Brien v Transco plc (formerly BG plc)* [2002] EWCA Civ 379, [2002] ICR 721. *Tullett Prebon Plc v BGC Brokers LP* [2011] IRLR 420 suggests the question is whether, looking at all the circumstances objectively, the party's intention was to refuse performance of the contract.

The implied term that the employer will not act in a manner calculated or likely to destroy or seriously to damage the relationship of trust and confidence is capable of being relevant in a very wide range of circumstances. Breaches of this implied term are often cited in constructive dismissal cases and a number of examples are given in that context (see **54.7** Unfair Dismissal – I).

The implied term includes a duty not to deliberately mislead the other party. This does not include a broader obligation to volunteer information, but where information is volunteered it must be done in good faith: *Rawlinson v Brightside Group Ltd* (2017) UKEAT/0142/17, [2018] IRLR 180.

It has been held that an employer's failure to adhere to statutory obligations may give rise to a breach of the implied term. Thus in *Nottinghamshire County Council v Meikle* [2004] IRLR 703 it was held that an employer's continuing failure to make the reasonable adjustments which were required to be made in order to accommodate the employee's disability was a breach of contract. (See also *Greenhof v Barnsley Metropolitan*

Borough Council [2006] IRLR 98.) This reasoning should not be pushed too far. It is wrong to suggest that every breach by an employer of his statutory obligations involves a breach of contract: *Doherty v British Midland Airways Ltd* [2006] IRLR 90.

Suspension of an employee may, in appropriate circumstances, also give rise to a breach of the implied term. This is certainly so where there are not reasonable grounds: *Gogay*. The test for whether there has been a breach of the implied term of trust and confidence is a "severe" one and is not answered by whether or not the employer acted "fairly": *North West Anglia NHS Foundation Trust v Gregg* [2019] EWCA Civ 387. Whether or not suspension is considered a "neutral act" is unlikely to assist in resolving the crucial question as to whether suspension in the context of the particular case constituted a breach of the implied term: *Lambeth LBC v Agoreyo* [2019] EWCA Civ 322, [2019] IRLR 560. The relevant considerations may include both the fact and manner of suspension, events preceding the suspension and whether or not the suspension was a "knee-jerk" reaction: *Lambeth*; *Gogay*; see also *Crawford v Suffolk Mental Health Partnership* [2012] IRLR 402.

In *Hill v General Accident Fire and Life Assurance Corpn plc* [1998] IRLR 641, 1999 SLT 1157, the Court of Session specifically rejected a submission that, as a result of *Malik*, a new approach had to be taken to the interpretation of contracts of employment and that they had to be construed in a way which furthered mutual trust. The English courts have shown similar restraint. In *University of Nottingham v Eyett* [1999] IRLR 87, it was held that there had been no breach of the implied term by an employer who failed to advise the employee that if he delayed his retirement by a short time, he would be paid a higher pension than that which he actually received.

In considering the scope of the implied term of trust and confidence, it is important to bear in mind that the obligation in question relates to the maintenance of the trust and confidence which should exist in an employment relationship. There is no implied obligation on the employer to act reasonably: see *Post Office v Roberts* [1980] IRLR 347. The Privy Council placed an important limit on the scope of the implied term. Where there is an untrammelled express power in a contract (for example, to dismiss without cause or to require an employee to move location) the implied term cannot operate to limit the scope of that power: *Reda v Flag Ltd* [2002] IRLR 747. Implied terms in contracts must give way to and may not contradict express terms.

There is a further important limitation on the efficacy of the implied term of trust and confidence. It is inoperative in connection with decisions to terminate employment: *Johnson v Unisys Ltd* [2001] ICR 480. This reasoning is informed by policy considerations. Since Parliament has enacted the right not to be unfairly dismissed, it would be an abuse of the judicial function to develop or apply an implied contractual term that in effect displaced, or usurped, the statutory provisions in regulating the manner of dismissal. It would be wrong, for example, for the common law to develop a right which overlapped with the right not to be unfairly dismissed but which was not subject to the same limitations, in respect of, for example, continuity of employment and time limits for the presentation of claims, which Parliament has decided should apply to unfair dismissal claims.

Thus, an employee cannot complain that his dismissal was in breach of the implied term of trust and confidence. It is, however, possible to formulate a claim for breach of the implied term of trust and confidence in respect of things done by the employer to the employee before dismissal. A line is drawn between unfairness in respect of the dismissal itself, which can only be the subject of a statutory claim of unfair dismissal and unfairness before the dismissal which gives rise to a separate cause of action in contract. Usually, it is the employer's decision to dismiss, rather than any earlier act, which gives rise to loss. However, there may be exceptional cases where this is not so. Examples might include cases of unjustified suspension (as in *Gogay v Hertfordshire County Council* [2000] IRLR 703) or cases where an employee suffers psychiatric illness as a result of pre-dismissal unfairness. Examples of the latter are *Eastwood v Magnox Electric plc* [2004] IRLR 733. In both cases employees alleged that they had suffered psychiatric illness as a result of the ways in which the employers had conducted investigations and disciplinary proceedings. The claims were originally struck out as having no basis in law in the light of *Johnson* but the House of Lords held that the claims, being based on allegations about pre-dismissal conduct, did disclose a cause of action and could proceed to trial.

In some cases, where a breach of the duty is alleged the question may arise whether the employer is liable for the act said to constitute the breach. Thus, in *Moores v Bude Stratton Town Council* [2001] ICR 271, [2000] IRLR 676 an individual councillor verbally abused an employee. When the employee resigned and claimed constructive dismissal, the issue arose whether the council was liable for the acts of the individual back-bench councillor. A majority of the EAT (Lindsay J dissenting) held that the council was liable. For the parameters of an employer's liability, see VICARIOUS LIABILITY (57). Even if the employer is not vicariously liable for the acts complained of, he may be directly liable for failing to supervise or prevent those acts: see *Waters v Metropolitan Police Comr* [2000] IRLR 720. In *Waters*, the House of Lords held that an employer might be liable to his employee in negligence if he knew of or foresaw acts being done by other employees which might cause physical or mental harm to the employee but did nothing to prevent or supervise such acts when it was in his power to do so. The argument in *Waters* was concerned with the tort of negligence. However, in that case there was no contract between the police officer and the commissioner. One can see how, in a case where there was a contract of employment, the implied term of trust and confidence would impose a similar duty in contract on the employer.

The implied term does not impose upon an employer a duty to its employees to conduct litigation in a manner which protects them from economic or reputational harm (*James-Bowen v Commissioner of Police of the Metropolis* [2018] UKSC 40, [2018] 1 WLR 4021) or to indemnify an employee or otherwise take steps to protect the employee from economic loss: *Benyatov v Credit Suisse Securities (Europe) Ltd* [2020] EWHC 85 (QB), [2020] IRLR 299.

The High Court has also held that there is no "justification for there being an implied term (whether free standing, or as part of a duty of good faith, trust and confidence) which prevents the employer from investigating whether there has been gross misconduct or acting upon any findings that there has been": *Wells v Cathay Investments 2 Ltd* [2020] EWHC 2996 (QB), [2020] IRLR 281. This finding was made in response to a submission by the Claimants that the investigation into their alleged misconduct was undertaken to avoid having to make payment they were entitled to under the contract of employment.

8.22e *Place of work—*

There must be a contractual term, express or implied, dealing with the place where the employee may be required to work. If there is no express term, that term will be implied which the parties would have agreed if they had directed their minds to the problem. All the circumstances of the case will be considered, including the nature of the business, the nature of the employee's duties and his status, what the employee was told when engaged and whether he has in fact been moved from time to time, and whether there is any provision for the payment of expenses for working away from home. The term implied may be that the employee can be required to work anywhere within reasonable daily travelling distance of his home (*O'Brien v Associated Fire Alarms Ltd* [1969] 1 All ER 93; *Jones v Associated Tunnelling Co Ltd* [1981] IRLR 477; *Courtaulds Northern Spinning Ltd v Sibson* [1988] ICR 451). See also *Little v Charterhouse Magna Assurance Co Ltd* [1980] IRLR 19 and *Rank Xerox Ltd v Churchill* [1988] IRLR 280. However, such a 'mobility clause' (whether express or implied) may be coupled with implied obligations to give reasonable notice of any move (see *United Bank Ltd v Akhtar* [1989] IRLR 507; *Prestwick Circuits Ltd v McAndrew* [1990] IRLR 191; and cf *White*, above). Although there must be a term which identifies where the employee is to work, it is not necessary in every case to imply a mobility clause. Whether or not it is necessary to imply such a clause will depend on the nature of the work and the other facts of the case (*Aparau v Iceland Frozen Foods plc* [1996] IRLR 119). It appears that an employer may only effectively rely upon a mobility clause if he makes it clear that he is doing so (*Curling v Securicor Ltd* [1992] IRLR 549).

In *Bass Leisure Ltd v Thomas* [1994] IRLR 104, the EAT held that the place where an employee works is a question of fact to be determined by considering where the employee in fact works rather than where she can be required to work (see **39.7** REDUNDANCY – I). This approach was approved by the Court of Appeal in *High Tables Ltd v Horst* [1997] IRLR 513. (Compare *Gale v Northern General Hospital NHS Trust* [1994] IRLR 292, which was concerned specifically with the construction of the *National Health Service and Community Care Act 1990, s 6(1)*.)

8.22f *Termination of the contract—*

In the absence of any express term governing the notice required to be given to terminate the contract, it is an implied term that reasonable notice of termination will be given. Reasonable notice will not be implied if to do so would contradict an express term, eg a term giving a party the right to terminate at any time without cause. The implication of the term is necessary in order to provide a means by which a contract of otherwise indefinite duration may be terminated. If the express terms make provision, there is no need to imply a term: *Reda v Flag Ltd* [2002] UKPC 38, [2002] IRLR 747. What is reasonable will depend on all the facts of the case (see **49.6** TERMINATION OF EMPLOYMENT). Where there is no contractual provision governing when a notice of termination served by an employer takes effect, the notice only takes effect when the employee has personally taken delivery of the letter containing the notice (*Newcastle upon Tyne NHS Foundation Trust v Haywood* [2017] EWCA Civ 153; affd [2018] UKSC 22, [2018] 1 WLR 2073).

8.22g Incorporated terms

These are terms which are incorporated into the contract rather than being agreed individually between the parties. The principal source of incorporated terms is collective agreements (see COLLECTIVE AGREEMENTS **(6)**). The *Equality Act 2010* incorporates into every contract of employment an 'equality clause'.

See also **8.13**.

8.23 Unenforceable terms

Certain terms, while not being unlawful in the sense of rendering an employer liable to criminal prosecution or a civil action, may be unenforceable, as set out in **8.24–8.30** below.

8.24 *Terms which are unlawful or contrary to public policy*

It has conventionally been the position that a contract that was unlawful (eg because it was entered into with the intention of committing an illegal act, because the contract was expressly or implicitly prohibited by statute aka "statutory illegality", or because the contract was being performed in an illegal fashion aka "common law illegality") was unenforceable.

The position as regards common law illegality may now be more flexible following the decision of the Supreme Court in *Patel v Mirza* [2016] UKSC 42, [2017] AC 467. Now, the correct approach is for the Court to assess whether the public interest would be harmed by enforcement of the illegal agreement, which requires it to consider (a) the underlying purpose of the prohibition which has been transgressed and whether that purpose will be enhanced by denial of the claim, (b) any other relevant public policy on which the denial of the claim may have an impact and (c) whether denial of the claim would be a proportionate response to the illegality, bearing in mind that punishment is a matter for the criminal courts. However, the view of the Court of Appeal in *Okedina v Chikale* [2019] EWCA Civ 1393, [2019] IRLR 905 was that *Patel* does not require a reconsideration of how the rule has previously been applied except where such an application is inconsistent with those principles (para 62).

The kinds of considerations that may be relevant include whether or not the employee was aware of the illegality, the employee's preparedness to perform the contract lawfully when and if the illegality was discovered and the centrality of the illegality to the contract: *ParkingEye Ltd v Somerfield Stores Ltd* [2012] EWCA Civ 1338, [2013] QB 840 (CA).

The typical employment situations in which the issue arises include:

Defrauding the revenue: see, eg, *Payne v Enfield Technical Services Ltd* [2008] EWCA Civ 393, [2008] ICR 1423, [2008] IRLR 500; *Connolly v Whitestone Solicitors* (UKEAT/0445/10/ZT) (24 June 2011, unreported); *Salveson v Simon* [1994] ICR 409.

Contracts for work performed in contravention of immigration laws: see, eg, *Sharma v Hindu Temple*, IDS Brief 464, p 5; *Vakante v Governing Body of Addey and Stanhope School* [2005] ICR 231, CA and *Zarkasi v Anindita* (UKEAT/0400/11/JOJ) (18 January 2012, unreported). Note, however, that working for less money than is stated on the employee's work permit application is not necessarily unlawful (*San Ling Chinese Medicine Centre v Lian Wei Ji* (UKEAT/0370/09) (25 January 2010, unreported). For work permits, see **27.4** FOREIGN EMPLOYEES.

Before the Supreme Court's decision in *Patel* there were a number of potential exceptions to the general rule. If the unlawful element of the contract could be severed, a court may in certain circumstances allow the employee to pursue a claim based on the lawful elements of the contract (*Blue Chip Trading Ltd v Helbawi* [2009] IRLR 128). Given the explanation of *Patel* given by the Court of Appeal in *Okedina v Chikale* [2019] EWCA Civ 1393, [2019] IRLR 905, CA, these exceptions should (in principle) not be affected by the Supreme Court's decision. Note, however, that such an argument has not been regularly accepted. Further, if the employee was not aware of the fact that the contract was being performed unlawfully by the employer (by, for example, not deducting tax from remuneration) the employee might rely on the contract for the purposes of claiming employment protection rights (*Newland v Simons and Willer (Hairdressers) Ltd* [1981] ICR 521).

However, ignorance of the law as opposed to the facts is no excuse (*Miller v Karlinski* (1945) 62 TLR 85). Nor is the fact that the parties did not intend to break the law relevant (*Salvesen v Simon* [1994] ICR 409). The mere fact that in the course of performing an otherwise lawful contract, the employee has committed an unlawful or immoral act does not bar him from bringing a claim for unfair dismissal (*Coral Leisure Group Ltd v Barnett* [1981] ICR 503; *Hewcastle Catering Ltd v Ahmed and Elkamah* [1992] ICR 626, [1991] IRLR 473, CA). Thus, the fact that an employee did not pay tax on occasional payments received outside his contract of employment did not have the effect of rendering the contract of employment illegal in *Annandale Engineering v Samson* [1994] IRLR 59. Further, the claim may be brought if the employer's conduct in participating in an illegal contract is so reprehensible in comparison with that of the employee that it would be wrong to allow the employer to rely on the illegality (cf *Euro-Diam*, above).

The distinction between unlawful tax evasion and lawful tax avoidance must be borne in mind. The fact that an employee lawfully arranges matters so as to minimise liability to tax does not render the contract of employment illegal (*Lightfoot v D & J Sporting Ltd* [1996] IRLR 64).

The fact that a contract might be unenforceable by reason of illegality does not preclude a person employed under such a contract from bringing claims of sex or race (or presumably disability or religion or age or belief or sexual orientation) discrimination. The reason for this is that such actions do not seek to enforce the unenforceable contract (*Leighton v (1) Michael and (2) Charalambous* [1996] IRLR 67) unless the claim arises out of or is inextricably bound up with the conduct which causes the contract to be illegal (see *Hounga v Allen* [2014] UKSC 47).

An appellate court should not interfere with a first instance decision about illegality merely because it would have taken a different view had it been undertaking the evaluation. An appellate court should only interfere if the first instance judge has proceeded on an erroneous legal basis, taken into account matters that were legally irrelevant, or failed to take into account matters that were legally relevant: *Singularis Holdings Ltd (In Official Liquidation) v Daiwa Capital Markets Europe Ltd* [2018] EWCA Civ 84, [2018] 1 WLR 2777, para 65; see also *Bank St Petersburg PJSC v Arkhangelsky* [2020] EWCA Civ 408, [2020] All ER (D) 137 (Mar).

8.25   *Terms automatically varied by statute*

Terms which, although they are agreed between the parties, are in breach of certain statutory provisions take effect as if varied to comply with those provisions. For example:

(a)   terms which are less advantageous than those which apply to a member of the opposite sex doing the same or like work, or work of equal value (see **23.8 Equal Pay**), or which infringe the law on sex discrimination; or

(b)   terms providing for the employment of directors for a guaranteed period of more than two years (see **9.3 Directors**).

8.26   *Restrictions upon contracting out of certain statutory provisions*

With some exceptions, for instance where a conciliation officer (see **2.3 Advisory, Conciliation and Arbitration Service**) has exercised his statutory powers in the settlement of certain claims or where there has been a valid compromise agreement (see **19.27 Employment Tribunals**), an employer or employee may not contract out of the following Acts. Any attempt to do so will be ineffective.

Equality Act 2010 (see *s 144*)

Equal Pay Act 1970

ERA 1996, Part II (see *s 203(1), (2)*)

Trade Union and Labour Relations (Consolidation) Act 1992 (see *s 288*)

Working Time Regulations 1998 (save insofar as the *Regulations* permit the parties to agree that the operation of the *Regulations* is to be excluded or limited)

8.27   *Discriminatory terms*

Terms in contracts which are contrary to the provisions of the discrimination legislation are void and unenforceable against the person discriminated against: see *Equality Act 2010, s 143*. Similarly, any term in a collective agreement which discriminates on grounds of sex, sexual orientation or religion or belief is void and unenforceable against the party discriminated against: see *Equality Act 2010, s 145*.

8.28   *Terms in restraint of trade*

Sometimes, a contract will contain a term restricting the employee's freedom to work after he leaves his employment. Such terms will be regarded as 'in restraint of trade' and therefore unenforceable if their main purpose is simply to restrain competition. However, if the main purpose is to protect something in which the employer has a legitimate interest, such as trade secrets or confidential information, or to protect the employer's goodwill or '*customer connection*' (as it is called in this context), then such a term may be enforceable. These questions are discussed in more detail in **Restraint of Trade, Confidentiality and Employee Interventions (42)**.

8.29 *Restrictions on industrial action*

Provisions in collective agreements which purport to restrict the right to take industrial action cannot form part of the individual contract of employment unless certain conditions are satisfied (see **6.5** COLLECTIVE AGREEMENTS).

8.30 *Unfair Contract Terms Act 1977*

The effect of the *Unfair Contract Terms Act 1977* ('*UCTA 1977*') is to render certain types of contractual term unenforceable, and others unenforceable unless they satisfy a test of reasonableness laid down in *UCTA 1977, s 11* (namely, that the term was a fair and reasonable one to be included having regard to the circumstances which were, or ought reasonably to have been, known to or in the contemplation of the parties when the contract was made; in applying this test the court is directed to have regard to certain specific considerations).

Despite earlier indications to the contrary, it has now been held that *UCTA* does not apply to contracts of employment. The reason for this is that *UCTA* applies only to those who either 'deal as a consumer' or deal 'on the other [party's] written standard terms of business'. In *Keen v Commerzbank AG* [2006] EWCA Civ 1536, [2007] ICR 623, *sub nom Commerzbank AG v Keen* [2007] IRLR 132, the Court of Appeal held that an employee neither dealt as a consumer nor on his employer's standard terms of business. Employers do not deal with their employees as consumers; the business of an employer is not employing its staff.

In the light of this judgment, no further consideration is given to *UCTA* in this work.

8.31 CHANGES TO CONTRACTUAL TERMS

The general principle is that no change in the terms of an employee's contract may be made without his consent. Consent can come either from an employee's (express or implied) agreement to the proposed change, or from a pre-existing contractual provision allowing the employer unilaterally to effect variations. Where neither of these forms of consent is in place, a change in terms is likely to amount to a breach of contract.

If the proposed change is of great importance to the employer, the only course of action open to him in circumstances in which the employee does not consent, is to give notice to terminate the original contract and offer new terms. Great care must be taken to adhere to a fair procedure when doing this so as to avoid a successful claim for unfair dismissal (see UNFAIR DISMISSAL – II **(55)**).

A particular question which has caused difficulty is whether a change in terms and conditions mutually agreed between the parties can be enforced in the context of the transfer of an undertaking under the *Transfer of Undertakings (Protection of Employment) Regulations 1981 (SI 1981/1794)* ('*TUPE 1981*'), which have now been replaced by the *Transfer of Undertakings (Protection of Employment) Regulations 2006 (SI 2006/246)* ('*TUPE 2006*'). This subject is considered fully in TRANSFER OF UNDERTAKINGS **(53)**.

8.32 **Agreement**

Consent may be express, by the employee agreeing to the change orally or, preferably, in writing (see *Judge v Crown Leisure Ltd* [2005] EWCA Civ 571, [2005] IRLR 823 on the importance, in discussions about contractual variation, of an intention to create legal relations). Consideration must be provided for any variation: see *Tenon FM Ltd v Cawley* [2018] EWHC 1972 (QB), [2018] All ER (D) 201 (Jul). On the question of consideration for agreed variations, see *Lee v GEC Plessey Telecommunications* [1993] IRLR 383, where the High Court held that there was good consideration for any pay rise which followed pay negotiations, so that the employer was legally bound by the increased rate of pay; but cf. *Reuse Collections Ltd v Sendall* [2015] IRLR 226 where the Court held that a 'general' pay rise did not provide consideration for insertion of a restraint of trade provision on the ground that there was an insufficient link between both matters.

Alternatively, consent may be *implied*, by the employee continuing to work for the employer without protest for a significant period of time whilst being aware of a change imposed by his employer. Where a change is imposed by the employer and the employee continues to work without objection, it may be that the employee will be held impliedly to have consented to the change: *Abrahall v Nottingham City Council* [2018] EWCA Civ 796, [2018] ICR 1425, CA. Where the change is one which has an immediate effect on the employee, continuing to work without protest may very well indicate consent. However, where the change is one which does not have an immediate practical effect, the court should exercise caution before inferring consent (*Jones v Associated Tunnelling Co Ltd* [1981] IRLR 477, *Aparau v Iceland Frozen Foods plc* [1996] IRLR 119, *Solectron Scotland Ltd v Roper* [2004] IRLR 4, *Cumbria County Council v Dow (No 2)* [2008] IRLR 109, EAT). In addition, the actual change in the employee's working conditions must be more than "trivial" under those changed conditions is to be regarded as implied consent: see the Court of Appeal decision in *Khatri v Co-operative Centrale Raiffeisen-Boerenleenbank BA* [2010] IRLR 715 applying *Solectron Scotland* (above). The conduct of the employee in continuing to work for the employer must give rise to the unequivocal inference of consent. Such conduct cannot be relied upon as implied consent if it is reasonably capable of a different explanation: *Abrahall*.

A further example of a variation is *Attrill & Other v Dresdner Kleinwort Limited & Anor* [2013] EWCA Civ 394, where the variation was effected by the employees' implicit acceptance of an offer (concerning the bonus pool to be made available to employees) made during a 'Town Hall' meeting broadcast over the internet. This was an offer to vary the terms of the employees' contract and, in the circumstances, the employer had waived any requirement for the employees to communicate acceptance (although, if this requirement had not been waived, such communication of acceptance could not be inferred from the employees' remaining in employment). There was consideration for this variation. *Attrill* should also be noted for its discussion of implied acceptance of variations. Where an employee protests but then continues to work for a considerable time, he may bear an evidential burden of showing that he did not impliedly agree to the new term (see *Henry v London General Transport Services Ltd* [2002] ICR 910, [2002] IRLR 472, where the employee continued to work for two years).

8.33   Variation clauses

In some contracts, the employer will expressly reserve a power to vary the terms. Such variation clauses are sometimes drafted in wide terms, purporting for example to allow the employer to make such changes as it sees fit from time to time. The answer to the question of whether or not such clauses are effective is a "qualified yes" (*Malone v British Airways* [2010] EWCA Civ 1225, [2011] ICR 125, [2011] IRLR 32; *Wandsworth London Borough Council v D'Silva* [1998] IRLR 193). These qualifications include the following. Courts take a strict approach to the interpretation of such clauses, and will construe them *contra proferentem*. Clear words are required to create a power unilaterally to alter the terms of the contract: *Norman and anor v National Audit Office* [2015] IRLR 634. Variation clauses specifying the terms that the employer is empowered to vary (as opposed to arrogating a general power to vary any term) are more likely to find favour with courts, although even more focussed variation provisions may be struck down: see *Hart v St Mary's School (Colchester) Ltd* UKEAT 0305/14 (where the Court held that a clause permitting variations to a teacher's working hours based on the requirements of the school timetable should not be accepted). The court is unlikely to favour an interpretation that does more than vary the contractual provisions with which the employer is required to comply. A court is unlikely to allow an interpretation which goes further and which may affect the rights of the employee under the contract: see, e.g. *Sparks v Department for Transport* [2016] ICR 695. Thus, the extent to which an employer will be permitted to rely on an express provision entitling him to vary the terms of a contract, and so to evade the general rule that changes to contracts must be mutually agreed, is likely to be limited.

8.34   Variation, breach and termination

Any change in terms to which the employee does not consent is *prima facie* a breach of contract. If the change is a significant one, the employee may be entitled to resign and allege that he has been constructively dismissed (see **49.19** TERMINATION OF EMPLOYMENT). However, where an employer unilaterally imposes radically different terms of employment, it may be that the correct interpretation is that the employer has terminated the original contract and replaced it with another. Accordingly, there would be a dismissal by the employer (and immediate re-employment) which entitled the employee to bring unfair dismissal proceedings (*Hogg v Dover College* [1990] ICR 39; *Alcan Extrusions v Yates* [1996] IRLR 327; and see UNFAIR DISMISSAL– I (54)). For guidance on the question of whether the situation is one of dismissal and reengagement or mere variation of terms, see *Cumbria County Council v Dow (No 2)* [2008] IRLR 109, EAT and *Potter v North Cumbria Acute Hospitals NHS Trust* [2009] IRLR 900: where the parties have not (expressly or impliedly) agreed to terminate the old contract, their intention is to be ascertained from all the circumstances, including the "elasticity" of the original contract and the cumulative effect of any minor variations.

8.35   EMPLOYEE'S REMEDIES FOR BREACH OF CONTRACT OF EMPLOYMENT

If an employer is in breach of contract, his employee may bring proceedings in the High Court or the county court for sums due under the contract and for damages. The employee can bring such an action while remaining in employment. However, if the employer's breach of contract is sufficiently serious, the employee may treat himself as dismissed, leave, and bring proceedings for his prospective loss (see WRONGFUL DISMISSAL (59)) as well as for any sums outstanding at the date of dismissal; though note that at common law an employee cannot accept a repudiation by resigning with notice: *Reuse Collections Limited v Sendall* [2015] IRLR 226. The courts are also able to grant declaratory relief. If the breach of contract involves a deduction from pay, the employee may present a complaint to the employment tribunal under *Part II* of the *ERA 1996* (which contains provisions formerly found in the *Wages Act 1986*) (see **35.6** PAY – I). However, unliquidated damages (for example, damages for pay in lieu of notice) are not capable of being recovered under *ERA 1996, Part II*: *Delaney v Staples (t/a De Montfort Recruitment)* [1992] 1 AC 687. However, as *Cortel Telecom Ltd v Shah* UKEAT/0252/18 demonstrates, close attention is required to the claim form and a claim for notice pay may well be said to be brought pursuant to an Employment Tribunal's contractual jurisdiction see (see below **8.44**).

8.36   Damages

Extent of damages which can be claimed

Where an employee is dismissed summarily in breach of contract, the *prima facie* measure of damages is the sum which the employer would have had to pay in order to bring the contract to an end lawfully – that is to say, the sum payable in respect of the notice period. However, it will often be a term of the contract that the employer must follow a prescribed disciplinary or other procedure prior to dismissal. In such cases, if the employee can show that the conduct of the disciplinary procedure would take time and, therefore, extend the period of employment, he may be able to claim as damages lost wages for the time which the disciplinary or other procedure would have taken, in addition to pay for the notice period (see *Boyo v Lambeth London Borough Council* [1994] ICR 727, [1995] IRLR 50, CA and *Focsa Services (UK) Ltd v Birkett* [1996] IRLR 325). However, in assessing compensation, the tribunal must work on the basis that the outcome of the pursuit of the disciplinary or other procedure would have been the same (*Janciuk v Winerite* [1998] IRLR 63). This means that an employee cannot be compensated in a breach of contract claim on the basis that, had a contractual disciplinary procedure been pursued, he would not have been dismissed. The limit of compensation is the time which would have been taken to complete the procedure.

Damages payable will include damages for loss of pension rights that would have accrued had the employee not been dismissed summarily in breach of contract: *Silvey v Pendragon plc* [2001] IRLR 685.

On the question of whether payment in lieu of notice should include bonus payments, see *Locke v Candy and Candy Ltd* [2010] EWCA Civ 1350, where the Court of Appeal held by a majority (based on the particular contractual terms in issue) that an employee who was summarily dismissed shortly before the payment date of a discretionary bonus was not entitled to the bonus as part of his payment in lieu of notice, because the bonus clause stated that employees had to be employed in order to receive the bonus. However, where there is no express term making the payment of a bonus conditional upon being employed at that time, one cannot simply be implied: *Rutherford v Seymour Pierce Ltd* [2010] EWHC 375 (QB), [2010] IRLR 606. There, the court found that such a term was not necessary for the contract to operate satisfactorily, was manifestly unreasonable, and was not customary in that area of business.

Of course, an employee need not actually have commenced duties in order to be able to bring a claim. So, for example, where an offer of employment is made and accepted, there is a valid contract of employment even if the start date is postponed. If the contract is terminated before the actual start date, the employee will have a claim for wrongful dismissal. He may also have other claims such as discrimination (see *Sarker v South Tees Acute Hospitals NHS Trust* [1997] IRLR 328 and **22.5 ENGAGEMENT OF EMPLOYEES**).

8.37 *No damages for loss of the chance to claim unfair dismissal*

Sometimes, employers dismiss employees summarily in order to prevent the employee from accruing a sufficient period of qualifying employment to bring a claim for unfair dismissal. Thus, for example, a person with a month's notice period might be summarily dismissed two weeks before accruing one year's continuous employment. However, it has been held that a claim for damages for breach of contract cannot include damages for the loss of a chance to bring an unfair dismissal claim: *Harper v Virgin Net Ltd* [2004] EWCA Civ 271, [2004] IRLR 390, CA.

8.38 *Damages for loss of reputation*

In *Malik v BCCI SA* [1997] IRLR 462, the House of Lords accepted that it might be possible to recover damages for loss of reputation caused by a breach of contract, provided that a relevant breach of contract could be established and that requirements of causation, remoteness and mitigation are satisfied. It was not necessary that the conduct relied upon be directed at the employees. In that case, the individual employees alleged that their employer had run a corrupt and dishonest business and that, as a result, the employees were tainted by their involvement with their former employer and were at a disadvantage in the job market. These facts were assumed to be true for the purposes of the argument, although no findings were made in respect of them. The House of Lords held that it would be a breach of the implied term of trust and confidence to operate a dishonest business and that the employees were entitled to argue that they could recover damages for any consequent loss as a result of damage inflicted on their employment prospects. The correct measure of damages where the breach affects employment prospects is to ask: but for the breach by the employer, what would prospective employers considering the claimant's application have done and what would have been the outcome for the employee? (*BCCI SA v Ali (No 3)* [2002] EWCA Civ 82, [2002] IRLR 460).

8.39   *Pecuniary loss only*

The *Malik* case does not alter the principle that damages are not recoverable for the manner of a dismissal, according to the House of Lords in *Johnson v Unisys Ltd* [2003] 1 AC 518. By a majority of four to one, their Lordships held that there was no right at common law to recover damages for injury to feeling (even in the case where that injury manifested itself as a psychological injury) caused by dismissal. Their Lordships held that it would be wrong to develop by judicial invention a right to compensation in circumstances where Parliament had already intervened by creating the right not to be unfairly dismissed. The courts therefore ought not to allow persons to side-step the limits on that right which Parliament had put in place by the creation of an inconsistent common law right. Lord Hoffmann expressed the view (obiter) that damages for unfair dismissal should extend beyond pecuniary loss to include 'in an appropriate case . . . compensation for distress, humiliation, damage to reputation in the community or to family life'. However, the House of Lords subsequently declined to follow Lord Hoffmann's *obiter* comment and has re-affirmed that damages for unfair dismissal are limited to financial losses: *Dunnachie v Kingston upon Hull City Council* [2004] UKHL 36, [2004] IRLR 727.

A number of cases in which employees alleged that they had suffered psychiatric injury as a consequence of the investigative or disciplinary process followed by their employer, rather than their dismissal, were struck out at first instance on the ground that they were barred by *Johnson*. However, the House of Lords subsequently held that the effect of *Johnson* is only to preclude common law claims where the employee seeks to recover damages consequent on dismissal: *Eastwood v Magnox Electric plc* and *McCabe v Cornwall County Council* [2004] IRLR 733. Where it is possible to claim that loss or injury has flowed not from dismissal but from pre-dismissal steps (such as suspension or the anterior conduct of disciplinary procedures), then *Johnson* does not prevent claims being brought: see for example *Gogay v Hertfordshire County Council* [2000] IRLR 703, CA (compensation awarded for psychological injury as a consequence of the manner in which an allegation of misconduct was investigated). The Supreme Court has confirmed the position: in the conjoined appeals of *Edwards v Chesterfield Royal Hospital NHS Foundation Trust* and *Botham v Ministry of Defence* [2011] UKSC 58, [2012] 2 WLR 55, [2012] 2 All ER 278, [2012] ICR 201, [2012] IRLR 129, it was held (by a majority of 5-2) that the effect of *Johnson* was to preclude damages for loss attributable to the unfair manner of a dismissal in breach of the terms of the employment contract. Where provisions of the employer's disciplinary code are incorporated into the contract, they are nonetheless not ordinary contractual terms, with breaches falling to be dealt with under the *ERA 1996* rather than as free-standing claims for breach of contract.

8.40   *'Stigma' damages*

The employee is under a duty to mitigate his pecuniary loss, for example (where he has been dismissed) by seeking alternative employment. In *Chagger v Abbey National plc* [2010] ICR 397, [2010] IRLR 47, the claimant (who had been employed as a risk analyst) contended that he had been stigmatised by prospective employers, who were unwilling to employ him because he had brought successful claims against his former employer for unfair dismissal, discrimination and breach of contract. He therefore retrained to work as a teacher on a substantially lower salary. His former employer argued that the claimant's damages should not include the ongoing financial consequences of stigmatisation by third parties, since that was too remote from the former employer's unlawful act. The Court of Appeal found for the claimant on this point: an employee has to be compensated for the full loss flowing from the unlawful act of his former employer, and the involvement of third party prospective employers did not sever the causal chain. Damages may now therefore in principle extend to such 'stigma' effects.

8.41   *Express terms regarding damages*

In some contracts, most usually those of senior executives, there is a term which provides for prescribed sums to be payable by the employer on breach. A question may arise whether such terms are penalties, which are unenforceable. In *Cavendish Square Holdings BV v Talal El Makdessi* [2016] AC 1172, three members of the Supreme Court indicated that the true test of a penalty was "whether the impugned provision is a secondary obligation which imposes a detriment on the contract-breaker out of all proportion to any legitimate interest of the innocent party in the enforcement of the primary obligation". The innocent party in such a situation "can have no proper interest in simply punishing the defaulter. His interest is in performance or in some appropriate alternative". Lord Hodge described the test as "whether the sum or remedy stipulated as a breach of contract is exorbitant or unconscionable when regard is had to the innocent party's interest in the performance of the contract".

Close attention needs to be paid to whether the obligation to pay arises from a breach of the contract (in which case, it may be – but is not necessarily – a penalty) or whether it arises for some other reason (in which case, it will not be a penalty): see, in the context of schemes making provision for the treatment of "bad leavers", *Richards v IP Solutions Group Ltd* [2016] EWHC 1835 (QB), [2017] IRLR 133; *Signia Wealth Limited v Vector Trustees Ltd* [2018] EWHC 1040 (Ch), [2018] All ER (D) 104 (May); *Nosworthy v Instinctif Partners Ltd* (2019) UKEAT/0100/18/RN.

8.42   **Injunctions**

Circumstances in which injunctions may be granted

In certain circumstances, the courts will grant an employee an injunction to restrain the employer from taking action in breach of contract. This may be done to restrain the implementation of a dismissal where a contractual disciplinary or disputes procedure has not been exhausted (see, eg, *Irani v Southampton and South-West Hampshire Health Authority* [1985] ICR 590 and observations in *R v BBC, ex p Lavelle* [1983] ICR 99). In *Barros D'Sa v University Hospital and Warwickshire NHS Trust* [2001] IRLR 691, there was a two-stage disciplinary procedure. The first stage involved an investigation by an inquiry panel. The second stage involved a disciplinary hearing at which decisions would be taken as to the appropriate course of action depending upon the circumstances and the inquiry panel's recommendations. At the second stage, the employer sought to introduce new material and new allegations against the employee which had not been considered at the inquiry panel stage. The Court of Appeal granted an injunction to prevent the new material and allegation being considered. An employer was not entitled to depart from a contractual disciplinary procedure on the ground that he considered that the relationship of trust and confidence had broken down.

In *Mezey v South West London and St George's Mental Health NHS Trust* [2007] IRLR 237, 244, the Court of Appeal upheld the grant of an injunction to restrain a suspension on full pay on the basis that the decision to suspend, even if permitted by the express terms of the contract, could involve a breach of the implied term of trust and confidence. A further development in that case saw the Court of Appeal uphold the grant of a further injunction against the employer taking capability proceedings against an employee who had already been cleared by an investigatory panel ([2010] EWCA Civ 293).

An injunction has also been granted to restrain the enforcement of an instruction the employer was not contractually entitled to give (see *Hughes v Southwark London Borough Council* [1988] IRLR 55) and to prevent a dismissal which would be in breach of a contractual redundancy selection procedure (*Anderson v Pringle of Scotland Ltd* [1998] IRLR 64, 1998 SLT 754, OH). However, an injunction will only be granted in the exceptional case where the employer still has full confidence in the employee's continuing ability and other necessary attributes (*Powell v Brent London Borough Council* [1988] ICR 176; *Alexander v Standard Telephones & Cables plc* [1990] ICR 291). In *Robb v Hammersmith and Fulham London Borough Council* [1991] ICR 514, it was suggested that this might not be necessary where the employee will merely be remaining at home under suspension pending a disciplinary hearing. The better view is that no injunction should be granted unless trust and confidence remain between the employer and the employee. To grant an injunction in circumstances where trust and confidence did not remain would be inconsistent with the general rule that there cannot be specific performance of a contract of service. However, within modern contracts of employment, there are often a number of provisions which may be enforced by an injunction without compelling the parties to a contract of employment to perform their obligations to employ and/or to work. Where the parties are in agreement that the contract of employment subsists, albeit in a qualified form (such as where the employee is suspended), then the court may enforce by order parts of the contract which do not compel the parties to co-operate any more than they would be prepared to do in any event. Thus if, for example, the parties agree that the contract subsists albeit that the employee is suspended, then the court may enforce contractual provisions relating to, for example, discipline. Enforcement of such provisions in those circumstances does not require a reluctant employer to employ or a reluctant employee to work (see *Peace v City of Edinburgh Council* [1999] IRLR 417).

The injunction may, if necessary, be made conditional upon the employee undertaking to work in accordance with instructions (*Wadcock v London Borough of Brent* [1990] IRLR 223). Similarly, if new working practices are introduced in breach of contract, an injunction will not be granted where, for practical purposes, the old system cannot be restored (*MacPherson v Lambeth London Borough Council* [1988] IRLR 470). See also *Dietman v Brent London Borough Council* [1988] ICR 842, *Ali v Southwark London Borough Council* [1988] ICR 567, [1988] IRLR 100 and *Wishart v National Association of Citizens Advice Bureaux Ltd* [1990] ICR 794.

Where an employer makes a claim to enforce a negative covenant, the ordinary remedy will be an injunction and proof of damage is not required: *Dyson v Pellery* [2016] ICR 688. However, it is a discretionary remedy and there may be cases in which it is inappropriate to refuse an injunction. Such cases will generally be exceptional and the employee will need to demonstrate that the granting of an injunction would be so prejudicial, and cause him such hardship, that it would be unconscionable for injunctive relief to be granted in the absence of damage. In such cases, the burden is on the employee to persuade the court that an injunction should not be granted: see also *Argus Media Limited v Halim* [2019] EWHC 42 (QB) at §215, [2019] All ER (D) 100 (Jan); see also *Affinity Workforce Solutions Ltd v McCann* [2019] EWHC 2829 (Ch), [2019] All ER (D) 185 (Oct).

8.43   *Interlocutory injunctions*

The court will usually first be asked to grant an *interlocutory* injunction, ie one which seeks to restrain the alleged breach of contract pending trial (which may not happen for several months or even longer). At the interlocutory stage, the judge does not hear oral evidence and will not have time to determine complex questions that may arise. The correct approach is therefore to decide, first, whether there is a serious question to be tried and, second, whether any injustice caused by granting or refusing to grant the injunction could be properly compensated by an award of damages later. A 'serious question to be tried' means that there is an arguable case that the claimant is entitled to the relief sought. There must be evidence which supports each of the constituent parts of the claimant's claim. The judge will not determine whether the claimant's evidence is true. He will, however, have to see that there is at that stage a sufficient basis in fact and law to mean that the claim has some merit. If there is a serious question and damages would not be an adequate remedy, the court may grant an injunction, and the decision whether to do so will depend upon the 'balance of convenience'. This will often lead it to preserve the *status quo* (see *American Cyanamid Co v Ethicon Ltd* [1975] AC 396). For an example of an interlocutory injunction against dismissal, see *Lauffer v Barking, Havering and Redbridge University Hospitals NHS Trust* [2009] EWHC 2360 (QB), [2010] Med LR 68, where the employer's failure to apply its disciplinary procedure deprived the employee of the opportunity to clear his name and avoid dismissal. See also *Mezey v South West London and St George's Mental Health NHS Trust* [2010] IRLR 512, where the Court of Appeal upheld the granting of an injunction to restrain an NHS Trust from taking capability proceedings in breach of its disciplinary procedures. The approach to be adopted to applications of this sort was considered by the Supreme Court in *West London Mental Health NHS Trust v Chhabra* [2013] UKSC 80, [2014] 1 All ER 943. While emphasising that the Courts should generally be cautious in intervening in on-going disciplinary proceedings, the Supreme Court overturned the Court of Appeal and granted an injunction preventing the Trust proceeding with the relevant disciplinary proceedings. The Court held that the irregularities in the case were serious and noted the limited nature of the damages to which the claimant would be entitled if an injunction was not granted. However, in *Hendy v Ministry of Justice* [2014] IRLR 856 the Court has re-emphasised that it will only intervene if any breach is sufficiently serious that it cannot be remedied within the disciplinary procedure and that it is not the Court's function to micro-manage a disciplinary procedure.

Somewhat different considerations may apply where the decision at the interlocutory stage will effectively determine the dispute in favour of one party or the other. In those circumstances, the court will do its best to form a view as to which party has the stronger case (see *Lansing Linde Ltd v Kerr* [1991] ICR 428). The *Lansing Linde* approach should also be applied on applications for interim springboard injunctions, unless the time gap between the application and trial is negligible: *Forse v Secarma Ltd* [2019] EWCA Civ 215, [2019] IRLR 587. Also, where the dispute turns upon a question of law or the construction of a document, the court has power to make a final determination of that question at an interlocutory stage (*Civil Procedure Rules, part 24*). For an example of this course being taken in an employment dispute, see *Jones v Gwent County Council* [1992] IRLR 521.

The courts will not generally make mandatory interlocutory orders for the continued payment of wages where these are sought as an indirect means of obtaining an injunction (see *Alexander*, above; *Jakeman v South West Thames Regional Health Authority and London Ambulance Service* [1990] IRLR 62).

8.44   Jurisdiction

Employment tribunals have jurisdiction to hear claims for breach of contracts of employment or contracts 'connected with employment' other than personal injury claims (*Employment Tribunals Extension of Jurisdiction (England and Wales) Order 1994 (SI 1994/1623)*).

The claim must be one which 'arises or is outstanding on the termination of the employee's employment' (*art 3(c)*). This means that the employee must have an enforceable but unsatisfied claim at the date of termination. This must be a claim against the employer, not a person other than the employer, even if the contract with the other person was somehow connected with the employee's employment: *Oni v Unison Trade Union* [2018] ICR 1111, [2018] IRLR 806. The formulation does not enable tribunals to determine claims which, at the termination of employment, are contingent: *Peninsula Business Services Ltd v Sweeney* [2004] IRLR 49, EAT. *Article 5* specifically excludes a claim relating to:

(a)   a term requiring the employer to provide living accommodation for the employee;

(b)   a term imposing an obligation on the employer or the employee in connection with living accommodation;

(c)   a term relating to intellectual property;

(d)   a term imposing an obligation of confidence; and

(e)   a term which is in restraint of trade.

Article 7 provides that an employee must present a contract claim:

(i)   within three months of the effective date of termination of the contract giving rise to the claim (see **54.13** UNFAIR DISMISSAL – I);

(ii)   where there is no effective date of termination, within three months of the date when the employee last worked in the employment which has been terminated; or

(iii)   within such further period as the tribunal considers reasonable, where it was not reasonably practicable for the employee to present a claim in time (see **19.20** EMPLOYMENT TRIBUNALS – I).

The tribunal has jurisdiction only in respect of contracts of employment or those connected with employment (*Employment Tribunals Act 1996, s 3(2)*). Thus, an agreement compromising a wrongful dismissal claim effected during employment falls within the tribunal's jurisdiction: *Rock-it Cargo Ltd v Green* [1997] IRLR 581.

The provisions as to the time when a claim must be made mean that the employment tribunal does not have jurisdiction to consider a claim made during the currency of employment. Its jurisdiction is limited to claims submitted after the termination of the employment: see *Capek v Lincolnshire County Council* [2000] ICR 878, CA. Further, the claim must arise or be outstanding on the termination of employment. This means that the tribunal does not have jurisdiction to entertain claims that only arise for the first time after the employment has terminated, eg a settlement of a dismissal claim made after the employment has ended: *Miller Bros and F P Butler v Johnston* [2002] IRLR 386. There are conflicting tribunal decisions on the question of whether the six year limitation period under *section 5* of the *Limitation Act 1980* for breach of contract claims in the civil courts also applies to claims in the tribunal.

Employers are entitled to counterclaim (*arts 4, 8*). Counterclaims must be made at a time when a contract claim by an employee is already before the tribunal and has not been settled or withdrawn. The counterclaim must arise out of a contract with the employee who has made the contract claim. The employee's contract claim must be brought by virtue of the *Employment Tribunals Extension of Jurisdiction (England and Wales) Order 1994* in the sense that it was necessarily brought under the Order or unequivocally brought under the Order. It cannot be a claim which could have been brought under *Part II* of the *ERA 1996*: *Read v Ryder Ltd* (2018) UKEAT/0144/18/BA. In *Ridge v HM Land Registry* (2014) UKEAT/0485/12, the EAT held that the defence of set-off is also available to an employer in the tribunal. The tribunal was therefore entitled to reduce the damages due to an employee in a claim for unpaid pension contributions by setting off the amount claimed by the employer for overpayment of wages, even though the tribunal had rejected the employer's contract claim as out of time.

The time limit for presenting counterclaims is six weeks from the date when the employer (or other respondent to the employee's contract claim) received a copy of the originating application in respect of that employee's contract claim. This period is subject to extension where it was not reasonably practicable for the employer's counterclaim to be presented in time (see **19.20** EMPLOYMENT TRIBUNALS – I).

The Order contains specific provisions relating to death and bankruptcy.

8.45   The maximum award which a tribunal may make in respect of a contract claim, or a number of contract claims relating to the same contract, is £25,000 (*art 10*). In many cases, the potential value of a contractual claim may exceed £25,000. The question may arise whether a successful employee in the tribunal who recovers the maximum award may then bring fresh proceedings in the High Court for the remainder of the value of the contractual claim. In *Fraser v HLMAD Ltd* [2006] IRLR 687, [2006] ICR 1395, the Court of Appeal held that no further claim may be brought in the civil courts once a tribunal has ruled on a wrongful dismissal claim. The key point is that, once the court has decided a matter, a claimant may not ask another court to deal with that same matter again. The reason for this is that the employee no longer has a cause of action which he is able to litigate. The cause of action – breach of contract – has been replaced by, or 'merged in' the judgment of the tribunal. The concept of a cause of action merging in a judgment, so precluding a further action being brought in respect of the same cause of action, is well established in law and is a topic that is beyond the scope of this work. Further, there are several cases in which a party who has succeeded in one forum which has a limited power to award damages has been precluded from seeking to institute fresh proceedings in respect of the same matter in another forum in order to recover the shortfall. In *Hills v Co-operative Wholesale Society Ltd* [1940] 2 KB 435, an employee brought an action in the High Court and in the county court against his employer in respect of the same complaint. A defence of common employment was available to the employer in the High Court but not in the county court. The employer paid into the county court the maximum sum which the employee could recover in that forum and the employee accepted that sum. The Court of Appeal held that the employee could not continue with the High Court proceedings. His cause of action had been completely satisfied when he accepted the payment made in respect of the county court proceedings, notwithstanding that there was a limit on the sum that the county court could award. See also *Wright v London General Omnibus Co* (1877) 2 QBD 271; *Clarke v Yorke* (1882) 52 LJ Ch 32.

For a comprehensive treatment of the application of estoppel principles in the context of Tribunal proceedings see **20.125** Estoppels and prevention of abuse of process and **20.126** Withdrawal and dismissal of claims.

8.46   Disclosure

This section is principally concerned with the remedies of the employee against the employer when the latter has acted in breach of contract. However, the situation may also arise when the employer has become mixed up in alleged wrongdoing by third parties. In *A v Company B Ltd* [1997] IRLR 405, an employee was dismissed by his employer after allegations of gross misconduct had been made to the employer by a third party. The employer did not identify the complainant or specify the nature of the complaints that had been made. The employee took the view that false allegations had been made about him and wished to institute an action against the third party alleging defamation. In order that the employee could prosecute that action, the High Court ordered that the employer disclose details of the allegations which had been made about him by the third party, following the principles laid down in *Norwich Pharmacal Co v Customs and Excise Comrs* [1974] AC 133.

8.47   EMPLOYER'S REMEDIES FOR BREACH OF CONTRACT OF EMPLOYMENT

Withholding or deduction of wages

If an employee does not perform any of his contractual duties, he is not entitled to his contractual wage. Thus, an employee is not entitled to be paid for days when he is on strike.

If the employee refuses to perform the full range of his contractual duties, particularly if this refusal is in pursuance of industrial action, the purpose of which is to disrupt the employer's business, the employee will not be entitled to his full contractual wage (see *Miles v Wakefield Metropolitan District Council* [1987] ICR 368). In *Wiluszynski v Tower Hamlets London Borough Council* [1989] IRLR 259, the Court of Appeal held that the Council was entitled to withhold the whole of the employee's wages when the employee refused to perform a substantial part of his duties and it was clear that the employer was not accepting the work which was performed as substantial performance of the contract. In *British Telecommunications plc v Ticehurst* [1992] ICR 383, it was held that a manager who intended to continue participating in a withdrawal of goodwill could be sent home without pay.

Alternatively, the employer may be able to deduct from the employee's wages a sum representing the financial loss suffered by him as a result of the employee's breach of contract (see *Sim v Rotherham Metropolitan Borough Council* [1986] ICR 897).

In *Cooper v Isle of Wight College* [2007] EWHC 2831 (QB), [2008] IRLR 124, it was held that the appropriate sum which an employer was entitled to deduct in respect of a one day strike was $1/260^{th}$ of a year's pay on the basis that there are 260 working days in the year.

In the case where the employee engages in action short of a strike, it is open to the employer to decline to make any payment on the basis that he is only prepared to accept full performance of the employee's obligations (*Miles* above). An employee who carries out only part of his duties does so at risk. There is no right to claim a quantum meruit. In *Spackman v London Metropolitan University* [2007] IRLR 744, the employee refused to perform some tasks and the employer deducted 30% of the employee's pay. Having held that the employer could lawfully have paid nothing, the court held that there was no breach of contract by deducting 30% of the employee's pay.

The employer's right to withhold pay may arise in many situations where the employee refuses to work. In *Luke v Stoke-on-Trent Council* [2007] EWCA Civ 761, [2007] ICR 1678, [2007] IRLR 777, the Court of Appeal held that an employer was entitled not to pay an employee who felt unable to attend her place of work after a breakdown in her relationship with her employer. The employer had reasonably required her to return to work. Since she had failed to do so, there was no entitlement to pay: see also *Sunrise Brokers LLP v Rodgers* [2014] EWCA Civ 1373.

However, note that deduction of wages may constitute an unlawful deduction under the *ERA 1996, s 13*.

(See also **35.14 PAY – I.**)

8.47a Acceptance of fundamental breach

If the employee is in fundamental breach of his contractual obligations, the employer can accept the breach and bring the contract to an end. Such a fundamental breach will generally consist of gross misconduct, extreme incompetence, or a major failure to carry out the work required of the employee. To go on strike will generally amount to a fundamental breach of contract. See also **46.2 STRIKES AND INDUSTRIAL ACTION** and **59.6, 59.7 WRONGFUL DISMISSAL**.

8.47b Damages

An employer may bring proceedings against an employee for damages for breach of contract (see, eg, *Janata Bank v Ahmed* [1981] ICR 791). Situations which may give rise to such proceedings are a breach of the employee's duty of fidelity, breach of his duty of care and failure to give the notice of termination he is contractually obliged to give. In practice, such claims are rare (but see *Cheltenham Borough Council v Laird* [2009] EWHC 1253 (QB), [2009] IRLR 621, an unsuccessful claim by a local authority against a former employee for the costs it would not have incurred if it had employed someone else). What is more common is an application for an injunction to restrain disclosure of confidential information or to enforce a restrictive covenant (see **RESTRAINT OF TRADE, CONFIDENTIALITY AND EMPLOYEE INTERVENTIONS (42)**).

Parties to contracts are entitled to make their own provision for compensation in the event of breach by one party. The law distinguishes between liquidated damages clauses (those containing genuine pre-estimates of loss and designed to compensate the innocent party) and penalty clauses (those designed to deter or punish a wrongdoer) – the former are enforceable, the latter are not. If the compensation provided for is "out of all proportion to any legitimate interest of the innocent party in the enforcement of the primary obligation", it will be a penalty and unenforceable. The question is really whether the sum payable is extravagant or unconscionable in comparison to the interest: see *Cavendish Square Holdings BV v Talal El Makdessi* [2016] AC 1172. For illustrations in the employment context see *Murray v Leisureplay plc* [2005] EWCA Civ 963, [2005] IRLR 946; *Giraud UK Ltd v Smith* [2000] IRLR 763; *Tullett Prebon Group Ltd v El-Hajjali* [2008] EWHC 1924 (QB), [2008] IRLR 760 (for an example of a liquidated damages clause successfully relied upon by an employer). Caution is required with these decisions. They should be read in light of the Supreme Court's judgment in *Cavendish Square Holdings BV*.

In *Gamatronic (UK) Ltd v Hamilton* [2016] EWHC 2225 (QB) (QBD), two directors were found to be in breach of fiduciary duty in taking steps to compete prior to joining a competitor's business. However, the claimant was not entitled to any remedy in respect of the breaches as the directors had continued to perform their duties diligently; nor would compensation be awarded in respect of their salaries paid by the competitor as there was no reasonable relationship between those salaries and their breach of fiduciary duty.

8.47c   Injunction or specific performance

In no circumstances may the employee be compelled to work by injunction or by an order of specific performance. That was the common law and the principle is enacted in *TULRCA 1992, s 236*. That applies also if such compulsion will be the practical result of granting an injunction against a third party, eg the only alternative employer (*Warren v Mendy* [1989] ICR 525); the court will not make an order which would prevent the employee from earning his living. However, the Court of Appeal held in *Evening Standard Co Ltd v Henderson* [1987] ICR 588 that it may be possible to restrain an employee who does not give proper notice (see **49.17** Termination of Employment) from working elsewhere during his notice period so long as the employer will provide him with all his contractual benefits without actually requiring him to work. The *Henderson* principle was approved in *Provident Financial Group plc and Whitegates Estate Agency Ltd v Hayward* [1989] ICR 160, where an express contractual prohibition was relied upon. However, the Court of Appeal indicated that no injunction would be granted if the plaintiff's business had nothing to do with that of the new employer. It also recognised that an employee might need to work and exercise his skills (the employer in *Hayward* had put the employee on 'garden leave' during his notice period, whereas in *Henderson* work was available if the employee wanted it), and refused to grant an injunction after considering the non-competitive nature of the job the employee wished to take up, and the length of the unexpired notice period (see also *Warren*).

In *William Hill Organisation Ltd v Tucker* [1998] IRLR 313, the Court of Appeal appeared to impose further limitations on the availability of the 'garden leave injunction' remedy. The court held that it was necessary to consider in each case whether the consideration moving from the employer obliged the employer to permit the employee to do work, or whether the full extent of the obligation is to pay the employee. If the employer was obliged to permit the employee to carry out work, then the court would be unlikely to grant a garden leave injunction in the absence of an express provision which entitled the employer not to provide work and/or required the employee to agree not to attend work during the notice period. It was unlikely that such a provision would be implied. However, even where an express term was present, the court would not grant relief to any greater extent than would be granted in respect of a justifiable covenant in restraint of trade (see **42.6** Restraint of Trade, Confidentiality and Employee Interventions).

8.47c   Contract of Employment

A garden leave injunction was granted in *SG&R Valuation Service Co LLC v Boudrais* [2008] IRLR 770 notwithstanding the absence of any express provision for garden leave in the employees' contracts. Although the employees had a right to work during their notice periods, this right was vitiated because the employees had, during their notice periods, committed wrongdoing by which they would or might profit. By those breaches of their contracts, they had "demonstrated in a serious way that they were not ready or willing to work, or that they had not rendered it impossible or reasonably impracticable for the employer to provide work". This principle – expressly described as a qualification to the right to work rather than an implied term of the employees' contracts – was approved by the Court of Appeal in *Standard Life Health Care Ltd v Gorman* [2009] EWCA Civ 1292, [2010] IRLR 233.

In *Sunrise Brokers LLP v Rodgers* [2015] ICR 272, however, the Court of Appeal held that there is no rule of law requiring an employer to pay an employee if it seeks an injunction preventing him from resigning in breach of contract. The question is whether the injunction would compel the employee to return to work for the employer. The court therefore held that an injunction restraining a broker, who had purported to resign without giving the required contractual notice, from joining a competitor or contacting clients during his notice period and a period thereafter covered by post-termination restrictive covenants, was properly granted. The reason the broker would be unpaid during this period was that he had refused to return to work.

The same general principles relating to the grant of interlocutory injunctions apply as are discussed under 'Employee's remedies', above (see also RESTRAINT OF TRADE, CONFIDENTIALITY AND EMPLOYEE INTERVENTIONS (42)).

In *Associated Foreign Exchange Ltd v International Foreign Exchange (UK) Ltd* [2010] EWHC 1178 (Ch), [2010] IRLR 964, the court refused to grant an interlocutory injunction to restrain a former employee from breaching a 12-month non-solicitation covenant, because the market changed at such a pace that such protection was unnecessary and because this covenant was unlikely to be enforceable.

8.47d Account of profits

In some cases, the appropriate remedy for a breach of contract may be the restitutionary remedy of an account of profits. An account was ordered by the House of Lords in *A-G v Blake* [2001] IRLR 36. Such a remedy will only be available in exceptional circumstances where the normal remedies of damages, specific performance and injunction do not provide an adequate remedy. The case of *Blake*, a spy who had published a book in breach of his contractual duties to the Crown, was such an exceptional case.

9   Data Protection

9.1   INTRODUCTION

This chapter was introduced in the 2018 edition of Tolley's Employment Law Handbook. It sets out the implications of the new European data protection regime for how employers handle their employees' personal data.

Although the term 'employee' is used throughout the chapter, none of the rights of the data subject depends on employment status. The rights are enjoyed equally by workers, contractors, and anyone else whose personal data is being processed.

The new regime has applied since 25 May 2018, when the *EU General Data Protection Regulation (GDPR)* entered into force. As an EU regulation, the *GDPR* takes effect in UK law without any requirement for domestic implementation. It will continue to have effect in UK law, whether the UK leaves the EU with or without a deal at the end of the transition period: see *European Union (Withdrawal) Act 2018, s 3*. The *GDPR* is supplemented by the *UK Data Protection Act 2018* ("*DPA 2018*"). The new regime replaces that previously contained in *Directive 95/46/EC* (the *Data Protection Directive*, "*DPD*"), as implemented in domestic law by the *Data Protection Act 1998* ("*DPA 1998*"), although claims alleging contraventions that occurred before 25 May 2018 will continue to be decided under the old regime.

Article 88 of the *GDPR* provides that Member States may pass more specific legislation to ensure the protection of the rights and freedoms in respect of the processing of employees' personal data in the employment context. Other than those in the *DPA 2018* as referred to below, the UK has not passed any such laws to date.

The purpose of the *GDPR* is to provide a stronger and more coherent data protection framework within the EU, in a context where rapid technological developments have brought new challenges for the protection of personal data, and the scale of its collection and sharing have increased exponentially. The *GDPR* reflects the fact that the protection of natural persons in relation to the processing of personal data is a fundamental right of the EU, protected by *Article 8* of the *Charter of Fundamental Rights of the European Union*. It aims to provide a consistent and high level of protection for personal data across the EU. Unlike the *DPD*, it applies to any and all processing of personal data in the context of the activities of an establishment of a controller or processor in the EU, regardless of whether the processing takes place in the EU or not. It also applies to the processing of personal data of data subjects within the EU by a controller or processor not established in the EU, where the processing is related to the offering of goods or services to them, or the monitoring of their behaviour within the EU.

There is still a relatively limited number of authorities interpreting the new regime. We have indicated where we consider that authorities decided under the *DPA 1998* or *DPD* will have continuing application, but practitioners should proceed with caution in this area.

In November 2011 the Information Commissioner issued, under *DPA 1998, s 51*, The Employment Practices Data Protection Code (in this chapter, "the ICO Code", available at https://ico.org.uk/media/for-organisations/documents/1064/the_employment_practices _code.pdf). The statutory purpose of the ICO Code is, of course, promoting compliance with the *1998 Act* rather than the *GDPR* and the *DPA 2018*, and employers should not assume that following the provisions of the Code will ensure compliance with *GDPR*. Where readers of this chapter are referred to the ICO Code for further details and practical guidance on aspects of employee data protection, this caveat should be borne in mind. However, until the

9.1 Data Protection

Information Commissioner publishes a GDPR-specific Code on employment and data protection, the ICO Code will continue to provide useful guidance on best practices for employers. Further detail is given in Supplementary Guidance published by the Information Commissioner (in this chapter, "the ICO Guidance", available at https ://ico.org.uk/media/for-organisations/documents/1066/employment_practice_code _supplementary_guidance.pdf).

Since the *GDPR* entered into force, the ICO has steadily developed its general guidance on the *GDPR* and *DPA 2018*. This provides a useful resource explaining the main concepts of the data protection regime, but it does not contain specific detail on its application in employment situations. See https://ico.org.uk/for-organisations/guide-to-data -protection/guide-to-the-general-data-protection-regulation-gdpr.

On 8 June 2017 the Data Protection Working Party established under *Article 29* of the *DPD* adopted 'Opinion 2/2017 on data processing at work' (in this chapter, "the Working Party Opinion"). The Working Party Opinion is chiefly concerned with the *DPD*, but also looks forward to the implementation of the GDPR.

Under the *GDPR*, the *Article 29* Working Party has been abolished. Its monitoring and guidance functions have now been taken over by the European Data Protection Board established under *Article 68* of the *GDPR*. Like the *Article 29* Working Party, the Board issues non-binding opinions, guidelines and best practice recommendations, which are a useful and informative source of general guidance on the application of the GDPR. Opinions and guidelines of *the Article 29* Working Party also continue to represent an important source of guidance, particularly in the absence of judicial authority interpreting the provisions of the *GDPR*. We also refer to other guidelines published by the European Data Protection Board or *Article 29* Working Party where relevant.

9.2 CONTENTS OF THIS CHAPTER

This Chapter is not a treatise on Data Protection law. It aims to consider common data protection issues that will arise in the course of the employment relationship. Specifically it considers:

(a) Basic concepts of data protection law as set out in the *GDPR* and *DPA 2018*;

(b) The principal rights and obligations contained within the *GDPR*, as applicable to employment;

(c) Data protection considerations for employers during the recruitment process of employees (for other considerations during recruitment, see CHAPTER 22);

(d) Data protection and the maintenance of employee records;

(e) Processing of special category data during the employment relationship, and in particular:

   (i) Employee Health Records; and

   (ii) Equal opportunities data;

(f) Monitoring of employees at work;

(g) Subject Access Requests and their use in Tribunal litigation;

(h) Common law privacy claims against the employer.

This chapter is not about:

(a) The numerous requirements of the *GDPR* that are not specific to the employer/employee relationship;

(b)   Disclosures required by TUPE (see CHAPTER 11)

(c)   Past criminal convictions (see CHAPTER 18)

(d)   Restraint of trade / confidential information (see CHAPTER 42)

9.3   BASIC CONCEPTS OF DATA PROTECTION LAW

There are certain key concepts of data protection law which are defined in the *GDPR* and *DPA 2018*, and which need to be appreciated in order for data protection issues properly to be understood.

9.4   Personal data

The *GDPR* and *DPA 2018* apply only to "personal data". "Personal data" means any information relating to an identified or identifiable living individual (a "data subject"). See *GDPR, Article 4(1)* and *DPA 2018, s 3(2)*. It should be noted that "information" can be in any form, whether (for example) a letter, an email, a photograph, an audio recording, CCTV footage, or anything else.

The expression "personal data" would cover information such as the name of a person, in conjunction with his telephone details or information about his working conditions or hobbies: see *Criminal Proceedings against Lindqvist* C-101 [2004] QB 1004; or his name and address: see *College van burgemeester en wethouders van Rotterdam v Rijkeboer* [2009] ECR I-3889. It would also cover for example the name, date of birth, nationality, gender, ethnicity, religion and language of an identifiable individual: *YS v Minister voor Immigratie, Integratie en Asiel* [2015] 1 WLR 609, [2014] All ER (D) 311 (Jul). It would cover his name and salary: *Rechnungshof v Österreichischer Rundfunk* (Joined Cases C-465/00, C-138/01 and C-139/01) [2003] ECR I-4989. An image of a person recorded by a camera is also his personal data: *Ryneš v Úřad pro ochranu osobních údajů* (Case C-212/13) [2015] 1 WLR 2607, [2014] All ER (D) 174 (Dec). A person's whereabouts on a particular day at a particular time may also amount to his personal data: *Ittihadieh v 5-11 Cheyne Gardens RTM Co Ltd* [2018] QB 256.

Some confusion as to what amounts to "personal data" has been caused by the Court of Appeal's judgment in *Durant v FSA* [2003] EWCA Civ 1746, [2003] All ER (D) 124 (Dec). In that judgment, Auld LJ referred to "two notions" which could provide guidance as to whether information was personal data, those being (i) whether the data is biographical in any significant sense, or records the data subject's involvement in a matter with no personal connotations; and (ii) whether the data subject is the "focus" of the information. The Court of Appeal has subsequently emphasised in *Edem v Information Commissioner* [2014] EWCA Civ 92, [2014] All ER (D) 50 (Feb) that it is unnecessary to apply those "notions" where information is "obviously about" or "clearly linked to" an individual, and that they will only be of assistance in borderline cases. A name of an individual, for example, would clearly be his personal data: although that would not mean that the whole of a document in which his name appeared would also be his personal data as a result. That having been said, it may be relevant to ask whether the interpretation of "personal data" in any particular case would further the purpose of guaranteeing the protection of an individual's right to privacy with regard to the processing of data relating to him: see *Ittihadieh* and *YS*.

The question of the "identifiability" of the data subject, and whether anonymisation prevents information from constituting "personal data", has been considered in a number of cases. Information which has been manipulated to conceal the identity of living individuals will remain personal data in the hands of the data controller, where the controller holds the "key" to reconstituting their identities. See eg *Common Services Agency v Scottish Information Commissioner* [2008] 1 WLR 1550, [2008] 4 All ER 851, HL. The *GDPR* sets out a concept of "pseudonymisation", which means the processing of personal data such that it can no longer be attributed to a specific data subject without the use of additional information, provided that such additional information is kept separately and is subject to technical and organisational measures to ensure that the personal data are not attributed to an identified or identifiable natural person: see *GDPR, Article 4(5)*. Where the data controller does not retain any "key" to reconstituting the identities of the persons whose data is anonymised, and there is no other means likely reasonably to be used which could enable identification of the data subjects, then it will no longer be personal data at all. This is a difficult area, and the Information Commissioner has published an extensive code on the position in the *DPA 1998*, "Anonymisation: managing data protection risk", at https ://ico.org.uk/media/for-organisations/documents/1061/anonymisation-code.pdf.

9.5   Processing

The *GDPR* and *DPA 2018* apply where personal data is "processed". "Processing" means any operation or set of operations which is performed on personal data, whether or not by automated means. It includes collecting it; recording it; storing it; retrieving it; consulting it; using it; disclosing it; or indeed destroying it. This is an extremely broad definition, that extends to 'passive' acts such as storing or accessing data, as well as the active manipulation of data. See *GDPR, Article 4(2)*.

One important limitation on the scope of the data protection legislation is that it does not apply to 'manual unstructured data'. There are two aspects to the definition of such data – firstly, it must be manual, that is, a paper record as opposed to an electronic one. Secondly, it must be 'unstructured', that is, not part of any filing system. A 'filing system' is given a broad definition in *GDPR, Art 4(6)* as '*any structured set of personal data which are accessible according to specific criteria, whether centralised, decentralised or dispersed on a functional or geographical basis*'. Guidance on whether a paper file is sufficiently structured to constitute a 'relevant filing system' (the equivalent term in the *DPA 1998* and *DPD*) may be found in the Court of Appeal's judgment in *Dawson-Damer v Taylor Wessing LLP* [2020] EWCA Civ 352, [2020] All ER (D) 104 (Mar) (the second appellate decision in that litigation).

The *GDPR* and *DPA 2018* do not apply to purely verbal communications. That is a necessary implication from the definitions of "processing" of data in *Article 4 GDPR* and *section 1(4)* of the *DPA 2018*, which refer to actions which only have meaning in relation to recorded information. That point is reflected at [60] of *Scott v LGBT Foundation Limited* [2020] EWHC 483 (QB), [2020] All ER (D) 44 (Mar), albeit that was a case where this issue arose under the previous regime in the *DPA 1998* and the *DPD*.

In the employment context, this might apply to, say, handwritten notes about an employee (which are 'manual'), although <u>not</u> where they are held as part of an employee's HR file (in which case they are not 'unstructured'). The *GDPR* does not apply at all to manual unstructured data held by private entities, and only in limited form to such data held by public authorities (defined as those bodies subject to the *Freedom of Information Act*), in which case many key *GDPR* provisions are disapplied by *DPA 2018, s 24(2)*. Furthermore, most of the remaining provisions setting out principles and rights of the data subject are disapplied in the case of personal data relating to '*appointments, removals, pay, discipline, superannuation or other personnel matters*' of public authorities' employees or contractors. These provisions are, however, complex, and care should be taken when determining whether any given data is exempt from a particular requirement of the legislation.

9.6   Data Controllers and Data Processors

The *GDPR* and *DPA 2018* impose obligations upon "data controllers" and "data processors". A "controller" means the natural or legal person, public authority, agency or other body which, alone or jointly, determines the purposes and means of the processing of personal data (see *GDPR, Article 4(7)*). A "processor" means a natural or legal person, public authority, agency or other body which processes personal data on behalf of the controller: *GDPR, Article 4(8)*. These are materially the same as the definitions in the DPD (implemented in domestic law by the *DPA 1998*).

The distinction between who is a "controller" and who is a "processor" is critical: guidance has been given by the Information Commissioner in relation to the same definitions of "controller" and "processor" contained in the *DPA 1998*: see https://ico.org.uk/media/for-organisations/documents/1546/data-controllers-and-data-processors-dp-guidance.pdf. This guidance will be of continuing relevance under the *GDPR*. It should be noted that an employee of the data controller is not a processor, but is treated (in effect) as part of the controller.

The data controller has primary responsibility for ensuring that data processing is carried out in accordance with the *GDPR* (and, where applicable, *DPA 2018*). See *GDPR, Article 24*. "Joint controllers" – ie controllers who jointly determine the purposes and means of processing – must in general have an arrangement between them determining their respective responsibilities for compliance with the *GDPR*: see *Article 26*.

Unlike the DPD, the *GDPR* places certain specific obligations on data processors. For instance, processors must maintain a record of all categories of processing activities carried out on behalf of a controller (*GDPR, Article 30*). Both controllers and processors are required to implement appropriate technical and organisation measures to ensure an appropriate level of data security (*GDPR, Article 32*). Public authorities, and organisations whose core activities consist of processing that is high risk because of its scale or nature, are obliged to appoint a designated data protection officer (*GDPR, Article 37*), who must have a certain standing in the organisation (*GDPR, Article 38*) and who is required to carry out certain tasks (*GDPR, Article 39*).

9.7 Conditions for processing

To be lawful, all processing of personal data must meet at least one specified condition (*GDPR, Article 6(1)*). The conditions for processing of personal data differ, depending upon whether or not the data is in a "special category", which entails particular sensitivity. "Special category" personal data is data revealing racial or ethnic origin, political opinions, religious or philosophical beliefs, or trade union membership, and the processing of genetic data, biometric data for the purpose of uniquely identifying a natural person, data concerning health, or data concerning a person's sex life or sexual orientation. See *GDPR, Article 9*. These categories correspond broadly to the familiar categories of 'sensitive personal data' under the *DPA 1998* (although data relating to criminal convictions and offences is now in a category of its own under the GDPR – see below).

In general terms, the processing of (non-special category) personal data must meet one of the conditions in *GDPR, Article 6(1)*. Those conditions are:

(a) The data subject has given consent to the processing for one or more specific purposes: *GDPR, Article 6(1)(a)*. "Consent" is defined by *Article 4(11)* in terms that mean consent is only valid if it is given with the utmost clarity: 'any freely given, specific, informed and unambiguous indication of the data subject's wishes by which he or she, by a statement or by a clear affirmative action, signifies agreement to the processing of personal data relating to him or her.' The concept of consent is importantly expanded upon in *GDPR Articles 7* and *8*. Among other matters, the controller must be able to demonstrate that a data subject has consented to processing of his or her personal data (*Article 7(1)*); the data subject must have the right to withdraw consent at any time (*Article 7(3)*); and when assessing whether consent is freely given, utmost account shall be taken of whether, inter alia, the performance of a contract, including the provision of a service, is conditional on consent to the processing of personal data that is not necessary for that performance (*Article 7(4)*). The provisions of *Article 7* limit the utility of consent as a condition for processing in the employment context, because consent will not be freely given where the data subject cannot withdraw it (which he cannot do if the employer requires that the processing take place), and/or where it is assumed as part and parcel of the performance of the employment contract. This view is confirmed by guidelines on consent issued by the Article 29 Working Party in July 2018 (paragraph 3.1.1). The *Article 29* Working Party's guidelines have been endorsed by the European Data Protection Board. If the processing is necessary for the performance of the contract, the employer may rely on *GDPR, Article 6(1)(b)* in any case (see below). The Working Party Opinion has already, in the context of the *DPD*, stated that for 'the majority of cases of employees' data processing, the legal basis of that processing cannot and should not be the consent of the employees' (page 6).

(b)   Processing is necessary for the performance of a contract to which the data subject is party or in order to take steps at the request of the data subject prior to entering into a contract: *Article 6(1)(b)*. As stated above, this will be the general basis for processing of non-sensitive category personal data in the employment context.

(c)   Processing is necessary for compliance with a legal obligation to which the controller is subject: *Article 6(1)(c)*.

(d)   Processing is necessary in order to protect the vital interests of the data subject or of another natural person: *Article 6(1)(d)*.

(e)   Processing is necessary for the performance of a task carried out in the public interest or in the exercise of official authority vested in the controller: *Article 6(1)(e)*.

(f)   Processing is necessary for the purposes of the legitimate interests pursued by the controller or by a third party, except where such interests are overridden by the interests or fundamental rights and freedoms of the data subject, in particular where the data subject is a child: *Article 6(1)(f)*. This basis for processing does not apply to processing carried out by public authorities in the performance of their tasks (which it is anticipated should generally fall within *Article 6(1)(c)* or *6(1)(e)*).

The processing of "special category" personal data must meet one of the conditions in *GDPR, Article 9(2)*, those being:

(a)   The data subject has given explicit consent to the processing, for one or more specified purposes.

(b)   Processing is necessary for the purposes of carrying out the obligations and exercising specific rights of the controller or the data subject in the field of employment and social security and social protection law, insofar as authorised by EU or Member State law or a collective agreement providing for appropriate safeguards.

The domestic legal authority for processing of "special category" personal data in the employment context is provided by *DPA 2018, Sch 1, Pt 1*, read with *s 10(2)*. *Paragraph 1(1)* of the *Schedule* provides that the employment condition is met if the processing is necessary for the purposes of performing or exercising obligations or rights imposed or conferred by law on the controller or data subject in connection with employment, and when the processing is carried out the controller has an "appropriate policy document" in place, as defined in *DPA 2018, Sch 1, Pt 4, para 34*. This is a document which (a) explains the controller's procedures for securing compliance with *GDPR, Article 5* in connection with the processing; and

(b) explains the controller's policies as regards retention and erasure of personal data processed in reliance on the condition. The policy document must be retained until at least 6 months after processing has ceased, reviewed and updated as appropriate, and provided to the Information Commissioner on request: *DPA 2018, Sch 1, Pt 4, para 35*.

(c) Processing is necessary to protect the vital interests of the data subject or another natural person, where the data subject is incapable of giving consent.

(d) Processing is carried out by a not-for-profit body, in certain specific conditions.

(e) Processing relates to personal data manifestly made public by the data subject.

(f) Processing is necessary for the establishment, exercise or defence of legal claims.

(g) Processing is necessary for reasons of substantial public interest, on the basis of EU or Member State law providing for appropriate safeguards.

The domestic legal authority for processing of "special category" personal data under this condition is provided by *DPA 2018, Sch 1, Pt 2*, read with *s 10(3)*. An appropriate policy document is required, unless the contrary is specified by the particular condition.

(h) Processing is necessary (broadly) for various medical purposes.

(i) Processing is necessary (broadly) for various public health purposes.

(j) Processing is necessary (broadly) for various research purposes.

Processing of personal data relating to criminal convictions and offences or related security measures based on *Article 6(1) GDPR* must be carried out only under the control of official authority or when authorised by EU or Member State law providing for appropriate safeguards: see *Article 10 GDPR*. The domestic legal authority for processing of this type of data under this condition is provided by *Parts 1, 2*, and *3* of *Schedule 1* to the *DPA 2018*, read with *s 10(5)*. For criminal convictions data, see further Chapter 17.

Processing of personal data must be undertaken in accordance with "principles" set out in *Article 5 GDPR*. Those principles broadly mirror the "data protection principles" previously set out in *Schedule 1* to the *DPA 1998*. They state that personal data must be:

(a) Processed lawfully, fairly and transparently: *Article 5(1)(a)*. The requirement of "lawful" processing means, among other matters, that processing must meet one of the conditions in *GDPR, Articles 6* or *9*.

(b) Collected for specified, explicit and legitimate purposes, and not further processed in a manner incompatible with those purposes (further processing for archiving or statistical purposes not, however, being inconsistent with the purposes): *Article 5(1)(b)*.

(c) Adequate, relevant and limited to what is necessary in relation to the purposes for which they are processed ("data minimisation"): *Article 5(1)(c)*.

(d) Accurate and, where necessary, kept up to date: *Article 5(1)(d)*.

(e) Kept in a form which permits identification of the data subject for no longer than is necessary for the purposes for which they are processed: *Article 5(1)(e)*.

(f) Processed in a manner ensuring appropriate security, including protection against unauthorised or unlawful processing and against accidental loss, destruction or damage, using appropriate technical or organisational measures: *Article 5(1)(f)*.

9.8 THE PRINCIPAL RIGHTS AND OBLIGATIONS WITHIN THE GDPR APPLICABLE TO EMPLOYMENT

This does not purport to be an exhaustive account of the rights and obligations within the GDPR that may arise in the employment context, but rather a brief introduction to the most important of those rights and obligations.

9.9 Transparency

The *GDPR* contains enhanced and far-reaching obligations of transparency. Individuals whose personal data are processed have the right to be informed about the collection and use of that data (a "privacy notice"). Unless they already have the information concerned, *GDPR, Article 13(1)* stipulates that where data are collected from the data subject, they must be provided with the identity and contact details of the data controller; the contact details of the controller's data protection officer (if applicable); the purposes for processing of their personal data, and lawful basis for processing; the categories of personal data obtained (if the personal data is not obtained from the individual to whom it relates); the recipients or categories of recipient of the data; and the details of its transfer to any third country (if applicable).

Article 13(2) then sets out 'further information necessary to provide for fair and transparent processing', including the period for which the data may be retained; the data subject's rights of access and rectification; the right to complain to a supervisory authority; and the existence of automated decision-making based upon the data. The information listed in *Article 13(1)* must always be provided; the best interpretation appears to be that the information listed in *Article 13(2)* should be provided insofar as necessary to ensure fair and transparent processing, taking into account the specific circumstances and context in which the personal data are processed (see *Recital (60)*). (It should be noted that the view of the *Article 29* Working Party is that the information listed in *Article 13(2)* should always be provided – see paragraph 24 of its Guideline on transparency, http ://ec.europa.eu/newsroom/article29/document.cfm?action=display&docid=51025 – but this view is less consistent with the wording of *Recital (60)* than that advanced above).

Article 13(3) states that where the controller intends to further process the personal data for a purpose other than that for which the personal data were collected, the controller shall provide the data subject prior to that further processing with information on that other purpose and with any relevant further information as referred to in *Article 13(2)*. None of *Articles 13(1)–(3)* applies where and insofar as the data subject already has the information (*Article 13(4)*).

Article 14 makes equivalent provision for information to be given, where personal data are collected otherwise than from the data subject (although the requirements are disapplied where they would involve disproportionate effort – *Article 14(5)(b)*).

GDPR, Article 12 indicates that the information must be provided free of charge, and in a concise, transparent and easily comprehensible form.

The information must be provided at the time when personal data are obtained, if obtained from the data subject: see *GDPR, Article 13(1)*. Where data are obtained from a third party, the relevant privacy information must be provided to the data subject within a reasonable period after obtaining it, not exceeding one month; where the personal data are to be used for communication with the data subject, at the latest at the time of the first communication to that data subject; or, if disclosure to another recipient is envisaged, at the latest when the personal data are first disclosed. See *GDPR, Article 14(3)*.

9.10 Subject Access Requests

Individuals have the right to access their personal data and supplementary information: see *GDPR, Article 15* (the "subject access right") (see further below **9.21**).

9.11   Rectification

Individuals have the right to obtain rectification of inaccurate personal data without undue delay. They also have the right to have incomplete personal data completed, taking into account the purposes of the processing. See *GDPR, Article 16*. If an individual contests the accuracy of the personal data, they also have the right to obtain restriction of its processing while the controller verifies its accuracy: *GDPR, Article 18*. The controller should communicate any rectification to each recipient to whom the personal data have been disclosed, unless this is impossible or involves disproportionate effort: *GDPR, Article 19*.

9.12   Erasure

Individuals can request erasure of their personal data (the "right to be forgotten"), where the conditions in *GDPR, Article 17* are met; and such erasure must similarly be communicated to recipients of the data in accordance with *GDPR, Article 19*. The conditions in *GDPR, Article 17* include where the personal data are no longer necessary in relation to the purposes for which they were collected or processed, or they have been unlawfully processed. There is a fast-developing body of case law on the right to be forgotten, including in the domestic courts, but it is outside the scope of this Chapter.

A data subject who considers his rights under the *GDPR* (or *DPA 2018*) have been infringed has the right to lodge a complaint with the Information Commissioner (see *GDPR, Articles 57* and *77* and *DPA 2018, s 165*). A person may also complain to court about a breach of the GDPR, and has the right to receive compensation for financial and other loss (including distress): see *GDPR, Article 82* and *DPA 2018, s 168*. Jurisdiction to consider such complaints is conferred on the High Court and County Court (and in Scotland, the Court of Session): see *DPA 2018, s 180*. The same facts that give rise to a data protection claim may of course also give rise to a potential claim for misuse of private information (as to which, see further below, in brief **9.22**).

An employer may be vicariously liable on a claim for the torts of misuse of private information, breach of confidence, or breach of the *DPA 1998* committed by an employee in the course of employment: see *Various Claimants v WM Supermarkets plc* [2020] UKSC 12, [2020] All ER (D) 02 (Apr). The same position would logically apply to a breach of the *GDPR* or of the *DPA 2018*. Strictly speaking, this issue was obiter in the Supreme Court's judgment, because it found on the facts that the employer was not vicariously liable for the employee's torts: it concluded that the employee, who deliberately released other employees' personal data onto the internet, in revenge against his employer, was acting on a "frolic of his own". However, the Supreme Court issued a fully reasoned opinion on the point, on the basis that it was "desirable that the court should express its view".

It can be seen that many of the basic rights and concepts of the *GDPR* are developments of similar rights and concepts applicable under the *DPA 1998*, albeit that in numerous ways the provisions of the *DPA 1998* have been amended to expand or strengthen the rights of the data subject. A distinct innovation of the *GDPR*, however, is that it imposes requirements on employers (as on all data controllers) to design procedures so as to minimise the processing of personal data and maximise the degree of protection for such personal data as is processed ('data protection by design and default' – see *GDPR, Article 25*) and to keep records of the categories of processing they are undertaking and how these comply with GDPR (*GDPR, Article 30*).

In other words, the *GDPR* requires employers not just to comply with its fundamental principles, but to plan for compliance, and furthermore to be able to demonstrate both their planning and their compliance. This is of fundamental importance to employers, who will need to maintain data protection policies, and/or build in data protection considerations to existing policies wherever those policies cover activities that involve the processing of personal data. The requirement for data protection policies is explored further below in specific contexts.

9.13   DATA PROTECTION CONSIDERATIONS DURING THE RECRUITMENT PROCESS

When an employer conducts a recruitment exercise, it will inevitably process a substantial amount of personal data about the applicants for any post. It must do so in accordance with the principles and conditions of processing set out in *Articles 5* and *6* of the *GDPR*, and the requirements that flow from them such as the requirement for transparency (*Articles 13* and *14*). So it is almost inevitable, given the requirements in the *GDPR* that employers plan for and demonstrate compliance, that employers will need written recruitment policies specifying how they will handle and protect personal data during the recruitment process.

In any case, if processing of special category data is taking place, and the employer wishes to rely on the condition in *GDPR, Article 9(2)(b)* (processing necessary for compliance with legal obligations relating to employment or social protection), the requirement for a policy document is made explicit by *s 10(2)*, read with *Part 1, Schedule 1* of the *DPA 2018. Paragraph 1(1)* of the *Schedule* authorises processing only if, at the time the processing is carried out, the controller has an "appropriate policy document" in place, as defined in *paragraph 34* of *Part 4, Schedule 1* to the *DPA 2018*.

Issues to consider when drawing up such a recruitment policy include:

(a)   The need for transparency about how personal data will be processed during the recruitment process. This will require job advertisements and application forms to specify how any personal data will be used, to whom it will be sent, how long it will be retained etc (the full checklist is in *GDPR, Article 13*). Employers should also set out their policies on verification of references, and background vetting checks (if any) – see further below.

(b)   Whether any special category or criminal convictions data will be processed as part of the application, and if so, what the justification is for such processing (which should be kept to a minimum).

(c)   Whether any automated processing will be used as part of the recruitment exercise.

(d)   How personal data will be kept secure: how application forms can be sent securely and how applications and other personal data can be stored securely, with access limited to only those employees with a business need to access the information.

(e)   Retention periods for personal data, in particular for the deletion of the personal data of unsuccessful candidates.

(f)   The extent to which the employer will verify the information provided, by taking up references, and carry out vetting of the candidate, by checking other sources of information about the candidate. As vetting is a more intrusive process, it should be kept to a minimum. It should be carried out as late as possible in the process (to minimise the number of candidates to whom it is applied) and should be justified for a reason that is specific both to the vacant role and to the type of information sought through vetting. Considerations of this type would apply, for example, to any decision to vet an employee by inspecting their social media profile, even where that profile is publicly available. For further detail on this issue see the Working Party Opinion, paragraph 5.1 (in relation to the *DPD*).

(g)   Employers may not wish to disclose the results of vetting and verification to candidates and they should think carefully about what, if any, exemptions would be available if they were faced with a subject access request from an unsuccessful candidate, or indeed a request to rectify personal data obtained as a reference that the candidate considered inaccurate.

For further detail in general on data protection during recruitment, see Part 1 of the ICO Code.

9.14   Recruitment agencies

Further data protection questions arise where an employer engages a recruitment agency. Such an agency is likely to be a data controller in its own right, since it contributes to determining the purposes and means of processing personal data (most clearly where it maintains a register of candidates to which it matches vacancies that arise with different employers). Furthermore, in most cases it will be prudent to assume that the employer and recruitment agency jointly determine the purposes and means of processing. In that case, they will be 'joint controllers' for the purposes of *GDPR, Article 26* and subject to the requirements of that Article: notably to have in place an arrangement determining their respective responsibilities for meeting their *GDPR* obligations, in particular to give effect to the data subject's rights. Thus the arrangement will need to specify who will issue privacy notices, who will respond to any SARs, etc. The 'essence of the arrangement' must be available to the data subject (*Art 26(2)*), who can exercise his rights against either controller (regardless of what the arrangements say).

9.15   Employment Agencies

As with recruitment agencies (see above), an employer is likely to be a joint controller with any employment agency it has engaged, in respect of the personal data of the agency worker being processed by either party. The requirements of *GDPR, Article 26* for an agreement between joint controllers would apply.

9.16   DATA PROTECTION AND THE MAINTENANCE OF EMPLOYEE RECORDS

Employers inevitably process significant amounts of employees' personal data, for a variety of legitimate reasons. Given the requirements of the GDPR that employers plan for and demonstrate compliance with the data protection principles and other aspects of the GDPR, employers will need to maintain written policies that set out how they will handle and protect their employees' personal data.

In particular, *GDPR, Article 30* will apply to the employee records kept by employers of all sizes. *Article 30(5)* contains a derogation for undertakings employing fewer than 250 employees, but it is only a partial exemption and it does not apply to processing that is 'not occasional'. In other words, any routine processing by an employer of any size will be caught by *GDPR, Article 30*. This point has been clarified by a position paper issued by the advisory '*Article 29* Working Party' (available at http://ec.europa.eu/newsroom/article 29/document.cfm?action=display&doc_id=51422) which gives the specific example of employee records of a small company as falling with *Article 30*.

The requirements of *Article 30* are highly prescriptive. The record of processing must contain:

(a)   the name and contact details of the controller and, where applicable, the joint controller, the controller's representative and the data protection officer;

(b)   the purposes of the processing;

(c)   a description of the categories of data subjects and of the categories of personal data;

(d)   the categories of recipients to whom the personal data have been or will be disclosed including recipients in third countries or international organisations;

(e)   where applicable, transfers of personal data to a third country or an international organisation (in which case additional safeguards apply);

(f)   where possible, the envisaged time limits for erasure of the different categories of data;

(g) where possible, a general description of the technical and organisational security measures referred to in *Article 32(1)*.

In addition, an employee data protection policy will need to consider how the employer will meet its other obligations as a controller of its employees' personal data, such as the transparency requirements (*Articles 13* and *14*), or the requirements of data minimisation and data protection by design and default (*Article 25*). The application of these requirements will vary according to the nature of the employer's business, but is likely to include:

(a) A mechanism for giving employees transparent information about how their personal data will be processed. This requirement will apply when a new employee joins, or when the scope or manner of processing changes significantly. Employees should also be told about their rights under the *GDPR*;

(b) Policies for ensuring that only the minimum amount of personal data is collected and retained, consistent with achieving the employer's purpose. In particular, special categories of personal data should be kept to a minimum (see further below in relation to health records and equal opportunities data);

(c) Policies for ensuring that employees' access to other employees' personal data is kept to the minimum necessary to discharge their roles. For instance, access privileges to electronic HR files should be strictly limited to HR personnel or others with a legitimate business need to access them. Likewise paper files should be locked and accessible only to those who require access in the course of their work. Where software permits maintaining an access audit trail, this functionality should be used and should be checked regularly to prevent unauthorised access;

(d) Grievance, capability and disciplinary policies in particular will need to take account of the fact that these processes involve processing, often of special category personal data, that goes beyond the processing undertaken as part of the everyday employment relationship. Additional employees are likely be granted access to personal data as part of these processes, and particular care must therefore be taken over confidentiality and security of data;

(e) Clear policies on providing references to prospective employers, and on responding to other requests for personal data from third parties. Policies should identify what information will be disclosed in what circumstances, and which employees have authority to disclose it;

(f) Regular training in data protection for employees who have access to significant amounts of employee personal data. Contracts of such employees should include appropriate confidentiality obligations;

(g) A mechanism for ensuring that personal data are kept up to date and accurate;

(h) Policies for ensuring that personal data is adequately protected when it is taken off site, for instance when company laptops or mobile devices are used;

(i) A commitment to review regularly the level of electronic and physical security to ensure that it is up to date and appropriate to the volume and nature of employee personal data that the employer is processing.

Employees have a right to access their own employee records. Subject Access Requests are dealt with in the context of Employment Tribunal litigation at **9.21** below. Many of the principles set out in that section apply equally to routine SARs in the course of employment. Employers should inform employees of their rights to access their personal data and have policies in place to facilitate access.

9.17   PROCESSING SPECIAL CATEGORY PERSONAL DATA DURING THE EMPLOYMENT RELATIONSHIP

Further consideration is required wherever the employer intends to process special category personal data. This section considers some general issues arising from the processing of special category personal data, and goes on to consider two areas where employers are particularly likely to be processing such data (maintaining records of sickness absence and health conditions, and carrying out equal opportunities monitoring: other areas may of course arise, depending upon the nature of the business in question).

Employers should identify areas within an overall data protection policy where additional provision may need to be made for special category personal data: for instance, whether the general level of security applied to personal data is adequate for handling employees' health data, given the particular distress that can be caused by unauthorised access to this type of information.

As to the conditions which must be met if the processing of special category personal data is to be lawful:

(a)   If the employer wishes to rely on the employee's consent for such processing, the consent must be 'explicit' consent to processing 'for one or more specified purposes'. This strongly suggests that separate, and specific consent is required for processing special category personal data. Employers should not rely on generic consent that covers processing of both 'ordinary' and special category personal data. Employees' consent must be freely given and they must be genuinely able to withdraw it, which indicates that consent may not be the most effective condition for an employer.

(b)   If the employer wishes to rely on the condition in *GDPR, Article 9(2)(b)* (employment social security and or social protection), a condition in *DPA 2018, Sch 1, Pt 1* is required, and an "appropriate policy document" as defined in *Schedule 1, Pt 4, para 34* is mandatory. See **9.13** above.

(c)   If the employer wishes to rely on the condition in *GDPR, Article 9(2)(g)* (processing necessary for reasons of substantial public interest), it must identify a condition within *DPA 2018, Sch 1, Pt 2* (by *DPA 2018, s 10(3)*). Unless the text of the particular condition states otherwise, an appropriate policy document is required (paragraph 5(1)).

Other than consent, all of the conditions on which an employer is likely to rely for processing special category data stipulate that the processing must be 'necessary' to achieve the purpose stated. This implies that the processing must go no further than is necessary to achieve the purpose, and must be justified in the light of the degree of privacy intrusion that it involves. Even where an employer relies on consent, the principle of data minimisation (*GDPR, Article 5(1)(c)* and *Article 25*) implies that data should only be processed to the extent necessary.

For the considerations that can arise when processing special category data in the context of a disciplinary investigation, see *Cooper v National Crime Agency* [2019] EWCA Civ 16, [2019] All ER (D) 12 (Feb). Mr Cooper was an employee of the Serious Organised Crime Agency ("SOCA", now the National Crime Agency) who was arrested following a late-evening brawl and accused of assaulting a police officer. His employer relied in part on information disclosed by the police in deciding to dismiss him. He brought proceedings alleging breach of the *DPA 1998*. His claims were dismissed, a decision upheld by the Court of Appeal. As he alleged contravention of a large number of DPA provisions, the decision provides useful guidance on various questions that might arise in this type of situation. Employers should note, however, that the Court's willingness to accept consent as a basis for processing both 'ordinary' and special category data would be unlikely to apply under the new regime.

9.18 Data Protection

9.18 Health and sickness absence

Employers may inadvertently be collecting and/or keeping excessive amounts of data relating to health. The justification for any processing of health data needs to be thought through carefully. Retention periods, and permissions to access health data, should be reviewed and limited to what is strictly necessary. Key areas that employers need to consider under the *GDPR* include:

(a) Sickness absence records: records of sickness absence often contain more information about the employee's medical condition than is actually necessary for the purposes of administering the sickness absence policy.

(b) Information from medical testing: the need for any such testing should be reviewed and the amount of medical information held by the employer should be minimised. For example, if it is necessary to assess employees' fitness for a physically demanding job, can this assessment be carried out by a medical profession who simply confirms the result to the employer, without disclosing all of the underlying medical data?

(c) Occupational health schemes: employers should be careful to minimise the medical information they hold on employees and to ensure the confidentiality of employees' interactions with occupational health professionals;

(d) Drug and alcohol testing: the need for any such testing must be established, and the testing kept to a minimum: for instance, is it required for all staff or just safety-critical employees? The purpose of testing should not be to identify activity in an employee's private life unless this is absolutely necessary given the nature of the role (for example law enforcement).

In relation to all of the areas above, employers will of course need to ensure they provide clear information to employees about how their health data is being processed.

For fuller detail, readers are referred to the helpful practical guidance in Part 4 of the ICO Code.

9.19 Equal opportunities

Information about an employee's ethnic origin, disability, religion or sexual orientation is special category personal data. Employers are likely to need to review their policies relating to the collection and processing of equal opportunity data to ensure compliance with the *GPDR*. In particular, it should be possible to anonymise much of this type of data (such that it is not personal data at all) while still meeting the purposes of equal opportunities monitoring. Where personal data are processed, employers must be transparent with their employees about the manner of processing.

If the employer wishes to rely on *GDPR, Article 9(2)(g)* (substantial public interest), a condition in *Schedule 1, Pt 2* is required. Two such conditions are "equality of opportunity or treatment" (*paragraph 8*) and 'racial and ethnic diversity at senior levels of organisations' (*paragraph 9*), although the provisions of these conditions are complex and may not apply in all situations.

9.20 MONITORING OF EMPLOYEES AT WORK

Employers monitor employees in a host of different ways. This section is concerned not with 'monitoring' in the sense of keeping records of performance or attendance (which is dealt with under 'employee records' at **9.16** but with what might be termed 'surveillance': monitoring of phones, email or the internet to detect excessive private use, which may be routine, through to more specific and more intrusive surveillance that might be carried out where an employee is suspected of wrongdoing.

This type of monitoring involves processing of personal data and may involve processing of special category personal data, or if an employee is suspected of criminal wrongdoing, data falling within *GDPR, Article 10*. In many cases, such monitoring will engage the employee's right to respect for private life under *ECHR, Article 8*.

A data privacy impact assessment ("DPIA") offers a structured way of working through the issues that arise from employee monitoring, and ensuring that special category personal data is only processed to the extent necessary. A DPIA is in any event mandatory by virtue of *Article 35(1)* of the *GDPR* wherever processing operations cause a high risk of harm to data subjects, taking into account the nature, scope, context and purposes of the processing. *GDPR, Article 35(7)* sets out minimum standards for a DPIA.

Guidance on carrying out DPIAs has been given by the *Article 29* Working Party (http ://ec.europa.eu/newsroom/article29/item-detail.cfm?item_id=611236) and, in the context of monitoring at work, at page 81 of the ICO Code.

Guidance relevant to video surveillance by employers has also been given by the European Data Protection Board: see *Guidelines 3/2019* on *processing of personal data through video devices* (adopted on 29 January 2020). At paragraph 37 of the guidance, the Board observes "*an employee in his/her workplace is in most cases not likely expecting to be monitored by his or her employer*", and at paragraph 47: "*Given the imbalance of power between employers and employees, in most cases employers should not rely on consent when processing personal data, as it is unlikely to be freely given*". The guidance considers a range of issues in this context, including (i) the basis for processing; (ii) disclosure of video footage to third parties; (iii) processing of special categories of data; (iv) the rights of the data subject; (v) transparency and information obligations; (vi) storage periods; (vii) technical and organisational measures to ensure e.g. the security of the information; and (viii) DPIAs.

As with other areas of data protection, employers will need to think about how monitoring activity interacts with the key principles of the *GDPR*:

(a)   Justification for the processing and data minimisation: the need for monitoring must be clearly identified; it must justify the intrusion into the employee's privacy; the degree of processing of personal data must be limited strictly to what is necessary to achieve the aim; and alternatives should be considered.

(b)   The condition for processing must be identified, bearing in mind that the conditions are more restricted where the processing is of special category data.

(c)   In particular, if data relating to criminal offences is being processed, employers should remember that processing is lawful only if it meets a condition in *DPA 2018, Sch 1, Pt 1, 2,* or *3* (see *DPA 2018, s 10(5)*). *Paragraph 10* with *part 2* of *Schedule 1* permits processing for the purposes of 'Preventing or detecting unlawful acts', provided that the processing must be carried out without the data subject's consent in order to be effective.

(d)   Transparency: employees should be made aware of what routine monitoring takes place. This will not apply to monitoring that needs to be covert to be effective, but as this type of monitoring is more intrusive, employers should consider whether to warn employees that it may take place.

Detailed guidance on monitoring employees at work can be found in Sections 4 and 5 of the Working Party Opinion (which deals in depth with a range of sophisticated technologies for tracking and monitoring employees), and in Part 3 of the ICO Code.

Monitoring that involves interception of electronic communications continues to be governed by the *Telecommunications (Lawful Business Practice) (Interception of Communications) Regulations 2000 (S.I. 2000/2699)*, made under the *Regulation of*

Investigatory Powers Act 2000, which are not repealed or amended by the *DPA 2018*. The Regulations provide a broad basis for lawful interception of communications over a private telecommunications system for business monitoring purposes. By *regulation 3* of the *Regulations*, conduct is authorised if it involves monitoring or keeping a record of communications in order to (a) establish the existence of facts or (b) ascertain compliance with regulatory or self-regulatory practices or procedures, which are applicable to the system controller in the carrying on of his business or applicable to another person in the carrying on of his business where that person is supervised by the system controller in respect of those practices and procedures. Such conduct is authorised only if the interception is effected solely for the purpose of monitoring or (where appropriate) keeping a record of communications relevant to the system controller's business; the telecommunications system in question is provided for use wholly or partly in connection with that business; and, importantly, the system controller has made all reasonable efforts to inform every person who may use the telecommunication system in question that communications transmitted over it may be intercepted: see *regulation 3(2)*. In other words, employees should be told if the system over which they communicate at work is being monitored. Any monitoring that involves processing of personal data will also have to satisfy the requirements of the *GDPR* and *DPA 2018*.

For issues that arise under *Article 8* of the *European Convention on Human Rights* concerning the monitoring of employees at work, see CHAPTER 31 – Human Rights.

9.21   SUBJECT ACCESS REQUESTS AND THEIR USE IN TRIBUNAL LITIGATION

Under *GDPR, Article 15*, employees (like any other data subject) have a right to gain access to the information about them held by the employer as data controller (the "subject access right"). Frequently, the purpose of such a request will be to use the data concerned in potential or current employment litigation against the employer. This section sets out the principles concerned.

Article 15(1) states that a data subject has the right to obtain confirmation from the data controller as to whether or not personal data concerning him or her are being processed, and where that is the case, has the right of access to the personal data and the information set out in *Article 15(2)*, viz:

(a)   the purposes of the processing;

(b)   the categories of personal data concerned;

(c)   the recipients or categories of recipient to whom the personal data have been or will be disclosed, in particular recipients in third countries or international organisations;

(d)   where possible, the envisaged period for which the personal data will be stored, or if not possible, the criteria used to determine that period;

(e)   the existence of the right to request from the controller rectification or erasure of personal data or restriction of personal data concerning the data subject, or to object to such processing;

(f)   the right to lodge a complaint with the supervisory authority;

(g)   where the personal data are not collected from the data subject, any available information as to their source;

(h)   the existence of any automated decision-making, including profiling, and meaningful information about the logic involved, and the significance and consequences for the data subject.

The data controller must provide a copy of the personal data undergoing processing: *GDPR, Article 15(3)*. Where the data subject makes the request electronically, and unless otherwise requested, the data should be provided in a commonly used electronic form. In contrast to the position under the *DPA 1998*, the controller must provide a copy of the information free of charge (*Article 12(5)*), although a reasonable fee for administrative costs can be charged where (i) a request is manifestly unfounded or excessive, in particular because it is repetitive; or (ii) the data subject wishes for further copies. The data controller can also choose to refuse a manifestly unfounded or excessive request: *Article 12(5)*. It may be expected that the Information Commissioner (and the courts) will apply a restrictive approach to whether a request is "manifestly unfounded or excessive", in line with the EU law position that any limitation of fundamental rights must be interpreted narrowly.

Information on a SAR under *GDPR, Article 15* must be provided to the data subject "without undue delay", and in any event, within one month of receipt of the request. That period may be extended by two further months where necessary, taking into account the complexity and number of requests. The controller must inform the data subject of any such extension within one month of receipt of the request, together with the reasons for delay. Where the data subject makes the request by electronic form means, the information must where possible be provided by electronic means, unless otherwise requested by the data subject. See *GDPR, Article 12(3)*.

If the controller does not take action on the request, the controller must inform the data subject without delay, and at the latest within one month of receipt of the request, of the reasons for not taking action and on the possibility of lodging a complaint with a supervisory authority and seeking a judicial remedy: *GDPR, Article 12(4)*.

The subject access right in *GDPR, Article 15* builds upon the subject access right in *DPA 1998, s 7/DPD, Article 12*, and authorities on the proper approach to the right under the *DPA 1998* will have continuing relevance to the right in the *GDPR*.

In the joined cases *Ittihadieh v 5-11*; *Cheyne Gardens RTM Co Ltd and Deer v University of Oxford* [2018] QB 256, the Court of Appeal has found in the context of the subject access right in *DPA 1998, s 7* that the Act imposed an implied obligation on a data controller to carry out a "reasonable and proportionate" search for personal data in response to a SAR. The principle of proportionality could not justify a blanket refusal to comply with a SAR; but it did limit the scope of the efforts which a data controller had to take in response. Accordingly, a search was not inadequate merely because it had not retrieved every single item of personal data relating to an individual. This principle was applied in the Deer case to explain why Oxford University had not breached the subject access right in relation to Ms Deer (an employee of the University), and is of particular relevance to SARs by employees generally, since an employer will ordinarily hold a very large amount of personal data in relation to any employee, in a variety of different forms and different places. The obligation is not to leave "no stone unturned", but to make a reasonable search in the sort of places where employee personal data could usually be expected to be found (employee personnel records; any places which the employee has flagged up as particularly relevant etc). That principle will continue to govern the subject access right under the *GDPR*, on the basis that proportionality is a general principle of EU law, and is in part reflected in the provision of the *GDPR* permitting an employer to refuse a "manifestly unfounded or excessive" request. However, once information has been retrieved, the data controller does not have similar latitude when determining whether personal data which have been retrieved as a result of a reasonable and proportionate search are subject to one or more of the exemptions from the subject access provisions: see *Rudd v Bridle* [2019] EWHC 893 (QB) per Warby J.

One issue that has arisen in a number of cases under the *DPA 1998* is whether the motive of an employee making a SAR is relevant: and in particular, whether a SAR can be refused where the employee intends to use the fruits of the request in litigation against the employer.

It is now firmly established that the answer is "no": see *Dawson-Damer v Taylor Wessing LLP* [2017] 1 WLR 3255, [2017] All ER (D) 208 (Feb). The Court of Appeal, considering the exercise of the Court's discretion under *DPA 1998, s 7(9)* whether to order compliance with a SAR, held that there was no rule to the effect that an order should be refused if the data subject proposed to use the information obtained for some purpose other than verifying or correcting data held about him. See also *Lin v Commissioner of Police of the Metropolis* [2015] EWHC 2484, [2015] All ER (D) 108 (Aug), and *Roberts v Nottinghamshire Healthcare NHS Trust* [2008] EWHC 1934 (QB), [2009] PTSR 415.

It will often be the case that an employee's personal data is mixed with the personal data of other individuals. The third party's personal data should not be disclosed without that individual's consent, unless it is reasonable to disclose in the circumstances. Specific factors relevant to balancing the rights of the requester against those of the third party are given in *paragraph 16(3)* of *Schedule 2* to the *DPA*. Employers faced with this situation will also draw guidance, and some comfort, from the Court of Appeal's decision in *DB v GMC* [2018] EWCA Civ 1497, [2019] 2 All ER 219, which confirmed that 'data controllers generally have a wide discretion as to which particular factors to treat as relevant to the balancing exercise'. DB was decided under the DPA 1998 but will be relevant under the new regime.

9.22   COMMON LAW PRIVACY CLAIMS AGAINST THE EMPLOYER

The same facts that give rise to breach of data protection legislation may also give rise to a claim by an employee against their employer for the tort of misuse of personal information or breach of confidence (or, in the event that their employer is a public body, for breach of *ECHR, Article 8*). The considerations applying to such claims are in large part outside the scope of this chapter, but some basic relevant principles are addressed below.

The civil wrong of misuse of personal information has only emerged recently as a tort distinct from traditional breach of confidence, following the entry into force of the *Human Rights Act 1998*: see *Campbell v MGN Ltd* [2004] 2 AC 457, [2004] 2 All ER 995 at [14] per Lord Nicholls. The essence of the tort lies in the right to respect for private life established under *ECHR, Article 8*, balanced (where applicable) against the right to freedom of expression under *ECHR, Article 10*. A cause of action for misuse of private information will exist whenever (i) the defendant's use of the claimant's information amounts to an interference with the claimant's right to respect for private life under *ECHR, Article 8(1)*; and (ii) there is no countervailing justification for the interference (i.e. it cannot be justified under *Article 8(2)*, whether because the defendant's own Article 10 rights outweigh the claimant's Article 8 rights, or for any other reason).

Unauthorised disclosure of an employee's information may also, of course, potentially give rise to a claim by the employee for breach of confidence. The ingredients of the tort of "classic" breach of confidence are: (i) the information at issue possesses the quality of confidentiality; (ii) it has been communicated in circumstances imposing an obligation of confidentiality; (iii) there is a use of it (or threatened use of it) which breaches that obligation, to the detriment of the confider; and (iv) there is no public interest defence to such use. In many if not most circumstances where an employee's information has been misused, however, such a claim may add nothing to a claim for the tort of misuse of private information.

An illustration of the sort of circumstances which may give rise to a common law claim for misuse of private information by employees against their employer is provided by *Various Claimants v Morrisons Supermarkets plc* [2018] EMLR 12. There, a disgruntled employee published a file of payroll information containing a significant amount of fellow employees' personal data on a file-sharing website, as an act of revenge. The Supreme Court has now held that the employer was not vicariously liable for the employee's tort, because he was acting on a "frolic of his own": [2020] UKSC 12; however, it has also held that in principle an employer can be vicariously liable both for the tort of misuse of private information, and for data protection wrongs.

Another recent claim for breach of confidence and misuse of private data in the employment context, on unusual facts, is *Axon v Ministry of Defence* [2016] EMLR 20. There, the claimant was the commanding officer of a Royal Navy ship, who had been removed from his command following bullying complaints. Articles concerning the matter appeared in the national press as a result of disclosures from a secret source, who supplied the stories in return for payment. The police informed the claimant of the source's involvement, and the source pleaded guilty to, and was imprisoned for, the offence of misconduct in public office. The claimant then began proceedings against the MoD for misuse of private information and breach of confidence, asserting that the source's disclosure amounted to an unlawful interference with his rights to privacy and confidentiality for which the MoD, as the source's employer, was vicariously liable. The claim failed on the basis that the claimant had no reasonable expectation of privacy in respect of the information concerned (and moreover, any duty of confidence the source owed was owed to the MoD, not the claimant). However, the Court stated that if the disclosures had been unlawful, it would have been just to impose vicarious liability on the MoD. Nicol J stated (*obiter*) that there was always a risk that individuals in the position of the source who were entrusted with confidential information would abuse the trust reposed in them, but that was a reason for imposing vicarious liability, not the reverse.

10   Directors

10.1   INTRODUCTION TO DIRECTORS

Directors of companies are office-holders. They are not necessarily employees. However, directors often enter into service agreements, thereby becoming employees in addition to holding office. The appointment of a director is independent of any contract of employment between a director and a company, although the contract of employment may contain provisions which have application to the office.

The provisions regulating the appointment to, and removal from, the office of a director are set out in the *Companies Act 2006* ('*CA 2006*'). The *Companies (Model Articles) Regulations 2008 (SI 2008/3229)*, as amended, ('*MA Regulations*') set out 'default' articles of association for different kinds of companies. The *MA Regulations* apply to all companies incorporated under *CA 2006* on or after 1 October 2009. A company may adopt for its articles the whole or any part of those default articles. Accordingly, it is necessary to look at the precise terms of a company's articles in order to determine the position in any particular case.

The old 'default' articles in *Table A* of the *Companies (Tables A to F) Regulations 1985 (SI 1985/805)* remain valid for any company incorporated under the Companies Act 1985 in the form they existed at the time of that company's incorporation.

CA 2006 also codifies the rules governing the duties directors owe to their companies.

This chapter concerns the position of directors as employees. It does not set out the numerous responsibilities of directors under company law, nor address the power of the courts to control delinquent directors.

10.2   APPOINTMENT

A director may be employed by the other directors of a company under the authority of one of the articles of association. Such a director is often referred to as an executive director. The relevant provisions of the model articles provide that:

(1)   Directors may undertake any services for the company that the directors decide;

(2)   Directors are entitled to such remuneration as the directors determine:

   (a)   for their services to the company as directors, and

   (b)   for any other service which they undertake for the company.

(For private companies limited by shares: *para 19* of *Sch 1* to the *MA Regulations*; for private companies limited by guarantee: *para 19, Sch 2, MA Regulations*; for public companies, it is *para 23* of *Sch 3*.)

The relevant provision in *Table A* was *art 84*. As explained above, *Table A* remains valid for companies incorporated prior to 1 October 20010. It provides:

'Subject to the provisions of the Act, the directors may appoint one or more of their number to the office of managing director or to any other executive office under the company and may enter into an agreement or arrangement with any director for his employment by the company or for provision by him of any services outside the scope of the ordinary duties of a director. Any such appointment, agreement or arrangement may be made upon such terms as the directors determine and they may remunerate any such director for his services as they think fit. Any appointment of a director to an executive office shall terminate if he ceases to be a director but without prejudice to any claim to damages for breach of the contract of service between the director and the company. A managing director and a director holding any executive office shall not be subject to retirement by rotation.'

As explained above, the model articles of association may or may not be incorporated into the articles of a particular company. Even where they are not incorporated into the articles, executive directors are not usually subject to retirement by rotation. However, where a company is listed, the Governance Code (about which see further **10.15** below) recommends (at para 18) that all directors should be submitted to annual re-election.

Usually, the terms of the director's appointment will be recorded in a letter written under the authority of the board of directors, or in a service agreement which the board has approved. Where a board resolution contains the terms of the appointment, this may be sufficient evidence of the terms of the contract between the director and the company.

Relationship between articles and contracts of employment

10.3   Where the articles do not confer the directors with a power to employ one of their number, or if that power is not properly exercised, the employment contract between the employed director and the company will be void for want of authority. An example of this situation is *Guinness plc v Saunders* [1990] 1 All ER 652, [1990] 2 AC 663. In *Guinness v Saunders*, a committee of the board purported to grant a director special remuneration pursuant to an alleged oral contract. The House of Lords held that this alleged contract was void. This was because the board had no power under the articles to delegate this power to the committee. Since there was no binding contract, their Lordships refused to permit the director to claim payment for actual services which he had performed (on a *quantum meruit* basis). He also could not claim an equitable allowance because it would be inequitable to permit the director to take advantage of his directorship in order to claim remuneration in such circumstances. This was in accordance with the general equitable principle that a director may not profit from the holding of his office. (This principle is often modified by the articles of association.) *Guinness v Saunders* was applied in the case of *Ball v Hughes* [2017] EWHC 3228 (Ch), [2018] BCC 196.

The articles and board resolutions are deemed to be known by each director. Accordingly, a director cannot rely on ostensible authority, implied authority or assume that another director, the committee or the board have powers which they do not have: *Guinness v Saunders*, above, at 658, per Lord Templeman. When considering the position of an employed director, it is necessary to examine carefully the relationship between the articles and terms of any service agreement. In order to avoid any doubt, service agreements should expressly provide for the circumstances in which they can be terminated. They must be drafted having regard to the articles which are then in force. (It should also be noted that the employers of directors are obliged to provide a written statement of the particulars of employment, see further below at **10.6**.)

In *Read v Astoria Garage (Streatham) Ltd* [1952] Ch 637, [1952] All ER 292, a managing director was appointed by a board resolution. This resolution contained no terms as to how the post might be terminated. A resolution of the board, later approved by the company in general meeting, removed the managing director from post. The relevant article provided that the appointment:

'shall be subject to determination *ipso facto* if he ceases for any cause to be a director or if the Company in general meeting resolves that the tenure of office as managing director . . . . be determined.'

In the absence of an express term in the original resolution, the director was taken to have contracted on the terms of the articles. He therefore had no claim for wrongful dismissal since the employment had been terminated in accordance with the articles. By contrast, the director in *Nelson v James Nelson & Sons Ltd* [1914] 2 KB 770, CA was appointed in accordance with an article which enabled the board to make an appointment 'for such period as they think fit, and may revoke such appointment'. The duration of the agreement by which the director was appointed was for an indefinite period. It was held that the board had an unfettered power to appoint for such period as it deemed fit. However, the right to revoke only existed if the contract so provided. Since the contract did not contain a power to revoke, the director was entitled to damages for wrongful dismissal when his appointment was terminated.

The position must be judged by considering the articles as they are at the date of entering into the contract of service with the director. In *Southern Foundries (1926) Ltd v Shirlaw* [1940] AC 701, [1940] 2 All ER 455, the company, subsequent to the appointment of a director, had adopted new articles which were less favourable to an employed director. It was held that the adoption of these new articles could not worsen the contractual position of an employed director. Accordingly, a dismissal taking place under the new articles was wrongful.

Service agreements may also contain implied terms. For example, in *Shindler v Northern Raincoat Co Ltd* [1960] 2 All ER 239, a director sold his shares in the company to a different company under a contract of sale which provided that he would be appointed managing director for a period of ten years. This second company was subsequently resold to a third company. The third company did not wish to retain the director's services. In the director's successful claim for wrongful dismissal, it was held that it had become an implied term of his contract of service that the company would not do anything of its own motion to cause him to be removed as managing director in breach of the contract of sale. Diplock J distinguished *Read v Astoria Garage* (above) on the basis that, in *Shindler* and unlike in *Read*, there was evidence of a contract between the company and the director which was inconsistent with the articles. On the basis of the reasoning in *Southern Foundries v Shirlaw*, the director had been wrongfully dismissed in breach of that contract.

10.4 Employed or not?

Articles, such as the model articles, usually give the directors a very broad discretion as to the terms of appointment of one of their number. In particular, articles often provide a power to employ a director pursuant to a contract of employment or, instead, to enter into an agreement for the provision of services. A director may, in respect of additional services, be engaged as either an employee or as an independent contractor. The question of whether the director is an employee or an independent contractor may be of great importance. Many statutory employment rights, such as the right to claim unfair dismissal, are only conferred on employees.

It should also be noted that whether or not an individual is 'employed' may depend on the purpose for which the question is asked. This is because the definition of an 'employee' is context specific.

This matter is addressed in detail in EMPLOYEE, SELF-EMPLOYED OR WORKER? (16)). However, the questions pertaining to directors are to some degree distinct and merit separate attention.

Where there is no formal agreement, evidence as to the employment status of a director may be gleaned from board resolutions or minutes, correspondence between the parties and the manner in which the individual is paid and taxed. The courts have tended to consider directors who work full-time for a company and are paid a salary to be employees: *Trussed Steel Concrete Co Ltd v Green* [1946] Ch 115. An example is *Folami v Nigerline (UK) Ltd* [1978] ICR 277, where an accountant from a holding company was appointed managing director of the company's subsidiary and it was held that, having been paid by the subsidiary, the managing director was an employee for the purposes of statutory employment rights. A director who was remunerated by way of director's fees and had not been treated as an employee for the purposes of national insurance was held not to be an employee for the purpose of exercising statutory employment rights in *Parsons v Albert J Parsons & Sons Ltd* [1979] IRLR 117.

A person who is a controlling shareholder can also be an employee of that company. In *Secretary of State for Business, Enterprise and Regulatory Reform v Neufeld (Richard)* [2009] EWCA Civ 280, [2009] IRLR 475, [2009] ICR 1183, the Court of Appeal considered the relevant authorities and confirmed that it is a question of fact whether or not such a shareholder/director is an employee. In domestic law, an employee's shareholding and/or degree of control of the company is not ordinarily relevant to the inquiry of whether a contract is one of employment, unless it gives rise to questions of whether the contract was genuine. For applications of *Neufeld*, see *Ashby v Monterry Designs Ltd* (UKEAT/0226/08/CEA) (18 December 2009, unreported), *Secretary of State for Business, Innovation and Skills v Knight* [2014] IRLR 605, and, in the Northern Irish Court of Appeal in *Department of Employment & Learning v Morgan* [2016] IRLR 350.

With regard to directors, the 'control test' is not particularly appropriate for determining whether a director is employed. This is because a director may be largely in control of the day-to-day running of the company or part of it (albeit that the 'control' in such a case is exercisable theoretically by the company: see *Secretary of State for Business, Enterprise and Regulatory Reform v Neufeld*, above). Indeed, a controlling shareholder, such as in *Neufeld*, can even ultimately decide whether or not he is dismissed. The 'organisation test', also known as the 'integration test' may be more appropriate. This test was set out by Denning LJ in *Stevenson (or Stephenson) Jordan and Harrison Ltd v MacDonald and Evans* (1952) 69 RPC 10, [1952] 1 TLR 101, CA as follows:

> 'Under a contract of service, a man is employed as part of the business and his work is done as an integral part of the business; whereas, under a contract for services, his work, although done for the business, is not integrated into it but is an accessory to it'.

Accordingly, a director who provides consultancy or advisory services to the company is likely to be an independent contractor, whereas an executive director who is engaged for the purposes of managing the business (or a part of it), and whose work forms an integral part of the business is likely to be an employee.

In *Crawford v Department for Employment and Learning* [2014] IRLR 626, the Northern Ireland Court of Appeal emphasised the importance of careful analysis of the contractual position. Clear written agreements may assist in clarifying the issues, however, courts are likely to look to the substance of the agreement rather than simply its form. In *Clark v Clark Construction Initiatives* [2008] ICR 635, [2008] IRLR 364, Elias J set out three circumstances in which a court would not give effect to a purported contract of employment: sham, ulterior purpose and where the parties do not conduct themselves in accordance with the contract. See also *Secretary of State for Business, Enterprise and Regulatory Reform v Neufeld*, above.

In *Secretary of State for Business, Innovation & Skills v Knight* [2014] IRLR 605, it was held that the fact that a managing director had decided not to require her salary to be paid did not necessarily mean that she was not an employee. See also *Stack v Ajar-Tec Ltd* [2015] IRLR 474, where the Court of Appeal overturned a finding that there was no employment contract despite the fact that a director had never been paid.

The legal tests are different in European law. In *Holterman Ferho Exploitatie BV v Spies van Bullenheim* C-47/14 [2016] IRLR 140, [2016] ICR 90, the CJEU considered this question in relation to the definition of an employee under European law. It was held that the answer would depend on whether there was the necessary relationship of "subordination". The CJEU applied this principle in *Bosworth v Aracadia Petroleum* [2019] IRLR 668, holding that directors who exerted control over by whom, where, and on what terms they were employed were not subordinate in the relevant sense. They had more than negligible ability to influence the company and thus were not "employees" within the meaning of the Lugano Convention.

10.5 Scope of employment

The scope of a director's employment will be determined by the terms of any service agreement, and any board resolutions which are in force from time to time which grant him or her authority. The powers and duties of a director may be subject to variation by the board. Directors may be appointed to an executive function such as finance director of the company or group. Subject to the terms of the service agreement, the scope of the employment is capable of being completely changed, expanded or narrowed. Even the executive function may be subject to change in some circumstances.

In *Harold Holdsworth & Co (Wakefield) Ltd v Caddies* [1955] 1 All ER 725, it was held that the board could confine the responsibilities of a managing director to the affairs of a subsidiary where the contract provided that he was:

> 'appointed a managing director of the Company and as such managing director he shall perform the duties and exercise the powers in relation to the business of the company and the business.. of its existing subsidiary company . . . .which may from time to time be assigned to or vested in him by the board of directors.'

(The court noted that Mr Caddies had been appointed 'a' rather than 'the' managing director.)

10.6 Written particulars

The employer of a director, like that of other employees (and, since 6 April 2020, other workers), is obliged to provide a written statement of the particulars of the employment. The provisions of *ss 1 to 6* of the *Employment Rights Act 1996* apply (see CONTRACT OF EMPLOYMENT (8)).

10.7 DIRECTORS' SERVICE CONTRACTS

A director's 'service contract' is defined, for the purposes of the relevant parts of *CA 2006*, in *s 227* as a contract under which:

(a)   a director of the company undertakes personally to perform services (as director or otherwise) for the company, or for a subsidiary; or

(b)   services (as director or otherwise) that a director of the company undertakes personally to perform are made available by a third party to the company, or to a subsidiary.

The definition is expressly stated not to be restricted to contracts for the performance of services outside the scope of the ordinary duties of a director.

10.8 Inspection

Under s *228* of *CA 2006*, a company must keep available for inspection a copy of every director's service contract with the company (or a subsidiary), or, if this is not in writing, a written memorandum setting out the terms of the contract. These documents must be

10.8 Directors

kept available for inspection at the company's registered office or at a place specified by regulations. If they are kept at a place other than the registered office, the company must give notice to the registrar of where they are kept: *s 228(4)*. The documents must be retained and kept available for at least one year from the date of termination or expiry of the contract: *s 228(3)*.

The provisions apply to a variation in a director's service contract as well as to the original contract.

Section 228 does not specify the terms which are to be included in any memorandum setting out the terms of a service agreement where this is not in writing. Nevertheless, a memorandum should specify the main terms of the employment pertaining to salary, benefits and duration. It could also contain all the written particulars required by *s 1* of the *Employment Rights Act 1996*.

There is no exception for service contracts with a short expiry date or for those who work wholly or mainly outside the United Kingdom.

All copies and memoranda which are required to be kept must be open to inspection to any member of the company without charge (*CA 2006, s 229(1)*).

If a company fails to comply with any of the above provisions, the company and every officer who is in default is liable to a fine and, for continued contravention to a daily default fine (*CA 2006, s 228(5), (6)*). If inspection of a copy or memorandum is refused, the court may order an immediate inspection or direct that a copy be sent to the person requiring it (*CA 2006, s 229(5)*).

10.9 Contracts with sole members who are also directors

Where, outside the ordinary course of the company's business, a limited company with only one member enters into a contract with that sole member who is a director, then, unless the contract is in writing, the terms must be set out in a written memorandum or recorded in the minutes of the first meeting of the directors following the making of the contract. A failure to comply is an offence punishable by a fine not exceeding level 5 on the standard scale: see *s 231* of *CA 2006*.

10.10 Listing Rule requirements

The Financial Conduct Authority ('FCA') is the United Kingdom's Listing Authority. (Prior to April 2013, the FCA was known as the Financial Services Authority or FSA). The FCA makes rules governing the admission and continuing obligations of listed companies. These are known as the *Listing Rules*. They can be found in the Handbook available on the FCA's website at www.fca.org.uk. These generally include provisions as to directors' service contracts. Companies should check the up-to-date provisions as they change from time to time.

In particular, according to the current version of the rules, a listed company must notify a Regulatory Information Service (RIS) of any change including:

(a)   the appointment of a new director stating the appointee's name and whether the position is executive, non-executive or chairman and the nature of any specific function or responsibility of the position;

(b)   the resignation, removal or retirement of a director (unless the director retires by rotation and is re-appointed at a general meeting of the shareholders);

(c)   important changes to the role, functions or responsibilities of a director; and

(d)   the effective date of the change if it is not with immediate effect (LR 9.6.11).

This notification must take place as soon as possible and in any event by the end of the business day following the decision or receipt of notice about the change by the company.

If the effective date of the change is not known, the notification should state this fact and the company should notify a RIS as soon as the date has been decided. (LR 9.6.12).

A listed company must also notify a RIS of the following information in respect of any new director appointed to the board:

(a)   details of all directorships held by the director in any other publicly quoted company at any time in the previous five years, indicating whether or not he is still a director;

(b)   any unspent convictions in relation to indictable offences;

(c)   details of any receiverships, compulsory liquidations, creditors voluntary liquidations, administrations, company voluntary arrangements or any composition or arrangement with its creditors generally or any class of its creditors of any company where the director was an executive director at the time of, or within the 12 months preceding, such events;

(d)   details of any compulsory liquidations, administrations or partnership voluntary arrangements of any partnerships where the director was a partner at the time of, or within the 12 months preceding, such events;

(e)   details of receiverships of any asset of such person or of a partnership of which the director was a partner at the time of, or within the 12 months preceding, such event; and

(f)   details of any public criticisms of the director by statutory or regulatory authorities (including designated professional bodies) and whether the director has ever been disqualified by a court from acting as a director of a company or from acting in the management or conduct of the affairs of any company (LR 9.6.13).

This notification must be given as soon as possible following the decision to appoint the director and in any event within five business days of the decision.

If there is no such information that is required to be disclosed about a director, then this should be notified to the RIS (LR 9.6.15).

Any changes in such information with respect to a current director should also be disclosed as well as any new directorships held by the director in any other publicly quoted company (LR 9.6.14).

10.11 Takeover Code

During the course of an offer, or even before the date of the offer if the board of an offeree company has reason to believe that a *bona fide* offer might be made imminently, *rule 21* of the *City Code on Takeovers and Mergers* issued and administered by the Panel on Takeovers and Mergers ('Panel') will apply. According to the 12th edition, published on 12 September 2016, where *Rule 21* applies, the board must not enter into contracts other than in the ordinary course of business without the approval of the shareholders of the company in general meeting (or with the consent of the Panel following consultation where the proposed action is in pursuance of a contract entered into earlier or another pre-existing obligation or an earlier decision).

Note 5 of the notes to *Rule 21* indicates that the Panel will regard amending or entering into a service contract with, or creating or varying the terms of employment of, a director as entering into a contract 'otherwise than in the ordinary course of business' for the purpose of *Rule 21* if the new or amended contract or terms constitute an abnormal increase in the director's emoluments or a significant improvement in the terms of service. Accordingly, during an offer period, extending the duration of a service agreement or increasing a director's salary should not be effected without the prior agreement of the Panel.

The notes go on to state that this will not prevent any such increase or improvement which results from a genuine promotion or new appointment. However, the Panel must be consulted in advance in such cases.

10.12 Disclosure

Directors have obligations to disclose their interests in some circumstances. *Section 177(1)* of *CA 2006* provides that 'if a director of a company is in any way, directly or indirectly, interested in a proposed transaction or arrangement with the company, he must declare the nature and extent of that interest to the other directors'. Such a declaration may (but need not be) made at a meeting of directors or by notice in accordance with specified procedures (see *ss 184* and *185* of *CA 2006*). Any declaration must be made before the company enters into the relevant transaction or arrangement: *CA 2006, s 177(4)*. Furthermore, where a director has an interest in an existing transaction or arrangement entered into by the company and has not declared the interest under *s 177*, he must do so (*CA 2006, s 182*). A failure to do so is an offence (*CA 2006, s 183*). The rules as to the nature of the declaration are the same as in *s 177*.

A director need not declare an interest if, or to the extent that, the other directors are already aware of it or ought reasonably to be aware of it (*CA 2006, s 177(6)*). The failure of a director to declare his interest renders a contract voidable at the instance of the company: see *Hely-Hutchinson v Brayhead Ltd* [1968] 1 QB 549, [1967] 3 All ER 98, CA at 589-90, 594. By contrast, where a director has complied with the duty to disclose an interest, the transaction or arrangement is not liable to be set aside by virtue of any common law rule or equitable principle requiring members' approval (*CA 2006, s 180*).

10.13 Duration of director's service agreement

The duration of a service agreement will largely be a matter of contract between the company and the director concerned. This may be subject, however, to any restrictions in the articles of association as well as to *s 188* of *CA 2006*, discussed further below.

10.14 *Section 188*

Pursuant to *s 188* of *CA* 2006, shareholder approval is required for any provision under which the guaranteed term of a director's employment with the company of which he is a director or, where he is the director of a holding company, within that group is, or may be, more than two years.

The provision applies wherever the employment is to continue, or may be continued, otherwise than at the instance of the company, for a period of more than two years during which the employment cannot be terminated by the company by notice, or can be terminated but only in specified circumstances (*CA 2006, s 188(3)*). The section therefore applies to contracts terminable by notice, and to contracts with a minimum duration but which are intended to continue thereafter upon notice, as well as to fixed-term contracts. Specified circumstances would include, for example, the right to terminate for gross misconduct or incapacity. Therefore, any right to terminate on these grounds would not avoid the need for shareholder approval of the term of the contract.

Section 188(3) sets out a situation in which serial contracts are, to some degree, aggregated in determining the duration of the agreement. Where, more than six months before the end of the guaranteed term of a director's employment, the company enters into a further service contract, then *s 188* applies as if the unexpired period of the guaranteed term of the original contract were added to the guaranteed term of the new contract. The aim of this provision appears to be to catch attempts to circumvent *s 188* by using a series of short term contracts.

Where *s 188* requires a term to be approved, it must be approved by a resolution of the members of the company (or, where the director is or is to be employed by the holding company, by a resolution of the holding company) (*CA 2006, s 188(2)*). Before a resolution is passed, a written memorandum setting out the proposed agreement incorporating the term must be made available to members. In the case of a written resolution, this is done by sending or submitting the provision to every eligible member at or before the time at which the proposed resolution is sent or submitted. In the case of a resolution at a meeting, this is done by making the provision available for inspection both at the company's registered office for not less than 15 days ending with the date of the meeting, and at the meeting itself (*CA 2006, s 188(5)*).

If a term is incorporated into an agreement in contravention of *s 188*, it is void, and the contract is deemed to contain a term entitling the company to terminate the employment at any time by giving reasonable notice (*CA 2006, s 189*). This provision incorporates the common law concept of reasonable notice which is discussed in WRONGFUL DISMISSAL (59).

10.15 *Recommendations*

Currently, there are no other statutory restrictions on the duration of a director's service agreement.

However, the UK Corporate Governance Code ('Governance Code', formerly the 'Combined Code on Corporate Governance') recommends that companies should set notice periods at one year or less.

The Governance Code sets out standards of good practice in relation to companies as well as more specific provisions. It is updated at regular intervals. The current edition of the Code was published in July 2018 and applies to financial years beginning on or after 1 January 2019. Listed companies must, in order to comply with the *Listing Rules*, report on how they have applied the Main Principles of the Governance Code, in a manner that would enable shareholders to evaluate how the principles have been applied. They must also either confirm that they have complied with all the provisions of the Governance Code, or, alternatively, state that they have not, setting out which provisions they have has not complied with, the periods within which they did not comply and the reasons for non-compliance (*LR 9.8.6(5)* and *(6)* of the *Listing Rules*). This is often described as 'comply or explain'.

Paragraph 39 of the Governance Code recommends that notice or contract periods should be set at one year or less. If it is necessary to offer longer notice or contract periods to new directors recruited from outside a company, such period should reduce to one year or less after the initial period.

Since a company is only required to 'comply or explain', departures may be made from these provisions in certain circumstances. A departure from the provisions may be justified, for example, where a new recruit is only prepared to contract with the company on terms other than those recommended. If a company decides to set a longer notice or contract period than the recommendation, an explanation for this must be given in the company's disclosure statement.

10.16   DIRECTORS' DUTIES

Whether or not a director is employed by the company, he or she owes it duties. The nature and extent of the duties will depend on the circumstances of an individual case. He or she will owe the general duties owed by all directors to their companies as well as any additional or specific duties imposed by reason of the articles of association or any relevant board resolution. There will also be relevant express and implied duties under the contract of employment or other service agreement.

CA 2006 codified the existing law in this area with effect from October 2008.

Further, executive directors of the largest banks, building societies, other credit institutions and insurers are senior managers for the purposes of the FCA Senior Manager and Certification Regime ("SMCR"). As from 9 December 2019, so too will be the executive directors all "solo regulated FCA firms" (ie those regulated only by the FCA). Under SMCR those executive directors will be subject to five general conduct rules and four specific senior manager conduct rule. They will also have a duty of responsibility under which they are personally accountable if there is a breach of a regulatory requirement in their area of responsibility and they failed to take such steps as a person in their position could reasonably be expected to take to avoid the breach. More details are set out in the FCA Handbook.

10.17   The Companies Act 2006

The background to *CA 2006* was a number of major reports which indicated the need for a statutory codification of directors' duties. This is the first time that the duties owed by directors to their company have been set out in statute. The hope was apparently to make the rules clearer and more accessible.

Sections 170 to *177* of *CA 2006* set out the general duties that are owed by a director to the company. It is expressly stated that these duties are based on certain common law rules and equitable principles and have effect in place of those rules and principles (*CA 2006, s 170(3)*).

There has been some discussion in the case law about whether the codification changed the scope or content of the common law and equitable duties upon which the statutory duties were based. In *Towers v Premier Waste* [2011] EWCA Civ 923, [2012] IRLR 73, Mummery LJ stated of the statutory rules that they 'extract and express the essence of the rules and principles which they have replaced'. See also *Eastford Ltd v Thomas Graham Gillespie* [2011] CSOH 12 in the Inner House of the Scottish Court of Session.

These general duties are to be interpreted and applied in the same way as common law rules or equitable principles and the courts will have regard to the corresponding rules and principles when interpreting and applying the general duties (*CA 2006, s 170(4)*). Where the duties have not been reformulated, the case law will assist in determining how these duties should be applied in individual cases. However, if there is any conflict, the new statutory provisions will clearly take precedence.

The consequences of a breach or threatened breach of *ss 170* to *177* are the same as would apply if the corresponding common law rule or equitable principle applied. They are enforceable in the same way as any other fiduciary duty owed to a company (*CA 2006, s 178*).

In a summary judgment application in of *Antuzis v DJ Houghton Catching Services* [2019] IRLR 629, Mr Justice Lane held that directors could potentially be peronsally liable where they were not acting bona fide and were in breach of *ss 172* and *174* of *CA 2006* (see further below). The case concerned the exploitative employment of chicken catchers.

The precise duties owed by an employed director will depend on the articles of association, memorandum, and relevant board minutes as well as the express and implied terms of the service agreement in addition to *CA 2006*.

The assessment of directors' conduct must be made without the benefit of hindsight: *Re Living Images Limited* [1996] BCC 112 at 116H per Laddie J and *Wessely v White* [2018] EWHC 1499 (Ch), 168 NLJ 7800 at para 43.

These general duties are not extinguished on the entry of the company into administration or creditors' voluntary liquidation (even though the *Insolvency Act 1986* imposes a series of additional duties in those circumstances): *Re System Building Services Group Limited (in liquidation)* [2020] EWHC 54 (Ch).

10.18 Duty to act within powers

A director of a company must act in accordance with the company's constitution, and only exercise powers for the purposes for which they are conferred (*CA 2006, s 171*). This duty replaced similar pre-existing duties.

In *Extrasure Travel Insurances Ltd v Scattergood* [2003] 1 BCLC 598 (applied in *Re HLC Environmental Projects Ltd (in liquidation)* [2013] EWHC 2876 (Ch)), it was held (at [92]) that the court must apply a four stage test:

First, identify the power whose exercise is in question;

Second, identify the proper purpose for which the power was delegated to the directors;

Third, identify the substantial purpose for which the power was in fact exercised; and

Finally, decide whether that purpose was proper.

See also *Madoff Securities International Ltd (in liquidation) v Raven* [2013] EWHC 3147 (Comm); [2014] Lloyd's Rep FC 95 at [196].

The Outer House of the Scottish Court of Session held in *Eastford Ltd v Thomas Graham Gillespie* [2009] CSOH 119 that this provision did not prevent the subsequent ratification of an act performed by a director.

For a recent example of a breach of this duty, see *Ball v Hughes* [2017] EWHC 3228 (Ch).

10.19 Duty to promote the success of the company

A director of a company is required to act in the way he considers, in good faith, would be most likely to promote the success of the company for the benefit of its members as a whole. In doing this, he must have regard to:

(a)   the likely consequences of any decision in the long term,

(b)   the interests of the company's employees,

(c)   the need to foster the company's business relationships with suppliers, customers and others,

(d)   the impact of the company's operations on the community and the environment,

(e)   the desirability of the company maintaining a reputation for high standards of business conduct, and

(f)   the need to act fairly as between members of the company.

(*CA 2006, s 172(1)*)

This duty replaces the common law duty to act in good faith in the company's interests. The duty also overlaps with the duty to avoid conflicts of interest, see below at **10.22**.

'Success' is not defined in *CA 2006*. The DTI guidance notes suggest that it should be taken to mean 'long-term increases in value'.

The duty is subjective in the sense that directors must act in a way which they honestly believe is likely to promote success: see *Regentcrest plc (in liquidation) v Cohen* [2001] 2 BCLC 80 at [120] – but see the qualifications set out in *Re Cosy Seal Insulation Ltd (In Administration)* [2016] EWJC 1255 (Ch); [2016] 2 BCLC 319 and paras 75 – 78 of *Ball v Hughes*, above and HLC at [91]-[92]. In *Wessely v White* [2018] EWHC 1499 (Ch), 168 NLJ 7800 it was held that there was no breach of *sections 171* or *172* where a managing director acted genuinely but mistakenly having taken professional advice. A similar finding was reached in *Re Vining Sparks UK Ltd (In Liquidation)* [2019] EWHC 2885 (Ch), where a director was held not to be liable who had adopted a tax avoidance scheme in good faith on the advice of experts, in the mistaken belief that it was in the best interests of the company.

Section 172 raises but does not answer a number of questions. It is not clear whether the company maintains its own interests separate from the interests of its current members at any time. This may be relevant, for example, to the question of whether a director can recommend the lower of two competing bids if it is considered that this is in the long term interests of the company albeit not in the interests of its existing members.

Another issue may arise if the factors to which the directors must have regard conflict. However, all that is required is that a director 'have regard to' the factors set out in *s 172*. Accordingly, so long as the factors are considered, it will not matter if some of the considerations point in different directions. It would be good practice for board minutes to refer to the factors in *s 172* when documenting the decision making process.

While the interests of a company are normally identified with those of its members, the interests of creditors as a class must be taken into account if the company is in financial difficulties: *GHLM Trading Ltd v Maroo* [2012] EWHC 61 (Ch), [2012] 2 BCLC 369 at [164]. Indeed, *s 172(3)* provides that the duty imposed by *section 172* has effect subject to any enactment or rule of law requiring directors, in certain circumstances, to consider or act in the interests of creditors. A useful summary of the law can be found in *Re HLC Environmental Projects Ltd (in liquidation)* [2013] EWHC 2876 (Ch) at [88], where it was held that the underlying principle is that directors are not free to take action which puts at real (as opposed to remote) risk the creditors' prospects of being paid, without first considering their interests rather than those of the company and its shareholders. This was described as the "clear" approach to be adopted by the court in *Ball v Hughes*, above, para 72. Guidance as to what should be considered in deciding whether creditors' interests should be taken into account is set out at para 73 of *Ball v Hughes*. However, in *BTI v Sequana* [2019] EWCA Civ 112, following an extensive consideration of the authorities, the Court of Appeal held that the duty to consider creditors' interests only arises when directors know or should know that the company is or is likely to become insolvent. (It should be noted that *Sequana* has been appealed to the Supreme Court and judgment is awaited.)

For an employed director, the duty of good faith arises both in his or her capacity as an employee, and as a director by which he or she owes various fiduciary duties to the company. There is a distinction between a director's fiduciary duties and an employee's obligation of fidelity.

10.20 Duty to exercise independent judgment

A company director is required to exercise 'independent judgment'. However, this duty is not infringed by acting in accordance with agreements entered into by the company or as authorised by the company's constitution (*CA 2006, s 173*).

This was to some extent a new duty and there is no exactly equivalent duty at common law (but see *Lonrho Ltd v Shell Petroleum* [1980] 1 WLR 627 at 634F).

The government stated in debate that this duty will not prevent directors from relying on the judgment of others in areas in which they are not expert and/or to delegate matters to committees. The duty is likely, however, to require individual directors to exercise independent judgment in deciding whether or not to accept advice or judgment from others even in such circumstances.

See *CF Booth Ltd, Re* [2017] EWHC 457 (Ch) for an example of a case of breach of this duty where directors had paid themselves excessive remuneration while following a policy of no dividends.

10.21 Duty to exercise reasonable care, skill and diligence

A director of a company must exercise 'reasonable care, skill and diligence' (*CA 2006, s 174(1)*). This is defined to mean the care, skill and diligence that would be exercised by a reasonably diligent person with the general knowledge, skill and experience that may reasonably be expected of a person carrying out the functions carried out by the director in relation to the company, and the general knowledge, skill and experience that the individual director has (*CA 2006, s 174(2)*). These provisions mean that the standard of care and skill required of a director will not be the same for all directors. It will depend not only on the nature of the company but also on the individual circumstances of the director in question (as well as on general, objective criteria: see [207] of *Madoff Securities International Ltd (in liquidation) v Raven* [2013] EWHC 3147 (Comm); [2014] Lloyd's Rep FC 95).

Prior to the coming into force of *CA 2006*, the classic exposition of the general (implied) duties of a director was stated by Romer J in *Re City Equitable Fire Insurance Co Ltd* [1925] Ch 407:

> 'In order therefore to ascertain the duties that a person appointed to the board of an established company undertakes to perform, it is necessary to consider not only the nature of the company's business but also the manner in which the work of the company is in fact distributed between the directors and other officials of the company, provided also that this distribution is a reasonable one in the circumstances and not inconsistent with any express provisions in the articles of association. In discharging the duties of his position thus ascertained, a director must, of course, act honestly; he must also exercise some degree of both skill and diligence. To the question of what is the particular degree of skill and diligence required of him, the authorities do not I think give any clear answers. It has been laid down that so long as a director acts honestly he cannot be made responsible in damages unless guilty of gross or culpable negligence in a business sense'.

Romer J went on to set out the following specific principles:

> '(1)   A director need not exhibit in the performance of his duties a greater degree of skill than may reasonably be expected from a person of his knowledge and experience. A director of a life insurance company, for instance, does not guarantee that he has the skill of an actuary or physician . . .
>
> (2)   A director is not bound to give continuous attention to the affairs of his company. His duties are of an intermittent nature to be performed at periodical board meetings, and at meetings of any committee of the board upon which he happens to be placed . . .
>
> (3)   In respect of all duties that, having regard to the exigencies of the business, and the articles of association, may properly be left to some other official, a director is, in the absence of grounds for suspicion, justified in trusting that official to perform such duties honestly.'

These principles were applied in *Northampton Regional Livestock Centre Co Ltd v Cowling* [2014] EWHC 30 (QB) (a point not considered in the appeal).

In *Madoff Securities International Ltd (in liquidation) v Raven* [2013] EWHC 3147 (Comm), it was held that directors' failure to apply their minds to whether a proposed act was in the interests of the company was a dereliction of the duty (see [265]).

Where a director is also an employee, the legal position is different. This is because an employee impliedly undertakes that he possesses, and will exercise, reasonable skill and competence in the work which he undertakes (*Harmer v Cornelius* (1858) 5 CBNS 236 and *Lister v Romford Ice and Cold Storage Co Ltd* [1957] AC 555, [1957] 1 All ER 125). He owes an implied duty to his employer to take such reasonable care and skill in his work. (For other implied duties of employees see CONTRACT OF EMPLOYMENT (8)). These duties go beyond those set out in *Re City Equitable* and in CA 2006. These higher duties would apply to a director who is also an employee. Any breach of these implied duties may constitute a repudiatory breach of the contract, and therefore justify a company in terminating the employment contract without notice. If the contract is terminated, the director will usually be under a contractual obligation to resign his office with the company.

10.22 Duty to avoid conflicts of interest

Section 175 of *CA 2006* imposes a duty on directors to avoid conflicts of interest. These are situations in which the director has or could have a direct or indirect interest that conflicts, or possibly may conflict with, the interests of the company. The duty is expressed to apply particularly to the exploitation of any property, information or opportunity. It is immaterial whether the company could itself take advantage of any of these (*CA 2006, s 175(2)*). The duty does not apply to a conflict arising in relation to a transaction or arrangement with the company.

There are two exceptions to the duty. First, it is not infringed if the situation cannot reasonably be regarded as likely to give rise to a conflict of interest. Secondly, there is no breach where the matter has been authorised (*s 175(4)* and see *Bristol and West Building Society v Mothew* [1998] Ch 1, [1996] 4 All ER 698 at [18] for the pre-existing law). For a private company, authorisation may be given by the matter being proposed to and authorised by the directors (unless this is invalidated by something in the company's constitution) (*s 175(5)(a)*). For a public company, where the constitution enables directors to authorise the matter, authorisation may be given by the matter being proposed and authorised in accordance with the constitution (*s 175(5)(b)*). (Public companies may wish to ensure that their articles of association allow for this.) Authorisation is only effective if any quorum requirement is met without including the potentially interested director and the matter was agreed without (or not counting) the vote of the interested director (*s 175(6)*). For a case where it was held that there was no liability as the shareholders acquiesced in what would otherwise have constituted a breach, see *Sharma v Sharma* [2013] EWCA Civ 1287, [2014] BCC 73.

A number of authorities have emphasised the strict application of the rules. For example, the case of *Towers v Premier Waste Management* [2011] EWCA Civ 923, [2012] IRLR 73, above, did not engage the new statutory duties. However, Mummery LJ emphasised the strictness of the no-conflict duty in that it does not depend on proof of fault on behalf of the director or of loss on behalf of the company. A director is in breach regardless of whether he acted in good faith or whether the company could not itself have exploited the opportunity. See also *Invideous v Thorogood* [2013] EWHC 3015 (Ch) (appealed on other grounds) and *Allnutt v Nags Head Reading Ltd* [2019] EWHC 2810 (Ch), [2020] BCC 70 where the director of a pub had a conflict of interest when he acquired an interest in another pub, and had failed to meet the disclosure requirements of *s 175*.

The duties of an executive director may be more extensive than the parallel duty of a director who is not employed. For example, in the very old case *London and Mashonaland Exploration Co Ltd v New Mashonaland Exploration Co Ltd* [1891] WN 165, it was held that a director (albeit a dummy director who did not attend board meetings) did not commit any breach of duty by being appointed a director of a competing company. By contrast, if a full time employee works for a competing company part-time without the consent of his full-time employer, this has been held to amount to a serious breach of his contract: see *Hivac Ltd v Park Royal Scientific Instruments Ltd* [1946] Ch 169, [1946] 1 All ER 350. This principle also applies to employed directors. For example, in *Thomas Marshall (Exports) Ltd v Guinle* [1978] IRLR 174, [1978] ICR 905, a managing director traded on his own account on behalf of two other companies which he had set up in competition with the company. His service agreement had expressly provided that, while employed as a managing director, he would not engage in any other business without the company's consent. He was held to be in breach of his obligation of fidelity and good faith as an employee and in breach of his fiduciary duty as a director.

There is no free-standing duty requiring an employed director to disclose his own wrongdoing (albeit that there is a duty to disclose their own interests in some circumstances, see **10.12**, above). However, the fundamental common law duty to act in good faith in the interests of the company may require an employed director to disclose his own wrongdoing in certain circumstances, particularly where the wrongdoing constitutes a breach of fiduciary duties. For example, in *Item Software (UK) Ltd v Fassihi* [2004] EWCA Civ 1244, [2005] ICR 450, [2004] IRLR 928, the Court of Appeal held that an employed director was under a duty to disclose his own misconduct in seeking to divert a contract from the company to another company which he himself owned. In these circumstances, the company could recover damages for loss caused by the breach of duty. (Such a duty may also apply to senior employees, see *Tesco Stores Ltd v Pook* [2003] EWHC 823 (Ch), [2004] IRLR 618 and *Helmet Integrated Systems Ltd v Tunnard* [2006] EWCA Civ 1735, [2007] IRLR 126.) Although *Fassihi* was described as a "controversial" decision in *Brandeaux Advisers (UK) Ltd v Chadwick* [2010] EWHC 3241 (QB), [2011] IRLR 224 at [47], it has been followed, see, for example the Court of Appeal in *Customer Systems plc v Ranson* [2012] EWCA Civ 841, [2012] IRLR 769. See also *GHLM Trading Ltd v Maroo* [2012] EWHC 61 (Ch); [2012] 2 BCLC 369 for a case in which the claimants failed to establish breach. In *Odyssey Entertainment Limited (in liquidation) v Kamp* [2012] EWHC 2316 (Ch), it was held that where a director is seriously considering carrying on a similar business to that of the company, and is recommending closing the business, those intentions must be disclosed.

Directors (and senior employees) may be under a duty not to prepare to compete with their existing employers and, if they do so, to disclose their wrongdoing to their employer. Whether or not such a duty exists and whether or not a director will be found to be in breach of the duty depends very much upon the circumstances of an individual case. For contrasting examples, see *Tunnard* (where the employee was not in breach), *Shepherds Investments Ltd v Walters* [2006] EWHC 836 (Ch), [2007] IRLR 110 (where the director was in breach) and *Crowson Fabrics Ltd v Rider* [2007] EWHC 2942 (Ch), [2008] IRLR 288. In *Attwood Holdings Ltd v Woodward* [2009] EWHC 1083 (Ch), an employed director was held to be in breach of duty by failing to alert a company to an impending threat of competition from him and a colleague, by taking preparatory steps including approaches to customers and by retaining confidential information. At first instance, in *Customer Systems plc v Ranson* [2011] EWHC 3304 (QB), Sir Raymond Jack held that an employee had owed fiduciary duties but had been entitled to discuss plans for his future with third parties, to set up a potential contracting company without advising the company but not to obtain contracting work or transfer his business contacts from his company mobile phone for his own purposes. However, the Court of Appeal ([2012] EWCA Civ 841, [2012] IRLR 769) overturned that decision, on the basis that the employee was not a fiduciary at all.

10.22 Directors

Directors are likely to be under a duty to disclose the wrongdoing of their colleagues, whether subordinate or superior (for an example, see *Walters*, above). This duty applies regardless of whether this would inevitably involve the disclosure of the director's own misconduct (*Sybron Corpn v Rochem Ltd* [1983] 2 All ER 707, [1983] IRLR 253).

In *QBE Management Services (UK) Ltd v Dymoke* [2012] EWHC 80 (QB), [2012] IRLR 458, Haddon-Cave J held that directors/senior employees were under a positive duty to inform the company in a timely manner of any activity, actual or threatened, which might damage the company's interest.

A breach of any duty to disclose may lead to a subsequent agreement for payment to a director being avoided on grounds of mistake. This could include, for example, a termination payment. The Court of Appeal accepted in *Horcal Ltd v Gatland* [1984] IRLR 288 that a director was not under a duty to disclose his own intended wrongdoing. Accordingly, the company was not entitled to recover a termination payment in a situation where the director had not committed any wrongful act at the date of the termination agreement. A company may even be liable to the director for any unpaid salary earned by the director from the time of a breach of duty until termination, even where the breach could have justified summary dismissal had the company been aware of it (*Healey v Francaise Rubastic SA* [1917] 1 KB 946).

In *Re Allied Business and Financial Consultants Ltd: O'Donnell v Shanahan* [2009] EWCA Civ 751, [2009] BCC 822, a case concerning facts prior to the coming into force of the statutory duties, the Court of Appeal held that a director who takes personal advantage of information or an opportunity which comes to him in his capacity as a director will be liable even if the information or opportunity regards a matter outside the scope of the company's business.

In *Foster Bryant Surveying Ltd v Bryant* [2007] EWCA Civ 200, [2007] IRLR 425, the Court of Appeal reviewed the law relating to a director's fiduciary duties during a period of notice after he had resigned but before he had left office. In general terms, the director must act towards his company with honesty, good faith and loyalty, and must avoid any conflict of interest. On the facts of *Bryant*, a director who had resigned in innocent circumstances was not in breach of fiduciary duty when he agreed to be retained by a company's main client after his resignation became effective. For a further recent consideration of the duties of a departing director, see *CJC Media (Scotland) Ltd v Sinclair* [2019] CSOH 8 in the Court of Session (Outer House).

10.23 Duty not to accept benefits from third parties

A company director must not accept a benefit from a third party which is conferred by reason of his being a director or his doing (or refraining from doing) anything as director (*CA 2006, s 176*). A third party is any person other than the company, an associated body corporate or a person acting on one of their behalves. Benefits received by a director from a person by whom his services are provided to the company are not regarded as conferred by a third party (*s 176(3)*). The duty is not infringed if the acceptance of the benefit cannot reasonably be regarded as likely to give rise to a conflict of interest (*s 176(4)*).

10.24 Continuing obligations

A person who ceases to be a director continues to be subject to the duty to avoid conflicts of interest (set out in *s 175*) as regards the exploitation of any property, information or opportunity of which he became aware at a time when he was a director (*s 170(2)(a)*). Such a person will also continue to be subject to the duty not to accept benefits from third parties (set out in *s 176*) as regards things done or not done by him before he ceased to be a director (*s 170(2)(b)*).

In *Thermascan v Norman* [2009] EWHC 3694 (Ch), [2011] BCC 535, the Court of Appeal held that *ss 170* and *175* could not be relied upon to extend the pre-existing law so as to support a blanket prohibition on canvassing or soliciting the business of any client of the company. The Court of Appeal analysed previous authority (*CMS Dolphin Ltd v Simonet* [2001] 2 BCLC 704, *Hunter Kane Ltd v Watkins* [2003] EWHC 722 (Ch), [2003] All ER (D) 144 (Feb) and *Foster Bryant Surveying Ltd v Bryant* [2007] EWCA Civ 200, [2007] IRLR 425) and summarised its effects as follows:

(a)   A director is precluded from taking any property or business advantage, especially where he was a participant in the negotiations, even after his resignation, if the resignation was prompted or influenced by a desire to acquire for himself any maturing business opportunity.

(b)   However, a director is entitled to resign and is then entitled to use his general fund of skill and knowledge acquired while a director. This may even include business contacts and personal connections.

10.25 Indemnity

An employee is entitled to be indemnified by his employer in respect of expenses, costs and claims incurred by him on behalf of his employer during the proper performance of his duties as an employee. An employed director is similarly entitled to such an indemnity. This entitlement may be expressly set out under the articles. For example, under the Model Articles for Private Companies Limited by Shares (*para 20* of *Sch 1* to the *MA Regulations*), the company may pay any reasonable expenses which the directors properly incur in connection with their attendance at meetings of directors or committees of directors, general meetings, or separate meetings of the holders of any class of shares or of debentures of the company, or otherwise in connection with the exercise of their powers and the discharge of their responsibilities in relation to the company. (For private companies limited by shares, see *para 20* of *Sch 2* and for public companies, see *para 24* of *Sch 3*.) In respect of companies incorporated before 1 October 2009, see *art 83* of *Table A*.

However, there is a statutory limit on the scope of indemnities that may be afforded to a director (whether or not he is employed). Any provision that purports to exempt a director from any liability in connection with any negligence, default, breach of duty or breach of trust in relation to the company is void unless at least one of the following three exceptions applies. The first exception is that a company may purchase and maintain insurance (*CA 2006, s 232 (2)(a), s 233*). The second exception is a 'qualifying third party indemnity provision'. A 'qualifying third party indemnity provision' is provision for indemnity against liability incurred by the director to a person other than the company (or an associated company) where the following two conditions are satisfied:

(1)   The indemnity is not against any liability to pay a fine imposed in criminal proceedings or a sum payable to a regulatory body by way of penalty in respect of non-compliance with any requirement of a regulatory nature.

(2)   The indemnity is not against any liability incurred by the director in defending any criminal proceedings in which he is convicted (and the conviction has become final) or in defending any civil proceedings brought by the company or an associated company in which judgment is given against him, or in connection with any application under any specified provisions in which the court refuses to grant him relief. These provisions are *s 661(3)* or *(4)* (acquisition of shares by innocent nominee) or *s 1157* of *CA 2006* (general power to grant relief in case of honest and reasonable conduct). (With regard to *s 1157* see further **10.26** below.)

(*CA 2006, s 234*)

The third exception is a 'qualifying pension scheme indemnity provision'. A 'qualifying pension scheme indemnity' is a provision indemnifying a director who is a trustee of an occupational pension scheme against liability incurred in connection with the company's activities as trustee of the scheme which meets the following conditions:

(1)   The indemnity is not against any liability of the director to pay a fine imposed in criminal proceedings or a sum payable to a regulatory body by way of penalty in respect of non-compliance with any requirement of a regulatory nature.

(2)   The provision does not provide any indemnity against any liability incurred by the director in defending criminal proceedings in which he is convicted (and the conviction has become final).

(*CA 2006, s 235*)

Qualifying third party indemnity provision and qualifying pension scheme indemnity provision must be disclosed in the directors' report. The rules governing this disclosure are set out at *s 236* of *CA 2006*. Copies of any qualifying indemnity provision must be kept available for inspection (*CA 2006, s 237*) and must be open to inspection by any member of the company without charge (*CA 2006, s 238*).

10.26 Relief from liability

Section 1157 of *CA 2006* applies where a director is facing proceedings for negligence, default, breach of duty or breach of trust. In such circumstances, if it appears to the court hearing the case that the director has acted honestly and reasonably and, in all the circumstances (including those connected with his appointment) he ought fairly to be excused, that court may relieve him either wholly or partly from his liability on such terms as it thinks fit. Where such a director is tried by a judge with a jury, the judge may withdraw the case in whole or in part from the jury if satisfied that relief should be granted, and direct that judgment be entered for the defendant on such terms as are considered appropriate (*CA 2006, s 1157(3)*).

If a director has reason to believe that any such proceedings will or might be brought against him, he may apply to the court for relief and the court has the same power of relief as set out above (*CA 2006, s 1157(2)*).

See *Towers v Premier Waste* [2011] EWCA Civ 923, [2012] IRLR 73 for a case where the court refused to relieve a director from liability pursuant to *section 1157* and *Northampton Regional Livestock Centre Co Ltd* [2014] EWHC 30 (QB) where a court would have been prepared to grant such relief. The relief may be available even where a director has failed to exercise reasonable care at common law: *Re D'Jan of London* [1994] 1 BCLC 561 per Hoffman LJ at [649]. In *McGivney Construction Ltd v Kaminski* [2015] CSOH 107, the Outer House of the Scottish Court of Session held that a director would require a strong case for relief where he or she had obtained a material personal benefit. The issue of honesty is to be tested subjectively, and the issue of reasonableness is to be tested objectively: *MDA Investment Management Ltd, Re* [2004] EWHC 42 (Ch), [2005] BCC 783 at paras 16–17 per Park J. The application of this provision was considered in the recent case of *Asset Co v Grant Thornton* [2019] EWHC 150 (Comm), [2019] All ER (D) 13 (Feb).

10.27 REMUNERATION

There is nothing in *CA 2006* to restrict or determine the amount of remuneration which may be paid to a director. The model articles set out in the *Schedules* to the *MA Regulations* provide that directors are entitled to such remuneration as the directors determine (a) for their services to the company as directors, and (b) for any other service which they undertake for the company. Subject to the articles, a director's remuneration may take any form and include arrangements in connection with the payment of a pension, allowance or gratuity or any death, sickness or disability benefits. Unless the directors decide otherwise, the remuneration accrues from day to day (see *para 19* of *Sch 1*, *para 19* of *Sch 2* and *para 23* of *Sch 3*, as appropriate).

Article 82 of *Table A*, for companies incorporated before 1 October 2009, provides in relation to non-executive directors that:

> 'The director shall be entitled to such remuneration as the company may by ordinary resolution determine and, unless the resolution provides otherwise, the remuneration shall be deemed to accrue from day to day.'

With regard to executive directors appointed in accordance with the model articles (see **10.2** above), the amount of remuneration is a matter for the board. So long as the board exercises its power in good faith in accordance with the relevant provisions of the model code (or *art 84*, as appropriate), the company will be unable to avoid the terms agreed for remuneration. However, if remuneration is set at an excessive level, this might provide evidence of a failure to exercise the power in good faith.

However, amendments made to *CA 2006* which have been in force since 1 October 2013 mean that a quoted company may not make a remuneration payment to a present, past or future director unless that payment is consistent with the approved directors' remuneration policy or an amendment to that policy authorising the company to make the payment has been approved by resolution of the members of the company (*CA 2006, s 226B*). The 'approved directors' remuneration policy' is the most recent remuneration policy to have been approved by a resolution passed by the members of the company in general meeting (*CA 2006, s 226B*). The same is true of payments for loss of office (*CA 2006, s 226C*).

A resolution approving an amendment for the purposes of *s 226B* or *s 226C* must not be passed unless a memorandum setting out particulars of the proposed payment to which the amendment relates (including its amount) is made available for inspection by the company's members at the registered office for not less than 15 days and at the relevant meeting itself (*CA 2006, s 226D*). It must be made available on the company's website (*CA 2006, s 226D(3)*). The memorandum must explain the ways in which the payment is inconsistent with the approved directors' remuneration policy but for the amendment (*CA 2006, s 226D(2)*).

An "obligation" to make a payment which would be in contravention of these rules has no effect (*CA 2006, s 226E(1)*). Any payment made in contravention of these rules is held by the recipient on trust for whoever is making the payment and, in the case of a company, any director who authorised the payment is jointly and severally liable to indemnify the company that made the payment for any loss resulting from it (*CA 2006, s 226E(2)*). However, a director may be relieved wholly or partly from liability if the director shows that he or she has acted honestly and reasonably and the court considers that, having regard to all the circumstances of the case, the director ought to be relieved of liability (*CA 2006, s 226E(5)*).

There are further detailed provisions in *s 226E* for payments made for loss of office in connection with transfers of undertaking, property or shares.

The excessive payment of remuneration to directors may also be in breach of the directors' other duties pursuant to *ss 170* to *176* of the *Companies Act 2006*. See, for example, *CF Booth Ltd* [2017] EWHC 457 (Ch).

10.28 Directors

10.28 Guidance: the Governance Code

A brief explanation of the operation of the Governance Code is set out at para **10.15** above. With regard to directors' remuneration, the Governance Code recommends that the board of directors establish a remuneration committee with delegated responsibility for setting remuneration levels for all executive directors and the chairman. Paragraph 5 of the Governance Code contains the relevant recommendations.

There are three principles dealing with Remuneration: Principles P, Q and R.

Principle P provides:

"Remuneration policies and practices should be designed to support strategy and promote long-term sustainable success. Executive remuneration should be aligned to company purpose and values, and be clearly linked to the successful delivery of the company's long term strategy."

Principle Q provides:

"A formal and transparent procedure for developing policy on executive remuneration and determining director and senior management remuneration should be established. No director should be involved in deciding their own remuneration outcome."

Principle R provides:

"Directors should exercise independent judgment and discretion when authorising remuneration outcomes, taking account of company and individual performance, and wider circumstances."

The Code then goes on to set out detailed provisions as to how these principles should be pursued. For example:

The Board should establish a remuneration committee of at least three independent non-executive directors (or two for smaller companies) (para 32).

The remuneration committee should have delegated responsibility for determining the policy for executive director remuneration and setting remuneration for the chair, executive directors and senior management. It should review workforce remuneration and related policies and the alignment of incentives and rewards with culture, taking these into account when setting the remuneration policy (para 33).

Remuneration schemes should promote long-term shareholdings by executive directors that support alignment with long-term shareholder interests. Share awards granted for this purpose should be released for sale on a phased basis and be subject to a total vesting and holding period of five years or more. The remuneration committee should develop a formal policy for post-employment shareholding (para 36).

Remuneration schemes and policies should enable the use of discretion to override formulaic outcomes. They should also include provisions that would enable the company to recover and/or withhold sums or share awards and specify when this would be appropriate (para 37).

Only basic salary should be pensionable and pension contributions should be aligned with those of the workforce. Pension consequences should be carefully considered (para 38).

The remuneration committee should ensure compensation commitments in directors' terms of appointment do not reward poor performance. They should be robust in reducing compensation to reflect departing directors' obligations to mitigate loss (para 39).

When determining executive director remuneration policy and practices, the remuneration committee should address clarity, simplicity, risk, predictability, proportionality and alignment to culture (para 40).

There should be a description of the work of the remuneration committee in the annual report, including a number of specific matters (para 41).

10.29 Guidance: the Stewardship Code

The UK Stewardship Code, substantially revised with effect from 1 January 2020, sets out the Financial Reporting Council's ('FRC') principles of effective stewardship by investors. The Stewardship Code consists of 12 principles for asset managers and asset owners, and six principles for service providers. Organisations who wish to be a signatory to the Code are required to produce an annual Stewardship Report explaining how they have applied the Code in the previous twelve months. When applying the principles, signatories are required to consider a number of matters including remuneration and the effective application of the UK Corporate Governance Code. This will include satisfying themselves that the company has complied with the provisions described in paragraph [10.28] above in relation to directors' remuneration.

10.30 The Remuneration Codes

It should also be noted that an executive director of any organisation which is authorised by the Financial Conduct Authority ('FCA') and/or the Prudential Regulation Authority ('PRA') may be subject to the FCA's Remuneration Codes or the remuneration part of the PRA Handbook. As such, provisions of those codes will apply to the assessment, method and timing of payment of that director's variable remuneration.

The details of these are outside the scope of this work.

10.31 Disclosure of directors' remuneration

The law on the disclosure of directors' remuneration changed with effect from 1 October 2013 for quoted companies with the introduction of a requirement to produce a new style remuneration report. (Quoted companies are defined as those registered in the UK with equity listed on the main market. AIM listed companies are not included). The relevant provisions are explained at [10.32] below. Even before that time, there were a number of requirements as to disclosure which apply to all companies and which continue to apply.

Section 412 of *CA 2006* empowered the Secretary of State to make regulations requiring certain information to be given in notes to a company's annual accounts about directors' remuneration.

The relevant regulations are the *Large and Medium-sized Companies and Groups (Accounts and Reports) Regulations 2008* (*SI 2008/410*) ('*2008 Regulations*'). They apply to all companies other than those subject to the small companies regime: see below at [10.33].

Companies are required to provide information about directors' remuneration in notes to the company's accounts (*reg 8* and *Sch 5, 2008 Regulations*). Some of the provisions apply to both quoted and unquoted companies. Quoted companies are exempted from some of these provisions but are instead subject to the regime described at [10.32] below.

Both quoted and unquoted companies must provide information as to:

(a)   the aggregate amount of remuneration paid to or receivable by directors;

(b)   the aggregate of the amount of gains made by directors on the exercise of share options;

(c)   the aggregate of the amount of money paid to or receivable by directors, and the net value of assets (other than money and share options) received or receivable by directors under long term incentive schemes; and

(d)   the aggregate value of any company contributions paid (or treated as paid) to a pension scheme in respect of directors and by reference to which the rate or amount of any money purchase benefits that may become payable will be calculated.

(Sch 5, para 1(1))

They must also provide information as to the number of directors (if any) to whom retirement benefits are accruing under money purchase schemes and under defined benefit schemes.

(Sch 5, para 1(2))

(The rules are slightly different for companies which are unquoted and whose equity share capital is not listed on AIM: see *para 1(3)*.)

Under these provisions, unquoted (but not quoted) companies must provide additional information in notes to the accounts as to details of the highest paid directors' emoluments (where the aggregates in (a), (b) and (c) above total £200,000 or more) (*para 2*). They are also required to provide information as to retirement benefits (*para 3*), compensation for loss of office (*para 4*), and sums paid to third parties in respect of directors' services (*para 5*).

A director, or anyone who has been a director in the last five years, is obliged to give notice to the company of those matters relating to himself that may be necessary for these purposes (*CA 2006, s 412(5)*). Any default is an offence which is punishable by a fine not exceeding level 3 on the standard scale (*CA 2006, s 412(6)*).

(For the application of *s 412*, with modifications, to unregistered companies, see the *Unregistered Companies Regulations 2009, SI 2009/2436*.)

10.32 *Quoted companies*

Quoted companies are required to prepare a directors' remuneration report which must be approved by the board of directors (see *s 420* and *422* of *CA 2006*). *Section 422A* of *CA 2006* permits changes to that report but only with board approval and in the manner specified. *Schedule 8* to the *2008 Regulations* sets out the information that must be contained in the report and requirements as to how it should be set out.

Since 1 October 2013, a new style of directors' remuneration report has been required for quoted companies. This report must contain the information specified in *Parts 2, 3,* and *4* of *Schedule 8* to the *2008 Regulations* as amended by the *Large and Medium-sized Companies and Groups (Accounts and Reports)(Amendment) Regulations 2013 (SI 2013/1981)*. In particular, it must contain:

(a)   a statement by the director who fulfils the role of chair of the remuneration committee (or, if there is no chair, by a director nominated by the directors to make the statement) summarising for the relevant financial year the major decisions on directors' remuneration, any discretion which has been exercised in the award of directors' remuneration, any substantial changes relating to directors' remuneration and the context in which those changes occurred and decisions have been taken (Part 2);

(b)   specified information in a table in the form set out in Part 3 setting out, for each director, the total amount of salary and fees, all taxable benefits, certain money or other assets received as a result of performance measures and targets, all pension related benefits and any other items in the nature of remuneration together with a total figure as well as a comparison with the previous year. (There are precise and detailed provisions setting out the meaning of each of these terms and what must be set out, to which the reader is referred);

(c)   specified information about pensions for those directors who have a prospective entitlement setting out the details of those rights, a description of any additional early retirement benefits and separate details relating to each type of pension benefit (para 13 of Part 3);

(d)   specified details of any scheme interest awarded to each director (para 14);

(e)   specified details of any payments of money or other assets to past directors (para 15);

(f)   specified details of any payments to directors for loss of office (para 16);

(g)   a statement of any requirements or guidelines for each director to own shares and whether these have been met and a table setting out the number of interests in shares of the director and any connected person (para 17);

(h)   a line graph showing shareholder returns on holdings (para 18(1);

(i)   for the director undertaking the role of chief executive officer, a table setting out total remuneration, and other information as set out in para 18(2);

(j)   specified percentage changes from previous years (para 19);

(k)   for companies with over 250 employees, certain pay ratio information comparing the remuneration of the directions (para 19A to 19G inclusive);

(l)   a graph or table showing the expenditure of the company and difference in spend on employee remuneration, shareholder distribution and any other significant distributions deemed to assist in understanding the relative importance of spending on pay in respect of the relevant financial year and the previous financial year (para 20);

(m)   a statement describing how the company intends to implement the approved directors' remuneration policy in the next financial year including, where applicable, performance measures and their relative weightings, performance targets and how awards will be calculated, as well as any significant changes in the way the remuneration policy will be implemented in the next financial year and any deviations from the implementation of the policy in that year (para 21);

(n)   details of any committee which has considered matters relating to directors' remuneration (para 22);

(o)   a statement setting out specified information about voting in respect of the directors' remuneration report and policy (para 23).

The report must also include a separate section setting out the directors' remuneration policy as required by *Part 4* of *Schedule 8*. The remuneration policy sets out how the company proposes to pay directors, including all forms of remuneration, and explains how that proposal supports the company's long-term strategy and performance. The remuneration policy must also include details of the company's proposed approach to payments relating to recruitment and loss of office. There are specific and detailed provisions as to the precise requirements in *Part 4*. Companies must take care to follow those precise requirements which are not set out in full here.

Shareholders have a binding vote on a resolution to approve the Remuneration Policy. Companies are required to put their remuneration policy to a shareholder resolution at the first AGM and thereafter at least every three years. If a company wishes to make changes to the remuneration policy, it has to put a new policy to shareholders for approval at a general meeting.

Once a remuneration policy has been approved, a company is only able to make remuneration and loss of office payments which are permitted within the limits of the policy, unless separately approved by shareholder resolution (see above at **[10.27]**).

Shareholders have an annual advisory vote on a resolution to approve the implementation report. If a company fails to pass this resolution in a year in which the remuneration policy was not put to a shareholder resolution, this will trigger a requirement to put the remuneration policy to shareholders the following year.

10.33 *Special provisions for small companies*

These requirements do not apply for companies which fall under the 'small companies regime' for financial years which commenced after 1 January 2016. A small company is a company in respect of which the following conditions are satisfied:

(a)   The turnover is not more than £10.2 million;

(b)   The balance sheet total is not more than £5.1 million;

(c)   The company has not more than 50 employees.

(*CA 2006, s 382*, as amended)

Detailed rules as to how these are calculated are found in *s 382* of *CA 2006*.

A parent company only qualifies as small if the group headed by it qualifies as a small group (*s 383(1)*). A group only qualifies as small if the following conditions are satisfied:

(a)   The aggregate turnover is not more than £10.2 million net (or £12.2 million gross);

(b)   The balance sheet total is not more than £5.1 million net (or £6.1 million gross);

(c)   The group has not more than 50 employees.

Again, there are detailed rules about how these should be calculated. They are found in *s 383* of *CA 2006*. It should be noted that these will be subject to some relatively minor amendments from 31 December 2020.

Some companies are ineligible to be small companies. These are any company that was at any time within the relevant financial year:

(a)   a public company;

(b)   a company which is an authorised insurance company, a banking company, an e-money issuer, a MiFID investment firm or a UCITS management company;

(c)   a scheme funder of a Master Trust scheme

(d)   a company that carries on insurance market activity; or

(e)   a member of an ineligible group.

(*CA 2006, s 384(1)*, as amended)

Again, some minor amendments are expected from 31 December 2020.

A group is ineligible if any of its members is:

(a) a public company;

(b) a body corporate (other than a company) whose shares are admitted to trading on a regulated market in an EEA State;

(c) a person (other than a small company) who has permission under *Part 4A* of the *Financial Services and Markets Act 2000* to carry on a regulated activity;

(ca) an e-money issuer;

(d) a small company which is an authorised insurance company, a banking company, a MiFID investment firm or a UCITS management company;

(e) a person who carries out insurance market activity; or

(f) a scheme funder of a Master Trust scheme.

(CA 2006, s 384(2), as amended)

10.34 *Listing Rules requirements*

Listed companies must make a disclosure statement stating whether they have complied with the Governance Code and, if not, set out those provisions with which they have not complied, the period of non-compliance and the reasons for it (see further above at **10.15**).

Rule 9.8.6 of the *Listing Rules* requires a company to include with its annual reports and accounts a report to the shareholders of the board containing a statement setting out all the interests of each director of the listed company (including the interests of all 'connected persons', as defined), including all changes in interests that have occurred between the end of the period under review and one month prior to the date of the notice of the annual general meeting; or a statement that there have been no such changes.

10.35 Pensions

Usually, the making of pension arrangements will be regulated by the company's articles of association. The model articles for companies incorporated on or after 1 October 2009 provide that a director's remuneration may take any form and include 'any arrangements in connection with the payment of a pension, allowance or gratuity, or any death, sickness or disability benefits, to or in respect of that director' (*para 19, Sch 1, MA Regulations, para 19 of Sch 2, MA Regulations* or, *para 23, Sch 3, MA Regulations*, depending on the type of company).

The making of pension arrangements for directors was expressly authorised by *Article 87* of *Table A. Article 87* of *Table A*, which applies to companies incorporated before 1 October 2009, provides:

> 'The directors may provide benefits, whether by the payment of gratuities or pensions or by insurance or otherwise, for any director who has held but no longer holds any executive office or employment with the company or with any body corporate which is or has been a subsidiary of the company or a predecessor in business of the company or of any such subsidiary, and for any member of his family (including a spouse and a former spouse) or any person who is or was dependent on him, and may (as well before as after he ceases to hold such office or employment) contribute to any fund and pay premiums for the purchase or provision of any such benefit'.

For unquoted companies, the notes of accounts must show the excess retirement benefits paid to or receivable by directors or past directors (*para 3 of Sch 5* to the *Large and Medium-sized Companies and Groups (Accounts and Reports) Regulations 2008* (*SI 2008/410*) ('*2008 Regulations*')). The notes must disclose the aggregate of:

(a)   the amount of retirement benefits paid to or receivable by directors under pension schemes; and

(b)   the amount of retirement benefits paid to or receivable by past directors under such schemes,

as, in each case, is in excess of the retirement benefits to which they were each entitled on the date the benefits first became payable or 31 March 1997, whichever is the later.

The aggregate need not include excess amounts if:

(i)   the funding of the scheme was such that the amounts were or could have been paid without recourse to additional contributions; and

(ii)   the amounts were paid to or receivable by all pensioner members of the scheme on the same basis.

Companies which are subject to the 'small companies regime' (see **10.32** above) are not obliged to disclose this information.

For quoted companies, detailed provisions as to the disclosure of retirement benefits in respect of the directors' remuneration report are contained in *para 13* of *Sch 8* to the *2008 Regulations*.

Furthermore, paragraph 38 of the Governance Code (see **10.15** above) recommends that:

(i)   only basic salary should be pensionable;

(ii)   pension contribution rates for executive directors should be aligned with those available to the workforce; and

(iii)   pension consequences and associated costs of basic salary increases and any other changes in pensionable remuneration, or contribution rates, particularly for directors close to retirement, should be carefully considered when compared with workforce arrangements.

10.36 TERMINATION OF DIRECTORS' OFFICE

A company may, by ordinary resolution at a meeting, remove a director from office under *section 168* of *CA 2006*. This power applies regardless of any contrary provisions in the articles of association or in any service agreement. However, the section does not deprive a person removed under it of compensation or damages payable to him in respect of the termination of his appointment, or as circumscribing from any other power to remove a director (*CA 2006, s 168(5)*). Such a power may, for example, derive its authority under the articles.

The ordinary resolution may only be proposed if special notice has been given (pursuant to *CA 2006, s 168(2)*). A director has specified rights to protest against a proposal to remove him from office (see *CA 2006, s 169*).

Any service agreement will usually be terminated by the removal of a director from office. However, this is not invariably so. The outcome will depend on the terms of the service agreement. A person cannot, for example, continue as managing director if he or she is not a director. By contrast, there may be situations in which the office of director is wholly separate from the employment relationship. This might be the case where a manager has no right under the employment contract to be appointed or remain as a director. Such a person may continue in employment as a manager despite the termination of the directorship. If the companies intend that the employment should end if the employee ceases to be a director, the service agreement expressly state this. The converse position may also occur where the employment of an executive director may terminate whilst he or she remains in office. Usually, the board is responsible for terminating the executive appointment of a director, by a majority. Again, if it is intended that the executive appointment should be co-terminous with the appointment as a director, the service agreement should so provide. Service agreements often provide that the executive is required to resign from office as a director (and all other offices held by him in the company) in the event that the employment terminates. Service agreements may also contain power of attorney clauses to effect a resignation if a director fails to resign when he is obliged to do so.

In *Richards v I P Solutions Group* [2017] IRLR 133, the EAT held that where, pursuant to a company's articles of association, a director could be dismissed for a 'material breach of a material statutory obligation', this meant a significant breach and not any breach of the duties set out in *CA 2006*.

10.37 Termination payments

It is not lawful for a company to make to a director any payment by way of compensation for loss of office, or as consideration for or in connection with his retirement from office, without particulars of the proposed payment (including the amount) being disclosed to members of the company and the proposal being approved by the company. This restriction is by virtue of s *217* of CA *2006*. It does not, however, prevent any payment made in good faith in discharge of an existing legal obligation, by way of damages for breach of an obligation, by way of settlement or compromise of any claim arising in connection with the termination or by way of pension in respect of past services (*CA 2006, s 220(1)*). Approval is not required where the amount concerned does not exceed £200 (*s 221*).

In *Taupo Totara Timber Co Ltd v Rowe* [1978] AC 537, [1977] 3 All ER 123, a director was given the right, under the terms of his service agreement, to resign his office following a takeover. Further, he would then be entitled to a payment equivalent to five times his annual salary to be paid tax free. Following a takeover, the director sought to enforce this provision by giving notice. The Privy Council held that the payment did not require shareholder approval since it had been contractually agreed by the company. In that case, there was no suggestion that this was a liquidated damages clause which might amount to an unenforceable penalty clause (and see also *Lander v Premier Pict Petroleum Ltd* [1998] BCC 248, 1997 SLT 1361 in the Court of Session (Outer House).

In the Australian case of *Lincoln Mills (Australia) Ltd v Gough* [1964] VR 193, it was held that a provision in Victorian companies legislation which was similar, but not identical, to the UK legislation applied only to payment to a director for loss of office and not in respect of loss of the employment.

In *Murray v Leisureplay plc* [2005] EWCA Civ 963, [2005] IRLR 946, the Court of Appeal considered an argument that a clause in a chief executive director's contract providing for the payment of one year's gross salary in the event of termination was unenforceable as a penalty. The Court of Appeal held that a clause will only be held to be a penalty if the party seeking to avoid it can demonstrate that the sum payable on breach is extravagant or unconscionable.

In respect of unquoted companies, details of compensation paid to directors for loss of office must be shown in notes to the accounts (under *Sch 5* to the *2008 Regulations*). There must be shown the aggregate amount of any compensation to director or past directors including compensation receivable for:

(a)   loss of office as a director of the company; or

(b)   loss, while a director of the company or on or in connection with his ceasing to be a director of it, of any other office in connection with the management of the company's affairs, or any office as director or otherwise in connection with the management of the affairs of any subsidiary undertaking of the company.

References to compensation include benefits otherwise than in cash and in relation to such compensation, references to its amount are to the estimated money value of the benefit. The nature of any such compensation must be disclosed. References to compensation for loss of office include:

(i)   compensation in consideration for, or in connection with, a person's retirement from office;

(ii)   where that retirement is as a result of a breach of the person's contract with the company or with a subsidiary undertaking, payments by way of damages or settlement in respect of the breach.

With regard to quoted companies, the directors' remuneration report must contain details of any 'significant award' made to any person who was not a director at the time but had previously been a director including compensation in respect of loss of office: *paras 15* and *16* of *Sch 8* to the *2008 Regulations*.

If a payment is made in contravention of *s 217*, it is held by the recipient on trust for the company making the payment and any director who authorised the payment is jointly and severally liable to indemnify the company that made the payment for any loss resulting from it.

Furthermore, any payments made to directors for loss of office will need to be consistent with the approved remuneration policy and disclosed in the remuneration report.

10.38 *Recommendations*

Paragraph 38 of the Governance Code recommends that the remuneration committee should be robust in reducing compensation to reflect departing directors' obligations to mitigate loss.

10.39 Company approval for property transfer

Payments to a director by way of compensation for loss of office, or as consideration for or in connection with retirement from office, where made in connection with the transfer of the whole or any part of the undertaking or property of a company, must have shareholder approval (*CA 2006, s 218*). Shareholder approval is not required, however, where payment is made of *bona fide* damages for breach of contract or by way of pension for past services (*s 220*). If approval is required but not obtained, the amount received is deemed to be held by the director in trust for the company (*s 222(2)*). Approval is not required where the amount concerned does not exceed £200 (*s 221*).

10.40 Payments on takeover

Payments to a director by way of compensation for loss of office, or as consideration for or in connection with a transfer of shares in the company resulting from a takeover bid, must also have the approval of the relevant shareholders (*CA 2006, s 219*). Again, there is an exception for *bona fide* damages for breach of contract or by way of pension for past services (*s 220*). If approval is required but not obtained, the amount received is deemed to be held by the director in trust for persons who have sold their shares as a result of the offer made. The director is also required to bear the expenses incurred in distributing that sum (*s 222(3)*).

10.41 TRANSFER OF UNDERTAKING

If an undertaking is sold or otherwise transferred or if there is a 'service provision change' (see Transfer of Undertaking), the employment of all those employed in the undertaking automatically transfers from the transferor company to the transferee under the *Transfer of Undertakings (Protection of Employment) Regulations 2006 (SI 2006/246) ('TUPE')*. For the purposes of *TUPE*, a contract of employment is defined as any agreement between an employee and his or her employer which determines the conditions of employment. An 'employee' is any individual who works for another person whether under a contract of service or apprenticeship or otherwise but does not include anyone who provides services under a contract for services. Accordingly, an employed director will be an employee for the purposes of *TUPE*. Therefore, if the undertaking or part of undertaking in which the director is employed is transferred, the directors' employment contract will transfer to the transferee.

If the director is entitled under the contract of employment to be appointed director of the company which employs him or her, then failure to appoint him as a director of the transferee will amount to a repudiatory breach of contract, entitling the director to resign and claim constructive dismissal. The director will also be required to resign as a director of the transferor company or otherwise be removed from office.

Service agreements often contain provisions dealing with reconstructions. A typical agreement will exclude any claim brought by a director if he or she is offered employment with the successor company on no less favourable terms and conditions. In any event, *TUPE* would be likely to apply in these circumstances to the same effect.

(*TUPE* is addressed in detail in Transfer of Undertakings (53).)

11 Disclosure of Information

11.1 An employer is under a duty to disclose certain information to his employees and their representatives, by virtue of the *Trade Union and Labour Relations (Consolidation) Act 1992* (*'TULR(C)A 1992'*) (see **11.2–11.5** below), the *Transfer of Undertakings (Protection of Employment) Regulations 2006 (SI 2006/246)* replacing the previous *1981 Regulations (SI 1981/1794)* (see **11.6** below) and the *Health and Safety at Work, etc Act 1974* (see **11.7–11.8** below). Information may also have to be disclosed for the purposes of consultation about forthcoming redundancies (see **40.2** REDUNDANCY – II). The trustees of occupational pension schemes are put under certain duties of disclosure by virtue of the *Occupational Pension Schemes (Disclosure of Information) Regulations 1996 (SI 1996/1655)* (see **11.9** below). Duties to afford access to certain records (as well as other obligations) arise from the *Data Protection Act 1988* (see DATA PROTECTION (**9**)), and the *Access to Medical Reports Act 1988* and *Access to Health Records Act 1990*.

Further, the employer is under a duty *not* to disclose certain types of information about his employees to third parties (see **11.14** below).

For the obligations of applicants to disclose information on matters of nationality and the like, see the *Asylum and Immigration Act 1996* and the *Immigration, Asylum and Nationality Act 2006* and see FOREIGN EMPLOYEES (**27**).

For the obligation to disclose information in relation to criminal convictions see EMPLOYEE'S PAST CRIMINAL CONVICTIONS (**18**).

As to disclosures of information made by employees concerning their employer or its business, the law of breach of confidence is relevant. (See RESTRAINT OF TRADE, CONFIDENTIALITY AND EMPLOYEE INTERVENTIONS (**42**).) Specific protection is also afforded in certain circumstances to employees who disclose information to third parties relating to wrongdoing by the *Public Interest Disclosure Act 1998*. This Act is considered in outline at the end of this chapter (see **11.14** below).

11.2 INFORMATION FOR COLLECTIVE BARGAINING

TULR(C)A 1992, Part IV Chapter I imposes an obligation on an employer to disclose information necessary for collective bargaining. He can no longer be in the advantageous position of withholding information about such matters as profits and wages when negotiating. The right to enforce such an obligation is given to trade unions recognised for the particular group of employees in whose interests the information is sought (for recognition, see **51.11** TRADE UNIONS – I). The sanctions for non-disclosure are wide: if the information required for negotiation is not disclosed, the Central Arbitration Committee ('CAC') may order that the terms and conditions under negotiation become part of the individual employee's contract of employment. The CAC may order these terms to take effect as claimed or in a modified form. If the employer refuses to implement these terms the employees affected may bring an action for breach of contract in the county court or High Court.

11.3 Duty to disclose

If, at any stage of collective bargaining, a representative of a trade union which is recognised by the employer requests, either orally or, if required by the employer, in writing, information which is both:

(a)   information without which the trade union representative would be, to a material extent, impeded in carrying on with the employer such collective bargaining; and

(b)   information which it would be in accordance with good industrial relations practice that the employer should disclose for the purposes of collective bargaining,

the employer must (in writing, if requested by the representative) disclose such information, unless it falls within one of the exceptions below (*TULR(C)A 1992, s 181*).

Exceptions. The employer need not disclose the information where:

(i)   it would be against the interests of national security;

(ii)   it is information which he could not disclose without contravening a prohibition imposed by or under an enactment;

(iii) it is information which has been communicated to the employer in confidence or which the employer has otherwise obtained in consequence of the confidence reposed in him by another person;

(iv)   it is information relating specifically to an individual and he has not consented to its being disclosed;

(v)   it is information the disclosure of which would cause substantial injury to the employer's undertaking for reasons other than its effect on collective bargaining; or

(vi)   it is information obtained by the employer for the purpose of bringing, prosecuting or defending any legal proceedings.

(*TULR(C)A 1992, s 182(1)*)

In the performance of his duty under *TULR(C)A 1992, s 181*, an employer will not be required:

(A)   to produce, or allow inspection of, any document (other than a document prepared for the purpose of conveying or confirming the information) or to make a copy of, or extracts from, any document; or

(B)   to compile or assemble any information where the compilation or assembly would involve an amount of work or expenditure out of reasonable proportion to the value of the information in the conduct of collective bargaining.

(*TULR(C)A 1992, s 182(2)*)

A union only has the right to information concerning matters which are relevant to collective bargaining for which it is recognised. Thus, although a union may have the right to represent a certain class of employee, unless it has a right to represent them *for the purpose of collective bargaining* it does not enjoy the statutory right to information (*R v Central Arbitration Committee, ex p BTP Tioxide Ltd* [1982] IRLR 60, [1981] ICR 843).

Furthermore, information which would not assist collective bargaining need not be disclosed. Thus, the High Court refused to order the disclosure of figures obtained by the Ministry of Defence showing detailed tenders submitted by contract labour cleaners (*Civil Service Union v Central Arbitration Committee* [1980] IRLR 274).

11.4   Code of Practice

ACAS issued its Code of Practice No 2, on 'Disclosure of Information to Trade Unions for Collective Bargaining Purposes' in 1977 (as subsequently revised in 1998 and 2003). The Code does not provide a complete list of items which should be disclosed, as these will vary according to the circumstances, but merely provides some examples of information which should be considered for disclosure (see also CODES OF PRACTICE (5)). Some of the categories of negotiations for which information may have to be disclosed are set out below.

(a)   Negotiations over pay and benefits.

(b)   Negotiations on conditions of service.

(c)   Negotiations over manpower.

(d)   Negotiations over performance.

(e)   Financial negotiations.

The extent of the duty, and the exceptions, will be matters for interpretation in individual cases. A common sense view of what information is necessary in all the circumstances will be taken.

11.5   Consequences of failure to comply with a request for information

Initial failure to give information. If an employer fails to comply with a request for information from an independent trade union, the union may present a complaint to the CAC. If conciliation seems a possibility, the CAC will refer the matter to ACAS. If ACAS fails in its attempt at conciliation, or if the complaint is not considered initially suitable for conciliation, the CAC will proceed to hear and determine the complaint. The trade union and employer concerned are entitled to be heard, as is any person whom the CAC considers to have a proper interest in the complaint (*TULR(C)A 1992, s 183(1)–(4)*).

If the CAC finds the complaint wholly or partly well-founded, it will make a declaration specifying the following:

(a)   the nature of the information which it considers should originally have been provided;

(b)   the date (or, if more than one, the earliest date) on which the employer refused or failed to disclose that information or to confirm it in writing; and

(c)   a period (not being less than one week from the date of the declaration) within which the employer must disclose the information or confirm it in writing.

(TULR(C)A 1992, s 183(5))

Continued failure to give information. If the employer persists in failing to disclose the information specified in the CAC's declaration within the specified time limit, the trade union may present a further complaint to the CAC who will hear and determine the further complaint. The trade union and employer concerned are again entitled to be heard, as is any person whom the CAC considers has a proper interest in the complaint. If it finds the complaint well-founded, the CAC will issue a declaration specifying the information in respect of which it so finds (*TULR(C)A 1992, s 184*).

On or after presenting such a further complaint, the trade union may also present a claim relating to the terms and conditions of employment of employees of a description specified in the original claim for information (*TULR(C)A 1992, s 185(1)*). If the CAC finds or has found the further complaint well-founded, it may make an award that there be incorporated into those employees' contracts of employment:

(i)   the terms and conditions specified in the claim; or

(ii)   other terms and conditions which it considers appropriate.

The award may be back-dated to the date on which the CAC declared that the employer refused or failed to disclose (or confirm in writing) the information (see (b) above) (*TULR(C)A 1992, s 185(3)*). It may only be made in respect of a description of employees and shall comprise only terms and conditions relating to matters in respect of which the trade union making the claim is recognised by the employer (*TULR(C)A 1992, s 185(4)*).

11.5 Disclosure of Information

However, if at any time after a trade union has presented a claim under *TULR(C)A 1992, s 185(1)* to the CAC, and before the CAC has made its award, the employer gives the union the required information, the claim is treated as withdrawn (*TULR(C)A 1992, s 185(2)*).

Terms incorporated by an award remain in force until they are superseded or varied:

(a)   by a subsequent award under this procedure;

(b)   by a collective agreement between the employer and the union; or

(c)   by express or implied agreement between the employees and the employer as far as it improves any terms and conditions awarded under this procedure.

(*TULR(C)A 1992, s 185(5)*)

11.6 TRANSFER OF UNDERTAKINGS REGULATIONS

The *Transfer of Undertakings (Protection of Employment) Regulations 2006 (SI 2006/246)* (which apply to relevant transfers of an undertaking or a service provision change taking place after 6 April 2006) impose obligations upon transferors to disclose to transferees 'employee liability information' (*reg 11*). Failure to make such disclosure is actionable in the employment tribunal by the transferee (*reg 12*). Transferor and transferee employers must also consult in relation to employees affected by a relevant transfer and disclose information to recognised trade unions or elected representatives when there is a transfer to which the *Regulations* apply. Both the transferor and transferee vendor must inform representatives of recognised trade unions, or elected representatives, of certain specified matters which arise on the transfer (*regs 13–16*). A failure to do so is actionable in the Employment Tribunal. See *Royal Mail Group Ltd v Communication Workers Union* [2009] IRLR 1046. The scope of the obligation to provide information under *regs 11* and *12* was considered in *Born London Ltd v Spire Production Services Ltd* [2017] IRLR 493 (See further, TRANSFER OF UNDERTAKINGS (53)).

It should be noted that the government consultation on Proposed Changes to the Regulations has, in addition to the proposal to abolish completely the concept of 'service provision change', proposed repealing the specific requirements regarding the notification of employee liability information, but making it clear that the transferor should disclose information to the transferee where it is necessary for the transferee and transferor to perform their duties regarding information and consultation.

11.7 INFORMATION NECESSARY FOR HEALTH AND SAFETY PURPOSES

Employers are obliged by the *Health and Safety at Work, etc Act 1974 ('HSWA 1974')* to provide their employees with information necessary to ensure, so far as is possible, their health and safety at work (*HSWA 1974, s 2(2)(c)*). An employer must prepare and, when appropriate, revise a written statement of his general policy with respect to the health and safety at work of his employees and the organisation and arrangements for the time being in force for carrying out that policy, and bring the statement and any revision of it to the notice of all his employees (*HSWA 1974, s 2(3)*; see also **28.18** HEALTH AND SAFETY AT WORK – I). Failure to provide such written information is an offence which carries a maximum fine of £20,000 on conviction in a magistrates' court, and an unlimited fine on conviction in the Crown Court (*HSWA 1974, s 33(1), (1A), (3); Magistrates' Courts Act 1980, s 32(2)*; and see **1.10** INTRODUCTION).

11.8 Safety representatives, and representatives of employee safety

Under *s 2(6)* of the *HSWA 1974* employers are required to consult with safety representatives from the workforce on health and safety matters. Safety representatives, appointed by a recognised trade union (see also **29.21** HEALTH AND SAFETY AT WORK – II), were given statutory powers to obtain certain information by the *Safety Representatives and Safety Committees Regulations 1977 (SI 1977/500), reg 7.* They are entitled, after giving the employer reasonable notice, to inspect and take copies of any document which the employer is legally obliged to keep, except a document consisting of or relating to any health record of an identifiable individual (*reg 7(1)*). In addition, an employer is obliged to make available to safety representatives any information within his knowledge relating to health, safety or welfare, which is necessary to enable them to fulfil their functions, *except*:

(a)   any information the disclosure of which would be against the interests of national security;

(b)   any information which he could not disclose without contravening a prohibition imposed by or under an enactment;

(c)   any information relating specifically to an individual, unless he has consented to its being disclosed;

(d)   any information the disclosure of which would, for reasons other than its effect on health, safety or welfare at work, cause substantial injury to the employer's undertaking or, where the information was supplied to him by some other person, to the undertaking of that other person; or

(e)   any information obtained by the employer for the purpose of bringing, prosecuting or defending any legal proceedings.

(*Regulation 7(2), (3)*)

Employees who are not covered by trade union-appointed safety representatives are entitled to be consulted by their employer on health and safety matters, by virtue of the *Health and Safety (Consultation with Employees) Regulations 1996 (SI 1996/1513)*. The consultation may be either with the employees directly or with representatives elected by the relevant employees (referred to in the *Regulations* as 'representatives of employee safety'). The employer must provide the necessary information to enable the employees or representatives to participate fully and effectively in the consultation. In the case of representatives, the information must also be sufficient to enable them to carry out their functions under the *Regulations*. Information within the categories – (a) to (e) above need not be provided. (See also **29.22** HEALTH AND SAFETY AT WORK – II.)

11.9   OCCUPATIONAL PENSION SCHEMES

Under the *Occupational Pension Schemes (Disclosure of Information) Regulations 1996 (SI 1996/1655)* the trustees of such schemes must make available to members and prospective members and (in most instances) to their spouses and to beneficiaries and independent recognised trade unions, various categories of information. These include the constitution of the scheme (*reg 3*), basic information about the scheme (*reg 4 and Sch 1*), information about entitlements (*reg 5 and Sch 2*) and audited accounts and annual reports (*reg 6 and Sch 3*). Each of these regulations details the categories of persons and (where applicable) trade unions to whom the information is to be furnished.

11.10   GENDER PAY GAP INFORMATION

Section 78 of the *EqA 2010* provides for regulations to be made requiring employers employing 250 or more employees to publish gender pay gap information. *Section 78* of the *EqA 2010* was brought into force by the *Equality Act 2010 (Commencement No 11) Order 2016 (SI 2016/839)* on 22 August 2016. The relevant regulations requiring the publication of gender pay gap information are the *Equality Act 2010 (Gender Pay Gap Information)*

11.10 Disclosure of Information

Regulations 2017 (SI 2017/172) which came into force on 6 April 2017 and apply to all employers with more than 250 employees. The extended definition of 'employee' under the *EqA 2010* applies in assessing whether the 250 employee threshold is crossed. Employers had up to 12 months to publish the gender pay gaps relating to their organisation. There are six calculations which must be carried out and the results must be published on the employer's website and also on a government website within 12 months from commencement. Employers have the option to provide a narrative account with their calculations. This narrative, if utilised, should, it is intended, explain the reasons for the results and give details about any action being taken to reduce or remove the relevant gender pay gap.

11.11 THE INFORMATION AND CONSULTATION OF EMPLOYEES REGULATIONS 2004 (SI 2004/3426)

On 11 June 2001, the EU Social Policy Council agreed a draft Directive on informing and consulting employees. In March 2002 *Directive 2002/14/EC* ('the *Information and Consultation Directive*') was adopted by the member states. The *Directive* gives employees a right to be informed about the undertaking's economic situation and employment prospects, and be informed and consulted with a view to reaching agreement about decisions likely to lead to substantial changes in work organisation or contractual relations. The *Directive* was implemented in the UK by the *Information and Consultation of Employees Regulations 2004, SI 2004/3426* ('the *Regulations*').

The *Regulations* came into force on 6 April 2005 in relation to undertakings with 150 or more employees and 6 April 2007 for undertakings with 100 or more employees. In the case of undertakings with 50 or more employees, the commencement date was 6 April 2008. The *Regulations* do not apply to undertakings employing fewer than 50 employees. It is particularly important to identify whether there is an undertaking employing the requisite number of employees for the provisions of the *Regulations* to apply. The definition of undertaking in the *Regulations* (taken from the *Directive*) is 'a public or private undertaking carrying out an economic activity whether or not operating for gain'. The issue of whether an employer is an "undertaking" was considered in *Advisory, Conciliation and Arbitration Service (ACAS) v Public and Commercial Services Union (PCS)* [2018] IRLR 1110. ACAS contended that the Regs did not apply on the basis it was not an "undertaking" as it was not carrying out an "economic activity". This argument was rejected by the EAT which concluded that it was sufficient if the relevant legal entity carried out an economic activity as part of its services which was not merely ancillary or de minimis. Part of the ACAS service was an economic activity (although others parts of the service were not) but this was sufficient to bring ACAS within the operation of the *Regulations*. As to calculating the number of employees engaged in the undertaking, this is averaged over a 12 month period. Further, only 'employees' are to be counted and accordingly subcontractors and temporary workers may be excluded from the calculation insofar as they are not 'employees'. The *Regulations* provide two ways in which information and consultation procedures may be established: first, by employee request and second, by the employer deciding to commence negotiations. If there is no existing mechanism for information and consultation in the undertaking then, for an employees' request to initiate the procedure, there must be a written request to the employer (or to the Central Arbitration Committee (CAC)) by not less than 10% of the employees employed in the undertaking. The undertaking is the whole business of the employer and is not to be equated with the body of workers working at a particular establishment or workplace. Accordingly, the 10% threshold properly understood applies to 10% of all of the employer's employees (*Moyer-Lee v Cofely Workplace Ltd* (2015) UKEAT/0058/15, [2015] IRLR 879). In cases where there is a pre-existing agreement, if a 10% request is made the employer must either enter into negotiations or ballot the employees on the issue of the continuance of the existing agreement. If 40% of the workforce (or a majority of those voting in the ballot) vote in favour of the request then the employer must enter into negotiations for a new agreement. The draft *Employment Rights*

(Miscellaneous Amendments) Regulation 2019 propose decreasing the percentage of the workforce necessary for there to be a valid request to negotiate an information and consultation agreement from the existing 10% to 2%.

In the case of pre-existing agreements relating to information and consultation, it must in any event be determined if that agreement satisfies the requirements of the *Regulations* (*reg 8(1)*). To be valid the agreement must be in writing, cover all the employees in the undertaking, have been approved by the employees and set out how the employer is to give information to the employees or their representatives and how their views will be sought on the information provided. The EAT in *Stewart (J) v Moray Council* [2006] ICR 1253, [2006] IRLR 592 for the first time considered the *Regulations* in determining whether pre-existing agreements which had been negotiated with trade unions satisfied the requirements of the *Regulations*. On the facts the trade union representatives had agreed and approved the agreements but the agreements had not been specifically put to non-union employees for approval. The CAC rejected an argument that in these circumstances employee approval had not been obtained. It was held that the approval of the representatives was sufficient to satisfy the requirements of the *Regulations*. On the facts, however, one of the agreements failed the statutory requirement of setting out adequately how the employer would give information to the employees and consult with them. The CAC's decision was upheld by the EAT which went on to give guidance on the issue of union involvement and the issue of coverage under *reg 8(1)(b)*. The EAT also found that the requirement of approval by the employees (*reg 8(1)(c)*) could be met by collective approval by trade unions so long as the *majority* of employees were union members. See also *University of London v Morrissey* [2016] IRLR 487 (UKEAT/0285/15) in which the EAT stressed that, notwithstanding the wide discretion afforded by the *Regulations*, the system chosen must ultimately give fair representation to all of the affected employees and, if it does not, it is open to challenge. In *Amicus v Macmillan Publishers Ltd* [2007] IRLR 378 the CAC upheld a complaint that the employer was in breach of the *Regulations* by failing to hold a ballot rejecting the employer's arguments that it was entitled to rely on pre-existing information and consultation agreements or that there was a negotiated agreement in place. The decision of the CAC entitled the union to apply for a penalty notice.

If there is no valid pre-existing agreement or no agreement at all and there has been an appropriate request and ballot, then the employer must enter into negotiations for an agreement with employees' representatives. Negotiations may last for up to six months (extendable by agreement).

For a negotiated agreement to be valid it must cover all the employees in the undertaking, be in writing and dated and signed by the employer, set out the circumstances in which the employer will inform and consult the employees and provide for the appointment or election of information and consultation representatives or for information and consultation directly with the employees (*reg 16(1)*). To be valid a negotiated agreement must also be approved by the employees by being signed by all or a majority of the negotiating representatives *and* by at least 50% of the employees in the undertaking *or* approved by 50% of the employees who vote in a ballot (*reg 16(2)*).

If the employer and representatives fail to reach a negotiated agreement (or if the employer fails to enter into negotiations following a 10% request) then the *Regulations* impose standard information and consultation procedures by default. In cases of a negotiated agreement, or where the standard procedures are imposed, the *Regulations* provide specific provisions in order to protect confidential information. By *reg 25* it will be a breach of statutory duty for an individual to disclosure confidential information subject to a right of challenge to the confidentiality in issue which will be heard by the CAC. In certain cases where the effect of disclosure would be potentially seriously prejudicial to the undertaking, the employer may be justified in withholding the information from employee representatives (*reg 26*). As to individual rights, the *Regulations* extend the standard rights to time off and protection against dismissal or detriment on the grounds of taking part in the activities of an information and consultation representative to the employees' representatives. The right to time off, however, does not apply to representatives who are exercising their functions pursuant to a pre-existing agreement. The enforcement of the *Regulations* on a collective level rests with the CAC which will be empowered to adjudicate on the issue of what is an 'undertaking', the number of employees employed in an undertaking, the employer's provision of data, validity of balloting and appointment or election of representatives and whether an employer has complied with obligations under a negotiated agreement or standard arrangement (as the case may be). The *Regulations* provide for substantial penalties for employers who default on their obligations: in cases of complaint of failure to comply with the terms of an agreement (which has been upheld by the CAC), there will be a right for employee representatives to apply to the Employment Appeal Tribunal for a penalty notice (of up to £75,000) to be issued against the employer. The time limit for such an application is three months from the date of the CAC's determination.

The consequences of failure to comply with the *Regulations* are likely to be substantial. In *Amicus v Macmillan Publishers Ltd* [2007] IRLR 378 the CAC upheld a complaint that the employer was in breach of the *Regulations* by failing to hold a ballot rejecting the employer's arguments that it was entitled to rely on pre-existing information and consultation agreements or that there was a negotiated agreement in place. The decision of the CAC entitled the union to apply to the EAT for a penalty notice and the EAT, issuing its first penalty notice in *Amicus v Macmillan Publishers Ltd* [2007] IRLR 885 fined the employer £55,000 commenting (Elias P.) that such a sum should 'deter others from adopting [a] . . . cavalier attitude to the obligations' imposed by the *Regulations*. See also *Darnton v Bournemouth University* [2010] ICR 524, [2010] IRLR 294 in which the EAT observed that previous cases on penalty would be likely to be of little assistance on the fixing of a penalty in another case. Following *Darnton*, some guidance on the approach to fixing a penalty in failure to ballot cases (see *regs 7* and *18*) was provided by *Brown v G4 Security (Cheltenham)* (UKEAT/0526/09/RN) [2010] All ER (D) 84 (Aug). When determining the penalty for a failure to ballot for employee representatives, as well as the non-exhaustive factors relevant to penalty set out in *reg 23(3)* (which comprise gravity of failure, period of time over which failure occurs, reasons for failure, number of employees affected and total number of employees employed) it is appropriate to take into account all additional relevant factors which should be weighted depending on the facts of the case. The proportion of employees affected is relevant as is the extent of any corrective measures taken by the employer following the CAC's determination of breach.

Guidance on the operation of the *Regulations* is available from: https ://www.gov.uk/government/publications/information-and-consultation-regulations-2004 (see, further, on the provisions of the *Directive* and *Regulations*: **17.2** EMPLOYEE PARTICIPATION). It should be borne in mind that the guidance is merely an interpretation of the law and not definitive. See *Darnton v Bournemouth University* [2009] IRLR 4 (CAC) in which the CAC concluded that the government guidance on the operation of *reg 14* of the *Regulations* was incorrect. The Employment Appeal Tribunal agreed with the CAC's interpretation, explaining that the guidance 'has no special status' and that, in relation to *reg 14*, the guidance was wrong. See *Darnton v Bournemouth University* [2010] ICR 524, [2010] IRLR 294, EAT. Specifically, in relation to disclosure of information, the Guidance at paragraphs 53–55 provides guidance on the information required to be provided under the *Regulations*. One matter which will often be of substantial concern to employers is disclosure of information which is also considered to be commercially confidential; whether the *Regulations* require the disclosure of such information and, if so, what protections are available to the employer to maintain confidence in the information. The Guidance explains (paragraph 76) that employers may: (1) restrict any information or document they provide to I&C representatives or others, so that it may not be passed on to anyone else (see *regulation 25*). The employer may do this where it is in the legitimate interest of the undertaking. This will include information that is share price sensitive; (2) withhold information or documents altogether that they would otherwise be required to give I&C representatives (see *regulation 26*). They may do this where disclosing it to them would seriously harm the functioning of the undertaking, or be prejudicial to it. In the event of a dispute in relation to confidential information the matter is to be resolved by the CAC. The guidance at paragraph 77 provides further information in relation to confidential information and the imposition of requirements of confidentiality upon the recipients.

11.12 ACCESS TO MEDICAL REPORTS

Medical reports obtained by an employer should obviously not be disclosed to third parties without the employee's consent.

The *Access to Medical Reports Act 1988* ('*AMRA 1988*') gives individuals a right of access to medical reports relating to them which are supplied by medical practitioners for employment purposes (*AMRA 1988, s 1*). An employer may not apply to a medical practitioner for such a report without the employee's consent (*AMRA 1988, s 3(1)*). The ACAS handbook 'Discipline at Work' includes a model letter of enquiry to an employee's doctor. The employee is entitled to see the report *before* it is supplied (*AMRA 1988, s 4*) and to withhold consent to the report being supplied (*AMRA 1988, s 5(1)*). There is also provision for the correction of errors (*AMRA 1988, s 5(2)*). If there is a failure to comply with the *Act*, an application may be made to the court (*AMRA 1988, s 8*).

The statutory definition of 'medical report' refers to a medical practitioner who is or has been responsible for the clinical care of the individual. Therefore, a report obtained from a company doctor after an examination carried out for a particular purpose is unlikely to be subject to the *Act*. Nor does an employer request a medical report within the meaning of the *Act* where he merely seeks confirmation of information already received (*McIntosh v John Brown Engineering Ltd*, IDS Brief No 441, p 3).

The *Access to Health Records Act 1990* came into force on 1 November 1991 and, in general, applies only to information recorded after that date. It applies to "health records" which are defined as information relating to the physical or mental health of an individual who can be identified from that information, or from that and other information in the possession of the holder of the record made by or on behalf of a health professional in connection with the care of that individual (AHRA 1990 s (1(1)). Individuals have a right to apply for access to records relating to them to the health professional who holds those records (AHRA 1990, s 3). There is also a right to apply for inaccurate records to be corrected (*AHRA 1990, s 6*). The right of access is subject to certain exclusions (*AHRA 1990, ss 4, 5*). A 'health professional' as defined by *AHRA 1990, s 2* includes any registered medical practitioner, so that the *Act* may be expected to apply to company doctors. An application may be made to the court if the holder of a health record fails to comply with the *Act* (*AHRA 1990, s 8*).

11.13 CONFIDENTIAL INFORMATION RELATING TO EMPLOYEES

An employer will normally be under a common law duty not to disclose to third parties confidential information which he holds concerning his employees. In *Dalgleish v Lothian and Borders Police Board* [1991] IRLR 422, there was held to be a *prima facie* case that employees' names and addresses were confidential.

However, it may well be that in a competitive tendering situation in which it is expected that there will be a transfer of an undertaking to the successful contractor (see further on this issue TRANSFER OF UNDERTAKINGS **(53)**), there is little option but to disclose details of the workforce to potential tenderers. In such a case, it will be preferable to disclose the information, so far as possible, in such a way as not to identify individual employees.

11.14 DISCLOSURE OF INFORMATION BY EMPLOYEES: THE PUBLIC INTEREST DISCLOSURE ACT 1998 AND PART IVA OF THE EMPLOYMENT RIGHTS ACT 1996

The *Public Interest Disclosure Act 1998 ('PIDA 1998')* received Royal Assent on 2 July 1998 and came into force on 2 July 1999. This somewhat complicated piece of legislation introduced specific rights into the *ERA 1996* for those who disclose information about alleged wrongdoings, including the right not to suffer detriment in employment (*PIDA 1998, s 2*, inserting *ERA 1996, s 47B*) and the right not to be unfairly dismissed for making such disclosures (*PIDA 1998, ss 5, 7*). Such a dismissal will be automatically unfair and there is no qualifying period of employment, nor upper age limit. (See UNFAIR DISMISSAL – I (54).) The provisions of *PIDA 1998* do not apply to employment in the Security Service, the Secret Intelligence Service or the Government Communications Headquarters (*PIDA 1998, s 11*) nor to police officers or persons employed under a contract of employment in the police service (*PIDA 1998, s 13*). Significant amendments to the provisions of *Part IVA* of the *ERA 1996* were introduced with effect from 25 June 2013 by amendments introduced by the *Enterprise and Regulatory Reform Act 2013 ('ERRA 2013')* and are considered below.

11.15 Protected disclosures by workers

In order for the protection afforded by the Act to apply, the disclosure must be made by 'a worker'. Worker is defined generally in *ERA 1996, s 230(3)* and, for the purposes of the protection against detriment for making protected disclosures, the definition of worker is further extended by *ERA 1996, s 43K* (as inserted by *PIDA 1998, s 1* and as variously amended) and includes contractors acting under the control of the employer, persons on training courses and doctors, dentists, opticians and pharmacists providing services under statutory schemes. Provision was made for Regulations to be made protecting applicants for employment in the health service from suffering detriment by reason of having made protected disclosures (*ERA 1996, s 49B* added by the *Small Business, Enterprise and Employment Act 2015, s 149*, as from 26 May 2015). Those *Regulations* are now in force with effect from 23 May 2018 and are the *Employment Rights Act 1996 (NHS Recruitment – Protected Disclosure Regulations 2018 (SI 2018/579)*. In *Clyde & Co LLP and another v Bates van Winkelhof* [2014] IRLR 641 the Supreme Court has held that a member of a Limited Liability Partnership ('LLP') is also a 'worker' for the purposes of *s 230(3)* of the *ERA 1996* and, accordingly, could bring claims relating to protected disclosures in the employment tribunal. Giving the leading Judgment Lady Hale observed 'That conclusion is to my mind entirely consistent with the underlying policy of those provisions, which some might think is particularly applicable to businesses and professions operating within the tightly regulated fields of financial and legal services.' The 'direction of travel' in the case law seems to favour extending protection against detriment and that protection will not be lost by a restrictive interpretation of 'worker' when that protection is consistent with the underlying policy of the legislation. This is further illustrated by *Keppel Seghers UK Ltd v Hinds* [2014] IRLR 754, a decision relating to *s 43K* (namely a worker who is 'introduced or supplied to do that work by a third person') in which the EAT emphasised that it was appropriate to adopt a purposive construction to provide protection rather than deny it where this was possible. Moreover, in *Roberts v Wilsons Solicitors LLP* [2016] IRLR 586 it was held that a member of an LLP could bring a claim for detriment under *ERA 1996, s 47B* where the loss in issue was post-termination financial loss. In *McTigue v University Hospital NHS Foundation Trust* [2016] IRLR 742 the EAT held that an agency worker could bring a claim against an end user client under the extended definition in *s 43K(1)* even though the agency worker was also an employee or worker of the relevant agency. The case provides helpful guidance on the operation of *s 43K*. The same conclusion was recently upheld, applying *McTigue*, by the Court of Appeal in *Day v Lewisham and Greenwich NHS Trust and Another* [2017] IRLR 623 permitting a junior doctor to bring, in principle, a complaint of detriment against a body with whom he had a training contract but who was not his employer. It was made clear in *Day* (and *McTigue*) that the fact that a person is an employee of one entity does not preclude worker status in relation to another entity. The matter was remitted to the employment tribunal to determine if the body with whom the doctor had the training contract 'substantially determined' the terms of the engagement for the purposes of *ERA 1996, s 43K*. As to the limits of the protection afforded in *Sharpe v The Bishop of Worcester* [2015] IRLR 663 the Court of Appeal held that there must be a contract in existence for *ERA 1996, s 43(1)(a)* to apply. In *Gilham v Ministry of Justice* [2020] IRLR 52, SC the claim was brought by a district judge claiming that she was a worker under for the purposes of *ERA 1996, s 230(3)*. The claim failed in the EAT and Court of Appeal on the basis of absence of a necessary contractual relationship. In the Supreme Court it was held that the failure to extend the protection of *Part IVA* of the *ERA 1996* to such officeholders was discrimination on grounds of status in violation of *art 14* of the *ECHR*. Accordingly, it was necessary to interpret the ERA 1996 to extend the protection to judicial office holders. The case is likely to be highly significant to other persons whose relationship lacks a contract and, accordingly, are prima facie outside of the protection as they are not workers within the definition of *ERA 1996, s 230(3)(b)*.

The protection is not without limits however. In *Sharpe v The Bishop of Worcester* [2015] IRLR 663 the Court of Appeal held that there must be a contract in existence for *ERA 1996, s 43(1)(a)* to apply and in *Gilham v Ministry of Justice* [2018] IRLR 315 the Court of Appeal held that a district judge was an officeholder but did not have a contract and, accordingly, was not a worker for the purposes of *ERA 1996, s 230(3)* .

Second, the disclosure must be a 'qualifying disclosure' as defined in *ERA 1996, s 43B* (*PIDA 1998, s 1*). A qualifying disclosure is a disclosure of information which, in the reasonable belief of the disclosing worker, is made in the public interest and tends to shows one or more of the following six categories of wrongdoing:

(a)   that a criminal offence has been committed, is being committed or is likely to be committed;

(b)   that a person has failed, is failing or is likely to fail to comply with any legal obligation to which he is subject;

(c)   that a miscarriage of justice has occurred, is occurring or is likely to occur;

(d)   that the health or safety of any individual has been, is being or is likely to be endangered;

(e)   that the environment has been, is being or is likely to be damaged; or

(f)   that information tending to show any matter falling within any one of the preceding paragraphs has been, is being or is likely to be deliberately concealed.

The requirement that the disclosure is, in the reasonable belief of the worker, in the public interest was added with effect from 25 June 2013 by *s 17* of the *ERRA 2013*. This is a significant amendment which may narrow to some extent the scope of disclosures which qualify for protection.

In *Geduld v Cavendish Munro Professional Risks Management Ltd* [2010] ICR 325, [2010] IRLR 38 the EAT considered what was required for a disclosure of 'information'. At issue was whether the contents of a solicitors' letter was a qualifying disclosure. The EAT there held that there was a distinction between communicating 'information' (which is protected) and making an 'allegation' which does not convey facts (and which is not protected). The distinction was illustrated by an example given in Mrs Justice Slade's judgment in relation to the state of a hospital. It was held that to say 'health and safety requirements are not being complied with' was an unprotected allegation. To say 'the wards of the hospital have not been cleaned for two weeks and sharps were left lying around' is conveying 'information' and was considered to be protected. On the facts the solicitor's letter contained only an allegation and was not a protected disclosure. In *Millbank Financial Services Ltd v Crawford*

11.15   Disclosure of Information

[2014] IRLR 18 the principles outlined in *Geduld* were further considered in the factual context of complaints alleging omissions to act. The EAT held that the disclosure in question was a qualifying one and that conveying facts for the purposes of the whistle-blowing provisions plainly included conveying facts about what had not been done as well as about what had been done. See also *Norbrook Laboratories (GB) Ltd v Shaw* [2014] All ER (D) 139 (Mar) which considered the effect of taking a series of complaints together in the analysis of whether a qualifying disclosure had been made out in the sense understood in *Geduld*. Wholly separate communications cannot, however, be aggregated to make out a protected disclosure (*Barton v Royal Borough of Greenwich* (2015) UKEAT/0041/14, [2015] All ER (D) 161 (May)). In *Kilraine v London Borough of Wandsworth* [2016] IRLR 422 the President of the EAT appeared to depart from the trend to apply strictly the distinction between 'information' and 'allegation' derived from *Geduld*, observing that the tribunals should be careful in applying the principle as the statute does not draw a distinction between information and allegation and the two concepts are often tied together. This approach has now been approved by the Court of Appeal (*Kilraine v London Borough of Wandsworth* [2018] IRLR 846). The concept of "information" can cover statements which might be characterised as "allegations". No rigid dichotomy between the two concepts should be introduced into consideration of *s 43B(1)*. For a statement to be a qualifying disclosure there must be sufficient factual content and specificity to show that one of the listed matters in *s 43B(1)* is engaged. Moreover, the context of the statement is relevant to the enquiry as to whether it is sufficient to be a qualifying disclosure. To return to the example derived from *Geduld* (above), pointing to sharps left lying around accompanied by the words "You are not complying with Health and Safety requirements" would, in the context the statement was made, be sufficient to amount to a qualifying disclosure.

An allegation that a worker had been defamed by others was held to fall within *s 43B(1)* (as an alleged breach of a legal obligation i.e. a tortious act) (*Ibrahim v HCA International* [2020] IRLR 224, CA). Generalised allegations of inappropriate behaviour have, however, been held to fall short of a disclosure of information (*Kilraine v London Borough of Wandsworth* [2016] IRLR 422). See also *Eiger Securities LLP v Korshunova* [2017] IRLR 115 in which the observations in *Kilraine* (at EAT level) on the "intertwining" of information and disclosure were applied and it was emphasised that the context and circumstances of the alleged disclosure must be carefully considered by the tribunal having heard all of the evidence. This is consistent with the approach now articulated by the Court of Appeal in *Kilraine* (above).

Helpful and detailed guidance on the approach to be taken by a tribunal in determining whether protected disclosures had been made is provided by *Blackbay Ventures Ltd v Gahir* [2014] IRLR 416. The tribunal should (i) separately identify each alleged disclosure by reference to date and content, (ii) identify each alleged failure to comply with a legal obligation or health and safety matter (as the case may be), (iii) identify the basis on which it is alleged each disclosure is qualifying and protected and (iv) identify the source of the legal obligation relied upon by reference to statute or regulations (save in obvious cases). Absent this exercise the tribunal will not know the particular disclosure said to have resulted in a particular detriment nor the relevant date of the alleged detriment. The tribunal should then go on to consider whether the claimant had the reasonable belief required under *ERA 1996, s 43B(1)*. The enquiry should then move to whether the disclosure was made in the public interest (for post 25 June 2013 disclosures) or whether made in good faith (for pre 25 June 2013 actions). The tribunal must identify the alleged detriment and the date thereof as part of its findings. A failure by an Employment Tribunal to identify a legal obligation by reference to its source (by referring, for example, to statute or regulations) when it is alleged that a protected disclosure has been made on this ground is an error of law (*Eiger Securities LLP v Korshunova* [2017] IRLR 115 and see also *Arjomand-Sissan v East Sussex Healthcare NHS Trust* UKEAT/0122/17 (17 April 2019 unreported).

In *Chesterton Global Ltd v Numohamed* [2015] IRLR 614 the EAT considered the public interest requirement for the first time. It was made clear that the disclosure need not be in the public interest per se – rather the question was whether the disclosing employee had a reasonable belief the disclosure was in the public interest. The EAT observed that the statutory objective of the addition of the public interest requirement was to reverse the decision in *Perkins v Sodexho* [2002] IRLR 109 and thus to prevent a worker from relying upon a complaint of a breach of his own contract of employment as a protected disclosure where that breach involves no wider public interest implications and held the disclosure in the instant case, which related to profit manipulation by the employer, passed the public interest test even though the motivation for raising the issue was the effect that manipulation had on the disclosing employee's (and some 100 other employees') rates of commission payment. In *Underwood v Wincanton* (2015) UKEAT/0163/15, [2015] All ER (D) 129 (Aug) an alleged disclosure by four employees about unfair allocation of overtime, which had been struck out, was remitted by the EAT for reconsideration to determine if it was capable of passing the hurdle of the public interest. See also *Morgan v Royal Mencap Society* [2016] IRLR 428 illustrating a broad and generous approach to the issue of when the public interest is engaged.

The Court of Appeal considered the public interest requirement on further appeal in *Chesterton Global Ltd v Numohamed* [2017] IRLR 837. The fact that a disclosure which is in the private interest of a worker making it does not become in the public interest merely because it serves the private interests of a number of other workers as well. Accordingly, the test is not one of merely numerical analysis but depends upon the character of the interest served. All the circumstances of the case must be considered including: (i) the numbers whose interests are served by the disclosure (ii) the nature of the interest affected and its importance (iii) whether the matter complained of was deliberate and (iv) the identity of the alleged wrongdoer. On the facts the employment tribunal did not err in concluding that the disclosure in that case satisfied the public interest test. The issue of reasonableness of belief in the public interest was considered post *Chesterton* by the EAT in *Parsons v Airplus International* UKEAT/0111/17 (13 October 2017). In that case it was determined that the worker had made disclosures in issue purely out of self interest and, accordingly, the test of reasonable belief in the public interest was not satisfied. The fact that in relation to the same disclosures a claimant could have had a reasonable belief in the public interest was not relevant to the enquiry – what mattered was whether the disclosing worker in fact had a reasonable belief that the public interest was engaged. In *Ibrahim v HCA International* [2020] IRLR 224, CA the Court of Appeal stressed that the two stage test of (a) did the claimant subjectively believe that the disclosure was made in the public interest and if so (b) was that belief reasonable should be applied separately by the tribunal and the two limbs of the test were not to be combined.

The geographical location of the wrongdoing (ie whether inside or outside the United Kingdom) is irrelevant (*ERA 1996, s 43B(2)* inserted by *PIDA 1998, s 1*). A disclosure is not a qualifying disclosure, however, if a person making the disclosure commits a criminal offence in so doing, or if the disclosure is made in breach of legal professional privilege (*ERA 1996, s 43B(3), (4)* inserted by *PIDA 1998, s 1*). The Court of Appeal has held that the requirements under *s 43B* are (i) that the employee believes that the information disclosed meets the requirements of the section (ii) that the employee's belief is objectively reasonable and (iii) that the disclosure is made in good faith (*Babula v Waltham Forest College* [2007] EWCA Civ 174, [2007] IRLR 346). It is important to note, however, that the "good faith" requirement in relation to any category of protected disclosure has been removed with effect from 25 June 2013 by the provisions of *s 18* of the *ERRA 2013*.

There is no absolute requirement that the legal obligation *in fact* exists, the objective reasonableness of the employee's belief is what is in issue (*Kraus v Penna plc* [2004] IRLR 260 disapproved). In *Korashi v Abertawe Bro Morgannwg University Local Health Board* [2012] IRLR 4, the EAT has given guidance on "reasonable belief". Although the test is objective this has to be considered taking into account the personal circumstances of the discloser. The question is whether it was reasonable for him to believe. Further, where an employee relies upon multiple alleged protected disclosures (as is very common), reasonable belief must be made out in relation to each of the disclosures and a general belief in the broad gist of the content of the disclosures is not enough.

Third, in order to be a 'protected disclosure', a qualifying disclosure must be made only to the category of persons contemplated in the *Act* and not to other persons (*ERA 1996, ss 43C–43H* inserted by *PIDA 1998, s 1*). There are six ways contemplated in which a worker may make a 'protected disclosure', the first four of which are as follows:

(i)   to the worker's employer or (in cases where the information relates to the conduct of another person or to matters for which a person other than the employer has legal responsibility) that other person (*ERA 1996, s 43C*);

(ii)   to a legal adviser in the course of obtaining legal advice (*ERA 1996, s 43D*);

(iii)   to a Minister of the Crown where the worker's employer is (a) an individual appointed under any enactment by a Minister of the Crown or (b) a body whose members are appointed by a Minister of the Crown (*ERA 1996, s 43E*);

(iv)   to a person prescribed by order made by the Secretary of State for the purposes of receiving qualifying disclosure information of relevant categories (*ERA 1996, s 43F*). The details of those persons and the relevant matters in respect of which they are prescribed are set out at length in the *Public Interest Disclosure (Prescribed Persons) Order 1999 (SI 1999/1549)* (as amended). Further, from 6 April 2010 the Employment Tribunal Service was empowered by the *Employment Tribunals (Constitution and Rules of Procedure) (Amendment) Regulations 2010 (SI 2010/131)* to provide a copy of the whole or part of any ET1 in which it is alleged a protected disclosure has been made to the relevant regulator. The consent of the claimant is required and the online form ET1 has been amended to provide for the claimant to indicate consent to disclosure. By the *Prescribed Persons (Reports on disclosures of Infromation) Regultions 2017 (SI 2017/507)* a prescribed person must publish a report on the workers' disclosures it has received in the relevant reporting year summarising the number of disclosures, the number of disclosures in relation to which it was decided to take further action, a summary of that action and how the disclosures have helped the organisation in the performance of its functions. This new obligation came into force on 1 April 2017.

The fifth category of protected disclosure will permit disclosures to be made to persons other than those contemplated in categories (i) to (iv) above but only if the worker reasonably believes the information to be substantially true, does not make the disclosure for the purposes of personal gain, one of a number of stringent conditions is satisfied, and in all the circumstances it is reasonable to make the disclosure (*ERA 1996, s 43G*). This category is "a last resort" and the test of the reasonableness of the disclosure in the circumstances is particularly important when this category of disclosure is being considered (*Jesudason v Alder Hay Children's NHS Foundation Trust* [2020] IRLR 374). It had previously been held that a disclosure is not made in good faith if an ulterior motive is the predominant purpose for making the disclosure even if the worker making the disclosure reasonably believed it was true (*Street v Derbyshire Unemployed Workers' Centre* [2004] IRLR 687). The burden of proving bad faith in relation to an employee's disclosure rests on the employer (*Bachnak v Emerging Markets Partnership (Europe) Ltd* (2006) UKEAT/0288/05, [2006] All ER (D) 211 (Jan). The fact that a protected disclosure is made during the course of disciplinary proceedings does not of itself indicate ulterior motive and absence of good faith (*Soh v Imperial College of Science Technology and Medicine* (2015) UKEAT/0350/14, [2015] All ER (D) 202 (Dec)).

As set out above, the absence of good faith does not prevent a qualifying disclosure being a protected disclosure. The issue of whether the protected disclosure was made in good faith remains relevant, however, at the stage of remedy. In assessing compensation for detriment the tribunal may reduce any award by up to 25% if it was not made in good faith and the tribunal considers it just and equitable to do so (*ERA 1996, s 49(6A)* as added by the *ERRA 2013, s 18(4)* from 25 June 2013). Thus the issue of good faith and the decided cases in relation to the concept will remain relevant in such cases where absence of good faith is in issue.

The conditions contemplated by this section are:

(A)   that the worker reasonably believes, at the time of making the disclosure, that he will be subjected to a detriment by the employer if the disclosure is made to the employer or a prescribed person (*ERA 1996, s 43G(2)(a)*); or

(B)   that, in cases where there is no prescribed person in relation to the relevant qualifying disclosure, the worker reasonably believes that evidence relating to the wrongdoing will be concealed or destroyed if a disclosure is made to the employer (*ERA 1996, s 43G(2)(b)*); or

(C)   that the worker has previously made a disclosure of substantially the same information to the employer or to a prescribed person (*ERA 1996, s 43G(2)(c)*).

Finally, in determining whether it was reasonable for the worker to make the disclosure under *ERA 1996, s 43G*, regard must be had to the identity of the person to whom the disclosure is made, the seriousness of the relevant failure, whether the relevant failure is continuing or likely to occur in the future, whether the disclosure is made in breach of a duty of confidence owed by the employer to another person, the action which the employer or person to whom a previous disclosure was made might reasonably have been expected to take as a result of the previous disclosure, and whether the worker complied with any procedure whose use by him was authorised by the employer (*ERA 1996, s 43G(3)–(4)*).

The final category of protected disclosure relates to disclosure of 'exceptionally serious failures' (*ERA 1996, s 43H*). In this situation the worker must make the disclosure, believing the information to be substantially true, not for personal gain in circumstances when the relevant failure is of an exceptionally serious nature and where in all the circumstances it was reasonable to make the disclosure. For an example of a disclosure to the local press being a protected disclosure see *Collins v National Trust* (2507255/05) (17 January 2006, unreported), EAT.

In determining reasonableness of the disclosure, particular regard shall be had to the identity of the person to whom the disclosure is made.

By *ERA 1996, s 43J* (inserted by *PIDA 1998, s 1*) a provision in an agreement (including a contract of employment) which purports to preclude a worker from making protected disclosures is rendered void.

In cases where an employee/worker has made a protected disclosure as defined in the *Act* and is subjected to a detriment or dismissal as a result by the employer, the remedy will be by way of complaint to an employment tribunal (*ERA 1996, ss 47B, 103A* inserted by *PIDA 1998, ss 2, 5*). It has been held by the EAT that an employee/worker could pursue a detriment claim under *s 47B* against his employer where the protected disclosure relied upon was made whilst employed by a previous employer (*BP Plc v Elstone and Petrotechnics Ltd* [2010] IRLR 558, EAT).

Consideration of the meaning of subjection to a detriment has been given by the EAT in *Abertawe Bro Mogannwg University Health Board v Ferguson* [2014] IRLR 14. In that case the EAT held that the employer does not have to be able to control the circumstances giving rise to the detriment and guidance was given on the concept of a deliberate failure to act by the employer. It should be noted that this case involved, in part, the issue of conduct of other workers for which employers can now be vicariously liable (see further below). In *Tiplady v City of Bradford MDC* [2020] IRLR 230 the Court of Appeal emphasised that although detriment is a broad concept the detriment must be suffered "in the employment field". Accordingly, an alleged detriment in relation to personal housing said to be suffered by a council employee by reason of protected disclosures were suffered qua resident rather than employee and were accordingly not suffered in the employment field for the purposes of *ERA 1996, s 47B*.

Protected disclosures made in bad faith are subject to the potential reduction in compensation by up to 25% (*ERA 1996, s 49(6A)* as added by the *ERRA 2013, s 18(4)* from 25 June 2013).

Under *ERA 1996, s 48(2)* it is 'for the employer to show the ground on which any act, or deliberate failure to act, was done'. In *NHS Manchester v Fecitt* [2012] IRLR 64, reversing the EAT, the Court of Appeal has held that the test in discrimination law of 'in no sense whatsoever' derived from *Wong v Igen Ltd* [2005] 3 All ER 812 was not to be imported into the statutory test for whistleblowing. The correct test is whether 'the protected disclosure materially influences (in the sense of being more than a trivial influence) the employer's treatment of the whistleblower'. In some cases it will be necessary to carefully analyse whether the detriment in issue is due to having made protected disclosures or whether the detriment is because of the way in which the employee makes the disclosure (eg in an unreasonable offensive or abusive way). If the latter is in fact the reason for the detriment then it will not be by reason of having made a protected disclosure (*Panayiotou v Kernaghan* [2014] IRLR 500. See also *Shinwari v Vue Entertainment* UKEAT/0394/14 (12 March 2015, unreported) and *Parsons v Airplus International Ltd* UKEAT/0111/17 (13 October 2017, unreported)).

Dismissal on grounds of having made a protected disclosure is automatically unfair and there is no qualifying period of employment or upper age limit. The protected disclosure must be the reason or principal reason for the dismissal – it is not sufficient that the disclosure was a material influence (as that test only applies to detriment cases and not dismissal) (*ERA 1996, s 103A* as explained in *Eiger Securities LLP v Korshunova* [2017] IRLR 115). If an employer dismisses because of a disclosure the question whether that disclosure is a protected one is a question for the employment tribunal. If so the employer's subjective belief that the disclosure was not protected will not avoid a finding of unfair dismissal (*Beatt v Croydon Health Services NHS Trust* [2017] IRLR 748).

It had been held that if dismissing officer was unaware of the protected disclosures relied upon (even though others in the organisation were aware) then the dismissal could not be by reason of the protected disclosures (*Royal Mail Group Ltd v Jhuti* [2018] IRLR 251, CA). If however the dismissal is a result of earlier detriments by reason of making protected disclosures the loss following from such detriments might include compensation for the loss of employment (A point raised in *Jhuti* which was considered to be "clearly arguable" but not finally determined). See also on loss flowing from earlier detriments possibly including compensation for loss of employment: *CFLIS (UK) Ltd v Reynolds* [2015] IRLR 562 (CA), *Malik v Cenkos Securities plc* UKEAT/0100/17 (17 January 2018) (EAT).

A clearer route to claiming unfair dismissal in such circumstances has now been identified by the Supreme Court. In *Royal Mail Group Ltd v Jhuti* [2020] IRLR 129, SC the Supreme Court holds that an employer can be liable for unfair dismissal on the basis of the employee having made protected disclosures even where the dismissing officer was unaware of the disclosures. In such cases where the decision maker adopts an invented reason for dismissal (from another in the organisation who is above the employee in the organisation's hierarchy and who is motivated to dismiss by reason of the protected disclosures ("the hidden reason")) then the real reason for the dismissal is the hidden reason not the invented reason.

In *Wilsons Solicitors LLP v Roberts* [2018] EWCA Civ 52, [2018] IRLR 1042 the Court of Appeal held that post termination loss properly attributable to pre termination detrimental treatment could be recovered under *s 49* if the test of "but for" causation is satisfied. In the important case of *Timis v Osipov* [2019] IRLR 52 the Court of Appeal held that compensation can be awarded against individual workers for losses following the imposition of detriments, including losses suffered in consequence of dismissal. Thus, where the detriment is a decision to dismiss, losses flowing from the dismissal are recoverable against the individual workers (and for which the employer will be vicariously liable). In addition, injury to feeling awards may be made (in contrast to compensation for automatically unfair dismissal under *s 103A*) and further, the test for imposition of a detriment is satisfied if the protected disclosure is a material influence on the decision (*NHS Manchester v Fecitt* above) as opposed, in dismissal cases, being required to be the reason or principal reason for the dismissal. In the light of this a significant increase in joinder of individuals to whistleblowing dismissal claims can be anticipated.

For the application of the burden of proof in *ERA 1996, s 103A* cases see *Kuzel v Roche Products Ltd* [2008] EWCA Civ 380, [2008] IRLR 530. As enacted, *PIDA 1998* contemplated that the compensation for unfair dismissal by reason of making a protected disclosure would be on the same basis as that applying to other categories of unfair dismissal. *PIDA 1998, s 8* kept open the possibility of introducing a different basis for assessment of compensation by way of regulations to be introduced by the Secretary of State prescribing the manner of calculation of compensation in such cases (see *ERA 1996, s 127B*, inserted by *PIDA 1998, s 8(4)*). The relevant *Regulations* (*Public Interest Disclosure (Compensation) Regulations 1999 (SI 1999/1548)*) remove the limit on an unfair dismissal compensatory award in relation to this category of dismissal (see *ERA 1996, s 124(1A)* and *s 103A*). By *ERA 1996, s 123(6A)*, in the event of an unfair dismissal where the reason or principal reason for the dismissal was a protected disclosure but one that was not made in good faith, then the compensatory award may be reduced by up to 25% if the tribunal considers it just and equitable to do so (as added by *s 18(5)* of the *ERRA 2013* from 25 June 2013). There is no similar provision applying to a basic award for unfair dismissal.

Awards for injury to feelings as a result of subjection to a detriment (but not dismissal) will be calculated on the same basis as in discrimination cases (ie applying the guidance in *Vento v Chief Constable of West Yorkshire Police (No 2)* [2002] EWCA Civ 1871, [2003] IRLR 102). See *Virgo Fidelis Senior School v Boyle* [2004] IRLR 268, EAT. Following a detailed review of the authorities, the EAT in *Commissioner of Police for the Metropolis v Shaw* [2012] IRLR 291 has held that, when making an award of aggravated damages in a whistleblowing claim, such damages are an aspect of injury to feelings as they refer to increasing the injury to feelings by some act in addition to the wrong itself. Tribunals are advised to express the award by identifying the ordinary injury to feelings element and the aggravated element as subheadings of the overall injury to feelings award. In the case of a dismissal which is automatically unfair by reason of making a protected disclosure, as in other areas of unfair dismissal, no award can be made for injury to feelings (cf *Dunnachie v Kingston upon Hull City Council* [2004] IRLR 727, HL).

Interim relief is available in appropriate protected disclosure cases where the claimant is 'likely' to succeed in the claim. See the *Employment Rights Act 1996, ss 128* and *129*. In *Dandpat v University of Bath* (UKEAT/408/09) (10 November 2009, unreported) and *Raja v Secretary of State for Justice* (UKEAT/0364/09/CEA) [2010] All ER (D) 134 (Mar) the EAT held that a claimant must show 'a pretty good chance of success' (*Taplin v C Shippam Ltd* [1978] IRLR 450 (EAT) – a case under *TULR(C)A, s 163* – applied). More recently in *Ministry of Justice v Sarfraz* [2011] IRLR 562, the EAT clarified that, in making an order for interim relief under *ss 128* and *129* of the *1996 Act*, the employment judge in a whistleblowing case must find that it was 'likely' that the employment tribunal at the final hearing would find five things: (i) that the claimant had made a disclosure to his employer; (ii) that he believed that that disclosure tended to show one or more of the things itemised at (a)–(f) under *s 43B(1)* of the *1996 Act*; (iii) that that belief was reasonable; (iv) that the disclosure was made in good faith; and (v) that the disclosure was the principal reason for his dismissal. In that regard, the word 'likely' does not mean 'more likely than not' (that is at least 51% probability) but connotes a significantly higher degree of likelihood. See also *Hancock v Ter-Berg* [2020] IRLR 97 where the EAT determined that where there was a dispute as to the claimant's employment status this did not preclude the grant of interim relief as employment status was one of the issues that could be considered on a summary basis at the interim relief hearing.

In a careful and detailed judgment the Court of Appeal decided that the principles outlined in *Relaxion Group plc v Rhys-Harper* [2003] IRLR 484 in relation to acts of victimisation occurring after the termination of the employment contract do apply to detriments suffered after the termination of the employment relationship, for example an unfavourable reference provided by reason of having made a protected disclosure (see *Woodward v Abbey National plc* [2006] IRLR 677). *Fadipe v Reed Nursing Personnel* [2001] All ER (D) 23 (Dec) (Note) which had held that post-employment victimisation under *s 44* of the *ERA 1996* (health and safety cases) was not protected should not now be followed after *Woodward*. In *Onyango v Adrian Berkeley t/a Berkeley Solicitors* [2013] IRLR 338, the issue was whether the protection against detriment could apply to the situation where the protected disclosure relied upon for the purposes of *s 43B, ERA 1996* occurred after the termination of the employment. The EAT, applying *Woodwood*, concluded that, as a post termination detriment was actionable, there was no reason to exclude the situation where the protected disclosure relied upon also occurred post termination.

The breadth of application of the protection afforded by the concept of a protected disclosure is further illustrated by two cases involving dismissal occurring *after PIDA 1998* came into force but in relation to disclosures of information made *before PIDA 1998* came into force. In circumstances where the dismissal or other detriment imposed by the employer by reason of the disclosure occurred after 2 July 1999 an Employment Tribunal had jurisdiction to hear a complaint (see *Stolt Offshore Ltd v Miklaszewicz* [2002] IRLR 344 and *Meteorological Office v Edgar* [2002] ICR 149). In *Pinnington v City and Council of Swansea* [2005] ICR 685, however, the Court of Appeal held that a suspension from work which had commenced prior to the coming into force of *PIDA 1998* but which continued for two days during which the *Act* was in force did not amount to a detriment under *ERA 1996, s 47B* in relation to the final two days as there was no distinct act or omission by the employer on those two days on the grounds of the employee having made a protected disclosure.

In *Hibbins v Hesters Way Neighbourhood Project* [2009] ICR 319, [2009] IRLR 198 the EAT held that the protection afforded to whistleblowers is not limited to cases where the wrongdoing relates to wrongdoing or failure by the employer but extends to a disclosure relating to the default of any legal person. Subject to the requirement that the disclosure is in the public interest this principle would appear to remain good law following the amendments introduced by the *ERRA 2013*.

The protection against detriment is, similarly, not without limits and does not extend to employees deciding to conduct an 'investigation' into possible misconduct by the employer by hacking into the employer's computer system or searching files for 'evidence'. Such activity does not amount to a 'disclosure'. See *Evans v Bolton School* [2006] EWCA Civ 1653, [2007] ICR 641, sub nom *Bolton School v Evans* [2007] IRLR 140 in which a disciplinary warning given to a teacher for hacking into a computer was held to be legitimate and not a detriment imposed by reason of a protected disclosure. *Bolton School* was applied in *Panayiotou v Kernaghan* [2014] IRLR 500 (above) drawing the important distinction between a detriment imposed by reason of a protected disclosure and one imposed by reason of the unreasonable way in which the employee makes the disclosure. It was held in *Waite v South East Coast Ambulance Service NHS Trust* [2009] All ER (D) 43 (Jan) that before a claimant may lodge a whistleblowing detriment claim under *s 48* of the *ERA 1996* a written grievance must be submitted pursuant to the statutory grievance procedures. This no longer applies after 6 April 2009 with the repeal of the statutory grievance procedure provisions of the *Employment Act 2002* by the *Employment Act 2008 (Commencement No 1, Transitional and Savings) Order 2008 (SI 2008/3232)*.

In *NHS Manchester v Fecitt* [2012] IRLR 64 (above) the Court of Appeal had held, applying *Majrowski v Guy's and St Thomas' NHS Trust* [2006] IRLR 695, that the employer cannot be vicariously liable for the acts of employees which are not themselves unlawful. Thus acts of victimisation on grounds of having made a protected disclosure were not in themselves unlawful and there was, accordingly, no basis for vicarious liability. The decision of the EAT in *Carlisle-Morgan v Cumbria County Council* [2007] IRLR 314, [2007] All ER (D) 248 (Jan) (EAT) to the contrary was considered to be wrongly decided. This lacuna in the statutory protection against detriment was addressed by amendments introduced by the *ERRA 2013* with effect from 25 June 2013. *Section 47B* of the *ERA 1996*, which provides the protection against detriment on grounds of having made a protected disclosure, had new subsections *(1A)–(1E)* added by *s 19(1)* of the ERRA 2013. These subsections extend protection against detriment by reason of having made a protected disclosure to detriments imposed by other workers in the course of that worker's employment or by agents of the employer acting with the employer's authority (*ERA 1996, s 47B(1A)*). The provisions are similar to those found in relation to liability of employees and agents in the *Equality Act 2010 ('EaA 2010')* and provide for a statutory defence for the employer to show that the employer took all reasonable steps to prevent the detriment (*ERA 1996, s 47B(1D)*). On the issue of potential extraterritorial application of these provisions see *Foreign and Commonwelath Office v Bamieh* [2019] IRLR 736, CA. The determining factor is the relationship between the workers in issue. In *Bamieh* that relationship was not sufficiently strong to displace the presumption that the tribunal did not have jurisdiction where the work was done outside Great Britain.

By *ERA 1996, s 47B(1E)* a worker or agent is not liable for doing something which subjects the disclosing worker to a detriment if the worker or agent does that thing in reliance on a statement by the employer that doing that thing does not contravene the *Act* and it is reasonable for the worker or agent to rely on that statement. If that defence is made out it does not prevent liability of the employer arising under *ERA 1996, s 47B(1B)* (*ERA 1996, s 47B(1E)*). On liability of individual workers for detriments resulting in dismissal pursuant to these provisions see *Timis v Osipov* (above)

12   Discrimination and Equal Opportunities – I

12.1   THE SCOPE AND APPROACH OF THIS CHAPTER

Scope

Over the course of the last half-century, UK employment law has seen the ongoing and often vigorous development of a body of equal opportunities law. The underlying concept is a straightforward one: people should not be subject to disadvantage in the job market or in the workplace for reasons that have nothing to do with the skills they have to offer or their performance of their duties. There has been a steady incrementing of characteristics of the employee upon which it is no longer accepted that an employer may base employment-related decisions. As the law stands they are: sex; marital or civil partnership status; race; disability; gender reassignment; religion or belief; sexual orientation; pregnancy or maternity leave; and age. These grounds are referred to below as the 'protected characteristics'.

On 8 April 2010, the *Equality Act 2010* ("*EqA 2010*") received Royal Assent. Many of its most important provisions came into force on 1 October 2010. The principal purpose of the Act was to consolidate the numerous individual pieces of legislation that had previously made up the patchwork of the earlier law. This edition of the Handbook does not set out the old law. It does, however, refer to caselaw decided under the former regime where it remains relevant to the interpretation of *EqA 2010*.

Discrimination on grounds of sex in respect of contractual terms and conditions, which is known more familiarly as "Equal Pay" or, to use the language of the *EqA 2010*, "Equality of Terms", is treated separately (see EQUAL PAY (23)).

Approach

The approach taken below is first to explain the relevant general principle and immediately thereafter to indicate where particular issues arise in the context of its application to one or more of the protected characteristics.

12.2   LEGAL SOURCES AND GUIDANCE MATERIAL

Each protection against discrimination has been introduced by a legislative instrument. Sometimes the Domestic law implements an obligation originally to be found in a European legislative measure. However, even those measures, such as protection against discrimination on grounds of sex or race, which have domestic origins have since been shaped by European Law. In addition to the individual European directives, a prohibition of "any discrimination based on any ground such as sex, race, colour, ethnic or social origin, genetic features, language, religion or belief, political or other opinion, membership of a national minority, property, birth, disability, age or sexual orientation" is to be found in *Art 21(1)* of the *European Charter of Fundamental Rights*. The ECJ determined in *Cresco Investigation GmbH v Achatzi*: C-193/17 [2019] IRLR 380, [2019] All ER (D) 108 (Jan), that the Charter creates horizontally enforceable rights. In other words, even if domestic legislation fails to implement the *Art 21(1)* prohibition, a complainant can rely on the Charter to found a claim against their employer (whether or not the employer is a so-called "emanation of the State"). It should be noted that the protected characteristics to be found in the Charter are broader than those found in the *EA 2010*. The significance of this development for

12.2 Discrimination and Equal Opportunities – I

English and Welsh Law will depend on the outcome of the present negotiations between the United Kingdom and the European Union and, in particular, what is agreed in respect of so-called "level playing field" and "non-regression" matters. However, it seems unlikely in the extreme that the employees will be able to rely directly on the Charter as a source of rights.

On 6 April 2011, the Employment and Human Rights Commission issued a Code of Practice on Employment (the "*EHRC* Code") which can be downloaded from the EHRC's website at the following address: www.equalityhumanrights.com/publication/employment-statutory-code-practice. Tribunals and courts must take into account any part of the Code that appears to them relevant to any questions arising in proceedings.

The Government produced a series of guides providing short, clear explanations of the impact of *EqA 2010* on different sectors. They may be found online at: https ://www.gov.uk/guidance/equality-act-2010-guidance.

BASIC DISCRIMINATION CONCEPTS

Set out immediately below is a summary of the legislative framework applicable to each of the protected characteristics:

12.3 Sex

Sex discrimination in employment is prohibited by the *EqA 2010*. Sex is identified as a protected characteristic at *EqA 2010, s 4*. Both men and women are protected (*EqA 2010, s 11*).

Men cannot complain of sex discrimination where a woman has received "special treatment . . . in connection with pregnancy or childbirth" (*EqA 2010, s 3(6)(b)*). However, in *Eversheds Legal Services Ltd v De Belin* [2011] IRLR 448, [2011] ICR 1137, EAT (a case brought under the *Sex Discrimination Act 1975* ("*SDA 1975*")), it was held that where the "special treatment" was disproportionate, in the sense of being more favourable treatment than was reasonably necessary to compensate the woman for the disadvantages occasioned by her pregnancy, a claim could be brought by a man using the woman as a comparator.

Equal treatment between the sexes in employment is (at least until the expiry of the transition period on 31 December 2020) within the scope of competence of the European Union. The *Equal Treatment Directive (2006/54/EC)* ('*ETD 2006/54/EC*') is vertically directly effective which means that public sector workers are, for the present, able to rely directly on its provisions. *EqA 2010* is interpreted, so far as possible, so as to be consistent with the requirements of the *Directive*.

On 1 May 1999, the *Amsterdam Treaty* came into force. It amended *art 119* of the *Treaty of Rome* (now *art 157* of the *Treaty on the Functioning of the European Union*) incorporating a principle of equal treatment into the *Treaty* itself. This, in turn, has opened up the possibility of a horizontally directly effective right to equal treatment conferred on both public and private sector employees (see also *Cresco* above).

12.4 Marital or civil partnership status

"Marriage and civil partnership status" is identified as a protected characteristic at *EqA 2010, s 4*. Marriage is to be interpreted as including the marriage of a same sex couple (*Marriage (Same Sex Couples) Act 2013, Sch 3, Pt 1, Para 1(1)(a)*). Only those who are married or who have a civil partner are protected (*EqA 2010, s 8(2)*). The *Act* does not protect those who are discriminated against on grounds of being single. Discrimination against unmarried partners was found to be precluded by Art 14, para 1 of the *European Convention on Human Rights* when read with Article 1 of the Protocol (ie the right to peaceful enjoyment of possessions) in a case concerning a survivor's pension (*Re Brewster's application for judicial review* [2017] UKSC 8, [2017] IRLR 366, [2017] ICR 434).

A protection against discrimination on grounds of marital or family status was included in the original *ETD 76/207/EEC* but is absent from the *ETD 2006/54/EC* which superseded it. It is unclear whether or not the intention was to push marital status outside the range of protected characteristics for the purposes of European Law (see *Dunn v Institute of Cemetery and Crematorium Management* [2012] All ER (D) 173 (Feb)).

12.5   Race

Race is identified as a protected characteristic by *EqA 2010, s 4*. For the definition of "race" see **12.20** below.

Article 18 of the *Treaty on the Functioning of The European Union* prohibits discrimination on grounds of nationality "within the scope of application of the Treaties". *Article 19* (formerly *art 13* of the *Treaty of Rome*) confers a power on the European Union to legislate to combat discrimination on a variety of grounds including 'racial or ethnic origin'. On 29 June 2000, the European Council issued the *Race Discrimination Framework Directive (Council Directive 2000/43/EC)*. The scope of the *Directive* is not identical to that of *EqA 2010*. For instance, *EqA 2010* treats nationality as a form of discrimination because of race. In contrast the *Directive* does not apply to discrimination on grounds of nationality (*art 3, para 2*).

12.6   Gender reassignment

Gender reassignment is identified as a protected characteristic at *EqA 2010, s 4*. For the definition of "gender reassignment" see **12.21** below.

12.7   Religion or belief

Adherence to a particular religion or holding a particular religious or philosophical belief is identified as a protected characteristic at *EqA 2010, s 4*. For the definition of "religion", "religious belief" and "philosophical belief" see **12.22** below. Lacking a particular religion or religious or philosophical belief is also a protected characteristic (*EqA 2010, s 10*).

The protection has its origins in *art 19(1)* of the *Treaty on the Functioning of the European Union* which provides that 'the Council . . . may take appropriate action to combat discrimination based on . . . religion or belief . . . '. On 27 November 2000, the Council issued *Directive 2000/78/EC* establishing a general framework for equal treatment in employment and occupation ('the *Framework Directive 2000/78/EC*'). The directive included a prohibition of religious discrimination.

12.8   Sexual orientation

Sexual orientation is identified as a protected characteristic at *EqA 2010, s 4*. For the definition of "sexual orientation" see **12.23** below.

The origin of the protection is, once again, *art 19* of the *Treaty on the Functioning of the European Union* and the *Framework Directive 2000/78/EC*.

12.9   Pregnancy or maternity leave

Pregnancy and maternity are identified as protected characteristics at *EqA 2010, s 4*. For the definitions of "pregnancy" and "maternity" see **12.24** below.

12.10 Discrimination and Equal Opportunities – I

12.10 Age

Age is identified as a protected characteristic at *EqA 2010, s 4*. For the definitions of "age" and "age group" see **12.25** below.

The *Act* is the present implementation of the age-related provisions of the *Framework Directive 2000/78/EC* which required member states to enact legislation prohibiting age discrimination in employment.

Following the case of *Mangold v Helm* [2006] IRLR 143 in the European Court of Justice, there is some question as to whether the *Directive* made it unlawful to discriminate on the grounds of age even prior to 1 October 2006 (that being the date on which the *Employment Equality (Age) Regulations 2006 (SI 2006/1031)* first implemented the *Directive*). This is a matter of some controversy and is not addressed in detail here. For a discussion by the Advocate General of the European Court of Justice which is somewhat critical of the judgment in *Mangold*, see *Félix Palacios de la Villa v Cortefiel Servicios* Case C-411/05 (Advocate General) at paras 79 to 100. In *Bartsch v Bosch und Siemens Hausgeräte (BSH) Altersfürsorge GmbH*: C-427/06 [2009] All ER (EC) 113, [2009] 1 CMLR 163, the ECJ held that the prohibition on age discrimination was not mandatory in a case where the allegedly discriminatory measure was not intended to implement the *Directive* at a time before the time limit for transposing the *Directive* had expired. However, in the case of *Seda Kucukdeveci v Swedex GmbH & Co KG*: C-555/07 [2010] IRLR 346, the ECJ reiterated that the principle of non-discrimination on the ground of age should be regarded as a general principle of European Law and held that the European provisions may be relied upon to challenge legislation which was enacted prior to the coming into force of the directive.

12.11 Disability

Disability is identified as a protected characteristic at *EqA 2010, s 4*. For the definition of "disability" see **12.26** below.

The *Act* is the present implementation in UK law of the prohibition against discrimination on grounds of disability to be found in the *Framework Directive 2000/78/EC*. In *HK Danmark*, acting on behalf of *Ring v Dansk Almennyttigt Boligselskab*: C-335/11 [2013] IRLR 571, the CJEU held that the *Framework Directive* had to be read, so far as possible, so as to be compatible with the *United Nations Convention on the Rights of Persons with Disabilities*.

12.12 MEANING OF DISCRIMINATION

There are four principal ways in which a person may discriminate against another:

(i)   by *directly* discriminating against them (**12.13** below);

(ii)   by *indirectly* discriminating against them (**12.34** below);

(iii)   by *victimising* them (**12.38** below); or

(iv)   by *harassing* them (**12.39** below).

In addition there are two forms of discrimination which are specific to disability discrimination:

(v)   failure to make reasonable adjustments (a close cousin of indirect discrimination) (**12.37** below); and

(vi)   discrimination arising from disability (**12.33** below).

There is also a discrete form of direct discrimination which prohibits unfavourable treatment of because of pregnancy or maternity leave (see **12.30** ff below).

12.13 DIRECT DISCRIMINATION

Direct discrimination is defined at *EqA 2010, s 13(1)*:

> "A person (A) discriminates against another (B) if, because of a protected character-istic, A treats B less favourably than A treats or would treat others."

Persons A and B may be any legal person, including a company (*EAD Solicitors v Abrams* [2016] ICR 380, [2015] IRLR 978).

When determining whether there has been direct discrimination, one focuses on an individual person. Thus, in *Her Majesty's Chief Inspector of Education, Children's Services and Skills v Interim Executive Board of C School* [2017] EWCA Civ 1426, [2018] IRLR 334, where a voluntary aided Islamic faith school segregated boys from girls, the correct approach was not to ask whether girls and boys as groups were subjected to the same disadvantage but to ask whether a girl who wanted to socialise with boys was precluded from doing so on because of her sex. If the same could also be said of an individual boy, the appropriate conclusion was that both were victims of direct discrimination rather than that neither were.

The basic definition is modified insofar as it relates to age discrimination. If the protected characteristic is age, A does not discriminate against B if A can show A's treatment of B to be a "proportionate means of achieving a legitimate aim" (see further below at **12.34**).

The definition differs from that which applied under the pre-existing law in that rather than the less favourable treatment having to be "on grounds of" the relevant protected characteristic, the treatment has to be "because of it". The explanatory notes accompanying the Act suggest that the change in language is intended to make the legislation easier to understand but not to bring about any material change in the law (*EqA 2010, EN Para 61*).

The account set out immediately below breaks the legislative tests into two elements: less favourable treatment and the reason for that treatment. Whilst that division reflects the manner in which a tribunal will usually approach the issue, in *Shamoon v Chief Constable of the Royal Ulster Constabulary* [2003] UKHL 11, [2003] ICR 337, [2003] IRLR 285 a number of their Lordships took the view that it may sometimes be appropriate to ask the latter question first. For an account of when it will be appropriate to do so, see **12.15** below.

Less favourable treatment

12.14 *Unfavourable and less favourable treatment distinguished*

Most people asked to summarise the overall aim of anti-discrimination legislation would likely begin by suggesting that people should not be treated badly because of their protected characteristic. However, the test for direct discrimination is not whether a person treats another "unfavourably". Instead, *EqA 2010, s 13* requires a complainant to show that they have been treated "less favourably" than another. The reason why the legislation takes this approach is that rather than trying to ensure that people are treated well, it is aimed at ensuring that people are treated equally. So, for instance, few would argue against the proposition that a pay rise is a good thing. However, if an employer gives his ethnic minority employees smaller pay rises than he gives white employees because of their race he commits an act of unlawful discrimination. The ethnic minority employees have been favourably treated (their pay has increased) but they have been less favourably treated. The flipside is that an employer who treats all of his employees equally badly will not normally be found to have discriminated. It is the equality rather than the quality of the treatment that matters. For that reason, the House of Lords has suggested that the conduct of a hypothetical reasonable employer is irrelevant to the question whether he has unlawfully discriminated:

'The fact that, for the purposes of the law of unfair dismissal, an employer has acted unreasonably casts no light whatsoever on the question whether he has treated an employee less favourably for the purposes of the [*EqA 2010*]'.

(*Glasgow City Council v Zafar* [1998] 2 All ER 953, [1998] ICR 120, [1998] IRLR 36. See also *Martins v Marks & Spencer plc* [1998] IRLR 326.) Despite the House of Lords' robust rejection of the suggestion that showing that an employer's conduct was unreasonable makes it more likely that they have treated an affected employee less favourably, other authorities have been prepared to give the unreasonableness of the employer's conduct a limited and indirect relevance. Thus in *Law Society v Bahl* [2003] IRLR 640, EAT, the Employment Appeal Tribunal took the view that the more unreasonable the treatment the more the credibility of any non-discriminatory explanation proffered may be called into question. The question was considered more closely by the Court of Appeal (*Bahl v Law Society* [2004] EWCA 1070; [2004] IRLR 799). The Court of Appeal reiterated that unreasonable behaviour cannot found an inference of discrimination. An employer is not obliged, therefore, to lead evidence that others have been treated equally unreasonably. However, if there is no explanation for the unreasonable treatment the absence of an explanation (as opposed to the unreasonableness of the treatment) might found an inference. The Court of Appeal returned to the issue in a later case in which no explanation was provided and held that whilst a tribunal should not be 'too ready' to infer unlawful discrimination from unreasonable conduct in the absence of evidence of other discriminatory behaviour, it was 'not wrong in law' to do so (*Wong v Igen Ltd* [2005] EWCA Civ 142, [2005] 3 All ER 812, [2005] IRLR 258, [2005] ICR 931). *Nelson v Newry and Mourne District Council* [2009] IRLR 548 approached the question from the opposite direction, appearing to suggest that the reasonableness of the employer's position pointed away from a conclusion of discrimination. In *Eagle Place Services Ltd v Rudd* [2010] IRLR 486, the EAT took yet another approach to the question of the relevance of the reasonableness of the employer's behaviour. The employer dismissed a disabled employee unreasonably. The employer said that the appropriate comparator would be someone towards whom they would have behaved equally unreasonably but who was not disabled. The EAT disagreed with the employer's analysis, holding that it was not open to the employer to say that they would have behaved unreasonably towards the comparator.

Even in cases where employees have plainly been treated differently, it may still be difficult immediately to determine whether there has been less favourable treatment. Thus, where male and female employees are subject to different but comparably restrictive dress requirements there is no less favourable treatment on grounds of sex (*Schmidt v Austicks Bookshops Ltd* [1977] IRLR 360, EAT; and see *Smith v Safeway plc* [1996] IRLR 456, [1996] ICR 868, CA and *Department for Work and Pensions v Thompson* [2004] IRLR 348, EAT).

The test of what amounts to less favourable treatment is an objective one (*Burrett v West Birmingham Health Authority* [1994] IRLR 7, EAT). However, there may be a limited role for the subjective preferences of the complainant. Thus, where a local education authority provided more places for boys than for girls in selective schools, the House of Lords held that it was not necessary for the complainant to demonstrate that selective education was, objectively, 'better' than non-selective education. It was enough that, by denying the girls the same opportunity as the boys, the council was depriving them of a choice which was valued by them (or at least by their parents) and which was a choice obviously valued, on reasonable grounds, by many others (*Birmingham City Council v Equal Opportunities Commission* [1989] AC 1155, [1989] IRLR 173, HL).

It is the treatment itself rather than its consequences which must be different and less favourable (*Balgobin v Tower Hamlets London Borough Council* [1987] IRLR 401, [1987] ICR 829, EAT).

Segregating a person from others on racial grounds is deemed to be less favourable treatment (*EqA 2010, s 13(5)*). Thus, it is not open to an employer to argue that the provision of segregated facilities for his black employees is not discriminatory even though the facilities provided for black workers are equal to, if not better than, those provided for his white employees. No similar provision is made in respect of the other protected characteristics (but see, in relation to sex: *Her Majesty's Chief Inspector of Education, Children's Services and Skills v Interim Executive Board of C School* [2017] EWCA Civ 1426, [2018] IRLR 334: A voluntary aided Islamic faith school which segregated boys from girls thereby directly discriminated against both).

In the case of a pre-operative transsexual, avoiding less favourable treatment does not necessarily require that the complainant be treated as if their gender had already been changed. What is required in any case will depend on the particular circumstances (*Croft v Royal Mail Group plc* [2003] EWCA Civ 1045, [2003] IRLR 592: pre-operative male to female transsexual not treated less favourably when not allowed to use female toilets).

12.15 *Comparators*

Identifying direct discrimination involves the making of a comparison. It is open to an employee either to demonstrate that another specific individual employee has been more favourably treated (in which case that other employee is known as the 'comparator') or to establish that, absent any concrete examples, the tribunal may nevertheless still be sure that the employer would have treated another employee more favourably. In the latter case, the Tribunal considers what is known as a 'hypothetical comparator'.

Identifying a suitable comparator

(a) General Requirement that there should be no material difference between the complainant and the comparator

The *EqA 2010* requires that the circumstances of the comparator should not be materially different:

> "On a comparison of cases for the purposes of section 13 [direct discrimination] . . . there must be no material difference between the circumstances relating to each case." (*EqA 2010, s 23(1)*)

The question whether a comparator is appropriate is one of "fact and degree" – the circumstances of the complainant and the comparator need not be identical (*Hewage v Grampian Health Board* [2012] UKSC 37, [2012] IRLR 870, [2012] ICR 1054). Although picking the wrong comparator will be an error of law (*Naeem v Secretary of State for Justice* [2014] IRLR 520, [2014] ICR 472).

For guidance on the question of when circumstances will be materially different see *Dhatt v McDonalds Hamburgers Ltd* [1991] 3 All ER 692, [1991] ICR 238, [1991] IRLR 130, CA: it was not discriminatory to treat potential employees differently according to whether they were or were not free to work in the United Kingdom without permission and, hence, it was legitimate to require evidence of such permission only from those who were not British or EU citizens. (See also *Wakeman v Quick Corpn* [1999] IRLR 424, CA: UK employees of a Japanese company could not complain about higher rates of pay enjoyed by colleagues seconded from Japan. The fact that they were secondees meant that their circumstances were materially different to those of the UK employees; but see *Spicer v Government of Spain* [2004] EWCA Civ 1046, [2005] ICR 213, [2004] All ER D 526 (Jul); *Bullock v Alice Ottley School* [1992] IRLR 564: The comparator selected in a sex discrimination case concerned with a disparity in retirement ages was inappropriate because he performed a different job to that performed by the complainant; *Shomer v B & R Residential Lettings Ltd* [1992] IRLR 317, *Leeds Private Hospital Ltd v Parkin* [1992] ICR 571 and *Brook v Haringey London Borough Council* [1992] IRLR 478.) Where a female prison officer complained about being made to search male prisoners the appropriate comparator was a man required to search female prisoners and not a man required to search men (*Saunders v Home Office* [2006] ICR 318, [2005] All ER (D) 83 (Nov), EAT. In a case where a Muslim school support worker was suspended for refusing to remove her veil when interacting with pupils the appropriate comparator was a woman who was not a Muslim who also covered her face: *Azmi v Kirklees MBC* [2007] IRLR 484, [2007] ICR 1154. In *Kelly v Covance Laboratories Ltd* UKEAT/0186/15 [2016] IRLR 338, where an animal testing laboratory was worried about infiltration by animal rights activists, an instruction to a Russian national to speak English called for a comparator who also spoke a language other than English at the workplace. Where the alleged less favourable treatment is said to be an inconsistency in decision-making, the mere fact that the decisions made in respect of the complainant and comparator were taken by different people does not mean that there is a material difference in their respective circumstances (*Olaleken v Serco Ltd* (2019) UKEAT/0189/18, [2019] IRLR 314), although the presence of additional factors such as the fact that the decision-makers were applying different policies or were at different levels may justify a tribunal concluding that the comparison is inappropriate.

Identifying an appropriate comparator has proven difficult in cases where employers have distinguished between different age groups when deciding what termination payments to make. *Lockwood v DWP* [2013] EWCA Civ 1195, [2013] IRLR 941, a younger employee complained that those older than 35 had voluntary redundancy payments calculated on a more generous basis. The EAT decided that those under 35 could not validly compare themselves with their older colleagues. Statistics suggested that older employees found it harder to get another job which made their circumstances materially different. The Court of Appeal overturned the EAT's decision. Since the reason that older employees found getting a new job harder was, the statistics suggested, their age, the supposed material distinction was, in truth, the protected characteristic itself. Applying *Lockwood*, the EAT in *Donkor v Royal Bank of Scotland* UKEAT/0162/15, [2016] IRLR 268 determined that where an employee was denied voluntary redundancy because he was old enough to qualify for early retirement he could be validly compared to a younger colleague who was not entitled to retire and whose voluntary redundancy package was consequently much cheaper. "But for" the claimant's age, the difference in entitlement would not have existed. Therefore, the cost was itself an age-related factor and not a material difference. The thrust of the domestic authorities is to treat age-related job market factors as being irrelevant to the question of the appropriate comparison but relevant to the question of justification. However, a somewhat different approach was taken by the ECJ in *O v Bio Philippe Auguste Sarl* C-432/14 [2015] IRLR 1017. The ECJ concluded that students doing vacation work could be excluded from an entitlement to receive a payment at the end of a fixed term period of employment. The students were not comparable to ordinary fixed-term workers. Vacation work was "temporary" and "ancillary" and students did not suffer from the same "job insecurity" as their older colleagues.

When dealing with hypothetical comparators it might be possible to construe the legislation so as to require the tribunal to construct a comparator who is 'in effect, a clone of the applicant in every respect (including personality and personal characteristics)' save that they are, for instance, of a different race. However, that approach was rejected in *Madden v Preferred Technical Group CHA Ltd* [2004] EWCA Civ 1178, [2005] IRLR 46 (per Wall LJ at paragraph 87). The effect of such an approach would be to run together the two relevant questions, namely whether the complainant was less favourably treated and whether they were less favourably treated on the prohibited ground. The reasoning would be that if the complainant and comparator are identical in all respects save, for instance, for their race any less favourable treatment must, logically, be on racial grounds. In practice, it can be very difficult to keep the two issues distinct. There are signs that this difficulty is being embraced by the appeal courts. In *Stockton on Tees Borough Council v Aylott* [2010] EWCA Civ 910, [2010] IRLR 994, [2011] ICR 1279, the Court of Appeal invokes the decision of the House of Lords in *Shamoon v Chief Constable of the Royal Ulster Constabulary* [2003] UKHL 11, [2003] 2 All ER 26, [2003] IRLR 285, [2003] ICR 337 and suggests that it will often be appropriate to start by identifying the reason for the treatment the employee complains of. If the answer is that the reason is a protected characteristic, the finding of less favourable treatment will likely follow as a matter of inevitability. Since the hypothetical comparator is designed to allow a tribunal to decide whether there has been less favourable treatment and that finding is, in turn, intended to be a signpost pointing to a prohibited and discriminatory reason for the employer's actions, the *Shamoon* approach effectively starts the journey at the point which had originally been identified as the destination. Adopting that approach will often make it unnecessary to identify a hypothetical comparator at all, as Mummery LJ made clear in *Stockton* (see also *JP Morgan Europe Ltd v Chweidan* [2011] EWCA Civ 648, [2011] IRLR 673, [2012] ICR 268). Where a tribunal determines, nevertheless, to identify one it should determine which circumstances are relevant by reasoning backwards from the reason for the treatment accorded to the complainant. As Mummery LJ puts it in *Stockton*:

> 'The relevant circumstances and attributes of an appropriate comparator should reflect the circumstances and attributes relevant to the reason for the action or decision which is complained of.'

The selection of the comparator is the responsibility of the complainant. However, in some circumstances, a tribunal that determines that the complainant's chosen comparator is inappropriate may be required to go on to make the comparison with a hypothetical comparator (see *Balamoody v UK Central Council for Nursing, Midwifery and Health Visiting* [2001] EWCA Civ 2097, [2002] IRLR 288: the complainant was unrepresented. The Court of Appeal appears to have felt that the tribunal had a rather better grasp of the nature of the complainant's case than he did himself).

(b) Comparators in cases of direct disability discrimination

Where the protected characteristic is disability, *EqA 2010, s 23(2)* requires that the "circumstances" that must not materially differ between complainant and comparator specifically include a person's abilities. In other words, the complainant and comparator must have the same abilities. This may mean that the appropriate comparator is also a disabled person. At first glance this might appear illogical. However, the rationale is that direct disability discrimination is not intended to protect against less favourable treatment received because the employee lacks certain abilities but rather against less favourable treatment because they have a "particular disability". An example would be an employee who is dismissed because they are HIV+. Their abilities may be indistinguishable from those of any other employee but the employer is not prepared to employ people with that particular disability. Discrimination on the grounds that an employee lacks a particular ability is the subject of a separate protection dealt with at **12.39** below. It is known as "discrimination arising from disability" and differs to direct discrimination in that it is engaged where the employee is treated unfavourably (rather than *less* favourably) and a defence of justification is potentially available.

Watts v High Quality Lifestyles Ltd [2006] IRLR 850, [2006] All ER (D) 216 (Apr), EAT was the first appellate decision to consider direct disability discrimination. The claimant was a support worker who had suffered a number of injuries including cuts and bites in the course of his work with persons with learning difficulties. Upon revealing to management that he was HIV+, he was suspended and later dismissed on the grounds that his position was untenable after a risk assessment concluded that injuries involving broken skin were commonplace. The employment tribunal found that such treatment was on the grounds of disability and upheld his claim. However, the EAT found that the employment tribunal had failed to consider whether he had in fact been less favourably treated than a hypothetical comparator would have been. The EAT also found that in identifying the appropriate comparator, the Employment Tribunal should have found that the comparator had 'some attribute, whether caused by medical condition or otherwise, which is not HIV+ . . . [which] must carry the same risk of causing to others illness or injury of the same gravity, here serious and possibly fatal'. It is thought that this approach to identifying comparators might be to construe 'relevant circumstances' too narrowly. A comparator with an attribute carrying precisely the same risk of causing illness or injury to others would almost always be likely to be treated in the same way as the claimant, in which case the claim of direct discrimination would fail. The EAT's approach to comparator in this case, which requires that the comparator is effectively someone who is HIV+ by another name, could also let discrimination based on the stigma of being HIV+ slip through the net. In *Aylott v Stockton-on-Tees Borough Council* [2010] EWCA Civ 910, [2010] IRLR 994, [2011] ICR 1278, the Court of Appeal considered that an employment tribunal had been entitled to exclude from the characteristics of its hypothetical comparator certain unsatisfactory aspects of the complainant's behaviour and performance on the basis that they stemmed from his particular disability. The tribunal had been entitled to exclude the particular disability itself from the comparison, but it seemed they could also exclude certain effects of the disability. The *Stockton* approach would appear, therefore, to take a more employee-friendly approach than *Watts*, though the latter authority has since been cited by the Court of Appeal with approval (see *Aitken v Commissioner of Police of the Metropolis* [2011] EWCA Civ 582, [2012] ICR 78, [2011] All ER (D) 165 (May) where *Aylott* was distinguished on its facts. The ET in *Aitken* considered threatening behaviour should be part of the circumstances applicable to a hypothetical comparator and the complainant did not suggest at that stage that the behaviour arose from his disability).

Whether and, if so, how the costs of supporting someone with a disability should be factored into the necessary comparison for direct discrimination purposes was at issue in *Cordell v Foreign and Commonwealth Office* [2012] ICR 280, [2012] All ER (D) 97 (Mar), EAT. The complainant was profoundly deaf. She was not appointed to a diplomatic post in Kazakhstan because of the cost and difficulty maintaining continuity of the services of a lip-speaker. Her case was the cost should be compared to cost of paying for diplomats posted overseas having their children educated in boarding school. The circumstances of those with children needing education was said to be materially different. A comparison that allowed the complainant to be compared with parents was too general to be useful. The EAT preferred to take the *Shamoon* approach (see **12.15** (a) above) and to ask the reason why the complainant was not appointed. The answer was not her disability but the costs of dealing with it, which meant that any less favourable treatment was not because of her disability and the claim for direct discrimination failed.

(c) Comparators in sexual orientation cases

Specific provision is made in relation to sexual orientation at *EqA 2010, s 23*:

(3) If the protected characteristic is sexual orientation, the fact that one person (whether or not the person referred to as B) is a civil partner while another is married to a person of the opposite sex is not a material difference between the circumstances relating to each case.

(4) If the protected characteristic is sexual orientation, the fact that one person (whether or not the person referred to as B) is married to a person of the same sex while another is married to a person of the opposite sex is not a material difference between the circumstances relating to each case.

(EqA 2010, s 23 as amended with effect from 13 March 2014 by the Marriage (Same Sex Couples) Act 2013, Sch 7 and SI 2014/93).

(d) Comparators in gender reassignment cases: absence due to undergoing a gender reassignment

EqA 2010, s 16 makes specific provision protecting transsexuals who are absent from work because of a gender reassignment. A person's absence is treated as being because of gender reassignment "if it is because the person is proposing to undergo, is undergoing or has undergone [a] process (or part of [a] process)" for the purpose of reassigning the person's sex by changing physiological or other attributes of sex (*EqA 2010, ss 7(1)* and *16(3)*). For the purposes of determining whether or not the employee has been treated less favourably because of their protected characteristic, *EqA 2010, s 16* provides that the employee should be their own comparator. The Tribunal asks whether they would have been treated more favourably if they had been absent because of sickness or injury (*EqA 2010, s 16(2)(a)*) or absent for some other reason where the Tribunal is satisfied that "it is not reasonable for [the employee] to be treated less favourably" (*EqA 2010, s 16(2)(b)*).

(e) Comparators in pregnancy and maternity leave cases

There is a specific prohibition on treating a person unfavourably (as opposed to less favourably) because of pregnancy or maternity leave (*EqA 2010, s 18*). Because what is prohibited is unfavourable treatment there is no need for a comparator. This reflects long-standing European authority to the effect that because only women may fall pregnant there is no appropriate male comparator. There is, in other words, no equivalent man whose circumstances could be said not to be materially different (see *Dekker v Stichting Vormingscentrum voor Jong Volwassenen (VJV - Centrum) Plus*: C-177/88 [1990] ECR I-3941, [1991] IRLR 27, [1992] ICR 325 and *Webb v EMO Air Cargo (UK) Ltd* [1994] IRLR 482, [1994] ICR 770, ECJ. For UK authority confirming the absence of a need for a comparator in pregnancy discrimination cases see *McGuigan v TG Boynes & Sons* [1999] 633 IDS Brief 6, EAT (EAT/1114/97); *Smith v Gardner Merchant Ltd* [1998] IRLR 510 per Ward LJ obiter and *Fletcher v NHS Pensions Agency* [2005] IRLR 689, [2005] ICR 1458, EAT). The *s 18* protection against unfavourable treatment on grounds of pregnancy is dealt with at **12.30** below.

However, *EqA 2010, ss 4* and *13* appear to have the effect that pregnancy and maternity are also amongst the protected characteristics which are prohibited from being the reason for less favourable treatment. Perhaps surprisingly, it seems to be open to an employee who can make out a claim under *EqA 2010, s 18* also to bring a claim under *s 13*. *EqA 2010, s 18(7)* expressly precludes an employee bringing both a *s 18* pregnancy claim and a *s 13* sex discrimination claim. However, it does not preclude a *s 13* pregnancy discrimination claim. Why would a complainant ever want to bring a *s 13* pregnancy discrimination claim given the express protection conferred by *s 18*? The answer may be that there are cases of pregnancy discrimination that would not fall within *s 18*. The *s 18* protection is only available to a complainant during the so-called "protected period" (broadly from conception to the end of maternity leave – see *EqA 2010, s 18(6)*). Thus, an employee who is discriminated against because she announces that she intends to become pregnant; because her employer discovers that she has miscarried; or because her employer mistakenly believes that she is pregnant cannot bring a *s 18* claim and will have to rely on *s 13*.

The uncertainty that remains is whether a complainant bring a *s 13* pregnancy discrimination claim has to identify a comparator. The need to establish less favourable treatment suggests that she does but since only women can announce an intention to get pregnant, miscarry or be mistakenly assumed to be pregnant, how can the apparent requirement for a comparator be reconciled with the European authorities referred to above? The legislation provides no answer and the matter awaits appellate consideration.

(f) Comparators in sex discrimination cases: is a comparison necessary where the conduct complained of is 'gender-specific'?

The short answer is 'yes'. At one point the courts and tribunals had come to accept that a comparative approach might not always be possible or appropriate in sex discrimination cases. As explained above, it has long since been accepted that a woman treated unfavourably on grounds of pregnancy has no valid male comparator. Attempts have been made to extend the principle to other instances of so-called "gender-specific" treatment, typically in cases of harassment where the female victim of harassment was treated in a way that a male victim would not have been.

The House of Lords in *Macdonald v Advocate General for Scotland* [2003] UKHL 34, [2004] 1 All ER 339, [2003] IRLR 512, [2003] ICR 937 (see also *Smith v Gardner Merchant Ltd* [1998] 3 All ER 852, [1998] IRLR 510) specifically reaffirmed the need for a comparator even where the alleged discriminatory behaviour could be said to be gender-specific.

(g) Irrelevance of whether the alleged discriminator shares the protected characteristic with the complainant

EqA 2010, s 24(1) makes it clear that it is irrelevant whether the alleged discriminator (referred to as "A") shares the relevant protected characteristic with the complainant:

> "For the purpose of establishing a contravention of this Act by virtue of Section 13(1), it does not matter whether A has the protected characteristic".

Thus, a woman may discriminate against another woman on grounds of sex, etc.

Performing the comparison

The burden of establishing that they have been less favourably treated falls upon the complainant.

In most cases involving an actual comparator the comparison will be relatively straightforward. For instance, a complainant who has not been appointed to a particular post may seek to compare themselves to the person who was. Evidence will then centre on the selection process. Similarly, an employee who is made redundant may seek to compare themselves to someone who was retained in employment.

Matters are more complex when dealing with hypothetical comparators because the Tribunal will be asked to infer that the necessary less favourable treatment. By definition one is dealing with a situation where there may be little direct evidence. In *Chief Constable of West Yorkshire v Vento* [2001] IRLR 124, the EAT suggested that a tribunal might look to see how 'unidentical but not wholly dissimilar cases' had been dealt with. Thus, someone whose circumstances differ sufficiently from those of the complainant to make them an inappropriate comparator may nevertheless have relevance in the context of the consideration of how a hypothetical comparator would have been treated.

In other cases a complainant may wish to lead evidence of, for instance, sexist comments made by the respondent on the basis that they tend to suggest a discriminatory attitude and thus that a male employee would have been treated more favourably. In such a case evidence principally relevant to the question whether less favourable treatment was on a prohibited ground may assist in establishing that the complainant would have been less favourably treated. Support for this approach may be found in *Shamoon v Chief Constable of the Royal Ulster Constabulary* [2003] UKHL 11, [2003] 2 All ER 26, [2003] IRLR 285, [2003] ICR 337, in which a number of members of the House of Lords suggested that rather than identify the less favourable treatment and only then ask whether the reason for the treatment was the protected characteristic, a tribunal could first ask whether the characteristic was the reason why the complainant was treated in the manner complained about. If the tribunal decides that the characteristic was part of the reason for the treatment it can then be inferred that someone without the characteristic would have been treated more favourably. The decision in *Shamoon* was concerned with the law as it was before the enactment of *SDA 1975, s 63A*. That section formally reversed the burden of proof in sex discrimination cases. The reverse burden of proof, which now applies to all of the protected characteristics (see **12.3**) is to be found at *EqA 2010, s 136*. As the burden only shifts where a prima facie case of discrimination has been established an exploration of the employer's reasons for actions as a first step would seem to jump the gun. However, the EAT has stressed the particular suitability of the *Shamoon* guidance when dealing with cases involving hypothetical comparators (see *Laing v Manchester City Council* [2006] IRLR 748, [2006] ICR 1519, EAT). The Court of Appeal has sought to allow tribunals the greatest flexibility, holding both that whilst it is generally good practice to follow the two stage test, there is no necessary error of law if a tribunal does not do so (*Brown v Croydon London Borough Council* [2007] EWCA Civ 32, [2007] IRLR 259) and that it cannot be said to be an error of law in cases involving hypothetical comparators to deal first with the question of less favourable treatment (see *Madarassy v Nomura International plc* [2007] EWCA Civ 33, [2007] IRLR 246, [2007] ICR 867 and *JP Morgan Europe Ltd v Chweidan* [2011] EWCA Civ 648, [2011] IRLR 673, [2012] ICR 268).

12.16 *Positive discrimination*

"Positive discrimination" involves favouring those with a particular protected characteristic for well-intentioned reasons. As explained below (see **12.17**), UK law largely disregards such intentions and motives. Well-intentioned discrimination is still unlawful. However, the law does allow a limited scope for positive discrimination. The essence of exception is that, in certain defined circumstances, positive discrimination may be lawful where the purpose is to redress the effect of pre-existing discriminatory disadvantage. A full consideration of positive discrimination may be found at **13.10** DISCRIMINATION AND EQUAL OPPORTUNITIES – II.

'Because of' the protected characteristic

12.17 *General principles*

EqA 2010, s 13 prohibits less favourable treatment "because of a protected characteristic". The use of the formula "because of" in preference to that used in the earlier legislation, (ie "on grounds of") was not intended materially to alter the law. The explanatory notes accompanying the Act suggest that the intention was simply to make the meaning of the legislation more readily accessible (*EqA 2010, EN, Para 61*). In *Onu v Akwiwu* [2014] EWCA Civ 279, [2014] ICR 571, [2014] IRLR 448, the Court of Appeal expressly accepted that the two formulations have the same meaning (Affirmed [2016] UKSC 31, [2016] IRLR 719, [2016] ICR 756).

Cases of direct discrimination may be usefully divided into two categories. In the first category the treatment in issue is discriminatory on its face. In the second category, the treatment with which the court is concerned is not objectively discriminatory – one has to know something about the respondent's reasons for their actions in order to know whether the less favourable treatment could be said to be "because" of the protected characteristic. (For an example of the court applying this categorization see *Khan v Royal Mail Group* [2014] EWCA Civ 1082, [2014] IRLR 947. See also *Amnesty International v Ahmed* [2009] IRLR 884, [2009] ICR 1450 and *Interserve FM Limited v Tuleikyte* UKEAT/0267/16 [2017] IRLR 615 where the two categories were referred to as "criterion" and "reason why" cases respectively and *Commissioner of Police of the Metropolis v Keohane* UKEAT/463/12 [2014] ICR 1073, [2014] All ER (D) 307 (Mar) where the EAT warns against the risk of letting such labels distract from the express statutory test).

A good example of the first type of case would be where an employer had an express policy of not appointing women to certain roles. Where the less favourable treatment is objectively discriminatory, the law does not require any investigation of the subjective motives of the discriminator. As the Court of Appeal put it in *Khan v Royal Mail Group*:

"It does not matter why he discriminated on the ground of sex; if in fact he did."

Thus unintentional direct discrimination is unlawful as are acts of direct discrimination performed for entirely non-discriminatory motives (see *R (on the application of E) v Governing Body of JFS (Secretary of State for Children, School and Families, interested parties) (United Synagogue intervening)* [2009] UKSC 15, [2010] IRLR 136 and *Ahmed v Amnesty International* [2009] IRLR 884, [2009] ICR 1450, EAT). See also *Martin v Devonshires Solicitors* UKEAT/86/10 [2011] ICR 352, [2011] All ER (D) 345 (Mar) which considers both *JFS* and *Ahmed* and proposes a distinction between "motive" which is irrelevant, and "motivation" which is not.

On the other hand, the presence of a discriminatory motive or intention will plainly be compelling evidence pointing to a finding of unlawful discrimination *Nagarajan v London Regional Transport* [2000] 1 AC 501 at 519, [1999] IRLR 572). The tribunal must bear in mind that a discriminatory motive may be sub- or unconscious (*Geller v Yeshurun Hebrew Congregation* UKEAT/190/15, [2016] ICR 1028, [2016] All ER (D) 229 (Mar)).

In some cases falling into the first category, less favourable treatment may be because of a characteristic which, while not itself a protected characteristic, is very closely related to one. For instance, in *James v Eastleigh Borough Council* [1990] 2 AC 751, [1990] IRLR 288, the claimant, a man, was charged to use a swimming pool whereas a woman of the same age would not have been. The difference in treatment arose from the fact that the local authority's policy was to allow pensioners to swim without charge and women had a lower State retirement age than men. Since retirement age depended directly upon gender, there was an exact correspondence between the characteristic relied upon by the claimant and the protected characteristic of sex. Similarly, in *Donkor v Royal Bank of Scotland* UKEAT/0162/15 [2016] IRLR 268, where voluntary redundancy was not offered to an older employee because he would have been entitled to take early retirement which would have been very costly, he was treated less favourably because of his age. The entitlement to retire and the associated cost arose from his age. In *Onu* (above), by contrast, the reason for less favourable treatment was the claimant's immigration status. The Supreme Court was not satisfied that that characteristic could be said exactly to correspond to the protected characteristic of nationality. Although all migrant domestic workers are non-British not all non-British people are migrant domestic workers. The test is whether the characteristic relied upon can be said to be "indissociable" from the protected characteristic (*Lee v Ashers Baking Company Ltd* [2018] UKSC 49, [2018] IRLR 1116). That test was not met (in the context of a goods and services case) where a bakery refused to make a cake with a slogan supporting same sex marriage. Although the client was gay, support for same sex marriage was not indissociable from his sexual orientation.

If a tribunal declines to making a finding of direct discrimination in a case where treatment is discriminatory on its face it should explain how it applied the burden of proof (see *Stefanko and others v Maritime Hotel Ltd and another* UKEAT/0024/18 [2019] IRLR 322).

An example of the second type of case is one where an ethnic minority employee is not promoted. It would not be sufficient for a tribunal to be satisfied that the employee has been less favourably treated than their chosen actual or hypothetical comparator. The tribunal will also want to consider *why* the complainant was not promoted. It is only if the protected characteristic is a substantive or operational reason for the less favourable treatment that liability will be established.

It might be said that in both categories the tribunal is still asking a causal question – what caused the less favourable treatment? Lawyers traditionally approach questions of causation by applying a "but for" analysis. They ask whether "but for" the protected characteristic the less favourable treatment would have occurred. The analysis works relatively straightfor-wardly with cases falling into the first category, like *James*. However, in *Onu* (above) the Court of Appeal suggested that in the second category of case it was better to avoid talk of causation altogether. A similar position was adopted by the House of Lords in *Chief Constable of West Yorkshire Police v Khan* [2001] UKHL 48, [2001] ICR 1065, [2001] IRLR 830, HL(E), where it was said that the real question was "what, consciously or unconsciously, was the [alleged discriminator's] reason". Unlike causation, the Court considered, that question required a subjective test. Causation is a legal question whereas a respondent's reasons for action are a question of fact.

In some cases, the tribunal has been criticised for using the but for test. One example is *Martin v Lancehawk Ltd (trading as European Telecom Solutions)* [2004] All ER (D) 400 (Mar) (UKEAT/0525/03) EAT: an employer dismissed a female employee when their affair concluded. It was argued that as the employer would not have slept with a man, it could be said that 'but for' the complainant's sex she would not have been dismissed. The EAT found that there had been no discrimination. They felt that the 'reason why' the complainant was dismissed was the end of the affair and not her sex. Her sex was causally relevant but not causally determinative. The Appeal Tribunal also considered that the appropriate comparator was a homosexual lover and that such a lover would have been treated no differently. On that analysis the 'but for' test would not have been made out. However, the Appeal Tribunal went on, in any event, to reject the 'but for' test formulating instead a test based on 'the reason why' the employer has acted as he had, relying on dicta in *Chief Constable of West Yorkshire Police v Khan* (above) and *Shamoon* (above). In *B v A* [2007] IRLR 576, EAT, the tribunal was said to have erred by applying the 'but for' test when, had they asked whether the claimant had been dismissed 'by reason' of her sex, they would have concluded that she had not been – rather she had been dismissed because her employer, who was also her lover, had been motivated by sexual jealousy on seeing her in the company of another man.

If a decision maker's reason for treating an employee less favourably is not directly influenced by a protected characteristic but, in reaching the decision, she relies upon views expressed by a colleague which are themselves tainted by discrimination the decision-maker does not treat the complainant less favourably because of their protected characteristic (*CLFIS (UK) Ltd v Reynolds* [2015] EWCA Civ 439, [2015] ICR 1010, [2015] IRLR 562. See also *Gallop v Newport City Council (No. 2)* UKEAT/0118/15, [2016] IRLR 395). Note, however, that the colleague upon whose views the decision-maker relied may themselves have acted unlawfully. There must also now be some doubt whether the approach adopted in CLFIS can be reconciled with that taken by the Supreme Court in *Royal Mail Group Ltd v Jhuti* [2019] UKSC 55, [2020] ICR 753, [2020] IRLR 139 to the question of the employer's reason for dismissal in unfair dismissal cases. In that case a line manager confected capability concerns as a result of the employee having made a protected disclosure. He fooled another manager into dismissing for capability. The employer's reason for dismissal was found to be the protected disclosure. If the line manager had been motivated by, say, the employee's race, the present authorities would mean that the employer's reason or principal reason for dismissal would be the employee's race for the purposes of the unfair dismissal claim but the dismissal would not because of race for the purposes of *EqA 2010, s 13*.

Discrimination will be treated as being because of the protected characteristic if the substantial or effective, although not necessarily the sole or intended, reason for the discriminatory treatment was the characteristic (see *R v Commission for Racial Equality, ex p Westminster City Council* [1984] IRLR 230, [1984] ICR 770; affd in part [1985] IRLR 426, [1985] ICR 827 – a race case). In *Barton v Investec Henderson Crosthwaite Securities Ltd* [2003] IRLR 332, [2003] ICR 1205, EAT, the Employment Appeal Tribunal went further in the context of sex discrimination holding that sex should not be 'any part of the reasons for the treatment in question' (approved by the Court of Appeal in *Igen v Wong* (above)). Even so, it must be a significant factor in the sense of being more than trivial. (See also *Villalba v Merrill Lynch & Co Inc* [2006] IRLR 437, [2007] ICR 469, EAT).

12.18   *Meaning of 'because of sex'*

EqA 2010, s 11 provides:

> "In relation to the protected characteristic of sex –
>
> (a)   a reference to a person who has a particular protected characteristic is a reference to a man or to a woman; and
>
> (b)   a reference to persons who share a protected characteristic is a reference to persons of the same sex."

'Sex' is not defined in *EqA 2010*. 'Woman' and 'man' are defined as being a female and male respectively of any age (*EqA 2010, s 212*).

An employer discriminates "because of sex" where their decisions rely on stereotypical assumptions. The Tribunal is entitled to take account of its own experience of such assumptions but should warn the parties where it proposes to do so (*Commerzbank v Rajput* UKEAT/0164/18 [2019] IRLR 722, [2019] ICR 1613).

Before the UK enacted specific protection for transsexuals, the European Court of Justice decided that discrimination against transsexuals was a form of sex discrimination. In *P v S*: C-13/94 [1996] All ER (EC) 397, [1996] IRLR 347, the European Court adopted a broad test which rendered unlawful any discrimination based 'essentially if not exclusively on the sex of the person concerned'.

At one point pregnancy discrimination was treated as falling within the scope of sex discrimination as only women may fall pregnant. It now has a discrete protection – for which see **12.24** below. Treating an employee less favourably because she is the commissioning mother in a surrogacy arrangement is neither discrimination because of pregnancy (because she has not herself been pregnant) nor discrimination because of sex (*CD v ST* C-167/12 [2014] IRLR 551). To succeed in a sex discrimination claim the mother would have to show that a commissioning father would have been treated differently.

12.19 *Meaning of 'because of marital or civil partnership status'*

EqA 2010, s 8 provides:

"(1)   A person has the protected characteristic of marriage and civil partnership if the person is married or a civil partner;

(2)   In relation to the protected characteristic of marriage and civil partnership –

(a)   a reference to a person who has a particular protected characteristic is a reference to a person who is married or a civil partner;

(b)   a reference to persons who share a protected characteristic is a reference to persons who are married or are civil partners."

"Marriage" is not defined in the Act. The *EHRC Code* does provide some further guidance, however. It says of "marriage" that it will cover any formal union of a man and woman which is legally recognised in the UK as a marriage. As a result of the *Marriage (Same Sex Couples) Act 2013, Sch 3, Pt 1, Para 1* it includes marriages between same sex couples. In *Bick v Royal West of England Residential School for the Deaf* [1976] IRLR 326, a tribunal decided (with very considerable reluctance) that the predecessor provisions in the *SDA 1975* did not protect employees who were merely engaged. That decision was not followed in *Turner v Turner* (ET/2401702/04) which concluded that the right to marry enshrined in *Art 12* of the *European Convention on Human Rights*, meant that the provision had to be interpreted so as to protect those dismissed because they are planning to marry.

Equally, civil partnership is not defined in *EqA 2010*, however a civil partner is someone who has been registered as the civil partner of another person of the same sex (see *Civil Partnership Act 2004, s 1*). The *EHRC Code* makes it clear that it also encompasses those whose civil partnerships have been registered abroad (Para 2.33).

For an example of direct discrimination on grounds of marital status see *Chief Constable of the Bedfordshire Constabulary v Graham* [2002] IRLR 239, EAT. In *Hawkins v Atex Group Ltd and Others* [2012] IRLR 807, [2012] ICR 1315, the EAT indicated that the appropriate comparator will usually be somebody who is in a relationship akin to (but falling short of) marriage. That comparator ensures that the focus is on the significance of the married status itself and not, for instance, on the question of which particular individual the employee is married to.

12.20 *Meaning of 'because of race'*

"Race" is defined by *EqA 2010, s 9(1)* to include: "colour", "nationality" and "ethnic or national origins". A "racial group" is "a group of persons defined by reference to race" (*EqA 2010, s 9(3)*).

In relation to the protected characteristic of race:

> "a reference to a person who has a particular protected characteristic is a reference to a person of a particular racial group" (*EqA 2010, s 9(2)(a)*)

A racial group can comprise two or more distinct racial groups (*EqA 2010, s 9(4)*). Thus, a French national will be a member of the racial group consisting of French people and of a racial group consisting of all foreign nationals.

EqA 2010, s 9(5) conferred a power on a Minister of the Crown to amend *s 9* by order to provide for caste to be an aspect of race. *Section 65* of the *Enterprise and Regulatory Reform Act 2013* ("*ERRA 2013*") amends *EqA 2010, s 9* by adding caste to the definition of race. The amendment is to take effect at a date that had not yet been appointed at the date of going to press (but see *Tirkey v Chandok* below). On 28 March 2017 the Government opened a consultation on caste discrimination. In July 2018, the indicated that it would not legislate but would rely on developments in case law instead.

A distinction is drawn between racial origin and citizenship: *Ealing London Borough Council v Race Relations Board* [1972] 1 All ER 105; *Tejani v Superintendent Registrar for the District of Peterborough* [1986] IRLR 502.

The House of Lords in *Mandla v Dowell Lee* [1983] IRLR 209, [1983] 1 All ER 1062 held that 'ethnic . . . origins' in the definition of 'racial group' meant a group which was a segment of the population distinguished from others by a sufficient combination of shared customs, beliefs, traditions and characteristics derived from a common or presumed common past, even if not drawn from what in biological terms was a common racial stock (see also *Para 2.39* of the *EHRC Code*). On that basis, it held that Sikhs were a racial group entitled to the protection of the *RRA 1976*. In *R (on the application of E) v Governing Body of JFS (Secretary of State for Children, School and Families, interested parties) (United Synagogue intervening)* [2009] UKSC 15, [2010] IRLR 136, SC, the Supreme Court, by a majority, determined that there was a discrete and "narrower sense" of discrimination on grounds of ethnic origin which applied to less favourable treatment on the ground of "lineage" or "descent". In the particular case a Jewish faith school applied an admission criterion that required that each pupil's mother should either be Jewish by birth or else have converted to Judaism under the auspices of an Orthodox synagogue. The application of the criterion was held to be an act of direct discrimination on grounds of ethnic origin.

In *Tirkey v Chandok* [2015] ICR 527, [2015] IRLR 195 EAT, the EAT upheld the refusal of an employment tribunal to strike out an argument that caste discrimination fell within the scope of race discrimination. Although not all caste discrimination would fall within the definition of race, the EAT considered (relying upon *JFS* above) that in some cases the link between descent and caste would be close enough to allow an argument that an act of discrimination was because of "ethnic or national origins".

The ECJ considered the meaning of "ethnic origin", which is used in the *Race Discrimination Framework Directive 200/43/EC* in *Jyske Finans A/S v Ligebhandlingsnaevnet* C-668/15; [2017] IRLR 665. The complainant alleged that he had been discriminated against by a Danish insurance company because it had asked him to provide more documentation that it would require from those born in EU or EEA member states before it would insure him. He had been born in Bosnia Herzegovina. In the UK this would be dealt with as a case of discrimination on grounds of national origins. However, the Directive does not prohibit discrimination on that specific ground. The ECJ determined that a person's country of birth could not justify a presumption that they were a member of a particular ethnic group. It might be one factor to be taken into account when assessing ethnicity which focused on "societal groups marked in particular by common nationality, religious faith, language, cultural and traditional origins and backgrounds."

Where 'racial group', is defined by 'colour' the group may comprise people of more than one ethnic origin (*Lambeth London Borough Council v Commission for Racial Equality* [1990] IRLR 231, [1990] ICR 768).

'National origins' means more than the legal nationality acquired at birth (*BBC Scotland v Souster* above). One may 'acquire' national origins by adherence. Whilst nationality is a protected characteristic, discrimination because of migrant domestic worker status is not discrimination because of nationality (*Onu v Akwiwu* [2016] UKSC 31, [2016] IRLR 719).

Jews are members of a racial group (see, for example, *Seide v Gillette Industries* [1980] IRLR 427). So are "gypsies" in the sense of those who belong to the Romany race, although mere habitual wanderers are not (*Commission for Racial Equality v Dutton* [1989] QB 783, [1989] IRLR 8). Rastafarians are not an ethnic group (*Crown Suppliers (Property Services Agency) v Dawkins* [1993] IRLR 284, [1993] ICR 517, CA). The Scots and the English are separate racial groups (*Northern Joint Police Board v Power* [1997] IRLR 610, EAT and *BBC Scotland v Souster* [2001] IRLR 150, Ct Sess).

In *Bradford Hospitals NHS Trust v Al-Shabib* [2003] IRLR 4, EAT, the tribunal decided that a grievance panel had treated the complainant less favourably on racial grounds when they formed an adverse impression of him as a result of his being 'difficult to control' and 'emotive'. The tribunal found that the respondent had erred by failing to take into account that, as an Iraqi, the complainant could not be expected to behave in a 'conventional Anglo-Saxon way'. However, the EAT found that it was not open to the tribunal to assume, in the absence of evidence, that there was a material difference in the manner in which 'Anglo-Saxons' and Iraqis might behave.

In *Simon v Brimham Associates* [1987] IRLR 307, [1987] ICR 596, the Court of Appeal reached the somewhat surprising conclusion that an employment tribunal was entitled to find that a Jew who had withdrawn a job application when he learned that to be Jewish might preclude his selection was not discriminated against in circumstances in which the interviewer had merely asked him the same question about his religion as he would have asked any candidate, not knowing whether or not he was Jewish.

Where an employee was dismissed for fighting, he was not dismissed on racial grounds merely because his employer applied a policy of not taking into account acts of provocation and thus ignored the fact that he had been provoked by acts of racial abuse and violence. The policy was applied consistently to employees of all races: *Sidhu v Aerospace Composite Technology Ltd* [2000] IRLR 602, [2001] ICR 167, CA.

The relevant race need not be the race of the employee that is the victim of the discrimination. For instance, in *Showboat Entertainment Centre v Owens* [1984] 1 All ER 836, [1984] IRLR 7, EAT a white employee was dismissed for refusing to carry out a discriminatory instruction. See the account of Associative Discrimination below at **12.27**.

In *Redfearn v Serco Ltd* [2006] EWCA Civ 659, [2006] IRLR 623, [2006] ICR 1367, the Court of Appeal refused to extend the approach taken in *Showboat* to a case in which a white bus driver whose passengers and colleagues were mainly Asian was dismissed, in essence, for being a member of the British National Party. It was a condition of membership of that party that one should be white. The employee contended that the race of his passengers and colleagues had substantially contributed to the decision to dismiss him. The Court of Appeal distinguished *Showboat* on the basis that whilst it was within the policy of *RRA 1976* that those affected by an employer's racist policies should be protected, it did not follow that racists should be protected from the anti-discriminatory policies of their employers. The Court of Appeal in *English v Thomas Sanderson Blinds Ltd* [2008] EWCA Civ 1421; [2009] ICR 543, [2009] IRLR 206 expressed doubts about whether *Redfearn* had been correctly decided but accepted that they were bound by it. Mr Redfearn subsequently brought proceedings in the European Court of Human Rights ([2013] IRLR 51). The Court did not focus on the question whether the dismissal had constituted an act of race discrimination. Instead it found that there had been a breach of his *Art 11* right to Freedom of Association. The Court considered that he should have had access to an unfair dismissal remedy without the need to serve a period of qualifying employment. The Government dealt with the ECtHR decision by amending *ERA 1996, s 108* to provide that a claim for unfair dismissal may be brought without the need for a qualifying period of service where the reason for dismissal "is or relates to the employee's political opinions or affiliation" (w.e.f. 25 June 2013, *ERRA 2013, s 13*).

12.21 *Meaning of 'because of gender reassignment'*

A transsexual person is defined by *EqA 2010, s 7(2)* to mean "a person who has the protected characteristic of gender reassignment". A person has the protected characteristic of gender reassignment if:

> "the person is proposing to undergo, is undergoing or has undergone a process (or part of a process) for the purpose of reassigning the person's sex by changing physiological or other attributes of sex" (*EqA 2010, s 7(1)*)

The *EHRC Code* emphasises that it is not necessary for an employee to have undergone any medical treatment before the protection is attracted (*Para 2.24*) – a proposal is sufficient. That is so, suggests the Code, even if the proposal is revoked (*Para 2.25*). Cross-dressing is covered only where "as part of the process of reassigning their sex, someone is driven by their gender identity to cross-dress" (*Para 2.26*).

In *Ashton v Chief Constable of West Mercia Constabulary* [2001] ICR 67, EAT considered a case concerning a transsexual undergoing a gender reassignment. As part of her treatment she received medication, which caused her to be depressed. Her depression affected her ability to work and she was dismissed on grounds of incapability. The EAT upheld the tribunal's finding that the fact that the incapability was a result of the side-effects of her medication did not establish a *causal* link between the dismissal and her sex and thus that she had not been unlawfully discriminated against.

In *A v Chief Constable of the West Yorkshire Police* [2002] EWCA Civ 1584, [2003] IRLR 32, [2003] ICR 161, the Court of Appeal considered that, for the purposes of employment law, post-operative transsexuals fall to be treated for all purposes as having their re-assigned sex. Thus, a post-operative male to female transsexual is to be treated as a woman rather than as a transsexual. The Court's reasoning was as follows: Post-operative male to female transsexuals are to be treated as women for the purposes of the European Convention on Human Rights (see *Goodwin v United Kingdom* [2002] IRLR 664). The *ETD 76/207/EEC* (since repealed and replaced by the *ETD 2006/54/EC*) had to be interpreted, so far as possible, as being compatible with the *ECHR*. *SDA 1975* (the predecessor of the *EqA 2010*), in turn, had to be interpreted, where possible, as being consistent with the *ETD 76/207/EEC*. However, the *Goodwin* case recognised that a departure from the normal rule may be required where 'significant factors of public interest . . .   weigh against the interests of the individual applicant in obtaining legal recognition of her gender reassignment'. The decision was affirmed by the House of Lords ([2004] UKHL 21, [2004] IRLR 573, [2004] ICR 806). The *Gender Recognition Act 2004* created a system of "gender recognition certificates". Anyone who holds a certificate must be treated according to their acquired gender.

The *EHRC Code* suggests that where a person has been diagnosed as having "Gender Dysphoria" or "Gender Identity Disorder" that may be an impairment within the meaning of the disability discrimination provisions of the *EqA 2010* (*Para 2.28*).

12.22 *Meaning of 'because of religion or belief'*

Meaning of 'belief'

"Belief" means any religious or philosophical belief and a reference to a belief includes a reference to a lack of belief (*EqA 2010, s 10(2)*).

A reference to a person who has a particular characteristic is a reference to a person of a particular religion or belief and a reference to persons who share a protected characteristic is a reference to persons who are of the same religion or belief (*EqA 2010, s 10(3)*). In *Gan Menachem Hendon Ltd v De Groen* UKEAT/0059/18 [2019] IRLR 410, the EAT applied *Lee v Ashers Baking Company Ltd* [2018] UKSC 49, [2018] IRLR 1116 and held that treatment is not because of religion or belief where it is because of the employer's belief and not the employee's belief (but see *IR v JQ* C-68/17 where a hospital run by the Catholic Church dismissed a doctor for re-marrying without having his first marriage annulled. The CJEU held that since the hospital employed doctors who were not catholic and did not require them to adhere to principle of lifelong marriage, there was no occupational requirement for the purposes of the *Framework Directive*. However, it is strongly arguable that it was the employer's belief that was the reason for the less favourable treatment).

Meaning of 'religion'

EqA 2010, s 10(1) defines "religion", with some circularity, to mean "any religion". It also provides that any reference to religion includes a reference to a lack of religion with the effect that an employer is no more free to discriminate against atheists than he is against Christians. No more detailed definition is given. This represents, it would appear, a deliberate decision on the part of the Government taken when the protection was first introduced by the now repealed *Employment Equality (Religion or Belief) Regulations 2003, SI 2003/1660 ("RBR 2003")*. The Government assumed that controversy about the scope of the definition will be rare and that in controversial cases it is best left to the courts and the tribunals to resolve the matter without further guidance.

It is tempting to suppose that it is the difficulty of defining 'religion' rather than the ease of doing so which has led the Government to avoid offering a more specific definition. The *EHRC Code* does not take matters very much further. It emphasises that a religion need not be "mainstream or well known". It does, however, have to have "a clear structure and belief system". Denominations or sects may be considered religions in their own right for the purposes of the *Act* (*EHRC Code, Para 2.54*)

Although not a matter which the *EHRC Code* touches upon, it is suggested that a religion will be concerned with the supernatural and, in particular, is likely to be theistic, ie it will be a belief about a god or gods.

The present context is not the only one in which this difficult definitional question has been faced and some assistance can be gained from consideration of those other contexts.

One context in which the issue has arisen is the law pertaining to charities. The advancement of religion is recognised as a charitable purpose (see *Income Tax Special Purposes Comr v Pemsel* [1891] AC 531, [1891–4] All ER Rep 28). In their decision of 17 November 1999 in relation to an application for charitable status made by the Church of Scientology, the Charity Commissioners reviewed the existing case law on the definition of religion and derived the following characteristics:

(i)   a belief in a god, deity or supreme being (*R v Registrar General, ex p Segerdal* [1970] 3 All ER 886 – though Buddhism qualified as a religion despite there being some doubt as to whether it required a belief in a supreme being);

(ii)   reverence and recognition of the dominant power and control of any entity or being outside their own body and life (*Segerdal* above); and

(iii)   faith and worship: faith in a god and worship of that god (*South Place Ethical Society* [1980] 3 All ER 918).

The Commissioners identified a further significant factor, absent from the express words of the *EqA 2010*; whilst the court will not consider the truth of the tenets of the relevant religion it will not treat as a religion everything which calls itself a religion. In practice the tribunal has adopted a similar approach. Because Charity Law is concerned with the 'advancement of religion', if the court is satisfied that the tenets of a particular sect 'inculcate doctrines adverse to very foundations of all religion and/or subversive of all morality' it will not be treated as 'advancing religion'. On its face the *EqA 2010* covers all religions whether or not they espouse morally repellent precepts. This is likely to lead to problems in which religious precepts conflict with the interests of other protected groups. As we shall see below, the tribunals have adapted Human Rights law to create a requirement that the belief at issue be "worthy of respect in a democratic society".

The *Segerdal* case upon which the Charity Commissioners placed reliance was given much less weight in *R (on the application of Hodkin) v Registrar of Births, Deaths and Marriages* [2013] UKSC 77, [2014] 1 All ER 737. The particular context of the decision was the proper interpretation of the Places of Worship Registration Act 1855. The issue was whether a chapel belonging to the Church of Scientology was a "place of worship". If it was then weddings could be performed there. The issue in turn prompted consideration of what was and was not a religion. Some guidance is given by Lord Toulson who seems to have felt that Lord Denning's approach in *Segerdal* was too narrowly theistic. Lord Toulson is careful to make clear that he is dealing with the particular legislation in issue and that he is not formulating a test, but his observations remain a helpful indication of the Supreme Court's likely approach to the definitional issue:

> "I would describe religion in summary as a spiritual or nonsecular belief system, held by a group of adherents, which claims to explain mankind's place in the universe and relationship with the infinite, and to teach its adherents how they are to live their lives in conformity with the spiritual understanding associated with the belief system. By spiritual or nonsecular I mean a belief system which goes beyond that which can be perceived by the senses or ascertained by the application of science. I prefer not to use the word "supernatural" to express this element, because it is a loaded word which can carry a variety of connotations. Such a belief system may or may not involve belief in a supreme being, but it does involve a belief that there is more to be understood about mankind's nature and relationship to the universe and can be gained from the senses or from science. I emphasise that this is intended to be description and not a definitive formula."

Another context in which the definition of religion arises as an issue is the *European Convention on Human Rights*. This second context has a more direct relevance because the *EqA 2010* implements a European Directive and European legislation has to be interpreted, wherever possible, so as to be compatible with the *European Convention on Human Rights*. *ECHR, art 9(1)* provides that 'everyone has the right to freedom of thought, conscience and religion'. The right also includes 'freedom to change . . . religion or belief . . . and freedom, either alone or in community with others and in public or in private, to manifest [one's] religion or belief, in worship, teaching, practice and observance'. However, whilst it might be hoped that a developed body of authority of the European Court of Human RIghts would be available to assist in interpreting the scope of the words 'religion or belief', in fact there is remarkably little helpful case law. The Commission has assumed that Scientology is a religion (*X and Church of Scientology v Sweden* (1979) 16 DR 68). The court decided that 'Wicca' was not a religion on the ground that it had no clear structure or belief systems (*X v United Kingdom* (1977) 11 DR 55) (but note Wicca appeared as an example of a religion in the *ACAS Code* issued to assist with the interpretation of the *RBR 2003*).

The *EHRC Code* lists (at *Para 2.53*) a number of what it describes as "commonly recognised religions": the Baha'i faith, Buddhism, Christianity, Hinduism, Islam, Jainism, Judaism, Rastafarianism, Sikhism and Zoroastrianism. However, the *EHRC Code* also stresses that a religion does not have to be "mainstream" or "well-known" and that "sects" and "denominations" may also be affected (*Para 2.54*).

Meaning of 'religious belief'

Religious belief is defined as follows:

> 'any religious . . . belief and a reference to belief includes a reference to a lack of belief'

(EqA 2010, s 10(2))

The Act distinguishes, therefore, between religion and religious belief. The distinction arises from the fact that religious beliefs are not exclusively about a god or gods. Most religions profoundly affect what might be described as one's 'world view'. In other words, religious adherence affects what one believes about the world as well as what one believes about the supernatural (but see *R (on the application of Williamson) v Secretary of State for Education and Employment* [2001] EWHC 860 (Admin), [2002] 1 FLR 493, [2001] All ER (D) 405 (Nov) where Elias J opined that a religious belief, for the purposes of the *ECHR* was not simply a belief which is 'in accordance with the religious faith' but which 'embod(ied) or define(d)' the belief or conviction itself). When *Williamson* came before the House of Lords, their Lordships felt it unnecessary to explore the definitional question as the *ECHR*, like *EqA 2010*, protects both religious and non-religious beliefs: [2005] 2 All ER 1).

In *Eweida v British Airways* [2009] ICR 303, [2009] IRLR 78 (affd without considering this issue in [2010] EWCA Civ 80, [2010] IRLR 322, [2010] ICR 890), the EAT decided that a belief could qualify as a religious belief even if it was unique to the employee (ie no-one else shared the same belief) and without it being a mandatory requirement of an established religion.

In *Eweida*, the belief at issue was the visible wearing of a crucifix. In *Azmi v Kirklees MBC* [2007] IRLR 484, [2007] ICR 1154, the belief was that of certain Muslims that Muslim women should only be in the presence of unrelated males when they are veiled. These are both examples of religious beliefs that deal not with whether there is a deity but how an adherent is expected to behave. A difficult question can arise as to whether the conduct that the employer is seeking to prevent should be treated as a religious belief or a "manifestation" of that belief. The latter concept is to be found in the *European Convention on Human Rights* (at *Art 9(2)*) and is dealt with separately below.

In refusing permission to appeal in the case of *Macfarlane v Relate Avon*, Lord Justice Laws touched upon a further distinction. The law, he said, protects "the right to hold and express a belief" but does not protect "that belief's substance" ([2010] EWCA Civ B1, [2010] IRLR 872). A similar position was adopted by the EAT in *Eweida* (above).

A belief in the sacrosanctity of Christian marriage was held to be a religious belief in *Pendleton v Derbyshire County Council* UKEAT/0238/15, [2016] IRLR 580.

In order to be protected, the belief must be genuine. That is a question of fact for the Employment Tribunal to determine. It is, however, a limited enquiry. The tribunal should look at whether the belief is asserted in good faith or whether it is an artifice (see *Gareddu v London Underground Limited* UKEAT/0086/16; [2017] IRLR 404; *R (on the application of Williamson) v Secretary of State for Education and Employment* [2005] UKHL 15, [2005] 2 AC 246, HL)

Meaning of 'philosophical belief'

Philosophical belief is defined as follows:

> 'any . . . philosophical belief and a reference to belief includes a reference to a lack of belief'

(EqA 2010, s 10(2))

As originally enacted *RBR 2003* protected those who held philosophical beliefs which could be said to be 'similar' to religious beliefs. The question how one identified a 'philosophical belief' which was sufficiently 'similar' to a religious belief as to fall within the scope of the legislation was harder to answer the more closely it was considered. Perhaps the defining characteristic of a religious belief is its theistic nature; it is a belief in a god or gods. If the belief is theistic it is a religious belief. If it is not, it is difficult to see how it could be said to be in any way 'similar' because the defining characteristic is absent.

An alternative approach was to assume that the similarity with which the legislation was concerned arose not from the essence of the belief but rather its ancillary characteristics. This would seem to be the approach adopted in the *ACAS Code* which stressed the likely importance of there being a 'clear belief system' and the belief being one which is 'profound' and which affects the adherent's 'way of life or view of the world'. The *ACAS Code* offered Humanism as an example of the sort of belief that might qualify. Other examples would include Confucianism and some commentators have even suggested that Vegetarianism might qualify.

With effect from 30 April 2007, *RBR 2003, reg 2(1)* was amended. The requirement that the philosophical belief be 'similar' to a religious belief was removed. Under *EqA 2010* simply holding a particular philosophical belief (or equally, not holding it) will suffice. The logical consequence of the present formulation might be thought to be that holding a belief that is philosophical but not similar to a religious belief will qualify for protection. However, in *Nicholson v Grainger plc* [2010] IRLR 4, [2010] ICR 360, EAT and *Gray v Mulberry Company (Design) Ltd* UKEAT/40/17 [2018] IRLR 893, [2019] ICR 175, EAT (upheld on other grounds by the Court of Appeal: [2019] EWCA Civ 2720, [2020] IRLR 29), the need for similarity was thought to be implicit in the amended provision. In Gray, the approach taken was that a philosophical belief would be treated as being "similar" to a religious belief it met certain threshold criteria. The relevant criteria are those set out in *McClintock v Department of Constitutional Affairs* [2008] IRLR 29 and further refined in Grainger and are described immediately below.

In *McClintock*, the EAT gave the following guidance:

> 'The test for determining whether views can properly be considered to fall into the category of a philosophical belief is whether they have sufficient cogency, seriousness, cohesion and importance and are worthy of respect in a democratic society: see *Campbell & Cosans v United Kingdom* [1982] 4 EHRR 293.'

McClintock was applied by the Employment Appeal Tribunal in *Nicholson v Grainger plc* [2010] IRLR 4, [2010] ICR 360, EAT, which upheld a finding by the Employment Tribunal that a belief in man-made climate change was capable of amounting to a philosophical belief for the purposes of the regulations. In addition to the matters specifically identified as relevant in the quotation from *McClintock* above, the Appeal Tribunal emphasised that the belief must be genuinely held and that it must not (as was the case in *McClintock*) be merely an opinion or viewpoint based on the present state of information available. It had also to be a belief as to a weighty and substantial aspect of human life and behaviour. The Appeal Tribunal rejected four proposed limitations on the types of beliefs that would qualify for protection, finding: (1) the belief does not need to be shared by anyone else; (2) it need not form part of a "fully-fledged system of thought"; (3) it may be a political belief so long as it otherwise qualifies and (4) a philosophical belief based upon science may qualify. Some refinements of the factors identified in *Nicholson* were suggested in *Harron v Chief Constable of Dorset Police* UKEAT/0234/15, [2016] IRLR 481: the reference to the need for a belief to be about a "substantial aspect of human life" is intended to exclude only beliefs about trivial aspects; and the requirement for the belief to be "coherent" requires only that it should be intelligible and capable of being understood. In *Gray* (above) the belief did not qualify because it lacked the necessary "cohesion". Rather than look at the belief in the abstract, the EAT suggested that cohesion needed to be analysed by reference to how the belief is manifested. If the belief is expressed inconsistently or not at all by the complainant, that would go to the question whether the belief was sufficiently cohesive or coherent. That would seem to replace a test of intelligibility with one of personal dedication.

In *Hashman v Orchard Park Garden Centre* [2011] EqLR 426 the Tribunal concluded that a belief in the sanctity of life and, more specifically, beliefs that fox-hunting and hare-coursing were incompatible with the sanctity of life were each beliefs qualifying for protection. The EAT dismissed an appeal on the basis that it had no reasonable prospect of success. In *Henderson v GMB* [2016] EWCA Civ 1049, [2017] IRLR 340, a tribunal had accepted that "left wing democratic socialism" was a qualifying belief. That finding went unchallenged before the EAT and subsequently the Court of Appeal, where the complainant lost on other grounds.

As an example of a belief that would not qualify the *EHRC Code* suggests a belief in a philosophy of racial superiority for a particular racial group. Such a belief would, it is suggested, be incompatible with human dignity and conflicts with the fundamental rights of others.

Philosophical beliefs are no less stringently protected than religious beliefs (*Henderson v GMB* above).

Manifesting a religious belief

The European Convention on Human Rights protects the manifestation of one's religion or beliefs at *Art 9(2)*:

> "Freedom to manifest one's religion or beliefs shall be subject only to such limitations as are prescribed by law and are necessary in a democratic society in the interests of public safety, for the protection of public order, health or morals, or for the protection of the rights and freedoms of others."

The Charter of Fundamental Rights of the European Union also protects manifestation of religion (at *Art 10(1)*). The ECJ has held that the since the *Framework Directive 2000/78* makes reference to the ECHR in its recitals and should be interpreted so as to be consistent with the Convention and the Charter, the Directive should also be taken to prohibit discrimination because of manifestation of religion (*Achbita v G4S Secure Solutions NV* Case C-157/15), [2017] IRLR 466, [2018] ICR 102).

The *EqA 2010* does not provide express protection for manifestation, although it must, of course, be interpreted so as to be consistent with the *Framework Directive* and therefore undoubtedly does. Before *Achbita*, the distinction between holding a belief and manifesting it had, however, arisen in the domestic law. It is a distinction which is expressly spelt out in the EHRC Code (at Paras 2.60 and 2.61). In *McConkey v Simon Community Northern Ireland* [2009] UKHL 24, [2009] IRLR 757, [2009] ICR 787, Lord Simon said in relation to the *Fair Employment and Treatment (Northern Ireland) Order 1998, (SI 1998/3162)*:

> ' . . . [T]he Order is concerned with discrimination against someone on the basis of the religious belief or political opinion that he holds. It is not concerned with discrimination on the ground of actions that the person may take in support of that religious belief or political opinion'

Insofar as *McConkey* might be thought to mean that manifestation of belief falls outside the scope of *EqA 2010*, that cannot be right in the light of the ECtHR's decision in four joined cases: *Eweida and others v United Kingdom* 48420/10, 59842/10, 51671/10 and 36516/10 and *Achbita*, above. In two of the cases (*Eweida* and *Chaplin*), the complainants were challenging policies that precluded them from wearing crucifixes over their work clothes. In *Eweida* the reason for the policy (which was later abolished) was the employer's corporate image. The European Court of Human Rights concluded that wearing a religious symbol was a manifestation of religious belief. Departing from the trend of earlier authority, the Court decided that the freedom was not protected merely by the fact that the complainant could obtain work with another employer with a less restrictive policy (though that was a factor that could be taken into account in determining whether the restriction to which she objected was a proportionate interference with her right). The Court took the view that concern about corporate image was an inadequate basis for restricting Ms Eweida's rights and found that the UK had failed to provide proper protection for them. This led to inaccurate press comment to the effect that there was now a "right" to wear a cross to work. In *Chaplin* however, the complainant's case was rejected. Her employer forbade the wearing of a cross on a necklace because it created health and safety concerns. The Court felt that that provided a defensible basis for restricting her right. The other two cases concerned employees whose religious beliefs meant that they did not wish to provide services to same sex couples. In *Ladele* a registrar of births, deaths and marriages did not wish to perform civil partnership ceremonies. In *Macfarlane* a Relate counsellor's employer concluded that he was not genuinely prepared to provide psychosexual counselling to same sex couples. In each case colleagues objected to the complainant's apparent unwillingness to comply with the employer's equality policies. Both complainants were unsuccessful in the domestic courts. The European Court of Human Rights recognised that the situation gave rise to a necessary balancing of interests and concluded that the United Kingdom had been within the margin of appreciation available to it in fixing the balance in the manner in which it had.

Achbita was concerned with an employer's policy that forbade the wearing of any signs of political, philosophical or religious beliefs by any customer-facing staff. Ms Achbita wanted to wear an Islamic headscarf whilst working on reception. She was dismissed. Since the policy was applied to all employees whatever their belief (or lack of belief), the ECJ determined that there was no direct discrimination. That suggests that a specific policy of forbidding, say, the niqab, might be taken to amount to direct discrimination and calls the decision in *Azmi*, above, into question. The ECJ also considered indirect discrimination arguments and decided that wanting to project neutrality in matters of belief to clients was a legitimate aim and, provided the policy was applied consistently and limited to customer-facing staff, it was likely justified.

As the express words of *Art 9(2)* make clear and the result in the *Chaplin* case demonstrates, the right to manifest one's religion is not limitless. That raises a difficult question: if an employee complains that they have been treated less favourably because they have manifested their religion, how is *Art 9(2)* to be reconciled with the fact that direct discrimination cannot be justified? *Wasteney East London NHS Foundation Trust* UKEAT/0157/15, [2016] IRLR 388, [2016] ICR 643 suggests that the answer is, in practice, likely to be by narrowly defining what the reason for the less favourable treatment is. In *Wasteney* itself, the complainant was alleged to have been trying to convert a junior Muslim colleague to Christianity. Proselytisation is a manifestation of religion. However, the Appeal Tribunal decided that because the complainant's behaviour had been unwelcome and she had been senior to the colleague she had been trying to convert, the manner of the manifestation was inappropriate and it was that inappropriateness that had been the real reason for the complainant being disciplined. In *Kuteh v Dartford and Gravesham NHS Trust* [2019] EWCA Civ 818, [2019] IRLR 716, the Court of Appeal drew from the ECtHR decision in *Kokkinakis v Greece* [1993] ECHR 14307/88, [1993] 17 EHRR 397, a distinction between manifestation and "improper proselytization". In *Kuteh* (an unfair dismissal case), the employee had been warned not to preach to patients, assured her employer that she would not, but then did so anyway.

In *Bougnaoui v Micropole SA* Case C-188/15; [2017] IRLR 447, [2018] ICR 139, an employee was dismissed when a client asked that she should not wear an Islamic headscarf when working at their premises and, when pressed by her employer, she refused to agree not to wear one. The ECJ assumed for the purposes of argument that it might be shown that she was being treated less favourably because she was manifesting her religion. They considered whether, in the circumstances, it might be said that there was a "genuine and determining occupational requirement" within *2000/78, Art 4(1)* and decided that there was nothing about the job itself which objectively required her not to wear the headscarf. A subjective desire on the employer's part to comply with the wishes of the client would not establish the defence.

12.23 *Meaning of 'because of sexual orientation'*

EqA 2010, s 12(1) provides that sexual orientation means a person's sexual orientation towards:

(a)   "persons of the same sex" (ie gay men or lesbians);

(b)   "persons of the opposite sex" (ie heterosexuals); or

(c)   "persons of either sex" (ie bisexual persons).

No definition is given of 'sexual orientation' *per se*. The *Oxford English Dictionary* defines 'orientation' as 'the state of being oriented', 'a person's attitude or adjustment in relation to circumstances'. It follows that there is no requirement that a person be sexually active in order to be regarded as being of a particular sexual orientation. The *EHRC Code* says that "sexual orientation relates to how people feel as well as their actions". *(Para 2.65).*

The *EqA 2010* does not cover asexuals or sexual orientation towards anything other than persons (eg bestiality), nor do they cover (regardless of orientation) sexual conduct or particular sexual preferences (eg sadomasochism, paedophilia, etc) or the absence of such conduct (eg celibacy).

Before the enactment of a specific protection, there were a number of attempts made to establish that sexual orientation discrimination was a species of sex discrimination. However, the House of Lords ultimately determined that it is not an act of sex discrimination to treat an employee less favourably on grounds of their sexual orientation (*MacDonald v Advocate General for Scotland* [2003] UKHL 34, [2004] 1 All ER 339, [2003] IRLR 512, [2003] ICR 937).

However, if an employer were to treat gay men less favourably than lesbian women (or vice versa), that would constitute sex discrimination on ordinary principles.

A reference to a person who has a particular protected characteristic is a reference to a person who is of a particular sexual orientation and a reference to persons who share a protected characteristic is a reference to persons who are of the same sexual orientation (*EqA 2010, s 12(2)*). Nevertheless, where an employee who was known to be heterosexual was subjected to innuendo that he was gay, he was harassed 'on the grounds of sexual orientation' (see *English v Thomas Sanderson Blinds Ltd* [2008] EWCA Civ 1421; [2009] ICR 543, [2009] IRLR 206).

12.24 *Meaning of 'because of pregnancy or maternity leave'*

For the purposes of *EqA 2010*, the protected characteristics are "pregnancy" and "maternity". Curiously, the Act omits to include a more detailed definition of the protected characteristic even though it has done so in respect of each of the others. In *Sahota v Home Office and another* [2010] ICR 772, the EAT opined that IVF treatment should be treated as equivalent to pregnancy only between the points in time at which follicular puncture and transfer of the embryo occurred. Commissioning a surrogate to have a child does not give an entitlement to maternity leave or fall within the scope of the protections against pregnancy or sex discrimination (*CD v ST* C-167/12 CJEU; [2014] 3 CMLR 272; [2014] IRLR 551; [2014] ICR D26).

EqA 2010, s 18(2)(b) ensures that a woman is protected against unfavourable treatment because of a pregnancy-related illness. It is unclear whether less favourable treatment because of a pregnancy-related illness would fall within *EqA 2010, s 13* as well and thus provide the basis for an allegation of direct discrimination. In the absence of clarification, the safest course would be to assume that it does.

The absence of more detailed definition of "maternity" is troubling as, on its face, "maternity" discrimination might be thought to have a broader scope than "maternity leave" discrimination (which is what was prohibited under the predecessor provisions in the *SDA 1975*). However, *EqA 2010, s 18*, though headed "Pregnancy and Maternity Discrimination: Work Cases", only prohibits discrimination because of compulsory maternity leave or because the employee exercises, has exercised or seeks to exercise her right to take ordinary or additional maternity leave. Whilst this may indicate that the protection against direct discrimination on grounds of maternity conferred by *EqA 2010, s 13* is intended to have a similarly limited scope, the question remains an open one until it has been considered by the courts.

12.25 *Meaning of 'because of age'*

For the purposes of *EqA 2010*, the protected characteristic is "age", a reference to a person having a particular protected characteristic is a reference to a person of a particular "age group" and an "age group" is defined as a "group of persons defined by reference to age, whether by reference to a particular age or to a range of ages" (*EqA 2010, s 5*).

In *Wooster v Mayor and Burgesses of the London Borough of Tower Hamlets* [2009] IRLR 980, the EAT upheld a tribunal finding that a local authority treated a 48-year-old employee less favourably on the grounds of his age by refusing to redeploy him where the consequence of doing so would have been to avoid having to pay him an early retirement pension to which he would become entitled once he reached the age of 50. (Such treatment may be justified in certain circumstances: see *Woodcock v Cumbria Primary Care Trust* [2012] EWCA Civ 330, [2012] IRLR 491 and DISCRIMINATION AND EQUAL OPPORTUNITIES – II (13).)

12.26 *Meaning of 'because of disability'*

EqA 2010 s 6(1) provides:

"A person (P) has a disability if–

(a)   P has a physical or mental impairment, and

(b)   the impairment has a substantial and long-term adverse effect on P's ability to carry out normal day-to-day-activities,"

The elements of the test are then further defined by *EqA 2010, Sch 1 Part 1*. That schedule substantially reproduces the former *DDA 1995, Sch 1* save that the former *paragraph 4(1)* is not reproduced so that the complainant does not have to show that one of the attributes formerly listed in that paragraph (ie mobility, manual dexterity, physical co-ordination, continence, the ability to lift, carry or otherwise move everyday objects; speech hearing or eyesight; memory or ability to concentrate, learn or understand; or perception of the risk of physical danger) is adversely affected. The exclusion of *paragraph 4(1)* makes the test a little less complicated to apply and arguably effects a modest broadening of its scope.

Guidance has been issued by the Secretary of State which applies to any case based upon a discriminatory act occurring (or, in the case of a continuing act, commencing) on or after 1 May 2011 (*Equality Act (Guidance on the Definition of Disability) Appointed Day Order 2011, SI 2011/1159*). The tribunal must take the guidance into account (*EqA 2010, Sch 1, Part 1, Para 12*). Advice as to how to take the guidance into account was given by the EAT in *Taylor v Ladbrokes Betting and Gaming Ltd* UKEAT/0353/15, [2017] IRLR 312:

"Tribunals should start with the statutory language, consider the guidance and decide, having looked at both, what the statute means, concentrating primarily on the language of the statutory provision itself."

The EAT in *Goodwin v Patent Office* [1999] IRLR 4 laid down detailed guidance as to the approach to be taken by employment tribunals in determining whether or not a claimant is disabled. Readers should refer to this case for the full details of the EAT's guidance. In summary, the EAT held that in determining whether or not a claimant is disabled, the tribunal should look carefully at what the parties have said in the pleadings and clarify the issues, in most cases after standard directions to this effect or at a directions hearing; they should take a purposive approach to the construction of the legislative protections; they should refer expressly to any relevant provisions of the Guidance which have been taken into account (see below); in determining whether or not an impairment has an adverse effect on a person's ability to carry out activities, they should bear in mind that the fact that a person can, with difficulty or great effort, carry out these activities does not mean that his ability to carry them out has not been impaired; they should bear in mind that disabled persons are likely to play down the effect that a disability has on their activities; in determining what is a day-to-day activity, the tribunal's inquiry should not focus only on a particular or a special set of circumstances such as activities carried on in the home; in determining whether an adverse effect is substantial the tribunal may, where the claimant still claims to be suffering from the same degree of impairment as at the time of the events complained of, take into account how the claimant appears to the tribunal to 'manage' his condition; where a claimant is or had been on medication, the tribunal should, in determining whether there is an adverse effect, examine how the claimant's abilities were affected whilst on medication and how those activities would have been affected without the medication; and when addressing each of the conditions under *EqA 2010, s 6(1)*, namely the 'impairment' condition, the 'adverse effect' condition, the 'substantial' condition and the 'long-term' condition, the tribunal should be careful not to lose sight of the overall picture.

The definition of disability used in *EqA 2010* must, of course, be read, so far as possible, as to be compatible with the *Framework Directive 2000/78/EC*. The Directive does not specifically define "disability". However, in *HK Danmark*, acting on behalf of *Ring v Dansk Almennyttigt Boligselskab* C-335/11: [2013] IRLR 571; [2014] ICR 851, the CJEU held that the *Framework Directive* had to be read, so far as possible, as to be compatible with the *United Nations Convention on the Rights of Persons with Disabilities*. The *Convention* contains the following definition at *Art 1*:

> "Persons with disabilities include those who have long-term physical, mental, intellectual or sensory impairments which in interaction with various barriers may hinder their full and effective participation in society on an equal basis with others".

The net effect is that the domestic provisions have to be read in the light of the Convention definition (confirmed in *Banaszczyk v Booker Ltd* UK/EAT/0132/15 [2016] IRLR 273).

In *Fag og Arbejde, acting on behalf of Kaltoft v Kommunernes Landsforening, acting on behalf of the Municipality of Bullund* C-354/13: [2015] IRLR 146, [2015] ICR 322, ECJ, the European Court of Justice determined, invoking the *Convention* test, that obesity may constitute a disability where it "hindered [a worker's] full and effective participation in professional life on an equal basis with other workers on account of reduced mobility or the onset, in that person, of medical conditions preventing him from carrying out his work or causing discomfort when carrying out his professional activity." Infertility does not, in contrast, meet the *Convention* test. In *Z v A Government Department* C-363/12: [2014] IRLR 563, the ECJ decided that a failure to grant maternity leave to the commissioning mother in a surrogacy arrangement did not amount to disability discrimination as "the inability to have a child by conventional means does not in itself, in principle, prevent the commissioning mother from having access to, participating in or advancing in employment".

Impairments

The *Guidance* deals with the definition of impairment at *Paras A3–A8*. It suggests that the terms should be given their "ordinary meanings". An impairment does not have to be the result of an illness, nor does the cause of an impairment have to be established, provided the tribunal is satisfied that it exists. According to the guidance (at *Para A7*), there is no need to consider the cause even if the likely cause is a condition which is excluded from the protective scope of the *Act*. So, for example, addiction to alcohol is deemed not to be an impairment (see below) but illnesses caused by alcohol addiction may cause other impairments which do fall within the scope of the protected characteristic. The Guidance provides that rather than focussing on the cause of the impairment, the focus should instead be on the effects of impairment on the person's ability to carry out normal day to day activities (*Para A4*).

In *College of Ripon and York St John v Hobbs* [2002] IRLR 185, the EAT held that the task of ascertaining whether there is a physical impairment did not involve drawing any rigid distinctions between an underlying fault or defect in the body on the one hand, and evidence of the manifestations or effects of that fault or defect on the other. Thus, an impairment can be something that consists simply of the effects of an illness as opposed to the illness itself. In that case, there was clear evidence that there was something physically wrong with the claimant's body. However, there was no conclusive medical evidence as to the precise cause. Notwithstanding this lacuna in the evidence, the EAT held that it was open to the tribunal to find that there was a physical impairment simply on the basis of the evidence that there was something wrong with the claimant physically (see also *Rugamer v Sony Music Entertainment UK Ltd* [2002] ICR 381, [2001] IRLR 644 and *Ministry of Defence v Hay* [2008] IRLR 928, [2008] ICR 1247). This rather relaxed approach to ascertaining a physical impairment is to be contrasted with the more rigid approach recommended in cases of mental impairment. In *Morgan v Staffordshire University* [2002] IRLR 190, the EAT held (no doubt to the relief of employers faced with a barrage of medical certificates merely citing 'stress' or 'anxiety' as the reason for absence) that the occasional use of terms such as 'anxiety', 'stress' or 'depression' even by GPs will not amount to proof of a mental impairment (See also *J v DLA Piper UK LLP* [2010] IRLR 936, EAT and *Igweike v TSB Banks plc* UKEAT/0119/19 [2020] IRLR 267). In particular, it was held that the occasional mention in medical notes of or reference in the World Health Organisation's International Classification of Diseases to such terms would not be sufficient in the absence of informed medical evidence that said more. The EAT in that case also provided some detailed guidance for those seeking to establish a mental impairment. Readers are referred to the report of the *Morgan* case for the full details. In essence, however, the guidance reiterates the importance of expert medical evidence in this area. Both the *College of Ripon* and *Morgan* cases were noted with approval by the Court of Appeal in *McNicol* (see above). (See also *De Keyser Ltd v Wilson* [2001] IRLR 324.) However, readers should also refer to the decision of *Dunham v Ashford Windows* [2005] ICR 1584, [2005] IRLR 608, in which the EAT held that a person might have a mental impairment (such as learning difficulties) which did not amount to a mental illness. The Guidance supports this distinction between a mental impairment and mental illness (*Para A5*). Where there is dispute between the parties as to whether or not the employee has an impairment, or as to the nature of that impairment, the employer is entitled to adduce expert evidence to disprove the existence of such an impairment: *Hospice of St Mary of Furness v Howard* [2007] IRLR 944.

In *Igweike* (above), the Employment Appeal Tribunal drew a distinction between the normal reaction to an adverse and tragic life event and an impairment. Someone whose concentration is adversely affected by grief may not have an impairment, although someone grieving could have that grief develop into a mental impairment.

It may not always be possible, nor is it necessary, to categorise a condition as either a physical or mental impairment (*Guidance Para A6*). It is sufficient that an impairment can be established.

There was formerly a requirement that a mental illness had to be a "clinically well-recognised illness" before it could be a mental impairment but that requirement was repealed as from 5 December 2005 (*DDA 2005, s 18(2)*).

Certain things are deemed by the *Equality Act 2010 (Disability) Regulations 2010 (SI 2010/2128)* not to amount to impairments:

(a)   Addiction to alcohol, nicotine or any other substance (*Reg 3(1)*) unless the addiction was originally the result of administration of medically prescribed drugs or other medical treatment (*Reg 3(2)*);

(b)   A tendency to: set fires; steal; physical or sexual abuse of other persons; exhibitionism; and voyeurism (*Reg 4(1)*);

(c)   Seasonal allergic rhinitis (or "hayfever") unless it aggravates the effect of any other condition (*Reg 4(2)* and *(3)*).

An employee may have a condition (eg a depressive illness) that does amount to a disability in its own right but which was caused by an excluded condition, (eg addiction to alcohol). The EAT has confirmed that an employee in these circumstances would be disabled notwithstanding the link with the excluded condition because it is not relevant to consider the cause of a particular disability (*Power v Panasonic (UK) Ltd* [2003] IRLR 151). Conversely, a person might have an excluded condition that is caused by or is a manifestation of an impairment that falls within the scope of *EqA 2010* (See *Edmund Nuttall Ltd v Butterfield* [2005] IRLR 751, where the excluded condition – in that case, exhibitionism – was caused by depression).

Adverse effect

Under the old law, an impairment was *only* to be taken to affect the ability to carry out normal day-to-day activities if it affected one of the following:

(a)   mobility;

(b)   manual dexterity;

(c)   physical co-ordination;

(d)   continence;

(e)   the ability to lift, carry or otherwise move everyday objects;

(f)   speech, hearing or eyesight;

(g)   memory or ability to concentrate, learn or understand; or

(h)   perception of the risk of physical danger.

(*DDA 1995, Sch 1 para 4(1)*)

The list set out above was not reproduced in the *EqA 2010*. The nearest one comes to such a list is to be found in the *Appendix* to the *Guidance*. There one finds two lists. The first is entitled "An illustrative and non-exhaustive list of factors which, if they are experienced by a person, it would be reasonable to regard as having a substantial adverse effect on normal day to day activities". There is a second list, equally extravagantly entitled, which focuses on factors that it would not be reasonable to regard as having the necessary substantial adverse effect. The examples are too numerous to list here. The first example included in the first list is "difficulty in getting dressed, for example, because of physical restrictions, a lack of understanding of the concept, or low motivation". The first example included in the second list is "inability to move heavy objects without assistance or mechanical aid, such as moving a large suitcase or heavy piece of furniture without a trolley". The *Guidance* stresses that the examples are indicators and not tests.

Substantial adverse effects

An effect is substantial if it is more than minor or trivial (*EqA 2010, s 212(1)* and *Guidance, Para B1*). Unless a matter can be classified as falling within the heading "trivial" or "insubstantial", it must be treated as substantial (*Aderemi v London and South Eastern Railway Ltd* [2013] ICR 591, [2013] All ER (D) 201 (Feb), EAT).

In assessing the effect, the Guidance suggests that the following should be looked at: the time taken to carry out an activity, the way it is carried out; and the cumulative effects of the impairment (*Guidance, Paras B2–B5*). The tribunal should also consider the extent to which a person could reasonably be expected to modify his or her behaviour by, for example, use of a coping or avoidance strategy (*Guidance, Para B7*).

Para B11 of the *Guidance* stresses the importance of keeping in mind the fact that environmental conditions may exacerbate or lessen the effect of an impairment.

The EAT in the case of *Leonard v Southern Derbyshire Chamber of Commerce* [2001] IRLR 19 emphasised that when considering whether an impairment had a substantial adverse effect on the ability to carry out normal day-to-day activities, the tribunal must concentrate on what the claimant cannot do or can only do with difficulty. An approach that looks mainly to what the applicant can do may lead to the erroneous conclusion that because the claimant can still do many things, the adverse effect cannot be substantial. This approach was supported by the EAT in *Paterson v Metropolitan Police Comr* [2007] IRLR 763, [2007] ICR 1522 where it held that, when assessing whether the effect of an impairment is 'substantial', the comparison to be made is between the way in which the individual in fact carried out the activity in question and the way he would have carried it out if not impaired. The mere fact that an employee can perform the duties of his job does not necessarily mean that he is not disabled. (See *Law Hospital NHS Trust v Rush* [2001] IRLR 611 and *Ekpe v Metropolitan Police Comr* [2001] IRLR 605.) In *Cruickshank v VAW Motorcast Ltd* [2002] IRLR 24, the EAT considered the position of an employee whose impairment (an asthmatic complaint) was such that he only appeared to suffer substantial adverse effects whilst present at the workplace. The employment tribunal had held that the employee was not a disabled person because it could not be said that there was an adverse effect on his normal day-to-day activities. The EAT disagreed and held that the tribunal had been wrong to confine its analysis to the claimant's activities outside of the work environment. (See *Chief Constable of Dumfries & Galloway Constabulary v Adams* [2009] ICR 1034, [2009] IRLR 612, where the EAT confirmed that an activity undertaken in the course of employment would be a normal day-to-day activity if it was common to different types of employment.) In general terms, the principle that normal day-to-day activities are not to be determined only on the basis of a particular environment must be correct. However, where there is evidence that an employee only suffers substantial adverse effects when in a particular work environment (in the form, say, of a severe allergic reaction to the carpets in a particular office) and nowhere else, it might still be possible to argue that there was no substantial adverse effect on normal day-to-day activities or that the effects were not long term. The better approach in these circumstances (as suggested by the EAT in *Cruickshank*) would be to consider whether any reasonable adjustments could be made rather than attempting to argue that there is no disability.

Where two impairments are relied upon, neither of which on its own would satisfy the substantial adverse effect requirement under *DDA*, account should be taken of whether the impairments together have a substantial overall effect on the person's ability to carry out normal day-to-day activities. (See *Ginn v Tesco Stores Ltd* [2005] All ER (D) 259 (Oct), applied in *Patel v Oldham Metropolitan Borough Council* [2010] IRLR 280, which addressed the question whether an impairment that had developed from an initial impairment could be aggregated with the original to determine whether the longevity requirement was satisfied.)

Long-term effects

By EqA 2010, Sch 1, para 2:

"(1) The effect of an impairment is long-term if –

(a)   it has lasted for at least 12 months,

(b)   it is likely to last for at least 12 months, or

(c)   it is likely to last for the rest of the life of the person affected."

Because the employee has to be a disabled person at the time at which the alleged discrimination occurs, the tribunal must ask whether the effect of the impairment had lasted 12 months by that date, or, if not, whether at that date it was likely that it would (*Tesco Stores Ltd v Tennant* UKEAT/0167/19 [2020] IRLR 363).

Even if an impairment ceases to have substantial adverse effect on the employee's ability to carry out normal day-to-day activities, it is treated as continuing to have that effect if it is likely to recur (*EqA 2010, Sch 1, para 2(2)*). The cumulative effect of related impairments should be taken into account (*Guidance, Para C2*). In assessing whether an effect is "likely" to last for the periods identified in *EqA 2010, Sch 1, para 2(1)(b)* and *(c)* above the tribunal should ask whether it "could well happen" (see *Guidance, Para C3* and *Boyle v SCA Packaging Ltd* [2009] UKHL 37; [2009] ICR 1056; [2009] IRLR 746).

European law looks to the UN Convention on the Rights of Persons with Disabilities when interpreting the *Framework Directive 2000/78* (see *HK Danmark* (above)). The Convention definition of disability refers to "long-term physical, mental, intellectual or sensory impairments". Two points of note arise: first, the UN definition differs from the *EqA 2010* definition in that the adjective "long-term" qualifies the impairment and not its effects. Second, there is no further more precise definition of what is meant by "long-term". These differences open the possibility of an argument that domestic law is not compatible with EU Law. The ECJ has looked at the UN definition in *Daouidi v Bootes Plus SL and others* C-395/15, [2017] IRLR 151, [2017] ICR 420. The court decided that the mere fact that a period of absence from work caused by injury was indeterminate did not mean it was "long-term". That was a question of fact to be judged on all of the evidence. There can be little doubt that the domestic courts and tribunals would take the same approach on that question of principle. *Daouidi* does not, therefore, create any specific concern that domestic law is incompatible with EU Law.

Normal day-to-day activities

The *Guidance* addresses "normal day-to day activities" in *section D*. General guidance is given at *Para D3*:

> "In general, day-to-day activities are things people do on a regular or daily basis, and examples include shopping, reading and writing, having a conversation or using the telephone, watching television, getting washed and dressed, preparing and eating food, carrying out and taking part in social activities. Normal day-to-day activities can include general work-related activities, and study and education-related activities, such as interacting with colleagues, following instructions, using a computer, driving, carrying out interviews, preparing written documents, and keeping to a timetable or a shift pattern."

The term is not intended to include activities which are normal only for a particular person or a small group of people (*Para D4*). However, a normal day-to-day activity does not have to be something that the majority of people do (*Para D5*). Specialised activities such as watch-making or playing an instrument to a high standard are not included (*Paras D8 and D9*).

Normal day-to-day activities can include activities engaged in at work (see *Chacón Navas v Eurest Coletivades* [2006] C-13/05 CJEU; [2007] ICR 1; [2006] IRLR 706; *Dumfries & Galloway Constabulary v Adams* [2009] ICR 1034; [2009] IRLR 612 and *Banaszczyk v Booker Ltd* UK/EAT/0132/15: [2016] IRLR 273).

In *Ekpe v Metropolitan Police Comr* [2001] IRLR 605, the EAT held that it was an error of law to conclude that an activity only done by women was not a normal day-to-day activity. However, a refusal to allow a person to progress in her professional life is not an adverse effect on normal day-to-day activities (see *Chief Constable of Lothian and Borders Police v Cumming* [2010] IRLR 109).

In *Leonard v Southern Derbyshire Chamber of Commerce* [2001] IRLR 19, [2000] All ER (D) 1327, the employment tribunal had considered the examples given in earlier guidance in determining whether or not the applicant's condition had a substantial adverse effect on her day-to-day activities. In deciding that the applicant was not disabled, the employment tribunal had balanced those examples in the Guidance that the claimant could do (such as being able to eat and drink) against those which the claimant could not do (such as negotiate pavement edges properly). The EAT held that this balancing exercise was inappropriate, 'since her ability to catch a ball did not diminish her inability to negotiate pavement edges safely'. As stated above, the correct approach involves considering all matters, but paying particular attention to those activities that the applicant cannot do.

Conducting litigation as a party is not a normal day-to-day activity, so that the fact that a complainant requires reasonable adjustments to tribunal procedures does not compel the Tribunal to find that he is disabled (*Herry v Dudley MBC and another* UKEAT/100/16 [2017] ICR 610).

Severe disfigurement

Severe disfigurement is deemed to have the necessary substantial adverse effect (*EqA 2010, Sch, para 3*). The Guidance gives the following examples of what might qualify to be protected under this provision: "scars, birthmarks, limb or postural deformation or diseases of the skin" (*Para B25*).

Tattoos and piercings are addressed at *Reg 5* of the *Equality Act 2010 (Disability) Regulations 2010, SI 2010/2128*. It is provided that they should not count as disfigurements having a substantial adverse effect on the ability of a person to carry out normal day-to-day activities.

Effect of medical treatment

The substantial adverse effects of an impairment may sometimes be avoided by medical treatment or other "measures". That does not have the effect, however, of removing the employee from the protective scope of the Act. *EqA 2010, Sch 1, para 5* provides:

"(1) An impairment is to be treated as having a substantial adverse effect on the ability of the person concerned to carry out normal day-to-day activities if:

(a)   measures are being taken to treat or correct it, and

(b)   but for that, it would be likely to have that effect.

(2) "Measures" includes, in particular, medical treatment and the use of a prosthesis or other aid

(3) Sub-paragraph (1) does not apply –

(a)   in relation to the impairment of a person's sight, to the extent that the impairment is, in the person's case, correctable by spectacle or contact lenses or in such other ways as may be prescribed

..."

The measures taken may, broadly, have one of three types of effect. First, it may temporarily alleviate the adverse effect. That is the set of circumstances with which the provision set out above is intended to deal. So, for instance, an asthmatic employee would probably be regarded as disabled within the meaning of the *Act* if his condition was such that if it were not controlled through the use of inhalers and medication, it would have a substantial adverse effect on his normal day-to-day activities. Similarly, an employee with a disabling depression still has a disability even if the effects of the depression are controlled with anti-depressants. Since the medical treatment means the adverse effect is prevented, the tribunal has to deduce what would happen if the medical treatment ceased. Where a deduced effect is alleged, the employee is required to prove the disability with some particularity and clear medical evidence will usually be necessary. A mere assertion by the employee as to what would happen if the treatment ceased will probably not be sufficient (*Woodrup v Southwark London Borough Council* [2003] IRLR 111, CA). When assessing what would happen if treatment or a corrective measure ceased to be taken, the tribunal must ask itself whether it is "likely" that the substantial adverse effect would resume. That outcome is sufficiently likely if the tribunal is able to say that it "could well happen" (*SCA Packaging Ltd v Boyle* [2009] UKHL 37, [2009] NI 317, [2009] IRLR 746).

The second type of effect that the measures might have is producing a permanent improvement such that it is unlikely that the substantial adverse effect will recur. In *Abadeh v British Telecommunications plc* [2001] IRLR 23, [2001] ICR 156, the EAT decided that where continuing treatment has produced a permanent improvement, that improvement must be taken into account. Put another way, the tribunal should ask would happen if treatment stopped now and not what would have happened if the claimant had never received treatment. The EAT further clarified that a "deduced effect" argument was only available at all if the medical treatment was continuing. *EqA 2010, Sch 1, para 5* does not apply where the treatment has ceased (see also *Carden v Pickerings Europe Ltd* [2005] IRLR 720).

The third type of effect that measures might have is curing the underlying impairment itself. Again, the claimant cannot argue that they are a disabled person on the basis that they would have been had they not been cured.

However, where a measure brings about a permanent improvement or a cure such that a claimant cannot argue they are still disabled that does not mean that the employee will not have the protected characteristic of disability, that is because less favourable treatment of those who disabilities in the past is also prohibited (see below and *Guidance, Para 17*).

The EAT in *Kapadia v Lambeth London Borough Council* [2000] IRLR 14 found that counselling sessions conducted by a consultant psychologist amounted to 'medical treatment', notwithstanding the fact that the counselling only comprised 'talking' to the claimant and the fact that no drugs were administered.

The EAT in *Vicary v British Telecommunications plc* [1999] IRLR 680, commented (*obiter*) that the words 'or other aid' (*EqA 2010, Sch 1, para 5(2)*) are probably intended to refer to aids such as Zimmer frames or sticks or wheelchairs and not to labour-saving household devices such as electric can-openers. An 'aid' in this context can also include surgically inserted plates and pins. (*Carden v Pickerings Europe Ltd* [2005] IRLR 720).

The Employment Appeal Tribunal considered the question of when an impairment to someone's sight could be considered to be "correctable" by contact lenses in *Mart v Assessment Service Inc* UKEATS/0032/18 [2019] IRLR 688, [2019] ICR 1414. An impairment is not "correctable" simply because the lens resolves the specific impairment if that resolution comes at the cost of unacceptable adverse consequences such as infection. Correctability is a "practical" issue.

Deemed disabilities

EqA 2010, Sch 1, para 6 deems Cancer, HIV infection and multiple sclerosis to be disabilities. All cancers are covered whether or not they are invasive (see *Lofty v Hamis t/a First Café* [2018] UKEAT/0177/17, [2018] IRLR 512 – Lentigo Maligna, a non–invasive, cancerous skin lesion - sometimes described a "pre-cancerous" condition - fell within the definition).

Para 7 confers a power to prescribe that other conditions should also be deemed to be disabilities. On 1 October 2010 the *Equality Act 2010 (Disability) Regulations 2010, SI 2010/2128* came into force. *Reg 3* deems that addiction to alcohol, nicotine or any other substance is to be treated as not amounting to an impairment unless the addiction is the result of the administration of medically prescribed drugs or other medical treatment. *Reg 4* deems certain other conditions not to amount to impairments: a tendency to set fires, to steal or to physical or sexual abuse of other persons; exhibitionism or voyeurism.

Seasonal allergic rhinitis ("hay fever") cannot amount to an impairment in its own right but can be taken into account if it aggravates another condition.

Reg 6 deals with babies and young children. Although, of course, neither are likely to be employees, whether or not a child is disabled may affect whether an associative discrimination claim will succeed. Where a child under six has an impairment which does not have a substantial long term adverse effect on the ability of the child to carry out normal day to day activities, the impairment is deemed to have that effect if it would have it on a child who was older than six.

Reg 7 deems to be disabled any person certified by a consultant ophthalmologist to be blind, severely sight impaired or partially-sighted.

For matters which are deemed by the Regulations not to amount to impairments, see the section on impairments above.

Progressive conditions

EqA 2010, Sch 1, para 8 deals with progressive conditions. The effect of the provision is that even if the employee's condition creates an impairment which has an adverse effect which is not yet sufficiently "substantial" to qualify as a disability, it is treated as doing so if "the condition is likely to result in [them] suffering such an impairment". In *Chief Constable of Norfolk v Coffey* [2019] EWCA Civ 1061, [2019] IRLR 805, [2020] ICR 145, Lord Justice Underhill comments that the requirement that there be some adverse effect, albeit not a substantial one, is illogical. There is no ready explanation as to why an employee should be unprotected if her progressive condition has not yet started to have an effect but protected as long as it has a trivial one. Nevertheless, that appears to be the law.

Mere diagnosis of a progressive condition (other than one of the conditions giving rise to a deemed disability) would not be sufficient in itself. In *Mowat-Brown v University of Surrey* [2002] IRLR 235, the EAT held that it is not even enough simply for an applicant to establish that he has a progressive condition and that it has or has had an effect on his ability to carry out normal day-to-day activities. A claimant with a progressive condition must go on to show that it is likely that at some stage in the future there will be a substantial adverse effect on his ability to carry out normal day-to-day activities. The *Guidance* (at *Para B19*) provides that in such cases, medical prognosis of the likely impact of the condition will be the normal route to establishing protection under the progressive conditions provisions. A person may be taken as having a disability even where the substantial adverse effect is as a result of the treatment for a progressive condition (eg an operation for prostate cancer that results in urinary incontinence) rather than the progressive condition itself (see *Kirton v Tetrosyl Ltd* [2003] EWCA Civ 619, [2003] ICR 1237, [2003] IRLR 353). Note that the decision in *Mowat-Brown* predates that in *SCA Packaging* (above). It interpreted "likely" to mean more likely than not. The EAT confirmed in *Taylor v Ladbrokes Betting and Gaming Ltd* UKEAT/0353/15, [2017] IRLR 312 that, in the light of *SCA Packaging*, it was sufficient if there was a "small possibility of deterioration in a population [affected by the relevant condition]".

Para B32 of the *Guidance* suggests the protection will not apply where the progressive condition is successfully treated so as to remove any adverse effect. More difficult is the question of the applicability of *Paragraph B7* (which is summarised in the section of this paragraph headed "Substantial Adverse effects" above). It suggests that when considering whether an effect is substantial one may take into account what might reasonably be expected of the claimant in terms of the modification of their own behaviour so as to avoid the effect. In *Taylor*, above, the EAT was urged to decide that the guidance should be taken into account when determining whether or not a deterioration is "likely". The EAT refused to decide the point.

Past disabilities

EqA 2010, s 6(4) provides that reference (however expressed) to a person who has a disability includes reference to a person who has had the disability. The *Guidance, Para B17* states that if medical treatment cures a condition, the employee may still be protected on the basis that they have had a disability in the past.

Disability "at the relevant time"

The EAT in *Cruickshank v VAW Motorcast Ltd* [2002] IRLR 24 confirmed that in determining whether a person is disabled, the court should apply the appropriate test to the claimant's condition at the date of the alleged discriminatory act and not at the date of the hearing. This approach could present difficulties particularly where the effects of a particular condition tend to fluctuate or last for uncertain periods. The fact that by the date of the hearing, an adverse effect had in fact lasted for 12 months is not necessarily conclusive of it having been likely to have lasted that long at the date of the discriminatory act. However, now that it has been confirmed that 'likely' in this context means 'could well happen', such difficulties will probably arise only rarely (see *SCA Packaging Ltd v Boyle* [2009] UKHL 37, [2009] IRLR 746, overruling *Latchman v Reed Business Information Ltd* [2002] ICR 1453, [2002] All ER (D) 287 (Feb)). In *Swift v Chief Constable of Wiltshire Constabulary* [2004] IRLR 540, the EAT had held that in determining whether at a particular point in time a substantial adverse effect was likely to recur, the Tribunal was entitled to take account of evidence of what had happened since that time. However, the effect of *Swift* was doubted by the Court of Appeal in *McDougall v Richmond Adult Community College* [2008] EWCA Civ 4, [2008] IRLR 227, [2008] ICR 431 (at paragraph 17). Rather, in *McDougall*, Pill LJ emphasised that a prediction as to the likelihood of recurrence must be made on the basis of the evidence available at the time of the act complained of. The central purpose of the legislation is to prevent discriminatory decisions and to provide sanctions if such decisions are made. Whether an employer has committed such a wrong is to be judged, therefore, on the basis of the evidence available at the time of the decision complained of. (See *Ministry of Defence v Hay* [2008] IRLR 928, [2008] ICR 1247, where *McDougall* was distinguished on the basis that it did not apply where the decision as to whether someone was disabled did not turn upon any predictive element to be established on the facts known at the time of the alleged act of discrimination. In *Hay*, the question was not one of recurrence of a condition but of whether the claimant was suffering from an impairment or impairments which had a substantial adverse effect upon his normal day-to-day activities.)

There is special provision made in relation to cases of past disability at *EqA 2010, Sch1, para 9* provides:

> "(1) A question as to whether a person has a disability at a particular time ("the relevant time") is to be determined, for the purposes of section 6, as if the provisions of, or made under, this Act were in force when the act complained of was done had been in force at the relevant time.
>
> (2) The relevant time may be a time before the coming into force of the provisions of this Act to which the question relates."

The *Guidance* provides that the protection would cover those who continue to experience debilitating effects as a result of treatment for a past disability (*Para A16*). Note that the wording of sub-paragraph 9(1) does not make sense on its face. The word "were" in the second line appears to have been inserted when the legislation was in draft form but without any obvious purpose and with the effect of obscuring the meaning of the provision. The purpose of the provision becomes clear if one ignores the "were".

12.27 Associative Discrimination – Cases where the member of the protected category is a third party

In most cases, a person who alleges that they have been discriminated against will be complaining that the have been treated less favourably because of their protected characteristic (ie because of their race, sex, sexual orientation, etc). However, where, for instance, a white employee is dismissed for refusing to comply with an instruction not to deal with black customers, it is the customers' protected characteristic that is in issue rather than that of the employee. Discrimination which is based upon a third person's protected characteristic is known as "associative discrimination". The label "associative" is not itself found in the legislation (either European or domestic) and no particular relationship is required between the complainant and the person with the protected characteristic. The question is simply a causal one – was the complainant treated less favourably because of the other person's protected characteristic? (see *Thompson v London Central Bus Company Ltd* (2015) UKEAT/0108/15, [2016] IRLR 9).

The coming into force of the *EqA 2010* represented a substantial expansion of the scope of associative discrimination. Whereas under the pre-existing law, associative discrimination claims could only be brought in respect of certain protected characteristics, *EqA 2010, s 13* extends the scope of protection to all of the protected characteristics save one. The exception is "marriage and civil partnership". A claim may only be brought where it is the person less favourably treated that is married or a civil partner (*EqA 2010, s 13(4)*).

In addition to associative direct discrimination, associative indirect discrimination and, it appears, associative victimisation are also prohibited (see **[12.34]** and **[12.38]** below).

A company could complain of associative discrimination where it was treated less favourably because of protected characteristic of the person whose services it supplied (*EAD Solicitors v Abrams* UKEAT/0054/15, [2015] IRLR 978). There was no associative discrimination where a bakery refused to supply a customer with a cake bearing a slogan in support of same sex marriage (*Lee v Ashers Baking Company Ltd and others* [2018] UKSC 49, [2018] IRLR 1116). The Supreme Court found that the reason for refusing to make the cake was not the customer's association with those with a same sex sexual orientation, but rather the bakery owner's religious scruples and that in the circumstances there was not a sufficiently close connection between the reason for the treatment and the protected characteristic of those with whom the customer was associated.

12.28 Perceived Discrimination – Cases where the complainant is assumed, incorrectly, to have the protected characteristic

The definition of direct discrimination adopted in *EqA 2010, s 13* has the effect that perceived discrimination is prohibited in relation to each of the protected characteristics. There was some doubt as to how that might operate in disability discrimination cases (see *J v DLA Piper UK LLP* [2010] IRLR 936 and *Peninsula Business Services Ltd v Baker* [2017] ICR 714, EAT). The issue was the complexity of the statutory test of disability and the difficulty that an employer might have in distinguishing disability from mere illness. That can make it hard to determine whether and at what point they might be said to have perceived someone as being a disabled person. However, the matter was considered by the Court of Appeal in *Chief Constable of Norfolk v Coffey* [2019] EWCA Civ 1061, [2019] IRLR 80. Lord Justice Underhill set out the test in the following terms:

> "In a case of perception discrimination what is perceived must, as a simple matter of logic, have all the features of the protected characteristic as defined in the statute."

In a disability case that meant that the employer had to perceive the employee as having an impairment with the features set out in the legislation. What is not required is any perception or knowledge that those features, taken together, constitute a disability for the purposes of the *Act*. To take a simple case, if an employer perceives an employee as having cancer that would be sufficient. They do not need to appreciate that cancer is deemed to amount to a disability as a matter of law.

12.29 Combined discrimination

Combined discrimination was a new form of discrimination that was to be introduced by *EqA 2010*. It would have occurred where an employee was treated less favourably because of two protected characteristics. For instance, if a driving school were to decide that the job of driving instructor was not a suitable one for an older woman and refused to appoint a woman in her sixties to a position, their reason would not be the candidate's sex or her age but the combination of her sex and age. On 23 March 2011, the Government Equalities Unit announced that it no longer intended to proceed with its proposals to bring *EqA 2010, s 14* into force. It is that provision which would otherwise have prohibited such discrimination.

In *Parris v Trinity College Dublin* C-443/15 [2017] ICR 313, the ECJ considered a complaint that a lecturer had been discriminated against because his employer's pension scheme only provided a survivor's pension if the marriage or civil partnership had been contracted before the employee reached the age of 60. The complainant had entered into a civil partnership when he was 63. However, he pointed out that civil partnerships had not come into existence until after he reached the age of 60. The ECJ concluded that the *Framework Directive 2000/78/EC* did not require that a claim for either sexual orientation or age discrimination should lie. It observed that whilst it was possible to rely on more than one of the protected characteristics, the Directive did not create a category of "combined" discrimination that might succeed where the characteristic-specific claims failed. It does not appear, therefore, that the UK's decision not to implement its proposal for combined discrimination involves any failure properly to implement the Directive.

12.30 Discrimination on the ground of pregnancy

EqA 2010 provides two discrete protections for women who are discriminated against because of their pregnancy. First, pregnancy is identified as a "protected characteristic" at *EqA 2010, s 4*. As a result, it would seem that it is possible for a woman to complain of direct discrimination where she is treated "less favourably" because of her pregnancy, relying on *EqA 2010, s 13(1)*. This is dealt with at **12.24** above.

The second protection provides is an express prohibition on employers treating employees unfavourably (as opposed to less favourably) because of their pregnancy (*EqA 2010, s 18(2)(a)*):

> 'A person (A) discriminates against a woman if, in the protected period in relation to a pregnancy of hers, A treats her unfavourably –
>
> (a) because of the pregnancy; . . . '

This formulation differs from that found in the earlier law in that, although it was clear that a pregnant employee was not required to identify a comparator, she was still required to show that she had been "less favourably treated" which unhelpfully implied a residual need for comparison. Now the *Act* simply prohibits "unfavourable" treatment. Otherwise, the provisions are materially the same.

As to what constitutes "unfavourable" treatment, the EAT suggested in *Interserve FM Ltd v Tuleikyte* UKEAT/0267/16; [2017] IRLR 615 that it is a question of fact to be "left to the good sense of tribunals". By analogy with the cases such as *Ministry of Defence v Jeremiah* [1980] QB 87, [1979] 3 All ER 83 on the meaning of "detriment", it is suggested that treatment will be unfavourable if a reasonable person in the complainant's position could have thought that it was.

In *New Southern Railways Ltd v Quinn* [2006] IRLR 266, EAT, an employer was found to have discriminated where it removed a pregnant employee from a trial position and returned her to her less senior and lower-paid position. The Tribunal was not prepared to treat the case as one of medical suspension. Where an employee is prevented, by reason of her pregnancy, from performing her usual job tasks, a failure to consider alternative employment may be discriminatory on the basis that the employer has treated the employee less favourably in relation to access to opportunities for transfer within *EqA 2010, s 39(2)(b)* (*Iske v P&O European Ferries (Dover) Ltd* [1997] IRLR 401, EAT).

A failure to comply with the obligation imposed by the *Management of Health and Safety Regulations 1999 (SI 1999/3242)* to carry out a risk assessment in respect of a pregnant employee may amount to an act of unlawful sex discrimination (see *Hardman v Mealon (t/a Orchard Lodge Nursing Home)* [2002] IRLR 516 and *Otero Ramos v Servici Galego de Saude and another* C-531/15; [2018] IRLR 159, [2018] ICR 965: failure to comply with risk assessment required by Pregnant Workers' Directive 92/85, Art 4(1) for a risk assessment in respect of a breast-feeding mother constituted direct discrimination contrary to *ETD 2006/54, Art 2(2)(c)*). However, there is no general obligation to carry out a risk assessment and there is only an obligation to do so where: (1) the employee notifies her employer in writing that she is pregnant; (2) the work is of a kind which could involve a risk of harm or danger to the health and safety of a new expectant mother or to the health and safety of her baby; and (3) the risk arises from either processes or working conditions or physical, biological or chemical agents in the workplace at the time specified in the non-exhaustive list at Annexes I and II of Directive 92/85/EEC (*O'Neill v Buckinghamshire County Council* [2010] IRLR 384, EAT). Where a risk assessment is carried out it must include a specific assessment taking into account the individual situation of the worker (*Otero Ramos* above).

The unfavourable treatment must be "because of" the complainant's pregnancy. As in cases of direct discrimination brought under *EqA 2010, s 13*, there must be a causal connection between the protected characteristic and the treatment complained of. The EAT confirmed in *Interserve FM Ltd v Tuleikyte* (above) the *s 13* and *s 18* tests of causation are the same.

Cases in which the reason for the employee being unfavourably treated is the pregnancy per se will be rare. More commonly, the employer points to a reason connected with the pregnancy. In *Dekker v Stichting Vormingscentrum voor Jong Volwassenen (VJV - Centrum) Plus*: C-177/88 [1990] ECR I-3941, [1991] IRLR 27, [1992] ICR 325, the complainant applied for a job as a teacher. Although suitable she was not appointed because the respondent would have had to pay her a maternity allowance, which, because she would have been pregnant when appointed, the respondent would have been unable to recover under their insurance policy. The reason for the refusal to appoint was thus not the pregnancy per se but the substantial irrecoverable costs of the appointment. However, the ECJ approached the case on the basis that the refusal to appoint was on ground of pregnancy. The domestic courts have adopted a similar approach. In *O'Neill v Governors of St Thomas More RCVA Upper School* [1996] IRLR 372, [1997] ICR 33, EAT, the Employment Appeal Tribunal considered a case where a Roman Catholic school dismissed a religious education teacher who was pregnant by a priest. The school argued that it was not the pregnancy itself but the circumstances of the pregnancy that provided the dominant motive for the decision to dismiss. The EAT held that the dismissal had been discriminatory and rejected the concept of dismissal for "pregnancy per se" as misleading. Instead the tribunal should simply ask itself whether, on an objective basis, the dismissal was on the ground of pregnancy. Pregnancy did not need, in the EAT's opinion, to be the sole or even the main ground for the decision to dismiss.

A common complaint made by employers is that an employee has 'deceived' them by not declaring that they are pregnant at a point at which an important decision is made. For example, in *Busch v Klinikum Neustadt GmbH & Co Betriebs-KG*: C-320/01 [2003] IRLR 625, ECJ, an employee absent on parental leave applied to return early. Having been allowed to do so, she declared she was pregnant and sought to take maternity leave which would have been unavailable to her during a period of parental leave. The employers tried to rescind their consent to her return from parental leave. The Court decided that the employee was not obliged to declare her pregnancy and, in any event, the employer would not have been entitled to take her pregnancy into account even if she had told them about it. That being so, they had discriminated against her.

In *Ministry of Defence v Pope* [1997] ICR 296, EAT, the Employment Appeal Tribunal held that where an employee terminated her pregnancy in order to avoid being dismissed for pregnancy, she could bring a claim against her employer for damages for injury to feelings. In its decision in *Webb v EMO Air Cargo (UK) Ltd* C-32/93: [1994] QB 718, [1994] ECR I-3567, [1994] ICR 770, [1994] IRLR 482 the ECJ had expressly referred to the need to prevent women feeling pressured into terminations as one of the policies underlying the maternity leave period.

In *Madarassy v Nomura International Plc* [2007] EWCA Civ 33, [2007] IRLR 246, (a case decided under the old law but after the requirement for a comparator had been abolished) the Court of Appeal indicated that even in pregnancy cases a comparator might still be of use. The Court had in mind a case where there is real doubt as to whether pregnancy was the reason for the treatment. Thus, where a pregnant employee is dismissed for dishonesty and claims that the employer only took the step of dismissing her (rather than disciplining her) because she was pregnant, it might be relevant to ask what had happened to male employees who had behaved in the same way. Where, however, the reason is a matter directly connected with the pregnancy (such as absence) it will not be appropriate to ask how a man with a similar absence record would have been treated.

There is a limit to how remote the reason can be from the pregnancy. Thus, in *Walter v Secretary of State for Social Security* [2001] EWCA Civ 1913, [2002] ICR 540, [2001] All ER (D) 71 (Dec), the *Jobseeker's Allowance Regulations 1996 (SI 1996/207)* did not offend against the *Social Security Directive 79/7/EEC* (which prohibited sex discrimination in access to social security entitlements; see **24.5** EUROPEAN UNION LAW) where a student breaking her studies to have a child was precluded from claiming the allowance. Those taking breaks from studies are treated under the Regulations as retaining their status as a student, a status which disqualifies them from making a claim. The Court of Appeal decided that the complainant's ineligibility to claim derived from her student status and not from her pregnancy.

The protection is specifically restricted to a "protected period" which begins when the woman conceives and ends, in cases where she is entitled to ordinary and additional maternity leave ("OML" and "AML"), either at the end of the additional maternity leave period or when she returns to work (if that is earlier) and in any other case at the end of the period of 2 weeks beginning with the end of pregnancy (*EqA 2010, s 18(6)*). Thus an employer who dismisses an employee who informs him that she intends to try for a child does not act in breach of *s 18* as the protected period has not begun. In such a case the complainant would have two options: (1) bringing a *s 13* pregnancy discrimination case; or (2) bringing a *s 13* sex discrimination case. The approach of treating pregnancy-related discrimination falling outside the period as sex discrimination was taken by the ECJ in *Mayr v Backerei und Konditorei Gerhard Flockner OHG* C-506/06, [2008] IRLR 387. A woman undergoing IVF treatment was dismissed between the removal of ova from her follicles and the replacement of a fertilised ovum in her uterus. The ECJ determined that she was not a pregnant worker for the purposes of *PWD 92/85* but could rely, instead on *ETD 76/207/EEC* (now the *ETD 2006/54/EC*).

On the other hand, once a protected period has begun *EqA 2010, s 18(7)* specifically requires that any pregnancy discrimination claim be brought under *s 18* rather than as a sex discrimination claim under *s 13*. If, during the protected period, the employee is treated less favourably because of her sex but not because of her pregnancy a claim under *EqA 2010, s 13* would of course still be available.

An employee may complain about the implementation of a decision taken during the protected period even if the implementation itself does not occur until after the period has come to an end (*EqA 2010, s 18(5)*). This, again, reflects the ECJ's approach: In *Paquay v Societe d'architectes Hoet + Minne SPRL*: C-460/06 [2008] ICR 420, [2007] All ER (D) 137 (Oct), ECJ, the protection against dismissal afforded during the 'protected period' provided for by *PWD 92/85* was held to apply where an employer advertised the employee's job during the protected period but gave notice only once the protected period had finished. The *PWD* was interpreted as requiring that steps preparatory to a decision to dismiss should also be unlawful.

As it is a form of direct discrimination, pregnancy discrimination cannot be justified. The strictness of the principle is well illustrated by the case of *Mahlburg v Land Mecklenburg-Vorpommern*: C-207/98 [2000] ECR I-549, [2000] IRLR 276. The ECJ considered the case of a pregnant woman who applied for and was refused a job intended to last for an indefinite period on the basis that, at the time at which she would otherwise have started the job, domestic law precluded her from working. Did the fact that the *ETD 76/207/EEC* (since repealed and replaced by *ETD 2006/54/EC*) was expressed to be without prejudice to such protective legislation mean that a refusal to appoint the claimant had not been discriminatory? The court decided that there had been an act of direct discrimination. The result pursued by the *ETD 76/207/EEC* was 'substantive, not formal, equality'. As a result, 'the application of provisions concerning the protection of pregnant women cannot result in unfavourable treatment regarding their access to employment'.

12.31 Discrimination on ground of maternity leave

EqA 2010, s 4 identifies "maternity" as a protected characteristic. *Part 2, Chapter 1* of the *Act* does not define what is meant by "maternity". The explanatory notes, equally, do not provide a definition. The significance of the lack of a definition is that "maternity" is a broader term than "maternity leave" and the earlier law only prohibited discrimination on the latter, narrower, ground. However, it is probable that *EqA 2010* intends to do no more than reproduce the existing maternity leave-related protection. That view is reinforced by *EqA 2010, s 18* which is headed "Pregnancy and maternity discrimination: work cases". Section 18 deals only with pregnancy discrimination (*EqA 2010, s 18(2)*) and maternity leave discrimination (*EqA 2010, ss 18(3) and (4)*). Despite the heading, there is no protection of maternity more generally.

EqA 2010, s 18(3) prohibits a person from discriminating against a woman by treating her unfavourably because she is on compulsory maternity leave. Compulsory maternity leave is the two week period provided for by *ERA 1996, s 72(1)* (*EqA 2010, s 213(3)*) (see MATERNITY AND PARENTAL RIGHTS **33.27**).

Unfavourable treatment because an employee "is exercising or seeking to exercise, or has exercised or sought to exercise [her] right to ordinary or additional maternity leave" is prohibited by *EqA 2010, s 18(4)*. Ordinary maternity leave ("OML") is the right conferred by *ERA 1996, s 71(1)* (*EqA 2010, s 213(4)* see MATERNITY AND PARENTAL RIGHTS **33.21**). Additional maternity leave ("AML") is the right conferred by *ERA 1996, s 73(1)* (*EqA 2010, s 313(7)* see MATERNITY AND PARENTAL RIGHTS **33.28**).

Discrimination for a maternity-related reason was, prior to October 2005, treated as a form of sex discrimination. In order to preclude overlapping claims *EqA 2010, s 18(7)(b)* disapplies *EqA 2010, s 13* (the prohibition on direct sex discrimination) where the unfavourable treatment is for a reason falling within *EqA 2010, s 18(3) or (4)*. However, since maternity is a protected characteristic in its own right (*EqA 2010, s 4*), it would seem that a *s 13* action would potentially still be available on that discrete basis. *Section 13* requires, however, that there should be "less favourable treatment" which would seem, on its face, to require a comparator to be identified which means that in most cases occurring during the protected period, there would be little point bringing a *s 13* claim rather than a *s 18* claim.

The scope of the protection is broad and the courts and tribunals have interpreted the provision purposively. For instance, early cases concerning maternity leave considered attempts by employers to narrow the protective scope of the provision by drawing a distinction between the taking of the leave and the consequences for the employer's business of the employee's absence. The ECJ rejected the distinction in *Dekker* (above) where an employer argued, unsuccessfully, that it did not discriminate against a pregnant applicant for employment by refusing to employ her since the real reason for not employing her was the adverse economic consequence of its inability to insure itself to recover the cost of the payments it would have to make to her during her maternity leave. Domestic authorities have taken the same line and establish, in general terms, that an employer may not use a maternity leave-related absence as either a reason for or (it would appear from the *Rees* and *Lewis Woolf* cases below) the occasion of treating a pregnant employee unfavourably.

However broad an interpretative approach is taken of the European and domestic provisions, there will still be some cases where *EqA 2010, s 18* is not engaged and a claimant will have to rely upon the sex discrimination provisions. An example might be where an employer discriminates against an employee because he believes that she wishes to start a family and anticipates that she may wish to take maternity leave in the future. His act is not, on the face of it, rendered unlawful by *EqA 2010, s 18*. It is likely, however, that his act will nevertheless amount to an act of unlawful sex discrimination falling within *EqA 2010, s 13*. The same would likely be true of discrimination on ground of taking contractual maternity leave which is also not covered by *s 18*.

Cases decided under the previous legal regime remain useful in helping to assess when liability will be incurred. Set out below, therefore, is an account of ECJ and domestic case law relating to discrimination on ground of sex in so far as the acts complained of were motivated by or occurred against a background of maternity absence.

One line of cases deals with women who are penalised for maternity absence in ways falling short of dismissal. In *Caisse Nationale D'Assurance Viellesse Des Travailleurs Salaries v Thibault*: C-136/95 [1998] IRLR 399, [1999] ICR 160, ECJ employees who had been present at work for at least six months in a particular year were entitled to a performance appraisal. A satisfactory appraisal would lead to a pay increase. Where the reason that an employee did not qualify for an appraisal was that she had been absent on maternity leave, it was an act of discrimination not to allow her an appraisal in any event. See also *Napoli v Minsterio della Giustizia, Dipartimento dell'Amministrazione penitenziaria*: C-595/12 [2014] ICR 487, [2014] All ER (D) 288 (Mar), CJEU – An Italian law that precluded trainee prison governors from further participation in the 12 month course required for promotion where they had been absent from the course for more than 30 days resulted in the Claimant, who was absent for three months because of compulsory maternity leave, being treated unfavourably. It was not enough that she was guaranteed a place on the next course as that still resulted in delay in her access to the higher rates of pay available to those who passed the course and there was no certainty as to when the next course would be arranged. Contrast, however, *Hoyland v Asda Stores* [2005] IRLR 438, [2005] ICR 1235, EAT; the claimant was not entitled to receive a bonus which had been earned by male colleagues during the period of her absence on maternity leave.

In *Land Brandenburg v Sass*:C-284/02 [2005] IRLR 147, the ECJ considered a different aspect of the effect of absence on benefits. Some benefits will be conditional on length of service. Should time spent absent on maternity leave count as service for those purposes? The ECJ held that the claimant should have been given credit for length of service for any period during which she had been on 'statutory maternity leave intended to protect women who have given birth'.

In *Blundell v Governing Body St Andrews Catholic Primary School* [2007] IRLR 652, [2007] ICR 1451, an employer acted unlawfully when it failed to consult with a teacher who was absent on maternity leave as to the class she wished to teach the following year – something that it would have done had she been at work.

In *Herrero (Sarkatzis) v Instituto Madrileno de la Salud (Imsalud)*: C-294/04 [2006] IRLR 296, the ECJ determined that an employer acts unlawfully where it counts continuous service only from the day on which an employee takes up her duties rather than on the date of her appointment where the reason for the delay was the taking of maternity leave.

A second line of cases deals with claimants who are either not recruited or who are dismissed for reasons relating to maternity leave absences. *Webb* was itself a case concerned with absence. It is significant that both the ECJ and the House of Lords placed considerable emphasis on the fact that Ms Webb had been employed for an indefinite period. The implication is that the case might have been decided differently had the contract of employment been for a fixed term over the whole or major part of which Ms Webb would have been unavailable. The distinction was refined in *Caruana v Manchester Airport plc* [1996] IRLR 378, EAT where it was decided that a further distinction had to be drawn between cases where a woman is employed for a single 'one-off' fixed period, and cases where she is employed on a series of fixed-term contracts. The latter type of case should be treated in the same way as employment for an indefinite period. In previous editions, we have opined that even in cases where the engagement is to be for a single fixed term, it would nevertheless be an act of discrimination not to appoint a pregnant candidate by reason of her pregnancy. The basis of our view has been that it is not open to an employer to justify an act of direct discrimination. In *Tele Danmark A/S v Handels-og Kontorfunktion-aerernes Forbund i Danmark (HK)*: C-109/00 [2001] IRLR 853, [2001] All ER (EC) 941, a woman was given a contract with a fixed maximum term of six months. The first two months of the contract would be spent being trained. The complainant was pregnant when she was offered the job. She did not tell the respondent. Her pregnancy had the effect that she was precluded from working for a substantial part of the fixed term. She was dismissed on the ground that she had failed to tell the respondent of her condition when applying for the job. The ECJ decided that the dismissal was contrary to *art 5(1)* of the *ETD 76/207/EEC* (since replaced by *Directive 2002/73/EC*). The non-discrimination principle it encapsulated is now to be found in *ETD 2006/54/EC*) and *art 10* of the *Pregnant Worker's Directive 92/85/EC*. The former provision is a general prohibition of less favourable treatment on grounds of sex. The latter is a specific prohibition on dismissal of pregnant workers during the period from conception to the end of maternity leave, 'save in exceptional cases not connected with their condition, which are permitted under national legislation and/or practice'. The court held:

> 'Since the dismissal of a worker on account of pregnancy constitutes direct discrimination on grounds of sex whatever the nature and extent of the economic loss incurred by the employer as a result of her absence because of the pregnancy, whether the contract of employment was concluded for a fixed or an indefinite period has no bearing on the discriminatory character of the dismissal. In either case, the employee's inability to perform her contract of employment is due to pregnancy.'

The court pointed out that neither directive distinguishes between those employed on fixed terms and those employed pursuant to contracts of indefinite duration. The European Court of Justice gave further consideration to the *Pregnant Worker's Directive* in *Jimenez Melgar v Ayuntamiento de Los Barrios*: C-438/99 [2001] ECR I-6915, [2001] IRLR 848. The court determined that:

(i)   the Directive has direct effect;

(ii)   where a member state wishes to enact legislation permitting dismissals in exceptional circumstances, it need not specify the particular grounds on which such workers may be dismissed; and

(iii)   a refusal to renew a fixed-term contract is not a dismissal. However, such a refusal may breach the provisions of the *ETD 76/207/EEC* (now the *ETD 2006/54/EC*).

12.31 Discrimination and Equal Opportunities – I

Where an employer refused to allow an employee to return after her maternity leave because he thought her temporary replacement was better at the job, the EAT considered that the employee's dismissal was discriminatory. The 'effective cause' had been the pregnancy as, had the employee not been absent as a result of her pregnancy, the replacement would never have been employed (*Rees v Apollo Watch Repairs plc* [1996] ICR 466, EAT. See also *Abbey National plc v Formoso* [1999] IRLR 222, EAT; an employee was dismissed for gross misconduct whilst absent on maternity leave. The lack of an opportunity to explain herself at a disciplinary hearing meant that the dismissal was discriminatory as her absence on maternity leave was the reason that she did not get a hearing).

The EAT seems to have gone further still in *Lewis Woolf Griptight Ltd v Corfield* [1997] IRLR 432, EAT. In the *Lewis* case, the tribunal found that the effective cause of the decision to dismiss was a breakdown in the relationship between the complainant and the respondent's Chief Executive. That reason was, of course, entirely gender-neutral. However, the respondent used an alleged failure by the complainant properly to exercise her right to return following maternity leave as a 'pretext' for the termination of her contract of employment. As this pretext was only available where the employee was a woman, the EAT reasoned, the dismissal was discriminatory.

12.32 Unfavourable treatment for reasons relating to a maternity-related illness

Under the earlier law, unfavourable treatment on grounds of a pregnancy-related illness was deemed to be discrimination on grounds of pregnancy (*SDA 1975, s 3A(3)(b)*). *EqA 2010, s 18(2)* adopts a slightly different approach making unfavourable treatment on grounds of a pregnancy-related illness a specifically prohibited form of discrimination:

> "A person (A) discriminates against a woman if, in the protected period in relation to a pregnancy of hers, A treats her unfavourably–
>
> . . .
>
> (b) because of illness suffered by her as a result of it."

In order to prevent overlapping heads of claim, *EqA 2010, s. 18(7)(a)* disapplies the protection against direct sex discrimination where the unfavourable treatment complained falls within *EqA 2010, s 18(2)(b)*.

For an explanation of the "protected period" see **12.30** above.

European case law provides helpful interpretative guidance: in *Brown v Rentokil Ltd*: C-394/96 [1998] All ER (EC) 791, [1998] IRLR 445, the following principles were established.

(a)   An employee may not be dismissed by reason of absence arising from a maternity-related illness at any point between conception and the end of her maternity leave period ('the protected period').

(b)   Where the maternity-related illness occurs after the end of the protected period, a dismissal will not be discriminatory if a man would have been dismissed had he been absent, because of illness, for a comparable period.

(c)   Where the illness arises during the protected period but persists thereafter, only days of absence which occur after the end of the protected period may be relied upon by an employer in deciding to dismiss (*William B Morrison & Son Ltd* (1999) 648 IDS Brief, EAT).

In a case decided before the ECJ's decision in *Brown* (and, thus, against the context of the former domestic protective regime), the EAT went further still and held that a dismissal effected after the end of the protected period was contrary to *SDA 1975* if it was for a maternity-related illness that arose during the employee's period of maternity leave (*Caledonia Bureau Investment and Property v Caffrey* [1998] IRLR 110, [1998] ICR 603). However, *Caledonia* was disapproved by the English EAT in *Lyons v DWP Jobcentre Plus* (UKEAT/348/13) [2014] ICR 668 which held that an employer dismissing an employee for sickness absence did not discriminate (either on grounds of sex or pregnancy) when it took into account periods of absence occurring outside the protected period that resulted from a pregnancy-related illness.

12.33   Discrimination arising from disability

EqA 2010 introduced a new form of discrimination: "Discrimination arising from disability". The explicit aim of the provision was to reverse the principal effect of the decision of the House of Lords in *London Borough of Lewisham v Malcolm* [2008] UKHL 43; [2008] 1 AC 1399; [2008] IRLR 700. That decision had concerned a predecessor tort defined in the *Disability Discrimination Act 1995*: "disability-related discrimination". Under the old law an employee had to establish that they had been treated less favourably for a reason relating to their disability. The requirement to demonstrate "less favourable treatment" meant that a comparator had to be identified. In *Clark v Novacold* [1999] IRLR 318, [1999] ICR 951, (a case decided on the old law) the Court of Appeal considered a case in which an employee was dismissed for sickness absence. The absence stemmed from his disability. Since the absence related to the disability, the Court decided that the reason for dismissal was disability-related. The appropriate comparator was someone in respect of whom that reason was not available. This meant essentially asking whether the employer would have dismissed for absence someone who had not been absent. The apparent absurdity of the test was mitigated by the fact that disability-related discrimination was capable of being justified. In *Malcolm* the House of Lords concluded that liability should be made out only when a tribunal could be satisfied that the disability itself was part of the reason for termination. The appropriate comparator was someone who had been absent but not for a reason relating to their disability. This was widely considered to have neutered the protection and the new tort was intended, in effect, to reinstate *Clark v Novacold*.

EqA 2010, s 15 provides:

"(1) A person (A) discriminates against a disabled person (B) if –

(a) A treats B unfavourably because of something arising in consequence of B's disability, and

(b) A cannot show that the treatment is a proportionate means of achieving a legitimate aim.

(2) Subsection (1) does not apply if A shows that A did not know, and could not reasonably have been expected to know, that B had the disability."

The claimant need only establish that they have been unfavourably treated. The test is not "less favourable treatment". No comparator is required.

A claimant cannot complain where they have been favourably treated but feel they should have been treated more favourably still. Therefore, where a claimant's working week was reduced to take account of her disability and her subsequent ill-health retirement pension was calculated by reference to her earnings whilst on reduced hours there was no breach of *section 15*. Ill health retirement was available only to those with a disability and was a benefit. The claimant could not complain that the benefit should have been calculated on a more generous basis (*Trustees of Swansea University Pension Scheme v Williams* UKEAT/0415/14: [2015] ICR 1197; [2015] IRLR 885, EAT, affirmed by the Court of Appeal [2017] EWCA Civ 1008, [2017] IRLR 882, [2018] ICR 233 and by the Supreme Court [2018] UKSC 65, [2019] IRLR 306, [2019] ICR 93). In the Supreme Court Lord Carnwath endorsed the guidance given in the *Code of Practice* emphasising that there is a relatively low threshold of disadvantage which is sufficient to trigger the requirement to justify under the *Act*.

Care must be taken to analyse whether something that, from one perspective, may seem like a benefit may nevertheless be unfavourable treatment. For instance, in *Bedi v Germany* C-312/17 [2019] IRLR 85, receipt of a disability pension founded a claim for indirect discrimination (for which see **12.34** below). The case concerned the payment of "bridging assistance" which was designed to help older employees who were made redundant make ends meet until their pension was payable. As disabled employees were entitled to receive a disability pension at a lower age than non-disabled colleagues were entitled to receive their ordinary state pension, disabled employees lost their entitlement to bridging assistance at a younger age. As the disability pension paid less than the bridging assistance, they were put at a disadvantage.

Section 15(1)(a) contains a double causation test: the unfavourable treatment must be "because of" the relevant "something" and that "something" must itself "arise in consequence" of the disability. The Tribunal must be careful not to elide the distinction between the two limbs of the test – it is not a question of whether the complainant was treated less favourably because of their disability (*Basildon and Thurrock NHS Foundation Trust v Weerasinghe* UKEAT/397/14 [2016] ICR 305, [2015] All ER (D) 397 (Jul)).

The EAT has provided guidance on the correct approach to *s 15* cases in *Pnasier* above:

"(a) A tribunal must first identify whether there was unfavourable treatment and by whom: in other words, it must ask whether A treated B unfavourably in the respects relied on by B. No question of comparison arises.

(b) The tribunal must determine what caused the impugned treatment, or what was the reason for it. The focus at this stage is on the reason in the mind of A. An examination of the conscious or unconscious thought processes of A is likely to be required, just as it is in a direct discrimination case. Again, just as there may be more than one reason or cause for impugned treatment in a direct discrimination context, so too, there may be more than one reason in a s.15 case. The 'something' that causes the unfavourable treatment need not be the main or sole reason, but must have at least a significant (or more than trivial) influence on the unfavourable treatment, and so amount to an effective reason for or cause of it.

(c) Motives are irrelevant. The focus of this part of the enquiry is on the reason or cause of the impugned treatment and A's motive in acting as he or she did is simply irrelevant ....

(d) The tribunal must determine whether the reason/cause (or, if more than one), a reason or cause, is 'something arising in consequence of B's disability'. That expression 'arising in consequence of' could describe a range of causal links. Having regard to the legislative history of s.15 of the Act . . . , the statutory purpose which appears from the wording of s.15, namely to provide protection in cases where the consequence or effects of a disability lead to unfavourable treatment, and the availability of a justification defence, the causal link between the something that causes unfavourable treatment and the disability may include more than one link. In other words, more than one relevant consequence of the disability may require consideration, and it will be a question of fact assessed robustly in each case whether something can properly be said to arise in consequence of disability.

(e) . . . . However, the more links in the chain there are between the disability and the reason for the impugned treatment, the harder it is likely to be to establish the requisite connection as a matter of fact.

(f) This stage of the causation test involves an objective question and does not depend on the thought processes of the alleged discriminator.

. . .

(i) . . . it does not matter precisely in which order these questions are addressed. Depending on the facts, a tribunal might ask why A treated the claimant in the unfavourable way alleged in order to answer the question whether it was because of 'something arising in consequence of the claimant's disability'. Alternatively, it might ask whether the disability has a particular consequence for a claimant that leads to 'something' that caused the unfavourable treatment."

In respect of the first element of causation (the "because" issue) the test is the same of that in respect of direct discrimination and focuses on the alleged discriminator's reasons for action (see *Dunn v Secretary of State for Justice* [2018] EWCA Civ 1998, [2019] IRLR 298). The "something" must more than trivially influence the treatment but it need not be the sole or principal cause (see *Hall v Chief Constable of West Yorkshire Police* UKEAT/0057/15 [2015] IRLR 893 and *Pnasier v NHS England and another* UKEAT/0137/15 [2016] IRLR 170). The required state of mind is simply that the unfavourable treatment should be because of the relevant something. There is no requirement that the alleged discriminator should have known that the relevant something arose from the Claimant's disability (*City of York Council v Grosset* [2018] EWCA Civ 1105).

In respect of the second element (the "in consequence" issue) there is no need to look at what was in the mind of the alleged discriminator (see *Pnasier*). It is a matter of objective fact to be decided in the light of the evidence (*Sheikholeslami v University of Edinburgh* UKEATS/0014/17 [2018] IRLR 1090). As the EAT suggests in the guidance set out above, there may be a number of links in the chain and "more than one relevant consequence of the disability may require consideration" (*Sheikholeslami* above). One consequence of the objective test is that if the unfavourable treatment is because of something that the claimant incorrectly believes arises in consequence of their disability, the claim will fail (see *IForce Ltd v Wood* UKEAT/0167/18 where an employee was disciplined for refusing to move to work at a different location. She refused because she incorrectly thought the new location would aggravate her osteoarthritis).

If an employee has a disability that causes him to be frequently absent from work, dismissing him for that absence record will amount to a breach of *s 15(1)* unless it can be justified. That is the same outcome that applying the former provisions of the *DDA 1995* would have produced had *Malcolm* (above) not overturned *Clark* (above). The EAT has suggested that where an employee wishes to complain that they have been dismissed for a disability-related absence, they should bring a claim under *s 15* rather than as a claim that the employer has failed to make a reasonable adjustment under *s 20* (for which see **12.37** below) (*General Dynamics Information Technology Ltd v Carranza* UK/EAT/107/14 [2015] ICR 169, [2015] IRLR 43, [2015] ICR 169, EAT). Absence policies with trigger points may also give rise to claims for indirect discrimination on the basis that those with disabilities are subject to a particular disadvantage as they are more likely to have periods of absence and hit the trigger points (see *Ruiz Conejero v Ferroser Servicios Auxiliares SA and another* C270/16; [2018] IRLR 372).

In cases where a dismissal arises from the application of a sickness absence policy, there is commonly argument about what needs to be justified by the employer. There are two possible views. The first view is that one has to justify the policy or procedure itself and that, so long as the policy is justified, its application in individual cases will be too. Lady Hale said in *Seldon v Clarkson Wright and Jakes* ([2012] IRLR 590 UKSC) "I would accept that where it is justified to have a general rule, then the existence of that rule will usually justify the treatment which results from it ...". However, the EAT has suggested that this general principle does not apply in cases concerned with sickness absence procedures that (as is typical) have a number of steps that are taken before an employee can be dismissed. In such cases the Appeal Tribunal held, it was the application of the policy at each individual stage that required justification – *Buchanan v Commissioner of Police of the Metropolis* UKEAT/0112/16, [2016] IRLR 918, [2017] ICR 184.

12.33 Discrimination and Equal Opportunities – I

For a detailed treatment of the justification defence see 13.9 DISCRIMINATION AND EQUAL OPPORTUNITIES – II.

An employer will not be liable where it did not know and could not reasonably have been expected to know that the employee had a disability. In *A Ltd v Z* UEAT/0273/18 [2019] IRLR 952 the Employment Tribunal concluded that although the employee concerned had taken steps to conceal her mental and psychiatric impairments, the employer could reasonably have been expected to have made some inquiry into her mental well-being. The Appeal Tribunal emphasised the importance of asking what the employer would have discovered had they made that inquiry and that since it was likely that employee would have continued to conceal her disability, the employer should not be treated as having constructive knowledge. Where the question of knowledge is in issue, the claimant must establish that the individual that took the decision being challenged either knew or ought to have known of the claimant's disability (*IPC Media Ltd v Millar* [2013] IRLR 707, EAT).

12.34 Indirect discrimination

The concept of indirect discrimination has always been easier to define than to apply in practice. It is often easiest to think first about direct discrimination and then consider how and why indirect discrimination differs. If an employer has a policy of never employing women, a female applicant who falls foul of that policy is the victim of an act of direct discrimination. There is a direct link between the application of the policy; the less favourable treatment that the woman receives and her protected characteristic. You do not need to know anything additional about the context in order to see the discriminatory impact. What if the employer instead insisted that all applicants should have post-graduate degrees? To use the language of *EqA 2010* (explained in greater detail below) that would be to apply a "provision, criterion or practice" that was on its face non-discriminatory. It is impossible to tell whether such a "PCP" would tend to disadvantage women without knowing more about the context – specifically about comparative rates of completion of higher degrees. If it turns out that far fewer women obtain post-graduate degrees, the apparently neutral PCP will in practice favour men. It is the combination of the PCP with what we will call below the "context factor", that explains the disparity. As Lady Hale observed in *Essop v Home Office (UK Border Agency); Naeem v Secretary of State for Justice* [2017] UKSC 27, [2017] 3 All ER 551, [2017] IRLR 558, [2017] ICR 640, the context factors may take a number of different forms. They may be genetic (minimum height requirements indirectly discriminate because women are on average shorter than men see *Ypourgos Esoterikon and another v Kalliri* C-409/16; [2018] IRLR 77, ECJ); or social (length of service provisions will tend indirectly to discriminate because women are expected to be the ones to interrupt their careers to take care of children); they may even be another PCP (so in *Chief Constable of West Yorkshire Police v Homer* [2012] IRLR 601, [2012] ICR 704 a requirement for a degree and a compulsory retirement age combined to produce an indirectly discriminatory effect).

Another way of understanding the difference between direct and indirect discrimination would be to look at what the different types of discrimination protection aim to achieve. This too was summarised eloquently by Lady Hale in *Essop*:

"the prohibition of direct discrimination aims to achieve equality of treatment. Indirect discrimination assumes equality of treatment—the PCP is applied indiscriminately to all—but aims to achieve a level playing field, where people sharing a particular protected characteristic are not subjected to requirements which many of them cannot meet but which cannot be shown to be justified. The prohibition of indirect discrimination thus aims to achieve equality of results in the absence of such justification. It is dealing with hidden barriers which are not easy to anticipate or to spot."

The dividing line between direct and indirect discrimination is not always an easy one to draw but the two forms of discrimination are distinct statutory torts and the distinction makes a material difference, particularly because a defence of justification is available in cases of indirect but not all cases of direct discrimination (*R v Secretary of State for Defence* [2006] EWCA Civ 1293, [2006] 1 WLR 3213, [2006] IRLR 934; For an account of the justification defence see **13.9** DISCRIMINATION AND EQUAL OPPORTUNITIES – **II**). It may be that the same broad set of facts may give rise both to a claim for direct and indirect discrimination. Thus, if a set of job requirements is indirectly discriminatory and, in addition, the interviewer favours members of one race over another, both claims may lie. However, in such a case the complainant will rely on different facts to make out each claim. A particular set of facts should normally (although not invariably) found one or other, but not both, sorts of claim (see *Jaffrey v Department of Environment Transport and the Regions* [2002] IRLR 688, EAT). In *Chief Constable of West Midlands Police v Harrod* (2015) UKEAT/0189/14, [2015] ICR 1311, [2015] IRLR 790, early retirement was only permitted to those whose length of service was long enough to have earned them an entitlement to a pension worth two thirds of average pensionable pay. That meant, in practice, one had to be at least 48 to qualify. The EAT considered, *obiter*, that a criterion that inevitably discriminated on grounds of age (even if it did not take that explicit form) should be treated as direct discrimination. The Court of Appeal specifically declined to consider the point ([2017] IRLR 539, [2017] ICR 869). In *Horgan v Minister for Education & Skills* C-154/18: [2019] IRLR 597, the Irish Government introduced salary arrangements which had the effect of entitling newly recruited teachers to 10% lower pay than that received by the cohort in the previous year. Whilst on the face of it that appeared to be a clear case of indirect age discrimination – an apparently neutral provision (date of appointment) was applied to all new recruits regardless of age but since 70% of those recruited were 25 or younger, it particularly disadvantaged younger teaches – the CJEU concluded that there was no indirect discrimination because the criterion was not "inextricably or indirectly linked to the age of the teachers". The decision appears to require that the PCP should have some inherently discriminatory element rather than simply having a disparate impact in practice. With respect to the CJEU, that is exceptionally difficult to reconcile with existing jurisprudence.

Before 2010, there were a number of subtly different statutory formulations of the test for indirect discrimination in operation. Since the coming into force of the *EqA 2010* there is a single, unified test. *EqA 2010, s 19(1)*, provides:

> "A person (A) discriminates against another (B) if A applies to B a provision, criterion or practice which is discriminatory in relation to a relevant protected characteristic of B's".

The relevant protected characteristics are all of those listed in *EqA 2010, s 4* with the single exception of "pregnancy and maternity" (*EqA 2010, s 19(3)*). This represents an extension of the protection afforded to those whose relevant characteristic is disability or gender re-assignment as neither were protected against indirect discrimination under the previous regime.

A provision, criterion or practice is discriminatory in relation to a relevant protected characteristic of B's if:

> "(a) A applies, or would apply, it to persons with whom B does not share the characteristic,
>
> (b) it puts, or would put, persons with whom B shares the characteristic at a particular disadvantage when compared with persons with whom B does not share it,
>
> (c) it puts, or would put, B at that disadvantage, and
>
> (d) A cannot show it to be a proportionate means of achieving a legitimate aim."

There is no definition of "provision", "criterion" or "practice" in the Act itself. The *EHRC Code* states:

"[the terms] should be construed widely so as to include, for example, any formal or informal policies, rules practices, arrangements, criteria, conditions, prerequisites, qualifications or provisions. A provision, criterion or practice may also include decisions to do something in the future – such as a policy or criterion that has not yet been applied – as well as a 'one-off' or discretionary scheme." (Para 4.5)

The phrase "provision, criterion or practice" is not a "term of art" (*Ishola v Transport for London* [2020] EWCA Civ 112, [2020] IRLR 368. The term 'provision' would be apt to include both contractual provisions and the provisions of non-contractual policies. It should be borne in mind that in cases of sex discrimination, unlawful discrimination in relation to contractual terms is combated by means of a separate legislative regime known, misleadingly, as 'Equal Pay' (see EQUAL PAY **(23)**). The term 'equal pay' is misleading because all discriminatory differences in contractual terms fall within the scope of that protective regime whether or not they are, strictly speaking, to do with pay. A provision may consist of a 'one-off decision' (*Starmer v British Airways plc* [2005] IRLR 862, EAT: decision not to allow an employee to reduce her work to 50% of normal hours constituted the application of a 'provision'). In *Ishola* (above) the Court of Appeal was cautious about being too ready to treat one-off decisions as PCPs. Simler LJ gave the following guidance:

"In context, and having regard to the function and purpose of the PCP in the Equality Act 2010, all three words carry the connotation of a state of affairs (whether framed positively or negatively and however informal) indicating how similar cases are generally treated or how a similar case would be treated if it occurred again. It seems to me that 'practice' here connotes some form of continuum in the sense that it is the way in which things generally are or will be done. That does not mean it is necessary for the PCP or 'practice' to have been applied to anyone else in fact. Something may be a practice or done 'in practice' if it carries with it an indication that it will or would be done again in future if a hypothetical similar case arises. . . . . I consider that although a one-off decision or act can be a practice, it is not necessarily one."

'Criterion' is self-explanatory and significant as many cases involving discrimination will be concerned with selection decisions whether for appointment, promotion or dismissal. There is no requirement (as there had been under the old sex and racial discrimination tests) for the discriminatory criterion to be an absolute bar to the member of the protected class. Thus a criterion that an applicant for a post should have English as a first language will be struck down if it disadvantages an employee of a particular race even if it appears on a list of desirable rather than required characteristics.

'Practice' naturally bears the widest of meanings. It enables the Tribunal to look past an employer's Human Resources policies and to look at the day-to-day experience of the employees. It is possible for a provision, criterion or practice "to emerge from evidence of what happened on a single occasion [but] there must be either direct evidence that what happened was indicative of a practice of more general application, or some evidence from which the existence of such a practice can be inferred" (see *Gan Menachem Hendon Ltd v De Groen* UKEAT/0059/18).

It is not necessary to decide whether a particular measure is specifically a provision, criterion or practice, as long as the apparent discrimination results from something that might properly be described by one or all of those labels (see Per Langstaff J in *Chief Constable of the West Midlands Police v Harrod* (2015) UKEAT/0189/14, [2015] ICR 1311, [2015] IRLR 790, approved by the Court of Appeal [2017] IRLR 539, [2017] ICR 869).

A PCP is applied where employees are required to enter into new terms and conditions if they are to avoid dismissal (*Edie v HCL Insurance BPO Services Ltd* UKEAT/0152/14; [2015] ICR 713, [2015] All ER (D) 264 (Feb)).

A claim may be based on more than one provision, criterion or practice (or "PCP") and relate to the impact the combined PCPs have on more than one protected characteristic. Thus, in *Ministry of Defence v DeBique* [2010] IRLR 471, EAT, a soldier who was unable to obtain the necessary visa to allow her sister to move from St Vincent to assist her with childcare was adversely affected by a PCP that required her to be available for duty twenty four hours a day and seven days a week (which indirectly discriminated against women as they are more likely to have childcare responsibilities) and a PCP which precluded members of family living overseas from coming to the UK so as to assist with childcare (which indirectly discriminated against foreign nationals).

In some cases, the relevant PCP may be expressly defined by the employer. In other cases, the tribunal may need to formulate a PCP by analysing the employer's practice or behaviour. There may be a number of different formulations which are consistent with the underlying circumstances of the case. If a complainant can 'realistically identify a [PCP] capable of supporting [their] case . . . it is nothing to the point that [their] employer can with equal cogency derive from the facts a different and unobjectionable requirement or condition' (*Allonby v Accrington and Rossendale College* [2001] EWCA Civ 529, [2001] IRLR 364, CA).

When is the PCP applied?

In *Little v Richmond Pharmacology Limited* UK/EAT/490/12 [2014] ICR 85, [2013] All ER (D) 204 (Sep) an employee's request to work flexibly, rather than full time, was initially refused but then granted (to the extent of a trial period) on appeal. The EAT determined that the original decision had been contingent on an appeal and, in the light of the employee's success at that stage, the requirement to work full time was not applied.

Disparity of effect - Group disadvantage

At the heart of indirect discrimination is the notion that a single measure taken by an employer may affect different groups of employees very differently. In *Eweida v British Airways Plc* [2010] EWCA Civ 80, [2010] ICR 890, [2010] IRLR 322, [2010] 09 LS Gaz R 19 Lord Justice Sedley defined the purpose of indirect discrimination protection as not to "deal with the problem of group discrimination" but rather to "deal with the discriminatory impact of facially neutral requirements". That task is approached by asking whether "an identifiable group is adversely affected, whether actually or potentially, by some ostensibly neutral requirement". The practical consequence is that a complainant has to show more than just that they have been disadvantaged by the relevant requirement. They have to show that others who share their protected characteristic would also be adversely affected. In *Eweida* itself, the complainant's indirect discrimination claim failed because she was unable to show that any other employee shared her religious belief that she should wear a crucifix visibly. Issues of justification never arose, because Ms Eweida could not establish she had been indirectly discriminated against. Ms Eweida took her case to Strasbourg. The European Court of Human Rights upheld her claim that the UK had failed to take adequate steps to protect her right to manifest her religion. The Court's analysis focused entirely on justification arguments which means that the Court must be taken to have believed that the Claimant should have been able to establish that she had been indirectly discriminated against. One possible reading of the ECtHR's decision, therefore, is that the requirement to show that the PCP particularly disadvantages others with whom you share your belief is incompatible with the convention right. In *Mba v Mayor and Burgesses of Merton LBC* [2013] EWCA Civ 1562; [2014] IRLR 145, [2014] ICR 357 Lord Justice Elias confirmed that: "The protection of freedom of religion conferred by . . . Article [9] does not require a claimant to establish any group disadvantage; the question is whether the interference of that individual right by the employer is proportionate given the legitimate aims of the employer". He goes on to say, however, that Article 9 rights cannot be directly enforced in the Tribunal and expresses his belief that it was "not possible to read down the concept of indirect discrimination to ignore the need to establish group disadvantage" so as to ensure compatibility with the Convention. Tribunals should assume, therefore, that group disadvantage is still required in religion and belief cases until Parliament deals with the incompatibility. Permission to appeal to the Supreme Court was subsequently denied ([2014] ICR 947). The need to establish group disadvantage was re-affirmed by the EAT in *Trayhorn v Secretary of State for Justice* UKEAT/0304/16/RN, [2018] IRLR 502 and again in *Gray v Mulberry Company (Design) Limited* [2019] EWCA Civ 1720, [2020] IRLR 29.

Causation

We suggested above that one way of understanding indirect discrimination was to think of it as discrimination which arises from the combination of a neutral PCP with a context factor. It is the context factor that provides the link to the protected characteristic. Both are "causes" of the disadvantage. To take the simple example of a height restriction: if the employer abandoned the minimum height requirement, there would be no disadvantage. Similarly, if the women and men were the same height on average (so that the context factor no longer existed), there would be no disadvantage. For the purposes of the *EqA 2010*, the legally relevant causal relationship is between the PCP and the particular disadvantage (see *Essop* (above) at paragraph 25 of the judgment). Another way of putting the same point is to say that the law is focused on whether the PCP is a cause of the disadvantage and not why it is. This point is dramatically illustrated by *Essop* itself. The Civil Service required those seeking promotion to sit a test. BAME civil servants tended to do less well on average. Similarly, older employees tended to do less well. Statistical analysis suggested that in each case the chances of the apparent connection between the protected characteristic and the lower average success rate being a matter of mere coincidence was 0.1%. There were plainly context factors related to protected characteristics in play. The difficulty was no-one could say what they were. The Supreme Court decided that that did not matter; the claimants did not have to establish why the PCP particularly disadvantaged those with the relevant protected characteristics, they just had to establish that the PCP was having that effect.

Meaning of 'particular disadvantage'

In cases of indirect discrimination the complainant must show that the PCP, puts persons who share the same protected characteristic as the complainant at a 'particular disadvantage'. This term is not defined. It was unclear whether the use of the word 'particular' was intended to convey something more than mere disadvantage. The same language is used in the *Race Discrimination Directive 2000/43*. In *Chez Razpredelenie Bulgaria AD v Komisia za Zashtita ot Diskriminatsia* C-83/14, [2015] IRLR 746, the ECJ rejected a contention that the use of the word "particular" connotes a "a serious, obvious and particularly significant case". The requirement for a "particular disadvantage" must be understood as meaning that "it is particularly persons [with the relevant protected characteristic] who are at a disadvantage because of the measure at issue". In other words, it is not a question of how grave a disadvantage might be but who suffers it (see also *Jyske Finans A/S v Ligebehandlingsnaevnet* C-668/15; [2017] IRLR 665, ECJ).

Assessing disadvantage

Assessing disparity of effect is a comparative process. Whereas, in a case of direct discrimination, one compares the treatment received by an individual with that received or which would have been received by another, indirect discrimination cases require comparisons between groups of employees. Taking, by way of example, a case of indirect sex discrimination, the Tribunal looks at the impact of the relevant PCP on the men and women affected by it. The first task of the Tribunal is to determine which group or groups of employees it is going to look at in order to perform the comparison. This is known as selecting the 'pool' for comparison. The task of identifying the relevant pool can be difficult and is often, in practice, determinative of the case (See, for example, *Chaudhury v British Medical Association* [2007] EWCA Civ 788, [2007] IRLR 800: In a case under the old test, the claimant complained that the BMA operated a policy (amounting to a requirement or condition) of refusing to support members in race discrimination claims against regulatory authorities. The Court of Appeal determined that had such a requirement or condition been applied the appropriate pool for assessing the disparity of its effect was not BMA members generally but those members who wished to bring such claims. Since all such members were equally disadvantaged, regardless of their race, no disparity of effect could be established).

EqA 2010, s 23(2) requires that on a comparison of cases for the purposes of *s 19* "there must be no material difference between the circumstances relating to each case". The EAT concluded in *Naeem v Secretary of State for Justice* UKEAT/215/13; [2014] IRLR 520, [2014] ICR 472 that the consequence of *s 23* is that the identity of the appropriate comparator group is a question of law (neither the Court of Appeal, nor the Supreme Court subsequently suggested otherwise, albeit that the EAT decision on pool was ultimately overturned).

The best starting point for determining the composition of the pool is the advice given in the Statutory Code of Practice (2011) issued by the EHRC. At paragraph 4.18 it says:

> "In general, the pool should consist of the group which the provision, criterion or practice affects (or would affect) either positively or negatively, while excluding workers who are not affected by it, either positively or negatively."

One should also bear in mind, however, what the purpose of the selecting the pool is. One should focus on the specific allegation that is being made. The pool should "realistically and effectively test the particular allegation" (*Ministry of Defence v DeBique* [2010] IRLR 471, EAT).

Because it may be possible in a particular case, to identify more than one potentially appropriate pool, the selection of the pool is, in the first instance, a matter for the claimant. However, the tribunal is not necessarily bound to adopt the pool suggested by the claimant and it may reject the claimant's pool where it considers that it is an artificial or arbitrary one (*Abbott v Cheshire and Wirral Partnership NHS Trust* [2006] EWCA Civ 523, [2006] IRLR 546, [2006] ICR 1267). If the Tribunal decides to reject the claimant's proposed pool, it should explain its reasons for doing so in its decision (*Secretary of State for Trade and Industry v Rutherford (No 2)* at the EAT, reported at [2004] IRLR 892, [2005] ICR 119 at 160). Once the Tribunal has resolved to determine the pool for itself, it does not have a broad discretion as to how the pool is identified. In most cases, the Court of Appeal suggested in *Allonby* ([2001] IRLR 364, CA, it should be a matter of logical deduction from the measure. Consistently with the EHRC guidance set out above, the starting point should be the whole of the group to which the provision, criterion or practice is applied, and the tribunal will be wary of any further sub-division (cf *London Underground Ltd v Edwards* [1995] IRLR 355, *Jones v University of Manchester* [1993] ICR 474, CA and *Rutherford v Secretary of State for Trade and Industry* [2006] UKHL 19, [2006] IRLR 551, [2006] ICR 785 – provisions precluding claims for redundancy payments and unfair dismissal by those over 65 applied to the whole working population and not just those older employees for whom the 'retirement had some meaning'). *Rutherford* was not authority, the Court of Appeal concluded in *Grundy v BA* [2008] IRLR 74, for the 'routine selection of the widest pool'. Sedley LJ instead preferred to allow the tribunal a discretion as to the pool considered:

> 'In discrimination claims the key determinant . . . is the issue which the claimant has elected to pose and which the tribunal is therefore required to evaluate by finding a pool in which the specificity of the allegation can be realistically tested. Provided it tests the allegation in a suitable pool, the tribunal cannot be said to have erred in law even if a different pool, with a different outcome, could equally legitimately have been chosen.'

Equally, an expansion of the pool to include those who were not even potentially subject to the provision, criterion or practice, would be inappropriate (cf *Briggs v North Eastern Education and Library Board* [1990] IRLR 181). However, where the provision, criterion or practice relates to recruitment criteria the relevant pool might be very large and in *Greater Manchester Police Authority v Lea* [1990] IRLR 372, the EAT held that the employment tribunal had not erred in accepting that the economically active population was an appropriate pool for the purpose of determining the proportion of men and women who could comply with a condition of not being in receipt of an occupational pension. In *Lord Chancellor v Coker* [2001] IRLR 116, the EAT considered a case where the Lord Chancellor had decided to appoint a particular individual to be his special adviser. The appointment was challenged by two complainants who alleged that the failure publicly to advertise the position had resulted in their having been the subjects of acts of indirect sex and race discrimination, respectively. As the criterion was, in effect, that the candidate should be the relevant specific individual, the EAT concluded that no pool could sensibly be identified. The EAT's decision was upheld by the Court of Appeal ([2001] EWCA Civ 1756, [2002] IRLR 80, [2002] ICR 321). The relevant criterion was identified before their Lordships as being a friend of the Lord Chancellor. The Court of Appeal concluded that the necessary disparity of impact could not be established. Looking at the pool of those qualified to perform the role, the criterion excluded almost the entirety of its members. The criterion could only be said to have a disproportionate effect where a significant proportion of the pool were able to satisfy it. That was not the case on the facts. Lord Phillips went on to opine that:

> 'Making an appointment from within a circle of family, friends and personal acquaintances is seldom likely to constitute indirect discrimination.'

Under the old law, the Claimant had to establish that a "considerably smaller proportion" of those who shared their protected characteristic could comply with the PCP. *EqA 2010* requires, instead, that the claimant establish that those in the pool who share the claimant's protected characteristic should be at a "particular disadvantage". The old test was explicitly concerned with numbers and the case law set out below, decided under the old provisions, understandably focus on figures. The new test is not expressly concerned with numbers but it seems from the EHRC Code that statistics will still be important. In defining "disadvantage", *EHRC Code, Para 4.12* says:

> 'Statistics can provide an insight into the link between the provision, criterion or practice and the disadvantage that it causes."

However, the *EHRC Code* recognises that the numbers of people involved may be too small or the evidence available too unreliable to allow for a statistical analysis. In such circumstances, the *EHRC Code* suggests (at *Para 4.13*), it would be neither practicable nor appropriate for a statistical approach to be taken and the tribunal may wish, instead, to rely upon expert evidence. Experts may also be appropriate where the tribunal requires some assistance in properly understanding the impact of a PCP on those with a particular protected characteristic (see *Para 4.14* which gives as an example expert evidence about the principles of a particular religious belief). It seems that even expert evidence may be unnecessary. In *Games v University of Kent* [2015] IRLR 202, EAT, the tribunal was unpersuaded by statistics relied upon by a claimant who alleged that a requirement for lecturers to have a PhD was indirectly age discriminatory. The EAT considered that evidence of the experience of the claimant or of other members of the affected group might provide "compelling evidence of disadvantage even if there are no statistics at all".

When the *EHRC Code* turns to providing guidance on carrying out the comparative exercise it turns again to numbers. The tribunal should ask (says *Para 4.21*) how many workers in the pool are (or would be) disadvantaged by the PCP despite not sharing the protected characteristic with the claimant. That number should be expressed as a proportion, which the guidance labels as "x". The same exercise is then repeated in relation to pool members who do share the protected characteristic. That proportion is labelled "y". The tribunal then compares "x" with "y" in order to determine whether the necessary particular disadvantage exists. *Para 4.22* advises:

'Whether a difference is significant will depend on the context, such as the size of the pool and the numbers behind the proportions. It is not necessary to show that the majority of those within the pool who share the protected characteristic are placed at a disadvantage.'

Turning to the case law on the old formulation, there was little guidance on how one determines whether a particular disparate impact is sufficient. The issue was referred to the European Court of Justice in *R v Secretary of State for Employment, ex p Seymour-Smith* [1999] IRLR 253, [1999] ICR 447. The guidance provided by the ECJ was disappointingly vague. The ECJ decision echoed the language of the *SDA 1975* as it was prior to 1 October 2005 in requiring that a 'considerably smaller percentage' of women than men were able to satisfy the relevant condition. A mere statistically significant disparity was insufficient. However, the ECJ went on to hold that a 'lesser but persistent and relatively constant disparity over a long period' might suffice. It was hoped that the House of Lords might feel able to put a little meat on these bones when the matter came back for their further consideration in the light of the reference ([2000] IRLR 263, [2000] ICR 244). The issue in *Seymour-Smith* was whether the requirement, introduced in 1985, that employees should have two years' continuous service before qualifying for protection against unfair dismissal indirectly discriminated against women. In 1985, 77.4% of men could comply with that requirement whereas only 68.9% of women could do so. In 1991, the year which their Lordships identified as being the critical one for the purposes of the particular case, the relevant percentages were 74.5% and 67.4%. None of their Lordships thought that those figures, on their own, suggested that a 'considerably smaller percentage' of women could comply. However, the majority felt that the disparity (which narrowed slowly to about 4.3% by 1993) fell into the category of the sort of 'persistent and relatively consistent' disparity that the ECJ had indicated might suffice. They determined, therefore, that the requirement was indirectly discriminatory although they went on to find that it was justified.

In practice, the tribunals are given a considerable margin of discretion in deciding when the percentages should be taken to indicate a sufficiently significant disparity. The courts had consistently rejected the adoption of a rule of thumb (see *McCausland v Dungannon District Council* [1993] IRLR 583 which was concerned with the construction of the *Fair Employment (Northern Ireland) Act 1976* which applied the same test of disparate impact to religious discrimination). In *Harvest Town Circle Ltd v Rutherford* [2001] IRLR 599, [2002] ICR 123, EAT, the EAT expressed the pious (if rather faint) hope that 'as more cases of indirect discrimination are heard a more soundly based assessment of what is or is not properly regarded as a considerable or substantial disparity will develop'. In *London Underground Ltd v Edwards (No 2)* [1998] IRLR 364, [1999] ICR 494, there was only one person in the pool of comparison who could not comply with the relevant requirement. 100% of the 2,023 men to whom the provision applied could comply. Of the 21 women affected, only the complainant could not comply. This meant that the proportion of women that could comply was 95.2%. Nevertheless, the Court of Appeal upheld the tribunal's decision that the proportion of women that could comply was considerably smaller.

The approach adopted in *Edwards* illustrates another general principle applicable to the assessment of disparate impact; one should not focus on the absolute numbers underlying the relevant proportions but on the percentages themselves. The principle was specifically endorsed by the ECJ in *Seymour-Smith* (but see *Harvest Town Circle Ltd* above, in which the EAT interpret *Seymour-Smith* as allowing a domestic court to look at either absolute numbers or relative proportions of those who could comply).

In many cases, the tribunal will look at the relevant proportions and simply subtract one from the other. In the *Edwards* case, for instance, one might say that 4.8% more men can comply than women. *McCausland* suggests taking a further mathematical step. Rather than subtracting the smaller percentage from the larger, one should calculate a ratio. In the *McCausland* case itself, 2.9% of Protestants could comply with the relevant requirement as compared with only 1.5% of Catholics. Simply subtracting one percentage from the other produces an unimpressive difference of only 1.4%. However, when one looks at the ratio of the two percentages one finds that the group of Catholics that could comply was only 71% of the size of the group of Protestants that could do so. A further variation was suggested by Lord Nicholls in *Barry v Midland Bank plc* [1999] IRLR 581, [1999] ICR 859 at page 869. He suggested that having calculated what proportion of men and women fell within the advantaged and disadvantaged groups respectively one should then calculate a ratio of the proportions of those falling within the disadvantaged group. His approach is thus akin to the *McCausland* approach save that it focuses on those who cannot comply rather than those who can. However, in *Secretary of State for Trade and Industry v Rutherford* above, the Court of Appeal indicated that it would be wrong to focus only on the disadvantaged group. When *Rutherford* came before the House of Lords, Lord Walker of Gestingthorpe took the view that, save where special circumstances justify it, attention should be focused on the 'advantaged' group (*Rutherford v Secretary of State for Trade and Industry* [2006] UKHL 19, [2006] IRLR 551, [2006] ICR 785). However, in *Grundy v British Airways plc* [2007] EWCA Civ 1020, [2008] IRLR 74, an equal pay case, the Court of Appeal held that an employment tribunal had been entitled to focus on the disadvantaged group. the position remains, therefore, somewhat unclear.

Not all PCPs produce a binary outcome in which someone will be found, for instance, either to be able to comply with a requirement or not. In *McNeil and others v R&C Comrs* [2019] EWCA Civ 1112, [2019] IRLR 915, [2020] ICR 515 the Court of Appeal looked (in the context of an equal pay claim) at whether the use of a length of service factor in determining pay put women at a particular disadvantage. The claimants ran a statistical case pointing out that women were "clustered" at the lower end of the pay scale. The Court of Appeal rejected that approach suggesting that the better course was to average the pay received by men and women across the pay band.

The EAT has sought to rely on *Seymour-Smith* as a basis for taking a much less mechanistic approach to the assessment of the sufficiency of disparity. In *Chief Constable of Avon and Somerset Constabulary v Chew* [2001] All ER (D) 101 (Sep), EAT, the EAT indicated that a 'flexible approach' could be adopted to assessing the sufficiency of any disparity. It was not always necessary to rely on statistics. Further, the tribunal was entitled to consider whether the objectionable provision was inherently more likely to produce a detrimental effect, which disparately affected a particular sex. Thus in *Chew*, a shift rota would likely be harder for those with childcare responsibilities to comply with, and women are more likely to have childcare responsibilities.

PCPs that distinguish between employees on the basis of length of service are often considered to adversely affect younger employees. However, not all such provisions will have the necessary disparity of effect, one example is *Tyrolean Airways Tiroler Luftfahrt Gesellschaft mbH v Betriebsrat Bord der Tyrolean Airways Tiroler Luftfahrt Gesellschaft mbH*: C-132/11 [2012] IRLR 781: A provision in a collective agreement which required flight and cabin crew to have three years' employment with the airline before achieving a particular grade was not sufficiently linked (either directly or indirectly) to age for it to be discriminatory. The rule excluded experience gained with other airlines it was not an age-related provision.

Disparity of effect - Personal disadvantage

The third element of the test is personal disadvantage. It does not matter if, for instance, persons of a particular religion or sex are disproportionately disadvantaged by a provision, criterion or practice, if the complainant is not. Thus a female employee cannot complain that she has been indirectly discriminated against as a result of an employer imposing a minimum height requirement if she is taller than the minimum requirement. Under the old test, inability to comply with the requirement or condition was not its own detriment (*Lord*

Chancellor v Coker [2001] IRLR 116, EAT). It is thought that a similar principle applies under the new test. The disadvantage must be the consequence of the application of the provision, criterion or practice and not the imposition of the measure itself.

In addition to being able to demonstrate that they are personally disadvantaged, the Act appears to require that the claimant demonstrate that they are subject to the same disadvantage as the group (hence the reference at *s 19(1)(c)* to "that disadvantage" rather than to "a disadvantage"). Usually, that will be obvious. However, there can be difficult cases. One is *Essop* (above). It was understood, in *Essop* that BAME candidates were more likely to fail the test. It was not understood why. It was argued on behalf of the Home Office that a black candidate who failed should have to show that the reason why they failed was the same reason that fewer black candidates on average succeeded. Unless the claimant could do that, it was argued, the tribunal could not know whether the claimant and the group were suffering from the same disadvantage. Otherwise, there was a danger of "coat-tailing". A candidate who failed because they were late to the exam could just say that they had suffered the same particular disadvantage (ie "failing") as the group. The Supreme Court rejected that approach. If it could be shown that the failure arose from lateness, it was not the PCP that was disadvantaging the candidate – the necessary causation was lacking. Another way of looking at it would be that their lateness amounted to a "material difference between the circumstances" of the candidate and the others in the pool for the purposes of *s 23*. A third suggestion made by Lady Hale was that the issue could be wrapped up in the consideration of justification.

If a causal connection must be established between the personal disadvantage and the protected characteristic, it seems that it does not have to be a characteristic of the complainant as it is possible to bring an associative indirect discrimination complaint. That was the view of the ECJ in *Chez Razpredelenie Bulgaria AD v Komisia za Zashtita ot Diskriminatsia* C-83/14, [2015] IRLR 746: An electricity company placed meters out of reach in predominantly Roma areas. This was to the complainant's detriment even though she was not herself of Roma origin. She lived in a Roma area and was not provided with a meter she could easily check. The ECJ considered that both associative direct and indirect discrimination claims were open to her.

Indirect discrimination: particular cases

12.35 *Sex discrimination and full-time work*

Provisions, criteria or practices which result in the less favourable treatment of part-time employees are frequently found indirectly to discriminate against women (cf *Bilka-Kaufhaus GmbH v Weber von Hartz*: 170/84 [1986] ECR 1607, [1986] IRLR 317; *Clarke v Eley (IMI) Kynoch Ltd* [1982] IRLR 482, [1983] ICR 165, EAT; *R v Secretary of State for Employment, ex p Equal Opportunities Commission* [1994] IRLR 176, [1994] ICR 317), although it cannot be assumed that such a condition would have a discriminatory effect (see, for example, *Sinclair, Roche & Temperley v Heard* [2004] IRLR 763, EAT). Each case turns on its own facts and claimants have to be prepared to lead evidence which establishes a disparate impact (*Kidd v DRG (UK) Ltd* [1985] IRLR 190, [1985] ICR 405).

Because the effects of a requirement to work full time are often complex, it is by no means always immediately obvious that the complainant had been less favourably treated. See, for instance, *Kachelmann v Bankhaus Hermann Lampe KG*: C-322/98 [2000] ECR I-7505, [2001] IRLR 49, ECJ, in which the ECJ wrestled with the question of whether a bank's decision, following the deletion of a part-time post, to limit the selection pool for redundancy to part-time workers amounted to less favourable treatment or (as it ultimately decided) that to have included full-timers would be to have conferred an advantage on part-timers by effectively entitling them to be offered a full-time post if a full-timer were selected for redundancy.

Historically, the predominance of women in the part-time sector has been assumed to be related to the fact that they have traditionally been expected to be the providers of homecare to young children. This assumption underpins the reasoning of the EAT in the case of *Price v Civil Service Commission (No 2)* [1978] IRLR 3 which held that imposing a maximum age limit of 28 for appointment as an Executive Officer in the Civil Service was, in practice, to the disadvantage of women as they were more likely to have had career breaks in order to start a family. Similarly, in *Meade-Hill and National Union of Civil and Public Servants v British Council* [1996] 1 All ER 79, [1995] ICR 847, [1995] IRLR 478, the Court of Appeal was persuaded that the exercise of a contractual mobility clause might be discriminatory as women were more likely than their partners to be the 'second earner' and thus less able to re-locate. Whilst it appears that the tribunals and courts are frequently comfortable making such assumptions, in practice it is dangerous for an employer to do so. In *Skyrail Oceanic Ltd v Coleman* [1981] IRLR 398, [1981] ICR 864, it was held that selection of a woman for redundancy on the assumption that men are more likely than women to be the primary supporters of their spouses and children could itself amount to unlawful discrimination.

The same issue arises in circumstances where a woman wishes to make changes to her work patterns following the birth of her child. In *Clymo v Wandsworth London Borough Council* [1989] IRLR 24, [1989] ICR 250, an employer declined to allow an employee to change to a job-sharing (ie part-time) arrangement. The EAT held that the employer, having merely declined to provide an advantage not proffered to any employees in that grade, had not 'subjected' the employee to anything, and that there was no detriment. By contrast, in *Robinson v Oddbins Ltd* [1996] 27 DCLD 1 an employment tribunal held that the employee's request to job-share had not been properly considered and the company's reliance on a contractual clause requiring employees, when asked, to work hours over and above the standard working week had indirectly discriminated against women who were more likely to have childcare responsibilities (cf also *Puttick v Eastbourne Borough Council* (unreported, 1995, COIT 3106/2)). In another case, the EAT held that a refusal to allow a woman to job-share was not directly discriminatory in the absence of evidence that a man making a similar request would have had it granted; however, it did not consider the issue of indirect discrimination (*British Telecommunications plc v Roberts* [1996] IRLR 601). In practice, employers will need to be able to establish that there is a sensible justification for requiring that employees work full-time if they are to be safe from claims. In *Lockwood v Crawley Warren Group Ltd* [2001] 680 IDS Brief 9 (EAT/1176/99), EAT, this approach was extended still further. A female employee encountered difficulties with her childcare arrangements. She offered to work full-time from home or else to take up to six months' unpaid leave with a view to resolving the difficulties. She was offered two weeks of leave instead and resigned. The EAT decided that the refusal to allow her either to work from home or to take the leave she had asked for, amounted to the application of a condition or requirement. For an example of the circumstances in which a refusal to allow an employee to work flexibly was justified, see *Georgiou v Colman Coyle* [2002] 705 IDS Brief 12, EAT: the office was small; there was a need for two full-time solicitors; commercial clients expected a prompt and efficient service; the need to consult files and to be supervised meant that the complainant had to attend the respondent's premises; and reduced fee income would adversely affect the respondent's profitability.

12.35a *Sex discrimination and absence on maternity or parental leave*

An employee who is absent on maternity or parental leave is unable to perform their work duties. That inability may have consequences where access to benefits or continued employment may depend on an assessment of work performed, targets achieved or income generated. There is, of course, a specific protection available where an employer treats an employee unfavourably because of maternity leave (see [12.31] above and 33.24 MATERNITY AND PARENTAL RIGHTS below) or parental leave. However, indirect sex discrimination may have a role to play too. In *Riezniece v Zemkopibas ministrija and another* C-7/12; [2013] IRLR 828; [2014] ICR 1096, the CJEU determined that a method of selecting employees for transfer or dismissal amounted to indirect sex discrimination. The employee was absent on parental leave when a post was abolished. An assessment was performed. Some of the criteria matched those used in annual appraisals but some did not. As the employee was on leave she was assessed on the basis of her last annual appraisal. This approach was thought to disadvantage her and she scored lowest in the assessment. A much higher number of women took parental leave than did men.

12.36 *Sexual orientation*

It is lawful to offer access to benefits, facilities or services to married persons and civil partners to the exclusion of all other persons. *EqA 2010, Sch 9, Part 3, Para 18(2)* specifically provides that that does not amount to an act of sexual orientation discrimination (but see *Maruko v Versorgungsanstalt der Deutschen Buhnen*: C-267/06 [2008] IRLR 450).

Many employers offered access to benefits, facilities or services exclusively to married persons which had the effect of excluding homosexual employees. *EqA 2010, Sch 9, Part 3, Para 18(1)* provides that no claim for sexual orientation discrimination lies in relation to any such practice in so far as the relevant right had accrued before 5 December 2005 (on which date civil partnerships came into being) or is a right to a benefit which is payable in respect of periods of service before that date. The Supreme Court held, however, in *Innospec Ltd and others v Walker* [2017] UKSC 47, [2017] IRLR 928, [2017] ICR 1077 that *Para 18* should be disapplied in so far as it authorises a restriction of payment of benefits based on periods of service before 5 December 2005.

To bring a claim of indirect discrimination, it will be necessary for a complainant to identify himself as being of a particular sexual orientation, something that is not necessary for a complaint of direct discrimination, victimisation or harassment.

12.37 Disability: Duty to make reasonable adjustments

Under the *DDA 1995*, there was no prohibition of indirect disability discrimination, instead there was a new creature: a duty to make reasonable adjustments where a disabled employee is placed at a "substantial disadvantage" as the result of a provision, criterion or practice, physical feature of the employer's premises or the absence of an auxiliary aid. That former single path to liability reflects EU Law. There is a duty of "reasonable accommodation" in the *Framework Directive 2000/78, Art 5*, which provides:

> 'In order to guarantee compliance with the principle of equal treatment for persons with disabilities, reasonable accommodation shall be provided. This means that employers shall take appropriate measures, where needed in a particular case, to enable a person with a disability to have access to, participate in, or advance in employment, or to undergo training, unless such measures would impose a disproportionate burden on the employer. This burden shall not be disproportionate when it is sufficiently remedied by measures existing within the framework of the disability policy of the Member State concerned.'

The CJEU in *DW Nobel Plastiques Iberica SA* C-397/18: [2019] IRLR 1104 read the duty along with the prohibition on indirect discrimination so that redundancy selection criteria that disadvantaged those with disabilities were unlawful unless reasonable accommodation had been made.

In our Domestic Law indirect discrimination and failure to make reasonable adjustments are distinct torts. The principal difference between the ordinary duty not indirectly to discriminate and the duty to make reasonable adjustments is that the former is simply a path to compensation whereas the latter imposes a positive duty upon an employer to remove barriers to the effective participation in its workforce of those with disabilities.

When does the duty arise?

The duty is set out at *EqA 2010, s 20* and is supplemented by a detailed schedule: *EqA 2010, Sch 8.*

EqA 2010, s 20 imposes a "requirement" on an employer:

(1)   whose provisions, criteria or practices puts a disabled person at a "substantial disadvantage" in relation to a relevant matter in comparison with persons who are not disabled (*s 20(3)*);

(2)   whose premises have a physical feature which puts a disabled person at a substantial disadvantage (*s 20(4)*); or

(3)   whose disabled employee will be put at a substantial disadvantage if they are not provided with an auxiliary aid (*s 20(5)*);

to "take such steps as it is reasonable to have to take to avoid the disadvantage" or to provide the auxiliary aid (as appropriate). A failure to comply with any of the requirements spelt out above is treated as a failure to comply with a duty to make reasonable adjustments (*EqA 2010, s 21(1)*) which, in turn, amounts to an act of discrimination (*EqA 2010, s 21(2)*). A tribunal considering whether or not the duty has been complied with should make explicit findings identifying: the relevant provision, criterion or practice; the persons who are not disabled with whom comparison is made; the nature and the extent of any substantial disadvantage suffered by the employee; and any step or steps it would have been reasonable for the employer to take (see *Secretary of State for Work and Pensions (Job Centre Plus) v Higgins* UKEAT/579/12, [2014] ICR 341, [2013] All ER (D) 351 (Oct)).

The Act does not further define the phrase "provisions, criteria or practices". *EHRC Code* suggests that the terms should be construed widely and would include: "any formal or informal policies, rules, practices, arrangements or qualifications including one-off decision and actions" (*Para 6.10*). "Physical feature" is defined at *s 20(10)* to include "a feature arising from the design or construction of a building; a feature of an approach to, exit from or access to a building; a fixture or fitting, or furniture, furnishings, materials, equipment or other chattels, in or on the premises; or any other physical element or quality". References to auxiliary aids include references to auxiliary services (*s 20(11)*). It would appear that a 'provision, criterion or practice' could include an implied condition that a person is fit for the job they are employed to do. If it transpires that a person through disability can no longer fulfil that condition (ie the person is no longer capable of doing the job for which they were employed) then there may be a duty to consider any adjustments that could be made to remove the disadvantage caused by that implied condition (see *Archibald v Fife Council* [2004] UKHL 32, [2004] IRLR 651, [2004] ICR 954, HL).

In *Nottingham City Transport Limited v Harvey* [2013] All ER (D) 73 (Apr), EAT, the Appeal Tribunal found that a procedurally-flawed disciplinary investigation which disadvantaged a disabled employee was not a "practice" as there was no evidence that investigations conducted by the respondent were generally inadequate. Similarly, in *Carphone Warehouse Limited v Martin* [2013] EqLR 481, EAT, the Appeal Tribunal decided that "incompetence or a woeful lack of application or a failure to stick to your own time limits [could not] . . . be properly characterised as a [PCP]". In *Griffiths v Secretary of State for Work and Pensions* [2015] EWCA Civ 1265, [2016] IRLR 216, [2017] ICR 160, the Court of Appeal considered the vexed and common question of adjustments to absence policies. The Court recommended care as to how the PCP is framed. The PCP in *Griffiths* itself was not the particular absence policy itself but rather the underlying requirement (reflected in the policy) to "maintain a certain level of attendance at work so as to avoid disciplinary sanctions".

The Act further defines what may be expected by way of adjustments:

(1)   Where the relevant provision, criterion or practice or auxiliary aid relates to the provision of information the steps that it is reasonable for an employer to take include steps for ensuring that the information is provided in accessible format (*s 20(6)*); and

(2)   Where the disadvantage arises from a physical feature, avoiding the disadvantage may include: "removing the physical feature in question; altering it; or providing a reasonable means of avoiding it" (*s 20(9)*).

EqA 2010, Sch 8 fleshes out the *s 20* test. In relation to employers two things are identified as "relevant matters": Deciding to whom to offer employment and employment itself (*EqA 2010, Sch 8, Part 2, para (1)*). In *General Dynamics Information Technology Ltd v Carranza* UKEAT/0107/14 [2015] ICR 169, [2015] IRLR 43, EAT suggested that adjustments should be understood as "practical actions which are taken to avoid the disadvantage". The EAT contrasted such actions with adjustments to "mere mental processes" which they felt the Act did not require. Specifically, they rejected an argument that it would have been a reasonable adjustment to disregard an earlier warning for absence when considering whether to dismiss. The EAT further suggested that where the essence of the complaint is someone has been dismissed for disability-related absence in accordance with an employer's absence management policy, the better course is to bring a claim under *s 15* (for which see **12.33** above) rather than suggesting that the policy should have been adjusted.

In order for the duty to arise the employee must be subjected to a "substantial" disadvantage in comparison with persons who are not disabled. "Substantial" is defined at *EqA 2010, s 212(1)* to mean "more than minor or trivial". The threshold is set deliberately low. The disadvantage is comparative, so it is no answer to a claim to show that persons who are not disabled are also disadvantaged by the PCP if the claimant's disadvantage is greater (*Sheikholeslami v University of Edinburgh* UKEATS/0014/17 [2018] IRLR 1090). The duty to make reasonable adjustments arises when the employer can take steps to avoid the relevant disadvantage (*Abertawe Bro Morgannwg University Local Health Board v Morgan* [2018] EWCA Civ 640, [2018] IRLR 1050, [2018] ICR 1194).

Is the claimant obliged to show that the reason for the comparative disadvantage is her disability? The EAT suggests not in *Sheikholeslami* (above). The EAT said of *EqA 2010, s 20(3)* that proving that a claimant was placed at a substantial disadvantage "*because of her disability*" was not what the statutory test required. It did not "*contain a strict causation test . . . Rather, a comparison exercise is required . . . to test whether the PCP has the effect of disadvantaging the disabled person more than trivially in comparison with others who do not have any disability*". That explanation of the purpose of the test is difficult to reconcile with *Para 6.16* of the *EHRC Code* which states that the purpose of the comparison is to "*establish whether it is because of disability that a particular provision, criterion, practice or physical feature or the absence of an auxiliary aid disadvantages the disabled person in question*". In contrast to the position with cases of direct and indirect discrimination, there is "*no requirement to identify a comparator or comparator group whose circumstances are the same or nearly the same as the disabled person's*" (*Para 6.16*). The disabled person affected must be the claimant. It is not possible to bring an "associative" reasonable adjustments claim. So in *Hainsworth v Ministry of Defence* [2014] EWCA Civ 763, [2014] IRLR 728 an employer did not have to transfer an employee back to the UK so as to ensure that her disabled son had access to education designed to meet his special needs.

No duty where employer lacks knowledge of disability or disadvantage

Limitations on the duty are set out *EqA 2010, Sch 8, Part 3*. An employer is not subject to a duty to make reasonable adjustments if he does not know and could not reasonably be expected to know:

(1)   In the case of an applicant or potential applicant for employment that the disabled person may be an applicant for the work in question;

(2)   In any other case, that an interested disabled person has a disability and is likely to be placed at the relevant substantial disadvantage.

In *Wilcox v Birmingham CAB Services Ltd* [2011] EqLR 810, the EAT departed from earlier authority (*Eastern and Coastal Kent PCT v Grey* [2009] IRLR 429) which had suggested that an employer could only rely on the exception if he could show that he lacked the actual or constructive knowledge referred to in both limbs of (2) above. That interpretation seemed to mean that an employer might be subject to the duty even where he was unaware (and could not reasonably have been expected to be aware) of the disability provided he could foresee that the employee might be subject to a disadvantage. In *Wilcox* the EAT took the view that unless the employer had actual or constructive knowledge of the disability, the question of substantial disadvantage did not arise. An employer will be taken to have the requisite knowledge provided they are aware of the impairment and its consequences. There is no need for them to be aware of the specific diagnosis of the condition that creates the impairment (*Jennings v Barts and the London NHS Trust* [2011] All ER (D) 73 (Aug), EAT).

Where a question as to whether an employee is a disabled person arises, an employer will often look to an occupational health practitioner for a view. However, an employer cannot simply "rubber stamp" an occupational health practitioner's opinion that an employee is not a disabled person. In *Gallop v Newport City Council* [2013] EWCA Civ 1583; [2014] IRLR 211 the fact that the employer had obtained a bare, unreasoned assertion by an occupational health doctor that an employee was not disabled did not mean that they did not have constructive knowledge of the claimant's disability. *Gallop* was distinguished in *Donelien v Liberata UK Ltd* [2018] EWCA Civ 129; [2018] IRLR 535 where the Court of Appeal warned against reading *Gallop* as suggesting that an employer could never rely on an OH opinion. In *Donelien* the opinion was reasoned; accorded with the employer's own experience and understanding; and the complainant had been unco-operative when the employer had tried to get to the bottom of the complainant's condition.

Where an employer had no actual knowledge of a disability the Tribunal must go on specifically to consider the question of constructive knowledge (*McCubbin v Perth and Kinross Council* UKEATS/0025/13).

Where an employer is fixed with constructive knowledge (on the basis that he ought to have known) it is open to him to argue that he has nevertheless complied with the duty on the basis either that no reasonable adjustments were possible or else that he had in fact taken steps that resulted in him unwittingly discharging the duty (see *British Gas Services Ltd v McCaull* [2001] IRLR 60). The test is an objective one. It is the steps taken or not taken that are to be tested and not the employer's state of mind in taking or not taking such steps.

The content of the duty

The employer must take such steps as it is reasonable to have to take either to avoid the disadvantage or, in auxiliary aid cases, to provide the aid (*EqA 2010, ss 20(3)* to *(5)*). The employer cannot require the employee to pay its costs of complying with the duty (*EqA 2010, s 20(7)*).

EqA 2010, s 22 allows for regulations to further define the duty including defining what would and would not be reasonable in particular circumstances. No regulations have yet been issued that apply in employment cases.

The *DDA 1995* had, at *s 18B*, guidance as to what sorts of measures might be required and what factors might be taken into account in determining reasonableness. The factors that were identified included:

(1)   the extent to which taking the step would prevent the effect in relation to which the duty is imposed;

(2)   the extent to which it is practicable for [the employer] to take the step;

(3)   the financial and other costs which would be incurred by [the employer] in taking the step and the extent to which it would disrupt any of his activities;

(4)   the extent of [the employer's] financial and other resources;

(5)   the availability to [the employer] of financial or other assistance with respect to taking the step; and

(6)   the nature of [the employer's] activities and the size of his undertaking.

The steps that might be taken included making adjustments to premises; allocating some of the disabled person's duties to another person; transferring him to an existing vacancy and altering his hours of work and training. The reasonableness factors and example adjustments do not appear to have been carried across to the *EqA 2010*. However, there is no doubt that they remain relevant and they have been substantially reproduced at Chapter 6 of the *EHRC Code*. Guidance is set out at *Para 6.23* ff of the *EHRC Code*. The EAT has suggested that tribunals would be wise to consider the factors identified in the Code whilst acknowledging that they are under no duty to address every factor contained in it (*Secretary of State for Work and Pensions (Job Centre Plus) v Higgins* above).

The first guidance factor – the extent to which the step would prevent the effect in relation to which the duty is imposed – has been the subject of some consideration in appeal cases. In *First Group plc v Paulley* [2017] UKSC 4, [2017] IRLR 258 Lord Neuberger held there has to be a "real prospect" that the step "would have made a difference" (see also *Lancaster v TBWA Manchester* UKEAT/0460/10 and *Foster v Leeds Teaching Hospital NHS Trust* [2011] All ER (D) 57 (Sep)). One has to be careful, however, precisely to identify the disadvantage in issue. In *Noor v Foreign and Commonwealth Office* [2010] UK/EAT/470/10, [2011] ICR 695, the EAT overturned a tribunal decision to the effect that since any proposed adjustment to an interviewing process would still not have resulted in the complainant having been appointed, there was no breach of the duty. The complainant had been at a disadvantage in the interview and there were steps that the respondent might have taken which would have reduced that specific disadvantage even if no step would have landed the applicant the job itself.

Employers should also be careful to identify what arrangement or what provision, criterion or practice is actually placing the disabled employee at a disadvantage in order that the appropriate adjustments can be considered. In *Paul v National Probation Service* [2004] IRLR 190, a tribunal rejected the claim of a claimant who had been refused a job after failing an occupational health assessment. The tribunal concluded that the claimant had not been placed at a disadvantage compared to others since all job applicants had to undergo an assessment. The EAT held that the tribunal had wrongly regarded the relevant arrangement as being the requirement to undergo an assessment. It was not the fact of the assessment that had placed the claimant at a disadvantage but the health adviser's assessment that the claimant's depressive illness rendered him unsuitable for the job. By focusing on the wrong 'arrangement' the tribunal omitted to consider whether there were any reasonable adjustments that the employer could have made (eg by obtaining specialist advice from the claimant's consultant on his fitness for the job). (See also *Smith v Churchills Stairlifts plc* [2005] EWCA Civ 1220, [2006] IRLR 41, where the Court of Appeal confirmed that the comparator for these purposes is readily identified by reference to the disadvantage caused by the relevant arrangements.)

The EAT has held that whether or not any adjustments were reasonable in the circumstances will be determined by the employment tribunal objectively (see *Morse v Wiltshire County Council* [1998] IRLR 352 and *HM Land Registry v Wakefield* [2009] All ER (D) 205 (Feb), EAT). Thus, it may not be sufficient for an employer simply to assert that adjustments were considered and thought to be unreasonable if the tribunal finds that there were other reasonable adjustments which could have been made by the employer (see also *Ridout v TC Group* [1998] IRLR 628). The employment tribunal will not be entitled, however, to rely upon a failure to make a reasonable adjustment where the particular adjustment in question was not raised as an issue and the parties have not had an opportunity to make submissions in relation to that adjustment (*Tarbuck v Sainsbury's Supermarkets Ltd* [2006] IRLR 664). Recognising that tribunals often fall into error when they fail to identify and address each of the separate elements of the 'failure to make reasonable adjustments' cause of action, the EAT has laid down useful guidance on the step-by-step process to be followed in such cases: *Environment Agency v Rowan* [2008] IRLR 20.

Clark v Novacold [1999] IRLR 318, EWCA was authority for the proposition that the duty to make reasonable adjustments did not apply to a dismissal. Following *Aylott v Stockton on Tees BC* [2010] IRLR 99, that would seem no longer to be the case. In an admittedly obiter consideration of the issue, Mummery LJ was inclined to accept that the effect of *Framework Directive 2000/78/EC, Art 3(1)(c)* was to require dismissals to fall within the scope of the duty. There would appear to be no duty to offer part-time employment as an alternative to dismissal in circumstances where the claimant had not asked to work part-time and where he was not fit for any form of work at the relevant time (*Callagan v Glasgow City Council* [2001] IRLR 724). Avoiding dismissal may involve offering the employee an alternative job at a higher grade which she is capable of doing without requiring her to undergo a competitive interview cf *Archibald v Fife Council* [2004] UKHL 32, [2004] IRLR 651, [2004] ICR 954 and in certain circumstances (eg where there is an on-going reorganisation) it could even involve the creation of an entirely new job (*Southampton City College v Randall* [2006] IRLR 18). However, there is no obligation on an employer to create a post specifically, which is not otherwise necessary, merely to create a job for a disabled person (*Tarbuck v Sainsbury's Supermarkets Ltd* [2006] IRLR 664 but see *Chief Constable of South Yorkshire Police v Jelic* [2010] IRLR 744 where in the context of a "disciplined service" the EAT held that employer should have considered a job swap, ie creating a vacancy by forcing the incumbent to transfer to another role). Nor is there an obligation to avoid dismissal by placing a disabled person into a role that the employer does not believe that they can perform (*Wade v Sheffield Hallam University* UKEAT/0194/12: [2013] All ER (D) 134 (Nov), EAT. Employers intending to adjust an employee's role should bear in mind that where an employee is moved to a role that would ordinarily be less well-remunerated, they may have at least to consider continuing to pay the employee at their former higher rate – see *G4S Cash Solutions (UK) Ltd v Powell* UKEAT/0243/15, [2016] IRLR 820. *G4S* also reminds employers that the duty to make reasonable adjustments is not a licence unilaterally to vary the employee's contract. If you want to make a change that would ordinarily require the employee's consent, that consent is still required.

In *Gomez v Glaxosmithkline Services Unlimited* [2011] EqLR 804, the EAT considered the case of a claimant who suffered from severe depression and panic attacks. The claimant was found to have been leaving the site at which he worked without authorisation and using a colleague's security pass. He was dismissed for gross misconduct. He argued that the penalty should have been "adjusted" and that he should have been given a warning instead. The EAT concluded that the employer could not be reasonably required to take such a step as it risked the employer appearing to condone the practice. *Burke v College of Law and another* [2011] All ER (D) 238 (Mar), EAT is a further example of an employer determining that a proposed adjustment would not have been reasonable. It is a case concerning a "qualification body" – one of the categories of non-employers covered by the Act. The claimant, who had MS, was re-sitting LPC exams. A series of adjustments were made including allowing them more time. However, the claimant had asked for still further time and the opportunity to take the exams at home. Those adjustments were declined. The EAT concluded that the examination's purpose was to "assess the ability of the candidate to demonstrate their competence and capability in the subject matter under time pressure." The time restriction was, therefore, a competence standard. See also: *Lowe v Cabinet Office* [2011] EqLR 803: The claimant had Asperger's Syndrome. She applied for admission to the Civil Service Fast Stream. The selection exercise involved application of a criterion that required a high standard of communication skills and assessment by group exercise. The tribunal accepted that no adjustment was reasonably required. The exercise was to find high quality applicants and the proposed adjustments would have destroyed the essence of the exercise. However, by contrast in *Government Legal Service v Brookes* UKEAT/0302/16; [2017] IRLR 780, the EAT found that the GLS should have allowed the complainant, who had Asperger's, to provide short narrative answers to exam questions rather than requiring her to take the test in multiple-choice form. Although that meant that the employer would have to administer more than one type of test, that was a proportionate requirement.

In *Clark v Newsquest Media* [2011] EqLR 932 an employer required a diabetic employee to test her blood and inject herself in private. The tribunal concluded that employer was acting in breach of the duty.

The following have been held by employment tribunals to be reasonable adjustments:

(i)   provision of subtitled training videos for Channel 5 Television re-tuners (*Williams v Channel 5 Engineering Services Ltd*, IDS Brief 609, p 13); and

(ii)   provision of a special 'Grahl' chair costing £1,000 for an employee with a club foot (*Tarling v Wisdom Toothbrushes Ltd*, 24 June 1997, COIT 1500148/97).

The employer's duty to make reasonable adjustments is confined to those which are 'job related' (see *Kenny v Hampshire Constabulary* [1999] IRLR 76). A disabled person may be in a position to obtain employment if he was provided with transport to get to the place of employment. However, the employer's duty in relation to that person, whilst extending to the making of adjustments to enable access to the employer's premises, would not extend to the provision of transport to get there from home. In *Kenny*, the job applicant had cerebral palsy and required assistance in carrying out his toilet functions. The EAT held that whilst there may be a duty to consider physical adjustments to enable access to the toilets, the employer was not under a duty to provide a personal carer to assist the claimant with his toilet needs. Such provision would address the claimant's personal needs but would not be job-related.

The extent to which tribunals should take into account the actual or assumed knowledge of an employer in the context of the duty to make reasonable adjustments has been considered by the EAT in *Ridout v TC Group* [1998] IRLR 628. In that case, a job applicant had disclosed in her application that she was disabled and had photosensitive epilepsy controlled by a daily dose of Epilim. She was shortlisted for an interview. Upon entering the room in which the interview was to be held, the claimant, who was wearing sunglasses around her neck, commented that she might be disadvantaged by the fluorescent lighting in the room. However, the claimant did not use the sunglasses during her interview nor did she say that she felt in any way disadvantaged. The claimant complained to the tribunal that the employer had failed in its duty to make reasonable adjustments in respect of the physical arrangements for the interview. The tribunal dismissed the complaint. The EAT held that the tribunal was correct to find that the employer was not in breach of its duty to make reasonable adjustments notwithstanding that it knew of the claimant's condition. The EAT added that the provisions of *DDA 1995, s 6* (the predecessor provisions) required the tribunal to measure the extent of the duty, if any, against the actual or assumed knowledge of the employer both as to the disability and its likelihood of causing the individual a substantial disadvantage in comparison with persons who are not disabled. In this case, no reasonable employer could be expected to know, without being told in terms by the claimant, that the arrangements which were made for her interview might disadvantage her. Thus, it would appear that the extent of the duty to make reasonable adjustments will depend partly on the amount of information volunteered by the disabled person as to any disadvantages being suffered. However, this does not mean that the employer can simply wait to be told of such disadvantages before a duty will arise. On the facts in *Ridout*, it may have been reasonable for the employer itself not to make further inquiries as to any disadvantage. Whether or not this will be so in other cases will be a question of fact for the tribunal. In *Mid-Staffordshire General Hospitals NHS Trust v Cambridge* [2003] IRLR 566, the EAT went so far as to hold that 'A proper assessment of what is required to eliminate the disabled person's disadvantage is . . . a necessary part of the duty imposed by *s 6(1)* since that duty cannot be complied with unless the employer makes a proper assessment of what needs to be done.' However, this decision (which was followed by the EAT in *Southampton City College v Randall* [2006] IRLR 18) was held by the EAT in *Tarbuck v Sainsbury's Supermarkets Ltd* [2006] IRLR 664 to have been incorrectly decided. Elias J concluded in Tarbuck that ' . . . there is no separate and distinct duty' to consult employees and that the single question under section 3A(1) was whether the employer had complied with his obligations there set out (see *Hay v Surrey County Council* [2007] EWCA Civ 93, [2007] All ER (D) 199 (Feb) in which the EAT's reasoning in *Tarbuck* was approved and it was held that there is, similarly, no separate duty to undertake a risk assessment, although an employer who had failed to conduct such an assessment could not use ignorance by reason of that failure to excuse non-compliance). The effect of these decisions is that consultation and/or risk assessments clearly remain prudent practice in any case where an employer is made aware of a disability, although the failure to take such steps would not of itself amount to a breach of the duty (see *Code of Practice, paras 5.12* and *7.29*). Indeed, the Court of Appeal has stated that a failure to conduct adequate investigations or assessments into the adjustments that can be made can amount to unjustified treatment of an employee. (See *Williams v J Walter Thompson Group Ltd* [2005] EWCA Civ 133, [2005] IRLR 376, which was not referred to in *Hay v Surrey County Council*.) In *Watkins v HSBC Bank plc* UKEAT/0018/18 [2018] IRLR 1015, a failure to monitor an employee's workload was found to be a failure to make a reasonable adjustment. Although such monitoring would not in and of itself avoid disadvantage it was, nevertheless, a "step" for the purposes of *EqA 2010, s 20(3)*. The distinction between what is and is not capable of amounting to a step seems, therefore, a fine one.

An employer may breach the duty to make reasonable adjustments by failing to take steps that the employee has never in fact asked should be taken (*Project Management Institute v Latif* [2007] IRLR 579 EAT and *Home Office (UK Visas and Immigration) v Kuranchie* UKEAT/0202/16). The duty is to make reasonable adjustments and not simply respond to reasonable requests.

An adjustment is more likely to be considered reasonable where it has been recommended in the employer's own disability policy (*Linsley v R&C Comrs* UKEAT/0150/18 [2019] IRLR 604).

The EAT has stated that there was almost bound to be a breach of the implied term of trust and confidence where the employer had over a period of time seriously breached its obligation to make reasonable adjustments (*Greenhof v Barnsley Metropolitan Borough Council* [2006] IRLR 98).

In *Griffiths v Secretary of State for Work and Pensions* [2015] EWCA Civ 1265, [2016] IRLR 216, Lord Justice Elias rejected a suggestion that an adjustment would only constitute a "step" for the purposes of S. 20 if it promoted "access to and progress in employment". It was contended that modifying an absence management procedure so as to discount periods of disability-related absence would not promote those goals. On the contrary, it would facilitate absence. Rejecting that contention, his Lordship warned against artificial narrowing of what would constitute a step and expressed the view that "any modification of, or qualification to, the PCP in question which would or might remove the substantial disadvantage caused by the PCP is in principle capable of amounting to a relevant step". His Lordship did suggest, however, that it may not be reasonable to expect an employer to take steps where the disadvantage was one which was "not directly related to the ability to integrate [the disabled person] into employment". He gave as an example of that latter sort of case *O'Hanlon v Revenue and Customs Comrs* [2007] EWCA Civ 283, [2007] IRLR 404, [2007] ICR 1359, in which the Court of Appeal determined that an employer had not failed to make a reasonable adjustment where it declined to modify a sick pay policy to provide for a longer period of absence on full pay for an employee whose absence was disability-related. The Court worried that avoiding financial hardship and stress might risk disincentivising return rather than enabling the employee to "play a full part in the world of work".

On the facts of *Griffiths* the particular adjustments sought were not thought to be reasonable. In *Jennings v Barts* (above) the EAT decided that he employer had not been obliged to produce a bespoke modification of its absence management procedures so as to discount from consideration disability-related absences. It accepted arguments that a modification would have been costly, disruptive and divisive (ie that would have caused resentment amongst colleagues). Discounting of disability-related absences in assessing absence record was, however, found to be reasonable in *Cox v Post Office*, IDS Brief 609.

When a complaint comes to the Tribunal and the complainant has alleged that certain adjustments should have been made, is it open to them to run an alternative case that other lesser, but unpleaded, adjustments would have been appropriate? In her partial dissent in *First Group v Paulley* (above) Lady Hale suggested that is open to a complainant to make that case.

12.38 Victimisation

In the United States, this form of discrimination is sometimes known as 'retaliation', a word which perhaps more accurately captures its essence than our own term 'victimisation'. There is little point conferring equal opportunity rights upon employees if their employers are free to punish them whenever they assert those rights. Thus the *EqA 2010* protects those who rely on its provisions from being subjected to a detriment.

The coming into force of *EqA 2010* marked a significant change to the law of victimisation. Under the previous law victimisation was treated as a form of discrimination, that is to say a claimant needed to establish that there had been "less favourable treatment" on a prohibited ground. However, rather than the prohibited ground being a protected characteristic, the previous law focused instead on the complainant having performed a so-called "protected act". *EqA 2010, s 27* adopts a different model – that of subjection to a detriment. As a result a complainant now needs only to show that he has been treated badly, not that others have been treated better. Furthermore, it may not be necessary for it to have been the complainant who has performed the protected act. If an employer subjects the complainant to a detriment because of a protected act performed by a colleague, that would suffice (*Thompson v London Central Bus Company Ltd* (2015) UKEAT/0108/15, [2016] IRLR 9 – although that is difficult to reconcile with the express words of the section itself (see immediately below) which requires the person subjected to the detriment to be the person who performed the protected act).

EqA 2010, s 27(1) provides:

> "A person (A) victimises another person (B) if A subjects B to a detriment because –
>
> (a)   B does a protected act, or
> (b)   A believes that B has done, or may do, a protected act."

"Protected act" is defined at *EqA 2010, s 27(2)*:

> "Each of the following is a protected act –
> (a)   bringing proceedings under this Act;

(b) giving evidence or information in connection with proceedings under this Act;

(c) doing any other thing for the purposes of or in connection with this Act;

(d) making an allegation (whether or not express) that A or another person has contravened this Act".

The reference in (d) above to contravening the Act includes committing a breach of an equality clause or rule (*EqA 2010, s 27(5)*).

If what is alleged would not be unlawful under the relevant legislation there is no protected act. For example, in *Waters v Metropolitan Police Comr* [1997] IRLR 589 (a case on the old law) a police officer, who was harassed by a colleague whilst both were off-duty, complained. She was later less favourably treated by her employer and alleged victimisation. As her harasser had been off duty, the employer was not vicariously liable for his actions. For that reason, the harassment was not unlawful. In those circumstances, the later act of less favourable treatment could not amount to victimisation.

Bringing an internal complaint does not constitute bringing proceedings (*British Telecommunications plc v Grant* (1994) 518 IDS Brief, EAT) although it may, nevertheless, involve alleging a breach of the Act on the part of the employer and qualify for protection on that basis instead.

An employee performs a 'protected act' by giving evidence even where the evidence given is not in support of the complaint (*Kirby v National Probation Service for England and Wales (Cumbria Area)* [2006] IRLR 508, [2006] All ER (D) 111 (Mar), EAT obiter). Nor need the evidence be given orally; providing a witness statement would be sufficient (*National Probation Service* above, again obiter).

Participating in an investigation into allegations of discrimination made by a third party would qualify as having done something by reference to the relevant anti-discrimination legislation (see *National Probation Service* above).

Giving false evidence or information, or making a false allegation, is not a protected act if the evidence or information is given, or the allegation is made, in bad faith (*EqA 2010, s 27(3)*). The test of bad faith focuses upon whether the complainant has "acted honestly" and whilst their motivation is part of the context relevant to making that determination the mere existence of a collateral motive will not require a finding that they acted in bad faith (*Saad v Southampton University Hospitals NHS Trust* UKEAT/0276/17 [2018] IRLR 1007, [2019] ICR 311. In *HM Prison Service v Ibimidun* [2008] IRLR 940, the EAT considered a case where an employee had brought a series of discrimination claims, some of which were upheld, others dismissed. One claim, the tribunal found, had been brought for the purpose of harassing the employer. The employer dismissed the employee for bringing that claim. The EAT accepted that, properly analysed, the reason for the employee's dismissal was the harassment that resulted from the bringing of the claim. The EAT considered whether the claim was false, asking itself whether it could be said to be 'not in accordance with the truth or facts'. However, that consideration was *obiter* as the EAT decided that the claim should fail, instead, for want of causation: the reason for the dismissal was not the claim but the fact that it had been brought to harass the employer. This approach appears to sidestep the requirements of *s 27(3)*; it means that claims brought in bad faith (but which may not be false) fail on causation grounds. In *Martin v Devonshires Solicitors* [2011] All ER (D) 345 (Mar), [2011] ICR 352, the EAT expressed the opinion that where an employee raises groundless complaints as result of a mental illness, the case would not fall within the bad faith exception. However, where the employee was dismissed for, amongst other factors, her inability to accept that her claims were groundless the dismissal would not be on grounds of her having performed protected act. In *Woodhouse v North West Homes Leeds Ltd* [2013] IRLR 773 the EAT stressed that Martin was an exceptional case and that the concept of victimisation might be "neutered" if the "irrationality and multiplicity of grievances" were to lead "as a matter of routine" to the case being treated as falling outside the scope of victimisation.

Only individuals are entitled to be protected against detriment (*EqA 2010, s 27(4)*).

It is important to note that the person doing the victimising need not be the person who was the subject of the original complaint of discrimination. Thus, if a prospective employer decides not to appoint a candidate because he had brought or given evidence in proceedings against his former employer, that will amount to an act of victimisation.

The employer must subject the employee to a detriment "because" the latter has performed a protected act. The language used in *EqA 2010, s 27* matches that in the definition of direct discrimination at *s 13*. It would seem to follow, therefore, that, the protected act has to be an effective and substantial cause of employer's detrimental actions but does not have to be the principal cause. Predecessor provisions required that the complainant should have been treated less favourably "by reason that" they had performed a protected act. Those words were closely analysed in *Chief Constable of West Yorkshire Police v Khan* [2001] IRLR 830, HL. It was decided that the provision did not "raise a question of causation as that expression is usually understood". One had to look at subjectively what was in the alleged discriminator's mind. Lord Scott observed that the words "by reason that" suggested that one was looking for "the real reason, the core reason . . ." Some caution needs to be exercised in relying on older authorities, therefore, since Lord Scott's comments would be difficult to reconcile with the proper approach to the test in direct discrimination cases and that is the approach which is now used in victimisation cases.

The sort of case in which the question of precisely why an employer subjected an employee to a detriment is likely to be most important is where there has been a protected act but the employer is contending that another related, but discrete, reason is their real reason for action. In *Aziz v Trinity Street Taxis Ltd* [1988] IRLR 204, [1988] 2 All ER 860, the Court of Appeal dealt with a number of points arising out of the construction of a predecessor provision in the *RRA 1976, s 2(1)*, and held in particular that it was necessary for a complainant to show that it was the very fact that his act had been done under, or by reference to, the race relations legislation that had influenced the unfavourable treatment. On the facts, the respondent association would have expelled any member who covertly recorded conversations, irrespective of whether that was done to support an allegation of racial discrimination and, therefore, the complaint of victimisation failed. It remains to be seen whether the courts will take a similarly narrow view of the new test.

There is no victimisation where the reason for the unfavourable treatment is the disruptive way in which complaints are made rather than the complaints as such (*Re York Truck Equipment Ltd*, IDS Brief 439, p 10). See also, *Martin v Devonshire Solicitors* [2011] ICR 352, [2011] All ER (D) 345 (Mar): An employee suffering from a mental illness repeatedly raised groundless complaints and was unable to accept that they were not well-founded. The employee was dismissed. The EAT upheld a finding that the reason for her dismissal was not the protected acts but a combination of "genuinely separable" factors including the risk to future management caused by her mental illness and her inability to accept that her complaints were groundless (but see *Woodhouse v North West Homes Leeds Ltd* above).

In *Woods v Pasab Ltd* [2012] EWCA Civ 1578, [2013] IRLR 305 an employee alleged that the pharmacy in which she worked was "a little Sikh Club" and was dismissed. The tribunal concluded that the comment amounted to a protected act but the Court of Appeal determined that the reason for the dismissal was her employer's belief that the comment was itself racist.

A line of authority on the old law addressed the question of whether respondents could be liable for steps taken in the context of defending legal proceedings. In *Khan* above, the House of Lords held that it was open to an employer faced with discrimination proceedings (and thus a protected act) to take honest and reasonable steps to protect its position in the relevant litigation even if that led to less favourable treatment. Thus, in *Khan* itself an employer could decline to issue a reference until the outcome of proceedings were known where the reference might otherwise have had to deal with matters that were in dispute. There are, however, limits. In *Derbyshire v St Helens Metropolitan Borough Council* [2007] UKHL 16, [2007] IRLR 540, it was stressed that the question whether the employer has acted in an honest and reasonable manner must be assessed from the perspective of the employee. On the facts, it was not open to an employer to write to claimants who had brought equal pay claims and to seek to persuade them to settle their claim by pointing out the possible negative consequences that the success of their claim might have for colleagues. In *South London & Maudsley NHS Trust v Dathi* [2008] IRLR 350, the EAT distinguished both *Khan* and *St Helens* and applied the principle of 'absolute immunity' to two letters written by representatives during the course of litigation. In one letter the representative refused certain disclosure, in the other the representative set out the grounds upon which it intended to resist a costs application. It was alleged that both letters amounted to acts of discrimination and/or victimisation. *Khan* was distinguished on the basis that the reference had been sent against the background of proceedings but could not be said to have 'come into existence for the purposes of the proceedings' themselves. *St Helens* was distinguished on the basis that the letter sent in that case had 'gone too far' and amounted to an exercise in intimidation rather than an appropriate step in litigation.

12.39 Harassment

Harassment relating to a relevant protected characteristic

EqA 2010, s 26(1) provides that:

"A person (A) harasses another (B) if –

(a) A engages in unwanted conduct related to a relevant protected characteristic, and

(b) the conduct has the purpose or effect of –
(i) violating B's dignity, or
(ii) creating an intimidating, hostile, degrading, humiliating or offensive environment for B."

The definition of harassment has a wide scope in that it covers harassment which "relates" to the relevant protected characteristic and not merely harassment which is "because of" the characteristic. In *GMB v Henderson* [2016] EWCA Civ 1049, [2017] IRLR 340, the Court of appeal suggested that deciding whether the unwanted conduct "relates to" the protected characteristic will require a "consideration of the mental processes of the putative harasser", though it is unclear from the decision whether the observation was intended to be limited to cases where the violation of dignity and/or the creation of the harassing environment is the alleged harasser's purpose rather than where it is merely the effect of the conduct in issue (see also *Bakkali v Greater Manchester Buses (South) Ltd* UKEAT/0176/17 [2018] IRLR 906, [2018] ICR 1481, where the EAT refer to the "broader enquiry" involved in deciding whether conduct relates to a protected characteristic and recommends "a more intense focus on the context of the offending words or behaviour").

In *Raj v Capita Business Services Ltd and another* UKEAT/0074/19; [2019] IRLR 1057, a female manager massaged the shoulders and neck of a male subordinate as he worked. The conduct was unwanted and created an harassing environment. However, the Tribunal found that the behaviour was not "related to" sex (although the Appeal Tribunal seems, at times, to have focussed on whether it related to the employee's sex which would be a very narrow reading of the statutory provision so that the decision needs to be approached with some caution).

The language is also not broad enough to mean that an employer can be held responsible for failing to prevent harassment by third parties. While the underlying harassment may relate to the protected characteristic, the employer's failure will only do so where the protected characteristic was part of the employer's motivation (see *Unite the Union v Nailard* [2018] EWCA Civ 1203, [2018] IRLR 730, [2019] ICR 28).

Although harassing conduct may cause an employee to resign and that resignation may amount to a constructive dismissal, the resignation cannot itself amount to "unwanted conduct" (*Timothy James Consulting Ltd v Wilton* (2015) UKEAT/0082/14, [2015] ICR 765, [2015] IRLR 368). On the other hand, where an employer expressly dismisses an employee, that act of dismissal can constitute unwanted conduct of the kind contemplated by *s 26(1)* (*Urso v Department for Work and Pensions* UKEAT/00045/16, [2017] IRLR 304).

In determining whether conduct has the effect of violating B's dignity or creating the relevant environment for the purposes of *EqA 2010, s 26(1)(b)* the Tribunal must take into account: B's perception; the other circumstances of the case; and whether it is reasonable for the conduct to have that effect (*EqA 2010, s 26(4)*). In *Land Registry v Grant* [2011] EWCA Civ 769, [2011] IRLR 748, [2011] ICR 1390, Elias LJ focussed on the words "intimidating, hostile, degrading, humiliating or offensive" and observed that:

> 'Tribunals must not cheapen the significance of these words. They are an important control to prevent trivial acts causing minor upsets being caught by the concept of harassment.'

The scope of the protection is limited in that not all of the protected characteristics defined at *EqA 2010, s 4* are included. Specifically, harassment relating to "marriage and civil partnership" and "pregnancy and maternity" are not covered. Does that mean that it is lawful to harass someone on those grounds? The answer is probably not. Before there was any specific protection against harassment in the *SDA 1975* and the *RRA 1976* an employee wishing to complain that they had been harassed was obliged to take an indirect route. If they could show that they had been harassed "on grounds of" their race or sex they would bring a claim for direct discrimination. Harassing someone was treated as subjecting them to a detriment which was, in turn, a form of less favourable treatment. *EqA 2010, s 212(1)* defines "detriment" so as specifically to exclude "conduct which amounts to harassment". The purpose is to ensure that someone who has been harassed is obliged to bring a *s 26* harassment claim rather than a *s 13* direct discrimination claim. However, the definition of "detriment" is said to be subject to *s 212(5)* which provides:

> "Where this Act disapplies a prohibition on harassment in relation to a specified protected characteristic, the disapplication does not prevent conduct relating to that characteristic from amounting to a detriment for the purposes of discrimination within section 13 because of that characteristic".

The effect of these rather roundabout provisions is that a complainant who has been harassed on grounds of marriage, civil partnership, pregnancy or maternity may be able to bring a direct discrimination claim under *EqA 2010, s 13* but only if they can show that the harassment was "because of" the relevant protected characteristic and, further, that they were less favourably treated than a comparator. These additional requirements are unnecessary where a claim is based directly upon *s 26*.

The test as to whether conduct has the relevant effect is not subjective. Conduct is not to be treated, for instance, as violating a complainant's dignity merely because he thinks it does. It must be conduct which could reasonably be considered as having that effect. However, the tribunal is obliged to take the complainant's perception into account in making that assessment. The intention of the alleged harasser may be relevant to determining whether the conduct could reasonably be considered to violate a complainant's dignity (*Richmond Pharmacology Ltd v Dhaliwal* [2009] IRLR 336, EAT). However, it is not necessary that the alleged harasser should have known that his behaviour would be unwanted (*Reed and Bull Information Systems Limited v Stedman* [1999] IRLR 299, EAT). Where the language of the alleged harasser is relied upon it will be important to assess the words used in the context in which the use occurred. In *Lindsay v London School of Economics* [2013] EWCA Civ 1650, [2014] IRLR 218, one employee used the word "gollywog" in conversation with a black colleague. The claimant argued that the term was inherently discriminatory and inevitably amounted to harassment. However, her colleague had not been describing the claimant as a gollywog. Instead she had been describing a jam manufacturer's former use of the doll in its branding. The particular context established that there was no harassment. The Court of Appeal gave guidance on the determining whether the statutory test has been met in *Reverend Canon Pemberton v Right Reverend Inwood, former acting Bishop of Southwell and Nottingham* [2018] EWCA Civ 564; [2018] IRLR 542, [2018] ICR 1291:

> "In order to decide whether any conduct falling within sub-paragraph (1)(a) has either of the proscribed effects under sub-paragraph (1)(b), a tribunal must consider *both* (by reason of sub-section (4)(a)) whether the putative victim perceives themselves to have suffered the effect in question (the subjective question) *and* (by reason of sub-section (4)(c)) whether it was reasonable for the conduct to be regarded as having that effect (the objective question). It must also, of course, take into account all the other circumstances – sub-section (4)(b). The relevance of the subjective question is that if the claimant does not perceive their dignity to have been violated, or an adverse environment created, then the conduct should not be found to have had that effect. The relevance of the objective question is that if it was not reasonable for the conduct to be regarded as violating the claimant's dignity or creating an adverse environment for him or her, then it should not be found to have done so.
>
> In order to decide whether any conduct falling within sub-paragraph (1)(a) has either of the proscribed effects under sub-paragraph (1)(b), a tribunal must consider both (by reason of sub-section (4)(a)) whether the putative victim perceives themselves to have suffered the effect in question (the subjective question) and (by reason of sub-section (4)(c)) whether it was reasonable for the conduct to be regarded as having that effect (the objective question). It must also, of course, take into account all the other circumstances – sub-section (4)(b). The relevance of the subjective question is that if the claimant does not perceive their dignity to have been violated, or an adverse environment created, then the conduct should not be found to have had that effect. The relevance of the objective question is that if it was not reasonable for the conduct to be regarded as violating the claimant's dignity or creating an adverse environment for him or her, then it should not be found to have done so."

"Outing" a lesbian or gay employee may itself amount to harassment: *HM Land Registry v Grant* (above).

Where an employer's action or inaction results in an intimidating, hostile, degrading or offensive environment becoming worse he may be said to have in part "created" the resulting environment: *Conteh* above.

A number of cases have considered variations of a situation where the victim of the harassment does not themselves have the relevant protected characteristic. In the first type of case the unwanted conduct relates to the protected characteristic of a third party, e.g. an employee who is harassed because of the religion of a colleague (where, for instance, he refuses to assist his employer in justifying the colleague's discriminatory dismissal) is himself unlawfully harassed (*Saini v All Saints Haque Centre* [2009] IRLR 74, EAT). In the second type of case, the harasser treats the employee as if they have the protected characteristic knowing that they do not actually have it. An employee was harassed on grounds of sexual orientation when he was subjected to homophobic abuse by colleagues who knew that he was not a homosexual *English v Thomas Sanderson Blinds Ltd* [2008] EWCA Civ 1421, [2008] IRLR 206, [2009] ICR 543. A third type of case is one concerned specifically with those who claim to have the protected characteristic of disability. In *Peninsula Business Service Ltd v Baker* UKEAT/0241/16, [2017] IRLR 39, [2017] ICR 714, the EAT was persuaded that this represents a special category of case (relying on *J v DLA Piper* (above) – where the EAT rejected the possibility of a perceived disability discrimination claim). Thus, a person who claimed, but had not established, that they were a disabled person could not claim that the unwanted conduct "related to" the protected characteristic of disability. However, in *Chief Constable of Norfolk v Coffey* [2018] IRLR 193, [2018] ICR 812, the EAT concluded that *EqA 2010, s 13* allowed perceived disability claims. On the facts, the complainant had a hearing problem that was not considered to amount to a disability, but the employer was concerned, incorrectly, that the condition would worsen.

An employer will be liable for acts of harassment committed by its employees against other employees (see below). A complainant will sometimes wish to take a further step and allege that there should be a discrete liability for the employer's failure to protect the employee from the harassment they suffered or properly to investigate the matter once it was raised with them. If the reason for the employer's failure to take steps to protect the employee was the employee's protected characteristic, the employer would be liable for an act of direct discrimination on ordinary principles. Thus, if employers allow both male and female employees to be subject to harassment by colleagues (or indeed by third parties), they do not discriminate. However, if they take steps to protect men but not women a liability will arise.

A mere failure to investigate a complaint of harassment will not in and of itself involve any unlawful action on the part of an employer. Again, the question is whether the reason for the employer's inaction was a protected characteristic (*Home Office v Coyne* [2000] IRLR 838, [2000] ICR 1443). Where a manager failed to take action following a complaint of racial abuse his inaction was capable of amounting to "unwanted conduct" but, on the facts, his decision not to investigate was not taken on the grounds of race and, for that reason, did not amount to harassment: *Conteh v Parking Partners Ltd* v Parking Partners Ltd UKEAT/288/10: [2011] ICR 341, [2011] All ER (D) 223 (Feb) (see also *Unite the Union v Nailard* UKEAT/0300/15, [2016] IRLR 906, [2017] ICR 121 affirmed [2018] EWCA Civ 1203, [2018] IRLR 730, [2019] ICR 28 and *Bessong v Pennine Care NHS Foundation Trust* UKEAT/0247/18 [2020] IRLR 4: *Art 2* of the *Race Directive 2000/43/EC* did not have the effect of requiring that an employer was liable for racial harassment by a third party where the employer's failure to prevent it was not itself related to the victim's race).

Harassment of a sexual nature

EqA 2010, s 26(2) provides that A harasses B if A engages in unwanted conduct of a sexual nature which has the effect of violating B's dignity or creating an intimidating, hostile, degrading, humiliating or offensive environment for B. The Act does not define what is meant by conduct being "of a sexual nature".

As with the general form of harassment, the Tribunal must take into account B's perception, the other circumstances of the case and whether it is reasonable for conduct to have the alleged effect when assessing whether the conduct complained of had the effect of violating B's dignity or creating the relevant hostile atmosphere (*EqA 2010, s 26(4)*).

Less favourable treatment of those who reject or submit to harassment

EqA 2010, s 26(3) defines a third form of protection. It deals with an employee's reaction to certain forms of harassment and how, in turn, the employer treats the employee. Where an employee is subjected either to harassment of a sexual nature or harassment relating to gender reassignment or sex and either rejects or submits to that conduct any less favourable treatment that results because of that rejection or submission is unlawful.

The fact that the protection is against "less favourable treatment" makes it a form of discrimination although the essence of the problem being dealt with seems more closely related to victimisation and might, therefore, have been expected to follow the "subjection to a detriment" model.

Employer's liability for harassment by third parties

EqA 2010, s 40(2) formerly made employers potentially liable for harassment by third parties. *Section 66* of the *Enterprise and Regulatory Reform Act 2013* ("*ERRA 2013*") repealed *EqA 2010, ss 40(2)* to *(4)* inclusive from 1 October 2013.

Art 2 of the *Race Directive 2000/43/EC* does not have the effect of rendering an employer liable for racial harassment by a third party where the employer's failure to prevent it was not itself related to the victim's race (see *Bessong v Pennine Care NHS Foundation Trust* UKEAT/0247/18 [2020] IRLR 4).

Harassment that is not specifically related to a protected characteristic

The *Criminal Justice and Public Order Act 1994* created an offence of 'intentional harassment'. It is committed where a person 'with intent to cause a person harassment, alarm or distress' uses threatening, abusive or insulting language or behaviour, or disorderly behaviour, or displays any writing, sign or other visible representation which is threatening, abusive or insulting, so that another person feels harassment, alarm or distress. The maximum penalties for the offence are six months in prison or a fine of £5,000. A further offence was created by the *Protection from Harassment Act 1997* (which came into force on 16 June 1997 (*SI 1997/1418*)). In addition to providing for harassers to be subject potentially to a fine or up to six months in prison, the Act creates a number of civil remedies, including damages and restraining orders backed by powers of arrest. In *Vaughan v London Borough of Lewisham* [2013] EWHC 795 (QB), [2013] IRLR 720 the High Court refused to injunct witnesses in a Tribunal claim from giving evidence. The claimant had alleged their evidence would be untrue and would amount to continuation of the harassment that she alleged she had suffered at work.

12.40 DISCRIMINATION IN EMPLOYMENT

Discrimination alone will not found liability. It is only certain forms of discrimination which are unlawful; principally discrimination in employment.

Discrimination and harassment is prohibited at every stage of employment: advertising vacancies; engagement of employees; promotion and other opportunities; and dismissal. For discrimination against non-employees, such as contract workers, office holders, etc, see **13.24** ff DISCRIMINATION AND EQUAL OPPORTUNITIES – **II**.

12.41 The meaning of 'employment'

EqA 2010 protects "employees" but defines "employment" broadly so as to include not just those employed under a contract of employment or apprenticeship but also those engaged pursuant to contracts "personally to do work" (*EqA 2010, s 83(2)*).

In *Mirror Group Newspapers Ltd v Gunning* [1986] ICR 145, [1986] IRLR 27, a case about the predecessor provision in the *SDA 1975*, the Court of Appeal held that the provision referred to a contract, the dominant purpose of which was the execution of personal work or services. *EqA 2010, s 83* would fall to be interpreted in the same way.

A sub-postmaster who was responsible for seeing that the work of the Post Office was carried out but was not obliged to carry out the work himself was also held not to be an employee even within the extended meaning of the *Act* (*Tanna v Post Office* [1981] ICR 374). A taxi driver was not employed under 'a contract personally to execute any work or labour' where there was no mutual obligation between himself and the cab firm to offer or to accept any work (*Mingeley v Pennock & Ivory* [2004] EWCA Civ 328, [2004] IRLR 373, [2004] ICR 727 – but see *Windle v Secretary of State for Justice* UK/EAT/339/13: [2014] IRLR 914, [2015] ICR 156 where the EAT took the view that mutuality was only relevant to cases concerned with employees and not where the issue was whether the claimant was engaged under a contract personally to provide services). Similarly, where the contract pursuant to which the claimant was engaged contained a right to send a substitute to perform work, they were not an employee *Halawi v WDFG UK Ltd* [2014] EWCA Civ 1387, [2015] IRLR 50.

An unpaid volunteer working at a Citizens' Advice Bureau was not an employee (*X v Citizens Advice Bureau (Equality and Human Rights Commission intervening)* ([2013] IRLR 146, [2013] ICR 249). Nor was the complainant a "worker" or someone pursuing an "occupation" for the purposes of the *Framework Directive 2007/78/EC*. Similarly, a locally elected trade union official is not an employee. They undertook responsibilities voluntarily. They did not agree to perform any particular amount of work and they had no right to remuneration: *Unite the Union v Nailard* UKEAT/0300/15, [2016] IRLR 906, [2017] ICR 121.

A person working under the Youth Opportunities Programme was also held not to be employed within the meaning of *RRA 1976, s 78* (another predecessor provision. See *Daley v Allied Suppliers Ltd* [1983] IRLR 14, [1983] ICR 90).

Wippel v Peek and Cloppenburg GmbH & Co KG: C-313/02 [2005] IRLR 211, [2005] ICR 1604, ECJ – the *ETD 76/207/EEC* protects workers who are engaged on an 'on demand' basis and who are not obliged to take on work offered. *EqA 2010* must, of course, be interpreted, wherever possible, to be consistent with the directive.

An associate minister in the Church of Scotland was employed under 'a contract personally to execute . . . work' despite being an office holder. The House of Lords concluded that she was both an office holder and an employee (*Percy v Board of National Mission of the Church of Scotland* [2005] UKHL 73, [2006] IRLR 195, [2006] ICR 134, HL(S)). The question (arising in a different context) as to whether part-time judges are workers has been determined by the CJEU: *O'Brien v Ministry of Justice* [2012] IRLR 421, [2012] ICR 955 – they are.

The definition of employment is broad enough to cover the personal provision of services by a professional and even the retention of a firm of solicitors, instructions to a firm being, in reality, a contract entered into with each partner (*Loughran and Kelly v Northern Ireland Housing Executive* [1999] 1 AC 428, [1998] 3 WLR 735, [1998] IRLR 593, [1998] ICR 828, HL(NI), distinguished in *Patterson v Legal Services Commission* [2003] EWCA Civ 1558, [2004] IRLR 153, [2004] ICR 312 where there was no obligation on the complainant to carry out the work personally). But see *Pimlico Plumbers and another v Smith* [2017] EWCA Civ 51, [2017] ICR 51 in which the Court of Appeal stated: "As a result of the jurisprudence of the European Court of Justice it is implicit that a relationship in which an independent contractor is doing work or providing services to another as a client or customer is excluded from the [*s 83(2)*] definition". *Loughran* does not appear to have been cited.

Discrimination in appointing an arbitrator falls outside the scope of *RBR 2003* (and thus the *EqA 2010*) – the arbitrator is engaged pursuant to a contract personally to provide services but is not subject to the necessary "control" of the parties to the arbitration (*Hashwani v Jivraj* [2011] UKSC 40, [2011] IRLR 827, [2011] ICR 1004). A beauty consultant whose services were provided to a respondent management company through a company she had herself set up was not, on the facts, subject to the control of the respondent (*Halawi* above). Professional interpreters who worked on an assignment by assignment basis for Her Majesty's Court and Tribunals Service in a relationship which involved no mutuality of obligation were not "employees" (*Windle and another v Secretary of State for Justice* [2016] EWCA Civ 459, [2016] IRLR 628). The Court of Appeal emphasised the need to consider all relevant factors and appeared to row back somewhat from any suggestion in *Jivraj* that the extent to which someone is acting "under direction" or is in a "subordinate position" is potentially decisive. The need to take into account all relevant factors in performing an essential evaluative exercise was re-emphasised in *Pimlico Plumbers* (above). See also *Capita Translation and Interpreting Ltd v Siacuinas and another* UKEAT/181/16; *[2017] ICR 887*, EAT.

A person discriminated against by being dismissed does not have to have been employed for a qualifying period before being entitled to bring a claim.

The Act applies to members of the armed forces "as it applies to employment by a private person" (*EqA 2010, s 83(3)*) save that references in the legislation to "associated employers" are "to be ignored". Also included within the scope of "employment" as defined are those in Crown employment (*EqA 2010, s 83(2)(b)*), certain members of the House of Commons and House of Lords staff (*EqA 2010, s 83(2)(c)* and *(d)* and police officers and cadets (*EqA 2010, s 42*)).

A person without employees can still be an employer provided they are "seeking to employ one or more persons" (*EqA 2010, s 83(4)*).

12.42   Territorial jurisdiction

Whereas the previous law contained an express territorial restriction (for which see above), the *EqA 2010* does not. *EqA 2010, EN Para 15* states:

> "As far as territorial application is concerned, in relation to Part 5 (work) and following the precedent of the Employment Rights Act 1996, the Act leaves it to tribunals to determine whether the law applies, depending for example on the connection between the employment relationship and Great Britain."

It seems, therefore, that the tribunals are intended to have regard to the guidance given by the House of Lords in *Lawson v Serco* [2006] IRLR 289, HL (see UNFAIR DISMISSAL I, para **54.15**). In *Bates Van Winkelhof v Clyde & Co LLP* [2012] EWCA Civ 1207, [2012] IRLR 992, [2013] ICR 883 the Court of Appeal suggested that expatriate employees may not need to meet the requirement identified in *Lawson* that the claim should have connections with Great Britain and with British Employment Law that were as strong as those with the country in which they worked if they could show that they lived and/or worked part of the time in Great Britain. All that is needed in such a case are connections to Great Britain that are sufficiently strong to enable it to be thought that Parliament would have regarded it as appropriate for the tribunal to deal with the claim. However, in *R (on the application of Hottak and another) v Secretary of State for Foreign and Commonwealth Affairs* [2016] EWCA Civ 938, [2016] IRLR 534, [2016] ICR 975, it was confirmed that there is a single test covering both unfair dismissal and discrimination cases.

Even where an employee works entirely outside Great Britain, they may still be able to bring a claim in the tribunal where their employment falls within certain European rules on jurisdiction and judgment. These were considered in the context of discrimination cases by the EAT in *Simpson v Intralinks* [2012] ICR 1343, [2012] All ER (D) 215 (Jun). The complainant lived and worked in Germany for a company registered in the UK. Her contract provided for German Law to be applicable and for disputes to be resolved in Germany. Nevertheless, the EAT concluded that the tribunal had jurisdiction to hear claims of sex discrimination and equal pay. The analysis was as follows: *EC Council Regulation 44/2001* ("the *Brussels Regulation*" now replaced by *Regulation (EU) No 1215/2012/EU* "the *Recast Brussels Regulation*") made provision for jurisdiction in civil matters including employment disputes. *Art 19* permitted an employer to be sued either in the state in which they are domiciled (in this case, in the UK) or in the state where the employee "habitually carries out [their] work" (in this case, Germany). The choice is the employee's and not that of the court. The choice of forum clause did not preclude UK proceedings because *Art 21* only allowed departure from jurisdiction by agreement where the agreement was entered into after the dispute had arisen (which was not the case here). The EAT then turned to the question of the applicable law. That was to be determined by reference to the *Rome Convention* (since superseded by *Rome II*). *Art 3* of the *Rome Convention* provided that a contract should be governed by the law chosen by the parties (ie in this case German Law). However, there was provision for certain mandatory employment protection provisions to be given effect. *Art 7(1)* provided:

> "When applying under this Convention the law of a country, effect may be given to mandatory rules of the law of another country with which the situation has a close

connection, if and insofar as, under the law of the other country, those rules must be applied whatever the law of applicable to the contract . . . "

The EAT was satisfied that the statutory provisions dealing with sex discrimination and equal pay were "mandatory provisions" as the underlying legislation provided that they may not be derogated from by agreement. If the *Brussels* rules pointed to Great Britain as having jurisdiction but the *Rome* rules point to foreign law being the applicable law, the EAT was prepared to countenance the tribunal having jurisdiction and applying foreign law save to the extent that mandatory provisions of domestic law took precedence. The *Brussels* and *Recast Brussels Regulations* cannot, however, create substantive rights. They simply determine which State has jurisdiction to consider claims. Thus, in *Nica v Xian Jiaotong Liverpool University and others* UKEAT/41/17; [2018] ICR 535, where the Tribunal was rightly satisfied that the employment fell outside the territorial scope of the *EqA 2010*, the *Recast Brussels Regulation* could not help the complainant sue his employer in the UK.

EqA 2010, s 81 provides that the protections to be found in *Part 5* of the *Act* only apply to work on ships or hovercraft and to seafarers in "such circumstances as are prescribed". Circumstances are prescribed by the *Equality Act 2010 (Work on Ships and Hovercraft) Regulations 2011 (SI 2011/1771)* as amended, with effect from 31 January 2020 by the *Merchant Shipping (Miscellaneous Provisions) (Amendments etc) (EU Exit) Regulations 2018, SI 2018/1221, Sch 1, Para 22*. The *2011 Regulations* distinguish between cases where seafarers work wholly or partly within Great Britain and adjacent waters and cases where they work wholly outside those waters. So far as those falling into the first category are concerned, the whole of *Part 5* applies if the seafarer is on either "a United Kingdom ship [whose] . . . entry in the register maintained under *section 8* of the *Merchant Shipping Act 1995* specifies a port in Great Britain as the ship's port of choice" or "a hovercraft registered in the United Kingdom and operated by a person whose principal place of business, or ordinary residence in Great Britain" (*Reg 3(1)*).

If the ship or hovercraft is registered in an EEA State other than the UK then *Part 5* applies except in relation to the protected characteristic of marriage and civil partnership and certain additional conditions apply (*Reg 3(2)*). The additional conditions are:

(a)   the ship or hovercraft is in United Kingdom waters adjacent to Great Britain,

(b)   the seafarer is a British citizen, or a national of an EEA State or of a designated state, and

(c)   the legal relationship of the seafarer's employment is located within Great Britain or retains a sufficiently close link with Great Britain. (*Reg 3(3)*)

The legal relationship of the seafarer's employment is located within Great Britain if the contract under which they are employed was entered into in Great Britain or if it takes effect in Great Britain (*Reg 2(2)(a)*). The legal relationship retains a sufficiently close link with Great Britain is determined by reference to "all relevant factors including – (i) where the seafarer is subject to tax; (ii) where the employer or principal is incorporated; (iii) where the employer or principal is established; where the ship or hovercraft on which the seafarer works is registered" (*Reg 2(2)(b)*).

For seafarers working wholly outside Great Britain and adjacent waters, the position is governed by *Reg 4* which provides:

4.—(1) Part 5 of the Act applies to a seafarer who works wholly outside Great Britain and United Kingdom waters adjacent to Great Britain if the seafarer is on—

(a)   a United Kingdom ship and the ship's entry in the register maintained under section 8 of the Merchant Shipping Act 1995 specifies a port in Great Britain as the ship's port of choice, or

(b)   a hovercraft registered in the United Kingdom and operated by a person whose principal place of business, or ordinary residence, is in Great Britain, and paragraph (2) applies.

(2) This paragraph applies if—

(a)   the seafarer is a British citizen, or a national of an EEA State or of a designated state, and

(b)   the legal relationship of the seafarer's employment is located within Great Britain or retains a sufficiently close link with Great Britain.

The "designated states" are the countries of the African, Caribbean and Pacific Group of States, the Kingdom of Morocco, Montenegro, the Most Serene Republic of San Marino, the People's Democratic Republic of Algeria, the Principality of Andorra, the Republic of Albania, the Republic of Croatia, the Republic of Macedonia, the Republic of Tunisia, the Republic of Turkey, the Russian Federation or the Swiss Confederation (*Reg 2(1)*).

The application of *Reg 4* was considered in *Wittenberg v Sunset Personnel Services Ltd and others* UKEATS/19/13 [2017] ICR 1012. The complainant, who was German, worked on a foreign-registered ship that serviced oil rigs off the coast of Nigeria. Since the ship was not a United Kingdom ship, the complainant could not bring a *Part 5* claim. That did not, in and of itself, rule out a claim based on the underlying directives, but the EAT was satisfied that that would have required a sufficiently close connection between the employment relationship and European Law. The Tribunal had been entitled to find that no such connection existed. In *Walker v Wallem Ship Management Ltd and another* UKEAT/0236/18 [2020] IRLR 257, the EAT rejected an argument to the effect that *Reg 4* should be read narrowly so as not to exclude the ability of those who are discriminated against in recruitment to complain of discrimination in the UK even where they were seeking to work wholly outside Great British and UK waters.

Reg 5 specifically excludes claims for discrimination in relation to pay on grounds of nationality where the complainant is not a British Citizen; a national of an EEA State; or a national of a "designated state" (for which see above).

EqA 2010, s 82 allows for "specified provisions" of *Part 5* to be applied to "offshore work". "Offshore work" is defined to mean:

"work for the purposes of:

(a)   activities in the territorial sea adjacent to the United Kingdom,

(b)   activities such as are mentioned in subsection (2) of section 11 of the Petroleum Act 1998 in waters within which subsection 8(b) or (c) of that section, or

(c)   activities mentioned in paragraphs (a) and (b) of section 87(1) of the Energy Act 2004 in waters to which that section applies.

The *Equality Act 2010 (Offshore Work) Order 2010, SI 2010/1835* provides that *Part 5* of *EqA 2010* applies to offshore work as if it were taking place in Great Britain unless it takes place in the Northern Irish Area (as defined by the *Civil Jurisdiction (Offshore Activities) Order 1987*) or is in connection with a ship which is in the course of navigation or a ship which is engaged in dredging or fishing (*Reg 2(1)*). Dredging is defined so as not to include excavation of the sea-bed or its subsoil in the course of pipe laying (*Reg 2(2)*). Jurisdiction is conferred on the English and Welsh Tribunals where the offshore work is being done in the "English Area" as defined in the *Civil Jurisdiction (Offshore Activities) Order 1987* and the offshore work consists of work falling within sub-paragraphs (a) or (b) of the definition set out above. If the work falls within sub-paragraph (c) the jurisdiction is conferred on the High Court.

12.43 Advertisements

There is no specific prohibition on discriminatory advertising in *EqA 2010*. However, the explanatory notes suggest that this is because the issue is dealt with elsewhere in the Act without, unhelpfully, identifying where else it is supposedly dealt with (*EqA 2010*, EN Para 1024). It is likely that discriminatory advertisements will be actionable by individuals as a form of direct discrimination contrary to *EqA 2010, s 13* consistent with the analysis of the ECJ in *Centruum voor Gelijkheid van kansen en voor racismebestrijding v Firma Feryn NV*: C–54/07, [2008] IRLR 732, [2008] ICR 1390.

12.44 Engagement

EqA 2010, s 39 provides that:

"An employer (A) must not discriminate against a person (B) –

(a)   in the arrangements A makes for deciding to whom to offer employment,
(b)   as to the terms on which A offers B employment,
(c)   by not offering B employment."

Refusing to employ someone because they have a protected characteristic is perhaps the most obvious example of employment-related discrimination. The equivalent protection in the *Framework Directive (2000/78/EU, Art 3(1))* and the *Equal Treatment Directive (2006/54/EU, Art 1)* requires equal treatment in respect of "access to employment". In *Kratzer v R+V Allegemeins Vershicherung AG* C–423/15, [2016] IRLR 888, [2016] ICR 967, there was found to be no breach of either directive where an applicant had applied not in order to get appointed but in order to try to bring discrimination proceedings. The ECJ considered that since he was not truly seeking employment, his case fell outside the scope of the directives. There is little doubt the UK courts would reach the same outcome although it would not necessarily be by saying that *s 39* was not engaged. It might instead be seen as an abuse of process.

Thus, if an employer offers a woman three weeks' holiday, whereas a man doing the same job is entitled to five weeks, he is guilty of discrimination. Also, the woman's contract will be modified by the equality of terms provisions of the Act to give her the same holiday entitlement as that of the man (see Equal Pay (23)).

Where a complainant's employment transfers by operation of the *Transfer of Undertakings (Protection of Employment) Regulations 2006, SI 2006/246*, there is no "offer" made by the new employer (*NHS Direct NHS Trust v Gunn* [2015] IRLR 799, which also suggested that an offer of "suitable alternative employment" where an employee is redundant will constitute such an offer).

In *Saunders v Richmond-upon-Thames London Borough Council* [1977] IRLR 362, [1978] ICR 75, it was assumed that questions asked at an interview constituted 'arrangements' within the meaning of (1) above. Whether or not the questions were unlawful was held to be a question of fact to be determined in each case. In *Brennan v JH Dewhurst Ltd* [1983] IRLR 357, [1984] ICR 52, the arrangements made for interviewing applicants were operated so as to discriminate against women, and were therefore unlawful.

A refusal to re-instate a former employee following a dismissal does not constitute 'refusing to offer employment' (*Post Office v Adekeye* [1997] IRLR 105, [1997] ICR 110, CA).

EqA 2010, s 60(1) prohibits employers from asking about the health of an applicant for employment before offering them work (either conditionally or unconditionally – see *EqA 2010, s 60(10)*) or, if the relevant person acting on behalf of the employer is shortlisting applicants, before including the applicant in the pool from which the employer intends to select the appointee. Breach can only be challenged by the EHRC (*EqA 2010, s 60(2)*). Offering work includes making a conditional offer (*EqA 2010, s 10*).

Merely asking the prohibited question does not in and of itself involve any disability discrimination, but it may be used as evidence to establish such discrimination (*EqA 2010, s 60(3)*).

EqA 2010, s 60(6) disapplies the prohibition in a surprisingly broad range of circumstances. In each case asking the question must be necessary for the specified purpose. Those purposes are:

(1)   Establishing whether the applicant will be able to comply with a requirement to undergo an assessment or establishing whether a duty to make reasonable adjustments is or will be imposed on the employer in relation to the applicant in connection with the requirement to undergo assessment. For this purpose, an assessment is an "interview or other process designed to give an indication of a person's suitability for the work concerned" (*EqA 2010, s 60(12)*);

(2)   Establishing whether the applicant will be able to carry out a function that is intrinsic to the work concerned. The exception is only available if the employer is satisfied that the function would still be intrinsic if the job were adjusted in accordance with the duty to make reasonable adjustments (*EqA 2010, s 60(7)*);

(3)   Monitoring diversity in the range of people applying to the Employer for work;

(4)   Taking action to which *section 158* (ie the Positive Action provisions) would apply if references to persons who share (or do not share) a protected characteristic were references to disabled persons (or persons who are not disabled) and the reference to the characteristic were a reference to disability; or

(5)   If the Employer applies in relation to the work a requirement to have a particular disability, establishing that the applicant has that disability. The requirement has to be an occupational requirement and its application has to be a proportionate means of achieving a legitimate aim (*EqA 2010, s 60(8)*).

The provision does not affect anything done for the purposes of national security vetting (*EqA 2010, s 60(14)*).

Is an unsuccessful candidate who meets the criteria for selection entitled to information from the employer about whether someone has been appointed and, if so, on what criteria? UK Law had, until recently, a questionnaire procedure (for which see below). In *Meister v Speech Design Carrier Systems*: C-415/60 [2012] ICR 1066, the CJEU decided that as a matter of European Law, a candidate was not entitled to such information but a refusal to provide it might be something that could be taken into account in deciding whether or not the complainant had been the victim of discrimination.

12.45 *Racial discrimination: engagement and asylum and immigration*

The *Immigration, Asylum and Nationality Act 2006, s 15* makes it an offence for an employer to employ those whose immigration status precludes them from working in the UK. The *schedule* to the *Immigration (Restrictions on Employment) Order 2007 (SI 2007/3290)* specifies a number of documents ('statutory documents') which, if produced prior to engagement, the employer may rely upon as establishing that the job applicant is entitled to work in the UK. Provided the employer has complied with the requirements of *reg 6* which included taking all reasonable steps to check the validity of the document, it has a defence to any prosecution under the *Act*. There is a danger that in seeking to avoid liability under the *Act*, employers may treat job applicants from ethnic minorities differently. This in turn creates the risk of discrimination claims. The Home Office has produced a code of practice which includes guidance on avoiding discrimination (www.gov.uk/government/publications/right-to-work-checks-code-of-practice-on -avoiding-discrimination).

A failure to comply with the provisions of the code may be taken into account by an employment tribunal considering a claim of race discrimination.

The EAT has suggested that a foreign national complaining of discriminatory treatment may only be able to compare herself with other foreign nationals rather than with British citizens (*Sheiky v Argos Distributions Ltd* (1997) 597 IDS Brief 16).

An employer that declined to consider applicants from outside the EEA on grounds that they would be unlikely to be able to obtain work permits committed an act of indirect discrimination (*Osborne Clarke Services v Purohit* [2009] IRLR 341, EAT).

12.46 *Sex discrimination: terms offered – special provisions for those on maternity leave*

EqA 2010, Sch 9, Part 3, Para 17 substantially reproduces the pre-existing law. *Para 17(1)* provides that a person does not contravene *EqA 2010, s 39(1)(b)* (discrimination as to the terms on which employment is offered) or *(2)* (discrimination as to the terms of employment, access to opportunities for promotion transfer or training or receiving any other benefit, facility or service, discriminatory dismissal or subjection to any detriment) by depriving a woman who is on maternity leave of any benefit from the terms of her employment relating to pay. However, "terms of employment" does not mean "contract of employment", *EqA 2010. Sch 9, Part 3, Para 17(4)* provides:

> "A reference to terms of her employment is a reference to terms of her employment that are not in her contract of employment, her contract of apprenticeship or her contract to do work personally".

The Act then creates an exception to the exception by providing that the reference to "benefit" from the terms of the woman's employment does not include a reference to –

(a)   maternity-related pay (including maternity-related pay that is increase-related),

(b)   pay (including increase-related pay) in respect of times when she is not on maternity leave, or

(c)   pay by way of bonus in respect of times when she is on compulsory maternity leave.

(*EqA 2010, Sch 9, Part 3, Para 17(2)*) with the effect that that there may be breaches of *EqA 2010, s 39(1)(b)* and *(2)* in relation to those matters.

Pay means benefits: (a) that consist of the payment of money to an employee by way of wages or salary; and (b) that are not benefits whose provision is regulated by the employee's contract of employment or apprenticeship or her contract personally to do work.

"Maternity-related pay" is pay to which the employee is entitled: (a) as a result of being pregnant; or (b) in respect of times when she is on maternity leave (*EqA 2010, Sch 9, Part 3, Para 17(6)*).

Pay is "increase-related" in so far as it is "to be calculated by reference to increases in pay that the woman would have received had she not been on maternity leave" (*EqA 2010, Sch 9, Part 3, Para 17(3)*).

12.47 Opportunities in employment

There is an express prohibition on discrimination "in the way A affords B access to opportunities for promotion, transfer or training or for receiving any other benefit, facility or service (*EqA 2010, s 39(2)(b)*).

In the case of receipt of a benefit, facility or service there is an exception to liability in the case of services which the employer offers to the public. The essence of the idea is that someone, for instance, who works for an airline, cannot bring a claim as an employee if she is treated less favourably when flying as a passenger on one of her employer's aircraft. She would be left to whatever remedies members the public would have, *EqA 2010, Sch 9, Part 3, Para 19(1)* provides that:

> "A person does not contravene [*EqA 2010, s 39(2)(b)*] in relation to the provision of a benefit, facility or service to B if A is concerned with the provision (for payment or not) of a benefit, facility or service of the same description to the public".

A reference to the public includes a section of the public which includes B (*EqA 2010, Sch 9, Part 3, Para 19(6)*).

There are exceptions to the general exclusion of liability in respect of benefits, facilities or services provided to the public. They, broadly, cover circumstances in which the fact that the complainant is an employee means that they are not sensibly to be treated as if they were simply another member of the public. The exceptions are set out at *EqA 2010, Sch 9, Part 3, Para 19(3)*:

> "Sub-paragraph (1) does not apply if –
>
> (a)   the provision by A to the public differs in a material respect from the provision by A to [other employees],
> (b)   the provision to B is regulated by B's terms, or
> (c)   the benefit, facility or service relates to training."

The reference in (c) to "B's terms" means "the terms of B's employment" (*EqA 2010, Sch 9, Part 3, Para 19(5)*. Similar provision is made in relation to contract workers, partners and office holders).

12.48 *Sex discrimination: opportunities afforded – special provisions for those on maternity leave*

There is a specific exception to liability under *EqA 2010, s 39(2)* in respect of the terms of employment of women on maternity which relate to pay (*EqA 2010, Sch 9, Part 3, Para 17(1)*). For a more detailed account of the exception see "Sex discrimination: terms offered – special provisions for those on maternity leave" above.

12.49 Dismissal

An express prohibition on discriminatory dismissal is to be found at *EqA 2010, s 39(2)(c)*. Dismissal is defined by *EqA 2010, s 39(7)* so as to include the termination of employment: (a) by the expiry of a period (including a period expiring by reference to an event or circumstance); and (b) by an act of B's (including giving notice) in circumstances such that B is entitled, because of A's conduct, to terminate the employment without notice. Termination by expiry of a period will not constitute dismissal if, immediately after the termination, the employment is renewed on the same terms (*EqA 2010, s 39(8)*).

Where an employee is prevented from performing their job by reason of a disability, the doctrine of frustration may apply so as to terminate their contract. However, the tribunal should first consider whether or not the employer has complied with any duty *Equality Act 2010, s 20* to make reasonable adjustments (*Warner v Armfield Retail & Leisure Ltd* UKEAT/376/12, [2014] ICR 239, [2013] All ER (D) 260 (Oct)).

An employer's breach of its duties under the anti–discrimination legislation may amount to a breach of the implied duty of trust and confidence so as to repudiate the contract of employment and entitle the victim to treat themselves as having been constructively dismissed (*Shaw v CCL Ltd* [2008] IRLR 284, EAT).

If an employee is dismissed for a combination of lawful and unlawfully discriminatory reasons, they are entitled to compensation, limited to injury to feelings, even where dismissal would have occurred even if there had been no discrimination (*GMBU v Henderson* [2015] IRLR 451, EAT, the dictum was not contradicted when the case was considered by the Court of Appeal ([2016] EWCA Civ 1049)).

12.50 Subjection to other detriment

EqA 2010, s 39(2)(d) contains a "catch all" obligation not to subject employees to a detriment. This reproduces the pre-existing law.

A complainant seeking to establish that he has been subjected to a 'detriment' need not demonstrate that he has suffered a physical or economic consequence. It is sufficient to show that a reasonable employee would or might take the view that they had been disadvantaged in the circumstances in which they had to work (*Shamoon v Chief Constable of the Royal Ulster Constabulary (Northern Ireland)* [2003] UKHL 11, [2003] 2 All ER 26, [2003] IRLR 285, [2003] ICR 337 and see *Ministry of Defence v Jeremiah* [1980] QB 87, [1979] 3 All ER 83 in which it was held that requiring only male supervisors to carry out dirty work was an unlawful detriment; see also *BL Cars Ltd v Brown* [1983] IRLR 193, [1983] ICR 143; *Jiad v Byford* [2003] EWCA Civ 135, [2003] IRLR 232).

In *De Souza v Automobile Association* [1986] IRLR 103, [1986] ICR 514, the Court of Appeal held that the Employment Appeal Tribunal had correctly concluded that Mrs De Souza had not been subjected to a 'detriment' as a result of overhearing a manager say to another manager, about her, to get his typing done by 'the wog'. The EAT in *Barclays Bank plc v Kapur* [1989] IRLR 57, [1989] ICR 142 (appeal allowed, [1989] IRLR 387, [1989] ICR 753) suggested, in a passage which was not a necessary part of its decision, that the words 'any other detriment' related to acts in connection with dismissal or disciplinary proceedings and were not wholly general in their scope. The correctness of this construction is, with respect, doubted. It is also open to argument whether *De Souza* was correctly decided, bearing in mind more recent cases dealing with harassment.

An employee was not subjected to a detriment where the employer failed, because of his race, to investigate complaints that he had fabricated against a colleague (*Cordant Security Ltd v Singh* UKEAT/0144/15 [2016] IRLR 4). However, there could be detriment where an employee's grievances were not properly investigated even though they would not have been upheld (*Deer v University of Oxford* [2015] EWCA Civ 52, [2015] ICR 1213, [2015] IRLR 481 – a victimisation case). There may, therefore, be a distinction to be drawn between fabricated and ill-founded complaints.

Failure, after the termination of the employment contract, to confer a non-contractual benefit on a former employee will only exceptionally constitute a 'detriment' (*Relaxion Group plc v Rhys-Harper* [2003] UKHL 33, [2003] IRLR 484).

12.51 *Harassment on grounds of marriage, civil partnership, pregnancy or maternity as a detriment*

EqA 2010 provides (somewhat obliquely) that harassing an employee on grounds of marriage, civil partnership, pregnancy or maternity is deemed to be direct discrimination. The method by which this result is achieved is not straightforward and is explained immediately below.

Before there was a specific prohibition of harassment, victims would bring claims instead for direct discrimination. To be harassed was to be subjected to a detriment (see *Porcelli v Strathclyde Regional Council* [1986] IRLR 134, [1986] ICR 564). That indirect protection was abandoned in favour of introducing a direct protection against harassment which is described at **12.39** above. However, the *EqA 2010*, specifically excludes two protected characteristics from the scope of its express prohibition of harassment: marriage and civil partnership and pregnancy and maternity (see *EqA 2010, s 26(5)*). It seems, however, that the intention is not to allow employees to be harassed on those grounds. The definition of "detriment" at *EqA 2010, s 212* excludes harassment save that there is provision made at *s 212(5)* in the following terms:

> "Where this Act disapplies a prohibition on harassment in relation to a specified protected characteristic, the disapplication does not prevent conduct relating to that characteristic from amounting to a detriment for the purposes of discrimination within section 13 because of that characteristic."

Therefore, harassing a woman because she is pregnant would amount to direct discrimination within *s 13*. The same would be true in the case of harassment because of marriage, civil partnership or maternity.

It should be noted that this indirect route does not entirely replicate the protection provided by the express prohibition on harassment. In particular, the employee will have to show that they have been "less favourably treated". This allows the employer to continue to run what has become known as the "bastard defence", ie because he is equally unpleasant to all employees an employee, though harassed, cannot establish that they have been less favourably treated.

Authorities which predate the introduction of the specific prohibition on harassment will be relevant to claims brought as direct discrimination claims. In *Reed and Bull Information Systems Ltd v Stedman* [1999] IRLR 299, the EAT gave guidance to tribunals dealing with three troublesome questions which commonly arise in harassment cases. The particular case was concerned was sexual harassment and the principles have been adapted below and expressed as matters of general principle:

(a)   *If an employee regards as harassment words or conduct to which many would not take exception or regard as harassment, has their claim been made out?*

The question is whether the behaviour has to be objectively offensive or whether it is sufficient that it should be offensive in the subjective opinion of the employee. The EAT steered a middle course. The fact that, objectively, the behaviour is not offensive does not dispose of the issue. If a particularly sensitive employee has made it clear that the conduct is unwelcome, any repetition may amount to harassment. Other forms of conduct are objectively hostile or offensive, and these do not require the employee to indicate that they are unwelcome before they may constitute harassment. This approach is consistent with that taken by *EqA 2010, s 26* in relation to the specific prohibition of harassment.

(b)   *If the alleged harasser does not appreciate that their words or conduct are unwelcome, has the claim been proved?*

The EAT restated the general principle that, as with all cases of direct discrimination, the fact that the alleged discriminator lacks a discriminatory motive or intention will not prevent a finding of direct discrimination. If the alleged harasser should have known that conduct is unwelcome either because that risk was obvious or else because the victim has made it clear to him, he will be liable even if he did not intend to harass.

(c)   *Is a 'one-off act' sufficient to constitute harassment?*

A one-off act may be sufficient. The clearer it is that objectively the conduct was hostile or offensive, the more likely it is that a one-off act will suffice to establish harassment (see also *Insitu Cleaning Co Ltd v Heads* [1995] IRLR 4).

Further guidance was given in *Driskel v Peninsula Business Services Ltd* [2000] IRLR 151, EAT. First, where there are a number of alleged incidents, the tribunal should be careful to focus on their cumulative effect rather than concentrating upon whether individual incidents are trivial in nature. Second, simply because a male superior engages in vulgar behaviour with male colleagues does not mean that a woman is not treated less favourably when she is subjected to such behaviour. Behaviour of that kind directed at a woman is more likely to be intimidatory and to undermine her dignity than similar behaviour directed at a male colleague. (On the question of the objective nature of the test, the Administrative Court expressed a preference for the guidance given in *Driskel* over that given in *Reed*; *EOC v Secretary of State for Trade and Industry* [2007] EWHC 483 (Admin), [2007] IRLR 327, [2007] ICR 1234 at para 33).

12.52 Post-employment discrimination

EqA 2010 reproduces the pre-existing application of post-termination protections against discrimination.

EqA 2010, s 108(1) provides: provides:

"A person (A) must not discriminate against another (B) if –

(a)   the discrimination arises out of and is closely connected to a relationship which used to exist between them,

(b)   conduct of a description constituting the discrimination would, if it occurred during the relationship, contravene the Act."

A similar provision is made in relation to harassment at *EqA 2010, s 108(2)*:

"A person (A) must not harass another (B) if –

(a)   the harassment arises out of and is closely connected to a relationship which used to exist between them, and

(b)   conduct of a description constituting the harassment would, if it occurred during the relationship, contravene the Act."

Since the Act is intended to be a consolidating measure, it does not matter whether the relationship ends before or after the commencement of *s 108* (*EqA 2010, s 108(3)*).

The requirement that the discrimination should arise out of and be closely connected with a "relationship that used to exist between [A and B]" means that where a former employee of a police authority was subjected to a detriment by a successor body by which she had never been employed, *s 108* did not apply (see *Butterworth v Police and Crime Commissioner's Office for Greater Manchester and another* UKEAT/0222/15: [2016] IRLR 280, EAT).

Conduct is not treated as breaching *s 108* "in so far as it also amounts to victimisation" (*EqA 2010, s 108(7)*). The statutory language appears on its face to suggest that post-employment victimisation is not actionable. However, the Court of Appeal has confirmed that proceedings can be brought (*Rowstock Ltd v Jessemey* [2014] EWCA Civ 185, [2014] ICR 550, [2014] IRLR 368).

Where a tribunal makes a reinstatement order as a remedy for unfair dismissal, a discriminatory failure to comply with the order was not 'discrimination in employment' for the purposes of the predecessor provision in *RRA 1976* (*D'Souza v Lambeth London Borough Council* [2003] UKHL 33, [2003] IRLR 484).

Other unlawful acts

12.53 *Instructions or pressure to commit unlawful acts*

EqA 2010, s 111 prohibits employers from instructing, causing or inducing (whether directly or indirectly) an employee to commit an unlawful act of discrimination (or from attempting to do so).

EqA 2010, s 111(1) creates a concept known as a "basic contravention" which involves the employee contravening any of the following in relation to a third party:

(a)   Part 3 of the Act (Services and Public Functions);

(b)   Part 4 of the Act (Premises);

(c)   Part 5 of the Act (Work);

(d)   Part 6 of the Act (Education);

(e)   Part 7 of the Act (Associations);

(f)   Section 108(1) (Post-employment discrimination);

(g)   Section 108(2) (Post-employment harassment); or

(h)   Section 112(1) (Knowingly helping another to commit a basic contravention).

EqA 2010, s 111(1) prohibits an employer from instructing an employee to commit a basic contravention. *EqA 2010, ss 111(2)* and *(3)* do the same thing in relation to causing or inducing a contravention respectively. Inducement may be either direct or indirect (*EqA 2010, s 111(4)*). It must be established that was an instruction, causation or inducement. It is insufficient to show, therefore, that a respondent was a "party to a decision" or "played a material part" in a decision (*NHS Trust Development Authority v Saiger and others* UKEAT/167/15; [2018] ICR 297).

Proceedings can be brought by the employee if they are subjected to detriment by their employer's conduct or by the third party that was the target of the employer's conduct. Proceedings may also be brought by the Commission (*EqA 2010, s 111(5)*). A claim may be pursued even if the basic contravention never occurs and whether or not other proceedings have been (or could be) brought in relation to the employer's conduct (*EqA 2010, s 111(6)*).

In *Weathersfield Ltd v Sargent (t/a Van and Truck Rentals) v Sargent* [1999] IRLR 94, [1999] ICR 425, CA, the receptionist at a truck rental company was instructed to tell black or Asian enquirers that no vehicles were available. As a result, she found her position intolerable and resigned. The respondent argued that as any employee would have been given the same instruction, the complainant could not establish that she had been less favourably treated. The EAT concluded that the instruction affected employees 'differentially' in that some, but not all, would regard themselves as 'victims of mistreatment'. The appropriate comparator, therefore, was somebody who was prepared to go along with the employer's unlawful instruction. The EAT's decision was affirmed by the Court of Appeal.

An attempt to instruct, cause or induce an employee to commit a basic contravention is also actionable (*EqA 2010, s 111(8)*).

In *Commission for Racial Equality v Imperial Society of Teachers of Dancing* [1983] IRLR 315, [1983] ICR 473, the Employment Appeal Tribunal held that a prospective employer acted unlawfully by telling the head of careers at a school that he would prefer that the school did not put forward any coloured applicants.

12.54   *Liability for unlawful act of employee*

EqA 2010, s 109 substantially reproduces the former regime of vicarious liability. *EqA 2010, s 109(1)* provides:

> "Anything done by a person (A) in the course of A's employment must be treated as also done by the employer".

A broad interpretation is given to the concept of "in the course of . . . employment" (*Jones v Tower Boot Co Ltd* [1997] IRLR 168, [1997] ICR 254, CA). It is a question of fact to be decided by having regard to all relevant circumstances (*Forbes v LHR Airport Ltd* UKEAT/0174/18 [2019] IRLR 890). The Tribunal should ask whether a lay person would understand the particular act to have occurred in the course of employment (*Forbes* above).

The Tribunal may consider, for instance, whether the act was done at or outside of work and, if outside, whether there is a sufficient "nexus or connection" with work (*Forbes* above).

Acts committed by colleagues away from the workplace are less likely to fall within the scope of the discrimination legislation (eg cf *Waters v Metropolitan Police Comr* [1997] IRLR 589, CA: sexual assault by one off-duty police officer on another in a police section house. Cf also *Sidhu v Aerospace Composite Technology Ltd* [2000] IRLR 602, CA: acts committed during the course of a 'family day' organised by an employer and held at an amusement park were not in the course of employment; and *HM Prison Service v Davis* (2000) 666 IDS Brief 14, EAT: harassment not in course of employment where employee visited colleague at her home, even though employer had power to discipline employees for misconduct committed away from the workplace) although that will not always be so; and *Forbes*, above: Posting racially offensive material on Facebook was not in the course of employment even if the images posted subsequently circulated in the workplace. *Chief Constable of Lincolnshire Police v Stubbs* [1999] IRLR 81, [1999] ICR 547, EAT, the EAT upheld a finding that drinks after work and an organised leaving party were sufficiently work-related to be treated as 'extensions of work'.

For an account of the vicarious liability more generally see Vicarious Liability (57) .

A police officer will not, for most purposes, be treated as an employee. However, police officers and police cadets are deemed, for the purposes of *Part 5* of the *Equality Act 2010*, to be employed by their chief officer (*s 42(1)*).

It does not matter whether the thing is done with the employer's knowledge or approval (*EqA 2010 s 109(3)*). Vicarious liability does not extend to cover the offences created under *EqA 2010* (with the exception offences under *Part 12* (disabled persons: transport)) (*EqA 2010, s 109(5)*).

The employee who commits the discriminatory act is fixed with liability by *EqA 2010, s 110(1)*:

"A person (A) contravenes this section if –

(a)   A is an employee . . .
(b)   A does something which by virtue of section 109(1) . . . , is treated as having been done by A's employer . . . , and
(c)   the doing of that thing by A amounts to a contravention of this Act by the employer . . . "

If the employer manages to establish the reasonable steps defence (for which see below), the employee may still be liable (*EqA 2010, s 110(2)*). Even under the former regime, it was possible to bring a claim of victimisation against an individual employee even where the employer was not sued (*Barlow v Stone* [2012] IRLR 898).

The employee has a defence where he reasonably relies on a statement by the employer that the doing the act in question would not involve a contravention of the Act (*EqA 2010, s 110(3)*). If the employer makes such a statement which is false or misleading in a material respect and does so knowingly or recklessly, he commits an offence liable to a fine not exceeding level 5 on the standard scale (*EqA 2010, s 110(5)*).

12.55 *Defence to vicarious liability*

EqA 2010, s 109(4) provides:

"In proceedings against A's employer (B) in respect of anything alleged to have been done by A in the course of his employment it is a defence for B to show that B took all reasonable steps to prevent A –

(a)   from doing that thing, or
(b)   from doing anything of that description."

See *Balgobin v Tower Hamlets London Borough Council* [1987] IRLR 401, [1987] ICR 829). In determining whether the defence is made out, the tribunal should focus on what the employer has done prior to the occurrence of the act and not how he reacts once it has occurred (*Haringey London Borough Council (Haringey Design Partnership Directorate of Technical and Environmental Services) v Al-Azzawi* (2002) 703 IDS Brief 7, EAT). An employment tribunal may have regard to such matters as whether the employer has issued a written policy to employees on equal opportunities, whether it has given its managers training in such matters and whether it has taken steps to discipline employees if they have been guilty of unlawful discrimination. Where there were steps which it would have been reasonably practicable to take, it seems that the respondent must take them if he is to escape liability even if it cannot be shown that those steps would have prevented the discriminatory acts from occurring (*Canniffe v East Riding of Yorkshire Council* [2000] IRLR 555, EAT).

Where an employee's discriminatory behaviour occurs outside the course of his employment, an employer may have a primary, as opposed to a vicarious, liability if he has a sufficient control over the circumstances in which the behaviour occurred to have prevented it from happening and the reason for not exercising that control is a prohibited ground.

12.56   *Liability for unlawful act of agent*

EqA 2010, s 109(3) treats the principal as having done anything that an agent has done with the principal's authority (*EqA 2010, s 109(2)*). That does not mean that the act must have been done with the principal's knowledge or approval (*EqA 2010, s 109(3)*).

The concept of agency used by the *Act* is the same as the common law concept (*Kemeh v Ministry of Defence* [2014] EWCA Civ 91, [2014] IRLR 377). In *Kemeh*, a cook employed by a third party contractor but working in an MoD kitchen was not the MoD's agent. Locally elected trade union officials were found to be agents by the Appeal Tribunal in *Unite the Union v Nailard* UKEAT/0300/15, [2016] IRLR 906, [2017] ICR 121 (affirmed by the Court of Appeal - *Unite the Union v Nailard* [2018] EWCA Civ 1203, [2018] IRLR 730, [2019] ICR 28).

In contrast to the position with employers there is no "reasonable steps" defence available to a principal.

EqA 2010, s 110(1) fixes the agent with liability where:

"A person (A) contravenes this section if –

(a)   A is an . . . agent

(b)   A does something which by virtue of section 109(2) . . . , is treated as having been done by A's . . . , principal . . . and

(c)   the doing of that thing by A amounts to a contravention of this Act by the . . . principal"

It is no answer for the principal to say that it did not give the agent authority to discriminate. It will be enough if the agent has authority to do an act which may be carried out in a lawful or a discriminatory manner (*Lana v Positive Action Training in Housing (London) Ltd* [2001] IRLR 501, EAT and *Kemeh v Ministry of Defence* [2014] EWCA Civ 91, [2014] IRLR 377).

The principal will only be liable where the agent's actions are a breach of the Act. If, for instance, an agent is unaware that a complainant has performed protected acts, the agent cannot victimise them and the principal will have no liability whatever they themselves knew – *Peninsula Business Service Ltd v Baker* UKEAT/0241/16, [2017] IRLR 394, [2017] ICR 714).

The agent has a defence where he reasonably relies on a statement by the principal that the doing the act in question would not involve a contravention of the Act (*EqA 2010, s 110(3)*). If the principal makes such a statement which is false or misleading in a material respect and does so knowingly or recklessly, he commits an offence liable to a fine not exceeding level 5 on the standard scale (*EqA 2010, s 110(5)*).

EqA 2010, s 109 does not render agents liable for the discriminatory acts of principals. So when an LLP committed an act of indirect discrimination, the individual partners were not liable (*Murray v Maclay Murray Spens LLP* UKEATS/0004/18 [2018] IRLR 710).

12.57   *Liability for act of other third party*

The *EqA 2010* formerly created a broad liability for failure to protect employees from harassment by third parties. However, this liability was abolished with effect from 1 October 2013; see Para **12.39** above.

In *Unite the Union v Nailard* [2018] EWCA Civ 1203, [2018] IRLR 730, [2019] ICR 28, the Court of Appeal rejected an argument that *EqA 2010 s 26* allowed an employer to be held responsible for harassment by third parties. The complainant contended that where an employer failed to prevent acts of harassment committed by third parties that failure "related to" the protected characteristic. The Court of Appeal concluded that: *"the mere use of the formula 'related to' is [in]sufficient to convey an intention that employers who are themselves innocent of any discriminatory motivation should be liable for the discriminatory acts of third parties, even if they could have prevented them".*

The actions of a third party purporting to exert influence over an employer may be treated as evidence of discrimination on the employer's part if they do not take steps to distance themselves from the behaviour (see *Asociatia ACCEPT v Combaterea Discriminarii* C-81/12; [2013] IRLR 660; [2013] ICR 938, CJEU – burden of proof reversed by evidence of a leading shareholder saying in a media interview that a football club would not recruit gay players).

12.58 *Aiding unlawful acts*

EqA 2010, s 112 makes it unlawful for a person knowingly to help another to commit what it calls a "basic contravention". A basic contravention is a breach of *Parts 3 to 7* of the *Act* inclusive (*Part 5* is the part that deals with work), *s 108(1)* or *(2)* (post-termination discrimination and harassment) or *s 111* (instructing, causing or inducing contraventions).

The act must be unlawful in the sense that it must be possible to sue the person who committed the *Act*. In *May & Baker Ltd (t/a Sanofi-Aventis Pharma) v Okerago* [2010] IRLR 394, EAT an employee was harassed by an agency worker that her employer had hired. The agency worker's act was not capable of founding liability since she did not employ the complainant. That being so, there was no unlawful act for the employer to aid.

Although the new language talks of "helping" rather than "aiding" an unlawful act, there is no reason to believe that the change in language is intended to bring about a different result. The guidance given by case law on the predecessor provisions is likely to remain authoritative.

Guidance on the circumstances in which a person might be said to 'aiding' a discriminator was given by the House of Lords in *Anyanwu v South Bank Student's Union* [2001] UKHL 14, [2001] IRLR 305, HL. Two paid student executives of a student union were dismissed by the union after an investigation into their activities had resulted in the University expelling them. The complainants alleged that their dismissals had been discriminatory and that, as their expulsion had meant that dismissal was inevitable, the University should be treated as having aided the discriminatory dismissals. The House of Lords upheld the claim and offered, in the course of Lord Bingham's judgment, the following guidance: First, the word 'aids' in the statutory provision should be given its ordinary meaning. Second, a person may knowingly aid another to do an unlawful act without inducing the wrongdoer to act unlawfully or procuring the act of discrimination. Third, provided that the assistance given is not so insignificant as to be negligible, it does not matter whether the help is substantive or productive.

The case of *Hallam v Avery* [2001] UKHL 15, [2001] IRLR 312, HL, draws an important distinction that limits the circumstances in which a person may be said to have aided another to discriminate. On the particular facts, a local authority had agreed to hire out rooms to a gypsy couple for their wedding reception. The police warned the local authority that they had experienced problems with gypsy weddings in the past. The local authority sought to impose further conditions on the hiring of the room, which, it was found, amounted to an act of discrimination. The House of Lords considered that the judge at first instance had been entitled to find that the police had not aided the local authority in its act of discrimination. Since it was the Police's warning that seemed to have prompted the discriminatory act one might, at first glance, conclude that the warning and the discrimination were sufficiently entangled to allow a finding that the Police had knowingly aided the local authority to discriminate. It was important, however, in the view of Lord Millet, to focus on what the discriminatory act actually was. In this case it was deciding to impose conditions. The Council had made the decision on its own and had neither 'needed or obtained the aid of the police' in doing so. Aiding someone to commit a discriminatory act required 'a much closer involvement in the actual act of the principal than   . . . encouraging or inducing on the one hand or causing or procuring on the other'. What was required was actual participation in the decision-making. It would seem from later cases (see immediately below) that even advising the local authority to impose conditions might not have been sufficient. The question whether a solicitor might be said to be aiding an act of discrimination in giving advice or in acting on instructions was considered in *Bird v Sylvester* [2007] EWCA Civ 1052, [2008] IRLR 232, [2008] ICR 208. An employee unsuccessfully sued her employer for race discrimination. The employer's solicitor advised his client to take disciplinary proceedings against the employee in part because of the claim. On instruction, the solicitor wrote to the employee informing her that disciplinary action would be taken against her. The employee claimed that she had been unlawfully victimised and that the solicitor had knowingly aided the employer to discriminate. The Court of Appeal decided that the solicitor was not liable. The decision to discipline the employee had been the employer's alone. The solicitor had advised the employer to perform the discriminatory act, but that was insufficient. Turning to the letter sent to the employee in which the threat of disciplinary action was made, the Court of Appeal considered that it was 'very difficult to see how a solicitor who confines himself to giving objective legal advice in good faith as to the proper protection of his client's interests, and acts strictly upon his client's instructions, could be at risk of an adverse finding'. Their Lordships were not prepared to go so far as to hold that a solicitor might never be liable. Liability might arise where 'the solicitor himself actively promotes, perhaps for a malign motive, oppressive actions, and actively carries them along'.

Being a "party to" or having "played a material part" in a decision will not amount, without more, to knowingly giving help (*NHS Trust Development Authority v Saiger and others* UKEAT/167/15; [2018] ICR 297).

A person does not 'aid' discrimination merely by creating an environment in which discrimination could occur. Fostering and encouraging a discriminatory culture may, however, suffice (*Gilbank v Miles* [2006] EWCA Civ 543, [2006] IRLR 538, [2006] ICR 1297).

A person cannot "aid" another to commit an act which the latter had already committed at the point at which the employer first becomes involved. Thus, a failure to investigate an allegation of harassment does not mean that the employer should be taken to have aided the harasser (*May & Baker Ltd v Okerago* [2010] IRLR 394, EAT).

When might someone be said to be knowingly aiding a discriminator?

Hallam (above) had been decided on a different basis by the Court of Appeal ([2000] ICR 583, CA). Whilst the imposition of further conditions was an act of discrimination, it was decided that there was insufficient evidence that the police had been aware that, as a result of their advice, the local authority would treat the couple less favourably on grounds of their race. That being so, they could not be said knowingly to have aided an act of discrimination. Recklessness was insufficient; the police had to know that they were aiding a discriminator. See also *Sinclair, Roche & Temperley v Heard* [2004] IRLR 763, EAT.

In *Shepherd v North Yorkshire County Council* [2006] IRLR 190, EAT a council was accused of knowingly aiding a trade union to delay the implementation of a collective agreement. The agreement had the effect of prolonging a disparity in pay between male and female employees. The EAT decided that even if the Council had been aware that the union was discriminating, they could not be said to have knowingly aided the discrimination. There was a material difference between taking advantage of a failure by another and aiding that party to discrimination. The Council had had its own interests to protect in any collective negotiation. Further, the union had not needed the employer's assistance to discriminate. Where, during the course of his employment, an employee commits an act of discrimination, his employer may be liable for it (see above). The employee may also be liable in a personal capacity.

Guidance on when the employee may be said to have knowingly aided his employer is given in *Allaway v Reilly* [2007] IRLR 864:

'If a fellow employee does an act in the course of employment which has the effect of discriminating against the claimant employee on grounds of sex and that is a result which can be concluded to have been within his knowledge at the time he carried out the act in question, the requirements of the subsection are met. Discrimination does not have to be what he intended nor does it have to have been his motive. It is enough that, on the evidence, the conclusion can be drawn that discrimination as the probable outcome was within the scope of his knowledge at the time. It would not need to be in the forefront of his mind nor would he need to have specifically addressed his mind to it. It must be enough if, in all the circumstances, it can properly be concluded that it was within the knowledge that was possessed by the alleged discriminator.'

The employee may be liable on this basis even in circumstances where the employer has succeeded in establishing the employer's defence (*Crofton v Yeboah* [2002] EWCA Civ 794, [2002] IRLR 634).

If a person found liable under the provision is an individual acting in the course of his employment, it may be proper for any award of compensation to be made only against the employer, who will generally be liable on the principles set out above (*Deane v Ealing London Borough Council* [1993] IRLR 209, [1993] ICR 329).

There is a defence to liability where A reasonably relies upon a statement by B that the act for which help is given does not contravene the Act (*EqA 2010, s 112(2)*). If B makes such a statement, it is false or misleading in a material respect and B either knew or was reckless as to its falsity, B commits an offence punishable to a fine of up to level 5 on the standard scale (*EqA 2010, s 112(3) and (4)*).

13   Discrimination and Equal Opportunities – II: Exceptions, Defences and Non-Employers covered by the Employment Rules

13.1   The *Equality Act 2010* (*'EqA 2010'*) came into force, for the most part, on 1 October 2010. It applies to all acts of discrimination occurring after 1 October 2010 or, in the case of 'acts extending over a period' (see **14.6** DISCRIMINATION AND EQUAL OPPORTUNITIES – III), to all acts that continue after 1 October 2010 even if they began before: see *art 7* of the *Equality Act 2010 (Commencement No 4, Savings, Consequential, Transitional, Transitory and Incidental Provisions and Revocation) Order 2010 (SI 2010/2317)*. The scope and application of the *EqA 2010* and the predecessor legislation, the *Sex Discrimination Act 1975* (*'SDA 1975'*), the *Race Relations Act 1976* (*'RRA 1976'*), *Employment Equality (Religion or Belief) Regulations 2003* (*'RBR 2003'*), the *Employment Equality (Sexual Orientation) Regulations 2003* (*'SOR 2003'*), the *Disability Discrimination Act 1995* (*'DDA 1995'*) and the *Employment Equality (Age) Regulations 2006* (*'AR 2006'*) is described in DISCRIMINATION AND EQUAL OPPORTUNITIES – I **(12)**.

This chapter deals with the exceptions to the scope, and defences to the application of, that legislation ('the equality legislation'). As a matter of principle, these exceptions ought to be narrowly or strictly construed: *Lambeth London Borough Council v Commission for Racial Equality* [1989] IRLR 379; upheld on appeal ([1990] IRLR 231, [1990] ICR 768) (although the principle of construction was not referred to in the judgments of the Court of Appeal). In summary, an employer (or non-employer covered by the rules) may have a defence to claims of both direct and indirect discrimination where he can show that being of a particular race, religion or belief, sex or sexual orientation is a genuine requirement or qualification for a particular job (see below **13.2** ff). A defence of justification is also available to certain forms of discrimination (see below **13.9**) and a defence of lack of knowledge of disability to certain forms of disability discrimination (see below **13.9A**). This chapter also covers the application of the equality legislation to non-employers covered by the employment rules, such as trade organisations, vocational training providers, partnerships, barristers, police officers, the Crown etc (see below **13.24** ff). Finally, the chapter deals briefly with the equality duties imposed on public authorities by the *EqA 2010* and the predecessor legislation (below **13.37**).

There are also a number of general exceptions (or limits) to the scope of the equality legislation. Broadly speaking, the legislation does not prohibit discrimination where the employee is employed outside Great Britain (below **13.18**), or works under an illegal contract (below **13.19**), or where the discrimination relates to benefits that the employer also provides to the public (below **13.20**), is authorised by another enactment (below **13.21**), is necessary for the purposes of national security (below **13.22**) or where the employer qualifies for immunity under the *State Immunity Act 1978* (below **13.23**). In addition, there are a number of exceptions that are specific to each of the different grounds of discrimination, such as where communal accommodation is provided, or where the employment is for the purposes of an organised religion, or where a particular benefit is dependent on the employee having marital or civil partnership status (see below **13.11–13.16**).

There are also circumstances in which a respondent is permitted to discriminate positively in favour of persons of a particular race, sex, etc (see below **13.10** ff) and certain exemptions that apply only to charities, which in some instances permit positive discrimination in relation to certain groups or (at least) enable charities to continue to pursue their charitable objectives without incurring liability for discrimination (**13.10A**).

13.1 Discrimination and Equal Opportunities – II

For the so-called 'reasonable steps' defence, which enables employers to avoid vicarious liability where they are able to show that they took all reasonable steps to prevent an employee from committing a particular act of discrimination see **12.54**, DISCRIMINATION AND EQUAL OPPORTUNITIES – I.

For enforcement of the equality legislation and remedies, see DISCRIMINATION AND EQUAL OPPORTUNITIES – III (14).

Note that because of its distinct legislative regime, discrimination on grounds of sex in respect of contractual terms and conditions is dealt with in a separate chapter (see EQUAL PAY (23)).

The equality legislation implements in domestic law a number of European Directives, specifically the *Equal Treatment Directive (2006/54/EC)* ('ETD 2006') (on sex discrimination), the *Race Discrimination Framework Directive (2000/43/EC)* ('the Race Directive') and the *Framework Directive (2000/78/EC)* (which covers discrimination on grounds of religion or belief, disability, sexual orientation and age) ('the Framework Directive'). In accordance with usual principles of EU law, until the UK completes withdrawal from the European Union the relevant provisions of the domestic equality legislation are to be interpreted in conformity with the governing European Directives. Where there are irreconcilable differences between the domestic legislation and the European Directives, public sector workers are able to rely on the Directives themselves under the principle of direct effect. In certain circumstances, EU law may require national courts to disapply provisions of national law even in the context of proceedings between private parties. Upon the UK withdrawing from the European Union, the provisions of *ss 2 to 8* of the *European Union (Withdrawal) Act 2018* will have effect and will, broadly speaking, maintain the effect of EU legislation in domestic law. See generally EUROPEAN UNION LAW (24).

13.2 OCCUPATIONAL REQUIREMENT OR QUALIFICATION

Broadly speaking, where being of a particular race, religion or belief, sex, sexual orientation, age or disability can be shown to be a genuine requirement or qualification for a particular job, a respondent may have a defence to certain forms of both direct and indirect discrimination.

Under the predecessor legislation to the *EqA 2010*, there were (save in relation to disability) a large number of specific genuine occupational requirement exceptions. These are detailed below. However, most of those are not available under the *EqA 2010*. Instead, the *EqA 2010* contains a general exception for occupational requirement in *paragraph 1* of *Schedule 9*. It applies only to discrimination taking the particular forms set out in *paragraph 1(2)*, ie discrimination in determining how and to whom to offer employment, in the way that persons are afforded access to opportunities for promotion, transfer or training or for receiving any other benefit, facility or service and to discrimination in relation to dismissal. It does not apply to discrimination in the terms of someone's employment (or offer of employment), or to discrimination in the form of subjecting someone to a detriment other than dismissal, or to a claim of harassment (as to the latter, see *Pemberton v Inwood* [2018] EWCA Civ 564, [2018] ICR 1291, [2018] IRLR 542). Under *paragraph 1* of *Schedule 9* a person will not contravene the *Act* by discriminating in one of the aforementioned ways if he applies in relation to work a requirement to have a particular protected characteristic and if he shows that, having regard to the nature or context of the work, it is: (a) an occupational requirement; (b) the application of the requirement is a proportionate means of achieving a legitimate aim; and, (c) the person to whom the requirement is applied does not meet it (or, for all protected characteristics except sex, the employer has reasonable grounds for not being satisfied that the person meets it).

In addition to this general exception, a handful of specific exceptions for occupational requirements or qualifications remain under the *EqA 2010*. These are set out at the appropriate points below.

It is likely that the various specific exceptions that were available under the predecessor legislation but are not available under the *EqA 2010* should now be regarded as examples of the sort of situation in which the new general genuine occupational requirement exception in the *EqA 2010* is likely to apply.

Note that the *DDA 1995* contained no occupational requirement/qualification exceptions. This exception is available for disability discrimination for the first time under the *EqA 2010*.

The domestic provisions reflect and, in accordance with usual principles (see EUROPEAN UNION LAW **(24)**), must be interpreted in conformity with the governing European Directives. *Article 4(1)* of the *Framework Directive 2000/78/EC* provides a general exception for discrimination on grounds of religion or belief, disability, sexual orientation and age 'where, by reason of the nature of the particular occupational activities concerned or of the context in which they are carried out, such a characteristic constitutes a genuine and determining occupational requirement, provided that the objective is legitimate and the requirement is proportionate'. *Article 14(2)* of the *Equal Treatment Directive 2006/54/EC* sets out the equivalent exception for sex discrimination (see further below **13.3**), and *Article 4* of the *Race Directive 2000/43/EC* sets out the equivalent exception for racial or ethnic origin (see further below paragraph **13.4**). *Article 4(2)* of the *Framework Directive* contains a specific exception for churches and other organisations with an ethos based on religion or belief (see further below **13.6**).

In *Egenberger v Evangelisches Werk fur Diakonie und Entwicklung eV* C-414/16: [2019] 1 CMLR 9, [2018] IRLR 762 the CJEU gave some guidance as to the proper application of *Article 4* of the *Framework Directive*. That case was a religious discrimination case, but the general principles will apply in all cases. The CJEU indicated in that case that (i) a requirement will be 'genuine' if it is objectively 'necessary' in relation to the particular job; (ii) it will be 'legitimate' if the requirement is not used to pursue an aim that has no connection with the object of the requirement; and (iii) it will be justified if it can be shown that, in the particular case, the harm that would result to the organisation if the requirement were not applied is 'probable and substantial, so that imposing such a requirement is indeed necessary', and the requirement is otherwise proportionate, applying usual principles (see below **13.9**). Although the text of the domestic legislation differs from that of the *Directive* (most notably by the omission of the word 'genuine'), a proper application of the proportionality test in the domestic legislation should encompass each of the elements identified by the CJEU in that case, i.e. (in summary) that there must be an objective assessment by the tribunal as to whether the requirement pursues a legitimate aim, is necessary to that aim (i.e. could not be achieved by other means) and is proportionate.

13.3   Sex: occupational qualification

In addition to the general exception set out above at **13.2**, the following occupational requirement exceptions relating to sex are available under the *EqA 2010*:

(a)   An exception for employment for the purposes of an organised religion where the application of the requirement engages 'the compliance or non-conflict principle' and the person to whom the requirement applies does not meet it (*para 2(1) of Sch 9*). The 'compliance principle' is engaged if the requirement is applied so as to comply with the doctrines of the religion (*para 2(5)*). The 'non-conflict principle' is engaged if, because of the nature or context of the employment, the requirement is applied so as to avoid conflicting with the strongly held religious convictions of a significant number of the religion's followers (*para 2(6)*).

(b)   An exception for service in the armed forces if it can be shown that a requirement for someone to be a man is a proportionate means of ensuring the combat effectiveness of the armed forces (*para 4, Sch 9*).

(c)   An exception for sporting events, specifically for acts done in relation to the participation of people as competitors in a 'gender-affected activity' (*s 195(1)*). A 'gender-affected activity' is a sport, game or other activity of a competitive nature where the physical strength, stamina or physique of average persons of one sex would put them at a disadvantage compared to average persons of the other sex as competitors in events involving the activity (*s 195(3)*).

Further, the exception set out at (a) immediately above also applies to requirements that a person not be married or a civil partner, that they not be married to, or the civil partner of, a person who has a living former spouse or civil partner, or to requirements relating to circumstances in which a marriage or civil partnership came to an end (*para 2(4)(c)–(e)*).

Note that, generally speaking, ministers of religion will be regarded as employees under employment legislation: see *Percy v Board of National Mission of the Church of Scotland* [2005] UKHL 73, [2006] IRLR 195, [2006] ICR 134, although cf *New Testament Church of God v Stewart* [2007] EWCA Civ 1004, [2008] IRLR 134, [2008] ICR 282 and *Moore v President of the Methodist Conference* [2013] UKSC 29, [2013] IRLR 646.

These exceptions reflect some of those that were available under the *SDA 1975*, although there were a much wider range of specific genuine occupational requirement exceptions relating to sex available under the *SDA 1975*.

The *SDA 1975* provided that where being a man (or, as appropriate, being a woman) is a genuine occupational qualification ('a GOQ') for a job, a respondent may have a defence to a complaint of discrimination in relation to determining who to offer employment, in refusing employment or in access to opportunities for promotion, transfer or training. The defence was not available where the complainant's complaint was that he had been dismissed or subjected to any other detriment.

Being a man was only capable of being a GOQ under the *SDA 1975* for a job in certain defined circumstances, namely:

(a)   Where the essential nature of the job calls for a man for reasons of physiology (excluding physical strength or stamina) or, in dramatic performances or other entertainment, for reasons of authenticity, such that the essential nature of the job would be materially different if carried out by a woman.

Thus, a woman may not be discriminated against simply because a job is perceived to require the physical strength and stamina of a man, provided that she is actually capable of performing the duties (ie provided the essential nature of the job would not be materially different if carried out by her). However, employers may discriminate for other physiological reasons, in particular where seeking male models or actors.

(b)   Where the job needs to be held by a man to preserve decency or privacy because:

(i)   it is likely to involve physical contact with men in circumstances where they might reasonably object to its being carried out by a woman; or

(ii)   the holder of the job is likely to do his work in circumstances where men might reasonably object to the presence of a woman because they are in a state of undress or are using sanitary facilities.

If an employer required his employees to work stripped to the waist, then in order to establish that he was justified in refusing to offer employment to women, a court hearing a complaint against him would, it is thought, decide whether that requirement was necessary for the performance of the task, or a mere whim on the part of the employer.

(c)   Where the job is likely to involve the holder of the job doing his work, or living, in a private home and needs to be held by a man because objection might reasonably be taken to allowing a woman:

    (i)   the degree of physical or social contact with a person living in the home; or

    (ii)   the knowledge of intimate details of such a person's life which is likely, because of the nature or circumstances of the job or of the home, to be allowed to, or available to, the holder of the job.

(d)   Where the nature or location of the establishment makes it impracticable for the holder of the job to live elsewhere than in premises provided by the respondent and:

    (i)   the only such premises which are available for persons holding that kind of job are lived in, or normally lived in, by men and are not equipped with separate sleeping accommodation for women and sanitary facilities which could be used by women in privacy from men; and

    (ii)   it is not reasonable to expect the respondent either to equip these premises with such accommodation and facilities, or to provide other premises for women.

(See, eg, *Sisley v Britannia Security Systems Ltd* [1983] IRLR 404, [1983] ICR 628.)

(e)   Where the nature of the establishment, or the part of it within which the work is done, requires the job to be held by a man because:

    (i)   it is, or is part of, a hospital, prison or other establishment for persons requiring special care, supervision or attention; and

    (ii)   those persons are all men (disregarding any woman whose presence is exceptional); and

    (iii)   it is reasonable, having regard to the essential character of the establishment or that part, that the job should not be held by a woman.

(f)   Where the holder of the job provides individuals with personal services promoting their welfare or education or similar personal services, and those services can most effectively be provided by a man.

(g)   Where the job needs to be held by a man because it is likely to involve the performance of duties outside the United Kingdom in a country whose laws or customs are such that the duties could not, or could not effectively, be performed by a woman.

(h)   Where the job is one of two to be held by a married couple or (with effect from 5 December 2005) civil partners: see *s 7, SDA 1975*, as amended by *s 251* of the *Civil Partnership Act 2004*. (See also below **13.14** for further discussion of civil partnership and same sex marriage.)

(*SDA 1975, s 7(2)*, as amended by the *Sex Discrimination Act 1986, s 1(2)* and the *Employment Act 1989, s 3(2)*)

These exceptions applied even where only some of the duties of the job fell within the above provisions, as well as where all of them did (*SDA 1975, s 7(3)*). However, where an employer already had female employees who were capable of carrying out the duties of a vacant post, and whom it would be reasonable to employ on those duties and whose numbers were sufficient to meet his likely requirements in respect of those duties without undue inconvenience, then he could not discriminate by filling the vacancy with another man, even if the vacancy fell within (*a*) to (*g*) above (*SDA 1975, s 7(4)*). (See, eg, *Etam plc v Rowan* [1989] IRLR 150 and also *Lasertop Ltd v Webster* [1997] IRLR 498, EAT.) It is existing employees that count. It was not open to a tribunal to find that the defence was defeated on the basis that it was open to the respondent to appoint new female employees capable of performing the relevant duties.

13.3 Discrimination and Equal Opportunities – II

For the exception under the *SDA 1975* for ministers of religion see below **13.11(g)**.

13.4 Race: genuine occupational requirement or qualification

There are no specific exceptions for race discrimination in the employment sphere under the *EqA 2010*. Only the general occupational requirement exception set out at **13.2** above is available.

The *RRA 1976*, as amended by the *Race Relations Act (Amendment) Regulations 2003 (SI 2003/1626)* ('*Race Relations Amendment Regulations*'), however, provided for two different genuine occupational exceptions. The first, the exception for genuine occupational requirement (*RRA 1976, s 4A*: 'the GOR exception'), applied with effect from 19 July 2003 in relation to discrimination on grounds of race or ethnic or national origins. Note that these grounds are a subset of the definition of 'racial grounds' used in the *Act* (see **12.20** DISCRIMINATION AND EQUAL OPPORTUNITIES – I). The second, the exception for genuine occupational qualification (*RRA 1976, s 5*: 'the GOQ exception'), applied where the first did not, ie in relation to discrimination on grounds of colour or nationality and to all racial discrimination occurring before 19 July 2003.

The GOR exception was available only where the discrimination related to a determination as to who to offer employment, a refusal to offer employment or dismissal. The exception was not available for discrimination in the way in which the complainant was afforded access to opportunities for promotion, transfer or training. Unlike the exception under the *SDA 1975*, however, it was available as a defence to a dismissal complaint.

The first exception (the GOR exception) applied where it was shown that:

> 'having regard to the nature of the employment or the context in which it is carried out:
>
> (a)   being of a particular race or of particular ethnic or national origins is a genuine and determining occupational requirement;
>
> (b)   it is proportionate to apply that requirement in the particular case; and
>
> (c)   either –
>
> (i)   the person to whom that requirement is applied does not meet it; or
>
> (ii)   the respondent is satisfied, and in all the circumstances it is reasonable for him not to be satisfied, that the person meets it.'
> (*RRA 1976, s 4A(2)*).

The second exception (the GOQ exception) was only available where the discrimination took the forms of discrimination in the arrangements made for the purpose of determining who should be offered employment; refusal or deliberate omission to offer employment; and discrimination in the way in which the complainant is afforded access to opportunities for promotion transfer or training. It was not available where the complainant's complaint was that he had been dismissed. In contrast to the general 'nature and context' principle that formed the basis of the GOR exception, the GOQ exception applied only in certain defined circumstances, namely where:

(a)   the job involves participation in a dramatic performance or other entertainment in a capacity for which a person of that racial group is required for reasons of authenticity; or

(b)   the job involves participation as an artist's or photographic model in the production of a work of art, visual image or sequence of visual images for which a person of that racial group is required for reason of authenticity; or

(c)   the job involves working in a place where food or drink is (for payment or not) provided to, and consumed by, members of the public or a section of the public in a particular setting for which, in that job, a person of that racial group is required for reasons of authenticity (thus, a respondent may lawfully discriminate in selecting waiters for an Indian or Chinese restaurant); or

(d)   the holder of the job provides persons of that racial group with personal services promoting their welfare, and those services can most effectively be provided by a person of that racial group (*RRA 1976, s 5(2)*).

The scope of the GOQ exception was discussed in *Tottenham Green Under-Fives' Centre v Marshall* [1989] IRLR 147, [1989] ICR 214 and in *Lambeth London Borough Council v Commission for Racial Equality* [1990] IRLR 231, [1990] ICR 768. In *Lambeth*, the Court of Appeal held that the use of the word 'personal' in *s 5(2)(d)* indicated that the identity of the giver and the recipient of the services is important. The Court of Appeal agreed with the Employment Appeal Tribunal that the *RRA 1976* appeared to contemplate direct contact between the giver and the recipient – mainly face-to-face or where there would be susceptibility to personal, physical contact.

The GOQ exception applied where some of the duties fell within (a) to (d) above as well as where all of them did (*RRA 1976, s 5(3)*), and also where those duties were merely ones which it was desirable that the post-holder should carry out and were not fundamental to the post. However, it did not apply where the duties were too trivial to be taken into account or where they had been deliberately put into the job description as a sham or smokescreen (*Tottenham Green Under Fives' Centre v Marshall (No 2)* [1991] IRLR 162, [1991] ICR 320).

It also did not apply where a respondent already had employees of a particular racial group who were capable of carrying out the duties of a vacant post and whom it would be reasonable to employ on those duties and whose numbers were sufficient to meet his likely requirements in respect of those duties without undue inconvenience, regardless of whether the vacancy fell within *s 5(2)* (*RRA 1976, s 5(4)*). As with cases of sex discrimination (see above **13.3**), it was existing employees who counted.

13.5   Gender reassignment: occupational qualification

In addition to the general exception set out at **13.2** above, the *EqA 2010* includes the following two specific exceptions for requirements that a person not be a transsexual person:

(a)   An exception for employment for the purposes of an organised religion where the application of the requirement engages 'the compliance or non-conflict principle' and the person to whom the requirement applies does not meet it (*para 2(1) of Sch 9*). The 'compliance principle' is engaged if the requirement is applied so as to comply with the doctrines of the religion (*para 2(5)*). The 'non-conflict principle' is engaged if, because of the nature or context of the employment, the requirement is applied so as to avoid conflicting with the strongly held religious convictions of a significant number of the religion's followers (*para 2(6)*).

(b)   An exception for service in the armed forces if it can be shown that a requirement is a proportionate means of ensuring the combat effectiveness of the armed forces (*para 4, Sch 9*).

These exceptions reflect some of the specific exceptions that were available under the predecessor legislation to the *EqA 2010*. Those exceptions were as follows.

Following the insertion of *ss 7A* and *7B* into the *SDA 1975* by the *Sex Discrimination (Gender Reassignment) Regulations 1999 (SI 1999/1102)* (*'Gender Reassignment Regulations'*) with effect from 1 May 1999 a genuine occupational qualification ('GOQ') defence was available in appropriate circumstances to allegations of sex discrimination brought by persons intending to undergo, undergoing or who have undergone gender reassignment ('transsexuals'). (See generally **12.21** DISCRIMINATION AND EQUAL OPPORTUNITIES – I.)

Broadly speaking, there were two circumstances where the GOQ defence might arise in relation to complaints by transsexuals. First, a gender reassignment might mean that the employee fell foul of a GOQ that the complainant be a man or, as appropriate, a woman. Second, there might be circumstances where the requirement was, in effect, not that the complainant should be a particular sex but that they should not be a transsexual.

(1)   *Where the requirement was that a complainant be a man or a woman*

Turning first to consider cases where the requirement was for a complainant of a specific sex, for the most part, *SDA 1975, s 7A* simply extended the GOQ exception for sex discrimination (see above **13.3**) to cases involving transsexuals. However, there were three differences between the scope of the defence in cases involving transsexuals and its scope in other cases of sex discrimination. First, there was a defence available to a respondent even in cases where a respondent discriminates:

(a)   in the terms in which he offers employment; or

(b)   by dismissing the complainant, or by subjecting him to any other detriment (*SDA 1975, s 7A(1)*).

Second, the defence was subject to an overarching requirement that treatment meted out to the complainant was reasonable in view of the circumstances giving rise to the GOQ (*SDA 1975, s 7A(1)(b)*).

Third, the limitation on the GOQ defence to a claim of sex discrimination imposed by *s 7(4)* (ie that a GOQ defence could not be used where a respondent already had female employees who were capable of carrying out the duties of a vacant post whom it would be reasonable to employ on those duties) applied to the dismissal of transsexuals as it did to the filling of vacant posts (*SDA 1975, s 7A(3)*).

Note, however, that the defence was not available where the complainant's sex had become the acquired gender under the *Gender Recognition Act 2004* ('*GRA 2004*'): *SDA 1975, s 7A(4)*, as inserted by *GRA 2004, s 14* with effect from 4 April 2005. The *GRA 2004* provides for the application by transsexuals for 'gender recognition certificates'. Where a gender recognition certificate had been issued to a person, this particular GOQ exception did not apply at all since the person becomes 'for all purposes' the acquired gender (*GRA 2004, s 9*).

(2)   *Where the requirement was that the complainant not be a transsexual*

SDA 1975, s 7B set out the variation of the defence which dealt with circumstances where it was thought that not being a transsexual was a GOQ. Those circumstances were in addition to those described above in relation to sex discrimination and were referred to as 'supplementary general occupational qualifications' ('supplementary GOQs'). The supplementary GOQs were as follows:

(a)   the job involves the holder of the job being liable to be called upon to perform intimate physical searches pursuant to statutory powers;

(b)   the job is likely to involve the holder of the job doing his work, or living, in a private home and needs to be held otherwise than by a person who is undergoing or has undergone gender reassignment, because objection might reasonably be taken to allowing such a person:

(i)   the degree of physical or social contact with a person living in the home; or

(ii)   the knowledge of intimate details of such person's life, which is likely, because of the nature or circumstances of the job or of the home, to be allowed to, or available to, the holder of the job;

(c)   the nature or location of the establishment makes it impracticable for the holder of the job to live elsewhere than in premises provided by the respondent, and:

(i)   the only such premises which are available for persons holding that kind of job are such that reasonable objection could be taken, for the purpose of preserving decency and privacy, to the holder of the job sharing accommodation and facilities with either sex whilst undergoing gender reassignment; and

(ii)   it is not reasonable to expect the respondent either to equip those premises with suitable accommodation or to make alternative arrangements; or

(d)   the holder of the job provides vulnerable individuals with personal services promoting their welfare, or similar personal services, and in the reasonable view of the respondent those services cannot be effectively provided by a person undergoing gender reassignment.

The supplementary GOQs set out in paras (c) and (d) above only applied where an employee intended to undergo or was undergoing a gender reassignment. They were not available where the employee had already undergone the reassignment (*SDA 1975, s 7B(3)*). Further, the supplementary GOQs could not be relied upon as a defence to discriminating against the employee:

(i)   in the terms on which they are offered employment (*SDA 1975, s 7B(1)(a)*);

(ii)   in the way in which the employee is afforded access to opportunities for promotion, transfer or training, other than where there is a deliberate refusal or a deliberate omission to afford such access to a job; or

(iii)   by subjecting him to any other detriment.

The case of *A v Chief Constable of West Yorkshire Police (No 2)* [2004] UKHL 21, [2004] IRLR 573, [2004] ICR 806, HL was a case that concerned, in effect, a requirement that a police officer not be a transsexual. It was decided on the basis of the *SDA 1975* as it stood prior to the coming into force of the *Gender Reassignment Regulations* on 1 May 1999. However, the decision is relevant to the GOQ defence under the *SDA 1975* and under the *EqA 2010*. *A* was a male-to-female transsexual who applied for a position as a police constable. Her birth certificate recorded her sex as 'male', but she had undergone gender reassignment surgery and was also in outward appearance female. The Chief Constable refused her application because he considered that in order to be a police officer it was necessary to be either a man or a woman, both in appearance and by birth. The Chief Constable relied for the genuineness of that requirement on *s 54(9)* of the *Police and Criminal Evidence Act 1984* ('*PACE*'), which stipulates that intimate searches must be carried out by a police officer of the same sex as the person searched. The House of Lords held that the jurisprudence of the European Court of Human Rights and the Court of Justice of the European Union required transsexuals to be recognised in their reassigned gender. Accordingly, *s 54(9)* had to be interpreted as applying to a transsexual's reassigned gender, thereby depriving the Chief Constable of his GOQ defence.

Note, however, that since the coming into force of the *GRA 2004* on 1 July 2004, transsexuals may apply for a gender recognition certificate. Where a gender recognition certificate has been issued to a person, that person becomes 'for all purposes' the acquired gender (*GRA 2004, s 9*). Where a person has not applied for a gender recognition certificate, it will be a matter for argument as to whether the reasoning of the House of Lords in *A* should apply to any provisions similar to *PACE 1984, s 54(9)*. On the one hand, if the decision in *A* is viewed as being driven by the CJEU's interpretation of the *Equal Treatment Directive*, it should make no difference where Parliament has chosen to draw the line on recognition, since EU law is supreme. On the other hand, if the decision in *A* is viewed as being driven by the jurisprudence of the European Court of Human Rights, it could be argued that, Parliament having now enacted the *GRA 2004* and determined the precise circumstances in which gender recognition should be accorded to transsexuals, that determination is to be respected as a matter that falls within the 'margin of appreciation' accorded to sovereign states.

Finally, it should be noted that, with effect from 1 October 2005, a further *caveat* to the supplementary GOQs was inserted into *SDA 1975, s 7B* by the *Employment Equality (Sex Discrimination) Regulations 2005 (SI 2005/2467)* ('the *2005 Sex Discrimination Regulations*'). That *caveat* was similar to provisions applying in respect of race (see above **13.4**) and sex (see above **13.3**): the supplementary GOQs did not apply where the employer:

(i)   already had transsexual employees who either had not undergone gender reassignment (and were not undergoing or intending to undergo gender reassignment) or (having already undergone reassignment) had become the acquired gender under *GRA 2004*; and,

(ii)   those employees were capable of carrying out the duties in question, were sufficient in number to meet the employer's likely requirements in respect of those duties without undue inconvenience and whom it would be reasonable to employ on those duties.

See also **13.6** below for the exception for requirements imposed in respect of employment by an organised religion that a person not be a transsexual.

13.6   Religion or belief: occupational requirement

In addition to the general exception set out at **13.2** above, under the *EqA 2010* the exception available under the predecessor legislation (see below) for organisations with an ethos based on religion or belief is preserved in *paragraph 3 of Schedule 9* to the Act. It applies where, having regard to the nature or context of the work, it is shown that a requirement to be of a particular religion or belief is: (a) an occupational requirement; (b) the application of the requirement is a proportionate means of achieving a legitimate aim; and, (c) the person to whom the requirement is applied does not meet (or the employer has reasonable grounds for not being satisfied that the person meets the requirement). This reflects the exceptions in the *Directives* referred to above (**13.2**), in particular *art 4(2)* of the *Framework Directive 2000/78* for 'occupational activities within churches and other public or private organisations the ethos of which is based on religion or belief . . . where, by reason of the nature of these activities or of the context in which they are carried out, a person's religion or belief constitutes a genuine, legitimate and justified occupational requirement, having regard to the organisation's ethos'. *Article 4(2)* continues: 'Provided that its provisions are otherwise complied with, this Directive shall thus not prejudice the right of churches and other public or private organisations, the ethos of which is based on religion or belief, acting in conformity with national constitutions and laws, to require individuals working for them to act in good faith and with loyalty to the organisation's ethos'.

The *EqA 2010* also contains a further exception under *paragraph 2 of Schedule 9* to the *Act* for employment for the purposes of an organised religion. (Note that, generally speaking, ministers of religion will be regarded as employees under employment legislation: see *Percy v Board of National Mission of the Church of Scotland* [2005] UKHL 73, [2006] IRLR 195, [2006] ICR 134, although cf *New Testament Church of God v Stewart* [2007] EWCA Civ 1004, [2008] IRLR 134, [2008] ICR 282 and *Moore v President of the Methodist Conference* [2013] UKSC 29, **[2013] IRLR 646**.) The exception applies to the application of the following requirements: (a) to be of a particular sex, (b) not to be a transsexual, (c) not to be married or a civil partner, (d) not to be married to a person of the same sex, (e) not to be married to, or the civil partner of, a person who has a living former spouse or civil partner, (f) relating to circumstances in which a marriage or civil partnership came to an end or (g) a requirement related to sexual orientation. The exception applies where the application of any such requirement engages 'the compliance or non-conflict principle' and the person to whom the requirement applies does not meet it (*para 2(1) of Sch 9*). The 'compliance principle' is engaged if the requirement is applied so as to comply with the doctrines of the religion (*para 2(5)*). The 'non-conflict principle' is engaged if, because of the nature or context of the employment, the requirement is applied so as to avoid conflicting with the strongly held religious convictions of a significant number of the religion's followers (*para 2(6)*). The exception also covers qualifications for employments covered by the exception: *para 2(3)*. This exception reflects specific exceptions available under the predecessor legislation. However, it is controversial because it does not include any proportionality requirement and is therefore arguably not compliant with the terms of the governing European Directives (above **13.2**). This argument was run, unsuccessfully, in *R (Amicus-MSF) v Secretary of State for Trade and Industry* [2004] EWHC 860 (Admin), [2004] IRLR 430 in relation to the equivalent provisions in the predecessor legislation. A European Commission Reasoned Opinion (RO 2006/2450) subsequently concluded that the absence of a proportionality requirement from the UK legislation meant that this provision did not comply with the *Directive*. At the time the Commission anticipated that this would be corrected in the *Equality Act 2010*, but it was not. This issue was not considered in *Pemberton v Inwood* [2018] EWCA Civ 564, [2018] ICR 1291, [2018] IRLR 542 (see below), but it is probable that, as a matter of statutory interpretation and application of principles of EU law, a requirement of proportionality falls to be read into the legislation: cf *Zaw Lin, Wai Phyo v Commissioner of Police for the Metropolis* [2015] EWHC 2484 (QB) at paragraph 80 per Green J.

In *Egenberger v Evangelisches Werk fur Diakonie und Entwicklung eV* C-414/16 [2019] 1 CMLR 9, [2018] IRLR 762 the CJEU emphasised that the *Framework Directive* aims, by providing in *art 4(2)* for the concept of 'genuine occupational requirement', to strike a fair balance between the right of autonomy of churches and other organisations whose ethos is based on religion or belief and the rights of workers not to be discriminated against. As such, it is not sufficient for the church or organisation to assert that the requirement is genuine, legitimate and justified, it is a matter for the national court to assess objectively whether each element is satisfied in the particular case. The CJEU indicated that: (i) a requirement will be 'genuine' if professing the religion or belief on which the ethos of the church or organisation is founded appears necessary in relation to the particular job because of the importance of the occupational activity in question for the manifestation of that ethos or the exercise by the church or organisation of its right of autonomy; (ii) it will be 'legitimate' if the requirement is 'not used to pursue an aim that has no connection with that ethos or with the exercise by the church or organisation of its right of autonomy'; and (iii) it will be justified if it can be shown that, in the particular case, the harm that would result to the organisation's ethos or right of autonomy of not applying the requirement is 'probable and substantial, so that imposing such a requirement is indeed necessary', and the requirement is otherwise proportionate, applying usual principles (see below **13.9**).

In *Pemberton v Inwood*, ibid, the Court of Appeal upheld the ET's decision that a refusal by the Bishop of Southwell and Nottingham to grant the licence necessary to allow the claimant to take up a post as an NHS chaplain fell within the scope of *para 2(3)* as the employment was 'for the purposes of an organised religion' even though the employer was the NHS: it sufficed if one of the purposes of the employment was for an organised religion even if there were other purposes to the employment. Further, since the reason for the refusal to grant the licence was because the claimant had entered into a same-sex marriage, which was against the teachings of the Church, a requirement related to sexual orientation had been applied (since the claimant would not have entered a same-sex marriage were he not gay) and had been applied in order to comply with 'the doctrines of the Church' within the meaning of that term in *para 2(3)*. 'Doctrines' in *para 2(3)* was to be interpreted objectively, rather than being restricted to what would actually be called 'doctrine' by the Church or to issues on which all members of the Church agreed. That case also highlighted the important point that the exception is not available for claims of harassment. The Court of Appeal confirmed that the *para 2(3)* exception did not apply to claims of harassment, and that accordingly a harassment claim could in principle be brought in a case where (as here) the respondent was entitled to rely on the *para 2(3)* exception in respect of the discrimination claims. However, the Court of Appeal observed that a tribunal should interpret 'harassment' in this context so as not to undermine the *para 2(3)* exception. It would not be 'reasonable' to regard conduct as harassment if it involved merely doing what was necessary to avoid conflict with the religious doctrine in question. If there were aggravating features, however, a claim for harassment could succeed. On the facts, the tribunal had been entitled to conclude that there was no such conduct.

In *IR v JQ* C-68/17 [2019] ICR 417 the CJEU considered a case where a senior medical manager at a Catholic hospital in Germany had been dismissed following the discovery that he had remarried without getting his first (Catholic) marriage annulled by the Pope. Although the arguments at the domestic level appeared to have been framed in terms of whether the medical manager had, by entering into the marriage, breached the German equivalent of the implied term of trust and confidence, the CJEU answered by reference to the concept of 'genuine, legitimate and justified occupational requirement'. While indicating that it was a matter for the national court to decide, the CJEU gave a strong steer that the defence was not made out in this case. The CJEU observed that adherence to the notion of marriage advocated by the Catholic Church did not appear to be necessary for the promotion of the Hospital's ethos due to the importance of the occupational activities carried out by the medical manager, namely the provision of medical advice and care in a hospital setting and the management of the internal medicine department which he headed. This was supported by the fact that similar posts were entrusted to employees who were not of the Catholic faith and, consequently, not subject to the same requirement.

Under the predecessor legislation, the *RBR 2003*, a genuine occupational requirement ('GOR') was available in two sorts of cases. The exception only applied where the discrimination related to the arrangements for determining who to offer employment, a refusal of employment, access to opportunities for promotion, transfer or training and dismissal.

The first type of case was like the GOR exception under the *RRA 1976* (see above **13.4**). In the first type of case the exception applied where, having regard to the nature of the employment or the context in which it was carried out, being of a particular religion or belief was 'a genuine and determining occupational requirement' (*reg 7(2)*).

The second type of case was where the respondent had an ethos based on a religion or belief and, having regard to that ethos as well as to the nature of the employment, or the context in which it was carried out, being of a particular religion or belief was a GOR (*reg 7(3)*).

In both types of case, the mere existence of a GOR did not take the complainant outside the protective scope of the *Regulations*. First, it had also to be shown that the complainant did not meet the requirement. Where it was not immediately clear whether the complainant met the requirement, it was sufficient that the respondent was not satisfied, on reasonable grounds, that the complainant met the requirement (*regs 7(2)(c)* and *(3)(c)*). Second, it had to be proportionate to apply the requirement in the particular case (*regs 7(2)(b)* and *(3)(b)*).

Note that in *Glasgow City Council v McNab* [2007] IRLR 476 it was held that a local education authority ('LEA') could not defend a discrimination claim in relation to a Catholic School for which it was responsible on the basis that it was an organisation with an ethos based on a religion or belief. Although the School had such an ethos, the employer and respondent to the claim was the LEA and it could not have a specific religious ethos.

See also **13.21** below for further specific provisions exempting from the *EqA 2010* acts of discrimination done pursuant to legislative provisions authorising discrimination on grounds of religious belief in relation to various appointments to educational establishments.

See also **13.11(G)** below for Ministers of Religion.

13.7   Sexual orientation: occupational requirement

In addition to the general exception set out at **13.2** the *EqA 2010* contains an exception for employment for the purposes of an organised religion where the application of a requirement related to sexual orientation engages 'the compliance or non-conflict principle' and the person to whom the requirement applies does not meet it (*para 2(1)* of *Sch 9*). The 'compliance principle' is engaged if the requirement is applied so as to comply with the doctrines of the religion (*para 2(5)*). The 'non-conflict principle' is engaged if, because of the nature or context of the employment, the requirement is applied so as to avoid conflicting with the strongly held religious convictions of a significant number of the religion's followers (*para 2(6)*). The exception also covers qualifications for employments covered by the exception: *para 2(3)*. This exception reflects specific exceptions available under the predecessor legislation.

The *SOR 2003* provided for two types of cases in which a respondent might rely on the genuine occupational requirement ('GOR') exception in defence to a claim of discrimination on grounds of sexual orientation. In both types of case the defence was only available where the discrimination related to the arrangements for determining who to offer employment, a refusal of employment, access to opportunities for promotion, transfer or training and dismissal.

The first type of case was like the first type of case under the *RBR 2003* (see above **13.6**), ie the exception applied where, having regard to the nature of the employment or the context in which it was carried out, being of a particular sexual orientation was a 'genuine and determining occupational requirement'. The respondent had to show that it was proportionate to apply the requirement in that particular case and that either the complainant did not meet the requirement as to sexual orientation or that it was reasonable, in all the circumstances, for the respondent to be satisfied that the complainant did not (*reg 7(2)*). In the absence of an express admission by the complainant, this involved the tribunal determining whether the respondent's conclusion or assumption about the complainant's sexual orientation was a reasonable one.

The second type of case was where the employment was for the purposes of an organised religion and the respondent applied 'a requirement related to sexual orientation' in order:

(a)   to comply with the doctrines of that religion, or

(b)   owing to the nature or context of that employment, to avoid conflicting with the strongly held religious convictions of a significant number of the religion's followers (*regs 7(3)(a)* and *(b)*).

As with the first type of case, the respondent had also to show that either the person to whom the requirement was applied did not meet that requirement or that it was reasonable for the respondent to have been satisfied that he did not (*reg 7(3)(c)*).

It was argued in *R (Amicus-MSF) v Secretary of State for Trade and Industry* [2004] EWHC 860 (Admin), [2004] IRLR 430 that *regs 7(2)* and *(3)* were incompatible with the governing European Directive (*Directive 2000/78/EC*) among other reasons because they contain no proportionality requirement. However, the High Court held that the *Regulations* were compatible. With regard to *reg 7(2)* (the first type of case), Richards J noted that, although the exception applied not only where the complainant did not in fact meet the requirement as to sexual orientation, but also where it was 'reasonable' for the respondent 'not to be satisfied' that the complainant met that requirement, the need for the respondent's decision to be 'reasonable' ensured that the decision could not be based on mere assumptions or social stereotyping. With regard to *reg 7(3)* (the second type of case), Richards J noted that the exception, as a derogation from the principle of equal treatment, had to be construed strictly. He noted that 'for the purposes of an organised religion' was a narrower expression than 'for the purposes of a religious organisation' or 'an ethos based on religion or belief', as used in the *RBR 2003*. Thus, employment as a teacher in a faith school was, he considered, likely to fall outside the exception as being 'for the purposes of a religious organisation' rather than 'for the purposes of an organised religion'. Further, he observed that the condition that the employer apply the requirement 'so as to comply with the doctrines of the religion' was an objective test and very narrow in scope. Similarly, the alternative condition that the exception be applied where required 'to avoid conflicting with the strongly held religious convictions of a significant number of the religion's followers' was also an objective test that would be difficult to satisfy in practice. He also noted that, although the phrase used in *reg 7(3)* 'a requirement related to sexual orientation' was linguistically wider in scope than the phrase 'being of a particular sexual orientation' used in *reg 7(2)*, it was difficult to see a practical difference between the two since 'being of a particular sexual orientation' necessarily encompassed matters relating to sexual behaviour, etc. A European Commission Reasoned Opinion (RO 2006/2450) subsequently concluded that the absence of a proportionality requirement from the UK legislation meant that this provision did not comply with the *Directive*. At the time the Commission anticipated that this would be corrected in the Equality Act 2010, but it was not. However, it is probable that, as a matter of statutory interpretation and application of principles of EU law, a requirement of proportionality falls to be read into the legislation: cf *Zaw Lin, Wai Phyo v Commissioner of Police for the Metropolis* [2015] EWHC 2484 (QB) at paragraph 80 per Green J.

Compare the exception for employment for purposes of an organised religion with the exception for ministers of religion in the *SDA 1975*: see below **13.11**(g).

13.8 Age: occupational requirement

There are no specific exceptions for age under the *EqA 2010*. Only the general occupational requirement exception set out at **13.2** above is available.

AR 2006 recognised that there might be circumstances in which being of a particular age group was a genuine requirement of the job. However, the existence of a genuine occupational requirement was no defence to discrimination taking one of the following forms under *AR 2006*:

(a)   discrimination in the terms on which employment was offered;

(b)   discrimination in the terms of employment afforded to an employee;

(c)   subjecting the employee to a detriment other than dismissal; and

(d)   harassing the employee.

The defence was *potentially* available where the discrimination took one or more of the following forms:

(a)   discrimination in the arrangements made for determining to whom employment should be offered;

(b)   discrimination by refusing to offer, or deliberately not offering, employment;

(c)   discrimination in the opportunities offered an employee for promotion, transfer, or training;

(d)   discrimination by refusing to afford, or deliberately not offering, an opportunity; and

(e)   discrimination by dismissal.

AR 2006 did not list the circumstances in which such a defence might apply. Instead, they set out a general defence where, having regard to the nature of the employment, or the context in which the employment is carried out, possessing a characteristic related to age was a genuine and determining occupational requirement, and it was proportionate to apply that requirement in the particular case (*reg 8(2)*).

In *Wolf v Stadt Frankfurt Am Main* [2010] IRLR 244, the CJEU found that legislation imposing an upper age limit of 30 for recruitment for frontline fire-fighting duties was justified as a genuine occupational requirement in accordance with the equivalent provision of the *Directive, Article 4(1)*. The genuine occupational requirement was physical fitness. The legislation was justified by the aim of preserving the operational capacity of the fire service and did not go beyond what was necessary to achieve that objective having regard to the number of years remaining following training during which officers could carry out physically demanding tasks.

13.8A Marriage and civil partnership: occupational requirement

In addition to the general exception set out at **13.2** above, there is an exception under *paragraph 2* of *Schedule 9* to the *Act* for employment for the purposes of an organised religion. It applies to the application of requirements: (i) not to be married or a civil partner, (ii) not to be married to a person of the same sex, (iii) not to be married to, or the civil partner of, a person who has a living former spouse or civil partner, or (iv) to requirements relating to circumstances in which a marriage or civil partnership came to an end. The exception applies where the application of any such requirement engages 'the compliance or non-conflict principle' and the person to whom the requirement applies does not meet it (*para 2(1)* of *Sch 9*). The 'compliance principle' is engaged if the requirement is applied so as to comply with the doctrines of the religion (*para 2(5)*). The 'non-conflict principle' is engaged if, because of the nature or context of the employment, the requirement is applied so as to avoid conflicting with the strongly held religious convictions of a significant number of the religion's followers (*para 2(6)*). This exception reflects specific exceptions available under the predecessor legislation. However, it is controversial because it does not include any proportionality requirement and is therefore arguably not compliant with the terms of the governing European Directive (*Directive 2000/78/EC*). This argument was run, unsuccessfully, in *R (Amicus-MSF) v Secretary of State for Trade and Industry* [2004] EWHC 860 (Admin), [2004] IRLR 430 in relation to the equivalent provisions in the predecessor legislation. A European Commission Reasoned Opinion (*RO 2006/2450*) subsequently concluded that the absence of a proportionality requirement from the UK legislation meant that this provision did not comply with the *Directive*. At the time the Commission anticipated that this would be corrected in the *Equality Act 2010*, but it was not. However, it is probable that, as a matter of statutory interpretation and application of principles of EU law, a requirement of proportionality falls to be read into the legislation: cf *Zaw Lin, Wai Phyo v Commissioner of Police for the Metropolis* [2015] EWHC 2484 (QB) at paragraph 80 per Green J.

13.9   JUSTIFICATION

A defence of justification is (and has always) been available to the following forms of discrimination:

- *Indirect discrimination* in respect of all the protected characteristics;

- *Discrimination arising from disability* under the *s 15* of the *EqA 2010*;

- *Direct discrimination* on grounds of age only.

13.9 Discrimination and Equal Opportunities – II

Under the *EqA 2010* a single formula applies for indirect discrimination in relation to all the protected characteristics. A provision, criterion or practice ('PCP') that is applied to all, but which puts (or would put) persons of a particular protected characteristic at a particular disadvantage when compared with others (and which puts the complainant at that disadvantage) will nonetheless be justified if the employer can show it 'to be a proportionate means of achieving a legitimate aim' (*s 19(2)*). The same test for justification applies on the face of the legislation for direct age discrimination (*s 13(2)*) and discrimination arising from a disability (*s 15(1)(b)*). However, so far as direct age discrimination is concerned, a slightly different test applies in *Directive 2000/78/EC* and *s 13(2)* of the *EqA 2010* must be 'read down' accordingly. Whereas there is no limitation on the aims that may be regarded as legitimate for the purposes of justifying indirect discrimination, or discrimination arising from disability, direct age discrimination can only be justified if the aim of the measure in question relates to 'employment policy, the labour market or vocational training' and not 'purely individual reasons particular to the employer's situation, such as cost reduction or improving competitiveness': see *art 6(1)* of *Directive 2000/78/EC* and *Seldon v Clarkson, Wright & Jakes* [2012] UKSC 16, [2012] IRLR 590, [2012] ICR 716 (see further below).

An issue that has arisen in the cases is whether it is necessary for the employer 'merely' to justify the PCP itself or whether it is also necessary to justify the application of the PCP to the claimant. The SC in *Seldon* accepted that it will normally suffice if the employer succeeds in showing that the PCP was a proportionate means of achieving a legitimate aim in general, although did not rule out that it might be necessary in certain cases for the employer to demonstrate that the application of the provision, criterion or practice to the particular employee was justified in that particular case. In *Homer v Chief Constable of West Yorkshire Police* [2012] UKSC 15, [2012] IRLR 601, [2012] ICR 704, however, the SC held that what needed to be justified was the rule itself and in *The City of Oxford Bus Services Limited t/a Oxford Bus Company v Mr L Harvey* UKEAT/0171/18/JOJ, the EAT held that it was an error of law for the Tribunal to have focused on the question of reasonableness of applying the rule to the claimant, rather than the proportionality of having a rule at all. (That case concerned the bus company's requirement for Saturday shift work, which conflicted with the Claimant's beliefs as Seventh Day Adventist.) See also *Rajaratnan v Care UK Clinical Services Ltd* [2015] All ER (D) 408 (Jul), UKEAT/0435/14/DA, UKEAT/0076/15/DA in which the EAT held that a requirement for GPs to work night-shifts was justified by the need to provide healthcare services 24 hours per day and the employer did not need also to justify the application of the rule to the claimant. Further support for this approach is to be found in *Chief Constable of West Midlands Police v Harrod and ors* where the EAT ([2015] IRLR 790, [2015] ICR 1311) and CA ([2017] IRLR 539) both took the view, in slightly differing terms, that provided the rule was justified (in that case a provision of the *Police Pensions Regulations 1987* that permitted compulsory retirement only of those who had become entitled to a pension), there was no need to justify the exercise of the discretion to apply the rule in any particular case. However, there is an important exception to this approach. Where a general rule or policy allows for a series of responses to individual circumstances, it will be the application of the rule or policy to the individual case – the treatment of the complainant themselves – that will need to be justified: see *Griffiths v Secretary of State for Work and Pensions* [2016] IRLR 216, *Buchanan v Commissioner of Police of the Metropolis* [2017] ICR 184 and *South Warwickshire NHS Foundation Trust v Lee* UKEAT/0287/17/DA. In *Buchanan*, HHJ Richardson observed that this would frequently be in claims of disability discrimination in relation to absence procedures, the issue will generally be whether the application of the procedure in the particular circumstances of the claimant's case was justified; asking whether it is justifiable for an employer to have sickness absence procedures at all simply does not address the discrimination claim at all.

Note that where an employer is able to show that what caused the disadvantage in the claimant's case was not the application of the PCP itself, but some sufficiently separate factor, unconnected to the protected characteristic, then the claim of indirect discrimination will fail and the employer will not be required to show that the PCP is justified: see *Essop v Home Office (UK Border Agency); Naeem v Secretary of State for Justice* [2017] UKSC 27, [2017] 3 All ER 551, [2017] IRLR 558, [2017] ICR 640 as further explained in *McCloud v Ministry of Justice* [2018] EWCA Civ 2844, [2019] ICR 1489. For example if in a case such as *Naeem* where it was apparent that the requirement to take civil service examinations was disadvantaging black and minority ethnic candidates as a group, an employer who shows that the reason why the particular claimant failed was because they turned up late to the exam would not have to justify the PCP, because the claim would fail on the basis that the claimant had been unable to show that they were disadvantaged by the PCP. See further **12.34** Discrimination and Equal Opportunities I **(12)**.

Under the predecessor legislation, the test for whether a provision, criterion or practice, was justified differed until recently depending on whether the complaint fell under the *SDA 1975*, related to discrimination on grounds of race or ethnic or national origins under the *RRA 1976*, or discrimination on grounds of colour or nationality under that *Act*, or fell under the *RBR 2003* or the *SOR 2003*, or the *DDA 1995*.

With the exception of discrimination on grounds of colour and nationality under the *RRA 1976*, the test had become the same in each of the Acts and Regulations as it is now under the *EqA 2010*, ie a 'proportionate means of achieving a legitimate aim' (*SDA 1975, s 1(2)*, as amended by the *Sex Discrimination Regulations 2005, reg 3; RRA 1976, s 1(1A)(c)*, as inserted by the *Race Relations Amendment Regulations* with effect from 19 July 2003; *RBR 2003, reg 3(1)(b)(iii); SOR 2003, reg 3(1)(b)(iii)*).

This contrasts with the 'old' test, which required respondents only to show that the application of the relevant provision, criterion or practice was 'justifiable irrespective' of the sex/race etc of the person to whom it was applied. The 'old' test still applies to indirect race discrimination on grounds of colour and nationality under the *RRA 1976* (*RRA 1976, s 1(1)(b)(ii)*), indirect race discrimination on any ground occurring prior to 19 July 2003 (*RRA 1976, s 1(1)(b)(ii)*) and indirect sex discrimination occurring prior to 1 October 2005 (*SDA 1975, s 1(2)(b)(ii)*).

The reason for the change in the test was so that the domestic legislation conformed with the governing European Directives (*Directive 76/207/EEC, art 2, para 2*, as amended by *Directive 2002/73; Directive* 2000/43/EC, *art 2, para 2(b)* and *Directive 2000/78/EC, art 2, para 2(b)*). It will be noted that the governing European Directives each provide that a respondent must demonstrate that the relevant provision, criterion or practice is 'objectively justified by a legitimate aim *and* the means of achieving that aim are appropriate and necessary'. Although the domestic legislation makes no mention of the requirements that the measure be 'appropriate and necessary', in line with the general principles for the application and interpretation of EC law (see **24.2** European Union Law) tribunals no longer accept that a measure is proportionate unless a respondent has shown that it is both appropriate and necessary.

Although the test for justification has changed, the case law on the 'old' test has continued to be regarded as relevant by tribunals. Care should be taken, however, to ensure that the specific requirements of the 'new' test are always met.

A defence of justification was also available in principle to claims of disability-related discrimination under the *DDA 1995* (see Discrimination And Equal Opportunities – I **(12)**). However, the position following *Lewisham London Borough Council v Malcolm* [2008] UKHL 43, [2008] IRLR 700, was that most such claims would in fact be complaints of direct discrimination. As such, the circumstances in which a justification defence to disability-related discrimination was available to employers became very limited indeed. Where the justification of disability-related discrimination was in issue, different considerations applied to those that are generally applicable to the defence of justification available to the types of discrimination set out in the bullet points above. In particular, first, the test for justification was whether the reason for the difference in treatment was both 'material to the circumstances of the particular case and substantial' (*DDA 1995, s 3A(5)*). In *Jones v Post Office* [2001] EWCA Civ 558, [2001] IRLR 384, [2001] ICR 805 Arden LJ explained that for a reason to be 'material', there must be a 'reasonably strong connection between that reason and the circumstances of the individual case', and for it to be 'substantial', it 'must carry real weight and thus be of substance' although it need not necessarily be the best possible conclusion that could be reached in the light of all known medical science. Unlike for other justification defences (see below), the 'range of reasonable responses' test (familiar to those dealing with unfair dismissals) applied to the question of justification in disability-related discrimination. The second main difference was that in the case of an employer who had not complied with his duty to make adjustments (see DISCRIMINATION AND EQUAL OPPORTUNITIES – I (12)), the defence of justification was only available if the treatment in question would have been justified even if the duty had been complied with (*DDA 1995, s 3A(6)*). Thus, where an employee using a wheelchair was not promoted solely because the workstation for the more senior post is inaccessible to wheelchairs, the refusal to promote would not be justified if the furniture could be rearranged to make the workstation accessible. For cases on justification of disability-related discrimination see *Jones v Post Office* [2001] EWCA Civ 558, [2001] IRLR 384, [2001] ICR 805; *Williams v J Walter Thompson Group Ltd* [2005] EWCA Civ 133, [2005] IRLR 376 and *O'Hanlon v Revenue and Customs Comrs* [2007] EWCA Civ 283, [2007] IRLR 404). Under the *EA 2010*, the concept of 'disability-related discrimination' was replaced with 'discrimination arising from disability' in *s 15*. The same approach to justification applies in such cases as for other forms of discrimination under the Act: see *South Warwickshire NHS Foundation Trust v Lee* UKEAT/0287/17/DA and *City of York Council v Grosset* [2018] EWCA Civ 1105, [2018] ICR 1492.

13.9a The general test for justification

The classic test for establishing whether or not discrimination may be justified is found in *Bilka–Kaufhaus GmbH v Weber Von Hartz (Case 170/84)* [1986] IRLR 317. There the Court of Justice of the European Union said that the national court (or tribunal) must be satisfied that the measures having a disparate impact 'correspond to a real need . . . are appropriate with a view to achieving the objectives pursued and are necessary to that end' (para 36). In subsequent cases (see especially *R v Secretary of State for Employment, ex p Seymour-Smith and Perez* [1999] IRLR 253 and also *Kutz–Bauer v Freie und Hansestadt Hamburg*: C-187/00 [2003] IRLR 368) the CJEU expanded on this, ruling that is for the national court (or tribunal) to ascertain:

(1)   whether the measure in question has a legitimate aim, unrelated to any discrimination based on any prohibited ground;

(2)   whether the measure is capable of achieving that aim; and

(3)   whether in the light of all the relevant factors, and taking into account the possibility of achieving by other means the aims pursued by the provisions in question, the measure is proportionate.

In *Bank Mellat v HM Treasury (No. 2)* [2013] UKSC 38, [2014] AC 700, the Supreme Court reviewed the domestic and European case law, and Lord Reed at para 74 (with which the other members of the Court agreed on this issue: see para 20) reformulated the three steps as four: (1) whether the objective of the measure is sufficiently important to justify the limitation of a protected right, (2) whether the measure is rationally connected to the objective, (3) whether a less intrusive measure could have been used without unacceptably compromising the achievement of the objective, and (4) whether, balancing the severity of the measure's effects on the rights of the persons to whom it applies against the importance of the objective, to the extent that the measure will contribute to its achievement, the former outweighs the latter.

While it is important for Tribunals to take the test in stages and consider each element (see *Homer v Chief Constable of West Yorkshire* [2012] UKSC 15, [2012] IRLR 601, [2012] ICR 704), in practice there can be overlap between the stages and below the elements of the test are addressed under headings as follows: (1) legitimate aim; (2) whether the measure is capable of achieving that aim; and (3) proportionality (encompassing the third and fourth elements of the *Bank Mellat* test).

13.9b General principles

The question of whether discrimination is justified is one of fact for the employment tribunal (*Singh v British Rail Engineering* [1986] ICR 22).

The burden of proof is on the respondent to satisfy the tribunal that the measure applied is objectively justified (*Rainey v Greater Glasgow Health Board* [1987] IRLR 26, [1987] ICR 129, an equal pay case in which the House of Lords held that the same principles are applicable to the *SDA 1975* as to the *Equal Pay Act 1970*; see **23.12** Equal Pay). (See DISCRIMINATION AND EQUAL OPPORTUNITIES – III (14) for general discussion of the burden of proof.)

The test to be applied by the tribunal is an objective one: while the tribunal should take into account the reasonable needs of the respondent's business, the tribunal has to make its own judgment as to whether the provision, criterion or practice applied by the respondent is reasonably necessary: there is normally no scope for 'margin of discretion' or 'range of reasonable responses' approach when considering whether an indirectly discriminatory provision, criterion or practice is justified (*Hardys & Hansons plc v Lax* [2005] EWCA Civ 846, [2005] IRLR 726, *MacCulloch v Imperial Chemical Industries plc* [2008] IRLR 846, [2008] ICR 1334). The exception is where the respondent is the state and the matter concerns social or employment policy, in which case a margin of discretion applies at all stages of the test (including whether the aim is legitimate), although it is for the Tribunal to determine what the appropriate width of that margin is in the particular case: *Ministry of Justice v McCloud and ors* [2018] EWCA Civ 2844, [2019] ICR 1489.

The tribunal must demonstrate that it has critically evaluated any defence of justification: its reasons for finding that a measure is a 'proportionate means of achieving a legitimate aim' must be apparent from the decision: *Redfearn v Serco Ltd*, above. In that case, the EAT held that the tribunal had not given sufficient reasons for finding that a requirement that no employee be a member of the British National Party was justified as a proportionate means of achieving the legitimate aim of protecting the health and safety of Asian passengers using the Respondent's services. See also *MacCulloch* ibid. Because the role of Tribunal in reviewing the employer's claimed justification is so intensive, the Court of Appeal has held that a commensurate degree of scrutiny of the Tribunal's reasons on appeal is appropriate: *Hardys* ibid at paragraph 34.

Although it rarely appears to have any practical impact, it has been accepted that some forms of discrimination (most notably age discrimination and other grounds that are not immutable personal characteristics) require a lesser degree of justification than others: see *R (Carson) v Secretary of State of Work and Pensions* at §§55-60, *R (on the application of the British Gurkha Welfare Society) v Ministry of Defence* [2010] EWCA Civ 1098, [2010] All ER (D) 131 (Oct) at §11 and *R (SC, CB and ors) v Secretary of State for Work and Pensions and ors* [2019] EWCA Civ 615 at §91. There is also another category of case in which a slightly different approach may be taken, and that is in cases concerning measures based on length of service. These are dealt with at the end of this section.

The time at which justification needs to be established is when the measure is applied, not when it was adopted (unless, of course, the challenge is to the adoption of the policy): *Trustees of Swansea University Pension & Assurance Scheme v Williams* [2015] IRLR 885, [2015] ICR 1197. This means that the employer needs to justify the measure by reference to the circumstances pertaining at the time of its application. Thus, in a case of dismissal because of something arising in consequence of disability under *EqA 2010, s 15*, the employer can only rely on matters known at the time of dismissal in justification, and not on what occurred subsequently: see *Reid v Lewisham LBC* UKEAT/0248-9/17/DA. However, that does not meant that the alleged discriminator needs to have given any express consideration to justification at the time. It is not necessary for the alleged discriminator to have identified the legitimate aim at the time of adopting the measure (*Air Products Plc v Cockram* [2018] EWCA Civ 346, [2018] IRLR 755 at [60]), nor to have analysed the proportionality question: see *Ministry of Justice v O'Brien* [2013] UKSC 6, [2013] IRLR 315, *Cadman v Health and Safety Executive* [2004] EWCA Civ 1317, [2004] IRLR 97 and the *Trustees of Swansea University* and *Elias* cases (above). Flaws in the employer's decision-making processes are irrelevant, what matters is the outcome, not how the decision was made: *Chief Constable of West Midlands Police v Harrod* [2015] IRLR 790 (upheld on appeal on slightly different grounds: [2017] EWCA Civ 191, [2017] IRLR 539). It is always open to the alleged discriminator to justify the rule or policy by factors not expressly taken into account at the time of adopting the rule or policy: see *Schönheit v Stadt Frankfurt* conjoined cases C-4/02 and C-5/02 [2004] IRLR 983 and *Seldon v Clarkson Wright & Jakes* [2010] EWCA Civ 899, [2010] IRLR 865, [2011] ICR 60 (affd on this point [2012] UKSC 16, [2012] IRLR 590, [2012] ICR 716). See also *Pulham and ors v London Borough of Barking & Dagenham* [2010] IRLR 184, [2010] ICR 333, in which the EAT held that an employer was not precluded from advancing a defence of justification in respect of pay protection arrangements merely because the arrangements had not been 'carefully costed and crafted' at the time of implementation. However, where the alleged discriminator has not even considered questions of proportionality at the time of adopting a rule or policy, it may be more difficult for him to establish justification (cf *Ministry of Justice v O'Brien* ibid, *Hockenjos v Secretary of State for Social Security* [2004] EWCA Civ 1749, [2005] IRLR 471 and the *Elias* and *Seldon* cases, above).

A respondent must normally produce cogent evidence of justification: see *Starmer v British Airways plc* [2005] IRLR 862, EAT and also the Court of Appeal's decision in *Hockenjos v Secretary of State for Social Security* [2004] EWCA Civ 1749, [2005] IRLR 471 (below). The Court of Appeal in *McCloud v Ministry of Justice* [2018] EWCA Civ 2844, [2019] ICR 1489 acknowledged that, following *R (Lumsdon) v Legal Services Board* [2016] AC 697, there may be cases in which aims based on moral or political considerations may be a matter of intuitive common sense in respect of which evidence was not required, in most cases, specific evidence was required in support of justification. In that case, the Court of Appeal did not accept that the Government's aim of protecting judges closes to retirement from the effect of transitional pension arrangements was an intuitively legitimate aim: it required evidence, and the Government had not produced sufficient. See also *Hampton v Lord Chancellor* [2008] IRLR 258, where the employment tribunal held that the government's decision to set the retirement age for part-time recorders at 65 was not proportionate as it considered that the government's evidence was insufficiently conclusive.

Where evidence is adduced, it must be aimed at the right issue. In *Whiffen v Milham Ford Girls' School* [2001] EWCA Civ 385, [2001] IRLR 468, the respondent attempted to justify a policy of responding to a redundancy situation by first allowing the contracts of temporary staff to lapse without renewal. The respondent argued that it needed to make redundancies and that the policy was gender-neutral. The Court of Appeal pointed out that all indirect discrimination cases concerned provisions which were gender-neutral on their face and that, where it had been found that an apparently gender-neutral provision had a disparate effect on a particular group (here, women), it was no justification that the policy might have operated non-discriminatorily in another situation. What required justification was that redundancies were first visited on temporary employees. See also *Garcia-Bello v Aviance UK Ltd* [2007] All ER (D) 318 (Dec): where there was no clear evidence that flexible shift patterns could not have been introduced, there was no justification for the disparate impact of the new shift patterns on those with childcare responsibilities (who were all female). Compare also *Mba v Mayor and Burgesses of the London Borough of Merton* [2014] IRLR 145, [2014] ICR 357 in which the Court of Appeal held that in considering whether a requirement for a care assistant to work on Sundays was justified when that put her at a disadvantage because of her Christian beliefs, the employment tribunal should not have taken into account (in the employer's favour) that the employer had previously tried to accommodate her wishes for two years, or that the employer had arranged her shifts so that she could attend Church on Sunday. Such general evidence of 'good will' on the part of the employer was not relevant to determining whether a present requirement for her to work on Sundays was justified (although, presumably, the tribunal could legitimately have taken into account the employer's evidence of the difficulty of accommodating the claimant's wishes over the previous two years as evidence of justification).

In particular, care must be taken in properly identifying and distinguishing the aim of the measure from the means used to achieve it. The fact that different measures with different aims could be introduced by an employer is not relevant in determining whether a particular measure with a legitimate aim is justified, what matters is whether there are more proportionate ways of achieving the aim of the measure in question: see *Blackburn and anor v Chief Constable of West Midlands Police* [2008] EWCA Civ 1208, [2009] IRLR 135 (aim of rewarding those who did night work was legitimate and therefore it was proportionate to pay those persons more – it did not matter that other police forces had decided not to reward night workers). Likewise, what the tribunal must evaluate is the employer's legitimate aim, not some other aim that it considers would have been preferable: thus in *XC Trains Ltd v D* [2016] IRLR 748 the EAT held that the ET had erred in law in concluding that the train company's shift system unjustifiably disadvantaged women where it had concentrated on an aim of its own, namely achieving a more gender-balanced workforce, rather than addressing the employer's legitimate aims of needing to run an efficient train service and minimise the anti-social hours worked by all drivers. Where there is no other way of achieving the identified aim, the means will inevitably be proportionate: *Harrod and ors v Chief Constable of West Midlands Police* [2017] EWCA Civ 191, [2017] IRLR 539 (a case that illustrates the importance of a well-crafted legitimate aim: once it was accepted that the legitimate aim was making as many officers redundant as possible, and there being only one way to make police officers redundant, it followed that all the redundancies were lawful. Had the legitimate aim been the less ambitious one of 'saving money' that would have opened up scope for argument as to the proportionality of the numbers of redundancies chosen). See also *Allen v GMB* [2008] IRLR 690. In that case the CA considered the situation of a union which had decided, in negotiating with an employer in relation to various pay issues, to adopt a policy whereby employees' interests in relation to future pay deals were prioritised over claims to back pay under the *Equal Pay Act 1970*. The result was that those employees who had equal pay claims (a predominantly female group) received less by way of settlement than they might otherwise have done. The Tribunal held that the union's objective (which it identified as being to achieve single status, avoiding privatisations, job losses, cuts in hours, and members receiving lower pay under the new system) was legitimate, but that the means used to achieve that aim amounted to 'manipulation' and were unjustified. One factor in the Tribunal's conclusion was that it was considered that the amount accepted by the Union in settlement of the equal pay claims was bordering on negligent. The EAT found that the Tribunal had taken the wrong approach to the question of objective justification. The EAT considered that, once it had been accepted that an aim was legitimate then if the means adopted to achieve that aim were the only means available then the policy would be justified. The CA disagreed and upheld the Tribunal's decision. The CA considered that the EAT had taken too narrow an approach to the concept of 'means'. The 'means' was not the balance struck by the union in the deal with the Council, but the methods used to persuade members to accept that deal. The Tribunal had been entitled to find that those methods had been manipulative and disproportionate to the legitimate aims pursued.

The fact that a discriminatory measure has been negotiated with the trade union or other workforce representatives will usually be a relevant factor in assessing whether or not the measure is justified. (This is consistent with the fact that achieving a stable workforce may be a legitimate aim, see *Rolls Royce Plc v Unite the Union* [2009] IRLR 576, [2010] ICR 1, CA.) However, the fact that a rule has been agreed in the process of collective bargaining will not render an otherwise unlawful scheme lawful, but nonetheless weight will be given to the fact that the parties have agreed to a scheme that they (presumably) consider to be fair: *Loxley v BAE Land Systems* [2008] IRLR 853. See also *Rosenbladt v Oellerking Gebaudereinigungsgesellschaft mbH*: C-45/09 [2011] 1 CMLR 32, [2011] IRLR 51. Similarly, the fact that the terms in question have been agreed by the members of a partnership will be a relevant factor (*Seldon v Clarkson Wright & Jakes (No. 2)* [2014] IRLR 748, [2014] ICR 1275. However, employers and tribunals cannot through negotiation and agreement with workforce representatives abdicate their responsibility to assess for themselves whether a measure is proportionate: see *Pulham and ors v London Borough of Barking & Dagenham* [2010] IRLR 184, [2010] ICR 333. Further, it has been held that where the discriminatory measure is included in legislation, leaving the individual employer with a discretion whether or not to adopt it, courts and tribunals should apply a lower standard of scrutiny to reliance on the measure by the individual employer since the fact that the measure has been approved by Parliament is an important justifying factor: see *Chief Constable of West Midlands Police v Harrod* [2015] IRLR 790 (concerning the compulsory retirement of police officers using a discretionary provision in the *Police Pensions Regulations 1987*: upheld on appeal on slightly different grounds: [2017] EWCA Civ 191, [2017] IRLR 539).

Note that the case law on justification of retirement and related measures is dealt with in a separate section below and in **(43)** RETIREMENT.

13.9c (1) Legitimate aim

To be legitimate, an aim must correspond to a 'real need' on the part of the employer's business: *Bilka-Kaufhaus* (ibid), *R (Elias) v Secretary of State for Defence* [2006] IRLR 934. This is not to be confused with a test of necessity: see *HM Land Registry v Benson* [2012] IRLR 373, [2012] ICR 627 at paragraph 37. Whatever the aim, it is important that the tribunal make clear findings as to the employer's aim and why it is legitimate: *Cockram v Air Products Plc* [2015] All ER (D) 290 (Nov), UKEAT/0122/15/LA (although note that the Court of Appeal considered that on the facts the EAT had been wrong to overturn the Tribunal's judgment in that case: [2018] EWCA Civ 346, [2018] IRLR 755).

13.9d *Direct age discrimination*

In relation to direct age discrimination only there is a limitation on the aims that may be regarded as legitimate. Direct age discrimination can only be justified if the aim of the measure in question relates to 'employment policy, the labour market or vocational training' and not 'purely individual reasons particular to the employer's situation, such as cost reduction or improving competitiveness': see *art 6(1)* of *Directive 2000/78/EC* and *Seldon v Clarkson, Wright & Jakes* [2012] UKSC 16, [2012] IRLR 590, [2012] ICR 716. So far as direct age discrimination is concerned, therefore, *s 13(2)* of the *EqA 2010* must be 'read down' accordingly. This does not mean, however, that an aim which happens to be of particular relevance and benefit to the individual cannot also be a legitimate employment policy aim: see *Air Products Plc v Cockram* [2018] EWCA Civ 346, [2018] IRLR 755 where consistency in retirement ages as between the two pension schemes was accepted as fulfilling the legitimate aim of achieving intergenerational fairness, even though it was also administratively convenient for the employer.

The *Directive* gives examples of the sort of age discriminatory measures that might be permitted in pursuit of such aims, including (a) the setting of special conditions on access to employment and vocational training, employment and occupation, dismissal and remuneration conditions, for young people, older workers and persons with caring responsibilities in order to promote their vocational integration or ensure their protection; (b) the fixing of minimum conditions of age, professional experience or seniority in service for access to employment or to certain advantages linked to employment; (c) the fixing of a maximum age for recruitment which is based on the training requirements of the post in question or the need for a reasonable period of employment before retirement. These examples are not to be regarded as exhaustive: *Rosenbladt (Gisela) v Oellerking Gebaud-ereinigungsges mbH*: C-45/09 [2011] 1 CMLR 1011, [2011] IRLR 51.

Aims that have been accepted as legitimate for the purposes of direct age discrimination include:

* encouraging better access to employment and better distribution of work between the generations (*Félix Palacios de la Villa v Cortefiel Servicios SA*: C-411/05 [2008] All ER (EC) 249, [2007] IRLR 989, *Petersen v Berufungsausschuss für Zahnärzte für den Bezirk Westfalen-Lippe* [2010] IRLR 254 and *Hörnfeldt v Posten Meddelande AB*: C-141/11 [2012] IRLR 785), including encouraging the reasonable flow of new applicants for judicial posts (*Hampton v Lord Chancellor* [2008] IRLR 258, ET) and ensuring promotion opportunities for associate solicitors (*Seldon* ibid) and generally pursuing intergenerational fairness (*Air Products Plc v Cockram* [2018] EWCA Civ 346, [2018] IRLR 755);

* the efficient planning of the departure and recruitment of staff (*Fuchs and another v Land Hessen*, Joined Cases C-159/10 and C-160/10: [2011] IRLR 1043; *Seldon* and *Hörnfeldt*);

* protecting acquired rights and legitimate expectations with regard to remuneration (*Specht v Land Berlin* (Joined Cases C-501, 506, 540 and 541/12), [2014] ICR 966, [2014] All ER (D) 39 (Jul) and *Schmitzer v Bundesministerin für Inneres* (Case C-530/13) [2015] IRLR 331; see further below and also **23.12 EQUAL PAY** for justification of pay protection arrangements generally);

* encouraging the recruitment of older persons (*Mangold v Helm* [2006] IRLR 143), 'modest refreshment' of the workforce, sharing of employment opportunities between generations, exchanging expertise and new ideas, enabling opportunities for promotion (*Re Early's Application for Leave to Appeal for Judicial Review* [2017] NIQB 48);

* improving access to vocational training for young people (*de Lange v Staatssecretaris van Financien* (C-548/15) [2017] IRLR 278;

* ensuring civil aviation safety: *Fries v Lufthansa CityLine GmbH* (C-190/16) [2017] IRLR 1003 (retirement age of 65 for pilots in Europe); and

* running an organisation in a collegiate way and avoiding the indignity of disciplining staff for underperformance (*Rosenbladt, Seldon* and *Hörnfeldt*) or the possibility of disputes about an employee's fitness for work after a certain age (*Fuchs*).

In the light of the SC's decision in *Seldon*, some earlier decisions may fall to be re-evaluated. Thus, in *MacCulloch v Imperial Chemical Industries plc* [2008] IRLR 846, [2008] ICR 1334 the CA accepted that 'rewarding loyalty' and 'encouraging turnover' could be legitimate aims of measures that were directly discriminatory on grounds of age. It is questionable whether aims thus expressed could be legitimate post *Seldon* for direct age discrimination.

For other cases on the justification of direct age discrimination see: *Lockwood v Department of Work and Pensions* [2013] EWCA Civ 1195, [2013] IRLR 941 (redundancy payments varying based on age were justified), *Ingeniorforeningen i Danmark, acting on behalf of Ole Andersen v Region Syddanmark*: C-499/08 [2012] All ER (EC) 342 and *Dansk Jurist- Og Okonomforbund, acting on behalf of Toftgaard v Indenrigs- Og Sundhedsministeriet*: Case

13.9d   Discrimination and Equal Opportunities – II

C–546/11 [2014] IRLR 37 (withholding termination payments from over 65s on grounds that they were eligible for a pension was not justified because the same aim could have been met by the lesser measure of withholding the payment only if the individual had actually decided to draw their pension); see also **13.15**(d) below.

13.9e   *Indirect discrimination*

So far as indirect discrimination of all forms is concerned, there is no restriction on the possible motivations that can in principle constitute legitimate aims. What constitutes a legitimate aim is a question of fact for the tribunal: see *Ladele v Islington London Borough Council* [2009] EWCA Civ 1357, [2010] IRLR 211, [2010] ICR 532 at [45]. It will therefore be open to employers to demonstrate that any aim they seek to pursue is legitimate. This is consistent with the fact that justification must be applied on a case-by-case basis and that it is very difficult to anticipate all possible justifications.

In addition to the aims identified above as legitimate for the purposes of direct age discrimination claims, examples of aims that have been accepted as legitimate aims for the purposes of justifying indirect discrimination include:

- facilitating the recruitment and retention of staff of appropriate calibre (*Homer v Chief Constable of West Yorkshire* [2012] UKSC 15, [2012] IRLR 601, [2012] ICR 704) or experience (*Peifer v Sullivan Upper School* [2019] NICA 51);

- recognising the legitimate expectations of employees who were already in receipt of a benefit or had otherwise acquired rights deserving of protection (*Pulham v Barking and Dagenham London Borough Council* [2010] IRLR 184, [2010] ICR 333, EAT, *Specht v Land Berlin* (ibid) and *Schmitzer v Bundesministerin für Inneres* (ibid));

- preventing a windfall or receipt of excessive compensation (*Loxley v BAE Systems Land Systems (Munitions & Ordnance) Ltd* [2008] ICR 1348, [2008] IRLR 853, EAT and *Kraft Foods Ltd v Hastie* (UKEAT/0024/10/ZT) [2010] ICR 1355, [2010] All ER (D) 100 (Aug), although this aim will not succeed where the numbers do not in fact add up to a windfall: *BAE Systems (Operations) Ltd v McDowell* [2018] ICR 214);

- achieving a stable workforce in the context of a fair process of redundancy selection (*Rolls Royce Plc v Unite the Union* [2009] IRLR 576, [2010] ICR 1, CA);

- avoiding the risk to the public of employing persons in the police force who have a criminal conviction (*RMC v Chief Constable of Hampshire* (UKEAT/0184/16/LA, 8 November 2016): the policy indirectly discriminated against men who are more likely to have criminal convictions, but the EAT upheld the ET's decision that it was justified);

- securing efficiencies, such as reducing the backlog of oral Parole Board hearings (*Greenland v Secretary of State for Justice* [2015] All ER (D) 258 (Jan), UKEAT/0232/14/DA, 20 March 2015) or other desirable management aims, such as achieving a coherent pay structure, avoiding privatisations, job losses, cuts in hours, and employees receiving lower pay (*Allen v GMB* [2008] IRLR 690) or securing the provision of a 24-hour health service (*Rajaratnan v Care UK Clinical Services Ltd* [2015] All ER (D) 408 (Jul) (7 October 2015, UKEAT/0435/14/DA, UKEAT/0076/15/DA));

- protecting those closest to retirement from the effects of pension reform on the basis that they are less likely to be able to make other arrangements: *Ministry of Justice v McCloud* [2018] EWCA Civ 2844, [2019] ICR 1489 (although note that on the particular facts of that case, the aim was held not to be legitimate because in fact younger members of the pension schemes were more adversely affected than those closer to retirement and insufficient evidence had been adduced in support of the claimed aim);

- making the maximum possible number of redundancies: *Harrod and ors v Chief Constable of West Midlands Police* [2017] EWCA Civ 191, [2017] IRLR 539 (although see commentary below on the lawfulness of using cost as a justification for discrimination);

- seeking to break even year-on-year: *Braithwaite v HCL Insurance BPO Services Ltd* [2015] ICR 713, [2015] All ER (D) 264 (Feb) (UKEAT/0152-3/14/DM);

- rewarding employees for specific work performed, eg night work (*Blackburn v Chief Constable of West Midlands Police* [2008] EWCA Civ 1208, [2009] IRLR 135);

- ensuring a teacher is able to communicate effectively with her pupils (a requirement not to wear a veil while teaching: *Azmi v Kirklees Metropolitan Borough Council* [2007] IRLR 484); and,

- ensuring the employer is able to fulfil its contractual requirements to a third party (eg by requiring a security guard to work on a Friday lunchtime and not attend Muslim prayers: *Cherfi v G4S Security Services Ltd* [2011] EqLR 825).

In addition, the legitimate aims accepted in *MacCulloch* (above) of 'rewarding loyalty' and 'encouraging turnover' are plainly capable of constituting legitimate aims for the purposes of indirect discrimination even if there is now some doubt about their legitimacy in the context of direct age discrimination.

13.9f *Cost-related aims*

One type of legitimate aim has proved particularly controversial – cost-related aims. Given the limitation on legitimate aims for the purposes of justifying direct age discrimination, cost reduction will plainly not be a legitimate aim in the context of direct age discrimination: see *Seldon* and *Schmitzer v Bundesministerin für Inneres* (C-530/13) [2015] IRLR 331. There is nothing express in the governing European legislation, or the domestic legislation, that imposes any such limitation on reliance on cost reduction as a legitimate aim when justifying indirect discrimination. Nonetheless, there is a line of cases in which it has been held that cost may only be relied on as justification if it is combined with other factors: *Cross v British Airways plc* [2005] IRLR 423, EAT; *R (Elias) v Secretary of State for Defence* [2006] EWCA Civ 1293, [2006] IRLR 934. In *Woodcock v Cumbria Primary Care Trust* [2011] IRLR 119 the EAT expressed the view (*obiter*) that, as a matter of principle and of common sense, there should be no rule that considerations of cost could never be sufficient on their own to justify indirect discrimination. On appeal, however, the Court of Appeal ([2012] EWCA Civ 330, [2012] IRLR 491, [2012] ICR 1126) confirmed what was then generally understood to be the orthodox position that justification by reference to costs alone was impermissible, although it could be taken into account with other factors – the 'costs plus' approach. The CA referred to the line of cases establishing this principle, including *Schönheit v Stadt Frankfurt*: C-4/02 and C-5/02 [2004] IRLR 983, CJEU and *Kutz-Bauer v Freie und Hansestadt Hamburg*: C-187/00 [2003] IRLR 368, CJEU, *British Airways plc v Grundy, Cross v British Airways Plc* [2005] IRLR 423 and *Redcar and Cleveland BC v Bainbridge* [2007] IRLR 91, [2008] ICR 249. See also *Osborne Clarke Services v Purohit* [2009] IRLR 341. However, in *Ministry of Justice v O'Brien* [2013] UKSC 6, [2013] IRLR 315, the Supreme Court reviewed the relevant authorities in the context of a claim under the *Part-time Workers (Prevention of Less Favourable Treatment) Regulations 2000* and reached the conclusion (at paragraph 69) that cost could not be relied on in order to justify discrimination (ie apparently even in combination with other factors). That said, the Court did not consider it needed to decide whether *Woodcock v Cumbria Primary Care Trust* had been wrongly decided. It also appeared to accept in principle that 'sound management of public finances' could be a legitimate aim. It thus remained to be seen whether the *O'Brien* decision would be regarded as outlawing altogether cost considerations. In *R (Unison) v Lord Chancellor (No. 2)* [2015] IRLR 99, [2015] ICR 390, the Divisional Court indicated that it regarded the law to be as stated in *Woodcock*, ie the 'costs plus' approach. The decision of the CJEU in *Schmitzer v Bundesministerin für Inneres* (Case C-530/13) suggests that the 'costs plus' approach is correct, although that case was a direct age discrimination case and thus a case in which cost saving could never be a legitimate aim, even if it can support the proportionality of a measure (see above). In *Schmitzer*, the CJEU made clear that budgetary considerations could be relied upon by way of justification, provided that they were relied on in conjunction with 'political, social or demographic considerations'. See also the discussion of this line of case law in *R(Unison) v Lord Chancellor (No. 3)* [2015] EWCA Civ 935, [2016] ICR 1.

Notwithstanding the statements of principle in the case law, it should be noted that there are in fact a number of cases where the Tribunals and Courts have reached conclusions that could be characterized as being findings that costs alone can justify discrimination and which may continue to be followed despite the Supreme Court's ruling. Thus, the courts appear to have had little difficulty with the notion that measures intended to avoid a 'windfall' or 'excessive compensation' to the employee – measures which the employer will inevitably have introduced to save itself money – have been held to be justified: *Loxley v BAE Systems (Munitions & Ordnance) Ltd* [2008] ICR 1348, [2008] IRLR 853 and *Kraft Foods UK Ltd v Hastie* [2010] ICR 1355, [2010] All ER (D) 100 (Aug). It should be noted that in those cases, the payments in question were held to serve some other legitimate purpose and so the courts were able to regard the quantum of the payment as being an aspect of the proportionality of the means of meeting the legitimate aim of (for eg in the case of severance pay) paying a reasonable sum of money on termination of employment to allow the employees time to find a new job. *HM Land Registry v S M Benson and ors* [2012] IRLR 373, [2012] ICR 627 is another apparently anomalous case. Here, the EAT found that the Tribunal had wrongly found an employer's use of a 'cheapness criterion' in a redundancy situation to be unjustified indirect age discrimination. The EAT held that the 'cheapness criterion' fulfilled a legitimate aim of saving the employer money, and that it was justified because there was no practicable alternative means of achieving the same aim and the measure was not disproportionate. It is notable, however, that the case seems to have been decided by the EAT without reference to the authorities for the general principle that costs alone cannot justify discrimination. See also *Braithwaite v HCL Insurance BPO Services Ltd* [2015] ICR 713, [2015] All ER (D) 264 (Feb) in which the EAT held, applying *Land Registry v Benson* that seeking 'to break even year-on-year' was a legitimate aim and that cost-saving changes to terms and conditions of employment (which employees had to accept or resign their employments) were justified. *Benson* and *Braithwaite* were followed in *Heskett v Secretary of State for Justice* [2020] ICR 359, where the EAT upheld the Tribunal's finding that the introduction of a new pay progression policy for the Probation Service, which lengthened the pay band from 8 years to 23 years was justified because it was, temporarily, necessary to enable the department to break even year on year given the reduced settlement from central government. Similarly, in *Harrod and ors v Chief Constable of West Midlands Police* [2017] EWCA Civ 191, [2017] IRLR 539, the CA (without referring to the 'costs alone' case law) accepted as legitimate the aim of making the maximum possible number of redundancies, which was in substance adopting an aim of saving as much money as possible.

Given these anomalous cases, and given that so far as disability discrimination is concerned cost can effectively justify indirect discrimination because it can be a reason why it is not reasonable to make an adjustment for a disabled person (see eg *Cordell v Foreign & Commonwealth Office* [2012] ICR 280 and **12.43** Discrimination and Equal Opportunities – I), prior to *O'Brien* (ibid) the time appeared to be ripe for the CJEU to consider again whether or not costs alone can be relied on as justifying indirect discrimination. However, following *O'Brien* there is little prospect of any reference on that point being made from the UK in the near future.

In past cases where cost was relied on as a justification, it was not necessary precisely to quantify the costs, it was usually sufficient for there to be evidence as to the 'broad scale' of costs: see *Pulham and ors v London Borough of Barking & Dagenham* [2010] IRLR 184,

[2010] ICR 333. In that case the EAT also observed that, although it is open to an employer to rely on the fact that the particular budget to which the cost in question has been allocated is exhausted, this should never be regarded as a determinative factor since the allocation of cost centres to particular budgets is a matter that it is within the employer's power to vary if necessary.

13.9g *Discriminatory aims*

An aim that is itself discriminatory, or is 'inextricably linked to' the forbidden ground of discrimination, will not be legitimate and it will not be possible for justification to be established: see *Orphanos v Queen Mary College* [1985] IRLR 349, HL, applied in *R (Elias) v Secretary of State for Defence and Commission for Racial Equality* [2006] EWCA Civ 1293, [2006] IRLR 934, save in the context of age discrimination where direct discrimination can be justified: see *obiter* comments in *Chief Constable of West Midlands Police and ors v Harrod and ors* [2017] EWCA Civ 145, [2017] IRLR 539. *Elias* concerned the requirement in a non-statutory compensation scheme for persons interned by the Japanese during the Second World War that, in order to qualify for compensation, internees had to have been born in the UK or have a parent or grandparent born in the UK. The Court of Appeal held that although the Government's desire to limit the scheme to those with a close connection with Britain was a legitimate aim, and cost factors could potentially justify such a limitation, the actual criteria imposed by the Government were so closely connected with the unlawful ground of discrimination (national origins) that their use could not be justified. See also *Ministry of Justice v O'Brien* [2013] UKSC 6, [2013] IRLR 315 (aims intended to reward the greater contribution of full-time judges and encourage better candidates to apply for full-time judicial appointment were held not to justify discrimination against part-timers in relation to pensions because, in effect, the aims were themselves discriminatory). See also *Lockwood v Department of Work and Pensions* [2013] EWCA Civ 1195, [2013] IRLR 941, applied in *Smith and Budgen v Ministry of Justice* [2014] All ER (D) 229 (Feb) (UKEAT/0308/12/RN, UKEAT/0309/12/RN) (where the EAT held that it had been impermissible for the Tribunal to find that the provisions were justified solely by reference to the difference in ages of the employees and remitted the matter to the Tribunal for further consideration).

For similar reasons, if an employer has recognised that a particular practice or policy may be discriminatory, the EAT has held that it will not be possible for the employer to justify continuing that practice or policy even on a transitional or phasing-out basis: see *Pulham and ors v London Borough of Barking & Dagenham* [2010] IRLR 184, [2010] ICR 333, [2014] All ER (D) 39 (Jul). However, in other cases the courts have accepted that transitional pay protection arrangements may be justified (even where past discrimination has been expressly recognised by the employer). Indeed, in *Specht v Land Berlin* (Joined Cases C-501, 506, 540 and 541/12), [2014] ICR 966, the CJEU found such arrangements to be justified even where they would perpetuate previous discrimination indefinitely. See further below *Other specific cases* and **23.12 Equal Pay**.

In a similar vein, it will not generally be possible to justify discrimination under *s 15* of the *EA 2010* where there has been a failure by the employer to comply with the duty to make reasonable adjustments under *s 20* of the *EA 2010*: see *Northumberland Tyne & Wear NHS Foundation Trust v Miss D Ward* (UKEAT/0249/18/DA) per Choudhury J at para 64 and *Griffiths v Secretary of State for Work and Pensions* [2014] EqLR 545, EAT at para 26. (As to the duty to make reasonable adjustments, see further **12.37 CHAPTER 12**).

Other examples of cases where the aim has been found to be itself discriminatory and therefore illegitimate include *Allonby v Accrington and Rossendale College* [2001] EWCA Civ 529, [2001] IRLR 364 (purpose of imposing the condition was to enable the employer to avoid a statutory protection against discrimination). Compare in this context *Osborne Clarke Services v Purohit* [2009] IRLR 341. That case concerned a firm of solicitors' practice of not offering training contracts to persons who required work permits. They sought to justify this indirect nationality discrimination on the grounds that: (i) they did not feel they could legitimately sign the work permit application form because that required the employer to certify that it was unable to fill the post with a national worker and in fact they were significantly over-subscribed with applicants for training contracts; and (ii) applications for work permits would increase the cost of the process of appointing trainees. The tribunal rejected the cost argument as being an 'unattractive way of justifying indirect discrimination'. As to the argument about the work permit criteria, the EAT ruled that in order to avoid unlawful discrimination, issues of requirement for work permits should only be considered once it had been decided on merit who should be awarded a training contract. Application should then be made to the British Immigration Authority ('BIA') and employers should leave it to the BIA to determine whether the work permit criteria were satisfied.

13.9h   (2) Whether the measure is capable of achieving the aim

It is not sufficient for an employer to convince a tribunal that the treatment (in the case of age) or PCP (in indirect discrimination) had a legitimate aim. He also needs to show that it was appropriate and reasonably necessary in order to achieve that aim. As noted above, the requirement that the treatment or measure be appropriate means that it must actually contribute to the pursuit of the legitimate aim. There must not be a mismatch between the aim and the means. There are few examples of cases where it has been held that the means employed are not at least capable of achieving the aim in question. However, one example which could be viewed as such is *Petersen v Berufungsausschuss für Zahnärzte für den Bezirk Westfalen-Lippe* [2010] IRLR 254, where the CJEU held that a maximum age limit of 68 for panel dentists was not justified as being necessary for the protection of health where there was an exception for those practising outside the panel system. This was because it could not be regarded as essential for the protection of health in the light of the broad exception. (In this respect, *Petersen* concerned an exemption in *Article 2(5)* of the *Framework Directive* for measures which are necessary for the protection of health rather than justification under *Article 6*. It therefore did not address the question of whether it was permissible to assume based only on 'general experience' that the performance of dentists declined after a certain age.) A better example is *Homer v Chief Constable of West Yorkshire* [2012] UKSC 15, [2012] IRLR 601, [2012] ICR 704 in which the SC accepted that a requirement to have a law degree in order to enter a higher pay band may facilitate the recruitment and retention of staff of appropriate calibre. However, the SC considered that where the member of staff in question had been recruited much earlier and under a different system where a law degree was not required, the requirement to have one before being allowed to cross a pay threshold was unlikely to fulfil the aim of retaining valued staff. Cf the similar case of *Games v University of Kent* [2015] IRLR 202 (concerning a requirement for university lecturers to hold a PhD) and also *Hennigs v Eisenbahn-Bundesamt; Land Berlin v Mai*, joined Cases C-297/10 and C-298/10: [2012] IRLR 83, CJEU (the aim of rewarding experience is not achieved by age-related pay scales which apply irrespective of experience) and *Kücükdeveci v Swedex GmbH & Co KG*: C-555/07 [2010] IRLR 346 (the aim of making it easier to recruit young people is not achieved by a measure which applies long after the employees have ceased to be young).

13.9i   (3) Proportionality

The requirement that a measure be proportionate means that tribunals must seek to balance the discriminatory effect of the requirement or condition against the legitimate aim in question (see *Ojutiku v Manpower Services Commission* [1982] IRLR 418, [1982] ICR 661; *Allonby v Accrington and Rossendale College* [2001] EWCA Civ 529, [2001] 2 CMLR 27, *Hardys & Hansons Plc v Lax* [2005] EWCA Civ 846, [2005] ICR 1565 and *Homer v Chief Constable of West Yorkshire* [2012] UKSC 15, [2012] 3 All ER 1287). The tribunal must consider both the quantitative and the qualitative effects of the discrimination, ie how many women or people of a particular racial group will suffer in consequence of it, and how seriously they will suffer (cf *Jones v University of Manchester* [1993] IRLR 218, [1993] ICR 474, *EC Commission v Belgium* [1991] IRLR 393 and *Bradley v London School of English and Foreign Languages Ltd* UKEAT/0011/18/LA). In general terms, the overall discriminatory effect of the measure will normally be greater in cases of direct (age) discrimination and this will be a material factor when applying the proportionality test: see *MacCulloch v Imperial Chemical Industries plc* [2008] IRLR 846, [2008] ICR 1334 and *Incorporated Trustees of the National Council on Ageing (Age Concern England) v Secretary of State for Business, Enterprise and Regulatory Reform*: C-388/07 [2009] IRLR 373, [2009] ICR 1080, CJEU. Where the discriminatory effect is particularly acute, the measure is more likely to be disproportionate. Thus in *Seda Kucukdeveci v Swedex GmbH & Co KG*: C-555/07 [2010] IRLR 346, the CJEU ruled that a German law was unlawful which provided that periods of employment completed by an employee before reaching the age of 25 were not taken into account in calculating the notice period for dismissal. The discrimination was significant and the link to the legitimate aim tenuous. *Ministry of Justice v McCloud and ors* [2018] EWCA Civ 2844 is a further example: those conjoined cases concerned the transitional arrangements for judges and firefighters moving to new public sector pension schemes. Although the judges had won before the EAT and the firefighters lost, ultimately the Court of Appeal upheld both claims, in part on the basis that the impact on younger judges, who bore the brunt of cost savings through substantial reductions in their pension entitlements, was disproportionate. In *Mba v Mayor and Burgesses of the London Borough of Merton* [2014] IRLR 145, [2014] ICR 357 (which concerned a requirement for a care assistant at a children's home to work on Sundays which put her at a disadvantage because she was a practising Christian who believed she should not work on Sundays) the Court of Appeal noted that the fact that only one or a minority of employees in the particular workplace would be affected by a requirement would not necessarily mean that it was easier for the employer to justify the discriminatory effect, since if only a few employees were affected it would in many cases be easier for the employer to accommodate their religious beliefs.

Measures that apply to all without taking sufficient account of the different circumstances of particular groups will generally be disproportionate. Thus, in *Ingeniorforeningen i Danmark, acting on behalf of Ole Andersen v Region Syddanmark*: C-499/08 [2011] 1 CMLR 1140 the CJEU considered a measure providing severance payments for all long-serving employees but not those over 65 was disproportionate because it applied to all employees over 65 regardless of whether they were actually drawing a pension. See, to similar effect, *Dansk Jurist-Og Okonomforbund, acting on behalf of Toftgaard v Indenrigs- Og Sundhedsministeriet*: C-546/11 [2014] IRLR 37, but note *BAE Systems (Operations) Ltd v McDowell* [2018] ICR 214 where the EAT upheld an appeal against a Tribunal's finding that a similar scheme was unlawful on the basis that the Tribunal had erred in considering the redundancy payment scheme in isolation from other measures relied on by the employer. In *Mangold*, a measure aimed to encourage the recruitment of older persons was held to be disproportionate as it applied to all old people, regardless of whether they had been out of employment. The CJEU took a more lenient approach in the case of *Félix Palacios*. It held that the enforcement of a compulsory retirement age under a collective agreement was justified as being proportionate. The CJEU noted that the national authorities had a broad discretion in social and employment matters and it was for them to strike the appropriate balance. In *R (Unison) v First Secretary of State* [2006] EWHC 2373 (Admin), [2006] IRLR 926, the Secretary of State had changed the Local Government Pension Scheme, considering this to be necessary in order to comply with the *Directive* and the *Regulations*. The Secretary of State considered that the scheme would not be justified by the aim of rewarding loyalty as it treated those who remained in service in the same way as those who had left. The Court held that this position was not irrational.

When determining whether or not a measure is proportionate, it will be relevant to consider whether or not any lesser form of the measure would nevertheless serve the employer's legitimate aim, although the fact that such a measure exists will not necessarily mean that the measure chosen is disproportionate: *Hardys & Hansons plc v Lax* [2005] IRLR 726, CA, *The City of Oxford Bus Services Limited t/a Oxford Bus Company v Mr L Harvey* UKEAT/0171/18/JOJ and cf *Gray v Mulberry Company (Design) Ltd* [2019] EWCA Civ 1720, [2020] IRLR 29 at para 50 (where the employer had offered the employee a less intrusive alternative which had been rejected by the employee). It will normally be for the parties to identify possible alternatives, although in *Naeem v Secretary of State for Justice* [2014] IRLR 520 EAT suggested, *obiter*, that a tribunal might be expected of its own motion to consider 'manifest' alternatives. The suggestion was not considered on appeal in that case ([2015] EWCA Civ 1264, [2016] IRLR 118, [2016] ICR 289 and [2017] UKSC 27; [2017] 1 WLR 1343) and in *Magoulas v Queen Mary University of London* [2016] All ER (D) 259 (Jan), UKEAT/0244/15/RN, the EAT declined to follow this suggestion. For example, in a case involving a dismissal for reason connected with a person's disability, it will often be relevant to consider whether some lesser alternative such as a reduction in working hours would be a proportionate response to the situation: see eg *Ali v Torrosian (t/a Bedford Hill Family Practice)* UKEAT/0029/18/JOJ. Evidence that alternatives have been explored (or not, as the case may be) is likely to be important to the Tribunal's analysis. Thus in *Azmi v Kirklees Metropolitan Borough Council* [2007] IRLR 484 (in which the Muslim claimant complained that she had been unlawfully discriminated against on grounds of her religious belief because she was not allowed to wear the veil while teaching at a primary school), the EAT held that the tribunal was right to have taken into account, in finding the requirement imposed by the school to be proportionate, the facts that (i) the respondent school had, before insisting on the claimant not wearing a veil, observed her teaching both with and without the veil and taken the view that she was much more effective without the veil, and (ii) the school had permitted her to wear the veil when moving around the school premises and had only required her not to wear the veil while teaching.

13.9j *Justification where the aim is to protect fundamental rights*

There is one possible exception to the requirement to consider the proportionality of a particular aim. This is where the aim is itself the protection of fundamental rights. The argument made in the cases in which this has been suggested appears to be that the aim is sufficiently legitimate to justify the use of any means to achieve it. See in this regard *Islington London Borough Council v Ladele* [2010] IRLR 211. That case concerned the Council's requirement that its services be provided on a non-discriminatory basis. It had accordingly disciplined a registrar who, owing to her religious beliefs, refused to carry out civil partnership ceremonies. The Tribunal found that the Council's aim of providing non-discriminatory services was legitimate but considered that the use of disciplinary measures to achieve this aim was disproportionate. The EAT (whose decision was approved by the CA) overturned this decision, holding that since the Council's aim was legitimate and could not be achieved other than by imposing disciplinary sanctions on employees who sought to pick and choose the duties that they would perform, the Council's actions had not been unlawful. The CA confirmed that in those circumstances it was not necessary to go on to consider the proportionality of the means: since the legitimate aim was itself the protection of fundamental rights, to ask whether a particular means to achieving that aim was disproportionate "might well be characterised as invoking the tail to wag the dog" (Lord Neuberger, [51]): see also *McFarlane v Relate Avon Ltd* [2010] EWCA Civ 880, [2010] IRLR 872. It should further be noted that the EAT in *Ladele* considered that, if the Council had wished to accommodate the claimant's religious beliefs, it would have been lawful for it to do so, but the fact that this could have been done did not mean that the policy the Council had in fact adopted was unlawful. However, the CA held (*obiter*) that where a registrar had been designated as a civil partnership registrar it would be unlawful under the *Equality Act (Sexual Orientation) Regulations 2007* for her to refuse to provide registration services to homosexual couples (for which unlawful act the Council would be liable).

Mrs Ladele, Mr McFarlane and two other claimants, Ms Eweida (whose complaint was that British Airways had refused to allow her to wear a cross at work, cf *Eweida v British Airways Plc* [2010] EWCA Civ 80, [2010] IRLR 322, [2010] ICR 890) and Ms Chaplin (a nurse who was refused permission to wear a necklace with a cross on it at work) took their cases to the ECtHR, complaining that the UK had unlawfully interfered with their rights under *Art 9* of the *ECHR* to manifest their religious belief and/or had unlawfully discriminated against them contrary to *Art 14* of the *ECHR*. In conjoined proceedings (*Eweida and ors v United Kingdom*, App nos 48420/10, 59842/10, 51671/10 and 36516/10, [2013] IRLR 231) the ECrtHR upheld Ms Eweida's complaint, but rejected the others. In each case the ECtHR considered that the applicant had established an interference with their rights under *Art 9* and/or *Art 14* and went on to consider whether that interference was justified. The test applied by the ECtHR when considering justification is indistinguishable from that which applies in domestic law under the *EqA 2010*. In each case the ECrtHR sought to balance the importance to the applicant of the right to manifest his or her religious belief against the business need / aim of the applicant's employer. The ECtHR did not take the view that just because an employer's aim was the protection of fundamental rights, there was no need to consider proportionality. Rather, in both the *Ladele* and *McFarlane* cases the fact that this was the employer's aim was merely treated as a factor that weighed heavily in the balance in favour of the interference being justified. The ECtHR also held that although it is relevant to the assessment of justification in the employment context that an employee can avoid the interference by resigning his or her job, this fact on its own could never justify discrimination or interference with an employee's fundamental rights. In *Ladele*, *McFarlane* and *Chaplin* the ECtHR considered that the UK had struck the right balance in holding the employer's action to be lawful. In *Eweida*, however, the ECtHR considered that although the employer's aim of projecting a uniform corporate image was a legitimate one, it was not weighty one (and not as weighty as the health and safety reasons for not allowing Ms Chaplin to wear a cross, for example) and the fact that the employer had subsequently amended the policy made clear that it had not been vital to have the policy in the first place. The interference with Ms Eweida's rights had therefore been disproportionate.

Another recent case to consider the impact of *Article 9* of the *ECHR* on domestic indirect discrimination law is *Mba v Mayor and Burgesses of the London Borough of Merton* [2014] IRLR 145, [2014] ICR 357. That case concerned a requirement for a care assistant to work on Sundays which conflicted with her Christian belief that she should not work on the Sabbath. In that case the Court of Appeal held that the tribunal had erred in taking into account, in the employer's favour, the fact that the belief that one should not work on a Sunday is not a 'core component' of Christian belief, since it is a belief shared only by some, not all, Christians. The Court of Appeal held that this did not mean that any less respect was to be accorded to the Claimant's belief (which was accepted to be genuine) in the context of *Article 9* and thus the fact that the belief was not a 'core component' of Christianity was to be regarded as largely irrelevant to the question of justification for the purposes of domestic law. In the context of a domestic law indirect discrimination claim, the only relevance of a claimant's belief not being a 'core component' of a particular religion was that it would be likely to mean that an employer would only encounter a few employees who may need to have that belief accommodated. In many cases this would make it harder for the employer to justify not accommodating the employee's belief.

13.9k *Length of service criteria*

Although generally speaking the same principles apply when considering justification of prima facie discriminatory measures regardless of the ground of discrimination relied on, it appears from the case law on equal pay that a slightly different approach is to be taken to cases involving disproportionate impact arising from the use of the criterion of length of service. There seems to be no reason why the same principles should not apply to indirect discrimination in relation to matters other than pay arising from the use of a length of service criterion. It will sometimes be the case that use of the criterion of length of service will have a disproportionate impact on women because women tend to have more career breaks or shorter working lives than men. However, the CJEU in *Danfoss* [1989] IRLR 532 held that, although the use of the criterion of length of service may involve some discrimination against women, the employer did not have to provide 'special justification' for that because, in essence, it could be assumed that length of service brings with it greater experience and improved job performance. In *Cadman v Health and Safety Executive*: C-17/05 [2006] IRLR 969, [2006] ICR 1623 the CJEU retreated slightly from this, saying 'where recourse to the criterion of length of service . . . leads to disparities . . . between the men and women to be included in the comparison, (i) since, as a general rule, recourse to the criterion of length of service is appropriate to attain the legitimate objective of rewarding experience acquired which enables the worker to perform his duties better, the employer does not have to establish specifically that recourse to that criterion is appropriate to attain that objective as regards a particular job, unless the worker provides evidence capable of raising serious doubts in that regard; (ii) where a job classification system based on an evaluation of the work to be carried out is used in determining pay, there is no need to show that an individual worker has acquired experience during the relevant period which has enabled him to perform his duties better'.

The CA in *Wilson v Health and Safety Executive* [2009] EWCA Civ 1074, [2010] IRLR 59, [2010] ICR 302 then clarified the approach that should be taken to domestic cases involving a length of service criterion in the light of the CJEU decision in *Cadman*. The CA ruled that, so far as domestic law is concerned, the 'serious doubts' test put forward by the CJEU in *Cadman* is only of relevance before trial (presumably as a ground for 'strike out'). The CA said that what a claimant needs to show, pre-trial, is that there is evidence from which, if established at trial, it can properly be found that the general rule in *Danfoss* and *Cadman* (that seniority and length of service are generally material differences other than sex) does not apply. The CA confirmed, however, that a claim involving a length of service criterion is to be approached in essentially the same way as any other claim involving indirect discrimination. The burden is on the claimant to show disparate impact and, if that is established, the burden shifts to the employer to justify the difference as necessary. The CA noted (at [52]) that the Tribunal had allowed the employer a 'margin of appreciation' in relation to objective justification in this case. The CA indicated that there was no error of law in that approach.

A measure based on length of service is also likely to be indirectly discriminatory on the grounds of age, although not necessarily: see *Horgan v Minister for Education and Skills* (C-154/18) in which the CJEU held that a measure introducing new pay arrangements from a particular date was not a measure based on age at all and therefore neither directly or indirectly discriminatory. See, to similar effect, *R (Harvey) v Haringey LBC* [2018] EWHC 2871 (Admin), [2019] Pens LR 3.

13.91

Until 6 April 2011 there was a specific exception in *reg 30* of the *AR 2006* (preserved by the *EqA 2010*) for retirement (see below **13.15** and also generally RETIREMENT **(43)**). Since 6 April 2011 the *Employment Equality (Repeal of Retirement Age Provisions) Regulations 2011 (SI 2011/1069)* have phased out the designated retirement age in reg 30 of the AR 2006 so that (at the latest from October 2012) there is no longer any automatically justified retirement age for employees and whether retirements and related provisions are justified falls to be considered in accordance with the standard principles for justifying indirect discrimination in relation to other protected characteristics (see above). There are, however, two important differences between the justification test as it applies to direct age discrimination and that which applies in relation to indirect discrimination. First, as set out above, direct age discrimination can only be justified if the aim of the measure in question relates to "employment policy, the labour market or vocational training" and not "purely individual reasons particular to the employer's situation, such as cost reduction or improving competitiveness": see *Art 6(1)* of Directive 2000/78/EC and *Seldon v Clarkson, Wright & Jakes* [2012] UKSC 16, [2012] IRLR 590, [2012] ICR 716. (In *Seldon* the Tribunal had not appreciated this distinction between direct age discrimination and indirect discrimination. Accordingly, the matter was remitted for the Tribunal to consider whether a compulsory retirement age of 65 for solicitors in a partnership was justified or not. On remission, the

Tribunal concluded that 65 was justified as a retirement age and the EAT upheld that decision: [2014] IRLR 748, [2014] ICR 1275.) Secondly, although normally it will suffice if the employer succeeds in showing that the provision, criterion or practice was a proportionate means of achieving a legitimate aim in general, it might be necessary in certain cases for the employer to demonstrate that the application of the provision, criterion or practice to the particular employee was justified in that particular case: see *Seldon*, ibid.

For further discussion of the case law on the justifications for retirements and related provisions see Retirement (43).

13.9m *Other specific cases*

For cases concerning justification of pay protection arrangements (ie arrangements made by an employer to protect employee's existing pay when introducing a new pay scheme, usually in response to a recognition that the previous pay scheme was, or might have been, discriminatory on grounds of age), see: *Specht v Land Berlin* (Joined Cases C-501, 506, 540 and 541/12), [2014] ICR 966, [2014] All ER (D) 39 (Jul) and *Schmitzer v Bundesministerin für Inneres* (C-530/13) [2015] IRLR 331. *Schmitzer* concerned the pay scheme for Austrian civil servants. Previously, the scheme had included an element whereby service prior to the age of 18 was disregarded, thus directly discriminating on grounds of age. A new system was introduced which allowed the full experience of workers, regardless of age, to be taken into account. However, those disadvantaged under the previous system continued to be disadvantaged under the new system. The CJEU accepted that on changing pay systems, pay protection arrangements intended to protect the rights of those acquired under the previous system pursued a legitimate aim. However, the CJEU emphasised that such arrangements would only be justified for a transitional period and that accordingly the Austrian arrangements (which perpetuated the previous discrimination indefinitely) were unlawful. In contrast, in *Specht*, the CJEU accepted that a new pay scheme was justified even though it perpetuated indefinitely the effects of discrimination under the previous scheme. *Specht* concerned the pay scheme for German civil servants. Pay had previously been determined by reference to a scale that depended on the employee's age at the date of appointment and was thus directly discriminatory on grounds of age. A new system was introduced so that pay was determined by reference to experience. The German civil service considered that it was not practical retrospectively to assess where all existing civil servants ought to sit on the new payscale, so existing civil servants were simply moved to the point on the new payscale that corresponded to their existing salary, thus perpetuating the directly discriminatory pay arrangements. The CJEU held that this was justified, essentially because it accepted that it was genuinely not practical to do anything else given the nature of the assessment of experience required under the new system and the numbers of civil servants. See also *Naeem v Secretary of State for Justice* [2017] UKSC 27, [2017] 1 WLR 1343 in which the Supreme Court, while declining to interfere with the Employment Tribunal's decision that the particular transitional pay protection arrangements for prison service chaplains were justified, nonetheless observed (at paragraph 47) that where a case concerned the lawfulness of a transitional scheme, 'the question was not whether the original pay scheme could be justified but whether the steps being taken to move towards the new system were proportionate. Where part of the aim is to move towards a system which will reduce or even eliminate the disadvantage suffered by a group sharing a protected characteristic, it is necessary to consider whether there were other ways of proceeding which would eliminate or reduce the disadvantage more quickly. Otherwise it cannot be said that the means used are 'no more than necessary' to meet the employer's need for an orderly transition. . . . The burden of proof is on the respondent, although it is clearly incumbent upon the claimant to challenge the assertion that there was nothing else the employer could do. Where alternative means are suggested or are obvious, it is incumbent upon the tribunal to consider them.' See further 23.12 Equal Pay for the case law on sex discrimination in similar circumstances.

For justification of differential treatment creating more favourable access to employment opportunities for UK students/employees than non-UK students/employees, see: *Daler-Rowney Ltd v Revenue and Customs Commissioners* [2015] ICR 632, [2014] All ER (D) 308 (Jul), concerning national minimum wage legislation.

For cases concerning justification of indirectly discriminatory requirements in relation to working practices in the armed forces, see *Macmillan v Ministry of Defence* [2004] All ER (D) 429 (Nov) (F.ATS/0003/04), EAT and *Boote v Ministry of Defence* (22 April 2004, unreported), IT(NI).

For justification of requirements or conditions that Sikhs who wear turbans should wear safety helmets on construction sites (a *prima facie* indirectly discriminatory provision) see below **13.13**.

For cases concerned with manifestations of religion or belief through clothing or jewellery, see *Eweida and ors v United Kingdom*, App nos 48420/10, 59842/10, 51671/10 and 36516/10, [2013] IRLR 231 (wearing of crucifix at work); *Azmi v Kirklees Metropolitan Borough Council* [2007] IRLR 484 (wearing a veil while teaching at a primary school), *R (on the application of Watkins-Singh) v Governing Body of Aberdare Girls' High School* [2008] EWHC 1865 (Admin), *[2008] All ER (D) 376 (Jul)* (school's policy forbidding jewellery not justified because it prevented Sikhs from wearing Kara bangles which were of great importance to them and yet so small and unostentatious that the discriminatory effect of the policy was disproportionate); *G v St Gregory's Catholic Science College Governors* [2011] EWHC 1452 (Admin), [2011] All ER (D) 113 (Jun) (prohibition on pupils wearing hair in corn-rows was indirectly discriminatory on racial grounds and not justified as it was disproportionate).

For cases concerned with justification of working days and hours, see *Williams-Drabble v Pathway Care Solutions Ltd* (ET, 10 January 2005, IDS Brief 776, p 8 and *Mba v Merton LBC* [2014] IRLR 145, [2014] ICR 357 (where a requirement to work Sundays was not justified discrimination against a Christian employee). See also *Cherfi v G4S Security Services Ltd* [2011] EqLR 825) (requirement to work on Friday lunchtimes justified despite disadvantage to Muslims wishing to attend Friday prayers), and *The City of Oxford Bus Services Limited t/a Oxford Bus Company v Mr L Harvey* UKEAT/0171/18/JOJ (concerning whether requirement to work on Saturdays indirectly discriminated against Seventh Day Adventists) and *Bradley v London School of English and Foreign Languages Ltd* UKEAT/0011/18/LA (concerning whether requirement to be at work by 8.45am indirectly discriminated against women as primary childcarers).

13.9N LACK OF KNOWLEDGE OF DISABILITY

A special defence is available to claims of discrimination arising from a disability under *s 15* of the *EqA 2010* and to claims of failure to comply with the duty to make reasonable adjustments under *s 20* of the *EqA 2010* (see generally DISCRIMINATION AND EQUAL OPPORTUNITIES – I (12)). Although not explicit in the statute, it appears that knowledge of disability is also a requisite element of a direct disability discrimination claim: see *Lewisham Borough Council v Malcolm* [2008] IRLR 700 and *Morgan v Armadillo Managed Services Ltd* (2014) UKEAT/0567/12, [2014] All ER (D) 113 (Aug), EAT. However, since this is as a result of a necessary element of liability being the requirement for a causal relationship between the treatment and the employee's disability, rather than by way of a defence or exception, this is not dealt with further in this chapter, but only in DISCRIMINATION AND EQUAL OPPORTUNITIES – I (12).

Under the *EqA 2010* there will be no unlawful discrimination arising from a disability if the employer shows that he did not know, and could not reasonably have been expected to know, that the employee had the disability (*s 15(2)*). There will be no duty to make reasonable adjustments if the employer: (a) did not know, and could not reasonably have been expected to know, that the employee had the disability; and (b) was likely to be placed at a disadvantage by the arrangements in question (*Sch 8, para 20(1)(b)*). In relation to claims made by applicants for employment (or partnership, or candidates for a contract position, etc), the defence also applies where the employer did not know and could not reasonably have been expected to know that an interested disabled person is or may be an applicant for the work in question.

A similar defence was available to a claim of a failure to make reasonable adjustments under the *DDA 1995, s 4A(3)* and it is likely that courts and tribunals will take the same approach to the defences available under the *EqA 2010*. In *Eastern and Coastal Kent Primary Care Trust v Grey* [2009] IRLR 429, the EAT held that the defence under the *DDA 1995, s 4A(3)* applies where the employer:

(i)   does not know that the disabled person has a disability;

(ii)   does not know that the disabled person is likely to be at a substantial disadvantage compared with persons who are not disabled;

(iii)   could not reasonably be expected to know that the disabled person had a disability; and

(iv)   could not reasonably be expected to know that the disabled person is likely to be placed at a substantial disadvantage in comparison with persons who are not disabled.

In *Secretary of State for Work and Pensions v Alam* [2010] IRLR 283, [2010] ICR 665 and *Wilcox v Birmingham Cab Services Ltd* [2011] All ER (D) 73 (Aug) the EAT emphasised again that it is necessary (for the purposes of the defence to a claim of failure to make reasonable adjustments) for the employer to show both that it did not know (actually or constructively) that the employee was disabled and that it did not know (actually or constructively) that the employee was placed at the relevant disadvantage by the disability. The EAT in *Wilcox* further confirmed that there was no conflict in this respect between *Grey* and *Alam* as some commentators appeared to have thought.

It is important to remember, though, that the same is not true of the defence to a claim of discrimination arising from disability under *s 15(2)*. To succeed on that defence it is only necessary to show that the employer did not know (actually or constructively) that the employee was disabled. If the employer does have actual or constructive knowledge of the disability then it does not matter whether or not the employer is aware that its reason for treating the employee as it does is something that arises in consequence of the disability or not: see *City of York Council v Grosset* [2018] EWCA Civ 1105, [2018] ICR 1492.

In considering whether an employer has the requisite knowledge of disability, the same principles should apply as to determining whether an employee is disabled, see **12.26** Discrimination and Equal Opportunities - I. Thus, for example, where there is an issue as to whether an employee's condition was likely at a particular juncture to last for more than 12 months, or likely to recur, that will be an issue to be judged by what was known to the employer at the time and not by reference to hindsight: see *McDougall v Richmond Adult Community College* [2008] EWCA Civ 4, [2008] IRLR 227, [2008] ICR 431. Indeed, generally, it will be an error of law for a Tribunal to take into account when determining whether an employer had the requisite knowledge matters that the employer could not have known at the time: *Northumberland Tyne and Wear NHS Foundation Trust v Geoghegan* [2014] All ER (D) 148 (Mar) (UKEAT/0048/13/BA).

It should be noted that employers are responsible for making their own judgment as to whether an employee is disabled or not and cannot necessarily rely on the opinion of a medical practitioner or the lack of formal confirmation by an employee. Where an employer has obtained advice from occupational health or a medical practitioner to the effect that an employee is not disabled, the Tribunal will need to consider whether it was reasonable for the employer to have relied on that advice or whether the Tribunal ought reasonably to have known that the employee was disabled, despite the advice to the contrary. *Gallop v Newport City Council* [2013] EWCA Civ 1583, [2014] IRLR 211 was a case in which the CA held that it was an error of law for the Tribunal to have held that an employer did not have the requisite knowledge of disability because it had relied on the unreasoned opinion of an occupational health adviser. The CA remitted the case to the Tribunal to consider again whether the employer had acted reasonably in relying on that advice. That is not to say, however, that an employer will not be able to rely on the opinion of a medical practitioner in order to make out a defence of lack of knowledge: indeed, the *Wilcox* case was one in which the EAT held that the Tribunal had been entitled to find that it was inappropriate to impute constructive knowledge to the employer prior to receipt of a formal medical report. In *Wilcox* the employee suffered from an unusual mental impairment and the EAT held that it had been open to the Tribunal to conclude that the employer could not reasonably have known both of that impairment and that its effects would be substantial and long term (so as to bring it within the definition of disability in *s 6* of the *EqA 2010*) prior to receipt of medical evidence to that effect. In *Donelien v Liberata UK Ltd* [2018] EWCA Civ 129, [2018] IRLR 535, the Court of Appeal clarified the law following Gallop, affirming the orthodoxy that in a case where a medical practitioner has expressed an appropriately reasoned opinion on the proper facts, the employer will be able to attach 'great weight' to that. See also *Peregrine (deceased) v Amazon.co.uk Ltd* (UKEAT/0075/13/SM) for a case in which medical professionals had not at the time appreciated that an employee's back pain was connected to his known disability (cancer) and the Tribunal found (and the EAT upheld) that in those circumstances the employer could not reasonably have known of the connection either.

Generally speaking, however, employers must be aware of the potential discriminatory impact of their decisions whenever less favourable treatment is meted out. As suggested by the EAT in *H J Heinz Co Ltd v Kenrick* [2000] IRLR 144 (in a passage cited with apparent approval by Baroness Hale in the non-dissenting part of her opinion in *Lewisham London Borough Council v Malcolm* [2008] UKHL 43, [2008] IRLR 700), an employer is required to pause before dismissing an employee or treating an employee in a less favourable way in order to consider whether the reason for the dismissal or treatment might relate to disability and, if it might, to reflect on the discrimination legislation and the EHRC *Code of Practice* before dismissing or treating the employee in that way. The employer's obligation is to do all that it reasonably can to find out whether an employee is disabled. An employer who has not done sufficient will be fixed with constructive knowledge. However, the test is one of reasonableness, not a 'counsel of perfection': see *Donelien v Liberata* ibid. Whether an employer has done all that can reasonably be expected is a question of fact for the tribunal: *Mutombo-Mpania v Angard Staffing Solutions Ltd* [2018] 7 WLUK 389, 17 July 2018.

13.10 POSITIVE DISCRIMINATION

Domestic law

Broadly speaking, positive discrimination was not permitted under the predecessor domestic equality legislation because discriminating in favour of one group of people generally involves unlawful discrimination against another group who are treated less favourably in comparison (*Lambeth London Borough Council v Commission for Racial Equality* [1990] IRLR 231, [1990] ICR 768; though compare *Arnold v Barnfield College* [2004] All ER (D) 63 (Jul), EAT: mere existence of a policy of attracting more ethnic minority candidates not sufficient to indicate that there had been unlawful discrimination). Disability discrimination has always been an exception to this, discrimination against non-disabled persons, on grounds of disability, not being in and of itself unlawful. The *EqA 2010* expressly provides that it is not an instance of unlawful discrimination for a disabled person to be treated more favourably than a non-disabled person is or would be treated: *EqA 2010, s 13(3)*. Moreover, the duty to make reasonable adjustments (see DISCRIMINATION AND EQUAL OPPORTUNITIES – I (12)) can also be regarded as a form of positive discrimination.

Under the *EqA 2010* there is now a generally applicable exception under *s 158* for 'positive action' and a specific exception under *s 159* for 'positive action' in relation to recruitment and promotion. The two exceptions are mutually exclusive (*s 158(4)(a)*), but they apply to any act done by anyone (ie by an employer or a trade union or an agency) that would otherwise be unlawful under the Act. The exception under *s 158* came into force on 1 October 2010 at the same time as the major part of the Act. The exception under *s 159* came into force on 6 April 2011 (*SI 2011/96, art 3*).

The general exception under *s 158* applies where a person reasonably thinks that: (a) persons who share a protected characteristic suffer a disadvantage connected to the characteristic; or (b) persons who share a protected characteristic have needs that are different from the needs of persons who do not share it; or (c) participation in an activity by persons who share a protected characteristic is disproportionately low (*s 158(1)*). In such circumstances the *EqA 2010* does not prohibit a person from taking any action which is a proportionate means of achieving the aim of: (a) enabling or encouraging persons who share the protected characteristic to overcome or minimise that disadvantage; or (b) meeting those needs; or (c) enabling or encouraging persons who share the protected characteristic to participate in that activity (*s 158(2)*).

The specific exception for recruitment and promotion under *s 159* applies where a person reasonably thinks that: (a) persons who share a protected characteristic suffer a disadvantage connected to the characteristic; or (b) participation in an activity by persons who share a protected characteristic is disproportionately low (*s 159(1)*). In such circumstances the *EqA 2010* will not prohibit a person from treating a particular candidate more favourably in connection with recruitment or promotion because they have a particular protected characteristic where that treatment is done with the aim of enabling or encouraging persons who share the protected characteristic to: (a) overcome or minimise that disadvantage; or (b) to participate in that activity (*s 159(2)*). However, the section only applies if 'all else is equal' (specifically if those who are being considered for recruitment or promotion are as qualified as each other) and if the employer does not have a general policy of preferring candidates of a particular protected characteristic for recruitment or promotion (*s 159(4)(a), (b)*). Further, in all cases the positive discrimination must be a proportionate means of achieving the statutory aims set out above (*s 159(4)(c)*).

In addition, there are exceptions under the *EqA 2010* for those providing supported employment for the disabled (*s 133(3)*) and for those providing training to non-EEA nationals who will not remain in the UK on completion of training (*para 4, Sch 23*).

See also **13.37** below for discussion of the equality duties imposed on all public authorities which, while not specifically authorising positive discrimination, do authorise and oblige public authorities to take positive action to eliminate unlawful discrimination.

Under the predecessor legislation there were a number of more specific exceptions for positive discrimination as follows, only some of which have been retained in the *EqA 2010*.

(a)   *Access to training*

There is no specific exception for access to training under the *EqA 2010*.

Under the predecessor legislation employers could discriminate positively in favour of a particular racial group or in favour of female or male employees in order to afford that group access to training and to encourage the members of that group to take advantage of opportunities for doing particular work, provided that, at any time within the 12 months immediately preceding the positive discrimination:

(i)   there were no persons of that group among those doing that work at that establishment; or

(ii)   the proportion of persons of that group among those doing that work at that establishment is comparatively small (*RRA 1976, s 38(1), (2)*; *SDA 1975, ss 48(1), (2)*).

The *RRA 1976* specified that the proportion of persons of that group must be 'small in comparison to':

(i)   all those employed by the respondent at that establishment; or

(ii)   the population of the area from which that respondent normally recruits persons for work in his employment at that establishment.

Other persons concerned with the provision of vocational training could also discriminate in favour of racial groups, men or women (as appropriate) where it reasonably appeared to that person that there were no, or a comparatively small number, of members of that particular race, sex, etc doing that work in Great Britain (*RRA 1976, s 37; SDA 1975, s 47*). This particular exception specifically did not apply to discrimination by employers (*RRA 1976, s 37(3)* and *SDA 1975, s 47(4)*).

Similar provision was also made for positive discrimination in favour of persons of a particular religion or belief or sexual orientation where it reasonably appears to the person discriminating that it will prevent or compensate for disadvantages, linked to religion, belief, sexual orientation or age (or age group), respectively, suffered by persons of that religion or belief or sexual orientation or age (or age group) (as appropriate) (*RBR 2003, reg 25(1); SOR 2003, reg 26(1); AR 2006, reg 29(1)*). The ACAS Guidance on the *SOR 2003* and *RBR 2003* suggested that the exception would allow advertisements encouraging applications from people of a particular sexual orientation, religion or belief, provided it was made clear that selection would be on merit without reference to sexual orientation, religion or belief. The *Regulations* did not permit quota systems.

(b)   *Membership etc of trade organisations*

There is no specific exception for membership etc of trade organisations under the *EqA 2010*.

Positive discrimination was permitted under the *SDA 1975* and the *RRA 1976* to encourage both membership of and post-holding in trade organisations (including discrimination in affording access to training for holding such posts) where, at any time during the previous 12 months, there were no or proportionally few postholders or members of the relevant racial group or sex in that organisation (*RRA 1976, ss 38(3), (4), (5); SDA 1975, ss 48(2), (3)*).

Similar provision was made by the *RBR 2003* and the *SOR 2003* to allow positive discrimination by trade organisations where it reasonably appeared to the organisation that the act prevents or compensates for disadvantages linked to religion, belief, sexual orientation or age suffered by those of that religion, belief, sexual orientation or age (or age group) who are members of the organisation, or are eligible to become members, or hold, or are likely to hold, posts within that organisation (*RBR 2003, reg 25(2); SOR 2003, reg 26(2); AR 2006, reg 29(2)*). The exception extended to 'encouraging' only people of a particular sexual orientation, religion or belief to become members of the organisation where it reasonably appeared to the organisation that doing so would prevent or compensate for disadvantages suffered by people of that sexual orientation, religion or belief (*RBR 2003, reg 25(3); SOR 2003, reg 26(3); AR 2006, reg 29(3)*).

Under the *SDA 1975* (but not under the *RRA 1976, SOR 2003, RBR 2003* or *AR 2006*), trade organisations were also permitted to discriminate positively by setting quotas reserving a certain number of elected seats to men only or women only where in the opinion of the organisation the quotas were in the circumstances needed to secure a reasonable lower limit to the number of members of that sex serving on the body (*SDA 1975, s 49(1)*). However, discrimination in the arrangements for determining who is entitled to vote in an election of members of the body or in any arrangements concerning membership of the union or organisation itself is *not* permitted: *SDA 1975, s 49(2)*.

Note that although a set of barristers chambers was a 'trade organisation' within the meaning of the equivalent provisions of the *DDA 1995*, a pupil is not a 'member' of that organisation (*Higham v Meurig Lestyn Horton* [2004] EWCA Civ 941, [2005] ICR 292, [2004] All ER (D) 261 (Jul)). (However, see **13.27** below for the general provisions relating to barristers.)

(c)   *Special treatment in connection with pregnancy or childbirth*

Special treatment afforded to women in connection with pregnancy or childbirth has always been permitted, and may not be taken account of when considering a claim of sex discrimination brought by a man: *SDA 1975, s 2(2)*. This rule is preserved under the *EqA 2010* by *s 13(6)(b)* in relation to direct sex discrimination and by para 2 of Part 1 of Sch 7 insofar as the sex equality clause is concerned. The effect of these provisions is to preclude claims brought by men seeking rights equivalent to maternity rights: see *Capita Customer Management Ltd v Ali* [2018] ICR 1591, [2018] IRLR 586. However, this does not prevent men bringing claims on the basis that an employer's parental leave arrangements (applicable to both women and men) are indirectly discriminatory against men. While a man cannot claim direct comparison with a woman on maternity leave, if more men than women make use of the parental leave arrangements (as will generally be the case because women will have access to the, usually more beneficial, maternity leave arrangements), a prima facie claim of indirect discrimination may be established: see *Hextall v Chief Constable of Leicestershire Police* [2018] ICR 1632. Further, in *Eversheds Legal Services Ltd v De Belin* [2011] IRLR 448, the EAT made clear that the exception is limited to such treatment as is necessary as a proportionate means of achieving the legitimate aim of compensating women for the disadvantages occasioned by their pregnancy or maternity leave. Thus, Eversheds had unlawfully discriminated against Mr De Belin when, in operating a redundancy selection procedure, they awarded his female colleague absent on maternity leave full marks for performance on the ground that she was not present at work to be assessed. The EAT held that Eversheds could have compensated the female colleague for the disadvantage she was under as a result of her maternity leave by assessing her performance during the period she was last at work. Since this would have been a fairer way of achieving the same aim, it followed that Eversheds had acted disproportionately and therefore unlawfully.

(d)   *Special treatment of Sikhs in relation to the wearing of helmets on construction sites*

See below **13.13**.

(e)   *Acts done to meet education, training or welfare needs of particular racial groups*

There is no specific exception in the *EqA 2010* for such acts. However, the *RRA 1976* contained a further general exception for acts done for the purposes of protecting a particular racial group or groups. *Section 35* of the *RRA 1976* provided that nothing done by any body would be unlawful if it was done in order to afford persons of a particular racial group ('the protected group') access to facilities or services to meet the special needs of persons of that group in regard to their education, training or welfare, or any ancillary benefits. While this may appear to have been a broad provision permitting positive discrimination, it is unlikely that *s 35* would have rendered lawful an act of (negative) discrimination against a particular person or racial group unless that act was specifically done in order to provide services for the protected group. For example, it is unlikely that a trade organisation could have relied on this provision in order to justify having a membership consisting of only one racial group (or excluding a particular racial group) since a refusal of membership would not be directly related to the provision of services to the protected persons (though, where funds were limited, it ought to justify a refusal to provide legal services to members of the organisation if that was a 'special need' of the protected persons). This is particularly so given the specific express (and limited) provision as to positive discrimination by trade organisations (see above).

Positive action under EC law

Broadly speaking, the position in relation to positive action under EC law is, as one would expect, parallel to that under domestic law. However, the CJEU has held that *art 2(4)* of the version of *Council Directive 76/207/EEC* that was in force until 5 October 2005 (ie before the amendments made by *Council Directive 2002/73/EC*) permitted certain positively discriminatory measures. Measures permitted are those to the effect that where 'all else is equal' a female should be preferred for an appointment or promotion, provided that the measure is qualified by a requirement that consideration is given to the individual circumstances of each applicant: *Marschall v Land Nordrhein-Westfalen*: C-409/95 [1998] IRLR 39, [2001] ICR 45, CJEU. However, where a national measure is not so qualified (*Kalanke v Freie Hansestadt Bremen*: C-450/93 [1995] IRLR 660, [1996] ICR 314, CJEU), or that qualification is too vague to prevent appointments being made on the basis of sex alone (*Abrahamsson v Fogelqvist*: C-407/98 [2000] IRLR 732, [2002] ICR 932, CJEU), the CJEU has held it to be incompatible with the *Directive* (cf also *EFTA Surveillance Authority v Norway*: E-1/02 [2003] IRLR 318, CJEU).

The wording of the old *art 2(4)* is wider than that of *art 2(8)*, which replaced it as from 5 October 2005 (compare 'measures to promote equal opportunity for men and women, in particular by removing existing inequalities' with the new version to be found in *art 2(8)* and *art 157(4)* of the Treaty: 'the principle of equal treatment shall not prevent any Member State from maintaining or adopting measures providing for specific advantages in order to make it easier for the under-represented sex to pursue a vocational activity or to prevent or compensate for disadvantages in professional careers'). However, it is likely that the type of positive discrimination permitted by *art 2(4)* will continue to be held by the CJEU to be permissible under the new wording of the *Treaty* and the *Directive*. Similarly, it is likely to be acceptable in relation to the other grounds of discrimination, as to which EC legislation currently provides that 'the principle of equal treatment shall not prevent any Member State from maintaining or adopting specific measures to prevent or compensate for disadvantages linked to' race, sexual orientation, etc (*Council Directive 2000/43/EC, art 5*; *Council Directive 2000/78/EC, art 7*). Further, with positive action now enshrined in *art 157(4)* of the *Treaty*, it is likely to be permissible for both private and public sector organisations positively to discriminate in this manner. Indeed, Parliament has assumed this to be the case by enacting *ss 158* and *159* of the *EqA 2010*.

CHARITIES

13.10a   *Section 193* of the *EqA 2010* sets out a number of exceptions to the Act for charities. By *ss 193(1)* and *(2)*, a person is deemed not to contravene the *Act* if he restricts the provision of benefits to persons who share a protected characteristic if he does so pursuant to a charitable instrument and the provision of the benefits is (a) a proportionate means of achieving a legitimate aim or (b) for the purpose of preventing or compensating for a disadvantage linked to the protected characteristic. However, save for the protected characteristic of disability, this exception does not apply where the benefit in question is vocational training: *ss 193(9)* and *(10)*.

There are also special rules about charitable instruments that refer to the provision of benefits by reference to 'colour'. By *s 193(4)* if a charitable instrument enables the provision of benefits to persons of a class defined solely by reference to colour, then henceforth the instrument has effect as if that reference were deleted and the instrument applied to persons generally. Where a charitable instrument refers to characteristics other than colour, it has effect as if the reference to colour were ignored. Further, the Charities Commission (or other charity regulator) does not contravene the *Act* only by exercising a function in relation to a charity in a manner which the regulator thinks is expedient in the interests of the charity, having regard to the charitable instrument.

By *s 193(3)* it is not a contravention of the *EqA 2010* for a person who provides supported employment to treat persons who have the same disability (or a disability of a prescribed description) more favourably than those who do not have that disability (or a disability of such a description).

By *s 193(5)* it is not a contravention of the *EqA 2010* for a charity that as of 18 May 2005 required members, or persons wishing to become members, to make a statement which asserts or implies membership or acceptance of a religion or belief to continue to do so. For this purpose, restricting the access by members to a benefit, facility or service to those who make such a statement is to be treated as imposing such a requirement. No new charity can impose such a requirement, however. Nor can a charity that formerly had such a requirement, but ceased to impose it for any period.

By *s 193(7)* it is not a contravention of the *Act* for a service provider, in relation to an activity which is carried on for the purpose of promoting or supporting a charity, to restrict participation in the activity to persons of one sex.

13.11 EXCEPTIONS SPECIFIC TO THE DIFFERENT GROUNDS OF DISCRIMINATION

Exceptions for sex discrimination

(a) *Where communal accommodation is provided*

The *EqA 2010* provides an exception for any act of sex discrimination or gender reassignment discrimination done in relation to the admission of persons to communal accommodation, or the provision of a benefit, facility or service linked to the accommodation (*para 3(1)* of *Sch 23*). 'Communal accommodation' is defined as 'residential accommodation which includes dormitories or other shared sleeping accommodation which for reasons of privacy should be used only by persons of the same sex (*para 3(5)*). It can also include residential accommodation all or part of which should be used only by persons of the same sex because of the nature of the sanitary facilities serving the accommodation (*para 3(6)(c)*). A benefit, facility or service is linked to communal accommodation if it cannot properly and effectively be provided except for those using the accommodation (*para 3(7)(a)*).

For the exception to apply, the accommodation must be managed in a way which is as fair as possible to both men and women (*para 3(2)* and *3(7)(b)*). In determining whether the exception applies, account must be taken of whether and how far it is reasonable to expect that the accommodation should be altered or extended or that further accommodation should be provided, and of the frequency of the demand or need for use of the accommodation by persons of one sex as compared with those of the other (*para 3(3)*). Where the discrimination is on grounds of gender reassignment, account must also be taken of whether and how far the conduct in question is a proportionate means of achieving a legitimate aim (*para 3(4)*).

The provision in the *EqA 2010* is substantially the same as that which applied under *ss 46(3)–(5)* of the *SDA 1975*.

The exception means that if, for example, a company provided a holiday home for its employees but the sleeping arrangements were only suitable for men, then provided that it was only used occasionally and it was impractical to modify it for the use of the women or to build additional accommodation for them, such discrimination may be lawful.

Similarly, if a firm ran a residential training course in northern Scotland and accommodation could only be provided for men and it was fair so to do, failure to make the course available to women would not be unlawful discrimination because the benefit (the residential training course) is linked to the communal accommodation and cannot be properly and effectively provided without it.

Arrangements to compensate for detriment

It should be noted that sex discrimination is only permitted in the above circumstances where such arrangements as are reasonably practicable have been made to compensate for any detriment caused by the discrimination (*EqA 2010, para 3(8)* of *Sch 23*; *SDA 1975, s 46(6)*). For example, training courses run by the ABC Company for a few days in the north of Scotland are not available to women employees because of the unsuitability of the accommodation: the company will *not* have a defence against a claim alleging discrimination unless it can show either that an alternative course had been provided or that, having been considered carefully, it was thought with good reason not to be practicable to provide it.

(b) *Pay and other contractual terms*

For all grounds of discrimination other than sex and maternity and pregnancy, differences in pay and other contractual terms fall to be considered under the general provisions on discrimination. Under the *SDA 1975, ss 6(5)* and *(6)*, however, offering or paying a woman less remuneration than a man was not an act of unlawful discrimination. Instead, it was, if certain conditions were satisfied, unlawful under the *Equal Pay Act 1970* ('*EPA 1970*'). Thus, if a woman was engaged on like work or on work rated as equivalent to that of a man or on work of equal value to that of a man, a woman's contract was modified by the *EPA 1970* (through the mechanism of a statutory implied equality clause) so that she could claim pay and other benefits equal to that which the man received (see Equal Pay (23)). Less favourable treatment in relation to contractual terms was still an act of unlawful discrimination under the *SDA 1975* if the victim was a transsexual (*SDA 1975, s 6(8)*).

The same exclusionary rule applies under the *EqA 2010* with one significant amendment. Differences in the contractual terms of men and women are covered by *ss 64–69* of the *EqA 2010* (which effectively re-enact the provisions of the *EPA 1970* by providing for a statutory implied sex equality clause in all contracts). Then, by virtue of *s 70* the 'ordinary' sex discrimination provisions are disapplied in circumstances where the claim relates to a term of the woman's contract that falls to be modified or included by virtue of the statutory sex equality clause, or would fall to be modified or excluded were it not for the fact that the employer is able to establish a defence of genuine material factor (see **23.10** Equal Pay), or because one of the various statutory exceptions in *Part 2* of *Sch 7* applies. They are also disapplied where the claim relates to contractual pay, but the statutory equality clause has no effect, unless – and this is the significant amendment on the position under the previous legislation – the difference in pay constitutes direct discrimination under *ss 13* or *14* of the *Act* (*s 71*). Complaints of direct discrimination in relation to contractual pay where there is no actual comparator and a hypothetical comparator only is relied on are thus dealt with under the 'ordinary' provision in relation to sex discrimination in *s 13* of the *Act*. All other complaints of sex discrimination in relation to contractual terms must be brought by reference to the sex equality clause in accordance with *ss 64–69* of the *Act*.

A similar exclusionary rule operates in respect of the new maternity equality clause created by the *EqA 2010*: see *ss 72–76* of the *Act* and below **13.11A**.

(c) *Retirement, death and related benefits*

Sex discrimination in relation to death and retirement benefits was partially excluded from the scope of the *SDA 1975* by *s 6(4)*. Instead, such discrimination was dealt with primarily by the *Pensions Act 1995*. *Sections 62* and *64* of the *Pensions Act 1995* implied into the rules of every occupational pension scheme an 'equal treatment rule' which operated in the same way as the more familiar 'equality clause' in the *Equal Pay Act 1970* (cf **13.35** below **23.5** EQUAL PAY). The partial exclusion under *SDA 1975, s 6(4)* applied to discrimination taking the following forms:

(i)   discrimination in the terms on which the woman is offered employment;

(ii)   discrimination in the way the woman is afforded access to benefits etc;

(iii)   discriminatory dismissals; and

(iv)   discriminatory subjection to any other detriment.

Where a person discriminated against a woman in one of those respects in relation to her membership of, or rights under, an occupational pension scheme, that discrimination would not be unlawful where, if provision had been made for that discrimination in the terms of the scheme, that term would have been compliant with the equal treatment rule in the *Pensions Act 1995*.

Although the provisions of the *Pensions Act 1995* and the *SDA 1975* have been brought together in the *EqA 2010*, there is still a similar division made between the general provisions prohibiting discrimination in relation to pensions and those prohibiting sex and maternity discrimination in relation to pensions. *Sections 61(1)* and *(3)* of the EqA 2010 provide that 'an occupational pension scheme must be taken to include a non-discrimination rule' and that the scheme will take effect 'subject to' that rule (see generally **13.35** below). However, where the equality rules apply (or would apply but for the exceptions in *Part 2* of *Sch 7*), the non-discrimination rule does not: *s 61(10)*. Thus, the general non-discrimination rule only applies to occupational pension schemes where the sex equality rule under *s 67* or the maternity equality rule under *s 75* does not.

By virtue of *para 5 of Part 2 of Sch 7* to the *EqA 2010*, a difference between men and women in relation to the calculation of employer's pension contributions or determination of benefits payable under the scheme is permitted if the difference results from the application of actuarial factors which differ for men and women (for example because of different life expectancies for men and women).

There are further specific temporal exclusions from the scope of the sex equality rule as it applies to pensions. By *s 67(9)*, the sex equality rule, so far as relating to the terms on which persons become members of an occupational pension scheme, does not have effect in relation to pensionable service before 8 April 1976 and by *s 67(10)* the sex equality rule, so far as relating to the terms on which members of an occupational pension scheme are treated, does not have effect in relation to pensionable service before 17 May 1990. This reflects the decisions in *Barber v Guardian Royal Exchange Assurance Group*: C-262/88 [1990] IRLR 240, [1990] ICR 616 and *Defrenne v Sabena*: C-43/75 [1981] 1 All ER 122, [1976] ICR 547. The CJEU held in *Ministry of Justice v O'Brien* C-432/17 [2019] 1 CMLR 40, [2019] ICR 505, [2019] IRLR 185 that part-time judges could, with effect from the coming into force of the *Part-Time Workers Regulations* on 7 April 2000, claim benefits equivalent to full-time judges with the same length of service, including periods of service prior to the coming into force of those Regulations. See further **23.16** EQUAL PAY.

By *s 69(4)* it is a defence to a claim that an occupational pension scheme breaches a sex equality rule for the trustees or managers to show that the difference between the treatment of men and women under the scheme is because of a material factor that is not the difference of sex. This is the same as the defence that is available to equal pay claims generally and is dealt with in **23.11–23.12** EQUAL PAY.

Note that it is unlawful to apply different compulsory retirement ages to men and women.

A fuller account of the equal opportunities issues relating to death or retirement benefits is set out in **23.15** EQUAL PAY and see also RETIREMENT (**43**). See also further below **13.35**.

(d) *Members of the armed forces*

Broadly speaking, since 1 October 1997, the equality legislation has applied to service in the armed forces as it does to other employment: cf the *Sex Discrimination (Complaints to Employment Tribunals) (Armed Forces) Regulations 1997 (SI 1997/2163)*, the *Race Relations (Complaints to Employment Tribunals) (Armed Forces) Regulations 1997 (SI 1997/2161)*; *RBR 2003, reg 36*; *SOR 2003, reg 36*; and see below **13.36**.

Under the *EqA 2010* there is a single exception for discrimination against women and transsexuals for service in the armed forces. The exception applies if it can be shown that the discrimination is a proportionate means of ensuring the combat effectiveness of the armed forces (*para 4, Sch 9*).

A similar exception for any act done 'for the purpose of ensuring the combat effectiveness of the armed forces' applied under the *SDA 1975, s 85(4)*. This was inserted into the *SDA 1975* by the *Sex Discrimination Act 1975 (Application to Armed Forces, etc) Regulations 1994 (SI 1994/3276)*. Its introduction raised a question as to whether the provisions of the *SDA 1975* complied with the *Equal Treatment Directive (Directive 76/207/EEC)*. The exemption was relied upon by the Army Board in *Sirdar v Army Board*: C-273/97 [2000] IRLR 47, [2000] ICR 130. A woman who had applied to work as a chef in the Royal Marines was refused a transfer on the grounds that chefs were expected, where necessary, to be capable of fighting as a member of a commando unit. The complainant argued that *SDA 1975, s 85(4)* was contrary to the *Directive 76/207/EEC*. The matter was referred to the European court, which decided that whilst it was true that there was no Treaty right to derogate from equality legislation on grounds of national security, *art 2(2)* of the *ETD* nevertheless allowed the Army Board to refuse the complainant her transfer. *Article 2(2)* provides that *Directive 76/207/EEC* is 'without prejudice to the right of Member States to exclude from [the Directive's] field of application those occupational activities and, where appropriate, the training leading thereto, for which, by reason of their nature or the context in which they are carried out, the sex of the worker constitutes a determining factor'. In effect, the CJEU seems to have decided that being male is a genuine occupational requirement for a Royal Marine.

Prior to 1 October 2005, there was another exception available under the *SDA 1975* for sex discrimination in admission to the Army Cadet Force, Air Training Corps, Sea Cadet Corps, Combined Cadet Force, or any other cadet training corps for the time being administered by the Ministry of Defence was not unlawful (*SDA 1975, s 85(5)*). However, this was deleted by *reg 34* of the *Sex Discrimination Regulations 2005*.

(e) *Police officers*

Discrimination in height requirements and uniform or uniform allowances, which would otherwise constitute sex discrimination, was specifically provided to be lawful in the employment of police constables under the *SDA 1975, ss 17(2), (3)*.

This exception is not included in the *EqA 2010*. Such discrimination will only be lawful if it falls within the general exception for occupational requirements: see above **13.2**.

See also **14.2** Discrimination and Equal Opportunities **III** for the exclusion from the jurisdiction of employment tribunals of claims against police disciplinary panels.

(f) *Prison officers*

Under the *SDA 1975* discrimination was lawful between male and female prison officers as to requirements relating to height (*SDA 1975, s 18(1)*). Men could be governors of women's prisons (*SDA 1975, s 18(2)*).

These exceptions are not included in the *EqA 2010*. Such discrimination will only be lawful if it falls within the general exception for occupational requirements: see above **13.2**.

(g) *Ministers of religion*

Generally speaking, ministers of religion will be regarded as employees under employment legislation: see *Percy v Board of National Mission of the Church of Scotland* [2005] UKHL 73, [2006] IRLR 195, [2006] ICR 134, although cf *New Testament Church of God v Stewart* [2007] EWCA Civ 1004, [2008] IRLR 134, [2008] ICR 282 and *Moore v President of the Methodist Conference* [2013] UKSC 29, [2013] IRLR 646. However, prior to 1 October 2005, there was an exception under the *SDA 1975* for employment for the purposes of an organised religion where a particular post-holder was required to be either male or female (or required not to be a transsexual) in order to comply with the doctrines of the religion or to avoid offending the religious susceptibilities of a significant number of its followers (*SDA 1975, ss 19(1), (3), (4)*). That exemption was preserved, but with some changes, by *reg 20* of the *Sex Discrimination Regulations 2005* (which amended *SDA 1975, s 19* with effect from 1 October 2005). The amended version of *s 19* provided an exemption for employment for purposes of an organised religion where a requirement was applied that:

(a)   the employee be of a particular sex;

(b)   the employee not be undergoing or have undergone gender reassignment;

(c)   the employee not be married, or not be a civil partner;

(d)   the employee not have a living former spouse or civil partner (or that the employee's spouse or civil partner not have a living former spouse or civil partner); or

(e)   as to how the person, or the person's spouse or civil partner has at any time ceased to be married or ceased to be a civil partner.

The exemption only applied if the requirement in question was applied either so as to comply with the doctrines of the religion or because of the nature of the employment and context in which it is carried out, so as to avoid conflicting with the strongly-held religious convictions of a significant number of the religion's followers.

For the current law, see above **13.2**, **13.3** and **13.7**.

(h) *Sports and competitions*

Section 44 excluded from the scope of the *SDA 1975* any act that related to participation as a competitor in a sport, game or other competitive activity, provided that the activity had been confined to competitors of one sex because the physical strength, stamina or physique of the average woman puts her at a disadvantage to the average man in carrying out that activity.

A similar exception applies under *s 195* of the *EqA 2010*: see above **13.3**.

(i) *Pregnancy and maternity discrimination*

Discrimination against women for pregnancy or maternity-related reasons was for some time dealt with as a type of sex discrimination. Specific provisions dealing with maternity and pregnancy discrimination were then introduced from 1 October 2005 and this separate provision is continued in the *EqA 2010* (see generally **12.30–12.32** Discrimination and Equal Opportunities – I). However, under the predecessor legislation discrimination in relation to pay on grounds of maternity or pregnancy was, as with sex discrimination in relation to all contractual terms, dealt with under the *EPA 1970* by way of a statutory equality clause rather than under the *SDA 1975* (see generally **23.13** Equal Pay). The same division is maintained in the *EqA 2010*.

Section 18(7) provides (in short) that where treatment would constitute pregnancy or maternity discrimination as defined in that section, then it cannot constitute direct sex discrimination under *s 13* of the *EqA 2010*. Where pregnancy-related unfavourable treatment does not fall within pregnancy or maternity discrimination as defined in *s 18* however (eg because the treatment occurs outside what the *Act* terms the 'protected period' of ordinary or additional maternity leave) a claim may still be dealt with as a claim of sex discrimination: see eg *Mayr v Backerei und Konditorei Gerhard Flockner OHG*: C-506/06 [2008] IRLR 387.

Whilst an employee is absent from work on maternity leave, an employer may lawfully cease paying her anything other than pay to which she is entitled by statute or contract as a result of being pregnant or on maternity leave: *EqA 2010, Sch 9, Part 3, para 17*. However, a woman remains entitled to any bonus in respect of a period when she is on compulsory maternity leave *(para 17(2)(c))*. She also remains entitled to be paid in accordance with the statutory maternity equality clause in *ss 73* and *74* of the *EqA 2010* and to be treated for the purposes of any occupational pension scheme in accordance with the statutory maternity equality rule in *s 75* of the *EqA 2010* (see further below (b)).

The statutory maternity equality clause (broadly speaking) requires a woman who is paid during maternity leave by reference to her normal salary to receive any salary increases (proportionately adjusted) as she would have received if she were working, and likewise to be paid any bonus (proportionately adjusted where appropriate) (see **23.13** Equal Pay for details of the effect of the maternity equality clause). By *s 76* it is then provided that where a term of a woman's employment relates to pay, no complaint of sex or pregnancy or maternity discrimination can be made in relation to it. Rather, the claim must be brought as an 'equal pay' claim based on the maternity equality clause under *ss 73* and *74*.

(j) *Special treatment in connection with pregnancy or child birth*

Section 13(6)(b) of the *EqA 2010* and *para 2* of *Part 1* of *Schedule 7* to the *EqA 2010* exclude from the provisions prohibiting (respectively) direct sex discrimination and unequal pay for men and women special treatment afforded to women in connection with pregnancy or child birth. In other words, although such treatment could constitute direct discrimination against men, no complaint may be brought about it under the *Act*. See further above **13.10(c)**.

(k) *Pay*

Prior to the coming into force of the *EqA 2010*, sex discrimination in relation to contractual terms was 'carved out' of the *Sex Discrimination Act 1975 ('SDA 1975')* by *s 6(5)* and *(6)* and instead covered by the *EqPA 1970*. *EqA 2010* consolidates the provisions previously found in the *EqPA 1970* and the *SDA 1975* into a single anti-discrimination statute alongside other aspects of discrimination law. However, the same separation between discrimination in relation to pay and discrimination in relation to other matters is maintained in the *EqA 2010* – with one important change. Differences in the contractual terms of men and women are covered by *ss 64–69* of the *EqA 2010* (which effectively re-enact the provisions of the EqPA 1970 by providing for a statutory implied sex equality clause in all contracts): see generally EQUAL PAY **(23)**. Then, by virtue of s 70 the 'ordinary' sex discrimination provisions are disapplied in circumstances where the claim relates to a term of the woman's contract that falls to be modified or included by virtue of the statutory sex equality clause, or would fall to be modified or excluded were it not for the fact that the employer is able to establish a defence of genuine material factor, or because one of the various statutory exceptions in *Part 2* of *Sch 7* applies. A claimant cannot succeed on both a discrimination and an equal pay claim in such cases: *BMC Software Ltd v Shaikh* [2017] IRLR 1074 (overruled on other grounds: [2019] EWCA Civ 267). As noted by the EAT in that case, the 'ordinary' sex discrimination provisions are also disapplied where the claim relates to contractual pay, but the statutory equality clause has no effect, unless – and this is the significant change on the position under the previous legislation - the difference in pay constitutes direct discrimination under *ss 13* or *14* of the *Act* (*s 71*). Complaints of direct discrimination in relation to contractual pay where there is no actual comparator and a hypothetical comparator only is relied on are thus dealt with under the 'ordinary' provision in relation to sex discrimination in *s 13* of the *Act* (see Discrimination and Equal Opportunities – I (12)). All other complaints of sex discrimination in relation to contractual terms must be brought by reference to the sex equality clause in accordance with ss 64–69 of the Act applying the statutory provisions and case law discussed in Equal Pay (23). Note that in *BMC Software Ltd v Shaikh* [2017] IRLR 1074 (UKEAT/0092/16/DM) (overruled on other grounds: [2019] EWCA Civ 267), Judge Hand considered it arguable that the effect of *EqA 2010, s 70* was to preclude a complaint of constructive discriminatory dismissal where the repudiatory conduct relied upon was alleged to be a breach of the sex equality clause.

(l) *Occupational pensions*

As with terms of a woman's employment related to pay, the right to equal treatment in respect of occupational pension schemes was 'carved out' of the *SDA 1975* and dealt with separately under the *Pensions Act 1995* (see generally **23.18** Equal Pay and **13.35** below). The same division is maintained in the *EqA 2010*. Thus *EqA 2010, s 75* creates a maternity equality rule that applies to all occupational pension schemes requiring them to treat time on maternity leave in the same way as time at work (save that any contributions may be reduced proportionate to any reduction in the pay that the woman receives during maternity leave). By *s 76* where a complaint concerns a matter that is covered by the maternity equality rule, no complaint of sex or pregnancy or maternity discrimination can be made in relation to it. Rather, the claim must be brought as an 'equal pay' claim based on the maternity equality rule under *s 75*.

13.12 Exceptions for race discrimination

(a) *Skills to be exercised outside Great Britain*

The predecessor legislation applied to training a person in skills intended to be exercised wholly outside Great Britain as it did to training for skills to be exercised in Great Britain, with one exception: discrimination on grounds of colour and nationality in the provision of such training fell outside the scope of the legislation: *RRA 1976, s 6*, as amended by the *Race Relations Act 1976 (Amendment) Regulations 2003 (SI 2003/1626)*).

This exception does not apply under the *EqA 2010*. There is, however, an exception (in *para 4* of *Sch 23* to the *EqA 2010*) for nationality discrimination in the provision of training to non-EEA residents where the trainer thinks that the non-resident does not intend to exercise in Great Britain skills obtained as a result.

(b) *Private household*

The predecessor legislation applied to employment for the purposes of a private household as it did to businesses, with one exception: discrimination on grounds of colour and nationality in relation to employment for the purposes of a private household was excluded from the scope of the *RRA 1976* by *s 4(3)*. The question was whether the employment is for the purposes of a private household 'to a substantial degree'. Thus, an applicant for a job as a chauffeur whose primary task was to drive a car for a company chairman could bring a complaint of racial discrimination (*Heron Corpn Ltd v Commis* [1980] ICR 713).

This exception is not available under the *EqA 2010*.

(c) *Seamen recruited abroad*

Under the predecessor legislation, seamen (whether employees or contract workers) recruited abroad to work on any ship could lawfully be discriminated against on grounds of their nationality unless their work concerned exploration of the sea bed or subsoil (or the exploitation of their natural resources) on the continental shelf, save for those parts of the continental shelf to which the law of Northern Ireland applied (*RRA 1976, ss 9(1), (3)*). If the ground for the discrimination is any of the other 'racial grounds' (for which see **12.20**

DISCRIMINATION AND EQUAL OPPORTUNITIES – I) they could lawfully be discriminated against in relation to their pay but not otherwise. 'Pay' included retirement or death benefits (*RRA 1976, s 9(5)*, as amended by the *Race Relations Act 1976 (Amendment) Regulations 2003 (SI 2003/1626)*).

This exception is not available under the *EqA 2010*.

(d) *Sports and competitions*

Discrimination on the basis of a person's nationality, place of birth, or length of time for which he had been resident in a particular area or place is not unlawful if it is done in selecting one or more persons to represent a country, place or area or related association, in a sport or game or other activity of a competitive nature, or if it consists of doing anything in pursuance of the rules of a competition so far as relating to eligibility to compete in a sport or game or other such activity: *EqA 2010, ss 195(5)* and *(6)*. A similar exception applied under the predecessor legislation: *RRA 1976, s 39*.

13.13 Exception for protection of Sikhs from discrimination in connection with requirements as to wearing of safety helmets

Under *s 11(1)* of the *Employment Act 1989* (*EA 1989*), a Sikh is generally exempt from any legal requirement to wear safety helmets in workplaces, provided that he is wearing a turban. The exemption does not apply to a Sikh who works, or is training to work, in an occupation that involves (to any extent) providing an urgent response to fire, riot or other hazardous situations, and is at the workplace to provide such a response in circumstances where the wearing of a safety helmet is necessary to protect the Sikh from a risk of injury, or to receive training in how to provide such a response in circumstances of that kind (*EA 1989, s 11(6A)*, as inserted by *Deregulation Act 2015, s 6*). It also does not apply to a Sikh who is a member of HM forces or a person providing support to HM forces and who is at the workplace to take part in a military operation in circumstances where the wearing of a safety helmet is necessary to protect the Sikh from a risk of injury, or to receive training in how to take part in such an operation in circumstances of that kind (*s 11(6B)*).

Where the Sikh turban/safety helmet exemption applies, then no discrimination claim can be brought in relation to that difference in treatment. Thus, where:

(a)   any person applies to a Sikh any provision, criterion or practice relating to the wearing by him of a safety helmet while he is at a workplace; and

(b)   at the time when he so applies the provision, criterion or practice that person has no reasonable grounds for believing that the Sikh would not wear a turban at all times when at such a workplace,

the provision, criterion or practice is taken to be one which cannot be shown to be a proportionate means of achieving a legitimate aim (*Employment Act 1989, s 12*, as amended). It follows that the act of indirect discrimination will not be justified (see **13.9** above).

Any special treatment afforded to a Sikh in consequence of the Sikh turban/safety helmet exemption is not to be regarded as giving rise, in relation to any other person, to any direct discrimination (*EA 1989, s 12(2)*).

13.14 Exception for sexual orientation discrimination: benefits dependent on marital or civil partnership status

Any benefit to which access is dependent on marital status was, prior to the coming into force of the *Marriage (Same-Sex Couples) Act 2013* on 13 March 2014, likely to be indirectly discriminatory against homosexuals as homosexuals were not permitted to marry under national law, but only to become civil partners under the *Civil Partnership Act 2004* (the *CPA 2004*). It was also likely to be direct discrimination: see *Hall v Bull* [2013] UKSC 73, [2013] All ER (D) 307 (Nov). Prior to 5 December 2005, however, *reg 25* of the *SOR 2003* provided expressly that nothing in the *SOR 2003* should make it unlawful for an employer to prevent or restrict access to a benefit by reference to marital status. It was argued in *R (Amicus-MSF) v Secretary of State for Trade and Industry* [2004] EWHC 860 (Admin), [2004] IRLR 430 that *reg 25* was incompatible with the governing European *Directive 2000/78/EC*). Richards J held that *reg 25* was compatible because it reflected the limitation in *Recital 2* of the *Directive* which says that 'this *Directive* is without prejudice to national laws on marital status and the benefits dependent thereon'.

The provision was then amended with effect from 5 December 2005 to reflect the coming into force of the *CPA 2004*. It provided for a complete exclusion from the SOR 2003 'for anything which prevents or restricts access to a benefit by reference to marital status where the right to the benefit accrued or the benefit is payable in respect of periods of service prior to the coming into force of the *Civil Partnership Act 2004*' (ie prior to 5 December 2005). Under the *EqA 2010* the exception in *reg 25* of the *SOR 2003* (as amended) was preserved by *para 18* of *Sch 9* to the *EqA 2010*. It was amended again by the *Marriage (Same-Sex Couples) Act 2013* so as to preserve the status quo regarding benefits notwithstanding the newly increased scope of marriage. Where the right to the benefit accrues, or the benefit is payable, after 5 December 2005, however, an employer is not permitted to make any distinction between married persons and civil partners, or between male-female married persons and same-sex married persons. *Section 23(3)* of the *EqA 2010* further makes explicit that for the purposes of identifying a comparator under the Act there is to be taken to be no material difference between marriage and civil partnership. An employer may still, however, make a particular benefit available to, say, married persons and civil partners, but withhold the benefit from other employees, including those in long-term heterosexual or homosexual relationships: see *para 18(2)* of *Sch 9* to the *EqA 2010*.

The decision of the CJEU in *Maruko v Versorgungsanstalt der deutschen Bühnen*: C-267/06 [2008] IRLR 450 showed that the amendment to the *SOR 2003* effected on 5 December 2005 was in fact required under EC law in any event. (In *Maruko* the CJEU held that it was unlawful for Germany to withhold a widower's pension from the widower of a civil partner, where it would have been payable to a married partner.) The *Maruko* judgment, and the subsequent judgment in *Jurgen Römer v Freie und Hansestadt Hamburg*: C-147/08 [2011] All ER (D) 212 (May), provided an indication, however, that under EU law it may not be permissible for UK legislation to limit the retrospective effect of the amendment made on 5 December 2005. In *Walker v Innospec Ltd* [2017] UKSC 47, [2017] ICR 1077 the Supreme Court upheld the decision of the Tribunal (reversing the EAT and the Court of Appeal) that a provision of a pension scheme that prevented the civil partner of a member from being entitled to the same benefit as the married partner of a member on the member's death breached the non-discrimination rule, even though the benefit had accrued as a result of a period of pensionable service that was wholly prior both to the coming into force of the *CPA 2004* on 5 December 2005 and the coming into force of the *SOR 2003* in December 2003. Although the Supreme Court upheld the conventional understanding that pensions are deferred pay, accrued during service, the Supreme Court considered that the position regarding survivor's benefits was different since the right to a survivor's benefit accrued regardless of the identity of the survivor and so what mattered was whether the refusal to pay the survivor's benefit was (or would be) discriminatory at the time of payment, not what the law was at the time that the entitlement to the pension was accrued through service.

Employers should note that 'civil partnership' is defined in detail in the *CPA 2004*. It includes not only those couples who have registered their partnership in the UK since the coming into force of that *Act*, but also those couples who have registered their partnership overseas whether before or after the coming into force of the *CPA 2004*. A large number of partnerships registered overseas are automatically to be recognised as 'civil partnerships' under the *CPA 2004*. These are listed in Sch 20 to the Act. Other partnerships may be recognised if the conditions in *ss 212* to *218* of the *CPA 2004* (readers are referred to the text of the *Act*). Where a 'civil partnership' is recognised under the *CPA 2004*, it must also be recognised by employers for the purposes of *reg 25* of the *SOR 2003* and *para 18* of *Sch 9* to the *EqA 2010*. Following the decision of the Supreme Court in *R (Steinfield) v Secretary of State for International Development* [2018] UKSC 32, [2018] 3 WLR 415 opposite sex couples are now permitted to enter civil partnerships.

13.15 Exceptions for age discrimination

(a) Retirement

Prior to 6 April 2011 there was an exception for retirement in the *AR 2006* as set out below. Under the *EqA 2010*, the exception for retirement dismissals was preserved until 6 April 2011 so that at or over the age of 65 if retirement was the reason for the dismissal the dismissal was not unlawful by virtue of *Part 10* of the *Employment Rights Act 1996* (*para 8, Part 2, Sch 9*). Further, it was not unlawful for an employer to discriminate against employees who were close to retirement in certain respects. In particular, under *para 9* of *Part 2* of *Sch 9* to *EqA 2010*, it was not unlawful for an employer to refuse to offer employment to an employee who was, or would be before the end of six months beginning with the date on which the application for employment had to be made, aged over 65, or, where this is higher, the normal retirement age for the employment concerned. These exceptions no longer apply. Since 6 April 2011 the *Employment Equality (Repeal of Retirement Age Provisions) Regulations 2011 (SI 2011/1069)* have phased out the designated retirement age in *reg 30* of the *AR 2006* so that (at the latest from October 2012) these exceptions are no longer available and whether or not retirements and related provisions are justified falls to be considered in accordance with the standard principles for justifying direct age discrimination. See **13.9** above for discussion of justification of retirement and related provisions under the general discrimination principles. See **43.3** RETIREMENT for the current law on retirement.

Prior to 6 April 2011, *reg 30(2)* of *AR 2006* provided that nothing in *Parts 2* or *3* of *AR 2006* 'shall render unlawful the dismissal of a person to whom this regulation applies at or over the age of 65 where the reason for the dismissal is retirement'. This exception, often dubbed the 'National Default Retirement Age' or 'NDRA', only applied to the dismissal of employees in the narrower sense of those employed on a contract of employment. There was no maximum age exemption for enforced retirement in other cases. An important example is that of partners, office holders and workers who are not employees. In such cases, any enforced retirement is unlawful unless the action can be justified. This can be illustrated by two recent decisions. In *Seldon v Clarkson Wright & Jakes* [2012] UKSC 16, [2012] IRLR 590, [2012] ICR 716, the claimant was an equity partner in a solicitors' firm. As he was not an employee, the respondent's only defence to a compulsory retirement age of 65 was objective justification. This defence succeeded before the Tribunal, but the EAT held that retirement at 65 was not justified by the assumption that performance would decline around that age – an older age could have been chosen. The CA upheld the EAT's decision, but observed that once it was accepted (as it was) that retirement had a legitimate aim, it was difficult to see how selection of the age of 65 was not justified, particularly as that was still at that stage the national default retirement age for employees. The SC, however, held that the Tribunal had taken the wrong approach to considering whether or not a retirement age of 65 was justified and accordingly remitted the matter. On remission, the Tribunal concluded that 65 was justified as a retirement age and the EAT upheld that decision: [2014] IRLR 748, [2014] ICR 1275. See further above **13.9** for the approach to be taken to considering whether or not direct age discrimination (including the application of retirement ages) is justified. For further examples of when retirement ages may or may not be justified see **13.9** above.

Whether or not the reason for dismissal was retirement depended on the application of specific criteria set out in detailed provisions of *AR 2006*. See **43.3** R*ETIREMENT*.

'Heyday', part of Age Concern, brought judicial review proceedings challenging the legality of *AR 2006* on the ground that the blanket exception for retirement over 65 did not properly transpose the *Equality Directive*. The Administrative Court referred the matter to the CJEU for a preliminary ruling. The CJEU held that *reg 30* was not necessarily unlawful but that it would be for the national court to determine whether the blanket exception for those dismissed at or over the age of 65 was justified. On its return to the Administrative Court (*R (on the application of Age UK) v Secretary of State for Business, Innovation & Skills* [2009] IRLR 1017, [2010] ICR 260), Blake J held that the NDRA was based upon a social policy aim of certainty, clarity and maintaining confidence in the labour market and that it was proportionate for there to be such a blanket exception. The judge further held that the choice of age of 65 was within the margin of appreciation when it was adopted in 2006 but that the conclusion might have been different had there been no suggestion of an upcoming government review. Blake J also indicated that he did not presently see how 65 could remain as the appropriate age after that review.

See **43.3** R*ETIREMENT* for the current law on retirement.

(b) National minimum wage

The National Minimum Wage ('NMW') legislation allows for lower sums to be paid to younger workers. *Para 11* of *Part 2* of *Schedule 9* to the *EqA 2010* (formerly *reg 31* of *AR 2006*) allows employers to retain different pay between the bands but only if the younger workers are being paid less than the adult NMW. Surprisingly, if the employer pays the younger workers more than the adult NMW, but less than older employees, this will require objective justification.

See also *para 12* of *Part 2* in relation to apprentices.

(c) Certain benefits based on length of service

Para 10 of *Part 2* of *Schedule 9* to the *EqA 2010* provides an exception for benefits, facilities or services based on length of service. The exception applies where a person ('A'), in relation to the provision of a benefit, facility or service, puts a worker ('B') at a disadvantage when compared to another worker ('C') if and so far as the disadvantage is because B has a shorter period of service than C (*para 10(1)*). A similar exception applied under the predecessor legislation: see *reg 32* of the *AR 2006*.

The exception is absolute where B's length of service does not exceed five years. Where B's length of service is longer than five years, it must reasonably appear to A that the way in which the criterion of length of service is used fulfils a business need. In the predecessor legislation examples of the types of business need that might be relied upon were given as encouraging loyalty or motivation, or rewarding experience (*reg 32(2), AR 2006*). No examples are given in the *EqA 2010* but such business needs will continue to be acceptable in principle.

For the purposes of this exception, the period of service may be counted from the start of B's employment with A, or from his employment above a particular level (the level being assessed by reference to the demands made on B and set at that which A reasonably regards as appropriate for the purposes of this exception): *para 10(3)*. The period of employment in question is the person's period of continuous employment as deemed by *s 218* of the *ERA 1996* or any other enactment (*para 10(6)* and see C*ONTINUOUS* E*MPLOYMENT* (7)).

The period of service must be based on the number of weeks during the whole or part of which B has worked for A (*para 10(4)*), but for that purpose A may, so far as reasonable, discount periods of absence and 'periods that A reasonably regards as related to periods of absence' (*para 10(5)*). Note that in the predecessor legislation specific reference was made in connection with treatment of periods of absence to a requirement that, in deciding whether it is reasonable for an employer to treat a period of absence in a particular way, regard must be had to the way in which other workers' similar absences have been treated (*AR 2006, reg 32(4)(b)*). Further, the reference to 'periods that A reasonably regards as related to periods of absence' was not included in the *AR 2006*, which instead included the more specific reference to 'any period during which the worker was present at work where that preceded a period of absence and, in all the circumstances including the length of the absence, the reason for the absence, its effect on the worker's ability to discharge his duties, and the way in which other workers are treated, it is reasonable for the period to be discounted' (*AR 2006, reg 32(4)(c)*). The provision in the *EqA 2010* is evidently somewhat broader, not being limited to periods that precede periods of absence, but it is difficult to envisage the circumstances in which resort may be had to this part of the exception.

Note that the exception does not apply to benefits, facilities or services that are provided only as a result of a person ceasing to work, whether through ill health, redundancy, retirement or other termination: *para 10(7)*.

In *Rolls Royce Plc v Unite the Union* [2009] EWCA Civ 387, [2009] IRLR 576, the Court of Appeal held that use of a length of service criterion in assessing employees for redundancy was capable of constituting 'the award of any benefit' within the meaning of *reg 32(1)* of the *AR 2006*. The majority further held that whether or not the employer had reasonably concluded at the time that the use of the length of service criterion fulfilled a business need of its undertaking for the purposes of *reg 32(2)* was to be assessed objectively and it did not matter that the employer had subsequently decided that the use of the length of service criterion did not fulfil a business need of its undertaking.

(d) Enhanced redundancy benefits

Para 13 of *Part 2* of *Schedule 9* to *EqA 2010* makes provision for employers to provide 'qualifying employees' with enhanced redundancy payments. Similar provision was made previously by *reg 33* of *AR 2006*.

The exception allows employers to give enhanced redundancy payments only to those 'qualifying employees' who are entitled to a redundancy payment by virtue of *ERA 1996, s 135*, or who would be so entitled but do not have the two year qualifying period, or to an employee who agrees to the termination of his employment in circumstances where, had he been dismissed, he would have fallen into one of the former two categories (*para 13(3)*).

There are rules as to how the amounts must be calculated. The amount must be calculated as in the relevant provisions of the *ERA 1996* (*ss 162(1)–(3)*). However, in making the calculation, the employer may treat a week's pay as not being subject to a maximum amount, and/or multiply the appropriate amount allowed for each year of employment by a figure of more than one (*para 13(5)*). Having made the calculation, the employer may also increase the amount calculated by multiplying it by a figure of more than one (*para 13(6)*).

Where an enhanced redundancy scheme does not fall within this exception, it is potentially discriminatory and will fall to be justified in the usual way. For examples of this, see *MacCulloch* and *Loxley* above. See also *Lockwood v Department of Work and Pensions* [2013] EWCA Civ 1195, [2013] IRLR 941, [2014] ICR 1257 in which redundancy payments under the Civil Service Compensation Scheme varying based on age depending on whether the individual was under or over the age of 35 were held to be justified in the light of statistical evidence produced by the employer as to the speed with which differing age groups could find alternative employment. Compare, however, *Heron v Sefton Metropolitan Borough Council* [2014] EqLR 130 where the application by the local authority of the provisions of the Civil Service Compensation Scheme which provide for enhanced redundancy payments made to employees over normal pension age to be subject to a cap not applied to employees below normal pension age was held to be unjustified direct age discrimination and compare

Smith v Ministry of Justice (UKEAT/0308/12/RN, UKEAT/0309/12/RN) (where the EAT held that it had been impermissible for the Tribunal to find that the provisions were justified solely by reference to the difference in ages of the employees and remitted that matter to the Tribunal for further consideration).

(e) Provision of life assurance cover to retired workers

Regulation 34 of *AR 2006* provided an exception for the provision of life assurance to retired workers. Where an employer arranged for workers to be provided with life assurance after their early retirement on grounds of ill health, it was not unlawful to arrange for such cover to cease when the workers reached a normal retirement age, if one existed, or age 65, where there was no retirement age (*reg 34(1)*).

'Normal retirement age' meant the age at which workers in the undertaking who held the same kind of position as the worker held at the time of his retirement were normally required to retire (*reg 34(2)*).

Similar provision was made in *para 14* of *Part 2* of *Schedule 9* of *EqA 2010*. However, this was repealed by the *Employment Equality (Repeal of Retirement Age Provisions) Regulations 2011 (SI 2011/1069), reg 2(3)* with effect from 6 April 2011.

(f) Child care

Paragraph 15 of *Part 2* of *Schedule 9* to *EqA 2010* provides that it is not unlawful age discrimination in a number of respects for a person to make arrangements for or to facilitate the provision of care for children of a particular age group. (Otherwise, this might give rise to a claim for 'associative discrimination', ie where a person is discriminated against because of someone else's age: see Discrimination And Equal Opportunities – I at **12.25**.) Facilitating the provision of care for a child includes paying for some or all of the cost of the provision, helping a parent to find a suitable person to provide care for the child, and enabling a parent to spend more time providing care or otherwise assisting the parent with respect to the care that they provide (*para 15(3)*). A 'child' is defined to be a person who has not attained the age of 17 (*para 15(3)*) and care includes supervision (*para 15(4)*).

There was no similar provision in *AR 2006*.

(g) Occupational pension schemes

The *AR 2006* provided a number of exceptions for age discrimination in relation to occupational pension schemes (in *Sch 2*). The *EqA 2010* does not itself contain any exceptions, but provides for exceptions to be set out in subordinate legislation. A Minister of the Crown may by order (following consultation) provide that it is not an age contravention for an employer or for the trustees and managers of an occupational pension scheme to use certain specified practices in relation to contributions to personal pension schemes (*para 16* of *Part 2* of *Schedule 9* to *EqA 2010* and *s 61(8)*).

The *Equality Act (Age Exceptions for Pension Schemes) 2010 Order (SI 2010/2133)* (as amended) made under that enabling power makes extensive and detailed provision for exceptions from the *EqA 2010* for certain practices in relation to pension schemes. See below **13.35**.

(h) Sport and other competitive activities

Section 195(7) of the *EqA 2010* provides an exception from the age discrimination provisions for participation in a competitive 'age-banded activity'. An 'age-banded activity' is a 'sport, game or other activity of a competitive nature in circumstances in which the physical or mental strength, agility, stamina, physique, mobility, maturity or manual dexterity of average persons of a particular age group would put them at a disadvantage compared to average persons of another age group as competitors in events involving the activity' (*EqA 2010, s 195(8)*). Discrimination in relation to such activities is permitted where it is 'necessary to secure in relation to the activity fair competition or the safety of competitors', or 'to comply with the rules of a national or international competition' or 'to increase participation in that activity' (*EqA 2010, s 195(7)*).

(i) Armed forces

Like the *AR 2006*, the *EqA 2010* does not apply to discrimination on grounds of age in service in the armed forces: *para 4 of Part 1 of Sch 9*. In *Child Soldiers International v Secretary of State for Defence* [2015] EWHC 2183 (Admin), [2015] All ER (D) 305 (Jul), the High Court determined that this exception was lawful and compatible with the governing *Framework Directive 2000/78/EC*. The context was a judicial review concerning the army's practice of requiring those recruited on their 16th birthday to serve six years before transfer to the reserves, while those recruited at 18 need only serve four years.

13.16 Exceptions for disability discrimination

(a) Armed forces

Paragraph 4(3) of *Schedule 9* to *EqA 2010* provides an exemption from the prohibition on disability discrimination in respect of service in the armed forces. The similar exemption for age discrimination in the armed forces was held by the High *Child Soldiers International v Secretary of State for Defence* [2015] EWHC 2183 (Admin), [2015] All ER (D) 305 (Jul) to be lawful and compatible with *art 3(4)* of the governing *Framework Directive 2000/78/EC*. It is likely that the same result would be reached if the disability discrimination exemption were to be considered.

A similar exemption applied under the predecessor legislation for those serving in the naval, military or air forces of the Crown (*DDA 1995, s 64(7)*).

(b) Exemption for small businesses

At one time small businesses were exempt from the *DDA 1995*. That exemption was repealed with effect from 1 October 2004 by *reg 6* of the *DDA 1995 (Amendment Regulations) 2004*.

(c) Charities

Any act done by a charity pursuant to any charitable purpose connected with categories of persons determined by reference to any physical or mental capacity was not unlawful under the employment provisions of the *DDA 1995* (*DDA 1995, s 18C*). This exception is not re-enacted in the *EqA 2010*. See **13.10A** above for the provisions on charities in the *EqA 2010*.

(d) Statutory office holders, police and prison officers, members of fire brigades

Whereas these and other categories of worker were excluded from the employment provisions of the *DDA 1995* prior to 1 October 2004, since that date there has been no such exception, save in relation to the armed forces (see above). See also now **13.25** below for office holders generally and **13.26** below for police officers.

13.17 GENERAL EXCEPTIONS TO THE EQUALITY LEGISLATION

A number of other exceptions or defences are available to discrimination claims in respect of all grounds of discrimination.

13.18 Employment out of the territorial jurisdiction

In the *EqA 2010* there are specific provisions applying the *Act* to employment on ships, hovercraft and other offshore work: see *ss 81–83*, the *Equality Act 2010 (Work on Ships and Hovercraft) Regulations 2011 (SI 2011/1771)* and *Hasan v Shell International Shipping*

Services (PTE) Ltd [2014] All ER (D) 15 (Feb) (UKEAT/0242/13/SM). In *Walker v Wallem Shipmanagement Limited* (UKEAT/0236/18/LA), 16 January 2020 the EAT (Kerr J) noted that the combined effect of these provisions does not prevent an offshore employment service provider from discriminating, on United Kingdom soil, in a way that would otherwise be unlawful under the *EA 2010* where the employment is for service on a foreign-flagged ship. The EAT noted that it was doubtful as to whether this state of affairs was compliant with the *Equal Treatment Directive*, but since that case involved only a private employer and not an emanation of the state, the claimant's only remedy would be against the United Kingdom itself.

Otherwise the *EqA 2010* does not include any specific provisions as to its territorial extent. It follows that whether or not a particular employment or act of discrimination falls under the jurisdiction of the *EqA 2010* has to be determined according to generally applicable principles on the conflict of laws: see generally FOREIGN EMPLOYEES, 27.9. The Court of Appeal accepted in *R (Hottak and anor) v Secretary of State for Foreign and Commonwealth Affairs and anor* [2016] EWCA Civ 438, [2016] IRLR 534 that courts and tribunals should apply the principles that have been developed in relation to claims of unfair dismissal brought under the *Employment Rights Act 1996* ('*ERA 1996*') as that statute too contains no specific provision about territorial extent. The CA rejected the employee's argument that the *EqA 2010* should be given a wider territorial scope than the *ERA 1996* (thus disapproving the suggestion of the Div Crt in that case ([2015] EWHC 1953, [2015] IRLR 827 and the EAT in *Olsen v Gearbulk Services Ltd* [2015] IRLR 818). In *Hottak* the CA concluded that local interpreters employed by British Forces in Afghanistan did not have a sufficient connection with the UK to bring their discrimination claims under the EqA 2010. See also *Smania v Standard Chartered Bank* [2015] IRLR 271 for a case in which the EAT considered, but rejected, an argument that the territorial extent of the public interest disclosure provisions of the *ERA 1996* should be given a wider scope than that of the unfair dismissal provisions.

The case law as it has developed in relation to claims under the *ERA 1996*, and now also the *EqA 2010*, may be summarised as follows.

The House of Lords in *Lawson v Serco Ltd* [2006] IRLR 289 held that an employment tribunal would have jurisdiction to consider a claim of unfair dismissal by an employee if he was 'employed in Great Britain'. Lord Hoffmann identified three potential categories of employee who would be regarded as 'employed in Great Britain' (ibid at paras 25–40):

The 'standard' case: an employee 'working in Great Britain' at the time of his dismissal (otherwise than on a casual visit);

The 'peripatetic' employee (such as an airline pilot): an employee based in Great Britain at the time of his dismissal;

The 'expatriate' case (ie an employee living, working and based abroad): normally such employment would be outside the territorial jurisdiction of the UK, unless the employee had 'strong connections' with Great Britain and British employment law.

Lord Hoffmann gave two examples of expatriate employees who would fall within the territorial jurisdiction of the *ERA 1996*: those posted abroad by a British employer for the purposes of a business carried on in Great Britain (such as a foreign correspondent on the staff of a British newspaper) and those expatriate employees of a British employer operating within what is in practice a British enclave in a foreign country (such as a British military base).

In *Ravat v Halliburton Manufacturing & Services Ltd* [2012] IRLR 315, [2012] ICR 389, the Supreme Court emphasised that Lord Hoffmann's three categories are merely examples of the application of the general principle that, in order for the Tribunal to have jurisdiction, the employee's employment must have much stronger connections with both Great Britain and with British employment law than with any other system of law. Their Lordships held that although the three categories were helpful, it was important to remember that there was no requirement of 'exceptionality' for expatriate employees. If they had strong connections with Great Britain and British employment law, then the Tribunal would have jurisdiction.

Ravat concerned an employee who lived in Preston, Lancashire, but who was employed by a British subsidiary of an American multinational corporation to provide services to that corporation's German company and as a result spent half his time living and working in Libya and half of it living and working in the UK. The employment tribunal held that the claimant had a sufficiently strong connection with the UK to fall within the jurisdiction of the *ERA 1996*. The Scottish EAT reversed that decision, but the Court of Session restored the decision of the Tribunal and the Supreme Court upheld the Court of Session's decision. Their Lordships considered it to be important that the employer's business was in truth based in Great Britain, and that the employee had been treated as a 'commuter', being given assurances that his posting to Libya would not affect the benefits to which he would have been entitled as a UK-based employee and that the law of his contract would remain that of Britain. In practice his employment had continued to be managed from the employer's human resources department in Aberdeen, and the employee had maintained his home in Great Britain. *Duncombe v Secretary of State for Children Schools and Families (No. 2)* [2011] ICR 1312 was another case in which employees working abroad, in this case in an expatriate community at an international school, were held to have a much stronger connection with England so as to bring them within the territorial jurisdiction. See also *Ministry of Defence v Wallis* [2010] IRLR 1035 and *Powell v OMV Exploration & Production Ltd* [2014] IRLR 80.

In *Bates van Winkelhof v Clyde & Co LLP* [2012] EWCA Civ 1207, [2013] ICR 883 (reversed on other grounds: [2014] UKSC 32, [2014] IRLR 641) the Court of Appeal had to consider whether or not UK employment tribunals had jurisdiction over discrimination claims brought by a solicitor who was a member of a UK LLP, but seconded to, and employed under, a contract with, a Tanzanian law firm. The employer argued that the Supreme Court in *Ravat* had held that in such cases it was necessary for a comparative exercise to be carried out by the Tribunal in order to ascertain whether the employee's connections with Great Britain were stronger than those with the territory in which he or she works. The Court of Appeal in *Bates*, however, clarified that such a comparative exercise is not required unless the employee is employed wholly abroad. In this case, where the claimant worked for at least part of her time in Great Britain, the only question was whether the connection with Great Britain was (to use Lord Hope's words in *Ravat*) 'sufficiently strong to enable it to be said that Parliament would have regarded it as appropriate for the tribunal to deal with the claim'.

In *R (Hottak and anor) v Secretary of State for Foreign and Commonwealth Affairs and anor* [2015] EWHC 1953 (Admin), [2015] IRLR 827 the Divisional Court held that Afghan interpreters employed by HM Government in the service of the armed forces in Afghanistan but on contracts subject to local law and local terms and conditions did not have a sufficient connection with the UK to enable them to bring claims under the *EqA 2010*. They had no physical contact or connection with the UK but were local staff, locally engaged. Their only connection with the UK was the identity of their employer. They had a much stronger connection with Afghanistan. See also *Nica v Xian Jiaotong Liverpool University* UKEAT/0041/17/JOJ.

For a recent statement of the law in this area, see: *British Council v David Jeffery and Jonathan Green v SIG Trading Ltd* [2018] EWCA Civ 2253. It should be emphasised that, despite the proliferation of appellate decisions, whether or not there is a sufficiently close connection is a question of fact for the Tribunal, susceptible to review on appeal only if the Tribunal has erred in law: *Olsen v Gearbulk Services Ltd* [2015] IRLR 818.

The approach to be applied where the employee is not working at the date of dismissal was considered in *YKK Europe Ltd v Heneghan* [2010] IRLR 563, [2010] ICR 611. The EAT held that in these cases a broader factual inquiry will be required. The Tribunal will need to consider (among other things): why the employee was absent from work, the length of his absence before dismissal, where he was working or based (and for how long) before his absence from work began, where the employee would have been working at the time of dismissal if he had not been absent from work, whether there was an active employment relationship between the date of his absence from work and the date of dismissal, from where the contract was being operated at dismissal, and whether the tribunal would have had territorial jurisdiction as at the date on which the claimant became absent from work. No factor is determinative and the weight to be given to the factors is for the tribunal. The EAT remitted the matter to the Tribunal to determine the question of jurisdiction.

The EAT in *Pervez v Macquarie Bank Ltd* [2011] IRLR 284, [2011] ICR 266 has confirmed that the principles discussed above are not 'cut down' in any way by *reg 19(1)* of the *Employment Tribunals (Constitution and Rules of Procedure) Regulations 2004* ('*the 2004 Regulations*'), which provides that an employment tribunal in England or Wales 'shall only have jurisdiction to deal with proceedings . . . where . . . one of the respondents resides or carries on business in England and Wales'. The EAT held that a respondent should be regarded as carrying on a business in England or Wales if it has (for eg) a peripatetic employee who is based here.

The above contrasts with the situation under the predecessor legislation, where specific provision was made as to the territorial extent of the Acts and Regulations. Broadly speaking, the predecessor equality legislation applied where a complainant did his work wholly or partly in Great Britain and did not apply where the complainant worked wholly outside Great Britain (*RRA 1976, ss 4, 8(1), (1A); SDA 1975, ss 6(1), 10(1)*, both as amended; *RBR 2003, reg 9(1); SOR 2003, reg 9(1); AR 2006, reg 10(10)*. The question was whether, viewing the complainant's employment as a whole, he did his work wholly outside Great Britain (*Saggar v Ministry of Defence* [2005] EWCA Civ 413, [2005] IRLR 618, [2005] ICR 1073). See also *Tradition Securities and Futures SA v X and Y* [2008] IRLR 934, [2009] ICR 88, *Deria v General Council of British Shipping* [1986] IRLR 108, [1986] ICR 172, *British Airways plc v Mak* [2011] EWCA Civ 184, [2011] All ER (D) 256 (Feb) for cases on the old provisions.

There are also specific provisions relating to employment on ships and hovercraft and to employment concerned with exploration or exploitation of the sea bed or subsoil, employment on the Frigg gas field and other parts of the Continental Shelf: see the *Equality Act 2010 (Work on Ships and Hovercraft) Regulations 2011 (SI 2011/1771)* and the *Equality Act 2010 (Offshore Work) Order 2010 (SI 2010/1835)* made under, respectively, *ss 81* and *82* of the *EqA 2010*.

See also **12.42** Discrimination and Equal Opportunities – I.

Note also that some cases will raise questions as to the Tribunal's international jurisdiction under the *Recast Brussels 1 Regulation (Regulation EU/1215/2012)*. See further *Ravisy v Simmons and Simmons* UKEAT/0085/18/OO and Foreign Employees **(25)**.

13.19 Employment under an illegal contract

The test for excluding a tribunal's jurisdiction on grounds of illegality in relation to discrimination claims is not as strict as that used in cases of breach of contract. In breach of contract cases, a court or tribunal will not enforce a claim where the employment is pursuant to an illegal contract, or if there was an intention at the time of the formation of the contract to perform it illegally, or if the complainant has to rely on his or her illegal conduct in order to found his claim (*Colen v Cebrian (UK) Ltd* [2003] EWCA Civ 1676, [2004] IRLR 210, [2004] ICR 568; though note that the court may in certain circumstances be prepared to 'sever' the legal and illegal parts of a contract: *Blue Chip Trading Ltd v Helbawi* [2009] IRLR 128 and see generally **8.24** Contract of Employment). By contrast, in discrimination cases, the fact that a contract is illegal or tainted by illegality will not exclude the tribunal's jurisdiction, unless the complainant's claim is so closely connected or inextricably bound up or linked with the complainant's illegal conduct that to allow the complainant to recover compensation would be to appear to condone that conduct (*Hall v Woolston Hall Leisure Ltd* [2000] IRLR 578, [2001] ICR 99, CA, approving *Leighton v Michael* [1996] IRLR 67, [1995] ICR 1091, EAT). In *Hall v Woolston Hall Leisure*, the CA held that where the complaint is concerned with a dismissal only, the fact of dismissal may not be sufficiently closely connected with the illegality as to preclude a claim. However, a claim in respect of discrimination relating to access to opportunities for promotion, transfer or training or any other benefits, facilities or services may be precluded: see *Governing Body of Addey and Stanhope School v Vakante* [2003] ICR 290, [2003] ICR 290, EAT. Further, the tribunal at the remitted hearing in that case decided that the dismissal as well as the manner in which the employer gave the employee access to training and other benefits were so inextricably linked with the employee's illegal conduct – obtaining employment in breach of immigration rules – that both claims were precluded. This decision was upheld on appeal: see [2004] EWCA Civ 1065, [2005] ICR 231, [2004] All ER (D) 561 (Jul). *Hounga v Allen and anor (Anti-Slavery International intervening)* [2014] UKSC 47, [2014] IRLR 811 was a case that concerned Ms Hounga, a 14-year-old from Nigeria, who the Allen family had offered to employ as a home help in return for schooling and £50 per month. They helped her obtain false identity documents with which she entered the UK and secured a six-month visitors' visa. Ms Hounga was then kept in the Allen's house, required to do the housework and look after the children, not paid, not enrolled in school and threatened with imprisonment should she try to leave. After 18 months, she had displeased Mrs Allen, who threw her out on the street. She brought a claim that her dismissal was discriminatory. The Tribunal upheld her complaint, and so did the EAT, but a unanimous CA ([2012] EWCA Civ 609, [2012] IRLR 685) held that the illegality of her conduct in working illegally was inextricably linked with her claim such that her claim was precluded as a matter of public policy. The SC reversed that decision, holding that Ms Hounga's illegal conduct merely provided the context for the claim and was not so inextricably linked with it as to bar the claim on public policy grounds. A majority (Lord Wilson JSC, Baroness Hale DPSC and Lord Kerr JSC) went further and held that, in the alternative, the 'inextricable link' test was not applicable because the public policy reasons for barring claims where the court might otherwise appear to be condoning illegality was trumped by the more significant public policy concern to stop human trafficking.

The burden of proof is on the party alleging illegality (*Colen v Cebrian (UK) Ltd*, above).

The Court of Appeal in *Woolston Hall Leisure* left undecided a question whether the limited grounds for derogation from the right not to suffer less favourable treatment conferred by *Directive 76/207/EEC* meant that illegality could not be used as a ground for refusing an employee a remedy. The point was also raised in *Vakante v Governing Body of Addey and Stanhope School (No 2)* [2004] ICR 279, [2003] All ER (D) 352 (Dec), EAT (in relation to the equivalent provision of the *Race Directive 2000/43/EC*). However, the Court of Appeal held that, since *Directive 2000/43* only came into force after the claimant's cause of action arose and, since it was clearly not intended to have retrospective effect, it could not assist the claimant ([2004] EWCA Civ 1065, [2005] ICR 231, [2004] All ER (D) 561 (Jul)). This point was not revisited in *Allen v Hounga* (ibid).

13.20 Benefits provided to the public

The provisions relating to discrimination with regard to access to benefits of any description (including facilities and services) do not apply if the respondent is concerned with the provision (for payment or not) of benefits of that description to the public, or to a section of the public comprising the complainant in question, unless:

(i)   that provision differs in a material respect from the provision of the benefits to his employees (or non-employees covered by the employment rules: see below **13.24** ff); or

(ii)   the provision of the benefits to the complainant in question is regulated by his contract of employment (or equivalent for non-employees covered by the employment rules); or

(iii)   the benefits relate to training.

(*Para 19* of *Sch 9* to the *EqA 2010*)

The same exception applied under the predecessor legislation: see *RRA 1976, ss 4(2)(b) and 4(4); SDA 1975, ss 6(2)(a) and 6(7); RBR 2003, regs 6(2)(b) and 6(4); SOR 2003, reg 6(2)(b) and 6(4); AR 2006, reg 7(6); DDA 1995, s 4(4)*.

Thus, for example, a bank which provides loans to members of the public and to most employees on the same terms may not be taken to an employment tribunal by an employee who is denied a loan on grounds of race, sex, religion or belief, gender reassignment, disability, age or sexual orientation if the employee is not entitled to the loan under his contract of employment. However, it will be liable to an action by that employee in the county court under the provisions relating to discrimination in the provision of goods, facilities or services: *Part 3* of the *EqA 2010*.

13.21   Discrimination in compliance with the law

Under *Sch 22, para 1* to the *EqA 2010* it is a defence to a claim of discrimination on grounds of age, disability, religion or belief that the act complained of was carried out in order to comply with a statutory requirement or (in the case of disability, religion or belief) in order to comply with a requirement or condition imposed by virtue of an enactment. A statutory requirement includes a reference to a Measure of the General Synod of the Church of England as well as an enactment passed or made on or after the date on which *EqA 2010* was passed: *Sch 22, para 1(3)*. Note that the defence will only succeed where the enactment actually requires the discrimination. The application by an employer of discriminatory provisions of an enactment (such as the provisions of the Civil Service Pension Scheme) will not be lawful if in fact the employer had the power or discretion not to apply the provisions in question: see *Heron v Sefton Metropolitan Borough Council* [2014] EqLR 130 and the decision of the ET concerning judicial pensions in *McCloud and ors v The Lord Chancellor and ors* (5 April 2016, Case No. 2201483/2015; not referred to in the EAT [2018] IRLR 284 or Court of Appeal [2018] EWCA Civ 2844, [2019] ICR 1489). For this reason the *obiter* suggestion in *Harrod and ors v Chief Constable of West Midlands Police and ors* [2017] EWCA Civ 191, [2017] IRLR 539 that the exception in *Sch 22, para 1* could have been relied upon by the Chief Constable in that case in relation to the decision to use *reg A19* of the *Police Pensions Regulations 1987* to retire all officers with over 30 years' service is probably incorrect: certainly it could not have been relied on to legitimise the decision to retire all such officers, even if it might have provided a partial defence since under the Police Pensions Regulations it is not possible to retire officers unless they have completed 30 years' service.

The defence is only available to claims of age, disability and religion or belief discrimination. Similar provision was made in respect of age and disability (but not religion or belief discrimination) under the predecessor legislation: *AR 2006, reg 27; DDA 1995, s 59*. No such defence is available in *EqA 2010* to claims of discrimination on grounds of race, sex or sexual orientation in the employment sphere, although this was not the case under the predecessor legislation (see below).

There is, however, a general exception in the *EqA 2010* for discrimination on grounds of nationality and/or indirect discrimination on the basis of a person's place of ordinary residence or the length of time a person has been present or resident in the UK or an area within it that is authorised by another enactment or statutory instrument: see *para 1* of *Sch 23* to the *EqA 2010*.

Racial discrimination

Prior to the amendments introduced with effect from 19 July 2003 by the *Race Relations Amendment Regulations*, there was a general defence available where the relevant act of discrimination was carried out pursuant to any enactment, Order in Council or statutory instrument, or in order to comply with a ministerial condition or requirement imposed pursuant to statute (*RRA 1976, s 41(1)*).

The scope of that provision was considered by the House of Lords in *Hampson v Department of Education and Science* [1990] IRLR 302, [1990] ICR 511. Their Lordships held that the application of the defence was restricted to acts done in the necessary performance of an express obligation contained in an instrument, and did not extend to discretionary acts carried out by the Secretary of State, even in circumstances where he had a positive public duty to exercise his discretion. (See also *Dhatt v McDonalds Hamburgers Ltd* [1991] IRLR 130, [1991] ICR 238.)

From 19 July 2003, the position was as follows (EqA 2010, para 1, Sch 23; formerly RRA 1976, s 41):

(a)   Where discrimination was on grounds of race, ethnic or national origins, no defence is available;

(b)   Otherwise, discriminatory acts were not unlawful if performed:

   (i)   in pursuance of any enactment or Order in Council;

   (ii)   in pursuance of any instrument made under any enactment by a Minister of the Crown; or

   (iii) in order to comply with any condition or requirement imposed by a Minister of the Crown by virtue of any enactment;

(c)   Where discrimination was on grounds of the complainant's nationality, place of ordinary residence or the length of time for which he has been present or resident in or outside the UK, the defence was available in the three circumstances set out in (b) immediately above but also:

   (i)   in pursuance of any arrangements made by or with the approval of, or for the time being approved by, a Minister of the Crown; or

   (ii)   in order to comply with any condition imposed by a Minister of the Crown.

For the application of the exemption for acts done pursuant to arrangements made by or with the approval of a Minister of the Crown, see *R (on the application of Mohammed) v Secretary of State for Defence* [2007] EWCA Civ 1023, [2007] All ER (D) 09 (May).

Sex discrimination

Save in certain respects intended to preserve the position as it was under previous enactments, or in order to ensure the health and safety of women, no defence is available under the *EqA 2010* for sex discrimination carried out in order to comply with a legal requirement. The exceptions on the grounds of statutory authority which relate to the protected characteristic of sex (*EqA 2010, Sch 22, para 1*) relate only to services and education.

However, it remains the case that a respondent is not guilty of an unlawful act if he discriminates in order to comply with a statute passed before the *SDA 1975*, or a statutory instrument made or approved (whether before or after the passing of the *SDA*) by or under an act passed before the *SDA*, or by a provision specified in *Sch 1* to the *Employment Act 1989*, in each case if such provision is one concerning the protection of women (*SDA 1975*, *s 51*, as substituted by *Employment Act 1989, s 3(3)*, now contained in *Sch 22, para 2* of the *EqA 2010*). Thus, discrimination in order to comply with college statutes enacted under a statute prior to *SDA 1975* was considered lawful in *Hugh-Jones v St John's College, Cambridge* [1979] ICR 848. Many such statutory requirements were removed as a result of *Employment Act 1989*.

Discriminatory action taken by an employer to ensure the health and safety of his employees will not be considered unlawful if it is taken in compliance with his statutory obligations and in order to protect the complainant (or class of women to which the complainant belongs): *SDA 1975, s 51(1)(c)(ii)* and now *Sch 22, para 2* of the *EqA 2010* and see *Page v Freight Hire (Tank Haulage) Ltd* [1981] IRLR 13, [1981] ICR 299.

Pregnancy and maternity

Para 2 of *Sch 22* to the *EqA 2010* further provides an exception from the maternity and pregnancy discrimination provisions for acts done in order to comply with a statute passed before *SDA 1975*, or by a provision specified in *Sch 1* to the *Employment Act 1989*, in each case if such provision is one concerning the protection of women, or in order to comply with other statutory obligations and in order to protect the complainant or class of women to which the complainant belongs.

Religion or belief

In addition to the general exception under para 1 (above), *paras 3* and *4* of *Sch 22* to the *EqA 2010* provide various exceptions for acts of religious discrimination in relation to appointments to positions in educational establishments, where that discrimination is authorised or required either by the constitution of the educational establishment or by statute.

The exceptions under *para 3* apply in relation to the appointment of (a) the head teacher or principal of an educational establishment (as defined in *sub-para (6)*), (b) the head, a fellow or other member of the academic staff of a college, or institution in the nature of a college, in a university; or (c) a professorship of a university which is a canon professorship or one to which a canonry is annexed. Discrimination on grounds of religion or belief is permitted in relation to such appointments where this is necessary to comply with a requirement of any instrument relating to the establishment that the head teacher or principle must be a member of a particular religious order, or that the holder of the position must be a woman (if the instrument was made before 16 January 1990) or an Act or instrument in accordance with which the professorship is a canon professorship or to which a canonry is annexed.

The exceptions under para 4 allow any discrimination that is permitted for the purposes of (a) *section 58(6)* or *(7)* of the *School Standards and Framework Act 1998* (dismissal of teachers because of failure to give religious education efficiently); (b) *section 60(4)* and *(5)* of that *Act* (religious considerations relating to certain appointments); (c) *section 124A* of that *Act* (preference for certain teachers at independent schools of a religious character); or (d) *section 124AA(5)* to *(7)* of that *Act* (religious considerations relating to certain teachers at Academies with religious character).

By a decision of 20 October 2014 (Ref. Ares (2014) 3466266) the European Commission dismissed a complaint about the width of the exceptions allowed for faith schools in UK law. However, on 20 February 2015, it was reported in the *Times Educational Supplement* that the European Commission had decided to re-open its investigation, although no outcome of any such investigation appears to have been published.

13.22 National security

Under the *EqA 2010* there is a single general exception to the *Act* for anything done for the purpose of safeguarding national security, provided it is proportionate to that purpose: *EqA 2010, s 192*. National security may also justify an exception to the rules on making enquiries about health and disability when vetting for employment: see *s 60(14)* of the *EqA 2010*. The meaning of 'national security' was considered by the House of Lords in *Secretary of State for the Home Department v Rehman* [2001] UKHL 47, [2003] 1 AC 153. The House of Lords held that "national security" means the security of the United Kingdom and its people; the interests of national security are not limited to actions by an individual which are targeted at the UK, its system of government or its people; the protection of democracy and the legal and constitutional systems of the state are part of national security as well as military defence; action against a foreign state may be capable indirectly of affecting the security of the UK; and reciprocal co-operation between the UK and other states in combating international terrorism is capable of promoting the United Kingdom's national security.

A similar exception applied under the predecessor legislation. Discrimination on grounds of sexual orientation, religion or belief, disability or age was not unlawful if it is done for the purpose of safeguarding national security, and the discriminatory act is justified by that purpose (*RBR 2003, reg 24*; *SOR 2003, reg 24*; *DDA 1995, s 59(2A)*; *EA 2006, reg 27*). An act of sex discrimination done for the purpose of safeguarding national security was also permitted by the *SDA 1975, s 52(1)*. However, it should be noted that no such derogation was available for sex discrimination in Community law, though cf *Sirdar v Army Board*: C-273/97 [2000] IRLR 47, [2000] ICR 130, CJEU and above **13.11**(d). The *RRA 1976* permitted race discrimination where the act in question was done for the purpose of safeguarding national security and was justified by that purpose: *RRA 1976, s 42*.

See also **13.11**(d) and **13.16**(a) above for the exceptions relating to sex and disability discrimination in the armed forces.

13.23 Employees working for those with state or diplomatic immunity

A number of provisions in principle confer state or diplomatic immunity in relation to employment discrimination claims, in particular the *State Immunity Act 1978* ('*SIA 1978*') and the *Diplomatic Privileges Act 1964* ('*DPA 1964*'), which incorporated the Vienna Convention on Diplomatic Relations 1961. It was at one time accepted that the provisions of the *SIA 1978* did not infringe *art 6(1)* of the *European Convention on Human Rights*: see *Holland v Lampen-Wolfe* [2000] 3 All ER 833, ECtHR and *Fogarty v United Kingdom* [2002] IRLR 148, ECtHR. However, more recent cases of the ECtHR (eg *Al-Adsani v UK* (2002) 34 EHRR 11) held that *art 6(1)* is engaged in such cases and will be infringed if the immunity is not justified by the need to comply with international law. On that basis, the Supreme Court in *Benkharbouche v Embassy of Sudan* [2017] UKSC 62, [2017] 3 WLR 957, [2017] ICR 1327 held that, in preventing employment claims being brought against embassies when that was not required by international law, the *SIA 1978* infringed *article 6* of the ECHR. Further, in *Al-Malki v Reyes* [2017] UKSC 61, [2017] 3 WLR 923, [2017] ICR 1417, [2018] IRLR 267 the Supreme Court held that a trafficking claim could be brought by persons employed in the domestic service of Saudi Arabian diplomats on the basis that this employment fell outside the Vienna Convention on Diplomatic Relations 1961 since by the time of the proceedings the diplomat was no longer in post (so *art 31* did not apply) and the diplomat was not entitled to immunity under *art 39(2)* as that immunity applied only to acts performed while the diplomat was in post in the exercise of diplomatic functions. The Supreme Court declined to determine whether, if the diplomat had remained in post, the employment would have fallen outside the scope of *art 31* on the basis that it related to 'commercial activity' outside a diplomat's official functions within *art 31(1)(c)*. The minority took the view it would not; the majority expressed doubts and invited the Law Commission to consider an amendment to the law to make clear that this sort of case would fall outside the scope of diplomatic immunity, given the strong public policy reasons for combatting human trafficking.

In the light of the Supreme Court's decision in *Benkharbouche*, earlier case law should be approached with care, but see *Warner v B&M Europe Ltd* [2016] All ER (D) 174 (Jul) (UKEAT/0081/15/RN, UKEAT/0139/16/RN), where the EAT held that the grant of immunity to the European Patent Office under the *European Patent Organisation (Immunities and Privileges) Order 1978* was compatible with *art 6 ECHR*. See also *Abusabib v Taddese* [2013] ICR 603, [2013] All ER (D) 121 (Mar) where the EAT held that a domestic servant employed solely in the diplomat's home was not part of the function of the mission and therefore he could not hide behind state immunity to avoid a discrimination claim. See further *Wokuri v Kassam* [2012] EWHC 105 (Ch), [2012] 2 All ER 1195.

13.24 NON-EMPLOYEES AND NON-EMPLOYERS COVERED BY THE EMPLOYMENT RULES

Contract workers

In recent times there has been a marked trend towards the use of contract workers. Contract workers are parties to a tri-partite arrangement. The first party is the person who has work which needs doing. He is known as the 'principal'. The principal enters into a contract with a second party who is obliged to supply employees to perform the work. The employees are known as 'contract workers' in relation to the principal.

Under the *EqA 2010*, contract workers are covered by *s 41*. *Sections 41(1)* and *(3)* prohibit discrimination and victimisation of contract workers by 'principals':

(i)   as to the terms on which the principal allows the worker to do the work;

(ii)   by not allowing him to do it or continue to do it;

(iii)   in the way he affords him access to any benefits or by refusing or deliberately not affording him access to them; or

(iv)   by subjecting him to any other detriment.

There is also a specific prohibition on harassment of contract workers by 'principals' (*s 41(2)*). A 'principal' is defined as 'a person who makes work available for an individual who is (a) employed by another person and (b) supplied by that other person in furtherance of a contract to which the principal is a party (whether or not that other person is a party to it) (*s 41(5)*). A 'contract worker' is an individual supplied to a principal in furtherance of such a contract.

Contract workers and reasonable adjustments. The duty to make reasonable adjustments applies to the hirer of contract labour as it does to an employer. However, it might not be reasonable for a hirer of contract labour to make certain adjustments if the period for which the contract worker works for the hirer of contract labour is short (*EHRC Code of Practice, para 9.8*). The provider of contract labour may also have a duty to make a reasonable adjustment where a similar substantial disadvantage is likely to affect a contract worker as a result of the arrangements or premises of all or most of the hirers of contract labour to whom he might be supplied. In such circumstances, the provider of contract labour would have to make any reasonable adjustment within his power which would overcome the disadvantage wherever it might arise. Thus, in a case of a blind word-processor operator working for an employment agency, it would be reasonable for the agency to provide her with a specially adapted computer to take with her to any temporary engagement to which she is sent because otherwise she would be suffering the same substantial disadvantage at all or most such engagements (*EHRC Code of Practice, para 9.10*).

In *Abbey Life Assurance Co Ltd v Tansell* [2000] IRLR 387, the applicant had set up his own company and was employed by it. That company supplied the applicant's services as a computer consultant to third parties under a contract with an employment agency, MHC. Abbey Life had an agreement with MHC to supply computer personnel. Abbey Life rejected the applicant's services and a complaint of disability discrimination was made to an employment tribunal. The tribunal held that the applicant was a contract worker for MHC and not Abbey Life. MHC appealed successfully to the EAT (see *MHC Consulting Services Ltd v Tansell* [1999] IRLR 677). The Court of Appeal dismissed Abbey Life's appeal against that decision, holding that Abbey Life was the 'principal' or the hirer of contract labour for the purposes of *DDA 1995*. The fact that Abbey Life's contract was with MIIC and not the applicant's employer did not preclude the application of *s 4B, DDA 1995* as there was a chain of unbroken contracts between the applicant and the 'end user', namely, Abbey Life.

The genuine occupational requirement exception (above para **13.2**) applies to contract workers in relation to not allowing them to do, or to continue doing, particular work: see *para 1(2)(b)* of *Sch 9* to the *EqA 2010*.

Similar provision was made in the predecessor legislation: see *SDA 1975, ss 9(2), (2A)*, as amended; *RRA 1976, ss 7(1), (3A)*, as amended; *RBR 2003, regs 8(1), (2); SOR 2003, regs 8(1), (2)*; and *EA 2006, regs 9(1), (2)*.

The provisions relating to the meaning of 'at an establishment in Great Britain' (above **13.18**) applied to principals as they did to employers under the predecessor legislation. So, too, did the genuine occupational requirement exceptions (*SDA 1975, ss 9(3), (3A) and (3B); RRA 1976, s 7(3); RBR 2003, reg 8(3); SOR 2003, reg 8(3); AR 2006, reg 9(3)*; see above **13.2** ff) and the exceptions for benefits provided to the public (*SDA 1975, s 9(4); RRA 1976, s 7(5); RBR 2003, reg 8(4); SOR 2003, reg 8(4); AR 2006, reg 9(4)*; see above **13.2**).

The provisions relating to contract workers are designed to prevent an employer from escaping its responsibilities under the equality legislation by bringing in workers on sub-contract and should therefore be given a broad construction so as to provide statutory protection to a wide range of workers (*Jones v Friends Provident Life Office* [2004] IRLR 783, NICA). In that case, Carswell LCJ held (para 17) that, in order to fall within the relevant provisions, it is necessary to show that: (i) the contract between the employer and the principal is one under which it is contemplated that employees will be supplied by the former to the latter; and, (ii) the principal is in a position to influence or control the conditions under which the employee worked. However, in *Leeds City Council v Woodhouse* [2010] EWCA Civ 410, [2010] IRLR 625 the Court of Appeal ruled that the second of those conditions was not necessary. What matters is that the worker works 'for' the principal. Influence and control does not have to be shown in all cases.

The notion of a 'contract worker' extends to cover a case where the complainant works for a company operating a 'concession' within a department store. Thus, where a department store withdrew, on racial grounds, the necessary permission for the complainant to work in the store, the latter was entitled to bring proceedings against the former under *RRA 1976, s 7* (*Harrods Ltd v Remick* [1997] IRLR 583, [1998] ICR 156, CA). However, it should be noted that the Northern Ireland Court of Appeal in *Jones v Friends Provident* considered that *Harrods Ltd v Remick* represented, possibly, too wide an interpretation of the relevant provisions. In particular, the Court in *Jones v Friends Provident* considered that it is unlikely to be sufficient for a complainant to establish merely that the principal benefited from the work done by them in order to bring that principal within the scope of the relevant provisions. Nevertheless, more complex contractual arrangements are probably covered by the provisions: see *MHC Consulting Services Ltd v Tansell* [2000] IRLR 387, [2000] ICR 789, CA, a case under the *DDA 1995*. In that case the complainant contracted with a company that he had set up which company then contracted with a service provider, which in turn contracted with the ultimate beneficiary of the services. The beneficiary was a principal for the purposes of the *DDA 1995* notwithstanding the inclusion of an additional link in the contractual chain. In all cases, however, there must in fact be a *contractual* relationship: where arrangements take effect under statute (as, for example, the obligations placed on general practitioners and local health authorities under the *National Health Service (General*

Medical Services) Regulations 1992) there may be no contractual relationship at all: *David-John v North Essex Health Authority* [2004] ICR 112, [2003] All ER (D) 84 (Aug), EAT. See also *Vidal-Hall v Hawley* (21 February 2008, UKEAT/0462/07/DA) where the claim failed for lack of a contract between principal and the supplier of the worker.

A contract worker is not limited to comparing the treatment he has received with the manner in which the principal treats contract workers of different sexual orientation, racial group etc; he may also compare himself to employees of the principal (*Allonby v Accrington and Rossendale College* [2001] EWCA Civ 529, [2001] IRLR 364). Thus, a company which refused to allow an agency worker to return to work for it after she had been on maternity leave discriminated against her on the grounds of her sex, contrary to *SDA 1975, s 9* (*BP Chemicals Ltd v Gillick* [1995] IRLR 128, EAT). Similarly, where a local authority appointed a permanent worker in place of a contract worker who had left to take maternity leave, it was argued on behalf of the principal that the contract worker could not rely upon the provisions of the equivalent Northern Irish legislation. The principal had not refused to allow her to continue to do the work (she had merely left to start maternity leave) and by the time that she wanted to return there was no work for a contract worker to do, a permanent worker having been appointed. Nevertheless, the NICA held that the principal was liable to the contract worker who had been subjected to 'other detriment' (*Patefield v Belfast City Council* [2000] IRLR 664, NICA).

13.25 Office holders

In addition to the general provisions applying the equality legislation to the Crown, etc (see below **13.36**), specific provision is also made in relation to discrimination against office holders. Overwhelmingly, office holders are public sector appointees, often those with specific statutory powers or responsibilities. They have historically been considered not to be employed in a post but, rather, as holding an office which exists independently of the terms of their appointment. An example would be Registrars of Births, Deaths and Marriages. Following the decisions of the CJEU and Supreme Court in *O'Brien v Ministry of Justice* (respectively, C-393/10, [2012] IRLR 421, [2012] ICR 955 and [2013] UKSC 6, [2013] IRLR 315) establishing that judges are 'workers' under European law, it is likely that many office holders will now also fall within the definition of 'employee' in *s 83* of the *EqA 2010* and thus be covered by the standard rules on employees. However, the provisions in relation to office holders are likely still to remain relevant to such people, and also to those who are genuinely office holders and not employees or workers in European law.

Under the *EqA 2010* office holders are covered by *ss 49–51*. *Section 49* makes provision in respect of appointments to personal offices (ie what are referred to below as 'general office holders'). *Section 50* makes provision in respect of 'public offices', prohibiting discrimination, victimisation and harassment in relation to appointments and dismissals. *Section 51* makes provision prohibiting discrimination, victimisation and harassment in relation to recommendations for appointment to public offices. An office or post which is both a personal office and public office is to be treated for the purposes of the *EqA 2010* as being a public office only (*s 52(4)*). Posts to which persons are elected rather than appointed are not covered (*s 52(5)*). There are also further excluded offices listed in *Schedule 6*. These include any office that would be covered by any of the other employment provisions (eg contract work, partnerships, etc) (see *para 1* of *Sch 6*), political offices (*para 2*) and honourable offices (eg life peerages or other dignities) (para 3). The genuine occupational requirement exception applies to office holders in the same way as to employees: see *para 1(2)(e)–(g)* of *Sch 9* to the *EqA 2010* and generally **13.2** above.

The predecessor legislation also applied to office holders: see *RRA 1976, ss 76* and *76ZA*, or *SDA 1975, ss 10A* and *10B*; *RBR 2003, reg 10*; *SOR 2003, reg 10*; *AR 2006, reg 12*; *DDA 1995, ss 4C–4F*.

13.26 Police

Police officers are office holders and not employees. However, *s 42(1)* of the *EqA 2010* deems holding the office of constable to be treated as employment by the chief officer (in respect of any act done by the chief officer in relation to a constable or appointment to the office of constable) and by the responsible authority (in respect of any act done by the authority in relation to a constable or appointment to the office of constable). The 'chief officer' is:

(a) in relation to an appointment under a relevant Act, the chief officer of police for the police force to which the appointment relates;

(b) in relation to any other appointment, the person under whose direction and control the body of constables or other persons to which the appointment relates is;

(c) in relation to a constable or other person under the direction and control of a chief officer of police, that chief officer of police;

(d) in relation to any other constable or any other person, the person under whose direction and control the constable or other person is.

The 'responsible authority' is:

(a) in relation to an appointment under a relevant Act (ie the *Metropolitan Police Act 1829*, the *City of London Police Act 1839*, the *Police (Scotland) Act 1967*, the *Police Act 1996*), the police authority that maintains the police force to which the appointment relates;

(b) in relation to any other appointment, the person by whom a person would (if appointed) be paid;

(c) in relation to a constable or other person under the direction and control of a chief officer of police, the police authority that maintains the police force for which that chief officer is the chief officer of police;

(d) in relation to any other constable or any other person, the person by whom the constable or other person is paid.

The predecessor equality legislation made similar provision: *SDA 1975, s 17; RRA 1976, s 76A; RBR 2003, reg 11; SOR 2003, reg 11; AR 2006, reg 13; DDA 1995, s 64A*.

The requirement that the act should be done by the chief officer (or, similarly, by the police authority) is not to be interpreted literally and will include acts performed by those to whom the chief officer has delegated authority (see *Chief Constable of Cumbria v McGlennon* [2002] ICR 1156, [2002] All ER (D) 231 (Jul), EAT).

In *P v Commissioner of Police of the Metropolis* [2017] UKSC 65, [2018] IRLR 66 the Supreme Court held, overruling *Heath v Commissioner of Police of the Metropolis* [2004] EWCA Civ 943, [2005] ICR 329, that decisions of police misconduct panels could be the subject of an appeal to an employment tribunal under *s 42* and were not subject to the doctrine of judicial immunity.

Further detailed provisions apply the legislation to cadets, employees and office holders of the Serious Organised Crime Agency and other police bodies (*EqA 2010, ss 42(2)–(6) and 43(4)–(7)*; see formerly *SDA 1975, ss 17(6), (7), (9); RRA 1976, s 76B; RBR 2003, reg 11(6), (7), 11A; SOR 2003, regs 11(6), (7), 11A; AR 2006, regs 13(6), (7), (14); DDA 1995, ss 64A(6), (7)*, and *s 56* of the *Serious Organised Crime and Police Act 2005*).

For circumstances in which police constables may lawfully be discriminated against see above **13.11(e)**.

See also **14.2** DISCRIMINATION AND EQUAL OPPORTUNITIES **III** for the exclusion from the jurisdiction of employment tribunals of claims against police disciplinary panels.

13.27 Barristers and advocates

Unlawful discrimination against applicants for pupillage or tenancy

It is unlawful for a barrister or barrister's clerk, in relation to any offer of a pupillage or tenancy, to discriminate against a person on any of the unlawful grounds:

(a)   in the arrangements which are made for the purpose of determining to whom the pupillage or tenancy should be offered;

(b)   in respect of any terms on which it is offered; or

(c)   by refusing, or deliberately not offering, it to him (*EqA 2010, s 47(1)*; see previously: *SDA 1975, s 35A(1); RRA 1976, s 26A(1); RBR 2003, reg 12(1); SOR 2003, reg 12(1); AR 2006, reg 15(1); DDA 1995, s 7A(1)*).

Unlawful discrimination against pupils or tenants

It is unlawful for a barrister or barrister's clerk, in relation to a pupil or tenant in the set of chambers in question, to discriminate against him:

(a)   in respect of any terms applicable to him as a pupil or tenant;

(b)   in the opportunities for training or gaining experience, which are afforded or denied to him;

(c)   in the benefits which are afforded or denied to him; or

(d)   by terminating his pupillage, or by subjecting him to any pressure to leave the chambers or other detriment (*EqA 2010, s 47(2)*; see previously: *SDA 1975, s 35A(2); RRA 1976, s 26A(2); RBR 2003, reg 12(2); SOR 2003, reg 12(2); AR 2006, reg 15(2); DDA 1995, s 7A(2)*).

Unlawful harassment of pupils, tenants or applicants for pupillage or tenancy

It is unlawful for a barrister or barrister's clerk, in relation to a pupillage or tenancy in the set of chambers in question, to subject to harassment a person who is, or has applied to be, a pupil or tenant (*EqA 2010, s 47(3)*; see previously: *SDA 1975, s 35A(2A)*, as amended with effect from 1 October 2005; *RRA 1976, s 26A(3A); RBR 2003, reg 12(3); SOR 2003, reg 12(3); DDA 1995, s 7A(3)*).

Unlawful victimisation of pupils, tenants or applicants for pupillage or tenancy

It is unlawful for a barrister or barrister's clerk, in relation to a pupillage or tenancy in the set of chambers in question, to victimise a person who is, or has applied to be, a pupil or tenant (*EqA 2010, ss 47(4) and (5)*).

Unlawful discrimination by those instructing barristers

It is unlawful for any person, in relation to the giving, withholding or acceptance of instructions to a barrister, to discriminate against any person by subjecting him to a detriment, or to subject him to harassment (*EqA 2010, s 47(6)*; see previously: *SDA 1975, s 35A(3); RRA 1976, s 26A(3); RBR 2003, reg 12(4); SOR 2003, reg 12(4); AR 2006, reg 15(4); DDA 1995, s 7A(4)*).

'Barrister's clerk' includes any person carrying out any of the functions of a barrister's clerk. 'Pupil', 'pupillage', 'set of chambers', 'tenancy' and 'tenant' have the meanings commonly associated with their use in the context of barristers practising in independent practice, but 'tenancy' and 'tenant' also include reference to any barrister permitted to work in a set of chambers who is not a tenant (ie a 'squatter') (*EqA 2010, ss 47(8) and (9)*; see previously: *SDA 1975, s 35A(4); RRA 1976, s 26A(4); RBR 2003, reg 12(5); SOR 2003, reg 12(5); AR 2006, reg 15(5); DDA 1995, s 7A(5)*).

The exceptions for genuine occupational requirements (above **13.2ff**) and benefits provided to the public (above **13.20**) do not apply to barristers.

The provisions in respect of barristers extend to England and Wales only. Similar provision is made for advocates and their pupils in Scotland (*EqA 2010, s 48*; see previously: *SDA 1975, s 35B; RRA 1976, s 26B; RBR 2003, reg 13; SOR 2003, reg 13; AR 2006, reg 16; DDA 1995, s 7C*).

13.28 Partnerships

Unlawful discrimination against partners and candidates for partnership

Prior to the decision of the Supreme Court in *Bates van Winkelhof v Clyde & Co LLP* [2014] UKSC 32, [2014] IRLR 641 it was thought that partners in firms were not only not 'employees', but that they could also not be 'workers' under EU or domestic law. In *Bates* the SC concluded that an equity partner in a limited liability partnership (LLP) could be a 'worker' for the purposes of a whistle-blowing claim under the *ERA 1996*. In principle, it would appear that such partners could therefore also be 'workers' for the purposes of the *EqA 2010*. However, whether they are or not, specific provision is made in the *EqA 2010* expressly prohibiting discrimination against partners and candidates for partnership. The legislation applies to limited partnerships and limited liability partnerships as it does to partnerships (with appropriate amendments of terminology) (*EqA 2010, ss 44(8), 45* and *46*; see previously: *SDA 1975, ss 11(5), (6); RRA 1976, ss 10(4), (5); RBR 2003, regs 14(5), (6); SOR 2003, regs 14(5), (6); AR 2006, reg 17(6); DDA 1995, s 6C(2)*). Note, however, that for discrimination on grounds of colour or nationality, the *RRA 1976* only applied to firms with six or more partners: *RRA 1976, s 10(1A)*:

(a)   in the arrangements they make for the purpose of determining to whom they should offer that position;

(b)   in the terms on which they offer him that position;

(c)   by refusing to offer, or deliberately not offering, him that position; or

(d)   in a case where the person already holds that position:

    (i)   in the way they afford him access to any benefits or by refusing to afford, or deliberately not affording, him access to them, or

    (ii)   by expelling him from that position, or

    (iii)   subjecting him to any other detriment (*EqA 2010, ss 44(1)* and *(2)*; see previously *SDA 1975, ss 11(1), (2); RRA 1976, ss 10(1), (2); RBR 2003, regs 14(1), (3); SOR 2003, regs 14(1), (3); AR 2006, reg 17(1); DDA 1995, s 6A(1)*).

Under *EqA 2010*, it is also unlawful to discriminate against a person who is already a partner as to the terms on which the person is a partner: *s 44(2)(a)*.

'Expulsion' of a person from a position as partner is defined additionally to refer to the termination of that person's position as partner by:

(a)   the expiration of any period (including a period expiring by reference to an event or circumstance), not being a termination immediately after which the partnership is renewed on the same terms; and

(b)   any act of his (including the giving of notice) in circumstances such that he is entitled to terminate it without notice by reason of the conduct of the other partners (*EqA 2010, s 1(6)*; see previously: *RRA 1976, s 10(6); DDA 1995, s 6A(4); RBR 2003, reg 14(8); SOR 2003, reg 14(8); AR 2006, reg 17(8)*).

Note that where one partner dissolves a two-person partnership the other partner is 'expelled' for the purposes of the provisions on partnerships and may sue the remaining partner (*Dave v Robinska* [2003] ICR 1248, [2003] All ER (D) 35 (Jun)).

It is also unlawful for a firm, in relation to a position as partner in the firm, to subject to harassment a person who holds or has applied for that position (*EqA 2010, ss 44(3), (4)*; see previously *SDA 1975, 11(2A)*, as inserted with effect from 1 October 2005 by the *Sex Discrimination Regulations 2005; RRA 1976, s 10(1B); RBR 2003, reg 14(2); SOR 2003, reg 14(2); AR 2006, reg 17(2); DDA 1995, s 6A(2)*).

It is also unlawful for a firm, in relation to a position as partner in the firm, to victimise a person who holds or has applied for that position (*EqA 2010, ss 44(5) and (6)*). Under the predecessor legislation victimisation was merely a form of discrimination and no separate provision was made for it.

Genuine occupational requirement defences (see above **13.2** ff) are available to partnerships under the *EqA 2010*: see *para 1(2)(c)* and *(d)* of *Sch 9*. For the position under the predecessor legislation see: *RBR 2003, reg 14(4); SOR 2003, reg 14(4); AR 2006, reg 17(4); SDA 1975, ss 11(3), (3A), (3B); RRA 1976, s 10(3)*.

13.29 Trade organisations

A 'trade organisation' is defined in the discrimination legislation as:

(i)   an organisation of workers,

(ii)   an organisation of employers, or

(iii)   any other organisation whose members carry on a particular profession or trade for the purposes of which the organisation exists.

(*EqA 2010, s 57(7)*; see previously: *SDA 1975, 12(1); RRA 1976, s 11(1); RBR 2003, reg 15(4); SOR 2003, reg 15(4); AR 2006, reg 18(4); DDA 1995, s 13(4)*).

'Profession' is defined so as to include 'any vocation or occupation', and 'trade' to include 'any business': *EqA 2010, s 212(1)*; see previously *SDA 1975, s 82(1); RRA 1976, s 78(1); RBR 2003, reg 15(4); SOR 2003, reg 15(4); AR 2006, reg 18(4)*.

The EAT has held that the National Federation of Self-Employed and Small Businesses Ltd is an 'employers' organisation': *National Federation of Self-Employed and Small Businesses Ltd v Philpott* [1997] IRLR 340. In *Medical Protection Society v Sadek* [2004] EWCA Civ 865, [2005] IRLR 57, [2004] ICR 1263, the Court of Appeal considered the status of the Medical Protection Society, a membership organisation which had provided the claimant with advice and representation in relation to a claim he had brought against his employer, an NHS Trust. The Court held that the Society was 'an organisation of workers' within the first category of the definition of 'trade organisation' in *s 11(1)* of the *RRA 1976*, because medical and dental practitioners were properly classified as 'workers' even though they were 'members [of] a profession' within the third category of the definition of 'trade organisation' and even though some of them may be employees and others independent contractors. The Court considered that the EAT had been wrong to conclude that the Society fell within *both* the first and third categories of the definition: the third category was only a residual one.

It is unlawful for a trade organisation to discriminate against a person:

(a)   in the terms on which it is prepared to admit him to membership of the organisation; or

(b)   by refusing to accept, or deliberately not accepting, his application for membership; (*EqA 2010, s 57(1)*; see previously *SDA 1975, s 12(2); RRA 1976, s 11(2); RBR 2003, reg 15(1); SOR 2003, reg 15(1); AR 2006, reg 18(1); DDA 1995, s 13(1)*).

Pursuant to *s 57(1)* of *EqA 2010*, it is additionally unlawful for a trade organisation to discriminate in the arrangements made for deciding to whom to offer membership of the organisation.

It is also unlawful for a trade organisation, in relation to a member of the organisation, to discriminate against him:

(a)   in the way it affords him access to any benefits or by refusing or deliberately omitting to afford him access to them;

(b)   by depriving him of membership, or varying the terms on which he is a member; or

(c)   by subjecting him to any other detriment (*EqA 2010, s 57(2)*; see previously: *SDA 1975, s 12(3); RRA 1976, s 11(3); RBR 2003, reg 15(2); SOR 2003, reg 15(2); AR 2006, reg 18(2); DDA 1995, s 13(2)*).

It is unlawful for a trade organisation, in relation to a person's membership or application for membership of that organisation, to subject that person to harassment (*EqA 2010, s 57(3)*; see previously: *SDA 1975, s 12(3A)*), as inserted with effect from 1 October 2005 by the *Sex Discrimination Regulations 2005; RRA 1976, s 11(4); RBR 2003, reg 15(3); SOR 2003, reg 15(3); AR 2006, reg 18(3); DDA 1995, s 13(3)*).

In *Fire Brigades Union v Fraser* [1998] IRLR 697 (Court of Session, Inner House), the union provided support and assistance for the alleged victim of the harassment, but refused to provide assistance to the alleged harasser. The Court of Session overturned a decision of the employment tribunal that the alleged harasser had been the victim of an act of discrimination on the part of the union. Whilst it was true that the union treated the alleged victims of harassment more favourably, the tribunal was making the wrong comparison in comparing harasser and harassee. The proper question was whether a female alleged harasser would have been treated differently.

The occupational requirement exception (above para **13.2**) does not apply to trade organisations.

Note that there is no express provision rendering the union liable for the discriminatory acts of its members. Where a union official is employed by the union, the union will be vicariously liable for the acts of that official under *EqA 2010, s 109*: see **12.54 Discrimination and Equal Opportunities – I**. However, elected union officials who undertake union duties during paid time off work from their 'normal' employer will (even if they do this on a full-time basis) not be employees of the union since they are not paid by the union. Rather, they will be agents of the union and thus the union will be vicariously liable for their actions on that basis if their actions would have fallen within the 'course of employment' test governing the liability of employers for employees' acts if the relationship were that of employer and employee: see *Unite the Union v Nailard* [2018] EWCA Civ 1203, [2019] ICR 28, [2018] IRLR 730 and **12.56 Discrimination and Equal Opportunities – I**.

13.30 Qualifications bodies

A qualifications body is an authority or body which can confer professional or trade qualifications: *EqA 2010, s 54(2)*. A 'professional or trade qualification' is an authorisation, recognition, enrolment, approval or certification, which is needed for, or facilitates, engagement in a particular profession or trade. 'Confer' is defined to include the renewal or extension of a qualification (see *EqA 2010, s 54(3)*; see previously *SDA 1975, s 13(1), (3); RRA 1976, s 12(1), (2); RBR 2003, reg 16(3); SOR 2003, reg 16(4); AR 2006, reg 19(3); DDA 1995, s 14A(5)*). Establishments of further and higher education and schools are excluded from the definition: *EqA 2010, 54(4)*. (Separate provision in relation to discrimination in education is made by both the *EqA 2010* and the predecessor legislation. Consideration of this is, however, outside the scope of this book.)

It is unlawful for a qualifications body to discriminate against a person:

(a)   in the terms on which it is prepared to confer a professional or trade qualification on him;

(b)   by refusing or deliberately not granting any application by him for such a qualification; or

(c)   by withdrawing such a qualification from him or varying the terms on which he holds it.

(*EqA 2010, ss 53(1)* and *(2)*; see previously *SDA 1975, s 13(1)*; *RRA 1976, s 12(1)*; *RBR 2003, reg 16(1)*; *SOR 2003, reg 16(1)*; *AR 2006, reg 19(1)*; *DDA 1995, s 14A(1)*))

Under *EqA 2010*, it is additionally unlawful for a qualifications body to discriminate against a person:

(a)   in the arrangements made for deciding upon whom to confer a relevant qualification; and

(b)   by subjecting him to any other detriment.

(*EqA 2010, ss 53(1), (2)*)

It is unlawful for a qualifications body, in relation to a professional or trade qualification conferred by it, to subject to harassment a person who holds or applies for such a qualification (*EqA 2010, s 53(3)*; see previously: *SDA 1975, s 13(1A)*, as inserted with effect from 1 October 2005 by the *Sex Discrimination Regulations 2005*; *RRA 1976, s 12(1A)*; *RBR 2003, reg 16(2)*; *SOR 2003, reg 16(2)*; *AR 2006, reg 19(2)*).

The *EqA 2010* also specifically prohibits victimisation by qualifications bodies: *ss 53(4)* and *(5)* of *EqA 2010*.

A number of cases have considered the definition of 'qualifications body' for the purpose of these provisions. In *British Judo Association v Petty* [1981] IRLR 484, [1981] ICR 660, it was held that a qualification would only fall within the predecessor provision in *SDA 1975, s 13* if it facilitated employment, ie remunerated work, not voluntary activity; on the facts, that requirement was satisfied in relation to a judo referee's certificate so that the discriminatory restriction it contained was unlawful. In *Pemberton v Inwood* [2018] EWCA Civ 564, [2018] ICR 1291, [2018] IRLR 542 the Court of Appeal agreed with the EAT [2017] IRLR 211 that whether or not something is a 'relevant qualification' is not to be determined by reference to the intention of the awarding body, but whether, as a matter of fact, the something may be properly characterised as a 'qualification' and is needed for, or facilitates engagement in, a particular trade or profession. The question of fact is one for the tribunal and the EAT will not normally interfere. In that case, which concerned the grant of licences by the Bishop of Southwold and Nottingham, the EAT upheld the Tribunal's determination (applying *British Judo Association*) that the grant of a 'Permission to Officiate' was not the grant of a qualification because it only qualified the priest for voluntary duties. However, the grant of an 'Extra parochial ministry licence' was necessary for the paid employment in the NHS sought by the claimant. Further, the grant of the licence was not a decision taken 'on a whim': it depended on the individual being 'of good standing': that was capable of objective assessment and could therefore properly be regarded as a 'qualification'. In refusing to grant the licence, the Bishop was therefore acting as a qualifications body.

The provisions relating to qualifications bodies are not to be so widely construed as to extend to the mere awarding of a contract, even by a body or authority which has a *de facto* monopoly in the particular trade (*Malik v Post Office Counters Ltd* [1993] ICR 93). The provisions are aimed at discrimination by professional bodies and not individual businesses.

Thus, where a private medical health insurer would only make payments in respect of treatment given by practitioners holding certain recognised qualifications, a plastic surgeon could not bring a claim where the insurer refused to recognise her Greek medical qualifications (*Tattari v Private Patients Plan Ltd* [1997] IRLR 586, CA; see also *Loughran and anr v Northern Ireland Housing Executive* [1998] IRLR 593). However, in *Patterson v Legal Services Commission* [2003] EWCA Civ 1558, [2004] IRLR 153, [2004] ICR 312 the Court of Appeal held that the conferral of a franchise by the Legal Services Commission enabling the applicant's firm to receive public funds for the provisions of services in certain categories of legal work was an 'authorisation' that 'facilitates engagement in' the profession of solicitor for the purposes of *RRA 1976, s 13*. The authorisation was conferred on both the applicant's firm and the applicant personally.

Being a Justice of the Peace is not 'engagement in a particular profession' (*Arthur v A-G* [1999] ICR 631). However, appointment as a Justice of the Peace would now be covered by the provisions relating to office holders (see above **13.25**).

A number of cases have considered the position of political parties. In *McDonagh and Triesman v Ali* [2002] EWCA Civ 93, [2002] IRLR 489, [2002] ICR 1026 the CA held (disapproving the EAT's decision in *Sawyer v Ahsan* [1999] IRLR 609) that the Labour Party is not a 'qualifications body' within the definition, at least in relation to the selection or nomination of candidates for elections. Although being an MP is a 'profession', the selection or nomination of candidates is not an 'authorisation' or 'qualification' for that profession. *Triesman* has now been approved by the House of Lords in *Watt (formerly Carter) v Ahsan* [2007] UKHL 51, [2008] IRLR 243. In that case, however, the House of Lords did confirm that although not a 'qualifications body', the Labour Party was an 'association' within the meaning of *s 25* of the *RRA 1976* (which applied to any association of persons of 25 or more members, regulated by a constitution, that did not fall within *s 11* of the *RRA 1976*. *Section 25* fell within *Part III* of the *RRA 1976*, is outside the jurisdiction of the employment tribunal and the scope of this work).

In *Kulkarni v NHS Education Scotland* [2013] EqLR 34 the EAT (Scotland) held that NHS Education Scotland was not a 'qualifications body' or, at least, was not covered by *s 53* of the *EqA 2010* in respect of its function of allocating trainees. Although having a trainee would facilitate a consultant surgeon's engagement in his profession, the EAT(S) was satisfied that the allocation of a trainee was not the conferral of 'an authorisation, qualification, recognition, registration, enrolment, approval or certification'.

Note that it is not possible to complain to an employment tribunal under this provision if the act complained of is one in respect of which an appeal, or proceedings in the nature of an appeal, may be brought under any enactment. In the predecessor legislation this exception was to be found in *SDA 1975, s 63(2); RRA 1976, s 54(2); RBR 2003, reg 28(2); SOR 2003, reg 28(2); AR 2006, reg 36(2); DDA 1995, s 17A(1A)*. The exception is now in *s 120(7)* of the *EqA 2010*. The scope and effect of this provision were considered in *R v Department of Health, ex p Gandhi* [1991] IRLR 431, [1991] ICR 805, *Khan v General Medical Council* [1994] IRLR 646, [1996] ICR 1032, CA, *Tariquez-Zaman v GMC* (UKEAT/0292/06), *Chaudhary v Specialist Training Authority Appeal Panel and ors* [2005] ICR 1086, [2005] All ER (D) 256 (Mar) and *Depner v GMC* (UKEAT/0457/11/KN). In *General Medical Council v Michalak* [2017] UKSC 71, [2017] 1 WLR 4193 the Supreme Court held, overruling *Jooste v General Medical Council* [2012] EqLR 1049, EAT, that the availability of a claim for judicial review of the decision of the qualifications body under *s 31* of the *Senior Courts Act 1981* does not operate so as to oust the jurisdiction of the employment tribunal in respect of complaints about qualifications bodies.

The occupational requirement exception (above para **13.2**) does not apply to qualifications bodies.

13.30a *Sex discrimination*

Uniquely, the *SDA 1975* provided that, if the qualifications body had to consider an applicant's character, if there was evidence to show that an applicant has practised unlawful discrimination in connection with the carrying on of any profession or trade, that must be taken into account by the body (*SDA 1975, s 13(2)*). No such provision appears in the *EqA 2010*.

13.30b *Disability discrimination*

Qualifications bodies benefit from an exception from the *EqA 2010* for disability discrimination in relation to the application of 'competence standards'. The application of a 'competence standard' is not unlawful unless it constitutes unlawful indirect discrimination under *s 19* (*s 53(7)*). A 'competence standard' is an academic, medical or other standard applied for the purpose of determining whether or not a person has a particular level of competence or ability (*s 54(6)*). By *para 15(2)* of *Part 2* of *Sch 8* to the *EqA 2010* the application of a competence standard by a qualifications body is not the application of a 'provision, criterion or practice' for the purpose of the duty to make reasonable adjustments.

A similar exception applied under the *DDA 1995*. Under the *DDA 1995* qualifications bodies benefitted from an exception to the duty to make reasonable adjustments for disabled people. If the provision, criterion or practice in question was a 'competence standard' then the duty to make reasonable adjustments did not arise: *DDA 1995, s 14B(1)*. A 'competence standard' was "An academic, medical or other standard applied by or on behalf of a qualifications body for the purpose of determining whether or not a person has a particular level of competence or ability" (*DDA 1995, s 14A(5)*). Further, insofar as a qualifying body applied a competence standard to those seeking qualification and sought to justify any disability-related discrimination against a disabled person, the application of the competence standard was only justified if the same standard was applied to persons that did not have the particular disability and its application was a proportionate means of achieving a legitimate aim (*DDA 1995, s 14A(3)*).

In *Burke v The College of Law* [2011] All ER (D) 238 (Mar) (UKEAT/0301/10/SM), the EAT considered the College of Law's requirement that Legal Practice Course exams be completed under timed conditions in an examination hall. The College of Law had already granted Mr Burke, who suffered from multiple sclerosis, 60% additional time. However, he contended that a reasonable adjustment would be that he be able to complete the exams over a number of days at home. The Tribunal (and the EAT) held that the requirement that the exam be completed under timed conditions was a competence standard. While the EAT recognised that there was a distinction to be made between an academic standard and the process by which it was assessed, and that in many cases the latter would be subject to the duty to make reasonable adjustments, the EAT accepted that, in the context of a professional examination which seeks to mimic (to some extent) conditions of practice, the time requirement was a competence standard. This was so even though the College of Law had already voluntarily made 'reasonable adjustments' to the time requirement: the fact that they had made the adjustment voluntarily did not mean they had been under a duty to so. Moreover, there was a qualitative difference between an extension of timed exam conditions and the home examination conditions proposed by the claimant. On appeal, the CA ([2012] EWCA Civ 37, [2012] All ER (D) 29 (Feb)) held that it was not necessary to decide whether or not the time requirement was a competence standard, the fact was that the Tribunal had looked at all the adjustments made by the College and had rightly concluded that reasonable adjustments had been made (including to the time requirement).

In addition to the competence standard exception, provision is made in *ss 96(7)–(9)* of the *EqA 2010* for the relevant regulators of qualifications bodies to specify certain provisions, criteria or practices in relation to which qualifications bodies are not to be subject to the duty to make reasonable adjustments in relation to specified qualifications. The identity of the relevant regulators, the specified qualifications and the means by which the regulators must publish their specified provisions, criteria or practices (principally on their websites) are prescribed for by regulations for England (*SI 2010/2245*), Scotland (*SI 2010/315*) and Wales (*SI 2010/2217*).

Sexual orientation discrimination

13.30c There is an exception equivalent to the occupational requirement exception for discrimination in employment (see above **13.7**). *Para 2(3)* of *Part 1* of *Sch 9* to the *EqA 2010* provides that the provisions relating to discrimination by qualifications bodies do not apply to 'professional or trade qualifications conferred for the purposes of an organised religion where a requirement related to sexual orientation is applied to the qualification so as to comply with the doctrines of the religion or to avoid conflicting with the strongly held religious convictions of a significant number of the religion's followers'. See *SOR 2003, reg 16(3)* for the exception under the predecessor legislation.

13.31 Providers of vocational training

The predecessor legislation contains specific provisions relating to providers of vocational training. The *EqA 2010* covers such persons by way of the provisions for employment service-providers (see below **13.34**).

Under the predecessor legislation, a 'training provider' was any person who provides, or makes arrangements for the provision of, training or facilities for training which would help fit another person for any employment: *SDA 1975, s 14(1); RRA 1976, s 13(1); RBR 2003, reg 17(4); SOR 2003, reg 17(4); AR 2006, reg 20(4)*. *DDA 1995* prohibited discrimination in the provision of 'work placements' (*s 14C*) and 'employment services' (*s 21A*, read with *ss 19* and *20*). 'Vocational training' and 'vocational guidance' were included within the scope of 'employment services' (*DDA 1995, ss 21A(1)(a), (b)*).

The *RBR 2003, SOR 2003* and *AR 2006* made clear that 'training' includes practical work experience provided by an employer to a person whom he does not employ; this is undoubtedly also within the meaning of 'training' in the *SDA 1975* (see especially *s 14(1B)*) and *RRA 1976* (training being defined under *s 78* of the *RRA 1976* as including '*any form of education or instruction*'). This point was confirmed by the EAT in *Chenge v Treasury Solicitor's Department* [2007] IRLR 386, in which the Department had sought to argue that the Government Legal Service vacation placement scheme (where successful applicants gain work experience placements for which they are paid only expenses) was not 'training' within the meaning of *RRA 1976, s 13(1)*. The EAT held that the phrase '*any form of education*' could include education by watching as well as education by doing and that was no need to analyse in detail the syllabus of a scheme in order to decide whether it was a training scheme or a work placement scheme. There was no principled reason why *RRA 1976* should not apply to work experience or work placement. Nor did it matter how long a course took, though the EAT did note that if it was '*merely an educational visit*' that might fall in a different category. Previously, the EAT held in *Fletcher v NHS Pensions Agency* [2005] IRLR 689, [2005] ICR 1458, that the NHS Pensions Agency, which provides bursaries to trainee midwives combining academic study at universities with practical training through clinical placements in the community and hospitals, is a 'training provider' within the meaning of *SDA 1975, s 14(1)* since the bursaries are a 'facility' for training.

However, where someone is appointed purely as a volunteer (even if they hope through that appointment to secure paid employment with the organisation), that is not 'vocational training'. Voluntary employment is outside the scope of the discrimination legislation: *X v Mid Sussex Citizens Advice Bureau* [2012] UKSC 59, [2013] IRLR 146, [2013] ICR 249.

The definition of 'training provider' excluded employers in relation to training for their own employees and also education establishments: *SDA 1975, s 14(2); RRA 1976, s 13(2); RBR 2003, reg 17(4); SOR 2003, reg 17(4); AR 2006, reg 20(4)*. This is because separate provision in relation to discrimination in education was made by both the Acts and the Regulations. Claims in relation to discrimination in education are excluded from the jurisdiction of the employment tribunals and are therefore outside the scope of this book. Note, however, that the mere fact that a provider of vocational training was acting as agent of an educational establishment did not mean that a claim against that provider was excluded from the jurisdiction of the employment tribunals, provided of course that the respondent otherwise fell within the definition of 'training provider' in the legislation: *Moyhing v Homerton University Hospitals NHS Trust* [2005] All ER (D) 03 (Sep) (UKEAT/0851/04/MAA).

It was unlawful, in relation to a person seeking or undergoing training which would help fit him for any employment for any training provider to discriminate against him:

(a)   in the terms on which the training provider affords him access to any training (or any facilities concerned with such training);

(b)   by refusing or deliberately not affording him such access;

(c)   by terminating his training; or

(d)   by subjecting him to any other detriment during his training (*SDA 1975, s 14(1)*; *RRA 1976, s 13(1)*; *RBR 2003, reg 17(1)*; *SOR 2003, reg 17(1)*; *AR 2006, reg 20(1)*; see also *DDA 1995, ss 19(1)* and *21A*).

RBR 2003, SOR 2003, AR 2006 and, with effect from 1 October 2005, the *SDA 1975* also applies expressly to 'arrangements' made 'for the purpose of selecting people to receive vocational training' (*SDA 1975, s 14(1)(a)*, as amended by the *Sex Discrimination Regulations 2005*; *RBR 2003, reg 17(1)(aa)*; *SOR 2003, reg 17(1)(aa)*; *AR 2006, reg 20(1)(a)*).

In *Fletcher* the bursaries were stopped during the trainees' maternity leave: since the bursaries were 'facilities concerned with training', which were stopped because the claimants were pregnant, this was unlawful sex discrimination. The EAT ruled that the tribunal had been wrong to conclude that there was no unlawful discrimination because employees absent for other reasons were treated the same way.

All the exceptions that applied to discrimination by employers applied in relation to discrimination by providers of vocational training. The *RBR 2003, SOR 2003* and *AR 2006* provided that the training provider would have a defence where the alleged discrimination only concerned training for employment which, by virtue of the fact that the exception for genuine occupational requirement applied, the respondent could lawfully refuse to offer the person seeking training (*RBR 2003, reg 17(3); SOR 2003, reg 17(3); AR 2006, reg 20(3)*). The exceptions in the *RBR 2003, SOR 2003* and *AR 2006* for national security, positive action and the protection of Sikhs from discrimination in relation to the wearing of safety helmets applied generally to Parts II and III of both sets of *Regulations* and therefore applied to training providers as they did to employers. The *SDA 1975* and *RRA 1976* provided, simply, that all the exceptions that applied in relation to discrimination by employers applied also to training providers (*SDA 1975, s 14(2)*; *RRA 1976, s 13(2)*). (For exceptions see above **13.3, 13.10, 13.11, 13.12** and **13.17** ff.)

It was also unlawful for a training provider, in relation to a person seeking or undergoing training which would help fit him for any employment, to subject him to harassment (*SDA 1975, s 14(1A)*, as inserted with effect from 1 October 2005 by the *Sex Discrimination Regulations 2005*; *RRA 1976, s 13(3)*; *RBR 2003, reg 17(2)*; *SOR 2003, reg 17(2)*; *AR 2006, reg 20(2); DDA 1995, s 21A(2)*).

13.32 Employment agencies, careers guidance, etc

The provisions relating to employment agencies applied in the predecessor legislation. The *EqA 2010* covers such person by way of the provisions for employment service-providers (see below **13.34**).

The *RBR 2003*, *SOR 2003* and *AR 2006* defined an employment agency as 'a person who, for profit or not, provides services for the purpose of finding employment for workers or supplying respondents with workers'.

Under *DDA 1995*, employment agencies were covered as providers of 'employment services', defined to include 'services to assist a person to obtain or retain employment, or to establish himself as self-employed' (*s 21A(1)(c)*).

No definition was given in the *SDA 1975* or the *RRA 1976*, though both those *Acts*, like the *RBR 2003* and *SOR 2003*, state that references to the services of an employment agency include 'guidance on careers and any other services related to employment' (*SDA 1975, s 15(3); RRA 1976, s 14(3); RBR 2003, reg 18(6); SOR 2003, reg 18(6); AR 2006, reg 21(6)*). Education establishments were excluded from the definition of employment agencies (impliedly in the *SDA 1975* and the *RRA 1976*, expressly in the *RBR 2003* and *SOR 2003: reg 18(6)* and in *AR 2006, reg 21(6)*). (Separate provision in relation to discrimination in education was made by both the Acts and the Regulations. Consideration of this is, however, outside the scope of this book.)

Note that users of employment agencies could also bring claims against the employer to whom they are supplied, either under the provisions relating to contract workers (see above **13.24**) or, in certain circumstances, as employees (see generally Employee, Self-Employed or Worker? (**16**)).

It was unlawful for an employment agency to discriminate against a person:

(a)   in the terms on which the agency offered to provide any of its services;

(b)   by refusing or deliberately not providing any of its services; or

(c)   in the way it provided any of its services (*SDA 1975, s 15(1); RRA 1976, s 14(1); RBR 2003, reg 18(1); SOR 2003, reg 18(1); AR 2006, reg 21(1)*).

All the exceptions that applied to discrimination by employers applied in relation to discrimination by employment agencies. The *RBR 2003*, *SOR 2003* and *AR 2006* provided that the agency would have a defence where the alleged discrimination 'only concerns employment which, by virtue of . . . (the) exception for genuine occupational requirement . . . the employer could lawfully refuse to offer the person in question' (*RBR 2003, reg 18(3); SOR 2003, reg 18(3); AR 2006, reg 20(3)*). The exceptions in the *RBR 2003*, *SOR 2003* and *AR 2006* for national security, positive action and the protection of Sikhs from discrimination in relation to the wearing of safety helmets applied generally to *Parts II* and *III* of both sets of *Regulations* and therefore applied to employment agencies as to employers. The *SDA 1975* and *RRA 1976* provided, simply, that the agency would have a defence where the alleged discrimination 'only concerns employment which an employer could lawfully refuse to offer the' person concerned (*SDA 1975, s 15(4); RRA 1976, s 14(4)*). (For circumstances in which an employer could lawfully refuse to offer employment see above **13.3**, **13.10**, **13.11**, **13.12** and **13.17** ff.)

A further defence was available that is peculiar to employment agencies. An employment agency would not be liable for unlawful discrimination where it proves that 'it acted in reliance on a statement made to it by the employer to the effect that, by reason of (the existence of a genuine occupational requirement) its action would not be unlawful', provided that it also proves that it was reasonable for it to rely on the statement (*SDA 1975, s 15(5);*

RRA 1976, s 14(5); *RBR 2003, reg 18(4)*; *SOR 2003, reg 18(4)*; *AR 2006, reg 21(4)*). Thus, if, for example, an employment agency relied on the statement of an employer who had been guilty of discrimination in the past, to the knowledge of the employment agency, it may be difficult for that agency to establish that it had acted reasonably in relying upon that statement.

If an employer knowingly or recklessly made a statement to that effect which 'in a material respect is false or misleading', they thereby committed an offence punishable by a fine not exceeding level 5 on the standard scale (*SDA 1975, s 15(6)*; *RRA 1976, s 14(6)*; *RBR 2003, reg 18(5)*; *SOR 2003, reg 18(5)*; *AR 2006, reg 21(5)* see also **1.10** INTRODUCTION).

It was also unlawful for an employment agency, in relation to the provision of its services, to subject to harassment a person to whom it provided such services, or who had requested the provision of such services: *SDA 1975, s 15(1A)*, as inserted with effect from 1 October 2005 by the *Sex Discrimination Regulations 2005, reg 18*; *RRA 1976, s 14(1A)*; *RBR 2003, reg 18(2)*; *SOR 2003, reg 18(2)*; *AR 2006, reg 21(2)*; *DDA 1995, s 21A(2)*.

13.33 State provision of employment-related services

The provisions relating to state provision of employment-related services applied in the predecessor legislation. The *EqA 2010* covers such person by way of the provisions for employment service-providers (see below **13.34**).

Under the predecessor legislation, the prohibitions on discrimination and harassment also applied to the provision of facilities or services by the Secretary of State under the *Employment and Training Act 1973, s 2* (arrangements for assisting persons to obtain employment) and by the Scottish Enterprise or Highlands and Islands Enterprise under the *Enterprise and New Towns (Scotland) Act 1990, s 2(3)* (the equivalent provision for Scotland) (*SDA 1975, ss 16(1), (1A)*; *RRA 1976, ss 15(1), (1A)*; *RBR 2003, regs 19(1), (2)*; *SOR 2003, regs 19(1), (2)*; *AR 2006, regs 22(1), (2)*).

Similarly, the prohibitions on racial and sex discrimination and harassment applied where a local authority provided services under the *Employment and Training Act 1973, s 10* (*SDA 1975, s 15(2)*; *RRA 1976, s 14(2)*).

The provisions relating to the provision of facilities or services under the *Employment and Training Act 1973, s 2* were default provisions, applying only where the Secretary of State would not be covered by the provisions relating to employment agencies (see above **13.32**) or providers of vocational training generally (see above **13.31**): *SDA 1975, 16(2)*; *RRA 1976, s 15(2)*; *RBR 2003, reg 19(3)*; *SOR 2003, reg 19(3)*; *AR 2006, reg 20(3)*).

13.34 Employment service-providers

The *EqA 2010* contains specific provision in relation to employment service-providers. This replaces the provision in the predecessor legislation on providers of vocational training, employment agencies and state provision of employment-related services, although case law on those types of provider (see above) will in the main continue to be relevant when construing the provision in the *EqA 2010* in respect of employment service-providers.

A non-exhaustive definition of employment service provision is given at *s 56(2)*. It includes the provision of vocational training, the provision of vocational guidance, the provision of a service for finding employment for persons, the supply of persons for work to employers, careers services and various other statutory services.

'Vocational training' is defined for the purposes of the section as 'training for employment' or 'work experience (including work experience the duration of which is not agreed until after it begins') (*s 56(6)*) and 'training' includes facilities for training (*s 56(8)*).

Section 55 makes it unlawful for any 'employment service-provider' to discriminate against, or victimise, persons:

(a)   in the arrangements they make for selecting persons to whom to provide, or to whom they offer to provide, their services;

(b)   as to the terms on which the service is provided;

(c)   by not providing, or not offering to provide, the service;

(d)   by terminating the provision of the service; or

(e)   by subjecting the individual to any other detriment (*EqA 2010, ss 55(1), (2), (4), (5)*).

There is also a specific prohibition on harassment by the employment service-providers: *EqA 2010, s 55(3)*.

The employment services provision is a residual one that applies only where the other provisions relating to employment do not apply (*s 56(3)*). Training that is covered by the parts of the *Act* relating to schools and higher education is also excluded: *ss 56(4)* and *(5)*. *Section 56(5)* provides that the employment services provision does not apply 'in relation to training or guidance for students of an institution to which section 91 (further and higher education) applies in so far as it is training or guidance to which the governing body of the institution has power to afford access'. In *Blackwood v Birmingham and Solihull Mental Health NHS Foundation Trust* [2016] IRLR 878, [2016] ICR 903 the CA considered the meaning of 'power to afford access' in *s 56(5)* and concluded that 'power' means 'the ability to do something' (even if that something requires third party co-operation and consent) and that 'afford access' means 'afford entry to a placement'. Thus, a student mental health nurse placed with the respondent Trust by her university was engaged in vocational training to which the university had 'power to afford access' even though the placement could only be arranged by the university with the consent of the Trust and even though the Trust had a unilateral power to terminate the placement (ie even though the university had no power to compel the Trust to continue to afford the claimant access to the placement). This meant that *s 56(5)* applied and accordingly *s 55* was disapplied. This in principle left the claimant only with a potential claim under the higher education provisions of the *Act* (*s 91*) against the University. This in effect left the claimant without a remedy since the only claim that could be made against the University under *s 91* was a claim in relation to 'access' to vocational training. The University could not under that provision be held responsible for the actions of the Trust in providing the vocational training. If the Trust had been the claimant's employer, a claim could have been brought straightforwardly under the employment provisions, but that was not the situation and in this case the *EqA 2010* on its face left the claimant without a remedy. The CA considered that this situation was incompatible with the requirements of EU Law (specifically *art 14(1)* of *Directive 2006/54*) and accordingly ruled that *s 56(5)* must be construed as reading 'This section does not apply to discrimination in relation to training or guidance for students of an institution to which section 91 applies to the extent that the student is entitled under that section to make a claim as regards that discrimination'. So read, *s 56(5)* did not prevent the tribunal from hearing the claimant's claim against the Trust under *s 55* as a vocational training provider. The Court of Appeal in Blackwood also gave guidance as to the circumstances in which the agency provisions in *ss 109* and *110* of the *EqA 2010* might be relevant in such claims. See **12.56 DISCRIMINATION AND EQUAL OPPORTUNITIES – I**. For a case in which it was determined that the university was not 'affording access' to vocational medical training for the purposes of *s 56(5)*, see *Garrard v University of London* [2013] EqLR 746.

The genuine occupational requirement exceptions (above para **13.2 ff**) are applied indirectly to employment service-providers. They may refuse to provide employment services to persons where the services relate to employment of a type the offer of which could lawfully be refused to that person by virtue of a genuine occupational requirement: see *para 5 of Sch 9* to the *EqA 2010*. An employment services provider will have a defence to any claim if he relies reasonably on a statement made by the person with the power to offer the work that a genuine occupational requirement would apply: *para 5(3)*. It is an offence for a person with the power to offer such work to knowingly or recklessly make a statement about a genuine occupational requirement that is false or misleading: *para 5(4)*. A person guilty of that offence is liable on summary conviction to a fine not exceeding level 5 on the standard scale: *para 5(5)*.

13.35   Trustees and managers of occupational pension schemes

The *EqA 2010* makes specific provision in relation to occupational pension schemes. *Section 61(1)* provides that an occupational pension scheme must be taken to include a non-discrimination rule. A non-discrimination rule is a provision by which a 'responsible person' (A):

(a)   must not discriminate against another person (B) in carrying out any of his functions in relation to the scheme;

(b)   must not, in relation to the scheme, harass B;

(c)   must not, in relation to the scheme, victimise B (*s 61(2)*).

'Responsible persons' are the trustees or managers of the scheme, employers whose employees are (or may be) members of the scheme and persons exercising an 'appointing function' in relation to an office the holder of which is, or may be, a member of the scheme (*s 61(4)*). An 'appointing function' includes the functions of appointing a person, terminating a person's appointment, recommending a person for appointment and approving an appointment (*s 61(6)*).

The non-discrimination rule does not operate in relation to a person who is a pension credit member of the scheme, ie the spouse or civil partner of a member of the scheme who has received a pension credit from the scheme on the death of the pensioner member: *s 61(5)*.

Section 62 makes specific provision to enable trustees and managers to make alterations to the scheme by resolution to conform with the non-discrimination rule, even if they do not have the power under the scheme to do so, or if the procedure for doing so would be liable to be unduly complex or protracted or involves obtaining consents which cannot be obtained or which can be obtained only with undue delay or difficulty.

The provisions in relation to occupational pension schemes in the predecessor legislation were similar: see the *RBR 2003* and *SOR 2003* (as amended with effect from 2 December 2003 by the *Employment Equality (Religion or Belief) (Amendment) Regulations 2003 (SI 2003/2828)* and The *Employment Equality (Sexual Orientation) (Amendment) Regulations 2003 (SI 2003/2827)* respectively) applied to trustees and managers of occupational pension schemes, as did the *DDA 1995* (as amended). *AR 2006* also applied to trustees and managers of pension schemes. However, there were detailed exceptions in relation to age set out in *Schedule 2* to *AR 2006*.

'Occupational pension scheme' has the same meaning as in the *Pensions Schemes Act 1993* (*EqA 2010, s 212*, see previously *RBR 2003, Sch 1A, para 1; SOR 2003, Sch 1A, para 1; AR 2006, Sch 2, para 1*).

Certain further provision is made in relation to occupational pension schemes so far as the protected characteristics of sex, pregnancy and maternity, sexual orientation, age and disability are concerned as follows.

Discrimination and Equal Opportunities – II

13.35a Sex discrimination

In the predecessor legislation sex discrimination in relation to pensions was dealt with in the *Pensions Act 1995* and not in the *SDA 1975*. Although the provisions of the *Pension Act 1995* and the *SDA 1975* have been brought together in the *EqA 2010*, there is still a similar division made between the general provisions prohibiting discrimination in relation to pensions and those prohibiting sex and maternity discrimination in relation to pensions. As set out above, *Sections 61(1)* and *(3)* of the *EqA 2010* provide that 'an occupational pension scheme must be taken to include a non-discrimination rule' and that the scheme will take effect 'subject to' that rule. However, the 'non-discrimination rule' only applies where an 'equality rule' does not have effect (or would have had effect but for the exceptions in *Part 2* of *Sch 7*): see *EqA 2010, s 61(10)*. Thus, the general 'non-discrimination rule' only applies to occupational pension schemes where the sex equality rule under *s 67* or the maternity equality rule under *s 75* (see below) does not.

See **23.14** ff EQUAL PAY for details of the sex equality rule in relation to occupational pension schemes and see also RETIREMENT **(43)**.

13.35b Pregnancy and maternity discrimination

In the predecessor legislation sex discrimination in relation to pensions was dealt with in the *Pensions Act 1995* and not in the *SDA 1975*. Although the provisions of the *Pensions Act 1995* and the *SDA 1975* have been brought together in the *EqA 2010*, there is still a similar division made between the general provisions prohibiting discrimination in relation to pensions and those prohibiting sex and maternity discrimination in relation to pensions. As set out above, *Sections 61(1)* and *(3)* of the *EqA 2010* provide that 'an occupational pension scheme must be taken to include a non-discrimination rule' and that the scheme will take effect 'subject to' that rule. However, the 'non-discrimination rule' only applies where an 'equality rule' does not have effect (or would have had effect but for the exceptions in *Part 2* of *Sch 7*): see *EqA 2010, s 61(10)*. Thus, the general 'non-discrimination rule' only applies to occupational pension schemes where the sex equality rule under *s 67* (see above) or the maternity equality rule under *s 75* does not.

See **23.17** EQUAL PAY for details of the maternity equality rule.

13.35c Sexual orientation

So far as the general non-discrimination rule applicable to occupational pension schemes is concerned, *section 67(7)* expressly provides that if the effect of a 'relevant matter' (ie a relevant term or the exercise of a relevant discretion permitted under the scheme: *s 67(8)*) differs according to a person's family, marital or civil partnership status, a comparison for the purposes of determining whether the trustees or managers have discriminated on grounds of sex contrary to *s 67* must be with persons of the opposite sex who have the same status, i.e. between male civil partners and female civil partners, not between male civil partners and female spouses, for example. It is to be noted, however, that in the light of the decision of the *Supreme Court in Hall v Bull* [2013] UKSC 73, [2014] 1 All ER 919 (see above **13.14**) such discrimination will generally constitute direct discrimination on grounds of sexual orientation.

There is, however, a further specific exception in *para 18* of *Part 3* of *Sch 9* to the *EqA 2010* for benefits dependent on marital status. This applies to pensions as to other benefits and is discussed in detail above at **13.14**. In short, it provides that a person does not contravene the Act, so far as relating to sexual orientation, by doing anything which prevents or restricts a person who is not married from having access to a benefit, facility or service (a) the right to which accrued before 5 December 2005 (the day on which *section 1* of the *Civil Partnership Act 2004* came into force), or (b) which is payable in respect of periods of service before that date. However, in *Walker v Innospec Ltd* [2017] UKSC 47, [2017] ICR 1077 the Supreme Court found that this exception was incompatible with EU law insofar as it precluded equal treatment in respect of survivor's pensions that come into payment after

5 December 2005 but the entitlement to the pension accrued by reference to service prior to that date. See, however, *Parris v Trinity College Dublin* (C-443/15) [2017] IRLR 173, [2017] ICR 313. That case concerned an occupational pension scheme with a rule to the effect that a survivor's pension would only be payable if the marriage (whether same-sex or opposite-sex) had taken place before the individual reached the age of 60. The claimant complained that this was indirectly discriminatory against homosexuals who under Irish law were not permitted to marry prior to 2011, by which time the claimant was already 60. Disagreeing with the Advocate General in that case, the CJEU rejected the claim, essentially on the basis that under EU law it is a matter for Member States if and when to provide legal recognition to same-sex partnerships and EU law does not require such legal recognition to be given retroactive effect. In *Walker v Innospec* the Supreme Court considered that disapplying the para 18 exception did not amount to giving retroactive effect to the *Directive* or the *Civil Partnership Act 2004* because entitlement to survivor's pension accrues regardless of the identity of the survivor so in the case of survivor's pensions what matters is what the law is at the time the pension is paid, rather than what it was at the time that the right to the pension accrued.

13.35d Age discrimination

The *AR 2006* provided a number of exceptions for age discrimination in relation to occupational pension schemes (in *Sch 2*). The *EqA 2010* does not itself contain any exceptions, but provides for exceptions to be set out in subordinate legislation. A Minister of the Crown may by order (following consultation) provide that it is not an age contravention for an employer or for the trustees and managers of an occupational pension scheme to use certain specified practices in relation to contributions to personal pension schemes (*para 16* of *Part 2* of *Schedule 9* to *EqA 2010* and *s 61(8)*).

The *Equality Act (Age Exceptions for Pension Schemes) 2010 Order (SI 2010/2133)* (as amended) made under that enabling power makes extensive and detailed provision for exceptions from the *EqA 2010* for certain practices in relation to pension schemes.

It is to be noted that the *2010 Order* states that the inclusion of a practice in the list of exceptions provided for in that *Order* does not mean that it would otherwise be unlawful: *art 5*.

It should also be noted that most of these exceptions go beyond the exceptions for age discrimination that are specifically referred to in the *Framework Directive* and would therefore need to be justified (in the event of a challenge) as being a proportionate means of achieving a legitimate aim. *Article 6(2)* of the *Framework Directive* does however specifically permit Member States to 'provide that the fixing for occupational social security schemes of ages for admission or entitlement to retirement or invalidity benefits, including the fixing under those schemes of different ages for employees or groups or categories of employees, and the use, in the context of such schemes, of age criteria in actuarial calculations, does not constitute discrimination on the grounds of age, provided this does not result in discrimination on the grounds of sex'. The scope of this exception was considered by the CJEU in *Dansk Jurist- Og Okonomforbund, acting on behalf of Toftgaard v Indenrigs- Og Sundhedsministeriet* C-546/11 [2014] IRLR 37, [2014] ICR 1. In that case the CJEU held that 'availability pay' paid to Danish civil servants when made redundant (up to three years further salary provided they remained available for assignment to another post during that period) did not constitute a form of occupational social security scheme. Exclusion of over 65s from receipt of availability pay because they were eligible for a state pension was therefore direct discrimination, and not justified.

Readers are referred to the text of the *2010 Order* for the detail of the provisions. In summary, however, the exceptions cover the following:

(a)   any rights accrued or benefits payable in respect of periods of pensionable service prior to 1 December 2006 (*art 3(b)*);

(b)   provisions which treat members or potential members of a scheme differently on the grounds of their length of service with an employer so long as that length of service is less than five years (and length of service may refer to length of service at or above a particular level, assessed by reference to the demands made on the member or worker, for eg, in terms of effort, skills and decision-making) (*art 6(2)*);

(c)   length of service criteria of greater than five years, if it reasonably appears to the employer that this meets a business need (for eg by encouraging the loyalty or motivation or rewarding the experience of some or all of its workers) (with regard to action by trustees or managers, they may rely on a confirmation by the employer) (*art 6(3)*);

(d)   setting minimum or maximum ages for admission to the scheme (*Sch 1, para 1(a)*), or for the commencement of payment of employer contributions (*Sch 2, paras 4* and *5*), including different ages for different groups or categories of worker;

(e)   setting a minimum level of pensionable pay for admission (provided this is not above one and a half times the lower earnings limit in s 5(1) of the Social Security Contributions and Benefits Act 1992, does not exceed an amount calculated by reference to the lower earnings limit where the aim is more or less to reflect the amount of the basic state retirement pension; or an amount calculated more or less to reflect the amount of the basic state retirement pension plus the additional state retirement pension) (*Sch 1, para 1(b)*);

(f)   the use of age criteria in actuarial calculations (*Sch 1, para 2*) (for a case in which this exemption was held to apply so as to preclude the claim see *Hadfield v Health & Safety Executive* UKEATS/0013/10/BI);

(g)   differences in employer or member contributions attributable to differences in pensionable pay (*Sch 2, para 2* and *Sch 1, paras 3, 18* and *21(3)*);

(h)   differences in the amount of any age related benefit or death benefit attributable to differences over time in the pensionable pay of those members (*Sch 1, para 20*) or the setting of a maximum amount of benefit by reference to a fraction, proportion or multiple of a member's pensionable pay (*Sch 1, para 21(3)*);

(i)   differences in employer or member contributions attributable to differences in age, but only in limited circumstances (broadly speaking where the aim of the payment of differential rates is to equalise the amount of benefits that persons of different ages whose circumstances are otherwise comparable will receive) (*Sch 1, paras 4, 5* and *6*);

(Note that, once an employee has passed the minimum age for admission to a scheme, there is no exception that enables an employer simply to pay different levels of contribution to employees based on their ages. Such arrangements would constitute prima facie age discrimination and would have to be justified by reference to a legitimate aim in the normal way: see *Handels- og Kontorfunktionaerernes Forbund Danmark v Experian A/S* C-476/11 [2014] ICR 27, [2013] All ER (D) 01 (Oct). In that case, the CJEU accepted that legitimate aims for paying different amounts of employer contribution by reference to the ages of workers could include enabling older workers entering late to build up a reasonable pension over a short period, or including younger workers in the scheme at an early stage while making it possible for them to have a larger proportion of their income at their disposal, or the need to cover risks the cost of which increased with age unless that is justified. The CJEU held that it was for the national court to determine whether the particular arrangements in question were justified by reference to those aims.)

(j) setting of early or late retirement ages including different ages for different groups or categories of member (including different ages for deferred and active members) (*Sch 1, para 11*);

(k) a minimum age for entitlement to or payment of any age-related benefit to a member, provided that this benefit is subject to actuarial reduction for early receipt, and the member is not credited with additional periods of pensionable service (except where certain other exemptions for minimum ages for entitlement apply) (*Sch 1, paras 7, 8, 9* and *12*);

(l) a minimum age for payment or entitlement to a particular age-related benefit on grounds of redundancy where it is enhanced in a specified manner (*Sch 1, para 10*);

(m) a minimum age for entitlement to age-related benefits on grounds of ill health, where the benefit is enhanced in a specified manner (*Sch 1, para 12*) and for the discontinuation of any life assurance cover for such members when they reach retirement age (*Sch 1, para 16*);

(n) for the purpose of equalising the amount of age-related benefit employees of different ages whose situations are otherwise comparable will receive as a result of historical arrangements, an employer may pay different rates of contribution according to the age of workers (*Sch 2, para 1*);

(o) an employer may always make equal rates of contribution irrespective of the age of the workers in respect of whom contributions are made (*Sch 2, para 6*);

(p) age-related benefits or death benefits may be calculated by reference to length of pensionable service, so long as members in a comparable situation are entitled to accrue rights based upon the same fraction of pensionable pay (*Sch 1, para 17*) and benefits may be limited by a maximum number of years of pensionable service (*Sch 1, para 21(2)*);

(q) pensions in payment may be increased for members over 55 (*Sch 1, para 28*), and may be increased for other members by reference to their ages (or the length of time the pension has been in payment) to the extent that the aim in setting the different rates is to maintain the relative value of members' pensions (*Sch 1, paras 29* and *30*);

(r) death benefit by reference to the number of years pensionable service that a member would have completed had they remained in employment to normal pension age (*Sch 1, para 13*), and any pension payable where the dependent is more than a specified number of years younger than the member may be actuarially reduced (*Sch 1, para 15*);

(s) benefits payable to members aged between age 60 and 65 may in certain circumstances be reduced by reference to the state retirement pension rate (*Sch 1, para 14*);

(t) certain differences in the fraction of pensionable pay at which any age-related benefit accrues, or the amount of death benefit, or age-related benefits, or setting a maximum amount of age-related benefits or death benefit equal to a fraction, proportion or multiple of the member's pensionable pay, or a minimum period of pensionable service, in each case where the aim is to give members in a comparable situation the right to the same fraction proportion or multiple of pensionable pay without regard to pensionable service (*Sch 1, para 18*);

(u) where (t) applies, setting different rates of member or employer contributions is also permitted (*Sch 1, para 19*);

(v) limiting age related benefits or death benefits to members entitled to short service benefit under s 71 of the Pension Schemes Act 1993 (*Sch 1, para 22*);

(w)   excluding from a calculation of pensionable pay an amount which does not exceed one and a half times the lower earning limit, aimed to reflect the basic state retirement pension, or calculated to reflect the basic state retirement pension plus the additional state retirement pension (*Sch 1, para 23*);

(x)   differences in age-related or death benefits attributable to accrual of age-related benefit at a higher fraction for pensionable pay over the upper limit to reflect the additional state retirement pension (*Sch 1, para 24*);

(y)   limiting the amount of a benefit (or employer contributions: *Sch 2, para 3*) where this relates to all members joining or eligible to join on, after or before a particular date and which results from imposing a maximum level of pensionable pay by reference to which such benefit is calculated (*Sch 1, para 25*);

(z)   closure of schemes, or parts of schemes, from certain dates (*Sch 1, paras 26* and *27*);

(aa)   an age limit for the transfer of the value of a member's accrued rights into or out of a scheme may be set provided that it is not more than one year before the member's normal pension age (*Sch 1, para 31*);

(ab)   anything necessary to secure any tax relief or exemption or to prevent any charge to tax arising under Part 4 of the Finance Act 2004 (*Sch 1, para 32*).

13.35e Disability discrimination

In addition to the general non-discrimination rule applicable to occupational schemes (see above) 'responsible persons' are also under a duty to make reasonable adjustments for persons with disabilities: *EqA 2010, s 61(11)*. *Section 63* further provides so far as communications are concerned (ie the provision of information and the operation of a dispute resolution procedure) the prohibition on disability discrimination applies to a disabled pension credit member as it does to someone who is a deferred member or pensioner member of the scheme.

Local authority members

Section 58 of the *EqA 2010* contains specific provision prohibiting local authorities from discriminating against a member of the authority in relation to the member's carrying out of 'official business' by not affording him access to training or other facilities or subjecting him to a detriment. By *s 59(4)*, 'official business' is anything the member does as a member of the authority, as a member of a body to which the member is appointed by the authority, or as a member of any other public body. A local authority must also not harass the member (*s 58(2)*) or victimise him (*s 58(3)*). However, *s 58(4)* provides that a member will not be subjected to a 'detriment' for these purposes only because the member is (a) not appointed or elected to an office of the authority, (b) not appointed or elected to, or to an office of, a committee or sub-committee of the authority, or (c) not appointed or nominated in exercise of an appointment power of the authority. By *s 58(6)* a duty to make reasonable adjustments also applies to a local authority (see also *paragraph 18* of *Schedule 8*). The occupational requirement exception (above **13.2**) does not apply to local authorities.

13.36 The Crown

As with the predecessor legislation, *EqA 2010* applies to employment by the Crown, House of Commons staff and House of Lords staff as it does to other employments: see *s 82(2)*. See *SDA 1975, ss 85–85B; RRA 1976, ss 75–75B; RBR 2003, regs 36–38; SOR 2003, regs 36–38; AR 2006, regs 44–46; DDA 1995, ss 64–65* for the relevant provisions of the predecessor legislation.

Save as set out above at **13.3**, **13.5**, **13.11**(d), **13.5**(i) and **13.16**(d), it also applies to service in the armed forces: see *s 82(3)*. As under the predecessor legislation, separate provision is made for enforcement of claims by members of the armed forces: see **14.2** DISCRIMINATION AND EQUAL OPPORTUNITIES – III.

13.37   GENERAL EQUALITY DUTIES ON PUBLIC AUTHORITIES

Sections 149–157 of the *EqA 2010*, which came fully into force on 6 April 2011, impose general equality duties on public authorities. Similar provision was to be found in the predecessor legislation at *RRA 1976*, *s 71*, *SDA 1975*, *s 76A* and *DDA 1995*, *s 49A*. Full discussion of these provisions is outside the scope of this work. However, in summary, section 149(1) creates a new, truly general public sector equality duty ('PSED') (in the sense that it applies to all protected characteristics apart from marital/civil partnership status: see *s 159(7)*), which requires public authorities and others exercising public functions (*s 149(2)*), in the exercise of their functions, to have 'due regard to the need to':

(a)   eliminate discrimination, harassment, victimisation and any other conduct that is prohibited by or under the *EqA 2010*;

(b)   advance equality of opportunity between persons who share a relevant protected characteristic and persons who do not share it;

(c)   foster good relations between persons who share a relevant protected characteristic and persons who do not share it.

Section 149(3) makes clear that the 'due regard' duty includes in particular a duty to have due regard to the need to remove or minimise disadvantages suffered by persons who share a relevant protected characteristic that are connected to that characteristic, to take steps to meet the needs of persons who share a relevant protected characteristic that are different from the needs of persons who do not share it, and to encourage persons who share a relevant protected characteristic to participate in public life or in any other activity in which participation by such persons is disproportionately low. *Section 149(5)* further stipulates that having due regard to the need to foster good relations between persons includes having due regard to the need to tackle prejudice and promote understanding. The section recognises that compliance with the PSED may involve treating some persons more favourably than others, but makes clear that this is not to be taken as permitting conduct that would otherwise be prohibited under the Act (*s 149(6)* and see **13.10** above for the exceptions for positive discrimination).

Note that the duty does not sanction treating some people more favourably than others where this would be conduct otherwise prohibited under the *EqA 2010* (see *s 149(6)*).

In addition to the PSED, the *EqA 2010* also imposes certain specific duties on public authorities for the purpose of enabling the better performance by the authority of its PSED: see *s 153*. Those specific duties are set out in the *Equality Act 2010 (Specific Duties and Public Authorities) Regulations 2017*, *SI 2017/353*. They require public authorities to publish information to demonstrate their compliance with the PSED and to set (and publish) specific equality objectives. They also require public authorities to report on their gender pay gap: see **23.32** EQUAL PAY (23).

An appraisal of the case law on the PSED is beyond the scope of this book.

13.38   Enforcement

Enforcement of the general duties is the responsibility of the Equality and Human Rights Commission (*ss 31* and *32* of the *Equality Act 2006*). *Section 156* of the *EqA 2010* further makes it clear that there is no 'cause of action at private law' in relation to an alleged breach of the GEDs or PSED. This leaves open the possibility of a judicial review claim by a private individual in relation to alleged breaches of these general duties, and many such claims have been brought (see **13.37** above). Permission to apply for judicial review may, however, be refused in such cases if the court considers that the option of complaint to the ECHR constitutes an adequate alternative remedy for the individual.

14   Discrimination and Equal Opportunities – III: Enforcement

14.1   The *Equality Act 2010* (*'EqA 2010'*) makes provision in relation to nine 'protected characteristics' defined in *s 4*, namely: age, disability, gender reassignment, marriage and civil partnership, pregnancy and maternity, race, religion or belief, sex, and sexual orientation (see further DISCRIMINATION AND EQUAL OPPORTUNITIES – **I (12)** above). The vast majority of the provisions of the *EqA 2010* in relation to employment and all those relevant to this chapter came into force on 1 October 2010. The *EqA 2010* provides a unified code covering all anti-discrimination law. Insofar as the contents of this chapter are concerned, the *EqA 2010* very largely replicates (and consolidates and simplifies) the provisions of the previous Acts and Regulations, namely the *Sex Discrimination Act 1975* (*'SDA 1975'*), the *Race Relations Act 1976* (*'RRA 1976'*), the *Employment Equality (Sexual Orientation) Regulations 2003 (SI 2003/1661)* (*'SOR 2003'*), the *Employment Equality (Religion or Belief) Regulations 2003 (SI 2003/1660)* (*'RBR 2003'*), the *Disability Discrimination Act 1995* (*'DDA 1995'*) and the *Employment Equality (Age) Regulations 2006 (SI 2006/1031)* (*'AR 2006'*). With effect from 1 October 2010 the *EqA 2010* repealed (so far as is relevant for this chapter) those Acts and Regulations. However, this chapter continues to refer to those Acts and Regulations because, as the *EqA 2010* largely replicates the old legislation, the vast majority of cases under the old legislation remain relevant to the interpretation of the equivalent provisions of the *EqA 2010* and the understanding of those cases is assisted by citation of the old legislation.

No civil or criminal proceedings may be taken against any person for a breach of any provision of the *EqA 2010*, except where such an action is expressly provided for by the *EqA 2010* (*EqA 2010, s 113(1)*). This does not restrict the making of quashing, mandatory or prohibiting orders (which are remedies obtained against public bodies upon an application for judicial review) or a complaint to the Pensions Ombudsman (*EqA 2010, s 113(3)*). Employment tribunals have jurisdiction in relation to certain complaints relating to occupational pension schemes under the *EqA 2010, s 120(2)–(5)*. The only means of direct enforcement open to an individual for discrimination, in relation to employment, is generally by application to an employment tribunal (see **14.2** below).

Since 1 October 2007 the Equality and Human Rights Commission ('EHRC'), established under the *Equality Act 2006* (*'EA 2006'*) (see **14.23 – 14.24** below) has had additional powers to hold investigations (see **14.25 – 14.27** below), issue unlawful act notices (see **14.28** below) and may apply for an injunction in certain cases (see **14.29 – 14.30** below). Previously, in the case of sex, race and disability discrimination only, the Equal Opportunities Commission ('EOC'), the Commission for Racial Equality ('CRE') and Disability Rights Commission ('DRC') respectively exercised similar powers.

The equality legislation implements in domestic law a number of European Directives, specifically the *Equal Treatment Directive (2006/54/EC)* (*'ETD 2006'*) (on sex discrimination), the *Race Discrimination Framework Directive (2000/43/EC)* ('the *Race Directive'*) and the *Framework Directive (2000/78/EC)* (which covers discrimination on grounds of religion or belief, disability, sexual orientation and age) ('the Framework Directive'). In accordance with usual principles of EU law, until the end of the transitional period on 31 December 2020 (or later if it is extended), the relevant provisions of the domestic equality legislation are to be interpreted in conformity with the governing European Directives. Where there are irreconcilable differences between the domestic legislation and the European Directives, public sector workers are able to rely on the Directives themselves under the principle of direct effect. In certain circumstances, EU law may require national courts to disapply provisions of national law even in the context of proceedings between private parties. Upon the UK withdrawing from the European Union, the provisions of *ss 2* to *8* of the *European Union (Withdrawal) Act 2018* will have effect and will, broadly speaking, maintain the effect of EU legislation in domestic law. See generally EUROPEAN UNION LAW **(24)**.

Reference can also be made to *Harvey on Industrial Relations and Employment Law* (HARVEYS – L (EQUAL OPPORTUNITIES) and PI (PRACTICE AND PROCEDURE)).

14.2   APPLICATIONS TO AN EMPLOYMENT TRIBUNAL

Under the *EqA 2010, s 120* an employment tribunal has jurisdiction to determine a complaint relating to (a) a contravention of *Pt 5* (work) and (b) a contravention of *ss 108* (relationship that has come to an end), *111* (instructing, causing and inducing contraventions) or *112* (aiding contraventions) that relates to *Pt 5*. An employment tribunal also has jurisdiction to determine various applications and questions in relation to occupational pension schemes which are outside the scope of this chapter (*EqA 2010, ss 120(2)–(5)*).

Despite the drafting of the legislation, a claim can be brought for victimisation (as well as discrimination and harassment) occurring after the employment relationship has ended: *Jessemey v Rowstock Ltd* [2014] EWCA Civ 185, [2014] 3 All ER 409, [2014] ICR 550, [2014] IRLR 368.

No claim can be brought by a person who is a volunteer rather than an employee or other 'worker' (*X v Mid-Sussex CAB and another* [2012] UKSC 59, [2013] IRLR 146, [2013] ICR 249).

The employer of a discriminator is also liable for the discrimination under the *EqA 2010, s 109*.

A complainant is entitled to include an individual respondent (eg a fellow employee) in his claim to see that that person is called to account as it is not correct to say that the primary liability for discrimination rests with the employer (see *Barlow v Stone* [2012] IRLR 898), but the complainant will need to plead a case that could prove that the individual respondent satisfies the requirements for liability under these provisions (see *Allaway v Reilly* [2007] IRLR 864, EAT). A tribunal was therefore wrong to rule that it could not hear a claimant's sexual harassment claim against a fellow employee unless the employer was also a respondent (see *Hurst v Kelly* [2013] ICR 1225, [2013] All ER (D) 15 (Aug), EAT). Where a claimant brings a claim against an unincorporated association it is permissible to do so either in the name of the association or in the name of a representative respondent, provided that the members of the board or management committee are actually aware of the proceedings and that where allegations are made against specific members those are joined as respondents (see *Nazir v Asim* [2010] ICR 1225, [2010] All ER (D) 113 (Aug), EAT). The members of an LLP are not, however, liable for the unlawful acts of an LLP unless they personally have done something on behalf of the LLP which renders the LLP in principle liable. They cannot therefore be joined as respondents to proceedings: *Murray v Maclay Murray and Spens LLP* [2018] IRLR 710.

In *Beresford v Sovereign House Estates* [2012] ICR D9 the EAT held that a tribunal could not exercise the power of joinder under *rule 10(2)(k)* or *rule 10(2)(r)* of the *Employment Tribunals (Constitution and rules of procedure) Regulations 2004 (SI 2004/1861), Sch 1*, to join a fellow employee as respondent at the request of the respondent employer where the claimant had disavowed any intention to pursue a claim against the fellow employee. Under the old rules, the power in question was a power to join any person whom the tribunal considered might be liable for the claim or who had an interest in the outcome of the claim. Under the new rules contained in *Schedule 1* to the *Employment Tribunals (Constitution and Rules of Procedure) Regulations 2013 (SI 2013/1237), rule 34* now empowers the tribunal to add any person as a party if it appears that there are issues between that person and any of the existing parties falling within the jurisdiction of the Tribunal which it is in the interests of justice to have determined in the proceedings. See further **20.71**, EMPLOYMENT TRIBUNALS – **II**.

In the case of sex and race discrimination members of the armed forces have also been able to bring claims in the employment tribunal since 1 October 1997. Previously, pursuant to the (now repealed) *Sex Discrimination (Complaints to Employment Tribunals) (Armed Forces) Regulations 1997 (SI 1997/2163)* (as amended by the *Armed Forces Act 2006 (Consequential Amendments) Order 2009 (SI 2009/2054), art 2* and *Sch 1*) and the (now repealed) *Race Relations (Complaints to Employment Tribunals)(Armed Forces) Regulations 1997 (SI 1997/2161)* (as amended by the *Armed Forces Act 2006 (Consequential Amendments) Order 2009 (SI 2009/2054), art 2* and *Sch 1*)) members of the armed forces had been subject to a separate statutory regime. Similar provisions were also contained in *SOR 2003, reg 36* and *RBR 2003, reg 36*, but not in *DDA 1995* and *AR 2006*, both of which expressly provided that they did not apply to service in any of the naval, military or air forces (*DDA 1995, s 64(7)*; *AR 2006, reg 44(4)*).

The *EqA 2010, s 121* makes similar provision to those previously made in relation to race, sex, sexual orientation and religion or belief in relation to complaints by members of the armed forces and does now include complaints of age discrimination. Where a member of the armed forces has the right to bring a claim, he may only present a complaint to the employment tribunal if he has made a complaint in respect of the same matter to an officer under the service complaints procedures prescribed by regulations made under the *Armed Forces Act 2006, s 334*, and that complaint has not been withdrawn. A complaint will be treated as having been withdrawn if, having made the complaint to an officer neither that officer nor a superior officer has decided to refer the complaint to the Defence Council, and the complainant fails to apply for such a reference to be made. Presenting a complaint to the employment tribunal does not prevent the continuation of the service redress procedures. An employment tribunal will not have jurisdiction to hear a claim from a member of the armed forces if a 'service complaint' has not been accepted as valid by the prescribed officer under the services complaints procedure (eg because it was made out of time) and this requirement does not breach EU law (see *Molaudi v Ministry of Defence* [2011] ICR D19, [2011] All ER (D) 72 (May), EAT). Similarly, there can be no claim if a complainant fails to appeal within time against the rejection of a service complaint (*Williams v Ministry of Defence* [2013] Eq LR 27, EAT).

An exception to the jurisdiction of the employment tribunals for employment-related claims exists for acts committed (or treated as committed) by qualifications bodies. It is not possible to complain to the employment tribunal if the act complained of is one in respect of which an appeal, or proceedings in the nature of an appeal, may be brought under any enactment (the *EqA 2010, s 120(7)*). The scope and effect of the equivalent provisions under the *RRA 1976* were considered in *R v Department of Health, ex p Gandhi* [1991] IRLR 431, [1991] ICR 805; *Khan v General Medical Council* [1994] IRLR 646, CA; and *Chaudhary v Specialist Training Authority Appeal Panel (No 2)* [2005] EWCA Civ 282, [2005] ICR 1086, [2005] All ER (D) 256 (Mar)). The availability of judicial review of a decision of a qualifications body does not oust the tribunal's jurisdiction (although judicial review is controlled by *section 31* of the *Senior Courts Act 1981*): *Michalak v General Medical Council* [2016] EWCA Civ 172, [2016] IRLR 458, [2016] ICR 628, the purpose of *section 120(7)* being to ensure that the most appropriate specialist body hears a complaint. In the case of a discrimination claim the employment tribunal is better equipped than the Administrative Court.

In *Watt (formerly Carter) v Ahsan* [2007] UKHL 51, [2008] 1 AC 696, [2008] IRLR 243, [2008] ICR 82, the House of Lords held that an employment tribunal had been a court of competent jurisdiction to decide that the Labour Party was a body conferring a qualification or authorisation needed for engagement in a profession or trade for the purposes of the *RRA 1976, s 12*, notwithstanding that a subsequent decision of the Court of Appeal had shown that decision to be wrong (and hence the claim should have been brought in the county court).

Tribunals also lack jurisdiction to hear complaints about discriminatory conduct in the course of judicial or quasi-judicial proceedings, and a police disciplinary board has been held to be a judicial body (*Heath v Metropolitan Police Comr* [2004] EWCA Civ 943, [2005] IRLR 270, [2005] ICR 329). That immunity from suit does not extend to the decision to commence disciplinary proceedings nor to a chief constable's decision to dismiss (*Lake v British Transport Police* [2007] ICR 47, [2006] All ER (D) 04 (Oct), EAT). Moreover, a police disciplinary board's immunity from suit is not impeached so as to oust the employment tribunal's jurisdiction where the claimant merely seeks to advance before the employment tribunal a case that had been rejected by the board (*Lake v British Transport Police* [2007] EWCA Civ 424, [2007] ICR 1293, reversing the EAT's decision on this issue). In *P v Commissioner of Police for the Metropolis* [2016] EWCA Civ 2, [2016] IRLR 301 it was decided that there is no inconsistency between *Heath* and *Lake* and that the employment tribunal has no jurisdiction to hear a claim of a discriminatory dismissal where a disciplinary panel is the effective dismissing agent.

In *South London & Maudsley NHS Trust v Dathi* [2008] IRLR 350, EAT, a claim for victimisation based on the respondent's letters in response to a costs application and an application for disclosure in the course of previous discrimination proceedings should have been struck out by the tribunal as the letters attracted absolute immunity as they had come into existence for the purpose of those proceedings. In *Parmar v East Leicester Medical Practice* [2011] IRLR 641, EAT, Underhill P confirmed that the absolute privilege identified in *Heath* applies also to a witness who prepares a witness statement, even if a trial never takes place, and applies also to claims of alleged victimisation as well as other forms of discrimination.

Discrimination claims do not lapse on the death of the complainant. The deceased's estate may commence or continue proceedings (*Lewisham and Guys Mental Health NHS Trust v Andrews* [2000] ICR 707, CA). A discrimination claim is a 'hybrid' claim and a bankrupt has standing to bring such a claim provided that he limits the remedy sought to a declaration or compensation for injury to feelings (*Khan v Trident Safeguards Ltd* [2004] EWCA Civ 624, [2004] IRLR 961). Where a claimant employed as a member of a diplomatic mission by a foreign state claims for personal injury in a discrimination claim the employment tribunal does have jurisdiction to hear such a claim as it falls within the exception from state immunity for claims in respect of personal injury under the *State Immunity Act 1978, s 5* (see *Federal Republic of Nigeria v Ogbonna* [2012] 1 WLR 139, [2012] ICR 32, [2011] All ER (D) 19 (Oct), EAT). (For further discussion of state and diplomatic immunity see DISCRIMINATION AND EQUAL OPPORTUNITIES – II, 13.23).

Where, following the transfer of business under the *Transfer of Undertakings (Protection of Employment) Regulations 1981 (SI 1981/1794)* (now the *Transfer of Undertakings (Protection of Employment) Regulations 2006 (SI 2006/2405)*), a complainant complained that the refusal of a reference by the transferor after the TUPE transfer was victimisation under the *RRA 1976, s 2*, any liability was that of the transferor and did not pass to the transferee (*Coutinho v Vision Information Services Ltd* [2008] All ER (D) 244 (Feb), (2008) 849 IDS Brief 12, EAT). In proceedings related to the latter case the Court of Appeal has held that an employment tribunal was wrong to strike out for want of jurisdiction a claim brought by the claimant in which he argued that the failure by the TUPE transferee to honour an award of compensation was itself victimisation for the purposes of the *RRA 1976, s 2* (see *Rank Nemo (DMS) Ltd v Coutinho* [2009] EWCA Civ 454, [2009] ICR 1296, [2009] IRLR 672).

The *EqA 2010, s 140* gives courts and employment tribunals the power to transfer cases between each other in certain circumstances. Where conduct has given rise to two or more separate proceedings under the *Act*, with at least one being for a contravention of *s 111* (instructing, causing or inducing contraventions), a court may transfer proceedings to an employment tribunal or an employment tribunal may transfer proceedings to a court (*EqA 2010, s 140(1), (2), (3)*). A court or employment tribunal is to be taken for the purposes of *Pt 9* of the *EqA 2010* to have jurisdiction to determine a claim or complaint transferred to it under the section (*EqA 2010, s 140(4)*). A court or employment tribunal may not make a decision that is inconsistent with an earlier decision in proceedings arising out of the conduct (*EqA 2010, s 140(5)*).

Final findings in previous relevant proceedings are treated as conclusive in proceedings under the *EqA 2010* (*EqA 2010, s 137(1)*). The 'relevant proceedings' are those under the *Race Relations Act 1968, ss 19* or *20*, the *EPA 1970*, the *SDA 1975*, the *RRA 1976*, the *Sex Discrimination Act 1986, s 6(4A)*, the *DDA 1995, Pt 2* of the *EA 2006*, the *SOR 2003*, the *RBR 2003, AR 2006*, and the *Equality Act (Sexual Orientation) Regulations 2007 (SI 2007/1263)* (*EqA 2010, s 137(2)*).

Important guidance on the case management of discrimination claims was given by the EAT in *Tarn v Hughes* [2019] ICR 76. In that case, which involved multiple allegations of discrimination, the Tribunal had ordered the claimant to select a maximum of ten recent and most serious matters from the claim form for consideration at a hearing, and to choose whether to rely on the other matters either as background to the ten selected complaints or to have them dealt with at a subsequent hearing. The EAT acknowledged that *Rule 29* gives a broad case management discretion which must be exercised in accordance with the Overriding Objective. However, the EAT emphasised that dealing with cases in a way that is proportionate to the complexity and importance of the issues does not permit the Tribunal to limit the claims a complainant may pursue, other than by striking out claims that have no reasonable prospect of success (see EMPLOYMENT TRIBUNALS – II, 20.74). The EAT held that the Tribunal's approach in this case was not a permissible approach for two reasons. First, it required the claimant of having to make the unfair choice of having ten selected complaints determined without the relevant background or abandoning the other claims and pursuing only the selected ten with the relevant background. Secondly, it would result in no saving of time and cost because all matters would have to be dealt with at some point. The EAT further gave guidance (at §28) as to the handling of discrimination claims as follows:

(1)   The tribunal has a broad discretion to manage cases justly, having regard to the overriding objective. It can expect the parties to assist it in that exercise, having regard to their obligation under the overriding objective.

(2)   A discrimination case may well involve a large number of allegations, pursued as different legal claims under different statutory provisions, and concerning events over a long period of time, perhaps involving a number of different people. The starting point for the tribunal must be to identify precisely what claims are made and on what basis; once that is done, it is possible to identify what is in issue. In this regard, the tribunal will be assisted by a list of issues—preferably drawn up and agreed by the parties, although it may be necessary to complete this exercise at a case management hearing.

(3)   There will be some cases—albeit rarely discrimination cases, involving disputes of fact—where it will be appropriate for the tribunal to consider striking out claims that can properly be said to have no reasonable prospect of success: see *rule 37* of the *Employment Tribunals Rules of Procedure 2013*. Save in such cases, however, the claims will stand to be determined after a full merits hearing on the evidence; it is not open to the tribunal to otherwise limit the claims a complainant can pursue—that would be to restrict her access to justice and to potentially deny an effective remedy in a case of unlawful discrimination.

(4)   That said, there may be cases where it will be possible to separate out a sample of complaints or issues, such that these might usefully be heard in advance of the remaining allegations. Where that would be an appropriate course, it would be hoped that the parties (consistent with their obligation under the overriding obligation)

would assist the tribunal by identifying and agreeing the complaints to be taken forward but, even if there were no such agreement, the tribunal would not be prevented from so directing, if that could properly be said to provide for the just determination of the particular case.

(5)   Allowing that a tribunal has such a power does not, however, suggest that this is a course that should be adopted, save in those cases where it is clear this would not endanger the just determination of the case —something that might be difficult for the tribunal to assess at a preliminary stage.

(6)   And this leads into the real problem with attempts to case manage discrimination claims in this way: in many such cases, it is necessary to consider the entire picture before any conclusion can be drawn as to whether, or not, there has been unlawful discrimination in respect of any particular allegation. There is an obvious temptation in directing the complainant to select her ten best points; no doubt, hoping that the determination of those matters will enable the parties to reach agreement in respect of the allegations that remain. In many discrimination cases, however, this will not be consistent with the just determination of the claims made: the tribunal will have to consider the complete picture if it is to fairly answer the question whether there has or has not been unlawful discrimination on the relevant protected grounds.

(7)   Moreover, the separate determination of selected allegations or issues may not be the proportionate course in a particular case; careful regard would need to be had as to whether it will really avoid delay and save expense in those proceedings.

Note also that guidance has been given in the case law on case management of cases brought by disabled persons who have difficulty attending hearings and participating in proceedings: see further **20.55 EMPLOYMENT TRIBUNALS – II**.

14.3   Burden of proof

The burden of proof has been an area that has generated much case law over previous years, particularly following the introduction of a 'reverse' burden of proof. The *EqA 2010, s 136(2), (3)* provides for a 'reverse' burden of proof but in slightly different (and simpler) terms than under the previous *Acts* and *Regulations*:

(a)   If there are facts from which the court could decide, in the absence of any other explanation, that a person (A) contravened the provision concerned, the court must hold that the contravention occurred (*s 136(2)*).

(b)   This does not apply if A shows that A did not contravene the provision (*s 136(3)*).

The change in wording from previous Acts and Regulations does not change the law: the effect is still that an initial burden of proof is on the employee: *Ayodele v Citylink Ltd* [2017] EWCA Civ 1913, [2018] IRLR 114, and *Royal Mail Group Ltd v Efobi* [2019] EWCA Civ 18, [2019] IRLR 352 overruling the EAT's decision in that latter case [2018] ICR 359 where the EAT had held that *s 136* created a neutral initial burden. The decision of the CJEU in *Otero Ramos v Servicio Galego de Saude* (C-531/15) [2018] IRLR 159 makes clear that the Court of Appeal's view is consistent with EU law.

The 'reverse' burden of proof applies to all the protected characteristics and proceedings for any type of contravention of the *Act* (*s 136(1)*). So the complications in relation to the potentially different treatment of race victimisation and colour and nationality claims discussed below is removed.

It is, however, important to understand the development of the burden of proof because much of the recent case law on burden of proof will remain relevant and because of the historic legacy of existing cases decided under the previous legislation.

But it is also important not to exaggerate the significance of the reverse burden of proof. Where the tribunal is in a position to make clear findings of fact in relation to allegedly discriminatory conduct, the reverse burden of proof has no effect, and the discussion below should be read with this in mind. See *Hewage v Grampian Health Board* [2012] UKSC 37, [2012] IRLR 870, [2012] ICR 1054 per Lord Hope, paragraph 32 and *Prasad v Epsom & St Helier University Hospitals NHS Trust* UKEAT/0111/18/RN.

SDA 1975 and *RRA 1976* originally gave the complainant the burden of showing both that they had been less favourably treated and that the less favourable treatment had been on grounds of sex or race. In practice, the burden proved difficult to discharge. Discrimination was very rarely overtly sexist or racist and the complainant had instead to persuade the tribunal to draw an inference. Complainants were assisted by case law (most famously *King v Great Britain-China Centre* [1991] IRLR 513, [1992] ICR 516, CA) in which the following approach was advocated. First, the complainant had to establish a difference in sex or race and that they had been less favourably treated. Once this prima facie case had been established the tribunal was entitled to turn to the employer and seek an explanation for this disparity in treatment. If the employer's explanation was unsatisfactory the tribunal was entitled but not obliged (see *Glasgow City Council v Zafar* [1998] IRLR 36, [1998] ICR 120, HL) to draw an inference that the less favourable treatment was on the relevant prohibited ground. The advantage of the guidance allowing rather than compelling the drawing of an inference is that it made allowance for the fact that humans are capable of acting inconsistently and unreasonably and yet not discriminatorily.

Eventually by way of a series of amendments to the Acts and in the *SOR 2003, RBR 2003* and *AR 2006* a new split burden of proof was introduced in discrimination cases. Except for race victimisation claims and possibly race discrimination claims on grounds of colour or nationality, the new burden of proof was applicable to all other discrimination and harassment claims under the *SDA 1975, RRA 1976, SOR 2003, RBR 2003, DDA 1995* and *AR 2006*, including claims where the respondent was vicariously liable or knowingly aided a prohibited act.

Where, on the hearing of the complaint, the complainant proved facts from which the tribunal could conclude in the absence of an adequate explanation that the respondent:

(a)   had committed an unlawful act against the complainant falling within the jurisdiction of the employment tribunal; or

(b)   was either vicariously liable for such an act or had knowingly aided the commission of such an act;

the tribunal had to uphold the complaint unless the respondent proved that he did not commit, or as the case may be, was not to be treated as having committed, the act.

There were conflicting decisions on whether the old test continued to apply in cases of discrimination on grounds of colour or nationality, and on whether the new reverse burden of proof applied to victimisation claims. These complexities should no longer be significant, thanks to the *EqA 2010*.

Seminal general guidance on the application of the reverse burden of proof test was provided by the EAT in *Barton v Investec Henderson Crosthwaite Securities Ltd* [2003] IRLR 332, [2003] ICR 1205, EAT at 1218F and by the Court of Appeal in *Wong v Igen Ltd* [2005] EWCA Civ 142, [2005] IRLR 258, [2005] ICR 931. The guidance is set out below in full under the heading 'the revised *Barton* Guidance'. Although couched by reference to the *SDA 1975, s 63A*, it applied equally to the *RRA 1976, SOR 2003, RBR 2003, DDA 1995* and *AR 2006*, and is likely to be highly relevant to the approach to be adopted under the *EqA 2010, s 136*. The Supreme Court in *Hewage v Grampian Health Board* [2012] UKSC 37, [2012] IRLR 870, [2012] ICR 1054 stated that this guidance had been very clearly expressed and no further guidance from the Supreme Court was needed. The revised Barton Guidance is as follows—

14.3 Discrimination and Equal Opportunities – III: Enforcement

(1) Pursuant to *SDA 1975, s 63A*, it is for the claimant who complains of sex discrimination to prove on the balance of probabilities facts from which the tribunal could conclude, in the absence of an adequate explanation, that the employer has committed an act of discrimination against the claimant which is unlawful by virtue of Part 2 or which, by virtue of *s 41* or *s 42* of *SDA 1975*, is to be treated as having been committed against the claimant. These are referred to below as 'such facts'.

(2) If the claimant does not prove such facts he or she will fail.

(3) It is important to bear in mind in deciding whether the claimant has proved such facts that it is unusual to find direct evidence of sex discrimination. Few employers would be prepared to admit such discrimination, even to themselves. In some cases the discrimination will not be an intention but merely based on the assumption that 'he or she would not have fitted in'.

(4) In deciding whether the claimant has proved such facts, it is important to remember that the outcome at this stage of the analysis by the tribunal will therefore usually depend on what inferences it is proper to draw from the primary facts found by the tribunal.

(5) It is important to note the word 'could' in the *SDA 1975, s 63A(2)*. At this stage the tribunal does not have to reach a definitive determination that such facts would lead it to the conclusion that there was an act of unlawful discrimination. At this stage a tribunal is looking at the primary facts before it to see what inferences of secondary fact could be drawn from them.

(6) In considering what inferences or conclusions can be drawn from the primary facts, the tribunal must assume that there is no adequate explanation for those facts.

(7) These inferences can include, in appropriate cases, any inferences that it is just and equitable to draw in accordance with *SDA 1975, s 74(2)(b)* from an evasive or equivocal reply to a questionnaire or any other questions that fall within *SDA 1975, s 74(2)* (see *Dattani v Chief Constable of West Mercia Police* [2005] IRLR 327, EAT – *RRA 1976, s 65* (the equivalent provision to *SDA 1975, s 74(2)*) also covers evasive or equivocal pleading in a response to a claim).

(8) Likewise, the tribunal must decide whether any provision of any relevant code of practice is relevant and, if so, take it into account in determining such facts pursuant to *SDA 1975, s 56A(10)* (now the *EA 2006, s 15(4)*). This means that inferences may also be drawn from any failure to comply with any relevant code of practice.

(9) Where the claimant has proved facts from which conclusions could be drawn that the employer has treated the claimant less favourably on the ground of sex, then the burden of proof moves to the employer.

(10) It is then for the employer to prove that he did not commit, or as the case may be, is not to be treated as having committed, that act.

(11) To discharge that burden it is necessary for the employer to prove, on the balance of probabilities, that the treatment was in no sense whatsoever on the grounds of sex, since 'no discrimination whatsoever' is compatible with the Burden of Proof Directive.

(12) That requires a tribunal to assess not merely whether the employer has proved an explanation for the facts from which such inferences can be drawn, but further that it is adequate to discharge the burden of proof on the balance of probabilities that sex was not a ground for the treatment in question.

(13)   Since the facts necessary to prove an explanation would normally be in the possession of the respondent, a tribunal would normally expect cogent evidence to discharge that burden of proof. In particular, the tribunal will need to examine carefully explanations for failure to deal with the questionnaire procedure and/or a code of practice.

The revised test is similar to the approach adopted in *King* in that the burden is initially on the complainant to make out what might be described as the '*prima facie case*'. The respondent then has to give an explanation. However, the revised test is stricter because once a *prima facie* case is established the respondent then has the burden of proving that he did not act unlawfully. If he fails to discharge the burden, the tribunal has to find in favour of the complainant.

As indicated above, under the old test the tribunal would decide, once a *prima facie* case had been made out, whether the case was in truth one of discrimination on a prohibited ground or whether it was perhaps unreasonable or inconsistent but nevertheless non-discriminatory treatment. Because discretion is replaced with compulsion, it becomes particularly important to determine when the *prima facie* case has been made out. Case law indicates that it is now harder for the complainant to make out a *prima facie* case than it was under the old *King* test.

In order to establish a *prima facie* case at stage one there must be something that raises a suggestion that a prohibited factor may have been at work. In *Igen v Wong* above, their Lordships addressed the issue in the context of the analysis of the *RRA 1976*:

'The relevant act is, in a race discrimination case . . . that (a) in circumstances relevant for the purposes of any provision of the 1976 Act (for example in relation to employment in the circumstances specified in section 4 of the Act), (b) the alleged discriminator treats another person less favourably and (c) does so on racial grounds. All those facts are facts which the complainant, in our judgment, needs to prove on the balance of probabilities.'

The Court of Appeal confirmed in *Madarassy v Nomura International plc* [2007] EWCA Civ 33, [2007] ICR 867, [2007] IRLR 246, that a claimant must establish more than a difference in status (eg sex) and a difference in treatment before a tribunal will be in a position where it 'could conclude' that an act of discrimination had been committed. See also *Adebayo v Dresdner Kleinwort Wasserstein Ltd* [2005] IRLR 514, [2005] All ER (D) 371 (Mar), EAT; *University of Huddersfield v Wolff* [2004] IRLR 534, EAT; *Fernandez v Office of the Parliamentary Commissioner* [2006] All ER (D) 460 (Jul), EAT; *Griffiths-Henry v Network Rail Infrastructure Ltd* [2006] IRLR 865, [2006] All ER (D) 15 (Jul), EAT; *Fox v Rangecroft* [2006] EWCA Civ 1112; *Islington London Borough Council v Ladele* [2009] ICR 387, [2009] IRLR 154, EAT (affd [2009] EWCA Civ 1357, [2010] IRLR 211, CA; and *Base Childrenswear Ltd v Otshudi* [2019] EWCA Civ 1648, [2020] IRLR 118. There does not have to be positive evidence that any difference in treatment was on a prohibited ground in order to establish a *prima facie* case (*Network Rail Infrastructure Ltd* above), but even if the tribunal believes that the respondent's conduct requires explanation, before the burden can shift there must be something to suggest that the treatment was due to the claimant's possessing a protected characteristic (see *B and C v A* [2010] IRLR 400, EAT). At the least, in a case of non-appointment where there is no evidence of overt discrimination, that means that the protected characteristics of other successful candidates must be put in evidence. The onus is on the claimant to do that, by seeking disclosure from the respondent if necessary: see *Royal Mail Group Ltd v Efobi* [2019] EWCA Civ 18, [2019] IRLR 352 where the claimant had not sought to obtain such evidence until the day of the trial and his application was refused as a matter of case management by the tribunal. It is not sufficient to shift the burden of proof that the conduct is simply unfair or unreasonable if it is unconnected to a protected characteristic (see *Comr of Police of the Metropolis v Osinaike* (2010) 907 IDS Brief 15, EAT; *St Christopher's Fellowship v Walters-Ennis* [2010] EWCA Civ 921, [2010] All ER (D) 03 (Aug)).

Whilst tribunals must be alert to the existence of, for example, racial or sexual stereotypes, the burden will only shift if there is sufficient reason to believe that the respondent could have been motivated by such a stereotype (see *B and C*, above). In *Canadian Imperial Bank of Commerce v Beck* [2009] All ER (D) 278 (Jun), EAT, an employment tribunal was held to have been entitled to regard the use of the word "younger" in a job specification as, in the circumstances, sufficient to shift the burden of proof onto the respondent in an age discrimination case relating to redundancy selection. Similarly, an employment tribunal had erred by not concluding that a manager's asking whether the claimant's age might be a reason why he could not work to the respondent's expectations had caused the burden of proof to shift (see *James v Gina Shoes Ltd* [2012] All ER (D) 166 (Mar), EAT). However, inferences about subconscious motivation of alleged discriminators can only be based on solid evidence. In *South Wales Police Authority v Johnson* [2014] EWCA Civ 73, [2014] All ER (D) 79 (Feb) a remark by an individual about her experiences in relationships with black men was insufficient basis for inferring that her treatment of a black employee was motivated by racial prejudice. Compare also *Chief Constable of Greater Manchester v Bailey* [2017] EWCA Civ 425 (where the Court of Appeal gave guidance as to the approach to be taken where there is evidence of institutional racism but no clear link to the particular case). In *Base Childrenswear Ltd v Otshudi* (above), the factor pointing to a decision to dismiss being prima facie discriminatory was the fact that the employer originally gave and then persisted until very late in the proceedings in giving a reason for termination that was not the real reason. Even where an employer does not retreat from the original reason given for their action, if the explanation is "unsustainable" that may also point towards the protected characteristic having played a part (*Iwuchukwu v City Hospitals Sunderland NHS Foundation Trust* [2019] EWCA Civ 498, [2019] IRLR 1022). What must be shown in any particular case is that it is possible that the treatment was unlawfully discriminatory. At this point, the burden shifts to the respondent to prove that it was not: *Governing Body of Tywyn Primary School v Aplin* (UKEAT/0298/17/LA). A tribunal will be setting an impermissibly high hurdle if it asks whether discrimination is the only inference which could be drawn from the facts before the burden shifts (*Pnaiser v NHS England and Coventry City Council* [2016] IRLR 170, EAT) or whether discrimination is proved (*Aplin* ibid).

In deciding whether or not a *prima facie* case has been made out, the tribunal should ignore the substance of any explanation proffered by the employer for the treatment, turning to it only once the burden has shifted (*Igen*, ibid; and *Madarassy* ibid and *Efobi* ibid). However, in *Veolia Environmental Services UK v Gumbs* [2014] EqLR 364, the EAT held that when considering whether the burden has shifted, the tribunal is entitled to take into account the fact of an employer giving inconsistent reasons for its conduct. Moreover, this does not mean that at the first stage the tribunal should consider only evidence adduced by the claimant and ignore the respondent's evidence. The tribunal should have regard to all the facts at the first stage to determine what inferences can properly be drawn (*Laing v Manchester City Council* [2006] ICR 1519, [2006] IRLR 748, EAT; approved by the Court of Appeal in *Madarassy* and *Appiah v Bishop Douglass Roman Catholic High School* [2007] EWCA Civ 10, [2007] ICR 897, [2007] IRLR 264; see also *Ayodele v Citylink Ltd* [2017] EWCA Civ 1913, [2018] IRLR 114). At this stage the tribunal will need to look at evidence that the act complained of occurred at all, evidence as to the actual comparator relied upon by the claimant, evidence as to whether the comparisons being made by the claimant were like with like, and available evidence as to the reasons for the differential treatment (*Madarassy* above). In *Madarassy* the Court of Appeal held that at the first stage the respondent may adduce evidence which: showed that the alleged acts did not occur; that, if they did occur, there was not less favourable treatment of the claimant; that the comparators chosen by the claimant or the situations chosen by the claimant were not like the claimant or the situations with which comparison was sought to be made; and that even if there was less favourable treatment it was not on prohibited grounds. So, in *Osoba v Chief Constable of Hertfordshire* [2013] All ER (D) 242 (Sep) the EAT held that where at the first stage the tribunal accepted that the employer had acted honestly, it would be wrong to require it to provide a further explanation. It is submitted that there may be some difficulty for tribunals in distinguishing between a respondent's evidence as to the reason for the treatment (which may be considered at the first stage) and its 'explanation' (which may not). *Kansal v Tullet Prebon Plc and ors* UKEAT/0147/16/DM provides a useful reminder that the fact that the employer has treated favourably others who share a protected characteristic with the claimant does not of itself demonstrate that the employer was not discriminating against the claimant.

The complainant must establish on the balance of probabilities that the employer has committed the potentially discriminatory act. It would not be appropriate to require an explanation from the employer for something that the employer *may* have done. Thus, where an act merely may have been committed by the employer or by a third party a *prima facie* case will not have been established (*Igen* above).

In a case of alleged indirect discrimination, it is necessary for a claimant to establish the existence of the relevant "provision, criterion or practice" before the burden can shift in relation to discriminatory impact (*Dippenaar v Bethnal Green and Shoreditch Education Trust* (2015) UKEAT/0064/15, [2015] All ER (D) 306 (Oct), EAT). It is not, however, necessary for a claimant to show that the reason why the PCP has disadvantaged the group is related to the protected characteristic, or that this is the reason why the individual claimant has suffered a disadvantage: all that is required is that there be a causal connection between the PCP and the disadvantage: *Essop v Home Office (UK Border Agency); Naeem v Secretary of State for Justice* [2017] UKSC 27, [2017] 3 All ER 551, [2017] IRLR 558, [2017] ICR 640, as further explained in *McCloud v Ministry of Justice* [2018] EWCA Civ 2844. Thus, in that case it was not necessary for the claimants to prove that the reason why more black and minority ethnic ("BME") civil servants fail the core skills test for promotion is related to their race or ethnicity: it was sufficient that a greater proportion of BME claimants failed and that there was a causal link between the test (the PCP) and the failure or likelihood of failure (the disadvantage), which was operative in the particular case (and the causative link not broken, for example, by the particular claim having turned up late to the exam or failed to do any work for it). Provided the causative link between the PCP and the disadvantage is established, the burden shifts to the respondent to justify the PCP.

In 'reasonable adjustments' cases under the *DDA 1995*, Elias J has suggested (see *Project Management Institute v Latif* [2007] IRLR 579, EAT) that the claimant is required, at the first stage: (a) to establish the provision, criterion or practice relied upon; and (b) to demonstrate substantial disadvantage. The burden then shifts to the respondent to show that no adjustment or further adjustment should be made.

In cases of 'discrimination arising from a disability', what is required at the first stage is that the Tribunal (1) identify the individual/s responsible for the treatment complained of and enquire into the reason for that treatment, undertaking this exercise as if determining the reason for conduct complained of in a direct discrimination claim; and (2) determine – applying an objective test – whether there is a connection between the disability and "the something" that provides the reason for the treatment in issue; there is no requirement that the ET determines these questions in any particular order, but the answers to the questions should be apparent from its reasoning: see *Pnaiser v NHS England and Coventry City Council* [2016] IRLR 170, EAT and *South Warwickshire NHS Foundation Trust v Lee* UKEAT/0287/17/DA.

Once the burden of proof has shifted, what is required is that the employer demonstrate that the act in question was not unlawful. Although in the revised Barton guidance (above), the Court of Appeal expressed this as a requirement that the employer demonstrate that the act was "in no sense whatsoever on the grounds of sex, since 'no discrimination whatsoever' is compatible with the Burden of Proof Directive", that does not mean that the employer has to show that the protected characteristic played no part at all in the treatment. What is required where there is more than one possible cause for the treatment is that the employer show that the protected characteristic did not have a significant or more than trivial influence on the unfavourable treatment so as to amount to an effective reason or cause of it: *Pnaiser v NHS England and Coventry City Council* [2016] IRLR 170, EAT and *South Warwickshire NHS Foundation Trust v Lee* UKEAT/0287/17/DA. In *Pnaiser* the EAT observed that a tribunal will be setting an impermissibly high hurdle if it asks whether discrimination is the only inference which could be drawn from the facts.

Logically the employer may offer one of a number of sorts of explanations at the second stage, if he offers one at all; those that confirm discrimination, those that explain the disparity in a manner which makes it clear that there was no unlawful discrimination but which, to use the words of the EAT in *Sinclair, Roche & Temperley v Heard* [2004] IRLR 763, EAT 'redound to the employer's discredit', and those which explain away discrimination and are themselves worthy reasons. It is not sufficient to establish discrimination that the tribunal considers that the explanation given is not one that is objectively justified or reasonable as unfairness is not sufficient to establish discrimination (see *Network Rail Infrastructure Ltd* above).

The explanation cannot simply be asserted but must be proved. As the facts supporting the explanation will be in the respondent's knowledge cogent evidence is expected in support of any explanation proffered (see *Barton* above). The Court of Appeal has emphasised in *EB v BA* [2006] EWCA Civ 132, [2006] IRLR 471 that where the burden of proof has shifted the respondent must be required to adduce the evidence necessary to discharge that burden, otherwise the protection afforded to a claimant by (in that case) the *SDA 1975, s 63A* is negated. If the explanation is unsustainable on the evidence, then the claim is made out: *Iwuchukwu v City Hospitals Sunderland NHS Foundation Trust* [2019] EWCA Civ 498. The weight of the burden imposed on the respondent at the second stage will depend on the strength of the *prima facie* case established by the claimant at the first stage (see *Network Rail Infrastructure Ltd* and *Ladele* above; *Khan & King v The Home Office* [2008] EWCA Civ 578, [2008] All ER (D) 323 (May), CA; *Virdi v Metropolitan Police Comr* [2009] EWCA Civ 477, [2009] All ER (D) 62 (Jun)). Once the burden of proof has shifted the tribunal is not required expressly to reject the respondent's explanation in order to make a finding of discrimination; it can merely not accept the explanation, though it is preferable if it does make positive findings one way or the other (see *Pothecary Witham Weld*, and *Beck*, above).

Before the new test many authorities emphasised the importance of making clear findings of fact and explaining why inferences were (or were not) being drawn (see *Anya v University of Oxford* [2001] IRLR 377, [2001] ICR 847, CA). The later authorities make the same point. There must be clear findings of fact in relation to less favourable treatment; a clear finding as to whether the burden has reversed (see *Wolff* above); clear findings of fact in relation to the explanation; and a clear finding as to whether the explanation offered has discharged the burden and, if not, why not (see *Sinclair, Roche & Temperley* above; *Bahl* below; and *Chatwal v Wandsworth Borough Council* [2011] All ER (D) 69 (Aug), EAT).

Where an employer advances an obviously non-discriminatory explanation, the tribunal's decision should show that it has recognised that an explanation has been provided and, if it still wishes to conclude that the act was unlawfully discriminatory, explain expressly why it is rejecting the explanation (*Bahl v Law Society* [2003] IRLR 640, EAT).

In a case where it is alleged that an act was on grounds of sex and/or on racial grounds and the evidence does not satisfy the tribunal that either ground, considered independently, is made out, it is not open to the tribunal to decide that 'taken together' the treatment was unlawful on both grounds (*Bahl* above) (and the same would hold true for any other attempt to combine other prohibited grounds). However, in *Ministry of Defence v DeBique* [2010] IRLR 471, EAT, it was held that an employment tribunal had been entitled, in a case of alleged indirect race and sex discrimination, to consider the combined effect of two PCPs (provision, criterion or practice). In that case a female single parent soldier from St Vincent and the Grenadines complained of indirect sex discrimination in relation to a requirement that she be available for duty 24 hours a day seven days a week, which the tribunal considered placed female soldiers at a particular disadvantage, and the effect of the immigration rules which meant that, unlike a UK soldier, she could not have a relative with her to assist with childcare.

EqA 2010, s 14 was to introduce the concept of combined discrimination where a claimant suffered less favourable treatment because of the combination of two (and only two) relevant protected characteristics (but not marriage and civil partnership or pregnancy and maternity). This was only to be available in relation to direct discrimination (not, as in *DeBique*, indirect discrimination). However, the Government has decided not to bring *s 14* into force and combined discrimination is not a concept recognised in EU law either: *Parris v Trinity College Dublin* C-443/15, [2017] IRLR 173, [2017] ICR 313.

The Court of Appeal has confirmed that it is not always necessary for a tribunal expressly to go through the two-stage test in sequence and it can instead focus on the respondent's reasons for the treatment, for example where the comparator is hypothetical and the facts are not fundamentally in dispute (*Brown v Croydon London Borough Council* [2007] EWCA Civ 32, [2007] ICR 909, [2007] IRLR 259; *Secretary of State for Work and Pensions v McCarthy* [2010] All ER (D) 209 (Mar), EAT; see also *Laing, Khan and Ladele* above). Although it is generally good practice to go through the two-stage test there are cases where the claimant is not prejudiced by the tribunal omitting the first stage and going straight to the second stage and concluding that the respondent has discharged the burden of proving that the treatment was not on a prohibited ground. However, in such cases the tribunal must take care to apply *s 136* correctly and consider whether the burden of proof had shifted to the respondent: *Country Style Foods Ltd v Bouzir* [2011] EWCA Civ 1519, [2011] All ER (D) 59 (Dec) and *Fennell v Foot Anstey LLP* (UKEAT/0290/15/DM, 28 July 2016).

See also HARVEYS – Division L.5.D.

14.4   Time limit

A complaint must be presented to a tribunal before the end of the period of three months beginning when the act complained of was done (*EqA 2010, s 123(1)(a)*; and previously *SDA 1975, s 76(1); RRA 1976, s 68(1); SOR 2003, reg 34(1), (1A); RBR 2003, reg 34(1), (1A); DDA 1995, Sch 3, para 3(1)*; and *AR 2006, reg 42(1)*, or such other period as the employment tribunal thinks just and equitable (*EqA 2010 s 123(1)(b)*).

Where the claim concerns, in whole or in part, a cross-border dispute to which *art 8(1)* of *Directive 2008/52/EC* ('the *Mediation Directive*') applies and a mediation (within the meaning of *art 3(a)* of the *Mediation Directive*) has started before the time limit expires but the time limit will expire before the mediation ends or less than four weeks after the mediation ends, the time limit under the *EqA 2010, s 123(1)(a)* is extended until four weeks after the mediation ends (*EqA 2010, s 140A(1), (5), (6)*). Where a tribunal has power to extend a time limit under the *EqA 2010, s 123(1)(b)* that power is exercisable in relation to the limitation period as extended by *s 140A* (*EqA 2010, s 140A(13)*). Insofar as it is still in force pursuant to transitional and saving provisions, the time limit under the *SDA 1976, s 76(1)* is now subject to similar extension provisions in relation to disputes to which *art 8(1)* of the *Mediation Directive* applies. Those provisions are contained in the *SDA 1976, s 76ZA*.

A six month time limit applies to complaints by members of the armed forces: *EqA 2010, s 123(2)*.

From 1 October 2004 the three month time limit could be extended by the 'extended period' under the *Employment Act 2002 (Dispute Resolution) Regulations 2004 (SI 2004/752)*, reg 15. However, following the repeal of the *EmA 2002, ss 29 to 33* and *Schedules 2 to 4* by the *Employment Act 2008, ss 1* and *20*, and subject to the transitional provisions under the *Employment Act 2008 (Commencement No 1, Transitional Provisions and Savings) Order 2008 (SI 2008/3232)*, *art 3* and *Schedule*, such an extension ceased to be available after 6 April 2009.

In computing the time limit, the clock is stopped during the period from the day after the claimant complies with the requirement to contact ACAS for early conciliation ('day A') until the day on which the claimant receives or is treated as receiving an early conciliation certificate ('day B'). If the time limit would otherwise expire between day A and one month after day B, it will instead expire at the end of that period. "One month" means on the 'corresponding date' so where day B is 30 June, the time limit will expire on 30 July (*Tanveer v East London Bus & Coach Co Ltd* [2016] ICR D11. Only one conciliation certificate can be, or needs to be, issued for each 'matter'. This means that a conciliation certificate issued in response to issues raised in the run-up to dismissal or resignation will also cover the subsequent dismissal or resignation: *Compass Group UK and Ireland Ltd v Morgan* [2016] IRLR 924, [2017] ICR 73. However, beware the mistaken issue of a second conciliation certificate in these circumstances: that will be invalid and will not give rise to any further extension of time: *HMRC v Garau* UKEAT/0348/16/LA. There is no need to seek a further conciliation certificate where amendments are made to a claim, even where the amendment is adding a different respondent provided the amended claim concerns the same 'matter': *Drake International Systems Ltd and ors v Blue Arrow Ltd* [2016] ICR 445. See further **14.10**.

Whether a claim in relation to benefits is properly characterised as concerning equal pay or sex discrimination will have significant consequences for the applicable time limit (see, for example, *Hosso v European Credit Management Ltd* [2011] EWCA Civ 1589, [2012] ICR 547, [2012] IRLR 235). See also HARVEYS – Divisions **L.5.E, PI.1.E**.

For the purposes of deciding when an act was done, in calculating the time limit:

(a)   where the inclusion of any term in any contract renders the making of the contract an unlawful act, that act shall be treated as extending throughout the duration of the contract;

(b)   any act extending over a period shall be treated as done at the end of that period: *EqA 2010, s 123(3)* (for an example, see *Calder v James Finlay Corpn Ltd* [1989] IRLR 55, [1989] ICR 157);

(c)   a deliberate omission shall be treated as done when the person in question decided upon it: *EqA 2010, s 123(3)*; and

(d)   in the absence of evidence establishing the contrary, a person is to be taken as having decided upon failure to do something when he does something inconsistent with the omitted act or when the period within which he would reasonably be expected to have done the act has expired: *EqA 2010, s 123(4)*.

Whether a claim form contains a complaint of a particular act (which may affect the time limit by being the last in a series of connected acts) is a question of construction of the document, and therefore an error by the tribunal in this regard can found an appeal to the EAT (*Gregory Charles v Tesco Stores Ltd* [2013] ICR D15, [2012] All ER (D) 141 (Dec), CA).

Where a claim had been struck out because it was brought outside the time limit, a second claim alleging that the claimant was the victim of an ongoing course of conduct was an abuse of process because it was in reality just an attempt to resurrect the first claim (*Agbenowossi-Koffi v Donvand Ltd t/a Gulliver's Travel Associates* [2014] EWCA Civ 855, [2014] All ER (D) 190 (Jun)).

Where the complaint relates to dismissal, time runs from the date of the dismissal, rather than (if earlier) the date on which notice was given: see the cases cited in *British Gas Services Ltd v McCaull* [2001] IRLR 60 at para 25. In *Derby Specialist Fabrication Ltd v Burton* [2001] 2 All ER 840, [2001] IRLR 69 this principle was followed in a race discrimination case where the claim was for constructive dismissal. The EAT held that this constituted a 'dismissal' within *s 4(2)* of the *RRA 1976* and it was not therefore necessary to rely on the discriminatory acts which had led to the employee's resignation as 'detriments' (in which case the claim would have been out of time). The same conclusion was reached by the Court of Appeal in relation to the *DDA 1995*: *Meikle v Nottinghamshire County Council* [2004] EWCA Civ 859, [2004] 4 All ER 97, [2005] ICR 1, [2004] IRLR 703, following *Catherall v Michelin Tyres plc* [2003] IRLR 61, EAT, and disapproving the earlier contrary view expressed by a different division of the EAT in *Metropolitan Police Comr v Harley* [2001] IRLR 263.

A point not directly arising in these cases, and on which there is no direct authority, is whether a claim alleging discrimination by way of dismissal may be presented before the claimant has been dismissed, in the sense applied in the cases cited above. There is nothing obvious in the wording of the statutory provisions on time limits to prevent this, as a claim is merely required not to be presented after the end of the period specified. Under the legislation on discrimination prior to the *Equality Act 2010*, the complaint to be presented was that the respondent 'has committed' an act of unlawful discrimination (see eg the *Sex Discrimination Act 1975, s 63(1)* wording which did preclude a complaint of dismissal being presented before the dismissal took effect, and there was (and is) no equivalent in the discrimination legislation of *ERA 1996, s 111(3)*, which specifically allows the presentation of a complaint of unfair dismissal during the notice period: see **19.19** EMPLOYMENT TRIBUNALS – I. However, the position is less clearly expressed in the *Equality Act 2010, ss 120(1)* and *123(1)*; the former provision refers to complaints 'relating to' a contravention of relevant parts of the Act, and 'not after the end' of a period does not necessarily mean also 'not before the beginning'. The prudent course, in the circumstances, is not to present a claim before the dismissal has taken effect.

14.5   *Omissions*

A difficulty of interpretation arose in cases where there was a delay between the point at which the discriminator decided upon a deliberate omission and the point at which he omitted to act. In *Swithland Motors plc v Clarke* [1994] IRLR 275, [1994] ICR 231, EAT, the appellant decided, whilst negotiating the purchase of a car sales business from receivers, that in the event that its bid was successful it would follow its usual practice of employing only female sales staff. It would omit, therefore, to offer the existing male staff the opportunity to continue in employment. The purchase was completed more than three months after the decision to apply the policy had been taken. On its face *SDA 1975, s 76(6)(c)* appeared to suggest that the male employees were out of time to complain before they even knew that there was something to complain about. The EAT decided that the section had to be read as meaning 'decides at a time and in circumstances when he is in a position to implement that decision'. Time ran, therefore, from the date on which the business was purchased.

The provisions of *s 123* of the *EqA 2010* have also caused difficulty. As noted above, *s 123(4)* provides that, in the absence of evidence to the contrary, a person (P) is to be taken to decide on failure to do something: (a) when P does an act inconsistent with doing it; or (b) if P does no inconsistent act, on the expiry of the period in which P might reasonably have been expected to do it. The Court of Appeal in *Matuszowicz v Kingston-Upon-Hull City Council* [2009] EWCA Civ 22, [2009] ICR 1170, [2009] IRLR 28, CA noted that ironically the effect of this is that, in the context of time limits, it is in the interests of a respondent employer to allege that it might reasonably have been expected to have dealt with the matter in question much earlier than it actually did, whereas it would be in the employee's interests to assert that it would have taken as long as it in reality did, so as not to give rise to an earlier date as the starting date *s 123(4)*. Such arguments would be likely to be entirely counter to the position the respective parties would take on the substance of the claim. The Court of Appeal suggested that there were two ways the problem might be eased: first, claimants and advisers may need to be prepared to issue proceedings more quickly once a potentially discriminatory omission has been brought to the employer's attention; secondly, when considering whether to extend time in such cases, tribunals 'can be expected to have sympathetic regard to the difficulty [*s 123(4)(b)*] will create for some claimants [since] its forensic effect is to give the employer an interest in asserting that it could reasonably have been expected to act sooner, perhaps much sooner, than it did, and the employee in asserting the contrary. Both contentions will demand a measure of poker-faced insincerity which only a lawyer could understand or a casuist forgive'. In *Matuszowicz* the Court of Appeal further noted that a complaint of disability discrimination by reason of failure to make reasonable adjustments is an act of omission and, usually, a continuing act of omission (see further below and also *Watkins v HSBC Bank Plc* [2018] IRLR 1015). Further consideration was given to these provisions in *Abertawe Bro Morgannwg University Local Health Board v Morgan* [2018] EWCA Civ 640, [2018] ICR 1194 where the Court of Appeal noted that ss *123(3)* and *(4)* were dealing with the question of when time starts to run for bringing proceedings, not with the question of when the employer first comes under a duty to act, which may (indeed, usually will) be earlier. The Court of Appeal held that the question to ask for the purposes of *s 123(3)* and *(4)* was to be determined from the point of view of the claimant and when the claimant might reasonably have expected the employer to take the step(s) in question.

14.6   *Acts extending over a period*

Applications in discrimination cases will often make reference to a number of alleged instances of discrimination stretching back over a period, only part of which is within three months of the date of submission of the claim. The tribunal must then assess whether the individual allegations together constitute an 'act extending over a period' or else are to be treated as a series of discrete events.

In *Barclays Bank plc v Kapur* [1991] IRLR 136, [1991] ICR 208, the House of Lords held that the bank's stipulation that service in Africa would not count for pension purposes, although originally made years before the complaints were brought, subjected the applicant employees to a continuing disadvantage which by virtue of *RRA 1976, s 68(7)(b)* was to be treated as an act done when the employees retired. It was necessary to distinguish a continuing rule such as this from an act which merely had continuing consequences. In *Sougrin v Haringey Health Authority* [1992] IRLR 416, [1992] ICR 650, a pay re-grading was held to fall into the latter category, but in *Littlewoods Organisation plc v Traynor* [1993] IRLR 154 the failure to take the remedial measures promised after an earlier act of discrimination was held to be a continuing act of omission (see also *Matuszowicz v Kingston-Upon-Hull City Council* [2009] EWCA Civ 22, [2009] ICR 1170, [2009] IRLR 28, CA and *Fairlead Maritime Ltd v Parsoya* (UKEAT/0275/15/DA, 30 August 2016)). However, in *Okoro v Taylor Wood Construction Ltd* [2013] ICR 580, [2012] All ER (D) 23 (Dec), CA, a construction company's decision to ban some contract workers from one of its sites was held to be a one-off act. In *Smith v Carillion and Secretary of State for Business, Innovation & Skills* [2015] EWCA Civ 209, [2015] IRLR 467, the Court of Appeal also applied *Okoro* holding that there could not be any more expansive interpretation by reference to the *Human Rights Act 1998* where the last incident complained of took place before the *Act* came into force.

A number of apparently discrete acts may provide evidence of a policy, rule or practice. The existence of such a policy or practice may itself constitute a 'continuing act' (*Owusu v London Fire and Civil Defence Authority* [1995] IRLR 574). In *Cast v Croydon College* [1998] IRLR 318, [1998] ICR 500, CA, an employee who was about to commence maternity leave asked to be allowed to return on a part-time basis. Her request was refused. She took her maternity leave, returned to work and repeated her request. When it was again refused she resigned, alleging that she was unable to comply with the requirement that she work full-time. She commenced proceedings in the tribunal. Only the second refusal was 'in time'. It was held that each refusal constituted a separate act of discrimination, because on each occasion the employer considered the matter afresh. Had it merely restated its earlier decision, the position might have been different. Further, the tribunal decided that the second refusal was merely a confirmation of the first and that the claim was out of time. However, the Court of Appeal determined, first, that the two refusals were discrete decisions and that the claim in relation to the second refusal was within time and, further, that the two refusals should have been treated as evidence of the existence of a 'policy' on the employer's part, the fact that the same decision was reached on each occasion was evidence of the existence of a discriminatory policy. The operation of such a discriminatory policy constituted an act 'extending over a period' within the meaning of *SDA 1975, s 76*. Similarly, where an employer fails to make a reasonable adjustment for a disabled employee and then keeps the refusal under review, there is a continuing act or omission and time does not run (*Jobcentre Plus v Jamil and others*, EAT (26 November 2013, unreported). In contrast, in another case, the Court of Appeal has held that the time limit begins to run again on each occasion on which the policy is applied. Thus, where a complainant was refused the same request on a number of occasions, each refusal caused the three-month time limit to start afresh (*Rovenska v General Medical Council* [1997] IRLR 367, [1998] ICR 85, CA). The EAT has held that an employment tribunal was entitled to conclude that a refusal by an employer to revoke a dismissal was entirely separate from the dismissal itself and not part of a continuing act (*Baynton v South West Trains Ltd* [2005] ICR 1730, [2005] All ER (D) 253 (Jun)).

The EAT has said, *obiter*, that complaints of different types of discrimination can in principle be taken together as constituting conduct extending over a period, giving the example of complaints of direct discrimination by giving a claimant undesirable shifts and a failure to make reasonable adjustments by giving the claimant different shifts (*Robinson v Royal Surrey County Hospital NHS Foundation Trust* [2015] All ER (D) 409 (Jul)).

Other authorities have used terms such as 'rule', 'scheme', 'regime' or 'practice' as well as 'policy'. However, the Court of Appeal has stressed that such terms are merely examples of acts which may extend over a period. Their Lordships have adopted a broader description of what the tribunal should look for: an 'ongoing situation' or a 'continuing state of affairs' which may be contrasted with 'a succession of unconnected or isolated specific acts' (*Hendricks v Metropolitan Police Comr* [2002] EWCA Civ 1686, [2003] IRLR 96, [2003] ICR 530, CA). The Court of Appeal confirmed the *Hendricks* approach in *Lyfar v Brighton and Sussex University Hospitals Trust* [2006] EWCA Civ 1548, [2006] All ER (D) 182 (Nov), emphasising the need to focus on the substance of the complaints when assessing whether they form a continuous act. However, in order to establish the existence of a policy or practice, the complainant must establish some degree of 'co-ordination' (*Metropolitan Police Comr v Hendricks* [2001] All ER (D) 57 (Nov), EAT). In *Moxam v Visible Changes Ltd* [2012] Eq LR 202, EAT, the employment tribunal had erred by not applying a broad approach to 'racial grounds' to recognise that earlier instances of the use of racist language revealed that a manager had the same mindset as he had in relation to later, in-time incidents and therefore time should have been extended to include the earlier incidents. Following the House of Lords' decision in *Relaxion Group plc v Rhys-Harper* [2003] UKHL 33, [2003] IRLR 484, [2003] ICR 867, the EAT has held that a series of acts constituting an act extending over time can include an act taking place after the complainant has ceased to be an employee of the respondent (*BHS Ltd v Walker* [2005] All ER (D) 146 (May)). It will be a relevant, but not conclusive, factor whether the same or different individuals were involved in the alleged incidents of discrimination over the period and where there is a break in contact of several months a tribunal may be entitled to conclude that continuity is not preserved (see *Aziz v FDA* [2010] EWCA Civ 304). However, it will be an error of law to regard the mere fact of the claimant being off work without incident as constituting a break in continuity: the legal question is whether the conduct is continuing. If the conduct complained of commences before and continues after the period of sick leave then the conduct may well be continuing, especially where the conduct is the cause of the absence: *Watkins v HSBC Bank Plc* [2018] IRLR 1015.

When considering whether there is, to use the language of *Hendricks* (above), a continuing discriminatory state of affairs, the complainant must be able to "anchor" that state of affairs with specific acts of discrimination. They cannot rely on a "floating or overarching" state of affairs. Further, if none of the specific acts is found to have occurred within the time limit, jurisdiction cannot be established (*South Western Ambulance NHS Foundation Trust v King* UKEAT/0056/19 [2020] IRLR 168).

It will generally be an error of law for a tribunal to seek to determine whether there is an act extending over a period on the basis of legal argument alone without hearing any evidence and making findings of fact (see *City of Edinburgh Council v Kaur* [2013] CSIH 32, and the 'public interest disclosure' case of *Arthur v London Eastern Rly Ltd (t/a One Stansted Express)* [2006] EWCA Civ 1358, [2007] IRLR 58). Even where some factual evidence is given at a preliminary hearing, care should be taken at that stage to consider the claimant's case at its highest and decide whether the acts alleged are capable of constituting continuing acts: *Mirek v Graysons Automotives Service* UKEAT/0198/18/RN. However, it is not enough for a claimant simply to assert that there is a continuing act or that there is an ongoing state of affairs, rather he or she must have an arguable basis for the contention that the complaints are so linked as to be a continuing act or an ongoing state of affairs (*Ma v Merck Sharp & Dohme Ltd* [2008] EWCA Civ 1426, [2008] All ER (D) 158 (Dec)). Conversely, a claimant is not required expressly to state in his claim form that there is a 'continuing act' if it is sufficiently clear to the respondent that such an argument would be raised in response to a limitation defence (see *Khetab v AGA Medical Ltd* (2011) 922 IDS Brief 9, EAT). In *Kerr v Ernst & Young Services Ltd* [2011] ICR D13, [2011] All ER (D) 146 (Feb), EAT, an employment judge was held to have erred in giving directions at a case management discussion that precluded a claimant from relying on complaints of discrimination against three individuals (on the grounds inter alia that too much time had elapsed) as she had no power at a case management discussion effectively to strike out parts of his claim. Further, even if she had had the power to do so, she had erred in not giving the opportunity for representations before making such an order.

In *Tyagi v BBC World Service* [2001] EWCA Civ 549, [2001] IRLR 465, the complainant sought to allege that he had been discriminated against in relation to an application for promotion. His claim was lodged 15 months after he had failed to obtain the promotion and a year after he had ceased to be employed by the respondent. He contended that the respondent operated a discriminatory recruitment policy which was still in place at the date of his application. That being so, he argued, his application was not out of time. The Court of Appeal found against him drawing a distinction between those who remained in employment at the time of complaint and those who did not. The former group was entitled to complain about discriminatory policies which affected the way in which their employer afforded them 'access to opportunities for promotion'. They could, therefore, complain about the existence of the policy itself. The latter were only able to complain about the arrangements made for the purpose of determining who should be offered a particular job and, thus, could not complain about the policy. See also *Ruhaza v Alexander Hancock Recruitment Ltd* [2012] EqLR 9, EAT.

In the case of a single act, time starts to run when the course of action is complete, that is when a complaint to a tribunal could first be made (*Clarke v Hampshire Electro-Plating Co Ltd* [1991] IRLR 490, [1992] ICR 312; see also *Adekeye v Post Office* [1993] IRLR 324, [1993] ICR 464). Where the alleged act of discrimination was the dismissal of an internal appeal relating to an unsuccessful promotion application time ran from the date of that decision, not the date that the claimant was notified of the decision (*Virdi v Metropolitan*

Police Comr [2007] IRLR 24, EAT). In the case of a constructive dismissal which is alleged to be discriminatory, time runs from the complainant's resignation, not from the employer's repudiatory breach (*Meikle v Nottinghamshire County Council* [2004] EWCA Civ 859, [2004] IRLR 703, [2005] ICR 1).

14.7   *Extension of time*

A tribunal may nevertheless consider a complaint or application which is out of time if, in all the circumstances of the case, it considers that it is just and equitable to do so (*EqA 2010, s 123(1)(b)*; and previously *SDA 1975, s 76(5); RRA 1976, s 68(6); SOR 2003, reg 34(3); RBR 2003, reg 34(3); DDA 1995, Sch 3, para 3(2)*; and *AR 2006, reg 42(3)*). In considering applications for extension, the correct approach for the tribunal to take is to bear in mind that employment tribunal time limits are generally enforced strictly and to ask whether a sufficient case has been made out to exercise its discretion in favour of extension. It is not a question of extending time unless a good reason can be shown for not doing so (*Robertson v Bexley Community Centre (t/a Leisure Link)* [2003] EWCA Civ 576, [2003] IRLR 434). The discretion to extend time is not at large and the time limit will operate to exclude otherwise valid claims unless the claimant can displace it, although this does not mean that the discretion has to be used sparingly (see *Chief Constable of Lincolnshire Police v Caston* [2009] EWCA Civ 1298, [2010] IRLR 327). For a recent summary of the legal principles, see *Thompson v Ark Schools* [2019] ICR 292.

In deciding whether or not it is just and equitable to grant an extension of time, the tribunal must take care first to consider the reasons why the claim was brought out of time and why the claim was not presented sooner than it was: *Abertawe Bro Morgannwg University Local Health Board v Morgan* (UKEAT/0305/13/LA, 18 February 2014). However, the failure to put forward a reason for the delay (whether a good reason or any reason at all) does not necessarily mean time should not be extended: all relevant factors including the balance of prejudice and the merits of the claim must be considered: *Abertawe Bro Morgannwg University Local Health Board v Morgan* [2018] EWCA Civ 640, [2018] ICR 1194, *Rathakrishnan v Pizza Express (Restaurants) Ltd* [2016] IRLR 278, doubting *Habinteg Housing Association Ltd v Holleran* (2015) UKEAT/0274/14, [2015] All ER (D) 353 (Feb), EAT.

One possible ground for extending time is that the complainant was unaware of his or her rights, another that she has received incorrect advice from her lawyer (*Hawkins v Ball and Barclays Bank plc* [1996] IRLR 258; *Chohan v Derby Law Centre* [2004] IRLR 685, EAT; *Virdi v Metropolitan Police Comr*, above; cf also *British Coal Corpn v Keeble* [1997] IRLR 336; *Bahous*; below, or where a complainant has delayed because she was awaiting the outcome of an internal appeal or grievance procedure (*Aniagwu v Hackney London Borough Council* [1999] IRLR 303, EAT). The undesirability of bringing a claim while still employed is a factor that a tribunal may legitimately take into account when determining whether it is just and equitable to extend time: *Fairlead Maritime Ltd v Parsoya* (UKEAT/0275/15/DA, 30 August 2016). However exhausting internal procedures will not always justify a delay (*Robinson v Post Office* [2000] IRLR 804), and the Court of Appeal has since decided that *Aniagwu* is limited to its own facts (*Apelogun-Gabriels v Lambeth London Borough Council* [2001] EWCA Civ 1853, [2002] IRLR 116, [2002] ICR 713). A tribunal is not required to accept a doctor's evidence that a claimant was unable due to psychiatric illness to present his claim in time where there was evidence that he had been fit enough to seek legal advice and had written coherent letters on unrelated matters within the limitation period (see *Chouafi v London United Busways Ltd* [2006] EWCA Civ 689, [2006] All ER (D) 33 (May)). In *Department of Constitutional Affairs v Jones* [2007] EWCA Civ 894, [2008] IRLR 128 (a case under the *DDA 1995*), the Court of Appeal held that a tribunal had been entitled to consider that the claimant's own inability to admit to himself that he was mentally ill and a disabled person for the purposes of the *DDA 1995* was a factor justifying delay in presenting a claim. In cases where medical reasons are relied on by a claimant as part of the reason why proceedings were not brought within the time limit, the question is not whether the claimant was prevented from bringing proceedings by the medical condition, but whether, in the round, it is just and equitable to extend time in the light of the claimant's medical difficulties, even if they were not such as actually to prevent the claimant commencing proceedings: see *Watkins v HSBC Bank Plc* [2018] IRLR 1015.

The tribunal may be assisted by considering the factors that the court is obliged to consider when extending time in personal injury cases (for which see the *Limitation Act 1980, s 33(3)* or *CPR rule 3.9(1)*). However, it is not obliged to do so. Its obligation is simply to ensure that no significant circumstance is left out of account (*Afolabi v Southwark London Borough Council* [2003] EWCA Civ 15, [2003] IRLR 220, [2003] ICR 800). One of the most significant factors which the tribunal should consider is whether a fair trial of the issue is still possible (*DPP v Marshall* [1998] IRLR 494, [1998] ICR 518). Whilst the fact that a fair trial is impossible will most likely preclude extension of time, it does not follow that merely because a fair trial is still possible time should be extended (*Simms v Transco plc* [2001] All ER (D) 245 (Jan), EAT). If a respondent wishes to establish that a fair trial is no longer possible, he should consider leading evidence to establish the point (*Southwark London Borough Council*, above). An employment tribunal will err if it fails to take account of the prejudice to the employer of allowing a claim out of time (*Abegaze v South East Essex College* [2006] ICR 468, [2005] All ER (D) 49 (Nov), EAT). Conversely, an employment tribunal will err if it fails to recognise the absence of any real prejudice to an employer when refusing to exercise its discretion to extend time (*Baynton v South West Trains Ltd* [2005] ICR 1730, [2005] All ER (D) 253 (Jun), EAT and *Watkins v HSBC Bank Plc* [2018] IRLR 1015). The merits of a case are an important factor and it will be an error of law for a tribunal not to take account of the merits of the case when considering the balance of prejudice (*Bahous v Pizza Express Restaurant Ltd* (2012) 945 IDS Brief 17, [2012] All ER (D) 191 (Jan), EAT and *Donald v AVC Media Enterprises Ltd* UKEATS/0016/14/JW, 9 November 2016). The Inner House of the Court of Session held in *Malcolm v Dundee City Council* [2012] CSIH 13, [2012] EqLR 363 that an employment tribunal had taken an overly strict approach in refusing to extend time *after* it had held a 21 day hearing and concluded that allegations of harassment were well-founded on their merits. Where time is extended an employee cannot rely on legislation that was not in force at the time of the act complained of if the act would not have been unlawful at the time that it was committed (see *Abegaze*, above).

Where there is more than one respondent, the employment tribunal should consider the position of each respondent separately when deciding whether it is just and equitable to extend time (*Harden v Wootlif and Smart Diner Group Ltd* (UKEAT/0448/14/DA, 15 April 2015)). Different claims brought within the same proceedings may also require separate consideration: *Abertawe Bro Morgannwg University Local Health Board v Morgan* [2014] All ER (D) 56 (May) (UKEAT/0305/13/LA).

In *Stevens v Bexley Health Authority* [1989] IRLR 240, [1989] ICR 224, the EAT appeared to consider that the statutory time limits were not applicable to claims brought directly under European law, but more recent decisions have shown that view to be incorrect (see **23.20–23.21** EQUAL PAY, and **24.2** EUROPEAN UNION LAW).

See also HARVEYS – Divisions **L.5.E**(4), (5), **PI.1.F**(1), (3).

14.8   Formulating the complaint

Care must be taken in drafting the complaint. In *Chapman v Simon* [1994] IRLR 124, the Court of Appeal held that an employment tribunal is limited to considering those matters complained of in the originating application (see also, *Akinmolasire v Camden and Islington Mental Health & Social Care Trust* [2004] EWCA Civ 1351, [2004] All ER (D) 59 (Oct)). However where general accusations of sex discrimination were made in relation to a redundancy dismissal, an employee was entitled to receive from the tribunal a finding on whether or not a failure to offer alternative employment was discriminatory even though she had not specifically relied on the point (*Prowse-Piper v Anglian Windows Ltd* [2010] EWCA Civ 428 [2010] All ER (D) 74 (Nov)). In the light of the Court of Appeal's decision in *Chapman* it is also advisable, when specifying the detriments to which it is alleged that the complainant was subjected, specifically to recite that employees who do not share the complainant's protected characteristic have not or would not be subjected to such detriments. In relation to racial discrimination, the EAT has held that the employment tribunal either at or before the substantive hearing needs to identify which categories of racial discrimination (ie colour, race, nationality or ethnic or national origin) are relied upon so that the correct comparator can be identified, although a claimant who is not sure may plead all or most of them (see *Okonu*, above; and also *Chagger*, above). The EAT held in *Baker v Metropolitan Police Comr* [2010] All ER (D) 17 (Apr), EAT, that it is not sufficient merely to tick the box on the ET1 form for the particular type of discrimination complained of (in that case disability) without pleading any details (although the EAT also held that the tribunal erred in not considering the claimant's application to amend the claim). An employment tribunal had been entitled to refuse to allow an amendment to a claim to plead associative disability discrimination where the tribunal had already made findings of fact which meant that the amended claim could not have succeeded (see *Brill v Interactive Business Communications Ltd* [2010] EWCA Civ 1604, [2010] All ER (D) 139 (Dec)). However, where an employee has not been able in advance of receiving the respondent's evidence (or in advance of oral evidence at the hearing) to identify an element of their case then an amendment at the hearing may be appropriate (see *Commissioner of Police for the Metropolis v Denby* UKEAT/0314/16/RN where the claimant could not have known until the hearing which officers were responsible for the discrimination and which were merely acting on 'tainted' information).

Where default judgment has been entered against a respondent for failure to file a response in time, in assessing compensation at a remedies hearing a tribunal may not make findings inconsistent with the case on liability pleaded in the claim form (see *Eaton v Spencer* [2012] ICR D7, EAT). In that situation, where alternative bases of liability are pleaded it is for the tribunal at a remedies hearing to decide which is appropriate (*Thomas and others v Taylors of St James Ltd* [2013] All ER (D) 16 (Sep) (UKEAT/0117/13/KN).

The Court of Appeal has determined that direct and indirect discrimination are separate claims which must be separately identified in a claim form (*Ali v Office of National Statistics* [2004] EWCA Civ 1363, [2005] IRLR 201). It is therefore essential fully to plead the facts on which different types of allegation of discrimination are based. Where a complainant believes that his dismissal was both discriminatory and unfair, it is essential that both are pleaded. If he first pursues a claim for unfair dismissal, he will not be entitled later to bring a fresh discrimination claim (*Divine-Bortey v Brent London Borough Council* [1998] IRLR 525, CA, applying *Henderson v Henderson* (1843) 3 Hare 100).

Where a complainant relies on more than one alleged act of discrimination, it is up to the complainant to ensure that each of them is pursued at the hearing itself. The tribunal is not obliged to make a finding in relation to everything raised in pleadings, only in relation to those matters which the complainant pursues at the hearing (*Mensah v East Hertfordshire NHS Trust* [1998] IRLR 531, CA). Where more than one incident is complained about, it is important for a tribunal to be clear which complaints are relied upon as distinct justiciable causes of action (and if necessary consider whether time should be extended in relation to those matters) and those complaints that are merely relied on as evidence (see *Aylott v Stockton-on-Tees Borough Council* [2009] IRLR 533, EAT).

A claim cannot be amended to include a complaint in relation to an act or omission that would not have been unlawful at the time that it took place (see *Standard Life Bank Ltd v Wilson* [2008] 1 ICR 947, EAT – a decision concerning age discrimination).

Where a claimant relies on an actual comparator in addition to a hypothetical comparator, this is an important detail of the claim and it should be set out in the claim form (if necessary by amendment) (see *Woodward v Santander UK plc* [2010] IRLR 834, EAT).

In general, discrimination cases should not be struck out at a preliminary stage on grounds that they stand no reasonable prospect of success. Normally, a full examination of the facts will be required. However, a strike out may be appropriate in cases where, taking the claimant's case at its highest, it is clear that it stands no reasonable prospect of success (see *Anyanwu v South Bank Students Union* [2001] UKHL 14, [2001] 1 WLR 638 and *Ezsias v North Glamorgan NHS Trust* [2007] EWCA Civ 330, [2007] 4 All ER 940. 'No reasonable prospects of success' is a high threshold which is not met where the judge merely considers it unlikely that a claimant will discharge the burden of proof: *Walters v Avanta Enterprise Ltd* UKEAT/0127/17/BA (in which the claimant contended being called a 'coconut', i.e. a black person who acts white, was evidence of race discrimination). However, a case will stand no reasonable prospect of success where it is conclusively disproved by, or is totally and inexplicably inconsistent with, undisputed contemporaneous documents: *Mechkarov v Citibank NA* [2016] ICR 1121. In that case, the EAT (Mitting J) further observed that if core issues of fact turned to any extent on oral evidence, there needed to be a full hearing and it was not appropriate for an employment judge to conduct a 'mini trial' on those issues at a preliminary hearing without consideration of relevant documents. Nonetheless, where all material facts are clear and there is unlikely to be further relevant evidence available at a full hearing, a strike out may be appropriate: see *RMC v Chief Constable of Hampshire* (UKEAT/0184/16/LA, 8 November 2016) (where it was agreed the facts were not in dispute and oral evidence was not required and *Shestak v Royal College of Nursing* (2008) 152 Sol Jo (no 37) 30, [2008] All ER (D) 193 (Oct), (2009) 873 IDS Brief 12, EAT (where the strike-out was based on undisputed documents and a failure to articulate an arguable basis for the claims). A strike out may even be appropriate in cases where there are disputed facts such as *Ahir v British Airways Plc* [2017] EWCA Civ 1392 (where the claimant's case was based on a 'speculative and highly implausible' theory about the fabrication of a letter). However see, in contrast, *A v B* [2010] EWCA Civ 1378, [2011] ICR D9, [2010] All ER (D) 101 (Dec), in which the Court of Appeal held that the EAT had correctly overturned a decision to strike out a sex discrimination victimisation claim where there was a more than fanciful prospect that the respondent would fail to discharge the reverse burden of proof; see also *Community Law Clinic Solicitors v Methuen* [2012] EWCA Civ 571, [2012] All ER (D) 23 (Apr), *Millbank Financial Services Ltd v Crawford* [2014] IRLR 18 and *Chandok v Tirkey* [2015] IRLR 195, [2015] ICR 527 (emphasising that strike-out will not be appropriate where there is further potentially material evidence to come).

Discrimination claims often create problems for case management because, as noted above, a claimant seeks to rely on a series of alleged incidents of discrimination, even if only as background material from which inferences can be drawn. Whilst the basic rule is that evidence is admissible if it is relevant and inadmissible if it is irrelevant, evidence may be logically or theoretically relevant but too marginal and unlikely to assist the tribunal to justify its admission (see *HSBC Asia Holdings BV v Gillespie* [2011] IRLR 209, [2011] ICR 192, EAT). In *Gillespie* the EAT held that an employment judge had erred in not excluding evidence which allegedly went to the background of discriminatory acts where the evidence was not sufficiently relevant to justify the burden that would be placed on the respondent in addressing it. Underhill P held that, while in many cases, the best approach is to address the question of admissibility during the course of the substantive hearing, in some cases, particularly discrimination cases, this may not be practicable or fair and it may be appropriate to decide questions of admissibility in advance of the hearing, for example when the issue affects the hearing length, disclosure or the need for witness orders. Underhill P also suggested (obiter) that where a claimant raises complaints in relation to a large number of incidents of alleged discrimination, and it cannot be agreed that the claimant proceed with a sample only of his allegations, it may be possible instead to deal with his allegations in tranches rather than at a single hearing. However, whilst an employment judge may direct a claimant to set out clearly in a schedule the acts and omissions he or she complains of, there is no power to require a claimant to 'self select' which complaints he or she will pursue at the final hearing (see *McKinson v Hackney Community College* (2012) 942 IDS Brief 16, [2012] All ER (D) 128 (Jan), EAT).

14.9   Questionnaire and disclosure

An important difficulty encountered by complainants has been obtaining the information necessary to assess the strength of their case and to conduct it successfully once they are satisfied of its merits. To assist a person who considers that they may have been unlawfully discriminated against or subjected to harassment to decide whether to institute proceedings and, if they do so, to formulate and present the case in the most effective manner, there used to be a procedure whereby such a person (whether an applicant or potential applicant) could serve, on the person against whom he or she has a complaint, a questionnaire in the form prescribed (*EqA 2010, s 138*) to gather information about their complaint. The questions and answers were admissible (subject to compliance with time limits) in tribunal proceedings and tribunals could draw inferences from a failure by the employer to answer the questions. However, *EqA 2010, s 138* was repealed with effect from 6 April 2014.

As a result of this repeal, claimants may now need to commence proceedings in order to obtain information which is not provided voluntarily. In pursuing a claim before an employment tribunal, a claimant may ask for the disclosure of documents by his employer or prospective employer. For the power of an employment tribunal to order the disclosure of documents which are relevant to the proceedings, see **20.60–20.62** Employment Tribunals – II. However, in *Science Research Council v Nassé* [1979] IRLR 465, [1979] ICR 921, the House of Lords held that tribunals should not order the disclosure of reports or references given and received in confidence, except when it is necessary for disposing fairly of the proceedings that the confidence should be overridden. In *Canadian Imperial Bank of Commerce v Beck* [2009] EWCA Civ 619, [2009] IRLR 740, the Court of Appeal summarised the position as being that an order for disclosure should be made if it was "necessary for fairly disposing of the proceedings" and that while relevance was a factor it was not sufficient on its own to warrant the granting of an order and conversely confidentiality does not, of itself, warrant refusal of an order.

In *West Midlands Passenger Transport Executive v Singh* [1988] IRLR 186, [1988] ICR 614, the Court of Appeal upheld an employment tribunal's order for discovery of a schedule of statistics showing the ethnic origins of candidates for promotion and those actually promoted during the period preceding the alleged discrimination. The decision also gives guidance as to when disclosure should be refused because, although relevant, it would be oppressive. The Court of Appeal further held that it might be possible, first, to infer from statistics that there had been discrimination against members of a racial group in general, and then to infer (in the absence of a satisfactory explanation in the particular case) that the applicant as a member of that group had been the victim of discrimination.

Under previously applicable tribunal rules, it was held that an employment tribunal did not have the power to require a schedule of statistics to be produced where the necessary information is not already in existence (*Carrington v Helix Lighting Ltd* [1990] ICR 125, [1990] IRLR 6, EAT). It remains to be seen whether this continues to be the case under the present rules.

The Court of Appeal has held that, where a respondent claimed to be prohibited by law from disclosing the reasons why a claimant failed a security vetting, or indeed from disclosing the legal basis for that prohibition, a tribunal erred in law by ordering the respondent to disclose the reason why the claimant was not appointed to a post (*Barracks v Coles* [2006] EWCA Civ 1041, [2007] ICR 60, [2007] IRLR 73). In a claim based on EU discrimination law, the Court of Appeal in *Kiani v Secretary of State for the Home Department* [2015] EWCA Civ 776, [2015] ICR 1179, [2015] IRLR 837 held that where national security considerations were invoked as a ground for withholding information from a claimant, the tribunal had to strike 'an appropriate balance between the requirements flowing from state security and the requirements of the right to effective judicial protection whilst limiting any interference with the exercise of that right to that which [was] strictly necessary'. The same approach was required by article 6 of the Human Rights Convention (see *Tariq v Home Office* [2011] UKSC 35, [2011] IRLR 843). The balancing of those competing interests had to take account of all the material facts of the particular case. The tribunal in *Kiani* did not err in refusing further disclosure where it had taken sufficient account of material seen at a closed hearing in which the claimant could not participate but was assisted by a special advocate, and had conducted a balancing exercise knowing that the material contained 'the very essence of the case'.

The EAT has held that evidence about a 'without prejudice' discussion with a complainant about bringing her employment to an end could be adduced as there was no dispute at the time attracting privilege and, in any event, the public interest in having discrimination allegations properly determined meant that it would be an abuse to apply the 'without prejudice' rule in that case (*BNP Paribas v Mezzotero* [2004] IRLR 508). However, in *Woodward v Santander UK plc* [2010] IRLR 834, the EAT sought to emphasise that *Mezzotero* did not create a new exception to the without prejudice rule and that the policy reasons behind the rule that parties be able to negotiate freely applied with particular force where parties were seeking to settle discrimination claims. The EAT held that the exception to the without prejudice rule for unambiguous impropriety applied only in the clearest cases, and was not engaged in the present case.

In *Vaseghi v Brunel University* (2006) 818 IDS Brief 10, EAT, the EAT held that discussions with two employees about settlement of their discrimination claims took place in circumstances where the without prejudice privilege was waived and that the importance of establishing the truth in discrimination cases may tip the scales of justice against maintaining the privilege where the claimants' case would be severely prejudiced by not being able to refer to the discussions. The Court of Appeal affirmed the EAT's judgment holding that in the particular and unusual circumstances of the case where the grievance procedure had in effect been a trial of the victimisation issue before an independent panel at which both parties gave evidence of the previous negotiations there was a waiver (*Brunel University v Vaseghi* [2007] EWCA Civ 482, [2007] IRLR 592). The Court of Appeal also held that by pleading its response in the way it did and attaching a copy of the grievance report the university had confirmed its intention to waive privilege and it was too late to amend the response to withdraw that waiver.

In disability discrimination cases there will often be a need for the claimant to be examined by a single jointly instructed medical expert to assist the employment tribunal to determine the question of whether the claimant is disabled. Persistent failure by a claimant to cooperate with a joint medical expert may justify the striking out of the claim (see *Chambers-Mills v Allied Bakers* [2011] EWCA Civ 277, [2011] All ER (D) 214 (Feb)).

See also HARVEYS – Divisions **L.5.C, PI.1.N**.

14.10 Conciliation

For tribunal claims lodged on or after 6 May 2014, it is compulsory, unless an exemption applies (eg for certain group or multiple claims), for a claimant to have made an Early Conciliation notification to ACAS.

Previously, when a complaint was presented to an employment tribunal, the conciliation officer was required to endeavour to promote a settlement of the complaint if:

(a)   he was requested to do so both by the complainant and the respondent; or

(b)   in the absence of requests by the complainant and the respondent, he considered that he could act with a reasonable prospect of success.

(*Employment Tribunals Act 1996* ('*ETA 1996*'), *s 18(1), (2)*). His services could also be sought by a prospective party before the presentation of a complaint (*ETA 1996, s 18(3)*).

From 6 April 2014, all such conciliation requests are treated as requests for Early Conciliation. From 6 May 2014, tribunal claims will not be accepted unless the complaint has been referred to ACAS and a conciliation certificate issued. This certificate confirms that the Early Conciliation requirements have been met (*Employment Tribunals Act 1996* ('*ETA 1996*'), *s 18A*).

Conciliation can also be requested by a person who anticipates having proceedings issued against them (ibid *s 18B*) or after the issue of proceedings (*s 18C*).

Information given to the conciliation officer in the performance of his duties is not admissible in evidence before the tribunal except with the consent of the giver of the information (*ETA 1996, s 18(7)*). Thus, frequently a conciliation officer will contact the employer to investigate the possibility of the removal of the cause of complaint. An employer is not obliged to give the conciliation officer information.

An ACAS conciliation officer has no responsibility to see that the terms of a settlement are fair to the employee and, indeed, a conciliation officer should not advise the parties on the merits of the case (see *Clarke v Redcar & Cleveland Borough Council* [2006] ICR 897, [2006] IRLR 324, EAT, for guidance on the role of a conciliation officer). The ACAS conciliation officer does not have to broker a settlement or record it in order for an agreement reached effectively to oust the employment tribunal's jurisdiction pursuant to the *ETA 1996, s 18(2)*, he merely needs to endeavour to promote settlement (*Allma Construction Ltd v Bonner* [2011] IRLR 204, EAT). Where one party makes an offer to another that is sufficiently definite to indicate an intention to be bound, covering the essentials of the contract in question, and it is accepted, then a contract is concluded which, if an ACAS conciliation officer has been involved, will be sufficient to oust the employment tribunal's jurisdiction. It does not matter if there are additional matters that could have been included in the agreement and what are the 'essentials' of the agreement will vary from case to case (see *Bonner* above).

See also **2.4** Advisory, Conciliation and Arbitration Service (ACAS). For the validity of settlements, see **14.33** below. For the effect of Early Conciliation on time limits, see **14.4** above.

See also Harveys – Divisions **PI.3**, **PI.1.T**.

14.11 Restriction of publicity

The *ETA 1996, s 11* empowered the Secretary of State to make regulations allowing for the restriction of publicity in cases where the commission of a sexual offence, or sexual misconduct, is alleged. In respect of cases involving an allegation of the commission of sexual offences, regulations may provide for "securing that the registration or other making available of documents or decisions shall be so effected as to prevent the identification of any person affected by or making the allegation". In addition, *section 1* of the *Sexual Offences (Amendment) Act 1992* provides for a lifetime prohibition on the publication of any matter that is likely to lead to members of the public identifying the alleged victims of sexual offences.

In respect of cases involving allegations of sexual misconduct, regulations may make provision for "enabling an employment tribunal, on the application of any party to proceedings before it or of its own motion, to make a restricted reporting order having effect (if not revoked earlier) until the promulgation of the decision of the tribunal."

Section 12 of the *ET 1996* allowed for the making of regulations enabling an Employment Tribunal to make restricted reporting orders in disability discrimination proceedings in which evidence of a "personal nature" was to be heard. Evidence of a personal nature would be evidence of a medical, or other intimate nature, which might reasonably be assumed to be likely to cause significant embarrassment to the complainant if reported (*ETA 1996, s 12(7)*).

The Employment Tribunal's powers are set out at *rule 50* of the *Employment Tribunal Rules* which are at *Sch 1* to the *Employment Tribunals (Constitution and Rules of Procedure) Regulations 2003 (SI 2013/1237)*. The scope and appropriate use of the powers are considered in detail at EMPLOYMENT TRIBUNALS – **II (20) 20.89** to **20.91** (see also HARVEYS – Divisions **PI.1.W(5)**, **(6)**, **PI.2.H(1)**, **(2)**).

The Employment Appeal Tribunal's powers are set out at *rule 23* of the *Employment Appeal Tribunal Rules SI 1993/2854*. The Appeal Tribunal's powers are discussed at EMPLOYMENT TRIBUNALS – **III (21)**: Appeals **21.26**.

14.12   Remedies

Where an employment tribunal finds that a complaint presented to it is well-founded, it must make such of the following orders as it considers just and equitable:

(a)   An order declaring the rights of the complainant and the respondent in relation to the act to which the complaint relates (*EqA 2010, s 124(1)(a)*; and previously *SDA 1975, s 65(1)(a); RRA 1976, s 56(1)(a); SOR 2003, reg 30(1)(a); RBR 2003, reg 30(1)(a); DDA 1995, 17A(2)(a)*; and *AR 2006, reg 38(1)(a)*). Such a declaration may state, for example, that the complainant is entitled to certain training facilities or should be considered for a certain position.

(b)   An order requiring the respondent to pay to the complainant compensation of an amount corresponding to any damages he could have been ordered by a county court to pay to the complainant if the complaint had fallen to be dealt with under the jurisdiction of the county court (*EqA 2010, s 124(1)(b)*; and previously *SDA 1975, s 65(1)(b); RRA 1976, s 56(1)(b); SOR 2003, reg 30(1)(b); RBR 2003, reg 30(1)(b); DDA 1995, s 17A(2)(b)*; and *AR 2006, reg 38(1)(b)*. Once a tribunal has decided to award compensation the amount must be computed on the basis of what damages would be recoverable in a county court, and not on the basis of what the tribunal thinks is just and equitable (the *EqA 2010, s 124(6); Hurley v Mustoe (No 2)* [1983] ICR 422).

(c)   An 'appropriate recommendation' pursuant to *EqA 2010, s 124(1)(c)*, namely a recommendation that within a specified period the respondent takes specified steps for the purpose of obviating or reducing the adverse effect of any matter to which the proceedings relate (a) on the claimant or (b) on any other person (*EqA 2010, s 124(3)*). Previously a tribunal could make a recommendation that the respondent take, within a specified period, action appearing to the tribunal to be practicable for the purpose of obviating or reducing the adverse effect on the complainant only of any act of discrimination to which the complaint relates (*SDA 1975, s 65(1)(c); RRA 1976, s 56(1)(c); SOR 2003, reg 30(1)(c); RBR 2003, reg 30(1)(c); DDA 1995, s 17A(2)(c)*; and *AR 2006, reg 38(1)(c)*).

The Tribunal's power under *s 207A* of the *Trade Union and Labour Relations (Consolidation) Act 1992* to uplift an award by up to 25% where the employer has failed to comply with a relevant ACAS Code of Practice, or decrease it by up to 25% where the employee has failed to comply, applies to discrimination claims as to other tribunal proceedings. The law on this is dealt with in EMPLOYMENT TRIBUNALS – **II, 20.119**A. Note that the power to make such an uplift raises different issues and needs to be considered separately to questions of injury to feelings and aggravated damages: see *Mr Q QU v Landis & GYR Limited* UKEAT/0016/19/RN.

See also HARVEYS – Divisions **L.6, L.7**.

14.13 Compensation: general principles

Until the mid-1990s, awards of compensation in cases of sex or race discrimination were subject to a statutory maximum like compensatory awards for unfair dismissals. However, following the decision of the ECJ in *Marshall v Southampton and South West Hampshire Regional Health Authority (No 2)* [1993] IRLR 445, that capping compensation meant victims of discrimination did not have an 'effective remedy', the upper ceiling on the size of awards was removed by the *Sex Discrimination and Equal Pay (Remedies) Regulations 1993 (SI 1993/2798)* (subsequently the *Employment Tribunals (Interest on Awards in Discrimination Cases) Regulations 1996 (SI 1996/2803)* – see below). Prior to 3 July 1994, compensation for employment-related acts of race discrimination was also subject to the same statutory maximum (by the former *RRA 1976, s 56(2)*). The *Race Relations (Remedies) Act 1994*, removed the limit.

It is important to remember that compensation is to be assessed on the same principles as apply to tort claims in the County Court: see *De Souza v Vinci Construction UK Ltd* [2017] EWCA Civ 879, [2018] ICR 433. The tortfeasor must 'take the victim as they find them': *BAE Systems (Operations) Ltd v Konczak* [2017] EWCA Civ 1188, [2018] ICR 1.

Where an employer is found to be vicariously liable for its employees' discriminatory acts, it will normally be required to make a payment in compensation. However, it does not follow that the individual discriminators should escape the consequences of liability. Where they have been named as individual respondents, it is open to the tribunal to make an order that they, too, should make a payment in compensation (see *Gbaja-Biamila v DHL International (UK) Ltd* [2000] ICR 730, [2000] All ER (D) 27, EAT). Tribunals are entitled to order that liability be on a joint and several basis or to make separate awards, but only if the respondents are responsible for separate unlawful acts or separate losses. It used to be the case that tribunals would apportion responsibility between co-respondents (see *Way v Crouch* [2005] IRLR 603), but in *London Borough of Hackney v Sivanandan* [2013] IRLR 408, [2013] ICR 672 the Court of Appeal held that where the same, 'indivisible', damage is done to a claimant by concurrent tortfeasors – ie either tortfeasors who are liable for the same act (joint tortfeasors) or tortfeasors who separately contribute to the same damage – each is liable for the whole of that damage. As between any particular tortfeasor and the claimant no question of apportionment arises. As between joint tortfeasors the position is determined under the *Civil Liability (Contribution) Act 1978* but this has no impact on the liability of any of them to the claimant. Following *Sivanandan* it was not clear whether the ET had jurisdiction to decide the position as between joint tortfeasors or whether this requires separate proceedings in the County Court, but in *Brennan v Sunderland City Council* [2012] ICR 1183, [2012] All ER (D) 275 (May) the EAT held emphatically that the tribunal had no jurisdiction to entertain a claim under the *1978 Act*; such a claim should be made in the civil courts. However, it remains the case that if the damage for which the claimant is to be compensated is the product of more than one unlawful act or other cause, then the Tribunal should make a sensible attempt to apportion responsibility: *BAE Systems (Operations) Ltd v Konczak* [2017] EWCA Civ 1188, [2018] ICR 1.

Exemplary damages became available in discrimination cases as a result of the decision of the House of Lords in *Kuddus v Chief Constable of Leicestershire Constabulary* [2001] UKHL 29, [2001] 3 All ER 193. See further below **14.18**.

The Court of Appeal overturned an employment tribunal's decision to strike out a successful claimant's claim as to remedy on the grounds that there had been a failure actively to pursue the claim and a fair hearing was no longer possible after a number of years had passed following the liability decision (see *Abegaze*, CA above).

For decisions relating to the assessment of compensation see *Alexander v Home Office* [1988] IRLR 190, [1988] ICR 685, *North West Thames Regional Health Authority v Noone* [1988] IRLR 195, [1988] ICR 813, *Sharifi v Strathclyde Regional Council* [1992] IRLR 259, and the cases summarised below. See also HARVEYS – Divisions **L.6.C, L.7**.

Care should be taken to ensure that the effect of tax on the award is taken into account. Compensation for pecuniary loss should be calculated in the first instance on the basis of net rather than gross loss of earnings (*Visa International Service Association v Paul* [2004] IRLR 42, EAT). However, compensation for loss consequent on the termination of employment will then be taxable above £30,000 since by virtue of *sections 401* and *403* of the *Income Tax (Earnings and Pensions) Act 2003*, a sum received in connection with the termination of a person's employment is tax-free up to £30,000 but is subject to income tax to the extent that it exceeds that sum. Contrary to the previous view of tribunals, this is not limited to compensation for financial loss, and compensation is taxable even where it is compensation for infringement of the right not to suffer discrimination where the discrimination relates to the dismissal: see *Moorthy v Revenue and Customs Commissioners* [2018] EWCA Civ 847, [2018] 3 All ER 1062, [2018] ICR 1326, overruling *Oti-Obihara v Revenue and Customs Comrs* [2010] UKFTT 568 (TC), [2011] IRLR 386. However, the Court of Appeal in *Moorthy* held that awards for injury to feelings were not taxable as they fell within the scope of the exemption for personal injury in *IT(EP)A 2003, s 406*. The practical effect of this ruling will, though, be short-lived as *s 406* was amended with effect from the 2018/19 tax year to exclude payments on account of injured feelings from its scope, so that they will fall to be taxed where they form part of compensation for loss of office within *ss 401* and *403*, subject to the £30,000 limit. Pension loss is also taxable on the same basis: *Chief Constable of Northumbria v Erichsen* (UKEAT/0027/15/BA). The same tax rules apply to compensation, or sums paid under a compromise agreement, for a discriminatory dismissal. In accordance with the principles in *British Transport Commission v Gourley* [1955] 3 All ER 796, it is therefore necessary, once the amount of the award has been calculated (using net figures for earnings and pension loss) to 'gross up' the award so as to ensure that the claimant is not left out of pocket once the tax on the award has been paid.

Compensation for discrimination during employment is however not taxable save to the extent that it is connected with remuneration so as to make it an 'emolument of the employment' (*Income Tax (Earnings and Pensions) Act 2003, s 62*). For a case where on the facts the First-tier Tribunal found a settlement payment to be referable to the discrimination claim and not to the employment, see *A v HM Revenue & Customs* [2015] UKFTT 189 (TC), [2015] IRLR 962. For a case where it was not, see *Moorthy* ibid.

There is no provision in the *EqA 2010* for the Tribunal to reduce any award of damages because of the 'contributory fault' of the claimant. However, in *Way v Crouch* [2005] ICR 1362 and *First Greater Western Limited v Waiyego* UKEAT/0056/18/RN, the EAT accepted that in principle *s 1(1)* of *The Law Reform (Contributory Negligence) Act 1945* could apply to discrimination cases. The EAT in *Waiyego* was, though, at pains to emphasise that this would rarely be an appropriate element to include in a discrimination award, in part because the concept of 'fault' on which *s 1(1)* of the *1945 Act* depends does not correlate with any particular concept under the *EqA 2010* and in part because there would be other ways in which a claimant's contribution could be reflected, such as at the causation stage or when assessing injury to feelings.

14.14 Compensation: indirect discrimination

In cases of intentional indirect discrimination a tribunal's power to award compensation is the same as for direct discrimination: *EqA 2010, s 124(2)(b)*. However, where the indirect discrimination is unintentional, the tribunal is required, before awarding compensation, first to consider whether to make a declaration and/or recommendation (*EqA 2010, s 124(4), (5)*). Provided it considers those remedies first, the tribunal has complete discretion as to whether it orders compensation in cases of unintentional indirect discrimination and may award compensation whether or not it also makes a declaration or recommendation. Previously there was no power to award compensation for unintentional indirect discrimination until the *Sex Discrimination and Equal Pay (Miscellaneous Amendments) Regulations*

1996 (SI 1996/438), which inserted a new *s 65(1B)* into the *SDA 1975*, gave tribunals, for the first time, a power to make awards of compensation in cases of unintentional indirect sex discrimination on a similar basis to that which now exists under the *EqA 2010*. The *SOR 2003, reg 30, RBR 2003, reg 30, DDA 1995, s 17A* and *AR 2006, reg 38* contained similar provisions. In the case of race discrimination there was no such mechanism for awarding compensation for unintentional indirect discrimination (*RRA 1976, s 57(3)*). In a case decided under the old rules, *JH Walker Ltd v Hussain* [1996] IRLR 11, [1996] ICR 291, it was held that intention may be inferred where it is established that the employer was aware that discriminatory consequences would flow from its actions. See also *London Underground Ltd v Edwards* [1995] IRLR 355, [1995] ICR 574 for the circumstances in which indirect discrimination may be said to have been intentional

14.15   Compensation: pecuniary loss

The measure of loss is tortious. In other words, a complainant must be put, so far as possible, into the position that he would have been in had the act of discrimination not occurred (*Ministry of Defence v Cannock* [1994] IRLR 509, [1994] ICR 918, EAT). Thus, the tribunal must ask itself, 'If there had been no unlawful discrimination, what would have happened?'

Where the act complained of is a discriminatory dismissal, the tribunal will have to decide whether the complainant would have been dismissed in any event if there had been no discrimination (see *O'Donoghue v Redcar and Cleveland Borough Council* [2001] EWCA Civ 701, [2001] IRLR 615, CA; *Abbey National plc v Chagger* [2009] ICR 624, [2009] IRLR 86, EAT; affd *sub nom Chagger v Abbey National plc* [2009] EWCA Civ 1202, [2010] ICR 397, [2010] IRLR 47). The tribunal often carries out a similar exercise when calculating compensation for unfair dismissal. However, in the context of discrimination proceedings, there is a significant difference of approach. In unfair dismissal cases, one asks whether a reasonable employer would have dismissed in any event. In discrimination cases, however, one asks whether the actual respondent would have dismissed (*Abbey National plc v Formoso* [1999] IRLR 222). As the unlawful act is the discrimination, not the dismissal itself, the question is whether (and when) the dismissal would have occurred on non-discriminatory grounds (or whether and when the employee would have left the respondent's employment of his own choice) (*Chagger*, above, and *Wardle*, below). In cases where the complainant alleges that her dismissal was both unfair and discriminatory, this difference may significantly complicate the process of calculation. However, a reduction of compensation to reflect the chance that the employee might have left under a compromise agreement, based on evidence of pre-hearing negotiations but without any evidence of waiver of privilege, is unfair (see *Gallop v Newport City Council* [2013] IRLR 23, a case in which an appeal was subsequently allowed on a different issue: [2014] Eq LR 141). In *Chagger*, above, the EAT stated that although there were conceptual differences between discriminatory and unfair dismissals it would be unsatisfactory if a radically different approach from the approach in *Polkey v A E Dayton Services Ltd* [1988] AC 344, [1988] ICR 142, [1987] IRLR 503, HL, were to be adopted in discrimination cases. While the starting point in analysing future loss may be the period during which the claimant would have remained employed with the respondent had there been no dismissal, a tribunal has to recognise that a discriminatory dismissal means that the dismissed employee enters the labour market not at a time or in circumstances of his or her choosing, thereby potentially altering the claimant's career path. The proper assessment of loss is determined by asking when the claimant might be expected to obtain another job with equivalent salary (*Chagger v Abbey National plc* [2009] EWCA Civ 1202, [2010] ICR 397, [2010] IRLR 47, reversing the EAT on this point).

The mere fact that there is an element of speculation involved in assessing whether a claimant would have been dismissed anyway is not a reason for an employment tribunal to refuse to engage with the assessment exercise if evidence is advanced by the employer that he might have been dismissed (see *Eversheds Legal Services Ltd v De Belin* [2011] ICR 1137,

[2011] IRLR 448, EAT). Determining what would have happened in the absence of discrimination may involve the tribunal in assessing percentage chances. For instance, in cases of pregnancy dismissal, the tribunal will usually have to assess the chance that the complainant would, but for the dismissal, have returned to work. It is not necessarily perverse for the tribunal to conclude that there is a 100% chance that the relevant event would have occurred (*Ministry of Defence v Hunt* [1996] ICR 544, EAT). A tribunal is not required to take account of contingencies that it regards as too remote or which are unlikely to arise during the period for which it considers that the claimant should be compensated (see *Wooster v Mayor and Burgesses of the London Borough of Tower Hamlets* [2009] IRLR 980, EAT and *Chief Constable of Northumbria v Erichsen* [2015] All ER (D) 204 (Dec) (UKEAT/0027/15/BA). Where there are a number of contingent possibilities, the proper approach is to cumulate the percentages (eg where there is a 75% chance that a woman would have returned to work following the birth of her child had she not been dismissed and a 50% chance of her having received a pay rise thereafter, her loss should be assessed on the basis of the chance of her having earned at the higher rate, that is 50% × 75% – see *Hunt* above). In *Wardle v Credit Agricole Corporate and Investment Bank* [2011] EWCA Civ 545, [2011] ICR 1290, [2011] IRLR 604 the Court of Appeal held that it is wrong for a tribunal to approach compensation for career loss by awarding damages until the point where it can be sure that the claimant will find an equivalent job, rather, in the normal case, if a tribunal assesses that a claimant is likely (ie it is more probable than not) to get an equivalent job by a specific date that is the date up to which loss is fairly to be assessed. See also *Colt Technology Services v Brown* UKEAT/00233-4/17/BA. Exceptionally a tribunal may be entitled to conclude on the evidence before it that there is no real prospect of the claimant ever securing an equivalent job, in which case the tribunal has to assess loss as continuing for the rest of the claimant's working life. (The Court of Appeal also delivered a supplemental decision in Wardle on the effect of an adjustment in the overall level of compensation awarded consequent upon an appeal on the level of statutory uplift under the *EmA 2002, s 31(3)* – [2011] EWCA Civ 770, [2011] IRLR 819.)

In *GM Packaging (UK) Ltd v Ottey* [2014] All ER (D) 69 (Sep) (UKEAT/0045/14/LA) it was held that a tribunal should have reviewed its remedy decision where an EAT ruling that another employee had been fairly dismissed in respect of the same incident could have supported a *Polkey* argument.

Where an employer has made an *ex gratia* payment on dismissal or any other payment which falls to be deducted from the award, the proper approach is to make the deduction before applying the percentage chance (*Hunt* above; *Ministry of Defence v Wheeler* [1998] IRLR 23, [1998] ICR 242; cf *Digital Equipment Co Ltd v Clements (No 2)* [1998] IRLR 134, CA).

In assessing percentage prospects of particular events occurring, the tribunal is encouraged to rely upon statistical evidence. However, such evidence is simply one factor to take into account. Thus in *Vento v Chief Constable of West Yorkshire Police (No 2)* [2002] EWCA Civ 1871, [2003] IRLR 102, [2003] ICR 318, the tribunal had been entitled to conclude that there was a 75% chance that the complainant would have remained in the police force until retirement (a period of 21 years of service) despite statistics suggesting that only 9% of female officers leaving the respondent's service had served for longer than 18 years. The fact that a claimant is in receipt of incapacity benefit does not, in itself, mean that he or she is incapable of working during the same period and therefore not eligible for compensation for loss of earnings during that period, rather an employment tribunal needs to consider all the evidence as to whether the claimant can work (*Sheffield Forgemasters International Ltd v Fox* [2009] ICR 333, [2009] IRLR 192, EAT). In *Brash-Hall v Getty Images Ltd* [2006] EWCA Civ 531, [2006] All ER (D) 111 (May), the Court of Appeal held that, where an employee had been dismissed constructively and in a discriminatory manner and the tribunal had decided that she would have been made redundant anyway, her compensation could only include the amount she would have received in contractual severance payment if she proved that she would have signed a severance agreement.

Percentage chances may also affect awards for injury to feelings: see *Das v Ayrshire and Arran Health Board* (below).

There will be cases where the evidence does not enable the calculation of loss to descend to the precise addition or subtraction of numerical values and a broad-brush assessment is necessary. The EAT will not interfere unless the resulting figure is manifestly excessive or manifestly too low on the evidence (*MoJ v Burton and Engel* [2016] IRLR 100, EAT).

In *Bullimore v Pothecary Witham Weld (No 2)* [2011] IRLR 18, EAT, Underhill P emphasised that questions of causation and remoteness are addressed according to different principles. Causation is a factual issue of whether the damage would have occurred 'but for' the wrongful act, whereas questions of remoteness involve a value judgment as to what was 'direct' or 'natural' or 'foreseeable' as a consequence. Where an employer for an illegitimate reason (in that case to victimise the claimant) gave an adverse reference leading to a prospective employer not offering a job or withdrawing an offer it was hard to see why that was too remote to attract compensation. The EAT held that there was no rule that a subsequent tortious act (eg the prospective employer itself unlawfully victimising the claimant) breaks the 'chain of causation'. In that case the employment tribunal had erred in not awarding compensation for loss of earnings stemming from victimisation by way of a damaging reference.

It is well established that a discriminator's motives are not relevant when it comes to deciding whether or not an act is discriminatory. However, a majority of the EAT (consisting of the two lay members) has decided that motives may be relevant when it comes to assessing compensation (*Chief Constable of Greater Manchester Police v Hope* [1999] ICR 338). Upholding the tribunal's decision that the complainant had been the victim of an act of direct race and sex discrimination, it nevertheless went on to decide that, in the absence of discriminatory intent, the tribunal should have made a nil award of compensation.

In *GM Packaging (UK) Ltd v Ottey* [2014] All ER (D) 69 (Sep) (UKEAT/0045/14/LA) it was held that a tribunal should have reviewed its remedy decision where an EAT ruling that another employee had been fairly dismissed in respect of the same incident could have supported a *Polkey* argument.

In *Chagger*, above, the EAT held that the risk that future potential employers might decline to employ the claimant because of his discrimination claim (so-called 'stigma loss') was too remote to be reflected in compensation payable by the respondent former employer. However, the Court of Appeal reversed the EAT on this point holding that there was no reason why a respondent should not be liable for so-called stigma losses resulting from the refusal of third party potential employers to employ the claimant, even if those refusals are unlawful. The Court held that a tribunal should take a sensible and robust approach and not simply rely on the assertion of stigma or speculation, but where there was very extensive evidence of attempted mitigation failing to result in a job the tribunal would be entitled to conclude that the claimant was unlikely to obtain future employment in the industry. The Court also considered that there could be exceptional cases where stigma loss was the only head of damage, for example where the respondent would have dismissed even had there been no discrimination, however the onus would be on the claimant to prove such loss.

Where a complainant receives a sum in respect of future loss, a discount should be made for accelerated receipt unless the sums concerned are so small as to make it an unnecessary complication (*Bentwood Bros (Manchester) Ltd v Shepherd* [2003] EWCA Civ 380, [2003] IRLR 364, [2003] ICR 1000). In *Chagger*, above, the EAT has suggested that if the Ogden Tables are used in complex calculations of future loss, tribunals should do so only with a proper understanding of their limitations and give proper consideration to the contingencies not reflected in the tables.

Any sums that have been received that would not have been received should be deducted, such as social security benefits received. See, for example, *Chan v Hackney London Borough Council* [1997] ICR 1014, the EAT decided that an employment tribunal had been right to deduct sums received by way of invalidity benefit from the compensatory award. However, there should be no such deduction when in fact the sums paid will be reclaimed by the state from the award in any event: *Olayemi v Athena Medical Centre and anor* [2016] ICR 1074, [2016] All ER (D) 175 (Jul). Loss that a claimant has managed to avoid (eg by obtaining alternative employment or securing an alternative pension) cannot be claimed on ordinary principles. However, the exception is where the loss is only avoided by dint of an insurance scheme for which the claimant has paid the premiums: see *Gaca v Pirelli General Plc* [2004] EWCA Civ 373, [2004] 1 WLR 2683 and *Colt Technology Services v Brown* UKEAT/00233-4/17/BA.

Pecuniary loss will often also include pension loss. In *Lambeth London Borough Council v D'Souza* [1999] IRLR 240, the Court of Appeal provided guidance in relation to the calculation of pension loss. Understandably reluctant to have to hear detailed and contested evidence from actuaries, tribunals sometimes adopt the less precise but less complicated approach of awarding the complainant a sum equivalent to the contributions that the respondent would have made into the pension scheme had the employee not been dismissed. In *D'Souza* a complication arose from the fact that the respondent was at that time enjoying a contributions holiday. The EAT makes it clear that the contributions holiday should not result in the complainant's compensation being reduced. Compensation should be calculated on the basis of contributions at what would have been the ordinary rate. The complainant is not being compensated for the loss of contributions but for the loss of a pension. The contributions method is a way of approximating the loss and should not be followed slavishly if it is plainly not going to compensate the complainant for the loss of his pension. The EAT in *Clancy v Cannock Chase Technical College* [2001] IRLR 331 again stressed the need for accurate assessment of pension loss to ensure that complainants are fully compensated. The Employment Tribunals Presidents publish detailed guidance on the calculation of pension loss, the most recent version of which (published in August 2017) is *Employment Tribunals: Principles for Compensating Pension Loss* (4th Edn). This wholly replaces the 3rd Edition, which was withdrawn in 2015 following the Court of Appeal decision in *Griffin v Plymouth Hospital NHS Trust* [2014] EWCA Civ 1240, [2014] IRLR 962. Tribunals should now refer to this guidance. Certain principles from previous cases will remain relevant, however. In *Greenhoff v Barnsley Metropolitan Borough Council* [2006] ICR 1514, [2006] All ER (D) 300 (Jun) the EAT held that a tribunal should set out why it adopted a particular approach to pension loss and why other approaches were rejected. The EAT also gave guidance about the steps that tribunals should go through in considering pension loss. See also *Chief Constable of West Midlands Police v Gardner* [2012] All ER (D) 39 (Mar), EAT, and *Chief Constable of Northumbria v Erichsen* [2015] All ER (D) 204 (Dec) (UKEAT/0027/15/BA) in which the need for a tribunal to give 'cogent, intelligible and appropriate' reasons as to why it was departing from the approach in the Booklet or the Ogden Tables was emphasised. The EAT in *Gardner* also noted that Ogden multipliers may be better suited to current economic conditions than those specified for the 'substantial approach' in the Booklet. The *Erichsen* case further serves as a salutary reminder that the *Gourley* principles apply to pension loss as well: loss should be calculated based on net figures and then grossed up to account for the incidence of taxation (see above *General principles*). In *Erichsen* the EAT also rejected the employer's argument that, as part of the employee's duty to mitigate his loss, he should have reinvested the compensatory award in a (tax-free) pension scheme.

Normal principles of mitigation apply in relation to compensation for pecuniary loss: the employee is under a duty to take reasonable steps to mitigate loss, but the burden of proving the employee has failed in that duty is on the employer: *Wilding v British Telecommunications plc* [2002] IRLR 524, [2002] ICR 1079; *Donald v AVC Media Enterprises Ltd* (UKEATS/0016/14/JW, 9 November 2016). The test of reasonableness is an objective and not too stringent one. In *Cannock* (above), the EAT gave a strong indication that a woman dismissed by reason of pregnancy ought not to recover compensation relating to a period more than six months after the date of the birth of her child unless she is actively engaged in looking for work at that date. However, tribunals must take care when assessing the evidence not to make assumptions (stereotypical or otherwise) about a woman's likely desire to return to work after maternity leave and must consider the facts presented: *Donald v AVC Media Enterprises Ltd* (UKEATS/0016/14/JW, 9 November 2016). The tribunal is entitled to bear in mind the difficulties which a woman with a small child may face in obtaining work (*Hunt* above). Her personal characteristics and the state of the labour market at the relevant time would also be relevant considerations. In *DeBique v Ministry of Defence (No 2)* (2012) 941 IDS Brief 7, EAT, an employment tribunal had been entitled to award no compensation for loss of earnings where the claimant was found to have unreasonably refused an offer of redeployment to a post where her child care obligations could be reconciled with her duties. In that case the EAT emphasised that the assessment of the reasonableness of a claimant's efforts to mitigate her loss were very much a matter of fact for the tribunal.

As with unfair dismissal an employee can mitigate their loss by setting up in business, in which case the tribunal should consider when calculating compensation both lost remuneration and the costs incurred in setting up the business (if reasonably incurred) (*Dove v Aon Training Ltd* [2005] EWCA Civ 411, [2005] IRLR 891).

See also Harveys – Division **L.6.C.**

14.16 Compensation: injury to feelings

The amount of compensation awarded may include a sum for injury to feelings resulting from an act of discrimination (*EqA 2010, ss 124(5) read with 119(4)*; and previously *SDA 1975, s 66(4); RRA 1976, s 57(4); DDA 1995, s 17A(4)*; and *AR 2006, reg 38(1)(b) read with reg 39(3)*).

For a sum to be awarded for injury to feelings it is not necessary for the claimant to be aware that the employer's reason for the treatment was discriminatory, although such knowledge might well serve to increase the hurt and therefore the award (see *Taylor v XLN Telecom Ltd* [2010] ICR 656, [2010] IRLR 499, EAT, explaining that this was not contrary to the Court of Appeal's judgment in *Skyrail Oceanic Ltd v Coleman* [1981] IRLR 398, [1981] ICR 864). See also *Wileman v Minilec Engineering Ltd* [1988] IRLR 144, [1988] ICR 318; *Murray v Powertech (Scotland) Ltd* [1992] IRLR 257. It follows that in a case concerned with a discriminatory dismissal, the fact that the complainant would have been dismissed at a later date in any event is not necessarily a ground for reducing the award for injury to feelings. The purpose of the award is to compensate the complainant for the 'anger, upset and humiliation' caused by the fact that he knows that he has been discriminated against. That upset is not displaced by the prospect that he might have been dismissed lawfully at a later date (*O'Donoghue v Redcar and Cleveland Borough Council* [2001] IRLR 615, EAT). However, in *Das v Ayrshire and Arran Health Board* (EAT 28/11/14) where the claimant had been denied only a 10% chance of being appointed to a post but was awarded £5,000 for injury to feelings, the EAT (though it did not overturn the award) considered it to be on the high side because injury to feelings from the loss of a limited chance of appointment would logically be less than injury to feelings from the loss of a post actually held.

Although evidence will be required of injury to feelings, a tribunal will readily conclude that some injury to feelings has arisen from a discriminatory act (see *Abegaze v Shrewsbury College of Arts & Technology* [2009] EWCA Civ 96, [2010] IRLR 238, CA). A tribunal erred in law in making no award at all for injury to feelings where it found that the claimant was merely angry and frustrated as a result of discrimination (*Assoukou v Select Services Partners Ltd* [2006] EWCA Civ 1442, [2006] All ER (D) 122 (Oct).

In *Munchkins Restaurant Ltd v Karmazyn* [2010] All ER (D) 76 (Jun), EAT, the EAT slightly uneasily accepted that an employment tribunal had not erred in awarding the same amount of compensation for injury to feelings to four claimants for sex discrimination despite their differing lengths of service. An increasing 'tariff' of compensation for injury to feelings for subsequent, repeat acts of discrimination is not automatically appropriate (*London Borough of Hackney v Sivanandan* [2011] ICR 1374, [2011] IRLR 740, EAT).

The assessment of the appropriate sum to award in any case is a difficult one. General guidance on assessing compensation for injury to feelings where an act of harassment results in psychiatric or physical injury was given in *HM Prison Service v Johnson* [1997] IRLR 162, [1997] ICR 275. Compensation for injury to feelings should be compensatory and not punitive, although it should not be set at so low a level as to 'diminish respect for the policy of the anti-discriminatory legislation'. It should also 'bear some similarity to the range of awards in personal injury cases and in exercising their discretion tribunals should remind themselves of the value in everyday life of the sum they had in mind' (*Johnson*, above). Subjecting the complainant to a disciplinary investigation, moving him to a different location and allowing a grievance procedure to drag on for 14 months were all factors a tribunal could take into account in awarding damages for injury to feelings (*British Telecommunications plc v Reid* [2003] EWCA Civ 1675, [2004] IRLR 327). The test of relevance was whether the matters arose from the act of discrimination and were consequential on it. The award must be based on evidence, so a tribunal's award was overturned where it was based merely on statements made in closing submissions (*Esporta Health Clubs and another v Roget* [2013] EqLR 877).

In the *Johnson* case, the EAT had made reference to the Judicial Studies Board's guidelines on compensation for post-traumatic stress disorder as a useful source of guidance. The guidelines adopt a four-band classification of cases as 'minor', 'moderate', 'moderately severe' and 'severe'. In *Zaiwalla & Co v Walia* [2002] IRLR 697, EAT, the EAT found that the tribunal had erred by treating the injury to feelings suffered by the particular complainant as analogous to a 'moderately severe' stress disorder. The complainant had been belittled, bullied and harassed over a three-month period, and was left feeling despair and suffering from panic attacks and prolonged tearfulness. Nevertheless, a moderately severe disorder is one which promises 'some recovery with professional help' but with a 'significant disability' being experienced for the 'foreseeable future'. The EAT considered the case was more closely analogous to the 'moderate category' (the victim will have 'largely recovered and any continuing effects will not be grossly disabling'). The effect of this analogy being drawn was to decrease the award from £15,000 to £10,000. The Court of Appeal in *Vento v Chief Constable of West Yorkshire Police (No 2)* [2002] EWCA Civ 1871, [2003] IRLR 102 and *De Souza v Vinci Construction UK Ltd* [2017] EWCA Civ 879, [2018] ICR 433 has confirmed the appropriateness of tribunals having regard to the Judicial College Guidelines on psychiatric personal injury when determining the appropriate injury to feelings award. As the JSB's four bands do not map precisely onto the Court of Appeal's three bands, reading them together may allow a more finely-tuned approach. Reference to awards made in defamation proceedings as a guideline for assessing the appropriate award for injury to feelings has, however, been deprecated by the EAT (*Vento v Chief Constable of West Yorkshire Police (No 2)* [2002] IRLR 177, [2003] ICR 318, EAT).

The Court of Appeal in *Vento (No 2)* identified three broad bands of compensation to assist the tribunals. The lower band is appropriate for 'less serious' cases where the act of discrimination is an 'isolated' or 'one-off' incident. The middle band should be used for 'serious cases which do not merit an award in the highest band'. The highest band is designed for use in the 'most serious' cases, eg where there has been a 'lengthy campaign of discriminatory harassment on the ground of sex or race'. In *Vento (No. 2)* the Court of Appeal indicated that awards of less than £500 should be 'avoided altogether' and that awards beyond the higher band range (at that point the range was £5,000 to £25,000) should be made in only the 'most exceptional' cases.

The upper limits of the bands were revised by the EAT in *Da'Bell v NSPCC* [2010] IRLR 19 to take account of inflation. In *De Souza v Vinci Construction UK Ltd* [2017] EWCA Civ 879, [2018] ICR 433 the Court of Appeal held that the general uplift of 10% on general damages in civil proceedings declared by the Court of Appeal in *Simmons v Castle* [2013] 1 All ER 334, [2013] 1 WLR 1239 should apply to injury to feelings awards made in accordance with the *Vento* bands. The Court of Appeal also affirmed the view taken by the Court of Appeal in *Vento* that reference could be made by Tribunals to the Judicial College Guidelines on psychiatric injury when considering injury to feelings awards. The noted that the Judicial College Guidelines on personal injury awards already include the 10% uplift so tribunals could rely on those without adjustment. The Court of Appeal recommended that revised guidance be issued by the EAT uplifting the *Vento* bands for inflation. The President of the Employment Tribunals for England and Wales has since issued annual guidance on the revised *Vento* bands. The revisions are set out in the table below. The first issue on 5 September 2017 set new ranges for claims presented on or after 11 September 2017. For claims presented before that date, the guidance indicated that an Employment Tribunal could uprate the bands for inflation by applying the formula x divided by y (178.5) multiplied by z and where x is the relevant boundary of the relevant band in the original *Vento* decision and z is the appropriate value from the RPI All Items Index for the month and year closest to the date of presentation of the claim (and, where the claim falls for consideration after 1 April 2013, then applying the *Simmons v Castle* 10% uplift).

Date claim presented on or after	Lower band	Middle band	Upper band
11 September 2017	800 – 8,400	8,400 – 25,200	25,200 – 42,000
6 April 2018	900 – 8,600	8,600 – 25,700	25,700 – 42,900
6 April 2019	900 – 8,800	8,800 – 26,300	26,300 – 44,000
6 April 2020	900 – 9,000	9,000 – 27,000	27,000 – 45,000

A question arises as to how a tribunal is to assess injury to feeling where there are a number of different discriminatory acts, possibly in relation to different grounds of discrimination. Generally, a broad brush approach should be adopted as an artificial attempt to assess injury to feelings in relation to each act would be a wholly unreal task. However, there may be cases that require a more nuanced approach where the tribunal does need separately to consider the level of injury to feelings caused by different individual acts whilst having overall regard to the magnitude of the global sum to be awarded (*Al Jumard v Clywd Leisure Ltd* [2008] IRLR 345, EAT).

For the purpose of setting the size of the award, the tribunal should ignore the fact that the complainant will receive interest on the sums awarded (*Ministry of Defence v Cannock*, above). In *Orlando v Didcot Power Station Sports and Social Club* [1996] IRLR 262, the EAT considered statistics which indicated that the removal of the statutory cap on compensation had not resulted in a significant increase in the average size of awards made for injury to feelings.

In terms of the range of awards made, the EAT in *Moonsar v Fiveways Express Transport Ltd* [2005] IRLR 9 has found that an award of £1,000 was not too low in a case where the female complainant's colleagues had viewed pornography on the internet in her presence. In another case, where the discrimination was not directed at the complainant personally, there was no slur on his reputation or character and he was only marginally inconvenienced an award of £750 was appropriate (*Moyhing v Barts and London NHS Trust* [2006] IRLR 860, EAT). The EAT in *Glasgow City Council v McNab* [2007] IRLR 476 held that an award of £2,000 for injury to feelings was at the upper end of the appropriate range of awards, but did not fall outside that range, in a case of religious discrimination where a teacher was not appointed to a temporary promotion because he was not a Roman Catholic. In *Ministry of Defence v O'Hare (No 2)* [1997] ICR 306, the EAT considered two pregnancy discrimination cases where employees had been faced with a choice of losing their job or aborting their pregnancies. £2,000 was suggested as a guideline figure for cases where an employee was required to make such a choice. Where the employee actually opted to abort, matters were more difficult, but a bracket of £1,500 to £3,000 was suggested for cases where the injury to feelings was 'relatively transient' with a further bracket of £3,000 to £7,500 where the injury was 'more durable'. This case would appear to be significantly out of line with current thinking. In *Vento (No 2)* above, the EAT overturned an award of £50,000 on the basis that it was 'manifestly excessive', substituting an award of £25,000. The complainant had suffered a 'moderate' psychiatric injury as a result of the discriminatory treatment received. The psychiatric injury had been compensated by an award of £9,000.

For guidance on avoiding double recovery in cases where complainants suffer both injury to feelings and a psychiatric injury, see 'Compensation: personal injury' immediately below. In *Voith Turbo Ltd v Stowe* [2005] IRLR 228, EAT, the EAT observed, *obiter*, that a dismissal on grounds of race discrimination was always very serious and could not be regarded as one-off and suitable for a lower band award. In *Miles v Gilbank* [2006] ICR 12, [2005] All ER (D) 355 (Oct), the EAT upheld an award of £25,000 for injury to feelings resulting from the bullying and harassment of a pregnant employee repeatedly and consciously inflicted with total disregard for the welfare of the employee or her unborn child. This was affirmed by the Court of Appeal ([2006] EWCA Civ 543, [2006] ICR 1297, [2006] IRLR 538), which held that if the discrimination involved the well-being of the claimant's unborn child, this increased the seriousness.

For guidance on the circumstances in which the appeal tribunal will be prepared to interfere with the amount of an award under this heading, see *ICTS (UK) Ltd v Tchoula* [2000] IRLR 643, EAT. An appellate court will only interfere if the award is so much out of line that it amounts to an error of law through a misdirection in principle or is for some other reason, such as an erroneous evaluation of the facts, plainly wrong (*R (Elias) v Secretary of State for Defence* [2006] EWCA Civ 1293, [2006] IRLR 934) or if the tribunal does not give adequate reasons for the size of the award (*NSL Ltd and another v Miller* UKEAT/0012/14/MC). Otherwise the EAT will not interfere, because such awards are 'not susceptible to close calculation' (*HM Land Registry v McGlue* [2013] EqLR 701). The EAT has demonstrated that it will overturn awards even if 'correctly categorised' so that its powers are not limited to correcting mis-categorisations (see *Doshoki v Draeger Ltd* [2002] IRLR 340, EAT). An example of this is *Massey v UNIFI* [2007] EWCA Civ 800, [2008] ICR 62, [2007] IRLR 902, a case of unjustified union discipline where the Court of Appeal raised the award for injury to feelings to £12,500 where it considered that an award of £7,500 was too far down the middle *Vento* category as the injury to feelings was intense and prolonged.

See also HARVEYS – Division L.7.B.

14.17 Compensation: personal injury

Where the injury to feelings is such that it results in the onset of psychiatric illness, the complainant may recover compensation for personal injury in the tribunal (*Sheriff v Klyne Tugs (Lowestoft) Ltd* [1999] IRLR 481, [1999] ICR 1170). It is thought that the same principle would apply where an employee is physically injured in the course of harassment. An award for personal injury may be made in addition to an award for injury to feelings (*Hampshire CC v Wyatt* (UKEAT/0013/16/DA, 13 October 2016)), although it may not always be easy to distinguish where injury to feelings stops and injury to mental health begins and there is consequently a danger of double recovery of which the tribunal must be aware and seek to avoid. In *HM Prison Service v Salmon* [2001] IRLR 425, the EAT suggested that in such cases it was open to a tribunal to make a single award for injury to feelings and to include an element for psychiatric harm. Tribunals may therefore make two awards or a combined award and, in either case, should make it clear what they are doing.

Damages for personal injury are recoverable for any harm caused by the discriminatory act and not simply harm which was reasonably foreseeable (*Essa v Laing Ltd* [2003] IRLR 346, [2003] ICR 1110, EAT). Although this decision was upheld on appeal by a majority of the Court of Appeal, there was some suggestion that the simple causation test may only apply to cases of racial abuse and not discrimination more widely ([2004] EWCA Civ 02, [2004] IRLR 313, [2004] ICR 746), although that suggestion has not gained wider acceptance. The 'eggshell skull' principle applies and the victim is entitled to recover damages notwithstanding that some pre-existing condition has predisposed him or her to that harm: *First Greater Western Limited v Waiyego* UKEAT/0056/18/RN. However, where there is evidence that the harm was likely to have occurred at some point in the future a discount for acceleration or exacerbation will be necessary (see *Massey v UNIFI*, above and *BAE Systems (Operations) Ltd v Konczak* [2017] EWCA Civ 1188, [2018] ICR 1). Further, when more than one event contributes to the harm suffered by a claimant then, save where the harm in question can be said to be 'indivisible' the extent of the respondent's liability is limited to the contribution to the harm made by its discriminatory conduct (see *Thaine v London School of Economics* [2010] ICR 1422, [2010] All ER (D) 105 (Sep), EAT – in that case only 40%; see also *Olayemi v Athena Medical Centre* [2016] ICR 1074, [2016] All ER (D) 175 (Jul) and *Konczak*, ibid). See further above **14.13** for the position of joint tortfeasors. The Court of Appeal remitted a case for rehearing when new evidence was obtained which might have materially affected the employment tribunal's assessment of the extent of the depressive illness that the tribunal had found had been exacerbated by the respondent's discriminatory conduct (see *Blundell v Governing Body of St Andrew's Catholic Primary School* [2011] EWCA Civ 427, [2012] ICR 295, [2011] All ER (D) 132 (Apr)). Although in most cases it will be necessary to have expert medical evidence to prove the nature and extent of a personal injury, its likely cause(s) and prognosis, it is not a prerequisite to making an award and in an appropriate case a tribunal can make an award for personal injury without expert medical evidence directed to the point: *Hampshire CC v Wyatt*, ibid.

In *De Souza v Vinci Construction UK Ltd* [2017] EWCA Civ 879, [2018] ICR 433 the Court of Appeal held that the general uplift of 10% on general damages in civil proceedings declared by the Court of Appeal in *Simmons v Castle* [2013] 1 All ER 334, [2013] 1 WLR 1239 should apply to personal injury awards by Tribunals and confirmed that awards by Tribunals should be made on the same basis as awards in the County Court. The Court of Appeal noted that the Judicial College Guidelines already incorporate the 10% uplift, so a tribunal following those guidelines need not make a further uplift.

See also HARVEYS – Division L.7.C.

14.18   Compensation: aggravated and exemplary damages

Aggravated damages may be awarded in discrimination cases where the complainant is able to establish a causal link between 'exceptional or contumelious conduct or motive' on the employer's part and her injury to feelings. Such damages may be appropriate, for instance, where an employer has failed properly to investigate the applicant's complaint of discrimination (*Johnson* above). The promotion of the alleged discriminator while he was still subject to disciplinary proceedings for his alleged discrimination was a matter a tribunal could take into account in awarding aggravated damages (see *British Telecommunications*, above). There has been some uncertainty over whether any sum awarded under this head should be incorporated into the award for injury to feelings. This approach was approved, *obiter*, by the EAT in *Gbaja-Biamila v DHL International (UK) Ltd* [2000] ICR 730, [2000] All ER (D) 273, EAT (adopting the approach of the Northern Ireland Court of Appeal in *McConnell v Police Authority for Northern Ireland* [1997] IRLR 625, NICA). However, in *ICTS (UK) Ltd v Tchoula* [2000] IRLR 643, EAT, the EAT declined to find that the tribunal had erred by making a separate award of aggravated damages. The Court of Appeal subsequently confirmed the approach in *ICTS* and overruled *McConnell* by holding that aggravated damages should not be aggregated with damages for injury to feelings (*Scott v IRC* [2004] EWCA Civ 400, [2004] IRLR 713). In *Commissioner of Police for the Metropolis v Shaw* [2012] ICR 464, [2012] IRLR 291, EAT, Underhill P stated that aggravated damages are an aspect of injury to feelings reflecting the making more serious of the injury to feelings by some additional element which would fall into one of three categories: (a) the manner in which the wrong was committed, (b) motive (but only if the claimant was aware of the motive), or (c) subsequent conduct (eg by the employer not taking the complaint seriously, failure to apologise or conduct at trial). The ultimate question would always be what additional distress was caused to a particular claimant in the particular circumstances of the case and tribunals should be cautious about focusing on the respondent's conduct. However, a tribunal should ask itself whether the conduct, objectively viewed, was capable of having that aggravating effect, and should be cautious to avoid awarding aggravated damages and compensation for injury to feelings for the same conduct: *HM Land Registry v McGlue* [2013] EqLR 701. Aggravated damages have been awarded where the respondents made a malicious and unfounded complaint to the police about the claimants after dismissal which the employment tribunal considered to be linked to the earlier discriminatory behaviour (see *Bungay v Saini* (2011) 938 IDS Brief 13, [2012] All ER (D) 40 (Mar), EAT). In *ICTS (UK) Ltd v Visram* UKEAT/0133/18/BA, UKEAT/0134/18/BA the EAT found that the Tribunal had erred in law in failing properly to consider whether the employer's private surveillance of the employee had warranted an award of aggravated damages separate to the injury to feelings award.

A tribunal awarding aggravated damages should seek to avoid double recovery by having regard to the overlap between the heads of damage (see *Ministry of Defence v Fletcher* [2010] IRLR 25, EAT and also *McGlue* above). The tribunal should look at whether the overall award is proportionate to the totality of the claimant's suffering and generally the large majority of awards would be in the range £5,000 to £7,500 (see *Shaw*, above). In *Shaw*, above, Underhill P confirmed that the only purpose of aggravated damages is compensatory and they should not be awarded in order to punish a respondent (in the process thereby doubting observations to the contrary in *Fletcher*). See also *First Greater Western Limited v Waiyego* UKEAT/0056/18/RN, approving the 'lack of enthusiasm' for aggravated damages demonstrated in *Shaw*.

Exceptionally, an award of aggravated damages may be appropriate where the manner in which a respondent has conducted proceedings has aggravated the harm caused by the original act of discrimination (*Zaiwalla & Co* and *Fletcher* above).

The position regarding the availability of exemplary damages is less clear. The law had been that exemplary damages were not available in discrimination cases because these are statutory torts that did not exist at the time of the House of Lords decision in *Rookes v Barnard* [1964] 1 All ER 367 (see *AB v South West Water Services Ltd* [1993] QB 507; *Deane v Ealing London Borough Council* [1993] IRLR 209, [1993] ICR 329; *Ministry of Defence v Meredith* [1995] IRLR 539). However, in *Kuddus v Chief Constable of Leicestershire Constabulary* [2001] UKHL 29, [2001] 3 All ER 193 (a case of alleged misfeasance in public office) the House of Lords confirmed that the availability of exemplary damages depends on the nature of the tortious behaviour rather than whether or not the precise cause of action relied upon was recognised prior to 1964. There are two categories of case where exemplary damages may be awarded: (1) where there is oppressive, arbitrary or unconstitutional action by servants of the Government; or (2) where the tortfeasor's conduct was calculated to make a profit for himself that may exceed any compensation payable to the claimant (see *Rookes v Barnard*, above). The award of exemplary damages in discrimination cases will be rare and will occur only where the conduct falls into one of the two categories identified in *Rookes v Barnard* and the award of compensatory damages (including aggravated damages) will not sufficiently punish the respondent's conduct (*Bradford City Metropolitan Council v Arora* [1991] IRLR 165, CA). Where the first limb of the *Rookes v Barnard* test is in issue careful consideration will need to be given to whether the respondent can be said to have acted as agent or servant of the Government, even at a local level. In *Virgo Fidelis Senior School v*

Boyle [2004] IRLR 268, the EAT held that the management of a voluntary-aided school were not agents or servants of the Government. In contrast, in *Arora* the Court of Appeal rejected the argument that the selection committee for a senior position in a college for which the respondent council had authority were exercising a private function of the council and could not be liable for exemplary damages. The principles governing the award of exemplary damages were considered by the EAT in *Fletcher*, above. While 'ordinary' employment law functions performed under statute by an official of a public body with sufficient seniority might, in principle, attract an award of exemplary damages the conduct must be conscious and contumelious and the award in that case was set aside where there was no finding by the tribunal that the failure to operate effective redress procedures was conscious. The EAT emphasised that such damages are punitive, not compensatory, and that the risk of double recovery must be avoided, especially where there is an award of both aggravated and exemplary damages. In *R (Elias) v Secretary of State for Defence*, above, the Court of Appeal held that on the facts the discrimination in that case was not of such a nature as to make aggravated or exemplary damages appropriate.

Exemplary damages will not be available in cases under the *EPA 1970* as such claims are contractual, rather than tortious (see *Allan v Newcastle-upon-Tyne City Council* [2005] IRLR 504, EAT). This principle presumably also applies to the 'equality of terms' provisions under the *EqA 2010, Pt 5 Chapter 3*, which replace the *EPA 1970*, as these are still framed by reference to the terms of a claimant's contract of employment.

See also HARVEYS – Division L.7.D.

14.19 Compensation: discrimination and unfair dismissal

Where a complainant has been the victim of a dismissal which is both discriminatory and unfair (ie contrary to the right not to be unfairly dismissed conferred on certain employees by the *ERA 1996*), the tribunal has a choice of two compensatory regimes. As compensation for unfair dismissal is subject to a statutory maximum, whilst awards made under the anti-discrimination legislation are unlimited, the tribunal will almost invariably use the latter regime. However, the one clear advantage of the unfair dismissal regime is that it allows the tribunal to order the respondent to reinstate, or to re-engage, the complainant. If the respondent does not comply with such a re-employment order, the matter is re-listed for a compensation hearing. A penal 'additional award' may be made (see **56.14** UNFAIR DISMISSAL – **III**). Although the statutory language states that where the matter returns for compensation issues to be considered, compensation should be awarded in accordance with the provisions of the *ERA 1996* the EAT has made it clear that the statute should not be taken to preclude the tribunal from using the *RRA 1976* regime (or that under the other discrimination regimes and now the *EqA 2010* regime) (*D'Souza v Lambeth London Borough Council* [1997] IRLR 677). Making a re-employment order does not take away a complainant's right to unlimited compensation for the act of discrimination. However, if a tribunal orders re-employment and awards compensation for injury to feelings at the first remedies hearing, there is a risk that it will be taken to have made a final order in relation to compensation for discrimination, thereby precluding it from making a further award for loss arising from the discrimination where the re-employment order is not complied with. If the tribunal wishes to keep open the possibility of further compensation under the anti-discrimination regime, it should say so expressly.

The outcome of an unfair dismissal claim is not automatically determined by the outcome of a successful discrimination claim in relation to dismissal (see *Eversheds Legal Services Ltd v De Belin* [2011] ICR 1137, [2011] IRLR 448, EAT). Where a dismissal is fair, even though also an act of victimisation, the complainant will only be entitled to compensation for injury to feelings (*Lisk-Carew v Birmingham City Council* [2004] EWCA Civ 565, [2004] All ER (D) 215 (Apr)). Conversely, a respondent cannot rely upon a subsequent unfair dismissal to break the chain of causation in relation to a complainant's continuing losses (*HM Prison Service v Beart (No 2)* [2005] EWCA Civ 467, [2005] IRLR 568, [2005] ICR 1206, upholding the EAT in *HM Prison Service v Beart (No 2)* [2005] IRLR 171).

14.20 Compensation: awards of interest

The *EqA 2010, s 139(1)* provides for regulations to be made enabling employment tribunals to include interest on an amount awarded in proceedings under the Act. Interest is payable on any sums awarded currently pursuant to the *Employment Tribunals (Interest on Awards in Discrimination Cases) Regulations 1996 (SI 1996/2803)* (now having effect under *EqA 2010, s 139* by virtue of the *Equality Act 2010 (Commencement No.4, Savings, Consequential, Transitional, Transitory and Incidental Provisions and Revocations) Order 2010 (SI 2010/2317), art 21(1), Sch 7*). Interest should be awarded on the complainant's net and not gross loss (*Bentwood Bros (Manchester) Ltd v Shepherd* [2003] EWCA Civ 380, [2003] IRLR 364, [2003] ICR 1000).

Where the tribunal is concerned with a sum other than an award for injury to feelings, it is required to identify a 'mid-point date'. This date is the halfway point between the date on which the act of discrimination complained of occurred and the date on which the interest is being calculated (*SI 1996/2803, reg 4*). Interest is then awarded in respect of the period from the mid-point date to the date of calculation (*reg 6(1)(b)*). A different rule applies to the calculation of interest on awards for injury to feelings. By *reg 6(1)(a)*, interest is awarded for the whole period from the date of the act of discrimination through to the date of calculation.

Interest is simple interest and accrues from day to day (*reg 3(1)*). By *reg 3(2)*, the rate to be applied in England and Wales is the rate fixed, for the time being, by *section 17* of the *Judgments Act 1838*. In Scotland, the relevant rate is that fixed for the time being by *section 9* of the *Sheriff Courts (Scotland) Extracts Act 1892*. Where the rate has varied over the relevant period the tribunal may, in the interests of simplicity, apply a median or average of the rates (*reg 3(3)*).

If a respondent has made a payment to the complainant prior to the date of calculation, the date of payment is treated as if it were the date of calculation for the purposes of calculating the interest to be awarded (*reg 6(2)*).

The tribunal is given a discretion to calculate interest by reference to periods other than those set out above, or even to use different periods for different elements of the award. The discretion may be exercised only where the tribunal is of the opinion that:

(a)   there are exceptional circumstances, whether relating to the claim as a whole or to a particular element of the award; and

(b)   those circumstances have the effect that serious injustice would be caused if interest were to be awarded by reference to the period or periods specified in *reg 6(1)(a)* or *(b)* or *6(2)*.

See also HARVEYS – Division L.6.C(10).

14.20a Financial penalties

The tribunal has a power (as of 25 April 2013) to order an employer to pay a penalty to the Secretary of State (but not to the claimant), where it concludes that the employer has breached any of a worker's rights to which the worker's claim relates and is of the opinion that the breach has one or more aggravating features (*Employment Tribunals Act 1996, s 12A*). See further EMPLOYMENT TRIBUNALS – II, 20.119D.

14.21 Recommendations

The *EqA 2010, s 124(2)(c)* empowers tribunals to make an appropriate recommendation. An appropriate recommendation is a recommendation that within a specified period the respondent takes specified steps for the purpose of obviating or reducing the adverse effect on the claimant of any matter to which the proceedings relate (*s 124(3)*). The predecessor provision to like effect was held not to give the tribunal power to recommend that an applicant for promotion who was discriminated against be promoted to the next open post as that was not a matter to which the proceedings related (*British Gas plc v Sharma* [1991] IRLR 101, [1991] ICR 19). Where statutory rules govern an appointment, a tribunal cannot recommend an applicant's appointment. It can merely recommend that the appointing body be made aware of the need to comply with the anti-discrimination legislation and of other relevant matters (*North West Thames Regional Health Authority v Noone* [1988] IRLR 530, [1988] ICR 813).

A tribunal should only make recommendations that are practicable but the exercise of that discretion will only be interfered with on appeal if exercised wholly wrongly, taking account of irrelevant considerations or failing to take account of relevant ones (*Lycée Charles de Gaulle v Delambre* [2011] EqLR 948, EAT). In *Vento (No 2)* (see above), the respondent was held vicariously liable for the actions of certain of the complainant's colleagues. The colleagues were not themselves parties. The tribunal recommended that the respondent should meet with the colleagues and raise with them the adverse findings made by the tribunal's decision. This recommendation was endorsed by the EAT. However, the EAT, whilst acknowledging the very broad discretion conferred upon the tribunal, overturned a further recommendation that the respondent should suggest to the colleagues that they should make an apology in writing to the complainant. The EAT considered the recommendation was inappropriate because:

(1)   the complainant had already had an apology from her 'employer';

(2)   the colleagues were not parties and had not been given an opportunity to put their side of the case to the tribunal;

(3)   the recommendation could not be enforced and if the colleagues refused to apologise, that would aggravate the situation; and

(4)   an ordered apology would have little worth as it would not appear sincere.

For examples of the type of recommendations that may be made in indirect sex discrimination cases see: *McFarlane and Ambacher v EasyJet Airline Company Ltd* (Case Nos 1401496/2015, 3401933/2015, ET, 5 October 2016) and for transgender cases see *Souza v Primark* where the Tribunal recommended that the employer consult a specialist organisation regarding the formulation of a written policy on dealing with transgender staff or those who wished to undergo gender reassignment.

Recommendations cannot be specifically enforced. However, if, without reasonable justification, the respondent to a complaint fails to comply with a recommendation made by an employment tribunal that he take certain action and it thinks it just and equitable to do so:

(i)   the tribunal may increase the amount of compensation required to be paid to the complainant in respect of the complaint by a compensation order; or

(ii)   if an order for compensation could have been made, but was not, the tribunal may make such an order.

(*EqA 2010, s 124(7)*; and previously *SDA 1975, s 65(3)(a), (b); RRA 1976, s 56(4)(a), (b); SOR 2003, reg 30(3); RBR 2003, reg 30(3); DDA 1995, s 17A(5); and AR 2006, reg 38(3).*)

See also HARVEYS – Divisions **L.6.D, L.7.F.**

14.22 Remedies in cases involving pension schemes

The *EqA 2010, s 126* makes similar provision for remedies in relation to complaints of discrimination involving pension schemes with respect to all protected characteristics as existed under the previous Acts and Regulations. An employment tribunal may grant remedies if it finds that there has been a contravention of a provision referred to in *EqA 2010, s 120(1)* in relation to either (a) the terms on which persons become members of an occupational pension scheme, or (b) the terms on which members of an occupational pension scheme are treated. In those circumstances, in addition to the remedies available under *s 124(1)*, the tribunal may also by order declare:

(a)   if the complaint relates to the terms on which persons become members of a scheme, that the complainant has a right to be admitted to the scheme; and

(b)   if the complaint relates to the terms on which members of the scheme are treated, that the complainant has a right to membership of the scheme without discrimination (*s 126(2)*).

An order under the *EqA 2010, s 126(2)* may make provision as to the terms on which or the capacity in which the claimant is to enjoy the admission or membership and may have effect in relation to a period before the order is made (*s 126(4)*).

A tribunal may only make an order for compensation in relation to an occupational pension scheme under the *EqA 2010, s 124(2)(b)* for compensation for injury to feelings or (by virtue of *s 124(7)*) for failure to comply with a recommendation (*s 126(3)*), and not for the loss caused by the unlawful discrimination. However, the effect of the power in *s 126(4)* to make a declaration as to the terms on which the claimant is to enjoy admission to or membership of the scheme for a period prior to the order is made should render the scheme liable to pay arrears to the claimant. In principle, the scheme would then be liable for the payment of arrears without limit of time by virtue of *s 21(1)(b)* of the *Limitation Act 1980*: see *Lloyds Banking Group Pensions Trustees Ltd v Lloyds Bank Plc* [2018] EWHC 2839 (Ch), [2019] Pens LR 5.

The Court of Appeal has confirmed that there was no incompatibility with EU law in a tribunal not granting a declaration of entitlement where part-time female employees who were indirectly discriminated against in accessing a pension scheme would in fact have opted out of membership of the scheme (see *Copple v Littlewoods plc* [2011] EWCA Civ 1281, [2012] 2 All ER 97, [2012] IRLR 121). The Court considered that the question was whether on the balance of probabilities the women would have joined the scheme during the closed period.

Previously the *SOR 2003, RBR 2003, DDA 1995* and *AR 2006* contained specific provisions relating to discrimination or harassment involving pension schemes. The numbering of the relevant provisions was identical under the *SOR 2003* and the *RBR 2003*. The provisions in *AR 2006* and *DDA 1995* were differently numbered. Claims against managers or trustees of pension schemes brought under *reg 9A* of *SOR 2003* or *RBR 2003*, under *ss 4G, 4H* of *DDA 1995*, or *reg 11* of *AR 2006* had (subject to the availability of a complaint to the Pensions Ombudsman and any right, where appropriate, to commence judicial review proceedings (see *reg 27(2)* of *SOR 2003* and *RBR 2003; DDA 1995, Sch 3, para 2;* or *reg 35(2)* of *AR 2006*) to be brought in the employment tribunal. This included cases where the claim was based on relationships which have come to an end (*SOR 2003, reg 21; RBR 2003, reg 21; DDA 1995, s 16A;* and *AR 2006, reg 24*), was a claim alleging vicarious liability, or was a claim alleging that a person had knowingly aided an unlawful act. The relevant employer was required to be a party to the proceedings (*SOR 2003, Sch 1A, para 6; RBR 2003, Sch 1A, para 6; DDA 1995, s 41(1);* and *AR 2006, Sch 2, Part 1, para 5*).

'Pensioner members' (for whom see *Pensions Act 1995, s 124(1)*) were not entitled to a remedy from the tribunal (*SOR 2003, Sch 1A, para 7(1)(b); RBR 2003, Sch 1A, para 7(1)(b); DDA 1995, s 4J(1)(c)*; and *AR 2006, Sch 2, Part 1, para 6(1)(b)*).

Otherwise, where the tribunal concluded that a claim was well-founded, it had the following remedy options:

(1)   In cases concerned with admission to membership, the tribunal could make an order declaring that the complainant be admitted to the scheme. The tribunal could make such provision as it considered appropriate as to the terms on or the capacity in which the complainant was to be admitted.

(2)   In cases concerned with the terms on which members are treated, the tribunal could make an order declaring that the complainant should be entitled to membership without discrimination. Again, the order could not have a retrospective effect and could make such provision as it considered appropriate as to the terms on or the capacity in which the complainant could enjoy membership.

(3)   The tribunal could make an order compensating the complainant for injury to feelings but not otherwise compensate the complainant, whether in relation to arrears of benefits or otherwise, unless the respondent refused to comply with a recommendation (though there was no specific power set out to make a recommendation).

The right to seek an investigation or determination by the Pensions Ombudsman was specifically preserved (*reg 9A(4)* of the *SOR 2003* and *RBR 2003* added by amendment in, respectively, the *Employment Equality (Sexual Orientation) (Amendment) Regulations 2003 (SI 2003/2827)*, the *Employment Equality (Religion or Belief) (Amendment) Regulations 2003 (SI 2003/2828), DDA 1995, Sch 3, para 2(2)*, and *AR 2006, reg 35(2)*).

ENFORCEMENT BY THE EHRC

14.23 Commission for Equality and Human Rights

Until the creation of the Commission for Equality and Human Rights or EHRC, there had been three commissions created by statute to promote equality and eliminate discrimination: the EOC, the CRE and the DRC. There were no corresponding bodies for sexual orientation, religious or age discrimination. However, Part I of the *EA 2006* created the single EHRC. The EHRC took over the functions of the DRC, EOC and CRE and also has responsibility for fighting discrimination on the grounds of sexual orientation, religion or belief, and age. The EHRC is also tasked with promoting human rights. The provisions of *Part I* of the *EA 2006* came fully into force on 1 October 2007 under the *Equality Act 2006 (Commencement No 3 and Savings) Order 2007 (SI 2007/2603), art 2*. The DRC, CRE and EOC were dissolved from the same date under the *Equality Act 2006 (Dissolution of Commissions and Consequential and Transitional Provisions) Order 2007 (SI 2007/2602), art 3* (made under the *EA 2006, ss 36–38*). *SI 2007/2603, art 3* and *SI 2007/2602, art 5* make saving and transitional provisions respectively. The *SDA 1975, ss 53–61, 67–73* and *Sch 3*, the *RRA 1976, ss 43–52* and *58–64* and *Disability Rights Commission Act 1999*, which set up and gave powers to the EOC, CRE and DRC respectively, now stand repealed (*EA 2006, s 40* and *Sch 3*). Readers who need to consider the transitional arrangements are referred to those orders and to the discussion of the functions of the EOC, CRE and DRC in previous editions of this work.

The responsibilities of the EHRC are wide-ranging and, to a considerable extent, fall outside the scope of this work, so the discussion below focuses on those aspects of the EHRC's enforcement powers that are relevant to discrimination in the employment field.

The functions of the EHRC, so far as they concern discrimination in employment, are broadly similar to those of the former EOC, CRE and DRC, although wider in scope. Below the functions of the EHRC alone are considered. However, due to the similarity between the functions of the EHRC and those of the EOC, CRE and DRC, where relevant, previous case law concerning the EOC, CRE or DRC is referred to.

On the EHRC see also Harveys – Division L.1.E.

14.24 The *EA 2006* came into force on 18 April 2006. *Part 1* of the *Act* established the EHRC (*EA 2006, ss 1, 2, Sch 1*). The EHRC has a general duty to encourage and support the development of a society in which:

(a)   people's ability to achieve their potential is not limited by prejudice or discrimination,

(b)   there is respect for and protection of each individual's human rights,

(c)   there is respect for the dignity and worth of each individual,

(d)   each individual has an equal opportunity to participate in society, and

(e)   there is mutual respect between groups based on understanding and valuing of diversity and on shared respect for equality and human rights.

(*EA 2006, s 3*)

The EHRC has a duty to prepare, and regularly review, a strategic plan of the activities that it will pursue in the exercise of its functions after it has consulted various parties (*EA 2006, ss 4, 5*).

The EHRC is required in exercising its powers to:

(a)   promote understanding of the importance of equality and diversity;

(b)   encourage good practice in relation to equality and diversity;

(c)   promote equality of opportunity;

(d)   promote awareness and understanding of rights under the *EqA 2010* (previously the equality enactments);

(e)   enforce the *EqA 2010* (previously the equality enactments));

(f)   work towards the elimination of unlawful discrimination; and

(g)   work towards the elimination of unlawful harassment.

(*EA 2006, s 8(1)*)

'Unlawful' is defined as contrary to the *EqA 2010* (previously the equality enactments) (*EA 2006, s 34* as amended). The equality enactments were (until they were repealed and replaced by the *EqA 2010*) the *EPA 1970*, the *SDA 1975*, the *RRA 1976*, the *DDA 1995*, *Part 2* of the *EA 2006*, regulations made under *Part 3* of the *EA 2006*, the *SOR 2003*, the *RBR 2003* and the *AR 2006* (*EA 2006, s 33(1)*, which was repealed when the *EqA 2010* came into force). In fulfilling its duties under *s 8*, the EHRC must take account of any relevant human rights (*EA 2006, s 9(4)*). The EHRC is required to monitor the effectiveness of the equality and human rights enactments and give advice and make recommendations to central government on changes to the law (*EA 2006, s 11*). The equality and human rights enactments are the *Human Rights Act 1998*, the *EA 2006* and the *EqA 2010* (*EA 2006, s 11(3)(c)* as amended). The EHRC is required to monitor progress in performing its functions under the *EA 2006, s 8* and 9, and issue a report on this progress every three years (*EA 2006, s 12*). The EHRC is also required to issue an annual report on its performance (*EA 2006, Sch 1, para 32*).

The EHRC may issue a code of practice in connection with a matter addressed by the *EqA 2010* (and previously the *EPA 1970, SDA 1975, Pts 2–4, s 76A* and orders under *ss 76B, 76C*, the *RRA 1976, Pts 2–4* and *s 71, DDA 1995, Pts 2–4* and *5A, EqA 2006, Pt 2* and regulations made under *Pt 3, SOR 2003, Pts 2, 3, RBR 2003, Pts 2, 3*, and *AR 2006, arts 2, 3* (*EA 2006, s 14(1)* as amended). Before issuing a code the EHRC must publish its proposals, consult such persons as it thinks appropriate and submit a draft to the Secretary of State for approval (*EA 2006, s 14(6), (7)*). A failure to comply with a code of practice does not make a person liable to criminal or civil proceedings but a code is admissible in evidence in such proceedings and shall be taken into account by a court or tribunal if it appears relevant (*EA 2006, s 15(4)*). The EHRC has published a Code of Practice on Employment, which is available on the EHRC website (See https://www.equalityhumanrights.com/en/advice-and -guidance/equality-act-codes-practice), and which reflects the new anti-discrimination law set out in the *EqA 2010*.

The EHRC has the power to institute or intervene in legal proceedings (including judicial review) if it appears to the Commission that the proceedings relate to a matter in connection with which it has a function (*EA 2006, s 30*). This makes explicit on the face of the statute a power that the EOC, CRE and DRC were held to have. In *R v Secretary of State for Employment, ex p Equal Opportunities Commission* [1994] 1 All ER 910, [1994] IRLR 176, [1994] ICR 317, the House of Lords considered that the EOC had *locus standi* to challenge by judicial review proceedings a refusal by the Secretary of State to accept that English law was sexually discriminatory in certain respects, and their Lordships also held (by a majority) that the Divisional Court was a proper forum for the challenge in question. The EHRC has already exercised this power to intervene in an number of discrimination cases in the employment field (see, for example, *Oyarce v Cheshire County Council* [2008] EWCA Civ 434, [2008] ICR 1179, [2008] IRLR 653; *Slack v Cumbria County Council* [2009] EWCA Civ 293, [2009] IRLR 463; *Bainbridge v Redcar and Cleveland Borough Council* [2008] EWCA Civ 885, [2009] ICR 133, [2008] IRLR 776; and *Seldon v Clarkson Wright & Jakes* [2012] UKSC 16, [2012] IRLR 590, [2012] ICR 716) and *Jessemey v Rowstock Ltd* [2014] EWCA Civ 185, [2014] 3 All ER 409, [2014] IRLR 368 and *R (UNISON) v The Lord Chancellor* [2017] UKSC 51 (see also **14.2** above).

14.25 Formal inquiries and investigations

The EHRC has an express power to conduct inquiries into any matter relating to its duties under the *EA 2006, ss 8* and *9* (*EA 2006, s 16(1)*). If, during an inquiry the EHRC begins to suspect that a person has committed an unlawful act it must: (a) in continuing the inquiry, so far as possible, avoid further consideration of whether the person has committed an unlawful act, (b) commence an investigation, (c) may use information acquired during the inquiry in the investigation, and (d) ensure that any aspect of the inquiry which concerns the person investigated is not pursued while the investigation is in progress (*EA 2006, s 16(2)*).

The EHRC has the power to investigate whether a person has committed an unlawful act or has not complied with an unlawful act notice issued under *s 21* or an undertaking made in an agreement made under *s 23*, but may only investigate whether a person has committed an unlawful act if it suspects the person to have done so (such suspicion may, but need not, arise as a result of an inquiry under *s 16*) (*EA 2006, s 20(1), (2), (3)*). In relation to the EOC, CRE and DRC it had been held that if they did not have a suspicion that the subject of an investigation had committed an unlawful act of discrimination, the investigation and any non-discrimination notice based upon it might be challenged (*Prestige Group plc, Re, Commission for Racial Equality v Prestige Group plc* [1984] 1 WLR 335, [1984] IRLR 166, [1984] ICR 473, HL; *Hillingdon London Borough Council v Commission for Racial Equality* [1982] IRLR 424).

Before settling the report of an investigation recording a finding that a person has committed an unlawful act or has failed to comply with an unlawful act notice or an undertaking, the EHRC is required to send a draft to the person and specify a period of at least 28 days in which the person may make written representations, which the EHRC must consider (*EA 2006, s 20(4)*). *Schedule 2* to the *EA 2006* sets out supplemental provisions concerning investigations (*EA 2006, s 20(5)*).

Where the EHRC conducts an inquiry it is required to publish the terms of reference in a manner that it considers likely to bring the inquiry to the attention of persons whom it concerns or who might be interested in it, and in particular to the attention of any person specified in the terms of reference (*EA 2006, Sch 2, para 2*). Before holding an investigation the EHRC is required to prepare terms of reference specifying the person to be investigated and the nature of the alleged unlawful act, give the person the notice, give that person the opportunity to make representations about the terms of reference, and having considered such representations publish the terms of reference once settled (*EA 2006, Sch 2, para 3*). The EHRC is required to make arrangements for persons to make representations (which may, but need not, include oral representations) in relation to inquiries, investigations and assessments and must give any person specified in the terms of reference the opportunity to make representations (*EA 2006, Sch 2, paras 6, 7*). The EHRC must consider any representations made but need not do so, if it considers it appropriate, where the representations are not made by a person specified in the terms of reference or by a 'relevant lawyer' (ie either (a) an advocate or solicitor in Scotland, or (b) a person who, for the purposes of the *Legal Services Act 2007*, is an authorised person in relation to an activity which constitutes the exercise of a right of audience or the conduct of litigation (within the meaning of that *Act*)) (*EA 2006, Sch 2, para 8*, as amended). In relation to formal investigations by the EOC, CRE or DRC it has been held that the persons concerned were not entitled to cross-examine witnesses (*R v Commission for Racial Equality, ex p Cottrell and Rothon* [1980] IRLR 279).

14.26 *Information*. The EHRC has powers to require persons to provide information by issuing a notice in the course of an inquiry, investigation or assessment (*EA 2006, Sch 2, para 9*). Such a notice may require a person to provide information in his possession, produce documents in his possession, or give oral evidence, and may specify the form of information, documents or evidence and the timing, but a notice may not require a person to provide information that he is prohibited from disclosing by an enactment, do anything that he could not be compelled to do in proceedings in the High Court or Court of Session, or require a person to attend at a place unless the EHRC undertakes to pay the expenses of his journey (*EA 2006, Sch 2, para 10*). A recipient of a notice may apply to a county court (in England and Wales) or a sheriff (in Scotland) to have the notice cancelled on the grounds that the requirement imposed by it is unnecessary having regard to the purpose of the inquiry, investigation or assessment, or is unreasonable (*EA 2006, Sch 2, para 11*). Where the EHRC believes that a person has failed, or is likely to fail, without reasonable excuse to comply with a notice it may apply to a county court (in England and Wales) or a sheriff (in Scotland) for an order requiring the person to take such steps as are specified in the order (*EA 2006, Sch 2, para 12*). A person commits an offence if he fails to comply with a notice under *para 9* or an order under *para 12(2)*, falsifies any document provided in accordance with such a notice or order, or makes a false statement in giving oral evidence in accordance with a notice under *para 9*, and such an offence is punishable on summary conviction by a fine not exceeding level 5 on the standard scale (*EA 2006, Sch 2, para 13*, and see **1.10** INTRODUCTION).

14.27 *The Commission's report*. The EHRC is required to publish a report of its findings following an inquiry, investigation or assessment and may make recommendations as part of the report or in respect of a matter arising in the course of the inquiry, investigation or assessment, which may be addressed to any class of persons (*EA 2006, Sch 2, paras 15, 16*). A tribunal or court may have regard to the findings of a report but shall not treat it as conclusive, and a person to whom a recommendation is addressed shall have regard to it (*EA 2006, Sch 2, paras 18, 19*).

It is an offence for a Commissioner, Investigating Commissioner or employee of the EHRC to disclose any information acquired by the EHRC by way of representations made in relation to, or in the course of, an inquiry under the *EA 2006, s 16*, an investigation under *s 20*, an assessment under *s 31* or a notice under *s 32*, or from a person with whom the EHRC enters into, or considers entering into, an agreement under *s 23* (*EA 2006, s 6(1), (2)*). Disclosure of such information is permitted only if the disclosure is:

(a)   for the purposes of a function of the EHRC under the *EA 2006, ss 16, 20, 21, 24, 25, 31,* or 32;

(b)   in a report of an inquiry, investigation or assessment published by the EHRC;

(c)   in pursuance of an order of a court or tribunal;

(d)   with the consent of the person to whom the disclosed information relates;

(e)   in a manner that ensures that no person to whom the disclosed information relates can be identified;

(f)   for the purposes of civil or criminal proceedings to which the EHRC is a party; or

(g)   if the information was acquired by the EHRC more than 70 years before the date of the disclosure.

(*EA 2006, s 6(3)*)

Contravention of these rules is made an offence punishable on summary conviction with a fine not exceeding level 5 on the standard scale (*EA 2006, s 6(6)*; and see **1.10** INTRODUCTION).

14.28 Unlawful act notices and other remedies

Remedies available to the EHRC. The EHRC has a wider range of remedies available to it than the EOC, CRE and DRC. Where, following investigation, the EHRC is satisfied that a person has committed an unlawful act it has the power to issue a notice specifying the unlawful act and the provision of the *EqA 2010* (or previously the equality enactments) that has been infringed – an 'unlawful act notice' – and the notice may require the person to prepare an action plan to avoid repetition or continuation of the unlawful act or recommend action to be taken for that purpose (*EA 2006, s 21(1), (2)* (as amended), *(4)*). A person in receipt of a notice may within six weeks beginning with the date on which the notice was given appeal to an employment tribunal or county court (depending on which of these would have jurisdiction to consider a claim in respect of the alleged unlawful act) on the grounds that either (a) the person did not commit the unlawful act specified in the notice or (b) the requirement to prepare an action plan was unreasonable (*EA 2006, s 21(5), (7)*). On such an appeal the court or tribunal may affirm, annul or vary the notice, affirm, annul or vary the requirement, or make an order for costs or expenses (*EA 2006, s 21(6)*). The *Employment Tribunals (Constitution and Rules of Procedure) Regulations 2013 (SI 2013/1237), Sch 1* now regulates the procedure to be adopted upon the hearing of appeals against unlawful act notices.

Where the EHRC issues a notice under *s 21* requiring a person to prepare an action plan the notice must specify the time within which the person must give the EHRC a first draft plan (*EA 2006, s 22(2)*). On the receipt of the first draft plan the EHRC may approve it or give the person notice that it is inadequate and require the person to submit a revised draft by a specified time, possibly with recommendations as to the content of the revised draft (*EA 2006, s 22 (3), (4)*). The EHRC is empowered to apply to a county court (in England and Wales) or (in Scotland) a sheriff for an order requiring a person to produce a first draft plan by a specified time, or a revised draft plan by a specified time and in accordance with any directions as to its contents (*EA 2006, s 22(6)*). Where, within six weeks of the person giving the draft plan to the EHRC, it has not issued a notice that the draft plan is inadequate or applied for an order under *s 22(6)(b)*, or where such an order is refused, the action plan will come into effect (*EA 2006, s 22(5)*). The EHRC may agree with the person who prepared it to vary an action plan (*EA 2006, s 22(7)*).

The EHRC is empowered to seek an order from the county court or sheriff within five years of an action plan coming into force requiring a person to act in accordance with the plan or to take specified action for a similar purpose (*EA 2006, s 22(6)(c)*). It is a criminal offence punishable on summary conviction by a fine not exceeding level 5 on the standard scale to fail to comply with an order under *s 22(6)* without reasonable excuse (*EA 2006, s 22(9); and see* **1.10** INTRODUCTION).

The EHRC has another remedy for potential unlawful acts contrary to the *EqA 2010* (or previously the equality enactments). Under the *EA 2006, s 23*, the EHRC may enter into an agreement with a person under which the person undertakes not to commit an unlawful act of a specified kind or to take, or refrain from taking, other specified action, and the EHRC agrees not to proceed against the person under *ss 20* or *21* in respect of any act of that specified kind (*EA 2006, s 23(1)*). The EHRC will only be able to enter into an agreement if it believes that the person has committed an unlawful act but a person will not be taken to have admitted to the commission of an unlawful act only by virtue of entering into an agreement (*EA 2006, s 22(2), (3)*).

INJUNCTIONS

14.29 Persistent discrimination

The EHRC is empowered, where it thinks that a person is likely to continue to commit an unlawful act, to apply (in England and Wales) to a county court for an injunction or (in Scotland) to the sheriff for an interdict to prevent the person from committing the act (*EA 2006, s 24(1)*). The EHRC is also able, if a person subject to an agreement under the *EA 2006, s 23* has failed, or is likely to fail, to comply with an undertaking, to apply to a county court or sheriff for an order requiring the person to comply with the undertaking or such other order as the court or sheriff may specify (*EA 2006, s 24(2), (3)*).

14.30 Advertisements and instructions or pressure to discriminate

Prior to the *EqA 2010* coming into force on 1 October 2010 only the EHRC had power to bring proceedings in relation to discriminatory advertising or instructions or pressure to discriminate contrary to the *SDA 1975, ss 38–40, the RRA 1976, ss 29–31*, the *DDA 1995, ss 16B* and *16C*, and the *EA 2006, ss 54, 55* (religious discrimination: advertising and instructions or pressure to discriminate) (*EA 2006, s 25(1), (2)*; and see *Ruhaza v Alexander Hancock Recruitment Ltd* [2012] EqLR 9, EAT). Where the EHRC believed that a person had committed an act to which *s 25* applied it could present a complaint to an employment tribunal where the alleged act was unlawful by reference to the *SDA 1975, Pt 2*, the *RRA 1976, Pt 2*, the *DDA 1995, Pt 3*, or the *EA 2006, Pts 2*, and *3* (in so far as it related to employment services), or otherwise in the county court (in England and Wales) or to a sheriff (in Scotland) (*EA 2006, s 25(3)*). Such a complaint or application was to be made within the six month period beginning with the date (or last date) on which the alleged unlawful act occurred, or with the permission of the tribunal, court or sheriff (*EA 2006, s 26(1)*). On an application under *s 25(3)* the court, sheriff or tribunal could determine whether the allegation was correct (*EA 2006, s 25(4)*).

The EHRC was also empowered to apply to a county court (in England and Wales) for an injunction or to a sheriff (in Scotland) for an interdict where a tribunal, court or sheriff had determined under *s 25(4)* that a person has done an act to which the section applied or the

EHRC considered that a person has done such an act, and the EHRC believed that if unrestrained the person was likely to do another such act (*EA 2006, s 25(5), (6)*). A court or sheriff could not rely upon a determination under *s 25(4)* while an appeal against that determination was pending or might be brought (disregarding the possibility of an appeal out of time with permission) (*EA 2006, s 26(2)*). Any application under the *EA 2006, s 25(5), (6)* had to be brought within five years of the unlawful act occurring or with the permission of the court or sheriff (*EA 2006, s 26(3)*).

The *EqA 2010* repealed *EA 2006, ss 25* and *26* (*EqA 2010, s 211, Sch 26, paras 6, 14* and *15, Sch 27, Pt 1*).

From 1 October 2010 *EA 2006, s 24A* made provision in relation to:

(a)   an act which is unlawful because, by virtue of any of *EqA 2010, ss 13* to *18*, it amounts to a contravention of any of *Pts 3, 4, 5, 6* or *7* of that *Act*,

(b)   an act which is unlawful because it amounts to a contravention of the *EqA 2010, s 60(1)* (or to a contravention of *ss 111* or *112* of that *Act* that relates to a contravention of *s 60(1)* of that *Act*) (enquiries about disability and health),

(c)   an act which is unlawful because it amounts to a contravention of the *EqA 2010, s 106* (information about diversity in range of election candidates etc),

(d)   an act which is unlawful because, by virtue of the *EqA 2010, s 108(1)*, it amounts to a contravention of any of *Pts 3, 4, 5, 6* or *7* of that *Act*, or

(e)   the application of a provision, criterion or practice which, by virtue of the *EqA 2010, s 19*, amounts to a contravention of that *Act*.

For the purposes of the *EA 2006, ss 20* to *24*, it is immaterial whether the EHRC knows or suspects that a person has been or may be affected by the unlawful act or application (*EA 2006, s 24A(2)*). An unlawful act includes making arrangements to act in a particular way which would, if applied to an individual, amount to a contravention mentioned in the *EA 2006, s 24A(1)(a)* (*EA 2006, s 24A(3)*). Nothing in the *EA 2006* affects the entitlement of a person to bring proceedings under the *EqA 2010* in respect of a contravention mentioned in the *EA 2006, s 24A(1)* (*EA 2006, s 24A(4)*).

14.31 ASSISTANCE FOR PERSONS DISCRIMINATED AGAINST

The EHRC is able to make grants to another person in pursuance of its duties under the *EA 2006, ss 8* and *9*, which may be subject to conditions (*EA 2006, s 17*). The EHRC may assist an individual who is, or may become, a party to legal proceedings where the proceedings relate to the *EqA 2010* (and previously the equality enactments) and the individual alleges that he has been the victim of behaviour contrary to that Act (or those enactments)) (*EA 2006, s 28(1)*, as amended). This assistance may take the form of legal advice, legal representation, facilities for settlement of a dispute, or any other form of assistance (*EA 2006, s 28(4)*). Where the proceedings partly relate to matters other than the *EqA 2010* (or previously the equality enactments) the assistance may be given in relation to any aspect of the proceedings but must cease if the proceedings cease to relate to the *EqA 2010* (or previously the equality enactments) (*EA 2006, s 28(6)*). The Lord Chancellor may by order disapply this restriction in specified kinds of cases (*EA 2006, s 28(7)*). For these purposes the section is taken to apply to any provisions of EU law that confer rights on individuals and relate to discrimination on the grounds of sex (including gender reassignment), racial origin, ethnic origin, religion, belief, disability, age or sexual orientation (*EA 2006, s 28(12), (13)*). Where an individual receives assistance from the EHRC under *s 28* and the individual becomes entitled to costs either as a result of settlement or an award by the court or tribunal the EHRC's expenses in providing assistance will be charged on any sum paid to the individual by way of costs (*EA 2006, s 29*).

14.32 EFFECT ON CONTRACTS

A term of a contract is unenforceable against a person in so far as it constitutes, promotes or provides for treatment of that or another person that is of a description prohibited by the *EqA 2010* (*EqA 2010, s 142(1)*). A relevant non-contractual term is unenforceable against a person in so far as it constitutes, promotes or provides for treatment of that or another person that is of a description prohibited by the Act, in so far as the Act relates to disability (*EqA 2010, s 142(2)*). A relevant non-contractual term is defined as a term which (a) is a term of an agreement that is not a contract, and (b) relates to the provision of an employment service within *ss 56(2)(a)* to *(e)* or to the provision under a group insurance arrangement of facilities by way of insurance (*EqA 2010, s 142(3)*).

Previously a term of a contract was void where:

(a)   its inclusion rendered the making of the contract unlawful by virtue of the *Acts* or *Regulations*;

(b)   it was included in furtherance of an act rendered unlawful by the *Acts* or *Regulations*; or

(c)   it provided for the doing of an act which would be rendered unlawful by the *Acts* or *Regulations*.

(*SDA 1975, s 77(1); RRA 1976, s 72(1); SOR 2003, reg 35 and Sch 4, part 1, para 1(1); RBR 2003, reg 35 and Sch 4, part 1, para 1(1); DDA 1995, s 17C and Sch 3A, part 1, para 1(1); and AR 2006, reg 43 and Sch 5, part 1, para 1(1)*)

Thus, a term in a contract for the provision of a discriminatory training programme would be rendered void by those provisions. A term in a contract for an advertisement which provided for the inclusion of a discriminatory expression would similarly be void. In *Jivraj v Hashwani* [2010] EWCA Civ 712, [2010] IRLR 797, [2010] ICR 1435, the Court of Appeal held that a provision in an arbitration clause that the appointed arbitrator had to be a member of the Ismaili community was void as it involved discrimination on the grounds of religion or belief contrary to the *RBR 2003, regs 2* and *6*, and as a result the whole arbitration clause was void because removal of the offending provision rendered the agreement substantially different from that originally intended (this decision was reversed by the Supreme Court on the basis that an arbitrator was not employed under a contract personally to do work such as to fall within the *RBR 2003* and, in any event, the requirement in question was a genuine occupational requirement – [2011] UKSC 40, [2011] ICR 1004, [2012] IRLR 827).

Also previously a term which constituted (or was in furtherance of or provided for) unlawful discrimination against a party to a contract was not made void, but was unenforceable against that party (*SDA 1975, s 77(3); RRA 1976, s 72(3); SOR 2003, reg 35 and Sch 4, part 1, para 1(2); RBR 2003, reg 35 and Sch 4, part 1, para 1(2); DDA 1995, s 17C and Sch 3A, part 1, para 1(2); and AR 2006, reg 43 and Sch 5, part 1, para 1(2)*). For example, a term in a contract with a woman which states that she cannot use a smoking room normally reserved for men was not enforceable in a court of law.

A party to the contract may apply to a county court in England and Wales or a sheriff court in Scotland which may remove or modify the discriminatory term, provided that all persons affected have been notified of the application (*EqA 2010, s 143(1), (2)*; and previously *SDA 1975, s 77(5); RRA 1976, s 72(5); SOR 2003, reg 35 and Sch 4, part 1, para 3(1); RBR 2003, reg 35 and Sch 4, part 1, para 3(1); DDA 1995, s 17C and Sch 3A, part 1, para 3(1); and AR 2006, reg 43 and Sch 5, part 1, para 3(1)*).

The *EqA 2010, s 145* provides that a term of a collective agreement is void in so far as it constitutes, promotes or provides for treatment of a description prohibited by the *Act*, and a rule of an undertaking is unenforceable against a person in so far as it constitutes, promotes or provides for treatment of the person that is of a description prohibited by the *Act*. A qualifying person (as defined by the *EqA 2010, s 146(5), (6)*) may make a complaint to an employment tribunal that a term is void, or that a rule is unenforceable, as a result of *s 145* (*s 146(1)*). A person will only be able to make such an application if either the term or rule may in the future have effect in relation to him, and where the complaint alleges that the term or rule provides for treatment of a description prohibited by the *Act*, he may in the future be subjected to treatment that would (if he were subjected to it in present circumstances) be of that description (*EqA 2010, s 146(2)*). If the tribunal finds that the complaint is well-founded, it must make an order declaring that the term is void or the rule is unenforceable (*EqA 2010, s 146(3)*).

This is similar to the position that obtained previously. By the *Sex Discrimination Act 1986, s 6* (as amended), *SDA 1975, s 77* was made to apply to any term of a collective agreement (see COLLECTIVE AGREEMENTS (6)) (even if not intended to be legally enforceable) or to any rule made by an employer for application to his employees or to applicants for employment. Similar provisions were contained in *RRA 1976, s 72A, SOR 2003, reg 35* and *Sch 4, part 2, RBR 2003, reg 35* and *Sch 4, part 2, DDA 1995, s 17C* and *Sch 3A, part 2*, and *AR 2006, reg 43* and *Sch 5, part 2*. These provisions also applied to any rule made by an organisation of workers, an organisation of employers, or an organisation whose members carry on a particular profession or trade for whose purposes it exists, for application to its members and prospective members. They also applied to any rule made by an authority or body which can confer an authorisation or qualification needed for, or facilitating, engagement in a particular profession or trade, for application to those who have received or seek to receive such authorisation or qualification. Persons who are (as the case may be) employees, members or the recipients of authorisations or qualifications, or who are genuinely and actively seeking to become such, and who have reason to believe that the offending term or rule may at some future time have effect in relation to them could complain to an employment tribunal. If the tribunal found the complaint well-founded, it would declare the term or rule void. In the context of multiple equal pay claims, the EAT has held that there was no alternative, consistent with the EU law obligation to provide an effective remedy, to the employment tribunal considering granting declarations under *SDA 1975, s 77* that a collective agreement was contrary to the principles of equal pay at the same time as considering the equal pay claims themselves, notwithstanding that the claimants could test the disputed terms in the context of the equal pay claims (*UNISON v Brennan* [2008] ICR 955, [2008] IRLR 492, EAT).

See also EQUAL PAY (23).

Local authorities used to be prohibited from inserting clauses into their contracts obliging the other party to comply with the discrimination legislation, because these are 'non-commercial matters' (*Local Government Act 1988, s 17*; and see *R v Islington London Borough Council, ex p Building Employers Confederation* [1989] IRLR 382). However, the *EqA 2010* amends the *Local Government Act 1988, s 17* so that the section does not prevent a public authority to which it applies from exercising any function regulated by the section with reference to a non-commercial matter to the extent that the authority considers it necessary or expedient to do so to enable or facilitate compliance with (a) the duty imposed on it by the *EqA 2010, s 149* (public sector equality duty), or (b) any duty imposed on it by regulations under the *EqA 2010, ss 153* or *154* (powers to impose specific duties) (the *Local Government Act 1988, s 17(10)*, inserted by the *EqA 2010, s 211(1), Sch 26, paras 1, 2(b)*).

See also HARVEYS – Division L.5.B.

14.33 SETTLEMENT OF A CLAIM

A term of a contract is unenforceable by a person in whose favour it would operate in so far as it purports to exclude or limit a provision of or made under the *EqA 2010* (*EqA 2010, s 144(1)*). A clause in a members' agreement in a firm of solicitors which purported to require any disputes between members to be referred for alternative dispute resolution and thence for final resolution through arbitration was held to be unenforceable by virtue of the *EqA 2010, s 144* in *Clyde & Co LLP v Bates van Winkelhof* [2011] EWHC 668 (QB), [2011] IRLR 467. Slade J held that the *EqA 2010, s 144(1)* was not just concerned with agreements to exclude the right not to be discriminated against but also agreements to exclude the enforcement of those rights in proceedings. The effect of the clause in the agreement was to preclude the continuation of sex discrimination proceedings in the employment tribunal and was therefore void and unenforceable. The Court of Appeal granted permission to appeal in that case [2011] EWCA Civ 947, [2011] Arb LR 18, but ultimately the claim did proceed in the employment tribunal, reaching the Supreme Court ([2014] UKSC 32, [2014] 1 WLR 2047, [2014] ICR 730, [2014] IRLR 641).

There is one exception to the rule against contracting out of the anti-discrimination legislation. Contracts or agreements settling or compromising a complaint relating to discrimination in employment (and previously complaints relating to the *Equal Pay Act 1970, s 2* (see **23.29** EQUAL PAY)) are enforceable against the complainant only where the contract is made with the assistance of a conciliation officer (see **2.4** ADVISORY, CONCILIATION AND ARBITRATION SERVICE (**ACAS**)), or where the contract is a compromise contract (now 'settlement agreement') meeting certain statutory conditions (see **ACAS** CONCILIATION (**3**)) (*EqA 2010, s 144(4)*; and previously *SDA 1975, s 77(4)(aa)* as inserted by *TURERA 1993, Sch 6, para 1*, and *Employment Rights (Dispute Resolution) Act 1998, s 9*; *RRA 1976, s 72(4)* as amended by *TURERA 1993, Sch 6, para 2(4A)* and *Employment Rights (Dispute Resolution) Act 1998, s 9*; *SOR 2003, reg 35* and *Sch 4, part 1, para 2*; *RBR 2003, reg 35* and *Sch 4, part 1, para 2*; *DDA 1995, s 17C* and *Sch 3A, Part 1, para 2*; and *AR 2006, reg 43* and *Sch 5, Part 1, para 2*).

It is most important to comply with these provisions when settling such a complaint, otherwise, despite a sum to settle the complaint having been paid, a complainant may still pursue his application to an employment tribunal. However, the EAT has held that there is nothing in law that requires a tribunal to ensure that a settlement agreement is binding within the *SDA 1975* or *RRA 1976* before it permits a claim to be dismissed where the parties have reached what is otherwise a contractual agreement (*Mayo-Deman v University of Greenwich* [2005] IRLR 845). An employment tribunal does have jurisdiction to consider whether a settlement agreement is a valid agreement (eg is not induced by a misrepresentation) (see *Industrious Ltd v Horizon Recruitment Ltd v Vincent* [2010] ICR 491, [2010] IRLR 204, EAT).

The requisite conditions for 'a qualifying settlement agreement' under the *EqA 2010, s 147(3)* (and also previously for a valid compromise agreement under the Acts and Regulations) are the following:

(a)   the contract must be in writing;

(b)   the contract must relate to the particular complaint;

(c)   the complainant must have received advice from an independent advisor (previously 'a relevant independent adviser') as to the terms and effect of the proposed contract and in particular its effect on his ability to pursue a complaint before an employment tribunal;

(d)   there must be in force, when the adviser gives the advice, a contract of insurance, or an indemnity provided for members of a profession or professional body, covering the risk of a claim by the complainant in respect of loss arising in consequence of the advice;

(e)   the contract must identify the adviser; and

(f)   the contract must state that the conditions (*c*) and (*d*) are satisfied.

Item (*f*) must not be ignored as the failure to include all the conditions in the relevant statutes in a settlement agreement will invalidate the agreement even if the substance of the requirements is met (*Lunt v Merseyside TEC Ltd* [1999] IRLR 458, [1999] ICR 17, CA; *Palihakkara v British Telecommunications plc* [2007] All ER (D) 131 (Jan), EAT). An employee was not precluded from bringing an equal pay claim despite signing a compromise agreement purporting to settle all claims that she 'believed' that she had which referred expressly to the *EPA 1970*, where the employee was not aware that she had an equal pay claim when she signed the compromise agreement (*Hilton UK Hotels Ltd v McNaughton* [2006] All ER (D) 327 (May), EAT). A claimant is not required to have presented a claim or articulated a grievance for a settlement agreement to relate to a 'particular complaint' (*McWilliam v Glasgow City Council* [2011] IRLR 568, EAT). An agreement that referred only to claims arising out of the termination of a claimant's employment did not cover discrimination claims arising prior to termination (*Palihakkara*, above). In *Bainbridge v Redcar and Cleveland Borough Council; Williams v Redcar and Cleveland Borough Council* [2007] IRLR 494, EAT, a COT3 which covered 'all claims . . . in connection with the terms of [the claimants'] contracts of employment' was held to be unambiguous and enforceable (see *Clarke v Redcar and Cleveland Borough Council*, above). The requirement for the claimant to receive advice on 'the terms and effect' of the agreement does not mean that the independent adviser is required to offer a view on whether the deal is a good one for the claimant (*McWilliam*, above).

A person was a 'relevant independent adviser' in relation to the previous Acts and regulations for the purposes of paragraph (*c*) immediately above if:

(a)   he is a qualified lawyer;

(b)   he is an officer, official, employee or member of an independent trade union who has been certified in writing by the trade union as competent to give advice and as authorised to do so on behalf of the trade union; or

(c)   he works at an advice centre (whether as an employee or a volunteer) and has been certified in writing by the centre as competent to give advice and as authorised to do so on behalf of the centre.

The *EqA 2010, s 147(4)* adopts this definition for 'an independent adviser' and adds (d) 'a person of such description as may be specified by order'.

A person is not an 'independent adviser' to the complainant if he is (*s 147(5)* as amended):

(a)   a person (other than the complainant) who is a party to the contract or the complaint;

(b)   a person who is connected to a person within paragraph (*a*);

(c)   a person who is employed by a person within paragraph (*a*) or (*b*);

(d)   a person who is acting for a person within paragraph (*a*) or (*b*) in relation to the contract or the complaint;

(e)   a person within subsection (4)(*b*) or (*c*), if the trade union or advice centre is a person within paragraph (*a*) or (*b*);

(f)   a person within subsection (4)(*c*) to whom the complainant makes a payment for the advice.

Any two persons are to be treated as connected if one is a company of which the other (directly or indirectly) has control, or else if both are companies of which a third person (directly or indirectly) has control (*EqA 2010, s 147(8)*).

The words 'to the complainant' and '(other than the complainant)' were inserted into the *EqA 2010, s 147(5)* with effect from 6 April 2012 by the *Equality Act 2010 (Amendment) Order 2012 (SI 2012/334)*. The original drafting of the *EqA 2010, s 147* caused a certain amount of debate because on a literal interpretation a solicitor acting for a claimant might be said to be acting for a party (ie the claimant) in relation to the complaint and therefore could not qualify as an independent adviser. The cautious view was that a claimant had to instruct a fresh solicitor to advise on a compromise contract (and even then might not escape from the problem) or else that only a settlement through ACAS could be effective. The alternative view was that the literal interpretation created an absurd result that Parliament plainly did not intend and that the reference to 'a party' in *s 147(5)(a)* must mean a party other than the claimant (this interpretation was preferred by the Government's Equality Office).

'Qualified lawyer' means (as respects England and Wales) a person who, for the purposes of the *Legal Services Act 2007*, is an authorised person in relation to an activity which constitutes the exercise of a right of audience or the conduct of litigation (within the meaning of that *Act*), and (as respects Scotland) an advocate (whether in practice as such or employed to give legal advice), or a solicitor who holds a practising certificate (*EqA 2010, s 147(6)*).

The definition of a 'qualified lawyer' was extended, with effect from 1 October 2004, to include a Fellow of the Institute of Legal Executives practising in a solicitors' practice (see: *Equality Act 2010 (Qualifying Compromise Contract Specified Person) Order 2010 (SI 2010/2192)*; and previously for the purposes of the *SDA 1975* and *RRA 1976*, the *Compromise Agreements (Description of Person) Order 2004 (SI 2004/754)*, as amended by the *Compromise Agreements (Description of Person) Order 2004 (Amendment) Order 2004 (SI 2004/2515)*; for the purposes of the *SOR 2003*, the *Employment Equality (Sexual Orientation) Regulations 2003 (Amendment) Regulations 2004 (SI 2004/2519)*); for the purposes of the *DDA 1995*, the *Compromise Agreements (Description of Person) Order 2005 (SI 2005/2364)*; and, for the purposes of the *RBR 2003*, the *Employment Equality (Religion or Belief) Regulations 2003 (Amendment) (No 2) Regulations 2004 (SI 2004/2520)*; all of which had been amended by the *Legal Services Act 2007 (Consequential Amendments) Order 2009 (SI 2009/3348), art 2*).

'Independent trade union' has the same meaning as in the *Trade Union and Labour Relations (Consolidation) Act 1992* (see **51.22** TRADE UNIONS – I).

See also HARVEYS – Division **PI.1.U**.

15   Education and Training

15.1   An employer has no general obligation at common law to provide facilities for the education and training of his employees unless they are engaged under a contract of apprenticeship or their contract of employment provides otherwise. Similarly, he does not have to allow employees time off for day-release or sandwich courses. However, with effect from 28 June 2013, young persons (ie 16 and 17 years olds) in England have a duty to participate in full-time education or training; participate in training in accordance with a contract of apprenticeship or an apprenticeship agreement; or, if they are in a full-time occupation, participate in "sufficient relevant training or education" (*Education and Skills Act 2008, s 2*). *ESA 2008* creates corresponding duties on local education authorities (*s 10*) and employers (*s 27*, from a date to be appointed) to enable and support participation in education and training . In Scotland and Wales, young persons in employment have the right to take time off from work in order to undertake study or training leading to a 'relevant qualification' (see **4.8** CHILDREN AND YOUNG PERSONS).

In addition, an employer should not ask his employee to carry out a task requiring a special skill unless he has ensured that the employee possesses those skills or unless the employer has undertaken to train the employee. (If he does so and an accident occurs he may be liable, see **28.5–28.7** HEALTH AND SAFETY AT WORK – I.)

Various bodies and schemes have been created by the Government to encourage the education and training of employees and those seeking employment.

From April 2017, the body responsible for funding the delivery of training and apprenticeships in England has been the Education and Skills Funding Agency. There are different arrangements in Wales and Scotland.

The *Apprenticeships, Skills, Children and Learning Act 2009* makes provision for the delivery of training in England. Amongst other matters, the Act has also made provision about apprenticeships in England and Wales, and has introduced a right for a 'qualifying employee' to apply to his or her employer to undertake study and/or training. Some of these changes took effect in April 2010, certain other changes took effect in 2011, and others are not yet in force; these provisions are dealt with in **15.9** onwards below.

For the income tax treatment of payment or reimbursement of training costs by an employer, see the *Income Tax (Earnings and Pensions) Act 2003, s 311*.

15.2   **APPRENTICESHIPS**

Apprenticeships offer what must be the oldest form of training in skilled trades for young people. There are two kinds of contracts that create apprenticeships. The first, and older, kind is a common law contract for apprenticeship. The second is an "apprenticeship agreement". The apprenticeship agreement is a creation of the *Apprenticeships, Skills, Children and Learning Act 2009* ("*ASCLA 2009*").

15.3   **Common Law Apprentices - Contracts for Apprenticeship**

An apprenticeship is normally for a fixed term of years or until a set qualification is achieved, the apprentice, his parent or guardian (if he is a minor), and the employer entering into a written agreement. The agreement will usually be in a form common to all apprenticeships for the trade concerned. In general, the apprentice will have time off work to attend college and take examinations.

15.3   Education and Training

A contract for apprenticeship may not be terminable for misconduct in the same way as an ordinary contract of employment; and in the event of wrongful termination, different principles apply to the assessment of damages (*Dunk v George Waller & Son Ltd* [1970] 2 All ER 630. See also *Revenue and Customs Commissioners v Jones* [2014] ICR D43 (UKEAT/0458/13/BA), in which the distinction between contracts of apprenticeship and contracts of employment was restated by the EAT and *McGrougher v Express Joinery Products* [2018] 11 WLUK 688).

In *Wallace v C A Roofing Services Ltd* [1996] IRLR 435, Sedley J in the High Court held that a contract of apprenticeship (unlike a contract of employment or training contract) cannot be terminated on the grounds of redundancy, falling short of closure or a fundamental change in the character of the employers' enterprise. He stated that a contract of apprenticeship remains a distinct entity at common law; its first purpose is training, and the execution of work for the employer is secondary. Thus, the ordinary law as to dismissal does not apply. The contract is for a fixed term and is not terminable at will, unlike a contract of employment at common law.

Wallace was applied in *Whitely v Marton Electrical Ltd* [2003] IRLR 197, in which the EAT held that a 'modern apprenticeship agreement', under which an employer agrees to employ an apprentice 'for the duration of the training plan', is different from an ordinary contract of employment and is not terminable on notice. The provision in the agreement requiring the apprentice to comply with the employer's terms and conditions of employment did not mean that the employer's terms as to notice of termination applied to the apprentice. Where any provision of the employer's terms and conditions were inconsistent with those of the agreement, the agreement must prevail because it was plainly the agreement which the parties intended should govern their relationship. However, in *Thorpe v Dul* [2003] ICR 1556, [2003] All ER (D) 14 (Jul), the EAT remitted the case for the employment tribunal to decide, as a question of fact, the legal status of the modern apprenticeship agreement in that case. See also *Revenue and Customs Commissioners v Jones* [2014] ICR D43 (UKEAT/0458/13/BA), where the EAT held that livery stable workers who trained for formal British Horse Society examinations were not engaged under a contract of apprenticeship because the training aspect was incidental and subsidiary to the contract. Moreover, there was an express power under the contract to dismiss for gross misconduct without notice which was inconsistent with a contract of apprenticeship.

In *Flett v Matheson* [2006] EWCA Civ 53, [2006] IRLR 277, some eight months after commencing employment at the age of 16, the employee entered into a tripartite individual learning plan (ILP) with the employer and a training provider, which was stated to be carried out under advanced modern apprenticeship arrangements (see also **15.9** below). The employee was subsequently dismissed without notice, and claimed unfair dismissal and/or breach of contract of employment. The EAT held that the employee was employed under a contract of employment but not under a contract of apprenticeship; the employee appealed against the latter finding.

Allowing the appeal, the Court of Appeal held that a modern tripartite apprenticeship arrangement can constitute a common law contract of apprenticeship. In its view, the important issue is the nature and duration of the employer's obligations under the agreement. The fact that part of the training is provided by a third party is not crucial to the analysis of those obligations. In the present case, the ILP had the essential features of an apprenticeship. The contract of employment was varied or overlaid by the ILP, and that variation gave rise to additional obligations on the employer. The individual learning plan was called an 'apprenticeship' and provided for a combination of off and on the job training for a lengthy period. What occurred at the workplace was part of the training. While the employer did not provide the more academic part of the training, he was required to give the apprentice time off to obtain it and to fund the cost of attendance at classes. It was not open to the employer to dismiss on reasonable notice, subject to making reasonable efforts to find another employer willing and able to continue the training. If attempts to find another employer failed, the obligations on the employer remained and, save in certain specified circumstances, the apprentice could not be dismissed within the period of training. *Flett* was considered by the EAT in *Revenue and Customs Commissioners v Jones* [2014] ICR D43 (UKEAT/0458/13/BA), where livery stable workers receiving training were held not to be engaged under a contract of apprenticeship.

If they satisfy the necessary qualifying conditions, apprentices enjoy the statutory employment protection rights (*Employment Rights Act 1996, s 230(2); Equality Act 2010, s 83(2)*).

The Employment Appeal Tribunal, on the basis of the evidence before it that the Law Society recommended the operation of a dual system whereby a clerk was articled to an individual partner in a firm of solicitors under a deed of articles but was employed by the firm under a contract of employment, held that an articled clerk was engaged under such a system (*Oliver v J P Malnick & Co* [1983] 3 All ER 795, [1983] IRLR 456, [1983] ICR 708).

In *Edmonds v Lawson* [2000] QB 501, [2000] ICR 567, [2000] IRLR 391, the Court of Appeal (allowing an appeal from Sullivan J: [2000] IRLR 18) held that, although a pupil barrister was employed under a contract by the set of barristers' chambers where she was taken on as a pupil, the contract was not a contract of apprenticeship or an equivalent contract. The pupil was, therefore, not a 'worker' for the purposes of the *National Minimum Wage Act 1998*, and was not entitled to be paid the national minimum wage ('NMW'). (For the NMW for apprentices, see **15.7** below; and see generally **35.9** Pay – I.)

Flett v Matheson was followed (and *Edmonds v Lawson* was considered) in *Lee v Chassis & Cab Specialists Ltd* (UKEAT/0268/10/JOJ) [2011] All ER (D) 178 (Feb), (Transcript) where the EAT, in allowing an appeal from the employment tribunal, held that on the evidence the claimant in that case was an apprentice and not an employee. He was therefore excluded from the NMW by virtue of *SI 1999/584, reg 12(2)* (now revoked). See also *Revenue and Customs Commissioners v Jones* [2014] ICR D43, where livery stable workers were held not to be engaged under a contract of apprenticeship in a complaint by the Revenue for failure to pay NMW. Since amendments to the legislation in 2014 and included in the consolidating National Minimum Wage Regulations 2015, participation in a traineeship (a short-term government-funded work experience placement for those aged between 16 and 25) in England does not qualify a worker for the NMW (*SI 2015/621, reg 54*).

"Modern" Apprentices - Apprenticeship Agreements

15.4 *Approved English apprenticeships*

An approved English apprenticeship is defined as an "arrangement" which either "takes place under an approved English apprenticeship agreement" or else "is an alternative English apprenticeship" (*ASCLA 2009, s A1(2)*).

Sections ZA1 to *ZA11* of the *Act* make provision for the establishment of the Institute of Apprenticeships (http://www.instituteforapprenticeships.org) whose functions include advising the Secretary of State in relation to apprenticeships in England and setting and publishing standards in respect of apprenticeships.

An "approved English apprenticeship agreement" is an agreement which provides for the apprentice to work for another person for reward in an occupation for which a standard has been published by the Institute for Apprenticeships (see *ASCLA 2009, s A1(3)* and *ZA11*); provides for the apprentice to receive training to assist the apprentice to achieve the approved apprenticeship standard and satisfies any other conditions specified in regulations made by the Secretary of State (*s A1(3)*). Certain other conditions are specified by the *Apprenticeships (Miscellaneous Provisions) Regulations SI 2017/1310 ("AMP Regulations*

2017"). The conditions came into effect from 15 January 2018. The regulations provide that an approved English apprenticeship must require off-the-job training which is to be received during normal working hours and which is for the purpose of achieving the relevant apprenticeship standard (*Reg 3(1)* and *(3)*). The agreement must specify the amount of time the apprentice is to receive off-the-job training during the period of the agreement (Reg 3(2)). The agreement must also specify the "practical period" (*Reg 4*) that being "the period for which the apprentice is expected to work and receive training under an approved English apprenticeship agreement" (*Reg 2*). The length of the practical period may differ from apprentice to apprentice and must take into account: the apprentice's knowledge and skills; whether the work and training is to be undertaken by the apprentice on a full-time or part-time basis; and the approved standard to which the agreement relates (*Reg 4(2)*). Unless, simplifying, the apprentice had already been working for an employer and receiving training under an earlier approved English apprenticeship which terminated less than 12 months before it was otherwise due to complete and has been engaged under a new apprenticeship which aims to achieve the same approved standard, the practical period cannot be less than 12 months in duration (*Reg 5*).

An alternative English apprenticeship is an arrangement of a kind described in regulations (*ALSCLA 2009, s A1(4)*). The relevant regulations are the *AMP Regulations 2017* (w.e.f. 15 January 2018). It is an arrangement under which a person works in order to achieve an approved standard, where that person either (a) was working for an employer and receiving training, under an approved English apprenticeship agreement but was dismissed by reason of redundancy less than six months before the apprenticeship would otherwise have completed (see *Reg 6(5)*); or (b) is working and receiving training to achieve an approved standard under an arrangement where the person is holding office as a minister or a trainee minister of a religious denomination; or as a constable of a police force in England (see *Reg 6(6)*).

Work may be for an employer; otherwise than for an employer; or otherwise than for reward (see *Reg 6(2)*).

There are certain additional formal requirements: The arrangement in paragraph must specify the amount of time the person is to receive off-the-job training during the period of the arrangement; the arrangement must terminate on a date specified in the arrangement (see *Reg 6(3)* and *(4)*).

An approved English apprenticeship agreement is deemed not to be a contract of apprenticeship and instead deemed to be a contract of service (*ASCLA 2009, s A5*).

An apprentice who successfully completes their apprenticeship can apply in writing for a certificate (*Apprenticeship Certificate (England) Regulations 2016/458, Reg 2* w.e.f. 29 April 2016). A fee of up to £25 may be charged (or £30 for a copy). Although it is the Secretary of State who has the power to issue the certificates, the application may be made online to "Apprenticeship Certificates England" (https://acecerts.co.uk/web/)

Apprenticeships in Wales

ASLCA 2009, ss 1 to *39* make provision about apprenticeships in Wales.

Apprenticeship frameworks may be issued by a "Welsh issuing authority", that being a person designated under the *Act* by the Welsh Ministers to issue frameworks (*ASLCA 2009, ss 12* and *18*).

ASCLA 2009, s 32 makes provision for statutory apprenticeship agreements. In order to qualify as an apprenticeship agreement it must meet four conditions: (a) a person (the "apprentice") undertakes to work for another (the "employer") under the agreement; (b) the agreement is in the prescribed form; (c) the agreement states that it is governed by the law of England and Wales; and (d) the agreement states that it is entered into in connection with a qualifying apprenticeship framework. The prescribed form is to be found in the *Apprenticeships (Form of Apprenticeship Agreement) Regulations 2012/844. Reg 2* provides:

"(1) The prescribed 1 form of an apprenticeship agreement for the purposes of section 32(2)(b) of the [*ASCLA 2009*] is—

(a)   a written statement of particulars of employment given to an employee for the purposes of section 1 of the 1996 Act; or

(b)   a document in writing in the form of a contract of employment or letter of engagement where the employer's duty under section 1 of [ERA 1996] is treated as met for the purposes of section 7A of [*ERA 1996*].

An apprenticeship agreement must include a statement of the skill, trade or occupation for which the apprentice is being trained under the apprenticeship framework."

Discrete provision is made for Crown Servants and Parliamentary Staff (*Reg 3*) and members of the Armed Forces (*Reg 4*).

As with English apprenticeships there are two "flavours" of Welsh apprenticeship. The first requires that the "standard Welsh completion conditions" are met (*ASLCA 2009, s 2(2)(a)*). Those conditions are that: the person has entered into an apprenticeship agreement in connection with an "apprenticeship framework"; at the date of that agreement the framework was a recognised Welsh framework; the person has completed a course of training for the competencies qualification identified in the framework; throughout the duration of the course, the person was working under the apprenticeship agreement; and the person meets the requirements specified in the framework for the purpose of the issue of an apprenticeship certificate (*s 3*).

The second flavour arises where the "alternative Welsh completion conditions" are met (*s 2(2)(b)*). Those conditions apply to someone who works "otherwise than under an apprenticeship agreement" (whether as a self-employed person or "otherwise than for reward" (see *ss 2(4)(a)* and *(6)*) and are presently specified by the *Apprenticeships (Alternative Welsh Completion Conditions) Regulations 2013/1468*. There are two conditions. Reg 3 provides that the conditions are that a person works as a self-employed person "in connection with a recognised Welsh apprenticeship framework" and that the requirements specified in that framework for the purpose of the issue of an apprenticeship certificate are met. Reg 4 deals with people who are made redundant whilst engaged under an apprenticeship agreement. Where they have started a course of training for the competencies qualification identified in the framework and, having been terminated, complete it within 6 months of dismissal whilst working or attending a recognised vocational training centre in connection with the framework then provided they meet the other requirements specified in the framework they meet the completion conditions and are entitled to their certificate.

Apprenticeship certificates are issued by the "Welsh Certifying authority" (see *ASCLA 2009, s 10(1)*). At present that is the Federation for Industry Sector and Skills & Standards (see http://fisss.org/) – *Apprenticeships (Designation of Welsh Certifying Authority) Order 2013/1191* as amended by the *Apprenticeships (Designation of Welsh Certifying Authority) (Amendment) Order 2015/1733* w.e.f 16 October 2015).

Apprenticeship levy

On 6 April 2017, the HMRC began to charge an apprenticeship levy on larger UK employers. The relevant provisions are contained in the *Finance Act 2016* and came into force from 15 September 2016. They provide for a levy to be charged on employers' pay bills at a rate of 0.5% for those employers having annual pay bills of more than £3 million. It was expected that the levy would be paid by less than 2% of UK employers. (See *Part 6* of the *Finance Act 2016*). See https://www.gov.uk/government/news/key-facts-you-should-know-about-the-apprenticeship-levy for information as to how the levy works.

15.4   Education and Training

The Government committed to an additional 3 million apprenticeship starts by 2020 which are to be funded by the levy

15.5   RECOVERY OF TRAINING COSTS

Problems are sometimes encountered in practice where an employer expends significant sums of money on training an employee, for example, by sending him on outside courses, and the employee then leaves his job shortly afterwards, in some instances without giving proper notice.

The wasted training costs will not usually be recoverable in the absence of an express agreement to that effect. That is so even if the employee leaves without giving proper notice, because the costs would have been incurred whether or not that breach of contract had occurred.

An agreement for the repayment of training costs in the event of an early departure will have to be very carefully drafted in order to be enforceable. If it applies where there is a breach of contract by the employee, it may be struck down as a 'penalty clause' unless it can be said to represent a genuine pre-estimate of loss suffered by the employer (*Giraud UK Ltd v Smith* [2000] IRLR 763; *Sands-Ellison v One Call Insurance* [2003] All ER (D) 389 (Mar); *Tullett Prebon Group Ltd v El-Hajjali* [2008] IRLR 760; *Imam-Sadeque v Bluebay Asset Management (Services) Ltd* [2013] IRLR 344; *Cavendish Square Holding BV v Talal El Makdessi* [2015] UKSC 67, [2016] 2 All ER 519). This will usually mean, for example, that the proportion of the costs to be repaid must depend upon how long the employee remains after being trained (a clause meeting that requirement was upheld in *Neil v Strathclyde Regional Council* [1984] IRLR 14). Another possible argument against an agreement to repay training costs is that it is in restraint of trade, although the contention in *Neil* that the clause in that case was also illegal and unenforceable as an unlawful restrictive covenant or, alternatively, as being contrary to public policy because it was an undue restraint on the employee's liberty, was rejected at first instance (*Strathclyde Regional Council v Neil* [1984] IRLR 11; the point was not pursued on appeal). The reasoning in *Neil* was upheld in *Transocean Maritime Agencies SA Monegasque v Pettit* 1997 SCLR 534.

15.6   INDUSTRIAL TRAINING BOARDS

Industrial Training Boards were established by the Secretary of State for Employment under the *Industrial Training Act 1982* ('*ITA 1982*'), as amended, which repealed and replaced the *Industrial Training Act 1964*, as amended. The Boards' role is to ensure that the quantity and quality of training are adequate to meet the needs of the industries for which they are established, and they may:

(a)   provide or secure the provision of such courses and other facilities (which may include residential accommodation) for the training of those persons as the Board considers adequate, having regard to any alternative courses or facilities available;

(b)   approve alternative courses and facilities;

(c)   publish recommendations regarding the length and nature of courses and standards to be attained in training;

(d)   make tests for ascertaining the standards recommended and award certificates of the attainment of those standards;

(e)   assist persons in finding facilities for being trained for employment in the industry;

(f)   carry out, or assist others to carry out, research into any matter relating to training for employment in the industry; and

(g)   provide advice about training connected with the industry.

(ITA 1982, s 5(1))

An Industrial Training Board may enter into contracts of service or apprenticeship with persons who intend to be employed in the industry and to attend courses or avail themselves of other facilities provided or approved by the Board *(ITA 1982, s 5(2))*.

Industrial Training Boards may provide advice on training. They may also:

(i)   pay maintenance and travelling allowances to persons attending courses provided or approved by the Board;

(ii)   make grants or loans to persons providing courses or other facilities approved by the Board, to persons who make studies for the purpose of providing such courses or facilities, and to persons who maintain arrangements to provide such courses or facilities which are not for the time being in use;

(iii) pay fees to persons providing post-school education in respect of persons who receive it in association with their training in courses provided or approved by the Board; and

(iv)   make payments to persons in connection with arrangements under which they or employees of theirs make use of courses or other facilities provided or approved by the Board.

(ITA 1982, s 5(4))

Forms are available from the relevant Industrial Training Board for the employer to provide the information enabling him to claim such a payment as is mentioned under (iv) above.

An Industrial Training Board, with the approval of the Secretary of State, may require employers in the industry to furnish returns and other information, to keep certain records and to produce them for examination by the Board *(ITA 1982, s 6(1))*. Penalties may be imposed for the infringement of any of these provisions. Penalties also exist for knowingly or recklessly furnishing false records or information.

Two statutory Boards remain: the Construction Industry Training Board ('CITB') and the Engineering Construction Industry Training Board ('ECITB').

Provision is made for the imposition of a levy from time to time on employers in the industry, for the purpose of raising money towards meeting the expenses of each Board *(ITA 1982, s 11)*. A levy is imposed by means of a 'levy order' made by the Secretary of State. The most recent levy orders include the *Industrial Training Levy (Construction Industry Training Board) Order 2018 (SI 2018/432)* (which took effect on 28 March 2018) and *Industrial Training Levy (Engineering Construction Industry Training Board) Order 2017 (SI 2017/485)* (which took effect on 29 March 2017). A claim that the CITB levy was ultra vires and operated unfairly towards the employer was dismissed by Kerr J in *R (Hudson Contract Services Ltd) v Secretary of State for Business Innovation and Skills* [2016] EWHC 844 (Admin), [2016] All ER (D) 116 (Apr). The Court held that the statutory purpose of the scheme was to fund the CITB's expenses, not just to fund courses, and the CITB incurred expenses in broader industry provision which could be recouped. Furthermore, as the statutory scheme did not prescribe any particular method of raising the levy or restrict how it could be raised, the CITB was entitled to raise the levy for payments other than just those made directly for labour.

In *Hudson Contract Services Ltd v Construction Industry Training Board* [2020] EWCA Civ 328, [2020] All ER (D) 72 (Mar) the Court of Appeal held that a company which directly employed, at its head office, only a small workforce, but which provided thousands of self-employed construction workers to employers in the construction industry, was an "employer in the construction industry", and its head office was a "construction establishment, for the purposes of the levy. Simler LJ said (paragraph 55) that there is nothing in the legislation that requires a focus on direct employees only, nor any reason for considering only a directly employed workforce and excluding activities performed by Hudson's self-employed operatives.

The CITB and the ECITB (as well as the non-statutory Film Industry Training Board) were subject to a Government review from 2013 and the final report was published in December 2015. Some changes to the ITBs were recommended but it was stated that final recommendations as to the future of the CITB and ECITB would be made once the future apprenticeship levy arrangements in respect of post-16 apprenticeships were clear. In October 2016, the Minister for Apprenticeships and Skills announced a review of ITBs to determine "whether market failures in construction still require a separate levy and grant system and if so, how this can operate alongside the apprenticeship levy". The review reported on 6 November 2017. No consequential legislative proposals have yet emerged.

15.7   SERVICES FOR SCHOOL-LEAVERS

The *Trade Union Reform and Employment Rights Act 1993* substituted new *ss 8–10A* in the *Employment and Training Act 1973* so as to place a duty on the Secretary of State to secure the provision of careers guidance and placing services ('relevant services') for people attending schools and colleges. The Secretary of State is also given power to arrange for the provision of relevant services for other people, and may direct local authorities to provide (or arrange for the provision of) relevant services. The *1973 Act* requires the providers of relevant services to provide them in accordance with the directions given by the Secretary of State. The Chief Inspector of Education, Children's Services and Skills in England must inspect and report on the provision of services in England in pursuance of *s 8* or *s 9* by any person or institution, when requested to do so by the Secretary of State; he may also undertake other inspections of the provision of those services as he thinks fit. However, any such inspection may not relate to services provided for persons who are over 20 years old (*ETA 1973, s 10B*, inserted by the *Learning and Skills Act 2000* and amended by the *Education Act 2005* and the *Education and Inspections Act 2006*).

15.8   WORK-BASED TRAINING

Work-based training opportunities are currently provided through various types of apprenticeships (currently known as Intermediate, Advanced , Higher and Degree Level Apprenticeships), and other training initiatives, all of which involve working and training with an employer, and studying for other qualifications (usually with a training provider). In the past, apprenticeships were aimed primarily at people aged between 16 and 24, but apprenticeship opportunities for people aged 25 or over were introduced in August 2007.

There is a national minimum wage (NMW) for apprentices. (*National Minimum Wage Regulations 2015 (SI 2015/621), reg 4A*). The wage applies to all apprentices aged under 19 (including those working under an 'approved English apprenticeship agreement' within the meaning of *section A5* of the *Apprenticeships, Skills, Children and Learning Act 2009* (see **15.11** below)), and apprentices aged 19 or over in the first year of their apprenticeship. (Apprentices aged 19 or over who have already spent a year on their apprenticeship must be paid at least the full NMW rate appropriate to their age.) As at 1 April 2018, the apprentice minimum wage is £3.70 per hour and applies to time working, plus time spent training that is part of the apprenticeship. If an apprentice is on a higher wage, the employer must continue to pay that amount for the remainder of the training or until the apprentice becomes eligible for the full NMW. (See **34.9 PAY – I.**)

For further information regarding apprenticeships, see https://www.gov.uk/apprenticeships-guide.

For the purposes of health and safety legislation, trainees are treated as the employees of the person whose undertaking is providing training (*Health and Safety (Training for Employment) Regulations 1990 (SI 1990/1380)*). For the application of discrimination laws see Discrimination and Equal Opportunities – I (12), II (13), and (14); an 'Equal Opportunities Toolkit' has also been produced for use in conjunction with training for young people.

15.9   SKILLS TRAINING

As from April 2017, the Education and Skills Funding Agency is responsible for funding and regulating adult skills training in England; for further information, see https://www.gov.uk/government/organisations/education-and-skills-funding-agency. As from 3 April 2017, the Institute for Apprenticeships was launched Its aims include ensuring high-quality apprenticeship standards and advising government on funding for each standard. The Institute of Apprenticeships is an executive non-departmental public body sponsored by the Department for Education. In Wales, the regulation and funding of adult skills training is the responsibility of the Welsh Assembly Government; for further information, see gov.wales/topics/educationandskills/?lang=en. In Scotland, since 2008 these functions are the responsibility of Skills Development Scotland; for further details, see www.skillsdevelopmentscotland.co.uk/our-services/services-for-individuals.aspx.

Another relevant service is *learndirect*, which provides courses (mainly on-line) and information through its network of learning centres; for further information, see www.learndirect.com. See also the Government website, which provides information and advice to adults who wish to earn new skills, gain new qualifications, or retrain; further information can be found on www.gov.uk/browse/working/finding-job.

15.10 Study and training

Section 40 of the *ASLCA 2009* inserted new *sections 63D* to *63K* (*Part VIA*) into the *ERA 1996*. These provisions came into force on 6 April 2010 (except in relation to small employers and their employees) (See *SI 2010/303, Sch 3*). A 'small employer' means an employer who employs fewer than 250 employees (for the detailed definition, see *SI 2010/303, Sch 3, col 2*). Originally, *SI 2010/303* stated that these provisions would come into force on 6 April 2011 in relation to small employers and their employees, but this was revoked by the *Apprenticeships, Skills, Children and Learning Act 2009 (Commencement No 2 and Transitional and Saving Provisions) Order 2010 (Amendment) Order 2011 (SI 2011/882)*.

15.11 *Statutory right to make request in relation to study or training*

A 'qualifying employee' (ie an employee who is not excluded by *section 63D(7)* (see below), and who has been continuously employed for a period of not less than 26 weeks: *Employee Study and Training (Qualifying Period of Employment) Regulations 2010 (SI 2010/800)*) may make an application under *section 63D* to his or her employer (*ERA 1996, s 63D(1)*). The application must state that it is an application under *section 63D* (*ERA 1996, s 63D(5)*), and must be made for the purpose of enabling the employee to undertake study or training (or both) within *section 63D(4)*, ie where its purpose is to improve:

(a)   the employee's effectiveness in the employer's business; and

(b)   the performance of the employer's business.

The following persons are excluded by *section 63D(7)*:

(i)   a person of compulsory school age (or, in Scotland, school age);

(ii)   a person to whom *Part 1* of the *Education and Skills Act 2008* (duty to participate in education or training for 16 and 17 year olds) applies;

(iii)   a person who, by virtue of *section 29* of that *Act*, is treated as a person to whom that *Part* applies for the purposes specified in that section (extension for person reaching 18);

(iv)   a person to whom *section 63A* of the *ERA 1996* (right to time off for young person for study or training — see **4.7** CHILDREN AND YOUNG PERSONS) applies;

(v)   an agency worker; or

(vi)   a person of a description specified by the Secretary of State in regulations.

Nothing in *ERA 1996, Part VIA* prevents an employee and an employer from making any other arrangements in relation to study or training (*ERA 1996, s 63D(8)*).

15.12 SECTION 63D APPLICATION: SUPPLEMENTARY PROVISIONS

A *section 63D* application may (a) be made in relation to study or training of any description (subject to what is stated below); (b) relate to more than one description of study or training (*ERA 1996, s 63E(1)*).

In particular, the study or training need not be intended to lead to the award of a qualification to the employee (*ERA 1996, s 63E(3)*), and may be such that it would:

(i)   be undertaken on the employer's premises or elsewhere (including at the employee's home);

(ii)   be undertaken by the employee while performing the duties of the employee's employment or separately;

(iii)   be provided or supervised by the employer or by someone else;

(iv)   be undertaken without supervision;

(v)   be undertaken within or outside the United Kingdom.

(*ERA 1996, s 63E(2)*)

A *section 63D* application must give the following details of the proposed study or training (*ERA 1996, s 63E(4)(a)*):

(A)   its subject matter;

(B)   where and when it would take place;

(C)   who would provide or supervise it;

(D)   what qualification (if any) it would lead to.

The application must also explain how the employee thinks the proposed study or training would improve (i) the employee's effectiveness in the employer's business, and (ii) the performance of the employer's business (*ERA 1996, s 63E(4)(b)*).

For detailed requirements as to the form of the application, and the information it must contain, see the *Employee Study and Training (Eligibility, Complaints and Remedies) Regulations 2010 (SI 2010/156)*.

15.13 EMPLOYER'S DUTIES IN RELATION TO SECTION 63D APPLICATION

Where an employer receives a *section 63D* application from an employee, and the employer has not received such an application from the employee within the previous 12 months, he must deal with the application in accordance with regulations made by the Secretary of State (*ERA 1996, s 63F(4)*). The employer may refuse the application (or, as the case may be, part of the application) only if he thinks that one or more of the permissible grounds for refusal applies in relation to the application (or, as the case may be, that part) (*ERA 1996, s 63F(1), (5), (6)*). The permissible grounds for refusal are:

(a)   that the proposed study or training to which the application, or the part in question, relates would not improve (i) the employee's effectiveness in the employer's business, or (ii) the performance of the employer's business;

(b)   the burden of additional costs;

(c)   detrimental effect on ability to meet customer demand;

(d)   inability to re-organise work among existing staff;

(e)   inability to recruit additional staff;

(f)   detrimental impact on quality;

(g)   detrimental impact on performance;

(h)   insufficiency of work during the periods the employee proposes to work;

(i)   planned structural changes;

(j)   any other grounds specified by the Secretary of State in regulations.

(*ERA 1996, s 63F(7)*)

For the detailed requirements imposed on the employer on receiving a *section 63D* application (including a requirement to hold a meeting with the employee within 28 days of receiving the application), see the *Employee Study and Training (Procedural Requirements) Regulations 2010 (SI 2010/155)*.

15.14 EMPLOYEE'S DUTIES IN RELATION TO AGREED STUDY OR TRAINING

Where an employer has agreed to a *section 63D* application (or part of one) made by an employee in relation to particular study or training, the employee must inform the employer if he (a) fails to start or complete the agreed study or training, or (b) undertakes, or proposes to undertake, study or training that differs from the agreed study or training in any respect (including those specified in *section 63E(4)(a)* — see **15.14** above) (*ERA 1996, s 63H*). For the requirements as to the way in which the employee is to comply with this duty, see the *Employee Study and Training (Procedural Requirements) Regulations 2010 (SI 2010/155), reg 20*.

15.15 COMPLAINT TO EMPLOYMENT TRIBUNAL

An employee who makes a *section 63D* application may present a complaint to an employment tribunal that:

(a)   the employer has failed to comply with *section 63F(4), (5)* or *(6)* (see **15.15** above), or

(b)   the employer's decision to refuse the application, or part of it, is based on incorrect facts.

15.15   Education and Training

(ERA 1996, s 63I(1))

No such complaint may be made in respect of an application which has been disposed of by agreement or withdrawn *(ERA 1996, s 63I(2))*. Where an application that has not been disposed of by agreement or withdrawn, a complaint under *section 63I* may only be made if the employer:

(i)   notifies the employee of a decision to refuse the application (or part of it) on appeal; or

(ii)   commits a breach of certain requirements set out in *SI 2010/155*, namely the failure to hold a meeting or a failure to notify a decision *(ERA 1996, s 63I(3);* *Employee Study and Training (Eligibility, Complaints and Remedies) Regulations 2010 (SI 2010/156), reg 5)*.

An employee also has a right to complain to an employment tribunal that the employer has failed, or threatened to fail, to comply with *reg 16(2), (3)*, or *(5)* of *SI 2010/155* (right of employee to be accompanied by companion at meeting to consider *s 63D* application; right of companion to address meeting or confer with employee; right of employee to have meeting postponed if companion unavailable) *(Employee Study and Training (Procedural Requirements) Regulations 2010 (SI 2010/155), reg 17)*.

An employment tribunal may not consider a complaint under *s 63I* unless the complaint is presented:

(A)   before the end of the period of three months beginning with the relevant date; or

(B)   within any further period that the tribunal considers reasonable, if the tribunal is satisfied that it was not reasonably practicable for the complaint to be presented before the end of that period of three months.

(ERA 1996, s 63I(5)). The new extension of time limits to facilitate conciliation before presenting a complaint apply to *ERA 1996, s 63I(5)* as of 6 April 2014 *(ERA 1996, s 63I(7))*.

The relevant date is the date on which the employee is notified of the decision on the appeal or (as the case may be) the date on which the breach was committed *(ERA 1996, s 63I(6))*.

15.16 REMEDIES

If an employment tribunal finds a complaint under *s 63I* well-founded it must make a declaration to that effect and may (a) make an order for reconsideration of the *s 63D* application; (b) make an award of compensation to be paid by the employer to the employee *(ERA 1996, s 63J(1))*.

The amount of any compensation must be the amount the tribunal considers just and equitable in all the circumstances, but must not exceed the permitted maximum of 8 weeks' pay *(ERA 1996, s 63J(2), (3); Employee Study and Training (Eligibility, Complaints and Remedies) Regulations 2010 (SI 2010/156), reg 6)*.

If an employment tribunal makes an order for reconsideration of the *s 63D* application, *s 63F* (see **15.15** above) and regulations under that section (ie *SI 2010/155*) apply as if the application had been received on the date of the order (instead of on the date it was actually received) *(ERA 1996, s 63J(4))*.

15.17   RIGHT NOT TO SUFFER DETRIMENT, AND RIGHT NOT TO BE UNFAIRLY DISMISSED

Detriment. An employee has the right not to be subjected to any detriment (ie an action short of dismissal) by any act, or any deliberate failure to act, by the employee's employer done on the ground that the employee:

(a)   made (or proposed to make) a *s 63D* application;

(b)   exercised (or proposed to exercise) a right conferred on the employee under *section 63F*;

(c)   brought proceedings against the employer under *s 63I*; or

(d)   alleged the existence of any circumstance which would constitute a ground for bringing such proceedings.

(ERA 1996, s 47F(1), inserted by the *Apprenticeships, Skills, Children and Learning Act 2009, s 40(1), (3))*

Unfair dismissal. An employee who is dismissed is to be regarded for the purposes of *Part X* of the *ERA 1996* as unfairly dismissed if the reason (or, if more than one, the principal reason) for the dismissal is that the employee took (or proposed to take) any of the actions specified in (a) to (d) under *Detriment* above.

(ERA 1996, s 104E, inserted by the *Apprenticeships, Skills, Children and Learning Act 2009, s 40(1), (4))*

16 Employee, Self-Employed or Worker?

Cross-reference. See also CONTRACT OF EMPLOYMENT (8), TEMPORARY AND SEASONAL EMPLOYEES 48.2, PUBLIC SECTOR EMPLOYEES (38).

16.1 INTRODUCTION

This chapter examines the distinction between who is an employee and who is self-employed, and considers the intermediate position of 'workers'.

It is important for many purposes to determine whether a person is an employee or not, and if not, whether they are a worker. The legal rights enjoyed by employees differ in many ways from the rights enjoyed by those who are not employees. For example, it is only employees who are entitled to bring claims of unfair dismissal, to recover redundancy payments and only employees transfer under TUPE. Workers may, in particular, bring discrimination claims under the *Equality Act 2010*, they have rights to paid holiday under the *Working Time Regulations 1998*, and they are entitled to be paid the minimum wage. Self-employed persons enjoy none of those rights. There are also consequences for 'employers' of having employees which relate to vicarious liability, the requirement for employers liability insurance, statutory duties as to health and safety, and data protection issues under the GDPR.

Different treatment by the tax authorities is another important distinction. An employee's earnings are liable to tax under *Schedule E* to the *Income and Corporation Taxes Act 1988*, and tax is deducted under the PAYE system, whereas a self-employed person is liable to tax under *Schedule D*. HMRC publishes a leaflet ES/FS1 'Employed or self-employed for tax and National Insurance contributions'.

The question of whether a person is an employee or self-employed is determined by reference to the contract under which he works – is it a contract of employment or a contract 'for services'? The unhelpfully fine distinction is often made between a contract "of service" (i.e. a contract of employment) and a contract "for services" (i.e. self-employment). The terms 'contract of service' and 'contract of employment' are identical in meaning. The former is the more archaic (and outdated) term that was used when the parties to the contract were known as 'master' and 'servant'.

As to the 'workers' category, the provisions of the *Employment Rights Act 1996* ('*ERA*') prohibiting unlawful deductions from wages apply to 'workers', who are defined in *section 230* to include those employed under a contract of service but also any contract:

> 'whereby the individual undertakes to do or perform personally any work or services for another party to the contracts whose status is not by virtue of the contract that of a client or customer of any profession or business undertaking carried on by the individual'.

The provisions of *ERA* dealing with protected disclosures apply to 'workers', as so defined. There is also an extended definition of worker in *section 43K*. As indicated above, the *National Minimum Wage Act 1998* and the *Working Time Regulations 1998* applies to workers.

The *Equality Act 2010* defines 'employment' in *section 83(2)(a)* as meaning "employment under a contract of employment, a contract of apprenticeship or a contract personally to do work". The definition is identical in legal terms to the definition of 'worker'. Consequently, often (and potentially confusingly) one may refer to 'workers' for the purposes of the *Equality Act 2010*, when in legal terms one means the expanded definition of 'employment' for the purposes of that Act.

16.1 Employee, Self-Employed or Worker?

This chapter will first consider the legal definition of employee before dealing with the concept of a 'worker'.

16.2 'Good work'

In response to the various high-profile 'gig economy' cases proceeding through the courts, the government commissioned Matthew Taylor to produce what became his report entitled 'Good work: the Taylor review of modern working practices' (July 2017) (the **"Taylor Review"**). On 7 February 2018, the government published its final response to the report. On 17 December 2018, the government published its policy paper entitled 'Good Work Plan', setting out its 'vision for the future of the UK labour market'.

The Taylor Review made a variety of recommendations concerning employment status, enforcement, tax status, zero hours contracts, holiday pay, statutory sick pay and other matters. The government's response made clear a number of changes would be made immediately, but that many more required consultation. Subsequently, four consultations were launched and completed in 2018 on: employment status, agency workers, enforcement of employment rights, and transparency in the labour market.

The legislative changes already brought into effect include:

- The *Employment Rights (Employment Particulars and Paid Annual Leave) (Amendment) Regulations 2018 (SI 2018/1378)*, which makes a the right to a written statement of particulars of employment a 'day 1' right and changes the reference period for the calculation of holiday from 12 weeks to 52 weeks under the *Working Time Regulations*.

- The *Agency Workers (Amendment) Regulations 2019*, which repeals the little-used 'Swedish derogation' and the *Conduct of Employment Agencies and Employment Businesses (Amendment) Regulations 2019 (SI 2019/725)* which require agencies to provide key information regarding positions to workers.

- The *Employment Rights (Miscellaneous Amendments) Regulations 2019*, discussed below, which extend the right to a written statement of particulars to all workers (not just employees), and increase the financial penalty for an 'aggravated' breach of employment law from £5,000 to £20,000.

The government has also committed to making various other changes, including:

- Extending the period required for a break of service for the purpose of calculating continuous service from one week to four weeks;

- Legislating for a right to request a more predictable and stable contract for those on zero-hours contracts and other flexible contracts;

- Repeal legislation that allows agency workers to opt out of equal pay legislation;

- Creating a state enforcement system for holiday pay; and,

- Making enforcement of ET awards easier, including naming and shaming employers who do not pay.

Additionally, *EU Directive 2019/1152* of 20 June 2019 proposes measures including a right to request more predictable and secure working conditions after six months, and to receive a reasoned reply within one month. However, as member states will have until 1 August 2022 to implement into national law, and this date falls after the Brexit transition period, it remains to be seen whether transposition into UK law will be required.

DISTINGUISHING A CONTRACT OF EMPLOYMENT FROM A CONTRACT FOR SERVICES

16.3 Introduction

The question of who is an employee is not straightforward. The starting point is to establish whether there is a contract at all between the alleged employer and alleged employee. There are contexts in which the analysis of precisely what, if any, contracts exist between the parties will require careful consideration. For example, when a person works for another through an employment agency, there will usually be two contracts: (i) between the agency and the worker on the one hand; and (ii) between the agency and the agency's client (the business for which the worker actually carries out his work) on the other. There will not ordinarily be an express contract between the worker and the end client. In the absence of a contract between worker and client, the worker cannot be an employee of the client: *Hewlett Packard Ltd v O'Murphy* [2002] IRLR 4. The effect of this is that the worker has no employment protection rights as against the end client for which he actually works. This has been recognised in a number of cases to be unsatisfactory. However, it has also been held that even if there is no express contract between the worker and the end client of the agency, in certain circumstances it may be possible to imply a contract between those parties through their conduct. See further below under the heading 'Employment agencies'.

Once the existence of a contract is established, the next question is whether the contract is a contract of employment or a contract for services (or indeed of some other sort). There are three essential elements that must be present to establish a contract of employment. These form the irreducible core of the contract of employment, without which a contract of employment will not arise:

(a)   the contract must impose an obligation on a person to provide work personally;

(b)   there must be mutuality of obligation between employer and employee; and

(c)   the worker must expressly or impliedly agree to be subject to the control of the person for whom he works to a 'sufficient' degree.

If any of these three elements is not present, the contract is not a contract of employment. If each element is present, the contract *may* be a contract of employment. Whether or not it is will depend on an assessment of all of the other circumstances of the case.

16.4 (a) Obligation to provide work personally

Dealing with those elements which must be present in order for a contract to be a contract of employment, the first element – that the person must be obliged to provide work personally – was made clear in *Express and Echo Publications Ltd v Tanton* [1999] IRLR 367. In that case, the contract provided that if the worker was unable or unwilling to do the work personally, he had to provide a substitute. The Court of Appeal held that the power to send a substitute meant that this could not be a contract of employment. The irreducible minimum of a contract of employment was an obligation on the worker to provide his services personally. The obligation to undertake work personally does not cease to exist where there is a power to send a substitute only where the worker is *unable* to do the work: *James v Redcats (Brands) Ltd* [2007] IRLR 296. The key point about *Tanton* was that the worker could send a substitute if he did not want to do the work as well as if he could not. Where the employee must do the work personally if he is able, then the requirement of personal obligation is satisfied.

However, where a contract contains a limited power to delegate, such power does not lead inescapably to the conclusion that the contract is not a contract of employment: *MacFarlane v Glasgow City Council* [2001] IRLR 7. According to the EAT in *MacFarlane*, the clause in

Tanton allowing the worker to send a replacement was 'extreme'. The worker in *Tanton* was not under any personal obligation ever to attend work. He was always entitled to send a substitute. In *Macfarlane*, the worker was entitled to send a replacement only in the event that he was unable to attend work. Therefore, the clause was of far more limited effect, and was not sufficient of itself to justify the conclusion that the contract was not a contract of employment (see also *Community Dental Centres Ltd v Sultan-Darmon* [2010] IRLR 1024).

In *Staffordshire Sentinel Newspapers Ltd v Potter* [2004] IRLR 752, the EAT provided guidance on the application of *Tanton* and *MacFarlane*. If there is a clear express contractual term that does not impose personal obligations on the individual, effect must be given to that term unless it is a sham or there has, on the facts, been a variation of the contract. In that case what happened in practice is not relevant. Where there is no clear express term, it is necessary to consider both the written terms of the contract and what happened in practice in order to determine what was the true agreement between the parties.

In considering 'delegation' and 'obligations' clauses in contracts of employment alleged to be a sham, the Court of Appeal in *Consistent Group Ltd v Kalwak* [2008] EWCA Civ 430, [2008] IRLR 505 held that a decision that the contract is in part a sham required a finding that both parties intended to paint a false picture as to the true nature of their respective obligations. However, the EAT held in *Redrow Homes (Yorkshire) Ltd v Buckborough & Sewell* [2009] IRLR 34 that a contractual term may be considered a sham not only where the parties intend to deceive a third party but also where the parties simply do not intend for the term to apply. The Court of Appeal looked at sham obligations again in *Protectacoat Firthglow Ltd v Szilagyi* [2009] EWCA Civ 98, [2009] IRLR 365 and decided that, in order for a court or tribunal to find that an agreement is a sham, there is no need for it to find that the parties intended to deceive a third party. If it is asserted that the document does not describe the true relationship between the parties, it is for the court to decide what the true relationship is. Smith LJ held that when determining the true legal relationship, the preferable approach is to ask whether or not the words of the written contract represent the true intentions or expectations of the parties, not only at the inception of the contract but, if appropriate, as time goes by.

In *Autoclenz Ltd v Belcher* [2011] UKSC 41, [2011] ICR 1157, [2011] IRLR 820, the Supreme Court confirmed that in the employment context the Court will look to the reality of the arrangements between the parties, as opposed to concentrating on the written terms of any agreement, in determining the true nature of the relationship. This meant that a written term purporting to permit the use of a substitute did not preclude the conclusion that a contract of employment existed when in practice the right was not exercised. In *Pulse Healthcare Ltd v Carewatch Care Services Ltd* [2012] All ER (D) 113 (Aug) (EAT 0123/12), the EAT held that written terms recording a 'zero hour' agreement with no mutuality of obligation did not reflect the true reality of the agreement between the parties. The claimants were carers providing critical care around the clock on a shift system to a particular patient. The EAT held that in the circumstances it was 'unrealistic' to suggest that no contract of employment arose.

16.5   (b) Mutuality of obligation

The second requirement – that there be a mutuality of obligations – means that for the entire duration of the contract under consideration, both the employer and the employee must be under legal obligations to one another. Of course, without the presence of an obligation towards another party, there would not be a contract at all. Thus, the requirement for mutual obligations is relevant to the question whether there is a contract at all: *Stephenson v Delphi Diesel Systems Ltd* [2003] ICR 471, [2003] All ER (D) 84 (Mar); *Cotswold Developments Construction Ltd v Williams* [2006] IRLR 181. In the ordinary case, the obligations in question will be an obligation on the employee to work and an obligation on the employer to pay for that work. It may not be necessary in every case for there to be obligations to work and to provide work. It may be sufficient if there is an obligation on the employee to accept and do such work as is offered to him and on the employer to pay the employee for the work that is done and, if there are periods when there is no work for the employee to do, to pay a retainer. In the absence of such a retainer in periods where there is no work to be done, there will be no contract of employment between the parties. The clearest exposition of this principle is to be found in *Clark v Oxfordshire Health Authority* [1998] IRLR 125. However, see also *O'Kelly v Trusthouse Forte* [1984] QB 90, [1983] 3 All ER 456, [1983] IRLR 369, [1983] ICR 728, *Nethermere (St Neots) v Gardiner* [1984] IRLR 240 and *Hellyer Bros Ltd v McLeod* [1987] 1 WLR 728, [1987] IRLR 232, CA. In *St Ives Plymouth Ltd v Haggerty* [2008] All ER (D) 317 (May) (Elias P) the EAT accepted, following *Nethermere* and *Airfix Footwear Ltd v Cope* [1978] IRLR 396, [1978] ICR 1210, that there may exceptionally be circumstances where the pattern of work is such that it may be possible to infer an obligation to work simply from the continual repetition of work being offered and accepted. Notably, the Court of Appeal has held that an absence of agreement as to pay for work done is not fatal to the existence of a contract of employment. Where there was an agreement that the individual would work for the company and had in fact done so the Court could imply a term for remuneration: *Stack v Ajar-Tec* [2015] EWCA Civ 46, [2015] IRLR 474.

In *Quashie v Stringfellow Restaurants Limited* [2012] EWCA Civ 1735, [2013] IRLR 99, the Court of Appeal affirmed that in the absence of any obligation on the employer to pay the worker for services provided there was no contract of employment. The claimant lap dancer was remunerated by the fees paid by visitors to the club and was therefore not an employee of the club itself.

The House of Lords has reiterated that the existence of mutual obligations between the parties is the irreducible minimum of a contract of employment (*Carmichael v National Power plc* [2000] IRLR 43). Hence, in a case where workers were engaged as power station guides on a 'casual as required' basis, there was no contract of employment. There was no obligation on the workers to work. Indeed, they had failed to attend on a number of occasions and had not been disciplined. Further, there was no obligation on the company to provide work.

Where the terms of a contract expressly negate mutuality of obligations, there cannot be a contract of employment: *Stevedoring and Haulage Services Ltd v Fuller* [2001] EWCA Civ 651, [2001] IRLR 627. In that case, the worker worked under a series of individual contracts, each of which recorded that there was no obligation to offer or accept any further contract. In those circumstances, it was impermissible to imply an over-arching or umbrella contract of employment pursuant to which each individual contract was issued.

In *Commissioners for HMRC v Professional Game Match Officials Ltd* [2020] UKUT 0147 (TCC), the Upper Tribunal (Tax and Chancery) determined an appeal by HMRC against a determination that referees engaged to officiate football matches (primarily in Leagues 1 and 2 but also in higher echelons in some circumstances). The case primarily turned on the question of mutuality of obligation in respect of an over-arching contract and individual contracts in respect of particular games. The parties were not obliged to offer nor accept work, and a referee could withdraw from an engagement post-acceptance without sanction. The Upper Tribunal found there was insufficient mutuality of obligation (and also of control) to find the existence of an employment contract either on an over-arching or individual contract basis.

16.6   (c) Sufficient degree of control

The third element – that the employer must have a sufficient degree of control over the employee – does not mean that work must necessarily be carried out under the employer's actual supervision or control. In a more general sense, it requires that ultimate authority over the employee in the performance of his work resides in the employer, so that the employee is subject to the latter's orders and directions.

The necessity of control derives from the judgment of McKenna J in *Ready Mixed Concrete (South East) Ltd v Minister of Pensions and National Insurance* [1968] 1 All ER 433 at 514. McKenna J's remarks on control have been cited with approval in the majority of subsequent important cases dealing with the essential ingredients of an employment contract. The Court of Appeal has re-affirmed that in the absence of sufficient control, there cannot be a contract of employment. What constitutes sufficient control – and whether that means the imposition of a framework within which a person works or direct supervision of the performance of a person's functions – will vary from case to case. But control is a necessary condition of a contract of employment: *Johnson Underwood Ltd v Montgomery* [2001] EWCA Civ 318, [2001] IRLR 269. Once there is mutuality of obligation such that there is a contract, control is relevant for deciding whether the contract is a contract of employment: *Stephenson v Delphi Systems Ltd* [2003] ICR 471, [2003] All ER (D) 84 (Mar). The Court of Appeal has emphasised that what is required is the 'ultimate' ability of the employer to control the manner in which work is carried out; it is not necessary that the employee is subject to detailed factual control on a day-to-day basis: *Troutbeck SA v White* [2013] EWCA Civ 1171, [2013] IRLR 949 (and see also *Catholic Child Welfare Society and Ors v Various Claimants* [2013] IRLR 219).

If the contract does not impose an obligation to provide services personally or if there is no mutuality of obligation throughout the period under consideration, or if there is no control present, then the contract in question cannot be a contract of employment. If all these elements are present, the contract *may* be one of employment. It will then be necessary to consider the surrounding circumstances to determine the nature of the relationship.

16.7   (d) the overall picture

In order to determine, once the irreducible minimum requirements are present, whether the contract is a contract of employment, it is necessary to paint a picture from the accumulation of relevant details. This means not only looking at specific matters, but also standing back and considering the overall picture. This approach derives from *Hall (Inspector of Taxes) v Lorimer* [1994] 1 All ER 250, [1994] IRLR 171, [1994] ICR 218. The matters that are capable of being relevant are too numerous to list in full. However, they might include payment by wages or salary; whether the worker provides his own equipment; whether he is subject to the employer's disciplinary and grievance procedures; receipt of sick pay or contractual holiday pay; provision of benefits traditionally associated with employment such as a pension scheme, health care or other benefits; whether the worker is a part of the employer's business; whether there are restrictions on working for others.

Some cases have focused on factors that distinguish an employee from a person in business on his own account. The sorts of details that may be relevant include whether (or how far) he:

(a)   is employed as part of the business of the employer and his work is done as an integral part of that business;

(b)   provides his own equipment;

(c)   hires his own helpers;

(d)   takes a degree of financial risk;

(e)   has responsibility for investment and management; and

(f)   has the opportunity of profiting from sound management in performing his task.

This list is derived from *Market Investigations Ltd v Minister of Social Security* [1968] 3 All ER 732, *per* Cooke J at 185. In *Lee Ting Sang v Chung Chi-Keung* [1990] 2 AC 374, [1990] IRLR 236, [1990] ICR 409, the Privy Council said that the best expression of the test was that stated in the *Market Investigations* case: is the person concerned in business on his own account? This test was again applied in *Andrews v King (Inspector of Taxes)* [1991] STC 481, [1991] ICR 846, where the Vice-Chancellor went on to say that the essence of business was that it was carried on with a view to profit (whereas it was not open to the employee there to make an increased profit from the way in which he carried out his tasks). The importance of this criterion has recently been emphasised by the Court of Appeal in *Quashie v Stringfellow Restaurants Limited* [2012] EWCA Civ 1735, [2013] IRLR 99. However, it is not a matter of running through these indicia as if they were an all-purpose checklist. Part of the function of painting the picture is to determine what are the significant details in the instant case and to look at the whole arrangement. Thus, in *Hall (Inspector of Taxes) v Lorimer* [1994] 1 All ER 250, [1994] ICR 218, a vision mixer who supplied no tools, equipment or money to his business and did not hire staff was still self-employed. The key factor was that he was a professional person who worked for a variety of people for short periods and was not dependent on any one paymaster (see also *Suhail v Barking Havering and Redbridge NHS Trust* [2015] All ER (D) 211 (Jul) (UKEAT 0536/13), where a similar analysis was applied to a locum working in the NHS). In *Pimlico Plumbers Ltd v Smith* [2014] All ER (D) 88 (Dec) (UKEAT 0495/12) the EAT held that a plumber was not an employee, a key point being that he assumed the financial risk of non-payment by customers (a case that was subsequently litigated to the Supreme Court on the different issue of whether Mr Smith was a 'worker').

It has been observed that one cannot safely rely on a simple dichotomy between the employed and those on business on their own account. There are categories of person who are not in business on their own account but who are not, for that reason alone, necessarily to be regarded as employees. In particular, many statutory provisions either contain a wider definition of employee than that which is used in the common law (for example, the discrimination legislation) or extend protection to a category of persons called 'workers' who are not employed but are not in business on their own account either: see *James v Redcats (Brands) Ltd* [2007] IRLR 296.

As a general rule, the greater the degree of personal responsibility an individual undertakes in any of the matters set out above, the more likely he is to be considered an independent contractor rather than an employee.

The way in which a person is treated for tax may be relevant but is not decisive. The tax and employment regimes are separate and do not necessarily have to give the same answer as to a person's status.

In assessing all of these factors, it is legitimate in a case where the contract is said to be based partly on oral exchanges and on conduct to consider evidence of the way in which the parties understood their relationship and the way in which they conducted themselves in practice (see *Carmichael v National Power plc* [2000] IRLR 43 and *Autoclenz* [2011] IRLR 820). However, the conduct of the parties cannot be relied upon for the purpose of implying a term that flatly contradicts an express term: *Stevedoring and Haulage Services Ltd*. In *Stevedoring and Haulage Services* [2001] IRLR 627, workers were engaged on terms that specifically negated mutuality of obligation in that they made it clear that there was no obligation to offer or accept employment beyond the individual engagement that was the subject of the contract. The conduct of the parties (which remained the same throughout several renewals of the contract) could not override those express written terms by creating mutual obligations to offer and to accept work outside the individual engagement. See also

Braine and ors v National Gallery (2019, ET Case 2201625/2018), in which the ET took into account the fact that the arrangements for the treatment of 'freelance educators' (who gave talks and lectures) were different from those of the National Gallery's salaried staff, as regards the application of policies and benefits such as pensions and sick pay. Whilst the individuals were 'workers', they were not employees.

Where the nature of the relationship between the parties is in doubt or is ambiguous, it is open to the parties, by agreement, to stipulate what the legal situation between them is to be (*Massey v Crown Life Insurance Co Ltd* [1978] 2 All ER 576, [1978] IRLR 31, [1978] ICR 590). However, all the circumstances of the relationship must be considered, and the courts will look behind the parties' intentions, and labels, to ascertain the true nature of the agreement (*Young & Woods Ltd v West* [1980] IRLR 201). Where a person worked for an employment agency and the tribunal found that there were mutual obligations and considerable control, it was incorrect to decide that there was no contract of employment on the basis that this is what the parties had originally intended. The label applied by the parties would only be decisive where all the other factors were evenly balanced: *Dacas v Brook Street Bureau (UK) Ltd* [2004] IRLR 358.

It is wrong to say that a person is an employee simply because he is not self-employed. There may also be intermediate categories of worker (*Dacas v Brook Street*). But to enjoy the statutory rights that apply only to employees (eg to claim unfair dismissal), the person must be an employee.

Note also that a full-time working director of his family firm (who drew fees rather than being paid a salary) was held to be self-employed (*Parsons v Albert J Parsons & Sons Ltd* [1979] IRLR 117, [1979] ICR 271), as were musicians with a London orchestra (*Winfield v London Philharmonic Orchestra Ltd* [1979] ICR 726) and a sub-postmaster (*Hitchcock v Post Office* [1980] ICR 100, *Wolstenholme v Post Office Ltd* [2003] IRLR 199, [2003] ICR 546). A police cadet was held not to be an employee or an apprentice (*Wiltshire Police Authority v Wynn* [1981] QB 95, [1980] 3 WLR 445, 79 LGR 591, [1980] ICR 649). A Presbyterian minister was held not to be an employee, as was a Sikh priest (*Davies v Presbyterian Church of Wales* [1986] 1 All ER 705, [1986] IRLR 194, [1986] ICR 280; *Singh v Guru Nanak Gurdwara* [1990] ICR 309, CA). But in *Percy v Board of National Mission of the Church of Scotland* [2005] UKHL 73, [2006] IRLR 195, [2006] ICR 134 a minister of the Church of Scotland was held to be employed within the wider definition of that term in the *Sex Discrimination Act* (see also *New Testament Church of God v Stewart* [2008] IRLR 134). There is no rule of law that a person who provides services via a company cannot be an employee (*Catamaran Cruisers Ltd v Williams* [1994] IRLR 386). It has been held that a volunteer is not an employee because of the absence of consideration moving from the recipient of the volunteer's services. There is no obligation on that party to make payment and, in the absence of payment, there is no consideration and no contract: *Melhuish v Redbridge Citizens' Advice Bureau* [2005] IRLR 419, EAT. It is necessary to consider the purpose of a contract in order to decide whether it is a contract of employment. Thus an arrangement by which a prisoner undertook work as part of his rehabilitation was not a contract of employment because that was not its purpose: *M&P Steelcraft Ltd v Ellis* [2008] IRLR 355, [2008] ICR 578.

The Court of Appeal considered the status of a modern apprenticeship agreement between a trainee, an employer and a Training and Enterprise Council or some other educational establishment in *Flett v Matheson* [2006] EWCA Civ 53, [2006] IRLR 277, [2006] ICR 673. The Court of Appeal overturned the EAT's decision that such an arrangement created a contract of employment between the individual and the employer. The Court held that the purpose of the arrangement was to provide practical aspects of training. The apprentice was to be released from work to attend academic training. The Court approved the distinction which had been drawn between an employment contract and a contract for apprenticeship in *Whitely v Marton Electrical Ltd* [2003] IRLR 197, [2003] ICR 495. In the event, the Court in *Flett* remitted the matter for the Tribunal to make further findings of fact.

A general practitioner is not employed by a health authority. GPs are under obligations in relation to the nature of the work they undertake. But since these obligations are imposed by statutory instrument and not by contract, those obligations do not make the GP an employee of the health authority: *David-John v North Essex Health Authority* [2004] ICR 112, [2003] All ER (D) 84 (Aug), EAT.

Equity partners are generally not employees. However, there are many different forms of partnership arrangements where individuals are not traditional equity partners. The *Partnership Act 1890, s 2(3)* provides that receiving a share of the profits is prima facie evidence of a partnership. But, there is old authority that suggests where an individual receives a salary as well as a share in the profits, there is strong evidence that he is an employee, not a partner (*Ross v Parkyns* (1875) LR 20 Eq 331). It is necessary to consider all the circumstances to determine whether or not an individual is an employee. In *Stekel v Ellice* [1973] 1 All ER 465 Megarry J considered that under a partnership agreement a salaried partner on a fixed salary, not dependent on profits, could still be a true partner at least if he was entitled to a share in the profits on a winding-up. There is no requirement for an individual to have a minimum share of profits or involvement in management decisions before they can be regarded as a partner. The fact that an individual has the rights and duties of a partner and an entitlement to a residue of the firm if wound up can be sufficient (see *Tiffin v Lester Aldridge LLP* [2011] IRLR 105). In *Kovats v TFO Management LLP* [2009] ICR 1140, [2009] All ER (D) 116 (May) the EAT examined *section 4(4)* of the *Limited Liability Partnerships Act 2000* which provides that a member of a limited liability partnership shall not be regarded for any purpose as employed by the limited liability partnership unless, if he and the other members were partners in a partnership, he would be regarded for that purpose as employed by the partnership. Judge Birtles held that "any purpose" includes *section 230* of *ERA 1996* and therefore the same test applied for partners in an LLP as in the case of traditional partnerships. See the section below on workers as to whether an equity partner can be a worker.

There may be contracts that are neither contracts of employment nor contracts for services but which fall into an intermediate category (*Construction Industry Training Board v Labour Force Ltd* [1970] 3 All ER 220; *Ironmonger v Movefield Ltd (t/a Deering Appointments)* [1988] IRLR 461, EAT). It is thought that a person who works under such a contract will, for most purposes, be in the same position as one who is self-employed. However, such persons may also be regarded as 'workers' for other statutory purposes such as the *Working Time Regulations* and the provisions in relation to unlawful deductions of wages.

In *O'Kelly v Trusthouse Forte plc* [1984] QB 90, [1983] 3 All ER 456, [1983] IRLR 369, [1983] ICR 728, the majority of the Court of Appeal held that an appellate court could only interfere with a decision of an employment tribunal on the question of whether an individual was an employee if it could be shown that the employment tribunal had erred in law or reached a perverse conclusion. See also *Lee Ting Sang v Chung Chi-Keung* [1990] 2 AC 374, [1990] 2 WLR 1173, [1990] ICR 409, [1990] IRLR 236; *Hall v Lorimer* [1994] ICR 218. However, when the issue whether a person is an employee or self-employed depends on the construction of a written document, this will involve questions of law (*Davies v Presbyterian Church of Wales* [1984] IRLR 194) but only to the extent that it appears that the parties intended all the express terms of their contract to be contained in the document (*Ministry of Defence HQ Defence Dental Service v Kettle* (UKEAT/0308/06/LA) [2007] All ER (D) 301 (Jan)). Whether or not that was their intention is a question of fact (*Carmichael v National Power plc* [2000] IRLR 43).

16.8   Can a controlling shareholder be an employee?

A question sometimes arises as to whether a person who controls the shareholding in the employing enterprise can also be employed by that enterprise. This arises often in cases where a company has become insolvent and a majority shareholder or director claims to be an employee and therefore entitled to payments from the Secretary of State under *section 182* of *ERA 1996*. The most recent guidelines on the issue were given in *Secretary of State for Business, Enterprise and Regulatory Reform v Neufeld (Richard) (2) Howe (Keith)* [2009] EWCA Civ 280, [2009] IRLR 475. There is no reason in principle why a controlling shareholder should not be an employee. The mere fact that a person is a shareholder or profits from the success of a business does not mean that he cannot be an employee. It is no answer to argue that the extent of the individual's control of the company meant that the control condition of a contract of employment could not be satisfied. There are three cases in which it would be legitimate not to give effect to a contract of employment between a controlling shareholder and his company. First where the contract is itself a sham. Second where the contract was entered into for an ulterior purpose (such as to obtain payment from the Secretary of State upon the company's insolvency). Third where the parties do not conduct themselves in accordance with the contract – either because they never intended to or because the relationship ceases to reflect the terms of the contract. Where a contract is in place, the onus is on the party seeking to deny it to show that it is not what it appears to be. If the parties conduct themselves in accordance with the terms of the contract, that is a strong indicator of a contract of employment. By contrast if their conduct is inconsistent, it may be held that there is no such contract.

16.9   Specific engagements

When one asks whether a person was employed or self-employed, the question usually concerns the general relationship between the parties to the contract. The question – although rarely framed in these terms – is whether the 'general engagement' between the parties was a contract of employment or a contract for services. Often it will be necessary to consider whether, over a period, a person was an employee. This will be the case, for example, when one is concerned to determine whether a person has sufficient continuity of service to bring an unfair dismissal claim.

However, in some cases it may be relevant to enquire whether a particular or specific engagement was a contract of employment or a contract for services. Thus, for example, in the case of a regular casual worker who is paid only when work is available but who is not paid in times when there is no work, it may be that the general engagement is not a contract of employment because of a lack of mutual obligations. However, it may be that, when the worker does actually work, the relationship is one of employment. Thus, it would be said that the worker was employed for each 'specific engagement' (for an example where the distinction was drawn, see *Clark v Oxfordshire Health Authority* [1998] IRLR 125). The process for analysing whether a specific engagement is a contract of employment is the same as that set out above. However, the focus is on each particular assignment when the worker does actually work and not on the general relationship.

There may be several reasons why it is necessary to determine whether there was a contract of employment for each specific engagement. For example, the regular casual worker may wish to claim unfair dismissal. Because there is no mutuality of obligations, he cannot establish sufficient continuity of employment by relying on the general relationship. However, if each specific engagement was a contract of employment then it may be that he could establish sufficient continuity by relying on the statutory provisions that allow for gaps in employment to be bridged (see CONTINUOUS EMPLOYMENT (7)). This was the case in *Prater v Cornwall County Council* [2006] EWCA Civ 102, [2006] 2 All ER 1013, [2006] IRLR 362, [2006] ICR 731 where a teacher was employed on a number of assignments. There was no overarching contract of employment because there were no mutual obligations between assignments. But the Court of Appeal held that this was irrelevant to determining the person's status when she was performing an assignment. If the conditions of employment were satisfied for each assignment, then the worker was an employee whilst undertaking them.

The question then was whether gaps when there was no contract could be bridged. *James v Redcats (Brands) Ltd* [2007] IRLR 296 also supports the point that a person's status between engagements is irrelevant to that person's status when an assignment is being performed.

An example in the case law where the court focused on the specific engagement is *McMeechan v Secretary of State for Employment* [1997] IRLR 353. The case concerned a person who worked via an employment agency for a number of different companies. The last company for which he worked went into insolvent liquidation without having paid him for his assignment. He made a claim against the Secretary of State in respect of those payments under *ERA 1996, s 182 et seq*. The question before the Court of Appeal was whether the worker could be regarded as an employee of the agency for the purposes of the *specific* engagement in respect of which he was not paid regardless of his status for the purpose of his *general* engagement by the agency. The Court of Appeal held that a person may be an employee for the purposes of specific engagements even though the general relationship between the parties is not one of employer and employee. It is then a question of assessing the person's status when he does in fact turn up for work regardless of the fact that there may be no general obligation on him to do so.

16.10 Employment agencies

Where a person is found work by an employment agency, there will be a contract between the worker and the agency (which may or may not be a contract of employment) and a separate contract between the agency and the person to whom the services are provided. But absent a further contract between the worker and the recipient of the services, the worker will not be an employee of that person (see *Costain Building and Civil Engineering Ltd v Smith* [2000] ICR 215, EAT). However, it may be possible to infer a contract between the worker and the recipient of services from the conduct of both those parties: *James v London Borough of Greenwich* [2008] IRLR 302; *Cable & Wireless plc v Muscat* [2006] IRLR 354. It is also possible that the contract with the agency may in truth be a contract of employment. In *Royal National Lifeboat Institution v Bushaway* [2005] IRLR 674, the EAT held that a tribunal had been entitled to ignore an entire agreement clause in finding that a person was employed by the client of an agency. (See also **48.2** TEMPORARY AND SEASONAL EMPLOYEES.)

The complexity of this area of the law is demonstrated by *Evans v Parasol Ltd* [2009] All ER (D) 52 (Dec) (UKEAT/0536/08/RN upheld by the Court of Appeal [2010] EWCA Civ 866, [2011] ICR 37, [2010] All ER (D) 240 (Jul)) in which the EAT noted it would be a bold employment judge who was willing to strike out a claim by an agency worker against a possible employer when an individual worked under agency type arrangements.

In *Motorola Ltd v (1) Davidson and (2) Melville Craig* [2001] IRLR 4, the EAT was concerned to consider whether a person taken on by a recruitment agency, Melville Craig, to work for Motorola, was to be regarded as employed by Motorola for the purposes of a complaint of unfair dismissal. The EAT upheld the decision of the tribunal that there was sufficient control by Motorola over Mr Davidson in fact to mean that the relationship was one of employer-employee even though Motorola had no direct legal control over Mr Davidson. It was sufficient that Motorola had indirect control over Mr Davidson in that it could give directions to Melville Craig, including a direction no longer to send Mr Davidson to work for Motorola. Further, at the site, there was a sufficient degree of control in fact. The appeal was unusual in that the only issue argued was that of control. Hence, the case does not lay down any wider propositions about persons engaged by employment agencies becoming employees of the agency's clients. The importance of the case is in the stress which it lays on 'practical aspects of control that fall short of direct legal rights' and the recognition that an employment relationship may be created by a combination of practical control and indirect legal control.

16.10 Employee, Self-Employed or Worker?

The Court of Appeal has reiterated in *Johnson Underwood Ltd v Montgomery* [2001] EWCA Civ 318, [2001] ICR 819, [2001] IRLR 269 that the essential test to apply in judging whether a person is employed by a recruitment agency (or, indeed, by a hirer) is the existence of irreducible minima of mutual obligation and control. To the extent that Waite LJ in *McMeechan* appeared to reduce mutual obligation and control to mere factors to be taken into account, the absence of which would not necessarily be decisive, Buckley J indicated that he was wrong to do so.

In *Montgomery*, the courts below had already determined that the applicant was not an employee of the hirer (a finding which the applicant did not challenge). The result of the Court of Appeal's finding was that the applicant was held not to be an employee of the respondent agency either, since the agency had little or no control over her. The court indicated its unhappiness with this state of affairs, which left the applicant without a remedy and in a state of legal limbo. However, it stated that the solution to her dilemma lay with Parliament. The government issued regulations governing the relationships between recruitment bureaux, work-seekers and hirers, *The Conduct of Employment Agencies and Employment Businesses Regulations 2003 (SI 2003/3319)*. The regulations require that recruitment businesses should be required to clarify whether their relation to work-seekers is one of an employment business or an agency (*reg 14*). (The distinction between agencies and employment businesses in the *Regulations* is derived from the *Employment Agencies Act 1973*. Under *section 13* of the *Act*, agencies find workers employment with employers; employment businesses supply persons to act for, or under the control of, other persons.) The Regulations also require that employment businesses must state in any agreement with work-seekers whether the work-seeker is engaged by them under a contract of service or contract for services (*reg 15*).

In *Bunce v Postworth Ltd (t/a Skyblue)* [2005] EWCA Civ 490, [2005] IRLR 557, the Court of Appeal held that an agency worker was not an employee of the agency either because of the general relationship between the parties or when the worker was engaged on a specific assignment. There were no mutual obligations as between agency and worker for the purposes of individual assignments nor was there sufficient control.

In *Dacas v Brook Street Bureau* [2004] EWCA Civ 217, [2004] IRLR 358, the Court of Appeal analysed the circumstances in which a person provided to another by an agency could be employed by the end user. The analysis was approved in *Cable & Wireless v Muscat* [2006] IRLR 354, [2006] ICR 975. However, the Court of Appeal added the important qualification that a contract could only be implied between the worker and the end user when it was 'necessary' to do so in order to give the relationship business reality. The question of necessity was considered in *Beck v Camden London Borough Council* (UKEAT/0121/08/ZT) [2008] All ER (D) 09 (Sep) and in *Sridhar v East Living Ltd* (UKEAT/0476/07/RN) [2008] All ER (D) 290 (Nov). It is only where express contractual arrangements do not adequately explain the legal relationship between the parties that the question of whether there is an implied contract between an agency worker and an end user might arise. The tribunal must specifically consider whether it is necessary to imply a contract rather than looking solely at whether the conduct of the parties was consistent with an employment relationship.

Later cases have indicated that it will be difficult to show that it is necessary to imply such a contract. In *James v Greenwich London Borough Council* [2008] IRLR 302, the Court of Appeal repeated the necessity test. The Court also approved observations in the EAT that in the usual agency relationship there were no mutual obligations between the worker and the end user: the end user was not obliged to pay the worker. The end user was also not able to insist on a particular worker being provided. It was the agency which was obliged to pay, but it did not control the worker. It would only be in exceptional circumstances that it was necessary to imply a contract. The express terms of the contract described the relationship and it would not be necessary to imply a contract. It might be possible to infer a contract from the parties' conduct if that departed from the express terms of the contracts. But the mere fact that an agency worker worked for an end user for a long time could not justify the implication of a contract. The judgment of the Supreme Court in *Autoclenz* does not refer to 'necessity' as a separate test to be applied when analysing the nature of the contractual relationship between the parties, and it may suggest that this requirement has been over-stated in *James* and other cases.

In *Cairns v Visteon UK Ltd* [2007] IRLR 175, [2007] ICR 616, the EAT toyed with the idea that there could be two contracts of employment – one with the agency and one with the end user. However, this could not resolve the problem that it would only be possible to imply a contract where it was necessary to do so. Also, there would be enormous practical problems – would both employers have to follow the dismissal procedures in the event of a dismissal?

The present state of the law is thus that it will only be in exceptional circumstances that an agency worker will be held to have a contract of employment with the end user.

The problems faced by agency workers have to some extent been ameliorated by the *Agency Workers Regulations 2010*, which came into force on 1 October 2011. Workers supplied by a temporary work agency to work "temporarily for and under the supervision and direction of a hirer" are covered by the *Regulations*. The definitions exclude the genuinely self-employed, those working through their own limited liability company (provided they are genuinely self-employed) and those working on "managed service contracts". Upon completion of a 12-week qualifying period, an agency worker is entitled to the same pay, holidays and other basic conditions as if he or she had been recruited directly by the hirer on day one of the assignment, whether as an employee or a worker. In identifying the "same basic working and employment conditions terms", agency workers may compare their terms with direct recruits of the hirer working in "the same" or "broadly similar" role, not necessarily in the same office or establishment. The *Regulations* reduce the need to infer a contract of employment between the worker and the recipient of services. In order to qualify for certain employment protection rights such as the right not to be unfairly dismissed agency workers will still need to demonstrate they are employees.

16.11 Employees and office-holders

Another distinction may be identified between employees who are employed under a contract of employment and 'office-holders' who may not be employees or have the rights of employees (such as the right to complain of unfair dismissal). In *Johnson v Ryan* [2000] ICR 236, the worker was a local authority rent officer appointed pursuant to the *Rent Act 1977*. It was argued that, as an office-holder, the worker was not entitled to present a claim of unfair dismissal. The EAT identified three categories of 'office-holder'. First, those whose rights and duties are defined by the office they hold and not by any contract. An example is police officers. Second, persons who are called office-holders but who in reality are employed under contracts of service. Third, those who are both employees and office-holders. An example is company directors. In determining whether a worker who is described as an office-holder is an employee, the factual situation must be considered. Relevant matters include whether the worker receives a salary, whether the salary was fixed and whether the worker's duties were subject to close control by the employer or whether the worker worked independently. The EAT held that a rent officer was an employee. In doing so, it noted that the recent approach of the appellate courts had been to take an inclusive approach to employee protection (see generally Public Sector Employees (38)).

In *Percy v Board of National Mission of the Church of Scotland* [2005] UKHL 73, [2006] ICR 134, [2006] IRLR 195, the House of Lords held that a minister of the Church of Scotland was employed within the broader meaning of that term in the Sex Discrimination Act. Holding an office and being an employee were not mutually exclusive. The legal question is whether there was an intention to create legal relations. The Court of Appeal adopted the same approach in *New Testament Church of God v Stewart* [2008] IRLR 134, but added that in deciding whether there was the necessary intention, one had to have regard to the religious principles of the church in question. If those principles precluded a legally binding relationship between the church and the minister, it could mean that no contract of employment would be found. This analysis has recently been affirmed by the Supreme Court in President of the *Methodist Conference v Preston* [2013] UKSC 29, [2013] IRLR 646, [2013] ICR 833 which emphasises the need to carefully analyse the specific rules and practices of the relevant church and the nature of the particular arrangements with the specific minister. On the facts, no contract of employment was established.

O'Brien v Ministry of Justice [2013] UKSC 6, [2013] ICR 499, [2013] IRLR 315 considers the position of part-time fee paid recorders. The Supreme Court has confirmed that although part-time fee paid recorders are not subject to any superior authority in the manner in which they perform their judicial functions, they are engaged in an employment relationship by the Ministry of Justice and are 'workers'. The court also held that there was no objective justification for not providing part-time fee paid record with *pro rata temporis* pension rights. In *Gilham v Ministry of Justice* [2019] UKSC 44, the Supreme Court held that a District Judge was a worker for the purposes of whistleblowing protections in *Part IVA* of the *ERA*. The Supreme Court decided this on the basis that the District Judge's exclusion from whistleblowing protections were an interference with her *Article 10 ECHR* rights read with *Article 14* (the relevant status being her role as a District Judge), such that *section 230(3)* of the *ERA* should be read so as to include the District Judge pursuant to *section 3* of the *Human Rights Act 1998*.

16.12 Workers

It has already been indicated that many of the provisions of employment legislation providing protection to individuals are not confined to those who are to be regarded in law as employees. Much protection is accorded to those who satisfy the definition of 'worker'.

That definition (found, for example, in *section 230* of *ERA 1996* and in similar form in the *Working Time Regulations 1998* and elsewhere) is wider than the definition of employee because it includes those who undertake to 'do or perform personally any work or services for another party to the contracts whose status is not by virtue of the contract that of a client or customer of any profession or business undertaking carried on by the individual'. The scope of this definition is currently highly topical because of the emergence of the so called 'gig economy', whereby businesses structure their arrangements in ways which prevent those who work from them acquiring employment rights and which transfer various commercial risks from the 'employer' to the worker.

This wider definition applies to a number of employment rights that are referred to in the start of this chapter. In particular, 'workers' are entitled to paid holidays pursuant to the *Working Time Regulations 1998, SI 1998/1833*, the national minimum wage pursuant to the *National Minimum Wage Act 1998* and protection from less favourable treatment if working part-time pursuant to the *Part-time Workers (Prevention of Less Favourable Treatment) Regulations 2000, SI 2000/1551*. Section 83(2)(a) of the *Equality Act 2010* has the effect that persons working 'under a contract of employment, a contract of apprenticeship or a contract personally to do work' are protected from discrimination under the *Equality Act 2010*. Importantly, whilst the term 'worker' is not used in the *Equality Act 2010* definition, the meaning of 'employee' in the Equality Act 2010 is essentially the same as the definition of 'worker' in the previously mentioned legislation (see *Pimlico Plumbers v Smith* [2018] UKSC 29). As of 6 April 2019, workers are entitled to itemised pay statements (see the amendments to *ERA 1996, sections 8–9, 11–12*), and from 6 April 2020, workers will be entitled to a written statement of initial employment particulars pursuant to further amendments of the *ERA* (see the *Employment Rights (Miscellaneous Amendments) Regulations 2019*).

The definition can be seen as comprising two elements. First the individual must be under an obligation personally to do work. Second, the person for whom the work is done must not be a client or customer of a business being run by the individual. The second limb is obviously necessary because otherwise the truly self-employed would be caught by a definition which required only that the person do work personally.

Several cases have considered what is meant by the definition of worker. The cases are decided under different provisions, but because the definition is the same at least under national law (the position under EU law is addressed shortly), no distinction needs to be drawn based on the legal context of the decision. It is legitimate to consider decisions under the discrimination legislation and under other provisions which use the term worker, such as the *National Minimum Wage Act 1998* and the *Working Time Regulations 1998*.

The position is, however, different when considering the position of 'workers' under EU law. The ECJ has made it clear that the definition of 'worker' has an autonomous meaning specific to EU law: see *Union Syndicale Solidaires Isere v Premier Ministre and ors* C-428/09; [2011] IRLR 84. The ECJ held that the concept must be defined in accordance with objective criteria which distinguish the relationship by reference to the rights and duties of the persons concerned. The essential feature of such a relationship are that for a certain period of time a person performs services for and under the direction of another person in return for which he receives remuneration. (However, in *O'Brien v Ministry of Justice* C-393/10; [2012] ICR 955, [2012] IRLR 421 the ECJ emphasised rather unhelpfully that there was no single definition of "worker" in European Union law; it varies according to the area in which the definition applied. The cases concerning EU-derived rights afforded to 'workers' may therefore not be on the same footing as purely national legislation.)

In *James v Redcats (Brands) Ltd* [2007] IRLR 296, the EAT held that one had to draw a careful distinction between employees, workers and those engaged in their own business. When a right extended to workers, it was only the last category that was excluded. The EAT referred to cases such as *Lee v Chung* (cited above) and said that the dichotomy suggested in those cases between employees and the self-employed could be too simple. It was necessary also to draw a further distinction between those in business on their own account and workers. The EAT suggested that it was useful to consider a 'dominant purpose' test, derived from discrimination cases. If the dominant feature of the arrangement was that the person was to provide personal service then, even if the prerequisites of employment were missing, the person was likely to be a worker. Where a genuine right to substitution exists, there is no personal service and there cannot be worker status. It is not sufficient that the individual might be obliged to personally find a substitute if unable to work (see *Community Dental Centres Ltd v Sultan-Darmon* [2010] IRLR 1024).

The leading case is now *Jivraj v Haswani* [2011] UKSC 40, [2011] ICR 1004, [2011] IRLR 827, in which the Supreme Court held that the correct test is whether the contract provides for services to be rendered by an independent contractor or whether the service provider consents to work under the control of another, and is therefore a worker. The Court concluded that an arbitrator was outside this definition, notwithstanding that he provided personal services and received fees, due to a lack of control or subordination. In *Halawi v WDFG UK Ltd t/a World Duty Free* [2015] IRLR 50, the Court of Appeal held that a beauty consultant who provided her services to a cosmetics company via a limited company and employment agency, and who had exercised her right to substitute performance, was not a worker and so was unable to bring a claim for discrimination. The Court emphasised the requirements of personal service and subordination.

Byrne Bros (Formworks) Ltd v Baird [2002] IRLR 96 was a case under the *Working Time Regulations*. The EAT concluded that labour-only sub-contractors had been correctly identified as workers notwithstanding that they had a limited power to send a substitute, the individuals were still under a personal obligation. Referring to the second part of the definition, the EAT said that the aim was to extend protection to an intermediate class of person between employees and those who are carrying on business on their own account. Such people, although not employees, are subordinate to the person for whom they work and hence in need of protection. The EAT said that a consideration of who was a worker would involve the same sorts of factors as are considered in deciding who is an employee 'but with the boundary pushed further in the putative worker's favour' In *Wright v Redrow Homes (Yorkshire) Ltd* [2004] EWCA Civ 469, [2004] 3 All ER 98, [2004] ICR 1126, [2004] IRLR 720 the Court of Appeal held that the question whether there was an obligation to undertake work personally depended on the terms of the contract and not what happened in practice. Pill LJ cautioned against relying too heavily on policy reasons when deciding who was a worker. The Court of Appeal has provided important guidance on the application of the test identified above in *Pimlico Plumbers Ltd v Smith* [2017] IRLR 323. The Court upheld the Tribunal's finding that a plumber who was self-employed for tax purposes, and whose written contract expressly provided that he was an independent contractor, was nevertheless a worker. While the conclusion was fact sensitive, the Court gave detailed guidance on the relevance of the obligation to provide personal services, emphasising that *limited* rights of substitution would not necessarily preclude the conclusion that a person is a worker. The Supreme Court ([2018] UKSC 29) upheld the Court of Appeal's decision in *Pimlico Plumbers*, emphasising the significance of the fact that any substitute put forward by the worker was required to be drawn from Pimlico Plumber's ranks of plumbers who were also subject to the same obligations, and that therefore Pimlico were far from "uninterested" in the identity of the substitute. The Supreme Court did not recast the applicable law in any significant way, finding that the ET was entitled to make the findings it did. It did, however, confirm that the definition of 'worker' in *section 230(3)* of the *ERA* is the same as the definition of "employment" in *section 83(2)(a)* of the *Equality Act 2010*.

As stated above, in *Clyde & Co LLP v Bates Van Winklehof* [2014] UKSC 32, [2014] IRLR 641, [2014] ICR 730 the Supreme Court held that an 'equity' member of a limited liability partnership could be a worker and therefore entitled to pursue a claim in respect of an alleged protected disclosure. Notably, the Court suggested that a relationship of subordination was not required in order to establish worker status. The Court left open the question of whether a partner in an ordinary partnership can be a worker.

In *Windle v Secretary of State for Justice* [2016] ICR 721, [2016] IRLR 628, the Court of Appeal restored a Tribunal's decision that two court interpreters who performed services for HM Courts and Tribunals Service on a case-by-case basis were not workers. The ultimate question is the nature of the relationship during the period when the work was being done. However, as a matter of common sense, and common experience, the fact that a person supplying services is only doing so on an assignment-by-assignment basis may tend to suggest a degree of independence, or lack of subordination, in the relationship while at work which indicates that the person is not a worker. The absence of a contract governing the periods between cases supported the conclusion that the interpreters acted as independent contractors.

In *Uber BV and others v Aslam and others* UKEAT/0056/17 the EAT held that Uber 'taxi' drivers are workers. The Tribunal rejected Uber's case that the drivers were self-employed, and that it merely provided a 'technology platform' that allowed drivers to find and agree work with individual passengers. The Court of Appeal by a majority upheld the EAT's judgment, Lord Justice Underhill dissenting ([2018] EWCA Civ 2748), but granted permission to appeal to the Supreme Court. In *Addison Lee Ltd v Gascoigne* UKEAT/0289/17 the EAT held that cycle couriers were workers, rejecting the Respondent's case seeking to rely on the written terms of contract between the parties, which described the couriers as 'independent contractors'. The EAT upheld the Tribunal's conclusion that this did not reflect the reality of the relationship. During the period when the couriers were 'logged on' to the Respondent's app, there was a contract with mutual obligations for work to be offered and accepted. See to similar effect *Addison Lee Ltd v Lange* UKEAT/0037/18/BA, in respect of private-hire drivers, in which the EAT found that an ET is entitled to use a "realistic and worldly wise" approach to determining employment status.

By contrast, in *Independent Workers' Union of Great Britain (IWGB) v RooFoods Ltd (t/a Deliveroo)* [2018] IRLR 84, the CAC considered that riders engaged by Deliveroo were not workers due to a genuine, and absolute, right to substitute performance of their duties. The CAC reached this conclusion notwithstanding that it accepted that it was difficult to see how the contractual right of substitution would have meaningful practical effect. In an extension of the *Deliveroo* decision, in *R(IWGB) v Central Arbitration Committee* [2019] EWHC 728 (Admin), [2019] All ER (D) 151 (Mar), the High Court rejected a judicial review challenge brought by IWGB against the CAC's decision that Deliveroo riders are not 'workers' and so cannot establish collective bargaining arrangements. The Court rejected the argument that the restriction of statutory collective bargaining rights to 'workers' breached *Article 11* of the *European Convention on Human Rights*, holding that *Article 11* was not engaged, and that even if it were, the challenge would still fail. Compare the decision in *Deliveroo* with that concerning *Hermes* and *CitySprint* couriers (*Leyland and ors v Hermes Parcelnet Ltd* (ET case 1800575/2017 and ors); *Dewhurst and ors v Revisecatch Ltd*; *CitySprint UK Ltd* (ET Case 2202512/2016) in which the individuals were found to be workers. For the purposes of the ERA, the EAT in *Stuart Delivery Ltd v Augustine* (UKEAT/0219/18/BA) found that the existence of a form of substitution clause, namely the opportunity to release another delivery slot to a pool of other delivery staff, precluded worker status: the EAT uphold the ET's decision that the claimant was a worker.

In the recent case in EU law of *B v Yodel Delivery Network Ltd* (judgment of 22 April 2020, Case C-692/19), the CJEU made key findings on worker status for the purposes of the Working Time Directive (2003/88/EC). Surprisingly, it did so pursuant to Article 99 of its Rules of Procedure, which permit a decision by reasoned order where the reply to a question referred for a preliminary ruling may be clearly deduced from existing case-law or where the answer to the question referred admits of no reasonable doubt (i.e. supposedly does not set out any new developments in the law). The key finding of the court was as follows:

> "[the directive] . . . must be interpreted must be interpreted as precluding a person engaged by his putative employer under a services agreement which stipulates that he is a self-employed independent contractor from being classified as a 'worker' for the purposes of that directive, where that person is afforded discretion:
>
> – to use subcontractors or substitutes to perform the service which he has undertaken to provide;
>
> – to accept or not accept the various tasks offered by his putative employer, or unilaterally set the maximum number of those tasks;
>
> – to provide his services to any third party, including direct competitors of the putative employer, and
>
> – to fix his own hours of 'work' within certain parameters and to tailor his time to suit his personal convenience rather than solely the interests of the putative employer,
>
> provided that, first, the independence of that person does not appear to be fictitious and, second, it is not possible to establish the existence of a relationship of subordination between that person and his putative employer. However, it is for the referring court, taking account of all the relevant factors relating to that person and to the economic activity he carries on, to classify that person's professional status under Directive 2003/88."

16.12   Employee, Self-Employed or Worker?

In other words, a person will not be a worker for the purposes of the Working Time Directive if those criteria are fulfilled – in short, genuine independence and lack of subordination precludes worker status.

In dealing with the second part of the definition (that the person for whom the work is done is not a client or customer of a business undertaken by an individual), the EAT in *Cotswold Developments Construction Ltd v Williams* [2006] IRLR 181 suggested that the paradigm case of a person who did work for clients was a professional such as a solicitor or barrister. The paradigm case of a person who did work for customers was the owner of a shop or a tradesman such as a domestic plumber. The EAT suggested that a helpful test would be to consider whether the individual marketed his services to the public generally (in which case he would not be a worker) or whether he was integrated into the business of his principal (in which case he would be a worker). See further *Varnish v British Cycling Federation* (ET Case 2404219/2017), in which the professional cyclist Jess Varnish was found not a worker for British Cycling because she was training and competing for her benefit.

The cases thus distinguish between those who are running their own business and those who, although not employed, are providing services as a part of another's business. In *Bacica v Muir* [2006] IRLR 35, the EAT suggested that factors such as working on the basis of a CIS certificate (in the construction industry), having accounts prepared for submission to the Inland Revenue, being free to work for others and in fact doing so, being paid a rate which included an overhead allowance and not being paid when not working were all factors indicating that a person was undertaking his own business.

In *Day v Lewisham and Greenwich NHS Trust* [2017] EWCA Civ 329, [2017] ICR 917, the Court of Appeal held that a 'worker' relationship was established simultaneously between junior doctors and both: (a) their employing NHS trust, and (b) Health Education England, for the purpose of *section 43K (1)(a)(ii)* of *ERA 1996*.

The Supreme Court has confirmed that unpaid volunteers are not workers: *X v Mid Sussex Citizens Advice Bureau* [2013] 1 All ER 1038, [2013] IRLR 146.

17   Employee Participation

17.1   OVERVIEW OF EMPLOYEE PARTICIPATION

The UK was slow to enact legislation providing for employees to participate or become involved in the affairs of the organisations in which they work. Unlike some European jurisdictions (Germany, for example, which requires a significant percentage of the supervisory boards of large public and private companies to be employee representatives), English company law has historically set its face against employee involvement in the running of companies. Some legislation in the 1970s (the *Health and Safety at Work Act 1974* and the *Employment Protection Act 1975*) compelled employers with recognised trade unions to consult with their employees on such matters as health and safety, disclosure of information and on redundancies. It is the influence of the United Kingdom's membership of the European Community (and subsequently the European Union) which has, over time, led to greater legislative initiative to increase employee participation. Obligations flowing from EC membership led to substantial implementing legislation, widening consultation requirements in the case of redundancies, transfers of undertakings, and health and safety. Further legislation was introduced by the Labour Government of 1997. For example, the *ERA 1999* requires employers to recognise trade unions where this is desired by a majority of the relevant workforce (see TRADE UNIONS – I **(51)**). Separately, workforce consultation was incorporated into the bidding process of the Private Finance Initiative.

The pace of legislative development has quickened since 1 May 1999, when the Treaty of Amsterdam came into effect, incorporating the Social Protocol into the *EC Treaty* (now the Treaty on the Functioning of the European Union) (see further EUROPEAN UNION LAW **(24)**). One effect of this has been to give increased emphasis to securing framework agreements on social legislation through negotiation between European-level trade union and employer bodies (the 'social partners').

The effect of Brexit on the legislation governing employee participation is therefore likely to be significant. The effect on the legislation discussed in this chapter is outlined further below.

There are currently five separate EU measures that deal with informing and consulting employees and employee participation:

(1)   The *European Works Council Directive (94/45)*, adopted in September 1994, was the first employment measure adopted under the *Social Protocol*. This places obligations on companies with more than 1,000 employees, including at least 150 employees in a second European member state, and was implemented in national legislation by the *Transnational Information and Consultation of Employees Regulations 1999 (SI 1999/3323)*. A recast *European Works Council Directive (2009/38/EC)* was agreed in May 2009 and came into force, in the main, in June 2011. The *1999 Regulations* were amended with effect, in the main, from 5 June 2011 to reflect this (see below **17.20**).

(2)   The original *European Works Council Directive* was followed by *Directive 2002/14/EC* 'establishing a general framework for informing and consulting employees in the European Community'. This places obligations on smaller, national companies and was implemented into domestic law by the *Information and Consultation of Employees Regulations 2004 (SI 2004/3426)*, as amended by *SI 2006/514* (see below **17.2**).

(3)   The *European Company Statute* (consisting of *EU Council Regulation 2157/2001* and *Directive 2001/86/EC*) enables companies operating in more than one member state to be established as a single company under EC law. This was originally implemented

domestically by the *European Public Limited-Liability Company Regulations 2004 (SI 2004/2326)* and is now implemented, in Great Britain, by the *European Public Limited-Liability Company (Employee Involvement) (Great Britain) Regulations 2009 (SI 2009/2401)* (see below **17.28**).

(4) Similar provisions apply to European Cooperative Societies under *Regulation 1435/03* and *Directive 2003/72/EC*, implemented domestically by the *European Cooperative Society Regulations 2006 (SI 2006/2078)* and the *European Cooperative Society (Involvement of Employees) Regulations 2006 (SI 2006/2059)*.

(5) Finally, EC rules in relation to employee participation following cross-border mergers between companies, contained in *Directive 2005/56/EC*, have been implemented domestically by the *Companies (Cross-Border Mergers) Regulations 2007 (SI 2007/2974)*.

Amendments have been made to the various sets of domestic implementing regulations to give effect to the *Agency Workers Regulations 2010 (SI 2010/93)*.

These various sets of regulations are detailed and complex, running cumulatively to many hundreds of pages. This chapter provides an overview of the main provisions. However, regard should be had to the regulations in their entirety. Practitioners advising on issues under any of the regulations will also, of course, be well advised to consider authorities decided under each set of regulations in relation to the comparable provisions of the other EU and domestic measures.

Decisions of the Central Arbitration Committee ('CAC') (and other information and consultation legislation) are available at: www.cac.gov.uk/index.aspx?articleid=2389.

NOTE: Because of the European origin of a number of the specific information and consultation regimes described below, they are affected by Brexit. At the date of publication, the United Kingdom has left the European Union ('exit day' being 31 January 2020) and is currently in the one year 'implementation period' fixed by part 4 of the withdrawal agreement between the EU and the UK, and implemented domestically by the *European Union (Withdrawal Agreement) Act 2020*. The implementation period ends at 11pm on 31 December 2020 (unless extended): see *EUWAA 2020, s 39* defining 'IP completion day'. The broad effect of *EUWAA 2020* is that during the implementation period most EU law will continue to have effect in domestic law in the same way that it did before.

It should also be noted that pursuant to *European Union (Withdrawal) Act 2018, s 8*, Ministers have the power to make provision for the repeal or amendment of EU-derived legislation which will be redundant or inappropriate after IP completion day. The Government has been seeking systematically to work through European measures deciding which to abandon and which to preserve, either in whole or in part. That process, although not complete, has significant implications for the legislation covered in this chapter. The effect on the five EU measures referred to above is, at the date of publication, as follows:

(1) The *Employment Rights (Amendment) (EU Exit) Regulations 2019 (SI 2019/535)* amend the *Transnational Information and Consultation of Employees Regulations 1999* to provide (in summary) that no new requests to set up a European Works Council can be made after IP completion day;

(2) The *Information and Consultation of Employees Regulations 2004* do not presently appear to be affected and will therefore remain in force after IP completion day pursuant to *EUWA 2018, s 2*;

(3)   The *European Public Limited-Liability Company (Amendment etc.) (EU Exit) Regulations 2018* partially revoke the *European Public Limited-Liability Company (Employee Involvement) (Great Britain) Regulations 2009* to cater for the fact that a Societas Europaea will become a 'UK Societas' after IP completion day and no new Societas Europaea will be able to be formed in the UK;

(4)   *Regulation 33(a)* of the *Financial Services (Miscellaneous) (Amendment) (EU Exit) Regulations 2019 (SI 2019/710)* revokes Regulation 1435/03 with effect from IP completion day and *regulation 25* thereof revokes the *European Cooperative Society Regulations 2006* also with effect from IP completion day. At present no domestic legislation has been made which specifically deals with the situation of the *European Cooperative Society (Involvement of Employees) Regulations 2006*;

(5)   *Part II* of the *Companies, Limited Liability Partnerships and Partnerships (Amendment etc.) (EU Exit) Regulations 2019 (SI 2019/348)* will repeal the *Companies (Cross-Border Mergers) Regulations 2007* in their entirety.

17.2   THE INFORMATION AND CONSULTATION OF EMPLOYEES REGULATIONS 2004

In February 2002, EC member states adopted *Directive 2002/14/EC* 'establishing a general framework for informing and consulting employees in the European Community'. The *Directive* provides for undertakings with at least 50 employees in any one member state to provide their employees with information and to consult with them over a wide range of issues concerning the operation of the organisation. As the ECJ noted in *Holst v Dansk Arbejdsgiverforening*: C-405/08 [2010] 2 CMLR 49, the *Directive* envisages that Member States may allow management and the workforce to play a leading role in its implementation, although it remains the responsibility of Member States to ensure that all workers are afforded the full protection for which the *Directive* provides.

The *Directive* has been implemented into domestic law by the *Information and Consultation of Employees Regulations 2004 (SI 2004/3426)*, as amended (the '*ICE Regulations*').

•   The *ICE Regulations* were made under *s 42* of the *Employment Relations Act 2004*. Their purpose, as explained by the EAT in *Darnton v Bournemouth University* [2010] IRLR 294, [2010] ICR 524 at [2], is "*to provide for the establishment of arrangements under which employees can be informed and consulted by their employers about matters of mutual concern*". Or as the EAT put it in *University of London v Morrissey* [2016] IRLR 487, [2016] ICR 893: "*to engage the workforce as a whole, to involve them all in the (often sensitive) process of obtaining information and engaging in consultation to a greater extent than had been the case prior to the 2002 Directive*", and "*to facilitate the engagement of employees – that is, all employees in the workforce – in general terms in that process*".

•   Guidance on the *ICE Regulations* is available on www.gov.uk/informing-consulting -employees-law. This includes the detailed guidance issued by the DTI (as was) in January   2006:   webarchive.nationalarchives.gov.uk/20121212135622/http ://www.bis.gov.uk/files/file25934.pdf. However, this guidance "has no special status ": see the EAT in *Darnton v Bournemouth University* [2010] IRLR 294, [2010] ICR 524 at [18] and the CAC in *Coombs & Holder v GE Aviation Systems Ltd* IC/43/(2012) at [55].

17.3

Employees in undertakings with 50 or more employees in the United Kingdom have a right to be informed and consulted on a regular basis about issues in the organisation for which they work: see *reg 3* and *sch 1* to the *ICE Regulations*. (The *ICE Regulations* applied originally only to undertakings with 150 or more employees, but this threshold has gradually been reduced.)

The number of employees in an undertaking is calculated by taking the average number of employees employed by the employer over the preceding 12-month period (*reg 4(1), (2)*). Employees who work for less than 75 hours in each month may count as 'half' an employee for this purpose (*reg 4(3)*).

From 1 October 2011, by virtue of the *Agency Workers Regulations 2011 (SI 2010/93)*, an agency worker who has a contract with a temporary work agency shall be treated as an employee of that agency for these purposes for the duration of his or her assignment (*reg 3A*).

Note that issues have arisen in other Member States as to the meaning of an "employee" within *article 3(2)* of the *Directive*. In *Association de Médiation Sociale v Union Locale des Syndicats CGT*: C-176/12 [2014] IRLR 310, [2014] ICR 411 workers engaged under particular atypical 'assisted contracts' (such as apprentices, or employees with professional training contracts) were required to be taken into account when calculating staff numbers in an undertaking. The Court held, further, that *Article 3(1)* of the *Directive* had direct effect. However, it could not be relied upon in a dispute between individuals, unlike for example, that in issue in *Kücükdeveci v Swedex GmbH & Co KG*: C-555/07 [2010] IRLR 346. The employees were left to claim *Francovich* damages from the French state (for which see *Francovich v Italy*: C-6/90 [1992] IRLR 84).

17.4 Undertakings

The *ICE Regulations* apply to 'undertakings' whose registered office, head office or principal place of business is situated in Great Britain (*reg 3*). Where the registered office is in Great Britain, and the head office or principal place of business is in Northern Ireland, or vice versa, the *ICE Regulations* only apply where the majority of employees are employed to work in Great Britain.

An undertaking is defined as a 'public or private undertaking carrying out an economic activity, whether or not operating for gain' (*reg 2*). This will cover almost all employers. However, there is uncertainty about whether particular parts of the public sector are carrying out economic activities: see eg *Henke v Gemeinde Schierke* and *Verwaltungsgemeinschaft Brocken*: C-298/94 [1996] ECR I-4989, [1996] IRLR 701, [1997] ICR 746, ECJ, *Mayeur v Association Promotion de l'Information Messine (APIM)*: C-175/99 [2000] IRLR 783, [2002] ICR 1316, ECJ and *Collino v Telecom Italia SpA*: C-343/98 [2000] ECR I-6659, [2000] IRLR 788, [2002] ICR 38, ECJ; cf the definition of 'undertaking' in the *Transfer of Undertakings (Protection of Employment Regulations 1981 (SI 1981/1794)* and the *Transfer of Undertakings (Protection of Employment) Regulations 2006 (SI 2006/246)* and the authorities in relation thereto and cf also the approach of the Court of Justice in the *USA v Nolan* litigation in relation to information and collective redundancies (**53.3 TRANSFER OF UNDERTAKINGS**). In *Public and Commercial Services Union v Advisory, Conciliation and Arbitration Service* [2017] IRLR 680 (affirmed by the EAT UKEAT/160/17; [2018] IRLR 1110, [2018] ICR 1793), the CAC placed reliance on the definition of undertaking adopted by the ECJ in *Scattolon v Ministerio dell'Instruzione, dell'Universita e della Ricera* (C-108/10 [2012] ICR 740 – a transfer of undertakings case), namely: "any economic entity organised on a stable basis, whatever its legal status and method of financing" and found that ACAS was a public undertaking carrying out an economic activity. Economic activity was not limited to commercial activity. Whilst offering goods and services for remuneration to a customer would be sufficient to mean that an undertaking was engaged in an economic activity, it was not necessary that it should be doing so.

The DTI Guidance (https://tinyurl.com/y7yund7z) suggests (in paragraph 5) that, in the case of a company, the definition of an undertaking in the *ICE Regulations* covers separately incorporated legal entities, rather than organisational entities such as an establishment, division or business unit. The CAC reached the same conclusion in *Coombs & Holder v GE Aviation Systems Ltd* IC/43/(2012) by reference to the language of the *ICE Regulations*, holding – without any enthusiasm – that an undertaking meant a single legal entity capable of being an employer, and that a group of legal entities was not itself an undertaking.

The CAC and then the EAT have considered the Guidance recently in *Cofeley Workplace Limited v Moyer-Lee* (CAC - IC/47(2014), 31 July 2014; EAT – [2015] IRLR 879, [2015] ICR 1333), determining that the relevant employee request did not satisfy the threshold in *reg 7(1)* of the *ICE Regulations*. The CAC held, *inter alia*, on the facts, that a particular contract (ie essentially, a particular site or subdivision of the business) was not a relevant "undertaking". Taking into account the terms of the DTI Guidance, it considered that the terms "undertaking" and "establishment" are mutually exclusive, that an undertaking means more than simply a unit of business and, so far as the *ICE Regulations* are concerned, that a public or private undertaking is not an "establishment". The EAT upheld that approach, noting in so doing that the Guidance is of persuasive weight. Langstaff J considered that an "undertaking", in this context, cannot mean any grouping smaller than that which is the legal employer of the employees concerned.

17.5   Employee requests for data

Employees or their representatives have the right to make a written request for their employer to supply them with data for the purpose of ascertaining the number of people employed by the employer in the UK (and therefore whether or not the *ICE Regulations* apply) (*reg 5*).

A complaint that an employer has failed to provide the data, referred to in *reg 5(3)*, or that the data is false or incomplete in a material particular, may be presented to the CAC up to one month after the date of the request (*reg 6*). Where the CAC finds the complaint to be well-founded, it will order the employer to disclose the data to the complainant (*reg 6(2)*).

17.6   Initiation of obligations under the ICE Regulations

The obligations under the *ICE Regulations* to inform and consult do not apply automatically, even where the employer has sufficient employees for the *ICE Regulations* to apply in principle. Instead, the obligations must be initiated by either the employer or the employees.

17.7   *Initiation by the Employer*

Employers may initiate negotiations under the *ICE Regulations* by giving notice in writing in accordance with *reg 11(1)*. Notice must be published in such a manner as to bring it to the attention of all the employees of the undertaking, so far as is reasonably practicable (*reg 11(2)*).

17.8   *Employee Requests*

In addition, an employer must generally initiate negotiations for an agreement in respect of information and consultation where it receives a valid employee request (*reg 7(1)*). To be valid, an employee request must be made by at least 2% of the employees in the undertaking (subject to a minimum of 15 and a maximum of 2,500 employees), either as a single request or a number of separate requests over a six-month period (*reg 7(1)–(3)*). (Note that *regulation 16* of the *Employment Rights (Miscellaneous Amendments) Regulations 2019 (SI 2019/731)* amended *regs 7(2)–(3)* as from 6 April 2020 to lower the threshold for an employee request from 10% to 2% of the employees in the undertaking). Requests must be in writing and sent to the registered office, head office or principal place of business of the employer, or to the CAC (*reg 7(4)*). A request must specify the names of the employee(s) making it and the date on which it is sent (*reg 7(4)*). Where the request is sent to the CAC, the CAC is then required to notify the employer of the request, request from the employer such information as it needs to verify the number and names of the employees who have made the request, and inform the employer and the employees who have made the request how many employees have made the request (*reg 7(5)–(6)*).

17.9   *General Considerations*

As a general rule, no employee may request negotiation (or renegotiation) of any agreement, and no employer may give notice of an intention to negotiate (or renegotiate) any agreement within three years of:

(a)   the date of the conclusion of any negotiated agreement under the *ICE Regulations* (see below **17.12**); or

(b)   the date when the standard information and consultation provisions began to apply (see below **17.13**, but note the provision in *reg 18(2)* for the renegotiation of the standard provisions 'at any time'); or

(c)   the date of the employee request, where the employer has held a ballot following an employee request which has resulted in endorsement of a pre-existing agreement (see below **17.15** (*reg 12(1)*).

There is an exception to the general rule where there are material changes in the undertaking during the three-year period having the result that an agreement in force no longer covers all the employees of the undertaking, or, if it is a pre-existing agreement (as to which see below **17.15**) can no longer be said to have been approved by all the employees of the undertaking (*reg 12(2)*).

If the employer considers that there was no valid employee request, or an employee (or employee's representative) considers that an employer notification was not valid, a complaint may be presented to the CAC (*reg 13(1), (2)*). Complaints must be presented to the CAC within one month of the date of the employee request or the date of the employer notification (*reg 13(3)*). If the CAC finds the complaint made out, it may make a declaration to that effect (*reg 13(1)–(2)*).

Note that in order to initiate negotiations for an agreement in relation to employees in more than one undertaking, it is necessary for there to be a valid employee request or employer notification in relation to each undertaking (*reg 14(6)*).

17.10   **Negotiated agreements**

Where a valid employee request has been made or employer notice has been given (see above **17.6–17.9**), the employer is obliged to initiate negotiations by taking the steps set out in *reg 14*. The employer must, as soon as reasonably practicable:

(a)   make arrangements satisfying the requirements of *reg 14(2)* for the employees of the undertaking to elect or appoint negotiating representatives;

(b)   inform the employees in writing of the identity of the negotiating representatives; and

(c)   invite the negotiating representatives to enter into negotiations to reach a negotiated agreement (*reg 14(1), (2)*).

Reg 14(1) requires an employer to take these steps as soon as reasonably practicable. In *Darnton v Bournemouth University* [2010] IRLR 294, [2010] ICR 524, the EAT rejected an argument that there is any implied requirement in *reg 14* for an employer to do so in any event within three months of the employee request. Whilst this appears to be what the DTI

Guidance issued in 2006 envisaged, and whilst the EAT recognised that it would be unusual for it not to be reasonably practicable to complete these steps within three months of the employee request, the statutory requirement is simply as stated in *reg 14(1)*: "as soon as reasonably practicable".

As to the election or appointment of negotiating representatives, there are only two express requirements in *reg 14(2)*: (i) the election or appointment must be arranged in such a way that all employees of the undertaking are represented by one or more representatives; and (ii) all employees of the undertaking must be entitled to take part in the election or appointment of the representatives and, if there is a ballot, all employees must be entitled to vote in the ballot. In *University of London v Morrissey* UKEAT/0285/15, [2016] IRLR 487, however, the EAT held that "the arrangements put in place should be with a view for the effective representation of *all* employees, and we would emphasis all employees rather than a section of employees." Moreover: *"Although the word "effective" does not appear in the Regulations . . . if [the CAC] concluded that effectiveness was absent, this would indicate that the Regulations had not been faithfully applied"*. There may be cases in which it is appropriate for an employer to enter discussions with recognised unions and evolve a process that satisfies *reg 14*. In other cases, that would not lead to effective representation; all will depend upon the particular facts. On the facts in *Morrissey*, the CAC had been entitled to hold that the process put in place by the employer – by inviting those unions which it recognised for the purposes of collective bargaining to nominate candidates – was not sufficient and did not comply with *reg 14*.

17.11   Complaints about the election or appointment of negotiating representatives

Complaints about the election or appointment of negotiating representatives may be made to the CAC within 21 days of the election or appointment (*reg 15(1)*). If the CAC finds the complaint well-founded it must make an order requiring the employer to arrange for the process of election or appointment to take place again (*reg 15(2)*).

17.12   Negotiated agreements

Once negotiating representatives have been appointed, the *ICE Regulations* are designed to encourage employers, employees and their representatives to agree information and consultation arrangements which suit their particular circumstances. Thus, the *ICE Regulations* specifically require employer and employee representatives to work in a spirit of co-operation (*reg 21*).

The *ICE Regulations* are notably non-prescriptive with respect to the substance of the arrangements for information and consultation, for example as to the subjects, method, timing or frequency of any information provision or consultation. Guidance as to the possible content of an agreement may be gained from the standard information and consultation provisions, which will apply in default if the parties fail to reach a negotiated agreement (see below **17.13**).

There are, however, some express requirements with which any negotiated agreement must comply (*reg 16(1)*). Any agreement must:

(a)   cover all employees of the undertaking (either in a single agreement or in different parts);

(b)   set out the circumstances in which the employer must inform and consult the employees to which it relates;

(c)   be in writing;

(d)   be dated;

(e)   be approved by the employees in accordance with the *ICE Regulations* (see below);

(f)   be signed by or on behalf of the employer;

(g)   either:

> (i)   provide for the appointment or election of information and consultation representatives to whom the employer must provide the information and whom the employer must consult; or

> (ii)   provide that the employer must provide information directly to the employees to which it relates and consult those employees directly; and

(h)   provide that where an employer is to provide information about the employment situation under any part of that agreement, that information shall include suitable information relating to the use of agency workers in that undertaking.

In addition, to be valid, a negotiated agreement must have been signed by all the negotiating representatives, or, if it is only signed by a majority of the negotiating representatives, it must have been approved by at least 50% of the employees in the undertaking either: (i) in writing, or (ii) in a ballot (*reg 16(3), (4)*).

If a ballot is held:

(a)   the employer must make such arrangements as are reasonably practicable to ensure that the ballot is fair, all employees must be entitled to vote, and the ballot must be conducted so as to secure that those voting do so in secret (again so far as is reasonably practicable) and the votes given in the ballot are accurately counted (*reg 16(5)*);

(b)   the employer must inform all employees entitled to vote of the result of the ballot as soon as is reasonably practicable (*reg 16(6)*);

(c)   a complaint may be presented to the CAC in circumstances where an employee representative considers that the ballot for approval of a negotiated agreement has not complied with the *ICE Regulations* (*reg 17(1)*). Complaints may only be made by a negotiating representative (and not by an employee). They must be made within 21 days of the date of the ballot. If the CAC finds the complaint well-founded it must order the employer to re-run the ballot (*reg 17(2)*).

A time limit is set on negotiations: they may last (in the first instance) for no more than six months commencing at the end of the period of three months beginning with the date on which the valid employee request was made or the valid employer notification was issued (*reg 14(3)*). However, time spent holding a ballot to determine whether or not to use a pre-existing agreement rather than negotiate a new one (see below **17.15**) or on making an application to the CAC is ignored when calculating the six-month negotiating period (see *reg 14(3), (4)* for the detailed provisions on the calculation of time). If the employer and a majority of the negotiating representatives agree, before the end of the six-month period to extend the period for negotiation, it may be extended by such further period(s) as the parties agree (*reg 14(5)*). In its decision in *Darnton v Bournemouth University* (IC/22/2009) (20 May 2009, unreported) the CAC held in paragraph 62 that it was crucial, to satisfy the requirements of the *ICE Regulations* that any agreement to extend the negotiation period was reached prior to the expiry of the time-limit, that the agreement to extend was itself explicit and that the period covered by the extension was made clear.

Whether or not particular policies fall within the scope of any negotiated agreement (or, by analogy) the standard provisions (see **17.13** below) will depend on the particular provisions of the agreement and the policy in question. In *Wright v Rolls Royce* IC/46/(2013), 24 January 2014, a travel policy was held not to be within the scope of 'contractual relations arrangements' under a negotiated agreement.

17.13 Standard information and consultation provisions

Where no arrangements are agreed, standard provisions on information and consultation will apply automatically from six months after the date on which negotiations should have started (if they did not start) or on which the negotiating period ended (if agreement was not reached): *reg 18(1)*. The standard provisions are set out in *reg 20*. In summary, they require the employer:

(a) to provide information and consultation representatives (as to the election and appointment of which, see below) with information on:

    (i) the recent and probable development of the undertaking's activities and economic situation;

    (ii) the situation, structure and probable development of employment within the undertaking and on any anticipatory measures envisaged, in particular, where there is a threat to employment within the undertaking (and from 1 October 2011 such information must include suitable information relating to the use of agency workers (if any) in that undertaking); and

    (iii) decisions likely to lead to substantial changes in work organisation or in contractual relations, including those referred to in *ss 188–192* of the *Trade Union and Labour Relations (Consolidation) Act 1992* (see generally REDUNDANCY – **II**: PRACTICE AND PROCEDURE **(40)**) and *regs 13–16* of the *Transfer of Undertakings (Protection of Employment) Regulations 2006* (see **53.18** TRANSFER OF UNDERTAKINGS) (*reg 20(1)*);

(b) to consult the information and consultation representatives as to developments, threats and changes to employment within the undertaking (*reg 20(3)*); and

(c) to ensure that the timing, method and content of the consultation are appropriate, that it takes place with the appropriate level of management and that a reasoned response is given by the employer to any opinion expressed by the representatives (*reg 20(4)*).

The information in *(a)* above must be given at a time, in a fashion and with such content as are appropriate to enable the information and consultation representatives to conduct an adequate study and, where necessary, to prepare for consultation (*reg 20(2)*).

Note that although there is an obligation to inform and consult on developments, threats and changes to employment within the undertaking, the obligation under the *ICE Regulations* ceases once the duties in *s 188* of *TULR(C)A 1992* or *reg 13* of *TUPE* or *regs 11–13* of the *Pension Scheme Regulations* apply, provided that the employer gives notification in accordance with *reg 20(5)*.

17.14 Whenever the standard provisions are going to apply, there is an obligation on the employer to arrange for the holding of a ballot of its employees to elect information and consultation representatives (*reg 19(1)*). There must be one representative for every 50 employees (or part thereof), provided that there are always at least two and not more than 25 representatives (*reg 19(3)*). The requirements for the holding of ballots under *reg 19* are set out in *Sch 2*.

Complaints in relation to the conduct of a ballot for the election of information and consultation representatives may be made to the CAC by any employee or employees' representative (*reg 19(4)*). Where the CAC finds the complaint well-founded, it must order the employer to arrange, or re-arrange and hold the ballot (*reg 19(5)*). If such an order is made, the complainant employee or employee's representative may also make an application to the Employment Appeal Tribunal, within three months of the CAC's decision, for a penalty notice to be issued against the employer (*reg 19(6)*). See **17.18** below for the issue of penalties.

17.15   Employee Participation

17.15 Pre-existing agreements

If a valid employee request to negotiate an agreement under the *ICE Regulations* is made by fewer than 40% of employees employed in the undertaking (see above **17.7**), but there is a pre-existing agreement which:

(a)   is in writing;

(b)   sets out how the employer is to give information to the employees or their representatives and seek their views on such information;

(c)   covers all the employees of the undertaking; and

(d)   has been approved by the employees,

the employer may, instead of initiating negotiations (see above **17.10**), hold a ballot to seek the endorsement of the employees for the employee request (*reg 8(1), (2)*). However, the option is only open to the employer where the employee request has been made by fewer than 40% of the employees employed in the undertaking (*reg 8(1)*).

Where the pre-existing agreement covers more than one undertaking, the employer may hold a combined ballot for all the undertakings so covered if the employee request either alone or aggregated with any requests made by employees in the other undertakings is made by fewer than 40% of the employees in all the undertakings (*reg 9(1), (2)*). However, even if the pre-existing agreement covers more than one undertaking, it is still open to the original undertaking to ballot only its own employees (*reg 9(3)*).

If the employer wishes to hold a ballot, he must inform the employees in writing within one month of the date of the employee request and arrange for the ballot to be held as soon as reasonably practicable thereafter (but no fewer than 21 days after the employer has informed the employees of its intention to hold a ballot) (*reg 8(3)*). The requirements for the ballot are the same as for the ballot for employee approval of a negotiated agreement where only a majority of the negotiating representatives have signed the agreement (see above **17.12**), save that the employees are only to be regarded as having endorsed the employee request if at least 40% of the employees employed in the undertaking and the majority of the employees who vote in the ballot have voted in favour of endorsing the request (*reg 8(4), (6)*).

If the employees endorse the employee request, the employer is under a duty to initiate negotiations as described in **17.10** above (*reg 8(5)(b)*). If the employees do not endorse the employee request, the employer is not under such an obligation (*reg 8(5)(c)*) and the pre-existing agreement will continue to govern information and consultation within the undertaking.

An employee or employees' representative who believes that the employer has not complied with the requirements of the *ICE Regulations* in relation to the holding of a ballot to endorse an employee request may complain to the CAC (*regs 8(7)–(8) and 10*). There is a time limit of 21 days for the bringing of complaints, which runs from the date the employer informed the employees of its intention to hold a ballot (if it is the employer's entitlement to hold a ballot that is disputed) or from the date of the ballot (if it is alleged that the employer has failed to comply with a ballot requirement) (*reg 10(1), (2)*). There is no time limit for complaints that an employer has failed to inform employees that it intends to hold a ballot, or (having announced that it intends to hold a ballot) fails to hold it within the requisite time period (*reg 8(7), (8)*). Where the CAC finds the complaint well-founded, it shall or may (as appropriate) order the employer to hold the ballot (*regs 8(9) and 10(3)(c)*) or commence negotiations in accordance with the procedure described at **17.10** above (*reg 10(3)(a), (b)* and *(c)(i)*).

From 1 October 2011, where information about the employment situation is to be provided by an employer under a pre-existing agreement, such information must include suitable information relating to the use of agency workers (if any) in that undertaking (*reg 8A*).

17.16 In *Stewart (J) v Moray Council* [2006] ICR 1253, [2006] IRLR 592 the EAT concluded that, where an undertaking had in place multiple agreements relating to the provision of information to its employees, the requirement under *reg 8(1)(b)* of the *ICE Regulations* that a pre-existing agreement should cover all the employees of that undertaking was met by all the agreements read together. However, each of the other requirements under *reg 8(1)* had to be met by each individual agreement so that the provisions relating to the holding of a ballot could apply. The EAT also held that employees are covered by the terms of a collective agreement within the meaning of *reg 8(1)(b)* if that agreement is intended to regulate their terms and conditions (whether or not they are union members) or if they fall within a category of employees intended to be regulated by that agreement. Further, *reg 8(1)(c)* does not prescribe any particular way in which employee approval needs to be demonstrated (eg by ballot or by written support): this is a matter of fact for the CAC. The EAT considered that it would usually (but not always) be legitimate to infer approval if, at the time the agreement was made, the majority of the employees covered by the agreement were members of the union or unions which are parties to that agreement.

17.17 Confidential information

An employer is not required to disclose any information or document for the purposes of the *ICE Regulations* where the nature of the information or document is such that, according to objective criteria, its disclosure would seriously harm the functioning of, or would be prejudicial to, the undertaking (*reg 26(1)*). Any dispute between an employer and information and consultation or employee representatives in relation to the nature of information or a document that an employer has refused to disclose may be referred to the CAC (*reg 26(2)*). The CAC has power to order the disclosure of the information or document where it considers that disclosure would not be seriously harmful or prejudicial, and has power to prescribe the terms on which it should be disclosed (*reg 26(3), (4)*).

If an employer discloses any information or document, pursuant to its obligations under the *ICE Regulations*, and requires that information or document to be held in confidence and not to be disclosed to others except, where terms permit him to do so, in accordance with those terms, then any disclosure by the recipient in breach of those terms will be actionable by the employer as a breach of statutory duty (*reg 25(1)–(3)*). This is in addition to any right which any person might have in relation to that disclosure otherwise than under the *ICE Regulations* (*reg 25(4)*). The employer will not, however, have any right of action for breach of statutory duty under the *ICE Regulations* if the recipient reasonably believed the disclosure to be a 'protected disclosure' within the meaning of *s 43A* of the *Employment Rights Act 1996* (*reg 25(5)*) and see **10.17** Disclosure of Information.

There is a right for a recipient to apply to the CAC for a declaration that it was unreasonable for the employer to require him to hold the information or document in confidence (*reg 25(6)*). If the CAC considers that disclosure of the information or document by the recipient would not, or would not be likely to, harm the legitimate interests of the undertaking, it must make a declaration to that effect (*reg 25(7)*). Where it does so, the information or document shall not be regarded as having been entrusted to any recipient on terms requiring it to be held in confidence (*reg 25(8)*).

17.18 Complaints

In addition to the various rights to bring complaints to the CAC mentioned above, a complaint may be presented to the CAC where an employee representative considers that an employer is not acting in accordance with an agreement negotiated under the *ICE Regulations* or with the standard arrangements. The time limit for presenting complaints is three months from the date of the alleged failure. If the complaint is upheld, the CAC may make a declaration and order the employer to take such steps as are reasonable for it to take in order to comply with the terms of the negotiated agreement or the standard arrangements (see *reg 22(1)–(5)*).

If the CAC makes such a declaration (whether with or without such an order) an application may be made to the Employment Appeal Tribunal for a penalty notice to be issued, under which the employer may be required to pay up to £75,000 (*regs 22(6), (7)* and *23*). The time limit for such applications is three months from the date of the CAC's declaration (*reg 22(6)*).

In *Darnton v Bournemouth University (No 2)* (UKEAT/0391/09/RN) (4 March 2010, unreported) the EAT rejected an argument that the University had reasonable excuse for its failure to comply with the *ICE Regulations* within the meaning of *reg 22(7)*, such that no penalty notice should be issued. It held that simply taking a wrong view about a material matter was not, without more, sufficient to constitute a reasonable excuse (paragraph 9). It was not necessary for the EAT to determine whether reliance on mistake expert advice would constitute reasonable excuse as there was no sufficient evidence before it that the University had in fact relied on such advice.

Matters to be taken into account by the EAT when setting the amount of the penalty include: the gravity of the failure; the period of time over which the failure occurred; the reason for the failure; the number of employees affected by the failure; and the number of employees employed by the undertaking or, where a negotiated agreement covers employees in more than one undertaking, the number of employees employed by both or all of the undertakings (*reg 23(3)*). In *Darnton (No 2)*, paragraph 12, the EAT indicated that "*the assessment of the right level of penalty is in the nature of a broad evaluation, and a nice analysis of the weight to be given to individual components is unrealistic*". It considered that it should have regard to all relevant considerations, which may cover a wide range and are not necessarily limited to those specific in *reg 23*. Moreover, assistance from other decided cases was not likely to be useful, including cases under the other jurisdictions. Similarly, in *Brown v G4 Security (Cheltenham)*, (UKEAT/0526/09/RN) [2010] All ER (D) 84 (Aug) the EAT reiterated that each case is fact-specific, that there is a need to take into account the matters listed in *reg 23* but that *reg 23* is not an exhaustive list: "Depending on the circumstances of the particular case additional factors may be taken into account and the weight of each of them will depend on the facts of the case under consideration." The EAT added, in *G4 Security*, that in its view, the number of employees in the undertaking was not particularly relevant in determining the gravity of the breach, as breach of obligations under the *ICE Regulations* affecting all employees in a small workforce may be almost as significant as a breach affecting a small proportion of a much larger workforce.

In *Amicus v Macmillan Publishers Ltd* [2007] IRLR 885, the EAT issued a penalty notice against Macmillan requiring it to pay £55,000. The penalty notice was issued in circumstances where the EAT found that Macmillan had adopted a 'wholly cavalier attitude' to its obligations under the *ICE Regulations* (see also the CAC decision reported at [2007] IRLR 378). In contrast, in *Darnton (No 2)*, the EAT imposed a penalty of £10,000. It held that the fact that the breach complained of was not deliberate and did not result from any deliberate disregard of the University's obligations under the *ICE Regulations* or even an attitude of carelessness or insouciance towards those obligations, was an important mitigating factor. In addition, on the facts, 'shadow' information and consultation procedures had been in place for a considerable period. Nevertheless, the EAT was concerned to ensure that any penalty was more than negligible. It held that the scheme of the *ICE Regulations* required unexcused errors by the University to be marked by a real penalty. In *Brown v G4 Security (Cheltenham)* [2010] All ER (D) 84 (Aug) (UKEAT/0526/09/RN), a penalty of £20,000 was imposed.

17.19 Employment protection

Employee representatives have the right to reasonable paid time off during working hours for the purpose of performing their functions as representatives (*regs 27, 28*). A complaint that an employer has unreasonably refused to permit the employee representative a reasonable amount of paid time off, or has failed to pay the whole or part of any amount to which the employee is entitled, may be presented to an employment tribunal (*reg 29(1)*). The time limit for bringing a complaint is 'three months beginning with the day on which the time off was taken or on which it is alleged the time off should have been permitted', with specific provision to facilitate early conciliation (*reg 29(1)(2)(a)* and *reg 29A* in relation to early conciliation and see **2.5 EARLY CONCILIATION**). If the tribunal is satisfied that it was not reasonably practicable for the complaint to be presented before the end of the initial time limit, then it may extend time for such further period as it considers reasonable (*reg 29(2)*). Where a tribunal finds a complaint well-founded, it must make a declaration and order the employer to pay the employee an amount equivalent to the amount of time off it should have allowed the employee, or the amount it should have paid the employee (as appropriate) (*reg 29(3)–(5)*).

In relation to the right to time off work, see generally TIME OFF WORK **(50)**.

An employee who is an employees' representative, negotiating representative, information and consultation representative or a candidate in an election to be any such representative, and who is dismissed is to be regarded as unfairly dismissed if the reason or (if more than one) the principal reason for dismissal is that the employee:

(a)   performed or proposed to perform any functions or activities as such a representative or candidate;

(b)   exercised or proposed to exercise an entitlement under *regs 27* or *28* to reasonable paid time off for performing any of those functions;

(c)   made or proposed to make a request to exercise such an entitlement (or did so through a person acting on his behalf).

        (Reg 30)

Such an employee is also protected from detriment on these grounds (*reg 32*).

In addition, an employee who is dismissed is to be regarded as unfairly dismissed if the reason or (if more than one) the principal reason for dismissal is that the employee:

(d)   exercised, or proposed to exercise, (in good faith) any entitlement to complain (or appeal) to an employment tribunal, the CAC or the EAT in connection with any rights conferred by the *ICE Regulations*;

(e)   requested, or proposed to request data in accordance with *reg 5* (above **17.5**);

(f)   acted with a view to securing that an agreement was or was not negotiated or that the standard information and consultation provisions did or did not become applicable;

(g)   indicated that he supported or did not support the coming into existence of a negotiated agreement or the application of the standard information and consultation provisions;

(h)   stood as a candidate in an election in which any person elected would, on being elected, be a negotiating representative or an information and consultation representative;

(i)   influenced or sought to influence by lawful means the way in which votes were to be cast by other employees in a ballot arranged under the *ICE Regulations*;

(j)   voted in such a ballot;

(k)   expressed doubts as to whether such a ballot had been properly conducted; or

(l)   proposed to do, failed to do, or proposed to decline to do, any of the things mentioned in sub-paragraphs (f) to (j) above.

(*Reg 30* and *ss 105(7H)* and *108(3) ERA 1996*)

Such an employee is also protected from detriment on these grounds (*reg 32*).

There is an exception where an employee has, in the performance of any of his functions or activities as a representative or candidate disclosed any confidential information in breach of the provisions of the *ICE Regulations* (*reg 30(4)* and see **17.17**). Such dismissals will be potentially fair, unless they also fall foul of the 'protected disclosure' provisions of the *Employment Rights Act 1996* (see **10.17–10.18** DISCLOSURE OF INFORMATION). See also generally **55.3** UNFAIR DISMISSAL- **II:** THE FAIRNESS OF THE DISMISSAL.

An employee also has the right not to be subjected to a detriment for any of the above actions (or inactions) (*reg 32*). This is subject to an identical exception for protected disclosures (*reg 32(4)*). A complaint that an employee has been subjected to a detriment in contravention of *reg 32* may be presented to an employment tribunal in the same manner as complaints under the *Employment Rights Act 1996* for subjection to a detriment on other grounds (*reg 33*). Compare **51.37** TRADE UNIONS – **I:** NATURE AND LIABILITIES.

These requirements reflect *art 7* of the *Directive*, by which Member States are required to ensure that employees' representatives, when carrying out their functions, enjoy adequate protection and guarantees to enable them to perform properly the duties which have been assigned to them. In *Holst v Dansk Arbejdsgiverforening*: C-405/08 [2010] 2 CMLR 49 the ECJ indicated that the *Directive* does not require that any more extensive protection against dismissal be granted to employees' representatives. However, any measure adopted to transpose the *Directive*, whether provided for by legislation or by collective agreement, must comply with the minimum protection threshold laid down in *art 7*.

17.20 EUROPEAN WORKS COUNCILS

The original *European Works Council (EWC) Directive (94/45)* applied in EEA states except the UK from 22 September 1996, and was subsequently extended to the UK by *Directive 97/74*. A recast *EWC Directive 2009/38/EC* (the '*Recast Works Council Directive*'), which was agreed on 6 May 2009 and came into force, in the main, on 6 June 2011, has made a number of substantive changes to the original.

The purpose of the *Directives* is to improve the right to information and to consultation of employees in Community-scale undertakings and Community-scale groups of undertakings.

They require the establishment of a European-level information and consultation procedure or a European Works Council ('EWC') in all undertakings (or groups of undertakings) employing:

(a)   at least 1,000 workers in the EEA, with

(b)   at least 150 workers in each of at least two member states.

(The EEA comprises the EU member states, Norway, Iceland and Liechtenstein.)

17.21 The *Directives* have been implemented in national legislation by the *Transnational Information and Consultation of Employees Regulations 1999 (SI 1999/3323)* (as amended) (the '*TICE Regulations*').

The original *TICE Regulations*, as previously amended, were further amended to give effect to the *Recast Works Council Directive* by the *Transnational Information and Consultation of Employees (Amendment) Regulations 2010 (SI 2010/1088)*, made under *s 2(2)* of the *European Communities Act 1972*. These amendments came into force, in the main, on 5 June 2011. This chapter refers to the amended form of the *TICE Regulations*, save where otherwise stated.

BIS issued detailed guidance on the Amendment Regulations in April 2010, which is available online: https://tinyurl.com/y8hbjrd4.

There are significant differences between the *TICE Regulations* as they stand now and as they stood before 5 June 2011. Practitioners need to consider carefully whether the issue before them falls under the *TICE Regulations* in their pre-amendment or amended form. In outline terms, the amended *TICE Regulations* will apply to all EWCs save to the extent specified in *Part IX* and especially amended *regs 44–45A* (which exempt from most of the newer provisions agreements establishing an EWC or information and consultation procedure which were signed between 5 June 2009 and 4 June 2011 or signed between 15 December 1999 and 4 June 2009 and then revised between 5 June 2009 and 4 June 2011, and certain forms of agreement in force prior to specified dates in the 1990s).

Note that the *TICE Regulations* do not apply to Community-scale undertakings which had pre-existing voluntary agreements in force before 23 September 1996 under the original *Directive* which cover the entire workforce, or to voluntary agreements made prior to 16 December 1999 by undertakings which are subject to the 15 January 2000 implementation date (*regs 44, 45*).

NOTE: Provision has been made substantially to amend the domestic regime by regulations – the *Employment Rights (Amendment) (EU Exit) Regulations 2019 (SI 2019/535)* ("the *Brexit Amendment Regulations*"). The amendments are to take account of the impact of a situation in which after IP completion day (31 December 2020), no further deal has been struck with the EU which takes account of European Works Councils. (Note that although the *Brexit Amendment regulations* continue to refer on their face to 'exit day', that reference is to be read as a reference to 'IP completion day' by virtue of *paragraph 1* of *Schedule 5* to *EUWAA 2020*). If that is the case, then the *Brexit Amendment Regulations* will amend the *TICE Regulations* in order (in the words of the Explanatory Memorandum) to "ensure the enforcement framework, rights and protections for employee representatives in the UK European Works Councils continue to be available, as far as possible". In short, this means that matters for existing EWCs will remain much as before, but no new requests to set up an EWC or information and consultation procedure will be able to made after 31 December 2020. In light of the fluidity of the political situation, readers should continue to check on the status of the *Brexit Amendment Regulations* in light of the progress of UK-EU negotiations.

17.22 Number of employees

In order to determine whether an undertaking (or group of undertakings) has the necessary number of employees to qualify as a Community-scale undertaking (or group of undertakings) for the purposes of the *Directive* and *TICE Regulations*, an average is taken of the two years preceding the relevant date (*reg 6*). For UK employees this means adding together the number of UK employees in each month in the two year period preceding the relevant date (as defined in *reg 6(4)*) and dividing the total by 24 (see *reg 6(2)–(3)*). For this purpose, employees who are contracted to work 75 hours or less in a normal month without overtime may be counted as half an employee for that month if the UK management so decides (*reg 6(3)*). For employees elsewhere, calculations are to be made according to the law and practice of the member state concerned (*reg 6(1)(b)*).

Proposed Amendments: the *Brexit Amendment Regulations* amend *reg 6(4)* so as to redefine the "relevant date" to take account of the end of the implementation period. In cases where, before IP completion day, a request has been made for information pursuant to *Reg 7* (see [**17.22**A] immediately below) the relevant date is the last day of the month immediately preceding that in which a request was made. Where the process is more advanced and a request has been made pursuant to *Reg 9* to negotiate an agreement for an EWC or an information and consultation procedure, the relevant date is the last in the month before that *Reg 9* request is made.

17.22a Number of employees

Reg 7 confers on an employee or an employees' representative an entitlement to receive certain information. The purpose of the entitlement is spelled out in *Reg 7(1)*: "An employee or employees' representative may request information from the management of an establishment, or of an undertaking, in the United Kingdom for the purpose of determining whether, in the case of an establishment, it is part of a Community-scale undertaking or Community-scale group of undertakings or, in the case of an undertaking, it is a Community-scale undertaking or is part of a Community-scale group of undertakings."

The information which may be requested is spelled out in *Reg 7(3)*. The first category is information "on the average number of employees employed by the undertaking, or as the case may be the group of undertakings, in the United Kingdom and in each of the other Member States in the last two years" (*Reg 7(3)(a)*). The second category is information "relating to the structure of (i) the undertaking, or as the case may be the group of undertakings, and (ii) its workforce in the United Kingdom and in each of the Member States in the last two years" (*Reg 7(3)(b)*). Where information disclosed includes information "as to the employment situation in the undertaking" (or group of undertakings) it must include information relating to any use of agency workers (*Reg 7(4)*).

The CAC may order disclosure where the employer has failed to comply (*reg 8*).

In *Betriebsrat der Bofrost Josef H Boquoi Deutschland West GmbH & Co KG v Bofrost Josef H Boquoi Deutschland West GmbH & Co KG*: C-62/99 [2001] ECR I-2579, [2004] 2 CMLR 53, [2001] IRLR 403, the ECJ stated, in relation to *Directive 97/74*, that an undertaking which is part of a group is required to supply information on number of employees, etc to workers' representatives, even where it has not yet been established that the management to which the request for information is addressed is the management of a controlling undertaking within the group (see also *Betriebsrat der Firma ADS Anker GmbH v ADS Anker GmbH*: C-349/01 [2004] ECR I-6803, [2004] 3 CMLR 14, [2004] All ER (D) 270 (Jul) ('*ADS Anker*')). Workers are entitled to have access to information enabling them to ascertain whether they have the right to request that negotiations on an EWC be opened with central management. The sorts of information that the group may be obliged to supply includes information on the average total number of employees, their distribution across the member states, the establishments of the undertaking and the group undertakings, and on the structure of the undertaking and of the undertakings in the group, as well as the names and addresses of the employee representatives which might participate in the setting-up of an EWC (*Gesamtbetriebsrat der Kühne & Nagel AG & CoKG v Kühne & Nagel AG & Co KG*: C-440/00 [2004] ECR I-787, [2004] 2 CMLR 54, [2004] IRLR 332). The group's obligation to supply information extends only to such information as is 'essential' (*Kühne & Nagel*, paragraphs 64 and 69) to the opening of negotiations for establishing an EWC. In *ADS Anker* (above), the ECJ ruled that it was for the national court to determine what information was 'essential'. In *Agyemang-Prempeh v Facilicom Service Group* [2016] EWCA Civ 14, [2017] IRLR 688, a complainant requested the information specified in *Reg 7(3)*. The Group declined to provide it, arguing that since it had conceded that it was a Community-scale undertaking, the purpose identified in *Reg 7(1)* was fulfilled and the duty to provide the information did not arise. The CAC disagreed. The respondent was a facilities provider. Employees worked in premises belonging to the respondent's clients. Each such premises was an establishment for the purposes of the *Regulations*. The complainant wanted to know where all of the employees had been assigned so that he could see whether there was support for the establishment of an EWC. The CAC concluded that the *Reg 7(1)* purpose was served by the information required by *Reg 7(3)(a)*. The *Reg 7(3)(b)* information, therefore, served a different purpose. Following *Kühne & Nagel* (above), the information should be disclosed if it is "essential to the opening of negotiations for the establishment of an EWC".

Where the central management of a Community-scale undertaking or group of undertakings is not located in an EU member state, the management ('the deemed management') required to provide information to employees and employees' representatives is the management of the undertaking employing the greatest number of employees in any member state: *art 4(2)* of the *Recast Works Council Directive* and see *Kühne & Nagel*. In order to fulfil its obligations under the *Recast Works Council Directive*, the deemed management must request the information from other undertakings in the group and the other undertakings must supply that information to the deemed management.

Note that only certain of the *TICE regulations* apply in relation to a Community-scale undertaking or group of undertakings whose central management is not situated in the UK: *reg 4* and for a recent example in practice see *Morgan & King v SAFRAN Group* EWC/8/2013, 26 July 2013.

Proposed Amendments: The *Brexit Amendment Regulations* will repeal *regs 7* and *8* in their entirety.

17.23 Requests for an EWC

Central management situated in the UK is required to initiate negotiations for the establishment of a European Works Council ('an EWC') or an information and consultation procedure if it receives either:

(a)   a valid request from 100 employees or from employees' representatives who represent at least that number in at least two undertakings or establishments in at least two different member states; or

(b)   separate requests by employees or employees' representatives which, taken together, mean that 100 employees or employees' representatives representing that number have made requests in at least two undertakings or establishments in at least two different member states.

(Reg 9(1), (2))

All such requests must be in writing, dated (with the date of sending) and sent to central or local management (*reg 9(3)*). Alternatively, central management may initiate negotiations on its own initiative (*reg 9(5)*).

Such requests must be in writing, dated and sent to central or local management (*reg 9(3)*). Central management may initiate negotiations on its own initiative (*reg 9(5)*). Disputes over the validity of requests to set up an EWC are to be referred to the CAC within three months, and undertakings which consider that they have a valid voluntary agreement but which receive a request to establish an EWC may also apply to the CAC to decide the point (*reg 10*).

These requirements also apply where the central management is not situated in a member state and the representative agent of central management is located in the UK and, in other cases, where a UK-based establishment or group has more employees than other establishments or groups in member states (*reg 5(1)*).

Proposed Amendments: The *Brexit Amendment Regulations* will repeal reg 9 in its entirety.

17.24 Special negotiating body

A 'special negotiating body' ('SNB') is to be established to represent employees in their negotiations with management on the setting up of an EWC or arrangements for implementing an information and consultation procedure (*reg 11*). It consists of representatives of employees from all Member States in which employees are employed to work (*reg 12*). For SNBs constituted on or after 5 June 2011, employees in each Member State shall elect or appoint one SNB member for each 10% (or fraction of 10%) of the total number of employees in all Member States which those employees represent (*reg 12(2)*). (Under the old *TICE Regulations*, the number of representatives for each member state had been decided by a formula set by the state in which the central management (or representative agent if the central management is outside the EEA) was located.) The SNB is then required to inform central management and local managements and the European social partner organisations of its composition and of the date on which it proposes to start negotiations (*reg 12(4)*).

UK members of the SNB are to be elected by a ballot of UK employees. Requirements for the ballot are set out in *regs 13* and *14*. There is no need for a ballot where there already exists a consultative committee carrying out an information and consultation function whose members were elected by a ballot of UK employees (*reg 15*). In these circumstances the committee may nominate from its number UK representatives for the SNB as set out in *reg 15*.

Central management and the SNB must negotiate in a spirit of cooperation, with a view to reaching written agreement on the detailed arrangements for informing and consulting employees (*reg 17(1)*).

In order to reach an EWC agreement, central management must convene a meeting with the SNB, informing local managements accordingly. SNBs are to take decisions by majority vote except that two-thirds of the votes are needed on a decision not to open, or to terminate, negotiations. The SNB may be assisted in these negotiations by experts, including representatives of European trade organisations (*reg 16(2)–(3)*). Any expert appointed by the SNB may, at the SNB's request, attend any meeting with central management under *reg 16(1)* in an advisory capacity.

SNB members are entitled to meet within a reasonable time both before and after any meeting with central management, without the central management or its representatives being present, using any means necessary for communication at those meetings (*reg 16(1A)*). Reasonable expenses relating to the negotiations necessary to enable the SNB to carry out its functions in an appropriate manner are to be borne by central management, including the expenses of one expert where applicable (*reg 16*).

In *Lean v Manpower Group* [2019] ICR 832, an appeal from the CAC, the EAT was required to determine whether the Claimant was a 'relevant applicant' to the CAC under *reg 20(3)(b)*, a question which in turn depended on whether an SNB existed at the relevant time. The Claimant had argued that the SNB ceased to exist upon the expiry of the three year time limit for negotiations with management set out in *regulation 18(1)(c)*. The EAT agreed with the CAC that whether an SNB continues to exist is essentially a question of fact, and it does not cease to exist automatically upon the termination of its negotiations with central management, whether undertaken voluntarily under *regulation 16(3)* or after expiry of the three year period in *regulation 18(1)(c)*.

Proposed Amendments: The *Brexit Amendment Regulations* will repeal *regs 11* to *16* in their entirety.

17.25 Setting up an EWC

Where the SNB and central management agree to establish an EWC, the agreement must specify:

(a)   the undertakings or establishments covered;

(b)   the composition of the EWC, number of members, allocation of seats (taking into account, so far as reasonably practicable, the need for balanced representation of employees by role, gender and sector) and term of office of the members;

(c)   the functions and procedure for information and consultation of the EWC and arrangements to link this with information and consultation of national employee representation bodies;

(d)   the venue, frequency and duration of meetings;

(e)   where the parties decide that it is necessary to establish a select committee, the composition of the select committee, the procedure for appointing its members, the functions and the procedural rules;

(f)   the financial and material resources allocated to the EWC;

(g)   the date of entry into force of the agreement and its duration, the arrangements for amending or terminating the agreement, the circumstances in which the agreement is to be renegotiated including where the structure of the Community-scale undertaking or Community-scale group of undertakings changes and the procedure for renegotiation of the agreement.

(*reg 17(4)*)

Central management and the SNB may decide in writing to establish an information and consultation procedure instead of an EWC (*reg 17(3)*). However, such agreement must specify a method by which the representatives can meet to discuss the information conveyed to them (*reg 17(5)*).

In addition, where information disclosed under an EWC agreement or an information and consultation procedure includes information as to the employment situation in the Community-scale undertaking or, as the case may be, the Community-scale group of undertakings, this must include suitable information relating to the use of agency workers (*reg 17(9)*).

Proposed Amendments: The *Brexit Amendment Regulations* will repeal *regs 17(1)* to *(8)* in their entirety, retaining only reg *17(9)*.

A statutory EWC, governed by the *Schedule* to the *TICE Regulations* (as opposed to an EWC as described in *reg 17(4)* and *(6)*), is to be set up if:

(a)   the parties agree;

(b)   central management refuses to start negotiations within six months of the date on which a valid request was made; or

(c)   no agreement has been concluded within three years of the request being made, provided the SNB has not taken a decision to terminate (or not to start) negotiations.

(*reg 18*)

In *Lean v Manpower Group* [2019] ICR 832 (above), the EAT held that application of the Schedule was not triggered under *reg 18(1)(c)* merely by expiry of the three year period without agreement being reached. The words "the parties have failed to conclude" should be understood as meaning "the parties are unable to conclude" rather than simply "*the parties have not concluded*". As Soole J put it "*If the parties consider that continued negotiation may result in agreement, there is no reason why the mere passage of time should prevent them continuing on that course.*"

Proposed Amendments: The *Brexit Amendment Regulations* will replace *reg 18* with the following:

"The provisions of the Schedule continue to apply on and after exit day in any case where they applied before exit day."

17.25 Employee Participation

The *Schedule* contains a 'statutory model' comprising a standard set of rules for the constitution of a statutory EWC governing its competence, composition, meetings and procedures. In particular, it lists topics about which the EWC is to be informed and consulted (see the *Schedule* at *para 7(3)–(4)*).

Central management and the EWC or information/consultation representatives are under a duty to work in a spirit of co-operation with due regard to their reciprocal rights and obligations (*reg 19*).

The amended *TICE Regulations* contain more detailed requirements as to the information to be provided by management to EWC members or to information and consultation representatives and as to consultation with such members or representatives than previously: see eg the new *reg 18A*. From 1 October 2011, however, they limit information and consultation to transnational matters (*reg 18A* - The *Brexit Amendment Regulations* will amend *reg 18A* so that it applies only to EWCs established before exit day). They also introduce requirements to link information and consultation of EWCs with information and consultation of national employee representation bodies (*reg 19E* – The *Brexit Amendment Regulations* will amend the requirement so that it applies only where failure to create the link occurred before exit day). At the same time, the amended *TICE Regulations* require EWCs to inform employees' representatives or, if there are no such representatives, employees themselves, of the content and outcome of the information and consultation procedure (with a right of complaint to the CAC if they fail to do so) (*regs 19C–19D*).

In *Hinrichs v Oracle Corporation UK Ltd* UKEAT/0194/18/RN [2019] IRLR 1051 the employer had consulted with the EWC but had gone on to make a final decision on redundancies without waiting to hear the EWC's opinion on the same (which it was entitled but not bound to express pursuant to *reg 18A(5)* and *paragraph 8(3)* of the *Schedule*). The EAT held that the obligation under *reg 18A* was merely to consult and that did not require the employer to wait for the EWC to render an opinion before it took and implemented a decision.

The amended *Regulations* also contain a new focus on the 'means' required by an EWC. Thus, they require central management to provide EWC members with the means to fulfil their duty to represent collectively the interests of the employees of the undertaking or group of undertakings concerned (*reg 19A*). They also require central management to provide EWC members and SNB members with the means required to undertake any necessary training (*regs 19B* and *25* – The *Brexit Amendment Regulations* abolish Special Negotiating Bodies and remove the obligation to assist with training provided for in *reg 25*).

Finally, the amended *Regulations* contain provision on 'adaptation' where there are significant changes in the structure of the Community-scale undertaking or group of undertakings (*reg 19F*). The *Brexit Amendment Regulations* repeal *reg 19F* in its entirety.

The CAC will rule on disputes about the operation of an EWC or the failure to establish an EWC. If a complaint is well-founded, the CAC must make a decision to that effect and may make an order requiring central management to take appropriate steps by a specified date. In addition, on an application by a relevant applicant within three months of a CAC decision, the EAT will issue a penalty notice requiring central management to pay an amount to the Secretary of State (*regs 20, 21, 21A* – Note that the *Brexit Amendment Regulations* adapt these regulations to take account of the amendments made to the other regulations). The maximum penalty to be imposed is £100,000 (*reg 22(2)*). The EAT also hears appeals on points of law from the CAC (*reg 38(8)*). Both the EAT and CAC may refer cases to ACAS if they believe that a dispute is reasonably likely to be settled by conciliation (*reg 39(1)*).

17.26 Confidential information

Present and former members of SNBs, EWCs, information/consultation representatives and relevant experts assisting them must not disclose information which central management requires to be kept confidential (*reg 23(1)*). Civil action may be taken by management for breach of this statutory duty of confidence except where the individual reasonably believed disclosure to be a protected disclosure within the meaning of *s 43A* of the *Employment Rights Act 1996*, as inserted by the *Public Interest Disclosure Act 1998* (*reg 23(1)–(5)*). Members or representatives can appeal to the CAC for a declaration if they believe UK central management is imposing confidentiality requirements unreasonably. A declaration will be made if the CAC considers that disclosure would not, or would not be likely to, 'prejudice or cause serious harm to the undertaking' (*reg 23(6)–(7)*).

Management may withhold any information which, according to objective criteria, would seriously harm the functioning of, or be prejudicial to, the undertaking. The CAC will rule on disputes over whether a document or information should be disclosed and will order disclosure where it considers, on objective criteria, that no serious harm or prejudice would result (*reg 24*).

17.27 Employment protection

Members of SNBs, EWCs, information/consultation representatives and candidates for election as such members are entitled to take reasonable time off work, with pay, to carry out their functions (*regs 25–27A* – the *Brexit Amendment Regulations* amend *reg 25* to remove time off rights for members of Special Negotiating Bodies). See TIME OFF WORK **(50)**.

Such employees also have the right not to be subjected to a detriment by the employer on the ground that they performed their functions or activities or made a request for statutory time off or payment for time off or proposed to do so (*reg 31*). Additional rights not to be victimised apply to any employee whether or not he or she falls within the above categories. It is unlawful (by *reg 31(5), (6)*) to subject an employee to a detriment on the grounds that the employee:

(a)   took proceedings in tribunal to enforce a right or entitlement under the *TICE Regulations* (provided any claim is made in good faith);

(b)   exercised any entitlement to apply or complain to the EAT or CAC;

(c)   requested information under *reg 7*;

(d)   acted with a view to securing (or not securing) the setting up of an SNB, an EWC or information/consultation procedure;

(e)   indicated that he supported (or did not support) the setting up of an SNB, an EWC or information/consultation procedure;

(f)   stood as a candidate for election to be an SNB or EWC member or information/consultation representative, influenced or sought to influence how votes are cast in a ballot under the *TICE Regulations*, voted in such a ballot or questioned the conduct of the ballot; or

(g)   proposed to do any of the above, or failed to do or proposed to decline to do, any of (d) to (f) above.

It is also automatically unfair under *reg 28* to dismiss an employee for such a reason (or for such a principal reason, where there is more than one reason) (see UNFAIR DISMISSAL – II **(55)**).

17.27 Employee Participation

Complaints of detrimental treatment may be made to an employment tribunal within three months of the act or failure to act or, if that is not reasonably practicable, within such further period as the tribunal considers reasonable (*reg 32*). Compensation may be awarded if the complaint is well-founded, see *ERA 1996, s 49*. Complaints may be settled by ACAS conciliation or by valid settlement agreements (*reg 41*).

17.28 EUROPEAN COMPANIES (SES)

Longstanding proposals for a European Company Statute ('ECS'), which would allow European Companies or 'Societas Europaea' ('SEs') to be formed under European law, came to fruition on 8 October 2001 with the adoption by the EU Council of Ministers of *Regulation 2157/2001*.

The ECS gives companies operating in more than one member state, with a share capital of more than 120,000 Euro, the option of being established as a single company under EU law, able to operate throughout the EU with one set of rules and a unified reporting system. The *Regulation* is accompanied by a *Directive* on worker involvement (*Directive 2001/86/EC*).

The SE form has not proven particularly popular in the UK. At the time of writing it appears that there are fewer than 20 in the UK with more than 5 workers (see https://www.worker-participation.eu/European-Company-SE/Facts-Figures), and only 49 overall (according to the Explanatory Memorandum accompanying the *European Public Limited-Liability Company (Amendment etc) (EU Exit) Regulations 2018*). For a recent example of the interaction of the SE provisions and the effect of Brexit in the context of a UK public company providing cross-border insurance services within the EEA seeking to convert to an SE in advance of Brexit see *Re Monarch Assurance plc* [2019] EWHC 979 (Ch).

NOTE: After IP completion day, those SEs which remain (i.e. which have not been voluntarily converted to another corporate form before or during the transition period) will automatically be converted to so-called "UK Societates" (see the *European Public Limited-Liability Company (Amendment etc) (EU Exit) Regulations 2018, SI 2018/1298* ("the *EU Exit Regulations 2018*"), *Reg 12*). A number of the provisions described below will then fall away on repeal and other provisions which refer to an SE will be amended to refer to a UK Societas.

17.29 The *Directive* and *Regulation* were originally implemented domestically by the *European Public Limited-Liability Company Regulations 2004 (SI 2004/2326)* (the '*EPLC Regulations*'). Under the *EPLC Regulations*, before an SE can be registered, the various companies or establishments involved in its creation must have complied with the requirements of *Regulation 2157/2001* in relation to the information, consultation and participation of employees (*reg 12*).

However, the *EPLC Regulations* were amended by *SI 2008/948* and, much more extensively, by *SI 2009/2400*, subject to transitional provisions in *SI 2009/2400 reg 2* and *Sch 2*. In particular, *SI 2009/2400* extended the reach of the *EPLC Regulations* to the entirety of the UK, and not just Great Britain. Most significantly for present purposes, *SI 2009/2400* revoked *Part 3* of the *EPLC Regulations* dealing with employee involvement.

Part 3 of the *EPLC Regulations* has been replaced since 1 October 2009 by the combination of:

(a)   the *European Public Limited-Liability Company (Employee Involvement) (Great Britain) Regulations 2009 (SI 2009/2401)*, applicable to SEs with a registered office in Great Britain (the 'GB Regulations'); and

(b)   the *European Public Limited-Liability Company (Employee Involvement) (Northern Ireland) Regulations (SI 2009/2402)*, applicable to SEs with a registered office in Northern Ireland.

This chapter addresses the *GB Regulations* only.

The Explanatory Memorandum states that there are no substantive differences between the *GB Regulations* and the prior provisions of *Part 3* of the *EPLC Regulations*.

The requirements of the *GB Regulations* apply whenever a company intends to establish an SE whose registered office is to be in Great Britain, or an SE has its registered office in Great Britain (*reg 4(1)*). The *EU Exit Regulations 2018* will amend *regulation 4(1)* to provide that they apply in respect of a UK Societas rather than an SE: see *reg 50*. In relation to the election or appointment of members of the 'special negotiating body' (below **17.31**) or employee representatives, the requirements apply whenever there are employees of the relevant company in Great Britain (*reg 4(2)*). In relation to matters of enforcement and employee protection, the GB Regulations also apply where any subsidiary or establishment of a relevant company or SE, or an employee or employees' representative, is registered or situated in Great Britain (*reg 4(3)*).

17.30 Employer's duty to provide information

Regulation 5 places a duty on the participating company (or companies) to provide information to employee representatives (or, if there are no such representatives, the employees themselves) whenever they decide to form an SE. The company must, as soon as possible after publishing the terms of any draft merger, or creating a holding company, or agreeing a plan to form a subsidiary or to transform into an SE, provide information to employees which, at least (by *reg 5(1), (2)*):

(a)   identifies the participating companies, concerned subsidiaries and establishments;

(b)   gives the number of employees employed by each participating company and concerned subsidiary and at each concerned establishment; and

(c)   gives the number of employees employed to work in each EEA State; and

(d)   provides specified information in relation to agency workers (from 1 October 2011).

Complaints that a company has failed to provide information, or has provided information that is false or incomplete in a material particular may be presented to the CAC by an employee's representative or (if there is no such representative) an employee (*reg 6(1)*). If the CAC finds the complaint well-founded, it must order the disclosure of the information in question (*reg 6(2)*).

There is a continuing obligation on the company to provide information as to progress in establishing an SE (*reg 5(3)*). The obligation is to provide that information to the 'special negotiating body' (see below **17.31**).

Regulation 5 is repealed with effect from IP completion day by the *EU Exit Regulations 2018, Reg 51.*

17.31 The special negotiating body

The company or companies proposing to form an SE are obliged to set up a 'special negotiating body' ('SNB') (*reg 8(1)*). The function of the SNB is to reach an 'employee involvement agreement' with the participating companies (see below **17.32**). The SNB consists of employee representatives elected from the employees in each member state. The employees from each member state have the right to elect one representative for each 10% or fraction of 10% which those employees represent (and so on, *reg 8(2)*). Where more than one company is involved there must be at least one representative from each company (*reg 8(3)*). Employees must be informed of the identity of the members of the SNB as soon as practicable and in any event within one month of the election (*reg 8(5)*). There is provision for appointing additional members and for changing members in certain circumstances (*reg 8(4), (6)*).

Complaints in relation to the establishment of (or failure to establish) an SNB may be presented to the CAC by a person elected or appointed to the SNB, an employees' representative (or, if there is no such representative, the employee) or a participating company or concerned subsidiary (*reg 9(1)–(2)*). Complaints must be made within one month of the last date on which the participating companies complied or should have complied with the obligation to inform employees of the identity of members of the SNB (*reg 9(3)*). Where the CAC finds an application well-founded it must make a declaration to that effect and the participating companies will continue to be under an obligation to comply with their duties under the *GB Regulations* (*reg 9(4)*).

The requirements of the ballot for the election of representatives are set out in *regs 10* and *11*. Any UK employee or UK employees' representative who believes that the arrangements for the ballot of the UK employees do not comply with the requirements of the *GB Regulations* may present a complaint to the CAC (*reg 10(4)*). Complaints must be presented within a period of 21 days beginning on the date on which the management published the final arrangements for the ballot (*reg 10(4)*). Where the CAC finds the complaint well-founded it must make a declaration to that effect and may make an order requiring the management to modify the arrangements it has made for the ballot of UK employees so as to comply with the requirements of the *GB Regulations* (*reg 10(5)*).

Where there is already a 'consultative committee' within the organisation concerned, the company is relieved of the obligation to arrange a ballot and instead the 'consultative committee' is permitted to appoint one or more of its own members to the SNB (*regs 12(1)* and *(3)*). A 'consultative committee' is defined as a body of persons which represents all the employees of the participating company, consists wholly of persons who are employees of the participating company or its concerned subsidiaries, whose normal functions include carrying out 'an information and consultation function', and which is able to carry out its functions without interference from the management of the participating company (*reg 12(4)*). 'Information and consultation function' is defined in *reg 12(5)* as 'receiving, on behalf of all the employees of the participating company, information which may significantly affect the interests of the employees of that company, but excluding information which is relevant only to a specific aspect of the interests of the employees, such as health and safety or collective redundancies; and being consulted by the management of the participating company on that information'. Most trade unions will be 'consultative committees' within the *GB Regulations*.

Where such a consultative committee exists, it is entitled to appoint so many of its number (or, with the permission of the management of the participating company, a trade union representative who is not an employee of the company) to the SNB as that company would be entitled to elect under a ballot (*reg 12(2)*). The consultative committee must then publish the names of those it has appointed to the SNB in such a manner as to bring them to the attention of the management of the participating company and, so far as reasonably practicable, the employees and employees' representatives (and those of its concerned subsidiaries) (*reg 12(5)–(6)*).

Where the management of a participating company, an employee or an employee's representative believes that a 'consultative committee' does not fulfil the requirements of *reg 12*, or that the representative appointed by that committee is not entitled to be appointed, they may complain to the CAC (provided they do so within 21 days of the publication of the names of the representatives purportedly appointed by the consultative committee) (*reg 12(7)–(9)*). If the CAC finds the complaint well-founded, it must make a declaration (*reg 12(8)*). Any appointment made by the consultative committee will then be of no effect and appointment of representatives must thereafter be by ballot (*reg 12(9)*).

Regulations 8–12 inclusive are repealed with effect from IP completion day by the *EU Exit Regulations 2018, reg 51.*

17.32 Negotiated employee involvement agreement

The task of the SNB is to reach an employee involvement agreement with the (proposed) SE (*reg 7*).

The parties are under a duty to negotiate in a spirit of co-operation (*reg 14(2)*). An initial six-month time limit is set within which to reach agreement, but with provision for extension for up to 12 months from the date the original time-limit began running by agreement between the parties (*reg 14(3)*).

There are no specific requirements as to the substance of the agreement to be reached on employee involvement, save that the elements of employee involvement at all levels must be at least as favourable as those which exist in the company to be transformed into an SE (*reg 15(4)*).

However, to be valid, the agreement must be in writing and must specify the agreement reached on certain key points (*by reg 15*):

(a)   the scope of the agreement;

(b)   the composition, number of members and allocation of seats on the representative body;

(c)   the functions and the procedure for the information and consultation of the representative body;

(d)   the frequency of meetings of the representative body;

(e)   the financial and material resources to be allocated to the representative body;

(f)   if, during negotiations, the parties have decided to establish one or more information and consultation procedures instead of a representative body, the agreement must specify the arrangements for implementing those procedures;

(g)   if, during negotiations, the parties have decided to establish arrangements for participation, the agreement must record the substance of those arrangements including (if applicable) the number of members in the SE's administrative or supervisory body which the employees will be entitled to elect, appoint, recommend or oppose, the procedures as to how these members may be elected, appointed, recommended or opposed by the employees, and their rights; and

(h)   in all cases, the date of entry into force of the agreement and its duration, the circumstances, if any, in which the agreement is required to be re-negotiated and the procedure for its re-negotiation.

In addition, from 1 October 2011, where under the employee involvement agreement the SE's competent organ is to provide information on the employment situation in that company, such information must include suitable information relating to the use of agency workers (*reg 15(3A)*).

There are specific rules as to how decisions must be taken by the SNB, and what level of majority is required for each sort of decision (an absolute majority generally, but two thirds where a decision would result in a reduction of participation rights) (*reg 16(1)–(3)*).

For the purpose of negotiations, the SNB may be assisted by experts of its choice (*reg 16(5)*). The participating company or companies must pay for any reasonable expenses of the SNB, though the company is not required to pay for the expenses of more than one expert (*reg 16(6)*).

The details of any decision taken by the SNB must be published to the employees represented on the body as soon as reasonably practicable and, in any event no later than 14 days after the decision has been taken (*reg 16(4)*).

Complaints in relation to decisions of the SNB may be presented to the CAC by a member of the SNB, an employees' representative, or where there is no such representative in respect of an employee, that employee *(reg 18(1))*. Complaints may only be presented on the grounds that (a) the decision was not taken by the requisite majority, or (b) that the SNB failed to publish a decision as required by the *GB Regulations*. The time limit for presentation of complaints is 21 days from the date the SNB did or should have published their decision. Where the CAC finds the complaint well-founded it must make a declaration that the decision was not taken properly and that it is to have no effect *(reg 18(2))*.

Regulations 14 to *16* and *18* inclusive are repealed with effect from IP completion day by the *EU Exit Regulations 2018, Regs 51* and *53.*

17.33 Standard rules on employee involvement

Where no employee involvement agreement has been reached within the six-month (or 12-month extended) time limit in *reg 14(3)*, or the parties have so agreed, the 'standard rules on employee involvement' will apply *(reg 19)*. These are detailed and complex and are set out in the *Schedule* to the *GB Regulations*. In summary, however, the standard rules provide as follows:

(a)   the management of the SE must arrange for the establishment of a 'representative body';

(b)   the representative body must be composed of employees of the SE and its subsidiaries and establishments (one member for each 10% or fraction thereof of employees of the SE, its subsidiaries and establishments employed for the time being in each member state). Its members must be elected or appointed by the EEA of the SNB, by whatever method the SNB decides;

(c)   once the representative body has been established for four years, it must decide whether to open negotiations with the management of the SE to reach an employee involvement agreement or whether the standard rules should continue to apply. If a decision is taken to open negotiations the procedure described at **17.32** above will apply, save that references to the SNB should be read as being references to the representative body;

(d)   for the purpose of informing and consulting on questions which concern the SE and any of its subsidiaries or establishments in another EEA state and questions which exceed the powers of the decision-making organ in a single EEA state, the management is obliged to:

    (i)   prepare and provide to the representative body regular reports on the progress of the business of the SE and the SE's prospects;

    (ii)   provide the representative body with the agenda for meetings of its administrative, management or supervisory committees and copies of all documents submitted to any general meeting of the SE's shareholders;

    (iii)   inform the representative body when there are exceptional circumstances affecting the employees' interests to a considerable extent, particularly in the event of relocations, transfers, the closure of establishments or undertakings or collective redundancies;

(e)   if the representative body so desires, the management must meet with it at least once a year to discuss the reports on the progress of the business. Such meetings should relate, in particular, to the structure, economic and financial situation, the probable development of business and of production and sales, the situation and probable trend of employment, investments and substantial changes concerning organisation, introduction of new working methods or production processes, transfers of production, mergers, cut-backs or closures of undertakings, establishments or important parts thereof and collective redundancies;

(f)   where there are exceptional circumstances affecting the employees' interests, the representative body (or, if it so decides, a select committee constituted in accordance with *paragraph 2* of the *Schedule* to the *GB Regulations*) must be permitted to meet with the most appropriate level of management and, if the SE does not act in accordance with the representative body's opinion as to what should be done in the circumstances, the representative body may request a further meeting to seek agreement;

(g)   the members of the representative body must inform the employees' representatives or, if no such representatives exist, the employees of the SE and its subsidiaries and establishments, of the content and outcome of the information and consultation procedures;

(h)   the representative body and the select committee of the representative body may be assisted by experts of its choice;

(i)   the costs of the representative body must be borne by the SE, which must also provide the members of that body with financial and material resources needed to enable them to perform their duties in an appropriate manner, including (unless agreed otherwise) the cost of organising meetings, providing interpretation facilities and accommodation and travelling expenses. However, again, where the representative body or the select committee is assisted by more than one expert the SE is not required to pay the expenses of more than one of them.

Again, since 1 October 2011, where under the standard employee involvement agreement the SE's competent organ is to provide information on the employment situation in that company, such information must include suitable information relating to the use of agency workers (*Schedule, para 8A*).

Regulation 19 and the *Schedule* are repealed with effect from IP completion day by the *EU Exit Regulations 2018, regs 53* and *65*.

17.34 Alternative arrangements

The members of the SNB may 'opt out' of any sort of employee involvement, in which case the usual national rules on employee involvement will apply, and the obligations to agree employee involvement procedures under the *GB Regulations* will fall away (*reg 17(3)*). The 'opt out' may be exercised by the SNB deciding, by a two thirds majority vote, not to open negotiations for an employee involvement agreement or to terminate any such negotiations (*reg 17(1)*). The SNB cannot, however, 'opt out' if the SE is to be formed by way of transformation of an existing company, and the existing company is one in which any of the employees have the right to participate in the board of that company (*reg 17(2)*). Procedures for agreeing employee involvement under the *GB Regulations* may, provided at least two years have passed since the decision to 'opt out' be 'reactivated' by an employee request that is:

(a)   in writing; and

(b)   made by at least 10% of the employees of, or by employees' representatives representing at least 10% of the total number of employees employed by the participating companies and its concerned subsidiaries, or (where the SE has been registered) the SE and its subsidiaries (*reg 17(4)*).

Where the SE has been registered, the SE may agree to the SNB being reconvened earlier than the specified two years.

17.35 Employee Participation

17.35 Disputes and complaints

Disputes about the operation of an employee involvement agreement or the standard rules on employee involvement may be referred to the CAC by a member of the representative body or (where no representative body has been elected or appointed) an information and consultation representative or employee of the SE (*reg 20(1)*). There is a three-month time limit, running from the date on which the defaulting party allegedly failed to comply with the agreed procedure (*reg 20(2)*). If the CAC finds a complaint well-founded it may make a declaration and an order requiring the defaulting party to take requisite steps to remedy the default (*reg 20(4)–(5)*).

In the event of the CAC making such a declaration, the aggrieved party has three months in which to apply to the Employment Appeal Tribunal for a penalty notice to be awarded against the defaulting party (*reg 20(6)*). Matters to be taken into account by the EAT when setting the amount of the penalty include: the gravity of the failure; the period of time over which the failure occurred; the reason for the failure; the number of employees affected; and the number of employees employed by the undertaking (*reg 21(3)*).

17.36 Employment protection

Similar provisions apply in relation to rights to reasonable paid time off (*regs 26–28*), protection from dismissal (*regs 29–30*) and protection from other detriment (*regs 31–32*) as apply under the *ICE Regulations* (see above **17.19**).

17.37 EUROPEAN CO-OPERATIVE SOCIETIES (SCES)

Directive 2003/72/EC, accompanying *Regulation 1435/03* on the establishment of European Co-operative Societies (or 'Societas Cooperativa Europaea') (SCEs), prescribed requirements as to employee involvement in SCEs, with effect from 18 August 2006. Together, these measures are known as the *Statute for a European Cooperative Society*.

Note that the *Financial Services (Miscellaneous) (Amendment) (EU Exit) Regulations 2019, SI 2019/710* ("the *EU Exit Regulations 2019*"), *reg 33(a)* revokes *Regulation 1435/03* insofar as it applies to the UK with effect with effect from IP completion day. Reg 25 of the *EU Exit Regulations 2019* revokes the *European Cooperative Society Regulations 2006* also with effect from IP completion day. This repeal is unlikely to have much practical effect – the Explanatory Memorandum to the *EU Exit Regulations 2019* says that there are no UK-based SCEs.

In *Validity of Regulation 1435/2003, Re: European Parliament v EU Council*: C-436/03 [2006] ECR I-3733, [2006] All ER (D) 12 (May), the ECJ held that the *Regulation* was correctly adopted under *art 308 EC*, as it has as its purpose the creation of a new form of co-operative society in addition to national forms, and leaves unchanged the different national laws already in existence (see [44]-[46]).

17.38 The *Directive* has been implemented domestically by the *European Cooperative Society (Involvement of Employees) Regulations 2006 (SI 2006/2059)* (the '*SCE Regulations*'), with effect from 18 August 2006. The *SCE Regulations* were implemented under *s 2(2)* of the *European Communities Act 1972* (unlike the *ICE Regulations*, which were made under *s 42* of the *Employment Relations Act 2004*).

An SCE is an organisation which has as its principal object the satisfaction of its members' needs and/or the development of their economic and social activities, in particular through the conclusion of agreements with them to supply goods or services or to execute particular work or commissions (*reg 3* read with *EC Regulation 1435/03, art 1(3)*).

The *SCE Regulations* apply to an actual or proposed SCE which will have its registered office in the UK, except where, at the relevant time:

(a)   the total workforce is less than 50;

(b)   the total workforce comprises employees employed to work in only one EEA state; and either—

(c)   if a participating individual (a natural person directly participating in the establishing of an SCE: *reg 3*) intends to form an SCE, all or all but one of the other parties to its formation are participating individuals, or

(d)   if a participating legal entity (as defined in *art 2* of the *Directive*) intends to form an SCE, all of the other parties to its formation are participating individuals.

(Regs 4(2) and 5(1)–(2))

The *SCE Regulations* do not apply where an SCE has been registered and, at the relevant time, paragraphs (*a*) to (*c*) above applied (*reg 5(3)*). However, the *SCE Regulations* will apply in modified form if a formerly exempt SCE sees its total workforce increase to 50 or more employees, including employees employed to work in at least two different EEA states (even if that does not continue to be so), or if a valid employee request is made to that effect (*reg 6*). Regard should be had to the detailed provisions as to exemption in *regs 5* and 6.

Note that particular provisions of the *SCE Regulations* apply to SCEs which have UK employees or other connections to the UK, but which do not fall within *reg 4(2)*, see *regs 4(3)–(4)*. Where the registered office of an SCE governed by participation transfers to the UK from another EEA state, at least the same level of employee participation rights must continue post-transfer (*reg 5(4)*).

Nothing in the *SCE Regulations* shall prejudice the rights of employees of an SCE, its subsidiaries or establishments to involvement (cf participation) as provided for by law or practice in the EEA state in which they were employed immediately prior to the SCE's registration (*reg 43*).

17.39 Duty to provide information

Reg 7 places a duty on the participating individual or the competent organ of a participating legal entity to provide information to employee representatives (or, if there are no such representatives, the employees themselves) as soon as possible after publishing draft terms of merger or conversion or agreeing a plan to form an SCE. The relevant employee representatives and employees are those of the participating individual or legal entity, any concerned subsidiaries and concerned establishments (*reg 7(1)*). The information must, as a minimum (*reg 7(2)*):

(a)   identify the participating individuals, legal entities, subsidiaries and establishments, and any concerned subsidiaries or establishments;

(b)   give the number of employees employed by each participating individual, legal entity, subsidiary and at each establishment (and, from 1 October 2011, provide specified information in relation to agency workers); and

(c)   give the number of employees employed to work in each EEA State.

Where there is a 'special negotiating body' (see below **17.40**), there is a continuing obligation on each participating individual and the competent organs of each participating legal entity to provide information to as to progress in establishing the SCE (*reg 7(3)*).

Complaints as to a failure to provide information, or provision of information that is false or incomplete in a material particular may be presented to the CAC by an employee's representative or (if there is no such representative) an employee (*reg 8(1)*). If the CAC finds the complaint well-founded, it must order the disclosure of the information in question (*reg 8(2)*).

17.40 The special negotiating body

The individuals or legal entities proposing to form an SCE are obliged to set up a 'special negotiating body' ('SNB') (*reg 10(1)*). The function of the SNB is to reach an 'employee involvement agreement' with the participating individuals and entities (*reg 9*).

The constitution of the SNB is complex, and is governed by *reg 10*. Employees must be informed of the identity of the members of the SNB as soon as reasonably practicable and in any event within one month of the election (*reg 10(5)*). The method used to elect or appoint representatives should seek to promote gender balance (*reg 10(1)*).

Complaints in relation to the establishment of (or failure to establish) an SNB may be presented to the CAC by a person elected or appointed to the SNB, an employees' representative (or, if there is no such representative, the employee) or a participating individual, legal entity or concerned subsidiary (*reg 11(1)–(2)*). Complaints must be made within one month of the last date on which the participating individuals and participating legal entities complied or should have complied with the obligation to inform employees of the identity of members of the SNB (*reg 11(3)*). Where the CAC finds an application well-founded it must make a declaration to that effect and the participating individuals and legal entities will continue to be under an obligation to comply with their duty under *reg 10(1)* to set up an SNB (*reg 11(4)*).

The requirements for ballots of UK employees to elect the UK members of the SNB are set out in *regs 12* and *13*. Any UK employee or UK employees' representative who believes that the arrangements for the ballot of the UK employees do not comply with the requirements of the *SCE Regulations* may present a complaint to the CAC (*reg 12(4)*). Complaints must be presented within 21 days from the date on which the relevant employers published the final arrangements for the ballot. Where the CAC finds the complaint well-founded it must make a declaration to that effect and may make an order requiring the relevant employers to modify their arrangements for the ballot of UK employees so as to comply with the requirements of the *SCE Regulations* (*reg 23(5)*).

However, the participating individual or participating legal entity is not obliged to arrange a ballot where it already has a relevant consultative committee (*regs 14(1)–(2)*). Instead, the committee is entitled to appoint the UK member or members of the SNB who would otherwise have been elected, having regard to the fact that the method used should seek to promote gender balance (*reg 14(2)(a)*). The committee can appoint either one of its number or, with the permission of the relevant participating individual or participating legal entity, a trade union representative who is not an employee of that individual or entity (*reg 14(2)(b)*). The consultative committee must then publish the names of those it has appointed to the SNB in such a manner as to bring them to the attention of the participating individual or legal entity and, so far as reasonably practicable, employees and employees' representatives (and those of concerned subsidiaries) (*reg 14(5)*).

Where the participating individual or legal entity, or an employee or an employee's representative believes that a consultative committee does not fulfil the requirements of *reg 14(3)*, or that the representative appointed is not entitled to be appointed, they may complain to the CAC within 21 days of the publication of the names of the purported representatives (*reg 14(6)*). If the CAC finds the complaint well-founded, it must make a declaration to that effect (*reg 14(7)*). Any appointment made by the consultative committee will then be of no effect and a ballot is required (*reg 14(8)*).

17.41 Negotiated employee involvement agreement

The task of the SNB is to reach an employee involvement agreement with the participating individuals and competent organs of the participating legal entities (*reg 16*). The parties must negotiate in a spirit of co-operation (*reg 16(2)*). There is an initial six-month time limit for agreement, but this can be extended for up to 12 months from the day on which the original time limit began running by agreement between the parties (*reg 16(3)*).

There are few specific requirements as to the substance of the agreement to be reached on employee involvement. To be valid, the agreement must be in writing and must specify the agreement reached on certain key points. These are broadly the same as those which apply in relation to SEs (see above, **17.32**) with, in addition, specification of the substance of any agreed arrangements for employees or their representatives to participate in and vote in the general meeting or any section or sectorial meetings of the SCE (*reg 17*). The standard rules on employee involvement (see below, **17.42**) will only apply if there is express provision to that effect (*reg 17(3)*). Note also that in relation to an SCE to be formed by conversion, the employee involvement agreement must preserve elements of employee involvement which are at least as favourable as those which exist in the cooperative to be converted into an SCE (*reg 17(4)*). From 1 October 2011, where under the employee involvement agreement information is to be provided on the employment situation in the SCE, such information must include suitable information relating to the use of agency workers (*reg 17(6)*).

There are specific rules as to how decisions must be taken by the SNB, what level of majority is required for each sort of decision, and the assistance of experts (*regs 18–19*). These are broadly similar to those which apply to SNBs established in relation to SEs (see above, **17.32**).

Members of the SNB, employees' representatives (or where there is no such relevant representative, employees) may complain to the CAC that an SNB decision was not taken by the requisite majority, or that the SNB failed to publish a decision as required by the *SCE Regulations*. The time limit for presentation of complaints is 21 days from the date the SNB did or should have published their decision (*reg 20(1)*). Where the CAC finds the complaint well-founded it must make a declaration that the decision was not taken properly and that it is to have no effect (*reg 20(2)*).

17.42 Standard rules on employee involvement

Detailed and complex 'standard rules on employee involvement' are set out in *reg 21* and *Sch 2* to the *SCE Regulations*. In general, these will apply where (*reg 21*):

(a)   the parties so agree; or

(b)   no employee involvement agreement has been reached within the six-month (or twelve-month extended) time limit in *reg 16(3)* and where: (i) the participating individual and legal entities agree that they should apply, and so continue with the registration of the SCE, and (ii) the SNB has not taken any decision under *reg 19(1)* to 'opt out' of negotiations.

Note that there are further detailed provisions in *reg 21(3)* and *(5)* as to when the standard rules on participation in *Pt 3* of *Sch 2* will apply. Where the standard rules on participation apply and more than one form of employee participation exists in the participating legal entities, the SNB shall decide which of the existing forms of participation are to exist in the SCE (*reg 21(4)*).

17.43 Alternative arrangements

The members of the SNB may 'opt out' of any sort of employee involvement, in which case the usual national rules on employee involvement will apply, and the obligations to agree employee involvement procedures under the *SCE Regulations* will fall away (*reg 19(3)*). The 'opt out' may be exercised by the SNB deciding, by a two thirds majority vote, not to open negotiations for an employee involvement agreement or to terminate any such negotiations (*reg 19(1)*). The SNB cannot, however, 'opt out' if the SCE is to be formed by way of conversion if any employees of the cooperative to be converted have participation (*reg 19(2)*). Procedures for agreeing employee involvement under the *SCE Regulations* may be 'reactivated' by an employee request in similar circumstances as applied in relation to SEs (*reg 19(4)* and see above, **17.34**).

17.44   Employee Participation

17.44 Disputes and complaints

Complaints that a participating individual or the competent organ of a participating legal entity or of the SCE has failed to comply with the employee involvement agreement or the standard rules on employee involvement may be referred to the CAC by a member of a representative body, or (in the absence of such a body) an information and consultation representative or an employee (*reg 22(1)*). There is a three-month time limit, running from the date of the alleged failure (*reg 22(2)*). If the CAC finds a complaint well-founded it must make a declaration and may make an order requiring the defaulting party to take requisite steps to remedy the default (*reg 22(4)–(5)*).

In addition, if an employees' representative (or, in the absence of such representative, the employees) believes that a participating individual, legal entity or SCE is misusing or intending to misuse the SCE or powers in the *SCE Regulations* for the purposes of depriving employees of their right to employee involvement, or withholding rights to employee involvement, he may present a complaint to the CAC (*reg 24(1)–(2)*). Where such a complaint is made either prior to registration or within a period of 12 months of the registration of the SCE, the CAC must uphold the complaint unless the respondent proves that it did not misuse or intend to misuse the SCE or the powers in the *SCE Regulations* (*reg 24(2)*). If the CAC finds the complaint to be well-founded, it shall make a declaration to that effect and may make an order requiring the participating individual, legal entity or SCE to take remedial action (*reg 24(3)*).

In the event of the CAC making either such declaration, the applicant has three months in which to apply to the Employment Appeal Tribunal for a penalty notice against the defaulting party (*reg 22(6)* and *reg 24(3)(b)*). Broadly similar provisions govern such applications as in relation to SEs (*regs 22(6)–(9), 23* and *24(3)(b)* and above, **17.35**).

17.45 Confidential information

Similar provisions apply in relation to confidential information (*reg 26*), and the withholding of information or documents which would seriously harm the functioning of or be prejudicial to the SCE or the participating legal entity or individual, or any subsidiary or establishment thereof (*reg 27*) as apply under the *ICE Regulations* (see above **17.17**).

17.46 Employment protection

Broadly similar provisions apply in relation to rights to reasonable paid time off (*regs 28* to *30*), protection from dismissal (*regs 31* and *32*) and protection from other detriment (*regs 33* and *34*) as apply under the *ICE Regulations* (see above, **17.19**).

17.47 CROSS-BORDER MERGERS

The *Companies (Cross-Border Mergers) Regulations 2007 (SI 2007/2974)* (the '*Merger Regulations*') came into force on 15 December 2007. They implement *Directive 2005/56/EC* on cross-border mergers between limited liability companies.

NOTE: The *Merger Regulations* are revoked in their entirety by the *Companies, Limited Liability Partnerships and Partnerships (Amendment etc) (EU Exit) Regulations 2019, SI 2019/348 , Reg 5(a)* with effect from IP completion day.

The *Merger Regulations* (as amended) contain detailed requirements applicable to cross-border mergers involving at least one company formed and registered in the UK and at least one company formed and registered in another EEA state or involving the formation of a new company which is to be a UK company (*regs 2, 3*). They apply to unregistered companies, as well as registered companies (*reg 5*).

Importantly, for present purposes, they prescribe minimum requirements as to the information to be provided to employees and their representatives prior to any merger, and as to employee participation following such a merger.

The requirements of the *Merger Regulations*, and in particular the provisions under which the UK courts may order meetings of members or creditors, have now been considered by the Courts in a number of cases. Those cases cast little light on employee information and participation requirements and an exhaustive review is thus beyond the scope of this chapter but see, *inter alia*, *Re Oceanrose Investments Ltd* [2008] EWHC 3475 (Ch), [2009] Bus LR 947, *Re Wood DIY Ltd* [2011] EWHC 3089 (Ch), [2012] BCC 67, [2012] BCC 67, *Diamond Resorts (Europe) Ltd, Re* [2012] EWHC 3576 (Ch), [2013] BCC 275, *In the Matter of Itau BBA International Limited* [2012] EWHC 1783 (Ch), [2012] All ER (D) 206 (Jun), *Re House-Clean Ltd* [2013] EWHC 2337 (Ch), [2013] All ER (D) 07 (Nov), *Re Nomura International plc* [2013] EWHC 2789 (Ch), [2013] All ER (D) 87 (Oct), *Re Sigma Tau Pharmaceutical Limited* [2013] EWHC 3279 (Ch), [2013] All ER (D) 31 (Oct), *Re Olympus* [2014] EWHC 1350 (Ch), [2014] All ER (D) 12 (May) and recently eg Birss J in *In the matter of International Game Technology Plc* [2015] EWHC 717 (Ch), [2015] BCC 866, Morgan J in *Re Livanova Plc* [2015] EWHC 2865 (Ch), [2015] All ER (D) 91 (Oct), *Re Easynet Global Services Ltd* [2018] EWCA Civ 10, [2018] 1 WLR 3913, and, specifically in the context of Brexit, in *Re AIG Europe Ltd* [2018] EWHC 2818 (Ch), [2019] Bus LR 307, *Re Monarch Assurance plc* [2019] EWHC 979 (Ch) and *Re Interoute Networks Ltd* [2019] EWHC 1030 (Ch).

17.48 A 'cross-border merger' means:

(a)   a merger by absorption, as defined in *reg 2(2)*;

(b)   a merger by absorption of a wholly-owned subsidiary, as defined in *reg 2(3)*; or

(c)   a merger by formation of a new company, as defined in *reg 2(4)*.

17.49

In the most part, the employee participation requirements contained in the *Merger Regulations* apply only when the *transferee company* is a UK company (as defined in *reg 3*). The entirety of *Part 4* ('employee participation') applies where the transferee company is a UK company and where:

(a)   in the six months before the publication of draft terms of merger, a merging company has over 500 employees on average, and has a system of employee participation (specific provision is made in *reg 22(1A)* as to the treatment of agency workers); or

(b)   a UK merging company has a proportion of employee representatives amongst its directors; or

(c)   a merging company has employee representatives amongst members of the administrative or supervisory organ or their committees or of the management group which covers the profit units of the company (*reg 22(1)*).

However, chapter 4 (election of UK members of the special negotiating board) and chapters 6–9 (confidential information, employee protection, complaints and enforcement) of *Part 4* of the *Merger Regulations* apply to a UK merging company, its employees or their representatives, regardless of whether the transferee company is a UK company (*reg 22(2)*).

The *Merger Regulations* apply in Northern Ireland in modified form (*reg 22(3)*).

17.50 Employee Participation

17.50 Employee participation is defined for the purposes of the *Merger Regulations* as the influence of the employees and/or employee representatives in the transferee company or a merging company by way of a right to elect or appoint some of the members of the company's supervisory or administrative organ (or recommend or oppose the appointment of some or all such members) (*reg 3(1)*).

An employee, for these purposes, is someone who has entered into or works under a contract of employment and includes, where the employment has ceased, an individual who worked under a contract of employment (*reg 3(1)*). Employee representatives are trade union representatives (if the employer recognises an independent trade union is recognised by their employer for the purpose of collective bargaining in respect of the relevant employees), or other employees who have been elected or appointed to positions in which they are expected to receive particular types of information (*reg 3(1)*). See further the definitions in *reg 3*.

17.51 The pre-merger process

Parts 2 and *3* of the *Merger Regulations* set out requirements in relation to the pre-merger process. In short, the *Merger Regulations* require certain information to be provided to employee representatives or employees of UK merging companies as part of the pre-merger process in cross-border mergers, and require the merging companies to consider any report by employee representatives (see, in particular, *regs 8* and *10*). In addition, the draft terms of merger (which must be certified by a court) must contain information on the procedures by which any employee participation rights are to be determined in accordance with *Part 4* of the *Merger Regulations* (see above **17.49**) (*reg 7(2)(j)*). Each UK company involved in a cross-border merger can apply for a court order certifying that the pre-merger requirements in *regs 7–10* and *12–15* have been complied with (*reg 6* and note also the amended *reg 16*).

17.52 Duty on merging company to provide information

As soon as possible after adopting draft terms of merger under *reg 7*, each merging company must provide certain minimum information to its employee representatives (or, if no such representatives exist, the employees themselves) (*reg 23(1)*). That information must as a minimum, by *reg 23(2)*:

(a)   identify the merging companies;

(b)   notify any decision taken by the merging companies pursuant to *reg 36* (ie a decision to apply statutory standard rules of employee participation); and

(c)   give the number of employees employed by each merging company.

From 1 October 2011 such information must include suitable information in relation to the use of agency workers (*reg 23(3)*).

Each merging company is also subject to a continuing obligation to provide information such as is necessary to keep the 'special negotiating body' (see below **17.53**) informed of the plan and progress of establishing the UK transferee company, up until the date upon which the consequences of the cross-border merger take effect (on which see *reg 17*) (*reg 23(3)*).

An employee representative (or, where no such representative exists, an employee) may complain to the CAC that a merging company has failed to provide information as required by *reg 23*, or that the information is false or incomplete in a material particular (*reg 24(1)*). If the CAC finds the complaint well-founded it must order the company to disclose information (*reg 24(2)*).

17.53 The special negotiating body

Unless the merging companies decide, pursuant to *reg 36*, that the statutory standard rules of employee participation applicable in cross-border mergers set out in *reg 38* are to apply to a UK transferee company, each merging company must make arrangements to establish a 'special negotiating body' ('SNB') (*reg 25(1)*). The task of the SNB will then be to reach an 'employee participation agreement' with the merging companies (*reg 25(2)* and see below **17.54**).

The composition (and election) of an SNB is prescribed by *reg 26*, the requirements in relation to a ballot to elect the UK members of an SNB are set out in *regs 33* and *34* and the representative role of each SNB member is defined by *reg 35*. Employees must be informed of the identity of the members of the SNB as soon as reasonably practicable and in any event within one month of the election (*reg 26(4)*). There is provision for appointing additional members and for changing members in certain circumstances (*reg 26(5)*).

Complaints in relation to the establishment of (or failure to establish) an SNB may be presented to the CAC (*reg 27(1)*). Where it is alleged that the failure is attributable to the conduct of the merging company, an application may be presented by a person elected to the SNB or by an employee representative (or, if there is no such representative, an employee) (*reg 27(2)*). Where it is alleged that the failure is attributable to the conduct of the employees or the employee representatives, an application may be presented by the merging company (*reg 27(3)*).

Complaints must be made within one month of the last date on which the merging companies complied or should have complied with the obligation to inform employees of the outcome of elections for membership of the SNB (*reg 27(4)*). Where the CAC finds an application under *reg 27(2)* well-founded it must make a declaration to that effect. If the complaint was made by an SNB representative, employee representative or employee, the merging companies will continue to be under an obligation to comply with their duty under *reg 25* (*reg 27(5)*). If it was made by a merging company, the companies no longer continue to be under that obligation (*reg 27(6)*).

17.54 Negotiated employee participation agreement

The merging companies and the SNB are to negotiate in a spirit of cooperation with a view to reaching an employee participation agreement (*reg 28(2)*).

There are no specific requirements as to the substance of the agreement to be reached. However, to be valid, the employee participation agreement must be in writing and must specify the agreement reached on certain key points:

(a)   the scope of the agreement;

(b)   the substance of any arrangements for employee participation (if, during negotiations, the parties decide to establish such arrangements), including (if applicable) the number of directors of the UK transferee company which the employees will be entitled to elect, appoint, recommend or oppose, the procedures as to how these directors may be elected, appointed, recommended or opposed by the employees, and their rights; and

(c)   the date on which the agreement enters into force, its duration and the circumstances of (and procedure for) any re-negotiation.

(*Reg 29(1)–(2)*)

From 1 October 2011, where under the employee participation agreement the transferee company is to provide information on the employment situation in that company, such information must include suitable information relating to the use of agency workers (if any) in that company (*reg 29(2A)*).

17.54 Employee Participation

The employee participation agreement will only be subject to the statutory standard rules of employee participation set out in *reg 38* if it contains a provision to that effect (*reg 29(3)*).

There is an initial six-month time limit within which they are to reach agreement (beginning one month after the last date on which SNB members were elected or appointed), but with provision for extension for up to 12 months from the date from which the original six-month time limit ran by agreement between the parties (*reg 28(3)*).

There are specific rules as to how decisions must be taken by the SNB, and what level of majority is required for each sort of decision (an absolute majority generally, but two thirds in certain circumstances where a decision would result in a reduction of participation rights) (*reg 30(1)–(4)*). The SNB may decide not to open negotiations to reach an employee participation agreement or to terminate negotiations already opened (in which case the duty of the parties to negotiate will cease) (*reg 31*). Such a decision must be taken by a 'particular prescribed' form of two thirds majority (*reg 31(1)*).

The details of any decision taken by the SNB must be published in such a manner as to bring the decision, so far as reasonably practicable, to the attention of the represented employees, as soon as reasonably practicable and within 14 days after the decision has been taken (*reg 30(5)*).

For the purpose of negotiations, the SNB may be assisted by experts of its choice (*reg 30(6)*). The merging companies must pay for any reasonable expenses of the SNB, though the company is not required to pay for the expenses of more than one expert (*reg 30(7)*).

Complaints in relation to decisions of the SNB may be presented to the CAC by a member of the SNB, an employee representative, or where there is no such representative in respect of an employee, that employee (*reg 32(1)*). Complaints may only be presented on the grounds that: (*a*) the decision was not taken by the requisite majority, or (*b*) that the SNB failed to publish a decision as required by the *Merger Regulations* (*reg 32(1)*). The time limit for presentation of complaints is 21 days from the date the SNB did or should have published their decision (*reg 32(2)*). Where the CAC finds the complaint well-founded it must make a declaration that the decision was not taken properly and that it is to have no effect (*reg 32(3)*).

17.55 Standard rules of employee participation in a UK transferee company

The *Merger Regulations* contain 'standard rules' on employee participation, in *reg 38*.

The merging companies may opt for these rules to apply to a UK transferee company from the date upon which the consequences of the cross-border merger take effect (on which see *reg 17*), without negotiating with the SNB, the employee representatives or the employees (*reg 36*).

In addition, these 'standard rules' apply to a UK transferee company where:

(a)   the parties agree that they should; or

(b)   the period specified in *reg 28(3)* has expired without the parties reaching an employee participation agreement and:

    (i)   the merging companies agree that they should; and

    (ii)   the SNB has not taken any decision either not to open or to terminate the negotiations under *reg 31* (*reg 37(1)*);

and provided that:

(c)   before registration of the UK transferee company, one or more forms of employee participation existed in at least one of the merging companies and either:

(i)   that participation applied to at least one third of the total number of employees of the merging companies, or

(ii)   that participation applied to less than one third of the total number of employees of the merging companies but the SNB has decided that the standard rules of employee participation should apply (*reg 37(2)*).

(*Reg 37*)

From 1 October 2011, for these purposes, agency workers whose contract within *reg 3(1)(b)* of the *Agency Workers Regulations 2010* was not a contract of employment with one or more temporary work agencies that were merging companies at the relevant time, are to be treated as having been employed by such an agency or agencies for the duration of their assignment with a hirer (*reg 37(2A)*).

Where the standard rules of employee participation apply and more than one form of employee participation existed in the merging companies, ordinarily the SNB shall decide (and inform the merging companies) which of those forms shall apply in the UK transferee company (*reg 37(3)*). However, if the SNB fails to make such a decision, the merging companies become responsible for determining the form of employee participation in the UK transferee company (*reg 37(4)*). In addition, the merging companies will also be so responsible where one or more forms of employee participation existed within them but they chose, without any prior negotiation, to be directly subject to the standard rules (*reg 37(4)*).

The standard rules of employee participation are set out in *reg 38*. They include that:

(a)   the employee representatives of the UK transferee company (or if there are no such representatives, the employees) have the right to elect, appoint, recommend or oppose the appointment of a number of directors of the transferee company, such number to be equal to the number in the merging company which had the highest proportion of directors (or their EEA equivalent) so elected or appointed (subject to *reg 39*, see below);

(b)   subject to (*c*) below, the employee representatives (or if there are no such representatives, the employees) shall decide, taking into account the proportion of employees of the transferee company formerly employed in each merging company, on the allocation of directorships, or on the means by which the transferee's employees may recommend or oppose the appointment of directors;

(c)   in making the decision in (*b*) above, if the employees of one or more merging companies are not covered by the proportional criterion set out in (*b*), the employee representatives (or if there are no such representatives, the employees) shall appoint a member from one of those merging companies including one from the UK, if appropriate; and

(d)   every director of the transferee company who was elected, appointed or recommended by the employee representatives or employees is a full director with the same rights and obligations (including the right to vote) as the directors representing shareholders.

From 1 October 2011, where under the standard rules of employee participation the transferee company is to provide information on the employment situation in that company, it must include suitable information relating to the use of agency workers (if any) in that company (*reg 38(5)*).

17.55 Employee Participation

Note that where the 'standard rules' apply following prior negotiation, the UK transferee company may choose to limit the proportion of directors elected, appointed, recommended or opposed through employee participation to a level which is the lesser of the highest proportion in force in the merging companies prior to registration, or one third of the directors (*reg 39*).

Specific protective provision is made in relation to subsequent domestic mergers (*reg 40*).

17.56 Disputes and complaints

Disputes about whether the transferee company has failed to comply with the terms of an employee participation agreement or the standard rules on employee participation may be referred to the CAC by an SNB, or (where no SNB has been elected or appointed, or an SNB has been dissolved) an employee representative or employee (*reg 53(1)–(3)*). There is a three-month time limit, running from the date of the alleged failure to comply with the agreed procedure (*reg 53(2)*). If the CAC finds a complaint well-founded it must make a declaration to that effect and may make an order requiring the transferee company to remedy the default (*reg 53(4)–(5)*).

In addition, if an employee representative (or where there is no such representative in relation to an employee, an employee) believes that a transferee or merging company is misusing or intending to misuse the transferee company or the powers in the *Merger Regulations* for the purpose of depriving the employees of that merging or transferee company of their rights to employee participation or withholding such rights, he may complain to the CAC (*reg 54(1)*). Such complaint must be made within 12 months from the date upon which the consequences of the merger take effect (on which, see *reg 17*) (*reg 54(2)*). The CAC must uphold the complaint unless the respondent proves that it did not misuse or intend to so misuse the transferee company or the powers in the *Merger Regulations* (*reg 54(3)*). If the CAC finds the complaint to be well-founded it must make a declaration to that effect and may make an order requiring the transferee company or merging company to take specified remedial action (*reg 54(4)*).

In the event of the CAC making either such declaration, the applicant has three months in which to apply to the Employment Appeal Tribunal for a penalty notice against the relevant company (*regs 53(6)* and *54(5)*). The EAT must issue a penalty notice unless satisfied that the failure resulted from a reason beyond the relevant company's control or that it has some other reasonable excuse for its failure (*regs 53(7)* and *54(6)*). When setting the amount of the penalty, up to a maximum of £75,000, the EAT must take into account: the gravity of the failure; the period of time over which it occurred; the reason for the failure; the number of employees affected by the failure; and the number of employees employed by the undertaking (*reg 55*).

Note that no order of the CAC under *regs 53* or *54* can suspend or alter the effect of any act done or of any agreement made by the transferee company or merging company (*regs 53(9)* and *54(7)*).

17.57 Confidential information

Similar provisions apply in relation to confidential information (*reg 41*), and the withholding of information or documents which would seriously harm the functioning of or be prejudicial to a transferring or merging entity (*reg 42*) as apply under the *TICE Regulations* (see above **17.26**).

17.58 Employment protection

The *Merger Regulations* also contain rights to reasonable paid time off for SNB members, directors of transferee companies or candidates as such (*regs 43* to *45*), protection from dismissal (*regs 46* and *47*) and protection from other detriment (*regs 49* to *51*).

17.59 OTHER NOTABLE CONSULTATION RIGHTS

Whilst the focus of this chapter is the specific legislative regimes described above, advisers will note that these are not the only provisions requiring particular information to be provided to employees or requiring consultation on particular issues, as a result both of domestic legislation and developments in EU law.

For example:

(a) Employers must consult with trade union representatives in certain cases where a large number of redundancies are planned (see eg. *section 188* of the *TULR(C)A* and REDUNDANCY – **II (40)**) and in relation to transfers of businesses (see eg the *Transfer of Undertakings (Protection of Employment) Regulations 2006 (SI 2006/246)*, *reg 13* and **53.18** TRANSFER OF UNDERTAKINGS).

(b) Employers must consult over certain health and safety issues (see eg the *Safety Representatives and Safety Committees Regulations 1977 (SI 1977/500)*, the *Health and Safety (Consultation with Employees) Regulations 1996 (SI 1996/1513)* and see HEALTH AND SAFETY AT WORK – **II (29)**).

(c) Where a trade union is statutorily recognised for collective bargaining purposes (see TRADE UNIONS – **I (51)**) an employer must consult the union regularly in relation to employee training, and to provide certain information to the union for such purposes (*TULR(C)A 1992, s 70B*).

(d) Employers must disclose certain information to employees and their representatives in relation to collective bargaining and occupational pension schemes: see DISCLOSURE OF INFORMATION **(10)**.

(e) By the *Large and Medium-sized Companies and Groups (Accounts and Reports) Regulations 2008 (SI 2008/410)* ('the *Reports Regulations*'), *reg 10* and *Sch 7, para 11* (together with the *CA 2006, ss 415* and *416*), the annual directors' report for medium and large-sized companies must contain a statement describing the action that has been taken by the company during that financial year to introduce, maintain or develop arrangements aimed at:

(i) providing employees systematically with information on matters of concern to them as employees;

(ii) regular consultation with employees or their representatives so that employee views can be taken into account in making decisions which are likely to affect their interests;

(iii) encouraging the involvement of employees in the company's performance through an employees' share scheme or by some other means; and

(iv) achieving a common awareness on the part of all employees of the financial and economic factors affecting the performance of the company.

18   Employee's Past Criminal Convictions

18.1   SPENT CONVICTIONS

The *Rehabilitation of Offenders Act 1974* ('*ROA 1974*') provides that, after a period of time, people who have been convicted of criminal offences and who have served their sentences are, with some exceptions (see **18.4** below), not obliged to disclose those convictions. The length of time which must elapse before a person's conviction becomes 'spent' in this way depends upon the nature of the sentence imposed and runs from the date of sentence. Certain sentences, such as imprisonment or custody for life, sentences of imprisonment, youth custody or detention in a young offender institution, or corrective training for a term exceeding 30 months, and detention during Her Majesty's pleasure, can never become spent (*ROA 1974, s 5(1)*; as amended by *Criminal Justice Act 1982, ss 77, 78, Sch 14 para 36, Sch 16*). An offender whose conviction has become spent is known as a 'rehabilitated person' (*ROA 1974, s 1(1)*).

18.2   Non-disclosure of spent convictions

Subject to certain exceptions, a rehabilitated person is to be treated for all purposes in law as a person who has not committed or been charged with or convicted of the offence in question.

Evidence of such matters may not be adduced in judicial proceedings and questions should not be asked in such proceedings which cannot be answered without revealing such matters; if asked, they need not be answered (*ROA 1974, s 4(1)*). This also applies to employment tribunal proceedings (*ROA 1974, s 4(6)*).

This all appears clear, however *A v B* (UKEAT/0025/13) reveals a possible further exception to this principle, namely a general exception contained in *s 7(3)* of the *ROA 1974* which appears to have been applied for the first time in the employment context in *A v B*. *Section 7(3)* provides that a judicial authority may admit or require evidence as to a person's spent convictions or circumstances ancillary thereto notwithstanding the provision of *s 4(1)* and may disregard those provisions if it is satisfied that "in the light of considerations which appear to it to be relevant ... that justice cannot be done in the case except by admitting or requiring evidence" on the spent convictions. *A v B* was a race discrimination case in which the employer had dismissed the employee. The employer contended the reason for dismissal was inappropriate comments to female members of staff and denied race discrimination. The employer wished to rely upon spent convictions of the claimant for kerb-crawling in defence of the claim. The tribunal held that the conviction was admissible by reason of the general exception in *ROA 1974, s 7(3)*. The tribunal's decision was upheld by the EAT. The EAT held that the first question is one of relevance of the conviction to the proceedings in question. Further the admission of the spent conviction must be the only way of doing justice. The tribunal must consider unfair prejudice to the convicted person but *s 7(3)* does not confer a discretion on the court. If justice can only be done by admitting the spent conviction then it must be admitted. *Art 8* of the *ECHR* (right to privacy) did not add anything to the exercise. In the circumstances the tribunal's decision to admit the conviction was upheld. It remains to be seen if this becomes a significant or frequently used exception to the general prohibition contained in *ROA 1974, s 4(1)* in employment claims.

Further, outside of the particular case of judicial proceedings, if questions about past convictions and related matters are put in other circumstances (such as at a job interview or on an application form), they may be answered on the basis that they do not refer to spent convictions, and the person questioned shall not be subjected to any liability or otherwise prejudiced in law by failing to acknowledge or disclose his spent convictions (*ROA 1974, s 4(2)*). Any obligation imposed on a person, by a rule of law or an agreement or arrangement (which would include a contract of employment), to disclose any matters does not require the disclosure of spent convictions or ancillary matters (*ROA 1974, s 4(3)(a)*).

A person who reveals another's spent criminal convictions may raise the defence of justification (ie truth) in any subsequent action for libel or slander, provided that the revelation was not made with malice (*ROA 1974, s 8(3), (5)*).

18.3 Spent convictions and dismissal

A spent conviction or a failure to disclose such a conviction are not proper grounds for dismissing or excluding a person from any office, profession, occupation or employment or for prejudicing him in any way in any occupation or employment (*ROA 1974, s 4(3)(b)*). Thus, an employer may not dismiss an employee merely because he discovers that the employee has a conviction which has become spent. In *Hendry v Scottish Liberal Club* [1977] IRLR 5, a Scottish employment tribunal held that a spent conviction for possession of cannabis had to some extent influenced the club's decision to dismiss the employee. Therefore, the reason for the dismissal could not fall within the range of permitted reasons and the dismissal was unfair (see **55.2** UNFAIR DISMISSAL – **II**). A security officer is not an occupation excluded from the benefit of the *ROA 1974* (see **18.4** below) and, consequently, an employer who dismissed two security officers for failing to disclose a spent conviction was held to have dismissed them unfairly (*Property Guards Ltd v Taylor and Kershaw* [1982] IRLR 175).

Furthermore, the fact that a person has a spent conviction is not a proper ground for an employer to refuse to engage that person, unless the person falls within a category to which the *Exceptions Order* applies (see below) (*ROA 1974, s 4(3)(b)*). However, it is not clear what remedy there would be for such a refusal: possibly it would be an action for breach of statutory duty.

18.4 EXCEPTIONS

The *Rehabilitation of Offenders Act 1974 (Exceptions) Order 1975 (SI 1975/1023)* (as variously amended) provides that people following certain occupations and professions are obliged (despite the provisions of *ROA 1974, s 4(2)*) to disclose any spent convictions and may be dismissed or excluded from employment because of such a conviction (despite the provisions of *ROA 1974, s 4(3)*). Those professions and occupations include: doctors, nurses, midwives, dentists, barristers, solicitors, accountants, teachers, police officers and (by virtue of *SI 1986/2268*, which amends the *(Exceptions) Order 1975*) directors or other officers of building societies. The *Rehabilitation of Offenders Act 1974 (Exceptions) (Amendment) Order 1986 (SI 1986/1249)* also amends the *(Exceptions) Order 1975* by substituting, for a number of specific excepted occupational groups, a general exception covering any office or employment which is concerned with the provision of accommodation, care, leisure and recreational facilities, schooling, social services, supervision or training to persons under 18 years, where the holder of the office or employment would have access to such minors in the normal course of his duties or if the duties are carried out wholly or partly on the premises where such provision takes place. Further amendments to the *(Exceptions) Order 1975* are made by the *Osteopaths Act 1993, s 39(2), (4)*, by the *Chiropractors Act 1994, s 40(2), (4)*, and by the *Insurance Companies (Third Insurance Directives) Regulations 1994 (SI 1994/1696)*. The application of the *(Exceptions) Order 1975* to work 'in connection with the provision of social services' was considered by the EAT in *Wood v Coverage Care Ltd* [1996] IRLR 264.

By virtue of the *1975 Order*, as amended, an applicant for, or candidate for admission to, any profession or occupation specified in the *Order*, or which falls within the general exception referred to above, is not statutorily excused from the obligation to disclose spent convictions where a question is asked in order to assess his suitability for any profession, occupation, office or employment in the circumstances described, if the question relates to the applicant for such a post or (where applicable) if it relates to a person who lives in the same household as the applicant, and the provision of the services mentioned would normally take place in that household.

The *Rehabilitation of Offenders Act 1974 (Exceptions) Order 1975* was further amended by the *Rehabilitation of Offenders Act 1974 (Exceptions) (Amendment) Order 2002 (SI 2002/441)*, which came into force on 29 February 2002. The professions to which the rehabilitative provisions of the *ROA 1974* do not apply are extended to include chartered psychologists, actuaries, registered foreign lawyers, legal executives and receivers appointed by the Court of Protection. Further employments subject to exemption from some of the provisions of the *ROA 1974* will now include the Crown Prosecution Service, Customs and Excise, the National Crime Squad, the National Criminal Intelligence Service, those working with vulnerable adults and certain employments in the RSPCA. Further exceptions relate to National Lottery Commission personnel, air traffic workers, and to the licensing of taxi drivers and National Lottery licences.

The *Rehabilitation of Offenders Act 1974 (Exceptions) (Amendment) (England and Wales) Order 2008 (SI 2008/3259)*, which came into force on 18 December 2008, further amended the *Exceptions Order* and extended the definition of a conviction to include a caution and made further extensions and modifications to the category of persons to whom the exemption provisions apply. Thus, in relation to the broad categories of persons to whom the exceptions to the *Act* apply, cautions as well as convictions were initially disclosable whatever the nature of the offence.

In addition, with the introduction of the *Safeguarding of Vulnerable Groups Act 2006* (see further **18.8** below) the *Rehabilitation of Offenders Act 1974 (Exceptions) Order* was further amended to confer the right to ask questions regarding spent convictions and spent cautions where a person seeks to work in a controlled activity with children or vulnerable adults within the meaning of the *Safeguarding of Vulnerable Groups Act 2006*. The right was, however, limited to circumstances where the person seeking such work is barred from regulated activity relating to children or vulnerable adults. See the *Rehabilitation of Offenders Act 1974 (Exceptions) (Amendment) (England and Wales) Order 2008 (SI 2010/1153)* which came into force on 31 March 2010.

The obligation to disclose all cautions and convictions whatever the nature of the offence and whenever occurring was challenged in *R (T) v Chief Constable of Greater Manchester* [2013] EWCA Civ 25. The Court of Appeal held that this was a breach of *Art 8* of the *ECHR*. The Exceptions Order was further amended by the *Rehabilitation of Offenders Act 1974 (Exceptions) Order 1975 (Amendment) (England and Wales) Order 2013 SI 2013/1198* introducing a filtering process so that certain spent convictions and cautions would not have to be disclosed. Certain offences which were serious remained always subject to disclosure and if a person had two or more convictions or cautions then full disclosure remained applicable (the multiple conviction rule).

In a recent challenge in *R (on the application of P) v Secretary of State for the Home Department and ors and other cases* [2019] UKSC 3, the Supreme Court found that the multiple convictions rule was not a necessary or proportionate way of indicating a criminal propensity to an employer and accordingly a further breach of Art 8. Secondly, the Supreme Court held that warnings and reprimands issued to young offenders (youth cautions) should not have been included in the scheme.

Accordingly it is anticipated that further amending legislation will be introduced amending the Exceptions Order so as to comply with the Supreme Court's judgment. To date no proposed amending legislation has been introduced.

18.4 Employee's Past Criminal Convictions

A further exception to the *Act* is set out in the *Financial Services Act 1986, s 189*, which provides that convictions for offences involving fraud or dishonesty, or for offences under legislation relating to companies (including insider dealing), various financial institutions, insolvency, consumer credit and consumer protection, shall not be regarded as spent for the purposes of certain proceedings, questions and actions specified in *FSA 1986, Sch 14*.

18.5 EFFECT OF PROVISIONS FOR REHABILITATION

If, for example, at an interview, an applicant is asked whether he has any criminal convictions, a negative answer may mean:

(i)   that he has no previous convictions;

(ii)   that he has convictions but they are spent; or

(iii)   that he has convictions which are not spent and he is not telling the truth.

If the employer subsequently discovers, after engaging the applicant, that he has previous convictions:

(a)   if these are not spent, he may consider the applicant for dismissal if such a dismissal would be fair in all the circumstances (see **55.4** U NFAIR D ISMISSAL **– II**); or

(b)   if these are spent, he may not take any action, unless there are other reasons which justify him in doing so.

If the applicant reveals at an interview that he has previous convictions:

(A)   if the convictions are spent, they do not form a good reason for refusing the applicant the job; or

(B)   if they are not spent, they may form good grounds for refusing the applicant the job (and there will be no legal redress if the applicant is refused the job on such grounds).

Any agreement or arrangement that an applicant must reveal past convictions is ineffective so far as spent convictions are concerned (see **18.2** above).

Applicants for any position in a profession or occupation excluded from the protection of the *Act* (see **18.4** above) must answer questions relating to previous convictions and may be refused or dismissed from such employment for a conviction or for failing to disclose such a conviction.

18.6 REHABILITATION PERIODS

The period of rehabilitation is related to the length of the sentence which was passed on the offender. The main rehabilitation periods presently applicable are set out below. These periods have been the subject of recent amendment by *s 139* of the *Legal Aid, Sentencing and Punishment of Offenders Act 2012* and came into force on 10 March 2014. The provisions of *s 5(2)* to *5(11)* of the *ROA 1974* have been replaced with new subsections *(2)* to *(8)*. By *ROA 1974, s 5(1)* certain sentences are excluded from rehabilitation under the *ROA 1974*. These are:

(a)   a sentence of imprisonment for life;

(b)   a sentence of imprisonment, youth custody detention in a young offender institution or corrective training for a term exceeding 48 months;

(c)   a sentence of preventive detention;

(d)   a sentence of detention during Her Majesty's pleasure or for life under *section 90* or *91* of the *Powers of Criminal Courts (Sentencing) Act 2000* or under *section 209* or *218* of the *Armed Forces Act 2006* or under *section 205(2)* or *(3)* of the *Criminal Procedure (Scotland) Act 1975*, or a sentence of detention for a term exceeding forty eight months passed under *section 91* of the said *Act* of *2000* or *section 209* of the said *Act* of *2006* (young offenders convicted of grave crimes) or under *section 206* of the said *Act* of *1975* (detention of children convicted on indictment);

(e)   a sentence of custody for life;

(f)   a sentence of imprisonment for public protection under *section 225* of the *Criminal Justice Act 2003*, a sentence of detention for public protection under *section 226* of that *Act* or an extended sentence under *section 226A, 226B, 227* or *228* of that *Act* (including any sentence within this paragraph passed as a result of any of *sections 219* to *222* of the *Armed Forces Act 2006*).

(ROA 1974, s 5(1))

The rehabilitation periods for non excluded sentences are set out in the table below (see further *ROA 1974, s 5(2)*). It is to be observed that very different rehabilitation periods apply depending upon whether the convicted person was over or under the age of 18 at the date of the relevant conviction:

Sentence	End of rehabilitation period for adult offenders	End of rehabilitation period for offenders under 18 at date of conviction
A custodial sentence of more than 30 months and up to, or consisting of, 48 months	The end of the period of 7 years beginning with the day on which the sentence (including any licence period) is completed	The end of the period of 42 months beginning with the day on which the sentence (including any licence period) is completed
A custodial sentence of more than 6 months and up to, or consisting of, 30 months	The end of the period of 48 months beginning with the day on which the sentence (including any licence period) is completed	The end of the period of 24 months beginning with the day on which the sentence (including any licence period) is completed
A custodial sentence of 6 months or less	The end of the period of 24 months beginning with the day on which the sentence (including any licence period) is completed	The end of the period of 18 months beginning with the day on which the sentence (including any licence period) is completed
Removal from Her Majesty's service	The end of the period of 12 months beginning with the date of the conviction in respect of which the sentence is imposed	The end of the period of 6 months beginning with the date of the conviction in respect of which the sentence is imposed
A sentence of service detention	The end of the period of 12 months beginning with the day on which the sentence is completed	The end of the period of 6 months beginning with the day on which the sentence is completed

Sentence	End of rehabilitation period for adult offenders	End of rehabilitation period for offenders under 18 at date of conviction
A fine	The end of the period of 12 months beginning with the date of the conviction in respect of which the sentence is imposed	The end of the period of 6 months beginning with the date of the conviction in respect of which the sentence is imposed
A compensation order	The date on which the payment is made in full	The date on which the payment is made in full
A community or youth rehabilitation order	The end of the period of 12 months beginning with the day provided for by or under the order as the last day on which the order is to have effect	The end of the period of 6 months beginning with the day provided for by or under the order as the last day on which the order is to have effect
A relevant order	The day provided for by or under the order as the last day on which the order is to have effect	The day provided for by or under the order as the last day on which the order is to have effect

(*ROA 1974, s 5* as amended by, in particular, the *Legal Aid, Sentencing and Punishment of Offenders Act 2012, s 139* with effect from 10 March 2014.)

See also on disclosure of old convictions and compatibility with *art 8* of the *ECHR T (and others) v Chief Constable of Greater Manchester and others* [2013] EWCA Civ 25, and *R (on the application of P) v Secretary of State for the Home Department and ors* [2019] UKSC 3 considered above and at the end of **18.7** below.

18.7   REFORM OF ACCESS TO PAST CRIMINAL CONVICTIONS: PART V OF THE POLICE ACT 1997

Part V of the *Police Act 1997* ('*PA 1997*'), which received Royal Assent on 27 March 1997, contains a number of provisions for access to the records of employees' past convictions. The *Act* provides for the issue of a number of certificates which may be sought by the employee or provided to an employer in order to satisfy a prospective employer of the accuracy of the employee's disclosure of criminal convictions (*PA 1997, ss 112–127*). See also the *Police Act 1997 (Criminal Records) Regulations 2002 (SI 2002/233)*.

An applicant may apply, upon payment of a fee, for a 'criminal conviction certificate' ('CCC') which records all convictions of the applicant (as defined in the *Rehabilitation of Offenders Act 1974* but excluding spent convictions) or states that there are no such convictions, as the case may be (*PA 1997, s 112*).

An application may be made for a 'criminal record certificate' ('CRC') in cases where *s 4(2)(a)* or *(b)* of the *Rehabilitation of Offenders Act 1974* have been excluded by order of the Secretary of State. The application must be countersigned by a 'registered person' within the meaning of the *Act* (*PA 1997, s 120*) who confirms that the information is sought in relation to a matter which is exempt from the provisions of the *Rehabilitation of Offenders Act 1974* (*PA 1997, s 113(2)*). The CRC is broader than the CCC in that it includes details of *all* convictions (including spent convictions) and also details of all cautions administered, or confirms the absence of any convictions or cautions, as the case may be (*PA 1997, s 113A*). Similarly, in the case of application for Crown employment, a CRC may be issued in cases of exempted questions concerning an applicant's suitability for Crown appointment (*PA 1997, s 114*).

An 'enhanced criminal record certificate' ('ECRC') may be obtained in relation to applications for certain sensitive employments (*PA 1997, s 115*). The application must be countersigned by a registered person who confirms that the certificate is sought in relation to considering the applicant's suitability for employment in a number of positions such as working with children or vulnerable adults (*PA 1997, s 113B*).

The ECRC (as in the case of the CRC) gives details of all convictions and cautions (or their absence) but, in addition, the Secretary of State will request the Chief Officer of every relevant police force to provide any information which the Chief Officer considers relevant to the issue of the applicant's suitability for such a position; this information will be included in the certificate (*PA 1997, s 113B(4)*). The application, meaning and effect of *s 115(7)* (the predecessor provision relating to relevant information prior to the enactment in materially identical terms of *s 113B(4)*) has been considered authoritatively in *R (X) v Chief Constable of the West Midlands Police* [2004] EWCA Civ 1068, [2005] 1 All ER 610, [2005] 1 WLR 65. It was held that the Chief Constable was under a duty to disclose if the information might be relevant, unless there was some good reason for not making such a disclosure, and that he was not required to afford the subject of the information a right to make representations. Further *s 115* (now *s 113(B)(4)*) has been held to engage *Art 8* of the *European Convention for the Protection of Human Rights and Fundamental Freedoms* but has been held to be compliant with that *Article* (see *R(X) v Chief Constable of the West Midlands Police* (above)). See also *R (L) v Metropolitan Police Comr* [2006] EWHC 482 (Admin), [2006] All ER (D) 262 (Mar), *R v Local Authority and Police Authority in the Midlands, ex p LM* [1999] All ER (D) 992), *R (on the application of Pinnington) v Chief Constable of Thames Valley Police* [2008] EWHC 1870 (Admin), [2008] All ER (D) 405 (Jul).

The discretion afforded by *s 113B* is broad and extends to any information which may, in the opinion of the Chief Officer, be relevant. It has been explained judicially that 'any' means just what it says and is not limited in its scope to information relating to criminal conduct: see *R (L) v Metropolitan Police Comr* [2006] EWHC 482 (Admin) [2006] All ER (D) 262 (Mar). By *s 116*, the issuing of ECRCs are extended to Crown employment.

In *Desmond v Chief Constable of Nottinghamshire Police* [2011] EWCA Civ 3, [2011] All ER (D) 37 (Jan) the Court of Appeal held that the police are not obliged in tort to take reasonable care when providing information under the *PA 1997* about a job applicant for the purposes of the ERRC certificate. The Court of Appeal held that statute does not confer a common law cause of action for breach of statutory duty in the information provided by the police or by refraining from providing information. The Court observed that the procedure's purpose of protecting vulnerable young people would be jeopardised if the police owed a tortious duty of care towards the person the subject of the check. The Court further observed that an aggrieved individual was not without alternative avenues of redress including the statutory remedy of correcting an inaccurate certificate contained in *s 117* of the *PA 1997*, a judicial review application and/or a claim under the *Human Rights Act 1998* for breach of *art 8*, breach of the *Data Protection Act 1998* or claims for misfeasance in public office and/or maladministration. The *Protection of Freedoms Act 2012* introduced a new *s 117A* to the *PA 1997* which provides for an independent monitor to whom application may be made to determine if information is not relevant or ought not to be included in a certificate.

In the case of each certificate outlined above, the Secretary of State may refuse to issue a certificate unless satisfied of the applicant's identity, which may involve the provision of fingerprints to confirm identity (*PA 1997, s 118*). If the applicant believes that any of the information contained in any certificate is inaccurate, he may apply in writing to the Secretary of State for a new certificate (*PA 1997, s 117*). On the utilisation of *s 117* see *R(B) v Secretary of State for Home Department and Metropolitan Police Comr* [2006] EWHC 579 (Admin), [2006] All ER (D) 370 (Mar). It is an offence to falsify or alter certificates or use certificates belonging to another (*PA 1997, s 123*). It is also an offence for employees of registered bodies or recipients of CRC or ECRC information to disclose the information contained in the certificates otherwise than in the course of their duties (*PA 1997, s 124* and see *s 124A* in relation to offences relating to delegated functions). There is a recently revised code of practice addressing relevant matters titled 'Revised Code of Practice for Disclosure and Barring Service Registered Persons November 2015' issued by the Secretary of State under the Act (*PA 1997, s 122(2)*). The Code is available from https ://www.gov.uk/government/publications/dbs-code-of-practice.

The *Protection of Freedoms Act 2012* made certain minor amendments to the provisions of *Part V* of the *PA 1997* and criminal record certificates are now obtained from the newly created Disclosure and Barring Service ('DBS').

The government announced in March 2013 that new legislation was to be enacted to filter out certain convictions from disclosure on a criminal record certificate. On 29 May 2013, by the *Rehabilitation of Offenders Act 1974 (Exceptions) Order 1975 (Amendment) (England and Wales) Order 2013 (SI 2013/1198)* and *Police Act 1997 (Criminal Record Certificates: Relevant Matters) (Amendment) (England and Wales) Order 2013 (SI 2013/1200)*, filtering rules were introduced to exclude certain convictions from disclosure on a criminal record certificate.

By the *Rehabilitation of Offenders Act 1974 (Exceptions) Order 1975 (Amendment) (England and Wales) Order 2013 (SI 2013/1198)* certain criminal matters are identified as either 'protected convictions' or 'protected cautions'.

A conviction is a 'protected conviction' if:

(i)   it does not relate to a 'listed offence', such as violent and sexual offences; and

(ii)   no custodial sentence was imposed; and

(iii)   the individual has no other convictions (where the individual has more than one conviction, all convictions will be included on the certificate); and

(iv)   it was received by a person aged under 18 at the time of the conviction and five and a half years or more have elapsed; or

(v)   it was received by a person aged 18 or over at the time of the conviction and 11 years or more have elapsed.

A caution is a 'protected caution' if:

(i)   it does not relate to a listed offence; and

(ii)   it was given to a person aged under 18 at the time of the caution and two years or more have elapsed; or

(iii)   it was given to a person aged 18 or over at the time of the caution and six years or more have elapsed.

These 'protected' categories are not to be disclosed on a DBS certificate. It should be noted that certain convictions will always be disclosed ('listed offences'). Further it is only if it is the individual's only conviction or caution (as the case maybe) that will attract the protection of being 'protected' and accordingly omitted from the DBS record. There are also certain excepted employments from the regime (eg employment which engages national security) where even protected convictions or cautions will be disclosed.

If a conviction or caution is 'protected' then, as well as being excluded from the DBS certificate, employers will not be legally entitled to ask questions about such convictions or cautions or rely on them to refuse employment or as grounds for dismissal as to do so would be unlawful under the *ROA 1974*.

These changes were made in response to the Court of Appeal's decision in *R (T and others) v Chief Constable of Greater Manchester and others* [2013] EWCA Civ 25, [2013] 2 All ER 813, in which the Court of Appeal held that the disclosure of all cautions and convictions, however old or minor, on a DBS Certificate was incompatible with Article 8 of the Convention for Human Rights. In that case the claimants contended that, in certain respects, the provisions of the *Police Act 1997*, the *Rehabilitation of Offenders Act 1974* and the *Rehabilitation of Offenders Act 1974 (Exceptions) Order* were incompatible with art 8 of the European Convention on Human Rights. The Court of Appeal held that the provisions of the *PA 1997*, requiring disclosure of all convictions, were incompatible with art 8 rights as the disclosure of all convictions and cautions relating to recordable offences was disproportionate to the legitimate aim of protection of the public. In a recent challenge in *R (on the application of P) v Secretary of State for the Home Department and ors* [2019] UKSC 3 the Supreme Court found that the multiple convictions rule (at subparagraph (iii) above) was not necessary or proportionate and, accordingly, a breach of *Art 8*. Secondly, the Supreme Court held that warnings and reprimands issued to young offenders (youth cautions) should not have been included in the scheme. Accordingly, it is anticipated that further amending legislation will be introduced amending the Exceptions Order and the categories of protected convictions and cautions so as to comply with the Supreme Court's judgment. To date no proposed amending legislation has been introduced.

As a consequence of the passing of the *Coronavirus Act 2020* in response to the Covid-19 pandemic, provisions have been made for expediting or "fast tracking" DBS checks for key workers such as nurse, midwives and social workers and also for facilitating DBS identity checks remotely. Under the current guidance, the person checking identity must be in physical possession of the original documents so they can be checked for indicators of fraud. As a consequence of difficulties in receiving the physical documents and delay to applications, with effect from 24 March 2020, the DBS identity checking guidance has been changed, for a temporary period, permitting identity documents to be viewed over video link and scanned images to be used in advance of the DBS check being submitted. The changes should only be applied to urgent cases where it is not possible to follow the normal identity checking guidelines. The applicant must present the original versions of the documents submitted electronically when they first attend their employment or volunteering role. Guidance on the new temporary measures can be found at https ://www.gov.uk/guidance/covid-19-how-dbs-is-supporting-the-fight-against-coronavirus.

18.8   THE SAFEGUARDING OF VULNERABLE GROUPS ACT 2006

The *Safeguarding Vulnerable Groups Act 2006* ('the *Act*') received Royal Assent on 8 November 2006 and significant provisions came into force on 12 October 2009. The Act provides that it is an offence to employ a person to work with children or vulnerable adults unless they were registered with the then Independent Safeguarding Authority ('ISA'). A main function of the ISA was the maintaining of two lists of persons barred from carrying out regulated activity in relation to children and, separately, vulnerable adults. From 12 October 2009 it was an offence for a barred individual to seek or undertake regulated activity with children and vulnerable adults and it was an offence for a Regulated Activity Provider (as defined in the *Act*) to knowingly employ a barred person in relation to regulated activity (*Safeguarding Vulnerable Groups Act 2006 (Commencement No 6, Transitional Provisions and Savings) Order 2009 (SI 2009/2611)*). A 'Regulated Activity' was any activity which involves contact with children or vulnerable adults, eg fostering and childcare, specified activities involving contact with children or vulnerable adults in specified places or at specified times or overnight and activities involving workers in defined positions of responsibility. A 'Controlled Activity' included support work in the health or further education field, support work in adult social care and work for specified organisations which would involve frequent access to sensitive records relating to children and/or vulnerable adults. Other provisions relating to registration under a vetting and barring scheme, which were due to commence in July 2010, were not brought into force and new legislation in the *Protection of Freedoms Act 2012* creates a new scheme considered in outline below.

In *R (Royal College of Nursing) v Secretary of State for the Home Department* [2010] EWHC 2761 (Admin), [2010] All ER (D) 103 (Nov), provisions of the *Act* providing for a person to be automatically placed on a barred list in the event of a caution or conviction were held to breach *art 6* of the *ECHR* and were incompatible with the *Human Rights Act* because the provisions did not permit representations to be made prior to being placed on the list. In other respects, in relation to appeal and minimum barring period, the Act was however found to be compliant with the *ECHR* and *HRA*.

18.9 THE PROTECTION OF FREEDOMS ACT 2012

The *Protection of Freedoms Act 2012* ('the *Act*') amended the *Safeguarding Vulnerable Groups Act 2006* and created a new corporate body, the Disclosure and Barring Service ('DBS'). The relevant amending provisions are found in *Part V* of the *Act*.

Sections 64–76 of the *Act* make amendments to the definition of regulated activity and the definition of vulnerable adults under the *Safeguarding Vulnerable Groups Act 2006* (see *ss 64–66*) and abolish the concept of controlled activity and monitoring (*ss 68–69*). Changes are made to the test for barring decisions (*s 67*) and the information required in order to make a barring decision is addressed in s 70. A power of review of barring decisions by the DBS of its own motion is provided for in *s 71* of the *Act*. By *s 72* an affected person may apply for information relating to a barring decision.

Section 73 of the *Act* introduces a new *s 34ZA* into the *Safeguarding Vulnerable Groups Act 2006* which requires a regulated activity provider to check that any relevant person is not barred prior to engaging that person. The duty also extends to suppliers of personnel.

Section 87 of the *Act* creates the DBS and by *s 87* the ISA is dissolved and its functions transferred to the DBS. *Schedule 8* of the *Act* provides further detail in relation to the constitution and operation of the DBS. Information in relation to the DBS may be obtained from its website www.gov.uk/government/organisations/disclosure-and-barring-service.

19   Employment Tribunals – I

19.1   HISTORY OF EMPLOYMENT TRIBUNALS

Employment tribunals (known until 1998 as 'industrial tribunals') are the principal forum for adjudicating disputes between employees (and prospective or former employees, and in some cases other workers) and employers. The tribunals, which were originally created in 1964 to decide disputes about liability to pay Industrial Training Levy, have over the years been given significant additional jurisdiction, increasingly so in recent years. Their future is now subject to the 13th Programme of Law Reform launched on 14 December 2017 by the Law Commission. The Law Commission published its report *Employment Law Hearing Structures* (LC 390) on 27 April 2020. It includes a number of significant proposals for reform which are outlined further below **19.3**.

The workload of the employment tribunals has, unsurprisingly, fluctuated over the 50 years of their operation. The number of cases rose from a low of 29,304 applications registered in 1988–89, to a high of 236,100 in 2009–10. The figures were affected in particular by significant numbers of multiple claims, mostly for equal pay, which have led to considerable variations in the total number of claims from year to year, and by large numbers of claims for holiday pay by air crew, reissued every three months. The underlying trend in single claims was for a gradual rise in the period prior to 2013, reaching a high point of over 70,000 such claims in 2009–10, but both the total number of claims (218,100) and the number of individuals bringing separate claims fell back in 2010–11 and again in 2011–12 (186,300). There was a slight rise in 2012–13 (191,541).

On 29 July 2013, the Government introduced a requirement for claimants to pay an issue fee when presenting their claim to the Employment Tribunal. This had a significant effect on the number of claims received by the Employment Tribunals. In the period September – December 2013, there was a 76% reduction in claims on the same period the year before for all claims combined. For January – March 2014 the reduction was 81%. Annually, in 2013-14 105,803 claims were received and 2014-15 saw only 61,308. The number then increased slightly to 83,031 in 2015-16 and 88,476 in 2016-17.

On 26 July 2017, however, the Supreme Court handed down its decision in *Regina (Unison) v Lord Chancellor* [2017] 3 WLR 409 finding the *Employment Tribunals and the Employment Appeal Tribunal Fees Order 2013* to be unlawful ab initio as an interference with access to justice under both domestic and European Union law. Since that judgment, and the abolition of fees, the number of claims has risen again, with receipts in single claim cases for 2017/18 totalling 109.685, and for 2018/19 totalling 121,111 .

Statistics of numbers of cases do not give the full picture of the volume and complexity of the tribunals' case load in recent years. The number of individual claims under separate jurisdictions raised in each case has been steadily rising over the years. The trend to more complex cases and lengthier hearings was reinforced by the extension of the tribunals' jurisdiction to cover discrimination on grounds of religion or belief, sexual orientation and age and claims by agency workers as well as the dramatic increase in the numbers of multiple equal pay claims.

The increase in workload since the 1990s, which was not matched by increases in resources, put a considerable strain on the tribunal system. This led to a number of measures intended to improve efficiency and effectiveness. Various changes to procedures were made by the *Trade Union Reform and Employment Rights Act 1993 ('TURERA 1993')* and new rules of procedure were made the same year; further reforms were enacted by the *Employment Rights (Dispute Resolution) Act 1998 ('ERDRA 1998')*. Since 2000, several further initiatives have been taken.

19.1 Employment Tribunals – I

(a) Back in July 2001, updated Rules of Procedure were introduced as from July 2001 (the *Employment Tribunals (Constitution and Rules of Procedure) Regulations 2001 (SI 2001/1171)* and their Scottish counterpart *(SI 2001/1170)*). Those rules embodied a number of changes, of which the most significant were:

    (i) The introduction of an Overriding Objective for tribunals, which must be taken into account in interpreting the rules of procedure and in deciding issues affecting the conduct of the proceedings. The Overriding Objective is 'to deal with cases justly', which includes so far as practicable ensuring that the parties are on an equal footing, saving expense, dealing with cases in ways proportionate to their complexity, and ensuring that they are dealt with expeditiously and fairly. The parties are required to assist in the achievement of this objective. The parties are required to assist in the achievement of this objective. See further **19.1** et sec.

    (ii) Tribunals were given powers to order a claim (or defence) to be struck out on the ground that it was 'misconceived', a term defined as including having 'no reasonable prospects of success'.

    (iii) The power to award costs was extended to cases where the bringing or conducting of proceedings was 'misconceived' (defined as above), and the amount that could be awarded on a summary assessment by the tribunal was raised from £500 to £10,000. In addition, the deposit that could be ordered at a pre-hearing review was increased to a maximum of £500; previously it had been £150.

These changes were retained and built on in further reforms of the rules in 2004, 2009, 2012 and 2013 (see below). During 2012, a comprehensive review of the rules was undertaken under the chairmanship of Underhill J (as he then was) and new rules contained in the *Employment Tribunals (Constitution and Rules of Procedure) Regulations 2013, SI 2013/1237* ('the *2013 Regulations*' and 'the *2013 Rules*') came into force on 29 July 2013.

(b) Following the recommendations of a Government Task Force which had been appointed to reassess the workings of the employment tribunal system as a whole, which recommended a greater emphasis on the early resolution of disputes, major changes in the procedure for making claims to employment tribunals were introduced by the *Employment Act 2002* and accompanying *Dispute Resolution Regulations*. The details of these procedures, which are now largely of historical interest following the repeal of the relevant provisions of the *2002 Act* by the *Employment Act 2008*, are briefly noted at **19.2** below. At the same time, various changes in tribunal procedure were made by Rules of Procedure which came into force on 1 October 2004 (the *Employment Tribunals (Constitution and Rules of Procedure) Regulations 2004, SI 2004/1861* ('the *2004 Regulations*'; the *Rules* themselves were in *Schedule 1* to the *2004 Regulations* ('the *2004 Rules*')). These rules were replaced on 29 July 2013 by the rules of procedure set out in the *2013 Regulations*.

(c) A major review of the tribunal system generally, under Sir Andrew Leggatt, a former Lord Justice of Appeal (*Tribunals for Users: One System, One Service*, TSO August 2000 (See http://webarchive.nationalarchives.gov.uk/+/http://www.tribunals -review.org.uk/leggatthtm/leg-00.htm)) led to the creation, by the *Tribunals, Courts and Enforcement Act 2007*, of a unified tribunal system, with a transfer of responsibility for employment tribunals from the DTI to the Ministry of Justice. Employment tribunals retained their separate identity as well as the existing tripartite structure of membership.

The *2007 Act* expressly preserved the separate identity of employment tribunals and the EAT, but not their administrative independence from the rest of the new tribunal system. The Tribunals Service was given the responsibility for the administration of employment tribunals and the Employment Appeal Tribunal, with BIS (as successor to the DTI) retaining responsibility for the Rules of Procedure. Subsequently the Tribunals Service has been merged with HM Courts Service to form HM Courts and Tribunals Service, which came into being on 1 April 2011. In Scotland, a Scottish Tribunals Service does not presently have responsibility for employment tribunals. A consultation in 2012 considered whether the employment tribunals and EAT in Scotland should transfer to that service; ultimately, however, no such proposals were contained in the *Tribunals (Scotland) Bill*, part of the Programme for Government 2012–13. However, more recently, a further consultation has completed and is being considered by Scottish Ministers concerning a draft Order in Council that would make provision to transfer specified functions of the Employment Tribunal to the First-tier Tribunal for Scotland pursuant to the *Scotland Act 2016*: see **19.6** below.

One change of detail made by the *2007 Act* (*Sch 8 para 36*, inserting a new *s 3A* into the *ETA 1996*) was the re-naming of employment tribunal chairmen (as they had been designated since 1964) as Employment Judges; Regional Chairmen became Regional Employment Judges. The change took effect on 1 November 2007.

(d)   There have been a number of other developments aimed at promoting the early resolution of employment disputes. A scheme for voluntary arbitration through ACAS in unfair dismissal cases, foreshadowed by *ERDRA 1998*, came into operation in 2001 for England and Wales and early 2004 in Scotland. It has subsequently been extended to cover disputes about the right to request flexible working arrangements. However, the scheme has had a very limited impact, with fewer than 100 cases referred to it since its inception. See further **19.25** below. Despite the limited impact of the voluntary arbitration service, there has been increasing interest in alternative dispute resolution schemes for employment disputes, and initiatives in this area include the development of mediation services by ACAS (the number of new cases has in general been on the rise, but the numbers are still relatively small; ACAS advertise a success rate of about 70%) and in January 2009 the introduction of a facility for judicial mediation within the employment tribunals themselves. Since 2016, judicial assessment has also been offered by the employment tribunal (see **19.24** below for details of judicial mediation and assessment).

A further initiative introduced by ACAS in 2009, with some initial success, was a facility for Pre-claim Conciliation, before a claim was presented to an employment tribunal. Nearly 10,000 cases were referred to this scheme in its first year, over 17,000 in 2010–11, some 23,700 in 2011/2012, reducing slightly to 22,630 in 2012/13 and 21,762 in 2013/14. Of these the number of cases recorded as successfully resolved has revolved around the 50% mark: more precisely 51.9% for 2012/13 and 57.1% for 2013/14. 77% (in 2012) and 82.6% (in 2013) were not followed by tribunal claims (a more generous measure of success). This scheme was discontinued in April 2014 with the introduction of Early Conciliation.

By *section 7* of the *Enterprise and Regulatory Reform Act 2013*, a new requirement for Early Conciliation was introduced in 2014 requiring prospective claimants under certain jurisdictions of the tribunal to provide information to ACAS prior to presenting their claim to the tribunal. This requirement was to remedy the fact that only around one fifth of claimants contacted ACAS for advice before submitting their claims. Provision is made for a certificate of compliance to be issued by an ACAS conciliation officer, and for consequential adjustments to the time limits for presenting the claims (see **19.8** et sec below for details).

19.2 The 2002 Act and its repeal

The changes affecting the powers and procedure of employment tribunals introduced via the *Employment Act 2002* and the *Employment Act 2002 (Dispute Resolution) Regulations 2004*, with effect from 1 October 2004, were largely reversed by the repeal of the relevant parts of that *Act* by the *Employment Act 2008*, with effect from 6 April 2009 and the consequential lapse of the *Regulations*. Consequently, only a brief summary of the features of the legislation is given below.

(a) A requirement for claimants to go through workplace grievance procedures where relevant, before a claim can be made to a tribunal, with power to reduce compensation if the claimant does not do so (and increase it if the employer does not provide a procedure, or dismisses or takes disciplinary action without following the applicable statutory procedure) (*2002 Act, s 31*).

(b) Changes in the time limits for commencing tribunal claims to allow time for internal procedures to be concluded without the necessity to present a claim to preserve the employee's rights; the employee is not permitted to present his or her claim to the tribunal in certain cases until after the employer has been given the opportunity to resolve it under the grievance procedure, and in certain circumstances the time limit for claiming is automatically extended by three months (*ss 32, 33*).

(c) Provision for a limited conciliation period for ACAS to attempt to secure a settlement; if the case was not settled within that period (or any extension of it), ACAS ceased to be under a duty to offer its assistance in any further attempts at settlement (*s 24*: this provision was repealed, and the implementing provisions in the *ET Rules* were revoked, with immediate effect both for new cases and those already before the tribunals, on 6 April 2009).

The changes introduced by the *2002 Act* proved to be widely disliked, and the approach of the courts to their interpretation has generally been based in the importance of preserving rights of access to justice rather than literal application of the legislation. In March 2007 the DTI instituted a consultation exercise on whether the procedures introduced by the *2002 Act* should be scrapped, as recommended by a Review commissioned by the Department. The consultation exercise confirmed the Government in its view that the procedures should be repealed, and the legislation to repeal the statutory dispute resolution procedures and associated procedural requirements, received Royal Assent as the *Employment Act 2008* in November 2008.

The relevant provisions of the *2008 Act* were brought into force on 6 April 2009, but subject to significant exceptions, contained in the *Employment Act 2008 (Commencement No 1, Transitional Provisions and Savings) Order 2008, SI 2008/3232*. This *Order* preserves the old law in cases where either of the statutory dismissal and disciplinary procedures applied, if the employer dismissed the employee, or initiated the statutory procedure, on or before 5 April 2009. The old law also applies in cases where either of the statutory grievance procedures applied, if the matter the subject of the claim occurred on or before 5 April 2009, or, if it extended over a period spanning that date, if the employee either presented a claim or submitted a written grievance before 5 July 2009 (or in certain cases 5 October 2009). For those cases where the old law applies, not only was the acceptance of a claim still subject to the preconditions in *s 32* of the *Employment Act 2002* (where applicable) but also the provisions of *s 31* giving tribunals powers to increase or decrease compensation by up to 50% where there has been a failure to comply with the applicable statutory procedure, continue to apply.

Other changes introduced at the same time as the repeal of the *2002 Act* included simplified tribunal claim and response forms. However, the procedure for screening claims prior to acceptance for compliance with procedural requirements such as using the prescribed claim form and providing the mandatory information on it, has also been retained, albeit the requirements of the new claim form are less prescriptive. New forms and new procedures for screening claims upon presentation are introduced by the Rules within the *2013 Regulations*.

One feature of the 2002 reforms that has been retained in modified form is the power given to tribunals to increase or decrease compensation in certain circumstances; the tribunal may increase or decrease the sum awarded by up to 25% if satisfied that the employer or employee, as the case may be, has unreasonably failed to comply with a provision of a relevant ACAS Code of Practice (*Trade Union and Labour Relations (Consolidation) Act 1992, s 207A*, inserted by the *Employment Act 2008, s 2*). See further EMPLOYMENT TRIBUNALS – II, [20.119A].

19.3   Developments since 2008

There have been a number of further developments affecting the operation and procedure of employment tribunals since the repeal of the *2002 Act* in 2008.

(a)   In January 2011, the Department for Business, Innovation and Skills (BIS, the successor to the DTI) launched a further round of consultation on proposals to reform the employment tribunal system to remove what the consultation document stated were regarded as unjustifiable burdens the working of the existing system places on business (*Resolving Workplace Disputes*). In addition to a change in substantive employment rights (the extension of the qualifying period of service for unfair dismissal claims to two years, since implemented for employees whose employment commences on or after 6 April 2012) the consultation paper proposed a requirement to submit all claims initially to ACAS, to then be presented to the tribunal only if not successfully conciliated; greater powers for tribunals to dispose of weak claims by striking out, including powers to do so on paper without a hearing; an increase in the maximum deposit that can be required (to £1,000) and the limit on costs orders (to £20,000); abolishing payments of expenses to witnesses; delegating to Legal Officers some of the interlocutory work now undertaken by employment judges; taking written witness statements as read at hearings; extending the provision for cases to be heard by a judge sitting alone to cover unfair dismissal; introducing penalties for employers found liable by a tribunal; and reducing the use of lay members in the EAT.

The outcome of this consultation was announced in November 2011; broadly, this was the Government's intention to proceed with all of the proposals summarised, and some, which could be implemented by secondary legislation, were brought into effect on 6 April 2012 by the *Employment Tribunals (Constitution and Rules of Procedure) (Amendment) Regulations 2012, SI 2012/468*. These changes are the addition of unfair dismissal claims to the categories of cases where an employment judge can sit alone (with a discretion to order a full panel under the *Employment Tribunals Act 1996, s 4(5)*: see the *Employment Tribunals Act 1996 (Tribunal Composition) Order 2012, SI 2012/988*); an increase in the maximum sum that can be ordered as a deposit to £1,000 and the maximum sum that can be awarded for costs to £20,000; ending the payment of travel expenses for witnesses, with a new power for the tribunal to order a party to pay these expenses; and a new rule providing that witness statements, where used, are to be taken as read unless the tribunal directs otherwise (this does not affect the position in Scotland that witness statements are generally not used). Although all these changes came into effect on 6 April 2012, all but the first only apply to cases presented on or after that date (see *reg 3* of the *2012 Regulations*). These changes have been retained within the *2013 Regulations* and *2013 Rules*.

Most of the other changes required legislation. The *Enterprise and Regulatory Reform Act 2013, Part 2* was enacted on 25 April 2013. The *Act* made provision for conciliation through ACAS prior to instituting proceedings (*s 7, s 8, s 9*); the prohibition on disclosure of information held by ACAS (*s 10*); the extension of decision making to legal officers (*s 11*); changes to the composition of the Employment Appeal Tribunal so that, by default, appeals are heard by a judge sitting alone but with power to direct that lay members sit on the case (*s 12*); no qualifying period of employment for dismissals for political opinions (*s 13*); confidentiality of negotiations before termination of employment (*s 14*); the Secretary of State to have power to order the increase or decrease in the limit of the compensatory award in unfair dismissal cases(*s 15*); the power of the Tribunal to award financial penalties payable to the Secretary of State of between £100 and £5,000 where the Tribunal concludes the employer has breached any of the worker's rights to which the claim relates and there are one or more aggravating features (*s 16*); various changes to the law on protected disclosures (*s 17–21*); and renaming compromise agreements (*s 23*).

(b)   In a separate but parallel development, in December 2011 the Ministry of Justice published consultation proposals for the introduction of fees for employment tribunal claims. Proposals were then based on a Government decision, announced in October 2012, that fees would be introduced, the consultation being limited to the levels of fees, when and how they would be payable, remission for those of limited means, and other issues arising. The Government aimed to save £10 million a year from the cost of the employment tribunals (just over £80 million in 2010–11) by levying fees, but questions were raised by those consulted about whether the level of exemptions and administrative cost of determining disputes about fees will affect this figure.

The consultation on fees closed in March 2012. There was a generally hostile response from professional bodies representing employment practitioners.

On 29 July 2013, the *Employment Tribunals and the Employment Appeal Tribunal Fees Order 2013* came into force. That order provided for the payment of fees for (i) issuing a claim, (ii) the listing of a final hearing (iii) the making of certain specified applications (the applications being: reconsidering a default judgment, reconsidering a judgment after a final hearing, dismissing a claim upon withdrawal, bringing an employer's contract claim), or (iv) by a Respondent upon a listing for judicial mediation.

The level of fees was specified in the order. Issue fees for single claims of either £160 or £250 and hearing fees for single claims of either £230 or £950, in each case dependant on whether the claim is of Type A or B respectively. The lower level of fee applied to straightforward claims (Type A) such as unauthorised deductions and claims for statutory redundancy payments. Type A claims are listed in *Table 2* of *Schedule 2* of the *Order*. The higher level applied to other claims (called Type B claims). This included most claims eg for unfair dismissal, discrimination, whistle-blowing etc. Different level of fees applied for grouped claims (but did not exceed the sum that would have been due had the claims been presented individually). Fees for the specified applications varied from £60 to £350 depending on the application and type of claim. The fee for judicial mediation was set at £600. *Schedule 3* of the *Order* set out the scheme for granting full and part remission in respect of the fees that would otherwise be payable.

In early 2017, the Government published its review into the introduction of fees in the Employment Tribunal noting that the scheme has "broadly met its objectives". This review recognised that there had been a significant fall in the number of claims made ("significantly greater than was estimated when fees were first introduced") and that claimants have been discouraged from bringing claims. However, the review stated that there was no conclusive evidence that claimants have been *prevented* from commencing claims. A proposal was included in the review for expanding the fee remission scheme by lifting the income threshold and by removing the requirement to pay fees in certain types of cases where the employer was insolvent.

On 26 July 2017, however, the Supreme Court handed down its decision in *R (Unison) v Lord Chancellor* [2017] 3 WLR 409. Disagreeing with the Government's assessment in that review of its fees regime, the Supreme Court found the *Employment Tribunals and the Employment Appeal Tribunal Fees Order 2013* to be unlawful ab initio as an interference with access to justice under both domestic and European Union law. A refund scheme was then introduced to provide refunds to those who had paid fees during the scheme's operation.

(c)   An additional announcement made by BIS on the occasion of the publication of the Government's response to the January 2011 consultation was the creation of a small group, chaired by Underhill J (as he then was), the immediate past President of the EAT, to conduct a 'root and branch' review of the *ET Rules*, with a view to the simplification both of the *Rules* and their operation. The group reported in July 2012. A further consultation on those proposed rules was launched in September 2012 and the Government's response to that exercise published in March 2013. As a result of the review, on 28 May 2013, the *Employment Tribunals (Constitution and Rules of Procedure) Regulations 2013, SI 2013/1237* ('the *2013 Regulations*') were made. The *2013 Regulations* contain the Rules in *Schedule 1*. The new rules came into force on 29 July 2013 and are covered comprehensively in the next chapter: see CHAPTER 20.

(d)   In July 2016, Lord Justice Briggs published his review into the Civil Courts Structure. The terms of reference for that review included a request to review the boundaries between the Civil Courts and the Tribunals Service. An interim report published in January 2016 specifically highlighted is the question of whether the Employment Tribunal and Employment Appeal Tribunal should be integrated into the structure of the civil courts. Three options were identified: "(a) To leave the ET (and the EAT) where they are, uncomfortably stranded between the civil courts and the main Tribunal Structure. (b) To bring both tribunals broadly under the wing of the structure of the civil courts. (c) To make both tribunals part of the Tribunal Structure, as First Tier and Upper Tribunals respectively." The interim report set out reasons why option (b) appeared to be the most attractive, albeit that this did not mean necessarily that the *Civil Procedure Rules 1998* would apply to employment disputes in place of specific rules, perhaps based on the *2013 Rules*. The final report declined to offer a firm recommendation, and notably there was no recommendation that a new Employment and Equalities Court should be created. Briggs LJ did offer some observations on how the jurisdiction of such a court might be set. He further expressed the view that whilst he was of the view that there was room for a body – such as the EAT – having a first instance jurisdiction in more complex cases (with a route of appeal direct to the Court of Appeal), he again declined to make specific recommendations.

A further potentially significant feature of Lord Justice Briggs' final report was the recommendation for the introduction of an on-line court (separate from the County Court) for the resolution of modest money claims (starting at £10,000 with the aim of lifting the threshold to £25,000) via a different online claims resolution process. The aim is to create a more investigative process, led by IT, which will critically be cheaper and therefore more accessible to ordinary people of more limited means. Costs recovery will be limited and fixed and modelled on the small claims track.

(e)   In September 2016, a joint statement prepared by the Lord Chancellor, Lord Chief Justice and Senior President of Tribunals set out an intention for digitising the entire claims process and delegating routine tasks from judges to case workers. Such changes would – for ETs – require amendments to primary legislation and a consultation was launched in December 2016. The Government's response was published in February 2017 and the intention is to bring forward measures as soon as Parliamentary time allows.

(f)   The *Tribunal Procedure (Coronavirus) (Amendment) Rules 2020, SI 2020/416* introduced to facilitate the continuing administration of justice during the coronavirus pandemic did not make any amendments to the Employment Tribunal procedure rules, apparently because the Employment Tribunal already had power in *Rule 46* to permit a hearing to be conducted, in whole or in part, by use of electronic communication (see further EMPLOYMENT TRIBUNALS – II, **20.83**), and power in many circumstances to make decisions without a hearing (see further EMPLOYMENT TRIBUNALS – II, **20.111**). A number of Presidential Practice Directions, Guidance and Directions have been published in connection with the pandemic, including guidance as to when and how hearings should take place and a Practice Direction permitting judgments and orders to be signed by judges electronically.

(g)   On 22 April 2020 important Presidential Guidance on Vulnerable Parties and Witnesses was issued. This is dealt with in more detail at **20.83A**.

(h)   The Law Commission report *Employment Law Hearing Structures* (LC 390) published on 27 April 2020 includes a number of significant recommendations for reform, including: that time limits for all claims should be six months with a 'just and equitable' test for extension, thus removing altogether the 'not reasonably practicable' 3-month time limit that can have quite harsh effects for claimants in unfair dismissal and other claims to which it applies; extending the Tribunal's contract jurisdiction to include more types of contract claims by employees against employers (i.e. in addition to the current types, also claims concerning living accommodation), with no restriction as to when the dispute must have arisen, and subject to an increased maximum of £100,000 (in line with the County Court); that tribunals should have power to interpret/construe contractual terms when exercising their jurisdiction under *Part I* of the *ERA 1996* to determine whether or not a particular term should be included in a written statement of particulars; extending the Tribunal's jurisdiction to enable them to hear complaints by workers that they are working hours in excess of the maximum working time limits contained in the *WTR 1998*; enabling Tribunals to order contributions as between join tortfeasors in discrimination claims as the ordinary courts can under the *Civil Liability (Contribution) Act 1978*; recommending that consideration be given to automatic fines for employers who fail to pay Tribunal awards; greater flexibility on deployment of Tribunal judges to the County Court and High Court to hear discrimination claims.

19.4   The 2013 Rules of Procedure

The *2013 Regulations* contain provisions providing for the continued establishment of employment tribunals (*reg 3*). They go on to provide for the appointment and tenure of office of the Presidents of the Tribunals (one for England and Wales and one for Scotland), the Vice-President (for Scotland only), Regional Employment Judges (in England and Wales only) and Employment Judges and members (see *regs 5* and *6*). These office holders are required to use the resources available to secure, so far as practicable, the speedy and efficient disposal of proceedings, determine the allocation of proceedings between Tribunals, and to determine when and where Tribunals shall sit. The President is able to make directions to Regional Employment Judges and the Vice President in Scotland (see *reg 7*).

The *2013 Regulations* also cover the composition of tribunals for particular cases, special rules for cases involving issues of national security, and a number of ancillary provisions which are referred to at relevant points in the text below. *Schedule 1* contains the rules of procedure applicable to most claims, and is referred to as the *Employment Tribunals Rules of Procedure 2013* ('the *2013 Rules*'). The other Schedules now cover the following:

(a)	*Schedule 2:*	Rules for National Security cases;
(b)	*Schedule 3:*	Rules for Equal Value cases.

Although the *2004 Regulations* and *2004 Rules* had made considerable changes in the substance of the procedure to be applied by tribunals, and had been intended to be drafted in simpler language more readily understandable by litigants without legal training, there had nonetheless been judicial criticisms of the quality of drafting. This was a central driver behind the development of the new *2013 Rules* contained within the *2013 Regulations*. The key terminology used by the *2013 Regulations* includes the following:

(i)   Those applying to a tribunal are referred to as 'claimants' (rather than 'applicants' as had been the case prior to 2004); those responding to claims are 'respondents'.

(ii)   The document by which an application is made to the tribunal is called a 'Claim Form' (instead of an 'originating application' which was the term used prior to 2004).

(iii)   The response by a respondent is called a 'Response Form' (rather than the old term, 'notice of appearance').

(iv)   Hearings are either final hearings or preliminary hearings (previous terminology, including directions hearings, interlocutory hearings, Case Management Discussions ('CMDs'), and Pre-hearing Reviews ('PHRs'), have been discarded).

19.5

Alongside the changes of terminology are changes of substance. Below is a brief summary of the principal changes of substance effected by the *2013 ET Rules* and related provisions:

(a)   There is a requirement for Early Conciliation via ACAS of certain claims prior to them being presented to an employment tribunal.

(b)   Differently designed Claim Forms (known as Form ET1) and Response Forms (Form ET3) were introduced to accompany the *2013 Rules* (there is a link to these forms at https://www.gov.uk/courts-tribunals/employment-tribunal). Use of the paper or electronic version of the prescribed forms is mandatory when presenting claims. Certain mandatory information is required to be given on the Claim Form. When presenting, a claimant must do so using one of the prescribed methods: online, in person or by post (fax is no longer available). The payment of an issue fee or application for a fee remission is required.

(c)   An initial administrative screening process will apply by which the tribunal secretariat will weed out and reject claims not containing the required minimum information, not enclosing a fee or remission application, or otherwise appearing to be outside the tribunal's jurisdiction. Where substantive defects are detected, the case is referred to a Judge for decision whether to refuse to accept and register the claim. Rejection decisions can be reconsidered by the claimant making an application for reconsideration.

(d)   Response Forms must be received by the tribunal within 28 days following the date that the Claim Form was sent to the respondent. Minimum information must be provided, otherwise the Tribunal can reject the response. A response will also be rejected if it is received late unless an application for an extension has been made or the response is accompanied by such an application. If the employer wishes to bring an employer's contract claim, this must be included within the response and a fee must be paid. If no response is received within the time, a Judge will issue a judgment covering the whole of the claim (if possible) or which part of the claim a judgment can properly cover, and then set a hearing before a judge alone to determine the rest. The respondent remains entitled to notice of hearings but (unless an extension of time for presenting a response is granted) is only entitled to participate in any hearing to the extent permitted by a judge.

(e) In every case, once the pleadings have closed, an employment judge will consider all the documents held by the Tribunal in order to determine whether the claims and defences are arguable and within the jurisdiction of the Tribunal. If so, case management orders will be made. If not (viz that a claim or defence, or part thereof, does not have reasonable prospects of success), a notice of dismissal will be issued by the Judge, requiring the relevant party to make written representations as to why the claim or defence, or part thereof, should not be dismissed. If no written representations are received by the date specified, the claim or defence or part thereof will stand dismissed. If the written representations do not satisfy the judge, then a hearing will be held to decide whether the claim or defence or part thereof should be allowed to continue. The other party may but need not participate in the hearing.

(f) Judges are required to consider facilitating ADR throughout the process of a claim.

(g) There are generally two types of hearing: preliminary hearings and final hearings. Preliminary hearings can be for case management only, or decide substantive points, called 'preliminary issues'. A preliminary issue is held in private unless a preliminary issue is to be decided, when that part of the hearing must be held in public. Final hearings are held in public. The Tribunal has powers to restrict the public disclosure of any aspects of the proceedings so far as it considers necessary in the interests of justice to protect convention rights, and in other circumstances.

(h) Decisions of tribunals can be in the form of orders and judgments. A written record of all decisions must be provided to the parties. Reasons must be given for any decision on any disputed issue, whether substantive of procedural, but must be proportionate to the significance of the issue and may be very short (particularly if the decision is other than a judgment). Where a decision is given in writing, the reasons must also be in writing. If reasons are given orally, a request for written reasons must be presented within 14 days of the sending of the written record of the decision.

(i) The Tribunal has powers to award costs, preparation time orders, and wasted costs. The Scottish term for costs is 'expenses'. The availability of preparation time orders enable a tribunal to make an award in favour of a party who is not legally represented, to cover the costs of his or her time in preparing for the hearing, covering such hours as the tribunal assesses as reasonable at a fixed hourly rate. This was set, initially, at £33 an hour, but with an automatic increase of £1 an hour each year from 6 April 2014, so that the current rate is £39 an hour. Preparation time orders cannot be made if a costs order is also made (or vice versa) and can only be made under the same conditions as a costs order. A wasted costs order, can be made against a representative, provided the representative is acting for profit, and is either an order to pay costs to the other party, or an order disallowing the representative's charges to his or her client in whole or in part. Tribunals may have regard to the means of the paying party in deciding whether, and if so how much, to award by way of costs. The Tribunal can summarily assess costs/preparation time up to £20,000, but can award more than this either by agreement of the parties, or by conducting a detailed assessment of costs, or by referring the case to the County Court for it to undertake a detailed assessment. The Tribunal also has a discretion 'at large' to order the reimbursement of a fee where the party who paid that fee has been wholly or partly successful. Such a reimbursement is a 'costs order' and is subject to the other general rules on costs.

(j) A number of other changes of detail were made, including widening the circumstances in which the Tribunal can make orders to restrict the disclosure to the public of any part of proceedings (including but not limited to restricted reporting orders), and wider powers to conduct hearings by telephone or video link. Changes were made to reconsideration of certain types of orders to remove some of the technical traps that existed in the *2004 Rules*. Further, a generalised power to make a case management order has been introduced, which covers many of the orders which were previously specified in terms in the *2004 Rules*. The generalised nature of the Case Management Powers is supplemented by Presidential Guidance which a Tribunal considering a matter is bound to consider, although is not bound to follow.

(k) The public register of applications was closed on 1 October 2004. The register of decisions (now a register of judgments) has been retained (*reg 14*), and judgments and written reasons remain available for public inspection. Final decisions in Employment Tribunal cases in England, Wales and Scotland from February 2017 onwards are available on-line at https://www.gov.uk/employment-tribunal-decisions. Information about parties will not be made available in advance of the hearing as such information falls within exemptions in the *Freedom of Information Act 2000*: *Peninsula Business Services Ltd v Information Commissioner and ors* [2014] UKUT 283 (AAC).

Reg 11 of the *2013 Regulations* confers power on the Presidents to issue Practice Directions regulating the procedure of tribunals and the manner of exercise of the powers conferred on tribunals and Employment Judges by the *2013 Regulations* and *Rules*. The first Practice Directions issued under the forerunner of this provision under the *2004 Regulations*, which apply in Scotland only, were issued in December 2006; they cover lists of documents, sists (the Scots Law term for stays) for mediation and the procedure for counterclaims in contract cases. Other Practice Directions are issued from time to time by both Presidents to give directions for particular categories of cases, such as staying (sisting in Scotland) claims affected by a pending reference to the Court of Justice of the European Union (CJEU), or transferring all cases against a particular respondent to the same tribunal office. More recently, Practice Directions have been issued both in England and Wales to cover the presentation of claims generally.

A facet of procedure, introduced for claims presented on or after 6 April 2010 where a claim has been made under the provisions of the *ERA 1996* introduced by the *Public Interest Disclosure Act 1998*, allows for the claimant's underlying 'whistleblowing' disclosure to be forwarded by the tribunal secretariat to the relevant Regulator for investigation, if the claimant has signified a wish for this to be done. This does not affect the procedure for hearing the claim itself. It now finds expression in Rule *14* of the *2013 Rules*. By *s 148* of the *Small Business, Enterprise and Employment Act 2015*, regulators are to be legally obliged to produce annual reports (and reports to Parliament) detailing the whistleblowing reports they receive.

19.6   ADMINISTRATION

The employment tribunals are constituted under the *Employment Tribunals Act 1996* ('ETA 1996') (a consolidating Act replacing equivalent earlier legislation) and the *Regulations* and *Rules of Procedure* made under the powers conferred by the *ETA 1996*. The overall responsibility for the running of the employment tribunals in England and Wales is vested in the President of the Employment Tribunals, a judicial officer appointed by the Lord

Chancellor (*2013 Regulations, reg 5*). The tribunal system is divided into 12 regions, each with a Regional Employment Judge appointed by the Lord Chancellor (*2013 Regulations, reg 6*). There is a separate President of the Employment Tribunals for Scotland, and a Vice-President, both appointed by the Lord President of the Court of Session (*2013 Regulations, regs 5, 6*). Tribunals sit at all the regional centres and at various other permanent centres and an increasing number of *ad hoc* centres.

The administration of tribunals (and of the EAT) is now the responsibility of HM Courts and Tribunals Service ('HMCTS'), which came into existence on 1 April 2011, merging the former Tribunals Service with HM Courts Service. The Tribunals Service itself came into existence in 2006 as an executive agency of the then Department for Constitutional Affairs, now the Ministry of Justice, and was given a statutory basis by the *Tribunals, Courts and Enforcement Act 2007*. The merger of the two services does not affect the office of Senior President of Tribunals created by the *2007 Act*. The Senior President (currently Lord Justice Ryder) has overall responsibility for all tribunals. HMCTS is responsible for the administration of some twenty separate statutory tribunals, including the provision of premises, staff and facilities such as computing.

The various tribunals within the remit of the Tribunals Service (and now HMCTS) have been brought together into a unified structure, with an Upper Tribunal replacing the various appellate tribunals and most of the first instance tribunals grouped into a number of Chambers reflecting their areas of jurisdiction. Employment tribunals and the Employment Appeal Tribunal have however retained their separate status, identity, judiciary and rules of procedure, although increasingly not their separate premises.

At present HMCTS is responsible for tribunals in Scotland as well as England and Wales. Section 39 Scotland Act 2016 allows for the transfer of competence over the functions of employment tribunals dealing with Scottish cases. Functions can be transferred to a Scottish Tribunal named in an Order in Council. A draft Order in Council has been promulgated and consulted upon which would enable the First-tier Tribunal to hear Scottish employment cases as defined under the order, along with certain specified other cases.

The proposed transfer of functions would allow the First-tier tribunal to hear Scottish employment cases (as defined in the draft Order), along with a number of cases that do not fit within that category but which have a sufficient link to Scotland and should therefore be heard in a Scottish tribunal. The challenges this proposal is likely to pose are discussed by the President of Employment Tribunals (Scotland), Judge Shona Simon, in the Senior President of Tribunal's Annual Report 2015 (see pp 80–82); and for 2016 (see pp 103-107). As at December 2017 (and apparently also May 2019), the Scottish Government was considering the consultation responses and awaiting a further draft of the Order in Council from the UK Government.

The Bury St Edmunds Office maintained the public Register of Judgments until February 2017 and applications for copies of judgments should be made to that office, enclosing the relevant fee (currently £10 per judgment plus £5 for each additional judgment). Judgments older than 6 years have been retained but are unavailable pending a decision as to the future administration of this archive. As noted above, since 2016, judgments and reasons have been available on-line at https://www.gov.uk/employment-tribunal-decisions.

There is a Central Office of Employment Tribunals for England and Wales and for Scotland (See https://www.gov.uk/guidance/employment-tribunal-offices-and-venues). Claims presented by post must be sent to the address set out in the Presidential Practice Direction. Online claims are also directed to that office automatically. Alternatively, presentation in person can be to a local office at the addresses (and within the times) set out in the Presidential Practice Direction. The relevant office which will determine the claim is determined by the postcode of the claimant's place of work or former place of work. The Central Office will automatically send the claim to be handled by the appropriate office.

19.7   COMPOSITION

Tribunals are drawn from three panels (*2013 Regulations, reg 8*):

(a)   Employment Judges, who are appointed by the Lord Chancellor on the recommendation of the Judicial Appointments Commission (a body established by the *Constitutional Reform Act 2005*), or in Scotland by the Lord President of the Court of Session (there is a Scottish Judicial Appointments Board, but its responsibilities do not extend to recommending appointments to the employment tribunals judiciary), and must have a five-year legal qualification (this was reduced from seven years in 2008). Appointments are both full-time and part-time.

(b)   Persons appointed by the Lord Chancellor after consulting organisations representative of employees.

(c)   Persons so appointed after consultation with organisations representative of employers.

The members drawn from panels (*b*) and (*c*) (variously referred to as 'lay members', 'wing members' and 'the industrial jury') all serve part-time. The Presidents are required to maintain separate panels of Judges, and of each of the two categories of lay members, who are considered suitable to hear cases involving issues of national security, and the tribunal assigned to such a case will be composed of a member of each special panel (*2013 Regulations, reg 10*). There is also a power to establish panels of Judges and members with specialist knowledge to hear particular categories of proceedings for which such knowledge would be beneficial (*reg 8(4)*). This power has been used to create specialist panels to hear equal pay cases, but there are no plans at present for other specialist panels.

The composition, and methods of appointment and reappointment to membership, of the employment tribunals have in the past given rise to a potential difficulty under the *Human Rights Act 1998 ('HRA 1998')*. *Article 6* of the *European Convention on Human Rights*, which the *HRA 1998* incorporates into UK law, confers the right to a determination of issues relating to civil rights (which includes most if not all issues brought before employment tribunals) at a fair and public hearing before an independent and impartial tribunal. The issue was raised whether employment tribunals could satisfy this requirement in cases where the Secretary of State for Trade and Industry was a party to the proceedings, as where claims were made against the Secretary of State because the employer was insolvent. Changes in the method of appointment of Judges and lay members in 2000 largely removed the potential conflicts of interest, and the creation of the Tribunals Service, together with the transfer of responsibility for recommending the appointment of Judges to the Judicial Appointments Commission (and appointments in Scotland being made by the Lord President), is thought to have resolved the problem, but this must remain open to possible judicial determination.

19.8   A full tribunal consists of one member from each panel (*2013 Regulations, reg 9(3)*). A tribunal with two lay members drawn from the same panel is not a properly constituted tribunal and any decision by such a panel would be a nullity. Decisions may be by majority, but if the Tribunal is composed of two persons (which by *ETA 1996, s 4(1)(b)* can occur where the parties consent), the Judge has a second or casting vote (*2013 Rules, Rule 49*). If agreement is sought to the tribunal sitting with only one lay member, the parties must be informed as to whether the lay member is from the employers' or employees' panel: *Rabahallah v British Telecommunications plc* [2005] IRLR 184, [2005] ICR 440 (following *De Haney v Brent Mind* [2003] EWCA Civ 1637, [2004] ICR 348, a case about the equivalent situation in the EAT). In *Rabahallah*, the EAT recommended that the parties be asked to sign a standard form to confirm that informed consent has been given to the tribunal sitting or continuing with only one lay member. If one party is absent, their consent may be sought, but if it is not practicable to obtain their consent, or it is refused, it will not be possible for the hearing to continue, unless the Tribunal is able to substitute a panel member, which is permissible in principle pursuant to *reg 9(3)* of the *2013 Regulations*. However, this will only be appropriate if it can be done without prejudicing the fairness of the hearing. If a Tribunal has already started hearing evidence, it may not be possible for a member to be substituted, but it will in many cases be acceptable to substitute a different member to determine remedy once a decision has been made on liability. This happened in *Monfort International plc v McKenzie* (UKEAT/0155/06/LA), where the EAT further clarified that the parties' consent is not required, nor are they necessarily required to be notified, that a member is to be substituted.

Tribunals normally sit in public; the circumstances in which they may sit in private or reporting of proceedings may be restricted are explained below (see **20.91–20.93**). The importance of a public hearing was reiterated in *Storer v British Gas plc* [2000] 2 All ER 440, [2000] 1 WLR 1237, [2000] ICR 603, [2000] IRLR 495, where the Court of Appeal set aside a decision on a preliminary issue reached at a hearing held in the private office of the Regional Employment Judge because no tribunal room was available. The court dismissed as irrelevant the argument that no members of the public had been prevented from attending the hearing.

19.9 Judges sitting alone

A full tribunal is required for the hearing of most claims: however, certain categories of proceedings must be heard by a tribunal consisting of a Judge sitting alone, unless a Judge (not necessarily the same person who hears the case) directs to the contrary considering factors such as the likelihood of a dispute on the facts, the likelihood of disputes of law, the views of the parties, and whether there are other proceedings which might be heard concurrently (*ETA 1996, s 4(2), (3)* and *(5)*). Where a case involves a number of claims, some which can be heard by a judge alone, and others which require a full tribunal, there is a duty on the Tribunal (in respect of the claims which can be heard by judge alone) to consider whether they should be heard together before a full tribunal: *Birring v Rogers and Moore t/a Charity Link* [2015] ICR 1001 (see below). An important change to the categories of cases which can be heard by a judge sitting alone was made by the *Employment Tribunals Act 1996 (Tribunal Composition) Order 2012, SI 2012/988*, adding unfair dismissal claims to the list with effect from 6 April 2012. (Since then, the EAT has felt the need to emphasise that the substantive law has not changed: see *Mitchell v St Joseph's School* [2013] All ER (D) 259 (Apr) (UKEAT/0506/12).)

The principal categories of case covered by these provisions are now as follows (see *ETA 1996, s 4(3)* for a complete list):

(a) applications for interim relief in relation to dismissal in health and safety and public interest disclosure cases (*ERA 1996, ss 128–132*) or for trade union reasons (*TULR(C)A 1992, ss 161, 165* and *166*);

(b) applications against the Secretary of State under *ERA 1996, ss 170* and *188* or *Pension Schemes Act 1993, s 126* (where the former employer is insolvent);

(c) applications under the *ERA 1996, s 23* or *TULR(C)A 1992, s 68A* (unlawful deductions from wages, etc);

(d) applications under the following provisions of *ERA 1996: s 11* (particulars of employment terms and itemised pay statements), *s 34* (guarantee payments), *s 70* (remuneration during suspension on medical grounds), *s 111* (unfair dismissal), *s 163* (redundancy payments), and *s 206(4)* (appointment of 'appropriate person' in proceedings, following the death of an employee);

(e)   applications under *TULR(C)A 1992, s 192* or *reg 15(10)* of the *Transfer of Undertakings (Protection of Employment) Regulations 2006 (SI 2006/246)* (failure to pay a protective award);

(f)   claims for breach of contract under the *Employment Tribunals Extension of Jurisdiction (England and Wales) Order 1994 (SI 1994/1623)* or the equivalent Scottish order;

(g)   claims under the *Working Time Regulations 1998, reg 30* (and equivalent provisions applying to certain categories of worker not covered by the *1998 Regulations*) for holiday pay or pay in lieu of holiday not taken prior to the termination of employment, but not other claims under the *1998 Regulations*;

(h)   proceedings where both or all parties have given their written consent to a hearing before a Judge alone (whether or not consent has been subsequently withdrawn); and

(i)   proceedings where the respondent (or all respondents if more than one) does not contest the claim, or no longer does so.

(ETA 1996, s 4(3))

For claims in categories not listed above, there is no power for a judge sitting alone to determine the case and any decision made following such a final hearing would be a nullity: *Nascimento v British Bakeries Ltd* [2005] All ER (D) 20 (Sep), EAT; *Insaidoo v Metropolitan Resources North West Ltd* [2011] All ER (D) 04 (May); *Birring* (above). This is to be contrasted with the ability of a judge sitting alone to conduct a preliminary hearing (whether for case management or to determine preliminary issues, subject to *2013 Rules, Rule 55*). In this connection it may be noted that whilst claims under *TULR(C)A 1992, s 192* for payment of a protective award already made under *s 189* can be heard by a judge sitting alone (as stated in (e) above), claims for a protective award to be made under *s 189* require a full panel, so a judgment upholding or refusing such a claim by a judge sitting alone is a nullity: *Weedon v Pinnacle Entertainment Ltd* [2012] All ER (D) 109 (Jan) (UKEAT/0217/11). It should be stressed that if any of the claims in a case where more than one claim has been made fall outside the list above, the case must be heard by a full panel (unless the claim requiring a full panel has been withdrawn or struck out before the hearing). As an example, in claims for unfair dismissal and for failure to provide written reasons for dismissal, the latter claim must be heard by a full tribunal, and the addition of such a claim will normally necessitate that the unfair dismissal claim is also heard by a full panel. Where a costs application is made after a substantive hearing, that may only be heard by judge alone if the substantive hearing had been conducted by judge alone. Where the substantive hearing had been before full tribunal, the judge alone had no power to determine the subsequent costs application: *Riley v Secretary of State for Justice* [2016] ICR 172.

The provision at (i) above was given greater significance by the decision of the EAT in *Parfett v John Lamb Partnership Ltd* (UKEAT/0111/08) [2008] All ER (D) 22 (Jul), holding that it covers cases where the Respondent either has not submitted a response or has not had the response accepted. In such cases a Judge may issue a judgment on such parts of the claim s/he can determine. If that does not cover the full scope of the claim (and frequently remedy will remain), the Judge will proceed to fix a hearing before a Judge alone: see *Rule 21(2)* of the *2013 Rules*.

In addition, preliminary hearings must be heard by a Judge sitting alone, regardless of the type or complexity of the claim (*Rule 55*) except where a notice has been given that preliminary issues are to be, or may be, decided at the hearing, and a party has requested in writing that the hearing be conducted by a full tribunal. In such cases an Employment Judge will make a decision whether this would be desirable (*Rule 55*). See the EAT's comments in *Sutcliffe v Big C's Marine Ltd* [1998] IRLR 428.

Until 2009, an important omission from the list of claims which could be heard by a Judge sitting alone was claims for holiday pay under the *Working Time Regulations 1998 ('WTR')*, *reg 30*. Following the ruling of the Court of Appeal in *IRC v Ainsworth* [2005] EWCA Civ 441, [2005] IRLR 465 that claims for unpaid holiday pay under the *WTR* could only be brought under *reg 30*, and not as a complaint of unlawful deductions under *Part II* of the *ERA 1996*, it became necessary for any claim for arrears of pay which included a statutory holiday pay claim to be heard by a full tribunal. As a result, the *ETA 1996, s 4(3)* was amended with effect from 6 April 2009 by the *Employment Tribunals Act 1996 (Tribunal Composition) Order 2009, SI 2009/789*, by adding holiday pay claims under the *WTR* to the list of categories of claim which may be heard by a judge sitting alone. However, the amendment does not extend to other claims under the *WTR*; claims in relation to rest breaks, rest periods and compensatory rest remain subject to the general requirement that a hearing must be before a full tribunal. The *2009 Order* also made equivalent amendments to the regulations conferring rights to paid holiday for sea fishermen, aircrew in civil aviation, and workers on inland waterways. However, the addition of claims for holiday pay under the *WTR 1998* has since largely lost its importance, following the decision of the House of Lords (under the name of *Revenue and Customs Comrs v Stringer* [2009] UKHL 31, [2009] ICR 985, [2009] IRLR 677), overruling the Court of Appeal's decision in *IRC v Ainsworth* and holding that such claims may be brought under *Part II* of the *ERA 1996*. This may afford advantages in terms of time limits, and claims under *Part II* may also be heard by a judge sitting alone (see paragraph (*c*) above).

An order can be made, in any case falling within *ETA 1996, s 4(3)*, for the hearing to be before a full panel. The power to make such orders has become much more significant with the addition of unfair dismissal to the categories of cases which can be heard by a judge sitting alone, a controversial change opposed by the majority of consultees in the consultation which preceded it. In an unfair dismissal case in which the members outvoted the judge, *McCafferty v Royal Mail Group Ltd* (UKEATS/0002/12), Lady Smith stated that tribunals should give 'careful consideration' to the parties' canvassed views.

Factors which must be considered in deciding whether to direct a full panel include whether there is a likelihood of a dispute of fact making this desirable (a point likely to be raised very commonly for unfair dismissal cases); whether there is a likelihood of a point of law arising making a hearing before a Judge alone desirable; the views of the parties; and the existence of any concurrent proceedings which have to be heard by a full tribunal (*ETA 1996, s 4(5)*).

There have been conflicting authorities in the past on the extent of the obligation to consider ordering a hearing before a full panel in cases within *s 4(3)*. The EAT has revisited its previous decisions, and the position, based on *Gladwell v Secretary of State for Trade and Industry* [2007] ICR 264, [2006] All ER (D) 154 (Nov) and *Sterling Developments (London) Ltd v Pagano* [2007] IRLR 471, [2007] All ER (D) 01 (May), is currently as follows:

(a)   Listing, including a decision whether to list a case before a Judge sitting alone or a full tribunal, is a judicial function, but it is permissible for a Regional Employment Judge to lay down a general policy on listing, subject to the consideration of individual cases.

(b)   There is a discretion to refer a case that may be heard by a Judge alone to a full panel, and the exercise or non-exercise of this discretion is open to challenge by an appeal. In the event of an appeal, if the Judge has not given reasons for the way the discretion was exercised, the EAT may ask for reasons. The implication of this is that the point must be considered, and a decision made, for each case.

(c)   The parties should be told of their right to request a full panel, either at a preliminary hearing for case management, if one is held, or in the notice of hearing; any request for a full panel should be judicially considered.

(d)   The Employment Judge responsible for the hearing should consider whether a full panel is needed, having regard to any developments in the case (such as that it has become clear that there are significant disputes of fact), but also having regard to the desirability of not creating delay or expense.

(e)   It may be necessary to canvass the views of the parties on whether the hearing should go ahead before the Judge alone, but it is not an error of law to fail to do so or to fail to give reasons for declining to order a full tribunal, and the Judge is not bound to accede to the wishes of the parties.

(f)   It may be necessary to at least consider ordering a full panel even if neither party asks for one, since unrepresented litigants may not appreciate the possibility of a full panel or why that would be desirable in the particular case.

The EAT in *Gladwell* declined to decide whether (as had been held in the earlier case of *Sogbetun v Hackney London Borough Council* [1998] ICR 1264, [1998] IRLR 676), a failure to exercise the discretion given by *s 4(5)* made the subsequent proceedings a nullity. It is this point in particular on which earlier cases differ, but in the light of the more recent guidelines the question has become largely academic, as a failure to follow the points indicated is likely to provide the basis for a successful appeal by the aggrieved party.

In *Birring v Rogers and Moore t/a Charity Link* [2015] ICR 1001, the EAT considered an appeal from the decision of a judge alone in a claim of both unfair dismissal and a trade union detriment. The unfair dismissal claim could be heard by a judge alone, whereas this was not the case in respect of the trade union detriment claim. The decision of a single judge was therefore a nullity in respect of the trade union detriment claim and the appeal allowed in that respect. However, Langstaff P went on to disturb the decision on the unfair dismissal complaint also. The judge below had failed to consider *s 4(5)* and decide whether the unfair dismissal complaint should be heard together with the trade union detriment claim. The EAT held he should have done, and there was a duty to do so, in cases involving a mixture of judge-alone and full tribunal jurisdictions (see para 18). The EAT also observed that it was a pity in the Notices of Hearing did not draw attention to the fact submissions might be made as to the composition of the Tribunal (para 20).

19.10 There is provision in the *ETA 1996, ss 4(6A)* and *7(3A)* (added respectively by the *ERDRA 1998, s 2* and the *Employment Act 2002, s 26*) for certain proceedings to be disposed of by an Employment Judge without a hearing. These powers have been implemented by the *2013 Rules*, which permit a Judge to issue a default judgment in favour of a claimant, either on liability only or including awarding the remedy claimed, if the respondent has failed to submit a Response Form within the time limit and to the extent this is possible (*2013 Rules, Rule 21(2)*).

A Judgment can also be issued without a hearing if all parties have agreed in writing as to its terms (*Rule 64*), and a Judgment dismissing the claim will be issued without the need for a hearing if it has been withdrawn by the claimant (*Rule 52*) unless the exceptions in that rule apply.

In certain circumstances also, a claim may be struck out for non-compliance by the claimant with an order of the tribunal without the right to a further hearing: see, under the old rules, *Sodexho Ltd v Gibbons* [2005] ICR 1647, [2005] IRLR 836, EAT (striking out for non-payment of a deposit ordered at a PHR), but such a step is a judicial act and therefore a judgment and therefore open to reconsideration: see now *Rule 70*.

In addition, there is provision for a case to be heard in the absence of a party who fails to attend (and is not represented) at the hearing (*2013 Rules, Rule 47*) or in the absence of a respondent who has been excluded from participating in the proceedings by virtue of *Rule 21(3)* for failure to submit a valid Response Form in time.

19.11 JURISDICTION

It is important to appreciate at the outset that employment tribunals are creatures of statute, and therefore have only such powers and jurisdiction as have been conferred on them by statutory provision. Jurisdiction cannot be conferred, or enlarged, by agreement between the parties to a case, or by the acquiescence or silence of a party. This does not mean that the tribunal cannot resolve a dispute about whether it has jurisdiction. Such disputes arise relatively frequently, and must be determined when they do arise; but if the tribunal erroneously holds that it has jurisdiction and proceeds to exercise it, the assertion of jurisdiction is open to challenge on appeal. Similarly, jurisdiction cannot be conferred simply by agreement, or a concession by one party which the party subsequently withdraws before there is a binding determination of the case: *Radakovits v Abbey National plc* [2009] EWCA Civ 1346, [2009] IRLR 307 (employer initially conceding claim in time, but later withdrawing concession; tribunal held bound to determine whether it had jurisdiction once the point was in dispute). (But, as was noted by Sedley LJ in *Clark v Clark Construction Initiatives Ltd* [2008] EWCA Civ 1466, [2009] ICR 718, at para 14, if the question determining jurisdiction is one of fact, there may be no practical grounds for appealing against an erroneous determination of the facts necessary to confer jurisdiction; and see *Kudjodji v Lidl Ltd* [2011] All ER (D) 165 (Jul) (UKEAT/0054/11): once tribunal has decided it has jurisdiction, and subject to any appeal, a different tribunal hearing the case at a later stage cannot reopen that decision.)

Tribunals have jurisdiction both under English and Scots law, and under EU law. The jurisdiction under English and Scots law is entirely statutory; jurisdiction under EU law derives from principles of EU law itself. The total number of separate jurisdictions is now in excess of 70, albeit many of these arise extremely infrequently in practice. The principal statutory provisions, which all apply equally to Scotland, are:

(a)   *Employment Rights Act 1996 ('ERA 1996')*, as amended (unfair dismissal, redundancy payments, disputes over written particulars of employment and itemised pay statements, unlawful deductions from wages or requirements to make payments to employers (formerly under the *Wages Act 1986*), breaches of the *National Minimum Wage Act 1998*, guarantee payments, rights to time off for public duties, protection from detriment in certain health and safety (and other) cases and as a result of a protected disclosure under the *Public Interest Disclosure Act 1998*, time off for family emergencies, maternity, paternity, adoption and parental leave issues, failure to pay during medical suspension, issues over requests for flexible working arrangements, written reasons for dismissal, claims (other than pension claims) against the Secretary of State in insolvency cases, interim relief in certain unfair dismissal cases and a number of minor and ancillary matters);

(b)   *TULR(C)A 1992* (unfair dismissal or action short of dismissal for trade union reasons or for participation in industrial action; offering inducements not to join a union or to opt out of collective agreements; blacklisting complaints; time off for union and other duties; failure to consult recognised unions or employee representatives over proposed redundancies; claims for payment of protective awards made for such failures to consult; failure to consult recognised unions over training; and disputes over union membership, disciplinary action against members and expulsions);

(c)   *Equality Act 2010, ss 120* (claims under *Part 5* of the *Act* (work)) and *127* (claims of breach of an equality clause or rule under the equality of terms provisions of the *Act*) and *ss 122* and *128* (cases referred to the tribunal by a court);

(d)   *Employment Tribunals Extension of Jurisdiction (England and Wales) Order 1994* and the equivalent Scottish Order (claims in contract and employers' counterclaims, subject to a maximum jurisdiction of £25,000) Note that the Law Commission in LC 390 *Employment Law Hearing Structures* (27 April 2020) recommended that this limit be increased to £100,000;

(e)   *Working Time Regulations 1998 (SI 1998/1833), regs 30–32* (complaints of dismissal or subjection to detriment for insisting on entitlements to breaks or rest periods, or refusing to agree to work hours in excess of the maximum, and of refusal to permit the exercise of rights to annual leave, rest breaks or rest periods conferred on workers by the *Regulations* or to provide compensatory rest, or to pay for annual leave or in lieu of accrued leave rights on termination of employment; also complaints of detrimental treatment or dismissal of those elected as representatives to negotiate workforce agreements, or standing as candidates for election);

(f)   *National Minimum Wage Act 1998, ss 22, 24* (appeals against penalty notices issued by compliance officers, and complaints of detriment by workers; complaints of underpayment are made under the *ERA 1996, Part II*);

(g)   *Employment Relations Act 1999 ('ERA 1999'), s 11* (failure to permit workers to be accompanied at grievance or disciplinary hearing or to postpone hearing for that purpose);

(h)   *Part-time Workers (Prevention of Less Favourable Treatment) Regulations 2000 (SI 2000/ 1551), reg 8* (infringement of right not to be less favourably treated; subjection to detriment for assertion of rights);

(i)   *Fixed-term Employees (Prevention of Less Favourable Treatment) Regulations 2002 (SI 2002/2034), reg 7* (infringement of right not to be less favourably treated; subjection to detriment for assertion of rights) and *reg 9(5)* (application for declaration of status as permanent employee);

(j)   *Transfer of Undertakings (Protection of Employment) Regulations 2006 (SI 2006/246), regs 12* (failure to notify employee liability information to transferee) and *15* (failure to inform or consult with trade unions or employee representatives, and associated claims for non-payment of protective awards);

(k)   *Equality Act 2006, ss 21, 25* (appeals against unlawful act notices issued by the Commission for Equality and Human Rights, and applications by the Commission to restrain certain unlawful acts under the discrimination legislation);

(l)   *Agency Workers Regulations 2010 (SI 2010/93), reg 18* (with effect from 1 October 2011, complaints of infringements of the rights conferred by the *Regulations*, including equality of treatment with directly employed staff);

(m)   *Employment Relations Act 1999 (Blacklists) Regulations 2010 (SI 2010/493), regs 5, 6, 9* (refusal to employ or provide agency services to, or subjecting to detriment, workers, by reference to blacklists);

(n)   miscellaneous legislation (including claims arising from failure to consult recognised union over application to contract out of occupational pension scheme and certain other claims under the *Pension Schemes Act 1993*; appeals against industrial training levies; appeals against improvement and prohibition notices; disputes over time off for safety representatives and union learning representatives and other employee representatives given statutory rights to paid or unpaid time off; proceedings against employment agencies under the *Deregulation and Contracting Out Act 1994*);

(o)   Claims under the *Third Parties (Rights Against Insurers) Act 2010*: see *Watson v Hemingway Design Limited* (UKEAT/0007/19/JOJ).

The jurisdictions under the *Equality Act 2010* replace several heads of jurisdiction under the various predecessor statutes and regulations, principally the *Equal Pay Act 1970, Sex Discrimination Act 1975, Race Relations Act 1976* and *Disability Discrimination Act 1995*, and the regulations on discrimination on grounds of sexual orientation, religion or belief and age. Part of the latter, the *Employment Equality (Age) Regulations 2006, SI 2006/1031*, providing for the procedure for requests to remain in employment after a notice to retire was issued remained in force after the revocation of the main regulations, but was revoked as from 6 April 2011 (see the *Employment Equality (Repeal of Retirement Age Provisions) Regulations 2011, SI 2011/1069*) but subject to transitional provisions which may result in claims arising after that date.

The EAT has held in relation to complaints of unlawful deduction from wages under *ERA 1996, Part II* that tribunals have no jurisdiction to hear complaints of non-payment or under-payment of Statutory Sick Pay, where the employer disputes liability to pay, as such disputes are reserved to the Inland Revenue (now HM Revenue and Customs): *Taylor Gordon & Co Ltd (t/a Plan Personnel) v Timmons* [2004] IRLR 180. The reasoning applies equally to disputes about entitlement to Statutory Maternity Pay, Statutory Paternity Pay and Statutory Adoption Pay. The tribunal also has no jurisdiction to determine the amount of an unquantified bonus claimed to be due in order to determine whether a failure to pay the bonus was an unlawful deduction from wages, since only a claim for non-payment of a specific sum said to be owed to the claimant can be made under *Part II*: *Coors Brewers Ltd v Adcock* [2007] EWCA Civ 19, [2007] ICR 983, [2007] IRLR 440; see also *Kingston upon Hull City Council v Schofield & Others* [2012] All ER (D) 342 (Nov). The definition of 'wages' in the *ERA 1996* provides further parameters to the Tribunal's jurisdiction to determine claims of this type. Notable exceptions from the definition are payments in respect of expenses: see *London Borough of Southwark v O'Brien* [1996] IRLR 420 and *Qantas Cabin Crew (UK) Ltd v Lopez and Hooper* [2013] IRLR 4.

A further limitation on the jurisdiction of tribunals is that they cannot interpret the contractual terms of employees in proceedings for a determination of whether a statement of the particulars of terms of employment given to the claimant were correct: *Southern Cross Healthcare Co Ltd v Perkins* [2010] EWCA Civ 1442, [2011] IRLR 247 (a case concerning a dispute over the amount of holiday entitlement the claimants' contracts conferred). There is a dispute within the EAT's case law as to whether this applies so as to prohibit the Tribunal interpreting contractual terms for the purposes of adjudicating upon an unauthorised deductions from wages claim. In *Agarwal v Cardiff University & Another* [2017] IRLR 600, Slade J held there was no jurisdiction to construe the contract for the purposes of a wages claim, applying Southern Cross with the consequence that a claim concerning whether the contract contained implied terms relevant to the wages payable would have to be determined in the civil courts. By contrast, in *Weatherilt v Cathay Pacific Airways Ltd* [2017] ICR 985 HHJ Richardson disagreed and considered that *Agarwal* should not be followed because the EAT in that case had not been referred to relevant Court of Appeal authority in *Delaney v Staples* [1991] IRLR 112 and *Camden Primary Care Trust v Atchoe* [2007] EWCA Civ 714, [2007] All ER (D) 145 (May). The EAT held in *Weatherilt* that it would be surprising if the tribunal could not construe a provision of the contract to see whether a deduction was authorised when that question might be central to the issue in an unauthorised deduction claim. In *Tyne and Wear Passenger Transport Executive (t/a Nexus) v Anderson* [2018] ICR 1207, Judge Hand QC followed *Weatherilt* on the same issue. Note that the Law Commission in its report on *Employment Tribunal Hearing Structures* (LC 390) (27 April 2020) has recommended that Tribunals be given the power to interpret contractual terms in the context of exercising this particular jurisdiction.

It should be noted that tribunals in England and Wales, and in Scotland respectively, only have jurisdiction over cases with the required territorial connection with the respective part of Great Britain. If a claim over which only the tribunals in Scotland have jurisdiction is presented in England or Wales, or vice versa, the claim is ineffective and the receiving tribunal has no jurisdiction to deal with it (or even to transfer the papers to the correct country): *McFadyen v PB Recovery Ltd* (UKEATS/0072/08) (31 July 2009, unreported).

The *2013 Rules* specify where a claim should be presented as between England and Wales and Scotland in *Rule 8(2)* and *(3)*. These provisions may allow for a claim to be brought in either jurisdiction. The test for Tribunals to apply gives a number of routes to jurisdiction (here set out by reference to England and Wales, but see *Rule 8(3)* for Scotland): where the respondent, or one of them, resides or carries on business in England and Wales, if one or more of the acts or omissions complained of took place in England and Wales, if the claim relates to a contract under which the work is or has been performed partly in England and Wales or where jurisdiction derives from a connection with Great Britain and the connection in question is at least partly a connection with England and Wales. A broad approach to the question whether the respondent carries on business within the jurisdiction was adopted in *Pervez v Macquarie Bank Ltd (London Branch)* [2011] ICR 266, [2011] IRLR 284, EAT, where it was held that the respondent (an Australian company) carried on business in England through the presence of the claimant who was working on secondment in London (having been based in Hong Kong), although the respondent had no other presence in the jurisdiction. *Rule 99* permits the Tribunal to transfer proceedings between England and Wales and Scotland provided that the tribunal receiving the claim would have had jurisdiction to receive the originally presented claim and the claim would be more conveniently determined there.

It should be noted that all of these points are separate from the jurisdictional issues which arise in relation to whether legislation conferring a substantive employment right applies to the particular circumstances of employment with an extra-territorial element; these issues are discussed elsewhere in this book in the context of the particular rights concerned, but see in particular **27.11** FOREIGN EMPLOYEES.

19.12 Jurisdiction over EU law

The legal position subsequent to the UK leaving the European Union

In common with all Courts and Tribunals, by *s 6(1)* of the *European Union (Withdrawal) Act 2018*, the Tribunal is not bound by any principles laid down, or any decisions made, on or after completion day by the CJEU, and cannot refer any matter to the CJEU under *article 234*. However, by *s 6(2)*, a Tribunal may have regard to anything done on or after completion by the CJEU, another EU entity (such as the Commission) or the EU so far as it is relevant to any matter before the Tribunal. By *s 6(3)*, any question as to the validity, meaning or effect of any retained EU law is to be decided, so far as that law is unmodified on or after completion and so far as they are relevant to it: (a) in accordance with any retained case law and any retained general principles of EU law, and (b) having regard (among other things) to the limits, immediately before completion, of EU competences. *Section 6(6)* clarifies that the same principle applies to law that has been modified after completion if that would be consistent with the intention of the modifications. However, by *s 6(4)(c)*, the Tribunal is not bound by any retained domestic case law that it would not otherwise be bound by. The Supreme Court has power to depart from retained EU case law (under *s 6(4)* and *(5)*); if it does so, then the Tribunal would be bound by the Supreme Court's decision. What is meant by 'retained domestic' and 'retained EU law' and 'retained general principles of EU law' is further defined in the Act. Of particular note: the general principle of the supremacy of EU law does not apply after exit day (*s 5(1)-(3)*); the Charter of Fundamental Rights is not part of domestic law on or after exit day (*s 5(4)*), (although the European Convention on Human Rights and the *Human Rights Act 1998* are not affected by withdrawal from the EU); no general principle of EU law is part of domestic law on or after exit day if it was not recognised as a general principle of EU law by the European Court in a case decided before exit day (whether or not as an essential part of the decision in the case) (*Sch 1, para 2*); there is no right of action in domestic law on or after exit day based on a failure to comply with any of the general principles of EU law and no court or tribunal or other public authority may, on or after exit day disapply or quash any enactment or other rule of law or decision because it is incompatible with any of the general principles of EU law (*Sch 1, para 3*); there is no right to *Francovich* damages (*Sch 1, para 4*).

The legal position prior to the UK leaving the European Union

Tribunals' jurisdiction is statutory, but there is no statutory provision giving the tribunal power to determine claims under EU law. The basis for tribunals hearing such claims has therefore been a source of legal difficulty.

There is clear authority recognising tribunals' jurisdiction where a claimant relies on *art 157* of the *Treaty on the functioning of the EU* (formerly *art 141* of the *Treaty of Rome* (equal pay claims)): *Pickstone v Freemans plc* [1989] AC 66, [1987] 3 All ER 756, [1987] IRLR 219. Claims relying on the *Equal Treatment Directive 76/207* (now replaced by the consolidating *Directive 2006/54*) against state authorities have been acknowledged to be within the jurisdiction of tribunals since the principle of direct effect was established by the European Court of Justice in *Marshall v Southampton and South West Hampshire Area Health Authority (Teaching)*: C-152/84 [1986] QB 401, [1986] IRLR 140 and are now relatively common. The position in relation to other *Directives* depends on whether the particular provision concerned is sufficiently 'clear, precise and unconditional' to have direct effect, a question of EU law and thus ultimately for the CJEU.

Rulings of the Court of Appeal to the effect that tribunals have no jurisdiction to hear 'freestanding' claims under EU law, and that any such claims must be made under the relevant statute with the offending provision disapplied (*Biggs v Somerset County Council* [1996] 2 All ER 734, [1996] IRLR 203, [1996] ICR 364; *Staffordshire County Council v Barber* [1996] IRLR 209) have since been overtaken by developments in the case law of the CJEU, in particular *Mangold v Helm*: C-144/04 [2006] IRLR 143, *Impact v Minister for Agriculture and Food*: C-268/06 [2008] IRLR 552, *Kücükdeveci v Swedex GmbH*: C-555/07 [2010] IRLR 346, and *Dominguez v Centre Informatique du Centre Ouest Atlantique*: C-282/10 [2012] IRLR 321. The effect of these and other decisions is that a claim may be made in a domestic forum to give effect to a right conferred by EU law, whether or not fully and correctly transposed into domestic law by the member state, once the date for transposition has passed; such enforcement may in some circumstances be against private sector respondents as well as public bodies. The basis for the employment tribunal being an appropriate forum for such claims can be derived from the *Impact* case, where the CJEU ruled that a specialist tribunal with power to determine claims under national legislation implementing a *Directive* must also have power to decide claims made directly under the *Directive*, if alternative means of pursuing the claim would involve sufficiently serious procedural disadvantages.

In addition, whether or not it is possible to maintain a claim in an employment tribunal directly under EU law, the EAT has held that the tribunal has power, even in proceedings against a non-state entity, to disapply, or read words into, a statutory provision, if this is necessary to give effect to a right conferred by EU law, and the rewriting of the statutory provision 'goes with the grain' of the domestic legislation: *Coleman v EBR Attridge Law LLP* [2010] 1 CMLR 846, [2010] IRLR 10; contrast the more restrictive approach (*obiter*) in *Hainsworth v Ministry of Defence* [2014] EWCA Civ 763, [2014] IRLR 728.

The Court of Appeal's decisions referred to above have two main effects (neither of which would appear to be affected by the *Impact* decision):

(a)   Procedural provisions, particularly those relating to time limits for making claims, contained in the relevant national legislation apply equally where that legislation is used as a basis for a claim relying on EU law. (The same principle applies to other procedural rules; for an example, see *Livingstone v Hepworth Refractories Ltd* [1992] IRLR 63.)

(b)   Claims against the Government for damages for failure to implement EU Directives cannot be brought in the tribunal; the claim must be made in the High Court against the Attorney-General, or in Scotland the Lord Advocate (*Secretary of State for Employment v Mann* [1997] ICR 209, CA; for an example of such a claim, see *R v A-G for Northern Ireland, ex p Burns* [1999] IRLR 315).

However, there are still considerations of EU law which may affect how any discretion under the national legislation has to be exercised (eg to extend time), whether time limits run against the claimant and whether restrictions on remedies available under the national statute are compatible with EU law (*Marshall v Southampton and South West Hampshire Area Health Authority (No 2)*: C-271/91 [1994] QB 126, [1993] IRLR 445 and *Levez v T H Jennings (Harlow Pools) Ltd*: C-326/96 [1999] IRLR 36, [1999] ICR 521 (both decisions of the CJEU)). For an interesting example see *Chief Constable of West Yorkshire Police v A* [2000] IRLR 465 (tribunal has power under EU law to make restricted reporting order protecting identity of transsexual claimant; see further **19.18** below and now *Rule 50* of the *2013 Rules*).

The CJEU has endorsed the principle of the application of national time limits to cases reliant on EU law, provided that the time limits are no less favourable than for those for similar claims in domestic law and do not render the exercise of rights under EU law impossible in practice: *Fisscher v Voorhuis Hengelo BV*: C-128/93 [1994] IRLR 662, [1995] ICR 635.

Separately from the European Convention of Human Rights (on which see below), the European Union's Charter of Fundamental Rights of the European Union, agreed in 2000 in Nice (OJ C 364, 19.12.2000, p1-22), is becoming a source of EU relied upon before national courts and tribunals. By Art 6(1) of the Treaty on European Union, it has the same legal value as a treaty. According to the CJEU, where it is necessary to interpret a provision of secondary Community law, preference should as far as possible be given to the interpretation which renders the provision consistent with the EC Treaty and the general principles of Community law: see eg *Schutzverband der Spirituosen-Industrie v Diageo Deutschland GmbH* (Case C-457/05) [2007] ECR I-8075, [2007] All ER (D) 109 (Oct). Further, domestic law must, as mentioned above, be interpreted as far as possible, in a manner to give effect to EU law, where necessary disapplying offending provisions of national law. In *R (NS) v Secretary of State for the Home Department* [2010] EWCA Civ 990, the UK Government accepted that in principle the rights set out in the Charter can be relied on as against the UK. See also the judgment of Mostyn J in *R (AB) v Secretary of State for the Home Department* [2013] EWHC 3453, [2013] All ER (D) 94 (Nov) at paras 13-14. A recent example of the Charter's effect can be seen in *Benkharbouche v Embassy of the Republic of Sudan* [2015] IRLR 301. There, the Court of Appeal recognised the direct effect of the Charter rights even in cases between private individuals (ie horizontally). Accordingly, the Court felt able to disapply sections of the *State Immunity Act 1978* as being contrary to art 47 of the EU Charter (guaranteeing an effective remedy, in that case with the same content as Art 6 ECHR). *Benkharbouche* is, at the time of writing, on appeal in the Supreme Court.

See further EUROPEAN UNION LAW (24).

19.13 Human Rights Act 1998

Proceedings under the *HRA 1998, s 7* can only be brought in those courts or tribunals designated as 'appropriate'. As no designation has been made for employment tribunals, it follows that no 'freestanding' claims can be brought in the tribunal under that *Act*. (See on this *Whittaker v Watson (P & D) (t/a P & M Watson Haulage)* [2002] ICR 1244, confirming that the EAT is in the same position, and cannot therefore issue a declaration that a statutory provision is incompatible with the *HRA 1998*.) However, tribunals are 'public authorities' within *s 6* of the *Act*, and thus are required not to act in a way which is incompatible with rights secured by the *European Convention on Human Rights* unless compelled to do so by legislation. This means that issues of alleged infringement of a party's human rights may be raised in the course of tribunal proceedings, and the tribunal may find it necessary to take the *Convention* into account in the course of deciding substantive or procedural issues in the case. To that extent the position is similar to that under EU law, but the power to overrule primary legislation incompatible with a directly applicable EU obligation does not have a direct parallel. For guidance on how the *Convention* affects the application of the general law of unfair dismissal see *X v Y* [2004] EWCA Civ 662, [2004] IRLR 625, CA, *Salford Royal NHS Foundation Trust v Roldan* [2010] EWCA Civ 522, [2010] ICR 1457, and *Turner v East Midlands Trains Ltd* [2013] IRLR 107, [2013] ICR 525.

As a separate point, the right under *art 6* of the *Convention* to a fair trial in the determination of one's civil rights imposes obligations on tribunals as the forum in which that right is afforded in most employment cases. In addition to the obligations of independence and impartiality, discussed at **19.7** above, tribunals are required to afford a determination 'within a reasonable time' in order to satisfy *art 6*. Even the relatively generous timescale applied by the European Court of Human Rights in its jurisprudence under *art 6* was held to have been exceeded in *Somjee v United Kingdom* [2002] IRLR 886, where a series of applications to the tribunal and appeals to the EAT, with lengthy delays at a number of stages, had led to a nine year delay between the initial application and its final determination. However delay is not in itself a ground of appeal: rather the question in any appeal where there has been serious delay, whether in issuing the tribunal's judgment or more generally, is whether there is a real risk that the party appealing has in substance been deprived of the right to a fair trial in accordance with *Art 6*: *Bangs v Connex South Eastern Ltd* [2005] EWCA Civ 14, [2005] 2 All ER 316, [2005] IRLR 389, where the Court of Appeal laid down guidance on the correct approach to such appeals. The earlier decision of the EAT in *Kwamin v Abbey National plc* [2004] IRLR 516, in which a broader approach was taken, was disapproved by the Court. In more mundane situations, compliance with the timeliness requirement of *Art 6* is a relevant factor for a tribunal in deciding whether to grant an adjournment, if the effect of doing so would be to create any significant delay or further delay in the proceedings.

Issues in relation to *Art 6* are frequently raised in employment tribunals (particularly by litigants in person) but in practice rarely add to the general principles of fairness embodied in the Overriding Objective (see **19.14** below for this), and given effect in more detail by the *ET Rules*. Two examples may be given. The Supreme Court held, in *Home Office v Tariq* [2011] UKSC 35, [2011] IRLR 843, that the special procedure for National Security cases laid down by *Sch 2* to the *2004 Regulations* (see now *Sch 2* to the *2013 Regulations*), under which a Special Advocate is appointed to advance the claimant's case and the claimant is denied access to sensitive evidence heard in private, does not breach the requirements of *Art 6*. In *Power v Greater Manchester Police Authority* [2010] All ER (D) 173 (Oct) (UKEAT/0087/10), the EAT held that there was no incompatibility with *Art 6* in a case where the claimant was denied the opportunity of cross-examining the person alleged to have discriminated against him (because the employer chose not to call her as a witness); the right under *Art 6* to cross-examine witnesses applies to criminal, not civil, proceedings. It is also worth noting the approach taken to *Art 6* in internal proceedings before the employer, clarified by the Supreme Court in *R (G) v Governors of X School* [2011] IRLR 756 and the Court of Appeal in *Mattu v University Hospitals Coventry and Warwickshire NHS Trust* [2012] IRLR 661.

In addition, *Art 6* is often cited in appeals based on the inadequacy of an employment tribunal's reasons; but in practice the higher courts' interpretation and application of the obligation to give reasons under *2013 Rules, Rule 62(1)* and general principles of common law fully meets the requirements derived from *Art 6*. See further **20.117–20.119**.

Issues of the right to privacy under *Art 8* of the *Convention* may arise in the context of what evidence a tribunal should admit, where it is asserted that the obtaining or use of the evidence involved or would involve an impermissible interference with that right. See further EMPLOYMENT TRIBUNALS – II, **20.60**A.

In *Woodrup v Southwark London Borough Council* [2002] EWCA Civ 1716, [2003] IRLR 111, the Court of Appeal considered an argument that employment tribunals are engaged in the provision of services to the public within *Part III* of the *Disability Discrimination Act 1995*, which would entail a duty to make reasonable adjustments in favour of disabled parties in the conduct of the proceedings. Without formally ruling on the point, both members of the Court (Simon Brown and Clarke LJJ) expressed strong doubts as to the suggestion that there is such a legal duty on tribunals. There is also an express exclusion of judicial acts, including things done on the instructions a person exercising judicial authority, from the general duty of public bodies not to discriminate against disabled persons in the exercise of any of their functions: *Equality Act 2010, Sch 3, para 3*, replacing equivalent provisions in the *Disability Discrimination Act 1995, ss 21B(1), 21C(1)*. Such acts may well attract judicial immunity from any claim that might be brought: see eg *Engel v PATROL* [2013] IRLR 787 (UKEAT/520/12). That said, it is well established that tribunals should make adjustments to accommodate disabled claimants: see further **20.55** EMPLOYMENT TRIBUNALS – II.

The Tribunal now has express ability in *Rule 50* to make an order preventing or restricting public disclosure of any aspects of proceedings so far as it considers necessary in the interest of justice or in order to protect Convention rights of any person. See further **20.89–20.90**, EMPLOYMENT TRIBUNALS – II.

TIME LIMITS FOR CLAIMS

19.14 General

All applications to employment tribunals must be presented within a certain time limit, which varies according to the particular statutory provision relied on. The statutory provisions as to time limits are relatively complex, as they differ according to the particular statutory provisions relied on. It is important to appreciate a number of basic points about time limits.

(a)   Time limits go to the jurisdiction of the tribunal. A claim presented after the time limit has expired cannot be considered at all on its merits, however strong these may be, unless the tribunal can be persuaded to extend time under the limited discretionary powers to do so conferred by the relevant statute. There is power to extend time in relation to almost all the statutory jurisdictions of the tribunals, but the criteria vary according to the particular type of claim; full details are given in **19.25–19.28** below.

(b)   Time limits do not only lay down the latest date for bringing a claim. In relation to some (though not all) jurisdictions, the tribunal is precluded from hearing a claim because it was brought prematurely, *before* the relevant time period began to run. In addition, under the *Employment Act 2002*, some claims could not be presented until 28 days had elapsed after a written grievance had been submitted to the employer, although this requirement was repealed in 2008 – for details please see the 23rd edition of this Handbook. There remains, however, a requirement to have engaged in early conciliation prior to commencing proceedings: see **19.8ff** below.

(c)   Time limits apply to the *presentation* of a claim, that is, its delivery (physically or electronically) to the relevant office of the tribunal (see (*e*) below for further details on how the date of presentation is calculated in marginal situations).

(d)   Time runs from a particular event, the nature of which varies depending on the particular jurisdiction. It may be both important and difficult to determine what is the relevant date in a particular case – notoriously so where it is the 'effective date of termination' that is in issue, as in an unfair dismissal claim. Normally it is the date of the event which starts the clock running, not the date (if later) on which the individual becomes aware of the event (eg an unlawful deduction from wages which the employee does not spot on first receiving the relevant payslip; or the learning of an employer taking detrimental action because of whistleblowing: see *McKinney v London Borough of Newham* [2014] All ER (D) 74 (Dec) in which the EAT held it was the date of the decision which started time running). However, some events, such as termination of employment, may require communication to the employee to be effective (cf *Gisda Cyf v Barratt* [2010] UKSC 41, [2010] IRLR 1073 and *Newcastle-upon-Tyne Hospitals NHS Foundation Trust v Haywood* [2018] UKSC 22, [2018] 1 WLR 2073, [2018] ICR 882, [2018] IRLR 644). See further **19.22** below. (This point may be important not just in determining when time starts to run for presenting a claim, but also whether there is a claim at all, as where legislation comes into force after the first point in time at which the right to complain arises: see for a good example *Coutts & Co plc v Cure* [2005] ICR 1098.)

(e)   The usual formulation of the time limit in employment legislation is that the complaint must be presented within a period (usually of three months) beginning with the date of the relevant event, such as the dismissal. This means that that date is the first day of the three-month period, which therefore ends one day earlier in the third following month. The correct way of calculating the three-month period is to take the day of the month of the day immediately prior to the date (eg of dismissal) and go forward three months. Thus, if the employee is dismissed on 1 June, the last date for presentation is 31 August, but if the date of dismissal was 30 April, the correct last date is 29 July; some anomalies may arise from months of different lengths. See further *Pruden v Cunard Ellerman Lines Ltd* [1993] IRLR 317 and *University of Cambridge v Murray* [1993] ICR 460.

(f)   The principal exceptions to the three-month time limit are claims for a statutory redundancy payment (six months from the 'relevant date', usually the date of dismissal) and equal pay (during, or within six months following the termination of, the relevant employment). One category of claims, for interim relief in certain categories of unfair dismissal claim (see *ERA, ss 128–132*; *TULR(C)A 1992, ss 161–163*), has a time limit of only seven days from the effective date of termination.

(g)   It is not necessarily possible to circumvent time limits for a particular claim by presenting an application under one jurisdiction and then applying to add further claims. The rules on amendment of claims (see **20.70** EMPLOYMENT TRIBUNALS - II) require tribunals to balance the prejudice or hardship that would be suffered by each party if the amendment is, or is not, allowed, taking into account, if it be the case, that the new claim has been raised for the first time after the time limit has expired. This may result in the application to amend being refused, particularly if made at the last minute before the Hearing (see further on amendments generally **20.72**). However, provided the proper test is applied, being out of time does not automatically mean that permission to amend should be refused: *Mist v Derby Community Health Services NHS Trust* [2016] ICR 543. See further **20.70**(F) EMPLOYMENT TRIBUNALS - II.

(h)   Since time points are a matter going to the jurisdiction of the tribunal, they may be raised at any time in the proceedings. The point may be (and quite frequently in practice is) raised by the tribunal itself, and in such cases it must be considered and decided on although the respondent is content to have the matter adjudicated on its merits. It is even possible (as an exception to the normal practice) for the issue of time to be raised for the first time in the course of an appeal: for an example see *Landon v Lill* (EAT/1486/00) (9 October 2002, unreported).

(i)   The time point is often considered as a preliminary issue separately from the substantive hearing; as it may raise questions of fact, evidence can be called by either or both parties. Under the *2013 Rules*, the time point (a 'preliminary issue') can be dealt with at a preliminary hearing (*Rule 53*). Sometimes it is inappropriate to determine the issue of jurisdiction separately, for example where it involves the same factual issues as have to be determined on the merits of the case: see *Ironsides Ray & Vials v Lindsay* [1994] ICR 384, [1994] IRLR 319. The general approach of the EAT before the introduction of the *2013* (and indeed the *2004 Rules*) was to discourage the separation of preliminary points unless they were clearly distinct from other issues arising in the case: see eg *Wellcome Foundation v Darby* [1996] IRLR 538 and *Sutcliffe v Big C's Marine Ltd* [1998] IRLR 428. The *2004 Rules* gave more weight to the pre-hearing review procedure, and the practice of ordering PHRs to determine time issues became more common, at least in unfair dismissal cases; however in discrimination cases, where evidence of alleged discrimination over a relatively extended period may be admissible even if the claims founded on that evidence are held to be out of time, and where arguments about whether acts continue over a period are frequent, tribunals were markedly more reluctant to deal separately with time points (see the Court of Appeal's judgment in *Hendricks v Commissioner of Police for the Metropolis* [2003] IRLR 96). This remains the position under the *2013 Rules*.

(j)   Special provisions apply to the presentation of claims by members or former members of the armed forces; see **31.4** for details.

(k)   Bringing a claim out of time does not mean necessarily that the claim is an abuse of process. Thus, in *Higgins v Home Office* [2015] All ER (D) 162 (May), the ET had erred in rejecting a claim 6 years out of time as an abuse of process under Rule 12(1)(b). The Judge ought to have had regard to the claimant's mental health issues which may have had a bearing on the late presentation.

19.15 Automatic extensions of the time limit

Subject to some complex transitional provisions, which in almost all cases do not apply to claims presented after 5 October 2009, the provisions of the *Employment Act 2002* and the *Dispute Resolution Regulations* which served to extend time automatically no longer apply following the repeal of *ss 29–33* of the *Employment Act 2002* and the associated Schedules with effect from 6 April 2009. For that reason the reader is referred to previous editions of this Handbook.

19.16   For jurisdictions in which there is an obligation to undergo Early Conciliation, there is an effect on the statutory time limits where a claimant, who is still within time, contacts ACAS to commence Early Conciliation. The provisions are discussed in the next chapter: see **20.14**.

19.17 COMPUTING AND EXTENDING TIME IN DIFFERENT JURISDICTIONS

Different statutes have provided different criteria for the extension of time. It is important to appreciate that the tribunal cannot extend time unless the relevant condition is satisfied; in addition, in relation to the first category of criteria noted below, even if it is satisfied, the tribunal must decide the further question whether the length of extension sought to validate the claim is reasonable. The principal categories of criteria, and the jurisdictions to which each applies, are as follows:

(i)   that it was not reasonably practicable to present the Claim Form within time: unfair dismissal; unlawful deduction from wages; subjection to a detriment for a reason within *ERA 1996* and *TULR(C)A 1992*; most other claims within *ERA 1996* and *TULR(C)A 1992*; claims under the *Working Time Regulations 1998*; claims for breach of contract;

(ii)   that it would be just and equitable to extend time: unlawful discrimination under the *Equality Act 2010, s 120*; less favourable treatment or subjection to detriment under the *Part-time Workers (Prevention of Less Favourable Treatment) Regulations 2000, reg 8* or the *Fixed-term Workers (Prevention of Less Favourable Treatment) Regulations 2002, reg 7*; redundancy payments (subject to a maximum extension of six months: *ERA 1996, s 164*); claims under the *Agency Workers Regulations 2010, reg 17*;

(iii)   no provision for extension (except in cases of concealment of the information on which the claim is based): equal pay claims (see the *Equality Act 2010, s 127*). See further **19.25** below.

The tests to be applied by the tribunals in relation to each of the first two criteria are considered below, at **19.25–19.26**

It should be noted that if there is a disputed issue as to whether a claim was presented in time, and/or whether, if not, time should be extended, it will be necessary, where the relevant facts are in dispute, that evidence is adduced at the hearing, whether this is the final hearing or a preliminary hearing: cf *Sodexo Health Care Services Ltd v Harmer* (UKEATS/0079/08).

19.18 Establishing when time starts to run in dismissal cases: the 'effective date of termination'

In claims alleging unfair dismissal, time starts to run from and including the 'effective date of termination' ('EDT': see *ERA 1996, s 97*). The EDT has been described judicially as a 'statutory construct' and normal contractual principles do not necessarily determine when the EDT falls. The (now relatively extensive) case law has established the following points.

(a)   If an employee is summarily dismissed, either orally or by notice in writing given to him or her at the time of dismissal, and whether or not the employer also makes a payment in lieu of the notice not given, the EDT is the date on which he or she is dismissed or ceases to work (*ERA 1996, s 97(1)*; *Dedman v British Building and Engineering Appliances Ltd* [1974] 1 All ER 520, [1974] 1 WLR 171, [1973] IRLR 379). Where an employee is dismissed without the statutory period of notice in *ERA 1996, s 86* being given, then the EDT is presumed by *s 97(2)* to be the day on which that statutory notice period would have expired, had the requisite notice been given. However, there is no entitlement to statutory notice in a case where an employer can lawfully dismiss without notice (i.e. for gross misconduct or equivalent) and accordingly, no statutory extension of the notice period counts to extend the EDT in such cases: *Lancaster and Duke Ltd v Wileman* [2019] ICR 125, [2019] IRLR 112.

(b)   However, if the employer gives notice to terminate a contract of employment and either requires or does not require the employee to work during the notice period, the EDT is not the date on which the employee ceases work but the date on which the notice expires. This situation is to be contrasted with where the employer dismisses and exercises a payment in lieu of notice clause so as to bring the contract to an end either immediately or on short notice accompanied by a payment instead of giving full notice. There, as described in (a) above, the EDT will be when the contract actually comes to an end. In *Societe Generale, London Branch v Geys* [2012] UKSC 63, [2013] IRLR 122, the Supreme Court held that to exercise the PILON clause in question it was not sufficient for the employee to receive their payment in lieu, but that they also receive notification from the employer in clear and unambiguous terms, that such a payment has been made and was made in the exercise of the contractual right to terminate the employment with immediate effect. If some notice of termination is given, and the parties subsequently agree to bring forward the date of termination (as may happen if the employee has another job to go to), the earlier date will be the EDT: an example in the redundancy context is *Palfrey v Transco Plc* [2004] IRLR 916.

(c)   If the employer dismisses summarily but communicates the decision by letter, the EDT is the date on which the employee receives and reads the letter, not the date on which the employer takes the decision to dismiss, or the date on which the letter is sent, or even received (if, for instance, the employee is away from home and does not see the letter until a few days later: *McMaster v Manchester Airport plc* [1998] IRLR 112). This conclusion was applied by the Supreme Court in a case with similar facts, *Gisda Cyf v Barratt* [2010] UKSC 41, [2010] IRLR 1073, with the caution that a claimant could not postpone the EDT by deliberately avoiding opening or reading a letter of dismissal. See further the discussion in *Newcastle Upon Tyne NHS Foundation Trust v Haywood* [2017] EWCA Civ 153, [2017] IRLR 629 in which the Court held that contractual notice was given on actual receipt rather than on delivery or the deemed date of receipt (although the reasoning of the different members of the court varied). The Supreme Court upheld the Court of Appeal, albeit for different reasons again: [2018] UKSC 22, [2018] ICR 882, [2018] IRLR 644. Where an employment agency employed an employee, and the employee's assignment ended, the burden was on the claimant to prove she had been dismissed. Dismissal did not fall to be implied even though the agency failed to take any steps to find other work and made assumptions about the employee's interest in further agency work: *Sandle v Adecco UK Ltd* [2016] IRLR 941.

(d)   If the employee resigns without notice (as in a constructive dismissal case), or by giving notice, and does so directly to the employer, the EDT will be the date on which the resignation without notice is communicated, or alternatively on the expiry of the period of notice given.

(e)   If the employee resigns without notice and communicates his or her resignation by letter to the employer, the EDT is the date on which the letter is received by the employer, and (probably) seen and read at least by someone in the employer's organisation, not necessarily the actual addressee: *Horwood v Lincolnshire County Council* [2012] All ER (D) 177 (Apr) (UKEAT/0462/11), following a decision to the same effect in *Potter v R J Temple (in Liquidation)* [2003] All ER (D) 327 (Dec) (UKEAT/0478,03), where the employee had resigned by fax, and *George v Luton Borough Council* [2003] All ER (D) 04 (Dec) (UKEAT/0311/03). If the employee gives, say, a week's notice, the week will run from the date of receipt of the notice, not (if later) the date on which the notice was seen and read by the relevant manager. (See further **19.24** below as to how the period of notice is calculated.)

(f)   If the employee is dismissed (or resigns) on notice, and during the currency of the notice the employer summarily dismisses the employee, the (earlier) date on which the summary dismissal occurs becomes the EDT in substitution for the (later) date on which the original notice would have expired: *Parker Rhodes Hickmott Solicitors v Harvey* [2012] All ER (D) 73 (Apr) (UKEAT/0455/11); if the result of the second dismissal is that the employee has less than the minimum period of service required to make a claim of unfair dismissal, that is the effect of the second dismissal and the employee cannot claim unfair dismissal (unless for a reason to which the qualifying service requirement does not apply): *M-Choice Ltd v Aalders* [2011] All ER (D) 145 (Oct) (UKEAT/0227/11), applying *Patel v Nagesan* [1995] IRLR 370.

The determination of the EDT is a question of fact which should be decided in a practical and common sense manner having regard to what the parties understood at the time: *Newman v Polytechnic of Wales Students Union* [1995] IRLR 72. However, the applicable date is a matter of law, and a date other than that derived from a correct application of legal principles to the facts cannot simply be agreed by the parties: *Fitzgerald v University of Kent at Canterbury* [2004] EWCA Civ 143, [2004] IRLR 300. Similarly, the EDT cannot be changed by the unilateral action of the employer in treating the date of the employee's resignation as later than it in fact was and paying her accordingly: *Horwood v Lincolnshire County Council* (above). Whilst the parties cannot themselves, unilaterally or by agreement, change what in fact is the EDT, they can of course set the EDT at a particular date by their actions, as where the parties agree to bring forward the date of termination so that the employee can leave to get another job, or the employee resigns without notice during the currency of notice of dismissal by the employer.

If the employee invokes an internal appeal procedure to appeal against his dismissal, time normally starts to run from the date of the original dismissal, *not* the date of the dismissal of the appeal, unless the contract provides for the employment to continue until the appeal is determined (*J Sainsbury Ltd v Savage* [1980] IRLR 109); for an example of a situation where the EDT was held to be the date of dismissal of the appeal, see *Drage v Governors of Greenford High School* [2000] IRLR 314, CA. This was also found to be the case in *Hawes & Curtis Ltd v Arfan, Mirza* [2012] All ER (D) 234 (Jun) (UKEAT/0229/12), where the EAT found that the parties had agreed after the employees appealed that their contracts would be kept open and in existence until the appeal hearing. For a case where the EDT was held to be affected by a decision to reinstate the employee following an appeal, which in turn was overruled by more senior management, see *London Probation Board v Kirkpatrick* [2005] IRLR 443; see also UNFAIR DISMISSAL – I (54). See also as to the potential complexities of identifying the EDT where the employer removes the employee from the payroll *Kirklees Metropolitan Borough Council v Radecki* [2009] EWCA Civ 298, [2009] IRLR 555 and compare *Societe Generale, London Branch v Geys*, above.

19.19   If notice of dismissal is given, the employee is not 'dismissed' until the notice expires: see *H W Smith (Cabinets) Ltd v Brindle* [1972] IRLR 125, CA. Thus, under ordinary principles a claim of unfair dismissal could not be presented during the notice period, and this was confirmed to be the case by the NIRC in *Penrose v Fairey Surveys Ltd* [1973] ICR 26. This led to a change in the law to allow applications in respect of dismissal with notice to be presented during the period the notice is running (the provision giving effect to this is now *ERA 1996, s 111(3)*). This facility has been held to apply equally in a case of a claim of constructive dismissal where the employee resigns with notice: *Presley v Llanelli Borough Council* [1979] IRLR 381. However, notice of dismissal must be unequivocal, and specify a date for the dismissal, in order to be effective; so an ultimatum to an employee who was absent from work that if he did not return by a stated deadline, his employment would be treated as terminated, was held by the EAT not to be a sufficiently unequivocal notice of dismissal to be effective as such, so that a complaint presented before the deadline had expired was premature and outwith the tribunal's jurisdiction: *Rai v Somerfield Stores Ltd* [2004] IRLR 124, [2004] ICR 656. On the other hand, a notice of dismissal which is to take effect on a stated date unless the employee appeals, and in that event on the date that the appeal is rejected, is sufficiently unconditional to constitute such a notice, and a complaint of unfair dismissal before the determination of the appeal is not premature: *Governing Body of Wishmorecross School v Balado* [2011] ICR D31 (UKEAT/0199/11). For the position relating to claims under the *Equality Act 2010* where the complaint is of dismissal, see **19.29** below.

A further complication is that it may be unclear when a notice of dismissal or resignation starts to run. Subject to any express statement to the contrary in the notice, the period of notice runs from the start of the day following the day on which the notice was communicated to the employee; this applies equally to written (including by email or text message) and oral notice and the position is not affected by the employer failing to pay the employee for the full period of notice: *West v Kneels* [1987] ICR 146, *Wang v University of Keele* [2011] IRLR 542. There is no equivalent authority on when notice of resignation starts to run, but it is submitted that the same approach should be adopted, by parity of reasoning.

If there is any ambiguity in a notice of dismissal as to when it is to take effect, this should be resolved against the employer, as the party giving the notice: *Chapman v Letheby and Christopher Ltd* [1981] IRLR 440, EAT, *Teva (UK) Ltd v Heslip* [2009] All ER (D) 277 (Jul); *Wang* (above).

For some purposes, the EDT is extended by a period equivalent to the employee's statutory notice entitlement, if the dismissal is summary; however, this does not apply for the purposes of computing the time limit for presenting a claim.

Different issues as to when time starts to run may arise in non-dismissal cases, particularly in relation to complaints about a continuing state of affairs or omissions. This point is addressed at **20.29** below.

19.20 'Not reasonably practicable' to present in time

An extension of time may be granted by the tribunal to validate a late complaint of unfair dismissal if, but only if, it is satisfied (the burden of proof being on the claimant) that it was 'not reasonably practicable for the complaint to be presented before the end' of the three-month period: *ERA 1996, s 111(2)*. The complaint must nevertheless have been presented 'within such further period as the tribunal considers reasonable' in order for an extension to be granted. The wording quoted is repeated in virtually identical terms in several other statutory provisions conferring jurisdiction on the tribunal: see **19.22** above. The EAT has confirmed that the principles and case law in relation to unfair dismissal claims apply equally to such other categories of claim: *GMB v Hamm* [2000] All ER (D) 1830 (claim for protective award); *Wandsworth London Borough Council v Covent Garden Market Authority* [2011] EWHC 1245 (QB), [2011] All ER (D) 173 (May) (appeal against health and safety Improvement Order). The comments which follow in this section accordingly apply equally to such claims.

It is a question of fact in each case whether it was reasonably practicable to present a claim in time. This question has generated extensive reported authority, but the Court of Appeal and EAT have repeatedly stressed that particular decisions should not be taken as laying down hard and fast rules (particularly as to the effect of the employee receiving advice). Following a review of the authorities, the Court of Appeal in *Palmer v Southend-on-Sea Borough Council* [1984] 1 All ER 945, [1984] 1 WLR 1129, [1984] IRLR 119 was able to offer no more specific test than that the tribunal should ask whether it was 'reasonably feasible' to present the claim in time – a test which May LJ acknowledged was easier to state than to apply. The general approach to be adopted was stated by the Court of Appeal in *Marks & Spencer plc v Williams-Ryan* [2005] EWCA Civ 470, [2005] IRLR 562 to be that the statute should be given a liberal interpretation in favour of the employee. In a subsequent case, *Theobald v The Royal Bank of Scotland plc* [2007] All ER (D) 04 (Jan), the EAT suggested that this is against the weight of other authority; however, the predominant view is that the liberal approach still applies: see *Northamptonshire County Council v Entwhistle* [2010] IRLR 740; *El-Kholy v Rentokil Initial Facilities Services (UK) Ltd* [2013] All ER (D) 137 (May) (UKEAT/0472/12). Where an otherwise valid claim has been rejected because of a minor error on the claim form, and a new corrected ET1 form has been presented out of time, the focus should be on the second claim when a Tribunal is considering its discretion to extend time: *Adams v British Telecommunications plc* [2017] ICR 382. The EAT also held in that case that the fact of the first (defective) claim did not automatically render it reasonably practicable to have presented in time.

The 'reasonably practicable' test is a more difficult one for a claimant to satisfy than the 'just and equitable' test that applies in discrimination and some other proceedings (see below **19.24**). The Law Commission recently consulted on the possibility of replacing the 'reasonably practicable' test with the 'just and equitable' test and in LC 390 Employment Law Hearing Structures (27 April 2020) the Commission recommends that this should happen, and that time limits for all employment tribunal claims should be set at six months, with a 'just and equitable' test for extension.

Some examples of the application of the test of whether it was reasonably practicable for the applicant to present his or her complaint in time are set out below. These should be treated as indicative rather than decisive. A full summary of the most important points and authorities can be found in para 5 of the judgment of Underhill J in *Northamptonshire County Council v Entwhistle*, above.

(i)   It is not reasonably practicable for an employee to bring a complaint of unfair dismissal until he or she has (or could reasonably be expected to have acquired) knowledge of the facts giving him or her grounds to apply to the tribunal (*Machine Tool Industry Research Association v Simpson* [1988] IRLR 212; *Marley (UK) Ltd v Anderson* [1996] IRLR 163; *Cambridge and Peterborough Foundation NHS Trust v Crouchman* [2009] All ER (D) 96 (May)); *Cullinane v Balfour Beatty Engineering Services Ltd* (UKEAT/0537/10)). An extreme example of the point is *Howlett Marine Services Ltd v Bowlam* [2001] IRLR 201, where the three-month time limit for claiming payment under a protective award had expired before the award was actually made by the tribunal.

(ii)   With the passage of time since unfair dismissal legislation was introduced and the publicity given to unfair dismissal cases, a claimant is unlikely to be able to show that it was not reasonably practicable for him or her to present a complaint because of ignorance of the right to claim for unfair dismissal. If the claimant ought reasonably to have known of his or her right to claim, then it will probably be held that it was reasonably practicable to present a complaint within the time limit, whether he or she in fact knew of the right or not (see *Porter v Bandridge Ltd* [1978] 1 WLR 1145, [1978] IRLR 271). However it is always necessary for the tribunal to consider what the claimant knew, and whether his or her lack of relevant knowledge was reasonable.

(iii)   Where an employee has knowledge of his or her rights to claim unfair dismissal, there is an obligation upon him or her to seek information or advice about the enforcement of those rights (*Trevelyans (Birmingham) Ltd v Norton* [1991] ICR 488), and accordingly ignorance of time limits may well be held not to be reasonable if the claimant was aware of the right to claim but made no further enquiries about how or when to do so: *Reed in Partnership Ltd v Fraine* (UKEAT/0520/10). In *Norton*, the EAT also held that a decision to await the outcome of related criminal proceedings did not render the presentation of a complaint within the three-month time limit not reasonably practicable. Similarly, in *Wandsworth London Borough Council v Covent Garden Market Authority* [2011] EWHC 1245 (QB), [2011] All ER (D) 173 (May), a decision to wait for a scheduled interview with the police to see if further relevant material emerged was held not to be a factor making it not reasonably practicable to comply with the time limit (for a health and safety appeal to which the same time limit applies).

(iv)   The fact that the employee has been re-employed as a consultant by the employer and is reluctant to jeopardise this arrangement by making a claim does not necessarily render it not reasonably practicable to claim in time (*Birmingham Optical Group plc v Johnson* [1995] ICR 459). Similarly, in *London Underground Ltd v Noel* [1999] IRLR 621, the fact that the employer had offered the dismissed employee another job but then withdrew the offer did not affect the question whether it was reasonably practicable for the employee to present her claim in time, since from the outset she had knowledge of the facts giving rise to a claim for unfair dismissal.

(v)   Before the introduction of the statutory dispute resolution procedures by the *Employment Act 2002*, it was well established, following *Palmer v Southend-on-Sea Borough Council*, above, that the fact that an internal appeal was pending did not render it not reasonably practicable to present the complaint before the final resolution of the appeal. This view was adopted by the EAT in *Bodhu v Hampshire Area Health Authority* [1982] ICR 200, and later confirmed by the Court of Appeal in *Palmer*. Following the coming into force of the *Dispute Resolution Regulations* and the related provisions of the *2002 Act*, this was called into question, and in *Ashcroft v Haberdashers' Aske's Boys' School* [2008] IRLR 375 (a case where the outcome of his appeal against dismissal had been notified to the claimant only five hours before the expiry of the three-month time limit), the EAT held that *reg 15* of the *Dispute Resolution Regulations*, had to be taken as overruling this line of authority. However, despite the policy attractions of this approach, it is submitted that following the repeal of the *2002 Act* and associated Regulations, *Palmer* again applies as binding authority; this view was expressed, *obiter*, by Underhill P in *John Lewis Partnership v Charman* [2011] All ER (D) 23 (Jun) (UKEAT/0079/11) and followed in *DHL Supply Chain Limited v Fazackerley* (UKEAT/0019/18/JOJ) and *Inchcape Retail Limited v Shelton* (UKEAT/0142/19/JOJ). In *Inchcape*, Richardson J summarised the position thus (at para 30): "*a mistaken belief that an unfair dismissal claim need not be brought until after an internal appeal procedure has been exhausted cannot of itself render it not reasonably practicable to commence proceedings. It will depend on what enquiries the Claimant ought to have made and what knowledge he ought to have acquired*". Richardson J went on to quote from the judgment of Browne-Wilkinson J in Bodhu: "*There may be cases where the special facts (additional to the bare fact that there is an internal appeal pending) may persuade an industrial tribunal, as a question of fact, that it was not reasonably practicable to complain to the industrial tribunal within the time limit. But we do not think that the mere fact of a pending internal appeal, by itself, is sufficient to justify a finding of fact that it was not 'reasonably practicable' to present a complaint to the industrial tribunal*".

It should also be appreciated that even if it only becomes practicable to present the claim within the dying days of the three month period, it may well be held to have been reasonably practicable to do so; claimants are expected to move quickly if they are aware that the time limit is nearly upon them (and hence it was an error of law for a tribunal not to consider whether it was reasonably practicable for the claimant to present her claim in the three days between being informed that police investigations (the existence of which she believed to be a bar to claiming) had ended and the expiry of the three months: *Kauser v Asda Stores Ltd*, [2007] All ER (D) 195 (Oct), EAT).

(vi)   The principles applicable where an application is posted immediately before the deadline were fully reviewed by the Court of Appeal in *Sealy v Consignia plc* [2002] EWCA Civ 878, [2002] 3 All ER 801, [2002] IRLR 624. Brooke LJ, with the concurrence of the other members of the court, set out guidance which can be summarised as follows. Reference should now also be made to *Rule 90* of the *2013 Rules*:

(1)   A complaint is 'presented' when it arrives at the tribunal office.

(2)   If it is proved that it was impossible to present the complaint in time, for example because the office was locked and did not have a letter-box, it is possible to argue that it was not reasonably practicable for the complaint to be presented in time.

(3)   If the complaint is presented by post, it will be assumed, unless the contrary is proved, to have been received at the time that a letter would have been delivered in the ordinary course of post.

(4)   If the letter was sent by first-class post it is legitimate to assume that this would be the second day after it was posted (excluding Sundays, Bank Holidays, Christmas Day and Good Friday: see on this point *Coldridge v HM Prison Service* (UKEAT/0728/04); the presumption is also now embodied in the *2013 Rules, Rule 90(a)* that a document duly posted will arrive in the ordinary course of post).

(5)   If the letter does not arrive at the expected time, but is delayed in the post, a tribunal may conclude that it was not reasonably practicable to present it in time.

(6)   If a form is date-stamped on a Monday by a tribunal office but the time limit expired on the preceding Saturday or Sunday, and it is found by the tribunal that it was posted by first-class post not later than the Thursday, it will be open to the tribunal to find as a fact that it arrived on the Saturday (and thus was in time), or alternatively to extend time as a matter of discretion.

(7)   There is no room for any unusual subjective expectation by the claimant that a letter may arrive earlier than the second working day after it is posted. The test is objective.

(8)   If despite being posted the day before the final day, the application arrives on the final day of the relevant period, it is in time.

If the application of the points set out above results in a finding that the claim would but for some unusual or unforeseen event have been received by the tribunal office in time, it does not matter that the claimant could have avoided the problem by sending the claim in earlier: see per Hart J at para 19. However, the risk of additional delay and cost being incurred in securing an extension of time for a claim that is delayed in the course of post makes it prudent to present claims earlier if possible. For an example of a case where delay in the post was accepted as justifying an extension of time, see *Lancaster v DEK Printing Machines Ltd* (EAT/623/99) (application sent by Royal Mail special delivery).

In relation to appeals to the EAT, there is express provision in the *EAT Rules 1993* that where time for the service expires on a non-working day, time is extended to the next working day (*Rule 37(2)*), but there is no equivalent provision in the *2013 Rules*, with the consequence that if the last day for presenting a claim is a Sunday, and it is posted on Friday, the presumed date of receipt will be too late to assist a claimant if the Claim Form is not in fact delivered until the Monday: *Coldridge v HM Prison Service* (UKEAT/0728/04). Burton P suggested in that case an amendment to the *ET Rules* to extend the time limit automatically to the next working day, but this was not implemented in the *2013 Rules*.

The guidelines at (4) and (5) above were applied by analogy to presentation by e-mail in *Initial Electronic Security Systems Ltd v Avdic* [2005] IRLR 671, where the Claim Form had been submitted by e-mail at 2.30 pm on the last day, but had not been received. The EAT held that there was a presumption that an e-mail will be received in the ordinary course of transmission within 30–60 minutes of being sent, and if it is not, the sender can argue that it was thereby not reasonably practicable to present the claim in time. (It would still be necessary in such a case to show that he or she had acted promptly in following up the matter when no acknowledgement was received, and had resubmitted the claim expeditiously.) *Rule 90(b)* of the *2013 Rules* now provides that there is a presumption that documents sent by means of electronic communication were delivered, unless the contrary is proved, on the day of transmission.

(vii)   Where the employee is prevented by serious illness from claiming in time, it will normally be held not to have been reasonably practicable to present the claim in time. In *Schultz v Esso Petroleum Ltd* [1999] 3 All ER 338, [1999] ICR 1202, [1999] IRLR 488, the employee became ill some six weeks before the time limit expired and was unable to instruct solicitors. The Court of Appeal rejected an argument that an extension of time should be refused since he could have claimed before he fell ill: the Court held that although the whole period of three months is relevant, it is necessary to focus particularly on the latter part of the period of three months. This decision was applied by the EAT in *Agrico UK Ltd v Ireland* (EATS/0042/05), in support of a finding that it had been perverse of a tribunal to hold that it had not been reasonably practicable to present the claim in time where the Claim Form had been left by the claimant's solicitor for his secretary to complete and send in on the last day for presentation, but she fell ill and was absent that day, and the matter was not attended to until she returned to work the following day. The tribunal's error was to focus exclusively on the end of the three months, and not consider the practicability of the claim having been presented earlier. It is difficult to reconcile this approach and that in the *Avdic* case, above, and it would be helpful to have further clarification from the Court of Appeal of the position where an intention to submit at the last moment goes wrong for unforeseen reasons.

(viii)   If the claimant instructs solicitors or advisers to act on his or her behalf and through their default the Claim Form is not presented in time, the tribunal will consider that it was reasonably practicable for the claim to be presented in time, and will not entertain the claim. As Lord Denning MR said in *Dedman v British Building and Engineering Appliances Ltd* [1974] 1 All ER 520, [1974] 1 WLR 171, [1973] IRLR 379:

> 'I would suggest that in every case the tribunal should inquire into the circumstances and ask themselves whether the man or his advisers were at fault in allowing [the time limit] to pass by without presenting the complaint. If he was not at fault, nor his advisers – so that he had just cause or excuse for not presenting his complaint within [the time limit] – then it was "not practicable" for him to present it within that time.'

See also *Walls Meat Co Ltd v Khan* [1979] ICR 52, [1978] IRLR 499, CA, *Riley v Tesco Stores Ltd* [1980] IRLR 103, *Croydon Health Authority v Jaufurally* [1986] ICR 4, and *El-Kholy v Rentokil Initial Facilities Services (UK) Ltd* [2013] All ER (D) 137 (May) (UKEAT/0472/12). The point is not limited to lawyers; if the claimant has placed his case in the hands of his trade union, he may be fixed with the consequences of delay on the union's part, as in *Cullinane v Balfour Beatty Engineering Services Ltd* (UKEAT/0537/10). However, in *Harvey's Household Linens Ltd v Benson* [1974] ICR 306 it was held that Department of Employment officials were not 'advisers' for this purpose, so their error ought not to be attributed to a claimant who followed their advice; this was followed in *Dixon Stores Group v Arnold* (EAT/772/93). The same applies to advice given by tribunal employees (*Rybak v Jean Sorelle Ltd* [1991] IRLR 153; and see *London International College v Sen* [1993] IRLR 333). In *Alexanders Holdings Ltd v Methven* (EAT/782/93), the EAT upheld a finding in the case of a claimant who believed, as a result of ambiguous advice from the Department of Social Security, that he was not permitted to present his claim for three months following dismissal, that it was not reasonably practicable for him to do so in time.

The question whether a claimant is fixed by the error of his or her adviser is sometimes said to turn on whether the adviser concerned was a 'skilled adviser'. That is a question of fact, depending on the particular circumstances of the case: *Theobald v Royal Bank of Scotland plc* [2007] All ER (D) 04 (Jan). The EAT in this case also makes the distinction between instructing an adviser to act on the employee's behalf, in which case it will usually be held to have been reasonably practicable to present the claim in time, and taking advice from an adviser but retaining control over the submission of the claim, where the fault of the adviser in giving erroneous advice will not count against the claimant; however this distinction was rejected by the EAT in the subsequent case of *T Mobile (UK) Ltd v Singleton* [2011] All ER (D) 12 (May), where it was held that the mere taking of advice from a solicitor was sufficient to fix the claimant with the solicitor's negligence in failing to alert him to the correct time limit. In the same case it was held that the employer is under no duty to take active steps to correct a misunderstanding by the employee of the correct time limit.

In *Marks & Spencer plc v Williams-Ryan* [2005] EWCA Civ 470, [2005] IRLR 562, however, the Court of Appeal upheld a finding that it was not reasonably practicable for the claimant to claim in time where she had been led by misleading information provided by the employer to understand that she could not present a tribunal claim until her internal appeal against dismissal had been concluded (and that process was in turn delayed beyond the three-month limit). The important distinction here is between inaction and actively (or unintentionally) misleading. See also *Aryeetey v Tuntum Housing Association*, [2007] All ER (D) 174 (Oct) (not reasonably practicable to present claim when claimant advised by Employment Judge during related proceedings that a further claim was not necessary).

In *DHL Supply Chain Ltd v Fazackerley* (UKEAT/0019/18/JOJ) the EAT upheld a Tribunal's decision that it was not reasonably practicable for the claimant to have presented his claim in time where he had been (erroneously) advised by ACAS that he should await the outcome of the internal appeal process before presenting his claim. The claimant had relied on that advice and the time limit expired while he followed it.

Although in most cases 'fault' by a legal representative in relation to presentation of a claim will mean that the *Dedman* principle applies, that is not always the case. The question is always whether it was 'reasonably practicable' to present a claim in time, whether it was 'reasonably practicable' for the legal representative or the individual personally. Where the 'fault' that leads to late presentation is something very minor, technical or otherwise excusable (such as a minor mistake in the ACAS EC number included on the claim form), it will still be necessary to consider whether the legal representative acted 'reasonably' or not: *North East London NHS Foundation Trust v Zhou* (UKEAT/0066/18/LA). See further **20.39** Employment Tribunals – II.

(ix)   A rather stricter view of ignorance of rights may be taken where the rights are based on principles of European law overriding restrictions in domestic law. Thus, in *Biggs v Somerset County Council* [1996] 2 All ER 734, [1996] 2 CMLR 292, [1996] IRLR 203, the Court of Appeal held as a matter of law that it was reasonably practicable for Ms Biggs to present a claim for unfair dismissal at a time when (as a part-time employee) she was expressly debarred by statute from the right to complain and the statute was only held to infringe EU law many years later.

19.21

If it is not reasonably practicable to present a claim in time, the tribunal may allow an extension of time of such further period as it considers reasonable. There is no fixed limit, and each case must be considered on its facts in the light of the employee's explanation for the delay: *Marley (UK) Ltd v Anderson* [1996] IRLR 163, CA. The EAT has commented that the tribunal has an unfettered discretion as to how long an extension of time to allow in the light of all the circumstances, albeit the discretion must be exercised judicially: *Howlett Marine Services Ltd v Bowlam* [2001] IRLR 201. In practice, however the starting point is that there is an obligation on claimants to act expeditiously in asserting their rights in the tribunal, so that even a relatively short delay beyond the point when it became reasonably practicable to present the claim may be more than is reasonable in the absence of an explanation for the further delay; in *Theobald v The Royal Bank of Scotland plc* (EAT/0444/06) [2007] All ER (D) 04 (Jan), a delay of 13 days was held on the facts to be too long, and in *Nolan v Balfour Beatty Engineering Services Ltd* [2011] All ER (D) 09 (Nov) (UKEAT/0109/11) a decision allowing an extension of 11 weeks from when the claimant became aware of the facts entitling him to claim was held to be perverse.

For the practical application of the process of assessing a reasonable time, see *James W Cook & Co (Wivenhoe) Ltd (in liq) v Tipper* [1990] IRLR 386, at 724–725, CA, as explained in *Marley (UK) Ltd v Anderson* (above). It has been suggested that the tribunal should consider the same questions as in applying the 'reasonable practicability' test, particularly as regards the claimant's state of mind and state of knowledge, but focusing on what was reasonable rather than what was practicable: *Thompson v Northumberland County Council*, [2007] All ER (D) 95 (Sep). More recently, the EAT has twice held that the same approach should be used to whether the extension sought is reasonable as to whether it was not reasonably practicable to present the claim in time: *Nolan*, above, and *Cullinane v Balfour Beatty Engineering Services Ltd* (UKEAT/0537/10), both claims under the trade union blacklisting legislation.

A claimant who loses the opportunity to have his or her case heard by the tribunal because of the negligence of professional advisers is able to sue them in the ordinary courts. The claim is for the loss of a chance of making a successful claim, so that an assessment of the prospects of success in the tribunal would have to be made when calculating damages.

If a claimant wishes to pursue his or her claim in another forum (eg in proceedings for wrongful dismissal (see WRONGFUL DISMISSAL **(59)**) but also wishes to preserve the right to proceed in the tribunal, he or she should submit a Claim Form, using the 'Further Information' section to explain the position, and seek to have the tribunal proceedings stayed (*Warnock v Scarborough Football Club* [1989] ICR 489; and see **20.83** below).

19.22 Redundancy payments

A time limit of six months applies. This period runs from the 'relevant date', which is defined in *ERA 1996, s 145* and is in most cases (where there has not been a trial period in alternative employment) the same as the EDT (see for details of this **19.18** and **19.19** above). The EAT in *Watts v Rubery Owen Conveyancer Ltd* [1977] 2 All ER 1, [1977] IRLR 112 held that a claim for a redundancy payment may not be presented until the dismissal has taken effect (unless the claim is based on the special procedure for claim in redundancy payments where the employee has been laid off or placed on short time working). However, the Court of Appeal in *Bon Groundwork Ltd v Foster* [2012] EWCA Civ 252, [2012] IRLR 517 acknowledged that the decision in *Watt* has since been heavily criticised, and declined to rule on whether it is still good law. In order to preserve the right to institute tribunal proceedings, it is sufficient that within the six-month period following the 'relevant date' the employee has made a claim by notice in writing to the employer; or referred the claim to a tribunal; or presented a claim of unfair dismissal to the tribunal; or that a payment (not necessarily the full entitlement) has been agreed and paid. The effect of any of these actions is to preserve the right to claim indefinitely (*ERA 1996, s 164(1)*). The six-month time limit may be extended by up to a further six months if the tribunal is persuaded that it is just and equitable to do so (*ERA 1996, s 164(2), (3)*). See **19.30** below for the principles applicable to a 'just and equitable' extension of time. There is no jurisdiction to extend time beyond the further period of six months: *Crawford v Secretary of State for Employment* [1995] IRLR 523.

19.23 Equal pay

The standard time limit laid down by *s 129* of the *Equality Act 2010* is six months from the date the employee ceased to be employed by the respondent employer (*ss 129(3), 130*). A claim may, of course, be made whilst the applicant is still employed. The time limit provisions are modified in cases about pension rights. All of these points applied equally to claims under the predecessor legislation, the *Equal Pay Act 1970*. The validity of the six-month time limit was challenged as contrary to EU law in *Preston v Wolverhampton Healthcare NHS Trust* [2001] UKHL 5, [2001] IRLR 237, but was upheld, subject to qualifications (see below) by the House of Lords.

Following amendments made by the *Equal Pay Act 1970 (Amendment) Regulations 2003 (SI 2003/1656)*, retained in the *Equality Act 2010*, there are three categories of case in which the time limit may be extended. First, whilst normally the limit applies to each contract where an employee is employed under a number of contracts, even if the contracts are immediately consecutive, where there is a succession of contracts at regular intervals forming part of a stable employment relationship (a 'stable employment case'), time only runs from the end of the last such contract (*Equality Act 2010, ss 129(3), 130(3)*). Second, where the employer deliberately concealed from the claimant a fact relevant to his or her claim and without knowledge of which he or she could not reasonably have been expected to institute the proceedings, and the claimant did not discover and could not with reasonable diligence have discovered the fact until after the end of the period of employment (a 'concealment case') time is extended to six months from the day on which the claimant discovered, or could with reasonable diligence have discovered, the fact (*ss 129(3), 130(4)*). Third, if at the date of the ending of his or her employment (or any later date from which time would otherwise run by virtue of either of the other exceptions) the claimant is under a disability, ie is a minor (or under 16 in Scotland) or is of unsound mind (a 'disability case'), time runs from the date that he or she ceases to be under such a disability (*ss 129(3), 130(7)*).

Subject to these exceptions, the tribunal has no jurisdiction to extend time. However, provided that a claim is presented in time, ie (usually) within six months following the termination of the employment, an equal pay claim relating to a job in which the employee had ceased to be employed some time previously may be pursued: *Young v National Power plc* [2001] 2 All ER 339, [2001] IRLR 32, CA: see further on this *Allan v Newcastle-upon-Tyne City Council* [2005] ICR 1170, [2005] IRLR 504, EAT.

The Court of Appeal has given guidance in *Slack v Cumbria County Council (Equality and Human Rights Commission intervening)* [2009] EWCA Civ 293, [2009] IRLR 463 on the position where a claimant was employed for a continuous period by the same employer but, because of changes in such matters as hours of work, new contracts were issued during that period. The Court's conclusion was that time would not start to run against the employee in relation to the prior period of employment simply because she signed a new contract, since the situation would normally fall within the scope of the 'stable employment relationship' exception in what is now *Equality Act 2010 ss 129(3), 130(3)*. In the light of that conclusion, the Court went on to hold that the time limits (then laid down by the *Equal Pay Act 1970*) were compatible with the requirements of European law.

The House of Lords has ruled that where an employee's employment has been transferred under the *Transfer of Undertakings (Protection of Employment) Regulations 1981*, time for making a claim in respect of employment with the previous employer runs from the date of the transfer, not the eventual end of the employment with the transferee employer: *Powerhouse Retail Ltd v Burroughs* [2006] UKHL 13, [2006] IRLR 381. The same principle would apply to a transfer under the replacement *2006 Regulations*. This limitation does not however apply where the claim is against the current employer, based on a term derived from the application of an equality clause during the previous employment but which then transferred with the claimant under the Regulations to her new employer: *Gutridge v Sodexo Ltd* [2009] EWCA Civ 729, [2009] IRLR 721.

It should be noted that claims for equal pay under the *Equality Act 2010* can also be brought in the High Court or County Court, based on the contractual equality clause implied into all employment contracts by the equality of terms provisions of the *2010 Act*. Like any contractual claim in the ordinary courts, such claims may be brought at any time within six years of the breach (the time limit in Scotland is five years). The Court has power to strike a claim out if it could 'more conveniently' be brought in the employment tribunal. In *Abdulla v Birmingham City Council* [2013] IRLR 38, the Supreme Court confirmed this position. The Court indicated that prior to the expiry of time to bring a claim in the tribunal, in most cases it would be more convenient to dispose of the case in the Tribunal. However, after that time period has expired, and the claim is time-barred in the tribunal, a Court could not conclude the claim would more conveniently be disposed of in the tribunal. Parliament had allowed the claims to be brought in the civil courts as well as in the tribunal. In *Asda Stores Ltd v Brierley* [2016] IRLR 709, the Court of Appeal considered whether an ET could impose a stay on its proceedings so as in effect to compel claimants to pursue High Court proceedings. Elias LJ held that whilst Rule 29 did confer a power to stay proceedings (including indefinitely), the ET could not use that power to relinquish jurisdiction to the High Court merely because it considered that court to be a more appropriate forum.

See further **23.22** EQUAL PAY.

19.24 Unlawful discrimination

A claim must be presented to the tribunal 'not after the end' of the period of three months 'beginning when the act complained of was done': *Equality Act 2010, s 123(1)*. There are specific provisions to deal with discrimination by omission, which is to be treated as occurring when the person in question decided upon it; and an act extending over a period is to be treated as done at the end of that period: see *s 123(3)*. The latter provision covers the maintenance of a continuing policy or state of affairs, as well as a continuing course of discriminatory conduct such as harassment: see *Barclays Bank plc v Kapur* [1991] 2 AC 355, [1991] 1 All ER 646, [1991] ICR 208, [1991] IRLR 136; and *Okoro v Taylor Woodrow Construction Ltd* [2013] ICR 580. The same provisions as to time limits and extensions of time apply to each of the *Part-time Workers (Prevention of Less Favourable Treatment) Regulations 2000*, the *Fixed-term Employees (Prevention of Less Favourable Treatment) Regulations 2002* and the *Agency Workers Regulations 2010*. See further **19.28** below.

In most cases it will be necessary for a Tribunal to hear evidence in order to determine whether conduct complained of constitutes a 'continuing act' and it will be an error of law for the Tribunal to reach a determination without doing so: *Caterham School Ltd v Rose* (UKEAT/0149/19/RN). The line between a continuing policy or course of conduct and a single act with continuing consequences is illustrated by cases on each side of the line in *Owusu v London Fire and Civil Defence Authority* [1995] IRLR 574. The leading case on what it is necessary to show to establish an act continuing over a period is now *Hendricks v Metropolitan Police Comr* [2002] EWCA Civ 1686, [2003] 1 All ER 654, [2003] IRLR 96. In this case the Court of Appeal emphasised that whilst a policy or practice of discrimination will normally provide a basis for a claim that there was a discriminatory act continuing over a period, it is not a necessary precondition, as earlier cases had appeared to indicate. The correct test is whether the acts complained of are linked, and are evidence of a continuing discriminatory state of affairs. In *Lyfar v Brighton and Sussex University Hospitals Trust* [2006] EWCA Civ 1548, [2006] All ER (D) 182 (Nov), the Court of Appeal confirmed that its decision in *Hendricks* was to be followed, in preference to *Robertson v Bexley Community Centre* [2003] EWCA Civ 576, [2003] IRLR 434, a case decided after *Hendricks* but which does not refer to it, and applies the requirement of a policy or practice. If an alleged act is found not to amount to unlawful discrimination, then it cannot form part of 'conduct extending over a period', so that if the only alleged act that is 'in time' does not succeed, other acts occurring previously will be out of time: *South Western Ambulance Service NHS Foundation Trust v King* [2020] IRLR 168, EAT.

A relevant factor in whether or not a series of acts is to be regarded as an act continuing over a period is whether the same person or persons is or are responsible for each of the acts: *Aziz v FDA* [2010] EWCA Civ 304, 154 Sol Jo (no 14) 29. As to the relevance of such matters as evidence that later events were acts of discrimination, see *HSBC Asia Holdings BV v Gillespie* [2011] IRLR 209. If the issue whether a number of incidents amounted to an act continuing over a period is being considered as a preliminary issue at a preliminary hearing (as may be the case when some but not all or the incidents would be out of time if treated separately) the test is whether the claimant has made out a prima facie case for the incidents being treated collectively as an act continuing over a period: *Lyfar v Brighton and Sussex University Hospitals NHS Trust* [2006] EWCA Civ 1548, *Aziz v First Division Association* [2010] EWCA Civ 304.

The fact that it has not been specifically pleaded in the claim that the various acts of alleged discrimination alleged form part of an act continuing over a period does not preclude the tribunal from treating them as such for the purpose of the running of time, at least if the respondent had been sufficiently alerted to the point: *Khetab v Aga Medical Ltd* (UKEAT/0313/10).

Where a discriminatory policy is operated by a respondent, time begins to run afresh each time the policy is operated to the detriment of the claimant: *Rovenska v General Medical Council* [1997] IRLR 367. If the complainant is an employee, the continued existence of the policy or practice, or state of affairs evidenced by the specific acts, postpones the running of time until the policy is discontinued or rescinded or (if earlier) the employment ends: *Cast v Croydon College* [1998] IRLR 319. This is not necessarily the case, however, where a claimant complains of repeated rejections of job applications: cf *Tyagi v BBC World Service* [2001] EWCA Civ 549, [2001] IRLR 465; each rejection is likely to be treated as a separate cause of action, with time running accordingly. Time does not start to run in respect of an act of discrimination until the discriminator is in a position to put into effect his or her discriminatory intention: *Swithland Motors plc v Clarke* [1994] IRLR 275 (as to the position in dismissal cases, see below).

The *Equality Act 2010* and the *Part-time Workers, Fixed-term Employees Regulations* and *Agency Workers Regulations* also make specific provision for when time runs where what is complained of is a deliberate omission (such as a refusal to make adjustments to the working arrangements for a disabled employee). In such cases the principle is that time runs from the date on which the employer decided not to act, rather than from the date of the employee becoming aware of this fact. As there will often be no direct evidence of the relevant date, there are further provisions treating the employer as having decided not to act when he does an act inconsistent with doing the act omitted, or at the end of a reasonable period within which he could be expected to have acted. These provisions were considered by the Court of Appeal in *Matuszowicz v Kingston-Upon-Hull City Council* [2009] EWCA Civ 22, [2009] 3 All ER 685, [2009] IRLR 288. The Court held that the statutory provisions must be taken to apply equally to a non-deliberate omission – as where the employer simply failed to make the required adjustment in a disability case (as this case was). Recognising the difficulty that employees may have in appreciating when time starts to run in these circumstances, the Court urged tribunals to allow some latitude to employees to take account of their difficulty in judging when a reasonable time had passed for the employer to act. In *Abertawe Bro Morgannwg University Local Health Board v Morgan* [2018] EWCA Civ 640, [2018] ICR 1194 the Court of Appeal observed that the question of when time starts to run in an 'omission' case should be determined from the point of view of the claimant and when the claimant might reasonably have expected the employer to take the step(s) in question.

Another difficult issue in relation to when time starts to run is where the complaint is of discrimination by way of, or leading to, dismissal. It is now clearly established (after earlier conflicting case law) that time runs from the date of the dismissal (rather than, if earlier, the date on which notice was given): see the cases cited in *British Gas Services Ltd v McCaull* [2001] IRLR 60 at para 25. In *Derby Specialist Fabrication Ltd v Burton* [2001] 2 All ER 840, [2001] IRLR 69 this principle was followed in a race discrimination case where the claim was for constructive dismissal. The EAT held that this constituted a 'dismissal' within *s 4(2)* of the *RRA 1976* and it was not therefore necessary to rely on the discriminatory acts which had led to the employee's resignation as 'detriments' (in which case the claim would have been out of time). The same conclusion has now also been reached by the Court of Appeal in relation to the *DDA 1995*: *Meikle v Nottinghamshire County Council* [2004] EWCA Civ 859, [2004] 4 All ER 97, [2005] ICR 1, [2004] IRLR 703, following *Catherall v Michelin Tyres plc* [2003] IRLR 61, EAT, and disapproving the earlier contrary view expressed by a different division of the EAT in *Metropolitan Police Comr v Harley* [2001] IRLR 263.

A point not directly arising in these cases, and on which there is no direct authority, is whether a claim alleging discrimination by way of dismissal may be presented before the claimant has been dismissed, in the sense applied in the cases cited above. There is nothing obvious in the wording of the statutory provisions on time limits to prevent this, as a claim is merely required not to be presented after the end of the period specified. Under the legislation on discrimination prior to the *Equality Act 2010*, the complaint to be presented was that the respondent 'has committed' an act of unlawful discrimination (see eg the *Sex Discrimination Act 1975, s 63(1)* wording which did preclude a complaint of dismissal being presented before the dismissal took effect, and there was (and is) no equivalent in the discrimination legislation of *ERA 1996, s 111(3)*, which specifically allows the presentation of a complaint of unfair dismissal during the notice period: see **19.19** above. However, the position is less clearly expressed in the *Equality Act 2010, ss 120(1)* and *123(1)*; the former provision refers to complaints 'relating to' a contravention of relevant parts of the *Act*, and 'not after the end' of a period does not necessarily mean also 'not before the beginning'. The prudent course, in the circumstances, is not to present a claim before the dismissal has taken effect.

19.25 'Just and equitable' extension of time

A tribunal has discretion to extend time where it would be 'just and equitable' to do so: *Equality Act 2010, s 123(3)*; *Part-time Workers (Prevention of Less Favourable Treatment) Regulations 2000, reg 8*, *Fixed-term Employees (Prevention of Less Favourable Treatment) Regulations 2002, reg 8*; *Agency Workers Regulations 2010, reg 19*. This is a broader discretion than the 'not reasonably practicable' test and the EAT has (albeit with limited success) discouraged the development of authorities on the application of the test: see *Hutchinson v Westward Television Ltd* [1977] ICR 279, [1977] IRLR 69. Where there is more than one Respondent, the Tribunal must consider the question of an extension of time for each one separately: *Harden v Wootlif & another* UKEAT/0448/14.

The Court of Appeal has emphasised that there is no presumption in favour of the extension of time. The onus is on the claimant to convince the tribunal that it is just and equitable to extend time, in the context that time limits in employment cases are intended to apply strictly: *Robertson v Bexley Community Centre* [2003] EWCA Civ 576, [2003] IRLR 434. However, in *Chief Constable of Lincolnshire Police v Caston* [2009] EWCA Civ 1298, [2010] IRLR 327, the Court of Appeal emphasised that the comments in *Robertson* merely indicated that there was a broad discretion, the question being one of fact and judgment rather than policy; 'there is no principle of law which indicates how generously or sparingly the power to enlarge time is to be exercised' (per Sedley LJ). Because of the breadth of the discretion, the appellate courts are reluctant to interfere with the exercise of the discretion if the issue is appealed. For a recent summary of the legal principles, see *Thompson v Ark Schools* [2019] ICR 292.

The fact that the onus is on the claimant to make out a case for an extension of time means that it is often necessary, or at least helpful, for the claimant to give evidence in support of the claim for an extension. However, the EAT has confirmed that evidence from the claimant is not a precondition for an extension; other material before the tribunal, such as documents, may be sufficient to establish the balance in favour of the claimant: *Accurist Watches Ltd v Wadher* [2009] All ER (D) 189 (Apr). See by analogy the approach of the EAT, requiring specific medical evidence relevant to the individual's condition, in order to justify an extension of time for appealing in *J v K* [2017] UKEATPA/0661/16.

If there are circumstances which otherwise render it just and equitable to extend time, the length of the extension required is not of itself a limiting factor, unless the delay would prejudice the possibility of a fair trial: *Afolabi v Southwark London Borough Council* [2003] EWCA Civ 15, [2003] IRLR 220, where the Court of Appeal upheld an extension of time of nearly nine years where the claimant had without fault on his part been unaware of the facts relied on to support his claim, and had acted reasonably promptly when those facts came to his knowledge. However, it will be exceptional that a delay of or approaching that order would not render a fair trial impossible, especially where facts are disputed and there is no clear contemporaneous documentation.

Other factors which a tribunal should take into account in the exercise of its discretion will depend on the facts of each case, and cannot be exhaustively listed. They will however include the reason for the delay, whether the claimant was aware of his or her rights to claim, and/or of the time limit, the conduct of the employer, the length of the extension sought, and the prejudice that would be suffered by the employer if the claim were permitted to proceed (necessarily balanced against the prejudice to the claimant if he or she is refused an extension of time). Tribunals are encouraged to consider by analogy the checklist of factors listed in the *Limitation Act 1980, s 33* (which confers discretion to extend time for personal injury claims in the courts) – see *British Coal Corporation v Keeble* [1997] IRLR 336 –, but the EAT has stated that this process is not mandatory (*Chohan v Derby Law Centre* [2004] IRLR 685). Tribunals do not need to follow a formulaic approach and set out a checklist of factors that may be relevant, in particular where no reliance is placed on them: *Hall v ADP Dealer Services Ltd* (UKEAT/00390/13). A failure to provide a good excuse for the delay in bringing a relevant claim will not inevitably result in an extension being refused: *Rathakrishnan v Pizza Express (Restaurants) Ltd* [2016] IRLR 278. There is authority for the proposition that the most important factor in whether to extend time is whether the delay has affected the ability of the tribunal to conduct a fair trial of the issues: *DPP v Marshall* [1998] IRLR 494. However it is suggested that this should not be relied on as a reason not to attach weight to other factors such as serious and avoidable delay by the claimant in claiming, or in obtaining advice about a possible claim.

An example of a specific factor being taken into account in favour of a claimant is *Department of Constitutional Affairs v Jones* [2007] EWCA Civ 894, [2008] IRLR 128, where the Court of Appeal accepted as a valid reason for extending time the claimant's inability or unwillingness to admit to himself or others that he was disabled (by clinical depression). In cases where medical reasons are relied on by a claimant as part of the reason why proceedings were not brought within the time limit, the question is not whether the claimant was prevented from bringing proceedings by the medical condition, but whether, in the round, it is just and equitable to extend time in the light of the claimant's medical difficulties, even if they were not such as actually to prevent the claimant commencing proceedings: see *Watkins v HSBC Bank Plc* [2018] IRLR 1015.

The EAT has held that where delay in presenting a claim is attributable to incorrect legal advice from the claimant's solicitor, this should not be visited on the claimant by refusing an extension of time, notwithstanding that the claimant may have a valid claim in negligence against the solicitor, since this would confer a windfall on the respondent: *Chohan v Derby Law Centre*, above. This does not mean that time *should* be extended in all such cases, but that all other factors must also be considered. See also *Hawkins v Ball* [1996] IRLR 258 for a more cautious approach to this point, and *Wright v Wolverhampton City Council* (UKEAT/0117/08) [2009] All ER (D) 179 (Feb), applying the principles to poor advice given by a trade union representative. By contrast, where the delay in presentation is down entirely to the claimant, a tribunal is more likely to refuse an application for a just and equitable extension of time: see *De Souza v Manpower UK Ltd* [2013] All ER (D) 199 (Feb), where the application was one day out of time.

Case law prior to the implementation of the *Dispute Resolution Regulations* had established that a decision by the employee to delay presenting a claim whilst an internal grievance procedure or appeal was being pursued would not necessarily be a sufficient reason to extend time under the 'just and equitable' principle, even if the delay had not prejudiced the employer. It was only one of the relevant factors to be taken into account, and the weight to be attached to it was a matter for the tribunal in the light of the facts of each case: *Apelogun-Gabriels v Lambeth London Borough Council* [2001] EWCA Civ 1853, [2002] ICR 713, [2002] IRLR 116 overruling *Aniagwu v Hackney London Borough Council* [1999] IRLR 303 and affirming *Robinson v Post Office* [2000] IRLR 804. It is probable that following the repeal of the dispute resolution legislation, the position as stated in *Apelogun-Gabriels* again applies.

The principle established in relation to unfair dismissal claims by the Court of Appeal in *Biggs v Somerset County Council* [1996] IRLR 203, that a failure to appreciate that European law confers a right to claim apparently excluded by the UK statute does not make it 'not reasonably practicable' to claim in time, does not apply to discrimination claims. The 'just and equitable' test is wider, and an understandable misapprehension as to the state of the law is a relevant factor in deciding whether to extend time: *British Coal Corpn v Keeble* [1997] IRLR 336. Not all misunderstandings of the law will be accepted as excuses however; see *University of Westminster v Bailey* [2009] All ER (D) 47 (Nov), where the EAT held that it was not an acceptable reason for a 19 month delay that the claimant, a senior lecturer in HR, did not realise that the *Sex Discrimination Act 1975* applied equally to men. It has been suggested that a change in the law could render it just and equitable to extend time to allow a claim which could not have been brought as the law had previously been understood to be: *Foster v South Glamorgan Health Authority* [1988] IRLR 277.

Whilst it is open to a tribunal to consider as a preliminary issue whether a discrimination claim is out of time, and if so whether it is just and equitable to extend time, in most cases tribunals will not accede to applications for a preliminary hearing, unless there is a clear point which would potentially dispose of the entire case. Discrimination cases are usually 'fact-sensitive', and it is therefore preferable to hear all the evidence before deciding issues as to the ambit of the tribunal's jurisdiction, particularly where at least part of the complaint is clearly in time. Matters which in themselves may be out of time may still be evidentially relevant, and the tribunal will in such cases have to hear evidence about the earlier matters, at least as background, in any event. In such cases there is little potential to save time or cost by holding a preliminary hearing, and indeed there may be a duplication of evidence over two hearings. The House of Lords in *SCA Packaging Ltd v Boyle* [2009] UKHL 37, [2009] IRLR 746 approved, in obiter comments, views expressed in earlier EAT cases to the effect that preliminary hearings should only be ordered sparingly, such as where 'there is a succinct, knockout point which is capable of being decided after only a relatively short hearing'. This is unlikely to be the case where at least some of the allegations made are in time. If the question whether to extend time is decided at the hearing of the substantive claim, and the tribunal finds the allegations concerned well-founded, it will require very significant reasons to refuse an extension of time, since the prejudicial effect of refusing an extension would be to deny the claimant a remedy for a proven wrong: see *Bahous v Pizza Express Restaurant Ltd* [2012] All ER (D) 191 (Jan) (UKEAT/0029/11).

19.26   Unlawful deductions from wages and claims arising from a failure to pay holiday pay or the National Minimum Wage

A complaint of unlawful deduction from wages must be presented within the period of three months beginning with the date of the deduction or enforced payment complained of, or such further period as the tribunal considers reasonable if it is satisfied that it was not reasonably practicable to present the claim within the three-month period: *ERA 1996, s 23(4)*. See **19.20** and **19.21** above for the application of the 'not reasonably practicable' test.

For the purpose of calculating the time limit, a failure to pay is not treated as an unlawful deduction until the last date on which the employer was contractually permitted to make the payment concerned, even if part payment was made earlier: *Group 4 Nightspeed Ltd v Gilbert* [1997] IRLR 398. It follows that a claim presented *before* the last date for payment may be outside the jurisdiction of the tribunal because it is premature: *Hyde v Lehman Brothers Ltd* [2004] All ER (D) 40 (Aug), EAT. Where the complaint is of a series of deductions or payments, time runs from the last such deduction or payment (*ERA 1996, s 23(3)*) and the tribunal can order repayment in respect of the entire series: see *Reid v Camphill Engravers* [1990] IRLR 268. Guidance as to the application of time limits both to single deductions and to a series of deductions was given by the EAT in *Taylorplan Services Ltd v Jackson* [1996] IRLR 184 in which the EAT identified the following questions which a Tribunal should consider: (1) Is this a complaint relating to one deduction or a series of deductions by the employer? (2) If a single deduction, what was the date of the payment of wages from which the deduction was made? (3) If a series of deductions, what was the date of the last deduction? (4) Was the relevant date under (2) or, alternatively, (3) above within the period of three months prior to the presentation of the complaint? (5) If the answer to question (4) is in the negative, was it reasonably practicable for the complaint to be presented within the relevant three-month period? (6) If the answer to question (5) is in the negative, does the tribunal consider that the complaint was nevertheless presented within a reasonable time? In *Bear Scotland Ltd v Fulton; Hertel Ltd v Woods; Amec Group Ltd v Law* [2015] ICR 221, the EAT held that as the Tribunal loses jurisdiction in respect of a deduction from wages unless it is brought within three months of the deduction, or last in the series of deductions, Parliament did not intend that jurisdiction could be regained simply because a later non-payment, occurring more than three months later, could be characterised as being part of the same series. Accordingly, if a series of deductions contains a gap of more than three months between deductions, this will cause the Tribunal to lose jurisdiction in respect of the earlier deductions.

Payments that would fall due after those complained of in the claim form do not form part of the series for these purposes: *Qantas Cabin Crew (UK) Ltd v Lopez and Hooper* [2013] IRLR 4 (where instalment 2 of a relocation payment due two years after the first instalment had not fallen due and was not complained about in the claim; the EAT held the complaint was about a single payment, instalment 1, and was out of time – see para 64). A separate issue is whether a Tribunal can order repayment in respect of deductions in a series that were made after the claim was presented but up to the date of the hearing. In *Arthur H Wilton Ltd v Peebles* (EAT/835/93), the EAT appears to have indicated that this would be possible, but the point was not argued and it is submitted the better view is that the Tribunal only has jurisdiction to order those deductions made to the date of presentation. There remains no direct authority on the question whether claims can extend back for longer than the contractual limitation period of six years (five in Scotland); it is suggested the better view is that the limitation period would apply. The position is, however, modified for claims in respect of wages falling outside *s 27(1)(b)* to *(j)* of the *ERA* (viz fees, bonuses, commission, holiday pay or other emoluments referable to employment which fall under *s 27(1)(a)* along with any residual categories of wages not falling within subsections (b) to (j)). For all unauthorised deduction claims of that sort presented on or after 1 July 2015, a Tribunal may only consider a complaint insofar as it relates to deductions made before the period of two years ending with the date of presentation of the complaint: see *ERA, s 23(4A)*.

Complaints by workers of a failure by their employer to pay the National Minimum Wage must be brought as claims for unlawful deductions from wages under *Part II* of the *ERA 1996* by virtue of the *National Minimum Wage Act 1998, ss 17, 18*, and the foregoing comments therefore apply equally to such claims. The Court of Appeal ruled in *Ainsworth v IRC* [2005] EWCA Civ 441, [2005] IRLR 465 that claims for holiday pay or payment in lieu for accrued but untaken holidays under the *Working Time Regulations 1998* could only be brought by way of a complaint under *reg 30* of the *1998 Regulations*, but this was reversed by the House of Lords when the case eventually reached it on appeal (sub nom *Revenue and Customs Comrs v Stringer* [2009] UKHL 31, [2009] ICR 985, [2009] IRLR 677). The difference between the two routes to the tribunal is that whilst essentially the same time limit provisions apply under *reg 30* as for a complaint of unlawful deductions, there is no equivalent in *reg 30* of the 'series of deductions' provision in *ERA 1996, s 23(3)*. Claims in respect of other provisions of the *1998 Regulations* which may be the subject of complaint to the tribunal are also subject to a three-month time limit, with any extension dependent on the 'not reasonably practicable' criterion.

19.27 Contract claims

Claims in contract brought under the *Employment Tribunals Extension of Jurisdiction (England and Wales) Order 1994 (SI 1994/1623)* or the equivalent Scottish Order may only be made if the claim arises out of, or is outstanding at the date of termination of, the employment concerned. The time limit for presentation is the same as in unfair dismissal cases and subject to the same 'not reasonably practicable' extension. The Law Commission has consulted on whether the six-year time limit for contract claims in the ordinary courts should also apply in the Tribunal, but has not recommended any change in this respect: see LC 390 *Employment Law Hearing Structures* (27 April 1990). The Commission does, however, recommend extending the Tribunal's contract jurisdiction to include more types of contract claims by employees against employers (i.e. in addition to the current types, also claims concerning living accommodation), removing the current restriction on when the dispute must have arisen so as to permit claims to be brought while employees are still employed, and claims arising after termination. The Commission also recommends increasing the maximum award that can be made to £100,000 (in line with the County Court).

Time runs from the EDT where the employee has been dismissed, and in other cases from the employee's last day of work in the employment concerned (*Art 7*). There is no provision equivalent to that for unfair dismissal cases permitting the claim to be presented during the notice period (*ERA 1996, s 111(3)*), and a breach of contract claim presented before the EDT is premature, with the result that the tribunal has no jurisdiction to determine it (*Capek v Lincolnshire County Council* [2000] IRLR 590, CA). The EAT has held (in *Miller Bros and F P Butler Ltd v Johnston* [2002] IRLR 386) that the tribunal has no jurisdiction to consider a claim for breach of contract where the contract was only concluded after the employment had terminated (in that case a compromise agreement which the employer had failed to implement).

Contract claims are the only class of claim in respect of which an employer may counterclaim. In the *2013 Rules* such a claim is called an 'Employer's Contract Claim'. An employer's contract claim may only be brought if presented at a time when the employee's claim is before the tribunal (ie it has been presented and not withdrawn) and is subject to a time limit of six weeks beginning with the day the employer received from the tribunal a copy of the employee's Claim Form (*Employment Tribunals Extension of Jurisdiction (England and Wales) Order 1994, art 8*). The same 'not reasonably practicable' test applies to any application for an extension of time. The validity of the employer's contract claim is not, however, affected by whether the claim itself was brought in time: all that is relevant is that a claim has been brought and a counterclaim is presented within the time limit running from the date of presentation of the claim (*Patel v RCMS Ltd* [1999] IRLR 161).

The *2013 Rules* specify that any employer's contract claim must be made as part of the response, presented in accordance with *Rule 16*: see *Rule 23*. Such a response is ordinarily due within 28 days of the date the copy of the claim form was sent by the Tribunal to the respondent: *Rule 16(1)*. Care must therefore be taken when seeking any extension of the 28–day period in order not to run into difficulties with the statutory limitation date for an employer's contract claim as set out in *Art 8* of the *1994 Order*. Having time extended for a response does not automatically grant an extension of the statutory time limit for bringing an employer's contract claim. The statutory time limit can only be extended on the 'not reasonably practicable' basis whereas there is a general discretion to extend the time for presenting a response.

The employer's contract claim can be rejected in the same way as a claimant's claim may be rejected under *Rule 12* of the *2013 Rules* – see *Rule 23*. The other procedural requirements for an employer's contract claim are covered in **20.52**. A Practice Direction issued by the President of the employment tribunals in Scotland (No 3 of December 2006) was revoked in February 2014 as a result of the new rules.

19.28 Other claims

For details of time limits for other classes of claim, and provisions as to extension of time, the relevant statutory provisions should be consulted. Three points of importance merit mention here:

(a) Claims under the *Part-time Workers (Prevention of Less Favourable Treatment) Regulations 2000*, the *Fixed-term Employees (Prevention of Less Favourable Treatment) Regulations 2002*, and the *Agency Workers Regulations 2010*, alleging either less favourable treatment or subjection to a detriment by way of victimisation, are subject to provisions as to the applicable time limit, when time runs and extensions of time which are substantially the same as those in the anti-discrimination statutes: see **19.24** and **19.25** above. This contrasts with claims of subjection to detriment under *Part IVA* of the *ERA 1996*, where the 'not reasonably practicable' test applies: *ERA 1996, s 48(3)(b)*. An application under *reg 9* of the *Fixed-term Employees (Prevention of Less Favourable Treatment) Regulations 2002* for a declaration that the employee is a permanent employee may be made at any time provided that the employee has requested a statement to that effect from the employer, and that he or she is still employed by the employer when the tribunal application is made: *reg 9(6)*. Time for bringing claims in respect of pension under the *Part-Time Workers Regulations* runs from the date of retirement, not the end of the part-time appointment: *Miller v Ministry of Justice* [2019] UKSC 60, [2020] IRLR 239.

(b) Complaints by trade unions or employee representatives, or in certain circumstances individual employees, under the *Transfer of Undertakings (Protection of Employment) Regulations 2006 ('TUPE'), reg 15*, of a failure to inform or consult over a relevant transfer, are subject to a three-month time limit, time running from the date of the transfer, and any extension is subject to the 'not reasonably practicable' criteria. However, the EAT has held that a complaint may also be presented before the transfer has occurred, where it is alleged that there has been a material breach of the duty to inform or to consult: *South Durham Health Authority v UNISON* [1995] IRLR 407. A similar position arises in relation to complaints of failure to consult recognised trade unions or employee representatives about proposed redundancies (*TULR(C)A*, *s 188*): a complaint must be presented either before the last of the dismissals the subject of the complaint takes effect or within the period of three months beginning with that date (*s 189(5)*) but there is no restriction on earlier presentation, provided that the employer is subject to an obligation to consult (ie the employer proposes redundancies) and it is alleged that there has been a breach of the obligation.

(c)   Complaints of failure to pay sums due under a protective award made under either of the two above provisions are subject to separate time limits. In a case under *TUPE*, the time limit is three months beginning with the date of the order for a protective award (with the possibility of an extension if presentation in time was not reasonably practicable: *reg 15(12)*). If the award is made, or varied, by the EAT following an appeal, the time for claiming runs from the date of the EAT's order: *Dillon v Todd* (UKEATS/0010/11). In redundancy cases, the period of three months runs from the last day in respect of which the protective award was made, again with the possibility of extension. However, it is possible that the protective award is not made (or confirmed on appeal) until after the time limit has expired. In such a case the claimant must rely on the 'not reasonably practicable' extension, and should therefore not delay in presenting his or her claim: *Howlett Marine Services Ltd v Bowlam* [2001] IRLR 201.

20   Employment Tribunals – II

20.1   THE OVERRIDING OBJECTIVE

The traditional approach to litigation in Britain was for the parties to prepare and present their respective cases with relatively little management of the proceedings by the court. That approach, which was to a considerable extent followed in the early years of the operation of employment tribunals, was superseded in the civil courts in England and Wales by the requirements of the *Civil Procedure Rules 1998* for the active management of cases to ensure that the principles embodied in the Overriding Objective are achieved in practice. The move towards much more active management of cases was followed in employment tribunals, both in England and Wales and Scotland, with the introduction of a similar Overriding Objective of dealing with cases justly. The Overriding Objective was first introduced in *reg 10* of the *2001 Regulations* and was said by *reg 10(1)* to be "to enable tribunals to deal with cases justly". The components of that objective were broken down in reg 10(2) to include, so far as practicable, (a) ensuring that the parties are on an equal footing; (b) saving expense; (c) dealing with the case in ways which are proportionate to the complexity of the issues; and (d) ensuring that the case is dealt with expeditiously and fairly. By *reg 10(3)* a tribunal was obliged to seek to give effect to the Overriding Objective when exercising powers under the rules and when interpreting the rules. There was further an obligation on the parties to assist the tribunal achieving the Overriding Objective. The objective thus framed followed, broadly, *Part 1* of the *Civil Procedure Rules 1998*, albeit without including specific reference to proportionality in terms of the amount of money involved in a case, the importance of the case or the financial position of each party; and further without reference to the need to allot to each case an appropriate share of the Court's resources, while taking into account the need to allot resources to other cases. By the time of the *2004 Regulations*, the Overriding Objective appeared as *reg 3*. Its content remained static, save for two minor adjustments: (i) including reference to dealing with cases in ways which are proportionate to the importance of the issues, as well as their complexity; and (ii) re-ordering the components of the objective so that saving expense was moved down the list to the last position.

20.2   The *2013 Regulations* and *2013 Rules* differ from their predecessors in that the Overriding Objective has been moved from its previous positioning as part of the *Regulations* to its new place as *Rule 2*. It provides as follows:

> 'The overriding objective to these Rules is to enable Employment Tribunals to deal with cases fairly and justly. Dealing with a case fairly and justly includes, so far as practicable –
>
> (a)   ensuring that the parties are on an equal footing;
>
> (b)   dealing with cases in ways which are proportionate to the complexity and importance of the issues;
>
> (c)   avoiding unnecessary formality and seeking flexibility in the proceedings;
>
> (d)   avoiding delay so far as compatible with proper consideration of the issues; and
>
> (e)   saving expense.
>
> A Tribunal shall seek to give effect to the overriding objective in interpreting, or exercising any power given to it by, these Rules. The parties and their representatives shall assist the Tribunal to further the overriding objective and in particular shall co-operate generally with each other and with the Tribunal.'

20.3

The Overriding Objective in the *2013 Rules* therefore differs in a number of respects from the previous formulations:

(i)   The requirement of dealing with cases "fairly" has been elevated from being a defined component part of the objective, to form a part of the expression of the objective itself. It is difficult to see that this change (and departure from the formulation in the *Civil Procedure Rules 1998*) is anything more than form over substance; no practical effect is likely given that it has always been a requirement to ensure that cases were dealt with fairly.

(ii)   *Rule 2* introduces for the first time a requirement to avoid unnecessary formality and to seek flexibility in the proceedings. This was not a feature of the objective as framed in the legacy Regulations, and nor is it to be found in the *Civil Procedure Rules 1998* (as amended). This may well give effect to a substantive change to the practice of Employment Tribunals.

(iii)   Rather than seeking expedition, *Rule 2* sets out to avoid delay, so far as that is compatible with proper consideration of the issues. Like point (i) above, this is likely to be a mere formal change.

(iv)   *Rule 2* extends the obligation to assist the Tribunal in furthering the Overriding Objective beyond the parties to representatives, and further requires the parties and representatives to co-operate generally with each other and the Tribunal. This change makes express that which was previously implicitly required by the objective.

20.4

Rule 2 also differs from the Overriding Objective as contained in the amended *Civil Procedure Rules 1998* (see the amendments in the *Civil Procedure (Amendment) Rules 2013*). The latter includes within the concept of dealing with a case justly specific reference to allotting an appropriate share of the Court's resources to a case, enforcing compliance with rules, practice directions and orders, and to dealing with cases in a way proportionate to the amount of money involved and the financial position of each party. The Overriding Objective in the *Civil Procedure Rules 1998* also refers to dealing with the case proportionately to the importance of the "case" rather than *Rule 2*'s reference to the importance of the "issues", although it may be difficult in practical terms to distinguish these concepts.

It should be noted that the need for compliance with rules, practice directions and orders has intensified in the Civil Courts since the change in the rules in April 2013: see eg *Mitchell v News Group Newspapers Ltd* [2013] EWCA Civ 1537, [2014] 1 WLR 795, *Fred Perry (Holdings) Ltd v Brands Plaza Trading* [2012] EWCA Civ 224, [2012] All ER (D) 77 (Jun), *M A Lloyd & Sons v PPC International Ltd* [2014] EWHC 41 (QB), [2014] All ER (D) 130 (Jan), *Holloway v Transform Medical Group (CS) Limited* [2014] EWHC 1641, *Hallam Estates Ltd v Baker* [2014] EWCA Civ 661, [2014] All ER (D) 163 (May) and Lord Dyson MR's Lecture to the Implementation Programme (22 March 2013, at para 27). Since then, however, the Court of Appeal has signalled a softening of that approach, explaining that Mitchell had been "misunderstood" and "misapplied" leading to "manifestly unjust and disproportionate" decisions: *Denton v TH White Ltd* [2014] EWCA Civ 906, [2014] 1 WLR 3926. Nonetheless the Court continued to emphasise the new "culture of compliance" that had come into being.

The EAT considered these developments in *Harris v Academies Enterprise Trust* [2015] ICR 617, [2015] IRLR 208. Langstaff P noted the difference in the terms of the Overriding Objective under the CPR and *Rule 2* (para 32-33) but considered that decisions in the Tribunal could accommodate wider considerations because the tribunal has to deal with a case fairly and justly. "Justice is a wide concept" which can include justice viewed from the perspective of the system of which the tribunals are part in ensuring that indulgence given to one party does not deprive another party of that justice to which they also are entitled (para 34). That said, whereas (a) the need for litigation to be conducted efficiently and at proportionate cost; and (b) the enforcement of compliance with rules, practice directions and orders, had been given "top seats at the table" in the civil courts, they were not singled out even as particular factors within *Rule 2*. *Rule 2* was drafted in full knowledge of the approach that the CPR were taking and therefore it was wrong to say that the Tribunal rules had "lagged behind, being overtaken by history". There was a conscious decision by Parliament to adopt a different regime in the Tribunal (see para 38). Nonetheless, the EAT underlined that "Rules are there to be observed, orders are there to be observed, and breaches are not mere trivial matters . . . Tribunal judges are entitled to take a stricter line than they may have taken previously, but it remains a matter to be assessed from within the existing rules and the principles in existing cases" (para 40).

This sentiment dovetails with the Presidential Guidance for General Case Management, which emphasises (at para 22) that Orders are important and that non-compliance may lead to sanctions. The Guidance encourages parties having difficulty in complying to discuss it with the other parties and then apply to the Tribunal to vary the Order. See further the discussion of *Rule 6* below. See also *Galilee v Commissioner of Police of the Metropolis* [2018] ICR 634, emphasising that although the principles underlying the CPR and those underlying the Tribunal rules are similar, they are not the same and the starting point must always be the wording of the particular Tribunal rule.

20.5 It is important to appreciate that, by *Rule 2*, the various powers of case management given to the tribunal, as described below, are required to be interpreted and exercised so as to give effect to the Overriding Objective. The extent to which the conduct of tribunal proceedings will be influenced by these overarching provisions will vary according to the circumstances, but it can generally be said that it would not be consistent with the Overriding Objective, or the duty of co-operation, for a party to seek to exploit technical or procedural points, or to drive up costs by excessive applications, for example, for additional disclosure or information. This is now underlined by the inclusion within the objective of the need to avoid unnecessary formality and to seek flexibility within proceedings. Deliberate delaying tactics, the concealment until the last minute of relevant evidence, or attempting to overload the tribunal with excessive and marginally relevant documentation are examples of behaviour that would be judged unreasonable by reference to the Objective, and which could result in an award of costs against the offending party. The "universal guiding principles" identified by Walker J in *Zazakhstan Kagazy Plc v Baglan Zhunus* [2015] EWHC 996 (Comm), [2015] All ER (D) 106 (Apr) are in principle equally applicable to litigation in the employment tribunal (para 3):

> "(1) The court expects solicitors and counsel to take appropriate steps to conduct the debate, whether in advocacy or in correspondence, in a way which will lower the temperature rather than raise it.
>
> (2) This remains the case even where – indeed particularly where – any concession is perceived as anathema by one or other or both sides. It is perfectly possible to be vigorous without being insulting.
>
> (3) Imputations on others, whoever they may be, should only be made if they are both necessary and justified. If they are not strictly necessary, or they are not objectively justified, they should be rigorously excluded. Sometimes they are necessary, for example when . . . an allegation of bad faith is necessary. They must be confined to what is necessary. As to what is objectively justifiable, regard should be had to the degree of proof that is needed. . . .

(4) Rather than focus on criticisms of the other side, the focus should be on working out a timetable which will enable opposing parties to consider what facts and issues can be agreed, and what information and revised estimates for reading and hearing time can be given to the court prior to the hearing so as to ensure that the court's time is used efficiently and productively.

(5) If it is likely that a point which might be taken by a party, or it becomes likely that a point previously taken by a party, will not significantly advance that party's case, or will require a disproportionate amount of time or resources if it is to be resolved, then notification should be given that the point will not be relied upon for present purposes. The notification can be accompanied by an appropriate reservation as to the position in future."

20.6   The case law on the provisions of pre-*2001 Rules*, where equivalent to the *2013 Rules*, should now be read subject to the effect of the Overriding Objective. An example of the impact of the Objective on previous interpretations of comparable provisions in previous versions of the *ET Rules* is *Williams v Ferrosan Ltd* [2004] IRLR 607, where the EAT held that the power of a tribunal to review its decisions 'in the interests of justice' (then contained in *rule 34(3)* of the *2004 Rules*) should not be restricted to cases where new facts had arisen subsequently or there had been a procedural mishap, but should be applied more widely to give effect to the Objective, effectively overruling the earlier and narrower approach taken by the EAT in *Trimble v Supertravel Ltd* [1982] IRLR 451, [1982] ICR 440. This approach was strongly endorsed in a case under the *2004 Rules*: *Sodexho Ltd v Gibbons* [2005] ICR 1647, [2005] IRLR 836, EAT. However, in *Serco Ltd v Wells* [2016] ICR 768 emphasised that the Overriding Objective was not to be regarded as having affected any change to the circumstances in which a judge could interfere with an earlier order by a different judge under *Rule 29* of the *2013 Rules*: although *Rule 29* also on its face gives the Tribunal power to vary or revoke any earlier case management order where necessary 'in the interests of justice', that power is to be interpreted through the prism of previous legal principle that, in light of the importance of finality and certainty in litigation, variation of an order made by a previous judge is only permissible where there has been a material change of circumstances since the order was made or where the order has been based on either a misstatement (of fact and possibly, in very rare cases, of law) or an omission to state relevant fact. Judge Hand QC observed that although there may be other situations, they would be 'rare' and 'out of the ordinary' and cases not falling within the principles should be the subject of appeal rather than application for review. Note however that a less restrictive approach was taken by the *Court of Appeal in Ministry of Justice v Burton* [2016] EWCA Civ 714, [2016] ICR 1128: see further **20.124** below.

Nonetheless, the Overriding Objective continues to have a role in shaping and updating procedural decisions taken by the EAT and the Courts. See for example *Burrell v Micheldever Tyre Services Ltd* [2014] EWCA Civ 716, [2014] IRLR 630, [2014] ICR 935 in which, but for contrary authority, the Court would have modified the traditional approach to remitting a case to the Tribunal following a successful appeal given the introduction of the Overriding Objective. See also *Chard v Trowbridge Office Cleaning Services Ltd* [2017] ICR D21, emphasising the importance of the Overriding Objective in avoiding unnecessary formality and seeking flexibility in relation to the requirements for completing claim forms.

20.7   ALTERNATIVE DISPUTE RESOLUTION

The importance now attached to alternative dispute resolution ("ADR") is reflected in the fact that *Rule 3* of the *2013 Rules* mandates that the Tribunal "shall wherever practicable and appropriate encourage the use by the parties of the services of ACAS, judicial or other mediation, or other means of resolving their disputes by agreement". This is underlined by other references in the *Rules*: upon the initial consideration of claims and defences for arguability, the Judge is empowered (as well as making case management orders) to propose judicial mediation or other forms of dispute resolution: *Rule 26(1)*. See also the Presidential Guidance on ADR.

ACAS Early Conciliation

20.8 *Introduction*

Following a consultation in January 2013, the ACAS Early Conciliation ('EC') scheme was introduced by the *Enterprise and Regulatory Reform Act 2013, s 7*. The background concern (see para 58 of the Enterprise and Regulatory Reform Act 2013's Explanatory Notes) was that less than one fifth of claimants contacted ACAS for advice before submitting their claims. The new scheme has predictably had the effect of substantially increasing those numbers. EC Notifications during the period 6 April 2014 to 31 March 2015 were 80,734 from employees, and 2,689 from employers (it should be noted that for the first month of those figures, the scheme was voluntary). Between 1 April 2015 and 31 March 2016 the numbers were 87,892 and 4,280 respectively. These numbers represent an approximately four-fold increase on the pre-claim conciliation scheme that ACAS operated from 2009 until the introduction of Early Conciliation. Numbers have continued to increase with a total of 109,364 EC notifications in 2017-18 and 132,711 notifications in 2018-19.

Further details of the scheme in practice can be found in the ACAS annual report, and the research papers *Evaluation of ACAS Early Conciliation 2015 (Ref 04/15)* and more recently, extending beyond the *EC experience, Evaluation of ACAS conciliation in Employment Tribunal Applications 2016 (Ref 04/16)*.

The relevant statutory provisions of the Early Conciliation scheme are to be found in *ETA 1996, ss 18, 18A, 18B, 18C*. The procedure for early conciliation is contained within the *Schedule* to the *Employment Tribunals (Early Conciliation: Exemptions and Rules of Procedure) Regulations 2014*. They are referred to below as the *EC Rules*.

For claims lodged on or after 6 May 2014, unless an exemption applies, there is a requirement that before a prospective claimant presents an application to a tribunal to institute "relevant proceedings", that prospective claimant must comply with the requirement for early conciliation: see *ETA 1996, s 18A(1)* and *Reg 4(1)* of the *Enterprise and Regulatory Reform Act 2013 (Commencement No 5, Transitional Provisions and Savings) Order 2014*. Such a prospective claimant will need an early conciliation certificate in order to institute those relevant proceedings: see *ETA 1996, s 18A(4)*. In *Cranwell v Cullen* [2015] UKEATPAS/0046/14, the EAT held the Early Conciliation scheme was mandatory and where the statutory exemption did not apply, there was no discretion on the Tribunal, whether applying Rule 6 or otherwise, to waive the requirements. This was so even in a case where the very thought of conciliation would be problematic (that was a case in which the claimant alleged "appallingly" bad treatment described as "demeaning, derogatory and discriminatory, culminating in a physical assault"). Similarly, in the first instance decision of *Thomas v Nationwide Building Society* (2014) Case No 1601342/2014, the initial rejection of the claim for failing to follow EC was upheld. There, the judge allowed a reconsideration of that rejection where the claimant had belatedly embarked on the procedure and rectified the defect (although there was then an effect on the presentation date – see **20.41** below). However, the EAT has been keen that the requirements of the EC scheme do not become a web of technical requirements and to avoid the "real risk that satellite litigation in respect of the provisions of early conciliation might proliferate, with the same stultifying effect that litigation under the *Employment Act 2002* had in respect of the provisions of the dispute resolution procedures for which it provided" (per Langstaff J in *Drake International Systems Ltd v Blue Arrow Ltd* [2016] ICR 445 (para 35); see also See HHJ Eady QC's comments in *Science Warehouse v Mills* [2016] IRLR 96, [2016] ICR 252 at para 26). The EAT has therefore emphasised in both of those cases that the *s 18A(1)* requirement on a prospective claimant is to provide information to ACAS before s/he "presents an application to institute relevant proceedings relating to any matter". A "matter" was not the same as a "claim" or "cause of action". As Langstaff J held in *Drake International*, a "matter" might involve an event or events, different times and dates, and different people. Similarly, in *Compass Group v Morgan* [2016] IRLR 924, [2017] ICR 73, Simler P emphasised the deliberate use of broad terminology: it was a matter of fact and degree as to whether the proceedings instituted related to "any matter" in respect of which the claimant had provided the requisite information to ACAS. The judge also observed that there was no indication of any temporal or other limitation on the validity of an EC Certificate. Thus in *Science Warehouse v Mills*, it was held that the Tribunal has a power to allow an amendment as a matter of judicial discretion to include a new cause of action in the ET1 as presented even if there had not been notification in respect of that new cause of action. Similarly in *Drake International Systems Ltd v Blue Arrow Ltd*, a TUPE case, new respondents could be substituted for the original respondent without there needing to be a further reference to ACAS under the EC procedures. Two other observations by Langstaff J in *Drake International* are of note. At para 26, he held that that once proceedings were on foot, it made no sense to talk of a "prospective" claimant in relation to the "matter". Further, and of more general application, at para 27, he remarked that what has been billed as the "obligation to engage in early conciliation" is overstated: "there is no such obligation but merely the need to obtain formal recognition that early conciliation has been considered by the claimant". As well as *Compass Group*, the approach in *Science Warehouse* and *Mills* was followed in *Mist v Derby Community Health Services NHS Trust* [2016] ICR 543, [2016] All ER (D) 252 (Jan).

Relevant proceedings for these purposes are defined by *ETA 1996, s 18*. That section contains a list of jurisdictions to which the early conciliation procedures apply. Almost all employment disputes within the jurisdiction of the tribunal are within the scope of ACAS conciliation, including breach of contract claims and claims for statutory redundancy payments (*ETA 1996, s 18(1)*).

20.9 *Notification*

By *Rule 1* of the *EC Rules*, a claimant satisfies the requirement for early conciliation if they either (i) present a completed early conciliation form to ACAS in accordance with *Rule 2* or (ii) telephone ACAS in accordance with *Rule 3*.

Rule 2 provides that an early conciliation form can be completed either on the ACAS website, https://ec.acas.org.uk/, or in hard-copy, which should then be posted to ACAS on the address shown on the early conciliation form (at the time of writing this is EC Notification, ACAS (Phoenix), PO Box 10279, Nottingham, NG2 9PE). The form must contain basic contact information for the claimant and employer (names and addresses) (*Rule 2(2)*), and ACAS may reject a form that does not contain the required information (*Rule 2(3)*) by returning it to the prospective claimant. In *Mist v Derby Community NHS Trust* [2016] ICR 543, [2016] All ER (D) 252 (Jan), the EAT held that the requirement to give the prospective respondent's name and address was not a requirement for the precise or full legal title and (by way of example) a trading name would be sufficient. There, the name given to ACAS had been "Royal Derby Hospital" yet in the subsequent ET1 form, the Respondent was named as "Derby Hospitals NHS Foundation Trust". The EAT held the Tribunal had been right not to reject the ET1 form (or alternatively to have treated it as a minor error under *Rule 12(2A)*). HHJ Eady QC held (para 54) that "[t]he requirement is designed to ensure ACAS is provided with sufficient information to be able to make contact with the prospective Respondent if the Claimant agrees such an attempt to conciliate should be made . . . . I do not read it as setting any higher bar." In addition to the mandatory information required by *Rule 2(2)*, the current early conciliation notification form asks for details of the claimant's employment (job title, dates of employment, date of incident about which complaint is made). On naming the correct respondent see also *Giny v SNA Transport Ltd* (UKEAT/0317/16) cf *Chard v Trowbridge Office Cleaning Services Ltd* [2017] ICR D21.

Rule 3 enables a prospective claimant to contact ACAS by telephone on the number set out on the early conciliation form (currently 0300 123 1122). The same mandatory basic information must be told to ACAS during the call (*Rule 3(1)*), and it is then down to ACAS to insert the information onto an early conciliation form (*Rule 3(2)*).

Separate notification forms under *Rule 2* (or oral notifications by telephone under *Rule 3*) are required for each prospective respondent: see *Rule 4*. This was a requirement introduced by amendment: The *Employment Tribunals (Early Conciliation: Exemptions and Rules of Procedure) (Amendment) Regulations 2014*. That said, a certificate which names two respondents is not to be regarded as unlawful, *De Mota v ADR Network and Cooperative Group Ltd* [2018] ICR D6.

20.10 *The Early Conciliation Process*

After ACAS has been notified, it is under a duty by *Rule 5(1)* of the *EC Rules* to make reasonable attempts to contact the prospective claimant. This will result in a conciliator speaking to the prospective claimant to find out what the claim is about, explain next steps and then ask whether they wish to proceed with conciliation.

If the prospective claimant consents, ACAS must then make reasonable attempts to contact the prospective respondent (*Rule 5(2)*). This is in order to hold a similar conversation with the respondent.

If ACAS is unable to make contact with either the prospective claimant, or the prospective respondent, then it is required to conclude that settlement is not possible (*Rule 5(3)*). This triggers the duty to issue an early conciliation certificate (see *Rule 7(1)* and below).

Assuming contact can be made with both parties, *Rule 6(1)* provides that for up to one calendar month, starting with either receipt by ACAS of the early conciliation form presented under *Rule 2*, or of the telephone call in accordance with *Rule 3*, ACAS is under a duty to "endeavour to promote a settlement" between the parties (see also *ETA 1996, s 18A(3)*). This period can be extended by the conciliation officer under *Rule 6(2)* provided the parties consent to the extension, and the conciliation officer "considers that there is a reasonable prospect of achieving a settlement before the expiry of the extended period". Such an extension can only occur once, and only be for up to a maximum of 14 days (*Rule 6(3)*).

The duty to promote settlement is not limited to financial remedies. Where the proposed proceedings are for unfair dismissal, and where the claimant has ceased to be employed, the conciliation officer may seek to promote reinstatement or reengagement as well as compensation (*ETA 1996, s 18A(9)*).

20.11 *Early Conciliation Certificate*

By *Rule 7(1)* and *ETA 1996, s 18A(4)*, if at any point during the period for early conciliation under *Rule 6(1)*, or any extension of that period under *Rules 6(2)* and *(3)*, the conciliation officer concludes that a settlement of a dispute (or part of a dispute) is not possible, ACAS is obliged to ("must") issue an early conciliation certificate.

In addition, by *Rule 7(2)* and *ETA 1996, s 18A(4)*, if the period for early conciliation under *Rule 6(1)*, or any extension of that period under *Rules 6(2)* and *(3)*, expires without settlement having been achieved, ACAS is again obliged to issue an early conciliation certificate.

The contents of the early conciliation certificate are mandated by *Rule 8*. It must contain:

(a)   the name and address of the prospective claimant;

(b)   the name and address of the prospective respondent;

(c)   the date of receipt by ACAS of the early conciliation form presented in accordance with *Rule 2* or the date that the prospective claimant telephoned ACAS in accordance with *Rule 3*;

(d)   the unique reference number given by ACAS to the early conciliation certificate; and

(e)   the date of issue of the certificate, which will be the date that the certificate is sent by ACAS, and a statement indicating the method by which the certificate is to be sent.

A copy of the certificate must be sent to the prospective claimant and, if contact has been had with the prospective respondent, that respondent (*Rule 9(1)*). Where an email address has been provided by the claimant and/or respondent, that must be used, failing which ACAS will send the certificate by post: see *Rule 9(2)*. The certificate is deemed to be received on the day it is sent (if sent by email), and on the day it would be delivered in the ordinary course of the post (if sent by post): see *Rule 9(3)*.

In *Galloway v Wood Group UK Ltd* [2019] ICR 995, EAT, the claimant had provided an incorrect address to ACAS as his email address in that he had omitted a crucial "dot" from the address. It was accepted by the parties that it was therefore not a valid email address (although in fact ACAS had not, when sending to it, received any 'bounceback' or other notice that it was undeliverable). On the basis that the email address was not valid, the EAT held that the claimant had not therefore provided an email address and ought accordingly to have been served by post under *Rule 9(2)*. Since this had not happened, the position was that no EC certificate had been sent and accordingly 'Day B' for the purposes of calculating time limits (see below **20.14**) had not been triggered. The EAT acknowledged that this outcome was somewhat anomalous, since a claimant who provided a valid, but incorrect email address (and thus did not receive the EC certificate) would nonetheless be deemed to have been 'sent' the EC certificate for the purposes of the time limit provisions.

Even though the period of early conciliation might have passed without settlement, and that ACAS has issued an early conciliation certificate in accordance with the provisions set out above, nonetheless, it is still open to a conciliator to endeavour to promote a settlement after the expiry of the prescribed period: see *ETA 1996, s 18A(5)*.

20.12 *Settlement*

If the matter can be successfully resolved by settlement, the conciliator will record the agreement in the form of a COT3 form (an ACAS settlement document). A COT3 is a legally binding contract; it will usually be part of that agreement that the claimant cannot pursue a Tribunal claim about the matter agreed (see further below at **20.18**).

20.13 *Exemptions*

There are a number of exemptions to the requirement to comply with early conciliation. By *ETA 1996, s 18A(7)* a person may institute relevant proceedings without complying with *ETA 1996, s 18A(1)* in those circumstances. The prescribed circumstances are set out in *Reg 3* of the *Early Conciliation Regulations 2014*. Relevant proceedings can be started by a person (referred to as A within *Reg 3*) without complying with the requirement for early conciliation where:

(a)   someone else (referred to as B within *Reg 3*) has complied with the requirement "in relation to the same dispute" and A wishes to institute proceedings on the same claim form as B (in this case, by *Reg 3(2)*, A benefits from any extension in time which B has achieved by complying with the requirement);

(b)   the relevant proceedings are instituted by A on the same claim form as proceedings which are not relevant proceedings;

(c)   A can show that the respondent has contacted ACAS in relation to a dispute, A has not provided early conciliation information to ACAS about that dispute, and the proceedings on the claim form relate to that dispute;

(d)   the proceedings are for unfair dismissal and are accompanied by an application for interim relief under *ERA 1996, s 128* or *TULR(C)A 1992, s 161*;

(e)   A is instituting proceedings against the Security Service, the Secret Intelligence Service or the Government Communications Headquarters.

20.14 *Effect on Time Limits*

Time limits for presenting a claim are affected by the Early Conciliation process. By way of general overview, when a claimant who is still within time contacts ACAS, the time limit for presenting their claim is "paused". The time limit then starts to run again when the Early Conciliation certificate is produced. Once Early Conciliation has ended, the claimant has at least one calendar month in which to present the claim.

The detailed legislative changes to time limits were made by *section 8* of the *2013 Act* and *Schedule 2* to that *Act*. They are now to be found in the amended *ERA 1996*, at *s 207B*. In general the following rules apply:

(i)   the time period beginning with the day after the day on which the prospective claimant complies with the requirement to provide information to ACAS ("Day A") and ending with the day on which the complainant receives or is treated as having received the conciliation officer's certificate ("Day B") is not to be counted when working out time limits. As has been seen above, the early conciliation period could be as long as one calendar month plus 14 days from the day on which ACAS is contacted;

(ii)   if a time limit would otherwise have expired during the period beginning with Day A and ending one month after Day B, the time limit expires instead one month after Day B. For example if dismissal occurred on 31 May, the original time limit would expire on 30 August. If conciliation is entered into on 15 August (day A), but this falls on 5 September (day B) then as the original time limit falls between days A and B, time is extended to one month after day B, ie 5 October;

(iii) if the time limit falls more than one month after day B, then time will be extended by a period equivalent to the early conciliation period. Thus for example, if dismissal occurred on 31 May and conciliation is entered into on 15 June (day A) but this fails on 5 July (day B), the original time limit (30 August) does not fall within these days. The early conciliation period took 20 days – the period between day A and B and therefore 20 days is added to the original time limit of 30 August so the date for presentation is extended to 19 September;

(iv)   if a time limit has already expired by the time of entering early conciliation, no extension will be available;

(v)   any power to extend time is exercisable in relation to a time limit as extended by these rules.

In *Luton Borough Council v Haque* [2018] ICR 1388 the EAT confirmed that these were sequential provisions and did not provide for alternative limitation periods. *Tanveer v East London Bus and Coach Company Ltd* [2016] ICR D11 (UKEAT/0022/16) provides a useful example of these provisions in practice and assists with the interpretation of the one month extension referred to above. The dates were these: a claimant was dismissed on 20 March 2015 (thus the time limit but for the provisions of *ERA 1996, s 207B* created a last day for presentation on 19 June 2015). The claimant made his notification to ACAS (ie Day A) on 18 June 2015 and the EC Certificate was received (Day B) on 30 June 2015. The ET1 was presented on 31 July 2015. By *ERA 1996, s 207B(3)*, the period beginning with the day after Day A and ending with Day B (19 June 2015 – 30 June 2015 inclusive – 12 days) is not to be counted. However, adding that period onto the date on which limitation would have applied (19 June 2015) did not render the claim in time. However, *ERA 1996, s 207B(4)* provides that where a time limit would (if not extended by that subsection) expire during a period beginning with Day A (18 June 2015) and ending one month after Day B (20 June

2015), then the time limit expires instead at the end of that period. But how does one calculate "one month after Day B"? In *Tanveer*, HHJ Eady QC held that the answer was that provided by the House of Lords in *Dodds v Walker* [1981] 2 All ER 609, applying the corresponding month date principle. In other words, "month" meant "calendar month" and the relevant time period ends upon the corresponding date in the appropriate subsequent month, ie the day of that month that bears the same number as the day of the earlier month on which the notice was given or the specified event occurred. Thus the period in *Tanveer* ended one month after 30 June 2015. This was 30 July 2015 so that the claim was out of time, having been presented the next day. One month after Day B did not mean (in this case) one month from 1 July 2015.

A number of ET decisions have considered whether time spent in early conciliation before the EDT should be added to the time limit. In *Fergusson v Combat Stress* (4105592/16), EJ Walker sitting in Scotland held that no account should be taken of the time after notification to ACAS but before the EDT when calculating the time limit for bringing a claim. There ACAS received the EC form (day A) on 14 July 2016, the EDT was 11 August 2016, the EC Certificate was received (day B) on 14 August 2016 and the ET1 was presented on 18 November 2016. The Judge held that *s 207B* was a "stop the clock provision" and that a clock cannot be stopped until it has started. Thus, it was only the days between the EDT and day B that fell not to be counted, rather than the entire period between day A and day B that fell to be 'added' to the primary time limit. The claim was therefore out of time. This approach differed from two English decisions in *Chandler v Thanet District Council* (2301782/14) and *Myers v Nottingham County Council* (2601136/15). Since all of those cases, in *Ullah v Hounslow LBC* (2302599/2015) EJ Baron sitting in England thought that the draftsman had probably not considered this type of case and without considering the previous cases, reached a result consistent with *Fergusson*.

The *Fergusson* and *Ullah* approach is supported by the reasoning of the EAT in *Revenue and Customs Commissioners v Garau* [2017] ICR 1121. Kerr J held that the EC provisions only allow for the provision of one EC certificate per matter to be issued. Issuing a second EC certificate has no impact on the limitation period as it does not trigger the modified limitation regime. There, the employee was told of the impending termination of his employment and contacted ACAS. An EC certificate was issued on 4 November 2015. The employment then ended on 30 December 2015. Ordinarily, the primary time limit would have ended on 29 March 2016. The employee had, however, contacted ACAS for a second time shortly before this and a second EC certificate was issued on 25 April 2016. The claimant presented his claims on 25 May 2016. Kerr J held that the second certificate was unnecessary and not a "certificate" within the meaning of *s 18A(4)*. Kerr J also reasoned that it was wrong to say that the time spent on EC would not count in calculating the date of expiry of the time limit (as the EJ had done). He observed that in *Tanveer*, limitation had already started to run when the claimant had contacted ACAS. In *Garau* the position was different: the limitation clock could not stop under the first certificate because it had never started. This reasoning is supportive of *Fergusson* and *Ullah*. In *Romero v Nottingham City Council* (UKEAT/0303/17/DM), the EAT followed *Garau* in holding that there was only one mandatory conciliation process and, while nothing prevented a claimant from contacting ACAS again to seek assistance on a voluntary basis, the rules on extending time applied to the single mandatory process and not to any subsequent process so that it was only the first EC certificate that was relevant for the purposes of computing the extension of time. *Garau* was applied again in *Peacock v Murreyfield Lodge Limited* [2020] ICR D3 where the EAT held that only the first of two EC certificates was relevant to the question of time limits and accordingly the claim, which had been presented following the issuing of the second certificate was out of time as it was the first certificate that was relevant (even though it included an incorrect address for the respondent).

20.15 *Beyond Early Conciliation: Other ACAS Duties*

ACAS also has a duty to endeavour to promote settlement where the prescribed information under the early conciliation procedure has not been received from the prospective claimant, and in circumstances where an exemption from the requirement to undertake early conciliation applies: see *ETA 1996, s 18B*. The duty under *s 18B* lasts until the conciliation officer concludes that a settlement is not possible, or until the early conciliation procedure is triggered so that the duty under *s 18A* applies.

A further duty on ACAS to endeavour to promote settlement is imposed by *ETA 1996, s 8C*: post-claim conciliation. This duty applies where, after the institution of relevant proceedings, ACAS is requested to endeavour to promote settlement by both parties to proceedings or the conciliation officer considers that he could act under that section with a reasonable prospect of success.

In order to assist with the discharge of the latter duty, *Rule 93* of the *2013 Rules* provides that where proceedings concern an enactment which provides for conciliation (ie those falling within the scope of *ETA 1996, s 18*), the Tribunal "shall" send a copy of the claim form and the response to an ACAS conciliation officer, as well as informing the parties of the services of an ACAS conciliation officer being available to them. Further, *Rule 93(2)* provides that a representative of ACAS may attend any preliminary hearing (subject to *Rules 50* and *94* – cases involving privacy and national security restrictions, see below).

20.16 *ACAS Conciliation in General*

The functions of conciliation officers are discussed in some detail in *Clarke v Redcar & Cleveland Borough Council* [2006] IRLR 324. It is not the conciliation officer's responsibility to ensure that the terms of any settlement are fair to the employee (or employer), and the conciliation officer should never advise a party as to the merits of the case, or advise the employee whether he could expect to get more compensation from the tribunal. The primary function is to promote a settlement by whatever legitimate means the officer thinks appropriate in the circumstances. These limitations are considered important to protect the impartiality of the conciliation service. In practice, some conciliation officers are more ready to express views on the value of claims or draw claimants' attention to typical levels of awards or the maximum that can be awarded for the claims being raised. Anything said to a conciliation officer is confidential and cannot, by statute, be disclosed to the tribunal without the consent of the communicator (*ETA 1996, s 18(7)*). If a settlement is reached with the aid of the conciliation officer it is recorded on a Form COT3. It is the policy of ACAS not to be involved in settlements where it has had no conciliation role whatsoever, ie the conciliation officer is merely asked to record a settlement reached privately.

Settlement Generally

20.17 *Prohibition on Contracting Out*

By *ERA 1996, s 203(1)* and *Equality Act 2010, s 144(1)* (and equivalent provisions in other statutes) any provision in an agreement is void insofar as it purports to (a) exclude or limit the operation of a provision in the relevant act, or (b) preclude a person from bringing any proceedings under the act before an employment tribunal. The High Court has confirmed that the words "bringing any proceedings" in subsection (b) includes "continuing any proceedings": see *Clyde & Co LLP v Bates van Winkelhof* [2011] IRLR 467 at para 16. The *Bates van Winkelhof* case illustrated the breadth of the section: there, a provision in a partnership agreement in a firm of solicitors which provided for binding arbitration of disputes between partners was held ineffective to prevent an equity partner from bringing whistleblowing and sex discrimination claims.

The legislative policy behind these measures was explained by Mummery LJ in *Hinton v University of East London* [2005] IRLR 552 (para 17): "to protect employees from signing away the right to bring employment tribunal proceedings . . . except in cases where a number of closely defined conditions are satisfied. The most obvious target of the section is the blanket or sweep-up form of general waiver or release covering all future claims and inserted in a contract of employment issued to an employee on his engagement. The elaborate code of employment protection in the *1996 Act* would be worthless, if, at the stroke of a pen, it could be removed by a general waiver or release of rights." Similarly, Smith LJ explained that the purpose was "to protect claimants from the danger of signing away their rights without a proper understanding of what they are doing".

The effect was examined by the EAT in *Sutherland v Network Appliance Ltd* [2001] IRLR 12. First, it was confirmed that a common law claim (such as a breach of contract claim) can be compromised by an agreement that does not comply with the statutory provisions. Secondly, the EAT explained that a non-compliant agreement is not totally void: at most it is only the provision within the agreement which purports to exclude/limit the operation of the relevant act or which precludes a person from bringing proceedings before an employment tribunal. Thus the EAT held that agreements were intended to be capable of surviving in part even if they had been struck out in part.

It is not the role of the Employment Tribunal to ensure that upon a compromise having been reached by the parties at the door of the Tribunal, a valid settlement agreement or other binding agreement has been reached by the parties. Thus no error of law is committed by a tribunal which dismisses a case when told that the dispute has been settled, even if the agreement is not compliant with the statutory provisions: see *Mayo-Deman v University of Greenwich* [2005] IRLR 845; see also *Times Newspapers Ltd v Fitt* [1981] ICR 637 and *Carter v Reiner Moritz Associates Ltd* [1997] ICR 881 (in which final orders were made by the Tribunal by consent). However, if, after terms of settlement are agreed, the Tribunal makes an order staying proceedings for a period to allow the terms of settlement to be put into effect, with liberty to apply to restore the proceedings, upon such an application to restore, a Tribunal should consider whether the agreement is a valid compromise of statutory rights, and is not entitled to dismiss the proceedings on the basis that the terms of a non-compliant settlement agreement have been complied with by one or more of the parties: see *Osaghae v United Lincolnshire Hospitals NHS Trust* [2013] UKEAT 0575/12; see also *Horizon Recruitment Ltd v Vincent* [2010] IRLR 204, [2010] ICR 491 discussed below.

Note that where the tribunal has given judgment in favour of the claimant on liability but adjourned the question of remedy, it is open to the parties to reach a private agreement as to the remedy, subject to a formal consent judgment being made by the tribunal. Such an agreement, provided that it is embodied in a judgment, is binding without the need to comply with the requirements for a settlement agreement (as to which, see **20.19** et seq above): *Carter v Reiner Moritz Associates Ltd* [1997] ICR 881. Alternatively, if the parties wish to keep the terms of the agreement confidential, the tribunal may be asked to make a consent order staying (or in Scotland sisting) the proceedings for a period to allow for payment of the agreed sum (the amount of which need not be set out in the order), with provision for the case to be dismissed if no application is made to restore it within a stated period.

20.18 *Compromise through ACAS Conciliation*

An agreement reached where a conciliation officer has taken action under one of the relevant statutes is a statutory exception to *s 203(1)*: the agreement will, subject to its terms, be binding on the parties. Endorsing an agreement on a Form COT3 is sufficient 'action': *Moore v Duport Furniture Products Ltd* [1982] IRLR 31, [1982] ICR 84. Provided that a conciliation officer has taken action there is no more formality required for a binding agreement that for any other contract; thus settlement can be reached orally (see *Duru v Granada Retail Catering Ltd* [2001] All ER (D) 97 (Jul) and *Allma Construction Ltd v Bonner* [2011] IRLR 204) but it is strongly advisable to reduce the terms of the agreement to writing as soon as possible, to avoid later disputes about the terms of the agreement (as occurred in *Duru*) or even whether an agreement was reached at all (as was in dispute in the *Allma* case). It is also important that any written record of the agreement made is properly worded to compromise all claims intended to be covered by it. Issues may also arise subsequently as to the meaning, scope or application of a COT3 agreement. The ordinary principles of law for the interpretation of contracts apply to such agreements. Unlike settlement agreements (see below) a settlement reached through ACAS conciliation may in principle cover any disputes between the parties, including disputes that have not arisen at the time of the settlement. However, as a matter of construction, a court or tribunal will expect very clear words to convey the parties' intention to compromise future disputes: *Royal National Orthopaedic Hospital Trust v Howard* [2002] IRLR 849; *McLean v TLC Marketing* [2009] All ER (D) 144 (Aug) (UKEAT/0429/08); see also by way of example *Department for Work and Pensions v Brindley* [2016] UKEAT/0123/16 (interpreting a COT3 which settled claims "arising from the facts of the Proceedings"). In an extreme case a conciliated settlement agreement may be set aside, eg if the conciliation officer acted in bad faith or adopted unfair methods to procure a settlement, but it would not be enough to justify setting aside the agreement that the conciliation officer had not adopted best practice, provided that he had acted in good faith: *Clarke v Redcar & Cleveland Borough Council* [2006] IRLR 324 (an unsuccessful attempt to set aside agreements to settle a large number of equal pay claims).

A party will normally be bound by a settlement signed by his authorised representative, even if not a lawyer: *Freeman v Sovereign Chicken Ltd* [1991] IRLR 408, [1991] ICR 853. However, this is only so if the party has held out the representative as being his or her representative (as by including details of the representative on the Claim Form or Response Form). If a representative merely holds himself out as having the requisite authority, an agreement reached by the opposing party with the representative will not bind the 'client': *Gloystarne & Co Ltd v Martin* [2001] IRLR 15.

20.19 *Settlement agreements*

In the absence of ACAS conciliation, before 1993 the only option to secure an effective compromise of a tribunal claim, in practice, was to include a term in the agreement that the claimant would apply to the tribunal to have his or her claim dismissed on withdrawal; or if the parties were at the tribunal when a settlement was reached, an application could be made to the tribunal for an appropriate order. The former procedure has the disadvantage that the claimant can change his or her mind before making the application; the practice therefore is to make any payment conditional on the application to withdraw being made. (It is important that the respondent also applies to have the claim dismissed, not merely withdrawn or stayed, since in the latter case – in the absence of a binding agreement to the contrary – the case can subsequently be reopened: for an example see *Osaghae v United Lincolnshire Hospitals NHS Trust* [2013] UKEAT 0576/12.)

Both of the procedures referred to above are still available, but *TURERA 1993* added a further and potentially more effective avenue of binding settlement, namely, a "compromise agreement". The scope for compromise agreements was extended by the *Employment Rights (Dispute Resolution) Act 1998* (*ERDRA 1998*). With effect from 29 July 2013, "compromise agreements" became known as "settlement agreements": see *SI 2013/1648, Art 2(c)*. The principal relevant statutory provisions are now in *ERA 1996, s 203*, *Equality Act 2010, s 147*, *TULR(C)A 1992, s 288*, *Working Time Regulations 1998, reg 35*, and *National Minimum Wage Act 1998, s 49*. The *Part-time Workers (Prevention of Less Favourable Treatment) Regulations 2000, reg 9* provides that *ERA 1996, s 203* applies as if the *Regulations* were contained in that *Act*, and there are similar provisions in the *Fixed-term Employees (Prevention of Less Favourable Treatment) Regulations 2002, reg 8* and in the *Transfer of Undertakings (Protection of Employment) Regulations 2006, reg 18* (rectifying the anomaly that there was no equivalent provision in the predecessor *1981 Regulations*). The *Equality Act 2010, s 147* used to refer to "compromise contracts" rather than "compromise agreements", however *SI 2013/1648, Art 2(c)* amended the language to "settlement agreements" in line with the other statutory provisions.

It is to be noted that some common claims cannot be settled by a settlement agreement, for example claims for the failure to inform and consult under *TUPE 2006*, claims for failure to consult in collective redundancy cases under *TULCRA 1992, s 188* and claims for the right to statutory maternity, paternity and adoption pay. A COT3 can be used to settle such claims (see **20.18** above).

20.20   A settlement agreement is an agreement to refrain from issuing or continuing proceedings under one of the statutes or regulations listed in the preceding paragraph. In order for a settlement agreement to be binding, the following conditions must now be satisfied:

(a)   The agreement must be in writing;

(b)   It must relate to the particular complaint or proceedings (see further below);

(c)   The claimant must have received advice from a relevant independent adviser as to the terms and effect of the proposed agreement and in particular its effect on his or her ability to pursue his or her rights before an employment tribunal;

(d)   There must be in force, when the adviser gives the advice, a contract of insurance, or an indemnity provided for members of a profession or professional body, covering the risk of a claim by the claimant in respect of loss arising in consequence of the advice;

(e)   The agreement must identify the adviser; and

(f)   The agreement must state that the conditions regulating settlement agreements under the relevant Act or Regulations are satisfied.

A provision in the Bill which became the *Employment Act 2002* removing the requirement at (b) above was withdrawn during the Bill's passage through Parliament because of fears that it could facilitate the misuse of the settlement agreement procedure by requiring prospective employees to sign such agreements as a condition of being offered employment. As a consequence it is not possible to compromise all and any potential future disputes or claims under this procedure. The requirements at (e) and (f) are applied strictly. It is not sufficient that there is an independent adviser and that the statutory requirements have been satisfied; it is essential that this be stated. In *Lunt v Merseyside TEC Ltd* [1999] IRLR 458, [1999] ICR 17, the EAT upheld a decision that a (then) compromise agreement which did not contain the statement required at (f) above was therefore void; this must apply equally to (e). In *Palihakkara v British Telecommunications plc* [2007] All ER (D) 131 (Jan), EAT, the EAT went further and held that a statement that the conditions under *ERA 1996, s 203* were satisfied was not effective to validate the agreement so far as it related to complaints of sex and race discrimination, although the requirements for such complaints were the same as those set out in *s 203* for complaints under *ERA 1996*. It is therefore necessary to state that the requirements for settlement agreements under the particular statute or statutes applicable for each claim intended to be compromised are satisfied; it is not completely clear following this decision whether it would be enough to say that the conditions under *s 203* 'and all similar statutory provisions' are satisfied, although it would be very surprising if this were not so. Advisors should also note the change in terminology from 'compromise agreements' to 'settlement agreements' when completing the statement required at (f).

The following are the categories of 'relevant independent advisers' who may act in settlement agreements:

(i)   Qualified lawyers;

(ii)   Fellows of the Institute of Legal Executives;

(iii)   Officers, officials, employees or members of an independent trade union; or

(iv)   Employees or volunteer workers at advice centres.

In each of the last two categories the individual must be certified in writing by the union or advice centre as competent and authorised to give advice. A 'qualified lawyer', means a barrister or advocate in practice as such or employed to give legal advice, or a solicitor holding a practising certificate.

In addition:

(A)   The adviser must not be, or be employed by, or be acting in the matter for, the employer or an associated employer;

(B)   In the case of a trade union or advice centre, that organisation must not be the employer or an associated employer; and

(C)   Advice from an advice centre worker must be free (but a union may apparently charge for its services).

There was initially widespread concern that there might be a drafting error in the former provisions of the *Equality Act 2010*, replacing the equivalents in the former discrimination statutes. The concern was that a lawyer who had acted for or advised a party during a dispute could not then act as the independent adviser required as a condition of the validity of a compromise contract under *s 147*. Conflicting advice was obtained from Leading Counsel by the Law Society, with the result that the Government, whilst maintaining that the section was fully effective, made an amendment to *s 147* to remove the perceived doubts, with effect from 6 April 2012 (see the *Equality Act 2010 (Amendment) Order 2012, SI 2012/334*). It is now clear that a lawyer who has advised the employee can act as the independent adviser for the purposes of a settlement agreement settling claims under the *2010 Act*.

A settlement agreement may be used to compromise more than one complaint, provided it clearly identifies each of the complaints being compromised and the relevant statutory provisions: *Lunt v Merseyside TEC Ltd* [1999] IRLR 458, [1999] ICR 17. This case also confirms that claims can be validly compromised without the need to commence tribunal proceedings; but there must be an actual complaint: as noted above, a settlement agreement cannot settle potential disputes which have not yet arisen. This last point is a significant restriction on the utility of settlement agreements where the parties wish to ensure a 'clean break'. Moreover, settlement agreements are likely to be strictly construed, and any ambiguity resolved against the employer, as in *Palihakkara v British Telecommunications plc*, above, where an agreement to compromise all claims arising out of the termination of the employment was held not to cover claims of discrimination against the claimant whilst she had been employed. The effective scope of settlement agreements was clarified and restricted by the Court of Appeal in *Hinton v University of East London* [2005] ICR 1260, [2005] EWCA Civ 532, and advice on the framing of agreements was also offered. The agreement must specifically identify the 'particular proceedings' (or the complaints which could lead to proceedings) being compromised. This entails for tribunal proceedings that the actual case be identified, and the agreement should identify complaints by a brief description of the complaint and a reference to the statutory provision under which the claim is asserted. A bare reference to the relevant statute is unlikely to be sufficient, especially if the statute is the *ERA 1996* or the *Equality Act 2010*, since these each cover a wide range of separate types of complaint. Mummery LJ added the advice that it is good practice to include a summary of the factual and legal basis of the complaint or proceedings to identify the subject matter of the compromise more clearly. It is also generally unwise to rely on standard form settlement agreements or simply include a list of all the statutory provisions in relation to which settlement agreements may be required under the statute. The policy underpinning these points is that settlement agreements are a device to protect employees when agreeing to relinquish their statutory rights, and the statutory provisions should be construed to give effect to that policy. The role of the independent adviser in the settlement of large multiple claims was considered by the EAT in *McWilliam v Glasgow*

City Council [2011] IRLR 568. In this case there were several thousand potential or actual claimants for equal pay, and a general settlement had been negotiated with the relevant trade unions. A panel of firms of solicitors was set up by the Council, with arrangements put in place to ensure that they were independent of any influence from the Council; group presentations were arranged, followed by individual meetings, and the individual claimants were given the opportunity to take away their agreements rather than signing on the spot. Advice given was limited to the binding effect of the agreements in preventing the employees from pursuing claims; no advice was given on the merits of their claims. The EAT held that these arrangements met the requirements for settlement agreements. In particular, advice as to the merits of a claim is not required by the statutes. A further restriction on the scope of settlement agreements was shown by the EAT's decision in *Hilton UK Hotels Ltd v McNaughton* [2006] All ER (D) 327 (May). This case decides that a compromise agreement will not be interpreted as compromising a claim referred to in the agreement if at the time of the agreement the claimant did not appreciate that she had a possible claim, even though the independent adviser should have advised on the possibility. (The case concerned a part-time pension claim, and the adviser had not appreciated that the claimant had previously worked part-time.)

It should also be remembered that settlement agreements are a particular kind of contract, and are subject to the general law of contract in relation to everything except the particular statutory framework under which they may override the general restriction on contracting out of statutory rights. Thus the ordinary rules of offer and acceptance apply (see by way of illustration *Newbury v Sun Microsystems* [2013] EWHC 2180 (QB), [2013] All ER (D) 84 (Aug)). Further, a settlement agreement procured by a misrepresentation by the employee may be rescinded under ordinary contractual principles: see *Crystal Palace FC (2000) Ltd v Dowie* [2007] EWHC 1392 (QB), [2007] IRLR 682 (where however the Court held that it was not possible in that particular case to set the agreement aside because it was no longer possible to restore the position to that prevailing before the agreement was made; the employer's remedy would therefore have to be in damages). If a claimant brings a claim in the employment tribunal and the respondent disputes the tribunal's jurisdiction on the ground that there is a valid settlement agreement, and the claimant in turn disputes the validity of the agreement, the tribunal has jurisdiction to determine whether the agreement is valid or not: *Horizon Recruitment Ltd v Vincent* [2010] IRLR 204, [2010] ICR 491, EAT, a case where the claimant sought to argue that the agreement was tainted by misrepresentation. In *Glasgow City Council v Dahhan* [2016] UKEATS/0024/15 the EAT held that this applied where the alleged invalidity of the agreement was due to a lack of mental capacity to enter into the settlement agreement. Lady Wise observed that the statutory provisions require a settlement agreement to be valid both in form and substance.

20.21 An agreement to refrain from instituting or continuing proceedings in a contract claim brought in the tribunal will be binding without the need for any special requirements to be satisfied. Where an agreement compromises both statutory and contractual claims and meets the requirements for a statutory settlement agreement it is clearly valid, and equally so for the claims which do not require the formality of a settlement agreement to be settled. Where the agreement does not satisfy the statutory requirements the EAT in *Sutherland v Network Appliance Ltd* [2001] IRLR 12 held that the contractual claim is nonetheless validly compromised (but contrast *Hoeffler v Kwik Save Stores Ltd* (EAT/803/97), a case where one of the issues settled by the agreement was the parties' respective rights of appeal to the EAT, which it was held are outside *ERA 1996, s 203*)).

A settlement agreement settling a prospective unfair dismissal claim, under which the employer agrees to make a payment to the employee, is a 'contract connected with employment' for the purposes of the tribunal's contract jurisdiction, so that the employee can bring a claim in the tribunal (subject to the relevant time limits) for money due under the agreement: *Rock-It Cargo Ltd v Green* [1997] IRLR 581. However, if the settlement agreement is not made until after the employment has terminated, the tribunal's contractual jurisdiction is not available to enforce it, since the claim is not outstanding on the termination and does not arise on termination: *Miller Bros and FP Butler Ltd v Johnston* [2002] IRLR 386. The same is presumably so if the complaint is of a breach of the agreement occurring after the employment has terminated.

In July 2013, ACAS produced a Code of Practice entitled "Settlement Agreements (under section 111A of the Employment Rights Act 1996)" and accompanying non-statutory guidance "Settlement Agreements: A guide". These documents provide guidance for the requirements of a settlement agreement, particularly in the context of *ERA 1996, s 111A* discussions (on which see **20.62** below).

20.22 *'Calderbank' offers*

Attempts to settle tribunal claims by negotiation are not always successful, and parties are sometimes inhibited from entering into negotiations by the fear that if the case is not settled, disclosure of offers made will weaken their case at the tribunal. However, negotiations conducted on a 'without prejudice' basis are not normally admissible in the tribunal, particularly where they amount to a genuine attempt to settle a dispute: see *Portnykh v Nomura International Plc* [2014] IRLR 251 and the authorities reviewed at **20.62**. This is so even if the term 'without prejudice' was not used, if it is clear that the parties intended the negotiations to be confidential (see *Rush & Tompkins Ltd v Greater London Council* [1988] 1 All ER 549 at 1299H–1300A). There are limited exceptions to that rule in the absence of agreement by both parties. A limited exception is where the party making an offer reserves the right to rely on the offer in support of an application for costs (or expenses in Scotland), if he is successful at the tribunal. Correspondence conducted 'without prejudice save as to costs' (known as '*Calderbank*' correspondence after the case in which its use was first sanctioned by the Court of Appeal: [1975] 3 WLR 586) is admissible in support of an application for costs after the tribunal has made its substantive decision. There is, however, considerable doubt as to how far such offers may be taken into account by the tribunal. The point was expressly left open by the Court of Appeal in *Kovacs v Queen Mary and Westfield College* [2002] EWCA Civ 352, [2002] IRLR 414, [2002] ICR 919. The EAT has since held that although the mere fact that the employer made an offer to settle for more than the tribunal awarded (or the claimant offered to accept less than he subsequently secured from the tribunal) is not a reason to award costs, the fact of rejecting a reasonable offer to settle may amount to unreasonable conduct, for which costs can be awarded, and *Calderbank* letters are admissible to establish that offers were made but not accepted in support of the claim of unreasonable conduct: *Kopel v Safeway Stores plc* [2003] IRLR 753. See further **20.129** as to the circumstances in which a costs order may be made.

20.23 *Mediation and Judicial Assessment*

An alternative to ACAS conciliation or private negotiations is mediation. This method of dispute resolution, which is increasingly favoured by the courts, and increasingly commonly used in civil litigation, has historically not been common in employment tribunal cases. Since the introduction of a judicial mediation scheme operated within the tribunal system, this position is changing (see **20.24** below). Mediation is becoming less unusual, particularly in relatively high value claims, and cases where there is the prospect of related civil litigation. Mediation is a method of structured negotiations led by an independent mediator, who meets with both parties in the course of the mediation and attempts to guide each to common ground and to make concessions to facilitate settlement. Unlike an arbitrator, a mediator cannot impose a decision on the parties; the extent to which mediators are prepared to express views on what would be suitable terms for settlement varies considerably. A number of organisations now offer the services of trained mediators, and mediation has a relatively high rate of success. It also has advantages of privacy, and often of speed. A further advantage is that, if the parties so agree, terms of settlement can be included which could not be obtained from the tribunal, such as an apology or a reference. Generally, mediations are set up as private arrangements between the parties and the mediator. The major disadvantage of this is that the parties must bear the cost of engaging the mediator, as well as their own costs of preparing for and attendance at the mediation, and this usually makes the option less attractive, and may make it impracticable, in claims for modest compensation, or where the employee is not in a position to meet his or her share of the mediation cost and the employer is not willing to meet the whole cost. One way of meeting this problem is to make use of one of the free mediation services now offered in employment cases.

ACAS offers free mediation where the matter at issue is about employment rights that could go to an employment tribunal. If the dispute is not about a statutory employment right, a charge is made for the mediation. This service, although relatively little known, has become well established with the number of cases rising. Some two thirds of cases referred for ACAS mediation are either settled or partially settled in the course of mediation, and in a total of over 90%, ACAS considers that some progress towards settlement is made.

20.24 There is also a facility for judicial mediation within the employment tribunals. A pilot scheme offering the services of an Employment Judge to mediate between the parties if they so wish was run in 2006–07, which was assessed as successful (but it should be noted that when the results of a research project based on the pilot scheme were finally published by the Ministry of Justice in March 2010, the report (Urwin et al, Evaluating the use of judicial mediation in Employment Tribunals) indicated that the success rate for mediations was no higher than the settlement rate for cases not referred to mediation, raising doubts about the cost effectiveness at least of the pilot). The Ministry of Justice Guidance Note indicates that over 65% of cases subject to judicial mediation reach a successful settlement on the day of mediation. Provision was made, by an amendment to the *ETA 1996* by the *Tribunals, Courts and Enforcement Act 2007*, for judicial mediation to be given more formal status, and a national scheme was introduced in January 2009. The scheme uses Employment Judges trained in mediation skills; the Judge is then excluded from any future involvement in the proceedings should the mediation not be successful. The parties must bear any costs incurred in preparing for the mediation, attendance of representatives etc, but subject to the point that reimbursement of such costs by the other party may form part of the terms of settlement. Because of resource considerations, mediation is only offered in a limited range of cases, generally those discrimination claims which are considered likely to involve a hearing of at least three days, and with priority given to cases where the claimant is still employed (although the practice in each region can vary). Both parties must agree to a reference to mediation. There is no guarantee that mediation will be offered even if the parties' views are canvassed (this is usually done at a Preliminary Hearing for Case Management) and both agree, because of the limited numbers of Judges who have been trained to undertake mediations. Any indication by a judge at a Preliminary Hearing is subject to the approval of the Regional Employment Judge, who will hold a telephone preliminary hearing with parties interested in judicial mediation to determine whether it should be offered. Parties are encouraged to produce an up-to-date schedule of loss or statement of remedy in advance of this hearing. If it is agreed that there will be a mediation, it will normally be scheduled for a full day, at the tribunal offices, and appropriate directions given to the parties about any documents etc. An order for the preparation and exchange of mediation position statements is becoming increasingly common. One point which is emphasised in the information given to parties invited to consider mediation is that it is essential that a person with the authority to agree terms of settlement is available to attend the mediation.

A further important point is that the proceedings are in private, and anything said in the course of the mediation is strictly confidential and will not be admissible in any tribunal proceedings that may follow in the event that the mediation does not achieve a settlement. If the mediation is successful, the agreed terms will be incorporated into a formal order of the tribunal.

The practice is that judicial mediators adopt a purely facilitative approach, and do not offer opinions on the merits of claims or what might be appropriate terms for settlement. This has led to criticism from some users of the scheme, but there is also concern that too interventionist an approach might be felt by some parties as undue pressure to settle on terms with which they are unhappy. Judicial mediation can in this way be contrasted with Judicial Assessment discussed in the following paragraph. The usual procedure is for the judicial mediation to be held at a tribunal office, for the parties to have separate rooms and for the mediator to liaise between them. Often joint sessions are held in a tribunal room at the start of the day and, if the mediation is successful, at the end. No statistics have been published for the numbers and outcomes of judicial mediations, but anecdotal evidence indicates that there is a relatively high success rate, and that demand for mediations fully meets, if not exceeds, the availability of appropriately trained employment judges.

Further guidance on judicial mediation can be seen from the Presidential Guidance Rule 3 – ADR (Appendix 3) (re-issued on 22 January 2018). The guidance indicates that an important factor in determining suitability is if there is an ongoing employment relationship. Cost effectiveness is also mentioned and as a result a working guide is that the hearing should be listed for at least 3 days for the case to qualify.

20.25   Presidential Guidance Rule 3 – ADR, Appendix 1 sets out a Protocol containing a formal framework for the Judicial Assessment of employment tribunal claims. Appendix 2 contains further information for the parties to assist them in deciding whether Judicial Assessment is appropriate for their case. The aim is to conduct with the parties a preliminary consideration of the claim and response at an early stage (viz at that stage when a case management preliminary hearing is conducted) so as to encourage the parties to resolve the dispute by agreement. The Guidance states that it will be particularly helpful (but not exclusively so) where a party is not professionally represented. The Protocol emphasises the impartial and confidential nature of the assessment which will cover the strengths, weaknesses and risks of the claims, allegations and contentions made by the parties. Judicial Assessment is generally offered at the first case management hearing, and at the stage after the issues have been clarified and the formal orders made. It is not expected to take place later in proceedings. Whilst an assessment can take place on the telephone, it will normally take place in person and at a hearing that has been listed for up to 2 hours. Judicial Assessment is aimed at most cases of any complexity, but a number of (non-exhaustive) factors are identified as making a case unsuitable:

(i)   the presence of multiple claimants, not all of whom request judicial assessment;

(ii)   presence of an insolvent party; and

(iii)   intimated High Court or other proceedings.

The parties must freely consent to Judicial Assessment and the Protocol is clear (para 14) that "no pressure should ever be placed on any party to agree to it". Where Judicial Assessment does take place, anything said by the parties or the Judge are non-attributable and must be kept strictly confidential. No reference may be made to things said in subsequent proceedings including the final hearing. Reference can be made in 'without prejudice' correspondence or in a judicial mediation. The assessment will consist of the Judge giving provisional, guarded, indications on the state of the allegations (without evaluating the evidence) as to the strength of the parties' cases, including the potential outcome. The Judge who conducts the assessment will then normally not be involved in any subsequent part of the proceedings (save for day-to-day case management). Whilst settlement might be reached immediately after the assessment, more usually the parties will wish to consider their positions and then enter into settlement discussions through ACAS, direct negotiation or judicial mediation.

20.26   ACAS arbitration schemes

Section 7 of the *Employment Rights (Dispute Resolution) Act 1998* (*ERDRA 1998*) provides for the making of a scheme by ACAS, subject to the approval of the Secretary of State, for the determination of unfair dismissal claims by private arbitration. The process of establishing a scheme proved unexpectedly protracted, but it was finally brought into effect, for England and Wales only, in May 2001. It was extended to Scotland in 2004. The ACAS Annual Reports have consistently recorded a disappointingly small take-up of the scheme, with only 61 cases registered in the six years to 31 March 2009, of which only four were registered in the years 2007–8 and 2008–9 together (ACAS Annual Reports, 2007–8 and 2008–9). Figures for the period from April 2009 onwards have not been published by ACAS. The Scheme is now contained in a *Schedule* to the *ACAS Arbitration Scheme (Great Britain) Order 2004 (SI 2004/753)*, and is given effect by *TULR(C)A 1992, s 212A*, as inserted by *ERDRA 1998, s 7*. The Scheme is lengthy (running to 227 paragraphs, including some containing separate provisions for England and Wales and for Scotland) and is supported by a separate Guide published by ACAS, which should be consulted by any party considering the submission of a dispute to arbitration under the Scheme. The Arbitration Scheme is entirely voluntary, in the sense that it requires the agreement of both parties, and it is available only for unfair dismissal claims. The *Employment Act 2002* amended *s 212A* to provide for a similar arbitration scheme in relation to disputes over requests for flexible working arrangements raised under the provisions of the ERA 1996 (as added by the 2002 Act) conferring the right to make such requests. A Scheme (for England and Wales only) was made by the *ACAS (Flexible Working) Arbitration Scheme (England and Wales) Order 2003 (SI 2003/694)*. This was repealed and a scheme extended to the whole of Great Britain by the *ACAS (Flexible Working) Arbitration Scheme (Great Britain) Order 2004, SI 2004/2333*.

The *Apprenticeships, Skills, Children and Learning Act 2009* amended *s 212A* to provide for an arbitration scheme in relation to disputes over requests for time off work in relation to study and training (see *ERA 1996, Part VIA, s 63D* ff). No such scheme has yet been enacted.

20.27 GENERAL PROVISIONS OF THE RULES

The *2013 Rules* contain a number of general provisions which provide for when compliance with orders and other rules must be achieved.

20.28 Computing time

The time for compliance with the provisions of the Rules, practice directions and Orders is governed by *Rule 4* of the *2013 Rules*.

Rule 4(1) provides that, unless otherwise specified by the Tribunal, an act required by the *Rules*, a practice direction or an order of the Tribunal to be done on a particular day, may be done at any time before midnight on that day. Where there is an issue as to whether the act has been done by that time, the party claiming to have done it shall prove compliance.

By *Rule 4(2)*, where the time for doing any act ends on a day other than a working day, the act is done in time if it is done on the next working day. A "working day" means any day except a Saturday, Sunday, Christmas Day, Good Friday or a bank holiday under *s 1* of the *Banking and Financial Dealings Act 1971*.

Where an act is required to be, or may be, done within a certain number of days of or from an event, by *Rule 4(3)*, the date of that event is not counted within the calculation. The example given in that sub-rule is of a Response which must be presented within 28 days of the date on which the respondent was sent a copy of the claim: if the claim was sent on 1 October, the last day for presentation of the response is 29 October. Similarly, where the formulation of the requirement is for an act to be done not less than a certain number of days before or after an event, by *Rule 4(4)* provides that the date of that event is also not included in the calculation. The example in the rules is of a party wishing to present representations in writing for consideration by a Tribunal at a hearing. The requirement under *Rule 40* is for these to be presented not less than 7 days before the hearing. If the hearing is fixed for 8 October, the representations must be presented no later than 1 October.

By *Rule 4(5)*, Tribunals are required "wherever practicable" to express the last date for compliance with an imposed time limit as a calendar date.

Time limits that run from the date when a document is sent to a person by the Tribunal are dealt with specifically by *Rule 4(6)*. In such cases, unless the contrary is proved, the date when the document is sent is to be regarded as the date endorsed on the document as the date of sending, or in the absence of such an endorsement, the date shown on the letter accompanying the document.

By *Rule 5*, the Tribunal may of its own initiative, or upon application by a party, extend or shorten any time limit specified in the Rules or in any decision, whether or not (in the case of an extension) it has expired.

20.29   Irregularities and Non-Compliance

Rule 6 caters for instances of irregularities and non-compliance with requirements of the *Rules* and orders of the Tribunal. It provides that, with exceptions, a failure to comply with any provision of the Rules or of an order of the Tribunal does not of itself render void the proceedings or any step taken in proceedings. Rather, in the case of such non-compliance, the Tribunal is given a discretion to take such action as it considers just. A non-exhaustive list of "such action" which the Tribunal "may take" is set out in the rule. It includes "all or any of" the following: (a) waiving or varying the requirement; (b) striking out the claim or the response, in whole or in part, in accordance with *Rule 37* (on which, see below); (c) barring or restricting a party's participation in the proceedings; and (d) awarding costs in accordance with *Rules 74* to *84* (on which, see below).

This Rule therefore gives the Tribunal considerable latitude to take action which it considers appropriate to the act of non-compliance concerned. In cases of proposed action which would limit a party's access to the Tribunal, or affect the ability of the party to have a fair hearing of its case, the discretion afforded by this Rule will need to be exercised in a manner which is proportionate so as to ensure compliance with *Art 6* of the *ECHR*.

Rule 6 does not apply in cases of failures to comply with:

(a)   *Rule 8(1)* – requirement to present a claim form using the prescribed form;

(b)   *Rule 16(1)* – requirement to present a response using the prescribed form and within 28 days of the day the copy of the claim form was sent by the Tribunal;

(c)   *Rule 23* – requirement for an employer's contract claim to be made as part of the response, presented in accordance with Rule 16;

(d)   *Rule 25* – requirement for a claimant to respond to an employer's contract claim within 28 days of the date the response was sent to the claimant.

Nor does *Rule 6* apply where there has been a failure to comply with an unless order made under *Rule 38* or a deposit order made under *Rule 39*.

Specific reference to *Rule 6* is given in *Rule 9* which provides that where two or more claimants wrongly include claims on the same claim form, this is to be treated as an irregularity within the terms of *Rule 6*.

The scope of *Rule 6* was considered by the EAT in *Cranwell v Cullen* [2015] UKEATPAS/0046. The EAT held that it offered no assistance to a claimant who had not complied with the requirements of the Early Conciliation scheme and whose claim therefore fell to be rejected by the Tribunal under *Rule 12*. *Rule 6* could not modify the requirement for Early Conciliation which was laid down in statute in the *ETA 1996*. Further, *Rule 6* was "plainly designed to allow a Tribunal to relieve litigants of the consequences of their failure to comply" and it made no sense to construe it as entitling the Tribunal to accept a claim which the Rules prohibited it from accepting. There also had to be non-compliance before *Rule 6* could apply and there had been no non-compliance with the Rules because the Tribunal had complied with its obligation under *Rule 12*. The non-compliance of the claimant with the statutory requirements under the *ETA 1996* was not enough to engage the Tribunal's discretion under *Rule 6*.

20.30   Delivery of Documents

The *2013 Rules* make specific provision for the delivery of documents both to the Tribunal and to the parties. The *Rules* further prescribe how the parties should communicate with the Tribunal and themselves.

Communication with the Tribunal

Rule 85 sets out how documents may be delivered to the Tribunal. Save for the delivery of a claim form, documents may be delivered to the Tribunal (a) by post; (b) by direct delivery to the appropriate tribunal office (including delivery by courier or messenger service); or (c) by electronic communication.

Specific treatment is given to a claim form, which must be delivered in accordance with the practice direction made under *Regulation 11*, which supplements *Rule 8*. The requirements are considered separately below.

In order to facilitate these requirements, *Rule 85(3)* requires the Tribunal to notify the parties after the presentation of a claim of the address of the Tribunal office dealing with the case, including by giving fax numbers and email. Thereafter, by that sub-rule, the parties must use the contact details so notified. The Tribunal may from time to time notify the parties of a change in contact details, after which the new details must be used.

When communicating with the Tribunal, parties should note the contents of *Rule 92*: where a party sends a communication to the Tribunal (except an application for a person to attend to give evidence, produce documents or produce information under *Rule 32*), it must send a copy to all other parties, and state that it has done so either by using "cc" or otherwise. The Tribunal may order a departure from *Rule 92* where it considers it is in the interests of justice to do so.

Relevant to electronic delivery of documents to the Tribunal is the EAT's decision in the (different) context of lodging a notice of appeal with the EAT. In *Majekodunmi v City Facilities Management* [2016] ICR D5 it was held that a notice of appeal was not lodged by sending a link to a Dropbox document. See also *J v K* [2019] EWCA Civ 5, [2019] ICR 815 where the Court of Appeal held that where an email with attachments had been rejected by the EAT's server as being too large, the appeal had not been received (although in that case the Court of Appeal held that it was just to grant an extension of time because the server file size limit had not been drawn to the appellant's attention). Contrast *Okotie v Newham LBC* [2019] EWCA Civ 2269 where the appellant had failed to respond promptly to emails notifying that his attempt to lodge his appeal electronically had failed because the emails and attached documents were too big.

Communication with Parties

By *Rule 86*, the Tribunal and the other parties are permitted to deliver documents to a party (a) by post; (b) by direct delivery to that party's address (including delivery by a courier or messenger service); (c) by electronic communication; or (d) by being handed personally to that party (if not represented), or to any individual representative named in the claim form or response, or, on the occasion of a hearing, to any person identified by the party as representing that party at that hearing. Where the methods listed at (a) to (c) above are used, the document in question shall be delivered to the address given in the claim form (if a representative is named in the claim form, their address shall be used) or to a different address as notified in writing by the party in question.

Where a party gives both a postal address and one or more electronic addresses, any of these may be used unless the party has indicated in writing that a particular address should or should not be used.

Communication with Non-Parties

Save in the special cases referred to below, by *Rule 87*, documents shall be sent to non-parties at any address for service which they may have notified and otherwise at any known address or place of business in the United Kingdom, or if the party is a corporate body, at its registered or principal office in the United Kingdom, or if permitted by the President, at an address outside the United Kingdom.

Special cases are governed by *Rule 88*. This provides that addresses for serving the Secretary of State, the Law Officers, and the Counsel General to the Welsh Assembly Government, in cases where they are not parties, are to be issued by practice direction. The Presidential Practice Direction – Addresses for Serving Documents in Special Cases (England and Wales) was issued under *Regulation 11* on 19 October 2017. It provides a schedule of addresses for the Redundancy Payments Service (UK), the Secretary of State (BIS), the Attorney General's Office (England), the Counsel General for Wales, the Advocate General for Scotland and the Lord Advocate (Scotland). A similar practice direction covers Scottish cases.

Substituted and Irregular Service

By *Rule 89*, where no address for service in accordance with *Rules 85–88* is known, or it appears that service at any such address is unlikely to come to the attention of the addressee, the President, Vice President or a Regional Employment Judge may order that there shall be substituted service in such manner as appears appropriate.

Even where there has been non-compliance with *Rules 86–88*, a Tribunal may nonetheless treat any document as delivered to a person, if it is satisfied that the document in question (or its substance) has in fact come to the attention of that person: see Rule 91.

Date of Delivery

Rule 90 provides for deemed dates of delivery of documents delivered in accordance with the provisions of *Rules 85* and *86* (communications with the Tribunal and with parties). The rule requires the Tribunal to treat the following deemed dates as the date of delivery, "unless the contrary is proved":

(a)   Document sent by post: on the day it would be delivered in the ordinary course of post.

(b)   Document sent by electronic communication: on the day of transmission.

(c)   Document delivered directly or personally: on the day of delivery.

It should be noted that on its face, *Rule 90* does not apply to communications with non-parties (under *Rule 87*).

20.31 Presidential Guidance

Pursuant to *Rule 7* of the *2013 Rules*, the Presidents of Employment Tribunals for England and Wales, and Scotland, may publish guidance as to how the powers conferred by the Rules may be exercised. *Rule 7* specifies, however, that Tribunals "must have regard to any such guidance, but they shall not be bound by it". The *Rule* requires the guidance to be published in an appropriate manner to bring it to the attention of claimants, respondents and their advisors.

The current practice is for Presidential Guidance to be published on the Judiciary website: www.judiciary.gov.uk/publications/employment-rules-and-legislation-practice-directions/. The guidance for England and Wales now covers:

•   making a statutory appeal falling within the jurisdiction of the Employment Tribunal (issued 11 September 2017);

•   general case management – issued 22 January 2018. The General Case Management guidance covers topics including: amendments to the claim and response (including adding and removing parties), disclosure of documents and preparing bundles, witnesses, witness orders and witness statements, disability issues, timetabling, remedies, costs, and concluding cases without a hearing;

•   issuing judgments under *Rule 21* (judgments issued in default of a response) – issued 4 December 2013;

•   seeking a postponement of a hearing – issued 4 December 2013;

•   principles for Compensating Pension Loss – 4th edition, issued 10 August 2017, revised and second addendum added December 2019;

•   quantum of injury to feelings awards (Vento bands) – issued 5 September 2017 (updated 23 March 2018, 25 March 2019 and 27 March 2020);

•   *Rule 3* Alternative Dispute Resolution – issued 22 January 2018; and

•   guidance on the conduct of employment tribunal proceedings during the Covid-19 pandemic (issued 18 March 2020).

The President has also issued Practice Directions covering (i) address for service in various special cases – issued 19 October 2017; and (ii) the presentation of claims – issued 2 March 2020.

The relevant parts of the Presidential Guidance are set out in the appropriate sections in this chapter. In some cases, separate Presidential Guidance is issued for Scotland.

STARTING A CLAIM

Presentation of a Claim Form

20.32 *Methods of Presentation*

Rule 8(1) mandates that a claim be started by presenting a completed claim form (using a prescribed form) in accordance with any practice direction made under *Reg 11* which supplements that rule. Presentation of a claim form is defined by *Rule 1(1)* as delivering to a Tribunal office by any means permitted by *Rule 85* (but see below concerning *Rule 85(2)*).

Rule 8(2) and *8(3)* govern where, as between the jurisdictions, claims may be presented. *Rule 8(2)* provides that a claim may be presented in England and Wales if:

(a)   the respondent, or one of the respondents, resides or carries on business in England and Wales;

(b)   one or more of the acts or omissions complained of took place in England and Wales;

(c)   the claim relates to a contract under which the work is or has been performed partly in England or Wales; or

(d)   the Tribunal has jurisdiction to determine the claim by virtue of a connection with Great Britain and the connection in question is at least partly a connection with England and Wales.

Rule 8(3) contains corresponding provisions permitting claims to be presented in Scotland.

Two practice directions have been made – one covering the presentation of claims in England and Wales, and the other presentation of claims in Scotland – to specify the permitted methods of presentation. The Presidential Practice Direction on the Presentation of Claims (England and Wales) sets out three ways in which a completed claim form may be presented to an Employment Tribunal (the additional information accompanying the practice direction encourages the use of the first):

(i)   online by using the online form submission service available at www.employmenttribunals.service.gov.uk;

(ii)   by post to Employment Tribunal Central Office (England and Wales) PO Box 10218, Leicester, LE1 8EG;

(iii)   in person to an Employment Tribunal Office listed in the schedule to the Practice Direction. The schedule to the Practice Direction sets out the addresses of the Tribunal offices by region.

A similar Presidential Practice Direction for Scotland provides for the same three methods of presentation (the postal address is Employment Tribunals Central Office (Scotland), PO Box 27105, Glasgow, G2 9JR).

Rule 85(2) underlines that a claim form may "only" be presented in accordance with the applicable practice direction. The three methods of presentation set out in the Presidential Practice Directions mark a significant shift away from the position under the previous Rules. The initial practice directions on the presentation of claims specified that presentation in person must be within tribunal business hours, but this has been removed. Before the 2013 Rules, claims could be presented by fax and by personal delivery at the Tribunal offices up until midnight so as to present within the limitation period (see the cases of *Hutchinson 3G UK Ltd v Francois* [2009] ICR 1323, [2009] All ER (D) 127 (May) and *Post Office v Moore* [1981] ICR 623 respectively). In respect of personal presentation, the removal of specific permissible hours marks a return to such an approach. Older authorities should still be read in light of the new more limited list of permitted methods of presentation. Statutory appeals where is no requirement to use a prescribed form may also be presented by email to the regional office in the schedule to the Practice Direction.

Where proceedings are transferred to a Tribunal by a Court, the *2013 Rules* still apply to proceedings as if the proceedings had been presented by the claimant: see *Rule 101*. In such cases the rules are applied *mutatis mutandis*.

20.33 *Date of Presentation*

The date of presentation of a Claim Form is an important date. It is by reference to that date that the question of whether the claim was presented within the statutory time limit will be resolved.

It has long been clear that a Claim Form is presented when it is received by the Tribunal, even if it is not dealt with immediately upon receipt: see *Hammond v Haigh Castle & Co Ltd* [1973] IRLR 91, [1973] ICR 148. The Tribunal office will usually stamp the claim form with a date stamp showing the date of presentation (there is now a box for this date on the form). It is the claimant's responsibility to ensure that the Claim Form is in fact received by the tribunal. Whilst generally acknowledgements of receipt of claims are sent out, it is important to check the position with the tribunal office as soon as practicable, if necessary by telephoning to confirm receipt.

It was formerly the position that where there was no authorised means by which a complaint could have been presented on a day when the tribunal office was closed, the time for presenting the complaint would be extended to the next working day (*Ford v Stakis Hotels and Inns Ltd* [1988] IRLR 46, [1987] ICR 943). However, the availability of electronic submission of the claim form in accordance with the practice direction makes it difficult to see how there is room for this possibility in the great majority of cases. In *Sealy v Consignia plc* [2002] IRLR 624, Brooke LJ considered that the Tribunal office being closed was not a ground for extending the time limit to the next working day, but rather a situation where a tribunal would need to consider whether the absence of a means of physical delivery of a hard copy of the claim had rendered it not reasonably practicable to present the claim in time. Further, whilst *Rule 4(2)* makes provision for an extension of time to the next working day where a deadline falls on a non-working day, it is important to appreciate that this Rule only applies to a time specified by the Rules, a practice direction or an order made by the Tribunal – it cannot be relied upon in relation to a limitation date set by another enactment.

Many older authorities deal with when a claim form should be treated as having been presented in light of the particular way in which presentation was effected in that case. There is, for example, a substantial body of case law dealing with when a claim form sent by fax should be treated as having been presented. The previous case law is considered in previous editions of this work. Here, the focus is upon the three permitted methods of presentation under the *2013 Rules*. The *2013 Rules* provide for deemed dates of delivery of documents at *Rule 90* (see above). *Rule 90* also governs the presentation of a claim form to the Tribunal as this is expressly included within the scope of *Rule 85*: see sub-rule (2).

Where a claim form is sent by post, *Rule 90(a)* provides that it will be deemed to be presented, unless the contrary be proved, on the day on which it would be delivered in the ordinary course of post. This was also the position under the old rules. The Court of Appeal gave general guidance about presentation by post in *Sealy v Consignia plc* [2002] IRLR 624. The Court held that where a complainant chose to present his/her complaint by sending it by post, presentation will be assumed to have been effected, unless the contrary is proved, at the time when the letter would be delivered in the ordinary course of post. In the case of a first class letter, it was legitimate to adopt the approach from the *CPR* and conclude that the ordinary course of post would mean that it would be delivered on the second day after which it was posted (excluding Sundays, Bank Holidays, Christmas Day and Good Friday). This regime, which was expressly said by the Court to hold good until a simpler regime for the service of documents was introduced in respect of employment tribunals (see now *Rule 90*) was in fact the approach adopted within the new Rules.

Electronically submitted claim forms are deemed (unless the contrary is proved) to be presented on the day of the electronic transmission (see Rule 90(b)). Authority under the previous Rules dealt with the question of what constituted presentation when a claim is submitted by email. In one case, *Mossman v Bray Management Ltd* [2005] All ER (D) 06 (Apr), EAT, it was held that where the claimant had clicked the 'submit' button for the completed form, but it had not been received on the tribunal website, it had not been presented. However, in *Tyne and Wear Autistic Society v Smith* [2005] ICR 663, the opposite conclusion was reached on the basis of only slightly different facts, and additional information. The claimant in that case had received an acknowledgement of receipt, and the Claim Form had reached the server of the company hosting the tribunals' website, but had not reached the tribunal office, for unknown reasons. The *Tyne and Wear* case was subsequently applied by analogy in other situations under the old rules (presentation by fax, which as noted above, is no longer permitted) and it is submitted that it is to be preferred to *Mossman*. This view is reinforced by the decision of the EAT in *Patel v South Tyneside Council* (UKEATPA/0917/11) that an appeal to the EAT was duly presented when sent by email to the correct address, followed by a notification of 'successful delivery' by the host server, Daemon, but did not (again for an unknown reason) reach the EAT's Inbox. The reasoning would seem to apply equally to the process of submitting a claim using the online submission form.

Under the previous *Rules*, a claim submitted electronically was treated as having been presented when it is received on the server used to receive claims and responses for the Tribunals Service. That may be a few seconds later than the time of sending. This may be important; in two cases the Court of Appeal and the EAT respectively upheld the dismissal of claims as out of time which were presented electronically, but received respectively 88 seconds and 8 seconds after midnight of the last day for presentation: *Beasley v National Grid* [2008] EWCA Civ 742, CA and *Miller v Community Links Trust* [2007] All ER (D) 196 (Nov), EAT. In the first case the delay was the result of incorrectly typing in the tribunal email address; in the second, the claim had been submitted at one second before midnight but took nine seconds to arrive. This approach is likely to hold good under the *2013 Rules*.

If online transmission to an employment tribunal office is successful, an email receipt is generated, and unless such a receipt is received, the claimant should contact the Tribunal service to check whether the Claim Form has in fact been received, and if necessary resubmit it.

The final method of presentation is by personal presentation at a Tribunal office. Unsurprisingly, *Rule 90(c)* provides that where the Claim Form is presented by this method, it will be deemed to be presented on the day of delivery. Until the Practice Direction was amended in December 2016, it was very precise about the times at which personal presentation could take place: it had to be within tribunal business hours of 9am – 4pm, Monday to Friday not including public holidays or weekends. This limitation has now been removed and it is perhaps likely that, like under the old rules, a Claim Form can be presented if it is placed through a letter-box or dealt with in some way held out by a Tribunal Office as a means whereby it will accept communications. Under the old rules, putting a Claim Form through the letterbox of the tribunal at any time prior to midnight counted as presentation on the day of posting.

Under the *2013 Rules*, the Tribunal is required to reject claim forms presented where they are not on the required form, do not contain the minimum specified information, or where they suffer from substantive defects (see discussion below). Where, however, upon an application for reconsideration under *Rule 13(1)*, the Tribunal accepts that a defect in the claim form has been rectified, but that the original rejection decision was correct, *Rule 13(4)* provides that the claim is to be treated as having been presented on the date that the defect was rectified. In these circumstances, the actual date of presentation will be replaced by this later date.

20.34 *Presentation to the Wrong Office*

A claim form presented by post or electronically will be sent by the Tribunal service to the correct Tribunal office in order to be managed and determined. Where personal presentation takes place, and the claimant presents to the wrong office it will simply be forwarded to the correct office. As under the previous regime, the date of presentation will be the date it reaches the first office.

It should be remembered, however that the jurisdictions north and south of the border are separate, and if the Claim Form is presented in England and Wales when the correct venue for the claim is Scotland, or vice versa, the claim will not be regarded as having been presented within the correct jurisdiction; it cannot simply be transferred, and the claimant is at risk of being out of time if he subsequently presents a fresh Claim Form in the correct jurisdiction. This was confirmed under the old rules by the EAT in Scotland in *McFadyen v PB Recovery Ltd* (UKEATS/0072/08), where a claim had been completed online giving the postal address of the employer as Bristol, but not including the address in Glasgow where the claimant had worked; this had led to the claim being automatically routed to the Bristol tribunal. Following the rejection of that claim, the claimant presented a fresh claim in Scotland giving the correct details, but out of time, and the dismissal of that claim was upheld by the EAT.

In order to determine whether to present in England and Wales or Scotland, the tests set out in *Rule 8(2)* and *8(3)* should be followed (see discussion above). Where a claim is pending before an employment tribunal in England or Wales which could be determined by a tribunal in Scotland, and it is more convenient to do so, the claim can be transferred to Scotland, and vice versa (*Rule 99*). However, this facility is only available if proceedings have been commenced in a tribunal which has jurisdiction to determine the claim, and could also have been commenced in the other jurisdiction in accordance with *Rule 8(2)* or *(3)* as the case may be. *Rule 99* indicates that such a transfer can take place of the Tribunal's own motion (acting through the President or Regional Employment Judge (England and Wales) or President or Vice President (Scotland)) or on application of a party. Depending on the direction of transfer, the consent of the President of Tribunals for England and Wales or Scotland must also be obtained.

20.35 *Multiple Claimants*

By *Rule 9*, two or more claimants may make their claims on the same claim form if their claims are based on the same set of facts. Where two or more claimants are wrongly included on the same claim form, this is treated as an irregularity falling within *Rule 6* (see above) and thereby allowing the Tribunal to take such action as it considers just, including the specific steps set out there (which notably include the making of a costs order).

In *Brierley v Asda Stores Ltd* [2019] EWCA Civ 8, [2019] ICR 910, the Court of Appeal held in the context of equal pay claims that multiple claimants cannot bring claims on a single ET1 where they perform different jobs, although what matters is the work they do, not the job title and it does not matter if there are variations such as working different hours or having different lengths of service. They also do not need to rely on the same comparators. However, the Court of Appeal in that case went on to make clear that the Tribunal has discretion to waive such an irregularity under *Rule 6*.

20.36 *The Prescribed Form*

Rule 1(1) defines the "prescribed form" as "any appropriate form prescribed by the Secretary of State in accordance with" *Reg 12*. The current ET1 form is available on paper and online.

20.37   Fees

One of the major changes in Tribunal procedure since 29 July 2013 was the introduction of the obligation on users of the Tribunal system to pay fees: see the *Employment Tribunals and Employment Appeal Tribunal Fees Order 2013*. Fees were to be paid on issue of a claim, a hearing fee, and various other fees for certain applications and judicial mediation. These fees were ultimately abolished by the Supreme Court's decision on 26 July 2017 in *Regina (Unison) v Lord Chancellor* [2017] 3 WLR 409. By that decision, the Supreme Court declared the fees regime unlawful and void ab initio. The Government thereafter introduced a refund scheme for those who had paid fees prior to that decision.

For details of the fees regime as it was, please see previous editions of this work.

Rejection of Claims

20.38 *The Bases for Rejection*

The *2013 Rules* provide for the Employment Tribunal to reject a presented claim in three different sets of circumstances.

Rule 10 deals with rejections for failure to use the prescribed form and failure to provide minimum information. Under *Rule 10(1)*, a Tribunal is required to reject a claim where (a) the claim has not been made on the prescribed form; and (b) where the minimum information is not supplied. The minimum information that must in all cases be included in the claim form is: (i) each claimant's name; (ii) each claimant's address; (iii) each respondent's name; (iv) each respondent's address; and (v) one of the following: (1) an early conciliation (EC) number, (2) confirmation that the claim does not institute any relevant proceedings, or (3) confirmation that one of the early conciliation exemptions applies. Where the claim is rejected under *Rule 10*, by *Rule 10(2)*, the form is to be returned to the claimant with a notice of rejection explaining why it has been rejected. The notice is to contain information about how to apply for a reconsideration of that rejection. In *Cranwell v Cullen* [2015] UKEATPAS/0046, the EAT held that a Tribunal had been right to reject a claim under *Rule 10* for failing to provide an early conciliation number when none of the EC exemptions applied. In *Sterling v United Learning Trust* (UKEAT/0439/14/DM) Langstaff P held that an Employment Tribunal had been obliged to reject the claim where an incorrect ACAS EC number had been given (see also *Adams v British Telecommunications plc* [2017] ICR 382, EAT and E.ON Control Solutions Ltd v Caspall [2020] ICR 552, EAT). However, in *Mist v Derby Community NHS Trust* [2016] ICR 543, [2016] All ER (D) 252 (Jan), the EAT took a broad view of the requirement to name the respondent so as not to require its full legal title and went on to point to the availability of *Rule 12(2A)* to correct minor errors (see below).

Rule 11 concerned rejections where the correct Tribunal fee has not been paid, however this is vestigial in nature following the decision in *Regina (Unison) v Lord Chancellor* [2017] 3 WLR 409. It is discussed in previous editions of this work.

Rule 12 is concerned with substantive defects in the claim form. *Rule 12(1)* permits the staff of the tribunal office to refer a claim form to an employment judge for a judicial decision concerning whether the claim form suffers from a substantive defect. Under *Rule 12(2)*, where the judge considers that the claim, or part of it, is (a) one which the tribunal has no jurisdiction to consider; (b) is in a form which cannot sensibly be responded to or is otherwise an abuse of process; (c) is one which institutes relevant proceedings and is made on a claim form that does not contain either an early conciliation number or confirmation that one of the early conciliation exemptions applies; or (d) is one which institutes relevant proceedings and is made on a claim form which contains information that one of the early conciliation exemptions applies, when none of those exemptions do apply; then the judge must reject the claim. This provision is mandatory and the tribunal has no discretion to accept claims falling within these categories: *E.ON Control Solutions Ltd v Caspall* [2020] ICR 552.

Under *Rule 12(2A)*, where the judge considers that the claim, or part of it, is (e) one which institutes relevant proceedings and the name of the claimant on the claim form is not the same as the name of the prospective claimant on the early conciliation certification to which the early conciliation number relates; or (f) is one which institutes relevant proceedings and the name of the respondent on the claim form is not the same as the name of the prospective respondent on the early conciliation certificate to which the early conciliation number relates; then the judge must reject the claim unless he considers that the claimant made a minor error in relation to a name or address and it would not be in the interests of justice to reject the claim. For an example where a minor error in the name of the respondent could have been rectified in this way, see *Mist v Derby Community NHS Trust* [2016] ICR 543,

[2016] All ER (D) 252 (Jan); and *Giny v SNA Transport Ltd* (UKEAT/0317/16) cf *Chard v Trowbridge Office Cleaning Services Ltd* [2017] ICR D21. In *De Mota v ADR Network and Cooperative Group Ltd* [2018] ICR D6, the EAT held there was no rule that rendered a certificate unlawful that named two respondents. In *Peacock v Murreyfield Lodge Ltd* (UKEAT/0117/19/JOJ), [2020] ICR D3 the EAT noted that the reference in *Rule 12(2A)* to 'name or address' is an 'oddity' and in fact a defect in the address of either claimant or respondent is not a ground on which a claim form may be rejected under *Rule 12(2)*.

Any rejected claim form under *Rule 12* must be returned to the claimant together with the notice of rejection giving the judge's reasons for rejecting the claim or part of it. The notice must contain information about how to apply for a reconsideration of the rejection decision.

Rule 12 was considered by the EAT in *Trustees of William Jones's School Foundation v Parry* [2016] ICR 1140. There, the ET1 form referred to attached sheets as containing the details of the claim, but the solicitor representing the claimant had mistakenly attached a document relating to a different case. The issue was whether the ET had been right to accept the claim, or whether it ought to have been rejected as being in a form which could not be sensibly responded to under *Rule 12(1)(b)*. Elisabeth Laing J held that although, contrary to the ET's finding, the claim could not sensibly be responded to, this was immaterial because *Rule 12(1)(b)* and *(2)* prescribed a procedure which allowed a claim to be rejected without hearing from any party (or only hearing one party) which was not authorised by primary legislation (*ETA 1996, s 7*) and was accordingly ultra vires. The EAT held that the correct procedure for enforcing compliance with *Rule 12(1)(b)* was that set out in *Rule 27* – giving the parties the opportunity to make representations and then to have a hearing before a claim is dismissed. The Judge remarked that *Rule 12(1)(a)* was the only part of the rule that was authorised by *ETA 1996, s 7*. This judgment put into doubt vires of the other provisions of *Rule 12(1)*, viz (c) to (f), concerning enforcement of the EC scheme and therefore it is no surprise that it was subsequently considered by the Court of Appeal, then known as *Secretary of State for Business, Energy and Industrial Strategy v Parry* [2018] EWCA Civ 672, [2018] ICR 1807. Bean LJ disagreed with the EAT and held that *rule 12(1)(b)* was a valid exercise of the rule-making power in *s 7* of the *ETA 1996*. The Court proceeded to give guidance that *rule 12* should be used sparingly, that the claimant should be given the benefit of the doubt and that in an appropriate case the respondent's knowledge of the matter could be taken into account in judging whether the claim could be sensibly responded to by that particular respondent. There was no rule that there must be a rejection of an unparticu-larised claim regardless of other facts of the case. Here, even though the claim here was unparticularised, it could be responded to because the school knew the claimant had been dismissed and what the circumstances of that dismissal were. Further particulars could be ordered subsequently. In similar vein, in *Birmingham City Council v Adams* (UKEAT/0048/17/LA), [2019] ICR 531 the EAT held that the Employment Judge had not erred in law in holding that nine equal pay claimants had complied with the requirement to provide details of their claim when in their claim form they referred to particulars submitted with a tenth (separate) claim.

20.39 *Reconsideration of Rejection*

Rule 13(1) gives an entitlement to a claimant whose claim has been rejected under either *Rule 10* or *Rule 12* to apply for reconsideration of that decision on the basis that (a) the decision to reject was wrong; or (b) the notified defect can be rectified.

A claimant wishing to avail themselves of such reconsideration, must apply in writing and present that application to the Tribunal within 14 days of the date that the notice of rejection was sent (*Rule 13(2)*). The application is required to ("shall") explain why the decision is said to have been wrong or the application must rectify the defect and if the claimant wishes to request a hearing, this must also be included in the application.

If a hearing is not requested, and an Employment Judge considering the application on the papers decides to accept the claim in full, then the Judge must determine that application without a hearing. Otherwise the application for reconsideration will be considered at a hearing attended only by the claimant (see *Rule 13(3)*).

Where the application for reconsideration is made on the basis that the notified defect can be rectified, and the Judge decides that the original rejection was correct, but that the defect has now been rectified, the claim is to be treated as having been presented on the date that the defect was rectified: *Rule 13(4)*. This can have harsh effects in many cases because a claim that must under the Rules be rejected for a minor defect will often be out of time by the time the employment tribunal issues a notice of rejection and the claimant has the opportunity rectify it, as was the case in *Adams v British Telecommunications plc* [2017] ICR 382, EAT (Simler J). Providing a glimmer of hope for claimants in such circumstances, however, Simler J remitted the matter to the Tribunal to reconsider its decision that the claims for unfair dismissal and discrimination were out of time. Simler J held that the Judge had failed properly to consider whether the claimant's assumption that she had made a valid and timeous application was reasonable, such that it was 'not reasonably practicable' for her to have presented a claim in time. Likewise, on the 'just and equitable' test Simler J held that the tribunal needed to consider the prejudice to the claimant of not having her case heard. Further guidance on the application of the 'not reasonably practicable' test was given by Eady J in *North East London NHS Foundation Trust v Zhou* (UKEAT/0066/18/LA). That case also concerned a mistake in the ACAS EC number, but this time made by the claimant's solicitors. Eady J noted that, unlike minor errors in a name or address (which can be corrected under *Rule 12(2A)*), there was no leeway in relation to the ACAS EC number. However, she held that although the claimant's legal advisers were 'at fault', it did not follow that they had acted 'unreasonably' so that the claimant was to be fixed with the consequences of their mistake under the *Dedman* principle: this was a matter that was remitted to the Tribunal to determine.

See generally **19.20** EMPLOYMENT TRIBUNALS – I for the 'not reasonably practicable' test and further guidance on time limits.

20.40 Notification to Regulators

Rule 14 of the *2013 Rules* concerns claims which allege that the claimant has made a protected disclosure. In such cases, the Tribunal has a discretion ("may"), if the claimant consents, send a copy of any accepted claim to a regulator listed in *Schedule 1* to the *Public Interest Disclosure (Prescribed Persons) Order 1999*. For these purposes, the term "protected disclosure" is said by *Rule 14* to have the defined meaning as set out in *ERA 1996, s 43A*.

RESPONDING TO A CLAIM

20.41 Sending the Claim Form to the Respondents

Where a claim is accepted, the Tribunal is required by *Rule 15* to send a copy of the claim form, together with the prescribed response form, to each respondent with a notice which includes the following information: (a) whether any part of the claim has been rejected, (b) how to submit a response to the claim, the time limit for doing so, and what will happen if a response is not received by the Tribunal within that time limit. *Rule 15* does not require that a claim form be sent to the registered office address (if the respondent is a company). Nor does it require that the documents should be received. It requires only that the claim form be sent to the address given in the claim form, or to a different address as notified in writing by the party in question (*Rule 86(1)–(2)*). A non-technical approach, consistent with the Overriding Objective is to be taken to determining whether as a matter of fact there has been compliance with *Rule 15*: *Campbell v Jamie Stevens (Kensington) Ltd* [2020] ICR D1.

Responding

20.42 *Response Form and Time Limit*

The rules governing the respondent's response are to be found in *Rule 16*. *Rule 16(1)* requires the response to be on the prescribed form. It also mandates that the response be presented to the Tribunal office within 28 days of the date that the copy of the claim form was sent by the Tribunal. The degree of detail to be contained in the response is a matter of judgment, but it needs to be remembered that the claimant may apply for an order for further information of the grounds set out by the respondent; and further information may also be required by order of the tribunal of its own motion. Given that initial consideration will be given to the response, respondents should also have in mind the need to advance only arguable defences.

It is important to emphasise that, like with the previous *Rules*, time runs from the date the claim form was sent to the respondent not the date it was received (this point was expressly confirmed by the EAT in *Bone v Fabcon Projects Ltd* [2006] IRLR 908, [2006] ICR 1421) and the response must be received by the tribunal office, not merely sent, by the end of the 28th day following the sending out of the claim form. Under the previous rules, a claim form was not regarded as having been 'sent' to a respondent if there were material inaccuracies in the name and address to which it was addressed by the tribunal, and as a consequence it is not in fact received by the respondent: *Chowles (t/a Granary Pine) v West* (UKEAT/0473/08) (claim sent to a Mr Charles instead of Chowles, and to address with incomplete postcode). However, the EAT has since held (see *Jarretts Motors Ltd v Wells* [2009] All ER (D) 350 (Jul)) that material errors in the name and/or address given for the respondent do not affect the position if the notice of the claim is in fact received by the respondent within the time for responding; the fact that it is delayed may provide grounds for an extension of time, but nothing more. See also *Campbell v Jamie Stevens (Kensington) Ltd* [2020] ICR D1, discussed above at **20.41**.

A single response form may include the response of more than one respondent if they are all responding to a single claim and they all resist the claim on the same grounds, or if they do not resist the claim (*Rule 16(2)*). Otherwise separate response forms should be used. Similarly, a single response form may include the response to more than one claim if the claims are based on the same set of facts and either the respondent resists all of the claims on the same grounds, or the respondent does not resist the claims (*Rule 16(3)*). Again, in other circumstances, separate response forms should be used.

There is no apparent sanction against the failure to observe *Rules 16(2)* or *(3)*, eg a joint response being submitted in a case where the respondents' grounds of resistance differ. The Tribunal is likely to apply *Rule 6* in such circumstances and may require the position to be rectified.

Whilst a blank prescribed form accompanies the notification of a claim under *Rule 15*, a respondent can choose to submit an online response. The respondent should set out with some care the grounds upon which he wishes to resist the claim, because if he omits a ground and wishes to raise it at any subsequent tribunal hearing, the claimant may successfully resist an application to amend the response or apply for an adjournment, possibly at the respondent's expense, to consider the additional matter (see also *Hotson v Wisbech Conservative Club* [1984] IRLR 422). In *Panama v London Borough of Hackney* [2003] IRLR 278, the Court of Appeal emphasised that serious allegations such as those of dishonesty must be put with sufficient formality at an early enough stage to provide a full opportunity for answer. Also, as with the claimant's Claim Form, any statement made by a respondent in the response may be challenged at the hearing.

20.43 *Extending the Time Limit for a Response*

Sometimes, a respondent will need longer than the 28 days provided for in *Rule 16* in which to respond to the claim. *Rule 20* permits such a respondent to apply for an extension of time to present a response either before the time limit has expired, or afterwards (although note the different requirements of the application in each case). This is a change from the position under the previous rules. *Rule 20(1)* requires any such application to be presented to the Tribunal in writing, copying in the claimant. The application must set out the reason why the extension of time is sought and must, except where the time limit has not yet expired, be accompanied by a draft of the response which the respondent wishes to present or an explanation of why that is not possible, and if the Respondent wishes to request a hearing, this must be requested in the application. The claimant then has 7 days in which to give reasons in writing explaining why the application is opposed (if this is indeed the case): *Rule 20(2)*.

Applications under *Rule 20* may be determined by the Employment Judge either with or without a hearing: *Rule 20(3)* expressly states that the application may be determined without a hearing.

If the decision is to refuse an extension, any prior rejection of the response under *Rule 18* (see below) shall stand. If, conversely, the decision is to allow an extension, any judgment issued under *Rule 21* must be set aside: see *Rule 20(4)*.

There is also an express power in *Rule 94(7)* for a Minister to apply for an extension of time to present a response in national security proceedings where the Minister has made a direction or an application under that *Rule*: see below **20.91**.

The principles in *Kwik Save Stores v Swain* [1997] ICR 49 apply where the Tribunal is required to consider whether to extend time for presentation of a response under *Rule 20*: see *Thornton v Jones* (UKEAT/0068 and 0018/11/SM) at para 18 per Underhill J (as he then was). Those authorities make clear that it is a discretion to be exercised taking into account the Overriding Objective and all relevant factors. The relevant factors include, as indicated in those authorities: the explanation for the delay (in general, the more serious the delay, the more important it is for an applicant for an extension of time to provide a satisfactory explanation for it); the prejudice that will be suffered by both parties if the extension is granted or refused; and the merits of the case.

Respondents are generally best advised to apply before the expiry of the time limit if this is possible, and as early as possible once the need to apply for an extension has become apparent. One obvious situation in which extensions will be sought is where the respondent did not receive the Claim Form until sometime after it was sent (either because of postal delays, or the respondent's absence, or because the claimant had given an incorrect address). If genuine, these reasons are likely to be compelling factors in favour of an extension of time: compare *Bone v Fabcon Projects Ltd* [2006] ICR 1421, EAT, where the claim was not received from the tribunal until, having heard of the claim through ACAS, the employer contacted the tribunal office and had it re-sent. However, as an alternative to applying for an extension, the respondent may be in a position to submit a response with the bare minimum of reasons for resisting the claim, and an offer to provide full particulars as soon as the necessary information can be obtained. This approach may also need to be adopted if there is insufficient information about the subject matter of the complaint in the Claim Form (although such cases might be less frequent now given the opportunity for the Tribunal to exercise powers under *Rule 12*); however, in most cases this will not necessarily be regarded as a compelling reason for an extension of time, since in most cases the respondent will be fully aware of the point in dispute because it will have been considered as a grievance or have been the subject of disciplinary proceedings. If the respondent did not receive the form because it was incorrectly addressed, he may be able to argue that it was not 'sent'. In these circumstances if the respondent becomes aware of the claim soon enough, it may be possible to tell the tribunal the claim has not been received and ask for it to be re-served. The tribunal will not automatically accede to such a request, and if a judgment has already been issued under *Rule 21(2)* by the time the respondent contacts the tribunal, the only practical remedy for the respondent is to apply for a review of that judgment under *Rule 70*: see *Chowles (t/a Granary Pine) v West* (UKEAT/0473/08/DM), for an example and **20.122** below.

See further **20.46** below.

20.44 *Acceptance of a Response*

Where the Tribunal accepts a response, it must send a copy of it to all other parties: *Rule 22*.

20.45 *Rejection of a Response*

There are two bases on which a respondent's response can be rejected: (i) the failure to use the correct form or supply minimum information (*Rule 17*) and (ii) late presentation (*Rule 18*).

By *Rule 17*, the Tribunal is required to ("shall") reject a response where it is not made on a prescribed form or if it did not contain all of the minimum information. The minimum information required is (i) the respondent's full name, (ii) the respondent's address and (iii) whether the respondent wishes to resist any part of the claim. Where the Tribunal rejects a response under *Rule 17*, it must return the form to the respondent with a notice of rejection explaining why it has been rejected. The notice must also explain what steps may be taken by a respondent, including the need (if appropriate) to apply for an extension of time, and how to apply for a reconsideration of the rejection.

If a respondent's response is received outside the time limit set out in *Rule 16*, or any extension granted within the original limit, then it must be rejected by the Tribunal unless an application for an extension of time has already been made under *Rule 20* and the response includes or is accompanied by such an application: *Rule 18(1)*. If no application for an extension of time is included, then rejection is mandatory: *Red Ninja Ltd v Succu* (UKEAT/0035/19/BA). Where the Tribunal rejects a response under this rule, it must return the response form to the respondent, together with a notice of rejection, explaining that the response was presented late. The notice sent to the respondent must explain how the respondent can apply for an extension of time and how to apply for a reconsideration: *Rule 18(2)*. If an application for an extension of time is made, then the response shall not be rejected pending the outcome of the application.

20.46 *Reconsideration of Rejection*

A respondent has an entitlement under *Rule 19(1)* to apply for a decision to reject its response under *Rules 17* or *18* to be reconsidered on the basis that the decision to reject was wrong, or in the case of a rejection under *Rule 17* (failure to use the prescribed form or provide the minimum information) on the basis that the notified defect can be rectified. These constitute the same grounds for reconsideration as appear in *Rule 13* concerning the claim form (see above).

The respondent must apply in writing and present the application to the Employment Tribunal within 14 days of the date that the notice of rejection was sent. It must explain why the decision is said to have been wrong or must rectify the defect and must state whether the respondent requests a hearing: *Rule 19(2)*. If the respondent does not require a hearing, and the Employment Judge decides after considering the application to accept the response in full, then the Judge shall determine the application without a hearing; otherwise the application must be considered at a hearing attended only by the respondent: *Rule 19(3)*.

Where a judge allows an application for reconsideration in circumstances where the original decision to reject was correct, but where the defect has subsequently been rectified, the response is treated as having been presented on the date that the defect was rectified (*Rule 19(4)*). *Rule 19(4)* goes on to provide, expressly, that a Judge may nonetheless extend time under *Rule 5* (see above).

A number of cases were decided under the previous editions of the rules concerning the rejection of a respondent's response. In *Butlins Skyline Ltd v Beynon* [2007] ICR 121, the EAT held that an administrative decision to reject a response is also open to appeal (as well as, under the then rules, a review – now reconsideration). Whilst the *2013 Rules* now provide specifically and expressly for the reconsideration of rejection decisions and the grounds on which this can be done, and the new rules are likely to be the focus for any decision taken by a Tribunal, nonetheless, the old case law is helpful in showing the likely approach of the EAT. In *Jarretts Motors Limited v Wells* [2009] All ER (D) 350 (Jul), for example, Underhill P emphasised that tribunals were obliged to adopt as flexible an approach as possible in order to mitigate the injustice than can be caused by what he described as the then "complex and rigid rules" (para 9). The scope for review of the non-acceptance of a response under the old rules was clarified by the EAT in *Moroak (t/a Blake Envelopes) v Cromie* [2005] IRLR 535 and *Pendragon plc v Copus* [2005] ICR 1671, [2005] All ER (D) 42 (Aug).

The EAT in *Moroak* held that if it was in the interests of justice to extend time and admit a late response, the tribunal should do so. The test to be applied was that set out (in relation to earlier Rules) by the EAT in *Kwik Save Stores Ltd v Swain* [1997] ICR 49, which requires the tribunal to balance all relevant factors, with particular weight being given to whether the respondent would suffer greater prejudice by being denied relief than the claimant would suffer if relief were granted to the respondent. The merits of the defence, so far as readily ascertainable at this stage in the proceedings, may also be relevant. (The *Moroak* case concerned a response sent in 44 minutes late following a malfunction of the respondent's representative's computer, which the EAT unsurprisingly regarded as causing no prejudice to the claimant.) In *Pendragon*, the EAT makes it clear that the absence of a good reason for the failure by the respondent to submit a response in time, whilst clearly an important consideration, is not on its own a bar to granting relief from the consequences: see also to this effect *Thornton v Jones* [2011] All ER (D) 122 (Sep) (UKEAT/0068/11). A failure on the part of a tribunal to consider an application for review of the non-acceptance of a response was found to be an error of law in *South East Leisure Group Ltd v Vachoumis* (UKEAT/0270/10). As a general point, the latitude towards respondents shown in these decisions is clearly much greater than that shown towards claimants whose claims are presented out of time and seek an extension of time under the 'not reasonably practicable' dispensation, and, to a lesser extent, to those seeking an extension on just and equitable grounds. The simple explanation for the apparent discrepancy is that it is the claimant who seeks to invoke the powers of the tribunal, and can therefore be expected to do so promptly, whereas the respondent has not initiated, and probably does not want to be party to, the litigation; and these differences of context lead to different expectations as to compliance with the requirements of the tribunal. Once proceedings have been fully initiated, there is less evidence of a difference of approach to the parties' conduct, and in particular to failure to comply with directions.

As *Butlins Skyline Ltd* made clear, the non-acceptance of a response is a decision open to appeal, and although there were particular reasons under the old rules which made that outcome just, it is likely to remain the position under the *2013 Rules*. Careful consideration should be given to whether to appeal rather than seek reconsideration – usually the latter will be the more appropriate route given the need to show an error of law on appeal.

20.47 Effect of No Response

Rule 21(1) provides for the Tribunal to issue a default judgment and/or to limit further participation in proceedings where:

(a)   on the expiry of the time limit for presenting a response under Rule 16 no response has been presented; or

(b)   any response that has been presented has been rejected and no application for a reconsideration is outstanding; or

(c)   where the respondent has stated that no part of the claim is contested.

It is to be noted that the wording of *Rule 21(1)(a)* speaks of the time limit for presenting a response under *Rule 16* without adding reference to any extension granted under *Rule 20* (contrast *Rule 18(1)* which does contain this additional wording). That said, it is most unlikely that the Tribunal would visit the consequences in *Rules 21(2)* and *(3)* where the Respondent was still within an extended time limit, or where a response had been presented after the 28 days but within an extension granted by the Tribunal.

20.48 *Judgment in Default*

In the circumstances set out in *Rule 21(1)*, by *Rule 21(2)*, an Employment Judge is required to ("shall") decide whether, on the available material (including further information which the parties are required to provide by the Judge) a determination can properly be made of the claim or part of it. To the extent that a determination can be made, the Judge is required to issue a judgment accordingly. Otherwise a hearing must be fixed before a Judge alone. *Rule 21* thus requires a employment judge to make a decision as to whether the claim can properly be determined and judgment entered; if not, a hearing should be fixed. The judge is not permitted to enter default judgment simply because the claim is not defended: *Limoine v Sharma* [2020] ICR 389, EAT. In that case, Auerbach J directed attention to the Presidential Guidance, which suggested that the judge should, at a minimum, consider whether the claim is clearly stated, where the burden of proof lies and whether there is any obvious jurisdictional problem with the claim.

It is clear that such a judgment may deal solely with liability, or also with remedy. Under the previous rules, in which the Tribunal had a discretion to issue a default judgment where no response was presented within time, it was common that default judgments were limited to liability; a default judgment on remedy was only appropriate where it is clear from the papers what the claimant is claiming, and this was unlikely except in claims for unlawful deductions or redundancy payments (and it was not be clear in many such cases what amount was being claimed). This is expected to the position under the *2013 Rules* also. The provision enabling Judges to order the provision of additional information is intended to enable more judgments under *Rule 21(2)* to deal also with remedy. In any case, a claimant who wishes to have a judgment covering remedy made is free to submit additional information without waiting for an Order to that effect, preferably by way of a Schedule of Loss; the Judge can necessarily only determine what remedy is appropriate in the light of the information available to him at the time of deciding.

As with the old rules, if the judgment under *Rule 21(2)* is for liability only, there is no provision in the *2013 Rules* for a second such judgment dealing with remedy. Rather *Rule 21(2)* provides for a hearing to deal with whatever matters are outstanding before a judge alone. The hearing must take place before judge alone even if it is a complaint of a type which, if it had been defended, would have been heard before a full three-person tribunal: *Limoine v Sharma* [2020] ICR 389, EAT. Again, at the hearing, the judge must only allow the claim if satisfied the claim is factually (and legally) made out.

The respondent will only be entitled to participate in any such hearing to the extent permitted by the judge: see *Rule 21(3)* below. It should be noted that even if a respondent is permitted to take part in a remedy hearing following a default judgment on liability, the tribunal cannot reopen any issues determined by the *Rule 21(2)* judgment, and issues relevant to remedy must therefore be decided on the basis of the claimant's claims as upheld in the earlier judgment. This was the position under the old rules: *Eaton v Spencer and others t/a/ Wiggles Experience* [2012] ICR D7 (UKEAT/0177/11). Under the current rules, it has been emphasised that this does not, however, mean that a respondent should not be permitted to contest issues as to remedy: *Hughes v Office Equipment Systems Ltd* [2019] ICR 201 and *Limoine v Sharma*, ibid.

Under the old rules, there was no requirement to give reasons for a default judgment issued under old *rule 8*. The *2013 Rules*, however, do not exempt judgments issued under *Rule 21(2)* from the general provisions of *Rule 62* – obligation to give reasons (see below). Either party may apply for reconsideration of the judgment in accordance with *Rule 70*. In the case of the claimant, this is likely to arise only in relation to remedy, if the tribunal has awarded less than he considers should have been awarded. The application must be made within 14 days of the date on which the judgment was sent to the parties (*Rule 71*). This time limit can be extended by the Judge under *Rule 5*. An example would be where the respondent only became aware of the proceedings, or the judgment, after the time limit for reconsideration had expired, because an incorrect address had been given by the claimant: see *Chowles (t/a Granary Pine) v West* (UKEAT/0473/08). The application must state the reasons for seeking the reconsideration (*Rule 71*). If it is the respondent who is applying, the application for reconsideration of the judgment issued under *Rule 21(2)* is likely to be accompanied by an application for an extension of time to present a response (or even in certain circumstances a reconsideration of the rejection of the response). It is important to remember the requirement of Rule 20(1) that an application for an extension after the time has expired must attach the proposed response to the claim as well as giving reasons for the applications made. Under the old rules, a failure to apply for an extension of time at the same time as a review of a default judgment was regarded as a technicality which should not be used to refuse an application for a review where there are good grounds for the review: *Bournemouth Borough Council v Leadbeater* [2011] All ER (D) 164 (Mar), [2011] ICR D15 (UKEAT/0010/11) (respondent had not received claim); and see *Jarretts Motors Ltd v Wells*, above, where a flexible approach by tribunals to applications for a review citing the wrong rule under the old rules was advocated by the EAT.

Please see **20.39** for commentary on the Rules regarding reconsideration generally. There are few criteria in the *2013 Rules* as to how applications for reconsideration of judgments issued under *Rule 21(2)* will be considered. The question under *Rule 70* is whether the interests of justice render it necessary to revoke the judgment (see below **20.122**). It is to be expected that Tribunals will have regard to the kinds of factors that were identified in the previous case-law, albeit with an eye to the fact that particular considerations under the old rules have been removed. On a respondent's application, these are likely to include the reason for any delay in presenting a response, the extent to which the respondent can show there were reasonable prospects of successfully defending the claim (or, as the case may be, successfully disputing the amount of compensation, or any other remedy, awarded). None of these matters is likely to trump a broad consideration of what the interests of justice necessitate: see under the old rules *Pendragon plc v Copus* [2005] ICR 1671, [2005] All ER (D) 42 (Aug); *Pestle and Mortar v Turner* [2006] All ER (D) 249 (Jan) (UKEAT/0652/05), and *Thornton v Jones* [2011] All ER (D) 122 (Sep) (UKEAT/0068/11), where a default judgment was revoked despite a finding that there was no good reason for the respondent's failure to present its response on time. The general approach adopted in the earlier cases was also reiterated by the EAT in *Jarretts Motors Ltd v Wells* [2009] All ER (D) 350 (Jul). A point not addressed by the EAT in *Moroak* or *Pendragon* is what test has to be applied in determining whether the respondent has reasonable prospects of successfully defending the claim (or part of it). There is as yet no appellate authority on this point. A subsidiary point is whether it is enough that the respondent has reasonable prospects of disputing the amount of compensation claimed or likely to be claimed, even if there is no reasonable prospect of defending on the issue of liability. It would not make sense to deny a respondent the right to contest remedy where there are real issues in dispute, merely because liability will probably be established.

If it is the respondent who has applied for the reconsideration, the effect of a successful application is likely to be that the response will be accepted, and the respondent will be able to defend the claim in the normal way, but this is not automatic. When the application is by a claimant, the question is whether there are good grounds which necessitate the varying the original award in the interests of justice. As an alternative to a review application, a party may appeal against a judgment issued under *Rule 21(2)*. However, in practice it is difficult to envisage circumstances in which it would be preferable to appeal rather than apply for reconsideration. Since permissible grounds of appeal are limited to points of law, it would be much more likely in the majority of cases that grounds for reconsideration could be identified.

20.49 *Further Participation*

A further consequence is set out in *Rule 21(3)*: whilst the respondent is entitled to notice of any hearings and of the decisions made by the Tribunal, unless and until any extension of time is granted to the Respondent for presenting its response, it shall only be entitled to participate in any hearing "to the extent permitted by the Judge".

The discretion to permit participation by the respondent in circumstances where a response has not been submitted marks a major shift in the *2013 Rules*. This reflects the disquiet over *rule 9* of the old *Rules* which, read literally, prohibited a respondent from participating in proceedings (irrespective of the proportionality of that limitation on *Art 6* ECHR rights) other than by way of appearing as a witness or applying for a review of a default judgment. In *D&H Travel v Foster* [2006] ICR 1537, [2006] All ER (D) 15 (Aug), Elias P held that were it not for the availability of a review, there would be a real question as to the compatibility of the old *Rule 9* with *Art 6* of the ECHR. In *D&H Travel v Foster*, the respondent failed to serve a response in time, and a default judgment on liability was issued. The respondent attended at the remedy hearing, but the tribunal declined to hear it; the EAT held that this was an error. The respondent's attendance was an implied application to review the rejection of its late response, and it would have been proportionate as between the parties to have allowed the review and permitted the respondent to take part in the remedy hearing. The EAT also accepted under the old rules that the exclusion of the respondent from participating in a hearing convened at his or her request to review a default judgment would be absurd, and that the rules should be interpreted so as to permit the respondent to be heard at the hearing of the review, and not merely to permit the respondent to apply for a review: *Terry Ballard & Co (a firm) v Stonestreet* [2007] All ER (D) 176 (Mar); *Jarretts Motors Ltd v Wells*, above.

Rule 21(3) of the 2013 Rules gives the Judge a discretion as to the future participation that the respondent might have. That discretion will have to be exercised not only in accordance with the Overriding Objective, but also in light of the fact that preventing a respondent from participating has the effect of limiting the respondent's ability to have access to the Tribunal to defend its civil rights (*Art 6 ECHR*). Under *HRA 1998, s 3* the Tribunal must interpret the rule to give effect to *Art 6*, and further under *HRA 1998, s 6*, the Tribunal is bound itself to give effect to *Art 6* in its decision-making. The upshot is that Tribunals will need to ensure that the extent of any limitation they impose is a proportionate one to give effect to the legitimate aim of the efficient and prompt resolution of employment claims. In *Office Equipment Systems Ltd v Hughes* [2018] EWCA Civ 1842, [2019] ICR 201, the Court of Appeal observed (at paras 19-20) that, where a respondent had been debarred from defending an employment tribunal claim on liability, it would "generally be wrong for the tribunal to refuse to read any written representations or submissions as regards remedy sent to it by the defaulting respondent in good time, but proportionality and the Overriding Objective do not entitle the respondent to a further hearing. . . . But in a case which is sufficiently substantial or complex to require the separate assessment of remedy after judgment has been given on liability, only an exceptional case would justify excluding the respondent from participating in any oral hearing; and it should be rarer still for a tribunal to refuse to allow the respondent to make written representations on remedy." See also *Talash Hotels v Smith* (UKEAT/0050/19/), applying Hughes. In *Limoine v Sharma* (ibid), Auerbach J emphasised that the guidance in Hughes should of course be followed in all cases, but observed that it was to the effect that "*the fact that a judgement has been given in respect of liability on an undefended claim should not be treated as an automatic bar to the respondent to that claim being entitled to contest issues in respect of remedy*" (para 35). He went on to express caution about permitting a defaulting party to participate fully in a hearing as if they had not been in default, especially on issues of liability. He observed (paras 38–39):

"The fact that there has been no written response at all is likely in most cases to be highly significant to the practical implications of a request to participate. Further, the fact that such a party can still potentially be permitted to participate under rule 21(3) should plainly not be treated as a ready substitute for the obligation to put in a timely response, or apply for, and obtain, an extension of time to do so, under rule 20. The rule 21(3) power cannot be lightly invoked in order to subvert or circumvent the essential framework of rules which support the obvious importance of defences to claims being properly set out in a timely pleading . . . If there is a rule 21(3) application to participate in a liability hearing in an undefended case, the tribunal will therefore need to give particularly close and careful consideration to the balance of prejudice and the practical implications of allowing such participation in one form or another, if at all, in that hearing. Certainly, it should not be assumed that the respondent to an undefended claim who simply turns up to a liability hearing of that claim will easily be able to persuade the judge to allow it to participate, even in a limited way." As examples of limited forms of participation, he suggested a party might be confined to written or oral submissions, or the cross-examination of witnesses, but not the introduction of evidence of their own. Note that where a respondent has been sent notice of the hearing at which remedy is to be determined but does not attend so that judgment is given without their having participated at all, that is not an error of law: the Tribunal is entitled to proceed in those circumstances: *Chelmsford Unisex Hair Salon Ltd v Grunwell* (UKEAT/0135/19/JOJ), 29 October 2019.

It is also noteworthy that read literally *Rule 21(3)* would seem not to apply where a respondent has been granted an extension of time, but has then failed to present its response within that extended period. It would be surprising if that were the result, and one would anticipate an interpretation of the Rule whereby it was avoided.

20.50 Employer's Contract Claim

If the claim, or one of the claims, brought by the claimant is for breach of contract, or for a sum due under a contract, the respondent may in addition to responding to the claim make an employer's contract claim. It is only in cases where the claim is made under the *Employment Tribunals Extension of Jurisdiction (England and Wales) Order 1994* or its Scottish equivalent, *Employment Tribunals Extension of Jurisdiction (Scotland) Order 1994*, that such a step is possible. Under the *2013 Rules*, an "employee's contract claim" is defined to be a claim brought by an employee in accordance with *articles 3* and *7* of the *1994 Order*. An "Employer's contract claim" means a claim brought by an employer in accordance with *articles 4* and *8* of the *1994 Order*. (See *Rule 1(1)*).

Rule 23 provides that any employer's contract claim must ("shall") be made as part of the response to the employee's contract claim and presented in accordance with *Rule 16*. It can be rejected on the same basis as a claimant's claim may be rejected under *Rule 12*, in which case the opportunity to seek reconsideration under *Rule 13* applies (see discussion above).

When the Tribunal sends a response containing an employer's contract claim to the other parties in accordance with *Rule 22*, it must notify the claimant that the response includes an employer's contract claim and include information about how to submit a response, the time limit for doing so, and what will happen if a response is not received by the Tribunal within that time limit: *Rule 24*.

The employee's response to an employer's contract claim must be submitted to the tribunal office within 28 days of the date that the response was sent to the claimant (*Rule 25*). *Rule 25* also provides that if no response is presented within that time limit, *Rules 20* and 21 apply (these allow the claimant to apply for an extension of time to present a response, and give powers to the Tribunal to issue a judgement in default under *Rule 21(2)* and limit the claimant's participation in the resolution of the claim under *Rule 21(3)*).

The *2013 Rules* do not contain any ability for a claimant's response to an employer's contract claim to be liable to be rejected under *Rules 17* or *18* (contrast *Rule 23*'s express reference to the potential for the employer's contract claim itself to be rejected under Rule 20).

20.51   INITIAL CONSIDERATION OF CLAIM FORM AND RESPONSE

The *2013 Rules* contain provisions under which every claim and response will undergo initial screening by an Employment Judge to assess the prospects of success of the claims and the defences and in order to decide whether the claim ought to be permitted to proceed.

20.52   Initial Consideration

As soon as possible after the acceptance of the response, *Rule 26(1)* requires a Judge to consider "all of the documents held by the Tribunal in relation to the claim" in order to confirm whether there are arguable complaints and defences within the jurisdiction of the Tribunal.

Rule 26(1) empowers the judge to order a party to provide further information to allow him to carry out that initial screening.

The mandatory language of *Rule 26(1)* should be noted: it appears that the Tribunal must consider all the documents it holds – it cannot conduct a more summary review. Further the assessment must happen "as soon as possible after the acceptance of the response". Where an employer's contract claim is presented in the response, it is likely that the Judge will conduct the assessment after the employee's response to that contract claim has been presented, because it is at that stage that the pleadings will have 'closed'.

The first task of the Judge on initial consideration is to determine whether the claims and defences are within the jurisdiction of the Tribunal. This ought to be a reasonably straightforward exercise. The second task requires the Judge to consider whether the claims and defences are "arguable" (*Rule 26(1)*). No definition of "arguable" is contained within *Rule 26(1)*, however it is apparent from the circumstances in which the whole or parts of the claim or response may be dismissed by the Judge the question is whether the claims and defences enjoy reasonable prospects of success. The use of the word "arguable" in *Rule 26(1)* is, however, sufficiently broad so as to allow the Judge conducting the initial consideration to make other observations as to the arguability of the claims and defences, which might be recorded in the case management order in accordance with *Rule 26(2)*, even where he is not satisfied that any part of the pleading should be dismissed at that stage as not enjoying reasonable prospects.

20.53   *Claims and Defences Arguable*

Where the Judge does not decide to dismiss the whole or part of a claim or response for not enjoying reasonable prospects of success, or not falling within the jurisdiction of the Tribunal, the Judge conducting the initial consideration must ("shall") make a case management order, unless one has already been made, which may deal with the listing of a preliminary or final hearing, and which may propose judicial mediation or other forms of dispute resolution (see *Rule 26(2)*). As noted above, it is likely that a Judge may at this stage make other observations as to the "arguability" of the claims and responses in this order.

The case management orders which might be made at this stage are considered in more detail below.

Where a devolution issue arises in the case, the Tribunal must as soon as practicable send a notice of that fact and a copy of the claim form and response to the bodies set out in *Rule 98*. It is likely that this will occur at the time of the initial consideration of claims.

20.54   *Dismissal of Claim or Response (or parts)*

If the Judge conducting the initial consideration considers either that the Tribunal has no jurisdiction to consider the claim (or part of the claim) or that the claim (or part of the claim) has no reasonable prospect of success, the Tribunal must send a notice to the parties: (a) setting out the Judge's view and the reasons for it; and (b) ordering that the claim, or part in question, shall be dismissed on such date as is specified in the notice, unless before that date, the claimant has presented written representations to the Tribunal explaining why the claim (or part of it) should not be dismissed: see *Rule 27(1)*.

Where no representations are received, the claim shall be dismissed from the date specified in the notice without further order, although the Tribunal must write to the parties to confirm that this has occurred: *Rule 27(2)*. If, however, representations are received within the specified time, an Employment Judge (the Rule does not require this to be the same Employment Judge who conducted the initial consideration) must consider them, and then will decide either to permit the claim (or part of the claim) to proceed, or to fix a hearing for the purpose of deciding whether the claim should be permitted to proceed: *Rule 27(3)*. A respondent is permitted to attend such a hearing, but *Rule 27(3)* expressly provides that it need not do so.

The question for the Judge either on receipt of the written representations, or at a hearing, per *Rule 27(3)* is whether the claim ought to be permitted to proceed (rather than a fresh consideration of the prospects of success of the claim). Whilst in most cases the two concepts are likely to be treated as identical, there is perhaps scope for claims with prospects falling below the threshold to be permitted to proceed for other reasons – for example, where the case is of particular importance, or where jurisprudence is developing.

Where, either after further written submissions, or after a hearing, the claim is permitted to proceed, the Judge must make a case management order: *Rule 27(4)*. It is likely that such an order will be similar in scope to that covered by *Rule 26(2)*.

A similar procedure applies to the response to the claim under *Rule 28*. Where an Employment Judge considers that the response or part of the response has no reasonable prospects of success, the Tribunal shall send a notice to the parties: (a) setting out the Judge's view and reasons for it, (b) ordering the response (or part) to be dismissed on a specified date unless the respondent has presented written representations to the Tribunal explaining why the response (or part) should not be dismissed, and (c) specifying the consequences of the dismissal of the response. That consequence is specified by *Rule 28(5)*: if a response is dismissed the effect shall be as if no response had been presented as set out in *Rule 21* (see discussion above). This therefore needs to be specified in the Tribunal's notice.

A similar procedure for the consideration of written representations, and the holding of a hearing if necessary, applies following a notice given under *Rule 28(1)*: see *Rule 28(2), (3)* and *(4)*.

CASE MANAGEMENT ORDERS AND OTHER POWERS

Case Management Orders

20.55 *General Power*

Rule 29 provides that the Tribunal may at any stage of the proceedings, whether on its own initiative or on application, make a case management order. The Rule expressly states that the particular powers identified in the various following rules do not restrict that general power (subject to *rules 30A(2)* and *(3)* concerning postponements). A case management order may vary, suspend or set aside an earlier case management order where that is necessary in the interests of justice, and in particular where a party affected by the earlier order did not have a reasonable opportunity to make representations before it was made.

The approach under the *2013 Rules* represents a significant change from that in the old rules, which contained a list of the various orders that could be made. Under the *2013 Rules*, there is a general power to make appropriate case management orders, without the minutiae being specified. The Presidential Guidance on Case Management provides non-binding guidance (which nonetheless must be considered) covering some of these situations. In *Tarn v Hughes* [2019] ICR 76, the EAT held that *Rule 29* gives a broad case management discretion which must be exercised in accordance with the Overriding Objective. However, the EAT emphasised that dealing with cases in a way that is proportionate to the complexity and importance of the issues does not permit the Tribunal to limit the claims a complainant may pursue, other than by striking out claims that have no reasonable prospect of success (see **20.74** below). See further **20.95** below on orders that may be made at Preliminary Hearings.

It is also important as a matter of case management that the Tribunal should consider and make appropriate directions to accommodate the needs of parties and witnesses with disabilities, where that disability is made known to the tribunal: see further below **20.83A**.

If an order is made against a party who has not had an opportunity to make representations before the order is made (as when the order is made on the Judge's own initiative, or is an order against a non-party), the order is subject to the right of the person subject to the order to apply to the tribunal to revoke or vary it. Any such application must be made in writing, (if possible) before the date for compliance with the order, and giving reasons for objecting to the order. In practice it can be expected that the tribunal will notify all parties of an application by a non-party to set aside an order against him. An application to set aside an order may be considered on the papers or at a hearing ordered for the purpose (see *Reddington v Straker & Sons Ltd* [1994] ICR 172).

In addition to applications to set aside orders made without notice to the party concerned, it is possible to apply for an order to be varied or revoked. The availability of the general power to vary or revoke orders made under *Rule 29* has been confirmed by the EAT: see *Onwuka v Spherion Technology UK Ltd* [2005] ICR 567, [2004] All ER (D) 153 (Dec) and *Hart v English Heritage* [2006] ICR 555. This is distinct from the power of reconsideration, which these cases also confirm was not available for orders under the old rules. However, it is important to note that as a matter of practice a tribunal or Judge will not vary or revoke an order unless there has been a material change of circumstances: *Goldman Sachs Services Ltd v Montali* [2002] ICR 1251, a decision affirmed in relation to the *2004 ET Rules* in *Hart v English Heritage* (above) and now under the *2013 Rules* in *Serco Ltd v Wells* [2016] ICR 768. In *Serco* the EAT observed that the *2013 Rules* must be taken to have been drafted with the principle of finality in mind such that challenges to an order would normally take place on appeal. Seeking the same Judge or another Judge of equivalent jurisdiction to look again at an order or decision, save in carefully defined circumstances, should be discouraged and the expression "necessary in the interests of justice" in *Rule 29* should be interpreted in light of the principle of finality. Case law under the *CPR* and in the Tribunal indicates that a variation or revocation of an order or decision may be necessary in the interests of justice where there has been a material change of circumstances after the order was made, or where the order has been based on either a misstatement, and there may be other occasions, which it is unwise to attempt to define but these will be "rare . . . [and] . . . out of the ordinary". The EAT further held that whether or not a subsequent event amounts to a material change in circumstances is a matter of "jurisdiction" and not a question of the exercise of discretion. It is to be decided from an objective standpoint. Note however that a less restrictive approach was taken by the Court of Appeal in *Ministry of Justice v Burton* [2016] EWCA Civ 714, [2016] ICR 1128: see further **20.124** below. Note further that it will generally be in the interests of justice for the Tribunal at the final hearing to review earlier case management orders made under *Rule 50* (see below 20.89) as the Tribunal at the final hearing is likely to be in a better position (different circumstances) than the Judge at the case management stage to assess where the balance between the privacy interests and principle of open justice should lie: see *The Home Secretary v Parr* (UKEAT/0046/20/BA). However, the case of *Payco Services Limited v Sinka* (UKEAT/0134/19/OO), 15 January 2020 demonstrates that this principle does not always hold good: in that case a judge had taken a case management decision to list certain issues for a preliminary hearing. A different judge sat on the preliminary hearing. She reserved judgment. In her reserved judgment, she decided that she could not determine the preliminary issues without adding two further respondents, which she did. The EAT (Auerbach J) held that this amounted to a variation or revocation of the earlier judge's case management decision which was an error of law unless there had been a material change of circumstances. The case thus makes clear that the mere fact that a subsequent judge or tribunal has heard evidence does not necessarily amount to a material change of circumstances. Auerbach J held that the second judge should have proceeded to determine the preliminary issues unless satisfied that there was a material change in circumstances. Further, if she considered there was such a change in circumstances, she should have notified the parties and given them an opportunity to make submissions on what should happen, including whether the additional respondents should be added.

Correspondence between a party or representative and the tribunal, such as an application for an order or a response objecting to the application, is afforded absolute immunity from claims based on it, in the same way as the claim and response are immune from being used as the basis of a further claim: *Dathi v South London and Maudsley NHS Trust* [2008] IRLR 350. Accordingly a letter from the respondent to the tribunal opposing an application for costs (and also a further letter to the claimant's representative declining to give voluntary disclosure) was immune from suit as an act of alleged victimisation.

20.56 *Applications for Case Management Orders*

Rule 30 governs the procedure under which the parties may apply for the Tribunal to make a case management order. *Rule 30(1)* provides that an application for a particular case management order may be made either at a hearing or by being presented in writing to the Tribunal. It is also clear from the ability of the Tribunal to make a case management order at any stage of the proceedings (*Rule 29*) that an application can similarly be made at any time. *Rule 30(3)* confirms that the Tribunal may determine the application in writing, or order it be dealt with at a preliminary or final hearing.

Even though an application can be made at any time, the Presidential Guidance on General Case Management encourages parties to make the application in writing or at a Preliminary Hearing and to do so as early as possible (paras 12–13). Where a hearing has been set, especially with the agreement of the parties, that fact must be considered by the Judge who determines the application. Applications should state the reason why it is made, why it is considered to be in accordance with the Overriding Objective to make the case management order sought (para 15). All relevant documents should be provided with the application (para 16). If the parties are in agreement, and the application is made by consent, this should be indicated to the Tribunal (para 17). Where an application is made in writing, as well as sending a copy to all other parties and indicating to the Tribunal that this has been done (see *Rule 92*), *Rule 30(2)* requires the party making the application to notify the other parties that any objections to the application should be sent to the Tribunal as soon as possible. Prior to the *2013 Rules* a similar obligation only applied to legally represented parties. In *Jones v Secretary of State for Business, Innovation and Skills* (UKEAT/0238/16), the EAT emphasised that communication from one party to the tribunal without copying in the other party should almost never occur and required specific justification.

The Presidential Guidance indicates that applications will be considered by the Employment Judge "as soon as practicable" (para 20) and the Judge may seek further information where this has not been supplied with the application (para 20). The decision of the Judge will be notified to all parties as soon as practicable after the decision has been made (para 21).

20.57 *Sanctions for Non-Compliance*

Any person (whether a party to the proceedings or not) who without reasonable cause fails to comply with a witness order or an order for disclosure commits a criminal offence punishable on summary conviction with a fine not exceeding £1,000 (*ETA 1996, s 7(4)*).

This fact must be conveyed by a penal notice attached to any such order made under *ET Rules*). In practice the sanction of prosecution is not used (although it may be threatened for a recalcitrant recipient of an order for disclosure or to attend as a witness); this has given added weight to the sanctions available to the tribunal itself (as distinct from being dependent on other agencies for enforcement), but these are of necessity only available where the default is that of a party to the proceedings.

The sanctions (other than referring the case to the relevant authority for possible prosecution, if applicable) available to the tribunal if a party fails to comply (or is late in complying) with an order, or with any requirement laid down by the *Rules* or a Practice Direction, are that the tribunal may make an order for costs, or a preparation time order, against the offending party, or, in more serious cases, order that the party's claim or part thereof be struck out, or that a response or part thereof be struck out and/or that the respondent be debarred from defending the claim (see below). The potentially drastic consequences for a party of the powers to strike out a claim or response necessitate that such powers are used sparingly and only for extreme cases of disregard of orders or cases where the consequences for the possibility of a fair trial are significant. See further **20.74** et sec below. *Rule 38* introduces an intermediate option, long available to the courts, of the making of an 'unless' order: unless the party complies with an order by a stated date, his or her case is to be struck out on the date for compliance without further order (*Rule 38(1)*). In practice such an order will only normally be made after there has been a failure to comply with an earlier order, and the specific power in the rules to revisit the consequential striking out of the claim or, in the case of a response, to vary or revoke orders, can be used to relieve the party concerned of the consequences of an 'unless' order if it is shown that the party would otherwise suffer serious injustice. See further **20.79** below.

Disclosure and Information

20.58 *The Rule and Disclosure Generally*

Rule 31 provides that the Tribunal may make an order that any person in Great Britain should disclose documents or information to a party (by providing copies or otherwise), or to allow a party to inspect such material as might be ordered by a County Court or, in Scotland, by a sheriff. It is clear by the formulation of the *Rule* that it is apt to include orders made against non-parties as well as parties. Although the *Rule* appears on its face to be restricted to persons physically present in Great Britain, the EAT in *Sarnoff v Weinstein and ors* [2020] (UKEAT/0252/19/LA) held that, properly interpreted, it is not so restricted and the Tribunal may order any person to provide disclosure, regardless of their geographical location.

Note, however, that where the subject is in a European Union country, consideration should be given to Rule 33 (see below).

Disclosure (formerly known as discovery) is the process in civil litigation where each party discloses to the other all documents relevant to the proceedings and not protected from disclosure. The tribunal's power to order disclosure is the same as that of the civil courts under *Part 31* of the *Civil Procedure Rules 1998* ('*CPR*'), or in Scotland that of the Sheriff Court. An important consequence of this is that the scope of disclosure should be consistent with the Overriding Objective of civil litigation.

There is no automatic disclosure in tribunals – unless given voluntarily or ordered by the tribunal it must be specifically asked for. However, it has increasingly become the practice of tribunals in England and Wales, although not in Scotland, to order mutual disclosure at an early stage of the proceedings. In Scotland Practice Direction No 1 issued in December 2006 requires the mutual notification by the parties of the documents each intends to rely on at least 14 days before the Hearing (these are referred to as Productions, and the list of documents as an Inventory). The Presidential Guidance on General Case Management deals with disclosure of documents and the preparation of documents and provides that even where there is no formal disclosure order, the Tribunal generally will prefer that documentary evidence is presented in an easily accessible hearing bundle with everyone involved having an identical copy.

The formal process of disclosure involves supplying a list of all the documents in a party's possession relevant to the proceedings and allowing the other party to inspect and take copies. In practice, the parties may agree simply to supply copies of all the documents concerned.

An increasingly important element in disclosure of documents is the retrieval of emails and other electronic documents. These are equally documents, and are disclosable not only if paper copies have been put on a file, but also if retained electronically within the party's computer system (this extends to deleted or archived emails/documents, if they can still be accessed). The civil courts are developing more sophisticated procedures to deal with large electronic disclosure exercises (see eg *CPR PD 31B* and the use of predictive coding in *Pyrrho Investments Ltd v MWB Property Ltd* [2016] EWHC 256 (Ch)) which, although not directly applicable in the Employment Tribunal, might provide a suitable analogy in an appropriate case, as might the Disclosure Pilot for the Business and Property Courts in *CPR PD51U*, for cases where standard disclosure may be disproportionate or otherwise inappropriate. Disclosure may be either general (ie covering the case as a whole) or specific (ie covering identified documents or classes of documents). Parties ordered to disclose documents need only undertake a reasonable search for relevant documents. A party giving voluntary disclosure need not disclose all documents; however, a document cannot properly be kept back if its non-disclosure would render a disclosed document misleading: *Birds Eye Walls Ltd v Harrison* [1985] IRLR 47, [1985] ICR 278, where the claimant was permitted to amend his claim to add new grounds part way through the hearing after coming into possession of a relevant document in the possession of the employer that had not been included in its earlier disclosure. The same point probably applies to documents the concealment of which would render oral evidence misleading. Failure to disclose a relevant document can lead to very serious consequences, as shown by *Aslam v Barclays Capital Ltd* (UKEAT/0405/10), where the subsequent production by the respondent of a crucial document not disclosed before the hearing led to an order by the EAT for the re-hearing of the entire case.

The obligation to disclose documents is a continuing one, so that if further documents come to light, or come into existence, during the course of the proceedings, they must be disclosed if they are relevant to material already disclosed, or within the terms of an order for disclosure. This principle was applied by the Court of Appeal in *Scott v IRC* [2004] EWCA Civ 400, [2004] IRLR 713 in relation to a new policy on permitting employees to continue to work beyond the normal retirement age, which was adopted whilst the claim was proceeding and which affected the basis on which the claimant's claim for compensation for future loss of earnings would fall to be calculated.

The normal and recommended practice, where either disclosure has not been ordered by the tribunal at an early stage in the proceedings or the disclosure given appears to be incomplete, is for disclosure, or additional specific disclosure, to be requested by correspondence in the first instance. If this request is refused, ignored or not fully complied with, an application should be made to the tribunal for an order.

20.59 The test for whether disclosure of a particular document or class of documents should be ordered is whether disclosure is necessary for disposing fairly of the proceedings. This involves more than just relevance; an application for disclosure of a large quantity of documents of marginal relevance is likely to be refused on the ground of excessive burden on the other party, in accordance with the Overriding Objective, which includes the requirement to act proportionately to the importance and complexity of the case. A good example of a refusal of excessive disclosure is *British Aerospace plc v Green* [1995] IRLR 433, [1995] ICR 1006, CA, where, in a case arising from a substantial redundancy selection exercise, disclosure of assessment records of several hundred employees was refused. See also *King v Eaton Ltd* [1996] IRLR 199.

The ambit of disclosure is likely to be widest in discrimination cases, because of the need to show evidence from which inferences can be drawn (*West Midlands Passenger Transport Executive v Singh* [1988] 1 WLR 730, [1988] IRLR 186, [1988] ICR 614). However, even in discrimination cases a test of relevance still applies; further guidance is given in *Ministry of Defence v Meredith* [1995] IRLR 539, *Canadian Imperial Bank of Commerce v Beck* [2009] EWCA Civ 619, [2009] IRLR 740, *HSBC Asia Holdings BV v Gillespie* [2011] IRLR 209, *Kalu v Brighton & Sussex University Hospitals NHS Trust* (UKEAT/0609/12), and *Dhanda v TSB Bank Plc* [2018] ICR D7.

Confidentiality is not as such a reason for refusing disclosure. In a doubtful case the tribunal may inspect the documents before deciding whether they are sufficiently relevant to overcome the need to respect confidentiality (see *Science Research Council v Nasse* [1980] AC 1028, [1979] 3 All ER 673, [1979] 3 WLR 762, [1979] IRLR 465, [1979] ICR 921). If disclosure is ordered, it must be disclosure to the other party or parties; the tribunal cannot order disclosure to itself alone: *Knight v Department of Social Security* [2002] IRLR 249. If necessary in order to preserve confidentiality, the tribunal can order disclosure subject to anonymising the document and/or deleting passages which would or might reveal the identity of the author or source of a statement, a procedure known as redaction: *Asda Stores Ltd v Thompson* [2002] IRLR 245 (a case concerning disclosure of witness statements taken under terms of confidentiality in an investigation of alleged drug dealing). Further guidance as to the procedure to be followed where a party wishes to disclose documents subject to redaction is given in *Asda Stores Ltd v Thompson (No 2)* [2004] IRLR 598. The tribunal also has power to restrict disclosure to the party himself and his or her representative, and to limit the purpose for which disclosure is given to the conduct of the particular case: see the *Knight* case, above. This is in any event an implied condition of any non-voluntary disclosure of documents that are not subsequently put into the public domain by being referred to in the course of a public hearing. This point is made in the Presidential Guidance on General Case Management. When dealing with the confidentiality of disclosed documents, the Guidance emphasises that they can only be used for the hearing and must only be shown to a party and that party's advisor or representative or another witness (insofar as necessary). The documents "must not be used for any purpose other than the conduct of the case". One class of documents the disclosure of which is commonly made subject to restrictions is the claimant's medical records, and medical reports on the claimant; the tribunal may limit disclosure to the legal representatives and medical advisers of the respondent to protect the confidentiality of the claimant's medical history.

The EAT gave a summary of the above guidance for the correct approach on a disclosure application in *Plymouth City Council v White* (UKEAT/0333/13) as follows: (a) the judge must first consider if the document sought is relevant (if not, no disclosure should be ordered); (b) if it is relevant, the Judge should consider if it is necessary for the fair trial of the case. In a case of objection, the Judge should examine the document itself: *Nassé*; (c) if the document is relevant and necessary and should be disclosed, the Judge should consider whether there is a more nuanced way of disclosing so as to respect the confidentiality (eg using redaction); (d) if the Judge has read the disputed documents, he should not conduct the full hearing unless the parties agree. See further *Birmingham City Council v Bagshaw & Others* [2016] All ER (D) 166 (Oct), [2017] ICR 263.

If, exceptionally, a party cannot disclose a document without acting unlawfully, it is wrong in principle to order disclosure: see *Barracks v Coles* [2006] EWCA Civ 1041, [2007] IRLR 73, [2007] ICR 60 (a case about a police officer refused security clearance for reasons the police force was unable lawfully to disclose) and *Northampton BC v Wolstenholme*

(UKEAT/0130/18/RN) (where the tribunal had wrongly ordered the employer to disclose information from HMRC concerning an employee which would have put it in breach of the *Anti-terrorism, Crime and Security Act 2001*). However, that would not be the case if the potential unlawfulness would be unlawfulness under a foreign law: see *Secretary of State for Health v Servier Laboratories Ltd* [2013] EWCA Civ 1234, [2014] 1 WLR 4383 and *Bank Mellat v HM Treasury* [2019] EWCA Civ 449. Disclosure can only be ordered of existing documents; it cannot be used to require the creation of a document (eg by compiling statistics): *Carrington v Helix Lighting Ltd* [1990] IRLR 6, [1990] ICR 125. The restricting effect of this point is considerably eased by the tribunal's general power to order a party to provide information, which can include in an appropriate case a table, chart or schedule containing relevant information (including a Schedule of Loss, or a table giving numbers of staff classified by grade and ethnic origin – the issue in the *Carrington* case).

20.60 *Documents Privileged from Disclosure*

Certain documents are immune from disclosure. These include those subject to legal professional privilege and (with qualifications) public interest immunity. Legal professional privilege covers both legal advice privilege and litigation privilege. The former applies only to communications with and from professional legal advisers, not, for instance, an accountant, a trade union official, or lay adviser (including a professional but not legally qualified consultant): as confirmed by the Supreme Court in *R (on the application of Prudential Plc) v Special Commissioner of Income Tax* [2013] 2 All ER 247; see also *New Victoria Hospital v Ryan* [1993] IRLR 202, [1993] ICR 201; *Howes v Hinckley and Bosworth Borough Council* [2008] All ER (D) 112 (Aug). Litigation privilege has wider application, covering communications with advisers who are not lawyers (see *Scotthorne v Four Seasons Conservatories (UK) Ltd* [2010] All ER (D) 17 (Sep) (UKEAT/0178/10)) but only in relation to communications the primary purpose of which is in relation to pursuing, defending or avoiding actual or anticipated litigation; for further details, specialist works on the subject should be consulted. Legal professional privilege can be waived; guidance was given by the EAT in *Brennan v Sunderland City Council* [2009] ICR 479, [2008] All ER (D) 192 (Dec) as to how to assess whether privilege has been waived. Public interest immunity is also a specialised area of law outside the scope of this work; the leading recent cases relevant to its application in tribunal proceedings are *Balfour v Foreign and Commonwealth Office* [1994] 2 All ER 588, [1994] ICR 277 and *R v Chief Constable of West Midlands, ex p Wiley* [1994] 3 All ER 420 (overruling *Halford v Sharples* [1992] 3 All ER 624, [1992] 1 WLR 736, [1992] ICR 583).

'Without prejudice' communications between the parties are in a slightly different category, as they are in their nature already known to both parties. They are, however, not admissible as evidence before the tribunal unless both parties agree, or to prove the contents of an agreement subsequently reached, or, exceptionally, where non-disclosure of the document would lead to the concealment of 'unambiguous impropriety' on the part of the party seeking to exclude the document, or where, if the content of the without prejudice communication was excluded, an abuse of the privileged occasion would occur. Something more is required than merely that one party would be put to a forensic disadvantage: see *Portnykh v Nomura International Plc* [2014] IRLR 251 in which the EAT confirmed that the exceptions to the without prejudice rule should not be applied too readily. See also *Savings and Investment Bank Ltd v Finken* [2004] 1 All ER 1125. For an example where the exception was held not to be made out, and disclosure was refused, see *Brodie v Ward (t/a First Steps Nursery)* [2008] All ER (D) 115 (Feb). The same principle applies to evidence of oral communications conducted without prejudice. A distinction can be drawn between the fact of negotiations and their content and the former might be admissible where the latter is not: see *Faithorn Farrell Timms LLP v Bailey* [2016] IRLR 839, [2016] ICR 1054.

However, the privilege against disclosure to the tribunal only applies to genuinely 'without prejudice' communications, ie those generated as or forming part of an attempt to settle a dispute. Usually, there must be a dispute, such that the parties must have contemplated that if not resolved, the matter might proceed to litigation, although it is not necessary that either party has actually threatened litigation. The dividing line has been described by the Court of Appeal as not always clear and highly dependent on the particular circumstances of each case: *Framlington Group Ltd v Barnetson* [2007] EWCA Civ 502, [2007] ICR 1439, [2007] IRLR 598.

This area has been examined by the EAT in *Portnykh v Nomura International Plc* [2014] IRLR 251. There, Nomura announced an intention to dismiss Dr Portnykh for misconduct. Discussions then ensued as to whether the termination could be framed as redundancy; ultimately in open correspondence Nomura confirmed that it would structure the exit as a redundancy. Thereafter, there were exchanges of correspondence marked "without prejudice" about the terms of a potential settlement agreement. A draft settlement agreement was prepared by Nomura and sent to Dr Portnykh again marked "without prejudice"; it proposed to settle various listed heads of claim that Dr Portnykh might have. The negotiations broke down and Dr Portnykh brought a claim in the Tribunal for unfair dismissal contending that the real reason for his dismissal was that he had made protected disclosures. He relied on the inconsistent reasons for dismissal set out by Nomura. At a preliminary hearing, Nomura argued that it should be allowed to refer at trial to the "without prejudice" correspondence because it contended (and this remained in dispute) this would show that Dr Portnykh had asked for his dismissal to be characterised as a redundancy. The Tribunal allowed Nomura to do so, but the EAT reversed this ruling. The EAT held firm to the *Framlington* approach as to what amounts to a 'dispute' in law; it found that there was clearly a dispute on the facts: "If the employer announces an intention to dismiss the employee for misconduct and there are then discussions around the question of the alternative of the dismissal being for redundancy, no matter how amicable all that might be, it seems to me beyond argument that it either demonstrates a present dispute or contains the potential for a future dispute". The whole purpose of the proffered settlement agreement was to resolve Dr Portnykh's potential employment claims and preventing him having access to an Employment Tribunal to litigate about his dismissal. Whilst the draft agreement covered a wide breadth, it was about the termination of Dr Portnykh's employment. There was also no need for the allegation that made up the subsequent claim to have been made, nor was a degree of objection to the course proposed, or a degree of hostility to the other party an essential ingredient of a dispute. The EAT stated that where parties reach the stage of proffering and considering a settlement agreement it would very often be the case that there will be a dispute. The EAT also raised the issue of whether the without prejudice rule might also apply absent a dispute, but where there had been "negotiations between the parties" of the necessary type. This possibility arose from language used in earlier cases: see *Unilever plc v The Procter and Gamble Co* [2001] 1 All ER 783 and *In re Daintry* [1891–4] All ER Rep 209. Ultimately it was not necessary to consider the "outer limits" of the without prejudice rule in *Portnykh* and the matter is left for another case.

A communication that might otherwise be covered by privilege may lose that status in certain circumstances. It was held by the High Court in BGBP Managing General Partner Ltd v Babcock and Brown Global Partners [2010] EWHC 2176 (Ch), [2011] Ch 296 the exception to the privilege rule would apply to any "circumstances . . . which the law treats as entirely contrary to public policy". This approach was followed by the EAT in *Curless v Shell International Ltd* (sub nom *X v Y Ltd* [2019] IRLR 516), but in the Court of Appeal [2019] EWCA Civ 1710, [2020] ICR 431 it was doubted (*obiter*) whether the exception was so broad. Referring to the exception as the 'crime/fraud exception', the Court of Appeal indicated (at para 59) that it may be that the exception is confined only to cases of dishonesty rather than applying more widely. *Curless* was concerned with legal advice privilege and no reference was made to the authorities on when 'without prejudice' privilege may be lost. It appears that 'without prejudice' privilege may be lost in a wider range of circumstances. In *BNP Paribas v Mezzotero* [2004] IRLR 508 the EAT refused to interfere with a Tribunal's decision that a grievance meeting called by an employer which was then used as the occasion to put proposals to the employee for a severance package was not within the privilege, with the result that the employee could rely on what was said at the meeting to support a complaint of sex discrimination. This was despite the fact that Ms Mezzotero was pursuing a grievance at the time. The EAT so held both because there was no dispute to which the proposals were directed, and also because it would be wrong to allow the employer to rely on the privilege when the status of the meeting was first raised unilaterally after it had begun, and had not been agreed in advance. A subsequent analysis of the law by the EAT in *Woodward v Santander plc* [2010] IRLR 834 led it to the conclusion that *Mezzotero* does not lay down any new exception to the 'without prejudice' rule, but is better understood as an application of the 'unambiguous impropriety' exception, the impropriety being the act of discrimination committed in the course of the allegedly without prejudice meeting. In *Woodward* itself, the EAT upheld the exclusion by the tribunal of evidence that in the course of without prejudice negotiations the respondent's solicitors had said that the respondent would not provide a reference for the employee, a point she wished to use in evidence to support her claim of victimisation by the giving of poor references.

The privilege attached to without prejudice discussions may be waived by the conduct of a party. Thus where a party provides voluntary disclosure of some legal advice, they also waive privilege in other legal advice which is part of the same 'transaction', and fairness may also require disclosure of other advice (whether or not part of the same 'transaction') to ensure the tribunal and parties have 'the full picture': see *Holyoake and or v Candy and ors* [2017] EWHC 387 (Ch). In this respect, fairness may not require further disclosure if the party that previously gave voluntary disclosure has not deployed it in court and does not intend to rely on the material at trial: see *R v Secretary of State for Transport ex p Factortame* [1997] WL 1106141 and *Vista Maritime Inc v Sesa Goa and anor* [1997] CLDC 1600. For specific examples in the employment context, see *Brunel University v Vaseghi* [2007] EWCA Civ 482, [2007] IRLR 592 (privilege waived by making reference to discussions during grievance hearing before independent panel, and by referring to them in response form); *National Centre for Young People with Epilepsy v Boateng* (UKEAT/0440/10) (dispute about validity of agreement reached at mediation based on allegations against party's own solicitor constituted waiver of privilege by that party); and *Faithorn Farrell Timms LLP v Bailey* [2016] IRLR 839, [2016] ICR 1054 (reference to privileged material in complaint and response without either party objecting). In *Gallop v Newport City Council* [2013] IRLR 23, the EAT considered a case in which, during evidence on remedy, one of the wing-members of the tribunal asked about negotiations over a proposed compromise agreement. The EAT held that the tribunal had erred: it was wrong in principle to have admitted evidence as to compromise negotiations absent a clear waiver by the parties. The Judge should have immediately intervened to cut off the wholly impermissible line of enquiry. (This particular issue was not considered on the subsequent appeal to the Court of Appeal in this case: [2013] EWCA Civ 1583, [2014] IRLR 211.)

A separate but related statutory provision excludes disclosure of any communication made (orally or in writing) to an ACAS conciliation officer to a tribunal without the consent of the party who made the communication: *ETA 1996, s 18(7)*. In addition, parties engaging in mediation will almost always agree that if the mediation is unsuccessful, any documents produced for the purpose of the mediation, as well as anything said during it, is confidential; this confidentiality will not be overridden by an order for disclosure in the absence of the most compelling reasons. The obligation of confidentiality is applied as a matter of course to any judicial mediation conducted in the Employment Tribunal.

It is possible to restrict the 'without prejudice' nature of communications by adding the qualification 'save as to costs', to the effect that such communications may be relied on in any issue as to costs, after the tribunal has determined the claim itself. See further **20.22** and **20.129**.

In addition to the above, and relevant to unfair dismissal complaints only, the *Enterprise and Regulatory Reform Act 2013, s 14* inserted *section 111A* into the *ERA* which makes evidence of "pre termination negotiations" inadmissible in proceedings on a complaint under *s 111* (unfair dismissal). As HHJ Eady QC said in *Faithorn Farrell Timms LLP v Bailey* [2016] IRLR 839, [2016] ICR 1054, *s 111A* must be viewed independently of common law without prejudice principles and a construction adopted that is informed by the language Parliament chose to use, not the language of the case law underpinning without prejudice privilege. "Pre-termination negotiations" are defined to mean "any offer made or discussions held, before the termination of the employment in question, with a view to it being terminated on terms agreed between the employer and employee". This definition includes negotiations and offers whether made by the employer or employee. It is designed to catch a wider range of discussions than those caught by the common law without prejudice rule set out above. The Explanatory Notes to the *Act* state (para 82): "The purpose of *section 14* is to provide a means for employers and employees to discuss settlement before any dispute has actually arisen, with certainty that the offer and any discussions about it cannot be used as evidence against them in a subsequent unfair dismissal claim." That said, if the common law rules include "negotiations" absent a dispute (see *Portnykh* above) there might not be much clear blue water between the scope of the section and the common law rule in many cases. In *Faithorn Farrell Timms LLP*, the EAT held that pre-termination negotiations extended both to the fact of the discussions (rather than just their content) and also to internal conversations within eg a corporate employer (rather than just discussions between the main protagonists).

There are three exceptions to the statutory provision: first, the rule does not apply where, on the complainant's case, the circumstances are such that a provision of an Act of Parliament requires the complainant to be regarded as unfairly dismissed – in other words, where the claimant alleges automatically unfair dismissal. Secondly, where the tribunal considers anything said or done was "improper, or was connected with improper behaviour", then the rule only applies to the extent that the tribunal considers just. The ACAS Code of Practice No 4 on Settlement Agreements (July 2013) suggests (para 21) that the common law concept of unambiguous impropriety (relevant to the common law rules) is "narrower". This was addressed in *Faithorn Farrell Timms LLP*. HHJ Eady QC held that "improper behaviour" allowed a potentially broader approach than "unambiguous impropriety": the ET had first to address the claimant's contention that the respondent had failed to engage in any genuine attempt to achieve a termination settlement (whether *s 111A* applied at all) and then the contention that its behaviour was improper. In that case, the latter issue was remitted. What is clear in relation to this exemption is that the Tribunal retains a great deal of discretion: it is for the Tribunal to consider whether what was said or done was improper and the exclusion is only to the extent that the Tribunal considers just. Third and finally, the rule does not affect the admissibility of evidence on the question of costs or expenses of evidence of an offer made on the basis that the right to refer to it on the question of costs or expenses is reserved. In other words, *Calderbank* offers can still be made and referred to on the question of costs.

One issue not covered by *s 14* is the issue of waiver. In *Faithorn Farrell Timms LLP*, the EAT held that where a conversation is protected pursuant to *s 111A*, that protection cannot be waived. This is because the statute prohibits admissibility in the circumstances specified. The EAT in *Faithorn Farrell Timms LLP* also expressed the view that the correct reading of the statute meant that inadmissibility for the purposes of an unfair dismissal complaint did not mean that such evidence would be inadmissible for the purposes of any other proceedings before the ET (eg a claim of discrimination): "in such circumstances, the ET would allow the evidence to be admitted for one claim (eg discrimination) but still treat it as inadmissible for the other (the unfair dismissal claim)" – see para 38. See also *Graham v Agilitas IT Solutions Ltd* (UKEAT/0212/17) and *Basra v BJSS Ltd* [2018] ICR 793.

In that latter case, the EAT held that where there was a preliminary dispute as to when termination occurred, the Tribunal must determine that issue on all the facts, including those which would otherwise have come within *ERA 1996, s 111A*. Thereafter, it may then be necessary for the Tribunal to exclude certain evidence under that section.

It remains to be seen whether *ERA 1996, s 111A* will be an attractive source of protection for those wishing to have negotiations about termination. Given the limited scope of the provisions as compared with the common law rules, and the greater width and discretionary nature of some of the exceptions to the statutory scheme, it is suggested that the common law without prejudice rule will continue to play a dominant role, particularly where a dispute (in the *Framlington* sense) has become evident.

20.60a *Otherwise inadmissible evidence*

Where evidence has been disclosed, a separate question may arise as to whether it may be used in the tribunal proceedings. In most cases issues about the admissibility of particular evidence will be decided by the tribunal hearing the case in the course of the hearing. However it is open to the tribunal in the exercise of its case management powers to rule in advance of the hearing on the admissibility of particular evidence which a party proposes to call. This may be done where there is a dispute about admissibility based on legal arguments, such as whether the evidence is covered by legal professional privilege (see above **20.60**), or is otherwise legally inadmissible (see below), but a ruling may also be based on proportionality. Thus in *HSBC Asia Holdings BV v Gillespie* [2011] ICR 192, [2011] IRLR 209, the EAT ruled that the tribunal should have excluded in advance evidence the claimant in a discrimination case intended to introduce at the hearing as background, in order to show a discriminatory culture within the respondent bank, covering a period of 10 years going back 18 years from the date of the claim, and involving departments of the bank, and individuals, who were not affected at all by the substantive allegations of harassment. Underhill P pointed out that whilst evidence that is irrelevant is inadmissible, relevance alone is not necessarily sufficient to justify admission; where the evidence is of marginal relevance, it may be disproportionate to admit it, as in this case where admission of the evidence would necessitate the calling of much additional evidence by the respondent to seek to rebut the allegations made, which were not the substantive complaints for which a remedy could be granted. See also the EAT's judgment in *Kalu v Brighton & Sussex University Hospitals NHS Trust* (UKEAT/0609/12), [2014] EqLR 488.

One issue that has arisen in a number of cases is whether evidence that has been obtained by way of covert surveillance and/or unlawfully, most commonly in breach of an individual's rights under the European Convention on Human Rights and/or data protection legislation should be admitted in proceedings. In general, cases have been decided on the basis that covert surveillance of a person in a public place does not involve a breach of their rights under Article 8 and whether or not the evidence thus obtained is admissible is decided on ordinary principles of relevance and proportionality: see *McGowan v Scottish Water* [2005] IRLR 167 and *City and County of Swansea v Gayle* [2013] IRLR 768 (UKEAT/0501/12). However, in *Antović v Montenegro* (70838/13) the European Court of Human Rights (Second Section) emphasised that video surveillance of employees at their workplace, even if non-covert, constituted a considerable intrusion into their private life. As such, it could only be justified under *Article 8* if it was: (a) in accordance with the law, (b) pursued one or more legitimate aims, and (c) was necessary in a democratic society in order to achieve any such aim. On the facts, the Court found that the video surveillance of teaching, in auditoriums at a university, was not in accordance with law and so was in breach of *article 8*. The Court did not determine whether it pursued a legitimate aim or was proportionate in the circumstances. In *López Ribalda v Spain* (1874/13 and 8567/13) the Third Section found a breach of *article 8* where the employer had installed surveillance cameras at work to address suspected theft. However, in the ordinary courts it has been held that evidence obtained illegally may still be admitted if it is of sufficient relevance: see, for example, *Singh v Singh* [2016] EWHC 1432 and *Jones v University of Warwick* [2003] EWCA Civ 151 (in the latter case the Court ordered the party who had acted unlawfully to pay the costs associated with the application to adduce the evidence, notwithstanding that the Court allowed the application, by way of deterring parties from such unlawful conduct). In *Vaughan v Lewisham Borough Council* [2013] All ER (D) 80 (Apr), in a discrimination claim the claimant had sought permission to rely on some 39 hours of covert recordings she had made of her conversations with managers and colleagues which she asserted went to the pleaded issues. The claimant did not supply any transcripts to the tribunal. The EAT held that the Judge had been correct to refuse to admit the recordings: it was not possible to form any view on the relevance or proportionality of the proposed evidence on the material that the claimant had produced. It was not enough to assert their centrality to pleaded allegations. The claimant was at liberty to make a fresh focused application to the tribunal, producing the transcripts and tapes which she wanted to rely on. The EAT went on to confirm that although the practice of making secret recordings is "to put it no higher, very distasteful", recordings are not inadmissible simply because of the way in which they were taken.

Slightly different considerations arise in relation to the covert recording of the deliberations of disciplinary panels. This has not generally been regarded as unlawful on the basis that the individuals sitting on disciplinary panels are not doing so as part of their private life, although they have a reasonable expectation of confidentiality and there is a strong public interest in maintaining privacy for panel deliberations. In some cases, such evidence has been excluded (see eg *Dogherty v Chairman and Governors of Amwell View School* [2007] IRLR 198, [2007] ICR 135; and *Williamson v Chief Constable of Greater Manchester Police* [2010] All ER (D) 03 (Sep) (UKEAT/0346/09)), but there is no strict rule and if the evidence is directly relevant to an issue in the proceedings, it may be admitted: and *Punjab National Bank (International) Ltd v Gosain* (UKEAT/0003/14) and *Fleming v East of England Ambulance Service NHS Trust* (UKEAT/0054/17/BA).

20.61   *Information*

Rule 31 also entitles the Tribunal to order a person in Great Britain to disclose "information" to a party. There has long been this power in a Tribunal and it is used to gain additional information about a claim or response which may be required because it fails to give sufficient details to enable the other party to know the case he has to meet; or the grounds stated may be ambiguous as to the facts or the basis in law of the claim. Orders to give additional information (previously referred to as 'further particulars') are designed primarily to spell out or clarify the party's case. The rules do not state particular criteria to operate when the Tribunal is considering making such an order, however, it is unlikely that there will be a particular change from the previous practice which involved considering how the provision of the information sought will assist the tribunal in dealing with the proceedings efficiently and fairly. This is wide enough to embrace the need for the applicant for the order to know the case he has to meet, since if that is not achieved it is difficult for the tribunal to deal with the proceedings fairly. A tribunal will not normally order the provision of additional information unless a written request has been made and either refused or ignored; the main exception is where an Employment Judge on reviewing the file considers that particulars or clarification are needed for the tribunal's own benefit as well as the parties'.

It should be noted that the Tribunal has the power at the initial consideration stage to order that additional information be provided concerning a claim or defence (see above). Under the old rules, similar orders against claimants before the response has been served were made, where the Judge reviewing the claim form considers that there is insufficient information to identify clearly the claims made or the issues raised by the claimant. These are likely to become more frequent following the initial consideration that must be given to all claims.

The EAT in *Byrne v Financial Times Ltd* [1991] IRLR 417 set out general principles governing the ordering of further particulars, which it is thought remain applicable to orders to provide additional information. These include the principle that the parties should not be taken by surprise at the last minute; that particulars should only be ordered when necessary to do justice in the case or to prevent adjournment; that the order should not be oppressive; that particulars are for the purposes of identifying the issues not for the production of evidence; and that complicated pleadings battles should not be encouraged.

Particulars of generalised allegations of discrimination may be ordered more readily than in other categories of case because of the potential seriousness of such allegations and the need for the tribunal to be able to identify clearly the allegations it is required to determine. In *Secretary of State for Work and Pensions (Jobcentre Plus) v Constable* [2010] All ER (D) 190 (Nov), where the claim was of automatically unfair dismissal for having made a protected disclosure under *ERA 1996, s 103A*, the EAT expressed the view that the respondent was entitled to know what the claimant claimed the disclosure was, when, how and to whom it had been made, and how it was alleged to have led to the dismissal, and ordered particulars to that effect to be provided. However, the EAT has also held in an equal pay case that it was not appropriate for a tribunal to order the respondent to provide particulars of its material factor defence before the claimants had identified whom they intended to rely on as comparators: *Amey Services Ltd v Cardigan* [2008] IRLR 279.

Additional information may be ordered not only in relation to the claim or response as served, but in relation to any other matter relevant to the proceedings – for instance the claimant's losses or attempts to find alternative work, or, in equal pay or discrimination cases, the kind of information that was commonly sought by way of statutory questionnaires (see below). Even prior to the *2013 Rules*, the practice of ordering claimants to provide a Schedule of Loss had become relatively standard practice in all tribunal regions. This is now reinforced by the Presidential Guidance on General Case Management which, in the section on Remedies, provides that the Tribunal will usually order a statement of remedy; that Guidance sets out how such documents might be put together (see para 10ff).

20.62 *Questionnaires*

Prior to 6 April 2014, an alternative procedure for obtaining information from the respondent, or from a prospective respondent before proceedings are started, was available in discrimination cases. The claimant or prospective claimant could serve a statutory questionnaire on the respondent in accordance with regulations made under the *Equality Act 2010, s 138*. A questionnaire ought normally to have been served within 21 days following presentation of the Claim Form, or before proceedings had been started but within three months following the alleged discrimination: see the *Equality Act (Obtaining Information) Order 2010 (SI 2010/2194)*; the *Order* also enabled the tribunal to give permission for a further questionnaire to be served in the course of the proceedings, or extend time for the service of an initial questionnaire. The *2010 Order* also prescribed a form of questionnaire for use in equal pay cases. There was no obligation on respondents to reply to such questionnaires, and the tribunal had no power to order answers. Its only direct power was to grant an extension of the time limit laid down in each case for serving a questionnaire or to grant leave to serve a further questionnaire. The sanction for not answering within a reasonable time (set as eight weeks) or answering inadequately or evasively, was that in certain circumstances the tribunal hearing the case could draw adverse inferences against the respondent: *Equality Act 2010, s 138(4)*. A tribunal was not however obliged to infer discrimination from a deficient response to a questionnaire, and the EAT repeatedly warned tribunals that inferences should only be drawn from failure to answer questionnaires, or the nature of the replies, if this is justified in the particular circumstances, and not simply because of the respondent's default: see for further guidance on this *D'Silva v NATFHE* [2008] IRLR 412 and *Deer v Walford* [2011] All ER (D) 58 (May) (UKEAT/0283/10).

Following a consultation, the Government decided to repeal this route to further information – it considered that many employee hours per year were being spent in answering questionnaires, and that in many cases they amounted to a "fishing expedition". *Section 138* was repealed by *Enterprise and Regulatory Reform Act 2013, s 66(1)* with effect from 6 April 2014, except in relation to proceedings that relate to a contravention occurring before that date.

Notwithstanding the repeal of the statutory questionnaire procedure, it is still open to claimants in discrimination cases to seek information from a respondent both prior to and after commencing proceedings. In *Dattani v Chief Constable of West Mercia Police* [2005] IRLR 327, the EAT held that the same power to draw adverse inferences from equivocal or evasive responses, or failure to respond, applied in discrimination cases in relation to questions outside the statutory questionnaire procedure. In *Kumar v DHL Services Ltd* (UKEAT/0117/17/LA), it was accepted that this principle still applies notwithstanding the subsequent enactment and repeal of *EA 2010, s 138(4)* and that adverse inferences can be drawn from failures to respond to questions or requests for information of all kinds. A claimant can certainly still seek an order from the tribunal for the provision of further information where this is necessary (see above **20.61**). ACAS has produced a Guide entitled "Asking and responding to questions of discrimination in the workplace" with suggestions as to how questions should be formulated and with an example form to use.

Similar procedures remain provided for part-time workers by the *Part-time Workers (Prevention of Less Favourable Treatment) Regulations 2000, reg 6*, and for fixed-term employees under the *Fixed-term Employees (Prevention of Less Favourable Treatment) Regulations 2002, reg 5*, to enable workers or employees respectively to ask their employers to explain the reasons for apparently less favourable treatment than that given to comparable full-time or, as the case may be, permanent workers. The consequences of failing to reply or deficient replies are as used to be the case under the *Equality Act 2010*. *Regulation 16* of the *Agency Workers Regulations 2010* makes similar provision for questions to be raised by agency workers of the agency or hirer, as appropriate, with similar consequences for failure to respond.

20.63 Requirement to Attend to Give Evidence

By *Rule 32*, the Tribunal may order any person in Great Britain to attend a hearing to give evidence, produce documents, or to produce information. Such orders are commonly referred to as a "witness order". It had long been thought that an application for an order under *Rule 32* did not need to be notified to the other parties when it is made on the basis that it might be inappropriate for the other party or parties to be aware that a witness order has been sought or granted in certain cases. In *Jones v Secretary of State for Business, Innovation and Skills* (UKEAT/0238/16), Kerr J held that although an application for a witness order could be made without notifying the other party to the proceedings (*Rule 92*), it was necessary for the Tribunal to notify the other party when a witness order was made, as the making of a witness order was a decision within the meaning of *Rule 1(3)(a)* and accordingly required to be notified in writing by *Rule 60*. However, the Presidential Guidance on General Case Management dealing with Witnesses and Witness Statements (see paras 5-9) makes clear that, exceptionally, if it is in the interests of justice the other party may need to be notified that an application for a witness order has been made. *Christie v Paul, Weiss, Rifkind, Wharton and Garrisson LLP* (UKEAT/0137/19/BA) is a case where the EAT upheld a Judge's decision that it was in the interests of justice to hear representations from the respondent before granting an application for a witness order made by a claimant. In that case, the witness in question had raised concerns about the proposed order relating to her pregnancy and a non-disclosure agreement (NDA) into which she had entered with the employer and the Tribunal needed to know the terms of the NDA in order to balance the interests at stake in deciding whether a witness order was appropriate.

Rule 32 can only be used to require a person in Great Britain to produce documents, information or to give evidence. Where the subject is in another country, see **20.64** below.

An order for the attendance of a witness can be sought if the witness is believed to have relevant knowledge or information to give and the party seeking the order believes he may not attend voluntarily. In practice a witness order can be needed where an employer would otherwise not be cooperative in releasing the witness. Orders are almost invariably required to secure the attendance of police officers. An ordered witness may apply before the hearing to set aside the order and the Tribunal has power to reconsider the order granted without the witness having reasonable opportunity to make representations before it was made: see *Rule 29*. There is no minimum period of notice of the order that has to be given to the witness. It is normally for the party obtaining the order to ensure it is served on the intended witness, although some tribunal offices undertake the service of witness orders.

The granting of witness orders is a matter of discretion; the tribunal must consider whether the witness is likely to be able to give relevant evidence and whether the giving of that evidence is necessary, and may refuse unjustified requests as a part of the general power to control and manage the proceedings and in the interests of proportionality to the issues in dispute: see *Dada v Metal Box Company Ltd* [1974] IRLR 251. It is essential to assess the relevance of the evidence of the proposed witness: *Remploy v Lowen-Bulger* (UKEAT/0027/18). It is also necessary to consider whether the evidence would be admissible and not, for example, subject to legal professional privilege, although of course if the privilege has been waived by the party to whom it belongs then that is not a reason for refusing to make an order: *National Centre for Young People with Epilepsy v Boateng* (UKEAT/0440/10/CEA).

The tribunal may also properly limit the number of witnesses who are to be heard on a particular issue of fact, especially where the issue is not central to case: *Noorani v Merseyside TEC Ltd* [1999] IRLR 184. In *McBride v Standards Board for England* [2009] All ER (D) 165 (Jun) (UKEAT/0092/09), the EAT held that it is open to the tribunal as part of its general case management powers to impose restrictions in advance on the number or identity of witnesses to be called at the Hearing, not just as part of the process of managing the proceedings in the course of the Hearing itself.

Evidence is admissible only if relevant to an issue in the proceedings, and is generally relevant only if it relates to issues which are in dispute between the parties, and where issues of fact are agreed (for instance a note of a meeting is agreed by both parties) it is not necessary to call a witness to 'prove' that which is not in dispute. This may apply equally to issues of character: claimants often assume, for instance, that evidence of their good character is an important part of their case, but it would only be relevant in practice if good character is an issue in the case, and then only if it is disputed by the employer.

The use of genuinely reluctant witnesses is a matter requiring considerable care. The party calling the witness cannot normally prompt him, dispute what he says, or cross-examine him, and so may be faced with an unsympathetic witness giving unhelpful or damaging evidence that cannot effectively be challenged. There is no guarantee that the tribunal will intervene to probe the witness to rectify this, and the concept of a witness being formally treated as a 'hostile witness' is all but unknown in employment tribunal litigation. It may also be difficult to establish in advance what evidence a reluctant witness is in a position to give. For these reasons an application by a claimant for witness orders in respect of managers of the employer is nearly always inadvisable, and likely to be refused.

One way around this difficulty is for the tribunal to be asked to call the witness concerned itself; the witness can then be offered for cross-examination by both parties. The EAT has confirmed that tribunals had this power under the old rules and there is no reason to think that the position is different under the *2013 Rules*: *Clapson v British Airways plc* [2001] IRLR 184, a case where the claimant himself was called by the tribunal after his representative indicated that he would not be called. However, the power is used very sparingly, and in general it remains the responsibility of the parties to put evidence before the tribunal and call any witnesses they rely on. It would be a serious matter, quite possibly amounting to contempt of court, for an employer to seek to prevent one of his or her employees from being called to give evidence or to influence his or her evidence (*Peach Grey & Co v Sommers* [1995] 2 All ER 513, [1995] ICR 549, [1995] IRLR 363), even if no witness order has been made. Any such attempt could also be regarded as scandalous or unreasonable conduct, entitling the tribunal to strike out the response in a sufficiently clear case. The employer may, however, seek to obtain a statement from such a witness as part of the preparation for the case; as a general principle, which applies to both parties, there is no 'property' in a witness.

The use of witness statements is discussed at **20.107** below.

Evidence from other states

20.64 *Introduction*

Rule 46 provides that a hearing may be conducted, in whole or in part, by use of electronic communication (including by telephone), provided that the Tribunal considers that it would be just and equitable to do so and provided that the parties and members of the public attending the hearing are able to hear what the Tribunal hears and see any witness as seen by the Tribunal (see further **20.83**). This power may be used to permit the giving of evidence by video link or other means of electronic communication from foreign countries. However, some care should be taken because although for most countries this presents no problem, the question whether a witness may be permitted to give evidence from a foreign country by video link may be affected by the law of that country. Some limited guidance is provided in the *White Book on Civil Procedure*, paragraph 32.3.1 and paragraph 4 of Practice Direction 32 to the *Civil Procedure Rules 1998*. The *Hague Convention of 1 March 1954 on Civil Procedure* and the *Hague Convention of 18 March 1970 on the Taking of Evidence Abroad in Civil or Commercial Matters*, provide for the taking of evidence between states who are parties to the Convention by way of letters of request between the judicial authority of one country and the competent authority of another state, and for the taking of evidence by diplomatic or consular agents and Commissioners. A form for making such requests, together with information about the position of the various states who are parties to the Convention, is provided on the Hague Convention website: https ://www.hcch.net/en/instruments/specialised-sections/evidence. The Convention does not itself provide for the giving of evidence by witnesses by video link voluntarily without involving the courts of the other country, but in practice this appears to be accepted as permissible by states who are party to the Hague Convention. *Preliminary Document No. 6 of December 2008 on The Taking of Evidence by Video-Link Under the Hague Evidence Convention* explains the view of the Permanent Bureau the law of the place where the evidence is taken should govern the proceedings; in particular the administration of oaths, the laws relating to perjury, and the laws relating to contempt of court. The *White Book* states that in case of any doubt about the lawfulness of taking evidence by video link from any country (whether or not party to the Hague Convention), enquiries should be directed to the Foreign Office: sopenquiries@fco.gov.uk. The White Book suggests that it is the party who is calling the particular witness who should take responsibility for ensuring that there are no legal difficulties, although Tribunals will also wish to be assured that there are no legal difficulties.

While the UK remains a functional member of the European Union, *Rule 33* provides that the Tribunal may use the procedures for obtaining evidence prescribed in *Council Regulation (EC) No 1206/2001* of 28 May 2001 on cooperation between the courts of the Member States in the taking of evidence in civil or commercial matters (referred to in this section as the *Regulation*). This will be repealed by the *Employment Rights (Amendment) (EU Exit) Regulations 2019, SI 2019/535, Sch 1, para 14* from a date to be appointed.

The Regulation prescribes procedures for judicial cooperation between the courts of the Member States for the taking of evidence. The *Regulation* was adopted in order to make it easier to take evidence in other Member States, for it was recognised that it will often be essential for a decision in a civil or commercial matter pending before a court in a Member State to take evidence in another Member State (see *recital 7*). The *Regulation* is applicable throughout the European Union with the exception of Denmark (*Art 1(3)*). The provisions of the Regulation prevail over other provisions contained in bilateral or multilateral agreements or arrangements concluded by the Member States and in particular the Hague Conventions in relations between the Member States party thereto (*Art 21*).

There are prescribed forms attached to the Regulation in an Annex which must be used when making, executing and refusing requests. These are referred to as applicable below. In addition, pursuant to *Art 19(1)*, the Commission has drawn up, and keeps updated, a Country Manual containing information provided by the Member States in accordance with *Art 22* relating to various of the articles of the *Regulation*. This is referred to where relevant below and is available at available at http://ec.europa.eu/justice_home/judicialatlascivil/html/te_documents_en.htm. Further, in 2006, in order to give guidance on the operation of the *Regulation*, the European Commission published a Practice Guide for the Application of the Regulation on the Taking of Evidence (available at ec.europa.eu/civiljustice/publications/docs/guide_taking _evidence_en.pdf).

The procedures prescribed by the *Regulation* apply only in "civil or commercial matters". As the Practice Guide makes clear, that notion is an autonomous concept of Community Law designed to apply to all civil and commercial proceedings whatever the nature of the court or tribunal in which they are taking place. Litigation based on employment law is given as a specific example of disputes which are included within the concept (Practice Guide para 7). It is also a pre-requisite of applicability of the *Regulation* that the evidence obtained by the request is intended for use in judicial proceedings, commenced or contemplated (*Art 1(2)*).

It should also be noted at the outset that although the Regulation uses the concept of a "court" of a Member State, it is clear from the Practice Guide (para 9) that this should be given a broad interpretation, including all authorities in the Member States with jurisdiction in the matters falling within the scope of the *Regulation*. This plainly includes Employment Tribunals, as is recognised by *Rule 33*.

20.65   *The Two Types of Request that may be made of EU Member States*

The basic scheme of the *Regulation* is to permit two types of request to be made by a court or tribunal of a Member State (known in the *Regulation* as the "requesting court"):

(1)   A request that the competent court of another Member State (known in the Regulation as the "requested court") takes evidence on its behalf in that other Member State (*Art 1(1)(a)*); or

(2)   A request that the requesting court itself takes evidence within another Member State (*Art 1(1)(b)*).

The concept of "evidence" under the *Regulation* and relevant to both types of request, is not defined. The Practice Guide (para 8) refers to it including, by way of examples, "hearings of witnesses of fact, of the parties, of experts, the production of documents, verifications, establishment of facts, expertise on family or child welfare". This paragraph has been cited with approval by the ECJ in *Lippens v Kortekaas* [2012] All ER (D) 67 (Sep) (footnote 16) and *Prorail BV v Epedys NV* [2013] All ER (D) 298 (Feb) (footnote 14). In The *MMR/MR Vaccination Litigation* [2004] All ER (D) 67 (Apr), Keith J also accepted (para 9) that a request could be limited to the inspection of documents and other objects, and referred to *Art 4(1)(f)* making express reference to such requests.

In respect of both types of request, *Art 1(1)* provides that the Regulation shall apply in civil or commercial matters "where the court of a Member State, in accordance with the provisions of the law of that State" makes the relevant request. In The *MMR/MR Vaccination Litigation* [2004] All ER (D) 67 (Apr), Keith J recorded that it was not disputed before him that this meant "that the courts of the foreign state can only be requested to make those orders which the courts of the requesting states can make against persons or bodies within its jurisdiction" (para 9). *Art 1(1)* mandates that it is the request which must be made "in accordance with the provisions of the law" of the Member State in which the requesting court is situated, but otherwise does not require that the content of the request is limited to orders which the requesting court could itself make against persons or bodies within its jurisdiction.

It is not, however, mandatory to use the procedure under the Regulation where parties from other Member States are involved. The domestic courts and tribunals may continue to use the ordinary domestic powers to order disclosure of documents and provision of information: see *Secretary of State for Health v Servier Laboratories Ltd* [2013] EWCA Civ 1234, [2014] 1 WLR 4383. Moreover, that case demonstrates that they may do so even where provision of the information may expose the party to criminal penalty under foreign law.

20.66 *Requirements of Requests of Either Type*

There are some common requirements for either type of request. First, requests must be made on Form A (which appears in an annex to the Regulation) and must contain the details set out in *Art 4*. These details are (a) the names of the requesting, and where appropriate, the requested court; (b) the names and addresses of the parties to the proceedings and their representatives, if any; (c) the nature and subject matter of the case and a brief statement of the facts; (d) a description of the taking of evidence to be performed; (e) where the request is for the examination of a person, the name(s) and address(es) of the person(s) to be examined, the questions to be put to the person(s) to be examined or a statement of the facts about which he is (they are) to be examined, where appropriate, a reference to a right to refuse to testify under the law of the Member State of the requesting court, any requirement that the examination is to be carried out under oath or affirmation in lieu thereof and any special form to be used, where appropriate, any other information that the requesting court deems necessary; (f) where the request is for any other form of taking of evidence, the documents or other objects to be inspected; (g) any request for the use of a special procedure or use of communications technology or for the presence and participation of the parties or representatives of the requesting court. Where the requesting court considers it necessary to enclose documents for the execution of the request, these should also be included with Form A.

Provided the request is on Form A and contains the necessary details, the request itself and all documents accompanying it are exempted from authentication or any equivalent formality by *Art 4(2)*.

Pursuant to *Art 5*, requests must be made in the official language of the requested Member State; or, if there are several official languages, in the official language (or one of the official languages) of the place where the requested taking of evidence is to be performed; or, alternatively, in another language which the requested Member State has indicated it can accept. The languages which each Member State has indicated it will accept are set out in the Country Manual maintained by the European Commission. Documents accompanying the request must also be translated into the language in which the request is written (*Art 4(3)*).

Requests (and other communications under the *Regulation*) must be transmitted by the swiftest possible means which the requested Member State has indicated it can accept (again, see the Country Manual): *Art 6*.

20.67 *(1) Requests under Art 1(1)(a)*

Requests under *Art 1(1)(a)* of the *Regulation* are made by the requesting court (in the present context, the Employment Tribunal) sending directly to the requested court the request on Form A, along with any other necessary documents and translations (see *Art 2(1)*). There is no involvement of third parties – the Tribunal communicates directly with the requested court. The appropriate requested court can be ascertained by consulting the appropriate Country Manual (see above) maintained by the European Commission and derived from the lists of competent courts provided by each Member State pursuant to *Art 2(2)* of the *Regulation*.

In addition to setting out in Form A the other details of the request required by *Art 4*, the requesting court may:

(a)   Call for the request to be executed in accordance with a special procedure provided for by the law of the requesting Member State (*Art 10(3)*).

(b)   Ask the requested court to use communications technology at the taking of evidence, in particular by using videoconference and teleconference (*Art 10(4)*).

In both cases, the requested court is obliged by the *Regulation* to comply with such a requirement unless the procedure is incompatible with the law of the Member State of the requested court, or by reason of "major practical difficulties" (see *Art 10(3)* and *(4)*). Whenever such a requirement is not complied with, the requested court must complete Form E attached to the Regulation.

The execution of a request "shall not give rise to a claim for any reimbursement of taxes or costs" (*Art 18(1)*). However, if the requested court so requires, the requesting court must ensure the reimbursement without delay of (i) fees paid to experts and interpreters; and (ii) costs occasioned by requesting the use of a special procedure or by using communications technology (*Art 18(2)*). Pursuant to *Art 18(2)*, the duty of the parties to bear these fees or costs is governed by the law of the Member State of the requesting court. Thus in a request emanating from an Employment Tribunal, any such fees or costs should be met by the party applying for a request to be made under *Rule 33*, subject to the application of the costs rules (discussed below). Where the opinion of an expert is required, the requested court is permitted to ask the requesting court for an adequate deposit or advance towards the expert's costs. In all other cases, however, a deposit or advance "shall not be a condition for the execution of a request" (*Art 18(3)*).

Where the law of the Member State of the requesting court provides for it, the parties and their representatives have the right to be present at the performance of the taking of evidence of the requested court (*Art 11(1)*). Thus save in exceptional cases where the presence of a party/representative is curtailed, a request from an Employment Tribunal will entitle the parties and their representatives to be present when the requested court takes evidence. The requesting court must inform the requested court that the parties/their representatives will be present and (where appropriate) that their participation is requested, either in Form A or at another appropriate time (*Art 11(2)*). It is for the requested court to determine, in accordance with *Art 10*, the conditions under which the parties/their representatives may participate (*Art 11(3)*). The requested court notifies the parties/their representatives of the time and place where the proceedings will take place and any conditions of participation using Form F (*Art 11(4)*). Even if not asked specifically by the requesting court, the requested court may ask the parties/their representatives to be present and participate in the taking of evidence where that possibility is provided for by the law of the requested Member State (*Art 11(5)*).

Similar provisions apply in respect of the presence and participation of representatives of the requesting court at the taking of evidence. Representatives are defined to include judicial personnel designated by the requesting court in accordance with the law of its Member State (*Art 12(2)*). Thus, if provided for by the law of the Member State of the requesting court, representatives of the requesting court have the right to be present (*Art 12(1)*). Thus the Employment Judge and Members of an Employment Tribunal have the right to be present at the taking of evidence performed by the requested court. The requesting court must inform the requested court that its representatives will be present and that their participation is requested, either in Form A or at another appropriate time (*Art 12(3)*). As with the parties/their representatives, it is for the requested court to determine, in accordance with *Art 10*, the conditions under which the representatives of the requesting court may participate (*Art 12(4)*). The requested court must notify the requesting court of the time when, and place where, the proceedings will take place and any conditions of participation using Form F (*Art 12(5)*).

Within 7 days of receipt of the request, the requested court must acknowledge receipt of the request on Form B (*Art 7(1)*). If the request is not in the correct language, or if the request or accompanying documents or translations are not legible, this must be noted on Form B (*Art 7(1)*). If the request is otherwise properly made, but has been sent to the wrong court in the foreign jurisdiction, viz the receiving court does not have jurisdiction to execute the request, the receiving court must forward the request to the competent court of its Member State and must inform the requesting court by completing the relevant section of Form A (*Art 7(2)*).

If a request cannot be executed because it does not contain all of the necessary information required by *Art 4*, the requested court must inform the requesting court "without delay and, at the latest, within 30 days of receipt of the request" using Form C (*Art 8(1)*). The requested court must request the missing information, which should be indicated as precisely as possible. If the request cannot be executed because a deposit or advance towards expert fees is necessary under *Art 18(3)* – see above – then the requested court shall inform the requesting court without delay and at the latest within 30 days of receipt of the request using Form C (*Art 8(2)*). It must also specify how the deposit or advance should be made. Once paid, the requested court must acknowledge receipt of the deposit or advance within 10 days of receipt, using Form D (*Art 8(2)*).

Pursuant to *Art 10(1)*, the requested Court "shall" execute the request "without delay and, at the latest, within 90 days of the receipt of the request". It must do so in accordance with the laws of the requested Member State (*Art 10(2)*). Any delay must be notified to the requesting court on Form G (*Art 15*). This must be accompanied by the grounds for the delay as well as an estimated time that the requested court expects it will need to execute the request. Where the requested court has informed the requesting court (under *Art 7(2)*) that the request is in the incorrect language or that the request/documents are not legible, or (under *Art 8(1)*) that the request does not contain all the necessary information under *Art 4*, the time limit pursuant to *Art 10* begins to run when the requested court receives the request duly completed (*Art 9(1)*). Similarly, where a deposit falls to be paid pursuant to *Arts 18(3)* and *8(2)*, the time runs from when the deposit or advance is made (*Art 9(2)*).

Where necessary, the requested court must apply the appropriate coercive measures in the instances and to the extent as are provided for by the law of the Member State of the requested court for the execution of a request made for the same purpose by its national authorities or one of the parties concerned (*Art 13*).

There are extremely limited circumstances in which the requested court can refuse to execute a request. As *recital 11* of the *Regulation* explains: "To secure the effectiveness of this *Regulation*, the possibility of refusing to execute the request for the performance of taking of evidence should be confined to strictly limited exceptional situations". *Art 14* specifies those limited situations. *Art 14(1)* is applicable to requests for the hearing of a person. It provides that such requests shall not be executed when the person concerned claims the right to refuse to give evidence or to be prohibited from giving evidence either (a) under the law of the Member State of the requested court; or (b) under the law of the Member State of the requesting court, where that right has been specified in the request, or, otherwise confirmed by the requesting court (at the instance of the requested court). *Art 14(2)* is applicable to all requests and is additional to *Art 14(1)*. It provides that a request "may be refused only if" (a) the request does not fall within the scope of the *Regulation* as specified in *Art 1*; (b) the execution of the request under the law of the Member State of the requested court does not fall within the functions of the judiciary; (c) the requesting court does not comply with the request of the requested court to complete the request pursuant to *Article 8* within 30 days after the requested court asked it to do so; or (d) a deposit or advance asked for in accordance with *Article 18(3)* is not made within 60 days after the requested court asked for such a deposit or advance. The limited scope of the right to refuse is underlined by *Art 14(3)* which provides: "Execution may not be refused by the requested court solely on the ground that under the law of its Member State a court of that Member State has exclusive jurisdiction over the subject matter of the action or that the law of that Member State would not admit the right of action on it." If any of the grounds in *Art 14(2)* are relied upon by a requested court to refuse to execute a request, the requested court must notify the requesting court within 60 days of receipt of the request using Form H (see *Art 14(4)*).

In *Werynski v Mediatel 4B Spolka zoo* (C–283/09) [2011] All ER (D) 239 (Mar), the ECJ held that the grounds on which a request could be refused were exhaustively listed in *Art 14* (see §45). Similarly, the Practice Guide emphasises that "the refusal of a request should be absolutely exceptional" (§43).

Pursuant to *Art 16*, the requested court is obliged to send the requesting court without delay the documents establishing the execution of the request and, where appropriate, return the documents received from the requesting court. This should be accompanied by completed Form H.

20.68   *(2) Requests under Art 1(1)(b)*

Requests pursuant to *Art 1(1)(b)* are of a different nature. They involve the requesting court (here the Employment Tribunal) itself taking evidence directly in another Member State. Another qualitative difference is that whereas in respect of requests under *Art 1(1)(a)*, the requested court must, where necessary, apply appropriate coercive measures, the direct taking of evidence may only take place if it can be performed on a voluntary basis, without the need for coercive measures (see *Art 17(2)*).

Requests to take evidence pursuant to *Art 1(1)(b)* must be made by the requesting court sending Form I to the central body or competent authority specified by the target Member State (*Art 17(1)*). Each Member State is required by *Art 3(3)* to designate a central body or one or several competent authority(ies) to be responsible for making such determinations. These are maintained by the Commission within the relevant Country Manual.

The central body or competent authority of the requested Member State must inform the requesting court if the request is accepted within 30 days of receiving the request (*Art 17(4)*). If necessary it must specify under what conditions, according to the law of its Member State, such performance is to be carried out, using Form J. *Art 17(4)* provides, in particular, for the central body or competent authority to assign a court of its Member State to take part in the performance of the taking of evidence to ensure the proper application of *Art 17* and any conditions that have been set out. The central body or competent authority must encourage the use of communications technology.

By *Art 17(5)*, requests under *Art 1(1)(b)* may be refused "only if": (a) the request does not fall within the scope of the *Regulation* as set out in *Art 1*; (b) the request does not contain all of the necessary information pursuant to *Art 4*; or (c) the direct taking of evidence requested is contrary to "fundamental principles of law" in the requested Member State.

If the request is accepted, the taking of evidence must be performed by a member of the judicial personnel (or by any other person such as an expert) who is designated by the law of the Member State of the requesting court (*Art 17(3)*). Subject to any conditions set by the requested Member State's central body or competent authority, the request is executed by the requesting court in accordance with the law of its Member State. Accordingly, subject to any conditions, the Employment Tribunal would apply the *2013 Rules* when taking evidence in another Member State.

20.69 Expert Evidence

The use of expert witnesses in tribunal proceedings is still relatively rare, but has become somewhat more common, especially in cases where a claim that the applicant is disabled is disputed, or there is a claim for compensation for personal injury in a discrimination claim. In *Hampshire County Council v Wyatt* [2016] UKEAT/0013/16, the EAT reiterated that there was no requirement for expert evidence in order for a claimant to claim personal injury damages arising from discrimination. That said, expert evidence in such cases can often identify "whether (i) all the injury or harm suffered by a claimant can be attributed to the unlawful conduct and (ii) that injury or harm is divisible. It may assist in determining the extent to which any treatment a claimant has undergone has been successful. It may also assist in dealing with questions of prognosis." (para 28). The EAT went on that where there are issues as to cause or divisibility of psychiatric or psychological harm it is advisable for medical evidence to be obtained and that a failure to produce such medical evidence risked a lower, or no, award being made. In unfair dismissal cases there may be technical issues affecting the computation of compensation, the calculation of pension loss in particular, which may on occasion require an expert witness. (In such cases it is advisable to apply to the tribunal for an order for issues of remedy to be heard separately, to avoid unnecessary costs being incurred on experts' fees.) Separate procedures apply in equal value cases, where the tribunal may be required to appoint an independent expert; details of the applicable rules are in *Sch 3* to the *2013 Regulations*.

The *2013 Rules*, like their predecessor rules, do not provide for how expert evidence should be dealt with in the Tribunal. In *Morgan v Abertawe BRP Morgannwg University Local Health Board* (UKEAT/0114/19/JOJ) the EAT (Auerbach J) in identified that Tribunals need to consider two questions when the possibility of expert evidence is raised. First, the Tribunal needs to consider whether, in principle, expert evidence will be permitted in principle. The second is what form that evidence will take. As to the first question, Auerbach J observed that the principal long-standing authority on expert evidence (*de Keyser Ltd v Wilson* [2001] IRLR 324) actually gives no guidance beyond saying that there is no presumption that expert evidence will be permitted simply because one party wishes to adduce it. Auerbach J ruled in that case that Tribunals should apply the same test as applies under the *Civil Procedure Rules 1998* in the ordinary courts, i.e. whether expert evidence is 'reasonably required'. That is a question to be considered taking into account the Overriding Objective. As to the second question, *de Keyser* remains the authoritative guide, the main points of which are that, where appropriate, the parties should use a joint expert, or at least if one party is calling an expert the other party should have an opportunity to agree to the terms of the instructions to the expert; and where there are experts on both sides, the tribunal should give directions setting out a timetable for the experts to meet to attempt to agree, or at least define, the issues in dispute. Guidance as to when a party may call its own expert to contradict the evidence of the joint expert was given by the EAT in *Hospice of St Mary of Furness v Howard* [2007] IRLR 944 (a case concerning medical evidence of the claimant's disability): the question for the tribunal is the same as that under *CPR 1998 Part 35* as explained in *Daniels v Walker* [2000] 1 WLR 1382.

An expert witness, even if instructed by one party and not jointly, has an overriding duty to the tribunal, which takes precedence over his or her duty to the party instructing him. There are also strict rules which govern how parties should interact with a joint expert: see *Peet v Mid-Kent Healthcare Trust: Practice Note* [2002] 3 All ER 688.

In practice, the use of joint experts may be inhibited by difficulties in agreeing who pays for the expert. As the EAT stated in *de Keyser*, the tribunal has no power, beyond its general powers to award costs, to order the parties to share the cost, or for one party to bear the cost, of an expert witness. This remains the case under the *2013 Rules*. In *City Facilities Management (UK) Ltd v Ling* (UKEAT/0396/13), the EAT confirmed that it is "wrong in law and perverse" for a Tribunal to have ordered a respondent to pay the full amount of fees due under a joint expert report. However, the tribunal itself has limited powers to pay for an expert where a joint appointment has been ordered; any party seeking the appointment of an expert should make enquiries as to the availability of funds for this purpose.

For guidance as to the scope of admissible expert evidence in civil cases see *Kennedy v Cordia (Services) LLP* [2016] UKSC 6, [2016] 1 WLR 597, [2016] ICR 325. There, in the context of a claim against an employer for injuries sustained by a home carer who slipped on an icy path, an engineering consultant provided expert evidence which, as well as unobjectionable parts, included statements as to how he would have carried out the risk assessment and as to the nature of the employer's legal duty. The Supreme Court held that the evidence was nonetheless admissible but that an experienced judge could readily treat the statements as the opinions of a skilled witness on health and safety practice, and make up his own mind on the legal question.

20.70 Amendments

There is no specific provision in the *2013 Rules* circumscribing the power that the Tribunal has to allow an amendment to a claim or response. This power forms part of the general case management power contained within *Rule 29*. Further, the Presidential Guidance on Case Management contains a section detailing the usual approach taken by the Tribunal to such applications.

It is open to any party to apply for permission to amend his or her claim or, as the case may be, response. Amendments may be necessary to correct or clarify details of the particulars already given, or to add information about a claim; sometimes amendments seek to go further, and to add to the claim, or put forward a new or different reason for resisting the claim. In practice it is also not uncommon that 'additional information' provided by a party, voluntarily or in response to a request, raises new allegations or heads of claim: in such cases the principles applicable to amendments apply. The same principles apply, with any necessary modifications, to applications by respondents to amend their response, for instance by adding a new ground of resistance to the claim or taking a point as to the tribunal's jurisdiction.

The principles applicable to amendments are summarised below. The leading case on the principles applicable is *Selkent Bus Co Ltd v Moore* [1996] IRLR 661, [1996] ICR 836. In this case Mummery J set out general principles both as to the procedure to be followed in relation to amendments and the criteria governing the tribunal's exercise of discretion whether to allow the amendment. Points of procedure are covered below. In relation to discretion, Mummery J emphasised that the tribunal: "should take into account all the circumstances and should balance the injustice and hardship of allowing the amendment against the injustice and hardship of refusing it."

The relevant factors include those listed in the Presidential Guidance (para 5 concerning amendments), which in turn emanate from *Selkent*: the nature of the amendment, the applicability of time limits (as to which see (f) and (g) below) and the timing and manner of application. Amendments should not generally be denied punitively where no real prejudice will be done by them being granted: *Sefton NBC v Hincks* [2011] ICR 1357, [2011] All ER (D) 122 (Aug). When considering an amendment, a tribunal should consider the all the circumstances and carry out the balancing exercise identified in *Selkent* or risk making an error of law (see eg *Thomas v Samurai Incentives & Promotions Ltd* [2013] All ER (D) 328 (May) (UKEAT/0006/13). The Presidential Guidance highlights that Tribunals must balance the injustice and hardship of allowing the amendment against the injustice and hardship of refusing it (see paras 4 and 10(2) of the section dealing with amendments). The discretion must be exercised in accordance with the Overriding Objective in *Rule 2*.

Further points relevant to the procedure for applying, and the criteria for the exercise of the tribunal's discretion, are set out below.

(a)   A party may only amend his or her claim or response with the permission of the tribunal. If permission is given on a written application without the other party having an opportunity to oppose the application, or without the amendment having been directly considered by the tribunal (as where permission to amend is given in general terms, although this practice is now disproved (see below)) the permission is provisional and the other party may apply to have it set aside: *Reddington v Straker & Sons Ltd* [1994] ICR 172, EAT. This is expressly confirmed by *Rule 29*. Guidance as to when an application to amend should be dealt with at a hearing (usually a preliminary hearing), and not simply on paper, is given in *Selkent* (above) and also now in the Presidential Guidance on General Case Management. Normally an application to amend should not be refused without affording the party applying the opportunity for an oral hearing of the application, but this is subject to any exceptional factors that may make it unnecessary to permit a hearing: *Mouteng v Select Services Partner Ltd* [2008] All ER (D) 25 (Jun). The Presidential Guidance envisages many decisions being taken on the papers after canvassing the views of the parties (para 1 concerning amendments); it acknowledges that "in some cases a hearing may be necessary".

(b)   It is important to appreciate that the tribunal only has jurisdiction to adjudicate on the acts complained of, so that it is necessary to amend the Claim Form to refer specifically to any further complaints (and to obtain permission to do so) if they are to be relied on: see *Chapman v Simon* [1994] IRLR 124, *Smith v Zeneca (Agrochemicals) Ltd* [2000] ICR 800, [2000] All ER (D) 163 and *Ahuja v Inghams (A Firm)* [2002] ICR 1485, [2002] All ER (D) 150 (Jul). The EAT emphasised the importance of the pleadings in relation to the issues that are properly before the Tribunal in *Chandhok v Tirkey* [2015] IRLR 195 where the Judge had considered part of the issue by reference to a witness statement rather than a pleading. Langstaff P observed (para 16) " . . . such an approach too easily forgets why there is a formal claim, which must be set out in an ET1. The claim, as set out in the ET1, is not something just to set the ball rolling, as an initial document necessary to comply with time limits but which is otherwise free to be augmented by whatever the parties choose to add or subtract merely upon their say so. Instead, it serves not only a useful but a necessary function. It sets out the essential case. It is that to which a respondent is required to respond. A respondent is not required to answer a witness statement, nor a document but the claims made – meaning, under the *Rules of Procedure 2013 (SI 2013/1237)*, the claim as set out in the ET1." After acknowledging that Tribunals were designed to be accessible and that undue formalism should be avoided, he went on to say (para 17): "the starting point is that the parties must set out the essence of their respective cases on paper in respectively the ET1 and the answer to it. If it were not so, then there would be no obvious principle by which reference to any further document (witness statement, or the like) could be restricted. Such restriction is needed to keep litigation within sensible bounds, and to ensure that a degree of informality does not become unbridled licence. The ET1 and ET3 have an important function in ensuring that a claim is brought, and responded to, within stringent time limits. If a 'claim' or a 'case' is to be understood as being far wider than that which is set out in the ET1 or ET3, it would be open to a litigant after the expiry of any relevant time limit to assert that the case now put had all along been made, because it was 'their case', and in order to argue that the time limit had no application to that case could point to other documents or statements, not contained within the claim form. Such an approach defeats the purpose of permitting or denying amendments; it allows issues to be based on shifting sands; it ultimately denies that which clear-headed justice most needs, which is focus. It is an enemy of identifying, and in the light of the identification resolving, the central issues in dispute." And at para 18 he went on: "In summary, a system of justice involves more than allowing parties at any time to raise the case which best seems to suit the moment from their perspective. It requires each party to know in essence what the other is saying, so they can properly meet it; so that they can tell if a tribunal may have lost jurisdiction on time grounds; so that the costs incurred can be kept to those which are proportionate; so that the time needed for a case, and the expenditure which goes hand in hand with it, can be provided for both by the parties and by the tribunal itself, and enable care to be taken that any one case does not deprive others of their fair share of the resources of the system. It should provide for focus on the central issues. That is why there is a system of claim and response, and why an employment tribunal should take very great care not to be diverted into thinking that the essential case is to be found elsewhere than in the pleadings." These views were considered of importance by a subsequent division in *Remploy Ltd v Abbott & others* (UKEAT/0405/14) in which it was recalled that a list of issues is not a pleading (see further at **20.84** and **20.95** below).

(c)   The tribunal has no power to amend a claim or response on behalf of a party; it can only grant or refuse permission on application being duly made: see *Margarot Forrest Care Management v Kennedy* (UKEATS/0023/10). Any application to amend should set out the precise wording of the amendment proposed, so that the other party can know the claim he has to meet: *Ladbrokes Racing v Traynor* (UKEATS/0067/06). Guidance as to the procedure to be adopted when an application to amend is made during the hearing is given in the *Ladbrokes* case, where the issue was the introduction of unpleaded allegations of procedural unfairness of the claimant's dismissal. Amongst other points, the decision in *Ladbrokes* emphasises the importance of any amendment being precisely formulated before a decision can be taken on whether to permit it, and, where an application to amend made during a hearing is disputed, of the tribunal giving reasons for its decision on the point. The EAT has emphasised that it is fundamental that any application to amend a claim must be considered in the light of the actual proposed amendment. In most cases this will require the amendment sought to be reduced to writing. Blanket permission to amend without the amendment having been drafted has now been depreciated. As the EAT put it, one of the dangers of permitting an amendment without seeing its terms is that, having been given the green light to draft an amendment, a party may go beyond the terms which the Judge was led to understand might be included in the amendment s/he was permitting. The EAT thought the position might be different if the amendment sought was very simple or a limited amendment was asked for by a litigant in person. See *Chief Constable of Essex Police v Kovacevic* (UKEAT/0126/13) and *Remploy Ltd v Abbott & others* (UKEAT/0405/14).

(d)   A distinction is made between amendments which add a new or different claim, and those which merely amend the factual or legal basis of an existing claim, for instance by adding further facts in support of a claim that a dismissal was unfair. Both can be made by way of amendment: the EAT in *Prakash v Wolverhampton City Council* [2006] All ER (D) 71 (Nov) held that a new claim can be "presented" by an application to amend an existing claim as well as by the issue of a separate originating application. Applications to amend the factual or legal basis of an existing claim are admissible whenever application is made, subject to the discretion of the tribunal, which is exercised in accordance with the principles laid down in the *Selkent* case. The timing of the amendment as well as its nature is likely to be of importance, but it is possible (and not uncommon in practice) for amendments to be allowed up to or even during the hearing, where no prejudice is caused to the other party; it is likely to be relevant to establish whether there was good reason for any delay in applying to amend. The same principles apply to an application by a respondent to amend the response: *Chadwick v Bayer plc* [2002] All ER (D) 88 (Jun) (a case involving an application to withdraw an admission of liability). The focus will often be on the extent to which the new pleading *"is likely to involve substantially different areas of enquiry than the old: the greater the difference between the factual and legal issues raised by the new claim and by the old, the less likely that it will be permitted"*: *Abercrombie and ors v AGA Rangemaster Ltd* [2013] IRLR 952.

(e)   There is a fine line between a new claim and a claim implicit in the facts already pleaded, but not expressly identified as a claim. The Presidential Guidance (para 6 dealing with amendments) draws a distinction between amendments seeking to add or substitute a new claim arising out of the same facts as the original claim, and those which add a new claim entirely unconnected with the original claim. When determining which of the categories the instant case falls into, the entirety of the claim form must be considered (para 7). The Presidential Guidance (para 11 dealing with amendments) invites a Tribunal to look for a link between the facts described in the claim form and the proposed amendment. Where there is no such link, the claimant will be bringing an entirely new cause of action. In such cases, the Tribunal must then consider whether the new claim is in time in light of the relevant statutory formula including any extensions of time (see (g) below). In *Reuters Ltd v Cole* Appeal No. UKEAT/0258/17/BA Soole J specifically considered what is necessary to make something a new claim and concluded that a relabelling of already pleaded facts with a new legal label does not make it a new claim, but if additional facts are pleaded with the new legal label such that the 'new' claim involves a different factual enquiry, then it will be a new claim. In that case, it was held that a different reason for treatment, and a different causation issue, made it a new claim, not a relabelling: see paras 28–30. Examples of what is a new claim can be found in *Housing Corpn v Bryant* [1999] ICR 123, CA (victimisation in addition to a claim of direct sex discrimination); *Harvey v Port of Tilbury (London) Ltd* [1999] IRLR 693, [1999] ICR 1030 (applicant alleging unfair dismissal seeking amendment to add claim that dismissal was disability discrimination); *Ali v Office of National Statistics* [2004] EWCA Civ 1363, [2005] IRLR 201 (complaint of direct racial discrimination does not cover indirect discrimination); *Potter v North Cumbria Acute Hospitals NHS Trust* [2008] ICR 910, [2009] IRLR 22 (addition of new comparators for equal pay claim); and *Reuters Ltd v Cole* (UKEAT/0258/17) (direct discrimination because of disability was not a relabelling of a claim for discrimination arising from disability). A case on the other side of the line is *Eltek (UK) Ltd v Thomson* [2000] ICR 689, where an amendment to a claim of pregnancy-related discrimination against an employee was permitted to base the claim on her status as a contract worker; the distinction was based on the same pleaded facts and was still an allegation of sex discrimination. However, this decision is difficult to reconcile with the decisions cited above, and should be regarded as confined to its own facts. The earlier EAT decision of *Quarcoopome v Sock Shop Holdings Ltd* [1995] IRLR 353, that an allegation of discrimination encompassed both direct and indirect discrimination and victimisation has effectively been overruled by *Ali* (above). In *Pruzhanskaya v International Trade and Exhibitors (JV) Ltd* (UKEAT/0046/18/LA), the EAT held that amendments to unfair dismissal claims to allege a new reason for dismissal, whether an 'ordinary' reason such as conduct or an 'automatic' reason such as the making of a protected disclosure did not involve the bringing of a new complaint with a new time limit.

(f)   Crucially, if a new claim is to be added by way of amendment (i.e. a new claim rather than a mere relabelling or addition of new facts: see above), then the Tribunal must consider whether the complaint is out of time or, at least, whether there is an arguable case that it is in time (*Galilee v Comr of Police of the Metropolis* [2018] ICR 634 and *Reuters Ltd v Cole* Appeal No. UKEAT/0258/17/BA at para 31). This to be considered on the basis that the new claim is deemed presented at the time that the amendment application is considered (*Reuters v Cole* at para 31). Where a claim is prima facie out of time at the time of the application to amend, the Tribunal will need to consider whether there is an arguable case that time should be extended applying the usual principles applicable depending on whether the claim is one to which the 'reasonably practicable' or 'just and equitable' tests apply (see **19.20** and **19.25** EMPLOYMENT TRIBUNALS - I). Although a view on arguability may be taken without hearing evidence, if a determination is to be made one way or the other that a proposed new claim is out of time, this will normally require the Tribunal to hear evidence: see Galilee at para 109(g). The same approach should be taken as with considering the application of the time limits generally, such that save in clear cases it may be inappropriate to determine as a preliminary issue whether a claim which is subject to the 'just and equitable' test is out of time, whereas this may be appropriate for claims subject to the 'reasonably practicable' test. If the claim is out of time, permission to amend should be refused as the claim will be outwith the Tribunal's jurisdiction. If the new claim is arguably out of time, then whether or the amendment is permitted will depend on consideration of all other relevant factors, but the fact that it is arguably out of time will be a factor against granting permission to amend. If the new claim is in time, or arguably in time, this does not mean that the amendment should be permitted: the other relevant factors will need to be considered: see *Patka v BBC & Another* (UKEAT/0190/17/DM). If, when deciding whether or not to grant permission to amend, the Tribunal does not determine definitively whether the claim is in or out of time, this will remain an issue for the full hearing. Note that if the proposed amendment does not constitute a new claim, but merely involves 'relabelling' or the addition of facts to existing claims, then there is no need to consider time limits: see *Foxtons Ltd v Ruwiel* UKEAT/0056/08 (18 March 2008) per Elias P at paragraph 13. This point remains good law following Galilee: see *Reuters v Cole* at paras 15 and 27.

(g)   The position is different for amendments to add or substitute parties to proceedings. The Employment Appeal Tribunal held in *Gillick v BP Chemicals Ltd* [1993] IRLR 437 and *Drinkwater Sabey Ltd v Burnett* [1995] ICR 328 that the Employment Tribunal under the Employment Tribunal Rules of Procedure then in force could add or substitute a party to the proceedings at any time. That is not a question to be determined by the rules of time bar. The Employment Tribunal has a discretion and should have regard to all the circumstances of the case, including any injustice or hardship which may be caused to any of the parties, including the party proposed to be added, if the proposed amendment were allowed, or as the case may be, refused. The same approach applies for adding or substituting claimants as well as respondents: *Enterprise Liverpool Ltd v Jonas* [2009] All ER (D) 115 (Aug) (UKEAT/0112/09) (a case where a trade union applied to be substituted for the individual claimant in a claim of failure to consult over a proposed transfer of an undertaking). The principle in *Drinkwater Sabey* was recently reaffirmed by the EAT (Lavender J) in *Pontoon (Europe) Limited v Shinh* (UKEAT/0094 and 0213/18/LA) at para 39. However, it is notable that Lavender J in *Pontoon v Shinh* does not appear to have been referred to either *Galilee* or *Reuters v Cole*. Likewise, neither *Gillick v BP Chemicals* or *Drinkwater Sabey* were referred to in *Galilee* or *Reuters v Cole*. In the absence of any apparently significant difference between the Tribunal's Rules of Procedure as they were at the time of the *Gillick* and *Drinkwater* cases, or any further guidance from the EAT, the law at present is that a party may (as a matter of judicial discretion) be added or substituted at any time without reference to any otherwise applicable time limit, but an amendment to add a new claim against an existing respondent must take into account the time limit.

A party may be added or substituted even at the hearing in an appropriate case, eg where a manager rather than the employing company had been identified as the employer in an unfair dismissal case: *Linbourne v Constable* [1993] ICR 698. Further, a respondent may be added even if his name and address had not been given to ACAS before commencing proceedings as required by *s 18A* of the *Employment Tribunals Act 1996*: see *Drake International Systems Ltd v Blue Arrow Ltd* [2016] ICR 445, although the fact that there is no ACAS certificate for a respondent who is to be added may be a factor that goes against permitting an amendment to add that respondent: *Payco Services Ltd v Sinka* (UKEAT/0134/19/OO), 15 January 2020 at para 56. One point raised, but not decided, in *Birch v Walsall Metropolitan Borough Council* (UKEAT/0376/10) is whether the effect of an amendment to add a respondent operates as from the time of permission to amend, or from when the claim was originally brought (as had generally been understood to be the position before this case). The point is of relevance to how far back claims for back pay can be made in equal pay cases (which *Walsall* was), as well as affecting whether a point on time limits can be taken by the party added by amendment. It remains to be seen how this question is to be resolved in the light of the decisions in Galilee and *Reuters v Cole* (above).

(h)   The general view of practitioners was for some time that only matters which could have been the subject of a claim at the time of presentation of the originating application could be added by an amendment to the original claim: allegations of matters occurring after the claim was presented could not be added (since they could not have been included at the time), and a fresh application would be needed to pursue such matters as substantive claims. This view now appears to be incorrect in the light of the EAT's decision in *Prakash v Wolverhampton City Council* [2006] All ER (D) 71 (Nov), that an amendment could be made to a claim of unfair dismissal to add a complaint of dismissal occurring after the original claim had been presented. It was also suggested by the EAT that this reflected the practice in discrimination cases. Independently of this decision, in discrimination cases subsequent events may, if relevant, be relied on as evidence supporting the inference of discrimination sought to be made in relation to the substantive allegations, and an amendment to this effect may be permitted. See also now *Galilee* (above).

(i)   The EAT has applied a similar approach as discussed in (f) above to introducing new claims by amendment without those causes of action having been subject to the ACAS EC requirements. In *Science Warehouse v Mills* [2016] IRLR 96, [2016] ICR 252, the EAT permitted a new claim of victimisation to be added without compliance with the EC requirements, but in circumstances where there had been compliance with the EC requirements in respect of the original claim. The EAT observed (para 31) that "had the subsequent claim been entirely unrelated to the existing proceedings . . . the tribunal might have declined to permit the amendment, but that decision would be informed by a variety of factors, not merely the fact that no early conciliation process could have been engaged in". See also *Drake International Systems Ltd v Blue Arrow Ltd* [2016] ICR 445 on substitution of parties (above).

(j)   Where the need for an amendment arises because of the 'fault' of the party or a legal adviser that is not necessarily a reason for the amendment to be refused: "it is not the business of the tribunals to punish parties (or their advisors) for their errors" (*Evershed v New Star Asset Management* UKEAT/0249/09 at para 33 per Underhill P, as he then was).

(k)   It has been somewhat controversial whether the tribunal can take into account the underlying merits when an amendment is proposed. It is often said that this is an appropriate consideration for the tribunal under 'all the circumstances' when considering an amendment which would add a new claim. In *Woodhouse v Hampshire Hospitals NHS Trust* (UKEAT/0132/12), the EAT held that the balance of hardship and prejudice may in all the circumstances include an examination of the merits: "there is no point in allowing an amendment to add an utterly hopeless case" (para 15).

However, otherwise it should be assumed that the case is arguable. There, the EAT held the tribunal had impermissibly taken into account the strength of the evidence relating to the proposed claims when at that stage there had been no disclosure given in relation to those claims. As to considering the merits of proposed claims, see also *Cooper v Chief Constable of West Yorkshire Police* [2006] All ER (D) 343 (Jul) (UKEAT/0035/06) at para 17.

Parties and Participation in Proceedings

20.71 *Addition, Substitution and Removal of Parties*

By *Rule 34*, the Tribunal may, on its own initiative, or on application of a party or any other person wishing to become a party, add any person as a party (by way of substitution or otherwise), if it appears that there are issues between that person and any of the existing parties falling within the jurisdiction of the Tribunal which it is in the interests of justice to have determined in the proceedings. The Tribunal may remove any party apparently wrongly included.

The Presidential Guidance on General Case Management (see from para 16–21 on the section concerning amendments) deals with adding or removing parties. The Guidance clarifies that asking to add a party is an application to amend the claim and the Tribunal will need to consider the type of amendment sought and particularly whether it is in response to a clerical error, an amendment which adds new labels to facts already set out, or whether it is a more fundamental amendment (para 17). The Guidance further indicates that applications to add parties should be done promptly (para 18). Applicants for such an order should set out in the application the name and the address of the party who it is wished to be added, and the application should say why they are liable for something that has been claimed. Also, the applicant should explain when s/he knew of the need to add the party and what action s/he took since that date (para 18). Similarly, applications to remove any party wrongly included should be made promptly after proceedings are served on them (para 19). A party can be removed from proceedings if the claimant has settled with them, or otherwise no longer wishes to proceed against them (para 20).

It is sometimes necessary for a claimant to apply to join one or more additional respondents to the claim. This may arise, for instance, where the respondent originally named disputes that it is or was the employer, or an issue arises as to whether the claimant's employment was transferred to a third party following a transfer of the former employer's undertaking. For other examples, see para 16 of the Presidential Guidance. The addition or substitution of parties by amendment is discussed further at **20.70(g)** above; note that normal time limits, and the normal requirement to notify ACAS before commencing proceedings, are no bar to adding an additional respondent (although the fact that there is no ACAS certificate for a respondent who is to be added may be a discretionary factor that goes against permitting an amendment to add that respondent: *Payco Services Ltd v Sinka* (UKEAT/0134/19/OO), 15 January 2020 at para 56).

Under the previous rules, a distinction was drawn between the ability to add a person on the basis that that person may be liable for the remedy claimed, and also a related power to join a person as a party, even though no remedy is claimed against the person if they have an interest in the outcome of proceedings (*Rule 10(2)(k)* and *(r)* of the old *2004 Rules*). The latter option was used for special cases where, for example, it was thought in accordance with justice for an interested third party such as a trade union to be joined where a claim is in the nature of a test case with implications for its members generally, or for press organisations to be joined in order to apply for the revocation of a restricted reporting order (see **20.90**).

Under the old rules, the EAT held that a Judge could not join a third party on his own initiative; such a party could only be joined on an application by an existing party to the proceedings who wishes to make a claim against the party to be joined, or on application by the person seeking to be joined: *Beresford v Sovereign House Estates Ltd* [2012] ICR D9, [2012] All ER (D) 159 (Jan). (The position was different if a claim had been brought by the wrong claimant and there was an application to substitute the correct claimant: an example is *Enterprise Liverpool Ltd v Jonas* [2009] All ER (D) 115 (Aug), where the correct claimant for compensation for failure to consult employees affected by the transfer of an undertaking was the union, not the individual employee who had brought the initial claim: see further **20.70**(k).)

Under the *2013 Rules*, the position is now clear. There are no limits to the exercise of the power under *Rule 34*. Indeed, the Presidential Guidance (para 21) states that a Tribunal may permit any person to participate in proceedings on such terms as may be specified in respect of any matter in which that person has a legitimate interest. This could involve where they will be liable for any remedy awarded, as well as other situations where the findings made directly affect them. When either the employer or the complainant claims that dismissal was due to union pressure (see UNFAIR DISMISSAL – III (56)) a tribunal must grant an application to join the union as a party to proceedings if it is made before the hearing of the complaint, and may do so if the application is made after the commencement of the hearing but before an award is made (*TULR(C)A 1992, s 160(1), (2)*); the tribunal then has the power to order that the party joined pay some or all of any compensation awarded. A similar procedure operates under the *Transfer of Undertakings (Protection of Employment) Regulations 2006, reg 15(5)*), where a transferor facing a complaint of failure to inform employee representatives of measures envisaged by the transferee, who intends to allege that this was due to the default of the transferee in breach of *reg 13(4)*), must notify the transferee of this intention; in this case, notification automatically makes the transferee a party and no order of the tribunal is necessary (but the tribunal must be advised of the joinder so that the transferee can be informed of the hearing, etc).

In deciding whether it is necessary to add or substitute a particular party in a discrimination case, consideration will need to be given to the nature of the liability of joint tortfeasors or co-respondents. See further **14.13** DISCRIMINATION AND EQUAL OPPORTUNITIES – III (14). It is open to a respondent, as well as the claimant, to apply to have a further respondent joined, as was done in *Finlay v Cyron* (UKEAT/0121/11) (employer applying to join former manager alleged to have been the person responsible for the discrimination alleged by claimant).

It should be noted that a substantive change in the name or identity of a party will necessitate an adjournment of the proceedings to enable the newly identified party to attend the hearing: see *Johanson t/a Kaleidascope Child Care* (UKEAT/0541/10), where the claim was against a limited company, but (in its absence) the tribunal agreed to change the name of the respondent to that of an individual trading in the name of the company. In general, it is better for all such applications to be dealt with in advance of the final hearing in order to avoid the risk of a postponement.

20.72 *Participation of Other Persons*

Rule 35 provides that the Tribunal may permit any person to participate in proceedings, on such terms as may be specified, in respect of any matter in which that person has a legitimate interest. This is a further power in the Tribunal to permit non-parties to participate in proceedings for particular purposes. It would be appropriate, for example, for non-parties potentially affected by orders sought to be permitted to make representations on the application, without necessarily needing to become a party to the action.

The Secretary of State is entitled to appear and be heard at any hearing in relation to proceedings which may involve a payment out of the National Insurance Fund and is to be treated as a party for the purposes of the *2013 Rules* in such cases: see *Rule 96*.

As to parties in claims relating to a term of a collective agreement under *Equality Act 2010, s 146(1)*, see *Rule 97* which deems persons to be respondents, whether or not identified in the claim. Such persons include the claimant's employer, every organisation of employers and organisations of workers which would negotiate a variation if the terms of the collective agreement were varied voluntarily.

20.73 *Multiple Parties and Lead Cases*

There are many cases which come to the Tribunal which involve more than two parties. These can span cases of a couple of claimants arising from the same facts, to claims brought by an entire workforce of many thousand employees against the same or a variety of respondents. The Tribunal will have to decide how best to manage such cases in light of the Overriding Objective and the particular features of the cases in question.

Consolidation

One option is for the tribunal to order that two or more claims be heard together. This power is part of the Tribunal's general case management power: *Rule 29*. This is often referred to as consolidation of the proceedings. In practice an order is likely to be made if the same question of law or fact arises in each case, or if the remedy claimed in them arises out of the same set of facts, such as if several workers claim redundancy payments on the closure of a business, or if for some other reason it is desirable to hear the claims together. Consolidation will also normally be appropriate if a claimant has brought more than one claim against the same respondent. The parties should have an opportunity to make representations before such an order is made.

Representative claimants or respondents

Where many people have the same interest in defending a claim, one or more of them may be cited as the person or persons against whom relief is sought, or may be authorised by the tribunal, before or at the hearing, to defend on behalf of all the persons so interested. This was formerly expressly provided for by the *2001 Rules, rule 19(3)*. There is no equivalent express provision in the *2013 Rules*, but the general case management powers of the tribunal are sufficiently wide to cover the point (and see *Affleck v Newcastle Mind* [1999] IRLR 405: claim against one member of a committee of unincorporated association on behalf of all the members of the committee).

Lead test cases

If there are a large number of claims raising the same question, some may be selected as lead, or test, cases. The large numbers of multiple claims for equal pay which have been brought against local authorities and NHS Trusts have usually required the selection of test cases, and a high level of active case management, to keep the issues to be heard by the tribunal within manageable limits. The general principles applicable to imposing a lead case regime can be found in *Ashmore v British Coal Corpn* [1990] IRLR 283, [1990] ICR 485, and contrast *Department of Education and Science v Taylor* [1992] IRLR 308. These general principles are now subject to the express provision contained in *Rule 36*. Pursuant to *Rule 36(1)*, where a Tribunal considers that two or more claims give rise to common or related issues of fact or law, the Tribunal or the President may make an order specifying one or more of those claims as a lead case and staying (or in Scotland sisting) the other claims, which are known as "the related cases". When the Tribunal later makes a decision in respect of the common or related issue in the lead case(s), it must send a copy of that decision to each party in each of the related cases: *Rule 36(2)*. That determination is binding on the parties in the related cases (*Rule 36(2)*) except where, within 28 days of the date on which the Tribunal sent a copy of the decision, a party in the related cases applies in writing for an order that the decision does not apply to, and is not binding on the parties to, a particular related case (*Rule 36(3)*). For an example, see *Engel v Ministry of Justice* [2017] ICR 277 rejecting an argument that the claim should be differentiated from the test case.

Rule 36(4) deals with lead cases dropping out during the course of group litigation. If a lead case is withdrawn before the Tribunal makes a decision in respect of the common or related issues, it shall make an order as to (a) whether another claim is to be specified as a lead case; and (b) whether any order affecting the related cases should be set aside or varied.

Striking Out

20.74 *The Rule in Outline*

Rule 37 permits a Tribunal to strike out all or part of a claim or a response, at any stage of the proceedings, and either on its own initiative or on the application of a party. The Tribunal can only however do so on one of the grounds set out in *Rule 37(1)*. The grounds are that:

(a)   the claim or response, (or part thereof) is scandalous or vexatious or has no reasonable prospect of success;

(b)   the manner in which the proceedings have been conducted by or on behalf of the claimant or the respondent (as the case may be) has been scandalous, unreasonable or vexatious;

(c)   there has been non-compliance with any of the Rules or with an order of the Tribunal;

(d)   that the claim or response has not been actively pursued;

(e)   that the Tribunal considers that it is no longer possible to have a fair hearing in respect of the claim or response (or the part to be struck out).

Rule 37(2) contains important procedural safeguards: a claim or response may not be struck out unless the party in question has been given a reasonable opportunity to make representations, either in writing or, if requested by the party, at a hearing (see *Beacard Property Management and Construction Ltd v Day* [1984] ICR 837). In practice any decision to strike out is likely to be taken at a preliminary hearing (although the issue may also arise at the hearing).

If a response is struck out, the effect is as if no response had been presented such that *Rule 21* applies (see above): *Rule 37(3)*. This provision is required because striking out a response does not by itself bring proceedings to an end.

It has been seen above (20.53) that upon initial consideration, an Employment Judge is required to consider the arguability of every claim and defence. A dismissal notice may be given where the Judge considers that the claim or defence does not enjoy "reasonable prospects of success". This procedure might well have a knock-on effect on the frequency with which applications for strike out are put before a Tribunal, although there is nothing in principle to prevent this even where – on the material then available, and without submissions from all the parties – the Judge on initial consideration did not make a proposal to dismiss the claim or defence.

20.75 *Prospects of Success*

The power to strike out a party's case as having no reasonable prospect of success was introduced by the *2001 Regulations*. The power is comparable to the power of the High Court under *Part 24* of the *CPR 1998* to give summary judgment where a case has no real prospect of success, as to which there is helpful guidance in *Swain v Hillman* [2001] 1 All ER 91, CA. The standard of "reasonable prospect of success" is, however, a higher threshold than that of a "real prospect". A tribunal is usually unlikely to entertain an application to strike out the claim or response at a preliminary hearing in factually contentious cases, since tribunals are reluctant to deny a party the opportunity to put his or her case to the tribunal except on the strongest grounds. The drastic nature of the power justifies caution in its exercise; the tribunal has a discretion to strike out, and is not required automatically to do so merely because it determines that the claim (or defence) has no reasonable prospects of success. It must also consider whether it is just to proceed to strike out in all the circumstances, rather than allowing the case to proceed to a full hearing or taking other, less draconian steps to elucidate the nature of the claims or making a deposit order: see *Parkin v Leeds City Council* (UKEAT/0178/19/RN) at para 8 per HHJ Shanks. In that case, having decided that the Tribunal Judge had been wrong to strike out a prolix and poorly pleaded claim, HHJ Shanks observed that in cases where a litigant in person has been unable properly to plead their case, but it is possible to discern matters that might in principle constitute proper claims, *"the best answer may be to just list them for a Full Hearing at the earliest opportunity and not keep making interim orders that are appealed . . . That way the Claimant is able to give evidence, tell her story facts are decided upon, and then the results of those can be adjudicated on"*.

The importance of not striking out discrimination cases in particular in any but the clearest of cases has been reinforced by dicta in the House of Lords: *Anyanwu v South Bank Students' Union* [2001] UKHL 14, [2001] IRLR 305 (see Lord Steyn at para 24, Lord Hope at para 39). See also *Balamoody v UK Central Council for Nursing, Midwifery and Health Visiting* [2001] EWCA Civ 2097, [2002] IRLR 288, [2002] ICR 646, paras 31–50; *HM Prison Service v Dolby* [2003] IRLR 694 and *Adebowale v Isban UK Ltd* (2015) UKEAT/0068/15, [2015] All ER (D) 127 (Aug) and, for a similar approach to whistle-blowing cases, *Boulding v Land Securities Trillium Ltd*, [2006] All ER (D) 158 (Nov), EAT, and *Ezsias v North Glamorgan NHS Trust* [2007] EWCA Civ 330, [2007] 4 All ER 940, [2007] ICR 1126, [2007] IRLR 603. The Court of Appeal in *Ezsias*, which has come to be regarded as the leading case on striking out claims as misconceived, emphasised that it would only be in exceptional cases that it would be appropriate to strike out a claim where the central facts were in dispute and the evidence relating to them had not been heard; an example of an exceptional situation might be where the facts asserted by one party were clearly and directly contradicted by contemporaneous documentation. The Court therefore emphasised that what mattered was the nature of the dispute of fact.

The approach applied in *Ezsias* was affirmed by the Court of Appeal in *A v B and C* [2010] EWCA Civ 1378, [2010] All ER (D) 101 (Dec), where the court refused to strike the claim out despite evident weaknesses in it, because there were significant factual issues which could only be resolved by evidence. In *Timbo v Greenwich Council for Racial Equality* [2012] All ER (D) 136 (Oct) (UKEAT/0160/12) the EAT overturned a decision to strike out in a discrimination claim as misconceived even though the application was made at the end of the Claimant's evidence at the final hearing and after the Respondent's statements had been read by the tribunal. The tribunal ought to have evaluated the core factual dispute in light of all the evidence. As the EAT said: "It is one thing to reach, at the half time stage, a provisional view that a witness's evidence is unsatisfactory and that it is unlikely to be accepted if there is evidence to the contrary. It is another thing altogether to reach a concluded view that a witness's evidence must inevitably be rejected in its entirety even if there is no evidence to contradict it" (para 48). In *Romanowska v Aspirations Care Limited* [2014] UKEAT/0015/14, there was an application to strike out a claim for automatic unfair dismissal based on the reason for the dismissal being the making of protected disclosures. The EAT held that "where the reason for dismissal is the central dispute between the parties, it will be very rare indeed that that dispute can be resolved without hearing from the parties who actually made the decision" (para 15).

The above having been said, the Court of Appeal has held that a Tribunal should not be deterred from striking out claims, even where there are disputed facts, provided that it can be established that there was no reasonable prospect of success: see *Ahir v British Airways Plc* [2017] EWCA Civ 1392. An example of the striking out of a discrimination claim where the factual basis for inferring discrimination was considered to be simply too weak to establish an arguable case is *ABN AMRO Management Services Ltd v Hogben* (UKEAT/0266/09), where a claim of age discrimination (in selecting employees for alternative posts in a redundancy situation) relied on comparators both younger and older than the claimant. Where the claim as pleaded is legally misconceived, striking out is fully justified; good recent examples are *Hadfield v Health and Safety Executive* (UKEATS/0013/10) and *Hawkins v Atex Group Ltd* [2012] IRLR 807. An exceptional case in which strike-out under *rule 37(1)(a)* part-way through a hearing was appropriate was *Leslie v Imperial College Healthcare NHS Trust* (UKEAT/0204/19/JOJ) where the Claimant had refused to continue to participate in proceedings. The burden of proof was on the Claimant so unless he gave evidence his claims were doomed to failure. The EAT held the claim could legitimately be struck out in those circumstances (although the Tribunal had in fact failed to identify that it was the strike-out power it was using).

A possible solution to the problem in cases involving factual disputes is exemplified by *Eastman v Tesco Stores Ltd* [2012] All ER (D) 264 (Nov). There, the tribunal heard evidence on the core area of factual dispute at the preliminary hearing dealing with the strike out application (the core issue was whether there had been express agreement to employment continuing through a four year career break). Having heard that evidence, and resolved it against the claimant, the tribunal struck out the complaint for having no reasonable prospects of success. The EAT endorsed that approach and distinguished the case from those where no evidence is heard at the preliminary hearing and the factual disputes remain unresolved at the preliminary hearing. In this respect, it should be remembered that evidence must be heard if an Employment Tribunal is to determine such questions as whether there is a 'continuing act' for the purposes of a discrimination claim: while a view as to the prospects of success may be taken on the basis of the pleadings (and thus in principle a case struck out where it is considered there is no reasonable prospect of establishing a 'continuing act'), ordinarily it will not be possible to determine such a question as a matter of fact without hearing evidence and it will be an error of law to purport to do so: *Caterham School Limited v Rose* (UKEAT/0149/19/RN).

The Court of Appeal has held that where the central issue is the construction of a written contract, one must be careful not to take the suggestion that the case should be determined at trial with fuller investigation into the facts too far. Whilst the factual matrix is key to understanding what the parties must have intended by the words they used, it far from follows that the need to know what that matrix was requires a full trial with discovery, evidence and cross examination: see Jacob LJ at paras 4–5 in *Khatri v Cooperateive Centrale RaifeisenBoerenleenbank BA* [2010] IRLR 715 (a case involving summary judgment under the *CPR 1998*); see also *Qantas Cabin Crew (UK) Ltd v Alsopp* [2013] All ER (D) 246 (Dec) (UKEAT/0318/13).

As striking out is a more drastic remedy – what has been described as showing the 'Red card' (as compared to the 'Yellow card' of a deposit order and costs warning: see *HM Prison Service v Dolby* [2003] IRLR 694) – tribunals can be expected to consider the merits of the case more rigorously when considering that sanction. It is open to a party (and advisable in practice) to apply for both a deposit and strike out in the alternative. *Deer v University of Oxford* [2015] EWCA Civ 52, [2015] IRLR 481 is an example of a case in which deposit orders were substituted by the Court of Appeal for a strike out of certain victimisation claims where there remained reasonable prospects of success.

20.76 *The Conduct of Proceedings; Compliance with Rules and Orders*

The Grounds for a strike out under *Rule 37(b)* and *(c)* are related: the former concerns the situation where the manner in which proceedings have been conducted by or on behalf of the claimant or respondent has been scandalous, unreasonable or vexatious, whereas the latter concerns specific identifiable non-compliance with Rules or Orders. As the EAT explained in *Harris v Academies Enterprise Trust* [2015] IRLR 208, "A party that does not observe an order is at the mercy of the tribunal. Though in many cases an unless order will be granted before there is a strike-out, it is not an essential prerequisite of an application to strike out and is no guarantee that one will not follow in an appropriate case." (para 35).

The conduct of a representative, as well as a party, may be grounds for striking out the party's case under *Rule 37(1)(b)* above, and it is not easily open to the party to 'disown' the representative: *Harmony Healthcare plc v Drewery* [2000] All ER (D) 1302 (EAT/866/00) (respondent's representative assaulting claimant's representative in waiting room). In *Harris*, the EAT reviewed the authorities (para 43) and noted that what is done in a party's name is done "presumptively, but not irrebuttably" on that party's behalf and that there were good reasons why a court should not ordinarily distinguish between a litigant and his advisors. There, the conduct of the respondent and representative viewed as a whole crossed the threshold for an award of costs, but the EAT upheld the Judge's decision to distinguish between representative and client when it came to the exercise of discretion (see below). The same is not necessarily true of a witness since 'not every witness is the personal responsibility of the party for whom he or she gives evidence': *E&O Laboratories v Miller* (UKEATS/0007/19/SS) at para 19 *per* Lord Summers.

The tribunal should only use the drastic sanction of striking out a claim or defence if this is a proportionate response to the offence: *Bennett v Southwark London Borough Council* [2002] EWCA Civ 223, [2002] IRLR 407, a case with helpful guidance on what constitutes 'scandalous' conduct. See also *Bolch v Chipman* [2004] IRLR 140, where guidance was given by the EAT both as to the procedure to be followed and the basis for making a strike-out order, in a case where the unreasonable conduct alleged was a threat of violence. The EAT stressed that the ground for striking out is not simply unreasonable behaviour but conducting the proceedings in an unreasonable manner. In *Gainford Care Homes Ltd v Tipple & Another* [2016] EWCA Civ 382, [2016] All ER (D) 112 (Apr), an employer was debarred from taking any further part in proceedings because of seriously intimidating conduct towards key witnesses. Whilst such a debarring order needed to be proportionate, an appeal to the EAT had only been based on a reasons challenge, and a subsequent appeal to the Court of Appeal could not go behind that limit. The reasons provided had been adequate.

Even where there has been unreasonable conduct on the part of a party or representative, the tribunal must still consider whether striking out the claim or response would be a proportionate sanction, and in particular whether a fair trial is still possible (in which case striking out would rarely be proportionate). The Court of Appeal has commented that it will only be in a very unusual case that it would be justified to strike out on procedural grounds a claim which has reached the point of trial: *James v Blockbuster Entertainment Ltd* [2006] EWCA Civ 684, [2006] IRLR 630. These sentiments were reiterated by the EAT in *Arriva London North Ltd v Maseya* [2016] UKEAT/0096/16. An example of a case where striking out was held to be justified because a fair trial was no longer possible (because of intimidation of the claimant by a director of the respondent outside the tribunal) is *Force One Utilities Ltd v Hatfield* [2009] IRLR 45, EAT. See also *Ahmed v Bedford Borough Council* [2013] All ER (D) 188 (Sep) (UKEAT/0064/13) where the EAT found an error of law where a Tribunal failed to consider whether a fair trial was still possible and whether a less draconian sanction was more appropriate in a case where the claimant in a multi-ground discrimination case failed to comply with an order that he undergo an examination by an appropriate expert relevant to the disability discrimination claim. In *Harris* (a case where witness statements in a discrimination case had not been exchanged in breach of the Tribunal's order), a Judge's decision to separate the actions of the respondent teachers, facing serious allegations of discrimination, from the acts of their representative, when refusing to strike out the response was upheld by the EAT. There was evidential material before the Judge that justified him concluding that the representative's actions were not a reflection of instructions from his clients and the prejudice of findings of discrimination without an opportunity to answer was seen as significant. In *Chidzoy v BBC* (UKEAT/0097/17), the EAT upheld a Tribunal's decision to strike out a claim based on the claimant discussing her case with a journalist during an adjournment whilst still under oath. The EAT considered that the Tribunal was entitled to find the conduct unreasonable, that a fair trial was no longer possible, and that a strike out was proportionate.

The Presidential Guidance on General Case Management (see paras 8–13 of the section concerning concluding cases without a hearing) emphasises that in some cases parties apply for a strike out of the opponent at every perceived breach of the rules. This is not a satisfactory method of managing a case and such applications are rarely successful. The Tribunal must exercise the power of strike out in light of the Overriding Objective and in proportion to what has occurred and the matters in dispute.

The question what amounts to unreasonable or vexatious conduct may arise in relation to the claimant's persistence in a claim when the respondent is prepared to concede all or part of the claim. In this connection it is important to remember that the remedies available to the claimant may include a declaration (that he has been unlawfully discriminated against, or unfairly dismissed) as well as compensation. Thus, it has been held not to be vexatious for a claimant to pursue his claim for unfair dismissal even after the respondent has offered to pay the maximum sum which the tribunal could award, so long as the respondent has not admitted that the dismissal was unfair (*Telephone Information Services Ltd v Wilkinson* [1991] IRLR 148). In *Nicolson Highlandwear v Nicolson* [2010] IRLR 859, the EAT held in awarding expenses to the respondent that it was unreasonable of a claimant to pursue a claim of unfair dismissal leading to a finding that the dismissal was procedurally unfair but with a nil award of compensation, but the *Wilkinson* case was not cited and the authority of *Nicolson* on this point is therefore doubtful. On the other hand, a claimant who decides at the last moment to withdraw a claim, thereby causing the respondent unnecessary work and expense in preparing for the case, may well be held to have acted unreasonably in delaying the withdrawal: *McPherson v BNP Paribas (London Branch)* [2004] EWCA Civ 569, [2004] 3 All ER 266, [2004] IRLR 558 (a case on liability for costs in such circumstances).

Where res judicata or issue estoppel (see **20.125** below) does not apply, the party seeking an order to strike out the other party's case must show that there is a special reason why relitigation of the issue would be an abuse of process and therefore vexatious (*Department of Education and Science v Taylor* [1992] IRLR 308; and see *Blaik v Post Office* [1994] IRLR 280 and *Staffordshire County Council v Barber* [1996] IRLR 209, [1996] ICR 379 on the principles applicable where a claimant who has failed in, or withdrawn, a claim under domestic law attempts to pursue the same point by way of a claim based on EU law).

20.77 *Not Actively Pursued; Fair Trial Not Possible*

The last two grounds for striking out are often closely related. The fifth ground – that a fair trial is no longer possible – was introduced by the *2004 Regulations* and is carried over to the *2013 Rules*. The occasions when it would be appropriate to strike out a claim on either ground will be very rare. An example of when a fair trial is no longer possible would be where a case has been adjourned on several occasions, over such a period that witnesses are either no longer available or liable to have no recollection of relevant events. To this extent it overlaps with the power to strike out a claim which has not been actively pursued: it is unlikely that such a claim would be struck out whilst the possibility of a fair trial remains, unless the claimant has clearly indicated that he no longer intends to pursue the claim.

The leading authority on the test to be applied where it is asserted that the claim has not been actively pursued is *Evans v Metropolitan Police Comr* [1993] ICR 151, [1992] IRLR 570 which held that *Birkett v James* [1977] 2 All ER 801, in turn the leading case on the equivalent rule in civil cases, applied to employment tribunals. *Birkett v James* holds that claims should not be struck out unless there has either been intentional or contumelious default by the claimant, or inordinate and inexcusable delay leading to a substantial risk that a fair trial will not be possible, or to substantial prejudice to the respondent. (Lesser prejudice to the respondent will be a relevant factor, albeit not necessarily determinative: *Itulu v London Fire Commissioner* (UKEAT/0298/18/BA)).

Four cases in which applications to strike the claim out because it had not been actively pursued are:

(1)   *Peixoto v British Telecommunications plc* [2008] All ER (D) 240 (May), where the hearing had been delayed for three years by the claimant's illness and there was no prognosis as to when she would be fit to give evidence; the EAT upheld the order striking out the claim made by the tribunal;

(2)   *Rolls Royce plc v Riddle* [2008] IRLR 873, where the claimant failed to attend a hearing and was unable to support his claim to have been too ill to attend with medical evidence; in this case the EAT overruled the tribunal's decision not to strike out the claim;

(3)   *Abegaze v Shrewsbury College of Arts and Technology* [2009] EWCA Civ 96, [2010] IRLR 238, where the claim had been struck out (both for this reason and because a fair trial was no longer possible) after a seven year delay, following a finding for the claimant on liability, caused in part by the claimant failing to take the steps necessary for the holding of a remedy hearing, but the Court of Appeal, reversing the EAT, held that the claim should not be struck out because rigorous case management orders could still achieve a fair hearing on remedy, and striking the claim out after liability had been established was therefore a disproportionate sanction; and

(4)   *Balls v Downham Market High School & College* [2011] IRLR 217, where the EAT held that the tribunal had been in error in striking out a claim which had been combined with a claim by the claimant's wife, also employed by the same respondent; the wife's claim had been struck out after she was imprisoned for theft from the respondent, but the EAT accepted that the claimant's case was separate from his wife's, and that he had been trying unsuccessfully to reactivate it after being exonerated in relation to the theft.

The Court of Appeal's view in *Abegaze* was significantly influenced by the fact that the claimant had already secured a finding in his favour on liability, and would therefore be deprived of his remedy if the claim was struck out. Nevertheless the contrast between the extreme delay of seven years in *Abegaze* and the 'mere' failure to attend a hearing without medical evidence of *Rolls Royce*, above, suggests that the decision of the EAT in the latter case is out of line with the later Court of Appeal decision and should not now be regarded as authoritative.

The striking out of a claim or response for non-compliance with an order short of an 'unless' order has been described by the Court of Appeal as a 'draconic power', not to be too readily exercised: *James v Blockbuster Entertainment Ltd* [2006] EWCA Civ 684, [2006] IRLR 630. The Court of Appeal has twice ruled that striking out as a sanction should only be applied where it is proportionate to the offence: *Bennett v Southwark London Borough Council* [2002] EWCA Civ 223, [2002] IRLR 407, where the issue was a party's conduct during the Hearing; and *Blockbuster*, where it was failure to comply with orders.

The guiding principle in deciding whether or not to strike out a party's case for non-compliance with an order is the requirements of the Overriding Objective. These require the tribunal to consider all relevant factors, including in particular what prejudice the other party has suffered, the issue of proportionality of the sanction, whether a lesser sanction could cure the prejudice, and as an overriding consideration, whether a fair trial remains possible. These points were articulated by the EAT in *Armitage v Weir Valves & Controls (UK) Ltd* [2004] ICR 371, [2003] All ER (D) 80 (Dec), where the employers successfully appealed against the striking out of their notice of appearance because they had been 10 days late in complying with a direction to exchange witness statements. (See also *Hazelwood v Eagle* [2009] All ER (D) 55 (May), where the EAT set aside a strike-out made because the claimant was in persistent breach of an order to supply medical evidence of a claimed disability. A case going the other way on similar facts is *Bennett v London Probation Service* (UKEAT/0194/09); however, in that case the claimant had indicated that she would never disclose the reports.) In *GCHQ v Bacchus* (UKEAT/0373/12) the EAT imposed an unless order rather than taking the draconian step of striking out where the claimant had refused to comply with an order requiring him to attend an appointment with a psychiatrist for the purpose of the respondent obtaining its own expert report, without which it would have been significantly disadvantaged in the litigation.

In *Maresca v Motor Insurance Repair Research Centre* [2004] 4 All ER 254, [2005] ICR 197, a case concerning the striking out of a claim for failure to comply with a case management order for mutual disclosure of documents, the EAT held that in considering whether to strike out a party's case, the tribunal should have regard to the factors listed in the pre-April 2013 version of *CPR 1998, rule 3.9*. (These included whether the application for relief was made promptly, whether the default was intentional, and whether the expected hearing date can still be met if the original order is now complied with.) The relevance of these considerations has been reiterated in several subsequent cases, but with the important proviso that it will not be an error of law for a tribunal to fail to refer to or consider each of the factors in the old *CPR rule 3.9* if the factors not considered are not relevant to the particular case. However, the more recent decision of the Court of Appeal in *Neary*, above, that it was not necessary to consider each of the factors in the old *CPR rule 3.9* where there had been a failure to comply with an 'unless' order is an indication that such an exercise is now rather less likely to be regarded as essential in other cases where the sanction for non-compliance with orders is under consideration. This position is further reinforced by the amendment of *CPR rule 3.9* post April 2013: the list of factors has been replaced by a requirement that the Court considers all the circumstances of the case, including the need for litigation to be conducted efficiently and at proportionate cost, and the need to enforce compliance with rules, practice directions and orders.

In *Blockbuster*, the Court of Appeal held that striking out could only be justified if either the offending party has been guilty of deliberate and persistent disregard of required procedural steps, or the unreasonable conduct of the case by that party (not necessarily deliberately so) has made a fair trial impossible. These are gateways to the exercise of the power; they do not necessitate the exercise of the power. Thus in *Osborne v Premium Care Homes Ltd* [2006] All ER (D) 272 (Oct), the sanction of debarring the respondent from defending the case on liability but permitting it to defend itself at the remedy stage was held to be a proper and proportionate response to breaches of orders that had made a fair trial on liability impossible (compare the similar sanction applied by the EAT where a response had not been submitted in time in *Foster v D & H Travel Ltd* [2006] ICR 1537, [2006] All ER (D) 15 (Aug)). The incorporation of *Art 6* of the *European Convention on Human Rights*, through the *Human Rights Act 1998*, provides a possible basis for challenges to striking-out decisions on the ground that the party (particularly a claimant) is deprived of the right to a determination of his civil rights by way of a fair and public hearing. However the case law of the European Court of Human Rights (which guides the decision-making of UK courts and tribunals) indicates that the proper judicial use of powers to control litigants, including striking out, does not in principle offend the *Convention*. (See also *Soteriou v Ultrachem Ltd* [2004] EWHC 983 (QB), [2004] IRLR 870 (striking out where contract of employment tainted by illegality not contrary to *Art 6*).)

Elliott v The Joseph Whitworth Centre Ltd [2013] All ER (D) 117 (Sep) (UKEAT/0030/13) is a further example of a case that was permissibly struck out because a fair trial was impossible in circumstances where there had been a two year delay in the Tribunal Service taking action on the claimant's ET1 claim form compounded by the inaction of his union representatives. The EAT considered the delay inexcusable and that it had made a fair trial impossible.

Delay may not be the only reason why a fair trial is no longer possible. In *E&O Laboratories v Miller* (UKEATS/0007/19/SS) the tribunal judge had struck out a respondent's case on grounds of unreasonable conduct and/or because a fair trial was no longer possible in circumstances where the respondent's witnesses had been observed discussing evidence during adjournments, and had been present in the tribunal room during other witnesses' evidence (contrary to the usual practice in Scotland), and because the tribunal judge formed the view that in the light of this conduct the witnesses were no longer 'impartial'. The Scottish EAT (Lord Summers) refrained from commenting on the appropriateness or otherwise of the judge's use of the word 'impartial' (surely, non-expert witnesses are under no obligation to be 'impartial'). Lord Summers acknowledged that this sort of conduct might result in a situation where a fair trial was no longer possible, but concluded that the judge had been wrong to regard the circumstances of that case as constituting such a situation. See the further discussion of this case at **20.87**.

20.78 *Application to Set-Aside the Strike Out*

Rule 38(2) provides that a party whose claim or response has been dismissed, in whole or in part, may apply to the Tribunal in writing, within 14 days of the date the notice was sent to have the order set aside on the basis that it is in the interests of justice to do so. Such an application is determined on the basis of written representations unless the application contains a request to the contrary. As to the criteria to be applied when the Tribunal considers such an application, the Court of Appeal in *Neary v Governing Body of St Albans Girls School* [2009] EWCA Civ 1190, [2010] IRLR 124, [2010] ICR 473 rejected the view expressed by the EAT that the tribunal must consider each of the factors listed in the pre April 2013 formulation of *CPR rule 3.9*, which set out the four factors to be considered in the High Court where there is an application for relief from sanctions (i.e. the reasons for the failure to comply with the order; the seriousness of the default; the prejudice to the other party; and whether a fair trial is still possible). The Court concluded that the decision whether to grant relief is simply a matter of discretion. In *Thind v Salvesen Logistics Ltd* [2010] UKEAT/0487/09 Underhill P held that, in the light of *Neary*, the Tribunal must decide whether it is right, in the interests of justice and the Overriding Objective, to grant relief to the party in default notwithstanding the breach of the unless order. This is now underlined by the formulation of the *2013 Rules* which renders the "interests of justice" the dominant test. As to what factors are likely to be relevant to the exercise of that discretion in particular cases the principles in the *James v Blockbuster Entertainment Ltd* [2006] EWCA Civ 684, [2006] IRLR 630 case are relevant (see above **20.76** and **20.77**); in particular it will be important for the tribunal to determine whether a fair trial of the case is still possible; thus if (as in the case of *North Tyneside Primary Care Trust v Aynsley* [2009] ICR 1333) the defaulting party has since complied with the 'unless' order, it may be disproportionate to deny that party a hearing, whether as claimant or respondent. However, where there has been a persistent and unexplained failure to comply with orders, the tribunal is entitled to say 'enough is enough' (as the Court of Appeal held was the case in *Neary*). Although it is clear from *Neary* and *Thind* that the factors in the *CPR rule 3.9* are not to be applied, in *Duncan Lewis Solicitors Ltd v Miss M Puar* (UKEAT/0175/19/RN) the Employment Appeal Tribunal held, with reference to a case on the CPR (*British Gas Trading Ltd v Oak Cash and Carry Ltd* [2016] EWCA Civ 153) that the fact that a party has failed to comply with an unless order (as opposed to an ordinary order) is undoubtedly a pointer towards seriousness and significance and that, at the least, the tribunal judge should have given adequate reasons as to the seriousness of the default before proceeding to consider other relevant issues.

20.79 Unless Orders

A less draconian option (as compared to striking out) for a Tribunal to secure compliance with rules and orders is for it to make an unless order. This is provided for by *Rule 38*. That *Rule* gives the Tribunal the power to make an order specifying "that if it is not complied with by the date specified the claim or response, or part of it, shall be dismissed without further order." Where such an order is made, and the party required to comply does not, the Tribunal must, by *Rule 38(1)* given written notice to the parties that dismissal has occurred. If a response is dismissed under the rule, the effect is to be as if no response had been presented, as set out in *Rule 21*.

As with strike out, under *Rule 38(2)*, a party whose claim or response has been dismissed, in whole or in part, as a result of an unless order, may apply to the Tribunal in writing, within 14 days of the date that the notice was sent, to have the order set aside on the basis that it is in the interests of justice to do so. Unless the application includes a request for a hearing, the Tribunal may determine it on the basis of written representations.

The operation of 'unless' orders under the old rules were described by the then President of the EAT, Underhill J, as a 'pig's breakfast': *North Tyneside Primary Care Trust v Aynsley* [2009] ICR 1333. The effect of the decisions in *Uyamnwa-Odu v Schools Office Services Ltd* [2005] All ER (D) 377 (Nov) (UKEAT/0294/05), *Neary v Governing Body of St Albans Girls' School* [2009] EWCA Civ 1190, [2010] IRLR 124, [2010] ICR 473, *EPI Coaches Ltd v Lafferty* [2009] All ER (D) 81 (Apr), the *North Tyneside case* and *Scottish Ambulance Service v Laing* (UKEATS/0038/12) was that if the order is not complied with by the due date (even if the non-compliance is partial), the claim, or as the case may be response, was struck out automatically, without the need for further judicial intervention. The effect of the automatic strike-out of a claim, although not of a response, was that the original unless order was converted into a judgment, which then opened the door to a review under the then applicable rules: *Uyanwa-Odu* and *Neary* (which reviews fully the relevant cases). *Neary* was the subject of a further appeal to the Court of Appeal, which reversed the decision of the EAT on the merits, but without disagreeing with the analysis of the effects of non-compliance with an 'unless' order (*Neary v Governing Body of St Albans Girls School* [2009] EWCA Civ 1190, [2010] IRLR 124, [2010] ICR 473). Note, however, that Smith LJ in *Neary* considered that the EAT's finding that the remedy of review was available in the case of a strike out taking effect for non-compliance with an unless order was not "wholly free from difficulty" (para. 5). In *Thind v Salvesen Logistics Ltd* [2010] All ER (D) 05 (Sep) (UKEAT/0487/09), the EAT applied the decision in *Neary*, but reached the opposite result, overturning the striking out of the claim, where the breach of an 'unless' order had resulted from a combination of delay by a medical expert in providing a report and inadvertence by the claimant's solicitors. As Lady Smith remarked in *Laing*, under the old rules, if the parties wished confirmation of their position in relation to an unless order, the onus was on them to communicate with the tribunal, but that ought not to be treated by the tribunal as an opportunity to revisit the question of whether the unless order should have been issued.

Under the *2013 Rules* the complications surrounding the availability of a 'review' (as it was called under the old rules) have been swept away by the ability of a party whose claim or response has been dismissed under an unless order to apply for the order to be set aside on the basis that it is in the interests of justice to do so. Similarly, to render that avenue of review available, the tribunal must send a notice if the sanction under an unless order is applied. The same approach on such an application is likely to be taken as that under applications to set-aside a decision to strike out (see above **20.78**).

A complicating factor in many cases where there has been an 'unless' order and it is asserted by the other party that there has been a failure to comply with it is that point may itself be in dispute (for instance there may be a dispute about whether the party has complied fully with an order to give particulars or disclose documents). In such cases the issue can only be fairly resolved by a hearing, leading to a judgment on the disputed issue of non-compliance, which may in turn be open to appeal. These procedural complications may remove much of the value of 'unless' orders as orders of last resort. In *Johnson v Oldham Metropolitan Borough Council* [2013] All ER (D) 187 (Sep) (UKEAT/0095/13), the EAT held that the question of whether there has been compliance with an unless order needs to be determined qualitatively rather than quantitatively. Accordingly, the Tribunal's view that there had been "substantial compliance" adopted the wrong test. In *Wentworth-Wood & Others v Maritime Transport Ltd* [2016] UKEAT/0316/15, an unless order in a multiple-claimant claim was held to apply severally to each claimant such that an ET's decision to confirm dismissal of all claims because some claimants had not complied with the unless order could not stand.

Being able to tell whether an unless order has been complied with is important, and is a guiding feature of the judicial guidance on how unless orders ought to be framed. In *Mace v Ponders End International Ltd* [2014] IRLR 697, the EAT overturned a decision to strike out a claim on the basis of failure to comply with an unless order which required the claimant to "provide disclosure of all relevant documents" by a given date. The claimant did not make a list, but did send some documents to the Tribunal and was informed at the last moment by the Tribunal that they should be sent to the respondent. HHJ Richardson held that the order lacked the necessary quality of clarity and certainty to take effect as an order striking out the claim. Unless orders under *Rule 38(1)* must identify with clarity what is required for compliance. In *Mace*, it was unclear whether the order was intended to require the claimant to provide a list of documents or provide copies and if so to whom, and it was not remedied by reading the unless order against the original case management order. At para 25 the EAT held: "Employment Judges have to deal with a great deal of what is commonly known as "box work": that is, correspondence asking for the making of an order on paper when the Employment Judge does not have the luxury of a hearing and full argument. The making of an unless order is one such kind of box work, but it requires particular care. Unless orders must be clear in their terms and are especially likely to result in injustice and satellite litigation if they are not. It is important to pay detailed attention to the wording and also to consider carefully whether the sanction is proportionate."

20.80 Deposit Orders

Rule 39 permits a Tribunal to make a 'deposit order'. This is an order requiring a party (known in the rule as "the paying party") to pay a deposit not exceeding £1,000 as a condition of continuing to advance a particular allegation or argument. *Rule 39(1)* provides that if, at a preliminary hearing (under *Rule 53*), a Tribunal considers that any specific allegation or argument in a claim or response has "little reasonable prospects of success" then it can make a deposit order. It is important to appreciate that 'little reasonable prospects of success' is not the same as the 'no reasonable prospect of success' test for striking out a claim: see *H v Ishmail* [2017] ICR 486 and *Arthur v Hertfordshire Partnership University NHS Foundation Trust* (UKEAT/0121/19/LA). The distinction between a deposit order and striking out was also highlighted in *H M Prison Service v Dolby* [2003] IRLR 694, where the EAT described the two sanctions respectively as 'the Yellow card' and 'the Red card'.

The question whether to make a deposit order must be dealt with at a preliminary hearing. This may be held on the application of the other party or as a result of an order made by the tribunal of its own initiative, and the issue of a deposit order may be referred for hearing at a preliminary hearing together with any other issues in the case which are judged appropriate for determination at that stage, or as the sole issue for determination. The tribunal will consider the Claim Form and Response, the representations (which may include relevant documents) and argument. Usually no evidence is heard, but in some cases this can also be done. In practice a deposit order is made most often against claimants.

Rule 39 applies to "allegations" or "arguments", not just claims or responses viewed as a whole. Therefore there is scope for a Tribunal to take a robust view to the individual contentions that are advanced by the parties. That said, a deposit order should not be made because the claimant's case is unclear and as a substitute to other case management orders such as ordering further particulars: *Tree v South East Coastal Ambulance Service* (UKEAT/0043/17). If the Tribunal determines that an allegation or argument in a claim or response has little reasonable prospects of success, a deposit order not exceeding £1,000 can be made. The EAT has held that in deciding what prospects of success a claim or response may have, the tribunal has a broad discretion and is not restricted to considering purely legal questions: *Wright v Nipponkoa Insurance (Europe) Ltd* (UKEAT/0113/14/JOJ) and *Arthur v Hertfordshire Partnership University NHS Foundation Trust* (UKEAT/0121/19/LA). The tribunal can take into account the credibility of the facts asserted, and the likelihood that they can be established at a hearing: *Jansen van Rensburg v Royal Borough of Kingston-upon-Thames* (UKEAT/0096/07).

There is no express power to reconsider a deposit order, however there is power to vary or revoke the deposit order (see *Rule 29* and, by analogy with the old rules, *Sodexho Ltd v Gibbons* [2005] IRLR 836). In *Sodexho*, the EAT upheld the use of this power to restart the time for payment of the deposit where it had transpired that the claimant had not received the order, having put an incorrect address for his solicitor on the Claim Form.

The tribunal must make reasonable enquiries in to the paying party's ability to pay the deposit. And must have regard to any such information when deciding the amount of the deposit (but not whether or not to make the deposit per se): *Rule 39(2)*. The *Rule* does not make clear how the tribunal may ascertain the party's means, but in practice this does not appear to cause difficulty. In *Oni v NHS Leicester City* [2012] All ER (D) 05 (Oct), [2013] ICR 91 (UKEAT/0144/12) the EAT recommended the completion of the County Court means form EX140 by the party whose means are to be taken into account. A party's means may include a student loan: *Simpson v Chief Constable, Strathclyde Police* (UKEATS/0030/11). In *Hemdan v Ishmail & Another* [2017] IRLR 228, [2017] ICR 486, the EAT underlined that the purpose of a deposit order was to identify at an early stage claims with little prospect of success and discourage their pursuit without making access to justice difficult or effecting a strike-out through the back door. The assessment of prospects should be made without a mini-trial of the facts and there should be a proper basis for doubting the likelihood of a party being able to establish essential facts at trial. Where misunderstandings as to the nature of allegations arose (eg where a party communicates through an interpreter) consideration of allowing an amendment might be appropriate when assessing prospects of success. It was further essential that a deposit order was proportionate and not set at a level that a party could not afford. In *Hemdan*, a victim of trafficking who received benefits with an income of around £125 per week was ordered by the ET to pay a deposit of £75 for each of three allegations. The EAT considered this was disproportionate and substituted an order of £1 per allegation.

The Tribunal must give its reasons for making a deposit order along with the order and the paying party must be notified about the potential consequences of the Order: *Rule 39(3)*. This includes giving reasons for the amount of the deposit order as well as the reasons why in principle an order is appropriate: *Adams v Kingdom Services Group Limited* (UKEAT/0235/18/LA) at para 42. In *Akanu-Otu v Secretary of State for Justice* [2014] ICR D13 (UKEAT/0295/13), the EAT noted that there are differences of terminology and content in *Rule 39* as compared with the previous rule. Under the old rule, in *Akanu-Otu* the EAT held that a deposit notice which stated that payment was required as a condition of being permitted to continue to take part in proceedings was adequate. Now the rule refers to the need to notify the paying party of the "potential consequences of the order" – in other words the content of *Rule 39(4)*. In *Akanu-Otu*, the EAT also held that regard could have been had to the guidance notes accompanying the order.

The consequence of not paying the deposit is set by *Rule 39(4)*: the specific allegation or argument to which the deposit order relates shall be struck out where the deposit is not paid by the date specified. This is a change to the old rules which provided for the party in question (whoever that was) not being permitted to take part in proceedings unless the deposit is paid.

What happens to the deposit is set by *Rule 39(5)*: if the Tribunal at any stage following the making of a deposit order decides the specific allegation or argument against the paying party for substantially the reasons given in the deposit order, then (i) the paying party shall be treated as having acted unreasonably in pursuing that specific allegation or argument for the purpose of costs, unless the contrary is shown, and *Rule 76*, unless the contrary is shown; and (ii) the deposit shall be paid to the other party (or, if there is more than one, to such other party or parties as the Tribunal orders). In all other cases, the deposit is to be refunded. The amount of a deposit order will off-set any costs award applied for: *Rule 39(6)*. The value of the deposit order procedure for respondents is that many claimants who are warned that they are at risk of a costs order do not pursue their claim. Such applications can also be considered as a lesser alternative to the striking out of a claim or response as misconceived, if the order for the holding of a preliminary hearing provides for this.

20.81 Stay of Proceedings

The power to order a stay (or sist in Scotland) of proceedings is a general power within *Rule 29*. A stay operates to suspend the proceedings, not to end them. Applications to stay tribunal proceedings are often made, and frequently granted, where there are concurrent proceedings in the High Court (or Court of Session) and the Employment Tribunal arising out of the same employment. Tribunal proceedings may also be stayed pending the outcome of foreign litigation (*JMCC Holdings Ltd v Conroy* [1990] ICR 179). Conversely, the tribunal might be seen as the more appropriate venue to determine the complaints before it, ahead of proceedings elsewhere (see eg *BUQ v HRE* [2012] EWHC 2827 where the tribunal was acknowledged to be better placed than High Court to determine the truth or otherwise of disputed claims of sexual harassment). The EAT should only interfere with the tribunal's decision to postpone or continue with the proceedings before it if that decision resulted from an error of law or if it was perverse (*Carter v Credit Change Ltd* [1980] 1 All ER 252, [1979] IRLR 361, [1979] ICR 908; *Automatic Switching Ltd v Brunet* [1986] ICR 542). An example of a case where the EAT was persuaded to overturn the refusal of a stay is *GFI Holdings Ltd v Camm* [2008] All ER (D) 74 (Sep), where the claimant was pursuing a claim in the High Court for unpaid bonuses, the determination of which would involve deciding issues that would also arise in his tribunal claim (for unfair dismissal). For further discussion of the factors to be taken into consideration, see *First Castle Electronics Ltd v West* [1989] ICR 72, *Bowater plc v Charlwood* [1991] IRLR 340, [1991] ICR 798 and *Chorion plc v Lane* [1999] All ER (D) 194 (where the High Court proceedings had been brought by the former employer). The position has been restated by the EAT in *Mindimaxnox LLP v Gover* [2011] All ER (D) 146 (May) (UKEAT/0225/10) and *Paymentshield Group Holdings Ltd v Halstead* [2012] ICR D5, both cases where a stay was ordered by the EAT on the basis that there was a significant overlap between the issues to be decided in the tribunal and High Court proceedings (and, in the first case, with court proceedings in Cyprus). Other factors which may affect whether or not a stay of the tribunal proceedings should be granted are the delay that this may cause, the degree of complexity of the issues (complexity being a factor favouring giving priority to the High Court proceedings), the nature of the issues (see *BUQ* above), and the different costs regimes in the two jurisdictions, as well the relative importance of each set of proceedings and the stage each has reached. In *Paymentshield*, the fact that the High Court action had not been commenced (only a formal letter before action had been served) was held not to be a sufficient reason to displace the other factors favouring giving priority to the Court proceedings.

It may sometimes be appropriate for proceedings to be stayed pending the outcome of an appeal, or a reference to the CJEU, the result of which is likely to determine, or at least influence, the outcome of the particular case. In *Johns v Solent SD Ltd* [2008] IRLR 88, the EAT ordered a stay of a claim for unfair dismissal and age discrimination where the claimant alleged that she had been forced to retire, because the issue of the validity of the relevant provisions of the *Employment Equality (Age) Regulations 2006* had been referred to the CJEU in another case, and the EAT's decision was followed by a Practice Direction by the President of Tribunals that all similar cases should be stayed pending the CJEU's ruling.

A different reason for seeking a stay of the proceedings is that the parties wish to attempt to settle their dispute by alternative means, such as through mediation (see further **20.23**). Tribunals generally encourage the use of such alternatives to litigation, although they will be wary about adding delay if there is no realistic prospect of a settlement being achieved. In Scotland this encouragement has been formalised into a Practice Direction on the sisting of cases for mediation, issued in December 2006. One reason for staying tribunal proceedings where related proceedings between the parties are anticipated is that the doctrine of res judicata (ie that issues decided in one set of proceedings cannot be relitigated) may apply so as to bind the High Court later. This will only be true if precisely the same issue arises in both sets of proceedings (see *Munir v Jang Publications Ltd* [1989] IRLR 224, [1989] ICR 1; *Crown Estate Comrs v Dorset County Council* [1990] 1 All ER 19; *Soteriou v Ultrachem Ltd* [2004] EWHC 983 (QB), [2004] IRLR 870) and the decision of the tribunal on the particular point was necessary to the determination of the issues before it, and within its jurisdiction (see for both points *Bon Groundwork Ltd v Foster* [2012] IRLR 517, and for a discussion of the principles of res judicata see **20.125** below). A stay can necessarily only be granted once the proceedings to be stayed have been commenced, and there is no equivalent procedure to suspend the running of time limits for the bringing of tribunal proceedings. A claimant who wishes to bring both High Court (or County Court) and tribunal proceedings, and to pursue the former first, should therefore present his or her claim to the tribunal within the statutory time limit and immediately apply for a stay pending the outcome of the other proceedings, explaining that the tribunal claim has been made at that time to ensure the claim is not time-barred (*Warnock v Scarborough Football Club* [1989] ICR 489).

Note *Watson v Hemingway Design Ltd* (UKEAT/0007/19/JOJ) in which Kerr J lifted a stay on proceedings imposed by the tribunal where the tribunal had wrongly concluded that it did not have jurisdiction under the *Third Parties (Rights against Insurers) Act 2010, s 2(6)* to make declarations as to the liability of the insurer as well as of the insured. In that case, Kerr J further noted that the respondent's reliance on an arbitration clause was misplaced as the clause was void against the claimant by reason of *s 203* of the *ERA 1996* and *s 144* of the *EqA 2010*.

For the position regarding stays necessitated by the insolvency of a party, see INSOLVENCY **(32)**.

20.82 References to the Court of Justice of the European Union

Rule 100 provides that where a Tribunal decides to refer a question to the Court of Justice of the European Union for a preliminary ruling under *Art 267* of the *Treaty on the Functioning of the European Union*, a copy of that decision shall be sent to the Registrar of the CJEU. This will be repealed by the *Employment Rights (Amendment) (EU Exit) Regulations 2019, SI 2019/535, reg 14* from a date to be appointed when the UK leaves the European Union.

Art 267 gives tribunals a discretion to refer questions concerning the interpretation of EU law to the CJEU where this is necessary. A reference is not appropriate where the issue is *acte clair* (as to the meaning of which, see *CILFIT Srl v Ministro Della Sanita* [1983] 1 CMLR 472). For guidance see the CJEU's Recommendations to National Courts and Tribunals on Initiation of Preliminary Ruling Proceedings (20.7.2018, OJ C257/1). The EAT has confirmed that in an appropriate case, a reference can be made on assumed facts: see *Attridge Law v Coleman* [2007] IRLR 88, [2007] ICR 654.

EMPLOYMENT TRIBUNAL HEARINGS

General Rules for All Types of Hearing

20.83 *General*

Tribunal hearings are usually conducted in modern rooms with the three members of the tribunal sitting at a table on a slightly raised dais and the claimant and respondent sitting at tables facing the tribunal. There is a table at which the witness sits to give evidence. A full tribunal is composed of a legally qualified Employment Judge, one member with management experience and one member with trade union experience; as to cases where the Judge may sit alone or with just one other member, see **19.8** and **19.9** EMPLOYMENT TRIBUNALS **– I**. The proceedings are public, although in practice members of the public not connected with the proceedings attend relatively infrequently. A 'public hearing' must be accessible to the public, even if no members of the public wished to attend the hearing: *Storer v British Gas plc* [2000] IRLR 495. For the power of the tribunal to sit in private, see **20.91** below.

Rule 46 of the *2013 Rules* provides that a hearing may be conducted, in whole or in part, by use of electronic communication (including by telephone) provided that the Tribunal considers that it would be just and equitable to do so and provided that the parties and members of the public attending the hearing are able to hear what the Tribunal hears and see any witness as seen by the Tribunal. Accordingly, hearings may be held by telephone or video link, so that it is possible, for instance, for evidence from a witness who is abroad to be heard by video link. In practice this happens infrequently, as most hearing centres are not equipped for video conferencing, and special arrangements therefore need to be made in advance; but if there are good reasons for such arrangements, an early application for a direction should be made to the tribunal. Some regions, such as London Central, have video conferencing facilities. At other hearing centres, directions can be made by the Tribunal for it to sit elsewhere so that the facilities are made available. The Presidential Guidance on conduct of employment proceedings in the context of the Covid-19 pandemic provides further information as to the mechanisms by which electronic hearings may be conducted and the circumstances in which that may be appropriate. The Presidential Guidance notes the difficulty in holding hearings that must be held in public (Open Preliminary Hearings and Final Hearings) on a fully remote basis. That will only be possible if the audio and video are accessible to members of the public in an open tribunal room, or if the same facility can be arranged virtually.

The Judge and members should be addressed as 'Sir' or 'Madam'. Proceedings are formal but considerably less so than in an ordinary court. Witnesses (including a party if giving evidence) are required to give their evidence on oath or under affirmation (see *Rule 43* below); the clerk will check on the preference of each witness in this respect. In Scotland, witnesses are excluded from the tribunal room until called to give their evidence (this does not apply to a party who is also a witness). Before the hearing starts, the clerk will speak to both parties and make a list of names of representatives and witnesses, and will collect copies of documents each party intends to rely on to give to members of the tribunal.

Rule 41 now gives voice to the general principle that Tribunals are free to regulate their own procedure to conduct the hearing in the manner it considers fair and having regard to the principles contained in the Overriding Objective. *Rule 41* specifically indicates that the following rules do not restrict that general power and that the Tribunal shall seek to avoid undue formality and may itself question parties or a witness so far as appropriate in order to clarify the issues or elicit the evidence. *Rule 41* also clarifies that the Tribunal is not bound by any rule of law relating to the admissibility of evidence in proceedings before the courts. Notwithstanding the apparent breadth of the ability on the Tribunal to regulate its procedure, the procedure in fact adopted must comply with *ECHR, Art 6* by virtue of *HRA 1998, s 6* and also be fair and comply with the rules of natural justice at common law. In *U v Butler* [2014] All ER (D) 34 (Sep), [2014] UKEAT/0354/13 (at para 72-3), the EAT applied the Supreme Court's dicta in *R (Osborn) v Parole Board* [2013] UKSC 61, [2014] AC 1115 (a case involving parole decisions) to the effect that the procedural fairness of hearing is not merely reviewable on *Wednesbury* grounds, but "The Court must determine for itself whether a fair procedure was followed . . . its function is not merely to review that reasonableness of the decision maker judgment for what fairness requires".

In *Hak v St Christopher's Fellowship* [2016] ICR 411, [2016] IRLR 342, the EAT considered the duties of a Tribunal to ensure a fair hearing for a litigant whose first language was not English. In general, where a party wishes to have an interpreter present, the Tribunal should facilitate it as best it can and should "strive to do so" (para 38). However, there may be circumstances in which the command of English is so poor that a litigant cannot give the account which they would wish to give to the Tribunal. There is, in such cases, a powerful argument that the Tribunal must take all reasonable steps – including funding – to secure the services of an interpreter (para 39). By contrast, where a litigant had a well-demonstrated ability to speak, write and read English, an interpreter would be unnecessary and the request should be refused (but the Tribunal should "think long and hard" before so concluding in respect of a person whose mother tongue may well not be English (para 40)). There were also cases, falling between these categories in which the Tribunal had to conduct an assessment of need, against achieving justice, fairness and equality of arms. This assessment was for the Judge bearing in mind that spoken and written language are different and that pressures in court are such that immediate comprehension and response are required (para 41). A useful test would be to ask whether the litigant's command of language was sufficient to enable him to give the best account to the tribunal which he would wish to give relating to the matters in dispute (para 45). See also *Lema v DHL Supply Chain Ltd* (UKEATPA/0315/17/LA), 21 March 2018 and *Ringway Infrastructure Services Ltd v Conlon* (UKEAT/0256/18/DA) in which it was determined that the claimant's command of English was sufficient that no interpreter was required.

The broad discretionary powers do, however, result in considerable variation in the extent to which particular tribunals conduct cases in an inquisitorial way or leave it to the parties to present their case as they think best; much depends on the style of individual Judges. Under the previous *Rules*, the EAT stressed that a degree of formality and structure is necessary; informality can be counter-productive and tribunals should normally adhere to the generally recognised rules of procedure (*Aberdeen Steak Houses Group plc v Ibrahim* [1988] IRLR 420, [1988] ICR 550). Although this case pre-dates the revisions of the *Rules* in 2001, 2004, and now 2013, it is still relevant. The same requirements as to fairness and absence of bias and appearance of bias apply to tribunal proceedings as to proceedings in other courts and tribunals (see further **20.92** below). Subject to the tribunal's power to control proceedings (see **20.84** below), parties are entitled to call such relevant evidence as they wish, and to cross-examine the witnesses of the other party. The general rule in adversarial proceedings (known as "the rule in *Browne v Dunn*"), as between the parties, is that one party should not be entitled to impugn the evidence of another party's witness if he has not asked appropriate questions enabling the witness to deal with the criticisms that are being made. However, this is not an absolute rule and failure to cross-examine will not necessarily amount to acceptance of a witness's testimony: the question is always whether it will be fair for the Tribunal to reach a conclusion adverse to that witness if the particular point has not been put to them: see *Deepak Fertilizers & Petrochemicals Corp Ltd v Davy McKee (UK) London Ltd* [2002] EWCA Civ 1396 at paras 49-50 and *NHS Trust Development Authority v Saiger and ors* (UKEAT/0167 and 0276/15/LA), at paras 99-102.

It is a general principle that decisions which require to be taken in the course of the hearing on points of case management (such as whether to grant a party's application for an adjournment) should not be taken by the judge without consulting the lay members, if there are lay members sitting: *Jones v Corbin* (UKEAT/0504/10).

The Tribunal has power to deal with points not identified by the parties, and to make findings of fact not contended for by either party, but it must act fairly, and it must be cautious where the parties are represented about advancing matters not put forward by the parties (although there is no prohibition on it doing so even where the parties are represented): *BAE Systems (Operations) Ltd v Paterson* UKEATS/0003/12/BI, [2013] ICR D3 at §31 per Langstaff P). Factual matters that the Tribunal considers relevant (and inferences the Tribunal may draw) must normally be put to the witnesses concerned, especially where the issue is one of bad faith, and the parties must be given an opportunity to make submissions on such facts (unless the legal effect is obvious and unarguably clear): *City of London Corp v McDonnell* (UKEAT/1096/17/JOJ), 28 February 2019. The Judge should alert the parties before taking a point on which they have not addressed the tribunal (McDonnell ibid and *Laurie v Holloway* [1994] ICR 32); and see *Launahurst Ltd v Larner* [2010] EWCA Civ 334, [2010] All ER (D) 282 (Mar) (error of law to base decision on point not raised by or with the parties during the hearing). It has also been held that the tribunal should not rely on cases discovered through its own researches without giving the parties an opportunity to make submissions on them: *Albion Hotel (Freshwater) Ltd v Maia e Silva* [2002] IRLR 200; but see also *Sheridan v Stanley Cole (Wainfleet) Ltd* [2003] EWCA Civ 1046, [2003] IRLR 885, adopting a less strict view on this point, and *Clark v Clark Construction Initiatives Ltd* [2008] EWCA Civ 1446, [2009] ICR 718, [2008] All ER (D) 191 (Dec), where it was held that the citation of cases was not in the circumstances material to the decision. See further below **20.84** for guidance as to the extent that the tribunal should assist parties in formulating lists of issues.

The Judge and members must also, unsurprisingly, remain attentive throughout the hearing: thus the Court of Appeal in *Stansbury v Datapulse plc* [2003] EWCA Civ 1951, [2004] IRLR 466 set aside the judgment of a tribunal reached after a hearing during which one of the lay members had fallen asleep after allegedly drinking alcohol during the lunch break. Contrast *Elys v Marks & Spencer Plc* [2014] ICR 1091 in which a lay member had apparently been sleeping for 15-20 seconds and had been observed to be drooling by the Judge (other instances of alleged sleeping by that member were rejected on the basis he had been attentive, but closing his eyes due to an eye condition). During the three week hearing the member had taken extensive notes, asked questions and had taken full part in discussions with the Tribunal. The EAT decided that it was for it to find facts as to what had happened and then consider whether a properly informed and impartial observer would regard there as having been inattention or the appearance of inattention. In that case, the EAT accepted that there was inattention during the 15-20 second incident (not otherwise) but this was not of sufficient materiality overall to amount to a procedural irregularity. More generally, the EAT emphasised the responsibility of those sitting in a judicial capacity for their own performance, and the entitlement of the parties to the attention of the entire panel for the entire case (trivial moments aside). If Judges and members have any reason to think they might be subject to inattention for extraneous reasons they should make that plain to the Tribunal and, if necessary, the parties should be told enough to make an informed decision as to their position. In the instant case, the EAT doubted whether the appeal would have proceeded had the member explained that he suffered from the eye condition he did. In *Healy v Slough Borough Council* (UKEAT/0125/19/JOJ) Auerbach J emphasised that the key question in cases where there is inattention by a member of the panel or judge is whether the fair-minded and informed observer would conclude that as a result of the inattention there was at least a real possibility that the fairness of the trial was affected. In that case, where he found a wing member had been asleep, or given every appearance of having fallen asleep, several times during the course of evidence, he held that there was a real possibility the fairness of the trail was affected and remitted the matter to a fresh tribunal.

The Court of Appeal has expressed the view that it is always desirable that any irregularity in procedure, such as the Judge or a member falling asleep, or the making of inappropriate comments, should be raised at the time, but failure to do so (particularly if the party subsequently complaining was not represented at the time) is not necessarily a bar to raising the point on appeal: *Stansbury v Datapulse plc* [2003] EWCA Civ 1951, [2004] IRLR 466, paras 23 and 27. Peter Gibson LJ acknowledged the difficulty that even a legal representative may have in raising such a point, since if the objection is unsuccessful the person complained about will continue to sit in the case.

The Court of Appeal has emphasised that despite the relative informality accorded to tribunal proceedings, employment tribunals are not inquisitorial bodies, so that where the burden of proof rests on a particular party, the onus is on that party to put evidence before the tribunal enabling that burden to be discharged: *McNicol v Balfour Beatty Rail Maintenance Ltd* [2002] EWCA Civ 1074, [2002] IRLR 711, [2002] ICR 1498, a case where the claimant's status as a disabled person was in dispute. However, the Court indicated that the tribunal should use its case management powers to ensure that a claimant appreciated the kind of medical evidence that might be needed to establish disability. In *Joseph v*

Brighton & Sussex University Hospitals NHS Trust (UKEAT/0001/15), a litigant in person failed to prove that she met the statutory definition of disability in respect of two conditions she suffered from. The EAT rejected the notion that the Tribunal had erred by failing to seek out evidence in a 580 page bundle which the claimant did not refer to at the hearing. The duty to assist litigants in person did not extend to referring to all the documents in the bundle. Equally, Tribunals should not search out evidence on their own. In *East of England Ambulance Service NHS Trust v Sanders* [2015] IRLR 277, [2015] ICR 293, after hearing evidence on disability, the Tribunal retired and conducted its own research as to the dosage of medication the claimant was taking by consulting Wikipedia and other websites. It then returned to the Tribunal room and provided copies to the parties. Langstaff P rejected the suggestion that *Rule 41* permitted a Tribunal to make its own enquiries. At para 29 he said: "The Tribunal may, in an appropriate case, ask the parties whether they have thought about particular evidence or even, possibly, whether in an appropriate case the parties or one of them would wish an adjournment in order to obtain it. But it is not, as the Judge appeared to think, for the Tribunal itself to investigate the evidence and rely upon its own investigations. The Tribunal is, as we said at the start of this Judgment, to act as the adjudicator not as advocate." The Tribunal had assumed the truth of that which it discovered and had demonstrated it would place improper weight upon it. The EAT went on to emphasise that this should not prevent a Tribunal appropriately making allowance for a party appearing as a litigant in person even if the degree of intervention in a Tribunal would "raise some eyebrows in civil courts" (para 31). Non-leading questions should be the form of choice when the Tribunal invokes *Rule 41* to ask questions to elicit evidence.

More generally, tribunals are not under a duty to ensure that every allegation in a Claim Form is dealt with, regardless of whether the claimant puts forward evidence or argument in support of it (*Mensah v East Hertfordshire NHS Trust* [1998] IRLR 531, CA; and see *Hyde-Walsh v Ashby* [2008] All ER (D) 225 (Feb), EAT: tribunal has discretion whether to draw attention to a head of claim apparently overlooked by the claimant). This point is particularly important because of the general rule that arguments and points not taken at the tribunal hearing cannot be raised for the first time by way of appeal: see **21.15** below. See further the discussion in relation to lists of issues at **20.84** below.

The EAT has held that the tribunal has discretion whether to permit a party to withdraw an admission: *Nowicka-Price v Chief Constable of Gwent Constabulary* (UKEAT/0268/09). The factors that should be taken into account in considering whether to exercise the discretion (and presumably also where it is the claimant who seeks to withdraw an admission or concession) are those listed for civil cases in *CPR Part 14*.

In some circumstances, it can be incumbent upon the Tribunal to grant a short adjournment of its own motion during a hearing. In *U v Butler* [2014] All ER (D) 34 (Sep), [2014] UKEAT/0354/13, the EAT held this applied where a claimant suffered from a mental disability, was a litigant in person and arrived after the hearing had started, and after the Tribunal had struck out his claims for failure to comply with case management orders. Although the Judge told him he could apply for a review (which he did, only for it to be dismissed because his submissions were not supported by medical evidence), the EAT held it was incumbent upon the Judge to have granted a short adjournment to allow the claimant to reflect and recover, and to gather material relevant to the review application. Further, the Judge should also have informed him that the review application could have been made within 14 days of receiving the reasons rather than immediately. See further below **20.83A** as to the steps a tribunal may have to take for vulnerable parties and witnesses.

More generally, Tribunals will take steps to assist litigants in person, but as the cases above show, when doing so, they must avoid stepping into the arena. The Court of Appeal in *Drysdale v Department of Transport* [2014] IRLR 892, [2015] ICR D2 identified the following general propositions:

"(1) It is a long–established and obviously desirable practice of courts generally, and employment tribunals in particular, that they will provide such assistance to litigants as may be appropriate in the formulation and presentation of their case.

(2) What level of assistance or intervention is "appropriate" depends upon the circumstances of each particular case.

(3) Such circumstances are too numerous to list exhaustively, but are likely to include: whether the litigant is representing himself or is represented; if represented, whether the representative is legally qualified or not; and in any case, the apparent level of competence and understanding of the litigant and/or his representative.

(4) The appropriate level of assistance or intervention is constrained by the overriding requirement that the tribunal must at all time be, and be seen to be, impartial as between the parties, and that injustice to either side must be avoided.

(5) The determination of the appropriate level of assistance or intervention is properly a matter for the judgment of the tribunal hearing the case, and the creation of rigid obligations or rules of law in this regard is to be avoided, as much will depend on the tribunal's assessment and "feel" for what is fair in all the circumstances of the specific case.

(6) There is, therefore, a wide margin of appreciation available to a tribunal in assessing such matters, and an appeal court will not normally interfere with the tribunal's exercise of its judgment in the absence of an act or omission on the part of the tribunal which no reasonable tribunal, properly directing itself on the basis of the Overriding Objective, would have done/omitted to do, and which amounts to unfair treatment of a litigant."

In *Jones v Secretary of State for Business Innovation and Skills* (UKEAT/0238/16/DM) the EAT noted that it would be good practice where one party was not represented for the judge to explain both that any counsel for the opposing party had a duty to ensure that any authority adverse to their case was drawn to the attention of the tribunal, and that it was the duty of the tribunal, in accordance with the Overriding Objective to ensure, so far as reasonably practicable, that both parties were on an equal footing. See also *EDF Energy Customers Ltd v Re-Energized Ltd* [2018] EWHC 652 (Ch) cautioning that assistance to a litigant in person should not result in unfairness to another party or place an unreasonable burden on another party or the court; further, that the fact that litigant was acting in person was not in itself a reason to disapply or excuse non-compliance with procedural rules, orders or directions, although some leeway may be given.

On the other hand, a Tribunal must also be careful not to place unfair pressure on a litigant in person: see *Gee v Shell UK Ltd* [2003] IRLR 82, CA (in that case the CA accepted that the Tribunal had not placed unfair pressure on a litigant in person by giving a costs warning). See also *Paul v Virgin Care Limited* (UKEAT/0104/19/RN), considering the Tribunal's obligations when faced with the withdrawal of a claim. She observed (para 45): "*the ET will need to be satisfied that the decision was clear, unambiguous, and unequivocal, but the level of inquiry required of the ET in any particular instance will depend upon whether the circumstances are such as to give rise to a reasonable concern that this may not be the case*". In that case, the EAT accepted that the Tribunal had acted with appropriate care in ensuring that the claimant understood the implications of withdrawing a claim for automatic unfair dismissal and accepted the factual basis which made that course appropriate in the particular case. The EAT further noted that by pausing and reading out to the claimant what the judge was recording about the withdrawal the judge had given an appropriate moment for reflection as envisaged by the EAT in *Segor v Goodrich Actuation Systems Ltd* UKEAT/0145/11/DM.

20.83a *Vulnerable parties and witnesses*

The Tribunal's general case management powers (see above **20.83**) give it wide powers to manage hearings to facilitate the participation of people with different needs and vulnerabilities in hearings. Presidential Guidance on the topic *Vulnerable parties and witnesses in Employment Tribunal proceedings* was published for the first time on 22 April 2020. This reflects and captures many of the principles developed in the case law discussed below. The Guidance is intended to "*focus the attention of all Employment Tribunal judges and members, parties, witnesses and representatives upon the issue of vulnerability, however that issue might arise or appear*". In particular, the Guidance should be considered where a person is likely to suffer fear or distress in giving evidence because of their own circumstances or those relating to the case, or their participation in proceedings is likely to be diminished by reason of vulnerability. The Guidance provides examples of the sorts of orders or arrangements that might be made to facilitate the participation of vulnerable witnesses and parties including the use of screens to prevent a party or witness from seeing or being seen by another party or witness, use of live link or pre-recorded video evidence, intermediaries, adjustments to language used or physical arrangements for the hearing, etc. The Guidance indicates that Tribunals may look to the Criminal Procedure Rules or the Family Procedure Rules for further guidance, but should remember that Tribunals do not have the same powers as the Civil Courts and cannot, for example, direct that public funding be made available to provide measures for parties, although if an Employment Judge orders the production of essential medical reports or evidence, repayment may be made in line with indicative HMCTS rates. Inquiry by the party or witness should first be made of HMCTS as a guide to what is possible or reasonable before incurring any costs.

As indicated, the Presidential Guidance reflects the principles developed in the case law, although there is much in the case law that it will still be valuable to consider. The key cases include *Royds LLP v Pine* [2012] EWCA Civ 1734, [2012] All ER (D) 184 (Dec) and *Pine v Cineven Ltd* [2016] EWCA Civ 1047. Further detailed guidance was given by the EAT in *Rackham v NHS Professionals Ltd* (2015) UKEAT/0110/15/LA, and expanded on in by the Northern Ireland Court of Appeal in *Galo v Bombardier Aerospace UK* [2016] NICA 25, [2016] IRLR 703, as follows (para 53):

(1)   It is a fundamental right of a person with a disability to enjoy a fair hearing and to have been able to participate effectively in the hearing.

(2)   Courts needs to focus on the impact of a mental health disability in the conduct of litigation. Courts must recognise the fact that this may have influenced the claimant's ability to conduct proceedings in a rational manner.

(3)   Courts and Tribunals can, and regularly do, have regard to the general, non-binding guidance and practical advice of the kind given in the Equal Treatment Bench Book published by the Judicial College (Revised 2013) (hereinafter called "the ETBB") in considering how best to accommodate disabled litigants in the court or tribunal process. It is clear therefore that courts and tribunals should pay particular attention to the ETBB when the question of disability, including mental disability, arises.

(4)   The ETBB provides helpful information for judges about the problems experienced by such litigants in accessing the courts or tribunals or participating in proceedings. The authors point out that "this may lead to erroneous perceptions such as that the person is being awkward or untruthful and inconsistent. In fact the problem may come down to a difficulty in communication or understanding." The ETBB has regularly been revised and updated. It has a section dealing with mental disabilities describing the different ways in which mental disability may arise and manifest itself. It points out that adjustments to court or trial procedures may be required to accommodate the needs of persons with such disabilities. Memory, communication skills and the individual's response to perceived aggression may all be affected.

Practical advice is given to particular situations when they arise. Decisions concerning case and hearing management " . . . . should address the particular needs of the individual concerned insofar as these are reasonable. The individual should be given an opportunity to express their needs. Expert evidence may be required". It is recognised that if a litigant has a condition that is worsened by stress, the difficulties will almost certainly become greater if he/she is acting in person.

(5)   The presence of a McKenzie Friend in civil or family proceedings or an independent mental health advocate in a Tribunal should be encouraged in order to help locate information, prompt as necessary during the questioning of witnesses and provide the opportunity for brief discussion of issues as they arise. A more tolerant approach to the use of a lay representative may assist.

(6)   A modified approach may be necessary when seeking to obtain reliable evidence from a person with mental health problems especially those who are mentally frail. It is necessary to ascertain whether any communication difficulties are the result of mental impairment. Section 7 of the ETBB stresses the need for particular assistance to be given in relation to those of mental disabilities, specific learning difficulties and mental capacity.

(7)   An early "ground rules hearing" is indicated in the ETBB at Chapter 5. Such a hearing would involve a preliminary consideration of the procedure that the tribunal or court will adopt tailored to the particular circumstances of the litigant. Thus for example the Tribunal may consider:

•   The approach to questioning of the claimant and to the method of cross-examination by him/her. Adaptions to questioning may be necessary to facilitate the evidence of a vulnerable person.

•   How questioning is to be controlled by the Tribunal.

•   The manner, tenor, tone, language and duration of questioning appropriate to the witness's problems.

•   Whether it is necessary for the Tribunal to obtain an expert report to identify what steps are required in order to ensure a fair procedure tailored to the needs of the particular applicant.

•   The applicant under a disability, if a personal litigant, must have the procedures of the court fully explained to him and advised as to the availability of pro bono assistance/McKenzie Friends/voluntary sector help available.

•   Recognition must be given to the possibility that those with learning disabilities need extra time even if represented to ensure that matters are carefully understood by them.

•   Great care should be taken with the language and vocabulary that is utilised to ensure that the directions given at the ground rules hearing are being fully understood.

•   As happened in the *Rackham* case, consideration should be given to the need for respondent's counsel to offer cross-examination and questions in writing to assist the claimant with the claimant being allowed some time to consult, if represented, with his counsel. These were deemed "reasonable adjust-ments".

•   The Tribunal must keep these adjustments needed under review.

In *Anderson v Turning Point Eespro* [2019] EWCA Civ 815, [2019] ICR 1362 the Court of Appeal emphasised that the guidance in *Galo* was helpful but there should not be a mechanistic approach. A ground rules hearing is not required in every case, and where parties are represented the Tribunal can generally rely on representatives to ensure that suitable adjustments are identified and requested (although there may be cases where the Tribunal should propose an adjustment not requested if it appears necessary in the interests of justice).

In *Heal v University of Oxford and ors* (UKEAT/0070 and 0183/19/DA) the EAT (Choudhury P) reviewed the above authorities again in the context of considering a case where the adjustment sought by the claimant was permission to record the hearing as, because of a disability, he had difficulty making notes. In that case, the Employment Judge had indicated that it would deal with the Claimant's application at the start of the full hearing. Part of the claimant's appeal was that the judge had erred in law in not deciding the application in advance of the hearing so that the claimant would know in advance what the position was, and also would not, when bringing a recording device to tribunal, be in contempt of the prohibition in *s 9* of the *Senior Courts Act 1981* on bringing a recording device to court. The EAT held there was no error on the part of the Judge. Choudhury P noted (at para 27) that although the Tribunal is under a duty to make reasonable adjustments to alleviate any substantial disadvantage related to a disability in a party's ability to participate in proceedings, there is no automatic entitlement to an adjustment. It is always a matter for the Tribunal to determine as a matter of case management, having regard to all relevant factors and the Overriding Objective. Choudhury P further held that it is a matter of discretion as to whether such an application is dealt with in writing or at a preliminary or final hearing. In relation to requests to record proceedings, Choudhury P held that the following (non-exhaustive) list of factors may need to be taken into account:

(1)   The extent of the inability and any medical or other evidence in support;

(2)   Whether the disadvantage in question can be alleviated by other means, such as assistance from another person, the provision of additional time or additional breaks in proceedings;

(3)   The extent to which the recording of proceedings will alleviate the disadvantage in question;

(4)   The risk that the recording will be used for prohibited purposes, such as to publish recorded material, or extracts therefrom;

(5)   The views of the other party or parties involved, and, in particular, whether the knowledge that a recording is being made by one party would worry or distract witnesses;

(6)   Whether there should be any specific directions or limitations as to the use to which any recorded material may be put;

(7)   The means of recording and whether this is likely to cause unreasonable disruption or delay to proceedings.

Choudhury P added that where an adjustment is made to permit the recording of proceedings, parties ought to be reminded of the express prohibition under *s 9(1)(b)* of the *1981 Ac*t on publishing such recording or playing it in the hearing of the public or any section of the public, which would include any upload of the recording (or part thereof) on to any publicly accessible website or social media or any other information sharing platform.

20.84   *Timetabling and Power to Control Proceedings*

Rule 45 provides that a Tribunal may impose limits on the time that a party may take in presenting evidence, questioning witnesses or making submissions, and may prevent the party from proceeding beyond any time so allotted. This, in conjunction with *Rule 41*, gives the Tribunal considerable ability to control the proceedings before it. Reference should also be made to the Presidential Guidance on General Case Management which contains a section on Timetabling. That Guidance underlines that the parties have a duty to conduct the case so that, wherever possible, the tribunal can complete the case within the time allowed. See also **20.55** above for the Tribunal's general powers of case management.

The usual procedure at a hearing is as follows:

(a)   the party upon whom the burden of proof rests is nominally responsible for 'opening' the case. This is the claimant in a discrimination case and the employer in an unfair dismissal claim where dismissal is conceded. If there are issues on which there is a burden of proof on both parties in turn, the tribunal is likely to hear submissions from the parties before deciding who should go first;

(b)   the party responsible for 'opening' the case: (i) may occasionally be permitted to make an opening statement giving an outline of the case (but this is increasingly rare except in the most substantial and complex cases and is not permitted in Scotland); and (ii) calls evidence first, each witness giving evidence on oath or under affirmation (with the witness's statement normally being taken as his evidence-in-chief, and being read by the tribunal before the witness is called: see below) and the witness then being cross-examined by the other party, with questions by the members of the tribunal either interposed in cross-examination or, more usually, at the end;

(c)   the other party:(i) calls his evidence; and (ii) goes first when making a closing speech (usually called submissions); and

(d)   the party who opened the case then makes submissions (in Scotland the order of making submissions is reversed). See further as to the content of submissions, and the use of written submissions, below.

A party does not have the right to cross-examine come what may. The tribunal has a duty to keep the inquiry before it within reasonable bounds, and it does not have to allow lengthy and detailed cross-examination on matters that do not appear to it to be of assistance. These points were emphasised by the EAT in *Zurich Insurance Co v Gulson* [1998] IRLR 118. It is for the parties to determine what evidence they wish to put before the tribunal, however the EAT has confirmed the tribunal has a discretion to exclude even relevant evidence, where for instance the evidence is unnecessarily repetitive or of only marginal relevance: *Digby v East Cambridgeshire District Council* [2007] IRLR 585 (and see for the power of the tribunal to exclude irrelevant and marginally relevant evidence in advance of the hearing *HSBC Asia Holdings BV v Gillespie* [2011] IRLR 209, [2011] ICR 192, EAT). This discretion must be exercised consistently with the parties' rights under *Art 6* of the *European Convention on Human Rights*, to a fair hearing of their respective cases. However, Art 6 does not give unlimited protection to whatever a party may want. It has been confirmed, for instance, in *Power v Greater Manchester Police Authority* (UKEAT/0087/10), that there is no general right for a claimant to cross-examine the person alleged to have discriminated against him under *Art 6*, so that it was not a ground of appeal that the respondent had not called the decision-taker concerned as a witness, thereby preventing the claimant from cross-examining her. See also *Khan v Vignette Europe Ltd* (UKEAT/0134/09), where the EAT upheld a tribunal's refusal of a request by the claimant for an adjournment part-way through a hearing to enable him to undertake religious observances for Ramadan.

The tribunal may also, in the interests of devoting a proportionate amount of time to issues within the case, curtail unnecessarily lengthy evidence or cross-examination. However, that discretion must be exercised judicially and is open to challenge on appeal if exercised by reference to irrelevant considerations or perversely, as in the *Digby* case. Even before the introduction of *Rule 45*, it was an increasingly common practice for tribunals to set time limits on stages in the proceedings, such as cross-examination of a particular witness or the making of a closing submission, usually as part of a timetable set at the start of the hearing to ensure that it is concluded within the time available. Such restrictions should not be so restrictive as to deny a party the opportunity to put his case. The general rule in adversarial proceedings (known as *"the rule in Browne v Dunn"*), as between the parties, is that one party should not be entitled to impugn the evidence of another party's witness if he has not asked appropriate questions enabling the witness to deal with the criticisms that are being made. However, the rule is not absolute and the need for a proportionate approach may mean that the Tribunal can or should curtail cross-examination even where there is an evidential dispute. Failure to cross-examine will not necessarily amount to acceptance of a witness's testimony: the question is always whether it will be fair for the Tribunal to reach a conclusion adverse to that witness if the particular point has not been put to them: see *Deepak Fertilizers & Petrochemicals Corp Ltd v Davy McKee (UK) London Ltd* [2002] EWCA Civ 1396 at paras 49-50 and *NHS Trust Development Authority v Saiger and ors* (UKEAT/0167 and 0276/15/LA), at paras 99-102. In some cases, where it is fair and appropriate to do so, the judge may indicate that there need not be cross-examination on a particular point and that this will not be taken as a concession.

In his judgment in *Bache*, Mummery LJ made the following statement of the principles governing the conduct of tribunal hearings:

> "(1) At the hearing the tribunal must follow a procedure which is fair to both sides. It must normally allow each party to call relevant evidence, to ask relevant questions of the other side's witnesses and to make relevant submissions on the evidence and the law.
>
> (2) The tribunal is responsible for the fair conduct of the hearing. It is in control. Neither the parties nor their representatives are in control of the hearing.
>
> (3) Procedural fairness applies to the conduct of all those involved in the hearing. Just as the tribunal is under a duty to behave fairly, so are the parties and their representatives. The tribunal is accordingly entitled to require the parties and their representatives to act in a fair and reasonable way in the presentation of their evidence, in challenging the other side's evidence and in making submissions. The rulings of the tribunal on what is and is not relevant and on what is the fair and appropriate procedure ought to be respected even by a party and his representative who do not agree with a ruling. If the party and his representative disagree with a ruling, an appeal lies against it if the tribunal has made an error of law."

As the Presidential Guidance on Timetabling makes clear, in simple cases it will be rare for a formal timetable to be issued, although the Judge might set out and agree at the outset how the hearing will proceed. For longer cases, a written timetable may be created. Fairness will be the touchstone, but this does not always require an equal division of the time between the parties: it will depend on the issues. If an interpreter is required, additional time will be required. Once the timetable has been set, a Tribunal will expect the parties to keep to it as part of their duty to assist. The Presidential Guidance states that if time is exceeded, a Tribunal can ultimately guillotine the evidence. Tribunals do not, however, like to take that step.

The procedure in practice is that the Judge (who, along with the lay members (where they are present), will have read the Claim Form and Response Form) may first seek to clarify what issues are, or remain, in dispute between the parties. A list of issues might have been agreed or set as a result of a Preliminary Hearing for Case Management, or upon Initial Consideration of the Claim. If there is an agreed list of issues, that will, as a general rule, limit the issues at the substantive hearing to that list: see *Land Rover v Short* (UKEAT/0496/10) as approved in *Parekh v London Borough of Brent* [2012] EWCA Civ 1630, [2012] All ER (D) 70 (Dec). Where the issues have been properly identified and formulated, the hearing will focus upon and only upon the issues as so identified: see *Tucker v Partnership in Care Ltd* (UKEAT/0455/09). This is particularly so if both sides are represented: see *Scicluna v Zippy Stitch* [2018] EWCA Civ 1320 in which Underhill LJ suggested that it would only be in "exceptional" cases where it would be legitimate for a tribunal not to be bound by the 'precise terms' of an agreed list of issues. However, the Court of Appeal in *Mervyn v BW Controls Ltd* [2020] EWCA Civ 393 considered that Underhill LJ's judgment in Zippy Stitch was not to be read as imposing a requirement of exceptionality in every case before a tribunal can depart from an agreed list of issues. In *Mervyn* the Court of Appeal observed that "*it is good practice for an employment tribunal, at the start of a substantive hearing with either or both parties unrepresented, to consider whether any list of issues previously drawn up at a case management hearing properly reflects the significant issues in dispute between the parties. If it is clear that it does not, or that it may not do so, then the ET should consider whether an amendment to the list of issues is necessary in the interests of justice*". Further, in that case, with the claimant in person, the Court of Appeal considered that it was an error of law for the Tribunal merely to have asked whether the parties confirmed the previous list of issues: the Tribunal should have specifically asked the claimant whether, if (contrary to her case) it found she had resigned rather than been dismissed, she wished the Tribunal to consider whether she had been constructively unfairly dismissed or not. The Court of Appeal's approach in *Mervyn*, while apparently departing from the strict approach in Zippy Stitch, reflects the more lenient approach taken in other cases. Thus both the Court of Appeal in *Parekh* and the EAT in *Price v Surrey County Council* (UKEAT/0450/10) (a judgment given, unusually, by the Senior President of Tribunals, Carnwath LJ, sitting as an EAT judge) emphasised the importance of the tribunal that hears the case satisfying itself as to precisely what issues do require to be decided, and not simply accepting what the parties may have agreed as the issues or sticking slavishly to a list of issues. Further, the EAT in *Millin v Capsticks Solicitors LLP* [2014] All ER (D) 12 (Dec), [2014] UKEAT/0093/14 emphasised that a list of issues is not to be construed as a formal contract, pleading, or statute; it is a useful tool to allow a Tribunal to case manage a hearing so as best to ensure justice as between the parties. In particular, where a legal label has been put on a factual claim as part of the process of agreeing a list of issues, the Tribunal may be required to consider whether it is the right legal label and, if need be, identify at the hearing alternative legal labels for the same issue and invite submissions on, and determine, the same: *Saha v Capita Plc* (UKEAT/0080/18/DM) at para 40 per Slade J. In that case, the claim had been identified as detriment for alleged infringement of a right under the *WTR 1998* under *s 45A(1)(f) ERA 1996*, but was held to fail because the allegation related to a future breach, rather than a past breach. Slade J held that the Tribunal should have considered the claim as a detriment for making a protected disclosure under *s 47B ERA 1996*, where the fact that the disclosure related to a future breach would not have prevented it from succeeding (although there would need to have been consideration of whether it was in the public interest). The claim was remitted to the Employment Tribunal to re-determine. Much the same situation might arise in relation to the overlap between victimization claims under the *EqA 2010* and public interest disclosure claims under *s 47B* or *s 43B ERA 1996*.

Particular care is required where, as in *Price*, the list agreed between the parties was not a helpful framework for deciding the case. The list in *Price* was attached to the judgment as an illustration of how not to prepare a list of issues not least because it failed to distinguish clearly between the central issues and the detailed factual allegations. Having said that, the tribunal hearing the case does not have carte blanche to decide new points: it is confined to deciding the pleaded issues and cannot when considering the evidence adjudicate upon additional allegations or complaints: see *Chapman v Simon* [1994] IRLR 124, *Foster v Bon Groundwork* [2012] IRLR 517 and *Chandhok v Tirkey* [2015] IRLR 195. To do otherwise will deny the party affected a fair hearing: *British Gas Services Ltd v McCaull* [2001] IRLR 60. A Tribunal may err in law if it decides issues that are not in dispute between the parties. An example can be seen in *Mr Clutch Auto Centres v Blakemore* [2014] All ER (D) 40 (Sep), [2014] UKEAT/0509/13 in which, whilst the parties disagreed as to how and when, they agreed that the employment relationship had ended. The EAT held in such circumstances it was not open to the judge to find that the employment relationship was still continuing.

The judge will also deal at the start of the hearing with any preliminary points that have not been dealt with by paper adjudication or at a previous hearing. This might include correcting the name of the respondent, considering any applications to amend the Claim Form or Response Form and ruling on any disputes about disclosure of documents or attendance of witnesses either party wishes to raise. Issues about admission of evidence may continue to be raised up until the end of the hearing. In *Sweeney v Merseyside Community Rehabilitation Company Limited* (UKEAT/0277/17/JOJ) the EAT (Auerbach J) held that a Tribunal erred in refusing to admit a new document in evidence in the course of the Claimant's closing submissions where it was relevant and the parties could properly deal with it in submissions.

The Presidential Guidance on General Case Management sets out in the section on timetabling these general steps in proceedings (see para 10).

20.85   *Rights of representation*

The right of a party to be represented at a hearing by whoever he chooses (whether or not professionally qualified) is expressly given by *s 6, ETA 1996*. In *Bache v Essex County Council* [2000] IRLR 251, the Court of Appeal ruled that the tribunal therefore has no power to 'sack' a party's representative under its general power to control the proceedings. If it does so, this is a ground of appeal notwithstanding the acquiescence of the party at the time. However, denial of representation by the chosen person did not render the hearing a nullity, and on the facts the decision was upheld.

The EAT has applied the principle in *Bache* in a case where the employers unsuccessfully sought an order forbidding the claimant from using a particular firm of solicitors to represent him at the hearing because of a claimed conflict of interest: *Dispatch Management Services (UK) Ltd v Douglas* [2002] IRLR 389. However, if the party's chosen representative behaves inappropriately, the tribunal's powers to act in response to the misbehaviour of a party (in an extreme case extending to the striking out of the claim or defence, provided that this is a proportionate response: see *Bennett v Southwark London Borough Council* [2002] EWCA Civ 223, [2002] IRLR 407) are equally available in respect of conduct of the representative acting on behalf of the party: *Rule 18(7)*. If the representative is acting for profit, the further sanction of a wasted costs order (see **20.135** for this) is available to the tribunal.

The tribunal has no express power to impose a representative on an unrepresented party. The EAT so held in *Johnson v Edwardian International Hotels Ltd* [2008] All ER (D) 23 (May), where the tribunal had sought to have the Official Solicitor appointed as the claimant's litigation friend, after he had made claims that he was the victim of a conspiracy involving the Prime Minister and the Jehovah's Witnesses to procure his dismissal. The EAT held that the tribunal's only recourse was to use its case management powers, including the power to strike out the claim on the ground that it had no reasonable prospects of success. However, in *AM (Afghanistan) v Secretary of State for the Home Department* [2017] EWCA Civ 1123 at para 48 Underhill LJ made clear his "strong provisional view" that his judgment in Johnson was not correct and in *Jhuti v Royal Mail Group Ltd* (UKEAT/0062/17) [2018] ICR 1077, Simler P that Johnson is not to be followed and that the *2013 Rules* do permit the employment tribunal to appoint a litigation friend where otherwise a litigant who lacks capacity to conduct litigation would have no means of accessing justice or obtaining a remedy. Simler P emphasised, however, that tribunals should tread carefully if invited to investigate a party's mental capacity. In such cases, it may well be that the tribunals powers to strike out misconceived or unreasonable claims should be considered. A tribunal should only embark on an assessment of capacity where there is clear evidence that there is a real issue as to whether an individual has capacity to conduct proceedings, and should never do so simply because the individual has been diagnosed as suffering from a mental illness. The principles for assessing capacity under the *Mental Capacity Act 2005* (*MCA 2005*) should be referred to in such cases, and also the principles in *CPR Part 21*. In *Jhuti* Simler P identified the most important principles to be as follows: (a) a person is assumed to have capacity unless it is established that they lack capacity: *ss 2(4)* and *3* of the *MCA 2005*, which provides a formula to be used in making a capacity assessment; (b) a person should not be permitted to act as a litigation friend unless he or she can fairly and competently conduct proceedings on behalf of the protected party and has no personal interest in the litigation or an interest adverse to that protected party; and (c) an application for an order appointing a litigation friend must be supported by evidence demonstrating that the person to be appointed is suitable and consents to act. Evidence must also be provided establishing the basis of the litigation friend's belief that the party lacks capacity to conduct the proceedings. In *Royal Bank of Scotland plc v AB* (UKEAT/0266/18/DA), 27 February 2020, the EAT (Swift J) held, applying *Jhuti* that the tribunal ought to have adjourned for an assessment of the claimant's capacity where she did not appear to recognise her counsel and appeared unable to respond to simple questions.

Although a party can choose anyone as a representative, any representative of a claimant (but not of a respondent) who is not a solicitor or barrister but who acts in a business capacity (which will be the case if the representative is paid) must be registered as a claims manager by the Financial Conduct Authority (FCA), thus regulated under the *Financial Services and Markets Act 2000* and the *Financial Services and Markets Act 2000 (Claims Management Activity) Order 2018 (SI 2018/1253)*. The *Act* makes it a criminal offence to provide regulated services other than in accordance with the *Act*. In *Miller v Community Links Trust* [2007] All ER (D) 196 (Nov), the EAT referred an unregulated representative to the regulator for possible action.

A person who is representing himself in a tribunal is known as a 'litigant in person'; this phrase is now to be preferred to 'self-represented litigant': see *Practice Guidance: Terminology for Litigants in Person* (issued by Lord Dyson MR, March 2013). The equivalent expression in Scotland is 'party litigant'.

20.86 *Written Representations and Skeleton Arguments*

Pursuant to *Rule 42*, the Tribunal shall consider any written representations from a party, including a party who does not propose to attend the hearing, if they are delivered to the Tribunal and to all other parties not less than 7 days before the hearing.

Written representations under *Rule 42* should not be confused with a skeleton argument that parties will often bring to a hearing setting out the central themes of their argument as to why they should succeed. Skeleton arguments are often provided to the Tribunal and other parties on the day of the hearing, sometimes at the outset of proceedings, and sometimes after the evidence has completed and the Tribunal is about to hear oral submissions. In the latter case, the Tribunal will often adjourn for a short period to read the written skeleton argument first and then proceed to hear oral submissions from the parties.

20.87 *Witnesses*

Rule 43 deals with witnesses. It provides that where a witness is called to give oral evidence, any witness statement of that person ordered by the Tribunal shall stand as that witness's evidence in chief unless the Tribunal orders otherwise. Acting under *Rule 43*, a Tribunal can decide to exclude parts of a witness statement (for example, if inadmissible in evidence). *Rule 43* requires witnesses to give their oral evidence on oath or affirmation.

Witnesses give their evidence seated at a table and should address the Judge as 'Sir' or 'Madam'. If, as is almost always required in England and Wales, a written witness statement has been prepared, the tribunal will normally have pre-read the statement themselves (for guidance as to the reading of witness statements see *Mehta v Child Support Agency* [2011] IRLR 305). Additional questions may then be asked if necessary, with the permission of the tribunal. In Scotland, evidence-in-chief is given by way of answers to questions from the party's representative, or if the party has no representative, by way of narrative or in answer to questions from the tribunal. *Rule 41* further provides that the Tribunal may itself question the parties or any witnesses so far as appropriate in order to clarify the issues or elicit the evidence. This may in particular be appropriate where one or both parties are unrepresented, in order to give effect to the Overriding Objective (*Rule 2*) of dealing with cases fairly and justly and, so far as practicable, ensuring that the parties are on an equal footing.

Documents should be introduced in the witness statements in chronological or other systematic order by the witness who can best deal with them. It is desirable, if possible, to cross-refer in the written witness statements to the page numbers of any relevant documents, and to invite the tribunal to read the documents or relevant parts together with the witness statement.

Detailed guidance is now provided in the Presidential Guidance on General Case Management concerning how a witness statement should be prepared. That guidance stresses the need for witness statements to be typed if possible, for the statement to be in logical, numbered paragraphs and should cover all the issues in the case and set out fully what the witness has to tell the Tribunal about their involvement in chronological order. The Guidance also underlines the fact that, as additional questions are only allowed in limited circumstances, the statement should be as full as possible. A supplemental statement should be prepared if something has been left out of a witness statement and should be exchanged with the other party "immediately". Otherwise, mutual exchange of witness statements is usual, although sometimes the Tribunal can order sequential exchange.

When the representative of one party cross-examines a witness of the other party, he should put questions to the witness and not make comments or statements. It must be remembered that there is a dual purpose to cross-examination. One is to test the truthfulness and reliability of the witness; the other is to put the questioner's version of the facts to the witness so far as it concerns him, so that he has an opportunity of commenting on it. A failure to do this may prejudice the cross-examiner's case. This is sometimes referred to as "*the rule in Browne v Dunn*", the rule being that a party who disputes the credibility of a witness on a particular matter must generally put that point to the witness as otherwise it will be unfair for the Tribunal to conclude that the witness is not telling the truth. This is not an absolute rule, however. In some cases fairness may not require that the case is 'put' in that way. See the lengthy discussion of "*the rule in Browne v Dunn*" by HHJ Hand QC in *NHS Trust Development Authority v Saiger and ors* (UKEAT/0167 and 0276/15/LA), especially at paragraphs 99–102. Note further that it is a general principle that a party or representative may not cross-examine his own witness; the concept of a 'hostile witness' is in practice almost unknown.

Parties acting in person, and non-legally qualified representatives, often have difficulty in cross-examining witnesses, through inexperience or unfamiliarity with what is required. In these circumstances the Judge may assist in giving guidance as to what questions can be asked and how they may be put, but should not take over the cross-examination of the witness, as this may lead to an appearance of bias in favour of the party being assisted. How far a Judge will be prepared to go in assisting a party in these circumstances is very much a matter of personal style, and therefore dependent on the particular Judge. As noted above, *Rule 2* (Overriding Objective) and *Rule 41* (Tribunal may itself question the parties or any witnesses 'so far as appropriate in order to clarify the issues or elicit the evidence') are relevant here.

Witnesses will not normally be permitted to refer to notes whilst giving evidence, unless these are agreed documents or a note taken by the witness at the time of an event or very soon thereafter; the witness may refer to such notes to refresh his memory of the event.

Where a witness is in the middle of giving evidence or being cross-examined when the tribunal adjourns for a break, the judge should normally warn the witness not to discuss their evidence with anyone during the break, although the judge is under no obligation to do so if the judge has no reason to anticipate that discussion of evidence will pose a threat to the truthfulness or reliability of the witness: *E&O Laboratories v Miller* (UKEATS/0007/19/SS) at para 21. In that case the Scottish EAT (Lord Summers) indicated that if a witness who is in the middle of giving evidence discusses their evidence with another witness during an adjournment (including short breaks), this may be unreasonable conduct (i.e. conduct that could be taken into account when considering a strike-out under *Rule 37(1)(b)* or an application for costs under *Rule 76*) if a prior warning has been given by the judge (ibid, para 19). However, it will not be unreasonable for a witness to discuss their evidence with another before or after giving evidence, nor will it in general be unreasonable for a witness to discuss their evidence during an adjournment if they have not been given a warning (ibid, para 20). In that case, Lord Summers appeared implicitly to accept that circumstances might arise in which a party's representative would be expected to warn witnesses not to discuss their evidence, but did not consider that it had been incumbent on the legal representative to do so in that case (ibid, paras 23–24). Lord Summers accordingly held in that case that the tribunal judge had been wrong to rely on the discussion between witnesses as a ground of unreasonable conduct in deciding to strike the case out under *Rule 37(1)(b)*. Lord Summers further noted in that case that 'not every witness is the personal responsibility of the party for whom he or she gives evidence', so even in cases where a witness has personally acted unreasonably, it may not amount to unreasonable conduct by a party to proceedings for the purposes of *Rule 76* or *Rule 37(1)(b)*.

Rule 43 also gives the tribunal a power to exclude from the hearing any person who is to appear as a witness in the proceedings until such time as that person gives evidence if it considers it in the interests of justice to do so. In Scotland it is the practice to require witnesses to wait outside the tribunal room until they are called to give their evidence; however, this is very infrequently done in English or Welsh proceedings. In *E&O Laboratories v Miller*, contrary to the Scottish practice, the witnesses for the respondent had sat in the tribunal room during the evidence of other witnesses (the respondent's counsel having been unfamiliar with the usual Scottish practice). This has also been regarded by the judge as unreasonable conduct and was part of the reason why the judge in that case had decided to strike out the respondent's case. However, Lord Summers in the EAT held that, given that *Rule 43* envisages that witnesses will be present in the tribunal room throughout unless excluded by the judge in the interests of justice, it could not possibly amount to unreasonable conduct for the witnesses to have remained in the tribunal room, notwithstanding the usual Scottish practice: ibid, para 11.

The powers of the tribunal extend to a power to call witnesses of its own initiative (or at the request of a party who is for some good reason unable or unwilling to call the witness): *Clapson v British Airways plc* [2001] IRLR 184. The evidence given by a witness in tribunal proceedings carries absolute privilege in the law of defamation, and is also within the principle of judicial immunity from suit which applies generally to judicial proceedings. Thus in *Parmar v East Leicester Medical Practice* [2011] IRLR 641 it was held that statements in a witness statement prepared for tribunal proceedings could not be used to found a claim of victimisation. However, the principle of judicial proceedings immunity is not wide enough to cover intimidating behaviour directed by a respondent at the claimant outside the tribunal room: *Nicholls v Corin Tech Ltd* [2008] All ER (D) 156 (May) (UKEAT/0290/07). The practice in the past has been that witnesses attending a hearing have been entitled to reclaim their travelling and subsistence expenses from the administration. However, the repayment of witness expenses was discontinued from 6 April 2012, for cases presented on or after that date; instead the tribunal has power to order a party to pay the witness's expenses (the paying party may either be the party calling the witness or the opposing party): see below in relation to costs **20.127**.

Rule 44 provides that, subject to any restrictive order the Tribunal makes on grounds of privacy or national security (under *Rules 50* and *94*: see below **20.89**), any witness statement which stands as evidence in chief shall be available for inspection during the course of the hearing by members of the public attending the hearing unless the Tribunal decides that all or any part of the statement is not to be admitted as evidence, in which case the statement or that part shall not be available for inspection. An illustration of *Rule 44* in operation is *Compass Group Plc v Guardian News and Media Ltd* [2014] UKEAT/0041/14 in which the EAT remitted to the Judge the issue of whether he had excluded the excised parts of the statement from evidence altogether, applying *Rule 43* (in which case those parts were not available for inspection by the public and media) or whether he had merely chosen to pay no attention to the parts in question (in which case inspection of the whole statement would be permitted under *Rule 44* with no further formality required).

20.88 *Non-Attendance and Postponements*

By *Rule 47*, if a party fails to attend or to be represented at the hearing, the Tribunal may dismiss the claim or proceed with the hearing in the absence of that party. Before doing so, it shall consider any information which is available to it, after any enquiries that may be practicable, about the reasons for the party's absence. The Tribunal may dismiss the claim or proceed with the hearing even if the party in question has not been expressly warned of the consequences of non-attendance or the right to apply for a postponement: the onus is on the party to attend or inform the Tribunal in a timely manner of the need for a postponement: *Dimitriu v Testerworld Ltd t/a De Pharmaceutical* (UKEAT/0088/19/OO).

An alternative course either on the non-attendance of a party, or on application of a party, is to postpone (or if started, adjourn) the hearing to another date under the general case management power of *Rule 29*. Special provision has now been made in the *Rules* for applications for postponements (which term includes adjournments which cause the hearing to be held or continued on a later date): see *Rule 30A*. These provisions (which are applicable to all proceedings which are presented to a tribunal on or after 6 April 2016) restrict the scope of the general case management power under *Rule 29*. *Rule 30A* provides that:

(a)   Any application for a postponement must ("shall") be presented to the Tribunal and communicated to the other parties as soon as possible after the need for a postponement becomes known (*Rule 30A(1)*);

(b)   If a party applies to postpone a hearing less than 7 days before the date on which the hearing begins, the Tribunal is constrained in its ability to allow a postponement. It may only order a postponement in one of three circumstances (*Rule 30A(2)*):

    (i)   All the other parties consent to a postponement and it is practicable and appropriate for the purposes of giving the parties the opportunity to resolve their disputes by agreement, or it is otherwise in accordance with the Overriding Objective;

    (ii)   The application was necessitated by an act or omission of another party or the Tribunal; or

    (iii)   There are exceptional circumstances (which may include ill health relating to an existing long term health condition or disability).

(c)   Where a Tribunal has ordered two or more postponements of a hearing in the same proceedings on the application of the same party, and that party makes an application for a further postponement, such an application may only be granted in the three circumstances listed in (b) above (*Rule 30A(3)*).

Further, amendments have been made to *Rule 76(1)* to provide that where a postponement or adjournment has been granted on application of a party made less than 7 days before the date on which the relevant hearing begins, the Tribunal may make an award of costs against that party.

Subject to those provisions, there are a wide range of circumstances in which the Tribunal will be called upon to exercise its discretion as to whether or not to adjourn or postpone proceedings. When considering whether or not to postpone, the Tribunal must also have regard to the Presidential Guidance issued concerning seeking a Postponement of a Hearing. That guidance provides as follows.

Applications for a postponement should be made in writing and should state why the application is made and why it would be in accordance with the Overriding Objective to grant the postponement. (One might now add that parties applying in the circumstances captured by *Rule 30A* should set out why they contend those provisions have been satisfied.) Where application is made in writing, the party must notify the other parties that they should send any objections to the tribunal as soon as possible. It is important for parties to appreciate the need to enclose all documents relevant to the application with the application. If these requirements are not complied with, then the application will ordinarily not be considered absent exceptional circumstances. Where exceptional circumstances are relied upon, they should be detailed in the application. The guidance also states that the party wishing to make an application for postponement should wherever possible discuss the proposal either directly with the other parties or through their representatives. If this discussion has taken place, then the detail should be provided to the Tribunal. Where agreement is reached, the Tribunal should be told of this fact. The Guidance draws parties' attention to the fact that where the hearing has been fixed with the agreement of the parties, this will be a factor which is taken into account by the Judge when considering the postponement application.

The Guidance goes on to provide specific examples of additional information that would be of assistance to the Tribunal in different circumstances. This is referred to where relevant in the discussion of the case law below.

One situation which arises relatively frequently is the failure of a party (often, but not always the claimant) to attend coupled with an application for an adjournment of the hearing on the grounds of the absent party's ill-health. Guidance has been given by the Court of Appeal prior to *Rule 30A* in two cases – *Teinaz v Wandsworth London Borough Council* [2002] EWCA Civ 1040, [2002] IRLR 721 and *Andreou v Lord Chancellor's Department* [2002] EWCA Civ 1192, [2002] IRLR 728 – as to how a tribunal should apply the conflicting considerations of justice when such an application is made on or immediately before the date of the hearing. Where *Rule 30A(2)* applies, the main issue will be whether or not there are "exceptional circumstances" entitling the tribunal to permit the postponement. The definition of "exceptional circumstances" in *Rule 30A(4)* is inclusive, specifically referring to ill health relating to an existing long term health conditions or disabilities. Short term or sudden ill health is not, however, excluded and where applicable is likely to be regarded as capable of amounting to an exceptional circumstance. It would therefore seem unlikely that *Rule 30A(2)* will make a substantive change in relation to this class of postponement applications. The Court of Appeal's guidance in *Teinaz* and *Andreou* emphasises that the tribunal is entitled to require clear medical evidence to satisfy it that the impediment to attendance is genuine, the burden being on the party making the application. If there is clear and uncontradicted evidence that a party is medically unfit to attend the hearing, it will often be an error of law to proceed with the hearing in the absence of a party, even if this causes considerable inconvenience or delay to the proceedings, since the absent party is in effect denied a fair hearing of his case: see *Chang-Tave v Haydon School* (UKEAT/0153/10). The *Teinaz* case itself also relied expressly on *ECHR, Art 6* as demanding nothing less than an adjournment in those circumstances (see eg para 21). That said, in *Transport for London v*

O'Cathail [2013] IRLR 310, [2013] ICR 614, the Court of Appeal held that it can be legitimate for a tribunal to take the exceptional step of rejecting an application for an adjournment on medical grounds, even in the face of unchallenged medical evidence supporting an adjournment. The Court emphasised that whilst the position of the potentially absent claimant is highly relevant, it is not determinative of every case. Overall fairness to both parties must be considered in the round and not pre-determined by the situation of one of the parties. *Art 6* of the *ECHR* does not compel the tribunal to the conclusion that it is always unfair to refuse an application for an adjournment on medical grounds, if it would mean that the hearing would take place in the party's absence: the tribunal must balance the adverse consequences of proceeding with the hearing in the absence of one party against the right of the other party to have a trial within reasonable time and the public interest in prompt and efficient adjudication of cases. See also *De Smith v Awe Plc and ors* (UKEAT/0292/16/BA), 11 April 2017 (upholding the Tribunal's decision to proceed with a 10-day hearing involving eight individual respondents in the absence of the claimant when granting his adjournment application would have delayed the hearing by 5 months).

The Presidential Guidance on Postponements, in line with this case law, states that where a party or witness is unable to attend for medical reasons, a medical certificate and supporting medical evidence should be provided in addition to an explanation of the nature of the health condition concerned. If medical evidence is supplied, it should include a statement from the medical practitioner that in their opinion, the applicant is unfit to attend the hearing, the prognosis of the condition and an indication of when that state of affairs may cease.

Where the evidence is unclear as to the applicant's fitness to attend or continue with the hearing, *Teinaz* emphasised that the tribunal has a power to give a direction to enable doubts to be resolved, eg by allowing for a short adjournment for further enquiries to be made. In *Iqbal v Metropolitan Police Authority* (UKEAT/0186/12), the EAT held that where an application for an adjournment on health grounds is made during the hearing, the tribunal should have regard to medical evidence including that in the bundle (eg expert and occupational health reports). Further, HHJ Richardson held when making further enquiries, a tribunal was entitled to entitled to ask the litigant to take with him a short letter drafted by the Tribunal explaining the assistance that the Tribunal can give to litigants in person and explaining what assistance and opinion it is that is required from the medical practitioner (para 20). Further enquiries will not, however always be required. In a "perhaps rare" case, the EAT in *Ejiofor t/a Mitchell & Co Solicitors v Sullivan* [2014] All ER (D) 77 (Sep), [2014] UKEAT/0268/13 upheld the Judge's decision to proceed without more, despite a sick note being produced (the Judge had found that a sick note had been "produced simply to add spurious weight to a weak and very late application for an adjournment"). Further guidance on the factors to be weighed up in determining last minute applications to adjourn was given in *D'Silva v Manchester Metropolitan University* (UKEAT/0336/09/LA) [2011] All ER (D) 05 (May), where the EAT upheld a decision to refuse an adjournment sought on the ground that the claimant claimed to be unfit to appear (but without supporting medical evidence) and sought an adjournment to arrange for representation, having lost his legal representation just before the hearing; the EAT held that the claimant was an educated and intelligent man with a full grasp of his claim and was therefore not sufficiently disadvantaged by the lack of representation to justify the cost and inconvenience to the respondent of an adjournment.

It is also not uncommon in practice that one party or the other does not attend without prior warning or explanation. The Court of Appeal has ruled that if the claimant fails to attend the hearing, the tribunal has a very wide discretion in the light of the available evidence whether to dismiss the claim, proceed in the claimant's absence or adjourn to another date: *Roberts v Skelmersdale College* [2003] EWCA Civ 954, [2004] IRLR 69, [2003] ICR 1127. The usual procedure in such a case, whether it is the claimant or respondent who has failed to attend, is for a member of the tribunal staff to telephone the party concerned to seek an explanation for their absence. This practice was endorsed by the EAT in *Cooke v Glenrose Fish Co* [2004] IRLR 866, [2004] ICR 1188, and the EAT has since held that a failure to attempt to contact the missing party would provide grounds for a review of any decision taken in that party's absence: *Euro Hotels (Thornton Heath) Ltd v Alam* [2009] All ER (D) 198 (Aug) (UKEAT/0006/09). The same approach was adopted by the EAT in a case where the parties had been ordered to lodge written submissions, the claimant's had not been received, and the tribunal proceeded to reach its decision without any attempt to contact him to find out what had happened: *Quashie v Methodist Homes Housing Association* [2012] All ER (D) 74 (May), [2012] ICR 1330. The EAT held that the tribunal was not entitled to assume that the claimant had decided not to make submissions, and its failure to investigate the matter deprived her of a fair hearing. See, to like effect, *Nyathi v Secretary of State for Justice* (UKEAT/0229/17/JOJ), 1 May 2018.

An option often adopted in practice when the claimant fails to attend, if the claim is of unfair dismissal, where the respondent has the initial burden of proof, is for the tribunal to hear the respondent's evidence and submissions before deciding the case on its merits, in the absence of the claimant. If the claimant does not attend for claimed medical reasons but without providing sufficient evidence of incapacity, the tribunal may refer the case to a PHR to consider striking the claim out as not being actively pursued; see *Rolls Royce Ltd v Riddle* [2008] IRLR 873; but see also *Abegaze v Shrewsbury College of Arts and Technology* [2009] EWCA Civ 96, [2010] IRLR 238 and **20.17** above.

In the case of non-attendance of a respondent, if when contacted by the tribunal an excuse or explanation for non-attendance is offered, the respondent should be told of the right to apply for an adjournment, and any such application must be considered before the tribunal decides how to proceed: *Beswick Paper Ltd v Britton* (UKEAT/0104/09); this would presumably equally be so if it is the claimant who fails to attend but proffers an explanation. See also *Southwark London Borough Council v Bartholomew* [2004] ICR 358, [2003] All ER (D) 190 (Dec), EAT. If the respondent fails to appear without good reason having been given, the tribunal will usually agree to hear the claimant's case and give a decision in the respondent's absence.

If a representative for the party attends, the representative is entitled to be heard even though the party has not attended (see *Astles v A G Stanley Ltd* (UKEAT/1275/95), IDS Brief 588). It is also not uncommon that both parties attend the hearing but an application is made for an adjournment because of a last minute development affecting the conduct of the case, most commonly the sudden illness of an important witness. As indicated above, such applications are likely now to be caught by *Rule 30A(2)*. In such a case, the tribunal will consider the matter in the light of the views of both parties, and balancing the interests of justice as between the parties. Where *Rule 30A(2)* applies, one of the three bases on which the application may be allowed must be made out. A pre-Rule 30A(2) example can be found in *North Bristol NHS Trust v Harrold* [2012] All ER (D) 13 (Oct) (UKEAT/0548/11), where the EAT endorsed a tribunal's decision to refuse a respondent's application to adjourn a hearing on the final day of a three-day hearing in order to allow the respondent to call further witnesses; the EAT held a tribunal should not accede automatically to the wishes of one of the litigants, but rather balance the interests of both parties.

Turning to other grounds for seeking a postponement, in *Firouzian v Metroline Travel Ltd* [2012] All ER (D) 298 (Oct) (UKEAT/0233/12), the EAT held the tribunal was entitled to refuse to adjourn what is now a preliminary hearing on the question of disability until after the claimant's criminal trial. That trial was in respect of causing death by dangerous driving arising out of his employment as a bus driver. The claims of disability and race discrimination arose from how the claimant was allegedly dealt with under internal proceedings as a result of the same driving incident. The EAT held there was no risk of prejudicing the criminal trial because of the lack of overlap between the issues on the preliminary hearing and that trial. The tribunal had been entitled to refuse to postpone the preliminary hearing.

The Presidential Guidance now covers this situation. It indicates where there are other court proceedings (whether civil or criminal) details should be given as to when these proceedings were commenced, what they entail, and how it is said that they will affect the Tribunal case, or how the Tribunal proceedings will affect those other proceedings.

If the case is determined in the absence of a party and it later transpires that that party had not received notification of the hearing date, the tribunal may reconsider its decision: see **20.72–20.73** above. An application for reconsideration may also be made, and would need to be considered on its merits, if there is any other reason for the absence of the party which had not been known to the tribunal when a decision to proceed with the hearing had been taken. The issue for the tribunal will in each case be what is the balance of the interests of justice as between the decision reached standing or being set aside and the case being referred for a hearing, or re-hearing. It may be relevant to the determination of this point that the expense and inconvenience to the attending party of a re-hearing can be compensated by an order for costs; but it is generally a factor of little weight against ordering a re-hearing that the party whose representative failed to attend the hearing may recover any losses from the representative: see *Euro Hotels (Thornton Heath) Ltd v Alam* (UKEAT/0006/09/DM), 20 April 2009.

The Presidential Guidance considers other situations. Where parties and witnesses are not available this should be notified to the Tribunal as soon as possible stating the details of the witness or party concerned; what attempts have been made to make alternative arrangements; the reason for the unavailability and in the case of a witness, the relevance of their evidence. Any supporting documents should be provided. The same approach should be followed where a representative has become unavailable or a newly appointed representative is unavailable. It sometimes happens that a party's representative will withdraw shortly before a hearing. Where this has occurred, the Presidential Guidance indicates that details should be given as to when this has happened and whether alternative representation has been or is being sought.

If an outstanding appeal to the EAT or other appellant court is relevant to the hearing, details of the dates of the appeal and the matters being appealed should be provided. This is frequently encountered where, for example, a liability determination of the tribunal is appealed and a postponement is sought of a listed remedy hearing. In such circumstances, Tribunals are often keen to know when the appeal was lodged and whether the appeal has been considered by the EAT on the preliminary sift process under *Rule 3(7)* of the *EAT Rules*. If an appeal has passed through the EAT's sift, the Tribunal will know that the appeal has reasonable prospects of success and this is likely to affect the decision to postpone. However it does not always mean that a postponement will be granted. There can be situations where it is more appropriate for the case to complete all parts of the first instance decision making so that all appeals can be heard in one go.

If the basis of an application is late disclosure of information or documentation, then details of the failure to disclose, and the contents of the documents or information, should be given. The applicant should also explain how the documents/information are relevant to the issues in the case and how the late provision relates to Orders which have already been given in the case, and any requests made by the parties for such information or documents, and the responses to those requests that have been received.

Finally, the Guidance indicates that Employment Judges are now encouraged to take a more pro-active approach to applications to postpone. If information has not been supplied, then an application may become the subject of a further enquiry from the Judge (although this will have the effect of delaying the determination of the application). Once all the relevant information is available, the Judge is to take into account all matters and information now available, and consider whether to grant or refuse the postponement. The decision remains in the discretion of the Judge concerned. The decision is notified to the parties as soon as possible after the decision has been made.

20.89 *Privacy and Restrictions on Disclosure: General*

Rule 50(1) gives a Tribunal a discretion, at any stage of the proceedings, on its own initiative or on application, to make an order with a view to preventing or restricting the public disclosure of any aspect of those proceedings so far as it considers necessary in the interests of justice or in order to protect the Convention rights of any person or in the circumstances identified in *ETA 1996, s 10A* (i.e. power to sit in private for the purpose of hearing confidential evidence). *Rule 50(2)* goes on to provide that in considering whether to make an order under this rule, the Tribunal shall give full weight to the principle of open justice and to the Convention right to freedom of expression.

The new formulation of *Rule 50* enables the Tribunal to make the orders that were previously available under the old rules, as well as widening the discretion to enable Tribunals to take action expressly to cover the protection of convention rights, albeit without losing sight of the principle of open justice. "Convention rights" within the meaning of this rule, has the same meaning as set out in *HRA 1998, s 1*: see *Rule 50(6)*. For the position prior to the enactment of *Rule 50* and the case law to similar effect, see the restricted reporting order section **[20.90]** below.

Rule 50(3) contains a list of the types of Order that a Tribunal can now make:

(a)   an order that a hearing that would otherwise be in public be conducted, in whole or in part, in private;

(b)   an order that the identities of specified parties, witnesses or other persons referred to in the proceedings should not be disclosed to the public, by the use of anonymisation or otherwise, whether in the course of any hearing or in its listing or in any documents entered on the Register or otherwise forming part of the public record;

(c)   an order for measures preventing witnesses at a public hearing being identifiable by members of the public;

(d)   a restricted reporting order within the terms of *ETA 1996, s 11* or *12* (see section below).

The *Rule* permits any party – or a person with a legitimate interest – to make representations to the Tribunal before such an order is made. If no such opportunity was granted, then such a person has the right to apply to the Tribunal in writing for the order to be revoked or discharged either on the basis of written representations, or, if requested, at a hearing: *Rule 50(4)*. *Rule 50(4)* does not, however, restrict the Tribunal's general power under *Rule 29* to vary a previous order when it is in the interests of justice to do so in the light of a material change of circumstances, as it may be where a provisional decision has been taken at the case management stage, but the Tribunal at the full hearing is in a better position to judge the appropriate balance between the competing interests in privacy and open justice: see *The Home Secretary v Parr* (UKEAT/0046/20/BA) and above **20.55**.

Note that the power in *Rule 50(3)(b)* includes the power for the Tribunal to anonymise any person 'in its listing or in any documents entered on the Register or otherwise forming part of the public record'. This used to be referred to as a 'register deletion order'. It was prior to 2004 available only in cases involving allegations of a sexual offence, as provided by *ETA 1996, s 11(1)(a)*. The power in *Rule 50* is now available in principle in all cases although it will normally be required only in cases where an RRO or other privacy order is required (see below **20.90** and **20.90**A). The requirement in *Rule 67* for judgments to be entered on the Register is expressly subject to any order made under *Rule 50*. *Rule 50* cannot, however, be used to prevent publication of a judgment altogether; that is only possible in cases raising issues of national security: *Q Ltd v L* [2019] EWCA Civ 1417, [2020] ICR 420. In that case, the Court of Appeal held that although it was appropriate in the particular and sensitive circumstances of that case for the names of all parties, witnesses and other persons referred to in the judgment to be anonymised, the judgment should otherwise be published in full; redaction of details of the claimant's disabilities would be inappropriate because it would mean that the judgment could not properly be understood. (See **20.91** below for the rules on national security.)

On its face, *Rule 50* is a wide power. Indeed, in *A, B v X, Y and Times Newspapers Ltd* Soole J observed (para 60) that in permitting orders where 'necessary in the interests of justice or in order to protect the Convention rights of any person' and requiring only 'full weight' to the principle of open justice and Article 10, it imposes a less onerous test for the derogation from the principle of open justice than the test of strict necessity which otherwise applies at common law. Nonetheless, the authorities (discussed below **20.90–20.90**A) indicate that very significant weight should be given to the principle of open justice (which includes the possibility of contemporaneous reporting of names as well as the proceedings more generally), so that in practice it is rare that an order under *Rule 50* will be appropriate.

It is important when considering orders under *Rule 50* to distinguish RROs as defined in *ss 11* and *12 ETA 1996* (see below **20.90**) and other orders that may be made under *Rule 50* (below **20.90**A). In particular, there are two significant differences between orders under *Rule 50* that are not RROs and RROs per se: first, an RRO by definition, deals only with the reporting of proceedings, not with how the hearing itself is conducted; and, second, an RRO can only have effect until promulgation of the final judgment on liability in the case. Accordingly, if an order is required that all or part of a hearing is conducted in private, or that no reference is made in open court to the identity of a particular person, or to particular evidence, or if an order is required protecting the identity of the parties or any other matter after the promulgation of the liability judgment, this can only be achieved by way of a wider order under *Rule 50* and not by way of an RRO.

If the tribunal decides to hold a hearing or part thereof in private, it will give reasons for doing so (*Rule 62(1)*).

For discussion of the equivalent provisions governing appeals to the EAT, see EMPLOYMENT TRIBUNALS – III: APPEALS, **21.26** below.

20.90 *Restricted Reporting Orders*

Some employment tribunal cases involving allegations of sexual misconduct attract considerable publicity in the media, all too often prurient and embarrassing to those involved. In order to diminish the adverse effect on the parties of such publicity, the *ET Rules* contain powers for tribunals to restrict publication of material identifying those involved in such cases. These were first given by the *1993 ET Regulations*, which introduced the power to make restricted reporting orders (RROs) and register deletion orders. Equivalent powers were introduced by the *Disability Discrimination Act 1995* for cases where evidence of a personal nature is to be given (see now the *ETA 1996, ss 12 and 32*).

The provisions relating to RROs are now contained in *Rule 50* of the *2013 Rules* and *ss 11* and *12* of the *ETA 1996*. Pursuant to *ETA 1996, s 11*, a RRO means an order made under that section 'prohibiting the publication in Great Britain of identifying matter in a written publication available to the public or its inclusion in a relevant programme for reception in Great Britain' (*s 11(6)*). Under *s 11(1)(b)* an RRO may be made 'for cases involving allegations of sexual misconduct, enabling an employment tribunal, on the application of any party to proceedings before it or of its own motion, to make a [RRO] having effect (if not revoked earlier) until the promulgation of the decision of the tribunal' By s 11(6), 'identifying matter', in relation to a person, means 'any matter likely to lead members of the public to identify him as a person affected by, or as the person making, the allegation' and 'sexual misconduct' means 'the commission of a sexual offence, sexual harassment or other adverse conduct (of whatever nature) related to sex, and conduct is related to sex whether the relationship with sex lies in the character of the conduct or in its having reference to the sex or sexual orientation of the person at whom the conduct is directed'.

By s 11(2) if any identifying matter is published in contravention of a RRO, any person responsible for the publication 'shall be guilty of an offence and liable on summary conviction to a fine not exceeding level 5 on the standard scale'. (There are detailed provisions in s 11(2) and (4) defining which individuals and corporations may be liable to conviction in connection with an offence.) By s 11(3), it is a defence to prove that at the time of the alleged offence the person was not aware, and neither suspected nor had reason to suspect, that the publication in question was of or included the matter in question.

The provision for making an RRO in disability cases in *ETA 1996, s 12* is similar. An RRO may be made in disability discrimination complaints brought under *EA 2010, s 120*, 'in which evidence of a personal nature is likely to be heard by the employment tribunal hearing the complaint' (*ETA 1996, s 12(1)*). As with RROs under s 11, they may only last until the promulgation of the decision of the tribunal (unless revoked earlier) (s 11(2)(a)). 'Evidence of a personal nature' is defined in s 11(7) as 'any evidence of a medical or other intimate, nature which might reasonably be assumed to be likely to cause significant embarrassment to the complainant if reported' and 'identifying matter' means 'any matter likely to lead members of the public to identify the complainant or such other persons (if any) as may be named in the order'. The provisions making it a criminal offence to breach an RRO made under s 12 are substantially identical to those under s 11 (ss 12(3)-(6)).

Where an RRO is made, a Tribunal may also order that it applies to any other proceedings being heard as part of the same hearing (*Rule 50(5)(d)*).

A notice drawing attention to the existence of the RRO must be placed on the tribunal door (*Rule 50(5)(c)*).

A RRO may be made by the tribunal of its own motion or on the application of a party. The primary purpose of a RRO is to protect parties, and sometimes witnesses, from being placed under inappropriate pressure when giving evidence by the fear of the publicity that may be given to their evidence.

The scope of the power to make a RRO enables protection to be given not only to the alleged victim and miscreant in a sexual misconduct case, but also the employer, and individual employee respondents to the claim, if not directly covered otherwise. However, the EAT has ruled (departing from a previous decision) that a body corporate cannot be the subject of a restricted reporting order (*Leicester University v A* [1999] IRLR 352, following *R v London (North) Industrial Tribunal, ex p Associated Newspapers Ltd* [1998] IRLR 569, [1998] ICR 1212 in preference to *M v Vincent* [1998] ICR 73). It should also be noted that the jurisdiction to make an RRO under s 11 is not limited to claims of discrimination by sexual harassment; it may include cases where the applicant's dismissal was for an alleged sexual offence (see eg *Securicor Guarding Ltd v R* [1994] IRLR 633) or any other proceedings in which allegations of sexual misconduct are expected to form part of the evidence, and regardless of whether or not the allegations can be substantiated: *X v Stevens* [2003] ICR 1031. In that latter case the EAT also held that it was not necessary in order to invoke the jurisdiction to make an RRO that the allegations should be the basis of the cause of action or even central to the decision-making; it is simply that the Tribunal has to reach a conclusion, on what it has heard or read, that the case will involve such allegations.

Where Convention rights are relied on as a reason for restricting public access to judicial proceedings or pronouncements, the Tribunal must first consider whether the particular Convention right is engaged. *Article 6* will always be engaged (right to a fair and public hearing), albeit that it will not generally require separate consideration as *Rule 50* already requires that the 'interests of justice' (fairness) must be balanced against the public interest in open justice. Likewise, *Article 10* will normally be engaged because public reporting is an aspect of the principle of open justice (see further below). If *Article 8* is relied on but not engaged, then it need not be considered further: see *Ameyaw v Pricewaterhousecoopers Services Ltd* [2019] ICR 976 at para 46, per Eady J in reliance on *McKennitt v Ash* [2008] QB 73, para 11, per Buxton LJ. It has been held that *Article 8* rights will inevitably be engaged in cases where there are allegations of sexual misconduct: *Fallows and ors v News Group Newspapers Ltd* [2016] ICR 801 at para 66 per Simler J. They may also be engaged where a person's reputation may be damaged as a result of the publicity, unless the damage is justifiable because the individual has brought the damage upon themselves through their own wrongdoing: *Turner v East Midlands Trains Ltd* [2012] EWCA Civ 1470, [2013] ICR 525. Impact on an individual's family relationships if the matter is made public will also engage *Article 8*: *Khuja v Times Newspaper Ltd* [2017] UKSC 49, [2019] AC 161, para 34.

There are a number of authorities that have given guidance on what factors may relevantly be taken into account when deciding whether to make an RRO and how the balancing exercise is to be undertaken as between the public interest in open justice and the Article 10 right to freedom of expression on the one hand and, on the other, the interests of justice and any Article 8 rights that are engaged. Particularly helpful are BBC v Roden [2015] ICR 985 per Simler J, Fallows and ors v News Group Newspapers Ltd [2016] ICR 801 per Simler J and A, B v X, Y, Times Newspapers Ltd [2019] IRLR 620 per Soole J. However, both judgments must now be read in the light of the judgment of the majority of the Supreme Court in Khuja v Times Newspaper Ltd [2017] UKSC 49, [2019] AC 161. The principles to be distilled from those authorities are as follows:

(i)   The burden of establishing any derogation from the fundamental principle of open justice or full reporting lies on the person seeking that derogation (*Fallows*, para 48(1));

(ii)   Derogations from the principle of open justice are only permitted where strictly necessary to secure the proper administration of justice (*Fallows*, para 48(1); *Roden*, para 22), or other Convention rights. Where *Article 8* rights are engage, clear and cogent evidence is required that harm will be done by reporting to the privacy rights of the person seeking the restriction on full reporting (*Fallows*, para 48(1));

(iii)   Where full reporting of proceedings is unlikely to indicate whether a damaging allegation is true or false, in *Fallows* (at para 48(ii)) it was suggested that courts and tribunals should credit the public with the ability to understand that unproven allegations are no more than that. It was noted that where such a case proceeds to judgment, courts and tribunals can mitigate the risk of misunderstanding by making clear that they have not adjudicated on the truth or otherwise of the damaging allegation. However, in *A, B v X, Y* (para 64), it was held that this did not mean the Tribunal could not take into account distress and damage to reputation likely from the reporting of unproven allegations of sexual offences, and that the Tribunal need not assume that the public must be taken to understand the difference between such allegations and their proof, or that if the judgment finds the allegations to be false that will necessarily provide sufficient vindication. A similar point was made in *Khuja* (para 9) where the majority of the Supreme Court accepted that "*It would be foolish for any court to ignore the extreme sensitivity of public opinion in current circumstances to allegations of the sexual abuse of children . . . the present appeal must be approached on the footing that there is a real risk that a person knowing of these matters would conclude that [x] had sexually abused the complainant notwithstanding that he had never been charged with any offence*";

(iv)   The open justice principle is grounded in the public interest, irrespective of any particular public interest the facts of the case give rise to. It is no answer therefore for a party seeking restrictions on publication in an employment case to contend that the employment tribunal proceedings are essentially private and of no public interest accordingly (*Fallows*, para 48(iii));

(v)   When undertaking the balancing exercise as between *Article 8* and *Article 10* rights, the approach to be followed is that described by Lord Steyn in *Re S (A Child)* [2005] 1 AC 593 at para 17: "*First, neither article has as such precedence over the other. Secondly, where the values under the two articles are in conflict, an intense focus on the comparative importance of the specific rights being claimed in the individual case is necessary. Thirdly, the justifications for interfering with or restricting each right must be taken into account. Finally, the proportionality test must be applied to each. For convenience, I will call this the ultimate balancing test*" (see *Fallows* at para 49). See also *Khuja*, para 23;

(vi)   The principle of open justice is not satisfied merely by the hearing being held in open tribunal. Full weight must be given to the point that contemporaneous press reporting of proceedings, including the names of parties, is an inseparable part of the concept of open justice. The public interest in the principle of open justice requires distinct consideration from the *Article 10* right to freedom of expression (*A, B v X, Y*, para 61 and Khuja, paras 16 and 29);

(vii)   However, this does not mean that will necessarily be a sufficient interest in the identification of individuals. Consideration must be given both to the likely impact on the administration of justice of reporting the name of the individual, and the public interest in publication of that name (*Khuja*, para 30);

(viii) In the balancing exercise, it must be assumed that reporting of proceedings will be lawful, namely fair and accurate. In the absence of a specific evidential basis, 'fear of misreporting' is not a relevant factor (*A, B v X, Y*, para 61);

(ix)   The Tribunal may take into account distress and damage to reputation likely from the reporting of unproven allegations of sexual offences, and need not assume that the public must be taken to understand the difference between such allegations and their proof, or that if the judgment finds the allegations to be false that will necessarily provide sufficient vindication (*A, B v X, Y*, para 64);

(x)   The public and social status of the parties in question is irrelevant: all persons are equal before the law (*A, B v X, Y*, paras 65-66);

(xi)   In permitting a RRO to be made protecting the identity of the alleged perpetrator as well as the victim, *Rule 50* potentially disturbs the balance set by Parliament in *s 1* of the *Sexual Offences (Amendment) Act 1992* which imposes a lifetime prohibition on publication of any matter which is likely to lead to members of the public identifying the alleged victims of sexual offences. It is impermissible for a Tribunal to take into account, when deciding whether or not to make an RRO, that making an RRO might rectify the imbalance in the *1992 Act*. As Soole J, put it (in *A, B v X, Y* at para 62) "the judgment of the legislature must be fully respected".

When making a RRO, by *Rule 50(5)*, the Tribunal must (a) specify the person whose identity is protected; and may specify particular matters of which publication is prohibited as likely to lead to that person's identification – this is not in order to protect their identity but because identifying them would lead to the identification of those for whose protection the order is made: *Tradition Securities & Futures SA v Times Newspapers Ltd* [2009] IRLR 354; (b) specify the duration of the order; (c) ensure that a notice of the fact that such an order has been made in relation to those proceedings is displayed on the notice board of the

Tribunal with any list of the proceedings taking place before the Tribunal, and on the door of the room in which the proceedings affected by the order are taking place; and (d) the Tribunal may order that it applies also to any other proceedings being heard as part of the same hearing.

Because of the wider public interest in justice being dispensed publicly, tribunals should not automatically order a restriction on publication simply – indeed especially – because both parties seek it: *X v Z Ltd* [1998] ICR 43, CA. The point was followed in *R v London (North) Industrial Tribunal, ex p Associated Newspapers Ltd* (above), in which Keene J stated that the words 'a person affected by the allegations of misconduct' should be interpreted narrowly, having regard to the principle of the freedom of the press to report court and tribunal proceedings fully and contemporaneously. In *Vatish v Crown Prosecution Service* [2011] EqLR 963 (UKEAT/0164/11), the EAT set aside an order made to protect a witness who had not asked for protection and whose evidence had already been given by the time the order was made.

The wider interest in public justice is reflected in both *Rule 50(2)* – see above – and the fact that interested parties (in practice this will almost always be media representatives) have the right to make representations at the hearing at which the decision is made whether to impose an order or the right to ask for the order to be revoked: *Rule 50(4)*. In *Fallows and others v News Group Newspapers Ltd* [2016] IRLR 827, [2016] ICR 801, Simler P held that *Rule 50(4)* had no temporal limitation and an application could be made even after the claim had been settled and withdrawn. A tribunal was not *functus officio* for these purposes after withdrawal of the claim. Under the old rules (which did not so provide), the Court of Session, overruling the EAT, held that tribunals can entertain applications from the press for an order to be revoked: *Davidson v Dallas McMillan* [2009] CSIH 70, [2010] IRLR 439. In addition, as the EAT noted in *Dallas McMillan*, it is open to press organisations to apply to be joined as parties to the proceedings for the purpose of making such an application; this was done in *Tradition Securities*, above.

Under the *2004 ET Rules* a new power was introduced enabling a Judge to make a temporary RRO, either on application by a party or of his own motion, and either without any hearing, or at a case management hearing. The parties were to be notified of a temporary order and informed of their right to apply for the continuance of the order; if no party applied within 14 days, the order lapsed, but if an application to continue it was made, the order remained in force until the question whether it should be continued could be determined at another hearing: see *Rule 50(2)–(5)* of the *2004 Rules*. Under the *2013 Rules* a tailored Order can still be made by the Tribunal creating the same effect: see the general discretion under *Rule 50*. This can be useful to deal with the situation where a party anticipates media interest in the case and seeks emergency protection from publicity.

A RRO remains in force until the promulgation of the final judgment in the case, unless revoked earlier. The EAT in the *Tradition Securities* case, above, held that an application to revoke, or vary the terms of, an order should only be entertained if there has been a change in the relevant circumstances since the order was made; but such changes may include the fact that a representative of the press, having become aware of the order, seeks to have the order revoked or varied (see now *Rule 50(4)*), or that a party for whose benefit the order was made now no longer wishes to have the protection afforded.

Once a final judgment has been given, the restriction on reporting the identities of those covered by the order falls away (unless the Tribunal has specified an earlier date in its order). This underlines the point that the purpose of the order is not to provide indefinite or permanent anonymity for the individuals covered by the order, but rather to ensure that they are not unduly pressured by the fear of publicity in giving their evidence. Where the judgment is given separately on liability and the tribunal will need to hold a further hearing to decide on remedy, the order expires once judgment on liability has been given. It cannot be extended to include any separate remedy hearing: *A, B v X, Y and Times Newspapers Ltd*

[2019] IRLR 620 at para 68. Under the old rules it was established that the tribunal had no power to entertain an application for the revocation of an order once the proceedings are at an end: see *Davidson v Dallas McMillan*, above, where the point was expressly confirmed by the Court of Session. This had the consequence that if the claim is settled before judgment, the order can remain in force indefinitely. See now *Fallows and others*, above, which also confirms that an RRO does not automatically expire upon withdrawal under the new rules and that an application under *Rule 50(4)* can be made post withdrawal.

Note that the fact that a RRO expires once judgment on liability has been given will make it an inappropriate order in cases where permanent anonymity is required in order to protect the Article 8 ECHR rights of those concerned: see further *A v Secretary of State for Justice* [2019] IRLR 108 and **20.90**A below.

20.90a *Other Privacy Orders: Anonymisation and Confidentiality*

As noted above (**20.89**) the range of orders that can be made under *Rule 50* is wider than the jurisdiction to make RROs as defined in *ss 11* and *12* of the *ETA 1996*. In particular, orders under *Rule 50* that are not RROs may deal with how the hearing itself is conducted and not just how it is reported. Further, an order under *Rule 50* that is not an RRO may have effect after promulgation of the final judgment on liability. Thus wider orders under *Rule 50* may include orders that all or part of a hearing is conducted in private, or that no reference is made in open court to the identity of a particular person, or to particular evidence, or an order permanently anonymising the parties. Prior to the introduction of the *2013 Rules* there was no express power for the Tribunal to make such wider orders, but in a series of cases, it was established that the Tribunal had jurisdiction to do so where that was required to give effect to EU law and/or Convention rights: see *X v Stevens* [2003] ICR 1031, *A v B* [2010] IRLR 844 and *B and C v A* [2010] IRLR 400. In *X v Stevens* the EAT held that the Tribunal could make restricted reporting orders where this was necessary in order to prevent a claimant from being deterred from pursuing a claim, and regardless of whether the statutory conditions for a restricted reporting order or register deletion order were met and whether the respondent was or was not a state authority. The *A v B* [2010] IRLR 844 (supplementary judgment at p 856) applied this principle to justify the making of a permanent anonymity order in relation to an appeal where the claimant had been the subject of unsubstantiated allegations of paedophile activities. A similar conclusion was reached in *B and C v A* [2010] IRLR 400, where the EAT considered a permanent anonymity order to be justified to protect a complainant of sexual violence (not the claimant in the case). The reliance in these cases on *Art 8* of the *Convention* provided a basis also for orders to be made protecting the identity of those who are not parties, or even witnesses, in the proceedings, where identification would be a sufficiently serious and unjustified interference with their privacy. This point was confirmed by the EAT in *F v G* [2012] ICR 246, [2011] All ER (D) 42 (Dec), where a permanent order was made to protect the identity of severely disabled students at the respondent college in circumstances where evidence about their sexual lives would be given in the course of the proceedings. The judgment of Underhill P in this case contains a full and helpful discussion of the range of orders that could be made and the basis for each.

This body of case law affected the drafting of the *2013 Rules*. As set out above, *Rule 50(1)* entitles the Tribunal to make wider orders than classic RROs where to do so would protect Convention rights of any person, or in circumstances under *ETA 1996, s 10A*. Essentially the same principles as have been discussed above at **20.90** in relation to the making of RROs apply to other types of *Rule 50* order. It should be borne in mind that although *Rule 50* permits a permanent anonymity order to be made (whereas an RRO cannot last beyond promulgation of the liability judgment), that does not mean that a permanent anonymity order should be granted in every case where there has been an RRO. As Simler J explained in *BBC v Roden* [2015] ICR 985, once judgment is published, there may be little ongoing public interest in protection of *Article 8* rights: *Roden*, paras 27 and 31.

An example of a permanent anonymity order made under the *2013 Rules* can be seen in *EF v AB* [2015] IRLR 619, a case involving lurid revelations and allocations of sexual misconduct made by an ex-employee against the CEO and his wife. Slade J undertook a helpful review of the authorities and held that all the sexual conduct in question took place in private and there was a reasonable expectation of privacy which applied even though some of the information might have been true, and some false (para 59). On the balancing exercise between open justice and the *Art 8 ECHR* rights, she held the latter must prevail, relying on a number of factors including the effect on relevant children, and the reasonable expectation of privacy (para 84). A somewhat contrasting approach can be seen in *BBC v Roden* [2015] ICR 985. There, during the course of an unsuccessful unfair dismissal complaint, allegations of sexual assault by the claimant emerged. A permanent anonymity order was made by the Employment Judge to protect the claimant's identity but this was lifted by the EAT. Simler J stressed the importance of open justice and that *Art 6* ECHR guaranteed a publicly proclaimed judgment. *Arts 8* and *10 ECHR* were also engaged. When values under different articles conflicted, an intense focus on the comparative importance of the specific rights being claimed in the particular case was required. In the present case the weight to be attached to the claimant's *Art 8* right was low and the Tribunal had failed to undertake the required balancing exercise. The only factor identified by the judge in that case as outweighing the principle of open justice was the risk of reputational damage to the claimant by public misunderstanding of the sexual allegations. However, Simler J held that the public should be "trusted to distinguish between an allegation and a finding of guilt" and there was no proper basis for the permanent anonymity order. This case should now be read in the light of the principles enunciated in subsequent cases concerned with RROs as described above at **20.90**.

In practice it is relatively common that privacy is afforded to individuals who feature in the evidence in a case, such as children or medical patients, by a direction that they are not to be identified by name in the course of evidence, and avoiding identification in the judgment. However, sometimes that is not sufficient as the case of *A v Secretary of State for Justice* [2019] IRLR 108 shows. In that case, the EAT noted that an anonymization order under *Rule 50(1)* could, by virtue of *Rule 50(3)(b)* protect the identity of any 'other person' and that included, in this case, a person with whom the claimant had had a previous relationship (J) (who was also a vulnerable person in the care of the respondent), and the child of that relationship (L). The EAT held the Judge had been wrong to regard the identities of J and L as 'unimportant' because they were not parties to proceedings and, indeed, in L's case did not even feature in the evidence. The EAT considered that, on the contrary, the interests of the child in particular were of paramount importance. The rights of both J and L under Article 8 of the ECHR should have been considered, especially in view of the fact that the child suffered from autism and anxiety. The EAT further emphasised the difference between an anonymization order and a RRO identified above, specifically that the RRO would end after promulgation of the tribunal's decision (by virtue if *ETA 1996, s 11(1)(b)*), whereas the anonymization order had indefinite effect. The EAT held that the Judge had erred in law in discharging an anonymization order and replacing it with an RRO and had given insufficient consideration to the rights of J and L, which in this case over-rode the interests in (fully) open justice. The EAT considered the interests in open justice were served by the facts of the case being made public and that the identities of those involved need not be revealed given the likely impact on J and L. The EAT made an AO preventing the identity of the employee and J from being disclosed, which would in practice have the effect of also protecting the identity of L.

A further category of orders that may be made under *Rule 50* are orders for the purpose of dealing with information or evidence alleged to be confidential. *Rule 50* expressly permits orders to be made in the circumstances set out in *s 10A* of the *ETA 1996*. *Section 10A* (in combination with *Rule 50*) provides that an Employment Tribunal may sit in private for the purpose of hearing evidence from any person which in the opinion of the tribunal is likely to consist of: (a) information which he could not disclose without contravening a prohibition imposed by or by virtue of any enactment, (b) information which has been communicated to him in confidence or which he has otherwise obtained in consequence of the confidence reposed in him by another person, or (c) information the disclosure of which would, for reasons other than its effect on negotiations with respect to any of the matters mentioned in *section 178(2)* of the *Trade Union and Labour Relations (Consolidation) Act 1992*, cause substantial injury to any undertaking of his or in which he works (see further below **20.91**). The EAT has also held that where the tribunal has to determine whether particular evidence relied on by one of the parties is privileged as a without prejudice communication, the test for whether the tribunal should sit in private to hear this aspect of the case will depend on whether it is likely that evidence will be given which is covered by the confidentiality attaching to without prejudice communications; if so, that factor has to be balanced against the general public interest in open justice: *Eversheds LLP v Gray* [2012] All ER (D) 111 (Feb) (UKEAT/0585/11). The same approach would apply where the confidentiality is sought for other reasons.

Rule 50 also enables Tribunals to make 'confidentiality club orders' of the type that have been developed in the High Court where documents or information are only disclosed to certain named individuals and not referred to in open court. Care should be taken in approaching both *s 10A*-type orders and confidentiality club-type orders. It will rarely be the case that Employment Tribunal proceedings are concerned with the sort of intellectual property matters that have classically required the development of confidentiality club orders in the High Court, i.e. proceedings where "*the whole object of the proceedings is to protect a commercial interest [so that] full disclosure may not be possible if it would render the proceedings futile*" (*Al Rawi v Security Service* [2011] UKSC 34, [2012] 1 AC 531 at para 64 per Lord Dyson). However, Employment Tribunal cases frequently require reference to medical evidence relating to parties or witnesses which it may be unfair (and unnecessary) to make public as part of the proceedings (see further below **20.91**). Employment Tribunal proceedings also sometimes touch on other matters that are confidential or commercially sensitive for one or more of the parties. In many cases (at least those not involving medical evidence), it will be possible for any such concerns to be addressed by a consideration of whether or not the information in question (whether contained in a document or to be given in oral evidence) is actually relevant to the proceedings. In some cases, it may be appropriate, as a stage on the way to determining relevance for the Tribunal to order disclosure of documents or provision of information by one party only to the Tribunal, or to the other party's representative or to a closed named group of individuals (see further below **20.91**). If the information or document is not relevant, then there is no need for the document (or that part of it) to be disclosed or for the oral evidence to be given. If it is relevant, then consideration may need to be given to the making of a *Rule 50* order, having full regard to the balancing exercise required by that rule (i.e. between the interests of justice and/or Convention rights and principle of open justice). In conducting that balancing exercise, the guidance in the authorities on RROs set out above at **20.90** will be relevant in general terms. The guiding principle is that, whatever order is made, it should involve the most minimal interference with the principle of open justice and the Article 6 right to a fair and public trial as is possible and commensurate with protecting the confidential interests at stake. However, it should be borne in mind that the right to a fair trial is paramount. If it is not possible to achieve that while also protecting the confidential interest, then the confidential interest must take second place. The observations of Aldous J in *Rouusell Uclaf v Imperial Chemical Industries plc* [1990] RPC 45 remain relevant: "*Each case has to be decided on its own facts and the broad principle must be that the court has the task of deciding how justice can be achieved taking into account the rights and needs of the parties. The object to be achieved is that the applicant should have as full a degree of disclosure as will be consistent with adequate protection of the secret. In so doing, the court will be careful not to expose a party to any unnecessary risk of its trade secrets leaking to or being used by competitors. What is necessary or unnecessary will depend upon the nature of the secret, the position of the parties and the extent of the disclosure ordered. However, it would be exceptional to prevent a party from access to information which would* *play a substantial part in the case as such would mean that the party would be unable to hear a substantial part of the case, would be unable to understand the reasons for the advice given to him and, in some cases, the reasons for the judgment. Thus what disclosure is necessary entails not only practical matters arising in the conduct of the case but also the general position that a party should know the case he has to meet, should hear matters given in evidence and understand the reasons for the judgment."* See further *TQ Delta LLC v Zyxel Communications UK Limited* [2018] EWHC 1515 (Ch) per Henry Carr J.

Subject to the provisions permitting a hearing in private, failure to hold the hearing at a place made accessible to the public renders any resulting judgment a nullity, even if no members of the public wished to attend the hearing: *Storer v British Gas plc* [2000] IRLR 495.

20.91 *Private Hearings: National Security*

Tribunal hearings are generally conducted in public and may be reported in the media. The requirement to sit in public applies to a final hearing (*Rule 59*) and to a preliminary hearing which determines a preliminary issue or a strike out application (*Rule 56*). Otherwise preliminary hearings are held in private.

The tribunal has power under *Rule 50* to direct that evidence or representations be heard in private if in the opinion of the tribunal it would be likely to consist of information which could not be disclosed without a breach of a statutory prohibition (see *ETA 1996, s 10A*) (see further above **20.90A**).

In addition, *Rule 94* makes specific provision in relation to 'national security proceedings'. Where the Tribunal considers it expedient in the interests of national security, it may order that all or part of the proceedings should be conducted in private, or may exclude a person from all or part of the proceedings or take steps to conceal the identity of a witness in the proceedings (*Rule 94(2)*); and see *AB v Ministry of Defence* [2009] All ER (D) 135 (Sep), [2010] ICR 54 (UKEAT/0101/09). A Minister may also direct a Tribunal to take such action (*Rule 94(1)*); alternatively, the Minister may apply to the Tribunal inviting the Tribunal to make such an order (*Rule 94(4)*). If the Minister makes a direction (rather than an application), then the Tribunal must comply, and (indeed) *s 10B* of the *ETA 1996* makes it a criminal offence to publish anything likely to lead to the identification of the witness that the Minister has directed be concealed, or the reasons for the Tribunal's decision or the part of its reasons which it is directed or has determined to keep secret. By *Rule 94(2)(b)* the Tribunal may also order a person not to disclose any document (or the contents of any document), where provided for the purposes of the proceedings to any person (save for any specified person). Where the Tribunal considers that it may be necessary to make an order under *Rule 94* in relation to particular proceedings, the Tribunal may consider any material provided by a party (or where a Minister is not a party, by a Minister) without providing that material to any other person. Such material shall be used by the Tribunal solely for the purposes of deciding whether to make that order (unless that material is subsequently used as evidence in the proceedings by a party).

Where the Tribunal decides not to make an order under *Rule 94(2)* (whether of its own motion or on application by the Minister), then the Tribunal must send a copy of the written reasons given under *Rule 62* to the Minister and allow 42 days for the Minister to make a direction as to whether, and if so to what extent, the reasons should be disclosed to specified persons or entered on the Register (*Rule 94(9)* and *para 6 of Schedule 2*). Where the Minister directs the Tribunal to prepare edited reasons, the Employment Judge must initial each omission (*para 6(4) of Schedule 2*). It is only by virtue of *para 6(6) of Schedule 2* that the written reasons of the Employment Tribunal may in principle be kept from entry on the Register at all: there is no such power in *Rule 50* for other cases: *L v Q Ltd* [2019] EWCA Civ 1417, [2020] ICR 420.

The Tribunal must ensure that in exercising its functions, information is not disclosed contrary to the interests of national security (*Rule 94(10)*).

An example of an order to sit in private under equivalent provisions in previous *Fry v Foreign and Commonwealth Office* [1997] ICR 512 (order did not extend to excluding claimant's husband who was assisting the presentation of her case). The EAT has suggested that there may be good reasons for 'closed evidence' (ie evidence heard in private session) to be heard before open evidence in cases involving Crown employment and/or national security: *Farooq v Commissioner of Police of the Metropolis* [2008] All ER (D) 187 (Jun). This point was endorsed by the Court of Appeal in *Home Office v Tariq* [2010] EWCA Civ 462, [2010] IRLR 1065, a case in which the Court held that the procedure laid down for cases involving national security (*Sch 2* to the *ET Regulations 2004*), involving the exclusion of the claimant from part of the proceedings with a Special Advocate appointed to represent his interests during that part of the hearing, was not incompatible with *Art 6* of the *European Convention on Human Rights*. The Court's decision in *Tariq* was upheld by the Supreme Court: *Home Office v Tariq* [2011] UKSC 35, [2011] IRLR 843.

For further information on national security proceedings, see **20.133** below.

20.92 *Bias or conflict of interest*

A judgment or order of a tribunal will be open to appeal if the circumstances give rise to an appearance of bias on the part of the Judge or a lay member of the tribunal. The test is an objective one: would a reasonable independent observer, in full possession of the facts, consider that there was a real possibility of bias, arising either from the relationship between the Judge or member and a party or witness, or the conduct of the hearing: Porter v Magill [2001] UKHL 67, [2002] 2 AC 357. See further **21.23–21.24** Employment Tribunals – III for the approach of the EAT to Guidance as to the circumstances in which bias may arise and what to do about it was given in the conjoined cases in *Locabail (UK) Ltd v Bayfield Properties Ltd* [2000] QB 451, [2000] 1 All ER 65, [2000] 2 WLR 870, [2000] IRLR 96. In that case, the Court of Appeal emphasised that where a judge has a direct personal interest (beyond the de minimis) in the outcome of the proceedings, bias is presumed and the judge is automatically disqualified. The Court held that it is for the judge in question to assess in the first instance whether bias has arisen, and the judge should recuse him- or herself wherever a 'real risk' of bias or apparent bias arises. However, the Court emphasised that a judge should not recuse her- or himself too readily, observing (at para 21): 'it will be the duty of the judge to consider the objection and exercise his judgment upon it. He would be as wrong to yield to a tenuous or frivolous objection as he would to ignore an objection of substance'. The Court further confirmed that there is no objection to judges sitting in cases in which other members of their current or former barristers' chambers appear (because of their independent employment status), but that the same is not true for solicitors and members of their firms who bear a responsibility for their partners and owe duties to the clients of their partners as well as their own. The Court also considered how bias might arise from extra-curricular comment by judges in textbooks and articles. The Court confirmed that such comments are not incompatible with the discharge of judicial functions and would not ordinarily give rise to a real danger of bias, unless the comments were intemperate (which in that case they were). The Court further considered the circumstances of an Employment Judge who had for a short period a number of years previously been employed by the respondent employer. The Judge had disclosed this at the time of the hearing and no objection was raised by the claimant, but she afterwards appealed. The Court of Appeal held that given the passage of time since the employment, no appearance of bias arose.

The Court of Appeal in *Locabail* further confirmed that it is always open to the parties, upon full disclosure being given, to waive any bias or possible bias that has arisen and elect to continue with the hearing. The requirements for a valid waiver in the employment tribunal context were further considered in *Jones v DAS Legal Expenses Insurance Co Ltd* [2003] EWCA Civ 1071, [2004] IRLR 218. In that case, the Employment Judge had indicated at the outset of the hearing that her husband was a barrister in chambers which did work for the respondent insurance company. The claimant agreed that proceedings could continue. The Court of Appeal that no presumed bias arose as a result of economic interest since the interest of the Judge's husband and, indirectly, her interest was in their own well-being not the fortunes of the respondent. Nor did any apparent bias arise. The Court of Appeal gave general guidance at para 35 on the handling of allegations of bias, emphasising that if there is any real as opposed to fanciful chance of objection being taken by the fair-minded spectator, the best course is to identify another judge able to hear the matter; if that is not possible, the judge must give full disclosure of the circumstances giving rise to potential bias and keep a careful note of what is said; the judge must also tell the parties what options there are for having the case heard by another judge, either on that day or by way of adjournment; the parties should then be given time to reflect before being put to their election as to whether to waive any apparent bias or seek the recusal of the judge; particular care should be taken to ensure that litigants in person understand the issues and are given an opportunity if reasonable to take advice from the Citizens Advice Bureau or the chief clerk or listing officer.

The principles on waiver discussed in Jones were applied by the EAT in *Adamson v Swansea University* [2010] All ER (D) 38 (May) (UKEAT/0486/09), where it was held that the claimant had given informed consent to the case being heard by an Employment Judge who had disclosed a personal acquaintance with a witness in the case. See also *Bhardwaj v FDA & others* [2016] IRLR 789, where the Court of Appeal held that an ET had provided the claimant with all material facts when it informed her that one of the respondents was a lay member in the same region and her waiver of her right to object was valid and irrevocable.

A fundamental point is that the Judge must not have any kind of financial interest in the proceedings. Technically, this would extend to minor interests such as holding a small shareholding in a large corporation that is the respondent to the proceedings; in practice parties would be unlikely to object to the Judge sitting in these circumstances, but the interest should be disclosed. Interests held in common with large sections of the population, such as being a resident and Council Tax payer in the area of a local authority that is a respondent, or a user of the services of a utility or transport company, need not be declared.

In *El-Farargy v El-Farargy* [2007] EWCA Civ 1149, [2007] 3 FCR 711, the Court of Appeal recommended that if concerns emerged about the impartiality of a judge during a hearing, it was preferable for the matter to be raised informally initially to give the judge an opportunity to recuse her- or himself without the need to determine whether apparent bias had arisen. (In that case, it was held that the judge had not overstepped the mark in expressing preliminary views the course of a lengthy pre-trial review, but the judge's comments about the appellant, a Saudi sheikh, 'departing on his flying carpet', 'every grain of sand [being] sifted', the case being 'a bit gelatinous . . . like Turkish Delight' and this being a 'relatively fast-free time of the year' were held to be discriminatory and insulting and gave rise to an appearance of bias.) *El-Faragy* was considered in *Balakumar v Imperial College of Health Care NHS Trust* (UKEAT/0252/16/RN), 25 September 2018. In that case, the EAT concluded that no apparent bias arose where, midway through a multi-day hearing, the Judge said to the claimant's counsel 'there is no need to lie'. The Judge was at that point under the impression that the claimant's counsel had lied about the reason for a short adjournment that had just been sought and granted. The Judge subsequently apologised on realising this was not the case. The EAT criticised the Judge's choice of language as intemperate and inappropriate, but concluded that in the circumstances they did not give rise to an appearance of bias.

Other cases where allegations of bias have been made include: *Hamilton v GMB* [2007] IRLR 391 and *Honey v Swansea City Council* [2008] All ER (D) 311 (Nov), where failure by one of the lay members of the tribunal to disclose that she was, in her capacity as a trade union official, involved in a current dispute with the respondent local authority led to the judgment of the tribunal being set aside. A finding of an appearance of bias was made in *Peninsula Business Services Ltd v Rees* [2009] All ER (D) 134 (Sep) (UKEAT/0335/08) where the (part-time) judge was in practice as a solicitor, and her firm had advertised its services as superior to those offered by consultants, of whom the appellant was one of the best known; by implication it could be thought her firm, and hence she, had an interest adverse to that of the appellant firm. It was also held that this point no longer applied in a second case involving the same judge and appellant heard after she had taken up a full–time appointment, as the conflict of interest could no longer apply. By contrast, the EAT rejected an allegation of apparent bias where the Judge's daughter was a partner in the firm representing the claimant: *South Lanarkshire Council v Burns* (UKEATS/0040/12).

Whilst a connection between the Judge (or a lay member) and a party or witness is likely, unless the parties consent to the Judge or member sitting, to provide grounds for appeal, this is much less likely to be so where the connection is with a representative of one of the parties; see for instance *Williams v Cater Link Ltd* [2009] All ER (D) 70 (Aug) (UKEAT/0393/08): no perception of bias where (full–time) Judge had whilst still in practice instructed counsel subsequently appearing for one of the parties in the case.

The fact that an accusation of bias has previously been made against a Judge by one of the parties, or that the Judge has in previous proceedings made adverse comments about a party or witness, is not of itself a reason for the Judge to withdraw from hearing a case (in technical language, to recuse himself): *Ansar v Lloyds TSB Bank plc* [2006] EWCA Civ 1462, [2007] IRLR 211, a case in which the Court of Appeal set out detailed guidance on the relevant principles to be applied. *WestLB AG London Branch v Pan* (UKEAT/0308/11) is an example of the application of *Ansar* by the EAT to overturn a decision by the Employment Judge to recuse herself after an objection by the claimant, taken without giving the other party a chance to be heard, and despite the Judge considering that the objection was not justified. In *Papajak v Intellego Group Ltd* (UKEAT/0124/12) the EAT held, unremarkably, that an allegation of bias founded upon the Judge having determined (different) issues against a litigant previously was without merit. However, note that where a firm conclusion on an issue is reached and the same issue is later re–heard by the same tribunal, the EAT has held that there is a real possibility of bias: *Menzies Distribution Ltd v Mendes* [2014] All ER (D) 143 (Aug) (UKEAT/0497/13). Whereas expressing a concluded view prior to the conclusion of proceedings can give grounds for a recusal application, the ET did not err in *Hussain v Nottinghamshire Healthcare NHS Trust* [2016] All ER (D) 88 (Aug), [2016] UKEAT/0080/16 where a costs warning was given to a claimant. An informed and impartial observer would not have thought the tribunal biased and the principles in *Oni v NHS Leicester City* [2013] ICR 91, [2012] All ER (D) 05 (Oct) had been complied with.

In *Begraj v Heer Manak Solicitors* [2014] IRLR 689 (UKEAT/0496/13), the EAT gave guidance as to the appropriate response from a Judge/tribunal who/that receives prejudicial information from a third party. In that case the Judge was approached by police officers part way through a lengthy hearing; the officers asked the Judge to keep the approach secret from the parties, which the Judge did for a week, but then revealed what had happened. Upon application the Tribunal recused itself. The EAT held that it was right to do so and offered the following guidance: (i) where a third party proffers information or opinion about the merits of a case, or the parties in it, to a Tribunal, without invitation, the parties must be made aware of what has happened without delay; (ii) Judges may continue to receive advice or warnings about peculiar risks from the police, security services, security guards and other relevant personnel. The parties should expect Judges to put that information to one side when reaching a decision on the merits; (iii) Judges must remain impartial and should re–buff and report approaches which interfere with their independence; (iv) in the event of doubt, Judges should discuss the issue with a more senior Judge (such advice should not relate to the merits of the case); (v) generally the Tribunal should not accept information on the basis that it remain confidential to the decision maker; (vi) there are exceptions to point (v) eg in national security cases; finally, (vii) there might be other exceptions to point (v) where there are serious risks to the security of an individual or where the revelation would be a significant breach of privacy to which a party might be entitled; usually, however, the approach should be mentioned to the parties with a request to keep it confidential.

The Different Types of Hearing

20.93 *General*

Under the *2004 Rules*, there were three types of hearing: Case Management Discussions (CMDs), Pre-Hearing Reviews and Final Hearings. There were complex rules governing which orders could be made at which type of hearing. Under the *2013 Rules* there are now two principal types of hearing: a preliminary hearing (PH) and a final hearing (FH). Preliminary hearings may be 'closed' (private) CPHs at which matters of general case management are dealt with, or 'open' (public) OPHs at which preliminary issues of substance are determined.

20.94 *Preliminary Hearings: General*

Rule 53 defines the scope of a preliminary hearing. A preliminary hearing is a hearing at which the Tribunal may do one or more of the following things:

(a)   conduct a preliminary consideration of the claim with the parties and make a case management order (including an order relating to the conduct of the final hearing);

(b)   determine any preliminary issue;

(c)   consider whether a claim or response, or any part, should be struck out under *Rule 37*;

(d)   make a deposit order under *Rule 39*;

(e)   explore the possibility of settlement or alternative dispute resolution (including judicial mediation).

By *Rule 53(2)*, there may be more than one preliminary hearing in any case.

20.95 *Preliminary Hearings: Case Management*

Preliminary hearings are convened in many cases in order to conduct case management with the parties. Such preliminary hearings are often labelled by the Tribunal "preliminary hearings for case management". They are have much in common with Case Management Discussions under the *2004 Rules*, save that there are not the same restrictions on deciding points of substance that existed with CMDs (for examples of previous restrictions, see *Way v Powercraft (Retail) Ltd* [2008] All ER (D) 151 (Aug) and *Kerr v Ernst & Young Services Ltd* [2011] All ER (D) 146 (Feb), [2011] ICR D13 (UKEAT/0567/10)).

The Presidential Guidance for General Case Management includes an Agenda for Case Management at a Preliminary Hearing (set out in the Annex). Para 23 of the Guidance states that the agenda should be completed in advance of the Preliminary Hearing and sent to the Tribunal. If possible, it should be agreed by the parties. It is open to a party to make applications on the agenda and care should be paid to what an unrepresented party is trying to say on the agenda form: see eg *Ministry of Defence v Dixon* (UKEAT/0050/17), 4 October 2017 concerning an unrepresented party making an application to add a claim of unfair dismissal on the agenda form.

The Court of Appeal has previously stressed the desirability of a directions hearing (a predecessor of the preliminary hearing for case management) in discrimination cases to enable the tribunal to deal with preliminary matters, identify the issues in dispute and establish a realistic time estimate for the hearing so that the case could be listed for long enough to avoid adjournments and delays in the substantive hearing: *Martins v Marks and Spencer plc* [1998] IRLR 326. These comments were reiterated, specifically in relation to claims based on the *Public Interest Disclosure Act 1998*, in *ALM Medical Services Ltd v Bladen* [2002] EWCA Civ 1085, [2002] IRLR 807, [2002] ICR 1444. Under the 2004 Rules no uniform practice on the ordering of CMDs existed and it was often left to the parties to identify the need for a CMD, even in discrimination cases and some relatively complex claims. Under the *2013 Rules*, the initial consideration given to claims and responses in every case is likely to assist the Tribunal judiciary get an early grip on the issues within a case. As has been seen above, where a claim proceeds, the Tribunal must make a case management order, unless one has been made already. It is likely that in future Judges will be able to identify at this stage where a preliminary hearing for case management is required, and make the necessary orders accordingly.

At a preliminary hearing for case management (CPH), the Tribunal will set out to identify the issues arising in the case with the parties. The parties are expected to attend with sufficient knowledge about the case to allow for this rigorous exercise to take place. Cost consequences might follow if the hearing cannot achieve its objectives (for an example, see *Wilsons Solicitors v Johnson* [2011] ICR D21). At many case management hearings, the issues will be reduced to writing and form an agreed list of issues. The case law on lists of issues is discussed at **20.84** above.

After the preliminary hearing for case management, the tribunal will send to the parties a copy of the orders made and a note of the discussion, which will include any list of issues. The Court in *Parekh* considered that where the issues were agreed, it would be difficult to see how the content of the list could ever be the proper subject of an appeal on a question of law. Alternatively, if the list was not agreed and it is contended that it is an incorrect record of the discussions, or there has been a material change in circumstances, the proper procedure is not to appeal, but to apply to the tribunal to reconsider the order in the interests of justice (para 32).

Orders for the preparation of chronologies, agreed facts, skeleton arguments etc are becoming increasingly common and parties should consider ahead of a case management hearing whether they would be appropriate to the circumstances of the individual case. Parties are prompted to do so on the Agenda for case management preliminary hearings which features in the Presidential Guidance.

One aspect of case management which is increasingly likely to be encountered, particularly in complex discrimination cases where numerous incidents have been raised by the claimant, is the application of the requirement in the Overriding Objective of proportionality: that the case be conducted in a manner proportionate to the importance and complexity of the issues in dispute. However, the Overriding Objective does not permit Employment Judges arbitrarily to limit the scope of the issues to be tried. Only the strike-out powers can be used to do that: see **20.74** et seq above. Thus in *McKinson v Hackney Community College* [2012] All ER (D) 128 (Jan) (UKEAT/0237/11) an order limiting the number of incidents the claimant was permitted to rely on to six was set aside on appeal. See also *Tarn v Hughes* [2019] ICR 76. In that case, which involved multiple allegations of discrimination, the Tribunal had ordered the claimant to select a maximum of ten recent and most serious matters from the claim form for consideration at a hearing, and to choose whether to rely on the other matters either as background to the ten selected complaints or to have them dealt with at a subsequent hearing. The EAT held this was not a permissible approach for two reasons. First, it required the claimant to make the unfair choice of having ten selected complaints determined without the relevant background or abandoning the other claims and pursuing only the selected ten with the relevant background. Secondly, it would result in no saving of time and cost because all matters would have to be dealt with at some point. The EAT further gave guidance (at §28) as to the handling of discrimination claims. This is set out in full in DISCRIMINATION AND EQUAL OPPORTUNITIES III (14), 14.2, but also provides helpful guidance that will be applicable in other cases where multiple claims are made.

Although the claims may not be cut down, directions may be given limiting the number of documents to be put before the tribunal, or the time to be allowed for particular witnesses or for the hearing as a whole; or requiring a claimant to identify and put forward at the hearing only the most important incidents forming part of his or her case, with the other incidents stayed to a later hearing (in the hope that a decision on the selected issues will enable the parties to resolve their differences on the outstanding matters): see *HSBC Asia Holdings BV v Gillespie* [2011] IRLR 209, [2011] ICR 192.

In certain cases, judicial assessment of a case as a means of facilitating ADR may take place at the end of a Preliminary Hearing for Case Management: see the discussion at **20.23**.

20.96 *Preliminary Hearings: Substantive Issues*

Preliminary hearings are also frequently convened in cases in order to determine preliminary issues. By *Rule 53(3)* a "preliminary issue" is defined to mean, as regards any complaint, any substantive issue which may determine liability, for example, an issue as to jurisdiction or as to whether an employee was dismissed. Other preliminary issues may include such matters as whether a claim was presented in time (and if not, whether time should be extended); whether the claimant is or was an employee or a worker, where the status of the claimant is in dispute; whether he had sufficient service to qualify for the right claimed; whether the claimant is or has been disabled; or whether a transfer amounted to a relevant transfer for the purposes of the *Transfer of Undertakings (Protection of Employment) Regulations 2006*.

The House of Lords has however indicated strongly, albeit in obiter comments, that it is in many cases not appropriate to hold a preliminary hearing, particularly to determine issues that are not completely separate from the issues that will remain to be decided at any full hearing: *SCA Packaging Ltd v Boyle* [2009] UKHL 37, [2009] IRLR 746, per Lord Hope at paras 9–10, Lord Rodger at para 45 and Lord Neuberger at para 82. Their Lordships cautioned against the holding of a preliminary hearing unless there is 'a succinct knockout point' to be decided. In particular, as in the *SCA* case, the issue whether a claimant is disabled is not necessarily sufficiently separable from the other issues in a claim of disability discrimination to justify it being made the subject of a separate hearing; nor are time points in discrimination cases where part at least of the claim is in time, since evidence of earlier incidents is likely to be admissible even if those incidents are as such out of time, as supporting evidence in relation to the matters which are in time; thus it is unlikely that any time would be saved by having a separate preliminary hearing. See also *Rossetti Marketing Limited v Diamond Sofa Company Limited* [2012] EWCA Civ 1021, [2012] All ER (D) 14 (Aug) in which Lord Neuberger MR warned that "while often attractive prospectively, the siren song of agreeing or ordering preliminary issues should normally be resisted" (para 1) and *English v Thomas Sanderson Limited* [2009] IRLR 206, [2009] ICR 543 in which the Court of Appeal held that a Tribunal should approach the use of a preliminary issue procedure with circumspection in any case where the result may be influenced by the details or nuance of the facts (paras 35, 36, 43). For an example of a case in which the EAT considered the ET's decision to hold a preliminary hearing was inappropriate, see *Wood v Durham County Council* (UKEAT/0099/18/OO), 3 September 2018, where the ET had held a preliminary hearing on the question of whether the claimant was disabled or whether the alleged disability involved an 'excluded condition' (tendency to steal). Since determining that issue inevitably left the free-standing unfair dismissal claim to go forward to a full hearing and evidence on that claim may be relevant to the disability issue as well, the EAT considered that it had been inappropriate to determine the matter as a preliminary issue. On the other hand in cases where it is arguable that the entire claim is out of time, a tribunal is likely to agree to that issue being addressed at a preliminary hearing because of the potential 'knockout' point involved.

Rule 56 governs when a preliminary hearing will be conducted in public. *Rule 53* provides that preliminary hearings must be conducted in private except where the hearing involves a determination of a preliminary issue or determination of a strike out application under *Rule 37*. In those circumstances, the part of the hearing dealing with such determinations is to be held in public (subject to the Tribunal having the ability to make orders for privacy reasons – *Rule 50* – and national security reasons – *Rule 94*). The Tribunal also may direct that the entirety of a preliminary hearing should be in public.

Rule 55 governs the constitution of the Tribunal for a preliminary hearing. It provides that preliminary hearings will be conducted by an Employment Judge sitting alone, except that where notice has been given that any preliminary issues are to be, or may be, decided at the hearing a party may request in writing that the hearing be conducted by a full tribunal. In such a case, an Employment Judge will then decide whether that would be desirable.

Unlike the old rules, there is no specific time limit for making the application for a full tribunal provided within *Rule 55*. Like the old rules, however, there would appear to be no power for the Judge on the day to convert the hearing to one before a full panel in the absence of a written application by a party. Any application for an adjournment to enable a party to make the necessary application is likely to be viewed with disfavour and may result in an application for the costs thrown away. It is therefore essential for a party wishing to have any preliminary issue decided by a full tribunal to apply promptly for an order to that effect. The fact that normally a preliminary hearing will be heard by an Employment Judge sitting alone is not generally regarded by tribunals as a good reason not to order the determination of factually complex preliminary points in this way.

The hearing of a preliminary hearing may be conducted by telephone or video link, provided that suitable arrangements are in place for members of the public to hear or see the proceedings: see above; however in practice this facility is very rarely used (as distinct from the practice of telephone preliminary hearings for case management, which is relatively common).

Preliminary hearings may be directed by a Tribunal on its own initiative following initial consideration under *Rule 26* or at any time thereafter, or as a result of an application by a party: *Rule 54*. When listing a preliminary hearing, the Tribunal shall give the parties reasonable notice of the date of the hearing and in the case of a hearing involving any preliminary issues at least 14 days' notice shall be given and the notice shall specify the preliminary issues that are to be, or may be, decided at the hearing.

20.97 *Interim Relief Hearings*

A Tribunal has the power to hear an application for interim relief (or to hear an application for its variation or revocation) under *TULR(C)A 1992, ss 161 and 165* (cases of unfair dismissal where the claimant alleges the dismissal is unfair because it is principally on grounds related to union membership or activities); and *ERA 1996, ss 128 and 131* (automatically unfair reasons for dismissal as listed in *s 128* including making protected disclosures).

If interim relief is granted, this involves either immediate reinstatement pending a full hearing, or if the employer will not reinstate, an order that the claimant be paid his normal pay until the hearing.

When such a hearing is held, *Rule 95* provides that *Rules 53* to *56* apply to the hearing, viz the rules relating to preliminary hearings: see above. This specifically includes the same rules for fixing a hearing – it must be done on reasonable notice, which may be very short if necessary. Under the primary legislation, a minimum of seven days' notice is required to hold an interim relief hearing: see the *ERA 1996 s 128(4)*, *TULR(C)A 1992, s 162(2)*). However, under *Rule 54*, 14 days' notice is required of a preliminary hearing which shall decide preliminary issues. An interim relief hearing should not be postponed "except where [the Tribunal] is satisfied that special circumstances exist which justify it in doing so" (*ERA 1996, s 128(5)*). The EAT has held that although not usually considered as such, counsel's availability can amount to a special circumstance. A special circumstance did not need to be 'exceptional': see *Lunn v Aston Darby Group Ltd* (UKEAT/0039/18).

Rule 95 also provides that the Tribunal shall not hear oral evidence unless it directs otherwise. There is no set procedure for an interim relief application other than that *Rule 95* provides that the default position is that evidence won't be heard. The practice as to whether the tribunal will agree to hearing witnesses varies as between tribunals. The exclusion of witness evidence may be regarded as a permissible exercise of case management powers in the interests of the expedition, which is given the highest priority in interim relief cases, but in an extreme case refusal to permit the calling of witnesses could be challenged on appeal as a procedural irregularity. The EAT has held that the tribunal is bound to hear and determine interim relief applications, however complex the underlying facts, if a timely application under one of the relevant jurisdictions has been presented: *Raja v Secretary of State for Justice* [2010] All ER (D) 134 (Mar) (UKEAT/0364/09); see also *London City Airport Ltd v Chacko* [2013] IRLR 610 (UKEAT/0013/13).

See further UNFAIR DISMISSAL, **54.18**.

20.98 *Final Hearing*

A final hearing is a hearing at which the Tribunal determines the claim or such parts as remain outstanding following the initial consideration (under *Rule 26*) or any preliminary hearing: see *Rule 57*. A claim can have more than one final hearing to cover different issues (for example, liability, remedy or costs).

A Tribunal must give the parties not less than 14 days' notice of the date of a final hearing: *Rule 58*. All final hearings must be held in public, although that requirement (see *Rule 59*) is subject to the ability of the Tribunal to make an order under *Rules 50* and *94*.

The Judge is required to keep a full note of the evidence given; this is normally done in longhand, or occasionally on a laptop computer; the taking of notes sometimes results in a speed of proceedings which many observers not used to tribunal proceedings find rather slow. The notes are important not only to assist the tribunal in reaching its judgment (especially if the hearing is adjourned part-heard, or judgment is reserved) but also for the benefit of the EAT, if necessary, on any subsequent appeal. A distinction is made, however, been the notes of the evidence (which constitute the record of the proceedings) and the judge's private reflections and observations which may be regarded as preliminary notes for the preparation of the judgment and which are therefore privileged from disclosure in all circumstances (and should therefore be redacted or excised where disclosure of the record of proceedings is required): see *R (McIntyre) v The Parole Board* [2013] EWHC 1969 (Admin). A judge's notes have been the subject of an ICO ruling which resulted in the notes being provided under data protection legislation: see *Percival* (ICO Case Reference RFA0582445). However, they are not disclosable under the *Freedom of Information Act 2000*: see the exemption in *s 32*.

Submissions, or closing speeches, are the opportunity to put to the tribunal the points the party considers should lead the tribunal to find in that party's favour, on each of the issues remaining in dispute. This may involve putting forward propositions as to what the relevant legal principles to be applied are, if necessary with the citation of relevant cases, as well as highlighting points of evidence, and reasons why it is submitted that the evidence of particular witnesses on disputed issues should be preferred. If cases are relied on, copies of the cases should be available to hand to the tribunal, and any particular passages in judgments that are relied on highlighted or drawn to the tribunal's attention. It is open to any party or representative to prepare written submissions or skeleton arguments and invite the tribunal to read them, and this is commonly done by legal representatives, particularly so in longer cases and cases where there are disputed points of law. Occasionally, the provision of written submissions may be directed in advance by the tribunal as part of its case management function, but this is rarely done except in lengthy cases. Written submissions are rarer in Scotland.

In addition, tribunals sometimes ask the parties to make their final submissions in writing, when there is not enough time to complete the case without an adjournment. The parties' representatives may sometimes suggest this. The EAT has given guidance to tribunals as to the procedure to be followed if written submissions are to be provided in place of, rather than in support of, oral submissions: *Barking and Dagenham London Borough Council v Oguoko* [2000] IRLR 179. The procedure should only be implemented with the consent of both parties, and each party must be served a copy of the other's submissions and given time to comment on them (comments being limited to correction of factual errors and responses to any new points of law not previously raised) before the tribunal proceeds to reach its decision. These points were reiterated by the EAT in *Blitz v Equant Integration Services Ltd (t/a Orange Business Services)* [2008] All ER (D) 203 (Jan), EAT, where the point was made that it is particularly important that each party should have the opportunity to comment, preferably orally, on the written submissions of the other. The EAT has held that where a tribunal ordered written submissions and those from the respondent were received in time, but the claimant's submissions were not (having gone astray) it was incumbent on the tribunal to make at least a telephone enquiry of the claimant before proceeding to reach a decision without her submissions: *Quashie v Methodist Homes Housing Association* [2012] All ER (D) 74 (May), [2012] ICR 1330 (UKEAT/0422/11).

In a lengthy or legally complex case, the tribunal may ask for written submissions in addition to oral submissions. In such cases, adequate time must be allowed for the other party's representative, and the tribunal, to read and digest the written submissions before the oral submissions are made: *Sinclair Roche & Temperley v Heard* [2004] IRLR 763.

It is open to a party to submit at the conclusion of the other party's evidence that there is no case to answer. This should be done without prejudice to the right to call evidence if the submission is rejected. However, the making of such submissions has increasingly been discouraged by the higher courts, especially in discrimination cases where it is necessary to weigh the circumstantial evidence of discrimination with the employer's explanation in assessing whether the evidence justifies an inference of discrimination: see *British Gas plc v Sharma* [1991] IRLR 101, where it was described as 'exceptional' for such a submission to be appropriate in a discrimination case. The principles were restated in *Clarke v Watford Borough Council* (EAT/43/99), in terms expressly approved by the Court of Appeal in *Logan v Customs and Excise Comrs* [2003] EWCA Civ 1068, [2004] IRLR 63, as follows:

(1) There is no inflexible rule of law and practice that a tribunal must always hear both sides, although that should normally be done.

(2) The power to stop a case at "half-time" must be exercised with caution.

(3) It may be a complete waste of time to call on the other party to give evidence in a hopeless case.

(4) Even where the onus of proof lies on the [claimant], as in discrimination cases, it will only be in exceptional or frivolous cases that it would be right to take such a course.

(5) Where there is no burden of proof, as under *s 98(4)* of the *Employment Rights Act*, it will be difficult to envisage arguable cases where it is appropriate to terminate the proceedings at the end of the first party's case.

It should be noted that the reference above to the burden of proof in discrimination cases pre-dates changes in the burden introduced from 2001 onwards; however the point made at (4) above is if anything stronger where only an initial burden is placed on the claimant.

For the sake of certainty, it is best to obtain a clear indication from the employment tribunal at the commencement of the hearing of whether it will consider liability and remedy separately, and if so, when it will consider evidence and argument on contributory fault and/or on whether a *Polkey* reduction in compensation should be made if a dismissal is found to be procedurally unfair. The EAT has held that it is an error of law for the tribunal to deal with the *Polkey* point without giving the parties an opportunity to make submissions on it: *Market Force (UK) Ltd v Hunt* [2002] IRLR 863; *Grace v BF Components Ltd* [2005] All ER (D) 06 (Oct) (UKEAT/0006/05). By analogy this would apply equally to the issue of contribution, or the amount of any uplift or reduction in compensation under *s 207A, TULR(C)A 1992*. The point is an illustration of the more general point that it would be an error of law for the tribunal to decide a case on a point the parties have not raised or had an opportunity to deal with; see *Launahurst Ltd v Larner* [2010] EWCA Civ 334, [2010] All ER (D) 282 (Mar) for an example of a case where this was held to have occurred and further **20.83** above. The usual practice, in the absence of a direction to the contrary, is that the tribunal will proceed to deal with remedy, if time permits, immediately following its decision on liability (and assuming that that decision is in the claimant's favour). However, it is unusual (at least in England and Wales) for a tribunal to hear evidence relating solely to compensation before it has reached a decision on liability. In *Iggesund Converters Ltd v Lewis* [1984] IRLR 431, [1984] ICR 544, the EAT suggested ways in which employment tribunals could deal with evidence and argument on the reduction of an award for contributory fault, and in *Ferguson v Gateway Training Centre Ltd* [1991] ICR 658 it suggested that the Judge should restate which issues are being considered prior to final submissions. The EAT has also emphasised that it is important that the tribunal gives the parties a chance to be heard on any issue of remedy before deciding the point: *Duffy v Yeomans & Partners Ltd* [1993] IRLR 368, [1993] ICR 862. The EAT has held that in unfair dismissal cases, the tribunal must consider the issue of contributory fault if it appears to arise on the evidence: *Swallow Security Services Ltd v Millicent* [2009] All ER (D) 299 (Mar). If the point is to be considered, the tribunal would have to alert the parties to this, to enable them to make submissions on the point.

The practice in Scotland is that unless there has been a prior direction that issues of remedy be dealt with separately, the tribunal will hear evidence on all issues together, and will give a single judgment covering both liability and remedy; the usual practice in all but the most straightforward cases is for the judgment to be reserved and delivered in writing. If there is good reason for keeping the issue of remedy separate (such as that there will be insufficient time within the period listed for the hearing to deal with all issues, or expert evidence will be needed in relation to issues of remedy) an early application should be made for a direction for the hearing to deal in the first instance with liability only.

Sometimes in the course of the hearing the Judge will give an indication to the parties of the tribunal's provisional view as to the merits of the case, or more commonly a particular issue in the case. This may be done for a number of reasons: to encourage the parties to settle, or give them assistance to settle by giving an indication as to the likely outcome on a particular point or the case as a whole; to identify which issues should be focused on in evidence or cross-examination; or to identify the issues on which submissions are particularly sought. Caution is needed in giving any kind of preliminary indication of the tribunal's view, since this may be interpreted as indicating that the decision has already been reached, or provide a basis for a later appeal on grounds of apparent bias. However the Court of Appeal has confirmed that, provided that it is made quite clear that any views expressed are provisional, there is no objection in principle to the Judge expressing a view in the course of the case: *Jiminez v Southwark London Borough Council* [2003] EWCA Civ 502, [2003] IRLR 477. By contrast, in *Gee v Shell UK Ltd* [2002] EWCA Civ 1479, [2003] IRLR 82, the Court of Appeal held that there had been procedural unfairness where the Judge had warned the claimant (who was acting in person) that she was at risk of an award of costs against her, in circumstances where there was no real basis for an award of costs, and she felt obliged to withdraw her claim to avoid the costs sanction. Contrast the position in *Hussain v Nottinghamshire Healthcare NHS Trust* [2016] All ER (D) 88 (Aug), [2016] UKEAT/0080/16 where a costs warning had not represented a concluded view and was an appropriate way of pointing out potential danger to the claimant. See further the section on bias at **20.92** above.

20.99 *Preparing for the hearing and Listing Arrangements*

The length of time from presentation of a claim to a Hearing varies considerably. HM Courts and Tribunals Service and its predecessors, the Tribunals Service, and before it the ETS, have for many years set performance targets for tribunals, one of which is that 75% of single cases will receive a first hearing within 26 weeks of receipt of the Claim Form, but success in achieving this figure has been variable, both over time and in different regions. For relatively simple cases many tribunal regions are now able to list a hearing date within a few weeks of the deadline for a response, but it is not unusual for there to be a delay of several months if a case needs to be listed for more than one day.

The tribunal must give the parties at least 14 days' notice of the date of a preliminary hearing which will decide preliminary issues and final hearing (see *Rules 54* and *58*). Otherwise reasonable notice of a preliminary hearing will be given (*Rule 54*). In practice, longer notice is usually (but not always) given. The usual practice for simple cases is to issue a notice of hearing without first checking with the parties whether the date is suitable (but in Scotland it is the practice to consult the parties before listing).

There is no automatic right to postponement of a hearing even if both parties request a postponement, and it is difficult on appeal to dispute a refusal to postpone (*Employment Service v Nathan* (EAT/1316/95), IDS Brief 568; *London Fire and Civil Defence Authority v Samuels* (EAT/450/00), IDS Brief 669); it is therefore important to apply as early as possible and with full reasons for the request. For an example of a successful appeal against the refusal of a postponement agreed by both parties, see *Chancerygate (Business Centre) Ltd v Jenkins* (UKEAT/0212/10). See postponements above at **20.88**.

Sometimes a listed hearing can be adjourned by the tribunal, often at short notice, for reasons of resource allocation (such as no Judge being available to take the case). In *University of East Anglia v Amaik Wu* [2012] All ER (D) 01 (Sep) (UKEAT/0361/12), the tribunal had listed a multiple day hearing which had to be adjourned on the working day before it was due to start because of a lack of judges to hear it. The tribunal then relisted the hearing without reference to the parties' available dates. This impacted upon one of the respondent's witnesses who was due to attend a wedding abroad. The respondent therefore applied for a relisting which was refused by the tribunal judge. The EAT found the judge erred by taking into account irrelevant circumstances and failing to take into account the fact that the tribunal had not sought dates to avoid. The EAT recorded that "in general the understanding is that a prompt response [to a listing] asking for another date based on witness availability is dealt with sympathetically" (para 14). Deciding the point *de novo*, the EAT granted the adjournment; central were the facts that: the witness was crucial, the application prompt, the tribunal did not seek dates to avoid, the witness had a significant role at the wedding.

20.100 Listing arrangements are normally made at a preliminary hearing for case management in more complicated cases. Information is gathered ahead of that preliminary hearing by the completion of the Agenda Questionnaire found in the Presidential Guidance on Case Management. Otherwise, upon initial consideration of a claim, the case can be listed for an appropriate hearing length. If a case is likely to take longer than the allowed time it is important to apply at an early stage for a longer listing; otherwise the tribunal will have to reconvene, possibly months later, if the case is not completed within the allotted day (it is very rare indeed that the case would be continued the following day in those circumstances). For cases to be listed for more than a day without a preliminary hearing, most regions write to the parties advising them of the intention to list the case and requiring notification to the tribunal if a party considers the proposed time allocation to be inappropriate. It is important to respond to such an invitation, since the tribunal may hold the parties to a time allocation even if at the hearing they suggest that the time allowed is insufficient, and this is also an opportunity to give the tribunal dates to be avoided because eg a witness will not be available. In Scotland parties are asked to identify the witnesses they intend to call and how long the evidence of each will take to be heard, and the time allocated to the case is based on the parties' responses.

The basis on which cases are listed, unless otherwise indicated, is that sufficient time should be allowed not only to hear the evidence and submissions of the parties, but also for the tribunal to reach and announce its decision, and to deal if appropriate with remedies. Anecdotally, a figure often mentioned by judges as the time required for deliberations with a full panel is around $1/3^{rd}$ of the time required to hear the evidence. Parties are now generally warned of this approach, and are advised also of the tribunal's power to set a timetable to ensure that the case is completed within the time available. Hearings are normally scheduled to take place at the Regional Office or other office of the tribunal at which the case has been presented (or to which the file has been transferred), but there are also a number of hearing centres at which cases are heard but which do not have a permanent staff presence. Increasingly, hearing centres shared with other tribunals are used, on the basis either of availability of tribunal rooms or of geographical convenience for the parties (the latter in particular in more rural areas); if travel to the tribunal office administering the case is likely to be difficult or expensive for a party, enquiries should be made of the tribunal as to whether it will be possible to list the case for hearing at a more convenient location. In Scotland, local Sheriff Courts are used for hearings in more remote locations.

Special priority is given to interim hearings of applications for interim relief (see 56.18 UNFAIR DISMISSAL – III). Only seven days' notice of the claim and of the hearing is required, and postponements will only be granted where special circumstances exist (the statutory provisions stipulating this are *ERA 1996, s 128(4), (5)* and *TULR(C)A 1992, s 162(2), (4)*). In *Lunn v Aston Darby Group Ltd* (UKEAT/0039/18), the EAT held that in principle counsel's availability could amount to a special circumstance, and that a special circumstance did not need to be 'exceptional' to qualify.

There are several steps a party should take prior to the hearing – preferably earlier rather than later. These are addressed in the following sections. The reader is also referred to the Presidential Guidance on General Case Management that has been issued.

20.101 A decision should be taken whether a legal or other representative is to be engaged; if so, this should be done in good time to enable the representative to prepare for the hearing and take any necessary interlocutory steps. There is no restriction on who may represent a party in the tribunal (see *Bache v Essex County Council* [2000] 2 All ER 847, [2000] IRLR 251). In general no legal aid is now available. Legal assistance for the preparation of the case used to be available to claimants of limited means, but (apart from in limited circumstances in Scotland) this ceased to be so on the coming into force on 1 April 2013 of the *Legal Aid, Sentencing and Punishment of Offenders Act 2012*. There are now only very limited circumstances in which legal aid assistance is available in England and Wales. It is limited to advice online, by telephone or post in discrimination cases (contact the Civil Legal Advice information line for details: 0345 345 4 345 or https://www.gov.uk/civil-legal-advice). In Scotland, a consultation is ongoing over plans to exclude civil legal assistance from various areas of civil law including employment law: see the paper "Legal Assistance in Scotland – Fit for the 21st Century".

Employers are often represented by an appropriate manager or a trade association official, employees by a union officer or a Citizens' Advice Bureau (CABx) or advice centre worker. The fact that no representative is given on the Claim Form or Response Form by no means necessarily indicates that the party concerned will not be represented. Whoever is to represent a party, it is desirable that the representative be consulted in good time before the hearing. It is also important that the tribunal is notified promptly of the appointment of a representative, with contact details, and of any change in arrangements for representation, to avoid the all too common situation that correspondence from the tribunal, including notice of hearings, does not reach the party or his current representative.

A number of organisations offer their services as representatives in tribunal proceedings, either as consultants offering a package of advice and representation to employers, or on a no win no fee basis for claimants. Concerns about the quality of representation offered by some of these organisations, and the lack of any professional or statutory regulation of their conduct, led to the introduction of a requirement, under the *Compensation Act 2006, Part 2*, for claims management services (including those providing representation in employment tribunals for reward) to be regulated. With effect from 1 April 2019, responsibility for regulation transferred to the Financial Conduct Authority (FCA) under the *Financial Services and Markets Act 2000 (FSMA 2000)*. It is a criminal offence for a person or organisation who, or which, is not registered with the FCA to provide representation for claimants (but not respondents) in employment tribunal proceedings for reward (including on a no win, no fee basis). In *Miller v Community Links Trust* [2007] All ER (D) 196 (Nov), the EAT referred an unregulated representative to the Regulator for possible action. A number of categories of representatives are exempt from regulation under the *FSMA 2000*, including solicitors, barristers, trade unions and the CABx; for full details see the *Financial Services and Markets Act 2000 (Claims Management Activity) Order 2018 (SI 2018/1253)*. The regulatory regime only applies to England and Wales, and there is no equivalent statutory regulation of representatives acting for reward in Scotland.

Before engaging a representative on a no win no fee basis, a prospective claimant needs to appreciate that the representative will normally have to be paid out of whatever compensation is awarded if the claim succeeds, since costs are not usually awarded, but compensation is assessed without regard to this liability. By way of further regulation of 'no win no fee' agreements, the *Damages-Based Agreements Regulations 2013 (SI 2013/609)*, which came into force on 1 April 2013, prohibit agreements in employment cases which provide for payment of more than 35% (including VAT) of the compensation recovered, whether by way of settlement or as an award of the tribunal: *reg 7*. This mirrored the provisions in the preceding *Damages-Based Agreements Regulations 2010*, which remain in force for agreements made before 1 April 2013. Neither set of Regulations extends to Scotland.

In an extreme case the conduct of a representative may lead to sanctions being imposed by the tribunal on the party represented, including striking out that party's case (see *Bennett v Southwark London Borough Council* [2002] EWCA Civ 223, [2002] IRLR 407). The tribunal also has the power to make a wasted costs order against a representative acting for profit (including under a no win, no fee agreement), ie an order that the representative must pay the other party's costs, or debarring the representative from recovering costs incurred from his client. See further **20.71**.

For those, particularly claimants, who cannot afford to pay for legal representation, free representation may be available through one or other of a number of organisations including the Citizens' Advice Bureaux (CABx), law centres, the Free Representation Unit (5th Floor, Kingsbourne House, 229-231 High Holborn, London WC1V 7DA, tel. 020 7611 9555, http ://www.thefru.org.uk/), the Employment Tribunal Litigant in Person Support Scheme (ELIPS) and Advocate (https://weareadvocate.org.uk/) and in discrimination cases application may be made for legal assistance to the Equality and Human Rights Commission, although the Commission's budget for legal assistance is limited, and funding is concentrated on cases with wider implications or meeting priority criteria.

Most trade unions provide a free representation service for members, either through union officials or union-appointed solicitors, and usually subject to being satisfied that the claim has some merit. An increasing number of claimants are represented by lawyers paid for under legal expenses insurance (often provided as an optional addition to household insurance) and it is important that a claimant should check at as early a stage as possible whether this facility may be available. Further advice on possible sources of free professional representation can be obtained through CABx.

20.102 Consideration should be given to whether an application for any case management orders, or a preliminary hearing, is needed. Orders may be any of those discussed in this chapter. A preliminary hearing for case management may be listed by the tribunal of its own motion. Most commonly this happens in discrimination cases; where the issues appear complex; or where a party's application for an order has been opposed. It may also be necessary to apply to the tribunal for a preliminary hearing to determine a particular preliminary point (such as whether it has jurisdiction over the claim). A party may wish to apply for permission to amend the claim or response. An application which is likely to be contested should not be granted by the tribunal without the opposing party being given an opportunity to resist the application (in writing or, if the tribunal so orders, at a preliminary or other hearing) and if an amendment is allowed ex parte, without such an opportunity, the opposing party may apply to the tribunal to have the order set aside (see *Reddington v S Straker & Sons Ltd* [1994] ICR 172). A tribunal should not normally decide an application to amend a Claim Form which raises an issue of substance, without giving the parties an opportunity to make representations (*Smith v Gwent District Health Authority* [1996] ICR 1044). The practice in relation to applications to amend was restated by the EAT in *Selkent Bus Co Ltd v Moore* [1996] IRLR 661, [1996] ICR 836. For more details, see **20.70** above.

20.103 It is sometimes necessary for a party to apply for a postponement of the hearing, either because a witness becomes unavailable or for a variety of other reasons. Any such application should if possible be made with the agreement of the other party. However, even agreed applications are not necessarily granted by the tribunal. It is important to give full reasons for the application, especially if it is opposed. The earlier the application is made, the more likely it is to be granted and special rules now restrict the Tribunal's ability to accede to an application made shortly before the hearing or if the party applying has already applied twice for a postponement: see *Rule 30A*. If the application is made on grounds of ill-health, medical evidence will be required by the tribunal. In deciding applications, tribunals are entitled to have regard to the public interest in cases being heard as promptly as reasonably practicable, now reinforced by the incorporation into domestic law of the right under *Art 6* of the *European Convention on Human Rights* to have a dispute decided within a reasonable time. See further **20.88** above.

20.104 The relevant documentary evidence should be identified. Documentation likely to be relevant will include the contract of employment or letter of engagement, statutory statement of particulars of employment, relevant parts of any staff handbook (such as a disciplinary procedure), any written warnings, records of performance or attendance (if these are relevant issues), the letter of dismissal and any correspondence notifying the employee of the disciplinary investigation or hearing, notes or minutes of any relevant meetings, appeal documents if applicable, documents demonstrating the need for a redundancy, and documents relevant to quantification of the claim, such as payments made to the employee and pension documentation. The employee may need to produce documentation showing his attempts to mitigate his loss and any earnings since dismissal, as well as evidence of pay and benefits prior to dismissal, and social security benefits received after termination. In cases where a grievance has been raised, the documentation relating to the grievance, grievance hearings and any appeal will be required.

The parties will be expected, particularly if both have professional representation, to agree a bundle of documents including those to be relied on by both sides. It is now standard practice for the tribunal to make an order to this effect, however even if no order is made, the Presidential Guidance on General Case Management emphasises that a single bundle should be prepared and that the parties must cooperate to this end. Such a bundle may be referred to as an 'agreed' bundle or the 'hearing bundle'; the word 'agreed' here means that the authenticity of the documents is not disputed, but not that their relevance or accuracy is necessarily conceded. The bundle should be paginated (ie each page should be consecutively numbered) and, if substantial, indexed. Six copies will be needed for the hearing (three for the tribunal, or one if an Employment Judge is sitting alone, and one each for each party and for the witnesses). Some tribunal regions in England have adopted a practice of limiting the number of pages of documentation parties may include, but practice on this varies, and is subject to consideration of any reasoned case a party may make to put in more than the maximum number of pages.

Where the parties fail to cooperate over bundles, they are in principle at risk of costs orders (see below). In *Smith-Twigger v Abbey Protection Group Ltd* [2014] ICR D33, [2014] All ER (D) 92 (Oct) the EAT (dealing specifically with the bundling requirements in the EAT) held that "it is in general unacceptable that the parties should fail to co-operate over the contents of a bundle" (para 47).

In Scotland, documents produced to the tribunal are referred to as 'productions'. Parties with legal representation are required by a Practice Direction to notify each other of what productions each party intends to rely on, and provide copies, 14 days before the hearing; in straightforward cases it is unusual for any specific orders to be made for disclosure or exchange of productions, but it is nevertheless important to prepare sufficient copies of the documents, numbered and indexed (this is referred to as an 'inventory of productions'), as failure to do so will inevitably extend the length of the hearing; if possible there should be a joint bundle of productions. The usual practice is to number each document (which may be more than one page) separately.

As the rules of evidence do not apply fully in tribunals, it is not necessary formally to prove the documents in the tribunal bundle, unless the genuineness or accuracy of a document is disputed (eg in the latter case, minutes of a meeting). If there is a dispute, a witness who can confirm the accuracy of the document from personal knowledge should be called. Where there may be issues of authenticity, originals of any documents should wherever possible be available at the hearing.

There are no formal rules as to who should produce the sets of documents needed for the hearing. The usual practice is for the party advancing a case to take this responsibility (ie the claimant in discrimination or breach of contract cases, but the employer in unfair dismissal cases where the dismissal is admitted). However, it has in recent years become increasingly common for the respondent to accept the burden of preparing the bundles, and the requirement of the Overriding Objective that the parties should so far as possible be put on an equal footing has led to it becoming part of the common practice of tribunals, at least in cases with substantial documentation, to require respondents to undertake this task. Often the tribunal will encourage agreement on the question of the cost of preparing and duplicating the bundle, but its powers to award costs are limited to those in the rules.

20.105 One category of documents is not normally admissible before a tribunal; this is 'without prejudice' correspondence. This means correspondence conducted in an attempt to reach a settlement of a dispute; it is only admissible either to prove an agreement reached as a result or if both parties agree. For further details of the limits of the 'without prejudice' privilege see **20.13** above. Correspondence is sometimes conducted under the heading 'Without prejudice save as to costs'. This preserves the right of the party putting forward proposals to refer to the correspondence after the substantive issues have been decided by the tribunal, solely in support of an application for costs – see further **20.34** above and **20.129** below. In unfair dismissal cases the effect of *ERA 1996, s 111A* should also be considered: pre-termination negotiations will, pursuant to that section become inadmissible in proceedings, subject to three exceptions. See further **20.13** above.

20.106 The relevant witnesses should be identified and their statements taken. An employer in an unfair dismissal case will usually need to call at least the manager who took the decision to dismiss the employee and, if applicable, the manager who decided the appeal. In a redundancy case, evidence of the redundancy situation, of the reasons for the decision to select the claimant, of consultation with the claimant and any recognised union, and of attempts to redeploy, may all be required. Where there has been a disciplinary hearing and the reason for the dismissal was that the manager decided on the evidence that the employee was guilty of misconduct, it is not the tribunal's function to re-try the case or decide for itself as to the employee's guilt; it should not therefore normally be necessary to call all those persons who were involved in the disciplinary hearing (apart from the manager conducting the hearing) or any earlier investigation. It may, however, be necessary to call the manager conducting any separate investigation prior to the disciplinary hearing, particularly so if there is any dispute as to the sufficiency or fairness of the investigation. In some cases it might be justifiable to call witnesses to the underlying allegations of misconduct as although this evidence does not go to liability for unfair dismissal, it can go to questions of contributory fault and liability for wrongful dismissal: see *London Ambulance Service v Small* [2009] IRLR 563, CA. As to the employee, whether any additional witness is to be called depends on the availability (and sometimes willingness) of those who have knowledge of relevant events.

Some caution should, however, be exercised when deciding whether to rely on a witness. Calling live evidence opens the door to cross examination and gives the opponent the opportunity to elicit other evidence helpful to their case. A careful judgment call is often required. When making that call, advisors should consider whether the oral evidence is really necessary. In some cases it will be, but in other cases, the documents might tell their own story. Such considerations now take place against an increasing judicial trend towards recognising the unreliability of human memory; as Tom Bingham put it in The Business of Judging (OUP, 2000, p15): "the human capacity for honestly believing something which bears no relation to what really happened is unlimited" (cited with approval by Mostyn J in *A County Council v M and F* [2011] EWHC 1804 (Fam) (para 30) and Leggatt J in *Brogden v Investec Bank Plc* [2014] EWHC 2785 (Comm), [2014] IRLR 924 (para 50)). More generally, see Leggatt J's longer analysis of the problems with relying on human memory in *Gestmin SGPS SA v Credit Suisse (UK) Ltd* [2013] EWHC 3560 (Comm), [2013] All ER (D) 191 (Nov) (paras 15 to 22) and *Blue v Ashley* [2017] EWHC 1928 (Comm) at paras 65-70. In *Suddock v Nursing and Midwifery Council* [2016] All ER (D) 53 (Jan), the Administrative Court cautioned against focusing overly on the demeanour of a witness when making findings. Whilst demeanour was not irrelevant, the way in which the person's evidence corresponded with non-contentious evidence or agreed facts, and with contemporaneous documents and the inherent probabilities and improbabilities of the account of events in question, as well as consistencies or inconsistencies, were likely to be far more reliable indicators of where the truth lay.

In most cases issues about the admissibility of particular evidence will be decided by the tribunal hearing the case in the course of the hearing. However it is open to the tribunal in the exercise of its case management powers to rule in advance of the hearing on the admissibility of particular evidence which a party proposes to call. This may be done where there is a dispute about admissibility based on legal arguments, such as whether the evidence is covered by legal professional privilege, but exceptionally a ruling may be based on proportionality. Thus in *HSBC Asia Holdings BV v Gillespie* [2011] ICR 192, [2011] IRLR 209, the EAT ruled that the tribunal should have excluded in advance evidence the claimant in a discrimination case intended to introduce at the hearing as background, in order to show a discriminatory culture within the respondent bank, covering a period of 10 years going back 18 years from the date of the claim, and involving departments of the bank, and individuals, who were not affected at all by the substantive allegations of harassment. Underhill P pointed out that whilst evidence that is irrelevant is inadmissible, relevance alone is not necessarily sufficient to justify admission; where the evidence is of marginal relevance, it may be disproportionate to admit it, as in this case where admission of the evidence would necessitate the calling of much additional evidence by the respondent to seek to rebut the allegations made, which were not the substantive complaints for which a remedy could be granted. See also now the EAT's judgment in *Kalu v Brighton & Sussex University Hospitals NHS Trust* (UKEAT/0609/12) and further above **20.60**A.

20.107   For hearings in England and Wales, witnesses will need to be asked to prepare written statements of their evidence (legal representatives will normally prepare drafts themselves following an interview with each witness). These should be typed or legibly written, using short, numbered paragraphs. It is important that all relevant matters of which the witness has knowledge are covered. Whilst the practice as to timing is not consistent between tribunal regions, the almost universal practice is that the tribunal will direct the parties to prepare witness statements, and to exchange them prior to the hearing. Sometimes the tribunal will also direct that the witness statements will be taken as the evidence-in-chief of the witness. This means that the party calling the witness will not be able to ask him additional questions without the permission of the tribunal. If there is good reason why a statement cannot be produced for a particular witness, it is advisable to apply to the tribunal for an order exempting that witness from the general requirement for statements to be exchanged in advance.

The practice as to how witness statements are used at the hearing was in the past that in most cases the tribunal would invite the witnesses to give their evidence by reading the statement; sometimes (usually where the facts did not appear to be substantially in dispute, or in more lengthy cases) the tribunal would pre-read the statements and simply ask the witnesses to confirm the truth of their contents. The practice has now been changed. *Rule 43* provides that if there is a witness statement, it stands as the witness's evidence-in-chief unless the tribunal directs otherwise. This means that the standard practice is that the witness will not have to read out the statement, but it will be read by the tribunal; and the witness will only be able to give additional evidence in chief if the tribunal agrees. The change reflects guidance given by the EAT in *Mehta v Child Support Agency* [2011] IRLR 305. In summary, Underhill P's guidance (which is likely to influence tribunals in deciding whether all or part of a statement should be read out) is that it is not a requirement of fairness that every witness statement is read out in full to the tribunal, but there may be cases where this is desirable, particularly if a party is unrepresented; it is not necessary for all statements to be treated in the same way: a witness may for instance be asked to read the key parts of his statement, the rest being read privately by the tribunal; and wherever possible, the tribunal should proceed with the agreement of the parties, taking care to ensure that any unrepresented party fully understands what is proposed, and agrees to the course proposed. In practice it will often be necessary for the tribunal to ask questions of the witness (or the representative of the party calling the witness) to clarify points in the statement, and to identify clearly documents referred to and the parts of documents the witness is referring to in the statement, so that these too can be read.

If it will not be possible to call a witness, evidence can be given by way of a signed statement, which should contain a statement confirming that the witness believes the facts stated in the statement to be true (a 'statement of truth'). Such evidence should be sent to the tribunal and the other party at least seven days before the hearing so that it can be considered as a written representation (see *Rule 42*) or by any other time limit set by the Tribunal for a witness statement. If tendered late, the tribunal may decline to consider it. In any case, however, the weight to be attached to evidence in this form is affected by the unavailability of the witness (for however cogent a reason) for cross-examination. Accordingly, unless the evidence is not in dispute, great caution should be used in relying on written evidence instead of a live witness.

The practice in Scotland is still that witness statements are not normally used as a means of giving evidence, or exchanged before the hearing. Instead, at least where there is legal representation, witnesses are usually interviewed before the hearing by the representative (a procedure known as 'precognosing' the witness), and a proof of evidence prepared, which can serve as a script for the advocate calling the witness. If there are particular reasons why it would be desirable for the evidence (or evidence of specific witnesses) to be given by way of written statements, early application should be made to the tribunal for directions on the point. Where witness statements are used, the new rules will apply equally.

20.108 It is open to any party to submit representations in writing to the tribunal; they must be submitted (and sent to each other party) at least seven days before the hearing date, unless the tribunal consents to a shorter period (*Rule 42*). Written representations may be made by a party attending the hearing, or in lieu of attendance. However, the latter course is extremely hazardous, since the absent party cannot deal with questions from the tribunal, points that arise unexpectedly or assertions made in evidence by the other party. In all but the simplest cases, attendance in person or by a representative is essential. The provision of written representations under the *ET Rules* outlined above is not to be confused with the practice of submitting a written skeleton argument; sometimes the tribunal will make an order for such skeletons to be exchanged and filed by a particular time, but otherwise, the parties are free to present them to the tribunal at the time of the hearing.

20.109 The current practice of tribunals in straightforward cases is to deal with all questions including, if appropriate, remedy, at one hearing. Accordingly, and unless the tribunal has directed that remedy will be dealt with subsequently, parties should come to the hearing prepared to deal with evidence relevant to remedy. This means that the claimant should include in his statement details of the earnings lost, any income received from new employment or state benefits, and information relevant to any claim that he has failed to take reasonable steps to mitigate his loss. In most regions the standard orders issued in unfair dismissal and discrimination cases include a requirement for the claimant to serve a Schedule of Loss detailing the amounts claimed, benefits received etc. The respondent should have the necessary information to put before the tribunal to establish take home pay (if disputed) and the value of any employment benefits. If there is likely to be a dispute about this, relevant documentation should be in the bundle. (It does not follow that the tribunal will have the time to deal with remedy, and it may agree to give the parties time to attempt to agree the remedy; however cases are listed on the basis that time is allowed for the tribunal to hear the case, reach and deliver its decision, and then deal with remedy if necessary.) If it is anticipated that additional evidence will need to be called in relation to remedy, particularly if expert evidence (eg on pension loss) will be needed, it may be advisable to apply well before the hearing for a direction that remedy will be dealt with separately at a second hearing. In Scotland the practice is that all issues including remedy will be dealt with together, before the decision on liability is given, if at all possible, although split hearings are becoming less uncommon, especially if expert evidence is required on the issue of remedy. See further above **20.98**.

20.110 *Conversion from Preliminary Hearing to Final Hearing and vice versa*

By *Rule 48*, a Tribunal that is conducting a preliminary hearing may order that it be treated as a final hearing, or vice versa if the Tribunal is properly constituted for the purpose and if it is satisfied that neither party shall be materially prejudiced by the change.

DECISIONS, REASONS, THEIR ENFORCEMENT AND RECONSIDERATION

Decisions and Reasons

20.111 *Making and Recording Decisions*

The *2013 Rules* provide at various points that decisions can be made by the Employment Tribunal both at or following a hearing and without a hearing.

If the Tribunal makes a decision without a hearing, by *Rule 60*, the decision must be communicated in writing to the parties, identifying the Employment Judge who has made the decision.

Where there is a hearing the Tribunal may either announce its decision in relation to any issue at the hearing or reserve it to be sent to the parties as soon as practicable in writing: *Rule 61(1)*. In Scotland the usual practice for all but the most straightforward cases is for the judgment to be reserved. If the Tribunal opts to announce the decision at the hearing, a written record (in the form of a judgment if appropriate) must still be provided to the parties (and, where the proceedings were referred to the Tribunal by a court, to that court) as soon as practicable: *Rule 61(2)*. This does not mean that reasons must be provided with that record. For the requirement to give reasons, see below **20.115**. *Rule 61(2)* further provides that decisions concerned only with the conduct of a hearing need not be identified in the record of that hearing unless a party requests that a specific decision is so recorded: see also *Ameyaw v PricewaterhouseCoopers Services Limited* (UKEAT/0292/18/LA) at para 85.

It is a general principle that decisions which require to be taken in the course of the hearing on points of case management (such as whether to grant a party's application for an adjournment) should not be taken by the judge without consulting the lay members, if there are lay members sitting: *Jones v Corbin* (UKEAT/0504/10).

Rule 61(3) requires the written record of decisions to be signed by the Employment Judge concerned. However, by *Rule 63*, if it is impossible or not practicable for the written record or reasons to be signed by the Employment Judge as a result of death, incapacity or absence, it shall be signed by the other member or members (in the case of a full tribunal) or by the President, Vice President or a Regional Employment Judge (in the case of a Judge sitting alone).

20.112 *Consent orders and judgments*

Rule 64 provides that where the parties agree in writing or orally at a hearing upon the terms of any order or judgment, a Tribunal may, if it thinks fit, make such order or judgment, in which case it shall be identified as having been made by consent. The rule makes clear that a Tribunal is not bound to make a consent order just because the parties have agreed, and it can still exercise its discretion to refuse to do so.

20.113 *Majority Decisions*

Rule 49 provides that where a Tribunal is composed of three persons any decision may be made by a majority and if it is composed of two persons the Employment Judge has a second or casting vote. The Court of Appeal in *Anglian Home Improvements Ltd v Kelly* [2004] EWCA Civ 901, [2005] ICR 242, [2004] IRLR 793 has given guidance that a tribunal should if at all possible avoid a majority decision, if necessary reserving its decision to give the members time to reflect and the Judge an opportunity to prepare reasons which accurately reflect the majority view (especially if he or she is in the minority). As a matter of good practice, the views of the minority member should be set out in the judgment: *Morgan v Welsh Rugby Union* [2011] IRLR 376. The Judge must sign the reasons even if in the minority: *Rustamova v Calder High School Governors* [2013] 11 WLUK 382. See also *Eyitene v Wirral Metropolitan Borough Council* [2014] EWCA Civ 1243, [2014] IRLR 944 in which Underhill LJ gave guidance generally on the process of deliberating and giving reasons when judges sit with lay members, observing that although it is not always necessary for a draft of the reasons to be agreed with the lay members, where there is a split decision, the reasons should be circulated for comment and agreement prior to promulgation (and see further below **20.115**).

20.114 *Effect of an Order or Judgment and Time for Compliance*

The normal rule is that a judgment or order takes effect from the day when it is given or made: *Rule 65*. However, *Rule 65* also provides that the Tribunal may specify a later date for it to take effect.

The *2013 Rules* introduce new provisions concerning compliance with judgments and orders.

If the order or judgment is for the payment of an amount of money, *Rule 66(1)* states that the party required to pay that sum must pay that amount within 14 days of the date of the judgment or order, unless (a) the judgment, order, or any of the *Rules*, specifies a different date for compliance; or (b) the Tribunal has stayed (or in Scotland sisted) the proceedings or judgment.

20.115 *Reasons*

Unlike the provisions of the old rules, the *2013 Rules* require a Tribunal to give reasons for a decision made on any disputed issue: *Rule 62(1)*. This is the case whether the issue is substantive or procedural. *Rule 62(1)* goes on to say that this includes any decision on an application for reconsideration, for orders for costs, preparation time or wasted costs.

Rule 62(2) goes on to specify how this duty should be discharged. If a decision has been given in writing, then the reasons must also be given in writing. In the case of a decision announced at a hearing the Tribunal may choose to give the reasons orally, or reserve them to be given in writing later. In the latter case, the reasons may (but need not be) part of the written record of the decision: see above **20.110**. Like the record of a decision, written reasons must be signed by the Employment Judge.

If oral reasons are given, the Judge must announce that written reasons will not be provided unless they are asked for by any party at the hearing itself, or by a written request presented by any party within 14 days of the sending of the written record of the decision. The written record of the decision must repeat that information: *Rule 62(3)*. If a request is received within that time period, the Tribunal will then produce, and send out, written reasons for the decision in question. If no request is received, the Tribunal will then only provide the written reasons if requested to do so by the Employment Appeal Tribunal or a court. The written reasons will normally be required as a prerequisite to an appeal against a judgment and so a litigant who intends to appeal against the decision in question should ask for written reasons in accordance with *Rule 62(3)* and the time limit mentioned above.

A proposal published in a December 2011 consultation for the introduction of a fee payable if reasons in writing are requested has been dropped. The provisions of *Rule 62* governing written reasons have the somewhat surprising consequence that if the judgment is not reserved, and neither party chooses to ask for reasons in writing, there will be no formal record of the reasons available to the press or other interested parties. Even in a case raising issues of wider public interest, there appears not only to be no duty, but even no power to give the reasons in writing, provided they have been given orally and none of the parties makes a request for written reasons and the matter is not appealed. This is particularly significant since judgments, and the written reasons for them, are matters of public record.

HM Courts and Tribunals Service sets a target for the promulgation of written judgments and reasons, which is currently that they must be promulgated within four weeks of the conclusion of the Hearing in 85% of cases; this target has been met consistently in recent years, although some tribunal offices have in some years fallen below the target. However occasionally there have been instances of serious delays in issuing the judgment in cases where the judgment was reserved at the end of the hearing. In one such case, *Bangs v Connex South Eastern Ltd* [2005] EWCA Civ 14, [2005] IRLR 389, the Court of Appeal, in the course of refusing to overturn the tribunal's decision, gave guidance as to how such delay is to be considered in the context of an appeal. Delay in issuing a judgment is not of itself an error of law and therefore not as such a ground of appeal. The key question, the Court held, is whether due to the delay there was a real risk that a party had been denied or deprived of the right to a fair trial.

In the related case of *Kwamin v Abbey National plc* [2004] IRLR 516, the EAT had taken a broader approach, which was disapproved by the Court of Appeal; it had also given strong guidance, which was implicitly approved by the Court of Appeal, as to the need to avoid lengthy delays in reaching and issuing reserved judgments. Three-and-a-half months is the longest acceptable time for the delivery of judgment following the conclusion of the hearing (or the delivery of written submissions, if later), and except in the most complex cases, longer delay without proper explanation (such as illness) would be regarded as culpable; it does not, however, follow that such delay justifies an appeal. An extreme example of delay occurred in *Carpenter v City of Edinburgh Council* (UKEATS/0038/07), where the judgment was issued over three years after the hearing had concluded; the EAT overturned the decision, not because of the delay itself, but because of a number of points on which it appeared from the terms of the reasons that the tribunal had forgotten relevant evidence.

In *Eyitene v Wirral Metropolitan Borough Council* [2014] EWCA Civ 1243, [2014] IRLR 944, the Court of Appeal explained how Tribunals should prepare written reasons when sitting with lay members. At para 11, Underhill LJ approved the practice of: (i) the Tribunal having a full discussion after the close of submissions either on the same day or during a subsequent chambers day(s) (which are noted in the reasons); (ii) during the discussions, Judges must identify with the lay members the issues that require determination and go through those issues in a structured fashion. Full notes of the decisions and essential reasoning, reflecting the view of all members and recording points of disagreement must be made. Some Judges will type or record passages of the judgment there and then for agreement, but that depends on the case and Judge in question. These materials form the basis of the Reasons, but it is not regarded as necessary for the detailed expression of the reasons to be agreed, which would substantially increase the time needed for deliberation. (iii) If the case is straightforward then the discussion will be short and the decision and reasons can be delivered orally on the basis of the notes, and the reasons recorded on tape as they are delivered. The tape will form the basis of the written reasons if they are then requested, subject to any editing by the Judge (see *The Partners of Haxby Practice v Collen* [2013] All ER (D) 11 (Feb) (UKEAT/0120/12), discussed below). (iv) If the case is more complex, the reasons may have to be reserved and drafted by the Judge on the basis of the notes. The lay members are entitled to see the text of the reasons prior to final promulgation, but circulation is not routine without a request (save that where there is a split decision, the Judge will always circulate a draft). Underhill LJ emphasised that "lay members should feel no inhibition about exercising that right if they wish to do so in a particular case".

For requirements in relation to reasons in national security cases, see above **20.91**.

20.116 *Adequacy of reasons*

Rules 62(4) and *(5)* contain some provisions concerning the nature of the reasons that Tribunals give. First, *Rule 62(4)* indicates that reasons for a decision must be proportionate to the significance of the issue and for decisions other than judgments may be very short. Case management decisions do not, therefore, require the Judge to give expansive reasoning. Often in practice a Judge will set out his reasoning on such a matter within a paragraph or so.

In the case of a judgment, *Rule 62(5)* provides a basic structure to the reasons. The reasons must identify the issues which the Tribunal has determined, state the findings of fact made in relation to those issues, concisely identify the relevant law, and state how that law has been applied to those findings in order to decide the issues. Further, where the judgment includes a financial award the reasons shall identify, by means of a table or otherwise, how the amount to be paid has been calculated. These requirements are similar to those which appeared in the previous rules – at *Rule 30(6)* of the *2004 Rules*.

There is an additional and specific duty to give an explanation of any award of interest, and reasons for any decision not to award interest, in discrimination and equal pay cases (*Employment Tribunals (Interest on Awards in Discrimination Cases) Regulations 1996 (SI 1996/2803), reg 7*); where the *Employment Protection (Recoupment of Jobseeker's Allowance and Income Support) Regulations 1996* apply, there is a requirement for the tribunal to state that they apply, and to specify the 'prescribed amount' (the part of the compensation covering the period during which benefits were received, which is then available for the DWP to recover the benefits before the balance is payable to the successful claimant).

It is an error of law on the part of the tribunal not to give reasons meeting the requirements of *Rule 30(6)* of the *2004 Rules: Greenwood v NWF Retail Ltd* [2011] ICR 896. The logic of this decision applies equally to *Rule 62(5)* of the *2013 Rules*: see *Vairea v Reed Business Information Ltd* [2017] ICR D9, [2016] UKEAT/0177/15 and *Dutton v Governing Body of Woodslee Primary School* [2016] UKEAT/0305/15. In *Greenwood*, however, the EAT quoted with approval comments of Buxton LJ in *Balfour Beatty Power Networks Ltd v Wilcox* [2007] IRLR 63, at para 25, that: " . . . the rule is surely intended to be a guide and not a straitjacket. Provided it can be reasonably spelled out from the determination of the employment tribunal that what [now *Rule 62(5)*] requires has been provided by that tribunal, then no error of law will have been committed."

The statutory requirements reflect and to some extent consolidate requirements increasingly emphasised by the appellate courts as a necessary part of the judicial process: see in particular *English v Emery Reimbold & Strick Ltd* [2002] EWCA Civ 605, [2003] IRLR 710. However in *Greenwood* the EAT said that the more relevant authority on sufficiency of reasons in employment tribunals is *Meek v City of Birmingham District Council* [1987] IRLR 250, CA.

The following statement by Bingham LJ in Meek is generally regarded as the leading statement of principle on inadequacy of reasons as a ground of appeal, and is regularly referred to for this purpose:

> "It has on a number of occasions been made plain that the decision of an [Employment] Tribunal is not required to be an elaborate formalistic product of refined legal draftsmanship, but it must contain an outline of the story which has given rise to the complaint and a summary of the Tribunal's basic factual conclusions and a statement of the reasons which have led them to reach the conclusion which they do on those basic facts. The parties are entitled to be told why they have won or lost. There should be sufficient account of the facts and of the reasoning to enable the EAT . . . to see whether any question of law arises; and it is highly desirable that the decision of an [Employment] Tribunal should give guidance both to employers and trade unions as to practices which should or should not be adopted."

Whilst the tribunal must reach a conclusion on all the issues required by the statute concerned to be decided, and at least consider all the relevant facts, its decision need only refer to the important and/or controversial points: *High Table Ltd v Horst* [1997] IRLR 513. It is, however, important that the tribunal properly identifies the legal rules and tests it has applied in reaching its decision: *Conlin v United Distillers* [1994] IRLR 169, para 6. Further guidance on the adequacy of reasons was given by the Court of Appeal in *Tran v Greenwich Vietnam Community Project* [2002] EWCA Civ 553, [2002] IRLR 735. Reasons need not be lengthy, but should be sufficient to explain to the parties how the tribunal got from its findings of fact to its conclusions (indeed, lengthy reasons can in certain circumstances still fail to tell the parties how the case was decided; for an example see *The Co-Operative Group Ltd v Baddeley* [2014] EWCA Civ 658). The reasons must explain why the evidence of one witness has been preferred over another on the relevant issue: see *Flannery v Halifax Estate Agents Ltd* [2000] 1 All ER 373 at 382 and *Kibirango v Barclays Bank plc* UKEAT/0234/14. In addition, whilst the reasons are primarily addressed to those already familiar with the context of the case, it is desirable that the reasoning can be ascertained from the face of the decision; in any case it is necessary that the decision is sufficiently reasoned to enable an appellate court or tribunal to ascertain what the tribunal's findings of fact and reasons for its conclusions were. The decision of the Court of Appeal in *Anya v University of Oxford* [2001] EWCA Civ 405, [2001] IRLR 377 contains important comments on the need for tribunals in discrimination cases to set out the findings reached on the issues of primary fact, and an explanation why the tribunal does or does not draw inferences of discrimination from the facts as found. In *Modha v Babcocks Airport Ltd* (UKEAT/0060/19/JOJ), 4 July 2019 Laing J emphasised the difference between a 'conclusion' (eg that something as 'no prospect of success') and the reasons why that conclusion had been reached. It was an error of law for the Tribunal Judge merely to have stated a conclusion in that form.

A number of cases have highlighted the need for tribunals to give reasons for specific elements in their judgments; these include the exercise of the discretionary power to increase or reduce compensation under *Employment Act 2002, s 31* (the same point presumably applies to the replacement power under *TULR(C)A 1992, s 207A*), and decisions on contributory fault (in relation to which the Court of Appeal has suggested that the tribunal should make findings of fact separate from those made in relation to the fairness of the dismissal: *London Ambulance Service v Small* [2009] EWCA Civ 220, [2009] IRLR 563). The alleged inadequacy of the tribunal's reasons (often put as a complaint that the judgment was not 'Meek-compliant') is one of the most frequent grounds of appeal. However, the EAT is in practice rarely prepared to overturn a tribunal's judgment simply on the grounds that the reasons given are inadequate. The Court of Appeal in the English case stressed that it is not a good ground of appeal that the reasons for a judgment are inadequate if it is clear from reading the judgment with knowledge of the evidence given and submissions made why the point in question was decided as it was. However a rather stricter approach was taken by the Court of Appeal in *Bahl v Law Society* [2004] IRLR 799 (a discrimination case), emphasising that only in a limited class of cases will it be possible to make good in that way inadequate reasons given by the tribunal. In *Northumberland Tyne & Wear NHS Foundation Trust v Miss D Ward* (UKEAT/0249/18/DA) Choudhury J at para 74 sounded a note of caution to Tribunals about 'truncating' analysis of a claim of unfair dismissal where a claim under *s 15* of the *EA 2010* had already been dismissed on the same facts. Such claims may have different outcomes: see *Scott v Kenton Schools Academy Trust* (UKEAT/0031/19/DA). In the *Ward* case, Choudhury J noted: "*Whether or not such an approach is appropriate will depend on the facts of the case, the factors relevant to the proportionality analysis, and the extent to which those factors overlap with those relevant to the unfair dismissal analysis. The better approach, possibly in the majority of cases, would be to set out the analysis of the claim under each head more fully.*"

The EAT has adopted a practice, in many but not all of the cases where an appeal is brought on the ground of inadequate reasons, of remitting the case to the tribunal for it to clarify or amplify its reasons, prior to the hearing of the substantive appeal. The legality of the practice (which had been in doubt because of conflicting decisions of the Court of Appeal on the EAT's powers) was initially confirmed by the EAT in *Burns v Consignia plc (No 2)* [2004] IRLR 425, and subsequently (but on a different basis) by the Court of Appeal itself in *Barke v SEETEC Business Technology Centre Ltd* [2005] EWCA Civ 578, [2005] IRLR 633, and the procedure is often referred to as a '*Burns/Barke* reference' accordingly. The power is to be found in the *2013 Rules* at *Rule 62(3)* which requires the tribunal to provide reasons for any order or judgment if requested by the EAT. The EAT also has the necessary power under a general provision giving it the power to regulate its own procedure (*ETA 1996, s 30(1)*). The Court added that the procedure should not be used in cases where the reasons were fundamentally deficient, or there is an allegation of bias, or a danger that the tribunal will tailor its response to shoring up the original decision rather than give its true reasons (a point taken up again by the Court in *Woodhouse School v Webster* [2009] EWCA Civ 91, [2009] IRLR 568, where it was stressed that the Judge should not in responding go beyond clarification of reasons to advocacy for the original decision). See further on the use of the *Burns/Barke* procedure *Korashi v Abertawe Bro Morgannwg University Local Health Board* [2011] EWCA Civ 187, [2011] All ER (D) 09 (Mar).

A Tribunal can also err in law by making findings on matters not properly before it (including by making findings about background facts that would not found an issue estoppel because they are not necessary to the decision): see *Baker v Peninsula Business Services Ltd* [2017] IRLR 394 at paras 81-82.

20.117 *Changing and correcting the decision and reasons*

A judgment given orally at the end of the hearing is a final decision. The powers of a tribunal to change its judgment subsequently, prior to promulgation in writing (eg where there is a subsequent change in the relevant case law), are very limited. In *Lamont v Fry's Metals Ltd* [1985] IRLR 470, [1985] ICR 566 the Court of Appeal assumed, without deciding the point, that a tribunal can recall its judgment before it is entered in the Register. However, it should then give both parties an opportunity of addressing further argument to the tribunal (see also *Arthur Guinness Son & Co (Great Britain) Ltd v Green* [1989] IRLR 288, [1989] ICR 241, EAT; *Gutzmore v J Wardley (Holdings) Ltd* [1993] ICR 581). More recent EAT decisions have emphasised the limits on the power of recall, and suggest that there is no power on recall to change the substantive judgment (*Spring Grove Services Group plc v Hickinbottom* [1990] ICR 111; *Casella London Ltd v Banai* [1990] ICR 215). However in *CK Heating Ltd v Doro* [2010] ICR 1449, the EAT held that a tribunal was entitled to recall for further consideration a decision, announced orally at the end of the hearing but which had not been issued as a written judgment, that the claimant's compensation would be reduced by 30% for contributory fault. Although in general the parties are entitled to regard an oral statement of the result of a hearing as final, until the written judgment is issued it is therefore open to the tribunal, if it considers it to be in the interest of justice to do so, to recall its decision. There is less objection to a decision being recalled in these circumstances if there will not be any requirement for reconsideration of the primary facts, or further evidence. A contrasting approach has been taken by the Court of Appeal to decisions reached by the Upper Tribunal where, under the different rules applicable there, decisions were effective as soon as the Judge had uttered the words: see *Patel v Secretary of State for the Home Department* [2015] EWCA Civ 1175, [2016] CP Rep 9.

Rule 69 contains a power which can be used by an Employment Judge at any time to correct any clerical mistake or other accidental slip or omission in an order, judgment or any other document produced by a Tribunal. If such a correction is made, any published version of the document shall also be corrected. If any document is corrected under *Rule 69*, a copy of the corrected version, signed by the Judge, shall be sent to all the parties.

A similar power existed in the previous versions of the rules and has been held to be limited; thus in *Bone v Newham London Borough Council* [2008] EWCA Civ 435, [2008] IRLR 546 the Court of Appeal held that the tribunal did not have the power to 'correct' its judgment by inserting a finding that the dismissal of the claimant was an act of sex discrimination, having recorded the opposite in its original written judgment.

It has been held by the EAT that if the form of the correction under what is now *Rule 69* is the substitution of a complete corrected version of the judgment and reasons for the original version, time for appealing starts to run from the date of the correction: *Kennaugh v Lloyd-Jones (t/a Cheshire Tree Surgeons)* [2006] All ER (D) 363 (Nov). The better practice is therefore only to identify the words or passage corrected; this will not affect the running of time.

The issue of deviation in the written reasons for a judgment (as opposed to the judgment itself) from oral reasons delivered by the Tribunal was considered by the EAT in *The Partners of Haxby Practice v Collen* [2013] All ER (D) 11 (Feb). Whilst the EAT accepted that normally written reasons supplied pursuant to *Rule 30(3)* will correspond closely to the oral reasons given at the conclusion of the hearing, it was acknowledged there will almost always be some degree of editing. Underhill J held that this editing process may, depending on the circumstances and temperament of the Judge, be more or less substantial; every now and then there will be cases where the process of revision is so extensive that the reasoning in support of a conclusion differs in substance from the oral reasoning. The EAT held there was "no shame in this" and a departure from initially expressed reasoning does not involve any error of law. The written reasons, where supplied, are the sole authoritative statement of the tribunal's reasons and the oral reasons are superseded. The oral reasons might, however, still remain relevant to allegations of apparent bias or where they might elucidate some ambiguity in the written reasons. See further the discussion of the process of crafting the reasons in *Eyitene v Wirral Metropolitan Borough Council* [2014] EWCA Civ 1243, [2014] IRLR 944 (above). *Haxby* was approved and applied in *Ministry of Justice v Blackford* [2018] IRLR 688 and *Patel v Specsavers Optical Group Limited* (UKEAT/0286/18/JOJ).

The power of reconsideration is considered at **20.122** below.

20.118 *The Register*

By *Rule 67*, a copy shall be entered in the Register of any judgment and of any written reasons for a judgment. In addition, where the proceedings were referred to the Tribunal by a court, a copy of any judgment and of any written reasons shall be provided to that court: *Rule 68*.

To give effect to this rule, there is a public register of tribunal judgments and written reasons: *Reg 14* of the *2013 Regulations*. All such judgments and reasons are entered in it and available for public (and press) scrutiny, except in cases of national security or where the tribunal has sat in private and it so orders (see *Rules 50* and *94*). The Tribunal has a discretion to delete matters from the public copy of a judgment and reasons by applying *Rule 50* see above **20.89**. Necessarily only written reasons can be included in the Register, a factor which parties should consider before deciding whether to ask for written reasons where the reasons have been given orally.

In complaints under *sections 120, 127* or *146* of the *Equality Act 2010*, the Tribunal must also send a copy of all judgments and written reasons to the Commission for Equality and Human Rights. This obligation does not apply in proceedings where a direction or order under *Rule 94*, relating to national security, has been given and either the Security Service, the Secret Intelligence Service or the Government Communications Headquarters is a party to the proceedings.

For details about the online database of judgments and reasons see **19.5–19.6**.

20.119 Remedies and enforcement

The remedies available in the tribunal depend on the particular jurisdiction covering the case, and are discussed together with the substantive law elsewhere in this book. A number of additional points require mention.

20.119a *Tax on tribunal awards*

Care should be taken to ensure that the effect of tax on any tribunal award is taken into account. Compensation for pecuniary loss should be calculated in the first instance on the basis of net rather than gross loss of earnings (*Visa International Service Association v Paul* [2004] IRLR 42, EAT). However, compensation for lost earnings will then be taxable in the same way as earnings under the *Income Tax (Earnings and Pensions) Act 2003* (*IT(EP)A 2003*). In accordance with the principles in *British Transport Commission v Gourley* [1955] 3 All ER 796, it is therefore necessary, once the amount of the award has been calculated (using net figures for earnings and pension loss) to 'gross up' the award so as to ensure that the claimant is not left out of pocket once the tax on the award has been paid. Compensation for loss consequent on the termination of employment is taxable above £30,000 since by virtue of *sections 401* and *403* of *IT(EP)A 2003*, a sum received in connection with the termination of a person's employment is tax-free up to £30,000 but is subject to income tax to the extent that it exceeds that sum. Contrary to the previous view of tribunals, this is not limited to compensation for financial loss, and compensation is taxable even where it is compensation for infringement of the right not to suffer discrimination where the discrimination relates to the dismissal: see *Moorthy v Revenue and Customs Commissioners* [2018] EWCA Civ 847, [2018] 3 All ER 1062, [2018] ICR 1326, overruling *Oti-Obihara v Revenue and Customs Comrs* [2010] UKFTT 568 (TC), [2011] IRLR 386. The same would presumably be true of compensation for infringement of other rights. However, the Court of Appeal in *Moorthy* held that awards for injury to feelings were not taxable as they fell within the scope of the exemption for personal injury in *IT(EP)A 2003, s 406*. The practical effect of this ruling will, though, be short-lived as s 406 was amended with effect from the 2018/19 tax year to exclude payments on account of injured feelings from its scope, so that they will fall to be taxed where they form part of compensation for loss of office within *ss 401* and *403*, subject to the £30,000 limit. Pension loss is also taxable on the same basis as earnings: *Chief Constable of Northumbria v Erichsen* (UKEAT/0027/15/BA). The same tax rules apply to compensation, or sums paid under a compromise agreement, for an unlawful dismissal. Compensation for discrimination or compensation for other unlawful acts during employment is however not taxable save to the extent that it is connected with remuneration so as to make it an 'emolument of the employment' (*Income Tax (Earnings and Pensions) Act 2003, s 62*). For a case where on the facts the First-tier Tribunal found a settlement payment to be referable to the discrimination claim and not to the employment, see *A v HM Revenue & Customs* [2015] UKFTT 189 (TC), [2015] IRLR 962. For a case where it was not, see *Moorthy* ibid.

20.119b *Increases or decreases to awards for failures to comply with ACAS Code of Practice*

The tribunal may increase or decrease the sum awarded in any proceedings relating to a claim by an employee under any of the jurisdictions listed in *Schedule 2* to the *Trade Union and Labour Relations (Consolidation) Act 1992* (which covers all claims that may be brought by employees) by up to 25% if satisfied that the employer or employee, as the case may be, has unreasonably failed to comply with a provision of a relevant ACAS Code of Practice (*s 207A*, inserted by the *Employment Act 2008, s 2*). The relevant ACAS Code is that on disciplinary and grievance procedures, which was reissued in a simplified and shortened form to accompany the legislative changes. This power is one of the few changes introduced via the *Employment Act 2002* and the *Employment Act 2002 (Dispute Resolution) Regulations 2004* which have been retained following the repeal of most of the changes introduced under that regime with effect from 6 April 2009: see further EMPLOYMENT TRIBUNALS – II, 19.2. Cases on that short-lived dispute resolution regime remain relevant to the consideration of uplifts and decreases on awards under the extant *s 207A*. In *Wardle v Credit Agricole Corporate and Investment Bank* [2011] IRLR 604 and *Abbey National v Chagger* [2010] IRLR 47, [2010] ICR 397, the Court of Appeal held that it was incumbent on tribunals when setting the percentage increase or decrease to have regard to the size of the award; it also considered that the maximum uplift should be reserved for the most exceptional and serious cases; there must be proportionality. Whilst the spirit of the ACAS Code of Practice should be followed even if the case is not strictly one of misconduct (see *Lund v St Edmunds School, Canterbury* [2013] All ER (D) 365 (May) (UKEAT/0514/12) – a 'some other substantial reason' dismissal), the EAT has now confirmed that the code itself does not apply (and therefore uplifts are not available) in cases of ill health dismissals (see *Holmes v QinetiQ Ltd* [2016] IRLR 664, [2016] ICR 1016) or 'some other substantial reason' dismissals (see *Phoenix House Ltd v Stockman* [2016] IRLR 848, [2017] ICR 84, disagreeing with provisional observations to the contrary in *Hussain v Jurys Inn Group Ltd* [2016] UKEAT/0283/15). Where a claimant is awarded compensation for both wrongful and unfair dismissal, and an uplift or decrease is to be applied to the unfair dismissal award, it is up to the Tribunal to decide whether this is done before or after deducting the compensation for wrongful dismissal applicable to the notice period: see *Shifferaw v Hudson Music Co Ltd* [2016] ICR D23. In *Qu v Landis and Gyr* (UKEAT/0016/19/RN), 8 March 2019 the Tribunal initially considered that an uplift would be inappropriate because it had already made an award of aggravated damages. However, on a review application, the Tribunal decided that it had wrongly concluded that the aggravated damages award covered the same territory: that award had been made because of the conduct of one individual, but in fact there had been other failures to follow procedure and on reflection the Tribunal considered a 10% uplift to be appropriate. The EAT held there was no error of law in this approach. Uplifts cannot be made in favour of workers as opposed to employees because of the terms of *s 207A*: see *Local Government Yorkshire and Humber v Shah* [2012] All ER (D) 20 (Nov) (UKEAT/0587/11).

20.119c *Financial penalties*

The tribunal has had power since 25 April 2013 to order an employer to pay a penalty to the Secretary of State (but not to the claimant), where it concludes that the employer has breached any of a worker's rights to which the worker's claim relates and is of the opinion that the breach has one or more aggravating features (*Employment Tribunals Act 1996, s 12A*). This power may be used in addition to, or as an alternative to, awarding compensation to the employee or ordering the employer to carry out an equal pay audit (see above). The maximum penalties were increased with effect from 6 April 2019 by the *Employment Rights (Miscellaneous Amendments) Regulations 2019, SI 2019/731* in light of the Government's 'Good Work Plan' response to the Matthew Taylor Review of Modern Working Practices and the consultation that followed that. The increases apply only to breaches of employee's rights beginning on or after 6 April 2019 *(reg 3)*. The minimum penalty that may be awarded under the section is £100, and the maximum is £5,000 (increased to £20,000 by the 2019 Order) (*s 12A(3)*). In deciding how much to award, the Tribunal must have regard to the employer's ability to pay, but not where the Tribunal has also decided to award compensation to the employee (*s 12A(2)*). Where the Tribunal makes an award against the employer and also orders the employer to pay a financial penalty, the amount of the penalty must be 50% of the amount of the award, save that if the amount of the award is less than £200, the amount of the penalty shall be £100, and if the amount is more than £40,000, the penalty is capped at £20,000 (*s 12A(4)* and *(5)*). In cases where two or more workers' claims have been considered together and the employer is ordered to pay a penalty in respect of any of those claims, the amount of the penalties in total shall be at least £100, the amount of a penalty in respect of a particular claim shall be no more than £5,000 (£20,000 following the increase) or no more than 50% of the amount of any compensation awarded to the employee (whichever is the lesser). If the total of the financial compensation awarded on all the conjoined claims is less than £200, then the penalty must be £100 (*ss 12A(6)* and *(7)*). Two or more claims in respect of the same act and the same worker are to be treated as a single claim for these purposes: (*s 12A(8)*). Once a penalty order is made, it cannot be reviewed simply because the tribunal is subsequently called on to award compensation for failure a failure by the employer to comply with an order of the tribunal (such as an order for a recommendation under *s 124(7)* of the *EqA 2010* or an order to carry out an equal pay audit) (*s 12A(9)*). This provision does not affect the Tribunal's general powers to review awards, however. Finally, it is to be noted that penalties awarded under these provisions operate like parking tickets: an employer who pays within 21 days of the order will have the amount of the penalty reduced by 50%: *s 12A(10)*. See *First Greater Western Ltd v Waiyego* UKEAT/0056/18/RN for a case where the EAT dismissed an appeal against the refusal by the Tribunal to order a penalty in circumstances where the Tribunal had found only two breaches of the legislation by the employer which the ET did not apparently regard as egregious.

20.119d *Enforcement*

A judgment ordering the payment of money made by a tribunal is enforceable as if it was a judgment of the County Court (or in Scotland the Sheriff Court). The fact that an appeal is pending does not itself suspend the remedy awarded, but if an application to enforce it is made to the County Court, the other party will usually be granted a stay of execution pending the appeal.

Tribunals have no power to enforce their own non-monetary judgments except by awards of compensation; the best examples are an additional award for failure to comply with an order for re-employment in an unfair dismissal case (*ERA 1996, s 117(3)–(5)*), and power to increase compensation if the employer has failed without reasonable justification to comply with a recommendation in a discrimination case (*Equality Act 2010, s 124(7)*). The absence of any enforcement machinery other than the County Court has led in a significant number of cases to real difficulties in the successful claimant recovering the compensation awarded, even disregarding cases where the employer is insolvent (in which case there may be a claim against the Secretary of State: see INSOLVENCY OF EMPLOYER (32)). Research commissioned by the Ministry of Justice (Research into the enforcement of employment tribunal awards in England and Wales, Ministry of Justice Research Series 9/09, May 2009) found that only 61% of those claimants interviewed who had received a tribunal award had received any payment; only 53% had been paid in full. Reasons for non-payment included 29% of non-paying employers simply refusing to pay, whilst 39% no longer existed or had gone bankrupt. This picture appears to have remained fairly constant: the Department for Business Innovation and Skills reported in 2014 that only 63% of claimants received their award (*Findings from the Survey of Employment Tribunal Applications 2013*, Research Series No 177, June 2014). The National Association of Citizens' Advice Bureaux had earlier proposed that awards of compensation should be paid by the State, with the right to recover the money from the employer passing to the Government (Hollow Victories, March 2005). This proposal was not accepted by the Government, but the *Tribunals, Courts and Enforcement Act 2007, s 142* (adding a new *s 19A* to the *ETA 1996*) introduced some improvement in the position. Once the judgment has been formally registered with the County Court, any of the various means of enforcement of County Court judgments can be initiated without the need first to apply for the Court to order the respondent to pay the sum awarded and then to allow time for payment. A similar but simpler procedure applies in Scotland, where the enforcement of a payment ordered by a judgment is undertaken by the Sheriff Court on the authority of the judgment of the tribunal.

In order to incentivise the payment of employment tribunal awards, *Section 150* of the *Small Business, Enterprise and Employment Act 2015* provided for the amendment of the *ETA* to include a new *Part 2A*: financial penalties for failure to pay sums ordered to be paid or settlement sums. With effect from 6 April 2016, the relevant provisions are now to be found at *sections 37A* to *37Q* of the *ETA 1996*. The provisions allow enforcement officers to issue warning notices to an employer in respect of defined sums awarded by a tribunal (including compensation and costs) and settlement sums that remain unsatisfied. If the sums remain unpaid, a penalty notice can then be issued requiring the employer to pay a financial penalty to the Secretary of State. The financial penalty will be 50% of the unpaid relevant sum, subject to a minimum of £100 and a maximum of £5,000. If, within 14 days of the penalty notice, the employer pays both the unpaid relevant sum and the penalty reduced by 50%, the employer will be treated as having complied with his obligations. If no payment is made, the full penalty will remain due and interest will be charged at the judgment rate. For the purposes of the statutory scheme, amounts in respect of financial awards are not regarded as outstanding during the time when the worker could make an application for costs (and if she has made that application, the period before it is finally determined) or where either party could appeal against the relevant tribunal judgment (and if a party has commenced appeal proceedings, the period before they have been finally determined). An employer to whom a penalty notice has been given may, before the end of the period within which the penalty must be paid, appeal against the penalty notice or the amount of a penalty to an employment tribunal on defined grounds (incorrect grounds stated on penalty notice, incorrect calculation or unreasonable for the enforcement officer to have issued the notice). The Department for Business, Innovation and Skills has published a form for claiming penalties which claimants can complete (see https ://www.gov.uk/government/uploads/system/uploads/attachment_data/file/ 524721/employment-tribunal-penalty-form.docx).

In response to the Matthew Taylor Review of Modern Working Practices, the Government held a consultation between 7 February 2018 and 16 May 2018 concerning the enforcement of employment tribunal awards. On 7 December 2018, the Government published a 'Good Work Plan' in the light of the consultation responses. The proposals outlined in that Plan include (so far as relevant to enforcement) state enforcement of holiday pay for vulnerable workers; state enforcement for the pay of agency workers where they have pay withheld by an umbrella company; the creation of an obligation for tribunals to consider sanctions where an employer has lost a previous case on broadly comparable facts; naming and shaming employers who fail to pay tribunal awards; and creating a new single labour market enforcement agency. Although some legislative amendments have been made in the light of that review (see eg the *Employment Rights (Miscellaneous Amendments) Regulations 2019*, the *Employment Rights (Employment Particulars and Paid Annual Leave) (Amendment) Regulations 2018* and the *Agency Workers (Amendment) Regulations 2019*) there has as yet been no legislation dealing with the enforcement proposals.

The Law Commission's Consultation Paper 239: *Employment Law Hearing Structures* (26 September 2018) asked the question as to whether tribunals should be given jurisdiction to enforce their own orders for compensation, but the Commission has not in its report (LC 390, 27 April 2020) recommended any change in this respect. It does, however, recommend consideration be given to introducing a system of automatic fines for employers who fail to pay Employment Tribunal awards.

The Court of Appeal has held that failure to pay compensation awarded to a claimant in a discrimination case may be made the subject of a claim of victimisation: *Rank Nemo (DMS) Ltd v Coutinho* [2009] EWCA Civ 454, [2009] IRLR 672.

20.120 *Interest on awards*

Post-judgment interest is payable on any compensation ordered by a tribunal which has not been paid when due. Interest on unpaid tribunal awards accrues from the day after the decision unless the award is paid in full within 14 days (see *Employment Tribunals (Interest) Order 1990*, as amended, and *Rule 66*). Interest is payable at the rate fixed from time to time under *s 17* of the *Judgments Act 1838* applicable at the date it starts to accrue. The current rate is 8% (this has not been changed despite the general collapse in interest rates in 2008–9 and rates remaining low in the ensuing period). There is no discretion to vary this. If compensation is subsequently increased or decreased on appeal, the new amount is subject to interest from the original date (*art 10, Employment Tribunals (Interest) Order 1990 (SI 1990/479)*).

Normally, tribunals cannot award pre-judgment interest as a remedy in its own right, however long the delay since the matters giving rise to the remedy. The principal exception to this is in discrimination and equal pay cases. The relevant regulations (which originate from regulations in sex discrimination and equal pay cases introduced in 1993 to give effect to a decision of the CJEU (*Marshall v Southampton and SW Hampshire Health Authority (No 2)* [1993] IRLR 445, [1993] ICR 893)) are currently the *Employment Tribunals (Interest on Awards in Discrimination Cases) Regulations 1996 (SI 1996/2803)* (the '*1996 Interest Regulations*'). There is no automatic right to interest under the *1996 Interest Regulations*, but the tribunal is required to consider the question even if not asked to do so (*reg 2(1)(b)*). In practice, in any case where there is a significant time lag between the discrimination and the decision, a tribunal may be expected to award interest unless there are special reasons for not doing so. It should do so of its own motion even if interest has not been claimed: *Komeng v Creative Support Ltd* (UKEAT/0275/18/JOJ), 5 April 2019.

The rate of interest is, since 29 July 2013, the rate fixed by *s 17* of the *Judgments Act 1838* and, in Scotland, the rate fixed by *section 9* of the *Sheriff Courts (Scotland) Extracts Act 1892*. The current rate is, as stated above, 8%, and there is no discretion to vary it. Prior to 29 July 2013, the rate was that laid down from time to time under *rule 27(1)* of the *Court*

Funds Rules 1987 (SI 1987/821) as the rate of interest for the Special Investment Account (reg 3(2)); this had, since 1 July 2009, been 0.5%, having been reduced in stages in 2009 from the former rate of 6%. Where the calculation period covers periods of varying rates of interest, an average rate can be taken (*reg 3(3)*). There were detailed rules as to the period in respect of which interest should be awarded (*reg 6*) and the normal rules as to interest on the total sum (including interest) awarded by the tribunal are varied, so that interest on the sum awarded (at the higher Judgment Act rate) runs from the day after the day on which the decision on remedy is issued, unless the respondent pays in full within 14 days (*reg 8*).

In an attempt to remedy the injustice to claimants that may arise from the lack of any power to award interest in, for instance, unfair dismissal cases, the Court of Appeal in *Melia v Magna Kansei Ltd* [2006] IRLR 117 held that compensation may be increased to reflect delay in receipt, by analogy with the reduction that may be made in calculating future loss to reflect accelerated payment. At the time of this case this was set at 2.5% a year, and the Court ruled that compensation could be increased at that rate for the delay between the date of dismissal and the date of the award. This principle applies primarily where there is also a discount for accelerated payment for future loss, but it is submitted that it is not limited to such cases, and thus amounts to a limited general power to award interest, at least where there has been significant delay between the dismissal and the decision on remedy. Since 20 March 2017, however, the Lord Chancellor reduced the discount rate from +2.5% to -0.75% (a reduction of 3.25%). This is likely to remove the incentive for claimants to pursue this line of argument, although in March 2019 the Lord Chancellor announced the rate was under review.

20.121 *Recoupment of benefits received*

Where an employee has received Jobseeker's Allowance, Income-related Employment and Support Allowance, Universal Credit or any Income Support between the date of dismissal and the date of the award of compensation for unfair dismissal (and certain other forms of compensation listed in *Sch 1* to the *Regulations* such as a protective award in redundancy consultation cases, but not compensation for loss of earnings in discrimination cases), there is a procedure for the Department for Work and Pensions to recover whatever amount of these benefits has been paid to the claimant during that period. This is known as 'recoupment', and is regulated by the *Employment Protection (Recoupment of Benefits) Regulations 1996 (SI 1996/2349)* (as amended). Recoupment only applies to the benefits listed above; other social security benefits are not affected. For details of how Employment and Support Allowance and other social security benefits may be taken into account in assessing compensation see **56.6 UNFAIR DISMISSAL – III**.

The system of recoupment is that the tribunal identifies the proportion of its award that relates to loss of income between dismissal and the date of the award; this is known as 'the prescribed element', and must be separately identified in the judgment and reasons. The employer should withhold this amount from any payment to the employee until notified by the Department for Work and Pensions how much it wishes to recoup from the award; notification must be given within 21 days, and the amount recoupable will be the amount of benefits paid, up to the maximum of the prescribed element. The employer must then pay the amount recouped to the DWP instead of the employee. If an award is made by the tribunal for future loss, the employee may lose relevant benefits during the period covered by the award, but this does not affect the amount or payment of the actual award.

The recoupment system applies only to an award by the tribunal. Whilst it ensures that neither the employer nor the employee benefits from the social security benefits paid to the employee, it may reduce quite considerably the value in the employee's hands of the tribunal's award. This does not apply to a payment agreed by the parties – a significant incentive to settle the amount of any compensation. Since recoupment does not apply to awards in discrimination cases, social security benefits received do have to be taken into account (subject to rather complex rules affecting particular benefits) in calculating the employee's net losses in such cases. See further **14.15** DISCRIMINATION AND EQUAL OPPORTUNITIES **(III)**.

Reconsideration

20.122 *General*

The previous position concerning the ability of a Tribunal to 'review' judgments it had made under the *2004 Rules* has been subject to rationalisation and simplification in the *2013 Rules*. The previous rules set out particular grounds on which judgments could be reviewed. The *2013 Rules* have opted simply for a test of the interests of justice.

By *Rule 70*, a Tribunal may now either on its own initiative (which may reflect a request from the Employment Appeal Tribunal) or on the application of a party, reconsider any judgment where it is necessary in the interests of justice to do so. In *TCO In-Well Technologies UK Ltd v Stuart* [2017] ICR 1175 it was held that an application for reconsideration and reconsideration of a Tribunal's own initiative were alternative processes and the rules did not provide for both to take place at the same time, nor for a hybrid process whereby an application made by a party would be taken over by the Tribunal. When reconsidering, the decision (referred to in *Rule 70* and the subsequent rules dealing with reconsideration as "the original decision") may be confirmed, varied or revoked. If it is revoked, it may be taken again.

As can be seen from the wording of *Rule 70*, it is also possible for a review to be instituted following an appeal to the EAT. The EAT has developed a practice in some cases of staying appeals to give the appellant an opportunity to apply for a review of the decision sought to be appealed. There is no obligation on the Judge who then receives a review application to grant a review, and each application will be considered on its merits; but in these circumstances, if the would-be appellant applies promptly for a review, it would be unlikely that the application would be refused solely on the ground that it is made out of time (see below). *Rule 70* also envisages a review request emanating directly from the EAT.

There is no power to reconsider orders other than judgments under *Rule 70*; in particular case management orders are not open to reconsideration. This will not normally present a problem, since there is a general power to vary or revoke such orders, which can be exercised without the formality of reconsideration (subject to there being a basis for varying or revoking a previous order: see **20.55** above). There are also separate powers of the Tribunal to reconsider decisions to reject claims and responses (see above **20.39**).

20.123 *Procedure*

Rule 71 requires an application for reconsideration to be presented in writing (and copied to all the other parties) within 14 days of the date on which the written record, or other written communication, of the original decision was sent to the parties or within 14 days of the date that the written reasons were sent (if later). There is a wide power to extend time: *Gosalakkal v University Hospitals of Leicester NHS Trust* (UKEAT/0223/18/DA), 4 July 2019 (potentially for three years in that case). The application must set out why reconsideration of the original decision is necessary. There is an exception for where an application for reconsideration is made in the course of a hearing. In such circumstances, it need not be presented in writing.

Once made, *Rule 72(1)* requires an application for reconsideration to be considered by an Employment Judge. If the Judge considers that there is no reasonable prospects of the original decision being varied or revoked (including, unless there are special reasons, where substantially the same application has already been made and refused), the application must be refused and the Tribunal must inform the parties of the refusal. Otherwise, *Rule 72(1)* requires that the Tribunal should send a notice to the parties setting a time limit for any response to the application by the other parties and seeking the views of the parties on whether the application can be determined without a hearing. The notice may also set out the Judge's provisional views on the application. Although the Judge may refuse an application for reconsideration under *Rule 72(1)* without inviting submissions from the other party, it is not permissible for the Judge to grant an application without giving notice inviting submissions from the other party: *The Practice Surgeries Ltd v Srivatsa* [2016] UKEAT/0212/15.

A decision on an application for reconsideration is a 'judgment' to which the requirement to give reasons in *rule 62* applies: *Modha v Babcocks Airport Ltd* (UKEAT/0060/19/JOJ), 4 July 2019.

If the reconsideration application has not been refused, by *Rule 72(2)*, the original decision must be reconsidered at a hearing, unless the Employment Judge considers (having had regard to the views of the parties on whether the application can be determined without a hearing elicited under *Rule 72(1)*) that a hearing is not necessary in the interest of justice. If the reconsideration proceeds without a hearing, *Rule 72(2)* provides that the parties must be given a reasonable opportunity to make further written submissions. A failure to afford such an opportunity can give rise to an error of law: see eg *Srivatsa* (above).

Where a hearing is held, this will be a formal oral hearing at which if necessary evidence can be called. The test for whether fresh evidence should be admitted on reconsideration is the same as that laid down by the EAT in *Wileman v Minilec Engineering Ltd* [1988] IRLR 144, [1988] ICR 318, adopting the established formulation as set out in *Ladd v Marshall* [1954] 3 All ER 745, i.e. whether the evidence have been obtained with reasonable diligence for use at the hearing; whether it is relevant and would probably have had an important influence on the hearing; and whether it is apparently credible: see **21.34** below. The EAT was clear that the *Ladd* test applied in *Outasight VB Ltd v Brown* [2015] ICR D11. HHJ Eady QC held that the change in the *2013 Rules* (removing specified categories under which a review could be granted) did not introduce a broader discretion as to when fresh evidence could be admitted. The approach in *Ladd* would in most cases encapsulate what is meant by "the interests of justice" and provided a consistent approach across the civil courts. The EAT did recognise, however, a residual category of case where the requirements of *Ladd* were not strictly met and when, that notwithstanding, the interests of justice might still require the admission of fresh evidence. HHJ Eady held that Tribunals have always had the ability to review judgments in such circumstances. *Outasight* was approved by the Court of Appeal in *Ministry of Justice v Burton* [2016] EWCA Civ 714, [2016] ICR 1128. See also *Dundee City Council v Margaret Gennelli Malcolm* (UKEATS/0019/15) in which Langstaff J held that a tribunal ought not to order reconsideration if its purpose was to permit a party to lead further evidence which could have been led earlier.

If the application is granted, the tribunal will either vary the decision or revoke it and order a re-hearing (*Rule 70*). If, on reconsideration, the tribunal concludes that the original decision was wrong, the power to vary is wide enough to allow variation by substitution of the opposite result, eg unfair rather than fair dismissal: *Stonehill Furniture Ltd v Phillippo* [1983] ICR 556. On the other hand, if the previous judgment is revoked, the matter must be re-decided, either without a hearing, if the judgment was originally issued without a hearing having been held, or at a fresh hearing.

The *2013 Rules* (*Rule 72(3)*) require, where "practicable", the initial consideration of an application to reconsider a judgment under *Rule 72(1)*, and the actual reconsideration under *Rule 72(2)*, to be taken by the Employment Judge who made the original decision, or, as the case may be, chaired the full tribunal which made it. Where that is not practicable, the President, Vice President or a Regional Employment Judge shall appoint another Employment Judge to deal with the application or, in the case of a decision of a full tribunal, shall either direct that the reconsideration be by such members of the original Tribunal as remain available or reconstitute the Tribunal in whole or in part. Under *Rule 35* of the *2004 Rules*, the EAT held that the similar requirement that where "practicable" the same Judge should conduct a review application was intended to deal with cases where the original Judge was physically unavailable, had died, or was too unwell to attend the application. "Practicable" meant feasible, not convenient; in that case, an allegation of bias against the Judge did not render it impracticable for the original Judge to consider the review application: see *Papajak v Intellego Group Ltd* [2013] UKEAT/0124/12. In *Benney v Department for Environment, Food and Rural Affairs* [2015] UKEAT/0252/13, the EAT held that the word "practicable" was to be properly construed by reference to dealing with the review application expeditiously, proportionately, fairly and in such a way as to save expense (ie by reference to the Overriding Objective). The word was not intended to be interpreted as it is in *ERA 1996, s 111(2)(b)*, governing when extensions of time for unfair dismissal claims can be granted by the Tribunal. Whether it is practicable for the original Judge to decide upon the application for a review is a question of fact to be decided in all the circumstances. In that case, the original Judge had moved to a different region, the application for a review was made very late (approx 2 years), the file had been destroyed and the application was made over 24 pages. The EAT found all of these to be legitimate factors justifying the Regional Judge determining the application. The EAT also commented in passing that it is possible that the merits of the application might also affect practicability: if an application is patently hopeless, it might be said to be impracticable to take up another Judge's time with what has already been considered by a Regional Employment Judge.

If a Tribunal proposes to reconsider a decision on its own initiative, *Rule 73* requires it to inform the parties of the reasons why the decision is being reconsidered and the decision shall then be reconsidered in accordance with *Rule 72(2)* as if an application had been made and not refused.

Under the old Rules, the EAT confirmed that the tribunal has no power to initiate a review of a judgment unless the procedural formalities are complied with: *CK Heating Ltd v Doro* [2010] ICR 1449. In *Srivatsa* (above) the EAT reached a decision to a similar effect under the *2013 Rules*.

20.124 *Commentary*

By *Rule 70*, a tribunal has power to reconsider a judgment. This will include any decision, including a determination of a preliminary point, which finally disposes of a particular issue, as well as a judgment on liability or remedy, or both. Under the old rules, it was held to include the striking out of a claim when a deposit was not paid (*Sodexho Ltd v Gibbons* [2005] IRLR 836), and on the same basis would include striking out a claim for other reasons such as unreasonable conduct. Under the old rules, there was the ability to "review" where a claim was struck out for non-compliance with an unless order: see *Tisson v Telewest Communications Group Ltd*, [2008] All ER (D) 42 (May), EAT and *Neary v Governing Body of St Albans Girls' School* [2009] EWCA Civ 1190, [2010] IRLR 124, EAT; where strictly, the effect of the striking out was to convert the conditional 'unless' order into a judgment, which could then be reviewed. See also *North Tyneside Primary Care Trust v Aynsley* [2009] ICR 1333, [2009] All ER (D) 125 (May). The approach is however different under the *2013 Rules* and the contortions seen under the previous rules are no longer necessary. *Rule 38(2)* provides the mechanism by which the unless order can be reconsidered and revoked if it is appropriate to do so: the interest of justice test applies there also.

The case law under the previous rules relating to 'review' must now be seen in light of the fact that the criteria for reconsideration have been reduced to one: that it is in the interests of justice. In *Williams v Ferrosan Ltd* [2004] IRLR 607 the EAT held that the power of a tribunal to review its decisions 'in the interests of justice' (then contained in *rule 34(3)* of the *2004 Rules*) should not (as was previously the case: see *Trimble v Supertravel Ltd* [1982] IRLR 451, [1982] ICR 440) be restricted to cases where new facts had arisen subsequently or there had been a procedural mishap, but should be applied more widely to give effect to the Overriding Objective. Under the earlier case law, it had also been held that the interests of justice include justice to the party which was successful at the hearing, and the public interest in the finality of litigation (see *Flint v Eastern Electricity Board* [1975] IRLR 277). In *Williams v Ferrosan* it was held that, where there is an obvious advantage in a mistake being addressed through reconsideration rather than requiring a party to appeal, it can be in the interests of justice to permit a review (in that case compensation had been awarded on a mistaken view on the part of both parties' representatives, and the Judge, as to whether it would be taxable). The approach in Williams v *Ferrosan* was strongly endorsed in *Sodexho Ltd v Gibbons* [2005] ICR 1647, [2005] IRLR 836, *Maresca v Motor Industry Repair Research Centre* [2004] 4 All ER 254 and *Southwark London Borough Council v Bartholomew* [2004] ICR 358. In *Council of the City of Newcastle upon Tyne v Marsden* [2010] ICR 743 the President of the EAT, Underhill J, reviewed the case law and concluded that the 'interest of justice' (as it featured as a ground of review under the old rules) confers a broad general discretion which should not be encrusted with too much case law, and that whilst the interests of finality in litigation remained important, this was not a conclusive argument. The President concluded that the principles underlying such decisions as *Trimble* remained valid as drawing attention to the underlying principles, which it would be wrong to ignore; but a liberal approach to the exercise of the discretion conferred by review (now reconsideration) in the interests of justice was nevertheless permissible.

This approach is reinforced by the framing of the new *2013 Rules*. However, as the Court of Appeal held in *Ministry of Justice v Burton* [2017] 4 All ER 603, [2016] ICR 1128, "the earlier case law cannot be ignored". While the Court in Burton did not suggest that the broad discretion apparently granted by the words 'in the interests of justice' needed to be 'cut down' by reference to the old case law, the Court of Appeal held that, as was the case previously (see *Ironsides, Ray and Vials v Lindsay* [1994] IRLR 318), the incompetence of a party's representative is not a sufficient reason for a review of a decision.

It should be noted, though, that the approach to be taken to 'interests of justice' reconsideration of case management orders under *Rule 29* (see above **20.55**) was reconsidered at length in *Serco Ltd v Wells* [2016] ICR 768, albeit without reference to *Williams v Ferrosan* or *Sodexho v Gibbons* and before the Court of Appeal's judgment in *Burton*. The principles discussed in *Serco* would appear to be equally applicable to the exercise of the power in *Rule 70*. In *Serco* the EAT observed that the *2013 Rules* must be taken to have been drafted with the principle of finality in mind such that challenges to an order would normally take place on appeal. Seeking the same Judge or another Judge of equivalent jurisdiction to look again at an order or decision, save in carefully defined circumstances, should be discouraged and the expression "necessary in the interests of justice" in *Rule 29* should be interpreted in light of the principle of finality. Case law under the *CPR* and in the Tribunal indicates that a variation or revocation of an order or decision may be necessary in the interests of justice where there has been a material change of circumstances after the order was made, or where the order has been based on either a misstatement, and there may be other occasions, which it is unwise to attempt to define but these will be "rare . . . [and] . . . out of the ordinary". The EAT further held that whether or not a subsequent event amounts to a material change in circumstances is a matter of "jurisdiction" and not a question of the exercise of discretion. It is to be decided from an objective standpoint. Two other EAT decisions have since followed *Serco* (see *Brettle v Dudley MBC* (UKEAT/0103/17/JOJ), and *Dobson v Pricewaterhousecoopers LLP* (UKEAT/0022/18/OO)) without reference to *Ministry of Justice v Burton*. On the other hand, *Ministry of Justice v Burton* was followed in *Qu v Landis and Gyr* (UKEAT/0016/19/RN), 8 March 2019, without reference to *Serco*.

Where a party wishes to rely on fresh evidence, the EAT has given very clear guidance to the effect that the most appropriate way to do so is by way of an application for (now) reconsideration of the tribunal's decision, rather than an appeal to the EAT, since the tribunal is better placed to decide whether the evidence would if available at the original hearing have made any difference to its conclusions: *Adegbuji v Meteor Parking Ltd* [2011] All ER (D) 39 (Dec) (UKEATPA/1570/09); *Korashi v Abertawe Bro Morgannwg University Local Health Board* [2012] IRLR 4. The President of the EAT, Langstaff J, has reinforced this point by a Practice Statement dated 17 April 2012, now incorporated at *paragraph 9* of the *Practice Direction (Employment Appeal Tribunal – Procedure) 2018*, which states that if an application to adduce fresh evidence is raised in an appeal to the EAT, the appeal will normally be stayed to allow the appellant to apply to the tribunal to reconsider its decision; if the tribunal refuses a reconsideration, that decision is of course open to appeal. Since *Outasight VB Ltd v Brown* [2015] ICR D11 (approved by the Court of Appeal in *Ministry of Justice v Burton* [2016] EWCA Civ 714, [2016] ICR 1128), it is clear that the same *Ladd v Marshall* test applies both on reconsideration and on appeal to the question of whether fresh evidence should be admitted i.e. the test is whether the evidence have been obtained with reasonable diligence for use at the hearing; whether it is and would probably have had an important influence on the hearing; and whether it is apparently credible. However, as the EAT made clear in *Outasight* (para 31), reconsideration may be permitted on the basis of fresh evidence not meeting the *Ladd v Marshall* test where it is in the interests of justice to do so. There is a separate power for the Judge to correct clerical errors or accidental slips (see above). This power is sometimes used to correct errors in the computation of compensation. It should not be used to make changes of substance to the judgment, such as the addition of a finding that the unfair dismissal of the claimant was also an act of unlawful discrimination: *Bone v Newham London Borough Council* [2008] EWCA Civ 435, [2008] IRLR 546. As indicated above, the Court of Appeal has now emphasised the importance of finality of litigation in *Burton*.

ESTOPPEL, ABUSE OF PROCESS AND WITHDRAWAL

20.125 Estoppel and prevention of abuse of process

One important aspect of preventing abuse of the tribunal's process is the prevention of the relitigation of issues previously decided, or which could have been decided by the tribunal in earlier proceedings between the parties. This requires consideration of the legal doctrine of estoppel. There are a number of relevant forms of estoppel which may be relied on in tribunal proceedings: these are cause of action estoppel, which prevents the relitigation of a claim which has already been decided between the parties; issue estoppel, which may prevent a party from seeking to pursue a claim dependent on facts which are the subject of a prior and contrary finding in proceedings between the same parties; and a wider form of issue estoppel (sometimes referred to as the rule in *Henderson v Henderson* (1843) 3 Hare 100) which lays down that parties to litigation must bring forward their whole case and, except in special circumstances, will not be permitted to bring fresh proceedings in a matter which could and should have been litigated in earlier proceedings, but was omitted through negligence, inadvertence or accident. The first two forms of estoppel (often referred to collectively as res judicata). For an explanation of the difference between the rule in *Henderson v Henderson* (which is subject to a discretion in special circumstances) and res judicata (which operates as an absolute bar), see *Patel v Governing Body of Lister Community School* (UKEAT/0289/16/JOJ), 1 March 2018.

The doctrines of cause of action and issue estoppel both apply to employment tribunals. The principle is that a decision on a specific claim or issue which has either not been appealed, or has been affirmed on appeal, is binding in any future litigation between the same parties, even if the decision was wrong in fact or law. Thus in *Watt (formerly Carter) v Ahsan* [2007] UKHL 51, [2008] 2 WLR 17, [2008] IRLR 243, the House of Lords held that a tribunal was bound to follow a previous decision in earlier proceedings between the parties although in the meantime the Court of Appeal had held in unrelated proceedings that the interpretation of the relevant law which the tribunal had applied in the first case was wrong; in the result the tribunal was bound in law to apply an incorrect interpretation of the law in the second proceedings.

The doctrine of cause of action estoppel applies equally to a judicial decision by an Employment Judge to dismiss a claim; this prevents the relitigation of the claim between the same parties where it has already been the subject of a binding determination dismissing the claim, even though that may have been as a consequence of withdrawal by the claimant, and not a considered conclusion reached after the hearing of the case. This kind of estoppel has been the subject of three decisions of the Court of Appeal, which are not easily reconciled.

(1)   In *Lennon v Birmingham City Council* [2001] IRLR 826, the claimant had brought tribunal proceedings alleging sex discrimination resulting in a stress-related illness. She withdrew the proceedings before the hearing, and they were dismissed by the tribunal at her request. She then commenced County Court proceedings in respect of stress-related ill health based on the same allegations (of offensive and intimidatory behaviour by fellow employees). The Court of Appeal, following *Barber v Staffordshire County Council* [1996] 2 All ER 748, [1996] IRLR 209, held that the County Court claim was rightly struck out as an attempt to relitigate matters which had been judicially determined by the tribunal's decision dismissing her earlier claim.

(2)   However in *Sajid v Sussex Muslim Society* [2001] EWCA Civ 1684, [2002] IRLR 113, a contrary conclusion was reached where the claimant had initially brought a breach of contract claim in the tribunal which he quantified well in excess of the maximum the tribunal could award, and then withdrew that claim specifically in order that he could pursue it in the High Court. *Barber* was distinguished because the withdrawal and subsequent dismissal of the claim was done with a view to pursuing the dispute elsewhere and not intended to determine the dispute.

(3)   Finally in *Ako v Rothschild Asset Management Ltd* [2002] EWCA Civ 236, [2002] 2 All ER 693, [2002] IRLR 348, on facts materially indistinguishable from *Lennon*, the court nevertheless held that it was necessary and permissible to look at the surrounding circumstances; tribunals, unlike courts, did not have a procedure for discontinuance of proceedings (which does not trigger an estoppel), and if in substance the withdrawal was a discontinuance it should not bar fresh proceedings based on the same facts.

The gap in the *ET Rules* identified in *Ako* has since been rectified by a new provision originally in the *2004 Rules* and maintained in the *2013 Rules*, allowing for withdrawal without dismissal of the proceedings necessarily following: see **20.126** below for details. The EAT has held that these changes remove the basis for the exception to the general principles of cause of action estoppel created by *Ako*: see *Cokayne v British Association of Shooting and Conservation* [2008] ICR 185, discussed below **20.126**. In any case where rights of future action may need to be preserved it is important for a claimant to make clear to the respondent and the tribunal why he is withdrawing his or her claim: see further below **20.126**. In *Patel v Governing Body of Lister Community School* (UKEAT/0289/16/JOJ), 1 March 2018, Simler P held that, where a claimant had raised in subsequent proceedings claims that had formed part of a claim previously withdrawn, and dismissed upon withdrawal, those claims were res judicata and the Tribunal had rightly held that they could not be raised again as heads of claim in the second proceedings (although they could be relied on as background matters in support of the new claims of discrimination raised in the second proceedings).

Issue estoppel is a narrower principle: where a court or tribunal of competent jurisdiction has decided an issue of fact in proceedings between parties, those parties are then bound by that finding in any subsequent proceedings between them. The principle applies to decisions of employment tribunals which either have been upheld on appeal or not appealed, but only if the determination of the particular issue was within the jurisdiction of the tribunal and necessary to its decision. A case where neither of these conditions was satisfied is *Bon Groundwork v Foster* [2012] IRLR 517, where the tribunal in earlier proceedings between the parties had held that the claimant had not been dismissed for redundancy in circumstances where it had no jurisdiction to decide the point because the claimant had not been dismissed at all at the time of his claim. See also *Nayif v High Commission of Brunei Darussalam* [2014] EWCA Civ 1521, [2015] IRLR 134 in which the Court of Appeal held the rejection of a race discrimination complaint on the jurisdictional time basis (claim out of time) did not prevent the claimant bringing a negligence claim in the high court based on the same matters. The doctrine of issue estoppel operates within a single set of proceedings as it does between proceedings, in that facts determined at a preliminary hearing cannot normally be re-opened at the final hearing. However, the doctrine only applies to facts that were necessary to the issue before the Tribunal at the preliminary hearing. Matters of background may be re-opened if necessary at the full hearing: *Aston v Martlet Group Ltd* [2019] ICR 1417, EAT. It also operates in relation to the decisions of an assistant certification officer in disciplinary proceedings, preventing the union from conducting further proceedings based on breaches of the same rule: *McFadden v Unite the Union* (UKEAT/0147/19/DA), 19 December 2019.

As indicated above, whereas the doctrines of cause of action and issue estoppel act as an absolute bar, the rule in *Henderson v Henderson* against abuse of process is subject to a discretion for special circumstances. The principle to be applied in deciding whether it is an abuse of process to pursue a claim which could have been raised in prior proceedings was reviewed and restated by the House of Lords in *Johnson v Gore Wood* [2001] 1 All ER 481, where Lord Bingham summarised the principles (at p 31) as being that the court or tribunal must consider whether in all the circumstances the bringing of proceedings is an abuse of process; the circumstances will include whether the proceedings are brought against the same defendant or respondent, whether the issue could, with reasonable diligence, have been discovered and raised in the previous proceedings and whether the later action involves unjust harassment or oppression of the party sued. The EAT has confirmed that it is these principles that should be applied, not a narrower approach based on an earlier decision of the Court of Appeal, *Divine-Bortey v Brent London Borough Council* [1998] IRLR 525: see *Parker v Northumberland Water* [2011] IRLR 652. The onus is on the respondent to establish abuse of process. See also *Sheriff v Klyne Tugs (Lowestoft) Ltd* [1999] IRLR 481 (action for personal injury allegedly caused by racial harassment struck out by the Court of Appeal, as this claim could and should have been pursued as part of the claimant's tribunal claim of racial discrimination against the same employers, which had been settled) and *Thomas v Devon County Council* [2008] All ER (D) 236 (Feb), EAT (where after withdrawing one claim, the claimant was permitted to proceed with a second claim in the absence of any prejudice to the respondent). In *Takhar v Gracefield Developments Ltd* [2019] UKSC 13, [2019] 2 WLR 984, the Supreme Court held that fraud is an exception to the requirement in *Henderson v Henderson* that the point not be one that could, with reasonable diligence, have been raised in the first proceedings. Provided the first proceedings did not include a fraud allegation, an allegation of fraud in respect of matters raised in the first proceedings could be raised in the second proceedings even if it could 'with reasonable diligence' have been raised in the first proceedings: 'fraud unravels all'. On the other hand, if fraud was raised in the first proceedings, but the new matter lends further support to that claim, then the Court indicated it should be dealt with in the same way as any other fresh allegation under the *Henderson v Henderson* rule. In *Butt v Reading Borough Council* (UKEAT/0040/19/JOJ) Lavender J had to consider whether a second equal pay claim covering part of the same ground as a first equal pay claim involving the same parties was an abuse of process. He noted (para 46) that although ordinarily a claim which duplicates an existing claim would be an abuse of process and should be struck out, if there was 'good reason' for bringing the second proceedings (which there was in that case because the first claim was outwith the Tribunal's jurisdiction for having been brought a day early) it should be permitted to proceed. In contrast, in *McFadden v Unite the Union* (UKEAT/0147/19/DA), 19 December 2019, the EAT held that the union was barred from bringing any further disciplinary proceedings against its member in respect of an allegation that he slapped a woman's bottom because the union should have brought forward its whole case in the first proceedings before the certification officer.

A related but equally venerable doctrine, of the merger of causes of action, arose in *Fraser v HLMAD Ltd* [2006] EWCA Civ 738, [2006] IRLR 687, where it was held that a successful claim under the tribunal's contractual jurisdiction precluded the claimant from then bringing High Court proceedings to recover the balance of the damages for wrongful dismissal. His claim had been valued by the tribunal at some £80,000, but its power to make an award under the *Extension of Jurisdiction Order 1994* was (and is) limited to £25,000, and the merger of his claim prevented him from pursuing the balance through separate proceedings.

The related Scots law doctrine of *lis alibi pendens*, under which a claim will be barred if it is the same as a claim already raised in litigation pending between the same parties, does not as such apply to employment tribunal proceedings: *Lynch v East Dunbartonshire Council* [2010] ICR 1094. However the fact of a second claim being brought in these circumstances may provide grounds for the striking out of the second claim under *Rule 37(1)(b)* as vexatious, a point which would apply equally in English proceedings. The case itself did not justify this characterisation, as the second proceedings had been brought to protect the claimants' position after the respondents had challenged the competency of the first proceedings on the question whether the claimants had complied with the statutory grievance procedure, as then required by the *Employment Act 2002, s 32*. For an example of the application of the principles of res judicata in Scots Law, and an explanation of the principles, see *Holmes v Greater Glasgow Health Board* (UKEATS/0045/11) (claim for sick pay struck out where previous claim in respect of an earlier period of the same absence had been dismissed).

In *Christou v London Borough of Haringey* [2013] EWCA Civ 178, [2013] IRLR 379, the Court of Appeal held that a decision taken by an employer on an internal disciplinary complaint did not constitute a determination of an issue which establishes the existence of a legal right. Accordingly, the doctrine of res judicata is not applicable to such decisions.

20.126 Withdrawal and dismissal of claims

A claimant may choose to withdraw his claim because, for example, a settlement has been reached, or because the claimant does not want to proceed with the claim, or wishes to pursue the issue through other proceedings. Prior to the coming into force of the *2004 ET Rules*, the practice if a claimant withdrew the claim was for the tribunal to issue a formal order dismissing it. Some of the potential difficulties that this could cause are set out at **20.125** above. The *2004 Rules* introduced a new procedure under what was *Rule 25* of the *2004 Rules*, but this rule was drafted in terms described by the Court of Appeal as 'lamentable' (*Khan v Heywood & Middleton Primary Care Trust* [2006] IRLR 793). *Rules 51* and *52* of the *2013 Rules* are designed to meet the problems that were detected with the earlier formulation.

A claimant may withdraw his claim at any time in accordance with *Rule 51*. That rule provides that where a claimant informs the Tribunal, either in writing or in the course of a hearing, that a claim, or part of it, is withdrawn, the claim, or part, comes to an end, subject to any application that the respondent may make for a costs, preparation time or wasted costs order.

Accordingly, to comply with *Rule 51*, the claimant must notify the tribunal in writing of his wish to withdraw the claim or a particular part of it, and as against which respondent or respondents (if there are more than one) it is withdrawn. Alternatively, a claim or part thereof may be withdrawn orally at a hearing. A withdrawal takes effect immediately and (to the extent of the withdrawal) brings proceedings to an end without any further action by the Tribunal (see *Khan* under the previous rules). This remains the position under *Rule 51*. (As to withdrawal of part of a claim, see *Verdin v Hurrods Ltd*, below.)

Under the *2004 Rules*, the claim would only be dismissed if the respondent applied for an order to that effect within 28 days from the notice of withdrawal being sent by the Tribunal. Under the *Rule 52* of the *2013 Rules*, however, the default position is that the Tribunal will dismiss a withdrawn claim. *Rule 52* provides that where a claim, or part of it, has been withdrawn under *Rule 51*, the Tribunal must issue a judgment dismissing it unless either of two exceptions can be made out. The *Rule* explains that an order dismissing the claim, or part of it, would mean that the claimant would be unable to commence a further claim against the respondent raising the same, or substantially the same, complaint. The two exceptions are: (a) the claimant has expressed at the time of withdrawal a wish to reserve the right to bring a further claim and the Tribunal is satisfied that there would be legitimate reason for doing so; or (b) the Tribunal believes that to issue such a judgment would not be in the interests of justice.

The fact that a claimant absents himself from a hearing does not necessarily amount to the withdrawal of the claim: *Smith v Greenwich Council* [2011] ICR 277, EAT. In that case the claimant had asked for an adjournment to give him time to work on the case; when this was (as he believed) refused, he indicated his intention to appeal and left the hearing. The EAT held that this was not withdrawal by conduct, not least because the statement that he intended to appeal was inconsistent with withdrawing the claim. The tribunal should only have treated the claim as withdrawn if the claimant had said expressly that he was withdrawing his claim. Tribunals have also been advised by the EAT not to treat a claimant as having withdrawn or abandoned part of his claim, or a particular contention, without making sure that that is the claimant's intention, and that he understands the consequences of doing so: *Segor v Goodrich Actuation Systems Ltd* (UKEAT/0145/11). Once notice of withdrawal of the claim has been given, it cannot be revoked by the claimant: *Khan* (above).

The test now endorsed by the EAT for withdrawal is that in *Segor* – did the claimant or his representative "clearly, unambiguously, and unequivocally" abandon the claim or part of the claim. This is a factual question. For an example of a withdrawal that meets this threshold, see *Osaghae v United Lincolnshire Hospitals NHS Trust* [2013] UKEAT/0576/12. See also *Drysdale v Department of Transport* [2014] IRLR 892 in which the claimant's wife (his lay representative) told the Tribunal that she was making an application to withdraw the claim, after which the tribunal (on application by the respondent) dismissed the claim. Later, the representative, sought a review. The Court of Appeal held that the tribunal did not fail in its duty to assist a lay representative by ensuring that the decision to withdraw was fully considered and not taken in the heat of the moment. The test has recently been approved in *Campbell v OCS Group UK Ltd* [2017] ICR D19 and was applied again in *Paul v Virgin Care Limited* (UKEAT/0104/19/RN).

The effect of withdrawal of a claim under the old rules was explained by the EAT in *Verdin v Harrods Ltd* [2006] ICR 396, [2006] IRLR 339. The consequence of withdrawal, without more, is that the proceedings automatically come to an end, but the claimant is not precluded from pursuing the claim in other proceedings (including further proceedings in the tribunal, subject to the applicable time limits); if the tribunal claim has been dismissed, however, the bringing of further proceedings (in the tribunal or elsewhere) is likely to be regarded as an abuse of process. Indeed, as stated above *Rule 52* states in terms that the consequence of a dismissal judgment is that the same, or substantially similar, claim cannot be recommenced against the respondent.

Where the claim is withdrawn, the claim must be dismissed under *Rule 52*, unless: (a) the claimant has expressed at the time of withdrawal a wish to reserve the right to bring a further claim and the Tribunal is satisfied that there would be legitimate reason for doing so; or (b) the Tribunal believes that to issue such a judgment would not be in the interests of justice.

The guidance on withdrawals under the old rules remains relevant to the exercise of that discretion. A claimant should explain to the tribunal when withdrawing the claim the basis on which it is being withdrawn, and whether there is any reason not to dismiss the claim. In *Cokayne v British Association for Shooting and Conservation* [2008] ICR 185, the claimant withdrew a constructive dismissal claim he had presented before the grievance procedure had been completed, and failed to explain that this was in order to re-present the claim after his grievance appeal was rejected. The first claim was dismissed and the EAT held that that presented a bar to the second claim, because the complaint of constructive dismissal was made res judicata by the dismissal of the first claim. It did not matter that the claimant had made clear to the respondent his intention to bring the second claim, or that the second claim was not in the general sense an abuse of process, since there are no exceptions to the operation of res judicata in this context. This clearly presents a trap for unwary claimants: the only solution in the particular case was for the claimant to apply for reconsideration of the dismissal of the withdrawn claim, a step encouraged by the EAT.

Under the old rules, the EAT in *Verdin* (above), identified the following two questions as being relevant to whether a dismissal order should be made. Is the withdrawing party intending to abandon the claim? If the withdrawing party is intending to resurrect the claim in fresh proceedings, would it be an abuse of process to allow that to occur? (see para 39).

Where a claim is withdrawn but not dismissed, the file will be closed and retained for a period by the Tribunal before being destroyed; however it is open to any party to make an application for costs, preparation time or wasted costs (see *Rule 51*).

Srivatsa v Secretary of State for Health [2018] EWCA Civ 936, [2018] ICR 1660 is an unhappy catalogue of the problems that arose as a result of the lack of clarity regarding withdrawals and dismissals under the *2004 Rules*, complicated by the Tribunal having in fact dismissed the claim in the face of the claimant indicating that he did not wish the claim to be dismissed as he intended to pursue the matter in the High Court. The EAT had ultimately determined that the claim had been rightly dismissed, which led to the High Court holding that the claimant was estopped from bringing his High Court claim. The Court of Appeal held that the Claimant was not so estopped. Since the *2004 Rules* lacked the clarity now to be found in the *2013 Rules* (which should mean that claims are not dismissed in these circumstances), what mattered was that the claimant had in fact evinced an intention to commence the High Court proceedings upon withdrawing the tribunal claim and accordingly he was not estopped from so doing notwithstanding the dismissal of his claim by the tribunal.

20.127 COSTS, PREPARATION TIME, AND WASTED COSTS ORDERS

Costs (referred to in Scotland as 'expenses') are awarded to a successful party only in relatively limited circumstances. The range of circumstances was somewhat broadened by changes in the relevant provisions of the *ET Regulations* made in 2001. Further changes in the powers of the tribunal to award costs came into effect on 1 October 2004, under the *2004 Regulations*. The maximum amount that may be awarded by a tribunal on summary assessment was increased by the *Employment Tribunals (Constitution and Rules of Procedure) (Amendment) Regulations 2012* ('the *2012 Regulations*') from £10,000 to £20,000, for cases first presented on or after 6 April 2012. The *2013 Rules* broadly recast the existing powers to make costs, preparation time and wasted costs orders. One notable change is the power for the Employment Tribunal now to conduct a detailed assessment of costs itself and order costs without limit after having done so. Whether this alternative to sending the case to the County or Sheriff Court for a detailed assessment will be used frequently remains to be seen, however anecdotal evidence suggests a willingness on the part of Tribunal Judges to embrace this new power.

The powers available to a tribunal under the *2013 Rules* are:

(a)   to make a costs order;

(b)   to make a preparation time order; and

(c)   to make a wasted costs order against a party's representative

By *Rule 75(1)*, a costs order is an order that the paying party make a payment to the receiving party which is either (a) in respect of the costs that the receiving party has incurred whilst legally represented or while represented by a lay representative; (b) in respect of a tribunal fee paid by the receiving party (although this is now only of historical interest); or (c) in respect of expenses incurred, or to be incurred for the purpose of, or in connection with, an individual's attendance as a witness at a Tribunal.

A preparation time order, by contrast, is an order that the paying party make a payment to the receiving party in respect of the receiving party's preparation time whilst not legally represented: *Rule 75(2)*. For these purposes, "preparation time" means time spent by the receiving party (including by employees or advisers) in working on the case, except for time spent at any final hearing.

A wasted costs order is an order made under *Rule 80* against a representative rather than a party, and in favour of any party (including the party that the representative represents).

A number of general points need to be made about these powers:

(a)   Orders may be made against or in favour of a respondent who has not had his or her response accepted, in relation to any part the respondent has taken in the proceedings. However if the respondent has not participated in the proceedings because it was prevented from doing so, having failed to have a response accepted, no costs can be awarded against it: *Sutton v The Ranch Ltd* [2006] ICR 1170; this is so even though the claimant may have incurred costs, eg in proving losses at a remedies hearing.

(b)   A costs order covering the costs of a representative can only be made in favour of a receiving party whilst represented (ie by a barrister, advocate or solicitor with a current practising certificate, or a registered claims manager). It can cover time when the receiving party has a damages based agreement: *Swissport Ltd v Exley* [2017] ICR 1288.

(c)   It is not possible to make both a costs order and a preparation time order in the same proceedings and in favour of the same party (*Rule 75(3)*). Thus a party represented initially by a non-practising solicitor, but by Counsel for the hearing, could only recover its costs of Counsel, and could not obtain a separate preparation time order for the cost of retaining the non-practising solicitor: *Ramsay v Bower-cross Construction Ltd* [2008] All ER (D) 131 (Aug) (UKEAT/0534/07). This point may also cause difficulties if a party obtains orders on more than one occasion during the proceedings, and either becomes or ceases to be legally represented between the making of the orders. To meet this potential difficulty, *Rule 75(3)* gives the tribunal power to make an order part way through the proceedings but to defer until the conclusion of the proceedings determining which category of order it should be. This will necessitate also deferring the decision as to the amount of the award; and it cannot meet the problem highlighted in *Ramsay*.

(d)   It used to be thought there was a strict rule that a costs order cannot be made in respect of costs incurred before the claim or (in favour of the respondent) the response was presented: see *Health Development Agency v Parish* [2004] IRLR 550 and *Sutton v The Ranch Ltd*, above. However, in *Sunuva Ltd v Martin* (UKEAT/0174/17) [2018] ICR D9 the EAT held that the wording of the *2013 Rules* did not limit the costs that could be awarded to those incurred at a particular stage of proceedings, or to costs after proceedings had begun.

(e)   Costs awards are intended to be compensatory, not punitive (a point confirmed by the Court of Appeal in *Lodwick v Southwark London Borough Council* [2004] EWCA Civ 306, [2004] IRLR 554). The EAT has held that this means that where costs are claimed because a party has acted unreasonably in conducting a case, the costs awarded should be no more than is proportionate to the loss caused to the receiving party by the unreasonable conduct: *Barnsley Metropolitan Borough Council v Yerrakalva* [2011] EWCA Civ 1255, [2012] IRLR 78.

(f)   Relevant definitions of "costs", "legally represented" and "represented by a lay representative" are to be found in *Rule 74*. In *Ladak v DRC Locums Ltd* [2014] IRLR 851, the EAT has held that the definition of "costs" (there under the *2004 Rules*, but applicable to the *2013 Rules*) is wide enough to include costs in respect of the time spent by a qualified in-house legal representative. The costs of an in-house legal department was a charge or expense upon the employer. The definition of costs in *Rule 74* includes costs incurred not only directly by the receiving party but also on their behalf (eg by their representative or a third party supporting their case): see *Taiwo v Olaigbe* [2013] ICR 770 and *Leeks v St George's University Hospitals NHS Foundation Trust* (UKEAT/0072/18/BA), 18 June 2018.

(g)   In respect of costs generally, regard should now be had to the Presidential Guidance on General Case Management.

The award of costs is still relatively unusual. The sections below set out the provisions as to each of the categories of orders available to the tribunal. For simplicity, references to costs and costs orders are intended to encompass expenses and expenses orders in Scottish proceedings.

Where the Tribunal makes a costs, preparation time or wasted costs order, it may also make an order that the paying party (or, in the case of a wasted costs order, the representative) pay to the Secretary of State, in whole or in part, any allowances (other than allowances paid to members of the Tribunal) paid by the Secretary of State under *ETA 1996, s 5(2)* or *(3)* to any person for the purposes of, or in connection with, that person's attendance at the Tribunal: *Rule 83*.

Note that if an application for costs is made where a claimant is represented by an unregistered claims manager (see above **21.85**) who is prohibited by the *Financial Services and Markets Act 2000* from charging for their services, then it may be appropriate for the Tribunal to refuse to award costs on the basis that to do so would be contrary to public policy: see, by analogy, *Hounga v Allen* [2014] UKSC 47, [2014] 1 WLR 2889.

20.128 Costs orders and Preparation Time Orders

A costs order, or a preparation time order, can be made in the circumstances of *Rule 76*. The relevant provisions of the *2013 Rules* governing the power to make, and the making and terms of, costs and preparation time orders are briefly as follows:

(a)   If the paying party has, in the opinion of the tribunal, acted vexatiously, abusively, disruptively or otherwise unreasonably in bringing or conducting proceedings, or his or her representative has so acted in bringing or conducting them, or if any claim or response had no prospects of success, the tribunal may make an order: *Rule 76(1)*. 'Conducting' proceedings applies equally to a respondent as to a claimant. Under the old rules, reference was made to the proceedings being "misconceived" which in turn was then defined as including 'having no reasonable prospect of success'. The *2013 Rules* now refer to the "no reasonable prospect of success" formulation directly, but it is helpful to note that references to claims or defences being "misconceived" in the older case-law refer to the same standard. For the meaning of 'vexatiously', see **20.129** below. Note that technically the tribunal is required to consider the award of costs, even if no application is made; but it has a discretion whether actually to make the award, and as to the amount (*Rule 76(1)*). In practice under the old rules it was unusual for a tribunal to exercise its discretion in favour of making a costs order in any case where the receiving party did not apply for costs.

(b)   An order can be made where a party has been in breach of any order or practice direction: *Rule 76(2)*. This basis for awarding costs is often prayed in aid alongside the unreasonable conduct ground.

(c)   An order can also be made if a hearing has to be adjourned or postponed on the application of a party (*Rule 76(2)*). In such cases, there is no requirement for this to be the fault of a party, although a costs order is more likely in those circumstances. Despite the wide discretion already present in this *Rule*, the Government has introduced, a new specific provision concerning postponements applicable to all proceedings which are presented on or after 6 April 2016. Where a hearing is postponed or adjourned on the application of a party made less than seven days before the date on which the relevant hearing begins, the Tribunal "may" make an order and "shall" consider whether or not to make one (see *Rule 76(1)(c)* and the *Small Business, Enterprise and Employment Act 2015, s 151*). The *Rules* also provided that in respect of certain complaints of unfair dismissal, costs "must" be awarded where the claimant has expressed a wish to be reinstated or re-engaged which has been communicated to the respondent at least seven days before the hearing of the complaint, and a postponement or adjournment of the hearing has been caused by the respondent's failure, without good reason, to adduce reasonable evidence as to the availability of the job from which the claimant was dismissed, or of comparable or suitable employment (*Rule 76(3)*).

(d)   When the fees regime was in place, a costs order to cover a tribunal fee was able to be made where a party has paid a Tribunal fee in respect of a claim, an employer's contract claim or application and that claim, counter claim or application is decided in whole or in part in favour of that party: *Rule 76(4)*. The case law relevant to the exercise of that discretion is set out in previous editions of this work and is not repeated here. Since 20 October 2017, a litigant who has paid a fee may seek a refund from the Government.

(e)   A costs order to cover witness expenses may be made on application of a party or witness, or of the Tribunal's own initiative where a witness has attended or has been ordered to attend to give oral evidence at a hearing: *Rule 76(5)*.

(f)   The procedure for making a costs or preparation time order is set out in *Rule 77*. An application may be made at any stage of proceedings up until 28 days after the date on which the final judgment is sent to the parties. No costs or preparation time order may be made until the paying party has had a reasonable opportunity to make representations in writing or at a hearing as the Tribunal orders, in response to the application.

(g)   A costs order may require the paying party to pay the whole or part of the other party's costs or expenses as assessed (by a County Court Costs Judge under the *CPR 1998* or by the Tribunal itself conducting a detailed assessment) if not otherwise agreed, or be for an agreed amount, or for a summarily assessed sum (not exceeding £20,000) fixed by the tribunal (*ET Rules, Rule 78(1)*). The limit on fixed costs was introduced by the *2001 Rules* and was retained in the *2004 Rules*; it does not apply to costs agreed between the parties or assessed by way of detailed assessment by the Tribunal itself or the County Court. When referring to the County Court for a detailed assessment, a Tribunal may specify that the assessment take place on an indemnity or standard cost assessment basis, however the Tribunal must properly consider the effect of the order it makes and the paying party's ability to pay when so doing (see *Howman v Queen Elizabeth Hospital King's Lynn* [2013] All ER (D) 262 (Apr) (UKEAT/0509/12); there the EAT held that an order for indemnity costs should be rare and the Tribunal failed to consider the effect of the order and the possibility of putting a cap on the overall order for costs). Similar considerations will no doubt apply to when the Tribunal itself conducts the detailed assessment. The maximum that can be awarded in a summary assessment was increased from £10,000 to £20,000 by the *Employment Tribunals (Constitution and Rules of Procedure) (Amendment) Regulations 2012 (SI 2012/468)* and has been retained in the *2013 Rules*. In assessing costs summarily, the tribunal is likely to refer to the guidelines used in summary assessments of costs in the High Court and County Court as to what are reasonable hourly rates for solicitors to claim in different parts of the country (these rates, which are published annually in the Supreme Court Practice, apply only to England and Wales). Similar criteria for the taxation of expenses in the Sheriff Court apply in Scottish proceedings. As stated above, under the (unlawful) fees regime, the amount of costs awarded could include reimbursement of all or part of a Tribunal fee paid, or witness expenses "necessarily and reasonably incurred" in attending proceedings. The Rules provide that such sums do not count towards the £20,000 limit: see *Rule 78(3)*.

(h)   When carrying out a detailed assessment of costs itself, the Tribunal must (by *Rule 78(1)(b)*) apply the same principles as the county court and follow the *CPR 1998*, especially *CPR, r 44.3*, which requires that (i) costs are disallowed if they are unreasonably incurred or unreasonable in amount; (ii) costs allowed are proportionate; (iii) any doubt is resolved in favour of the paying party; and (iv) all the circumstances are taken into account include the conduct of the parties at all stages, any efforts to resolve the dispute, the amount of any property involved, the importance of the matter to the parties, the complexity of the matter, the skills of those involved and the time spent on the case: *Monfared v Spire Healthcare Ltd* UKEAT/0131/18/RN, 30 October 2018 (where the Tribunal reduced a costs schedule of £121,210.80 to £85,143). Further, the costs of the detailed assessment may be included within the costs assessed: *Monfared* ibid.

(i)   In deciding whether to make an order for costs or preparation time (and indeed wasted costs), and if so in determining the amount to be awarded, the tribunal is permitted but not required to have regard to the means of the party against whom the order is made (*Rule 84*, reversing the decision of the Court of Appeal in *Kovacs v Queen Mary and Westfield College* [2002] EWCA Civ 352, [2002] IRLR 414 that there was no power to take means into account under an earlier iteration of the *Rules*). It was observed by Simon Brown LJ in *Kovacs* that logically, the discretion to have regard to the paying party's means would require the tribunal also to consider the means of the receiving party (para 10), and by Chadwick LJ that if means are a relevant factor, it would not be reasonable for a tribunal to make an award that it was satisfied the paying party could not meet (para 32). Neither of the points raised in *Kovacs* remains good law under the current *Rules*. *Rule 84* is specific that it is the "paying party's" ability to pay that may be taken into account and not the means of the receiving party and the EAT in *Brooks v Nottingham University Hospitals NHS Trust* (UKEAT/0246/18/JOJ), 17 October 2019 has confirmed that there are good policy reasons for not taking into account the means of the receiving party. Further, it is clear from the cases cited below that the other point determined in *Kovacs* is also no longer good law: it is clear that means is only one consideration in the exercise of discretion, and there is no prohibition on making an award even if there is no ability to pay provided that means to pay has been considered.

Two further points were made by the EAT in *Jilley v Birmingham and Solihull Mental Health NHS Trust* [2008] All ER (D) 35 (Feb), EAT. First, the tribunal should state clearly whether or not it has taken the paying party's means into account in making its order as to costs. Secondly, if payment of all the receiving party's costs would be beyond the claimant's means, it may order payment of a specified proportion of the costs. In *Kuwait Oil Company v Dr Jamal Al-Tarkait* (UKEAT/0210/19/00) Kerr J confirmed that this permits an order for costs to be assessed (whether by a Tribunal judge or a County Court judge), subject to a maximum liability of a stated amount.

The EAT has also held that even if the claimant does not raise the issue of means, it should be raised by the tribunal, particularly before a very large order is made: *Doyle v North West London Hospitals NHS Trust* [2012] All ER (D) 205 (Jun) (UKEAT/0271/11), a case where an order to pay all the respondent's costs, estimated at £95,000, had been made. Contrast *Osonnaya v Queen Mary University of London* (UKEAT/0225/11) in which the EAT held that the tribunal is required, if the matter is raised, to consider ability to pay, but if the matter is not raised, there is no authority imposing a legal duty on the Judge to raise the question, even with a litigant in person. It is not necessary to take the claimant's means into account if she was voluntarily absent from the proceedings when the point arose (*Mirikwe v Wilson & Co Solicitors* (UKEAT/0025/11), or if the evidence of means given by the claimant is contradictory or unreliable (*Shields Automotive Ltd v Greig* (UKEATS/0024/10)). The last mentioned case is also authority for the point that 'means' can include equity in a home, even if not readily realisable. Similarly in *Chadburn v Doncaster and Bassetlaw Hospital NHS Foundation Trust* [2015] UKEAT/0259/14, the EAT upheld an award of costs even though the claimant currently could not afford to pay: affordability was "not the only criterion for the exercise of discretion". In that case there was also evidence that her financial position was likely to improve based on the realistic prospect of the claimant returning to employment. In *Oni v NHS Leicester City* [2012] All ER (D) 05 (Oct), [2013] ICR 91 (UKEAT/0144/12) the EAT held that there should be a proper consideration of means where the claimant asserted limited means and where the costs claimed were anticipated to be large. The EAT recommended the completion of the County Court means form EX140 by the party whose means are to be taken into account. In *Abaya v Leeds Teaching Hospital NHS Trust* [2017] UKEAT/0258/16, Singh J held that an ET had erred in taking into account the means of the claimant's ex-wife without explaining how that impacted the claimant's ability to pay. The ET also failed to explain how it had reached the sum it had decided to award.

It is not completely clear how far the power to take into account the paying party's means extends to taking the means of an organisation, such as a trade union, representing him into account. In a case decided before the *ET Rules* were amended to allow the conduct of a representative to be taken into account in deciding whether to make a costs order, the EAT held that the conduct of the case by a trade union representative did not entitle the tribunal to take the union's means into account in deciding the issue of a costs order against the claimant: *Omar v Worldwide News Inc* [1998] IRLR 291. This approach was however later doubted in *Beynon v Scadden* [1999] IRLR 700; it may in any case no longer be applicable following the change in the *ET Rules* permitting the award of costs on account of the unreasonable conduct of the proceedings by a party's representative. However any costs order would only be enforceable against the party against whom it is made, and it does not necessarily follow that a union would accept liability to reimburse its members in such a situation; this may make a tribunal reluctant to disregard the limited means of the claimant, even if permitted to do so.

(j)   If there has been a preliminary hearing, and a party was ordered to pay a deposit, and that party loses, *Rule 39(5)* imposes a presumption that the paying party is to be treated as having acted unreasonably in pursuing that specific allegation unless the contrary is shown and the deposit order shall be paid to the other party. However the tribunal is not required to make such an order solely on this ground unless, having considered the reasons given for the making of the deposit order, it considers that the reasons given were substantially the same as the reasons for finding against the party at the hearing. If costs are awarded, the deposit is used to pay, or in part payment of, the costs; if not, or if the costs awarded are less than the deposit, the deposit or balance is refunded to the party concerned (*Rule 39(6)*). An example under the old rules is *Deer v Walford* [2011] All ER (D) 58 (May), [2011] UKEAT /0283/10. See, however, *Oni v Unison* [2015] ICR D17, [2015] UKEAT/0370/14 under the *2013 Rules* in which the EAT held that a tribunal erred by assuming that once there was unreasonable conduct in persisting with proceedings following a deposit order, a costs order should follow subject only to considering means. Simler J held that even where unreasonable conduct has been found on that basis, a tribunal has a discretion as to whether or not costs should be awarded, and if so, in what amount; the tribunal must consider all relevant circumstances when exercising that discretion.

(k)   An application for costs may be made at any time at a preliminary hearing, or at the conclusion of a hearing, or subsequently in writing. If an application for costs is made after judgment is given finally determining the claim, it must be received by the tribunal no later than 28 days from the date the judgment was sent to the parties: *Rule 77*.

(l)   If an application for costs is made at the hearing, the other party will be given an opportunity to oppose the application orally. In any other case, an order cannot be made unless the intended paying party has been given an opportunity to give reasons why the order should not be made. This may be by way of a further hearing, or on paper, as the Judge may direct (*Rule 77*). The EAT recently underlined that the putative paying party should be given a reasonable opportunity to oppose a costs award: see *Gwara v Mid Essex Primary Care Trust* [2013] All ER (D) 229 (Sep) (UKEAT/0074/13). The party claiming costs should, if the sum claimed is more than nominal, prepare a schedule showing the costs incurred and the amount claimed.

(m)   If within 14 days of the date of the order either party requests written reasons for a costs order, reasons must be given in writing (*Rule 62*). This codifies the Court of Appeal's comments in *Lodwick v Southwark London Borough Council* [2004] EWCA Civ 306, [2004] IRLR 554 as to the importance of a tribunal giving sufficient reasons for both the fact and the amount of an award of costs.

(n)   There is in principle a power under *Rule 38* for the tribunal to make an 'unless' order for the payment of costs (*Criddle v Epcot Leisure Ltd* [2005] All ER (D) 89 (Aug)). The effect of this would be that if the costs are not paid by the date required, the party's case would automatically be struck out; for a claimant this means that the proceedings would be at an end, whilst a respondent in that position would be debarred from further participation in the case.

20.129

There have been several decisions on the scope of the power to award costs, when and how the discretion to do so should be exercised, and what costs should be awarded if an order is made. The basic principles were restated in *Hossaini v EDS Recruitment Ltd* [2020] ICR 491 at para 64. There are three stages involved in the determination of a costs application: (1) the tribunal needs to determine whether or not its jurisdiction to make a costs award is engaged (i.e. whether the circumstances provided by rule 76(1), such as 'unreasonable conduct' exist); if so, (2) it must consider the discretion afforded to it by the use of the word "may" at the start of that rule and determine whether or not it considers it appropriate to make an award of costs in that case; only then should it turn to question (3), that is to determine how much it should award

It is important to bear in mind that costs orders are relatively rare, but a tribunal is not obliged to refer to that fact in its reasoning, provided that it follows the statutory, two-stage procedure of first determining whether there has been unreasonable conduct etc, and then exercising a discretion whether to make an award, and if so of what amount or proportion of costs incurred: *Power v Panasonic (UK) Ltd* [2005] All ER (D) 130 (Jul), EAT, following

Salinas v Bear Stearns International Holdings Inc [2005] ICR 1117. On the other hand, the mere fact that the tribunal makes an award of aggravated damages against the respondent does not justify making an order for costs: *Saiger v North Cumbria Acute Hospitals NHS Trust* (UKEAT/0325/10).

As noted, the first question for the Tribunal is whether one of the jurisdictional tests is met. The key question for the Tribunal where it is alleged there has been unreasonable conduct of the proceedings (*Rule 76(1)(a)*) is whether the course taken by the party is reasonable. In this respect the Tribunal must not substitute its own view, but must review the decision taken by the litigant (a 'range of reasonable responses test', in effect). The test of unreasonable conduct is a 'wide and objective' one and it may include having an 'unreasonably distorted perception of matters': *Brooks v Nottingham University Hospitals NHS Trust* (UKEAT/0246/18/JOJ), 17 October 2019.

The Tribunal must also bear in mind that it is not to judge a person who is representing him- or herself or has a lay representative by the standards of a legal professional: see *Solomon v University of Hertfordshire* (UKEAT/0258/18/DA_and UKEAT/0066/19/DA) at para 107 and *Vaughan v London Borough of Lewisham and ors* [2013] IRLR 713 at para 25. Whilst a litigant in person might receive a more sympathetic response from a tribunal considering whether conduct of litigation was unreasonable, they are not shielded from such a finding: see eg *Liddington v 2gether NHS Foundation Trust* [2016] UKEAT/0002/16. The conduct of a party's representative, as well as that of the party himself, can provide the basis for an award of costs; the party is in effect fixed with the consequences of his choice of representative: see *Taiwo v Olaigbe* [2013] ICR 770 and *Leeks v St George's University Hospital NHS Foundation* (UKEAT/0072/18/BA), 18 June 2018. The same is not necessarily true of a witness since 'not every witness is the personal responsibility of the party for whom he or she gives evidence': *E&O Laboratories v Miller* (UKEATS/0007/19/SS) at para 19 per Lord Summers. Further, not all conduct of tribunal proceedings by a representative which causes additional cost to the other party is necessarily unreasonable; thus it was held by the EAT in *Francois v Castle Rock Properties Ltd* (UKEAT/0260/10) that the incompetent presentation of the claimant's case by her representative, an inexperienced solicitor, which had unnecessarily prolonged the hearing, was nevertheless on the facts not unreasonable conduct of the case, and there was therefore no justification for an award of costs.

There is no rule that the discretion to award costs will only be exercised where there has been deliberate dishonest conduct: *Brooks*, ibid, para 47. However, where a tribunal finds on the evidence that a party has deliberately lied in evidence to the tribunal, that is necessarily at least unreasonable conduct, and should usually result in a costs order: *Daleside Nursing Home Ltd v Mathew* [2009] All ER (D) 99 (Aug) (UKEAT/0519/08) (a case where the tribunal had found that the racially abusive words alleged by the claimant had not in fact been used) and *Dunedin Canmore Housing Association Ltd v Donaldson* (UKEATS/0014/09). These cases were followed and applied in *Nicolson*, above, where the claimant had in evidence admitted what amounted to fraudulent conduct against his employer; the EAT held that it was an error of law for the tribunal not to award expenses. These cases must however now be read in the light of a number of subsequent decisions most notably, *Barnsley Metropolitan Borough Council v Yerrakalva* [2011] EWCA Civ 1255, [2012] IRLR 78, *Arrowsmith v Nottingham Trent University* [2011] EWCA Civ 797, [2012] ICR 159, *HCA International Limited v JL May-Bheemul* (UKEAT/0477/10) and *Kapoor v Governing Body of Barnhill Community School* [2014] All ER (D) 261 (Feb) (UKEAT/0352/13). In *Kapoor*, the EAT confirmed that giving false evidence is not, automatically, unreasonable conduct warranting a costs order.

In *Yerrakalva*, the tribunal had awarded the respondent council all of its costs after the claimant withdrew her claim part-way through the Proceedings. It found that she had lied, in particular in exaggerating her claimed disability, but also criticised the council for the way it had defended the case. The Court of Appeal held that the tribunal was entitled to find the claimant's conduct was unreasonable, but not to award 100% of the council's costs, and reduced the award to 50%. Mummery LJ said (at para 41): "The vital point in exercising the discretion to order costs is to look at the whole picture of what happened in the case and to ask whether there has been unreasonable conduct by the claimant in bringing and conducting it, and in doing so, to identify the conduct, what was unreasonable about it and what effects it had." The costs awarded need not be precisely calculated to reflect the additional cost to the respondent caused by the claimant's unreasonable conduct, but should broadly reflect what had been caused by the erring party (the same points would apply equally to an unreasonable respondent). Mummery LJ also clarified that his Lordship's comments in *Macpherson v BNP Paribas (London Branch)* [2004] IRLR 558, which had been widely taken as indicating that a causal link need not be established, were not intended to have that effect but only to indicate that a precise correlation need not be established.

In *Arrowsmith*, the tribunal had applied the *Daleside* case on the basis that the fact that (as it had found) the claimant had told untruths as part of her case was evidence that she had conducted the case unreasonably. The Court of Appeal, in upholding a costs order against the claimant, emphasised that *Daleside* does not create a rule, and each case depends on its own facts; on the facts of this case, it was fully open to the tribunal to find her conduct to be unreasonable and award costs against her. In both of the Court of Appeal judgments the Court emphasises that it is a question of fact whether conduct is unreasonable, and therefore provided the tribunal correctly directs itself as to the law, its decision on that point, and equally on whether to exercise its discretion to award costs, will rarely be open to challenge on appeal.

Where a party's unreasonable conduct, such as by failing to comply with orders for disclosure, exchange of witness statements or other case management orders, leads to a case having to be adjourned, the tribunal may award the other party its costs thrown away because of the 'lost' hearing. These are in effect wasted costs, but an order for costs thrown away is not the same as an order for 'wasted costs' under *Rule 80*, which is an award against a representative; see **20.131**. Guidance as to the computation of costs thrown away has been given by the EAT in *Carruthers v London School of Economics Student Union* [2011] All ER (D) 51 (May) (UKEAT/0183/10). In *Schaathun v Executive & Business Aviation Support Ltd* [2015] All ER (D) 388 (Jul) (UKEAT/0615/11) the EAT held that it was not unreasonable conduct of proceedings for a claimant whose first language was not English and whose command of English was good but not perfect to enquire by email a few days before a hearing as to whether an interpreter would be available. Even though the Tribunal postponed the hearing, the email could not have been read as an application for a postponement, nor was it foreseeable that a postponement would inevitably result. A good example of a finding of unreasonable conduct (by the respondent) leading to an unnecessary hearing is *Godfrey Morgan Solicitors Ltd v Marzon* (UKEAT/0465/11).

It has been accepted by the Court of Appeal that deliberately delaying notification of a decision to withdraw a claim can constitute unreasonable behaviour (*McPherson v BNP Paribas (London Branch)* [2004] IRLR 558); the same would be true of unjustifiable delay in conceding liability, or an issue in the claim such as whether the claimant is disabled. This should not be relied on to penalise a party who, perhaps in the light of disclosure of documents or seeing the other party's witness statements, or the failure of settlement negotiations, takes a pragmatic decision to abandon a claim or defence. The unreasonable behaviour lies in then failing to inform the other party and the tribunal of the decision promptly, thereby allowing the other party to incur further costs (and possibly preventing the tribunal from listing another case for the date listed for the hearing).

A party may also be found to have acted unreasonably if he has rejected an offer to settle the proceedings, either made openly or 'without prejudice save as to costs', but it is not unreasonable behaviour to reject an offer simply because the tribunal's decision is more favourable to the party making the offer (eg the claimant is awarded less than the respondent had offered, or even nothing at all): *Kopel v Safeway Stores plc* [2003] IRLR 753. This decision has the effect that the tribunal may take into account offers made without prejudice save as to costs (often referred to as '*Calderbank*' offers; see **20.34** above), but costs do not automatically follow in the way that would be the case in equivalent situations in the High Court. See also *Power v Panasonic (UK) Ltd*, above, where a costs order was upheld on appeal in circumstances where the claimant was found by the tribunal to have put an unrealistically high value on her claims, rejected offers substantially in excess of what she was eventually awarded, and acted intransigently in negotiations; and see *G4S Security Services (UK) v Rondeau* (UKEAT/0207/09), where costs were awarded by the EAT on the basis of an appellant having unreasonably rejected offers to settle an appeal until he accepted the same offer on the morning of the hearing. A further recent example is *Sud v London Borough of Ealing* [2013] EWCA Civ 949, [2013] All ER (D) 386 (Jul), where offers were rejected out of hand by a claimant and the Court of Appeal noted that an argument that she was entitled to seek declarations or reinstatement did not have substantive credibility given her response to offers focussed on an exorbitant sum by way of suggested compensation. In *Solomon v University of Hertfordshire* (UKEAT/0258/18/DA_and UKEAT/0066/19/DA), it was argued by the respondent that part of the reason why the claimant's refusal to accept a settlement offer was unreasonable was because the respondent had paid for her to take legal advice on that offer. However, the respondent's payment had been limited to £500+VAT. Richardson J took the view that while that might have been sufficient to take advice on the terms of the settlement agreement, it was plainly insufficient to enable a claimant to take advice on the merits of the claim and thus not a factor that pointed towards a cost award in that case.

In a case involving a claim of discrimination, one of the remedies is a declaration by the tribunal that the claimant was discriminated against. It will not necessarily be unreasonable conduct for a claimant to refuse a reasonable monetary offer where he is seeking such a declaration and the respondent is not prepared as part of the terms of settlement to admit liability. This principle was applied to unfair dismissal in *Telephone Information Services Ltd v Wilkinson* [1991] IRLR 148, EAT, but the opposite view was taken by the EAT in the later case of *Nicolson Highlandwear Ltd v Nicolson* [2010] IRLR 859, EAT, where the claimant had succeeded in obtaining a finding of unfair dismissal but the EAT considered that he had had no reasonable basis for pursuing the claim, since it was inevitable on the facts that he would not be awarded any compensation (he had admitted to defrauding his employers, and the tribunal had made a nil award). However *Wilkinson* was not cited, and the case cannot therefore be regarded as excluding the argument in other cases that it may be reasonable to pursue a claim of unfair dismissal purely to establish a finding to that effect.

Awards of costs on the basis that the paying party has acted vexatiously in the bringing or conduct of the proceedings are rare, since it is not necessary to show such extreme conduct in order to make a case for an award of costs. However a tribunal would be much more likely to exercise its discretion in favour of such an order if it found vexatious conduct. The essential difference between vexatious and merely unreasonable conduct is that the party concerned need not be aware that his claim has no reasonable prospect of success in order for it to be misconceived (and therefore the bringing of it to be unreasonable), but if a party pursues a claim knowing it has no reasonable prospect of success, or depends on false evidence, or pursues the claim out of malice towards the other party or for some other ulterior reason, his conduct may be found to be vexatious. See further *E T Marler Ltd v Robertson* [1974] ICR 72. For a party's conduct in bringing or pursuing a case to be labelled as 'vexatious', or even 'misconceived', it will normally be necessary, at least where the factual issues are disputed, for the tribunal to have heard and determined the dispute, and accordingly a tribunal should not award costs on this basis where the claim has been struck out on jurisdictional grounds: *Dean & Dean (a Firm) v Dionissiou-Moussaoui* [2011] EWCA

Civ 1332, [2011] All ER (D) 142 (Nov). Further helpful guidance on what constitutes vexatious conduct of litigation can be found in the judgment of Lord Bingham CJ in *A-G v Barker* [2000] 2 FCR 1, [2000] 1 FLR 759, at 763–4, and in *A-G v Roberts* [2005] All ER (D) 138 (Jul).

Where a tribunal is considering an award on the basis of Rule 76(1)(b) (i.e. that the claim 'had no reasonable prospect of success'), the tribunal must focus on the question of how things would have looked to the party in question at the outset of the proceedings and any relevant juncture in the course of proceedings: it should not have regard to any information which would not have been available to the party in question at the relevant point: *Radia v Jefferies International Ltd* (UKEAT/0007/18/JOJ), 21 February 2020. That said, the mere fact that there were factual disputes which could only be resolved by hearing evidence, and there was fact finding at the final hearing, did not necessarily mean that the tribunal could not properly conclude that the claim had no reasonable prospects from the outset: ibid at paras 67-69. However, if the Tribunal is able fairly to find as a fact (after giving the party an opportunity to address the point in evidence and submissions) that the party did not consider there was genuine merit in their allegations costs may be appropriate: ibid, paras 113-130.

In *Topic v Hollyland Pitta Bakery* [2012] All ER (D) 250 (Nov) (UKEAT/0523/11), the EAT confirmed that a claim can be found to have no reasonable prospects of success, and costs awarded, even if the party concerned genuinely believed in the merit of their case. There the claimant had genuinely believed she suffered discrimination, although her beliefs had no basis in reality. The genuineness of her beliefs was not relevant to whether the claim was misconceived but was relevant to the exercise of discretion whether or not to award costs, and if so, how much. There is no general principle from the above cases that an award of costs must follow when a party fails to establish a central allegation in their case: *HCA International Ltd v May-Bheemul* [2009] All ER (D) 154 (Jun). Similarly, in *Ghosh v Nokia Siemens* [2013] All ER (D) 293 (Jun) (UKEAT/0125/12) the EAT confirmed that it was not necessary to have an express finding of dishonesty before making an award of costs in respect of a large number of failed allegations of discrimination. In *Millin v Capsticks Solicitors LLP* [2014] All ER (D) 12 (Dec), [2014] UKEAT/0093/14, the EAT noted that although discrimination cases have special difficulties for a claimant arising from the personal nature of the case and the difficulties of proof, they frequently involve the consideration over a long period of time by a tribunal of many allegations, facts and documents. The EAT held "[w]here a claim is truly misconceived and should have been appreciated in advance to be so, we see no special reason why the considerable expense to which a respondent will needlessly have been put (or a claimant in a case in which a response is misconceived) should not be reimbursed in part or in whole" (para 67). In *Brooks v Nottingham University Hospitals NHS Trust* (UKEAT246/18/JOJ), 17 October 2019 the EAT (Choudhury J) observed that tribunals need not afford the same latitude to represented litigants as to litigants in person as represented litigants in person can be expected to receive appropriate advice and, if acting reasonably, to take that advice.

It is a factor relevant to the exercise of the tribunal's discretion whether to award costs that the tribunal has warned the party concerned that he is at risk of a costs order, but such a warning is not a prerequisite to the making of an order; nor is it a prerequisite that the receiving party has put the paying party on notice that there may be an application for costs. (See *Millin v Capsticks Solicitors LLP* [2014] All ER (D) 12 (Dec), [2014] UKEAT/0093/14 (para 68) and *Deer v Walford* [2011] All ER (D) 58 (May) (UKEAT/0283/10), where the respondent was awarded its full costs, following a four-day hearing, on the grounds both that the claim had been misconceived from the outset and that a deposit had been ordered on substantially the grounds that the claim failed; the award was upheld by the EAT.)In deciding whether or not award costs, the Tribunal may have regard to correspondence marked "without prejudice save as to costs", but not to other "without prejudice" material that is not so marked (unless both parties consent): *Hossaini v EDS Recruitment Ltd and anor* [2020] ICR 491.

There is no rule of public policy that prevents costs awards being made in whistleblowing claims as in other cases: *Brooks v Nottingham*, ibid.

20.130 Preparation time orders

Preparation time orders are intended to compensate a party who is not legally represented at the Hearing (or the conclusion of proceedings which do not reach a Hearing) for time spent preparing the case. This covers time spent by the receiving party personally, or (where applicable) by his employees, by a representative who is not a practising lawyer, or by a legal representative who was engaged at an earlier stage in the proceedings. Preparation time orders can be made in the same circumstances as an order for legal costs: see *Rule 76* and the commentary above.

The hourly rate is fixed by *Rule 79(2)*. The rate was initially fixed at £33 an hour, but subject to an automatic increase of £1 an hour each year. The same hourly rate applies regardless of whose time is being compensated; it will thus be the same for a claimant who had been dismissed from a job paid at the National Minimum Wage as for a solicitor engaged to prepare the case for hearing but not used to conduct the case at the Hearing.

By *Rule 79(1)*, the time allowed is what the tribunal assesses to be a reasonable and proportionate amount of time to spend on preparation having regard to such matters as the complexity of the case, the number of witnesses and the amount of documentation involved. Only time spent in preparation for the hearing will be compensated, not time spent attending the hearing itself: *Andrew v Eden College* [2011] All ER (D) 08 (Oct) (UKEAT/0438/10) and see *Rule 75(2)*.

Awards for preparation time were limited to a maximum of £10,000 but this sum was increased in line with the increase in the maximum award of costs to £20,000 (*Rule 78*). The principle that the tribunal may have regard to the paying party's means in deciding whether to make an order and if so the amount, applies equally to preparation time orders (*Rule 84*); however it is not clear how this principle is to be applied in determining the amount – in particular whether the tribunal can reduce the hourly rate, or make an award for fewer hours' preparation time, or both.

20.131 Wasted costs orders

The power to make wasted costs orders was entirely new within the tribunal system when it was introduced in 2004. The power continues to exist in the *2013 Rules*: see *Rule 80*. Equivalent provisions have existed for many years in the civil courts, where experience has been that they are rarely made, no doubt in considerable part because of the necessary procedural safeguards for representatives potentially subject to such orders.

A wasted costs order is an order against a party's representative in favour of any party where the party has incurred costs as a result of any improper, unreasonable or negligent act or omission on the part of a representative or which, in the light of any such act or omission occurring after they were incurred, the Tribunal considers it unreasonable to expect the receiving party to pay (*Rule 80(1)*).

The tribunal must exercise a discretion at two stages: it must first decide whether the circumstances render the application justified and proportionate, in which case (but only if so) it can proceed to hear the application. Having done so, there is a further discretion to be exercised whether to make an order (and in what terms).

The judgment in *Mitchells Solicitors* contains a helpful and detailed analysis of both substantive and procedural issues likely to arise on a wasted costs application. The necessity to consider first whether the application should be entertained at all was emphasised by the Court of Appeal in *Gill v Humanware Europe Ltd* [2010] EWCA Civ 799, [2010] IRLR 877, where the Court concluded that the application (which had resulted in an award of only £750) should not have been entertained at all on grounds of proportionality of the time and cost involved in determining the application. The decision is also authority for the points that normally there should be a hearing unless the parties agree to the matter being decided on the papers, particularly so where there are contested issues of fact; and that costs should only be awarded to compensate for additional costs incurred by the receiving party, not for costs that would have been incurred in any event (the costs in issue being of an appeal to the EAT). The strict causation requirement was highlighted by the EAT in *Isteed v London Borough of Redbridge* [2017] ICR D1, Simler P holding (at para 57): "As to causation, in *Ridehalgh* the Court of Appeal emphasised that the jurisdiction to make a wasted costs order extends only to impugned conduct that has caused a waste of costs and only to the extent of such wasted costs. The Court of Appeal held that demonstration of a causal link is essential and that where the conduct is proved but no waste of costs is shown to have resulted, the case may be referred to a disciplinary body or other authority, but it is not one for the exercise of the wasted costs jurisdiction."

Further helpful guidance on the procedure to be followed is given in *Godfrey Morgan Solicitors Ltd v Cobalt Systems Ltd* [2012] ICR 305 and more recently in *Single Homeless Project Ltd v Abu* (UKEAT/0519/12) and *Wentworth-Wood v Maritime Transport Ltd* (UKEAT/0184/17).

The need for causation between the act and the costs was stressed by Langstaff J in *Hafiz & Haque Solicitors v Mullick* [2015] ICR 1085. The term 'representative' is defined to exclude any representative who is not acting for profit, such as a trade union official or CAB adviser, or a representative who is employed by the party, such as a manager of the employing company (*Rule 80(3)*). However the term is not limited to legal representatives, and is expressly applied to a representative acting under a conditional fee agreement (*Rule 80(2)*). A wasted costs order can be made in favour of a party whether or not that party is legally represented and can also be made in favour of a representative's own client (*Rule 80(3)*). The procedure is set out in *Rule 82*: the application for wasted costs can be made at any stage up to 28 days after the date of the final judgment in the proceedings. There is a requirement that the tribunal must give the representative a reasonable opportunity to make oral or written representations before making a wasted costs order. In addition the tribunal may (but is not obliged to) take into account the representative's ability to pay (*Rule 84*); it is submitted that where the representative is a company or firm, it is the means of that entity, not the individual representative, that is to be considered, and it is the company or firm against which any order should be made, but these points are not made clear by the *Rules*. As with costs orders, reasons must be given if requested within 14 days of the order. The Tribunal must also inform the representative's client in writing of any proceedings for a wasted costs order and of any order made against the representative: *Rule 82*.

Wasted costs applications pose a number of potential practical difficulties. The first and most basic is that there may be a conflict of interest between a representative and his client. In these circumstances (eg where the tribunal is considering disallowing the representative's fees), the client will have to be advised to consider obtaining separate representation, and the representative will have to be given the opportunity to engage his own advocate; this will almost inevitably necessitate an adjournment of the hearing. Second, the question whether a representative was negligent may turn on what instructions were given by the client, and/or what advice was given by the representative. In the case of legal representatives, such matters are covered by legal professional privilege, which can only be waived by the client. (Non-lawyer representatives may also be subject to litigation privilege preventing them from disclosing their client's instructions without the consent of the client:

Scotthorne v Four Seasons Conservatories (UK) Ltd [2010] All ER (D) 17 (Sep) (UKEAT/0178/10).) The client will be deemed to have waived privilege if he claims wasted costs against the representative, but not in other cases, such as where the other party has made the application. The tribunal will not be able to draw inferences against the representative from the refusal of the client to waive privilege.

The leading case on wasted costs in the civil courts is *Ridehalgh v Horsefield* [1994] Ch 205, [1994] 3 All ER 848. The EAT in *Mitchells Solicitors v Funkwerk Information Technologies York Ltd* [2008] PNLR 717, [2008] All ER (D) 99 (Apr) held that the guidelines laid down in *Ridehalgh* should equally be applied by a tribunal in considering whether the make a wasted costs order. The principles to be followed are:

(a)   The wasted costs jurisdiction should only be exercised with great caution and as a last resort.

(b)   An order should only be made if the tribunal is satisfied that the representative's conduct was improper, unreasonable or negligent. (For an example of what constitutes such conduct see *Wilsons Solicitors v Johnson* [2011] ICR D21 where the failure of the claimant's solicitors to produce coherent particulars of his claims justified an order).

(c)   A legal representative should not be held to have so acted simply because of having acted for a party who has pursued a hopeless case; an order can only be made on this basis if it is shown that the representative presented a case he regarded as bound to fail, and in doing so has failed in his duty to the court, and the proceedings amounted to an abuse of process.

(d)   The tribunal must take into account that unless the representative's client has waived privilege, the representative will be likely not to be able to explain why the case has been conducted in the manner it was. Accordingly, in *Hafiz & Haque Solicitors v Mullick* [2015] ICR 1085 the EAT held that a Tribunal should be slow to conclude that representatives have insufficient material to justify pleadings or schedules of loss where legal professional privilege prevents instructions from being revealed.

(e)   It must be shown that the representative's conduct caused the person applying for costs to incur unnecessary costs.

Although the *Ridehalgh* principles indicate that the need to consider whether a representative has breached a duty to the court applies only where the alleged unreasonableness concerns the pursuing of a hopeless case, in *KL Law Ltd v Wincanton Group Ltd and anor* [2018] 5 Costs LO 639 Simler P held that this was a requirement of the wasted costs jurisdiction more generally and that the tribunal was wrong in that case to have held it could make a wasted costs order where it found the representative merely to have been negligent in relation to disclosure rather than in breach of duty to the court.

In contrast to an ordinary costs order, there is no express provision for the employment tribunal to refer the assessment of a wasted costs order made under *Rule 80* to the County Court. The tribunal itself must therefore deal with the assessment and make an order for a specified sum. So held the EAT in *Casqueiro v Barclays Bank* [2012] ICR D37, a decision under the old rules in which Slade J also observed that this may reflect a drafting oversight in the rules. It would appear likely therefore that a decision has been taken under the *2013 Rules* not to extend this power to the Tribunal.

20.132 VEXATIOUS LITIGANTS

The EAT has power, upon an application by the Attorney General, to make a restriction of proceedings order against a person who has habitually and persistently and without any reasonable ground either instituted vexatious proceedings in an employment tribunal or before the EAT (whether against the same person or against different persons), or made vexatious applications in tribunal or EAT proceedings. The effect of such an order, which may be for a limited or an indefinite period, is that employment tribunal and EAT proceedings may not be commenced or continued, and applications in such proceedings may not be made, without the leave of the EAT. The EAT may not give leave unless satisfied that the proceedings or application are not an abuse of process and that there are reasonable grounds for them; there is no appeal from a refusal of leave (*ETA 1996, s 33*).The first order made under *s 33* was made in *A-G v Wheen* [2000] IRLR 461; the decision gives guidance as to the scope of the power and how the EAT should exercise the discretion conferred by it. The order was subsequently upheld by the Court of Appeal ([2001] IRLR 91); the court rejected an argument that an order was in breach of the litigant's rights under *Art 6* of the ECHR. A useful review of the criteria for making a restriction of proceedings order can be found in the judgment in *A-G v Roberts* [2005] All ER (D) 138 (Jul).

Rule 102 of the *2013 Rules* provides for the Tribunal to provide any information or documents requested by the Attorney General, the Solicitor General, or the Lord Advocate for the purpose of preparing an application or considering whether to make an application under *Senior Courts Act 1981, s 42* (see below); *Vexatious Actions (Scotland) Act 1898, s 1*; the *Courts Reform (Scotland) Act 2014, s 100*; or *ETA 1996, s 33*. As mentioned above, the right to petition the EAT for a restriction of proceedings order only lies with the Attorney General. This contrasts with the position in the High Court where civil restraint orders ("CROs") may be sought by litigants pursuant to *Civil Procedure Rules, r 3.11* and *Practice Direction 3C*. The High Court's power to make a CRO under those statutory provisions extends only to proceedings in the High Court or County Court (although in *Vidler v UNISON* [1999] ICR 746, an Employment Tribunal decided in relation to the power within the *Senior Courts Act 1981, s 42(1A)* that "any court" included a Tribunal so that the claimant was prevented by the High Court's order from bringing proceedings in the Tribunal).

In the important decision of *Nursing & Midwifery Council v Harrold* [2015] EWHC 2254 (QB), [2016] IRLR 30, however, Elisabeth Laing J decided that the High Court had an inherent jurisdiction to make a CRO covering proceedings before the Employment Tribunal. This decision followed that in *Law Society of England and Wales v Otobo* [2011] EWHC 2264 (Ch) which highlighted the Tribunal's status as an inferior court and the inherent jurisdiction of the High Court relating to proceedings before an inferior court: see also *SCA 1981, s 42*. In the subsequent judgment in *Nursing & Midwifery Council v Harrold* [2016] EWHC 1078 (QB), [2016] IRLR 497, Elisabeth Laing J applied the statutory provisions by analogy when making a CRO covering tribunal proceedings.

Civil Restraint Orders can be limited, extended or general civil restraint orders and can be made against a party who has issued claims or made applications which are totally without merit. For an example see *London Borough of Redbridge, Governing Body of Trinity Catholic High School v Johnson* [2012] EWHC 4224 (QB); *HM Attorney General v Johnson* [2017] EWHC 979 (Admin). For the meaning of "totally without merit" see *R (Grace) v Secretary of State for the Home Department* [2014] 1 WLR 3432 and *Wasif v Secretary of State for the Home Department* [2016] EWCA Civ 82, [2016] 1 WLR 2793. In *Harrold*, Elizabeth Laing J accepted the correct test to be whether the claim was "bound to fail" and indicated that (para 139) " . . . it would be desirable for ETs, when they make decisions in weak claims, expressly to consider, and to make a finding on, the question whether the claim (or application) is TWM [totally without merit]. . . . It will greatly help to have the views of the ET on the TWM issue in any case in which a respondent to ET claims applies for a CRO in this court. It may also be that those who draft the rules governing the procedures in the ET and in the EAT may wish to give some thought to this topic." *Harrold* was followed by Jay J in *The Law Society of England and Wales v Anal Sheikh* [2018] EWHC 1644 (QB).

20.133 PROCEDURE IN CERTAIN SPECIALIST JURISDICTIONS

The procedures described above apply to proceedings covered by *Sch 1* to the *ET Regulations 2013*. Other Schedules set out complementary rules of procedure in claims involving national security (*Sch 2*) and claims for equal pay for work of equal value (*Sch 3*; see EQUAL PAY (23)). These rules of procedure should be consulted if relevant.

The Employment Tribunal also has jurisdiction to determine a variety of statutory appeals. These include appeals against an assessment to levy imposed under *s 11* of the *Industrial Training Act 1982*; an improvement notice issued under *s 21* of the *Health and Safety at Work etc Act 1974* and a prohibition notice issued under *s 22* of that *Act*; an unlawful act notice issued by the Commission for Equality and Human Rights under *s 21* of the *Equality Act 2006*; and a notice of underpayment issued under *s 19* of the *National Minimum Wage Act 1998*. In respect of such statutory appeals, *Rule 104* states that *Sch 1* applies to levy appeals for which purpose a reference to a claim and claimant shall be read as references to a levy appeal or to an appellant. *Rule 105* applies *Sch 1* to appeals against improvement and prohibition notices and *Rule 106* applies *Sch 1* to appeals against unlawful act notices. *Reg 12* of the *2013 Regulations* is clear that it is not necessary to use a prescribed ET1 form in such statutory appeals, however to enable the Tribunal to deal with appeals expeditiously and fairly, appellants should now use the form attached in the appendices to the Presidential Guidance on making a Statutory Appeal. Appellants should consult the relevant Presidential Guidance (for England and Wales, or for Scotland as appropriate) for details.

21   Employment Tribunals – III: Appeals

21.1   THE EMPLOYMENT APPEAL TRIBUNAL

Status and jurisdiction

Any appeal from a decision of an employment tribunal is heard by the Employment Appeal Tribunal ('EAT'), save for appeals in health and safety cases against improvement and prohibition notices, which go to the High Court or Court of Session, and in certain special jurisdictions outside the scope of this book. An appeal can only be brought on a point of law (see further below).

The EAT is a tribunal created by statute, and its substantive jurisdiction is statutory: *ETA 1996, s 21*. It also has both statutory (by *s 30(3) ETA 1996*) and (limited) inherent jurisdiction to regulate proceedings before it, as a superior court of record (ie of equivalent status to the High Court): see in particular *X v Stevens* [2003] IRLR 411, discussed at **21.26** below.

In addition to its appellate functions the EAT has certain limited jurisdictions as a court of first instance, in relation to information and consultation of employees; these rarely arise in practice and are not considered in detail in this chapter.

The EAT is not a 'court' within the meaning of *s 4* of the *Human Rights Act 1998*, and it therefore does not have the power to make a declaration that a statutory provision is incompatible with a Convention right guaranteed by the *Human Rights Act 1998:* see *Whittaker v Watson (P & D) (t/a P & M Watson Haulage)* [2002] ICR 1244, [2002] All ER (D) 424 (Feb), where it was suggested that in a case where there was a serious issue of compatibility the EAT should dispose of the appeal on paper, giving permission to appeal to the Court of Appeal. However, the EAT is, like other public bodies, subject to the duty to give effect to Convention rights imposed by *section 3* of the *Act*: see eg *EF v AB* [2015] IRLR 619 (imposition of a permanent restriction on identifying parties to protect privacy rights).

The EAT is a single appellate court which sits in divisions and may sit anywhere in Great Britain (in fact, it normally sits in London and Edinburgh, and occasionally also in Cardiff). Both judicial and lay members may, and occasionally do, sit in both principal centres. Following questions being raised by some commentators as to how far a decision of the EAT given in Scotland binds English tribunals, and vice versa, the status and effect of decisions was the subject of a public statement by its then President, Morison J, on 3 April 1998 ([1998] IRLR 435). The statement makes it clear that all tribunals are equally bound by decisions of any division of the EAT wherever given.

Despite the foregoing, the EAT sitting in England or Wales is not formally bound by decisions of the Court of Session on appeals from the EAT sitting in Scotland, and the EAT sitting in Scotland is not bound by decisions of the Court of Appeal on appeals from the EAT in England or Wales. The consequences of this were starkly demonstrated in *Marshalls Clay Products Ltd v Caulfield* [2003] IRLR 552, a case on 'rolled up' holiday pay under the *Working Time Regulations 1998,* where the EAT refused to follow a decision of the Court of Session (*MPB Structures Ltd v Munro* [2002] IRLR 601); the Court of Appeal ([2003] IRLR 350) held that it had been entitled to do so, and that its decision was right, thereby raising the prospect of a different interpretation of the same legislation binding tribunals north and south of the border. A further example of an apparent conflict is between the decisions of the EAT sitting in England (on the interpretation of the *Fixed-term Employees (Prevention of Less Favourable Treatment) Regulations 2002*) in *Sharma v Manchester City Council* [2008] IRLR 336 and *Carl v University of Sheffield* [2009] IRLR 616, and the earlier decision of the Inner House in *McMenemy v Capita Business Services plc* [2007] IRLR 400, reaching a different interpretation, which appears not to have been drawn to the attention of the EAT in *Sharma* but was in *Carl*. The only way to resolve such differences is by way of further appeal to the Supreme Court, a United Kingdom Court, whose decisions are binding in both jurisdictions, or, as happened in the *Marshalls Clay Products* case, by a reference to the CJEU (see *Robinson-Steele v RD Retail Services Ltd*: C-131/04 [2006] ECR I-2531, [2006] IRLR 386, [2006] ICR 932, a decision supporting the Scottish approach).

Decisions of the EAT are not formally binding on the EAT itself. They are normally followed, even if in a later case the EAT has doubts about the correctness of the previous decision, unless the EAT is satisfied after argument that the first decision is clearly wrong, or there are exceptional circumstances; see for a full review of the circumstances in which a prior EAT decision may not be followed *British Gas Trading Ltd v Lock* (2016) UKEAT/0189/15, [2016] IRLR 316, [2016] All ER (D) 273 (Feb), EAT. However, on occasion the EAT has overruled a previous decision; good examples are *Woodward v Abbey National plc* [2005] IRLR 782, overruling *Clark v Midland Packaging Ltd* [2005] 2 All ER 266, on the question when a Notice of Appeal is taken as received by the EAT, and *OTG Ltd v Barke* [2011] IRLR 272, overruling *Oakland v Wellswood (Yorkshire) Ltd* [2009] IRLR 250, on whether the exception in *reg 8(7)* of the *Transfer of Undertakings (Protection of Employment) Regulations 2006* applied to a company in administration. (The *Barke* decision was subsequently held by the Court of Appeal to be correct: *Key2Law (Surrey) LLP v De'Antiquis* [2012] IRLR 212.)

In addition, the range of representation means that the EAT's attention is not always drawn to relevant reported decisions, resulting on occasion in mutually inconsistent decisions, which the EAT in a subsequent case must choose between; this problem has become greater since the unreported decisions of the EAT have become publicly available on its website (https ://www.gov.uk/employment-appeal-tribunal-decisions; in addition, all final judgments of the EAT issued since 1992 are now freely available on www.bailii.org).

21.2   Questions of Law

The jurisdiction of the EAT to hear appeals from decisions of employment tribunals is conferred principally by *ETA 1996, s 21*. This provides that an appeal lies to the EAT on any question of law arising from any decision of, or arising in any proceedings before, an employment tribunal under any of a large number of statutory provisions listed in the section (see **21.10** below on the question who is entitled to institute an appeal). The statutory nature of the EAT's jurisdiction, the itemisation of the statutory provisions in s 21, and the proliferation of statutes and regulations conferring additional jurisdictions on employment tribunals, has led on occasions to errors of drafting being found to have failed to confer jurisdiction on the EAT over a particular class of appeal; an example is appeals concerning the statutory right of accompaniment under the *Employment Relations Act 1999, s 10* (*Refreshment Systems Ltd (t/a Northern Vending Services) v Wolstenholme* [2004] All ER (D) 185 (Mar) (UKEAT/608/03)). This oversight was corrected by the *Employment Relations Act 2004, s 38*.

However subject to this point (which has arisen only very infrequently) any decision of an employment tribunal or judge which determines a claim or issue in the case is in principle open to appeal, not just a formal judgment or decision given after a hearing. Even a failure to act, or delay in making a decision, may be the subject of an appeal: see *Paw v HM Revenue and Customs*, (UKEATPA/0703/11), where HHJ McMullen QC held that a letter written on the instructions of a judge stating that the tribunal could not give advice and stating the procedure for making a complaint could be the subject of an appeal if a point of law could be identified, as the letter arose in the course of proceedings before the tribunal. However, the EAT has no jurisdiction to entertain an appeal against incidental findings of fact adverse to the appellant, as these are not 'decisions' within *s 21*: see *Wolfe v North Middlesex University Hospital NHS Trust* [2015] ICR 960, [2015] All ER (D) 195 (May), and **21.16** below. *Para 2.1* of the *2018 Practice Direction* provides that "the parties must expect any decision of fact made by the Employment Tribunal, Certification Officer or Central Arbitration Committee to be decisive".

In addition an appeal which has become entirely academic is likely to be rejected as an abuse of process: *TIC International Ltd v Ali* (UKEAT/0284/15).

21.3   Fees

During the period from 29 July 2013 to 26 July 2017, fees of £400 were charged for the presentation of appeals to the EAT, with a further fee of £1,200 payable before the full hearing of an appeal presented on or after 29 July 2013: see the *Employment Tribunals and the Employment Appeal Tribunal (Fees) Order 2013*. However the Supreme Court in *R (on the application of UNISON) v Lord Chancellor* [2017] UKSC 51, [2017] IRLR 911, [2017] ICR 1037 held that the Fees Order was unlawful, and it was quashed in its entirety. With effect from the date of that judgment (26 July 2017), therefore, no fees are chargeable in connection with proceedings in the EAT (whether commenced before or after the Supreme Court's decision).

21.4   Composition

The composition of the EAT has traditionally mirrored that of the employment tribunals. Until relatively recently this meant that the great majority of full appeals were heard by a panel of both judicial and lay members, but for appeals referred to a full hearing since 25 June 2013, all hearings are before a judicial member sitting alone unless the EAT has directed that there be a full panel with lay members; see further below. There is a pool of 10 High Court Judges and 6 Deputy High Court Judges.

The judicial members of the EAT are High Court or Circuit Judges, with one High Court Judge appointed as President for three years at a time. One Court of Session judge is also allocated to the EAT and presides over most Scottish, and some English, appeals. The lay members are formally appointed by the Queen on the recommendation of the Lord Chancellor and the Secretary of State (*ETA 1996, s 22(1)(c)*), and are selected for their experience in employment matters. They are generally very senior and experienced in their respective fields. The Judicial Appointments Commission has since 2006 been responsible for selection of candidates for lay membership in England and Wales.

21.5   The position before June 2013 was that the EAT normally sat in divisions of three, although there was (and still is) is provision for a panel of five (one judicial member and two from each of the panels of lay members). Full appeals from decisions of employment tribunals constituted of an employment judge sitting with lay members were required to be heard by a judge sitting with lay members. Where the decision under appeal was taken by an employment judge sitting alone, the appeal would usually be heard by a judge alone, but with a discretion, albeit rarely exercised, to constitute a full panel of three for such cases (*ETA 1996, s 28(4)*).

The Government in November 2011 announced a significant change in the composition of the EAT, as part of the package of reforms of the employment tribunal system which were the subject of consultations earlier that year. The change was implemented by the *Enterprise and Regulatory Reform Act 2013, s 12*, with effect from 25 June 2013 (with an exception for appeals 'in the process of being heard' on that date). *Section 12* removes the requirement for the EAT to be constituted with lay members altogether, replacing this with a discretion to convene a panel with lay members for specific cases. Even before this change, the increased number of cases heard in the employment tribunals by an employment judge sitting alone had already resulted in a considerable increase in the proportion of appeals heard by a judge sitting alone, a trend accentuated by the change in the composition of employment tribunals for hearings since 6 April 2012, whereby unfair dismissal cases are heard by an employment judge sitting alone, unless the discretion to order a full tribunal under *ETA 1996, s 4(5)* has been exercised or the claim includes another claim which requires to be heard by a full tribunal.

The practice of the EAT has been to use the power to order a full panel in cases where the judge considering the papers anticipates that the issues in the appeal are such that the judge hearing the appeal will be assisted by the contribution made by lay members with considerable experience of the working environment. An example of a case in which judicial discretion was exercised to order a full panel is *McGrath v Ministry of Justice* [2015] All ER (D) 71 (Apr) (UKEAT/0247/14), an appeal by a lay member of the employment tribunal claiming that his work was comparable with that of employment judges for the purposes of the *Part Time Workers (Prevention of Less Favourable Treatment) Regulations 2000*. Under provisions contained in the *Prisons and Courts Bill 2017*, the Senior President of Tribunals would be given powers to determine the composition of the EAT for particular classes of appeal. However this Bill lapsed on the dissolution of Parliament following the announcement of a General Election in June 2017, and had not, as at 1 May 2018, been reintroduced.

In addition, issues arising in the EAT after a notice of appeal has been lodged but prior to the full hearing of an appeal have for many years been determined by a judicial member (often the President) sitting alone. Such matters include hearings for directions (when held) and appeals from decisions of the Registrar on preliminary points taken under *rule 20* (eg on extending time for a Notice of Appeal). References under *rule 3(10)* arising from a decision that an appeal should not be admitted at the preliminary sift (see below for this) have since the introduction of this procedure also been required to be heard by a Judge alone; such cases have become increasingly common following a tightening of the practice of rejecting apparently hopeless appeals at the sift stage.

Where an appeal is required to be heard by a panel of three, the hearing may proceed in the absence of one of the lay members, but only with the agreement of all parties to the appeal (*ETA 1996, s 28(3)*). The Court of Appeal has ruled that it is a prerequisite to proceeding under this rule that the parties are informed as to which of the panels (employer or employee) the missing member belongs to: *De Haney v Brent Mind* [2003] EWCA Civ 1637, [2004] ICR 348, [2003] All ER (D) 444 (Oct).

Legal aid was in the past available to individuals for appeals from employment tribunals, subject to the normal conditions, although in practice it was very rarely granted. However with effect from 1 April 2013 the *Legal Aid, Sentencing and Punishment of Offenders Act 2012* removed this facility for cases in England and Wales. Legal aid is, however, still available for appeals in Scotland.

21.6 Practice and administration

The abolition of the Tribunal fees regime provoked a 30% increase in the number of appeals in the year from April 2018 to 2019.

A significant proportion of potential appeals are screened out at the preliminary sift (see **21.17** for an explanation of this) and are never registered as full appeals.

21.7 The procedures of the EAT are regulated by *Rules* made under the *ETA 1996 s 30*; the current rules are the *Employment Appeal Tribunal Rules 1993 (SI 1993/2854)* (the '*EAT Rules*') as amended, most recently by the *Employment Appeal Tribunal (Amendment) Rules 2013 (SI 2013/1693)*. The changes made by the 2013 amendments address the introduction of fees for appeals (see **21.3** above; there has been no formal amendment to the Rules to remove these provisions, but they are no longer effective following the Supreme Court decision that fees in the EAT were unlawful) and a tightening of the procedure for further appeals after a Notice of Appeal has been rejected at the sift stage.

As part of the process of regulating its own procedure, and also as a means to improve the appellate process, the EAT has from time to time issued Practice Directions. The presently applicable *Practice Direction* was issued on 19 December 2018 ([2019] IRLR 221). The text of the *2018 Practice Direction* is available on the EAT website (now part of the Judicial website, www.justice.gov.uk), and it is strongly advised that this be read carefully by anyone involved as a party to an appeal or as a representative. It applies to all appeals, whenever instituted. The EAT has however held that it is not mandatory for the EAT to follow the Practice Direction, and in the event of any inconsistency between its provisions and those of the EAT Rules, it is the latter which prevail: *Zinda v Governing Body of Barn Hill Community High* [2011] ICR 174.

The President of the EAT may also issue *Practice Statements* for the guidance of practitioners; a *Practice Statement* issued by Langstaff P on 17 April 2012 gives guidance on applications to admit fresh evidence, and the citation of authorities, and a further *Practice Statement* was issued on 13 May 2015 dealing with the format and length of Notices of Appeal and Skeleton Arguments. *Practice Statements* are posted on the EAT's website. The 2012 *Statement* included the announcement that copies of the most commonly cited authorities would be available for reference at all EAT hearings and copies need not therefore be provided by the parties; a list of these authorities is annexed to the President's *Statement* on the EAT website. The 2015 Statement stresses the importance of representatives marking up bundles of authorities to highlight the passages to be relied on.

The *Practice Directions* of 2002 and 2004 introduced significant changes in procedure, including the adoption of the Overriding Objective (see **21.14** below and **20.1** above) and a duty for parties to co-operate with the EAT in achieving it, new obligations on the parties (rather than, as hitherto, the staff of the EAT) to prepare and submit the documentation to be considered at each appeal, and new 'tracks' to which different categories of appeal are allocated. All of these features are retained in the *2013 Practice Direction*. The Overriding Objective was formally incorporated into the *EAT Rules* in 2004.

21.8   Administratively the EAT falls within the responsibilities of HM Courts and Tribunals Service (an agency of the Ministry of Justice and the successor to the Tribunals Service) but it remains separate from those appellate tribunals which have been grouped together into Chambers of the Upper Tribunal, starting from November 2008, under the reforms to the tribunal system generally introduced by the *Tribunals, Courts and Enforcement Act 2007*. Ministerial responsibility for the EAT Rules lies, rather confusingly, with BEIS; as noted above, this will transfer to the Tribunal Procedure Committee if the proposals in the *Prisons and Courts Bill 2017* are reintroduced.

The position of the EAT in Scotland is also somewhat anomalous, as HMCTS is responsible principally for the Courts and tribunals in England and Wales, but also for tribunals with jurisdiction in non-devolved areas of the law, including the EAT. One of the proposals made by the Smith Commission in November 2014 was for the devolution of the administration of reserved tribunals (including the EAT, as well as employment tribunals) to the Scottish Parliament. Powers to bring this proposal into effect by Order in Council are given in *s 39* of the *Scotland Act 2016*, which amends the restrictions on the powers of the Scottish Parliament contained in *Schedule 5* to the *Scotland Act 1998*. Initial proposals for the exercise of this power were issued for consultation by the Scottish Government in early 2016, but have not been implemented.

21.9   APPEALS

The procedure for appeals to the EAT is governed by the *EAT Rules*, as amended, supplemented by the *2018 Practice Direction*. The *EAT Rules* also contain modifications to the procedure for appeals in the (very infrequent) cases where the modified procedure for national security cases in *Sch 2* to the *ET Regulations* applies. These modifications are too specialised to be covered in detail in this chapter.

As part of the consultation preceding the making of the *2004 Amendment Rules*, the DTI solicited views on whether a statutory requirement should be introduced that permission would be required to appeal to the EAT; however this proposal was widely opposed and was not pursued (and was not resurrected in the January 2011 consultation paper on tribunal reform issued by its successor, BIS). Instead, however, a new procedure was introduced for weeding out obviously hopeless appeals without a hearing. This was introduced by amendments made in 2004 to the EAT Rules, with associated changes in the Practice Direction. This sifting procedure has been further tightened by amendments to the EAT Rules made in July 2013 (see **21.17** below for details of the sift).

21.10   Who may appeal?

Any party to the proceedings in an employment tribunal may appeal against an adverse decision (for the scope of what decisions may be the subject of an appeal see **21.2** above). Those who may appeal include a respondent to the original claim who has not presented a response, or whose response was not accepted by the tribunal (eg because it was out of time) and who has therefore not been permitted to take part in the proceedings: *Atos Origin IT Services UK Ltd v Haddock* [2005] ICR 277, [2005] IRLR 20, EAT; *Butlins Skyline Ltd v Beynon* [2007] ICR 121 (and see the *Practice Direction, para 19*, for the procedural steps required of such an appellant); and a claimant whose Claim Form has been rejected, either by an Employment Judge or by the secretariat, and who wishes to appeal against its rejection: see respectively for appeals against rejection by an Employment Judge and by the secretariat *Richardson v U Mole Ltd* [2005] IRLR 668 and *Grant v In 2 Focus Sales Development Services Ltd* [2007] All ER (D) 281 (Jan), EAT.

The right to appeal is not limited to parties to the proceedings from which an appeal is pursued. *Section 21* of the *Employment Tribunals Act 1996* gives the EAT jurisdiction to entertain appeals from decisions of employment tribunals, without specifying who may bring the appeal. The EAT confirmed in *Martineau v Ministry of Justice* [2015] ICR 1122 that this meant that a non party could in principle bring an appeal. The EAT commented that whilst it would usually be an abuse of process for a third party to bring an appeal (and any such appeal would be struck out for that reason) there could be circumstances in which a non-party had a sufficient interest to bring the appeal. In the instant case a large number of similar claims had been brought, and a lead claimant identified for a hearing. The lead claimant decided not to appeal against the rejection of his claim, but one of the other claimants, whose claim stood to be dismissed in consequence of the rejection of the lead claim, brought an appeal. The EAT held that it had jurisdiction to hear the appeal, and should do so in these circumstances. Another example of a non-party having a sufficient interest in the proceedings to be permitted to appeal would be a press organisation aggrieved at the terms of an order restricting the reporting of the tribunal's judgment.

21.11   Institution and content of appeals

Appeals to the EAT must be instituted by presenting a Notice of Appeal on, or substantially in accordance with the prescribed form (Form 1) to the EAT within 42 days from the date on which the written reasons were sent to the parties or, in a case where the reasons for the judgment were not reserved and written reasons were not requested when the judgment and reasons were given orally or within 14 days thereafter, within 42 days of the judgment being sent to the parties. An appeal from an order or other decision not in the form of a judgment must be presented within 42 days of the date of the order etc (*rule 3(3)*). For the purpose of calculating the 42 day period, the date of the judgment appealed against does not count, so that if for instance that date is a Friday, the last date for lodging an appeal is the Friday 6 weeks later (by 4 pm – see below).

A notice of appeal may be delivered to the EAT "by any method" (see *2018 Practice Direction, Para 3.1*).

The requirement for presentation means that the Notice of Appeal must be received by the EAT within the prescribed time. *Rule 37(1A)* requires that any act required to be done on or before a particular day must be done before 4 pm on that day; this includes the lodging of a Notice of Appeal: *Woodward v Abbey National plc* [2005] IRLR 782. It was also held in that case that the whole of the documentation required as part of a Notice of Appeal must be received by the EAT office by the deadline; this means that an appeal submitted by fax is only in time if the whole of the fax has been received on the EAT machine by 4 pm on the final day. With this important proviso, service may be by fax as well as by post or personal delivery; there is as yet no formal provision in the *EAT Rules* permitting a Notice of Appeal (or other documents) to be served by email, but the EAT website confirms that appeals may be lodged by email (with the required accompanying documents attached) and this method of service is now routine. However appellants should be aware that the EAT has limited capacity to receive large scanned documents, and the alternative of sending an electronic link to the documents required to be lodged is not accepted: see further **21.14** below. In *Patel v South Tyneside Council* (UKEATPA/0917/11), the EAT ruled that an appeal submitted by email was validly presented when the appellant received a 'successful delivery' notification from Daemon, the host server for the EAT, although no trace of the Notice of Appeal could be found at the EAT itself.

The EAT Rules permit service of notices, including a Notice of Appeal, at any office of the EAT (there are only two, in London and Edinburgh), so technically, and in contrast to the position governing presentation of a claim, a Notice of Appeal would be validly lodged if received in time at the Scottish office in respect of an appeal from a tribunal in England, and vice versa. However, it is not sufficient that the Notice of Appeal is sent in error to the tribunal whose decision is to be appealed, if it is not in fact received by the EAT within the applicable time limit, and such an error is unlikely to be considered a sufficient reason to extend time: *Pierre-Davis v North West London Hospitals NHS Trust* (UKEATPA/1496/08). In practice appeals should always be sent to the office in the country in which the decision under appeal was taken, and are then administered by that office. There is no separate office in Wales, although a limited number of appeals from tribunals sitting in Wales are heard in Cardiff; the appropriate EAT office for appeals from Wales is the London office. The London address is now Rolls Building, 7 Rolls Building, Fetter Lane, London, EC4A 1NL . The telephone number is 0207 273 1041. The new email address is LondonEAT @Justice.gov.uk.

The date from which time for appealing starts to run is the day after the date on which the judgment or reasons is or are sent to the parties or, in the case of an order, the day following the date of the order; the applicable date is recorded on the document containing the judgment, reasons or order itself. 'Sent' means sent and not received: *Gdynia America Shipping Lines (London) Ltd v Chelminski* [2004] EWCA Civ 871, [2004] IRLR 725, [2004] ICR 1523. A decision is treated as having been sent on the day the document was actually sent by the tribunal office, even if is never received, for instance because it was sent to the wrong address: *Carroll v Mayor's Office for Policing and Crime* [2015] ICR 835, [2015] All ER (D) 209 (Feb). The only recourse of a party wishing to appeal who does not get to see the decision until very near the end of the 42 day period (as in the *Dodd* case: see **21.14** below), or after it has expired, is to apply for an extension of time, which will only be granted if the prospective appellant acted with due diligence when he or she became aware that the decision had been sent out.

The period for lodging an appeal is automatically extended to the next working day if it expires on a day on which the offices of the EAT are closed; in practice this will only apply to public holidays, since it is not the practice of tribunals to make orders or send out judgments on a Saturday or Sunday.

21.12 Format and Content of the Notice of Appeal

There is a prescribed form for Notices of Appeal, Form 1, set out in the *Schedule* to the *EAT Rules*. It was stated in an early case that the use of a document other than the prescribed form will be permitted only in exceptional cases (*Martin v British Railways Board* [1989] IRLR 198, [1989] ICR 24); however, in practice this requirement is no longer enforceable, not least since there is as yet no online version of the Form; it is sufficient that the Notice of Appeal, in whatever format submitted, contains the information required to complete Form 1 and is accompanied by the required documents.

The *2018 Practice Direction* sets out requirements (and some pointed advice) as to how grounds of appeal should be identified:

'3.6 Notices of appeal should set out the grounds relied on in numbered paragraphs, in line with the forms set out in the [*EAT Rules*], Rule 3 and Schedule.

3.7 A point of law should be easy to identify in a few words. Whatever the paragraph numbering of the surrounding text is, the grounds of appeal themselves:

3.7.1 should begin with the heading "Numbered Grounds" and be numbered consecutively, starting at (1);

3.7.2 each be headed by a brief description – underlined or in bold or both – of the points of law relied upon (e.g. "Misinterpreted Section XX of the Equality Act 2010"; "Reached a decision on a point which had not been argued"; etc) followed only by what is needed to enable a Judge of the EAT to understand the point and identify what the error of law(s) is/are said to be;

3.7.3 should (except in the case of appeals alleging either perversity or bias) usually occupy in total no more than 2 sides of A4 paper – a well-directed notice of appeal is usually more persuasive than along one, and in general, the more points raised the more it suggests that none is a good one;

3.7.4 in the case of appeals alleging either perversity or bias, or both, should comply with [the specific guidance given elsewhere in the *2018 Practice Direction*];

3.7.5 should not include any quotation from either the Tribunal judgment under appeal (which can and will be read by the EAT) or any authority (though if it is important and relevant to refer to an authority, the reference should allow it to be identified, and the relevant page and paragraph number should be stated);

3.7.6 should not contain any footnote, nor incorporate any other document."

Any introductory or explanatory text considered necessary should also be brief. The *2018 Practice Direction* warns that a Notice of Appeal that gives insufficient grounds of, or lacks clarity in identifying, a point of law, or fails to comply with the directions may be sent back to be re-submitted, with adverse consequences, including the possibility of the appellant being made to attend a hearing to persuade the EAT there are reasonable grounds for appeal and a possible liability for costs, for any consequential delay (*Para 3.9*)

It is however important that each of the grounds for the appeal that the appellant intends to rely on are clearly set out. The *2018 Practice Direction* makes it clear (*para 3.10*) that there is no automatic right to add to or amend grounds of appeal, and permission to pursue a ground of appeal may be refused if it has not been set out in the original Notice of Appeal; even if permission to amend is given, there may be adverse costs consequences for the appellant. Delay in applying to amend a Notice of Appeal is likely to lead to permission to amend being refused; for a detailed review of considerations affecting applications to amend see **21.27** below. On the other hand a Notice of Appeal is not the same as the skeleton argument that is usually required for the appeal hearing itself.

21.13 Documentation to be submitted with the Notice of Appeal

In addition to the Notice of Appeal, the appellant must submit (i) a copy of the judgment, decision, or order which is the subject of the appeal; (ii) a copy of the written reasons for that judgment, decision or order, if any; (iii) in the case of an appeal against a judgment, if written reasons are not enclosed, an explanation of why not; and (iv) also in the case of an appeal against a judgment copies of the claim and response forms (ET1 and ET3) or an explanation of why they are not included (*EAT Rules, rule 3(1)*). Form 1 also specifies the additional documentation required where there has been an application to review the decision the subject of the Notice of Appeal (see below). If there are no written reasons for the judgment being appealed, the appellant must include in the Notice of Appeal an application for the EAT to exercise its discretion to hear the appeal without written reasons, or to request the tribunal to supply them (*2018 Practice Direction, para 3.4*).

A *Practice Statement* issued by the President in February 2005 ([2005] IRLR 189) makes it clear that all the required documentation must be received by the EAT in order for an appeal to be treated as lodged; so, for instance, if the judgment under appeal and any written reasons are not submitted by the deadline, the Notice of Appeal will be treated as out of time. If two or more cases initially presented on separate ET1s are heard together, each of the ET1s and, if applicable, ET3s, must be enclosed with the Notice of Appeal, or an explanation given for not enclosing them; if this is not done the Notice of Appeal will be treated as not properly constituted, and will be rejected: see *Carroll v Mayor's office for Policing and Crime* [2015] ICR 835, [2015] All ER (D) 209 (Feb).

The requirement for all the documentation to be lodged within the time limit for appealing is very strictly applied: in *Woods v Suffolk Mental Health Partnership NHS Trust*, (UKEATPA/0360/06), an extension of time was refused where the Notice of Appeal was submitted on the last day with an incomplete copy of the claim form, and the missing pages were not received until after the time for appealing had expired; the refusal of an extension of time was subsequently upheld by the Court of Appeal ([2007] EWCA Civ 1180). Occasionally a more lenient view may be taken of failure to include all documents, as in *Singh-Rathour v Taylor* (UKEATPA/0879/10) [2011] All ER (D) 64 (May), where a respondent appealing a costs order failed to include the response forms of other respondents to the original proceedings who had no interest in the appeal, and *Hine v Talbot* (UKEATPA/1783/10), where the documents had been scanned and emailed to the EAT but two pages of the judgment had been fed through the scanner together; see also *Desmond v Cheshire West and Chester Council*, at **21.14** below. However, it would be very unwise to rely on such an exercise of leniency occurring. If the Notice of Appeal is submitted by email, the documents which are required to be sent together with it must be sent as an attachment; it is not acceptable to provide a link to documents contained in a file elsewhere, such as a Dropbox zip file: see *Majekodunmi v City Facilities Management UK Ltd* [2016] ICR D5 (UKEATPA/0157/15). It may be necessary, if the accompanying documents are lengthy, to send them as attachments to a series of emails; in that case all the emails and attachments must be received by 4.00 pm on the last date for receipt of the appeal: see the facts of *J v K and L* (UKEATPA/0661/16).

If there has been an application for a reconsideration of the judgment under appeal, the application, and if available the judgment or order determining it, must be included with the Notice of Appeal (*Practice Direction, para 3.2*), but it appears from the wording of the *Practice Direction* that failure to do so will not lead to the appeal being treated as not validly lodged.

21.14   Time limits and extension of time

Appeals against orders, directions or decisions (which fall short of being judgments) must be instituted within 42 days of the date of the relevant order, direction or decision. The EAT treats a Tribunal's refusal to make an order, direction or decision as itself constituting one. The relevant date is the date recorded on the order, direction or decision as the date it was sent to the parties (*2018 Practice Direction, Para 4.2*).

Appeals against judgments must be instituted within 42 days of the date on which the written record of the Judgment was sent to the parties, subject to four exceptional cases: (1) where written reasons were requested orally at the hearing before the Tribunal; (2) where written reasons were requested in writing within 14 days of the date on which the written record of the judgment was sent to the parties; (3) where the Tribunal itself reserved its reasons and gave them subsequently in writing; or (4) where a request to the Tribunal for written reasons is made out of time and granted. In each of those four cases, the appeal must be instituted within 42 days from the date when written reasons were sent to the parties (*2018 Practice Direction, Para 4.3*).

The time limit for instituting appeals is very strictly enforced (see eg *Mock v IRC* [1999] IRLR 785: last minute failure of computer of counsel preparing the Notice of Appeal not sufficient excuse for appeal being lodged one day late; *Woodward v Abbey National plc* [2005] IRLR 782: last page of faxed Notice not received until 4.06 pm on final day for appealing; extension only allowed because previous authority had suggested it was sufficient if the *first* page arrived in time). Every appeal lodged out of time must be accompanied by an application for an extension of time under *EAT Rules, rule 37* setting out the reasons for the delay. The time limit for an appeal applies even though there may be a pending application to the tribunal to reconsider its decision (*Practice Direction, para 5.4*). Nor is the fact that an application for public funding for the appeal is pending a reason for exceeding the time limit: *2018 Practice Direction, para 4.8*.

The strict approach to the time limit adopted by the EAT has been upheld by the Court of Appeal, notwithstanding that a less rigorous approach applies to appeals to that court: *Aziz v Bethnal Green City Challenge Co Ltd* [2000] IRLR 111; *Jurkowska v Hlmad Ltd* [2008] EWCA Civ 231, [2008] IRLR 430 (where, however, a decision to grant an extension of time of 33 minutes in respect of a missing accompanying document was upheld on the particular facts: see further below for this).

General guidance as to the criteria for allowing appeals out of time has been given in *United Arab Emirates v Abdelghafar* [1995] IRLR 243, [1995] ICR 65, a decision endorsed by the Court of Appeal in *Jurkowska* (and see *2018 Practice Direction, para 4.7*). The principles re-summarised by the EAT in *Muschett v Hounslow London Borough Council* [2009] ICR 424, and again, in more detail, in *J v K and L* (UKEATPA/0661/16).

In summary, the principles to be applied are that:

(a)   There is an interest in the finality of litigation, so stricter rules apply at the appeal stage than before a case has been heard. Adherence to the 42 day time limit is fundamental, and compliance essential.

(b)   The grant of an extension of time is an indulgence, and will only be granted in rare and exceptional cases.

(c)   Generally speaking no distinction is drawn between an unrepresented litigant and one with professional representation (but if a legal adviser has been at fault that may be a relevant consideration).

(d)   Neither ignorance of the time limit, nor failure within the time limit to assemble the relevant documents, justifies a relaxation of the time limit.

(e)   The EAT must first be satisfied that it has been given a full, honest and acceptable explanation for the delay in submitting the appeal (or documents omitted).

(f)   The EAT will have regard to the length of the delay, but the crucial issue is the excuse, or explanation, for the delay. Consequently, the whole period from the date of the decision under appeal must be considered.

(g)   The merits of the appeal are rarely relevant (but if it is clear that the appeal raises no point of law, an extension will be refused).

(h)   Lack of prejudice to the other party will not normally be a relevant factor in favour of extending time (but any prejudice to the proposed respondent *would* be a factor against an extension).

(i)   The foregoing points are guidelines, not intended to fetter the discretion of the Registrar and Judge in each case.

The EAT has rejected in terms an argument that these criteria for the application of the time limit for appeals are inconsistent with the Overriding Objective: *Waller v Bromsgrove District Council* (UKEATPA/0019/07). Indeed, the objective of the overriding objective is to secure the efficient handling and disposal of disputes. Compliance with time limits helps to further that aim.

The decision of the Court of Appeal, *O'Cathail v Transport for London* [2012] EWCA Civ 1004, [2012] IRLR 1011, affirms the established approach, emphasising also that whilst the length of the extension of time sought is relevant, the primary focus is on whether there is a good excuse for the delay, that the strict requirement to lodge in time applies equally to the requirement to lodge all the specified accompanying documents as to the Notice of Appeal itself, and that the EAT must balance the interests of both parties. The Court in that case upheld the refusal by the EAT of a one day extension to validate the late submission of the judgment and reasons of the employment tribunal, despite the fact that the appellant, acting in person, was disabled and had suffered a panic attack on the final day for submission of the appeal.

For examples of exceptional circumstances held by the EAT to justify an extension of time, see *Dodd v Bank of Tokyo–Mitsubishi Ltd*, [2005] All ER (D) 74 (Dec) (tribunal judgment not received by appellant's solicitor until the 42nd day following its issue); *Jurkowska* (solicitors for appellant had not received judgment and mistakenly believed reasons, issued later, included the judgment; this decision was upheld by the Court of Appeal); *Hakim v Italia Conti Academy of Theatre Arts* (UKEATPA/1444/08) (application supported by medical evidence of claimant's dyslexia); *Hancocks v Cambian Education Services Ltd* (UKEATPA/0824/10) [2011] All ER (D) 64 (May) (combination of appellant's ignorance of right of appeal and misleading information given by employment tribunal office) and *Farmer v Heart of Birmingham Teaching Primary Care Trust* (UKEATPA/0896/14) (final attachment received 10 minutes late after a series of unusual and unforeseeable problems followed by internet failure).

A further example of the exercise of discretion on exceptional facts is *Desmond v Cheshire West and Chester Council* (UKEATPA/0027/12), where the appellant had tried to submit his appeal electronically on day 41 but it had been rejected because the attached files were too large for the EAT server to accept, and he then resubmitted the appeal with an electronic link to the ET1 and judgment, unaware of the EAT policy of not accepting documents sent via links (albeit the policy is stated on the EAT website). However, in *Majekodunmi v City Facilities Management UK Ltd* [2016] ICR D5 (UKEATPA/0157/15) an extension of time was refused where the prospective appellant had submitted the Notice of Appeal by email with a link to a Dropbox zip file containing the required additional documentation; the documentation had not been 'received' at the point when the link was notified, as it would have been if sent in an attachment with the email attaching the Notice of Appeal.

In *Peters v Sat Katar Co Ltd* [2003] IRLR 574, the Court of Appeal allowed an appeal against a refusal to extend time where a litigant in person had posted her Notice of Appeal 14 days before the deadline but it had been lost in the post. It was, in the Court's view, not reasonable to expect an unrepresented party to realise the need to check with the EAT that the Notice had been received. However, it is very unlikely that this much indulgence would be shown to a professionally represented party.

Some indulgence may be given to an appellant who has greater difficulty appealing because of a disability, but even in such cases a very strict approach is taken: see *Lungu t/a Len Fowler Trophies v Shell (deceased)* (UKEATPA/1178/14) (appellant blind but had software that enabled him to 'read' Word documents: not entitled to extension so that time only ran from when a braille copy of judgment received). In *J v K and L* (above), the appellant was refused an extension of an hour despite disabilities including being HIV positive, as the EAT was not satisfied that his disabilities prevented him from submitting a timely appeal.

An appeal out of time will not necessarily be permitted merely because a decision of a higher court has changed what was generally understood to be the law in favour of the intending appellant: *Setiya v East Yorkshire Health Authority* [1995] IRLR 348, [1995] ICR 799.

Exceptionally a short extension may be granted where there is a wider public interest in the issue raised by the appeal: *Ministry of Justice v Burton* (UKEATPA/1215/14) (no good reason for being 11 minutes out of time, but case was a test case the outcome of which would determine a large number of other pending claims).

The Registrar of the EAT will determine any application for an extension of time to validate the Notice of Appeal or Respondent's Answer/cross-appeal (see below for these) on the basis of written representations from the parties (*Practice Direction, para 5.6*). Any party aggrieved by the Registrar's decision (including a respondent to the appeal, if the decision is to extend time) may appeal to a judge of the EAT within five days of the date the Registrar's decision is sent to the parties (*EAT Rules, rule 21; Practice Direction, para 6.3*). Appeals against decisions of the Registrar not to extend time are by way of a re-hearing, and evidence may be (and not uncommonly is) given, particularly where there is an issue as to the sufficiency of the explanation for the lateness of the appeal.

A more general power to extend time (used in relation to extending the time for compliance with later steps in the appeal process, including orders made on the sift) is given by *rule 37* of the *EAT Rules*; applications for extensions are considered in the first instance by the Registrar, with a right of appeal against a refusal. Time limits are not as strictly enforced at later stages of an appeal as in relation to the submission of the appeal, but are still applied relatively strictly, and failure to comply with a deadline without seeking an extension of time is highly risky, as the sanctions include the striking out of an appeal or debarring the respondent to the appeal from participating in the hearing; see further **21.15** below.

21.15 Responding to the Notice of Appeal

The procedure for responding to an appeal depends initially on how the appeal itself is treated by the EAT. All appeals are subject to a sift, as explained at **21.17** below, and only if the appeal is accepted at the sift, or subsequently on an appeal under *rule 3(10)* or after a preliminary hearing, is the respondent to the appeal required to respond formally. (There is an exception to this in some cases where a preliminary hearing has been ordered: the respondent may be directed to provide a concise statement giving reasons why the appeal should be rejected at the preliminary stage. However, this is not the formal response to the appeal referred to below.)

If the appeal is allowed to proceed to a full hearing, a respondent to an appeal who wishes to resist the appeal must set out his or her grounds of resistance, and cross-appeal where applicable (see below), in or substantially in accordance with Form 3 (this is referred to as a 'Respondent's Answer') and deliver it to the EAT within the time specified by the Registrar (*EAT Rules, rule 6*; the form is set out in the *Schedule*, and the time limit for filing the response has, since the introduction of the *2018 Practice Direction*, been set at 28 days (see *Para 11.1*)). The respondent may rely on the reasons given by the tribunal, or (alternatively or additionally) other grounds put forward to the tribunal but not relied on by it in support of its findings. These should be set out fully at the outset; the same considerations as to amendments to the Notice of Appeal (as to which see **21.27** below) apply equally to any application to amend the Respondent's Answer.

If an appeal is registered, the respondent is given the opportunity to cross-appeal, that is, to appeal against any elements of the judgment or order under appeal that are adverse to him or her. Directions as to the time for filing the cross-appeal will be notified to the respondent at the same time that he or she is directed to file a Respondent's Answer. If there is a cross-appeal, the procedure applicable to appeals under *rule 3(7)* applies equally to the cross-appeal (*rule 6(12), (12A), (16)*); see **21.17** below for details. If the cross-appeal is accepted following scrutiny under *rule 3(7)*, it will be dealt with in accordance with directions given by a Judge or the Registrar; these can be expected to follow broadly the same procedures as for the appeal; further details are given in the *Practice Direction*. There is no separate fee for cross-appeals.

The EAT has confirmed that a cross-appeal may be made against any part of the decision of the tribunal which is the subject of the original appeal which is adverse to the cross-appellant, not just the part or parts of the decision that are the subject of the appeal: *Weerasinghe v Basildon & Thurrock NHS Foundation Trust* [2015] All ER (D) 397 (Jul), [2016] ICR 305, [2015] All ER (D) 397 (Jul) (a case where the claimant had succeeded in some but not all his claims, and following an appeal by the respondent against one of the findings in favour of the claimant, he cross appealed against some of the findings against him; this was held to be a valid cross-appeal). The same case also confirms that it is not a good ground of objection to a cross appeal that the time limit for appealing had expired by the time it was lodged. However, it is not possible to use the device of a cross appeal to challenge a decision made in the proceedings on a different occasion to that on which the decision the subject of the original appeal was made; *Asda Stores Ltd v Thompson (No 2)* [2004] IRLR 598.

The time limit for submitting a Respondent's Answer is not as strictly enforced as that for submitting a Notice of Appeal, partly because the period for compliance is shorter, and partly because the debarring of a respondent to an appeal might lead to the appeal being allowed without the EAT being aware of the full picture, whereas striking out the appeal means that there is no decision on the merits of the appeal. However, the fact that there is a discretion to extend time does not mean that an extension will be granted readily; matters relevant to the exercise of the discretion include the length of and reasons for the delay, and the extent of any prejudice the other party would suffer if an extension is granted. If a response is not lodged in time and no extension is granted, the respondent will be debarred from taking any further part in the appeal. The prudent course is therefore always to comply with the deadline set, and if it is anticipated that that will not be possible, to apply as soon as possible for an extension of time. The principles are discussed in *Slingsby v Griffiths Smith Solicitors (a firm)* [2009] All ER (D) 150 (Feb); this case is also authority for the point that the principles applicable to extension of time for a Notice of Appeal apply equally stringently to any cross-appeal. The May 2015 *Practice Statement* (see **21.12** above) also gives guidance as to the importance of brevity in Respondent's Answers. Unless additional arguments are to be raised, it is usually sufficient to say that the respondent to the appeal relies on the reasoning of the employment tribunal.

21.16   Grounds of appeal

The EAT's jurisdiction is limited to appeals on points of law. In practice, one of the three most common grounds of appeal is 'perversity' (the other two are bias and insufficiency of reasons, both discussed below). Perversity is recognised to be a separate head of appeal but is narrowly construed and rarely successful. See *Piggott Bros & Co Ltd v Jackson* [1991] IRLR 309, [1992] ICR 85, *East Berkshire Health Authority v Matadeen* [1992] IRLR 336, [1992] ICR 723 and *Yeboah v Crofton* [2002] EWCA Civ 794, [2002] IRLR 634, and the discussion of these cases at **21.35**. It is not acceptable for an appellant to contend that 'the decision was contrary to the evidence' or that 'there was no evidence to support the decision', or to advance similar contentions, unless full and sufficient particulars identifying the particular matters relied upon are set out in the Notice of Appeal (*2018 Practice Direction, para 3.10*). Equally however, the Notice of Appeal should avoid prolixity, and should not be as full as the skeleton argument which will generally be required for the full hearing of the appeal: see *Salmon v Castlebeck Care (Teesdale) Ltd* [2015] IRLR 191, [2015] ICR 735, and the May 2015 *Practice Statement*.

There are also specific requirements to be observed where a ground of appeal is bias or similar unfairness: see **21.23–21.25** for details. It is not a valid ground of appeal that the decision appealed against was a majority decision (even where the Employment Judge was the minority): *Chief Constable of Thames Valley Police v Kellaway* [2000] IRLR 170. However, a serious procedural irregularity, leading to a hearing which was unfair to the appellant, may be the subject of an appeal on that ground, as may a failure to give adequate reasons for the tribunal's conclusions (see **21.36**).

The EAT will not normally entertain appeals which are, or have become, academic: for an example see *Evans v University of Oxford* (UKEATPA/1510/09) (appeal against refusal to adjourn hearing; by the time appeal due to be heard, hearing had been adjourned). Further, an otherwise successful party cannot appeal against an immaterial finding of the tribunal, or indeed any finding of fact; and if the prospective appellant considers that the tribunal has omitted to make a particular finding (having otherwise found for that party) the correct course is to apply to the tribunal to make a finding on the point, not to appeal: see *Wolfe v North Middlesex University Hospital NHS Trust* [2015] ICR 960, [2015] All ER (D) 195 (May).

21.17   Preliminary sifting of appeals

All Notices of Appeal are subject to a preliminary paper sift by either the Registrar or a Judge, in accordance with *rule 3(7)*. In practice the sifting is undertaken by a Judge in almost all cases. If it appears to the Judge reviewing the Notice that it discloses no reasonable grounds for bringing the appeal, or is an abuse of the EAT's process or otherwise likely to obstruct the just disposal of proceedings, the prospective appellant is notified that no further action will be taken on the appeal. Under the procedure in place before July 2013, a prospective appellant could either serve an amended Notice of Appeal (which would again be scrutinised under *Rule 3(7)*) or apply for a hearing before a judge. Changes in the *EAT Rules* as from 29 July 2013 have removed the former option. The only recourse for the prospective appellant whose Notice of Appeal has been rejected at the sift is therefore to apply within 28 days of the rejection for what is referred to as a 'Rule 3(10) hearing', before a judge sitting alone. This may (but rarely does) lead to the appeal being permitted to go forward to a full hearing.

In some cases, under a new provision in the EAT Rules (*Rule 3(7A)*) introduced in July 2013, a prospective appellant may be denied even the limited right to apply for a *Rule 3(10)* hearing, if the judge sifting the Notice of Appeal determines that the appeal is 'totally without merit' (this follows an equivalent procedure introduced some years ago in the Court of Appeal).

The time limit for appealing under *Rule 3(10)*, is enforced strictly, applying the same principles as for the time limit for the initial Notice of Appeal, a practice approved by the Court of Appeal in *Morrison v Hillcrest Care Ltd* [2005] EWCA Civ 1378. An example of a case where an extension of time for a *rule 3(10)* appeal was granted is *Mitchell v Barratt Homes (Leeds) Ltd* (UKEATPA/0903/08), where the delay was attributable to the appellant having erroneously appealed from the rejection of his appeal on the sift to the Court of Appeal, which had refused his appeal as premature. It is not permissible to circumvent the limits on challenging the rejection of an appeal under *rule 3(7)* by applying for a review of that decision: *Zinda v Governing Body of Barn Hill Community High* [2011] ICR 174.

As an indication of the prospects of a successful challenge to the refusal to allow an appeal to proceed under *rule 3(7)*, HHJ McMullen QC in the course of his judgment in *Haritaki v South East England Development Agency* [2008] IRLR 945 stated that in 2007–8, of a total of 917 appeals initially sifted out, there were applications under *rule 3(10)* in 210 cases, of which 29 were wholly or partly successful. An adverse decision of the Judge at a *rule 3(10)* hearing may be further appealed (with permission, either of the EAT or the Court of Appeal) to the Court of Appeal (in Scotland such an appeal would be to the Court of Session, also subject to obtaining permission to appeal). Applications for permission to appeal further are relatively frequent, but very rarely successful.

A hearing under *rule 3(10)* is effectively a re-hearing, and the judge will take a decision on the application on the basis of the material before him or her, not the more limited material that may have been available at the sift stage. However *rule 3(10)* hearings are usually quite short; the *2018 Practice Direction* states that such hearings will not normally last for more than one hour, including time for an oral judgment (*para 10.8*). The prospective respondent to the appeal is not entitled to participate in *rule 3(10)* hearings.

It is open to the Judge hearing an application under *rule 3(10)* to permit only one, or some, of the grounds of appeal to proceed to a full or preliminary hearing, and this is in practice a common outcome of successful *rule 3(10)* hearings. In that event only the permitted ground or grounds will be entertained at the later hearing, and an appellant wishing to pursue further any of the grounds disallowed would have to seek permission to appeal to the Court of Appeal (or in Scotland to the Court of Session): see further **21.19** below. The judge may also permit the appellant to amend the Notice of Appeal at this stage. As the respondent will not have had an opportunity to oppose any proposed amendment, any such permission is provisional, and subject to the right of the respondent to apply to have the permission to amend set aside: see *Readman v Devon Primary Care Trust* (UKEAT/0116/11) and **21.27** below.

A decision taken on the sift to allow an appeal to proceed to a full hearing is normally final; the respondent's opportunity to argue that the appeal has no merit is at the full hearing. However, it is possible in exceptional circumstances for the EAT to review a decision taken on the sift, in the interests of justice; this was done (for the first and, to date only, recorded time) in *Jamieson v Nationwide Building Society* (UKEAT/0028/13), where the respondent complained that the decision to allow the appeal to proceed had been influenced by an untruthful statement made by the appellant about the facts of the case. (In the event the appeal was allowed to proceed, because it remained arguable even without the benefit of the false supporting statement.) Langstaff P pointed out that because a successful review would result in the appeal not being allowed to proceed further, the appellant in turn would be able to apply for a hearing under *rule 3(10)* – a reason why a review at this stage is likely to remain a rarity.

The Registrar also deals with interim applications, which must be made by notice in writing (*EAT Rules, rules 19, 20*). She disposes of such applications herself or refers them to a Judge, who may him or herself refer them for hearing before the EAT. An appeal lies against a decision of the Registrar (*EAT Rules, rule 21*). There are separate procedures for applications for restricted reporting orders; see further below for these.

21.18 For a period between 1997 and 2002, it was the practice for all appeals to be referred first to a preliminary hearing involving the appellant only. However, this was replaced, following a recognition that it was not an efficient use of the EAT's resources to hold preliminary hearings in cases where there was clearly an arguable point of law, by a much greater use of the sift, as described above, to weed out hopeless cases, and a more sparing use of preliminary hearings for appeals which fall between being clearly arguable and clearly hopeless. The outcome, if a case is permitted to proceed on the sift, is therefore either that it is referred to a full hearing, or that it is to be considered at a preliminary hearing involving (usually) the appellant only (if there is a cross-appeal, or if so directed, the preliminary hearing may also be open to the respondent to the appeal).

If the appeal is permitted to go forward, whether to a full or preliminary hearing, directions for the steps needed to prepare the appeal for hearing will be given on paper. If the direction is that the appeal proceed to a full hearing, it will also be given a listing category. These (as set out at *para 10.20* of the *2018 Practice Direction*) are:

P - recommended to be heard in the President's List

A - complex, and raising point(s) of public importance

B - other cases.

In an appropriate case the judge undertaking the sift may also direct that the appeal be expedited or fast-tracked; examples of the kinds of cases likely to be considered for expedition are given at *para 10.22* of the *2018 Practice Direction*. Either or both parties may make a reasoned application for expedition of the appeal.

A number of other matters are routinely covered by directions given at the sift, including steps to be taken if either party wishes to rely on a note of any part of the evidence given in the tribunal, and arrangements for the lodging of appeal bundles and skeleton arguments. Directions made on paper are subject to the right of any party to the appeal to apply for a variation of the terms of the directions, an extension of time, or additional directions. If a party wishes to have directions varied, or seeks additional directions, the procedure is to apply by letter; see the final paragraph of **21.17** for how such applications are considered.

21.19 Preliminary hearings

Where a preliminary hearing is to be held, it is now the practice to order or invite the respondent to the appeal to make concise written submissions as to why the appeal should not be allowed to proceed to a full hearing (*2018 Practice Direction, para 10.10*). The standard directions for preliminary hearings include a requirement for the respondent to lodge any cross-appeal, which will then also be considered at the preliminary hearing (with the consequence that both parties will have the opportunity to put their respective cases). In any case, the appellant will be required to submit a skeleton argument in support of the appeal in advance of the preliminary hearing. Standard directions for preliminary hearings also deal with such matters as applications to admit fresh evidence, or for notes of the evidence before the tribunal to be produced (see **21.21** below), and requiring an appellant alleging bias or a procedural defect to provide evidence on affidavit to support the allegation (see further **21.23–21.25** below). It is usual that the latter direction is expressed in terms that amount to an 'unless' order: if the appellant fails to comply within the time limit (typically 14 days from the date of the order) the relevant parts of the Notice of Appeal will be dismissed.

The outcome of a preliminary hearing may be that the appeal is dismissed, referred to a full hearing, or permitted to proceed but only on some of the grounds advanced in the Notice of Appeal. In the latter category of case, the EAT may not consider any other ground of appeal at the substantive hearing of the appeal, unless there are exceptional reasons to do so, but the appellant may seek permission to appeal to the Court of Appeal against what is effectively the dismissal of part of the appeal: *Miriki v General Council of the Bar* [2001] EWCA Civ 1973, [2002] ICR 505, [2001] All ER (D) 364 (Dec). Permission may also be given at this stage to amend the Notice of Appeal, but the respondent (unless present at the hearing and thus given an opportunity to object to the proposed amendment) will in such cases have the opportunity to apply to have the amendment set aside (see generally *2018 Practice Direction, para 10.16*, and **21.33** below).

Hearings for directions may also be held under *EAT Rules, rule 24*, and there is a general power to give directions under *EAT Rules, rule 25* and to waive compliance with the normal rules under *EAT Rules, rule 39*. A new power to strike out a Notice of Appeal, or a Respondent's Answer, has been given by *rule 26(2)*, added from July 2013. This is subject to the right of the party affected to make representations, either on paper or, if requested, at a hearing. This has been followed by a significant increase in the proportion of appeals struck out, from 30 in 2012-13 to 186 in 2014-15, but dropping to 58 in 2016-17. It is most likely to be used when there has been serious or persistent failure to comply with procedural requirements or orders.

21.20 Where a separate hearing is held by the employment tribunal on a preliminary issue and the tribunal gives a judgment (for instance on whether the claimant is disabled, or whether time should be extended for a claim presented out of time), it is open to the losing party to appeal, and time for appealing runs from the date the reasons for the judgment on the preliminary issue are sent to the parties (or the date the written judgment is sent, if reasons have not been given in writing). However, the EAT has stated that it is only in exceptional cases that such an appeal will be *heard* before the final determination of the case by the tribunal: *Sutcliffe v Big C's Marine Ltd* [1998] IRLR 428, [1998] ICR 913. One reason for this approach is that there may be a second appeal from the final decision of the tribunal, and in that event it is a better use of judicial resources for both appeals to be heard together. Appeals against interlocutory case management orders, by contrast, often need to be, and are, heard very speedily.

Conversely, where a party applies to the employment tribunal for a reconsideration of a judgment, and the application is refused, time for appealing against the original decision is not suspended, but if the refusal to reconsider, or the outcome of the reconsideration, is to be challenged a separate appeal must be lodged, with time for this running from the date of the refusal, or judgment, as the case may be. Such double appeals are not uncommon, and are whenever practicable taken together at a single hearing.

21.21 Notes of evidence

An issue often arising on an appeal is what evidence the tribunal had heard on a particular point. Normally, the only admissible evidence of this is the Employment Judge's note of the evidence given. These notes are not produced automatically or on the direct request of a party to the tribunal but only if ordered by the EAT. Reasons must be given in support of any application for an order for the production of the notes. The *2018 Practice Direction, para 8*, sets out the procedure to be followed in, and the criteria applicable to, an application for production of the Employment Judge's notes. Applications must be made promptly, giving reasons in accordance with the criteria set out in the *Practice Direction*. Appellants should make their application together with the Notice of Appeal; if this is not done, and the case is referred to a preliminary hearing, the application for notes must be made at that hearing. In other cases, applications will be considered on paper by the Registrar or a Judge.

21.21   Employment Tribunals – III: Appeals

The practice is that if an appeal is allowed through the sift, the directions given at that stage will include a standard direction which applies if either party intends to rely on notes of evidence (and whether or not any such application has been intimated). The Standard Direction requires the parties if possible to agree a note of the evidence in question; normally they are given 21 days to do so, and (if this does not prove to be possible) any further application for the Employment Judge's notes must be accompanied by evidence of the steps taken to agree the evidence (such as relevant correspondence).

There is no automatic right to production of the Employment Judge's notes simply because the appellant alleges that the decision was perverse: *Hawkins v Ball and Barclays Bank plc* [1996] IRLR 258, EAT. 'Fishing expeditions' are specifically disapproved by the *Practice Direction* (see *para 8.6*), with a warning that unreasonable applications may lead to an order for costs against the offending party.

21.22   Reference back to tribunal for clarification of reasons

A relatively recent innovation in the EAT's procedure is the reference back of appeals which are based on the inadequacy of the tribunal's reasons, for amplification or clarification of the reasons under challenge. It had been thought that there was no power for the EAT to refer a case back to the tribunal, whether for reconsideration of its findings or to clarify or amplify its reasons, except as part of the disposition of the case after hearing and deciding the appeal; this view was based on obiter comments by the Court of Appeal in *Tran (Kien) v Greenwich Vietnam Community Project* [2002] EWCA Civ 553, [2002] IRLR 735 on the ambit of *ETA 1996, s 35(1)*. However, a different view was expressed, in relation to civil appeals generally, in the later case of *English v Emery Reimbold & Strick Ltd* [2002] EWCA Civ 605, [2002] 3 All ER 385, [2002] 1 WLR 2409, [2003] IRLR 710, and following that decision, the EAT held in *Burns v Consignia (No 2)* [2004] IRLR 425 that there is such a power.

This view was subsequently endorsed by the Court of Appeal, but on different grounds, in *Barke v SEETEC Business Technology Centres Ltd* [2005] EWCA Civ 578, [2005] IRLR 633. The view expressed in *Tran* was held to be correct, but it was held that there is power to remit derived from the provision (newly introduced in 2004) in the *ET Rules, rule 30(3)(b)*, for tribunals to be required to provide reasons if requested by the EAT (see now *rule 62(3)* of the *2013 Rules*); alternatively, the inherent jurisdiction of the EAT allowed this course to be adopted. The procedure for referral back has become known by reference to the leading cases as a '*Burns/Barke*' order. The power may be exercised on a Judge's initiative or at a preliminary hearing; the appeal then proceeds on the reasons as clarified or amplified. The Court of Appeal has stated that a *Burns/Barke* reference should not be made where the reasons given by the tribunal are too deficient to be remedied by amplification, and also that the judge responding to a request for clarification or amplification of reasons should limit him or herself to doing that, and should not attempt to justify or argue in support of the original decision: *Woodhouse School v Webster* [2009] EWCA Civ 91, [2009] IRLR 568. For further guidance on the use of procedure see *Korashi v Abertawe Bro Morgannwg University Local Health Board* [2011] EWCA Civ 187, [2011] All ER (D) 09 (Mar).

The most recent guidance given by the EAT, in *Wolfe v North Middlesex University Hospital NHS Trust* [2015] ICR 960, [2015] All ER (D) 195 (May), is that if it is claimed by the appellant that the tribunal has failed to deal at all with an issue which was before it, or to give adequate reasons for part of its decision, the proper course is to apply to the tribunal for it to rectify the failure (by way of reconsideration of its judgment and reasons), and it is the duty of advocates to take this course before appealing. If such a case is the subject of an appeal without the point having first been referred back to the tribunal, the EAT will adjourn the appeal for a reference to be made to the tribunal, and the appeal will not proceed until the tribunal has clarified its decision.

In a case where there is an appeal against a judgment or order for which the tribunal has not given written reasons, *ET Rules, rule 62(3)* implicitly gives the EAT power to ask the tribunal or Employment Judge to supply written reasons for the purpose of the appeal. This is frequently used where the appeal is against a decision taken without a hearing, for which written reasons may not be required by the *ET Rules*.

The EAT also has the power to stay an appeal; this is sometimes used (in addition to the circumstances covered by *Wolfe*, above) to enable the appellant to apply for a reconsideration of the tribunal's decision, where it is thought that a decision following reconsideration might obviate the need for an appeal; the procedure is formally sanctioned by the *2018 Practice Direction, para 10.3*.

21.23 Allegations of bias

The EAT will not normally consider complaints of bias or of the conduct of an employment tribunal unless full and sufficient particulars are set out in the grounds of appeal. In any such case the Registrar may inquire of the party making the complaint whether it is the intention to proceed with the complaint, in which case the Registrar will give directions. Such directions may include the filing of affidavits dealing with the matters upon the basis of which the complaint is made, or for giving further particulars. The Employment Judge (and in appropriate cases the other members) will be given the opportunity of commenting upon the complaints made against him or her (*2018 Practice Direction, para 12*). It has been held that this procedure should also be followed where a ground of appeal is that the tribunal refused or failed to adjourn the proceedings: *Knight v Central London Bus Co Ltd* (EAT/443/00).

The Court of Appeal has confirmed that the EAT has jurisdiction to hear an appeal based on an allegation of bias, unless the allegation was on its face so lacking in substance that it could not be said to amount to a real challenge: *Lodwick v Southwark London Borough Council* [2004] EWCA Civ 306, [2004] IRLR 554, [2004] ICR 884, a case where the appellant had objected to the Judge but the latter had declined to recuse himself. Further detailed guidance as to how appeals alleging bias by the tribunal should be conducted, particularly where there is a dispute of fact as to what occurred at the hearing, has been given in *Facey v Midas Retail Security* [2001] ICR 287, [2000] All ER (D) 1306. The guidance provides for affidavits or witness statements to be served by each of the parties, comments to be provided by the judge and tribunal members, and if necessary the witnesses (but not the judge or tribunal members) to attend the EAT for cross-examination on their evidence.

A high proportion of appeals alleging bias are sifted out at the initial stage. Those allowed to proceed further are generally made subject to quite strict case management, including orders for the filing of affidavits within 14 days on an 'unless' basis. This means that the relevant parts of the appeal are automatically dismissed if the appellant fails to file an affidavit giving details of the allegations within the time allowed; however, the appellant may apply retrospectively for a review of the original order: the criteria for reviewing such orders are considered in *Roberts v Carling* (UKEAT/0183/09).

21.24 Where there is an allegation of bias based on the conduct of the judge or one of the lay members of a tribunal at a hearing, the test is an objective one: whether, having regard to the relevant circumstances 'a fair minded and informed observer who had considered the facts would conclude that there was a real possibility that the tribunal was biased' (*Porter v Magill* [2001] UKHL 67, [2002] 2 AC 357, [2002] 1 All ER 465). Bias of this kind on the part of one tribunal member is sufficient (*Lodwick v Southwark London Borough Council*, above). Examples of cases where the EAT found that there was an appearance of bias are *Diem v Crystal Services plc* [2006] All ER (D) 84 (Feb), EAT, where, in a claim of race discrimination, the Employment Judge made comments about the colour of the claimant's skin, *Gill v Humanware Europe Ltd* (UKEAT/0312/08) [2009] All ER (D) 77 (Aug), where the Employment Judge was alleged to have had private discussions about aspects of the case with counsel for the respondent in the absence of the claimant, who was representing himself (for the subsequent wasted costs proceedings in this case see [2010] IRLR 877) and *Governing Body of St Michael's Church of England Junior & Infant School v Smith* (UKEAT/0165/14) (excessive and confrontational questioning of witnesses by judge gave rise to a perception of bias).

In *Ansar v Lloyds TSB Bank plc* [2006] EWCA Civ 1462, [2007] IRLR 211, the Court of Appeal gave guidance on when the fact that a complaint of bias had been made against an Employment Judge makes it inappropriate for the Judge to continue to hear the case, or to deal with any later application by the person complaining. The mere fact of an allegation of bias having been made is not in itself a reason for the Judge to stand aside (the technical term is recusal). See also *Bennett v Southwark London Borough Council* [2002] EWCA Civ 223, [2002] IRLR 407 (allegations made against Judge during course of hearing). On the other hand if the tribunal has made comments, whether in the course of the hearing or in a judgment, which indicate that it has reached a conclusion on an issue still to be decided, it may be disqualified from continuing to deal with the case; a good example is *Oni v NHS Leicester City* [2013] ICR 91, [2012] All ER (D) 05 (Oct) (tribunal had made findings making it inappropriate for it to hear a costs application). See also *Begraj v Heer Manek Solicitors* [2014] IRLR 689, [2014] ICR 1020, in which the EAT held that a tribunal was right to recuse itself after the police had contacted the judge and given information about a party which they asked her not to disclose to the claimant; this rendered an unprejudiced hearing no longer possible.

For the position where a tribunal member is directly associated with a party to the case, or a body with an interest in the outcome of the proceedings (such as a pressure group) see *R v Bow Street Metropolitan Stipendiary Magistrate, ex p Pinochet Ugarte (No 2)* [1999] 1 All ER 577, HL and *Helow v Secretary of State for the Home Department* [2008] UKHL 62, [2009] 2 All ER 1031. In *Honey v Swansea City Council* [2008] All ER (D) 311 (Nov), an appearance of bias was found to be established where one of the tribunal members was at the time of the hearing involved, in his capacity as a union official, in an unrelated dispute with the appellant local authority. The opposite conclusion was reached by the Court of Appeal in *Galloway v Barnet Enfield and Haringey Mental Health NHS Trust* [2010] EWCA Civ 1368, [2010] All ER (D) 120 (Dec) with respect to a lay member of the tribunal who had previously been employed for several years as HR Director of another NHS Trust; amongst other reasons for concluding that there was no basis for an allegation of apparent bias on these facts, Gross LJ made the point that the tribunal system benefits from the relevant knowledge and experience of lay members who have worked in the particular industry or sector to which the proceedings relate. See also *Taylor v Governing Body of the Potters Gate CE Primary School* [2015] All ER (D) 31 (Apr) (UKEAT/0227/14) (fact that judge was a governor of another school in the same local education authority area as the respondent Governing Body, but had not had dealings with any of the persons involved in the case, did not create an appearance of bias).

A somewhat different situation which led to a finding of a perception of bias arose in *Peninsula Business Services Ltd v Rees* (UKEAT/0335/08) [2009] All ER (D) 134 (Sep), where the firm of solicitors for which the (part-time) employment judge worked had issued an advertisement for its services criticising the services offered by consultants, of which the appellant company was the best known. However, in a second case heard together with *Rees*, it was held that there was no basis for a perception of bias where the judge had subsequently become full time and no longer worked for the firm concerned. A similar conclusion was reached in *Williams v Cater Link Ltd* (UKEAT/0393/08) [2009] All ER (D) 70 (Aug).

The foregoing examples are of cases where the connection with a party was either not disclosed or not fully disclosed; if a connection has been fully disclosed and the parties have consented to the judge or member concerned hearing the case, the relationship will normally not provide a ground of appeal: *Jones v DAS Legal Expenses Insurance Co Ltd* [2003] EWCA Civ 1071, [2004] IRLR 218. For an example where consent was held to have been given (which includes consideration of the requirements for informed consent) see *Adamson v Swansea University* (UKEAT/0486/09) [2010] All ER (D) 38 (May). Both cases stress the need for fully informed consent, and therefore a full disclosure by the judge or member of any relevant interest or connection.

21.25 Procedural unfairness to a party in the course of the hearing is also a permissible (and relatively common) ground of appeal: see further **21.37**. There have been conflicting decisions of the EAT as to whether any issue of allegedly improper conduct by the judge or a lay member arising in the course of the proceedings had to be raised at the time of its occurrence if it was to be the subject of an appeal (see *Peter Simper & Co Ltd v Cooke* [1986] IRLR 19 and *Red Bank Manufacturing Co Ltd v Meadows* [1992] IRLR 209, [1992] ICR 204). The Court of Appeal reviewed the position and gave general guidance in *Stansbury v Datapulse plc* [2003] EWCA Civ 1951, [2004] IRLR 466, a case where the original decision was set aside for procedural irregularity on evidence that one of the lay members had fallen asleep during the proceedings after having consumed alcohol during the lunch break. The test where the issue was not raised with the tribunal at the time is one of reasonableness, recognising in particular that while it is desirable that the matter should be raised at the time, so that if possible corrective action can be taken, it is difficult even for a legal representative, let alone an unrepresented party, to raise a complaint against a member of the tribunal who, if the complaint is not accepted, will proceed to adjudicate on the case. Where it is claimed that there was procedural unfairness as a result of a ruling of the tribunal in the course of the hearing, the failure of the disadvantaged party to object at the time does not necessarily prevent the point from being taken on appeal, especially if the appellant had not been professionally represented: *Bache v Essex County Council* [2000] 2 All ER 847, [2000] IRLR 251.

It is for the EAT, not the tribunal itself, to decide any disputed issue as to whether a judge or lay member was asleep during the proceedings (or any other disputed issue about what was said or done during the hearing): *Elys v Marks and Spencer plc* [2014] ICR 1091.

Other circumstances may lead to allegations of procedural unfairness, which in principle is a permissible ground of appeal. One such was raised in *McGrath v Ministry of Justice* [2015] All ER (D) 71 (Apr) (UKEAT/0247/14), where the employment judge took into account his personal experience of working with lay members in deciding whether a lay member had a valid claim that his work was comparable to that of employment judges for the purposes of the *Part time Workers (Prevention of Less Favourable Treatment) Regulations 2000*; this was held not to be procedurally unfair as the judge had given the claimant a full opportunity to comment. In *East of England Ambulance Service NHS Trust v Sanders* [2015] IRLR 277, the EAT stated that the tribunal should not undertake its own researches on the internet to supplement the evidence adduced by the parties, particularly if the parties are not given an opportunity to comment on any material found in this way.

Another category of procedural irregularity is illustrated by *NHS Trust Development Agency v Saiger* [2018] ICR 297, EAT (appeal allowed where tribunal had made inferences derived from respondents' witnesses' evidence, without the inferences having been put to the witnesses for their comments).

21.26 Restricted Reporting and Anonymity Orders

Rule 23 of the *EAT Rules* contains provisions which closely follow those of *rule 50* of the *ET Rules* conferring powers on tribunals to make restricted reporting orders and other orders protecting the identity of parties, witnesses and third parties. It should be noted that although the provisions of the *ET Rules* on this have been recast in the *2013 Rules*, there have been no corresponding amendments to the *EAT Rules*, which thus mirror the provisions formerly in the *ET Rules* more closely than the provisions in the new *ET Rules*. In particular, *rule 23(2)* of the *EAT Rules* provides that if an appeal appears to involve allegations of the commission of sexual offence, the Registrar must withhold from the Register of judgments, and delete from other documents available to the public, any identifying matter likely to lead members of the public to identify any person making or affected by the allegations. The latter is treated as an administrative responsibility of the Registrar, and does not require an application by a party. This mirrors the procedure formerly applicable in employment tribunals under the *2004 ET Rules, rule 49*, now replaced by a wider power for the tribunal itself to grant anonymity to parties, witnesses or affected third parties.

In cases involving allegations of sexual misconduct (not amounting to an offence), a restricted reporting order, prohibiting the publication prior to the final judgment on the appeal of identifying matter likely to lead to the identification of any person named in the order, may be made either on a temporary basis or, on the application of a party or of the EAT's own motion, having given the parties an opportunity to be heard on the matter (*rule 23(3), (5)*). A temporary order lasts for 14 days unless a party applies for it to be extended, in which case the order continues in force until that application has been heard and determined (*rule 23(5A)–(5C)*).

There are other important differences in the scope of the powers of the EAT in comparison with those of the employment tribunal. There is no equivalent provision in *rule 23* to the provision in *rule 50* of the *ET Rules* enabling interested third parties such as press representatives to be given an opportunity to make representations before an order is made, or for it to be revoked. In addition, the power to make orders securing the permanent anonymity of a party is restricted by the express wording of the *ETA 1996, s 31* (which is the statutory authority for *rule 23*) to appeals against the making or refusal by a tribunal of restricted reporting orders and certain interlocutory appeals: appeals against final judgments of a tribunal are therefore not covered.

The last point has led to a series of cases in which the EAT has held that it nevertheless has power to order the anonymisation of public documents relating to the case, including judgments. In *Chief Constable of West Yorkshire Police v A* [2000] IRLR 465, [2001] ICR 128 and *X v Stevens* [2003] IRLR 411 the reason for anonymity was that the claimant in each case would otherwise have been inhibited in pursuing a claim based on an EU right, and protection was thus considered necessary to ensure that that right could be given full effect. In the first case, the EAT under Lindsay P relied on the direct effect of the *EU Equal Treatment Directive*, while in the second, Burton P preferred to base the power on the inherent jurisdiction of the EAT as a superior court of record (see **21.1** above for this). In two further cases not involving any EU right, *B v A* [2010] IRLR 400 and *A v B* [2010] IRLR 844, the EAT, in both cases under Underhill P, held that where it was necessary to make an order in order to protect the rights of the party concerned to privacy under *art 8* of the *European Convention on Human Rights*, this could be done. The basis for doing so was clarified in a supplemental judgment in *A v B* [2010] IRLR 844 at 856) as the application of the EAT's general power to regulate its own procedure, conferred by *ETA 1996, s 30(3)*. The cases concerned claims of unfair dismissal; the dismissal in *A v B* had followed a report to the employer by the police of allegations that the claimant had been engaged in paedophile activities overseas and in *B v A* an allegation of rape made against the claimant by a fellow employee.

It is the duty of both the employment tribunal and the EAT, as public bodies, to ensure that effect is given to Convention rights: see *section 3* of the *Human Rights Act 1998*. This provides a basis for an order protecting the anonymity of a non-party whose privacy rights would otherwise be compromised by public disclosure of his or her identity: the anonymity requiring protection in *B v A* was that of the victim of the alleged rape, who was not herself a party to the proceedings but whose rights under *art 8* were asserted by the employer, which was. See further *F v G* [2012] ICR 246, [2011] All ER (D) 42 (Dec) (anonymity order made by tribunal on privacy grounds for the protection of vulnerable students of the respondent college upheld on appeal). In *EF v AB* [2015] IRLR 619 a permanent Restricted Reporting Order was made by the EAT on this basis to protect the privacy of the wife of a respondent in the original tribunal proceedings, and her young son, in the context of lurid allegations of sexual activity involving her having been made in the tribunal proceedings. In each of these cases, the countervailing rights of the press and the general public in the reporting of public judicial proceedings under *art 10* of the *Convention* had to be balanced against the individual interests of those whose privacy would be adversely affected by the reporting of the proceedings.

For further details of the scope of and case law relating to restricted reporting orders and other orders restricting publicity in employment tribunals, see **20.91–20.92**.

21.27 Amendments to the Notice of Appeal

Appellants frequently seek to amend their Notice of Appeal. This may be because they have advice that was not available before the Notice of Appeal was lodged, typically when an ELAAS representative (see **21.28** below) is made available to a previously unrepresented appellant at a preliminary or *rule 3(10)* hearing. Permission is required for any amendment, and the respondent to the appeal has the right to resist any application for permission. For this reason, if permission is given at a hearing at which the respondent is not present the permission is expressed as provisional, and is subject to the respondent's right within a set time (usually 14 days) to apply to have the permission set aside.

Permission to amend to add a ground of appeal will not be given unless the EAT is satisfied that the amendment raises a point of law which is at least arguable. There is also an important difference between amendments which clarify a ground of appeal already in the Notice of Appeal and amendments which raise entirely new points. The other factors the EAT will take into account in deciding whether to give permission to amend are set out in *Khudados v Leggate* [2005] IRLR 540, [2005] ICR 1013, at para 86:

(a)   Whether the application for permission was made as soon as the need for amendment was known;

(b)   Whether a full, honest and acceptable explanation has been given for any delay in applying;

(c)   The extent to which permitting the amendment would delay the appeal;

(d)   Whether permitting the amendment will cause prejudice to the respondent (over and above the inevitable prejudice of having to deal with a ground of appeal that it would not otherwise have to meet), and conversely whether denying permission will cause prejudice to the appellant;

(e)   In some cases the merits of the proposed additional or amended ground will be relevant;

(f)   The public interest in the expeditious conduct of the EAT's business and efficient use of its resources.

These factors are further considered in *Readman v Devon Primary Care Trust* (UKEAT/0116/11), where Underhill P makes the point that a less stringent approach to permission to amend is taken at *rule 3(10)* hearings, since they are often the first point at which the appellant has legal advice about the potential points of law that could be pursued in the appeal, and because there will be no prejudice to the respondent since it will not up to that point have been required to take any action on the appeal. A similar point is made in *King v Royal Bank of Canada* [2012] IRLR 280 in relation to appeals by litigants in person, who should be given more latitude in relation to a failure to identify all the potential grounds of appeal at the outset, particularly in the light of the difficulty many lay persons have in obtaining legal advice. *King* contains a full and helpful summary of the considerations relevant to whether permission to amend should be given: see paras 31–44.

Whilst most applications to amend the Notice of Appeal are made, and determined, before the matter proceeds to a full hearing, there is in principle no restriction on how late in the proceedings an application for permission to amend may be made and granted. An extreme example of this is *BMC Software Ltd v Shaikh* [2017] IRLR 1074 (UKEAT/0092/16), where the appellant employer was given permission to amend its Notice of Appeal after the close of submissions. The issue raised by the amendment was a point of law affecting the jurisdiction of the tribunal whose decision was under appeal, and which had been raised by the EAT itself, and the EAT concluded that the balance of prejudice, including prejudice to the good administration of justice if permission was refused, was in favour of permitting the amendment.

21.28 CONDUCT OF THE APPEAL

Representation

As in employment tribunals, there is no restriction as to the persons who may represent a party to an appeal (*ETA 1996, s 29(1)*). In the nature of the proceedings, legal representation is more common than in the employment tribunals, but by no means universal. A scheme known as ELAAS has existed since 1996 for the provision of professional advice for, and, if desired, representation of, unrepresented appellants at preliminary hearings. This is operated with the active encouragement of the EAT by experienced barristers and solicitors who provide free representation on a rota basis. The Free Representation Unit and the Bar Pro Bono Unit also provide free representation in an increasing number of cases. There are as yet no equivalent services available for hearings in Scotland.

Concerns about the prevalence of organisations offering representation to parties in employment litigation, often on a no win no fee basis, but which were not subject to external scrutiny of their competence or professional standards, led to the introduction by the *Compensation Act 2006* of a scheme of regulation of claims management bodies, including those which provide representation in employment tribunals or the EAT for reward. It is a criminal offence for an unregulated person or body to undertake regulated claims management services for reward (including under conditional fee arrangements); those exempt from regulation include lawyers and trade unions, as well as those, such as the CAB, not acting for reward. The term 'regulated claims management services' covers the representation of claimants (but not respondents) in employment tribunal proceedings and any subsequent appeal to the EAT. The regulator is the Secretary of State for Justice. The *2006 Act* does not apply to Scotland, and there is currently no equivalent regulation of representatives who are not practising lawyers in Scotland.

21.29 Preparation for the hearing

Following the decision of the Supreme Court in *R (on the application of UNISON) v Lord Chancellor* [2017] UKSC 51, [2017] IRLR 911, [2017] ICR 1037 that the legislation imposing fees for employment tribunal claims and appeals was unlawful, there is no longer any requirement to pay a fee prior to an appeal being listed for hearing, and the references in the *EAT Rules* to fees are no longer effective.

21.30 The EAT will have before it at the substantive hearing the Notice of Appeal, the Respondent's Answer, the decision of the employment tribunal and any documents which were before the employment tribunal and which are relied on by the parties as relevant to the appeal. It is the responsibility of the appellant to lodge copies of a core bundle of documents (if possible this should be an agreed bundle, and it should be in the format set out in *para 7* of the *2018 Practice Direction* and contain the documents listed there, together with any other documents relevant to the appeal). The *2018 Practice Direction* suggests, at *Para 7.1* that a represented Respondent "may be willing to take [the] responsibility [for preparing and lodging the bundle] from an unrepresented Appellant". Irrelevant documents should not be included. Permission is required for the submission of a bundle exceeding 50 pages in addition to the documents required to be included under the *2018 Practice Direction* (which include the Notice of Appeal and Respondent's Answer, the judgment under appeal and reasons, the ET1 and ET3, any orders made by the EAT, and a number of other documents specified in the *Practice Direction, para 7.3*). The Employment Judge's notes must be included in the appeal papers if their production was ordered.

It is not acceptable for the parties to fail to co-operate in agreeing the content of the appeal bundle. If however there is a dispute about what documents should be included, the appellant should prepare and lodge a core bundle containing the documents required under the *2018 Practice Direction* to be included and any other documents the inclusion of which is agreed; any documents the relevance of which is disputed should also be included (within the overall limits set by the *Practice Direction*) but with the risk to a respondent to the appeal who insists on the inclusion of inappropriate or unnecessary documents that there may be a costs sanction. See *Smith-Twigger v Abbey Protection Group Ltd* [2014] All ER (D) 92 (Oct), [2014] ICR D33 (UKEAT/0391/13).

A party seeking to show that no reasonable tribunal could have reached the conclusion it reached on the evidence will almost certainly require the notes of evidence, or a jointly agreed note supplied by the parties (*Piggott Bros & Co Ltd v Jackson* [1991] IRLR 309, [1992] ICR 85 at 96). (This view was qualified by the EAT in *Hawkins v Ball and Barclays Bank plc* [1996] IRLR 258, where the evidence was clearly recorded in the tribunal's decision and the issue was whether the conclusions reached from that evidence were perverse.) Any application for an order to produce all or part of the notes must be made in accordance with *para 8* of the *2018 Practice Direction*; see **21.21** above.

Most cases are listed for a fixed date. It is the practice of the EAT that the listing office consults the parties, or as appropriate their representatives, over dates to avoid, and as a consequence once a hearing is listed, cogent reasons will be needed to secure a postponement. It is the duty of the parties to advise the EAT if for any reason the time estimate given for the hearing is likely to be inadequate or too long. Parties are also required to notify the EAT immediately of any settlement which results in the appeal being withdrawn; the Court of Appeal has stated that it is a strict professional duty of legal representatives to avoid waste of judicial time by notifying settlements of cases under appeal immediately, particularly if a settlement is achieved in the immediate run up to the hearing of the appeal: *Yell Ltd v Garton* [2004] EWCA Civ 87, [2004] All ER (D) 80 (Feb). Shorter, and urgent, appeals may be called on at short, sometimes very short, notice.

21.31   Skeleton arguments

In accordance with *para 15* of the *2018 Practice Direction*, skeleton arguments are required to be lodged with the EAT and exchanged between the parties' representatives, normally 14 days in advance of any full or preliminary hearing (precise timing varies depending on the length of notice of the hearing) – see *2018 Practice Direction, Para 15.13*; appellants may lodge a skeleton argument with the Notice of Appeal, and should prepare an agreed chronology of relevant events which should, if possible, be agreed with the other party (*2018 Practice Direction, Para 15.8*). In cases that are fast-tracked or in the warned list, skeletons should be lodged "as soon as possible" and "unless the hearing date is less than seven days later, in any event within seven days after the parties have been notified that the cases is expedited or in the warned list (*2018 Practice Direction, Para 15.13*) The format and content of skeleton arguments are prescribed in some detail in *para 15* of the *2018 Practice Direction*. This is supplemented by guidance in the May 2015 *Practice Statement*, which explains that 'skeleton arguments are not expected to be full written arguments, but instead are intended to provide the framework within which oral submissions will be made, and should be as short as the nature of the case permits'.

The requirements for skeleton arguments do not apply in Scotland unless specifically directed; however, it is increasingly common that skeleton arguments are directed in Scotland, and even when not directed, parties' representatives are encouraged to provide them.

Parties intending to rely on authorities are expected to provide copies for the use of the judge and (if present) members. The *2018 Practice Direction, para 16* gives detailed guidance on the presentation of authorities. Parties are expected to co-operate in agreeing a joint list of authorities; the authorities should be presented in a ring binder, in chronological order and separately tabbed, using the officially reported versions with headnotes wherever available, and with the relevant passages highlighted; and only cases which are authority for a legal principle, rather than merely illustrative, should be relied on. Normally no more than 10 authorities should be cited unless the scale of the appeal warrants more extensive citation. If the EAT is presented with bundles of authorities which have not been marked up, it may require the party responsible to mark them up before the hearing begins, and if this results in additional costs for the other party, an order may be made against the party failing to provide marked up bundles in the first place: see *East of England Ambulance Service NHS Trust v Sanders* [2015] IRLR 277.

The EAT has available for reference its own copies of the most frequently cited cases, and it is not necessary to provide copies of any of the listed cases for the hearing. The full list of cases to which this practice applies is posted on the EAT website.

It is the practice of the EAT to read the papers, and skeleton arguments, in advance and representatives can expect to be asked questions arising from their and the other party's skeleton arguments as well as points arising in the course of their oral submissions.

21.32 The hearing

The hearing before the EAT consists of legal argument; it is not the practice to hear evidence again, and therefore witnesses who attended the tribunal do not need to attend the appeal. Exceptions to this, where witnesses may be required to give evidence, include where there is an appeal against a refusal by the registrar to extend time for a late notice of appeal: in such cases, evidence may be given to explain the delay in submitting the Notice of Appeal; and in relation to allegations of bias or improper conduct in the course of the hearing, where if the events in issue are disputed, the EAT may wish to hear live evidence from those present (other than the Employment Judge and members, who will never be required to give evidence). If fresh evidence is put forward this is done by way of affidavit, or a witness statement with a signed Statement of Truth.

21.33 Raising points not taken at the tribunal hearing

A party is not normally permitted to raise points of law which were conceded or abandoned, or never raised at all, before the employment tribunal, especially where such points would require further investigation of the facts. The law and practice on this issue was reviewed by the EAT in *Glennie v Independent Magazines (UK) Ltd* [1999] IRLR 719, following the decision of the Court of Appeal in *Jones v Governing Body of Burdett Coutts School* [1998] IRLR 521, which established that the EAT's discretion to allow a new point of law to be raised, or a conceded point to be reopened, should be exercised only in exceptional circumstances, for compelling reasons. This was especially so if the result would be to open up fresh issues of fact which, because the point was not in issue, were not sufficiently investigated before the employment tribunal. The facts that the point is of wider importance, or that the amount at stake in the claim is very significant, are not reasons to depart from the general practice: *UNISON v Leicestershire County Council* [2006] EWCA Civ 825, [2006] IRLR 810 (where the tribunal had made a protective award totalling several million pounds). An example of an exceptional case is *Lipscombe v Forestry Commission* [2007] EWCA Civ 428, [2007] All ER (D) 132 (May), where a litigant in person was permitted by the Court of Appeal to rely on a point not taken at the hearing, which involved undisputed facts and was decisive of whether the tribunal had jurisdiction.

The various authorities were again reviewed by the EAT, and the principles fully set out, in *Rance v Secretary of State for Health* [2007] IRLR 665. There is a discretion whether to allow the raising of new points or the reopening of conceded points, but it will be exercised only in exceptional cases, particularly so where the effect of taking the point would be that fresh issues of fact would have to be investigated; on the other hand the fact that the point goes to the tribunal's jurisdiction is not a trump card. Within these general principles, the earlier cases provide examples of the sort of case in which the discretion is, or is not, likely to be exercised in favour of the party seeking to raise the point.

In *London Borough of Wandsworth v Vining* (UKEAT/0234/13), the EAT allowed a new point to be taken by the respondent to the appeal (the claimant in the original hearing) because the point went to jurisdiction, involved no additional evidence if successful, and engaged the issue whether there had been a denial of an effective remedy by reference to *art 6* of the *European Convention on Human Rights*. The claimant had been successful in the employment tribunal but a subsequent decision of the Court of Appeal had effectively overruled the legal basis for the decision in his favour. The point was subsequently considered, and rejected, by the EAT at the full hearing of the appeal (see [2016] ICR 427, [2015] All ER (D) 266 (Dec)), and the appellant's further appeal to the Court of Appeal was also unsuccessful (see [2017] EWCA Civ 1092, [2017] IRLR 1140).

21.34 Fresh evidence

Appellants not infrequently seek to put additional evidence before the EAT to undermine the basis for the decision under appeal. It is at least arguable that this is not a permissible ground of appeal, since the tribunal cannot be said to have erred in law in failing to take account of evidence which was not put before it; this point was noted, but not decided, by the EAT in *Adegbuji v Meteor Parking Ltd* [2011] All ER (D) 39 (Dec) (UKEATPA/1570/09). Irrespective of that point, the EAT has repeatedly urged that the usual way of seeking to have additional evidence considered is by applying to the tribunal itself to reconsider its decision: see for example *Korashi v Abertawe Bro Morgannwg University Local Health Board* [2012] IRLR 4.

The matter was made the subject of a Practice Statement by the President, Langstaff J, in 2012 which has since been incorporated in the *2018 Practice Direction*. This explains that there is a strong preference for fresh evidence applications to be pursued by way of reconsideration by the tribunal which took the decision under appeal since this is quicker than an appeal, which if successful would result in the matter being referred back to the tribunal to consider the evidence, and more suitable since the tribunal which took the original decision is better placed to assess whether the proposed fresh evidence would have affected its decision. Accordingly, it is likely that if an appeal includes an application to admit fresh evidence, the appeal will be stayed for the appellant to apply to the tribunal to reconsider its original decision, based on the fresh evidence. This does not of course preclude a subsequent appeal on the ground that the tribunal erred in refusing to admit the evidence. Alternatively, if no application for a review has been made prior to the hearing of the appeal, the EAT may dismiss the appeal, leaving it to the appellant to apply to the tribunal for reconsideration of its decision, with the possibility of a further appeal to the EAT if that application is unsuccessful: see *Noor v Metroline Travel Ltd* (UKEAT/0059/14).

Despite the general approach, it may still exceptionally be more appropriate for an application for the admission of fresh evidence to be considered by the EAT, for instance if this is one of a number of issues in the appeal and it would delay or unnecessarily complicate matters for the fresh evidence point to be referred back to the tribunal for reconsideration.

Whether the point is dealt with by way of reconsideration by the tribunal, or appeal, the principles of the admissibility of fresh evidence are essentially the same. A party will not be permitted to adduce factual matters before the EAT which it chose not to put before the employment tribunal (*Bingham v Hobourn Engineering Ltd* [1992] IRLR 298). The test for the admission of fresh evidence is as set out in *Wileman v Minilec Engineering Ltd* [1988] IRLR 144, [1988] ICR 318, adopting the established formula applied in appeals from the civil courts to the Court of Appeal, as set out in *Ladd v Marshall* [1954] 3 All ER 745. The three requirements, which are cumulative, are set out in the *2018 Practice Direction, para 9.3*, as follows:

'9.3.1   the evidence could not have been obtained with reasonable diligence for use at the Employment Tribunal hearing; and

9.3.2   it is relevant and would probably have had an important influence on the hearing; and

9.3.3   it is apparently credible.'

The application of these requirements is fully reviewed in the judgment of the EAT in *Korashi v Abertawe Bro Morgannwg University Local Health Board* (above). A good example of a successful application to admit fresh evidence is *SQR Security Solutions Ltd v Badu* (UKEAT/0329/15). The claimant in that case had given evidence that he had been unable to mitigate his loss because a number of job offers he had secured had been withdrawn. The appellant employers investigated these claims and sought to introduce evidence to show that they were false. The EAT accepted that this evidence could not reasonably have been adduced before the claimant had made the allegedly false claims, and that the evidence was material and important not just to rebut the claims but also as going to the credibility of the claimant's evidence as a whole.

The procedure if the issue is pursued before the EAT is that the evidence sought to be admitted should be submitted in the form of one or more sworn affidavits or witness statements with a signed Statement of Truth, or exhibited to an Affidavit or witness statement if the evidence is in documentary form. The evidence should normally be submitted together with the Notice of Appeal or Respondent's Answer (*2018 Practice Direction, para 19*). If leave to admit the evidence is given, the case will usually be remitted for a rehearing, but the cogency of the evidence may occasionally be such that the original decision is simply reversed.

21.35 Errors of law and perversity

The EAT can only overturn the decision of an employment tribunal if the tribunal can be shown to have erred in law. Where an appeal succeeds, the point of law on which the tribunal erred should be identified in the EAT's decision (*British Gas plc v McCarrick* [1991] IRLR 305). The error of law may be an express misdirection or it may be inferred from the fact that the conclusion of the tribunal was one which no reasonable employment tribunal, properly directing itself as to the relevant legal principles, could have reached; in other words, that the decision of the tribunal was so inconsistent with the correct application of the law that it was either a perverse decision or reached applying incorrect legal principles.

Even if the EAT would have come to a different conclusion, it must not interfere with the decision of the employment tribunal unless an error of law is identified (*Retarded Children's Aid Society Ltd v Day* [1978] ICR 437, [1978] IRLR 128). Misunderstanding or misapplication of the facts does not of itself amount to an error of law unless the tribunal proceeds upon a basis contrary to the undisputed or indisputable facts (*British Telecommunications plc v Sheridan* [1990] IRLR 27).

Perversity is recognised as a separate ground of appeal, and is often relied on, but rarely successfully so, because of the high standard required to establish that a decision was perverse. Unless the employment tribunal has misdirected itself in law, its decision should not be disturbed on the ground of perversity unless the decision under appeal was not a permissible option (*Piggott Bros & Co Ltd v Jackson* [1991] IRLR 309, [1992] ICR 85). In *Piggott*, the Court of Appeal held (at 92) that in concluding that the decision under appeal was not a permissible option, the EAT will almost always have to be able to identify a finding of fact which was unsupported by *any* evidence or a clear self-misdirection in law by the employment tribunal (see also *Hough v Leyland DAF Ltd* [1991] IRLR 194, [1991] ICR 696, in which the EAT pointed out that a finding of fact was not perverse merely because the tribunal had reached it by way of inference and without any direct evidence). However, the EAT in *East Berkshire Health Authority v Matadeen* [1992] IRLR 336, [1992] ICR 723 held that a conclusion drawn from unassailable facts could be attacked as perverse. The approach adopted in *Piggott* represented a departure from the test of whether one could say of a decision, 'My goodness, that was certainly wrong', formulated in *Neale v Hereford and Worcester County Council* [1986] IRLR 168, [1986] ICR 471.

Subsequently, Mummery J has categorised perversity as including a decision that on the evidence before the tribunal is 'irrational', 'offends reason', 'must be wrong', 'is not a permissible option', or 'flies in the face of properly informed logic': *Stewart v Cleveland Guest (Engineering) Ltd* [1994] IRLR 440 at 443.

The Court of Appeal gave further guidance as to the correct approach to deciding perversity appeals in what has come to be regarded as the leading case on perversity appeals, *Yeboah v Crofton* [2002] EWCA Civ 794, [2002] IRLR 634:

> 'Such an appeal ought only to succeed where an overwhelming case is made out that the employment tribunal reached a decision which no reasonable tribunal, on a proper appreciation of the evidence and the law, would have reached.'

(Mummery LJ at para 93)

The court also warned of the danger of turning an appeal on a point of law into a rehearing of parts of the evidence.

21.36 Inadequacy of reasons

The alleged inadequacy of the reasons given by a tribunal is a frequently raised ground of appeal. A failure by an employment tribunal to give adequate (or any) reasons for a judgment or order, or a substantive finding in the proceedings, may amount to an error of law rendering the decision liable to be set aside on appeal. As to the adequacy of reasons, see the citation from *Meek v City of Birmingham District Council* [1987] IRLR 250, CA in **20.118** above and the cases cited there. It should be noted that the decision in *Meek* predates the introduction of a more prescriptive approach to the content of reasons for judgments by *rule 30* of the *ET Rules 2004* (now replaced by similar wording in *rule 62(5)* of the *2013 ET Rules*), and a somewhat less tolerant approach to inadequately expressed reasons is apparent in EAT decisions, particularly in cases involving allegations of discrimination, than was formerly the case. In *Greenwood v NWF Retail Ltd* [2011] ICR 896, the EAT held that failure to comply with *ET Rule 30(6)* was in itself an error of law. However, the EAT went on to confirm that this does not require the tribunal to follow precisely or rigidly the format prescribed by *Rule 30(6)*, provided that each of the matters specified in the rule was addressed. The EAT noted with approval the comment of Buxton LJ in *Balfour Beatty Power Networks v Wilcox* [2006] EWCA Civ 1240, [2007] IRLR 63 that:

> 'the rule is surely intended to be a guide and not a straitjacket. Provided it can be reasonably spelt out from the determination of the employment tribunal that what rule 30(6) requires has been provided by that tribunal, then no error of law will have been committed.'

These comments apply equally to the equivalent provisions of the *2013 ET Rules*. The EAT may also, if inadequacy of reasons is given as a ground of appeal, remit the case to the tribunal for it to clarify or amplify its reasons, prior to hearing the substantive appeal: see **21.22** above.

21.37 Procedural failures

A separate category of error of law is a failure by the tribunal to afford the parties a fair hearing, whether through some serious procedural failure or through bias, or where the circumstances have created a real danger, or a perception, of bias. Cases falling within this general categorisation would include, for instance, those where relevant evidence was unjustifiably excluded or a party was prevented from putting forward part of his or her case, or the tribunal failed to invite the parties to deal with a particular point before deciding it or relied on a point of law not canvassed at the hearing; the Employment Judge or a member sitting despite a potential conflict of interest; and inappropriate conduct by the Judge or a member in the course of the hearing (see generally as to these potential grounds **21.23–21.25** above). Excessive delay in delivering judgment following the hearing is not of itself an error of law, and will only provide grounds for appeal if in the circumstances there is a real risk that the appellant was deprived of the right to a fair trial: *Bangs v Connex South Eastern Ltd* [2005] EWCA Civ 14, [2005] 2 All ER 316, [2005] IRLR 389. Thus in *Grosvenor v Governing Body of Aylesford School* (UKEAT/0001/08) a delay of a year in promulgating the judgment was held not to provide a ground of appeal on the basis that the judgment, albeit excessively long, was adequately reasoned.

It may also be a ground of appeal that the tribunal has decided the case on a point not relied on by the parties and on which the losing party has not been given the opportunity to make submissions. An example is *Launahurst Ltd v Larner* [2010] EWCA Civ 334, [2010] All ER (D) 282 (Mar), where the tribunal held that the contract under which the claimant was held out to be self-employed was a sham, a point not advanced by him or raised with the respondent at the hearing. In addition, it may be a ground of appeal that the tribunal relied in reaching its decision on legal authorities not cited by the parties and on which they have not been given an opportunity to make submissions: *Clark v Clark Construction Initiatives Ltd* [2008] EWCA Civ 1446, [2009] ICR 718, [2008] All ER (D) 191 (Dec); however this does not prevent the citation of authority to support uncontentious or incidental points in the tribunal's judgment: *Stanley Cole (Wainfleet) Ltd v Sheridan* [2003] EWCA Civ 1046, [2003] IRLR 885, [2003] ICR 1449. A further ground of appeal is that the tribunal supplemented the evidence presented to it by conducting its own researches on the internet, without giving the parties an opportunity to deal with the additional information thus discovered: *East of England Ambulance Service NHS Trust v Sanders* [2015] IRLR 277.

21.38 Disposal of the appeal

There are essentially two possible outcomes if an appeal is successful. Either the matter may be remitted (to the original tribunal or a fresh tribunal), to be considered further in the light of the EAT's judgment or for a complete rehearing; or the EAT may substitute a decision in favour of the appellant, eg that the dismissal was fair, rather than unfair. In cases not involving a specific point of statutory construction, which may necessarily determine the result, the EAT is careful not to usurp the tribunal's role as arbiter of facts. It will therefore not substitute a decision unless there is only one decision that a tribunal correctly directing itself in law could have reached (*Morgan v Electrolux Ltd* [1991] IRLR 89, [1991] ICR 369).

Where a material error of law is identified, the EAT must allow the appeal unless the conclusion of the employment tribunal was plainly and unarguably right, notwithstanding the misdirection (*Dobie v Burns International Security Services (UK) Ltd* [1984] 3 All ER 333, [1984] ICR 812, [1984] IRLR 329). Equally, unless the decision was plainly and arguably wrong, the EAT should not substitute a different decision but should remit the matter for rehearing. It is also possible for an appeal to fail despite a finding of a material error of law, where the tribunal's conclusions on other points are upheld and are decisive of the case. An example is *Sargeant v London Fire and Emergency Planning Authority* [2018] IRLR 302, EAT, an age discrimination case where the tribunal's conclusion that the respondent had failed to make out a legitimate aim for the admittedly discriminatory pension rules was held to be erroneous in law, but the tribunal's finding in the alternative that the means adopted were not proportionate, was correct, and decisive against the appeal.

Following conflicting decisions of the Court of Appeal as to the desirability of the EAT deciding a point rather than remitting it to the tribunal to decide (*Buckland v Bournemouth University Education Corporation* [2010] EWCA Civ 121, [2010] IRLR 445, [2010] ICR 908 and *Tilson v Alstom Transport* [2010] EWCA Civ 1308, [2011] IRLR 169), the position was restated in two further decisions of the Court, *Jafri v Lincoln College* [2014] EWCA Civ 449, [2014] IRLR 544, [2014] ICR 920 and *Burrell v Micheldever Tyre Services Ltd* [2014] EWCA Civ 716, [2014] IRLR 630, [2014] ICR 935. The Court concluded (with reluctance) that it was bound by previous authority to hold that the EAT could only substitute a different conclusion from that reached by the tribunal if it considered that the result to be substituted followed from the findings made by the tribunal, supplemented by any undisputed or indisputable facts. The EAT cannot make additional findings of fact in order to avoid remitting the case to the tribunal (or a fresh tribunal).

However, as Underhill LJ pointed out in *Jafri*, the EAT can, if all parties consent, exercise the power conferred on it by *section 35(1)* of the *Employment Tribunals Act 1996* to decide the point itself rather than remit. It should also be noted that the Court in *Burrell*, whilst considering itself obliged to follow *Jafri*, explicitly encouraged the EAT to be robust in its approach to determining whether only one outcome of the original proceedings was possible, and if not, and if the parties were not willing to agree to the EAT determining the matter itself, to limit the scope of any necessary remission.

This point was reinforced by Elias LJ in *Kuznetsov v Royal Bank of Scotland plc* [2017] EWCA Civ 43, [2017] IRLR 350. It was suggested that the consent of the parties to the point being decided by the EAT rather than remitted should be sought before the hearing in any case where it was likely that the issue would arise; it was also noted that there is no advantage in remittal where the issue is not one of fact but of the correctness of a case management order (as in that case). See also *GMB v Henderson* [2016] EWCA Civ 1049, [2017] IRLR 340, where the Court of Appeal held that the EAT was entitled to refuse to remit a case, having allowed the appeal on the ground of inadequate reasoning, where it was clear on the tribunal's findings of fact that the claim was bound to fail; the EAT had therefore been entitled to substitute a finding to that effect.

Nicholson v Hazel House Nursing Home Ltd [2016] All ER (D) 189 (Jun) (UKEAT/0241/15) is a further example of a case where the EAT, applying *Jafri*, concluded that it was able to substitute its own finding (that the appellant had been constructively dismissed) for that of the tribunal (that he had not been).

The same principles apply to appeals from interlocutory orders or judgments as to appeals from final judgments (*Adams and Raynor v West Sussex County Council* [1990] IRLR 215, [1990] ICR 546). A good example of a case where an interlocutory order, fixing a hearing, was overturned because the employment judge had taken into account an irrelevant factor, is *Gillingham Football Club v McCammon* [2012] All ER (D) 218 (May) (UKEAT/0625/11); as often occurs in urgent appeals, in that case the EAT, with the parties' agreement, proceeded to re-decide the issue on the material before it rather than remit it to the tribunal.

The EAT in *Sinclair Roche & Temperley v Heard* [2004] IRLR 763 gave guidance which is frequently cited as to the factors to be considered in determining whether a case should or should not be remitted to the same tribunal. The principal factors to be taken into account are proportionality (it will almost always be more expensive and time consuming for a case to be remitted to a freshly constituted tribunal than to the tribunal which first decided the case); the passage of time (if a significant amount of time has passed since the hearing below, there may be a risk that that tribunal has forgotten the case); bias or partiality (remission to the same tribunal is inappropriate if there has been an issue of possible bias); whether the decision under appeal was totally flawed (in which case remission should be to a different tribunal); the risk of the tribunal having a second bite at getting to the same decision for different reasons; and a presumption of professionalism (favouring remission to the original tribunal, other things being equal). See para 46 of the judgment for details.

21.39 If a case is ordered by the EAT to be remitted (to the same or a fresh tribunal) following a successful appeal, the tribunal which hears the case on remission only has jurisdiction by reason of the remission. It cannot, therefore, even with the agreement of the parties, reopen or deal with issues other than those remitted for its consideration. This conclusion was reached by the Court of Appeal in *Aparau v Iceland Frozen Foods plc* [2000] 1 All ER 228, [2000] IRLR 196, where (in a constructive dismissal case) the issue remitted to the tribunal was whether a term had been incorporated in the contract of employment. This was then conceded, with the consequence that the constructive dismissal claim was made out, but the employers persuaded the tribunal to deal with the fairness of the dismissal, which had not been disputed at the original hearing. The Court of Appeal held that its decision on that point was a nullity. These principles would not, however, prevent the tribunal from dealing with a point affecting its jurisdiction to deal with the matters remitted.

21.40 Where both the parties to an application to an employment tribunal agree that the decision of the tribunal was in error and reach a proposed settlement, the parties may not themselves reverse that decision but must refer the matter to the EAT. The EAT is cautious about allowing an appeal without hearing argument on the issue of law, since any decision may have implications more generally than for the particular case. The parties should draw up a formal order and request the EAT to accept it, ratify it and make it part of the order of the Appeal Tribunal. However, unless the consent order is part of an overall settlement of the proceedings (in which case the EAT will usually agree to the order without hearing full argument – see *British Publishing Co Ltd v Fraser* [1987] ICR 517) a consent order will not be granted unless the EAT is persuaded by argument at a hearing that the decision appealed against was wrong in law; and if the effect of the proposed order is to remit the case to the tribunal for further consideration, the EAT will give a reasoned judgment on the appeal: *J Sainsbury plc v Moger* [1994] ICR 800; *Dozie v Addison Lee plc* [2013] All ER (D) 172 (Sep), [2013] ICR D38 (UKEAT/0328/13). See also *2018 Practice Direction, para 17*. The *Practice Direction* also deals with withdrawal of appeals where there has been a settlement, and warns that if an application for permission to withdraw an appeal is made close to the hearing date, the appellant may be summoned to explain the delay in deciding not to pursue the appeal.

21.41 OTHER POWERS OF THE APPEAL TRIBUNAL

For the purpose of disposing of an appeal, the EAT may exercise any powers of the body or officer from whom the appeal was brought (*ETA 1996, s 35*). It also has the same general powers as the High Court in relation to production of documents, attendance of witnesses, contempt of court and other matters incidental to its jurisdiction (*ETA 1996, s 29(2)*). As to the EAT's powers to make restricted reporting orders, and orders preserving anonymity, see **21.26** above.

The *2002 Practice Direction* introduced new procedures regarding the transcription of judgments of the EAT, and these have been retained in the subsequent revisions. Unless the decision is reserved or the EAT so directs as part of its judgment given orally, or, in the case of a preliminary hearing, the judgment is given in the absence of the appellant, a transcript will only be drawn up if requested by one or both parties within 14 days, or the judge so directs (eg because of the public importance of the points decided) (*2018 Practice Direction, paras 20.3, 20.4*). The *Practice Direction* gives more detailed information about the arrangements for handing down reserved judgments and any consequential applications (for permission to appeal, for costs etc). In Scotland the practice is that judgments are normally reserved. Judgments given following full hearings which are ordered to be transcribed, or are reserved and handed down, are posted on the EAT website as are judgments given in appeals under *rule 3(10)*, but in this case only if a judge or the Registrar so directs: *2018 Practice Direction, para 20.6*. The website address is https://www.gov.uk/employment -appeal-tribunal-decisions. Final judgments issued since 1992 are also available on http ://www.bailii.org/.

21.42 COSTS RELATING TO THE EMPLOYMENT APPEAL TRIBUNAL

The powers of the EAT to award costs (expenses in Scotland) were significantly recast by the *2004 Amendment Rules*. The provisions are now contained in *rules 34–34D*. The scheme of the new provisions follows that of the *ET Rules* in providing separately for the costs incurred by unrepresented parties, and in introducing wasted costs orders.

Additional powers to order a respondent to an appeal to pay as costs to the successful appellant the fees paid by the appellant to pursue the appeal were added as one of the changes in the EAT Rules consequential on the introduction of fees; however whilst these powers remain in force, and the point may arise in an appeal instituted before fees were abolished in July 2017, the EAT is likely to refuse to make such an order on the ground that the Government has undertaken to reimburse any fees paid, and the successful appellant need not therefore be out of pocket.

Until recently there was no authority to suggest that the EAT has power to award costs or expenses incurred in the employment tribunal, as against those incurred in the appeal. However in *Soll (Vale) v Jaggers* (UKEAT/0218/16), the EAT held that costs incurred in the tribunal proceedings could in principle be awarded by the EAT (in the particular case, the costs incurred by the respondent, which had won both at the tribunal and on the claimant's appeal); however the EAT went on to hold that in the particular circumstances of the case it was better for the tribunal itself to decide whether to exercise its discretion to award costs incurred in the proceedings before it.

A party may apply for a costs order at any stage during the appeal, or within 14 days of the date the order finally disposing of the proceedings is sent to the parties (*rule 34(4)*). However, unless the paying party is given an opportunity at the hearing to make representations against the making of an order, it can only be made after an opportunity to make such representations has been afforded by notice to the party concerned (*rule 34(5)*). The representations will normally be dealt with on the papers, but if it is considered appropriate, they can be referred for a further hearing. Written reasons must be given for a costs order if a party so requests within 21 days of the date of the order (*rule 34(6)*).

The statistics published by the Ministry of Justice do not include details of the numbers and amounts of awards of costs or expenses; experience in practice is that awards are relatively uncommon but far from unknown.

21.43 Grounds for costs orders

The principal circumstances in which a costs order can be made against a party are that the paying party has brought proceedings that were unnecessary, improper, vexatious or misconceived, or that there has been unreasonable delay or other unreasonable conduct by the paying party. Without prejudice to the general application of those criteria, costs may be ordered in four specific cases, namely where the paying party has not complied with a direction of the EAT, or has amended a Notice of Appeal, Respondent's Answer or similar document, or has caused an adjournment of the proceedings (*rule 34A(1), (2)*; or, following the introduction of fees, where the receiving party has paid a fee, the paying party may be ordered to reimburse all or part of the fee (*rule 34A(2A)*; but see **21.42** above).

The most important of these conditions is the bringing of an appeal which is misconceived (ie has no reasonable prospect of success), and unreasonable conduct by a respondent, which may include resisting an appeal on misconceived grounds. In practice, however, there will rarely be grounds for an award of costs under either head, since misconceived appeals are likely to be screened out, at latest at the preliminary hearing, before the respondent to the appeal needs to incur significant costs in resisting it. It will also only very rarely be the case that it can be said that defending a decision of a tribunal against an appeal is as such unreasonable conduct (a view confirmed by the Court of Appeal in *Afolayan v MRCS Ltd* [2009] EWCA Civ 796, [2009] All ER (D) 256 (Jul)).

The *manner* in which an appeal is pursued or defended may however be unreasonable even though the party concerned has a case with some merit. An example of a case where expenses were awarded on the ground that the appeal was so lacking in merit as to be misconceived is *Morgan v Greater Glasgow Health Board* (UKEATS/0044/11). In *Faithorn Farrell Timms LLP v Bailey* [2016] IRLR 839, [2016] ICR 1054 (UKEAT/0025/16), costs were awarded against the appellant employer, which had succeeded in part of its appeal, because its unreasonable conduct of the appeal had put the respondent to the appeal to unnecessary expense.

One ground for an award of costs is that the appellant has pursued an appeal until just before it is due to be heard and then abandoned it.

There are limits on the making of an order for costs against the respondent to an appeal who has not had an answer accepted by the EAT: in such a case *rule 34(3)* allows for a costs order in relation to his or her conduct of any part of the proceedings in which he or she has taken part; the necessary limitation implied by this is that if a respondent takes no part in the appeal, there is no power to award costs against that respondent (compare in relation to costs in the employment tribunal *Sutton v The Ranch Ltd* [2006] ICR 1170, [2006] All ER (D) 195 (Jun)). Costs may be awarded in favour of a respondent who has taken only a limited part in the appeal, but in practice it is unlikely that such a respondent will have incurred significant costs, and only costs actually incurred can be claimed.

Further guidance on when the bringing or pursuit of an appeal can be categorised as unreasonable is given in *Iron and Steel Trades Confederation v ASW Ltd (in liquidation)* [2004] IRLR 926. In *G4S Security Services (UK) v Rondeau* (UKEAT/0207/09/DA), the EAT awarded costs against the respondent to the appeal, who had refused a reasonable offer of settlement by the appellant, only to accept it at the door of the court. An example of a case where costs were awarded against a successful appellant because the proceedings were 'unnecessary' is *Fowler v British School of Motoring* [2006] All ER (D) 93 (May), where the appellant employer had failed for no good reason to present its response to the original claim in time, and successfully appealed against the tribunal's refusal to review a decision that it should not be permitted to take part in the proceedings. The appeal was 'unnecessary' because the appellant could and should have submitted its response in good time.

The fact that the preconditions for an award of costs exist does not entitle the receiving party to an order. The EAT has a discretion whether to award costs (and its exercise of that discretion will rarely be disturbed on appeal: see *Afolayan*, above). If it decides to do so, it has a further discretion to take into account the means of the paying party (*rules 34A(3), 34B(2)*). The powers available subject to this discretion are to award a sum determined by the EAT itself by summary assessment, or an agreed sum, or to award costs subject to a detailed assessment by the High Court or taxation by the Auditor of the Court of Session (*rule 34B(1)*).

21.44 Litigants in person

There are separate rules as to the amount that may be awarded where the receiving party is a litigant in person (in Scotland a party litigant), equivalent to the powers of the tribunal to make a preparation time order. It should however be noted that, in contrast to the position in employment tribunals, the general power to award costs is not confined to an award to legally represented parties; any party who does not fall within the definition of a litigant in person or a party litigant is eligible for an award of costs in accordance with *rule 34B*. A litigant in person is defined to include a company or corporation which is acting without a legal representative, and a solicitor, barrister, advocate or other person qualified to conduct litigation who is appearing for him or herself (*rule 34D(7)*). This does not cover a company represented by an in-house lawyer, or an individual represented by a non-legal representative, including a relative or friend, or a professional consultant who is not a lawyer; the latter are therefore eligible for ordinary costs orders under *rule 34A*.

The conditions for an award of costs in favour of a litigant in person are the same as for any other party. The costs recoverable may not exceed two thirds of the costs that would be payable if the party had had legal representation (with an exception for any disbursements, such as a payment for legal advice, which may be recovered in full if a full award is made and the payment was of a reasonable amount) (*rule 34D(2)*). Within this overall restriction, the costs recoverable are payments for advice, and for expert assistance in assessing the claim for costs, and expenses incurred in the proceedings (eg for photocopying or travel to the hearing), and compensation for time spent preparing the case and attending the hearing (*rule 34D(3)*). In relation to this head, the rate of payment will either be the amount the party can prove he or she has lost (eg lost wages) or a flat rate of £40 an hour (from 6 April 2020; this rate increases annually by £1 an hour, in the same way as the equivalent rate for preparation time orders: see **20.132** for further details) (*rule 34D(4), (5)*). The amount awarded will be subject to the EAT's assessment of what was a reasonable and proportionate amount of time to spend preparing for the hearing. Litigants in person are treated no differently from legally represented litigants in relation to recovering fees paid to pursue the appeal.

21.45 Wasted costs orders

The powers to make wasted costs orders and the procedures to be followed are set out in new *rule 34C*. This is for all practical purposes in exactly the same terms, with necessary modifications of terminology, as *rule 48* of the *ET Rules*, and reference should therefore be made to the discussion of that *Rule* at **20.132** above for details. Guidance on the procedure to be followed in the EAT when considering a wasted costs application (as distinct from the hearing of an appeal against an order made by a tribunal) was given by the Court of Appeal in *Gill v Humanware Europe Ltd* [2010] EWCA Civ 799, [2010] ICR 1343, [2010] IRLR 877.

21.46 Reimbursement of fees

Following the introduction of fees, payable by the appellant, for appeals, the EAT Rules were amended to give powers to the EAT to order a respondent to an appeal to pay all or part of the fees incurred by the appellant: see *rule 34A(2A)*. Following the abolition of fees in July 2017, the only relevance of this rule is for cases where an appeal had been lodged, and a fee paid, before 26 July 2017 (the date of the Supreme Court's decision that fees were unlawful). The Ministry of justice agreed that all fees paid should be reimbursed, and set up procedures for parties that had paid fees to apply for reimbursement. Any application for an order for costs under *rule 34A(2A)* is therefore likely to be met by the EAT drawing attention to this facility.

21.47 REVIEW

The EAT may review any order made by it on the grounds that:

(a)   the order was wrongly made as the result of an error on the part of the EAT or its staff;

(b)   a party did not receive proper notice of the proceedings leading to the order; or

(c)   the interests of justice require such review.

(*EAT Rules, rule 33*)

(The terminology used has not changed in line with the change in the *2013 ET Rules* from 'review' to 'reconsideration'.) Orders which may be reviewed are not limited to final determinations of appeals; it may on occasion be appropriate for the EAT in the course of a hearing to review an order made earlier in the proceedings, such as an order specifying the grounds of appeal which may be considered (see *Khan v Vignette Europe Ltd* (UKEAT/0350/08)). The circumstances in which the review procedure can be invoked are rare (see *Stannard & Co (1969) Ltd v Wilson* [1983] ICR 86). In *Jenkins v P & O European Ferries (Dover) Ltd* [1991] ICR 652, the EAT on its own initiative was prepared to review its earlier decision on the ground that it recognised that there was a fundamental error of law in that decision, but in *Blockleys plc v Miller* [1992] ICR 749 it appeared to prefer a narrower approach. In *Digital Equipment Co Ltd v Clements (No 2)* [1997] IRLR 140, [1997] ICR 237 the EAT reviewed, and reversed, its initial decision in circumstances where that decision had been given in ignorance of another decision on essentially the same point of law; the review thus enabled the EAT to resolve the law on a point on which there would otherwise have been conflicting authorities. There is as yet no reported decision of the EAT on whether its powers of review in the interests of justice have been enlarged by the addition to the *EAT Rules* of the Overriding Objective, but this would be consistent with the view taken by the EAT of the equivalent change in the *ET Rules* (see eg *Williams v Ferrosan Ltd* [2004] IRLR 607).

However, there is no jurisdiction to review a decision not to register an appeal taken under *Rule 3(7)* on the sift; the appropriate course for an aggrieved appellant to take is to apply for a hearing under *Rule 3(10)*: see *Zinda v Governing Body of Barn Hill Community High* [2011] ICR 174. The EAT in that case accepted, however, that it might exceptionally be appropriate to permit a review of a decision taken under one of the procedures in *Rule 3* on the basis of fresh evidence having become available, if the point first arose after any time limit for appealing had expired. By contrast it has been held that there is power in exceptional circumstances to review a decision under *rule 3(7)* to allow the appeal to proceed to a hearing, where the decision to do so has been taken on the basis of false or misleading information given by the appellant: *Jamieson v Nationwide Building Society* (UKEAT/0028/13).

Where the EAT has not formally drawn up and issued the order embodying its decision, it has a wider power of review based on its inherent jurisdiction as a superior court of record, and need not confine itself to the *Blockleys* approach: *Bass Leisure Ltd v Thomas* [1994] IRLR 104 at 108–109. Exceptionally, the EAT may reach a provisional decision, notify the parties accordingly and invite further submissions before pronouncing final judgment; this was done in *Rubenstein and Roskin (t/a McGuffies Dispensing Chemists) v McGloughlin* [1997] ICR 318, [1996] IRLR 557. This only occurs in rare circumstances.

21.48 FURTHER APPEALS

A further appeal may be taken to the Court of Appeal (or in Scotland, the Court of Session) on a point of law, but only with permission from the EAT or the Court of Appeal or Court of Session (*ETA 1996, s 37(1), (2)*). Permission should be sought initially from the EAT.

If the EAT refuses permission, an application may be made to the Court of Appeal (or the Court of Session, as the case may be). The principles to be applied upon such an application were considered by the Court of Session in *Campbell v Dunoon and Cowal Housing Association Ltd* [1992] IRLR 528. The restrictions on 'second appeals' to the Court of Appeal introduced by the *Access to Justice Act 1999, s 55* do not apply to appeals from the EAT, and the introduction of more restrictive criteria in relation to other areas does not appear significantly to have affected the Court of Appeal's practice in granting permission to appeal in employment cases.

In appeals from the EAT, the Court of Appeal is a second-tier appellate court and is concerned with whether the decision of the employment tribunal was right, not with whether the EAT was right (*Hennessy v Craigmyle & Co Ltd* [1986] IRLR 300, [1986] ICR 461; *Campion v Hamworthy Engineering Ltd* [1987] ICR 966). However, the Court of Appeal itself expressed serious reservations about the correctness of this approach in *Gover v Propertycare Ltd* [2006] EWCA Civ 286, [2006] 4 All ER 69, [2006] ICR 1073, and it may fairly be regarded as arguable in the light of these reservations. Where the EAT has allowed an appeal from the original decision of the tribunal, the focus of a further appeal to the Court of Appeal is inevitably directed more to whether there was sufficient basis for the EAT to have interfered with the first instance decision.

The time limit for lodging an appeal to the Court of Appeal with the permission of the EAT is 14 days from the date on which the order or judgment of the EAT was drawn up, unless the EAT gives a longer period; if permission is refused, an appellant's notice must be served on the court, by way of application for permission to appeal, within the same 14-day period (*Civil Procedure Rules 1998, r 52.3*).

The normal practice of the Court of Appeal is that costs follow the event, so that a successful appellant is usually entitled to, and will be awarded, his or her costs. Until 2013 this was equally the case for appeals from the EAT despite the general principle that the employment tribunals and EAT are costs-free jurisdictions in which an award of costs requires specific justification. However recent developments have reduced the risks to litigants of more modest means of the usual costs regime of the Court. In *Governing Body of St Albans Girls' School v Neary (No 2)* [2009] EWCA Civ 1214, the Court of Appeal refused to award costs to the employers, who had successfully appealed against the refusal of the EAT to strike out the claimant's claim for breach of an unless order. The fact that the employee had been taken to the Court by his ex-employer, rather than the other way round, coupled with the employee's impecuniosity, was considered by the Court to be in the circumstances a reason to depart from the normal rule that costs follow the event. Costs are ultimately always in the discretion of the Court.

An amendment to the *Civil Procedure Rules 1998*, applicable from 1 April 2013, gives the court power on an appeal from a jurisdiction where costs are not normally awarded to make an order in advance of the appeal limiting the costs recoverable by the successful party, having regard to the means of the parties, the circumstances of the case and the interests of justice (*CPR Rule 52.9A*). The use of this power was foreshadowed by the decision in *Manchester College v Hazel* [2013] EWCA Civ 281, [2013] IRLR 563 that the employee respondents to an appeal by the employer should be protected from an award of costs against them if the appeal succeeded (the employees having agreed not to seek costs if the appeal was refused). There is not as yet any equivalent provision protecting parties of limited means in appeals to the Court of Session.

A further appeal lies to the Supreme Court if the Court of Appeal, or the Supreme Court itself, gives permission. A number of special rules govern Supreme Court appeals. Further, *ETA 1996, s 37A* (as amended) permits the EAT to grant a certificate allowing an appeal directly from the EAT to the Supreme Court (a so-called "leapfrog" appeal). The procedure to be adopted in such cases is to be found at *2018 Practice Direction, Paras 24.5–24.7*. An application should either be made at the hearing, at the "hand-down" hearing if the reasons were reserved, or within seven days thereafter.

21.48   Employment Tribunals – III: Appeals

In Scotland, the appeal from the EAT is to the Inner House of the Court of Session, and thence, with permission, to the Supreme Court. In Northern Ireland, appeals lie directly from the tribunal to the Northern Ireland Court of Appeal, and thence to the Supreme Court. Leave to appeal is required at each stage, except that appeals to the Northern Ireland Court of Appeal (which involve the stating of a case by the tribunal) are a matter of right.

21.49 ISSUES OF EU LAW

Britain left the European Union on 31st January 2020. By *Section 6(1)* of the *European Union (Withdrawal) Act 2018* neither a Court nor a Tribunal is bound by any principles or decisions made on or after exit day. The ability to refer any matter to the European Court ceased on the same day. Nevertheless, Courts and Tribunals may have regard to anything done by the European Court after exit day says *section 6(2)* of the *2018 Act*.

22   Engagement of Employees

Cross-reference. See REFERENCES **(40)** for employment made conditional on references.

22.1   ADVERTISING

When advertising for prospective employees, an employer must be careful not to infringe the provisions of the equality legislation (see **14.12** DISCRIMINATION AND EQUAL OPPORTUNITIES – III). For example, the advertisement should avoid use of gender-specific phrases and should not indicate that applicants of a particular race or age are required (subject to this being a genuine occupational requirement). An example of this in the age discrimination field is *Canadian Imperial Bank of Commerce v Beck* [2010] All ER (D) 102 (Sep) where the EAT held that an advertisement seeking someone with a 'younger, entrepreneurial profile' was sufficient to establish a prima facie case of age discrimination. *Section 39* of the *Equality Act 2010* provides that A must not discriminate against or victimise B in the arrangements made for deciding to whom to offer employment; as to the terms on which A offers B employment; or by not offering B employment. *Section 40* provides that an employer must not harass an applicant for employment.

However, it has been held that these provisions do not apply to an employee who is already in post and who is, for example, responding to an internally advertised vacancy: *Clymo v Wandsworth London Borough Council* [1989] IRLR 241, [1989] ICR 250, EAT (cf *Timex Corpn v Hodgson* [1981] IRLR 530, [1982] ICR 63, EAT). Moreover, the protection does not apply to an applicant who was not intending to take the job even if offered it, on the basis that there would have been no detriment in being rejected: *Keane v Investigo* (UKEAT/0389/09) (11 December 2009, unreported) and *Berry v Recruitment Revolution* (UKEAT/0190/10) (6 October 2010, unreported). *Section 39(1)* does, however, apply where a TUPE transfer of employment is taking place but the employee is being offered suitable alternative employment (and therefore potential redundancy): *NHS Direct NHS Trust v Gunn* [2015] IRLR 799, EAT.

An advertisement indicating that a job is open only to persons who are or who are not union members will lead to a conclusive presumption that work has been refused on union membership grounds and thus, in general, unlawfully (see **22.3**(d) below, and the reference there cited).

22.2   INTERVIEWING AND SELECTION

An employer may use any interviewing and selection procedures he wishes, provided that they are not discriminatory within the meaning of the equality legislation (see DISCRIMINATION AND EQUAL OPPORTUNITIES – I (12), II (13), III (14)). Particular care should be exercised in wording job application forms and other documents in which applicants may be asked to provide personal information. There is no obligation on the candidate to disclose information potentially adverse to them as though there were a duty of good faith: *Nottingham University v Fishel* [2000] IRLR 471.

Discrimination claims arising out of alleged discriminatory reasoning for non-selection following an interview are not uncommon. For a recent unsuccessful example, see *Kumar v DHL Services Ltd* (UKEAT/0117/17/LA) (8 September 2017, unreported).

In *Cheltenham Borough Council v Laird* [2009] EWHC 1253 (QB), [2009] IRLR 621 an employer sued a former employee for having made allegedly fraudulent or negligent misrepresentations in her job application for a senior position and in particular in her responses to a pre-employment medical questionnaire. The claim was unsuccessful because the questions asked had been too ambiguous, not because no such cause of action could arise. *Section 60* of the *Equality Act* relates to enquiries about disabilities or health. *Subsection (1)* provides:

> '(1) A person (A) to whom an application for work is made must not ask about the health of the applicant (B) –
>
> (a)   before offering work to B, or
>
> (b)   where A is not in a position to offer work to B, before including B in a pool of applicants from whom A intends (when in a position to do so) to select a person to whom to offer work.'

Subsection (6) provides that enquiries about disability or health are allowed in so far as asking the question is necessary for the purpose of (a) establishing whether B will be able to comply with a requirement to undergo an assessment or establishing whether a duty to make reasonable adjustments is or will be imposed on A in relation to B in connection with a requirement to undergo an assessment, (b) establishing whether B will be able to carry out a function that is intrinsic to the work concerned, (c) monitoring diversity in the range of persons applying to A for work, (d) taking action to which *s 158* [positive action] would apply if references in that section to persons who share (or do not share) a protected characteristic were references to disabled persons (or persons who are not disabled) and the reference to the characteristic were a reference to disability, or (e) if A applies in relation to the work a requirement to have a particular disability, establishing whether B has that disability. The effect of *subsection (6)* is that employers may, and often do, ask applicants to complete a type of Equal Opportunities Monitoring Form, but that Form (or similar) must be detached or removed from the application before it is seen by those taking the hiring decision: *Patel v Lloyds Pharmacy Ltd* [2013] All ER (D) 215 (Sep) (UKEAT/0418/12/ZT).

Sections 158 and *159* relate to positive action. *Section 159* applies if a person (P) reasonably thinks that (a) persons who share a protected characteristic suffer a disadvantage connected to the characteristic, or (b) participation in an activity by persons who share a protected characteristic is disproportionately low. *Subsection (2)* provides that *Part 5* of the *Equality Act* (work) does not prohibit P from taking action within *subsection (3)* with the aim of enabling or encouraging persons who share the protected characteristic to (a) overcome or minimise that disadvantage, or (b) participate in that activity. Action within *subsection (3)* is treating a person (A) more favourably in connection with recruitment or promotion than another person (B) because A has the protected characteristic but B does not. *Subsection (4)* provides that *subsection (2)* applies only if (a) A is as qualified as B to be recruited or promoted, (b) P does not have a policy of treating persons who share the protected characteristic more favourably in connection with recruitment or promotion than persons who do not share it, and (c) taking the action in question is a proportionate means of achieving the aim referred to in *subsection (2)*.

Appendix 2 to the *EHRC Statutory Code of Practice on Employment* provides recommendations on the monitoring of diversity by employers.

22.3   In arranging an interview for a disabled person, it may be necessary for the employer to make reasonable adjustments to enable that person to attend. The employer is free to select for employment whomsoever he chooses, subject to the following:

(a)   the restrictions on the employment of CHILDREN AND YOUNG PERSONS (4);

(b)   the restrictions on the employment of FOREIGN EMPLOYEES (27);

(c)   the restriction on excluding a person from any office, profession, occupation or employment by reason of a spent conviction (see EMPLOYEE'S PAST CRIMINAL CONVICTIONS (18));

(d)   the bar on refusing a person employment because he is or is not a trade union member (see TRADE UNIONS – I (51)).

22.4

In *R (T & others) v Chief Constable of Greater Manchester & others* [2014] UKSC 35, [2014] 4 All ER 159 the Supreme Court considered the blanket requirement in the *Rehabilitation of Offenders Act 1974, s 113B* of the *Police Act 1997* and *articles 3* and *4* of the *Rehabilitation of Offenders Act 1974 (Exceptions) Order 1975* that criminal convictions and cautions must be disclosed in an enhanced criminal record check in the context of particular types of employment (such as with children or vulnerable adults), even if those convictions or cautions would otherwise be deemed spent by the *1974 Act*. The Supreme Court had no difficulty in finding that the criminal records regime pursued a legitimate aim, generally of protecting employers and children or vulnerable adults in their care, and particularly of enabling employers to make an assessment as to whether an individual is suitable for a particular kind of work. However, the Court held that the disclosure of all convictions and cautions relating to recordable offences was disproportionate to that aim. The regime implemented by the *1997 Act* was declared incompatible with *art 8 ECHR*, although the Court held that *articles 3* and *4* of the *1975 Order* should not have been declared ultra vires by the Court of Appeal because it was inconsistent with the non-effect on validity that a declaration of incompatibility is intended to have under the *Human Rights Act 1998* to declare void subordinate legislation made under the provision subject to that declaration. The Government had in any event enacted the *Rehabilitation of Offenders Act 1974 (Exceptions) Order 1975 (Amendment) (England and Wales) Order 2013* and the *Police Act 1997 (Criminal Record Certificates: Relevant Matters) (Amendment) (England and Wales) Order 2013*, which came into force on 29 May 2013, which applies a more nuanced filtering system distinguishing between offenders under and over the age of 18, types of offences which must always be disclosed relevant to safeguarding, the time elapsed and whether a custodial sentence resulted. That amended scheme was largely upheld by the Supreme Court *R (P) v Secretary of State for Justice* [2019] UKSC 3, [2019] 2 WLR 509, which emphasised the importance of an assessment of risk posed by the individual with a past criminal record be a matter for the employer and not the State in the abstract. Aspects which were found to be incompatible with *ECHR, article 8* were the rule that if an individual has two convictions of whatever type, all conviction information is disclosable, and the absence of a specific rule excluding from disclosure youth warnings and reprimands. For strong judicial criticism of employers failing to reflect the changes in the law on criminal record disclosures, and operating blanket bans on hiring individuals with even very minor records, see: *R (R) v National Police Chiefs Council & Secretary of State for Justice* [2017] EWHC 2586 (Admin), [2018] 1 WLR 1651.

An employer may not avoid the restrictions on disclosure of spent convictions by requiring a prospective employee obtain a full criminal record under a subject access request made to the police (or any other person). *Section 184* of the *Data Protection Act 2018* makes it a criminal offence to require job applicants (or existing employees) to produce a copy of their criminal record through a subject access request.

Where an employment tribunal has made a finding in relation to an incident, it is not necessarily unreasonable for the police to form their own view, unrestricted by the tribunal, and to disclose the incident to a prospective employer: *R (W) v Chief Constable of Warwickshire* [2012] EWHC 406 (Admin), [2012] All ER (D) 38 (Mar).

22.5   ENGAGEMENT

An employer should inform a new employee of the terms and conditions under which he is to work and his commencement date and time. This should be done by letter (if not by a formal signed agreement), although a purely verbal agreement may be sufficient to found an employment relationship (as in *Ferguson v John Dawson & Partners (Contractors) Ltd* [1976] IRLR 346). He is obliged by law to give the employee written particulars of those terms and conditions within two months of the commencement of his employment (see **8.6** CONTRACT OF EMPLOYMENT). An offer may be made 'subject to satisfactory references' and in *Wishart v National Association of Citizens Advice Bureaux Ltd* [1990] IRLR 393, [1990] ICR 794 the Court of Appeal considered that this meant only satisfactory to the employer, subject to an obligation of good faith. If a conditional offer subject to satisfactory references is withdrawn upon receipt of that reference, the decision to withdraw the offer is subject to challenge as an act of discrimination. For an example of a successful claim against both the former employer which provided a reference, and the putative employer which withdrew the offer of employment, under *s 15* of the *Equality Act 2010* arising out of a reference which had noted a high level of sickness absence, see: *Pnaiser v NHS England & Coventry City Council* [2016] IRLR 170, EAT.

In *Barclays Bank v Various Claimants* [2020] UKSC 13, [2020] All ER (D) 04 (Apr) the Supreme Court held, overturning the Court of Appeal, that a bank was not vicariously liable for the misconduct – in the form of sexual assaults – of an independent medical practitioner with whom the bank had contracted to carry out medical assessments as part of the recruitment process.

The actual day on which employment commences has importance under the rules for computing continuity of employment (see **7.3** CONTINUOUS EMPLOYMENT) irrespective of whether the employee actually performs any duties on that day, and determination of that day is a matter of fact (see *General of the Salvation Army v Dewsbury* [1984] IRLR 222, [1984] ICR 498 and *Boufoy-Bastick v University of the West Indies* [2015] UKPC 27, [2015] IRLR 1014). The employment must start under the contract itself: *Koenig v Mind Gym Ltd* (2013) UKEAT/0201/12/RN, [2013] All ER (D) 261 (May), EAT.

22.6   EMPLOYMENT AGENCIES

For the law regulating employment agencies, and the status of those recruited through such agencies, see **48.2** TEMPORARY AND SEASONAL EMPLOYEES.

22.7   WITHDRAWAL OF OFFERS OF EMPLOYMENT

Once an offer of employment has been made and accepted, a valid contract exists even though the date when the employee is due to start work may be delayed or does not commence immediately. The contract governs the relations between the parties accordingly: *Welton v Deluxe Retail Ltd* [2013] IRLR 166. If in these circumstances the employer retracts the offer or terminates the contract prior to the actual commencement of work, the employee will not be without a remedy. There are three remedies which may potentially be available to the employee depending on the circumstances. First, there may be a claim for wrongful dismissal (see WRONGFUL DISMISSAL **(59)**). Under ordinary contractual principles, such a scenario will be an anticipatory breach where one party has given unequivocal notice that it will not comply with the agreement: see the old authority of *Hochster v de la Tour* (1853) 2 E&B 678. That claim may be brought before the employment tribunal or the county court. Second, if the reason for the dismissal is an inadmissible reason, there may be a claim of unfair dismissal. No period of qualifying employment is necessary when the reason for dismissal is an inadmissible reason (see **55.3** UNFAIR DISMISSAL – II). The authority for both of these propositions is *Sarker v South Tees Acute Hospitals NHS Trust* [1997] IRLR 328, [1997] ICR 673. Third, it may be possible to bring a claim alleging that the dismissal was discriminatory on grounds of age or sex or race or disability or religion or belief or sexual orientation (see DISCRIMINATION AND EQUAL OPPORTUNITIES – **I (12)**, **II (13)**, **III (14)**). An example in the discrimination context is *Mamedu v Hatten Wyatt Solicitors* [2008] All ER (D) 76 (Apr), EAT.

The Court of Appeal has confirmed that obligations of trust and confidence can apply to both employer and employee from the outset of the contract where the agreement is one to take up employment at a future date (a so-called forward contract): *Tullett Prebon Plc v BGC Brokers LP* [2011] EWCA Civ 131, [2011] IRLR 420. In forward contract situations, an individual may have acquired contractual obligations to his future employer, but this does not absolve him of his contractual obligations (and fiduciary obligations if applicable) to his existing employer, even if those obligations are mutually inconsistent: *Imam-Sadeque v Bluebay Asset Management (Services) Ltd* [2012] EWHC 3511 (QB), [2013] IRLR 344; *Hilton v Barker Booth & Eastwood* [2005] UKHL 8, [2005] 1 All ER 651.

23   Equal Pay

23.1   Since the coming into force on 29 December 1975 of the *Equal Pay Act 1970* (*'EqPA 1970'*), women have been able to claim equal pay with men, and vice versa. The accession of Great Britain to the *Treaty of Rome* on 1 January 1973 also affected women's rights to equal pay since *art 157* (formerly *art 141*) provides that 'Each Member State shall ensure that the principle of equal pay for male and female workers for equal work or work of equal value is applied'. *Article 157* and *Directive No 75/117* ('the *Equal Pay Directive*') provide a European underpinning of the domestic rights to equal pay (see below **23.3**). The European Commission has also published a *Code of Practice on the Implementation of Equal Pay for Work of Equal Value for Women and Men* (COM(96)336) (See https ://core.ac.uk/download/pdf/5076938.pdf). The provisions of domestic legislation which currently provide for equal pay between men and women are found in the *Equality Act 2010* (*'EqA 2010'*).

Although the right to equal pay in the UK was introduced in domestic law before the UK was required by the European Union to implement any such right, subsequent developments in equal pay law have very much been driven by the European Union and accordingly the provisions of the *European Union (Withdrawal) Act 2018* (the *Withdrawal Act*) will need to be taken into account when considering the continued application of the law set out in this chapter after the UK completes withdrawal from the European Union. In general terms, little will change. Since the *EqA 2010* is domestic legislation it is not itself affected by withdrawal from the European Union. However, the interpretation of the *EqA 2010* may change over time as the provisions of the *Withdrawal Act* introduce new rules on the way the European law, and the decisions of the CJEU, should be taken into account in future in interpreting EU-derived domestic legislation such as the *EqA 2010*.

In particular, in common with all Courts and Tribunals, by *s 6(1)* of the *European Union (Withdrawal) Act 2018*, the Tribunal is not bound by any principles laid down, or any decisions made, on or after completion day by the CJEU, and cannot refer any matter to the CJEU under *article 234*. However, by *s 6(2)*, a Tribunal may have regard to anything done on or after completion by the CJEU, another EU entity (such as the Commission) or the EU so far as it is relevant to any matter before the Tribunal. By *s 6(3)*, any question as to the validity, meaning or effect of any retained EU law is to be decided, so far as that law is unmodified on or after completion and so far as they are relevant to it: (a) in accordance with any retained case law and any retained general principles of EU law, and (b) having regard (among other things) to the limits, immediately before completion, of EU competences. *Section 6(6)* clarifies that the same principle applies to law that has been modified after completion if that would be consistent with the intention of the modifications. However, by *s 6(4)(c)*, the Tribunal is not bound by any retained domestic case law that it would not otherwise be bound by. The Supreme Court has power to depart from retained EU case law (under *s 6(4)* and *(5)*); if it does so, then the Tribunal would be bound by the Supreme Court's decision. What is meant by 'retained domestic' and 'retained EU law' and 'retained general principles of EU law' is further defined in the Act. Of particular note: the general principle of the supremacy of EU law does not apply after exit day (*s 5(1)-(3)*); no general principle of EU law is part of domestic law on or after exit day if it was not recognised as a general principle of EU law by the European Court in a case decided before exit day (whether or not as an essential part of the decision in the case) (*Sch 1, para 2*); and there is no right of action in domestic law on or after exit day based on a failure to comply with any of the general principles of EU law and no court or tribunal or other public authority may, on or after exit day disapply or quash any enactment or other rule of law or decision because it is incompatible with any of the general principles of EU law (*Sch 1, para 3*).

See further European Union Law (**24**).

23.2 Equal Pay

23.2 THE LEGISLATIVE FRAMEWORK

Domestic legislation

Discrimination in relation to pay (and other contractual terms) on grounds of age, disability, gender reassignment, marriage and civil partnership, race, religion or belief and sexual orientation is dealt with in the same way as discrimination in relation to other matters: see DISCRIMINATION AND EQUAL OPPORTUNITIES – I (12). However, sex discrimination in relation to pay (and other contractual terms) is generally dealt with separately. Prior to the coming into force of the *EqA 2010*, sex discrimination in relation to contractual terms was 'carved out' of the *Sex Discrimination Act 1975* ('*SDA 1975*') by s 6(5) and *(6)* and instead covered by the *EqPA 1970*. As described further below, the *EqPA 1970* provided for a statutory equality clause to be implied into all contracts of employment. Thus, if a woman was engaged on like work or on work rated as equivalent to that of a man or on work of equal value to that of a man, a woman's contract was modified by the *EqPA 1970* so that she could claim pay equal to that which the man received.

EqA 2010 consolidates the provisions previously found in the *EqPA 1970* into a single anti-discrimination statute alongside other aspects of discrimination law. The key provisions are found in *Chapter 3* of *Part 5* of the *EqA 2010*. Although the *EqPA 1970* and the *SDA 1975* have been consolidated in the *EqA 2010*, the same separation between discrimination in relation to pay and discrimination in relation to other matters is maintained in the *EqA 2010* – with one important change. Differences in the contractual terms of men and women are covered by *ss 64–69* of the *EqA 2010* (which effectively re-enact the provisions of the *EqPA 1970* by providing for a statutory implied sex equality clause in all contracts). Then, by virtue of *s 70* the 'ordinary' sex discrimination provisions are disapplied in circumstances where the claim relates to a term of the woman's contract that falls to be modified or included by virtue of the statutory sex equality clause, or would fall to be modified or excluded were it not for the fact that the employer is able to establish a defence of genuine material factor (see below), or because one of the various statutory exceptions in *Part 2* of *Sch 7* applies. A claimant cannot succeed on both a discrimination and an equal pay claim in such cases: *BMC Software Ltd v Shaikh* [2017] IRLR 1074 (overruled on other grounds: [2019] EWCA Civ 267, [2019] ICR 1050). As noted by the EAT in that case, the 'ordinary' sex discrimination provisions are also disapplied where the claim relates to contractual pay, but the statutory equality clause has no effect, unless – and this is the significant change on the position under the previous legislation – the difference in pay constitutes direct discrimination under *ss 13* or *14* of the *Act* (*s 71*). Complaints of direct discrimination in relation to contractual pay where there is no actual comparator and a hypothetical comparator only is relied on are thus dealt with under the 'ordinary' provision in relation to sex discrimination in s 13 of the Act (see DISCRIMINATION AND EQUAL OPPORTUNITIES – I (12)). All other complaints of sex discrimination in relation to contractual terms must be brought by reference to the sex equality clause in accordance with *ss 64–69* of the *Act* applying the statutory provisions and case law discussed in this chapter.

As with terms of a woman's employment related to pay, the right to equal treatment in respect of occupational pension schemes was 'carved out' of the *SDA 1975* and dealt with separately under the *Pensions Act 1995*. The same division is maintained in the *EqA 2010*. Thus *EqA 2010, s 75* creates a maternity equality rule that applies to all occupational pension schemes requiring them to treat time on maternity leave in the same way as time at work (save that any contributions may be reduced proportionate to any reduction in the pay that the woman receives during maternity leave). By *s 76* where a complaint concerns a matter that is covered by the maternity equality rule, no complaint of sex or pregnancy or maternity discrimination can be made in relation to it. Rather, the claim must be brought as an 'equal pay' claim based on the maternity equality rule under *s 75*.

Note that the *EqA 2010* also contains a prohibition on pay confidentiality clauses which prevent employees from discussing their pay with colleagues (*EqA 2010, s 77*) and a power to require employers with 250 or more employees to provide reports on the gender pay gap in their business (*EqA 2010, s 78*): see **23.32** below.

Prior to 1 October 2010 the *EqPA 1970* provided the domestic legal framework for the elimination of discrimination between the sexes in the terms of their contracts of employment. Because a large number of equal pay cases (including local authority 'multiples') continue to be heard under the *EqPA 1970*, and because the case law under *EqPA 1970* continues to be relevant under the *EqA 2010*, this chapter continues to include reference to the *EqPA 1970* as well as *EqA 2010*.

The *EqPA 1970* and the examples set out below are framed with reference to women but they are to be read as applying equally to men. The *EqA 2010* is framed in gender neutral language.

Maternity and pregnancy

A similar exclusionary rule operates in respect of complaints about discrimination in relation to pay and pensions on grounds of maternity and pregnancy. Whilst an employee is absent from work on maternity leave, an employer may lawfully cease paying her anything other than pay to which she is entitled by statute or contract as a result of being pregnant or on maternity leave: *EqA 2010, Sch 9, Part 3, para 17*. However, a woman remains entitled to any bonus in respect of a period when she is on compulsory maternity leave (*para 17(2)(c)*). She also remains entitled to be paid in accordance with the statutory maternity equality clause in *ss 73* and *74* of the *EqA 2010* (see **23.13** below) and to be treated for the purposes of any occupational pension scheme in accordance with the statutory maternity equality rule in *s 75* of the *EqA 2010* (dealt with at **13.35**B DISCRIMINATION AND EQUAL OPPORTUNITIES – II). The statutory maternity equality clause (broadly speaking) requires a woman who is paid during maternity leave by reference to her normal salary to receive any salary increases (proportionately adjusted) as she would have received if she were working, and likewise to be paid any bonus (proportionately adjusted where appropriate). By *s 76* it is then provided that where a term of a woman's employment relates to pay, no complaint of sex or pregnancy or maternity discrimination can be made in relation to it. Rather, the claim must be brought as an 'equal pay' claim based on the maternity equality clause under *ss 73* and *74* (see further below **23.13** and **23.28**).

Part-time workers

Discrimination against part-time workers was for some time (and is still to a certain extent) dealt with by way of the protection against indirect sex discrimination in the *SDA 1975* and now in *Chapter 1* of *Part 5 EqA 2010* (see **12.34** DISCRIMINATION AND EQUAL OPPORTUNITIES – I). Part-time workers can also bring equal pay claims under the provisions discussed in this chapter (see especially **23.20** below). However, since 1 July 2000, part-time workers have also been specifically protected in relation to pay and other detriments by the *Part-time Workers (Prevention of Less Favourable Treatment) Regulations 2000 (SI 2000/1551)* ('*Part-time Workers Regulations*') (PART-TIME WORKERS (34)).

Transsexuals

In 1996, the European Court of Justice, now the Court of Justice of the European Union (CJEU) decided that discrimination against transsexual employees constituted sex discrimination (*P v S and Cornwall County Council: C-13/94* [1996] IRLR 347). The *Sex Discrimination (Gender Reassignment) Regulations 1999 (SI 1999/1102)* inserted into the *SDA 1975* provisions relating to discrimination against those who intend to undergo, are undergoing or have undergone a gender reassignment (see, in particular, *SDA 1975, ss 2A* and *4*), and these provisions were re-enacted in the EqA 2010 (see DISCRIMINATION AND EQUAL OPPORTUNITIES – I (12)). However, unlike for sex discrimination, there was no 'carve out' from the *SDA 1975* in respect of discrimination in relation to pay for transsexuals, which fell to be dealt with as an 'ordinary' discrimination rather than equal pay claim: see *SDA 1975, s 4(8)*. The same is true under the *EqA 2010*.

Code of Practice. Note that a code of practice prepared by the EOC came into force on 26 March 1997 and was re-issued by the Equal Opportunities Commission in 2003 and was admissible as evidence in *EqPA 1970* and *SDA 1975* proceedings. A new *Equal Pay: Statutory Code of Practice* (See https://www.equalityhumanrights.com/en/publication-download/equal-pay-statutory-code-practice) has now been issued by the Equalities and Human Rights Commission under the *EqA 2010*.

23.3   EU Provisions

The foundation of the right to equal pay in EU law is contained in what is now *art 157* of the *Lisbon Treaty* (formerly *art 141* of the *Treaty of Rome*) (the '*Treaty*') which provides:

'Each Member State shall ensure that the principle of equal pay for male and female workers for equal work or work of equal value is applied.

For the purposes of this Article, "pay" means the ordinary basic or minimum wage or salary and any other consideration, whether in cash or in kind, which the worker receives, directly or indirectly, in respect of his employment from his employer.

Equal pay without discrimination based on sex means:

(*a*)   that pay for the same work at piece rates shall be calculated on the basis of the same unit of measurement;

(*b*)   that pay for work at time rates shall be the same for the same job.'

Article 157 and *Directive No 2006/54/EC* ('the *Recast Directive*' which replaced *Directive No 75/117* from 15 August 2009) provide a European underpinning to domestic rights to equal pay. These provisions have been relied upon as an aid to construction of domestic law and as a basis for disapplying inconsistent provisions of domestic legislation (cf *Scullard v Knowles* [1996] IRLR 344 and below). However, it is not possible in all circumstances to enforce *art 157* claims directly before the domestic courts (see EUROPEAN UNION LAW (24)). Where it is possible, *article 157* creates a directly enforceable right to equal pay where the comparator is doing the same or similar work, or work rated as equivalent, but not necessarily where the question of whether the jobs are of equal value is in dispute. On this latter point, the Court of Appeal in *Asda Stores Ltd v Brierley* [2019] EWCA Civ 44, [2019] IRLR 335 considered that a reference to the CJEU would be necessary if the point was material in a particular case (which in that case, it was not).

The Council of the EU has also adopted *Directive 86/378/EEC* on the progressive implementation of the principle of equal treatment for men and women in occupational social security schemes, including pension schemes. *Directive 96/96/EC* (which came into effect on 1 July 1997) amended *Directive 86/378/EC* to take account of the CJEU's decision in *Barber v Guardian Royal Exchange Assurance Group* [1990] IRLR 240, [1990] ICR 616. *Directive 86/378/EEC* has also been repealed and replaced by the provisions of the Recast Directive from 15 August 2009.

The *Recast Directive* provides at *Article 14* (which replaces *Article 5.1* of *Directive No 76/207* (the '*Equal Treatment Directive*')):

'There shall be no direct or indirect discrimination on grounds of sex in the public or private sectors, including public bodies, in relation to:

...

(c) employment and working conditions, including dismissals, as well as pay as provided for in Article 141 (now *art 157*) of the Treaty...'

Upon the UK withdrawing from the European Union, the provisions of *ss 2* to *8* of the *European Union (Withdrawal) Act 2018* will have effect and will, broadly speaking, maintain the effect of EU legislation in domestic law. See generally EUROPEAN UNION LAW **(24)**.

See also **12.2** DISCRIMINATION AND EQUAL OPPORTUNITIES – I.

The meaning of 'work' in EU law

Article 157 enshrines the right to equal pay for equal work. The definition of 'work' for this purpose has proven to be wider than might initially be imagined. In *Davies v Neath Port Talbot County Borough Council* [1999] IRLR 769, [1999] ICR 1132, EAT, the issue was whether attending a union–organised course for elected health and safety representatives constituted 'work' for the purposes of *art 157*. Relying on an analogy with the CJEU cases of *Botel*: C–360/90 [1992] IRLR 423 and *Lewark*: C–457/93 [1996] IRLR 637, the EAT determined that:

> 'Attending a training course organised by a recognised trade union is still related to the employment relationship and is safeguarding staff interests which is ultimately beneficial to the employer.'

The effect of this finding was that the complainant, who ordinarily worked part-time, was able to claim full-time pay as she was attending the course on a full–time basis. Reliance on *art 157* enabled the EAT to avoid applying *TULR(C)A 1992, s 169* which would otherwise have required her to be paid her normal part-time pay. *Section 169* had an indirectly discriminatory effect and was thus contrary to *art 157* and was not applied. Note, however, that not all trade union activities are 'work' for this purpose: see, eg, *Manor Bakeries Ltd v Nazir* [1996] IRLR 604 (attending trade union conference not 'work').

The meaning of 'pay' in EU law

It is now well established that 'pay' in *art 157* is to be given a broad meaning. In *Barber v Guardian Royal Exchange Assurance Group*: C–262/88 [1990] IRLR 240, [1990] ICR 616, it was held that a benefit is in the nature of pay if the worker is entitled to receive it from his employer by reason of the existence of the employment relationship. Thus, it included benefits paid by the employer upon compulsory redundancy, even where they consisted of pension payments made after the termination of employment. It did not matter that the payment was received only indirectly from the employer (eg through the trustees of a pension scheme). The CJEU reached a similar decision in *Kuratorium Für Dialyse und Nierentransplantation eV v Lewark* [1996] IRLR 637, ruling that compensation paid pursuant to a German statute for loss of earnings whilst attending training sessions for participants in staff councils is pay. (Contrast, however, *Manor Bakeries Ltd v Nazir* [1996] IRLR 604, EAT: employee entitled to paid time off pursuant to a collective agreement to attend a trade union conference. The paid time–off was not 'pay' for the purposes of *art 157* as attending the conference was not 'work' and pay is remuneration for work.) In *Barber*, the CJEU also observed that pensions from both contributory and non–contributory schemes were 'pay' within *art 157*. (See also *Bilka-Kaufhaus GmbH v Weber von Hartz*: 170/84 [1986] IRLR 317, [1987] ICR 110.) The CJEU, unusually, specifically limited the effect of its decision by stating that it could not be relied upon to claim entitlement to a pension prior to 17 May 1990 (the date of the decision). This matter is considered in greater detail at **23.14** *et seq* below.

Compensation for unfair dismissal is pay for the purposes of *art 157*: *R v Secretary of State for Employment, ex p Seymour-Smith and Perez*: C–167/97 [1999] IRLR 253, [1999] ICR 447. The CJEU decided that the basic and compensatory awards (for which see **56.7** and **56.10** UNFAIR DISMISSAL – III) are deferred pay to which the worker is entitled (ultimately) by reason of his employment. The fact that the compensation consisted of a judicial award did not invalidate that conclusion. However, neither an order for reinstatement nor for re–engagement (for which see **56.2** and **56.3** UNFAIR DISMISSAL – III) is 'pay'. The CJEU does not seem to have considered the status of the monetary award made in cases where re–employment is ordered.

Pay includes sums paid in lieu of notice and also covers payments made by the Secretary of State on the insolvency of an employer in respect of the employee's contractual entitlement to notice (*Clark v Secretary of State for Employment* [1996] IRLR 578, [1997] ICR 64, CA).

Further, 'pay' within *art 157* includes a statutory redundancy payment or an *ex gratia* payment upon redundancy (see *McKechnie v UBM Building Supplies (Southern) Ltd* [1991] IRLR 283, [1991] ICR 710 for entitlement to equal statutory and contractual redundancy payments).

In *Rinner-Kühn v FWW Spezial-Gebäudereinigung GmbH & Co KG*: 171/88 [1989] IRLR 493, 'pay' was held to include the statutory sick pay which an employee was entitled to receive from her employer; see also *EC Commission v Belgium*: C-173/91 [1993] IRLR 404.

The CJEU also expanded the definition of 'pay' to cover contractual terms which relate to the calculation of entitlements or to requirements imposed as prerequisites to the granting of entitlements. In *Hill v Revenue Comrs and Department of Finance*: C-243/95 [1998] IRLR 466, [1999] ICR 48, CJEU, the CJEU considered the employment conditions of certain Irish civil servants. Salary was dependent on length of service. Employees who worked half-time earned half of the full-time rate. However, when they moved to full-time employment their pay did not double. Instead, they were placed on the full-time pay spine at a level that gave them credit for only half of the actual period that they had worked for their employer. In other words, their length of service was pro-rated to reflect their previous part-time status. The CJEU decided that the method adopted by the employer for converting part-timers to full-time status constituted 'pay' within *art 157* and that it was, in the particular circumstances, discriminatory and not justified. However, terms with a less direct connection to pay rates may be treated differently. In *Gerster v Freistaat Bayern*: C-1/95 [1997] IRLR 699, [1998] ICR 327, Bavarian civil service regulations, which required that periods of part-time service should (depending on the number of hours worked) either be entirely or partly discounted when assessing eligibility for consideration for promotion, were held not to offend *art 157*. The CJEU distinguished *Nimz*: C-148/89 [1991] IRLR 222, in which a complainant had successfully challenged a similar rule which gave part-time workers only partial credit for their periods of service. In *Nimz*, promotion was practically automatic on completion of the relevant period of service. As the provision in *Gerster* was only concerned with eligibility for promotion, the connection to pay was insufficiently direct to bring the case within the scope of *art 157* which was not concerned with inequalities relating to 'access to career advancement'. The CJEU opined, however, that the rule was potentially contrary to the *Equal Treatment Directive (EEC/76/2007)*. It was left to the national court to decide whether or not the respondent's contention that the requirement was intended to ensure that employees had sufficient experience (and was therefore objectively justified) was made out.

The dividing line between what constitutes 'pay' and what is a 'working condition' that falls to be considered under the *Equal Treatment Directive* (and now, the *Recast Directive*) has been addressed by the CJEU in a number of cases. *Kording v Senator für Finanzen*: C-100/95 [1997] IRLR 710 concerned German legislation which exempted employees with sufficient length of service from having to take certain examinations. Part-time workers had to work a longer period which was pro-rated to the proportion of full-time hours that they worked. The CJEU considered that the provision was not 'pay', but that it was nevertheless indirectly discriminatory (though capable of objective justification). Similarly, the provision of subsidised nursery places to female staff only is to be regarded as a 'working condition' within the meaning of the *Equal Treatment Directive* rather than 'pay' within *art 157*: *Lommers v Minister van Landbouw Natuurbeheer en Visserij*: C-476/99 [2002] IRLR 430. The CJEU held that the fact that the fixing of certain working conditions may have pecuniary consequences is not sufficient to bring such conditions within the scope of *art 157*, which is a provision based on the close connection between the nature of the work done and the amount of pay. However, the CJEU went on to hold that measures giving a specific advantage to women with a view to eliminating inequality (such as providing nursery places for working mothers only) was not contrary to the *Equal Treatment Directive*, in particular where male single parents were given places on the same conditions. (See also *Steinicke v Bundesanstalt für Arbeit*: C–77/02 [2003] IRLR 892: schemes of membership that may have pecuniary consequences not 'pay', though they were indirectly discriminatory contrary to the *Equal Treatment Directive*).

23.4   THE RIGHT TO EQUAL PAY IN DOMESTIC LAW

The equal pay provisions in *Chapter 3* of *Part 5* of *EqA 2010* apply by reason of *s 72 EqA 2010* to persons who are employed or who hold 'a personal or public office'. Employment is defined by *s 83* of *EqA 2010* as including 'employment under a contract of employment, a contract of apprenticeship or a contract personally to do work' (cf **16.3** EMPLOYEE, SELF-EMPLOYED OR WORKER?) as well as Crown employment and employment as a 'relevant member' of House of Commons or House of Lords staff. Service in the armed forces is deemed to be employment by *s 83(3)* of *EqA 2010*. For the territorial scope of the *EqA 2010*, see **13.18** DISCRIMINATION AND EQUAL OPPORTUNITIES – **II**.

The position under the *EqPA 1970* was similar. The right to equal pay applied:

(a)   to women employed in an establishment in Great Britain whether they were British or not and regardless of the law governing their contract of employment (*EqPA 1970*, *s 1(1)*, *(11)*);

(b)   to men as well as women (*EqPA 1970*, *s 1(13)*).

'Employed' under *EqPA 1970* was defined as 'employed under a contract of service or of apprenticeship or a contract personally to execute any work or labour' (*EqPA 1970*, *s 1(6)(a)*).

Office-holders

As set out above, the equal pay provisions in *Chapter 3* of *EqA 2010*, *Part 5* apply to personal or public office holders. Personal office holders are defined by *EqA 2010*, *s 49* as those holding an office or post to which a person is appointed to discharge a function personally under the direction of another person, and in respect of which an appointed person is entitled to remuneration. Public office holders are defined by *EqA 2010*, *s 50(2)* as those holding an office or post appointment to which is made by a member of the executive, or subject to the approval of a member of the executive, or in relation to which appointment is made on the recommendation of, or subject to the approval of the House of Commons, the House of Lords, the National Assembly for Wales or the Scottish Parliament. Following the decisions of the CJEU and Supreme Court in *O'Brien v Ministry of Justice* (respectively, C–393/10, [2012] IRLR 421, [2012] ICR 955 and [2013] UKSC 6, [2013] IRLR 315) establishing that judges are 'workers' under European law, it is likely that many office holders will now also fall within the definition of 'employee' in *s 83* of the *EqA 2010* and thus be covered by the standard rules on employees. However, the provisions in relation to office holders are likely still to remain relevant to such people, and also to those who are genuinely office holders and not employees or workers in European law.

The position under *EqPA 1970* was that statutory office-holders were formerly excluded from the provisions of the *EqPA 1970*. However, with effect from 1 October 2005, office-holders (with the exception of holders of political office) were expressly brought within the scope of the *Act*: *EqPA 1970*, *s 1(6A)–(6C)* as amended by *reg 35* of the *Employment Equality (Sex Discrimination) Regulations 2005*. *Section 1(6A)* of the *Act* extended the right to equal pay to those holding an office or post to which persons were appointed to discharge functions personally under the direction of another person, and in respect of which they were entitled to remuneration, or any office or post to which appointments are made by (or on the recommendation of or subject to the approval of) a Minister of the Crown, a government department, the National Assembly for Wales or any part of the Scottish Administration. This amendment followed the decision of the Northern Ireland Court of Appeal in *Perceval-Price v Department of Economic Development* [2000] IRLR 380, holding that an identically worded provision in the *Equal Pay Act (Northern Ireland) 1970* was incompatible with *art 157* as the right to equal pay conferred by the *EC Treaty* extends to all 'workers' as defined by the CJEU in *Lawrie-Blum v Land Baden-Wurttemberg*: 66/85 [1986] ECR 2121 (a case about *art 48* of the *EC Treaty*). In *Lawrie-Blum*, the CJEU identified the 'essential feature' of an employment relationship as being that 'for a certain period of time a person performs services for and under the direction of another person in return for which he receives remuneration'. The NICA concluded that the tribunal chairmen fell within that definition despite their status as statutory office-holders, and disapplied the exclusion.

Employees posted abroad

Employment in an establishment in Great Britain formerly required that the employee should not work 'wholly or mainly outside Great Britain'. However, the *Equal Opportunities (Employment Legislation) (Territorial Limits) Regulations 1999 (SI 1999/3163)* removed the words 'or mainly' from the relevant provision. The effect is that the legislation now covers workers posted abroad. The *Regulations* came into effect on 16 December 1999. With effect from 1 October 2005, for the purposes of the *EqPA 1970*, employment is regarded as being at an establishment in Great Britain if (a) the employee does her work wholly or partly in Great Britain, or (b) if she does her work wholly outside Great Britain but her employer has a place of business at an establishment in Great Britain, her work is for the purposes of the business carried on at that establishment, and she is ordinarily resident in Great Britain at the time when she applies for or is offered the employment, or at any time during the course of the employment: *SDA 1975, s 10* as amended by the *Employment Equality (Sex Discrimination) Regulations 2005, reg 11(2)*.

For the current law and provisions dealing with the territorial extent of the *EqA 2010* see generally **13.18** Discrimination and Equal Opportunities – **II**.

Women suspended on maternity grounds

Women whose pay is reduced when they are suspended on maternity grounds may not seek to challenge the reduction by bringing claims under the general provisions of the *EqA 2010* or under the predecessor provisions in *EqPA 1970*. *ERA 1996, ss 66–70A* represent a complete code governing the contractual entitlements of such women (*British Airways (European Operations at Gatwick) Ltd v Moore* [2000] IRLR 296, EAT) and see further (33) Maternity and Parental Rights.

Special treatment of women in connection with pregnancy or childbirth

Paragraph 2 of *Schedule 7* to the *EqA 2010* provides that the 'sex equality clause' will not apply in respect of special treatment of women in connection with pregnancy or childbirth. However, there are circumstances in which women absent on maternity leave may bring challenges in relation to pay and benefits paid to them while on maternity leave: by virtue of the statutory maternity equality clause and rule in *ss 73* and *74* of the *EqA 2010*: see further below **23.13** and **23.28** and **13.35B** Discrimination and Equal Opportunities – **II**. The effect of *paragraph 2* of *Schedule 7* to the *EqA 2010* is also to preclude claims brought by men seeking rights equivalent to maternity rights: see *Capita Customer Management Ltd v Ali* [2018] ICR 1591, [2018] IRLR 586. This also prevents men bringing claims on the basis that an employer's parental leave arrangements (applicable to both women and men) are indirectly discriminatory against men on the basis that more men than women make use of the parental leave arrangements and are therefore disadvantaged as these are generally less beneficial than maternity leave arrangements. As the Court of Appeal held in *Hextall v Chief Constable of Leicestershire Police* [2019] EWCA Civ 900, [2020] ICR 87, such a claim is in substance a claim that maternity entitlements accorded to women are discriminatory against men. The effect of *s 70(1)(b)* to the *EqA 2010*, read together with *para 2* of *Schedule 7*, is to preclude any sex discrimination claim (whether direct or indirect) in relation to the special treatment of women in connection with pregnancy or childbirth. However, it should be noted that the CJEU in *RE v Praxair MRC SAS* (C-486/18) [2019] 3 CMLR 29 (a French case, not referred to in *Hextall*) held that it was unlawful for compensation payments for dismissal and redeployment of an employee to be paid on a part-time basis where the employee was normally employed full-time, but taking part-time parental leave, Since the evidence was that in France more women than men are likely to take part-time leave, this breached art 157. This would appear to provide support at the European level for the conclusion of the EAT in the *Hextall* case ([2018] ICR 1632) (overturned by the Court of Appeal) that men on parental leave may have prima facie indirect discrimination claims in relation to any identifiable less favourable treatment (at least where the comparison is with the workforce as a whole).

Members of the armed forces

Members of the armed forces were formerly expressly excluded from the scope of *EqPA 1970*. However, *EqPA 1970* was amended by the *Armed Forces Act 1996, s 24* to allow claims to be brought. This was brought into force on 1 October 1997 by the *Armed Forces Act 1996 (Commencement No 3 and Transitional Provisions) Order 1997 (SI 1997/2164)* and the *Equal Pay (Complaints to Employment Tribunals) (Armed Forces) Regulations 1997 (SI 1997/2162)*. The position under *EqA 2010* is dealt with by a deeming provision, deeming members of the armed forces to be employees: see *EqA 2010, s 83(3)*.

23.5   The equality clause

Neither the *EqPA 1970* or the *EqA 2010* straightforwardly prohibit direct and indirect discrimination in matters of contractual entitlement. Instead, the *EqPA 1970* adopted a rather oblique and artificial approach. By *s 1(2)* it implied an 'equality clause' into any contract of employment that does not already include one. The equality clause operated whenever a woman was doing like work, work of equal value or work rated as equivalent to that of a man (*s 2(1)*). The *EqA 2010* adopts a similar approach. *Section 66(1)* creates a 'sex equality clause'. The clause has the effect that:

(a)   any term of a person's contract which is less favourable than that of an appropriate comparator is modified so as to be not less favourable (*s 66(2)(a)*);

(b)   where a person's contract does not have a term which corresponds to a beneficial term in the contract of an appropriate comparator, the person's contract is modified so as to include such a term: *(s 66(2)(b))*;

(c)   unless the employer does not seek to, or fails to, establish that the difference between the person's contract and the comparator's is genuinely due to a material factor which is not the difference of sex and which is not indirectly discriminatory and cannot be justified (*EqA 2010, s 69*) (see **23.11** below).

Appropriate comparators are those doing 'equal work' as defined in *EqA 2010, s 65*, ie those doing:

(a)   *like work* (see below **23.6**); or

(b)   *work rated as equivalent* (see below **23.7**); or

(c)   work of *equal value* (see below **23.8**).

Thus, for example, if a man and a woman are engaged on like work and the man is paid £500 per week for that work, but the woman only £400, the equality clause will operate so as to entitle the woman to £500 per week. Also, if the man's contract contains a clause which entitles him to be paid during absence from work due to sickness, but the woman's contract contains no such clause, the woman's contract will be deemed by law to include such a clause. (For appropriate comparators see below **23.9**.)

The sex equality clause in *EqA 2010* is framed in gender neutral language. That in the *EqPA 1970* was not, but by virtue of *s 1(13)* applied equally to men. It is also established in the case law that the operation of the equality clause allows 'piggyback' contingent claims. Thus, where a group of female claimants bring equal pay claims, male colleagues of those claimants may simultaneously bring 'piggyback' contingent claims using the female claimants as comparators and to recover sums equivalent to those awarded to such comparators (if they are successful) by way of arrears: *Llewellyn v Hartlepool Borough Council* [2009] ICR 1426, [2009] IRLR 796.

The equality clause applies to all terms and conditions of employment and not only to pay (eg *Sun Alliance and London Insurance Ltd v Dudman* [1978] IRLR 169, [1978] ICR 551, relating to a contractual term granting a mortgage interest allowance). The provisions of the *SDA 1975* and the *EqPA 1970* were considered to contain an interlocking but mutually exclusive prohibition on discrimination on grounds of sex: *SDA 1975, s 6(6)* and *Peake v Automotive Products Ltd* [1977] IRLR 105, [1977] ICR 480. The *EqPA 1970* applied where the contract regulated the provision of benefits in the form of money: *Grundy v British Airways plc* [2005] All ER (D) 94 (Aug), EAT; reversed on other grounds by the CA [2007] EWCA Civ 1020, [2008] IRLR 74). It was not necessary for the payment in question to be expressly provided for in the contract. Provided that the contract 'regulated' the payment it would fall under *EqPA 1970* and not under the *SDA 1975*: thus a so-called 'discretionary' bonus scheme would fall to have been considered under *EqPA 1970* if the discretionary element of it was in fact only as to the amount paid to all employees in any one year and not as to whether or not the employee is entitled to a bonus at all: *Hoyland v Asda Stores Ltd* [2006] IRLR 468. In that case the Court of Session expounded a 'but for' test in order to determine whether or not the payment fell to be considered under *EqPA 1970* or the *SDA 1975*, ruling that if the payment would not have been made 'but for' the existence of the contract of employment, then *EqPA 1970* applied. However, it is doubtful whether this is the correct approach since on that basis any benefit conferred on an employee *qua* employee would have to be regarded as covered by the *EqPA 1970*. The better approach is perhaps to be found in *Hosso v European Credit Management* [2012] IRLR 235, [2012] ICR 547. In that case, Stanley Burnton LJ found that where the contract granted an employer a discretion as to whether and in what amount to confer a benefit, then the exercise of that discretion was not 'regulated' by the contract of employment and so any claim for discriminatory exercise of the discretion had to be pursued under the *SDA 1975* and not the *EqPA 1970*. Stanley Burton LJ considered that the difficulty with pursuing an equal pay claim where the term in question provided for a contractual discretion was that there was no difference in the terms of the complainant and the comparator's contracts of employment such that the equality clause could operate. Mummery LJ did not express a view on this reasoning preferring to confine his reasoning to the facts of *Hosso* which related to a share option scheme where the claimant and her comparator had the benefit of the same scheme (on the same terms). However, if Stanley Burnton LJ is correct, *Hoyland v Asda Stores Limited* has been effectively confined to its facts.

Section 70 of the *EqA 2010* preserves the mutual exclusion of 'ordinary' sex discrimination and equal pay claims formerly contained in *s 6(6)* of the *EqPA 1970*, with one significant change. Where the 'sex equality clause' operates, or would operate but for the success of the employer's 'genuine material factor' defence (see below **23.10**) or the application of one of the exceptions in *Part 2* of *Sch 7* to the *Act* (see generally **13.11** DISCRIMINATION AND EQUAL OPPORTUNITIES - II), no claim for 'ordinary' sex discrimination may be made in relation to a contractual term relating to pay. However, and this is the significant change on the position under the *EqPA 1970*, where the 'sex equality clause' has no effect on a contractual term relating to pay (eg because no real comparator can be identified), then a direct (but not an indirect) discrimination claim may be brought in relation to that term under the 'ordinary' direct discrimination provisions: see *s 71* and Discrimination and Equal Opportunities - I (12). Note that in *BMC Software Ltd v Shaikh* [2017] IRLR 1074 (overruled on other grounds: [2019] EWCA Civ 267, [2019] ICR 1050), Judge Hand considered it arguable that the effect of *EqA 2010, s 70* was to preclude a complaint of constructive discriminatory dismissal where the repudiatory conduct relied upon was alleged to be a breach of the sex equality clause.

It is, however, clear that the equality clause cannot operate so as to give the complainant a more favourable term than that contained in her comparator's contract. Where, for instance, qualified female employees are paid at the same rate as male trainees, the employee cannot rely on the clause to secure a premium over the rate paid to a trainee selected as a comparator (see *Enderby v Frenchay Health Authority (No 2)* [2000] IRLR 257, [2000] ICR 612, CA), but a sex discrimination claim could now be brought using the male trainees as evidence to help establish the position for a hypothetical comparator: see 23.2 above.

In *Hayward v Cammell Laird Shipbuilders Ltd* [1988] IRLR 257, [1988] ICR 464, the House of Lords rejected the argument that the 'total remuneration package' must be taken into account when making the comparison between a woman's pay and a man's. What must be compared is each distinct provision of the contract dealing with pay and benefits in kind. The applicant was thus entitled to the same rate of basic pay and overtime pay as her male comparator even if she was more favourably treated in other respects, in this case paid meal breaks, additional holidays and better sickness benefits. However, it can be difficult to determine what constitutes a distinct provision or term of the contract. In *Degnan v Redcar & Cleveland Borough Council* [2005] EWCA Civ 726, [2005] IRLR 615, the Court of Appeal held that attendance allowances paid to male employees were all part of a single term of the contract together with their hourly rate and fixed bonuses for the purposes of the comparison of the terms in the woman's contracts. This approach was held to be consistent with *Hayward* in that it did not lump together different terms but instead looked at the reality of the situation by classifying all these payments which related to the same subject-matter as coming under the same contractual term, being 'provision for monetary payment for the performance of the contract by employees during normal working hours'. All monetary payments received by the men should be aggregated and divided by the number of hours in the working week to give an hourly rate which, if lower for women than men, should be increased for women to eliminate the difference. This approach, of treating different payments as different elements of a single contractual term, does sit uneasily with the prohibition on taking a 'swings and roundabouts' approach in *Hayward*. This approach is also difficult to reconcile with the CJEU's decision in *Elsner-Lakeberg v Land Nordrhein-Westfalen* [2005] IRLR 209 in which it held that, in order to determine whether the principle of equal pay is being complied with, genuine transparency permitting an effective review is assured only if that principle applies to each aspect of remuneration, excluding any general overall assessment of the consideration paid. In that case, the CJEU held that it was necessary for there to be separate comparison in respect of the pay for regular hours and the pay for additional hours. Following *St Helens & Knowsley Hospital NHS Trust v Brownbill* [2011] IRLR 815 the scope for applying the approach taken in the *Degnan* case has been further limited. In *Brownbill*, the Court of Appeal, upholding a decision of the EAT, held that the tribunal should have carried out a comparison between the rates paid to the complainants and their comparators for unsocial hours work. Broadly speaking, the comparators received lower rates of pay, but higher rates for unsocial hours. Overall, most of the complainants were better paid than their comparators. The tribunal noted that if the claims succeeded the complainants would be even more highly paid than their comparators and held that the claims failed. The EAT and Court of Appeal disagreed, holding that the pay for unsocial hours was a distinct term for distinct work, present in both the contracts of the claimants and their comparators, and the proper approach was to compare the pay received by the complainants and comparators for unsocial hours work and determine whether there was a genuine material factor other than the difference in sex justifying the inequality (see **23.11** below). The matter was remitted to the tribunal. In so deciding Maurice Kay LJ held that *Degnan* was not an exception to the principles set out in *Hayward*. It was merely a particular application of Hayward by looking at the reality of the contractual provisions on the facts of the particular case.

Section 66(2) of *EqA 2010* appears to have accepted the analysis of the law as set out in *Hayward v Cammell Laird Shipbuilders Ltd* [1988] IRLR 257, [1988] ICR 464 by requiring a comparison as between the term in a woman's contract and the 'corresponding term' of the contract of the relevant comparator rather than by comparing the term in a woman's contract with 'a term of a similar kind' as was required by *s 1* of *EqPA 1970*. However, the requirement to consider each term separately does not mean that every element of a contract falls to be considered separately. In some cases, a contract may make provision for a particular component of pay to be calculated by reference to two or more elements. Whether or not those elements constitute 'terms' in their own right is a matter for assessment by the tribunal, but if the reality is that they are calculation factors in the calculation of a single component of pay, then they should be treated together as a single 'terms' for equal pay purposes. See in this regard: *McNeil v Revenue and Customs Commissioners* [2019] EWCA Civ 1112, [2020] ICR 515 ('basic pay' could not be divided into 'grade boundary pay' plus 'length of service element': 'basic pay' was both elements together under the contractual terms) and *Lloyds Banking Group Pension Trustees Ltd v Lloyds Bank plc* [2018] EWHC 2839 (Ch), [2019] Pens LR 5 ('terms' relating to indexation, revaluation, guaranteed minimum pension and 'excess' were regarded as in reality calculation factors in the single 'term', being basic pension).

It was suggested in *Hayward* that the 'material factor' defence under *EqPA 1970, s 1(3)* and now found in *section 69 EqA 2010* (see **23.10–23.12** below) might be available to an employer who could show that the unfavourable character of the term in the woman's contract was due to the more favourable character of the other terms. Broadly, the same approach is taken by the CJEU in relation to claims based upon *art 157* (see *Barber v Guardian Royal Exchange Assurance Group: C-262/88* [1990] IRLR 240, [1990] ICR 616 and *Jämställdhetsombudsmannen v Örebro läns landsting: C-236/98* [2000] IRLR 421, [2001] ICR 249, CJEU).

Note, however, that once it has been established that there is a 'genuine material factor' (see **23.10–23.12** below) that justifies a difference in pay, the equality clause will not operate so as to 'correct' a particular term of an employee's contract simply because that employee is, by the date of the hearing, a member of a group of women who are being paid less than a group of men: see *Armstrong v Newcastle Upon Tyne NHS Hospital Trust* [2005] EWCA Civ 1608, [2006] IRLR 124.

For indirect discrimination under the *EqPA 1970* and *EqA 2010*, see below **23.11**.

23.6 Like work

A woman is regarded as employed on like work with men if, but only if, her work and theirs is of the same or of a broadly similar nature and the differences (if any) between the things she does and the things they do are not of practical importance in relation to the performance of her contract of employment. 'Like work' is defined by *s 65(2)* of *EqA 2010* as meaning that 'A's work and B's work are the same or broadly similar and such differences as there are between their work are not of practical importance in relation to the terms of their work'. *Section 65(3)* of *EqA 2010* states that in considering differences between the work of a claimant and her comparator, for the purposes of determining whether or not the two are engaged on 'like work' 'it is necessary to have regard to the frequency with which differences between their work occur in practice and the nature and extent of the differences'. Similar provisions were formerly contained in *s 1(4)* of the *EqPA 1970*.

Thus, although the job descriptions of male and female employees or their written job specifications may be different, if the differences in their duties are of no practical importance, the women will be considered to be employed on like work with the men. The question of what is or is not a difference of practical importance will always be one of fact and degree depending upon the particular circumstances of the case. If, for example, male guillotine operators in a paper mill are required once in two weeks to lift reams of paper whereas women are not, the lifting is purely incidental to their main employment and is not of practical importance. Accordingly, it is not a difference which would prevent the women's right to equal pay.

The EAT has stated in *Capper Pass Ltd v Lawton* [1976] IRLR 366, [1977] ICR 83, that 'in deciding whether the work done by a woman and the work done by a man is 'like work' the employment tribunal has to make a broad judgment. The intention is that the employment tribunal should not be required to undertake too minute an examination, or be constrained to find that work is not like work merely because of insubstantial differences. In order to be like work within the *Act*'s definition the work need not be of the same nature; it need only be broadly similar.' In that case, a cook in the directors' dining room was held to be engaged on like work with the assistant chefs of the company's factory canteen. The fact that women do their work at a different time of the day from men may not prevent them from claiming that they are engaged upon like work (*Dugdale v Kraft Foods Ltd* [1976] IRLR 368, [1977] ICR 48; *National Coal Board v Sherwin* [1978] IRLR 122, [1978] ICR 700; contrast with *Thomas v National Coal Board* [1987] IRLR 451, [1987] ICR 757 in which the EAT held that a male canteen worker on permanent night-shift was not employed on like work with female day-shift canteen workers).

However, the duties actually performed are not the only considerations to be taken into account in deciding whether a woman is engaged on like work. In *Eaton Ltd v Nuttall* [1977] IRLR 71, [1977] ICR 272, the EAT held that 'In considering whether there is like work, though the most important point is what the man does and what the woman does, the circumstances in which they do it should not be disregarded. One of the circumstances properly to be taken into account is the degree of responsibility involved in carrying out the job.'

Article 157 uses the term 'same work' rather than 'like work'. However, the case law on the European provision suggests that a tribunal should not simply confine its consideration to the duties actually performed. In *Angestelltenbetriebsrat der Wiener Gebeitskrankenkasse v Wiener Gebeitskrankenkasse* [1999] IRLR 804, the CJEU considered a case concerning psychotherapists. Whilst the psychotherapists were all engaged in 'seemingly identical activities', they could be divided into those who had had training in psychology to graduate level and those who had been trained as general practitioners. The graduate psychologists, the majority of whom were women, were paid less. The CJEU decided that training and qualifications could be matters which were relevant to the determination whether the work and/or job were the same and were not merely relevant to a possible material factor defence. It should be noted, however, that although the CJEU purported to proceed on the basis that the applicants and their comparators were engaged in the same activity, it also observed that the former general practitioners, who were better qualified, could be called on to perform 'different tasks or duties'. It is not a case, therefore, where it could be said that the applicants and their comparators necessarily performed identical tasks. The CJEU seems to have had a broader notion in mind when it referred to the 'activity' in which both groups were engaged. In *Brunnhofer v Bank der Osterreichischen Postsparkasse AG: C–381/99* [2001]

23.6 Equal Pay

IRLR 571, CJEU, the CJEU followed *Angestelltenbetriebsrat*, to draw the conclusion that the existence of an identical collective agreement governing the employment of two employees was not in itself sufficient to show that they performed the same work, or work of equal value.

Helpful guidance on the fact-finding process was given by Lavender J in the High Court in *Beal v Avery Homes (Nelson) Limited* (Case No. HQ16X01000, 6 June 2019), following a review of the authorities. He noted that, in determining the facts relevant to the work of the employee and their comparator, it is (para 30): "*appropriate to look at what the employee actually did, and not simply at documents (such as contracts, job descriptions or work manuals), even if they had contractual force. Such documents are relevant, but not necessarily determinative, when considering what constitutes someone's work. Likewise, what the employee actually did is an important consideration, but is not necessarily determinative. To take an obvious example, an employee who loafs around during work hours does not thereby convert loafing into part of their work. Likewise, as the parties agreed, if an employee refused or neglected to do something which they were supposed to do, that activity would remain part of their work*". He went on (para 32): "*Of course, where an employee is contractually required to do something (and that requirement has not fallen into desuetude or otherwise been varied), then that activity will form part of their work (even if, in practice, they neglect or refuse to perform it). . . . In general terms, therefore: (1) Where an employee is instructed by their manager to do something, then, if they do it, that is surely part of their work. Moreover, that is so, even if they might have been entitled to say, "But that is not something I am obliged to do." (2) The same is likely to be the case where the manager does not instruct, but requests or encourages, the employee to perform the activity in question. On the other hand, in such a case, it may be relevant to note for the expert's benefit (if it is the case) that the employee could not be required to perform that activity. (3) Where an employee does something which they have not been instructed, requested or encouraged to do, it may still constitute work if, for instance: (a) it is simply a way of doing something which forms part of their work; and/or (b) their manager knows that they are doing it, but does not object and thereby tacitly approves of their doing it. (4) On the other hand, something may not be part of an employee's work if they have not been instructed, requested or encouraged to do it, their doing it has not been approved by their employer and it does not simply constitute a way of doing something which forms part of their work.*" Lavender J stressed (para 33) that these are merely general considerations, which are not intended to place a gloss on the *Act* and that each disputed issue has to be considered on the basis of its own particular facts.

If a woman's work is more onerous or more responsible than a man's, she may not be considered to be engaged on like work, even though less well paid (*Waddington v Leicester Council for Voluntary Service* [1977] IRLR 32, [1977] ICR 266). However, she may be able to obtain equal pay by bringing an equal value claim (see below **23.8** and *Murphy v Bord Telecom Eireann* [1988] IRLR 267, [1988] ICR 445) or a direct sex discrimination claim under *EqA 2010, s 13* using a hypothetical comparator.

23.7 Work rated as equivalent

A woman may claim equivalence with a man even though she is not engaged on like work, if a job evaluation study has been carried out in respect of his work and hers, and her job has been rated as equivalent to the man's in terms of the demands made on a worker, or would have been rated as equivalent but for the evaluation being made on a sex-specific system (*EqA 2010, s 65(4)*). A system is sex-specific 'if for the purposes of one or more of the demands made on a worker, it sets values for men different from those it sets for women' (*s 65(5)*). Similar provision was made in *EqPA 1970, s 1(5)*, although that Act gave examples of the ways in which demands made in jobs may differ in terms of 'effort, skill, decision'.

By *EqA 2010, s 80(5)* a job evaluation study is 'a study undertaken with a view to evaluating, in terms of the demands made on a person by reference to factors such as effort, skill and decision-making, the jobs to be done (a) by some or all of the workers in an undertaking or group of undertakings, or (b) in the case of the armed forces, by some or all of the members of the armed forces'. By *EqA 2010, s 131(5)–(7)* if under a job evaluation study the claimant's work has been given a different value to that of the comparator, a tribunal must determine that the work in question is not of equal value (see below **23.8**), unless 'it has reasonable grounds for suspecting that the evaluation contained in the study: (a) was based on a system that discriminates because of sex, or (b) is otherwise unreliable'. For these purposes, a system discriminates because of sex if a difference (or coincidence) between values that the system sets on different demands is not justifiable regardless of the sex of the person on whom the demands are made. Similar provision was previously contained in *s 2A(2A)* of the *EqPA 1970*. The validity of a job evaluation study may thus be challenged if reliance is placed on such a study to claim or to resist a claim for equal pay. There have been remarkably few such challenges. *McDonald and ors v Glasgow City Council* [2017] CSIH 56, [2017] IRLR 993 provides a useful illustration of one such challenge, in which the Court of Session held that the burden of proof of showing a job evaluation study to be lawful was always on the employer and that this would not be satisfied by simply placing the study before the tribunal: the employer must usually bring expert evidence as to the scheme's efficacy and lawfulness. Only then did the burden shift to the claimant to adduce evidence of grounds for suspecting the study.

Advice on job evaluation is set out in ACAS Advisory Booklet 'Job evaluation: Considerations and Risks' available at www.acas.org.uk (See http://www.acas.org.uk/media/pdf/3/d/Job-evaluation-considerations-and-risks-advisory-booklet.pdf). See also the *Equal Pay : Statutory Code of Practice* available at www.equalityhumanrights.com (See https://www.equalityhumanrights.com/sites/default/files/equalpaycode.pdf).

It has been held that the comparison of jobs must be done by reference to the same job evaluation study (*Paterson (KD) v Islington London Borough* (23 April 2004, UKEAT/0347/03/DA), but it is submitted that what is crucial is that the same system is applied, not that the evaluation is carried out by the same people or at the same time. A job evaluation must be carried out on an objective basis. The principles were set out in *Eaton Ltd v Nuttall* (see above **23.6**). The job of each worker covered by the study must be valued in terms of the demand made on the worker under various headings (eg effort, skill, responsibility) in the study (*Bromley v H & J Quick Ltd* [1988] IRLR 249, [1988] ICR 623). Thus, it will not suffice simply to compare 'whole jobs'. The assessment should be qualitative, not quantitative – matters such as a difference in the number of hours worked go to the defence of material factor (see **23.10–23.12** below), not to evaluation of the job (*Leverton v Clwyd County Council* [1989] IRLR 28, [1989] ICR 33). Whilst the study as a whole must be objective, it is permissible for it to contain certain subjective elements, so long as they are not themselves inadvertently discriminatory. It is for the employer to explain how any job evaluation study worked and what was taken into account at each stage (see also *Rummler v Dato-Druck GmbH* [1987] IRLR 32, [1987] ICR 774).

In determining whether two jobs have been given an equal value by a job evaluation study, it is necessary to look at the full results of the study, including the allocation to grade or scale at the end of the evaluation process. Thus, in *Springboard Sunderland Trust v Robson* [1992] IRLR 261, [1992] ICR 554, the EAT held that the applicant and a male comparator were employed on work rated as equivalent because each of their scores resulted in an allocation of the same grade, albeit their scores in a job evaluation study had been different.

If no job evaluation study has been carried out, there is no legal requirement for an employer to conduct one. However, once a job evaluation study has been undertaken and has resulted in a conclusion that the job of a woman is of equal value to that of a man, the woman may claim equal pay, despite the fact that the employers may not have implemented the scheme (*O'Brien v Sim-Chem Ltd* [1980] IRLR 373, [1980] ICR 573). Where a valid job evaluation study has been carried out and a woman's job has been rated as slightly lower than her male comparator, it is not permissible for a tribunal, by reliance on extraneous expert evidence, to find that the difference is insignificant: *Home Office v Bailey* [2005] IRLR 369, [2005] ICR 1057. But, for work to be rated as equivalent there must be a *completed* job evaluation study, and there is no complete job evaluation study unless and until the parties who have agreed to the carrying out of the study have accepted its validity (*Arnold v Beecham Group Ltd* [1982] IRLR 307, [1982] ICR 744). The outcome of a job evaluation study cannot be applied retrospectively: it values the jobs from the point it is agreed and going forward only: *Redcar and Cleveland Borough Council v Bainbridge* [2008] EWCA Civ 885, [2009] ICR 133, applied in *Co-Operative Group Limited v Walker* (UKEAT/0087/19/RN).

23.8 Work of equal value

Where a woman is employed on work which is not like work or work which has been rated as equivalent to that of a male comparator, she may claim equal pay with a man if her work is of equal value to his, in terms of the demands made on her, eg under such headings as effort, skill and decision (*EqA 2010, s 65(1)(c) and (6)* and formerly *EqPA 1970, s 1(2)(c)*). Relying upon EU law, she may also claim equal pay where she is doing work of *greater* value (*Murphy v Bord Telecom Eireann*: 157/86 [1988] IRLR 267, [1988] ICR 445 and *Bainbridge v Redcar & Cleveland Borough Council (No 2)* [2008] EWCA Civ 885, [2008] IRLR 776, [2009] ICR 133). Employees of one sex may use *EqA 2010, s 65(1)(c)* to claim equal pay with those of the other sex doing a quite different job. Using this provision, a female cook employed as a canteen assistant succeeded in a claim for equal pay with male skilled tradesmen (see *Hayward v Cammell Laird Shipbuilders Ltd* [1988] IRLR 257, [1988] ICR 464). The fact that one man is being paid the same as a woman for doing like work to hers is no longer a bar to the woman claiming equal pay with another man doing a different job of equal value to hers (see *Pickstone*). In that case, the House of Lords held that the construction of *EqPA 1970* which enabled them to achieve this result was consistent with EU law. (For the procedure to be adopted on claims based on work of equal value see **23.29** below.)

A woman will not be able to succeed in an equal value claim if a valid job evaluation study has concluded that she and her male comparator do work which is not of equal value (*EqA 2010, s 2A(2)* and previously *EqPA 1970, s 2A(2)*). In such cases the employment tribunal must determine that the work is not of equal value unless it has reasonable grounds for suspecting that the study discriminated on the grounds of sex, or there are other reasons why it is not suitable to be relied upon *EqA 2010, s 131(5) and (6)* (see previously *EqPA 1970, s 2A(2) and 2A(2A)*). For these purposes, a system discriminates because of sex if a difference (or coincidence) between values that the system sets on different demands is not justifiable regardless of the sex of the person on whom the demands are made (*s 131(7)*).

It was suggested by the EAT in *Dibro Ltd v Hore* [1990] IRLR 129, [1990] ICR 370 at 377 that a job evaluation study carried out at the request of the employer after the institution of proceedings which evaluates the jobs of the applicants and the comparator may be relied upon for the purposes of *s 2A(2)* (see also *Avon County Council v Foxall* [1989] IRLR 435, [1989] ICR 407). In *McAuley v Eastern Health and Social Services Board* [1991] IRLR 467, the Northern Ireland Court of Appeal held that an employment tribunal had correctly concluded that the work of the applicants and that of their comparator could not be regarded as having been given different values under a job evaluation study so as to preclude their equal value claim, in circumstances in which the job evaluation study was prepared in respect of health boards in Great Britain and its results applied in Northern Ireland only through a policy of maintaining parity of remuneration with Great Britain.

A claimant may use a new job evaluation study which rates her as equivalent to a man as evidence in support of an equal value claim in relation to the period pre-implementation of the job evaluation study but a tribunal cannot necessarily work back from the fact that two jobs are now rated as equivalent to assume that they had equal value prior to implementation; see *Redcar & Cleveland BC v Bainbridge (No 2)* [2008] EWCA Civ 885, [2008] IRLR

776, [2009] ICR 133. A job evaluation study is of evidential value only in an equal value claim and does not even raise a presumption of equal value for the employer to rebut: see *Hovell v Ashford and St Peter's Hospital NHS Trust* [2009] IRLR 734, [2009] ICR 1545. However, it is not the case that an employment tribunal must always have the benefit of an independent expert report before finding equality where a woman's job has been marked lower than a comparator's job in a job evaluation study.

For guidance on how 'equal value' claims should be assessed where the woman's (or the man's) job has changed over time, see *Potter v North Cumbria Acute Hospitals NHS Trust* [2009] IRLR 22, [2008] ICR 910, EAT and *Reading Borough Council v James and ors* [2018] ICR 1839. For guidance on the approach the Tribunal should take to determining the facts on the basis of which an assessment of equal value may be made, see below **23.28** and above **23.6**.

23.9   Persons with whom an employee may claim equivalence

The man with whom a woman seeks to compare herself is known as the 'comparator'. Under the EqA 2010 the comparator must be employed by the same employer or an associated employer and (a) work at 'the same establishment' (*s 79(3)*); or *(b)* if not working at the same establishment, 'common terms' must apply at each establishment (*s 79(4)*). For office holders (including police officers), the same person must be responsible for paying the claimant and her comparator (*s 79(5)* and *(8)*). There are also specific provisions for members of the House of Commons (*s 79(6)*) and House of Lords (*s 79(7)*). Similar provision was made in *EqPA 1970, s 1(6)* which allowed a complainant to compare herself with others in the 'same employment' which was defined as follows:

'   . . .   men shall be treated as in the same employment with a woman if they are men employed by her employer or any associated employer at the same establishment or establishments in Great Britain which include that one and at which common terms and conditions of employment are observed either generally or for employees of the relevant classes.'

The general principles about comparators developed in the case law under the *EqPA 1970* about comparators employed in the 'same establishment' thus remain relevant under the *EqA 2010*. The questions of (i) what constitutes the 'same establishment' and (ii) in what circumstances employees at different establishments are to be regarded as employed on 'common terms and conditions of employment' are more complicated and are returned to below.

General rules about comparators

In contrast to direct and indirect discrimination cases brought under *SDA 1975* (now under *Chapter 1* of *Part 5 EqA 2010*), the orthodox position prior to the coming into force of the *EqA 2010* was that an employee could not use a 'hypothetical' comparator. In other words, she could not base a claim on an allegation that if a man were employed, for instance, on like work, he would be paid more (cf **12.15** DISCRIMINATION AND EQUAL OPPORTUNITIES – **I**). Nor could a woman absent on maternity leave rely on an actual male comparator to bring a claim under the equal pay provisions in the *EqPA 1970* since there is no appropriate comparator for a pregnant woman, although in *Alabaster v Barclays Bank plc and Secretary of State for Social Security* [2005] EWCA Civ 508, [2005] IRLR 576 the CA held that in a claim for a pay increase received before the beginning of maternity leave to be taken into consideration when calculating statutory maternity pay, it was appropriate to disapply those parts of *s 1* of the *EqPA 1970* which impose a requirement for a male comparator (see further below **23.13** for maternity leave and pay arrangements). However, under the *EqA 2010* a woman may only bring a claim where there is no 'actual' comparator as a direct (but not an indirect) sex discrimination claim: see *EqA 2010, s 71*. The previous case law on comparators for the purposes of the *EqPA 1970* will nevertheless remain relevant to the identification of 'evidential' comparators, whose circumstances may be considered by tribunals in determining (i) whether or not the woman is being paid less than a hypothetical male comparator; and, if so (ii) whether the reason for the difference in treatment is sex such that a complaint of sex discrimination under *EqA 2010, s 13* is made out.

It should be noted that although the *EqA 2010* and the *EqPA 1970* on their face require a woman to identify an actual comparator if she wishes to bring an equal pay claim, there may be a class of cases where this requirement will need to be 'read down' in order to comply with EU law. Thus, in *Allonby v Accrington and Rossendale College*: C–256/01 [2004] IRLR 224, [2004] ICR 1328, the CJEU was asked to decide whether a male comparator with the right to join a pension scheme was necessary in a claim brought by part-time employees who had been dismissed and re-engaged as self-employed contractors to lecture at their former college. The complainant could not identify a male comparator who, like herself, was not an employee. The question was whether the statutory requirement that, in order to join the pension scheme, a teacher be employed under a contract of employment, should, if found to have a differential impact on women, be set aside. The CJEU set out the orthodox position that a worker cannot rely on *art 157* in order to claim pay to which she could be entitled if she belonged to the other sex unless, now or in the past, there were workers in the undertaking concerned who perform or performed comparable work. However, where national legislation was the cause of the differential impact (the statutory requirement to be an employee in order to join the pension scheme being a provision of domestic law) the CJEU held there is no need to point to a comparator: it will be sufficient to show a statistical disadvantage. In the absence of objective justification for the national legislation, the requirement to be an employee should be set aside where it is shown that, among the teachers who are workers within *art 157* and fulfil all other conditions for membership of the pension scheme, a much lower percentage of women than men is able to fulfil that condition. In short, the CJEU held that where it is the national legislation that is the sole source of the different treatment, there is no need to identify a particular comparator, as the comparison can be done by examining the position nationally using statistics. This decision sits uncomfortably with the *EqA 2010*, which requires an 'actual' comparator for equal pay claims. Further, although *s 70* of the *EqA 2010* permits a claimant to bring an 'ordinary' direct sex discrimination claim in relation to pay under *s 13* of the *Act* where he or she has no actual comparator, the *EqA 2010* does not permit recourse to be made to an 'ordinary' indirect sex discrimination claim under *s 19* in such circumstances.

Where a comparator is required, selection of an appropriate comparator is a matter for the employee (*Ainsworth v Glass Tubes and Components Ltd* [1977] IRLR 74, [1977] ICR 347). She may select more than one individual, although tribunals have been warned by the House of Lords to be alert to prevent abuse of the procedure by applicants who 'cast their net over too wide a spread of comparators' (*Leverton v Clwyd County Council* [1989] IRLR 28, [1989] ICR 33). There is no requirement that the comparator should be in any way 'typical' of his class (although the Court of Appeal in *North Yorkshire County Council v Ratcliffe* [1994] IRLR 342, [1994] ICR 810 considered that such a requirement might be thought to be implicit in the *EqPA 1970*. The issue was not considered by the House of Lords when it heard the subsequent appeal: [1995] IRLR 439, [1995] ICR 833.)

There is nothing to prevent a complainant from selecting as a comparator a male employee whom she believes is engaged in work of a lesser value than her own. However, if she is successful in her claim she will only receive the pay awarded to her comparator. A complainant cannot use the *EqPA 1970* to establish a salary differential in her favour (*Enderby v Frenchay Health Authority (No 2)* [2000] IRLR 257, [2000] ICR 612, CA), (although a sex discrimination claim could now be brought under the *EqA 2010* using the male employee as evidence to help establish the position for a hypothetical comparator).

In *Hartlepool Borough Council v Llewellyn* [2009] IRLR 796 the EAT found that male claimants could pursue contingent 'piggyback' claims citing female comparators whose terms and conditions of employment had been modified by operation of *s 2(1)* of *EqPA*

1970. However, since the *EqPA 1970* required a real comparator, such claims could only be pursued in respect of periods where female comparators had actually received greater sums than the male claimants either by reason of terms found in the employment contract or alternatively by reason of a declaration of the employment tribunal.

Even under the *EqPA 1970* it was well-established that (provided the comparator was employed prior to the claimant) there is no requirement for contemporaneous employment between the complainant and her chosen comparator and express provision to this effect is made in *s 64(2) EqA 2010*. Lindsay P, giving the judgment of the EAT in *Kells v Pilkington plc* [2002] IRLR 693, held that the effect of the CJEU's decision in *Macarthys Ltd v Smith* was that there was no requirement for contemporaneous employment and once the need for that has gone, there was, on the face of things, no specified period under the *EqPA 1970* within which comparisons can or cannot be made. This was confirmed by the Court of Appeal in *Gutridge v Sodexo* [2009] IRLR 721 where it was accepted that after a TUPE transfer, a transferring employee could continue to compare herself with a comparator whose employment did not transfer. The six-year period of limitation in *EqA 2010, s 132* and *EqPA 1970, s 2(5)* (see **23.21** below) is concerned with the period of default which can be compensated for, rather than the period during which comparison is acceptable. Likewise, the fact that the claimant's comparator is promoted part-way through the period in respect of which the claim is made does not mean that the claim fails from that point on: the contractual right to equal pay with a particular comparator crystallises from the time that an appropriate comparator exists and does not disappear if the comparator moves on. This is so even if from that point on there are other potential comparators available with whom the claimant has not sought to compare herself: see *Reading Borough Council v James and ors* [2018] ICR 1839. Although considerable difficulties may arise in claims based on comparisons with predecessors from many years ago, these are difficulties of fact and evidence and not difficulties of law: see *Kells v Pilkington*. However, none of this means that a complainant can compare herself with a successor in her role: see *Walton Centre for Neurology and Neurosurgery NHS Trust v Bewley* [2008] IRLR 588, [2008] ICR 1047 in which the EAT held that an earlier decision of the EAT that had held that comparison with a successor was permissible (*Hallam Diocese Trustee v Connaughton* [1996] IRLR 505, [1996] ICR 860) was wrongly decided. The comparison must involve a 'concrete appraisal' of the work actually performed and using a successor as a comparator would be akin to using a hypothetical comparator which is not permitted under Community law: *Bewley*. Compare also *Horgan v Minister for Education and Skills* (C-154/18) and *R (Harvey) v Haringey LBC* [2018] EWHC 2871 (Admin), [2019] Pens LR 3, which make clear that where new, more beneficial pay arrangements are introduced, predecessors may not compare themselves with successors in post.

The same establishment

As set out above, under *EqA 2010, s 79(3)* (and formerly under *EqPA 1970, s 1(6)*) it is not sufficient for a complainant to be employed by the same employer as her comparator in order to claim equivalence. She must also either be employed at the 'same establishment' as her comparator or be able to show commonality of terms and conditions of employment (as to the latter see below). 'Establishment' was not defined in the *EqPA 1970*, and is not defined in the *EqA 2010*, nor is it expressly used in *art 157*. In *Defrenne v Sabena*: C-43/75 [1981] 1 All ER 122, [1976] ICR 547 the CJEU stated that the then *art 119* (now *art 157*) applied where men and women carried out work 'in the same establishment or service'. In *South Ayrshire Council v Morton* [2002] IRLR 256 Lord Justice Clerk observed that it was apparent from this paragraph of *Defrenne* that 'the scope of the enquiry is not always confined to the claimant's own workplace or his own employer'. In *Edinburgh City Council v Wilkinson* [2012] IRLR 202 the Court of Session was of the view that whether or not a complainant and comparator worked at the same establishment was a question of fact requiring an evaluation of the relevant facts and circumstances. The term 'establishment' was not intended to refer to a 'body' or an 'undertaking'. It was primarily directed to the place of work such as a particular complex or group of buildings and the organisational structure would also be a particularly important definitional element. The existence of a mobility clause in a contract of employment may suggest that the employer runs different establishments. On the facts of that case, where the complainants were local authority employees employed in schools, hostels and libraries and sought to compare themselves with male manual employees, the complainants and their comparators were employed in different physical locations and distinct entities. Those entities had a high degree of permanence and stability, different organisational structures and their own workforces which performed specific tasks. The employment tribunal was therefore entitled to conclude that the employees worked at different establishments.

Different establishments – common terms and conditions of employment

If the complainant and her comparator are employed at different establishments then in order to claim equivalence, the complainant must show that 'common terms and conditions of employment' are observed by the employer at the establishments in question 'either generally or as between A and B' (*EqA 2010, s 79(4)*, previously *EqPA 1970, s 1(6)*). Note that (as the Supreme Court observed in *North v Dumfries and Galloway Council* [2013] IRLR 737, [2013] ICR 993) this requirement is not to be confused with the requirement for the complainant to identify a like term in the comparator's contract with which to claim equality (as to which see above **23.5**), nor with the requirement to establish that the work of claimant and comparator are equal (as to which see above **23.5**). The object is simply to identify whether the class of employees that includes the claimant would, if employed at the same establishment as the class of employees that includes the comparator, still be employed on broadly similar terms and conditions. A simple example is where both groups of employees are covered by the same collective agreement, even if by slightly different provisions within that agreement: cf *Leverton v Clwyd County Council* [1989] IRLR 28, [1989] ICR 33, CA. Note that it is not necessary to show that the terms and conditions of the claimant and comparator are similar to each other, just that they would each be employed on broadly similar terms and conditions as they are in fact employed if they were co-located in the same establishment: *North*, ibid, as further explained in *Asda Stores Ltd v Brierley* [2019] EWCA Civ 44, [2019] IRLR 335. In that case the Court of Appeal made clear that the Tribunal should not have carried out an exercise in comparing the claimants' and their comparators' terms and conditions. Although *s 79(4)* of the *EA 2010* provides that 'common terms' must apply at the establishments "either generally or as between A and B", that does not require a comparison of A's and B's terms. The question in that case was just whether, if an Asda Store had been co-located with one of its depots, then cashiers and depot workers would still have been employed on the same terms and conditions as currently. The Tribunal had determined as a matter of fact they would be and accordingly the claimants' claims could proceed.

It was at one stage held (see *Dumfries and Galloway Council v North* [2009] IRLR 915, *[2009] ICR 1363*, EAT) that it was necessary for a complainant to show that there was a 'real possibility' of the comparator actually being employed at the same establishment as the claimant. However, the Supreme Court in *North* (*[2013] UKSC 45, [2013] IRLR 737, [2013] ICR 993*) ruled, and the Court of Appeal in *Asda Stores* confirmed, that there is no such requirement: the claimant and comparator may be doing very different types of job which could never be carried out at the same establishment (because, eg, one is messy manual labour and the other involves working in an office). It is thus immaterial whether co-location had ever, or would ever, happen in practice. See also *British Coal Corpn v Smith* [1996] IRLR 404, [1996] ICR 515, *South Tyneside Metropolitan Borough Council v Anderson* [2007] EWCA Civ 654, [2007] IRLR 715, [2007] ICR 1581, *Beddoes v Birmingham City Council* [2011] EqLR 838, EAT (affd on other grounds [2012] EWCA Civ 585, [2012] All ER (D) 28 (May)) and *City of Edinburgh Council v Wilkinson* [2012] IRLR 202.

Associated employers

If two or more employers are associated (ie if one is a company of which the other directly or indirectly has control or if both are companies of which a third person directly or indirectly has control; see **7.9** CONTINUOUS EMPLOYMENT) a woman working in a factory owned by Company A can claim equivalence with a man working in another factory owned by an associated company, Company B, provided that broadly similar terms and conditions of employment apply either generally or for employees of the class of which the comparator is a member (*EqA 2010, s 79(3)(a)* and *79(4)(a)*; formerly *EqPA 1970, s 1(6)(c)*). It has long been established that, in the case of two companies controlled by a third person, it is not necessary for the third person to be a company. They may, for eg, be a local authority or government agency: see *Hasley v Fair Employment Agency* [1989] IRLR 106. Because the statutory language requires at least one of the allegedly associated employers to be a 'company' (see now *EqA 2010, s 79(9)*), it appeared to exclude the possibility of two public sector employers being associated. However, in *Scullard v Knowles* [1996] IRLR 344 the EAT held that such an exclusion would be contrary to *art 157* and should be treated as 'displaced' by the broader European approach. Further, in *Fox Cross Claimants v Glasgow City Council* [2014] CSIH 27, [2014] EqLR 271, the Scottish Court of Session held that the word 'company' was not limited to companies formed under the *Companies Act 2006*. The Court of Session followed the dictum of Lord Hoffmann in *O'Neill v Phillips* [1999] 2 All ER 961 in holding that a company 'is an association of persons for an economic purpose, usually entered into with legal advice and some degree of formality' and therefore included a limited liability partnership and a community interest company.

The 'single source' test

Challenges made under European Union law to the validity of the requirement in *s 1(6)* of the *EqPA 1970* (reproduced in material respects in the *EqA 2010, ss 79(3)* and *(4)*) that comparators be in the 'same employment' have resulted in the development of an additional 'single source' test for equal pay comparisons: *Lawrence v Regent Office Care Ltd* [2002] IRLR 822, [2003] ICR 1092. It should be noted that this is an alternative route to a comparison that applies only under art 157. It is not a necessary element to be established for the purposes of a comparison under *EA 2010, s 79* (formerly *EqPA 1970, s 1(6)*): see *North Cumbria Acute Hospitals NHS Trust v Potter* [2009] IRLR 176.

The CJEU in *Lawrence v Regent Office Care Ltd* held that although there was nothing in the wording of *art 157* to suggest that its application was limited to situations in which men and women worked for the same employer, where, as in *Lawrence*, the differences in pay of workers of different sex performing equal work or work of equal value could not be attributable to a single source, such as a collective agreement, there was no one body responsible for the inequality which could restore equal treatment. Such a situation did not come within the scope of *art 157* and the work and pay of the different sets of workers could not be compared on the basis of *art 157*. See also *South Ayrshire Council v Morton* [2001] IRLR 28. This approach has been confirmed by the CJEU in *Allonby v Accrington and Rossendale College*: C-256/01 [2004] IRLR 224, [2004] ICR 1328, CJEU. In *Allonby*, the applicant worked as a lecturer in the respondent college, but was a self-employed worker, hired by the college through an agency holding a database of lecturers. She claimed comparison with a named, salaried teacher at the college. The issue was whether working in the same establishment or service, for the benefit of a single employer, but under different contracts with different employers, was nevertheless working in the same employment for the purposes of *art 157*. The Court of Appeal ([2001] EWCA Civ 529, [2001] IRLR 364, [2001] ICR 1189) referred the issue to the CJEU. The CJEU reiterated that *art 157* did not require the applicant to be employed by the same employer as her comparator and that a 'single source' would suffice. However, the CJEU considered on the facts of that case that there was no 'single source'. The fact that her pay as an employee of the agency was influenced by the rates of pay paid by the College did not mean that her pay and her comparator's was set by a 'single source'. This was so even though she may provide the same services as the man and for the benefit of the man's employer.

The 'single source' test was also considered by the Court of Appeal in *Robertson v Department for Environment, Food and Rural Affairs* [2005] EWCA Civ 138, [2005] IRLR 363, [2005] ICR 750. In that case, the complainant and her comparator were both civil servants in common employment (all employed by the Crown). The CA held this was neither a necessary nor sufficient basis for an equal pay comparison. The bare fact of common employment is not enough: it is necessary to consider whether the terms and conditions were traceable to one source. The relevant body is the one which is responsible for the inequality and which could restore equal treatment. This will often, but not always, be the same employer. As responsibility for negotiating civil servant pay had been delegated down to the individual departments, an inter-department comparison did not involve comparison of pay from a single source and was not permissible. See also *Armstrong v Newcastle upon Tyne NHS Hospital Trust* [2005] EWCA Civ 1608, [2006] IRLR 124: in that case, although both sets of employees were employed by the same NHS Trust, which had endeavoured to a certain extent to harmonise terms and conditions across the hospitals for which it was responsible, the Court of Appeal held that the tribunal was right to find that the Trust had not assumed responsibility for the setting of terms and conditions of employment across all its hospitals and that therefore female employees in one hospital could not compare themselves with male employees in another. It remains to be seen what approach will be taken to employers hiving off their pay negotiations for different departments to different decision-making bodies or companies in order to avoid a 'single source' for cross-departmental comparison. Note, however, the cautionary observations of the Scottish EAT ([2013] ICR 954) and Court of Session in *Fox Cross Claimants v Glasgow City Council* [2014] CSIH 27, [2014] EqLR 27: careful consideration must be given to the power or authority alleged to be the 'single source' in order to ascertain whether it does constitute a 'single source' or whether the powers of the direct employer of claimant or comparator in relation to pay exclude or restrict the power of the alleged 'single source' in some material way. In this respect, it is immaterial that the alleged single source does not choose to exercise any power it has. What matters is whether it has the power.

In *Beddoes v Birmingham City Council* [2011] EqLR 838 the position of non-teaching staff in community schools was considered. The local authority employed those staff, but acting on the requirements of the governing body of the school. It was asserted, therefore, that there was no single source as between the complainants and their comparators, the terms and conditions of employment in relation to the comparators being set by the local authority. The EAT rejected the argument. First, the argument failed by reason of the decision in *North Cumbria Acute Hospitals NHS Trust v Potter* [2009] IRLR 176 where the EAT had held that it was not necessary to 'read down' *EqPA 1970, section 1(6)* so as to include the 'single source test': if complainant and comparator are in 'the same employment' for the purposes of *s 1(6)*, that is sufficient, their terms and conditions do not also have to emanate from a single source. Secondly, the argument failed on the facts (and on an application of the decision of the Court of Appeal in *South Tyneside MBC v Anderson* [2007] IRLR 715, [2007] ICR 1581). Finally, the EAT considered that in most cases the requirement of a 'single source' was unlikely to be any different to the requirements of *EqPA 1970, s 1(6)* since in most cases, a complainant will be able to compare herself with the employer's other employees (subject to satisfying the establishment criterion) and there will be a 'single source' because the employer will have the power to determine the terms and conditions of each its own employees. This part of the EAT's decision was not appealed to the Court of Appeal ([2012] EWCA Civ 585, [2012] EqLR 695), which upheld the EAT's decision on other grounds. In *Asda Stores Ltd v Brierley* [2019] EWCA Civ 44, [2019] IRLR 335 the Court of Appeal noted that the fact that the claimants and their comparators were employed by the same employer which was responsible for determining their terms and conditions and therefore that the 'single source' test was met was a further reason for finding that they were valid comparators despite being employed at different establishments.

In all cases where the question of 'single source' arises it is important to remember that the principle as enunciated in *Lawrence* requires both that a single body is responsible for the inequality and that it is capable of restoring equal treatment: *North Cumbria Acute Hospitals NHS Trust v Potter* [2009] IRLR 176 and *Fox Cross Claimants v Glasgow City Council* [2014] CSIH 27, [2014] EqLR 27.

23.10 Material factor defence – general approach

Although a woman may establish that she is engaged on like work, work rated as equivalent to that of a man or work of equal value, she will not be able to claim equivalence with that man if the employer can establish a 'material factor' defence. By *s 69* of *EqA 2010* a 'sex equality clause' will not have any effect where the 'responsible person' is able to show that the difference is because of a material factor. (A 'responsible person' is defined at *s 80* of *EqA 2010* as the employer of a person or alternatively the person responsible for paying remuneration to that person.) That material factor must: (i) be a material difference between the claimant's case and her comparator's (s 69(6)); (ii) not be a factor which is directly discriminatory (*s 69(1)(a)* of *EqA 2010*); nor (iii) one which is indirectly discriminatory (*s 69(1)(b)* and *(2)* of *EqA 2010*). An indirectly discriminatory factor is defined as being a factor which results in 'persons of the same sex doing work equal to A's' being 'put at a particular disadvantage when compared with persons of the opposite sex doing work equal to A's' and where that factor is not 'a proportionate means of achieving a legitimate aim'. For this purpose, the long-term objective of reducing inequality between men's and women's terms of work is always to be regarded as a legitimate aim (*s 69(3)*).

Under the *EqPA 1970* a similar defence of 'genuine material factor' ('GMF') was available. It was a defence for the employer to show that the variation between the woman's contract and the man's contract was genuinely due to a material factor which was not the difference of sex (*EqPA 1970, s 1(3)*). In the case of equality claimed on the basis of *like work* or *work rated as equivalent*, that factor *must* be a material difference between the woman's case and the man's (*EqPA 1970, s 1(3)(a)*). In the case of equality claimed on the basis of *work of equal value*, that factor *may* be a material difference between the woman's case and the man's (*EqPA 1970, s 1(3)(b)*). Thus, in establishing a defence to a claim based on like work or work rated as equivalent, any difference in terms had to be explained (and, in some cases, objectively justified: see below) by a difference between the woman's case and the man's case. In a claim based on work of equal value the defence includes, but is not limited to, such differences.

The question whether an employer could succeed in a 'GMF' defence by relying upon a factor which did not objectively justify the difference in pay between the employee and her comparator received considerable judicial attention prior to the coming into force of the *EqA 2010*. The 'old law' on this issue is set out below. The *EqA 2010* has clarified the position. Under the *EqA 2010* the employer will be required to justify pay differentials where it relies, to explain such differentials, on a factor which is prima facie indirectly discriminatory, ie which puts persons of one sex at a particular disadvantage as compared to those of another sex doing the work (*s 69(1)(b)* and *(2)*). 'Particular disadvantage' will likely be established by reference to statistical information. Following *Essop v Home Office (UK Border Agency); Naeem v Secretary of State for Justice* [2017] UKSC 27, [2017] 3 All ER 551, [2017] IRLR 558, [2017] ICR 640, it is clear that the line of defence to an indirect discrimination equal pay claim identified in *Armstrong, Gibson* and *Hamilton* (see the 'Pre *EqA 2010* approach' section below) that an employer can avoid the need to justify a pay differential if it is able to show that statistics which on their face establish a prima facie case of indirect sex discrimination are in fact wholly explained by factors unrelated to sex is no longer available. Once a prima facie case of indirect discrimination is made out by reference to statistical evidence, then an employer has no alternative but to justify it in order to make out the defence in *s 69(1)(b)* and *(2)* of the *EqA 2010*: see *McNeil v Revenue and Customs Commissioners* [2018] IRLR 398, EAT (a point not in dispute in the Court of Appeal in that case: [2019] EWCA Civ 1112, [2020] ICR 515). Following *Essop*, it does not matter why the disadvantage has arisen: it is sufficient if group disadvantage is shown. The employer must then establish justification or, in the equal pay context, a GMF defence. However, as the Court of Appeal explained in *McCloud v Ministry of Justice* [2018] EWCA Civ 2844, [2019] ICR 1489, there is still scope for an employer to show that in the case of a particular individual the reason for the disadvantage was nothing to do with sex. For example, where a pay scheme is shown to operate to the general detriment of women, it is still open to the employer to show that in an individual case the reason why the individual is paid less is, for example, because she missed out on pay rises as a result of taking a four-year sabbatical to complete a PhD. In such a case, the woman would have failed to show that it was the scheme that disadvantaged her and consequently the indirect discrimination claim would not get off the ground. Equally, of course, the same facts would lead to the conclusion that a GMF defence would succeed.

Pre EqA 2010 approach

There was for some time a marked difference in the approach taken to the scope of the defence at European and domestic levels. The European approach was set out in *Enderby v Frenchay Health Authority* [1993] IRLR 591, [1994] ICR 112: it requires that a difference in pay be objectively justified. Further, *Enderby* requires, subject to a de minimis principle, that the whole of the difference must be justified.

The approach taken by the UK courts was, traditionally, less demanding. The domestic approach has been simply to require the employer to be able to account for the difference by reference to a factor which is material but is not the sex of the employee. Thus, in *Yorkshire Blood Transfusion Service v Plaskitt* [1994] ICR 74, the employer succeeded in establishing a defence in circumstances where the disparity in pay was due to a mistake. Whilst an error may explain an unlawful disparity, it clearly cannot be said to justify it. Nevertheless, if a factor provides no sensible basis for justifying the disparity, domestic tribunals have tended to conclude that the factor is not 'material'. In *Tyldesley v TML Plastics Ltd* [1996] IRLR 395, [1996] ICR 356, the EAT made an ambitious attempt to reconcile the domestic and European approaches. The principle which the EAT developed may be summarised as follows: if the factor relied upon by the employer is one which may itself be tainted by sex discrimination, it must be shown that the factor objectively justifies the difference; however, if it is not tainted by sex discrimination, the factor need only explain the difference. The EAT decision in *Tyldesley* was approved by the House of Lords in *Strathclyde Regional Council v Wallace* [1998] IRLR 146, HL and *Glasgow City Council v Marshall* [2000] IRLR 272, HL) and applied by the EAT in *Parliamentary Comr for Administration v Fernandez* [2004] IRLR 22; *King's College London v Clark* [2003] All ER (D) 118 (Oct) (in which the EAT held that a mistake and a *TUPE* transfer adequately explained the difference in pay); and *Armstrong v Newcastle Upon Tyne NHS Hospital Trust* [2005] EWCA Civ 1608, [2006] IRLR 124. In *Armstrong*, the Court of Appeal held that the need to provide objective justification does not arise in cases in which the bare *Enderby* statistics, taken in isolation, suggest *prima facie* discrimination but there are other factors which suggest that the statistics are not good evidence of such prima facie discrimination so that the pay differential can be said not to be the difference of sex. Although the 'not tainted by sex' defence is still the appropriate way of approaching a direct discrimination claim, it is no longer good law for indirect discrimination following *Essop v Home Office (UK Border Agency)*; *Naeem v Secretary of State for Justice* [2017] UKSC 27, [2017] 3 All ER 551, [2017] IRLR 558, [2017] ICR 640, and *McNeil v Revenue and Customs Commissioners* [2018] IRLR 398, EAT and [2019] EWCA Civ 1112, [2020] ICR 515, and below **23.11**. In *Sharp v Caledonia Group Services Ltd* [2006] IRLR 4, [2006] ICR 218, the EAT proceeded to eschew the *Glasgow CC v Marshall* approach in favour of the more stringent European approach in the *Enderby* and *Brunnhofer* cases, the latter of which the EAT considered 'provides clear guidelines in equal pay cases as to the need for objective justification in all cases'. However, in *Armstrong* Lord Justice Buxton warned that, 'once the House of Lords has determined the meaning of [European Union rules] it is not open to domestic courts to resort to the decisions of the Court of Justice on which the House of Lords based its analysis in order to find a different or wider meaning'. Although Lord Justice Buxton does not appear to have been referred to the *Sharp* case, this would appear to be a condemnation of the approach taken by the EAT in that case and a reaffirmation that *Glasgow CC v Marshall* should continue to be applied unless and until the issue is reconsidered by the Supreme Court or the CJEU.

This the EAT did in *Villalba v Merrill Lynch & Co Inc* [2006] IRLR 437, [2007] ICR 469 and *Surtees v Middlesbrough Borough Council* [2007] IRLR 869, [2007] ICR 1644, holding that once an employer has established that a difference in pay was owing to factors other than sex, the employer is not required to go further and objectively justify the difference in pay. In *Villalba*, which concerned bonus payments based on performance assessments, it held it to be sufficient that the employer had shown that sex was not a factor in its decision-making. (Or, rather, that it was not a 'significant influence' on its decision-making, as per Lord Nicholls in *Nagarajan v London Regional Transport* [1999] IRLR 572, HL.) In *Surtees* Elias P referred to the formulation set out in Villalba and observed that if the argument that 'the mere fact that a woman is making a comparison with a man whose job is of equal value itself automatically requires that any difference in pay is objectively justified, even though the employer shows that the difference has nothing to do with sex' is correct, then 'equal pay has broken loose from its moorings in discrimination law'. In that case, Elias P ruled that, where the employer has succeeded in explaining the difference in pay by reference to a factor that is not tainted by sex discrimination, he does not need to go further and objectively justify the use of that factor. On appeal from Elias P's judgment, the Court of Appeal in *Bainbridge/Surtees* [2008] IRLR 776, [2009] ICR 133 considered arguments about the approach adopted by the Court of Appeal in *Armstrong* (supra) but held that it was not the right case to analyse that case.

In *Gibson v Sheffield City Council* [2010] EWCA Civ 63, [2010] IRLR 311, [2010] ICR 708, the CA examined the issue again. That case concerned bonus schemes which had been introduced in the 1960s for manual workers in the Council (street cleaners, refuse collectors, maintenance, etc) and subsequently consolidated into salary. As a result, the manual workers were paid over 30% more basic salary than the claimants who worked as care workers and school meals supervisors. The manual workers were overwhelmingly male, the care workers and school meals supervisors overwhelmingly female. The Tribunal found that the bonus schemes had initially been introduced for genuine productivity reasons, but since consolidation into basic pay the additional money was being paid without reference to productivity. The Tribunal found that it would not have been possible, because of the nature of their work, for similar bonus schemes to have been introduced for the claimants' roles and, in any event, that their work ethic had always been good. The Tribunal held that the reason for the difference in pay was the need to provide payments for increased productivity, and that this was unrelated to gender. Accordingly, the Tribunal held, following *Marshall* and *Armstrong*, that it was not necessary for it to go on to determine whether the difference in pay was objectively justifiable. Smith LJ and Kay LJ in the Court of Appeal (although not Pill LJ) expressed the view that *Armstrong* was correct in principle and that an employer can avoid the need for objective justification if it can show that, notwithstanding that statistics have been produced which show that the pay practice in question has an adverse impact on women, the adverse impact has arisen as a result of factors wholly unrelated to gender. On the facts of the particular case, however, the CA ruled that the Tribunal had been wrong to find that the schemes were not sex-tainted. The matter was remitted to the Tribunal to consider the question of objective justification.

In *Newcastle-upon-Tyne NHS Hospitals Trust v Armstrong* [2010] ICR 674 (the 'second round' of *Armstrong* litigation) and *Bury Metropolitan Borough Council v Hamilton* [2011] IRLR 358, the EAT (Underhill P presiding) gave the clearest guidance to date on the approach that should be taken by tribunals to the *GMF* defence and the question of objective justification. The 'structured approach', as the EAT has termed it, is as follows (*Bury v Hamilton*, para 14):

•   It is necessary first to identify the explanation for the differential complained of. The burden of proof is on the employer.

• It is then necessary to consider whether that explanation is 'tainted with sex'. What that not altogether happy metaphor means is that the explanation relied on must not itself involve sex discrimination, whether direct or indirect.

• In considering whether the explanation involves direct or indirect discrimination, the ordinary principles of the law of discrimination apply. That means that:

    – If the differential is the result of direct discrimination the defence under *s 1(3)* will fail;

    – If the differential involves indirect discrimination of either the PCP-type or the *Enderby*-type (as to this distinction, see **23.11** below) the defence will fail unless the employer proves that the differential is objectively justified as being a proportionate means of achieving a legitimate aim;

    – If the employer's explanation involves neither direct nor indirect discrimination the defence will succeed, even if the factor relied on cannot be objectively justified.

• In considering the employer's explanation, the ordinary principles governing the burden of proof in discrimination claims will apply. Thus if the claimant shows a prima facie case of discrimination (in the sense explained in *Madarassy v Nomura International plc* [2007] IRLR 246), the burden shifts to the employer to prove the absence of such discrimination. (See generally DISCRIMINATION AND EQUAL OPPORTUNITIES – III (14)).

The 'structured approach' advanced by the EAT must be correct as a matter of legal principle. It is also clear and readily capable of application by employment tribunals. In omitting the line of defence that in a case of prima facie indirect discrimination an employer need not establish objective justification if it can show that the reason for the disparate impact is not 'tainted by sex' (i.e. the approach approved twice at Court of Appeal level in the *Armstrong* and *Gibson* cases (supra)), Underhill P's formulation also survives the decision of the Supreme Court in *Essop v Home Office (UK Border Agency)*; *Naeem v Secretary of State for Justice* [2017] UKSC 27, [2017] 3 All ER 551, [2017] IRLR 558, [2017] ICR 640, the effect of which is establish that the 'not tainted by sex' defence does not work where prima facie indirect discrimination is established and *Armstrong* is no longer good law in this respect: *McNeil v Revenue and Customs Commissioners* [2018] IRLR 398.

23.11 'Prima facie' indirect discrimination and the 'material factor' defence

The model adopted by the *EqPA 1970*, in which an employee compares her terms and conditions with those of a specific comparator, worked well enough in relation to cases of direct discrimination. Indeed, it favoured the complainant in that, once she had established that her male colleague enjoyed different and more favourable terms, the employer had then to establish that the difference was due to a material factor which was not a difference in sex. In effect, to use the language of *SDA 1975*, the employee needed only to establish that she had been 'less favourably treated'. She did not need to show that the less favourable treatment was 'on the ground of her sex'; it was for the employer to show that the difference in sex was not the ground of the difference in treatment (see **23.10** above and **12.34** DISCRIMINATION AND EQUAL OPPORTUNITIES – I.) Nonetheless, the 'structured approach' to the 'material factor' defence that was enunciated by the EAT in *Bury Metropolitan Borough Council v Hamilton* [2011] IRLR 358 (above, **23.10**) required the tribunal, as a step in considering an employer's defence, to determine whether or not a 'prima facie' case of indirect discrimination had arisen. However, this issue has caused the courts and tribunals significant difficulties.

The *EqA 2010* attempts to codify the law on indirect discrimination in equal pay claims. However, it does so through a circuitous route. First, a real comparator of the opposite sex must be identified by the complainant who is doing equal work (as defined by *s 65*), but being paid more: see *s 66*. The employer must then show both that the difference in treatment is not the difference in sex (*s 69(1)(a)*) and, if the factor that is causing the difference in pay puts persons of one sex at a particular disadvantage (*s 69(2)*), that the factor is a proportionate means of achieving a legitimate aim (*s 69(1)(b)*). See further above **23.10**.

Although there has been considerable doubt on the issue (cf, for eg, *Bailey v Home Office* [2005] EWCA Civ 327, [2005] IRLR 369) it is now generally recognised that there are two forms of indirect discrimination that arise in relation to equal pay (see *Bury Metropolitan Borough Council v Hamilton and ors* [2011] IRLR 358, EAT):

•   where the employer applies a provision, criterion or practice which puts or would put women at a particular disadvantage when compared with men (the 'PCP'-type of discrimination or *Seymour-Smith* type discrimination after *R v Secretary of State, ex p. Seymour-Smith* [1999] ICR 447 (ECJ));

•   where two groups of employees doing work of equal value receive different pay and there is a sufficiently substantial disparity in the gender break-down of the two groups (referred to as discrimination arising from a 'state of affairs', or *Enderby*-type discrimination, having first been recognised in the decision of the CJEU in *Enderby v Frenchay Health Authority* [1993] IRLR 591).

These two forms are not mutually exclusive: *Cooksey (GMB Claimants) v Trafford BC* [2012] EqLR 744. It is important to remember, following *Essop v Home Office (UK Border Agency); Naeem v Secretary of State for Justice* [2017] UKSC 27, [2017] 3 All ER 551, [2017] IRLR 558, [2017] ICR 640, that for an indirect discrimination claim to succeed there is no need to show a causal link between the particular disadvantage and the protected characteristic: it suffices that there is a causal link between the PCP and the particular disadvantage. As such, much of the previous case law on indirect discrimination must be approached with caution. In particular, the line of authority based on *Armstrong v Newcastle upon Tyne NHS Hospital Trust* [2005] EWCA Civ 1608, [2006] IRLR 124 (see above **23.10**) which has been understood as holding that it is open to a respondent to rebut a finding of particular disadvantage by showing that the underlying reason for it was not related to or 'tainted by' sex is inconsistent with *Essop* and no longer to be regarded as good law: *McNeil v Revenue and Customs Commissioners* [2018] IRLR 398, EAT – a point not in dispute in the Court of Appeal: [2019] EWCA Civ 1112, [2020] ICR 515). Nonetheless, the two forms of discrimination (*Seymour-Smith* and *Enderby*) remain relevant following *Armstrong*. (A third type, argued for in *McNeil*, based clusters of distribution of male and female employees within civil service pay grades was held by the EAT and CA in that case not to be a legitimate way of establishing a case of prima facie indirect discrimination.)

In cases of the first type of indirect discrimination (PCP or *Seymour-Smith* type discrimination), the employee's terms will often be identical to those of her male comparator. In such cases, the issue will centre instead on a benefit which, whilst theoretically available to the complainant, is contingent on her satisfying a provision, criterion or practice ('PCP') which fewer women than men are able to satisfy. For instance, the contracts of both employees may provide that they are entitled to join their employer's pension scheme only if they work full-time. It is difficult to apply the equality clause to such cases. What is needed in order to eliminate the discrimination is not the addition to the complainant's contract of a clause already present in her comparator's, but the replacement of the term common to both contracts with one which does not have a discriminatory effect. For this reason, there was initially some doubt as to whether or not *EqPA 1970* prohibited indirect discrimination at all although it has now long been established that indirect discrimination is contrary to both UK and European law (*Jenkins v Kingsgate (Clothing Productions) Ltd* [1980] IRLR 6, EAT, *Bilka-Kaufhaus GmbH v Weber von Hartz*: C-170/84 [1986] IRLR 317, CJEU).

Thus, if pay criteria are adopted which apparently tend to favour men, it is for the employer to justify those criteria. Such criteria would include ones less favourable to part-time workers (see, eg *Arbeiterwohlfahrt der Stadt Berlin eV v Botel*: C-360/90 [1992] IRLR 423 and *Vroege v NCIV Institut voor Volkshuisvesting BV*: C-57/93 [1994] IRLR 651, CJEU and generally **23.20** below).

In cases of the second type of indirect discrimination (*Enderby*-type), it is not necessary for the complainant to follow the formal steps of identifying a provision, criterion or practice, choosing a pool for comparison and establishing a disparate impact. Thus in *Enderby v Frenchay Health Authority*: C-127/92 [1993] IRLR 591, CJEU (the case in which the second type of discrimination was first recognised) the CJEU decided that the employer could be called upon objectively to justify a difference in pay once the complainant had demonstrated that 'significant statistics disclosed an appreciable difference in pay between two jobs of equal value, one of which was carried out almost exclusively by women and the other predominantly by men'. Whilst this approach focuses on disparities in pay, it plainly does not require the identification of any condition or requirement (now PCP). In *Ministry of Defence v Armstrong* [2004] IRLR 672, the EAT favoured the Enderby approach, holding that there is no need for a tribunal always to adopt the formulaic approach of the *SDA 1975* when considering whether there is a disparate impact for the purposes of *EqPA, s 1(3)*.

Nonetheless, this has caused confusion in practice and the distinction between the two types of indirect discrimination has been doubted. Thus in *Bailey v Home Office* [2005] EWCA Civ 327, [2005] IRLR 369 the Court of Appeal held that the tribunal's attempt to fashion a condition or requirement out of the circumstances of the case had led it into error. It rejected the EAT's attempt to distinguish between condition and requirement/PCP cases on the one hand and cases which did not have an obvious condition or requirement/PCP but which involved a disparity of pay between two groups on the other. In each case, the Court of Appeal ruled that the tribunal is concerned to determine whether what on its face is a gender-neutral practice may be disguising the fact that female employees are being disadvantaged as compared with male employees to an extent that signifies that the disparity is *prima facie* attributable to a difference of sex (although note this requirement for a causal link to sex is no longer good law following *Essop*). The Court of Appeal held that the statistical approach in *Seymour-Smith* could be used in either case. A common approach to both types of cases has the merit of ensuring that the Act is applied consistently to all forms of indirect discrimination. On the facts of *Bailey*, the Court of Appeal held that the tribunal could conclude that there was sufficient disparate impact requiring justification where there was one group of employees which contained a significant number, even though not a clear majority, of female workers whose work is rated as equal to that of another group of employees who are predominantly male and who receive greater pay. The fact that the disadvantaged group contained a significant number of men was not a bar to a claim.

It is certainly the case that in relation to both types of indirect discrimination there will often be an issue as to whether there is a sufficiently substantial disparity in the gender make-up of the two groups to give rise to a *prima facie* case of indirect discrimination.

In particular, the 'almost exclusively by women' formula used by the CJEU in *Enderby* has given rise to a number of difficulties of interpretation. The Court of Appeal in *British Road Services Ltd v Loughran* [1997] IRLR 92, CA, having carefully considered *Enderby*, took the view that it would suffice if there were a 'significant proportion of women' in the claimant's group. Later cases have attempted to establish a more precise formula, though with little success.

When it made its reference to the CJEU in *R v Secretary of State for Employment, ex p Seymour-Smith and Perez* [1999] IRLR 253, the House of Lords asked for guidance on the circumstances in which a court is entitled to conclude that a provision has an indirectly discriminatory effect. Characteristically, in giving guidance, the CJEU posed as many questions as it answered. The CJEU declined to give any precise guidance as to the assessment of disparate impact; it merely observed that the national court must be satisfied that the proportion of women that can comply must be 'considerably smaller' than the proportion of men who can do so. In that case, which was concerned with the upper age limit on the availability of the right to claim unfair dismissal, the particular period with which the court was concerned was 1985, the date on which the former requirement of one year's service was increased to two years. At that point, the proportion of men who could comply with the requirement was 77.4%, whereas the proportion of women who could comply was 68.9%. Since that time the gap has narrowed. The CJEU observed that these figures did not suggest a sufficient disparity of impact to result in a discriminatory effect. However, the Court also observed that a small but persistent difference may result in a finding of discrimination. No guidance was given as to how this new, alternative test will operate. The majority of the House of Lords found the relevant provision to be discriminatory on the basis of this 'alternative' test. They do not appear to have seen it as an alternative, however (see **12.34** DISCRIMINATION AND EQUAL OPPORTUNITIES – I).

In assessing whether a statistically relevant difference in pay has been established, the CJEU in both *Enderby* (at para 17) and *Seymour-Smith* and *Perez* (at para 62) emphasised that it is for the national court to decide whether the pools of employees selected for comparison 'cover enough individuals, whether they illustrate purely fortuitous or short-term phenomena and whether, in general, they appear to be significant'. Further guidance on the proper test to be applied can be gleaned from *Barry v Midland Bank* [1999] IRLR 581, HL. Lord Nicholls remarked at 869 that a comparison between the proportions of men and women disadvantaged by a particular provision could on its own be misleading, because those proportions would be affected by the comparative sizes of the disadvantaged and non-disadvantaged groups. (For an example of a case where the tribunal was so misled, see *Best v Tyne and Wear Passenger and Transport Executive (t/a Nexus)* [2007] ICR 523, [2006] All ER (D) 362 (Dec), EAT in which the EAT ruled that the tribunal had been wrong to find that a disparate impact had been established in circumstances where the disadvantaged group was mainly male, albeit that there were more women in the disadvantaged group than there were women in the advantaged group – in such circumstances there was no disparate impact on women generally.) In *Barry v Midland Bank*, Lord Nicholls suggested that the better guide would often be found by expressing the proportions of men and women in the disadvantaged groups as a ratio of each other. Moreover, the absolute size of numbers of those disadvantaged remains relevant, since a low ratio may be of little significance in a small company, but of considerable significance in a large company. Thus in *Audit Commission v Haq (S)* (UKEAT/0123/10/LA) (18 March 2011, unreported) the EAT held that the numbers involved were insufficient to give rise to a *prima facie* case of discrimination. In that case senior and junior administrative roles had been amalgamated and a pay protection policy implemented which meant that former senior administrators were paid more in the new role because they had previously been paid more. Two of the four former senior administrators were male (and both the senior administrators retained were male), whereas all nine former junior administrators were female. The tribunal found that there was unjustified indirect discrimination. The EAT overturned that decision, holding that the numbers involved were too small to give rise to a *prima facie* case of indirect discrimination on that ground alone. The CA ([2012] EWCA Civ 1621, [2013] IRLR 206) reversed the EAT on this point, upholding the Tribunal decision. The CA took the view that the numbers were sufficient. Post the amalgamation the numbers were sufficient to establish a prima facie case of discrimination. The employer could not rebut that case because, historically, the fact that all nine former junior administrators were female was itself evidence of a sex taint. In the absence of evidence of any other source of discrimination, the claims must fail. Cf also *Armstrong v Newcastle Upon Tyne NHS Hospital Trust* [2005] EWCA Civ 1608, [2006] IRLR 124 where it was held that a failure by a tribunal to make a finding that the employer's arrangements have a 'considerable' impact on women prior to concluding that an arrangement is discriminatory will be an error of law: (although cf *Gibson v Sheffield City Council* [2010] EWCA Civ 63, [2010] IRLR 311, [2010] ICR 708).

Care must also be taken in selecting the appropriate pools for comparison. In *Abbott v Cheshire & Wirral Partnership NHS Trust* [2006] EWCA Civ 523, [2006] IRLR 546 the Court of Appeal ruled that, while it was for the claimant in the first instance to select a pool for comparison, it was open to the employer to dispute the appropriateness of that pool, and it was for the tribunal to determine the appropriate pool for comparison purposes. The CJEU has noted that it is not permissible for a claimant to create the appearance of a difference in pay between groups of male and female employees by arbitrarily identifying as 'pools' a number of male employees who are paid more, and a number of female employees who are paid less. There has to be some connection between the employees in each group that means their circumstances can meaningfully be considered collectively: *Specialarbejder-forbundet i Danmark v Dansk Industri, acting for Royal Copenhagen A/S*: C-400/93 [1995] IRLR 648, CJEU, paragraph 36.

The proper approach to selection of the pool and statistical evidence was considered in *Secretary of State for Trade and Industry v Rutherford (No 2)*. This concerned a challenge to the upper age limit of 65 for unfair dismissal claims in *ss 109* and *156 ERA 1996* on the basis that it had a disparate impact on men which could not be objectively justified. The tribunal selected a pool consisting of those employees for whom retirement at 65 had 'some real meaning', being those aged 55 to 74. The Court of Appeal ([2004] EWCA Civ 1186, [2004] IRLR 892, [2005] ICR 119) held that the tribunal had erred in law in concentrating on the 'disadvantaged group'. The Court of Appeal considered that the tribunal should have based its assessment of adverse impact on the statistics for the entire workforce to which the requirement of being under 65 applied and then primarily compared the respective proportions of men and women who could satisfy that requirement. Adopting this approach, the statistics clearly established that the difference in the working population between the proportion of men aged under 65 who could comply and the proportion of women under 65 who could comply was very small indeed. Accordingly, the complainants had failed to establish that there was any indirect sex discrimination against men in the imposition of the upper age limit. On appeal, the House of Lords ([2006] UKHL 19, [2006] IRLR 551) disagreed with the Court of Appeal's approach, but the judgments of their Lordships are not models of clarity as to the approach that is to be preferred. A majority of their Lordships rejected the classification of the case as one of (even potential) indirect discrimination. They each considered that this was not a case where one could speak coherently of those who are 'able to satisfy' a rule or requirement and those who are not. Since the rule in question simply imposes a disadvantage on those who stay in employment after the age of 65, there was therefore no comparison to be made since all men and all women over the age of 65 were equally disadvantaged. Lord Nicholls and Lord Walker, however, took a statistical approach as the Court of Appeal had done. However, unlike the Court of Appeal, they focused on the disadvantaged group (ie on the percentage of the workforce over 65), but emphasised how small this group was in comparison to the workforce as a whole. They noted that the proportion of the entire workforce affected by the age limit was 1.2%. 1.4% of the male workforce was affected, and 1% of the female workforce. Lords Walker and Nicholls considered that those proportions were simply too small to indicate a 'substantial' disadvantage to the male workforce.

In *Grundy v British Airways Plc* [2007] EWCA Civ 1020, [2008] IRLR 815 the Court of Appeal considered *Rutherford* and emphasised that the issue of whether or not there was a disparate impact was a question of fact in each case to be determined by the Tribunal. The Court observed that there was no rule as to what pool would or would not be appropriate, though care should be taken that the pool was not so small as to be unrepresentative or so large that like was not being compared with like. Similarly, there was no rule that one must always look at the advantaged or the disadvantaged groups. The job for the Tribunal is to identify a cohort within which the genuine material factor defence can be objectively tested. That means that employees within each pool chosen must share relevant characteristics and not exclude employees who also share those characteristics: *Cooksey (GMB Claimants) v Trafford BC* [2012] EqLR 744 and *R (Unison) v Lord Chancellor (No 2)* [2015] IRLR 99, [2015] ICR 390, DC.

While the Tribunal enjoys some latitude in its selection of pools, a Tribunal can still err in law by selecting the 'wrong' pool. In *Abbott v Cheshire* (supra), claims were brought by hospital domestic workers (almost entirely female) whose terms and conditions did not include a right to a bonus. They sought to compare themselves to hospital porters (entirely male) whose terms and conditions included a right to a bonus. The employers had argued that the proper comparator pool was not just the porters, but the porters and the catering staff. The catering staff were predominantly female and had also received bonuses. The Court of Appeal ruled that the tribunal had been wrong to reject the employer's argument as to pool: the three groups were plainly comparable. However, the Court of Appeal considered that the right result had been reached in any event because the porters and catering staff together were still 65% male in comparison to the domestic staff who were almost exclusively female: that was sufficient to establish a prima facie case of discrimination. The Court of Appeal also rejected an argument (based on *Specialarbejderforbundet i Danmark v Dansk Industri, acting for Royal Copenhagen A/S*: C-400/93 [1995] IRLR 648, CJEU) that the comparator group (of 37) was too small in order to establish a valid statistical difference in the proportions of male and female workers. The Court of Appeal considered that it would be wrong to set minimum numerical requirements because that would mean that indirect discrimination could never be established for small employers.

In *Pike v Somerset County Council* [2009] IRLR 870, [2010] ICR 46, the CA considered a claim by a retired teacher who had returned to teaching part-time. She was unable to rejoin the Teachers' Pension Scheme and her service from then on did not count towards her pensionable employment. However, if she had returned to teaching full-time, she would have been able to rejoin the scheme. The competing pools comprised: (a) retired teachers who had returned to work, and (b) all members (whether or not retired) of the pension scheme. The CA held that the correct pool included retired teachers only. The pool was to be defined as a group in which all the members wanted a particular benefit, but the benefit was denied to some members because of a criterion applicable to the benefit. The members of the claimant's proposed pool, namely teachers returning after retirement, all wanted the benefit of their service being pensionable, but that benefit was denied to part-timers. Those who were members of the pension scheme but had not retired were uninterested in the post-retirement rules. They derived no advantage from the post-retirement rule favouring full-timers; it simply did not apply to them.

The introduction of equal pay questionnaires under the *Equal Pay (Questions and Replies) Order 2003* (see **23.29** below) assisted complainants with gathering appropriate statistics to show disparate impact and to enable complainants to pierce the culture of secrecy. However, the questionnaire procedure is not available for claims commenced after 25 April 2013 as *s 138* of the *EqA 2010* was repealed by *s 66* of the *Enterprise and Regulatory Reform Act 2013*. The importance of transparency is nonetheless emphasised in the Equal Pay: Statutory Code of Practice published by the Equality and Human Rights Commission. Complainants may also find assistance in the results of 'equal pay audits' (below **23.24**) and 'gender pay gap reporting' (below **23.32**).

Note that under *s 77* of the *EqA 2010* individuals are also protected from retaliation or victimisation where they seek, or provide, disclosures about the terms of their work (including how much they are paid) (*ss 77(4)* and *(5)*). Contractual terms purporting to restrict such disclosures will be void (*ss 77(1)* and *(2)*).

23.12 Equal Pay

23.12 Specific considerations in relation to the 'material factor' defence

The House of Lords in *Rainey v Greater Glasgow Health Board* [1987] IRLR 26, [1987] ICR 129 resolved earlier doubts upon the matters which may be taken into account in considering a 'genuine material factor' (GMF) defence under *s 1(3)* of the *EqPA 1970* in favour of holding that it is open to a tribunal to consider the merits of any factor advanced by an employer in support of such a defence, and the observations made in that case remain good law. At 140, Lord Keith stated:

> 'The difference must be "material", which I would construe as meaning "significant and relevant", and it must be between "her case and his". Consideration of a person's case must necessarily involve consideration of all circumstances of that case. These may well go beyond what is not very happily described as "the personal equation", ie the personal qualities by way of skill, experience or training which the individual brings to the job. Some circumstances may on examination prove to be not significant or not relevant, but others may do so, though not relating to the personal qualities of the employee. In particular, where there is no question of intentional sex discrimination whether direct or indirect (and there is none here) a difference which is connected with economic factors affecting the efficient carrying on of the employer's business or other activity may well be relevant.'

He held that the defence available in *EqPA 1970, s 1(3)* was equivalent in scope to the defence of justification held by the European court in *Bilka-Kaufhaus Gmbh v Weber von Hartz* C-170/84: [1986] IRLR 317, [1987] ICR 110 to be available under *art 157*.

Although each case will therefore turn on its particular facts and circumstances, certain general points of principle have been considered in the cases as set out below.

Note that where, applying the 'structured approach' set out by the EAT in *Bury v Hamilton* (above, **23.10**), and now codified in *EqA 2010, s 69*, it is necessary for the tribunal to consider whether a particular indirectly discriminatory situation or PCP is objectively justified, the approach to the question of justification should be the same as for any other case of discrimination, ie the employer must show that there is a legitimate aim and that the means used to achieve that aim are proportionate: see DISCRIMINATION AND EQUAL OPPORTUNITIES – II (13).

Factors relevant to equal value as well as the 'material factor' defence

In *Davies v McCartneys* [1989] IRLR 439, [1989] ICR 705, the EAT held that a defence was made out under s 1(3) despite the fact that some of the matters relied upon, such as circumstances in which the job was performed, were relevant to an assessment of whether the jobs were of equal value. In *Christie v John E Haith Ltd* [2003] IRLR 670, the EAT held that the mere fact that a particular factor may be relevant in the evaluation exercise to determine the question of equal value was not a ground for excluding it as part of a *s 1(3)* defence: the principle in *Davies v McCartneys* was not limited to cases where there had not actually been a determination of equal value taking into account the factors in question. Once an employee has shown that she is engaged on like work, work rated as equivalent to that of a man, or work of equal value to that of a man it is for the employer to prove that he has a defence under *s 1(3)* (*Financial Times Ltd v Byrne (No 2)* [1992] IRLR 163). See also *Kenny and ors v Minister for Justice, Equality and Law Reform* Case C 427/11 [2013] ICR D27 at §29 and *Angestelltenbetriebsrat der Wiener Gebeitskrankenkasse v Wiener Gebeitskrankenkasse* [1999] IRLR 804 at §29, where the CJEU holds that the fact that one group of employees doing a job has professional training and the other does not can both be a factor pointing to a finding that the employees are not doing 'like work' and a factor justifying any differential in pay.

The 'genuine' requirement

Although the word 'genuine' (used in *EqPA 1970, s 1(3)*) does not appear in *EqA 2010, s 69*, it is submitted that this is because the word is superfluous. Plainly an employer cannot establish a 'material factor' defence under the *EqA 2010* unless there is genuinely (or truly) a material difference between a claimant's case and her comparator's that is not directly or indirectly discriminatory. The 'genuine' requirement simply means that the factor relied on must truly be the reason for the difference in pay. Thus, for example, if there is evidence that women are systematically disadvantaged, it will not be acceptable to say simply that pay awards are based on the quality of work – it would be plain from the result that the system was being abusively applied (*Danfoss*). The factor relied upon must not be a 'sham'; see *Hartlepool Borough Council v Dolphin* [2009] IRLR 168 in which the EAT held the tribunal was entitled to find that productivity bonuses paid to men were a sham. The employer's assertion that an explanation was all that needed to be shown could not be accepted. The tribunal's task had been to determine whether the schemes had been genuine, by deciding whether they were intended to achieve and in fact achieved productivity improvements; its approach, in holding that the monitoring measures were not enough to satisfy it that the schemes were genuinely intended to improve productivity, was correct. Note, however, that tribunals should guard against using the word 'sham' unless there has actually been dishonesty on the part of the employer. If it is the case, for example, that productivity bonuses were justified when first introduced but cease to be so, that does not mean they are a 'sham', but merely that they are no longer justified: see *Bury Metropolitan Borough Council v Hamilton* [2011] IRLR 358, [2011] ICR 655.

The distinction between the legitimate aim and the means used to achieve it

In considering whether a *prima facie* indirectly discriminatory measure is objectively justified (see above **23.11**), care must be taken in properly identifying and distinguishing the aim of the measure from the means used to achieve it. The fact that different measures with different aims could be introduced by an employer is not relevant in determining whether a particular measure with a legitimate aim is justified, what matters is whether there are more proportionate ways of achieving the aim of the measure in question: see *Blackburn v Chief Constable of West Midlands Police* [2008] EWCA Civ 1208, [2009] IRLR 135 (aim of rewarding those who did night work was legitimate and therefore it was proportionate to pay those persons more – it did not matter that other police forces had decided not to reward night workers). See also *Allen v GMB* [2008] IRLR 690. In that case the CA considered the situation of a union which had decided, in negotiating with an employer in relation to various pay issues, to adopt a policy whereby employees' interests in relation to future pay deals were prioritised over claims to back pay under the *EqPA 1970*. The result was that those employees who had equal pay claims (a predominantly female group) received less by way of settlement than they might otherwise have done. The Tribunal held that the union's objective (which it identified as being to achieve single status, avoiding privatisations, job losses, cuts in hours, and members receiving lower pay under the new system) was legitimate, but that the means used to achieve that aim amounted to 'manipulation' and were unjustified. One factor in the Tribunal's conclusion was that it was considered that the amount accepted by the Union in settlement of the equal pay claims was bordering on negligent. The EAT found that the Tribunal had taken the wrong approach to the question of objective justification. The EAT considered that, once it had been accepted that an aim was legitimate then if the means adopted to achieve that aim were the only means available then the policy would be justified. The CA disagreed and upheld the Tribunal's decision. The CA considered that the EAT had taken too narrow an approach to the concept of 'means'. The 'means' was not the balance struck by the union in the deal with the Council, but the methods used to persuade members to accept that deal. The Tribunal had been entitled to find that those methods had been manipulative and disproportionate to the legitimate aims pursued.

23.12   Equal Pay

Timing of the justification/explanation

The material difference or factor relied upon must be one which exists throughout the period during which there is a difference in pay. For example, where a woman was appointed at a lower rate of pay than existing male employees because of financial constraints, there was no defence to her equal pay claim after those constraints had ceased to exist (*Benveniste v University of Southampton* [1989] IRLR 122, [1989] ICR 617). In *Co-operative Group Limited v Walker* (UKEAT/0087/19/RN) Lord Summers regarded *Benveniste* as supportive of an argument that there had to be a new 'decision' by an employer about pay levels which is tainted by discrimination before a prior justification can be regarded as having ceased to exist, but it is submitted that this reading of *Benveniste* must be wrong since liability for breach of the equality clause does not (unlike liability for direct sex discrimination) depend on their being some specific 'act' or 'omission' by an employer: where a term of a woman's contract operates less favourably to her, the employer is required to justify that differential and it is no defence for the employer to say that it had not taken a decision about the woman's pay. What matters is whether there remains objective justification for any continuing differential. Thus, where employees are on appointment placed at different points on a pay scale as a result of having different qualifications or experience, a continuing difference in pay as the employees move up that payscale as a result of annual increments will be lawful, provided that the continuing difference is wholly explained by the operation of the payscale and there was no discrimination in the initial decision as to where the employee was placed on the payscale on appointment: *Secretary of State for Justice (sued as National Offenders Management Service) v Bowling* [2012] IRLR 382. In that case the EAT said that that would even be the case if the employees' subsequent experience in the job meant that the man's initial advantage as a result of his qualifications and experience had been entirely wiped out by the woman's personal development in the role.

An initial difference in pay between male and female employees performing the same work cannot be justified on the basis of factors, such as a difference in performance levels, which become known only after the employees concerned have taken up their duties and which can only be assessed during the employment relationship (*Brunnhofer v Bank der Osterreichischen Postsparkasse AG*: C-381/99 [2001] IRLR 571, CJEU). However, such factors will obviously be relevant when what is complained about is the level of an annual bonus which is based on an assessment of an employee's performance during the year: *Villalba v Merrill Lynch & Co* [2006] IRLR 437.

'Red-circling' of existing pension entitlements will not amount to a genuine material factor where, although justifying an initial difference in pension entitlement, it does not provide justification for maintaining the differential over twenty years: *Home Office v Bailey* [2005] IRLR 369, [2005] ICR 1057. See also *Cumbria County Council v Dow (No 1)* [2008] IRLR 91, EAT (difference in pay which arose from a bonus scheme originally designed to improve productivity was not objectively justified where the scheme had ceased to be effective and the bonus payments had in practice become automatic additions to the pay of the male comparators).

After-the-event justification

The Court of Appeal in *Cadman v Health and Safety Executive* [2004] EWCA Civ 1317, [2004] IRLR 971, [2005] ICR 1546 reiterated that 'after the event' justification is permissible so that an employer may rely on matters which did not consciously and contemporaneously feature in its decision making at the time of introducing the pay arrangements. The CJEU adopted the same approach in *Schönheit (Hilde) v Stadt Frankfurt am Main*: C-4/02 and C-5/02 [2003] ECR I-12575, [2004] IRLR 983. See also *Pulham v Barking and Dagenham London Borough Council* [2010] IRLR 184, [2010] ICR 333 where the EAT held that an employer was not prevented from advancing a justification defence in respect of pay protection arrangements merely because they had not been 'carefully costed and crafted' at the time of implementation. However, on usual principles, the factual matters relied on in justifying the policy must be matters that are contemporaneous with the application of the policy: compare *Trustees of Swansea University Pension & Assurance Scheme v Williams* [2015] IRLR 885, [2015] ICR 1197 and *Reid v Lewisham LBC* UKEAT/0248-9/17/DA. Differences in hours worked

Differences in hours worked

The House of Lords held in *Leverton v Clwyd County Council* [1989] IRLR 28, [1989] ICR 33 that, if there was no significant difference between the hourly rates of pay of the applicant and her male comparator, it would be a legitimate, if not a necessary, inference that the difference between their total salaries was due to, and justified by, the difference in the number of hours worked. This approach was adopted by the CJEU in *Stadt Lengerich v Helmig* [1995] IRLR 216, [1996] ICR 35 which held that, prima facie, there is unequal treatment wherever the overall pay of full-time employees is higher than that of part-time employees for the same number of hours worked. The CJEU determined that there was no discrimination where part-time employees only received pay at overtime rates once they had worked the equivalent of a full-time worker's ordinary weekly hours rather than once they had completed the number of hours which they themselves ordinarily worked each week.

Qualifications / training

In *Angestelltenbetriebsrat der Wiener Gebeitskrankenkasse v Wiener Gebeitskrankenkasse* [1999] IRLR 804, [2000] ICR 1134 and *Kenny and ors v Minister for Justice, Equality and Law Reform* Case C 427/11 [2013] ICR D27 the CJEU accepted that differences in levels of professional training between the two groups of employees could justify differing levels of pay. Although a case concerned with alleged indirect race discrimination in relation to pay (and therefore not brought under the equal pay provisions of the *EqA 2010*), *Greenland v Secretary of State for Justice* (UKEAT/0232/14/DA, 28 January 2015) is helpful here. That case concerned differences in pay between lay members of the Parole Board and the retired judges (all white males) who had been recruited to the Board. Among other things, the EAT considered that the differences in qualification, and the fact that the retired judges were able to chair oral hearings in a wider range of cases, meant that there were material differences between the retired judges and the lay members. See also the similarly unsuccessful case of *McGrath v Ministry of Justice* (UKEAT/0247/14/LA, 27 February 2015) concerning a claim by an employment tribunal lay member to a pension equivalent to that of the legally qualified tribunal judges.

The importance of transparency

The CJEU in *Danfoss* held that where an undertaking applies a system of pay which is totally lacking in transparency, it is for the employer to show that his practice concerning wages is not discriminatory. The Court of Appeal in *Calder v Rowntree Mackintosh Confectionery Ltd* [1993] IRLR 212, [1993] ICR 811 apparently accepted that the transparency principle applied in English law, but held that it did not require the employer to explain exactly how a figure for shift premium was achieved. By contrast, in an important decision on City bonus payments, *Barton v Investec Henderson Crosthwaite Securities Ltd* [2003] IRLR 332, [2003] ICR 1205, the EAT held that the tribunal erred in appearing to condone the lack of transparency in the employer's bonus system on the basis of its 'industrial knowledge' that the City 'bonus culture' was one of secrecy. Although the bonus claim was brought under the *SDA 1975*, the lack of transparency was also relevant to the material factor defence in the *EqPA* claim.

Note also that there have been obiter indications in UK authorities that, in cases where there is a challenge to a pay system which is alleged to be indirectly discriminatory, the clarity and simplicity of the system may amount to a material factor. Put another way, the material factor may consist of the 'administrative convenience' of operating a simple and straightforward system, or equally, the administrative inconvenience of having to alter it (cf Dillon and Hirst LJJ in *R v Secretary of State for Employment, ex p Equal Opportunities Commission*

[1993] IRLR 10, [1993] ICR 251, CA, and *Barry v Midland Bank plc* [1998] IRLR 138, [1999] ICR 319, CA; the Court of Appeal's decision in *Barry* was upheld by the House of Lords ([1999] IRLR 581, [1999] ICR 859), but on a different basis: their Lordships looked at the 'primary object' of the redundancy scheme in considering whether it was discriminatory, rather than reserving such issues to a consideration of whether the scheme could, if it had a disparate impact, be justified.

'Productivity bonuses' and attendance allowances

A number of cases have involved so-called 'productivity bonuses' and/or attendance allowances paid to male manual workers. See, for eg, *Degnan v Redcar & Cleveland Borough Council* [2005] EWCA Civ 726, [2005] IRLR 615; *Armstrong v Newcastle Upon Tyne NHS Hospital Trust* [2005] EWCA Civ 1608, [2006] IRLR 124; *South Tyneside Metropolitan Borough Council v Anderson* [2007] EWCA Civ 654, [2007] IRLR 715, [2007] ICR 1581; *Bainbridge/Surtees* [2008] EWCA Civ 885; [2008] IRLR 776; *Cumbria County Council v Dow and ors* [2008] IRLR 91; *Bury Metropolitan Borough Council v Hamilton* [2011] IRLR 358, [2011] ICR 655; and *Gibson v Sheffield City Council* [2010] EWCA Civ 63, [2010] IRLR 311, [2010] ICR 708; and *Sunderland City Council v Brennan* [2012] EWCA Civ 413, [2012] IRLR 507, [2012] ICR 1216. Those cases show that in general employers have in practice found it difficult to justify bonuses that have applied to groups of (mainly) male workers but not to groups of (mainly) female workers. In such cases the tribunal will consider whether or not there was when the bonus was introduced, and whether there continues to be, a good reason for the payment of the bonus (eg performance improvement or maintaining productivity) or whether the bonus is in reality an 'attendance allowance' paid simply because the employee attends work (in which case it will not be justified). The tribunal will also consider whether or not a similar scheme could have been introduced for the female workers. However, even a finding that no similar scheme could have been introduced will not prevent the tribunal concluding that having the bonus for the male workers is not justified: see, eg, *Gibson v Sheffield City Council* [2010] EWCA Civ 63, [2010] IRLR 311, [2010] ICR 708 (although note that in that case the tribunal had found that what were originally productivity bonuses had effectively become mere attendance allowances).

Seniority and length of service as factors

The CJEU has held that differences in seniority and length of service are generally material differences (not requiring special justification), at least where the employer is distinguishing between full-time workers (*Handels-Og Kontorfunktionaerernes Forbund i Danmark v Dansk Arbejdsgiverforening ('Danfoss')* [1989] IRLR 532, [1991] ICR 74). In two subsequent cases, however, the CJEU appeared to doubt the correctness of *Danfoss* or at least have second thoughts as to its general application: see *Nimz v Freie und Hansestadt Hamburg*: C-184/89 [1991] ECR 1-297 and *Gerster v Freistaat Bayern*: C-1/95 [1997] IRLR 699, [1998] ICR 327. In *Cadman v Health and Safety Executive* the Court of Appeal therefore referred the issue to the CJEU again. The CJEU (Case C-17/05, [2006] IRLR 969, [2006] ICR 1623) affirmed that, as a general rule, an employer may rely on seniority and length of service as being genuine material differences not requiring special justification or (at least where pay is based on a job evaluation system) evidence that the individual in question has indeed acquired experience during his or her years in service. However, the CJEU made clear that, if the complainant provides evidence capable of giving rise to 'serious doubts' as to whether the criterion of length of service is, in the circumstances, appropriate to attain the legitimate objective of rewarding experience which enables the worker to perform his duties better, then the burden will shift to the employer to justify in detail reliance on the criterion of length of service by proving, as regards the job in question, that length of service goes hand in hand with experience and that experience enables the worker to perform his duties better. The CA in *Wilson v Health and Safety Executive* [2009] EWCA Civ 1074, [2010] IRLR 59, [2010] ICR 302 clarified the approach that should be taken to domestic cases involving a length of service criterion in the light of the CJEU decision in *Cadman*. The CA ruled that, so far as domestic law is concerned, the 'serious doubts' test put forward by the CJEU in *Cadman* is only of relevance before trial (presumably as a ground for 'strike out'). The CA said that what a claimant needs to show, pre-trial, is that there is evidence from which, if established at trial, it can properly be found that the general rule in *Danfoss* and *Cadman* (that seniority and length of service are generally material differences other than sex) does not apply. The CA confirmed, however, that a claim involving a length of service criterion is to be approached in essentially the same way as any other equal pay claim involving indirect discrimination. The burden is on the claimant to show disparate impact and, if that is established, the burden shifts to the employer either to explain or justify the difference as necessary (see further the discussion at **23.10** above). The CA noted (at 52) that the Tribunal had allowed the employer a 'margin of appreciation' in relation to objective justification in this case. The CA indicated that there was no error of law in that approach.

In *Secretary of State for Justice v Bowling* [2012] IRLR 382 the EAT (Underhill P presiding) held that a salary point scale applied by the civil service amounted to a good GMF defence. The salary scale explained the difference in pay between the claimant and her comparator. It continued to explain the differential throughout the claimant's employment and there was no reason to suppose that there was any sex taint in the application of the salary scale. A similar approach was adopted in *Skills Development Scotland Co Limited v Buchanan and others* [2011] EqLR 955 in which the EAT (Lady Smith presiding) held that transferred terms and conditions of employment which required future increases in salary amounted to a genuine material factor which explained the difference in pay throughout the period and which were not sex-tainted. Note that in order to prove that a length of service criterion is prima facie indirectly discriminatory it is not sufficient to show that there are clusters of female employees at the bottom of a pay grade and clusters of males at the top: what matters is whether there are actually significant differences between male and female basic pay: *McNeil v Revenue and Customs Commissioners* [2018] IRLR 398.

Market forces

One 'extrinsic factor' which may, in certain circumstances, justify a difference in pay is the scarcity of suitably qualified employees to fill a particular post. In such circumstances, an employer may be able to justify a resultant difference in pay as consisting of a necessary premium paid to obtain the scarce skills which the more highly paid employee has to offer (*Enderby v Frenchay Health Authority* [1993] IRLR 591, [1994] ICR 112). See also *Greenland v Secretary of State for Justice* (UKEAT/0323/14/DA, 28 January 2015), a claim in relation to race discrimination in pay, which shows that similar considerations apply to justification of 'prima facie' indirect discrimination. In that case, the EAT accepted that the higher pay paid to retired judges recruited to the Parole Board was justified by the urgent need to recruit more Board members with those qualifications in order to deal with the backlog of oral hearings. In *BMC Software Limited v Shaikh* [2019] EWCA Civ 267, [2019] ICR 1050, the Court of Appeal emphasised that where an employer seeks to justify a difference in pay by reference to market forces, it must be able to explain with particularity what those market forces are and how they apply in the circumstances of the case. That case shows that an employer that lacks a transparent pay system in the first place will be unlikely to be successful in establishing a market forces defence.

Note that it is for the employer to show that the market dictated the higher rate of pay and not for the claimant to show that the pay was too high: see *Cumbria County Council v Dow and ors* [2008] IRLR 91, EAT. In *Ratcliffe v North Yorkshire County Council* (above) the women concerned, who were catering assistants, had been the subject of a job evaluation exercise. Their job had been rated as equivalent to that of certain other employees engaged in very different jobs and they had received the same pay. Their function was subject to competitive tendering. A competing company had much lower overheads as it paid its (largely female) staff lower wages than those paid by the Council. In order properly to compete, the Council believed it needed to reduce the pay of its own catering assistants. The majority of the tribunal found that whilst there was a material difference between the circumstances of the women and their comparators, namely that the women were employed in functions which had to be subjected to the market, the market itself was not sexually neutral and therefore the material difference was 'due to [a] difference in sex'. The catering sector was regarded as 'women's work' and the pay of those employed by the competing company, was discriminatorily low. The Court of Appeal disagreed ([1994] IRLR 342, [1994] ICR 810). It found that the defence was made out on the controversial basis that even if the competing company's pay rates were discriminatory it did not follow that the Council discriminated if it lowered its own rates in order to compete. The decision of the House of Lords in *Ratcliffe* ([1995] IRLR 439, [1995] ICR 833) is not a model of clarity. What is clear is that their Lordships found that the tribunal was entitled to reach the view that the defence had not been made out. It does not appear, however, that the basis of the decision was that the pay reduction was tainted by the competing company's discrimination. Lord Slynn noted (ibid, at 442): 'The fact, if it be a fact, that [the competing company] discriminated against women in respect of pay and that the [Council] had to pay no more than [the competing company] in order to be competitive does not however conclude the issue'. Unfortunately, it is not clear, from what follows, what their Lordships considered to be the conclusive factor. Lord Slynn continued: 'The basic question is whether the [Council] paid women less than men for work rated as equivalent. The reason they did so is certainly that they had to compete . . . The fact, however, is that they did pay women less than men engaged on work rated as equivalent. The employment tribunal found and was entitled to find that the employers had not shown that this was genuinely due to a material difference other than a difference of sex.' It appears therefore that their Lordships simply took the view that the tribunal had been entitled to find the employer had not discharged the burden of proof on the facts.

Pay protection arrangements

In some cases where an employer has identified that there is an 'equal pay issue' as between two groups of employees, the employer has sought to equalise pay over the course of a number of years, by gradually reducing the pay of the highest-paid group, but in the meantime offering 'pay protection' to existing employees within that group. In *s 69(3)* of *EqA 2010* a statutory basis for the lawfulness of 'pay protection' policies is provided. *Section 69(3)* provides that 'the long-term objective of reducing inequality between men's and women's terms of work is always to be regarded as a legitimate aim'. However, it does not follow that an employer who has made use of a pay protection policy will be able to succeed in the material factor defence. Employment tribunals are likely to scrutinise carefully a pay protection policy, in order to determine whether or not it is proportionate as to achieving any legitimate aim, particularly where the employer has already recognised that differentials in pay are tainted by historic discrimination.

In *Bainbridge v Redcar and Cleveland Borough Council/Surtees v Middlesbrough Borough Council (Bainbridge/Surtees)* [2008] EWCA Civ 885, [2008] IRLR 776, [2009] ICR 133, the Council sought to justify a four-year 'pay protection' scheme introduced in the aforementioned circumstances on grounds that may broadly be described as cost (ie because it would have been too expensive to pay the predominantly female group more) and employee relations (ie in relation to the predominantly male group). However, the CA (and EAT) approved the Tribunal's finding that the Council had failed to establish the genuine material factor defence because the 'pay protection' policy was irredeemably tainted by sex discrimination as it amounted to perpetuating the benefit of the past sex discrimination. The Council's argument was that there was nothing inherently discriminatory in providing a 'soft landing' to protect employees from a sudden and drastic drop in pay. The Court of Appeal rejected the claimants' argument that as a matter of law, giving pay protection to the beneficiaries of past pay discrimination was always a breach of the *EqPA 1970*. However, the Court of Appeal also rejected the Council's argument that there was no *prima facie* sex discrimination in respect of the pay protection and held that the tribunal was right to look at the underlying reason for the pay protection and to find that it was causally related to historic unlawful sex discrimination. The burden of proof then shifted to the Council to objectively justify this *prima facie* discrimination. The Court of Appeal's judgment is not wholly clear as to when and how this can be justified, holding both that: (a) justification will be difficult where the employer knew or strongly suspected that there was past pay discrimination (see paragraph 133 of *Bainbridge/Surtees*), and/or (b) where the employer knows it is perpetuating past discrimination this can be justified if it considers the matter carefully and there is a good reason for pay protection to be offered only to the losers (paragraphs 149, 156 and 173 of *Bainbridge/Surtees*). Although the Court of Appeal in *Bainbridge/Surtees* was keen to stress the point made in the EAT that its decision did not rule out all 'pay protection' policies, its decision in practice left employers conducting a job evaluation scheme in a Catch 22 situation; the 'losers' will be unhappy if they do not receive 'pay protection' but the 'winners' will be unhappy at what they now see as historic pay discrimination.

In *Bury Metropolitan Borough Council v Hamilton* [2011] IRLR 358, [2011] ICR 655 the EAT sought to clarify the approach that should be taken to pay protection cases. The EAT ruled that in any case where past direct discrimination has been 'recognised', the continuation for the future of such discrimination in the form of transitional or phasing-out arrangements cannot be justified. However, transitional arrangements that continue past indirect discrimination (as to which see below) will not be unlawful if they can be justified. In order to establish justification, the employer will need in all cases to advance cogent and specific reasons for the pay protection arrangements. Where cost is relied on as a reason for justifying the arrangements, evidence of the costs themselves and the financial context must be adduced. Mere assertions of unaffordability will not suffice. The tribunal will need to apply the proportionality test. In doing so it will be relevant to consider the employer's state of knowledge about the discriminatory effect of his provisions and the extent to which he tries to minimise that effect. See also *Macdonald and ors v Glasgow City Council* (12 May 2015), UKEATS/0008/14/BI, UKEATS/0009/14/BI and UKEATS/0011/14/BI and, on appeal, *Glasgow City Council v UNISON claimants* [2017] CSIH 34, [2017] IRLR 739.

Audit Commission v Haq (S) [2012] EWCA Civ 1621, [2013] IRLR 206 is another case in which pay protection arrangements were held to be pursuing a legitimate aim and to be justified. In that case, the EAT overturned the ET's decision on this point, and the EAT's judgment on this issue was upheld by the CA on appeal. The CA held that the ET had been wrong in law in rejecting the Commission's aims in this regard as illegitimate. The CA also considered that it was legitimate for an employer to take into account that without the pay protection arrangements the Commission might have been prejudiced as a result of losing the services of the employees in question.

See also *Naeem v Secretary of State for Justice* [2017] UKSC 27, [2017] 1 WLR 1343 which was a religious discrimination case rather than an equal pay case, but the Supreme Court's observations about the transitional pay protection arrangements for prison service chaplains are potentially relevant to equal pay too, albeit somewhat out of line with existing authority in this field. The Court observed (at paragraph 47) that where a case concerned the lawfulness of a transitional scheme, 'the question was not whether the original pay scheme could be justified but whether the steps being taken to move towards the new system were proportionate. Where part of the aim is to move towards a system which will reduce or even eliminate the disadvantage suffered by a group sharing a protected characteristic, it is necessary to consider whether there were other ways of proceeding which would eliminate or reduce the disadvantage more quickly. Otherwise it cannot be said that the means used are "no more than necessary" to meet the employer's need for an orderly transition. . . . The burden of proof is on the respondent, although it is clearly incumbent upon the claimant to challenge the assertion that there was nothing else the employer could do. Where alternative means are suggested or are obvious, it is incumbent upon the tribunal to consider them.'

23.12 Equal Pay

Two CJEU cases on the justification of pay arrangements and transitional pay arrangements that are directly discriminatory on grounds of age also provide relevant guidance in this area. *Schmitzer v Bundesministerin für Inneres* (Case C-530/13) [2015] IRLR 331 concerned the pay scheme for Austrian civil servants. The CJEU accepted that on changing pay systems, pay protection arrangements intended to protect the rights of those acquired under the previous system pursued a legitimate aim. However, the CJEU emphasised that such arrangements would only be justified for a transitional period and that accordingly the Austrian arrangements (which perpetuated the previous discrimination indefinitely) were unlawful. In contrast, in *Specht v Land Berlin* (Joined Cases C-501, 506, 540 and 541/12), [2014] ICR 966, [2014] All ER (EC) 111, which concerned pay arrangements for German civil servants, the CJEU accepted that a new pay scheme was justified even though it perpetuated indefinitely the effects of discrimination under the previous scheme. Pay had previously been determined by reference to a scale that depended on the employee's age at the date of appointment and was thus directly discriminatory on grounds of age. A new system was introduced so that pay was determined by reference to experience. However, existing civil servants were simply moved to the point on the new payscale that corresponded to their existing salary, thus perpetuating the directly discriminatory pay arrangements. The CJEU held that this was justified, essentially because it accepted that it was genuinely not practical to do anything else given the nature of the assessment of experience required under the new system and the numbers of civil servants.

In the light of the above authorities, the EAT decision in *Pulham and ors v London Borough of Barking & Dagenham* [2010] IRLR 184, [2010] ICR 333 (an age discrimination case), should probably be regarded as wrongly decided insofar as the EAT held that if an employer has recognised that a particular practice or policy may be discriminatory, it will not be possible for the employer to justify continuing that practice or policy even on a transitional or phasing-out basis. The case does, though, make the important point that the fact that the pay protection arrangements have been agreed with a trade union or workforce representatives will be relevant to the question of the whether the arrangements are justified, but it does not relieve the employer and, in turn, the Tribunal from independently considering whether the arrangements are justified.

Industrial relations

Good industrial relations may be taken into account as one factor among others in deciding whether a difference in pay is objectively justified by factors unrelated to any discrimination on grounds of sex: *Kenny and ors v Minister for Justice, Equality and Law Reform* Case C 427/11 [2013] ICR D27 at para 50. Good industrial relations cannot be used as a factor on its own justifying discrimination, however, because the interests of good relations are also subject to the observance of the principle of non-discrimination (*Kenny* ibid para 48). Further, collective agreements, like individual worker contracts, and legislative provisions, must not discriminate unlawfully between men and women: *Enderby v Frenchay Health Authority* [1993] IRLR 591, [1994] ICR 112 at para 21.

However, in equal value claims, differences in contractual entitlements sometimes arise from the complainant and her comparator having been represented by different negotiating bodies. The justificatory force of this factor was considered by the CJEU in *Enderby*. In *Enderby* a woman employed as a speech therapist sought to establish an inequality of pay by comparing herself with two men – a clinical psychologist and a pharmacist. It having been established that the woman was engaged in work of equal value to that of the comparators, the employer sought to justify the difference in pay by showing that the pay rates had resulted from different collective bargaining processes, each of which was free from any sex bias. The CJEU found, in effect, that whilst this explained the difference in pay it did not, where the complainant's job was 'carried out almost exclusively by women and the [comparator's] . . . predominantly by men', objectively justify it and in those circumstances the employer did not have a defence. This 'almost exclusively by women' formula has given rise to a number of difficulties of interpretation (see above **23.11**). In relation to the question of the significance of representation by different negotiating bodies, the Court of Appeal in *British Road Services Ltd v Loughran* [1997] IRLR 92, CA made it clear that the *Enderby* decision does not decide that the factor can never justify a difference in pay. They also rejected an argument that the mere fact of there being different bargaining structures would always justify a disparity in pay, provided that the group of employees engaged to perform the complainant's job is not comprised 'almost exclusively' of women. Instead, they decided that if there is a 'significant proportion of women' in the claimant's group, the tribunal is obliged to look carefully at the bargaining structures in order to satisfy itself that there was no discriminatory effect.

In *Bainbridge/Surtees* (supra), the Court of Appeal rejected an argument that the difference in pay (an attendance allowance paid to a predominantly male group of employees) was the result of separate collective bargaining which was a non-sex-based reason for the difference. The Court of Appeal held that separate collective bargaining could be a GMF defence but that the tribunal had been entitled to infer that there was a sex-taint where there was a marked difference in the sex balance between the two groups and there was no other reason to explain the difference in pay so that the fact of separate collective bargaining would not, of itself, be likely to disprove the possibility of sex discrimination. See also *Grundy v British Airways plc* [2008] EWCA Civ 875, [2008] IRLR 815 where the Court of Appeal held that attention had to be paid by negotiators of collective agreements to the possibility that such differentials would have a disparate impact on employees of one gender. If that was overlooked, with a consequent breach of one group's equality clauses, the oversight could not logically be justified by reference to the collective agreement which resulted.

In *Coventry City Council v Nicholls* [2009] IRLR 345, Elias P rejected an argument that the pay differential was adequately explained by a 'supervening cause', namely the alleged intransigence of the trade unions to reaching an agreement on single status pay arrangements which would have equalised pay. The EAT held that 'union hostility to change is incapable of constituting a new explanation for the difference in pay such that it can be said that a pay differential whose roots lay firmly in sex discrimination, has at some indeterminate point ceased to have anything to do with sex . . . properly analysed, the union's stance may be said to explain why the discrimination was not removed earlier than it was, but it does not supersede, in the sense of replacing, the original discriminatory explanation for the difference in pay'. In any event, 'ultimately the ability to remedy unequal pay was always in the council's own hands . . . '.

Cost

It was for a long time established that budgetary factors alone cannot justify discrimination against one of the sexes (*Schonheit v Stadt Frankfurt Am Main* [2004] IRLR 983), although it was widely accepted that cost considerations could be prayed in aid where the difference in pay was objectively justified by some other factor (*Cross v British Airways plc* [2006] EWCA Civ 549, [2006] IRLR 804, [2006] ICR 1239, *Redcar & Cleveland Borough Council v Bainbridge* [2007] IRLR 91, [2008] ICR 249, EAT and *Osborne Clarke Services v Purohit* [2009] IRLR 341). See also *Pulham and ors v London Borough of Barking and Dagenham* [2010] IRLR 184, [2010] ICR 333 in which the EAT accepted that cost could form part of a defence of justification for pay protection arrangements and that in such cases it is not necessary for there to be precise evidence on costs: some indication of the 'broad scale' of costs will do. In that case the EAT also observed that, although it is open to an employer to rely on the fact that the particular budget to which the cost in question has been allocated is exhausted, this should never be regarded as a determinative factor since the allocation of cost centres to particular budgets is a matter that it is within the employer's power to vary if necessary. The EAT also observed that, although relevant, it is not sufficient for an employer to rely on the fact that a particular budget has been exhausted since the budget to which a particular cost is allocated is a matter for the employer. In *Woodcock v Cumbria Primary Care Trust* [2011] IRLR 119, [2011] ICR 143 the EAT expressed the view (*obiter*) that, as a matter of principle and of common sense, there should be no rule that considerations of cost could never be sufficient on their own to justify indirect discrimination. However, on appeal the Court of Appeal ([2012] EWCA Civ 330, [2012] IRLR 491, [2012] ICR 1126) reaffirmed the then orthodox position that justification by reference to costs alone is impermissible, although it can be taken into account with other factors – the 'costs plus' approach. Then, in *Ministry of Justice v O'Brien* [2013] UKSC 6, [2013] IRLR 315 the Supreme Court reviewed the relevant authorities in the context of a claim under the *Part-time Workers (Prevention of Less Favourable Treatment) Regulations 2000* and reached the conclusion (at paragraph 69) that cost could not be relied on in order to justify discrimination (i.e apparently even in combination with other factors). That said, the Court did not consider it needed to decide whether *Woodcock v Cumbria Primary Care Trust* had been wrongly decided. It also appeared to accept in principle that 'sound management of public finances' could be a legitimate aim. It thus remains to be seen whether the *O'Brien* decision will be regarded as outlawing altogether cost considerations, or whether cost will continue to be regarded as relevant to justification, provided a legitimate aim other than cost-saving can be identified. In *R (Unison) v Lord Chancellor (No 2)* [2015] IRLR 99, [2015] ICR 390, the Divisional Court indicated that it regarded the law to be as stated in *Woodcock*, ie the 'costs plus' approach. The decision of the CJEU in *Schmitzer v Bundesministerin für Inneres* (Case C-530/13) [2015] IRLR 331 suggests that the 'costs plus' approach is correct, although that case was a direct age discrimination case and thus a case in which cost saving could never be a legitimate aim, even if it can support the proportionality of a measure (see above). In *Schmitzer*, the CJEU made clear that budgetary considerations could be relied upon by way of justification, provided that they were relied on in conjunction with 'political, social or demographic considerations'. See also the discussion of this line of case law in *R (Unison) v Lord Chancellor (No 3)* [2015] EWCA Civ 935, [2016] ICR 1.

Notwithstanding the statements of principle in the case law, it should be noted that there are in fact a number of cases where the Tribunals and Courts have reached conclusions that could be characterized as being findings that costs alone can justify discrimination and which may continue to be followed despite the Supreme Court's ruling. Thus, the courts appear to have had little difficulty with the notion that measures intended to avoid a 'windfall' or 'excessive compensation' to the employee – measures which the employer will inevitably have introduced to save itself money – have been held to be justified: see *Loxley v BAE Systems (Munitions & Ordnance) Ltd* [2008] IRLR 853, [2008] ICR 1348 and *Kraft Foods UK Ltd v Hastie* [2011] 3 All ER 956, [2010] ICR 1355. In those cases, the payments in question were held to serve some other legitimate purpose and so the courts were able to regard the quantum of the payment as being an aspect of the proportionality of the means of meeting the legitimate aim of (for eg in the case of severance pay) paying a reasonable sum of money on termination of employment to allow the employees time to find a new job. *HM Land Registry v S M Benson and ors* [2012] IRLR 373, [2012] ICR 627 is another apparently anomalous case. Here, the EAT found that the Tribunal had wrongly found an employer's use of a 'cheapness criterion' in a redundancy situation to be unjustified indirect age discrimination. The EAT held that the 'cheapness criterion' fulfilled a legitimate aim of saving the employer money, and that it was justified because there was no practicable alternative means of achieving the same aim and the measure was not disproportionate. It is notable, however, that the case seems to have been decided by the EAT without reference to the authorities for the general principle that costs alone cannot justify discrimination. See also *Edie and others v HCL Insurance BPO Services Ltd* [2015] ICR 713, [2015] All ER (D) 264 (Feb) in which the EAT held, applying *Land Registry v Benson*, that seeking 'to break even year-on-year' was a legitimate aim and that cost-saving changes to terms and conditions of employment (which employees had to accept or resign their employments) were justified. *Benson* and *Braithwaite* were followed in *Heskett v Secretary of State for Justice* [2020] ICR 359, where the EAT upheld the Tribunal's finding that the introduction of a new pay progression policy for the Probation Service, which lengthened the pay band from 8 years to 23 years was justified because it was, temporarily, necessary to enable the department to break even year on year given the reduced settlement from central government. Similarly, in *Harrod and ors v Chief Constable of West Midlands Police* [2017] IRLR 539, the CA (without referring to the 'costs alone' case law) accepted as legitimate the aim of making the maximum possible number of redundancies, which was in substance adopting an aim of saving as much money as possible

Given these anomalous cases, and given that so far as disability discrimination is concerned costs can effectively justify indirect discrimination because it can be a reason why it is not reasonable to make an adjustment for a disabled person (see eg *Cordell v Foreign & Commonwealth Office* [2012] ICR 280, [2012] All ER (D) 97 (Mar) and **12.43** DISCRIMINATION AND EQUAL OPPORTUNITIES – I), prior to *O'Brien* (ibid) the time appeared to be ripe for the CJEU to consider again whether or not costs alone can be relied on as justifying indirect discrimination. However, following *O'Brien* there is little prospect of any reference on that point being made from the UK in the near future.

Mistake

In the absence of direct or prima facie indirect discrimination, a mistake may provide a good material factor defence: see **23.10** above. See *Yorkshire Blood Transfusion Service v Plaskitt* [1994] ICR 74, *Tyldesley v TML Plastics Ltd* [1996] IRLR 395, [1996] ICR 356 (approved by the House of Lords in *Strathclyde Regional Council v Wallace* [1998] IRLR 146, [1998] ICR 205, HL and *Glasgow City Council v Marshall* [2000] IRLR 272, [2000] ICR 196, HL); *Parliamentary Comr for Administration v Fernandez* [2004] IRLR 22, [2004] ICR 123; and *King's College London v Clark* [2003] All ER (D) 118 (Oct) (in which the EAT held that a mistake and a TUPE transfer adequately explained the difference in pay).

23.13 MATERNITY PAY

(See generally MATERNITY AND PARENTAL RIGHTS (33).)

Reflecting, the established person that there is no appropriate comparator for a woman so far as pregnancy and childbirth are concerned (cf *Alabaster v Barclays Bank plc and Secretary of State for Social Security* [2005] EWCA Civ 508, [2005] IRLR 576) the 'sex equality clause' does not apply in respect of special treatment of women in connection with pregnancy or childbirth: *paragraph 2* of *Schedule 7* to the *EqA 2010*. See further above **23.4**. However, reflecting developments in the case law in cases such as Alabaster, the *EqPA 1970* had been amended (with effect from 1 October 2005) to expressly provide for the equality clause to apply to maternity-related pay in certain circumstances: *reg 36* of the *Employment Equality (Sex Discrimination) Regulations 2005*. *Section 1(2)* of the *EqPA 1970* then provided for the equality clause to apply to pay increases and bonus in certain circumstances. The *EqA 2010* was not intended to make substantive changes to the law. *Section 73* provides for a 'maternity equality clause' to be included in a contract of employment. Under *s 74* the maternity equality clause operates on a contract of employment in the same manner as *s 1(2)(d)* to *(f)* of *EqPA 1970* previously operated.

The maternity equality clause has four aspects:

Maternity-related pay during the protected period – First, it applies to 'maternity-related pay', ie pay (other than statutory maternity pay) to which a woman is entitled as a result of being pregnant, or in respect of times when she is on maternity leave (*s 74(9)*, see formerly *s 5A* of the *EqPA 1970*). Where a term of a woman's employment provides for her maternity-related pay to be calculated by reference to her pay at a particular time (*s 74(1)*) the maternity clause modifies it so as to provide that any pay increases in her salary during the 'protected period' (ie during the pregnancy and compulsory, ordinary or additional maternity leaves), or pay increases she would have received had she not been on maternity leave, must be reflected accordingly in her maternity-related pay (*s 74(2)*, *(5)*, *(10)* and *s 18* of the *EqA 2010*). The maternity equality clause only operates, however, where the maternity-related pay to which the woman is entitled under the terms of her employment is neither what her pay would have been had she not been on statutory maternity leave nor the difference between what her pay would have been had she not been on statutory maternity leave and any statutory maternity pay to which she is entitled (*s 74(3)*).

Pay before maternity leave – Secondly, the maternity equality clause applies to pay (including pay by way of bonus) in respect of times before the woman is on maternity leave. By *s 74(7)(a)* and *(6)* if a term of her employment provides for her to receive any such pay or bonus, but does not provide for her to be given the pay in circumstances in which she would have been given it had she not been on maternity leave at the time of payment, then the maternity equality clause modifies that term so as to provide for the woman to be paid accordingly (see formerly *s 1(2)(e)* of the *EqPA 1970*);

Bonuses during compulsory maternity leave and after maternity leave – Thirdly, the maternity equality clause applies to pay by way of bonus in respect of times when she is on compulsory maternity leave, and pay by way of bonus in respect of times after the end of the protected period (*s 74(7)(b)* and *(c)*). By *s 74(6)* if a term of her employment provides for her to receive any such forms of pay or bonus, but does not provide for her to be given the pay in circumstances in which she would have been given it had she not been on maternity leave, then the maternity equality clause modifies that term so as to provide for the woman to be paid accordingly (see formerly *s 1(2)(e)* of the *EqPA 1970*);

Pay after the end of the protected period – Fourthly, where a term of a woman's work provides for pay after the end of the protected period, but does not provide for it to be subject to an increase to which it would have been subject had she not been on maternity leave, then the maternity equality clause modifies that term so as to provide for such an increase: *s 74(8)* (and see formerly *s 1(2)(f)* of the *EqPA 1970*).

The maternity equality clause as enacted in the *EqPA 1970* and the *EqA 2010* is intended to reflect certain principles established by the case law under *art 157* decided prior to 2005. Other aspects of that case law have not been incorporated into the maternity equality clause and thus the case law discussed below remains relevant.

The story begins with the decision of the CJEU in *Gillespie v Northern Health and Social Services Board: C-342/93* [1996] IRLR 214, [1996] ICR 498. At that time women whose pay was reduced when they were suspended on maternity grounds could not seek to challenge the reduction by bringing claims under *EqPA 1970*. The CJEU held that this position was compatible with *art 157*: a woman absent on maternity leave is not entitled to full pay. Women taking maternity leave are in a unique position which is not comparable with that of a man actually at work (see **12.9** Dɪsᴄʀɪᴍɪɴᴀᴛɪᴏɴ ᴀɴᴅ Eǫᴜᴀʟ Oᴘᴘᴏʀᴛᴜɴɪᴛɪᴇs – **I**). However, the CJEU has confirmed that this does not mean that a woman is excluded from all equal pay rights while on maternity leave.

Thus increases in pay awarded during a woman's maternity leave must be taken into account when calculating the amount of maternity pay to which a woman is entitled, regardless of whether that increase is backdated to the reference period for calculating statutory maternity pay (as it was in *Gillespie*) or is awarded with only prospective effect at any time up until the end of the maternity leave (*Alabaster v Woolwich plc and Secretary of State for Social Security*: C-147/02 [2004] IRLR 486, [2005] ICR 695 and *Alabaster v Barclays Bank (No 2)* [2005] EWCA Civ 508, [2005] IRLR 576, [2005] ICR 1246). This principle is reflected in the now statutory maternity equality clause.

In *Edwards v Derby City Council* [1999] ICR 114, the EAT considered an unusual case in which the male comparator was in receipt of full pay even though he was not at work. The complainant was a teacher absent on maternity leave and in receipt of half-pay. Her maternity leave overlapped with a half-term holiday. Had she not been absent on maternity leave, she would have received full pay without having to attend work. The EAT rejected her claim that she should have received full pay during the half-term period, relying on *Gillespie* as authority for the proposition that a woman absent on maternity leave was in a unique position which could not be compared with that of those working normally even if, in the particular circumstances, that might include periods in which no actual duties were performed. The decision was made, however, before the CJEU gave its ruling in *Boyle v Equal Opportunities Commission*: C-411/96 [1998] IRLR 717, [1999] ICR 360. In that case, EOC employees absent on maternity leave were entitled to three months' full pay and thereafter a period at a reduced rate. Those absent as a result of sickness were entitled to six months' full pay. In the fourth month of an absence, therefore, an employee absent through sickness would receive more than an employee absent on maternity leave. An employee fell sick during her maternity leave and wished to be put on sick leave. The EOC's contract of employment allowed the employee to move onto sick leave but only on the basis that the maternity leave was terminated. The CJEU decided that the provision was discriminatory. The employee had to be allowed to swap into a period of sick leave and then to swap back. *Boyle* is an example of a case where it has been decided, in effect, that though a pregnant woman is not comparable to a man with an illness, a pregnant woman with an illness may be treated as being comparable (see also *Handels-og Kontorfunktionaernes Forbund I Danmark, acting on behalf of Hoj Pederson v Faelesforeningen for Danmarks Brugsforninger, acting on behalf of Kvickly Skive*: C-66/760 [1999] IRLR 55: national legislation providing that men who are unfit to work through illness should receive full pay but women absent from work as a result of a pregnancy-related condition should not, is contrary to *art 157*; *Osterreichischer Gewerkschaftsbund v Wirtschaftskammer Osterreich* [2004] All ER (D) 03 (Jun): period of voluntary parental leave not comparable to compulsory military or civilian service; cf also *P & O European Ferries (Dover) Ltd v Iverson* [1999] ICR 1088).

In *Abdoulaye v Regie National des Usines Renault SA*: C-218/98 [1999] IRLR 811, [2001] ICR 527, the CJEU had to consider a provision in a collective agreement which governed the terms and conditions of Renault employees. Female employees not only continued to receive their full salary whilst on maternity leave but also received a lump sum to compensate them for the 'occupational disadvantages' that arose from their absence. Male employees argued that new fathers should receive the same bonus. However, the court decided that men were not subject to the same disadvantages. Unlike the women, they did not lose the chance of promotion or the right to performance-related pay for the period of maternity leave, nor did they suffer the resulting loss in the length of service.

The CJEU considered yet another variation on the theme of payments due or refused to those on maternity leave in *Lewen v Denda*: C-333/97 [2000] IRLR 67, [2000] ICR 648. A firm paid Christmas bonuses to those in 'active' employment on 1 December each year. The complainant was absent on maternity leave on the relevant date. She was refused a bonus and claimed that her employers had breached *art 157*. The court felt that the result hinged upon the nature of the payment. A requirement that an employee should be in active employment was not discriminatory if the purpose of the payment was to encourage those at work to be loyal and to work hard in the following year. If, on the other hand, the purpose of the payment was to reward the employees for having worked hard in the previous year, it would be discriminatory to refuse to make any payment at all to those absent on parental leave. An employer could legitimately pro-rate the bonus to take account of the employee's absence from work, provided no account was taken of any period during which, by reason of her pregnancy, the employee was prohibited from attending work. For an example of a permissible proportionate reduction in bonus paid in recognition of work undertaken by the workforce during a period of ordinary maternity leave, see also, *Hoyland v Asda Stores Ltd* [2006] IRLR 468 (Court of Session). Specific provision in relation to bonuses is now made in the maternity equality clause.

Gruber v Silhouette International Schmeid GmbH & Co KG: C-249/97 [1999] All ER (D) 1013 was a case concerned with termination payments. In Austria, those who simply resign from employment receive no payment. However, those who resign for 'important reasons' and who have been employed for more than three years receive a payment. The European court determined that the 'important reasons' justifying payments had in common that they were all either concerned with poor working conditions or with misconduct on the part of the employer. Those who work for longer than five years and resign within a certain period after childbirth receive smaller payments. The complainant, who resigned after having had a child, argued that she should be entitled to compare herself with those who resigned for 'important reasons' and to pay her a reduced sum resulted in discrimination contrary to *art 157*. The court rejected her argument. Her situation was not analogous to that of someone who resigned because of poor working conditions or employer misconduct. That being so, her proposed comparison, and thus her claim, was ill-founded.

The suggestion in *Gillespie* that women absent on maternity leave are not entitled to receive pay is subject to an important qualification. The CJEU did suggest in *Gillespie* that 'the amount payable [to a woman absent on maternity leave] could not . . . be so low as to undermine the purpose of maternity leave, namely the protection of women before and after giving birth'. The *Pregnant Workers Directive EEC/92/85* requires Member States to provide that women absent from work on maternity leave receive an 'adequate allowance' for 14 weeks (*arts 8(1)* and *11(2)(b)*). An allowance will be adequate provided that it is at least equivalent to what the employee would receive if she were absent through illness. In effect it requires that SMP should be at least as generous as SSP. A number of cases have since raised claims that sums received by the complainants during maternity leave did not amount to an 'adequate allowance'. In *Iske v P & O European Ferries (Dover) Ltd* [1997] IRLR 401, the EAT was asked to consider the adequacy of SMP. It declined to do so, although it suggested that it might have been prepared to consider the issue had the respondent been an emanation of the state. In *Gillespie v Northern Health and Social Services Board (No 2)* [1997] IRLR 410, the Northern Ireland Court of Appeal rejected a complaint that an employee's contractual maternity payments were less generous than contractual sick pay on the ground that the *Directive* merely required the payment to be more than SSP. In *Banks v Tesco Stores Ltd* [1999] ICR 1141, the EAT considered a case where an employee received no SMP at all. This was because, as her previous earnings were less than the lower earnings limit, she did not qualify for SMP. Notwithstanding that she was receiving nothing at all, the EAT declined to conclude that this was a case in which the amount received was so low as to undermine the purpose of maternity leave. The EAT relied on the fact that *art 11* of the *Pregnant Worker's Directive* allows Member States to impose conditions upon entitlement to maternity pay. If the *Directive* allowed it, reasoned the EAT, it could not be read as contravening *art 157*. Where the maternity pay received by the employee is determined by reference to full pay, pay rises should be reflected in the level of maternity pay, even where the rises take place while the woman is away on maternity leave and after the reference period used to calculate the level of maternity pay (*Alabaster v Woolwich plc and Secretary of State for Social Security: c-147/02* [2004] IRLR 486, [2005] ICR 695 and *Alabaster v Barclays Bank (No 2)* [2005] EWCA Civ 508, [2005] IRLR 576, [2005] ICR 1246; though cf *Clark v Secretary of State for Employment* [1996] IRLR 578, [1997] ICR 64, CA).

Note also that women whose pay is reduced when they are suspended from work on maternity grounds may not seek to challenge the reduction by bringing claims under the general provisions of the *EqA 2010* or under the predecessor provisions in *EqPA 1970. ERA 1996, ss 66–70* represent a complete code governing the contractual entitlements of such women (*British Airways (European Operations at Gatwick) Ltd v Moore* [2000] IRLR 296, EAT) and see further **(33)** MATERNITY AND PARENTAL RIGHTS.

23.14 EQUAL PAY AND PENSIONS

The principles applicable to retirement and pensions have evolved slowly and continue to evolve. Prior to the decision in *Barber v Guardian Royal Exchange Assurance Group: C-262/88* [1990] IRLR 240, [1990] ICR 616 domestic legislation on the matter was piecemeal. Following *Barber* (and the flurry of CJEU decisions which followed it: see below **23.5**) the UK was forced to rethink its approach. The fruits of this re-consideration were the *Occupational Pension Schemes (Equal Access to Membership) Amendment Regulations 1995 (SI 1995/1215)* and, subsequently, the *Pensions Act 1995* ('*PA 1995*'). Now those provisions are consolidated in the *EqA 2010*. (For the position under the previous legislation, readers are referred to earlier editions of this book.)

The first part of this section is devoted to describing the statutory regime which was in force prior to the implementation of the *EqA 2010* since a considerable number of cases are still in the employment tribunal system that relate to periods of service before either *SI 1995/1215* or *PA 1995* came into force or are based instead, like *Barber*, on *art 157*.

23.15 The legislation

There has, traditionally, been an inequality between men and women in the age at which they are expected to retire. The State pension was, until recently, payable to women who were aged 60 or older, whereas men did not receive corresponding benefits until aged 65. *PA 1995* provides for the progressive implementation of a common age of entitlement to State retirement benefits of 65 over a period of 10 years beginning on 6 April 2010 (*PA 1995, s 126*). Employers, however, have been prohibited from discriminating, either directly or indirectly, in relation to the age at which employees are required to retire since 7 February 1987 (*SDA 1986, s 2(1)*; see now *EqA 2010, s 13* and DISCRIMINATION AND EQUAL OPPORTUNITIES – I (12)). If an employer chooses to adopt a retirement age (and many do not, given this is now direct age discrimination which must be justified: see generally RETIREMENT (43)), an employer is not obliged to have a common retiring age for all its employees. It can provide for different ages to apply to different jobs if it can justify that direct age discrimination, but it should be aware that if the employees performing a particular job are predominantly of one sex, there is a risk of a claim of indirect sex discrimination (as well as direct age discrimination).

Where an employer provides its employees with access to an occupational pension scheme (see RETIREMENT (43)), a 'non-discrimination rule' in *s 61* of the *EqA 2010* prohibits discrimination in relation to access to membership of the scheme and to the benefits payable thereunder in respect of nearly all the protected characteristics covered by the *EqA 2010*, ie age, disability, gender reassignment, marriage and civil partnership, race, religion or belief and sexual orientation. (See **13.35** DISCRIMINATION AND EQUAL OPPORTUNITIES – II (13) and *EqA 2010, s 61*.) As with pay, however, slightly different provision is made in respect of sex and pregnancy/maternity discrimination in the operation of pension schemes. The legislation creates statutory sex equality and maternity equality rules as set out below. Where these rules apply (or would apply but for the exceptions in *Part 2* of *Sch 7*), the general non-discrimination rule does not: see *s 61(10)* and *Parker v MDU Services Ltd* UKEAT/0113/17/DA). Thus the general non-discrimination rule only applies to occupational pension schemes where the sex equality rule under *s 67* or the maternity equality rule under *s 75* does not.

23.16 *Sex discrimination*

Section 67 of *EqA 2010* provides for a 'sex equality rule' to be implied into all occupational pension schemes that do not already contain such a rule (*s 67(1)*). The sex equality rule applies both to terms on which people become members of the scheme, and the terms on which members of the scheme are treated, or any dependant who may benefit from the scheme (*s 67(3)* and *67(5)*). It also applies to the exercise of any discretion in relation to the way in which persons become members of the scheme or the way in which members of the scheme are treated, or any dependant who may benefit from the scheme (*s 67(4)* and *67(6)*).

The sex equality rule modifies any term of a scheme that would result in less favourable treatment of a man in comparison to woman (or vice versa) so as to ensure that the treatment is not less favourable (*s 67(2)(a)* and *s 64*). Similarly, it modifies any discretion so that it cannot be exercised in a way that would result in less favourable treatment (*s 67(2)(b)* and *s 64*).

As with the provisions relating to equal pay, the sex equality rule only operates where there is an actual comparator and the man and woman are:

(i)   Employed in the same employment or on common terms and conditions: see *EqA 2010*, *s 79* and above **23.9**; and

(ii)   Do equal work, ie like work, work rated as equivalent or work of equal value: see *ss 64* and *65* of the *EqA 2010* and above **23.5**.

Again, as with the provisions relating to equal pay, the sex equality rule has no effect if the trustees or managers of the scheme in question are able to show that the difference in treatment between the man and the woman is because of a material factor that is not the difference of sex: *s 69(4)*. In other words, the material factor defence is available to a complaint of sex discrimination in relation to an occupational pension scheme as it is in relation to pay and the case law discussed above at **23.10–23.11** will apply equally here. For cases in which the requirement for an actual comparator does not apply, see further **23.9** above. For a case considering the requirements for a valid comparator in a pensions case, see *Parker v MDU Services Ltd* UKEAT/0113/17/DA.

By *s 67(7)* it is expressly provided that if the effect of the term or the discretion differs according to a person's family, marital or civil partnership status, then the comparison for the purposes of the sex equality rule must be with persons of the opposite sex who share the same status (thus preventing the section from applying 'by the back door' to sexual orientation or marital status discrimination).

In accordance with the decisions of the CJEU in *Barber v Guardian Royal Exchange Assurance Group* (see below) and *Defrenne v Sabena* (see below) the sex equality rule does not operate on discriminatory terms relating to access to the pension scheme in respect of pensionable service prior to 8 April 1976 (*s 67(9)*) or on discriminatory terms relating to the way in which members of the scheme are treated in respect of benefits accruing from pensionable service prior to 17 May 1990 (*s 67(10)*). However, note that the CJEU has made it clear that the temporal limitation to 17 May 1990 in the Barber case does not apply to a 'benefits' claim which is made ancillary to an 'admissions' or 'access' claim (*Dietz v Stichting Thuiszorg Rotterdam*: C-435/93 [1996] IRLR 692). In the light of this decision, a question arises as to whether the *EqA 2010* (and the *PA 1995* before that) properly implements EU law.

Section 68 of the *EqA 2010* further provides a power for trustees and managers of an occupational pension scheme to make alterations to the scheme (including retrospective alterations: *s 68(4)*) to make it compliant with the sex equality rule. The power is available if the trustees and managers do not already have such power under the terms of the scheme, or if they do have such power under the terms of the scheme, but the procedure for using it would be unduly complex or protracted, or involve obtaining consents which cannot be obtained or which can be obtained only with undue delay or difficulty. For a discussion of what *section 68* permits, and its relationship with the 'principle of minimum interference' which applies in domestic law relating to pension schemes governed by trusts, see: *Lloyds Banking Group Pension Trustees Ltd v Lloyds Bank plc* [2018] EWHC 2839 (Ch), [2019] Pens LR 5.

By virtue of *para 4* of *Part 2* of *Sch 7* to the *EqA 2010* the Secretary of State may prescribe circumstances in which a man and woman may lawfully receive different amounts by way of pension where that difference is attributable only to differences in the state retirement pension to which men and women are entitled. The *Equality Act 2010 (Sex Equality Rule) (Exceptions) Regulations 2010 (SI 2010/2132)* duly prescribes for differences in pension to be permitted for bridging pensions and where differences remain after pensions have been indexed in certain circumstances. Readers are referred to the text of *regs 2* and *3* of those *Regulations* for details.

Further, by virtue of *para 5* of *Part 2* of *Sch 7* to the *EqA 2010*, a difference between men and women in relation to the calculation of employer's pension contributions or determination of benefits payable under the scheme is permitted if the difference results from the application of prescribed actuarial factors which differ for men and women. *Reg 4* of the *Equality Act 2010 (Sex Equality Rule) (Exceptions) Regulations 2010/2132* further prescribes that different actuarial factors may be applied in respect of the average life expectancy of men and women where they are applied with a view to providing equal periodical pension benefits for men and women. However, it is widely accepted that, following the decision of the CJEU in *Association Belge des Consommateurs Test-Achats ASBL v Conseil des Ministres* C-236/09 [2012] 1 WLR 1933, [2011] Eq LR 409 that sex-specific factors may not lawfully be used when determining insurance premiums, although sex-specific factors can be used by pension schemes in determining funding requirements and employer contributions, they should not have any impact on the level of benefits that an individual receives, or the level of contributions they are required to pay. For example, when calculating the level of benefits payable to an individual from a particular fund, men and women in comparable situations must receive the same even though the woman is statistically likely to live longer.

23.17 *Pregnancy and maternity discrimination*

The maternity equality rule in *EqA 2010, s 75* has effect as follows in relation to any occupational pension scheme that does not already contain such a rule:

(a)   If a 'relevant term' of the scheme does not treat time when the woman is on maternity leave as it treats time when she is not, the term is modified so as to treat time when she is on maternity leave as time when she is not (*s 75(3)*);

(b)   If a term confers a 'relevant discretion' capable of being exercised so that time when she is on maternity leave is treated differently from time when she is not, the term is modified so as not to allow the discretion to be exercised in that way (*s 75(4)*).

A term is 'relevant' for this purpose if it is: (a) a term relating to membership of the scheme, (b) a term relating to the accrual of rights under the scheme, or (c) a term providing for the determination of the amount of a benefit payable under the scheme (*s 75(5)*). A discretion is 'relevant' for this purpose if its exercise is capable of affecting (a) membership of the scheme, (b) the accrual of rights under the scheme, or (c) the determination of the amount of a benefit payable under the scheme (*s 75(6)*).

The maternity equality rule does not, however, require the woman's contributions to the scheme in respect of time when she is on maternity leave to be determined otherwise than by reference to the amount she is paid in respect of that time (*s 75(7)*) (pay for this purpose includes statutory maternity pay: see *s 75(10)*).

There are also temporal limitations on the application of the maternity equality rule. First, so far as relating to time when she is on ordinary maternity leave but is not being paid by her employer, the maternity equality rule applies only in a case where the expected week of childbirth began on or after 6 April 2003 (i.e. after the coming into force of the *Maternity and Parental Leave (Amendment) Regulations 2002*) (*s 75(8)*). Secondly, so far as relating to time when she was on additional maternity leave but not being paid by her employer, the maternity equality rule (a) does not apply to the accrual of rights under the scheme in any case; and (b) applies for other purposes only in a case where the expected week of childbirth began on or after 5 October 2008 (ie after the amendments made on that date to the *Maternity and Parental Leave Regulations 1999* and the *Paternity and Adoption Leave Regulations 2002*).

23.18 *Enforcement and remedies*

Complaints of breach of the sex or maternity equality rules may be made in the same way as complaints of breach of the sex equality clause and the provisions in relation to enforcement set out below at **23.21**ff apply equally to pension complaints. In addition, by *s 127(4)* an employment tribunal has jurisdiction to determine an application by the trustees or managers of an occupational pension scheme for a declaration as to their rights and those of a member in relation to a dispute about the effect of an equality rule. In any proceedings before an employment tribunal relating to a breach of an equality rule, the employer is to be treated as a party (i.e. in addition to the trustees and managers of the occupational pension scheme) and is accordingly entitled to appear and be heard (*s 127(8)*).

The remedies available in a 'pensions case' are governed by *ss 133* and *134* of *EqA 2010*. By *s 133(2)* if a court or tribunal finds there has been a breach of an equality clause or rule in relation to an occupational pension scheme, the court or tribunal may make a declaration as to the rights of the parties, but must not order arrears of benefits or damages or any other amount to be paid to the complainant unless the complainant is already a 'pensioner member' (ie in receipt of pension under the scheme): *s 133(3)*. Where the complainant is a pensioner member then they may be awarded arrears of benefits or compensation (*s 134(2)(b)*). The *Act* provides that any such award is limited to the period of 6 years before the day on which the proceedings were commenced in a 'standard case', or the day on which the breach first occurred in a 'concealment' or 'incapacity' case (*s 133(3)* and *(5)* and see below **23.22**). However, in *Lloyds Banking Group Pensions Trustees Ltd v Lloyds Bank Plc* [2018] EWHC 2839 (Ch), [2019] Pens LR 5 the High Court held that this 6-year limitation period is incompatible with EU law. This was on the basis that, by virtue of *s 21(1)(b)* of the *Limitation Act 1980*, no limitation period applies to claims for recovery of trust property. The High Court held that accordingly the 6-year limitation period in *s 134* offended the EU principle that the rules laid down by the domestic legal system for enforcement of EU law rights must not be less favourable that those governing similar domestic actions (see *Totel Ltd v Revenue and Customs Commissioners* [2018] UKSC 44, [2018] 1 WLR 4053). The High Court so held notwithstanding that, as the Supreme Court made clear in *Totel*, EU law does not require that states afford EU law rights equivalence with the most favourable elements of the domestic regime. It should further be noted that the High Court's reasoning applies only to private sector pension schemes governed by trust law. It would not apply to public sector pension schemes established by legislation, which would under domestic law be subject to the six-year limitation period in *s 9* of the *Limitation Act 1980* for the recovery of sums due under statute. However, see **14.22**, Dɪsᴄʀɪᴍɪɴᴀᴛɪᴏɴ ᴀɴᴅ Eǫᴜᴀʟ Oᴘᴘᴏʀᴛᴜɴɪᴛɪᴇs – II for the position regarding discrimination on other grounds in relation to pension schemes.

Where a declaration is made, it may relate to a specified period or time, provided that (in the case of declarations as to whether a person should be admitted to the scheme) the time in question is not before 8 April 1976 (*s 133(4)* and *(5)*), or (in the case of declarations as to terms on which a person may become a member of a scheme) the period in question does not begin before 17 May 1990 (*s 133(6)* and *(7)*). If the court or tribunal makes such a declaration, or awards arrears of benefit to a pensioner member, then the employer is required to contribute to the scheme whatever amount is necessary to enable the complainant to receive a pension on the declared terms, or to receive the arrears of benefit awarded, without the complainant or any other member being required to make further contribution: *s 133(8)* and *s 134(4)*.

See also **14.22** Dɪsᴄʀɪᴍɪɴᴀᴛɪᴏɴ ᴀɴᴅ Eǫᴜᴀʟ Oᴘᴘᴏʀᴛᴜɴɪᴛɪᴇs – III

23.19   Barber and claims based on art 157

The impetus for the statutory scheme described above, and now consolidated in the *EqA 2010*, came from Europe. *Directive 86/378/EEC* required Member States to introduce measures providing for equal rights to membership of occupational pension schemes by 1 January 1993. The UK had drafted legislation which was set out at *Social Security Act 1989, Sch 5* but before it could be brought into force it was overtaken by events, specifically the decision of the CJEU in *Barber*. The CJEU decided that pensions from both contributory and non-contributory schemes were 'pay' within the meaning of *art 157* in that they were deferred pay for services rendered during employment. The effect of the decision was that an obligation not to discriminate in relation to access to (which includes age of access to), or benefits under, a pension scheme was found already to exist without the need for implementing domestic legislation. A recent Polish case unsurprisingly confirms that this remains the law and that it is not legitimate positive discrimination for women to be required or permitted to retire earlier than men: *European Commission v Poland* (C-192/18) [2020] 2 CMLR 4.

The potential consequences of the decision were so great that the CJEU took the unusual step of specifically limiting the effect of its decision by stating that it could not be relied upon to claim entitlement to a pension with effect from a date prior to 17 May 1990 (the date of the decision) unless the applicant had already commenced proceedings by that date. It was not initially clear whether the limitation excluded all claims relating to periods of service before the stipulated date or only those where the benefits arising out of such service were also payable prior to 17 May 1990. The precise scope of the limitation was later clarified in *Ten Oever v Stichting Bedrijfspensioenfonds voor het Glazenwassers- en Schoonmaakbedrijf*: C-109/91 [1993] IRLR 601, [1995] ICR 74, in which the CJEU determined that *Barber* only applied to benefits payable in respect of periods of service after 17 May 1990 (but cf *Dietz v Stichting Thuiszord Rotterdam*: C-435/93 [1996] IRLR 692 below).

The *Barber* decision is now reflected in Protocol no. 33 to the consolidated (Lisbon) Treaty on the Functioning of the European Union as follows:

> 'For the purposes of Article 157 of the Treaty on the Functioning of the European Union, benefits under occupational social security schemes shall not be considered as remuneration if and in so far as they are attributable to periods of employment prior to 17 May 1990, except in the case of workers or those claiming under them who have before that date initiated legal proceedings or introduced an equivalent claim under the applicable national law.'

The *Barber Protocol* applies only to claims relating to the level of benefit provided and not to claims alleging denial of access to benefits. For instance, the formerly commonplace refusal of pension schemes to admit part-time workers was indirectly discriminatory on grounds of sex. Where a former part-time employee complains that she was refused access to membership, the *Protocol* does not apply and her claim may, subject to any other domestic limitations, go back as far as 8 April 1976, that being the date on which the CJEU gave its decision in *Defrenne* (*Deutsche Telekom AG v Schröder*: C-50/96 [2000] IRLR 353) (see also below **23.21**). Surprisingly, the CJEU has also held that the *Barber* limitation does not apply to any ancillary claim for non-payment of benefits (*Dietz v Stichting Thuiszorg Rotterdam*: C-298/94 [1996] IRLR 692). A woman seeking a remedy in respect of such a denial of access to membership must pay the contributions which she would have paid had she been admitted to membership at the appropriate time if she is to be entitled to any benefits under the scheme in respect of the period of her exclusion (*Fisscher v Voorhuis Hengelo BV*: C-128/93 [1994] IRLR 662, [1994] IRLR 651, [1995] ICR 635).

The temporal limitations established in the *Barber* and *Defrenne* judgments are now reflected in specific provisions in the *EqA 2010, s 67(9)* and *(10)*. However, the principles established in the *Dietz* and *Fisscher* judgments have not been reflected in the *EqA 2010* (nor were they reflected in the legislative scheme that preceded the *EqA 2010*). The CJEU held in *Ministry of Justice v O'Brien* C-432/17 [2019] 1 CMLR 40, [2019] ICR 505, [2019] IRLR 185 that part-time judges could, with effect from the coming into force of the *Part-Time Workers Regulations* on 7 April 2000, claim benefits equivalent to full-time judges with the same length of service, including periods of service prior to the coming into force of those *Regulations*.

Following the *Barber* decision, a number of cases were referred to the CJEU with the intention of clarifying the difficult issues left unresolved by the Barber decision itself. The following matters have now been settled. Benefits payable to survivors fall within *art 157* (*Ten Oever v Stichting Bedrijfspensioenfonds voor het Glazenwassers en Schoonmaakbedrijf*: C-109/91 [1993] IRLR 601, [1995] ICR 74) as do benefits payable under non-contracted out supplementary schemes (*Moroni v Collo GmbH*: C-110/91 [1994] IRLR 130, [1995] ICR 137). Benefits payable under schemes which have at all times been 'single sex' are not within art 157, nor are benefits payable as a result of contributions made by employees on a voluntary basis (*Coloroll Pension Trustees Ltd v Russell*: C-200/91 [1994] IRLR 586, [1995] ICR 179).

In *Quirk v Burton Hospitals NHS Trust* [2002] EWCA Civ 149, [2002] IRLR 353, [2002] ICR 602, the Court of Appeal had to consider the effect of a provision in the *National Health Service Pension Scheme Regulations 1995* (*SI 1995/300*). Formerly, female members of the NHS Pension scheme could, in certain circumstances, retire early at 55. Men could only take early retirement once they were 60. The *1995 Regulations* corrected this discriminatory situation by providing that both men and women could retire at 55. However, whereas a woman retiring at 55 received a pension calculated by reference to her whole period of service, a man doing the same would receive a pension calculated by reference only to his service since 17 May 1990. Unsurprisingly, the woman's pension would be greater than that of a man with a comparable length of service. A male complainant sought to argue that the *1995 Regulations* were incompatible with *art 157*. He contended that the provision had the effect of precluding him from access to benefits in respect of his pre-1990 service. The Court of Appeal decided that, properly analysed, the case was not an 'access to benefits' case at all. The complainant was a member of the scheme. The contentious provision simply resulted in his receiving less money. It was, therefore, a 'level of benefit' case and the *Barber Protocol* applied. Lord Justice Buxton opined that the 'access'/'level of benefit' dichotomy was an unhelpful basis for analysis. The tribunal should ask itself whether the alleged discrimination relates to an age condition which varies according to sex. If it does, it is a case to which the *Barber Protocol* applies.

Where a Member State provides for men and women to become entitled to a State pension at different ages (eg in the UK women used to become so entitled at 60 whereas men became entitled at 65, although the *Pensions Act 1995* provides for progressive implementation of a common age of entitlement of 65 over a period of 10 years beginning on 6 April 2010), occupational pension schemes sometimes provide for payment of a 'bridging pension', the purpose of which is to ensure that employees, of whichever sex, receive the same total sum by way of pension when their State entitlements are aggregated to their entitlements under the scheme. Between the ages of 60 and 65 in the UK male and female employees would, under such a scheme, receive the same total sum but the male employees would receive substantially more from their employers. It follows, therefore, that under a 'bridging pension' male employees will receive more 'pay' than their female colleagues over the period. However, the State pension is not 'pay' for the purposes of *art 157* (see further **23.3** above). In *Roberts v Birds Eye Walls Ltd*: C-132/92 [1994] IRLR 29, [1994] ICR 338 the CJEU held that it is not contrary to *art 157* to take account of an employee's entitlement to a State pension when calculating benefits payable under a bridging pension, provided that the purpose is to achieve overall equality between men and women; see also *Trustees of Uppingham*

School Retirement Benefit Scheme for Non-Teaching Staff v Shillcock [2002] EWHC 641 (Ch), [2002] IRLR 702, *Hlozek v Roche Austria GmbH* C-19/02 [2005] 1 CMLR 28, and *Vergani v Agenzia Delle Entrate, Ufficio di Arona* C-207/04 [2006] 1 CMLR 5.

Inequality of employer's contributions to a scheme (as opposed to the benefits payable to the employee under the scheme) which result from the use of different actuarial factors for men and women is not contrary to *art 157* (*Neath v Hugh Steeper Ltd*: C-152/91 [1994] IRLR 91, [1995] ICR 158 and *Coloroll Pension Trustees Ltd v Russell*: C-200/91 [1994] IRLR 586, [1995] ICR 179). See now *para 4* of *Part 2* of *Sch 7* to the *EqA 2010* and the *Equality Act 2010 (Sex Equality Rule) (Exceptions) Regulations 2010/2132, regs 2* and *3*. However, note that, following the decision of the CJEU in *Association Belge des Consommateurs Test-Achats ASBL v Conseil des Ministres* C-236/09 [2012] 1 WLR 1933, [2011] Eq LR 409 that sex-specific factors may not lawfully be used when determining insurance premiums, although sex-specific factors can be used by pension schemes in determining funding requirements and employer contributions, they should not have any impact on the level of benefits that an individual receives, or the level of contributions they are required to pay.

The CJEU has also given guidance on how a scheme should approach the task of modifying its rules so as to provide for equality. No action need be taken in relation to benefits payable in respect of periods of service prior to 17 May 1990 by reason of the temporal limitation established in *Barber*. Benefits payable in respect of the period between 17 May 1990 and the date on which the scheme is amended to provide for equality should be rounded up to the higher of the differential rates. After entitlements have been equalised, however, the scheme may reduce benefits overall provided that it is done in a way which involves no discrimination and which is consistent with the obligations of the employer and/or trustees under national laws and the contract of employment or rules of the scheme. Equalisation must be done in one step; it is not lawful for the employer or trustee to equalise benefits progressively over a transitional period (*Smith v Advel Systems Ltd*: C- 409/92 [1994] IRLR 602, [1995] ICR 596). It has been held that schemes which reduced male entitlements to match female entitlements between 17 May 1990 and the date on which the discriminatory scheme was actually amended ('the *Barber* window') will be unlawful for that period, and male employees will be entitled to claim the difference in pension benefits attributable to any difference in pension entitlement arising during the *Barber* window: *Harland and Wolff Pension Trustees Ltd v Aon Consulting Financial Services Ltd* [2006] EWHC 1778 (Ch), [2006] All ER (D) 216 (Jul), [2007] ICR 429. However, in *Safeway Ltd v Newton* [2017] EWCA Civ 1482, [2018] Pens LR 2, the Court of Appeal referred to the CJEU the question of whether it is permissible to 'level down' rather than up in the light of the decision of the CJEU in *Smith v Avdel Systems Ltd*, and whether it is possible to do so with retroactive effect. In the *Safeway* case the Trust Deed governing the pension scheme had in 1996 been amended to as to retroactively 'level down' NPA from 1991 onwards (by increasing the retirement age for women to the same as that for men). The CJEU (C-171/18) [2020] 1 CMLR 40 answered that 'levelling-down' is permissible, provided that it is not done retroactively. If retroactive, it will only be lawful if there is an overriding reason in the public interest for the measure to have retroactive effect, and the legitimate expectations of those concerned are duly respected. Further, any retroactive measure must comply with the principle of legal certainty, in that it must be implemented in a way that is sufficiently precise, clear and foreseeable to enable an individual to know precisely their rights and obligations, to take steps accordingly and to rely on those rights. Note that *Section 68* of the *EqA 2010* makes provision empowering the trustees and managers of occupational pension schemes to make changes to the scheme to bring it into line with the sex equality rule (if they do not already have that power under the scheme): see above **23.16**.

The decision of the CJEU in *Bestuur van het Algemeen Burgerlijk Pensioenfonds v Beune*: C-7/93 [1995] IRLR 103 settled a long-running controversy over whether benefits payable under schemes established by statute and applicable to State employees are 'pay' for the purposes of *art 157*. There was domestic authority to the effect that they were not (*Griffin v London Pensions Fund Authority* [1993] IRLR 248, [1993] ICR 564, which concerned a Local Government Superannuation Scheme). In *Beune* benefits payable under the statutory scheme applicable to the Dutch civil service were held to fall within *art 157* on the basis that they complied with what the CJEU termed the 'only possible decisive criterion', namely, whether the pension is paid to the worker by reason of the employment relationship between himself and his former employer. Whilst being 'decisive' the criterion is not, according to the court, 'exclusive'. Some consideration of the balance between the relative importance to the determination of the benefits payable of social policy on the one hand, and employment-related questions on the other may still be necessary. Employment related questions will include whether the scheme applies to a particular category of worker only and whether the benefits are directly related to length of service.

23.20   The part-time workers litigation

The *Preston* litigation concerns claims brought by many thousands of part-time workers before employment tribunals alleging that they have been indirectly discriminated against as a result of having been refused membership of their occupational pension scheme on the ground that they worked part-time. Until it was amended by *PA 1995*, the *EqPA 1970* only prohibited directly discriminatory exclusion from membership. In the circumstances, each applicant relies upon *art 157* and the *Barber* decision to found his or her claim.

The cases raise many questions about whether employees may enforce rights based on European legislation in the domestic courts and tribunals and, if so, as to the appropriate procedural rules which apply to such claims. Such questions are dealt with in greater detail at **23.19** above in the context of a more general consideration of the application of *art 157* in the UK. In the *Preston* litigation, two particular points have been resolved: first, the claims are brought in the employment tribunal on the basis that the incompatible domestic legislation should be disapplied rather than as a 'free standing' *art 157* claim (see further **23.29** below); and, secondly, the claimant's remedy is limited to a declaration of entitlement to membership of the relevant scheme and to benefits whilst a member.

The first series of test cases was considered by the Birmingham Employment Tribunal, and appeals from those decisions were decided by the EAT (*Preston v Wolverhampton Healthcare NHS Trust* [1996] IRLR 484), the Court of Appeal ([1997] IRLR 233, [1997] ICR 899), the House of Lords ([1998] IRLR 197, [1998] ICR 227), the CJEU on a referral from the House of Lords ([2000] IRLR 506) and the House of Lords on its return from the CJEU ([2001] UKHL 5; [2001] IRLR 237).

The CJEU in *Preston* held that the two-year limitation period for arrears of pay contained in *EqPA 1970, s 2(5)* was incompatible with Community law. On return to the House of Lords, their Lordships concluded that due to this incompatibility, the respondent employers could not rely on that section to defeat a claim for periods prior to the two years to be taken into account, subject to the employee paying contributions owing in respect of the period for which membership was claimed retroactively. Future pension benefits therefore had to be calculated by reference to full and part-time periods of service subsequent to 8 April 1976 as the date when the CJEU held in *Defrenne v Sabena*: C-43/75 [1981] 1 All ER 122, [1976] ICR 547 that *art 157* had direct effect. See now **23.18** above. Note that for claims based on the *Part-time Workers Regulations* and governing directive (98/23) the CJEU held in *Ministry of Justice v O'Brien* C-432/17 [2019] 1 CMLR 40, [2019] ICR 505, [2019] IRLR 185 that part-time judges could, with effect from the coming into force of those Regulations on 7 April 2000, claim benefits equivalent to full-time judges with the same length of service, including periods of service prior to the coming into force of those Regulations.

In respect of the six-month limitation period formerly contained in *EqPA 1970, s 2(4)*, the CJEU held that the requirement to bring proceedings within six months of the termination of employment was not incompatible so long as such limitation period was not less favourable for actions based on Community law than for those based on domestic law. The CJEU decided that an action alleging a breach of the *Act* was not a domestic action 'similar' to a claim for infringement of *art 157*. The House of Lords on return held that the claim in Community law was to establish the right of retroactive access to the pension schemes. That was not similar in form to a claim in contract for damages but in substance the eventual benefit to the employee was sufficiently similar for the purposes of testing equivalence. Although the limitation period for a claim in contract was six years, that period did not run from the termination of employment. Since a claim in contract could only go back six years, whereas a claim brought within six months of termination could go back to the beginning of employment or 1976, it could not be said that the provisions of *EqPA 1970, s 2(4)* were less favourable than those applying to a claim in contract despite the apparent difference in length of the limitation periods. Therefore the provisions of *s 2(4)* did not violate Community law as to effectiveness and equivalence. See now **23.18** above for the current rules on enforcement.

In relation to employees on successive short-term contracts, the House of Lords held that it was clear from the CJEU's judgment that where there were intermittent contracts of service without a 'stable employment relationship' the period of six months ran from the end of each contract, but where such contracts were concluded at regular intervals in respect of the same employment in a stable employment relationship the period ran from the end of the last contract. Their Lordships referred the question of which applicants were in stable employment relationships back to the employment tribunal.

After the employment tribunal's decisions in the test cases, a second round of appeals reached the Court of Appeal (*Preston v Wolverhampton Healthcare NHS Trust (No 3)* [2004] IRLR 979, [2005] ICR 222 ('*Preston (No 3)*'). Three issues on appeal to the EAT related to the circumstances in which there would be a breach of the equality clause. The EAT held:

(1)   The equality clause is breached where part-time employees are excluded from a pension scheme that is available to full-time employees, irrespective of whether the part-time employee would have joined the scheme if it had been made available to her. However, in such a case, although there will always be a breach of the equality clause, where an employee would not in fact have joined the pension scheme had she had the option to do so, no remedy will be granted. This 'opt out' principle has since been held to be compliant with EU law: see *Copple and others v Littlewoods Plc* [2011] EWCA Civ 1281, [2012] IRLR 121, [2012] ICR 354, CA. In that case, the CA also emphasised that the burden is on the employee to show that she would have joined the scheme if it had been made available to her. In this respect, the CA noted that a Tribunal would be entitled to infer from failure to join the scheme once eligible to do so that the employee would not have joined the scheme during an earlier period had she not been wrongly excluded in breach of the equality clause. (See also *Andrews v Kings College Hospital NHS Foundation Trust* [2012] EqLR 1032.)

(2)   However, there is no breach of the equality clause where membership of the scheme is obligatory for full-time employees but only optional for part-time employees.

(3)   Although it had been (rightly) accepted before the tribunal that the imposition of a qualifying hours threshold in relation to membership of an occupational pension scheme was a breach of the equality clause, where an employer removed that threshold but failed to inform his employees that was not itself either a breach or a continuing breach of the equality clause. It may well, however, be a breach of an implied term of the employment contract (see *Scally v Southern Health and Social Services Board* [1991] IRLR 522, [1991] ICR 771, *Andrews v Kings College Hospital and anor* [2012] Eq LR 1032 and **8.9, 8.13** CONTRACT OF EMPLOYMENT).

A fourth issue concerned the limitation period: the EAT held that a 'stable employment relationship' consisting of a succession of short term contracts (see further below **23.21**) ceased, and the six-month limitation period began to run, where one of the two essential features of the relationship was no longer present, ie the same employment or periodicity of employment. These features will not be present where there is no longer an intention to employ, or to work, on a regular basis.

A fifth issue concerned the point at which the time limit begins to run where an employee's employment has been transferred from one employer ('the transferor') to a new employer ('the transferee') under the *Transfer of Undertakings (Protection of Employment) Regulations 2016* ('*TUPE*'; see Transfer of Undertakings (**53**)). The EAT held that time begins to run against the transferor from the end of the employee's employment with the transferee, and not from the date of the transfer. Only this last issue was appealed to the Court of Appeal in *Powerhouse Retail Ltd v Burroughs* [2004] EWCA Civ 1281, [2004] IRLR 979, [2005] ICR 222. The Court of Appeal (affd [2006] UKHL 13, [2006] IRLR 381, [2006] ICR 606) reversed the EAT's decision and held that time runs for the purposes of a pensions claim from the date of the transfer, pensions being the one element of the contract of employment that does not transfer under *TUPE*. The EAT in *Sodexo Ltd v Gutridge* [2008] IRLR 752, [2009] ICR 70 (upheld on appeal: [2009] IRLR 721) confirmed that time runs from the date of the transfer for the purposes of all equal pay claims involving a *TUPE* transfer and that a transferred employee can claim against the transferee in respect of a pay inequality which arose during employment with the transferor (and see also *Trimble v North Lanarkshire Council* (20 November 2012) UKEATS/0048/12/BI). The decision in *Sodexo* was applied in *Foley and ors v NHS Greater Glasgow & Clyde* [2013] ICR 342. However, in *Foley*, the appellant employees sought to argue for the first time on appeal that this rule breached the principle of 'effectiveness' under EU law because it was excessively difficult or virtually impossible in practice for a claimant to comply with it. The EAT refused to entertain this argument because there had been insufficient findings of fact by the ET for it to be properly considered. The argument therefore remains open for another day.

Note that (successful) equal pay claims constitute "arrears of pay" under the *ERA 1996, s 184(1)(a)* following a TUPE transfer, so that if the employer becomes insolvent, the Secretary of State will be liable to make a guarantee payment: *Graysons Restaurants Ltd v Jones* [2019] EWCA Civ 725, [2019] ICR 1342.

A further limitation issue was determined by the tribunal, but not appealed to the EAT or Court of Appeal. The tribunal held that, where a series of employments are covered by an overarching pensions scheme, time starts to run from the end of each employment and not from the end of the series (unless, of course, they are *TUPE* transfers, in which case they count as a single employment). It should also be noted that it was conceded before the tribunal that a male part-time worker could bring a claim if he could identify a female comparator with the right to join the pension scheme by operation of her equality clause (for another example of such a case, see *Pepper v Lancashire County Council* [2008] All ER (D) 122 (Jan)). In such cases, the part-time worker is permitted to join the scheme for the period during which he or she was forbidden to join the pension scheme by dint of the operation of the then rules on part-time workers. Whether or not such employees are entitled to make claims in respect of the period *after* the rules preventing part-time workers from joining the scheme had been amended will depend on the worker's reason for not joining the scheme at the point: see *Pepper*, ibid.

One of the questions referred to the CJEU in *Allonby v Accrington and Rossendale College* [2004] IRLR 224, [2004] ICR 1328 was whether or not the requirement for a comparator was incompatible with EU law. The CJEU limited its ruling to the facts of that particular case, which concerned access to the statutory Teachers' Superannuation Scheme. It ruled that, where state legislation (such as the Teachers' Superannuation Scheme) was at issue, there is no need for an employee to point to a comparator: it will be sufficient to show statistical disadvantage. It seems that a comparator will still be necessary where state legislation is not in issue. However, under the *EqA 2010* a complainant now has the possibility of bringing a direct sex discrimination claim under *s 13* of the *Act* where he or she has no actual comparator on which to rely: see above **23.2** and **23.9**.

Information Bulletins and up-to-date information on the case management of the part-time pension claims can be found on the part-time worker pension cases section of the tribunal service website (www.justice.gov.uk/tribunals/employment/part-time-workers/current).

REMEDIES FOR UNEQUAL PAY

23.21 Jurisdiction of the employment tribunals

See also generally DISCRIMINATION AND EQUAL OPPORTUNITIES – III (13).

Any claim brought by virtue of the *EqPA 1970* or now under the equal pay provisions in the *EqA 2010*, whether for arrears of remuneration or damages, may be brought before an employment tribunal (*EqA 2010, s 127*; see previously *EqPA 1970, s 2(1)*).

A tribunal can hear a case in the following circumstances:

(a)   Where the employee is complaining about the breach of an equality clause or rule (*EqA 2010, s 127(1)*; see previously *EqPA 1970, s 2(1)*).

(b)   An employer may apply to the tribunal for an order declaring his and the employee's rights in relation to an equality clause (*EqA 2010, s 127(3)*; see previously *EqPA 1970, s 2(1A)*).

(c)   Under the *EqPA 1970, s 2(2)* the Secretary of State could refer a question to the tribunal on behalf of an aggrieved employee where it is not reasonable to expect the parties to take steps to have the question determined. No similar power is contained in the *EqA 2010*.

(d)   Under the *EqA 2010, s 127(4)* an employment tribunal also has jurisdiction to determine an application by the trustees or managers of an occupational pension scheme for a declaration as to their rights and those of a member in relation to a dispute about the effect of an equality rule).

(e)   Where an equal pay claim is proceeding in the civil courts (see below **23.26**), a court may on application of any party or of its own motion refer a question to an employment tribunal and stay the proceedings meanwhile (*EqA 2010, s 128(2)*; see previously *EqPA 1970, s 2(3)*).

Note that it will not necessarily be an abuse of process (and nor will a claim necessarily be *res judicata* or otherwise precluded by the rule in *Henderson v Henderson*) where a claimant, having been successful in one claim under the *EqPA 1970*, subsequently brings a second claim identifying a different (and more highly paid) comparator in respect of the same period of employment: *Bainbridge v Redcar and Cleveland Borough Council* [2007] IRLR 494, EAT.

23.22 Time limits

Prior to 19 July 2003, no equal pay claim could be brought to an employment tribunal unless the woman had been employed in the employment within the six months preceding the date of the reference (although that time limit did not apply where a question was referred from the civil courts pursuant to (*e*) above). The question of the compatibility of this limitation period was referred to the CJEU by the House of Lords in *Preston v Wolverhampton*

Healthcare NHS Trust [1998] IRLR 197, [1998] ICR 227. The CJEU decided (C–78/98, [2000] IRLR 506) that the limitation was not, in principle, contrary to Community law. However, that decision was qualified in two respects. First, the CJEU stated that the national court would have to be satisfied that the limitation was not less favourable than the limitations applied to comparable domestic law claims. Second, the CJEU addressed the application of this limitation period to circumstances where an employee has been employed pursuant to a series of discrete contracts of employment. In *Preston* the CJEU held that the limitation should not apply from the date of termination of each employment contract in a case where the employee is engaged pursuant to a series of such contracts so that it can be said that a 'stable employment relationship' existed across the period of time covered by the individual contracts. On return to the House of Lords ([2001] UKHL 5, [2001] IRLR 237), the six-month limitation period was held to be compatible with Community law but the issue of what constitutes a 'stable employment relationship' was remitted back to the employment tribunal: see **23.20** above for the progress of the *Preston* part-time workers pensions litigation.

With effect from 19 July 2003, *EqPA 1970* was amended by the *Equal Pay Act 1970 (Amendment) Regulations 2003* so that no equal pay claim can be brought in an employment tribunal (again otherwise than by virtue of (*e*) above) unless the proceedings are instituted on or before the 'qualifying date' (*EqPA 1970, s 2(4)*). These provisions have been replicated in tabular form in *EqA 2010, ss 129–130*. The 'qualifying date' before which a claim must be brought varies depending on which of the following five categories applies to the circumstances of the claim (*EqA 2010, s 129*; see previously *EqPA 1970, s 2ZA*):

A stable employment case

(a)   A 'stable employment case' means a case where the proceedings relate to a period during which a stable employment relationship subsists between the woman and the employer, notwithstanding that the period includes any time after the ending of a contract of employment when no further contract of employment is in force. In a stable employment case, the qualifying date is the date falling six months after the date on which the stable employment relationship ended. See *EqA 2010, ss 129* and *130(3)*. The CJEU in *Preston* indicated that a 'stable employment case' would be a case where the woman works regularly, but periodically or intermittently, for the same employer, under successive legally separate contracts. The CJEU indicated that in such cases the starting point for the limitation period should be fixed as 'the date on which the sequence of such contracts has been interrupted through the absence of one or more of the features that characterise a stable employment relationship of that kind, either because the periodicity of such contracts has been broken or because the new contract does not relate to the same employment or that to which the same pension scheme applies' (*ibid*, [70]). What is required is that there be a succession of contracts, with or without gaps between them: *North Cumbria University NHS Hospitals Trust v Fox* [2010] EWCA Civ 729, [2010] IRLR 804, *Slack v Cumbria County Council* [2009] EWCA Civ 293, [2009] IRLR 463). In *Dass v College of Haringey Enfield and North East London* UKEAT/0108/12/MC, 27 November 2014, Slade J (sitting in the EAT) observed 'it is apparent that the CJEU considered that a stable employment relationship could continue beyond the end of a particular contract. It would however come to an end if no new contract were entered into by the time expected in accordance with the established pattern, or periodicity, of the parties entering into such contracts'. There is no requirement that there should be an 'umbrella contract' (express or implied) covering the whole period of the stable employment: that is a feature that is required to establish continuity of employment for the purposes of *s 212* of the *Employment Rights Act 1996*, but not to establish 'stable employment' for the purposes of the time limit for bringing an equal pay claim (*Slack* and *Dass* ibid). Nor is the concept of 'temporary cessation of work' in *s 212* of the *ERA 1996* relevant (*Dass*, ibid). Changes of job or promotions while working for the same employer will not normally break the link in a stable employment case unless the nature of the change is fundamental or radical: see *Preston v Wolverhampton Healthcare NHS Trust (No. 3)* [2004] ICR 993, *Potter v North Cumbria Acute Hospitals NHS Trust* [2009] IRLR 900 and *Barnard v Hampshire Fire and Rescue* [2019] ICR 602, EAT. A 'broad and non-technical' approach is to be taken to that question, as the EAT emphasised when *Barnard v Hampshire* returned to the EAT: [2020] IRLR 176 at para 69.

A concealment case

(b)   A 'concealment case' is a case where the employer deliberately concealed from the woman any fact (referred to as a 'qualifying fact') which is relevant to the contravention to which the proceedings relate, and without knowledge of which the woman could not reasonably have been expected to institute the proceedings, and the woman did not discover the qualifying fact (or could not with reasonable diligence have discovered it) until after the last day on which she was employed in the employment, or the day on which the stable employment relationship between her and the employer ended (as the case may be). In a concealment case, the qualifying date is the date falling six months after the day on which the woman discovered the qualifying fact in question (or could with reasonable diligence have discovered it). See *EqA 2010, ss 129* and *130(4)–(6)*.

A disability case (referred to as an incapacity case under EqA 2010)

(c)   A 'disability case' means a case where the woman was under a disability at any time during the six months after the last day on which she was employed in the employment, the day on which the stable employment relationship between her and the employer ended, or the day on which she discovered (or could with reasonable diligence have discovered) the qualifying fact deliberately concealed from her by the employer (if that day falls after the day(s) referred to above, as the case may be). In a disability case, the qualifying date is the date falling six months after the day on which the woman ceased to be under a disability. See *EqA 2010, ss 129* and *130(7)–(9)*.

A case which is both a concealment and a disability case

(d)   In such a case, the qualifying date is the later of the two dates which would otherwise apply if it were just disability or just a concealment case. See *EqA 2010, s 129*.

A standard case

(e)   A 'standard case' is a case which is not a stable employment case, a concealment case, a disability case or a case which is both a concealment and a disability case: see *EqA 2010, s 139(2)*. In a standard case, the qualifying date is the date falling six months after the last day on which the woman was 'employed in the employment'. The meaning of that phrase was determined by the House of Lords in *Preston v Wolverhampton NHS Trust (No.1)* [1998] IRLR 197. Lord Slynn, with whose judgment Lords Goff, Lloyd, Nolan and Hope agreed, approved the analysis of Otton LJ delivering judgment in the Court of Appeal in that case ([1997] IRLR 233, [1997] ICR 899) who said that the time limit runs 'from the end of the contract of employment alleged to contain the equality clause in respect of which the claim is made'. In *Slack v Cumbria County Council (Equality and Human Rights Commission intervening)* [2009] EWCA Civ 293, [2009] IRLR 463, [2009] ICR 1217, CA (under the name of *Cumbria County Council v Dow (No.2)* in the EAT [2008] IRLR 109), the Court of Appeal upheld the EAT's decision that where it was clear from the contractual documents that employer and employee had agreed to effect a change to the contract by means not of a variation but rather by means of a termination and re-engagement (in contrast to the decision of the EAT in *Potter v North Cumbria Acute Hospitals NHS Trust* [2009] IRLR 900 where a change to contractual documents was found to be a variation) then time will start to run in respect of the previous contract from the date of termination where this is in accordance with the mutual intention of the parties. The potential harshness of this approach was alleviated in the Court of Appeal by the (new) argument that these were stable employment cases as there were a series of uninterrupted contracts and the cases were remitted back to the tribunal on this question: *Fox v North Cumbria University Hospitals NHS Trust* [2010] EWCA Civ 729, [2010] IRLR 804. See also *Winder v Aston University* [2007] All ER (D) 45 (Nov), EAT.

The tribunal has no discretion to extend time in a claim under *EqPA 1970* or under *EA 1010*. In this respect the time limit for sex discrimination claims is more generous as it allows for an extension of time where the tribunal considers it to be just and equitable: see **14.3 DISCRIMINATION AND EQUAL OPPORTUNITIES – III**. Nor can the time limit be waived or varied by agreement between the parties: *Secretary of State for Health v Rance* [2007] IRLR 665. However, the time limit may be extended by the early conciliation procedures as set out below at **23.28**.

23.23 Compensation

Where a court (see **23.26** below for the jurisdiction of the civil courts) or tribunal upholds a complaint relating to a breach of an equality clause or rule (other than a breach with respect to membership of or rights under an occupational pension scheme) it may (a) make a declaration to that effect; and/or (b) order the employer to pay compensation to the employee in the form of an award by way of arrears of pay or damages (*EqA 2010, s 132(1)* and *(2)*). Note, however, that awards of damages or arrears of benefits are only available to pensioner claimants in pension cases: see above **23.18**.

If the claim is successful, the amount awarded will be the difference in pay between that of the claimant and the 'equal' or 'equivalent' employee. In certain cases, such as those involving performance-related pay or bonuses, that may require the tribunal to engage in the speculative exercise of devising an equivalent performance-related bonus scheme to apply to the group of workers to which the claimant belongs in order to determine the appropriate level of award: see *South Tyneside Metropolitan Borough Council v Anderson* [2007] All ER (D) 410 (Mar) (not appealed on this point: [2007] EWCA Civ 654, [2007] IRLR 715, [2007] ICR 1581).

Compensation for non-economic loss was not recoverable in a claim under the *EqPA 1970*: *Degnan v Redcar and Cleveland Borough Council* [2005] IRLR 504, [2005] ICR 1170. There is no reason to suppose that the position is any different under the *EqA 2010*.

Note also, that the tribunal will not grant a declaration that there has been discrimination where in fact the employee has suffered no loss: see *Copple and others v Littlewoods Plc* [2011] EWCA Civ 1281, [2012] IRLR 121, [2012] ICR 354. That case concerned a large number of part-time pensions claims. However, the EAT held that since most of the claimants would not actually have joined the scheme even if it had been open to them to do so, although there had been discrimination, no declaration would be granted since that would be to put the claimants in a better position than, say, a man who, despite having the option to join the scheme in his contract of employment, had not done so at the time.

The limitation provisions under the *EqA 2010* stipulate that a court or tribunal may not award compensation in respect of any time before the 'arrears day' (*s 132(3)*). The 'arrears day' in a 'standard case' (see above **23.22**) is the day falling 6 years before the day on which proceedings were instituted. The 'arrears day' in a concealment or incapacity (formerly, disability) case is the day on which the breach first occurred (*s 132(4)*).

Formerly, the *EqPA 1970* contained a two-year limitation period. This was also held by the CJEU in *Preston v Wolverhampton Healthcare NHS Trust* to be incompatible with Community law. On return to the House of Lords ([1998] IRLR 197, [1998] ICR 227, HL), it was held that the respondent employers could not rely on this two-year limitation which must be disapplied. The respondent employers could not therefore defeat a claim for periods prior to the two years to be taken into account, subject to the employee paying contributions owing in respect of the period for which membership was claimed retroactively. Future pension benefits had to be calculated by reference to full and part-time periods of service subsequent to 8 April 1976 as the date when the CJEU held in *Defrenne v Sabena*: 43/75 [1981] 1 All ER 122, [1976] ICR 547 that *art 157* had direct effect. See now the *Equal Pay Act 1970 (Amendment) Regulations 2003*.

Following the CJEU's declaration of incompatibility in *Preston*, with effect from 19 July 2003, *EqPA 1970, s 2ZB* provided that arrears of pay may be recovered up to six years back from the 'arrears date'. As noted above, these provisions have now been replicated in the *EqA 2010*, (although also found to be incompatible with EU law so far as pensions are concerned: see *Lloyds Banking Group Pensions Trustees Ltd v Lloyds Bank plc* [2018] EWHC 2839 (Ch), [2019] Pens LR 5 and **23.18** above).

Note that where the claim is based on the job having been rated as equivalent by the employer, there can be no claim for back pay: the employee will be entitled to equal wages only from the date that the job was rated as equivalent: *Bainbridge v Redcar and Cleveland Borough Council* [2007] IRLR 494.

The meaning of the words 'proceedings were instituted' which set the relevant arrears date in a 'standard case' was considered by the EAT in *Prest and others v Mouchel Business services and another* [2011] ICR 1345. The issue in that case was that proceedings had been amended so as to include new comparators. The tribunal found that the arrears date was the date on which the application to amend the ET1 had been made. The EAT disagreed, holding that the original and amended claims were, in substance, the same claims as both of the comparators were in one of the two classes of comparators named in the original claim. Consequently, proceedings were instituted on the date that the ET1 was originally presented to the employment tribunal. However, the matter may have been different in circumstances where the work done by the new comparator had been different from the work done by the comparators originally named in the ET1.

Exemplary damages are not available in cases under the *EqPA 1970* as such claims are contractual, rather than tortious (see *Allan v Newcastle-upon-Tyne City Council* [2005] IRLR 504, EAT).

The *Sex Discrimination and Equal Pay (Remedies) Regulations 1993 (SI 1993/2798)* (now replaced by the *Employment Tribunals (Interest on Awards in Discrimination Cases) Regulations 1996 (SI 1996/2803)*) conferred on the employment tribunal a power to award interest on sums awarded under the *EqPA 1970*. The tribunal is required to identify a 'mid-point date'. This date is the halfway point between the date on which the act of discrimination complained of occurred and the date on which the interest is being calculated (*reg 4*). Interest is then awarded in respect of the period from the mid-point date to the date of calculation (*reg 6(1)(b)*), except that interest on any sum for injury to feelings is to be awarded for the whole of the period from the date of the act of discrimination to the date of calculation (*reg 6(1)(a)*). Interest is simple interest and accrues from day to day (*reg 3(1)*). By *reg 3(2)* the rate to be applied in England and Wales is the rate fixed, for the time being, by *section 17* of the *Judgments Act 1838*. In Scotland the rate is the rate fixed, for the time being, by *section 9* of the *Sheriff Courts (Scotland) Extracts Act 1892*. Both rates are currently 8%.

If a respondent has made a payment to the complainant prior to the date of calculation, the date of payment is treated as if it were the date of calculation for the purposes of calculating the interest to be awarded (*reg 6(2)*).

The tribunal is given a discretion to calculate interest by reference to periods other than those set out above, or even to use different periods for different elements of the award (*reg 6(3)*). The discretion may be exercised only where the tribunal is of the opinion that:

(a)   there are exceptional circumstances, whether relating to the claim as a whole or to a particular element of the award; and

(b)   those circumstances have the effect that serious injustice would be caused if interest were to be awarded by reference to the period or periods specified in *reg 6(1)(a)* or *(b)* or *6(2)*.

23.24 Equal Pay Audits

Section 132 of the *EqA 2010*, which deals with equal pay cases, contains no specific power to make a 'recommendation' such as is contained in *EqA 2010, s 124(1)(c)* for other discrimination claims: see **14.21 DISCRIMINATION AND EQUAL OPPORTUNITIES – III**. However, it is arguable that equal pay cases also fall within the scope of *s 124(1)(c)* since that section applies to all contraventions of *Part 5* of the *Act*, which includes in principle contraventions of the equality clause: see *ss 120(1)* and *124(1)*. Nonetheless, *s 98* of the *Enterprise and Regulatory Reform Act 2013* created a new power for employment tribunals to make a very specific type of 'recommendation' in an equal pay case. That *Act* inserts a new *s 139A* into the *EqA 2010. Section 139A* gives the Secretary of State the power to make regulations requiring employment tribunals to order a respondent to carry out an equal pay audit in any case where the tribunal finds that there has been a breach of the equality clauses in the *EqA 2010* or a contravention of the sex discrimination provisions relating to pay. This power is additional to the power to award compensation to the individual claimant (above), and to the power to impose a financial penalty on an employer (below). The purpose of such audits is 'to identify action to be taken to avoid equal pay breaches occurring or continuing' (*s 139A(3)*). The *Act* requires the regulations to provide for an equal pay audit not to be ordered where the tribunal considers that: (a) an audit completed by the respondent in the previous 3 years meets requirements prescribed for this purpose; (b) it is clear without an audit whether any action is required to avoid equal pay breaches occurring or continuing; (c) the breach the tribunal has found gives no reason to think that there may be other breaches; or (d) the disadvantages of an equal pay audit would outweigh its benefits (*s 139A(5)*). Otherwise, the *Act* allows for the regulations to make further provision as to the content of an audit, any circumstances in which an audit may be required to be published or disclosed to any person, the powers and duties of the tribunal for deciding whether an order has been complied with, and for the tribunal to have power, where a person fails to comply with an order to carry out an equal pay audit (*s 138A(2), (6)* and *(8)*). In the first regulations to be made under the section, the amount of such a penalty may not exceed £5,000 (*s 139A(8)*). That limit will not apply to subsequent regulations. Similarly, the statute gives power in the first regulations (but not in subsequent regulations) made under the section to provide for an exemption from the equal pay audit provisions for small and/or new businesses.

The *Equality Act 2010 (Equal Pay Audits) Regulations 2014 (SI 2014/2559)* made under that section came into force on 1 October 2014. Subject to certain exceptions, the Regulations require a tribunal, where it finds that there has been an equal pay breach, to order the respondent to carry out an audit (*reg 2*). There are exceptions where: (i) an audit covering the required matters has been carried out in the previous three years (*reg 3(1)(a)*); (ii) it is clear without an audit whether any action is required to avoid equal pay breaches occurring or continuing (*reg 3(1)(b)*); (iii) the breach which the tribunal has found gives no reason to think that there may be other breaches (*reg 3(1)(c)*); (iv) the disadvantages of an audit would outweigh its benefits (*reg 3(1)(d)*). There are also exceptions for existing micro-businesses and new businesses (*reg 4*). Micro-businesses are businesses with fewer than 10 full-time equivalent employees (*Sch, para 1*; full-time equivalence is calculated by reference to the formula in *para 6*), as determined immediately before the date of judgment (*Sch 1, para 2*). New businesses are businesses which are less than 12 months old when the claim is presented to the tribunal (*Sch, para 3(1)* and *reg 1(2)*). However, there is detailed provision in *Sch, para 3(2)–(8)* dealing with the circumstances where businesses have been transferred and are therefore not to be regarded as 'new businesses'. The exceptions for micro-businesses and new businesses are not going to be in force indefinitely. The Regulations only prohibit a tribunal from ordering such businesses to undertake an audit 'within the applicable exemption period' (*reg 4(1)*). The 'backstop' is ten years from the date the Regulations came into force (ie 1 October 2024) for both micro-businesses (*Sch, para 4*) and new businesses (*Sch, para 5*). Micro-businesses may lose the protection of the exception earlier if, during a six month 'assessment period', the number of days when their employees exceed 10 is greater than the number of days when they have fewer than 10 employees (see *Sch, para 4(2)* and *(3)* for the detailed provisions on 'assessment periods').

Where a tribunal makes an order under *reg 2* requiring an audit to be carried out, it must specify (by description) the employees who must be covered by the audit and the period of time to which the audit must relate (*reg 5(1)(a)*). The tribunal must also specify a date, which must be at least three months hence, by which the audit must be received by the tribunal (*reg 5(1)(b)* and *(2)*). The audit must then include relevant gender pay information for the categories of employees specified by the tribunal, identify any differences in pay between male and female employees and the reasons for those differences, including the reasons for any potential equal pay breach identified by the audit and must set out the respondent's plan to avoid equal pay breaches occurring or continuing (*reg 6*).

Where an audit is received by the tribunal by the time specified in the order, the tribunal must (of its own motion) determine whether the audit complies with the requirements of *reg 6* and, if so, make an order to that effect (*reg 7(1)* and *(2)*). If the tribunal is not satisfied that the audit complies, or if no audit has been received, then the tribunal must fix a hearing, and give the respondent notice of that (*reg 7(3)*). Where an audit has been received, the tribunal must also notify the respondent employer of the reasons why it is not satisfied with the audit and inform the respondent of its right to make representations at the hearing. If the employer does not provide the audit within the time specified, then the tribunal must specify a new date for compliance, which must be no later than the date fixed for the hearing (*reg 7(3)(c)*).

At the hearing, the tribunal must (if the audit has been received) determine whether it complies with the requirements of *reg 6*. If it does, it must make an order to that effect (*reg 8(3)(a)*). If the tribunal determines that the audit does not comply then the tribunal must notify the respondent of its reasons for that determination, make an order requiring the respondent to amend the audit and consider whether or not to order the respondent to pay a penalty under *reg 11* (*reg 8(4)*). Even if a compliant audit has been supplied by the date of the hearing, the tribunal may order the respondent to pay a penalty under *reg 11* if the respondent failed to provide the audit by the date originally set by the tribunal (*reg 8(3)(b)*). Where an audit has not been received by the date of the hearing, the tribunal must make an order specifying a new date by which the tribunal must receive the audit and consider whether or not to order the respondent to pay a penalty under *reg 11* (*reg 8(5)*). Where a respondent fails to comply with any of these orders, then the tribunal must fix a further hearing and notify the response of the date of the hearing and right to make representations (*reg 8(6), (7)*).

Where a tribunal is satisfied that a compliant audit has been completed, and has made an order to that effect, the respondent must (not less than 28 days after the date of the order) publish the audit on its website (if it has one) for a period of three years and inform all people about whom gender pay information was included in the audit where they can obtain a copy (*reg 9(2)*). If the respondent considers that publication in this way would result in a breach of a legal obligation, then they must publish the report with such revisions as it considers necessary to ensure compliance with that legal obligation (*reg 9(3)(a)*). Only if it is not possible to make revisions that would avoid breach of the legal obligation is it permissible not to publish the audit (*reg 9(3)(b)*). Where the audit has been published, the respondent must, not more than 28 days after publication, send evidence of the publication to the tribunal and, where it has not published the report, or has published it in revised form, adequate written reasons why it considers that publication would result in breach of a legal obligation (*reg 9(5)* and *(6)*).

The tribunal must then consider (of its own motion) whether or not the respondent has complied with the publication requirements (*reg 10(2)*). If the tribunal concludes that the respondent has complied, or is not required to comply because of a legal obligation, it must issue a decision in writing to that effect (*reg 10(3)*). If the tribunal considers on the papers that the respondent has not complied, then it must fix a hearing to determine the matter, notifying the respondent of the reasons why it is not so satisfied and its right to make representations (*reg 10(4)*). If at the hearing, the tribunal determines that the respondent has complied, then it must issue a decision to that effect (*reg 10(6)*). If not, the tribunal must make an order setting a new date for compliance (*reg 10(7)*). If the respondent still does not comply, then a further hearing must be fixed (*reg 10(8)*, *(9)*).

Where a tribunal finds that a respondent has failed to comply with an order to carry out an audit (under *reg 2*) or an order to amend an audit (under *reg 8*), then the tribunal may, if satisfied that the respondent has no reasonable excuse for failure to comply, order the respondent to pay a penalty to the Secretary of State under *reg 11*. Repeated penalties may be awarded for repeat offences (*reg 11(2)*). The maximum amount of any individual penalty is £5,000 (*reg 11(4)*). There is no limit on the number of penalties that can be awarded.

Guidance on equal pay audits is available on the Equalities and Human Rights Commission website (See https://www.equalityhumanrights.com/en/multipage-guide/equal-pay-audit -larger-organisations).

23.25 Other financial penalties for employers

The tribunal has a power (as of 25 April 2013) to order an employer to pay a penalty to the Secretary of State (but not to the claimant), where it concludes that the employer has breached any of a worker's rights to which the worker's claim relates and is of the opinion that the breach has one or more aggravating features (*Employment Tribunals Act 1996, s 12A*). See further EMPLOYMENT TRIBUNALS – II, **20.119B**.

23.26 Equal Pay Claims and the Civil Courts

Because the right to equal pay in the *EqPA 1970* and the *EqA 2010* is given effect by way of the deemed inclusion of an equality clause in the worker's contract (see above **23.5**), it is possible for claims for equal pay to be brought in the civil courts by way of a claim for breach of contract. The *EqA 2010* explicitly preserves the jurisdiction of the civil courts in respect of equal pay (*s 127(9)* of *EqA 2010*), subject to provisions permitting the striking out of claims where such claims could be more conveniently dealt with by an employment tribunal and for the transferring of issues to the employment tribunal: see *s 128* of *EqA 2010*. Note that there is not an equivalent power for the employment tribunal to transfer an equal pay claim to the County Court and the tribunal has no power to achieve the same ends by using its power to stay proceedings in *rule 29* of the *Employment Tribunals (Constitution and Rules of Procedure) Regulations 2013* even if it considers the High Court would be the more appropriate forum for the claim: *Asda Stores Ltd v Brierley and ors* [2016] EWCA Civ 566, [2016] ICR 945. The doctrine of *forum non conveniens* does not apply. The Law Commission's report on *Employment Law Hearing Structures* (LC 390), published 27 April 2020, includes a proposal to permit the County Court to transfer entire cases, not just issues to employment tribunals.

The *EqPA 1970* contained identical provision to *s 128(2)* of the *EqA 2010* at *s 2(3)* as follows: 'Where it appears to the court in which any proceedings are pending that a claim or counter-claim in respect of the operation of an [equality clause] could more conveniently be disposed of separately by an [employment tribunal], the court may direct that the claim or counter-claim shall be struck out; and (without prejudice to the foregoing) where in proceedings before any court a question arises as to the operation of an [equality clause], the court may on the application of any party to the proceedings or otherwise refer that question, or direct it to be referred by a party to the proceedings, to an [employment tribunal] for determination by the tribunal, and may stay or sist the proceedings in the meantime.' This section of the *EqPA 1970* suggested that the civil courts have jurisdiction over equal pay claims but raised the question of whether or not an equal pay claim which would be out of time in the employment tribunal, could be pursued by making use of the longer limitation periods permitted in contract claims in the civil courts or whether such claims fall to be struck out, under *EqPA 1970, s 2(3)* on the basis that it would be more convenient to hear them in the employment tribunal (having regard to the expertise of the employment tribunals in equal pay cases and the specialist rules of procedure).

In *Abdulla v Birmingham City Council* [2010] EWHC 3303 (QB), [2011] IRLR 309 Colin Edelman QC (sitting as a deputy High Court Judge) declined to strike out an equal pay multiple under *EqPA 1970, s 2(3)*. He considered that a construction of *EqPA 1970, s 2(3)* which permitted claims to be struck out on the basis that they could be more conveniently disposed of in the employment tribunal, even though they could not be heard in the employment tribunal (by reason of the time bar) would amount to the imposition of the employment tribunal time limit on claims in the civil courts even though Parliament had chosen not to enact the same time limit in the different sets of proceedings. He also considered that the European principle of equivalence was engaged and required that equal pay proceedings in the civil courts should have equivalent time limits to contract claims in the civil courts. A rather different approach was suggested by Slade J in *Ashby v Birmingham City Council* [2011] EWHC 424 (QB), [2011] IRLR 473, [2012] ICR 1. Slade J drew on the jurisprudence which applied in the context of staying claims in this jurisdiction on an application of the *forum non conveniens* principles. She concluded that it was essential in applying *EqPA 1970, s 2(3)* to consider the reason why the claims had been pursued in the civil courts and why timely claims were not issued in the employment tribunal. Where the failure to issue a timely claim in the employment tribunal was reasonable, she opined that 'the interests of justice are likely to be served by enabling claimants to continue litigating in a forum which has jurisdiction to hear their claims. Such considerations could affect the decision as to whether the claims could be more conveniently disposed of in the Employment Tribunal or, if a judge so concluded, whether discretion should be exercised to strike out the claims in the County Court.' When the question came before the Court of Appeal in *Birmingham City Council v Abdulla* [2011] EWCA Civ 1412, [2012] IRLR 116, [2012] ICR 20 the Court of Appeal preferred the approach of Colin Edelman QC to that of Slade J. Mummery LJ considered that the purpose of *section 2(3)* was to enable claims to be dealt with in the most appropriate forum and not to leave claimants without any remedy. Consequently, it would not be appropriate to strike out equal pay claims pursued in the civil courts exercising the section 2(3) power when the claims would be out of time such that the employment tribunal would have no jurisdiction to entertain them. The Court of Appeal did not therefore need to express an opinion upon the question of the European principle of equivalence. Mummery LJ did not find the comparison with the staying of claims on an application of the *forum non conveniens* principles, which had influenced the decision in *Ashby*, helpful. However, he did accept that the reasons why a claimant had allowed the time limit in the employment tribunal to expire, may be relevant in the exercise of judicial discretion given by *EqPA 1970, s 2(3)* albeit that he opined that it would be in exceptional case that it would be an abuse of process for claimants to continue with claims in the civil courts where they could not be pursued in the employment tribunal. On appeal to the Supreme Court in *Abdulla* ([2012] UKSC 47, [2013] IRLR 38, [2012] ICR 1419) a majority of the Supreme Court (Lords Wilson and Reed and Lady Hale) favoured the approach of Colin Edelman QC. The majority considered that although in most cases it will be more convenient for the tribunal to dispose of a claim in respect of the operation of an equality clause, if such a claim would be out of time in the employment tribunal, it would never be more convenient for it to be brought there and the civil court should not strike the claim out. Nor were the reasons why the claim had not been brought in time in the employment tribunal relevant to the question of whether it should be struck out by the High Court. However, in the view of the majority, those reasons might be relevant to the question of costs, since such claims should normally be dealt with in the employment tribunal, where each side would normally bear its own costs. The SC further noted that the power under *s 2(3)* of the *EqPA 1970* (now *EqA 2010, s 128(2)*) for a civil court to refer any issue in an equal pay claim for determination by a tribunal is not subject to any time limit and should not be forgotten.

23.27   Agricultural Wages Orders

Under the *EqPA 1970* if any such order contained a discriminatory term, it could be referred by the Secretary of State to the Central Arbitration Committee ('CAC') for amendment. He may be requested to do so by employer or worker representatives on the Agricultural Wages Board, or may do so on his own motion. If the CAC decides that the amendments should be made, the Agricultural Wages Board must make an order giving effect to those amendments not later than five months from the date of the decision *EqPA 1970, s 5*).

The *EqA 2010* does not replicate *s 5* of *EqPA 1970*.

23.28   PROCEDURE IN EQUAL PAY CLAIMS

See also generally DISCRIMINATION AND EQUAL OPPORTUNITIES – III (14).

The *Employment Tribunals (Constitution and Rules of Procedure) Regulations 2004 (SI 2004/1861)* ('the *2004 Regulations*') governed the procedure relating to all claims before employment tribunals with effect from 1 October 2004 to 29 July 2013 (see EMPLOYMENT TRIBUNALS – I (19)). With effect from 29 July 2013, employment tribunal procedure is governed by the *Employment Tribunals (Constitution and Rules of Procedure) Regulations 2013 (SI 2013/1237)* ('the *2013 Regulations*'). The *2013 Regulations* apply to all proceedings before employment tribunals from that date, save that the *2004 Regulations* continue to apply in relation to respondent's counterclaims where the claim form was received before 29 July 2013: see *reg 15*.

Proceedings in equal pay claims are started in the same way as all proceedings before employment tribunals, by the filing of a Claim (*2013 Regulations, Sch 1, rule 8*). The respondent enters a Response (*2013 Regulations, Sch 1, rule 15*). The tribunal has power to order the discovery and inspection of documents, and the attendance of witnesses (*2013 Regulations, Sch 1, rules 29, 31* and *32*).

Multiple claims

The new rules also contain specific provisions relating to the making of claims by multiple claimants whose claims are based on the same set of facts (*rule 9*) and to responding to such claims (*rule 16(3)*). These will often be relevant in group equal pay claims. In addition, there is specific provision in the new *rule 36* for lead cases to be identified 'where a Tribunal considers that two or more claims give rise to common or related issues of fact or law'. In such cases, the other claims will be stayed while the lead case will go forward to a preliminary or substantive hearing. Any decision made in the lead case 'shall be binding' on each of the parties to the other cases stayed behind the lead case (*rule 36(2)*) unless, within 28 days of the Tribunal's decision any party successfully applies for an order that the decision does not apply to, and is not binding on the parties to, a particular related case. Note that multiple claimants cannot bring claims on a single ET1 where they perform different jobs, although they need not all rely on the same comparators: *Brierley v Asda Stores Ltd* [2019] EWCA Civ 8, [2019] IRLR 327, although the Court of Appeal in that case went on to make clear that the Tribunal has discretion to waive such an irregularity under *rule 6*. See also *Birmingham City Council v Adams* (UKEAT/0048/17/LA) for what may be sufficient by way of details of claim where claimants whose claims could potentially have been brought as multiple claims in fact file separate claims.

Disciplinary and grievance procedures

Note that the, now repealed, statutory grievance and disciplinary procedures in *Sch 2* to the *Employment Act 2002* continue to apply to claims under the *EqPA 1970* until 4 October 2009 in the case of an equal pay claim that relates to a period prior to 6 April 2009. Accordingly, for claims governed by these old procedures, an employee must have set out her complaint in writing and sent a copy of it to her employer at least 28 days prior to commencing proceedings in the employment tribunal. In *Hurst v Suffolk Mental Health Partnership NHS Trust* [2009] EWCA Civ 309, [2009] IRLR 452, [2009] ICR 1011, the Court of Appeal confirmed that it is sufficient for the first step of an equal pay grievance to inform the employer that the claim was brought under the *1970 Act* and further detail is not required. As such, where comparators are named in a grievance and a subsequent claim seeks to rely on different comparators it is very likely that the claim will not be barred from proceeding by reason of *EmA 2002, section 32*: see *Amery v Perth and Kinross Council* [2012] ICR 1067, *Sefton Metropolitan Borough Council v Hincks* [2011] ICR 1357, [2011] All ER (D) 122 (Aug) and *Abendshine v Sunderland City Council* [2012] ICR 1087.

Early conciliation requirements

Similarly, the new provisions in *EqA 2010, s 140B* providing (from 6 April 2014) for extensions of time limits to facilitate conciliation before institution of proceedings apply to equal pay claims as they do to other claims under the *EqA 2010*: see *s 140B(1)*. By virtue of *s 18A* of the *Employment Tribunals Act 1996* all would-be claimants must normally now contact ACAS before instituting proceedings. The only exceptions to this which may be relevant to equal pay claims are where:

(a)   Another person (B) has complied with the requirement to contact ACAS and the claimant wishes to institute proceedings as a multiple claim on the same claim form as B (*reg 3(1)(a)* of the *Employment Tribunals (Early Conciliation: Exemptions and Rules of Procedure) Regulations 2014/254* ('the *2014 Regulations*');

(b)   The claimant institutes the equal pay claim on the same claim form as a claim that is not covered by the early conciliation provisions (ie not listed in *s 18(1)* of the *Employment Tribunals Act 1996*) (*2014 Regulations, reg 3(1)(b)*);

(c)   The claimant is able to show that the respondent has contacted ACAS in relation to the same dispute previously (*2014 Regulations, reg 3(1)(c)*);

(d)   The claim is against the Security Service, the Secret Intelligence Service of the Government Communications Headquarters (*2014 Regulations, reg 3(1)(e)*).

Where the exception in *reg 3(1)(a)* above is relied on, then the time limit for bringing claims is extended for all claims in the multiple (*reg 3(2)*). If one of the other exceptions applies, there is no requirement to contact ACAS before instituting proceedings but, equally, no extension of time is available for instituting proceedings either.

In proceedings to which the conciliation provisions apply, broadly speaking, the ordinary time limit for bringing a claim is extended by the time spent in attempting conciliation through ACAS. The period between the would-be claimant contacting ACAS in the prescribed manner (see below) and the day after ACAS issuing a certificate confirming that the conciliation period is at an end (again in the prescribed manner, see below) does not count for the purposes of calculating whether the ordinary time limit has expired. Specifically, the time period that is not counted runs from the day on which the claimant contacts ACAS to the day after the claimant receives or is deemed to have received the early conciliation certificate (*EqA 2010, s 140A(3)* and see further below). Further, if the ordinary time limit has expired within that conciliation period then the time for presenting the complaint is extended by one month: *EqA 2010, s 140A(4)*. 'One month' means on the 'corresponding date' so where day B is 30 June, the time limit will expire on 30 July (*Tanveer v East London Bus & Coach Co Ltd* [2016] ICR D11).

Where the would-be claimant is required to contact ACAS, he or she must do so in the manner prescribed by the *Schedule* to the *2014 Regulations*, ie using the online or postal form (*para 2*), or by telephone (*para 3*), providing in each case the claimant's and the respondent's name and address (*para 2(3)* or *para 3(1)*). Note that, where there is more than one potential respondent, only one name and address need be provided (*para 4*). ACAS must then make reasonable attempts to contact the prospective claimant and (if the claimant consents) the respondent (*paras 4(1)* and *(2)*). If ACAS is unable to make contact with the prospective claimant or respondent, it must conclude that settlement is not possible (*para (3)*).

Otherwise, then for up to one calendar month starting on the date of receipt by ACAS of the early conciliation form, or telephone call from the claimant, the ACAS officer must endeavour to promote a settlement (*para 6(1)*). The ACAS officer may extend the one-month period if the ACAS officer considers that there is a reasonable prospect of achieving a settlement within that extended period and both parties agree (*para 6(2)*). If at any point during the period for early conciliation, or during any extension of that period, the conciliation officer concludes that a settlement of a dispute, or part of it, is not possible, ACAS must issue an early conciliation certificate (*ETA 1996, s 18A(4)* and *2014 Regulations, para 7(1)*). If the period for early conciliation, including any extension of that period, expires without a settlement having been reached, ACAS must issue an early conciliation certificate (*para 7(2)*).

The early conciliation certificate must comply with the requirements of *para 8* and must be sent to the claimant and (if contact has been made with the respondent) the respondent by e-mail (if an e-mail address has been provided) or otherwise by post (*para 9(1)* and *(2)*). An early conciliation certificate is deemed received on the day it is sent if sent by e-mail and on the day on which it would be delivered in the ordinary course of the post if sent by post (*para 9(3)*). Note that this means that it is not necessary for the certificate actually to have been read or received by the claimant in order for time to start running. The consequences of this may be harsh in equal pay cases where (unlike in most other employment tribunal claims) the tribunal does not have a discretion to extend the time limit).

Only one conciliation certificate can be, or needs to be, issued for each 'matter'. This means that a conciliation certificate issued in response to issues raised in the run-up to dismissal or resignation will also cover the subsequent dismissal or resignation: *Compass Group UK and Ireland Ltd v Morgan* [2016] IRLR 924, [2017] ICR 73. However, beware the mistaken issue of a second conciliation certificate in these circumstances: that will be invalid and will not give rise to any further extension of time: *HMRC v Garau* UKEAT/0348/16/LA. There is no need to seek a further conciliation certificate where amendments are made to a claim, even where the amendment is adding a different respondent provided the amended claim concerns the same 'matter': *Drake International Systems Ltd and ors v Blue Arrow Ltd* [2016] ICR 445.

See generally Employment Tribunals – II, 20.70.

Amendments to equal pay claims

As with other types of claim, a tribunal faced with an application to amend an equal pay claim must take all relevant circumstances into account and balance the relative injustice and hardship of allowing or refusing the amendment (*Selkent Bus Co Ltd v Moore* [1996] IRLR

661, [1996] ICR 836). In such applications, the fact that an amendment includes a new claim which would be out of time if brought separately is a relevant but not determining factor, to be taken into account along with other relevant factors, including the nature of the amendment, the time of the application, etc. The fact that there is no discretion to extend time in equal pay cases makes no difference to the application of the principles on amendment to such claims: *Walsall Metropolitan Borough Council and anor v Birch and ors* (17 February 2011), UKEAT/0376/10 and *2 Sisters Food Group Ltd v Abraityte* [2015] All ER (D) 304 (Nov) (UKEAT/0209/15/MC). A number of cases have considered in what circumstances an amendment to an equal pay claim constitutes a new claim. Where a claimant seeks to amend her claim to cover periods during which she did a different role, that will be a new cause of action: *2 Sisters Food Group Ltd v Abraityte* [2015] All ER (D) 304 (Nov) (UKEAT/0209/15/MC). Similarly, the amendment of proceedings by the addition of new comparators in an equal pay claim does add a new cause of action: *Bainbridge v Redcar and Cleveland Borough Council* [2008] EWCA Civ 885, [2008] IRLR 776 and *Potter v North Cumbria Acute Hospitals NHS Trust* [2009] IRLR 22, [2009] IRLR 900, EAT (which held further that the new cause of action was not necessarily out of time and that the complexities of litigation under the *EqPA 1970* should be taken into account when deciding whether to permit an amendment to add new comparators).

Like work or work rated as equivalent. If a claim for equal pay is brought asserting that the claimant is employed on like work or work rated as equivalent with a male comparator, the issues to be determined by the tribunal are, first, whether the work is like work, or has been rated as equivalent under a valid job evaluation study. Secondly, if it is raised, the tribunal will then decide whether the respondent has a genuine material factor defence under *EqPA 1970, s 1(3)* or *EqA 2010, s 69*. These claims are determined under the ordinary rules of procedure in schedule 1 to the *2013 Regulations*.

Work of equal value. Equal pay claims in which it is alleged that the work done was work of equal value were the subject of complementary rules of procedure contained in *Sch 6* to the *2004 Regulations* and now largely replicated in *Sch 3* to the *2013 Regulations*.

By *EqA 2010, s 131(2)*, where a dispute arises as to whether any work is of equal value, the Tribunal may proceed to determine that question itself. Alternatively, it may require a member of the panel of independent experts to prepare a report on that issue before the Tribunal determines the matter. (The panel of independent experts is appointed by ACAS: see *s 131(8)*). See further below for the procedure to be adopted by the Tribunal in relation to the appointment of an expert.

In a case where there has already been a job evaluation study which has given different values to the work of the claimant and the comparator, the employment tribunal must determine that the work is not of equal value unless it has reasonable grounds for suspecting that the study discriminated on the grounds of sex, or there are other reasons why it is not suitable to be relied upon *EqA 2010, s 131(5)* and *(6)* (see previously *EqPA 1970, s 2A(2)* and *2A(2A)*). For these purposes, a system discriminates because of sex if a difference (or coincidence) between values that the system sets on different demands is not justifiable regardless of the sex of the person on whom the demands are made (*s 131(7)*). (See further above **23.8**.)

In response to widespread concerns about the costs and delay involved in the independent expert procedure, *Sch 3* to the *2013 Regulations* makes provision for a two-stage procedure with an 'indicative timetable'. In cases not involving an independent expert, the indicative timetable takes a total of 25 weeks and allows for a Stage 1 equal value hearing within 3 weeks of the Response with the merits hearing to follow within 18 weeks. In cases where an expert is appointed, the indicative timetable takes 37 weeks and provides for a Stage 1 equal value hearing within 3 weeks of the Response, a Stage 2 hearing within 10 weeks of Stage 1, the expert's report within 4 weeks of Stage 2, written questions to the expert 4 weeks after his or her report and the merits hearing within a further 8 weeks. However, the requirement to hold a Stage 1 or a Stage 2 equal value hearing does not preclude holding more than one of each of those types of hearing or other hearings from being held in accordance with the ordinary Tribunal rules of procedure in *Sch 1* to the *2013 Regulations: rule 12(2)* of *Sch 3* to the *2013 Regulations*.

The procedure for equal value claims provides as follows.

In making all directions in relation to equal value claims, the Tribunal is required to have regard to the indicative timetable (see *rule 2(2)* of *Sch 3* to the *2013 Regulations*).

Stage 1 Equal Value Hearing. Where there is a dispute as to whether one person's work is of equal value to another's (referred to as 'the question' in the *Regulations*), the Tribunal shall conduct a hearing called a 'Stage 1 Equal Value Hearing'. At this hearing the Tribunal must consider whether and how to exercise its powers under *EqA 2010, s 131*. By *EqA 2010, s 131(2)*, where a dispute arises as to whether any work is of equal value, the Tribunal may proceed to determine that question itself. Alternatively, it may require a member of the panel of independent experts to prepare a report on that issue before the Tribunal determines the matter. (The panel of independent experts is appointed by ACAS: see *s 131(8)*). At the Stage 1 hearing the Tribunal shall (*rule 3* of *Sch 3* to the *2013 Regulations*):

(a)   strike out the claim if, by virtue of the claimant's and her comparator's work having been rated differently in a valid job evaluation study, their work is not of equal value;

(b)   determine whether or not the claimant and her comparator's work are of equal value, or alternatively require an independent expert to prepared a report on the question (and hear evidence and submissions for the purpose of deciding these issues);

(c)   if the Tribunal decides to require an independent expert to prepare a report on the question, the Tribunal must fix a date for a 'Stage 2 Equal Value Hearing';

(d)   if the Tribunal decides not to require an independent expert to prepare a report, then a date for a final hearing must be fixed.

Under the *2004 Regulations* there was also a specific power in *rule 4* to order disclosure to the expert of all documents and evidence relevant to the question of equal value disclosed between the parties. This power is now contained in *rule 2(1)(b)* of *Sch 3* to the *2013 Regulations*. *Rule 2* also gives the Tribunal specific power to limit the parties to facts that they have put in evidence and disclosed by a date set by the Tribunal (*rule 2(1)(a)*).

At the Stage 1 Equal Value Hearing, the tribunal shall also, unless it considers it inappropriate, make the following 'standard orders' (*rule 4* of *Sch 3* to the *2013 Regulations*):

(a)   before the end of the period of 14 days after the date of the Stage 1 hearing the claimant shall:

    (i)   disclose in writing to the respondent the name of any comparator, or, if the claimant is not able to name the comparator he shall instead disclose such information as enables the comparator to be identified by the respondent; and

    (ii)   identify to the respondent in writing the period in relation to which he considers that the claimant's work and that of the comparator are to be compared;

(b)   before the end of the period of 28 days after the date of the Stage 1 hearing:

    (i)   where the claimant has not disclosed the name of the comparator to the respondent, if the respondent has been provided with sufficient detail to be able to identify the comparator, he shall disclose in writing the name of the comparator to the claimant;

(ii)   the parties shall provide each other with written job descriptions for the claimant and any comparator;

(iii)   the parties shall identify to each other in writing the facts which they consider to be relevant to the question;

(c)   the respondent is required to grant access to the claimant and his representative (if any) to his premises during a period specified by the tribunal or chairman in order for him or them to interview any comparator;

(d)   the parties shall before the end of the period of 56 days after the date of the stage 1 equal value hearing present to the tribunal a joint agreed statement in writing of the following matters:

(i)   job descriptions for the claimant and any comparator;

(ii)   facts which both parties consider are relevant to the question;

(iii)   facts on which the parties disagree (as to the fact or as to the relevance to the question) and a summary of their reasons for disagreeing;

(e)   the parties shall, at least 56 days prior to the hearing, disclose to each other, to any independent or other expert and to the tribunal written statements of any facts on which they intend to rely in evidence at the hearing; and

(f)   the parties shall, at least 28 days prior to the hearing, present to the tribunal a statement of facts and issues on which the parties are in agreement, a statement of facts and issues on which the parties disagree and a summary of their reasons for disagreeing.

Where the Tribunal has decided to appoint an independent expert to prepare a report on the question, the Tribunal or a Chairman may if it or he considers it appropriate (for example where a party is not legally represented etc) at any stage of the proceedings order an independent expert to assist the tribunal in establishing the facts on which the independent expert may rely in preparing his report: *rule 5 of Sch 3 to the 2013 Regulations*. *Rule 2(1)(d) of Sch 3 to the 2013 Regulations* also makes specific provision in relation to joint reports being produced by experts where more than one expert is instructed in proceedings.

See generally the decision of the Scottish EAT in *Amey Services Ltd v Cardigan* [2008] IRLR 279 for discussion of the need for the claimant to identify comparators before the respondent is required to give details of any genuine material factor defence.

Stage 2 Equal Value Hearing. At the Stage 2 hearing the Tribunal shall make a determination of facts on which the parties cannot agree which relate to the question and shall require the independent expert to prepare his report on the basis of facts which have (at any stage of the proceedings) either been agreed between the parties or determined by the tribunal (referred to as 'the facts relating to the question'): *rule 6(1) of Sch 3 to the 2013 Regulations*. The facts relating to the question shall be the only facts on which the tribunal shall rely at the hearing, subject to an application by the independent expert for some or all of the facts relating to the question to be amended, supplemented or omitted: *rule 6(2) and (3) of Sch 3 to the 2013 Regulations*. Helpful guidance on the fact-finding process was given by Lavender J in the High Court in *Beal v Avery Homes (Nelson) Limited* (Case No. HQ16X01000, 6 June 2019), following a review of the authorities. See above **23.6**.

At the Stage 2 hearing the Tribunal shall, unless it considers it inappropriate to do so, make the following 'standard orders' having regard to the indicative timetable (*rules 6(1)(b) and 7 of Sch 3 to the 2013 Regulations*):

(a)   make any orders which it considers appropriate;

(b)   fix a date for the hearing, having regard to the indicative timetable;

(c)   order, by a date specified by the Tribunal (with regard to the indicative timetable) the independent expert to prepare his report on the question and shall (subject to any special provision made in national security proceedings) have sent copies of it to the parties and to the tribunal; and

(d)   order the independent expert to prepare his report on the question on the basis of the facts relating to the question.

The merits hearing. In proceedings in relation to which an independent expert has prepared a report, unless the Tribunal determines that the report is not based on the facts relating to the question, the report of the independent expert shall be admitted in evidence in those proceedings: *rule 8(1) of Sch 3 to the 2013 Regulations.* If the Tribunal does not admit the report of an independent expert, it may determine the question itself or require another independent expert to prepare a report on the question: *rule 8(2) of Sch 3 to the 2013 Regulations.* The Tribunal may refuse to admit evidence of facts or hear argument as to issues which have not been disclosed to the other party as required by these rules or any order made under them, unless it was not reasonably practicable for the party to have so complied: *rule 8(3) of Sch 3 to the 2013 Regulations.*

The role of the independent expert. When a Tribunal requires an independent expert to prepare a report with respect to the question or to assist in establishing the facts, it shall inform that independent expert of the duties and powers he has under this rule: *rule 9(1) of Sch 3 to the 2013 Regulations.* The independent expert shall have a duty to the Tribunal to:

(a)   assist it in furthering the overriding objective in *rule 2 of Sch 1 to the 2013 Regulations;*

(b)   comply with the requirements of the rules and any orders made by the Tribunal in relation to the proceedings;

(c)   keep the Tribunal informed of any delay in complying with any order in the proceedings (with the exception of minor or insignificant delays in compliance);

(d)   comply with any timetable imposed by the Tribunal or chairman in so far as this is reasonably practicable;

(e)   inform the Tribunal or a chairman on request by it or him of progress in the preparation of the independent expert's report;

(f)   prepare a report on the question based on the facts relating to the question and (subject to the provisions for national security cases) send it to the Tribunal and the parties; and

(g)   attend hearings in the proceedings.

An expert is under a duty to assist the Tribunal on matters within his expertise and this duty overrides any obligation to the person from whom he has received instructions or by whom he is paid: *rule 10(2) of Sch 3 to the 2013 Regulations.* The independent expert may make an application for any order or for a hearing to be held as if he were a party to the proceedings: *rule 9(3) of Sch 3 to the 2013 Regulations.* An independent expert shall be given notice of all hearings, orders or judgments in those proceedings as if a party to those proceedings and when a party is required to provide information to another party, such information shall also be provided to the independent expert: *rule 12(1) of Sch 3 to the 2013 Regulations.* At any stage of the proceedings the Tribunal may, after giving the independent expert the opportunity to make representations, withdraw the requirement on the independent expert to prepare a report. If it does so, the Tribunal may itself determine the question, or it may determine that a different independent expert should be required to prepare the report: *rule 9(4)* of *Sch 3* to the *2013 Regulations*. When a Tribunal determines that an independent expert is no longer required, the expert shall provide the Tribunal with all documentation and work in progress relating to the proceedings by a date specified by the Tribunal in a form which the tribunal is able to use: *rule 9(5)* of *Sch 3* to the *2013 Regulations* (see also *EqA 2010, s 131*). Such documentation and work in progress may be used in relation to those proceedings by the Tribunal or by another independent expert.

When it is alleged that the claimant's or comparator's jobs changed over the period in which equal value is claimed, a tribunal may, in the exercise of its case management powers, commission an expert's report based on the claimant's and comparator's jobs as they stood on the date the claims were presented and defer consideration of changes in job content to a later stage in the proceedings: see *Potter v North Cumbria Acute Hospitals NHS Trust* [2009] IRLR 22, [2008] ICR 910, EAT.

Use of expert evidence. See generally EMPLOYMENT TRIBUNALS – II, **20.69**. Expert evidence shall be restricted to that which, in the opinion of the tribunal, is reasonably required to resolve the proceedings: *rule 10(1)* of *Sch 3* to the *2013 Regulations*. No party may call an expert or put in evidence an expert's report without the permission of the Tribunal and no expert report shall be put in evidence unless it has been disclosed to all other parties and any independent expert at least 28 days prior to the hearing: *rule 10(3)* of *Sch 3* to the *2013 Regulations*. (See generally *Baines v Blackpool Borough Council* [2008] All ER (D) 95 (Jan), EAT, on the use of expert evidence in an equal value case.) In proceedings in which an independent expert has been required to prepare a report on the question, the Tribunal shall not admit evidence of another expert on the question unless such evidence is based on the facts relating to the question: *rule 10(4)* of *Sch 3* to the *2013 Regulations*. (See, in this regard, *Middlesbrough Borough Council v Surtees (No 2)* [2007] IRLR 981, [2008] ICR 349, EAT: this rule gives the discretion to admit the expert evidence of a second party's expert, but the words 'unless such evidence is based on the facts' mean that what the expert can give evidence about must exclude the facts which are not challenged and which represent a sacrosanct position following findings or agreement at an earlier stage in the proceedings.) Unless the Tribunal considers it inappropriate to do so, any such expert report shall be disclosed to all parties and to the Tribunal on the same date on which the independent expert is required to send his report to the parties and to the Tribunal: *rule 10(4)* of *Sch 3* to the *2013 Regulations*. If an expert (other than an independent expert) does not comply with these rules or an order made by the Tribunal or a chairman, the Tribunal may order that the evidence of that expert shall not be admitted: *rule 10(5)* of *Sch 3* to the *2013 Regulations*. Where two or more parties wish to submit expert evidence on a particular issue, the Tribunal may order that the evidence on that issue is to be given by one joint expert only. When such an order has been made, if the parties wishing to instruct the joint expert cannot agree who should be the expert, the Tribunal may select the expert: *rule 10(6)* of *Sch 3* to the *2013 Regulations*.

Written questions to experts. *rule 11* of *Sch 3* to the *2013 Regulations* makes provision for written questions to be put to experts (including an independent expert) on their report. The question must be: put once only; put within 28 days of the date on which the parties were sent the report; for the purpose only of clarifying the factual basis of the report; copied to all other parties and experts involved in the proceedings at the same time as they are sent to the expert who prepared the report; and answered within 28 days of receiving the question. An expert's answers to questions shall be treated as part of the expert's report: *rule 11(3)* of *Sch 3*. Where a party has put a written question to an expert instructed by another party and the expert does not answer that question, or does not do so within 28 days, the Tribunal may order that the party instructing the expert may not rely on the evidence of that expert: *rule 11(4)* of *Sch 3*.

Burden of proof

The same burden of proof provisions apply to equal pay claims as to other discrimination claims: see *EqA 2010, s 136(1)–(4)*. The burden of proof is on the claimant. However, if there are facts from which the court could decide, in the absence of any other explanation, that the employer has contravened the provision concerned, the tribunal must hold that the contravention occurred, unless the employer shows that it has not contravened the provision. See further DISCRIMINATION AND EQUAL OPPORTUNITIES III, 14.3.

Help for complainants

With effect from 6 April 2003, claimants or potential claimants in equal pay claims were able to serve questionnaires in the same manner as under the other discrimination statutes. The *Equal Pay (Questions and Replies) Order 2003 (SI 2003/722)*, provided for such questionnaires to be served before a claim was presented to a tribunal or within 21 days after such a claim or such longer period as the tribunal may on application allow. The tribunal could then draw adverse inferences, including an inference that the equality clause has been breached, where an employer deliberately and without reasonable cause failed to reply in the eight-week period specified by *reg 4* of the *Order* or where an employer's reply was evasive or equivocal: *EqPA 1970, s 7B*. Such questionnaires were particularly useful to complainants who bore the burden of establishing a disparate impact by reference to statistics: see *Nelson v Carillion Services Ltd* [2003] EWCA Civ 544, [2003] IRLR 428, [2003] ICR 1256, CA.

These provisions were re-enacted in *s 138* of the *EqA 2010*. However, the questionnaire procedure is not available for claims commenced after 25 April 2013 as *s 138* of the *EqA 2010* was repealed by *s 66* of the *Enterprise and Regulatory Reform Act 2013*.

Note also that relevant information may be found in the gender pay gap information that employers with 250 or more employees are now required to publish as a result of regulations made under *s 78* of the *EqA 2010* (see further **23.32** below).

Further, the provisions in *EqA 2010, s 132* in relation to equal pay audits have now been brought into force by the *Equality Act 2010 (Equal Pay Audits) Regulations 2014* (see above **23.24**).

In the meantime, employees of public sector employers may well be able to obtain relevant information about the pay of other employees by means of a request under the *Freedom of Information Act 2000*: see *South Lanarkshire Council v The Scottish Information Commissioner* [2013] UKSC 55, [2013] IRLR 899.

Help may also be available by way of disclosure orders within proceedings: *rule 31* of the *Employment Tribunals Rules of Procedure 2013* provides that the tribunal has the same powers as the County Court to order any person to disclose documents. In *Birmingham City Council v Bagshaw and ors* [2017] ICR 263, [2016] All ER (D) 166 (Oct), the EAT held the ET had been entitled to use this power to get the Council (against whom proceedings by the claimants had been settled) to disclose judgments, orders and other material relating to those settled claims where that material was relevant to claims the claimants were still pursuing against an employer to whom they had transferred. See generally **20.60** EMPLOYMENT TRIBUNALS – II.

23.29 EFFECT ON CONTRACTS

A term in a contract which purports to exclude or limit any provision of the *EqPA 1970* is unenforceable by any person in whose favour the term would operate (*EqA 2010, s 144(1)*; and see generally **14.32** DISCRIMINATION AND EQUAL OPPORTUNITIES – III). However, a contract settling a complaint to an employment tribunal will be upheld if it was made with the assistance of a conciliation officer and is a 'qualifying settlement agreement' (*EqA 2010, s 144(4)(a)* and *(5)* and see **2.3** ADVISORY, CONCILIATION AND ARBITRATION SERVICE). It will also be upheld if it meets the statutory conditions for a compromise agreement or 'qualifying settlement agreement' entered into after the employee has had independent advice (*EqA 2010, s 144(4)(b)* and *(5)* and *s 147*; and see **19.20** EMPLOYMENT TRIBUNALS and **14.33**

DISCRIMINATION AND EQUAL OPPORTUNITIES – III). In other circumstances, an agreement by a complainant that he or she will not bring a claim for equal pay will be void, and the payment of any sum to compromise such a claim will not prevent her from continuing with her complaint.

23.30 Collective agreements

Terms of collective agreements (whether they would otherwise be legally enforceable or not) are deemed automatically unenforceable and void insofar as they constitute, promote or provide for treatment that would contravene the *Act*: *EqA 2010, s 145(1)* and see generally **14.32** DISCRIMINATION AND EQUAL OPPORTUNITIES – III. Employees (or persons seeking to be employees of) an employer who is party to the collective agreement or a member of an association/organisation of employers that is party (*s 146(5)*) have the right to complain to an employment tribunal about any term that is void or unenforceable under *s 145*. To be eligible to make a complaint the employee must be able to show that the term may affect them now or in the future (*s 146(2)*).

It was held that a tribunal may grant a declaration of incompatibility in existing proceedings before it under the *EqPA 1970* without the need to issue separate proceedings; see *UNISON v Brennan* [2008] IRLR 492, [2008] ICR 955. The same must be true now of the tribunal's power under *s 146(3)*. In *Nimz v Freie und Hansestadt Hamburg*: C-184/89 [1991] IRLR 222, the CJEU held that where there is indirect discrimination in a provision of a collective agreement, the national court is required to disapply that provision, without requesting or awaiting its prior removal by collective negotiation (see also *Kowalska v Freie und Hansestadt Hamburg*: C-33/89 [1990] IRLR 447, [1992] ICR 29, CJEU).

23.31 Protection for complainants

Under *s 77* of the *EqA 2010* individuals are protected from retaliation or victimisation where they seek, or provide, disclosures about the terms of their work (including how much they are paid) (*s 77(4)* and *(5)*). Contractual terms purporting to restrict such disclosures are void (*s 77(1)* and *(2)*).

23.32 GENDER PAY GAP REPORTING

Section 78 of the *EqA 2010* makes provision enabling the making of regulations requiring employers with 250 or more employees (and other employers who may be specified) to publish information relating to the pay of employees for the purpose of showing whether there are differences in the pay of male and female employees. Two sets of regulations have been made bringing these requirements into force: the *Equality Act 2010 (Gender Pay Gap Information) Regulations 2017, SI 2017/172* (which apply to private sector employers) and the *Equality Act 2010 (Specific Duties and Public Authorities) Regulations 2017, SI 2017/353* (which apply to public sector employers covered by the public sector equality duty in *EqA 2010, s 149*: see **13.37** DISCRIMINATION AND EQUAL OPPORTUNITIES – II). The effect of the regulations is that employers with more than 250 employees must publish six metrics by April 2018, and annually thereafter, specifically: the difference between (1) the mean and (2) the median hourly rates of pay of male and female employees; the difference between (3) the mean and (4) the median bonus pay of male and female employees; (5) the proportions of male and female employees who are paid bonus pay; and (6) the proportions of male and female employees in the employer's lower, lower middle, upper middle and upper quartile pay bands. The regulations contain detailed provision as to how each of these metrics is to be calculated. Pay gap metrics are to be taken as at a 'snapshot date' of 31 March for public sector employers and 5 April for private sector employers. The bonus gap metrics refer to the 12-month period running up to that date. The information must be published on both the employer's own website and the government's website (the *Gender Pay Gap Viewing Service*) and must be left on the employer's website for a period of at least three years. The information must be accompanied by a report signed by director or other responsible person verifying report is accurate. Employers may publish a commentary with the data, but there is no requirement to do so. The regulations require the government to conduct a review of their operation at least every five years. Although *EqA 2010, s 78(5)* permits the regulations to make provision for failure to comply with the regulations to constitute a criminal offence, punishable on summary conviction by a fine not exceeding level 5 on the standard scale, the regulations have made no such provision. There are therefore no specific penalties for non-compliance, although the Equality and Human Rights Commission would have power to take enforcement action under the *Equality Act 2006* (see generally **14.23** Discrimination and Equal Opportunities – III).

24   European Union Law

24.1   BREXIT

European Union ('EU') law has applied in the UK since its accession to the European Communities on 1 January 1973. However, on 31 January 2020, the UK formally left the EU and began the process of changing the way in which this body of law applies domestically.

This departure followed from the result of an advisory referendum on 23 June 2016 in which the UK public voted to leave the EU. After this, on 29 March 2017, the then Prime Minister, acting with the authority given to her by the *European Union (Notification of Withdrawal) Act 2017*, notified the European Council in accordance with Article 50(2) of the Treaty on European Union ('TEU') of the UK's intention to withdraw from the EU. Under the Article 50 TEU procedure, there was a two-year period for conclusion of an agreement on the terms of the UK's withdrawal, after which it was envisaged that the EU Treaties (defined and discussed below) would cease to apply to the UK. This period was originally due to end of 29 March 2019. However, Article 50(3) provides for the possibility to extend this period, which occurred several times during 2019 to various dates, the last of which was 31 January 2020.

At the end of that period, the UK left the EU. However, the immediate effects of this on the UK's legal system were at a constitutional rather than a practical level. This was because the UK and EU had ratified a Withdrawal Agreement shortly beforehand, which provided for a transition period that preserved the application of (almost all) EU law to and within the UK. The transition period is due to end of 31 December 2020 (*Article 126* of the *Withdrawal Agreement*). *Article 132* of the Withdrawal Agreement provides that this period may be extended once, 'for up to 1 or 2 years', if the UK and the EU (through a joint UK-EU Committee) agree to do so before 1 July 2020. If this date is missed, an extension would only be possible through the ratification of a further agreement replacing or amending *Article 126* of the *Withdrawal Agreement*.

During the transition period, three pieces of legislation make up the constitutional structure through which EU law continues to apply in the UK:

(i)   The European Communities Act 1972;

(ii)   The European Union (Withdrawal) Act 2018; and

(iii)   The European Union (Withdrawal Agreement) Act 2020.

Until 'exit day' on 31 January 2020, EU law had effect in the UK because of the *European Communities Act 1972* ('*1972 Act*') (see **24.3** below). This provided in *s 2* that EU law would be applicable and enforceable in the UK without need for further incorporation. The entirety of the 1972 Act was repealed on 'exit day' by *s 1* of the *European Union (Withdrawal) Act 2018* ('*2018 Act*'). As originally enacted, 'exit day' was defined in *s 20* as 29 March 2019. Following the various extensions of the Article 50 TEU process noted above, this definition was changed on a number of occasions, ending with the existing date of 31 January 2020. However, during the transition period, the effect of the *1972 Act* is almost entirely preserved through a convoluted way by *ss 1A* and *1B* of the *2018 Act*. These sections were inserted into the *2018 Act* by the *European Union (Withdrawal Agreement) Act 2020*. The consequence is that, while 'exit day' led to an important constitutional change by moving the basis on which EU law applies from s 2 of the 1972 Act to *ss 1A* and *1B* of the *2018 Act*, the immediate practical changes for the legal system are minimal.

24.1 European Union Law

At the end of the transition period, however, more dramatic changes are in store. After this date, EU law will cease to apply in the manner it has up until then. In its place, the *2018 Act* will freeze EU law as it was on the last day of the transition period and convert that body of law into the UK's domestic law. EU law as of that date will therefore remain in force in the UK unless and until repealed, revoke or amended under the procedures in the *2018 Act* for these purposes. This body of law will be known as 'retained EU law'. Significantly, however, any new developments in EU law after that date will not automatically be part of UK law. Significant also is the express exclusion of the Charter of Fundamental Rights from domestic law by *s 5(4)* of the *2018 Act*.

There are, therefore, two important dates that provide turning points in the application of EU law within the UK:

(i) 'exit day', 31 January 2020, on which the *1972 Act* ceased to apply on its own terms, but EU law retained its effect through *ss 1A* and *1B* of the *2018 Act*;

(ii) End of the transition period, currently scheduled for 31 December 2020, on which EU law as currently understood will cease to apply and a new concept of 'retained EU law' will come into being.

Continuity of EU Law after the end of the transition period

Following the transition period, *ss 2–4* of the *2018 Act* will provide the basis on which retained EU law will apply in the UK:

(i) Section 2 will provide for 'EU-derived domestic legislation' to have effect;

(ii) Section 3 will provide for 'direct EU legislation' to have effect;

(iii) Section 4 will provide a general basis for rights and obligations under s 2(1) of the 1972 Act to have effect.

At the time of writing, these provisions are not yet in force (i.e. during the course of the transition period). When it comes into force, *s 2(1)* will provide:

'EU-derived domestic legislation, as it has effect in domestic law immediately before IP completion day, continues to have effect in domestic law on and after IP completion day.'

This principally relates to domestic legislation (both primary and secondary) used to implement EU directives (in relation to which, see **24.2** below).

Section 3(1) will provide:

'Direct EU legislation, so far as operative immediately before IP completion day, forms part of domestic law on and after IP completion day.'

The most obvious examples of direct EU legislation are EU regulations (in relation to which, see **24.2** below). Notably, EU directives are not retained by this provision.

Similarly, *s 4(1)* will provide:

'Any rights, powers, liabilities, obligations, restrictions, remedies and procedures which, immediately before IP completion day —

(a) are recognised and available in domestic law by virtue of section 2(1) of the European Communities Act 1972, and

(b) are enforced, allowed and followed accordingly,

continue on and after IP completion day to be recognised and available in domestic law (and to be enforced, allowed and followed accordingly).'

Section 4(1) provides the route through which some EU directives may become retained EU law. They are excluded from *s 3*, but directives that have direct effect in domestic law (as to which see **24.3** below) may be retained through the broad retention of rights and obligations in *s 4(1)*.

The *2018 Act* will thus provide for the conversion of the body of EU law as it stands at the end of the transition period into UK law. Collectively, this body of law will be known as 'retained EU law'. In general, therefore, the same laws will apply on the day after Brexit is finally concluded as the day before. The aim thereby is to provide as much legal certainty as possible as the end of the transition period approaches, to avoid the huge gaps in the UK statute book which would otherwise be left by the repeal of the *1972 Act*, and to deal with the fact that Parliament simply does not have the time or capacity to review and replace that enormous body of law.

The *2018 Act* does not only provide for the continuity of EU law after Brexit; it also provides various legislative processes through which that the retained EU law can be amended, and sets down general rules about how it is to be interpreted.

Process by which retained EU law may be amended

A novel (and thorny) legal problem created by Brexit is the question of how to amend retained EU law. At present, amendments to EU law are dealt with by the normal processes for the creation of EU law. Upon its conversion into domestic law, however, it will need to be amended through entirely domestic processes. Retained EU law will need to be categorised as either primary or secondary legislation, with the processes for amendment determined by this categorisation.

The *2018 Act* deals with this in a number of ways. In relation to EU-derived domestic legislation (e.g. primary and secondary legislation implementing an EU directive), *s 7* provides that the domestic instrument can be amended according to the usual rules for primary or secondary legislation. The significance of this is that secondary legislation originally used to implement an EU directive can, at the end of the transition period, be amended by secondary legislation without reference the constraints imposed by the EU directive (as EU directives are not retained EU law in their own right).

In relation to retained direct EU legislation, *s 7* creates two categories of 'principal' and 'minor' direct EU legislation. *Section 7* defines direct principal EU legislation so as to include (most) EU regulations, leaving most other pieces of direct EU legislation in the minor category. For the purposes of amendments, retained direct principal EU legislation will be treated as though it were primary legislation, with retained direct minor EU legislation treated as secondary legislation.

The approach of the *2018 Act* to this issue means that the Government's ability to repeal or amend retained EU law will be constrained in relation to some categories of law, but notably broad in relation to others.

Status and Interpretation of retained EU law

The *2018 Act* makes specific provision for the status and approach to interpretation of retained EU Law in *ss 5, 6* and *7*. In their present form, they each refer to nature and content of EU law on 'exit day'. However, amendments are pending in relation to each that will change the relevant date to the end of the transition period ('IP completion day'; see *s 1A(6)* of the *2018 Act* and *s 39* of the *2020 Act*). On the assumption that these amendments will come into force by the required date, the references to the relevant timeframes in these sections below is to the end of the transition period. *Section 6(1)(b)* provides that courts and tribunals cannot, after the end of the transition period, refer any matter to the ECJ and are not bound by any of its decisions. A court or tribunal may, however, have "regard" to "anything done on or after IP completion day by the [ECJ], another EU entity or the EU so far as it is relevant to any matter before the court or tribunal" (*s 6(2)*). This provision means that, while future ECJ judgments, for example, are not binding on UK courts and tribunals, they can be considered and relied upon as relevant to the interpretation of retained EU law.

Section 6(3) contains the general statement of principle that, where a question as to the "validity, meaning or effect" of a retained EU law arises, it is to be decided, so far as the law is unmodified and so far as they are relevant to the question, "in accordance with any retained case law and any retained general principles of EU Law"; and having regard to what were EU competences immediately before the end of the transition period. Put simply, this means that retained EU law is not just the strict letter of the retained provisions; it also includes the established principles and values that are so influential in the interpretation of EU law.

This inclusion of principles and values within the body of retained EU law is given more detail by *s 6(7)*. It provides the definitions of 'retained case law' and 'retained general principles of EU law' that are binding on courts and tribunals because of *s 6(3)*:

(i)   'retained case law' mean "retained domestic case law" and "retained EU case law" relating to any retained EU law as they have effect in EU law immediately before IP completion day. This means that any domestic or EU case law existing before the end of the transition period will continue to be binding on the UK's courts and tribunals.

(ii)   "Retained general principles of EU Law" are "the general principles of EU law, as they have effect in EU law immediately before IP completion day".

The *2018 Act* does not make retained case law any more binding than other categories of apex-court case law; it is not indelible and (broadly) can be departed from according to normal principles. Retained EU case law is not binding on the Supreme Court which may depart from it if it satisfies the "same test it would apply in deciding whether to depart from its own case law" (*s 6(5)*). As to what that test is, see the House of Lords' Practice Statement on Judicial Precedent [1966] 1 WLR 1234, which has been adopted by the Supreme Court. Save in circumstances irrelevant to this work, retained EU case law binds all other courts and tribunals. The High Court is also not bound when sitting in certain capacities (*s 6(4)*) and, potentially of significance to the Employment Tribunals, *s 6(5A)* allows for ministerial regulations to change the extent to which courts or tribunals are bound by or may depart from retained EU case law. In general however, departures from retained EU case law will be a matter for the Supreme Court; this is a sensible attempt to balance legal certainty with the UK's common law constitutional system which allows for evolution of the law through case law. The ministerial power in *s 6(5A)*, therefore, has the potential to shift that balance dramatically away from legal certainty. It remains to be seen how and whether this power will be exercised.

One of the hallmarks of the government's Brexit policy has been to end the supremacy of EU (as to which principle, see **24.3** below). *Section 5(1)* of the *2018 Act* contains the broad statement that the principle of supremacy does not apply to any future enactments or rules of law made after the end of the transition period (based on the pending amendments noted above as to when this principle will apply). In order to preserve legal certainty in relation to retained EU law, however, *s 5(2)* provides that supremacy continues to apply in relation to laws made before the end of the transition period (again, subject to pending amendments). The *s 5(2)* retention of the principle of supremacy creates a slight confusion in relation to EU directives, which are not expressly included as retained EU law (instead, the domestic implementing measures are retained in their place as EU-derived domestic legislation). However, the principle of supremacy means that such domestic implementing measures have to be interpreted consistently with EU directives, which means that EU directives necessarily retain their status in the UK's legal system despite not formally being included in the body of retained EU law.

As is clear from the above, a proper understanding of EU law remains essential for UK lawyers. During the transition period (due to last at least until 31 December 2020), EU law remains applicable in the UK. After the transition period the huge body of retained EU law will have to be interpreted in accordance with present EU law principles and case law, and "regard" may be had to any subsequent developments in EU law. Consequently, the remainder of this chapter sets out the current state of EU law in the UK (which is likely to remain directly relevant for a significant period of time).

24.2   SUBSTANTIVE EU LAW

There are three basic sources of EU law:

(i)   The Treaties: the *Treaty on European Union ('TEU')* and the *Treaty on the Functioning of the European Union ('TFEU')*, previously known as the *EC Treaty* or the *Treaty of Rome*;

(ii)   EU legislation; and

(iii)   decisions of the Court of Justice of the EU ('CJEU').

Changes to key terminology were introduced by the *Treaty of Lisbon*, which came into force on 1 December 2009. The *Lisbon Treaty* amended both the *Treaty of Rome*, changing its name to the *TFEU*, and altering the numbering of the Articles contained in it; and the *Maastricht Treaty*, changing its name to the *TEU*. The *Lisbon Treaty* also abandoned the term 'the European Community' ('EC'), replacing it for all purposes with 'the European Union', which was part of a move to give the EU a single legal personality. Additionally, the *Lisbon Treaty* put the EU's *Charter of Fundamental Rights* on a legal basis for the first time. *Art 6(1)* of the *TEU* provides that the EU Charter has the "same legal value as the Treaties".

The *Treaty of Rome* was made in 1957. It has been substantially amended since. The *Single European Act* of 1986, the *Maastricht Treaty* of 1991, the *Treaty of Amsterdam* of 1997, the *Treaty of Nice* of 2001 and the *Lisbon Treaty* have all introduced significant changes. The *Treaty of Amsterdam* resulted in a renumbering of the Articles of the *EC Treaty*; and the *Lisbon Treaty* resulted in a further renumbering. The new numbering is used below (but the old numbering is included in square brackets for ease of reference, with the post-*Amsterdam* numbering appearing first, followed by the original numbering). The *TFEU* sets out the fundamental principles of the EU. The provisions that are particularly relevant to the EU's powers in the employment law field are *Arts 19 [13], 115 [94, 100], 114 [95, 100A], 151 [136, 117], 153 [137, 118], 154 [138, 118A], 155 [139, 118B], 156 [140, 118C], 157 [141, 119], 294 [251, 189B] and 220 [302, 235]*.

Other treaties entered into by the EU also form part of the substance of EU law without being part of the EU's constitutional architecture. The UK-EU Withdrawal Agreement, for example, is now a matter of substantive EU law.

EU legislation takes the form of regulations and directives. Regulations are the closest equivalent to an Act of Parliament (in that they are 'directly applicable', ie they do not need to be implemented by national legislation) whereas directives are instructions to member states to bring their national legislation into conformity with EU requirements.

The EU also promulgates 'recommendations'. Recommendations have no legal effect, but ought, as a matter of European law, to be taken into account when construing national legislation adopted in order to implement them or where they are designed to supplement binding EU measures (*Grimaldi v Fonds des Maladies Professionnelles*: 322/88 [1989] ECR 4407, [1990] IRLR 400, ECJ). The EAT adopted this approach to the *Recommendation on the Dignity of Men and Women at Work* (see **24.7** below) in *Wadman v Carpenter Farrar Partnership* [1993] IRLR 374.

The EU has its own court, the CJEU, which sits in Luxembourg, and is not to be confused with the European Court of Human Rights in Strasbourg (see HUMAN RIGHTS (30)). The CJEU consists of two courts, the Court of Justice ("ECJ") and the General Court. In deciding each case, the ECJ is assisted by an Advocate General, who gives an opinion upon the issues for decision after the ECJ has heard the arguments of the parties. Beneath the ECJ, there is the General Court (which was previously named the Court of First Instance), but its role in employment matters is limited to dealing with disputes between the EU and its own employees (see **38.7** PUBLIC SECTOR EMPLOYEES).

24.3   THE EFFECT OF EU LAW

Early in the history of the European Communities, before the UK's accession, the ECJ developed the principles of the 'supremacy' and 'direct effect' of EU law. Under the 'supremacy' principle, if there is a conflict between a provision of EU law and a provision of domestic law, EU law takes precedence (see eg *Costa v ENEL*: C-6/64 [1964] ECR 585). Under the 'direct effect' principle, individuals may, in certain circumstances, rely directly on a provision of EU law as giving rise to rights which are enforceable before domestic courts (see the ECJ's ruling in *van Gend en Loos*: C26/62 [1963] ECR 1).

A provision of EU law usually has direct effect only if it fulfils certain threshold criteria. First, it must be sufficiently clear and precise. Second, it must be unconditional and leave no room for discretion in its implementation by the EU or member states. Third, the deadline for implementation of the provision must have expired (see eg *Reyners:* C-2/74 [1974] ECR 631).

Historically, UK law has been reluctant to accept that obligations arising from treaties have any effect on domestic law. British jurists have insisted that for a treaty to produce rights or obligations within the domestic legal context there must be some implementing domestic legislation (for example see *Civilian War Claimants Association Ltd v R* [1931] All ER Rep 432). A doorway into domestic law was created by *European Communities Act 1972, s 2(1)* which provides:

> 'All such rights, powers, liabilities, obligations and restrictions from time to time created or arising by or under the Treaties, and all such remedies and procedures from time to time provided for by or under the Treaties, as in accordance with the Treaties are without further enactment to be given legal effect or used in the United Kingdom shall be recognised and available in law, and be enforced, allowed and followed accordingly; and the expression "enforceable Community right" and similar expressions shall be read as referring to one to which this subsection applies.'

Section 2(2) authorises secondary legislation to implement any EU obligations of the UK, which includes the implementation of directives, even if the effect is to repeal primary legislation. *Section 2(4)* requires future legislation to be interpreted in the light of *section 2* of the *Act*. *Section 3* provides for questions of EU law to be determined in accordance with decisions of the ECJ.

The UK courts have relied on these provisions to accommodate the EU principles of direct effect and supremacy: see especially *R (Factortame) v Secretary of State for Transport (No 2)* [1991] 1 All ER 70 at 658 per Lord Bridge; and *Thoburn v Sunderland City Council* [2002] EWHC 195 (Admin), [2002] 4 All ER 156 at §69 per Laws LJ.

Numerous domestic statutes and statutory instruments have been introduced or amended so as to give effect to EU obligations. These include, for example, the *Transfer of Undertakings (Protection of Employment) Regulations 2006 (SI 2006/246)* (see TRANSFER OF UNDERTAKINGS (53)), and changes made to the law on the CONTRACT OF EMPLOYMENT (8), MATERNITY AND PARENTAL RIGHTS (33) and REDUNDANCY —II (40) by the *Trade Union Reform and Employment Rights Act 1993*.

It may be that the implementing legislation clearly and unequivocally implements the relevant European law. Such legislation will usually define the right conferred, state the remedy available for breach and identify the jurisdiction in and procedures by which the right may be enforced. However, all too often the domestic legislation does not clearly and unequivocally implement the relevant law.

In such circumstances the principle that European law has primacy is expressed first through a principle of interpretation. Courts and tribunals are required, so far as possible, to interpret national law in the light of the wording and purpose of any relevant EU directive (*Marleasing SA v La Comercial Internacional de Alimentacion SA*: C-106/89 [1992] 1 CMLR 305). The House of Lords has been prepared to go so far as to read additional words into the domestic legislation (*Litster v Forth Dry Dock and Engineering Co Ltd* [1989] IRLR 161, [1989] ICR 341). There is, however, a limit to how far the court or tribunal is able to go. The House of Lords has held that *Marleasing* applies only where the wording of the domestic provision is capable of being interpreted consistently with the directive, and not where consistency could be achieved only by distorting the meaning of the domestic legislation (*Webb v EMO Air Cargo (UK) Ltd* [1993] IRLR 27, [1993] ICR 175; see also *Duke v GEC Reliance Ltd (formerly Reliance Systems Ltd)* [1988] IRLR 118, [1988] ICR 339, HL, *Re Hartlebury Printers Ltd* [1992] IRLR 516, [1992] ICR 559 and *Porter v Cannon Hygiene Ltd* [1993] IRLR 329). In some circumstances, the court will be required to interpret a piece of legislation which, though it deals with the same subject matter as a directive, was not intended to implement European law. While there had been controversy as to whether, in those circumstances, the principle of interpretation described above should be applied, *Marleasing* decided that it should. Most examples of purposive interpretation lead to extension of the scope of the domestic legislation; but, conversely, where a literal interpretation of domestic implementing legislation would confer rights which go beyond what is required by EU law, it may be held that the domestic legislation includes by implication such limitations as are contained in EU law (eg *Risk Management Partners Ltd v Brent LBC* [2011] UKSC 7, [2011] 2 All ER 209); but not where the domestic legislation clearly intends to go beyond what is required by EU law (eg *USA v Nolan* [2014] IRLR 302).

R (Factortame) v Secretary of State for Transport (No 2) [1991] 1 All ER 70, HL illustrated a second principle: any provision of domestic law, including primary legislation, should be disapplied insofar as it is contrary to a directly effective provision of EU law. The approach has since been used to disapply a number of the provisions of the *Equal Pay Act 1970* (now succeeded by *Chapter 3* of *Part 5* of the *Equality Act 2010*) including, by way of example, the provisions which excluded complaints by those indirectly discriminated against in relation to access to occupational pension schemes (*Preston v Wolverhampton Healthcare NHS Trust* [2001] IRLR 237, CA) and which provided that two employers could be treated as 'associated' for the purposes of determining whether a complainant and her comparator are in the same employment only where one of the two employers was a company (*Scullard v Knowles and Southern Regional Council for Education and Training* [1996] IRLR 344, EAT). For further examples of provisions in domestic legislation being disapplied see *Perceval-Price v Department of Economic Development* [2000] IRLR 380, NICA, *Allonby v Accrington and Rossendale College*: C-256/01 [2004] IRLR 224, *Alabaster v Barclays Bank plc and Secretary of State for Social Security* [2005] EWCA Civ 508, [2005] IRLR 576 and *R (on the application of Manson (Finian)) v Ministry of Defence* [2005] EWCA Civ 1678, [2006] ICR 355, [2005] All ER (D) 69 (Nov).

24.3   European Union Law

A directive enters into force in the sense of producing legal effects in the member states from the date of its publication in the Official Journal of the EU or from the date of its notification to member states (*Adeneler v Ellinikos Organismos Galaktos*: C-212/04 [2006] IRLR 716). During the period prescribed for transposition of a directive, member states must refrain from taking any measure liable seriously to compromise the attainment of the result prescribed by it, whether or not the national measure is concerned with transposition of the directive: *Mangold v Helm*: C-144/04 [2006] IRLR 143 and *Adeneler v Ellinikos Organismos Galaktos* (above). During this period, domestic courts must refrain as far as possible from interpreting domestic law in a manner which might seriously compromise, after the period for transposition has expired, attainment of the objective pursued by the directive: *Adeneler v Ellinikos Organismos Galaktos*. Where the relevant provisions of the directive do not have direct effect (see below), the general obligation owed by national courts to interpret domestic law in conformity with the directive exists once the period for its transposition has expired.

What if the state has failed to introduce legislation which properly and fully implements the EU law by the date specified in the directive? In those circumstances the Commission is empowered by *Art 258 [226, 169]* to bring enforcement proceedings against the defaulting member state (see for example *EC Commission v United Kingdom*: C-382/92 [1994] ECR I-2435, [1994] IRLR 412, [1994] ICR 664). *Article 259 [227, 170]* contains a related but rarely used power for other member states to bring similar proceedings. Within our own jurisdiction legislation purporting to implement EU law has been successfully challenged using judicial review (for instance *R v Secretary of State for Employment, ex p Equal Opportunities Commission* [1994] IRLR 176, [1994] ICR 317, HL and *Equal Opportunities Commission v Secretary of State for Trade and Industry* [2007] IRLR 327, [2007] ICR 1234).

In addition, there are three mechanisms by which EU law may be given effect in British courts and tribunals, even where national law fails properly to implement it or would otherwise breach it: (1) a *Francovich* claim against the government for failure to implement; (2) reliance on the direct effect of EU law to bring a claim to enforce a European right; and (3) reliance on the direct effect of EU law to disapply an inconsistent domestic provision.

(1) *Francovich claims*

First, the landmark decision of *Francovich and Bonifaci v Italy*: C-6/90 and C-9/90 [1991] ECR I-5357, [1992] IRLR 84, [1995] ICR 722, ECJ decided that an individual may have an EU law claim for damages against the state for failure properly to implement a directive. *Francovich* claims should be brought in the High Court; employment tribunals do not have jurisdiction to hear such claims (*Secretary of State for Employment v Mann* [1996] IRLR 4, [1996] ICR 197, EAT, affirmed by the Court of Appeal [1997] ICR 209). The appropriate defendant is the Attorney General (*Mann; R v Secretary of State, ex p EOC* above). In order to bring a claim, the claimant will have to show that the unimplemented EU law provision is intended to confer rights on individuals. He must also establish that the breach is sufficiently serious and that the failure to implement it is causally connected to the loss incurred (*Francovich* above). The ECJ's decision in *Brasserie du Pêcheur SA v Germany*: C-46/93 [1996] IRLR 267 provides useful guidance as to the scope of the substantive and procedural rights of an individual wishing to bring a *Francovich* claim. Where the relevant provision is enacted in an area of policy in relation to which a wide discretion is reserved to the member state the breach must be 'manifest' and 'grave'. Factors relevant to deciding whether a particular failure to implement is sufficiently serious include: the clarity and precision of the EU law provision, the breadth of the discretion reserved to the member state and the question whether the default was intentional. A breach will almost certainly be 'sufficiently serious' where a member state fails to implement a provision in circumstances where the ECJ has already ruled that there is an infringement or where it fails to take any steps to implement the directive before the date specified for implementation (*Dillenkofer v Germany*: C-178/94 [1997] IRLR 60, ECJ).

The member state cannot:

(a)   restrict the right to damages to cases where intentional or negligent default can be established;

(b)   adopt procedural rules governing the bringing of *Francovich* claims which are less favourable than those applying to analogous domestic claims or which have the effect of making it impossible or excessively difficult for individuals to obtain damages;

(c)   impose limits on the amount of damages recoverable which would have the effect that the compensation available was not commensurate with the loss suffered.

(2) *Claims to enforce a directly effective European right*

Secondly, the ECJ's doctrine of 'direct effect' means that, in some circumstances, an enforceable right may be conferred on an individual whether or not there has been any implementing legislation. There are three sources of directly effective rights: Articles of the Treaty, EU regulations and EU directives. An example of the first is the right to equal pay conferred by *Art 157 [141, 119]*. The ECJ decided that this particular provision was directly effective in the case of *Defrenne v Sabena*: 43/75 [1981] 1 All ER 122, [1976] ICR 547.

Not all treaty provisions or directives are directly effective. The precise requirements for direct effect to be established are complex, but the provision concerned must be clear, unconditional and precise.

In *Gharehveran*: C-441/99 [2001] ECR I-7687, [2001] All ER (D) 245 (Oct) the ECJ established an exception to the rule that a directive may have direct effect only if it is clear, unconditional and precise. The problem in that case was that Swedish legislation excluded from employee protection on employer's insolvency (mandated under a directive) not only employees who owned the undertaking (permissible under the directive) but also those whose relatives owned the undertaking (impermissible). The ECJ held that, whilst the member state had a broad discretion as to the system of protection adopted, Sweden had fully exercised that discretion in the system that it had established. That meant that the individual had a precise and unconditional right, capable of being directly effective, to protection under that system. The principle therefore appears to be that, where a provision of EU law would lack direct effect because it offers too much choice to the member state to be clear, unconditional and precise, then if the state in question has in fact decided how it will exercise that choice, but has done so in some way that has a specific deficiency, direct effect can be used to remedy that deficiency. The *Gharehveran* principle has been discussed in a number of recent English cases (for example *Byrne v Motor Insurers' Bureau* [2008] 4 All ER 476, and *Duncombe v SoS for Children, Schools and Families* [2010] IRLR 331, [2010] ICR 815, overturned on other grounds).

A directly effective provision may be either horizontally or vertically directly effective. A provision which has only vertical direct effect is one which creates rights which an individual may enforce against the state but not against other individuals. A provision which has horizontal direct effect creates a right which may be enforced against other individuals.

Some, though not all, directly effective Treaty provisions have horizontal direct effect. An example of the application of horizontal direct effect is the case of *Barber v Guardian Royal Exchange Assurance Group*: C-262/88 [1990] IRLR 240, [1990] ICR 616. When *Barber* was decided, domestic anti-discrimination legislation broadly excluded matters relating to pensions. In *Barber* the ECJ decided that occupational pensions were 'pay' within the meaning of *Art 157 [141, 119]*. As a result, individuals were able to bring a claim under *Art 157* if they suffered sex discrimination in relation to the benefits paid under a pension scheme. EU law filled the gap left by the domestic legislation.

Where a member state fails properly to implement a directive by the due date, a directive may be the source of directly effective rights. However, these rights have only vertical direct effect (*Faccini Dori v Recreb Srl*: C-91/92 [1995] All ER (EC) 1; but cf *CIA Security*

International SA v Signalson: C-194/94 [1996] ECR I-2201, [1996] All ER (EC) 557, ECJ in which a defendant to a counterclaim was entitled to have the domestic provision upon which the counterclaim was based disapplied on the basis that it had not been notified to the European Commission as required by *Directive 83/189/EEC*, thus arguably giving some limited horizontal effect to the directive). The rationale is that the state cannot rely on its own failure to implement the right to defend itself against those who might have been able to exercise the right against it. See also *R v Durham County Council, ex p Huddleston* [2000] 1 WLR 1484, [2000] All ER (D) 297, CA.

For this purpose the 'state' includes any body, whatever its legal form, which has been made responsible by the state for providing a public service under the control of the state, and which has special powers for that purpose (*Foster v British Gas plc* [1990] IRLR 353, [1991] ICR 84 and 463 and see *National Union of Teachers v St Mary's Church of England (Aided) Junior School (Governing Body)* [1997] IRLR 242, [1997] ICR 334, CA – a voluntary aided school is an emanation of the state; see further **38.7** Public Sector Employees). The individual seeking to rely upon the directive must be a citizen of an EU member state *(Bernstein v Immigration Appeal Tribunal* [1988] Imm AR 449), and must be a person of a kind within the scope of the directive (*Verholen*, above).

Direct effect can arise only after expiry of the time allowed for implementation of a directive (*Suffritti v Istituto Nazionale della Previdenza Sociale (INPS)*: C-140/91, C-141/91, C-278/91 and C-279/91 [1992] ECR I-6337, [1993] IRLR 289), though during the transition period, a member state may not adopt a measure that would seriously compromise the result of the directive: *Inter-Environnement Wallonie ASBL v Région Wallone*: C-129/96, [1997] ECR I-7411.

A directly effective right may, in theory, operate in one of two main ways. The right may be used in order to disapply a bar to an existing domestic remedy, or it may create a 'free-standing' right to a remedy. In many cases both types of operation may be appropriate. For instance, in a case similar to *Barber* (above) a claimant may argue either that the EU right works to disapply the exclusion of pension-related discrimination from the existing domestic legislation or that there is a free-standing right to an equal pension under *Art 157 [141, 119]* which, being horizontally directly effective, may be enforced against other individuals. The distinction between the two affects the question of what court or tribunal may consider cases based on EU law, and what time limits apply to them.

It was at one point simply assumed that the employment tribunal had jurisdiction to hear claims based directly upon *Art 157* (*Stevens v Bexley Health Authority* [1989] IRLR 240; *Secretary of State for Scotland and Greater Glasgow Health Board v Wright and Hannah* [1993] 2 CMLR 257, [1991] IRLR 187, EAT). The difficulty was that employment tribunals have a statutory jurisdiction. In other words, they can hear only the cases which statute has specifically conferred jurisdiction upon them to hear. No statute has ever conferred jurisdiction on the employment tribunals to hear cases which are directly based upon *Art 157*. In two cases (*Biggs v Somerset County Council* [1996] IRLR 203 and *Barber v Staffordshire County Council* [1996] IRLR 209) the Court of Appeal stated very clearly that the tribunal does not have jurisdiction to hear 'free-standing' *Art 157* claims. However, the ECJ and EAT have since held that, in the context of enforcing rights based on a directive, a national specialist court which is granted jurisdiction in matters relating to transposing legislation must have jurisdiction to hear claims arising directly from the directive thereby transposed: *Impact v Minister for Agriculture and Food*: C-268/06 [2008] IRLR 552 and *UNISON v Brennan* [2008] IRLR 492, [2008] ICR 955, EAT. This is so provided that it is established that the obligation on the claimant to bring, at the same time, a separate claim based directly on the directive before an ordinary court would involve procedural disadvantages liable to render excessively difficult the exercise of the rights conferred on him by EU law. This principle probably applies to claims based directly on *Art 157*, since employment tribunals' equal pay jurisdiction is derived from domestic equal pay legislation which aims to transpose *Art 157*.

The question of what time limits apply to claims based directly on *Art 157* is not straightforward. Broadly speaking, EU law has left the question of time limits to the member state subject to the following general principles of equivalence and effectiveness:

(i) the time limits applied to the enforcement of EU law rights should be no more restrictive than those which apply to analogous domestic claims (see *Preston v Wolverhampton Healthcare NHS Trust* [2000] IRLR 506, ECJ and [2001] UKHL 5, [2001] IRLR 237, HL);

(ii) the time limits should not make the enforcement of the rights impossible in practice (see *Rewe-Zentralfinanz GmbH v Landwirtschaftskammer für Saarland*: 33/76 [1977] 1 CMLR 533 and *Fisscher v Voorhuis Hengelo BV*: C-128/93 [1994] IRLR 662); and

(iii) provisions which seek to limit the amount of compensation recoverable by restricting the extent to which a claim may be back-dated are less likely to be considered to make enforcement of rights impossible than more straightforward time limits (*Steenhorst-Neerings v Bestuur van de Bedrijfsvereniging voor Detailhandel, Ambachten en Huisvrouwen: C-338/91* [1993] ECR I-5475, [1994] IRLR 244; *Johnson v Chief Adjudication Officer (No 2): C-410/92* [1994] ECR I-5483, [1995] IRLR 157 and *Preston v Wolverhampton Healthcare NHS Trust* [2001] IRLR 237).

There was formerly thought to be a fourth principle, namely that where the right which the claimant seeks to enforce is a vertically directly effective right, time will not begin to run until the directive has been properly implemented (*Emmott v Minister for Social Welfare: C-208/90* [1991] IRLR 387, [1993] ICR 8). But in *Fantask A/S v Industriministeriet (Erhvervsministeriet): C-188/95* [1997] ECR I-6783, [1998] All ER (EC) 1 the ECJ decided that *Emmott* was restricted to its own facts and applied the *Rewe* criteria. See also *Danske Slagterier v Bundesrepublik Deutschland: C-445/06* [2010] All ER (EC) 74.

(3) *Reliance on directly effective European legislation to disapply a domestic bar to a claim*

The third mechanism by which unimplemented European legislation may be given effect in domestic courts and tribunals derives from the decision in *Biggs v Somerset County Council* [1995] IRLR 452, [1995] ICR 811 (affirmed by the Court of Appeal at [1996] IRLR 203, [1996] ICR 364) which concerned a woman who did not qualify for protection against unfair dismissal because she worked part-time. The claim was prompted by the decision of the House of Lords in the *EOC* case (above) that the hours thresholds contained in *Employment Protection (Consolidation) Act 1978* were indirectly discriminatory and could not be justified, contrary to the *Equal Treatment Directive*. The claim was submitted many years after the relevant dismissal. An issue arose, therefore, as to what the relevant time limit was. The claimant argued, inter alia, that her claim was for equal pay under *Art 157 [141, 119]*. The 'pay' in question was compensation for unfair dismissal. Though once a matter of considerable controversy, the ECJ has now decided that unfair dismissal compensation is pay for the purposes of *Art 157 [141, 119]* (*Seymour-Smith* [1999] IRLR 253, [1999] ICR 447, ECJ). The applicant relied upon *Rankin v British Coal Corpn* [1993] IRLR 69 to support an argument that there was no time limit for EU rights other than a requirement that they be brought within a reasonable time. In her submission this meant within a reasonable time of the decision in *EOC* which was the point at which it first became clear that she might have a claim.

The decision of the EAT in *Biggs* was to the effect that the claim was not brought under *Art 157 [141, 119]* but rather under the domestic legislation. The significance of the EU right was that it operated to override and disapply what would otherwise have been a bar to the bringing of proceedings under the domestic law. As the claim was under domestic law the domestic time limit (three months from the date of dismissal) applied unless it was itself inconsistent with EU law which it was not. A radically 'free-standing' European right of the sort argued for by the claimant would not have been enforceable in the employment tribunal as its jurisdiction is strictly defined by statute. No statute has conferred on the industrial tribunal any jurisdiction to consider claims based solely on EU law, which are independent of the operation of any domestic legislation (cf also *McManus v Daylay Foods Ltd* (unreported) EAT/82/95 and *Preston v Wolverhampton Healthcare NHS Trust* [1997] IRLR 233, CA for the application of the same reasoning to claims for a redundancy payment and in relation to the indirectly discriminatory exclusion of part-timers from access to membership of occupational pension schemes respectively). The decision was expressly limited to a consideration of cases based upon *Art 157 [141, 119]*.

The jurisdiction of employment tribunals to determine whether a domestic provision is in fact incompatible with EU law was confirmed by the Court of Appeal in *R (on the application of Manson (Finian)) v Ministry of Defence* [2005] EWCA Civ 1678, [2006] ICR 355, [2005] All ER (D) 69 (Nov).

The direct effect of 'general principles' of EU law

In *Mangold v Helm*: C-144/04 [2006] IRLR 143, the ECJ held that the domestic court was obliged to set aside provisions of national legislation which were incompatible with a directive even before the expiry date for implementation of the directive had passed. This conclusion was based in part on a controversial finding by the ECJ that non-discrimination on grounds of age is a 'general principle' of EU law, the source of which was held to be found in various international instruments and in the constitutional traditions common to the Member States.

There was considerable doubt amongst commentators as to whether *Mangold* was correct. The soundness of this approach and the existence of a general principle of non-discrimination on grounds of age were doubted expressly by the Advocate General in *Palacios de la Villa v Cortefiel Servicios SA* [2007] IRLR 989. However, in *Seda Kucukdeveci v Swedex GmbH & Co KG*: C-555/07 [2010] IRLR 346, [2010] All ER (D) 126 (Feb) the ECJ followed *Mangold*. It held that the *Equal Treatment Framework Directive* is a specific application of a general principle of EU law which prohibits age discrimination; and that this principle was breached by a German law providing that employment before the age of 25 was to be disregarded when calculating service-related notice periods. On this basis, the ECJ held that the national court was required, even in a dispute between private individuals, to disapply the offending national law which was incapable of interpretation in line with the directive. In effect, and controversially, because of the conflict with established principles, this decision gave horizontal direct effect to a directive.

The direct effect, in some circumstances, of the EU Charter of Fundamental Rights

The *EU Charter of Fundamental Rights* has legal effect by *Art 6* of *TEU*, at least until the end of the Brexit transition period (after which see above, **24.1**). The Charter repeats many of the rights contained in the *European Convention on Human Rights* ('*ECHR*'), but also contains additional rights. *Art 6(3)* of the *TEU* provides that fundamental rights, as guaranteed by the *ECHR* and arising from the constitutional traditions of the member states, "shall constitute general principles of the Union's law". On the basis that the *Charter* expresses general principles of EU law, and in the light of the ECJ's decision in *Kucukdeveci* that general principles of EU law should be given horizontal direct effect, it now appears that domestic courts are, in some circumstances, obliged to give direct effect to the rights recognised in the *Charter*, even insofar as they are inconsistent with provisions of national law.

Many commentators initially believed, and the High Court stated at §§155 and 157 in *R (S) v SSHD* [2010] EWHC 705 (Admin), [2010] All ER (D) 16 (Apr), that the UK and Poland had negotiated an effective 'opt out' from the EU Charter, contained in *Protocol 30* to the

Treaty of Lisbon. However, the ECJ in *NS v SSHD* (Case C-493/10) held that the opt-out has no legal effect (§§116-122), and that the *Charter* reflects pre-existing general principles of EU law which themselves have direct horizontal effect.

Art 51(1) of the *Charter* states that the *Charter* applies to member states only when they are implementing EU law. According to the EU Commission, the situations in which the application of the Charter is triggered under *Art 51(1)* include: (1) where national legislative activity and judicial and administrative practices are designed to fulfil obligations under EU law; (2) where a member state authority exercises a discretion which is vested in it by virtue of EU law; and (3) where national measures are linked to the disbursement of EU funds. (See the Commission's '2013 Report on the Application of the EU Charter of Fundamental Rights' (COM(2014) 224 final)). In *R (Zagorski) v BIS* [2010] EWHC 3110 (Admin), [2010] All ER (D) 295 (Nov) the High Court held that *Art 51(1)* requires consideration of whether, in taking a decision, a defendant is acting within the material scope of EU law. The case concerned exportation of drugs. The government had chosen not to legislate on the particular area in question. However, the fact that it was empowered to do so under EU law was a sufficient basis for finding that it was implementing EU law for the purposes of *Art 51(1)*.

It also seems that only some of the rights which are set out in the *Charter* have direct effect. In *Association de Mediation Sociale v Union Local Des Mediation Sociale Synidcats CGT* (case C-176/12) [2014] IRLR 310 the ECJ found that *Art 27* of the *Charter*, on workers' right to information and consultation, did not have horizontal direct effect. It distinguished *Kucukdeveci* on the basis that *Art 27* is qualified by reference to "the conditions provided for by EU law and national laws and practices"; whereas *Art 21*, the right to non-discrimination on grounds of age, is not similarly qualified.

In *Benkharbouche v Embassy of Republic of Sudan* [2015] EWCA Civ 33, [2015] IRLR 301 the Court of Appeal disapplied the immunity from suit conferred by the *State Immunity Act 1978* on the ground that it was incompatible with *Art 47* of the *Charter*, which sets out the right to an effective remedy and a fair trial. This meant that the claimants were able to bring claims which, on their face, were expressly excluded by primary legislation. However, the *State Immunity Act* was disapplied only in relation to rights derived from EU Directives, in relation to discrimination and working time. The effect of the *Charter* was limited to claims "within the scope of EU law", which meant that it did not apply to employment rights, such as unfair dismissal, which are not derived from EU law.

The importance of the Charter was vividly illustrated in *Benkharbouche* by the fact that the Court of Appeal held that the *State Immunity Act 1978* also breached *Arts 6* of the *ECHR* (which is similar to *Art 47* of the *Charter*), as well as *Art 14* of the *ECHR*, but that *s 3* of *Human Rights Act 1998* ('*HRA*') (which requires legislation to be read compatibly with the ECHR so far as possible) did not enable it to be interpreted compatibly with *Art 6*. The *HRA* does not permit primary legislation to be disapplied; whereas the *Charter* does.

The Court of Appeal's decision was upheld by the Supreme Court (see [2017] UKSC 62; [2017] ICR 1327).

For an expression of judicial surprise at the far-reaching effects the *Charter* may now have, see §14 of Mostyn J's judgment in *R (AB) v SSHD* [2013] EWHC 3453: "The constitutional significance of this can hardly be overstated. The Human Rights Act incorporated into our domestic law large parts, but by no means all, of the European Convention on Human Rights. Some parts were deliberately missed out by Parliament. The Charter of Fundamental Rights of the European Union contains, I believe, all of those missing parts and a great deal more. Moreover, that much wider Charter of Rights would remain part of our domestic law even if the Human Rights Act were repealed."

24.4 EU REQUIREMENTS AFFECTING EMPLOYMENT LAW

EU employment legislation has been enacted or proposed in relation to a wide variety of different areas, notably the following:

(a)   free movement of labour;

(b)   equal access to social security benefits;

(c)   equal pay and equal treatment;

(d)   information on terms of employment;

(e)   redundancy procedure;

(f)   rights on the transfer of an undertaking;

(g)   health and safety at work;

(h)   information and consultation;

(i)   agency workers;

(j)   posted workers;

(k)   employees of insolvent employers;

(l)   fixed-term workers;

(m)   the regulation of pay in the financial services sector.

These are examined briefly in the following paragraphs. More detailed expositions of these areas may be found elsewhere in this book: see the cross-references below.

24.5 FREE MOVEMENT OF LABOUR

Articles 45–48 [39–42, 48–51] of the *TFEU* require member states to permit the free movement of workers between member states. No discrimination based on nationality may be exercised against EU citizens in relation to employment, remuneration or other conditions of work and employment. Free access to employment is a fundamental right, and there must be a judicial remedy against decisions which refuse the benefit of that right to EU citizens (*Union Nationale des Entraîneurs et Cadres Techniques Professionnels du Football (UNECTEF) v Heylens*: C-222/86 [1987] ECR 4097, [1989] 1 CMLR 901, ECJ). Directives and regulations relating to these Articles have been passed. The UK has complied with these requirements so that EU citizens have a right to enter the country to take or seek work without the necessity of obtaining a work permit.

Article 45 [39, 48] of the *TFEU*, as a directly enforceable provision, was relied upon by the EAT in its decision in *Bossa v Nordstress Ltd* [1998] IRLR 284, [1998] ICR 694 to disapply *ss 4* and *8(1)* of the *Race Relations Act 1976*. These sections had excluded those whose work was wholly or mainly outside Great Britain from bringing claims in the employment tribunal.

Directives regulate the mutual recognition of qualifications in member states for professions such as medicine and dentistry. *Directive 2005/36/EC* deals with mutual recognition of professional qualifications. EU nationals employed or seeking work here have the right to remain and to bring their families with them (see also FOREIGN EMPLOYEES (**27**)).

24.6 EQUAL ACCESS TO SOCIAL SECURITY BENEFITS

TFEU Art 48 [42, 51] provides for the passing by the Council and Parliament of the EU of such measures in the field of social security as are necessary to provide freedom of movement to workers. Such regulations, which provide for the aggregation of social security benefits which may have been paid in different member states, and for the payment of benefit in one member state where contributions have been made in another member state, have been passed (*Regulation 883/2004*; *Regulation 987/2009*). Equal treatment between men and women in matters of social security, including occupational social security schemes, is largely dealt with by *Directive 79/7/EEC* and *Directive 2006/54/EC*; however, the ECJ has also held certain domestic social security provisions to be contrary to the *Equal Treatment Directive 76/207/EEC* (*Meyers v Adjudication Officer*: C-116/94 [1995] IRLR 498, a UK case about 'Family Credit'). This issue, and "citizens' rights" more generally, has been a thorny issue in the Brexit negotiations. The Withdrawal Agreement provides for some existing rights to be retained beyond the transition period, but many aspects remain to be negotiated between the UK and the EU. A detailed account of this area is beyond the scope of this book.

24.7   EQUAL PAY AND EQUAL TREATMENT

Equality between men and women is an explicit objective of the EU (*Art 8 [3(2)]*). In all its activities, the EU must aim to eliminate inequalities, and to promote equality between men and women (*Art 8*). *Art 157 [141, 119]* obliges each member state to ensure and maintain the principle that men and women should receive equal pay for equal work. Further, *Council Directive 76/207/EEC* required member states to take the measures necessary to implement the principle of equal treatment for men and women in relation to the following stages of employment: engagement, training, promotion, working conditions and dismissal; and *Directive 75/117/EEC* required member states to take measures necessary to achieve equal pay between the sexes. *Directives 76/207/EEC* and *75/117/EEC* were repealed and replaced by *Directive 2006/54/EC*.

The UK sought to comply with the requirements imposed by *Art 157* and *Council Directives 75/117/EEC* and *76/207/EEC*. However, in a number of cases, the ECJ held that the UK had failed to comply fully with its EU obligations and further legislation had to be introduced. See eg *EC Commission v United Kingdom of Great Britain and Northern Ireland*: 61/81 [1982] ECR 2601, [1982] IRLR 333, [1982] ICR 578, ECJ. The domestic courts have also proven to be willing to find, without a reference to the ECJ, that domestic legislation is incompatible with European provisions. See eg *Equal Opportunities Commission v Secretary of State for Trade and Industry* [2007] IRLR 327. Domestic law protection from sex discrimination is now contained in the *Equality Act 2010*. See also EQUAL PAY (23) and DISCRIMINATION AND EQUAL OPPORTUNITIES – I (12).

In October 1992 a *Directive on the Protection of Pregnant Women at Work* (*Directive 92/85/EEC*) was adopted, which has led to the inclusion of a number of new and improved maternity rights provisions in the *Employment Rights Act 1996*. See also MATERNITY AND PARENTAL RIGHTS (33).

Parental leave. The government sought to implement the *Parental Leave Directive* (*Directive 96/34/EC*, now replaced by *Directive 2010/18/EC*) by bringing into force the *Maternity and Parental Leave Regulations 1999 (SI 1999/3312)*. The domestic provisions confer a right to leave only on parents of children born on or after 15 December 1999. The compatibility of this restriction with EU law was referred to the ECJ (*R v Secretary of State for Trade and Industry, ex p Trades Union Congress* [2000] IRLR 565). Consequent amendments were made to ensure compliance with the directive: see the *Maternity and Parental Leave (Amendment) Regulations 2001 (SI 2001/4010)*. The *Parental Leave (EU Directive) Regulations 2013* implemented *Directive 2010/18/EC* by amending provisions relating to parental leave in the *Employment Rights Act 1996* and the *Maternity and Parental Leave Regulations 1999*.

Part-timers. The *Part-time Workers (Prevention of Less Favourable Treatment) Regulations 2000 (SI 2000/1551)* implement the *EU Part-time Work Directive (97/81/EC)*.

In December 1991 the Commission adopted a *Recommendation on the Protection of the Dignity of Men and Women at Work (92/131/EEC)*, which is not legally binding, but will be taken into account by courts and tribunals (see **24.1** above). It may be especially relevant to complaints of sex discrimination founded upon incidents of sexual harassment (see DISCRIMINATION AND EQUAL OPPORTUNITIES – I **(12)**). A further *Recommendation on Child Care* was adopted in March 1992.

Discrimination on grounds other than sex. Article 19 [13] of the *TFEU* confers a power on the EU to legislate against discrimination on grounds of racial or ethnic origin, religion or belief, disability, age and sexual orientation. The European Council has adopted two directives which are intended to give effect to the broad anti-discrimination principles found in *Art 19* of the *TFEU*.

The first is *Council Directive 2000/43/EC* of 29 June 2000 implementing the principle of equal treatment between persons irrespective of racial or ethnic origin. The directive prohibits direct and (unless it is objectively justified) indirect discrimination on grounds of racial or ethnic origin in both the public and private sectors. It does not prohibit discrimination on grounds of nationality. Harassment is expressly to be treated as an act of direct discrimination. Victimisation is also prohibited. There is a genuine occupational requirement defence. The provisions of the directive are now implemented by the *Equality Act 2010*.

The second directive is *Council Directive 2000/78/EC* of 27 November 2000 establishing a general framework for equal treatment in employment and occupation. The directive prohibits direct and unjustified indirect discrimination on grounds of 'religion or belief, disability, age or sexual orientation'. It applies to both public and private sectors, prohibits harassment and victimisation, and includes an 'occupational requirement' defence. *Article 5* of the directive introduces a duty to take proportionate and appropriate measures to enable disabled persons to have access to, participate in or advance in employment or to undergo training which is analogous to the obligation imposed to by the *Equality Act 2010, ss 20* and *39(5)* to make reasonable adjustments: see *Navas (Chacon) v Eurest Colectividades SA*: C-13/05 [2006] ECR I-6467, [2006] IRLR 706, [2007] ICR 1, ECJ. *Article 6* creates a defence of objective justification in cases of direct age discrimination. The directive is now implemented in Great Britain by the *Equality Act 2010*.

24.8   INFORMATION ON TERMS OF EMPLOYMENT

Directive 91/533/EEC (the *Information on Conditions of Employment Directive*) was adopted in October 1991. As a result of this directive, the United Kingdom, by means of amending the *Employment Protection (Consolidation) Act 1978* (now the *Employment Rights Act 1996*), extended the rights which already existed for employees to receive written particulars of the terms of their employment (see **8.4** CONTRACT OF EMPLOYMENT).

24.9   REDUNDANCY PROCEDURE

Directive 98/59/EC contains requirements for the approximation of the laws of member states relating to collective redundancies. This was complied with by the enactment of provisions now to be found in *TULR(C)A 1992, ss 188–198*. See **40.2–40.6** REDUNDANCY – II.

The ECJ found that by restricting the obligation to consult prior to collective redundancies to circumstances where the employer recognises a trade union in respect of the class of employees affected, the UK had failed properly to implement the predecessor to *Directive 98/59/EC, Directive 75/129/EEC (EC Commission v United Kingdom*: C-383/92 [1994] ECR I-2479, [1994] IRLR 412, [1994] ICR 664, ECJ). In order to remedy this, the *Collective Redundancies and Transfer of Undertakings (Protection of Employment) (Amendment) Regulations 1995 (SI 1995/2587)* were enacted (see also **24.10** below).

24.10 RIGHTS ON TRANSFER OF BUSINESS

The *Transfer of Undertakings (Protection of Employment) Regulations 1981 (SI 1981/1794)* (now repealed and replaced by the *Transfer of Undertakings (Protection of Employment) Regulations 2006 (SI 2006/246)* were intended to implement the requirements of *Directive 77/187/EEC* (the *Acquired Rights Directive*). In fact, the *1981 Regulations* proved to be defective in several respects, and various amendments were made by the *Trade Union Reform and Employment Rights Act 1993* in an attempt to bring them into line with the directive. However, subsequent to those amendments being made, a further failure properly to comply was identified in *EC Commission v United Kingdom*: C–382/92 [1994] ECR I-2435, [1994] IRLR 412, [1994] ICR 664 when the ECJ found that by restricting the obligation to consult prior to a transfer to circumstances where the employer recognises a trade union in respect of the class of employees affected, the UK had failed properly to implement *Directive 77/187/EEC*. In order to remedy this, the *Regulations* mentioned in **24.9** above *(SI 1995/2587)* were enacted.

On 12 March 2001, a new *Transfers Directive (2001/23/EC)* came into force. It was intended to codify the *Acquired Rights Directive (77/187/EEC)* and the amendments thereto adopted in 1998 (which are described in the main text). The *Transfer of Undertakings (Protection of Employment) Regulations 2006 (SI 2006/246)* came into force with effect from 6 April 2006 and are intended to implement the *Transfers Directive*.

(See Transfer of Undertakings **(53)**.)

24.11 HEALTH AND SAFETY

Between 1977 and 1986, the EU adopted directives on various aspects of health and safety, including safety signs, lead, asbestos and noise. A framework directive, *Directive 89/391/EEC* on the introduction of measures to encourage improvements in the safety and health of workers at work, was adopted in 1989. A number of statutory instruments have implemented the framework directive in national law (eg the *Management of Health and Safety at Work Regulations 1999 (SI 1999/3242)*, the *Health and Safety (Consultation with Employees) Regulations 1996 (SI 1996/1513)*, the *Control of Substances Hazardous to Health Regulations 2002 (SI 2002/2677)*).

The framework directive also provides for further directives, known as 'daughter' directives, to be made in particular areas (eg work equipment, personal protective equipment). A number of daughter directives have been made (eg *Directive 89/654/EEC* concerning the minimum safety and health requirements for the workplace, *Directive 2009/104/EC* concerning the minimum safety and health requirements for the use of work equipment by workers at work) and implemented in national law by health and safety regulations (eg the *Workplace (Health, Safety and Welfare) Regulations 1992 (SI 1992/3004)*).

(See **28.25** Health and Safety at Work – I.)

24.12 WORKING TIME

One directive which was adopted despite the objections of the UK is the *Working Time Directive 93/104/EC* (now repealed and replaced by *Directive 2003/88/EC*). It provided, with certain exceptions, for a maximum 48-hour week including overtime, averaged over four months. There was also provision for a minimum daily rest period of 11 consecutive hours, for a weekly break of not less than 35 consecutive hours, and for restrictions upon the length of night shifts. Finally there was provision for a minimum of four weeks' paid holiday per annum.

Whilst the directive was adopted under the provisions of the *TFEU* relating to Health and Safety at Work, the view of the UK government was that, in substance, it was an attempt to regulate conditions of employment, a matter which is outside the EU's competence. The UK brought a challenge to the directive in the European Court of Justice which was rejected by the Court (*United Kingdom v EU Council*: C-84/94 [1997] IRLR 30, [1997] ICR 443).

In *Dominguez v Centre Informatique du Centre Ouest Atlantique* [2012] IRLR 321 the ECJ held that the right to four weeks' paid annual leave in *Art 7(1)* of the directive has vertical direct effect. Thus, the claimant was to be able to rely directly on *Art 7(1)*, but only if the referring court was satisfied that her employer, which dealt with social security, was an emanation of the state.

The *Working Time Regulations 1998 (SI 1998/1833)* came into force on 1 October 1998. The provisions of the *Regulations* relating to annual leave are summarised in HOLIDAYS **(30)**; as to the provisions relating to hours of work and rest breaks, see **29.15** HEALTH AND SAFETY AT WORK – II. In *R (on the application of the Broadcasting, Entertainment, Cinematographic and Theatre Union) v Secretary of State for Trade and Industry*: C-173/99 [2001] IRLR 559, [2001] ICR 1152 the ECJ held that *reg 13* of the *Regulations*, restricting entitlement to paid annual leave to workers continuously employed for 13 weeks by the same employer, constituted an impermissible restriction on the rights conferred by the *Working Time Directive*. Consequential alterations to the *Regulations* were made by the *Working Time (Amendment) Regulations 2002 (SI 2002/3128)* with effect from 6 April 2003: see HOLIDAYS **(30)**. In *European Commission v United Kingdom*: C-484/04 [2006] ECR I-7471, [2006] IRLR 888, [2007] ICR 592, the ECJ held that the UK had failed to fulfil its obligations under the *Working Time Directive* by issuing guidance on the *Regulations* which advised employers that they must make sure that workers can take their rest, but were not required to make sure they do take their rest.

The *Working Time Directive (93/104/EEC)* excluded employment in certain sectors from its scope. The sectors were: road, rail, air, inland waterway and lake transport, sea fishing, other work at sea, and doctors in training. *Directive 2000/34/EC* extended the application of the directive to non-mobile workers in the excluded sectors (with a special transitional period for its application to doctors in training). A consolidating *Directive 2003/88/EC* was adopted on 4 November 2003 and this is now the *Directive* governing this area (see WORKING TIME **(58)**). This has been implemented by the *Working Time (Amendment) Regulations 2003 (SI 2003/1684)*.

A specific directive covering the organisation of the working time of seafarers (*1999/63/EC*) was adopted on 21 June 1999. Domestic provision is made for sea fishermen and the inland water way sector by the *Fishing Vessels (Working Time: Sea Fishermen) Regulations 2004 (SI 2004/1713)* and the *Merchant Shipping (Working Time: Inland Waterways) Regulations 2003 (SI 2003/3049)*.

24.13   INFORMATION AND CONSULTATION

The *European Works Councils Directive 94/45/EC* (now repealed and replaced by *Directive 2009/38/EC*) was adopted under the Social Protocol procedure. See EMPLOYEE PARTICIPATION **(17)**. The original *Directive* was implemented with effect from 15 January 2000 by the *Transnational Information and Consultation of Employees Regulations 1999 (SI 1999/3323)*. *Directive 2009/38/EC* was implemented by way of amendment to the *1999 Regulations*: see the *Transnational Information and Consultation of Employees (Amendment) Regulations 2010 (SI 2010/1088)*.

The *Directive of the European Parliament and of the Council 2002/14/EC* establishing a general framework for informing and consulting employees in the EU has been implemented in the UK by the *Information and Consultation of Employees Regulations 2004 (SI 2004/3426)*.

24.14 AGENCY WORKERS

The *EC Temporary Workers Directive (Directive 2008/104/EC)* provides for, amongst other things:

- equal treatment between temporary agency workers and permanent workers from the commencement of their work in terms of basic working and employment conditions (including working time, overtime, breaks, rest periods, night work, holidays and pay);

- the ability for member states to derogate from this by way of collective agreements or through agreements between social partners at national level (which the UK has done by implementing a 12-week qualifying period for agency workers' rights to equal basic working and employment conditions, which has been agreed by the TUC and the CBI); and

- temporary agency workers to be informed about permanent employment opportunities with the hirer.

The UK implemented the directive through the *Agency Workers Regulations 2010 (SI 2010/93)* which came into force in October 2011.

See TEMPORARY AND SEASONAL EMPLOYEES **(47)**.

24.15 POSTED WORKERS

The *Posted Workers Directive (Directive 96/71/EC)* aims to strike a balance between workers' rights on the one hand, and freedom of movement of services and freedom of establishment on the other. It aims to address lack of clarity about which law applies to workers who are posted from one undertaking within the EU to another; to avoid local terms and conditions being undermined by the use of "cheaper" foreign workers; and to avoid abuse of foreign workers. Broadly, it provides that temporarily posted workers should enjoy the same basic minimum employment rights as workers in the country to which they are posted. The rights covered by the directive include maximum work periods, minimum paid holidays, minimum rates of pay, health and safety and hygiene at work, and protective measures for pregnant women or those who have recently given birth. It does not cover all statutory employment rights; for example, the right not to be unfairly dismissed is outside the scope of the directive.

See FOREIGN EMPLOYEES **(27.3)**.

24.16 EMPLOYEES OF INSOLVENT EMPLOYERS

Minimum rights for the employees of insolvent employers were specified by *Directive 80/987/EEC*, which has now been repealed and replaced by *Directive 2008/94/EC* (see **32.1** INSOLVENCY OF EMPLOYER).

24.17 FIXED-TERM WORKERS

On 28 June 1999, the Council adopted a directive transposing into European law a framework agreement on fixed-term work (*1999/70/EC*). The directive was implemented in the UK by the *Fixed-term Employees (Prevention of Less Favourable Treatment) Regulations 2002 (SI 2002/2034)*. It prohibits less favourable treatment of fixed-term workers on account of their fixed-term status, save where such treatment is objectively justified; and restricts successive renewals of fixed-term contracts (see **48.8** TEMPORARY AND SEASONAL EMPLOYEES).

24.18 THE REGULATION OF PAY IN THE FINANCIAL SERVICES SECTOR

Pay in the financial services sector is regulated by remuneration codes in the Financial Conduct Authority Handbook and in the Prudential Regulation Authority Rulebook. Most of the rules on pay contained in the handbooks are required by EU law, namely the *CRD IV Directive (2013/36/EU)* and accompanying *Capital Requirements Regulation (Regulation 575/2013)*; the *Alternative Investment Fund Managers Directive (2011/61/EU)*; and the *UCITS V Directive (Directive 2014/91/EU)*.

The detailed rules contained in these instruments are beyond the scope of this chapter. Their overall purpose is to ensure that remuneration is consistent with and promotes sound and effective risk management. In other words, they are designed to de-incentivise excessively risky and short-termist behaviour by bankers and other financiers. One of the more important rules is the so-called 'bonus cap' for bankers. The cap is required by the *CRD IV Directive*. The value of an individual's variable pay (or bonus) should be no greater than the value of his or her fixed pay (or basic salary); in other words, the ratio of bonus to basic salary should not exceed 1:1. However, the ratio can be raised to 1:2 with the express permission of shareholders.

25   Financial penalties on employers

25.1   In relation to claims presented on or after 6 April 2014 a new power has been granted to employment tribunals to impose financial penalties on employers: *s 12A* of the *Employment Tribunals Act 1996*, introduced by *s 16* of the *Enterprise and Regulatory Reform Act 2013* (the implementation date being dealt with by *s 24* of that *Act*).

An employment tribunal may do so where it concludes that the employer has breached any of the worker's rights and it is of the opinion that the breach has 'one or more aggravating features'.

25.2   There is no guidance in the *Act* as to what is an aggravating factor. However, the explanatory notes suggested that a tribunal might consider 'the size of the employer; the duration of the breach; or the behaviour of the employer and employee', as well as whether the action was 'deliberate or committed with malice, the employer was an organisation with a dedicated human resources team, or where the employer had repeatedly breached the employment right concerned'. On the other hand, it might be less likely to find an aggravating factor where the business is new or small or the breach was the result of a genuine mistake.

25.3   Having found one or more aggravating factors, the tribunal must decide whether to order the employer to pay a penalty. In considering this question, it must have regard to the employer's ability to pay.

The level of the penalty is to be:

- Where no financial award is made against the employer on the claim, in the range £100 and £5,000;

- In relation to any other single claim where a financial award is made against the employer, the penalty is 50% of that award (subject to a minimum and maximum of £100 and £5,000); for these purposes:

    – the amount of the award to be taken into account ignores any uplift made by reason of a failure to comply with an order of the tribunal;

    – two or more claims in respect of the same act and the same worker are to be treated as a single claim;

- Where the tribunal considers two or more claims involving different workers (but the same employer), then the penalty shall be no more than £5,000 for each claim, provided that it should be no more than 50% of any financial award on that claim.

Any penalty which is imposed is payable to the Secretary of State. There is a discount of 50% for payment within 21 days after the day on which the penalty notice is sent to the employer. The Government has indicated (in its Good Work Plan) an intention that the maximum level of the award should be increased from £5,000 to £20,000.

25.4   A further and entirely separate penalty regime was introduced by *Part 2A* of the *Employment Tribunals Act 1996* (as inserted from 6 April 2016 by the *Small Business, Enterprise and Employment Act 2015*). This allows for a financial penalty to be imposed upon an employer if it fails to pay a sum awarded by an employment tribunal (including an award of costs) or a sum agreed on a conciliated settlement (in each case including interest), or an instalment due in relation to such sums. The process is one for an enforcement officer (appointed by the Secretary of State under *s 37M*) and first requires a warning notice to be issued. The penalty may be 50% of the unpaid amount of the relevant sum on the date specified in the warning notice (subject to a minimum of £100 and a maximum of £5,000).

Financial penalties on employers

An employer may challenge the issue of a penalty by an appeal to an employment tribunal. A form for these purposes, "Employment tribunal: penalty enforcement" is available on the Department for Business, Energy & Industrial Strategy website. However, the penalty is payable to the Secretary of State, rather than to the unpaid claimant (*s 37F(2)*).

25.5 Where an award is registered by a claimant on or after 18 December 2018, there is the option to engage in a "naming scheme" (provided that the award is greater than £200). The naming scheme was introduced following a recommendation of the Taylor Review of Modern Working Practices, which referred to "the huge success of the naming and shaming regime for employers who fail to pay the [National Minimum Wage]". The Department for Business, Energy and Industrial Strategy Guidance describes the naming scheme as providing "a new incentive, alongside any financial penalty, for employers to settle outstanding employment tribunal awards quickly". There is a "naming round" every quarter. Once an award is registered, a naming notification letter is sent to the employer allowing written representations to be made as to why naming should not take place. Those reasons may be one of the following: proof that the payment has been made in full; that there is a risk of personal harm to an individual, their family or other employees; that there are national security risks; or that there are other reasons why it would not be in the public interest to name the employer. The naming scheme does not presently extend to ACAS conciliated settlements.

25.6 A response to a written Parliamentary question given on 4 January 2017, revealed that since April 2016 the Department for Business, Energy and Industrial Strategy had issued 60 penalty notices as a result of 164 warning notices to employers for failure to comply with employment tribunal orders to pay compensation to applicants. As a result of the employment tribunal penalty regime £83,000 in previously unpaid awards had been secured for claimants. A more recent response, dated 21 January 2020, stated that this figure had increased to over £2.5 million (of which £1.3m followed only a warning letter and a further £1.2m followed a warning letter and penalty notice).

26   Financial regulation in the UK

26.1   RECENT HISTORY OF FINANCIAL REGULATION IN THE UK

The bedrock legislation of financial regulation in the United Kingdom is the *Financial Services and Markets Act 2000*, usually abbreviated to '*FSMA*' (pronounced fizz-ma) – or occasionally, depending on the context, 'the Act'. As part of New Labour's regulatory overhaul, the various regulatory streams (including self-regulatory organisations) that had operated in parallel (and in some cases overlapping) were superseded by and consolidated into the Financial Services Authority ('FSA'). A company limited by guarantee, the FSA had originally been incorporated as the Securities and Investments Board ('SIB') in 1985 and was renamed in 1997.

Following the global financial crisis of 2007–08, there was a concerted effort by governments and regulators, both domestically and on a global scale, to diagnose shortcomings in the existing regulatory system. In the UK, the Government conducted several consultations before issuing its White Paper, 'A new approach to financial regulation: the blueprint for reform' in June 2011. This White paper, together with some recommendations made by the Independent Commission on Banking ('ICB') in September 2011, culminated in the *Financial Services Act 2012* ('*FSA 2012*'). The *FSA 2012* left *FSMA* in force, albeit subject to substantial amendments.

The report of the Parliamentary Commission on Banking Standards ('PCBS') followed shortly after, in June 2013, with a range of criticisms and recommendations. In December 2013, the *Financial Services (Banking Reform) Act 2013* ('*FS(BR)A 2013*') obtained Royal Assent. The *FS(BR)A 2013*, influenced in large part by the PCBS report, introduced the senior managers and certification regime ('SMCR'), again by amending *FSMA*. This has three main components: the senior managers regime ('SMR'); the certification regime; and the Conduct Rules. It transforms the regulatory landscape, imposing substantial additional burdens on firms within scope (currently, deposit takers and the largest investment firms). The *FS(BR)A 2013* also introduced, to somewhat less fanfare, the Senior Insurance Managers Regime ('SIMR') (which is beyond the scope of this Chapter). The SMCR and SIMR went live on 7 March 2016 for certain firms, and the scope has now been expanded to all firms since 9 December 2019.

26.2   THE REGULATORS

On 1 April 2013, the *FSA 2012*'s most significant structural reform came into effect when the FSA was replaced by three 'new' regulators: the Financial Conduct Authority ('FCA'); the Prudential Regulatory Authority ('PRA'); and the Financial Policy Committee ('FPC'). For these purposes, it will suffice to describe the roles of the FCA and PRA.

26.3   The FCA

The FCA stepped into the shoes of the late FSA: section 1A(1) FSMA explicitly provides that '*The body corporate previously known as the Financial Services Authority is renamed as the Financial Conduct Authority.*' What is now the FCA is, therefore, the same company that was incorporated as the SIB in 1985. As such, the FCA is not a creature of statute, and is therefore not limited by the scope of its statutory powers but rather by its constitution: *R v Rollins* [2010] UKSC 39, [2010] 4 All ER 880.

The FCA is the 'conduct of business' regulator, ensuring that 'regulated activities' are carried out (i) only by persons with permission to do so and (ii) in compliance with applicable rules. The former role is often described as policing the 'regulatory perimeter'.

26.3 Financial regulation in the UK

The FCA also has responsibility for financial crime, such as the high profile LIBOR-rigging fraud prosecutions. Another large aspect of the FCA's remit is quasi-criminal breaches such as market abuse (currently a directly applicable EU regime in the *Market Abuse Regulation 594/2014*) and, since April 2015, anticompetitive practices in financial services. In these criminal and quasi-criminal spheres, the FCA's powers are not limited to regulated persons but may be exercised against the world at large. As a rule, the FCA's powers tend to be broader and less inhibited within the regulatory perimeter, on the basis that regulated persons have voluntarily undertaken to be subject to regulatory oversight.

26.4 The PRA

The PRA, part of the Bank of England (and for that reason sometimes referred to as 'the Bank' in regulatory contexts), is the micro-prudential regulator of deposit-takers, insurance companies and a small number of systemically important investment firms. These are the firms whose failure or capital inadequacy would have a serious detrimental impact on the UK financial market more broadly. All such firms are concurrently regulated by the FCA as well, and are therefore known as 'dual-regulated firms'. By a similar token, all regulated individuals at such firms are subject to regulation by both the FCA and the PRA. To facilitate the co-ordinated exercise of powers over the same firms, each regulator is required to consult the other before taking certain steps, such as varying permissions or taking disciplinary action. The regulators are also required by *section 3E* of *FSMA* to maintain a memorandum of understanding.

26.5 WHO IS REGULATED

Regulated activities are defined by *section 22* of *FSMA* and the Regulated Activities Order ('RAO'), secondary legislation under FSMA. The FCA has also issued guidance on the 'regulatory perimeter' in its Handbook, Chapter 'PERG', which explains the FCA's understanding of certain terms used in the statutory definitions, including illustrative examples. It is a criminal offence, known as a breach of the 'general prohibition', to carry out regulated activities without either having permission to do so pursuant to *Part 4A* of *FSMA* or being exempt: *section 19* of *FSMA*. A person who has *Part 4A* permission is an "authorised person" (not to be confused with 'approved person' – see below) – for convenience, these are often referred to simply as "firms" which is an interchangeable term in most contexts. It should be noted that *Part 4A* permissions relate to specified activities, and indeed specified products: an authorised person who carries out activities beyond the scope of its *Part 4A* permission does so in breach of the general prohibition.

All firms are now subject to the SMCR. The vast majority operate under a 'core regime'. Most of these will have switched from the old Approved Persons Regime ("APR") to the SMCR on 9 December 2019. Particularly large or complex business, comprising less than one percent of all FCA-regulated firms as well as dual-regulated firms, are subject to the more stringent requirements of the 'enhanced regime'. Most of these firms have been subject to the SMCR since March 2016). A 'limited scope' regime applies to certain types of firms, most notably sole traders and EEA branches. (In some circumstances, firms may 'opt up' to a more onerous tier.) Firms in each of these tranches are usually referred to in brief as 'enhanced firms', 'core firms' and 'limited scope firms'.

For the avoidance of doubt, it should be noted that the statutory language remains unchanged, inasmuch as the regulators still 'approve' persons to perform certain functions under *section 61*: under the SMCR, these persons are generally referred to as 'senior managers', despite technically being 'approved persons' for the purposes of FSMA and the regulators' rulebooks. The terms 'approved person', 'senior manager' and 'SMF manager' are therefore interchangeable, at least for the purposes of this chapter.

While the APR no longer applies to firms, it will continue to have potential relevance, as the limitation period for the FCA to bring regulatory proceedings is two years from the date of constructive knowledge, having regard to the rules in force at the time of any breach. (The APR also has continuing relevance to appointed representatives and benchmark administrators, although the latter will come within the SMCR from 7 December 2020.)

26.6   THE SENIOR MANAGERS AND CERTIFICATION REGIME

As set out above, the SMCR was introduced by the *FS(BR)A 2013* and came into force on 7 March 2016. The purpose of the SMCR was to ensure that responsibility for important parts of the business would be tied to specified individuals. The hope was not only that such a system would facilitate enforcement proceedings when things have gone wrong, but also that responsible individuals would be in a position to decrease the risk of failure in the first place – and would be incentivised to do so.

The SMCR has three main components. First, the SMR, which governs the performance of senior management functions by individuals who are required to be appropriately approved by the regulators. Secondly, the certification regime, whereby firms themselves ensure that individuals who carry out 'significant harm functions' are 'fit and proper' to do so. Finally, all 'employees' are bound by the Code of Conduct rules, even if they are neither approved nor certified.

26.7   Senior Management Responsibilities and Functions

The statutory architecture of the SMR – ie the senior management aspect of the SMCR – is fundamentally the same as the APR: there are particular functions which can only be carried out by individuals with express approval by the appropriate regulators: *section 59* and *Part 5* of *FSMA* more broadly.

Under *section 59* of *FSMA*, firms must take reasonable care to ensure that no person performs a controlled function under an arrangement entered into by it, or by its contractor, in relation to the carrying on by A of a regulated activity, unless that person is acting in accordance with an approval: in other words, they must not only be approved but approved for that specific function. 'Arrangement' is defined at *subsection (10)* as *'any kind of arrangement for the performance of a function of A which is entered into by A or any contractor of his with another person'* and expressly includes – but is not limited to – appointing someone to an office, making her a partner or employing her (whether under a contract of service or otherwise).

Subsection (3) leaves it to the regulators to determine what those controlled functions – which for present purposes is synonymous with 'senior management functions', or 'SMFs' – should be, and only individuals carrying out such functions require approval. (Other functions formerly requiring approval under the APR may require certification under the SMCR: see below.) These are set out at SUP 10C.4, 'Specification of functions'.

It is the firm who applies for approval ('the applicant'), not the prospective approved person ('the candidate'). Firms must vet candidates to ensure that they are fit and proper before applying: *section 60A* of *FSMA*. The regulator may only grant the application where it is satisfied that the candidate is a fit and proper person to perform the function to which the application relates: *section 61(1)*. *FSMA* gives a flexible definition of 'fit and proper', allowing (not requiring) both applicant and regulator to have regard to whether the candidate (a) has obtained a qualification, (b) has undergone, or is undergoing, training, (c) possesses a level of competence, or (d) has the personal characteristics, for the functions to which the application relates. Both regulators have issued rules elucidating the matters which will be taken into account: the FCA in its Handbook, Chapter 'FIT', and the PRA in its Rulebook, Chapter 'Fitness and Propriety'. These both set out three limbs. The first is 'honesty, integrity and reputation': this compasses criminal and regulatory offences, adverse civil or disciplinary findings, and connections to firms with such. The second is 'competence and capability', which takes into account training, experience and availability, as well as drug or alcohol abuse inasmuch as it affects the individual's ability to perform the relevant function. The third is financial soundness: whether the individual is bankrupt or has failed to satisfy a judgment debt or award – this is not aimed at those of limited financial means. The regulator may attach conditions or a time limitation to the approval when granting it: *section 61(2B)* of *FSMA*.

Different forms apply for different types of application: a new approved person submits Long Form A, a current approved person whose fitness and propriety is unchanged from their previous application (but is now applying for a new function, say) uses Short Form A, whereas an internal transfer calls for Form E. Form A requires the candidate to sign a declaration to the effect that: the information in the application relating to her is accurate; the FCA is authorised to make further enquiries; and she understands the regulatory requirements applicable to her.

Most firms which were, until 9 December 2019, under the APR, will have had their APR functions converted to the corresponding SMF automatically, ie without the need for any paperwork. Enhanced firms, and those core firms which have a Non-Executive Chair, ought to have completed a conversion notification form (Form K).

Whereas usually the FCA and PRA only have jurisdiction over regulated individuals, they are empowered to impose financial penalties on individuals who perform a controlled function without approval, if they could reasonably be expected to have known that they were doing so: *section 63A*. The limitation period is 6 years from the day when the regulator became aware of the unapproved performance of a controlled function (or 3 years, if the performance took place before 8 June 2010).

Senior management functions should not be confused with senior management responsibilities. Some of these have been prescribed by the regulators ('prescribed responsibilities'), depending on the applicable regime: see the table at SYSC 24 Annex 1 4.2R. Enhanced firms are also required to allocate 'overall responsibility' for each of their activities, business areas and management functions: SYSC 26.3.1R (SYSC 26 only applies to enhanced firms: SYSC 26.1.1R). Each responsibility must be allocated to a named senior manager. Attached to the application for approval must be a 'statement setting out the aspects of the affairs of the authorised person concerned which it is intended that the person will be responsible for managing in performing the function': *section 60(2A)* of *FSMA*. This is known as a 'statement of responsibilities'. Any significant change to the individual's responsibilities, such as addition, removal or re-allocation, will require the firm to submit a revised statement of responsibilities: SUP 10C.11.

Enhanced firms must also construct and keep up-to-date a management responsibility map, which comprehensively sets out the apportionment of responsibility, reporting lines and "reasonable details" about each senior manager: SYSC 25.2.1R. Where responsibilities are shared, eg on a job share arrangement, the map should show this clearly. While one of the map's main purposes is to enable the regulators to know who is the appropriate person to speak to in respect of a specific matter, the regulators have emphasised that this is also a tool to help the firm itself understand its own business structure to identify potential failings or risks.

Some of the senior management responsibilities correspond to specific SMFs: eg the responsibility for safeguarding the independence of, and oversight of the performance of, the risk function ('Risk control') corresponds to SMF10, Chair of the Risk Committee. Others are less obvious, in particular the 'overall responsibility' under SYSC 26. One senior manager may be responsible for more than one responsibility. An individual does not need to be on the governing body to have overall responsibility for a given matter, and so could in theory be someone quite junior, but the FCA does expect that the person will be sufficiently senior and credible, and will have sufficient resources and authority, to be effective. The FCA is resistant to splitting responsibilities between more than one individual, but it accepts that this could be justified as part of a job sharing arrangement or during a handover period: SYSC 24.3.9G.

The 'miscellaneous' SMF18 applies where an individual has a senior management responsibility which does not correspond to one of the specific SMFs identified by the regulators, and is not also approved for one of those SMFs. This will be particularly relevant where a firm has identified an activity, business area or management function which falls outside the responsibilities prescribed by the regulators. The FCA has now confirmed, after several years of consideration and consultation, that Head of Legal is not a SMF, but will be subject to the certification regime and Conduct Rules (see below): PS19/20 at [2.12ff.]. The 'oversight SMFs', such as SMF10, must be carried out by a non-executive director, who (it is hoped) is in a more independent position to provide that oversight. The '12-week rule' allows firms to appoint a non-approved individual to an SMF to provide up to 12 weeks' cover for a temporarily or unforeseeably absent senior manager: SUP 10C.3.13. For the duration of the Covid-19 crisis, the FCA has said that FCA-regulated firms may extend this to 36 weeks; at time of writing, the PRA and FCA were still considering whether to offer this extension to dual-regulated firms: https://www.fca.org.uk/news/statements/smcr -coronavirus-our-expectations-solo-regulated-firms;   https ://www.fca.org.uk/news/statements/joint-fca-pra-statement-smcr-coronavirus-covid-19.

26.8   Certification

Firms are required to certify that 'employees' who carry out certain functions ('certification functions' or, in the statutory language, 'specified functions': *section 63E of FSMA*) are "fit and proper" to carry out their roles. An employee for these purposes is someone who (a) personally provides, or is under an obligation personally to provide, services to the firm in question under an arrangement made between the firm and the person providing the services or another person; and (b) is subject to (or to the right of) supervision, direction or control by the firm as to the manner in which those services are provided: *section 63E(9) of FMSA*. In other words, some distance from the definition of employment status familiar to employment lawyers.

The regulators are empowered to specify functions as certification functions if they are not controlled functions, but the relevant regulator is satisfied that they are nevertheless significant-harm functions ('SHFs'): section 63E(3)(4) of FSMA. SHFs are defined at *section 63E(5) of FSMA* as those which (a) require the person performing them to be involved in one or more aspects of the firm's affairs, so far as relating to the activity, and (b) involve, or might involve, a risk of significant harm to the firm or any of its customers. At time of writing, the FCA has specified eight SHFs as certification functions, including 'significant management', 'material risk takers' and 'client-dealing' (the last of which now excludes individuals who have no scope to choose, decide or reach a judgement on what should be done in a given situation, and whose tasks do not require them to exercise significant skill), with explanations, at SYSC 27.7.3R. Any non-approved person who directly or indirectly manages certified staff must also be certified. The PRA has taken a slightly different approach: any function (other than a controlled function) that is performed by a significant risk taker for a firm is a certification function to the extent that the function requires the significant risk taker to be involved in one or more aspects of the firm's affairs, so far as relating to a regulated activity carried on by the firm: Certification 2.2.

FSMA sets out the same mandatory considerations for determining fitness and propriety as for a senior manager: the firm must have regard, in particular, to whether the person (a) has obtained a qualification, (b) has undergone, or is undergoing, training, (c) possesses a level of competence, or (d) has the personal characteristics, required by general rules made by the appropriate regulator in relation to employees performing functions of that kind: *section 63F(2)*. The firm should also follow the same regulatory guidance as if it was vetting a senior manager – always bearing in mind that the requirements of the certification role will almost inevitably be markedly different from that of a senior manager. The certificate is valid for only twelve months (*section 63F(5)* of *FSMA*), so must be renewed annually to allow an individual to continue carrying out his function. The regulators have endorsed the sensible approach of building the recertification process into any existing annual performance review procedure.

Under *section 63E*, such firms must take reasonable care to ensure that no employee of it performs a specified function under an arrangement entered into by it in relation to the carrying on by it of a regulated activity, unless the employee has a valid certificate. Both regulators do, however, allow a four-week grace period, where an appointment to a certification function is (PRA adds: 'solely') to provide cover for a certified employee whose absence is reasonably unforeseen. The FCA also operates a '30-day rule', which allows individuals based outside the UK to perform most certification functions for up to 30 days in a year without being certified. As with approval, it is often prudent for the relevant contract (usually but not necessarily an employment contract) to expressly provide for termination in the event of a lack of certificate.

To replace the existing information of the financial services register about individuals who would previously have been approved but are now, or will be, certified by their firm instead, the FCA will launch "the Directory": The *Directory*, PS19/7. When complete, the Directory will list all certified staff and executive and non-executive directors who are not senior managers. This came after "substantial feedback on the public value of the certified staff and certain other individuals", and a consultation in July 2018 (CP18/19). The responsibility will be on firms to update details by making notifications within seven days (and the relevant Senior Manager will be accountable for inaccurate data and failures to update). In turn, the conduct rules provide that individuals are responsible for providing accurate information to their employers. FCA-regulated firms are required to submit their data for inclusion in the Directory by 9 December 2020.

26.9 **Code of Conduct**

The SMCR also brings individuals who are neither approved nor certified within its regulatory scope, to the extent that 'employees' are bound by the 'Code of Conduct', set out by the FCA at Handbook Chapter 'COCON'. Again, the definition of 'employee' departs from employment law: *section 64A(6)* defines an employee as someone who (a) personally provides, or is under an obligation personally to provide, services to the firm in question under an arrangement made between the firm and the person providing the services or another person; and (b) is subject to (or to the right of) supervision, direction or control by the firm as to the manner in which those services are provided (identical to the definition in the context of certification employees). There are two sets of conduct rules: those which apply to all employees save for those in non-financial roles (eg post room staff, catering staff, HR, etc), also referred to as 'conduct rules staff', and those which apply to senior managers. The five basic conduct rules are:

Rule 1: You must act with integrity.

Rule 2: You must act with due skill, care and diligence.

Rule 3: You must be open and cooperative with the FCA, the PRA and other regulators.

Rule 4: You must pay due regard to the interests of customers and treat them fairly.

Rule 5: You must observe proper standards of market conduct.

Senior managers are subject to four further rules, which are (as one might expect) more onerous, in that they require the senior manager to take active steps:

SC1: You must take reasonable steps to ensure that the business of the firm for which you are responsible is controlled effectively.

SC2: You must take reasonable steps to ensure that the business of the firm for which you are responsible complies with the relevant requirements and standards of the regulatory system.

SC3: You must take reasonable steps to ensure that any delegation of your responsibilities is to an appropriate person and that you oversee the discharge of the delegated responsibility effectively.

SC4: You must disclose appropriately any information of which the FCA or PRA would reasonably expect notice.

Breach of these rules is misconduct (*sections 66A* and *66B* of *FSMA*), which may attract a disciplinary sanction from either regulator. SC4 does not require the disclosure of legally privileged communications.

26.10 NOTIFICATIONS

Principle 11 of the FCA's Principles for Business ("PRIN") require firms to "deal with its regulators in an open and cooperative way, and must disclose to the FCA appropriately anything relating to the firm of which that regulator would reasonably expect notice." As above, Rule 3 and SC4 of COCON impose similar general requirements on individuals. However, certain matters are subject to specific notification obligations (though these do not limit the application of the general obligations).

Firms must notify the relevant regulator where it takes disciplinary action against an employee (according to the expanded definition at *section 64A(6)* of *FSMA*), a director or any other senior manager (which could be a contractor, for example), and one of the reasons for that action is breach of a regulatory rule: *section 64C* of *FSMA*. Disciplinary actions is defined as 'the issuing of a formal written warning', 'the suspension or dismissal of the person' or 'the reduction or recovery of any of the person's remuneration'. The FCA has emphasised (if it needed to be emphasised) that notification requirements under *section 64C* apply notwithstanding any COT3 or other exit agreement, and firms should not enter into such arrangements which 'could conflict' with its obligations: SUP 15.11.19G. From an employment law perspective, of course, a suspension is not typically viewed as a disciplinary measure. Both regulators have confirmed that suspensions imposed to facilitate or pending an investigation, prior to any finding of wrongdoing, need not be reported under *section 64C*: FCA PS16/6, [2.7]; PRA PS9/16, [2.18]. The FCA does not expect a firm to notify COCON breaches which occurred before the application of COCON to that firm: SUP 15.11.11G.

If a senior manager ceases to perform an SMF function, the firm must notify the FCA within ten business days via Form C: SUP 10C.14.4R. If, however, the reason for that cessation of performance is dismissal, suspension, resignation while under investigation (by the firm or any regulator), might reasonably affect the FCA's assessment of the individual's fitness and propriety, it will be what is called a 'qualified Form C'. A firm must notify the FCA in advance, as soon as practicable, once it has information which reasonably suggests a qualified Form C will be necessary: SUP 10C.14.7.

Firms must also notify the regulators of any change in details relating to a senior manager, via Form D. This includes everything from personal details such as their title or name and their working arrangements to information about their fitness and propriety. Information which would reasonably be material to the assessment of a senior manager (and does not fall to be mentioned in Form C) must be notified to the FCA as soon as practicable and in any case within seven business days (which may be by email if more practical and with the FCA's agreement): SUP 10C.14.18R.

It is a criminal offence to knowingly or recklessly give a regulator information which is false or misleading in a material particular in purported compliance with a notification requirement: *section 398 of FSMA*.

26.11 INVESTIGATIONS

The regulators have a broad range of investigatory powers, under *Part 11 of FSMA*. These allow them to require firms and individuals to produce existing documents and to answer questions (both in writing and in compelled interviews). Usually this will be in the context of a formal investigation, but the regulators do have a power under *section 165 of FSMA* to require, at any time, information or documents reasonably required in connection with the exercise of their functions under *FSMA*. More commonly, the regulator will appoint investigators (invariably internal staff) to carry out either "general investigations" into the nature, conduct or state of an authorised person's business under *section 167* or 'investigations in particular cases' under *section 168* where it appears to the regulator that there has been a contravention of a specific provision. The nature of the suspected breach determines various aspects of the duties and powers of the investigators. For example, if a civil (as opposed to criminal or quasi-criminal) investigation is launched, the relevant regulator must give written notice to the subject of the investigation, specifying the suspected breach and reason for appointing investigators, unless such notification would be likely to result in the investigation being frustrated: *section 170 of FSMA*.

The regulators may become aware of potential breaches in a wide variety of ways. Very commonly, it will be self-reporting: Principle 11 of PRIN requires firms to deal with its regulators in an open and cooperative way, and to disclose to the appropriate regulator appropriately anything relating to the firm of which that regulator would reasonably expect notice. Alternatively, a whistleblower from within a firm who has either exhausted internal processes or has no faith in them (assuming, indeed, that the firm has such internal processes) may tip the regulator off. The regulators may also respond to other bodies' findings, for example adverse judicial dicta in courts or tribunals, or to complaints from the public.

The investigators may use compulsory information-gathering powers against two groups of people: (1) the subject of the investigation and persons connected with them; and (2) any other person. If seeking information from the former category, the statutory threshold is lower: it merely requires that the investigator reasonably considers the question, provision of information or production of the document to be relevant to the purposes of the investigation: *section 171*. For these purposes, an individual is connected to the subject of the investigation if she is (depending on the corporate structure) an officer, manager, employee, agent or member – this includes being an employee or agent of an individual who is under investigation: *Schedule 15, Part I of FSMA*. Meanwhile, if the information is sought from someone unconnected to the subject of the investigation, a requirement may only be imposed if the investigator is satisfied that the requirement is necessary or expedient for the purposes of the investigation: *section 172 of FSMA*.

Section 176 of FSMA sets out the consequences of non–compliance with a Part 11 information requirement. If someone subject to a requirement fails without reasonable excuse to comply with it, the regulator may refer that to the court who may in turn treat the defaulter as if he were in contempt. In the case of a body corporate, this would include a director or other officer: case law on the Civil Procedure Rules contempt provision suggests that the individual in question must be aware of the order, and that failure to supervise or investigate, or wilful blindness, will be sufficient even in the absence of active participation in the breach: *Templeton Insurance Ltd v Thomas* [2013] EWCA Civ 35, [2013] All ER (D) 32 (Feb). Meanwhile, it is a criminal offence to falsify, conceal, destroy or dispose of a relevant document, or to permit or cause such behaviour, as well as to knowingly or recklessly provide false or misleading information.

Another option for the regulators is to obtain a 'skilled persons' report under *section 166*. This involves a third party – usually one of the leading accountancy firms but occasionally solicitors or consultants – to independently review an authorised person's business or an aspect thereof. The scope of the review is set by the regulator but the costs (including those incurred by the FCA) are borne by the firm under review. Depending on the scope, this can be a substantial sum: the median cost of reviews in 2015/16 was £155,000, according to the FCA's annual report. The FCA and PRA both publish quarterly statistics on their use of this power describing the type of suspected misconduct and the type of firm (the FCA also includes the identity of the skilled person retained).

26.12 SANCTIONS

The regulators have a 'toolkit' of powers under FSMA with which to carry out their functions. These can broadly be categorised as: (1) disciplinary or punitive; and (2) supervisory or protective. This is an important distinction for issues such as double jeopardy and limitation. They also arise in different ways: disciplinary responses tend to be where a person has breached a regulatory requirement which applies to them. For a firm, this could be a breach of any of the rules in the FCA Handbook or PRA Rulebook, including those set out in this Chapter, and including in particular the Principles for Business set out in PRIN. For an individual, this could be: a breach of the conduct rules; being knowingly concerned in a firm's contravention; a senior manager who breaches the 'duty of responsibility' under Condition C of *sections 66A* or *66B* of *FSMA*; or market abuse. Protective measures, on the other hand, tend to be applied where a person is failing to reach a given standard of fitness and propriety. Depending on the context, this could be someone falling short of the very high standard required for a senior manager at a large bank, or (at the other end of the spectrum) so lacking in integrity that they cannot be permitted to perform any function in connection with regulated activities. Clearly, there will be cases where both disciplinary and supervisory measures are appropriate.

The lightest disciplinary measure is a public censure (ie a 'statement of misconduct'), although this can have serious, and in some cases deleterious, effects on an individual's career. The regulators may also impose a condition, limitation or suspension in respect of an individual's approval, or a part thereof. By far the most common sanction is, however, the financial penalty, or 'fine', imposed under *section 66* (for individuals) or *section 206* (for firms) of *FSMA*.

The amount of a financial penalty is decided according to set policies, which are updated from time to time. The regulators are required to have regard to the policy as worded at the time that the misconduct occurred (and not when action is taken): *section 69(8)*. Both regulators' policies consist of five steps: (1) disgorgement (ie ensuring that the wrongdoer retains no benefit from the breach); (2) seriousness of the breach (a fraction of the gross income from the breach up to 40%, depending on the seriousness); (3) mitigating and aggravating factors (which may relate to the nature of the breach or the conduct post-breach, including during the investigation); (4) a potential adjustment to ensure appropriate deterrence; and (5) a settlement discount of 30%, if settlement is reached during the Stage 1 of the investigation. (The FCA may also enter into a partial settlement – formally a "focussed resolution agreement" – where there is scope for agreeing certain issues but other issues remain in dispute.) There are similar policies in respect of the duration of conditions and suspensions. The regulators may also take into account serious financial hardship which might be caused by the fine, upon receipt of verifiable evidence that the subject is below the relevant threshold of income and capital holding. A firm may not pay a fine imposed by the FCA on a present or former employee, director or partner of the firm or of an affiliated company (unless it is a sole trader): *GEN 6.1.4R*. Firms may not take out insurance which indemnifies any person against fines (*GEN 6.1.5R*), but may indemnify against costs of defending regulatory proceedings (*GEN 6.1.7G*).

The most draconian protective tool is a prohibition order under *section 56* of *FSMA* (or 'ban'), whereby an individual is barred from carrying out functions in relation to a regulated activity. This may be a 'full ban' or it may be limited to specified functions, activities or firms. Individuals will be banned if they are deemed not to be fit and proper to perform functions. The purpose of this is not only to preclude those individuals from carrying out functions when they are unfit to do so, but may also be *'to send out messages to the financial services industry and to the public about unacceptable conduct in the financial markets and in order to deter others'*: *Davies v Financial Services Authority* [2003] EWCA Civ 1128, [2003] 4 All ER 1196 at [28]. Firms have a statutory duty to 'take reasonable care to ensure that no function of his, in relation to the carrying on of a regulated activity, is performed by a person who is prohibited from performing that function by a prohibition order': *section 156(6)* of *FSMA*. As is clear from the statutory wording, this applies regardless of the relationship with the individual (ie whether the function is performed by an employee, worker, contractor etc.) but what is 'reasonable' in the circumstances may vary. Meanwhile, it is a criminal offence for a banned individual to breach (or agree to breach) a prohibition order, punishable by a fine: *section 56(4)* of *FSMA*.

Senior managers may also have their permissions removed or varied, either on the regulator's own initiative or voluntarily. Firms must therefore take reasonable steps to ensure that all controlled functions are at all times carried out by individuals with the appropriate approval (unless taking advantage of the '12 week rule'). To this end, it is often advisable to include express contractual terms which provide for the eventuality that an individual becomes unable to perform his role due to his lack of approval.

A regulator may also require a bank, building society or MiFID investment firm to remove or replace a director or senior executive, and to take any necessary step to do so eg to call a shareholders' meeting: *section 71B*. It is subject to two conditions: (1) there is a significant deterioration in the firm's financial situation or serious infringement of a regulatory requirement or its own constitution; and (2) no less intrusive measure would be reasonably likely to reverse the deterioration or end the infringement. If merely removing or replacing the manager would itself not be sufficient to reverse the deterioration or bring the infringement to an end, the regulator may appoint a person to act (or one or more persons to act jointly) as a temporary manager of that firm: *section 71C*. These relatively new powers, implementing the *Banking Recovery and Resolution Directive 2014/59*, came into force on 16 December 2016.

The regulator will give the subject a 'warning notice' in the first instance, following which the subject may make representations (the FCA would usually have furnished a preliminary investigation report prior to this, but that is not a statutory requirement). The relevant decision maker will then issue a 'decision notice'. If that is not appealed, a final notice is issued. Appeals go to the Upper Tribunal, which, depending on the nature of the reference, may either substitute its own decision or refer the matter back to the regulator with findings of fact. Where the notices identify a third party, they also have rights to see the notices, make representations and refer the matter to the Upper Tribunal: *section 393* of *FSMA*. The Supreme Court has held that a person may be identified by name or by a synonym, such as his office or job title, which makes it apparent from the notice itself that it could apply to only one person; extraneous information will be relevant where it enables one to interpret, but does not supplement, the language of the notice: *Financial Conduct Authority v Macris* [2017] UKSC 19, [2017] 4 All ER 1027.

Details of the measure taken, and the reasons for doing so, will usually be published by the relevant regulator pursuant to *section 391* of *FSMA*. This will involve publishing the final notice, and in some cases the warning notice as well. The regulator *must* publish such information about the matter as it considers appropriate, but *may not* publish information in certain circumstances, eg where it would be unfair to the subject of the action (FCA and PRA), prejudicial to the interests of consumers or detrimental to the stability of the UK financial system (FCA) or prejudicial to the safety and soundness of PRA-authorised persons (PRA).

Where the regulator decides not to take formal action using one of its statutory powers, it may issue a 'private warning', ie a letter (identifying itself as a private warning) which sets out the concerns and reprimands the person in question. Other powers are the regulators' disposal include applying to the court for an injunction (*section 380* of *FSMA*) or a restitution order (*section 382* of *FSMA*), or requiring a firm to pay restitution without recourse to the courts (*section 384* of *FSMA*).

26.13 REMUNERATION

One of the factors identified as contributing to the financial crisis was 'inappropriate' remuneration policies, which allowed individuals to receive vast sums of money, often in the form of bonuses, irrespective of the eventual effects of their behaviour. It incentivised short-termism, since large profits in one fiscal year would yield large personal rewards, even if those profits were later revealed to be illusory or toxic. Accordingly, one of the earliest policy responses was a remuneration code, being the subject of an FSA Policy Statement in August 2009 (PS09/15), 'Reforming remuneration practices in financial services', and one of the focuses of the G20 Pittsburgh Summit in September 2009 (which used the terminology of 'compensation practices'). It is clear, however, from the PCBS report in 2013 that the problem remained unsolved: see especially Chapter 8 of that report, 'Remuneration'.

There are currently six remuneration codes applicable in the UK, depending on the type of investment firm. (In addition, insurance firms are subject to remuneration requirements pursuant to the directly applicable *Solvency II Regulation EU 2015/35*.) The codes are rules made by the FCA and PRA pursuant to their *Part 9A* of *FSMA* powers, appearing at Sections 19A-19E of the FCA Handbook Chapter 'Systems and Controls', or 'SYSC', and the 'Remuneration' section of the PRA Rulebook as it applies to CRR firms (that is, banks, building societies and PRA-designated investment firms). It is beyond the scope of this chapter to adumbrate the differences between each of the various codes. The focus of this section will be on the rules applicable to dual-regulated firms, set out at SYSC 19D. (These are largely similar to two other codes: namely the PRA's and FCA's respective codes which relate to institutions covered by the *EU Capital Requirements Regulation 575/2013*.) The code contains three types of provisions: rules, indicated by the letter 'R'; guidance, indicated by 'G'; and evidential, indicated by 'E', meaning that a contravention may be relied on as tending to establish contravention of such other rule made by that regulator as may be specified: *section 138C* of *FSMA*. Rules will also use the word 'must', whereas guidance and evidential provisions will use 'should'.

Breach of the codes, given their status as regulatory rules, will render a firm liable for disciplinary action by the regulators but will not ordinarily render any transaction void or unenforceable: *section 138E(2)* of *FSMA*. The FCA has, however, carved out an exception for individuals who work at a firm which has total assets of greater than £50bn, whereby any provision which contravenes the rules on either guaranteed remuneration, deferral or clawback will be void. In addition, firms are required by the codes to take reasonable steps to remove contractual provisions which are incompatible with the codes.

The 'general requirement' of the remuneration code is that firms '*must establish, implement and maintain remuneration policies, procedures and practices that are consistent with, and promote, sound and effective risk management.*' This is in order to achieve the codes' purpose of ensuring that policies are '*risk-focused,*' '*consistent with and promote effective risk management*' and '*do not expose [firms] to excessive risk*'.

The code then goes on to enumerate 12 'Remuneration Principles'. Whereas the general requirement applies to all staff, the remuneration principles apply only to 'material risk takers'. An individual may be a material risk taker by virtue of her role or by virtue of the amount she is paid. She may, however, be exempt if she earns less than a '*de minimis*' amount (total remuneration of at least £500,000 or bonus more than 33% of total remuneration). Moreover, under the proportionality principle, smaller firms may disapply some of the remuneration rules.

(1)   Risk management and risk tolerance. A firm must ensure that its remuneration policy is consistent with, and promotes, sound and effective risk management and does not encourage risk-taking that exceeds the level of tolerated risk of the firm.

(2)   Supporting business strategy, objectives, values and long-term interests of the firm. A firm must ensure that its remuneration policy is in line with the business strategy, objectives, values and long-term interests of the firm.

(3)   Avoiding conflicts of interest. A firm must ensure that its remuneration policy includes measures to avoid conflicts of interest.

(4)   Governance. A firm must ensure that its management body in its supervisory function adopts and periodically reviews the general principles of the remuneration policy and is responsible for overseeing its implementation. It must ensure that the implementation of the remuneration policy is, at least annually, subject to central and independent internal review for compliance with policies and procedures for remuneration adopted by the management body in its supervisory function.

(5)   Control functions. This regulates the employment employees in control functions, who must be: (1) independent from the business units they oversee; (2) vested with appropriate authority; and (3) remunerated adequately both to attract qualified and experienced employees and commensurately with the importance of their role.

(6)   Remuneration and capital. This requires firms to ensure that total variable remuneration does not limit its ability to strengthen its capital base. A firm should have variable remuneration arrangements that are sufficiently flexible to allow it to direct the necessary resources towards capital building.

(7)   Exceptional government intervention. A firm that benefits from exceptional government intervention must ensure that: (1) variable remuneration is strictly limited as a percentage of net revenues when it is inconsistent with the maintenance of a sound capital base and timely exit from government support; (2) it restructures remuneration in a manner aligned with sound risk management and long-term growth, including (when appropriate) establishing limits to the remuneration of members of its management body; and (3) no variable or discretionary remuneration of any kind is paid to members of its management body unless this is justified. Guidance provides that this will normally apply only to members of the management body who were in office at the time that the intervention was required.

(8)   Profit-based measurement and risk adjustment. This requires firms to ensure that any measurement of performance used to calculate bonuses allows for risk adjustment. The guidance notes the importance of applying judgment and common sense.

(9)   Pension policy. This requires a firm's pension policy to be in line with its business strategy, objectives, values and long-term interests; and governs how discretionary pension benefits should be held (before retirement) and paid (after retirement).

(10)   Personal investment strategies. This requires a firm to ensure that its employees undertake not to use personal hedging strategies or insurance contracts to undermine the risk alignment effects embedded in their remuneration arrangements. Firms must also maintain effective arrangements designed to ensure that employees comply with their undertaking.

(11)   Non-compliance with the dual-regulated firms Remuneration Code. A firm must ensure that variable remuneration is not paid through vehicles or methods that facilitate non-compliance with remuneration obligations.

(12)   Remuneration structures. This is split into eight sections:

(a)   General requirement: A firm must ensure that the structure of an employee's remuneration is consistent with, and promotes, effective risk management.

(b)   Assessment of performance: This requires firms to take into account the performance of the business unit and firm as a whole, as well as the individual, and to take into account financial as well as non-financial criteria.

(c)   Guaranteed variable remuneration, buy-outs: Guaranteed bonuses are forbidden unless it is exceptional, the firm has a strong and sound capital base and it is limited to the first year of a new employee's service. Remuneration when buying out new employees' old contracts must align with the firm's long-term interests including appropriate retention, deferral and performance and clawback arrangements.

(d)   Ratios between fixed and variable components of total remuneration: ie the bonus cap. In general, the ratio of bonus to salary should not exceed 1:1, or 2:1 where approved by shareholders, owners or members.

(e)   Payments related to early termination: Payments relating to the early termination of a contract must reflect performance achieved over time and be designed in a way that does not reward failure or misconduct.

(f)   Retained shares or other instruments: At least 50% of a bonus must be an appropriate balance of (i) ownership interests in the firm and (ii) other instruments tied to the credit quality of the firm.

(g)   Deferral: At least 40% of a bonus (or 60% if the bonus is more than £500,000 or the firm is significant) must be deferred for a number of years (7 if PRA-designated SMF, 3–5 otherwise).

(h)   Performance adjustment (affordability, malus, clawback): Variable remuneration should be paid only if doing so is sustainable according to the financial situation of the firm as a whole, and justified on the basis of the performance of the firm, the business unit and the individual concerned. Firms must be able to clawback an amount equivalent to the bonus for at least seven years in appropriate circumstances. The firm must have policies for the application of malus and clawback which cover at least cover situations where the employee (i) participated in, or was responsible for, conduct which resulted in significant losses to the firm; or (ii) failed to meet appropriate standards of fitness and propriety.

When making decisions about malus and clawback, employers will be bound by ordinary principles of acting in good faith when exercising a contractual discretion: see CHAPTER 8 in this volume, but in particular *Keen v Commerzbank AG* [2006] EWCA Civ 1536, [2007] IRLR

132 and *Braganza v BP Shipping* [2015] UKSC 17, [2015] IRLR 487. The courts will undoubtedly take into account the important policy considerations which underlie the remuneration codes, but an irrational or unfair decision may be the subject of a contractual claim for damages.

26.14 REGULATORY REFERENCES

The common law governing the contents of references, considered in detail at CHAPTER 11 of this volume, applies to the financial services sector just as it does to any other industry. This is explicitly acknowledged by both regulators in recent policy statements. The FCA acknowledged in September 2016 that 'Firms are subject to common law and employment law, which apply independently of regulatory requirements,' and 'a firm's compliance with the regulatory referencing requirements [needs] to be consistent with firms' common law duties'. In addition to endorsing that acknowledgment, the PRA had also in February 2016 noted the employer's 'duty to their former employees and to the recipient firm to exercise due skill and care in the preparation of the reference'.

Indeed, it may be noted that many of the common law authorities in this area involved employers in the financial services industry. This should come as no surprise, given that it is the sector in which the paramountcy of integrity and competence intersects with substantial amounts of compensation. This (as foreshadowed in the case law) led to a chilling effect, whereby risk-averse employers have either toned down their references to the point of blandness or avoided giving them altogether (where possible). The regulators have therefore made it a priority to prevent 'rolling bad apples' – individuals with poor conduct records who move from firm to firm undetected – with regulatory references. These are mandatory in two ways: first, certain firms are required to both seek and to give such reference; secondly, there are minimum requirements as to the contents of the reference. These requirements are set out in the PRA Rulebook Fitness and Propriety 2 and 5 and the FCA Handbook SYSC 22.

When proposing to make an appointment which requires approval, certification or a directorship, firms are required to take reasonable steps to obtain appropriate references covering the previous six years of employment when assessing an individual's fitness and propriety. "Employment" has a special meaning in this context, and as well as the broader definition used elsewhere in the SMCR (see above) includes being an approved person or director (including non-executive director): FCA Handbook Glossary. A sole trader is not considered her own employer, so there is no obligation to seek a reference from her about herself. References must be sought from all institutions, regardless of whether they are regulated or even in the financial services industry, and regardless of whether they are in the UK. Failure to obtain the reference will not in itself be a breach, as long as the requesting firm has taken reasonable steps.

Meanwhile, when receiving a request for a regulatory reference, a firm must provide one to another firm as soon as reasonably practicable, disclosing all information of which it is aware that it reasonably considers to be relevant to the requesting firm's assessment of whether the individual in question is fit and proper. The information only needs to go back six years before the date of the request, unless it relates to 'serious misconduct', but a firm may disclose more if it wishes, so long as to do so would not breach any other obligation (eg of fairness).

Firms are also required, up to six years after employing an individual, to update references when it becomes aware of matters, or reaches a conclusion or takes an action, which would have required them to draft their original reference differently. This will involve making reasonable inquiries as to the individual's current employer and forwarding details of those differences to the original requester as soon as reasonably practicable, unless the matter has become academic, for example because that firm is no longer the individual's employer.

SYSC 22.5 governs what information should be included in the reference for FCA purposes. Firms are not required to disclose information that has not been properly verified, eg as a result of unfinished disciplinary proceedings. However, the rules do not prohibit a firm from including such information if it wishes to. A firm should provide as complete a picture of an employee's conduct record as possible to new employers, while keeping within the bounds of its duty to exercise due skill and care in the preparation of the reference. The firm may give frank and honest views, but only after taking reasonable care both as to factual content, and as to the opinions expressed. References should be true, accurate, fair and based on documented fact.

A firm must not enter into any arrangements or agreements with any person that limit its ability to disclose information pursuant to its regulatory requirements. This will be most relevant in exit agreements and settlement agreements. While there should not be any problem with warranting that the firm is not aware of any disclosable information, if that is the position, the firm may not undertake not to revise a reference should new information or conclusions come to light.

26.15 WHISTLEBLOWING

Protection for whistleblowers is provided by the *Employment Rights Act 1996*, as amended by the *Public Interest Disclosure Act 1998*: see CHAPTER 11 of this volume. This statutory regime applies to workers in the financial services industry just as it does to any other worker. Given the importance of whistleblowing to the regulatory system, and by extension to the financial markets in general, there are various additional requirements which pertain to banking firms (and insurers).

First, banking firms are required to establish, implement and maintain appropriate and effective arrangements for the disclosure of reportable concerns by whistleblowers: PRA General Organisational Requirements 2A; SYSC 18.3. A 'reportable concern' is, in fact, wider than a 'qualifying disclosure' in the *Employment Rights Act 1996*, since it also includes (i) breaches of the firm's policies and procedures and (ii) behaviour that harms or is likely to harm the reputation or financial well-being of the firm. The firm's internal arrangements: must allow for confidentiality and a range of communication methods; must allow for effective assessment and escalation where appropriate; must ensure no victimisation; must provide feedback to the whistleblower where appropriate; and appropriate records must be kept.

Although these obligations only apply to banking firms, all firms remain subject to PRIN11: "A firm must deal with its regulators in an open and cooperative way, and must disclose to the FCA appropriately anything relating to the firm of which that regulator would reasonably expect notice." Moreover, if any firm is found to have acted to the detriment of a whistleblower, the FCA says it could call into question the fitness and propriety of the firm or relevant members of its staff: SYSC 18.3.9G.

It should also be borne in mind that every senior manager, regardless of the type of firm, is subject to Conduct Rule SM4: "You must disclose appropriately any information of which the FCA or PRA would reasonably expect notice." This does not, however, require the disclosure of legally privileged communications.

One of the regulators' prescribed responsibilities for banking firms (and insurers) is that of 'Whistleblowers' Champion', who has responsibility for ensuring and overseeing the integrity, independence and effectiveness of the firm's policies and procedures on whistleblowing. This must therefore be allocated to a senior manager: the FCA expects that the firm will appoint a non-executive director as whistleblowers' champion if it has at least one: SYSC 18.4.

In May 2018, in their first regulatory action under the SMCR, the FCA and PRA jointly imposed a fine of £641,200 (after settlement discount) on Jes Staley, the Chief Executive of Barclays, for failing to act with due skill, care and diligence in the way he acted in response to an anonymous letter received by Barclays in June 2016. They also imposed special requirements on Barclays itself, whereby it must report annually to the regulators detailing how it handles whistleblowing, with personal attestations from those Senior Managers responsible for the relevant systems and controls.

27 Foreign Employees

27.1 ENTITLEMENT TO WORK IN THE UK

The first issue which arises in respect of employees who are not nationals of the UK is whether they are lawfully entitled to work in this country. The existing regime draws a broad distinction between nationals of Member States of the European Economic Area ('EEA'), which (as of 1 February 2020) comprises the 27 European Union Member States as well as Iceland, Liechtenstein and Norway. Switzerland is not a member of the EEA but Swiss nationals have the same rights to live and work in the UK as EEA nationals.

- **To 31 December 2020** *Migrant workers from within the EEA* — Employees who are nationals of countries within the EEA are generally entitled to work in the UK, see further the *Immigration (European Economic Area) Regulations 2016 (SI 2016/1052)* which came into force on 1 February 2017 (repealing and replacing the *Immigration (European Economic Area) Regulations 2006 (SI 2006/1003)* and clarifying the UK's implementation of more recent CJEU case law). Between 2004 and 2011, an exception to this general rule was in effect pursuant to the *Accession (Immigration and Worker Registration) Regulations 2004 (SI 2004/1219)* (as amended). Under the 2004 Regulations, individuals who are nationals of recently acceded Member-States (apart from Cyprus and Malta) and who wanted to work in the UK for more than one month were required to register with the home office 'Worker Registration Scheme' as soon as they found work. The Worker Registration Scheme closed on 30 April 2011 and the 2004 Regulations were revoked. As from 1 January 2014, Bulgarian and Romanian nationals are no longer required to apply for permission to work. Croatian nations must obtain authorisation to work (see the scheme set out in the *Accession of Croatia (Immigration and Worker Authorisation) Regulations 2013, SI 2013/1460*).

- **From 1 January 2021** *Migrant workers from within the EEA* — the *Immigration (European Economic Area) Regulations 2016* will cease to have effect on 31 December 2020. EU, EEA and Swiss citizens resident in the UK by 31 December 2020 are eligible to apply for settled status (for those who have lived in the UK for five years or more) or for pre-settled status (for those who have lived in the UK for a shorter period) under the settled scheme until 30 June 2021.This status preserves the entitlement to work. EEA workers entering the UK from 1 January 2021 will be treated the same way as migrant workers from non-EEA States (see the final bullet point below). [Note: *In light of the COVID-19 outbreak in early 2020, it is possible that these dates may change.*]

- **To 31 December 2020** *Migrant workers from outside the EEA* — With the exception of Swiss nationals, individuals who are not nationals of a Member State of the EEA currently have their entitlement to work in the UK decided by the points-based system which came into force in the UK in November 2008. The points-based system largely replaced the long-standing work permits scheme. Swiss nationals are exempted from the points-based system and are accordingly free to work in the UK.

- **From 1 January 2021** Migrant workers from outside the EEA — Details of a new points-based immigration system that will apply to all migrant workers entering the UK from 1 January 2021 were announced on 19 February 2020. At the time of writing primary legislation was in the process of being enacted but no draft regulations had been produced. A Policy Statement has been released and is available

at   https://www.gov.uk/government/publications/the-uks-points-based
-immigration-system-policy-statement/the-uks-points-based-immigration-system
-policy-statement. Again, it is conceivable that the COVID-19 outbreak could delay
introduction of this scheme.

27.2   NATIONALS OF THE EUROPEAN ECONOMIC AREA

The below information continues to apply until the end of the transition period for the UK's exit from the European Union. That is expected to occur on 31 December 2020 (although the COVID-19 outbreak in early 2020 may delay this). From the end of the transition period, it is not expected that nationals of the EEA or Switzerland will be treated any differently that citizens of other countries seeking to live or work in the UK. For the information currently known about the post-transition period arrangements, see 27.1 Entitlement to Work in the UK.

The principle of free movement of labour, which is currently applicable to all members of the EEA, is derived principally from *Art 45* of the *Treaty on the Functioning of the European Union (TFEU)*, and *Regulation 1612/68*. Other relevant pieces of European legislation include *Directive 68/360, Regulation 1251/70* (repealed by *Regulation 635/2006*), *Directive 90/365* and *Directive 90/364*. Although Turkey and certain other states have Association Agreements with the EU, these confer no general right of free movement upon individuals (*R v Secretary of State for the Home Department, ex p Narin* [1990] 2 CMLR 233; but see also *Sevince v Staatssecretaris van Justitie*: C-192/89 [1992] 2 CMLR 57). Until 30 June 2018, restrictions requiring Croatian workers to have work permits existed. These have expired and Croatian workers are now treated the same as other EU citizens.

The family of an EEA worker may also come to this country without any restriction on their right of entry. EEA nationals are entitled to the same treatment as UK nationals with regard to pay, working conditions, access to housing and property, training, social security and trade union rights. They are free, if unemployed but seeking work, to claim jobseeker's allowance for up to three months if they have been claiming benefit in their own country for at least four weeks. There is also a considerable body of EU legislation directed towards establishing equivalence of mutual recognition of professional qualifications by member states (see **24.4** EUROPEAN UNION LAW). More restrictive rules however apply to the families of Croatian nationals.

Pursuant to the *Immigration (European Economic Area) Regulations 2016*, EEA nationals (and Swiss nationals) may, along with their families, reside in the UK for an initial period of three months, provided that they have a valid passport or identity card and do not become an unreasonable burden on the domestic social security system. After the initial three-month period has expired, the EEA/Swiss national may continue to reside in the UK along with their family for so long as they continue to be a 'qualified person'. A person will be a 'qualified person' for the purposes of the Regulations if he or she is: a job-seeker, a worker, a self-employed person, a self-sufficient person or a student. EEA and Swiss nationals will acquire a permanent right of residence if they have both resided and worked in the UK for more than five years.

Member states are entitled to except employment in the public service from the general requirement of free movement, and to reserve such employment for their own nationals (*TFEU, art 45(4)*); see also PUBLIC SECTOR EMPLOYEES (38). These provisions have given rise to a substantial number of reported cases in national courts and in the ECJ (now CJEU), a detailed discussion of which is beyond the scope of this book.

Collective agreements must take account of comparable employment completed in the public service of another member state for the purposes of seniority and promotion (*Schöning-Kougebetopoulou v Freie und Hansestadt Hamburg*: C-15/96 [1998] All ER (EC)

97). A clause in a collective agreement which treats foreign nationals differently in this respect breaches *art 45* of the *TFEU* and *Regulation 1612/68* on freedom of movement. For an ECJ ruling concerning the relationship between *art 45* and national legislation denying termination payments to a worker who left employment in order to take up work in another member state, see *Graf v Filzmoser Maschinenbau GmbH*: C-190/98 [2000] All ER (EC) 170.

See also EUROPEAN UNION LAW **(24)**.

27.3   EUROPEAN UNION: POSTED WORKERS

The below information continues to apply until the end of the transition period for the UK's exit from the European Union. That is expected to occur on 31 December 2020 (although the COVID-19 outbreak in early 2020 may delay this).

Measures have been taken to implement in the UK the *Posting of Workers Directive (96/71)* which came into force on 16 December 1999. The UK has implemented the *Directive* through various pieces of statutory employment law, rather than through a single instrument. The *Directive* now applies to all EEA States. Broadly, it provides that minimum terms and conditions laid down by national laws, regulations or collective agreements should apply to workers posted temporarily by their employer to work in another State.

Article 1 provides that the *Directive* applies to undertakings which:

(a)   post workers to another member state on their account and under their direction under a contract concluded between the undertaking and a party in the other state for whom the services are intended;

(b)   make intra-company postings; or

(c)   are temporary employment undertakings or agencies which hire out workers to undertakings established or operating in an EU member state.

A further requirement in each case is that there must be an employment relationship between the undertaking making the posting and the worker during the period of posting. The terms and conditions of employment covered by the *Directive* are set out exhaustively in *art 3(1)*, as follows:

(i)   maximum work periods and minimum rest periods;

(ii)   minimum paid annual holidays;

(iii)   minimum rates of pay, including overtime rates (but not supplementary occupational pension schemes);

(iv)   conditions of hiring out workers, in particular the supply of workers by temporary employment undertakings;

(v)   health, safety and hygiene at work;

(vi)   measures to protect at work pregnant women, new mothers, children and young people; and

(vii)   equality of treatment between men and women and other provisions on non-discrimination.

Various flexibilities are permitted under the *Directive*, such as not applying the minimum rate of pay to postings of less than one month. However, the UK Government has decided not to take advantage of any of the exemptions.

Workers may enforce their rights under the *Directive* in the territory of the member state to which they were posted without prejudice to their rights in the country where they are normally employed (*art 6*).

27.3 Foreign Employees

In *Mazzoleni*: C-165/98 [2001] All ER (D) 182 (Mar), the ECJ ruled (15 March 2001) that the principle of freedom of movement did not preclude one member state from requiring an undertaking established in another state which provides services in the territory of the first state to pay its workers the minimum remuneration fixed by the national rules of that state. However, application of these rules might prove to be disproportionate where the workers operate in a frontier region and are required to carry out their work, on a part-time basis and for brief periods, in more than one member state. It is for the host member state to decide the extent to which the imposition of a minimum wage is necessary and proportionate to protect the workers in question. In a number of cases emanating from Germany, the ECJ has examined the compatibility of certain domestic laws governing posted workers with the principle of freedom of movement. These cases include: *Finalarte Sociedade de Construcao Civil Lda v Urlaubs- und Lohnausgleichskasse der Bauwirtschaft*: C-49/98 [2001] All ER (D) 361 (Oct); *European Commission v Germany*: C-341/02 [2005] All ER (D) 172 (Apr), ECJ; *Ruffert (Dirk) v Land Niedersachsen*: C-346/06 [2008] ECR I-1989, [2008] IRLR 467, ECJ; and *Hudzinski v Agentur fur Arbeit Wesel - Familienkasse*: C-611/10 [2012] 3 CMLR 23. For guidance on the minimum rates of pay see *Sahkaolajen ammattilitto ry v Elektrobudowa Spolka Akcyjna*: C-396/13. The *Posting of Workers Directive* was considered by the High Court in *R (on the application of Low) v Secretary of State for the Home Department* [2009] EWHC 35 (Admin), [2009] All ER (D) 175 (Jan). In that case, an Irish company had hired non-EU nationals to work in certain catering establishments in the UK. The Secretary of State refused to confirm that these workers had a right to work under EU law. The applicants applied to have that decision judicially reviewed. They sought to argue that they had a right to work in the UK on an application of *art 49* of the Nice Treaty and/or under the *Posting of Workers Directive*, particularly because the Irish company which employed them had a right to provide services in the UK. The High Court rejected the claim. It held that the arrangements constituted an unlawful attempt to circumvent enforceable UK immigration laws. The Court of Appeal upheld the High Court's judgment, [2010] EWCA Civ 4, [2010] ICR 755.

The UK has sought to incorporate the *Directive* by making amendments to statutory employment rights. Most existing UK legislation relevant to the *Directive* applies to all workers, whether they are employed on a temporary or permanent basis in the UK (eg the *Working Time Regulations 1998*, the *National Minimum Wage Act 1998*, and health and safety legislation). For a discussion of the effect of the *Directive* on the application of the *Employment Rights Act 1996* see the Court of Appeal's judgment in *Lawson v Serco Ltd* [2004] EWCA Civ 12, [2004] IRLR 206 and the opinion of Lord Hoffmann in the House of Lords [2006] UKHL 3, [2006] IRLR 289 at 256 para 13.

In March 2012, the European Commission proposed new rules designed to increase the protection of posted workers by complementing the *Posting of Workers Directive*. The rules are aimed in particular at improving levels of monitoring and compliance with the requirements imposed by the *Directive*. The new *Posting of Workers Enforcement Directive* was adopted by the EU's Council of Ministers in May 2014 (*Directive 2014/67*). The *Directive* has been implemented in England, Wales and Scotland by the *Posted Workers (Enforcement of Employment Rights) Regulations 2016, SI 2016/539* which entered into force on 18 June 2016. For the position in Northern Ireland see the *Posted Workers (Enforcement of Employment Rights) Regulations (Northern Ireland), SI 2016/242*. The 2016 Regulations make provision for a posted worker in the construction sector to have the right to make a claim, and bring proceedings before the Employment Tribunal or early conciliation, against their employer's contractor for the non-payment of wages (up to the national minimum wage). These Regulations continue to have effect until the end of the implementation period for the UK's withdrawal from the EU (ie. until, at this stage, 31 December 2020: *European Union (Withdrawal) Act 2018, s 2*).

27.4   NON-EEA NATIONALS

Up until November 2008, nationals from outside the EEA and Switzerland who were subject to immigration control were generally obliged to obtain work permits in order to be able to take up employment in the UK. On 26 November 2008, the work permit system was largely abolished and replaced by tier 2 of the points-based system. This system is operated by UK Visas and Immigration (UKVI), a department of the Home Office. Under the points-based system, migrant workers need to pass a points-based assessment before they are given permission to enter or remain in the United Kingdom. As originally constituted, the points-based system consisted of five tiers, with each tier having different points requirements. Points are awarded to reflect the migrant's ability, experience, age and, where appropriate, the level of need within the sector in which the migrant will be working. For up to date information on work visas for non-EEA nationals, see https ://www.gov.uk/browse/visas-immigration/work-visas.

Details of a new points-based immigration system that will apply to all migrant workers entering the UK from 1 January 2021 were announced on 19 February 2020. At the time of writing primary legislation was before the House of Commons but no draft regulations were available. However, a Policy Statement has been released and is available at https ://www.gov.uk/government/publications/the-uks-points-based-immigration-system -policy-statement/the-uks-points-based-immigration-system-policy-statement.   The COVID-19 outbreak may delay introduction of this scheme.

27.5   IMMIGRATION, ASYLUM AND NATIONALITY ACT 1996

Since 27 January 1997, it has been an offence to employ a person who is not entitled, under the Immigration Rules, to work in the UK. Originally, this offence was provided for under s 8 of the *Asylum and Immigration Act 1996* ('*AIA 1996*'). However, on 29 February 2008, *AIA 1996, s 8* was repealed and replaced by provisions in the *Immigration Asylum and Nationality Act 2006* (IAN 2006).

27.6   The statutory scheme governing the treatment of employers who employ persons not lawfully entitled to work in the UK is found in *sections 15–26* of *IAN 2006*. Under *s 15*, the Secretary of State may issue a penalty notice to employers who employ persons: (a) who have no leave to enter or remain in the UK; or (b) whose leave is invalid, has ceased to have effect or does not entitle them to work in the UK. The penalty notice will require the employer to pay a specific amount subject to a statutory maximum. The employer will be excused from paying the penalty if he complied with certain 'prescribed requirements' relating to the employment, unless he knew at the time that the employment was unlawful despite his having complied with the requirements. The 'prescribed requirements' are provided for under the *Immigration (Restrictions on Employment) Order 2007, SI 2007/3290*. The requirements imposed under the Order include that employers must scrutinise the passports and biometric immigration documents held by their potential employees and keep copies of those documents. Under *s 16*, the employer has a right to object to the notice by sending an objection to the Secretary of State. *Section 17* provides that the employer also has a right of appeal to the court against the penalty notice. The introduction of a penalty notice regime is one of the key novelties of the scheme introduced under *IAN 2006*. Under *s 19*, the Secretary of State must issue a Code of Practice relating to the giving of penalties. Pursuant to *s 21*, a person who employs someone who is subject to immigration control knowing that he or she is either in the UK unlawfully or is not lawfully entitled to work in the UK will be guilty of an offence and liable, on conviction, to imprisonment and/or a fine. *Section 22* provides that an employer (whether corporate or not) shall be treated as knowing a fact about an employee for the purposes of *s 21* if a person within the employing body has responsibility for an aspect of the employment and knows that fact. *Section 22(2)* makes provision for officers of the employer to be liable to conviction along with the employer itself in circumstances where the offence is committed with the consent or connivance of the officer. Under *s 23*, the Secretary of State is required to issue a Code of Practice to assist employers in avoiding racially discriminatory behaviour in the context of their complying with their obligations under *IAN*. The current 2019 version of the Code of Practice issued pursuant to *s 19* and the 2014 version of the Code of Practice issued pursuant to *s 23* can be found on the UKVI website, along with general guidance for employers on the application of *IAN*.

Claims under the ERA 1996

In order to bring a claim under the Employment Rights Act 1996, a claimant must show that he is an employee. A breach of immigration law may render the contract of employment unlawful such that it should not be enforced as a matter of public policy. Statutory protections usually depend on the existence of an enforceable contract and, accordingly, should not be provided in cases where the contract of employment is itself unlawful. There are three clear cases of unlawful contracts: (1) a contract entered into for the purposes of committing an illegal act; (2) a contract expressly or implicitly prohibited by statute ("statutory illegality"); and (3) a lawful contract performed illegally where the party seeking to enforce knowingly participated in the illegal performance ("common law illegality"): see *Hall v Woolston Hall* [2000] IRLR 578; [2001] ICR 99, CA at §§30–31; see also *Vakante v Governing Body of Addey & Stanhope School* [2004] EWCA Civ 1065, [2004] 4 All ER 1056; *Hounga v Allen* [2014] UKSC 47, [2014] IRLR 811; *Okedina v Chikale* [2019] EWCA Civ 1393, [2019] IRLR 905.

Blue Chip Trading Ltd v Helbawi (A) (UKEAT/0397/08/LA) [2009] IRLR 128 was a case of common law illegality. There, a foreign student had breached the Immigration Rules by working more than 20 hours per week for his employer. The EAT held that the fact that some of the work done by the student was unlawful did not render the entire contract of employment illegal. Instead, the contract was severable from the unlawful arrangements so that the student could pursue a claim under the contract in respect of those times when he was working lawfully and in accordance with the Immigration Rules. In another case of common law illegality, the Supreme Court in *Patel v Mirza* [2016] UKSC 42, [2017] AC 467 at para 101 concluded that a Court needed to consider (a) the underlying purposes of the prohibition transgressed; (b) whether any other relevant public policies may be rendered ineffective or less effective by denial of the claim; and (c) whether there was the possibility of overkill unless the law was applied with a due sense of proportionality. The Court of Appeal in *Okedina v Chikale* [2019] EWCA Civ 1393, [2019] IRLR 905 concluded that *Patel v Mirza* did not require a reconsideration of how the rule had been applied in earlier case law except where the earlier case law was inconsistent with those principles and that, in cases of common law illegality in the employment context, the established approach in *Hall v Woolston Hall Leisure Ltd* [2000] IRLR 578, [2001] ICR 99, CA was unaffected.

A case of "statutory illegality" was relied upon in *Okedina v Chikale* [2019] EWCA Civ 1393, [2019] IRLR 905. There, the employer resisted various claims under the *ERA* on the basis that the employee did not have the right to work in the UK at the relevant time, but in circumstances where the employer had told the employee that an application for an extension to her visa was being made on her behalf. It was suggested that, on the proper construction of *sections 15* and *21* of the *Immigration, Asylum and Nationality Act 2006*, that a contract of employment with a person whose leave to remain in the United Kingdom had ceased was prohibited by statute. The Court of Appeal considered that an intention to render a contract of employment entered into by a person without the appropriate immigration status could not be implied into either section. In reaching that conclusion, the Court balanced the fact that it was contrary to public policy for a person without the relevant immigration status to be employed in the UK against the public policy in ensuring that innocent employees have a contractual remedy (noting that common law illegality was available in a case where the employee knowingly participated in the illegal performance): at paras 47–50.

In a slightly unusual case, the EAT allowed an appeal from a decision that dismissal for failure to provide documentation evidencing an entitlement to work was not unfair. There, the employee (who in fact had a right to work) was not given the opportunity to appeal his dismissal, which could have given the employee a further opportunity to prove his entitlement: *Afzal v East London Pizza Ltd (t/a Domino's Pizza)* [2019] IRLR 119.

EEA nationals and their family members have an unqualified right to work in the UK (at least until 31 December 2020 – see **27.1** Entitlement to Work in the UK). Therefore, their contracts of employment cannot be rendered void by reason of a failure to produce evidence of entitlement to work ((see *Okouimose v City Facilities Management (UK) Ltd*, UKEAT/0192/11 (13 September 2011, unreported); employee suspended without pay; claim for unlawful deduction from wages upheld). However, in *Kurumuth v NHS Trust North Middlesex University Hospital* UKEAT/0524/10/CEA, despite the fact that the employee had a right to work while awaiting the determination of a timely immigration application, the EAT held that it was acceptable for an employer to rely upon the Home Office guidance on preventing illegal working in deciding to dismiss the employee. Note that even a contractual requirement to provide evidence of a right to work will not necessarily justify refusing to pay an employee who fails to provide such evidence and could, potentially, be considered a provision, criterion or practice which was not justifiable and therefore indirectly discriminatory: *Badara v Pulse Healthcare Ltd* UKEAT/0210/18/BA.

Discrimination claims

In *Vakante v Governing Body of Addey & Stanhope School* [2004] EWCA Civ 1065, [2004] 4 All ER 1056, the Court of Appeal considered the question of whether a claimant could pursue complaints of race discrimination against the respondent employer in circumstances where, as a person who was subject to immigration control, he had entered into an employment with the respondent knowing that the employment was unlawful. The Court of Appeal found that the claim was barred on an application of the 'inextricably linked' test. The Court also appeared to place reliance on the fact that the claimant had misled his employer as to his immigration status. The same result was reached by the Court of Appeal in *Allen v Hounga* [2012] EWCA Civ 609, [2012] IRLR 685 which concerned a race discrimination claim brought by a Nigerian national who had illegally posed as a member of the respondents' family in order to obtain entry into the United Kingdom. Compare those judgments with the judgment of the Employment Appeal Tribunal in *Wijesundera v Heathrow 3PL Logistics Ltd* (UKEAT/0222/13/DA) [2014] ICR 523. In that case, Langstaff P held that the crucial question is whether the form of the respondent's action giving rise to the claim is inextricably bound up with the illegal conduct. Whereas dismissal was inextricably linked to the claimant's employment status, sexual harassment was not.

The leading authority is now *Hounga v Allen* [2014] UKSC 47, [2014] IRLR 811 in which the Supreme Court reversed the Court of Appeal's decision and held that the claimant's race discrimination claim was not defeated by illegality. The Supreme Court split 3:2 on the reasoning. The majority judgment was delivered by Lord Wilson (with whom Lady Hale and Lord Kerr agreed). After reviewing the relevant authorities, Lord Wilson observed that the prevailing 'inextricable link' test has been subject to certain criticism but did not express a clear view on the matter. On the facts, all members of the Court agreed that the claim was not inextricably linked to the illegality. The illegal contract of employment provided no more than the context for the respondent's actions. However, the majority decided the appeal on the separate basis that the public policy aim of upholding immigration law was outweighed by the countervailing policy objective of supressing human trafficking. To allow the illegality defence to succeed would place the UK in breach of its international obligations under the United Nations 'Palermo Protocol' on forced labour and servitude, the Council of Europe Convention on Action against Trafficking in Human Beings and *Article 4* of the *ECHR*. The majority's failure to formulate a clear test introduces significant uncertainty. It is unclear whether the inextricable link test was disapplied in favour of an alternative public policy test or whether the inextricable link test is subject to policy exceptions.

27.7 JURISDICTION, APPLICABLE LAW AND THE TERRITORIAL SCOPE OF LEGISLATION DISTINGUISHED

Where a particular employment relationship has a foreign element, questions may arise as to whether the claim can be brought before English courts (the jurisdiction question). Depending on the circumstances, the allocation of jurisdiction between the courts of different states may be governed by EU law or common law rules.

The question may also arise as to what law governs the claim (the applicable law question). For example, where an employee who is based in France seeks to sue his British-based employer for breach of contract, a question may arise as to whether the claim is to be decided under English or French law. Alternatively, where a British-based employee is injured whilst travelling for work abroad, a question may arise as to whether any tortious claim for personal injury brought by the employee is governed by English law or the law of the country where the accident took place.

Importantly, the jurisdiction question is distinct from the applicable law question. For example, a contract may be governed by the laws of Saudi Arabia. This is not in itself determinative of whether the English courts have jurisdiction to hear the claim. Choice of law may, however, be a relevant factor in determining jurisdiction at common law, the logic being that courts are best placed to apply the domestic law of their own systems.

It is also important to be aware that, so far as statutory employment claims are concerned, the following additional question needs to be posed: 'Is this a claim which falls within the territorial scope of the particular legislation?' (the territorial scope question). Whether or not the statute applies to the facts of any given case is a question of statutory construction. Did Parliament intend that the relevant statutory protections should apply to a person in the relevant employee's specific circumstances? This issue is often said to concern the 'territorial jurisdiction' of the employment tribunals. However, the territorial scope question is entirely distinct from the jurisdiction question. Moreover, the territorial scope of legislation is not necessarily dependent on English law being the governing law of the contract of employment (although this is likely to be a relevant factor). These issues are examined in further detail below.

27.8 JURISDICTION

Where an employee brings a claim and the events about which the employee complains have a connection with more than one country, questions may arise as to whether the defendant can properly be served with proceedings and, further, whether England is the country in which claims can or must be brought.

Civil Courts Generally

The civil courts of England and Wales have jurisdiction to hear claims in personam (for present purposes, such claims include most claims in contract or torts) where (a) the defendant is served with process in England and Wales (whether or not they have a connection with England and Wales other than physical presence or not, but note the relevance of the doctrine of *forum non conveniens* discussed below); or (b) they are served with process abroad as authorised by statute.

In the context of claims brought against foreign defendants in the ordinary courts, reference must be made to *Part 6* of the *CPR* which contains detailed provisions on the question of when a foreign defendant may be served with proceedings. Service out of the jurisdiction will require the permission of the courts, save where the requirements of *CPR 6.33* have been met. If permission is required, the court will only consider granting permission in circumstances where the requirements contained in *CPR PD 6B paragraph 3.1* have been met. The courts will not grant permission where the domestic courts are clearly not the most appropriate forum for the claim. For an example of a case in which the domestic courts were considering whether they were the proper forum for tortious claims brought by foreign employees see *Lubbe v Cape plc* [2000] 4 All ER 268.

A common law claim which is brought by an employee in the ordinary courts will usually be subject to the doctrine of forum non conveniens with the result that claim will not be allowed to proceed before the domestic courts if there is another more appropriate (foreign) forum for the claim (see further *Spiliada Maritime Corpn v Cansulex Ltd* [1986] 3 All ER 843, HL). However, following the judgment of the ECJ in *Owusu v Jackson* [2005] All ER (D) 47 (Mar), it is clear that the *forum non conveniens* doctrine cannot be applied in a case where the English court automatically has jurisdiction to hear the claim under the *Brussels I Regulation* (as to which, see the section below entitled "Employer or employee domiciled in an EU Member State"). The Court of Appeal affirmed this in *Lungowe v Vedanta Resources plc* [2017] EWCA Civ 1528, [2018] 1 WLR 3575 paras 28–39; and see also *Vedanta Resources plc* [2019] UKSC 20, [2019] 2 WLR 1051 at §16. Note that, following the end of the transition period for the UK's exit from the EU, currently scheduled for 31 December 2020, the Brussels I Regulation will cease to apply in the UK and recourse to the doctrine of forum non conveniens should be available more broadly.

Employment Tribunals

The employment tribunal rules contained in *Schedule 1* to the *Employment Tribunals (Constitution and Rules of Procedure) Regulations 2013*, which came into force in July 2013, contain specific provisions as to the circumstances in which an employment tribunal claim may lawfully be presented in England and Wales. If the requirements of these provisions are met then, in effect, the employment tribunal will have jurisdiction to hear the claim. In summary, a claim may lawfully be presented *under rule 8* if: (a) the respondent or one of the respondents resides or carries on business in England or Wales; (b) one or more of the acts or omissions complained of took place in England or Wales; (c) the claim relates to a contract under which the work is or has been performed partly in England or Wales; or (d) the Tribunal has jurisdiction to determine the claim by virtue of a connection with Great Britain and the connection in question is at least partly a connection with England and Wales. The proper application of *rule 8(2)*, which does not on its face expressly mirror the requirements as to service contained in the *CPR*, has yet to be considered in any detail by the appellate courts or tribunals.

The employment tribunals have no jurisdiction to hear common law tortious claims brought by employees, whether foreign or domestic. However, they do have jurisdiction to hear breach of contract claims brought in respect of particular contracts of employment under the *Employment Tribunals Extension of Jurisdiction (England and Wales) Order 1994*. *Article 3* of that *Order* provides that the tribunal will have jurisdiction to hear the particular claim in circumstances where, had the claim been brought in the ordinary courts, the courts would have been jurisdiction to hear and determine the claim. The effect and scope of art 3 in respect of foreign employment was considered by the Court of Appeal in *Crofts v Cathay Pacific Airways Ltd* [2005] EWCA Civ 599, [2005] IRLR 624, [2005] ICR 1436.

The *forum non conveniens* doctrine can generally be applied equally by the Employment Tribunals in the context of breach of contract claims which are brought before them: see generally, *Crofts* (above).

27.8　Foreign Employees

Employer or employee domiciled in an EU Member State

This information applies until the end of the transition period for the UK's exit from the EU, currently scheduled for 31 December 2020.

Where the defendant is domiciled in an EU member state, the *Civil Jurisdiction and Judgments Act 1982* ('CJJA 1982') applies. CJJA 1982 originally gave effect to the *Brussels Convention*. It was then amended to give effect to *Regulation 44/2001* (the '*Brussels I Regulation*'), which came into force on 1 March 2002. More recently, the CJJA gives effect to *Regulation 1512/2012* (the '*Brussels I Regulation* (recast)') which came into force on 10 January 2015. Changes to the existing law in the UK required by the *Brussels I Regulation* and the *Brussels I Regulation* (recast) are contained in the *Civil Jurisdiction and Judgments Order 2001 (SI 2001/3929)*). The CJJA deals not only with jurisdiction, but also with the enforcement of judgments in other member states. Questions of interpretation arising under the *Convention*, the *Brussels I Regulation* or the *Brussels I Regulation* (recast) may be referred to the CJEU (see EUROPEAN UNION LAW (**24**)). Similar provisions apply under the *Lugano Convention* where the defendant is domiciled in an EFTA member state (*Civil Jurisdiction and Judgments Act 1991*).

Under the *Brussels I* regime, the normal rule is that the defendant must be sued in the state in which he is domiciled (*art 2*). However, special rules apply to claims relating to contracts of employment. These rules are contained in *s 5* (*arts 18–21*) of the *Brussels I Regulation* (see now *arts 20–23 Brussels I Regulation* (recast)). The terms "employer", "employee" and "employment" must be given an autonomous meaning. In *Bosworth v Arcadia Petroleum Ltd* Case C-603/17 (a decision on a reference from the UK Supreme Court), the CJEU observed (at para 26) that, for the purposes of the Brussels I Regulation (recast) ' . . . an employment relationship implies the existence of a hierarchical relationship between the worker and his employer, and that the issue whether such a relationship exists must, in each particular case, be assessed on the basis of all the factors and circumstances characterising the relationship between the parties'. Further, the absence of a formal contract does not preclude the existence of an 'individual contract of employment' but there must be a 'relationship of subordination' between the putative employer and employee: *Bosworth* at paras 26–27. The ability by a putative employee employee to influence the putative employer to an extent that is not negligible will prevent a finding of subordination: cf *Bosworth* at para 31.

The phrase "relating to" should be given a broad interpretation. A dispute may "relate to" a contract of employment even though the claim itself is tortious in nature: see *Alfa Laval Tumba AB v Separator Spares International Ltd* [2013] 2 All ER 463; *James Petter v EMC Europe Ltd & Anor* [2015] IRLR 847; but see *Bosworth v Arcadia Petroleum Ltd* [2016] EWCA Civ 818 and (following the preliminary reference from the Supreme Court) the significantly more expansive interpretation of Advocate General Saugmandsgaard Øe in *Bosworth v Arcadia Petroleum Ltd* Case C 603/17 (24 January 2019) at para 101, in relation to equivalent provisions under the Lugano Convention:

'In short, leaving aside cases where there can be no connection with the employee's duties, there will be, between an employer's claim for compensation and the obligations arising under an 'individual contract of employment', a sufficiently material link to justify that claim relating to that 'contract', as required by the terms of that provision.'.

The CJEU ultimately did not decide this issue, finding in the first instance that there was no individual contract of employment which the dispute could "relate to" (see above).

Under *Section 5* of the *Regulation*, an employer domiciled in a member state may be sued by his employee either: in the courts of the state where the employer is domiciled; or in the courts of the place where the employee habitually carries out his work or in the courts of the last place where he did so; or, if the employee does not or did not habitually carry out his work in any one country, in the courts of the place where the business which engaged the employee is or was situated (*Brussels I Regulation art 19* and *Brussels I Regulation (recast) art 21*) (In *Weber v Universal Ogden Services Ltd*: C-37/00 [2002] IRLR 365, the ECJ held that the relevant criterion for establishing the employee's habitual place of work was, having regard to the whole duration of employment, the place where he or she has worked the longest on the employer's business. See also: *Rutten v Cross Medical Ltd* [1997] IRLR 249, ECJ and *Mulox IBC Ltd v Geels*: C-125/92 [1994] IRLR 422, ECJ. In *Harada Ltd (t/a Chequepoint UK) v Turner* [2001] EWCA Civ 599, [2001] All ER (D) 82 (Apr), the Court of Appeal held that an employment tribunal had jurisdiction to hear a wrongful dismissal claim made by an English employee working in Spain for an Irish offshore company since the central management and control of the company was exercised in England). Thus, the *Regulation* is fairly generous when it comes to claims brought against the employer by the employee (although compare *Powell v OMV Exploration & Production Ltd* [2014] IRLR 80: employee who resided in the UK but habitually carried out his work outside the EU was not entitled to bring a claim in the English employment tribunal against an EU domiciled employer).

The *Regulation* is rather less generous when it comes to claims brought against the employee by the employer. The employer may bring proceedings only in the courts of the Member State in which the employee is domiciled, although he may counter-claim in the courts of another Member State in response to a claim brought by the employee (*Brussels I Regulation art 20*; *Brussels I Regulation (recast) art 22*). The Brussels I regime makes clear that exclusive jurisdiction clauses can only be enforced against an employee when those clauses are entered into after the particular dispute has arisen (*Brussels I Regulation art 21(1)*; *Brussels I Regulation (recast) art 23(1)*). Under *Brussels I Regulation art 18(2)/Brussels I Regulation (recast) art 20(2)* an employer will be 'deemed to be domiciled' in a member state if it has a branch, agency or other establishment in that member state and the dispute arises out of the operations of that branch, agency or establishment.

In *Samengo-Turner v J & H Marsh & McLennan (Services) Ltd* [2007] EWCA Civ 723, [2007] 2 All ER (Comm) 813, [2008] IRLR 237, the Court of Appeal was called upon to apply the provisions of *s 5* of the *Brussels I Regulation* in a case where the employees were claiming that they were entitled to an anti-suit injunction to restrain breach of contract claims brought against them in New York. The employees were both domiciled and employed to work in the UK. When they notified their UK-based employer that they were terminating their employment in order to go and work for a competitor, claims were brought against them in New York for repayment of bonuses which had been awarded to them under a bonus agreement. The employees argued that they were entitled to the anti-suit injunction because, although the companies who could sue under the bonus agreement included US-based companies other than their employer, the reality was that the bonus agreement formed part of their contract of employment with the UK employer and, accordingly, on an application of *arts 18* and *20*, claims under that agreement would have to be brought in the UK, where the employees were domiciled. The Court of Appeal agreed with these arguments, holding that the employees were entitled to anti-suit injunctions restraining the New York proceedings.

For a decision on jurisdiction concerning proceedings involving employers located in two different Member states see *Glaxosmithkline v Rouard*: C-462/06 [2008] ICR 1375, [2008] All ER (D) 312 (May). In that case, the claimant was employed in the first instance by a French domiciled employer. His employment was then transferred to a UK domiciled employer, albeit that his contract with the UK employer imported certain entitlements which the claimant had enjoyed under his contract with the French company, including entitlements as to continuity of service. When the claimant was dismissed from his employment with the UK company, he sought to bring claims in France against both the French and the UK company. He asserted that he was entitled to proceed against the UK company on an application of *art 6(1)* of the *Brussels 1 Regulation* (*art 6(1)* entitles a claimant to sue a number of defendants in the place where any one of them is domiciled, provided that the claims are so closely connected that it is expedient to hear and determine them together to avoid the risk of irreconcilable judgments resulting from separate proceedings). The ECJ held that the claimant could not rely on *art 6(1)* to draw the UK company into the French proceedings for the simple reason that there was a comprehensive code to deal with claims brought in respect of employment contracts which was contained in *s 5* of the *Brussels I Regulation*; on an application of that code, no claim could be brought by the employee against the UK company in the French courts.

The rules for employment disputes under the *Brussels I Regulation* (recast) very closely mirror those in the *Brussels I Regulation*. However, employees' rights have been strengthened as a result of three important changes:

(a)   an employee is now able to sue a non–EU domiciled employer in the courts of the employee's habitual place of work or where the business which engaged the employee is situated (*art 21(2)*);

(b)   the place where an employee habitually works is clarified to include the place where or from where the employee carries out his work (*art 21(1)(b)(i)*). This clarification achieves consistency with the approach under the Rome I Regulation; and

(c)   the rules of jurisdiction on joining co–defendants have been extended to employment claims (*art 20(1)*). This change reverses the decision of the ECJ in *Rouard*.

In matters relating to tort, the *Brussels I Regulation* provides that the employer may be sued either in the courts of the member state where he is domiciled (*art 2(1)*) or in the courts of the place where the harmful event occurred (*art 5(3)*). These rules are maintained under the *Brussels I Regulation* (recast) (see *arts 4(1)* and *7(2)*).

Where proceedings involving the same cause of action and between the same parties ('parallel proceedings') are brought in the courts of different contracting states, a court other than the court 'first seised' is to stay proceedings and where the jurisdiction of the court first seised is established, other courts are to decline jurisdiction (*art 27* of the *Brussels I Regulation*). In the case of *Turner v Grovit*: C–159/02 [2004] IRLR 899, the ECJ was called upon to decide whether it was possible under the Brussels Convention for the English courts to grant restraining orders in respect of proceedings in another Convention country on the ground of abuse of process. The ECJ concluded that the functioning of the Convention was underpinned by the necessity for the contracting state to place mutual trust in the judicial systems and institutions of other states and that, accordingly, it did not permit the jurisdiction of a court to be reviewed by a court in another contracting state other than in the special cases enumerated in *art 28*. These principles apply with equal force to the provisions of the *Brussels I Regulation*. However, in cases to which the *Brussels I Regulation* (recast) applies the first seised rule has been partly reversed by *art 31(2)*. The court designated in an exclusive jurisdiction agreement has priority to decide on the validity of the agreement and on the extent to which the agreement applies to the dispute pending before it.

The *Brussels I Regulation* (recast) introduced revised rules applicable where parallel proceedings have been initiated in the courts of a non Member State (*art 33*). In such cases, the English courts now have a discretion to stay proceedings if: (a) it is expected that the court of the third State will give a judgment capable of recognition and, where applicable, of enforcement in that Member State; and (b) the court of the Member State is satisfied that a stay is necessary for the proper administration of justice. The court should take into account all the circumstances of the case including: the degree of connections between the facts and parties; how far advanced the third state proceedings are; and whether the third State's court can be expected to give a judgment within a reasonable time (*Recital (24)*). There are also new rules governing related proceedings in non Member State courts (*art 34*).

APPLICABLE LAW

27.9   Contract claims

Where an employer and employee are both English, and the work is done in England, it will generally be clear that the contract of employment is governed by English law, and there will normally be no doubt as to the jurisdiction of the English courts to deal with any contractual disputes which may arise. However, where there is a foreign element of some kind, difficult questions may arise concerning the system of law which governs the contract, and as to where any proceedings may be brought in this country. This is an extremely complicated area of law, and what follows is intended only as a simplified outline guide.

The *Contracts (Applicable Law) Act 1990* was enacted to give force in the United Kingdom to the *Rome Convention on the Law Applicable to Contractual Obligations* of 1980. That was a treaty between the EC member states, and provision is made for the ECJ to be given jurisdiction to determine questions concerning its interpretation (see EUROPEAN UNION LAW **(24)**). However, the Act applies to all contracts, not merely to those with an EC connection. With effect from 17 December 2009, the *Convention* ceased to apply in the UK and was replaced by a new *Regulation EC No 593/2008*, known as the *Rome I Regulation*. So far as "individual employment contracts" are concerned, the provisions of the *Rome I Regulation* broadly mirror those contained in the *Convention* (see in particular *art 8*). Therefore, the earlier case law on the interpretation and application of the *Convention* remains relevant. The *Rome I Regulation* continues to apply in the UK, notwithstanding its withdrawal from the EU, and will continue to apply in the UK to contracts which are concluded before the end of the transition period (currently scheduled to end on 31 December 2020) after the UK withdraws completely from the EU: *Withdrawal Agreement, Art 66*. Rome I will be retained in domestic law after the transition period ends. The *Law Applicable to Contractual Obligations and Non-Contractual Obligations (Amendment etc.) (UK Exit) Regulations 2019* convert the rules in the Rome Convention into domestic law (insofar as it relates to contracts entered into between 1 April 1991 and 16 December 2009) and gives effect to the *Rome I Regulation*.

A contract is governed by the system of law chosen by the parties, such choice being either expressed or demonstrated with reasonable certainty by the terms of the contract or the circumstances of the case (*art 3(1)*). However, in the case of a contract of employment, a choice of law made by the parties may not deprive an employee of the protection afforded to him by the "non-derogable provisions" or "mandatory rules" of the system of law which would apply if no such choice had been made (*art 9(2), Regulation* and *art 6(1), Convention*).

Mandatory rules are those which cannot be derogated from by contract in the law of the country concerned (*art 3(3)*). Mandatory rules consist not only of provisions relating to the contract of employment, but also provisions such as those concerning industrial safety and hygiene which are regarded in certain Member States as being provisions of public law. Hence, for example, under the *Convention*, if an English employee worked in Great Britain for an English employer, it is not possible to deprive him of the right to claim unfair dismissal **(54), (55), (56)** by providing that the contract shall be governed by, say, Hong Kong law (see further *Base Metal Trading Ltd v Shamurin* [2003] EWHC 2419 (Comm), [2004] 1 All ER (Comm) 159; see also *Employment Rights Act 1996, s 204*).

If the parties to a contract of employment have not chosen the system of law which is to govern the contract, then it will be governed by:

27.9 Foreign Employees

(a)   the law of the country in which or failing that from which the employee habitually carries out his work in performance of the contract, even if he is temporarily employed in another country (*art 8(2)* and *Recital (36)*); or

(b)   if the employee does not habitually carry out his work in any one country, the law of the country in which the place of business through which he was engaged is situated (*art 8(3)* and *Voogsgeerd v Navimer SA*: C-384/10, [2012] I.L.Pr 341, ECJ),

unless it appears from the circumstances as a whole that the contract is more closely connected with another country, in which case the contract shall be governed by the law of that country (*art 8(4)*).

The concept of the country in which the work is habitually carried out must be interpreted broadly (see *Koelzsch v Luxembourg*: C-29/10, [2012] QB 210, [2011] IRLR 514 at paras 43, 45 considering the narrower terms of *art 6(2)* of the Convention). As *art 8(2)* of the *Rome I Regulation* clarifies, this criterion must be understood as referring to the place in which or from which the employee carries out his working activities. For recent guidance on the application of *art 8(4)* see *Schlecker v Boedeker*: C-64/12, [2014] IRLR 151, CJEU.

The application of a rule of foreign law specified by *art 8* of the *Regulation* is subject to a number of limitations.

Firstly, *art 8* does not restrict the application of overriding mandatory provisions of the law of the forum (*art 7(2)*, *Convention* and *art 9(2)*, *Regulation*). *Article 9* of the *Regulation* defines "overriding mandatory provisions" as provisions the respect for which is regarded as crucial by a country for safeguarding its public interests, such as its political, social or economic organisation, to such extent that they are applicable to any situation falling within their scope, irrespective of the law otherwise applicable to the contract under the *Regulation*.

Secondly, under *art 7(1)* of the *Convention*, even if one system of law applies (eg English law), effect could be given to the mandatory rules of the law of another country with which the contract has a close connection (eg France), provided that those mandatory rules would be applied under French law whatever system of law governed the contract, and depending upon the nature and purpose of those rules and the consequences of their application or non-application. However, importantly, *art 7(1)* did not have the force of law in the United Kingdom (*Contracts (Applicable Law) Act 1990, s 2(2)*). *Art 9(3)* of the *Regulation* adopts a narrower approach, providing that effect may be given to the mandatory rules of the law of the country where the obligations arising out of the contract have to be or have been performed, in so far as those mandatory rules render the performance of the contract unlawful.

Thirdly, in addition to showing deference to mandatory rules of the forum, the *Regulation* makes it clear that the application of a rule of foreign law specified by the *Regulation* may be refused if it is 'manifestly incompatible with the public policy (*ordre publique*) of the forum' (*art 21, Regulation* and *art 16, Convention*)). In *Duarte v Black and Decker Corpn* [2007] EWHC 2720 (QB), [2007] All ER (D) 378 (Nov), the High Court was called upon to consider whether English common law principles relating to the enforcement of restrictive covenants in a contract of employment effectively overrode the governing law of the contract, which was in that case the law of Maryland. The court held that English common law rules relating to the enforcement of restrictive covenants in employment contracts did not constitute mandatory rules of the English forum and, hence, *art 6.1* of the *Convention* was not engaged in respect of the covenants. However, the court also decided that those common law rules enshrined public policy principles which should be applied to the contract under *art 16* of the *Convention*. As it happens, the court found that the law of Maryland in any event operated so as to ensure that the covenants were too wide to be enforceable.

Under *art 7(1)* of the *Convention*, even if one system of law applies (eg English law), effect could be given to the mandatory rules of the law of another country with which the contract has a close connection (eg France), provided that those mandatory rules would be applied under French law whatever system of law governed the contract, and depending upon the nature and purpose of those rules and the consequences of their application or non-application. However, importantly *art 7(1)* did not have the force of law in the United Kingdom (*Contracts (Applicable Law) Act 1990 Act, s 2(2)*).

Fourthly, *art 8* of the *Regulation* is without prejudice to the application of overriding mandatory provisions of the country to which a worker is posted in accordance with *Directive 96/71* (*Recital (34), Regulation*).

27.10 Tort claims

The rules determining what law applies to tortious claims arising out of employment disputes (such as conspiracy and unlawful interference) have evolved over time. Originally, non-statutory common law rules applied, see, eg *Sayers v International Drilling Co NV* [1971] 3 All ER 163 and *Johnson v Coventry Churchill International Ltd* [1992] 3 All ER 14. From 1 May 1996 until 11 January 2009, the common law rules were abolished and superseded by provisions contained in the *Private International Law (Miscellaneous Provisions) Act 1995* ('*PIL(MP)A*'). Under *PIL(MP)A*, the general rule was that the applicable law would be the law of the country in which the events constituting the tort in question occur (*s 11(1)*). That rule was displaced where, viewed overall, it appeared that the tort was more closely connected to a country other than that which would be appropriate if the general rule were applied (*s 12(1)*). See further *Harding v Wealands* [2006] UKHL 32, [2006] 4 All ER 1 where the House of Lords decided, in respect of an accident which took place in New South Wales, that the provisions of *PIL(MP)A* did not operate to enable the capping provisions contained in New South Wales personal injury legislation to apply to quantification by the UK courts of personal injury damages. However, with effect from 11 January 2009, the provisions of PIL(MP)A, insofar as they relate to torts in the employment context were superseded by *Regulation EC No 864/2007*, known as the *Rome II Regulation*. The *Rome II Regulation* continues to apply in the UK, notwithstanding its withdrawal from the EU, and will continue to apply in the UK to events giving rise to damage occurring before the end of the transition period (currently scheduled to end on 31 December 2020) after the UK withdraws completely from the EU: *Withdrawal Agreement, Art 66*. Rome II will be retained in domestic law after the transition period ends: the *Law Applicable to Contractual Obligations and Non-Contractual Obligations (Amendment etc.) (UK Exit) Regulations 2019*. Under *art 4* of *Rome II Regulation*, the general rule is that the law which applies to the tort is the law of the country where the damage occurred. This general rule may be displaced in circumstances where the parties are habitually resident in another country at the time the damage occurs (*art 4(2)*) or where it is clear from all the circumstances that the tort is manifestly more closely connected with another country (*art 4(3)*). Specific provision is made in the *Rome II Regulation* for particular non-contractual obligations in *arts 5–13*. Those relevant to the employment context are *art 6* (unfair competition), *art 8* (intellectual property rights, for example database rights) and *art 9* (industrial action).

TERRITORIAL SCOPE OF EMPLOYMENT LEGISLATION

27.11 Discrimination claims

Where an employment relationship incorporates a foreign element (eg the employee has worked for his employer abroad), a question will often arise as to whether, in view of that foreign element, the employee has the right to bring a discrimination claim against his employer in the domestic employment tribunal. This question is often referred to as the 'territorial jurisdiction', 'territorial application' question. In order to distinguish the international jurisdictional question, the phrase 'territorial scope' is preferred here.

27.11   Foreign Employees

Prior to the coming into force of the *Equality Act 2010*, answering the territorial scope question entailed applying the express territorial scope provisions contained in the relevant anti-discrimination enactments see further: *s 1* of the *Equal Pay Act 1970*; *ss 6* and *10* of the *Sex Discrimination Act 1975* (as amended by the *Employment Equality (Sex Discrimination) Regulations 2005 (SI 2005/2467)*; *ss 4* and *8* of the *Race Relations Act 1976*; *ss 4(6)* and *68* of the *Disability Discrimination Act 1995*; and *reg 9* of the *Employment Equality (Religion and Belief) Regulations 2003*, *Employment Equality (Sexual Orientation) Regulations 2003* and *reg 10* of the *Employment Equality (Age) Regulations 2006*. Whilst there were some differences in how these provisions were framed across the different enactments, in general the employee would enjoy the protection of British anti-discrimination legislation provided that he or she worked 'wholly or partly in Great Britain'. On 1 October 2010, the new *Equality Act 2010* came into force. A principal aim of that Act was to consolidate all the myriad discrimination enactments into a single piece of legislation. One effect of the introduction of the *Equality Act* is that the territorial application question now has to be considered afresh. Below, consideration is given both to the territorial scope principles which applied under the original anti-discrimination enactments and to the position which now obtains under the new *Equality Act*.

The Pre-Equality Act position

As was indicated above, in cases involving an employment relationship which incorporated a foreign element, the question whether the employee could bring discrimination claims in Great Britain against his or her employer generally turned on whether the employee had done his work either 'wholly or partly in Great Britain'. In the case of *Saggar v Ministry of Defence* [2005] EWCA Civ 413, [2005] IRLR 618, the Court of Appeal was obliged to determine the meaning of the expression 'does his work wholly or partly in Great Britain' in the context of a claim brought under the *Race Relations Act 1976*. The issue arose in the context of certain complaints of racial discrimination which had been brought by an MOD employee who had initially been based in the UK for 16 years but had then been permanently stationed abroad. The issue for the Court of Appeal was whether the fact that the employee had, in the early phase of his employment, been based in the UK was sufficient to establish that he had worked 'wholly or partly in Great Britain' for the purposes of the Act. The Court of Appeal held that the correct approach was to focus not on the employment relationship as a whole, from its beginning to end, rather than merely on the time when the discrimination was alleged to have occurred. Subsequently, in *Tradition Securities and Futures SA v X* [2009] ICR 88, [2008] IRLR 934, the Employment Appeal Tribunal considered the concept of 'doing work wholly or partly in Great Britain' in the context of an employee who worked initially in France but then transferred to work in the UK. The employee went on to bring claims of sex discrimination in the English employment tribunal in respect of the period when she worked in France. The issue for the EAT was whether the *Sex Discrimination Act 1975* applied to the French phase of the employee's employment. The EAT concluded that it did not. It arrived at this conclusion based on the following analysis: during the period the employee was employed in France there would have been no question of her bringing claims under the *Sex Discrimination Act 1975* in the English employment tribunal as she would have not have worked wholly or partly in Great Britain during any part of this period; it could not be accepted that the right to claim discrimination in respect of this earlier period could, in effect, be retrospectively created as a result of the employee latterly coming and working in Great Britain. In *British Airways Plc v Mak* [2010] All ER (D) 162 (Jan) (UKEAT/0055/09/SM), a question arose as to whether certain cabin crew members who were based in Hong Kong could pursue claims of age and race discrimination against British Airways in the English employment tribunal. It was not in dispute that, as part of their duties, the claimants flew in and out of London airports and, further, that, whilst they were in the UK they performed certain airport duties and also undertook training. The employment tribunal decided that the work done by the claimants in Great Britain was sufficient to establish that they worked 'partly in Great Britain' and, hence, they could pursue their age and race discrimination claims.

British Airways appealed the tribunal's judgment on the basis that the work done in Great Britain was *de minimis* and, hence, was insufficient to found jurisdiction. The EAT, having considered the Court of Appeal's judgment in *Saggar v Ministry of Defence*, accepted that jurisdiction could not be established if the work done here was *de minimis*. However, it rejected British Airways' case on the basis that the tribunal had properly found as a fact that the work done by the claimants had not been *de minimis* in all the circumstances. The Court of Appeal rejected British Airways' appeal against the EAT's judgment, [2011] EWCA Civ 184, [2011] All ER (D) 256 (Feb). The Supreme Court granted permission to appeal but the case subsequently settled ([2011] ICR 895).

EU law considerations

Where employees have been working exclusively in another Member State of the European Union, a question may arise as to whether they may pursue discrimination claims in the domestic employment tribunals, notwithstanding that they have never actually done any work in the UK. This was an issue which arose in the case of *Ministry of Defence v Wallis & Grocott* [2011] EWCA Civ 231, [2011] All ER (D) 97 (Mar). In that case, two female claimants who had formerly been employed by the Ministry of Defence at NATO headquarters in Belgium brought claims of sex discrimination (and unfair dismissal) in the English employment tribunal. It was not in dispute before the tribunal that, whilst employed by the MOD, the claimants had worked exclusively in Belgium. The MOD argued that, in the circumstances and pursuant to the express provisions of the *Sex Discrimination Act 1975*, the tribunal had no jurisdiction to hear the claimants' sex discrimination claims as their employment with the MOD had not entailed them working 'wholly or partly in Great Britain'. The claimants, relying on a judgment of the EAT in *Bleuse v MBT Transport* (as to which see further below), argued that the tribunal did have jurisdiction to hear their discrimination claims, particularly because any other result would amount to an unlawful denial of the rights which they enjoyed under the directly effective *EU Equal Treatment Directive 76/207*. The tribunal accepted the claimants' arguments and held that it had jurisdiction to hear the discrimination claims (it also concluded that it had jurisdiction to hear the unfair dismissal claims – see further below). The tribunal's decision was upheld first by the EAT and then by the Court of Appeal. The Court of Appeal, agreeing with the EAT, held that the claimants enjoyed the protection of the directly effective rights afforded under the *Directive* and that, in order to give effect to those rights, the provisions of the SDA would have to be read down so as to afford the tribunal jurisdiction to hear the claims.

A related question faced the Supreme Court in *Duncombe v Department for Education & Skills* [2011] IRLR 498, [2011] ICR 495. The Supreme Court considered the application of the *Fixed Term Employees (Prevention of Less Favourable Treatment) Regulations 2002* to employees of English employers, who had always worked in another EU country. Like the equality legislation explored above, the *Regulations* also enacted EU law. The Court found that it was unnecessary for it to reach a conclusion on whether the *Regulations* applied in this situation. However, it commented that if it had had to do so, it would have needed to make a reference to the CJEU. It found that, intuitively, employees ought to be protected in other EU countries, but that this issue was not yet *acte clair*.

See also *Williams v University of Nottingham* [2007] IRLR 660, where the EAT concluded that principles derived from the House of Lords' judgment in *Lawson v Serco* (discussed further below) should inform the Tribunal's approach to the application of certain express territorial scope provisions in the *Disability Discrimination Act 1995*.

Following the conclusion of the transition period for the UK's withdrawal from the EU (currently expected to occurr on 31 December 2020), the Employment Tribunal will not continue to have regard to EU law in determining whether claims fall within its jurisdiction.

27.11 Foreign Employees

Territorial scope of the Equality Act 2010

Whilst many practitioners may have expected the new *Equality Act 2010* to embody express territorial scope provisions similar to those contained in the original discrimination enactments, in fact the *Equality Act* contains no express territorial scope provisions at all. It is simply silent on the subject. The Explanatory Notes to the Act do not themselves shed much light on how the tribunals are to approach questions of territorial scope in respect of claims brought under the Act. They merely state that: 'the Act leaves it to tribunals to determine whether the law applies, depending for example on the connection between the employment relationship and Great Britain'. It remains unclear what kind of 'connection' is needed to fall within the *Equality Act's* territorial scope. In 2012, the Employment Appeal Tribunal held that determining whether claims fell within the jurisdictional ambit of the *EqA 2010* required the application of the test outlined by the House of Lords in *Lawson v Serco* (as to which see further below) – see *Bates Van Winklehoff v Clyde & Co LLP* (UKEAT/0169/12/RN). However, importantly the EAT reached this conclusion in circumstances where it was accepted by both parties that *Lawson v Serco* principles, which were devised in the context of a number of claims brought under the *Employment Rights Act 1996 ('ERA 1996')*, applied equally under the *EqA 2010* as they did under *ERA 1996*. This decision was appealed to the Court of Appeal ([2012] EWCA Civ 1207, [2012] IRLR 992), but there was no challenge to the judgment on this point. In *Ministry of Defence v Holloway* (2015) UKEAT/0396/14, [2015] All ER (D) 391 (Jul), EAT, a discrimination claim brought by civilian employees of the MOD in Cyprus, Langstaff P held that the applicable test depends upon the closeness of the connection, and raises much the same issue as raised by application of the *Ravat* principle regarding the *ERA 1996*.

Most recently, in *R (Hottak and AL) v Secretary of State for Foreign and Commonwealth Affairs and anor* [2016] EWCA Civ 438, [2016] IRLR 534, the Divisional Court considered a judicial review challenge to the protection redundancy package for Afghan nationals who had been employed as interpreters for British Forces in Afghanistan. The claimants claimed that the Afghan scheme was less generous than the equivalent scheme introduced when British Forces withdraw from Iraq. The claimants argued that their less favourable treatment amount to discrimination on grounds of nationality in relation to employee benefits and public functions, contrary to *sections 39(2)* and *29(6)* of the *Equality Act*. Both the claimants and the Foreign Secretary at least implicitly accepted that the approach to the territorial scope of the *ERA 1996* applied by analogy. The Court accepted this approach, reasoning that no intention may be imputed to Parliament that the territorial scope of the protection against discrimination be wider than unfair dismissal or other employment rights, and that there is much to be said for symmetry between the two statutes. Applying this approach, the Court held that *section 39(2)* did not apply on the facts since their employment relationship did not have a closer connection with Great Britain and with British employment law than with Afghanistan and Afghan law. The claimants could not be considered to be expatriate workers or peripatetic workers, however widely those terms might be understood. Their contracts of employment were not governed by English law. The connection with Great Britain was limited to the identity of their employer. Although they worked in and from both Camp Bastion and the British Embassy, this was far removed from operating in an international enclave. Their position was substantially the same as locally employed staff in a British embassy. The claimants continued to live and work in Afghanistan, and they did or could go home when not working. The Court of Appeal dismissed the claimants' appeal, finding that the Divisional Court's analysis correctly identified the principles, correctly assessed the relevant facts, was soundly based and arrived at a conclusion that was not only open to it on the evidence but was the correct one.

Claims under the Employment Rights Act 1996

Section 204 of the *ERA 1996* provides that the Act applies irrespective of the law which, apart from the *Act*, governs any person's employment. Accordingly, the *ERA 1996* contains non-derogable provisions for the purposes of *art 8(1)* of the *Rome I Regulation*. Where, in the absence of a choice, English law would be applicable the employee may not be deprived of rights under the *ERA 1996*.

The question whether foreign employees enjoy the rights afforded under the *ERA 1996*, particularly the right to claim unfair dismissal, was addressed by the House of Lords in the joined cases of *Lawson v Serco Ltd, Botham v MOD and Crofts v Veta Ltd* [2006] UKHL 3, [2006] IRLR 289, [2006] ICR 250 ('*Lawson v Serco*'). The following principles were enunciated by the House of Lords in *Lawson v Serco*:

(a)   the question whether a particular claim falls within the territorial ambit of the unfair dismissal provisions contained in the *Employment Rights Act 1996* will depend on the nature of the particular employment arrangements in issue in the case;

(b)   in 'standard cases' (ie cases where the employee works in Great Britain), the employee will be able to pursue their claim of unfair dismissal if they were 'working in Great Britain at the time of the dismissal';

(c)   in cases involving 'peripatetic employees' (eg airline pilots and international travelling salespersons), the employee will be able to pursue their claim of unfair dismissal if they were 'based in Great Britain' during the employment (cf *Hunt v United Airlines Inc* [2008] ICR 934, [2008] All ER (D) 35 (Apr), EAT);

(d)   in cases involving 'expatriate employees' (ie employees who work and live abroad), the employee will not be able to pursue their claim of unfair dismissal in the absence of 'exceptional circumstances'. Those exceptional circumstances could include, for example: where the employee was posted abroad by a British-based employer to work on behalf of or as a representative of that employer (such a situation might arise in the case of a foreign correspondent posted to a foreign country by a British newspaper); or where the employee is working abroad but within a 'political or social enclave' (for example a British military base).

The question as to whether the connection between an employee's employment and the United Kingdom is sufficiently strong to found jurisdiction is an evaluative judgment to be made on the basis of the underlying facts but the evaluation is itself a question of law. An appellate court or tribunal will not interfere with the judgment unless the first instance tribunal took into account irrelevant matters, failed to take into account relevant matters, made some error or was otherwise wrong: *Jeffery v British Council* [2018] EWCA Civ 2253 (per Longmore and Peter Jackson LJJ, Underhill LJ dissenting).

In practice, the greatest difficulties in applying the *Lawson v Serco* principles tend to arise in the context of 'expatriate employee' cases. However, see *Fuller v United Healthcare Services Inc* [2014] All ER (D) 41 (Sep) (UKEAT/0464/13/BA) in which the EAT held that a US citizen employed by a US company who worked in London almost half the time fell outside the territorial scope of the statutory protections against unfair dismissal and sexual orientation discrimination.

In *Duncombe v Department for Education & Skills (No. 2)* [2011] UKSC 36, [2011] 4 All ER 1020, [2011] IRLR 840, the question arose whether teachers who were employed by the Department for Education and Skills to work in European schools throughout the European Union enjoyed the protection from unfair dismissal conferred by *ERA 1996*. The Supreme Court concluded that they did. The Supreme Court took the view that the test approved in *Lawson v Serco* was whether the employment had "much stronger connections" with Great Britain and with British employment law than with and any other system of law.

In *Duncombe*, whilst the teachers were classic expatriate employees in that they lived and worked abroad, the facts of their cases were sufficiently exceptional to bring them within the scope of the legislation. Relevant factors here included that the teachers were employed to work in effect within international enclaves; they had no particular connection with the countries within which they were working and they did not pay local taxes.

The question was next considered by the Supreme Court in *Ravat v Halliburton Manufacturing & Services Ltd* [2012] UKSC 1, [2012] IRLR 315. In *Ravat*, an English national was employed by a subsidiary of a multinational corporation. The subsidiary was based in Scotland. However, the employee discharged his duties in Libya. The work done by Mr Ravat was done for the benefit of a German subsidiary of the multinational corporation. Mr Ravat continued to live in England during the period of his employment and commuted to his work in Libya, spending 28 days there followed by 28 days in England. Consistent with his commuter status, Mr Ravat's contract of employment afforded him the same benefits which he would have enjoyed had he been employed in England. Moreover, his employer had assured him that English law would govern the contract. Mr Ravat was dismissed from his employment by a manager employed by another British-based subsidiary who was based in Cairo. The Supreme Court concluded that the Scottish employment tribunal had been entitled to conclude that it had jurisdiction to hear Mr Ravat's claim for unfair dismissal. On the wider question of when an expatriate employee's case would be sufficiently exceptional to fall within the scope of *ERA 1996*, the Supreme Court took the view that, in order to amount to an exceptional case, the employment would have to have a "stronger connection" with Great Britain than with the place where the employee worked. The place where the employee discharged his duties was highly relevant to but not necessarily determinative of the application of this test. Other relevant factors would include: the nationality of the employee; the place of recruitment and the location of the employer. In every case, it would be a question of fact and degree whether an expatriate employee's case was sufficiently exceptional such that it fell outside the general rule. In cases where the employee was, in effect, only a quasi-expatriate employee (ie because they worked abroad but continued to live in Great Britain) the general rule should in any event be applied more loosely. In cases where the employment involved a number of subsidiary companies of a larger multinational, it was important to be aware of the foreign elements which any foreign subsidiaries introduced into the employment relationship. However, those elements should not be relied upon so as to ignore the reality of the employee's situation. In Mr Ravat's case, it was unrealistic to treat his employment as falling outside the scope of *ERA 1996*. This was particularly in view of the facts that: Mr Ravat was British and had been recruited in Great Britain; the employer's business was based in Great Britain; the employer had chosen to treat Mr Ravat as a commuter and, accordingly, had preserved all his contractual entitlements as though he had been employed in Great Britain; the employer had given Mr Ravat assurances to the effect that he would continue to enjoy the protection of English law; and, further, Mr Ravat had continued to live in England throughout his employment.

In *Bates Van Winklehoff v Clyde & Co LLP* [2012] EWCA Civ 1207, [2012] IRLR 992, the Court of Appeal confirmed that it is only in the case of expatriate workers who both live and work wholly abroad that it is necessary to undertake an extensive comparative exercise to work out with which country the employment has the closest connection. Where the claimant lives and/or works for at least part of the time in the UK, a less strict test applies. The circumstances need not be truly exceptional before the connection with UK employment law can be identified. All that is required is that the tribunal should satisfy itself that the connection is sufficiently strong to enable it to be said that Parliament would have regarded it as appropriate for the tribunal to deal with the claim. Ms Bates van Winkelhof was a partner of a UK LLP who had been recruited to work in Africa but visited London for work on a regular basis. The Court of Appeal held that these facts involved a sufficient connection with the UK.

What *Lawson*, *Ravat* and *Duncombe* all confirm is that, whilst in the majority of cases expatriate employees will not fall within the scope of *ERA 1996*, there will be exceptional cases where the general rule does not apply. In *Duncombe*, Lady Hale emphasised that there is no hard and fast rule and that it is a mistake to try and torture the circumstances of one employment to make it fit one of the examples given in *Lawson*. In marginal cases, *Ravat* suggests it will be particularly important to consider a whole range of factors affecting the location of the employment relationship including not least: the nature and location of the employer's business, including whether the employer is a UK company and where the employment was administered; the nationality of the employee; where the employee was recruited; where the employee worked; where the employee lived during the period of the employment; whether the employee commuted from Great Britain; where the employee was taxed; whether the employee was paid in foreign currency; whether the contract was designed to afford the employee benefits which were peculiar to the foreign jurisdiction or to the domestic jurisdiction; whether the employee had any particular connection to the place where the duties were discharged and whether the employer gave assurances to the effect that the employee would be protected by domestic employment law. Considerable uncertainty remains regarding the relevance of particular factors, and the weight to be given to each factor, in any given case. Ultimately, the approach to the territorial scope question in *Ravat* resembles closely the *forum conveniens* stage of the jurisdiction question at common law. This conflation of methodology threatens to obscure the important conceptual distinction between the two questions. Moreover, not all of the connecting factors under the jurisdictional enquiry are (or should be) of equal relevance to the territorial scope question. Indeed, two of the factors relied on in *Ravat* are particularly problematic. First, absent any express statutory limitation, it is difficult to see why the employee's nationality should be of any relevance. Secondly, any reliance on the choice of law governing the contract of employment is seemingly precluded by *ERA 1996, s 204*.

In *Dhunna v Creditsights Ltd* [2013] ICR 909, [2013] All ER (D) 133 (May), the EAT considered the case of an employee who lived and worked in Dubai for the UK subsidiary of a global organisation operated from the US and was line managed from Delhi and paid in US dollars. The EAT held that it was not enough that his employment had a greater connection with Great Britain and British employment law than with the foreign jurisdiction. The litmus test was whether the links were sufficiently strong to enable it to be said that Parliament would have regarded it as appropriate for the English tribunal to deal with the claim. The EAT rejected the argument that the tribunal should consider the substantive differences between any competing systems of law. The decision was upheld by the Court of Appeal who confirmed that the employee's connection with the UK were tenuous (see *Creditsights Ltd v Dhunna* [2014] EWCA Civ 1238, [2014] IRLR 953; followed in *Foreign and Commonwealth Office and ors v Bamieh* [2019] EWCA Civ 803, [2019] IRLR 736 at paras 63 and 82). Secondly, in *Powell v OMV Exploration & Production Ltd* [2014] IRLR 80, [2014] 1CR 63, Langstaff J reaffirmed that the starting point, which must not be forgotten, is that the statute will have no application to work outside the UK. There must be a 'sufficiently strong connection' to displace that position.

In *Olsen v Gearbulk Services Ltd & Anor* [2015] IRLR 818, the EAT held that a Danish national who was an 'internationally mobile' employee of a Bermudian company, living in Switzerland, who spent more time working in the UK than anywhere else, fell outside the territorial scope of *ERA 1996, s 204*. The EAT agreed with the ET's finding that the claimant had taken great steps to distance himself from having any permanence in the UK. After taking advice on his tax position, the claimant had freely chosen to be governed by a contract governed by Bermudian law and not to live in the UK.

In *Jeffery v British Council* [2018] EWCA Civ 2253, [2018] ICR 929, the Court of Appeal considered that the inclusion of a choice of law provision in the contract selecting the law of England and Wales was a factor that was relevant to assessing the strength of the connection of the employment relationship with British employment law, but was not decisive and would only be relevant where it had been drawn to the attention of the employee. However, where a standard form contract is used, this might undermine the significance of the choice of law provision. Similarly, the Scottish Employment Appeal Tribunal concluded that provisions of a contract nominating Scots law as the governing law and conferring jurisdiction on the courts of Scotland was a relevant factor to be taken into account in assessing the strength of the connection: *Hexagon Sociedad Anonima v Hepburn* [2020] IRLR 263.

Whilst the House of Lords in *Lawson v Serco* did not decide the point, it is generally accepted that the *Lawson v Serco* principles apply not merely to unfair dismissal provisions but also to all the other provisions of the *Employment Rights Act 1996*. A number of other types of claims have been considered to be potentially available in this context:

- provisions in the *Working Time Regulations 1998*: *Bleuse v MBT Transport Ltd* [2008] IRLR 264 and, *Dhunna v Creditsights Ltd* [2013] All ER (D) 133 (May) (UKEAT/0246/12/LA);

- whistleblowing claims: *Bates Van Winklehoff v Clyde & Co LLP* [2012] EWCA Civ 1207, [2012] IRLR 992; *Jeffery v British Council* [2018] EWCA Civ 2253, [2018] ICR 929 and *Foreign and Commonwealth Office and ors v Bamieh* [2019] EWCA Civ 803, [2019] IRLR 736; and

- claims under the *Trade Union and Labour Relations (Consolidation) Act 1992*: *Netjets Management Ltd v CAC and Skyshare* [2012] IRLR 986.

Additional considerations

Where an employee works in another Member State of the European Union, a question may arise as to whether that employee can rely on directly effective EU rights in order to pursue claims in the domestic employment tribunals. This question has been considered in a number of recent. In *Bleuse v MBT Transport Ltd* [2008] IRLR 264, the EAT held that an expatriate employee who had worked in other Member States of the EU was entitled to bring claims under the *Working Time Regulations 1998* against his UK based employer. This was despite the fact that he had never worked in the UK. The EAT reached this conclusion on the basis that this was the result which was required by directly effective provisions of the *Working Time Directive 2003/88*. A similar conclusion was reached by the Court of Appeal in the context of a claim brought under the *Fixed-term Employees (Prevention of Less Favourable Treatment) Regulations 2002* ('the 2002 Regulations'): *Duncombe v Department for Education & Skills* [2009] EWCA Civ 1355, [2010] IRLR 331. However, the Court of Appeal's judgment in *Duncombe* was subsequently overturned by the Supreme Court, albeit on other grounds, *Duncombe v Department for Education & Skills* [2011] UKSC 14, [2011] 2 All ER 417, [2011] IRLR 498. The Supreme Court found that it was unnecessary for it to reach a conclusion on whether the *Regulations* applied in this situation. However, it commented that, if it had had to do so, it would have needed to make a reference to the CJEU since this issue was not yet *acte clair*. In the circumstances, query whether the Court of Appeal's analysis in *Duncombe* can properly be relied upon. It should be noted that the *Duncombe* case subsequently came before the Supreme Court for a second time, *Duncombe v Department for Education and Skills (No. 2)* [2011] 4 All ER 1020, [2011] IRLR 840. On this second occasion, the claimant teachers succeeded in persuading the Supreme Court that their cases did fall within the scope of the *ERA 1996* on an application of *Lawson v Serco* principles (see above).

In *Holis Metal Industries Ltd v GMB and Newell Ltd* [2008] IRLR 187, the EAT concluded that the *Transfer of Undertakings (Protection of Employment) Regulations 2006* had the potential to apply to the transfer of undertakings which were situated in the UK prior to the transfer but were then transferred outside of the EU.

Following the judgment of the House of Lords in *Lawson v Serco*, it would seem that domestic employment tribunals cannot apply the common law doctrine of *forum non conveniens* in the context of statutory claims which come before it (see in particular per Lord Hoffmann at para 24). Thus, where the domestic employment tribunal has territorial jurisdiction to hear a particular statutory claim, it cannot then refuse to hear the claim on the basis that there is arguably some more appropriate forum in which the claim could be heard. This is simply because no foreign court has jurisdiction to hear a claim under UK employment legislation.

When bringing a claim against a foreign respondent in the Employment Tribunal, the rules of service provided for in *rule 8(2)* of the Tribunal Rules (as set out in *Schedule 1* to the *Employment Tribunals (Constitution & Rules etc) Regulations 2013*) must be considered. No authoritative guidance as to how this rule should be applied in the case of a foreign respondent has yet been provided by the appellate courts or tribunals. However, in the case of *Pervez v Macquarie Bank Ltd (London Branch)* (UKEAT/0246/10/CEA) [2011] ICR 266, [2011] IRLR 284, the EAT held that *rule 19(1)* of the predecessor to the current *Tribunal Rules*, could not be relied upon to oust the tribunal's jurisdiction in circumstances where that jurisdiction was afforded under primary legislation. Thus, in *Pervez*, the fact that the claimant's employer was based in Hong Kong and, hence, could not apparently be sued in the tribunal pursuant to *rule 19(1)* of the *Tribunal Rules*, did not operate to prevent the tribunal hearing the claimant's claims of unfair dismissal and race and religious discrimination. The tribunal had jurisdiction to hear these claims under the relevant primary enactments and that jurisdiction could not be excluded through the application of a rule contained in secondary legislation. For further discussion of *rule 19(1)* and *Pervez v Macquarie* see *Hasan v Shell International Shipping Services (PTE) Ltd & Ors* [2014] All ER (D) 15 (Feb) (UKEAT/0242/13/SM).

27.12 STATE IMMUNITY, DIPLOMATIC IMMUNITY AND DOMESTIC WORKERS

Particular problems of state immunity or diplomatic immunity may arise in cases where individuals are employed by foreign state embassies or foreign diplomatic agents. In practice, many of these posts are filled by foreign nationals. It is important to distinguish these two different types of immunity under international law. Difficult questions may also arise in the context of employment by international organisations but there is so far little English authority on this topic, which is beyond the scope of this book: for a recent decision of the EAT see *R Warner v B&M Europe, European Patent Office* [2016] All ER (D) 174 (Jul) (UKEAT/0139/16/RN) finding that the grant of immunity to an international organisation does not engage *Art 6* of the *ECHR* insofar as such immunity is required by a rule of international law and/or is compatible with that provision.

State immunity

The law on state immunity is set out in the *State Immunity Act 1978*, which implements the *European Convention on State Immunity 1972*. The starting point under s 1 is that foreign states enjoy general immunity from suit before UK courts. *Section 4* introduces a specific exception for proceedings relating to a contract of employment where either (a) the contract was made in the UK, or (b) the work is to be wholly or partly performed in the UK (*s 4(1)*). However, this exception is itself subject to various exceptions. Two of these are of particular relevance to foreign employees. First, a state is immune if: (a) at the time when the proceedings are brought the individual is a national of the state concerned; or (b) at the time the contract was made the individual was neither a national of the UK nor habitually resident there (*SIA 1978, s 4(2)*). Secondly, a state is immune from proceedings concerning the employment of the members of the mission (*SIA 1978, s 16(a)*). This includes claims brought by administrative and technical staff and members of service staff in the domestic service of the mission such as cleaners and cooks (see *Vienna Convention on Diplomatic Relations 1961, Art 1,* which is incorporated in UK law by the *Diplomatic Privileges Act 1964*).

In the conjoined cases of *Benkharbouche v Embassy of the Republic of Sudan* and *Janah v Libya* [2015] EWCA Civ 33, [2015] IRLR 301, the Court of Appeal considered the application of the *SIA 1978* to a range of claims under UK and EU law including unfair dismissal, racial discrimination and breach of the *Working Time Regulations 1998* brought by two Moroccan nationals employed as domestic service staff in foreign embassies. In the case of Ms Janah, the exception in *s 4(2)(b)* also applied as she was not habitually resident in the UK at the time the contract was made. Affirming the decision of EAT ([2013] IRLR 918), the Court of Appeal held that *ss 4(2)(b)* and *16(1)(a)* amounted to a disproportionate (and in the case of *s 4(2)(b)*, discriminatory) interference with the right of access to a court under *ECHR, Art 6* and *EU Charter, Art 47*. After conducting a comparative review, the Court of Appeal concluded that the breadth of immunity prescribed by *s 16(1)(a)* fell outside the range of tenable views of what is required by international law. Since the relevant provisions could not be read down, the Court of Appeal issued a declaration under *HRA 1998, s 4* for breach of *ECHR, Arts 6* and *14*. As far as the EU law claims were concerned, it was common ground that the substantive content of *Art 47* of the *EU Charter* is identical to that of *ECHR, Art 6* (see also *EU Charter, Art 52(3)*). However, relying on the CJEU's line of case law on the effect of general principles of EU law (see *Mangold v Helm*: C-144/04 [2006] IRLR 143 and *Küküdeveci v Swedex*: C-555/07 [2010] IRLR 346), the Court of Appeal held that the right to an effective remedy guaranteed by *Art 47* has 'horizontal' direct effect. Thus, Ms Janah was able to rely on *Art 47* even though Libya is not an EU Member State. The Court of Appeal therefore disapplied *ss 4(2)(b)* and *16(1)(a)* of the *SIA 1978* to the extent necessary to enable employment claims (other than for recruitment, renewal or reinstatement) falling within the scope of EU law by members of the service staff, whose work does not relate to the sovereign functions of the mission staff. While the Court of Appeal's urge to confine state immunity to proceedings concerning core sovereign functions is understandable, state practice on the rule embodied in *s 16(1)(a)* remains mixed. The Court of Appeal's conclusion that the approach taken in the SIA 1978 falls outside the tenable range of views may therefore be thought to have been a bold one. Similarly, the sweeping approach to 'horizontal direct effect' may be thought to apply to all fundamental rights found in the EU Charter. However, the Supreme Court [2017] UKSC 62 unanimously upheld the Court of Appeal's decision, reasoning that *ss 4(2)(b)* and *16(1)(a)* of the *SIA 1978* were not consistent with international law. Whereas international law only accords immunity from claims based on sovereign acts, the Court held that the employment of purely domestic staff in a diplomatic mission is a private act. The relevant provisions are therefore incompatible with *ECHR, Art 6* and *EU Charter, Art 47*. The EU law claims were remitted to the ET to be determined at trial.

EJ Foxwell, in *Webster and Wright v United States* (3327693/2017), considered that the United States was entitled to state immunity in respect of two discrimination claims brought by employees of the United States Air Force Europe. EJ Foxwell considered Ms Webster's role, record-keeping, to be a function of the State and that litigation of the claim was likely to involve judicial consideration of the policies and objectives of the United States in its management of record keeping and the staff working within it, including if the US was called upon to justify treatment which might otherwise be unlawful under the Equality Act. EJ Foxwell came to the same conclusion with respect to Ms Wright, a firefighter.

Diplomatic immunity

On the same day as it gave judgment in *Benkharbouche*, the same bench of the Court of Appeal handed down its judgment in *Reyes and Anor v Al–Maliki and Anor* [2015] EWCA Civ 32, [2015] IRLR 289. In that case, a domestic worker sued her Saudi diplomatic agent employer alleging that she was a victim of mistreatment and trafficking. In contrast to the result in *Benkharbouche*, the Court of Appeal held that Ms Reyes' claim was barred by diplomatic immunity pursuant to the *Vienna Convention on Diplomatic Relations 1961*. The fact that the employer diplomat derived an economic benefit was not sufficient to bring the activity of employment within the *art 31(1)(c)* exception for commercial activities outside official functions. Indeed, the court found that the employment of domestic workers is incidental to a diplomat's official functions. The court therefore concluded that the international law obligation to grant diplomatic immunity represents a legitimate and proportionate restriction on the right of access to court under *art 6* of the *ECHR*.

Following the Court of Appeal's judgment, the employer's diplomatic status was terminated when his post ended. In these different circumstances, the Supreme Court [2017] UKSC 61 unanimously allowed the employees appeal, finding that the defendants were not entitled to rely on the residual immunity in respect of official actions which is afforded to diplomatic agents who have left the UK. Although the employment of Ms Reyes to carry out domestic tasks assisted the employer diplomatic agent in the performance of his official functions, it was not an act in the exercise of the diplomatic functions of the mission or on behalf of Saudi Arabia. The Court left open the question whether the diplomatic agent would have been immune had he remained in his post.

Reyes confirms that it is possible to bring claims against former diplomatic agents who enjoy residual immunity only. However, the Supreme Court left open the question whether, as far as serving diplomats are concerned, diplomatic immunity remains a jurisdictional bar to employment claims irrespective of the gravity of abuse alleged. While Lord Sumption (with whom Lord Neuberger agreed) suggested that immunity would have been available, Lord Wilson expressed doubt given the allegations of human trafficking. Where this is not an option, *Benkharbouche* suggests that claims should instead be pursued against the foreign embassy.

In *Basfar v Wong* (2020) UKEAT/0223/19, [2020] IRLR 248 (EAT), the Employment Appeal Tribunal was faced with a case in which the facts were assumed to be identical to *Reyes* save that the employer remained a diplomatic agent in post. The EAT concluded that, although the Court of Appeal's decision in *Reyes* on the scope of the Article 31(1)(c) exception was not strictly binding, it nonetheless considered that it (in conjunction with the views expressed by Lords Sumption and Neuberger in the Supreme Court in *Reyes*) represented the current state of the law. The diplomatic immunity defence was allowed. The case has been certified as appropriate for a leapfrog appeal to the Supreme Court (the first time that the EAT has used this power).

28   Health and Safety at Work – I: The Legal Framework

The law relating to health and safety is both long-established and rapidly developing. To that end, keeping track of it is difficult, like most other legal subject-matter. However, the Health and Safety Executive ('HSE') produces a wide range of free and priced information on health and safety in the workplace. See also www.hse.gov.uk.

Cross-reference. See HEALTH AND SAFETY AT WORK – II (29) for specific legislation and health and safety issues.

28.1   THE LEGISLATIVE FRAMEWORK

An employer is under a common law duty to have regard to the safety of his employees. He is also liable at common law for accidents caused by acts of his employees where the employees were acting in the course of their employment. The assessment of damages in personal injury actions is beyond the scope of this book. In addition to these common law duties, statutory obligations have been imposed upon employers in certain circumstances by such enactments as the *Occupiers' Liability Act 1957*, the *Occupiers Liability Act 1984* (see **28.12** below) and the *Health and Safety at Work, etc Act 1974* (see **28.16** below). An employer owes specific statutory duties to his own employees, members of the public who are affected by the activities of the employer, and other people's employees working on the employer's premises. A breach of an employer's statutory duties under the *Health and Safety at Work, etc Act 1974* ('*HSWA 1974*') imposes only criminal liability, although a breach of health and safety regulations made thereunder, insofar as damage is caused, will give rise to civil liability unless the regulations provide otherwise (see **28.43** below). The *Enterprise and Regulatory Reform Act 2013*, by *section 69*, substantially amends *section 47* of the *1974 Act*. The consequence is that in cases where previously strict liability attached to an employer, it will become necessary for the claimant to show direct fault, ie negligence, on the part of the employer. The mere occurrence of an accident without more will not sound in liability. The reform was not retrospective and is only applicable to accidents after implementation, which was on 1 October 2013.

An employer is obliged to have in place insurance in respect of injury claims brought by employees. This duty was created by the *Employers' Liability (Compulsory Insurance) Act 1969*. In *Campbell v Gordon* [2016] UKSC 38 the Supreme Court decided, by a majority of 3 to 2, that the director of a company which had failed to take out cover was not personally liable to compensate an injured employee. The company would of course be liable to pay compensation but that would be subject to it having adequate assets to discharge the claim.

Under provisions in the *Employment Rights Act 1996*, employees are protected from dismissal or victimisation by the employer in health and safety cases (see **55.3** UNFAIR DISMISSAL – II and **29.8** HEALTH AND SAFETY AT WORK – II). In addition, an employer who fails to fulfil his legal duties may face a claim for constructive dismissal should an employee resign as a result of an alleged breach of the employer's duty of care. For example, in *British Aircraft Corpn v Austin* [1978] IRLR 332, an employer's obstinate and unjustified refusal to deal with a safety grievance was held to justify a complaint of constructive dismissal when the employee resigned (see **29.11** HEALTH AND SAFETY AT WORK – II).

28.2   THE COMMON LAW DUTY

An employer is obliged to take such steps as are reasonably necessary to ensure the safety of his employees. The definition of 'employee' is given a wide interpretation by the courts (*Lane v Shire Roofing Co (Oxford) Ltd* [1995] IRLR 493, [1995] PIQR P 417, CA). In

Autoklenz v Belcher [2011] UKSC 41, [2011] IRLR 820 the Supreme Court explained that the question of status was to be determined by having regard to the true nature of the arrangement between the parties rather than by slavishly accepting documentation which might not be accurate. In *Cox v Ministry of Justice* [2016] UKSC 10, [2016] IRLR 370 the Supreme Court unanimously held that an employer was vicariously liable for injury inflicted upon the claimant, their employee, by a prisoner who was helping in the kitchens at the workplace, Swansea prison. The defendant contended that since the prisoner was not their employee it could not be held answerable for his clear negligence in dropping a heavy sack on Mrs Cox. The pragmatic view of the Court was that the prisoner was doing work which benefitted the claimant. In his absence a conventional employee would have been required to perform the task. It was fair, just and reasonable to extend liability. The orthodox approach to status was unanimously upheld by the Supreme Court in *Pimlico Plumbers Ltd v Smith* [2018] UKSC 29, [2018] 4 All ER 641, [2018] IRLR 872. Meanwhile, a challenge in respect of so called ' gig economy ' personnel appears destined for the Supreme Court after the Court of Appeal divided on how to categorise taxi drivers in *Uber BV v Aslam* [2018] EWCA Civ 2748, [2019] IRLR 257.

Delivery couriers who enjoyed total autonomy over their working hours and who were free to delegate work to others have been held by the High Court in *R (on the application of Independent Workers Union of Great Britain) v Central Arbitration Committee* [2018] EWHC 3342 (Admin), [2019] IRLR 249 to be outside the scope of worker status .

The duty to ensure safety is not an absolute one and the mere occurrence of an accident does not of itself necessarily impose liability on the employer (see *McCook v Lobo* [2002] EWCA Civ 1760, [2003] ICR 89, [2002] All ER (D) 272 (Nov)). All the circumstances of the accident will be investigated in deciding whether the employer acted reasonably or not. If an accident occurs as a result of the employer's failure to comply with his duty to his employees, he is liable for any resulting injury or damage. The Court of Appeal held in *Carroll v Greater Manchester Police* [2017] EWCA Civ 1992 that the claimant had an arguable case against his former employer and so his claim should proceed to a full trial. Mr Carroll , a Police Officer, was sent undercover to infiltrate drug dealings. He alleged that this lead to him becoming a heroin addict , an outcome for which the defendant ought to be liable.

Where a job has inherent risks to health and safety which are not commonly known but of which the employer is or ought to be aware, and if the employer cannot guard against those risks by taking precautionary measures, then he has a duty to inform prospective employees of the risks if knowledge of them would be likely to affect a sensible and level-headed person's decision on whether or not to accept the job (*White v Holbrook Precision Castings* [1985] IRLR 215). The employer must keep abreast of contemporary knowledge in the field of accident prevention (*Baxter v Harland and Wolff plc* [1990] IRLR 516; *Bowman v Harland and Wolff plc* [1992] IRLR 349). In *Williams v University of Birmingham* [2011] EWCA Civ 1242, [2011] All ER (D) 25 (Nov) the Court of Appeal emphasised that one must look to the knowledge of risk at the time of exposure, here to asbestos in the early 1970s, and must not make the error of applying hindsight.

The employer's compliance with his common law duty of care is usually tested under the following headings:

(a)   providing a safe place of work;

(b)   providing a safe means of access to the place of work;

(c)   providing a safe system of work;

(d)   providing safe plant and equipment;

(e)   employing competent fellow employees; and

(f)   protecting employees from unnecessary risk of injury.

However, these are simply specific aspects of the employer's overall general duty not to be negligent, and so should be viewed as examples of ways in which employers can take steps to ensure that their employees are reasonably safe at work.

The Supreme Court in *James-Bowen and others v Metropolitan Police Commissioner* [2018] UKSC 40, [2018] 4 All ER 1007 rejected an argument that the employer owed a duty to defend legal proceedings in order to protect the economic, psychiatric and reputational interests of her employees. The claimants were Police Officers who had arrested a suspected terrorist .He sued alleging that he had been subjected to gratuitous violence in the course of the arrest. This litigation was settled 3 days into trial. The officers asserted that the settlement impugned their integrity and it was contrary to their personal interests .Lord Lloyd-Jones, delivering the only reasoned judgment said " it would not be fair, just or reasonable to impose on an employer a duty of care to defend legal proceedings so as to protect the economic or reputational interest of his employees".

28.3   Safe place of work

An employer is obliged to see that the place where his employees work is reasonably safe in all the circumstances. A place of work must be safely constructed and adequately maintained in a reasonable state of repair. An employer would be as guilty of failing to provide a safe place of work if, for example, a platform high above the ground on which men were required to stand was not adequately fenced as if one of the planks provided for the platform were rotten and liable to give way.

So far as construction of the workplace is concerned, it is not sufficient to show that the employer engaged a competent contractor to provide a safe place (*Paine v Colne Valley Electricity Supply Co Ltd and British Insulated Cables Ltd* [1938] 4 All ER 803, *per* Goddard LJ at 807). This reflects the general principle that the employer's duty of care to his employees is non-delegable. If, however, an employer maintains an adequate system of inspection of the workplace and despite inspection, a part of the workplace becomes inadequate or defective, the employer will probably not have been in breach of his common law duty. (He may nevertheless be in breach of a statutory provision which imposes a stricter duty.)

Temporary conditions affecting the workplace. A place of work which is intrinsically safe may become unsafe by the occurrence of certain events. Liquid may be spilt on a workshop floor making it slippery, a fence may be temporarily removed or an object placed in an unfamiliar position. All these events could cause accidents. The employer's liability will depend upon whether a reasonable employer would in the particular circumstances have taken measures to avoid the accident or different measures from those in fact taken. What is reasonable will vary according to the facts of the case. If a man slips on an oil slick at his workplace and thereby injures himself, his employer's potential liability may well vary according to how long the oil had been present (or according to the frequency with which such spillages occur, as in *Bell v Department of Health and Social Security* (1989) Times, 13 June). If the oil had been spilt just a few minutes before the accident there may well be no liability, whereas if it had been there for half a day, the position would be different. In *Thomas v Bristol Aeroplane Co Ltd* [1954] 2 All ER 1, an employer was held not to be in breach of the common law duty of care in failing to take steps to remove from the entrance to the factory frozen snow which had fallen about a quarter of an hour before the factory opened.

Employee working on other premises. An employer owes a general duty to his employee to provide him with a safe place of work whether he is employed on the employer's own premises or elsewhere; see the House of Lords judgment in *McDermid v Nash Dredging and Reclamation Co Ltd* [1987] AC 906, [1987] IRLR 334, [1987] ICR 917. However, the extent of that duty when the employee is on other premises may well be less than when he is on his employer's premises. The test again is: did the employer in question act as a reasonable employer would have acted in the circumstances? Thus, if an employer sends a window-cleaner to premises he knows to be unsafe, he may well be held liable for any accident caused as a result of the state of the premises. If he does not know whether the premises are safe or not, then, depending on the convenience of inspection and the degree of risk involved, he may be held negligent in failing to inspect and, if necessary, make those premises safe (*General Cleaning Contractors Ltd v Christmas* [1952] 2 All ER 1110).

The Supreme Court in *Kennedy v Cordia Services LLP* [2016] UKSC 6, [2016] All ER (D) 99 (Feb) gave an illuminating unanimous judgment as to risk assessment and avoidance. The claimant was a carer employed by the defendant. Her work entailed visiting patients at their homes. She was injured when, in the midst of a bitter spell of bad weather, she slipped on ice that had accumulated on the path leading up to the door of the patient upon she was about to call. The employer was aware of other similar incidents having occurred. A competent risk assessment would have lead to the issue of shoe attachments which could well have avoided the incident. The judgment is also helpful in explaining when and how expert evidence should be relied upon by a court.

The extent of an employer's duty in relation to employees working on other premises was considered by the Court of Appeal in *Square D Ltd v Cook* [1992] IRLR 34. An employer must take all reasonable steps to ensure the safety of his staff and this includes the premises where the staff are required to work (whether occupied by the employer or by a third party). This duty cannot be delegated. However, the duty is not an absolute one and considerations such as the place where the work is to be done, the nature of the building on the site concerned, the experience of the employee who is sent to work at such a site, the nature of the work he is required to do, the degree of control that the employer can reasonably be expected to exercise in the circumstances and the employer's own knowledge of the defective state of the premises are all factors to be taken into account. These considerations apply whether the third party's premises are in the UK or abroad. However, the court may take a different view of the employer's duty where staff are sent to work abroad for a considerable period of time. The Court of Appeal suggested that in such an instance, the employer may be expected to inspect the site personally and satisfy himself that the occupiers are conscious of their obligations concerning the safety of people working there.

28.4   Safe means of access

It is the duty of every employer to provide his employees with a safe means of access to their place of work. Thus, if access to a factory is by means of a footpath, that footpath should be kept in a reasonable state of repair.

Sometimes it is hard to distinguish the means of access to the place of work from the place of work itself. A painter may use a ladder to reach a position from where to carry on his decorating. The ladder may in certain circumstances be considered the means of access and in others the place of work. In any event the common law duty of care in relation to both is the same.

28.5   Safe system of work

A system of work is the method used for carrying out the work, the sequence of events followed. It includes such things as manning of operations, provision of equipment, and supervision. It may be that the system used by an employer is intrinsically unsafe or it may be that there is in existence a suitable system of work but that the system itself is applied unsatisfactorily. For example, an employer who provides insufficient workers to carry out a task may be held liable for any accident caused thereby.

One defect in an otherwise unimpeachable system may render the whole system unsafe. If, for example, the procedures for carrying out blasting in a quarry were adequate but the warning given to workers in the quarry to leave was too short, the whole system would thereby be rendered unsafe. Similarly, it would be considered an unsafe system to require men who had insufficient training or supervision to carry out a task which would otherwise be considered safe.

Where an operation is so inherently dangerous that it should not be performed at all, the employer must provide explicit instructions banning employees from carrying it out (*King v Smith* [1995] ICR 339). It would be incumbent upon the employer to police and uphold the prohibition.

Employers who require their workers to carry out manoeuvres which involve several actions should first check to see whether there are any relevant statutory requirements relating to the procedure. Before devising a system of working they should consult the employees who are to work the system or their representatives. Where the workforce is unionised, the employer has a duty to consult with union-appointed safety representatives. Non-unionised groups of workers or their representatives must also be consulted (see **29.20** HEALTH AND SAFETY AT WORK – **II**). If the procedure is at all complicated, employers should consult the Health and Safety Executive (see **28.26**).

Duty based on reasonable steps. The duty to provide a safe system of work is not an absolute one. The duty is to take reasonable steps to provide a system which will be reasonably safe, having regard to the dangers necessarily inherent in the operation. In deciding what is reasonable, long-established practice in the trade (although not necessarily conclusive) is generally regarded as strong evidence in support of reasonableness (*General Cleaning Contractors Ltd v Christmas* [1952] 2 All ER 1110 *per* Lord Tucker at 195). Nevertheless, acceptable standards of safety change over the years and the courts will have regard to current best practice. In deciding the extent of the duty the courts will take into account: (i) the size of the danger; (ii) the likelihood of an accident occurring; (iii) the possible consequences of the occurrence of an accident; and (iv) the steps needed to eliminate all risk and the cost of doing so (*Edwards v National Coal Board* [1949] 1 All ER 743).

Ensuring implementation of safety measures. It is not sufficient to provide a safe system of work. An employer should take such steps as are reasonably practicable to see that the system is implemented. If it is within his knowledge that a piece of safety equipment is persistently not used, he should take reasonable steps to encourage his workers to use it (*Bux v Slough Metals* [1974] 1 All ER 262). However, this duty is not so onerous as the duty to provide the safety equipment, etc in the first place. As Lord Radcliffe said in *Qualcast (Wolverhampton) Ltd v Haynes* [1959] 2 All ER 38 at 753: 'the courts should be circumspect in filling out that duty with the much vaguer obligation of encouraging, exhorting or instructing workmen or a particular workman to make regular use of what is provided'. In *Crouch v British Rail Engineering Ltd* [1988] IRLR 404 it was held to be insufficient on the facts merely to make safety goggles available for collection from a point about five minutes away. The failure to have them available where they were needed encouraged the taking of risks.

28.6   Safe equipment and materials

An employer is under a common law duty to provide equipment, materials and clothing to enable his workmen to carry out their duties in safety. As with the system of work, the duty is not an absolute one. It may be, for example, that goggles costing £300 per pair are marginally safer than those costing £50 per pair. In deciding whether an employer was in breach of his duty in failing to provide his employees with the more expensive goggles, the court would have regard to the difference in effectiveness between the cheaper and the more expensive goggles, the degree of risk involved, and the additional cost.

When an employer bought materials from a reputable supplier, and injury was caused by an undetected defect in those materials, his failure to examine the materials would not render him liable for the accident at common law. However, under the *Employers' Liability (Defective Equipment) Act 1969*, if an employee is injured by reason of a defect in the equipment, the injury is by statute deemed to be attributable to the fault of the employer. This does not affect the employer's right to allege that the accident was wholly or partly due to negligence on the part of the employee; nor does it affect any remedy the employer may have against his supplier. Thus, if an employee is injured by a piece of metal flying from a defective high-pressure hose, supplied to him by his employer, he could succeed in a claim against the employer for his injury. The employer could only seek to reduce the damages awarded against him by showing that the accident was caused or contributed to by the fault of the employee and/or by claiming against the supplier of the hose.

Under *s 1(3)* of the *Employers' Liability (Defective Equipment) Act 1969* 'equipment' includes any plant, machinery, vehicle, aircraft and clothing. A ship is 'equipment' for the purposes of *s 1(3)* (*Coltman v Bibby Tankers Ltd, The Derbyshire* [1987] 3 All ER 1068, [1988] ICR 67). 'Equipment provided by the employer' includes materials (in this case a flagstone) which an employee is given by the employer to do the job (*Knowles v Liverpool City Council* [1993] IRLR 588). The contention that 'equipment' was confined to the tools of the job was rejected; a nail, a brick and a piece of timber all amount to equipment.

28.7 Fellow workers

An employer is under a duty to provide competent fellow workers. Thus, if an employee of his is injured because of the known inadequacy of a fellow worker, the employer is liable to that employee in damages for the injury caused by the fellow worker. Even if the employee's action is untypical, the employer may nevertheless be held liable by reason of his VICARIOUS LIABILITY (57). This principle also applies to the employer's duty not to engage or continue to employ employees who are known to indulge in dangerous 'horseplay' (*Hudson v Ridge Manufacturing Co Ltd* [1957] 2 All ER 229). Liability on the part of an employer where one employee assaults another in the workplace has been considered in the conjoined appeals of *Wallbank v Wallbank Fox Designs Ltd* and *Weddall v Barchester* [2012] EWCA Civ 25, [2012] IRLR 307. Lord Phillips in *The Catholic Care Child Welfare Society and others v Various claimants and The Institute of Brothers of the Christian Schools* [2012] UKSC 56, [2013] IRLR 219 [at 19] wisely observed that the law was on the move. The absence of a conventional contract of employment between a religious body and some members of it who abused children did not prevent a finding of vicarious liability. The relationship was akin to employment and so the body was liable. One can anticipate interesting arguments about liability arising for the acts of volunteers and others who do not fulfil conventional employment criteria and yet, arguably, come within the ambit of quasi-employment.

The Supreme Court in *Various Claimants v Barclays Bank plc* [2020] UKSC 13, [2020] All ER (D) 04 (Apr) held that the defendant Bank was not liable for acts of abuse perpetrated by an independent contractor. The claimants were teenage girls who had applied to the Bank for employment. The bank insisted that they first had to undergo a medical examination by a male doctor who was not their employee. He abused each victim at the examination. No female doctor was offered and nor was a chaperone made available. The defendant contended that since the doctor was an independent contractor who invoiced for his fees it could not be liable for any impropriety on his part. The Supreme Court unanimously agreed that the bank was not responsible. There was no retainer between it and the errant doctor who had a range of working commitments. He was under no obligation to accept a given instruction and as such was far removed from the concept of a quasi-employee In *WM Morrison Supermarkets plc v Various Claimants* [2020] UKSC 12, [2020] All ER (D) 02 (Apr) the Court unanimously accepted that the employer was not liable for an unauthorised data breach. This was a classic frolic of his own and bore no relationship whatsoever with his working obligations. The Court has reined in what appeared to be a relentless expansion of liability.

The mere fact that an incident occurs at the premises of an employer will not in itself generate liability. In the Scottish case of *Vaickuviene v J Sainsbury plc* [2013] CSIH 67, [2013] IRLR 792, Ct of Sess, one employee murdered a workmate in the workplace. It was held that there was no liability on the part of the employer for the unprovoked and extreme act. This case was not addressed in the Supreme Court judgment of *Mohamud V WM Morrison Supermarkets plc* [2016] UKSC 11, [2016] IRLR 362. Mr Mohamud was the victim of an unprovoked attack perpetrated by an employee of the defendant. The incident occurred at a petrol station. The late claimant entered and asked if the employee manning the till could print off some documents for him from a USB stick. The employee chased Mr Mohamud out to his vehicle and assaulted him. A supervisor standing nearby implored the culprit to desist but to no avail. Having lost both at first instance and in the Court of Appeal, the claim succeeded before the Supreme Court. A close connection was held to exist between the job and the attack. The assailant was employed to attend to customers and was doing so, albeit in a despicable manner, when he carried out the attack.

With some reluctance the Court of Appeal held that an employer was liable where a company director struck an employee in the early hours of the morning after an office Christmas party. The two men had left the party venue and returned to the hotel where they were staying. An argument about work related matters triggered the assault which left the claimant badly injured. See *Bellman v Northampton Recruitment Ltd* [2018] EWCA Civ 2214, [2019] 1 All ER 1133This decision was affirmed by the Supreme Court in *WM Morrison Supermarkets plc v Various Claimants* [2020] UKSC 12, [2020] All ER (D) 02 (Apr). This decision was distinguished by Lane J in *Shelbourne v Cancer Research UK* [2019] EWHC 842 (QB), [2019] All ER (D) 68 (Apr). The claimant employee was injured at a Christmas party held at the premises of her employer. A visiting scientist not employed by the defendant attempted to lift up Mrs Shelbourne on the dance floor. He lost his balance and dropped her. This was held to be a frolic of his own and was utterly unconnected with his work which was not with the defendant anyway.

An employer may not contract out of his liability to his employees for the negligence of fellow workers. The *Law Reform (Personal Injuries) Act 1948, s 1(3)* renders void any agreement to that effect.

28.8   Protection from risk of injury

An employer is under a duty to take reasonable care to see that his employees are not subjected to any unnecessary risks of injury. In *Charlton v Forrest Printing Ink Co Ltd* [1980] IRLR 331, the Court of Appeal held that an employer has a duty to take steps to eliminate a risk which he knows or ought to know is a real risk and not a mere possibility which would never influence the mind of a reasonable man. The Court of Appeal in *Coxall v Goodyear Great Britain Ltd* [2002] EWCA Civ 1010, [2002] IRLR 742, [2003] ICR 152, considering whether or not an employer was under a duty to prevent an employee from doing work which he was willing to do because of a risk to his health, depended largely on the actual nature and extent of the risk. Consequently, if on the facts the employer were negligent in failing to either move the employee from the job in question or dismiss him in order to protect him from the danger, the employer would become liable.

What though constitutes "an injury?" This issue was addressed by the Supreme Court in *Dryden and others v Johnson Matthey plc* [2018] UKSC 18, [2018] 3 All ER 755, [2018] IRLR 963. The claimants were exposed at work to platinum salts and as a result became sensitised to them. This meant that they had developed antibodies so that any subsequent exposure to the salts would trigger allergic reactions. Provided they no longer came into contact with platinum salts their health would not be affected. The claimants were either dismissed or redeployed to prevent further exposure. Injury claims were brought. The defendant contended that sensitisation was not in itself harmful. It did not manifest any adverse consequences. By keeping the claimants away from the salts it followed that no identifiable injury existed.All that remained was an action for pure economic loss.

The Supreme Court, in a unanimous judgment delivered by Lady Black held that a viable cause of action existed for personal injury. An injury, which could be hidden and symptomless, was a physical rendering the claimant worse off in their health or capabilities. The capacity to work was plainly impaired and so the claimants were significantly worse off.

An argument that platinum salts were not encountered in normal day to day life so that sensitisation was inconsequential was rejected.

Where a risk is not obvious, the employee will succeed only if he can show that the state of knowledge in the relevant industry at the relevant time was such that the employer knew or ought to have known of that risk. But an employer must keep reasonably abreast of developing knowledge, and if he has greater than average knowledge of the risks, he may have to take greater than average precautions (*Stokes v Guest Keen & Nettlefold (Bolts and Nuts) Ltd* [1968] 1 WLR 1776).

An employer may also be liable in certain circumstances for psychiatric illness caused by work if it is reasonably foreseeable (see *Page v Smith* [1995] 2 All ER 736 for the principles involved, and *Walker v Northumberland County Council* [1995] IRLR 35 and *Cross v Highlands and Islands Enterprise* [2001] IRLR 336 at **29.24** HEALTH AND SAFETY AT WORK – **II**). The House of Lords in *White v Chief Constable of South Yorkshire Police* [1999] IRLR 110 overturned the ruling of the Court of Appeal in *Frost v Chief Constable of South Yorkshire Police* [1997] IRLR 173 relating to an employer's liability for work-related psychiatric illness. The case concerned police officers who sustained psychiatric damage as a result of tending to victims of the Hillsborough football stadium disaster which was caused by the employer's admitted negligence. Compensation for physical injury caused by negligence was recoverable if it was reasonably foreseeable that the conduct would cause such injury. Where this situation does not apply (ie the claimant is not within the range of foreseeable physical injury), individuals are 'secondary victims' and, in order to recover compensation for psychiatric injury, it was necessary that the conditions set out in *Alcock v Chief Constable of South Yorkshire Police* [1991] 3 All ER 88 should be satisfied:

(a)   there must be a close tie of love and affection between the claimant and the victim;

(b)   the claimant must have been present at the accident or its immediate aftermath; and

(c)   the psychiatric injury must have been caused by direct perception of the accident or its immediate aftermath and not by hearing about it from someone else.

Since the officers did not have sufficiently close ties to the victims, their claim failed. The House of Lords concluded that the employment relationship did not put the officers in a special position in this regard. See also *Robertson and Rough v Forth Road Bridge Joint Board* [1995] IRLR 251, *Young v Charles Church (Southern) Ltd* (1997) 33 BMLR 101, CA and *Hunter v British Coal Corpn* [1998] 2 All ER 97, CA.

The House of Lords in *Corr (Administratrix of Corr dec'd) v IBC Vehicles Ltd* [2008] UKHL 13, [2008] 2 All ER 943, [2008] ICR 372 held an employer liable for the suicide of their employee who had been badly injured in an accident at work six years before. Mr Corr had become severely depressed as a result of his injuries. His death was attributable to the accident for which the employer had been to blame. This is an example of the classic maxim that one must take the claimant as one finds him. Whilst extreme depression was not an inevitable consequence of injury it happened to have been so here and thus the defendant was liable.

In mainstream stress cases it had been the conventional approach to apportion liability where there were a combination of causes, some of which were non-tortious, that lead to injury. This would occur, for example, where it was accepted that the employer was culpable but the claimant had other non work related problems too. No more. In *Dickins v O2 Plc* [2009] IRLR 58 the Court of Appeal accepted, obiter, that stress was an injury incapable of division and so the claimant would be entitled to full compensation where the employer had made a material contribution to the injury. In BAE Systems (Operations) Ltd V Konczak [2017] EWCA Civ 1188 the Court of Appeal drew back from *Dickins* and directed that Courts should seek to apportion damages where there might be various factors, some of which were not the fault of the defendant, leading to psychiatric damage. Underhill LJ at paragraph 93 of the Judgment emphasised the need for reporting medical experts to address this point. Nevertheless, the Appeal Court held that the damage here was indivisible and so the defendant was liable in full.

In cases of industrial disease, it may often be difficult to determine whether the employee's illness was *caused* by the employer's breach of duty. The decision of the House of Lords in *Fairchild v Glenhaven Funeral Services Ltd* [2002] UKHL 22, [2002] IRLR 533 contains a comprehensive review of the relevant authorities. The Supreme Court decided in *Sienkiewicz v Greif (UK) Ltd* [2011] UKSC 10, [2011] 2 All ER 857, [2011] ICR 391 that the *Fairchild* principle can equally apply where there was only one relevant defendant and also that a claim may succeed without the need to prove that guilty exposure doubled the risk of harm. Here, the evidence was that the employer negligently exposed the victim to 18% more asbestos than would be found in the general environment. Accordingly, the employer was liable. In cases of mesothelioma only, *s 3* of the *Compensation Act 2006* enables a claimant to recover in full from any culpable employer even though the victim was exposed to asbestos in more than one job.

In *Chandler v Cape Industries Ltd* [2012] EWCA Civ 525, [2012] 3 All ER 640 the Court of Appeal upheld a finding that a parent company was liable for the negligence of a subsidiary which was now defunct. The parent was liable because the respective businesses were similar (asbestos production), it had or ought to have had superior knowledge of health risks, it knew of an unsafe system of work at the subsidiary and it had intervened in the business of the subsidiary.

In *Vedanta Resources Plc v Lungowe* [2019] UKSC 20, [2019] All ER (D) 57 (Apr) the Supreme Court unanimously held that individuals exposed to toxic emissions by a by a local company in Gambia could sue its parent company which was incorporated and domiciled in the UK.This would ensure that substantial justice was secured . Funding considerations and the ability of the English legal system to cope with large numbers of claimants were identified by the Court as significant factors .

28.9   Vicarious liability for acts of employees

An employer is liable for the acts of his employee if they are committed in the course of the employee's employment. This is known as vicarious liability. The modern test is whether the incident was job related or job connected. An incident can be job related even if it forms no part of the employee's authorised work. In *Lister v Hesley Hall Ltd* [2001] IRLR 472 it was found that a teacher who abused a pupil was acting in the course of employment even though what he did was criminal, unauthorised and something that no teacher should ever have done. Thus, if a van delivery driver drives negligently while in the normal course of his duties and causes an accident, his employer is held liable for the resulting damage or injury. Sexual abuse of a child by a priest was held to be the responsibility of the Archdiocese in *Maga v Roman Catholic Archdiocese of Birmingham* [2010] EWCA Civ 256, [2010] All ER (D) 141 (Mar). Likewise, the Court of Appeal held the employer liable when an employee stole silver bullion which was to be transported abroad from a secure compound which he was authorised to enter. This question is dealt with in more detail in Vɪᴄᴀʀɪᴏᴜs Lɪᴀʙɪʟɪᴛʏ **(57)**.

28.10 Employee working under direction of third party

The primary employer remains liable for the safety of an employee who is working under the direction of a third party. However, where the employee suffers an accident which is wholly due to the third party's negligence in breach of its duty of care, the primary employer may be able to recover full indemnity from the third party in accordance with the *Civil Liability (Contribution) Act 1978* (*Nelhams v Sandells Maintenance Ltd* (1995) Times, 15 June, CA).

28.11 Independent contractors

With the exception of the statutory occupier's liability (see **28.12** below), in general an employer is not liable for acts of an independent contractor engaged by him, provided that he exercised due diligence in selecting the contractor for the task. (For criminal liability in respect of the negligence of an independent contractor, see **28.19** below.)

28.12 OCCUPIERS' LIABILITY ACT 1957

Apart from the common law duties of an employer to provide his employees with a safe place of work, as an occupier of premises he owes his employees, and other visitors, the common duty of care imposed by the *Occupiers' Liability Act 1957* ('*OLA 1957*'). The extent of the duty which is owed to trespassers is defined by the *Occupiers' Liability Act 1984*. An outline is given below of the duties imposed on an employer, as the occupier of premises, to employees and other visitors by the *OLA 1957*.

28.13 Meaning of 'occupier'

An occupier of premises may be the owner, the lessor, or the licensee (a person who merely has permission to occupy). An occupier need not have exclusive control over premises in order to have a duty to persons who visit those premises; more than one person may owe a duty in respect of the same premises. For example, both an employer and an independent contractor may be held to be occupiers of premises where the employer has engaged the independent contractor to carry out work on the premises.

28.14 Duty of occupier

The extent of the duty of care is defined in *OLA 1957, s 2(2)* as:

> 'a duty to take such care as in all the circumstances of the case is reasonable to see that the visitor is reasonably safe in using the premises for the purposes for which he is invited or permitted by the occupier to be there.'

In defining the extent of the duty, the courts will take into account the *degree of control over the premises actually enjoyed* by the occupier and, if applicable, the division of duties between the two occupiers of the same premises. Thus, if a harbour authority leases a certain wharf to a shipping company and an employee of that company suffers an accident due to the state of repair of the wharf, the apportionment of blame will depend on the actual degree of control exercised by the harbour authority and the shipping company.

Children and persons pursuing a calling. OLA 1957, s 2(3) provides a little help in defining the extent of the duty of care to be exercised in relation to children and to persons on the premises in pursuance of a particular calling.

'The circumstances relevant for the present purpose include the degree of care, and of want of care, which would ordinarily be looked for in such a visitor, so that (for example) in proper cases:

(*a*)   an occupier must be prepared for children to be less careful than adults; and

(*b*)   an occupier may expect that a person, in the exercise of his calling, will appreciate and guard against any special risks ordinarily incident to it, so far as the occupier leaves him free to do so.'

The duty under *OLA 1957, s 2(2)* is to see that the visitor is reasonably safe in using the premises for the purpose for which he or she is there. This covers the static state of the premises and does not extend to dangers occurring to employees of contractors as a result of activities they are performing on the premises. The House of Lords, in its landmark ruling in *Fairchild v Glenhaven Funeral Services Ltd* [2002] UKHL 22, [2002] IRLR 533, overruled the Court of Appeal's decision ([2002] EWCA Civ 1881, [2002] IRLR 129) that claimants were not entitled to recover damages from their former employers in relation to mesothelioma, a form of cancer which develops as a result of negligent exposure to asbestos.

Unanimously, their Lordships held that the victim, on grounds of so-called 'justice', should not be deprived of a remedy because it cannot be established which of a series of different employers caused the alleged harm. As Lord Nicholls put it: '*Any other outcome would be deeply offensive to instinctive notions of what justice requires and fairness demands.*' Consequently, employers may now be held liable for damage which they did not cause. The House of Lords established a right to damages by departing from the orthodox test of causation where justice so requires, by establishing a notion of joint liability. For instance, on the facts of this case, it was sufficient that the employer's breach of duty materially increased the risk that the claimants would contract mesothelioma. Therefore, the *Fairchild* ruling presupposes negligence by all employers. Clearly, the impact of this historic ruling is that once a breach of duty can be established, then each employer becomes liable for the full damages.

28.15 Faulty work by independent contractor

If an accident occurs as a result of faulty work by an independent contractor employed at the premises which the employer occupies, *OLA 1957, s 2(4)(b)* provides that:

'the occupier is not to be treated without more ["without more" in the sense of "on those facts alone"] as answerable for the danger if in all the circumstances he had acted reasonably in entrusting the work to an independent contractor and had taken such steps (if any) as he reasonably ought in order to satisfy himself that the contractor was competent and that the work had been properly done.'

Thus, if injury is caused to a visitor to the premises by the fault of an independent contractor, the occupier will not be held liable for the injury or damage so caused if he can show that:

(a)   he acted reasonably in entrusting the work to the independent contractor (it may be held to be reasonable to employ an independent contractor where the work to be done is of a skilled or specialist nature and is beyond the capabilities of the employer);

(b)   he exercised a reasonable degree of care in selecting the independent contractor to see that he was competent to do the task entrusted to him; and

(c)   he checked so far as was possible to see that the work was properly carried out.

For example, an employer may need to have his factory rewired. He may have no electricians in his employ and, therefore, need to engage an outside firm. If he has reasonable grounds for regarding that firm as competent, he will not ordinarily be expected to supervise the firm's activities in order to ensure that a safe system of work is being used. But if he knows or has reason to suspect that the firm is using an unsafe system of work, it may well be reasonable for him to take steps to see that it is made safe. If he does not, he might be liable to one of his own or the firm's employees injured, eg by receiving an electric shock (*Ferguson v Welsh* [1988] IRLR 112, on different facts). He may also be liable to the employee for breach of other statutory provisions.

In 2011, a review entitled 'Reclaiming Health and Safety for All', of all existing health and safety legislation was undertaken by an advisory panel chaired by Professor Lofstedt, director of King's College Centre for Risk Management. The general consensus of the reports was that occupational health law – and the *Health and Safety at Work etc Act 1974* in particular – was not broken and was fit for purpose. Specifically, there have been several repeals/revocations of outdated legislation, eg *RIDDOR 1995*, consolidation of several pieces of legislation, eg Pressure Systems and Dangerous Substances, and reviews/discontinuation of certain Approved Codes of Practice (ACoPs), eg the ACoP associated to the *Management of Health and Safety at Work Regulations 1999*.

In essence, Lofstedt recommended a simplification of much of the guidance associated with primary legislation, rather than a root and branch change to what is working well in practice.

28.16   THE HEALTH AND SAFETY AT WORK, ETC ACT 1974

The *Health and Safety at Work, etc Act 1974* ('*HSWA 1974*') lays down general principles to be followed by employers governing the health and safety at work of employees. It also establishes the Health and Safety Commission ('the Commission') and the Health and Safety Executive ('the Executive') (note: the HSC has now been devolved; only the HSE now exists); gives powers to inspectors to issue improvement notices and prohibition notices; and imposes certain civil and criminal liabilities upon employers. The Executive publishes many explanatory guides and booklets. In the autumn of 2010 the Government published and accepted the report of Lord Young who concluded that the law was unduly onerous and a more proportionate approach should be taken. It is highly probable that the law will be simplified with lower burdens being imposed upon those in low risk environments. Rescue workers should also be put beyond the risk of prosecution where they take heroic actions when striving to save life and limb.

28.17   Health, safety and welfare

The provisions of *HSWA 1974, Part I* (as expressed in s *1(1)*) are designed to have the effect of:

(a)   securing the health, safety and welfare of persons at work;

(b)   protecting persons other than persons at work against risks to health or safety arising out of, or in connection with, the activities of persons at work; and

(c)   controlling the keeping and use of explosive or highly flammable or otherwise dangerous substances, and generally preventing the unlawful acquisition, possession and use of such substances.

Regulations and codes of practice are issued under *HSWA 1974* to give effect to the general principles set out and also to enforce the provisions of a large body of health and safety legislation which is set out in *Sch 1* to the *Act*. Among the more important regulations made under *HSWA 1974* are the *Health and Safety (First-Aid) Regulations 1981 (SI 1981/917)*, the *Reporting of Injuries, Diseases and Dangerous Occurrences Regulations 1995 (SI 1995/3163)* (*RIDDOR* has been amended/revised in 2013; *RIDDOR 2013*, is *SI 2013/1471*) and the *Electricity at Work Regulations 1989 (SI 1989/635)*. There are also many regulations dealing with specific problems such as asbestos at work. From 1 October 1989 a large number of outdated Statutory Instruments were replaced upon the coming into force of the *Control of Substances Hazardous to Health Regulations 1988* ('*COSHH*'). The *1988 Regulations* were subsequently amended and replaced by the *2002 Regulations* (*SI 2002/2675*) of the same name. *COSHH* has been described as 'the most far-reaching health and safety legislation since 1974'. Further important changes have taken place with the implementation of EC Directives on health and safety issues by regulations made under *HSWA 1974*. These regulations cover, *inter alia*, noise at work, management of health and safety, display screen equipment (VDUs), manual handling, work equipment, and workplace health, safety and welfare.

Further details of regulations made under *HSWA 1974* are contained in HEALTH AND SAFETY AT WORK – II (29) under specific subject headings.

As will be seen below, inspectors appointed under the *Act* have powers to enforce the legislation set out in *Sch 1* as well as the provisions of the *Act* itself, and health and safety regulations.

The protection of *HSWA 1974* is extended by *Health and Safety (Training for Employment) Regulations 1990 (SI 1990/1380)* to those receiving work experience provided pursuant to a training course or programme, or training for employment, or both, except if the training is received on a course run by an educational establishment.

28.18 Employer's obligations under HSWA 1974

HSWA 1974 contains provisions broadly equivalent to the common law duty of care of an employer to his employees (see **28.2** above) (*HSWA 1974, s 2(1), (2)*). Criminal liability under *HSWA 1974* can arise even where senior management has taken all reasonable steps to protect employees. A failure at local management level may be attributable to the employing organisation (*R v Gateway Foodmarkets Ltd* [1997] IRLR 189). A failure by an employer to comply with the requirements relating to the safety of his employees may also in certain circumstances constitute a fundamental breach of contract entitling the employee to resign and claim that he was constructively dismissed (*British Aircraft Corpn Ltd v Austin* [1978] IRLR 332).

Health and safety policy statement. Employers are obliged to prepare (and, if necessary, revise) a written statement of their general policy with respect to the health and safety at work of their employees and the organisation and arrangements for carrying out that policy. In addition, employers must bring such information to the notice of all of their employees (*HSWA 1974, s 2(3)*). The length and complexity of the notice required will depend on the nature of the employer's undertaking. Such information should in all cases be placed on an easily accessible notice board. In addition, information relating to health, safety and welfare must be given to employees by means of posters and leaflets approved and published by the Health and Safety Executive. From 1 July 2000 employers are required to use a revised version of the poster; additional detail is provided on aspects of the *Management of Health and Safety at Work Regulations 1999 (SI 1999/3242)* and new sections have been incorporated for the insertion of the names and locations of safety representatives and competent persons together with their health and safety responsibilities. Copies of the form of approved poster or leaflet may be obtained from HSE Books (see the *Health and Safety Information for Employees Regulations 1989 (SI 1989/682)*). Alternative health and safety posters may be approved by the HSE provided certain criteria are met (the *Health and Safety Information for Employees (Modifications and Repeals) Regulations 1995 (SI 1995/2923)*).

Employers who carry on undertakings in which for the time being they employ fewer than five employees are exempted from the requirement of *s 2(3)* by the *Employers' Health and Safety Policy Statements (Exception) Regulations 1975 (SI 1975/1584)*.

28.19 Employers and the self-employed

Employers and self-employed people are obliged to conduct their undertakings, so far as is reasonably practicable, in a way which will ensure that persons who may be affected, not being their employees, are not exposed to risks to health or safety (*HSWA 1974, s 3(1), (2)*). The conduct of the undertaking extends to the manner in which equipment is made available for use by employees outside business hours (*R v Mara* [1987] IRLR 154, [1987] ICR 165). The Court of Appeal has ruled that it is not necessary to prove actual danger to members of the public for criminal liability to arise. It is sufficient to show that there is a risk which might be run (*R v Science Museum (Board of Trustees)* [1994] IRLR 25, 158 JP 39).

Subject to reasonable practicability, s *3(1)* creates an absolute prohibition on exposing non-employees to risk. It is no defence to argue that the employer is not liable because senior management was not involved in the incident (*R v British Steel plc* [1995] IRLR 310). It may not be sufficient to show that the employer has issued a code of instructions on a safe system of work. In certain circumstances tangible technical equipment may be necessary to ensure safety (*R v Rhône-Poulenc Rorer Ltd* [1996] ICR 1054, CA).

Nevertheless, employers should not necessarily be held criminally liable under s *3(1)* for an isolated act of negligence by the employee performing the work (*R v Nelson Group Services (Maintenance) Ltd* [1999] IRLR 646). It is a sufficient obligation to require the employer to show that everything reasonably practicable was done to see that the person doing the work had the appropriate skill and training, was adequately supervised and provided with safe equipment, and that a safe system of work was laid down.

In February 1997 Port Ramsgate, together with others, was convicted of a breach of *s 3(1)* and heavily fined following the collapse of a ferry passenger walkway which caused the death of six people. The port had employed highly reputable contractors and designers and made arrangements for safety checks but, according to the judge, it had not ensured that proper quality assurance provisions were included in the contract or given detailed thought to its own responsibilities for the design, construction and installation of the walkway.

In *R v Associated Octel Co Ltd* [1997] IRLR 123 the House of Lords held that an employer was criminally liable under s *3(1)* for the negligence of an independent contractor in respect of injuries sustained by an employee of the contractor while undertaking maintenance and repair work for the employer. The conduct of the employer's undertaking could cover ancillary activities carried out by independent contractors, particularly when the activity was carried out on the employer's premises.

Regulations may be introduced compelling employers and self-employed people to give information relating to health and safety to people (not being their employees) who may be affected by the way in which they conduct their undertakings (*HSWA 1974, s 3(3)*).

28.20 Duties of occupiers

Obligations are imposed on occupiers of 'non-domestic' premises in respect of persons who are not their employees but who are working on their premises or using plant or substances provided for use on the premises (*HSWA 1974, s 4*). They must take such measures as are reasonable for persons in their position to ensure, so far as is reasonably practicable, that the premises, plant and machinery are safe and without risks to the health of the non-employees working there. These provisions would apply to protect workers who were sent by their employer, for example, to re-decorate a client's factory. The nature of the duties imposed by *HSWA 1974, s 4* was considered by the House of Lords in *Austin Rover Group Ltd v HM Inspector of Factories* [1989] IRLR 404, [1990] ICR 133.

Operators in control of an establishment or installation which involves the use of dangerous substances are required to take all measures necessary to prevent major accidents and to limit their consequences to people and the environment, under the *Control of Major Accident*

Hazards Regulations 1999 (SI 1999/743), which came into force on 1 April 1999. Known as '*COMAH*', the *1999 Regulations* (which primarily affect the chemical industry) revoke and replace the *Control of Industrial Major Accident Hazards Regulations 1984 (SI 1984/1902)*. Under the *1999 Regulations*, operators are obliged to notify the competent authority about their activities and prepare a major accident prevention policy.

28.21 Duties of manufacturers

Manufacturers, designers, importers and suppliers of articles or substances for use at work are placed under a duty to ensure so far as is reasonably practicable that the design of their product is safe, to carry out necessary tests for so ensuring and to provide adequate information about the use of the product and the conditions necessary for its safe use (*HSWA 1974, s 6*, as amended by the *Consumer Protection Act 1987, s 36* and *Sch 3*). The manufacturers, designers, importers or suppliers of articles for use at work are exempt from such duties if they obtain a written undertaking from their customers that the customer will take specified steps sufficient to ensure, so far as is reasonably practicable, that the article will be safe and without risk to health when properly used (*HSWA 1974, s 6(8)*). This exemption is qualified where the goods are imported (*HSWA 1974, s 6(8A)*).

28.22 Duties of employees

Every employee while at work has the duty:

(a)   to take reasonable care for the health and safety of himself and of other persons who may be affected by his acts or omissions at work; and

(b)   to co-operate with his employer, or any other person, in ensuring that requirements or duties imposed by the relevant statutory provisions (including those specified in *Sch 1*) are complied with.

(*HSWA 1974, s 7*)

Thus, if an employer is required to provide his workers with goggles, supervisors should, if that task is delegated to them, ensure that adequate goggles are available. Also, the workers themselves are under an obligation to wear them.

There are additional duties placed on employees by the *Management of Health and Safety at Work Regulations 1999, regulation 14*.

28.23 Interference with safety measures

No person may intentionally or recklessly interfere with or misuse anything provided in the interests of health, safety or welfare in pursuance of any of the relevant statutory provisions (*HSWA 1974, s 8*). Thus, an employee who removes a safety guard provided by his employer, in breach of the regulations, is in breach of *s 8* and is guilty of an offence for which in a magistrates' court he may be fined up to level 5 on the standard scale and in the Crown Court there may be an unlimited fine (*HSWA 1974, ss 33(1)(b), (3)(b)*; see **1.10** Introduction).

Such conduct may also justify dismissal, provided the employee was properly instructed about the safety measures and had been made aware that interference could lead to dismissal (*Martin v Yorkshire Imperial Metals Ltd* [1978] IRLR 440).

28.24 No charge for safety measures

An employer may not charge any employee of his for anything done or supplied in compliance with any specific requirement of the relevant statutory provisions (*HSWA 1974, s 9*). If, for example, an employer is required to provide an employee of his with a mask, he may not require that employee to contribute towards the cost of that mask. This applies to all personal protective equipment, including safety footwear.

28.25 EU LEGISLATION

The influence of European-derived legislation in the health and safety field is substantial. The original *Treaty of Rome*, as amended by the subsequent Treaties of Maastricht, Amsterdam and Nice (see **24.1** EUROPEAN UNION LAW), provides in *art 137* (formerly *art 118A*) for the adoption of Directives in connection with improvements to the working environment to protect workers' health and safety. Such Directives are subject to the co-decision procedure whereby the European Parliament jointly adopts proposals with the Council of Ministers. Health and safety *Directives* are normally implemented in UK law by means of regulations made under *HSWA 1974*. The future position after the Brexit referendum means that the future shape of the law is utterly uncertain.

A surge in EU health and safety legislation occurred following the adoption of the so-called *Framework Directive* (*89/391*), implemented on 1 January 1993. The *Directive* imposes a number of general obligations upon both employers and employees. Whereas much English legislation uses the standard of what is 'reasonably practicable', the EC approach is to set absolute standards and to permit a defence of *force majeure* for non-compliance (see *art 5(4)* of the *Directive*).

Five further Directives, laying down detailed requirements, were initially adopted pursuant to the *Framework Directive*. They relate to minimum requirements for safety and health in the workplace (*89/654*), the use of machines and equipment (*89/655*), the use of personal protective equipment (*89/656*), the use of visual display units (*90/270*) and the handling of heavy loads (*90/269*).

In addition, Directives have been adopted on, *inter alia*: carcinogens (*90/394, 97/42, 99/38*), biological agents (*90/679*), construction sites (*92/57*), health and safety signs (*92/58*), and protection of pregnant workers (*92/85*).

Regulations have been made by statutory instrument to implement the EC Directives referred to above. For further details of Regulations within the scope of this book, see HEALTH AND SAFETY AT WORK – II **(29)** under the specific subject heading.

It remains to be seen what the Legislature will do once Brexit takes effect as it is presently intended to do at the end of 2020 although there is provision for an extension of up to 2 years to be agree. Those promulgating departure argued, amongst other things, that the weight of EU Directives was oppressive and ought to be reduced.

28.26 THE HEALTH AND SAFETY COMMISSION AND EXECUTIVE

HSWA 1974, s 10 establishes the Health and Safety Commission and the Health and Safety Executive. The Commission is made up of both employer and employee representatives and the Executive is made up of three of the Commission's appointees approved by the Secretary of State for the Environment, one of whom is first chosen as the director of the Executive and who is consulted as to the appointment of the other two members. The Commission's chief function is to advise, authorise research and make suggestions for the implementation of the provisions of the *HSWA 1974*. It may make suggestions for the passing of regulations. The Executive also has the duty of providing information and advice to any Government minister who requests it.

The Commission may either direct the Executive or authorise any other person to investigate and make a special report on any accident, occurrence, situation or other matter that the Commission thinks is necessary or expedient to investigate, or (with the consent of the Secretary of State) direct an inquiry to be held into any such matter (*HWSA 1974, s 14(1)(2)*). The *Health and Safety Inquiries (Procedure) Regulations 1975*, as amended *(SIs 1975/335; 1976/1246)* lay down the procedure for the conduct of such inquiries. Since civil or criminal liability for an accident may depend on the outcome of such an inquiry, proper representation is essential.

The HSC and the HSE were merged on 1 April 2008 to form a single regulatory body called the Health and Safety Executive (HSE), formerly tasked with the general responsibilty of promoting improved health and safety in the workplace. The decision to merge followed consultation with interested parties and was arrived at pursuant to the process set out in the *Legislative and Regulatory Reform Act 2006.*

28.27 Information

HSWA 1974, s 27 enables the Commission to obtain information necessary for the discharge of its functions, or for provision to an enforcing authority (eg the Executive or an inspector) of information necessary to discharge its duties. Since April 2008, this has passed to the Executive (HSE).

28.28 Codes of Practice

The Commission is empowered by *HSWA 1974, s 16* to approve and issue Codes of Practice for the enforcement of *ss 2–7* or of health and safety regulations introduced under the *Act*, or any other existing statutory provisions. Approved Codes give guidance on methods of complying with regulations and on what is considered reasonably practicable.

28.29 ENFORCING AUTHORITIES AND INSPECTORS

The Health and Safety Executive and local authorities are responsible for the enforcement of the *Health and Safety at Work Act 1974*. From 1 April 1998 the *Health and Safety (Enforcing Authority) Regulations 1998 (SI 1998/494)* re-enact, with amendments, the *1989 Regulations* of the same name (*SI 1989/1903*) which are revoked. *Schedule 1* sets out the main activities which determine whether local authorities will be enforcing authorities.

The enforcement powers under *HSWA 1974* cover all the 'relevant statutory provisions', which comprise the provisions of *HSWA 1974, Part I*, all the enactments specified in *HSWA 1974, Sch 1* and regulations made under them, and any health and safety and agricultural health and safety regulations (*HSWA 1974, s 53(1)*).

In January 2002 the Health and Safety Commission published its revised enforcement policy statement which, for the first time, sets out specific criteria to enable enforcement officers to decide when to investigate health and safety incidents, and to prosecute breaches of the law. The statement may be viewed on the HSE's website at http ://www.hse.gov.uk/enforce/enforcepolicy.htm. This policy provides clarity on offences and the penalties available, as well as the HSE's role in investigations and inquiries. Since 2001 the HSC has published a list of health and safety offenders convicted and a prosecutions database.

28.30 Powers of inspectors

Every enforcing authority has the power to appoint inspectors. An inspector has many powers to enforce the statutory provisions for which his enforcing authority has responsibility. He may enter premises, if necessary accompanied by a police constable, take measurements and photographs and make other records, and take samples of articles or substances found in any premises which he has power to enter and of the atmosphere in or near such premises. If he fears that an article or substance found on premises which he has power to enter has caused or is likely to cause danger to health or safety, he may have it dismantled or subjected to any process or test. He may not destroy it unless that action is necessary for the performance of his duties. The inspector may take possession of a dangerous or potentially dangerous article or substance to examine it, to ensure that it is not tampered with or to ensure that it is available for use as evidence in any proceedings under the *HSWA 1974*. When he takes possession of any article, the inspector must fix, in a conspicuous position, a notice giving particulars of the article or substance and stating that he has taken possession of it (*HSWA 1974, ss 20(2)(a)–(i), (4)*).

An inspector may require persons to answer questions in the course of his investigations and to sign a declaration of the truth of their answers. He may require the production of books and documents and take copies of them. If he requires any facilities or assistance in the course of his investigations, he may require the person able to do so to provide him with such facilities (*HSWA 1974, s 20(2)(j)–(l)*). No answer given by a person to an inspector is admissible in evidence against that person or the husband or wife of that person (*HSWA 1974, s 20(7)*). The section does not compel a person to disclose a document which could be withheld on grounds of legal professional privilege in High Court proceedings (such as an opinion of counsel) (*HSWA 1974, s 20(8)*).

Where an inspector has reasonable cause to believe that an article or substance on premises he is empowered to enter is a cause of imminent danger of serious personal injury, he may seize it and cause it to be rendered harmless (*HSWA 1974, s 25(1)*).

28.31 IMPROVEMENT AND PROHIBITION NOTICES

Improvement notices

If an inspector is of the opinion that a person:

(a)   is contravening one or more of the relevant statutory provisions (see **28.29** above); or

(b)   has contravened one or more of those provisions in circumstances that make it likely that the contravention will continue or be repeated,

he may serve on that person a notice (referred to as 'an improvement notice') (*HSWA 1974, s 21*).

An improvement notice must: (i) state that he is of that opinion; (ii) specify the provisions which in his opinion are being or have been contravened; (iii) give particulars of the reasons for his opinion; and (iv) require that person to remedy the contravention within a specified period.

The specified period in (iv) above is not to be shorter than that allowed for an appeal to an employment tribunal (which is 21 days from the date of the service on the appellant of the notice appealed against; see *Employment Tribunals (Constitution and Rules of Procedure) Regulations 2001, Sch 5 (SI 2001/1171)*).

28.32 Prohibition notices

If an inspector regards any activities as involving or potentially involving *a risk of serious personal injury, or risk of imminent danger*, he may serve on the person in control of those activities a notice known as 'a prohibition notice' (*HSWA 1974, s 22*).

A prohibition notice must:

(a)   state the opinion of the inspector;

(b)   specify the matters which in his opinion give or, as the case may be, will give rise to the risks;

(c)   where in his opinion any of those matters involves or will involve a contravention of any of the relevant statutory provisions, state that he is of that opinion, specify the relevant provision or provisions, and give particulars of the reasons why he is of that opinion; and

(d)   direct that the activities to which the notice relates shall not be carried on by or under the control of the person on whom the notice is served unless the matters specified in the notice and any associated contraventions so specified have been remedied.

A direction given in pursuance of (d) above takes effect immediately if the inspector is of the opinion, and states it, that the risk of serious personal injury is or will be imminent. For example, in *BT Fleet Ltd v McKenna* [2005] EWHC 387 (Admin), [2005] All ER (D) 284 (Mar), QBD, Evans-Lombe J held that an improvement notice served by a health and safety Inspector, pursuant to *HSWA 1974, s 21*, should be clear and easily understood for it to be operative.

Improvement and prohibition notices may make reference to any approved Code of Practice (see **28.28** above) (*HSWA 1974, s 23(2)(a)*).

28.33 Withdrawal of notices

Where an improvement notice or a prohibition notice which is not to take immediate effect has been served, the notice may be withdrawn by an inspector at any time before it takes effect and the period before it takes effect may be extended or further extended by an inspector at any time when an appeal against the notice is not pending (*HSWA 1974, s 23(5)*).

28.34 APPEALS AGAINST THE NOTICES

A person on whom an improvement or prohibition notice is served may, within 21 days, appeal to an employment tribunal (*Employment Tribunals (Constitution and Rules of Procedure) Regulations 2001 (SI 2001/1171), Sch 5, rule 2(1)*). A tribunal may extend the period for lodging an appeal (on an application made in writing to the Secretary of the Tribunals either before or after the expiration of the time limit) if it is satisfied that it is not or was not reasonably practicable for an appeal to be brought within that time (*rule 2(2)*).

One or more assessors may be appointed for the purposes of any such appeals brought before an employment tribunal (*HSWA 1974, s 24(4)*).

The tribunal may either cancel or affirm the notice and, if the tribunal affirms it, may do so either in its original form or with such modifications as the tribunal may in the circumstances think fit (*HSWA 1974, s 24(2)*).

28.35 Suspension of notices pending appeal hearing

Where an appeal is brought within the time limit allowed:

(a)   *Improvement notice*: the bringing of the appeal has the effect of suspending the operation of the notice until the appeal is finally disposed of or, if the appeal is withdrawn, until the withdrawal of the appeal (*HSWA 1974, s 24(3)(a)*); and

(b)   *Prohibition notice*: the bringing of the appeal will not affect the notice unless, on application by the appellant, the tribunal so directs, in which case the prohibition notice will be suspended from the time that the tribunal gives its direction (*HSWA 1974, s 24(3)(b)*).

28.36 Cost of remedy required

In deciding whether an improvement notice which required the cleaning and repainting of walls should be cancelled or not, an employment tribunal sitting at Shrewsbury held that the company's financial position was irrelevant and evidence relating to its financial position would not be admitted (*T C Harrison (Newcastle-under-Lyme) Ltd v Ramsey (K) (HM Inspector)* [1976] IRLR 135). It may therefore be no ground for appeal against such notices that the company cannot afford to remedy the defects.

28.37 CRIMINAL PROCEEDINGS

The HSE publishes an annual report naming companies and individuals convicted in the previous 12 months of flouting health and safety law. The names of those convicted are also listed on the HSE's website.

HSWA 1974, s 33 lists various offences including:

(a)   failure to discharge a duty under *ss 2–7* (see **28.18–28.22** above) (*HSWA 1974, s 33(1)(a)*);

(b)   contravention of any health and safety regulations or any requirement or prohibition imposed under such a regulation (*HSWA 1974, s 33(1)(c)*);

(c)   contravention of any requirement or prohibition imposed by an improvement notice or a prohibition notice (including any such notice as modified on appeal) (*HSWA 1974, s 33(1)(g)*);

(d)   intention to obstruct an inspector in the exercise or performance of his powers or duties (*HSWA 1974, s 33(1)(h)*).

Criminal offences are triable either summarily (ie in the magistrates' court) or on indictment (ie in the Crown Court) or 'either way' (ie where the defendant may normally elect the mode of trial). In respect of offences committed on or after 6 March 1992, *HSWA 1974, s 33(1A) and (2A)* (inserted by *Offshore Safety Act 1992, s 4*) empowers a magistrates' court to impose a fine of up to £20,000 for breaches of *HSWA 1974, ss 2–6* (see (*a*) above), failure to comply with an improvement or prohibition notice (see (*c*) above), and failure to comply with a court remedy order under *HSWA 1974, s 42* (see **28.39** below).

On indictment the penalty may be a fine unlimited in amount and/or, for certain offences, imprisonment for up to two years (*HSWA 1974, s 33(2)–(4); see* **1.10** INTRODUCTION).

In two cases, the courts have emphasised that where a company is convicted of offences under the *HSWA 1974* the financial penalties imposed should reflect the seriousness of the case. In *R v F Howe & Son (Engineers) Ltd* [1999] IRLR 434, the Court of Appeal indicated that the general level of fine for health and safety offences was too low and outlined some of the factors which should be taken into account by the courts when setting the level of fines. These observations were subsequently given unqualified support by the Court of Appeal in *R v Rollco Screw and Rivet Co Ltd* [1999] IRLR 439.

In *R v Davies (David Janway)* [2003] IRLR 170, [2003] ICR 586, an employer was convicted and fined for being in breach of *ss 3(1)* and *33(1)* of the *HSWA 1974*, having failed to discharge the duty to conduct his undertaking in such a way as to ensure that he did not expose his employees to risks to their health and safety. The Court of Appeal, dismissing the employer's appeal, ruled that the *HSWA 1974* was regulatory and designed to protect and that the defence of 'reasonably practicable' was not incompatible with the *Human Rights Act 1998*. Consequently, £15,000 fine and £22,544.32 costs were upheld.

Current maximum penalties for offences specified in the Health and Safety at Work etc Act 1974, section 33 (HSWA)

HSWA SECTION	HSW(O)B, Schedule 6A, Item	CURRENT MAXIMUM
33(1)(a) Sections 2, 3, 4 and 6 – the general duties on employers and others	1	**Summary** - a fine not exceeding £20,000 **Indictment** - an unlimited fine
33(1)(a) Section 7 – duty on employees	2	**Summary** - a fine not exceeding £5,000 **Indictment** - an unlimited fine
33(1)(b) Section 8 – duty not to interfere with or misuse things provided for health and safety	3	**Summary** - a fine not exceeding £5,000 **Indictment** - an unlimited fine
33(1)(b) Section 9 – duty not to charge employees for things done to meet requirements of relevant statutory provisions	4	**Summary** - a fine not exceeding £5,000 **Indictment** - an unlimited fine
33(1)(c) Contravening requirements of health and safety regulations, licences or authorisations	5	**Summary** - a fine not exceeding £5,000 **Indictment** - an unlimited fine

HSWA SECTION	HSW(O)B, Schedule 6A, Item	CURRENT MAXIMUM
33(1)(d) Contravening requirements imposed specifically in relation to public inquiries or special investigations	6	**Summary only** – a fine not exceeding £5,000
33(1)(e) Contravening any requirement imposed by an inspector under section 20 (eg to give information for an investigation, or to leave premises undisturbed after an incident) or under section 25	7	**Summary** – a fine not exceeding £5,000 **Indictment (section 25 breaches only)** – an unlimited fine
33(1)(f) Preventing another person from appearing before an inspector, or from answering an inspector's question	7 (continued)	**Summary only** – a fine not exceeding £5,000
33(1)(g) Contravening an improvement or prohibition notice	7 (continued)	**Summary** – 6 months' imprisonment, or a fine not exceeding £20,000, or both **Indictment** – 2 years' imprisonment or an unlimited fine or both
33(1)(h) Obstructing an inspector	8	**Summary only** – a fine not exceeding £5,000

HSWA SECTION	HSW(O)B, Schedule 6A, Item	CURRENT MAXIMUM
33(1)(i) Contravening any notice issued under section 27(1) (general powers of HSC/E to obtain information)	9	**Summary** - a fine not exceeding £5,000 **Indictment** - an unlimited fine
33(1)(j) Disclosing information in breach of HSWA section 27(4) or 28	10	**Summary** - a fine not exceeding £5,000 **Indictment** - 2 years' imprisonment, an unlimited fine, or both
33(1)(k), (l) and (m) Offences relating to deception	11	**Summary** - a fine not exceeding £5,000 **Indictment** - an unlimited fine
33(1)(n) Falsely to pretend to be an inspector	12	**Summary only** - a fine not exceeding £5,000
33(1)(o) Failure to comply with a court remedy order (section 42)	13	**Summary** - 6 months' imprisonment, or a fine not exceeding £20,000, or both **Indictment** - 2 years' imprisonment or an unlimited unlimited fine or both
33(3) (in so far	14	**Summary**

HSWA SECTION	HSW(O)B, Schedule 6A, Item	CURRENT MAXIMUM
as no other penalty is specified)		– a fine not exceeding £5,000
Penalties for health and safety offences arising from 'existing statutory provisions' (pre-1974 enactments) set out in HSWA Schedule 1		**Indictment** – an unlimited fine
33(4)(a), (b) and (c) Offences of breaching licensing or explosives requirements	Covered under Bill items above	**Summary** – a fine not exceeding £5,000 **Indictment** – 2 years' imprisonment or an unlimited fine or both

Any explosive article or substance may be forfeited by order of the court and may be destroyed (*HSWA 1974, s 42(4)*).

Breaches of Codes of Practice approved by the Health and Safety Commission (see **28.28** above) are not in themselves criminal offences. However, if in a prosecution for a contravention of the *Act* or the Regulations, it is shown that there was a failure to observe any relevant Code, then that contravention will be considered proven unless the court is satisfied that the requirement or prohibition was complied with in an alternative, acceptable manner (*HSWA 1974, s 17(2)*).

28.38   Personal liability of directors and other company officers

Under *HSWA 1974, s 37*, personal liability is imposed on any director, manager, secretary or other similar officer of a company (or any person who was purporting to act in that capacity) if an offence is committed by the company under *HSWA 1974*, or any of the other health and safety legislation specified in *HSWA 1974, Sch 1*, with the consent or connivance, or due to the neglect, of any such person.

In practice, such prosecutions are rare. However, several successful prosecutions of directors and senior managers have resulted, for example, in *Armour v Skeen* [1977] IRLR 310 (the director of roads and bridges for a Scottish regional council) and *R v Mara* [1987] IRLR 154 (the director of a cleaning company). A director who fails to take out compulsory employers' liability insurance is, however, not liable to a victim who is injured but unable to recover damages from the company which might have negligible assets or cannot otherwise satisfy a judgment.

Defining who is responsible. In *Tesco Supermarkets Ltd v Nattrass* [1971] 2 All ER 127, in a prosecution of a company for a breach of the *Trade Descriptions Act 1968*, Lord Reid observed that:

' . . . a board of directors can delegate part of their functions of management so as to make their delegate an embodiment of the company within the sphere of delegation.'

In that case, the company was held not to have delegated any of its functions, so that the acts or omissions of the store manager were not acts of the company itself; the House of Lords therefore quashed the company's conviction. However, the Court of Appeal decision in *R v British Steel plc* [1995] IRLR 310 has cast doubt on whether the approach of the House of Lords in a consumer protection case is sufficiently stringent for health and safety legislation.

In *R v Boal* [1992] IRLR 420, the Court of Appeal defined 'manager' in relation to personal liability under the *Fire Precautions Act 1971*. The Court held that the relevant provision was intended:

' . . . to fix with criminal liability only those who are in a position of real authority, the decision-makers within the company who have both the power and responsibility to decide corporate policy and strategy. It is to catch those responsible for putting proper procedures in place; it is not meant to strike at underlings.'

Where directors have been convicted of offences under the *HSWA 1974*, the Court of Appeal has said that the penalties imposed should make it clear that directors had a personal responsibility which could not be shuffled off to the company (*R v Rollco Screw and Rivet Co Ltd* [1999] IRLR 439). See also, *R v Transco* [2006] All ER (D) 416 (Mar), CA, where in assessing the level of fine, the Court takes account of the employer's knowledge regarding their responsibility for any breach of health and safety.

Company Directors Disqualification Act 1986. A director found guilty of an indictable offence under *HSWA 1974* (whether on indictment or summarily) may be disqualified from holding office as a director under the *Company Directors Disqualification Act 1986, s 2(1)*. The first such disqualification occurred in 1992 when a director was disqualified for two years after being found guilty of serious breaches of *HSWA 1974*. The director had been fined £5,000 for refusing to comply with a prohibition notice in relation to dangerous rock falls where men were working. In September 1998, the managing director of a recycling company was disqualified under the *Company Directors Disqualification Act 1986* following a breach of the *Provision and Use of Work Equipment Regulations 1992* (see **29.12 HEALTH AND SAFETY AT WORK – II**) which had resulted in a serious injury to an employee operating an unguarded machine.

In July 2001 the HSC published guidance on health and safety responsibilities for company directors and board members (IND(G) 343, HSE) of public sector and voluntary organisations. In particular, the guidance specifies that Boards need to:

(a) accept joint responsibility and leadership for their organisations' health and safety performance;

(b) appoint one Board member as a health and safety director;

(c) ensure that each Board member accepts his or her individual role in providing health and safety leadership;

(d) ensure that all Board decisions reflect their health and safety intentions;

(e) encourage the active participation of workers in improving health and safety; and

(f) keep up-to-date with all health and safety issues affecting the organisation and review performance regularly.

28.39 Order to remedy default

If a person is convicted of an offence and it appears to the court that the matter is one which it is in his power to remedy, the court may, in addition to or instead of imposing any punishment, order him (within such time as may be fixed by the order) to take such steps as may be specified in the order to remedy the situation. The time fixed by such an order may be extended or further extended by order of the court on an application made before the end of the time originally fixed or as extended (*HSWA 1974, s 42(1), (2)*). Failure to comply with an order under *HSWA 1974, s 42* is an offence (*HSWA 1974, s 33(1)(o)*), which is punishable: (i) on summary conviction, by up to six months' imprisonment and/or a fine of up to £20,000; and (ii) on indictment, by up to two years' imprisonment and/or an unlimited fine (*HSWA 1974, s 33(2A)*, inserted by *Offshore Safety Act 1992, s 4*).

28.40   Time for bringing proceedings

Summary proceedings may be brought at any time within six months from the date on which there comes to the knowledge of an enforcing authority evidence to justify a prosecution (*HSWA 1974, s 34(3)*). A failure to do something required by the Act is treated as continuing until the requirement is complied with, so that the six-month period runs from the last day on which the requirement was not complied with (*HSWA 1974, s 34(2)*). The time limit is extended in cases where there is a special report under *s 14(2)(a)*, a report of an inquiry under *s 14(2)(b)*, a coroner's inquest, or a public inquiry (in Scotland) into a death, to three months from the making of the report or three months from the conclusion of the inquest or inquiry (*HSWA 1974, s 34(1)*).

28.41   Defence

Many of the statutory provisions contain the modification 'so far as is reasonably practicable', or 'practicable' or to use 'the best practicable means to do something'. In those cases the onus is on the accused to prove that it was not practicable or not reasonably practicable to do more than was in fact done to satisfy the duty or requirement, or that there was no better practicable means than was in fact used to satisfy the duty or requirement (*HSWA 1974, s 40*). However, where proceedings are brought under *HSWA 1974, s 33(1)(g)* for contravention of an improvement notice, the offence is established if there has been a non-compliance with a requirement of the notice irrespective of whether compliance was reasonably practicable (*Deary (HM Inspector of Factories) v Mansion Hide Upholstery Ltd* [1983] IRLR 195).

In addition, since 11 July 2001 the defence that UK health and safety provision did not apply in the part of the business outside the jurisdiction (ie not situated in the UK) was abolished by the *Health and Safety at Work etc Act 1974 (Application outside Great Britain) Order (SI 2001/2127)*.

28.42   Corporate killing

The successful prosecution for manslaughter following the death of 23 cocklers on Morecambe Bay in February 2004, and consequential sentencing on 21 counts of manslaughter, re-emphasised the need to tighten up existing laws on corporate manslaughter. Under the Common Law a conviction for corporate manslaughter is obtainable only where a senior individual in a company (the 'controlling mind') is shown to have been grossly negligent and thereby responsible for the fatal accident. This is difficult to prove where managerial responsibilities are divided as is typical in a large organisation. Tragic incidents involving major train crashes and the sinking of a cross-channel ferry failed to yield convictions.

The *Corporate Manslaughter and Corporate Homicide Act 2007*, implemented in April 2008, seeks to make it easier to secure convictions against organisations. The Act creates no new duties and nor does it render individuals liable to prosecution. Liability for the new offence depends on a finding of gross negligence in the way in which the activities of the organisation are run. In summary, the offence is committed where, in particular circumstances, an organisation owes a duty to take reasonable care for a person's safety and the way in which activities of the organisation have been managed or organised amounts to a gross breach of that duty and causes the person's death. How the activities were managed or organised by senior management must be a substantial element of the gross breach. The likely impact of the Act should not be exaggerated. The Government estimated that there would be about one prosecution a month. In fact, barely any prosecutions have been launched.

Section 1(1) defines the new offence, which is called corporate manslaughter in England and Wales and Northern Ireland and corporate homicide in Scotland.

The elements of the new offence are:

(a)   The organisation must owe a 'relevant duty of care' to the victim. The relevant duties of care are set out in *section 2*.

(b)   The organisation must be in breach of that duty of care as a result of the way in which the activities of the organisation were managed or organised. This test is not linked to a particular level of management but considers how an activity was managed within the organisation as a whole. *Section 1(3)* stipulates that an organisation cannot be convicted of the offence unless a substantial element of the breach lies in the way the senior management of the organisation managed or organised its activities.

(c)   The way in which the organisation's activities were managed or organised must have caused the victim's death. This means that the management failure need not have been the sole cause of death; it need only be a cause.

(d)   The management failure must amount to a gross breach of the duty of care. *Section 1(4)(b)* sets out the test for whether a particular breach is 'gross'. The test asks whether the conduct that constitutes the breach falls far below what could reasonably have been expected. *Section 8* sets out a number of factors for the jury to take into account when considering this issue. There is no question of liability where the management of an activity includes reasonable safeguards and a death nonetheless occurs.

Since only an organisation can be guilty the penalty upon conviction is a fine without limit. The court can also order that remedial measures be taken and it may make a publicity order requiring the defendant to publicise the conviction. The *Act* is extensive in application; employers, suppliers, Government departments, transport providers and others face liability. Valuable guidance may be found on the HSE website and the Government guidance notes upon the Act are exemplary.

In the first conviction under the *Act* in February 2011 Cotswold Geotechnics (Holdings) Ltd, a small company with 8 employees, was fined £385,000 after an employee was killed when a trench caved in. The company was allowed to pay the fine at the rate of £38,500 per annum as else it would have been forced out of business. This is a clear indication that massive penalties will be applied upon conviction.

Prosecutions are rare and convictions few and far between.

November 2011:	PS and JE Ward — Case pending
May 2012:	JMW Farms — £187,000 fine
July 2012:	Lion Steel Equipment — £480,000 fine
December 2012:	MNS Mingin — Case pending
February 2013:	Prince's Sporting Club — Case pending

March 2013: Mobile Sweeperds (Reading) — Case pending

28.43 CIVIL LIABILITY

Breaches of *HSWA 1974, ss 2–8* cannot form the basis of a civil action (*HSWA 1974, s 47(1)(a)*) but breach 'of a duty imposed by health and safety regulations . . . shall, so far as it causes damage, be actionable except in so far as the regulations provide otherwise' (*HSWA 1974, s 47(2)*). In other words, a civil action can be brought where a breach of the health and safety regulations causes damage, unless the regulations prevent such an action from being brought.

Any provision in any agreement to contract out of liability for such breaches is void unless the health and safety regulations provide otherwise (*HSWA 1974, s 47(5)*).

28.44 CONTRIBUTORY NEGLIGENCE

In any successful action against the employer for breach of duty at common law or under some enactment, the amount of damages may be reduced in proportion to the degree to which the employee failed to take reasonable steps for his own safety (*Law Reform (Contributory Negligence) Act 1945, s 1(1)*). The *Act* applies where both the employer and employee have contributed to the damage. For example, in *Bux v Slough Metals Ltd* [1974] 1 All ER 262 the employee's failure to use the goggles with which he was provided contributed to the extent of the injury he suffered and reduced his damages by 40%. It is for the employer to allege and establish contributory negligence. In *Dziennik v CTO Gesellschaft Fur Containertransport MBH* [2006] EWCA Civ 1456, [2006] All ER (D) 157 (Nov) the Court of Appeal held that since the employer had not pleaded the issue it was wrong of a Trial Judge to deduct 60% of the compensation awarded even though there was overwhelming evidence to justify that decision. The Court of Appeal indicated in *Pitts v Hunt* [1991] 1 QB 24, [1990] 3 All ER 344 that there was no such thing as 100% contributory fault. The purpose of contribution was to apportion blame, not to put it all at the door of the claimant and the tenor of the *1945 Act* anticipated that, after deduction, the claimant would be left with something. This very point was reiterated by the same court in *Brumder v Motornet Services and Repairs Ltd* [2013] EWCA Civ 195, [2013] All ER (D) 159 (Mar).

28.45 CORONER'S INQUESTS

In some health and safety incidences, interaction with the coroner is necessary. A coroner enquires into reported deaths. It is the coroner's duty to find out the medical cause of the death, if it is not known, and to enquire about the cause of it if it was due to violence or otherwise appears to be unnatural. In most cases the deceased's own doctor, or a hospital doctor who has been treating him or her, is able to give a cause of death. However, there are a number of circumstances under which a death will be reported to the coroner. For example, when no doctor has treated the deceased during his or her last illness or when the death was sudden or unexpected or unnatural. Yet deaths are usually reported to the coroner by the police or by a doctor called to the death if it is sudden. A doctor will also report a patient's death if unexpected. In other cases, the local registrar of deaths may make the report. Whenever the death has been reported to the coroner the registrar must wait for the coroner to finish his or her enquiries before the death can be registered.

28.46 CORONER'S FINDINGS

The coroner may decide that death was natural and that there is a doctor who can sign a form saying so. In this case the coroner will advise the registrar. The coroner may ask a pathologist to examine the body. If so, the examination must be done as soon as possible.

The coroner or his or her staff will, unless it is impracticable or cause undue delay, give notice of the arrangements to, amongst others, the usual doctor of the deceased and any relative who may have notified the coroner of his or her wish to be medically represented at the examination. If the examination shows the death to have been a natural one, there may be no need for an inquest and the coroner will send a form to the registrar of deaths so that the death can be registered by the relatives and a certificate of burial issued by the registrar. If the person is to be cremated, the certificate may be issued by the coroner.

28.47 INQUESTS

An inquest is not a trial. It is a limited inquiry into the facts surrounding a death. It is not the job of the coroner to blame anyone for the death, as a trial would do. The inquest is an inquiry to find out who has died, and how, when and where they died, together with information needed by the registrar of deaths so that the death can be registered. Most inquests are held without a jury. There are particular reasons when a jury will be called, including if the death occurred in prison or in police custody or if the death resulted from an incident at work. In every inquest which is held with a jury, it is the jury, and not the coroner, which makes the final decision. The High Court has decided in *Roach v Home Office* [2009] EWHC 312 (QB), [2009] 3 All ER 510 that in principle the costs of attending an inquest or indeed a Health and Safety prosecution may be recoverable in subsequent civil proceedings where a claim for damages is pursued. In *Lynch v Chief Constable of Warwickshire Police* [2014] JR 130517 it was declared that the inquest costs must be proportionate to the overall value of the subsequent civil claim. Consequently, significant inquest costs were disallowed as they were out of all proportion to the value and importance of the civil litigation.

28.48 'INTERESTED PERSONS'

An 'interested person' is someone who can question a witness at an inquest. They can be:

(a) a parent, spouse, child and anyone acting for the deceased;

(b) anyone who gains from a life insurance policy on the deceased;

(c) any insurer having issued such a policy;

(d) anyone whose actions the coroner believes may have contributed to the death, accidentally or otherwise;

(e) the chief officer of police (who may only ask questions of witnesses through a lawyer);

(f) any person appointed by a government department to attend the inquest;

(g) anyone else who the coroner may decide also has a proper interest.

29   Health and Safety at Work – II: Specific Legislation and Health and Safety Issues

Cross-reference. See HEALTH AND SAFETY AT WORK – I (28) for safety duties at common law and the general legislative framework.

29.1   ACCIDENT REPORTING

Notification of accidents, diseases and dangerous occurrences. The current regulations governing the notification and recording of accidents are the *Reporting of Injuries, Diseases and Dangerous Occurrences Regulations 2013 (SI 2013/1471)*. The reporting rules have been amended with effect from 6th April 2012. Whereas before it was obligatory to report an occurrence, as defined below, where the individual was incapacitated for 3 days or more that period has been extended to only apply to incapacity for 7 days or more (excluding the day of the incident). The employer now has 15 days to report the incident from the date it occurred. Note that an incident involving incapacity must still be recorded albeit not reported by the employer. The HSE has issued explicit guidance that an entry in a workplace accident book will satisfy this obligation.

An employer must notify the Health and Safety Executive ('HSE') or local authority, whichever is in the circumstances the enforcing authority (see **28.29** HEALTH AND SAFETY AT WORK – I), of:

(a)   an accident arising out of or in connection with work resulting in:

　　(i)   the death of any person;

　　(ii)   a specific injury to any person at work:

- a fracture, other than to fingers, thumbs and toes

- amputation of an arm, hand, finger, thumb, leg, foot. or toe

- permanent loss of sight or reduction of sight

- crash injuries leading to internal organ damage

- serious burns (covering more than 10% of the body) or damaging eyes, respiratory system or other vital organs

- scalpings (separation of skin from head) which require hospital treatment

- unconsciousness caused by head injury or asphyxia

- any other injury arising from working in an enclosed space which leads to hypothermia, heat-induced illness or requires resuscitation or admittance to hospital for more than 24 hours.

　　(iii)   hospital treatment of a person not at work; or

　　(iv)   major injury to a person not at work as a result of an accident in connection with work at a hospital;

(b)   a dangerous occurrence

The list of reportable dangerous occurrences that have to be reported in all industrial and commercial sectors has been reduced and simplified. The full list is available at www.legislation.gov.uk/uksi/2013/1471/made. DOs removed include those involving the carriage of dangerous substances by road, failure of fairground equipment, and failure of load-bearing parts of freight containers. The revised list contains 27 specified dangerous occurrences;

(c)   an accident connected with work as a result of which a person at work is incapacitated for work for more than seven days;

(d)   the death of an employee within one year of being injured as the result of a notifiable accident or notifiable dangerous occurrence (this applies whether or not the accident was reported at the time it occurred);

(e)   any person suffering from a reportable work-related illness as specified.

The former schedule of 47 industrial diseases has been replaced by eight categories of work-related illness: These include:

- occupational dermatitis

- occupational asthma

- occupational cancer

- diseases due to work exposure to biological events

- carpel tunnel syndrome

- severe cramp of the hand or forearm

- hand/arm vibration syndrome

- tendonitis or tenosynovitis of the hand or forearm.

These are reportable wherever at work they occur.

(f)   any 'gas incident' as specified.

(*Regulations 3–6*)

In cases under (*a*) and (*b*) the enforcing authority must be notified by the fastest practicable means in the first instance, and a report on the prescribed form must be sent to that authority within 15 days (*reg 3*).

In cases under (*c*) a report must be sent on an approved form within 15 days of the accident. Category (*d*) requires notification in writing as soon as the employer becomes aware of the death. Under (*e*) a report on an approved form must be made forthwith and for cases falling within (*f*) notification is required immediately, followed by a report within 14 days. Accident reports must be made on Form F2508 and disease reports on Form F2508A. For notification to the HSE, an online notification regime is now in place. The HSE website contains links to the various report forms.

Road accidents are not covered by the *Regulations*, except where they result from exposure to a substance which is being transported, the loading or unloading of vehicles, specified roadworks or where a train is involved (*reg 10*). See *Road Safety Act 2005*.

The definition of 'accident' includes acts of non-consensual physical violence done to a person at work.

They must be kept at the place of work to which they relate, or at the usual place of business of the responsible person as defined in the *Regulations*, for a period of three years from the date the details were entered in the records.

Accidents to self-employed persons are covered if they were working under the control of someone else, in which case the obligations attach to the person in control of the premises where the accident occurred.

Major accident hazards. Operators of premises liable to major accident hazards are, in addition, subject to a special regime under the *Control of Major Accident Hazards Regulations 1999 (SI 1999/743)* from 1 April 1999 (see **28.20** HEALTH AND SAFETY AT WORK – I).

Notification of industrial injuries. An employee who suffers an 'industrial injury' must report the accident to his employer. Notice of the accident may be given orally or in writing, and may be given by someone else on the employee's behalf. It is sufficient notice if the accident is recorded in the accident book (see below). The employer is required to take reasonable steps to investigate the accident and must, on request, provide all information uncovered to the Department for Work and Pensions. Failure by an employee to notify an accident may jeopardise his entitlement to industrial injury benefits.

Accident book. Every employer who normally employs 10 or more persons on or about the same premises in connection with a trade or business must keep an accident book (Form BI 510) in which specified particulars of accidents may be recorded, as must (however few employees they have) all employers who are owners or occupiers of a mine or quarry or of a 'factory' within the meaning of the *Factories Act 1961, s 175* (*Social Security (Claims and Payments) Regulations 1979 (SI 1979/628), reg 25*). The significant data reforms of 2018 are dealt with elsewhere in this book. The Employment Practices Code and Supplementary Guidance issued by the Information Commissioner's Office are illuminating and available without charge online .

29.2   ALCOHOL AND DRUG MISUSE

Problems arising from consumption of alcohol and misuse of drugs are seen as an increasing problem in the workplace. Employers have a duty of care, both at common law and under *HSWA 1974, s 2*, to ensure, so far as reasonably practicable, the health, safety and welfare at work of their employees. In addition, they are required to assess risks to health and safety under the *Management of Health and Safety at Work Regulations 1999* (see **29.17**). An employer who allows a person under the influence of drink or drugs to continue working could be in breach of its duty of care by putting the employee or others at risk.

Under the *Transport and Works Act 1992* it is a criminal offence for certain transport workers in safety-sensitive posts, primarily in the railway industry, to be unfit through drink or drugs while working. Transport system operators are required to show all due diligence in order to prevent an offence being committed.

It is an offence for occupiers of premises (such as employers) knowingly to allow the production or supply of controlled drugs on their premises or to permit the smoking of cannabis (*Misuse of Drugs Act 1971, s 8*).

Dependency on alcohol or drugs is an illness. Where an employee's performance or misconduct is found to be a result of alcohol dependency this should normally be handled as a capability issue (see **55.6** UNFAIR DISMISSAL – **II**). ACAS advises that drug dependency should be treated in the same way. However, the fact that use of non-prescription drugs is illegal may justify disciplinary action depending on the circumstances. One-off incidents of excessive consumption of alcohol by employees who are not alcohol-dependent would normally be dealt with according to disciplinary procedures. Off-duty use of alcohol or drugs is not normally the legitimate concern of the employer unless it has a connection with the workplace, damages the reputation of the employer's business or undermines trust and confidence in the employee.

As part of an overall health and safety policy, employers are advised to have a written policy on alcohol and drug misuse. Once a policy is in place, it should be applied consistently (*Angus Council v Edgley* EAT/289/99).

29.3   Drug testing

Drug testing is a controversial and sensitive issue. The HSE warns that testing is only likely to be acceptable if it is part of an organisation's health policy and is clearly designed to prevent risks to the misuser and others. Testing programmes should be introduced only with the consent of existing employees. Otherwise this may be seen as a breach of the implied term of trust and confidence, leading to constructive dismissal (see **54.7 UNFAIR DISMISSAL – I**). Pre-employment testing where applicants are asked to take a test voluntarily raises fewer legal problems. In all cases individuals need to be assured of the integrity of the screening process and medical confidentiality. Company policies should indicate the action which will be taken if testing yields a positive result.

Drug testing (except in highly safety-critical areas) is unlikely to be justified unless there is a reasonable suspicion of drug use that has an impact on safety. Employers should also bear in mind the effect on protection of privacy of the *1950 European Convention on Human Rights* and the *Human Rights Act 1998* (see **31.6 HUMAN RIGHTS**).

In *Swansea v Gayle* [2013] IRLR 768, an unfair dismissal claim, the EAT held it proper for an employer to have had an employee put under video surveillance. The claimant had been observed visiting a gym during working hours. The man was followed on five occasions and was surreptitiously filmed. At first instance this was found to be oppressive and dismissal was declared unfair. In a robust reversal, the EAT declared that the claimant had been watched whilst in public areas and the degree of surveillance demonstrated how thoroughly the local authority employer had investigated before electing to dismiss.

29.4   CONSTRUCTION SITE MANAGEMENT

Some 2.9 million workers make up the UK's construction industry. The *Construction (Design and Management) Regulations 1994 (SI 1994/3140)* gave effect to the EC Directive on temporary or mobile construction sites *(92/57)*. The *Regulations* impose detailed requirements with respect to design and management aspects of construction work, placing new obligations on all parties involved in construction projects. The *1994 Regulations* were amended by the *Construction (Design and Management) (Amendment) Regulations 2002 (SI 2002/2380)*. A revised Approved Code of Practice ('ACOP') and guidance on the *Construction (Design and Management) Regulations 1994 (SI 1994/3140)* have been published by the Health and Safety Commission and came into force on 1 February 2002. The revised ACOP is designed to clarify roles and responsibilities, placing emphasis on managing health and safety throughout the life of a project.

Further effect has been given to *Directive 92/57* by the *Construction (Health, Safety and Welfare) Regulations 1996 (SI 1996/1592)* as amended by *SI 1999/3242)* which also incorporate three sets of existing Regulations which have been modernised and simplified.

In 2007, the revised *Construction (Design and Management) Regulations* incorporated the *Construction (Health, Safety and Welfare) Regulations 1996* into one set of regulations: *CDM 2007 (SI 2007/320)*.

Note that no statutory provision or rule of law is to be taken as imposing, upon a Sikh on a construction site, any requirement to wear a safety helmet at any time when he is wearing a turban (*EA 1989, s 11*). However, a Sikh who does not comply with a requirement that would otherwise have been imposed, and is injured, may recover damages in tort only to the extent that he would have suffered injury even if wearing a helmet (*EA 1989, s 11(5)*). A person who does require a Sikh to wear a safety helmet on a construction site will probably be guilty of indirect racial discrimination, and if he has no reasonable grounds to believe that the Sikh would not wear a turban at all times when on site, he will not be permitted to justify that requirement (*EA 1989, s 12(1)*). Nor will special treatment afforded to a Sikh in consequence of s *11* constitute racial discrimination against anyone else (*EA 1989, s 12(2)*). See *Construction (Head Protection) Regulations 1989 (SI 1989/2209)*.

29.5 DISPLAY SCREEN EQUIPMENT

The *Health and Safety (Display Screen Equipment) Regulations 1992 (SI 1992/2792)* give effect to the *EU Directive* relating to the use of display screen equipment (eg VDUs) (*90/270*). Broadly, the *Regulations* require every employer, after making a suitable and sufficient analysis of each workstation (ie display screen equipment, its accessories and the surrounding work environment) to ensure that it meets the detailed requirements set out in the *Schedule* to the *Regulations*. Users of display screen equipment must: (i) be provided with eye and eyesight tests on request, both initially and at regular intervals thereafter; (ii) be provided with adequate health and safety information relating to the equipment; and (iii) have their daily work routine planned in such a way that they have periodical interruptions from using the equipment. See also **29.29** on work-related upper limb disorders.

The ECJ gave a ruling on the application of *Directive 90/270* in *Dietrich v Westdeutscher Rundfunk*: C-11/99 [2000] ECR I-5589. *Article 2(a)* of the *Directive* and *reg 1(2)* of the *Health and Safety (Display Screen Equipment) Regulations 1992* provide that 'display screen equipment' means 'an alphanumeric or graphic display screen, regardless of the display process involved'. The court concluded that the term 'graphic display screen' had to be interpreted broadly and therefore included screens that display film recordings, whether in analogue or digital form. A film cutter in a television production studio was therefore entitled to the protection of the provisions of the Directive.

Regulation 3 of the *Health and Safety (Miscellaneous Amendments) Regulations 2002 (SI 2002/2174)*, by removing the limitation in relation to workstation users and operators, so as to widen the remit to all users, amends *reg 3* of the *DSE Regulations 1992*.

29.6 ELECTRICITY AT WORK

The *Electricity at Work Regulations 1989 (SI 1989/635)* place a duty on employers to assess all foreseeable risks associated with work activities involving electricity which might give rise to personal injury or danger. Electrical equipment covers everything from power lines to electric kettles.

Employers are required to install safe systems of working with well-maintained equipment (*reg 4*). Steps must be taken to avoid danger in the use of equipment where it is reasonably foreseeable that it will be exposed to adverse or hazardous environments (*reg 6*). Specific precautions are laid down with regard to the insulation and protection of conductors (*regs 7–9*).

Regulations 12 and *13* lay down requirements for cutting off the supply, isolation and for working on dead equipment. No person should be engaged in work near a live conductor except where it is reasonable in all the circumstances and suitable precautions are taken to prevent injury (*reg 14*). Special attention should be paid to adequate working space, means of access and lighting where work is to be done on electrical equipment (*reg 15*), and no person should work on electrical equipment unless he or she possesses appropriate technical knowledge or is adequately supervised (*reg 16*).

29.7 EMPLOYMENT PROTECTION

The *Employment Rights Act 1996 ('ERA 1996')* provides that certain dismissals in health and safety cases are to be deemed automatically unfair (see **55.3** Unfair Dismissal – II below), and confers protection on employees in such cases from unfavourable treatment. Two EAT decisions are illuminating. In *Oudahar v Esporta Group Ltd* [2011] IRLR 730 an employee refused to mop behind a fridge because maintenance work had taken place and electrical wires were protruding from the wall. It was no answer to his legitimate and reasonable belief in a danger being present for the employer to show objectively that the perceived danger did not exist. His refusal should have been taken seriously. In *Jaoa v Jurys Hotel Management Ltd* (2011) UKEAT/210/11 an employee was found to have a reasonable belief that it was dangerous to his health to require him to work on nine successive night shifts even though this was strictly lawful and within the provisions of the *Working Time Regulations*.

29.8 Detriment in health and safety cases

ERA 1996, s 44 confers on an employee the right not to be subjected to any detriment by any act (short of dismissal), or any deliberate failure to act, by his employer done on the ground that:

(a) having been designated by the employer to carry out activities in connection with preventing or reducing risks to the health and safety of employees at work, he carried out, or proposed to carry out, any such activities;

(b) being a health and safety representative or member of a safety committee, in accordance with any statutory arrangements or by reason of being acknowledged as such by the employer, he performed or proposed to perform any functions as such a representative or member;

(c) he took part (or proposed to take part) in consultation with the employer in accordance with the *Health and Safety (Consultation with Employees) Regulations 1996 (SI 1996/1513)* or in an election for representatives of employee safety;

(d) where there is no representative or it is not possible to raise the matter by this means, he brought to his employer's attention, by reasonable means, circumstances which he reasonably believed were harmful or potentially harmful to health and safety;

(e) in circumstances of serious or imminent danger which he could not reasonably be expected to avert, he left, or proposed to leave, his place of work or any dangerous part of his place of work; or

(f) in circumstances of serious or imminent danger, he took, or proposed to take, appropriate steps to protect himself or other persons from the danger. 'Other persons' includes members of the public (*Masiak v City Restaurants (UK) Ltd* [1999] IRLR 780).

'Circumstances of danger' is not confined to dangers arising out of the workplace itself. It can include dangers caused by the misbehaviour of fellow employees (*Harvest Press Ltd v McCaffrey* [1999] IRLR 778). For the purposes of (*f*) above, whether the steps which the employee took, or proposed to take, were appropriate will be judged by reference to all the circumstances including, in particular, his knowledge and the facilities and advice available to him at the time (*ERA 1996, s 44(2)*). An employee will not be regarded as having suffered any detriment on the ground specified in (*f*) above if the employer shows that it was, or would have been, so negligent for the employee to take the steps which he took, or proposed to take, that a reasonable employer might have treated him as the employer did (*ERA 1996, s 44(3)*).

Provided a safety representative acts in good faith when pursuing a genuine health or safety matter, there is no duty to act reasonably (*Shillito v Van Leer (UK) Ltd* [1997] IRLR 495). In *Goodwin v Cabletel UK Ltd* [1997] IRLR 665 the Employment Appeal Tribunal held that the manner in which designated employees carry out health and safety activities can fall within the statutory protection. Tribunals must consider whether the way in which such employees approach their concerns about safety takes them outside the scope of health and safety activities.

29.9   Whistleblowing on safety

ERA 1996 provides further protection against victimisation by employers in specified circumstances if workers who ordinarily work in Great Britain raise concerns about, *inter alia*, health and safety issues (*ERA 1996, s 47B*, inserted by *Public Interest Disclosure Act 1998*, ('*PIDA 1998*'), *s 2*). The legislation protects not only direct employees but also most other workers including, specifically, agency workers, homeworkers, NHS practitioners and trainees on vocational or work experience schemes (*ERA 1996, s 43K* inserted by *PIDA 1998, s 1*). Provided certain conditions are met, workers will be protected against detrimental treatment or dismissal where they disclose information, they reasonably believe that disclosure is in the public interest and, further, they reasonably believe that the information tends to show that there has been, is, or will be a criminal offence; failure to comply with a legal obligation; a miscarriage of justice; endangering of health and safety; or damage to the environment. A full account of this protection may be found at **11.13** and following Disclosure of Information.

The *Public Interest Disclosure Act 1998* ('*PIDA 1998*') provides further protection against victimisation by employers in specified circumstances if workers who ordinarily work in Great Britain raise concerns about, *inter alia*, health and safety issues (*ERA 1996, s 47B*, inserted by *PIDA 1998, s 2*). The legislation protects not only direct employees but also most other workers including, specifically, agency workers, homeworkers, NHS practitioners and trainees on vocational or work experience schemes (*ERA 1996, s 43K* inserted by *PIDA 1998, s 1*). Provided certain conditions are met workers will be protected against detrimental treatment (or dismissal, see **55.3** Unfair Dismissal – II) if they reveal information about the workplace relating to: a criminal offence; failure to comply with a legal obligation; a miscarriage of justice; endangering health and safety; or damage to the environment. Information disclosed which tends to show that any of the above matters is being deliberately concealed would also qualify for protection (*ERA 1996, s 43B* inserted by *PIDA 1998, s 1*). Workers are required to raise their concerns initially with the employer or prescribed regulator. External disclosures are protected only if stringent conditions are met; an exception is made for 'exceptionally serious cases' (*ERA 1996, ss 43C–43H*, inserted by *PIDA 1998, s 1*). In *Goode v Marks And Spencer plc* (2010) UKEAT/442/09 the mere expression of disquiet by way of opinion about what an employer was proposing to do (change certain employment terms and conditions) was held not to be a protected disclosure at all.

29.10   The remedy

An employee has the right to complain to an employment tribunal for a declaration and compensation if he has suffered a detriment by an act, or failure to act, done on any of the grounds specified in (*a*) to (*f*) in **29.8** above. On such a complaint it is for the employer to show the ground on which any act, or deliberate failure to act, was done (*ERA 1996, s 48(1), (2)*). Workers who have suffered detrimental treatment for making a protected disclosure are able to make a complaint to an employment tribunal (*ERA 1996, s 48(1A)*, inserted by *PIDA 1998, s 3*).

The employee may make a complaint within three months of the act, or failure to act, complained of (or the last act or failure, where that act or failure is part of a series of similar acts or failures). Where the tribunal is satisfied that it was not reasonably practicable for the complaint to be presented within three months, it may be presented within such further period as the tribunal considers reasonable (*ERA 1996, s 48(3)*; as to the meaning of 'the date of the act' and 'a deliberate failure to act', see *ERA 1996, s 48(4)*).

If the tribunal finds the complaint well-founded it will make a declaration to that effect and order compensation to be paid to the employee. The compensation will be such amount as it considers just and equitable in the circumstances, having regard to the right infringed and any loss which is attributable to the act or failure which infringed his right (*ERA 1996, s 49*). In the case of workers penalised for making a protected disclosure the tribunal may award such compensation as it considers just and equitable.

29.11 Breach of safety regulations and unfair dismissal

A failure by an employer to have regard for the safety of his employees can be considered a fundamental breach of contract entitling the employee to resign and claim that he has been constructively dismissed. In *British Aircraft Corpn Ltd v Austin* [1978] IRLR 332, the Employment Appeal Tribunal held that the employer's failure to give consideration to the employee's request that she should be provided with protective goggles incorporating the prescription lenses of her spectacles amounted to conduct entitling the employee to resign and, when she did resign, to claim that she had been constructively dismissed under what is now *ERA 1996, s 95(1)(c)*.

Where employees refuse to work with materials which in the past have adversely affected their health, and as a consequence are dismissed, the dismissals will be held to be unfair if the employer has not taken adequate steps to remedy the danger (*Piggott Bros & Co Ltd v Jackson* [1991] IRLR 309).

An employer may fairly dismiss an employee for breach of safety regulations if he brought the regulations to the attention of the employee and made clear to him the fact that such a breach would lead to dismissal (*Martin v Yorkshire Imperial Metals* [1978] IRLR 440).

29.12 EQUIPMENT FOR WORK

The law has been utterly transformed by *section 69* of the *Enterprise and Regulatory Reform Act 2013*. It is imperative to, appreciate that the *Act* only applies to accidents occurring on or after 1st October 2013 and so the authorities cited below remain good law for claims arising before that date.

What the *Act* does is to reverse the presumption that a breach of statutory duty such as the Manual Handling Regulations would be actionable as a breach of statutory duty. Now, no such claim is viable unless the legislative measure expressly provides that a civil claim is permitted. None of the key measures do so. Consequently, a claimant who would have been able to rely upon he strict duties imposed by workplace legislation is now compelled to prove fault. The claim for breach of statutory duty becomes a claim in common law negligence thus firmly putting the onus upon the claimant to establish breach, causation and foreseeability. Put simply, it will be harder for claimants to win.

The *Employers Liability (Defective Equipment) Act 1969* will become relevant again since it does expressly recognise a civil claim. Under the *Act*, an employer is held liable for injury caused by defective equipment which the employer has supplied. It matters not that the defect was incapable of detection. The scope of 'equipment' has been held to be enormous. It captures a 90,000 ton ocean going tanker; *Coltman v Bibby Tankers Ltd* [1987] 3 All ER 1068. Also, it includes materials used in performing a task such as paving slabs in the Law Lords decision of *Knowles v Liverpool City Council* [1993] IRLR 588 where a submission that equipment ought to be confined to the tools of the trade, say a shovel or pick, was unanimously rejected.

The Government has announced its intention to increase the personal injury small claims limit applicable here from £1,000 to £2,000. Remarkably, the Association of British Insurers has agreed with Thompsons, the claimant injury law firm, at an event held on 26 February 2020 at the House of Lords that the existing small claims limit of £1,000 for employer's liability claims should not be increased. The Ministry of Justice has now announced that the intended reforms will not be implemented until April 2021.

The *Provision and Use of Work Equipment Regulations 1998 (SI 1998/2306) ('PUWER')* give effect to the EC Directive relating to the use of machines and equipment *(89/655)* and amending *Directive 95/63*. The *Regulations* came into force on 5 December 1998, replacing *1992 Regulations* of the same name *(SI 1992/2932)*. *Regulations 4–10* set out general requirements with which employers must comply, for example in relation to suitability, maintenance and inspection. The requirement contained in *reg 5(1)* of the *1998 Regulations* for work equipment to be maintained in an efficient state and working order and in good repair imposes an absolute duty on employers (*Stark v Post Office* [2000] ICR 1013, [2000] All ER (D) 276, CA). The very purpose of the *Regulations* is to make the employer liable for the unexplained and indeed inexplicable incident held the Court of Appeal in *Ball v Street* [2005] EWCA Civ 76, [2005] All ER (D) 73 (Feb). There are limits to the ambit of the *Regulations*. In *Smith v Northamptonshire County Council* [2009] UKHL 27, [2009] 4 All ER 557 the claimant had to collect a patient from home. The NHS had installed a wooden wheelchair ramp at the property. The ramp collapsed injuring Mrs Smith who relied on *Regulation 5* in a claim against her local authority employer. Since the employer had not installed the ramp and had no control over it, it would be wrong to treat it as work equipment and so the claim failed.

More specific requirements, concerning, for example, specific hazards, extremes of temperature, lighting, maintenance operations and dangerous parts are set out in *regs 11–24* (see *Horton v Taplin Contracts Ltd* [2002] EWCA Civ 1604, [2003] ICR 179, [2002] All ER (D) 122 (Nov)). In *Horton* the Court of Appeal emphasised that the target of achieving suitability of work equipment for its purpose was to be measured by reference to such hazards to anyone's health and safety as were reasonably foreseeable (Bodey J). In addition, the *1998 Regulations* impose requirements relating to mobile work equipment and power presses. The provisions relating to mobile work equipment did not apply until 5 December 2002 to equipment provided for use in an undertaking before 5 December 1998. Since 14 April 1999, certain duties set out in the *Regulations* are modified by the *Police (Health and Safety) Regulations 1999 (SI 1999/860)*. The effect is to take account of the special circumstances in which police officers sometimes have to work. For provisions applying to UK ships and to others when in UK waters, see the *Merchant Shipping and Fishing Vessels (Personal Protective Equipment) Regulations 1999 (SI 1999/2205)*, in force since 25 October 1999.

Since 5 December 1998 the *Lifting Operations and Lifting Equipment Regulations 1998 (SI 1998/2307)* ('LOLER') gather together requirements relating to lifting equipment formerly contained in industry-specific legislation, and implement certain provisions of EC *Directives 89/655* and *95/63*. *Directive 2001/45* of 27 June amends *Directive 89/655* concerning the minimum health and safety requirements for the use of work equipment, so that it covers worker safety when using equipment to carry out work at height.

The *Personal Protective Equipment at Work Regulations 1992 (SI 1992/2966)* ('PPE') give effect to the *EC Directive* relating to the use of personal protective equipment *(89/656)*. Personal protective equipment is defined as all equipment (including clothing giving protection against the weather) which is intended to be worn or held by a person at work and which protects the employee against health and safety risks. Broadly, the *Regulations*, which came into force on 1 January 1993, require employers to ensure that suitable personal protective equipment is provided for their employees and impose various other requirements, for example in relation to maintenance and storage of the equipment. Personal protective equipment supplied from 1 July 1995 must bear the 'CE' marking. Under *HSWA 1974, s 9* employers are barred from charging employees for equipment provided in accordance with a specific statutory requirement. The then House of Lords clarified in *Fytche v Wincanton Logistics plc* [2004] UKHL 31, [2004] IRLR 817, [2004] ICR 975, a majority (3:2) ruling (Lady Hale and Lord Hope dissenting), that *reg 4* of the *1992 Regulations* required employers to provide suitable equipment to protect employees against an identified risk. Such a duty was further maintained by repairs required under *reg 7(1)*. Yet the latter duty only extended to repairs for the purposes of ensuring that assessed risks under *reg 4* are met.

PPER 1992 were amended by the *Health and Safety (Miscellaneous Amendments) Regulations 2002 (SI 2002/2174)*.

These *2002 Regulations* stressed the importance that ppe should be seen as 'last resort' protection and its use should only be prescribed when all else fails, ie when engineering and management solutions and other safe systems of work do not effectively protect the employee from danger where the risk of injury is still foreseeable after other controls have been implemented.

See also *Gerrard v Staffordshire Potteries* [1995] PIQR P169.

In *Threlfall v Hull City Council* [2011] ICR 209, [2010] All ER (D) 184 (Oct) the claimant employee suffered lacerations when clearing garden waste. The employer had supplied conventional gardening gloves whilst appreciating that stronger, but more expensive, ones were available. Smith LJ held that the duty to risk assess meant that the employer should have given positive thought to the hazards that might be encountered and the failure to actively consider alternatives put the employer in breach.

The Court of Appeal in *Hyde v The Steeplechase Company (Cheltenham) Ltd* [2013] EWCA Civ 545, [2014] 1 All ER 405 reiterated that the thrust of these provisions is intended to be stringent and onerous upon an employer. The Judge at first instance had wrongly applied a common law approach in finding that, since the defendant had acted reasonably, it was not liable for an accident.

For further details, see www.hse.gov.uk/work-equipment-machinery/.

29.13 FIRE PRECAUTIONS

The *Regulatory Reform (Fire Safety) Order 2005 (SI 2005/1541)* introduced in October 2006 has greatly simplified fire safety legislation, with many Acts being repealed and regulations being revoked. Other pieces of legislation have been amended to streamline the legislative basis of fire safety in non-domestic premises. However, the FSO sit comfortably alongside the *Dangerous Substances and Explosive Atmospheres Regulations 2002 (SI 2002/2776)* which are still in force.

The FSO 2005 replaces fire certification under the *Fire Precautions Act 1971 ('FPA 1971')* with a general duty to ensure, so far as it is reasonably practicable, the (fire) safety of employees, general duty in relation to non-employees to take such fire precautions as may reasonably be required in the circumstances to ensure that premises are safe, and a duty to carry out a fire risk assessment ('FRA').

The FSO 2005 imposes a number of specific duties in relation to fire precautions and their enforcement. The Order applies to all non-domestic premises. The main duty holder in relation to the premises is the 'responsible person' who should be identified in the fire risk assessment.

The responsible person means the employer or any person in control of the premises.

Duties imposed on the responsible person include:

- taking suitable fire precautions to ensure the safety of employees and others not in his employment (eg general public) and to ensure the fire safety of the premises

- making a suitable a sufficient fire risk assessment of the risk to which relevant persons are exposed for the purpose of identifying the general fire precautions to be taken.

29.14 FIRST AID

First aid requirements are contained in the *Health and Safety (First Aid) Regulations 1981 (SI 1981/917)*, supplemented by an Approved Code of Practice (revised 2013). The *1981 Regulations* and revised Guidance (L74) are available at www.hse.gov.uk/pubns/priced/L

74.pdf. Employers are placed under a duty to make adequate and appropriate provision for first aid (*reg 3*). The *2013 Code of Practice* and Guidance stress the duty of the employer to make an assessment of first aid needs appropriate to the circumstances of each workplace. A checklist is included for evaluating first aid requirements and guidance given on criteria for deciding on the extent of first aid equipment, first aid boxes and facilities which are necessary and on the number of first aiders required. The guidance notes explain how first aid provision should be related to the level of risk. Employers must inform their employees of the arrangements that have been made in connection with the provision of first aid, including the location of equipment, facilities and personnel (*reg 4*). *Regulation 2* of the *Health and Safety (Miscellaneous Amendments) Regulations 2002 (SI 2002/2174)* amends *reg 2* of the existing *1981 Regulations* so as to require that a first-aid room must be easily accessible and sign-posted. This amendment gives effect to *Annex II* of *Directive 89/654/EEC* (OJ L393 30.12.1989).

From 1 October 2013, *regulation 3(2)* of the *1981 Regulations* has been amended to remove the requirement for HSE to approve first aid training and qualifications. Advice on selecting a First Aid Training Provider (GEIS3) has been made available at www.hse.gov.uk/pubns/geis3.pdf.

29.15 HOURS OF WORK

The *Working Time Directive (93/104)*, as amended *2000/34*, imposes requirements relating to hours of work, night work, breaks and holidays. Provisions restricting the working hours of children and young persons are contained in the *Young Workers' Directive (94/33)*. From 1 October 1998 the *Working Time Regulations 1998 (SI 1998/1833)* implement the *Working Time Directive* together with aspects of the *Young Workers' Directive* which relate to young persons (ie those who have reached minimum school leaving age but are under 18). For details of provisions relating to working hours, night work and breaks, see WORKING TIME (58). For statutory holiday provisions, see HOLIDAYS (30).

29.16 INSURANCE AGAINST LIABILITY

The *Employers' Liability (Compulsory Insurance) Act 1969*, as amended, obliges every employer carrying on a business in Great Britain to maintain insurance, under one or more approved policies with an authorised insurer, against liability for bodily injury or disease sustained by employees and arising out of and in the course of their employment in Great Britain. An employer is not obliged to insure members of his family (*s 2(2)(a)*). Insurance companies issue annual certificates which must be displayed at every place where the employer carries on business so that they may be easily seen and read by every person employed there. From 1 January 1999 the *Employers' Liability (Compulsory Insurance) Regulations 1998 (SI 1998/2573)* fix the limit of the sum to be insured at not less than £5m in respect of any one occurrence. The *Regulations* require employers to keep certificates for 40 years and give powers to inspectors to inspect past certificates.

There is generally no duty upon the employer to protect his employees from economic loss as opposed to physical injury. Hence it was not a breach of duty to fail to arrange or advise insurance for an employee sent to work in a country without compulsory motor insurance (*Reid v Rush & Tompkins Group plc* [1989] IRLR 265).

29.17 MANAGEMENT OF HEALTH AND SAFETY AT WORK

The *Management of Health and Safety at Work Regulations 1999 (SI 1999/3242)* came into effect on 29 December 1999, re-enacting *1992 Regulations* of the same name, with modifications. The *Regulations* give effect to the EC '*Framework Directive*' (*89/391*), the '*Temporary Workers' Directive*' (*91/383*), and certain provisions of the '*Pregnant Workers' Directive*' (*92/85*) and '*Young Workers' Directive*' (*94/33*).

The *Health and Safety (Miscellaneous Amendments) Regulations 2002 (SI 2002/2174)* which came into force on 17 September 2002 amended various long-established regulations, including the *1981 First Aid, 1992 Display Screen Equipment, 1992 Manual Handling Operations, 1992 Protective Personal Equipment, 1992 Workplace, 1998 Lifting Operations and Lifting Equipment*, and *1999 Quarries Regulations*. Whilst many of these amendments are minor, they seek to ensure full European compliance with their requisite *Directives*.

Every employer (and self-employed person) must make a risk assessment relating to his premises, so as to identify the measures he needs to take to comply with the health and safety and fire precautions requirements applicable to him; the assessment must be reviewed when necessary and (where there are more than five employees) recorded. Assessment of the risks to young people must be made before they start work, taking their immaturity and other specified factors into account (*reg 3*). When an employer implements any preventive and protective measures, it is to be done on the basis of the following principles:

(a)   avoiding risks;

(b)   evaluating the risks which cannot be avoided;

(c)   combating the risks at source;

(d)   adapting the work to the individual, especially as regards the design of workplaces, the choice of work equipment and the choice of working and production methods, with a view in particular to alleviating monotonous work and work at a predetermined work rate and to reducing their effect on health;

(e)   adapting to technical progress;

(f)   replacing the dangerous with the non-dangerous or the less dangerous;

(g)   developing a coherent overall prevention policy which covers technology, organisation of work, working conditions, social relationships and the influence of factors relating to the working environment;

(h)   giving collective protective measures priority over individual protective measures; and

(i)   giving appropriate instructions to employees.

(*Regulation 4, Sch 1*)

This *Schedule* is, in effect, a risk control hierarchy: the best control measures are at the top of the hierarchy and, generally, do not involve people. To achieve the best available controls, start at the top of the hierarchy and work down until a reasonably practicable solution is found.

It is interesting to note that the issue and use of personal protective equipment (ppe) does not feature in this risk control hierarchy.

Every employer must also make, and give effect to, adequate health and safety arrangements, including the effective planning, organisation, control, monitoring and review of the preventive and protective measures. Where there are five or more employees, these arrangements must be recorded in writing (*reg 5*).

Every employer must ensure that his employees are provided with appropriate health surveillance (*reg 6*), and must appoint one or more competent persons to assist him in undertaking the preventive and protective measures. Where there is a 'competent person' in the employer's employment then that person must be appointed as the competent person to assist in undertaking health and safety measures, in preference to a competent person from another source (*reg 7*).

Every employer must, *inter alia*:

(a)   establish (and where necessary, give effect to) procedures to be followed in the event of serious and imminent danger to persons working in his undertaking; and

(b)   nominate a sufficient number of competent persons to implement such procedures in relation to the evacuation of the premises.

The procedures referred to in (*a*) above must:

(i)   so far as is reasonably practicable, require persons at work who are exposed to serious and imminent danger to be informed of the nature of the hazards and the steps to be taken to protect them from it;

(ii)   enable the persons concerned to stop work and proceed to a place of safety in the event of being exposed to serious, imminent and unavoidable danger; and

(iii)   require the persons concerned to be prevented from resuming work where there is still a serious and imminent danger.

(Regulation 8)

Employers are required to ensure that any necessary contacts with external services are arranged, particularly as regards first aid, emergency medical care and rescue work (*reg 9*).

Employees must be provided with comprehensible and relevant health and safety information (*reg 10*), as must non-employees working in the employer's undertaking (*reg 12*) and temporary workers (*reg 15*). When employing school-age children, employers must inform their parents or guardians of the risks and control measures introduced (*reg 10*). Where two or more employers share a workplace, they must co-operate as necessary to enable them to comply with the applicable health and safety and fire precautions requirements, and co-ordinate measures they are taking to comply with such requirements (*reg 11*).

Employers must take into account employees' capabilities as regards health and safety in entrusting tasks to them. Employees must be provided with adequate health and safety training within working hours, which must be repeated where appropriate (*reg 13*). Employees must use all machinery and equipment in accordance with the training they have received. They must inform the employer of: (i) any work situation which represents an immediate danger to health and safety; and (ii) any shortcoming in the employer's protection arrangements for health and safety (*reg 14*).

An assessment must be made of workplace risks to new and expectant mothers, and measures must be taken to avoid any risk by altering working conditions or hours of work. Where it is not practicable to take these steps the woman should be suspended from work (subject to *ERA 1996, s 67*). Where it is necessary for her health and safety, a new or expectant mother must be removed from night work (*regs 16, 17*). (See also the *Suspension from Work (on Maternity Grounds) Order 1994 (SI 1994/2930)*.) In *Day v T Pickles Farms Ltd* [1999] IRLR 217, the EAT emphasised that employers must undertake an assessment of the workplace risks to pregnant women as soon as a woman of child-bearing age is employed. It is not sufficient to wait until an employee becomes pregnant.

Young persons must not be employed in certain dangerous or harmful work activities unless it is necessary for their training, the risks are reduced to the minimum, and they are competently supervised. Children must never be permitted to do such work (*reg 19*).

In criminal proceedings employers have no defence for a contravention of their health and safety obligations by reason of any act or default caused by an employee or by a person appointed to give competent advice (*reg 21*).

Since October 2003, the *Management of Health and Safety at Work Regulations 1999 (SI 1999/3242)* have been amended to allow employees to claim damages from their employer if they suffer illness or injury as a result of a breach of the *Regulations*. Amending *reg 22*, the lifting of the civil liability exclusion will ensure full compliance with the *Health and Safety Framework Directive 89/391*. Guidance can be found at www.hse.gov.uk/services/education/information.htm.

29.18 MANUAL HANDLING OF LOADS

The HSE estimates that some 12.3 million working days have been lost due to work-related musculoskeletal disorders. As a result, some 1.1 million people a year are affected, making manual handling the most common cause of occupational illness in the UK. According to HSE statistics, some 37% of reported accidents are related to manual handling incidents. The *Manual Handling Operations Regulations 1992 (SI 1992/2793)* as amended by *SI 2002/2174*, give effect to the *EU Directive* relating to the manual handling of loads *(90/269)*. Broadly, the *Regulations* require each employer, so far as reasonably practicable, to avoid the need for his employees to undertake manual handling operations involving a risk of injury. That is a real risk, a foreseeable possibility of injury, not a probability (see *O'Neill v DSG Retail Ltd* [2002] EWCA Civ 1139, [2003] ICR 222, [2002] All ER (D) 500 (Jul)). It is important to be able to show that consideration has been given to ways of avoiding such operations. Where it is not reasonably practicable, the employer is required to assess such operations and reduce the risk of injury arising from them to the lowest practicable level. For a case interpreting 'reasonably practicable' in this context, see *Hawkes v Southwark London Borough Council* (20 February 1998, unreported), CA. Emphasising the importance of providing, where practicable, information to employees on the weight of loads they are required to handle was noted in *Swain v Denso Marston Ltd* [2000] ICR 1079, CA.

Regulation 4 of the *Health and Safety (Miscellaneous Amendments) Regulations 2002 (SI 2002/2174)* amends the *1992 Regulations* by adding *reg 4(3)* by specifying factors to be taken account of, in determining whether operations involve risk, particularly of back injury to workers. The new regulation adds that particular regard should be given to: (a) the physical suitability of the employee to carry out the task; (b) the clothing and footwear the person is wearing; (c) the person's knowledge and training; and (d) the results of any relevant risk assessments. This amendment gives full effect to *Annex II* of *Directive 90/269/EEC* (OJ L156 25.6.90).

The *Regulations* also contain, in *Sch 1*, a list of the factors to which an employer must have regard (tasks, loads, working environment, individual capability and other factors) and the relevant questions which must be considered in each case when making an assessment of manual handling operations. Guidance on the *Regulations* has been published by the HSE (L23, revised 2016).

Since 31 December 1998, the *Merchant Shipping and Fishing Vessels (Manual Handling Operations) Regulations 1998 (SI 1998/2857)* give effect to *Directive 90/269* in respect of shipping activities in the UK. The *Regulations* apply to UK-registered ships and, in part, to ships registered outside the UK when they are in UK waters.

The HSE has developed an online manual handling chart tool (MAC Tool) to help identify high risk workplace manual handling activities.

29.19 NOISE AT WORK

According to the HSE, over 170,000 people in the UK suffer deafness, tinnitus or other ear conditions as a result of exposure to excessive noise at work. The *Control of Noise at Work Regulations 2005 (SI 2005/1643)* (the *'Noise Regulations'*), in force since 6 April 2006 (except for the music and entertainment sectors where they come into force on 6 April 2008), replace the long-standing *Noise at Work Regulations 1989 (SI 1989/1790)* which came into force on 1 January 1990. The aim of these new *Noise Regulations* is to ensure that workers' hearing is protected from excessive noise at their place of work, which could cause them to lose their hearing and/or to suffer from tinnitus (permanent ringing in the ears). There has been a significant increase recently in the number of industrial deafness claims being made. In part this is due to the fact that legal costs remain at large in the event of success whereas fixed costs are now applicable to fast track public and employers' liability claims worth up to £25,000. In July 2017 Sir Rupert Jackson put forward proposals to fix costs recoverable in claims worth between £25,000 and £100,000. To date , no Government consultation has been commenced.

The level at which employers must provide hearing protection and hearing protection zones is now 85 decibels (daily or weekly average exposure) and the level at which employers must assess the risk to workers' health and provide them with information and training is now 80 decibels. There is also an exposure limit value of 87 decibels, taking account of any reduction in exposure provided by hearing protection, above which workers must not be exposed.

There is a general duty upon the employer to reduce the risk of damage to the hearing of his employees from exposure to noise to the lowest level reasonably practicable.

The Supreme Court has decided, by a bare 3–2 majority, that claimants exposed to noise levels of 85 decibels during the 1970s and 1980s could not recover damages for noise induced deafness since the employer was neither negligent nor in breach of the duty imposed by *section 29* of the *Factories Act 1961*. See *Baker v Quantum Clothing Group Ltd* [2011] UKSC 17, [2011] 4 All ER 223.

On 28th March 2018 the High Court held, in a Judgment running to 125 pages, that the Royal Opera House was liable for hearing loss suffered by an employee during rehearsals. The claimant, Chris Goldscheider , suffered acoustic shock as a result of being exposed to over 130 decibels generated by the brass section of the orchestra. This was a significant decision for it held that the solitary incident had caused damage. Overwhelmingly, noise induced hearing loss cases are brought because of prolonged exposure to excessive noise. The Court of Appeal has on April 17th 2019 dismissed an appeal by the defendant.

In *Keefe v Isle of Man Steam Packet Co Ltd* [2010] EWCA Civ 683, [2010] All ER (D) 137 (Jun) the Court of Appeal declared that where an employer had failed to monitor noise levels, evidence of which would clearly determine whether exposure was unlawful, the evidence of the employer should be treated with some scepticism and that of the claimant should be treated benevolently.

The *Schedule* to the *Regulations* contains formulae for calculating an employee's 'daily personal noise exposure' and its weekly average. These are to be applied without taking into account the effect of ear protectors. If any employees are likely to be exposed to noise or sound pressure in excess of certain specified levels, the employer must ensure that a competent person makes a noise assessment identifying which employees are so exposed and providing such information with regard to the noise to which they may be exposed as will facilitate compliance with various duties imposed by the *Regulations*. Noise assessments must be reviewed if there is reason to suspect that they are no longer valid, or if there has been a significant change in the relevant work.

Where any employees are likely to be exposed to certain specified noise or sound pressure levels, their exposure to noise must so far as is reasonably practicable be reduced, other than by the provision of personal ear protection, and also so far as practicable be provided with suitable personal ear protectors to keep the risk of damage to below that arising from exposure to those levels. Employers must also, so far as reasonably practicable, identify by signs 'ear protection zones' where such exposure is likely and prevent employees from entering them without personal ear protectors.

At certain specified lower levels of noise, an employee must so far as practicable be provided with suitable and efficient personal ear protectors at his request.

There are also duties relating to ensuring the proper use and maintenance of equipment provided and to informing and training employees.

The HSE may grant exemptions from certain requirements where average weekly exposure does not exceed given levels.

Employees themselves are under a duty to use personal ear protectors and other protective measures and to report defects to the employer, and the self-employed are brought within the scope of the *Regulations*.

29.20 SAFETY REPRESENTATIVES

Employers are obliged to consult with employees over health and safety matters. Two different régimes operate: one for groups of workers in respect of which a union is recognised and the other where there is no union recognition.

For union-appointed safety representatives the *1977 Regulations* apply (*SI 1977/500* – see **29.21** below), and for non-unionised workers the *1996 Regulations* apply (*SI 1996/1513* – see **29.22** below)

29.21 Union-appointed safety representatives

Employers must recognise, afford facilities and allow time off for the training of safety representatives appointed in accordance with the *Safety Representatives and Safety Committees Regulations 1977 (SI 1977/500* as amended by *SI 1992/2051, SI 1996/1513, SI 1999/860)* made under the *HSWA 1974, s 2(4)*. Safety representatives are appointed by a trade union recognised by an employer from among the employees of a unionised workforce, with certain exceptions, eg members of the British Actors' Equity Association or of the Musicians' Union who need not be employees (*regs 3(1), 8(2)*). The representative should, if possible, either have been employed by his employer throughout the preceding two years or have had at least two years' experience in similar employment (*reg 3(4)*).

Safety representatives represent the employees in consultations with the employer over arrangements for their health and safety at work. Every employer is under a duty to consult safety representatives regarding such arrangements (*HSWA 1974, s 2(6)*); without prejudice to that general duty, employers are now required to consult safety representatives with regard to a number of specified health and safety matters, and to provide safety representatives with such facilities and assistance as they may reasonably require for the purposes of carrying out their functions under *HSWA 1974, s 2(4)* and the *Regulations* (*reg 4A*, inserted by the *Management of Health and Safety Regulations 1992 (SI 1992/2051)*). See also the Code of Practice and guidance notes, *Safety representatives and safety committees* (third edition 1996).

In addition, safety representatives have other functions, including the investigation of potential hazards and complaints about health, safety or welfare. They can make representations about such matters and attend meetings of safety committees (*reg 4(1)*). (See also **11.8** Disclosure of Information.) Employers must allow safety representatives time off with pay to perform these functions (*reg 4(2)*). An employer must also permit safety representatives time off with pay to undergo training to fulfil these duties. (See **50.9–50.10** Time Off Work and the *Code of Practice on Time off for the Training of Safety Representatives*.) A safety committee must be established if two or more safety representatives request one in writing (*reg 9*). Safety representatives and others enjoy special protection from dismissal and action short of dismissal (see **29.9** above, **55.3** Unfair Dismissal – II).

29.22 Non-unionised workers

From 1 October 1996 the obligation on employers to consult over health and safety matters was extended to employees who are not covered by trade union-appointed safety representatives (*Health and Safety (Consultation with Employees) Regulations 1996 (SI 1996/1513)*).

Employers may consult either with their employees directly or through elected representatives (*reg 4*). Employees will be entitled to receive such information as is necessary to participate fully and effectively in the consultation process (*reg 5*). The functions of elected representatives are to make representations to the employer on health and safety issues and to represent employees in consultations with inspectors (*reg 6*). Elected representatives are entitled to time off with pay for training and to carry out their duties, and are protected against dismissal and victimisation (*regs 7, 8*).

29.23 SMOKING AT WORK

The EAT, in *Waltons and Morse v Dorrington* [1997] IRLR 488, held that there is a term implied into employment contracts that 'the employer will provide and monitor for his employees, so far as is reasonably practicable, a working environment which is reasonably suitable for the performance by them of their contractual duties'. In this particular case, a non-smoker was held to have been constructively dismissed when she was required, despite her protests, to work in a smoke-affected atmosphere.

The *Health Act 2006* prohibited smoking in the workplace from 2 April 2007 in Wales, from 30 April 2007 in Northern Ireland and from 1 July 2007 in England, (*SI 2006/3368*) via the *Smoke-Free (Premises and Enforcement) Regulations 2006*.

'Suitable 'smoking prohibited' notices should be displayed in accordance with the *Smoke-free (Signs) Regulations 2007 (SI 2007/923)*.'

29.24 STRESS

Stress-related illness connected with work remains a controversial and topical issue for employers. According to the HSE, nearly 1 in 3 of workers across the EU (some 40 million people, estimated 5 million Britons) report that they are affected by stress at work (see www.hse.gov.uk/stress/resources.htm), losing an estimated 9.8 million working days in 2009–2010.

To tackle the problem of absence/ill-health caused or made worse by occupational stress, the HSE has produced a set of Management Standards (see http ://www.hse.gov.uk/pubns/wbk01.pdf) that employers should achieve in practice. Compliance is not a legal requirement but will assist employers in reducing stress at source.

These Management Standards are based around six key areas:

Standard 1:	Demands — includes issues such as workload, work patterns and the working environment.
Standard 2:	Control — concentrates on how much or little) involvement or autonomy a person has in the way they work.
Standard 3:	Support — consider the level of encouragement and assistance provided by the organisation and the resources made available to provide support where additional assistance is needed.

Standard 4:	Relationships — promotes positive behaviours and co-operation at work and identifies if there are systems in place to respond to unacceptable behaviour.
Standard 5:	Role — considers how clearly job descriptions and organisational structures are defined, whether there are conflicts in workers' roles and whether there are clear and unambiguous reporting lines.
Standard 6:	Change — assess how organisational change is managed and communicated to the workforce.

29.25   Common law liability

'Many, alas, suffer breakdowns and depressive illnesses and a significant proportion could doubtless ascribe some at least of their problems to the strains and stresses of their work situation: be it simply overworking, the tension of difficult relationships, career prospect worries, fears or feelings of discrimination or harassment, to take just some examples. Unless, however, there was a real risk of breakdown which the claimant's employers ought reasonably to have foreseen and they ought properly to have averted there can be no liability.' This statement from Simon Brown LJ in *Garrett v Camden London Borough Council* [2001] EWCA Civ 395, [2001] All ER (D) 202 (Mar) sets out the relevant legal test to be applied by the Court when considering a common law action in negligence.

In *Sutherland v Hatton* [2002] EWCA Civ 76, [2002] IRLR 263 the Court of Appeal has set out guidelines for determining employer liability for psychiatric injury caused by stress at work, summarised below.

The ordinary principles of employers' liability apply. First, the kind of harm to the particular employee must be reasonably foreseeable. Foreseeability depends on what the employer knows (or ought reasonably to know) about the individual. It may be harder to foresee mental conditions than physical injury, but may be easier in a known individual. Unless the employer knows of a particular problem or vulnerability, it is usually entitled to assume that the employee can withstand normal job pressures. No occupations should be regarded as intrinsically dangerous to mental health. The court listed a number of factors likely to be relevant in establishing foreseeability, such as the nature and extent of the work done by the employee. In general, an employer does not need to make detailed inquiries of the employee or his or her medical adviser.

To trigger the employer's duty to take steps, the indications of likely harm to the employee's health must be obvious enough for the reasonable employer to realise that something should be done. An employer will only be in breach of duty if it fails to take steps which are reasonable in the circumstances. Where an employer offers a confidential advice service with referral to counselling, it is unlikely to be in breach of its duty. It will not amount to a breach of duty to allow a willing employee to continue in a job if the only reasonable step involves dismissal or demotion.

The steps an employer could and should have taken need to be identified. For the employee, it must be shown that the breach of duty caused or materially contributed to the harm suffered. So long as the breach by the employer was material rather than merely negligible the employer will be liable in full for the injury sustained. See the discussion in *Bailey (by her father and litigation friend) v Ministry of Defence* [2008] EWCA Civ 883, [2008] All ER (D) 382 (Jul), 103 BMLR 13.

Where stress risks are a feature of a particular job, a risk assessment should be made under the *Management of Health and Safety at Work Regulations 1992* (see **29.17** above) in the same way as for the risk of physical injury. It is important that complaints of working conditions or workloads causing stress are dealt with quickly and thoroughly and efforts made to reduce the risk of future health problems.

In cases of bullying the claimant might be able to rely on the civil cause of action established by *s 3* of the *Protection from Harassment Act 1997* as was the case in *Green v DB Group Services (UK) Ltd* [2006] EWHC 1898 (QB), [2006] IRLR 764. A secretary bullied by fellow employees established both negligence and breach of duty under the *1997 Act*. A significant advantage of the *Act* is that it provides for a six year limitation period. The common law time limit to institute proceedings is three years. However, the Court of Appeal in *Conn v Sunderland City Council* [2007] EWCA Civ 1492, [2008] IRLR 324, [2007] All ER (D) 99 (Nov) has taken a restrictive approach to civil claims under the *Act*. Conduct must be criminal in nature to found a valid civil claim. The same court took a more lenient approach in *Ferguson v British Gas Trading Ltd* [2009] EWCA Civ 46, [2009] 3 All ER 304 and refused to strike out a claim made under the *1997 Act* where the claimant alleged that she had been pursued aggressively by a utility company for payment of unjustified bills. In *Dowson v Chief Constable of Northumbria Police* [2010] EWHC 2612 (QB), [2010] All ER (D) 191 (Oct) a group of police officers failed in their claims. They alleged that a Detective Chief Inspector had constantly criticised and undermined them and subjected them to vulgar abuse. It was held that this was not sufficiently oppressive to cross the threshold on liability. Simon J did state, obiter, that unjustified and abusive arguments with an employee could be actionable. It is submitted that the court was influenced considerably by the notion that police officers are to be seen as robust and what might be acceptable here could well be unlawful in, say an office or hospital. In *Jones v Ruth* [2012] 1 All ER 490 the Court of Appeal awarded the claimant damages of £28,750 for harassment injury.

As well as claims for damages, it is also possible that employees whose complaints of excessive stress have gone unheeded could resign and claim constructive dismissal on the basis that the employer failed in the duty of care or breached the implied term to maintain the relationship of trust and confidence.

The High Court in *Sayers v Cambridgeshire County Council* [2006] EWHC 2029 (QB), [2007] IRLR 29 rejected a stress claim based upon a breach of the *Working Time Regulations*. The claimant established that she was working 55 hours a week and had never signed an individual opt–out agreement. Since a breach is a criminal matter the court decided that no civil remedy was intended by the legislature.

29.26 SUBSTANCES HAZARDOUS TO HEALTH

References in this section are to provisions of the *Control of Substances Hazardous to Health Regulations 2002 (SI 2002/2677)*, which replaced the *1999 Regulations* of the same name (except for *regs 4* and *20*, which came into force in 2004). Employers' duties remain unaffected. The main change is the removal of the *Schedule* listing maximum exposure limits ('MELs') from the *Regulations*. These appear instead in the HSE's publication *EH40* which is revised annually.

The definition of a substance hazardous to health is contained in *reg 2(1)*, and includes:

(a)   substances designated as very toxic, toxic, corrosive, harmful or irritant under product labelling legislation (the *CHIP Regulations*);

(b)   substances for which the Health and Safety Commission (now Executive) has approved a Workplace Exposure Limit (WEL);

(c)   biological agents (microorganisms, cell cultures or human endoparasites);

(d)   dust of any kind, when present at a concentrations in air equal to or greater than 10 mg/m^3 (inhalable dust) or 4 mg/m^3 (respirable dust) as a time–weighted average (twa) over an eight-hour period;

(e)   other substances creating a risk to health because of it chemical or toxicological properties and the way it is used or is present within the workplace.

Employers owe duties under *COSHH Regulations 2002* to their employees and, so far as reasonably practicable and with certain exceptions, to other persons who may be affected by the work which they carry on (*reg 3*). The Executive has powers to grant exemption certificates (*reg 14*).

An employer may not carry on any work liable to expose any employees to any substance hazardous to health unless he has made a suitable and sufficient assessment of the risks to their health and of the steps necessary to meet the requirements of *COSHH* (*Dugmore v Swansea NHS Trust* [2002] EWCA Civ 1689, [2003] IRLR 164, [2003] ICR 574). The assessment must be reviewed forthwith if there is reason to suspect that it is no longer valid or if there has been a significant change in the work to which it relates (*reg 6*).

The employer must ensure that the exposure of his employees to hazardous substances is either prevented or, where this is not reasonably practicable, adequately controlled (*reg 7(1)*). So far as reasonably practicable, that objective is to be secured by measures *other* than the provision of personal protective equipment, although that is also to be provided where necessary. Special measures apply to exposure to carcinogens (*reg 7(2), (3), (4)*).

Employers are under a duty to take all reasonable steps to ensure that control measures, protective equipment etc are properly used or applied, and employees are under a duty to make full and proper use of such facilities, to return them after use and to report any defects to their employer (*reg 8(1), (2)*). The employer must maintain control measures and equipment in an efficient state, in efficient working order and in good repair, and keep records of tests carried out on them (*reg 9*).

In appropriate cases the employer must ensure that the exposure of employees to hazardous substances is monitored (*reg 10*) and/or that the relevant employees are under suitable health surveillance. In certain specified cases that must include medical surveillance, as a result of which the employer may be barred from engaging an employee for the work concerned (*reg 11*).

Employees whose work may expose them to hazardous substances are to be provided with suitable and sufficient information, instruction and training to enable them to know the risks of exposure and the precautions which should be taken (*reg 12*).

The Health and Safety Commission has approved a number of relevant Codes of Practice: 'Control of Substances Hazardous to Health', 'Control of Carcinogenic Substances' and 'Control of Biological Agents' are published in a single volume (L5, 6th Edition published 2013). See also the COSHH Essentials website at www.coshh-essentials.org.uk. Codes of Practice on the control of vinyl chloride at work, control of substances hazardous to health in pottery production, prevention or control of legionellosis and on the safe use of pesticides for non-agricultural purposes are also available. The Executive has published 'COSHH assessments: a step by step guide to assessment and the skills needed for it' and 'Health Surveillance under COSHH'. EH40, which lists the occupational exposure limits for use in complying with *COSHH*, is updated annually.

The *COSHH Regulations 2002* do not cover asbestos or lead which are subject to specific legislation, including the *Control of Asbestos at Work Regulations 2006 (SI 2006/2739)* and the *Control of Lead at Work Regulations 2002 (SI 2002/2676)*.

The *COSHH Regulations* have been extended in Northern Ireland – see *COSHH (Amendment) Regulations (NI) 2005, SI 2005/165*.

29.27 VIBRATION AT WORK

The *Control of Vibration at Work Regulations 2005 (SI 2005/1093)* came into force on 6 July 2005. These *Regulations* will help both employers and employees to take preventive action from vibration risks in the workplace. These *Regulations* comply with *European Physical Agents (Vibration) Directive (Directive 2002/44)* which seeks to deal with the control of diseases caused by vibration at work from equipment, vehicles and machines.

Hand Arm Vibration (HAV) is a major cause of occupational ill health and it is estimated around five million workers are exposed to HAV in the workplace. Two million of these workers are exposed to levels of vibration where there are clear risks of developing disease.

See www.hse.gov.uk/vibration/index.htm. Also, see the HAV Health Surveillance scheme and vibguide.

Whole Body Vibration (WBV) has four principal effect:

- health risks

- impaired ability to perform duties

- impaired comfort

- motion sickness

Exposure to WBV causes a complex distribution of oscillatory motions and forces within the body. These may cause unpleasant sensations giving rise to discomfort or annoyance, resulting in impaired performance — eg loss of balance, degraded vision, or present a health risk. The most widely reported WBV injury is back pain.

The HSE has produced guidance on HAVS (L140, 2005) and WBV (L141, 2005).

29.28 VIOLENCE AND BULLYING AT WORK

The employer's duty of care at common law and under *HSWA 1974, s 2* means that an employer needs to provide adequate security precautions where it is reasonably foreseeable that employees may suffer violence in the course of their work (which, given the escalation of violent incidents at work, probably covers every workplace). When making the risk assessment required under the *Management of Health and Safety at Work Regulations 1992*, as amended in 1999, (see **29.17** above) the possibility of violence to employees must be evaluated. When an employee has been the victim of an attack and the employer has taken inadequate safety measures, the employee may resign and claim constructive dismissal (*Dutton & Clark Ltd v Daly* [1985] IRLR 363), or claim damages for negligence.

The HSE leaflet *Violence at Work: a guide for employers* sets out a strategy for the effective management of violence.

Employees must also be safeguarded against bullying or harassment at work either by members of the public or fellow employees. Such behaviour, if not causing actual physical harm, may have a detrimental effect on an employee's morale and health. Where insufficient action is taken to stamp out the problem it is possible that the employer may be held liable for personal injury even if psychological damage only is caused. Intentional harassment is a criminal offence under the *Public Order Act 1986, s 4A* (as inserted by the *Criminal Justice and Public Order Act 1994*). From 16 June 1997, the *Protection from Harassment Act 1997* creates two new criminal offences of harassment and provides a civil remedy whereby an individual can apply for an injunction and damages against the harasser. Racially aggravated harassment constitutes a separate offence from 30 September 1998 (*Crime and Disorder Act 1998, ss 31, 32*).

It is imperative that all complaints from employees of violence, bullying or harassment are investigated fully and prompt action taken where necessary. The failure to do so could provoke a constructive dismissal claim before the Employment Tribunal. It could also found the basis of a claim in negligence as it did in *Green v DB Group Services (UK) Ltd* [2006] EWHC 1898 (QB), [2006] IRLR 764 where allegations of workplace bullying were not acted upon and the victim was awarded over £800,000 in damages.

The Court of Appeal delivered a confused and confusing judgment in *Weddall v Barchester Healthcare Ltd* [2012] EWCA Civ 25, [2012] IRLR 307. The case was conjoined with *Wallbank v Wallbank Fox Designs Ltd*. Both claimants were the unfortunate victims of assault perpetrated by a fellow employee. In the former case the court held that the act of violence was gratuitous and unconnected with employment so the defendant was not liable. With respect, it would appear that the assault arose because the claimant had given a fellow employee a lawful instruction to come in and work so as to cover someone who was absent. In the latter case the claimant was attacked after giving an employee a direction to turn on an oven in the factory where they worked. This incident was held to be one for which the employer was liable, it being job related. The distinction is fine if not imperceptible.

29.29 WORKPLACE STANDARDS

The *Workplace (Health, Safety and Welfare) Regulations 1992 (SI 1992/3004)* give effect to the EC Directive concerning the minimum health and safety requirements for the workplace (*89/654*). The *Regulations* came into force on 1 January 1993 in respect of any new workplace, and apply to any modification, extension or conversion of an existing workplace on or after that date. In respect of any other existing workplace, the requirements came into effect on 1 January 1996. *Regulation 6 of the Health and Safety (Miscellaneous Amendments) Regulations 2002 (SI 2002/2174)* amends the *1992 Regulations* to give complete or clearer effect to the technical definitions of its key terms, such as the meaning of 'workplace'. These requirements supersede provisions in the *Factories Act 1961 (ss 1–7, 18, 28, 29, 57–60* and *69), Offices, Shops and Railway Premises Act 1963 (ss 4–16)*, and *Agriculture (Safety, Health and Welfare Provisions) Act 1956 (ss 3, 5, 25(3)* and *(6))*.

The requirements under the *Regulations* are imposed on employers, persons having control of a workplace, and any person who is deemed to be the occupier of a factory by virtue of s *175(5)* of the *Factories Act 1961 (reg 4)*. The requirements relate to the following matters:

(a)   maintenance of workplaces, and of equipment, devices and systems (*reg 5*);

(b)   ventilation of enclosed workplaces (*reg 6*);

(c)   temperature in indoor workplaces (including provision of thermometers) (*reg 7*);

(d)   lighting (*reg 8*);

(e)   cleanliness and waste materials/storage (*reg 9*);

(f)   room dimensions and space (*reg 10*);

(g)   workstations and seating (*reg 11*);

(h)   conditions of floors and traffic routes, and organisation of traffic routes (*regs 12, 17*);

(i)   falls or falling objects (*reg 13*);

(j)   windows, doors, gates, walls, skylights and ventilators (*regs 14–16, 18*);

(k)   escalators and moving walkways/travelators (*reg 19*);

(l)   sanitary conveniences (*reg 20*);

(m)   washing facilities (*reg 21*);

(n)   drinking water (*reg 22*);

(o)   accommodation for clothing, and facilities for changing clothing (*regs 23, 24*); and

(p)   facilities to rest and to eat meals (*reg 25*).

Regulation 24 requires facilities to be provided for changing clothes when workers have to wear special clothing for work and, for reasons of health or propriety, cannot be expected to change in another room. 'Special clothing' in this context means any clothing which would not ordinarily be worn other than for work, such as a distinctive uniform (*Post Office v Footitt* [2000] IRLR 243).

29.30 Safety signs

The *Health and Safety (Safety Signs and Signals) Regulations 1996 (SI 1996/341)* implements the EC Directive on safety signs and signals *(92/58)*. All workplace safety signs are required to be of a type referred to within the Regulations.

Basically, there are four recognised safety colours:

Red —	Prohibition sign: Danger, Firefighting equipment
Yellow/Amber —	Warning sign: Be careful, Take precautions
Blue —	Mandatory sign: Specific behaviour or action, Wear protective equipment
Green —	Safe place, No Danger: Emergency Escape Routes, First Aid Equipment.

29.31 WORK-RELATED UPPER LIMB DISORDERS ('WRULDS')

Work-related upper limb disorders or 'RSI' (repetitive strain injury) as they are commonly known, are becoming an increasingly worrying issue for employers, particularly in relation to keyboard users. Although there have only been a small number of claims successfully pursued through the courts, a number of employers have settled claims for large sums of money.

In 1996 a secretary who had developed 'writer's cramp' (a WRULD disorder) as a result of an excessive typing workload succeeded before the Court of Appeal in a claim that her employer had been negligent in allowing her to type for long periods on a word processor without breaks. The court held that it was reasonably foreseeable that a WRULD condition could occur with the amount of typing involved and that the company had negligently failed to warn the employee of the need to take breaks. This ruling was overturned by the House of Lords in *Pickford v Imperial Chemical Industries plc* [1998] IRLR 435, primarily because of inconclusive medical evidence. In addition, the employer was held not to be in breach of the duty of care in failing to warn of the need to take breaks because, unlike a typist, a secretary could organise the workload to avoid continuous working on a word processor. (A statutory requirement to provide information to workers on health and safety risks associated with VDUs is contained in the *Health and Safety (Display Screen Equipment) Regulations 1992 (SI 1992/2792)* (see **29.6** above).)

The possibility of contracting WRULDs can be minimised by paying attention to posture, ergonomics, job design and working methods and conditions.

More recently, the term musculoskeletal disorders (MSDs) has been introduced to cover a range of conditions including WRULDs and RSI which adversely affect the skeletal system and its associated muscles, tendons and ligaments.

These conditions are usually separated into those affecting the upper limbs (from the shoulder to the fingertips), the lower limbs (from the hip to the toes) and the back.

Among people who have ever worked, 2.7% suffer from some form of musculoskeletal disorder, resulting in 10.7 million lost working days (2006–07). On average, each affected person took 16.7 days off in a twelve-month period.

29.31 Health and Safety at Work – II

The HSE has produced a useful guidance publication – HSG60, 2nd Edition, 2002 – entitled *Upper Limb Disorders in the Workplace.* It is possible to download a free copy through the HSE website.

30   Holidays

30.1   The right of an employee to a period of paid holiday is regulated by his contract of employment (see **30.8** below) and the *Working Time Regulations 1998 (SI 1998/1833)* (see **30.2–30.6** below). The *Deduction from Wages (Limitation) Regulations 2014* amended *reg 16* of the *Regulations* to confirm that they do not confer a contractual right to paid holiday: the regime under the *Regulations* is simply statutory (although a contract of employment could, in principle, expressly incorporate the *Regulations*). In addition, in certain fields of employment, separate statutory provision is made (see **30.7** below).

30.2   STATUTORY RULES

Working Time Regulations 1998

The *Working Time Regulations 1998 (SI 1998/1833)* came into force on 1 October 1998. They implemented the *Working Time Directive 93/104/EC* which has now been replaced by the *Working Time Directive 2003/88/EC*. The *Regulations* confer a right on workers to take paid annual leave (*reg 13(1)*). There is no continuous service requirement to qualify for paid annual leave.

Working Time Directive and Direct Effect

In *Dominguez v Centre Informatique du Centre Ouest Atlantique*: C-282/10 [2012] IRLR 321 the ECJ held that *art 7* of the *Directive* had direct effect and could be relied upon by workers where their employer was an emanation of the state. Subsequently, in *NHS Leeds v Larner* [2012] ICR 1389, [2012] IRLR 825, the Court of Appeal confirmed that *art 7* of the *Directive* was directly effective (i.e. vertical direct effect in cases where the employer is a state entity). However the *Directive* will not have "horizontal" direct effect (between a worker and a private employer). In this context, in recent decisions the ECJ reached the controversial conclusion that rights to annual leave in *article 31* of the *EU Charter of Fundamental Rights* may be relied upon directly against private employers in certain situations regardless of domestic law: see *Max-Planck-Gesellschaft v Shimizu*: C-684/16 [2019] CMLR 35. The implications of this decision (and indeed whether it is a correct interpretation of EU law) will take some time to work out at a domestic level. However it seems likely that this issue will be raised in holiday pay claims against non-state employers where it is unclear whether the *Regulations* can be interpreted consistently with the *Directive*.

Key Definition - Worker

'Worker' is defined in the *Regulations* to include employees and those employed under a contract pursuant to which they undertake personally to provide services. However, those who are in business on their own account and whose 'employer' is in reality their customer or client are not workers (*reg 2(1)*). There is a constant stream of case law on the definition of worker and a detailed review can be found earlier in this book in EMPLOYEE, SELF-EMPLOYED OR WORKER **16.9**.

Children under the age for compulsory schooling are not workers and, therefore, are not entitled under the *Regulations* to paid holiday: *Ashby v Addison* [2003] ICR 667, [2003] IRLR 211, EAT.

For further discussion of the *Working Time Regulations* and *Directive* see WORKING TIME (**58**), EUROPEAN UNION LAW (**24**) and HEALTH AND SAFETY AT WORK – II (**29**).

30.3 Holidays

30.3 Period of leave – Number of Days' Leave in a Leave Year

Annual Entitlements: Annual Leave and Additional Annual Leave

Annual entitlements under the *Regulations* are based upon the concept of a 'leave year'. A leave year commences on the date set out in a relevant agreement. A relevant agreement means a workforce agreement, a collective agreement which is incorporated into the contract of employment, or any other agreement in writing which is legally enforceable as between the worker and his employer (normally this will simply be the contract of employment). In the absence of such an agreement, the leave year commences on 1 October 1998 and on the anniversary of that date for those workers already in employment on that date, and, for workers who started work after 1 October 1998, on the date their employment commenced (*reg 13(3)*).

When the *Regulations* were introduced, they entitled a worker to four weeks' annual leave in each leave year (*reg 13(1)*). For a worker working a five day week this amounted to 20 days' annual holiday. Public holidays (of which there are normally eight each year) may count towards the worker's annual leave entitlement. The fact that an employer could count public holidays towards the four week entitlement was much criticised by workers and trade unions. The Department for Trade and Industry (as it then was) sought to address this criticism by introducing the concept of additional annual leave (*reg 13A*). As additional leave reflects a domestic policy decision rather than the implementation of the *Directive*, decisions of the ECJ or domestic courts on the *Directive* will not technically apply to the interpretation of the right to additional annual leave.

The total entitlement to annual leave (*reg 13*) and additional annual leave (*reg 13A*) is 5.6 weeks per year. For a person working five days a week, this increases the entitlement to 28 days' annual leave per year. *Reg 13A(3)* further provides that the aggregate entitlement to annual leave and additional annual leave is subject to a maximum of 28 days. So an employee working six days a week would only be entitled to a total of 28 days' annual leave. When considering the entitlement to leave under the *Regulations*, it should not be forgotten that the *Regulations* set only minimum requirements: more generous provision relating to annual leave may be, and often is, made in the contract of employment.

The distinction between annual leave and additional annual leave is also relevant to the treatment of leave at the end of the leave year. A worker may not carry forward from one leave year to the next any of the four weeks' annual leave (*reg 13(9)(a)*) (save in cases of sickness absence, various types of maternity and parental leave, or certain other situations where the worker was unable to exercise the right to paid annual leave including as a result of the current Coronavirus epidemic– see **30.3A–30.3D** below). Nor may an employer pay a worker in lieu of permitting him to take annual leave except on termination of his employment (*reg 13(9)(b)*). The prohibition of payment in lieu of annual leave is intended to remove any incentive for workers to accept additional payment rather than taking leave as this would undermine the health and safety objectives of the *Directive*: see *Federatie Nederlandse Vakbeweging v Netherlands State*: C-124/05 [2006] ECR I-3423, [2006] ICR 962, [2006] IRLR 561, ECJ. The position with additional annual leave is different. A relevant agreement may provide for any additional annual leave to be carried forward into the immediately following leave year (ie leave carried over under this regulation should not then be carried over into the subsequent leave year) (*reg 13A(7)*). However, an employer is not permitted to make a payment in lieu of additional annual leave.

Finally, to add to the complexity of the current statutory provisions, *reg 26A* provides that the entitlement to additional annual leave under *reg 13A* does not apply where, subject to certain conditions, as at 1 October 2007, a relevant agreement provided that all workers engaged by an employer were entitled to annual leave of at least the equivalent to the now extended statutory entitlement (ie 5.6 weeks or 28 days).

Accruing Annual Leave

The leave entitlement is based on the entire leave year. However, save for workers in their first year of employment, the *Regulations* do not make provision for leave to be accrued incrementally on a month by month basis. So, for example, subject to agreement with the employer (which is discussed at **30.5** below), a worker would be entitled under the *Regulations* to take all his or her annual and additional annual leave at the very start of the leave year. By contrast, workers in their first year of employment accrue entitlement to leave at the rate of one-twelfth of their entitlement on the first day of each month and leave under the *Regulations* may only be taken after it has been accrued (*regs 13(5)* and *13A(5)*).

In *Zentralbetriebsrat der Landeskrankenhauser Tirols v Land Tirol*: C–486/08 [2010] IRLR 631 the ECJ gave important guidance on dealing with accrued annual leave when a worker changes from full time to part time employment during the leave year. It held that the combined effect of the *Part Time Workers Directive* and the *Working Time Directive* was that a reduction of working hours when moving from full time to part time employment does not reduce the right to annual leave that the worker has accrued during the period of full time employment if the worker did not have the opportunity to take that accrued leave. In *Land Tirol* it was rather unclear what the ECJ meant by referring to a worker 'not having the opportunity to exercise the right' to take accrued leave. More recently in *Greenfield v The Care Bureau Ltd*: C-219/14, [2016] ICR 161, [2016] IRLR 62, the facts of which are considered in more detail below, the ECJ affirmed that "annual leave accrued during a reference period can be taken during a subsequent period" without referring to a need to enquire into whether a worker "had the opportunity to exercise the right" to take accrued leave. In the circumstances, it now seems clear that annual leave accrued as a full time worker may be carried over into a period of part time employment (provided it is in the same leave year).

The facts of *Greenfield* were that an employee took 7 days' annual leave early in the leave year at a time when she was working one day a week. Accordingly, the leave taken was equivalent to 7 weeks' leave, and so above the annual leave entitlement under the *Regulations*. Around 2 months into the leave year, she significantly increased her days of work to 12 days every 2 weeks. Later in the leave year she asked to take annual leave, but this was refused on the basis that she had exhausted her entitlement by taking 7 days' leave earlier in the leave year. The employer's argument was that as she had exhausted her annual leave entitlement while working one day a week, she could take no more annual leave that year, irrespective of her hours of work for the rest of the leave year. The ECJ, unsurprisingly in view of the decision in *Land Tirol*, held that a new calculation of annual leave entitlement must be carried out for periods when working time is increased. Accordingly, the calculation of the employee's annual leave entitlement in that case should have been based upon the entitlement accrued while working one day a week, plus the leave accrued while working 12 days out of 14. The 7 days' leave she had taken early in the leave year would be deducted from that total.

To give another example, based on simple facts, a worker working 5 days a week for 6 months of the leave year will accrue 2 weeks – or 10 days – paid annual leave under the *Regulations* (the leave accrued would be 14 days including additional annual leave; this example, however, refers only to annual leave as the ECJ decisions would not technically apply to additional annual leave). If the worker then chose to take that accrued leave at a time when he or she had changed to working 3 days a week, he or she would still be entitled to 10 days' paid leave, rather than just 6 days' (which would be two weeks' leave based on the worker's reduced hours). The same principles would apply in the reverse situation. While working 3 days a week for 6 months, the worker would accrue 6 days' leave. If the worker then changed to full time work, he or she would only be entitled to carry over the leave actually accrued but untaken as a part time worker. The accrued but untaken holiday would not be recalculated based on the new full time hours.

30.3 Holidays

The question of how entitlement to leave is accrued is particularly relevant to workers who do not work for the entire leave year. How is leave entitlement calculated in these cases? Three particular scenarios are commonly encountered in the workplace. First, as mentioned above, a worker may commence employment part-way through the leave year. Where this happens, in that leave year the worker is entitled to the proportion of the annual leave entitlement equal to the proportion of the leave year for which he is employed (*regs 13(5) and 13A(5)*).

The second scenario is that the worker leaves the employment part way through the leave year. In this situation, *reg 14* provides a mechanism to compare the amount of leave taken by a worker in that part of the leave year which he worked with the amount of leave accrued. So, for example, if a worker left the employment exactly six months through the leave year, he would have accrued half his annual leave entitlement; this can be compared to the amount of leave actually taken. *Reg 14* then sets out procedures for dealing with any difference between leave accrued and leave taken. These procedures are discussed at **30.4A** below.

30.3A Annual Leave, Absence from Work and Illness

The third scenario occurs where, although the worker remains employed throughout the leave year, he is absent for part or all of the year due to, for example, illness. Neither the *Regulations* nor the *Directive* expressly address this situation or the relationship between illness and annual leave. Accordingly, it has been left to the courts to seek a solution. In 2011, the Government's Modern Workplaces consultation proposed that these issues would be addressed in amended *Regulations*. However, it is not clear if, or when, such amendments will be introduced.

Until clarification is provided in amended *Regulations*, employers, workers and Tribunals will need to find answers from an increasingly complex collection of decisions of both the ECJ and the domestic courts on the relationship between annual leave and sick leave. A detailed review of those cases is beyond the scope of this chapter. However, the summary below seeks to draw out the key principles of those cases.

The key points to be taken from the decisions of the ECJ in relation to interpretation of the *Working Time Directive* are:

- Paid annual leave "is a particularly important principle of Community social law from which there can be no derogations".

- The purpose of the right to paid annual leave (ie to provide a period of rest, relaxation and leisure) is different from the purpose of sick leave (ie to enable a worker to recover from illness): reaffirmed in *Sobczyszyn v Szkola Podstawowa w Rzeplinie*: C-178/15 [2016] IRLR 725. As a result, entitlement to annual leave continues to accrue during sickness absence.

- Workers must be given the opportunity to take annual leave. Accordingly, workers should not lose their entitlement to annual leave simply because they are unable to take that annual leave as a result of sickness. This was initially decided by the ECJ's decisions in the joined cases of *HMRC v Stringer and Schultz-Hoff v Deutsche Rentenversicherung Bund*: C-502/06, [2009] ICR 932, [2009] IRLR 214. The ECJ specifically noted that the aims of the *Directive* could be achieved in more than one way. For example, workers could be permitted to take annual leave while they are on sick leave. In addition or alternatively, where a worker has been unable to take annual leave because he is sick, he could be permitted to take that leave later, even if that meant carrying the untaken leave over into the next leave year.

- In *Pereda v Madrid Movilidad SA*: C-277/08, [2009] IRLR 959 the ECJ held that where a worker does not wish to take annual leave during a period of sick leave, the employer must grant him annual leave for a different period, if necessary, by permitting him to carry leave over to a new leave year. Subsequently in *Asociación Nacional de Grandes Empresas de Distribución (ANGED) v Federación de Asociaciones Sindicales (FASGA) and others*: C-78/11, [2012] ICR 1211, [2012] IRLR 779 the ECJ held that a worker who falls ill during a period of annual leave must be permitted to interrupt that annual leave and take the untaken annual leave at a later date (even if that resulted in the leave being carried over to a new leave year). In such a case the employer would clearly be entitled to require the worker to provide proof of illness during the holiday.

•   Entitlement to annual leave cannot be made conditional on a worker carrying out a minimum amount of work in the leave year. In *Dominguez v Centre Informatique du Centre Ouest Atlantique*: C-282/10, [2012] IRLR 321 the ECJ held that a French provision making entitlement to paid annual leave conditional upon an employee doing one month of actual work during the leave year was inconsistent with the *Directive*.

•   Where a worker's employment terminates, he is entitled to be paid in lieu for annual leave which has accrued but which the worker was unable to take due to sickness (even where that is annual leave accrued over more than one leave year): see *HMRC v Stringer*.

•   Issues also commonly arise in relation to carrying over annual leave while on maternity and parental leave. For example in *Zentralbetriebsrat der Landeskranken-hauser Tirols v Land Tirol*: C-486/08, [2010] IRLR 631 the ECJ held that the effect of the *Working Time Directive* and the *Framework Agreement on Parental Leave* was that a worker who took parental leave could carry over, until after the parental leave, any annual leave accrued prior to the worker taking parental leave.

A major difficulty thrown up by the ECJ's decisions is the apparent inconsistency between the decision in *Pereda* (recognising that in certain cases workers must be permitted to carry leave over into the next leave year) and *reg 13(9)* of the *Regulations* which provides that leave cannot be carried over from one leave year to the next.

In *NHS Leeds v Larner* [2012] ICR 1389, [2012] IRLR 825, the Court of Appeal (Mummery LJ) suggested that *reg 13(9)* of the *Regulations* could be interpreted consistently with the ECJ decisions referred to above in the following way (the words in italics have been added by the Court of Appeal to ensure consistency with the *Directive*):

"Leave to which a worker is entitled under this regulation may be taken in instalments, but— (a) it may only be taken in the leave year in respect of which it is due, *save where the worker was unable or unwilling to take it because he was on sick leave and as a consequence did not exercise his right to annual leave* . . . ."

While the *Larner* case was decided by the direct application of *art 7* of the *Working Time Directive* (as the claimant was employed by an emanation of the state) rather than under the *Regulations*, the approach of the Court of Appeal in *Larner* was followed by the EAT in *Sood Enterprises Ltd v Healy* [2013] ICR 1361, [2013] IRLR 865. Accordingly, employers should permit workers to carry over annual leave if they have not been able to, or have chosen not to, take it due to illness. In this regard, in *Plumb v Duncan Print Group Ltd* [2016] ICR 125, [2015] IRLR 711 the EAT emphasised that a worker who is absent from work on sick leave is entitled to choose not to take annual leave while on sick leave; he is not required to demonstrate that he is physically unable to take annual leave by reason of his medical condition before being permitted to carry it over into the next leave year.

A further issue then arises in relation to how long a worker will retain the right to carry over leave, before that entitlement lapses. In *KHS AG v Schulte*: C-214/10 [2012] IRLR 156 the ECJ held that national rules or relevant agreements could limit the period for which annual leave could be accrued during long term absence. In *Schulte* a provision of a

German Collective Agreement provided that any entitlement to annual leave which accrued during sickness absence would lapse 15 months after the end of the leave year in which it was accrued. The ECJ gave guidance that any carry over period must be "substantially longer" than the leave year but accepted that the period of 15 months in the case before it was permissible. In a subsequent case, *Neidel v Stadt Frankfurt am Main*: C-337/10, [2012] ICR 1201, [2012] IRLR 607 the ECJ held that a 9 month carry over period was insufficient.

The *Regulations* do not address the issue of the period of carry over in respect of annual leave which cannot be taken in the leave year in which it accrued (although they do provide in *reg 13A(7)* that a relevant agreement may permit additional annual leave to be carried over into the immediately following leave year). However, in *Plumb v Duncan Print Group Ltd* [2016] ICR 125, [2015] IRLR 711 the EAT concluded, by reference to the International Labour Organisation – Holiday and Pay Convention, that a carry-over period of 18 months should be read into *reg 13(9)*: see paragraph 45 of the decision. Accordingly, until there is an amendment to the *Regulations*, or a further judicial decision, workers should be permitted to carry over for 18 months from the end of the leave year any annual leave that they were unable or unwilling to take in that leave year because of illness.

Annual Leave and Giving Notice during Illness

As explained in **30.5** below, *reg 15* of the *Regulations* sets out a procedure for the employer and worker to agree or determine when annual leave is taken. Where a worker wishes to claim entitlement to be paid in respect of annual leave during a period of sickness absence, the worker would have to give notice to the employer and would then be entitled to receive paid annual leave: see *Larner* at paragraph 87 and *Fraser v Southwest London St George's Mental Health Trust* [2012] ICR 403, [2012] IRLR 100 at paragraph 30. A worker on long term sick leave who has exhausted sick pay may well want, or need, to be paid in respect of annual leave while they remain ill, rather than carrying that annual leave over.

In other cases, as the ECJ noted in *Stringer*, a worker may simply wish to keep annual leave which she could not take because she was ill until after she has recovered (even if that means carrying it over into a new leave year). It has now been confirmed that the worker is not required to give notice of the intention to carry that annual leave over to the next leave year: see *NHS Leeds v Larner* [2012] ICR 1389, [2012] IRLR 825 and *Sood Enterprises Ltd v Healy* [2013] ICR 1361, [2013] IRLR 865.

Taking Annual Leave on Return to Work after Sick Leave

A further difficulty arises in cases where a worker is unable to take leave due to sickness but returns to work in the same leave year. In such a case, is the worker permitted to carry leave over, or is she required to take her leave in the current leave year? In *NHS Leeds v Larner* Mummery LJ hinted, by reference to the EAT decision in *Fraser v Southwest London St George's Mental Health Trust*, that there would be no entitlement to carry over annual leave where the worker was able to take it in the current leave year. Accordingly, the focus in such cases is likely to be on whether the worker was reasonably able do so. This will be fact specific and will depend on the amount of accrued but untaken leave and the period between the worker returning to work from sickness absence and the end of the leave year.

Annual Leave and Additional Annual Leave: Should they be treated in the same way?

As explained below, the Government has proposed that annual leave under *reg 13* and additional annual leave under *reg 13A* should be treated differently when considering the right to carry over annual leave which cannot be taken due to illness. This reflects that the leave under *reg 13* is the leave required by the *Directive*, while leave under *reg 13A* goes beyond the *Directive* and is a national policy. Pending amendment of the *Working Time Regulations*, how should the current provisions – as interpreted in *Larner* – be applied? In *Neidel v Stadt Frankfurt am Main*: C-337/10, [2012] ICR 1201, [2012] IRLR 607, the ECJ confirmed that the *Directive* did not require national law to permit additional leave to be carried over in cases of illness. The ECJ made a similar point in *Dominguez v Centre*

Informatique du Centre Ouest Atlantique: C-282/10 [2012] IRLR 321. In *Larner* the Court of Appeal refused to determine this point, but strongly hinted that it considered that *Neidel* had already provided the answer. In *Sood Enterprises Ltd v Healy* [2013] ICR 1361, [2013] IRLR 865, the EAT took up the Court of Appeal's hint and expressly held that a worker could not carry over additional annual leave accrued while off sick, unless there was a relevant agreement with the employer which permitted this. This analysis was recently restated by the ECJ in *Terveys- ja sosiaalialan neuvottelujärjestö (TSN) ry v Hyvinvointialan liitto ry v Fimlab Laboratoriot Oy*: Joined Cases C-609/17 and C-610/17, [2020] ICR 336, [2020] IRLR 141. In that decision the ECJ confirmed that the right to paid annual leave beyond the minimum required by the *Directive* was governed by national law. Therefore, member states could decide the conditions for, and limitations on, additional days of paid annual leave (beyond the four weeks required by the *Directive*). Accordingly, a national provision which precluded the carry over of additional annual leave which could not be taken due to illness did not contravene the *Directive*.

One further caveat must be borne in mind in relation to the treatment of annual leave and additional annual leave. Where other Directives are also in play such as those governing maternity leave, it would appear to be unlawful not to permit the carryover of additional annual leave. For example, in *Gomez (Merino) v Continental Industrias del Caucho SA*: C-342/01 [2004] ECR I-2605, [2005] ICR 1040, [2004] IRLR 407, the ECJ held that, in relation to maternity leave, where a Member State had provided for a longer entitlement to annual leave than the minimum prescribed by the *Working Time Directive*, the Pregnancy *Directive 92/85* also applied to the entitlement to that additional annual leave. Accordingly, that additional annual leave could not be operated in a way which undermined the taking of maternity leave (see further discussion of the *Merino Gomez* case at **30.5** below).

Proposed Amendments

As the above summary illustrates, the relationship between annual leave and sick leave is complex. Part of the difficulty has been that neither the *Directive* nor the *Regulations* provided any guidance on these issues. As a result the ECJ and domestic courts were left to provide solutions on a case by case basis – typically in response to cases with relatively unusual facts.

Amendment of the *Regulations* was proposed as part of the Modern Workplaces consultation. In summary, the initial key proposals in the consultation document were:

- The 4 weeks' annual leave under *reg 13* and the 1.6 weeks' additional annual leave under *reg 13A* will continue to accrue during sickness absence.

- The *Regulations* will allow annual leave to be rescheduled where the worker has been unable to take annual leave due to illness (whether he fell ill before or during the leave). This will include a right to carry over untaken leave where there is no opportunity to reschedule that annual leave in the current leave year.

- However, the right to reschedule and carry over will be limited to the 4 weeks' annual leave under *reg 13*. It will not apply to the 1.6 weeks' additional annual leave under *reg 13A* (or any further contractual leave to which a worker is entitled). This will require employers and workers to know under which provision each particular period of leave is being taken. The Government has proposed that this could be determined by a local agreement, failing which the amended *Regulations* will specify the order in which leave is deemed to be taken (the suggestion is that *reg 13* leave would be deemed to be taken first followed by all other types of annual leave).

- The carry over rights will also apply where leave cannot be taken due to maternity, paternity, parental or adoption leave. However, this right will extend to both annual leave under *reg 13* and additional annual leave under *reg 13A*.

30.3A   Holidays

The implementation of these proposed amendments has not only stalled (perhaps due, initially, to the need to take into account the on-going stream of cases from the ECJ and domestic courts and more recently as a result of Brexit) but has also been overtaken by new case law (considered below) on the calculation of holiday pay. However, at some future point amended *Regulations* will hopefully resolve many of the uncertainties addressed in this chapter.

Conclusion on Annual Leave and Illness

Until the *Regulations* are amended, to avoid costly legal disputes, it would be prudent for employers to give a worker, who is sick during a period of annual leave, the option of still taking annual leave during the period of sickness or taking annual leave at a later date, even if this means carrying the annual leave missed through sickness over to the next leave year, and beyond where the worker is absent for a very long time.

One source of comfort for employers and workers is that while complex issues do arise when considering sickness absence and annual leave, the reality is that these issues will only arise in exceptional cases: typically where workers are on long term sick leave, or they have left taking their annual leave until the end of the leave year and then fallen ill. In most cases, where workers fall sick during or shortly before a period of annual leave, and request that the period be treated as sick leave, they will be able to take the annual leave which they missed as a result of sickness later in the same leave year.

30.3B Accruing Annual Leave during Absences or Reasons other than Illness or Maternity

Workers may, of course, be absent from work for reasons other than illness and maternity leave. Under the Regulations, leave accrues as a consequence of having the status of worker (i.e. being under a contract of employment or a contract to provide personal services). In the UK the relevant statutory provisions for maternity, paternity, adoption, parental and shared parental leave make it clear that the contract continues during periods of such leave. Accordingly leave will accrue under the Regulations during such family leave. However, the ECJ decision in *Botoşani, Ministerul Justiţici v Dicu*: C-12/17, [2018] IRLR 1175 illustrates that in this respect UK law goes further than required by the *Directive*, at least in respect of parental leave. In this case the ECJ confirmed that the *Parental Leave Directive* did not require that annual leave accrued during parental leave (unlike during sick leave or maternity leave).

Another common reason for absence from work arises where a worker takes a period of unpaid leave or a sabbatical. Do they continue to accrue annual leave entitlement during such absences? Again the *Directive* and *Regulations* do not provide an answer. However, some guidance can be found in the ECJ decision in *Heimann and another v Kaiser GmbH*: C-229/11 [2013] IRLR 48. In that case, the employer dismissed a number of employees due to financial difficulties. However, it then agreed with its works council to extend the employment contracts of the dismissed workers for one year from the date of their dismissal on a zero hours short-time working basis. This suspended the workers' obligation to work and the employer's obligation to pay them a salary. The purpose of that extension was to give the workers the opportunity of receiving, for the year following their dismissal, a statutory allowance payable during periods of zero hours short-time working. The ECJ held that the *Working Time Directive* permitted national law or relevant agreements to provide that annual leave accrued in proportion to the time actually worked during the leave year (as it would for part time workers). Accordingly, such a law or agreement could provide that annual leave did not accrue during periods where no work was being performed. In reaching this conclusion the ECJ explained that the situation of a worker unable to work as a result of an illness, and that of a worker on short-time working, are fundamentally different. In particular, the ECJ noted, during the period of short-time working, the worker was free to rest or to devote himself to recreational and leisure activities, whereas a worker on sick leave would be subject to physical or psychological constraints caused by illness.

The approach in *Heimann* was followed in *Hein v Albert Holzkamm GmbH*: C–385/17, in which the ECJ confirmed that annual leave would normally only accrue under the *Directive* when work was actually performed. Accordingly no leave was accrued under the *Directive* during short time working when no work was performed. However the ECJ noted that national laws or agreements could provide for more paid annual leave than guaranteed by the *Directive*.

The reasoning of the ECJ in *Heimann* ought to apply equally to other absences not caused by illness, or maternity leave, such as unpaid leave and sabbaticals. However, in such cases employers should be advised to agree expressly with the worker (and to record that agreement in writing) that the worker will not accrue annual leave during the period of absence and that in this respect, at least, the contract of employment will be suspended during the period of unpaid leave or sabbatical.

30.3C Carry Over of Annual Leave Where Paid Leave is not Offered by the Employer

As explained above, in *NHS Leeds v Larner* [2012] ICR 1389, [2012] IRLR 825, the Court of Appeal suggested that *reg 13(9)* of the *Regulations* could be interpreted to allow annual leave to be carried over to a new leave year "where the worker was unable or unwilling to take it because he was on sick leave and as a consequence did not exercise his right to annual leave . . . ." This will also apply to maternity and other parental leave.

To what extent might a similar analysis apply where a worker is prevented from taking paid annual leave due to reasons other than illness or maternity etc? This might commonly occur where the employer considers that its staff are not workers, and so do not qualify for the right to paid annual leave under the Regulations, or where the employer simply does not permit workers to exercise their rights to annual leave.

This issue was considered by the ECJ in *King v Sash Window Workshop Ltd*: C–214/16 [2018] IRLR 142. Mr King worked as a commission only salesman from 1999 to 2012. He was not regarded as a worker and was not given paid annual leave by his employer. However over the years of his employment he had taken various periods of unpaid holiday (although often less than the 4 weeks' a year provided for by the Regulations). After his employment ended, Mr King brought various claims in the Tribunal including in relation to holiday pay. The Tribunal determined that he was a worker, and therefore he had been entitled to paid annual leave under the *Regulations*. The claims in relation to holiday pay fell into three categories: the first was a claim for holiday accrued but untaken in relation to the leave year 2012/2013 (i.e. the last year of his employment); the second was a claim for a series of unlawful deductions of wages in respect of leave which Mr King had taken and for which he was not paid; and the third related to leave to which he had been entitled under the Regulations over his years of employment but which he had not taken even as unpaid leave. Before the Employment Tribunal Mr King succeeded on all 3 categories of claim.

The EAT allowed an appeal in relation to category three (i.e. leave not taken at all in the earlier years of his employment) on the ground that Mr King had been able to take holiday during his employment (albeit unpaid – as he had done for part of his annual entitlement): in effect he could have taken leave and then brought a claim in respect of not being paid for it. As he was not prevented from taking annual leave, any untaken leave lapsed at the end of each leave year and could not be carried over into the following leave year.

The ECJ rejected this analysis. It noted the importance of providing an effective remedy under Article 47 of the EU Charter, as well as the importance of the right to paid annual leave. It held that, in a case in which the employer granted only unpaid leave, requiring the worker to take that leave and then bring a claim for holiday pay meant that the worker was not receiving the right to take paid leave. This might also dissuade the worker from taking leave, as it was unpaid. The employer was obliged to "provide adequate facilities" to permit a worker to take paid annual leave, and if it did not do so, the right to leave could be carried over into future leave years. The ECJ noted that in cases where paid leave was not offered, this was the responsibility of the employer and "an employer that does not allow a worker to exercise his right to paid annual leave must bear the consequences." Accordingly, as the employer was at fault, there was no need to balance the interests of employer and worker and place a temporal limit on the period for which leave could be carried over (unlike the sickness cases considered above). Accordingly, Mr King was entitled to a payment on the termination of his employment for all the leave which he had accrued but not taken during his employment from 1999 to 2012. It was irrelevant to this analysis that Mr King had refused the offer to work under an employment contract which provided for paid leave (presumably because he felt that there were financial, tax or other benefits of remaining on a "self-employed" contract).

The decision in *King* has huge ramifications for employers who have considered that their staff were not workers and did not qualify for the right to paid annual leave but who are later found by a Tribunal to be workers. King was concerned with a claim where the worker had left employment, and was seeking a payment of accrued but untaken leave on termination (under reg. 14 which is considered in more detail below). The ECJ's analysis that the right to paid annual leave can rollover indefinitely in cases where the employer has not provided adequate opportunity to take such leave must also apply to workers who remain employed. However will these workers be entitled to seek to agree to take lengthy periods of continuous leave while remaining a worker, or must they wait until the termination of employment and receive a payment in lieu? The answer is probably somewhere between these two extremes, with a worker gradually reducing the period of accrued leave and receiving a payment in lieu of any outstanding leave on termination. In practice, some employers may also seek to pay workers in lieu of any accrued leave, and seek to avoid the prohibition on such payments in lieu by the use of settlement agreements.

A further issue may arise over what in the King case was referred to category 2: i.e. leave which was taken but unpaid. Mr King recovered pay in respect of this leave through an unlawful deductions claim. However the scope for such a claim has now been limited (as explained below) by the imposition of a 2 year limitation period and a restrictive approach to the definition of "series of deductions". It is suggested that in cases where unpaid leave has been taken, and no claim made for payment within 3 months of that leave, there is a strong argument that a worker should be entitled to claim that the unpaid leave which was taken is irrelevant to his entitlement under the *Regulations*, and that the right to 4 weeks' paid annual leave remains in existence and rolls over until finally taken as paid leave, or paid out on termination. Otherwise, on the analysis of the ECJ in *King*, the worker may be denied an effective remedy for the employer's breach.

Of course the circumstances in which a worker is unable to take annual leave may vary: the employer's refusal to pay holiday pay may be the most common situation, and the approach in King will apply. However, there may also be cases in which, while the right to paid annual leave is in theory offered, the employer has indicated that it will not look favourably at requests to take that leave: if the worker chooses not to rock the boat and does not request leave, should his entitlement lapse? In such cases, following the ECJ decision in *King* the Tribunal should carefully scrutinise whether the worker's right to request leave was undermined by the employer's attitude towards such requests.

The approach to these issues may also depend on the recent ECJ decision in *Kreuziger v Land Berlin*: C-619/16 [2019] CMLR 34. While this case related to payment in lieu of accrued but untaken annual leave on the termination of employment (see further **30.4A** below), the ECJ's comments on the opportunity to take leave are also relevant to taking leave while employment continues. In *Kreuziger* the ECJ stated that the loss of a right to leave (at the termination of employment or the end of a leave year) should not be automatic but should only occur if "the worker who has lost his right to paid annual leave has actually had the opportunity to exercise the right conferred on him by the directive" (paragraph 42) and that "employers must . . . ensure that workers are given the opportunity to exercise such a right [to paid annual leave]" (paragraph 51).

The ECJ also noted that the "worker must be regarded as the weaker party in the employment relationship, and it is therefore necessary to prevent the employer from being in a position to impose upon him a restriction of his rights. On account of that position of weakness, such a worker may be dissuaded from explicitly claiming his rights vis-à-vis his employer where, in particular, doing so may expose him to measures taken by the employer likely to affect the employment relationship in a manner detrimental to that worker . . . " (paragraph 48).

Finally the ECJ held that "the employer is in particular required . . . to ensure, specifically and transparently, that the worker is actually given the opportunity to take the paid annual leave to which he is entitled, by encouraging him, formally if need be, to do so, while informing him, accurately and in good time so as to ensure that that leave is still capable of procuring for the person concerned the rest and relaxation to which it is supposed to contribute, that, if he does not take it, it will be lost at the end of the reference period or authorised carry-over period, or upon termination of the employment relationship where the termination occurs during such a period. In addition, the burden of proof in that respect is on the employer... should the employer not be able to show that it has exercised all due diligence in order to enable the worker actually to take the paid annual leave to which he is entitled, it must be held that the loss of the right to such leave, and, in the event of the termination of the employment relationship, the corresponding absence of a payment of an allowance in lieu of annual leave not taken" would amount to a breach of the *Working Time Directive* (paragraphs 52 and 53).

While the ECJ in *Kreuziger* started from a position similar to that in *King*, with a focus on whether a worker had the opportunity to take annual leave, the approach in *Kreuziger* then went a lot further placing a requirement on employers to ensure that workers know about their rights to annual leave, to encourage them to take such leave, and to inform them of the effect of not taking it.

It is not yet clear how the decision in *Kreuziger* will play out in Employment Tribunals. It seems clear that the ECJ intended to impose an obligation that employers specifically and transparently provide the opportunity for annual leave. However in many businesses holiday entitlements and the "use it or lose it principle" are well known. In such cases, reference to the leave policy in contracts of employment or staff handbooks may be sufficient to persuade a Tribunal that sufficient opportunity was given to take annual leave. However it would be sensible for employers to encourage workers to take annual leave through either general or individual communications. A failure to this could lead to a Tribunal concluding that workers did not have the opportunity to take annual leave. The result of this could be that workers accrue significant holiday entitlements due to untaken leave rolling over at the end of a leave year.

30.3D Carry Over of Annual Leave and the Working Time (Coronavirus) (Amendment) Regulations 2020

The *Working Time (Coronavirus) (Amendment) Regulations 2020, SI 2020/365*, were made and brought into force with immediate effect on 27 March 2020. They amend *reg 13(9)* of the *Working Time Regulations* to permit the carry over of annual leave (but not additional annual leave) in the circumstances set out in new *regs 13(10)* and *13(11)*. *Reg 13(10)* provides that leave may be carried over where it was 'not reasonably practicable' for a worker to take some or all of his annual leave in the correct leave year as a result of the effects of coronavirus (including on the worker, the employer or the wider economy or society) and *reg 13(11)* provides that the period of carry forward is the two leave years immediately following the leave year in respect of which the leave was due. The *2020 Coronavirus Regulations* also:

- Add *reg 13(12)* to the *Working Time Regulations* to provide that an employer may only require a worker not to take leave carried over under *reg 13(10)* on particular days (as provided for in *reg 15(2)*) where the employer has good reason to do so; and

- Amend *reg 14* of the *Working Time Regulations* to ensure that payment in lieu of annual leave on termination of employment includes leave carried over under *regs 13(10)* and *(11)*.

The government has issued guidance on the effect of the *2020 Regulations* (https ://www.gov.uk/guidance/holiday-entitlement-and-pay-during-coronavirus-covid-19). This indicated that when considering whether it was not reasonably practicable for a worker to take leave as a result of the coronavirus an employer should consider various factors including the demands on the business, disruption to its workers, the health of the worker and his need to have a period of rest and relaxation, the length of time remaining in the leave year, the impact of taking leave on the societal response to the coronavirus situation and the ability of the remainder of the employer's available workforce to provide cover for the worker going on leave.

This guidance also confirmed that:

- Workers on furlough (under the Coronavirus Job Retention Scheme) continue to accrue statutory holiday.

- Workers on furlough can take holiday without disrupting their furlough. However, if an employer wishes to require its workers to take leave while on furlough, the employer should consider whether any restrictions on movement due to coronavirus would prevent the workers from resting, relaxing and enjoying leisure time, which is the fundamental purpose of holiday.

- Where a worker on furlough takes annual leave, he is entitled to his normal pay. Where this is above the pay the worker receives while on furlough, the employer must pay the difference.

30.4 Payment for Annual Leave

A worker is entitled to be paid for any period of leave at the rate of a week's pay for each week of leave. In *British Airways plc v Noble* [2006] EWCA Civ 537, [2006] ICR 1227, [2006] IRLR 533 the Court of Appeal reiterated that pay while on holiday should be the same as pay while at work. The application of this simple principle to various employment situations is not, however, as straightforward as it sounds.

Calculating a Week's Pay

Calculating the amount of holiday pay a worker should receive has become the new area of substantial, sustained litigation under the *Working Time Regulations*, following hot on the heels of the cases discussed above which dealt with the relationship between sickness and annual leave entitlements. In fact, calculation of holiday pay is likely to be far more significant than the holiday/sickness issues as it will potentially affect all workers who currently receive lower holiday pay than their normal pay (because for example when working they work overtime or receive shift premia), not just those few who are on long term sick leave.

The starting point is that under the *Regulations* a week's pay is calculated in accordance with the rules in *ERA 1996, ss 221–224 (reg 16)*. These rules distinguish between workers who have normal working hours and those that do not. The provisions are themselves complex and are discussed in more detail in Redundancy – I (39) and Pay– I (35)).

Where a worker does not have normal working hours a week's pay, until 5 April 2020, was calculated under *ERA 1996, s 224*, by averaging his pay over the last 12 weeks in which he worked. From 6 April 2020, the reference period was increased to 52 weeks for workers who had been employed by their employer for at least 52 weeks, and for workers who had been employed by their employer for less than 52 weeks, the reference period will be the number of weeks for which the workers have been employed: see the *Employment Rights (Employment Particulars and Paid Annual Leave) (Amendment) Regulations 2018*.

The use of a 12 week reference period led to fluctuations in the amount paid during annual leave for workers whose weekly hours changed over the year. The introduction of the 52-week reference period should provide a better reflection of normal pay over the entire leave year.

The case of *Brazel v Harpur Trust* relates to the calculation of holiday pay and is a particularly important case for term time workers, or others who only work part of the year. The claimant was a music teacher who worked term time only (between 32 and 35 weeks per year) but was contractually entitled (under a permanent contract) to receive 5.6 weeks' paid holiday per year. She was effectively treated more favourably in relation to holiday pay than full time workers who worked 46.4 weeks per year (i.e. 52 weeks less 5.6 weeks' annual leave under the Regulations). However, the Court of Appeal ([2019] EWCA Civ 1402, [2019] IRLR 1012) held that there was no requirement in the *Working Time Regulations* to pro-rate holiday pay for part-year employees to ensure that full-time employees were not treated less favourably. In particular, the Court of Appeal held that:

- While EU law had applied an accrual approach to entitlement to annual leave, there was no requirement as a matter of EU law to give effect to the pro rata principle or, more particularly, to pro-rate the entitlement of part-year workers to that of full-year workers.

- Under domestic law "on any natural construction" the *Working Time Regulations* make no provision for pro-rating. They simply require the straightforward exercise of identifying a week's pay in accordance with the provisions of *ERA 1996, ss 221–224*, and multiplying that figure by 5.6.

- In the circumstances, the claimant was entitled to 5.6 weeks' paid annual leave each leave year, with a week's pay calculated in accordance with the provisions of the *ERA 1996*.

- The Court of Appeal accepted that this approach could lead to odd results in extreme cases but noted that general rules do sometimes produce anomalies when applied in untypical cases and that if employers choose to retain, on permanent contracts, workers whom they could have engaged freelance, because doing so had particular advantages, it was reasonable that the employers should have to accept the additional costs that came with that choice.

Another issue frequently raised by the application of *ERA 1996, ss 221–224* is that the calculation of a week's pay under these provisions may not be the same as the actual pay earned by a worker in a typical working week. For example, where an employee does have normal working hours, overtime only qualifies as part of a week's pay where the overtime is fixed under the contract of employment. The effect is that only contractual hours are included when calculating a week's pay and, for example, non-contractual overtime hours are not. This is illustrated by the decision in *Bamsey v Albion Engineering and Manufactur-*

ing plc [2004] EWCA Civ 359, [2004] ICR 1083, [2004] IRLR 457 in which the employee worked significant overtime. However, as his contractual hours were only 39 this lower number of weekly hours formed the basis of his entitlement to holiday pay. He argued that this was contrary to the *Working Time Directive* which required workers to be paid during holiday periods at the same or similar level to their normal income when actually at work and that the *Working Time Regulations, reg 16* should be interpreted purposively to ensure that this was achieved. The Court of Appeal rejected this argument and confirmed that non-contractual overtime did not form a part of a week's pay for workers. It also concluded that this interpretation was not contrary to the purpose of the *Directive* which did not require Member States to guarantee more pay during a holiday period than a worker was contractually entitled to even if the worker regularly worked periods of non-contractual overtime.

A further impact of the application of the rules in *ERA 1996, ss 221–224* is that commission payments were, in many cases, not taken into account when determining a week's pay: see *Evans v Malley Organisation Ltd* [2002] EWCA Civ 1834, [2003] ICR 432, [2003] IRLR 156. As explained below, *Bamsey v Albion Engineering and Evans v Malley* no longer represent the law in relation to calculating holiday pay under the *Regulations*.

The long standing approach to calculating holiday pay in accordance with *ERA 1996, ss 221–224* was thrown into doubt by the ECJ's decision in *Williams v British Airways*: C-155/10, [2011] IRLR 948. In that case, the claimant pilots argued that while on holiday they should receive basic salary plus 2 supplements which they received while working. The first was a flying pay supplement (or 'FPS') which was an additional payment of around £10 per hour spent flying. The second was a time away from base allowance (or 'TAFB') which British Airways regarded as a payment to cover expenses (but which HMRC regarded as overgenerous for this purpose and a portion of which was taxable as remuneration). The ECJ decided that pay during annual leave must be comparable or equivalent to pay normally received when working but that remuneration intended to cover expenses incurred while working need not be paid during annual leave. That strongly suggested that payments such as overtime needed to be included when calculating holiday pay, as overtime is a part of normal remuneration for work done.

The ECJ's decision was considered by the Supreme Court [2012] ICR 1375, [2012] IRLR 1014, which remitted the case to the Employment Tribunal to determine (i) the average value of the FPS over a representative period (as the FPS was clearly part of normal remuneration); and (ii) whether the TAFB was genuinely intended exclusively to cover expenses (in which case it would not be payable during annual leave). Although *Williams* was brought under the *Civil Aviation (Working Time) Regulations 2004*, the ECJ's reasoning applies equally to cases under the *Working Time Regulations* and *Directive*.

Subsequently in *Lock v British Gas Trading Ltd*: C-539/12, [2014] ICR 813, [2014] IRLR 648, the ECJ decided that holiday pay should take into account commission payments (effectively meaning that the Court of Appeal decision in *Evans v Malley Organisation Ltd* was inconsistent with the *Directive*). In *Lock*, as is typical in commission cases, Mr Lock's pay was not affected while he was on holiday because during that period he was paid commission for earlier sales. However, his future commission payments were affected as he made no sales during his period of leave. The ECJ, following *British Airways v Williams*, noted that the sales which earned Mr Lock commission were an intrinsic part of the work he performed. Accordingly, that commission needed to be taken into account when calculating remuneration in respect of annual leave. In reaching this conclusion the ECJ was influenced by the fact that losing future commission payments as a result of sales not being made during a period of annual leave could deter workers from taking annual leave. Accordingly, following *Lock*, commission that would notionally have been earned during a period of annual leave should be treated as being payment "in respect of" the period of annual leave, and this commission will fall to be paid at a later date. The ECJ went on to state that it was for the national court or Tribunal to determine how to calculate the amount that should be paid in respect of the commission that would have been earned but for annual leave. However, based on comments of Advocate General Bot, it seems likely that one lawful approach would be to calculate the commission payable on sales that would notionally have been made during a period of leave by reference to the average commission over a representative period (such as 12 months).

Following the ECJ decisions in *Williams* and *Lock*, the expected challenge that the *Regulations* did not correctly implement the *Directive* was considered by the EAT in *Bear Scotland Ltd v Fulton* [2015] ICR 221, [2015] IRLR 15. The EAT concluded that:

- The *Directive* required that a worker should receive normal pay during periods of annual leave. Normal pay will need to be determined by considering average remuneration over a reference period determined by each member state (paragraph 44). Remuneration will amount to normal pay where there is an intrinsic or direct link between the remuneration and the tasks which a worker is required to carry out (paragraph 45). This effectively draws the distinction identified in *Williams* between payment for work and payment of expenses.

- Pay for non-guaranteed overtime was part of normal pay and, therefore, the *Directive* required this to be taken into account when calculating holiday pay.

- The *Regulations* could be interpreted to achieve this result by adding words to *reg 16(3)(d)* so that it reads: "(d) as if the references to *sections 227* and *228* did not apply and, in the case of the entitlement under *regulation 13, sections 223(3)* and *234* do not apply." The EAT also commented that as long as the *Regulations* are interpreted to implement the *Directive*, it did not matter exactly what words were read into the *Regulations*.

The decision in *Bear Scotland* was followed in March 2015 by the Employment Tribunal decision in *Lock*, reported at [2015] IRLR 438 (following remission from the ECJ). As in *Bear Scotland*, the Employment Tribunal in *Lock* felt able to construe the *Regulations* purposively so that they were compatible with the *Directive*. In doing so, the Tribunal could not simply adopt exactly the same approach as the EAT in *Bear Scotland* (as the words added to *reg 16(3)(d)*) in *Bear Scotland* dealt only with the overtime issues relevant to that case). In order to ensure that commission was taken into account when calculating holiday pay the Tribunal in *Lock* concluded that a new *reg 16(3)(e)* should be added to the *Regulations* which reads: "as if, in the case of the entitlement under *regulation 13*, a worker with normal working hours whose remuneration includes commission or similar payment shall be deemed to have remuneration which varies with the amount of work done for the purpose of *section 221*".

The EAT decision in *Bear Scotland* was not appealed to the Court of Appeal. However, the Employment Tribunal decision in *Lock* was appealed to the EAT ([2016] IRLR 316). In that appeal, the EAT held that although *Lock* and *Bear Scotland* concerned commission and overtime respectively, it was not possible to distinguish the cases. Further the EAT held that, while it had been argued that *Bear Scotland* was wrongly decided and should not be followed, the EAT would not depart from its practice that it would normally follow one of its earlier decisions. As the EAT stated at the end of its judgment in *Lock*, "if *Bear Scotland* was wrongly decided, then it must be for the Court of Appeal to say so."

The Court of Appeal in *British Gas v Lock* [2017] ICR 1, [2016] IRLR 946, agreed with the EAT's decisions in that case, and also in *Bear Scotland*, and held that the *Working Time Regulations 1998* can be interpreted compatibly with the *Directive*, with the result that the holiday pay of a worker should include an element referable to the amount of contractual results-based commission the worker normally earned that he would otherwise not earn during his holiday period: as the Court of Appeal explained the *Regulations* must be interpreted on the presumption that the UK Government intended "to fulfil *entirely* the obligations arising under the *Directive*". The Supreme Court refused permission for British Gas to appeal against that decision. However, that is not the end of the matter for two reasons. First, the Court of Appeal expressly stated that its decision was limited to the facts before it: ie where Mr Lock had a contractual results based entitlement to commission and the same approach would not necessarily apply to other forms of commission scheme. So there will almost certainly be future cases which consider different forms of commission scheme. Secondly, *Lock* has now returned to the Employment Tribunal so that it can determine the actual financial impact of including commission in Mr Lock's holiday pay (which will also require consideration of the appropriate reference period). The fact that the Court of Appeal, EAT and ET have all felt able to interpret the *Regulations* consistently with the *Directive* means that there is no immediate requirement for the Government to revisit how holiday pay is calculated under the *Working Time Regulations*. In addition, a clear principle has now been established by the ECJ, willingly followed and applied by the domestic courts and Tribunals, that holiday pay should be the same as normal pay for tasks intrinsically or directly linked to work performed.

Nonetheless, a number of uncertainties remain, which will need to be clarified in future decisions or by amendment of the *Regulations*. These areas of uncertainty include:

• What forms of variable pay should be treated as normal pay? Normal pay clearly includes overtime which the employee was required to perform if offered (*Bear Scotland*) and contractual results based commission (*Lock*). Similarly, *Patterson v Castlereagh Borough Council* [2015] IRLR 721, (Northern Ireland Court of Appeal) and *Dudley MBC v Willetts* [2018] ICR 31, [2017] IRLR 870 (EAT) held that, in principle, voluntary overtime could be included when determining holiday pay. In Dudley the EAT explained that it will be a question of fact for each Tribunal to determine whether or not voluntary overtime was normally carried out by the worker over a sufficient period of time to be included in the calculation of holiday pay: "[t]his will be a question of fact and degree. Items which are not usually paid or are exceptional will not count [for the purposes of calculating holiday pay]" (paragraph 40).

• In *Flowers v East of England Ambulance Trust* UKEAT/0235/17/JOJ the EAT applied the approach in *Dudley MBC v Willetts*: i.e. that voluntary overtime should be included in the calculation of holiday pay where it is normally carried out.

• In *Hein v Albert Holzkamm GmbH and Co KG*: Case C-385/17, [2019] 2 CMLR 19 the ECJ threw a spanner in the works of what had become settled law on overtime by suggesting that (at paragraph 46) "given its exceptional and unforeseeable nature, remuneration received for overtime does not, in principle, form part of the normal remuneration that the worker may claim in respect of the paid annual leave" under the *Directive*. When *East of England Ambulance Service NHS Trust v Flowers* reached the Court of Appeal, [2019] ICR 1454, [2019] IRLR 798, [2019] EWCA Civ 947, the employers argued that *Hein* showed that *Fulton*, *Willets* and the EAT in *Flowers* were wrongly decided. After noting that the ECJ "is notorious for making pronouncements resembling those of the oracle at Delphi" but that "even by their oracular standards para 46 is hard to understand", the Court of Appeal concluded that in paragraph 46 of *Hein* the ECJ only intended to refer to overtime which was "exceptional and unforeseeable" rather than all overtime. That being the case, the position set out in *Fulton*, *Willets* and the EAT in *Flowers* remains the same. The saga is not yet over, however, as the Supreme Court has referred this issue to the ECJ.

• In addition to overtime, it is suggested that normal pay would be likely to include, shift-premia, unsocial hours payments, acting up payments, most forms of commission and certain types of bonuses, provided they are "normally received". As made clear in the Court of Appeal's decision in *Lock*, this will need to be decided on a case by case basis.

- As noted above, in *Bear Scotland* and *Lock* the EAT and the Employment Tribunal had to read different words into the *Regulations* to ensure that overtime and commission respectively were included in the calculation of holiday pay. Other types of variable payment may need additional amendments to be read into the *Regulations*. It is far from ideal for Employment Tribunals to have to engage in a constant process of rewriting the *Regulations* in order for them to correctly implement the *Directive*.

- As both the EAT in *Bear Scotland* and the ET in *Lock* were able to construe the *Regulations* consistently with the Directive, the calculation of a week's pay is still based on the rules in *ERA 1996, ss 221–224* (albeit with some amendments). Accordingly, it is suggested that, where it is necessary to calculate a week's pay using a reference period, that period would remain 12 weeks.

In the circumstances, notwithstanding the clarification provided by the decisions in *Bear Scotland* and *Lock*, the full implications of the ECJ decisions in *Williams* and *Lock* are still in the process of being worked out at a domestic level. What is now clear beyond doubt is that certain regular payments need to be taken into account when calculating holiday pay. Accordingly, employers would be wise to adopt systems which reflect the *Williams*, *Lock*, *Bear Scotland*, and *Dudley* decisions sooner rather than later to avoid the risk of accruing significant future liabilities.

Finally, it is worth noting that, because these issues on calculating holiday pay arise as a result of ECJ decisions on the *Working Time Directive*, they will not apply to any holiday over the minimum 4 weeks' annual leave under the *Directive*. This was confirmed by the EAT in *Bear Scotland*. Accordingly, subject to amendment of the *Regulations*, holiday pay for additional annual leave can still be calculated by reference to *ERA 1996, ss 221 to 224*, without any of the provisions being disapplied, or additional words read in.

Remuneration under the Working Time Regulations and the Contract of Employment

The right to annual paid holiday does not affect the right of a worker to remuneration under his contract. However, any contractual remuneration paid during a period of leave will be offset against leave payments due under the *Regulations*, and similarly any payment for a period of leave under the *Regulations* will be offset against a claim for contractual remuneration for the same period (*regs 16(4)* and *(5)*). In addition, as the EAT's decision in *Crossland v Corps of Commissionaires Management Ltd* (UKEAT/0014/10/LA) (18 August 2010, unreported) shows, the terms of the contract of employment may make provision for holiday pay to be calculated in a more favourable way than permitted by *ERA 1996, ss 221–224*. In such cases, a claim under the contract will be more valuable than a claim under the *Regulations*.

Holiday Pay must be Paid at the Time Holiday is Taken

For some time there was debate and dispute about whether an employer could 'roll up' holiday pay: ie whether the *Regulations* allowed the rate of pay while actually working to be enhanced to include an element referable to holiday pay so that no additional pay was due when the worker took leave. The ECJ decided in *Robinson-Steele v RD Retail Services Ltd*: C-131/04, [2006] ICR 932, [2006] IRLR 386 that the *Directive* required that workers were paid for annual leave at the time they took it. Accordingly, 'rolling up' holiday pay is contrary to the *Regulations* and *Directive*. The ECJ explained this decision on the basis that, although the *Directive* did not expressly lay down when payment for leave should be made, the purpose of the requirement of payment for annual leave is to put the worker, during annual leave, in a position which is, as regards remuneration, comparable to periods of work. Therefore, the entitlements to annual leave and to payment for that leave are two aspects of a single right. The rationale which underlies this conclusion is that workers may be discouraged from taking leave if they will receive no remuneration during that period of leave.

30.4 Holidays

The ECJ's decision in *Robinson-Steele* resolved earlier inconsistent decisions in England and Scotland in favour of the approach of the Court of Session in Scotland which had concluded that rolled up holiday pay was unlawful: see *Munro v MPB Structures Ltd* [2003] IRLR 350. By contrast the Court of Appeal and the EAT in England had held that, subject to certain restrictions, rolling up holiday pay into pay for periods when the worker was actually working did comply with the *Regulations*: see, as background, *Marshalls Clay Products v Caulfield* [2004] ICR 1502, [2004] IRLR 564, CA and *Smith v AJ Morrisroes & Sons Ltd* [2005] ICR 596, [2005] IRLR 72, EAT.

Bearing in mind that, prior to the ECJ decision in *Robinson-Steele*, rolled up holiday pay was thought to be lawful (at least in England and Wales), it is unsurprising that the practice had been commonly adopted in a number of industries where working patterns are irregular and/or unpredictable (for, example, industries with certain shift patterns and recruitment businesses providing temporary staff). It is now clear that this will not comply with the *Regulations*. However, this does not necessarily mean that any workers who have benefited from rolled up holiday pay can gain a windfall by claiming payment for leave at the time they take it notwithstanding that they have already been paid for that leave through rolled up holiday pay. In this regard, the ECJ held that the *Directive* did not preclude sums paid transparently and comprehensibly as rolled up holiday pay being set off against the payment due for specific leave which is actually taken by a worker. *Lyddon v Englefield Brickwork Ltd* [2008] IRLR 198 is an example of a case where the Employment Tribunal and EAT applied such a set off because the agreement between Mr Lyddon and his employer in relation to rolled up holiday pay, whilst contrary to the *Regulations*, was sufficiently clear and transparent.

Notwithstanding this decision, Employment Tribunals are likely to be far less willing to apply a set off today, given that employers have had plenty of time to put in place systems for paying holiday pay at the time holiday is taken.

30.4A Payment on termination of employment

Where a worker's employment is terminated and he has accrued but untaken leave to which he is entitled under the *Regulations*, the employer must pay him in lieu of that untaken leave (*reg 14*). As set out in **30.3D** above, the *Working Time (Coronavirus) (Amendment) Regulations 2020* amended *reg 14* of the *Working Time Regulations* to ensure that payment in lieu of annual leave on termination of employment includes leave carried over under *regs 13(10)* and *(11)*.

In *Kreuziger v Land Berlin*: C-619/16 [2019] CMLR 34 the ECJ confirmed that the right to payment in lieu of untaken annual leave on the termination of employment was a fundamental right. Accordingly a worker should not automatically lose the right to a payment in lieu of untaken annual leave on termination of employment simply because he had failed to take that leave during his employment.

This is unlikely to have a significant impact in the UK on payments in lieu on termination under the Regulations, as *reg 14(3)* provides that, in the absence of a relevant agreement, payment is made based on a simple calculation to determine the amount the worker would have been paid under *reg 16* for the period of leave accrued but untaken (ie the period of leave which, in proportion to the leave year, he is entitled to take), less the period of leave he has in fact taken (*reg 14(3)*).

Alternatively to the application of this formula, the amount payable to the worker who has accrued but untaken leave may be specified in a relevant agreement: see *reg 14(3)(a)*. A relevant agreement may not, however, specify that no sum is to be paid: see *Witley and District Men's Club v Mackay* [2001] IRLR 595, EAT, in which an agreement that no sum was to be paid for accrued holiday where the worker was dismissed on grounds of dishonesty was void under *reg 35(1)(a)*. Following *Kreuziger v Land Berlin*: C-619/16

[2019] CMLR 34 (referred to above) there is a risk that any agreement providing for payment in lieu which is less than the value of accrued but untaken holiday will be found to be incompatible with the *Working Time Directive*.

Compensation for failure to pay for accrued but untaken holiday on termination of employment is not limited by principles of justice and equity under *reg 30(4)*; *reg 30(5)* requires a Tribunal to make an award for the actual sum due: *Witley and District Men's Club v Mackay* (above).

The ECJ has also confirmed that the right to be paid in lieu of accrued but untaken annual leave on the termination of employment will apply where the employment ends as a result of the worker's death: see *Bollacke v Klaas & Kock*: C–118/13, [2014] ICR 828, [2014] IRLR 732. Similarly, the heir of a worker who dies while employed will be entitled to payment in lieu of the worker's accrued but untaken leave: see *Stadt Wuppertal v Bauer* C-569/16.

However, in *Maschek v Magistratsdirektion der Stadt Wien* [2016] IRLR 801, the ECJ concluded that where a worker continues to be paid but is not required to attend work (similar to garden leave in the UK), that period can be treated as annual leave, with the result that any entitlement to accrued but untaken leave is reduced or extinguished by the period of garden leave. The ECJ based its decision on the dual purposes of annual leave, namely to give a worker a period of rest from carrying out work and a period of relaxation and leisure, and the fact that these purposes can be achieved during a period of garden leave. The corollary of this, however, is that if a worker is ill during garden leave, the period could not be treated as annual leave, and the worker would retain the right to be paid for accrued but untaken leave on termination.

The case law considered above in relation to the accrual of annual leave during sick leave is often relevant under *reg 14*: ie in determining how much leave a worker has accrued but not taken and in respect of which he is entitled to a payment in lieu on termination of employment. In particular, this issue may arise where a worker is dismissed on the ground of capability after a prolonged period of absence due to ill-health. In such cases, the Court of Appeal held in *Larner* that the accrued annual leave should include annual leave from previous leave years which the worker could not take due to ill-health. In particular Mummery LJ proposed that, in order to ensure consistency with the *Working Time Directive* a new *reg 14(5)* could be read into the *Regulations* to provide that:

> "Where a worker's employment is terminated and on the termination date he remains entitled to leave in respect of any previous leave year which carried over under regulation 13(9)(a) because of sick leave, the employer shall make him a payment in lieu equal to the sum due under regulation 16 for the period of untaken leave."

While this comment was *obiter* as the case was decided by the direct application of *art 7* of the *Working Time Directive*, it is almost certain to be followed in practice by Tribunals.

An employer may specify in a relevant agreement that, where a worker has at the date of his dismissal taken more than his accrued leave entitlement, he reimburse his employer, for example, by making a payment or undertaking additional work (*reg 14(4)*). In the absence of a relevant agreement, the employer will not be entitled to claw back payment for holidays taken but not accrued and no term can be implied which would allow such a claw back: see *Hill v Chapell* [2003] IRLR 19, EAT.

30.5   Notice requirements and when leave is taken

The procedures which must be complied with when a worker requests, or an employer refuses, annual leave, may be specified in a relevant agreement (*reg 15(5)*). In the absence of such an agreement, the provisions of *reg 15(1)–(4)* apply as follows. A worker must give notice of the dates he intends to take leave. The notice period must be equivalent to at least twice the period of leave he is proposing to take. An employer may refuse leave on the requested dates by serving a counter-notice on the worker at least as many days before the proposed leave commences as the number of days' leave refused. The employer may also require a worker to take all or part of his leave on certain dates by giving him notice of that requirement; the length of notice must be at least twice the period of leave he requires the worker to take. However the employer's right to require a worker not to take leave on particular days is restricted under *reg 13(12)* (see **30.3D** above) where it relates to leave carried over under the *Working Time (Coronavirus) (Amendment) Regulations 2020* – in such cases the employer must have a "good reason" for requiring leave not to be taken on a particular day. Good reason is not defined in the *2020 Regulations* and, in practice, Tribunals are likely to apply the concept of reasonableness in deciding whether there was a good reason for requiring leave carried over under the *2020 Regulations* not to be taken on particular days.

It is important to recognise that the notice provisions set out in *reg 15* may be varied or excluded by a relevant agreement (*reg 15(5)*): see *Industrial and Commercial Maintenance Ltd v Briffa* [2008] All ER (D) 105 (Sep). In *Briffa* the contract of employment provided that, following notice of the termination of employment, the employee would be required to take any outstanding annual leave during the notice period. The employee's notice period was only a week, and he had accrued 4 days' leave (so proper notice of leave could not be in accordance with *reg 15* which requires the advance notice of leave to be given at least twice as long before the leave is to be taken as the length of the period of leave). However, the EAT held that the contract amounted to a relevant agreement which varied *reg 15*. Accordingly, the employer was entitled to require the employee to take all his outstanding annual leave during his notice period.

The recent ECJ decision in *Kreuziger v Land Berlin*: C-619/16 [2019] CMLR 34 (as set out in section **30.3** above) might lead to a more flexible approach to taking annual leave. *Kreuziger* was a case about payment in lieu of accrued but untaken leave on termination of employment. However the ECJ made a number of comments about the importance of employers ensuring that workers have the opportunity to take annual leave.

Sumsion v BBC (Scotland) [2007] IRLR 678 is an extreme example of how an employer might make use of the entitlement to require a worker to take leave on certain days. Mr Sumsion was contracted to work a six day week (Monday to Saturday) during a fixed term contract. He was entitled to six days leave during this time and he requested that the leave be taken in a block. The BBC refused this request and required that he take a day's leave every second Saturday. The Employment Tribunal and EAT concluded that this was lawful and Mr Sumsion was receiving the annual leave to which he was entitled. The EAT may have been influenced in this decision by the short term nature of the contract as it commented that in certain cases this approach may have been unlawful if it did not permit a worker to take 'real' leave.

A similar conclusion was reached by the Supreme Court in *Russell v Transocean International Resources Ltd* [2012] ICR 185, [2012] IRLR 149 which related to the annual leave entitlements of oil field workers who worked a shift pattern of two weeks offshore, two weeks onshore. They were not required to work during the onshore periods. The Supreme Court upheld the decisions of the Court of Session and EAT that: (i) onshore periods could be treated as annual leave and (ii) the workers had been given notice, in accordance with *reg 15*, that annual leave was to be taken during the onshore periods. Accordingly, the workers' entitlement to annual leave was met during their 26 weeks onshore, and they could not claim a further 4 weeks' leave out of the periods they were scheduled to be on the rigs.

The decision in *Lyons v Mitie Security Ltd* [2010] ICR 628, [2010] IRLR 288 provides a further example of the operation of the notice requirements under the *Regulations*. Although the facts of the case were unusual, the EAT did have to decide an issue of more general importance, namely whether an employer was entitled, under the *Regulations*, to deny a worker's request for leave where this prevented the worker exercising his right to annual leave because, for example, the worker could not then take his or her remaining leave before the end of the leave year. This type of situation would commonly arise in cases where the worker requests annual leave towards the very end of the leave year. Will the employer be obliged either to grant the request to enable the worker to take their annual leave or to permit leave to be carried over? Or will the worker lose his or her entitlement at the end of the leave year? In *Lyons* the EAT held that, while an employer could not operate the notice requirements in an unreasonable, arbitrary or capricious way so as to deny any entitlement lawfully requested, there was no inalienable right to leave. Accordingly, a worker may lose their entitlement under the *Regulations* if he or she requests leave very late in the leave year and the employer genuinely cannot accommodate that request. Again, these issues are unlikely to arise that regularly in practice. Nonetheless, workers would be well advised to request holiday early. At the same time, as the EAT noted in *Lyons*, employers should consider whether any refusal of a request for leave may be unreasonable or lead to grievances and litigation. Following the ECJ decision in *Kreuziger v Land Berlin*: C-619/16 [2019] CMLR 34 it is distinctly possible that a Tribunal today would conclude that Mr Lyons did not have that opportunity to take his annual leave on these facts.

The right of an employer to require leave to be taken at certain times may, however, be restricted in certain situations. For example, in *Gomez (Merino) v Continental Industrias del Caucho SA*: C-342/01 [2004] ECR I-2605, [2005] ICR 1040, [2004] IRLR 407, the ECJ concluded that a worker returning from maternity leave had to be allowed to take her statutory leave entitlement even though it meant that she would take the leave outside the established periods for leave set out in a workforce agreement. See also, *Pereda and Landtirol*, considered at paragraph **30.3** above.

Finally, it should be noted that in *Bear Scotland Ltd v Fulton* [2015] ICR 221, [2015] IRLR 15 the EAT suggested at paragraph 82 that, in the absence of contractual agreement, the first four weeks of annual leave in any leave year should be treated as constituting the annual leave provided for by *reg 13(1)* of *Regulations*, and the subsequent 1.6 weeks as constituting additional annual leave under *reg 13A*.

30.6 Remedies

There are two potential statutory remedies available to workers whose rights to paid annual leave have been infringed: a claim under *reg 30* of the *Regulations*, or a claim for unlawful deductions of wages under *ERA 1996, Part II*. However, *reg 16* confirms that the *Regulations* do not confer a contractual right to paid holiday, so rights under the *Regulations* cannot be enforced by a breach of contract claim.

Reg 30 of the Working Time Regulations

A worker may complain to an Employment Tribunal that his employer has refused to allow him to take annual leave (*reg 30(1)(a)*) or has failed to pay him sums due in respect of leave which he has taken (*reg 30(1)(b)*). A complaint must be presented to the Tribunal within three months of the date of the act complained of. The Tribunal may also extend time where it considers it was not reasonably practicable for the worker to submit his claim within three months (*reg 30(2)*).

If the Employment Tribunal finds that a claim under *reg 30(1)(a)* (refusal to allow a worker to take annual leave) is well-founded, the Tribunal must make a declaration to that effect and, in addition, may order payment of such compensation as it considers just and equitable in all the circumstances, having regard to the employer's default in refusing to permit the worker to exercise his right, and any loss sustained by the worker as a consequence of that refusal (*regs 30(3)* and *30(4)*). In *Santos Gomes v Higher Level Care Ltd* [2018] EWCA Civ

418 the Court of Appeal confirmed that a Tribunal was not entitled to make an award for compensation for injury to feelings in respect of a breach of the *Working Time Regulations*. However, an award may be made for personal injury: see *Grange v Abellio London Ltd* UKEAT/0304/17/JOJ.

If the complaint is made under *reg 30(1)(b)* (failure to make a payment for leave taken during employment or leave accrued but untaken on termination), and the Tribunal finds that the complaint is well-founded it must order payment of the sum due for that period of leave (*reg 30(5)*).

Unlawful Deduction of Wages

In *Revenue and Customs v Stringer* [2009] UKHL 31, [2009] ICR 985, [2009] IRLR 677, the House of Lords confirmed that a claim for holiday pay to which a worker was entitled under the *Regulations* could be brought as a claim for unlawful deduction of wages under *ERA 1996, Part II*. In reaching this conclusion the House of Lords overturned the decision of the Court of Appeal ([2005] ICR 1149, [2005] IRLR 465) who had held that *reg 30* was intended to provide a single and exclusive regime for the enforcement of the statutory rights in the *Regulations*.

The right to bring a claim for unlawful deductions of wages under *ERA 1996, Part II* in relation to holiday pay was significant as *ERA 1996, Part II* provides that the time limit for presenting a claim where there has been a series of deductions of pay is 3 months from the date of the last deduction in the series (see *ERA 1996, s 23(3)*). Accordingly, a worker could potentially have brought a claim for a number of failures to permit paid holiday stretching back over a significant period of time (all the way back to introduction of the *Regulations* in 1998 – see *Coletta v Bath Hill Court* UKEAT/0200/17, a case in relation to the minimum wage which confirmed that the *Limitation Act 1980* did not apply to limit unlawful deductions claims to 6 years' back pay, as the *ERA 1996* provided its own time limit for such claims). By contrast to unauthorised deductions claims, *reg 30* does not have a provision dealing with a series of failures to pay holiday pay, so a separate claim has to be brought within 3 months of each failure.

There are, however, now two very significant limits on the extent to which a worker is entitled to recover the failure to pay for holidays over a period of time as a "series of deductions". These limits are:

• In *Bear Scotland Ltd v Fulton* [2015] ICR 221, [2015] IRLR 15 the EAT held that, for there to be a series of deductions, there had to be "a sufficient factual, and a sufficient temporal, link" between the deductions (paragraph 79). Accordingly, if there is a gap of 3 months or more between deductions, the passage of time will break the "temporal link" with the result that there is no "series" of deductions and the Tribunal's jurisdiction to consider the earlier deduction or deductions will be extinguished. This interpretation of "series of deductions" was novel, and it potentially greatly reduces the retrospective liability of employers for unpaid holiday pay (or indeed any other unauthorised deductions of pay). The claimants in these appeals (supported by their trade unions) did not seek to appeal this point to the Court of Appeal. However, given its ramifications, it is almost certain that the Court of Appeal (and possibly the Supreme Court) will be asked to consider this issue in the future. In the meantime in *Chief Constable of the Police Service of Northern Ireland v Agnew* [2019] IRLR 782, [2019] NICA 32, the Northern Ireland Court of Appeal did not follow the EAT's decision in the *Bear Scotland* and held that a series of deductions is not ended, as a matter of law, by a gap of more than 3 months between unlawful deductions, nor is it ended by a lawful payment. While a decision of the Northern Ireland Court of Appeal is not binding in Great Britain (while a decision of the EAT is binding) this decision is likely to be persuasive if this issue is again considered by the EAT or a higher court.

• The *Deduction from Wages (Limitation) Regulations 2014 (2014/3322)* amended *ERA 1996, s 23* to provide that a Tribunal can only consider unauthorised deductions claims in relation to holiday pay (and certain other payments including claims for fees, bonuses, commission, or other emoluments referable to employment) where payment fell due within the two–year period prior to the presentation of the claim. In effect this introduced a two–year cap on recovery of unauthorised deductions from wages. This new rule came into force for any claims presented to the Employment Tribunal on or after 1 July 2015. It has been suggested that this amendment may be either ultra vires (as the *Regulation* amending the *ERA 1996* was made under *European Communities Act 1972, s 2(2)* and it is arguable that these amendments do not arise out of the UK's obligations under European law) and/or that it is unlawful because it undermines the EU law principle of effectiveness.

In addition, as mentioned above, an unlawful deductions claim must be made within 3 months of the last in the series of deduction. Accordingly, in a holiday pay claim a Tribunal will need carefully to consider when the last deduction of holiday pay was made. The Employment Tribunal decision in *Khan v Martin McColl* (ET/1702926/09) (22 March 2010, unreported) illustrates the point. Mr Khan had been on long term sick leave. He resigned due to his illness in mid–2009 (at which point he had accrued but not taken leave from 2008 and 2009). The employer paid him in respect of his accrued but untaken leave for 2009. He brought a claim for payment of his untaken leave from 2008. The Tribunal held that Mr Khan's claim for unlawful deductions from wages in respect of the 2008 leave was out of time. As the employer had paid Mr Khan his 2009 holiday entitlement on termination of employment, the last of the series of deductions was prior to the start of 2009. This issue has not yet been tested on appeal. However, it is suggested that the argument that the last deduction was made on 31 December 2008 is questionable, given that under the *Regulations* payment in lieu of annual leave may only be made on the termination of employment. On that basis, the date for the payment of Mr Khan's leave which he could not take in 2008 due to illness (and which therefore could have been carried over to 2009) was the date his employment ended, rather than 31 December 2008.

A further issue arises in relation to whether unauthorised deductions claims can only be made where a worker has taken holiday and not been properly paid for it or whether such claims can also be made where a worker is not permitted to take holiday at all. The House of Lords in *Stringer* plainly envisaged that a worker could bring an unlawful deduction of wages claim in the former category – ie if the worker had taken holiday but not been paid for it. However, it is less clear whether such a claim should be available where the employer refuses to permit a worker to take paid holiday and the worker decides to work rather than take the holiday in order to avoid a loss of earnings. In such a case, as the worker has continued to attend work and be paid for doing so, he will earn the same as normal and there would be no deduction from wages. Instead the loss suffered by the worker would be the loss of the health, relaxation and other benefits associated with taking a period of annual leave. The *Regulations* recognise the distinction between these two scenarios and in the latter a Tribunal is entitled to award just and equitable compensation (see *regs 30(1)(a)* and *30(4)* of the *Regulations*). Where, however, a worker is not paid for holiday which is actually taken, the *Regulations* provide that the compensation must be the amount of money which ought to have been paid to the worker during the period of leave (see *regs 30(1)(b)* and *30(5)*).

Despite this distinction, in *Canada Life Ltd v Gray* [2004] ICR 673, [2004] All ER (D) 36 (Jan) the EAT concluded that a worker could bring an unlawful deductions claim in respect of his or her annual leave entitlement regardless of whether or not the leave had actually been taken, and that the series of deductions could extend back into previous leave years. More recently in *Fraser v Southwest London St George's Mental Health Trust* [2012] ICR 403, [2012] IRLR 100 the EAT took a different approach and suggested that a worker could not recover unpaid holiday as a deduction from wages where he or she had not actually taken the leave in question. A similar analysis was also adopted by the EAT in *Sash Window*

30.6 Holidays

Workshop Ltd v King [2015] IRLR 348: at paragraphs 37 and 38 the EAT noted that it was not obvious that an unauthorised deductions claim could be made in relation to a complaint based on refusal to permit a worker to take annual leave as the worker would have been paid his wages for the periods he worked which he would otherwise have taken as annual leave, and what had been lost was the health and welfare benefits of taking annual leave, not wages. It is suggested that the EAT's conclusions in *Fraser* and *King* on this issue were correct, and that the ECJ decision in *King*, which disagreed with part of the EAT's analysis, does not affect the EAT's approach to the scope of the remedy afforded by an unlawful deductions claims. (However, as set out above, the ECJ decision in King does mean that, where a worker has not taken holiday because he would not be paid, the worker will now be permitted to treat that holiday as rolling over into subsequent leave years and be entitled to receive payment in lieu on termination – or, arguably, to take that leave in subsequent leave years, rather than being required to bring a claim under *reg 30(1)(a)* during each leave year that his employer has refused to allow him to take paid annual leave.)

In addition to claims based on entitlements to annual leave under the *Regulations*, a worker may also be entitled to bring a claim for unlawful deduction of wages or breach of contract on the basis that, under his contract of employment, he was entitled to holiday pay or payment in lieu of accrued but untaken holiday. This will depend on the interpretation of the contract of employment and is discussed at paragraph **30.9** below.

30.7 Civil aviation, shipping and agricultural workers

Statutory leave entitlements for crew members employed in civil aviation are governed by the *Civil Aviation (Working Time) Regulations 2004, SI 2004/756* which implement the *Aviation Working Time Directive (2000/79/EC)*.

Regulation 4 provides that 'a crew member is entitled to paid annual leave of at least four weeks, or a proportion of four weeks in respect of a period of employment of less than one year'. As with the *Working Time Regulations*, this leave may be taken in instalments and may not be replaced by a payment in lieu, except where the crew member's employment is terminated, and the right is enforceable through a claim to the Employment Tribunals.

However, the *Civil Aviation (Working Time) Regulations 2004* do not contain any of the detailed mechanisms in the *Working Time Regulations* for determining when annual leave may be taken and the rate of pay during leave. They also have different provisions in relation to remedies.

These lacunae have been the source of a number of claims, most notably, *Williams v British Airways plc*: C-155/10 [2011] IRLR 948 (ECJ) and [2012] ICR 1375; [2012] IRLR 1014 (Supreme Court) (referred to in **30.4A** above) which concerned a claim by pilots who only received basic pay when they took annual leave despite the fact that when they were actually working they had a contractual entitlement to additional remuneration in the form of two supplements. The issue was what payment the pilots should receive during annual leave given that the *Civil Aviation (Working Time) Regulations 2004* did not make any provision for how pay should be calculated (unlike the *Working Time Regulations 1998* which expressly refer to *ERA 1996, ss 221–224*). The ECJ concluded that during annual leave workers must receive comparable or equivalent pay to what they receive when actually working, but that this did not include payments to cover expenses.

A further consequence of the lack of detailed provisions for calculating pay in the *Civil Aviation (Working Time) Regulations 2004* is that there is no definition of the period over which average or normal pay should be calculated (under the *ERA 1996*, the reference period is 12 weeks). However, the Supreme Court in *Williams* gave guidance that in cases under these *Regulations* the relevant reference period could be determined by the employer (and/or included a relevant agreement) provided that it was representative. Failing that, the Employment Tribunal should determine the length of the representative reference period so that the level of "normal" remuneration to be paid during annual leave could be calculated.

Specific regulations have also been made for certain other industries: see the *Fishing Vessels (Working Time: Sea-fishermen) Regulations 2004 (SI 2004/1713);* the *Merchant Shipping (Working Time: Inland Waterways) Regulations 2003 (SI 2003/3049)*; and the *Merchant Shipping (Hours of Work) Regulations 2002 (SI 2002/2125)*. In relation to agricultural workers, historically their holiday entitlements were set by the *Agricultural Wages Board* under the *Agricultural Wages Act 1948, s 3*, as substituted by *EPA 1975, s 97(1), Sch 9 Pt 1*. However, the Agricultural Wages Board was abolished in 2013 pursuant to the provisions of the *Enterprise and Regulatory Reform Act 2013*. Currently there are different provisions governing holiday entitlements for agricultural workers in each of England, Wales, Scotland and Northern Ireland.

30.8   CONTRACT

The *Working Time Regulations 1998* lay down a minimum paid annual holiday entitlement. The contract of employment may, however, make more generous provision than provided for by the *Regulations*. In such circumstances, the contract will determine the employee's rights in respect of that more generous provision.

Authorities on the common law on employee's rights to holidays which were decided before the *Regulations* came into force must now be read subject to those *Regulations*.

Employers who grant more than the statutory leave entitlements under the Directive should be aware of the risks of providing different amounts of annual leave to different classes of workers. For example, in *Kocur v Angard Staffing Solutions Limited* UKEAT/0181/17, the EAT held that the failure to provide an agency worker with the same annual leave entitlement as that enjoyed by the hirer's permanent employees could not be compensated for by an enhanced hourly rate of pay, and amounted to a breach of the *Agency Workers Regulations 2010*.

Particulars of holiday entitlement are among those the employer is obliged by the *Employment Rights Act 1996, s 1(4)(d)(i)* to supply in writing to the employee (see **8.7(g)** CONTRACT OF EMPLOYMENT). In the absence of express provisions, certain terms relating to holidays have been implied by the courts.

It is thought likely that in most industries, in the absence of express provision, it will be held to be an implied term of the contract of employment that bank holidays may be taken as paid holiday: see *Tucker v British Leyland Motor Corpn Ltd* [1978] IRLR 493 at 496, in which a County Court judge decided that ' . . . if no express contractual provision or regular usage to the contrary is established an hourly paid employee is entitled to a day's holiday on recognised public holidays without fear of dismissal as an absentee; and that if he is entitled to a guaranteed minimum weekly wage he is entitled to be paid for that day without having to work additional hours in that week.'

It was held in *Hurt v Sheffield Corpn* (1916) 85 LJKB 1684, that the right to a holiday accrued only at the end of the year in the absence of any express provision to the contrary. Although this does not accord with the normal modern practice, the Court of Appeal in *Morley v Heritage plc* [1993] IRLR 400 declined to disapprove the decision in *Hurt*.

In *Morley*, it was held that there was no implied term in the contract that the employee should be paid for accrued but untaken leave when he left part-way through the year. However, in an appropriate case it might be possible to imply such a term as a matter of custom and practice. The decision of the EAT in *Janes Solicitors v Lamb-Simpson* (1996) 541 IRLB 15 suggests that in the case of an oral contract where there is nothing in writing, there is a wide area over which terms could be implied on the basis of business efficacy, including one as to accrued holiday pay. In addition, in *Wang v Beijing Ton Ren Tang (UK) Ltd* (UKEAT/0024/09/DA) [2010] All ER (D) 84 (Jan), the EAT held that a provision in a worker's contract that, on the termination of her employment, the worker could recover pay in lieu of all untaken holiday (ie not just untaken holiday from the final leave year) was valid and not contrary to the *Regulations* (which, as explained above, prohibit in most cases the carrying over of leave from one year to the next). Accordingly, where a worker's contact includes such a term, and the worker has untaken leave from a number of leave years, he or she should claim under the contract rather than the *Regulations*. However, in the absence of any term on the payment of accrued but untaken leave, a claim could be brought under the *Regulations* in respect of untaken leave in the last leave year (see **30.4** above).

The contract may also provide that the employer is entitled, on the termination of employment, to claw back payment for holidays taken by the worker but not accrued. However, in the absence of an express provision of the contract of employment, no term can be implied which would allow such a claw back: see *Hill v Chapell* [2003] IRLR 19, EAT. Not only would a deduction in the absence of express agreement be contrary to the *Regulations*, it could also be an unlawful deduction from wages under *section 13* of the *Employment Rights Act 1996*, and a breach of contract.

Where there is a contractual entitlement to pay due under the contract for accrued but untaken holiday the contract may also make express provision as to how that entitlement is calculated. In the absence of such provision, there is inconsistent EAT authority as to how the rate of a day's pay should be calculated where the worker is paid an annual salary. The two approaches adopted have been to divide annual salary by 365 or to divide it by the actual number of working days. Obviously the former calculation will mean that the worker is entitled to lower payment for each untaken day of accrued holiday. In *Thames Water Utilities v Reynolds* [1996] IRLR 186 the EAT concluded that the *Apportionment Act 1870* applied with the result that a day's pay was to be calculated by dividing annual salary by 365. In *Taylor v East Midlands Offender Employment Consortium* [2000] IRLR 760 the EAT accepted that the *Apportionment Act* did apply in calculating a day's pay. However, on the facts of the case, the pay for the employee's 10 days accrued but untaken holiday were 'grossed up' to 14 days pay to take account of weekends necessarily included in the 10–day holiday period. Thus the EAT found a way to mitigate the apparent harshness of the decision in *Thames Water*.

Subsequently (at a preliminary hearing) in *Leisure Leagues UK Ltd v Maconnachie* [2002] IRLR 600 the EAT concluded that the approach in *Thames Water* was wrong for two reasons. First, the approach was at odds with the virtually universal practice in industry in respect of the calculation of holiday pay in respect of holiday entitlement which is by reference to a day's work rather than calendar days per year. Second, *Thames Water* predated the *Working Time Regulations*. The issue was resolved by *Yarrow v Edwards Chartered Accountants* [2007] All ER (D) 118 (Aug), in which HHJ Peter Clarke (who had also sat on *Thames Water*) declined to follow his own decision in *Thames Water* and, instead, applied *Maconnachie*. His reasons for doing so were that: (i) judicial comity required him to follow the more recent decision, and (ii) in any event the advent of the *Regulations* required a different approach than that which had been adopted in *Thames Water*.

31   Human Rights

31.1   INTRODUCTION TO HUMAN RIGHTS AND EMPLOYMENT

The employment relationship may give rise to issues involving human rights law. At the individual level, human rights law may give an employee important protection against acts of discrimination or protect the employee's privacy or right to a fair hearing. Similarly, in relation to collective labour relations, human rights law is relevant to the right of members of a trade union to associate, to join a trade union of their choice and to take part in industrial action.

From 2 October 2000, with the coming into force of the *Human Rights Act 1998*, the domestic courts have been required to interpret United Kingdom law in accordance with the provisions of the European Convention on Human Rights and Fundamental Freedoms ('the Convention'). Prior to the *Act* coming into force, the Convention did not form part of the domestic law of the UK but was an international obligation which could, in appropriate cases, be used as an aid to the interpretation of unclear UK statutory provisions. An aggrieved individual seeking to rely upon the Convention was required to seek to present a case to the European Court of Human Rights ('ECtHR') for the determination of that court. This process could be expensive and very slow. Whilst the right of petition to the European Court remains as the final source of determination and jurisprudence on Convention Rights, issues of Convention rights are now be determined directly in the UK domestic courts.

This chapter presents an overview of the Convention and the historical development of the rights most relevant to the employment relationship, identifying some of the key decisions of the European Court of Human Rights and instances where Convention principles have assisted the UK courts in interpreting statutory provisions. The chapter goes on to consider, in outline, the key provisions of the *Human Rights Act* and its application and recent UK decisions in the employment sphere raising issues under the *Act*.

31.2   THE CONVENTION

Effect of the Convention

The European Convention on Human Rights and Fundamental Freedoms is an international treaty which was drawn up in 1950 and came into force in 1953. The Convention sets out in broad terms a number of fundamental rights and freedoms. It also established the European Commission of Human Rights and the European Court of Human Rights, both based in Strasbourg. It should be emphasised that the Convention and its institutions are entirely separate from the law and institutions of the European Community. The subscribing states are the members of the Council of Europe. Also, unlike European Community Law, the provisions of the Convention are not part of domestic law; they only bind the Government. The main text of the Convention, which has been amended by several protocols, can be found in Command Paper *Cmd 8969* (1953), published by the Stationery Office.

If a state which is a party to the Convention interferes with or abrogates any of the rights or freedoms enshrined in the Convention, a complaint may be made by any other party state. More importantly, the Convention allows for a right of direct complaint by an *individual* affected by an alleged breach of the Convention (such an individual right of complaint is very rare in international law). The Government of the United Kingdom ratified the Convention in 1950. However, it was not until 1966 that the UK Government recognised the jurisdiction of the European Court of Human Rights and accepted the right of an individual in the UK to petition the court.

31.3 Procedure for petition by an individual

In outline the procedure is as follows. The aggrieved individual must pursue every remedy available under UK law. When he has exhausted these 'domestic' remedies, without having his complaint satisfactorily resolved, he may present his petition to the European Commission of Human Rights. The Commission investigates the complaint. If it decides that there is, or may be, a breach of the Convention and that the complaint is admissible, it will endeavour to obtain a settlement between the parties. If no settlement is reached, the Commission will refer the case, together with its report, to the European Court of Human Rights. The court will then proceed to decide on the complaint.

UK legal aid is not available for petition, but limited legal aid is available from the Council of Europe. ECtHR cases are now also among the limited categories of litigation in which English lawyers are now permitted to work on a conditional fee basis.

31.4 KEY DECISIONS OF THE ECTHR ON FREEDOM OF ASSOCIATION, THE RIGHT TO PRIVATE LIFE AND OTHER RELEVANT PROVISIONS

One of the most significant cases concerning UK collective employment law to reach the European Court of Human Rights was the British Rail closed shop case, *Young, James and Webster v United Kingdom* [1981] IRLR 408, [1983] IRLR 35.

Article 11 of the Convention provides:

'1.   Everyone has the right to . . . freedom of association with others, including the right to form and to join trade unions for the protection of his interests.
2.   No restrictions shall be placed on the exercise of these rights . . . [certain exceptions permitted].'

In the *Young, James and Webster* case, the court held that the requirement on the applicants to join one of the unions specified in the closed shop agreement between British Rail and the railway unions, in circumstances where there had been no such requirement at the time when they were engaged, amounted to a restriction on the freedom guaranteed by *art 11* because the alternative to their joining was that they would lose their jobs ([1981] IRLR 408 at 409). The court made substantial monetary awards to the applicants.

The decision left the general question of the consistency of closed shop agreements with *art 11* unclear. Now that the right of individuals not to join a specified trade union has been entrenched and the pre-entry closed shop has been outlawed (see TRADE UNIONS – I (51)), it has become less important to resolve that issue. However, in *Sibson v United Kingdom* (1993) 17 EHRR 193, the court held that there was no breach of *art 11* where the complainant had no objection based on conviction to being a member of the union concerned, and where non-membership would not lead to dismissal (but rather to a move to another depot at which he could be required to work under his contract); contrast *Sigurjonsson v Iceland* (1993) 16 EHRR 462.

In a further important decision of collective employment rights (*Wilson and NUJ v United Kingdom*; *Palmer, Wyeth and RMT v United Kingdom*; *Doolan v United Kingdom* [2002] IRLR 568) the ECtHR ruled that the UK was in breach of the right of freedom of association under *art 11* by permitting employers to use financial incentives to persuade employees to surrender trade union rights (see *TULR(C)A 1992, s 146(1)(a)*). This is the first case in which the ECtHR has upheld a claim relating to trade union rights under *art 11*.

(For example, in the past, a complaint by workers at GCHQ that they were not permitted to belong to trade unions was not referred to the court by the Commission, which accepted the Government's argument based upon national security.) The *Wilson* decision prompted the introduction of *s 29* of the *Employment Relations Act 2004* which introduced new sections into *TULR(C)A 1992* conferring a right upon workers not to have an offer made by the employer for the purpose of inducing the worker not to be a member of a union or to take part in the activities of the union.

The corollary of the right to associate is the right to disassociate, which arose for consideration in *Associated Society of Locomotive Engineers and Firemen v United Kingdom (Application No 11002/05)* [2007] IRLR 361, ECtHR. The case involved the expulsion of a trade union member who was a member of the BNP. The Court held that the issue was the balance between the individual's right to associate and the right of the union to disassociate. *Article 11* did not place an obligation on the union to admit anyone who wished to join, particularly as an individual's livelihood was not dependent upon membership of a union and collectively bargained benefits would apply to all employees whether union members or not. Accordingly, the expulsion did not breach the ECtHR.

The substantive nature of the associative rights protected by *art 11* was significantly expanded by the decision of the ECtHR in *Demir v Turkey* [2009] IRLR 766. Previous decisions, whilst upholding the right to join (or not join) trade unions, had not held that the associative right extended to a right to bargain collectively or enter into collective agreements. In *Demir* the ECtHR held that such a substantive right must now be recognised as "the right to bargain collectively with the employer has, in principle, become one of the essential elements of the right to form and join trade unions". Moreover, the ECtHR stated that there may in addition be "positive obligations" on the State to secure effective enjoyment of the right to collectively bargain.

Another area of employment law to which the Convention might be relevant is picketing (see STRIKES AND INDUSTRIAL ACTION **(46)**), given that *arts 10* and *11* protect freedom of expression and assembly (see *Middlebrook Mushrooms Ltd v TGWU* [1993] IRLR 232 at para 25). In *Unison v United Kingdom* [2002] IRLR 497, the ECtHR dismissed an application in relation to an alleged breach of *art 11* rights by the imposition of an injunction restraining a strike which fell outside the definition of a 'trade dispute' (see STRIKES AND INDUSTRIAL ACTION **(46)**). The ECtHR concluded that a prohibition upon a strike was a restriction on the freedom of association right in *art 11(1)*. The restraint was, however, in compliance with *art 11(2)* as a proportionate measure necessary in a democratic society for the protection of others (in this case, the employer). The point of significance in the case is the recognition that restraint upon the right to strike may, in appropriate circumstances, be a breach of *art 11*. In *Guler v Turkey* [2018] IRLR 880 a disciplinary warning imposed for absence from work without permission whilst taking part in a trade union demonstration was found to breach *Art 11* as the employee was exercising his right to freedom of assembly and the sanction was such as to dissuade participation in trade union activities. In *Association of Academics v Iceland* [2019] IRLR 189 a prohibition on further strikes and imposition of compulsory arbitration in the context of an ongoing trade dispute was found not to breach *art 11* as the particular restrictions were necessary in a democratic society as there was a risk to public safety in the context of strike action in the hospital and healthcare sectors. In *Ognevenko v Russia* [2019] IRLR 195 the dismissal of a train driver for taking part in industrial action in circumstances where strikes by those providing train service was prohibited by legislation, breached *art 11* as the prohibition did not satisfy the test of a pressing social need.

In *Redfearn v United Kingdom* [2013] IRLR 151 the ECtHR held that the dismissal of a bus driver, who was dismissed by his employer when he was elected as a local councillor representing the British National Party and in relation to whom there was no remedy in UK law for dismissal on grounds of political opinion or affiliation, was a contravention of *art 11* read in the light of *art 10*. In that case unfair dismissal would have provided a remedy but the claimant did not have the requisite period of qualifying service. The UK government's arguments on justification for the qualifying period failed as, in other areas requiring protection (for example whistleblowing), no qualifying period was required. Thus the exclusion of the claimant from the protection of unfair dismissal was not proportionate and, hence, an infringement of *art 11* rights.

Article 10 has also been invoked (unsuccessfully) as part of a challenge to the statutory restrictions upon the political activities of certain local government employees (*NALGO v Secretary of State for the Environment* (1992) 5 Admin LR 785 and see **38.2** PUBLIC SECTOR EMPLOYEES). However, in *Vogt v Germany* (1995) 21 EHRR 205, the court held that the dismissal of a teacher employed in a state school on the grounds of membership of the German Communist Party breached *arts 10* and *11* of the Convention. In *Heinisch v Germany* [2011] IRLR 922, ECtHR the ECtHR considered a dismissal following an instance of "whistleblowing". It was held that *art 10* was engaged and, accordingly, the employer had a legitimate interest in protecting its business reputation, and so the question became whether the sanction of dismissal used against the employee had been proportionate. The court held on the facts that it was not. In *Szima v Hungary* [2013] IRLR 59 the ECtHR held that the demotion and fining of a union official who posted articles critical of the police on a website was not a breach of *art 10* as the actions pursued the legitimate aim of preserving order in the police force and was necessary in a democratic society. In *Herbai v Hungary* [2020] IRLR 159 the ECtHR held that the protection of *art 10* applied to statements made to a professional audience (in that case a knowledge sharing website). Relevant to whether *art 10* was engaged and breached was the nature of the speech in issue, the author's motives and the damage (if any) caused by the speech contrasted with the severity of any sanction imposed by the employer. In that case dismissal of the employee absent evidence of specific harm caused to the employer was a violation of *art 10*.

Article 14 provides that the rights conferred by the Convention are to be exercised without any discrimination on grounds of *inter alia* race or sex (see, eg *Schuler-Zgraggen v Switzerland* (1993) 16 EHRR 405).

In *Halford v United Kingdom* [1997] IRLR 471, *art 8* of the Convention which protects private and family life was successfully invoked by a United Kingdom employee before the European Court of Human Rights. The court held that the applicant, a former Police Assistant Chief Constable, had been subjected to telephone tapping by her employer in an attempt to gather material to be used against her in a sex discrimination claim she was pursuing against her employer. The court in an important judgment held that such recording, without the knowledge of the employee, was a breach of the right to private life and correspondence. The applicant was awarded £10,000 compensation for non-pecuniary loss. *Halford* was considered in *Copland v United Kingdom* [2007] 45 EHRR 37 where the ECtHR held that *art 8(1)* was infringed when a public sector employer monitored, collected and stored personal information relating to an employee's telephone, e-mail and internet usage at work.

Further, in the important case of *Smith and Grady v United Kingdom* [1999] IRLR 734, the European Court of Human Rights concluded that a ban on homosexuals in employment contravenes the right to respect for private life (*art 8*). As is well known, the UK armed forces did not permit homosexual men or women to serve. Persons known to be homosexual were the subject of an 'administrative discharge' from the armed services. The applicants brought test cases challenging their discharges by way of judicial review in the UK courts, alleging that the policy banning homosexuals was a breach of the *ECtHR* and the *EC Equal Treatment Directive*. The domestic challenges were ultimately unsuccessful. Before the European Court of Human Rights, however, the applicants were successful, the court finding that the investigation into their homosexuality and their subsequent discharge from the armed forces violated *art 8*. The court concluded that such investigations were not 'necessary in a democratic society' (*art 8(2)*). The court further found that there was an infringement of *art 13* in that there was 'no effective remedy' before a national authority in relation to the violation of the right to respect for their private lives. A supplementary alleged violation of *art 3* ('degrading treatment or punishment') was not, however, made out on the facts. The court stated, nevertheless, that treatment on the basis of a bias against a homosexual minority could, in principle, fall within the scope of *art 3* but a minimum level of severity of treatment was required to bring such action within the scope of that article. The court held that it was not necessary to examine an alleged violation of *art 10* (right to freedom of expression) but commented that the silence imposed on the applicants in relation to their sexual orientation could not be ruled out as a potential interference with freedom of expression. In a further case, *Salgueiro da Silva Mouta v Portugal* [2001] 1 FCR 653, ECtHR, the ECtHR found that denial of the right to visit the child by a male homosexual was a breach of *arts 8* and *14*. In *Goodwin v United Kingdom* [2002] IRLR 664, the ECtHR held that the UK's failure to give legal recognition to gender reassignment was a breach of *arts 8* and *12* (the right to marry). *Goodwin* was considered by the House of Lords in *A v Chief Constable of West Yorkshire Police* [2004] UKHL 21, [2004] IRLR 573, [2004] 3 All ER 145, a case involving discrimination by the police against a transsexual. The House of Lords held that such discrimination was contrary to the provisions of the *EC Equal Treatment Directive* and, accordingly, recourse was not needed to reliance upon human rights law.

In *Pay v United Kingdom* (Application 32792/05) [2009] IRLR 139, the ECtHR considered *art 8* in the context of a United Kingdom dismissal case. The claimant, a probation officer working with sex offenders, had brought an unfair dismissal claim. His employers having discovered his involvement in the merchandising of bondage and sadomasochistic products and other matters took the view that these activities were incompatible with his position as a probation officer and in particular one working with sex offenders. The issue before the ECtHR was whether this dismissal was an infringement of the claimant's right to respect for his private life. The ECtHR concluded that notwithstanding the 'public' nature of the activities in question, *art 8* protection still applied but that the dismissal was proportionate to the legitimate aim pursued, namely protecting the reputation of the probation service. In the light of this decision it would seem that the ambit of what is private life will not be subject to a simple division between a private and public place but that, even when *art 8* is engaged, it is likely that dismissal will be justified on the reputational damage basis in many cases, although such a response must be a proportionate one in the circumstances.

Monitoring of an employee's email and other correspondence in employment by the employer is an important issue and has been considered by the ECtHR in *Barbulescu v Romania* [2016] IRLR 235. The employer had an express prohibition against the use of computers for private purposes. The claimant breached this rule by using a messenger account for private purposes and was dismissed. The breach of policy was disclosed by the employer's monitoring of the relevant account. The ECtHR found that *art 8* was engaged on the facts as the applicant's private life and correspondence were affected. The ECtHR further held that the employer's access to the account was legitimate on the assumption that the material contained related to work activities and that it was not unreasonable for an employer to seek to verify that professional tasks were being completed during working hours and that the extent of monitoring involved was limited in scope and proportionate. The majority of the ECtHR placed particular emphasis on the fact that the employer had an express policy forbidding personal use of the account or the company's computers (although the company did not have an express internet surveillance policy) and that the employee had not put forward any convincing reason for his personal use. Accordingly, a fair balance was struck between respect for the applicant's private life and the employer's legitimate interests. *Art 8* may also be engaged in relation to an employer's use of information relating to the employee's health. *Barbulescu v Romania* returned to the Grand Chamber of the ECtHR ([2017] IRLR 1032) on a further appeal and. by a majority, the applicant's complaint was upheld as, notwithstanding the prohibition on personal internet use which had been brought to the applicant's notice, he was unaware of the extent of the monitoring and also unaware that the employer might have access to the content of the communications. It was held that *art 8* was to be given a wide interpretation applying to private communications within or from the workplace. The ECtHR set out a number of factors to be considered including (i) the extent to which the employee was aware of the nature of monitoring, (ii) the extent of the monitoring, (iii) the legitimacy of the employer's reasons for monitoring, (iv) the extent to which other less intrusive measures could be adopted, (v) the consequences to the employees and (vi) the extent of safeguards in place.

In *Surikov v Ukraine* [2017] IRLR 377, ECtHR, an employer, in refusing promotions to an employee, considered old medical evidence relating to the employee's mental health, which information predated the promotion decisions by at least 15 years. The court held that there was a breach of *art 8*. Whilst an employer had a legitimate interest in assessing an employee's fitness, in that case a fair balance was not struck between that interest and the employee's interest in the privacy of his personal information.

The issue of covert surveillance was considered in *Vukota-Bojic v Switzerland* [2017] IRLR 94. Following surveillance of the applicant by private investigators engaged by an insurance company, the insurance company stopped making payments to the applicant. The ECtHR found that *art 8* was certainly engaged. Significantly the court found that such surveillance was not "in accordance with law" for the purposes of *art 8(2)* and accordingly the claim succeeded without the need to consider the proportionality of the interference. This decision may be of considerable significance in the employment context. Similarly, in *Lopez Ribalda v Spain* [2018] IRLR 358, a case which did arise in the employment context, the issue was the use of hidden surveillance cameras in the workplace (a supermarket) to monitor stock losses. The employees were informed of the introduction of visible surveillance cameras but were not informed of the introduction also of hidden surveillance cameras to monitor possible employee thefts. The ECtHR held that *art 8* was breached as the surveillance was not proportionate. On appeal to the Grand Chamber of the ECtHR (*Lopez Ribalda v Spain* [2020] IRLR 60 held that there was no breach of *art 8*. Drawing on *Barbulescu v Romania* [2016] IRLR 235 (above) the court held that relevant factors included whether the employee had been notified of the possibly of surveillance measures, the extent of the monitoring and the degree of intrusion into the employee's privacy and whether the employer had provided a legitimate reason to justify the monitoring holding that the more intrusive the surveillance the more weighty the justification required would be.

Denial of access to the courts and the rights conferred by *art 6* have also arisen in the employment context before the ECtHR. In *Fogarty v United Kingdom* [2002] IRLR 148 an employee of the US Embassy in London had successfully brought a sex discrimination claim. In relation to subsequent victimisation proceedings following non-appointment to other posts, the US claimed immunity under the *State Immunity Act 1978*. The complainant complained of a breach of *art 6(1)* on the grounds of denial of access to the courts. The ECtHR held that the claim fell within *art 6(1)* but that sovereign immunity was an aspect of international law and within the margin of appreciation allowed to states to limit access to the courts. By contrast the ECtHR ruled that there was a contravention of the *art 6* right to a fair hearing in *Sabeh El Leil v France* [2011] IRLR 781 where a French court dismissed the unfair dismissal claim of an employee of the Kuwaiti embassy (a French national employed as an accountant) because Kuwait had State immunity against court actions in France. Exclusion from the jurisdiction had to be justified and here it was not. As such this decision may have implications for the UK and the general immunity conferred by the *State Immunity Act 1978*. In *Devlin v United Kingdom* [2002] IRLR 155 the ECtHR held that, in the context of a discrimination claim, the issue by the Secretary of State of a national security certificate blocking proceedings in the tribunal was a disproportionate restriction on the applicant's right of access to the courts and, accordingly, a breach *of art 6(1)*. Damages of £10,000 were awarded. See also *Devenney v United Kingdom* (2002) Times, 11 April, [2002] ECHR 24265/94 where a similar judgment was given by the ECtHR and the same sum awarded by way of damages.

In *Somjee v United Kingdom* [2002] IRLR 886 the judicial process in the Employment Tribunal and the Employment Appeal Tribunal was found wanting. At the end of various hearings it had taken eight years for Ms Somjee's discrimination and unfair dismissal complaints to be fully dealt with and more than seven years in the case of her victimisation claim. The ECtHR held that a significant proportion of the blame for the delay rested with the Employment Tribunal and the Employment Appeal Tribunal and that such delay constituted a violation of the right to a fair hearing 'within a reasonable time' under *art 6* of the Convention. Ms Somjee was awarded 5,000 euros plus costs.

Article 3, although headed "prohibition on torture", has recently been applied in the employment context as it prohibits *"inhuman or degrading treatment or punishment"*. In *Hovhannisyan v Armenia* [2019] IRLR 99 the ECtHR held that workplace harassment could be a violation of *art 3* on this basis if the treatment attains a minimum level of severity which depends on all of the circumstances including the nature and context of the treatment, the duration and effects and also the age, health and sex of the victim.

31.5   THE POSITION PRIOR TO THE HUMAN RIGHTS ACT 1998: THE CONVENTION AS AN AID TO INTERPRETATION

Prior to the coming into force of the *Human Rights Act 1998*, as the Convention was not incorporated in UK law, it could not be relied upon directly in domestic courts and tribunals. However, it was, like other treaties, cited on the basis that Parliament is presumed to have intended to legislate consistently with the UK's international obligations unless the contrary intention appears. But there was no scope for such a presumption to operate where the statutory words were clear. The position was reviewed by the House of Lords in *R v Secretary of State for the Home Department, ex p Brind* [1991] 1 All ER 720 and in *Derbyshire County Council v Times Newspapers Ltd* [1993] AC 534, [1993] 1 All ER 1011.

In a number of cases the UK courts showed a willingness to apply Convention principles as an aid to interpretation of domestic law. By way of example, in *Camelot Group plc v Centaur Communications Ltd* [1998] IRLR 80, [1998] 1 All ER 251 the Court of Appeal upheld an order for the delivery up to the plaintiff of confidential information sent to a journalist (employed by the defendant) by an employee of Camelot. The purpose of Camelot seeking the order was to identify their disloyal employee. The Court of Appeal in applying *s 10* of the *Contempt of Court Act 1981* (which gives certain protections to journalists from disclosure of their sources of information) held that the domestic court would give the greatest weight to the judgments of the European Court of Human Rights in cases where the facts are similar to the case before the domestic court, and considered in detail the ECtHR's decision in *Goodwin v United Kingdom* [1996] 22 EHRR 123. Under the *Human Rights Act 1998*, the courts are required to adopt such an approach where issues of Convention rights are raised (see **31.6** and **31.7** below).

It is also material to note that the jurisprudence of the European Court of Justice, applying EUROPEAN UNION LAW (25) (which *is* part of English law), is heavily influenced by the Convention (see eg *R v Kirk*: 63/83 [1985] 1 All ER 453). See also *Grant v South-West Trains Ltd*: C-249/96 [1998] IRLR 206, ECJ, a case on discrimination against homosexual persons brought under *art 141* (formerly *art 119*) of the EC Treaty in which the ECJ considered some of the jurisprudence on, and relevant articles of, the European Convention on Human Rights.

31.6   HUMAN RIGHTS ACT 1998

The *Human Rights Act 1998* (which received Royal Assent on 9 November 1998) came into force on 2 October 2000 and is a radical reform of the status of the Convention in domestic law. The *Act* requires that the courts interpret United Kingdom law in accordance with the Convention. *Section 1* of the *HRA 1998* lists those articles of the Convention to which the *Act* is to apply and those articles are set out as *Sch 1* to the *Act*. By *HRA 1998, s 2* a court or tribunal determining a question in connection with a Convention right must take into account relevant judgments, decisions, declarations and opinions made or given by the Commission and Court of Human Rights and the Committee of Ministers of the Council of Europe. Primary and subordinate legislation are to be read, wherever possible, as being compatible with Convention rights but are not rendered void if incompatible (*HRA 1998, s 3*). Certain courts will be given the power to make a declaration of incompatibility when satisfied that the provision of primary legislation is incompatible with a Convention right (*HRA 1998, s 4*). This power does not, however, extend to an employment tribunal or the EAT. Accordingly, a detailed consideration of the *Act* is beyond the scope of this work.

The effect of the *Act*, as more cases are brought in domestic law relying upon Convention rights, is likely to be considerable in many fields; not least employment law, where *art 6* (the right to a fair hearing), *art 8* (the right to respect for private and family life), and also *arts 10, 11* and *14* (considered in **31.4** above) are likely to be of the greatest importance. The *Act* makes it unlawful for a 'public authority' to act in contravention of the Convention (*HRA 1998, s 6*). Those aggrieved will be able to bring proceedings against the authority in question (*HRA 1998, s 7*). The definition of 'public authority' is broad and includes any body whose function is of a public nature (*HRA 1998, s 6(3)*) and includes, expressly, courts and tribunals. The definition would appear to be sufficiently broad to apply to, for example, privatised public utilities.

The *Act* provides for remedies including an award of damages analogous to the principles applied by the European Court of Human Rights in relation to compensation (*HRA 1998, s 8*). Ministers of the Crown are given the power to amend offending legislation following a declaration of incompatibility (*HRA 1998, s 10*). Finally, in relation to any new legislation, a Minister of the Crown is required in either House prior to the second reading of the Bill to make a statement that the provisions of the Bill are compatible with the Convention rights or to state that, despite incompatibility, the Government wishes the House to proceed with the Bill in any event (*HRA 1998, s 19*).

31.7   THE APPLICATION OF THE HUMAN RIGHTS ACT 1998 IN EMPLOYMENT CASES

A number of cases have arisen in employment law raising issues under the *Human Rights Act 1998* particularly in relation to the right to a fair hearing (*art 6*) and the right to private and family life (*art 8*). The paragraphs below provide illustrations. As a point of procedure, it is to be observed that the Court of Appeal has sought to discourage a perceived tendency for Employment Tribunals to treat EC and human rights issues as appropriate for determination as preliminary issues (see *Barracks v Coles (Secretary of State for the Home Department intervening)* [2006] EWCA Civ 1041, [2007] IRLR 73, [2007] ICR 60). In the light of this, it is likely that such arguments will have to be raised as part of the full hearing of the claim rather than at a preliminary point.

(a) Article 6

Article 6 provides for 'a fair and public hearing within a reasonable time by an independent and impartial tribunal.' Its application has been considered in a variety of employment related contexts with the issue of its application to disciplinary proceedings in particular generating a substantial body of law. In summary the majority of internal disciplinary proceedings will not engage *art 6* if the employee has the right to bring proceedings in the employment tribunal in satisfaction of the requirements of *art 6*.

A-G v Wheen [2001] IRLR 91 concerned *s 33* of the *Employment Tribunals Act 1996* which permitted the Attorney General to make a restriction of proceedings order against a litigant barring him from bringing further proceedings without the leave of the EAT on the grounds of vexatious institution of proceedings. The Court of Appeal held that *s 33* did not conflict with the right to a fair hearing under *art 6(1)* of the *Convention*. The Court of Appeal stated that the right under *art 6(1)* was not an absolute right but was to be balanced between the rights of the citizen to use the courts and the rights of others (and the court) to avoid wholly unmeritorious claims. Further, the order made *did* provide for access to the Employment Tribunal system but required permission first. As access was not prohibited, but was provided on terms, there could be no breach of *art 6(1)*.

In *Tehrani v United Kingdom Central Council for Nursing, Midwifery and Health Visiting* [2001] IRLR 208, 2001 SLT 879, the issue was to what extent *art 6* of the *Convention* (namely, the entitlement 'to a fair and reasonable public hearing within a reasonable time by an independent and impartial tribunal established by law') applied to disciplinary proceedings other than in a court of law. Whilst *art 6* may not apply to purely internal disciplinary inquiries, it was held in *Tehrani* that, when disciplinary proceedings determine the right to practise a profession, *art 6* may apply, as the decision of the Council's Professional Conduct Committee fell within a 'determination' of 'civil rights and obligations' for the purposes of *art 6*. It followed that there was an entitlement to a hearing before an independent and impartial tribunal. However, the Court of Session held that a professional disciplinary tribunal was not required to meet all the requirements of an independent and impartial tribunal if the disciplinary procedures provided for a right of appeal to a court of law. The Court of Session, following a review of relevant authorities, concluded that the case law of the ECtHR established that there was no breach of the Convention if the disciplinary tribunal is subject to the control of a court of full jurisdiction, which court complies with the requirements of *art 6(1)*. This case raises important questions in relation to professional disciplinary bodies which do not have a statutory right of appeal to a court. If the disciplinary body is not sufficiently independent or important to satisfy *art 6(1)*, it is not clear whether a right to present subsequent complaints in an Employment Tribunal will be sufficiently akin to a statutory right of appeal to satisfy the exception recognised in the jurisprudence of the ECtHR.

In *Kulkarni v Milton Keynes Hospital NHS Trust* [2009] IRLR 829 the Court of Appeal held, in the context of a doctor facing serious disciplinary charges, that the doctor was entitled to be represented by a lawyer instructed by the Medical Protection Society. The facts of the case were unusual in that there was an express contractual term permitting representation by various persons, including a legally qualified person who "will not be representing the practitioner formally in a legal capacity". Holding the words quoted above to be devoid of meaning the Court of Appeal concluded that the doctor was entitled contractually to be represented by a lawyer instructed by the MPS. Of broader significance, it appeared, were Lady Justice Smith's (*obiter*) observations on *art 6*. Whilst *art 6* would not be engaged in ordinary disciplinary proceedings, where the effect of the disciplinary proceedings could deprive the employee of the right to practise his or her profession *art 6* could, in Smith LJ's view, be engaged conferring the right to legal representation. Thus where the outcome could be effectively barring from employment in the NHS the right would be engaged. This reasoning if correct would, *prima facie*, be applicable to a large number of occupations where a decision to dismiss by an employer would have the effect of freezing the employee out of employment in his chosen field. See, however, the discussion of *Mattu v University Hospitals of Coventry and Warwickshire NHS Trust* [2012] EWCA Civ 641, [2012] IRLR 661, [2012] 4 All ER 359 below.

The scope of application of *Kulkarni* was, in practice, very limited (and see, in *R (on the application of Kirk) v Middlesbrough Borough Council* [2010] IRLR 699, a case involving a disciplinary hearing in relation to a social worker, in which *art 6* was held not to be engaged).

Similarly, in *Hameed v Central Manchester University Hospital NHS Foundation Trust* [2010] EWHC 2009 (QB), [2011] All ER (D) 11 (May) the High Court held that *Kulkarni* (above) was exceptional and that each case must be considered on its own facts in the light of the gravity of the charge, the likelihood of dismissal and the individual's chance of practising their profession in the future if dismissed. On the facts this was not a case where the practising of the profession would be lost. Accordingly, there was no right to rely upon *art 6* in relation to the disciplinary process. Leave to appeal on the *art 6* point was, however, granted.

In an important decision, *R (on the application of G) v Governors of X School* [2011] IRLR 756, [2011] 4 All ER 625, the Supreme Court effectively limited the expansion of the *Kulkarni* principle. The case involved disciplinary proceedings against a teacher accused of misconduct. If the charges were upheld there was an obligation to report the findings to the Independent Safeguarding Authority ('ISA') (see EMPLOYEE'S PAST CRIMINAL CONVICTIONS **18.8**) for consideration whether the teacher was to be included on the list of persons considered to be unsuitable to work with children. The decision was to be taken by the ISA but the outcome of the disciplinary process would have a significant influence or effect on the ISA's decision. On this basis the Court of Appeal concluded that *art 6* was engaged so as to entitle the teacher to legal representation. This was overturned by the Supreme Court which did not consider that there was a sufficient connection between the disciplinary proceedings and the ISA proceedings for *art 6* to apply at the disciplinary hearing concluding that the ISA would exercise its independent judgment on the issue of barring. Although the case appears restrictive of further development in this area it is important to note that the reasoning in *Kulkarni* was not expressly disapproved and was explained as involving circumstances where the employer's disciplinary process would be determinative of the employee's right to work in his chosen profession.

A number of further cases have considered the extent to which the composition of a disciplinary panel can be challenged relying upon *art 6* and the right to an independent and impartial tribunal established by law. Applying the same principles as articulated in *Kulkarni*, reliance on *art 6* on this basis has proved unsuccessful. See *R (on the application of Puri) v Bradford Teaching Hospitals NHS Foundation Trust* [2011] IRLR 582; *Hameed v Central Manchester University Hospital NHS Foundation Trust* [2010] EWHC 2009 (QB), [2011] All ER (D) 11 (May) (above).

The most recent example is *Mattu v University Hospitals of Coventry and Warwickshire NHS Trust* [2012] IRLR 661, [2012] 4 All ER 359 in which the Court of Appeal concluded that an NHS trust's disciplinary decision to dismiss an employee under his contract of employment did not determine any civil right of his within the meaning of *art 6*. The case is particularly significant in that the majority of the Court of Appeal expressly disapproved Smith LJ's *obiter dicta* in *Kulkarni* (above) that *art 6* could be engaged where the effect of upholding the disciplinary charges would, effectively or in practice, bar the practitioner from practising his chosen profession in the future. The Court of Appeal held that a contractual decision to dismiss did not determine civil rights and obligations (which could only be determined by public or professional bodies; compare *Tehrani* above) even if the practical effect of that contractual decision was to "freeze-out" the employee from his chosen employment. *Article 6* would only be engaged at the stage of determination of the question of whether the dismissal was in breach of contract or unfair (ie at the judicial determination stage). Leave to appeal to the Supreme Court in *Mattu* was refused. Accordingly, it is now clear that the "*Kulkarni* principle" of the potential application of *art 6* in disciplinary decisions simply has no application to contractual disciplinary decisions by employers (which are, of course, the vast majority of cases).

In the context of disciplinary procedure, *R (on the application of Bonhoeffer) v General Medical Council* [2011] EWHC 1585 (Admin), [2012] IRLR 37, is significant in that the High Court concluded, drawing upon *art 6* jurisprudence, that a professional conduct body erred in law in admitting hearsay evidence in relation to serious allegations of child abuse.

The Court concluded that the more serious the allegation, the more important it was to ensure that the accused be afforded fair and proper procedural safeguards. This is a potentially important development and it remains to be seen how broadly it may be applied in other disciplinary proceedings involving serious allegations of wrongdoing.

As to the Employment Tribunal system itself and *art 6(1)*, it had been suggested in *Smith v Secretary of State for Trade and Industry* [2000] IRLR 6 that the Employment Tribunals may not be independent when determining matters on redundancy payments from the DTI as the DTI appointed lay members of the tribunals. The case was not appealed. In *Scanfuture UK Ltd v Secretary of State for Trade and Industry* [2001] IRLR 416, the EAT revisited the question of whether the mechanism of appointment of lay members to the Employment Tribunal breached *art 6(1)* of the *Convention*. It is significant to note that the procedures for the appointment of lay members have changed since the procedures which were in place in 1999 (the time of the Employment Tribunal decision in *Scanfuture*). The EAT found that the new procedures complied with the ECtHR. As to the position in 1999, the EAT concluded that the procedures for the appointment of lay members breached *art 6(1)* of the *Convention*. The application of *art 6* has also led to successful appeals against decisions of the employment tribunal which have been issued after a lengthy period of delay. See also the consideration of *art 6* in the context of allegations of bias in relation to an employment tribunal in *Jones v DAS Legal Expenses Insurance Co Ltd* [2003] EWCA Civ 1071, [2004] IRLR 218. In *Kwamin v Abbey National plc* [2004] IRLR 516 the EAT emphasised that it is a fundamental principle of natural justice that a fair trial includes the absence of excessive or avoidable delay by the tribunal and that the same principle is enshrined in the right to a fair trial within a reasonable period in *art 6*. In *Kwamin* the decisions under appeal had been delivered 7.5, 12 and 14.5 months after the end of the hearings respectively. The EAT gave guidance that, whilst it remained for an appellant to show that the result was unfair as a consequence of delay, employment tribunal decisions must be delivered within 3.5 months (after which there would, in the view of the EAT be 'culpable delay'). The issue of whether *arts 6* and *8* may require certain tribunal hearings to be conducted in private (beyond the categories of cases for which statutory provision for the tribunal sitting in private is already made) has been raised in *XXX v YYY*. The EAT had held that *arts 6* and *8* required the tribunal to sit in private. On appeal (*XXX v YYY* [2004] EWCA Civ 231, [2004] IRLR 471) the Court of Appeal reached its decision on different grounds relating to relevance of the evidence in issue. Accordingly the *art 6* and *8* points on the need for a tribunal to sit in private (outside the existing categories of claims) remain undecided at Court of Appeal level.

In *Home Office v Tariq* [2011] UKSC 35, [2011] IRLR 843 the Supreme Court considered whether the use of closed proceedings in an employment law context was compatible with *art 6*. The claimant, an immigration officer, brought claims of race and religious discrimination following his suspension because of national security concerns. The employment tribunal adopted the closed material procedure in the interests of national security under *rule 54(2)* of *Schedule 1* of the *ET Rules* and the claimant contended that the procedure was contrary to *art 6*. The Supreme Court concluded that the closed material procedure did not violate *art 6* and was necessary on grounds of national security. Further there was no absolute requirement that the claimant see the allegations against him in order to challenge them. *Art 6* did not prescribe a uniform approach to all cases and the character of the proceedings (eg a civil claim as opposed to criminal charges) and the circumstances of a particular case can justify derogating from the right to see the allegations in issue. *Rule 49* of the *Employment Tribunal Rules of Procedure* (permitting anonymity orders) was considered in *A v B* [2010] IRLR 844 and the EAT concluded that it also had the power to anonymise a judgment if the loss of a claimant's anonymity would involve a breach of his *art 8* rights. See also *B and C v A* [2010] IRLR 400.

31.7 Human Rights

In *R v Securities and Futures Authority, ex p Fleurose* [2002] IRLR 297 the Court of Appeal held, in relation to disciplinary proceedings of the SFA (which could result in a fine and/or suspension), that such proceedings were not a criminal charge or offence for the purposes of *art 6* of the Convention. Nevertheless, the SFA were required to prove the allegations, to permit the accused to prepare a defence in the knowledge of the 'charges' and to allow a proper opportunity to give evidence and call evidence and to question witnesses giving evidence in support of the allegations.

In *R (on the application of Wright) v Secretary of State for Health* [2009] UKHL 3, [2009] 2 All ER 129 a declaration of incompatibility with the *HRA 1998* was issued in relation to *Part VII* of the *Care Standards Act 2000*. That *Act*, for the purposes of protecting vulnerable persons, made provision for a list to be kept of persons considered unsuitable to work with vulnerable adults. The *Act* also provided for workers to be placed provisionally on the list where concerns arose about their conduct pending final determination in relation to their conduct. The Court held these provisions, for provisional listing without the right to be heard, to be incompatible with the workers' right to a fair hearing under *art 6* of the Convention and also the right to respect for private and family life under *art 8*. The House of Lords subsequently confirmed on appeal that these so called POVA and POCA lists were indeed incompatible with *art 6* (see *R (on the application of Wright) v Secretary of State for Health* [2009] UKHL 3, [2009] 2 All ER 129).

The *Rehabilitation of Offenders Act 1974 (Exceptions) (Amendment) (England and Wales) Order 2008 (SI 2008/3259)*, which came into force on 18 December 2008, the Exceptions Order further amended and extends the definition of a conviction to include a caution and made further extensions and modifications to the category of persons to whom the exemption provisions apply. Thus, in relation to the broad categories of persons to whom the exceptions to the *Act* apply, cautions as well as convictions were initially disclosable whatever the nature of the offence. In addition, with the introduction of the Safeguarding of Vulnerable Groups Act 2006 (see further **18.8** below), the *Rehabilitation of Offenders Act 1974 (Exceptions) Order* was further amended to confer the right to ask questions regarding spent convictions and spent cautions where a person seeks to work in a controlled activity with children or vulnerable adults within the meaning of the *Safeguarding of Vulnerable Groups Act 2006*. The right was, however, limited to circumstances where the person seeking such work is barred from regulated activity relating to children or vulnerable adults. See the *Rehabilitation of Offenders Act 1974 (Exceptions) (Amendment) (England and Wales) Order 2008 (SI 2010/1153)* which came into force on 31 March 2010.

The obligation to disclose all cautions and convictions under the *Rehabilitation of Offenders Act 1974 (Exceptions) (Amendment) (England and Wales) Order 2008 (SI 2008/3259)*, which originally applied whatever the nature of the offence and whenever occurring, was challenged in *R (T) v Chief Constable of Greater Manchester* [2013] EWCA Civ 25. The Court of Appeal held that this was a breach of *Art 8* of the *ECHR*. The Exceptions Order was further amended by the *Rehabilitation of Offenders Act 1974 (Exceptions) Order 1975 (Amendment) (England and Wales) Order 2013, SI 2013/1198* introducing a filtering process so that certain spent convictions and cautions would not have to be disclosed. Certain offences which were serious remained always subject to disclosure and if a person had two or more convictions or cautions then full disclosure remained applicable (the multiple conviction rule). In a recent challenge in *R (on the application of P) v Secretary of State for the Home Department and ors* [2019] UKSC 3, the Supreme Court found that the multiple convictions rule was not a necessary or proportionate way of indicating a criminal propensity to an employer and accordingly a further breach of *Art 8*.

In *Dispatch Management Services (UK) Ltd v Douglas* [2002] IRLR 389, the EAT considered the situation where an application was made to remove representatives in Employment Tribunal proceedings on the grounds of conflict of interest. The Court of Appeal in *Bache v Essex County Council* [2000] IRLR 251, [2000] 2 All ER 847 had held that there was no power in an Employment Tribunal to interfere with a party's choice of representative. In *Douglas*, the EAT held that this principle of non-interference was not inconsistent with the right to a fair hearing under *art 6* of the Convention.

In *Whittaker v Watson (P & D) (t/a P & M Watson Haulage)* [2002] ICR 1244, [2002] All ER (D) 424 (Feb) the EAT confirmed that it was not a 'court' for the purposes of hearing a submission that domestic legislation was incompatible with Convention rights. Referring to the definition of 'court' in *s 4(5)* of the *Human Rights Act 1998*, the EAT held that the conclusion was clear but puzzling (not least when the EAT was composed of a High Court judge sitting with lay members) and was, perhaps, a result which had not been intended in the drafting of the legislation.

On the issue of adjournment of hearings, the Court of Appeal held in *Teinaz v Wandsworth London Borough Council* [2002] EWCA Civ 1040, [2002] IRLR 721 that, in order to comply with the right to a fair trial under *art 6*, a litigant whose presence is needed for the fair trial of a case and who is unable to attend through no fault of his own will usually have to be granted an adjournment regardless of the inconvenience of such adjournment to the court or other parties (see also *Andreou v Lord Chancellor's Department* [2002] EWCA Civ 1192, [2002] IRLR 728). The practice of part-time EAT judges appearing as counsel before lay members of the EAT with whom they had previously sat in a judicial capacity and the compatibility of that practice with *art 6* reached the House of Lords in *Lawal v Northern Spirit Ltd* [2003] UKHL 35, [2003] IRLR 538, [2004] 1 All ER 187. Overturning the decision of the Court of Appeal (which had upheld the decision of the EAT), the House of Lords held that such a practice tended to undermine confidence in the judicial system and ought to be discontinued. In determining whether there is bias in terms of the right to a hearing before an impartial tribunal under *art 6(1)* or the common law test of bias, the principle to be applied was that stated by the House of Lords in *Porter v Magill* [2001] UKHL 67, [2002] 1 All ER 465 namely whether a fair minded and informed observer, having considered the given facts, would conclude that there was a real possibility that the tribunal was biased. The key to this test is public perception of the possibility of unconscious bias. On apparent bias of tribunal members and *art 6* see *City and County of Swansea v Honey* UKEAT/0465/09.

The principle that illegal contracts will not be enforced by the Courts was the subject of an *art 6* challenge in *Soteriou v Ultrachem Ltd* [2004] EWHC 983 (QB), [2004] IRLR 870. A claim of wrongful dismissal was struck out by reason of illegality. The claimant contended that this contravened the right to a fair hearing and also that the strike out was contrary to *art 1* of the *First Protocol* to the Convention. These arguments were rejected. The Court held that *art 6* was not breached as the issue of illegality was part of the substantive law of contract and not a mere procedural bar and that, in any event, the strike out would have been legitimate under *art 6(2)*. As to the claim based upon the *First Protocol* right (in relation to 'possessions'), it was held that, although a claim of breach of contract could indeed be a 'possession', there was no deprivation of a possession here as the contract was unenforceable (on the grounds of illegality) and therefore conferred no 'possession' which the claimant could complain that he was deprived and that the claimant had had his case considered substantively as part of the strike out application.

(b) Article 8

In relation to the right to private life, in the context of employment litigation, this right must be balanced with the right of the parties to have a fair trial of the issues between them. In *De Keyser Ltd v Wilson* [2001] IRLR 324, the EAT considered the *art 8* right to respect for private and family life in the context of an unfair dismissal claim in which the applicant alleged she suffered from a depressive illness caused by stress at work. In the course of the proceedings, the applicant agreed to be seen by the employer's medical expert and a letter of instruction was drafted on behalf of the employer to the expert which letter included certain details of the applicant's private life. The employment tribunal struck out the employer's notice of appearance on the basis that the employer's conduct of the proceedings was scandalous and in breach of the applicant's Convention right to privacy. Allowing the employer's appeal, the EAT held that there was no breach of *art 8* and that in relation to the need, in the context of the case, for a medical examination, the right to privacy was qualified as far as necessary by the right of both parties to have a just trial of the issues between them. In judicial review proceedings, the provisions of the *Employment Equality (Sexual Orientation) Regulations 2003* were found to be compatible with the convention rights in *art 8* and *art 14* (see *R (on the application of Amicus – MSF section) v Secretary of State for Trade and Industry* [2004] EWHC 860 (Admin), [2004] IRLR 430).

In *Whitefield v General Medical Council* [2002] UKPC 62, [2003] IRLR 39, the Privy Council considered the extent to which *art 8* was engaged in circumstances where the respondent, the General Medical Council, made it a condition of the applicant's continued practice as a doctor that he 'abstain absolutely from the consumption of alcohol'. The Privy Council held that the condition was not a breach of *art 8(1)* and in any event would, in the circumstances, have been justified under *art 8(2)*.

The provisions of the *Human Rights Act* are only directly applicable against public authorities. However, in the context of proceedings before the employment tribunal, Convention rights (and in particular the rights contained in *art 8*) may nonetheless be relevant in proceedings before the employment tribunal even where the employer is in the private sector. This is illustrated by the decision of the Court of Appeal in *X v Y* [2004] EWCA Civ 662, [2004] IRLR 625. The case concerned a dismissal by the employer for the employee's failure to disclose a caution. The employee contended that the dismissal was unfair as breaching the Convention right to respect for family life. While the claim failed on the facts, the Court of Appeal accepted that, if a dismissal was on grounds of an employee's private conduct within *art 8*, and was an interference with the right to respect for private life, that fact would be relevant to the determination of a claim of unfair dismissal whether the employer was a public authority or not. This is because the employment tribunal must, under *s 3* of the *Human Rights Act* read and give effect to relevant legislation (in this case the general provisions as to fairness of dismissal in *s 98* of the *ERA 1996*) in a way which is compatible with Convention Rights such as *art 8*. In such circumstances there is no basis to treat a public employer differently from a private employer. Accordingly, say the Court of Appeal, it would not normally be fair to dismiss an employee for a reason which was an unjustified interference with the employee's private life. For a consideration of the role of *art 8* in relation to the fairness of the dismissal of an employee employed by a public sector employer see *Pay v Lancashire Probation Service* [2004] IRLR 129, EAT where the EAT held that a tribunal should effect consideration of Convention rights in the context of the fairness or otherwise of a dismissal by interpreting the words 'reasonably or unreasonably' in *s 98(4)* of the *ERA 1996* as including the words 'having regard to the applicant's Convention rights'. Accordingly, in assessing the fairness in all the circumstances, consideration must be given to whether there had been an interference with the applicant's Convention rights and also any matters advanced by the employer as justification for such an interference. On the facts of *Pay*, in the EAT the applicant was unsuccessful in establishing that the *art 8* right to private life was engaged and, in relation to the *art 10* right of freedom of expression, the interference in issue was found to be justified in the circumstances. Notwithstanding the outcomes on the facts of both *X v Y* and *Pay*, the cases provide important indications of the likely relevance of Convention rights to the issue of the substantive fairness of dismissals both in the private and public sector. See **31.4** above in relation to *Pay* in the ECtHR.

On the (generally limited) relevance of *art 8* to the general enquiry as to fairness of dismissal under *ERA 1996, s 98(4)* see *Turner v East Midlands Trains Ltd* [2012] EWCA Civ 1470, [2013] IRLR 107, [2013] 3 All ER 375 in which the Court of Appeal held that the application of *art 8* (where engaged) did not result in any higher standard of procedural fairness than that which was required under the range of reasonable responses test. See also *X v Y* [2004] IRLR 625 (CA), *Leach v OFCOM* [2012] IRLR 839 (CA) and *Garamukanwa v Solent NHS Trust* [2016] IRLR 476 (below) which each suggest, in summary, that *art 8* arguments will add little to the application of the test under *ERA 1996, s 98(4)*.

Issues of surveillance of employees arose in *McGowan v Scottish Water* [2005] IRLR 167, EAT. The employee, suspected of falsely claiming on time sheets, was put under surveillance by private investigators engaged by the employer. The employee was dismissed in the light of evidence obtained on the surveillance. In an unfair dismissal claim the employee alleged the surveillance was a breach of *art 8*. This was rejected by the Scottish EAT on the facts of the case. The EAT held that *art 8* was indeed engaged in circumstances of covert surveillance but the central issue was that of proportionality. In the circumstances of suspected serious fraud, the surveillance was undertaken for legitimate reasons and was held to be proportionate. The case is significant in illustrating that, where employers do engage in covert surveillance of employees by whatever means, *art 8* is engaged and a 'strong presumption' (per Lord Johnston) of invasion of the right to family life will arise. Accordingly, it will be of central importance for an employer to be able to show that the interference arising was for a legitimate purpose and also 'proportionate' in all the circumstances which will involve consideration of the seriousness or gravity of the issue which prompted the surveillance and the extent of the surveillance exercise undertaken. Consider, however, the ECtHR's recent decision in *Vukota-Bojic v Switzerland* [2017] IRLR 94 (at [31.4] above) in which the ECtHR held that covert surveillance by an insurance company was not on the facts of that case "in accordance with law" and so the claim succeeded without the need to consider the issue of proportionality at all. This has potential application in the employment context as well.

The admissibility of covert recordings of a disciplinary hearing was considered in *Chairman and Governors of Amwell View School v Dogherty* [2007] IRLR 198. On the facts the EAT held that an employment tribunal had not, in allowing some of the covert recordings to be admitted in evidence, breached the school's governors' *art 8* rights. Recording of the private deliberations of the panel were, however, excluded on public policy grounds. In *City and Council of Swansea v Gayle* [2013] IRLR 768 the EAT further considered covert video surveillance evidence of a claimant in the context of an unfair dismissal appeal. The ET had held the dismissal unfair by reason of the use of covert surveillance. This was held by the EAT to be an error of law, holding that an employee has no right of privacy when doing acts which were defrauding the employer. In *Garamukanwa v Solent NHS Trust* [2016] IRLR 476 an employer was provided by the police with copies of malicious emails sent by an employee to other employees from, it appeared, the employee's private mobile telephone. The claimant was dismissed for gross misconduct and contended that the employer had breached his *art 8* rights. This was rejected by the EAT which held that *art 8* was not engaged on the facts as the employee had no reasonable expectation of privacy in relation to such communications. On appeal to the ECtHR (*Garamukanwa v United Kingdom* [2019] IRLR 853) the ECtHR dismissed the application again concluding tat the employee had no reasonable expectation of privacy in relation to the recordings used by the employer at the disciplinary hearing leading to dismissal.

In *Argus Media Ltd v Halim* [2019] EWHC 42 (QB) the High Court held that access by an employer to a departing employee's emails did not breach *art 8* as the employer had a clear email policy which had been sufficiently communicated to the employee and accordingly there was no breach of the employee's expectation of privacy in such communications.

Art 8 may also be relied upon in support of confidentiality and privacy orders in the context of employment tribunal proceedings. However, this must be balanced against the principle of open justice when considering private hearings. An order for non-registration of a judgment based upon *art 8* was considered to be wrong in *L v Q* [2019] EWCA Civ 1417 the Court of Appeal observing that it was difficult to see how such an order could ever be appropriate.

31.7 Human Rights

Rule 49 of the Employment Tribunal Rules of Procedure (permitting anonymity orders) was considered in *A v B* [2010] IRLR 844 and the EAT concluded that it also had the power to anonymise a judgment if the loss of a claimant's anonymity would involve a breach of his *art 8* rights. See also *B and C v A* [2010] IRLR 400.

Closely related to the right to family and private life is the right to peaceful enjoyment of possessions. In *Nerva v United Kingdom* [2002] IRLR 815 the ECtHR held that the decision of the UK High Court and the Court of Appeal that tips included in cheque and credit card payments were the property of the employer and could be used by them to discharge their statutory obligations to pay the applicant waiters a minimum level of remuneration did not amount to a breach of the applicants' rights under *art 1* of the *First Protocol to the Convention* to the peaceful enjoyment of their possessions (see **35.21 PAY – I**). See also *Legal & General Assurance Ltd v Kirk* [2001] EWCA Civ 1803, [2002] IRLR 124 in which the Court of Appeal held that a right to seek a particular employment cannot constitute a possession for the purposes of *art 1* of the *First Protocol to the Convention*. Similarly, in *R (Malik) v Waltham Forest NHS Primary Care Trust (Secretary of State for Health, interested party)* [2007] EWCA Civ 265, [2007] 4 All ER 832, [2007] IRLR 529, [2007] ICR 1101, the Court of Appeal (reversing the decision of the Administrative Court at [2006] IRLR 526) held, in essence, that the right to practice a profession cannot be regarded as a 'possession' for the purposes of *art 1* of the *First Protocol*. In that case a medical practitioner had been unlawfully suspended and contended that his inclusion on an NHS medical performers list was a possession (inclusion on the list being a requisite for practice akin to a licence) and the suspension had interfered with the peaceful enjoyment of that 'possession'. The Court of Appeal rejected the contention that inclusion on the list was a possession for the purposes of *art 1*. *Art 1*, the Court of Appeal held, does not cover an anticipated future right to income and thus the decision represents a substantial limitation upon the applicability of *art 1* in employment claims.

(c) Other Convention rights in the employment context

Article 9 protects freedom of thought, conscience and religion and the right to manifest religion or belief in worship, teaching, practice and observance. Its application to the requirement of Sunday working was considered in *Copsey v WWB Devon Clays Ltd* [2005] EWCA Civ 932, [2005] IRLR 811. In that case a change in shift pattern giving rise to an obligation to work on a Sunday led to the dismissal of the claimant for whom Sunday working was incompatible with his religious beliefs. The claimant brought a claim for unfair dismissal and alleged a breach of *art 9*. His claim was dismissed by the employment tribunal. On appeal to the Court of Appeal the decision of the Tribunal was upheld. Mummery LJ held that *art 9* was not in any event engaged as the employee was not compelled to work on a Sunday – he could always leave and get alternative employment (*Stedman v United Kingdom* [1997] 23 EHHR CD 168 applied). Rix and Neuberger LJJ held that *art 9* might be engaged but, applying the test of reasonableness and *s 98(4)* of the *ERA 1996*, reasonable steps had been taken to accommodate the employee and accordingly the employment tribunal had not erred in reaching the decision which it did. This approach to human rights issues being engaged at the level of the general fairness of a dismissal under *s 98(4)* of the *ERA* is consistent with the approach adopted in relation to *art 8* in *Pay v Lancashire Probation Service* [2004] IRLR 129 and in *X v Y* [2004] EWCA Civ 662, [2004] IRLR 625 (see **31.7(b)** above).

In *Eweida v British Airways plc* [2010] IRLR 322, [2010] ICR 890 the Court of Appeal held that an employer's policy forbidding visible jewellery, which prevented displaying a cross on a necklace while at work, had not amounted to indirect discrimination under the *Employment Equality (Religion or Belief) Regulations 2003 SI 2003/1660* (see now *s 19* of the *EqA 2010*). The Court rejected the argument that *art 9* was relevant to the employee's case. Relying on *Kalac v Turkey* [1997] 27 EHRR 552, the Court held that *art 9* did not protect all acts motivated or inspired by religion or belief. If there are other ways in which an employee can practise or observe his or her religion then a breach of *art 9* is unlikely. In *Wasteney v East London NHS Foundation Trust* [2016] IRLR 388, which involved a complaint of direct discrimination on grounds of religion or belief, the EAT observed that, where the issue was whether treatment was because of manifestation of religion or because of "inappropriate" manifestation of that religion, the issue of "inappropriateness" could be tested by reference to *art 9(2)* and the relevant case law under that article.

Article 9 has been relied on, so far without success, in cases of employees refusing to carry out certain aspects of their work on the ground that it conflicted with their religious beliefs and where that refusal conflicted with the rights of others and thus could not be accommodated. In *Ladele v London Borough of Islington* [2010] IRLR 211, [2010] ICR 532, CA the claimant refused to conduct civil partnership services in relation to same-sex couples. The Court of Appeal held that the employer Council did not discriminate against the claimant on the ground of religion when it threatened her with dismissal for refusing to carry out the services. The claimant's *art 9* rights should not override the Council's need to ensure equality. A similar conclusion was reached in *McFarlane v Relate Avon Ltd* [2010] IRLR 196, [2010] ICR 507 which raised very similar issues. In *McClintock v Department for Constitutional Affairs* [2008] IRLR 29 the EAT held that a Justice of the Peace, who resigned from the Family Panel when his request to be excused from cases that might lead to the adoption of a child by a same-sex couple was rejected, was not discriminated against on the ground of his religious belief and nor were his *art 9* rights infringed and/or any infringement would have been justified under *art 9(2)*.

In *Eweida v United Kingdom* [2013] IRLR 231 the ECtHR has given judgment in relation to the claims in *Eweida, Ladele, McFarlane* and also in relation to *Chaplin* (a case involving a nurse who was prohibited from wearing a cross at work in accordance with hospital policy). In Ms Eweida's case the ECtHR held that the prohibition in issue did breach her *art 9* rights. The wearing of the cross was a manifestation of religion and the interference was not justified or proportionate. Conversely in *Chaplin*, although interference with religious manifestation was made out, the prohibition in a nursing context of jewellery on health and safety grounds was justified. The claims in *Ladele* and *McFarlane* each failed before the ECtHR, with the court concluding that the interference in issue was justified. The ECtHR stressed that the aim of the employer was to secure the implementation of its policy of providing a service without discrimination to others. This was considered by the ECtHR to be the most important factor in justifying the requirements in issue, given that the ECtHR generally allows national authorities a wide margin of appreciation when striking the balance between competing Convention rights. Thus, where the manifestation of religious belief will conflict with the rights of others (or where eg health and safety obligations are engaged) a prohibition on the manifestation is likely to be justified. Where, however, there is no such competing interest or right it is likely (as in Ms Eweida's case) to fail to be a justified interference with the *art 9* rights of the complainant. Similarly, in *Mba v Mayor and Burgesses of the London Borough of Merton* [2014] IRLR 145, [2014] 1 All ER 1235 a requirement to work on a Sunday was held by the Court of Appeal to be justified. Whilst the size of the group affected by a particular measure was relevant to indirect discrimination it was not a relevant consideration in a case where *art 9* was engaged and the question was whether the policy in question can be justified in the light of the difficulty or otherwise of accommodating the particular religious practices of the individual claimant.

Articles 10 and *11* on freedom of expression and association respectively were engaged in *Gate Gourmet London Ltd v Transport and General Workers Union* [2005] EWHC 1889 (QB), [2005] IRLR 881. This case involved applications for injunctions restraining picketing at Heathrow Airport. Fulford J held that in deciding whether to grant such an injunction appropriate weight must be given to the 'right to picket' (as a consequence of the *art 10* and *art 11* rights). On the facts of the case an order was granted limiting the number of pickets but the decision is significant in its express recognition in the domestic courts of effectively the right to picket in relation to an employment dispute (see also *Unison v United Kingdom*

[2002] IRLR 497 above at **31.4**). *Redfearn v Serco Ltd (t/a) West Yorkshire Transport Service)* [2006] EWCA Civ 659, [2006] IRLR 623 involved the dismissal of an employee because of him standing as a candidate for the British National Party. The claim was brought under the *Race Relations Act 1976* (the claimant having insufficient continuous employment to bring an unfair dismissal claim) raising claims of direct and indirect discrimination which were both rejected. Issues of freedom of expression were raised under the *Human Rights Act* relying upon *art 10* but these were rejected by the domestic court on the basis of applying *art 17* of the Convention which provides that nothing in the Convention gives a right to engage in activities which themselves are aimed at destroying Convention rights and freedoms. See however *Redfearn v United Kingdom* (above) in which the ECtHR has held the dismissal in *Redfearn* and the absence of effective remedy in UK law was a breach of *art 10* and *art 11* rights of the complainant. Confidentiality provisions in a contract of employment have been held by the ECtHR to be in violation of the right to freedom of expression under *art 10* (*Matuz v Hungary* [2015] IRLR 74).

In *Hill v Governing Body of Great Tey Primary School* [2013] IRLR 274 *art 10* was in issue in an unfair dismissal claim. In that case a school employee had contacted parents and the press in relation to a child being hurt in the playground. An employment tribunal found her subsequent dismissal unfair having regard to *art 10*. On appeal the EAT confirmed that *art 10* was engaged and an employment tribunal must adopt a structured approach to the issue including making a structured assessment of proportionality.

In *Ministry of Justice v Prison Officers Association* [2008] EWHC 239 (QB), [2008] ICR 702, [2008] IRLR 380 the issue of the 'right to strike' in the context of *art 11* was considered by a domestic court. The Prison Officers Association had been subject to an injunction restraining their strike action (in circumstances of a no strike agreement being in force). In seeking to discharge the injunction various arguments based on *art 11* were unsuccessful before the Court. The Court held that *art 11*, whilst protecting freedom of association, contains no express right to strike and, even if it did, *art 11(2)* gave considerable freedom to a member state to restrict such a right. Accordingly, the injunction restraining strike action was maintained. In the context of the statutory process for trade union recognition by the Central Arbitration Committee, *s 178* and *Schedule 1* of the *Trade Union and Labour Relations (Consolidation) Act 1992 (TULR(C)A)* has been construed purposively to give effect to *art 11* rights by reading a limitation into the exclusion of a recognition application where another trade union is recognised for very limited collective bargaining purposes (*Pharmacists' Defence Association Union v Boots Management Services* [2013] IRLR 262).

The question of whether the complex balloting and notice provisions contained in *Part V* of the *Trade Union and Labour Relations (Consolidation) Act 1992 (TULR(C)A)* infringe the right to freedom of association under *art 11* has been considered in *Metrobus Ltd v Unite the Union* [2009] IRLR 851, [2010] ICR 173. The Court of Appeal rejected the Union's contention that the provisions of *TULR(C)A* presented obstacles so numerous and so complex that errors by unions were almost inevitable, and that for this reason the rights under *art 11* were so constrained as not to be effectively exercisable in respect of industrial action. A similar argument was rejected in *EDF Energy Powerlink Ltd v National Union of Rail, Maritime and Transport Workers* [2010] IRLR 114. The ECtHR has now considered some *art 11* issues in a trade union context in *National Union of Rail, Maritime and Transport Workers v United Kingdom* [2014] IRLR 467. The union contended that its ability to protect its members interests was subject to excessive statutory control and this, it was alleged, gave rise to breach of the *art 11* right of freedom of association. Two key matters were under consideration. First the complexity of strike ballot requirements (arising from the *EDF Energy Powerlink Ltd* case above) and, second, the prohibition on secondary action. The first issue was determined to be inadmissible on the facts and, accordingly, was not the subject of a substantive determination. As to secondary action, the ECtHR held that strike action was clearly protected by *art 11* and that secondary action by its nature may well have broader ramifications than primary action and effect upon persons not party to the dispute.

The court held that the ban on secondary action did not strike at the core of trade union activity and thus member states were to be afforded a wide margin of appreciation and that the ban was not an unjustified interference with the union's right of freedom of association. In *Vining and others v London Borough of Wandsworth* [2017] IRLR 1140 the Court of Appeal held that the police service exception in *TULR(C)A 1992, s 280* whereby the operation of the act did not apply to the police service and accordingly excluded collective consultation in circumstances of redundancy was a breach of *art 11*. The Court of Appeal held that the right to be consulted "falls squarely within the 'essential elements' protected by *Article 11*." As such, any provision of the legislation which restricted its availability to particular classes of workers had to be justified, and the Secretary of State had failed to advance any such justification for the exclusion in this case. Accordingly, there was a breach of *Article 11*. The protection under *art 11* is, however, dependent upon an employment relationship and, accordingly, "worker" status. The issue in *Independent Workers Union of Great Britain v Central Arbitration Committee* [2019] IRLR 249 was an application for union recognition for Deliveroo delivery riders. Those riders had been found not to be workers. In a judicial review application from the CAC's decision rejecting the recognition request, the Court found that an employment relationship was essential for *art 11* to be engaged and, accordingly, the rejection of the recognition request did not breach *art 11*.

31.8 OTHER INTERNATIONAL OBLIGATIONS RELEVANT TO HUMAN RIGHTS

The Council of Europe has also promulgated, and the United Kingdom has ratified, the *European Social Charter*, which contains provisions relating to, for example, annual holidays and the right to strike. This should not be confused with the Social Charter and the Social Chapter to the Maastricht Treaty agreed by the EC (see **24.3** EUROPEAN UNION LAW). There is an Additional Protocol which has not been signed by the UK.

The International Labour Organisation ('ILO') is a specialist body of the United Nations. It has issued a number of conventions, some of which have been ratified by the United Kingdom. They deal with matters such as health and safety, freedom of association and racial discrimination. UK law has been held by the ILO to infringe these conventions in a number of respects. However, there is no remedy for any such breaches in English courts or tribunals.

32   Insolvency of Employer

32.1   A detailed analysis of the law of insolvency is beyond the scope of this book, however, it should be noted that the global COVID-19 pandemic has already triggered the insolvency of several large, household-name employers, including Debenhams and Carluccio's. With effect from 1 March 2020, the Government announced a temporary suspension of wrongful trading legislation for three months, in order to give directors a breathing space in which to assess the impact of the pandemic and of the Government's response upon their organisations. At the time of writing, the draft new insolvency legislation has still not yet been published (see *House of Commons Briefing Paper Number 8877*, 31 March 2020 "*Coronavirus: changes to insolvency rules to help businesses*"). In many cases, based on the Government's announcement, directors of businesses which have been affected by the pandemic may continue to employ staff in the period 1 March 2020-31 May 2020 without risk of personal liability.

On 13 April 2020, the High Court in *Carluccio's Ltd (in administration)* [2020] EWHC 886 (Ch) held that if an administrator places employees on furlough under the Coronavirus Job Retention Scheme ("the CJRS"), the contracts of employment will be adopted by the administrator when the administrator applies for the grant under the CJRS, and the employees will have super-priority over other creditors and be entitled to receive the payments made under the CJRS grant. Snowden J said, "*The COVID-19 pandemic is a critical situation which carries serious risks to the economy and jobs in addition to the obvious dangers to health. I think that it is right that, wherever possible, the courts should work constructively together with the insolvency profession to implement the government's unprecedented response to the crisis in a similarly innovative manner*". On 15 April 2020, the Chancellor made a Treasury Direction under *sections 71* and *76* of the *Coronavirus Act 2020*, setting out that HMRC are responsible for the payment and management of amounts to be paid under the CJRS. On 17 April 2020 Trower J gave judgment in *Debenhams Retail Limited (in administration)* [2020] EWHC 921 (Ch), which likewise found that administrators will be taken to have adopted the contracts of employment of any employees in respect of whom at any time after 14 days from the time of their appointment they paid sums due under the contract of employment, including sums which may be reimbursed through the CJRS, or made an application in respect of the employees under the CJRS, however, the case concerned an administration involving a workforce which had largely already been furloughed but without clear consent, meaning that adoption of the contracts would expose the company to super-priority claims for the remaining 20% of the wages which would not be covered by the CJRS, a risk which could in practice reduce the prospects of saving the business and mean that dismissing the employees would be the better course of action for the administrators. At the time of writing, various questions in connection with how the CJRS will interact with the *Insolvency Act 1986* remain unanswered.

In the event of insolvency, an employer is likely to have limited funds which are insufficient to pay all its debts. These debts may include sums due to employees, for example payment of wages. Some statutory protection is afforded to employees in this situation.

First, under the *Insolvency Act 1986*, employees' rights to payment of certain sums due to them from their employer take precedence over payment of debts to other creditors. Second, under the *ERA 1996* (which in part implements the *EC Directive on Insolvency Protection 2008/94/EC*), the Secretary of State offers a limited guarantee to pay certain sums due to employees from their employers, and to make up unpaid employer pension contributions, out of the National Insurance Fund. Third, statutory maternity, paternity, adoption and sick payments may be claimed from HM Revenue and Customs. Fourth, under the *Pensions Act*

2004, compensation for loss of pension entitlements following insolvency of an employer may be payable from the Pension Protection Fund. Finally, in certain circumstances, a receiver or administrative receiver of a company may take on personal liability under an employee's contract of employment.

See *Tolley's Company Law* for a detailed treatment of corporate insolvency. A brief outline of the provisions affecting employees is set out below.

32.2 CLAIMS GIVEN PRECEDENCE BY THE INSOLVENCY ACT 1986

Under the *Insolvency Act 1986, s 386* and *Sch 6* any claim to remuneration payable to an employee, in respect of the four-month period immediately preceding the insolvency of the employer, is treated as a preferential debt and given precedence over other creditors' claims. 'Remuneration' is defined to include:

(a)   wages or salary (including commission);

(b)   a guarantee payment under *ERA 1996, Part III* (see Pay– I (35));

(c)   a payment for time off work under *ERA 1996, ss 53* (time off to look for work or training in the event of redundancy), and *56* (time off for ante-natal care) or *TULR(C)A 1992, s 169* (time off for trade union activities) (see generally Time Off Work (50));

(d)   a payment on medical suspension or on maternity grounds under *Part VII* of *ERA 1996* (see Maternity and Parental Rights (33) and Pay – I (35));

(e)   a protective award made under *s 189* of *TULR(C)A 1992* (see Redundancy – II (40));

(f)   accrued holiday pay (see Holidays (30)); and

(g)   remuneration payable in respect of a period of holiday or absence from work through sickness or good cause.

(*Insolvency Act 1986, Sch 6, paras 9–15.*)

The maximum total sum which may be treated as a preferential debt under *s 386* is £800 (save that remuneration for accrued holiday pay under *para 10* of *Sch 6* is not subject to this cap) (*Insolvency Proceedings (Monetary Limits) Order 1986 (SI 1986/1996), art 4*). If the employer's assets are insufficient to pay claims for remuneration, each individual claim ranks equally and is to be paid in equal proportions to other such claims.

The test whether an employee is an employee for the purposes of *s 386* and *Sch 6* falls to be determined by whether the employee has a contract for services or a contract of employment: see *Eaton v Robert Eaton Ltd* [1988] ICR 302, [1988] IRLR 83, *Secretary of State for Business Innovation and Skills v Knight* ([2014] IRLR 605), and Employee, Self-Employed or Worker? (16).

An employee may have other contractual or statutory claims against his employer which are not treated as preferential debts under *s 386* and *Sch 6* (including any claim for sums in excess of £800 which are owed as remuneration, etc). Such claims must be proved in the normal way under the *Insolvency Rules 1986 (SI 1986/1925)* as amended.

Recent cases of relevance include *Day v Haine* [2008] EWCA Civ 626, [2008] ICR 1102, [2008] IRLR 642, where it was found that protective awards granted to a number of employees after a company had gone into liquidation were provable debts of the company as they were liabilities to which the company might become subject after the date of the liquidation by reason of an obligation incurred before that date (see 32.5 below for payment of protective awards by the Secretary of State). Also see *Leeds United Association Football*

Club Ltd, Re [2007] EWHC 1761 (Ch), [2007] ICR 1688, [2007] All ER (D) 385 (Jul), which clarified that there is no priority given to damages for wrongful dismissal when claimed by employees as creditors against their employer's insolvency.

32.3   PAYMENTS OUT OF THE NATIONAL INSURANCE FUND: EMPLOYMENT RIGHTS ACT 1996

Where their employer is insolvent, employees may claim redundancy payments from the Secretary of State for Trade and Industry under *ERA 1996, Part XI* and certain other debts owed to employees under *ERA 1996, Part XII*. Payments are made by the Redundancy Payments Office from the National Insurance Fund on behalf of the Secretary of State. The statutory provisions, in part, implement the *Insolvency Protection Directive 2008/94/EC*. Under the *Directive*, where an employer has its registered office in one member state but also employs workers in another member state, it is the guarantee institution of the member state in which the employee is employed which must pay out in the event of an insolvency (*Everson and Barrass v Secretary of State for Trade and Industry and Bell Lines Ltd*: C-198/98 [2000] IRLR 202, ECJ). *Article 8a* of the *Insolvency Protection Directive* provides 'when an undertaking with activities in the territories of at least two Member States is in a state of insolvency . . . the institution responsible for meeting employees' outstanding claims shall be that in the Member State in whose territory they work or habitually work'. In *Sweden v Holmqvist*: C-310/07 [2009] ICR 675, [2008] IRLR 970 the ECJ held that 'activities', for this purpose, means a stable economic presence in the latter State, featuring human resources which enable it to perform activities there.

Any debts which fall outside the scope of these statutory provisions (or any excess above the statutory maximum payable) may be claimed by the employee as a creditor against his employer's insolvency.

Depending on events, it may become relevant to note that on 6 June 2019, the European Council adopted a Directive on preventive restructuring frameworks, second chance and measures to increase the efficiency of restructuring, insolvency and discharge procedures and amending *Directive 2012/30/EU* (COM) (2016) 72 (the *Restructuring and Second Chance Directive*). At the time of writing, the UK has left the EU on 31 January 2020 and is currently in a transition period which is due to end on 31 December 2020.

32.4   Redundancy payments

Where an employer is insolvent, and has failed to pay in whole or in part:

(a)   a statutory redundancy payment;

(b)   a payment under a formal settlement agreement made in respect of a claim to a statutory redundancy payment; or

(c)   a redundancy payment under a collective agreement approved under the collective contracting out provisions (*ERA 1996, s 157*),

to which an employee is entitled, the employee may apply to the Redundancy Payments Office for payment (*ERA 1996, ss 166–167*).

'Insolvency' for these purposes is defined in *ERA 1996, s 166(5) to (8)*. The mere fact of insolvency (in the sense of not being able to meet debts) is not enough (*Secretary of State for Employment v McGlone* [1997] BCC 101). *Section 166(6)* defines insolvency where the employer is an individual. Where the employer is a traditional partnership, the test as to whether or not the employer is insolvent will only be satisfied if every partner has been adjudged bankrupt (*Secretary of State for Trade and Industry v Forde* [1997] ICR 231, [1997]

32.4 Insolvency of Employer

IRLR 387). Where the employer is a company, insolvency is defined in *ERA, s 166(7)*. It is not sufficient that a company has been struck off the register: *Secretary of State for Trade and Industry v Walden* [2000] IRLR 168. *Section 166(8)* applies where the employer is a limited liability partnership. In each case, the employee seeking payment out of the National Insurance Fund must show that the employer falls within the relevant definitions of insolvency. If the employee fails to do so, there is no discretion to make a payment and the employee will not be entitled to payment (*Secretary of State for Trade and Industry v Walden* [2000] IRLR 168). The employer (even if a foreign company) must have entered insolvency proceedings in Great Britain. The same definitions of insolvency are used to determine whether the Secretary of State is obliged to make a payment under *ERA 1996, Part XII*: see **32.5** below.

An individual who is a controlling shareholder (or director) of the company he or she works for may also be an employee of that company for the purposes of obtaining a redundancy payment from the Secretary of State: see *Secretary of State for Business, Enterprise and Regulatory Reform v Neufeld (Richard)* [2009] EWCA Civ 280, [2009] IRLR 475, [2009] 3 All ER 790, CA. For the position of self-employed workers see *Alade v Secretary of State for Trade and Industry* [2007] All ER (D) 08 (May), EAT.

There is no express time limit for making an application to the Secretary of State for a redundancy payment, but if the employee is out of time to claim the payment from his employer (see *ERA 1996, s 164*), the employee may not claim it from the Secretary of State (*Crawford v Secretary of State for Employment* [1995] IRLR 523).

Where an employee applies for a payment under *s 166*, the amount payable is determined in accordance with *s 168*. This will normally be the amount of a statutory redundancy payment. However, where there is a settlement agreement or collective agreement under *s 157* in relation to the redundancy payment, the Secretary of State will pay out whichever is the lesser of a statutory redundancy payment or the amount payable under the settlement agreement/ collective agreement.

The Secretary of State, where an employee applies for a payment under *s 166*, has the power to request in writing that the employer provide information and documents to allow the Secretary of State to decide whether the application is well founded. Failure to comply with such a request without reasonable excuse is a criminal offence (*ERA 1996, s 169*). In addition, in cases where the Secretary of State makes a payment, he or she will assume the rights of the employee as against the employer, and any monies recovered from the employer pursuant to this right are paid into the National Insurance Fund (*ERA 1996, s 167(3) and (4)*).

Disputes relating to payments by the Redundancy Payments Office are to be referred to the employment tribunal under *ERA 1996, s 170*. The employee may refer a dispute to a tribunal without joining his employer as a party to the proceedings (*Jones v Secretary of State for Employment* [1982] ICR 389). However, the EAT has suggested that it may be proper on such occasions to join the company in liquidation for the purposes of disclosure (*Bradley v Secretary of State for Employment* [1989] ICR 69).

32.5 Other guaranteed debts: arrears of pay, notice and holiday pay etc

If, on an application made to him in writing by an employee, the Secretary of State is satisfied:

(a)   that the employer of that employee has become insolvent;

(b)   that the employment of the employee has been terminated; and

(c)   that on the appropriate date the employee was entitled to be paid the whole or part of any debt set out in (i) to (v) below, the Secretary of State must pay the employee the entitlement out of the National Insurance Fund (*ERA 1996, s 182*). 'Insolvency' for these purposes is defined in *ERA 1996, s 183* in the same terms as the definition in *s 166* relating to the Secretary of State's obligation to pay redundancy payments in the event of an employer's insolvency: see **32.4** above.

This right applies to the following debts:

(i)   any arrears of pay in respect of one or more (but not more than eight) weeks; arrears of pay are deemed to include the following statutory payments: a guarantee payment under *ERA 1996, Part III* (however, this will not include contractual guarantee payments in excess of the statutory scheme: *Benson v Secretary of State for Trade and Industry* [2003] ICR 1082, [2003] IRLR 748, EAT), any payment for time off for trade union duties, remuneration for suspension on medical or maternity grounds, and remuneration under a protective award (*ERA 1996, s 184(2)*);

(ii)   any amount which the employer is liable to pay the employee for the statutory minimum period of notice under *ERA 1996, s 86*, or for any failure of the employer to give the period of notice required;

(iii)   any holiday pay due for a period or periods of holiday not exceeding six weeks in all, both for holidays already taken and holiday entitlement accrued but not taken, and to which the employee became entitled during the 12 months ending with the appropriate date;

(iv)   any basic award of compensation for unfair dismissal (see **56.7** UNFAIR DISMISSAL – III);

(v)   any reasonable sum by way of reimbursement of the whole or any part of any fee or premiums paid by an apprentice or articled clerk.

(*ERA 1996, s 184(1)*.)

'Appropriate date' in relation to arrears of pay and holiday pay means the date on which the employer becomes insolvent. An employee may therefore only claim unpaid wages and holiday pay which accrued before the insolvency of the employer. In relation to a protective award and to a basic award of compensation for unfair dismissal, the appropriate date is the latest of:

(1)   the date on which the employer became insolvent;

(2)   the date of the termination of the employee's employment; and

(3)   the date on which the award was made.

In relation to any other debt, the appropriate date is the later of the dates mentioned in (1) and (2) above (*ERA 1996, s 185*).

The total amount payable to an employee in respect of any debt referred to above, where that debt is calculated according to a period of time, may not exceed £538 for any one week (or proportionately less for a period less than one week) (*ERA 1996, s 186* as amended by *SI 2020/206* with effect from 6 April 2020). The House of Lords held, *obiter*, that the cap is not contrary to *EC Directive 80/987: Mann v Secretary of State for Employment* [1999] IRLR 566. Assessment of the amount due to the employee for arrears of pay and holiday should be made on the basis of salary net of tax and National Insurance contributions. When applying the statutory cap, tax and National Insurance contributions should be deducted from the sum payable *after* it has been capped, rather than deducting them from the total sum owing to the employee and then applying the cap (*Morris v Secretary of State for Employment* [1985] ICR 522, [1985] IRLR 297, EAT, followed in *Titchener v Secretary of State for Trade and Industry* [2002] ICR 225, [2002] IRLR 195, EAT).

32.5 Insolvency of Employer

The eight-week limit in respect of which an employee may claim arrears of pay under *s 184(1)(a)* is a permitted derogation to the *EC Directive* and, as a derogation, it must be interpreted restrictively, so as to afford maximum benefit to the employee. Accordingly, it must be construed as permitting an employee to choose the eight weeks in respect of which the claim is most valuable: see *Mann v Secretary of State for Employment* [1999] IRLR 566, HL and *AGR Regeling v Bestuur van der Bedrijfsvereniging voor de Metaallnijverheid*: C-125/97 [1998] ECR I-4493, [1999] ICR 605, [1999] IRLR 379, ECJ (a case on the meaning of the *EC Directive* which *ERA 1996, s 182* partly implements). See further *Mau v Bundesanstalt fur Arbeit*: C-160/01 [2003] ECR I-4791, [2004] 1 CMLR 1113, [2003] All ER (D) 197 (May).

Where an employee claims notice pay under *s 184(1)*, the amount he or she may recover depends on whether the employee worked out the notice period or was unlawfully dismissed without notice. In the former case, the employee may recover the arrears of pay from the Secretary of State as a liquidated sum. In the latter case, he or she is subject to the normal rules on mitigating his loss. Thus, the Secretary of State may in those circumstances, in assessing the amount he or she is liable to pay, take into account any earnings of the employee during the notice period, or, where the employee has failed to mitigate his or her loss properly, any earnings he or she should have received (*Secretary of State for Employment v Cooper* [1987] ICR 766, EAT; *Secretary of State for Employment v Stewart* [1996] IRLR 334, EAT). He or she may also deduct from the amount payable the amount of state benefits the employee has received during the notice period, which he or she would not have received but for the dismissal (see *Westwood v Secretary of State for Employment* [1985] ICR 209, [1984] IRLR 209, [1984] 1 All ER 874, HL).

The liability of the Secretary of State to make payments under *s 182* cannot exceed that of the insolvent employer. Thus, where the insolvent employer would be entitled to set-off against the debt owed by him to the employee sums owed by the employee to him, the Secretary of State is entitled to deduct from the amount he or she pays the employee the amount of the employer's set-off (see *Secretary of State for Employment v Wilson* [1997] ICR 408, [1996] IRLR 330, EAT).

Where an insolvency practitioner such as a trustee in bankruptcy, liquidator, administrator or receiver has been (or is required by law to be) appointed, the Secretary of State will not normally make any payment from the National Insurance Fund until the insolvency practitioner sends the Secretary of State a statement of what is due to the employee. The Secretary of State may, however, at his or her discretion, satisfy himself or herself that the employee's claim is valid and that he or she does not need a statement before paying the claim *(ERA 1996, s 187)*. Once payment has been made to the employee by the Secretary of State, the employee's rights to claim the debt against his employer are transferred to the Secretary of State. In addition, any sums payable as the result of a subsequent decision of an employment tribunal requiring an employer to pay the debt to the employee must be paid to the Secretary of State *(ERA 1996, s 189)*. Following an application under *s 183*, the Secretary of State has the power to request in writing that the employer provide information and documents to allow the Secretary of State to decide whether the application is well founded. Failure to comply with such a request without reasonable excuse is a criminal offence *(ERA 1996, s 190)*.

32.6 Remedy under ERA 1996 Part XII

A person who has applied for payment of other guaranteed debts may, within the period of three months beginning with the date on which the decision of the Secretary of State on that application was communicated to him or her (or if that is not reasonably practicable, within such further period as is considered reasonable), present a complaint to an employment tribunal that:

(a)   the Secretary of State has failed to make any such payment; or

(b)   any such payment by him is less than the amount which should have been paid.

(*ERA 1996, s 188.*)

If the employment tribunal finds the complaint well-founded, it will make a declaration to that effect and state the amount due from the Secretary of State. See *Secretary of State for Employment v Reeves* [1993] ICR 508 for the law relating to interest upon the tribunal's award in such a case (for interest generally, see **19.28** EMPLOYMENT TRIBUNALS – I).

32.7   Unpaid contributions to occupational pension schemes

The Secretary of State may make payments out of the National Insurance Fund into an occupational pension scheme if he or she is satisfied that an employer has become insolvent and that, at the time it became insolvent, there remained unpaid relevant contributions falling to be paid by the employer to the scheme. Application for payment is to be made by the person competent to act in respect of the pension scheme (*Pension Schemes Act 1993* ('*PSA 1993*'), s 124(1)). 'Relevant contributions' are defined as contributions to be paid by the employer on its own behalf or on behalf of a worker from whose pay a deduction has been made for that purpose (*PSA 1993, s 124(2)* and *124(6)*).

The amount payable in respect of contributions of an employer on his own behalf is the least of the following:

(a)   the balance of relevant contributions remaining unpaid on the date when the employer became insolvent and payable by the employer on his own account to the scheme in respect of the 12 months immediately preceding that date;

(b)   the amount certified by an actuary to be necessary for the purpose of meeting the liability of the scheme on dissolution to pay the benefits provided by the scheme to or in respect of the workers of the employer;

(c)   an amount equal to 10% of the total amount of remuneration paid or payable to those workers in respect of the 12 months immediately preceding the date on which the employer became insolvent.

The sum payable is the lesser of the amounts in (a) and (c) above in any case where the pension scheme is a defined contributions scheme, a shared risk scheme under which all the benefits that may be provided are money purchase benefits, or a shared risk scheme under which all the benefits that may be provided are money purchase benefits or collective benefits.

(*PSA 1993, ss 124(3) and (3A)* (as inserted by the *Pension Schemes Act 2015, s 46, Sch 2, paras 1, 4*).)

The sum payable in respect of unpaid contributions on behalf of a worker may not exceed the amount deducted from the pay of the worker in respect of the worker's contributions to the occupational pension scheme during the 12 months immediately preceding the date on which the employer became insolvent (*PSA 1993, s 124(5)*).

The trustee in bankruptcy, liquidator, administrator, receiver or manager or trustee under a composition or arrangement between the employer and the employer's creditors or under a trust deed for the creditors executed by the employer (the 'relevant officer') must make a statement to the Secretary of State of the amounts so owing before any payment out of the National Insurance Fund may be made (*PSA 1993, s 125(3), (4)*). However, the Secretary of State may make a payment from the National Insurance Fund if he or she is satisfied that he or she does not require such a statement in order to determine the relevant amounts (*PSA 1993, s 125(5)*).

32.7 Insolvency of Employer

The rights and remedies of the persons competent to act in respect of the scheme will be transferred to the Secretary of State (*PSA 1993, s 127(1)*).

A person who has applied to the Secretary of State for payment of pension contributions may present a complaint to the Employment Tribunal that the Secretary of State has failed to make any such payment or that any such payment by the Secretary of State is less than the amount which should have been paid (*PSA 1993, s 126*). The provisions in relation to remedy are the same as those for claims for payment of guaranteed debts under *ERA 1996, Part XII:* see **32.6** above.

Following the decision of the ECJ in *Robins and another v Secretary of State for Work and Pensions* C–278/05 [2007] 2 CMLR 269, [2007] IRLR 270, that UK legislation did not provide the minimum degree of protection of accrued occupational pension rights required by *art 8* of *EC Directive 80/987*, the *Financial Assistance Scheme (Miscellaneous Amendments) Regulations 2007/3581* (and subsequent regulations made under *s 286* of the *Pensions Act 2004* (as amended by the *Pensions Acts 2007, 2008* and *2011* and the *Pension Schemes Act 2015*)) were enacted to determine the pension protection provided for qualifying employees upon an 'insolvency event' occurring in respect of their employer.

32.8 Pensions Act 2004

The *Pensions Act 2004* provides protection for employees of employers which become insolvent. The *Act* established a new body corporate, the Pensions Regulator, together with the Pension Protection Fund, the Board of the Pension Protection Fund and the Pension Protection Fund Ombudsman.

Chapter 3 of *Part 2* to the *Act (ss 126–181A)* provides for pension protection for 'eligible' pension schemes in the event that the employer suffers an 'insolvency event'. The complex details of the protection offered are set out in detail in the *Act* and also in the *Pension Protection Fund (Compensation) Regulations 2005 (SI 2005/670)*, the *Financial Assistance Scheme (Miscellaneous Amendments) Regulations (SI 2007/3581)* and subsequent regulations made under *s 286* of the *Pensions Act 2004* (as amended by the *Pensions Acts 2007, 2008* and *2011* and the *Pension Schemes Act 2015*). However, in summary the Board of the Pension Protection Fund will, in defined circumstances, be under a duty to assume responsibility for eligible schemes following an insolvency event. The Board may pay compensation to members of the pension scheme whose pensions are affected by the insolvency pursuant to the pension compensation provisions set out in *Sch 7*. In *Hampshire v Board of Pension Protection Fund* C–17/17 ECLI:EU:C:2018:674 [2018] ICR 327, [2018] IRLR 1128 the European Court of Justice held that the *Insolvency Protection Directive* requires members states to guarantee each individual employee, without exception, compensation corresponding to at least 50% of the value of their accrued entitlement under their occupational pension scheme.

The *Pension Protection Fund and Occupational Pension Scheme (Levy Ceiling and Compensation Cap) Order 2020 (SI 2020/101)* caps the relevant compensation at £41,461.07, with effect from 1 April 2020.

32.9 Statutory maternity, paternity, adoption and sick pay

An employee who, due to the insolvency of his or her employer, is unable to obtain statutory maternity pay, paternity pay, adoption pay, sick pay or statutory shared parental pay may claim such payment from HM Revenue and Customs: see *Statutory Maternity Pay (General) Regulations 1986 (SI 1986/1960), regs 7* and *30*, the *Statutory Paternity Pay and Statutory Adoption Pay (General) Regulations 2002 (SI 2002/2822), reg 43,* the *Statutory Sick Pay (General) Regulations 1982 (SI 1982/894), reg 9B,* and the *Statutory Shared Parental Pay (General) Regulations 2014, reg 45,* respectively. See also MATERNITY AND PARENTAL RIGHTS (33) and SICKNESS AND SICK PAY (45).

32.10 OTHER CONSEQUENCES OF INSOLVENCY AND RELATED EVENTS

Insolvency frequently necessitates the dismissal of the employees formerly engaged by the insolvent business. Insolvency itself does not absolve employers from the duty to have consultation with the unions and employees before the dismissal notices are sent out (see the cases cited in **40.6** REDUNDANCY – **II**).

The *Transfer of Undertakings (Protection of Employment) Regulations 2006 (SI 2006/246)*, *regs 8 and 9* make special provision with regard to employee rights where at the time of a relevant transfer the transferor is subject to relevant insolvency proceedings. See **53.11** TRANSFER OF UNDERTAKINGS. The special provision for the (partial) disapplication of *TUPE* in insolvency situations applies only when the *TUPE* transfer occurs after insolvency proceedings have been formally 'instituted' and when the insolvency practitioner is acting in that capacity and has been appointed as such; see *Secretary of State for Trade and Industry v Slater and others* [2007] IRLR 928. The effect of *TUPE* is partially disapplied where the employer is in insolvency proceedings which are 'relevant insolvency proceedings' within *reg 8(6)* of *TUPE*. The effects of *TUPE* are disapplied almost in their entirety (NB but not in respect of the information and consultation obligations in *regs 11* and *13–16* of *TUPE*) if the insolvency proceedings fall within *reg 8(7)* of *TUPE*. Whether insolvency proceedings are 'relevant' insolvency proceedings within *reg 8(6)* or *(7)* of *TUPE* depends on whether they were instituted 'with a view to the liquidation of the assets' of the employer.

The EAT held that as the primary object of an administration is to rescue the company as a going concern that purpose is inconsistent with the liquidation of the assets of the company so that an administration can never fall within *reg 8(7)* of *TUPE*; *OTG Ltd v Barke* [2011] IRLR 272. The Court of Appeal in *Key2Law (Surrey) LLP v De'Antiquis* [2011] EWCA Civ 1567, [2012] IRLR 212 has confirmed that the "absolute" approach to administration proceedings applies and not the "fact-based" approach. Administration proceedings instituted pursuant to *Insolvency Act 1986, Sch B1* never fall within *TUPE, reg 8(7)*. *TUPE* applies to companies in administration and there is no scope for argument on the individual facts of each case.

Reg 8(7) does not apply to the purchase of a business or assets from a company in administration, including sales using pre-pack arrangements, so that in such a case the employees of the insolvent transferor will transfer to the purchaser. In *Pressure Coolers Ltd v Molloy* [2011] IRLR 630 the EAT considered the effect of *TUPE* on liability to pay compensation in a pre-pack administration, where the claimant, after having been dismissed by the transferee on redundancy grounds, had brought successful employment tribunal claims. Adopting a purposive approach to *TUPE, reg 8(3)*, the EAT concluded that liability lay with the transferee, not the Secretary of State, because the dismissal had occurred after the transfer date. The same reasoning was used by the EAT in *Dobrucki v Secretary of State for Business, Innovation and Skills* ([2015] All ER (D) 30 (Apr)).

Subject to the application of the *Transfer of Undertakings (Protection of Employment) Regulations* (see TRANSFER OF UNDERTAKINGS **(53)**), the effect of a winding-up order made by the court is to terminate the contracts of employment made by the company (*Re General Rolling Stock Co* (1866) LR 1 Eq 346; *Measures Bros Ltd v Measures* [1910] 2 Ch 248, [1908–10] All ER Rep Ext 1188). The same occurs where a receiver is appointed by the court (*Reid v Explosives Co Ltd* (1887) 19 QBD 264; *Midland Counties District Bank Ltd v Attwood* [1905] 1 Ch 357, [1904–7] All ER Rep 648), and if employees continue to work for the business they will be deemed to have entered into new contracts of employment with the receiver.

However, a voluntary winding-up does not terminate contracts of employment, because the liquidator is an officer of the company and the personality of the employer does not change (*Midland Counties District Bank*, above). Nor does the appointment of a (contractual) receiver who is an agent of the company otherwise than by the court (eg under a loan security agreement) have that effect, at any rate unless the employees concerned are directors or managers who could not continue to perform their functions without a conflict with the exercise of the receiver's powers (*Re Foster Clark Ltd's Indenture Trusts* [1966] 1 WLR 125, [1966] 1 All ER 43; *Re Mack Trucks (Britain) Ltd* [1967] 1 WLR 780, [1967] 1 All ER 977; *Griffiths v Secretary of State for Social Services* [1974] QB 468, [1973] 3 All ER 1184; *Nicoll v Cutts* [1985] PCC 311, [1985] BCLC 322; *Re Ferranti International plc* [1994] 4 All ER 300 (Ch D), [1995] 2 All ER 65, [1995] IRLR 269 (HL)). See also *Deaway Trading Ltd v Calverley* [1973] 3 All ER 776; and *Pambakian v Brentford Nylons Ltd* [1978] ICR 665, 122 Sol Jo 177, EAT. The appointment of an administrator, as agent of the employer, does not automatically terminate contracts of employment.

The institution of insolvency proceedings gives rise to a statutory moratorium on commencing or pursuing proceedings against the insolvent employer without the consent of the insolvency practitioner or the court; *Insolvency Act 1986, Sch B1*. Exceptional circumstances will be required before the courts will only lift the moratorium to permit employees seeking to enforce money claims for protective awards, unfair dismissal etc; see *Unite the Union v Nortel Networks UK Ltd (in administration)* [2010] EWHC 826 (Ch), [2010] IRLR 1042.

32.11 Liability of administrative receivers and administrators

An administrative receiver is, essentially, a receiver or manager of substantially the whole of a company's property appointed on behalf of the holders of debentures secured by a floating charge (*Insolvency Act 1986, s 29(2)*). By contrast, a person may be appointed as the administrator of a company by an administration order of the court, by the holder of a floating charge or by the company or its directors (*Insolvency Act 1986, Sch B1 paras 10, 14 and 22*, respectively). The administrative receiver or administrator will be treated as adopting the contract of employment of an employee if he continues the employment relationship for 14 days after appointment (*Insolvency Act 1986, s 44(2)* and *Sch B1, para 99(5)(a)*). An administrative receiver or administrator will not be able to avoid adoption of the contract simply by writing to employees expressly to state that he is not adopting the contracts. If he takes advantage of the services of existing employees without negotiating new contracts of employment for more than 14 days he will be regarded as having adopted their contracts (*Powdrill v Watson* [1995] 2 AC 394, [1995] IRLR 269; see also *Re Antal International Ltd* [2003] EWHC 1339 (Ch), [2003] 2 BCLC 406, [2003] All ER (D) 56 (May)).

An administrative receiver will be personally liable on any contract of employment adopted by him in carrying out his functions. Any such liability is limited to 'qualifying liabilities', essentially contractual liabilities for payment of a sum by way of wages or salary or contribution to an occupational pension scheme where that liability is incurred while the administrative receiver is in office and in respect of services rendered wholly or partly after the adoption of the employment contract. However, the administrative receiver is entitled to be indemnified out of the company's assets (*Insolvency Act 1986, s 44* as amended by *Insolvency Act 1994*). For the law prior to 15 March 1994, see *Powdrill v Watson* [1995] 2 AC 394, [1995] IRLR 269.

An administrator does not undertake a personal liability. 'Qualifying liabilities' for wages, salary and pension contributions after the adoption of the contract are, however, given 'super priority' in that they are charged on the company's property in their custody or control in priority to most other charges and securities including the fees and expenses of the administration (*Insolvency Act 1986, Schedule B1, para 99*; see also *Re Allders Department Stores Ltd (in administration)* [2005] ICR 867, [2005] 2 All ER 122). In *Krasner v McMath* [2005] EWCA Civ 1072, [2006] ICR 205, [2005] IRLR 995 the Court of Appeal concluded that an administrator's liabilities to employees of a company in administration for protective awards and payments in lieu of notice were not payable in priority to the expenses of the administration (save that any payments in lieu of notice where an employer did not require an employee to work during his notice period and paid his wages attributable to that period in a lump sum would be payable in priority as such payments constitute wages as set out in *Delaney v Staples (RJ) (t/a De Montfort Recruitment)* [1992] 1 AC 687, [1992] ICR 483, [1992] IRLR 191, HL).

In *Larsen v Henderson* [1990] IRLR 512 an important suggestion was made by the Scottish Court of Session that a receiver owes a duty of care to the employees of a company in receivership to adopt such method of achieving his desired end as will have the least adverse effect upon them. There is considerable doubt as to whether this suggestion is, in fact, correct.

33 Maternity and Parental Rights

Cross-references. See Unfair Dismissal – I (54) and II (55) for the general rules on unfair dismissal; Equal Pay (23) and Discrimination and Equal Opportunities – I (12) for the rules prohibiting discrimination on the ground of pregnancy and maternity.

INTRODUCTION TO MATERNITY AND PARENTAL RIGHTS

33.1 Chapter structure and scope

This chapter has the following structure:

(i) Introduction [33.1].

(ii) Ante-natal care & adoption appointments [33.9].

(iii) Maternity-related suspension, dismissal and detriment [33.24].

(iv) Maternity leave [33.35].

(v) Statutory maternity pay [33.54].

(vi) Unpaid parental leave [33.62].

(vii) Shared parental leave and pay [33.68].

(viii) Paternity and adoption leave & pay [33.106].

(ix) Parental Bereavement leave and Pay [33.117].

33.2 This chapter provides an overview of maternity and parental rights in UK law, concentrating on those aspects that are most often litigated in the employment tribunal. Topics that are not addressed in this chapter in detail include:

- Discrimination on the grounds of pregnancy and maternity under the *Equality Act 2010 (EA 2010)* (but see [33.25] and Discrimination and Equal Opportunities – I (12), II (13), and III (14)).

- Specific health & safety requirements relating to pregnancy & maternity rights, such as risk assessments (however, see *O'Neill v Buckinghamshire County Council* [2010] IRLR 384 and C 531/15).

- The detail and practicalities of administering statutory payments to entitled individuals.

- Equal pay (see Equal Pay (23)).

33.3 *Summary of maternity and parental rights*

Parents and adopters enjoy the following rights:

- *Ante-natal care & adoption appointments*: pregnant women are entitled to paid time off to attend ante-natal appointments, and their partners are entitled to unpaid time off work to accompany the mother. A similar scheme applies for adoption appointments; one parent may take paid time off, and the other unpaid time off.

33.3 Maternity and Parental Rights

- *Maternity-related suspensions* must be justified, employers must offer suitable alternative work and generally must continue to remunerate the employee. Dismissal on grounds relating to maternity, pregnancy or the exercise of other family-leave rights will usually be automatically unfair, and any detriment imposed for any of those reasons will be unlawful.

- *Maternity leave*: mothers are entitled to 52 weeks of maternity leave (26 weeks ordinary maternity leave ("**OML**"), 26 weeks additional maternity leave ("**AML**")), without any need for a qualifying period of service. The first two weeks of maternity leave are 'compulsory maternity leave' ("**CML**") and an employer cannot allow a mother to return to work within that period.

- *Statutory maternity pay*: mothers with at least 6 months continuous service generally qualify for 39 weeks of statutory maternity pay ("**SMP**"), at the rate of 90% of average weekly earnings for the first six weeks and the remaining 33 weeks at the lower of the statutory rate of £151.20 or 90% of normal weekly earnings. Many employers provide enhanced contractual maternity entitlements. Mothers who do not qualify for SMP may qualify for maternity allowance ("**MA**"), a social security benefit.

- *Shared parental leave and pay*: mothers with at least six months continuous service may generally curtail their statutory maternity leave and SMP, and (flexibly) share the balance of leave and pay between herself and her partner as shared parental leave ("**SPL**") and statutory shared parental pay ("**SSSP**"). The rate of SSPP is the lower of the statutory rate of £151.20 or 90% of normal weekly earnings. SPL and SSPP is also available to adopters, surrogate parents and others, and replaces 'additional paternity leave' ("**APL**")

- *Unpaid parental leave*: employees with a year's service may take up to 18 weeks of unpaid leave for each natural or adopted child up to the child's 18th birthday, but such leave can only be taken in blocks of one week at a time (unless the contract of employment provides otherwise).

- *Paternity and adoption leave and pay*: statutory paternity leave (birth) is two weeks in length, with a qualifying requirement for 26 weeks' continuous service. Statutory paternity pay, with the same qualifying requirement, is payable at either £151.20 per week or 90% of the employee's normal weekly earnings. Adoption leave for a primary adopter is 52 weeks in length with no qualifying period of service. Statutory adoption pay ("**SAP**"), which generally requires six months' continuous service, is set at 90% of average weekly earnings for the first six weeks, then the remaining 33 weeks are paid at the lower of the statutory rate of £151.20 or 90% of normal weekly earnings. There is also shared parental leave and pay in adoption cases which confer essentially the same entitlements as in the case of birth.

- *Parental bereavement leave and pay*: statutory parental bereavement leave ("**SPBL**") is available in respect of the death of any child or in the event of a stillbirth after 24 weeks of pregnancy. There is no period of qualifying service. The maximum leave period is two weeks. The employee can take either one week (it cannot be taken in shorter periods); two continuous weeks; or two discontinuous weeks. The leave must be taken within 56 weeks of the date on which the relevant child died. Statutory parental bereavement pay ("**SPBP**") is payable at either £151.20 per week or 90% of the employee's normal weekly earnings. The employee must have been continuously employed for 26 weeks by the end of the week immediately preceding that in which the relevant child died and still be employed on the date of the child's death.

33.4 *Abbreviations*

Abbreviations peculiar to this chapter include:

- AML – additional maternity leave.

- APL – additional paternity leave.

- ACAS Guide – 'Shared Parental Leave: a good practice guide for employers and employees' (14 October 2014), ACAS.

- BIS Guide – 'Employer's Technical Guide to Shared Parental Leave and Pay' (December 2014), Department for Business, Innovation and Skills.

- EWC – expected week of childbirth.

- Leave Curtailment Regulations – the *Maternity and Adoption Leave (Curtailment of Statutory Rights to Leave) Regulations 2014 (SI 2014/3052).*

- MA – maternity allowance.

- MA Curtailment Regulations – the *Maternity Allowance (Curtailment) Regulations 2014 (SI 2014/3053).*

- MPL Regulations – the *Maternity and Parental Leave etc. Regulations 1999 (SI 1999/3312).*

- OML – ordinary maternity leave.

- PAL Regulations – *Paternity and Adoption Leave Regulations 2002 (SI 2002/2788).*

- Pay Curtailment Regulations – the *Statutory Maternity Pay and Statutory Adoption Pay (Curtailment) Regulations 2014 (SI 2014/3054).*

- PBA 2018 – The *Parental Bereavement (Leave and Pay) Act 2018.*

- SAL – standard adoption leave.

- SAP – statutory adoption pay.

- SMP – statutory maternity pay.

- SMP Regulations – the *Statutory Maternity Pay (General) Regulations 1986 (SI 1986/1960).*

- SML – statutory maternity leave.

- SPBL – statutory parental bereavement leave.

- SPBP – statutory parental bereavement pay.

- SPL – shared parental leave.

- SPL Regulations – the *Shared Parental Leave Regulations 2014 (SI 2014/3050).*

- SSPP – statutory shared parental pay.

- SSPP Regulations – the *Statutory Shared Parental Pay (General) Regulations 2014 (SI 2014/3051).*

- SSCBA 1992 – *Social Security Contributions and Benefits Act 1992.*

33.5 Maternity and Parental Rights

33.5 *The development of maternity & parental rights*

Historically, the *Employment Protection Act 1975* created statutory rights for female employees. These provisions were re-enacted in the *Employment Protection (Consolidation) Act 1978*. An additional right, the right to paid time off for ante-natal care, was conferred by the *Employment Act 1980*, which also amended the existing provisions, and statutory rights were further extended by the *Trade Union Reform and Employment Rights Act 1993*.

With the exception of the law relating to statutory maternity pay (which is contained in the *Social Security Contributions and Benefits Act 1992*), all the relevant legislation was consolidated into the *Employment Rights Act 1996* ("**ERA 1996**"). Most of the rights and principles set out in the *ERA 1996* which relate to maternity leave have found their way into the *Employment Relations Act 1999* ("**ERA 1999**"), or appear in the regulations made under the *ERA 1999*, principally the *Maternity and Parental Leave etc Regulations 1999 (SI 1999/3312)*.

The *Employment Act 2002* ("**EmA 2002**") and accompanying regulations ushered in significant changes to the law on maternity and paternity rights, extending the period of ordinary maternity leave from 18 weeks to 26 weeks, and the period of additional maternity leave to 26 weeks from the date when ordinary maternity leave has ended. The *Work and Families Act 2006*, and accompanying regulations, introduced further changes, including a right (now abolished) to additional paternity leave to enable parents, in effect, to share the right to additional leave to care for their child (see **33.63** below), a move which was taken a step further by the introduction of shared parental leave and pay under the *Children and Families Act 2014* ("**CFA 2014**") (see **33.68** below).

The *Social Security Act 1989, Sch 5 paras 2, 5, 6*, contains provisions which deal with unfair maternity and family leave provisions in employment-related benefits schemes. These provisions are intended to implement *Directive 86/378/EEC* (see **24.5** EUROPEAN UNION LAW) and were brought into force to a limited extent on 23 June 1994 (*Social Security Act 1989 (Commencement No 5) Order 1994 (SI 1994/1661)*).

33.6 The law as to sex discrimination (see DISCRIMINATION AND EQUAL OPPORTUNITIES – I (12), II (13), and III (14)) has also historically been extremely important in defining the extent of the protection which the law confers on women in connection with pregnancy or childbirth and, indeed, in connection with IVF treatment (on which see *Mayr v Backerei und Konditorei Gerhard Flockner OHG*: C-506/06 [2008] IRLR 387 and *Sahota v Home Office* [2010] ICR 772).

33.7 In 2008, the European Commission proposed a number of new rights in relation to maternity leave as part of proposed revisions to the *Pregnant Workers Directive EC 1992/85*. The Government consulted on those proposals during 2009 and published a response in 2010. In October 2010 the European Parliament adopted amendments to the *Directive* which went beyond even those proposed by the Commission, including a right to 20 weeks' paid maternity leave, two weeks' paid paternity leave and breastfeeding leave. These were politically controversial and were broadly rejected by the European Council in late 2010.

In June 2010 the European Parliament agreed a new *Directive 2010/41/EU* to provide for increased protections for self-employed workers, including a right to maternity leave for self-employed women and their partners. The UK has taken the view that existing domestic legislation already provides sufficient compliance for the purposes of the new Directive. As to the right to maternity allowance in UK law, see **33.61** below.

33.8 In December 2009, EU Charter of Fundamental Rights (the "**Charter**") came into effect. Article 33 of the Charter provides:

> Family and professional life
>
> 1. The family shall enjoy legal, economic and social protection.

2. To reconcile family and professional life, everyone shall have the right to protection from dismissal for a reason connected with maternity and the right to paid maternity leave and to parental leave following the birth or adoption of a child.

Similarly, Article 34(1) provides:

Social security and social assistance

1. The Union recognises and respects the entitlement to social security benefits and social services providing protection in cases such as maternity, illness, industrial accidents, dependency or old age, and in the case of loss of employment, in accordance with the rules laid down by Community law and national laws and practices.

It remains to be seen what, if any role the Charter will play in the development of maternity and paternity rights. See *R(NS) v Secretary of State for the Home Department* [2010] EWCA Civ 990 and *Association De Mediation Sociale v Union Locale Des Syndicats Cgt*; (Case C-176/12) [2014] IRLR 310 as to the applicability of the Charter.

On 13 March 2014, the *Children and Families Act 2014* received Royal Assent. It made three important changes to the law:

- *Part 7* provides for statutory rights to shared parental leave and pay;

- *Part 8* provides for a new right to time off to accompany on ante-natal appointments; and

- *Part 9* abolishes the requirement to be a carer in order to request flexible working (see **[50.17]**).

Shared parental leave is discussed in detail below at **[33.68]**. Accompanying on ante-natal appointments is discussed at **[33.14]** and the new right to request flexible working is addressed at **[50.17]**.

In March 2016 the Equality and Human Rights Commission and HM Government published 'Pregnancy and maternity-related discrimination and disadvantage: Experiences of mothers', which set out stark findings. Some 77% of women reported a potentially discriminatory or negative experience, 10% of mothers said that their employer discouraged them from attending antenatal appointments and 11% of mothers reported being dismissed, made compulsorily redundant or treated so poorly they had to leave their job. On 12 July 2016, the House of Commons Women and Equalities Committee published a report entitled 'Pregnancy and maternity discrimination', noting that the March 2016 research, when compared with equivalent research in 2005, showed that pregnancy and maternity discrimination was getting worse. The report set out a range of recommendations. The Government's response notably included a commitment to review the position in relation to making new and expectant mothers redundant, as well as commenting on a range of other practical measures. On 19 February 2018, capping a series of damning reports by a range of bodies throughout 2017-2018, the Equality and Human Rights Commission published its view: "Employers in the dark ages over recruitment of pregnant women and new mothers".

The *Parental Bereavement (Leave and Pay) Act 2018* received Royal Assent on 13 September 2018 and was brought into force with effect from 18 January 2020 by the *Parental Bereavement (Leave and Pay) Act 2018 (Commencement) Regulations 2020, SI 2020/45*. As the name suggests, it creates rights for employees who lose a child to take a period of "Parental Bereavement Leave" and to receive "Statutory Parental Bereavement Pay". The rights are addressed at Paragraph **[33.117]** and following below.

Maternity and Parental Rights

ANTE-NATAL CARE & ADOPTION APPOINTMENTS

33.9 Paid time off for ante-natal care

An employee who is pregnant and who has, on the advice of a registered medical practitioner, registered midwife or registered nurse, made an appointment to attend at any place for the purpose of receiving ante-natal care, is entitled: (a) not to be unreasonably refused time off during her working hours to enable her to keep the appointment (*ERA 1996, s 55(1) and 57(1)*); and (b) to be paid for the period of absence at the appropriate hourly rate (*ERA 1996, s 56(1)*). (See also *art 9* of the *Pregnant Workers Directive 92/85/EEC*.) See [33.14] below in relation to the right to accompany a pregnant woman to an ante-natal appointment and [33.19] in relation to adoption appointments.

33.10 *Qualifying requirements*

There is no minimum qualifying period of employment for the enjoyment of this right. However, in respect of all save the first appointment for ante-natal care for which she seeks time off work, the employee must, if requested to do so by her employer, produce for his inspection:

(a)   a certificate from a registered medical practitioner, registered midwife or registered nurse stating that she is pregnant; and

(b)   an appointment card or some other document showing that the appointment has been made.

(ERA 1996, s 55(2)–(3) and s 55(5).)

If an employer could reasonably refuse to allow an employee time off to attend an ante-natal appointment – for example, if she were a part-time employee and could arrange to attend during her time off – yet he allows her time off, it is thought that he is not obliged to pay her during the period of her absence provided that he obtains her agreement and makes it clear that the time is not being given in satisfaction of a statutory obligation. This qualification is an important one: if an employee is entitled to take time off in accordance with the provisions of *ERA 1996, s 55(1)*, she is automatically entitled to be paid for the time taken (*ERA 1996, s 56(1)*). (See *Gregory v Tudsbury Ltd* [1982] IRLR 267.)

33.11 *Right to remuneration*

The employee is entitled to payment from her employer for the period of her absence, at the appropriate hourly rate. That rate is the amount of one week's pay divided by:

(a)   the number of normal working hours in a week for that employee when employed under the contract of employment in force on the day when the time off is taken;

(b)   where the number of such normal working hours differs from week to week or over a longer period, the average number of such hours, calculated by reference to the hours worked during the period of 12 weeks ending with the last complete week before the day on which the time off is taken; or

(c)   where the number of hours worked in a week differs, but the employee has not been employed long enough for the 12-week calculation to be made, a number which fairly represents the number of normal working hours in a week taking into account (as appropriate in all the circumstances) the average number of hours which the employee could expect under her contract and the average number of hours worked by other employees of the same employer in comparable employment.

(ERA 1996, ss 56(2)–(6) and 225(3); and see PAY – I (35).)

33.12 *Remedies*

An employee may present a complaint to an employment tribunal to the effect that her employer has unreasonably refused her time off as required by *s 55(1)* of the *ERA* or has failed to pay her the whole or part of any amount to which she is entitled under *s 56(1)* (see *ERA 1996, s 57(1)*). Such a complaint must be presented within the period of three months beginning with the date of the appointment concerned, or within such further period as the tribunal considers reasonable in a case where it is satisfied that it was not reasonably practicable for the complaint to be presented within the period of three months (*ERA 1996, s 57(2)*; for reasonable practicability see **19.20** EMPLOYMENT TRIBUNALS – I). The extension of time limits under section 207B, to facilitate conciliation before institution of proceedings, apply. Where an employment tribunal finds a complaint well-founded, it will make a declaration to that effect and make an order for payment of twice the amount of money due under the statutory provisions (*ERA 1996, s 57(3)–(5)*). The employee's statutory right to remuneration does not affect her contractual right, but any contractual remuneration will go to discharge her statutory entitlement, and vice versa (*ERA 1996, s 56(5)–(6)*).

A dismissal for a reason relating to ante-natal appointments may relate to pregnancy, and so be automatically unfair under *ERA 1996, s 99*. See [**33.31**].

33.13 *Agency Workers*

From 1 October 2011 agency workers who have worked for the qualifying period prescribed in *reg 7* of the *Agency Workers Regulations 2010 (SI 2010/93)* (ie working in the same role with the same hirer for 12 continuous calendar weeks), have comparable rights as against both their temporary work agency and their hirer (*ERA 1996, ss 57ZA–57ZD*). Following the *CFA 2014, s 129*, agency workers also have the right not to be subject to detriment for exercising their rights to attend ante-natal care appointments.

33.14 ACCOMPANYING FOR ANTE-NATAL CARE: UNPAID TIME OFF

The *CFA 2014* by *Part 8* created a new right for certain employees to take unpaid time off work to attend up to two ante-natal appointments if they have a "qualifying relationship" with a pregnant woman, by inserting new *sections 57ZE–57ZI* into the *ERA 1996*. In September 2014 the Department for Business, Innovation and Skills published an employer guide entitled 'Time off to accompany a pregnant woman to ante-natal appointments'. The government brought *ERA 1996, ss 57ZE–57ZI* into force on 1 October 2014.

32.15 Qualifying requirements

The employee claiming the right to take unpaid time off work to attend an ante-natal appointment must be in a "qualifying relationship" with a pregnant woman or her expectant child, as defined by *ERA 1996, s 57ZE(7)*. A person is in such a qualifying relationship if:

- they are the husband or civil partner of the pregnant woman;

- the person lives with the pregnant woman in an "enduring family relationship", regardless of the person's sex. That person cannot, however, be a relative (as defined by *ss 557ZE (8)* and *(9)*);

- the person is the father of the expectant child; or,

- the person is in a surrogacy situation and meets the conditions set out in *ss 57ZE (7)(d)* or *57ZE(7)(e)* read with *s (10)*.

The appointment must have been made on the advice of a registered medical practitioner, registered midwife or registered nurse: *ss 57ZE(4)* and *(11)*.

32.15 Maternity and Parental Rights

There is (as above) no minimum qualifying period of employment for the enjoyment of these rights. However, for all the ante-natal appointments (including the first, unlike the above) the employee must, if the employer requests, produce a signed declaration that states: that the person is in a qualifying relationship (as set out above); that their purpose is the specified purpose set out in the paragraph below; that the appointment was made on medical advice (as set out above); and the date and time of the appointment (*ss 57ZE(5)* and *(6)*). The declaration may be in electronic form.

33.16 Limitations on time off work

ERA 1996, s 57ZE(1) provides that the time off work must be for the purpose of accompanying the woman when she attends by appointment at any place for the purpose of receiving ante-natal care.

The employee is entitled to take time off in accordance with *s 57ZE(1)* on only two occasions (*s 57ZE(2)*), and on each occasion the maximum time off during working hours which the employee is entitled is six and a half hours (*s 57ZE(3)*). Working hours means, in accordance with the employee's contract of employment, the time the employee is required to be at work (*s 57ZE(12)*).

33.17 Remedies

The remedies scheme is the same as in paragraph [**33.12**] save for the following. It is set out in *ERA 1996, s 57ZF*.

- As the right is to unpaid time off, a person can complain only that his or her employer has unreasonably refused to let him or her take time off as required by *section 57ZE*.

- The compensation due to the employee for the employer's unreasonable refusal is set out at *ss 57ZE(5)* to *(8)*. In short, the amount payable is the number of working hours the employee would have been entitled to under *s 57ZE* but for the unreasonable refusal multiplied by twice the employee's hourly rate of pay.

A dismissal for a reason relating to accompanying for ante-natal care is automatically unfair: see *ERA 1996, s 99(3)(aa)* and *reg 3* of the *Paternity and Adoption Leave Regulations 2002 (SI 2002/2788)* ("**PAL Regulations**"). See *ERA 1996, s 47C* and *reg 28* of the *PAL Regulations* as to detriment. (See *reg 14* of the *Paternity and Adoption Leave (Amendment) Regulations 2014 (2014/2112)* as to commencement dates.)

33.18 Agency workers

Agency workers who have worked the qualifying period specified in [**33.13**] have comparable rights as against both their temporary work agency and their hirer (*ERA 1996, ss 57ZG–57ZI*). Following the *CFA 2014, s 129*, agency workers also have the right not to be subject to detriment for exercising their rights to accompany on ante-natal care appointments.

33.19 ADOPTION APPOINTMENTS

The *CFA 2014* also created a right to paid time off work for adopters to attend meetings in advance of a child being placed with them for adoption, by inserting new *sections 57ZJ–57ZS* into *ERA 1996*. The government brought these sections into force on 5 April 2015.

33.20 Qualifying requirements

It is a requirement of *section 57ZJ* that the employee has been "notified by an adoption agency that a child is to be, or is expected to be, place for adoption" with that employee: *ss 57ZJ(1)–(2)*.

Where an employee is adopting a child jointly, that employee may elect to take time off with pay (in which case *s 57ZG(2)* applies) or without pay (in which case *s 57ZL(1)* applies). That employee's election is constrained by the election of their co-parent: in effect, those subsections provide that one of the joint-adopters is entitled to paid time off and the other to unpaid time off. They cannot both have paid time off, and they cannot both have unpaid time off: once parent A has elected to take paid time off, only the election to take unpaid time off is available to parent B. Pay for time off under *section 57ZJ* is calculated in accordance with *section 57ZK*.

Again, there is no minimum qualifying period of employment for the enjoyment of these rights. However, for all adoption appointments the employee must (if requested by the employer):

- If adopting alone, give the employer a document showing the date and time of the appointment; and that it has been arranged at the request of the same adoption agency that notified the employee that a child was to be placed with them (*s 57ZJ(8)*);

- If adopting jointly, two documents are required. The first document is the same as set out in the above bullet point. The second is a declaration signed by the employee stating that they have made a declaration for the purposes of *ss 57ZJ(2)(b)* or *57ZL(1)(a)* in connection with the adoption (*ss 57ZJ(9)* and *57ZL(7)*).

Sections 57ZJ(11) and *57ZL(9)* make provision in respect of adoptions of more than one child.

33.21 Limitations on time off work

Section 57ZJ of *ERA 1996* provides that the time off work must be for the purpose of attending an appointment at any place for the purpose of having contact with the child to be adopted or for any other purpose connected with the adoption. The employee is not entitled to take time off under *section 57ZJ* on or after the date of the child's placement for adoption with the employee (*s 57ZJ(4)*).

The employee is entitled to take paid time off in accordance with *section 57ZJ* on a maximum of five occasions (*s 57ZJ(5)*); and a joint-adopter is only entitled to take unpaid time off work on two occasions (*s 57ZL(4)*). On each occasion the maximum time off during working hours to which the employee is entitled is six and a half hours (*s 57ZJ(6)*).

33.22 Remedies

The remedies scheme is the same as in paragraph [**33.12**] [above] save that a person may complain either that his or her employer has unreasonably refused him or her time off; or that his or her employer has failed to pay the whole or part of any amount to which the employee is entitled. See *ERA 1996, s 57ZM*.

A dismissal for a reason relating to an adoption appointment is automatically unfair: see *ERA 1996, s 99(3)(ab)* and *reg 3* of the *PAL Regulations*. See *ERA 1996, s 47C* and *reg 28* of the *PAL Regulations* as to detriment. (See *reg 14* of the *Paternity and Adoption Leave (Amendment) Regulations 2014 (2014/2112)* as to commencement dates.)

33.23 Agency workers

Agency workers who have worked the qualifying period specified in [33.13] have comparable rights as against both their temporary work agency and their hirer (*ERA 1996, ss 57ZN–57ZR*). Following the *CFA 2014, s 129*, agency workers also have the right not to be subject to detriment for exercising their rights to attend adoption appointments.

MATERNITY-RELATED SUSPENSION, DISMISSAL AND DETRIMENT

33.24 Introduction

This section considers:

*   The protections in discrimination law arising from the *Equality Act 2010*;

*   Suspension on maternity grounds;

*   Protection from dismissal by reason of pregnancy or maternity; and,

*   Protection from detriment by reason of pregnancy or maternity.

33.25 Equality Act 2010

See DISCRIMINATION AND EQUAL OPPORTUNITIES – I (12) for the rules under the Equality Act 2010 relating to pregnancy and maternity.

33.26 Suspension from work on maternity grounds

The domestic regime of suspension from work on maternity grounds comprises, in part, implementation of obligations set out in the *EU Pregnant Worker's Directive 92/85*. An employee will be taken to be suspended from work on maternity grounds if her employer suspends her on the ground that she is pregnant, has recently given birth, or is breastfeeding a child, and he does so in consequence either of a relevant statutory requirement, or of a recommendation contained in a relevant provision of a Code of Practice issued or approved under *s 16* of the *Health and Safety at Work Act 1974* (see **28.17** HEALTH AND SAFETY AT WORK – **II**), which means a provision specified in an order made by the Secretary of State (*ERA 1996, s 66*). Suspension may only be invoked if removing the hazard to health or transferring to an alternative role is not available or would be insufficient to remedy the risk to health and safety: *Gassmayr v Bundesminister fur Wissenschaft und Forschung*: C-194/08 [2010] ECR I-6281.

The *Suspension from Work (on Maternity Grounds) Order 1994 (SI 1994/2930)* specified the following provisions for these purposes:

(a)   *reg 13A(3)* of the *Management of Health and Safety at Work Regulations 1992 (SI 1992/2051)* (suspension from work of new or expectant mother to avoid risk from any processes or working conditions, or physical, biological or chemical agents); this provision is now set out in *reg 16* of the *Management of Health and Safety at Work Regulations 1999 (SI 1999/3242)* (the "**MHSW Regulations**");

(b)   *reg 17* of the *MHSW Regulations* (certificate from a registered medical practitioner).

In addition, *regs 8(3)* and *9(2)* of the *Merchant Shipping and Fishing Vessels (Health and Safety at Work) Regulations 1997 (SI 1997/2962)* are specified for these purposes by the *Suspension from Work on Maternity Grounds (Merchant Shipping and Fishing Vessels) Order 1998 (SI 1998/587)*.

Article 7 of the *EU Pregnant Worker's Directive* requires that pregnant workers; those who have recently given birth; and those that are breast-feeding should not be obliged to perform "night work" (which would be treated as entailing risks from working conditions, to use the language of *Reg 16* of the *MHSW Regulations*). There is an obligation to transfer the worker to daytime work or to place them on leave if such a transfer is not "technically and/or objectively feasible or cannot reasonably be required on duly substantiated grounds". In *Gonzáles Castro v Mutua Umivale and others* C-41/17 [2018] IRLR 1142, the CJEU concluded that if a worker works a shift any part of which involves night work, they are a night worker and *Art 7* applies to them. As a matter of domestic law, they would have either to be transferred or suspended.

Other provisions as to suspension include those in the *Suspension from Work on Maternity Grounds (Merchant Shipping and Fishing Vessels) Order 1998 (SI 1998/587)*. For discussion of the concept of 'suspension' see *New Southern Railway Ltd v Quinn* [2006] IRLR 266, [2006] ICR 761, EAT.

33.27 *Right to alternative work*

Before being suspended on maternity grounds, the employee must be offered suitable alternative work if the employer has it available. This means work which is of a kind both suitable in relation to her and appropriate for her to do in the circumstances, and to which terms and conditions not substantially less favourable than her own apply (*ERA 1996, s 67(1), (2)*).

If the employer fails to offer the employee such work as is available she may complain to an employment tribunal, which has power, if it finds the complaint well-founded, to award such compensation as is just and equitable having regard to the infringement of the employee's right and to any loss which she has sustained because of it (*ERA 1996, s 70(4), (6), (7)*). The complaint must be presented before the end of the period of three months beginning with the first day of the suspension, or within such further period as the tribunal considers reasonable where it is satisfied that it was not reasonably practicable to present the complaint within three months (*ERA 1996, s 70(5)*; see **19.7** Employment Tribunals – I).

In *British Airways (European Operations At Gatwick) Ltd v Moore* [2000] IRLR 296, [2000] ICR 678, the EAT upheld a finding that airline cabin crew who were employed on ground-based work only during their pregnancy had not been offered suitable alternative work while they were pregnant. The terms and conditions offered to them were substantially less favourable: they were given their basic pay only, not the flying allowances which they would normally have received had they been airborne.

33.28 *Right to remuneration*

If an employee is suspended from work on maternity grounds, she is entitled to remuneration at the rate of a week's pay for each week of suspension, unless she has been offered suitable alternative work which she has unreasonably refused (*ERA 1996, ss 68, 69(1)*; **39.12** Redundancy – I). This statutory right does not affect any contractual rights to remuneration during her suspension which the employee may have, and any contractual payments which are made go towards discharging the statutory obligation and vice versa (*ERA 1996, s 69(2), (3)*).

If the employer fails to pay the whole or part of the remuneration which is due under *ERA 1996, s 68*, the employee may complain to an employment tribunal. If it finds the complaint well-founded, the tribunal will order payment of the amount due (*ERA 1996, s 70(1), (3)*). The complaint must be presented before the end of the period of three months beginning with the unremunerated day to which it relates, or within such further period as the tribunal considers reasonable where it is satisfied that it was not reasonably practicable to present the complaint within three months (*ERA 1996, s 70(2)*; **19.7** Employment Tribunals – I).

33.29 *Agency Workers*

From 1 October 2011 agency workers who have worked for the qualifying period prescribed in *reg 7* of the *Agency Workers Regulations 2010 (SI 2010/93)* (ie working in the same role with the same hirer for 12 continuous calendar weeks), have comparable protections where the supply of that worker to a hirer is ended on maternity grounds pursuant to one of the measures in **33.26** above or *reg 20* of the *Conduct of Employment Agencies and Employment Businesses Regulations 2003 (SI 20013/3319) (ERA 1996, ss 68A–68D, 69A and 70A).*

33.30 *Pregnant Workers Directive*

In *Parviainen v Finnair Oyj* (Case C-471/08) [2011] ICR 99, [2010] ECR I-6533, the CJEU has held that where an employer transfers a pregnant employee to another job to avoid health risks during her pregnancy, *art 11* of the *Pregnant Workers Directive* requires that she receive her basic pay together with any compensation or allowances related to her status (eg related to her seniority, qualifications or length of service). *Gassmayr v Bundesminister fur Wissenschaft und Forschung* (Case C-194/08) [2010] ECR I-6281 held that *art 11* is directly enforceable in national courts.

33.31 Protection from dismissal by reason of pregnancy

An employee will automatically be held to have been unfairly dismissed if the reason or principal reason for his or her dismissal relates to any of the following matters (which range more widely than pregnancy alone but all of which have been included here for completeness):

(a)   her pregnancy, childbirth or maternity;

(b)   the fact that she has given birth to a child, where her ordinary or additional maternity leave period is ended by the dismissal;

(c)   the application of a requirement or recommendation such as is referred to in *ERA 1996, s 66(2)* (suspension from work on maternity grounds; see **33.9** above);

(d)   the fact that she took, sought to take or availed herself of the benefits of ordinary or additional maternity leave;

(e)   the fact that he or she took or sought to take parental leave or time off under the *ERA 1996, s 57A* (time off to care for dependants);

(f)   the fact that she failed to return to work after a period of ordinary or additional maternity leave in circumstances where her employer did not notify her of the date on which the period in question would end, and she reasonably believed that the period had not ended, or he gave her less than 28 days' notice of the relevant end date, and it was not reasonably practicable for her to return on that date;

(g)   the fact that she undertook, considered undertaking or refused to undertake work during her statutory maternity leave period in accordance with *reg 12A* of the *MPL Regulations*;

(h)   the fact that he or she declined to sign a workforce agreement for the purposes of the *MPL Regulations*;

(i)   the fact that he or she performed (or proposed to perform) any functions or activities as a workforce representative or as a candidate to be such a representative;

(j)   taking time off under *section 57ZE* (accompanying to ante-natal appointments);

(k)   time off under *sections 57ZJ or 57ZL* (adoption appointments);

(l)   ordinary or additional adoption leave

(m)   shared parental leave (see [**33.68**]);

(n)   parental leave;

(o)   paternity leave;

(p)   parental bereavement leave (see [33.121]).

(*Reg 20* of the *MPL Regulations*; *ERA 1996, s 99.*)

An employee will also be treated as having been unfairly dismissed if the reason for the dismissal is that he or she is redundant, but where the circumstances constituting the redundancy applied equally to one or more employees in the same undertaking who held similar positions and who have not been dismissed, and it is shown that the reason or the principal reason for which he or she was selected for dismissal is a reason connected with the above matters (*reg 20(2)*).

In addition, a woman will be treated as having been automatically unfairly dismissed even if there is a genuine redundancy situation if the employer fails to comply with the requirements set out in *reg 10* for dealing with redundancies during ordinary or additional maternity leave (*reg 20(1)(b)*, and see *Simpson v Endsleigh Insurance Services Ltd* [2011] ICR 75, [2010] All ER (D) 95 (Sep)). The dismissal for redundancy must, however, end the maternity leave period. See [**33.50**].

There is no longer a small employers' exemption for automatically unfair dismissal. However, there is an exemption in non-redundancy situations, if the employer can show that it is not reasonably practicable (for a reason other than redundancy) to permit the employee to return to a job which is both suitable for her and appropriate for her to do in the circumstances; and an associated employer offers her a job of that kind, and she accepts or unreasonably refuses that offer (*reg 20(7)*). It is for the employer to establish that he has satisfied this statutory defence (*reg 20(8)*).

Even though the dismissal may not be treated as automatically unfair, however, it may still be unfair according to ordinary principles of the law of unfair dismissal. If the employee is dismissed because another employee has been engaged in her position, that will not be an acceptable reason for her dismissal (*McFadden v Greater Glasgow Passenger Transport Executive* [1977] IRLR 327).

Under the previous legislation, it was held that the words 'or any other reason connected with her pregnancy' were to be interpreted broadly (*Clayton v Vigers* [1989] ICR 713, [1990] IRLR 177). This included a pregnancy-related illness, such as post-natal depression arising in the period of maternity leave following childbirth (*Caledonia Bureau Investment and Property v Caffrey* [1998] ICR 603, [1998] IRLR 110, EAT). The same broad interpretation is likely to apply under the present legislation, but see also *Atkins v Coyle Personnel plc* [2008] IRLR 420, EAT in relation to paternity leave (see below, **33.63**).

In *Ramdoolar v Bycity Ltd* [2005] ICR 368, [2004] All ER (D) 21 (Nov), the EAT held that for a dismissal to be automatically unfair for a reason connected with pregnancy, the employer must know, or believe in the existence, of the pregnancy. It is not sufficient that symptoms of pregnancy existed which the employer ought to have realised meant that the employee was pregnant. The EAT left open the possibility, however, that a dismissal may be automatically unfair if an employer, detecting the symptoms of pregnancy and fearing the consequences, dismisses the employee before his suspicion could be proved right. See also *Really Easy Car Credit Limited v Thompson* (UKEAT/0187/17/DA).

A dismissal in connection with pregnancy and the taking of maternity leave may also amount to sex discrimination (see DISCRIMINATION AND EQUAL OPPORTUNITIES – 1 (12)) and, for an example, *Eversheds Legal Services Ltd v De Belin* [2011] IRLR 448, [2011] ICR 1137 where a man succeeded in a sex discrimination claim in respect of preferential treatment given to a woman on maternity leave in redundancy selection scoring which went beyond what was reasonably necessary to compensate a woman for the disadvantages occasioned by her pregnancy/maternity leave.

33.32 *Qualifying period for protection from dismissal*

There is no qualifying period for a complaint of unfair dismissal where the dismissal is for any of the reasons set out in *ERA 1996, s 99* (see above, **33.31**), nor (although less common!) is there any upper age limit (*ERA 1996, s 108(3)*). See also **49.14** TERMINATION OF EMPLOYMENT for the obligation to give reasons for dismissal of pregnant employees.

33.33 Protection from detriment by reason of pregnancy

Reg 19 of the *MPL Regulations* (and the *ERA 1996, s 47C*) confers a statutory right an employee from being subject to any detriment (other than dismissal) by any act, or any deliberate failure to act, by their employer if it is done for a reason which relates to:

(a) her pregnancy;

(b) the fact that she has given birth to a child, if the act or failure to act takes place during the employee's ordinary or additional maternity leave period;

(c) the fact that she is the subject of a relevant requirement, or a relevant recommendation, as defined by s *66(2)* of the *ERA 1996*;

(d) the fact that she took, sought to take or availed herself of the benefits of, ordinary or additional maternity leave; or

(e) the fact that she took or sought to take parental leave or time off under the *ERA 1996, s 57A*;

(f) the fact that she failed to return to work after a period of ordinary or additional maternity leave in circumstances where her employer did not notify her of the date on which the period in question would end, and she reasonably believed that the period had not ended, or he gave her less than 28 days' notice of the relevant end date, and it was not reasonably practicable for her to return on that date;

(g) the fact that she undertook, considered undertaking or refused to undertake work during her statutory maternity leave period;

(h) the fact that she declined to sign a workforce agreement for the purposes of the *MPL Regulations*;

(i) she performed (or proposed to perform) any functions or activities as a workforce representative or as a candidate to be such a representative.

(j) taking time off under *section 57ZE* (accompanying to ante-natal appointments);

(k) time off under *sections 57ZJ* or *57ZL* (adoption appointments);

(l) shared parental leave (see [**33.68**]);

(m) paternity leave;

(n) parental bereavement leave (see [**33.121**]).

CFA 2014, s 129 also introduces new protections from detriment for agency workers by inserting a new *subsection (5)* into *section 47C* of the *ERA 1996*.

A woman is treated as availing herself of the benefits of ordinary or additional maternity leave if, during that period, she avails herself of the benefit of any of the terms and conditions of her employment preserved by *s 71* or *s 73* of *ERA 1996*: *reg 19(3)–(3A)*.

The failure of an employer to pay a woman on maternity leave wages, salary or a bonus which she would have earned had she been at work cannot be a 'detriment' within the meaning of *reg 19*: see *Hoyland v Asda Stores Ltd* [2005] IRLR 438, [2005] ICR 1235.

33.34 *Remedies*

Where an employee has suffered such a detriment, she may claim to an employment tribunal pursuant to *ERA 1996, s 48*. On such a complaint, it is for the employer to show the ground on which any act, or deliberate failure to act, was done. The complaint must be presented within the period of three months beginning with the date of the act or failure to act, or the last of the series of similar such acts. Time for presenting a complaint can be extended where (as in the case for unfair dismissal) the employment tribunal is satisfied that it was not reasonably practicable for the complaint to be presented within the period of three months.

If the complaint is well-founded, the employment tribunal shall make a declaration to that effect, and may make an award of compensation. The amount of compensation shall be such as the tribunal considers to be just and equitable in all the circumstances, having regard to the infringement to which the complaint relates, and any loss attributable to the act in question (*ERA 1996, s 49*).

33.35   MATERNITY LEAVE

ERA 1996, Pt VIII (ss 71–75), and the *MPL Regulations* made thereunder, provide for a statutory right to maternity leave. It is necessary to distinguish between three types of maternity leave: (a) compulsory maternity leave; (b) ordinary maternity leave ("OML"); and (c) additional maternity leave ("AML").

In summary, compulsory maternity leave is a two-week period in which a mother is not permitted to return to work; OML is a 26 week period; and AML is an additional 26 week period of leave. Taken together, these periods of leave are known as 'statutory maternity leave'.

Church of England clergy have the right to maternity, paternity, parental, adoption leave and shared parental leave in accordance with directions given by the Archbishops' Council: see the *Ecclesiastical Offices (Terms of Service) Regulations 2009 (SI 2009/2108), reg 23*.

See [**33.54**] in relation to statutory maternity pay. This section concerns statutory maternity leave only.

33.36   Compulsory maternity leave

An employee entitled to OML in accordance with *ERA 1996* shall not be permitted by her employer to work for a period of two weeks commencing with the day on which childbirth occurs. (This is described as 'compulsory maternity leave' (*ERA 1996, s 72*, and the *MPL Regulations, reg 8*). Failure to comply with this prohibition renders the employer liable on summary conviction to a fine (*ERA 1996, s 72(5)*).

Note that an occupier of a factory will be subject to a fine if he knowingly allows a woman to be employed therein within four weeks after she has given birth: *Public Health Act 1936, s 205*.

33.37   Ordinary maternity leave

The OML period commences with the date which the employee notifies as the date on which she intends her absence to commence (see below **33.39**), or if earlier, the first day on which she is absent from work wholly or partly because of pregnancy or childbirth after the beginning of the 4th week before the Expected Week of Childbirth ("EWC") (*reg 6(1)–(2)*).

If childbirth occurs before the relevant date, OML commences on the day after the day of the birth (*reg 6(2)*). 'Childbirth' means the birth of a living child or the birth of a child whether living or dead after 24 weeks of pregnancy (*reg 2(1)*).

33.38 The OML period continues for 26 weeks or until the latest of the end of the compulsory maternity leave period, the expiry of any period during which there is any statutory prohibition on the employee working by reason of her recently having given birth, or upon her dismissal (*reg 7*).

33.39 In order to enjoy the right to OML, the employee must generally:

(a)   notify her employer of:

(i)   her pregnancy;

(ii)   the 'EWC'; and

(iii)   the date on which she intends her OML period to start;

no later than the 15th week before her EWC or, if that is not reasonably practicable, as soon as is reasonably practicable; and

(b)   if requested to do so by her employer, produce for his inspection a certificate from a registered medical practitioner or a registered midwife stating the EWC (*reg 4(1)*).

The notification of the date on which the employee intends her OML period to start must be in writing, if the employer so requests (*reg 4(2)*). Note that OML cannot start any earlier than the beginning of the 11th week before the EWC (*reg 4(2)*). As to these notification provisions, and for an example of a case in which it was found to have been not reasonably practicable for the employee to comply with *reg 4*, see the decision of the EAT in *St Alphonsus RC Primary School v Blenkinsop* (UKEAT/0082/09) [2009] All ER (D) 54 (Aug).

However:

(a)   where the period of OML commences the day following the first day after the beginning of the 4th week before the EWC on which she is absent from work wholly or partly because of pregnancy, by *reg 6(1)(b)*, the employee must notify her employer as soon as is reasonably practicable that she is absent wholly or partly because of pregnancy and of the date on which her absence on that account began (*reg 4(3)*); and

(b)   where childbirth occurs before the notified leave date or before the employee has notified such a date (see *reg 6(2)*), the employee must notify her employer that she has given birth (and on which date) as soon as is reasonably practicable after the birth (*reg 4(4)*).

Such notice must be given in writing if the employer so requests (*reg 4*).

The date upon which the employee commences OML may be varied if she gives 28 days' notice before the date that is being varied, or 28 days' notice before the new date, whichever is earlier (or if those dates cannot be complied with, she gives notice as soon as it is reasonably practicable to do so) (*reg 4(1A)*). Such notice must be in writing if the employer so requests.

There is no service requirement for OML.

33.40 An employee who is absent from work at any time during her OML period is entitled to the benefit of the terms and conditions of employment which would otherwise have been applicable to her, such as holiday entitlement, even if they do not arise under her contract of employment, although this does not confer any entitlement to remuneration (*ERA 1996, s 71* and *reg 9*). The *MPL Regulations* define 'remuneration' as wages or salary only (*reg 9(3)*).

In *Peninsula Business Services v Donaldson* (UKEAT/0249/15) (9 March 2016) the EAT held that *reg 9* of the *MPL Regulations* did not require a salary sacrifice scheme for childcare vouchers, whereby a portion of a person's remuneration was diverted in exchange for the aforesaid vouchers, to be continued during maternity leave. The vouchers provided under the scheme were not a benefit as such, but remuneration that had been diverted for the tax-efficient provision of childcare. The EAT disapproved HMRC guidance providing to the contrary in its judgment. Revised guidance is to be found at: https ://www.gov.uk/guidance/salary-sacrifice-and-the-effects-on-paye. However, the EAT noted *obiter* at [35] that if the vouchers had merely been given as such, as an additional benefit, *reg 9* would require the continued provision of the vouchers. Clearly, the distinction drawn by the EAT is of significance for all salary sacrifice benefits during maternity leave.

The employee is also bound during this period by any obligations arising under these same terms and conditions (*ERA 1996, s 71* and *reg 9*).

In *Gomez (Merino) v Continental Industrias del Caucho SA* (C-342/01) [2004] ECR I-2605, [2004] IRLR 407, [2005] ICR 1040, the ECJ held that a worker must be able to take the paid annual leave to which she is entitled under the *Working Time Directive* during a period other than the period of her maternity leave.

33.41   An employee returning after an isolated period of OML is ordinarily entitled to return to the job in which she was employed before her absence (*reg 18*). 'Job' means the nature of the work that she is employed to do in accordance with her contract, and the capacity and place in which she is so employed (*reg 2(1)*). See **33.50** below for the considerations relating to a redundancy situation.

The purpose of this provision is to put the returning employee back into a situation as near as possible to that which she left: see *Blundell v Governing Body of St Andrews Catholic Primary School* [2007] ICR 1451, [2007] IRLR 652, EAT. In that case, it did not mean that the returning teacher had to be offered the job of teaching the particular class that she had taught before her maternity leave. The work that she was employed to do was that of a teacher, her capacity was viewed as a class teacher rather than the teacher of a particular reception class, and her place of work was the school and not a particular classroom. Note that the right to return to the job carries with it the right to return on terms and conditions no less favourable than those that the employee would have enjoyed had she not been absent, and with her seniority, pension and similar rights as they would have been had she not been absent (*reg 18A*).

33.42   An employee who has a contractual or other right to maternity leave may not exercise both that and the statutory right separately, but may take advantage of whichever right is in any particular respect more favourable. The provisions of *ERA 1996* and of the *Regulations* then apply, modified as necessary, to the exercise of the composite right (*reg 21*).

33.43   The position in relation to surrogacy arrangements, up to 5 April 2015, was that in two cases (*Z v A Government Department* (Case C-363/12) and *CD v ST* (Case C-167/12) [2014] IRLR 551) the CJEU held that women who receive children under a surrogacy arrangement are not entitled to maternity leave, even where the receiving mother breast feeds the child. However, the CJEU also held that this does not prevent a member state introducing a provision that is more favourable to commissioning mothers who receive babies through surrogacy. The *CFA 2014* did just that from April 2015: it provided for surrogacy parents to receive the same rights to leave and pay as those adopting children (see **[33.68]**).

33.44   Additional maternity leave

An employee who qualifies for OML now qualifies automatically for AML as well (*reg 4*). There is no qualifying period of employment for this right. She will continue to have the benefit of her terms and conditions of employment during AML (and is bound by any obligations), in the same way as during OML (*reg 9* and see above **33.29**).

The AML period commences on the day after the last day of the employee's OML period (*reg 6(3)*). Importantly, where the employee notifies her employer under reg 4 of the date on which her OML period will commence or has commenced, the employer shall notify her of the date on which her AML period shall end either within 28 days of the date on which he received the notification (where the notification is under *reg 4(1)(a)(iii), (3)(b)* or *(4)(b)*) or within 28 days on which the employee's OML period commenced (where the notification is under *reg 4(1A)*) (*reg 7(6),(7)*).

The right to AML continues until the end of the period of 26 weeks from the date upon which it commences, unless the employee is dismissed before that date (*reg 7(4)*).

33.45   An employee who is entitled to AML may return to work before the end of the AML period. To do so, she has to give her employer not less than eight weeks' notice of the date on which she intends to return (*reg 11(1)*). If she does give this notice, then it would appear that her employer cannot seek to postpone her return date.

Where an employee does not give eight weeks' notice of her intended return date and attempts to return to work earlier than the end of her AML period, then her employer is entitled to postpone her return to such a date as will mean that they have eight weeks' notice of her return (*reg 11(2)*). The only exception to this is that the postponement cannot extend beyond the date of the end of the AML period (*reg 11(3)*). During the period of postponement, the employer is under no contractual obligation to pay any remuneration until the date to which the employee's return was postponed, save where they have failed to notify her of when the AML period was due to end (*reg 11(4)–(5)*).

An employee is entitled to change her mind as to when to return to work during the AML period, if she has already given notice of return before the end of that period or if the employer has (in line with the procedure above) postponed her return date (*reg 11(2A)–(2B)*). If the employee wishes to return to work later than the original return date, she must give her employer not less than eight weeks' notice ending with the original return date. If she wishes to return earlier than the original return date, she must give at least eight weeks' notice of the new return date.

The employee does not need to inform her employer that she intends to exercise her right to return at the end of the AML period unless she is specifically requested to do so by her employer. In addition, an employer is no longer entitled to request confirmation that the employee will be returning to work at the end of the AML period (the former *reg 12* has been revoked).

33.46   The right on redundancy is the same as for employees seeking to return after OML (see **33.50** below).

33.47   The returning employee has the right to return to the job in which she was employed before her absence or, if it is not reasonably practicable for the employer to permit her to return to that job, to another job which is both suitable for her and appropriate for her to do in the circumstances (*reg 18(2)*). The definition of 'job' is the same as for returnees from OML: see *Blundell v Governing Body of St Andrews Catholic Primary School* [2007] ICR 1451, [2007] IRLR 652, EAT and see above **33.40**. The right is also to return on terms and conditions no less favourable than would have applied if the employee had not been absent. She is entitled to the same seniority, pension rights and similar rights as she would have enjoyed if she had not taken any AML (*reg 18A*). There is no right as such to return to work on a part-time basis, or on terms preferable to the returning employee: see *British Telecommunications plc v Roberts* [1996] IRLR 601, [1996] ICR 625, EAT. Nevertheless, an employer's refusal to permit an employee to job share or return part-time might constitute indirect sex discrimination (*Hardys & Hansons plc v Lax* [2005] IRLR 726, [2005] ICR 1565, CA).

33.48   Save for the limited circumstances described by *reg 20* of the *MPL Regulations*, the legislation has nothing to say about the difficult question of mothers who do not return to work on the return date. *Reg 20* states that a mother will be automatically unfairly dismissed if the reason for the dismissal relates to the fact that she failed to return to work after a period of ordinary or additional maternity leave in circumstances where her employer did not notify her of the date on which the period in question would end, and she reasonably believed that the period had not ended, or he gave her less than 28 days' notice of the relevant end date, and it was not reasonably practicable for her to return on that date.

In other circumstances, it may well be that the law under the previous legislation will prevail. It may be useful therefore to consider the decision of the House of Lords in *Halfpenny v IGE Medical Systems Ltd* [2001] IRLR 96, [2001] ICR 73, construing the former legislation.

The facts of *Halfpenny* are relatively straightforward. The employee failed to return to work on the notified return date for reasons of ill-health, supported by a medical certificate. As she had not exhausted her contractual entitlement to sick leave and had a good reason for her absence, her employer was found to have dismissed her wrongfully by refusing to extend her period of leave. In addition, the employer was found to have discriminated against the employee on grounds of her sex as it would have allowed a male employee to continue sick leave with pay.

In the Court of Appeal ([1999] IRLR 177, [1999] ICR 834), it was held (confirming the earlier decision of *Crees v Royal London Mutual Insurance Society Ltd* [1998] IRLR 245, [1998] ICR 848) that to avail herself of the right not to be unfairly dismissed following maternity leave, an employee need not physically return to work on the notified day of return. An employee was held to have exercised the right to return to work following maternity leave (and also preserved her continuity of employment) merely by giving the appropriate notice of return before the notified date of return.

This aspect of the decision was overturned by the House of Lords, where it was held that an employee did not avail herself of the 'return to work' merely by giving the appropriate notice of return if she did not actually return to work on the notified day. Rather, the employee had to give the appropriate notice and also demonstrate that, on the notified date for return, she had done something consistent with the due performance by her of her revived contract of employment. Normally, this would mean that she actually returned to work physically. If, however, under the contract she would not be bound to return on that day (eg as a result of an accident, a strike, or poor weather conditions) she merely had to have done something to demonstrate that she would have returned to work otherwise. If she were ill, she would have to provide the necessary certificates that would be required of her under the contract.

The House of Lords went on to decide that where the employee had demonstrated the appropriate conduct for a 'return to work', she would be treated as having been 'dismissed' by her employer if he refused to let her return, for the purposes of the law of unfair dismissal only. She had no right, however, to claim that she had been wrongfully dismissed as the contract of employment would be treated as having been suspended until her actual return. This aspect of the decision may have been overtaken by the fact that the period of AML during which the contract continues ends pursuant to the legislation.

See *Rashid v Asian Community Care Services Ltd* (EAT/480/99, 16 November 2000) [2000] All ER (D) 2344 for a case in which an employment tribunal found that a mother had terminated the contract of employment by failing to return to work, a finding reversed by the EAT.

33.49   An employee who has both a statutory and a contractual right to return to work may not exercise the two rights separately, but may take advantage of whichever right is the more favourable in any particular respect (*reg 21*).

33.50 Maternity and Parental Rights

33.50 Redundancy during maternity leave

As described above the *EU Pregnant Workers Directive, 92/85* prohibits the dismissal of workers who are pregnant; have recently given birth; or who are breast-feeding during the period from the beginning of their pregnancy to the end of the 14 week period of maternity leave required by the Directive "save in exceptional cases not connected with their condition which are permitted under national legislation". In *Jessica Porras Guisado v Bankia SA* C–103/16 [2018] IRLR 563, the CJEU took the view that redundancy could constitute such an exceptional case. European Law permits redundancy dismissals during maternity leave. The position, as is explained immediately below, is a somewhat different as a matter of Domestic law. Those on maternity leave are special cases.

If, during the OML or AML period, redundancy makes it impracticable to continue to employ an employee under her existing contract, she is entitled to be offered alternative employment with her employer, his successor (as defined by *ERA 1996, s 235(1)*) or an associated employer (see **7.9(a)** CONTINUOUS EMPLOYMENT) if a suitable available vacancy exists. The offer must be made before the old employment ends, and the new employment must commence immediately the old employment ends. It must involve work of a kind suitable in relation to the employee and appropriate for her to do in the circumstances, and the terms and conditions as to capacity, place of employment and otherwise must not be substantially less favourable than under the old contract (*MPL Regulations, reg 10*).

These provisions have been considered by the EAT in *Simpson v Endsleigh Insurance Services Ltd* [2011] ICR 75, [2010] All ER (D) 95 (Sep). Amongst other things, the EAT indicated that: (i) the requirement of suitability in *reg 10(2)* can only sensibly be tested by the requirement that it is coupled with a new contract of employment which complies with *reg 10(3)* – the provisions should not be looked at in isolation; (ii) there is no requirement on the employee to engage in this process and it is up to the employers, knowing what they do about the employee, to decide whether or not a vacancy is suitable; and (iii) the EAT was "by no means satisfied" that an employer could choose to test suitability by assessment and interview, contrary to the suggestion in the IDS Handbook on Redundancy. More recently, in *Wainwright v Sefton Borough Council* [2015] IRLR 90, [2015] ICR 652, the EAT considered how *reg 10* may operate depending upon the particular redundancy process chosen. The EAT reiterated that the obligation under *reg 10* arises once the employee is redundant within the meaning of *ERA 1996, s 139*, and does not depend on any label imposed by the employer (such as 'displacement' or 'redeployment'). The tribunal also emphasised that a breach of *reg 10* does not necessarily also entail discrimination under *section 18* of the *EqA*.

More favourable treatment of a woman for a reason related to her pregnancy can be less favourable treatment of a man for sex-related reasons and unlawful discrimination: *Eversheds Legal Services v De Belin* [2011] IRLR 448, [2011] ICR 1137. In that case the EAT considered that the protection of special treatment afforded to women in connection with pregnancy or childbirth under *paragraph 2* of *Schedule 7* to the *2010 Act* must be proportionate, and in *De Belin* the employer could have compared periods for the purposes of redundancy scoring where both employees had been at work.

In *Riezniece v Zemkopibas ministrija (Republic of Latvia)* (Case C-7/12) [2013] ICR 1096, [2013] IRLR 828 the CJEU held that the Framework Agreement on Parental Leave precluded a worker being put in a less favourable position in a redundancy selection exercise because they had taken parental leave; and stated that a person returning from parental leave cannot be dismissed merely because the post to which the person would be returning to work is due to be abolished. See also AG Sharpston's opinion in *Jessica Porras Guisado v Bankia SA* C-103/16 concerning collective redundancies and the 'exceptional cases' exception in *art 10* of the *Maternity Directive (Directive 89/391/EEC)*.

33.51 Dismissal of replacement

Where an employer engages an employee to take the place of one who is absent due to pregnancy, the subsequent dismissal of that employee upon the resumption of work by the original employee will be considered to be a dismissal for a (potentially fair) some other substantial reason (see **55.14 Unfair Dismissal – II**) only if the employer informs the employee in writing, on engaging her, that her employment will be terminated on the resumption of work by another employee who is, or will be, absent wholly or partly because of pregnancy, childbirth, adoption leave, APL or SPL, or the end of a period of suspension from work on maternity grounds, and if the employee is dismissed in order to make it possible to give work to the returning employee (*ERA 1996, s 106*). The language used in the written information must be clear and unambiguous: see *Victoria and Albert Museum v Durrant* [2011] IRLR 290.

However, this fact does not, in itself, make the dismissal fair. The employment tribunal will consider whether the dismissal was fair in all the circumstances (see further **55.4 Unfair Dismissal – II**). The EAT in *Victoria and Albert Museum v Durrant* also indicated, *obiter*, that *s 106* does not operate in all cases to deem the reason for dismissal to be for some other substantial reason. In some cases the reason for dismissal might be (for example) redundancy, notwithstanding that *s 106* is engaged.

33.52 Right to written statement of reasons for dismissal

Without having to request it, and irrespective of how long she has been employed, an employee is entitled to a written statement giving particulars of the reason for her dismissal if she is dismissed whilst pregnant, or after childbirth in circumstances in which her OML or AML period ends by reason of the dismissal: *ERA 1996, s 92(4)*.

33.53 Work during statutory maternity leave

An employee may carry out up to 10 days' work for her employer during her statutory maternity leave period without bringing her maternity leave to an end (*reg 12A(1)*), known as 'keeping in touch' or 'KIT' days. Work means any work done under the contract of employment and may include training or any activity undertaken for the purposes of keeping in touch with the workplace (*reg 12A(3)*). Such work does not extend the total duration of the statutory maternity leave period (*reg 12A(7)*).

Any work carried out on any date constitutes a day's work for these purposes (*reg 12A(2)*). However, reasonable contact from time to time between an employee and her employer (eg to discuss her return to work) does not bring the maternity leave period to an end (*reg 12A(4)*). There is no right for an employer to require that an employee work during the statutory maternity leave period, and no right for an employee to work during this period (*reg 12A(6)*). The employee does not lose her entitlement to SMP during the 10 keeping in touch days and any additional payment for the work done is a matter of contract between her and the employer.

33.54 STATUTORY MATERNITY PAY

The statutory provisions relating to the system of statutory maternity pay ("SMP"), first introduced by the *Social Security Act 1989*, have been consolidated into the *Social Security Contributions and Benefits Act 1992* ("SSCBA 1992"). The relevant provisions have been the subject of significant amendments to reflect the *Pregnant Workers Directive* (*Directive 92/85/EEC*). The general position is that the employer pays SMP, but the employer may recoup a significant proportion of the SMP paid from the government (see [**33.60**]).

The legislative scheme governing payment of SMP and, in particular, the rules on when the SMP period commences were considered by the Upper Tribunal in *Wade v North Yorkshire Police Authority* [2011] IRLR 393, UT (TCC).

It is not possible to contract out of the obligation to pay SMP. Consequently, for the purposes of a settlement agreement, it is not sufficient to settle 'all claims' (in the normal way) by the payment of a sum unless the part of the total sum constituting SMP is specifically identified in the settlement agreement: see *Campus Living Villages UK Ltd v Commissioners for HMRC* [2016] UKFTT 0738 (TC). In that case, despite making a payment of £60,000 by way of settlement, the FTT held that a further £42,325.26 was payable by way of SMP due to the drafting of the settlement agreement.

There may also be a contractual right to maternity pay under a woman's contract of employment. This is often known as 'enhanced' maternity pay. If the employee fails to return to work and contractual maternity pay becomes repayable to the employer pursuant to a term of the contract, either the employer or the employee may be able to recover the National Insurance contributions on such pay from the Secretary of State.

33.55 Qualifying requirements

An employee must normally satisfy the following conditions before she can qualify for SMP:

(a)   she must have been continuously employed by her employer for at least 26 weeks ending with the week immediately preceding the 14th week before the EWC, but have ceased to work for him (see CONTINUOUS EMPLOYMENT (7)). (Note that she will have normally have 'ceased to work for him' by reason of her pregnancy, but there is no requirement to prove this (see further the repealing provisions in the *Employment Act 2002, Sch 8, para 1*));

(b)   her normal weekly earnings, for the period of 8 weeks ending with the week immediately preceding the 14th week before the EWC, must be not less than the lower limit for the payment of National Insurance contributions (£116 per week from 6 April 2018);

(c)   she must have become pregnant and reached, or been confined before reaching, the start of the 11th week before the expected week of confinement.

(SSCBA 1992, s 164(1), (2).)

'Confinement' is defined as labour resulting in the issue of a living child, or labour after 24 weeks of pregnancy resulting in the issue of a child whether alive or dead *(SSCBA 1992, s 171(1))*. 'Employee' is defined as meaning a woman who is gainfully employed in Great Britain either under a contract of service or in an office (including elective office) with general earnings *(SSCBA 1992, s 171(1))*. (Note that this definition is subject to various other statutory provisions, including those in *s 171(1)* itself and in *reg 17* of the *Statutory Maternity Pay (General) Regulations 1986 (SI 1986/1960)* (the "**SMP Regulations**")).)

There are certain exceptions to the above requirement of continuous employment. For example, the employer remains liable to pay SMP if the period of continuous employment was not less than eight weeks and he brought the contract of employment to an end solely or mainly for the purpose of avoiding his liability for SMP *(reg 3 of the SMP Regulations)*. In addition, the right to SMP survives if the woman is confined more than 14 weeks before the expected date of confinement, and would, but for her confinement, otherwise have qualified *(reg 4 of the SMP Regulations as amended by SI 1994/1367, reg 3)*.

For the purpose of calculating continuity of employment, it is the existence of the contract of employment which is crucial, and not whether the employee is in fact working. In *Secretary of State for Employment v Doulton Sanitaryware Ltd* [1981] ICR 477, [1981] IRLR

365, EAT (decided under the previous law relating to maternity pay), it was held on the facts that the parties intended the contract to continue even though the employee had stopped working (she had been put on a list of 'prolonged absentees'). In *Rosselle v Institut national d'assurance maladie-invalide* (Case C-65/14) [2015] All ER (D) 51 (Jun) the CJEU held that the six month period of employment required to establish entitlement to a maternity allowance could not be re-started merely because a worker's employment status or the post of the worker has changed at that particular employer.

It is clearly intended that the right to SMP should not be conditional upon an intention to return to work after the confinement.

There is no entitlement to SMP in respect of any week in which the employee is in legal custody or sentenced to a term of imprisonment, other than a suspended sentence, or in respect of any subsequent week within the maternity pay period (*reg 9 of the SMP Regulations*).

Members of Her Majesty's forces are excluded from the right to SMP (*SSCBA 1992, s 161(2)*). The right extends to persons working for the Crown (*s 161*), within the EU, to employees who are absent from Great Britain on holiday or for business purposes at any time during the maternity pay period, as well as to certain mariners (see the *Statutory Maternity Pay (Persons Abroad and Mariners) Regulations 1987 (SI 1987/418)*, as amended by *Social Security Contributions, Statutory Maternity Pay and Statutory Sick Pay (Miscellaneous Amendments) Regulations 1996 (SI 1996/777), reg 4*).

SSCBA 1992, s 164(6) provides that any agreement is void in so far as it purports to exclude or limit the right to SMP.

33.56 Procedure for making a claim

The employee must give her employer (or the person liable to make payments of SMP) 28 days' prior notice of the date from which she expects his liability to pay SMP to begin, or if that is not reasonably practicable, such notice as is reasonably practicable (*s 164(4)* and *reg 23 of the SMP Regulations*). That notice must be in writing if the liable person so requests (*SSCBA, s 164(5)*).

The employee must also provide the liable person with a maternity certificate signed by a doctor or midwife as evidence of her pregnancy and of the expected date of confinement and there is a prescribed form for such certificates (*reg 22 of the SMP Regulations; Social Security Administration Act 1992, s 15; Statutory Maternity Pay (Medical Evidence) Regulations 1987 (SI 1987/235)*).

33.57 Period of entitlement

SMP is payable in respect of each week during the 'maternity pay period'. The maternity pay period will be a period of 39 consecutive weeks (*reg 2(2) of the SMP Regulations*). In general, when it starts depends upon when the employee gives notice and stops work (*reg 2(1) of the SMP Regulations*). However, ordinarily the first day of the period will not be earlier than the 11th week before the expected week of confinement, nor later than the day immediately following the day of confinement. Note that *reg 2 of the SMP Regulations* contains other specific rules on the start of the maternity pay period. The *SMP Regulations* do not permit payment to cease upon dismissal.

These rules were considered by the Upper Tribunal in *Wade v North Yorkshire Police Authority* [2011] IRLR 393, UT (TCC). The UT provided detailed guidance on the start date for SMP and observed that a woman could nominate a date from which she wished to claim SMP and would be ceasing to work "in conformity with [a] notice" for the purposes of *reg 2(1)* even if she has previously ceased to work on some other basis (in a way analogous to her right to claim statutory maternity leave from a date of her choosing, even if she had previously been away from work for eg annual leave or sick leave).

SMP is not ordinarily payable by an employer in respect of a week during any part of which the woman works under a contract of service with him (*SSCBA, s 165(4)*).

33.58 Amount of payments

SSCBA 1992, s 166 provides for two rates of payment. (Note: the application of *s 166* is modified by *SI 1986/1960, reg 4(3)* (as amended by *SI 1994/1367, reg 3*) where the employee is confined more than 14 weeks before the expected date of confinement, and would, but for her confinement, otherwise have qualified; see **33.48** above.)

For the first six weeks of the maternity pay period, the rate is calculated as being 90% of the employee's normal weekly earnings for the period of 8 weeks immediately preceding the 14th week before the EWC (there is no minimum rate of payment) (*SSCBA, s 166(2)*). The calculation is made by reference to actual earnings, regardless of any abnormal amounts in those eight weeks. After the first six weeks, the payment for the remaining 33 weeks is set at the lesser of £151.20 per week or the rate payable during the first six weeks (*SCCBA, s 166(1)(b)*; *reg 6* of the *SMP Regulations*). The rate of SMP is amended annually, and the stated rate is correct as of 7 April 2020.

In any case where a woman is awarded a pay increase (or would have been awarded such an increase had she not then been absent on statutory maternity leave) and the pay increase applies to the whole or any part of the period between the beginning of the relevant period and the end of her period of SML, her normal weekly earnings should be calculated as if such sum was paid in that period: *reg 21(7)* of the *Statutory Maternity Pay (General) Regulations 1986 SI 1986/1960*. This regulation was amended in order to give effect to the decision of the ECJ in *Gillespie v Northern Health and Social Services Board: C-342/93* [1996] ICR 498, [1996] IRLR 214. Thus the EAT had held in *Alabaster v Woolwich plc* [2000] 1 IRLR 754, [2000] ICR 1037 that in calculating maternity pay, a woman was entitled to the benefit of all increases in her basic salary which took effect between the start of the 'relevant period' (the period of eight weeks immediately preceding the 14th week before the EWC) and the end of her maternity leave, and not just backdated pay increases. The EAT also held that the proper remedy for failure to make appropriate payments of maternity pay was an action for unlawful deduction of wages. The matter was referred to the ECJ, which held ([2004] IRLR 486, [2005] ICR 695) that a woman who receives a pay increase before the start of her maternity leave is entitled to have the increase taken into consideration even though the pay rise was not backdated to the relevant reference period for the purposes of the relevant regulations.

SMP should be paid in the like manner and at the same time as the employee would normally be paid, or if there is no agreement as to a pay day, or no normal pay day, on the last day of a calendar month (*regs 27, 29* of the *SMP Regulations*). It does not exclude any contractual benefits to which the employee may be entitled, but the employer is entitled to set off SMP against contractual remuneration in respect of the same period and vice versa (*SSCBA, Sch 13 para 3*). In other words, the employer has to meet the more onerous of the contractual and statutory burdens, but not both of them. Similarly, tax, National Insurance contributions and any other regular deductions fall to be deducted from SMP.

In *Peninsula Business Services v Donaldson* (UKEAT/0249/15) (9 March 2016) the EAT disapproved certain sections of previous HMRC Guidance entitled 'SMP – Salary-Sacrifice and Non-cash Benefits' (August 2008) relating to childcare vouchers. Revised guidance has been issued (with the latest update being made in October 2018) and can be found at: https ://www.gov.uk/guidance/salary-sacrifice-and-the-effects-on-paye. See Para **[33.40]** above.

33.59 Remedy for non-payment

If the employer fails to make payments of SMP to which the employee believes herself to be entitled, the employee may first of all require the employer within a reasonable time to supply her with a written statement of the position which he is adopting (*Social Security Administration Act 1992, s 15(2)*). Where an employer decides that he has no liability to pay SMP or further SMP, he must also furnish her with the details of and reasons for his decision, and with other information, in connection with the making of a claim by her for a maternity allowance or incapacity benefit or employment and support allowance (*reg 25A* of the *SMP Regulations* (inserted by *SI 1990/622*)). If the dispute is not resolved, either the employee or the DWP may refer the matter to an HMRC officer (*Statutory Sick Pay and Statutory Maternity Pay (Decisions) Regulations 1999 (SI 1999/776)*: *Taylor Gordon & Co Ltd v Timmons* [2004] IRLR 180 (on SSP); *Hair Division Ltd v Macmillan*, EAT (12 October 2012, unreported). An employer's continued refusal to pay after an adverse determination is an offence.

If the employee is unable to obtain her entitlement from the employer (which may be because he has become insolvent), she is entitled to look to the Secretary of State for payment (*regs 7, 30* of the *SMP Regulations*).

However, if her employer does not dispute the entitlement to SMP, and the complaint is that the payment has not been paid (or not paid in the correct amount), this may be brought as a wages claim because SMP is within the definition of wages in *ERA 1996, s 27*.

33.60 Recoupment by employer

The employer is able to recoup from the government at least a substantial proportion of SMP. In short, the employer deducts the relevant moneys from its National Insurance contributions which would otherwise fall to be remitted. Employers will be able to recover only 92% of each payment of SMP, save for 'small employers' who may recoup 100%. Indeed, small employers are entitled to receive an additional 3% to cover the estimated cost of secondary Class 1 contributions in respect of SMP. The system of recoupment is governed by regulations made under *SSCBA 1992, s 167* (substituted by *EmA 2002, s 21(1)*). These are the *Statutory Maternity Pay (Compensation of Employers) and Miscellaneous Amendment Regulations 1994 (SI 1994/1882)*, as amended.

Employers can, in certain circumstances, obtain advance recovery of SMP from HMRC (*EmA 2002, s 21(2); Statutory Maternity Pay (Compensation of Employers) and Miscellaneous Amendment Regulations 1994 (SI 1994/1882), reg 5* (as amended by *SI 2003/672*)).

33.61 Maternity allowance

Women who do not qualify for SMP may be entitled to receive the social security benefit of maternity allowance instead: see the *SSCBA, s 35(1)*.

33.62 UNPAID PARENTAL LEAVE

Any employee with one year's continuous service who has, or expects to have, responsibility for a child is entitled to be absent from work on parental leave for the purpose of caring for that child: *MPL Regulations, reg 13(1)*. 'Responsibility' means 'parental responsibility' or registration as the child's father: *reg 13(2)*. Enforcement of this right is by complaint to an employment tribunal (*ERA 1996, s 80(1)*).

The original entitlement under *reg 14* was to thirteen weeks of leave in respect of any individual child. In March 2010 the EU Council adopted a further Directive extending the period of parental leave to eighteen weeks: the *Parental Leave Directive 2010/18/EU*. This was implemented by the *Parental Leave (EU Directive) Regulations 2013 (SI 2013/283)* with effect from 8 March 2013. The period of parental leave remains at 18 weeks for each child (*reg 14(1)*), but each parent is limited to four weeks for each individual child in any one year.

From 5 April 2015, the right to take parental leave may be exercised in respect of a child up until (and including) the date of the child's 18th birthday: *reg 15(1)* of the *MPL Regulations*, which were amended by the *Maternity and Parental Leave etc. (Amendment) Regulations 2014/3221*. Prior to 5 April 2015, leave generally could only be taken up to the child's fifth birthday, with special provision for disabled children and children born before 15 December 1999.

The *MPL Regulations* gave effect to provisions contained in the *EU Parental Leave Directive (96/34)*. They created a right to unpaid parental leave in respect of children born or adopted on or after 15 December 1999. A number of amendments have been made to the *MPL Regulations* to ensure compliance with the *Directive*: see the *Maternity and Parental Leave (Amendment) Regulations 2001 (SI 2001/4010)*; the *Maternity and Parental Leave (Amendment) Regulations 2002 (SI 2002/2789)*; the *Maternity and Parental Leave etc and the Paternity and Adoption Leave (Amendment) Regulations 2006 (SI 2006/2014)*; the *Maternity and Parental Leave etc and the Paternity and Adoption Leave (Amendment) Regulations 2008 (SI 2008/1966)*; and the *Parental Leave (EU Directive) Regulations 2013 (SI 2013/283)*.

33.63 The *MPL Regulations* envisage that parental leave arrangements will be governed by contract in most workplaces. Where there is no such agreement, default provisions apply: *reg 16* and *Sch 2*.

Under the default provisions, leave can only be taken in blocks of one week at a time (except in a case where the child in question is entitled to a disability living allowance): *Sch 2, para 7*. A week's leave is defined in *reg 14*. It is not open to an employee to take one day's parental leave (unless this is agreed to by his employer as part of a *Workforce Agreement*): see *New Southern Railways Ltd (formerly South Central Trains Ltd) v Rodway* [2005] IRLR 583, [2005] ICR 1162, CA. The maximum that can be taken is four weeks' leave in respect of any individual child during a particular year: *Sch 2, paras 8* and *9*. The default provisions also contain 'conditions of entitlement' for the taking of parental leave. These include the provision of evidence of responsibility if required, notice to the employer of the leave dates, and the ability of the employer to postpone leave in certain circumstances (see *Sch 2, paras 1 to 5*).

33.64 The *Regulations* provide protection against victimisation. An employee is protected against detriment by reason of taking or seeking to take parental leave, declining to sign a workforce agreement or performing any function or activity as a workforce representative or candidate (or proposing to do so): *reg 19(2)* and *ERA 1996, s 47C*. He or she will have been automatically unfairly dismissed if dismissed for such a reason: *reg 20(3)* and *ERA 1996, s 99*. There are also further protections in relation to asserting a statutory right in the *ERA 1996, s 104*.

In *New Southern Railways Ltd* (above), an employee sought to take one day's leave to look after his son. This was refused by the employer. The employee took the day off anyway and was subsequently issued with a disciplinary warning for being absent without permission. The EAT and Court of Appeal overturned the decision of an employment tribunal that he had been victimised because the disagreement as to whether or not he was entitled to take one day's parental leave was for 'a reason related to parental leave'. The Court of Appeal held that victimisation by the employer must be 'done for a prescribed reason', which is one prescribed by the *MPL Regulations*. As the employee could not lawfully take one day of parental leave under the 'Default Provisions', the disciplinary action was not for a prescribed reason, and was therefore lawful.

33.65 Certain contractual provisions continue to apply during the parental leave period, including the implied obligations of trust and confidence and good faith (*reg 17*). As a matter of EU Law, there is no requirement that a worker should be treated as continuing to accrue entitlement to statutory paid annual leave when on parental leave: *Tribunal Botoşani, Ministerul Justitiei v Dicu* C-12/17 [2018] IRLR 1175.

33.66 There is also a right to return to work after parental leave. An employee who takes parental leave for a period of four weeks or less, which was an isolated period of leave or the last of two or more consecutive periods of statutory leave which did not include any period of statutory leave which when added to any other period of statutory leave (excluding parental leave) taken in relation to the same child means that the total amount of statutory leave taken in relation to that child totals more than 26 weeks, or a period of parental leave of more than four weeks, is entitled to return from leave to the job in which he or she was employed before the absence: *reg 18(1)*. Otherwise, or where an employee takes parental leave for a period of more than four weeks, the employee is entitled to return from leave to the job in which he or she was employed before her absence or, if it is not reasonably practicable for the employer to permit her to return to that job, to another job which is both suitable and appropriate for her to do in the circumstances: *reg 18(2)*. The returning parent has a right to return with the seniority, pension rights and similar rights as if they had not been absent, and on terms and conditions not less favourable than those which would have applied if they had not been absent: *reg 18A(1)*. The provisions are analogous to those for mothers returning after maternity leave (see **33.35** above).

33.67 In *Meerts v Proost NV*: C 116/08 [2009] ECR I-10063, [2009] All ER (D) 259 (Oct) the CJEU held, by reference to clauses 2.6 and 2.7 of the *Framework Agreement on Parental Leave*, that an employer who dismisses a full-time employee without giving statutory notice or having 'urgent cause' whilst that employee is taking part-time parental leave is obliged to pay compensation on the basis of that employee's full-time salary (not the reduced salary paid during his parental leave). The CJEU accepted the Advocate General's view that national legislation which entailed a reduction in employment rights in the event of parental leave could discourage workers from taking such leave and could encourage employers to dismiss workers who are on parental leave rather than other workers. This would run directly counter to the aim of the *Framework Agreement*, one of the objectives of which is to make it easier to reconcile working and family life.

There remains a real question whether UK law properly implements the *Framework Agreement*, in light of the decision in *Meerts*. By *reg 17* of the *MPL Regulations*, an employee who takes parental leave is entitled, during that leave, to the benefit of her terms and conditions of employment relating to notice of termination given by her employer. However, under the enabling provision for the *MPL Regulations* in *section 77* of the *ERA*, 'terms and conditions' for these purposes do not include terms and conditions as to remuneration. At least arguably therefore, an employee dismissed whilst taking parental leave is entitled only to statutory notice pay, not contractual.

In *Zentralbetriebsrat der Landeskrankenhauser Tirols v Land Tirol*: C-486/08 [2010] IRLR 631 the CJEU ruled that *clause 2.6* of the *Framework Agreement* on Parental Leave precludes a national provision whereby workers on parental leave lose their right to paid annual leave accumulated during the year preceding the birth of their child. *Clause 2.6* requires that rights acquired or in the process of being acquired by the worker on the date on which parental leave starts are to be maintained as they stand until the end of parental leave and apply after that leave. It covers all the rights and benefits, whether in cash or in kind, derived directly or indirectly from the employment relationship, which the worker is entitled to claim from the employer at the date on which parental leave starts, including the right to paid annual leave.

In *Chatzi v Ipourgos Ikononikon*: C-149/10 [2010] All ER (D) 84 (Sep), the CJEU confirmed that the right to leave is that of the parent rather than the child, so that multiple births do not entitle an additional period of leave, albeit that national law should permit flexibility to take account of the needs of having, for example, twins.

See also C-174/16 *H v Land Berlin* [2017] All ER (D) 48 (Sep) in relation to questions of promotion and parental leave.

SHARED PARENTAL LEAVE AND PAY

33.68 Introduction

Shared parental leave was introduced by the *Children and Families Act 2014* ("**CFA 2014**"), replacing and abolishing additional paternity leave. The legislative scheme came into effect on 1 December 2014 but applies only to children due to be born on or after 5 April 2015 (note that it is the 'due date' that is key, rather than actual birth date). The scheme allows a woman who fulfils certain conditions to bring her statutory maternity leave and statutory maternity pay to an end by curtailing it, and share the balance with her partner (or as the case may be, her spouse, civil partner or the father of her child). SPL and pay may only be shared with one other person, and the amount that may be shared between the two partners is the amount foregone by the mother following her curtailment. Equivalent rights are afforded to adoptive parents and parents who adopt through a surrogacy arrangement. The right is expressly presented as SPL so as to differentiate it from EU-derived concepts of flexible leave (a distinction affirmed by the CJEU in *Sanchez* Case C-351/14).

On 5 October 2015, the government announced its intention to legislate to extend SPL to working grandparents by 2018, the consultation in relation to which was expected in May 2016. As at April 2020, the proposal has still not been consulted upon. Instead, the Government, is understood to be proposing to review SPL more generally in the light of very low take up rates.

For the purposes of presentation, throughout this chapter the person who shares in SPL or pay but who is not the mother or primary adopter is referred to as the mother or primary adopter's "**partner**". The partner is referred to in the masculine gender throughout. It is also assumed that the primary adopter is female. The following key abbreviations are used:

- "**SPL**" – shared parental leave.

- "**SSPP**" – statutory shared parental pay.

The right to shared parental leave and pay respectively were created by inserting new *sections 75E* to *75K* into the *ERA 1996*, and *sections 171ZU* to *171ZZ5* into the *Social Security Contributions and Benefits Act 1992* ("**SSCBA 1992**"). Those sections came into effect on 30 June 2014, primarily for the purpose of making regulations. The substance of the SPL and SSPP schemes are set out in those regulations. The principal regulations, and the abbreviations used for them in this chapter, are:

- The *Shared Parental Leave Regulations 2014 (SI 2014/3050)*: the "**SPL Regulations**";

- The *Statutory Shared Parental Pay (General) Regulations 2014 (SI 2014/3051)*: the "**SSPP Regulations**".

- The *Maternity and Adoption Leave (Curtailment of Statutory Rights to Leave) Regulations 2014 (SI 2014/ 3052)*: the "**Leave Curtailment Regulations**".

- The *Maternity Allowance (Curtailment) Regulations 2014 (2014/3053)*: the "**MA Curtailment Regulations**";

- The *Statutory Maternity Pay and Statutory Adoption Pay (Curtailment) Regulations 2014 (SI 2014/3054)*: the **"Pay Curtailment Regulations"**.

The Department for Business, Innovation and Skills published 'Employer's Technical Guide to Shared Parental Leave and Pay' in December 2014 (the **"BIS Guide"**), the majority of which is helpfully set out in a 'Frequently Asked Questions' format. ACAS has also published 'Shared Parental Leave: a good practice guide for employers and employees' (the **"ACAS Guide"**). Both are referred to below.

Shared parental leave

33.69 *Eligibility for shared parental leave: birth cases*

If both partners are to take up SPL, both partners must fulfil the relevant qualification criteria set out in the *SPL Regulations*. The criteria for a mother's entitlement to SPL is set out at *reg 4* of the *SPL Regulations*, and the partner's entitlement to SPL is set out in *reg 5* of the *SPL Regulations*. The criteria for the mother under *reg 4* are:

- The mother is an employee (see *sections 75E* to *75K* of the *ERA 1996*, under which 'employee' is defined by *ERA 1996, s 230(1)*).

- The mother satisfies the continuity of employment test set out in *reg 35* of the *SPL Regulations*. *Reg 35* requires the mother to have been in continuous employment with the same employer for 26 weeks immediately before the 'relevant week' (which is the 15th week before the EWC), and to have remained in continuous employment at that employer until the week before any period to be taken as SPL. Note that by contrast, there is no such requirement for statutory maternity leave.

- The mother has the main responsibility for the care of the child (along with her partner). This requirement is not further defined.

- The mother is entitled to SML in respect of the child (see [33.35]).

- The mother has curtailed her SML (see [33.73] below) and complied with the relevant notice and evidential requirements (see [33.81] below]).

- The mother's partner (a) fulfils the employment and earnings test set out in *reg 36* of the *SPL Regulations* ([33.70] below)), (b) with the mother, the partner has the main responsibility for the care of the child, and (c) falls within the relevant class of persons under the definition of 'P' in *reg 4* of the *SPL Regulations* (see the next paragraph)

A mother may share her leave with the child's father, her spouse, civil partner or her **"partner"** (see the definition of "P" in *reg 3* of the *SPL Regulations*). Partner is defined in *reg 3* of the *SPL Regulations* as someone of either sex who lives with the mother and child "in an enduring family relationship" but is not the mother's child, parent, grandchild, grandparent, sibling, aunt, uncle, niece or nephew. There is no indication in the *SPL Regulations* of what an 'enduring family relationship' is.

33.70 The employment and earnings test under *reg 36* requires the partner to fulfil two conditions:

- To have been an employed earner or self-employed earner (see *section 2* of *SSCBA 1992*) for at least 26 weeks of the last 66 weeks before the EWC (which do not need to be continuous); and,

- To have average weekly earnings of not less than the amount specified in *section 35(6A)* of the *SSCBA 1992* in the tax year before the tax year in which the EWC falls, which as at 1 April 2020 remains at £30.

See *reg 36* and the relevant sections of the *SSCBA 1992* referred to therein for further details.

33.71 It is also possible for the partner of a mother or primary adopter to take SPL, notwithstanding the fact that the mother or primary adopter cannot take SPL (see FAQ 10 of the BIS Guide). The requirements for a partner to take SPL in such a situation (and indeed, generally) are set out in *reg 5* of the *SPL Regulations*. An example of this situation, in the case of birth parents, is where the mother is entitled to SMP or MA which she curtails, and the partner fulfils the criteria set out in *reg 36* of the *SPL Regulations* (employment and earnings test), the partner may take SPL even if the mother or primary adopter does not fulfil the requirements of *reg 35* (continuity of employment test). This may be the case if the mother is self-employed or her employment terminated after she acquired the right to SMP. The possibility of the partner being eligible for SPL despite the mother's ineligibility for SPL arises from the differences between *reg 4(2)* and *5(3)* in the *SPL Regulations*. Generally, if the mother qualifies for SML, the partner will be entitled to SPL; but if the mother only qualifies for SMP or MA, she cannot receive SPL but the partner may be entitled to it.

33.72 *Eligibility for shared parental leave: adoption, surrogacy and special cases*

Part 3 of the *SPL Regulations* (*regs 20* to *34*) sets out the entitlement of adopters (*Part 2*, *regs 4* to *19*, makes equivalent provision in respect of birth mothers and their partners). The criteria for adopters under regulation 20 are much the same as those for mothers under *reg 4* of the *SPL Regulations*, as is the scheme for adoptive parents generally. The primary adopter (defined as 'A' in *reg 3* of the *SPL Regulations*) is the person with whom the child is or is expected to be placed for adoption; special provision is made in *reg 3* for cases in which two people have been matched jointly.

The provisions in respect of adopters include local authority foster parents who have a child placed with them with a view to adoption in accordance with *section 22C* of the *Children Act 1989*: see the definition of 'placed for adoption' in *reg 3* of the *SPL Regulations*.

The following regulations make special provision for adoptions from overseas:

- the *Employment Rights Act 1996 (Application of Sections 75G and 75H to Adoptions from Overseas) Regulations 2014 (SI 2014/3091)*;

- the *Shared Parental Leave and Paternity and Adoption Leave (Adoptions from Overseas) Regulations 2014 (SI 2014/3092)*, and

- the *Statutory Shared Parental Pay (Adoption from Overseas) Regulations 2014 (SI 2014/3093)*.

The *Statutory Shared Parental Pay (Persons Abroad and Mariners) Regulations 2014 (SI 2014/3134)* makes provision for certain individuals who work outside the UK and seafarers.

Finally, the *Paternity, Adoption and Shared Parental Leave (Parental Order Cases) Regulations 2014 (2014/3096)* extend the right to adoption leave to intended parents under a surrogacy agreement, and by that route also extend to them the right to SPL. The conditions for taking SPL are the generally same as those for adoptive parents, albeit modified by the regulations. Surrogate parents are not mentioned again in respect of SPL in this chapter. Note that the birth mother of a child given up for adoption or under a surrogacy agreement may also be entitled to SPL. See further the following regulations:

- The *Social Security Contributions and Benefits Act 1992 (Application of Parts 12ZA, 12ZB and 12ZC to Parental Order Cases) Regulations 2014 (SI 2014/2866)*;

- The *Employment Rights Act 1996 (Application of Sections 75A, 75B, 75G, 75H, 80A and 80B to Parental Order Cases) Regulations 2014 (SI 2014/3095)*;

- The *Statutory Paternity Pay and Statutory Adoption Pay (Parental Orders and Prospective Adopters) Regulations 2014 (SI 2014/2934)*;

•   *Statutory Shared Parental Pay (Parental Order Cases) Regulations 2014 (SI 2014/3097).*

33.73 *Curtailment of leave*

In order to take SPL, a mother must curtail her entitlement to SML, or in the case of adoption, the adopter must curtail her entitlement to statutory adoption leave ("SAL"). There are two methods of doing so: (1) returning to work early, with the relevant notice requirements (see next paragraph); or (2) giving a curtailment notice in accordance with the *Maternity and Adoption Leave (Curtailment of Statutory Rights to Leave) Regulations 2014 (SI 2014/3052)*: the **Leave Curtailment Regulations**. Note that the first two weeks of SML are compulsory for a mother: see *section 72(1)* of the *ERA 1996*, *reg 8* of the *MPL Regulations*, and *reg 6(2)(a)* of the *Leave Curtailment Regulations*.

33.74 Returning to work early entails following the relevant notice requirements under the regulations for SML or statutory adoption leave. The relevant regulations are *reg 11* of the *MPL Regulations*, and *reg 25* of the *PAL Regulations*. Generally, those regulations provide that the employee must give the employer at least eight weeks' notice of the date that she intends to return to work.

33.75 A leave curtailment notice must be issued in accordance with the procedure set out *Part 2* (in the case of SML; *regs 5–8*) or *Part 3* (in the case of statutory adoption leave; *regs 9–12*) of the *Leave Curtailment Regulations*.

A leave curtailment notice must be in writing and state the date on which the mother or adopter's leave is to end. That date is known as the 'leave curtailment date': see the definition in *reg 3(1)* of the *SPL Regulations*. The leave curtailment date must be at least eight weeks after the date on which the leave curtailment notice was given to the employer: *regs 6(2)(b)* and *10(2)(a)* of the *Leave Curtailment Regulations*. See *regs 6(2)* and *10(2)* for further conditions. If the person is employed by more than one employer, the leave curtailment notice must be given to all her employers at the same time: *reg 5(3)* and *9(3)* of the *Leave Curtailment Regulations*.

When a leave curtailment notice is provided to an employer, the notice and evidential requirements must be complied with: specifically, a notice of entitlement to SPL, or a declaration of consent and entitlement must be provided. A notice of entitlement to SPL is required where the mother herself intends to take SPL. The evidential requirements relating to a notice of entitlement are burdensome; the declaration of consent and entitlement provides a less burdensome option that permits the partner to take SPL (as the mother's leave will be curtailed), even though the mother will have to give a notice of entitlement later if she wishes to take SPL herself. See **[33.82]** for further details.

A leave curtailment notice may be revoked only in accordance with *regs 8* (birth) or *12* (adoption) of the *Leave Curtailment Regulations*, by means of a 'revocation notice'. Those regulations set out three circumstances in which a leave curtailment notice may be revoked: (1) neither parent is entitled to SPL or SSPP; (2) the death of the mother or adopter's partner; (3) in the case of birth only, the notice was provided before the birth of the child. See the BIS Guide for further detail.

33.76 *Rules on how SPL may be taken*

Regs 7 and *23* of the *SPL Regulations* for birth and adoption cases respectively make general provision as to how SPL must be taken. First, SPL may only be taken between the date of birth or adoption and the first birthday/anniversary of the child's adoption. Consequently, a partner could take SPL from the date of birth of a child, so long as a mother has fixed her curtailment date (and even though the mother would still be on SML until the curtailment date). Second, SPL must be taken in complete weeks. Third, SPL may be taken in continuous or discontinuous periods (see **[33.78]** below). Fourth, the minimum amount of time taken as SPL is one week. Fifth, SPL may be taken concurrently. Specifically, one parent may be absent on SPL whilst the other is absent for the particular child on any of the types of parental leave provided for under *Part 8* of the *1996 Act* (ie SPL, SML, SAL, statutory paternity leave or unpaid parental leave) or in receipt of pay under *section 35* or *Part 12, 12ZA* or *12ZC* of the *SSCBA 1992* in respect of the same child (ie MA, SMP, SAP, statutory paternity pay or SSPP).

33.77   The total amount of leave available to be taken as SPL is determined by *regs 6* (in the case of birth) and *22* (in the case of adoption) of the *SPL Regulations*. In both the calculations set out below, the following must also be deducted from the total SPL available: (a) any periods of leave booked or taken by the other parent; (b) any periods of leave required to be taken under *reg 18* or *33* (see **[33.80]**); (c) any weeks of SSPP to which the other parent is entitled but during which the other parent is not absent on SPL. In other words, the amount of SPL available to a particular parent / adopter depends to a large degree on what is agreed between them.

Where a mother or adopter returns to work early, the amount of SPL available is 52 weeks minus the number of weeks of SML or statutory adoption leave already taken: *regs 6(1)(b)* and *22(1)(b)* of the *SPL Regulations*. The total amount of SPL available in the case of birth cannot be more than 50 weeks, because the first two weeks of SML are compulsory for a mother: see *section 72(1)* of the *ERA 1996, reg 8* of the *MPL Regulations*, and *reg 6(2)(a)* of the *Leave Curtailment Regulations*. The period is four weeks in the circumstances described by *s 205* of the *Public Health Act 1936*.

Where a mother or adopter curtails her SML or statutory adoption leave, the total amount of SPL available is 52 weeks minus the number of weeks between the first day of SML or statutory adoption leave and the date specified in the leave curtailment notice: *regs 6(1)(a)* and *22(1)(a)* of the *SPL Regulations*. The total amount of SPL available in the case of adoption is 50 weeks: see *reg 10(2)(b)* of the *Leave Curtailment Regulations* and *reg 22(1)(b)* of the *SPL Regulations*.

Employees are also entitled to work for 20 'keeping in touch' or SPLiT days: see **[33.101]** for details.

33.78   *Regs 12* to *19* (birth) and *28* to *34* (adoption) make provision in respect of the methods for booking leave. Leave must be booked through a period of leave notice: see **[33.81]** below as to the formal requirements relating to period of leave notices.

The crucial limiting issue in respect of booking leave is that an employee may only issue three period of leave notices to each of his or her employers: *reg 16(1)* of the *SPL Regulations*. That limit includes variation of period of leave notices (see **[33.79]** below). However, the limit in *reg 16(1)* may be waived by agreement between the employer and employee, and the limit does not include: (a) notices given in response to an employer request to vary the period of leave (*regs 16(2)(c)* and *32(2)(c)*); (b) notices given due to changes in the expected birth date or date of adoption (*regs 16(2)(b)* and *32(2)(b)*); (c) notices withdrawn within 15 days and before being agreed by the employer in respect of discontinuous leave (*regs 16(2)(a)* and *32(2)(a)*). The fact that three notices may be given means that an employee may take three separate (continuous) blocks of leave.

An employee may book either a continuous or discontinuous period of leave. There is considerable flexibility as how discontinuous periods of leave may be structured. An employee may propose a 'week-on, week-off' arrangement, or that they take two-months leave, work for four weeks, then take another two-months of leave (with the partner taking the balance of the leave at various times arranged with his own employer). However, employers do not have to accept an employee's proposal of discontinuous leave: *reg 14* and *30* of the *SPL Regulations* (see below for further details). Employers are, however, required to accept the employee's request for continuous leave: *regs 13* and *29* of the *SPL Regulations*.

After an employee requests discontinuous leave, the employer has two weeks to decide whether to: (a) consent to the periods of leave requested; (b) propose alternative dates for the periods of leave; (c) refuse the periods of leave without proposing alternative dates (*regs 14(2)* and *30(2)* of the *SPL Regulations*). If no agreement is reached between the employee and employer, the employee is entitled to take the total amount of leave requested (in the period of leave notice) as continuous block of leave: *regs 14(4)* and *30(4)*. The start date of that continuous period of leave must be nominated by the employee within 5 days of the end of the two-week negotiation period (and that date must be eight weeks before the period of leave notice was given to the employer), failing which the original start-date will have effect: *regs 14(5)* and *30(5)*. However, if alternative dates are agreed during the two-week negotiation period, the employee is entitled to take that leave (*regs 14(3)* and *30(3)*). The employee may also withdraw the period of leave notice requesting discontinuous leave if there is no agreement so long as it is withdrawn before the two week period ends: *regs 14(6)* and *30(6)*. (That withdrawal will not count towards the three permitted period of leave notices: *regs 16(2)(c)* and *32(2)(c)*).

However, as the employee may give three notices to take continuous leave, the fact that an employer can refuse (other types of) discontinuous leave may be of limited significance: the employee is entitled to take three 'blocks' of leave, making the total SPL period 'discontinuous' in that the employee can insist on returning to work for two periods during the SPL period (see further FAQ 46 of the BIS Guide). For discontinuous leave proper (ie within the meaning of *regs 14* and *30*), the difficulty for employers will be likely to be ensuring they are consistent as between employees in responding to requests for discontinuous leave.

33.79 After the employee has given notice of a continuous period of leave or a discontinuous period of leave has been agreed with the employer, the employee may submit a notice to vary those periods of leave (a 'variation notice'): see *regs 15* and *31* of the *SPL Regulations*. A variation notice may request changes to continuous leave, in which case *regs 13* and *29* of the *SPL Regulations* apply. In other words, so long as the dates to be varied are more than eight weeks away (including the start and end date, even if that cancels a period of leave), the employer cannot refuse the variation. However, the employer can refuse a request to convert continuous leave into discontinuous leave, or to vary the dates of discontinuous leave, in accordance with the process set out in the paragraph above relating to *regs 14* and *30* of the *SPL Regulations*. A variation notice must state the periods of leave which the employee is already entitled to (whether continuous or discontinuous: *regs 15(3)* and *31(3)*), and the rules relating to the number of notices that may be given by the employee apply to the variation notice (see [33.78]). If the amount of SPL to be taken by each of the parents / adopters changes, a variation notice of entitlement will be have to be submitted to the employer: see [33.85] below.

33.80 *Regs 18–19* and *33–34* make provision for certain changes of circumstances.

Regs 18 and *33* relate to an employee ceasing to care for a child or the mother/primary adopter revoking their notice of curtailment. In such circumstances, if those events occur more than eight weeks before the SPL in question, the leave need not be taken. If those events occur less than eight weeks before SPL is due to be taken, the employer may require the employee to take the period of leave as SPL if it is not reasonably practicable for the employer to accommodate the change in circumstances by allowing the employee to work during the planned period of SPL. Note that as the period is taken as SPL, the leave reduces the overall amount of SPL that is available to be taken.

Regs 19 and *34* relate to the death of the child or one of the parents/adopters. *Reg 19* and *Part 1* of the *Schedule* to the SPL Regulations make provision for circumstances in which the mother, partner or child dies before the end of the period in which SPL may be taken. *Reg 34* and *Part 2* of the *Schedule* make equivalent provision in the case of death or disruption of the child's placement for adoption.

33.81 *Notice and evidential requirements*

The main notice and evidential requirements relating to SPL are as follows:

- A notice of entitlement must be provided with certain signed declarations: *regs 8, 9* (birth) and *24, 25* (adoption) of the *SPL Regulations*. (Alternatively, a declaration of consent and entitlement may be provided by the mother so as to enable her partner to take SPL: see *reg 5* and *9* of the *Leave Curtailment Regulations*.)

- Certain additional information must be provided upon request: *regs 10* (birth) and *28* (adoption) of the *SPL Regulations*.

- A variation notice of entitlement must be given to the employer if the amounts of SPL to be taken by each of the parents changes: *regs 11* and *27* of the *SPL Regulations*.

- A period of leave notice must be provided to book the periods of leave: *regs 12* (birth) and *28* (adoption) of the *SPL Regulations*.

33.82 The requirements to provide a notice of entitlement and signed declarations are set out in *regs 8, 9* (birth) and *24, 25* (adoption) of the *SPL Regulations*. *Regs 8* and *24* address the mother or primary adopter's notice of entitlement, and *regs 9* and *25* address the partner's notice of entitlement. The notice of entitlement serves also as the notice that the employee intends to take SPL: see the subtitle of each of the regulations cited in this paragraph. A notice of entitlement must be provided to the employer at least eight weeks before the first period of SPL, and must be in writing.

A declaration of consent and entitlement may be provided by the mother/adopter to her employer to curtail her SML or SAL (which she would do so as to enable her partner to take SPL) without complying with the onerous requirements of a notice of entitlement. See *regs 5* and *9* of the *Leave Curtailment Regulations*. A declaration of consent and entitlement means a written declaration signed by the mother or primary adopter stating that (a) her partner has given a notice of entitlement to his or her employer and (b) that the mother / primary adopter consents to the amount of leave her partner proposes to take. See the definition provided by *reg 3* of the *Leave Curtailment Regulations*.

In the case of birth, the notice of entitlement must contain the following information (*regs 8(2)* and *9(2)* of the *SPL Regulations*):

- The names of the mother and partner;

- The start and end dates of any SML taken or to be taken;

- The total amount of SPL available;

- The expected week of birth and the date of birth (to be provided as soon as reasonably practicable after the child's birth and in any event before the first period of SPL is taken);

- A binding indication of how much SPL each of the mother and partner each intend to take (a notice to vary entitlement may later be provided under *reg 11*: see [33.85]);

- A non-binding indication of when the employee intends to take SPL, including specific dates.

In the case of adoption, the notice of entitlement must contain the following information (*regs 24(2)* and *25(2)* of the *SPL Regulations*):

- The names of the primary adopter and his or her partner;

- The date that the primary adopter was notified that she was matched for adoption;

- The date that the child is expected to be placed, and the date the child was placed (to be provided as soon as reasonably practicable after the child is placed and in any event before the first period of SPL is taken);

- The start and end dates of any statutory adoption leave or pay taken or to be taken by the primary adopter;

- The total amount of SPL available;

- A binding indication of the amount of SPL each adopter intends to take (a notice to vary entitlement may later be provided under *reg 27*: see [33.85]);

- A non-binding indication of when the employee intends to take SPL, including specific dates.

33.83 The signed declarations that must accompany the notice of entitlement must contain the following:

- **Declarations accompanying mother's notice of entitlement to her employer:** in the case of birth, a mother must provide a signed declaration from her and must also provide a signed declaration from the mother's partner (herein, the partner). The mother's signed declaration must state that: (A) she satisfies or will satisfy the conditions in *reg 4(2)* of the *SPL Regulations*, that is, that she is entitled to take SPL; (B) that the information in her notice is accurate; (C) that she will immediately inform her employer if she ceases to care for the child. A signed declaration from the partner must be provided to the mother's employer stating: (A) his name, address, and national insurance number (or a declaration that he does not have one); (B) that he satisfies or will satisfy the conditions in *reg 4(3)* of the *SPL Regulations* which enable the mother to take SPL; (C) that he is the father / spouse / civil partner / partner of the mother; (D) that the partner consents to the amount of SPL which the mother intends to take; (E) that he consents to the mother's employer processing the information in the declaration.

- **Declarations accompanying partner of mother's notice of entitlement to his employer:** in the case of birth, the partner of a mother (herein, the partner) must provide to his employer a signed declaration from him and a signed declaration from the mother. The partner's signed declaration must: (A) state that he satisfies or will satisfy the conditions set out in *reg 5(2)* of the *SPL Regulations*, that is, that he is entitled to SPL; (B) that the information in his notice is accurate; (C) that he is the father / spouse / civil partner / partner of the mother; (D) that he will immediately inform his employer if the mother tells him that she has revoked her curtailment notice; (E) that that he will immediately inform his employer if he ceases to care for the child. A signed declaration from the mother must be provided to the partner's employer: (A) stating the mother's name, address and national insurance number (or a declaration that she has none); (B) that the mother satisfies the conditions in *reg 5(3)* which enable the partner to take SPL; (C) that the mother consents to the amount of SPL which the partner intends to take; (D) that the mother will immediately inform the partner if she revokes her curtailment notice; (E) that the mother consents to the partner's employer processing the information in the mother's declaration.

- **Declarations accompanying a primary adopter's notice of entitlement to her employer:** in the case of adoption, the primary adopter must provide a signed declaration from her and must also provide a signed declaration from her partner (herein, the partner). The primary adopter's signed declaration must state that: (A) she satisfies the conditions in *reg 21(2)*, that is, that she is entitled to take SPL; (B) the information given in her notice is accurate; (C) she will immediately inform her employer if she ceases to care for the child. The primary adopter must also provide a signed declaration from her partner: (A) that states his name, address, and national insurance number (or a declaration that he has none); (B) that that the partner satisfies the conditions in *reg 20(3)* which entitle the primary adopter to take SPL; (C) that the partner is the spouse / civil partner / partner of the primary adopter; (D) that the partner consents to the amount of leave which the primary adopter intends to take; (E) that the partner consents to the primary adopter's employer processing the partner's information.

- **Declarations accompanying notice of entitlement from the partner of the primary adopter to his employer:** in the case of adoption, the partner of the primary adopter (herein, the partner) must provide a signed declaration from him and must also provide a signed declaration from the primary adopter. The partner's signed declaration must: (A) state that the partner satisfies the conditions set out in *reg 21(2)* that entitle him to take SPL; (B) that the information given in his notice is accurate; (C) the partner is the primary adopter's husband / civil partner / partner; (D) that the partner will immediately inform his employer if he ceases to care for the child or if the primary adopt revokes her notice of curtailment. The partner must also provide to his employer a signed declaration from the primary adopter that: (A) specifies the primary adopter's name, address and national insurance number (or a declaration that he has none); (B) that the primary adopter satisfies or will satisfy the conditions in *reg 21(3)* which entitle the partner to take SPL; (C) that the primary adopter consents to the amount of leave which the partner intends to take; (D) that the primary adopter will immediately inform her partner if she revokes her notice of curtailment; (E) that the primary adopter consents to the partner's employer processing the primary adopter's information.

Clearly, those declarations are very complicated and bureaucratic. The dangers are as follows. For the parents / adopters, if they fail to provide the requisite declarations, the right to SPL falls away. For the employer, a failure to hold the correct paperwork leaves them open to their rebate of SSPP being challenged by HMRC if there is an audit. Overall, perhaps, the dangers are greater for the employees, and it is difficult to see what justification there is for entitlement to SPL to depend on the completion of such complex paperwork.

33.84 Additional information that may be requested by the employer in the case of birth includes the following (see *reg 10* of the *SPL Regulations*):

- A copy of the child's birth certificate;

- The name and address of the mother/adopter's or partner's employer (as the case may be).

The employer may must make the request within 14 days of receiving the relevant notice, and the employee must provide the information within 14 days of receiving the request.

In the case of adoption, the additional information that may be requested includes the following (see *reg 26* of the *SPL Regulations*):

- The name and address of the adoption agency;

- The date that the adopter was notified of having been matched for adoption with the child;

- The date on which the adoption agency expects to place the child; and,

- The name and address of the partner's employer.

The timescales are the same as above.

33.85 A variation notice of entitlement is required if the parents intend to change the amount of SPL to be taken by either of the parents: *regs 11* and *27* of the *SPL Regulations*. A variation notice of entitlement must contain the following:

•   A description of the periods of SPL notified by each of the parents under a period of leave notice or variation notice;

•   A non-binding indication of when the employee giving the notice to his or her employer intends to take the SPL, including specific dates;

•   A description of the periods of SSPP that have been notified by each of the parents;

•   A declaration signed by both parents or adopters that they agree the variation.

There is no limit to the number of notices that may be given.

33.86 A period of leave notice must meet the requirements of *reg 12* (in the case of birth) or *28* (in the case of adoption) of the *SPL Regulations*. The period of leave notice must be in writing, and contain the start and end dates of each period of leave requested. It must be given to the employer at least eight weeks before the start dates of the first period of leave requested. The period of leave notice may also specify a date relative to the birth or adoption of the child: see *regs 12(4)(c)* and *28(4)(c)* of the *SPL Regulations*. The period of leave notice cannot be given before the notice of entitlement, and cannot state dates outside the range in which SPL may be taken: *regs 12(5)* and *28(5)* of the *SPL Regulations*.

33.87   Statutory shared parental pay

Statutory shared parental pay or "**SSPP**" is governed by *sections 171ZU* to *171ZZ5* of the *SSCBA 1992*, and the *Statutory Shared Parental Pay (General) Regulations 2014 (2014/3051)* (the "**SSPP Regulations**"). The general principles applicable to SSPP are much the same as SPL: a mother or primary adopter must curtail her entitlement to SMP, maternity allowance or statutory adoption pay, and the remaining balance may be taken by either parent as SSPP.

A government rebate of 92% applies to payments by the employer of SPPP: see the *Statutory Shared Parental Pay (Administration) Regulations 2014 (2014/2929)*, which make equivalent provision for SSPP as for SMP including the entitled of small employers to recover up to 103% of the SPL (see **[33.60]**).

> *Can paying men SSPP result in unlawful discrimination where women on maternity leave are paid more?*

During 2018, the Employment Appeal Tribunal heard two cases in which it was alleged that men taking SPL were discriminated against where they received less pay than female colleagues taking maternity leave. In *Capita Customer Management Ltd v Ali* UKEAT/0161/17 [2018] IRLR 586 the Appeal Tribunal rejected an argument that it was an act of direct sex discrimination to pay men taking SPL less than was paid to women taking ordinary maternity leave ("OML"). The EAT found that the correct comparator for a man taking SPL was a woman taking SPL. Since men and women on SPL receive the same pay, there was no discrimination. The basis of the conclusion was that the purpose of OML is in part to allow a woman to recover from childbirth and to form a bond with her child. The reason for Additional Maternity Leave (or "AML") might be different in that it might be more simply focussed on ensuring the child was cared for. For that reason, the EAT did not rule out the possibility that a complaint might succeed where a man on SPL was paid less than a woman on AML. The decision was upheld by the Court of Appeal ([2019] EWCA Civ 900, [2019] IRLR 695, [2020] ICR 87).

The second case, *Hextall v Chief Constable of Leicestershire Police* UKEAT/0139/17 [2018] IRLR 605 was a case of indirect discrimination. It again concerned a man on SPL being paid less than a woman on OML. The EAT considered that an indirect discrimination claim might succeed and remitted it for determination. The argument was that the PCP was paying those on SPL less. A woman could choose to avoid the lower pay by taking OML. The man could not do so. That being so, men were put at a particular disadvantage. When the case came before the Court of Appeal ([2019] EWCA Civ 900, [2019] IRLR 695, [2020] ICR 87), the court considered that the claim was more properly characterised as a claim for breach of an equality clause pursuant to *EqA 2010, s 66* (in other words, it was really an "equal pay" claim). That claim failed because *EqA 2010, Sch 7, para 2* specifically excludes claims concerned with "terms of work affording special treatment to women in connection with pregnancy or childbirth". Because the claim was properly an equal pay claim, it could not be brought as an indirect discrimination claim because *EqA 2010, ss 70* and *71* preclude that. The Court went on to hold that even if an indirect discrimination claim had been permissible it would have failed, first because the EAT had incorrectly identified the pool for comparison – women on maternity leave are in materially different circumstances to either men or women taking SPL and they should not all be put into the same pool – and, second, because they considered that any indirect discrimination would in any event have been justified.

33.88 *Eligibility for SSPP*

The conditions of eligibility for SSPP for a particular employee are very similar to those for SPL. See in particular the *SSPP Regulations* at *regs 4* and *5* (birth cases), *17* and *18* (adoption cases), and *29–31* (general provisions).

- The individual must be an employee, although the term is defined more widely than for SPL. *Section 171ZZ4(2)* of the *SSCBA 1992* provides the relevant definition: "in this Part, 'employee' means a person who is gainfully employed in Great Britain either under a contract of service or in an office (including elective office) with general earnings (as defined by *section 7* of the *Income Tax (Earnings and Pensions) Act 2003)*". *Reg 33* of the *SSPP Regulations* make provision for certain special cases and *section 171ZZ2* provides that Crown servants are to be treated as employees for these purposes.

- The employee must have 26 weeks continuous employment with the same employer by the end of the 'relevant week' (immediately before the 14th week before the EWC, or in adoption cases, the week on which the adopter is matched with the child): *regs 4(2)(a), 5(2)(a)* and *30* in the case of birth and *regs 17(2)(a), 18(2)(a)* and *31* in the case of adoption. See *regs 34–38* as to 'continuous employment'.

- The employee must have normal weekly earnings of at least £120 a week for eight weeks immediately preceding the relevant date: *regs 4(2)(a), 5(2)(a)* and *30(1)(b)* (birth) and *17(2)(a), 18(2)(a)* and *31(1)(b)* (adoption).

- The employee must share the main caring responsibility for the child with the other parent at the date or birth or adoption: *regs 4(2)(b), 4(3)(a), 5(2), 5(3)(a)* in the case of birth and *regs 17(2)(b), 17(3)(a)* and *18(3)(a)* in the case of adoption.

- The employees must have complied with the relevant notice requirements eight weeks before leave begins (see **[33.92]** below).

- The mother/adopter must be entitled to SMP or statutory adoption pay and have curtailed that entitlement: *regs 4(2)(d), 4(3), 5(3)(c)* and *5(3)(d)* in case of birth, and *17(2)(d), 17(2)(e)* and *18(3)(c)* in case of adoption.

- During each week of SSPP, the individual must intend to care for the child, and be absent from work (although see *regs* 15 and 27 for certain exceptions). If the individual is an employee within the meaning of *section 230* of the *ERA 1996* (as opposed to the wider meaning for the purposes of SSPP), he or she must be absent from work by means of SPL. See *regs 4(2)(f)–(h), 5(2)(d)–(f)* in case of birth, and *17(2)(f)–(h), 18(2)(d)–(f)* in case of adoption.

- The other parent must satisfy the 'employment earnings test' set out in *regulation 29* of the *SSPP Regulations*: *regs 4(3)(b)*, *5(3)(b)* in case of birth, and *17(3)(b)*, *18(3)(b)* in case of adoption. This test is identical to that which applies under SPL: see [33.70] above.

Women who do not qualify for SMP but who do qualify for the social security benefit of MA cannot create a shared entitlement to SSPP. However, a woman who is eligible for MA may create an entitlement to SSPP for her partner by curtailing her MA (see *reg 5(3)(d)* of the *SSPP Regulations*); she will not herself be entitled to SSPP because one of the conditions of entitlement for her is eligibility for SMP or SAP (see *regs 4(2)(d)* and *17(2)(d)* of the *SSPP Regulations*).

33.89 *Curtailing maternity pay or allowance*

A mother must curtail her SMP or MA for each parent to be entitled to SSPP. The procedures for doing so in the case of SMP and SAP are set out in *regs 7* and *12* respectively of the *Statutory Maternity Pay and Statutory Adoption Pay (Curtailment) Regulations 2014 (2014/3054)* (the "**Pay Curtailment Regulations**") and for MA, they are set out in *reg 5* of the *Maternity Allowance (Curtailment) Regulations 2014 (2014/3053)* (the "**MA Curtailment Regulations**").

Those provisions require the provision of a 'maternity pay period curtailment notice', 'adoption pay period curtailment notice' or a 'maternity allowance period curtailment notification' respectively, which all have the following requirements:

- They must be given to the prescribed person: in the case of SMP and SAP, the person liable to pay the SMP or SAP, and in the case of MA, the Secretary of State. In the cases of SMP and SAP, they must be in writing.

- They must specify the date on which the SMP, SAP or MA is to end, which must be the last day of a week.

- The date chosen for the curtailment must be at least eight weeks after the curtailment notice was given.

- If the mother has the right to ordinary maternity leave under *section 71* of the *ERA 1996*, then the date chosen to curtail must be at least one day after the end of the period of compulsory maternity leave, and if not, at least two weeks after the end of the pregnancy or adoption date.

- The curtailment date must be at least one week before the last day or the SMP, SAP or MA period.

Readers should consult the regulations referred to above for information as to their detailed operation, such as where a curtailment notice is provided when the employee has already returned to work.

Provisions as to the revocation of a curtailment notice may be found at *regs 8* and *13* of the *Pay Curtailment Regulations* (in respect of birth and adoption respectively), and *reg 6* of the *MA Curtailment Regulations*. In short, in the case of SMP or MA a revocation notice may only be provided if the curtailment notice was provided before the birth of the child (and given within six weeks of the child's birth), or the mother's partner dies. In the case of SAP, a revocation notice may only be provided if the primary adopter's partner dies.

33.90 *SSPP: how much and when?*

The weekly rate of payment of SSPP is the smaller of (a) £151.20 or (b) 90% of the normal weekly earnings of the individual claiming SSPP: see *reg 40(1)* of the *SSPP Regulations*. *Reg 43* provides that payments of SSPP may be made in a "like manner to payments or remuneration but shall not include payment in kind of by way of the provision of board and lodgings". Payments are normally to be made on the day on which it was normal practice for the employee to be paid, or if there is no such practice, on the last day of a calendar month: *reg 44(5)*. *Subsection 171ZY(6)* of the *SSCBA 1992* provides that SSPP may be calculated at a daily rate (see also *reg 40(2)* of the *SSPP Regulations*). *Section 171ZX* makes provision for the person liable to make payments, and see *regs 44* and *45* of the *SSPP Regulations* as to determinations by HMRC as to an employer and HMRC's liability to pay SSPP. *Reg 41* provides that any contractual remuneration (including sick pay) goes towards discharging an employer's liability to pay SSPP. See *regulation 42* in respect of dismissals and SSPP; *reg 48* as to issues relating to the capacity of the person receiving SSPP; and *reg 39* as to issues relating to an individual being employed in two or more separately jobs.

33.91 The amount of SSPP available to be shared depends on the remaining SMP, SAP or MA, and is governed by *reg 10* and *22* of the *SSPP Regulations*. The maternity pay period for SMP is 39 weeks, but due to the requirements relating to curtailment set out above, the maximum SMP that may be taken as SSPP is 37 weeks. The same applies to SAP. The minimum amount of SSPP that may be taken is one week: *regs 7(2)(d)* and *12(2)(d)* of the *Pay Curtailment Regulations*. It should be noted that it is not sufficient for the mother merely to return to work to curtail her entitlement, because her maternity pay period will continue to 'run in the background'. Rather, she must specifically curtail her SMP or SAP: see the BIS Guide at FAQ 30. See similarly *reg 10(1)(a)* in respect of MA. *Regs 11* and *23* of the *SSPP Regulations* provide that SSPP will not be payable after the first birthday of the child or the first anniversary of the adoption. Finally, SSPP cannot be taken by a mother or primary adopter when they are receiving SMP/SAP/MA, but if the curtailment date has been set, her partner may receive SSPP even whilst the mother/primary adopter is in receipt of SMP/SAP/MA.

Section 171ZY(4) of the *SSCBA 1992* provides that SSPP is not payable in respect of a week during any part of which the employee works for an employer, with the exception provided by *reg 12* and *24* of the *SSPP Regulations* relating to 'keeping in touch' or SPLiT days (see those regulations more generally as to obligations that arise when work is undertaken for an employer). See *subsection 171ZY(3)* and *regs 13* to *15*, and *25* to *27* of the *SSPP Regulations* as to other circumstances in which SSPP is not payable due to the actions of the employee.

33.92 *Notice and evidential requirements*

The notice and evidential requirements for SSPP are much the same as those for SPL. However, as the length of time the SSPP is shorter than for SPL, parents and adopters must make a separate decision as to how to divide their SSPP. Whilst the regulations are silent on the matter, the ACAS Guide suggests that the notice of claim for SSPP may be included in the notice of entitlement for SPL. The relevant regulations within the SSPP Regulations are *reg 6* for claims by a mother; *reg 7* for claims by the partner; *reg 19* for claims by the primary adopter; and *reg 20* for claims by the partner of the adopter.

One of the purposes of the notice and evidential requirements is to prevent both parents fraudulently taking (up to) 50 weeks of SPL, rather than sharing that pay / leave. There is, however, no provision in the regulations for communication between the respective employers of the two employees. The BIS Guide states at FAQ 67 that employers are not expected to perform detailed checks, and specifically, that they are not expected to contact the employer of the other employee to satisfy themselves regarding the eligibility of the partner to SPL. However, whilst the BIS Guide then states *"[e]mployers are entitled to rely on the information about the other parent provided to them by their employee"*, it goes on to say (in accordance with the regulations) that *"employers who want to check can ask their employee for the name of the other parent's employer and contact them if they wish."* The BIS Guide also states that HMRC will attempt to identify any parents defrauding the system.

33.93 The requirements in respect of birth are as follows (for convenience, the person liable to pay the mother's SSPP is refereed to below as her 'employer'):

- **Notice provided by a mother to her employer**: the mother must provide her employer with notice of: (A) the total number of weeks that the mother would be entitled to claim SSPP if no claim for SSPP were made by her partner; (B) the number of those weeks that each of the mother and her partner intend to take as SSPP; (C) the period or periods during which the mother intends to claim SSPP; (D) a written and signed declaration from the mother's partner that consents to the mother's intended claim for SSPP; that the partner meets the required conditions for the mother's eligibility for SSPP under *reg 4(3)*; that sets out the partner's name, address, and national insurance number (or a declaration that he has no national insurance number); and consents to the mother's employer processing the partner's information; (E) the child's EWC, and as soon as is reasonably practicable, the child's date of birth; (F) the mother's name; (G) a written declaration from the mother stating that the information in the notice is correct; that the mother meets the conditions for eligibility for SSPP; that the mother will immediately inform the person who will be liable to pay SSPP if she ceases to curtail her SMP or maternity allowance; the date on which the maternity pay period or maternity allowance period began and the number of weeks by which it is or will be reduced.

- **Notice provided by a partner of a mother to his employer**: the partner of the mother (the 'partner') must provide his employer with notice of: (A) the total number of weeks that the partner would be entitled to claim SSPP if no claim for SSPP were made by the mother; (B) the number of those weeks that each of the mother and her partner intend to take as SSPP; (C) the period or periods during which the mother intends to claim SSPP; (D) a written and signed declaration from the mother that consents to the partner's intended claim for SSPP; states that the mother meets the required conditions for the partner's eligibility for SSPP under *reg 5(3)*; that the mother will immediately inform the partner if she ceases to curtail her SMP or MA; specifies the mother's name, address and national insurance number (or a declaration that she has no national insurance number); specifying the date on which the mother's SMP period or MA period began and the number of weeks by which it is or will be reduced; and consents to the partner's employer processing the mother's information; (E) states the EWC, and as soon as reasonable practicable after the birth, the child's date of birth; (F) the partner's name; (G) a written declaration signed by the partner that the information given by the partner is correct; that the partner meets the conditions for eligibility of SSPP in *reg 5(2)* SSPP; and that the partner will immediately inform his employer if the mother ceases to curtail her SMP or maternity allowance.

Save where otherwise specified above, the employer must receive this information at least eight weeks before the beginning of the first period of SSPP.

The employer may also request a copy of the child's birth certificate (or if one has not been issued, a declaration signed by the mother which states that one has not been issued); and the name and address of the partner's employer (or if the partner has no employer, a written declaration signed by the mother that states the partner has no employer). In both cases, the information must be provided to the employer within 14 days of the information being requested; and the employer has only 14 days from the date of the notice to request that information.

33.94 The requirements in respect of adoption (set out in *regs 19* and *20* of the *SSPP Regulations*) are the same as those in respect of birth, with the following adjustments: (1) the date of placement, rather than of birth, is required; (2) the date on which the primary adopter was matched with the child, rather than the EWC; (3) the date of placement for adoption, instead of the date of birth; and finally, (4) in respect of the information that may be requested by the employer, that information is the name and address of the adoption agency;

the date on which the primary adopter was notified that she had been matched with the child; the date on which the adoption agency was expecting to place the child with the primary adopter; and this is in place of the child's date of birth as set out above.

33.95 Parents and adopters may vary a notice to claim SSPP in accordance with *regs 8* (birth) and *21* (adoption) of the *SSPP Regulations*. Such a variation notice must be given at least eight weeks before the first period of SSPP specified in the original notice. A variation notice may vary the number of weeks that they intend to claim SSPP in the notice, under the same time constraints, if the notice sets out how many weeks both parents have claimed SSPP and includes a signed declaration from both parents/adopters to the effect that they consent to the variation.

Employment protection and SPL / SSPP

33.96 *Introduction*

Employees taking SPL enjoy the following protections (see *regs 37* to *44* of the *SPL Regulations*):

* Protection from dismissal;

* Protection from detriment;

* Protection from discrimination;

* Redundancy protection;

* Keeping in touch or 'SPLiT' days;

* Protections in resect of terms and conditions of employment during SPL;

* Returning to work after SPL.

Each is addressed in turn below.

33.97 *Protection from dismissal*

Section 99(1) of the *ERA 1996* makes provision that an employee will be regarded as unfairly dismissed if the principal reason for dismissal is one of a prescribed kind, known as 'automatically unfair dismissal'. See generally Unfair Dismissal – I (54) and II (55). *Section 99(3)(bb)* of the *ERA 1996* provides that reasons relating to SPL are of that prescribed kind.

Reg 43 of the *SPL Regulations* makes further provision in respect of the reasons that will result in an employee being unfairly dismissed for the purposes of *section 99* of the *ERA 1996*. *Reg 43(1)* states that the employee will be regarded as unfairly dismissed if the reason or principal reason is of a kind specified in *reg 43(3)*, or where the employee is redundant, that regulation 39 of the *SPL Regulations* has not been complied with (see [33.100] in respect of redundancy).

Reg 43(3) states that if the reason for the dismissal are reasons relating to any of the following, the employee will be unfairly dismissal:

* That the employee took, sought to take, or made use of the benefits of, SPL;

* That the employer believed that the employee was likely to take SPL;

* That the employee undertook, considered undertaking, or refused to undertake work in accordance with regulation 37 (in respect of keeping in touch or 'SPLiT' days; see [33.101]).

Reg 43(2) also provides that an employee who is dismissed will be regarded as unfairly dismissed for the purposes of *Part 10* of the *ERA 1996* if they were dismissed for redundancy because of one of the matters set out in *reg 43(3)*, and the circumstances constituting the redundancy applied equally to one or more employees in the same undertaking who held positions similar to that held by the dismissed employee who had not been dismissed by the employer.

Reg 42 of the *SSPP Regulations* provides that a former employer will be liable to pay SSPP to a former employee where the employee was employed on a continuous basis for at least eight weeks and the employee's contract of services was brought to an end solely or mainly for the purpose of avoiding liability to pay SSPP.

33.98 *Protection from detriment*

Section 47C(2)(bb) of the *ERA 1996* provides that an employee has a right not to be subjected to any detriment by any act or deliberate failure to act by his employer for a reason set out in *reg 42(1)* of the *SPL Regulations*. Those reasons are:

- the employee took, sought to take, or made use of the benefits of, SPL;

- the employer believed that the employee was likely to take SPL; or

- the employee undertook, considered undertaking, or refused to undertake work in accordance with reg 37 ('keeping in touch' or SPLiT days).

Reg 42(2) states that an employee makes use of the benefits of SPL if during a period of SPL the employee benefits from any of the terms and conditions of employment persevered by *reg 38* during that period (see [**33.102**]).

33.99 *Protection from discrimination*

There are a range of potential claims arising from SPL under the *Equality Act 2010*. The most difficult relate to indirect discrimination on grounds of sex, and is discussed below at [**33.105**]. There is also the possibility of discrimination on grounds of maternity or civil partnership status as well as sexual orientation. Finally, there is also a range of more common but less legally novel complaints that may arise from the introduction of SPL, such as harassment, direct discrimination on grounds of sex and so on. See generally DISCRIMINATION AND EQUAL OPPORTUNITIES – I (12), II (13), and III (14).

33.100 *Redundancy protection*

Reg 39 makes provision in respect of redundancy during a period of SPL. *Reg 39(2)* requires an employer to offer any suitable alternative vacancy with the employer, the employer's successor or an associated employer under a new contract of employment that takes effect immediately after the end of the employee's previous employment contract. *Reg 39(3)* requires the new contract of employment to be suitable in relation to the employee and appropriate work for the employee to do in the circumstances; and that the terms and conditions and provisions as to the capacity and place in which the employee are employed are not substantially less favourable to the employee than if she had not been redundant. A failure to fulfil this duty will result in a finding of unfair dismissal, but subject to *section 141* of the *ERA 1996*.

33.101 *Keeping in touch or 'SPLiT' days*

Reg 37 makes provision for 'keeping in touch' days (equivalent to those in respect of maternity leave), which are labelled 'SPLiT' ('shared parental leave in touch') days in the BIS Guide at FAQ 85. The nature of SPLiT days is set out in *reg 37(1)*: they permit the employee to carry out work for the employer without the employee bringing the period of SPL to an end. The employee has no right to undertake such work, and the employer no right to require that the employee undertake the work: *reg 37(6)*. The employee may work for up to 20 keeping in touch or 'SPLiT' days "for each employer" (*reg 37(2)*), but such days do not have the effect of extending SPL (*reg 37(7)*). *Reg 37(4)* provides that keeping in touch or 'SPLiT' days constitute work under the contract of employment, which may create an entitlement to pay for that work depending on the terms of the contract (that may in turn be set off against entitlement to SSPP). However, contact to discuss an employee's return to work or any reasonable contact from time to time between the employer and employee does not constitute work: *reg 37(5)*.

33.102 *Terms and conditions during SPL*

Reg 38 provides that during SPL an employee is entitled to the benefit of all of his or her terms and conditions of employment, within the meaning of *ERA 1996, s 75I(2)* (in other words, excluding the right to remuneration by way of wages and salary). The employee is also bound by any obligations arising from those terms and conditions, subject to *ERA 1996, s 75I(1)(b)*.

33.103 *The effect of more favourable contractual rights*

If the employee has a contractual right to SPL in addition to his or her statutory rights, *reg 45(a)* of the *SPL Regulations* provides that the employee may not exercise those rights separately, but may take advantage of whichever right is more favourable, "in any particular respect", in taking leave. *Reg 45(b)* provides that the provisions in the *SPL Regulations* as regards the *ERA 1996* are modified to protect the 'composite right' (i.e. presumably, the contractual and statutory rights combined).

33.104 *Returning to work after SPL*

Regs 40 and *41* make provision in respect of returning to work after SPL. *Reg 41(1)* provides that an employee has the right to return to work to the job that he or she had before the absence if:

- the employee's statutory leave in respect of the particular child is less than 26 weeks; and,

- if the period of SPL was the last of two or more consecutive periods of statutory leave (under *Part 8* of the *1996 Act*), and that consecutive period does not include any period of additional maternity leave, additional paternity leave or unpaid parental leave that itself lasted for more than four weeks.

Otherwise, the employee's right to return to the same job is subject to whether it is reasonably practicable for the employer to permit the employee to return to that job; if it is not reasonably practicable, the employee has only a right under *reg 40(2)* to a job which is both suitable for the employee and appropriate for the employee to do in the circumstances.

Note that by *reg 41(1)*, the job is the one specified in the contract of employment (which is not necessarily precisely what the employee was doing before taking SPL), and the capacity and place the employee was employed before the absence. However *reg 41(3)* provides that the right under *reg 40* is a right to return:

- with the employee's seniority, pension rights and similar rights as they would have been if there was no absence; and

- on terms and conditions not less favourable than those which would have applied if there had been no absence.

A refusal to permit the employee to return in accordance with her *reg 40* rights may constitute a detriment or a (unfair) dismissal.

PATERNITY AND ADOPTION LEAVE & PAY

33.106 Paternity Leave

The law in relation to 'paternity leave' has developed as follows:

(a)   The *Employment Act 2002* introduced an entitlement to a short period of 'paternity leave'. This is described in this chapter as 'ordinary' paternity leave. The details are set out in the *Paternity and Adoption Leave Regulations 2002 (SI 2002/2788)* (the "**PAL Regulations**").

(b)   There was a right, now abolished, to 'additional' paternity leave under the *Additional Paternity Leave Regulations 2010 (SI 2010/1055)* (the "**Additional PL Regulations**"), which came into force on 6 April 2010 (in relation to children whose expected week of birth begins on or after 3 April 2011). The *Additional PL Regulations* implement powers in the *Work and Families Act 2006*. In effect they allow parents to share additional leave between them. The rights to additional paternity leave and pay were abolished from 5 April 2015.

(c)   See [33.68] above in relation to the introduction of shared parental leave from 5 April 2015.

33.107 Entitlement to 'ordinary' paternity leave

An employee is entitled to paternity leave under *reg 4* of the *PAL Regulations* (ie to be absent from work for the purpose of caring for a child or supporting the child's mother) if:

(a)   he has been continuously employed for a period of not less than 26 weeks ending with the week immediately preceding the 14th week before the expected week of the child's birth (note the provisions in *reg 4(3), (5)* where the child is born early or is stillborn);

(b)   he is either the child's father or is married to or is the civil partner or partner of the child's mother (note that this definition may include a female civil partner or partner of the child's mother);

(c)   he has or expects to have responsibility for bringing up the child (main responsibility, if he is not the child's father); and

(d)   he has complied with the requirements to give notice (and, in certain cases, provide evidence) set out in *reg 6* of the *PAL Regulations*.

An employee is not entitled to take paternity leave if the employee has taken any shared parental leave in respect of the child: *reg 4(1A)* of the *PAL Regulations*.

33.108 *'Ordinary' paternity leave*

The employee may take either one week's leave, or two consecutive weeks' leave: *reg 5(1)*. This leave may only be taken during the period commencing with the child's birth or the date on which the child is placed with the adopter and ending either 56 days later or, if the child is born before the first day of the expected week of its birth, 56 days after that date: *reg 5(2)*.

Before taking 'ordinary' paternity leave, the employee must notify his employer that he intends to do so, specifying the expected week of childbirth, the length of leave that he has chosen to take (see *reg 5(1)*), and the date on which he has chosen to take such leave (see *reg 5(3)–(4)*): *reg 6(1)*. Such notice must be given in or before the 15th week before the expected week of the child's birth or as soon as reasonably practicable if notice could not have been given sooner: *reg 6(2)*. In addition, if requested by the employer, the employee must sign a declaration that he is taking leave for the purpose of caring for the child or supporting the child's mother (per *reg 4(1)*) and that he satisfies the eligibility requirements in *reg 4(2)(b)–(c)*: *reg 6(3)*.

There is a mechanism in the *PAL Regulations* to vary the date on which 'ordinary' paternity leave will begin, including where the birth is late: *reg 6(4)–(8)*.

33.109 *Benefits during 'ordinary' paternity leave*

During the course of paternity leave, an employee is entitled to the benefit of all the terms and conditions that would have applied if he or she had not been absent (save for those in relation to remuneration, ie wages or salary), and remains bound by the obligations that arise out of those terms and conditions: *reg 12*.

An employee is entitled to return to the same job at the end of an isolated period of paternity leave or the last of two or more consecutive periods of statutory leave which did not include any period of statutory leave which when added to any other periods of statutory leave (excluding parental leave) taken in relation to the same child means that the total amount of statutory leave taken in relation to that child totals more than 26 weeks, or a period of parental leave of more than four weeks (*reg 13(1)*). In all other cases, he or she is entitled to return to the same job or, if this is not reasonably practicable, to another job which is suitable and appropriate for him or her to do in the circumstances (*reg 13(2)*). The employee's return to work broadly carries with it the same seniority, pension and similar rights and the right to no less favourable terms and conditions than he would have enjoyed had he not taken leave (*reg 14*).

33.114 Adoption Leave

Entitlement to adoption leave was introduced:

(a)   under the *PAL Regulations*, both as adoption leave per se (see especially *regs 8–14*) and as a form of paternity leave in relation to an adopted child (see especially *regs 15–27*);

(b)   under the *Additional PL Regulations*, as a form of APL in relation to adopted children who are matched to a person who is notified of having been matched on or after 3 April 2011 (see especially *reg 3* and *regs 14–23*), although these rights were abolished as of 5 April 2015 in favour of shared parental leave. See **[33.68]** above;

(c)   under the *Additional Paternity Leave (Adoptions from Overseas) Regulations 2010 (SI 2010/1059)* (the **"Overseas Adoptions Additional PL Regulations"**) and the *Employment Rights Act 1996 (Application of Section 80BB to Adoptions from Overseas) Regulations 2010 (SI 2010/1058)*, as APL in relation to employees married to or the civil partner or partner of an adopter whose child enters Great Britain on or after 3 April 2011, but these rights were abolished as of 5 April 2015 in favour of shared parental leave. See **[33.68]** above;

(d)   the *CFA 2014* and accompanying regulations make provision for shared parental leave. See **[33.68]** above;

(e)   the *Paternity and Adoption Leave (Amendment) (No. 2) Regulations 2014 (2014/3206)* create new rights to adoption leave and paternity leave for local authority foster parents who are prospective adopters if they have been notified that a child is to be placed with them under *section 22C* of the *Children Act 1989* following consideration in accordance with *section 22C(9B)(c)* of that *Act*.

An employee is not entitled to take adoption leave if the employee has taken any shared parental leave in respect of the child or exercised a right to take time off under *section 57ZJ* of the *1996 Act* (adoption appointments): *reg 8(1A)* of the *PAL Regulations*.

The detailed rules applicable to adoption leave are broadly similar to those applicable to the comparable provisions for ordinary and additional maternity leave. Those applicable to paternity leave in relation to adopted children are broadly similar to those applicable to ordinary and additional paternity leave.

33.115 Protection against detriment in relation to paternity or adoption leave

As with employees taking maternity leave, employees are protected against suffering detriment in certain circumstances in relation to paternity or adoption leave: *reg 28* of the *PAL Regulations*, *reg 33* of the *Additional PL Regulations*, *reg 23* of the *Overseas Adoptions Additional PL Regulations* and *ERA 1996, s 47C*. Dismissal of an employee for a reason connected with the fact that he took, or sought to take, paternity or adoption leave, or for a series of other specified related reasons, will be an automatically unfair dismissal, save in prescribed circumstances, as will the dismissal of a person on APL for the reason that he is redundant where *reg 28* of the *Additional PL Regulations* or *reg 18* of the *Overseas Adoptions Additional PL Regulations* as appropriate have not been complied with: *reg 29* of the *PAL Regulations*, *reg 34* of the *Additional PL Regulations*, *reg 24* of the *Overseas Adoptions Additional PL Regulations* and *ERA 1996, s 99*. The protections in relation to APL in the *Additional PL Regulations* came into effect on 6 April 2010; and those of the *Overseas Adoptions Additional PL Regulations* on 9 April 2010 (and the same applies to the protection from detriment/dismissal provisions therein).

In *Atkins v Coyle Personnel plc* [2008] IRLR 420, the EAT observed that there had to be a causal connection between the dismissal and the taking of paternity leave in a claim under *reg 29* of the *PAL Regulations*, rather than some vague, less stringent connection. The mere fact that a dispute between employee and manager originated in an incident when the employee was on paternity leave will not be sufficient by itself to establish the causal connection.

33.116 Statutory paternity and adoption pay

Employees who satisfy certain qualifying conditions are entitled to statutory paternity pay for up to two weeks in the sum of the lesser of £151.20 per week as of 6 April 2018 or 90% of his normal weekly earnings, and employees adopting children after 5 April 2015 are entitled to 90% of their gross average weekly earnings for the first six weeks, after which the same position as statutory paternity pay applies (see the *Statutory Paternity Pay and Adoption Pay (General) Regulations 2002 (SI 2002/2822)*): *Statutory Paternity Pay and Statutory Adoption Pay (Weekly Rates) Regulations 2002 (SI 2002/2818)*, as regularly amended.

In addition, employees who satisfy the relevant qualifying conditions are entitled to additional statutory paternity pay in accordance with the detailed requirements of the *Additional Statutory Paternity Pay (General) Regulations 2010 (SI 2010/1056)* or the *Additional Statutory Paternity Pay (Adoptions from Overseas) Regulations 2010 (SI 2010/1057)* and the *Additional Statutory Paternity Pay (Weekly Rates) Regulations 2010 (SI 2010/1060)*. See also variously the *Additional Statutory Paternity Pay (Birth, Adoption and Adoptions from Overseas) (Administration) Regulations 2010 (SI 2010/154)*, the *Statutory Paternity Pay (Adoption), Additional Statutory Paternity Pay (Adoption) and Statutory Adoption Pay (Adoptions from Overseas) (Persons Abroad and Mariners) Regulations 2010 (SI 2010/150)* and the *Additional Statutory Paternity Pay (National Health Service Employees) Regulations 2010 (SI 2010/152)*.

33.117 PARENTAL BEREAVEMENT

The *Parental Bereavement (Leave and Pay) Act 2018* ("the **PBA 2018**") received Royal Assent on 13 September 2018 and was brought into force with effect from 18 January 2020 by the *Parental Bereavement (Leave and Pay) Act 2018 (Commencement) Regulations 2020*,

SI 2020/45. It creates rights to leave and pay for bereaved parents. It does so, principally, by amending the *Employment Rights Act 1996* and the *Social Security and Benefits Act 1992* and conferring a power on the Secretary of State to make regulations. At the date of publication two sets of regulations have been drawn up: the *Statutory Parental Bereavement Pay (General) Regulations 2020, SI 2020/233* ("the *PB Pay Regulations*") and the *Parental Bereavement Leave Regulations 2020, SI 2020/249* ("the *PB Leave Regulations*"). Both sets of regulations came into force with effect from 10 March 2020.

33.118 Parental Bereavement Leave

The *Act* adds a new *section 80EA* to the *ERA 1996.* The section (at *s 80EA(1)*) requires the Secretary of State to make regulations "entitling an employee who is a bereaved parent to be absent from work on leave". The *PB Leave Regulations* are made under that power. Statutory Parental Bereavement Leave is referred to below as "SPBL".

33.119 *Who qualifies?*

The Act confers entitlement to leave on any "bereaved parent". Note, it is an entitlement conferred on employees and not workers more generally.

The *Act* left it to the anticipated regulations more precisely to define who is to be taken to be a bereaved parent. It stipulates that regulations must specify conditions "as to the relationship with a child who has died" (*s 80EA(2)*). Those conditions "may be framed, in whole or in part, by reference to the employee's care of the child before the child's death" (*s 80EA(3)*).

The *PB Leave Regulations* set out a list of those who qualifies as a "bereaved parent" at *Reg 4.* Throughout the list it refers to the deceased child as "C". A bereaved parent is someone who, at the date of C's death, is:

(a)   C's parent;

(b)   C's natural parent and named in an order made pursuant to *section 51A(2)(a)* of the *Adoption and Children Act 2002* provided that the order has not been revoked or discharged;

(c)   a person with whom C has been placed for adoption, for so long as the placement has not been disrupted (disruption being further defined at sub-paragraph (3) of *Reg 4*);

(d)   an adopter –

   (i)   with whom C was living, following C's entry into Great Britain from outside the United Kingdom in connection with or for the purposes of adoption which does not involve the placement of C for adoption under the law of any part of the United Kingdom, and

   (ii)   who has received official notification in respect of C;

(e)   an intended parent of C;

(f)   C's parent in fact (for a definition of which, see below); or

(g)   the partner of anyone who qualifies under (a) to (f) above.

A child is "a person under the age of 18" (*s 80EA(9)*) and includes a child stillborn after 24 weeks of pregnancy (*s 80EA*). In the case of a stillborn child, references to death are treated as being references to their birth (*s 80EE*).

A person is C's "parent in fact" if, for a continuous period of 4 weeks ending with the date on which C dies, C was living with that person in that person's own home and they had day to day responsibility for C's care (*Reg 4(4)*). The continuous period will not be broken by any "absences of a temporary or intermittent nature" (*Reg 4(5)*). There are, however, two exceptions. The first is where, although the potential "parent in fact" has day to day responsibility for care, one (or more) of C's parents or anyone who has parental responsibility for C is also living in the home (*Reg 4(6)(a)* and *4(7)*). The second is where the putative "parent in fact" is or was entitled to receive remuneration, whether by way of wages or otherwise, in respect of the care of C (*Reg 4(6)(b)*). Remuneration is further defined at *Reg 5(8)* so as to exclude: any fee or allowance paid by a local authority to a foster parent; payments wholly or mainly intended to reimburse the person for expenses which arise from, or are expected to arise from, the person's care of C; and amounts received pursuant to the terms of a will, trust or similar instrument which makes provision in respect of C's care.

A person is C's "intended parent" if, in the context of a surrogacy arrangement, they have applied, or intended to apply during the period of 6 months beginning with the day of C's birth either with another person or as sole applicant for an order under *ss 54* and *54A* respectively of the *Human Fertilisation and Embryology Act 2008* in respect of C and they expected the court to make such an order (*Reg 3*).

Reg 5(9) makes provision for who is to count as the "partner" of a qualifying parent. The provision is, to put it mildly, complicated. The starting point is that the partner must be someone who lived with the qualifying parent, P and with C. The partner can be of the same sex as P. The partner, P and C must live together in an "enduring family relationship". However, a person cannot be P's partner if they are their parent, grandparent, sibling, aunt or uncle. Those excluded family relationships apply whether they are full or half blood or, in the case of an adopted person, one of those relationships would have existed but for the adoption. Also excluded is the relationship of a child with his adoptive, or former adoptive, parents (but not any other adoptive relationship).

33.120 *What is the leave entitlement?*

ERA 1996, s 80EA(5) will provide that regulations must "secure that where an employee is entitled to leave . . . in respect of a child the employee is entitled to at least two weeks' leave". The PB Leave Regulations provide for a minimum period of 1 week (*Reg 5(1)*) and a maximum period of two weeks (*Reg 5(2)*). It is left to the employee to decide whether they want to take one or two weeks. If they decide to take two weeks leave, they can either take it all in one go or take two discrete, non-consecutive periods of one week (*Reg 5(3)*).

Where the parent loses more than one child, they are to be entitled to leave in respect of each child (*s 80EA(7)* and *PB Leave Regulations, Reg 4(10)*).

The leave will have to be taken (which seems to suggest will have to been completed by) the end of a specified period commencing with the date of the child's death. The Act requires that the Regulations should secure that the period during which leave is to be taken is at least 56 days (*s 80EA(6)*). However, the *PB Leave Regulations* go much further and provide that the leave may be taken at any time within a period of 56 weeks from the date of C's death.

Reg 8 of the *PB Leave Regulations* makes provision for where SPBL overlaps with other statutory leave. So, for instance, an employee on SPBL may start a period of SML. *Reg 8* provides that in the event of overlap the SPBL immediately comes to an end and the remainder of any SPBL is carried over until the end of the other leave at which point it must be taken in one block. When the remainder is taken, a new notice must be given under *Reg 6* (for which see **[33.122]** below).

Where the employee has both a statutory and a contractual right to SPBL, they cannot both be taken. However, the employee can take whichever is more beneficial and where they take the contractual right they are treated for the purposes of the *ERA 1996* and the *PB Leave Regulations* as if they were taking the statutory right so that they are no less well-protected (*Reg 15*).

33.121 *Rights during and at the end of Parental Bereavement Leave*

When does PBL begin?

Leave begins on the date specified in any notice given under *Reg 6* (for which see [33.122] below) unless notice of cancellation is given or unless notice is given at a point at which the employee is already at work in which case it starts the following day (*Reg 7*).

Contractual Rights and Obligations during PBL

ERA 1996, s 80EB makes provision for regulations stipulating the bereaved parent's rights during leave.

Section 80EB(1) requires that regulations should provide:

"(a) that an employee who is absent on leave under that section is entitled, for such purposes and to such extent as the regulations may prescribe, to the benefit of the terms and conditions of employment which would have applied but for the absence,

(b) that an employee who is absent on leave under that section is bound, for such purposes and to such extent as the regulations may prescribe, by obligations arising under those terms and conditions (except in so far as they are inconsistent with subsection (1) of [*s 80EA*]), and

(c) that an employee who is absent on leave under that section is entitled to return from leave to a job of a kind prescribed by regulations, subject to section 80EC(1)."

The relevant provision of the *PB Leave Regulations* is *Reg 9(1)*, which provides:

"An employee who takes parental bereavement leave, is, during any period of leave—

(a) entitled to the benefit of all of the terms and conditions of employment which would have applied if the employee had not been absent, and

(b) bound by any obligations arising under those terms and conditions, subject only to the exception in section 80EB(1)(b) of the 1996 Act(18)."

The reference to *s 80EB(1)(b)* brings one back to *s 80EA(1)* which is the power to make regulations entitling a bereaved parent to be absent from work. The presumed effect of this piece of legislative hopscotch is that a bereaved parent is not, whilst on SPBL, bound by any contractual obligation to attend work.

"Terms and conditions of employment" is defined to include "matters connected with an employee's employment whether or not they arise under the contract of employment" but the definition excludes "terms and conditions about remuneration" (*s 80EB(3)* and *Reg 9(2)*). The *PB Leave Regulations* further define remuneration so that "*only sums payable to an employee by way of wages or salary are to be treated as remuneration*" (*Reg 9(3)*). Special provision is made in respect of "employment-related benefit schemes". *Social Security Act 1989, Sch 5, Para 5D* provides, simplifying, that for the purposes of membership of any such scheme, accrual of benefits under it and the calculation of benefit paid from it, someone on parental bereavement leave should be treated as if they were at work. *Reg 9(4)* provides that nothing in *Reg 9(1)* imposes a requirement which exceeds the requirements of *Para 5D* of the *1989 Act*.

Protection from Detriment

ERA 1996, s 47C confers a right on an employee not to be subjected to any detriment by any act, or any deliberate failure to act, by their employer done for any of a number of "prescribed reasons". Those reasons "relate" to the various rights to leave for family and domestic reasons and specifically include (at *s 47C(2)(cb)*) PBL. The relevant prescription is found at *Reg 12(1)* of the *PB Leave Regulations* which provides:

"An employee is entitled under section 47C of the 1996 Act not to be subjected to any detriment by any act, or any deliberate failure to act, by an employer because—

(a) the employee took, sought to take, or made use of the benefits of, parental bereavement leave, or

(b) the employer believed that the employee was likely to take parental bereavement leave."

An employee "makes use of the benefits of" SPBL if, during a period of SPBL they benefit from any of the terms and conditions of the employment preserved by *Reg 9* (for which see immediately above) (*Reg 12(2)*).

The protection does not apply where the detriment "amounts to dismissal within the meaning of *Part 10* of [*ERA 1996*] (*Reg 12(3)*)

The Right to Return to Work

Where the right to return to work provided for by *s 80EB(1)(c)* and *Reg 10* is concerned, the reference to "absent on leave" includes a continuous period of leave only part of which is parental bereavement leave. The other part may consist of maternity; paternity; adoption; shared parental; or parental leave (*s 80EB(2)*). Where the only leave taken is *SPBL, Reg 10* refers to it as an "isolated period of parental bereavement leave". An employee has a right to return to the job in which they were employed before their absence in two sets of circumstances:

(a) where they have taken an isolated period of parental bereavement leave; or

(b) where they are returning after the last of two or more consecutive periods of statutory leave which did not include any—

    (i) period of parental leave (within the meaning of *MPL 1999, Reg 13* – for which see [**33.62**] above) of more than four weeks; or

    (ii) period of statutory leave which when added to any other periods of statutory leave (excluding parental leave) taken in relation to the same child as the period of parental bereavement leave the employee is returning from means that the total amount of statutory leave taken in relation to that child totals more than 26 weeks. (*Reg 10(1)*).

The position is slightly different where they return to work following a period of SPBL that does not fall into one of the two categories set out above. In that case, where it is not "reasonably practicable" for the employer to allow the employee to return to the job in which they were employed before they took leave, the employee is entitled to return to another job that is "both suitable and appropriate for the employee to do in the circumstances" (*Reg 10(2)*).

How does one determine what job the employee was doing before they took leave? Where they take isolated SPBL, one looks at what they were doing immediately before they took the leave. Where they are returning from consecutive periods of statutory leave one looks at what they were doing immediately before they took the first of those periods of leave (*Reg 10(3)*).

"(a) with the employee's seniority, pension and similar rights as they would have been if the employee had not been absent, and

(b) on terms and conditions not less favourable than those which would have applied if the employee had not been absent." (*Reg 11*)

Protection from Unfair Dismissal

If the reason (or principal reason) for dismissing an employee is "connected with" the fact that the employee: (a) took, sought to take, or made use of the benefits of SPBL; or (b) the employer believed that the employee was likely to take PBL, the dismissal will be unfair (*Reg 13(1)* and *(3)*). The dismissal will equally be unfair if that reason was why an employee was selected for redundancy (*Reg 13(2)*).

An employee "makes use of the benefits of" SPBL if, during a period of SPBL they benefit from any of the terms and conditions of the employment preserved by *Reg 9* (for which see immediately above) (*Reg 13(4)*).

Where the employee's pay varies and the tribunal has to calculate a week's pay for the purposes of a redundancy payment or the basic award under *Chp 2* of *Pt 14* of *ERA 1996*, any averaging of the employee's pay must treat take account of SPBL by ensuring that their pay for weeks of PBL are calculated on the basis of what they would have received had they not been on leave.

33.122 *Notices and evidence*

In order to take SPBL, the employee must give notice to their employer. The notice requirements are set out in *PB Leave Regulations, Reg 6*. What notice must be given depends on when the employee intends to take it. The *Regulations* call the first 56 days from the C's death "Period A". "Period B" covers day 57 through to the end of the 56 week period from C's death during which SPBL must be taken (see **[33.120]** above).

Notice requirements during Period A: Notice does not need to be provided in writing. The employee must provide three pieces of information: (1) the date of C's death; (2) the date on which the employee wants their leave to begin; and (3) whether the employee intends to take one or two weeks of parental bereavement leave (*Reg 6(1)*).

The notice must be given "before the employee is due to start work on the employee's first day of absence from work" in the proposed week of SPBL unless that is not reasonably practicable in which case notice should be given as soon as reasonable practicability allows (*Reg 6(2)*).

Notice requirements during Period B: The same information is required as in Period A. However, a longer period of notice is required. The employee must give notice "at least one week before the start of" the week's leave (*Reg 6(3)*).

Cancellation: Leave can be cancelled by the employee but only if it has not already begun (*Reg 6(5)*). The employee must give notice of cancellation. *Reg 6(4)* provides that:

> "(a) in Period A, the employee may cancel that week's parental bereavement leave by giving notice to the employer no later than the time on the first day of that week at which the employee would have been due to start work if the employee was not taking parental leave;
>
> (b) in Period B, the employee may cancel that week's parental bereavement leave by giving notice to the employer at least one week before the start of that week."

33.123 Parental Bereavement Pay

A right to "statutory parental bereavement pay" ("SPBP") was created by a new *section 171ZZ6* which is to be inserted into the *SSCBA 1992*. The regime has been spelled out in greater detail in the *PB Pay Regulations*. The provisions are complex and only a summary is set out below.

33.124 *Who qualifies?*

In order to qualify for SPBP, the person claiming has to be a bereaved parent. The categories of relationships that qualify are the same as those to be found in the *PB Leave Regulations*, for which see **[33.119]** above.

SSCBA 1992, s 171ZZ6(2) sets out other conditions that must be met in order for an employee to be entitled to SPBP. They are not dealt with in detail in this work but may be summarised as follows:

(1)   the person has to be an employee. A very specific definition is set out at *Reg 11* by reference to the *Social Security (Categorisation of Earners) Regulations 1978, SI 1978/1689* (as amended). It includes those employed under a contract of apprenticeship;

(2)   the person has to have been in employed earner's employment with an employer for a continuous period of at least 26 weeks ending with the week immediately before the one in which the child dies (the "relevant week"). Special provision is made in relation to continuous employment (*Regs 12 to 18*);

(3)   the person's normal weekly earnings for the period of 8 weeks ending with the relevant week are not less than the lower earnings limit in force under *SSCBA 1992, section 5(1)(a)* at the end of the relevant week. Detailed provision is made in respect of "normal weekly earnings" at *Reg 19*. At the date of publication, the LEL is £120 gross per week; and

(4)   the person has been in employed earner's employment with the employer by reference to whom the condition at (2) above is satisfied for a continuous period beginning with the end of the relevant week and ending with the day on which the child dies.

Where the parent satisfies the conditions as a result of the death of more than one child, they are "entitled to [SPBP] in respect of each child" (*s 171ZZ6(6)*). As with Parental Bereavement Leave (see para [33.119] above) "child" includes a child stillborn after 24 weeks of pregnancy (*s 171ZZ15*). Considerable scope is given for regulations to modify the entitlement conditions (see *s 171ZZ7(4)*).

The provisions apply to Crown Employees (*s 171ZZ12*).

The Secretary of State (with the concurrence of the Treasury) can make regulations modifying provisions in their application to people:

"(a) employed on board any ship, vessel, hovercraft or aircraft;

(b) outside Great Britain at any prescribed time or in any prescribed circumstances; or

(c) in prescribed employment in connection with continental shelf operations, as defined in section 120(2)"

(*Section 171ZZ13*)

In exercise of that power, the Secretary of State made the *Statutory Parental Bereavement Pay (Persons Abroad and Mariners) Regulations 2020, SI 2020/252* which came into force on 6 April 2020.

33.125 *Notices, evidence and liability to make payment*

The notice requirements for SPBP differ from and are more demanding than those that apply to SPBL (see [**33.122**] above). The notice has to be given to the person liable to pay the SPBP and must be given either before the end of the period of 28 days beginning with the first day of the period in respect of which payment of SPBP is to be made, or where that is not reasonably practicable as soon as is reasonably practicable thereafter (*Reg 8(1)*).

In addition, and at the same time as notice is given, "a person" (so not necessarily the bereaved parent themselves) must provide, in writing, certain information and a declaration. The information is the name of the person claiming SPBP and the date of their child's death (*Reg 8(3)*). The declaration is a declaration that person meets the qualifying criteria in *Reg 4* (i.e. that they are, broadly, a parent) (*reg 8(2)(a)*).

A notice can be withdrawn provided that it is given before start of the week or weeks specified as being the ones in respect of which SPBP is claimed (*Reg 8(6)*). Notice of withdrawal has to be given in writing. Where the notice is for two weeks of SPBP, the withdrawal may cover either or both weeks. It does not matter whether the two weeks are continuous or discontinuous (*Reg 8(7)*). The timing of the notice of withdrawal depends on whether it relates to a week falling within a period of 56 days from C's death ("Period A") or in the period after the end of Period A and before the end of a period of 56 weeks from C's death ("Period B"). If it relates to a week in Period A, it must be given no later than the first day of the relevant week. If it relates to a week in Period B, it must be given no later than one week before the start of the relevant week (*Reg 8(8)* and *(9)*).

33.126 *Rate and Period of Pay*

The *PB Pay Regulations* provide for an entitlement to two weeks of SPBP (*Reg 5*) and that the pay may be taken for a single period of either one or two weeks or for discontinuous periods of a week each (*Reg 6*). As one would expect, that mirrors precisely the entitlement to SPBL conferred on employees by the PB Leave Regulations (see **[33.120]** above).

Reg 7 provides that the SPBP must be taken within a period of 56 weeks beginning with the date of the child (C)'s death. Rather confusingly (and by reference to *SSCBA 1992, s 171ZZ9(5)*) this is referred to as the "qualifying period". However, it is not a period that has to elapse before the entitlement is conferred. It is, instead, a period during which the employee continues to qualify to receive the pay.

The weekly rate of payment is the lower of £151.20 or 90% of the normal weekly earnings of the person claiming SPBP (*Reg 20*).

SPBP received can be set off against contractual pay received in a period of Parental Bereavement Leave and vice versa (*s 171ZZ11* and *Reg 21*) Contractual remuneration for this purpose is sums payable under the contract of service: (a) by way of remuneration; (b) for incapacity for work due to sickness or injury; or (c) by reason of birth, adoption, care or death of a child.

SPBP cannot be paid in kind or by providing board or lodgings (*Reg 23*).

33.127 *Contracting Out and Avoidance*

To the extent to which any agreement seeks to "exclude, limit or otherwise modify any provision of the [part of ERA 1996 that deals with SBPB]" it is void. The same is true of any agreement that requires "a person to contribute (whether directly or indirectly) towards any costs incurred by that person's employer of former employer [under that part]" (*s 171ZZ10(1)*). It possible, however, for a deductions agreement to cover SPBP provided it applies equally to contractual remuneration (*s 171ZZ10(2)*).

If an employee has been employed for at least 8 weeks and their contract of service is brought to an end by the former employer solely, or mainly, for the purpose of avoiding liability for SPBP, the employer remains liable to make payments to their now former employee (*Reg 22*).

34   Part-Time Workers

34.1   LEGAL FRAMEWORK

Part-time workers are protected from discrimination under both European and domestic law.

- *Directive 97/81/EC* on part-time work (implementing 'the *Framework Agreement*') was concluded by the European Social Partners and adopted by the European Council on 15 December 1997. It was extended to the United Kingdom by *Directive 98/23/EC*. The *Framework Agreement* is aimed at eliminating discrimination against part-time workers and contributing to the encouragement, development and quality of part-time work.

- The prohibition on discrimination in *cl 4* of the *Framework Agreement* is a specific expression of the principle of equality, which is a fundamental principle of EU law. See, for example paragraph 58 of the judgment of the CJEU in: *Istituto Nazionale della Previdenza Sociale v Bruno*: C-395/08 & C-396/08, [2010] 3 CMLR 45, [2010] IRLR 890.

- The Directive is implemented domestically in the *Part-Time Workers (Prevention of Less Favourable Treatment) Regulations 2000 (SI 2000/1551)* ('the Regulations'), as since amended. Note, however, that the *Regulations* were made under *s 19* of the *Employment Relations Act 1999* and not *s 2* of the *European Communities Act 1972* and that, in some respects, the protections in the *Regulations* go beyond those mandated by the *Directive* (see further **34.20** below).

The *Regulations* provide a relatively simple, gender-neutral route for tackling discrimination against part-time workers. A part-time worker may still, however, have a claim in the alternative under the *Equality Act 2010*. In *Voss v Land Berlin*: C-300/06 [2007] ECR I-10573, [2008] 1 CMLR 49, [2007] All ER (D) 87 (Dec), for example, the ECJ held that a difference in treatment which is detrimental to part-time workers could be contrary to the principle of equal pay and therefore require objective justification. See also, for example, *Pike v Somerset County Council* [2009] EWCA Civ 808, [2010] ICR 46, [2009] IRLR 870 (in relation to a provision of the *Teachers' Superannuation (Consolidation) Regulations 1988* which disadvantaged part-time workers); *Meerts v Proost NV*: C-116/08 [2010] All ER (EC) 1085, ECJ (in relation to notice pay for workers who are taking part-time parental leave); and *Copple v Littlewoods plc* [2012] ICR 354, [2012] IRLR 121, [2012] 2 All ER 97 (in relation to occupational pension schemes). This chapter is concerned with the *Regulations* only.

As to the application of sex discrimination legislation to part-time workers, see DISCRIMINATION AND EQUAL OPPORTUNITIES I (12), II (13), and III (14) and EQUAL PAY (23).

34.2   Guidance Material

Sections 20 and *21* of the *Employment Relations Act 1999* empower the Secretary of State to issue a Code of Practice in relation to part-time work and the *Framework Agreement*. A Code issued under that power would be admissible in evidence in proceedings before an Employment Tribunal and shall be taken into account by the Tribunal in any case where it appears relevant, but the failure to observe it would not render a person liable to proceedings: *s 20(3)* and *(4)*. To date, however, no Code has been issued. BERR (as it then was) issued Guidance Notes to accompany the *Regulations* which provide advice on the law as well as on how employers can widen access to part-time work, although these do not appear to have been updated (https://tinyurl.com/ydbarpsh). Some limited guidance is also provided in the Explanatory Note to the *Regulations*.

34.3 Part-Time Workers

34.3 Direct effect

In *Zentralbetriebsrat der Landeskrankenhauser Tirols v Land Tirol*: C-486/08 [2010] 3 CMLR 30, [2010] IRLR 631, the ECJ held that *cl 4(1)–(2)* of the *Framework Agreement* (i.e. the non-discrimination provision) is unconditional and sufficiently precise for individuals to be able to rely upon it before a national court (see paragraphs 21–25). This is consistent with the approach taken in *R (on the application of Manson (Finian)) v Ministry of Defence* [2005] EWHC 427 (Admin), [2005] All ER (D) 270 (Feb), in which Moses J considered, *obiter*, that *cl 4* of the *Framework Agreement* has direct effect (an appeal was dismissed on a separate issue: [2006] ICR 355). In *Christie v Department for Constitutional Affairs and Department for Work and Pensions* [2007] ICR 1553, [2007] All ER (D) 355 (Jul), however, an appeal against a decision that there was no directly enforceable right did not get through the EAT 'sift'. The President did not express any opinion on the point (see [23]).

34.4 WHO HAS THE RIGHT?

Workers

The majority of rights under the *Regulations* are granted to 'workers'. The definition of 'worker' in *reg 1(2)* is the same as that in *s 230(3)* of the *Employment Rights Act 1996*. It covers individuals who have entered into, work or worked under a contract of employment or any other contract, whether express or implied and (if it is express) whether oral or in writing, whereby the individual undertakes to do or perform personally any work or services for another party to the contract, whose status is not by virtue of the contract that of a client or customer of any profession or business undertaking carried on by the individual (see EMPLOYEE, SELF-EMPLOYED OR WORKER? **(16)**).

Applicants for employment are not within the scope of the *Regulations*. In addition, it is important to note that *reg 7(1)* (unfair dismissal) applies only to 'employees' (see **34.21**).

The *Regulations* apply to those in Crown employment and to House of Lords and House of Commons staff: *regs 12, 14* and *15*. They also apply to persons appointed as police cadets or holding the office of constable other than under a contract of employment, who are treated as employed under a contract of employment for these purposes: *reg 16*. Special provisions apply to constables who are seconded to the Serious Organised Crime Agency: *regs 16(1A)–(1B)*.

The *Framework Agreement* applies to 'workers who have an employment contract or employment relationship as defined by the law, collective agreement or practice in force in each Member State'. In *O'Brien v Ministry of Justice*: C-393/10 [2012] IRLR 412, [2012] All ER (EC) 757, [2012] 2 CMLR 25, [2012] ICR 955, the CJEU explained:

- None of the terms 'worker', 'employment contract' or 'employment relationship' are defined in the *Framework Agreement*. The *Directive* and the *Framework Agreement* do not aim at complete harmonisation of national laws in this area, but only to establish a general framework for eliminating discrimination against part-time workers. Member States are free to define those terms in accordance with national law and practice. It is for national law to determine whether a person in part-time work has a contract of employment or an employment relationship.

- However, Member States may not apply rules which are liable to jeopardise the achievement of the objective pursued by the *Framework Agreement* and deprive it of its effectiveness. In particular, a Member State cannot remove certain categories of people from the scope of the protection offered by the *Framework Agreement* at will, violating its effectiveness.

• The exclusion of fee-paid judges from the protection of the Regulations would be permitted only if the nature of the employment relationship concerned is *"substantially different"* from that between employers and their employees who are 'workers' under national law.

In *Ministry of Justice (formerly Department for Constitutional Affairs) v O'Brien* [2013] UKSC 6, [2013] 2 All ER 1, [2013] 1 WLR 522, [2013] IRLR 315, the Supreme Court held that fee-paid judges are 'workers' for the purposes of the *Regulations*. Recorders were not self-employed free agents who could make their own choices as to the work they would do, and where and when that work was to be done. As a consequence *reg 17* (see **34.6**) was disapplied so as to bring the meaning of "worker" in the *Regulations* into line with the *Directive*.

34.5   Casual workers and members of the armed forces

In *Wippel v Peek & Cloppenburg GmbH & Co KG* C-313/02 [2004] ECR I-9483, [2005] ICR 1604, [2005] 1 CMLR 9, [2005] IRLR 211, the ECJ considered the status of 'framework contracts of employment' or 'work on demand' contracts, which set out applicable rates of pay, but provide no fixed working hours, no guarantee of income, and that the worker can accept or refuse the job offered each week without having to give any reason for doing so. The ECJ considered that such contracts do fall within the scope of the *Directive*, provided that the following conditions are met: (a) that such workers have a contract or employment relationship recognised by law, collective agreement or practices in force in the member state; (b) that they work 'part-time', ie their normal working hours are less than those of a comparable full-time worker; and (c) that in regard to part-time workers working on a casual basis, the member state has not excluded them from the benefit of the terms of the *Framework Agreement*, pursuant to *cl 2(2)*.

Under UK law, a framework contract would probably lack the mutuality of obligation necessary to amount to a contract of employment (see EMPLOYEE, SELF-EMPLOYED OR WORKER? **(16)**). Depending on the precise terms of the framework contract, an individual may also fall outside the domestic definition of a 'worker' if he or she has not 'undertaken to perform any work or services', e.g. if the individual is not obliged to accept any work offered to her under the framework contract.

As to the armed forces:

• The *Regulations* apply to members of the armed forces, subject to specific exceptions: *reg 13(1)*. They apply to individuals employed by Reserve Associations established for the purposes of *Part XI* of the *Reserve Forces Act 1996* ('the 1996 Act'): *reg 13(1)*. However, they do not apply to service as a member of the reserve forces in so far as that service consists of undertaking training obligations under *ss 38, 40* or *41* of the *Reserve Forces Act 1980, s 22* of the *1996 Act*, regulations made under *s 4* of the *1996 Act* or voluntary training or duties under *s 27* of the *1996 Act*: *reg 13(2)*.

• *Reg 7(1)* (unfair dismissal) does not apply to members of the armed forces: *reg 13(1)*. In addition, a complaint concerning the service of any person as a member of the armed forces may only be presented to an employment tribunal under *reg 8* of the *Regulations* if that person has already made a complaint in respect of the same matter to an officer under the service redress procedures, and that complaint has not been withdrawn: *reg 13(3)–(6)*.

Is the exclusion in respect of reservists in *reg 13(2)* compatible with the Directive? At first instance in *R (on the application of Manson (Finian)) v Ministry of Defence* [2005] EWHC 427 (Admin), [2005] All ER (D) 270 (Feb), Moses J expressed the obiter view that it is compatible. *Cl 2(2)* of the *Framework Agreement* permits member states to exclude part-time workers who work on a casual basis from the protections of the *Framework Agreement*, provided that they do so for objective reasons and after prescribed consultation. Moses J noted that 'casual worker' is not defined: it is a term left to member states to define pursuant to *recital 16* and to the *Framework Agreement* (although any definition must not diminish the class of part-time worker so as to deprive the *Directive* of any force). The result in that case was not disturbed on appeal: [2006] ICR 355.

34.6 Fee-paid holders of judicial office

The *Regulations* do not apply to any individual in his capacity as the holder of a judicial office if he is remunerated on a daily fee-paid basis: *reg 17*.

The scope and effect of *reg 17* has been extensively litigated in the past five years, both domestically and in Europe, in the ongoing 'judicial pensions' proceedings.

In 2010, the Supreme Court (in *O'Brien v Department for Constitutional Affairs* [2010] UKSC 34, [2010] 4 All ER 62, [2010] IRLR 883) referred the compatibility of *reg 17* with European law to the CJEU. The Supreme Court noted: (1) that there was no single definition of 'worker' for all Community law purposes; (2) that in contrast to the position under other Directives (where references to workers have an autonomous European meaning), the effect of *cl 2(1)* of the *Framework Agreement* read with *recital 16* of the *Directive* was to make domestic law relevant to the interpretation of the expression 'worker'; but also (3) that domestic law must respect the underlying purposes of the EU legislation and must not oust or "trump" the principles underlying that legislation in such a way as to frustrate them. It considered, however, that the application of these principles to *reg 17* required a reference.

In 2012, the CJEU gave judgment in the case (*O'Brien*: C-393/10 [2012] IRLR 412, [2012] 2 CMLR 25), holding that:

• It is for each Member State to define the concept of 'workers who have an employment contract or an employment relationship' for the purposes of the *Framework Agreement*. However, Member States may not apply rules which are liable to jeopardise the achievement of the objective pursued by the *Framework Agreement* and deprive it of its effectiveness, by arbitrarily excluding a category of persons from the protection the *Framework Agreement* offers.

• The exclusion of fee-paid judges from the protection of the *Regulations* would be permitted only if the nature of the employment relationship concerned is "*substantially different*" from the that between employers and their employees who are 'workers' under national law.

• The term 'worker' is used in the definition of the scope of the *Framework Agreement* to draw a distinction from a self-employed person, and the national court would have to bear in mind that this distinction is part of the spirit of the *Framework Agreement*. It would be necessary for the national court to consider the rules for appointing and removing judges, and the way in which their work is organised. For example, judges are expected to work during defined times and periods, and are entitled to sick pay, maternity or paternity pay and other similar benefits. The CJEU also noted that the fact that judges are subject to terms of service and might be regarded as workers within the meaning of *cl 2.1* of the *Framework Agreement* docs not undermine the principle of the independence of the judiciary or the right of Member States to provide a particular status for the judiciary. It merely aims to extend to those judges the scope of the principle of equal treatment and to protect them against discrimination as compared with full-time workers.

•   Full-time judges and recorders perform essentially the same activity. Accordingly, if fee-paid judges are workers for these purposes, the *Framework Agreement* precludes discrimination between full-time judges and fee-paid part-time judges for the purposes of access to the relevant retirement pension scheme, unless such a difference in treatment can be justified by objective reasons. Again, whether or not that is so would be a matter for the national court. However, the CJEU noted that "*budgetary considerations cannot justify discrimination*".

In 2013, the Supreme Court held in light of the CJEU's judgment, that fee-paid judges are 'workers' for the purposes of the *Regulations* (in *Ministry of Justice (formerly Department for Constitutional Affairs) v O'Brien* [2013] UKSC 6, [2013] IRLR 315, [2013] 2 All ER 1, [2013] 1 WLR 522. Recorders are not self-employed free agents who can make their own choices as to the work they do, and where and when they do that work. They are expected to observe the terms and conditions of their appointment, and may be disciplined if they fail to do so. The Court noted that the very fact that most recorders are self-employed barristers or solicitors merely serves to underline the different character of their commitment to the public service when they undertake the office of recorder. They are in an employment relationship within the meaning of *cl 2.1* of the *Framework Agreement* and so must be treated as 'workers' for the purposes of the *Regulations*. Consequently, *reg 17* was disapplied to bring the meaning of "worker" in the *Regulations* into line with the *Directive*.

34.7   QUALIFYING PERIOD

There is no qualifying period for entitlement to the rights conferred by the *Regulations*.

A further issue that arose in *O'Brien v Ministry of Justice* concerned the fact that Mr O'Brien had been a part-time Recorder from 1978 to 2005 but the UK was only required to transpose the Directive from 7 April 2000. When calculating his pension rights, should the tribunal only consider sitting days after 7 April 2000? The Court of Appeal ([2015] EWCA Civ 1000, [2016] IRLR 1005, [2016] ICR 182) held that only the period 2000 – 2005 was to be taken into account. The principle of non-retrospectivity applied and pension rights attributable to a particular period of service were acquired during that period and the legal situation created by that period of service was "definitively fixed", as a matter of EU law, and to ensure legal certainty, when that period expired. When the matter reached the Supreme Court, it referred the question to the CJEU: [2017] UKSC 46, [2017] IRLR 939, [2017] ICR 1101. The CJEU (*O'Brien v Ministry of Justice (No. 2)* (C-432/17) [2019] IRLR 185, [2019] ICR 505, [2019] 1 CMLR 40) adopted a different approach to the Court of Appeal and held the calculation of pension rights also had to take into account the periods of service prior to the entry into force of the *Directive*. This was because it was only subsequently by reference to the earlier periods of service, that the worker could effectively avail himself of the right. The *Directive* applied immediately to the future effects of a situation arising under the previous law. The CJEU did hold, however, that the situation was different where a worker retired before the expiry of the period for transposition of the *Directive*.

34.8   DISCRIMINATION

Less favourable treatment

A part-time worker has the right not to be treated by his employer less favourably than a comparable full-time worker: (a) as regards the terms of his contract; or (b) by being subjected to any other detriment by his employer: *reg 5(1)*. However, the right applies only if the treatment is on the ground that the worker is a part-time worker, and if it is not objectively justified: *reg 5(2)*.

34.8   Part-Time Workers

A person is being treated less favourably 'as regards the terms of his contract' if those contractual terms are less favourable. He or she does not have to wait until that term is triggered to his detriment before beginning proceedings: see *Sharma v Manchester City Council* [2008] ICR 623, [2008] IRLR 336, at [45].

It is likely that the same approach will be taken to 'detriment' as has been adopted in relation to other anti-discrimination provisions (see DISCRIMINATION AND EQUAL OPPORTUNITIES – I (12)). Pressuring an individual to work full time, issuing an ultimatum to that effect, or selecting him or her for redundancy are all examples of potential less favourable treatment. Requiring a part-time worker to work a higher proportion of 'standby' to rostered hours than a full-time worker can also constitute a detriment: *Gibson v Scottish Ambulance Service* (EATS/0052/04) (16 December 2004) at [3]. Where the Ministry of Justice assumed that a Recorder who maintained his private practice would be less likely to be able to sit at short notice and flexibly, he was treated less favourably when he was not permitted to continue sitting on reaching retirement age when a comparable full-time Circuit Judge was (*Ministry of Justice v Blackford* UKEAT/0053/17 [2018] IRLR 688).

34.9   *The pro rata principle*

The *Regulations* require that the 'pro rata principle' be applied to determine whether a part-time worker has been treated less favourably than a comparable full-time worker unless it is inappropriate: *reg 5(3)*. That principle – which is defined in *reg 1(2)* – means that where a comparable full-time worker receives or is entitled to receive pay or some other benefit, a part-time worker is to receive or be entitled to receive not less than the proportion of that pay or other benefit that the number of his weekly hours bears to the number of weekly hours of the comparable full-time worker. 'Weekly hours' means, by *reg 1(3)*: (a) the number of hours a worker is required to work under his contract of employment in a week in which he has no absences from work and does not work any overtime; or (b) where the number of such hours varies according to a cycle, the average number of such hours.

The original source for the 'pro rata principle' is *cl 4(2)* of the *Framework Agreement*.

A tribunal considering *reg 5* should always consider whether it is 'appropriate' to apply the pro rata principle. It will usually be appropriate to do so where the claim is based on a difference in pay for hours worked in the ordinary course of events: *James v Great North Eastern Railway* [2005] All ER (D) 15 (Mar), EAT. However, in *Matthews v Kent and Medway Towns Fire Authority*, a tribunal held that it was inappropriate to apply the pro rata principle over the whole range of a financial package for fire fighters which included pension benefit, sick pay and pay for additional duties. This conclusion was not challenged on appeal (House of Lords decision reported at [2006] ICR 365, [2006] IRLR 367, [2006] 2 All ER 171). See further *British Airways plc v Pinaud* [2018] EWCA Civ 2427, [2019] IRLR 144 – cabin crew member had a work pattern that was 14 days on and 14 days off. When she was "on" she had to be available to work on 10 days. She suffered less favourable treatment because although she had to be available for work for 130 days per year – which was 53.5% of the figure for full-time workers – she only received 50% of full-time pay.

The role of the pro rata principle was further considered by the EAT and then the Court of Session in *McMenemy v Capita Business Services Ltd* [2007] IRLR 400 (CS). Employees at a call centre which operated seven days a week were entitled to public holidays which 'fell on [their] normal working day'. The claimant worked part-time, Wednesday to Friday. He was not allowed time off in lieu when public holidays fell on a Monday, although full-time workers in his team who normally worked on Mondays were given the day off. He argued that he had a stand-alone right to pro rata treatment as regards holidays, and that he could demonstrate that he received less holiday than a comparable full-time worker. The tribunal, EAT and Court of Session dismissed his claim. The EAT held that the tribunal had been entitled to conclude that the reason that the claimant was receiving the treatment complained of was not because he was a part-time worker but because he did not work on a Monday. The tribunal did not err in failing to have regard to the pro rata principle because *reg 5(3)* is not an independent right, and is not something that a tribunal must have in mind when considering whether any less favourable treatment is on the ground that the employee is a part-time worker (see **34.16** below). The Court of Session agreed: the pro-rata principle relates only to the logically first question whether or not a part-time worker has been treated less favourably than a full-time worker.

Where a part-time worker is more favourably treated, there is no requirement to apply the pro rata principle so as to remove that advantage: *Brazel v Harpur Trust* UKEAT/0102/17, [2018] All ER (D) 116 (Apr), upheld by the Court of Appeal: [2019] EWCA Civ 1402, [2020] ICR 584.

34.10 *Overtime*

Where part-time workers only receive overtime rates once they have worked the equivalent of a full-time worker's weekly hours, not once they have completed the hours they themselves ordinarily work each week, there is no less favourable treatment: *reg 5(4)*. This reflects the orthodox position with regards to equal pay: see *Stadt Lengerich v Helmig* C-399/92 [1995] IRLR 216, [1995] 2 CMLR 261, [1996] ICR 35, CJEU and **23.12** EQUAL PAY. It does not affect the right of part-time workers to receive other payments such as unsocial hours payments, weekend payments or other forms of enhanced pay on comparable terms to full-time workers.

In James v Great North Eastern Railways [2005] All ER (D) 15 (Mar), the EAT held that the *reg 5(4)* exception did not apply to an 'additional hours payment' made to full-time workers. Full-time employees were contractually obliged to work a 40 hour week judged over the length of an 8-week roster cycle. Employees could also be required to work overtime. Pay for the first 35 hours was paid at basic rate; they then received an 'additional hours payment' for the next five hours, being 1¼ times basic pay, and any overtime over and above the 40 hours was paid at 1¼ times basic pay. Pay for the set hours for part-time workers was at the same basic rate as full-time equivalent posts, with pay for any overtime up to 35 hours being at the same basic rate. Pay for additional hours over 35 hours was at 1¼ times basic pay but part-time workers did not receive an 'additional hours payment'. The EAT held that the payment in question must amount to a 'true' overtime payment to fall within the *reg 5(4)* exception. The 'additional hours payment' made to full-time workers was pay for the contractual rostered hours that they worked and, accordingly, the *reg 5(4)* exception was not applicable.

34.11 *Paid annual leave*

In *Zentralbetriebsrat der Landeskrankenhauser Tirols v Land Tirol* C-486/08 [2010] IRLR 631, [2010] 3 CMLR 30 the CJEU held that the pro rata principle in *cl 4(2)* of the *Framework Agreement* could not be applied to reduce ex post facto annual leave which had been accumulated (but not yet taken) during a period of full-time work. EU law, and in particular *cl 4(2)*, precluded a national provision under which a worker who moved from full- to part-time either suffered a reduction in the paid annual leave which he had accumulated but not been able to exercise while working full-time, or was required to take that leave with a reduced level of pay. *Land Tirol* was endorsed by the CJEU in *Heimann v Kaiser GmbH* C-229/11 [2013] IRLR 48, [2013] 1 CMLR 52. As to the converse situation, see the similar approach in *Greenfield v The Care Bureau Ltd* C-219/14 [2016] IRLR 62, [2016] ICR 161.

34.12 *Occupational Pensions*

In *Istituto Nazionale della Previdenza Sociale v Bruno* C-395/08 & C-396/08, [2010] IRLR 890, [2010] 3 CMLR 45, the CJEU held that the *Framework Agreement* precluded national legislation under which part-time vertical-cyclical workers (ie workers working only during certain periods of the year) were treated less favourably than comparable full-time workers in relation to the qualifying period for accruing pension rights, unless that treatment could be objectively justified. The Court held, in particular, that the prohibition of discrimination in relation to "employment conditions" found in the *Framework Agreement* and *Directive* extended to occupational pensions dependent on an employment relationship (and the ECJ gave guidance as to when social-security type pensions would fall within that definition) and confirmed that that prohibition extended to the future effects of situations which arose prior to the *Framework Agreement* and *Directive* coming into force (eg periods of employment before the *Directive* came into force which were qualifying service requirements for future retirement pensions).

In *O'Brien v Ministry of Justice* [2015] EWCA Civ 1000, [2016] IRLR 1005, [2016] ICR 182, the Court of Appeal held that when calculating the pension rights of a part-time Recorder, the tribunal should consider only sitting days after 7 April 2000 (ie the date by which the UK was required to transpose the Directive). See **34.7** above. However, The ECJ has subsequently held that, for the purposes of *Cl 4* of the *Framework Agreement*, sitting days that occurred before that date also had to be taken into account (*O'Brien v Ministry of Justice (No. 2)* C-432/17 [2019] IRLR 185, [2019] 1 CMLR 40, [2019] ICR 505). Whilst *Cl 4* could not apply to "legal situations that arose and became definitive prior to [its] . . . entry into force" that was not the case in *O'Brien*. The legal situation only became "definitive", in effect, when the judge sought to avail himself of his pension right.

34.12A *Allowances*

In *Österreichischer Gewerkschaftsbund v Verband Österreichischer Banken und Bankiers*: C-467/12 [2015] IRLR 67, the CJEU held that a dependent child allowance paid by employers in Austria pursuant to a collective agreement fell within the scope of *Cl 4* of the *Framework Agreement* and could be paid pursuant to the principle of *pro rata temporis*. Such allowance was "pay", not a social security benefit.

34.12B *Discretion*

In *Ministry of Justice v Burton* [2016] IRLR 100, the EAT held that there was less favourable treatment where part-time judges of the Residential Property Tribunal were paid for writing-up time as a matter of discretion, whilst full-time tax judges received such payments as a matter of entitlement. This was not in issue when the case went to the Court of Appeal: [2016] ICR 1128 at [4].

34.13 Comparators

The *Regulations* involve the making of a comparison between a part-time worker and a 'comparable' full-time worker, unless *regs 3* and *4* apply. Special provisions apply in relation to a full-time worker who drops down to part-time, or someone returning from less than 12 months' maternity leave.

34.14 *Actual comparator*

Do the *Regulations* require an 'actual' comparator (as was the orthodox position under the *Equal Pay Act 1970*: see **23.9** EQUAL PAY), or will a hypothetical comparator suffice (as under the *Equality Act 2010*: see **12.15** DISCRIMINATION AND EQUAL OPPORTUNITIES – I)?

- The wording of the *Regulations* suggests that a narrow comparison is all that is envisaged, and that if there is no full-time comparator employed by the same employer, any claim will fail. However, the wording of the *Directive* is somewhat wider, stating that 'where there is no comparable full-time worker in the same establishment, the comparison shall be made by reference to the applicable collective agreement or, where there is no applicable collective agreement, in accordance with national law, collective agreements or practice'.

- In *Carl v University of Sheffield* [2009] ICR 1286, the EAT confirmed that a part-time worker must show that he or she has been treated less favourably than an *actual* full-time comparator. The definition of a comparable full-time worker in *reg 2(4)* does not include the "or would" formula found in *s 1(1)(a)* of the *Sex Discrimination Act 1975* or *s 1(1)(a)* of the *Race Relations Act 1976* (ie "*a person discriminates against a woman if ... on the ground of her sex he treats her less favourably than he treats or would treat a man*"). The EAT noted that a hypothetical comparator is expressly permitted in certain circumstances under *regs 3* and *4* and that this suggests that these two exceptional categories are the only cases in which reliance on a hypothetical comparator is permissible. In addition, the EAT endorsed the dicta of Lady Smith in *McMenemy v Capita Business Services Ltd* [2006] IRLR 761 to the effect that a hypothetical comparator was probably 'not apposite' under the *Regulations* and that the *Framework Agreement* does not require any other conclusion. In *McMenemy*, Lady Smith had noted that the ECJ had held in *Wippel v Peek & Cloppenburg GmbH & Co KG* [2005] IRLR 211, [2005] 1 CMLR 9, [2005] ICR 1604 that a particular part-time contract was not in breach of the *Directive* when there was no full-time worker in the establishment with the same type of contract or employment relationship to enable a comparison and had not gone on to construct a hypothetical comparator.

•   The decision in *Carl* is consistent with the early observations of the EAT in *Tyson v Concurrent Systems Inc Ltd* [2003] All ER (D) 09 (Sep) and *Lynch v Royal Mail Group plc* [2003] All ER (D) 11 (Sep). In *Advocate General for Scotland v Barton* [2016] IRLR 210, the Inner House of the Court of Session held that a comparator who had worked only 70% of available hours was not a permissible comparator, even though he had been treated by the Secretary of State as working "full time" for certain pension purposes. The effect of this restriction is likely to be that the *Regulations* will not provide protection for the many part-time workers who do jobs only done by part-timers.

34.15 *Identifying 'part-time' and 'full-time' workers*

The first step is to identify 'full-time workers' and 'part-time workers'.

•   A worker is a part-time worker if he is 'paid wholly or in part by reference to the time he works and, having regard to the custom and practice of the employer in relation to workers employed by the worker's employer under the same type of contract, is not identifiable as a full-time worker': *reg 2(2)*.

•   By contrast, he is a full-time worker if he is 'paid wholly or in part by reference to the time he works and, having regard to the custom and practice of the employer in relation to workers employed by the worker's employer under the same type of contract, is identifiable as a full-time worker': *reg 2(1)*.

These definitions are structured by reference to workers employed under "*the same type of contract*". *Reg 2(3)* provides that each of the following groups shall be regarded as being employed under different types of contract, for the purposes both of determining whether a worker is full- or part-time in the first place and of comparing the treatment of full- and part-time workers: (a) employees employed under a contract that is not a contract of apprenticeship; (b) employees employed under a contract of apprenticeship; (c) workers who are not employees; and (d) any other description of worker that it is reasonable for the employer to treat differently from other workers on the ground that workers of that description have a different type of contract. As to the authorities on the meaning of "*the same type of contract*" in this context, see further **34.16** below.

The *Regulations* used to provide that those working under fixed term contracts were employed under different types of contract to those who worked under permanent contracts. However, the distinction between fixed-term and permanent contracts was removed by the *Part-Time Workers (Prevention of Less Favourable Treatment) Regulations 2000 (Amendment) Regulations 2002, SI 2002/2035* with effect from 1 October 2002 in order to give effect to the *Fixed-Term Employees (Prevention of Less Favourable Treatment) Regulations 2002, SI 2002/2034*, which prohibit discrimination between fixed term employees and comparable permanent employees.

In *Hudson v University of Oxford* [2007] EWCA Civ 336, [2007] All ER (D) 356 (Feb) the Court of Appeal allowed an appeal against a tribunal decision to strike out Mr Hudson's claim of less favourable treatment on the basis that it had no reasonable prospects of success. Mr Hudson was employed by the University under two part-time contracts. He claimed that, in reality, he had had one full-time job and that he had been less favourably treated when compared with other full-time employees. The Court of Appeal considered it arguable that (1) his contention that the reality was that he had a single full-time job did not necessarily preclude him from having been a part-time worker as defined in *reg 2(2)* of the *Regulations*; (2) to the extent that he was a part-time worker under one of his contracts, he was, on account of his job, treated less favourably than relevant full-time comparators; and (3) he was so treated on the ground that he was contractually and within the terms of *reg 2* a part-time worker. He was therefore permitted to pursue his claims under the *Regulations*. The Court of Appeal left open the question whether the comparison should be between a part-time worker doing two jobs and a full-time worker doing both jobs together, or whether each part-time contract had to be looked at separately and compared with a full-time worker under separate contracts.

In *Augustine v Econnect Cars Ltd* (2019, UKEAT/0231/18), the EAT held ([75–80]) that a private hire car driver was a part-time worker within *reg 2(2)*. His driving work was not piecework. Although he was paid on a commission basis by reference to the fare paid by the passenger, that meant he was paid in part by reference to the time he worked (the time taken to complete a journey). Further, he was not identifiable as a full-time worker.

34.16 *Identifying a 'comparable full-time worker'*

The second step is to determine whether the part-time workers' full-time colleagues are 'comparable full-time workers' within the meaning of *reg 2(4)*.

A full-time worker will be a 'comparable full-time worker' in relation to a claimant part-time worker within the meaning of *reg 2(4)* where, at the time that the less favourable treatment occurs:

(a)   both workers are employed by the same employer under the same type of contract, and both are engaged in the same or broadly similar work (having regard, where relevant, to whether they have a similar level of qualification, skills and experience); and

(b)   the full-time worker works or is based at the same establishment as the part-time worker.

If there are no full-time workers who satisfy the requirements in (a) above, a full-time worker who satisfies those requirements but who works or is based at a different establishment may be considered: *reg 2(4)(b)*.

In *O'Brien v Ministry of Justice*: C-393/10 [2012] IRLR 412 the CJEU noted that 'comparable full-time worker' is defined in *cl 3* of the *Framework Agreement* as 'a full-time worker in the same establishment having the same type of employment contract or relationship, who is engaged in the same or a similar work/occupation, due regard being given to other considerations which may include seniority and qualification/skills' and that "*those criteria are based on the content of the activity of the persons concerned*". Accordingly, the CJEU concluded that full-time judges and recorders were in a comparable situation, notwithstanding that they have different careers as recorders retain the opportunity to practise as barristers, because they perform essentially the same activity.

34.17 *'Same type of contract'*

What does the requirement that a comparable full-time worker be employed by the same employer as the part-time worker "*under the same type of contract*" actually mean?

Reg 2(3) provides that the following categories of workers are employed under different types of contract: (a) "*employees employed under a contract that is not a contract of apprenticeship*"; (b) "*employees employed under a contract of apprenticeship*"; (c) "*workers who are not employees*"; and (d) workers in a long-stop category - "*any other description of worker that it is reasonable for the employer to treat differently from other workers on the ground that workers of that description have a different type of contract*".

The leading authority is *Matthews v Kent and Medway Towns Fire Authority* [2004] ICR 257, [2003] IRLR 732 (in the EAT); [2005] ICR 84, [2004] IRLR 697 (in the Court of Appeal) and [2006] ICR 365, [2006] IRLR 367 (in the House of Lords). This was a test case brought by part-time ('retained') firefighters who claimed that they were treated less favourably than comparable full-time firefighters in that they were denied access to statutory pension arrangements, they were denied increased pay for additional responsibilities and their sick pay arrangements were calculated on a less favourable basis. The Courts decided as follows:

(a)   The ET and the EAT considered that the retained firefighters were employed under a different type of contract from full-time firefighters, as it was reasonable for the employer to treat them differently within the meaning of *reg 2(3)(d)*. The ET had found many differences and special features in working patterns as between the two groups.

(b)   The Court of Appeal took a different approach. It held that both retained and full-time firefighters belonged to category (a) in *reg 2(3)*, being employees employed under a contract that was not a contract of apprenticeship.

(c)   A majority of the House of Lords (Lord Mance dissenting) upheld the approach of the Court of Appeal. They held that the requirement that the part-time worker and the full-time worker proposed as a comparator be employed under the same type of contract is directed to comparable types of employment relationship rather than comparable terms and conditions of employment. The categories set out in *reg 2(3)* are defined broadly in a way that allows for a wide variety of different terms and conditions within each category. The categories are mutually exclusive. Under *reg 2(3)(d)* the courts are asked to examine a type of worker who is different from any of those previously mentioned in *reg 2(3)(a)–(c)*. While it is difficult to think of a type of contract which is different to those mentioned in *reg 2(3)(a)–(c)*, a contract will only fall within *reg 2(3)(d)* if a worker does not fall into one of the other categories. It is a long-stop or residual category. It is not designed to allow employers to single out particular kinds of part-time working arrangements and treat them differently from the rest.

Further guidance was provided by the EAT in *Roddis v Sheffield Hallam University* [2018] UKEAT/0299/17, [2018] IRLR 706. At [18] the Appeal Tribunal sought to set out comprehensive guidance drawing on the existing body of authority, including *Matthews*, *Wippel* and *O'Brien*:

•   "*Reg 2(3)* provides a comprehensive list of categories of different types of contract for the purposes of *paragraphs 2(1), (2)* and *(4)*;

•   The categories in *reg 2(3)* are broadly defined and, since the purpose of the Regulation is to provide a threshold to require a comparison of full and part-time workers to take place, the threshold is deliberately set not too high;

34.17   Part-Time Workers

- A contract cannot be treated as being of a different type from another just because the terms and conditions that it lays down are different, nor because an employer chooses to treat workers of a particular type differently;

- Where a worker and his or her comparator are both employed under contracts that answer to the same description given in the same paragraph in *reg 2(3)*, they are both to be regarded as employed under the same type of contract for the purposes of *reg 2(4)*;

- In order to satisfy the requirements of *reg 2(4)(a)(i)*, it is not necessary to go further than to find that both workers are employed under contracts that fit into one or other of the listed categories;

- The categories are designed to be mutually exclusive;

- The category in *reg 2(3)(d)* is a residual category. It refers to a description of worker who is different from those mentioned in categories (a) to (c) and does not apply to a worker who falls into one of those categories. An example of a description of worker who would fall within category (d) has yet to be identified. A zero-hours contract is not, of itself, a type of contract."

In *Wippel v Peek & Cloppenburg GmbG & Co KG* [2005] ICR 1604, [2005] IRLR 211 (see **34.4**), the ECJ considered the position of part-time workers who worked according to need under 'framework contracts'. It held that as there was no full-time worker who worked according to need under a 'framework contract', there was no comparable full-time worker who worked under the same type of employment contract or relationship as the part-time worker within the meaning of the *Framework Agreement*. The employment relationship differed, as to subject matter and basis, between a full-time worker (working under a 'traditional' contract) and the claimant (working under a 'framework contract'). However, *Wippel* was distinguished in *Roddis v Sheffield Hallam University* [2018] UKEAT/0299/17, [2018] IRLR 706 which held that a university lecturer employed on a zero hours contract was employed on the 'same type of contract' as a lecturer on a full-time contract.

34.18   'The same or broadly similar work'

Matthews v Kent and Medway Towns Fire Authority (see **34.17**) also provided guidance on what is meant by "*the same or broadly similar work*". The tribunal had held that retained firefighters were not engaged in the same or broadly similar work as full-time firefighters. That finding was upheld by the EAT and the Court of Appeal, but then rejected by the House of Lords:

(a)   The EAT and Court of Appeal found that full-time firefighters carried out measurable additional job functions, such as educational, preventive and administrative tasks which were not carried out by retained firefighters. There were differences in entry standards, probationary standards and on-going training, which led to differences in the level of qualification and skills. They noted that differences in recruitment procedures and promotion prospects also served to illustrate the different work carried out by full-time firefighters compared to retained firefighters, as full-time firefighters are recruited to do a job with measurable additional functions and overwhelmingly constitute the recruitment pool for promotion to higher grades. In short, the EAT and Court of Appeal did not accept that firefighting was the central role of all operational fire fighters, such that retained and full-time firefighters must be engaged in broadly similar work.

(b)   The House of Lords disagreed. The majority (Lord Nicholls, Lord Hope and Baroness Hale) held that the tribunal had erred in concentrating on the differences in the work carried out by retained and full-time firefighters, rather than assessing the weight to be given to the similarities in such work. The question is not whether the work is different, but whether it is the same or broadly similar. The *Regulations* are inviting a comparison between two types of workers whose work will almost inevitably be different to some extent. The tribunal must look at the work that both the full-time and part-time worker are engaged in, and ask whether it is the same work or if not, whether it is broadly similar. To answer that question, the tribunal must look at the whole of the work, leaving nothing out of account. Regard must be had to the question whether they have a similar level of qualification, skills and experience when judging whether work which at first sight appears to be the same or broadly similar does indeed satisfy the test in the *Regulations*. But this question must be directed to the whole of the work that the two kinds of workers are actually engaged in at the relevant time, not to some other work for which they may be qualified. In carrying out the assessment, particular weight should be given to the extent to which the work of part-time and full-time workers is exactly the same. If a large component of the work is exactly the same, the question is whether any differences are of such importance as to prevent the work of the two groups being regarded overall as 'the same or broadly similar'. Where both full- and part-timers do the same work, but the full-timers have extra activities with which to fill their time, this does not mean that the work under consideration is not nevertheless the same or broadly similar overall. The importance of the work which the workers do to the work of the enterprise as a whole is also of great importance in this assessment. If full-timers do the more important work and part-timers are brought in to do the more peripheral tasks, it is unlikely that the work of the two groups is the same or broadly similar. However, where full-timers and part-timers spend much of their time on the core activity of the enterprise, the fact that full-timers may do some extra tasks will not prevent their work being the same or broadly similar to that of the part-timers.

The case was remitted to the tribunal for reconsideration of whether the retained and full-time firefighters are engaged in the same or broadly similar work, where the ET determined that the part-time firefighters were carrying out the same or broadly similar work to the full-time firefighters. There was a substantial body of work comprising the firefighter's 'central duties' that were the same for both roles, and the full-timers' additional skills and experience, while relevant, did not contribute 'something different to the work'.

These issues have been explored in two cases in relation to part-time Judges and lay members: *Moultrie v Ministry of Justice* [2015] IRLR 264 and *McGrath v Ministry of Justice* (UKEAT/0247/14/LA; permission to appeal refused – [2016] EWCA Civ 379). In *Matthews v Kent and Medway Towns Fire Authority*, Lord Hope had said, at paragraph 15 that:

> "It is important to appreciate that it is the work on which the workers are actually engaged at the time that is the subject matter of the [regulation 2(4)] comparison. So the question whether they have a similar level of qualification, skills and experience is relevant only insofar as it bears on that exercise. An examination of these characteristics may help to show that they are each contributing something different to work that appears to be the same or broadly similar, with the result that their situations are not truly comparable. But the fact that they may fit them to do other work that they are not yet engaged in, in the event of promotion for example, would not be relevant."

Against that backdrop, in *Moultrie*, Lewis J held in the EAT that a Tribunal had been entitled to conclude that the position of part-time fee-paid medical members of tribunals such as the mental health tribunal (who were not entitled to an occupational pension) was not the same or broadly similar to the work of full-time, salaried regional members (who were so entitled). Some 85% of the work done by the two groups was the same, that work was of the highest importance to the work of the relevant tribunals, and there was no different between the two groups' respective levels of qualifications, skills and experience. Nevertheless, the Tribunal had been entitled to conclude that full-timers performed a role which was qualitatively different from that of part-timers. The additional work performed by full-timers, including appraisal, recruitment and training work, and other tasks delegated by chief medical members of the tribunals and Chamber Presidents, was sufficiently important to mean that the two groups' work was not the same or broadly similar. In *McGrath*, decided shortly afterwards, the EAT (HHJ Peter Clark presiding) held that the situation of an Employment Judge and the lay members of an employment tribunal were, similarly (indeed, a fortiori), not truly comparable for the purposes of *reg 2(4)*.

34.19   *The scope of the comparison*

The EAT in *Matthews v Kent and Medway Towns Fire Authority* [2004] ICR 257, [2003] IRLR 732, EAT (see **34.12** above) followed the approach of the House of Lords in *Hayward v Cammell Laird Shipbuilders Ltd* [1988] AC 894, [1988] IRLR 257 and held that each specific term of the contract must be compared, rather than a 'broad brush' comparison. In the House of Lords in *Matthews*, Baroness Hale (with whom Lord Nicholls and Lord Hope agreed) did not rule out the possibility that a less favourable term might be so well balanced by a more favourable one that it could not be said that part-timers were treated less favourably overall. Nor did she rule out the possibility that more favourable treatment on one point might supply justification for less favourable treatment on another. On the facts, however, she found it difficult to see how a differently structured pay package for retained fire-fighters could justify total exclusion from the pension or sick pay schemes, unrelated to the hours actually worked.

34.20   *Specific circumstances where a comparator is not required*

There are two circumstances in which the *Regulations* do not require a strict comparative approach.

First, if an individual becomes a part-time worker having previously worked in a job on a full-time basis, he can compare his part-time conditions with his previous full-time contract. *Reg 3* applies where the worker was a full-time worker within the meaning of *reg 2(1)* but, following a termination or variation of his contract, he continues to work under a new or varied contract, whether of the same type or not, that requires him to work for a lower number of weekly hours than the number he was required to work immediately before the termination or variation. The effect of *reg 3(2)* is that *reg 5* applies to such a worker as if he were a part-time worker and as if there were a comparable full-time worker employed under the terms that applied to him immediately before the termination or variation.

Secondly, if an individual who had previously worked in a job on a full-time basis returns to a part-time role after a period of absence of up to 12 months, such as maternity leave, he or she can compare their new part-time conditions with their previous full-time contract: *reg 4*.

•   This regulation applies where the worker was a full-time worker within the meaning of *reg 2(1)* immediately before the period of absence (irrespective of whether the absence followed a termination of her contract), and where she returns to work for the same employer within 12 months of the date on which her absence started. The worker must return to the same job or a job at the same level under a contract in which she is required to work for a number of weekly hours that is lower than the number she was required to work immediately before the period of absence, regardless of whether the new contract is a different contract or a varied contract, or whether it is of the same type as the original contract or not: *reg 4(1)*.

•   *Reg 5* applies to such a worker as if she were a part-time worker and as if there were a comparable full-time worker employed under: (a) the contract under which she was employed immediately before the period of absence; or (b) where it is shown that, had she continued to work under the original contract, a variation would have been made to its term during the period of absence, the original contract including that variation: *reg 4(2)*.

When calculating the worker's period of absence, time spent on annual leave does not count towards the total (*Fidessa plc v Lancaster* UKEAT/0093/16).

34.21 'On the ground that the worker is a part-time worker'

It is not sufficient for a tribunal to be satisfied that a claimant part-time worker has been less favourably treated than his or her full-time comparator. Liability will lie only if the less favourable treatment is "*on the ground that the worker is a part-time worker*": *reg 5(2)(a)*.

Unfortunately, there is a division between English and Scottish authority as to the meaning of "*on the ground that*" in *reg 5* of the *Regulations*. In England and Wales, the EAT held in *Carl v University of Sheffield* [2009] ICR 1286, [2009] IRLR 616 that 'on the ground that' means that part-time work must be the effective and predominant cause of the less favourable treatment complained of; it need not be the only cause. This had similarly been the conclusion of the EAT in *Sharma v Manchester City Council* [2008] ICR 623, [2008] IRLR 336, but the EAT in *Sharma* had not had cited to them a contrary decision of the Court of Session, *McMenemy v Capita Business Services Ltd* [2007] IRLR 400. In Scotland, *McMenemy* remains authority for the proposition that the less favourable treatment of part-time workers will only be prohibited where it is for the sole reason that the workers work part-time (following an earlier decision of the Scottish EAT in *Gibson v Scottish Ambulance Service* (EATS/0052/04)). In *Carl*, the EAT noted that it was not bound by decisions of the Court of Session and declined to follow the approach taken in *McMenemy*. Judge Peter Clark noted that the expression "on the ground that" or "on the grounds of" appears frequently in domestic legislation and agreed with Elias J in *Sharma* that domestic legislation may go further than the protection contained in the *Framework Agreement*. The same approach as *Carl* was taken in *Ministry of Justice v Edge and Burton* (2016, UKEAT/0247/15), albeit without reference to previous authority. However, the uncertainty has been further deepened by the decision of the EAT in *Engle v Ministry of Justice* UKEAT/337/15, [2017] ICR 277. The decision appears to have been reached without reference to any of the previous authorities. The learned judge noted that the language of the *Framework Directive* suggested that a remedy was to be available to those who were treated less favourably "solely because they work part-time"; acknowledged that the wording of the *Regulations* was wider but then held that their purpose was the same: "the purpose of the legislation is not to redress any and all injustices that may exist; it is to redress the less favourable treatment of part-time workers if and only if that treatment occurs because they are part-time workers". It is unclear what the EAT has decided. On one view it has taken the *McMenemy* line but the reference to "because of" echoes the test for direct discrimination in *EA 2010, s 13* which only requires that the protected characteristic should be a substantive and not the sole cause of the less favourable treatment.

It is respectfully submitted that the approach in *Carl* and *Sharma* is to be preferred. It was conceded in *McMenemy* that the *Regulations* should be construed consistently with the *Framework Agreement* and that they did not go further than the *Framework Agreement*. The Court of Session referred to the wording of *cl 4(1)* of the *Framework Agreement* to the effect that 'part-time workers shall not be treated in a less favourable manner than comparable full-time workers solely because they work part-time . . . .' and held that 'solely' means that less favourable treatment must be for the reason that workers work part-time and for that reason alone. It is submitted that the EAT in *Carl* was right to doubt the correctness of the original concession. The *Regulations* were made under *s 19* of the *Employment Relations Act 1999* and not under *s 2* of the *European Communities Act 1972*. It was therefore open to Parliament to go further than the *Framework Agreement*. It is further submitted that the absence of the word 'solely' in the *Regulations* is crucial to the analysis and that, properly construed, the *Regulations* do go further than the *Directive* in this regard. The phrase 'on the grounds that' in the *Regulations* should be interpreted in the same way as the 'on the prohibited grounds' test in other discrimination legislation (see **12.3–12.11** DISCRIMINATION AND EQUAL OPPORTUNITIES – I for application of the 'on the prohibited grounds' test in other contexts).

In *Komeng v Sandwell MBC* [2011] EqLR 1053 the EAT commented, at [45], that tribunals should take care before accepting an explanation that the reason for less favourable treatment lies merely in general poor administration, because of the risk that this masks discrimination on prohibited grounds.

34.22 Objective justification

Any less favourable treatment may be justified on objective grounds: *reg 5(2)(b)*.

The concept of objective justification is treated in the same way under the *Regulations* as in other anti-discrimination contexts (see **13.9** DISCRIMINATION AND EQUAL OPPORTUNITIES – II and **23.11** EQUAL PAY). Less favourable treatment will be objectively justified only if it can be shown that the treatment: (1) has a legitimate objective, such as a genuine business objective; (2) is necessary to achieve that objective; and (3) is an appropriate way of achieving that objective.

In *O'Brien v Ministry of Justice*: C-393/10 [2012] IRLR 412 the CJEU commented that the concept 'objective grounds' within the meaning of *cl 4* of the *Framework Agreement* must be understood as not permitting a difference in treatment between part-time workers and full-time workers to be justified on the basis that the difference "*is provided for by a general, abstract norm*" and, on the contrary, that the unequal treatment must "*respond to a genuine need be appropriate for achieving the objective pursued and be necessary for that purpose*" (see paragraph 64). The CJEU added, in this context, that "*budgetary considerations cannot justify discrimination*" (see paragraph 66).

When *O'Brien* was remitted to the Supreme Court, the Court rejected the Ministry of Justice's attempts to justify a difference in treatment in pension provision for part-time and full-time judges, holding that they were not made out on the evidence. It adopted the guidance given by Advocate General Kokott [2012] ICR 955, [2012] IRLR 421 to the effect that the unequal treatment at issue must be justified "*by the existence of precise, concrete factors, characterising the employment condition concerned in its specific context and on the basis of objective and transparent criteria for examining the question whether that unequal treatment responds to a genuine need and whether it is appropriate and necessary for achieving the objective pursued*". It concluded that the aims of giving a greater reward to those who are thought to need it most or to those who make the greatest contribution, or recruiting a high quality judiciary might all be legitimate aims – but that the Government had failed to make out the specific basis for such justification on the evidence. For example, an employer might devise a scheme which rewarded its workers according to need rather than to their contribution, but the criteria would have to be precise and transparent, but that was not the case in relation to the provision for part-time judges, some of whom would need occupational pension provision, others of whom would not. Equally, the proper approach to differential contributions is to make special payments for extra responsibilities – which was not the case here. There was (the Court found) blanket discrimination between part-time and full-time judges which had not been justified. *O'Brien* concerned a recorder, but the Court noted that it seemed unlikely that the ministry's argument could be put any higher than it has been in relation to any other holder of part-time judicial office.

34.23 RIGHT TO RECEIVE A WRITTEN STATEMENT OF REASONS FOR LESS FAVOURABLE TREATMENT

A worker who considers that his employer may have treated him in a manner which infringes a right conferred upon him by *reg 5* may request in writing from his employer a written statement giving particulars of the reasons for the treatment: *reg 6*. The employer must provide such a statement within 21 days of the worker's request and such written statements will be admissible as evidence in any proceedings under the *Regulations*. A tribunal may draw inferences from an employer's refusal to answer or provision of an evasive or equivocal response: *reg 6(3)*.

Reg 6 does not apply where the treatment in question consists of the dismissal of an employee, and that employee is entitled to a written statement of reasons for his dismissal under *s 92* of the *Employment Rights Act 1996* (see **49.14, 49.15** TERMINATION OF EMPLOYMENT).

34.24 PROTECTION FROM DETRIMENT

A worker has the right, by *regs 7(2)–(3)*, not to be subjected to any detriment by an act, or deliberate failure to act, by his employer done on the ground that:

(i)   he has brought proceedings against the employer under the *Regulations*;

(ii)   he has requested a written statement under *reg 6*;

(iii)   he has given evidence or information in connection with any proceedings under the *Regulations* brought by any worker;

(iv)   he has done anything under the *Regulations* relating to his employer or any other person;

(v)   he has alleged that his employer has infringed the *Regulations*;

(vi)   he has refused or proposed to refuse to forego any right under the *Regulations*; or

(vii)   the employer believes or suspects that he has done or intends to do any of these things.

However, neither *reg 7(1)* (unfair dismissal) nor *reg 7(2)* (protection from detriment) applies in relation to an allegation that the employer has infringed the *Regulations* (or that the employer believes or suspects that the worker has made or intends to make such an allegation) if the allegation made by the worker is false and not made in good faith: *reg 7(4)*.

34.25 RELATIONSHIP WITH UNFAIR DISMISSAL

Reg 7(1) provides that an employee who is dismissed is to be regarded as unfairly dismissed for the purposes of *Part X* of the *Employment Rights Act 1996* if the reason or principal reason for his dismissal is that:

(i)   he has brought proceedings against the employer under the *Regulations*;

(ii)   he has requested a written statement under *reg 6*;

(iii)   he has given evidence or information in connection with any proceedings under the *Regulations* brought by any worker;

(iv)   he has done anything under the *Regulations* relating to his employer or any other person;

(v)   he has alleged that his employer has infringed the *Regulations*;

(vi)   he has refused or proposed to refuse to forego any right under the *Regulations*; or

(vii)   the employer believes or suspects that he has done or intends to do any of these things.

Save as set out in *reg 7*, a breach of the *Regulations* does not make any dismissal automatically unfair: *Pipe v Hendrickson Europe Ltd* [2003] All ER (D) 280 (Apr), EAT. In such cases, a tribunal must ascertain the reason for the dismissal, and then determine whether the dismissal was unfair within the terms of *s 98(4)* of the *Employment Rights Act 1996* (see Unfair Dismissal – II (55)). The act of discrimination may be an important factor for the tribunal to take into account when carrying out this evaluation, but it does not automatically follow that the dismissal is unfair.

34.26 APPLICATIONS TO AN EMPLOYMENT TRIBUNAL

A worker may present a complaint to an employment tribunal that his employer has infringed a right conferred on him by *reg 5* (less favourable treatment) or *reg 7(2)* (victimisation): *reg 8(1)*. Where a worker presents a complaint to a tribunal under the *Regulations*, it is for the employer to identify the ground for the less favourable treatment or detriment: *reg 8(6)*. A claim for breach of the *Regulations* that includes an allegation that the *Regulations* themselves are incompatible with *Directive 97/81* cannot be brought by way of judicial review, and must be brought in the tribunal: *R (on the application of Manson) v Ministry of Defence* [2005] EWCA Civ 1678; [2006] ICR 355, [2005] All ER (D) 69 (Nov).

34.27 TIME LIMITS

A claim must ordinarily be presented to a tribunal before the end of the period of three months beginning with the date of the less favourable treatment or detriment to which the complaint relates, save that the time limit will be extended as set out in *reg 8A* of the *Regulations* to reflect the rules on early conciliation: *reg 8(2)*, *reg 8(2A)*, *reg 8A* and Chapter 3: ACAS Conciliation. A six month time limit applies to complaints by members of the armed forces: *reg 8(2)*.

Where an act or failure to act is part of a series of similar acts or failures comprising the less favourable treatment, the time runs from the last of those acts. For the purposes of calculating the date of the less favourable treatment or detriment, *reg 8(4)* and *8(5)* provides that:

(a)   where a term in the contract is less favourable, that treatment shall be treated, subject to (b) below, as taking place on each day of the period during which the term is less favourable;

(b)   where an application relies on *regs 3* or *4* the less favourable treatment shall be treated as occurring on, and only on, in the case of *reg 3*, the first day on which the applicant worked under the new or varied contract and, in the case of *reg 4*, the day on which the applicant returned; and

(c)   a deliberate failure to act contrary to *reg 5* or *7(2)* shall be treated as done when it was decided on. In the absence of evidence establishing the contrary, a person shall be taken to decide not to act when he does an act inconsistent with doing the failed act, or if he has done no such inconsistent act, when the period expires within which he might reasonably have been expected to have done the failed act if it was to be done.

In *Miller v Ministry of Justice* [2019] UKSC 60, [2020] IRLR 239, the Supreme Court considered the application of this time limit to fee-paid judges seeking to bring less favourable treatment claims on the basis of lack of entitlement to a judicial pension. Lord

Carnwarth noted that the provisions of the *Regulations* needed to be construed in a "highly artificial context", namely the need for the *Regulations* to confirm to EU law and the special characteristics of judicial appointments and pensions in domestic law [31]. The reference in *reg 8(4)* to "a term of a contract" had to be applied by analogy as a judicial officer was not employed under a contract (see *Gilham v Ministry of Justice* [2019] UKSC 44, [2019] 1 WLR 5905). Further, the judicial pension scheme was based not on individual appointments, but on qualifying judicial office. The Court held that the three-month period imposed by *reg 8(2)* ran from the date of the fee-paid judge's retirement, not from the end date of the relevant part-time appointment.

A tribunal may consider a complaint which is out of time if, in all the circumstances of the case, it considers that it is just and equitable to do so: *reg 8(3)*. At an earlier stage in the *Miller v Ministry of Justice* litigation, when (prior to the Supreme Court's judgment discussed above it was thought that time ran from the end of each part-time appointment), the EAT (UKEAT/0003/15/LA and UKEAT/0004/15/LA) upheld the decision of an employment judge to refuse extensions of time. The fact that other litigation was proceeding as a test case did not relieve these claimants of their own duty to make a claim in time; nor did a moratorium which had been established by the Secretary of State after these claims were issued. (See **34.6** above). In *Ibarz v Sheffield University* (2015) UKEAT/0018/15, the consistent application of the same rules, policies and practices across a number of separate contracts (where there was no contractual continuity) was capable of being 'a series of similar acts' with sufficient linkage so that, if the latest of that series is in time, it would be just and reasonable for the claims in respect of the earlier acts to be treated as in time.

34.28 REMEDIES FOR PART-TIME WORKERS

Where an employment tribunal finds that a complaint presented to it under *reg 8* is well-founded, it shall take such of the following steps as it considers just and equitable:

(a) *Making a declaration as to the rights of the complainant and the employer in relation to the matters to which the complaint relates: reg 8(7)(a).*

(b) *Ordering the employer to pay compensation to the complainant: reg 8(7)(b).*

Where a tribunal orders compensation, the amount of the compensation awarded shall be such as the tribunal considers just and equitable in all the circumstances having regard to (a) the infringement to which the complaint relates, and (b) any loss which is attributable to the infringement having regard, in the case of an infringement of the right conferred by *reg 5*, to the pro rata principle, except where it is inappropriate to do so: *reg 8(9)*. The loss shall be taken to include any expenses reasonably incurred by the complainant in consequence of the infringement and loss of any benefit which he might reasonably be expected to have had but for the infringement: *reg 8(10)*. Concurrent reasons for the treatment can be relevant to the assessment of loss at the remedy stage: see *Ministry of Justice v Edge and Burton* (2016, UKEAT/0247/15) per Elisabeth Laing J at [41–42]. In *Ministry of Justice v Burton* [2016] IRLR 100, the EAT held that an employment judge was entitled to make a "broad brush assessment" when calculating the appropriate compensation. The assessment was allowed to stand on appeal: [2016] ICR 1128. See further the approach in *Engal v Ministry of Justice* (2019, UKEAT/0279/18), in which Slade J also observed that the jurisdiction of the ET was to determine compensation; it was not tasked to determine the Claimant's entitlement to membership of a judicial pension scheme under the relevant pension regulations.

Compensation in respect of less favourable treatment on the grounds of part-time status (ie less favourable treatment contrary to *reg 5* of the *Regulations*) will *not* include compensation for injury to feelings: *reg 8(11)*.

In *Tyson v Concurrent Systems Inc Ltd* [2003] All ER (D) 09 (Sep), EAT, the appellant sought to argue that stigma damages and stigma compensation were not excluded by *reg 8(11)*. The EAT doubted whether stigma damages which did not include loss of earnings produced by the stigma could be brought within the provisions of *reg 8*.

Normal principles of mitigation apply: *reg 8(12)*. Where the tribunal finds that the act, or failure to act, to which the complaint relates was to any extent caused or contributed to by the action of the complainant, it shall reduce the amount of the compensation by such proportion as it considers just and equitable having regard to that finding: *reg 8(13)*.

(c)   *Recommending that the employer take, within a specified period, action appearing to the tribunal to be reasonable, in all the circumstances of the case, for the purpose of obviating or reducing the adverse effect on the complainant of any matter to which the complaint relates: reg 8(7)(c).*

If the employer fails, without reasonable justification, to comply with a recommendation made by an employment tribunal under *reg 8(7)(c)* the tribunal may, if it thinks it just and equitable to do so, increase the amount of compensation required to be paid to the complainant in respect of the complaint where an order for compensation has already been made, or may make such an order for the first time: *reg 8(14)*.

(For a more detailed discussion of these rules in relation to other anti-discrimination legislation, see DISCRIMINATION AND EQUAL OPPORTUNITIES – III (14).)

34.29   RESTRICTION ON CONTRACTING OUT

The restriction on contracting out of employment rights contained in *s 203* of the *Employment Rights Act 1996* applies in relation to the *Regulations* as if they were contained in the *1996 Act: reg 9* (see **54.19, 54.20** UNFAIR DISMISSAL – I).

(The requirements for a valid settlement agreement which satisfies the statutory conditions are addressed at **20.18–20.20** EMPLOYMENT TRIBUNALS – **II.**)

34.30   LIABILITY OF EMPLOYERS AND PRINCIPALS

As in other anti-discrimination legislation, anything done by a person in the course of his employment is treated for the purposes of the *Regulations* as also done by his employer, whether or not it was done with the employer's knowledge or approval: *reg 11(1)*. Anything done by a person as agent for the employer with the authority of the employer is treated as also done by the employer: *reg 11(2)*.

In proceedings under the *Regulations* against any person in respect of an act alleged to have been done by a worker of his, it shall be a defence for that person to prove that he took such steps as were reasonably practicable to prevent the worker from (a) doing that act, or (b) doing, in the course of his employment, acts of that description: *reg 11(3)*.

(See further **12.54** DISCRIMINATION AND EQUAL OPPORTUNITIES – **I.**)

35   Pay – I: Payments, Pay Statements and Miscellaneous Statutory Pay Rights

Cross-references. See Pay – II (36) for statutory deductions from pay; Equal Pay (23) for the rules against sex discrimination in pay; Trade Unions – II (52) for deduction of trade union subscriptions.

35.1   INTRODUCTION TO PAY – I

An employee's right to payment for his services is, of course, fundamental to the employment relationship and is principally governed by the particular terms of the contract of employment between the individual employee and employer. For example, the rate of pay and the intervals at which payment is made are governed by the individual employee's contract of employment, which also provides for any bonuses, commission, overtime, holiday pay or sick pay which may be payable. Such matters must be included in the written particulars of the contract of employment given by the employer to the employee (see 8.4 Contract of Employment). There is, however, a substantial overlay of statutory rights and protection afforded to employees in relation to payment for their services in the form of the right not to suffer unauthorised deductions from wages, the right to a National Minimum Wage and the right to itemised pay statements. These important rights are considered below.

Various other statutory rights to payment, such as statutory sick pay (see Sickness and Sick Pay (45)) and statutory maternity pay (see Maternity and Parental Rights (33)) are considered in other chapters in this work. Certain miscellaneous statutory rights to payment, namely, guarantee payments and medical suspension payments are outlined towards the end of this chapter. In addition there is an overview of the principles applicable to the calculation of 'a week's pay' – a statutory concept relevant to calculation of the sums payable under a number of the statutory employment rights such as the right to a redundancy payment and the payment of a basic award in a claim for unfair dismissal.

35.2   PAYMENT OF WAGES AND DEDUCTIONS FROM WAGES

Deductions from employees' pay were originally regulated by the *Wages Act 1986 ('WA 1986')*. The *WA 1986* had replaced the *Truck Acts*, which had formerly restricted payment of wages other than in cash (but see 35.3 below). The *WA 1986* made special provision for employees in retail employment affording them greater protection against deductions from their wages. The provisions of the *WA 1986* are all consolidated in *Part II* of the *Employment Rights Act 1996*. In this section of this chapter, references below are to the *Employment Rights Act 1996 ('ERA')* unless otherwise stated.

35.3   PAYMENT OF WAGES

WA 1986, s 11 (now repealed) removed restrictions on the way in which payment of wages to manual and other workers could be made. The method of payment is now determined solely by the terms of the contract. It will be either the subject of express agreement or determined by an implied term. If no express agreement is reached it is likely that the method of payment impliedly agreed will be that which is customary in the industry.

The provisions of *WA 1986* replaced the old restrictions on the payment of wages contained in the *Truck Acts* and the *Payment of Wages Act 1960*. *Section 11* came into force on 1 January 1987 (*The Wages Act 1986 (Commencement) Order 1986 (SI 1986/1998)*).

35.4 DEDUCTIONS FROM WAGES: PART II OF THE ERA

No deduction from a worker's wages may be made unless either:

(a)   it is required or permitted by a statutory or contractual provision; or

(b)   the worker has given his prior written consent to the deduction.

(ERA 1996, ss 13(1), 15(1).)

It is extremely important that deductions are not made in breach of this provision. Not only may sums wrongfully deducted be ordered to be repaid, but the employer may lose the right to recover the sums which he was seeking to deduct by any means at all (see **35.8** below).

If the deduction is made pursuant to a contractual provision, the terms of the contract must have been shown to the worker or, if not in writing, its effect notified in writing to the worker before the deduction is made (*ERA 1996, ss 13(2), 15(2)* and see *Kerr v Sweater Shop (Scotland) Ltd; Sweater Shop (Scotland) Ltd v Park* [1996] IRLR 424, EAT). In *Mennell v Newell & Wright (Transport Contractors) Ltd* [1997] IRLR 519 the Court of Appeal held that an employment tribunal had no jurisdiction to deal with *threatened* deductions from wages as the *Act* stated that a tribunal could only hear complaints where an employer had actually made a deduction. Accordingly, a threat of dismissal in order to impose a variation of the contract of employment so as to enable an employer to make deductions from wages did not amount to a breach of the relevant wages provisions of the *ERA 1996*. In *Discount Tobacco and Confectionery Ltd v Williamson* [1993] ICR 371, [1993] IRLR 327, it was held that for there to be prior written consent, the consent must precede not only the deduction itself, but also the event or conduct giving rise to the deduction. What has to appear in writing in either case is not merely provision for repayment of the sum concerned but for it to be deducted *from wages* (*Potter v Hunt Contracts Ltd* [1992] ICR 337, [1992] IRLR 108).

The above provisions do not apply to deductions:

(i)   made in order to reimburse the employer for any overpayment of wages or expenses made for any reason;

(ii)   made pursuant to any statutory disciplinary proceedings;

(iii)   which are statutory payments due to a public authority. In *Patel v Marquette Partners (UK) Ltd* [2009] IRLR 425, [2009] ICR 569, EAT, the (unsurprising) application of this exclusion to a deduction in the form of a taxation decision in relation to a bonus was considered. The policy underlying the exclusion of such matters from the general provision of *s 13* of the *ERA* is that challenges to a statutory authority's decision that money is owing must be made under the specific legislation empowering the deduction (eg the tax legislation) and thus the exclusion in *s 14(3)* was to be generally construed in a non technical way;

(iv)   payable to third parties, for example, trade union dues, made either pursuant to a contractual term to the inclusion of which the worker has agreed in writing, or otherwise with his prior written agreement or consent (but as to union dues, see **50.1** Trade Unions – II for restrictions on the deduction of union dues);

(v)   made from a worker's wages for taking part in a strike or other industrial action; or

(vi)   made, with the worker's prior written agreement or consent, for the purpose of satisfying an order of a court or tribunal for the payment of an amount by the worker to the employer.

(ERA 1996, ss 14, 15.)

It is irrelevant whether deductions made for a purpose falling within these exceptions are in fact lawful and justified. Such issues are outside the jurisdiction of the tribunal under the *ERA 1996* in any event (*Sunderland Polytechnic v Evans* [1993] ICR 392, [1993] IRLR 196, in which the EAT disapproved its own earlier reasoning in *Home Office v Ayres* [1992] ICR 175, [1992] IRLR 59; see also *SIP (Industrial Products) Ltd v Swinn* [1994] ICR 473, [1994] IRLR 323). In an important clarification, however, in *Gill v Ford Motor Co Ltd; Wong v BAE Systems Operations Ltd* [2004] IRLR 840, the EAT held that where an exception provided by *s 14* is relied upon by an employer, the employment tribunal must make findings of fact as to whether the *s 14* ground is actually engaged on the facts of the case. This does not, however, oblige the tribunal to make findings as to whether, as a matter of contract, such deductions are lawful as the enquiry is limited to whether the factual basis for reliance upon a *s 14* exception is made out. On the scope of the "industrial action" exception see *Norris v London Fire and Emergency Planning Authority* [2013] IRLR 428. An employee refusing to carry out a task which he did not believe he was obliged under his contract to do is not, without more, "industrial action". Industrial action also connotes action taken by more than one worker acting together. Accordingly, a lone employee cannot "take part" in industrial action for the purposes of the exclusion under *ERA 1996, s 14(5)*.

Equivalent restrictions apply to the receipt of payments by an employer, from a worker employed by him, in his capacity as the worker's employer (*ERA 1996, s 15(1), (5)*).

The scope of the wages provisions of the *ERA 1996* is dependent upon the meaning given to the crucial terms 'wages', 'deduction' and 'worker'.

Wages. Wages are defined by *ERA 1996, s 27(1)* to mean any sums payable to the worker by his employer in connection with his employment, including:

(A)   any fee, bonus, commission, holiday pay or other emolument referable to his employment (or unpaid commission; see *Robertson v Blackstone Franks Investment Management Ltd* [1998] IRLR 376, CA below);

(B)   sums payable pursuant to orders for reinstatement or re-engagement (see UNFAIR DISMISSAL – III (56));

(C)   sums payable pursuant to interim orders for the continuation of a contract of employment (see 56.21 UNFAIR DISMISSAL – III);

(D)   PAY – I (35), guarantee payments, medical suspension payments (see further below), remuneration on suspension on maternity grounds (see MATERNITY AND PARENTAL RIGHTS (33)), certain payments for TIME OFF WORK (50) and remuneration under protective awards (see 40.6 REDUNDANCY – II);

(E)   statutory sick pay (see SICKNESS AND SICK PAY (45)); and

(F)   statutory maternity pay, paternity pay and adoption pay (see MATERNITY AND PARENTAL RIGHTS (33)).

A non-contractual bonus also counts as wages when payment is made (*ERA 1996, s 27(3)*). The EAT in *Kent Management Services Ltd v Butterfield* [1992] ICR 272, [1992] IRLR 394 appeared to suggest that the *WA 1986* extended to any sums of the relevant kinds which would normally be expected to be paid, even if there was no strict contractual entitlement to receive them (see also *Farrell Matthews & Weir v Hansen* [2005] IRLR 160 below). Further, an employment tribunal has no jurisdiction, in relation to a claim of unlawful deduction from wages, to determine an applicant's *entitlement* to statutory sick pay where that entitlement was disputed by the employer. In relation to statutory sick pay, the exclusive jurisdiction for the determination of disputes as to entitlement rests with HR Revenue & Customs and, on appeal, the HMRC Commissioners. The employment tribunal only has jurisdiction in relation to statutory sick pay where the employer admitted entitlement to statutory sick pay but had withheld all or part of that pay. The same limitation will apply in relation to statutory maternity, paternity or adoption pay. See *Taylor Gordon & Co Ltd v Timmons* [2004] IRLR 180, EAT.

However, the following payments are excluded from the definition of wages by *s 27(2)*:

(I)   advances under loan agreements or by way of an advance of wages;

(II)   payments in respect of expenses incurred in carrying out the employment (for example a car mileage allowance; see *Southwark London Borough v O'Brien* [1996] IRLR 420 EAT but compare *Mears v Salt* UKEAT/0522/11 EAT where it was held on the facts that a longstanding "travel allowance" was in fact the payment of an emolument and not caught by the exclusion for expenses);

(III)   payments by way of pension, allowance or gratuity in connection with the worker's retirement or as compensation for loss of office;

(IV)   any payment referable to the worker's redundancy; and

(V)   any payment otherwise than in his capacity as a worker.

Benefits in kind are not treated as wages unless they are vouchers, stamps or similar documents of a fixed monetary value capable of being exchanged for money, goods or services (*ERA 1996, s 27(5)*). This would embrace, for example, luncheon vouchers.

Particular doubts arose as to whether a payment in lieu of notice amounts to wages. However, the House of Lords in *Delaney v Staples* [1992] ICR 483 held that it did not. Wages were payments in respect of the rendering of services during the employment, so all payments in respect of the termination of the contract are excluded, save to the extent that they are expressly caught by *s 27(1)*.

In *Robertson v Blackstone Franks Investment Management Ltd* [1998] IRLR 376, the Court of Appeal, upholding the decision of the EAT, held that commission payments which become payable after the termination of employment are 'wages' within the definition of *ERA 1996, s 27* and, accordingly, are protected against unauthorised deductions made by the employer. The statutory requirement was that the sum was payable 'in connection with the employee's employment' but it did not require the sum to be payable *during* the currency of the employee's contract. The Court of Appeal further held that the employer was entitled to set off sums paid as an advance against future commission in assessing the amount payable. To hold to the contrary would contravene *ERA 1996, s 25(3)* which obliges a tribunal to take into account sums 'already paid or repaid' by the employer to the worker. In *New Century Cleaning Co Ltd v Church* [2000] IRLR 27, the Court of Appeal held that the employer did not breach the provisions of *Part II* of the *ERA 1996* in reducing the amount of money paid to teams of employees for each job done by the team. On the facts of the case, which concerned a window-cleaning business, there was no express or implied contractual term for identifying the amount of money which each team would be paid nor any such term relating to the distribution of the money among the team. Accordingly, there was no breach of *ERA 1996, s 13(3)* which relates to the amount of wages 'properly payable' to each employee. The amount payable to each member of the team was not sufficiently certain to allow the wages to be ascertained prior to allocation of the money to each individual.

In *Farrell Matthews & Weir v Hansen* [2005] IRLR 160 the issue of discretionary bonuses as 'wages' was further considered. In that case a solicitor was paid an annual discretionary bonus in instalments. The claimant left her employer in circumstances where £9,000 of the bonus was still outstanding. The EAT held that a deductions from wages claim under s 13 had been rightly allowed. The employer's argument relying upon *ERA 1996, s 27(3)* that non-contractual bonus could only become wages when actually paid was rejected by the EAT which held that once the bonus payable had been declared by the employer the sum became payable and amounted to wages within the meaning of *ERA s 27(1)*. Similarly, in *Tradition Securities and Futures SA v Mouradian* [2009] EWCA Civ 60, [2009] All ER (D) 100 (Feb) it was held by the Court of Appeal that claims for deductions from bonus payments could be brought under the unlawful deductions jurisdiction, even where there is a dispute over alleged variations to the bonus scheme, provided the employer has fully exercised its discretion to make a payment under the scheme and the amount claimed is quantified, and payment is due.

The issue of quantification of the sum in issue is crucially relevant to whether a claim may be brought under the deduction from wages provisions of the *ERA*. In *Adcock v Coors Brewers Ltd* [2007] EWCA Civ 19, [2007] IRLR 440, [2007] All ER (D) 190 (Jan), *sub nom Coors Brewers Ltd v Adcock*, the Court of Appeal considered whether a claim in relation to an *unquantified* discretionary bonus could be advanced under the provisions of *Part II* of the *ERA*. While such claims could be brought under the employment tribunal's *contractual* jurisdiction after termination of employment (by analogy with the discretionary bonus cases such as *Clark v Nomura plc* [2000] IRLR 766 which had been brought as a contractual claim in the High Court) that jurisdiction is limited to £25,000 whilst the jurisdiction under the provisions of *Part II* of the *ERA* is unlimited. The Court of Appeal held (applying *Delaney v Staples* [1992] ICR 483, [1992] IRLR 191, HL) that the jurisdiction under *Part II* of the *ERA* is limited to claims brought on the premise that a *specific amount of money* by way of wages is owing. Accordingly, the jurisdiction does not extend to an unquantified claim in relation to an unidentified sum (such as a claim to a discretionary bonus). Such claims will remain limited to the contractual jurisdiction and, in relation to claims with a potential value of in excess of £25,000, or whether the employee remains in the employer's employment, will still have to be brought in the Courts rather than the employment tribunal. See also, applying the principle of the requirement of quantifiability as a precondition to a claim under *s 13* of the *ERA*, *Mouradian v Tradition Securities and Futures SA* [2009] EWCA Civ 60, [2009] All ER (D) 100 (Feb), *Allsop v Christiani and Neilsen Ltd* (UKEAT/0241/11) and *Kingston-upon-Hull CC v Schofield* UKEAT/0616/11 (6 November 2012).

Deductions. A broad definition of deductions is contained in *ERA 1996, s 13(3), (4)*. Where the total amount of any wages that are paid on any occasion by an employer to any worker employed by him is less than the total amount of the wages properly payable on that occasion (after deductions), the amount of the deficiency counts as a deduction, unless it is attributable to an error of computation as defined by *s 13(4)*. A conscious decision not to pay a particular sum which is caused by the employer's mistaken interpretation of the contract of employment is not such an error of computation (*Yemm v British Steel plc* [1994] IRLR 117; *Morgan v West Glamorgan County Council* [1995] IRLR 68).

In determining whether there been a deduction it is necessary to calculate the sum "properly payable" to the worker considering the definition of wages in *s 27* of the *ERA* and then compare it to the sum actually paid. It is an error to apply the "week's pay" calculation provisions in *Chapter II* of *Part XIV* of the *ERA* in this exercise as *s 13(3)* of the *ERA* has its own calculation regime (*Davies v Droylsden Academy* (UKEAT/0044/16)).

There were originally doubts as to whether *s 13(3)*, *ERA 1996* applies only to cases where there is some amount due as wages and the employer has sought to recover some *other* sum allegedly due to him by setting it off against those wages, or whether it also extends to the case where the employer has simply refused to pay the wages allegedly due or some part of them (usually because he denies that they are due at all). In *Delaney v Staples* [1991] ICR 331, [1991] IRLR 112, the Court of Appeal held that a total non-payment *was* a deduction. The House of Lords ([1992] ICR 483, [1992] IRLR 191) did not have to consider this point on appeal. In *Francis v Elizabeth Claire Care Management Ltd* [2005] IRLR 858 the EAT held that 'deduction' had a wide meaning and can include a case of failure to pay wages on time (rejecting robustly the employer's argument that there was no right to be paid on time). In that case, the employee was dismissed for complaining about the late payment. Unsurprisingly, that dismissal was held to be automatically unfair as a dismissal for asserting a statutory right (ie the right not to suffer deductions from wages. See also *s 104* of the *Employment Rights Act 1996* and **55.3**(d) UNFAIR DISMISSAL – **II**). In *Lucy v British Airways plc*

[2009] All ER (D) 58 (Jan) the distinction between a claim to a deduction from wages and a breach of contract claim was helpfully illustrated. The issue was whether a claim for loss of a flying pay supplement was an unlawful deduction from wages or a breach of contract claim which should be pursued in the civil courts. The claimant had previously been paid a supplement when carrying out flying duties. Following closure of the base at which the claimants worked, they continued to be paid basic pay but not flight supplements (as they were not flying). The EAT held that for the claims to fall within *Part II* of the *ERA* they must be quantifiable and held that the claims could be quantified. The claimants failed, however, on the issue whether the sums in question were wages. The EAT held they were not as they were only payable when the claimants were actually undertaking flying duties. Accordingly, there could be no claim to a deduction from wages but there might be a claim for contractual loss based upon breach of contract arising from the withdrawal of a contractual scheme.

In *Bruce v Wiggins Teape (Stationery) Ltd* [1994] IRLR 536, the *WA 1986* (as it then was) was held to cover a situation in which the employer, in breach of contract, reduced the employee's wages. In *Morgan* (above), the wages provisions of the *ERA 1996* were similarly applied where the employer had demoted the employee without having power to do so. In *Hussman Manufacturing Ltd v Weir* [1998] IRLR 288, the employer had a contractual right to change the employee's working hours. After the employee was moved from night shift he was worse off as a result of loss of unsocial hours pay. The EAT held that a reduction in income which is the result of a lawful act by the employer is not a deduction. The EAT acknowledged, however, that in exceptional cases the unilateral exercise of such a contractual right by the employer might breach the implied term of mutual trust and confidence. In a situation where there is no contractual right to change the hours of work, a unilateral change by the employer, without the consent of the workers, to short-time working and, consequently, a reduction in remuneration, will amount to an unlawful deduction from wages: *International Packaging Corpn (UK) Ltd v Balfour* [2003] IRLR 11. In *Beveridge v KLM UK Ltd* [2000] IRLR 765, the EAT considered whether it was an unlawful deduction from wages to fail to pay any salary to an employee (who, following a period of sickness absence, claimed to be fit and willing to return to work) during a six-week period when the employer wished to satisfy itself that the employee was in fact fit to return. The EAT held that, in the absence of express provision to the contrary, an employee who offers his services is entitled to be paid wages. Accordingly there was an unlawful deduction from wages for the purposes of *Part II* of *ERA 1996* (see **54.7 UNFAIR DISMISSAL – I**). In *Rice Shack Ltd v Obi* UKEAT/0240/17 a worker on a zero hours contract succeeded in a claim for unlawful deductions in relation to a period when the worker was suspended and offered no hours.

An illustration of the sometimes complicated exercise of determining entitlement to payment for the purposes of *s 13* of the *ERA 1996* is the Court of Appeal decision in *Dunlop Tyres Ltd v Blows* [2001] EWCA Civ 1032, [2001] IRLR 629 which involved the construction of ambiguous contractual terms in a collective agreement as to rates of pay. The Court of Appeal concluded that, on the proper construction of the agreement, the employees were entitled to triple pay for public holidays and, accordingly, the claim for unlawful deduction of wages was well founded. See also *Henry v London General Transport Services Ltd* [2002] EWCA Civ 488, [2002] IRLR 472. An example of the requirement of employee consent to variations to the rate of remuneration is provided by *Davies v MJ Wyatt (Decorators) Ltd* [2000] IRLR 759. In that case, the employer, in an attempt to meet its obligations to provide paid holiday under the *Working Time Regulations*, unilaterally reduced the employees' hourly pay in order to fund the holiday payment. Unsurprisingly, this amounted to an unlawful deduction from wages. In relation to holiday pay to which an employee is entitled under the *Working Time Regulations*, there may be an overlap between the right to recover these sums (in the event of non payment) under the *Working Time Regulations* and under the *ERA 1996, s 13*. In *List Design Group Ltd v Douglas* [2003] IRLR 14 it was held that even though the claim to holiday pay was out of time under the relevant provisions of the *Working Time Regulations*, it was recoverable pursuant to the *ERA 1996* as an unauthorised deduction from wages. This conclusion was upheld by the House of Lords in *HM Revenue and Customs v Stringer* [2009] IRLR 667 which confirms that failure to pay holiday pay under the WTR can constitute an unauthorised deduction from wages under the *ERA 1996*.

In *Mears v Salt* UKAT/0522/11 the EAT had held that, in determining whether there had been an unlawful deduction from wages, as the employment tribunal was required by *s 13(3)* of the *ERA* to determine the "total amount of wages properly payable" this required the tribunal to construe and interpret the relevant contract including identifying any applicable implied terms. The argument, by analogy with the provisions in *Part I* of the *ERA* (to the effect that, in relation to statements of terms and conditions, the tribunal may only declare the terms and conditions but not interpret them) was accordingly rejected. See also *Fairfield Ltd v Skinner* [1992] ICR 836, [1993] IRLR 4. More recently, however, in *Agarwal v Cardiff University* [2017] IRLR 600 the EAT held, relying upon *Southern Cross Healthcare v Perkins* [2011] IRLR 247 (which held that there was no power of interpretation under *Part I* of the *ERA*) that the same principle applies equally to *s 13* of the *ERA* and *Part II*. Very shortly thereafter, a different division of the EAT in *Weatherilt v Cathay Pacific Airways Ltd* [2017] IRLR 609 expressly disagreed with the decision in *Agarwal* concluding that the employment tribunal was, in a deduction from wages claim, permitted to engage in a process of interpretation of the contract and that such a process was central to the operation of *s 13* of *ERA 1996*. In *Anderson v Tyne & Wear Passenger Transport Executive* [2018] ICR 1207, [2018] All ER (D) 92 (Jan) the point was revisited again by the EAT which concluded that *Weatherilt* was correct. Clarity has now been provided by the Court of Appeal in the combined appeals in *Agarwal v Cardiff University; Tyne & Wear Passenger Transport Executive v Anderson* [2018] EWCA Civ 2084, [2019] IRLR 657. The Court of Appeal has unequivocally affirmed that the employment tribunal can, if necessary, construe the claimant's contract of employment.

If a contract provides for an express power to make a deduction then the deduction will not be lawful if it is in fact a penalty and not a genuine pre-estimate of loss (*Cleeve Link Ltd v Bryla* [2014] IRLR 86). It must be determined as a matter of construction if the provision in issue was intended to deter breach or to compensate for it. The EAT gave helpful guidance on the process to be adopted by tribunals in addressing this issue. The contract must be construed at the time it was entered into on an objective basis. In assessing the question of deterrence and compensation it is relevant to have regard to the difference between the sum to be deducted and that which could be recovered in an action for breach. If the difference is extravagant then this may indicate that it is only explicable as a penalty. See also *Murray v Leisureplay plc* [2005] IRLR 946 (CA) which was applied and analysed in *Cleeve Link Ltd v Bryla*.

Finally, the fact that the government declares a public holiday does not necessarily give rise to a right to additional payment for that day. In *Campbell and Smith Construction Group Ltd v Greenwood* [2001] IRLR 588, the EAT held that the failure by an employer to pay an additional day's pay for the Millennium public holiday (which, on the facts, the employees were already contractually entitled to take as holiday) was not an unlawful deduction from wages. The EAT stated that a government declaration of an additional so-called public holiday does not, of itself, entitle employees to an additional day's paid holiday.

Worker. By *s 230(3)*, *ERA 1996* those entitled to the protection from deductions from wages include persons working under contracts of apprenticeship and contracts for services as well as contracts of employment (see Employee, Self-Employed or Worker? (16)). The contract for services must be one whereby the individual undertakes to do or perform personally any work or services for another party to the contract whose status is not, by virtue of the contract, that of a client or customer of any profession or business undertaking carried on by the individual.

35.5   Deductions from wages of, and receipt of payments from, workers in retail employment

Special provisions apply to deductions from the wages of workers in retail employment and to payments by such workers, on account of cash shortages or stock deficiencies. Retail employment is defined as employment involving the carrying out by workers of retail transactions – the sale or supply of goods, or the supply of services (including financial services) – directly with members of the public (*ERA 1996, s 17(1)–(3)*).

The employer of a worker in retail employment may not deduct for cash shortages or stock deficiencies more than one-tenth of gross wages payable to the worker on a particular pay day (*ERA 1996, s 18(1)*). The employer must make such a deduction not more than 12 months after the date when he discovered or ought reasonably to have discovered the shortage or deficiency (*ERA 1996, s 18(2), (3)*).

If such a worker's pay is calculated by reference to cash shortages or stock deficiencies, the difference between the payment made when there are shortages and when there are not is treated as a deduction and the difference may not be more than one-tenth on any pay day (*ERA 1996, s 19(1)*).

In addition, the employer of a worker in retail employment may not receive from the worker any payment on account of a cash shortage or stock deficiency, unless certain requirements are met. The employer must:

(a)   notify the worker in writing of his total liability to him in respect of that shortage or deficiency; and

(b)   make a demand for payment which is:

   (i)   in writing; and

   (ii)   on a pay day.

(*ERA 1996, s 20(1), (2)*.)

The demand must be made not earlier than the first pay day on or after the date of the written notification and not later than 12 months after the date when the employer discovered or ought reasonably to have discovered the shortage or deficiency (*ERA 1996, s 20(3)*).

The amount demanded on a particular pay day must not exceed one-tenth of the gross wages payable to the worker on that day, or the balance of that one-tenth remaining after any deductions on account of cash shortages or stock deficiencies (*ERA 1996, s 21(1)*).

The restriction of deductions and payments to one-tenth of gross wages (and the requirements referred to in (*a*) and (*b*) above) do not apply to deductions or payments made from the final payment of wages. Nor do *ss 20* and *21* apply to payments made after the final payment of wages (*ERA 1996, ss 20(5), 21(3), 22(1)–(4)*). However, after the 12-month time limit referred to above has expired, the employer may neither receive payments (even after the final payment of wages), nor bring legal proceedings for recovery unless he has made a demand in accordance with *ss 20* or *21* within that time limit (*ERA 1996, ss 21(3), 22(4)*).

Even if legal proceedings are taken against a worker still in retail employment, a court which finds him liable to pay sums in respect of a shortage or deficiency must make provision so that the rate of payment does not exceed that which the employer could recover under *s 20* or *s 21* (*ERA 1996, ss 21(3), 22(4)*).

35.6   Remedies

The worker's exclusive remedy for breach by his employer of the statutory provisions outlined above is to present a complaint to an employment tribunal (*ERA 1996, s 23(1)*). The remedy of a worker for any contravention of *ss 13(1), 15(1), 18(1)* or *21(1)* is by way of a complaint to an employment tribunal under *s 23(1)* and not otherwise (*ERA 1996, s 205(2)*). However, the Court of Appeal has held in *Rickard v PB Glass Supplies Ltd* [1990] ICR 150 that what is now *s 205(2)* was not intended to prevent an employee from pursuing a claim in contract before the county court or High Court for moneys due to him where the non-payment is alleged by the employer to be due to the fact that no payment is due at all. Such a claim may now also be brought in the employment tribunal, within certain limits (see **8.23** CONTRACT OF EMPLOYMENT).

A complaint may be made that:

(a)   an unauthorised deduction has been made contrary to *s 13(1)* or *s 15(1)*;

(b)   an unauthorised payment has been received by the employer contrary to *ss 15(1)* or *20(1)*;

(c)   deductions exceeding the limit set by *s 18(1)* have been made; or

(d)   the employer has received more than the limit set by *s 21(1)*.

(*ERA 1996, s 23(1)*.)

The time limit for presenting a complaint to an employment tribunal under these provisions is three months beginning with the date of the deduction or the receipt of which complaint is made. The tribunal has jurisdiction to extend the time limit where it is satisfied that it was not reasonably practicable for the complaint to be presented within the relevant period of three months (see **19.8** EMPLOYMENT TRIBUNALS – I). Guidance on dealing with limitation points arising under those provisions was given by the EAT in *Taylorplan Services Ltd v Jackson* [1996] IRLR 184. It is to be noted that the right to make a complaint relates only to 'unauthorised' deductions. Deductions made by an employer in accordance with a direction given by a public authority pursuant to statute are authorised deductions, therefore the right not to suffer unlawful deductions does not apply, and a tribunal has no jurisdiction to hear a claim in respect of them (*Patel v Marquette Partners (UK) Ltd* [2009] ICR 569, [2009] IRLR 425).

Where a series of deductions or payments are made, in certain circumstances, the time limit runs from the date of the last payment (*ERA 1996, s 23(3)*). A complaint may then be made about the entire unlawful series (*Reid v Camphill Engravers* [1990] IRLR 268). See also *Group 4 Nightspeed Ltd v Gilbert* [1997] IRLR 398, EAT. In *Arora v Rockwell Automation Ltd* [2006] All ER (D) 112 (May), EAT the EAT held (applying *Group 4 Nightspeed Ltd v Gilbert*) that, in relation to an unlawful deductions claim, time starts to run, not from the date of termination of the contract, but from the date of the payment of wages containing the shortfall. In *Bear Scotland Ltd v Fulton* [2015] IRLR 15 (the much publicised holiday pay case) the EAT held that for the purposes of a series of deductions claim under *ERA 1996, s 23(2)* and *23(3)* that a previous underpayment which occurred more than three months before the next in the alleged series could not form part of the series of deductions for the purposes of *s 23(3)*. As Langstaff P explained (at paragraph 81): "The sense of the legislation is that any series punctuated from the next succeeding series by a gap of more than three months is one in respect of which the passage of time has extinguished the jurisdiction to consider a complaint that it was unpaid." This is a significant limitation of the historic application of *s 23(3)* to a series of deductions claim. Further, by the *Deduction from Wages (Limitation) Regulations 2014 (SI 2014/3322)* which came into force on 8 January 2015 a further limitation upon claims for a series of deductions is imposed. By *Reg 4* new *subsections 4A* and *4B* are added to *ERA 1996, s 23* to the effect that for deductions from wages falling within the definition of wages contained in *ERA 1996, s 27(1)(a)* any series of deductions is limited to the maximum period of two years preceding the date of presentation of the complaint to the employment tribunal. Thus this "longstop" provision will apply to all claims for "any fee, bonus, commission, holiday pay or other emolument referable to his employment, whether payable under his contract or otherwise" (*ERA 1996, s 27(1)(a)*) but will not apply to the other categories of wages as listed in *ERA 1996, s 27(1)(b)–(j)* (see *ERA 1996, s 23(4B)*). Moreover, the new provisions are subject to transitional arrangements as set out in *Reg 4* of *Deduction from Wages (Limitation) Regulations* so that the two year "longstop" provision will only apply to claims presented to the employment tribunal on or after 1 July 2015. For claims presented before that date under *Part II* of the *ERA 1996* there is, however, no applicable limitation period and the period of six years under the *Limitation Act 1980, s 9* does not apply as s 23 of the *ERA 1996* contains its own (albeit open ended period) of limitation (*Bath Hill Court (Bournemouth) Property Management Co v Coletta* [2020] IRLR 124, CA).

Where an employment tribunal finds that a complaint under *s 23(1)* is well-founded, it will make a declaration to that effect and, where an unlawful deduction or payment has been made, will order the employer to pay (or, as the case may be, repay) to the worker the amount of the deduction or payment (*ERA 1996, s 24*).

If the wages provisions of the *ERA 1996* have been satisfied in respect of an amount less than the deduction, the employer will be ordered to pay the worker the difference between the amount actually deducted and that which could lawfully have been deducted (*ERA 1996, s 25(1), (2)*).

In making the order, the tribunal will take into account payments or repayments already made to the worker (*ERA 1996, s 25(3)*). *Section 25(3)* applies to any payment made by an employer in respect of a deduction at any time prior to the date on which the tribunal makes its order and is not limited to amounts paid *before* the deduction (see *Robertson v Blackstone Franks Investment Management Ltd* [1998] IRLR 376).

Where a tribunal has ordered an employer to pay or repay a worker any amount (the relevant amount), the amount which the employer is entitled to recover by whatever means in respect of the matter which gave rise to the deduction or payment (including cash shortages or stock deficiencies) is reduced by the relevant amount (*ERA 1996, s 25(4), (5)*). In other words, sums wrongfully deducted cannot later be recovered at all, even if they were properly owing to the employer. The correctness of this far-reaching proposition was confirmed by the EAT in *Potter v Hunt Contracts Ltd* [1992] ICR 337, [1992] IRLR 108.

Where an order is made under *ERA 1996, s 11* and *ss 23–25* (see **35.18** below) the aggregate of the amount ordered to be paid by the employer to the worker will not exceed the amount of the deduction (*ERA 1996, s 26*).

Parties cannot, by agreement, exclude or limit the operation of *ERA 1996, ss 23–25* except where agreement has been reached to refrain from presenting or continuing with a complaint where a conciliation officer has taken action in accordance with *s 18(2)* or *(3)* of *ERA 1996* or where the employee has entered into a settlement agreement which meets certain conditions, principally that legal advice has been taken (*ERA 1996, s 203(1), (2)*; for settlement agreements, see **19.22** EMPLOYMENT TRIBUNALS – I).

These provisions do not apply to employment where under his contract the person employed ordinarily works outside Great Britain (*ERA 1996, s 196(2), (3)*; and see **54.15** UNFAIR DISMISSAL – I).

35.7   THE NATIONAL MINIMUM WAGE ACT 1998

The *National Minimum Wage Act 1998* ('*NMWA 1998*') received Royal Assent on 31 July 1998 and came fully into force on 1 April 1999. The majority of the detailed provisions as to the operation of the National Minimum Wage ('NMW') are contained in the relevant Regulations. The *National Minimum Wage Regulations 1999* (*SI 1999/584*) ("the 1999 Regs") were issued in March 1999 and came into force on 1 April 1999. The *1999 Regs* have now been replaced by the *National Minimum Wage Regulations 2015 (SI 2015/621)* ("the *2015 Regs*") with effect from 6 April 2015. The *1999 Regs* will continue to apply to any issue relating to the NMW arising prior to 6 April 2015 and so there is likely to be a considerable transitional period during which the *1999 Regs* will continue to be applicable. In the text below reference is made to the relevant provisions of the *1999 Regs* and also to the equivalent provisions of the *2015 Regs*. The *2015 Regs* are not intended to make substantive changes to the relevant law but are, according to the explanatory note to the *2015 Regs*, a "remake" of the *1999 Regs* consolidating the amendments to those Regs. Accordingly they involve a rewriting of the existing law as contained in the *1999 Regs* and not merely a renumbering of the relevant regulations.

All 'workers' (see *NMWA 1998, s 54* and below) are to be paid at a rate which is not less than the NMW. As to the level of the NMW, the main points as now enacted in the *Regulations* are as follows:

(a)   with effect from 1 April 2020 workers aged 25 and over qualify for the National Living Wage of £8.72 per hour (previously £8.21 per hour) (*Reg 4* of the *2015 Regs* as substituted by the *National Minimum Wage (Amendment) Regulations 2020 (SI 2020/338)* and *section 1(3)* of the *NMWA 1988*);

(b)   from 1 April 2020 the NMW for workers aged 21 and over (but less than 25) is £8.20 per hour (previously £7.70 per hour) (*Reg 4A(1)(a)* of the *2015 Regs* as substituted by the *National Minimum Wage (Amendment) Regulations 2020 (SI 2020/338)*);

(c)   from 1 April 2020 the NMW for workers aged 18–21 is £6.45 (previously £6.15 per hour) (*Reg 4A(1)(b)* of the *2015 Regs* as substituted by the *National Minimum Wage (Amendment) Regulations 2020 (SI 2020/338)*);

(d)   from 1 April 2020 the NMW for workers under 18 is £4.55 per hour (previously £4.35 per hour) (*Reg 4A(1)(c)* of the *2015 Regs* as substituted by the *National Minimum Wage (Amendment) Regulations 2020 (SI 2020/338)*);

(e)   workers aged under 19 engaged on a contract of apprenticeship or workers aged over 19 but employed on the first 12 months of a contract of apprenticeship are entitled, from 1 April 2019, to the new rate of £4.15 per hour (previously £3.90) (*Reg 5* of the *2015 Regs* determines when the apprenticeship rate applies).

Certain categories of workers are expressly excluded by *reg 12* of the *1999 Regs* (as amended) from entitlement to the NMW. In summary, the excluded categories for the purposes of the *1999 Regs* are as follows:

(i)   workers engaged on certain "Government arrangements" (such as "Programme Led Apprenticeships") and schemes designed to provide training, work experience or temporary work (such as "Apprenticeships or Advanced Apprenticeships"). See *reg 12(4A)–12(7)* of the *1999 Regs*;

(ii)   workers engaged in work experience of less than one year pursuant to a course of higher education are excluded from the NMW by *reg 12(8), (9)* and *(9A)* of the *1999 Regs*;

(iii)   workers who were homeless persons working in return for shelter and benefits pursuant to a not for profit scheme are not entitled to the NMW provided all of the conditions of *reg 12(10),(11)* and *(12)* of the *1999 Regs* are satisfied; and

(iv)   workers participating in the European Community Leonardo da Vinci programme or the European Community Youth in Action Programme or the European Community Erasmus Programme or Comenius Programme are not entitled to the NMW (*reg 12(13)–(16)* of the *1999 Regs*).

Part 6 of the *2015 Regs* sets out the rewritten categories of exclusions from the right to the NMW in *regs 51–56* and comprises: schemes for training, work experience, temporary work or obtaining work (*reg 51*); schemes for trial periods of work (*reg 52*); work experience as part of a higher or further education course (*reg 53*); government funded traineeships in England not exceeding six months (*reg 54*); work schemes for provision of accommodation to the homeless (*reg 55*); and European Union programmes (*reg 56*).

Guidance and up to date information on the NMW may be found from links on the gov.uk website at www.gov.uk/national-minimum-wage.

Detailed provisions are contained in each of the *1999* and *2015 Regulations* for the purpose of calculating whether a worker has been paid the NMW. Thus, the individual's hourly rate of pay must be determined by reference to total remuneration over a 'relevant pay reference period' and the hours worked during that period. The pay reference period is one month or a shorter period if the worker is paid by reference to such shorter period (eg a week) (see *reg 10* of the *1999 Regs* and *reg 6* of the *2015 Regs*). Regulations exist for allocation of pay to relevant periods (*reg 30* of the *1999 Regs* and *regs 8* and *9* of *Part 4* of the *2015 Regs*). As to determining the actual remuneration received in the relevant period, *regs 30–37* of the *1999 Regs* (and *Regs 9–15* of the *2015 Regs*) set out in detail the treatment of various types of payment. Gross pay must be determined and the following payments will be included for the purpose of calculation:

(i)   incentive payments including commission; and

(ii)   bonuses.

It is important to note that since 1 October 2009 tips, service charges, gratuities and cover charges cannot be used to make up National Minimum Wage pay by amendments made to the *NMW Regulations* by the *National Minimum Wage Regulations 1999 (Amendment) Regulations 2009 (SI 2009/1902)*. See also *reg 10(m)* of the *2015 Regs* which is to the same effect. Previously it had been held that tips and gratuities paid through the payroll system could be used in discharge of the *NMWA 1998* remuneration obligations (see *Nerva v United Kingdom* [2002] IRLR 815, ECtHR, (see **31.7** Human Rights) but that tips distributed through a "tronc" system (and not directly through the employer's payroll) did not count towards the national minimum wage (*Annabels (Berkeley Square) Ltd v Revenue and Customs Comrs* [2009] EWCA Civ 361, [2009] 4 All ER 55, [2009] ICR 1123). The position has now been simplified (and helpfully clarified) so that eligible workers will receive at least the National Minimum Wage in base pay with any tips being paid in addition. In addition a voluntary code of best practice on service charges, tips, gratuities and cover charges has been introduced with the aim to improve the information provided to customers and workers. The code is intended to provide practical guidance to businesses on how to operate in a fair and transparent way and aims to ensure that businesses are able to provide their customers with sufficient information to make an informed choice before they leave a tip or gratuity or pay a service charge. The relevant guidance and code of practice may be accessed from https://www.gov.uk/government/publications/national-minimum-wage-code-of-best -practice-on-service-charges-tips-gratuities-and-cover-charges.

A worker's basic pay, from which enhancements such as time and a half payments are calculated, must comply with the NMW and the enhanced rate of pay is not the relevant hourly rate of pay for the purposes of the *Regulations*. This remains that case even if the worker never receives only the basic pay, but is always paid at the enhanced rate, for example where the worker always works night shifts which are remunerated at the enhanced rate (*Hillier v Hamilton House Medical Ltd* (2009) EAT UKEAT/0246/09), [2009] All ER (D) 319 (Nov).

Certain deductions are ignored for the purpose of calculating the remuneration in the relevant period (eg tax and National Insurance deductions, deductions in respect of the worker's conduct in relation to which he is contractually liable, deductions in respect of loans or overpayment, deductions in relation to accidental overpayment and deductions in relation to the purchase of shares, options or other securities (*reg 33* of the *1999 Regs* and *reg 12* of the *2015 Regs* as amended by the *National Minimum Wage (Amendment) (No 2) Regulations 2020 (SI 2020/339)*). The general principle is that benefits in kind are not to be included for the purpose of calculating the remuneration (*reg 9* of the *1999 Regs* and *reg 10* of the *2015 Regs*). The exception to this is living accommodation provided by the employer. The 'value' of the accommodation is set by *reg 36* of the *1999 Regs* (as amended by the *National Minimum Wage Regulations 2019 (SI 2019/603)*) and cannot exceed, with effect from 1 April 2020, £8.20 for each day the accommodation is provided, giving a maximum of £57.40 per week. This is reflected in *regs 14–16* of the *2015 Regs*. Travel expenses to a temporary workplace and related subsistence costs paid by an employer and eligible for tax relief are also excluded from the calculation of payments for the purposes of the NMW with effect from 1 January 2011 by amendments made to *reg 31* of the *1999 Regs* by the *National Minimum Wage (Amendment) (No. 2) Regulations 2010 (SI 2010/3001)* and see *reg 10(n)* of the *2015 Regs*.

Regulations 31 and *36* of the *1999 Regs* (and see now *regs 14–16* of the *2015 Regs*) in relation to accommodation and deductions have been considered by the Court of Appeal in *Leisure Employment Services Ltd v Revenue and Customs Comrs* [2007] EWCA Civ 92, [2007] IRLR 450. Upholding the decision of the EAT, the Court of Appeal held that, in relation to holiday resort workers living on site in accommodation provided by the employer, it was not permissible to count a £6 sum per fortnight which they had agreed to pay for gas and electricity as counting towards the minimum wage as the total permitted by *reg 36* in relation to accommodation had already been exhausted by their rent payments. Accordingly, the employer was in breach of the NMW. See also *R&C Comrs v Middlesborough Football and Athletic Company (1986) Ltd* UKEAT/0234/19 (20 March 2020 unreported). Conversely, a "sleep-in payment" paid to a care worker was held not to amount to an allowance within the meaning of *reg 31 (1)(d)* of the *1999 Regs* and could therefore be taken into account when calculating whether the worker had received the minimum wage (*Smith v Oxfordshire Learning Disability NHS Trust* (2009) EAT Appeal No. UKEAT/0176/09), [2009] ICR 1395, [2009] All ER (D) 170 (Aug). On "sleep in" working and entitlement to the NMW see *Royal Mencap Society v Tomlinson-Blake* [2018] IRLR 932 at **[35.10]** below.

The provisions for the calculation of the number of hours worked by the worker in the relevant pay reference period are similarly complicated. There are four types of work which can be carried out:

(A)   time work (*reg 3* of the *1999 Regs* and *reg 17(b)* and *regs 30–35* of the *2015 Regs*) which is paid by reference to the time which a worker works;

(B)   salaried hours work (*reg 4* of the *1999 Regs* and *reg 17(a)* and *regs 21–29* of the *2015 Regs* as amended by the *National Minimum Wage (Amendment) (No 2) Regulations 2020 (SI 2020/339)*) which deals with the situation where a worker is paid under the contract for a fixed number of hours a year and is paid an annual salary in instalments;

(C)   output work (*reg 5*) which covers piece-work and commission-related working (as amended by the *National Minimum Wage Regulations 1999 (Amendment) Regulations 2004 (SI 2004/1161)* with effect from 1 October 2004 with further amendments coming into force on 6 April 2005). Output work is addressed in the *2015 Regs* in *reg 17(c)* and *regs 36–43*); and

(D)   unmeasured work (*reg 6* of the *1999*) which provides a residual category. Unmeasured work is addressed in the *2015 Regs* in *reg 17(d)* and *regs 44–50*)

35.7 Pay – I

The actual hours worked must be calculated in accordance with the detailed calculation provisions of the *1999 Regulations* or the *2015 Regulations* (for matters after 6 April 2015). A detailed consideration of these provisions is beyond the scope of this work. For the detail of the provisions and the methods of calculation the reader is referred to *Tolley's National Minimum Wage: A Practical Guide* (ISBN: 075450 226-0).

35.8 Coverage of the Act

Section 54(3) defines 'worker' for the purpose of the *NMWA 1998* as 'an individual who has entered into or works under (or where employment has ceased worked under):

(a)   a contract of employment (which is defined to include a contract of apprenticeship);

(b)   or any other contract, whether express or implied and (if it is express) whether oral or in writing, whereby the individual undertakes to do or perform personally any work or services for another party to the contract whose status is not by virtue of the contract that of client or customer of any profession or business undertaking carried on by the individual.'

Regulation 12 of the *National Minimum Wage Regulations 1999 (SI 1999/584)* and *s 54* (the definition of 'worker') of the *National Minimum Wage Act 1998* were considered by the Court of Appeal in the context of a pupil barrister in *Edmonds v Lawson* [2000] IRLR 391. The claimant was a pupil in the defendant's chambers and was over the age of 31. Accordingly, she did not fall within *reg 12(2)* which, at that time, excluded only workers under the age of 26 on the first 12 months of a contract of apprenticeship from the NMW. At first instance Sullivan J held that the applicant was entitled to the NMW on the basis that during her pupillage there was a contract of apprenticeship between the applicant and the barristers' chambers (see [2000] IRLR 18). On appeal, the Court of Appeal held that the pupillage arrangement between the applicant and the chambers had the essential characteristics of an intention to create legal relations and, accordingly, there was a legally binding contract between the applicant and the chambers. The Court of Appeal held, however, allowing the appeal, that the contract was not a contract of apprenticeship and did not fall within the definition of a contract of employment within *s 54(3)* of the *NMWA 1998*. In relation to *s 54(3)(b)* (which relates to any other contract whereby the individual undertakes to do or perform personally any work or services for another party) the Court of Appeal held that the pupil did not undertake to perform work or services for the members of the chambers and in the event that the pupil did any work for which she was paid, the person for whom the work was done was the pupil's professional client. Accordingly, the pupil was not entitled to the benefit of the National Minimum Wage. In *Lee v Chassis & Cab Specialists Ltd* (UKEAT/0268/10/JOJ) [2011] All ER (D) 178 (Feb) the EAT held that apprentice status at common law (not a case where the specific exceptions for government arrangements in *reg 12* applied) was not negated by the involvement of a third party in the provision of training and, accordingly, the claimant worker was properly subject to the (then) exception excluding apprentices from the coverage of the NMW. See also *Flett v Matheson* [2006] IRLR 277.

Prisoners, share fisherman and voluntary workers working for no remuneration are expressly not covered (*NMWA 1998, ss 43–45*). Persons who are covered by the Act include Crown employment (*NMWA 1998, s 36*), most work on board ships registered in the United Kingdom (*NMWA 1998, s 40*), work in the armed services (*NMWA 1998, s 37*) and in the House of Commons and House of Lords (*NMWA 1998, ss 38, 39*). Additionally (and importantly), home workers are expressly included in the coverage of the *Act* (*s 35*) as are agency workers (*NMWA 1998, s 34*). The definition of 'home worker', in *s 35* of the *NMWA 1998*, is intended to cover persons whose place of work is not materially under the control of the person for whom the work is being done: *IRC v Post Office* [2003] IRLR 199.

The coverage of the *NMWA* was further considered in *James v Redcats (Brands) Ltd* [2007] IRLR 296 in which the EAT had to determine if a parcel courier was a 'worker' or a 'home worker' or not covered by the *NMW* at all (as had been held by the employment tribunal). The decision of the EAT provides important and helpful guidance on the issue of 'worker' generally, the requirement of mutuality of obligation, and emphasises that in marginal cases a person is *presumed* to qualify for the *NMW* unless the contrary is established (*NMWA 1998, s 28*). As to the issue of 'homeworker', a submission that to qualify a person must have some identified 'place' from which they work (albeit not necessarily their own home) was rejected in the light of the general policy of the *NMWA*. Thus a person engaged in delivery or distribution of items could nevertheless be a 'homeworker' for the purposes of the *NMWA*.

By *Reg 2(2)* of the *National Minimum Wage Regulations 1999* an employer is exempt from the obligation to pay the NMW where the worker lives with the family and is treated as a family member "in particular as regards to the provision of accommodation and meals and the sharing of tasks and leisure activities", so long as there is no deduction from wages for food or accommodation. This exclusion is now contained in the similarly worded *regs 57* and *58* of the *2015 Regs*. The provision was intended to apply to eg au pairs, nannies and companions. In *Julio v Jose* [2012] IRLR 180, the EAT considered this exemption for live-in domestic workers. The claimants were foreign domestic workers employed in the respondents' households. The EAT held that the exemption must be narrowly interpreted and it must be shown that the relevant individual was genuinely being treated as a family member. On the facts *reg 2(2)* of the *1999 Regs* applied in respect of all the claimants and accordingly they were not entitled to the NMW. In *Nambalat v Taher* [2012] IRLR 1004 (Court of Appeal), on appeal from the decision of the EAT in *Julio v Jose* [2012] IRLR 180, the Court of Appeal upheld the decision of the EAT that the claimants fell within the exclusion in *reg 2(2)* of the *1999 Regs*. Pill LJ confirmed that the exception should be carefully and narrowly construed and cautioned that employment tribunals must be astute to ensure that the exception was not used as a device for obtaining cheap domestic labour. The same result would appear to arise under *reg 57* of the *2015 Regs*. In *Ajai v Abu* [2017] IRLR 1113 it was held that the exception was not engaged in the case of a domestic worker who was found effectively to be subject to a diminution in the rate to pay on the basis of the value of living accommodation and food.

The Secretary of State is afforded an additional power to make regulations applying the minimum wage to persons not otherwise covered (*NMWA 1998, ss 41* and *42*). By the *National Minimum Wage (Offshore Employment) Order 1999 (SI 1999/1128)* the operation of the *NMWA 1998* has been extended to workers in offshore employment, defined as employment in United Kingdom territorial waters, exploring or exploiting natural resources in the UK sector of the continental shelf or (in a foreign sector) a cross boundary petroleum field. *Section 22* of the *Employment Relations Act 1999* inserted a new *s 44A* into the *NMWA 1998*. By this section the exclusion from the entitlement to the NMW (see *ss 43–45*) is extended to cover residential members of religious communities. Accordingly, it would appear that nuns and monks will be excluded from entitlement to the NMW. The relevant provisions came into force on 25 October 1999.

The power to set the rate is conferred by *NMWA 1998, s 2* (for the current rates, see above). *NMWA 1998, s 3* gives the power to the Secretary of State to exclude persons under 26 from the operation of the National Minimum Wage or to apply a different hourly rate to such persons. The statutory role of the Low Pay Commission ("LPC") and the obligations of the Secretary of State to refer matters to the LPC are set out in *ss 5–8* and *Sch 1*.

35.9   Written records and pay statements

In addition to the fixing of the minimum wage, the *Act* casts further obligations upon employers of maintaining records in relation to hours worked and payments made to workers in a manner to be prescribed by the regulations (*NMWA 1998, s 9*). By *reg 38(1)* of the *1999 Regs* the employer is obliged to keep records 'sufficient to establish that [the worker] is remunerated at a rate at least equal to the national minimum wage'. This is reflected in the *2015 Regs* in *reg 59* generally and *reg 59(1)* in particular. The records must be kept in such a way that the information about a worker in respect of a pay reference period may be produced in a single document (*reg 38(2)* of the *1999 Regs* and see to like effect *reg 59(2)* of the *2015 Regs*). The relevant records must be kept for a period of three years (*reg 59(8)* of the *2015 Regs* formerly *reg 38(7)* of the *1999 Regs*). The records may be stored on computer (*reg 59(9)* of the *2015 Regs* and *reg 38(8)* of the *1999 Regs*). The obligation to maintain records continues to apply in the event of the *TUPE* transfer of the employment (*Mears Homecare Ltd v Bradburn* [2019] IRLR 882). Workers may require the employer to produce the records and the worker may take a copy in order to determine if the worker is in fact being paid the minimum wage (*NMWA 1998, s 10*). Failure to comply with such a request may lead to a complaint being made to an employment tribunal (*NMWA 1998, s 11*). If the tribunal upholds the complaint it shall make a declaration to that effect and order that the employer pay the worker a sum equivalent to 80 times the hourly rate of the relevant National Minimum Wage then in force (*NMWA 1998, s 11(2)*). The *Act* in *s 12* provides a power for regulations to be made to provide workers with a National Minimum Wage statement which would be similar to the right an itemised statement under the provision of *ERA 1996* (see below). Following widespread opposition to this proposal the *Regulations* in their present form contain no obligation to provide a National Minimum Wage statement.

35.10 Failure to pay the National Minimum Wage: individual remedies

A failure to pay to an employee the National Minimum Wage entitles the employee to commence proceedings in the employment tribunal or the county court to recover the difference between what has been paid and what ought to have been paid under the National Minimum Wage. By amendments to *s 17* of the *NMWA* (introduced by the *Employment Act 2008, s 8*), where a worker has been paid at a rate less than the national minimum wage he can claim the difference based upon the rate of the national minimum wage applying at the time of the arrears being determined as if it had been at that rate throughout the periods the employer was in default. The claim may be brought either as a breach of *Part II* of the *ERA 1996* as an unlawful deduction from wages or as a breach of contract claim. For claims of unlawful deductions of wages presented after 1 July 2015 the claim will be subject to a cap of two years back pay by the *Deduction from Wages (Limitation) Regulations 2014 (SI 2014/3322)* (see, further, **35.6** above). For claims presented before that date under *Part II* of the *ERA 1996* there is, however, no applicable limitation period and the period of six years under the *Limitation Act 1980, s 9* does not apply as *s 23* of the *ERA 1996* contains its own (albeit open ended period) of limitation (*Coletta v Bath Hill Court (Bournemouth) Property Management Co* [2018] IRLR 886). In relation to workers (as defined in *NMWA 1998, s 54(3)*) who are not covered by the provisions of *Part II* of the *ERA 1996* (see above) because they do not satisfy the particular definition of worker in *ERA 1996, s 230(3)*, they are deemed to be covered by the provisions by *s 18* of the *National Minimum Wage Act 1998*. An employee has a right not to suffer a detriment (*NMWA 1998, s 23*) nor to be dismissed by reason of bringing proceedings relating to the enforcement of the National Minimum Wage (*NMWA 1998, s 25* which inserts *ERA 1996, s 104A*). (See also **55.3** UNFAIR DISMISSAL – **II**.) As to proceedings in the employment tribunal, claims relating to non-payment of the NMW, may be heard by an employment tribunal chairman sitting alone (*NMWA 1998, s 27* amending *ETA 1996, s 4*). The burden of proof in such cases is unusual: it will be presumed that the employee is paid less than the minimum wage unless the employer establishes the contrary (*NMWA 1998, s 28*). This principle applies whether the proceedings are brought in the employment tribunal under *Part II* of the *ERA 1996* or for breach of contract claims whether in the county court or in the employment tribunal. Accordingly, this will be an added incentive for employers to keep proper records as required in order to be able to establish that a worker has in fact been paid, at least, the National Minimum Wage. The worker's right to present a complaint that he has been subjected to a detriment in contravention of *s 23* is contained in *s 24* which extends the powers in *ss 48* and *49* of the *ERA 1996* to detriment cases arising in relation to the National Minimum Wage. On a related point, the EAT held in *Paggetti v Cobb* [2002] IRLR 861 that, in assessing a compensatory or basic award for unfair dismissal, calculations pursuant to *ss 221–229* of the *ERA 1996* were automatically subject to the NMW. This principle applies even if the claimant has not made a specific NMW claim as it is sufficient if, prior to the dismissal, he was remunerated at a rate less than the NMW. On the facts of the instant case, the applicant was only paid £120 for a 63-hour week. Compensation was, accordingly, to be assessed based upon the NMW rate. In *Blue Chip Trading Ltd v Helbawi* [2009] IRLR 128 a student subject to immigration restrictions on working was only permitted to work up to 20 hours per week during term time but could work without restriction during vacations. He knowingly worked more than the 20 hours he was permitted to work during term time. He claimed that he had not been paid the NMW. The EAT held that it would be contrary to public policy to allow the claimant to recover for any work done during the period he was knowingly in breach of the working limits. However, he could recover the NMW in relation to those periods when he was not subject to limitations on periods of work (such as the vacations) as in that case the unlawful elements of his performance could be severed.

Devices adopted by employers to attempt to meet the minimum wage obligation without additional expenditure are unlikely to succeed in practice. In *Laird v AK Stoddart Ltd* [2001] IRLR 591, the EAT considered whether there was a breach of the *NMWA 1998* or an unlawful deduction from wages contrary to *s 13(1)* of *ERA 1996* in circumstances where the employer consolidated part of an employee's attendance allowance into the basic hourly rate for the job in order to comply with the NMW requirement (at that time £3.60 per hour). By *reg 31* of the *National Minimum Wage Regulations 1999 (Amendment) Regulations 2000 (SI 2000/1989)*, certain payments are not to be taken into account in calculating the total remuneration. This exclusion includes an attendance allowance. Accordingly, the employer sought to reduce the attendance allowance and increase the basic pay to comply with the NMW. The employees were not consulted. The EAT held that there was no breach of the *NMWA 1998*. The EAT went on, however, to hold that the reduction in the attendance allowance was an unlawful deduction from wages for the purposes of *s 13* of the *ERA 1996* as there was no consent to the change and *s 27* of the *ERA 1996* required attendance allowances to be taken into account in determining whether there was any unlawful deduction from wages. Moreover, an employer cannot minimise his obligations by attempting to exclude certain work time from the calculation of hours worked. By way of example, in *British Nursing Association v Inland Revenue (National Minimum Wage Compliance Team)* [2002] IRLR 480, the Court of Appeal upheld the decision of the EAT ([2002] EWCA Civ 494, [2001] IRLR 659) that nurses providing a night service by telephone from home were working throughout the shift period for the purposes of the *NMWA 1998*, although free to do whatever they wanted between telephone calls. The fact that there was an obligation to be ready to answer the call throughout the night shift meant that the nurses were working throughout the shift and were engaged on 'time work' within the meaning of the *NMWA 1998* (see 35.7 above). It is also worthy of note that this case was an appeal from an enforcement notice served by the Inland Revenue – an example of a State as opposed to individual remedy in relation to the *NMWA 1998* (see below). The *British Nursing Association* case was followed by the Court of Session in *Scottbridge Construction Ltd v Wright* [2003] IRLR 21. That case concerned a nightwatchman, who was permitted by his employer to sleep on the employer's premises whilst at work. It was held that he was engaged on 'time work' for the purposes of the *NMWA 1998* and, accordingly, was entitled to the NMW for all the hours he was required to be on the premises, including time asleep as, even if asleep, he could respond to an alarm when he awoke and was thus liable to perform functions at every stage during the night. Conversely, in *Walton v Independent Living Organisation Ltd* [2003] IRLR 469 the Court of Appeal held that a live-in carer, required to be on the client's premises for a consecutive period of 72 hours each week, was only entitled, under the *NMWA 1998*, to payment in respect of the time that she was actually carrying out her duties as her work was properly characterised as 'unmeasured work' (with a daily average agreement falling within *reg 28* of the *1999 Regs*) and not 'time work' and, accordingly, *British Nursing Association* and *Scottbridge Construction* (above) were distinguished (see **35.7** above). In *McCartney v Oversley House Management* [2006] ICR 510, [2006] IRLR 514 (EAT) *British Nursing Association* was applied in relation to 'on-call' work holding that a manager at a residential home with 'on call' obligations was engaged on 'salaried hours work' with the result that it was found that the employee was remunerated at a rate below that permitted by the *NMW*. In *Burrow Down Support Services Ltd v Rossiter* [2008] ICR 1172, [2008] All ER (D) 49 (Oct), the EAT applied the *British Nursing Association* decision and *Scottbridge Construction Ltd v Wright* to conclude that notwithstanding changes introduced to *reg 15* of the *NMW Regulations 1999* the previous cases remained good law so that a night sleeper at a care home who was permitted to sleep but had to be available throughout the night shifts to deal with emergencies was entitled to the NMW for each hour of the shift. The issue of time asleep was further considered in *South Manchester Abbeyfield Society Ltd v Hopkins* (UKEAT/0079/10/ZT) [2011] ICR 254, [2011] IRLR 300. The Claimants were employed in housekeeping roles with "on call" periods overnight. The EAT held that such periods when the employee was sleeping did not qualify for the NMW (although the same periods might count for the purposes of the working time regulations). The provision of *regs 15(1A)* and *16(1A)* of the *1999 Regs* would only apply to the periods that the worker was "awake for the purposes of working". This is reflected in the *2015 Regs* in *reg 32* which provides that time work includes hours when a worker is available and required to be available but that hours when a worker is "available" only includes hours when the worker is awake for the purposes of working, even if a worker by arrangement sleeps at or near a place of work" (*reg 32(2)* of the *2015 Regs* and see also *Reg 27*). In *City of Edinburgh Council v Lauder UK* EATS/0048/11 the EAT held that "on-call" time of a sheltered housing residential warden provided with accommodation was not time which qualified for the NMW, applying *British Nursing Association, Scottbridge Construction Ltd v Wright* and *South Manchester Abbeyfield Society Ltd v Hopkins* (above). In *Whittlestone v BJP Support Ltd* [2014] IRLR 176 the issue of "sleep over" work was further considered. The EAT held, applying *Burrow Down Support Services Ltd v Rossiter* (above) that the claimant qualified for the NMW. The EAT gave guidance on the approach to be adopted in distinguishing between an employee working (but permitted to sleep) and the different situation of being "on call". See also *Esparon v Slavikovska* (UKEAT/0217/12) [2014] IRLR 598 in which the EAT observed the difficulty in reconciling the previous case law but reached a decision consistent with that in *Whittlestone v BJP Support Ltd*. The issue returned to the EAT in *Shannon v Rampersad* [2015] IRLR 982. The claimant was employed as an on-call night care assistant and was permitted to sleep during the period of attendance. Applying *Reg 16(1A)* the EAT concluded that this was an "on-call" situation and, accordingly, the time spent sleeping did not qualify for the NMW. In *Governing Body of Binfield Chuch of England Primary School v Roll* [2016] IRLR 670 the EAT emphasised that the key issue in such MMW cases was the determination of the relevant terms of the contract.

Clarity (for now) has been provided in relation to sleep in work by the Court of Appeal in the important case of *Royal Mencap Society v Tomlinson-Blake* [2018] IRLR 932. Having considered *reg 32* (which provides that time work includes hours when a worker is available and required to be available but that hours when a worker is "available" only includes hours when the worker is awake for the purposes of working, even if a worker by arrangement sleeps at or near a place of work") and the previous case law, including *British Nursing Association v Inland Revenue, Scottbridge Construction Ltd v Wright* and, significantly, *Burrow Down Support Services Ltd v Rossiter* (the latter of which the Court of Appeal concluded was wrongly decided), the Court of Appeal held (Underhill LJ) that sleeping workers are available for work rather than actually working and thus come within the terms of the exception for sleep in *Reg 32*. Accordingly, the only time that counts for the NMW is time when the worker is required to be awake for the purposes of working. This is a significant shift from the earlier cases summarised above which the Court of Appeal described as "difficult and intractable" and could be now be "put to one side". An appeal to the Supreme Court is anticipated on this important issue.

35.11   Failure to pay the National Minimum Wage: state remedies

The *Act* also provides a system whereby the right to minimum wage may be enforced by state officials rather than individuals. The enforcement mechanisms were substantially modified by the *Employment Act 2008* which introduced new *s 19–19H* into the *NMWA* replacing the old *ss 19–22F* with a new regime of enforcement notices with effect from 6 April 2009. The relevant officers are HM Revenue & Customs (see *NMWA 1998, s 13*). Officers may require an employer to produce records, allow access to premises and provide information in order to determine an issue under the *Act* (*NMWA 1998, s 14*). Officers may take copies of records produced. Information which is so obtained may be used only for the purposes of the *Act* or for criminal or civil proceedings relating to the *Act* if authorised by the Secretary of State (*NMWA 1998, s 15*). By a further amendment contained in the *Employment Act 2008* the information may, however, be supplied to officers acting for the purposes of the *Employment Agencies Act 1973* and may thereafter be used for the purposes of that Act. Similarly, the information may be disclosed to a relevant worker or agency worker for the purpose of assisting the officer in the enforcement of the obligations under the *Act*.

In cases where it appears that an employer is paying less than the National Minimum Wage *s 19* of the *NMWA* provides for the issue of a 'notice of underpayment' requiring the employer to pay to the worker, within a 28-day period, sums due in accordance with the provision for calculation of arrears of the NMW under *s 17* of the *Act*.

By *s 19A*, the employer may be required to pay a financial penalty because of the failure to pay the NMW within 28 days. The amount of the penalty was originally 50% of the arrears of the NMW as calculated subject to a minimum of £100 and a maximum of £5000 (*s 19(6), (7)*) but this has increased substantially in recent years. First, in March 2014 the penalty increased to 100% of the total arrears and a cap of £20,000 per notice of underpayment (*National Minimum Wage (Variation of Financial Penalty) Regulations 2014 (SI 2014/547)*). The penalty has increased now to 200% of the arrears from 1 April 2016 (see the *National Minimum Wage (Amendment) Regulations 2016 SI 2016/68, reg 2* amending *NMWA 1998, s 19A(5A)*). Further, from 26 May 2015 the cap of £20,000 now only applies per affected worker (and not per notice of underpayment) (see the *Small Business, Enterprise and Employment Act 2015, s 152* and *Small Business, Enterprise and Employment Act 2015 (Commencement No 1) Regulations 2015 (SI 2015/1329)* which amended *NMWA 1998, s 19A*). The combination of the increase in the percentage penalty (to 200%) and the modifications to the applicable cap to a per worker cap is intended to have a strong deterrent effect on any employer failing to pay the NMW and the quantum of penalty for those who continue to fail to do so is likely to be severe. If, however, the employer complies with the notice within 14 days of its service the financial penalty is reduced by 50% (*NMWA 1998, s 19A*).

It is Government policy since 2011 to "name and shame" employers who break NMW Law. A policy document titled "Policy on HM Revenue & Customs Enforcement, Prosecutions And Naming Employers Who Flout National Minimum Wage Law" was first promulgated with effect from January 2011 by BIS in relation to the operation of the regime introduced by the *Employment Act 2008*. . The November 2017 version can be found at www.gov.uk/government/uploads/system/uploads/attachment_data/file/316652/bis -14-621-national-minimum-wage-policy-on-hm-revenue-and-customs-enforcement -prosecutions-and-naming-employers-who-break-national-minimum-wage-law -updated.pdf. The Policy was intended to identify when employers who have breached the NMW will be publicly named and is intended to raise awareness of the NMW enforcement mechanisms and to deter employers who may seek to breach the NMW obligations. The policy in sections 5.2 and 5.3 set out the general criteria to be applied for naming employers (eg knowing breach, failure to keep NMW records, obstruction of compliance officers or previous failure to pay arrears) and provision was made for employers to make representations before they were named (section 5.5).

A tougher and simpler policy was introduced in late 2013 whereby all employers who have been issued with a notice of underpayment and have not appealed or have had an appeal dismissed are to be considered for naming by means of a press release. Employers have 14 days to identify exceptional circumstances why they should not be named. The exceptions are narrowly circumscribed and limited to a risk of personal harm to an individual or their family; national security; or that naming would not be in the public interest. It follows that in a normal case naming will follow as a matter of course.

A right of appeal against a notice of underpayment lies to the employment tribunal (*s 19C*). In the event of non-compliance with a notice of underpayment, an officer may present a complaint for unlawful deduction of wages on behalf of relevant workers (*s 19D*). Non-compliance with a notice to pay a penalty may be enforced in the county court by the relevant officer (*s 19E*). Provision is also made for withdrawal and replacement of notices of underpayment (*ss 19F, 19G*).

In *IRC v Bebb Travel plc* [2002] IRLR 783 the EAT had held that, on a proper construction of the legislation, compliance officers were not entitled, pursuant to *s 19* of the *NMWA 1998*, to serve an enforcement notice on the respondent employer requiring it to pay arrears of wages in respect of employees who had ceased employment before the notice was issued. This unsatisfactory result was reversed by the passage of the *National Minimum Wage (Enforcement Notices) Act 2003* which came into force on 8 July 2003. As a result *s 19* of the *NMWA 1998* provides that an enforcement notice may be served on an employer who has not paid an employee a rate of pay at least equal to the NMW whether or not the worker is still employed. The further revisions introduced by the *Employment Act 2008* maintained this position. Thus *s 19(1)* provides that a notice of underpayment may relate to any period for which the worker *at any time* qualified for the NMW.

Finally, if the preceding enforcement measures are to no avail, there is a criminal offence created for employers who wilfully breach their obligations to workers under the Act. It is an offence:

(i)   to fail to refuse or wilfully neglect to pay the minimum wage (*NMWA 1998, s 31(1)*);

(ii)   to fail to keep records as required by *s 9* (*NMWA 1998, s 31(2)*);

(iii)   to falsify *s 9* records (*NMWA 1998, s 31(3)*);

(iv)   to knowingly provide false information to an officer (*NMWA 1998, s 31(4)*); or

(v)   to obstruct or delay an officer or to refuse to answer questions or furnish information (*NMWA 1998, s 31(5)*).

Each offence under *s 31* was originally only punishable on summary conviction with a fine not exceeding level 5 on the Standard Scale (see **1.10 INTRODUCTION**) (*NMWA 1998, s 31(9)*). In the case of a body corporate, if an offence is committed with the consent, connivance or by the neglect of an officer of the company, that officer, as well as the body corporate, is guilty of the offence (*NMWA 1998, s 32*). Proceedings for offences under the *Act* were limited to the Magistrates Court but with amendments introduced by the *Employment Act 2008*, the potential for greater penalties is introduced as the offence, in serious cases, may be tried on indictment as well as summarily.

The ability to effectively police whether employers are abiding by their obligations to pay the NMW is enhanced by the provisions of *s 39* of the *Employment Relations Act 1999* which permits revenue officials to disclose information which comes into their possession in the course of carrying out the function of Commissioners of the Inland Revenue to other agencies for the purposes of the *National Minimum Wage Act 1998*. The information may be disclosed to the Secretary of State for any purpose relating to the *National Minimum Wage Act 1998*. That information may be supplied by the Secretary of State for any purpose relating to the *National Minimum Wage Act 1998*. That information may be supplied by the Secretary of State to any person acting under *s 13(1)(b)* of the *NMWA 1998* or to the agricultural wages inspectors.

35.12   OTHER DEDUCTIONS FROM WAGES

In *Sim v Rotherham Metropolitan Borough Council* [1986] ICR 897, [1986] IRLR 391, it was held that the principle of equitable set-off applied to contracts of employment. In other words, where an employee's breach of contract has caused the employer loss, the employer is in principle entitled to retain for himself sums representing the amount of that loss when he pays the employee's wages. This saves the employer from paying the full wage and suing for damages for breach of contract. However, the court retains a discretion to disallow the set-off. Further, if there is no contractual provision or written consent permitting a deduction by way of set-off, for the employer to make such a deduction may contravene the wages provisions of the *ERA 1996* (see **35.4** above; this will not be an obstacle where the deduction is made for taking part in industrial action).

The leading authority on the employer's right to pay less than the full contractual wage where the employee refuses to carry out all his contractual duties is the decision of the House of Lords in *Miles v Wakefield Metropolitan District Council* [1987] ICR 368, [1987] IRLR 193. A superintendent registrar with a normal working week of 37 hours, including three hours on Saturday mornings, took industrial action and refused to conduct weddings on Saturdays. He worked normally during the rest of the week. It was held that the council was entitled to deduct $^3/_{37}$ths from his normal salary, even though the registrar would have been willing to perform duties other than the conduct of weddings on Saturdays (in fact, the council instructed him to work normally or not at all).

Lord Brightman and Lord Templeman took the view that a worker not performing the full range of his contractual duties was not entitled to his full wages but to a *quantum meruit* payment based upon the value of the work actually done. The other law Lords in *Miles* did not, however, express a view on the *quantum meruit* point. An employer placed in such a position by a partially performing employee must make it clear to the employee that he is not waiving that employee's breach of contract in failing to perform the full range of his contractual duties. He should state that, whilst the breach continues, he will make a specified adjustment to the employee's wages.

However, an employer cannot be *compelled* to accept and pay for something significantly less than the efficient performance of all the employee's contractual duties (*MacPherson v Lambeth London Borough Council* [1988] IRLR 470). In *Wiluszynski v Tower Hamlets London Borough Council* [1989] IRLR 259 the Court of Appeal, dealing with a council employee who had refused to perform a material part of his duties, held that the council was entitled to withhold the whole of his pay. This decision was arrived at only because the council had clearly informed the employee that if he attempted to undertake limited work, he would not be paid for it. See also *British Telecommunications plc v Ticehurst* [1992] ICR 383, [1992] IRLR 219. In *Spackman v London Metropolitan University* [2007] IRLR 744 (Co Ct) - a test case relating to claimant lecturers - some of the issues raised by *Sim, Miles* and *Wiluszynski* arose again for consideration. In *Spackman* recovery was sought of deductions made by the university in respect of days in which the lecturers participated in industrial action short of strike and thus provided partial performance. Rejecting the claim to full pay on the basis that an employer is not obliged to accept partial performance, the judge went on to hold that employees participating in collective industrial action have no right to remuneration at all by way of *quantum meruit* and if they present for work and undertake some duties or even the substantial majority of those duties they run the risk of being paid nothing by the employer. The fact that the university had paid anything at all was more than the employees were legally entitled to expect. In *Luke v Stoke-on-Trent City Council* [2007] EWCA Civ 761, [2007] ICR 1678, [2007] IRLR 777 an employee refused to return to their job unless conditions were met and refused a temporary transfer to a different location, following an investigation into the employee's allegations of bullying. The employer's decision to stop wages was upheld by the Court of Appeal on the application of the principle, recognised in *Miles* (above) of 'no work, no pay'.

In *Ekwelem v Excel Passenger Services* (UKEAT/0438/12) the EAT considered the effect of the inability to work due to a criminal charge. The orthodox position is that wages are payable to an employee if the employee is ready and willing to work but is prevented from doing so by reason of unavoidable impediment. In *Burns v Santander UK plc* [2011] IRLR 639 an employee was not entitled to wages during a period on remand which had resulted in conviction as the impediment was avoidable. In *Ekwelem* the employee was, however, acquitted. The EAT remitted the case to the tribunal for further consideration on the issue of whether the employee was entitled to wages for the relevant period he was unable to work due to the pending charge. From the EAT's judgment (UKEAT/0291/15/DA, UKEAT/0292/15/DA, [2016] All ER (D) 288 (Feb)) it appears possible that different conditions may apply so as to distinguish *Burns* in cases where the employee is acquitted of the charge which caused the inability to carry out work. In *North West Anglia NHS Foundation Trust v Gregg* [2019] EWCA Civ 387 the issue under consideration was a suspension and the right to be paid. The Court of Appeal held that if an employee does not work they must show that they were willing to work to avoid deduction. If the employee is willing to work and the inability to work was the result of a third-party decision or external constraint, any deduction of pay may, in the particular circumstances, be unlawful. However, an inability to work due to a lawful suspension imposed by way of sanction will permit deduction of pay. Conversely, inability to work due to an unavoidable impediment may render the deduction unlawful. In the case of an employee accused of a criminal offence the issue cannot be determined merely by reference to ultimate guilt or innocence or whether bail was subsequently granted.

Where an employee is actually required to work only on, say, 245 days in the year, and that employee participates in a one-day strike, the question frequently arises as to whether the employer is entitled to deduct $^1/_{245}$ or only $^1/_{365}$ of the annual salary in respect of that day. It is thought that this may depend upon the precise terms of the contract of employment, and upon the nature of the work done (eg does it require extensive preparation outside actual working hours?). In *Smith v Bexley London Borough Council*, IDS Brief 448, p 5, a county court judge took the approach more favourable to the employer. However, in *Re Bank of Credit and Commerce International SA* [1994] IRLR 282, Evans-Lombe J, although approving this approach where the question was what a lost day had cost the employer, held that, when considering what part of a monthly salary had accrued by the date of a dismissal, the total number of days in that month had to be taken into account, and not merely working days; this point was not considered on appeal. (See also *Thames Water Utilities v Reynolds* [1996] IRLR 186, EAT applying *Re Bank of Credit and Commerce International SA*.) In *Leisure Leagues UK Ltd v Maconnachie* [2002] IRLR 600, however, in the context of holiday pay, the EAT held that the correct denominator was the number of working days in the year (in this case, 233 days) and the *Thames Water* decision was distinguished on the basis it predated the *Working Time Regulations*. The issue of holidays working days and deductions arose for determination in *Cooper v Isle of Wight College* [2007] EWHC 2831 (QB), [2008] IRLR 124 in the context of apportioning annual salary in order to calculate a day's pay for the purpose of deductions to be made for participation in days of industrial action. The employer contended that the employees only provided actual services on 228 days of the year (deducting 32 days of statutory and contractual holiday) and that this should be used for calculating the value of a day's pay. Rejecting this argument it was held that the paid holidays had to be brought into account for the apportionment exercise so that the wage payable for any one day was $^1/_{260}$th of the annual wage and not $^1/_{228}$th as the employer had contended. In *Amey v Peter Symonds College* [2014] IRLR 206 (QBD) the issue arose again in the context of industrial action. The case involved a teacher who had participated in two days of strike action. The employer made deductions based on 1/260th for each strike day (based on working days). The teacher contended, relying on the *Apportionment Act 1870, s 2* and *Leisure Leagues UK Ltd v Maconnachie* and *Re BCCI* (above), that $^1/_{365}$ths should be used. It was held, applying both *s 2* and *s 7* (stipulations that apportionment does not apply) of the *Apportionment Act 1870* and applying *Cooper v Isle of Wight College* (above) that *s 7* would apply where the terms of the contract were inconsistent with apportionment on a calendar day basis under *s 2*. Here the contract expressly stipulated the working hours and days and holidays. Accordingly, the employer was correct to use $^1/_{260}$ths as the basis for deductions. The Supreme Court has now had the opportunity to consider the effect of the *Apportionment Act 1870* in *Hartley v King Edward VI College* [2017] IRLR 763, [2017] UKSC 39. This was another strike case and the issue was whether pay should be deducted for strike days at the rate of $^1/_{365}$ or $^1/_{260}$ (reflecting the number of working days). At first instance it was determined that $^1/_{260}$ths should be used applying *Amey v Peter Symonds College* (*supra*). This was the correct result said the Court of Appeal but for different reasons. The Court of Appeal held that the Apportionment Act 1870 applied to employment and remuneration (applying Item *Software (UK) Ltd v Fassihi* [2004] EWCA Civ 1244, [2004] IRLR 928) but that *s 2* of the *Act* does not compel apportionment on a calendar day basis (ie $^1/_{365}$ths). The form of appointment to be applied was to be determined in each case from the proper construction of the contract. In that case the proper construction required a $^1/_{365}$ths apportionment.

The court will not normally make mandatory interlocutory orders for the payment of wages; in clear cases, the employee's remedy is to apply for summary judgment (*Jakeman v South West Thames Regional Health Authority and London Ambulance Service* [1990] IRLR 62).

35.13 OVERPAYMENT

Payments made under a mistake of law or fact are, in principle, recoverable by the party who made the payment. This would extend to a mistaken overpayment of wages. However, if the employee in good faith changes his position by incurring expenditure which he would not otherwise have incurred, he may have a defence in whole or part to any subsequent claim to recover the overpayment (*Lipkin Gorman (a firm) v Karpnale Ltd* [1991] 2 AC 548, [1992] 4 All ER 512; see also *Avon County Council v Howlett* [1983] 1 All ER 1073, [1983] 1 WLR 605, [1983] IRLR 171).

35.14 ITEMISED PAY STATEMENTS

An employer is required to give any employee or worker of his, at or before the time at which any payment of wages or salary is made to him, a pay statement in writing containing the following particulars:

(a)   the gross amount of the wages or salary;

(b)   the amounts of any variable and any fixed deductions from that gross amount and the purposes for which they are made, unless a statement of fixed deductions has been given to the employee (see **35.15** below);

(c)   the net amount of wages or salary payable; and

(d)   where different parts of the net amount are paid in different ways, the amount and method of payment of each part payment.

(e)   where the amount of wages varies by reference to time worked the total number of hours worked in respect of the variable amount of wages or salary as either a single aggregate figure or separate figures for different types of work or rates of pay.

(*ERA 1996, s 8.*) The application of the section was extended to workers (previously limited to employees) from 6 April 2019 by the *Employment Rights Act 1996 (Itemised Pay Statement) (Amendment) (No 2) Order 2018 (SI 2018/529)*). The requirement to itemise variable pay in relation to time worked in *ERA 1996 s 8(e)* was introduced with effect from April 2019 by the *Employment Rights Act 1996 (Itemised Pay Statement) (Amendment) Order 2018, SI 2018/147*.

Tips paid by customers to a waiter in a restaurant were held not to be wages within the meaning of *EPCA, s 8* (now *ERA 1996, s 8*), and his employers were therefore not required to give particulars of such tips or of payments from them to the manager of the restaurant (*Cofone v Spaghetti House Ltd* [1980] ICR 155).

35.15   Statement of fixed deductions

Provided that the employer has given in writing a standing statement of fixed deductions, there is no need to itemise fixed deductions on a worker's pay statement, but simply to state the total amount of the deductions. This standing statement should give the following information:

(a)   the amount of each deduction;

(b)   the intervals at which the deduction is to be made; and

(c)   the purpose for which it is made.

(*ERA 1996, s 9(1)–(3)*).

A statement of fixed deductions may be amended, whether by the addition of a new deduction or by a change in the particulars or cancellation of an existing deduction, by notice in writing containing particulars of the amendment given by the employer to the employee (*ERA 1996, s 9(3)*).

It must be remembered that a standing statement of fixed deductions only remains effective for 12 months from the date on which it is given to the employee. Before the expiry of the 12-month period, the employer must re-issue the statement, together with any amendments, in consolidated form (*ERA 1996, s 9(4)*).

35.16   Exclusions

The requirement for an employer to provide an employee with a pay statement does not apply:

(a)   to persons engaged in police service (*ERA 1996, s 200(1)*);

(b)   to employment as a merchant seaman, or as a master or member of the crew of a fishing vessel where the employee is remunerated only by a share in the profits or gross earnings of the vessel (*ERA 1996, s 199(2)(4)*).

(c)   to members of the armed forces (*ERA 1996, s 192*).

35.17   Application to an employment tribunal

If an employer or worker does not give any employee of his a pay statement, the employee may refer the matter to an employment tribunal to determine what particulars ought to have been included in a statement so as to comply with the requirements in **35.9** above (*ERA 1996, s 11(1)*). An employee or worker may also apply to a tribunal, as may an employer, to determine provisions which should have been included in a pay statement or a standing statement of fixed deductions, but which have been omitted (*ERA 1996, s 11(2)*).

Any application concerning a pay statement must be brought while the employee is still employed by the relevant employer, or within three months of the date on which the employment ceased (*ERA 1996, s 11(4)*) or within such further period as the tribunal consider treasonable where satisfied that it was not reasonably practicable for the application to be made before the end of the period of three months (*ERA s 11(4)(b)*).

35.18 Tribunal order

Where, on a reference under these provisions, an employment tribunal finds that an employer has failed to give an employee or worker a pay statement or that a pay statement or standing statement of fixed deductions does not, in relation to a deduction, contain the particulars required to be included in that statement, the tribunal will make a declaration to that effect.

Where the tribunal further finds that any unnotified deductions have been made from the pay of the employee during the period of 13 weeks immediately preceding the date of the application (whether or not such deductions were made in breach of the contract of employment), the tribunal may order the employer to pay the employee a sum not exceeding the aggregate of the unnotified deductions so made (*ERA 1996, s 12(3)–(5)*; see **35.6** above for the relationship between *ERA 1996, s 11* and *ss 23–25*).

For example, an employee may be required by his contract of employment to pay subscriptions to a sports club of £10 per week. If the employer does not notify the employee of this deduction, either in a note with his pay packet or in a statement of fixed deductions, then, on an application to an employment tribunal, the tribunal may order the employer to repay the employee a sum of up to £130, which is equivalent to the employee's subscriptions for the previous 13 weeks.

In *Milsom v Leicestershire County Council* [1978] IRLR 433, an employment tribunal held that an employer was in breach of the requirement to give an itemised pay statement. A sum had been deducted from the employee's wages, the only explanation being that it was a 'miscellaneous deduction/payment'. The tribunal ordered the employer to pay £25 to the employee for the failure to give a proper statement, despite the fact that the employee was well aware of the reason for the deduction and that the employer was entitled under the contract between the parties to make such a deduction.

However, in *Scott v Creager* [1979] ICR 403, [1979] IRLR 162, the EAT held that where an employer had made unnotified deductions, an employment tribunal had not erred in awarding a sum to the employee equal to the amount by which the pay she actually received fell short of the net pay she should have received.

35.19 GRATUITIES AND TRONCS

The authorities relating to a system whereby customers' gratuities are pooled in a 'tronc' and distributed among employees (typically, restaurant staff) were reviewed by the Court of Appeal in *Nerva v RL & G Ltd* [1996] IRLR 461. This was a case dealing with whether payments out of a tronc counted towards the minimum remuneration required under a Wages Council order; it establishes that a gratuity left by a customer as a cash tip is normally held on trust for the benefit of the restaurant's employees, whereas payments received by those employees in respect of such a gratuity added to a customer's cheque or credit-card payment are not held on trust, but instead form part of their remuneration. The case, under the name *Nerva v United Kingdom* (Application 42295/98) [2002] IRLR 815, went to the European Court of Human Rights (see **31.7** HUMAN RIGHTS). The ECHR upheld the decision of the Court of Appeal concluding that an employer could use such payments in discharge of remuneration obligations to the waiter employees and that such a practice did not amount to a breach of the applicants' rights (under Article 1 of Protocol No 1 to the

European Convention on Human Rights) to peaceful enjoyment of their possessions. On the exclusion with effect from 1 October 2009 of such payments from the calculation of whether there has been compliance with the NMW and for the government's code of practice on such payments, see **35.7** above.

35.20 PAY ON TERMINATION OF EMPLOYMENT

Upon termination of employment, an employer should pay to the former employee any of the following sums which may be due, depending upon the circumstances: wages in lieu of notice (see **49.9** TERMINATION OF EMPLOYMENT); accrued holiday pay (see **30.4A** HOLIDAYS); reimbursement of expenses; other contractual payments; and redundancy pay (see REDUNDANCY – I **(39)**).

If the employee is paid weekly or monthly and the employment has terminated part–way through the week or month, he will be taken to have earned a rateable proportion of his wages or salary for that period. This is the result of applying the *Apportionment Act 1870*, which provides by *s 2* that (*inter alia*) all annuities and other periodical payments in the nature of income shall be considered as accruing from day to day, and shall be apportionable in respect of time accordingly. 'Annuities' are defined by *s 5* to include salaries and pensions. It is possible to exclude apportionment by an express stipulation to the contrary (*Apportionment Act 1870, s 7*). The *Act* is also capable of being applied to a payment such as an annual bonus when the employee leaves part–way through the year (see, on the application of the *Apportionment Act 1870, Thames Water Utilities v Reynolds* [1996] IRLR 186, EAT and *Re Bank of Credit and Commerce International SA* [1994] IRLR 282) and compare *Leisure Leagues UK Ltd v Maconnachie* [2002] IRLR 600 and *Amey v Peter Symonds College* [2014] IRLR 206 (QBD) at **35.12** above. See also *Item Software (UK) Ltd v Fassihi* [2004] EWCA Civ 1244, [2004] IRLR 928 and now *Hartley v King Edward VI College* [2015] IRLR 650 (at **35.12** above).

35.21 GUARANTEE PAYMENTS FOR WORKLESS DAYS

The *Employment Protection Act 1975* created certain rights to payment when no work is done owing to circumstances beyond the control of the employee. These provisions are now contained in the *Employment Rights Act 1996 ('ERA 1996')*. These are of benefit, chiefly, to hourly paid employees and to workers on piece rates.

35.22 RIGHT TO GUARANTEE PAYMENT

Workless day

Where any employee, throughout a day during any part of which he would normally be required to work in accordance with his contract of employment, is not provided with work by his employer by reason of:

(a)   a diminution in the requirements of the employer's business for work of the kind which the employee is employed to do; or

(b)   any other occurrence affecting the normal working of the employer's business in relation to work of the kind which the employee is employed to do,

he is, subject to certain exceptions, entitled to a guarantee payment (*ERA 1996, s 28(1)–(3)*).

A threatened power cut is such an occurrence (*Miller v Harry Thornton (Lollies) Ltd* [1978] IRLR 430).

If a worker can turn down work given to her she is not normally 'required to work' within the meaning of the section and is not entitled to a guarantee payment when not provided with any work (*Mailway (Southern) Ltd v Willsher* [1978] ICR 511, [1978] IRLR 322; *York and Reynolds v Colledge Hosiery Co Ltd* [1978] IRLR 53). It had been held in a series of old cases at employment tribunal level that variations to the contract to reduce the days worked may mean that the employee would no longer normally be required to work on the workless days. See *Clemens v Peter Richards Ltd (t/a John Bryan)* [1977] IRLR 332 and *Daley v Strathclyde Regional Council* [1977] IRLR 414. Until recently there was no consideration of these provisions by the higher courts. In *Abercrombie v Aga Rangemaster Ltd* [2013] IRLR 953 this issue was, for the first time, considered by the Court of Appeal. In that case there was a formal agreed variation to the employees' contracts of employment, albeit for a fixed temporal period (in that case a 6 month period in which Fridays were not to be worked with an equivalent reduction in pay). The EAT had held that the effect of this was that Friday ceased to be a day on which the employees would be normally be required to work for the purposes of *ERA 1996, ss 28(1)* and *30(1)* and that there was no requirement in *s 28(1)* of the *ERA 1996* for any variation of the employees' contract to be permanent in order to change the employees' normal working hours and thus disentitle the employees to guarantee payments. Reversing the decision of the EAT, the Court of Appeal held that the issue under *s 28(1)* was that of the meaning of "normally". On the facts, notwithstanding a temporary, albeit formal, variation of the contracts, Friday remained a day on which the employees were "normally required to work" and thus were entitled to guarantee payments.

If an employer provides some although not the usual amount of work during a day, that is not considered a 'workless day' for which an employee is entitled to a guarantee payment. Examples of situations which may cause a day to be 'workless' are a lack of orders, under (*a*), or any other occurrence such as a power cut affecting the normal working of the employer's business in relation to work of the kind which the employee is employed to do, under (*b*).

Where employment begins before midnight and extends into the next day, the period of employment for the purpose of deciding which is the workless day is defined as follows:

(i)   if the employment before midnight is, or would normally be, of longer duration than that after midnight, that period of employment is treated as falling wholly on the first day; and

(ii)   in any other case, that period of employment is treated as falling wholly on the second day.

(*ERA 1996, s 28(4), (5)*.)

35.23 Qualifying period

In order to qualify for the entitlement, an employee must have been continuously employed for one month ending with the day before the workless day (*ERA 1996, s 29(1)*). (See CONTINUOUS EMPLOYMENT (7).)

An employee who is employed:

(a)   under a contract for a fixed term of three months or less; or

(b)   under a contract made in contemplation of the performance of a specific task which is not expected to last for more than three months,

is not entitled to a guarantee payment unless he has been continuously employed for a period of more than three months ending with the day before that in respect of which the guarantee payment is claimed (*ERA 1996, s 29(2)*).

35.24 Exclusions

Trade disputes. An employee is not entitled to a guarantee payment in respect of a workless day if the failure to provide him with work occurs in consequence of a strike, lock–out or other industrial action involving any employee of his employer or of an associated employer (*ERA 1996, s 29(3)*; for 'associated employer' see **7.9**(a) Continuous Employment). Thus, a dispute with his employer involving members of another union at his workplace or of employees of his employer at a factory in another part of the country, which causes a halt in production, disentitles an employee from receiving a guarantee payment.

Offer of suitable alternative work. An employee is not entitled to a guarantee payment in respect of a workless day if:

(a)   his employer has offered to provide alternative work for that day which is suitable in all the circumstances (whether or not it is work which the employee is employed to perform under his contract) and the employee has unreasonably refused that offer; or

(b)   he does not comply with reasonable requirements imposed by his employer with a view to ensuring that his services are available.

(*ERA 1996, s 29(4), (5)*.)

Both objective and subjective tests are involved in deciding what is 'suitable' and 'reasonable' within the meaning of (*a*) above. No general rules can be laid down, but what tribunals will have in mind are pay, hours, geographical location and skill required. So far as (*b*) is concerned, clearly, if an employer asked an employee to telephone to find out whether work was available, that would be considered a reasonable requirement. It has been held that a wide variety of alternative work may be suitable if it is only temporary. See *Purdy v Willowbrook International Ltd* [1977] **IRLR** 388, IT; *Meadows v Faithful Overalls Ltd* [1977] **IRLR** 330, IT.

35.25 Amount of payment

The amount of the guarantee payment payable in respect of any day is the sum produced by multiplying the *number of normal working hours* in that day by the *guaranteed hourly rate* (*ERA 1996, s 30(1)*).

The 'guaranteed hourly rate' is the amount of one week's pay (see below **35.32**) divided by the number of normal working hours in that week. In calculating 'normal working hours' where the number of working hours in a week fluctuate, one takes the average number of working hours over the 12 weeks ending with the last complete week before the day in respect of which the guarantee payment is payable. If the employee has not been employed for 12 weeks, a calculation is made having regard to:

(a)   the average number of normal working hours in a week which the employee could expect in accordance with the terms of his contract; and

(b)   the average number of such hours of other employees engaged in relevant comparable employment with the same employer.

(*ERA 1996, s 30(2)–(4)*).

If any employee's contract has been varied or a new contract has been entered into for short–time working, the calculation is made by reference to the last day that the original contract was in force (*ERA 1996, s 30(5)*).

The amount of a guarantee payment payable to an employee in respect of any day will not exceed £30.00 (with effect from 6 April 2020: *Employment Rights (Increase of Limits) Order 2020, SI 2020/205*). The previous maximum was £29.00. Further, such payments cannot exceed five days in any period of three months. The present maximum annual liability is therefore £600 (*ERA 1996, s 31*). Any contractual remuneration paid to an employee in respect of a workless day goes towards discharging any statutory liability of the employer to pay a guarantee payment in respect of that day and, conversely, any guarantee payment paid in respect of a day goes towards discharging any liability of the employer to pay contractual remuneration in respect of that day (*ERA 1996, s 32*). Thus, if any employee is paid on a weekly or monthly basis, irrespective of the work actually done, these payments will go towards discharging any statutory liability. Contractual payments made in respect of any workless days are to be taken into account when calculating the maximum number of days within the three-month period for which the employee is entitled to a payment (*Cartwright v G Clancey Ltd* [1983] ICR 552, [1983] IRLR 355).

The Secretary of State may by order exempt certain industries from these provisions where there is in force a collective agreement or an agricultural wages order which complies with certain conditions (*ERA 1996, s 35*).

35.26 Remedy for failure to make payment

An employee may present a complaint to an employment tribunal that his employer has failed to pay the whole or any part of a guarantee payment to which he is entitled. The tribunal, if it finds the complaint well-founded, will order the employer to pay the complainant the amount of guarantee payment which it finds due to him (*ERA 1996, s 34(1), (3)*). Such a complaint must be presented to a tribunal before the end of the period of *three months* beginning with the workless day (or within such further period as the tribunal considers reasonable, when it is satisfied that it was not reasonably practicable for the complaint to be presented within the period of three months; see **19.20** EMPLOYMENT TRIBUNALS – **I**) (*ERA 1996, s 34(2)*).

35.27 MEDICAL SUSPENSION PAYMENTS

Statutes and regulations safeguard workpeople from exposure to health hazards. They may provide, for example, that a factory be closed when the atmosphere in it becomes contaminated. At common law, if a factory closed down in compliance with regulations relating to the health of the factory workers, the workers were not entitled to be paid for the time lost unless their contracts provided otherwise. However, now where an employee is suspended from work by his employer on medical grounds in compliance with any law or regulation concerning the health and safety of workers, he may be entitled to be paid remuneration by his employer while he is so suspended for a period not exceeding 26 weeks. The provision which leads to him being suspended must be one of those for the time being specified in *ERA 1996, s 64(3)*. At present only the *Control of Lead at Work Regulations 1980 (SI 1980/1248), reg 16*, the *Ionising Radiations Regulations 1985 (SI 1985/1333), reg 16* and the *Control of Substances Hazardous to Health Regulations 1988 (SI 1988/1657), reg 11*, are so specified. (See also **33.47** MATERNITY AND PARENTAL RIGHTS for an employee's right to remuneration when suspended on maternity grounds.)

35.28 Qualifying conditions

An employee will be regarded as suspended from work only if, and so long as, he continues to be employed by his employer but is not provided with work or does not perform the work he normally performed before the suspension (*ERA 1996, s 64(5)*).

In order to be entitled to claim a medical suspension payment, the employee must have been continuously employed for a period of one month ending with the day before that on which the suspension begins (*ERA 1996, s 65(1)*).

An employee who is employed:

(a)   under a contract for a fixed term of three months or less; or

(b)   under a contract made in contemplation of the performance of a specific task which is not expected to last for more than three months,

is not entitled to a medical suspension payment unless he has been continuously employed for a period of more than three months ending with the day before that on which the suspension begins (*ERA 1996, s 65(2)*).

For continuity of employment, see Continuous Employment (7).

35.29 Exclusions from right to payment

These are:

(a)   An employee will not be entitled to a medical suspension payment in respect of any period during which he is incapable of work by reason of disease or bodily or mental disablement (*ERA 1996, s 65(3)*).

(b)   An employee is not entitled to a medical suspension payment in respect of any period during which:

    (i)   his employer offered to provide him with suitable alternative work, whether or not it was work the employee was engaged to perform; and

    (ii)   the employee unreasonably refused to perform that work.

    (*ERA 1996, s 65(4)(a)*.)

If, for example, an employee is engaged as a machine operator in the toolroom of a factory and the toolroom has to be closed for medical reasons for a few weeks, it may be considered unreasonable for the operative to refuse to work on a similar type of machine in a different part of the factory, provided he is offered the same rate of pay as that which he had previously received.

(c)   An employee is not entitled to a medical suspension payment in respect of any period during which he did not comply with reasonable requirements imposed by his employer with a view to ensuring that his services were available (*ERA 1996, s 65(4)(b)*).

Therefore, if an employer sent a man home because his workplace was medically unsafe but asked him to telephone each day to find out whether his services were required, and the employee failed to do so, he may be deprived of his right to a medical suspension payment.

35.30 Amount of payment

The employee is entitled to a week's pay in respect of every week of suspension (with proportionate reduction for part of a week) (*ERA 1996, s 69(1)*). A week's pay is calculated in accordance with *ERA 1996, ss 220–229* (see below **35.32**). If an employee is entitled to payment during suspension on medical grounds by a term of his contract, he will only be able to claim from the employer the additional amount by which his statutory entitlement exceeds the contractual entitlement. Any payment under a contract goes to discharge the statutory liability and vice versa (*ERA 1996, s 69(2), (3)*). Thus, if an employee's week's pay is £538 (the same as the statutory week's pay; see the *Employment Rights (Increase of Limits) Order 2020 (SI 2020/205)* with effect from 6 April 2020 and, on suspension from work on medical grounds, he is contractually entitled to £300, he can claim £238 as a statutory medical suspension payment. If, however, the week's pay is £600 and the contractual entitlement £300, the statutory medical suspension payment will still be capped at £238.

35.31 Remedy for failure to make payment

If an employer fails to make a medical suspension payment, an employee may present a complaint to an employment tribunal in respect of that payment (*ERA 1996, s 70(1)*).

The complaint must be presented to the tribunal within three months beginning with the day in respect of which the claim is made (or within such further period as the tribunal considers reasonable, in a case where it is satisfied that it was not reasonably practicable for the complaint to be presented within the period of three months) (*ERA 1996, s 70(2)*; for reasonable practicability, see **19.20** EMPLOYMENT TRIBUNALS – I).

Where an employment tribunal finds a complaint well founded, it will order the employer to pay the complainant the amount of remuneration which it finds is due to him (*ERA 1996, s 70(3)*).

35.32 'A WEEK'S PAY'

The amount of money payable under several of the statutory employment protection rights depends upon a calculation based on the week's pay of the employee concerned. For example, a week's pay is the basis for the calculation of a redundancy payment and of the basic award in a claim for unfair dismissal.

The calculation of a week's pay differs according to whether the employee is in employment for which there are normal working hours or whether he is in employment for which there are no normal working hours.

The statutory rules governing 'a week's pay' are set out in *ERA 1996, ss 221–229*.

35.33 EMPLOYMENTS FOR WHICH THERE ARE NORMAL WORKING HOURS

If the employee's normal working hours are the same every week and his remuneration for employment in normal working hours does not vary with the amount of work done in the period, the amount of a week's pay is the amount which is payable by the employer under the contract of employment in force on the calculation date if the employee works throughout his normal working hours in a week (*ERA 1996, s 221(2)*). One possible complication is illustrated by *Agard v Westminster Kingsway College* (UKEATPA/0767/10/SM) (14 December 2010, unreported). Here the employee worked 20 hours per week for 40 weeks of the year but could not take holiday during this (term–time) 40 week period. The holiday was 5.39 weeks. The EAT held that in such circumstances the calculation of a week's pay should add in the holiday weeks giving 45.39 working weeks by which the annual salary would be divided. See also *Gilbert v Barnsley Metropolitan Borough Council* (UKEAT/674/00) [2002] All ER (D) 45 (Apr).

Where the amount of the remuneration varies with the amount of work done but the number of normal working hours does not vary, the amount of a week's pay is the amount of remuneration for the number of normal working hours in a week calculated at the *average* hourly rate of remuneration payable by the employer to the employee in respect of the period of 12 weeks:

(a)   where the calculation date is the last day of a week, ending with that week;

(b)   in any other case, ending with the last complete week before the calculation date.

(*ERA 1996, s 221(3)*.)

This is the provision which must be applied even where the variation may be attributable to the amount of work done by other employees (*Keywest Club Ltd (t/a Veeraswamys Restaurant) v Choudhury* [1988] IRLR 51, EAT).

Where the employee is required under his contract to work during normal working hours on days of the week or at times of the day which differ from week to week or over a longer period so that the remuneration payable for or apportionable to any week varies, the amount of a week's pay is based upon the average remuneration paid and the average number of hours worked in the last 12 weeks before the calculation date (*ERA 1996, s 222*).

For the purposes of these calculations, weeks in which the employee was not paid because he was not working are excluded, and a previous working week is brought into account (*ERA 1996, s 223(1), (2)*).

35.34   Overtime

In a case where remuneration for employment in normal working hours is unaffected by any variable element in the pay structure, overtime hours and payment for them only fall within the calculation if the employer is obliged to provide, and the employee is obliged to work, the overtime (*Tarmac Roadstone Holdings Ltd v Peacock* [1973] 2 All ER 485, [1973] 1 WLR 594, [1973] ICR 273, [1973] IRLR 157; *Gascol Conversions Ltd v Mercer* [1974] ICR 420, [1974] IRLR 155). Thus, where overtime is voluntary and there is no such variable element, a week's pay is simply the contractual amount payable for the normal working hours in a full week, excluding overtime (*ERA 1996, ss 221(2), 234(1), (2)*). The same definition of a week's pay applies where a minimum number of hours of overtime is fixed by the contract of employment except that, in such a case, 'normal working hours' include that minimum number of hours of compulsory overtime (*ERA 1996, s 234(3)*).

However, where there is a variable element in the employee's remuneration dependent on results, eg piece rates, productivity bonus, or commission, the amount of a week's pay is to be calculated in accordance with *ERA 1996, s 221(3)* and *223(3)*. Section *223(3)* provides as follows:

> 'Where, in arriving at the (average) . . .   hourly rate of remuneration, account has to be taken of remuneration payable for, or apportionable to, work done in hours other than normal working hours, and the amount of that remuneration was greater than it would have been if the work had been done in normal working hours (or, in a case within *s 234(3)* falling within the number of hours without overtime), account shall be taken of that remuneration as if –
>
> (*a*)   the work had been done in normal working hours, falling within the number of hours without overtime in a case within *s 234(3)*; and
>
> (*b*)   the amount of that remuneration had been reduced accordingly.'

In *British Coal Corpn v Cheesbrough* [1990] 2 AC 256, [1990] 1 All ER 641, [1990] 2 WLR 407, [1990] ICR 317, [1990] IRLR 148, the House of Lords had to consider the situation where there was a variable element, namely, a weekly bonus paid to the employee for work done during normal working hours. The employee also regularly worked voluntary overtime, which was paid at time and a half, but no additional bonus was paid in respect of overtime. In such a case, the effect of *ERA 1996, s 223(3)* was that the total hours worked in the relevant weeks (including overtime) had to be taken into account, but the overtime premium was to be disregarded, and the overtime was to be treated as having been worked in normal working hours. The House of Lords held that the overtime was to be treated as having been paid at the basic hourly rate, without the addition of an amount to reflect the employee's weekly bonus. On the particular facts, this worked against the employee because his bonus had to be spread over more hours, thereby reducing his average rate of remuneration and the amount of his 'week's pay'.

35.35   EMPLOYMENTS FOR WHICH THERE ARE NO NORMAL WORKING HOURS

The amount of a week's pay is the amount of the employee's average weekly remuneration in the period of 12 weeks:

(a)   where the calculation date is the last day of a week, ending with that week;

(b)   in any other case, ending with the last complete week before the calculation date.

In arriving at the average weekly rate of remuneration no account shall be taken of a week in which no remuneration was payable by the employer to the employee, and remuneration in earlier weeks is brought in so as to bring the number of weeks of which account is taken up to 12 (*ERA 1996, s 224*).

35.36 THE CALCULATION DATE

In ascertaining the 'calculation date' for the purpose of the calculations described above, it is necessary to look to *ERA 1996, ss 225, 231*. Different calculation dates apply for the various purposes for which it may be necessary to ascertain the amount of a week's pay.

35.37 THE AMOUNT OF A WEEK'S PAY

For the purposes of calculating the amount of a week's pay, remuneration includes wages, salaries and expenses insofar as they represent profit in the employee's hands (*S & U Stores Ltd v Wilkes* [1974] 3 All ER 401, [1974] IRLR 283, [1974] ICR 645). It also includes an incentive bonus, irrespective of whether the bonus is identifiably related to the particular employee's efforts (*British Coal Corpn v Cheesbrough* [1990] 2 AC 256, [1990] 1 All ER 641, [1990] 2 WLR 407, [1990] ICR 317, [1990] IRLR 148). The amount of remuneration without deduction of tax is taken into account for the purposes of calculating a basic award and a redundancy payment (*Secretary of State for Employment v John Woodrow & Sons (Builders) Ltd* [1983] ICR 582, [1983] IRLR 11). In *W A Armstrong & Sons v Borril* [2000] ICR 367, the EAT held that a week's pay for the purpose of a redundancy payment payable to an agricultural worker was the amount specified in the *Agricultural Wages Order* without deduction of board and lodging.

The amount of a week's pay for certain calculations is subject to statutory maxima. The present limit on the amount of a week's pay for the purpose of calculating a basic award of compensation for unfair dismissal and for calculating a redundancy payment is, with effect from 6 April 2020, £538 (*Employment Rights (Increase of Limits) Order 2020 (SI 2020/205)*). The previous limit, for matters arising prior to 6 April 2020, was £525.

36   Pay – II: Attachment of Earnings

36.1   An *attachment of earnings order* is a means of enforcing a court order that a person must pay a sum of money. The order is made by the court and operates as an instruction to that person's employer to deduct sums from his earnings and pay them directly to the court office. The employer must also notify the court of certain matters. The *Attachment of Earnings Act 1971* ('*AtEA 1971*'), as amended, sets out the obligations of employers and the methods of calculating the deductions. Similar systems for attachment of earnings are enacted in order to assist with the enforcement of the council tax (see **36.10** below) and of child support maintenance under the *Child Support Act 1991* or the *Child Support, Pensions and Social Security Act 2000* ('*CSPSSA 2000*') as the case may be (see **36.11** below).

An attachment of earnings order may be made by a court if it appears to it that a person has failed, or is likely to fail, to pay in a satisfactory way sums due from him. Orders may be made for the payment of:

(a)   **maintenance:**

    (i)   if under a High Court maintenance order, an attachment of earnings order may be made in the High Court or the county court;

    (ii)   if under a county court maintenance order, an order may be made in the county court;

    (iii)   if under a magistrates' court maintenance order, an order may be made in a magistrates' court;

(b)   **payments under an administration order** (dealing with a number of debts owed by the same person) – county court;

(c)   **payment under a legal aid contribution order** pursuant to *section 17(2)* of the *Access to Justice Act 1999* and Regulations under that Act – magistrates' court.

(*AtEA 1971, s 1(1)–(3)* as amended.)

Where a county court makes an administration order in respect of a debtor's estate, it may also make an attachment of earnings order to secure the payments required by the administration order (*AtEA 1971, s 5(1)*).

The person who is obliged to make the deduction is the employer. No obligation rests on someone who as servant or agent makes payments to the employee (*AtEA 1971, s 6(2)*).

36.2   EARNINGS FROM WHICH THE DEDUCTIONS ARE MADE

Earnings, for the purposes of attachment of earnings, include wages or salary together with bonuses, commission, overtime pay and other emoluments payable under a contract of employment in addition to wages or salary. Pensions, annuities and compensation for loss of office are also included as is statutory sick pay (*AtEA 1971, s 24(1)* as amended by, *inter alia*, *Social Security Act 1985, s 21, Sch 4 para 1; Social Security Act 1986, Sch 10 para 102; Pension Schemes Act 1993, s 190, Sch 8 para 4*).

The following payments are not treated as earnings:

(a)   sums payable by any public department of the Government of Northern Ireland or a territory outside the United Kingdom;

(b)   income or allowances payable to the debtor as a member of Her Majesty's forces other than pay or allowances payable by his employer to him as a special member of a reserve force (see the *Reserve Forces Act 1996*);

(c)   pensions, allowances or benefits payable under any social security enactment (including, in particular, statutory maternity pay);

(d)   pensions or allowances payable in respect of disablement or disability;

(e)   except in relation to a maintenance order, wages payable to a person as a seaman, other than wages payable to him as a seaman of a fishing boat;

(f)   guaranteed minimum pension within the meaning of the *Pensions Schemes Act 1993*;

(g)   a tax credit within the meaning of the *Tax Credits Act 2002*.

(*AtEA 1971, s 24(2)* as amended by, inter alia, *Social Security Pensions Act 1975, s 65; Merchant Shipping Act 1979, s 39; Merchant Shipping Act 1995, s 314(2), Sch 13 para 46; Pension Schemes Act 1993, s 190, Sch 8 para 4; Tax Credits Act 2002, s 47, Sch 3, para 1*).

In order to determine whether payments made by him are earnings, an employer may apply to the court which made the order (*AtEA 1971, s 16(1), (2)*). While such an application, or an appeal from the finding on such an application, is pending, an employer will not incur any liability for non-compliance with the order to which the application relates (*AtEA 1971, s 16(3)*).

36.3 DEDUCTIONS FROM PAY

Where an employer receives an attachment of earnings order which relates to one of his employees, he must make such deductions from his employee's pay as are specified in the order (*AtEA 1971, s 6* as amended by *Courts and Legal Services Act 1990, Sch 17 para 5; Access to Justice Act 1999, s 90, Sch 13 paras 64, 66, Tribunals, Courts and Enforcement Act 2007; Collection of Fines (Final Scheme) Order 2006 (SI 2006/1737)*).

The court may use the following terms.

(a)   '*Attachable earnings*': that part of the employee's earnings to which an attachment of earnings order applies (usually income after statutory deduction).

(b)   '*Normal deductions*': the sum to be deducted from the employee's income on each pay day.

(c)   '*Protected earnings*': the earnings below which no deduction may be made.

36.4 Calculating the deduction

If an attachment of earnings order is made, then the employer must, on pay day:

(a)   if the attachable earnings are greater than the protected earnings:

    (i)   deduct the lesser of the normal deduction and the amount of the excess; and

    (ii)   in the case of orders *not* made to secure the payment of a judgment debt or payments under an administration order, deduct any *arrears* still outstanding, insofar as the excess allows;

(b)   if the attachable earnings are equal to or less than the protected earnings, take no action (but the arrears are increased by the amount due).

(*AtEA 1971, Sch 3 Pt I; ERA 1996, s 240, Sch 1 para 3.*)

Example. An employee working part-time earns, on average, £90 per week after tax, National Insurance, etc. but because the employee is on piece-work her weekly earnings may vary. The court has ordered the employee to pay £300 at a *normal deduction rate* of £15 per week and has decided that his *protected earnings rate* is to be £60 (ie, the employee will always be allowed to take home £60, provided that he earns that much). The order does not relate to a judgment debt or an administration order.

The following table shows his pay, and the deductions over a five-week period.

Week no.	Attachable earnings	Deductions under the order	Take home	Comments
	£	£	£	
1	90	15	75	Normal deduction
2	95	15	80	Normal deduction
3	70	10	60	Only £10 deducted, Jones takes home his protected earnings
4	95	20	75	Normal deduction plus £5 of arrears
5	100	15	85	Normal deduction

See also *Pepper v Pepper* [1960] 1 WLR 131, [1960] 1 All ER 529.

36.5 Priority of orders

Where there are two or more orders in existence, which are not to secure either the payment of judgment debts or payments under an administration order, then the employer must deal first with the first in time and apply the residue of the debtor's earnings over and above his protected earnings to subsequent orders, dealing with them in date order. Where there are several types of orders in existence, those to satisfy judgment debts or administration orders must be dealt with after the rest (*AtEA 1971, Sch 3 Pt II paras 7, 8*).

36.6 Time limits

It should be noted that the following notices should be complied with, within seven days:

(a)   an attachment of earnings order (*AtEA 1971, s 7(1)*);

(b)   a variation (*AtEA 1971, s 9(2)*);

(c)   a notice of cessation or discharge (*AtEA 1971, s 12(3)*).

36.7 EMPLOYER'S OBLIGATIONS TO NOTIFY COURT

An employer must notify the relevant court as follows.

(a)   Where a person is served with an attachment of earnings order directed to him and the debtor is not in his employment, *or* subsequently ceases to be in his employment, he must within 10 days give notice of that fact to the court (*AtEA 1971, s 7(2)*). In relation to a deductions from earnings order (see 33.11 below) there is a similar obligation to notify the Secretary of State (*SI 1992/1989 Reg 16(1), (2)*).

(b)   If the court orders him to do so, the employer must give the court, within a specified period, a statement signed by him or on his behalf of the debtor's earnings and anticipated earnings (*AtEA 1971, s 14(1)(b)*).

(c)   If he becomes the debtor's employer and knows that the order is in force and by what court it was made, he must within seven days of his becoming the debtor's employer or acquiring that knowledge (whichever is the later) notify that court in writing that he is the debtor's employer and include in his notification a statement of the debtor's earnings and anticipated earnings (*AtEA 1971, s 15(c)*). In relation to a deductions from earnings order (see **36.11** below) similar obligations are imposed (*SI 1992/1989 Reg 16(3)*).

36.8 PENALTIES FOR NON-COMPLIANCE

If an employer, required to comply with any of the above provisions relating to deductions or notice, fails to do so, he may be liable on conviction in a magistrates' court to a fine of not more than level 2 on the Standard Scale (see **1.10** INTRODUCTION) or he may be fined up to £250 by a judge of the High Court or the county court (*AtEA 1971, s 23*, as amended). Furthermore, if he gives a notice or makes any statement on these matters which he knows to be false in a material particular then, in addition to being fined, he may be imprisoned for not more than 14 days. It should be noted that the *Legal Aid, Sentencing and Punishment of Offenders Act 2012* makes provision in *ss 86–87* for the Secretary of State to increase the levels 1–4 of the Standard Scale fines to such sums considered appropriate. These provisions are, however, not yet in force (see **1.10** INTRODUCTION).

It will be a defence for an employer to prove:

(a)   that he took all reasonable steps to comply with the attachment of earnings order; or

(b)   that he did not know and could not reasonably be expected to know that the debtor was not in his employment, or had ceased to be so, and that he gave the required notice as soon as reasonably practicable after that fact came to his knowledge.

(*AtEA 1971, s 23(5)*.)

36.9 OTHER MATTERS CONCERNING ATTACHMENT OF EARNINGS

Clerical costs. When an employer makes a deduction in compliance with an order from an employee's earnings, he is entitled to deduct £1 (or such sum as is currently applicable) for clerical and administration costs (*AtEA 1971, s 7(4)(a); Attachment of Earnings (Employer's Deduction) Order 1991 (SI 1991/356), art 2*). The employer must give the employee a statement in writing of the deduction (*AtEA 1971, s 7(4)(b)*).

Pay statements. The employee must be given a pay statement showing, among other things, deductions from his pay. An employer need not, on each occasion upon which a payment of wages is made, give separate particulars of a fixed deduction. It is sufficient if he supplies a statement of the aggregate amount of fixed deductions having supplied a standing statement in writing of each fixed deduction stating:

(a)   the amount of the deduction; and

(b)   the intervals at which the deduction is to be made; and

(c)   the purpose for which it is made.

Any such standing statement is valid for 12 months. It may be amended (by adding a new deduction or altering or cancelling an existing one) by a written notice to the employee, detailing the amendment. If the employer wishes to continue to rely on the statement, it must be reissued in a consolidated form, incorporating any amendments previously notified to the employee, at intervals not exceeding 12 months.

(*ERA 1996, ss 8, 9*.) (See further **35.17** PAY – **I**.)

If an employer requires advice or information concerning an attachment of earnings order or subsequent procedures he should contact the court where the order was made.

36.10 COUNCIL TAX

Attachment of earnings for failure to pay the council tax is provided for by the *Council Tax (Administration and Enforcement) Regulations 1992 (SI 1992/613)*, as amended (by, inter alia, the *Local Government Changes for England (Community Charge and Council Tax, Administration and Enforcement) Regulations 1995 (SI 1995/247)*, the *Local Authorities (Contracting Out of Tax Billing, Collection and Enforcement Functions) Order 1996 (SI 1996/1880)*, the *Community Charge and Council Tax (Administration and Enforcement) (Amendment) (Jobseeker's Allowance) Regulations 1996 (SI 1996/2405)*, the *Council Tax (Administration and Enforcement) (Amendment) Regulations 1998 (1998/295)* and the *Council Tax (Administration and Enforcement) (Amendment) (England) Regulations 2004 (SI 2004/927)* and the *Council Tax (Administration and Enforcement) (Amendment) (No. 2) (England) Regulations 2012 (SI 2012/3086)*. There must first be an outstanding sum in respect of which the relevant billing authority (in general, a district or borough council) has obtained a liability order from magistrates pursuant to *reg 34*. The authority is then itself empowered by *reg 37(1)* to make an attachment of earnings order to secure the payment of any outstanding sum covered by the liability order.

The attachment order is directed to the debtor's employer and is in a prescribed form (*reg 37(2)*). A duty to comply with an order served upon him is imposed on the employer by *reg 37(3)*. Non-compliance is an offence unless the employer proves that he took all reasonable steps to comply with the order and is punishable by a fine not exceeding level 3 on the Standard Scale (*reg 56(2)*; and see **1.10** INTRODUCTION).

The amount to be deducted under the order is regulated by *reg 38* and *Sch 4*. An amount is specified for any given level of net earnings. 'Earnings' has the same meaning as in the *AtEA 1971* (see **36.2** above and see *reg 32(1)*), and the net earnings are arrived at by the deduction of income tax, primary class 1 contributions under the *Social Security Act 1975* and certain amounts deductible for the purposes of a superannuation scheme (*reg 32(1)*).

The employer must notify the debtor in writing of the total sum deducted up to the date of each notification (*reg 39(2)*). The notice should be provided at the same time as a pay statement (*reg 39(3)*) The employer may deduct the sum of £1 towards administrative costs for each deduction made (*reg 39(1)*).

While such an order is in force, the debtor is under a duty to notify the authority of changes in his employment pursuant to *reg 40*. The ex-employer is under a similar duty (*reg 39(4)*), as is the new employer if he knows of the order (*reg 39(6)*).

If two or more orders are made under these provisions (or such an order is made following the making of an order under the *AtEA 1971*), the priority between them is governed by *reg 42*.

36.11 CHILD SUPPORT MAINTENANCE

A similar system to that under the *AtEA 1971* operates in relation to the enforcement of the payment of child support maintenance by an absent parent, under the *Child Support Act 1991* ('*CSA 1991*') and under the *Child Support, Pensions and Social Security Act 2000* ('*CSPSSA 2000*'). Orders under the *CSA 1991* or *CSPSSA 2000* (which apples to orders made after 3 March 2003) are referred to as 'deduction from earnings orders', and the procedure is set out in the *Child Support (Collection and Enforcement) Regulations 1992 (SI 1992/1989)*, as amended by, inter alia, the *Child Support (Collection and Enforcement and Miscellaneous Amendments) Regulations 2001 (SI 2001/162)* and the *Child Support (Miscellaneous Amendments) (No. 2) Regulations 2008 (SI 2008/2544)* and the *Child Support Collection and Enforcement (Deduction Orders) Amendment Regulations 2009 (SI 2009/1815)* and the *Child Support (Deduction Orders and Fees) (Amendment and Modification) Regulations 2016 (SI 2016/439)*. The regime is similar to that under the *AtEA 1971* and is therefore not dealt with separately in this chapter. Priority between deduction from earnings orders, and between one or more such orders and one or more attachment of earnings orders, is governed by *reg 24* of the *Child Support (Collection and Enforcement) Regulations 1992*. See also **36.7** ante.

37   Probationary Employees

37.1   LEGAL STATUS

Many employers when engaging new employees state that they will initially be employed for a 'probationary' period. An employee may have reduced contractual rights (for example, a shorter contractual notice period) during their probationary period, but their status as a probationer has no effect on their statutory rights. For example, unless their employment continues for less than a month, a probationer will have to be given written particulars of the main terms of their employment (see **8.4** CONTRACT OF EMPLOYMENT). During the probation period, it is an implied contractual term that the employer will take reasonable steps to maintain an appraisal, giving guidance by advice or warning where necessary: *White v London Transport Executive* [1981] IRLR 261, [1982] 1 All ER 410.

37.2   DISMISSING A PROBATIONER

It is a commonly held but mistaken belief that giving a new employee the status of probationer enables the employer to dispense with that employee's services, if he is found to be unsatisfactory, without the normal hazards of dismissal, such as a claim for unfair dismissal. The labelling of an employee as a 'probationer' has virtually no effect on the employer/employee relationship. If a probationer with the necessary length of service is dismissed, he may bring a claim for unfair dismissal as may any other employee in a similar situation. The fact that he only had probationer status will not automatically make the dismissal fair. It is merely a circumstance which the tribunal will take into account in deciding whether the dismissal was fair or unfair.

In *Post Office v Mughal* [1977] ICR 763, [1977] IRLR 178 at 768, the Employment Appeal Tribunal laid down guidelines for employment tribunals considering the fairness of the dismissal of an employee during a probationary or trial period. They considered that the following question should be asked: 'Have the employers shown that they took reasonable steps to maintain appraisal of the probationer throughout the period of probation, giving guidance by advice or warning when such is likely to be useful or fair; and that an appropriate officer made an honest effort to determine whether the probationer came up to the required standard, having informed himself of the appraisals made by supervising officers and any other facts recorded about the probationer?'. In *Anandarajah v Lord Chancellor's Department* [1984] IRLR 131, the EAT cautioned against reliance on previous authority – in that case *Mughal* – in assessing the fairness of a dismissal. The preferred approach was to apply the statutory test now set out in *Employment Rights Act 1996, s 98(4), (6)* to the circumstances of each case. However, in *British Heart Condition v Harrison* EAT/1354/96 the EAT found the *Mughal* guidelines useful. In particular, in *Harrison* the EAT noted that a probationer must be taken to know that they are on trial and that they can expect to be judged strictly against a reasonable standard. Where a probationer has been unfairly dismissed, there may be particular *Polkey* issues for the employment tribunal to consider when assessing the compensatory award. For example, would the probationer have passed the probation period if they had not been unfairly dismissed and, if so, what difference would that have made to their employment prospects if they had subsequently resigned: *Davidson–Hogg v Davis Gregory Solicitors and Howarth* (UKEAT/0512/09/ZT) (15 November 2010, unreported).

The above considerations apply where a probationer has the qualifying length of service to bring an unfair dismissal claim. Note that in the case of dismissals for certain impermissible reasons (including trade union activities, union membership or non-membership, health and safety activities, pregnancy or childbirth, refusal of a protected shop worker or betting worker or opted-out shop worker or betting worker to do shop work on a Sunday, the assertion of a statutory right) there is no qualifying period (see Unfair Dismissal – I (54)). Further, employees who claim that their dismissal was discriminatory, can bring claims under the *Equality Act 2010* without establishing any qualifying period of employment.

37.3   EXTENDING A PROBATION PERIOD

If the end of the contractual probation period is approaching and an employer is not yet sure whether to dismiss the employee or not, the probation period can be extended if the contract includes an express right for the employer to do so or if the employee agrees to an extension. If the employer fails to exercise any such right before the end of the probation period, then the employee automatically passes the probation period; an employer does not have an implied right to extend an employee's probationary period for a reasonable time in order to assess their suitability (*Przybylska v Modus Telecom Ltd* (UKEAT/0566/06/CEA) [2007] All ER (D) 06 (May)). If an employee is placed on garden leave before the end of their probation period and subsequently dismissed without having been formally confirmed in post, they have nevertheless passed their probation period: *Cornell (Lynne) v Revenue and Customs Comrs* (TC00108) [2009] UKFTT 140 (TC), [2009] STI 2199.

Note that as a probationer often has different terms and conditions, status and benefits, the extension of an employee's probationary period of employment is generally a detriment: *N v Lewisham London Borough Council* (UKEAT/156/09) [2009] ICR 1538, [2009] All ER (D) 74 (Aug).

In *Millbank Financial Services v Crawford* [2014] IRLR 18, an employee who complained to her employer about the extension of her probationary period, asserting that there had been no feedback during the probationary period, no consultation with the person recruited to carry out the HR function, no consultation with the director and just a single meeting at the end of the probation period with no plan of action and no idea how long the probation period would last, was held to have disclosed "information" for the purpose of a whistleblowing claim (see paragraph **11.13**: Disclosure of Information by Employees).

In *Okwu v Rise Community Action* (2019) UKEAT/0082/19, an employee was subject to an initial 3-month probation period towards the end of which the employer raised a number of issues regarding her performance and extended her probation period for a further 3-month period; two weeks later the she was dismissed. She contended that nothing had happened since the extension of her probationary period save that she had sent a letter to her employer which she said made protected disclosures, and relied on this in her claim for automatically unfair dismissal. The EAT held that in dismissing the claim the tribunal had failed to engage with the employee's contention and remitted the matter for reconsideration. The decision is unremarkable legally but notable as a rare EAT case in this area which illustrates how probationary periods can lead to claims.

37.4   In *H v Land Berlin* (C-174-16) [2017] All ER (D) 48 (Sep) the employee was promoted to a higher grade but subject to a two-year probationary period. She never took up her duties in the new post, being first on sick leave for reasons linked to pregnancy, then on maternity leave, and then on parental leave for the remainder of the probationary period. She was informed by her employer that under the applicable national rules her probationary period had ended and could not be extended and as she had not successfully completed the probationary period, she would be returned to her former (lower) post. The ECJ held that the national rules in question were precluded by Clauses 5(1) and (2) of the revised Framework Agreement on parental leave set out in the *Annex* to *Council Directive 2010/18/EU* (see **33.67**) and the infringements of those clauses were not justified by the objective of the probationary period, ie to enable the assessment of suitability for the new post to be assigned permanently. The ECJ further held that: (1) the issue for the national

court was whether it was objectively possible for the employer to enable the person concerned to return to her post at the end of her parental leave, (2) if not, to ensure she is assigned to an equivalent or similar post consistent with her employment contract or relationship and without a new selection procedure beforehand, and (3) it was also for the national court to ensure that the person may, at the end of parental leave, continue (in the post returned to or newly assigned) a probationary period under conditions that comply with clause 5(2) of the Framework Agreement.

38 Public Sector Employees

38.1 Many people are employed in the public sector, for example in the Civil Service, the police, as teachers or by local authorities. Much of the law described in other chapters of this book applies equally to such people. However, there may sometimes be special factors to bear in mind when dealing with or advising upon public sector employment.

In many cases, there are specific statutory provisions which affect employment in particular areas of the public sector. The provisions set out below are among the most important, but it will be important to look carefully at all the relevant statutes and Statutory Instruments when dealing with an individual case.

38.2 CROWN SERVANTS

The civil service is made up of all permanent but non-political offices and employments (except for those in the armed forces) held under the Crown. Crown servants have a special status in the eyes of the law, albeit that the common law position has been much changed by statute.

At common law, the Crown servant is employed at the pleasure of the Crown. That is, he can be dismissed at will – without notice and without the need to show cause or to follow any particular procedure (see *Dunn v R* [1896] 1 QB 116, [1895–9] All ER Rep 907; *Council of Civil Service Unions v Minister for the Civil Service* [1985] AC 374, [1985] IRLR 28, [1985] ICR 14).

There has for many years been a controversy as to whether Crown servants in fact have a CONTRACT OF EMPLOYMENT (8) at all. The question was considered by the Divisional Court in *R v Civil Service Appeal Board, ex p Bruce* [1988] 3 All ER 686, [1988] ICR 649 (the Court of Appeal did not express an opinion when it considered the case). It was suggested that there was nothing unconstitutional in a Crown servant having a contract of employment: the question was whether that was the intention of the Crown when the employment began. In *Bruce*, it was said that the evidence suggested no such intention in relation to civil servants prior to 1985 (which was the case in question), but a likelihood that future civil service appointments *would* be on the basis of contract. However, in *R v Lord Chancellor's Department, ex p Nangle* [1992] 1 All ER 897, [1991] ICR 743, [1991] IRLR 343, the Divisional Court upon similar facts concluded that *Bruce* was wrong and that a contract *did* exist for current civil servants. This decision was applied by the High Court to civil servants appointed by the Postmaster General: in *British Telecommunications Plc v Royal Mail Group Ltd* [2010] EWHC 8 (QB), [2010] All ER (D) 10 (Jan). See also *McClaren v Home Office* [1990] ICR 824, [1990] IRLR 338.

Whilst the Crown may terminate an employment contract at will, it cannot enter into one quite so easily. Restrictions on the manner by which a Crown servant may be employed are imposed by the *Constitutional Reform and Governance Act 2010, s 10(2)*. That section provides that selection of persons for "appointment" to the civil service (save for excepted selections set out in *subsection (3)*) must be on the basis of fair and open competition. That is a mandatory requirement, and has been held by the EAT to apply both the appointment of a person to the office of a civil servant and to the employment of any civil servant (see *Secretary of State for Justice v Betts* [2017] ICR 1130, [2017] IRLR 804). Any employment contract entered into in contravention of *s 10* will be ultra vires, albeit the Crown servant in question may still qualify for certain protections as a worker.

The employment statutes avoid the question of whether there is an employment contract, by deeming that there is such a contract for specific purposes or by explicitly including or excluding civil servants from their scope. An example of the former approach is *TULR(C)A*

1992, s 245, which deems Crown servants to have a contract of employment for the purpose of liability for torts involving the inducement or threatened inducement of a breach of contract (see **46.2 STRIKES AND INDUSTRIAL ACTION**), and of certain provisions of *TULR(C)A 1992.*

Civil servants enjoy most of the normal statutory rights by virtue of *ERA 1996, s 191*. This provision applies many of the sections of ERA 1996, including the right to pursue a claim for UNFAIR DISMISSAL – I **(54)**, to individuals employed under or for the purposes of a government department or any officer or body exercising on behalf of the Crown functions conferred by a statutory provision. The main exceptions are the right to a minimum notice period (because of the doctrine that employment by the Crown is terminable at will) and the right to a statutory redundancy payment (although redundancy payments are in fact made to civil servants when appropriate: see *R (Public and Commercial Services Union) v Minister for the Civil Service* [2010] EWHC 1027 (Admin), [2010] ICR 1198, [2011] 3 All ER 54).

A civil servant may, however, acquire an enforceable right to redundancy payments through the operation of the *Human Rights Act*. The High Court has held that a civil servant's right under a scheme to a redundancy payment can constitute a possession for the purposes of *Article 1 Protocol 1* of the *ECHR*: *R (Public and Commercial Services Union) v Minister for the Civil Service* [2011] EWHC 2041 (Admin), [2012] 1 All ER 985, [2011] IRLR 903, and more recently *R (Public and Commercial Services Union) v Minister for the Cabinet Office* [2017] EWHC 1787 (Admin), [2018] ICR 269, [2017] IRLR 967, a judgment of the divisional court (Sales LJ, as he then was, and Whipple J) which highlights the importance of procedural rights to consultation which representative trade unions for civil servants enjoy under certain statutory schemes.

There are limits to the scope of *Article 1* of *Protocol 1*, however. Compulsory retirement has been found not to engage *Article 1 Protocol 1*, as it does not deprive the employee of any accrued rights: *The Police Superintendents Association of England and Wales and others v Chief Constable of Bedfordshire Police* [2013] EWHC 2173 (Admin), [2013] All ER (D) 11 (Aug) at [89]–[93]). Not only does *ERA 1996, s 191* fail to apply the statutory redundancy payment rights to such employees, any employee whose employment is treated for the purposes of pensions and other superannuation benefits as being in the civil service of the state, is explicitly prevented from claiming a statutory redundancy payment by *ERA 1996, s 159*. For continuity of employment see *ERA 1996, s 191.*

Similarly to the approach regarding rights under *ERA 1996*, civil servants have rights by virtue of *TULR(C)A 1992, s 273*, with the exception of the collective redundancy procedures in *Chapter 2* of *Part IV* of that Act.

The *Transfer of Undertakings (Protection of Employment) Regulations 2006 (SI 2006/246)* (*TUPE*) apply to transfers of undertakings from the public sector to the private sector, but not to the administrative reorganisation of public administrative authorities or to the transfer of administrative functions between public administrative authorities (*reg 3(5)*). However, the Cabinet Office's non-statutory Statement of Practice 'Staff Transfers in the Public Sector' in effect guarantees 'TUPE-equivalent' treatment for public sector employees who are transferred within the public sector. The Cabinet Office has also adopted Principles of Good Employment Practice, which set out voluntary principles designed to encourage best practice amongst private sector employers who employ employees transferred from the public sector.

Further, the *Employment Relations Act 1999, s 38* enables the Secretary of State to make regulations extending the *TUPE* protections to other staff. To date, this power has been exercised in relation to the creation of OFCOM, the Greater London Authority, the Rent Officer Service, the Research Councils UK Shared Services Centre, the transfer of police staff to the National Crim Agency, some staff transferring to the Department for Work and Pensions and various staff in public health units. From 31 December 2020, *s 38* will provide the Secretary of State to make "TUPE-like provision" in relation to employment which does not fall within the scope of the *TUPE Regulations.*

Civil servants enjoy much of the protection afforded by the *Equality Act 2010. Section 83(2)* provides that "employment" for the purposes of *Part 5* of the *Act*, Work, includes Crown employment. *Section 83(5)* provides that in the case of a person in Crown employment (defined in *s 83(9)* as bearing the same meaning as in *s 191* of *ERA 1996*) a reference to the person's dismissal is a reference to the termination of the person's employment.

The *Equality Act 2010* does not apply in full, however. *Paragraph 5* of *Schedule 22* provides an important exception to the prohibition on discrimination. It provides that a person does not contravene the Act by virtue of making, continuing in force, publishing, displaying or implementing rules (or gists of such rules) which restrict Crown Employment to persons of particular birth, nationality, descent or residence. The applicable rules are the *Race Relations (Prescribed Public Bodies) (No. 2) Regulations 1994 (SI 1994/1986)*.

In relation to industrial action in the public sector, there is an extension to the statutory immunity from claims in tort for action taken in contemplation or furtherance of a trade dispute (see **46.3** STRIKES AND INDUSTRIAL ACTION). Whereas the dispute must normally be between the workers concerned and their employer in order to attract the immunity, a dispute between a Minister of the Crown and any workers is treated as a dispute between those workers and their employer if the dispute relates to matters which:

(a)   have been referred for consideration by a joint body on which statutory provision is made for the Minister to be represented, or

(b)   cannot be settled without the Minister exercising a statutory power.

(TULR(C)A 1992, s 244(2).)

38.3 ARMED FORCES

The armed forces are not part of the civil service and, to date, the statutory protections have not been applied to them so extensively. The main statutory provisions specific to service in the armed forces include the *Armed Forces Acts 1991, 1996* and *2001*, so far as they have not been repealed, and the *Armed Forces Act 2006* (the *2006 Act* is due to expire on 11 May 2021, its repeal having been delayed by successive statutory instruments: see the *Armed Forces Act (Continuation) Order 2020*), the *Armed Forces Redundancy Scheme Order 2006 (SI 2006/55)* (as amended by *SI 2011/208* and *2011/3013*), the *Armed Forces (Redundancy, Resettlement and Gratuity Earnings Schemes) (No. 2) Order 2010 (SI 2010/832)* and *Armed Forces (Service Complaints and Financial Assistance) Act 2015*. The *Armed Forces (Flexible Working Act) 2018* was adopted on 8 February 2018, and is expected to come into force by April 2019.

Members of the armed forces have the protection of the equality legislation by virtue of the *Equality Act 2010, s 83(3)*, which provides that *Part 5, Work* applies to service in the armed forces as it applies to employment by a private person. *Paragraph 4* of *Schedule 9* to the *Equality Act 2010* provides for various exceptions relating to the armed forces. In particular, the armed forces are not prohibited from discriminating in specified respects in relation to service in armed forces if they can show that requiring the employee to be male or not transsexual is a proportionate means of ensuring the combat effectiveness of the armed forces. *Part 5* of the *Equality Act 2010* does not apply to service in the armed forces at all in relation to age or disability.

Under *s 121* of the *Equality Act 2010*, if a member of the armed forces fails to exercise a right to apply to the Defence Council to determine their complaint, this will bar the jurisdiction of the Employment Tribunal to determine that complaint: *Equality Act 2010, s 121* and *Duncan v Ministry of Defence* (UKEAT/0191/14/RN) [2014] All ER (D) 101 (Oct).

38.3 Public Sector Employees

Interesting issues concerning the territorial scope of the law have arisen from recent cases about the rights of those employed by the British armed forces abroad: *R (Hottak) v Secretary of State for Foreign and Commonwealth Affairs* [2015] IRLR 827 (upheld on appeal: [2016] 1 WLR 3791, [2016] IRLR 534, [2016] ICR 975); *Ministry of Defence v Holloway* UKEAT/0396/14/BA [2015] All ER (D) 391 (Jul) (see **[27.11]** FOREIGN EMPLOYEES).

Members of the armed forces have the right to make a complaint about any matter relating to their service (*Armed Forces (Redress of Individual Grievances) Regulations 2007 (SI 2007/3353)*). The High Court has considered the scope of this right, including human rights issues: *Crosbie v Secretary of State for Defence* [2011] EWHC 879 (Admin), [2011] All ER (D) 64 (Apr), see also *Clayton v Army Board of the Defence Council* [2014] EWHC 1651 (Admin), [2014] All ER (D) 13 (Jun). The *Armed Forces (Service Complaints and Financial Assistance) Act 2015* introduced a new complaints ombudsman.

If and when *ERA 1996, s 192* comes into force, on a date to be fixed by regulations (*ERA 1996, Sch 2, para 16*), most of the rights enjoyed by other Crown servants, e.g. unfair dismissal, will be extended to members of the armed forces, although not any rights associated with trade union membership.

38.4 POLICE

Police officers are officers of the peace and, as such, are not Crown servants. The main statutes are the *Police Act 1996* (a consolidating statute), the *Police Reform Act 2002*, the *Police Reform and Social Responsibility Act 2011* and the *Police (Complaints and Conduct) Act 2012*. The *Police Act 1996* includes provisions barring membership of trade unions other than the Police Federation (*s 64*) and making it a criminal offence to induce or attempt to induce breaches of discipline, which would include the taking of industrial action (*s 91*).

Police officers are generally excluded from the benefit of various statutory rights, including the right to complain of UNFAIR DISMISSAL – I, II, III (54, 55, 56) and the right to complain of an unlawful deduction of wages (see *Metropolitan Police Comr v Lowrey-Nesbitt* [1999] ICR 401), by *ERA 1996, s 200(1)*. They may, however, claim in relation to detriment on the ground that, or dismissal by reason that, they made a protected disclosure: *ERA 1996, s 43KA* (and see *Lake v British Transport Police* [2007] EWCA Civ 424, [2007] ICR 1293, [2007] All ER (D) 77 (May)). Further, the power of the police and crime commissioner for a police area under *Police Reform and Social Responsibility Act 2011, s 38* to suspend or call upon a chief constable of the police to resign or retire is amenable to judicial review (see **38.6** further below).

Police officers also have the protection of the discrimination legislation by virtue of the *Equality Act 2010, s 42* which provides that holding the office of constable and appointment as police cadet (with some exceptions) are treated as employment by the chief officer or relevant authority for the purposes of *Part 5, Work*.

It should be noted that, at least in the context of claims based on EU law rights, judicial immunity will not bar employment tribunal challenges decisions arrived at by the Police Misconduct Board (for example, on the grounds that the decision was discriminatory). That was the conclusion of the Supreme Court in *P v Commissioner of Police of the Metropolis* [2017] UKSC 65, [2018] 1 All ER 1011 (overturning the judgment of the Court of Appeal ([2016] EWCA Civ 2, [2016] IRLR 301)) at [30]. It remains to be seen whether the inroads into judicial immunity recognised by the Supreme Court will remain open following the repeal of the *European Communities Act 1972*.

Some other bodies, such as local authorities, employ constables who are not subject to the general statutory scheme for police officers. The position of those constables as a matter of domestic law was considered by the Court of Appeal in *Redbridge LBC v Dhinsa* [2014]

EWCA Civ 178, [2014] ICR 834, [2014] All ER (D) 10 (Mar). It was held there that, as in the case for police officers, the constable was excluded from bringing dismissal proceedings as his service with the local authority constituted a "constabulary maintained by virtue of an enactment" within the meaning of *s 200* of the *ERA 1996*.

Redbridge was followed by the EAT in *Wandsworth LBC v Vining* UKEAT/0234/13/LA [2016] ICR 427, [2015] All ER (D) 266 (Dec). The appellants in that case advanced various EU and human rights law arguments which had not been before the Court of Appeal in *Redbridge*, arguing in effect that the domestic legislation, as interpreted by the Court of Appeal in that case, was incompatible with the ECHR rights of the appellants.

Those arguments were rejected by the EAT, and the case went on appeal. The Court of Appeal ([2017] EWCA Civ 1092, [2017] IRLR 1140) upheld the appeal, in part. It rejected the appellants' human rights challenge against the exclusion of the right to bring claims for unfair dismissal. However, it upheld their argument that the bar on employees in police service from the collective redundancy consultation rights conferred by *section 280* of *TULR(C)A 1992* breached the appellants', and the appellants' union's, right to free association under *Article 11*. That finding is nuanced, however, by the Court of Appeal's (albeit *obiter*) acceptance that certain categories of employee in police service could lawfully be excluded from the collective redundancy consultation rights under *TULR(C)A* (see [73]).

38.5 LOCAL GOVERNMENT

Local government employees generally have a contract of employment (with the exception of some officers, such as coroners) and they generally enjoy the panoply of employment rights. However, it should be remembered that the local authority is a creature of statute, and thus its powers are limited to those provided by statute.

Local authorities have the power to appoint such staff as they think are necessary for the proper discharge of their statutory functions on such reasonable terms and conditions as the local authority thinks fit, under the *Local Government Act 1972, s 112*. This power is subject to the *Localism Act 2011, s 41* which requires local authorities to comply with their respective pay policy statement. Terms and conditions are agreed at a national level (with some scope for local variations) with the National Joint Council, incorporated in the collective agreement known as the Green Book. Also see the *Local Authorities (Standing Orders) (England) Regulations 2001 (SI 2001/3384)*.

Local authorities face some restrictions on who they can appoint. By *s 116* of the *Local Government Act 1972*, members of an authority, and any person who in the preceding twelve months had been a member of an authority, may not be appointed to any paid office with that authority. Further restrictions are contained in the *Local Government and Housing Act 1989*: certain posts are 'politically restricted', which means that their holders may not be members of *any* local authority without express exemption (*ss 1–3*); with certain exceptions, all appointments must be made on merit (*s 7*); and authorities must ensure so far as practicable that they are not represented in negotiations about terms and conditions of employment by members of the authority who are also in local authority employment or who are officials or employees of trade unions whose members include local authority employees (*s 12*). The *Local Government Officers (Political Restrictions) Regulations 1990 (SI 1990/851)* have been held not to contravene the European Convention on Human Rights (*Ahmed v United Kingdom* (Application 22954/93) (1998) 29 EHRR 1, [1999] IRLR 188, European Court of Human Rights).

There are further rules in relation to specific posts (chief officers), including the local authority's Head of the Paid Service and monitoring officer. All employees of a local authority are also officers, but an officer (including a chief officer) does not have to be an employee: *Pinfold North Ltd v Humberside Fire Authority* [2010] EWHC 2944 (QB). The *Local Authorities (Standing Orders) Regulations 1993 (SI 1993/202)* require local authorities to incorporate in standing orders provision relating to their staff. These must include provision for the appointment of chief officers and for investigation by a designated independent person (known as a DIP) in case of alleged misconduct by a chief officer.

The *Transfer of Undertakings (Protection of Employment) Regulations 2006 (SI 2006/246)* do not apply to the administrative reorganisation of public administrative authorities or to the transfer of administrative functions between public administrative authorities (*reg 3(5)*). See **53.9** TRANSFER OF UNDERTAKINGS.

The position is more complicated in respect of school staff. School teachers' pay and conditions of employment are subject to control by the Secretary of State for Education by virtue of the *Education Act 2002, ss 119–130*; and compensation for redundancy is subject to regulations made under the *Public Service Pensions Act 2013*, and now the *Teachers (Compensation for Redundancy and Premature Retirement) Regulations 2015 (SI 2015/601)*. The identity of the employer (in practice) depends on which of the following two categories the school falls within: (*a*) community, voluntary controlled, community special and maintained schools; or (*b*) foundation, voluntary aided and foundation special schools. The former category have delegated budgets and, by virtue of the *Education (Modification of Enactments Relating to Employment) (England) Order 2003 (SI 2003/1964)*, the *ERA 1996* generally applies as if the governing body were the employer.

More detail is given on the complicated interrelationship of the employment responsibilities of the local education authority and the governing body in the *School Staffing (England) Regulations 2009 (SI 2009/2680)*. These relationships were considered by the Court of Appeal in *Murphy v Slough Borough Council* [2005] EWCA Civ 122, [2005] ICR 721, [2005] IRLR 382 and (in relation to comparators under the *EqPA*) by the CA in *South Tyneside Metropolitan Borough Council v Anderson* [2007] EWCA Civ 654, [2007] ICR 1581, [2007] IRLR 715. *Murphy* was considered by the Employment Appeal Tribunal in *Butt v Bradford Metropolitan District Council* (UKEAT/0210/10/ZT) [2010] All ER (D) 92 (Oct) and *Birmingham City Council v Akhtar* [2011] 3 CMLR 42, [2011] Eq LR 838 *Davies v London Borough of Haringey* [2014] EWHC 3393 (QB), [2015] ELR 18, [2014] All ER (D) 266 (Oct).

38.6 AVAILABILITY OF JUDICIAL REVIEW

Generally, an employment tribunal will be the appropriate forum for an employee to bring a claim against a public sector employer. However, those who work in the public sector may sometimes seek to assert their rights, not simply in an employment tribunal or in an action for tort or breach of contract in the ordinary courts, but by way of an application for judicial review. This is a means of challenging the unlawful actions and decisions of public authorities and bodies exercising statutory power. The possible grounds for such challenge include procedural unfairness, acting outside the statutory powers (this is often referred to as acting "ultra vires") and irrationality. Applications are heard in the Administrative Court and the procedure is governed by the *Civil Procedure Rules, Part 54* (note also the *Practice Direction*, the *Pre-Action Protocol* and the *Administrative Court Judicial Review Guide*). Its features include a need to obtain permission to proceed from the court and a strict time limit (applications must be brought promptly, and *in any event* within three months of the action challenged).

Historically there has been much academic debate about the circumstances in which a claim must (or cannot) be brought by way of judicial review (see eg *O'Reilly v Mackman* [1983] 2 AC 237, [1982] 3 All ER 680 and *Roy v Kensington and Chelsea and Westminster Family Practitioner Committee* [1992] 1 AC 624, [1992] 1 All ER 705, [1992] 2 WLR 239, [1992]

IRLR 233). Whilst in recent years (and particularly since the introduction of the *Civil Procedure Rules*), the categorisation of claims has become less important, it remains the case that only claims involving a public law element can proceed by way of judicial review.

A helpful statement of the position in the employment context is to be found in the judgment of Woolf LJ in *McClaren v Home Office* [1990] ICR 824, [1990] IRLR 338. His Lordship held that judicial review was generally an unnecessary and inappropriate remedy for public sector employees, but that there were two types of case where it might be available. One was where the decision impugned was that of a tribunal or other body (such as the Civil Service Appeal Board) which had a sufficient public law element and was not wholly domestic or informal. The other was where the employee was adversely affected by a decision of *general* application which was alleged to be flawed (the decision to bar trade union membership at GCHQ was an example of this).

This decision was applied in *R (Davies) v Pennine Acute Hospitals* [2010] EWHC 2887 (Admin) and *R (Kirk) v Middlesbrough Borough Council* [2010] EWHC 1035 (Admin), [2010] IRLR 699 and in both cases the High Court found that judicial review was not available because the issues were essentially private law matters. In *R (Lock) v Leicester City Council* [2012] EWHC 2058 (Admin), the claimant applied for judicial review of the defendant local authority's decision to dismiss her from her post as chief executive. The Court found that it could consider the decision to terminate her statutory role as designated head of paid service. However, it could not consider the termination of her contractual role as chief executive.

However, it will not always be the case that judicial review is inappropriate. *R (Shoesmith) v Ofsted* [2011] EWCA Civ 642, [2011] IRLR 679, [2011] ICR 1195 concerned the dismissal of the Director of Children's Services at Haringey Council. The Claimant issued a claim for judicial review challenging an Ofsted report, the action of the Secretary of State in removing the Claimant from her statutory office based upon that report and the actions of Haringey in subsequently dismissing her from its employment. In this case, the Court of Appeal found that the issues were amenable to judicial review because the position of Director of Children's Services had been created, required and defined by statute.

The Court of Appeal confirmed that in the great majority of cases proceedings in the employment tribunal will be the better, if not the only, remedy where a local authority employee has been dismissed. It suggested that the exceptions would be cases where the remedy available in the employment tribunal was inadequate because of the statutory cap on compensation or where the case raised significant issues falling outwith the scope of an employment tribunal's inquiry.

On the facts of *Shoesmith*, the Court of Appeal found that there was a benefit in the Claimant being able to bring all her claims (against Ofsted, the Secretary of State and her local authority employer) in one set of proceedings and that success in judicial review proceedings would be more valuable in financial and reputational terms, due to the cap on compensation in the employment tribunal. For these reasons, the right to bring an unfair dismissal claim in the employment tribunal was not an equally convenient and effective alternative remedy for the Claimant. Indeed, in *R (Lock)* (cited above) the High Court distinguished *Shoesmith* on the basis that, unlike in that case, the claimant's position was not wholly a statutory one.

An application for judicial review was also considered in *Crosbie v Secretary of State for Defence* [2011] EWHC 879 (Admin), [2011] All ER (D) 64 (Apr), where the claimant was an army chaplain whose fixed term contract had not been renewed and who (unsuccessfully) alleged various breaches of public law principles and *Article 6, ECHR*.

In *R (Crompton) v Police and Crime Commissioner for South Yorkshire* [2018] 1 WLR 131, the Divisional Court granted a claim for judicial review brought by a chief constable who was suspended and subsequently required to resign by the Police and Crime Commissioner for

38.6   Public Sector Employees

South Yorkshire. The chief constable had made a public apology following verdicts in the Hillsborough inquests, but followed that apology up with a further statement to which the Commissioner took objection, and for which he was criticised by Members of Parliament. The Commissioner's suspend and ultimately required the chief constable's resignation on the basis of his second statement pursuant to *s 38* of the *Police Reform and Social Responsibility Act 2011*.

Although the claim proceeded by way of judicial review, the Divisional Court's analysis of the Commissioner's decision rested upon principles that will be familiar to employment lawyers. The Court concluded that the chief commissioner's conduct in issuing the second decision was within the range of reasonable responses available to him, and the Commissioner's decision to require his resignation was therefore irrational. The Court held further, *per curiam*, that the Commissioner's decision had violated the chief constable's rights under *ECHR, Article 8*.

It should also be remembered that the court hearing an application for judicial review has an overriding discretion as to whether any relief should be granted. One possible reason for refusing to consider a claim or to grant relief is that some alternative remedy was available and should have been pursued. Thus, in *Bruce* ([1988] 3 All ER 686, [1988] ICR 649) the Divisional Court accepted that there was a sufficient public law element for an unsuccessful appeal against dismissal to the Civil Service Appeal Board to be judicially reviewable, but held that only in exceptional cases would it be right not to confine the applicant to his remedy in an industrial tribunal. The Court of Appeal upheld the refusal of relief on the facts without expressing a view on the general proposition. In *R v Hammersmith and Fulham London Borough Council, ex p NALGO* [1991] IRLR 249, it was held that a local authority's redundancy selection policy should be tested by way of cases brought in the tribunal alleging unfair dismissal or discrimination, and not by way of judicial review.

If available, judicial review can provide a powerful remedy to the employee, as it did in *R v Civil Service Appeal Board, ex p Cunningham* [1991] 4 All ER 310, [1992] ICR 816, [1991] IRLR 297, where a decision of the Board was struck down because of the Board's failure to give adequate reasons. In *R (Shoesmith) v Ofsted* [2011] EWCA Civ 642, [2011] IRLR 679, [2011] ICR 1195 (discussed above) the Court of Appeal declared that the Claimant's dismissal had been unlawful and ordered the local authority to pay compensation.

38.7   LITIGATING AGAINST PUBLIC AUTHORITIES

A local authority has an express power under the *LGA 1972, s 222* to prosecute, defend or appear in legal proceedings, and an implied power to compromise litigation. However, a public body can lawfully compromise a dispute with an employee (or ex employee) only in circumstances where it is acting within the scope of its statutory powers in doing so.

One application of the *ultra vires* doctrine is that any sum paid to settle a claim must not be excessively generous. See *Gibb v Maidstone and Tunbridge Wells NHS Trust* [2009] EWHC 862 (QB), [2009] All ER (D) 209 (Apr), [2009] IRLR 707 where an NHS Trust paid its Chief Executive £100,000 in excess of what she could have been awarded by an employment tribunal in return for her leaving its employment. The High Court found that this was excessive generosity, which led to a finding that the payment was irrational and therefore the compromise agreement was void. However, this decision was overturned by the Court of Appeal, which found that the sum was not excessively generous because the NHS Trust was entitled to take into account the employee's length of service and chances of re-employment: [2010] EWCA Civ 678, [2010] IRLR 786.

In litigation against public authorities, in particular government departments, attempts to obtain documents by way of an order for disclosure may sometimes be met by a claim that those documents should not be disclosed because they are subject to public interest immunity. This means that the interest in preventing the disclosure of such documents outweighs the interest in the court or tribunal having all the relevant evidence. The court may itself examine the documents in order to decide whether they ought to be disclosed. See in particular *Conway v Rimmer* [1968] AC 910, [1968] 1 All ER 874, *Air Canada v Secretary of State for Trade* [1983] 2 AC 394, [1983] 1 All ER 161, *R v Chief Constable of West Midlands Police, ex p Wiley* [1995] 1 AC 274, [1994] 3 All ER 420, *R (Corner House Research) v Director of the Serious Fraud Office (BAE Systems plc, interested party)* [2008] UKHL 60, [2009] AC 756, [2008] 4 All ER 927, *R (Mohamed) v Secretary of State for Foreign and Commonwealth Affairs* [2010] EWCA Civ 65, [2010] 4 All ER 91, *R (on the application of Evans) v Secretary of State for Defence* [2013] EWHC 3068 (Admin), [2013] All ER (D) 251 (Oct) and *Amin v Director General of the Security Service* [2014] EWCA Civ 598.

Occasionally employment disputes will also raise questions of national security (see, eg *Council of Civil Service Unions v Minister for the Civil Service* [1985] AC 374, [1985] IRLR 28). Provision is made for requiring or enabling tribunals and the EAT to sit in private in cases involving national security or confidential information (*ETA 1996, ss 10* and *10A* respectively). See also *Employment Tribunals (Constitution and Rules of Procedure) Regulations 2013 (SI 2013/1237), reg 10* and *para 94* of *Sch 1, Sch 2*, and *para 13* of *Sch 3* and *Employment Appeal Tribunal Rules 1993 (SI 1993/2854), rule 30A*. The Supreme Court held that the former Employment Tribunal Rules were not intrinsically unlawful, provided that sufficient safeguards were in place and the procedure was used flexibly in the context of the case, as it progressed: *Home Office v Tariq* [2012] 1 AC 452, [2011] IRLR 843, [2011] ICR 938. The Employment Appeal Tribunal gave guidance on the correct approach when an application is made for a closed hearing before the EAT on national security grounds in *AB v Ministry of Defence* [2010] ICR 54, [2009] All ER (D) 135 (Sep). The application of *Tariq* was considered by the Court of Appeal in *Kiani v Secretary of State for the Home Department* [2016] 2 WLR 788, [2015] IRLR 837, [2015] ICR 1179.

Where in the opinion of any Minister of the Crown the disclosure of any information would be contrary to the interests of national security, disclosure of that information will not be required by certain provisions of *ERA 1996*, and no person may disclose that information in any court or tribunal proceedings relating to any of those provisions (*ERA 1996, s 202*). The rights generally available to employees who have made a protected disclosure do not apply in relation to employment in the Security Service, the Secret Intelligence Service, or the Government Communications Headquarters. (*ERA 1996, s 193*).

38.8   EUROPEAN UNION LAW

Prior to the UK's withdrawal from the European Union, the EU Law doctrine of direct effect provided an additional layer of complexity for public sector employees. That layer of complexity will be removed following the expiry of the implementation period on 31 December 2020.

The doctrine of direct effect provided, as the name suggests, for the direct enforcement in domestic courts of rights arising under EU law which would otherwise require domestic enabling legislation. Some categories of EU legislation (the Treaties themselves, and regulations) become applicable once promulgated without any need for further action by member states. In the *Directives*, however, the intention is that member states should, within a given time, take such steps as they consider appropriate to implement the *Directive* in their territory.

A central feature of EU Law, developed by the European Court of Justice,, provided that if a member state fails to comply with its obligation to implement a *Directive* (either because it does nothing or because what it does is held not to achieve all that the *Directive* requires), then, although that *Directive* cannot be relied upon in proceedings against private persons, it may be relied upon against that State. The theory underpinning the doctrine was that the State may not take advantage of its own wrong in failing to introduce measures to implement the *Directive*. In order for a person to be able to rely on a *Directive* against the state, the terms of the *Directive* must be clear and it must be unconditional, ie it must require no further implementing measures or time before it is intended to have effect.

It was this doctrine which enabled the applicant in *Marshall v Southampton and South West Hampshire Area Health Authority (Teaching)* [1986] ICR 335, [1986] IRLR 140 to succeed in her claim of unlawful sex discrimination based on discriminatory retiring ages at a time before the *Sex Discrimination Act 1986* was passed. The health authority which employed her was agreed to be an organ of the state, so that she could rely directly upon *Directive 76/207/EEC*, unlike private sector employees (see **24.6** EUROPEAN UNION LAW).

This doctrine was controversial, and it was a prominent target for those advocating the UK's withdrawal from the European Union. It is now significantly curtailed by the *European Union (Withdrawal) Act 2018*. *Section 1* of the *Withdrawal Act* repealed the *European Communities Act 1972*, and *ss 2–6* make provision for the retention of certain provisions, rules and principles of EU Law, defined collectively in the *Act* as Retained EU Law. *Section 2* provides for the retention of EU-derived domestic legislation. *Section 3* makes provision for the incorporation into domestic law of direct EU legislation. It does not include directives. *Section 4(2)(b)* goes further and provides that rights arising under an EU directive do not continue to be recognised and exist in available in domestic law if they *"arise under an EU Directive... and are not of a kind recognised by the European Court or any court or tribunal in the United Kingdom in a case decided before exit day"*.

Accordingly, following exit day, only those Directives that were (i) implemented through domestic legislation or (ii) recognised by the Courts as having direct effect will continue to influence domestic employment law. The law is, in this respect, frozen as at exit day.

39   Redundancy – I: The Right to a Redundancy Payment

Cross-references. TRANSFER OF UNDERTAKINGS (53). See **55.11** UNFAIR DISMISSAL – II for dismissal on grounds of redundancy, and PAY – I (35) for details of the calculation of the employee's weekly pay. See CONTRACT OF EMPLOYMENT (8) for principles applicable to enhanced redundancy payments claimed under the contract of employment.

39.1   The *Redundancy Payments Act 1965* ('*RPA 1965*') introduced the right of employees who lost their jobs in certain circumstances to a payment from their employers irrespective of whether they had another job to go to. The *RPA 1965* was amended by the *Employment Protection Act 1975* ('*EPA 1975*') and the provisions, as amended, were re-enacted in the *Employment Protection (Consolidation) Act 1978* ('*EPCA 1978*'). The provisions are now contained in the *Employment Rights Act 1996* ('*ERA 1996*').

39.2   PRE-CONDITIONS FOR PAYMENT

The conditions which must be fulfilled for a person to be entitled to a redundancy payment are:

(a)   that he was an employee;

(b)   that he had been continuously employed for the requisite period;

(c)   that he was dismissed (as defined); and

(d)   that the dismissal was by reason of redundancy.

(*ERA 1996, ss 135, 155.*)

Certain employees are excluded from the right to a redundancy payment (see **39.10** below).

39.3   APPLICANT MUST HAVE BEEN AN EMPLOYEE

Only 'employees' are entitled to claim a redundancy payment. Thus, those engaged under a contract for services are not entitled to make such a claim. 'Employee' is defined as:

'   . . .   an individual who has entered into or works under (or, where the employment has ceased, worked under) a contract of employment.'

(*ERA 1996, s 230(1).*)

See EMPLOYEE, SELF-EMPLOYED OR WORKER? (16).

If the respondent to an application for a redundancy payment (ie the employer) disputes the fact that the applicant was an employee, it is for the applicant to prove that he was.

39.4   Continuous employment for the requisite period

In order to be entitled to a redundancy payment, an applicant must have been *continuously employed for a period of two years ending with the relevant date* (see below for 'relevant date') (*ERA 1996, s 155*).

The rules for computing continuous employment are dealt with in detail in CONTINUOUS EMPLOYMENT (7).

The relevant date. The relevant date in relation to the dismissal of an employee:

(a) where his contract of employment is terminated by notice, whether given by his employer or by the employee, means the date on which that notice expires;
(b) where his contract of employment is terminated without notice, means the date on which the termination takes effect; and
(c) where he is employed under a limited-term contract which terminates by virtue of the limiting event without being renewed under the same contract, means the date on which the termination takes effect.
(*ERA 1996, s 145.*)

This provision corresponds to the definition of the 'effective date of termination' for the purposes of unfair dismissal contained in *ERA 1996, s 97(1)*; for a discussion of its application see **54.13** Unfair Dismissal – I.

If an employee is dismissed with no notice or less than the statutory minimum period of notice, for the purposes, *inter alia*, of calculating the qualifying period of employment, the relevant date will be the date upon which the statutory minimum period of notice would have expired had it been given (*ERA 1996, s 145(5)*). (See **49.7** Termination of Employment.) However, this provision does not affect the employer's right to dismiss without notice for an employee's gross misconduct (*ERA 1996, s 86(6)*). In the event of such a dismissal, the statutory minimum period of notice will not be added on for the purpose of computing the length of continuous employment.

39.5   Changes in the ownership of the business

The *Transfer of Undertakings (Protection of Employment) Regulations 2006 (SI 2006/246)* are discussed fully in Transfer of Undertakings (53). By virtue of the *Regulations*, on a 'relevant transfer' of an undertaking, the existing employees' contracts of employment are not terminated. On completion of such a transfer all the transferor's rights, powers, duties and liabilities under or in connection with any such contract are transferred to the transferee (*Transfer of Undertakings Regulations, reg 4(2)(a)*). Therefore, such an employee will be deemed not to have been dismissed by the transferor and the continuity of his employment will be preserved.

39.6   The employee must have been 'dismissed'

There is no presumption of dismissal and, if the employer disputes the fact, it is for the employee to prove it. For redundancy payments purposes, dismissal has a statutory meaning instead of merely meaning termination of the contract by the employer. Sub-paragraph (*a*) below reflects the common law position (see **49.5** Termination of Employment), and occurs most frequently in practice, while (*b*) would not be a dismissal at common law. In addition, certain forms of termination of the contract at common law are disregarded for redundancy payments purposes (see below).

An employee will be taken to be dismissed by his employer if, but only if:

(a) the contract under which he is employed by the employer is terminated by the employer, whether it is terminated by notice or without notice;
(b) where under that contract he is employed for a limited term, the contract terminates by virtue of the limiting event without being renewed under the same contract; or
(c) the employee terminates that contract with or without notice in circumstances such that he is entitled so to terminate it without notice by reason of the employer's conduct (not being termination by reason of a lock-out).
(*ERA 1996, s 136(1), (2).*)

The statutory definition of dismissal for redundancy payments purposes is the same as for the purposes of unfair dismissal (see Unfair Dismissal – I (54)).

Where in accordance with any enactment or rule of law any act on the part of an employer, or any event affecting an employer, operates so as to terminate a contract of employment, that is treated for redundancy payments purposes as a termination by the employer, even if it would not otherwise amount to such a termination (*ERA 1996, s 136(5)*; and see *Pickwell v Lincolnshire County Council* [1993] ICR 87).

Situations where no dismissal occurs. An employee is deemed not to have been dismissed in certain circumstances where a dismissal by reason of redundancy has in fact taken place. Two examples are given below.

(i)   *Renewal or re-engagement.* If an employee's contract is renewed or he is re-engaged under a new contract of employment and:

(A) the offer, whether in writing or not, is made before the ending of the existing contract; and
(B) it is to take effect either immediately on the ending of the original employment or within a period of not more than four weeks thereafter (if the contract ends on Friday, Saturday or Sunday, the new employment must take effect four weeks from the following Monday),

no dismissal will be deemed to have taken place in respect of the termination of the original contract (*ERA 1996, s 138(1)*).

If the terms and conditions of the new employment differ wholly or in part from the original contract, the employee has a trial period of four weeks from the ending of the original employment, or such longer period as may be agreed in writing, within which to decide whether to accept or reject the offer (see **39.12** below). If he rejects the offer or if the employer terminates or gives notice to terminate the contract for a reason connected with the change in contractual terms, within that period, the employee will be taken to have been dismissed on the date of termination of the original contract for the reason that contract was terminated (*ERA 1996, s 138(2)–(6)*).

(ii)   *Offers of employment by associated companies.* It should be noted that where the employer is a company, any reference to re-engagement by the employer is construed as including a reference to re-engagement by *that company or by an associated company*, and any reference to an offer made by the employer is construed as including a reference to an offer made by an associated company (*ERA 1996, s 146(1)*). For the meaning of 'associated company', see **7.9**(a) CONTINUOUS EMPLOYMENT.

Employee who leaves prematurely. An employee who leaves his employment before his employer's notice of dismissal expires may lose his right to a redundancy payment. If the employee gives written notice to terminate his employment on a date earlier than that given by his employer, he will not lose his right to a redundancy payment if the employer does not object to his premature departure. If, however, the employer does object and serves on the employee a written request to withdraw his notice, warning him that if he does not do so the employer will contest any liability to make a redundancy payment, he may lose the right to such a payment. If the employer withholds the redundancy payment, the employee may apply to an employment tribunal which will decide whether the employee is entitled to the full payment, or no payment, or part of the payment. The tribunal will consider whether the employee's action in leaving prematurely was reasonable or unreasonable in the circumstances (*ERA 1996, ss 136(3), 142(1), (2)*). If, however, the parties agree by mutual consent to substitute some other date of termination for the date specified by the employer, no such question arises (*CPS Recruitment Ltd v Bowen and Secretary of State for Employment* [1982] IRLR 54).

39.7 Redundancy must be the reason for dismissal

In order to be entitled to a redundancy payment, the employee must be dismissed by reason of redundancy. An employee who has been dismissed by his employer is, unless the contrary is proved, presumed to have been dismissed by reason of redundancy for the purposes of any claim for a redundancy payment (*ERA 1996, s 163(2)*). There is, however, no formal burden of proof upon the employer. The tribunal must decide whether the presumption has been rebutted on the basis of all the evidence before them: see *Greater Glasgow Health Board v Lamont* UKEATS/0019/12.

'Redundancy' is defined as follows:

'For the purposes of this Act an employee who is dismissed shall be taken to be dismissed by reason of redundancy if the dismissal is wholly or mainly attributable to –

(*a*)   the fact that his employer has ceased or intends to cease:
(i) to carry on the business for the purposes of which the employee was employed by him, or
(ii) to carry on that business in the place where the employee was so employed, or

(*b*)   the fact that the requirements of that business:
(i) for employees to carry out work of a particular kind, or
(ii) for employees to carry out work of a particular kind in the place where the employee was employed by the employer,
have ceased or diminished or are expected to cease or diminish.'

(*ERA 1996, s 139(1)*; note that a different definition applies for the purposes of the redundancy consultation provisions of *TULR(C)A 1992* (see **40.3** REDUNDANCY – **II**).)

Sub-paragraph (*a*) covers the closure of the employer's business as a whole, or, alternatively, just at the place where the employee is employed. The test for determining 'the place where the employee was employed' is primarily a factual one, although the employee's contractual terms may provide evidence of the place of work where the employee did go from place to place (see *High Table Ltd v Horst* [1998] ICR 409, [1997] IRLR 513, CA). Thus, if an employee had as a matter of fact worked in only one location, then the existence of a contractual mobility clause (entitling the employer to transfer him) will not widen the definition of the place where the employee was employed under *ERA 1996, s 139(1)* (see also *Bass Leisure Ltd v Thomas* [1994] IRLR 104).

Under sub-para (*b*) it must be considered whether the business requires so many employees to carry out certain work. In deciding whether there has been a cessation or diminution in the requirements of the business for employees to carry out 'work of a particular kind', it was uncertain whether the work is defined by what is required under an employee's contract of employment ('the contract test'), or by what an employee is actually doing ('the function test'), or by a blend of the two. Until 1997, it was assumed that the Court of Appeal in *Cowen v Haden Ltd* [1983] ICR 1, [1982] IRLR 314 had established that the proper test was the contract test. However, the EAT in *Safeway Stores plc v Burrell* [1997] ICR 523, [1997] IRLR 200 disagreed with this interpretation of *Cowen v Haden* and stated that the terms of an employee's contract of employment were irrelevant when determining whether there was a redundancy situation within the meaning of *ERA 1996, s 139(1)*. The House of Lords confirmed in the case of *Murray v Foyle Meats Ltd* [2000] 1 AC 51, [1999] 3 All ER 769, [1999] IRLR 562, [1999] ICR 827 that both the 'contract test' and the 'function test' are an unnecessary gloss on the plain wording of the statute. Further, the Court of Appeal held in *Shawkat v Nottingham City Hospital NHS Trust (No 2)* [2001] EWCA Civ 954, [2001] IRLR 555 that whether there was less need for employees to carry out work of a particular kind was always a question of fact for a tribunal to decide.

The House of Lords in *Murray* approved the reasoning of the EAT in *Safeway Stores v Burrell* (see above), one of whose conclusions was that 'bumped employees' will be dismissed by reason of redundancy. A 'bumping' situation will exist where Smith, whose job is no longer required, is put by his employer into Brown's position, so that Brown is dismissed instead of Smith. The reasoning in *Safeway Stores v Burrell* would mean that Brown was redundant, because the employer's requirement for work of a particular kind had diminished, and because Brown was dismissed as a result. It is not necessary that any reduction in the employer's requirements for work of a particular kind should be a reduction in the type of work that Brown himself carried out. *Safeway Stores v Burrell* follows earlier authority (see *W Gimber & Sons Ltd v Spurrett* (1967) 2 ITR 308; applied by the EAT in *Elliott Turbomachinery Ltd v Bates* [1981] ICR 218) in reaching this conclusion. The EAT decision in *Church v West Lancashire NHS Trust* [1998] ICR 423, [1998] IRLR 4 initially created some uncertainty as to whether *Safeway Stores* was correct, but those doubts were dispelled by *Murray*, and more recently, by the EAT in *Stankovic v City of Westminster* [2001] All ER (D) 340 (Oct), EAT. Indeed, the EAT specifically stated in *Stankovic* that *Church* was no longer good authority on the point.

A redundancy situation within the meaning of *ERA 1996, s 139(1)(b)* will also exist where the amount of work available for the same number of employees has reduced. So, for example, where an employer offers employees reduced working hours following a downturn in business, and an employee is dismissed for refusing to accept reduced working hours, the dismissal is for redundancy: see *Packman v Fauchon* [2012] ICR 1362, [2012] IRLR 721. (In *Packman*, Langstaff P considered in detail the EAT's decision to the opposite effect in *Aylward v Glamorgan Holiday Homes Ltd* UKEAT/167/02 [2003] All ER (D) 249 (Apr), and declined to follow it.)

Where an employee is employed on a succession of fixed-term contracts this can, in principle, give rise to a dismissal by reason of redundancy on the expiration of each fixed-term contract (*Pfaffinger v City of Liverpool Community College* [1997] ICR 142, [1996] IRLR 508).

39.8   Redundancy payments for lay-off and short time

Special provisions relating to redundancy claims by piece-workers who are laid off or put on short time are contained in *ERA 1996*. An employee is considered to be *laid off* during a particular week if under his contract he gets no pay of any kind from his employer for that week because there is no work for him to do although he is available for work (*ERA 1996, s 147*). An employee is considered to be on short time for a week if during that week he gets less than half a week's pay (*ERA 1996, s 147(2)*).

A redundancy payment may only be claimed by a worker laid off or on short time if he gives notice in writing to his employer of his intention to claim and the claim is submitted within four weeks of:

(a) the end of a continuous period of lay-off or short time of four or more weeks' duration; or
(b) the end of a period of six weeks' lay-off or short time out of 13 weeks (where not more than three weeks were consecutive).
(*ERA 1996, s 148*.)

He must then terminate his contract of employment by giving the contractual period of notice or one week's notice, whichever is the greater (*ERA 1996, s 150(1)*).

The notice to terminate must be given within the following time limits:

(a) if the employer does not give a counter-notice (see **39.9** below) within seven days after the service of the notice of intention to claim, that period is three weeks after the end of those seven days;

(b) if the employer gives a counter-notice within those seven days, but withdraws it by a subsequent notice in writing, that period is three weeks after the service of the notice of withdrawal; and

(c) if the employer gives a counter-notice within those seven days and does not so withdraw it, and a question as to the right of the employee to a redundancy payment in pursuance of the notice of intention to claim is referred to a tribunal, that period is three weeks after the tribunal has notified to the employee its decision on that reference.

(*ERA 1996, s 150(3)*.)

Even if an employee fails to comply with these statutory requirements, he may claim that he has been constructively dismissed for redundancy if he is laid off in fundamental breach of his contract of employment (*A Dakri & Co Ltd v Tiffen* [1981] ICR 256, [1981] IRLR 57; cf *Kenneth McRae & Co Ltd v Dawson* [1984] IRLR 5). However, no term should be implied into an employee's contract that any period of lay-off will be for no longer than is reasonable, in circumstances where Parliament has provided a detailed scheme which sets out the appropriate balance between the rights of the employee and the interests of the employer: *Craig v Bob Lindfield & Son Ltd* (UKEAT/0220/15) [2016] ICR 527, [2015] All ER (D) 307 (Nov).

39.9   Counter-notice

An employee who gives a notice of intention to claim pursuant to *ERA 1996, s 148* will not be entitled to a redundancy payment if, on the date of service of that notice, it was reasonably to be expected that he would (if he continued to be employed by the same employer), not later than four weeks after that date, enter upon a period of employment of not less than 13 weeks during which he would not be laid off or kept on short time (*ERA 1996, s 152(1)*).

However, an employer cannot take advantage of this rule unless, within seven days after service of the notice of intention to claim, he gives the employee notice in writing that he will contest liability to make a redundancy payment (*ERA 1996, s 152(1)(b)*). If the employee wishes to pursue his claim after the service of a counter-notice, an employment tribunal must be asked to determine whether he is entitled to a redundancy payment (*ERA 1996, s 149*).

39.10 Exclusions from right to payment

The following are excluded from the right to a redundancy payment.

(a)   Masters or crew of a fishing vessel who are not remunerated otherwise than by a share of the profits or gross earnings of the vessel (*ERA 1996, s 199(2)* (see *Goodeve v Gilsons (a firm)* [1985] ICR 401)).

(b)   Civil servants and other public employees (*ERA 1996, s 159*).

(c)   Persons employed in any capacity under the Government of any territory or country outside the United Kingdom (*ERA 1996, s 160*).

(d)   Domestic servants in a private household where the employer is the parent (or step-parent), grandparent, child (or step-child), grandchild or brother or sister (or half-brother or half-sister) of the employee. References to step-parent or step-child include relationships arising through civil partnership: see the *Civil Partnership Act 2004, ss 246, 247, Sch 21* (*ERA 1996, s 161*).

(e)   Employees who have been offered employment on the same terms and conditions as their original employment or offered *suitable alternative employment* and in either case have *unreasonably refused the offer* (see **39.12** below) (*ERA 1996, s 141(1)–(3)*).

(f)   Employees who have been offered suitable alternative employment, and have unreasonably terminated their contracts during the statutory trial period (see **39.12** below) (*ERA 1996, s 141(4)*).

(g)   Employees who are dismissed for misconduct. If notice is given for this reason it must be accompanied by a statement in writing that the employer would, because of the employee's conduct, be entitled to terminate the contract without notice. If the employee is dismissed without notice, there is no need to give any statement in writing that dismissal was on the ground of misconduct (*ERA 1996, s 140(1)*). The employer is entitled to terminate when the employee has been in fundamental breach of his contract of employment (*Bonner v H Gilbert Ltd* [1989] IRLR 475). This provision does not apply where the dismissal is for taking part in a strike (*ERA 1996, s 140(2)*). The tribunal, in any event, has a discretion to award the whole or part of a redundancy payment to the dismissed employee where it is just and equitable to do so (*ERA 1996, s 140(3)*).

(h)   Employees who are dismissed if an *exemption order* is in force (*ERA 1996, s 157*). An exemption order is an order made by the Secretary of State for Business, Innovation and Skills exempting an employer or a group of employers from liability to make redundancy payments under the *Act* where they have similar or more advantageous agreements with their employees for making payments on redundancy.

39.11 Time limit for claims

Employees are not entitled to a redundancy payment unless, before the end of the period of six months beginning with the relevant date:

(a) the payment has been agreed and paid;
(b) the employee has made a claim for the payment by notice in writing given to the employer;
(c) a question as to the right of the employee to the payment, or as to the amount of the payment, has been referred to an employment tribunal; or
(d) a complaint of unfair dismissal has been presented by the employee to a tribunal.
(*ERA 1996, s 164(1)(c)*.) (For the meaning of 'relevant date', see **39.4** above.)

If, however, within the *next* six months, the employee takes the action in (*b*), (*c*) or (*d*), a tribunal may award a redundancy payment if it considers it just and equitable to do so having regard to the reason for the delay (*ERA 1996, s 164(2)*).

An application for a redundancy payment is 'referred' to an employment tribunal when it is received by the tribunal office and not when it is sent by the employee (*Secretary of State for Employment v Banks* [1983] ICR 48).

The time limits for a complaint under *ERA 1996, s 164(1)(c)* or *s 164(2)* are subject to *ERA 1996, s 207B* (extension of time limits for facilitate conciliation before institution of proceedings).

See also **39.14** below.

39.12 UNREASONABLE REFUSAL OF SUITABLE ALTERNATIVE EMPLOYMENT

An employee who is dismissed by reason of redundancy loses his right to a redundancy payment if he unreasonably refuses an offer of suitable alternative employment. The offer of alternative employment:

(a)   must be made by his original employer or an associated employer (*ERA 1996, s 141(1)*; and see **7.9**(a) Continuous Employment);

(b)   must be made before the ending of his employment under his previous contract (*ERA 1996, s 141(1)*);

(c)   may be oral or in writing;

(d)   must take effect either immediately on the ending of the employment under the previous contract or after an interval of not more than four weeks thereafter (*ERA 1996, s 141(1)*). The alternative employment will be treated as taking effect immediately on the ending of the employment under the previous contract if that employment ends on a Friday, Saturday or Sunday, and the alternative employment is to commence on or before the next Monday. The interval of four weeks is calculated accordingly (*ERA 1996, s 146(2)*). An offer which is not ongoing and which would take effect prior to the dismissal will not satisfy *ERA 1996, s 141(1)* (*McHugh v Hempsall Bulk Transport Ltd*, IDS Brief 480, p 6); and

(e)   must be either:
(i) on the same terms and conditions as the previous contract; or
(ii) suitable employment in relation to the employee.
(*ERA, s 141(3)*.)

If the terms and conditions of the renewed or new contract of employment differ (wholly or in part) from the corresponding provisions of his previous contract, the employee has a statutory trial period of four weeks, beginning with the ending of his previous employment, in which to decide whether the alternative employment is suitable for him. The four-week trial period means four calendar weeks. Thus, 11 days when the factory was closed over Christmas had to be taken into account (*Benton v Sanderson Keyser Ltd* [1989] ICR 136, [1989] IRLR 19). This four-week period may be extended by agreement, for the purpose of retraining the employee for employment under the new or renewed contract. Such an agreement must:

(i) be made before the employee starts work under the renewed or new contract;
(ii) be in writing;
(iii) specify the date of the end of the trial period; and
(iv) specify the terms and conditions of employment which will apply in the employee's case after the end of that period.
(*ERA 1996, s 138(6)*.)

Although the employer is no longer required, in making the offer, to give the employee details of the changes in terms and conditions in writing, where applicable, employers may still find it useful to do so. The employer, however, remains obliged to give written particulars of the main terms of an employee's employment within one month of the change (*ERA 1996, s 4(1)*). (See **8.7 CONTRACT OF EMPLOYMENT**.)

An employee whose contract was repudiated by his employers is entitled, in accordance with the common law, to a reasonable period in which to decide whether to enter into a new contract or to treat himself as dismissed (see TERMINATION OF EMPLOYMENT (**49**)). So an employee whose contract is repudiated, and who is given alternative employment which does not fall within the terms of *ERA 1996, s 138(1)*, has a reasonable period within which to decide whether to accept the repudiation and claim a redundancy payment: see *Turvey v C W Cheney & Son Ltd* [1979] ICR 341, [1979] IRLR 105. However, the *Turvey* case should not be seen as authority for the proposition that the common law can operate to extend the statutory four-week period under *ERA 1996, s 136*. If alternative employment is offered within the terms of *ERA 1996 s 138(1)*, the four-week period cannot be extended save under s 138(6): see *Optical Express Ltd v Williams* [2008] ICR 1, [2007] IRLR 936.

If the employee accepts the alternative employment, which was offered before the termination of his original employment and which takes effect not more than four weeks thereafter, he is deemed not to have been dismissed on the termination of the original employment for the purposes of determining any liability of the employer for redundancy payments (*ERA 1996, s 138(1)*; see *Jones v Governing Body of Burdett Coutts School* [1997] ICR 390, EAT, cf *Ebac Ltd v Wymer* [1995] ICR 466). If, during the trial period, the employee terminates the contract or gives notice to terminate it, or if the employer, for a reason connected with or arising out of any difference between the renewed or new contract and the previous contract, terminates the contract or gives notice to terminate it, the employee is treated as having been dismissed on the date on which his original contract came to an end (*ERA 1996, s 138(2), (4)*).

If, during the trial period, the employer dismisses the employee for a reason unconnected with or not arising out of the change, the employee can bring an unfair dismissal claim on the basis of the fairness of the dismissal in the trial period (*Hempell v W H Smith & Sons Ltd* [1986] ICR 365, [1986] IRLR 95).

If the terms of the new contract are suitable and the employee unreasonably terminates the contract during the trial period, he will not be entitled to a redundancy payment by reason of his dismissal under the original contract (*ERA 1996, s 141(4)*).

The question of the suitability of an offer of alternative employment is an objective matter, whereas the reasonableness of the employee's refusal depends on factors personal to him and is a subjective matter to be considered from the employee's point of view. This means that the importation of a "reasonable band of responses" test analogous to that used in unfair dismissal is not appropriate: see *Readman v Devon Primary Care Trust* [2013] IRLR 878. So, for example, the offer to a butcher's shop manager of a job as a supermarket butchery department manager may be suitable alternative employment, but his perceived loss of status may make it reasonable for him to refuse it (*Cambridge & District Co-operative Society v Ruse* [1993] IRLR 156). The Court of Appeal in *Spencer and Griffin v Gloucestershire County Council* [1985] IRLR 393 has said that in evaluating the separate questions of suitability of employment and reasonableness of refusal, the employment tribunal is entitled to look at factors which may prove, on analysis, to be common to both. In that case, the Court of Appeal, in upholding a decision of an employment tribunal, considered that a refusal by an employee to do work of a lower standard than the employee considered reasonable, may be a reason for holding that the work offered is not suitable or has been reasonably refused. Before the tribunal, an employee can rely on a reason for refusal that he or she has not expressly raised with the employer when refusing the offer: see *Dunne v Colin & Avril Ltd* UKEAT/0293/16 (8 March 2017).

39.13 AMOUNT OF THE PAYMENT

The amount of the redundancy payment is based upon the employee's age, length of continuous employment and gross average wage.

The calculation of continuity is made in accordance with rules set out in *ERA 1996, ss 210 to 219*; see **39.4** above and CONTINUOUS EMPLOYMENT (7).

Contractual agreements relating to continuity of employment cannot affect an employer's statutory liability to make a redundancy payment (*Secretary of State for Employment v Globe Elastic Thread Co Ltd* [1980] AC 506, [1979] 2 All ER 1077, [1979] IRLR 327, [1979] ICR 706). Therefore, if an employer agrees to preserve an employee's continuity of employment where there is no continuity in accordance with the statutory provisions, he will be contractually liable to make a redundancy payment calculated in accordance with his agreement, but not liable to make any payment under statute.

Provisions for an enhanced contractual redundancy payment will usually provide that the statutory payment is offset against any contractual entitlement. In *Ugradar v Lancashire Care NHS Foundation Trust* UKEAT/0301/18 (20 June 2019), a question arose as to whether this precluded an employee receiving a statutory redundancy payment, when the Tribunal had allowed her claim in respect of a contractual redundancy payment, but had capped the award at £25,000 pursuant to the statutory cap in the *Employment Tribunals (Extension of Jurisdiction)(England and Wales) Order 1994*. The Employment Appeal Tribunal held that the employee was entitled to receive her statutory redundancy payment in addition to the award of £25,000. The cap of £25,000 was to be imposed upon the contractual award after the employee's loss had been assessed; and her contractual loss was £43,000 minus the amount of any statutory redundancy payment. The Employment Appeal Tribunal also commented that the statutory cap was out of step with the Employment Tribunal's powers generally, and should be reviewed.

The amount of the redundancy payment is calculated by reference to the period, ending with the relevant date, during which the employee has been continuously employed. (For the meaning of 'relevant date' see **39.4** above.) There is then allowed:

(a) one and a half week's pay for each such year of employment which consists wholly of weeks in which the employee was not below the age of 41;
(b) one week's pay for each such year of employment (not falling within (*a*) above) which consists wholly of weeks in which the employee was not below the age of 22; and
(c) half a week's pay for each such year of employment not falling within either of the preceding sub-paragraphs.

(*ERA 1996, s 162(1), (2)*.) Where an employee has been continuously employed for 20 years ending with the relevant date, no account is taken of any year of employment earlier than those 20 years (*ERA 1996, s 162(3)*). In other words, the maximum number of years to be taken into account in calculating a redundancy payment is 20, reckoning back from termination of his contract. A previous redundancy payment breaks continuity for this purpose (*ERA 1996, s 214(2)*).

A week's pay is calculated in accordance with *ERA 1996, ss 221–229*. The calculation is based on average wages without deduction of tax, not taking into account overtime, unless the employer is contractually bound to provide and the employee to work such overtime. Where an employee is on short-time working on the calculation date, "a week's pay" should be that provided for by the original contract of employment, notwithstanding the short-time working: see *Dutton v Jones* UKEAT/0236/12 [2013] ICR 559, [2013] All ER (D) 317 (Feb). (See Pay – I (35) for full details.)

With effect from 6 April 2020, the maximum amount of a week's pay allowed in computing a statutory redundancy payment is £538 (*ERA 1996, s 227* and the *Employment Rights (Increase of Limits) Order 2020 (SI 2020/205)*). Thus, the current maximum statutory redundancy payment is £16,140.

39.14 REFERENCES TO EMPLOYMENT TRIBUNAL AND RESTRICTION ON CONTRACTING OUT

Any question arising as to the right of an employee to a redundancy payment, or as to the amount of a redundancy payment, is to be referred to and determined by an employment tribunal (*ERA 1996, s 163(1)*). Where an employment tribunal determines that an employee has a right to a redundancy payment, it may also order the employer to pay to the employee such amount as it considers appropriate in all the circumstances to compensate him for any financial loss which is attributable to the non-payment of the redundancy payment (*ERA 1996, s 163(5)*).

Any provision in any agreement (whether a contract of employment or not) is *prima facie* void insofar as it purports to exclude or limit any provisions relating to redundancy, or to preclude any person from bringing any proceedings in respect of a redundancy payment before an employment tribunal (*ERA 1996, s 203(1)*).

However, an employee will be bound by a settlement agreement reached following action by a conciliation officer, or by a compromise contract which satisfies the statutory conditions, including that the employee should have had independent advice (*ERA 1996, s 203(2)*; and see **2.4** ADVISORY, CONCILIATION AND ARBITRATION SERVICE and **19.20** EMPLOYMENT TRIBUNALS – I).

39.15   Ready Reckoner for Redundancy Payments

To use the Table — Read off employee's age and number of complete years' service. The Table will then show how many weeks' pay the employee is entitled to. It should be noted that although the Table runs only between the ages of 20 and 64, service before and after these ages does count for redundancy purposes, and there is no age below or above which redundancy payments cannot be claimed.

The Table may also be used to calculate the basic award for unfair dismissal.

AGE (years)	\multicolumn{19}{c}{SERVICE (years)}																		
	2	3	4	5	6	7	8	9	10	11	12	13	14	15	16	17	18	19	20
20	1	1½	2	2½	—														
21	1	1½	2	2½	3	—													
22	1	1½	2	2½	3	3½	—												
23	1½	2	2½	3	3½	4	4½	—											
24	2	2½	3	3½	4	4½	5	5½	—										
25	2	3	3½	4	4½	5	5½	6	6½	—									
26	2	3	4	4½	5	5½	6	6½	7	7½	—								
27	2	3	4	5	5½	6	6½	7	7½	8	8½	—							
28	2	3	4	5	6	6½	7	7½	8	8½	9	9½	—						
29	2	3	4	5	6	7	7½	8	8½	9	9½	10	10½	—					
30	2	3	4	5	6	7	8	8½	9	9½	10	10½	11	11½	—				
31	2	3	4	5	6	7	8	9	9½	10	10½	11	11½	12	12½	—			
32	2	3	4	5	6	7	8	9	10	10½	11	11½	12	12½	13	13½	—		
33	2	3	4	5	6	7	8	9	10	11	11½	12	12½	13	13½	14	14½	—	
34	2	3	4	5	6	7	8	9	10	11	12	12½	13	13½	14	14½	15	15½	—
35	2	3	4	5	6	7	8	9	10	11	12	13	13½	14	14½	15	15½	16	16½
36	2	3	4	5	6	7	8	9	10	11	12	13	14	14½	15	15½	16	16½	17
37	2	3	4	5	6	7	8	9	10	11	12	13	14	15	15½	16	16½	17	17½
38	2	3	4	5	6	7	8	9	10	11	12	13	14	15	16	16½	17	17½	18
39	2	3	4	5	6	7	8	9	10	11	12	13	14	15	16	17	17½	18	18½
40	2	3	4	5	6	7	8	9	10	11	12	13	14	15	16	17	18	18½	19

	2	3	4	5	6	7	8	9	10	11	12	13	14	15	16	17	18	19	20
41	2	3	4	5	6	7	8	9	10	11	12	13	14	15	16	17	18	19	19½
42	2½	3½	4½	5½	6½	7½	8½	9½	10½	11½	12½	13½	14½	15½	16½	17½	18½	19½	20½
43	3	4	5	6	7	8	9	10	11	12	13	14	15	16	17	18	19	20	21
44	3	4½	5½	6½	7½	8½	9½	10½	11½	12½	13½	14½	15½	16½	17½	18½	19½	20½	21½
45	3	4½	6	7	8	9	10	11	12	13	14	15	16	17	18	19	20	21	22
46	3	4½	6	7½	8½	9½	10½	11½	12½	13½	14½	15½	16½	17½	18½	19½	20½	21½	22½
47	3	4½	6	7½	9	10	11	12	13	14	15	16	17	18	19	20	21	22	23
48	3	4½	6	7½	9	10½	11½	12½	13½	14½	15½	16½	17½	18½	19½	20½	21½	22½	23½
49	3	4½	6	7½	9	10½	12	13	14	15	16	17	18	19	20	21	22	23	24
50	3	4½	6	7½	9	10½	12	13½	14½	15½	16½	17½	18½	19½	20½	21½	22½	23½	24½
51	3	4½	6	7½	9	10½	12	13½	15	16	17	18	19	20	21	22	23	24	25
52	3	4½	6	7½	9	10½	12	13½	15	16½	17½	18½	19½	20½	21½	22½	23½	24½	25½
53	3	4½	6	7½	9	10½	12	13½	15	16½	18	19	20	21	22	23	24	25	26
54	3	4½	6	7½	9	10½	12	13½	15	16½	18	19½	20½	21½	22½	23½	24½	25½	26½
55	3	4½	6	7½	9	10½	12	13½	15	16½	18	19½	21	22	23	24	25	26	27
56	3	4½	6	7½	9	10½	12	13½	15	16½	18	19½	21	22½	23½	24½	25½	26½	27½
57	3	4½	6	7½	9	10½	12	13½	15	16½	18	19½	21	22½	24	25	26	27	28
58	3	4½	6	7½	9	10½	12	13½	15	16½	18	19½	21	22½	24	25½	26½	27½	28½
59	3	4½	6	7½	9	10½	12	13½	15	16½	18	19½	21	22½	24	25½	27	28	29
60	3	4½	6	7½	9	10½	12	13½	15	16½	18	19½	21	22½	24	25½	27	28½	29½
61	3	4½	6	7½	9	10½	12	13½	15	16½	18	19½	21	22½	24	25½	27	28½	30
62	3	4½	6	7½	9	10½	12	13½	15	16½	18	19½	21	22½	24	25½	27	28½	30
63	3	4½	6	7½	9	10½	12	13½	15	16½	18	19½	21	22½	24	25½	27	28½	30
64	3	4½	6	7½	9	10½	12	13½	15	16½	18	19½	21	22½	24	25½	27	28½	30

40   Redundancy – II: Practice and Procedure

(See ACAS advisory booklet "How to manage collective redundancies" (published April 2013)).

Cross-reference. See REDUNDANCY – I (38) for the right to a redundancy payment.

40.1   If an employer dismisses an employee by reason of redundancy, he has a number of statutory obligations in addition to that of making the employee a redundancy payment.

He may be liable in a claim of unfair dismissal unless he acts fairly. He must allow the employee reasonable time off work to look for alternative employment. If the proposed dismissal is of 20 or more employees at one establishment within 90 days, the employer must consult 'appropriate representatives' of the employees concerned. For the meaning of 'appropriate representatives' in this context, see **40.4** below.

This chapter considers the following.

(a)   The requirements for consultation before making an employee redundant (see **40.2–40.7** below).

(b)   The requirement for notification to the Department for Business, Innovation and Skills (see **40.8** below).

(c)   The basic 'fair dismissal' considerations relating to proposed redundancies (see **40.9** below).

The chapter ends with a checklist of redundancy dismissal procedure (see **40.10** below).

40.2   CONSULTATION AND NOTIFICATION REQUIREMENTS

The *Trade Union and Labour Relations (Consolidation) Act 1992* ('*TULR(C)A 1992*'), as amended by the *Trade Union Reform and Employment Rights Act 1993* ('*TURERA 1993*') and relevant regulations, imposes far-reaching obligations on employers to notify and consult appropriate employee representatives about proposed redundancies. *TULR(C)A 1992, s 193* imposes obligations on employers to notify the Secretary of State for Employment about proposed redundancies. The statutory provisions give effect to the *EC Collective Redundancies Directive 98/59/EC*, amending *Directive 75/129/EEC* and *Directive 92/56/EEC* (see **24.8** EUROPEAN UNION LAW). For the use of the Directive as an aid to construction of the statute, see *Hough v Leyland DAF Ltd* [1991] ICR 696; but cf *Re Hartlebury Printers Ltd* [1993] 1 All ER 470, [1992] ICR 559. Above and beyond the requirements of the *Directive*, *TULR(C)A 1992* also empowers employers to whom employees will, or are likely to, transfer under the provisions of the *Transfer of Undertakings (Protection of Employment) Regulations 2006* ("*TUPE*") to engage in consultation with the representatives of those employees prior to transfer: see *TULR(C)A 1992, ss 198A, 198B*.

40.3   Meaning of 'redundancy' and 'dismissal'

In *TULR(C)A 1992, Part IV Chapter II*, which contains the statutory consultation and notification requirements, references to 'dismissal as redundant' are references to dismissal for a reason not related to the individual concerned or for a number of reasons all of which are not so related (*TULR(C)A 1992, s 195(1)*). This is a substantially different definition from that which applies for redundancy payments purposes (see **39.7** REDUNDANCY – I). A reason 'relates to' an individual if it is something to do with him such as something he is or something he has done, and is to be distinguished from a reason relating to the employer, such as his need to effect business change in some respect: see *University and College Union* *v University of Stirling* [2015] UKSC 26, [2015] ICR 567, [2015] IRLR 573. For the purposes of any proceedings under *TULR(C)A 1992*, where an employee is or is proposed to be dismissed, it shall be presumed that he is or is proposed to be dismissed as redundant unless the contrary is proved (*TULR(C)A 1992, s 195(2)*). It follows from the definition of 'dismissal as redundant' in *TULR(C)A 1992, s 195(1)* that the collective consultation and notification provisions in *TULR(C)A 1992* can apply to proposed dismissals, notwithstanding the fact that there is no intention to lose jobs or workers. Thus, where an employer seeks to change the terms and conditions of employment of a part or group of the workforce by giving notice of termination to the employees concerned and offering them re-engagement on new terms, the employer may be under a duty to consult in accordance with *TULR(C)A 1992, s 188* (*GMB v MAN Truck & Bus UK Ltd* [2000] IRLR 636). This reflects the position under *Directive 98/59/EC*. If an employer intends to make a unilateral amendment to employees' contracts which, if refused, will result in termination of the employment relationship, and which is made for economic reasons not related to the individuals concerned, the obligation to consult collectively under the Directive may be engaged: see *Socha v Szpital Specjalistyczny im A Falkiewicza we Wroclawiu* C-149/16 [2018] ICR 260, [2018] IRLR 72 and *Ciupa v Szpital Ginekologiczno-Polozniczy im dr L Rydygiera* C-429/16 [2018] ICR 249, [2017] All ER (D) 89 (Sep).

A 'redundancy' within the meaning of *Directive 98/59/EC* means the declaration by an employer of its intention to terminate the contract of employment rather than the actual cessation of the employment relationship upon the expiry of the period of notice. See *Junk v K Kühnel*: C-188/03 [2005] IRLR 310. This affects the timing of collective consultation under *TULR(C)A 1992* (see further **40.5** below).

The term 'dismissal' in *TULR(C)A 1992* is to be construed in accordance with *Part X of ERA 1996* (see *TULCRA 1992, s 298*). So the applicable definition of "dismissal" includes a constructive dismissal (see *ERA 1996, s 95(1)(c)*). This is consistent with EU law. A constructive dismissal can in principle amount to a dismissal for the purposes of *art 1(1)* of *Directive 98/59/EC*: see *Pujante Rivera v Gestora Clubs Dir SL and another* C-422/14 [2016] ICR 227. In *Pujante*, the CJEU stated that where an employer made significant unilateral changes to an employee's contract for reasons not related to the individual concerned, and the individual resigned as a consequence, the circumstances would fall within the definition of "redundancy" in the *Directive*.

The provisions of *TULR(C)A 1992, Part IV, Chapter II* do not apply to employment under a contract for a fixed term, unless the employer proposes to dismiss an employee on a fixed-term contract before the term has expired: see *TULR(C)A 1992, s 282* as amended with effect from 6 April 2013. That position is consistent with *Directive 98/59/EC*: see *Rabal Canas v Nexea Gestion Documental* C-392/13 [2015] IRLR 577.

Under *Directive 98/59/EC*, obligations to inform and consult upon collective redundancies apply irrespective whether the decision regarding collective redundancies is taken by the employer or by an undertaking controlling the employer: see *Directive 98/59/EC, art 2(4)*. There is no equivalent provision in UK law. The CJEU has held in *Bichat v Aviation Passage Service Berlin GmbH* C-61/17 [2018] IRLR 1074, [2018] All ER (D) 77 (Aug) that the concept of a "controlling undertaking" covers "*all undertakings linked to that employer by shareholdings in the latter or by other links in law which allow it to exercise decisive influence in the employer's decision-making bodies and compel it to contemplate or to plan for collective redundancies.*" However, purely de facto control will not suffice.

40.4   Notification to appropriate representatives

Where an employer is proposing to dismiss as redundant at least 20 employees at an establishment within a period of 90 days or less, he must consult about the dismissals 'appropriate representatives' of the affected employees (*TULR(C)A 1992, s 188(1)*). The class of 'affected employees' includes not only those who may be dismissed, but also any employee affected by the proposed dismissals or who may be affected by measures taken in connection with those dismissals (*TULR(C)A 1992, s 188(1)*). An employer has to include employees whom it is hoped to redeploy in calculating the number it proposes to dismiss as redundant, if what is proposed amounts to a termination of the employee's existing contract of employment (*Hardy v Tourism South East* [2005] IRLR 242, EAT). This is because the applicable definition of dismissal for the purposes of *TULR(C)A s 188* (that in *ERA 1996, s 95*) refers to the termination of an employee's contract, with or without notice. Employees who volunteer for redundancy pursuant to an invitation from the employer should be included in the numbers of those the employer proposes to dismiss as redundant: see *Optare Group v Transport and General Workers' Union* [2007] IRLR 931.

The 'appropriate representatives' of any affected employees are:

(a)   if the employees are of a description in respect of which an independent trade union is recognised, representatives of the trade union; or

(b)   in any other case, either:

    (i)   employee representatives appointed or elected by the affected employees for other purposes but who have authority to receive information and to be consulted about the proposed dismissals on their behalf; or

    (ii)   employee representatives elected by the affected employees for the purposes of *TULR(C)A 1992, s 188* and in accordance with the statutory procedure set out in *TULR(C)A 1992, s 188A*.

(*TULR(C)A 1992, s 188(1B)* as amended by *SI 1999/1925*.)

'Representatives of a trade union' are officials or other persons authorised by the union to carry on collective bargaining with the employer (*TULR(C)A 1992, s 196(2)* as substituted by the *Collective Redundancies and Transfer of Undertakings (Protections of Employment) (Amendment) Regulations (SI 1995/2587)*). 'Recognition', in relation to a trade union, is defined by *TULR(C)A 1992, s 178(3)* as meaning the recognition of the union by an employer, or two or more associated employers, to any extent, for the purpose of collective bargaining (as defined by *TULR(C)A 1992, s 178(1)*). In *National Union of Gold, Silver and Allied Trades v Albury Bros Ltd* [1979] ICR 84, [1978] IRLR 504, the Court of Appeal held that recognition should not be held to be established unless there was clear and unequivocal evidence of an express agreement, or conduct from which recognition should be inferred which involved not a mere willingness to discuss but a positive decision to negotiate on one or more of the issues specified in what is now *TULR(C)A 1992, s 178(2)*. See also *Working Links (Employment) Ltd v Public and Commercial Services Union*: UKEAT/0305/12 [2013] All ER (D) 74 (Apr).

40.5   The timing and content of the consultation

It had long been understood that, in order to comply with the requirements of *TULR(C)A 1992, s 188*, the employer must begin consultations before giving individual notices of dismissal (*National Union of Teachers v Avon County Council* [1978] IRLR 55). However, in *Junk v Kühnel*: C-188/03 [2005] IRLR 310, the CJEU ruled that, for the purposes of *Directive 98/59/EC*, consultation must in fact already have been completed before employees are given notice of dismissal. This is because a 'redundancy' for the purposes of the Directive means the declaration of an employer of its intention to terminate the contract of employment (ie the giving of notice), rather than actual dismissal on the expiry of notice.

Consultation must not be a sham exercise; there must be time for the representatives, who are consulted, to consider properly the proposals that are being put to them (*Transport and General Workers' Union v Ledbury Preserves (1928) Ltd* [1985] IRLR 412). Fair consultation involves consultation when the proposals are still at a formative stage; adequate information on which to respond; adequate time in which to respond; and conscientious consideration by an employer of the response. However, the process of consultation is not one in which the employer is obliged to adopt any or all of the views expressed by the person or body whom he is consulting (*R v British Coal Corpn and Secretary of State for Trade and Industry, ex p Price* [1994] IRLR 72). Further, the consultation envisaged by *s 188* cannot begin until the information required by the section, as set out below, has been given (*E Green & Son (Castings) Ltd v Association of Scientific, Technical and Managerial Staffs* [1984] ICR 352, [1984] IRLR 135; see also *GEC Ferranti Defence Systems Ltd v MSF* [1993] IRLR 101 and [1994] IRLR 104).

The employer does not 'propose' to dismiss until he has reached the stage of having formulated a specific proposal (*Hough v Leyland DAF Ltd* [1991] ICR 696, [1991] IRLR 194). Thus, the word 'propose' connotes an intention in the mind of the employer (*Scotch Premier Meat Ltd v Burns* [2000] IRLR 639). Significantly, the EAT held in the *Burns* case that where an employer had determined a plan of action which had two alternative scenarios only one of which necessarily included redundancies then this was capable of amounting to the employer 'proposing to dismiss' employees. It was, however, emphasised that this was essentially a question of fact for the employment tribunal to determine. In addition, a 'proposal' to dismiss does not necessarily have to be made by the person with power to carry out the dismissal (*Dewhirst Group v GMB Trade Union* [2003] All ER (D) 175 (Dec), EAT). For further consideration of what is meant by a 'proposed' dismissal, and for the application of *TULR(C)A 1992, s 188* where administrators have been appointed, see *Re Hartlebury Printers Ltd* [1993] 1 All ER 470, [1992] ICR 559, [1992] IRLR 516, *R v British Coal Corpn, ex p Vardy* [1993] ICR 720, [1993] IRLR 104 and *MSF v Refuge Assurance plc* [2002] IRLR 324. In *MSF* the EAT held that *s 188* did not have the same meaning as *Directive 75/129* (now, *Directive 98/59*), which requires consultation when collective redundancies are first 'contemplated'. 'Contemplation' means 'having a view', and refers to a relatively early stage in the decision-making process, whereas 'proposes' relates to a state of mind which is much more certain (see also *Scotch Premier Meat Ltd v Burns* [2000] IRLR 639 and *R v British Coal Corpn, ex p Vardy* [1993] ICR 720, [1993] IRLR 104). More recently the EAT in *Unison v Leicestershire County Council* [2005] IRLR 920 approved the tribunal's finding that a 'proposal' meant 'something less than a decision that dismissals are to be made and more than a possibility that they might occur'. While not inconsistent with *Vardy* or *MSF*, this ruling suggests that an employer may "propose" to dismiss employees at an earlier stage of the decision-making process than previously understood. Of course, insofar as there is any difference between the requirements of the *Directive* and that of *TULR(C)A 1992*, employees of 'the State' may be able to rely directly on the *Directive* insofar as the UK remains a member of the EU: *Griffin v South West Water Services Ltd* [1995] IRLR 15) (see **24.2 EUROPEAN UNION LAW**; **38.7 PUBLIC SECTOR EMPLOYEES**).

In circumstances where decisions on collective redundancies are taken within a group of companies with a parent company and subsidiaries, the obligation to consult always lies with the subsidiary company which employs the workers, and never with the parent, irrespective of whether the decision in connection with collective redundancies is made by the parent or the subsidiary. Where the parent company makes decisions on redundancy across the group, consultation obligations are only triggered once the subsidiary in which collective redundancies would be made has been identified: see *Akavan Erityisalojen Keskusliitto AEK ry v Fujitsu Siemens Computers Oy*: C-44/08 [2010] ICR 444, [2009] IRLR 944, CJEU.

Where a consultation is required, it must begin 'in good time', and in addition:

(a)   if an employer is proposing to dismiss *at least 100* employees at any one establishment within a period of 90 days or less, the consultation must begin at least 45 days before the first of the dismissals takes effect; and

(b)   in any other case in which consultation is required, consultation must begin at least 30 days before the first of the dismissals takes effect.

(TULR(C)A 1992, s 188(1A)), as substituted by *SI 1995/2587,* and as amended by *SI 2013/763* with effect from 6 April 2013.)

The phrase 'before the first of the dismissals takes effect' obviously refers to the proposed date of the first dismissal, not the actual date, otherwise the provisions would be unworkable (see *E Green & Son (Castings) Ltd v ASTMS* [1984] IRLR 135, following *GKN Sankey Ltd v National Society of Motor Mechanics* [1980] IRLR 8). On the basis of *Junk v Kühnel*: C-188/03 [2005] IRLR 310, consultation for the purposes of *Directive 98/59/EC* must be completed before notice of dismissal is given (see above). The EAT in *Unison v Leicestershire* [2005] IRLR 920 held *obiter* that it was possible to read *TULR(C)A 1992 s 188(1)* consistently with EC law by construing the phrase "proposing to dismiss" as meaning "proposing to give notice of dismissal". The effect of this construction is that the full consultation must be completed before notices of dismissal are issued. Whether consultation has begun "in good time" is a matter of fact and degree for the employment tribunal: see *UNISON v Leicestershire County Council* [2006] EWCA Civ 825, [2006] IRLR 810, CA.

The term 'establishment' for the purposes of *TULR(C)A 1992, s 188* is to be interpreted in line with its meaning in *Article 1(1)(a)* of *Directive 98/59*: see *MSF v Refuge Assurance plc* [2002] IRLR 324 and *Renfrewshire Council v Educational Institute of Scotland* [2013] IRLR 76.

The CJEU held in *Rockfon A/S v Specialarbejderforbundet i Danmark*: C-449/93 [1996] ICR 673, [1996] IRLR 168 that the word 'establishment' under *Directive 75/129* (the predecessor to *Directive 98/59*) referred to the local employment unit, that is the unit to which the workers made redundant are assigned to carry out their duties. Thus, for example, the fact that a contract contains a mobility clause allowing the worker to be moved elsewhere is not relevant: see *Renfrewshire Council v Educational Institute of Scotland* [2013] ICR 172, [2013] IRLR 76. Although the term 'establishment' connotes a distinct entity assigned to perform particular tasks, an 'establishment' need not have any legal, economic, or administrative autonomy, nor have a management that can independently effect collective redundancies, nor be geographically separate from other units of the undertaking in question: see *Athinaiki Chartopoiia AE v Panagiotidis*: C-270/05 [2007] IRLR 284, interpreting *Directive 98/59*. The ascertainment of an "establishment" focuses on functional and organisational characteristics – essentially, whether the putative establishment constitutes a unit – and also, which is related, whether it is a single "place". It does not depend upon whether the establishment is operated by the employer. In *Seahorse Maritime Ltd v Nautilus International* [2018] EWCA Civ 2789, [2019] IRLR 286, the Court of Appeal reversed a finding of the ET that separate ships were not each a separate establishment, made in part because the employer did not operate the ships, but simply employed crew members working on them.

The CJEU confirmed in *USDAW and Ethel Austin Ltd and ors* C-80/14 [2015] ICR 675 and in *Lyttle v Bluebird UK Bidco 2 Ltd* C-182/13 [2015] IRLR 577 that the interpretation of 'establishment' in the *Rockfon* case is correct; that the same interpretation applies wherever the term 'establishment' is used in Directive 98/59; and that the threshold test in *TULR(C)A 1992, s 188(1)* that proposed dismissals concern at least 20 employees at a single establishment is consistent with EU law. Thus, no reliance can be placed on the controversial decision of the EAT in *USDAW v Ethel Austin Ltd* [2013] ICR 1300, [2013] IRLR 686 that the phrase 'in one establishment' in *TULR(C)A, s 188(1)* should effectively be ignored in order properly to reflect EU law.

For the purposes of the consultation, the employer must disclose in writing to the appropriate representatives:

(i) the reasons for his proposals;

(ii) the number and descriptions of employees whom it is proposed to dismiss as redundant;

(iii)   the total number of employees of any such description employed by the employer at the establishment in question;

(iv)   the proposed method of selecting the employees who may be dismissed;

(v)   the proposed method of carrying out the dismissals with due regard to any agreed procedure, including the period over which the dismissals are to take effect;

(vi)   the proposed method of calculating the amount of any redundancy payments otherwise than in compliance with a statutory obligation;

(vii)   the number of agency workers working temporarily for and under the supervision and direction of the employer,

(viii)   the parts of the employer's undertaking in which those agency workers are working, and

(ix)   the type of work those agency workers are carrying out.

(TULR(C)A 1992, s 188(4).)

Where the employer has invited affected employees to elect representatives, but the affected employees fail to do so within a reasonable time, then the employer must give the requisite information to each affected employee individually *(TULR(C)A 1992, s 188(7B))*.

The information must be provided in proper form: it will not do to say that it may be gleaned from the surrounding circumstances and from a number of documents (*Sovereign Distribution Services Ltd v TGWU* [1990] ICR 31, [1989] IRLR 334).

The consultation must include consultation about ways of avoiding the dismissals, reducing the number of employees to be dismissed and mitigating the consequences of the dismissals, and must be undertaken by the employer with a view to reaching agreement with the appropriate representatives *(TULR(C)A 1992, s 188(2))*. The fact that consultation must be undertaken with a view to reaching agreement means that it is tantamount to negotiation (*Junk v Kühnel*: C-188/03 [2005] IRLR 310). An employer must consult on all the matters set out in *TULR(C)A 1992, s 188(2)*, which are to be viewed disjunctively. Furthermore, it is not open to an employer to argue that consultation would, in the circumstances, be futile or useless (*Middlesbrough Borough Council v TGWU* [2002] IRLR 332).

Until 2007, the domestic courts held that *TULR(C)A 1992, s 188* did not require consultation about the reasons for the redundancy, including whether or not a plant should close (see *Vardy*, and two cases following *Vardy*: *Middlesbrough v TGWU* and *Securicor Omega Express Ltd v GMB* [2004] IRLR 9). However, the EAT took a different approach in *UK Coal Mining Ltd v National Union of Mineworkers (Northumberland Area)* [2008] ICR 163, [2008] IRLR 4. In the *UK Coal Mining* case, the Employment Appeal Tribunal observed that at the time *Vardy* was decided, *TULR(C)A 1992, s 188* required consultation only 'about the dismissal'. After amendments made in 1995, *TULR(C)A 1992, s 188* now required consultation over 'ways of avoiding dismissals'. This inevitably involved engaging with the reasons for dismissals. So, where dismissals were inextricably linked with the closure of a plant, a duty to consult over the closure would arise. The EAT in *UK Coal Mining* followed *Vardy* and *MSF* in holding that the wording 'proposing to dismiss' in *TULR(C)A 1992, s 188* connoted a more certain state of mind than the wording 'contemplating dismissals' in *Directive 98/59*. Nevertheless, the EAT indicated that this would not prevent the consultation obligation from extending to the closure of a plant: in a closure context where it is recognised that dismissals will inevitably, or almost inevitably, result from the closure, dismissals will be proposed at the point when closure itself is proposed.

The question whether the *Vardy* or *UK Coal* approach should be preferred is at present unclear. In *United States of America v Nolan (Christine)* [2011] IRLR 40, the Court of Appeal referred to the CJEU the issue whether *Directive 98/59* gives rise to consultation obligations when the employer is proposing, but has not yet made, a strategic business decision that will inevitably lead to redundancies; or whether it gives rise to consultation obligations only when such a strategic decision has actually been made, and the employer then proposes consequential redundancies. The Court of Appeal stated that it was referring the question because it was unclear from the CJEU's judgment in *Akavan Erityisalojen Keskusliitto Alek RY and others v Fujitsu Siemens Computers OY* C-44/08 [2009] IRLR 944 which approach was to be preferred. The Court also stated that *TULR(C)A 1992, s 188* was not intended to impose a wider consultation obligation than that contained in *Directive 98/59* (so that the proper approach to *TULR(C)A 1992, s 188* would be determined by the meaning of the *Directive*). The CJEU, however, declined to rule on the reference on the basis that *Directive 98/59* did not apply to workers employed by public administrative bodies or by establishments governed by public law, and this included civilian staff at a military base: *United States of America v Nolan* C-583/10 [2013] ICR 193, [2012] IRLR 1020 (Note that the Court of Appeal on remission from the CJEU, and the Supreme Court on appeal, have nevertheless held that *TULR(C)A 1992, s 188* should not be interpreted so as to mirror the exclusion of public administrative bodies from *Directive 98/59*: *United States of America v Nolan* [2014] EWCA Civ 71 [2014] ICR 685, [2014] IRLR 302 CA, [2015] ICR 1347 SC.) Effectively the same question was referred in *Bichat v Aviation Passage Service Berlin GmbH & Co KG* C-61/17 [2018] IRLR 1074, but again, the CJEU considered it unnecessary to answer it in the context of that case.

Specified employers may also be obliged to inform and consult appropriate representatives about economic decisions likely to lead to changes in work organisation or contractual relations under the *Information and Consultation of Employees Regulations 2004, SI 2004/3426*.

Failure to consult with the appropriate representatives, or to do so within the stipulated time when it was reasonably practicable to do so, may lead to the employer being held liable to pay each redundant employee a protective award (see **40.7** below). Such a failure is also likely to render the dismissals unfair (*Kelly v Upholstery and Cabinet Works (Amesbury) Ltd* [1977] IRLR 91; *North East Midlands Co-operative Society Ltd v Allen* [1977] IRLR 212; *Polkey v A E Dauton (or Dayton) Services Ltd* [1988] AC 344, [1988] ICR 142, [1987] IRLR 503, HL; but cf *Hough*, above).

40.6   Election of employee representatives

If elections are held for employee representatives they must be held in accordance with the provisions of *TULR(C)A 1992, s 188A*. This provides that:

(a)   the employer shall make such arrangements as are reasonably practical to ensure that the election is fair;

(b)   the employer shall determine the number of representatives to be elected so that there are sufficient representatives to represent the interests of all the affected employees having regard to the number and classes of those employees;

(c)   the employer shall determine whether the affected employees should be represented either by representatives of all the affected employees or by representatives of particular classes of those employees;

(d)   before the election the employer shall determine the term of office as employee representatives so that it is of sufficient length to enable information to be given and consultations under this section to be completed;

(e)   the candidates for election as employee representatives are affected employees on the date of the election;

(f)   no affected employee is unreasonably excluded from standing for election;

(g)   all affected employees on the date of the election are entitled to vote for employee representatives;

(h)   the employees entitled to vote may vote for as many candidates as there are representatives to be elected to represent them or, if there are to be representatives for particular classes of employees, may vote for as many candidates as there are representatives to be elected to represent their particular class of employee; and

(i)   the election is conducted so as to secure that:

   (i)   so far as is reasonably practicable, those voting do so in secret; and

   (ii)   the votes given at the election are accurately counted.

(TULR(C)A 1992, s 188A(1).)

Further, if after an election held in accordance with this procedure, an elected representative ceases to act as a representative so that employees are no longer represented then they shall elect another representative by an election held in accordance with the requirements at *(a)*, *(e)*, *(f)* and *(i)* above *(TULR(C)A 1992, s 188A(2))*.

An employer is not necessarily obliged to hold a formal election if it simply accepts all candidates as appropriate representatives: *Phillips v Xtera Communications Ltd* [2012] ICR 171, [2011] IRLR 724. An "election" for the purposes of *s 188A(1)* occurs when, pursuant to fair arrangements, the number of candidates matches the number of representatives to be elected, and no further candidates are proposed. In such circumstances, there is no need for a ballot or vote.

40.7   Pre-transfer consultation

With effect from 31 January 2014, the provisions of *TULR(C)A* were amended by the addition of new *ss 198A* and *198B*, permitting an employer to whom employees will, or are likely to, transfer under *TUPE* to engage in pre-transfer consultation with the representatives of those employees (see Transfer of Undertakings (53)).

Where there is to be, or is likely to be, a relevant transfer, and the transferee is proposing to dismiss as redundant 20 or more employees at one establishment within a period of 90 days or less, and the individuals who work for the transferor and who are to be (or are likely to be) transferred to the transferee's employment under the transfer include one or more individuals who may be affected by the proposed dismissals or by measures taken in connection with them, the transferee may elect to consult, or to start to consult, representatives of affected transferring individuals before the transfer takes place ("pre-transfer consultation"): *TULR(C)A 1992, s 198A(1)–(2)*. A "relevant transfer" is a transfer under *TUPE*, or any other transfer which by virtue of any enactment is either deemed to be a TUPE transfer, or is of the same or similar effect: see *TULR(C)A 1992, s 198A(7)*.

An election to engage in pre-transfer consultation may be made only if the transferor agrees to it, and must be made by way of written notice to the transferor: *TULR(C)A 1992, s 198A(3)*. On any complaint, if a question arises as to whether notice of an election has been given or agreed to by the transferor, it is for the transferee to show those matters: *TULR(C)A 1992, s 198B*.

If the transferee elects to carry out pre-transfer consultation, the consultation requirements in *TULR(C)A 1992, ss 188–198* apply from the time of the election as if the transferee were already the transferring individuals' employer, and as if any transferring individuals affected by the proposed dismissals were already employed at the relevant establishment: *TULR(C)A 1992, s 198A(4)*. The transferor is empowered to provide information or other assistance to help the transferee meet those consultation requirements. However, a failure on the part of the transferor to provide information or other assistance to the transferee does not constitute special circumstances rendering it not reasonably practicable for the transferee to comply with any consultation requirement: *TULR(C)A 1992, s 198B(1)(d)*.

A transferee who elects to carry out pre-transfer consultation may cancel that election at any time by written notice to the transferor. However, if he does so, nothing he has done prior to that cancellation is of any effect for the purposes of *TULR(C)A 1992, ss 188–198*, and he cannot make another election: *TULR(C)A 1992, ss 198A(5)–(6)*.

The appropriate representatives of transferring individuals for the purposes of *TULR(C)A 1992, s 188(1B)* are, where the transferor recognises an independent trade union, representatives of that union: *TULR(C)A 1992, s 198B(1)(a)*.

40.8   Protective award

If an employer fails to comply with any of the statutory requirements for consultation or fails to do so within the appropriate time, a complaint may be made to an employment tribunal by the trade union where the failure relates to trade union representatives, or by any of the affected employees or by any of the employees who have been dismissed as redundant where the failure relates to the election of employee representatives, or in the case of any other failure relating to employee representatives, by any of the employee representatives to whom the failure related and, in any other case, by any of the affected employees or by any of the employees who have been dismissed as redundant (*TULR(C)A 1992, s 189*).

A protective award is an award in respect of one or more descriptions of employees who have been dismissed as redundant, or whom it is proposed to dismiss as redundant, and in respect of whose dismissal or proposed dismissal the employer has failed to comply with a requirement of *s 188*: *TULR(C)A 1992, s 189(3)*. So, for instance, it cannot cover employees whom the employer originally proposed to dismiss, but subsequently decided to keep on (whether as a result of consultation or otherwise). They may be employees whom it was originally proposed to dismiss, but they are not employees whom it "is proposed" to dismiss: see *Securicor Omega Express v GMB* [2004] IRLR 9.

A protective award can only be made in favour of those in respect of whom a complaint of breach has been proved by themselves or their representative. So, where a claim is made by a trade union, the protective award will benefit only those employees within the bargaining unit in respect of which the union is recognised: *TGWU v Brauer Coley Ltd (in administration)* [2007] IRLR 207. Similarly, where a claim is made by an individual employee, the employment tribunal can only make an award in the individual claimant's favour, and cannot make an award that benefits other redundant employees: *Independent Insurance Company Ltd v Aspinall* [2011] IRLR 716. Note also that an individual employee who is not an employee representative cannot bring a claim in respect of a failure relating to employee representatives (other than a failure relating to the election of representatives): see *Northgate HR Ltd v Mercy* [2007] EWCA Civ 1304, [2008] ICR 410, [2008] IRLR 222.

If a question is raised on any such complaint as to whether or not any employee representative was an appropriate representative for the purposes of *s 188*, the burden of proof will be on the employer to show that the employee representative had the authority to represent the affected employees (*TULR(C)A 1992, s 189(1A)*). Also, where the alleged failure relates to the election of employee representatives, the burden will be on the employer to show that the statutory election procedure in *s 188A* has been complied with.

The complaint must be presented before the date on which the last of the dismissals to which the complaint relates takes effect, or during the period of three months beginning with that date, or within such further period as the tribunal considers reasonable in a case where it is satisfied that it was not reasonably practicable for the complaint to be presented during the period of three months (*TULR(C)A 1992, s 189(5)*; and see **19.20** EMPLOYMENT TRIBUNALS – I).

It is a defence to such an application for an employer to show (the burden being upon it) that there were special circumstances which rendered it not reasonably practicable for him to comply with the requirements, and that he took all such steps as were reasonably practicable in those circumstances (*TULR(C)A 1992, s 188(7)*). For example, an unforeseen financial crisis may make it necessary to close down a plant at short notice so that consultations can only take place during a shorter period than that prescribed by law. The test focuses upon the actual events that occurred, and not upon what an employer might with hindsight have thought about consultation if it had addressed its mind to the question at the relevant time: see *E Ivor Hughes Educational Foundation v Morris* [2015] IRLR 696.

In *Clarks of Hove Ltd v Bakers' Union* [1979] 1 All ER 152, [1978] 1 WLR 1207, [1978] ICR 1076, [1978] IRLR 366, the Court of Appeal held that insolvency is not on its own a special circumstance and that it depends entirely on the course of the insolvency whether the circumstances can be described as special or not. It is a fact-specific test. What might be special circumstances in one case might not be in another if the employer could, or should, have seen what was to come. (See also *Angus Jowett & Co Ltd v National Union of Tailors and Garment Workers* [1985] ICR 646, [1985] IRLR 326, EAT; *Re Hartlebury Printers Ltd* [1993] 1 All ER 470, [1992] ICR 559, [1992] IRLR 516, *GMB v Rankin* [1992] IRLR 514 and *Keeping Kids Company (in Compulsory Liquidation) v Smith* UKEAT/0057/17 [2018] IRLR 484.) The employer may not neglect his duty under TULR(C)A 1992, s 188 merely because he considers that consultation will achieve nothing (*Sovereign Distribution Services Ltd v TGWU* [1990] ICR 31, [1989] IRLR 334).

Section 188(7) precludes the employer from relying upon a failure to provide information by the person whose decision led to the proposed dismissals if that person directly or indirectly controls the employer. The meaning of this provision was considered in *GMB and Amicus v Beloit Walmsley Ltd* [2004] IRLR 18. The EAT determined that: (i) the mischief at which this provision is aimed is a controlling entity's delay in providing the employer with information. Any period of delay in providing information must therefore count against the employer, for the purposes of determining whether or not the duty under *TULR(C)A 1992, s 188* could have been complied with; (ii) there must be a causal link between the decision, and the proposed dismissals. However, it is not necessary that the person making the decision contemplates any particular number of dismissals, at any particular establishment; (iii) the 'information', required to be provided by *TULR(C)A s 188(7)*, is not confined to the 'information' required to be disclosed by *TULR(C)A s 188(4)*. It includes information necessary to begin the process of consultation.

An employer would appear to escape its information and consultation obligations under *s 188* if he invites any affected employees to elect representatives and has given enough time to allow for an election but such election is not organised (*TULR(C)A 1992, s 188(7A)*; and see *R v Secretary of State for Trade and Industry, ex p UNISON* [1996] IRLR 438).

Where a tribunal finds the complaint well-founded it makes a declaration to that effect and may also make a protective award (*TULR(C)A 1992, s 189(2)*). A protective award is an order that an employer make payments for the protected period in respect of specified employees who have been dismissed, or whom it is proposed to dismiss, as redundant without complying with the statutory requirements for consultation. The length of the period will be what is considered to be just and equitable by the tribunal in the circumstances having regard to the seriousness of the employer's default and will be up to 90 days, beginning on the date on which the first of the dismissals to which the complaint relates was proposed to take effect, or the date of the award, whichever is the earlier (*TULR(C)A 1992, s 189(4)*). See *Transport and General Workers' Union v Ledbury Preserves (1928) Ltd* [1986] ICR 855, [1986] IRLR 492; *E Green & Son (Castings) Ltd v Association of Scientific, Technical and Managerial Staffs* [1984] ICR 352, [1984] IRLR 135. The purpose of the award is to provide a sanction for breach by the employer of the obligations in *TULR(C)A s 188*, not to compensate employees for any loss suffered: hence the futility of consultation is not relevant to the making of a protective award (*GMB v Susie Radin Ltd*

[2004] EWCA Civ 180, [2004] 2 All ER 279, [2004] ICR 893, [2004] IRLR 400, reversing *Spillers-French (Holdings) Ltd v USDAW* [1980] 1 All ER 231, [1980] ICR 31, [1979] IRLR 339). Nor is the employer's insolvency relevant to the size of any protective award: the employment tribunal should focus simply upon the seriousness of the employer's default in failing to comply with its statutory duty (*Smith v Cherry Lewis Ltd* [2005] IRLR 86). In the *Susie Radin* case, the Court of Appeal stated that how the length of the protected period is assessed is a matter for the tribunal, but a proper approach in a case where there has been no consultation is to start with the maximum period and reduce it only if there are mitigating circumstances justifying a reduction. Mitigating circumstances may, however, include any steps taken by the employer before proposals have crystallised in relation to keeping employees informed or consulted, even if there has been no consultation under *TULR(C)A s 188* itself (*AMICUS v GBS Tooling Ltd (in administration)* [2005] IRLR 683). A union's obstructive approach to statutory consultation may also be taken into account when assessing the correct level of a protective award: see *GMB v Lambeth Service Team; TGWU v Lambeth Service Team* [2005] All ER (D) 153 (Jul), EAT. Furthermore, when assessing the seriousness of the default, it is relevant to consider both the culpability of the employer and the harm or potential for harm of the default: see *Shanahan Engineering Ltd v Unite the Union* UKEAT/0411/09 [2010] All ER (D) 108 (Mar). There is no connection between the length of the statutory consultation period, and the length of the protective award. Even if the employer proposed to dismiss fewer than 100 employees, so that the minimum consultation period was 30 days before the first dismissal took effect, the proper protective award for a complete failure to consult is 90 days: see *Hutchins v Permacell Finesse Ltd (In Administration)* [2008] All ER (D) 112 (Jan).

Where a tribunal has made a protective award, every employee to whom it relates is entitled to be paid remuneration by the employer for the protected period at the rate of a week's pay (see PAY – I (35)) for each week of the period (*TULR(C)A 1992, s 190(1), (2), (5)*). There is no upper limit on the amount of a week's pay for this purpose.

If an employee, specified in the award, receives payments under his contract of employment during the protected period, those payments do not go to discharge his employer's liability under the protective award, nor vice versa: see *Cranswick Country Foods plc v Beall* [2007] ICR 691, [2006] All ER (D) 315 (Dec).

Liability for protective awards will transfer as a result of a transfer of an undertaking under the *Transfer of Undertakings (Protection of Employment) Regulations 2006 (SI 2006/246)* (*Alamo Group (Europe) Ltd v Tucker* [2003] ICR 829, [2003] IRLR 266, following *Kerry Foods Ltd v Creber* [2000] ICR 556, [2000] IRLR 10 and not following *TGWU v McKinnon* [2001] ICR 1281, [2001] IRLR 597 – see also TRANSFER OF UNDERTAKINGS (53)).

Disallowance of payment under award. If an employee remains employed during a protected period and:

(i)   he is fairly dismissed by his employer for a reason other than redundancy;

(ii)   he unreasonably terminates the contract of employment; or

(iii)   he unreasonably refuses an offer of suitable alternative employment made to take effect before or during the protected period,

he will not be entitled to payment under the protective award in respect of any period during which he would have been employed but for the dismissal, termination or refusal of employment (*TULR(C)A 1992, s 191(1)–(3)*). If the offer of alternative employment embodies terms which differ from those under which he previously worked, the employee has a trial period of four weeks beginning with the commencement date of the new contract (or by agreement in writing, a longer period) (*TULR(C)A 1992, s 191(4)–(6)*; see also **39.6** REDUNDANCY – I). If during the trial period, the employment is terminated by the employer for a reason connected with the change to the new or renewed employment, or by the employee, the employee remains entitled to his protective award unless he acted unreasonably in terminating or giving notice to terminate the contract (*TULR(C)A 1992, s 191(7)*).

Remedy for non-payment of award. If an employer fails to pay a protective award, the employee concerned may present a complaint to an employment tribunal which will order the employer to make the payment (*TULR(C)A 1992, s 192(1), (3)*). The time limit for the presentation of a complaint by an individual employee for failure to pay a protective award is three months from the day or last day of the failure to make the payment, or such further period as the tribunal considers reasonable in a case where it is satisfied that it was not reasonably practicable for the complaint to be presented within the period of three months (*TULR(C)A 1992, s 192(2)*; and see **19.20** EMPLOYMENT TRIBUNALS – I).

The Employment Appeal Tribunal held in *Howlett Marine Services Ltd v Bowlam* [2001] IRLR 201 that the three months' time limit for bringing a complaint in respect of non-payment of a protective award under *TULR(C)A 1992, s 192(2)* runs from the last day of the protected period. Moreover, this remains the case even when the protective award was made by a tribunal well after the expiry of the protective period. However, the EAT held in *Howlett* that in these circumstances it would obviously not have been 'reasonably practicable' to present a complaint within the three months' time limit so that the tribunal would still have jurisdiction to hear it provided that it was presented in such further period of time as was reasonable.

40.9 NOTIFICATIONS TO THE DEPARTMENT FOR BUSINESS, INNOVATION AND SKILLS

An employer must send written notification of certain redundancies to the Redundancy Payments Service, (an executive agency of the Department for Business, Innovation and Skills, 'BIS'). If he proposes to make 100 or more employees redundant at one establishment within a period of 90 days or less, the employer must notify the Secretary of State in writing at least 45 days before giving notice to terminate an employee's contract in respect of any of those dismissals (*TULR(C)A 1992, s 193(1)*). If he proposes to make 20 or more employees redundant at one establishment within a period of 90 days or less, the employer must give at least 30 days' notice (*TULR(C)A 1992, s 193(2)*).

The notice must be in a prescribed form and sent to the specified office. The applicable form (Form HR1) is available on the government's website. If consultation with appropriate representatives is required, the representatives concerned must be identified and the date when consultations began must be stated (*TULR(C)A 1992, s 193(4)*). Where consultation with appropriate representatives is required, he must give a copy of the notice to those representatives (*TULR(C)A 1992, s 193(6)*). If there are special circumstances which make it impossible for the employer to comply with any of the requirements of notifying BIS or the representatives concerned, he must take such steps to comply as are reasonably practicable in the circumstances (*TULR(C)A 1992, s 193(7)*). Ignorance of the statutory obligation to notify BIS cannot constitute such special circumstances (*Secretary of State for Employment v Helitron Ltd* [1980] ICR 523); see also **40.8** above.

In *Vauxhall Motors Ltd v TGWU* [2006] IRLR 674, the employer sent written notification of proposed redundancies twice in respect of a single redundancy exercise, because the length over which redundancy proposals were considered (approximately two years) meant that the first notification had expired. The union argued that following the second notification, fresh consultation should have occurred under *TULR(C)A 1992, s 188*. The EAT disagreed, stating that the lodging of notification was immaterial to the question of whether the employers were in breach of *TULR(C)A 1992*.

Failure to notify BIS may lead to a conviction and fine of up to level 5 on the Standard Scale in a magistrates' court (*TULR(C)A 1992, s 194(1); and see **1.10** INTRODUCTION).

(The cap of £5,000 on fines at level 5 was removed in March 2015 by *Legal Aid, Sentencing and Punishment of Offenders Act 2012, s 85*, so that a fine under *TULR(C)A 1992, s 194(1)* may in principle be of an unlimited amount.)

40.10 FAIRNESS OF THE DISMISSAL

Where redundancy is the reason for a dismissal the employer will be liable in a claim for unfair dismissal in addition to the redundancy payment if he fails to act fairly. The principles governing the fairness of dismissals for redundancy are set out in full in UNFAIR DISMISSAL – II (55), and in particular in 55.11. The main points to bear in mind are that the dismissal may either be automatically unfair, or unfair because the employer has failed to act reasonably in all the circumstances.

Automatic unfairness arises, subject to certain exceptions, where an employee is selected for an inadmissible reason. Circumstances where the employer may be held to have acted unreasonably include where he has failed to consult the trade unions or individuals involved (his obligations in this respect may go beyond the express statutory obligations dealt with in 40.4 above), where selection criteria are inadequate or have been improperly applied, or where inadequate efforts have been made to find alternative employment for those whose jobs have disappeared.

40.11 CHECKLIST OF REDUNDANCY DISMISSAL PROCEDURE

In practical terms, the first step in the redundancy dismissal procedure is the business decision on the necessity of making one or more employees redundant. Thereafter the following actions should be considered and undertaken as necessary.

(a)   *Preliminary procedure* (not necessarily in chronological order)

  (i)   Where the proposal is to issue notices of dismissal for redundancy to at least 20 employees at an establishment within 90 days or less, consult with the appropriate representatives of the employees concerned within the appropriate time limits on the measures to be taken which are set out below. Provide them with all necessary information. (Provide each affected employee with the necessary information where the affected employees fail to elect representatives within a reasonable time.)

  (ii)   Decide on the number of employees to be made redundant.

  (iii) Invite volunteers for redundancy.

  (iv)   Consider whether alternative jobs are available within the organisation or group. If it should be necessary to retrain employees for those jobs, consider the practicability of doing this.

  (v)   Select employees to be made redundant in accordance with any customary arrangement or agreed procedure. If no such arrangement or procedure exists, establish, if possible with the agreement of the relevant unions or employee representatives, objective criteria for selection, and apply them.

  (vi)   Consult with individuals affected before a final decision is taken.

  (vii) Inform those employees as soon as possible of their impending redundancies.

  (viii) Allow them time off to look for other employment.

  (ix)   Notify BIS of impending redundancies within the appropriate time limits.

(b)   *Dismissal notices* (taking due note of the time limits – see below)

40.11   Redundancy – II: Practice and Procedure

NB Consultations must be completed before notices of dismissal are sent out.

Time limits. The date on which the dismissal is to take effect should be fixed having regard to the obligations of the employer as regards notice (see TERMINATION OF EMPLOYMENT (49)) and with an eye on the following time limits.

For step (*a*)(i):

(A)	'in good time'	in all cases in which consultation is required and in any event:
(B)	45 days before first notice of dismissal	100+ employees in one establishment to be dismissed within 90 days
(C)	30 days before first notice of dismissal	20–99 employees in one establishment to be dismissed within 90 days

For step (*a*)(ix), as (B) and (C) for step *(a)*(i) above.

41   References

41.1   An employer may be requested to provide a general reference or specific details about an employee or ex-employee. The request may come from the employee, a prospective employer or any other person interested in obtaining such information (for example, the employee may need a reference in order to obtain a mortgage or a lease of residential premises.) The request may be for a reference to be given over the telephone, but more usually it will be for a written document.

41.2   OBLIGATIONS TO GIVE A REFERENCE

Generally, an employer is not obliged to provide an employment reference, under statute or at common law, regardless of whether the employee was dismissed: see for example *Ros and Angel v Fanstone* [2007] UKEAT/0372/07, [2008] All ER (D) 46 (Jan) and *Legal and General Assurance Ltd v Kirk* [2001] EWCA Civ 1803. Accordingly, many employers adopt an approach that minimalises litigation-risk, namely by provision of a 'factual reference' that details information concerning dates of employment, job titles and confirmation of the fact that the person was employed, without providing any further commentary.

However, as one of the terms of settlement of a claim or a potential employment tribunal claim, an employer may agree to provide a reference, and he will then be bound to do so, assuming the agreement to be enforceable. Further, in certain regulatory contexts, an employer is required to provide a reference, for example in the financial services industry (see CHAPTER **26**) and in certain circumstances, state schools. In *Byrnell v British Telecommunications plc* [2009] EWHC 727 (QB), the High Court considered that there could in such industries be an implied term to the effect that an employer will provide a reference upon request.

Further, the job centre has the authority to demand information concerning a benefit applicant's previous employment: *section 109B* of the *Social Security Administration Act 1992. Section 111* makes it a criminal offence not to comply with the demand.

41.3   CONTENT OF A REFERENCE

References often request that certain specific matters are addressed. If, however, the request is a general one, for example, from a prospective employer, the following matters will commonly be dealt with:

(a)   Length of service;

(b)   Positions held;

(c)   Competence in the job;

(d)   Honesty;

(e)   Time-keeping;

(f)   Reason for leaving;

(g)   Any other particular remarks about the employee, such as long periods of absence due to sickness;

(h)   Any relevant remarks of a more personal nature about the employee.

For references relating to junior employees, some employers request that a form dealing with these matters be completed. However, for a more senior employee such a form may give an inadequate picture, and a fuller letter may be more appropriate.

1.4   EMPLOYER'S POTENTIAL LIABILITIES

Liability to the employee

A reference provided by an employer in respect of a former (or current) employee may give rise to the following possible causes of action:

(1)   Tortious claims: negligent misstatement, deceit, malicious falsehood, libel; and/or

(2)   Statutory claims.

In addition, the EAT has held that the implied term of trust and confidence in a contract of employment requires the employer to provide a reference meeting certain standards ('fair and reasonable' was the standard set by the EAT, although that particular test was articulated prior to much of the case-law set out below). If the employer fails to provide the requisite reference, the employee may resign and claim constructive dismissal (see *TSB Bank plc v Harris* [2000] IRLR 157).

(1) Tortious claims

The primary tort is negligent misstatement. Deceit, malicious falsehood and libel are generally not litigated in relation to references due to the requirement to show malice, whereas negligent misstatement only requires negligence.

In relation to libel, references given by one employer to a prospective employer may not be made the grounds for a libel action by the employee even if the information given proves to be inaccurate, provided that the employer believes the information to be correct and gives it without malice. This is because the employer (or ex-employer) and the prospective employer have a common interest in the statement made about the employee, and the statement is protected by what is known as 'qualified privilege'. As Lord Ellenborough CJ said in 1818: 'In the case of master and servant, the convenience of mankind required that what is said in fair communication between man and man, upon the subject of character, should be privileged, if made *bona fide* and without malice. If, however, the party giving the character knows what he says to be untrue, that may deprive him of the protection which the law throws around such communications' (*Hodgson v Scarlett* (1818) 1 B & Ald 232; see also *Sutherland v British Telecommunications plc* (1989) Times, 30 January). The defence of qualified privilege may, however, be lost if the statement is not merely passed between people having a mutuality of interest in the subject matter but falls into the hands of a third person. Thus, all references should be carefully marked 'private and confidential'.

The leading case concerning negligent misstatement is *Spring v Guardian Assurance plc* [1994] ICR 596, [1994] IRLR 460, [1994] 3 All ER 129. In that case the House of Lords held that an employer owes a duty of care to an employee about whom he writes a reference. The employer's duty is to take reasonable care in the preparation of the reference, and he will be liable to the employee in negligence if he fails to do so and the employee thereby suffers damage. The case reached the House of Lords on the issue of recovery of pure economic loss for negligent misstatement.

The obligation on the employer is to provide a true, accurate and fair reference. The reference must not give a misleading impression. However, as long as the reference is accurate and does not tend to mislead, there is no obligation on the employer to set great detail or to be comprehensive. In *Bartholomew v London Borough of Hackney* [1999] IRLR 246, the employer stated that the employee had been suspended and was subject to disciplinary action, which action ceased upon an agreed termination of the employee's employment. The employee complained that a reference was negligent because it failed to say that he strongly disputed the charges. The reference was held not to be negligent. It was accurate and fair and did not cease to be so simply because it did not recite chapter and verse.

In *Kidd v Axa Equity and Law Life Assurance Society plc* [2000] IRLR 301, the High Court held that the duty of care on an employer did not require the employer to provide a reference which was fair, full and comprehensive. The duty is to take reasonable care. That means not giving misleading information whether by selective provision of information or by the inclusion of information in a manner that would lead a reasonable recipient to draw a false or mistaken inference. However, there is no duty to give a full or comprehensive reference, nor to refer to all material facts. See also *Byrnell v British Telecommunications Plc* [2009] EWHC 727 (QB), where the High Court rejected an argument that a purely factual reference (referring only to dates of employment and the former employee's role) was so inadequate as to constitute no "reference" at all.

Subsequent to *Bartholomew*, the Court of Appeal has further considered the requirements of accuracy and fairness in a reference for an employee who has resigned while under investigation, so that the investigation was never completed: *Cox v Sun Alliance Life Ltd* [2001] EWCA Civ 649, [2001] IRLR 448. In *Cox*, the employer provided an inaccurate and unfair reference, suggesting that it would have had a reasonable basis for dismissing the employee on the grounds of dishonesty amounting to corruption. Mummery LJ drew an analogy between the principle to be applied and the proper approach of a tribunal to dismissal for misconduct, as set out in *British Home Stores Ltd v Burchell* [1978] IRLR 379. If an employee is to be fairly dismissed for misconduct, the employer must genuinely believe in the employee's guilt, must have reasonable grounds for that belief, and must have carried out a reasonable investigation. The same principles will render negligent a reference that alludes to an employee's misconduct, when the employer has not carried out an investigation, and does not have reasonable grounds for believing in his misconduct.

On this latter issue, see *Jackson v Liverpool* [2011] IRLR 1009. The ex-employer had provided a partial reference, in that it had not answered two of the questions posed by the prospective new employer. The ex-employer had a telephone conversation with the prospective new employer in which he explained that there were certain unresolved allegations concerning discrepancies in the ex-employee's record-keeping, but had made it clear that these were only allegations. Contrary to the finding of the first-instance judge, the Court of Appeal held that the ex-employer had not behaved unfairly or otherwise negligently.

In *Hincks v Sense Networks Limited* [2018] EWHC 533 (QB), [2018] IRLR 614, the High Court held that unless there was a 'red flag' prompting a need for further inquiry, the duty would not extend to re-opening investigations that had previously been conducted in respect of a former employee on account of alleged procedural unfairness.

In order to succeed in an action based on an allegedly negligent reference, a claimant will have to show first that the information contained in the reference is misleading, second, that it would be likely to have a material effect on a reasonable recipient and, third, that the defendant was negligent in compiling the reference. In *Bullimore v Pothecary Witham Weld Solicitors* (UKEAT/0189/10/JOJ) [2011] IRLR 18, an employer gave a former employee an unfairly adverse reference which led to the withdrawal of a subsequent offer of employment. The EAT held that the employee's loss was not too remote from the employer's actions, and the employee could recover for loss of earnings and injury to feelings. Compare this with *Brown v Baxter (T/A Careham Hall)* UKEAT/0354/09/SM (7 July 2010, unreported), where it was found that the employer would have given an unfavourable reference even if it had not dismissed the employee. The unfavourable reference therefore was not "a consequence" of the dismissal, and should not have been reflected in the damages awarded to the employee. The employee sought to rely on the "stigma damages" principle arising from *Chagger v Abbey National plc* [2009] EWCA Civ 1202, [2010] ICR 397, [2010] IRLR 47 (see CONTRACTS OF EMPLOYMENT (8)), but this was dismissed as irrelevant: the usual principles of causation applied. *Abdel-Khalek v Ali* [2016] EWCA Civ 80, [2016] IRLR 358 is a case that emphasises that the negligence must be the cause of the loss. In that case, the employer negligently misdescribed the employee's (actual) incompetence. The court found it was the employee's incompetence that caused the loss, not the negligent misdescription.

In *McKie v Swindon College* [2011] IRLR 575, the High Court extended the principle established in *Spring* to hold that a former employer could be liable to a former employee in damages for negligent misstatement where it had sent an email about him to a subsequent employer which resulted in his dismissal (i.e. the principle applied well after the employee had begun his employment with his new employer, without any request for a reference having been made, and therefore not merely in pre-employment checks).

(2) Statutory claims

A former employee who is refused a reference or given a bad reference because he or she had made a complaint of discrimination or done some other protected act under the *Equality Act 2010* would be entitled to sue for victimisation provided that the claim arose out of the incidents of the employment relationship or was sufficiently proximate to the employment or that there was a substantive connection between the complaint and the employment. See *section 108* of the *Equality Act 2010*, which prohibits discrimination and harassment which (inter alia) "arises out of and is closely connected to a relationship which used to exist between them". In *Jessemey v Rowstock Ltd* [2014] EWCA Civ 185, [2014] 3 All ER 409, the Court of Appeal confirmed that post-employment victimisation was prohibited by section 108, notwithstanding a drafting error in the legislation.

This entitlement was first recognised (prior to the *Equality Act 2010*) in the context of sex discrimination law by the decision of the European Court of Justice in *Coote v Granada Hospitality Ltd: C-185/97* [1999] ICR 100, [1998] IRLR 656. It was there held that an employer who refused to provide a reference to an ex-employee on the grounds that the employee had brought legal proceedings to enforce the right to equal treatment of men and women would be liable for victimisation. At the time of this decision the position under domestic law was that the discrimination legislation only applied to events occurring during employment and not afterwards: *Adekeye v Post Office (No 2)* [1997] IRLR 105. The EAT has held that the *Sex Discrimination Act 1975* ('*SDA 1975*') can be construed consistently with this decision (*Coote v Granada Hospitality Ltd (No 2)* [1999] IRLR 452). More recently the House of Lords has overturned *Adekeye* and held that the protection afforded to employees by the discrimination legislation is not coterminous with the existence of a contractual relationship. Therefore claims may be brought by former employees so long as there is a substantive connection between the discriminatory conduct alleged and the employment relationship, whenever the discriminatory conduct arises: *Relaxion Group plc v Rhys-Harper* [2003] UKHL 33, [2003] 4 All ER 1113, [2003] IRLR 484. See also *Bullimore* (reference above).

An employee who was refused a reference after employment had ended or who was provided with a poor reference because he had made a protected disclosure under *Part IVA* of the Employment Rights Act 1996 (see DISCLOSURE OF INFORMATION (11)) would be able to allege that the failure to provide the reference to or the content of it involved the employee being subjected to a detriment on the ground that the employee had made a protected disclosure, contrary to *s 47B*: *Woodward v Abbey National plc* [2006] IRLR 677, CA. The protected disclosure may even have been made after his employment terminated: *Onyango v Berkeley (t/a Berkeley Solicitors)* UKEAT/0407/12.

In *Pnaiser v NHS England* [2016] IRLR 170, the EAT held that giving a negative reference in connection with absence arsing from disability could constitute an unlawful act of discrimination. See similarly *Lee v South Warwickshire NHS Foundation Trust* (UKEAT/0287/17/DA, 11 July 2018).

41.5 Liability to the recipient

The recipient of a negligent reference may also be able to sue the person giving the reference for any loss suffered. It is reasonably foreseeable that the recipient of a reference will act on its contents and if he relies on a reference which is inaccurate because it was carelessly drawn up and thereby suffers loss, the giver of the reference may be held liable to pay the recipient damages on account of his negligence (cf *Hedley Byrne & Co Ltd v Heller & Partners Ltd* [1964] AC 465, [1963] 2 All ER 575).

There is no sure way of avoiding the possibility of liability for negligent mis-statements in references since the *Unfair Contract Terms Act 1977* ('*UCTA 1977*') applies. Disclaimers such as 'The above information is given in confidence and in good faith. No responsibility, however, can be accepted for any errors, omissions or inaccuracies in the information or for any loss or damage that may result from reliance being placed upon it' may have been effective to exclude liability before the *UCTA 1977* came into force, but now such a disclaimer will only be effective insofar as it 'satisfies the requirement of reasonableness' (*UCTA 1977, s 2(2)*). The 'explanatory provisions' of the *Act* state that such a notice of disclaimer will satisfy this requirement of reasonableness where it is 'fair and reasonable to allow reliance upon it, having regard to all the circumstances obtaining when the liability arose or (but for the notice) would have arisen' (*UCTA 1977, s 11(3)*). If the reference purports to give facts which are ordinarily within the knowledge of an employer, it is thought that liability cannot now be excluded for negligent mis-statement of those facts. If, however, it contains an opinion as to the employee's suitability for a certain post which he has not filled in the past, it may arguably be considered reasonable to insert a disclaimer for such a statement of opinion.

41.6 Data protection issues

The *General Data Protection Regulation* (*GDPR*) and *Data Protection Act 2018* ("*DPA 2018*") came into force on 25 May 2018, replacing the *Data Protection Act 1998* ("*DPA 1998*"). The UK's Information Commissioner's Office publishes 'The employment practices code' (the "ICO Guide") to assist employers/employees and which, amongst other things, recommends that employers should have a clear policy relating who give reference and that the consent of the person who is the subject of the reference should be secured prior to providing a reference. The ICO Guide has not been updated for the *GDPR* but remains a helpful guide to the applicable principles.

Under the *DPA 2018* and *GDPR*, there is a prohibition on processing 'special categories' of personal data (previously sensitive personal data), which includes data concerning health. Data concerning health may be communicated in a reference in relation to the issue of a person's absence record. *GDPR, Article 9* provides exemptions from this prohibition in circumstances in which the data subject consents or where "processing is necessary for the purposes of carrying out the obligations and exercising specific rights of the controller or of the data subject in the field of employment . . . law".

As regards subject access requests, the ICO Guide summarised the position under the *DPA 1998* as follows (*Sch 7, para 1*): "Under a specific exemption in the Act, a worker does not have the right to gain access to a confidential job reference from the organisation which has given it. However, once the reference is with the organisation to which it was sent then no such specific exemption from the right of access exists. That organisation is though entitled to take steps to protect the identity of third parties such as the author of the reference." By contrast, under the *DPA 2018, Sch 24, para 24* provides an exemption for both the provider and receiver of the reference in specified circumstances.

However, under both the *DPA 1998* (esp *s 10*) and *DPA 2018* (esp *s 99*) the data subject has rights to object to the processing of their data in certain circumstances. A very unusual example of a person successfully preventing the processing of their data in an employment reference context is *AB v A Chief Constable* [2014] EWHC 1965 (QB), [2014] IRLR 700.

41.7   LIABILITY OF PERSONS OTHER THAN THE EMPLOYER

It is frequently the case that employment will be dependent on a satisfactory medical report being presented to the prospective employer. In *Kapfunde v Abbey National plc and Daniel* [1998] IRLR 583, the claimant was refused employment on the basis of a medical report. She sought to sue the author of the report alleging that it was negligent. The Court of Appeal dismissed the claim holding that a medical practitioner who compiles a report about a prospective employee does not owe a duty of care to the prospective employee. There is insufficient proximity between the author of the report and the prospective employee. It may well be, however, that the medical practitioner owes a duty of care to the prospective employer.

The Scottish case of *Glasgow City Council v First Glasgow (No 1) Ltd* [2019] CSOH 101 considered whether a previous employer who gave a reference to a new employer could be liable in negligence to a third party who was injured by the employee during the course of his new employment. The facts revolved around a bin lorry driver who loft consciousness at the wheel, resulting the multiple deaths. The Court of Session decided that there was no applicable duty of care in negligence first due to the lack of proximity between those third parties and the former employer. Second, because it would not be fair just and reasonable to impose such a duty, because it render former employers unwilling to provide references for former employees if the potential liability were widened so significantly in scope.

41.8   REFERENCES AND EMPLOYMENT PROTECTION RIGHTS

Although employees do not have a statutory or common law right to a reference, references may be relevant to proceedings in employment tribunals. A good reference may be powerful evidence against an employer who tries to justify the dismissal of an employee on grounds of misconduct or incompetence. Similarly, a reference which is inconsistent with written reasons for a dismissal supplied to an employee may be persuasive in enabling the employee to show that those written reasons were inadequate or untrue, thus entitling him to an award under *ERA 1996, s 93* (see **49.15** Termination of Employment).

A reference may sometimes be negotiated as part of compromising a claim for unfair dismissal, because a reference is not something an employment tribunal has the power to order an employer to provide.

41.9   EMPLOYMENT CONDITIONAL UPON REFERENCES

Sometimes, a contract of employment may be offered 'subject to satisfactory references'. In *Wishart v National Association of Citizens' Advice Bureaux Ltd* [1990] ICR 794, [1990] IRLR 393, the Court of Appeal was strongly of the opinion that such a provision was satisfied only if the references supplied were subjectively satisfactory to that particular employer. However, it recognised that it was arguable that the requirement was an objective one. It is prudent therefore to expressly state in any offer letter that references are conditional upon receipt of 'references satisfactory to' the new employer.

41.10   ACAS GUIDANCE

On 4 September 2018, ACAS published guidance relating to employment references which reflects the case-law set out above. The guidance also states, amongst other things:

- "Employers should have a policy to help them handle reference requests, telling them what information they and their employees can provide."

- "Employees should consider waiting until they get an unconditional offer before handing in their notice."

- "References must not include misleading or inaccurate information. They should avoid giving subjective opinions or comments that are not supported by facts."

- "Potential employers should remember a referee may not provide a reference or might inaccurately suggest the applicant is unsuitable. In these circumstances it may help to discuss any concerns with the job applicant directly first."

These principles will no doubt be taken into account by the courts in future proceedings relating to references.

42   Restraint of Trade and Confidential Information

42.1   INTRODUCTION TO RESTRAINT OF TRADE AND CONFIDENTIAL INFORMATION

Considerations of restraint of trade operate in employment law in two distinct ways: first, there is the common law doctrine of restraint of trade comprising a body of rules under which certain contractual restraints must be justified before the court will enforce them. Secondly, a court will have regard to the impact of restraints on trade in any form in situations where the common law doctrine does not apply, or cannot be applied in accordance with its rules, as a factor influencing its discretion to grant or withhold the remedy of an injunction and in framing the terms of any injunction granted. The latter operation of what may be called 'considerations' of restraint of trade is seen most clearly in so-called 'garden leave' and 'springboard' injunction cases. Confusion between restraint of trade as a narrow doctrine of the law of contract and as a factor in the exercise of judicial discretion as to whether or not to grant an injunction, has led to considerable confusion in the law and, on occasion, to judicial error: see *J A Mont (UK) Ltd v Mills* [1993] IRLR 172. That confusion still persists: see *Tullett Prebon plc v BGC Brokers LP* [2010] IRLR 648 and *JM Finn & Co Ltd v Holliday* [2014] IRLR 102.

Obligations of confidentiality that arise in the employment situation are also apt to cause confusion and, again, a clear distinction must be drawn between those obligations which underpin, in part, the doctrine of restraint of trade and those which give rise to relief and remedies which lie outside that doctrine altogether.

It is impossible in a work of this nature to do more than briefly sketch the main principles of these large and partially interlocking fields of law which apply specifically to the employment relationship. Hence we do not deal in this chapter with restraint of trade principles as they apply to business sale agreements, shareholder agreements or partnerships, etc, even where there may be partial overlaps of principle. It should, however, be noted that the statutory regulation of competition in the United Kingdom has relatively recently undergone major changes to bring it into line with European models: see *Competition Act 1998* and *Enterprise Act 2002*. These reforms affect the common law doctrine of restraint of trade and, in certain circumstances, displace it altogether: see *Days Medical Aids Ltd v Pihsiang Machinery Manufacturing Co Ltd* [2004] EWHC 44 (Comm), [2004] 1 All ER (Comm) 991. The domestic statutory controls, over restraints ancillary to mergers and acquisitions of businesses, however, apply to individuals only if they may be treated as 'undertakings', i.e. if they have a controlling interest in the business merged or acquired. The vast majority of employees will not, therefore, fall within the provisions of *Part I* of the *Competition Act 1998* or *Art 101* of the *Lisbon Treaty*. For this reason, we do not attempt a review of competition law in this chapter. However, although the principles of competition law do not apply directly to most employees, they may have an indirect impact in shaping public policy, from which the common law doctrine itself springs (see further below **42.5**).

Proceedings in relation to the enforcement or breach of covenants in restraint of trade must in almost all cases be brought in the ordinary courts, and not in the employment tribunals. This is because most disputes in relation to the enforcement or breach of such covenants will fall outside the jurisdiction of the employment tribunals, since any claim in respect of such a covenant will not (as a general rule) be one that 'arises or is outstanding' on the termination of the employee's employment so as to bring it within the scope of the *Employment Tribunals Extension of Jurisdiction (England and Wales) Order 1994*. (This Order extended the jurisdiction of the employment tribunals so as to encompass breach of contract claims by employees and, where the employee has brought such a claim, counterclaims for breach of contract by the employer: see *Peninsula Business Services Ltd v Sweeney* [2004] IRLR 49 and generally **8.22c** and **8.22d** CONTRACT OF EMPLOYMENT). Further, the employment tribunals' contractual jurisdiction (as set out in the *Extension of Jurisdiction Order*) only extends to the power to award damages for breach of contract: the employment tribunals have no power to issue injunctions, which is the usual remedy sought by the claimant in restraint of trade cases (see below **42.16**).

There have been a handful of cases in which the question of the enforceability of covenants in restraint of trade has been raised as part of a claim falling within the jurisdiction of the employment tribunals, for example where an employee's refusal to sign up to covenants in restraint of trade is relied on by an employer as a reason for dismissing an employee, or where sums deducted pursuant to a covenant in restraint of trade are claimed as an unlawful deduction from wages. However, the Court of Appeal has now confirmed that, in both those situations, the employment tribunal need not determine whether or not the covenant in question is reasonable and enforceable. Thus in *Willow Oak Developments Ltd (t/a Windsor Recruitment) v Silverwood* [2006] EWCA Civ 660, [2006] IRLR 607 the Court of Appeal confirmed previous authority to the effect that a refusal on the part of an employee to sign up to new terms and conditions of employment that included covenants in restraint of trade was capable (whether or not the restraints were reasonable) of being a potentially fair reason for dismissing an employee. However, the Court of Appeal observed that the reasonableness (or otherwise) of the restraints was a (non-determinative) factor which the employment tribunal could take into account when determining whether or not it was in fact fair to dismiss the employee for that reason under *ERA 1996, s 98(4)* (see generally **55.14** UNFAIR DISMISSAL – II). The Court of Appeal disapproved the earlier decision of the EAT in *Forshaw v Archcraft Ltd* [2006] ICR 60, [2005] IRLR 600 in which it was held that, if the new term sought to be imposed by the employer was in fact an unreasonable restraint of trade, then an employee dismissed for failing to sign up to that term had been unfairly dismissed. As to unlawful deductions from wages claims under *s 23* of the *Employment Rights Act 1996*, the EAT in *Peninsula Business Services* (above) confirmed that deductions pursuant to clauses in restraint of trade are to be treated in the same way as deductions pursuant to any other clause in the employee's contract: provided the covenant is set out in writing, and the employee has agreed to it in writing, the employer will have a defence to any such claim in the employment tribunal. The employee's remedy in such circumstances lies in a claim for breach of contract in the ordinary courts: see generally PAY – I: PAYMENTS, PAY STATEMENTS AND MISCELLANEOUS STATUTORY PAY RIGHTS (35).

We propose to review first the law in relation to the common law doctrine of restraint of trade (below **42.2**), then to review confidential information (below **42.13**) and to consider restraint of trade as a discretionary element in granting injunctive relief outside of the narrow common-law doctrine of restraint of trade (including so-called 'garden leave' and 'springboard' injunctions) (below **42.14, 42.15**). Finally, we consider procedural issues and remedies (below **42.16**).

42.2 THE COMMON LAW DOCTRINE OF RESTRAINT OF TRADE

Although of ancient origin the doctrine in its modern form may be traced to the speech of Lord McNaghten in *Nordenfelt v Maxim Nordenfelt Guns and Ammunition Co Ltd* [1894] AC 535, 565, [1891–4] All ER Rep 1:

'All interference with individual liberty of action in trading, and all restraints of trade of themselves, if there is nothing more, are contrary to public policy, and therefore void. That is the general rule. But there are exceptions: restraints of trade and interference with individual liberty of action may be justified by the special circumstances of a particular case. It is a sufficient justification, and indeed it is the only justification, if the restriction is reasonable – reasonable, that is, in reference to the interests of the parties concerned and reasonable in reference to the interests of the public, so framed and so guarded as to afford adequate protection to the party in whose favour it is imposed, while at the same time it is in no way injurious to the public.'

It follows that in applying the common law doctrine of restraint of trade it is necessary to consider the following fundamental issues:

(1)   what restraints of trade are covered by the doctrine?

(2)   what are the legitimate interests of the parties?

(3)   is the restraint injurious to the public interest?

42.3   What restraints are covered?

A very large number of contracts or contractual provisions will impose some limits on a person's freedom to trade (for example, a contract to sell specific goods or a lease of a property prohibiting the use of the premises for business purposes). Such contracts or provisions are not subject to the restraint of trade doctrine: see *Esso Petroleum Co Ltd v Harper's Garage* [1968] AC 269, [1967] 1 All ER 699 .

Various tests have been propounded to identify restraints which do, or do not, fall within the doctrine. The best of these tests, it is submitted, is contained in the speech of Lord Pearce in the *Esso* case:

'The doctrine does not apply to ordinary commercial contracts for the regulation and promotion of trade during the existence of the contract, provided that any prevention of work outside the contract, viewed as a whole, is directed towards the absorption of the parties' services and not their sterilisation. Sole agencies are a normal and necessary incident of commerce and those who desire the benefits of a sole agency must deny themselves the opportunities of other agencies. So, too, in the case of a film star who may tie herself to a company in order to obtain from them the benefits of stardom . . . parties habitually fetter themselves to one another.

When a contract only ties the parties during the continuance of the contract and the negative ties are only those which are incidental and normal to the positive commercial arrangements at which the contract aims, even though those ties exclude all dealing with others, there is no restraint of trade within the meaning of the doctrine and no question of reasonableness arises. If, however, the contract ties the trading activities of either party after its determination, it is a restraint of trade and the question of reasonableness arises. So, too, if *during* the contract one of the parties is too unilaterally fettered so that the contract loses its character of a contract for the regulation and promotion of trade and acquires the predominant character of a contract in restraint of trade. In that case . . . the question whether it is reasonable arises.'

Applying this to a contract of employment, it is clear that the doctrine will apply to restraints imposed on the employee's working activities or fields of work after the original contract has ended. It is also clear from that test, however, that the doctrine can apply to some employment contracts, or provisions within those contracts, intended to operate during the currency of the employment relationship. Thus extravagantly oppressive and one-sided employment contracts may be held unenforceable during their lifetime: see *Young v Timmins* (1831) 1 Cr & J 331. The doctrine may also apply where, for example, other contractual provisions may be imposed which have the substantive effect of restraining the freedom of the employee to move jobs (for example, provisions clawing back bonuses if an employee goes to work for a rival or depriving an employee of commission which he has earned during the currency of his employment if he leaves to work for a rival). Some cases have considered such clauses solely by reference to the common law penalty doctrine (eg *Imam-Sadeque v BlueBay Asset Management (Services) Ltd* [2012] EWHC 3511 (QB), [2013] IRLR 344). Where the restraint of trade doctrine has been relied upon, the courts have not been consistent in their treatment of these kinds of provisions. In *Sadler v Imperial Life Assurance Co of Canada Ltd* [1988] IRLR 388, HC the doctrine was held to apply to a covenant depriving an employee of commission payable post termination of his employment if he went to work for a rival. The provision in question was held unenforceable and severed from the agreement, thereby entitling the employee to recover the commission payments (see also *Marshall v NM Financial Management Ltd* [1997] 1 WLR 1527, [1997] IRLR 449, CA). However, in *Peninsula Business Services Ltd v Sweeney* [2004] IRLR 49 the EAT held that a provision in an employee's contract denying him post-termination commission was not a restraint of trade since it did not impose any restraint on him as to whom he might work for or what he might do: it was merely an 'economic disincentive' to discourage the employee from leaving his employment. The EAT's decision in *Peninsula* seems far too restrictive in its refusal to apply the doctrine of restraint of trade to the provision in question. The doctrine is not based upon the form of the contractual restraint, but upon its substantive effect: 'whether a particular provision operates in restraint of trade is to be determined not by the form the stipulation wears but . . . by its effect in practice. . . . The clause in question here contains no direct covenant to abstain from any kind of competition or business, but the question to be answered is whether, in effect, it is likely to cause the employee to refuse business which otherwise he would take or, looking at it in another way, whether the existence of this provision would diminish his prospects of employment' (*per* Lord Wilberforce, *Stenhouse Australia Ltd v Phillips* [1974] AC 391, [1974] 1 All ER 117, PC at 402F-H). In the *Stenhouse* case the clause held to be unenforceable as an unreasonable restraint of trade was a profit-sharing clause imposed on an employee of an insurance broker as part of a settlement agreement entered into on the termination of his employment. The clause provided that, in the event that any client of the employer within a period of five years from the date of termination of the employment placed any insurance business (of the type transacted by the employer) with the departing employee, the departing employee would be entitled to a one-half share of the commission received in respect of such transaction. See also *22.20 London Ltd v Reilly* [2012] EWHC 1912 (Ch), [2012] All ER (D) 134 (Jul) where the judge refused to follow *Peninsula v Sweeney* (ibid).

It is of crucial importance to distinguish between post-termination restraints and garden leave provisions. An exclusive services provision in an employment contract operating during the currency of the employment relationship will not have the doctrine applied to it. Nonetheless, if, during the currency of the employment contract, the employer puts the employee on garden leave and seeks an injunction to prevent the employee, during that notice period, from working for a competitor, the court will pay heed to the restrictive effect of the exclusive services provision in determining whether to grant such an injunction and, if so, for what period. This is not the application of the doctrine of restraint of trade but the application of considerations of restraint of trade in the exercise of a judicial discretion: see *Symbian Ltd v Christensen* [2001] IRLR 77, *Provident Financial Group plc and Whitegates Estate Agency Ltd v Hayward* [1989] 3 All ER 298, [1989] ICR 160, [1989] IRLR 84, CA and *Mont v Mills* (supra).

It is a cardinal principle of the application of the common law doctrine of restraint of trade that the court must determine the enforceability of the contract or contractual provision concerned as at the date the contract was entered into, not at the date when it comes to be enforced (see *Gledhow Autoparts Ltd v Delaney* [1965] 1 WLR 1366, [1965] 3 All ER 288, *Home Counties Dairies Ltd v Skilton* [1970] 1 WLR 526, [1970] 1 All ER 1227, *Commercial Plastics Ltd v Vincent* [1965] 1 QB 623, [1964] 3 All ER 546, *Allan Janes LLP v Balraj Johal* [2006] EWHC 286 (Ch), [2006] ICR 742, [2006] IRLR 599 and *Patsystems Holdings Ltd v Neilly* [2012] EWHC 2609 (QB), [2012] IRLR 979). Thus if a restrictive covenant is adjudged to be invalid at the date it was entered into, it cannot be saved by a subsequent renegotiated contract of employment referring to an agreement or general acknowledgment by an employee that his previous terms 'remain unchanged' (*Patsystems*, ibid). It is accordingly apparent that the restraint of trade doctrine in its pure form may be readily applied to an employee's post-termination restraints, but cannot in its 'pure' form be applied to disputes which arise in relation to garden leave injunctions. In the case of exclusive service provisions in contracts of employment their reasonableness at the date the contract is entered into is obvious: they are there to provide the employer with the means of ensuring that the employee's skills and endeavours are fully absorbed. Thus they satisfy Lord Pearce's test at that stage. It is only when they are deployed during notice periods as the basis for seeking injunctive relief to enforce garden leave that they cease to have the character of a provision to absorb skills and endeavours and take on the character of a provision aimed at sterilising the employee. At that stage the doctrine of restraint of trade still cannot be applied in its pure form. The court embarks on a more flexible exercise of determining what, if any, harm the employee on garden leave may do to the employer's business if freed during his notice period to work for a rival and weighing against that harm considerations of restraint of trade in imposing an injunction restricting what the employee is permitted to do during his notice period or part of it (see *Symbian Ltd v Christensen* above). Because the court is engaged on a more flexible exercise than that permitted under the doctrine of restraint of trade it is able, for example, to impose injunctions for a period of time less than the contractual period of notice and, it would seem, can take into account interests of the employer that would not be considered legitimate under the doctrine of restraint of trade (see below **42.14**). In *JM Finn & Co* (above), the judge, Simler J, recognised the distinction between the judicial approach to enforcing contractual post-termination restraints and exercising a discretion to enforce by injunction negative contractual obligations of employee during notice periods. However, it appears that she believed that the latter exercise was an application of the restraint of trade doctrine. The danger of this confusion is that the courts will become less flexible in relation to discretionary relief in garden leave cases or will become too flexible in relation to granting relief in post-termination restraint cases, in effect re-writing the contractual restraint as happened in the *Tullett* case (see below). It appears that the Court of Appeal decision in the *Symbian* case (above) was not cited to the Court in the *JM Finn* case.

It also follows from the aforementioned cardinal principle that in judging the reasonableness of contractual restraints the court cannot consider events occurring after the contract containing the restraints is entered into. There is a limited exception to this rule in relation to events or matters subsequent to the outset of the contract where such events or matters throw a general light on what might have been fairly contemplated on a reasonable view of the meaning of the restrictive covenant in question (see *Coppage v Safety Net Security Ltd* [2013] IRLR 970). In *Coppage* the Court of Appeal upheld the first instance judge's approach to the issue of the enforceability of a covenant where he had taken into consideration the stability of the customer base of the employer during the last 12 months of the employee's employment as one factor in holding the covenant to be reasonable. However, when judging whether a covenant has been breached the court will, of course, look at the circumstances at the date of the alleged breach. A good illustration of the distinction between judging whether a covenant is valid and judging whether it is breached is furnished by *Phoenix Partners Group LLP v Asoyag (Maurice)* [2010] EWHC 846 (QB), [2010] IRLR 594. In that case (an interim injunction application) the judge held that it was likely that the restrictive covenants would, at trial, be held enforceable. However, those restrictive covenants prohibited the covenantor from joining a business "which competes with" the business of the covenantee and from soliciting or dealing with clients "in competition with" the business of the covenantee. At the date of the alleged breach, as the judge held, the covenantee had discontinued doing business of the particular kind covered by the covenants and, accordingly, the judge held that there was no breach of the covenant. A further example of this approach is to be found in *Stallergenes (UK) Ltd v Stern & Anor* [2013] EWCA Civ 1249.

There is one area of potential difficulty in applying this rule as to the date when the court must consider the reasonableness of any covenant in restraint of trade, namely that caused by the effect of the *Transfer of Undertakings (Protection of Employment) Regulations 2006* ('the *2006 TUPE Regulations*', which replace the *1981 TUPE Regulations* with effect from 6 April 2006: see generally TRANSFER OF UNDERTAKINGS (53)). The effect of those *Regulations* is that, where there is a 'relevant transfer' of an undertaking or part of one, employees whose contracts would otherwise be terminated by that transfer are instead subject to a statutory novation of their existing employment contract so that the transferee company is substituted for the transferor company. *Regulation 4(1)* of the *TUPE Regulations* provides that, following a transfer, an employee's contract of employment 'shall have effect after the transfer as if originally made between the person so employed and the transferee'. If *reg 4(1)* were to be applied literally then it would have the effect of rendering certain restrictive covenants (which prohibit dealing with customers of a specified business) imposed by the specified business (the transferor) upon its employees nugatory if the transfer that takes place had the result of substituting <u>in every respect</u> (and at all material times) the transferee for the transferor. In *Morris Angel & Son Ltd v Hollande* [1993] IRLR 169, [1993] 3 All ER 569 the court considered the effect of *reg 5(1)* of the *1983 TUPE Regulations* (now *reg 4(1)* of the *2006 TUPE Regulations*) on a restrictive covenant in the employee's contract of employment which prohibited him, for a period of one year after the contract came to an end, from seeking 'to procure orders from or do business with any person, firm or company who has, at any time during the one year immediately preceding the cesser done business with [Group Y]'. The business of Group Y was sold to X Ltd and on the date of sale the employee's contract of employment with Group Y was terminated. The employee sought to contend that the effect of the transfer was to substitute in the restrictive covenant for clients of Group Y the clients of X Ltd. Accordingly, the employee contended that he could not be in breach of the covenant by canvassing or soliciting persons who had been clients of group Y during the period one year prior to the termination of his contract because the effect of the old *reg 5(1)* was to alter the wording of the covenant 'clients of X Ltd' which, as a matter of fact, he had not solicited or dealt with after the termination of his employment. At first instance, it was held that the old *reg 5(1)* applied so that, although the transferee company could enforce the covenant, the customers with whom he was prohibited from doing business after termination were those of the transferee X Ltd. It followed that there was no breach of the covenant in question. On appeal, the Court of Appeal preferred a construction of the rules under which the transferee company was deemed to have been the owner of the transferor's business during the relevant 12-month period (i.e. the 12 months prior to the termination of the employment contract). Thus, the customers with whom the employee was prohibited from dealing under the covenants were those of the part of the business transferred (ie those of Group Y prior to the transfer). It followed that the employee was in breach and an interim injunction was ordered.

Any attempt to impose a new restrictive covenant upon employees following a *TUPE* transfer was, prior to 6 April 2006, almost bound to fail. Such variations to an employee's contract of employment were unenforceable under *reg 5(1)* of the *1983 TUPE Regulations* even if they formed part of a 'package' which was to the overall benefit of the employee (see *Credit Suisse First Boston (Europe) Ltd v Lister* [1998] IRLR 700). However, under the *2006 TUPE Regulations* variations to an employee's contract that are implemented for 'economic, technical or organisational' reasons entailing changes in the workforce will be valid even if the reason for the variation is the transfer. So if in a particular case the reason for seeking to change the restrictive covenants is an 'ETO' reason, then such a variation will be valid. Further, from 31 January 2014 variations to an employee's contract will be valid where, even where the reason for them is the transfer, if the employer has the contractual right to make the amendment (see *reg 5(b)*). Under the *2006 TUPE Regulations* employees should be informed of the identity of the transferee employer prior to the transfer. If they are not, then their entitlement to object under *reg 4(7)* may be exercised after the transfer so that the transferee cannot enforce post-termination restrictive covenants in their contracts of employment (see *New ISG Ltd v Vernon* [2007] EWHC 2665 (Ch), [2008] ICR 319, [2008] IRLR 115). See also TRANSFER OF UNDERTAKINGS (53).

42.4 The interests of the parties

In order to justify a contract or provision in restraint of trade it must be proved that it is reasonable in the interests of the parties. This does not mean that the provision in question must support the interests of both parties equally. Rather, it means: 'For a restraint to be reasonable in the interests of the parties it must afford *no more than* adequate protection of the party in whose favour it is imposed . . . though in one sense no doubt it is contrary to the interests of the covenantor to subject himself to any restraint, still it may be for his advantage to be able so to subject himself in cases where, if he could not do so, he would lose other advantages, such as . . . the possibility of obtaining employment or training under competent employers' (*Herbert Morris Ltd v Saxelby* [1916] 1 AC 688, 707, [1916–17] All ER Rep 305*per* Lord Parker). It is now firmly established that the burden of proof in relation to this first step in the justification process is on the party seeking to enforce that covenant: see *Mason v Provident Clothing and Supply Co Ltd* [1913] AC 724, [1911–13] All ER Rep 400 *per* Viscount Haldane, LC at 733 and Lord Shaw at 741 and *Herbert Morris*, above, at 700, 707 and 715. This will normally, but not invariably, be the employer (see, for example, *Wyatt v Kreglinger and Fernau* [1933] 1 KB 793, [1933] All ER Rep 349, where it was the employee who sought to enforce the covenant in question because that covenant was the sole consideration supporting the employee's pension entitlement).

The courts will not enforce any provision against mere competition (such covenants are generally referred to as 'covenants in gross'). It is of the essence that an employer demonstrates that he has a legitimate interest to protect. Preventing competition *per se* is not a legitimate interest. Covenants in restraint of trade are upheld not on the ground that the employee 'would, by reason of his employment or training, obtain the skill and knowledge necessary to equip him as a possible competitor in the trade, but that he might obtain such personal knowledge of and influence over the customers of his employer or such an acquaintance with his employer's trade secrets as would enable him, if competition were allowed, to take advantage of his employer's trade connection or utilise information confidentially obtained' (*per* Lord Parker in *Herbert Morris*, above, 709). This quotation from Lord Parker demonstrates that, historically, the courts had recognised two legitimate interests of the employer justifying the imposition of a reasonable restraint: (a) trade secrets (and confidential information); and, (b) customer connection.

The categories of legitimate interest that may be protected by an employer are not, however, confined to the two interests mentioned by Lord Parker. The modern approach to the identification of interests justifying provisions in restraint of trade is not based on a narrow categorisation: ' . . . the employer's claim for protection must be based upon the identification of some advantage or asset inherent in the business which can properly be regarded as, in a general sense, his property and which it would be unjust to allow the employee to appropriate for his own purposes, even though he, the employee, may have contributed to its creation. For while it may be true that an employee is entitled and is to be encouraged to build up his own qualities of skill and experience, it is equally his duty to develop and improve his employer's business for the benefit of his employer. These two obligations interlock during his employment: after its termination they diverge and mark the boundary between what the employee may take with him and what he may legitimately be asked to leave behind to his employers' (per Lord Wilberforce *Stenhouse Australia Ltd v Phillips*, ibid at p 400). Thus, in recent years new interests of an employer have been identified by the courts as justifying the protection of provisions in restraint of trade. In *Office Angels Ltd v Rainer-Thomas* [1991] IRLR 214, CA the court recognised as a legitimate interest of an employment agency the pool of workers on the agency's books. See also *East England Schools CIC (t/a 4MySchools) v Palmer and anor* [2014] IRLR 191. In *Dawnay, Day & Co Ltd v de Braconier d'Alphen* [1997] IRLR 285, affd [1998] ICR 1068, [1997] IRLR 442, CA the court recognised as a legitimate interest the stability of an employer's workforce, holding that a covenant imposed on an employee prohibiting him from soliciting his former colleagues to leave their employment was a reasonable restraint. Nevertheless, some caution needs to be exercised in framing contractual provisions in restraint of trade. Client connection is an important aspect of the goodwill of any business, but it is not the exclusive component of that goodwill. A competent and hard-working employee who does not have any dealings with clients may enhance the reputation of his employer's business, and the reputation of the business is part of its goodwill, but an employer cannot prohibit an employee from going to work for a competitor upon termination of his employment merely to protect the enhanced reputation of his business to which the employee has contributed: the employee is entitled to take with him his own skills and knowledge, even where those skills and knowledge have contributed to the reputation enjoyed by the employer (see *Countrywide Assured Financial Services Ltd v Smart* [2004] EWHC 1214 (Ch)).

Another interest that in practice one frequently sees employers seeking to protect are their suppliers. Thus one sees covenants aimed at prohibiting a former employee from dealing with suppliers of his former employer or, in extreme cases, from seeking to solicit or entice the supplier to cease to be a supplier of the former employer. The latter kind of covenant was considered in *Landmark Brickwork Ltd v Sutcliffe and ors* [2011] IRLR 976. In that case Slade J granted an interim injunction to enforce it, without giving reasons. However, while an employer is of course entitled to restrain an employee from inducing a supplier to break an existing contract with the employer (since that is in any event a tort to induce or procure the breach of a contract), it is hard to see what legitimate interest an employer has in preventing its employees from dealing with its suppliers generally. Such a covenant merely inhibits the suppliers' ability to trade and has no impact on the employer's business. The only situation in which an employer might have a legitimate interest in protecting its suppliers would be if the supplies in question were scarce so that if an employee took supplies from the supplier there would be insufficient to supply the employer. Even a covenant such as that considered in the *Landmark* case (ie prohibiting the employee from seeking to dissuade a supplier from continuing to supply the employer) might not be protecting a legitimate business interest if the supplies are readily obtainable elsewhere and the employee was not (in approaching the supplier) misusing the employer's confidential information. In *Energy Renewals Ltd v Borg* [2014] IRLR 713, a restriction on contacting suppliers of the former employer was considered to be too wide to be enforceable where those suppliers comprised all of the six national energy suppliers in the energy brokerage sector and would effectively preclude the employee from acting in competition.

Having identified a legitimate interest to protect, the contract or contractual provision in question must be no more than adequate to protect that interest. Clearly the reasonableness of the ambit or duration of any restraint is tied to the nature of the interest in question. If it is sought by an employer to protect his customer connection, that may be achieved by post-termination restraints which prohibit for a reasonable period of time the ex employee from soliciting or dealing with those customers with whom the employee had contact during the course of his employment. *Prima facie* there would be no justification for imposing on that employee a post-termination restraint which prohibited him from entering into employment with a competitor. However, if an employer wishes to protect trade secrets or confidential information he may be justified in imposing a post-termination restraint prohibiting the employee from joining a competitor for a reasonable period of time. It is dangerous for an employer to seek too wide a protection for a limited interest because a court is entitled to look at the nature of the restraints imposed with a view to determining whether a lesser restraint would have been adequate to protect the employer's interest: see *Office Angels*, above. We return to the various forms of restraint and issues of reasonableness in more detail below.

Difficulties can arise in relation to corporate groups. Sometimes the employer company within the group will be a mere holding company which does not itself conduct any business. In such an instance, provided that the group is vertically aligned, the court will readily hold that the holding company has a legitimate interest to protect arising from the business conducted by its subsidiaries and can therefore enforce the covenant if valid (see *Stenhouse v Phillips*, ibid and *Beckett Investment Management Group Ltd v Hall* [2007] EWCA Civ 613, [2007] ICR 1539, [2007] IRLR 793). In such cases the parent or holding company is treated as conducting its business through the agency of its subsidiaries. However, in relation to horizontally organised groups, such an analysis is not possible (see *Henry Leetham & Sons Ltd v Johnstone-White* [1907] 1 Ch 322). In light of the fact that many persons employed within corporate groups are employed by a service company, close attention should be paid to the drafting of any restrictive covenants in employment contracts entered into by the service company to ensure that they properly embrace the legitimate interests of the subsidiaries for whom the employees will in fact be working.

Another case on restructuring of a business arose in *Towry EJ Ltd v Barry William Prosser Bennett and ors* [2012] EWHC 224 (QB), [2012] All ER (D) 148 (Feb). In that case Company A purchased shares of Company B. A number of employees then left. Company B was restructured and ceased to have any employees. It then commenced proceedings against the departed employees seeking to enforce post-termination restrictive covenants, both for the period whilst it was still in business and also for a period after that. Counsel for the employees submitted that there is a free-standing principle that a covenantee cannot enforce a covenant if he no longer has a legitimate business interest to protect. There is some force in that submission since the doctrine of restraint of trade is one founded in public policy (see above **42.2**) and it is hard to see why as a matter of public policy a covenant in restraint of trade should be enforceable in the absence of a protectable legitimate interest. At least, where an employer is no longer trading it should be the case that neither interim nor final injunctions will be granted since if the employer is not trading it can be suffering no more than nominal damage. However, in *Towry* Cox J held that the covenant was enforceable and that there was no free-standing principle that a restrictive covenant only remained enforceable for as long as the employer continued to have a legitimate business interest to protect. However, that case concerned only claims for breach of contract and inducement (which failed on the facts) and there was no claim for an injunction. (Cf *Phoenix Partners Group LLP v Asoyag* [2010] IRLR 594 for a case in which a post-termination covenant was not enforceable where an employer had ceased to do business because it was framed in terms preventing the employee from competing; since the employer had ceased to do business, the employee was not competing; see also *BFCA Ltd v Butt* [2013] EWHC 326 (QB)).

It is important to note that an interest of an employer in his customer connection can be protected even if the employee is not moving to a competitor business. Cases such as *Caterpillar Logistics Services (UK) Ltd v Paul Huesca de Crean* [2012] EWCA Civ 156, [2012] ICR 981, [2012] IRLR 410 and *Generics (UK) Ltd v Yeda Research and Development Co Ltd and anor* [2012] EWCA Civ 726, [2012] CP Rep 39, [2012] All ER (D) 01 (Jun) support, in principle, the protection of customer connection by prohibiting employees on reasonable terms from going to work with a customer. Such covenants are important in the area of service industries where employees are seconded to, or spend substantial periods of time, working for, or within the premises of, clients and can therefore establish strong relationships with those clients who may choose to poach those employees to save themselves the costs of paying the employer's fees for providing services through those employees. It may also be that these kind of 'customer' covenants can be justified on the basis of confidential information (although it must be recognised that there will be a substantial overlap, or sharing, of information between the customer and employer in these kinds of cases).

42.5   The public interest

Much confusion has arisen about the second step in the justification process enunciated by Lord McNaghten in the *Nordenfelt* case (see above, **42.2**). Problems arise for two reasons: first, the doctrine of restraint of trade is a creation of public policy which collides head on with another public policy, namely the sanctity of contract; secondly, in some cases (particularly those decided in the early part of the 20th century) judges tend to use the expressions 'public policy' and 'public interest' interchangeably (see for example Cozens-Hardy MR in *Sir WC Leng & Co Ltd v Andrews* [1909] 1 Ch 763). This confusion has led in more recent times to judicial debate about whether the doctrine of restraint of trade has been properly applied in the past in distinguishing between the private interest of the parties and public policy in the sense of public interest (see, for example, *per* Lord Reid in the *Esso Petroleum* case (above, at p 300E)). It is submitted that the true analysis of the doctrine is as follows:

(a)   It is contrary to public policy for parties to a contract to enter into restraints which go beyond the reasonable protection of legitimate private interests (the first limb of Lord McNaghten's test).

(b)   It is also contrary to public policy for parties to a contract to enter into restraints which are no more than adequate to protect a private legitimate interest recognised by the law, if those restraints are contrary to the public interest (the second limb of Lord McNaghten's test).

(c)   It follows that, in theory at least, a covenant which satisfies public policy to the extent that it is no more than adequate to protect a private legitimate interest may fail to satisfy public policy because it is not in the public interest.

Unfortunately, it is not possible to identify any cases in the employment field which clearly illustrate proposition (c). In a number of cases, eg *Sir WC Leng* (above), *Herbert Morris v Saxelby* (above), *Strange (SW) Ltd v Mann* [1965] 1 WLR 629, [1965] 1 All ER 1069, *Countrywide Assured Financial Services Ltd v Smart* (above) and *Commercial Plastics Ltd v Vincent* [1965] 1 QB 623, [1964] 3 All ER 546, the courts have held covenants to be against 'public policy' (and sometimes against the 'public interest') where, it is submitted, the real basis for the decisions in those cases is that there is no legitimate interest of the covenantee to protect or, alternatively, that the restraints go beyond what is reasonable to protect that interest. This is against public policy in the sense set out in (a) above, but is not illustrative of the principle in (c) above. (The only exception in these cases would appear to be the, (perhaps) *obiter*, statement of Farwell LJ in the *Sir WC Leng* case above at p 334.)

In a number of cases the public interest (as distinct from public policy) has been raised as a discrete ground of attack on contractual restrictions, but with a marked lack of success. Although Lord Denning MR in *Oswald Hickson Collier & Co v Carter-Ruck* [1984] AC 720n, [1984] 2 All ER 15 appeared to hold that it was contrary to 'public policy' that a fiduciary (a solicitor) should be precluded by a restrictive covenant from acting for a client who wanted him to act, that decision was swiftly departed from: see *Edwards v Worboys* [1984] AC 724n, [1984] 2 WLR 850n; *Bridge v Deacons* [1984] AC 705, [1984] 2 All ER 19 and *Allan Janes LLP v Balraj Johal* [2006] EWHC 286 (Ch), [2006] ICR 742, [2006] IRLR 599. See also, in relation to the medical profession, *Kerr v Morris* [1987] Ch 90, [1986] 3 All ER 217.

Probably the real reason why issues of public interest do not generally arise for decision, at least in employment cases, is because restraints which customarily appear in employment contracts normally have no impact on the public at large and hence the public interest. Moreover the onus of proving that a restraint is injurious to the public interest is upon the person (normally the employee) who is making that allegation. The burden is a heavy one: *A-G Commonwealth of Australia v Adelaide Steamship Co Ltd* [1913] AC 781, [1911–13] All ER Rep 1120 at 797 *per* Lord Parker. It is, however, submitted that one area in which the issue of public interest is of great significance in the employment field is where an employee challenges an <u>indirect</u> restraint upon his freedom. These kind of restraints arise where the employee has no direct restraint imposed upon him in his contract of employment but nonetheless is fettered by contractual restraints which his employer has entered into with other parties. In these cases the private interests of the parties are not in issue because the parties are not challenging the enforceability of the restraints: a third party (the employee) is challenging the restraints in so far as they affect him and not the parties to the contract. (See *Eastham v Newcastle United Football Club Ltd* [1964] Ch 413, [1963] 3 All ER 139 and *Greig v Insole* [1978] 3 All ER 449 and compare *Kores Manufacturing Co Ltd v Kolok Manufacturing Co Ltd* [1957] 3 All ER 158 which involved an agreement between two employers not to employ each other's employees for a period of five years after their leaving the employment of the respective parties. In fact, however, in that case, the challenge to the agreement was not made by an employee but by one of the parties. Nonetheless, the Court of Appeal opined, *obiter*, that such an agreement could not be justified under the restraint of trade doctrine because of its indirect effect upon employees.)

It was suggested by Lord Hodson in the *Esso* case that issues of the burden of proof in relation to the interests of the parties and the public interest will seldom arise because, once the agreement is before the court, it is open to the scrutiny of the court in all its surrounding circumstances 'as a question of law': *Esso*, above, 319. It is submitted that this is not right. In the employment situation the employer must (if he seeks to enforce a restraint) establish that the covenant is in the interests of the parties in the narrow sense required by the doctrine. If the employee wishes to challenge the restraint on the ground that it is injurious to the public interest he cannot rely on the employer to furnish the court with the evidence required to prove injury to the public: the onus is on him to do that. The evidence which would require the court to consider the impact of a restraint upon a particular market is likely to be voluminous and to require expert opinion. Most employees would lack the financial means to undertake the provision to the court of that kind of evidence themselves. It is therefore extremely improbable that a court will have furnished to it in an employment case all the evidence that is required to deal properly with the issue of the public interest. It may be, however, that restraint of trade law is entering into a new era where issues of public interest will become more prominent. In the case of *Dranez Anstalt v Hayek (Zamir)* [2002] EWCA Civ 1729, [2003] 1 BCLC 278, [2002] All ER (D) 377 (Nov) restrictive covenants entered into by the inventor of a new ventilator for use in hospitals were held to constitute unreasonable restraints of trade by the Court of Appeal amongst other grounds on the basis that they offended against the public interest in restricting the inventor from making further developments which would be of great benefit to the public. There are, too, the developments in competition law to which reference has already been made (see above **42.1**). Competition law will not normally have any relevance to employees as they are not 'undertakings' for the purposes of competition law. However, the European Commission has issued guidance in Commission Notice [2005] OJ C-56/24 as to its position in relation to ancillary restraints taken upon the merger or acquisition of a business as follows: '*Non-competition clauses are justified for periods of up to three years, when the transfer of the undertaking includes the transfer of customer loyalty in the form of both goodwill and know-how. When only goodwill is included, they are justified for up to two years.*' This Guidance was adopted by the OFT in its previous Mergers Assessment Guidance, but the most recent joint OFT

/ Competition Commission guidance does not refer to this. Nonetheless, it is possible that these periods may be taken as a 'benchmark' for public policy in cases involving the common law of restraint of trade.

42.6 Judging the reasonableness of restraints

Construction of covenants in restraint of trade

The principles which a court should apply to the construction of covenants in restraint of trade do not materially differ from the principles applicable to the construction of any other written terms. Those principles are derived from the speech of Lord Hoffmann in *Investors Compensation Scheme v West Bromwich Building Society* [1998] 1 WLR 896, [1998] 1 All ER 98 at 912H–913E (see *Beckett Investment Management Group Ltd v Hall*, ibid). The approach of the Court is exemplified in the case of *Clarke v Newland* [1991] 1 All ER 397. In that case, the Court concluded that the following approach should be adopted. First, the court should consider the construction of the term in question without having regard to the issue of validity or invalidity of the covenant, ie the court must decide what the contractual provision means before it decides whether the provision is reasonable or not. Second, the court must have regard to the object of such restraints, namely the protection of one of the parties against trade rivalry. Finally, the court must construe the provision in context, that is to say, having regard to the factual matrix at the date when the contract was made. By following this approach, a court ought to avoid the worst excesses of an over-literal construction or of an over-purposive approach. The vice inherent in the over-literal construction of a covenant in restraint of trade is that the court ignores the intent of the parties and construes the covenant so that it extends to situations not contemplated by the parties:

> 'Another matter which requires attention is whether a restriction on trade must be treated as wholly void because it is so worded as to cover cases which may possibly arise, and to which it cannot be reasonably applied . . . Agreements in restraint of trade, like other agreements, must be construed with reference to the object sought to be obtained by them. In cases such as the one before us, the object is the protection of one of the parties against rivalry in trade. Such agreements cannot be properly held to apply to cases which, although covered by the words of the agreement, cannot reasonably be supposed ever to have been contemplated by the parties, and which on a rational view of the agreement are excluded from its operation by falling, in truth, outside and not within its real scope.'

Haynes v Doman [1899] 2 Ch 13, [1895–9] All ER Rep Ext 1468, CA, *per* Lindley LJ at 24–25. (See also *Coppage v Safety Net Security* (above) where the Court of Appeal decried the use, in attacking a covenant as too wide, of arguments based on merely theoretical or fanciful possibilities.)

In this respect much criticism has been levelled at the decision in *Commercial Plastics v Vincent* [1965] 1 QB 623, [1964] 3 All ER 546. A purposive approach to construction is well illustrated by the following cases. In *Moenich v Fenestre* (1882) 67 LT 602 the expression 'any trade or business' in a restrictive covenant was held to mean, contextually, 'any trade or business as commission merchant'. In *G W Plowman & Son Ltd v Ash* [1964] 1 WLR 568, [1964] 2 All ER 10 a covenant requiring an employee after termination of the employment 'not [to] canvass or solicit for himself or any other person . . . any farmer or market gardener who shall . . . have been a customer of the employers' was construed by the court as meaning, in the context of the employment agreement read as a whole, 'not to canvass or solicit with respect to the goods which the employee dealt with during his employment'. In *Home Counties Dairies Ltd v Skilton* [1970] 1 WLR 526, [1970] 1 All ER 1227 the words 'dairy produce' were construed by the court as being limited to only that sort of dairy produce with which the employee had been concerned whilst in employment. (See also *Hollis & Co v Stocks* [2000] IRLR 712.) In *TFS Derivatives Ltd v Morgan* [2004]

EWHC 3181 (QB), [2005] IRLR 246 'business' was held to refer to a particular business activity of the investment company in question, and not to the whole of the 'business entity' that was the company: see also *Dyson Technology Ltd v Strutt* [2005] EWHC 2814 (Ch), [2005] All ER (D) 355 (Nov), but compare the approach taken in *Wiggle Ltd v Burge* which appears to be out of line with these authorities (9 May 2012, QB, unreported). In the recent case of *Croesus Financial Services Ltd v Bradshaw and anor* [2013] EWHC 3685 (QB), [2013] All ER (D) 347 (Nov) the judge held that the expression 'personal contact in the course of their duties' (in relation to defining a class of clients which the employees were barred from dealing with by a restrictive covenant) when properly construed meant business contact that was more than trivial or de minimis and was personally undertaken by the employee covenantee. Compare this generous approach to construction with the approach adopted by Andrew Smith J in *Ashcourt Rowan Financial Planning Ltd v Hall* [2013] IRLR 637 which was far more restrictive.

However, the Court can be guilty of, in effect, re-writing a covenant by an over-purposive approach (see *Littlewoods Organisation Ltd v Harris* [1977] 1 WLR 1472, [1978] 1 All ER 1026, CA). The court ought not to be over indulgent when faced with ill-drafted and ambiguous provisions in restraint of trade. In *J A Mont (UK) Ltd v Mills* [1993] IRLR 172, CA a sales and marketing director of a paper mill entered into a severance agreement with his employer to terminate his employment. Under this agreement the employee received one year's remuneration although he was not required to work for the employer during that period. The severance agreement contained the following restraint: 'This total payment is made on condition that you do not join another company in the tissue industry within one year of leaving our employment'. The Court of Appeal held that the wording of the covenant was too wide because it operated worldwide and restrained the defendant from working in any capacity whatsoever in any sector of the tissue industry. The employer argued that the court should apply a purposive construction to the covenant to cut down its ambit. The Court of Appeal refused to do so, holding that it was clear that the employer had made no attempt whatever 'to formulate the covenant so as to focus upon the particular restraint necessary to guard against [the employee's] possible misuse of confidential information, the only legitimate target for imposing any restraint on his future employment'. The Court of Appeal relied heavily on the consideration that if covenants, *ex facie* too wide, could always be 'rescued' by the court implying restrictions to the restraint in order to render it enforceable then employees would be trapped into accepting excessive restraints or facing expensive litigation. This vice has long been recognised by the courts:

> 'It would in my opinion be *pessimi exempli* if, when an employer had exacted a covenant deliberately framed in unreasonably wide terms, the courts were to come to his assistance and, by applying their ingenuity and knowledge of the law, carve out of this void covenant the maximum of what he might validly have required. It must be remembered that the real sanction at the back of these covenants is the terror and expense of litigation, in which the servant is usually at a great disadvantage, in view of the longer purse of his master. It is sad to think that in this present case this appellant, whose employment is a comparatively humble one, should have had to go through four courts before he could free himself from such unreasonable restraints as this covenant imposes, and the hardship imposed by the exaction of unreasonable covenants by employers would be greatly increased if they could continue the practice with the expectation that, having exposed the servant to the anxiety and expense of litigation, the Court would in the end enable them to obtain everything which they could have obtained by acting reasonably.'

(*Mason v Provident Clothing and Supply Co Ltd* [1913] AC 724, [1911–13] All ER Rep 400, *per* Lord Moulton at 745.)

Accordingly, in construing provisions in restraint of trade the courts must establish a balance between extreme literalism and extreme liberalism. However, the approach to construction enunciated in *Clark v Newland* leads to one difficulty. It is a principle of contractual construction that in resolving ambiguities a court must strive to render the contractual term in question legal rather than illegal. Faced with an ambiguity which on one construction would render it too wide to be enforceable under the restraint of trade doctrine (thereby rendering the contractual provision 'illegal') and an alternative construction which would render the provision of narrower impact (and therefore legal), the court must choose the latter. It is not clear how, if the court is not permitted to have regard to the consequences of its construction exercise, it is able at the same time to comply with this principle (see *Mills v Dunham* [1891] 1 Ch 576). This principle has been confirmed in more recent cases where the courts have accepted that if, having examined the restrictive covenant in the context of the relevant factual matrix, there remains an element of ambiguity, the court should adopt the construction that would render the covenant lawful under the restraint of trade doctrine: see *Turner v Commonwealth and British Minerals Ltd* [2000] IRLR 114 at para 14 *per* Waller LJ and *TFS Derivatives Ltd v Morgan* [2004] EWHC 3181 (QB), [2005] IRLR 246 at para 43 *per* Cox J. By contrast, if a contractual provision is not truly ambiguous, then there can be no scope for recasting the parties' bargain by the insertion of words so as to given commercial efficacy to an otherwise toothless restrictive covenant: see *Prophet plc v Huggett* [2014] IRLR 797. In that case the literal reading of a clause prohibiting the departing employee from being engaged in connection with products which he had dealt with whilst with his employer was pointless because only the employer was engaged in such products. However, the Court of Appeal refused to uphold the trial judge's conclusion that something had "gone wrong" with the drafting and held that, in the context where it could be assumed that the draftsman had chosen his words with deliberate and specific care, the provision was to be applied as it read notwithstanding the fact that it would have no practical effect.

42.7   *Severance*

An English court is not permitted to uphold a covenant in restraint of trade by reducing its ambit or duration for that is to impose a new bargain upon the parties: see *J A Mont (UK) Ltd v Mills* (supra) and *Provident Financial Group plc and Whitegates Estate Agency Ltd v Hayward* (supra). (In many foreign jurisdictions courts do have this power.) Under English law, the covenant either satisfies the test of reasonableness as drawn and properly construed or it does not. Any provision in a contract (and one frequently sees them) stating that the covenants in question 'if held to be unenforceable, but would be enforceable if the ambit or duration of them were reduced, may be reduced accordingly' are of no effect and probably constitute an unlawful attempt to oust the jurisdiction of the court (see *Living Design (Home Improvements) Ltd v Davidson* [1994] IRLR 69). Moreover, a covenant imposing restraints of trade: 'so far as the law would allow' will be held too vague to be enforceable (see *Davies v Davies* (1887) 36 Ch D 359, CA. In the recent case of *Tullett Prebon plc v BGC Brokers LP* [2010] EWHC 484 (QB), [2010] IRLR 648 the learned judge at trial (point not considered on appeal: [2011] EWCA Civ 131, [2011] IRLR 420) appeared to overlook this fundamental principle and we deal further with this error below at **42.14**.

Nonetheless, the English court does have the power of severance. That is to say, to sever the whole or parts of contractual provisions too wide to be enforceable leaving in place those parts which the court considers reasonable. A contractual provision imposing a restraint of trade may be in simple or compound form. Very frequently seen in employment contracts are covenants which proscribe a number of separate activities thus: '[the employee] shall not, for a period of twelve months after termination of this contract, solicit, or canvas, or entice away, or deal with any client of the employer' (or words to that effect). A court may take the view that in the circumstances of any particular case it would be reasonable for an employer to protect himself against solicitation of his clients, but that, for example, it is unreasonable for the employer to require protection against the employee dealing with his clients. The common law, as part of the exercise of construction of a provision in restraint of trade, permits the court to uphold part of the restrictions imposed whilst holding invalid other restrictions in such composite clauses. The process by which the court does this is colloquially referred to as 'blue-pencilling' in respect of those parts of a covenant struck out as unreasonable.

For some years there was a debate in the authorities as to whether or not the 'blue pencil' test could be applied to parts of a single covenant, or only to separate covenants: see *Attwood v Lamont* [1920] 3 KB 571, [1920] All ER Rep 55 *per* Younger LJ at 593, *Sadler v Imperial Life Assurance Co. of Canada Ltd* [1988] IRLR 388, *Marshall v NM Financial Management Ltd* [1997] 1 WLR 1527, [1995] ICR 1042, [1996] IRLR 20, *Beckett Investment Management Group Ltd v Hall* (ibid) and *Egon Zehnder v Tillman* [2018] ICR 574, [2017] IRLR 906.

This debate was resolved by the Supreme Court in *Egon Zehnder Ltd v Tillman* [2020] AC 154, [2019] ICR 1223, [2019] IRLR 838 where it was held (overruling *Attwood v Lamont*) that parts of a covenant could be satisfied provided that a three part test was satisfied (see para 85–88):

(a)   the unenforceable provision must be capable of being removed without the necessity of adding to or modifying the wording of what remains;

(b)   the remaining terms must continue to be supported by adequate consideration;

(c)   the removal of the unenforceable provision must not generate any major change in the overall effect of all the post-employment restraints in the contract – the burden being on the employer to show that its removal would not do so.

In that case the Supreme Court severed the words "or interested" from a non-compete covenant which would otherwise have been too wide to be enforceable since it would have prevented the employee from taking a minority shareholding in a competing business.

The test set out in *Egon Zehnder* helpfully resolves difficult questions which previously arose in this area and in most cases ought to be capable of application without difficulty: see, by way of example, *Wells v Cathay Investments 2 Ltd* [2020] IRLR 281. One potential area of ambiguity, however, is what is meant by a "major change" to a restraint.

42.8   *Testing reasonableness*

General approach

The court's approach to enforcement of restraints in employment contracts is far less sympathetic than its approach to restraints arising in commercial transactions such as business sale agreements, agency agreements, distribution agreements, shareholder agreements and agreements between equity partners (see *Herbert Morris Ltd v Saxelby* [1916] 1 AC 688, [1916–17] All ER Rep 305, *Systems Reliability Holdings plc v Smith* [1990] IRLR 377 and *Allied Dunbar (Frank Weisinger) Ltd v Weisinger* [1988] IRLR 60). It is frequently suggested that the reason for the closer scrutiny paid by English courts to employment contracts than to other forms of commercial bargain is because employees are by and large not in a strong bargaining position when compared to employers. Whereas this may no doubt have some veracity, it is not a full explanation of the rigour with which the court approaches covenants in restraint of trade in employment contracts. Indeed, the courts recognise that not all employees are in an unequal bargaining position: 'Managing directors can look after themselves' (see *M and S Drapers (a firm) v Reynolds* [1957] 1 WLR 9, [1956] 3 All ER 814, CA; see also *Hanover Insurance Brokers Ltd v Schapiro* [1994] IRLR 82; *Merlin Financial Consultants Ltd v Cooper* [2014] IRLR 610; and *TFS Derivatives*, above). The principal reason why courts are more generous towards restraints between equity partners, for example, is because those restraints are <u>mutual</u> and because a partnership resembles (to some extent, at least) a 'business' sale agreement: see *Bridge v Deacons* [1984] AC 705, [1984]

2 All ER 19, PC. A business sale agreement creates intrinsically different interests for protection than those that exist between employer and employee (see *Herbert Morris v Saxelby*). In addition, the vendor of the business will receive an enhanced consideration if he is prepared to undertake not to compete with the business he sells. Shareholder agreements may also bear many of these features (depending on the type of agreement): see *Ideal Standard International SA v Hoover* [2019] IRLR 431, *Kynixa Ltd v Hynes* [2008] EWHC 1495 (QB), [2008] All ER (D) 30 (Jul) and *Guest services Worldwide Ltd v Shelmerdine* [2020] IRLR 392.

In employment contracts the position is likely to be different. There is no mutuality of obligation: an employer does not undertake not to compete with the employee if the employee were to set up a rival business on the termination of his employment. Neither is there any enhancement, necessarily, of the remuneration that an employee receives during the currency of the employment contract because he assumes obligations under a restrictive covenant operative only post termination of his employment. In this latter respect, an employer who pays a sum of money to an employee in consideration of the employee accepting provisions in restraint of trade as part of a settlement for the termination of his contract of employment, is not absolved from having to justify the restraints imposed on the employee under the ordinary principles of the restraint of trade doctrine (see *J A Mont (UK) Ltd v Mills* [1993] IRLR 172 and *Turner v Commonwealth and British Minerals Ltd* [2000] IRLR 114). In *Turner* the court stated that regard may be had to the additional payment made to the employee on settlement as one factor in considering reasonableness. (See also *Thurstan Hoskin & Partners v Jewill Hill & Bennett* [2002] EWCA Civ 249, [2002] All ER (D) 62 (Feb).) It is submitted that if this means that the more money that is paid to an employee the greater the restraint that may be imposed, then this is wrong in principle. Restraints of trade cannot be purchased outright (see *J A Mont (UK) Ltd v Mills*, ibid).

Having ascertained what the proper meaning of the provisions imposing restraints may be (see above **42.6**) the court must next determine whether on that proper construction the covenants are reasonable in the sense of being no more than adequate to protect that legitimate interest.

Covenants may be unreasonable in the following respects:

(a)   the nature of the restraint;

(b)   the ambit of the restraint;

(c)   the duration of the restraint.

Nature of the restraint

The approach of the court is first to identify the legitimate interest or interests which the employer is seeking to protect by the restraints in question. Restraints can take a wide variety of forms, but broadly fall into two categories:

(a)   Restraints against conducting or being engaged or interested in a competing business (whether specifically identified or not in the covenant) for a period of time; and

(b)   Restraints which prohibit a limited kind of competitive activity, such as soliciting or dealing with customers.

The former category of restraint (a non-compete restraint) may be in a wide form prohibiting an employee from joining a competitor's business regardless of the field of that business in which he is proposing to work, or it may be limited to prohibiting him working for a competitor in the particular field in which the employee has been engaged by the former employer imposing the covenant. The more limited form of non-compete provision is now more frequently encountered in modern contracts of employment, but the wider form of restraint is sometimes still upheld by the courts: see *Norbrook Laboratories (GB) Ltd v Adair* [2008] EWHC 978 (QB), [2008] IRLR 878. It is to be observed that considerable care must be taken in drafting even the more limited form of non-compete restraint: see *Ashcourt Rowan Financial Planning v Hall* (above).

The court, having identified an interest of the employer justifying protection, is entitled to look at the nature of the restraint deployed to determine whether the legitimate interest could have been protected by a narrower restraint than, for example, either a wide or narrow non-compete provision (see *Office Angels Ltd v Rainer-Thomas* [1991] IRLR 214, CA). In identifying the legitimate interest to be protected the court is entitled to look at any express words in the contract which may identify that interest (*Office Angels*). If the employer has categorically identified the interest he seeks to protect (for example, client connection) he cannot, when the covenant comes to be tested in court, claim that the restraint in fact is aimed at protecting a different interest (for example, confidential information: see *Office Angels*). This, however, is a matter of construction: see *Patsystems Holdings Ltd v Neilly* [2012] EWHC 2609 (QB), [2012] IRLR 979. Again, if the interest to be protected is, for example, client connection or the stability of the employer's workforce a covenant in the nature of a non-compete provision risks being held to be disproportionate for such interests may be protected by a covenant directed at the prohibition of specific competitive acts, such as the soliciting or dealing with customers, or the soliciting or enticing away of staff. It follows that the nature of the interest to be protected will dictate the nature of the restraint which should be employed by the employer to protect the interest. Non-compete provisions are generally only justifiable if the nature of the interest to be protected is trade secrets and confidential information: see *per* Simon Brown LJ in *J A Mont (UK) Ltd v Mills* [1993] IRLR 172. This is because it is notoriously difficult to police covenants which merely restrain the disclosure or use of confidential information. Moreover, it is notoriously difficult for a covenantee to know what information is truly confidential and which he cannot use or disclose and what information is merely part of his stock of accumulated knowledge and experience which he is entitled to disclose or use. Accordingly an employer may protect his trade secrets and confidential information by imposing on an employee a covenant restraining that employee for a reasonable period of time from joining a competitor, at least in the same field of activity in which he was engaged for the former employer (see *Littlewoods Organisation Ltd v Harris* [1977] 1 WLR 1472, [1978] 1 All ER 1026, CA; *Printers & Finishers Ltd v Holloway* [1964] 3 All ER 54n, [1965] RPC 239; and *David (Lawrence) Ltd v Ashton* [1991] 1 All ER 385, [1989] ICR 123, CA). Nevertheless, caution must be exercised in drafting non-compete restraints so as to ensure that the definition of 'competitor' is not too widely drawn, thereby rendering the covenant unenforceable: see *Norbrook Laboratories*, ibid.

In some cases the court has upheld non-compete provisions where the interest to be protected is client connection. The basis for this is that in some instances it may be impossible, or, at least, very difficult for the employer to 'police' a more limited covenant restraining soliciting or dealing with clients (see *Scorer v Seymour-Johns* [1966] 1 WLR 1419, [1966] 3 All ER 347, *per* Salmon LJ, p 1427C-E, *Turner v Commonwealth and British Minerals Ltd* [2000] IRLR 114, *per* Waller LJ at para 18 and *TFS Derivatives Ltd v Morgan* [2004] EWHC 3181 (QB), [2005] IRLR 246).

It is, however, submitted that the courts should be suspicious of assertions that it is difficult to police non-solicitation and non-dealing covenants. If it is difficult to do so, it is likely to be because there is no firm connection between the client and the employer in the first place, and the justification sometimes advanced for area non-compete restraints (namely that they are intended to protect what is in effect passing trade) is surely, for that reason, wrong in principle. If trade is passing it is difficult to see how the employee can gain any material knowledge of, or influence over, such clientele. In the *TFS Derivatives* case the court appeared to assume that it would be difficult to police non-solicitation and non-dealing covenants in circumstances in which the only evidence proffered by the employer to support this assertion was their experience of losing clients when an employee had previously left their employment. However, the employer did not at the same time suggest that that other employee had surreptitiously breached his non–solicitation and non–dealing covenants. If clients leave an employer in circumstances in which the employer is not asserting that their departure is consequent upon breaches of restrictive covenants by a former employee, it is difficult to see how the conclusion may be drawn that the covenants in question cannot be effectively policed. It is equally, if not more, plausible that the covenants were simply ineffective to achieve their purpose.

In *Thomas v Farr Plc* [2007] EWCA Civ 118, [2007] IRLR 419 the Court of Appeal held that a covenant prohibiting the solicitation of clients would not be sufficient to protect confidential information relating to those clients because such a covenant could not be policed. This was because the covenantor did not, in his work for the competitor company which he had joined, actually deal with clients himself. Prohibiting him from soliciting clients would not in any way inhibit his ability to pass on confidential information about those clients learnt whilst working for the covenantee to those members of staff in the competing company who *were* actually dealing with clients. Whereas it is extremely difficult to police covenants merely restraining the disclosure or use of confidential information, it is submitted that it is very far from self–evident that non–solicitation or non–dealing covenants taken to protect customer connection cannot be policed and no such assumption ought to be made without evidence of some sort to that effect. The fact is that breaches (or alleged breaches) of non–solicitation/–dealing covenants are regularly uncovered by covenantees: see for example *Allan Janes LLP v Johal (Balraj)*, above, and *Advantage Business Systems Ltd v Hopley (James)* [2007] EWHC 1783 (QB), [2007] All ER (D) 399 (Jul). See also the cautious approach taken by the court to 'policing' arguments in *Ashcourt Rowan* (above) and *Brake Brothers Ltd v Ungless* [2004] All ER (D) 586.

The court also held in the *TFS Derivatives* case that a non–compete provision was justified to protect confidential information. However, the court does not appear to have fully analysed the restraint in question to determine whether its duration was in fact commensurate with the length of time in which such information may have been of continuing use to a competitor. Compare *Duarte v Black and Decker Corpn*, ibid, where the judge, in determining that a two–year restraint on joining a competitor to protect confidential information would be unlawful under English law, considered the likely 'shelf–life' of the confidential information in question (cf *Norbrook Laboratories*, ibid).

Recently, however, the rationale adopted in the *TFS Derivatives* case, was adopted by Foskett J in *Tradition Financial Services v Gamberoni* [2017] EWHC 768 (QB), [2017] IRLR 698. In that case, he stated, in broad terms, that he agreed with Counsel for Tradition that '*the necessity for non–compete provisions arises where non–solicitation and non–dealing covenants and confidential information restrictions are difficult to police or where there are material disputes as to what information is confidential*'. The analysis in the *Gemberoni* and *TFS* cases has also been cited with approval and applied recently by Jon Turner QC (sitting as a deputy judge of the High Court) in *Square Global Ltd v Leonard* [2020] EWHC 1008 (QB), [2020] All ER (D) 188 (Apr).

The ambit of the restraint

The ambit of a restraint will comprise the following elements:

(a)   the geographical area within which the restraint is to operate;

(b)   the proscribed actions (eg non–solicitation or non–dealing with clients and the class of client not to be solicited or dealt with).

Geography

Restraints may be worldwide (and will be so construed) if they contain no express or, perhaps, implied geographical limitation (see *Commercial Plastics Ltd v Vincent*, above). Worldwide non-compete restraints may be justifiable on the basis that they are necessary to protect trade secrets or confidential information: see *Scully UK Ltd v Lee*, above. Conversely, a restraint against soliciting or dealing with clients will not require an express geographical limitation (see *G W Plowman & Son Ltd v Ash* [1964] 1 WLR 568, [1964] 2 All ER 10), even if clients may be located throughout the world, because the restraint is limited by the class of proscribed person. In many employment contracts radial or other area restraints are frequently employed. These are extremely clumsy instruments and appear to be a hang-over from the old common-law 18th and 19th-century rules about 'general' and 'partial' restraints. Area restraints must have a functional correspondence with the legitimate interest to be protected (see *Office Angels* and *Landmark Brickwork Ltd v Sutcliffe and Ors* [2011] IRLR 976). Thus, a local business whose customers are drawn exclusively or substantially from a radius of, say, five miles from the place of that business cannot justify a radial restraint of ten miles. Equally, the area in which a restraint is to operate will be considered carefully by the court. Thus, a radial restraint of five miles, for example, may be justifiable in rural or lightly populated areas, but could not be justified in a major conurbation where it may cover populations of a million or more: see *Fellowes & Son v Fisher* [1976] QB 122, [1975] 2 All ER 829 and *Spencer v Marchington* [1988] IRLR 392. The real difficulty with radial or area restraints is that they are unnecessary if the protection is sought for the purposes of, say, customer connection because a non-solicit or non-compete covenant will suffice. It is difficult to see how they can be justified on the basis that they are necessary to protect confidential information or trade secrets since such interests are not confined to territorial boundaries (see *Scully UK Ltd v Lee*, above). Neither can radial restraints be justified on the basis of an interest in the stability of the workforce because solicitation of employees can readily be conducted from outside the radius imposed and, again, a more focused form of protection is afforded by a non-solicitation/non-enticement of staff covenant. The only practical effect of an area restraint, over and above that of a more limited non-solicitation or non-dealing covenant, is that it will prevent an ex employee from competing with his ex employer for new customers, ie customers who have not dealt with the former employer before (see *Allan Janes LLP v Balraj Johal*, above). Accordingly, radial restraints of the non-compete provision variety extend the protection afforded to an employer beyond that element of good will, namely existing client connection which he is entitled to protect. In business sale agreements it may be legitimate for the purchaser to protect himself against the vendor acquiring future business which ought otherwise to go to the business sold (see *Allied Dunbar (Frank Weisinger) Ltd v Weisinger* [1988] IRLR 60). The acquisition of new clients by reason of recommendation of existing clients is, however, based on the <u>reputation</u> of the business which, although it forms part of the goodwill on a business sale, forms no part of a legitimate interest to protect in the case of employer/employee covenants (see *Countrywide Assured Financial Services Ltd v Smart* [2004] EWHC 1214 (Ch)). See also *Merlin Financial Consultants Ltd v Cooper* [2014] IRLR 610, where a UK-wide restriction was upheld in circumstances where the employer's clients were predominantly in London and the South East, on the basis that the financial market was a single geographical market which was particularly true in the age of electronic communication. The latter point does highlight the increasingly outmoded nature of geographical restraints in some sectors.

The proscribed actions

If the proscription is against conducting, or joining, or being employed in (or being otherwise interested in) another business then the covenant will be too wide if the proscribed business is described as 'a similar business' to that of the employer. An employer may be entitled to protect himself from unfair competition by the employee, but he is not permitted to prohibit the ex employee from joining or setting up a business which is merely 'similar' and not competitive (see *Scully v Lee* [1998] IRLR 259, CA, but cf *Spafax Ltd v Harrison* [1980] IRLR 442, CA, where the court reached the opposite conclusion). It is sometimes held by the courts that it is not legitimate to bar an employee from working in a competitive business in an area of work in which he has not been engaged in the employer's business (see, for example, *Commercial Plastics v Vincent*, above) or in a part of a competitor's business which does not compete with the former employer. Given, however, that a non-compete covenant may generally only be justified on the basis that it protects trade secrets or confidential information, it is difficult to see the logic behind such decisions: a former employee may impart confidential information of his former employer to a competing business after he leaves his employment and joins that competing business, regardless of the capacity in which he is working with the competitor or the department in which he may be engaged: see *Symbian Ltd v Christensen* [2001] IRLR 77 and *Norbrook Laboratories* ibid at para 81.

A prohibition on being "interested in" a competing business is likely to be too wide without further qualification permitting the holding of a minority shareholding: see Scully v Lee, above and *Egon Zehnder v Tillman* [2018] ICR 574, [2017] IRLR 906 but cf *Tradition Financial Services Ltd v Gamberoni* [2017] IRLR 698 where a different conclusion appears to have been reached (and where permission to appeal was refused) and *Ideal Standard International S.A. v Herbert* [2018] EWHC 3326 (Comm), [2019] IRLR 431 where a different conclusion was reached at an interim stage.

Lesser forms of restraint, such as non-solicitation or dealing with customers, may be too wide if the class of customer with which the ex employee may not deal is drawn too widely. For example, covenants which prohibit soliciting or dealing with any client of the employer will be too wide if the employer has many hundreds or thousands of customers and the employee covenantor has dealt with only a limited number of them whilst employed: see *Marley Tile Co Ltd v Johnson* [1982] IRLR 75 and *Office Angels*, above. However, courts have upheld covenants that are not limited to dealings with clients which the employee has dealt with whilst employed: see *Gilford Motor Co. Ltd v Horne* [1933] Ch 935, [1933] All ER Rep 109, CA, *Plowman v Ash* (above), *Business Seating (Renovations) Ltd v Broad* [1989] ICR 729, *Allan Janes LLP v Balraj Johal*, above, *Thurstan Hoskin & Partners v Jewill Hill & Bennett* [2002] EWCA Civ 249, [2002] All ER (D) 62 (Feb) and *Safetynet Security Ltd v Coppage* [2013] IRLR 970. The better view is, however, that proscribed classes of customers should be limited to those that the employee has dealt with or, at least, may have knowledge about because the employee in question has overseen the work of other employees dealing with them (see *Spafax v Harrison*, above). Similarly, the class of customer ought to be limited to those persons who were clients of the employer for a defined period of time prior to the termination of the employee's contract of employment. In this way the covenant will not embrace persons who may have been clients prior to the employment of the employee, but were not clients of the employer at any time during the period of the employee's employment. However, in *Plowman v Ash* (above) the Court of Appeal held that an employer is entitled to protect by a non-dealing covenant customers who have ceased to deal with that employer during the currency of the employment contract in which that restraint appeared. This seems contrary to principle. It is of the essence of a reasonable restraint that it should protect the employer only against unfair competition by the employee, which means the exploitation by the employee of his knowledge about, and influence over customers that he has acquired during his employment (see *per* Lord Parker in *Herbert Morris v Saxelby*, above). The recent case of *White Digital Media Ltd v Weaver and anor* [2013] EWHC 1681 (QB), [2013] All ER (D) 122 (Jul) emphasises the danger of not restricting non-solicitation or non-dealing covenants to those clients about whom the covenantee has knowledge or over whom he can exercise influence. A covenant will be too wide in its ambit if it purports to prohibit the ex employee from soliciting or dealing with persons who only become customers of the employer after the employee has left his employment (see *Konski v Peet* [1915] 1 Ch 530). There is a limited exception to this, namely prospective customers. An employer is entitled to protect himself against solicitation or dealing with prospective customers, at least where those prospective customers have been in negotiation with the employer prior to the employee leaving his employment and the employee has had contact with that prospective customer in the course of the negotiations (see *International Consulting Services (UK) Ltd v Hart* [2000] IRLR 227 and *Advantage Business Systems Ltd v Hopley* ibid, but compare *Associated Foreign Exchange Ltd v International Foreign Exchange UK Ltd* [2010] EWHC 1178 (Ch), [2010] IRLR 964).

The problem posed by the existence of contradictory authorities on whether the class of clients not to be solicited or dealt with ought to be closed by reference to clients actually dealt with by the employee remains to be resolved, the Court of Appeal having failed to grapple with the issue in *Dentmaster (UK) Ltd v Kent* [1997] IRLR 636. It would seem from the recent decisions cited above that ultimately the reasonableness of non-solicitation and non-dealing covenants is so fact sensitive that authorities can provide little guidance. The Court of Appeal in the *Coppage* case (above) observed that cases in this area turn so much on their own facts that the citation of precedent is not of assistance.

Difficulty can arise even with limited restraints on dealing with customers where the market may be small and the customers therefore limited in number. This difficulty may be exacerbated by the use of ambiguous phraseology (see *Austin Knight (UK) Ltd v Hinds* [1994] FSR 52). The courts regard a non-solicitation covenant as being the least form of restraint and therefore more readily justifiable (see *Stenhouse Australia Ltd v Phillips*, above, *Scully v Lee*, above and also *Premier Model Management Ltd v Bruce* [2012] EWHC 3509 (QB), [2012] All ER (D) 05 (Dec)). Similarly, a restriction on dealing with suppliers of the employer was not upheld where all of the principal suppliers in the market were covered and it had the effect of preventing any competition: see *Energy Renewals Ltd v Borg* [2014] IRLR 713.

There is remarkably little authority on what constitutes 'solicitation'. In *Wessex Dairies Ltd v Smith* [1935] 2 KB 80, [1935] All ER Rep 75 a milkman, prior to the termination of his employment contract, informed his customers, that he was leaving his existing employment, but would be available to do business with them again after a specified date in the future. The Court of Appeal held that this constituted solicitation of his employer's customers. In *Taylor Stuart & Co v Croft (Timothy)* (1998) 606 IRLB 15 an employee subject to a non-solicitation restraint despatched a letter to clients on the headed notepaper of a new firm he was proposing to establish as follows:

'Dear X,

This is to inform you that I left the Partnership of Taylor Stuart & Co on 18 November 1994. With effect from 1 December 1994 I shall be establishing my own professional practice and can be contacted as above.'

The court held that it was of the essence of solicitation that the client should be requested to transfer his custom. Accordingly, the letter would have been unobjectionable if it had been limited to its first sentence, but constituted a solicitation because of the second, which invited the addressees to contact him. Other forms of solicitation less direct than that involve advertising. In *Trego v Hunt* [1896] AC 7, [1895–9] All ER Rep 804 it was held that an advertisement not directed specifically to the clients of the business concerned, but more generally, did not constitute 'solicitation'. In *Towry EJ Ltd v Bennett and ors* [2012] EWHC 224 (QB), [2012] All ER (D) 148 (Feb) the learned judge held, as must be right, that solicitation can occur even though a client or customer makes the first approach to the employee. It is of the essence of a solicitation that the employee engages in requesting, persuading or encouraging a person to place business with them or on behalf of their employer. It is plain that a customer who makes a first approach to the employee along the lines of 'what are you doing now, having left your former employer?' can be solicited with the response 'I'm in the same line of business as before. Have you got any work that my new employer could do for you?' In that situation who makes the first approach is irrelevant, it is the substance of the conversation that matters. See *Croesus Financial Services Ltd* (above). See also the discussion of the meaning of 'solicitation' in *QBE Management Services (UK) Ltd v Dymoke* [2012] IRLR 458 at paragraphs 184 to 185. There must be a 'direct and specific' appeal, whether by advertisement or otherwise.

Further difficulties arise where, in addition to a prohibition on 'solicitation', a draughtsman of a restrictive covenant adds other expressions such as: 'enticing away' or 'interfering with' the clients or customers of the employer. The word 'canvass' is synonymous with soliciting (see *QBE Management Services* and *Customer Systems Plc v Ranson* [2012] EWCA Civ 841, [2012] IRLR 769). In other such cases, it is difficult for the court to know whether the covenant merely prohibits solicitation in the sense of making the first approach or whether acts beyond making the first approach are also prohibited such as to render the covenant a prohibition against dealing with customers even if those customers make the first approach to the employee: see *Austin Knight (UK) Ltd v Hinds* [1994] FSR 52 and *Hanover Insurance Brokers v Schapiro*, above, *per* Dillon LJ, but *cf* Nolan LJ. In *Hydra plc v Anastasi* [2005] EWHC 1559 (QB), [2005] All ER (D) 276 (Jul) Royce J held in respect of a covenant 'not to solicit or entice away any employee of the employer for a period of twelve months following the termination of the covenantor's employment' that the word 'entice' meant 'tempt, lure, persuade and inveigle'. In that case the facts established were that the covenantee employer company was a small business with few employees and it was therefore entitled to protect the entirety of its employees from poaching by a former employee and, further, on the facts the employee who had left to join the covenantee's rival business had himself approached the covenantor and sought to persuade him to let him join the new venture. In those circumstances, there was no breach of the covenant not to entice away an employee. It seems therefore that, even in the extended meaning of the word 'entice' given by Royce J, the essential ingredient of that term is making the first approach.

It is to be observed that the views of the client cannot affect or influence the court in determining whether to enforce a non-solicitation or non-dealing covenant. In *John Michael Design plc v Cooke* [1987] ICR 445, [1987] 2 All ER 332 a client intervened in an application by a claimant employer for interim injunctive relief against former employees to restrain them from dealing with former clients of the employer. The client protested that the interim injunction should not extend to prohibit the former employees from dealing with the intervenor because the intervenor had no intention whatsoever of doing any further business with the claimant. At first instance, the judge acceded to the intervenor's argument. The Court of Appeal, however, held that there should be no qualification of the interim injunction to enforce the restrictive covenants in question so as to exclude from its ambit an individual client. Rather, the Court of Appeal held that the restrictive covenant was most necessary to the claimant in the cases of clients refusing to do future business because, manifestly, if a client proposed to remain loyal to the claimant employer there was no need for the protection of the restrictive covenant.

Until the case of *Dawnay, Day & Co Ltd v de Braconier d'Alphen* [1998] ICR 1068, [1997] IRLR 442 there was conflicting authority at Court of Appeal level as to whether an employer could justify a restraint on soliciting his employees to leave his employment. In the *Dawnay, Day* case it was held that an employer had a legitimate interest in the stability of his workforce, at least so far as senior employees were concerned. However, in *Dawnay, Day* there were two restraints relating to the protection of the workforce in the employment contracts in question. The first restraint prohibited soliciting senior employees to leave their employment. The second restraint prohibited the covenantor employing the covenantee's senior employees. The claimants sought relief only in respect of the first of these covenants which the judge held to be reasonable. The judge, however, opined *obiter* that the second form of restraint would be too wide to be enforceable. This *obiter* opinion was followed by Tugendhat J in *White Digital Media Ltd* (above) where he held a covenant restricting one former employee from employing another former employee unenforceable. The objection to any form of restraint prohibiting an ex employee from employing in his business, or in a business that he has joined, a colleague of his at his former employers is that it amounts to a restraint on that colleague from seeking or obtaining work with whom he pleases. In *Kores Manufacturing Co Ltd v Kolok Manufacturing Co Ltd* (above) two employers in the same industry entered into an agreement that they would not employ members of each other's staff for a period of time after those employees had left their respective employment. The Court of Appeal held that this provision was unenforceable because it was not limited to senior employees who might carry away trade secrets or confidential information to the competitor. However, the Court of Appeal also opined, *obiter*, that the covenant was against public policy because it would prevent employees of each of the parties from seeking employment with the other in circumstances in which those individual employees did not have in their employment contracts any restraint prohibiting them from joining a competitor. The effect of the covenant in *Kores Manufacturing Co Ltd v Kolok Manufacturing Co Ltd* was to enable the two employers to achieve through the back door what they had failed to achieve through the front.

However, in *TFS Derivatives* (above) one of the restrictive covenants in the employee's contract was as follows: '[you will not] for six months employ, engage or work with an employee for the purpose of the supply of relevant services or a business which competes, or which plans to compete with, or is similar to a relevant business'. The learned judge held that this covenant went 'no further than is reasonably necessary in all the circumstances to protect [a legitimate interest] of the employer'. The judge did not, however, grant an injunction to enforce this restraint on the grounds that there was no evidence of breach. However, the judge's attention does not appear to have been drawn to the decision in *Dawnay, Day* (above) or to *Kores Manufacturing Co Ltd v Kolok Manufacturing Co Ltd* (above). Employers seeking to impose restrictions on the solicitation of their staff should be cautious about distinguishing for the purposes of such protection those staff occupying positions of importance to the covenantor's business or have training or business or technical knowledge and experience from those members of staff who do not: see *TSC Europe (UK) Ltd v Massey* [1999] IRLR 22. In small organisations, however, it may be that all the staff will have the necessary qualities or importance to justify protection against solicitation by an ex employee.

Duration

Whether the length of any restraint renders it unreasonable is a matter of impression for the judge. In *Stenhouse Australia Ltd v Phillips* [1974] AC 391, [1974] 1 All ER 117 (above) Lord Wilberforce stated that the question of a reasonable duration for a covenant in restraint of trade could not 'advantageously form the subject of direct evidence. It is for the judge, after informing himself as fully as he can of the facts and circumstances relating to the employer's business, the nature of the employer's interest to be protected, and the likely effect on this of solicitation, to decide whether the contractual period is reasonable or not. An opinion as to the reasonableness of elements of it, particularly of the time during which it is to run, can seldom be precise, and can only be formed on a broad and commonsense view' (*Stenhouse*, 402). The question that the court must ask itself is: 'what is a reasonable time during which the employer is entitled to protection against solicitation of clients with whom the employee had contact and influence during employment and who were not bound to the employer by contract or by stability of association' (ibid). Thus even limited restraints, such as non-solicitation of client covenants, will be subject to close scrutiny to determine whether their duration is too long given the circumstances of the covenantee's business and the covenantor's role in that business: see *Associated Foreign Exchange Ltd v International Foreign Exchange UK Ltd* [2010] EWHC 1178 (Ch), [2010] IRLR 964. So far as the protection of confidential information is concerned acute problems are likely to arise in relation to fixing a reasonable duration for a post-termination covenant restraining an employee from engaging in competition with the employer. Logically, if the covenant is designed to protect trade secrets or equivalent confidential information in the sense of information that would never be disclosed by the employer and could not be 'reverse engineered' by a rival then it would be reasonable to impose a lifetime prohibition on the employee working for a competitor. Yet the courts constantly refer to the necessity, even when protecting trade secrets and equivalent confidential information, of keeping the non-compete provision to a reasonable duration: see, for example, *per* Cross J in *Printers and Finishers Ltd v Holloway (No 2)* [1965] 1 WLR 1, [1964] 3 All ER 731. Where a covenant over a limited geographical area is taken to protect confidential information, the courts have, in the past, accepted a non-compete provision of unlimited duration: *Haynes v Doman* [1899] 2 Ch 13, [1895–9] All ER Rep Ext 1468, CA. But, as the Court of Appeal has recently observed in *Scully v Lee* (above), confidential information knows no territorial boundaries and, accordingly, the imposition of an area blanket restraint to protect confidential information is, in itself, illogical. All that can be said about the duration of covenants to protect confidential information is that it must be an issue of fact in every case as to the reasonableness of the duration of the covenant and it is submitted that the covenant's duration must necessarily be a function of how long the information to be protected is likely to remain confidential, or, at least, useful to a competitor (see *Norbrook Laboratories v Hopley* ibid and *Duarte v Black and Decker Corpn* ibid). Thus, if the confidential information to be protected is information relating to a proposed business strategy the covenant cannot endure for longer than the period during which the strategy is to remain confidential before being implemented (in effect, made public) by the employer. This, however, does not resolve the essential problem presented by extremely confidential technical information (for example, the secret of the recipe for the manufacture of Coca-Cola – anecdotally the most treasured and most protected trade secret in the world). Would it be permissible for that company to impose a lifetime ban on an employee who knew what the recipe was from joining a competitor like Pepsi-Cola? The law has yet to grapple with this problem. It is, however, clear that a judge is <u>not</u> bound by precedent to uphold as reasonable a restraint of the same duration and in the same field as a previous judge: see *Dairy Crest Ltd v Pigott* [1989] ICR 92, CA. It is equally clear that the more limited the ambit of the restraint, the greater the period of duration that will be upheld: see *Stenhouse v Phillips*, above, and *Fitch v Dewes* [1921] 2 AC 158, [1921] All ER Rep 13. However, it must be doubtful that the latter case would, on the same facts, nowadays be followed (see, for example, *Allan Janes LLP v Balraj Johal*, above). It seems clear that where both the ambit of the restraint is narrow and the duration is short the covenant will a fortiori be held enforceable. Thus a non-solicitation restraint for a period of six months was upheld by the Court of Appeal in the *Coppage* case (above). Moreover there seems to be a trend toward upholding covenants where the duration of the covenant appears to be an industry standard, for example non-solicitation and non-dealing covenants imposed on insurance brokers for 12 months (see for example *Romero Insurance Brokers Ltd v Templeton and anor* [2013] EWHC 1198 (QB), [2013] All ER (D) 142 (May), *Tradition Financial Services v Gamberoni* [2017] EWHC 768 (QB), [2017] IRLR 698 and *Square Global Ltd v Leonard* [2020] EWHC 1008 (QB), [2020] All ER (D) 188 (Apr)). Such industry 'standards' for restrictive covenants should be approached with suspicion by the Courts. The fact that an industry imposes similar restraints does not mean that they will be justifiable. It remains the case that the court must scrutinise each case on its own facts.

(Subject always to the caveat that judges should not slavishly follow precedent in restraint of trade cases, but rather examine the reasonableness of covenants in the light of the facts of each case, for a convenient compendium of cases where covenants have been upheld, or not, see *Restrictive Covenants Under Common and Competition Law* (4th edn, Sweet & Maxwell), Kamerling & Osman, p 381ff.)

42.9   *What is the consequence of a finding of unreasonableness?*

Many judges (see, for example, Lord McNaghten in *Nordenfelt*, above, and Cox J in *TFS Derivatives*, above) have erroneously described a covenant in restraint of trade which is not justifiable as being 'void'. This is not correct. A covenant in unreasonable restraint of trade is merely unenforceable. The significance of this distinction is that a covenant in restraint of trade is not illegal in the sense of it being a criminal offence to enter into or perform the obligations so imposed: *Apple Corpn Ltd v Apple Computer Inc* [1992] FSR 431, Ch D. Accordingly, covenants in restraint of trade, the proper law of which is English law will be enforced by an English court by, for example, a worldwide injunction even if the restraint may be invalid under the law of other jurisdictions. Equally, whole contracts may be found to be in restraint of trade (see, for example, *A Schroeder Music Publishing Co Ltd v Macaulay* [1974] 1 WLR 1308, [1974] 3 All ER 616).

42.10   Other elements

Consideration

There is considerable debate as to whether a court is permitted to look at the adequacy of the consideration which supports any contract or provision in restraint of trade as part of the court's investigation into the reasonableness of the covenant. Authorities against the court considering adequacy of consideration include: *M and S Drapers (a firm) v Reynolds* [1957] 1 WLR 9, [1956] 3 All ER 814, CA *per* Hodson LJ and *Allied Dunbar (Frank Weisinger) Ltd v Weisinger* [1988] IRLR 60, paras 30–32 *per* Millett J. Contradicting these authorities are: Lord McNaghten in *Nordenfelt* (above) at 565, Lord Hodson (apparently dissenting from his own earlier judgment in *M and S Drapers*) in *Esso Petroleum v Harper's Garage* (above) at 318D–F and Lord Pearce in the same case at 323E–F. (See also *Reuse Collections Ltd v Sendall* [2015] IRLR 226 at [71], where HHJ Stephen Davies considered, *obiter*, that the adequacy of the consideration was a factor relevant to the reasonableness of the restrictive covenant.) The better view, it is submitted, is that the court cannot look to the adequacy of the consideration in the sense of determining whether the value of the bargain to the party restrained is the same as the value imparted to the covenantee. The court does not ask 'whether the consideration is equal in value to that which the party gives up or loses by the restraint under which he has placed himself . . . it is impossible for the court . . . to say whether, in any particular case, the party restrained has made an improvident bargain or not'. Rather the test is whether 'the restraint of a party from carrying on a trade is larger and wider than the protection of the party with whom the contract is made can possibly require': (*per* Tindale CJ, *Hitchcock v Coker* (1837) 6 Ad & El 959). It is therefore submitted that the issue of consideration has become confused because in many cases the courts have elided the issue of consideration in the technical sense of the contractual rule that there must be adequate consideration to support a bargain enforceable by the courts with consideration in the sense of a balance of benefit between the parties bestowed under a contract. The latter form of consideration may be considered only to the extent that the covenantee does not under the bargain struck extract more protection from the covenantor than is reasonable to protect the covenantee's legitimate interests. If it were legitimate to consider the adequacy of consideration, then it would follow that covenants in restraint of trade could be purchased outright, which is clearly not the law (see *Mont v Mills* ibid). The more money paid to the covenantor, either specifically as consideration to support a restrictive covenant, or by way of salary or other emoluments of employment, the longer the restraint that could be imposed upon him. This cannot be right because the nature, ambit and duration of a covenant can never be greater than is merely adequate to protect a legitimate interest. The legitimate interest does not change as a function of the amount of money paid to a covenantor. Equally, taking into account the adequacy of consideration would mean that low-paid employees could never have valid restrictions imposed upon them, even although the employer might have legitimate interests to protect. The court has rejected in a recent case the notion that low pay vitiates a restrictive covenant: see *Norbrook Laboratories* ibid. Extreme cases do, however, arise in which the courts will indulge in balancing the benefit and burden as between the two parties: see *Schroeder v Macaulay* (above) and *M and S Drapers (a firm) v Reynolds* [1957] 1 WLR 9, [1956] 3 All ER 814, CA. There must be some consideration to support the restraint and it should be noted that in this respect a deed will not be sufficient if it is a seal alone: see *Hutton v Parker* (1839) 7 Dowl. 739. Equally, restrictive covenants cannot be supported where the only consideration for them is a promise to perform an existing contract: see

WRN Ltd v Ayris [2008] EWHC 1080 (QB), [2008] IRLR 889. The introduction of restrictions after the commencement of employment should normally be supported by consideration. In *Reuse Collections Ltd v Sendall* (ibid), the High Court held that a restrictive covenant introduced during employment was unenforceable for want of consideration in that there was no express benefit or payment associated with the variation, and continued employment did not suffice as consideration where the variation was not proposed on the basis that a failure to accept would lead to dismissal or other sanction. A similar view was taken in *Tenon FM Ltd v Cawley* [2018] EWHC 1972 (QB), [2019] IRLR 435.

42.11 *Repudiatory breach*

An employer in repudiatory breach of an employment contract, where that breach is accepted as terminating the same by the employee, cannot enforce any post-termination restraints: *General Billposting Co Ltd v Atkinson* [1909] AC 118, [1908–10] All ER Rep 619. However, the fact that a restrictive covenant purports to apply upon termination of the contract of employment, 'howsoever caused, whether lawfully or unlawfully', does not itself render the covenant too wide and unenforceable: cf *Rock Refrigeration v Jones and Seward Refrigeration Ltd* [1997] 1 All ER 1, [1996] IRLR 675. There was a period when this proposition was doubted by the courts and it was held that restrictive covenants purporting to apply upon termination of the contract of employment 'howsoever caused, whether or lawfully or unlawfully' were held to be too wide. However, in the *Rock Refrigeration* case this argument was resolved in favour of upholding covenants expressed to apply even to a termination of the employment contract occasioned by a repudiatory breach by the employer. The Court of Appeal held that the doctrine of restraint of trade does not become engaged unless and until the contract of employment containing the restraints is lawfully terminated. Thus, if the employer repudiates the contract, which is then terminated by the acceptance of that repudiation by the employee, the restrictive covenant does not fall to be considered at all under the restraint of trade doctrine because both parties to the contract which has been repudiated are discharged from future performance of their express contractual obligations: see *Photo Production Ltd v Securicor Transport Ltd* [1980] AC 827, [1980] 1 All ER 556. The principle of *Securicor* is that upon acceptance of repudiatory breach express future obligations upon both parties (the innocent and the guilty) to a contract are discharged, whereupon implied secondary obligations (such as the obligation to pay damages for breach) come into force. However, despite the (minority) views expressed by Phillips LJ in *Rock Refrigeration* (above), it is submitted that the court cannot at this stage imply obligations in restraint of trade because they are, *prima facie*, contrary to public policy and unenforceable (see *Wallace Bogan & Co v Cove* [1997] IRLR 453). (To this principle there are the very narrow exceptions of an implied obligation in business sale agreements on the part of the vendor not to solicit customers of the business sold (see *Trego v Hunt*, above) and an implied obligation on the part of employees not to make use of or disclose trade secrets or equivalent confidential information of their employers after the termination of the employment contract (see *Faccenda Chicken v Fowler*, above).) It is inconceivable beyond these two implied obligations that a court will impose by implication any other provisions in restraint of trade because it is contrary to public policy in the broad sense to do so. The decision in *Rock Refrigeration* does, however, reveal a real danger for employers (identified by Phillips LJ). If an employer accepts a repudiatory breach by an employee as terminating the contract of employment he will (under the principle in the *Securicor* case) be in danger of losing the protection of any post-termination restraints in the contract of employment. It should be noted, however, that the majority of the court in *Rock Refrigeration* considered that a repudiatory breach did not discharge an employee from his obligations of confidentiality (see also *Campbell v Frisbee* [2002] EWHC 328 (Ch), [2002] EMLR 656). It is for this reason that it is crucial for employers to provide expressly in any contract of employment for a right to terminate the contract (ie in accordance with its terms) in the event of any conduct of the employee which would constitute a repudiatory breach (for example, gross misconduct). If the contract of employment is terminated in accordance with an express term of that kind then the rules relating to repudiatory breach do not apply because the employer will have terminated the contract in accordance with its express terms and will not have to rely on any implied obligation arising under common law but can rely instead on the obligations expressed in the contract of employment as applying post-termination of the same. It should be noted that an employer's decision to cease paying an employee who had failed to give due notice of resignation under the contract does not necessarily amount to an acceptance of the employee's repudiatory breach so as to bring the contract to an end: see *Sunrise Brokers LLP v Rogers* [2014] IRLR 780, where the High Court held that the employer had the option of affirming the contract where an employee had refused to continue working and that the failure to pay the employee did not automatically bring the contract to an end. The employer was therefore entitled to seek injunctive relief to keep the employee on garden leave notwithstanding the absence of the usual requirement that the employee continues to be paid for the duration of the notice period.

Controversially, in *RDF Media Group Plc v Clements* [2007] EWHC 2892 (QB), [2008] IRLR 207, the judge held that an employee against whom the employer had committed a breach of the implied duty of trust and confidence was not entitled to treat the contract as repudiated because that employee had committed a prior breach of that same implied duty which was not known to the employer at the date on which the employer breached that duty. Because the employee could not treat the contract as repudiated, covenants he had entered into in a shareholders agreement continued to operate. Not only does this decision fly in the face of long-established principles of repudiatory breach of employment contracts (see *Healey v Francaise Rubastic SA* [1917] 1 KB 946, which was upheld in the House of Lords in *Ramsden v David Sharratt & Sons Ltd* (1930) 35 Com Cas 314, HL, and *Howard v Pickford Tool Co Ltd* [1951] 1 KB 417), but it is based upon an authority relating to commercial arbitrations (*Bremer Vulkan Schiffbau und Maschinenfabrik v South India Shipping Corpn Ltd* [1981] AC 909, HL) which although a decision of the House of Lords was much criticised at the time and has subsequently been superceded in any event by statutory reforms of arbitration. In *Food Corpn of India v Antclizo Shipping Corpn, The Antclizo* [1988] 2 All ER 513, [1988] 1 WLR 603, HL Lord Goff commented on the *Bremer* case as follows: 'It is not understating the position to record that the effect of this decision and, indeed, the reasoning upon which it is based, has provoked serious disquiet among the whole commercial community. In particular, it has been suggested that the mutual obligation resting upon both parties to proceed with their reference to arbitration, as expressed by Lord Diplock, bears no relation to commercial reality . . . '. In *Tullett Prebon plc v BGC Brokers LP* [2010] EWHC 484 (QB), [2010] IRLR 648 the judge refused to follow the *RDF* case (decision affd on appeal [2011] EWCA Civ 131; [2011] IRLR 420). The same judge (Jack J) again refused to follow the RDF case subsequently: see *Brandeaux Advisers (UK) Ltd v Chadwick* [2010] EWHC 3241 (QB), [2011] IRLR 224 holding that an unaccepted repudiation was a "thing writ in water" (see the *Howard* case supra). Subsequently, judges sitting in the Court of Session and the EAT have declined to follow the *RDF* case: see *McNeill v Aberdeen City Council (no. 2)* [2014] IRLR 113 and *Atkinson v Community Gateway Association* [2014] IRLR 834.

In *Lonmar Global Risks Ltd v West* [2011] IRLR 138 an employee was subject to 12 months post termination non-solicitation and dealing covenants set out in clause 14A of his employment contract. Clause 14B stated: "Clause 14A shall apply in the event of termination of the . . . employment in all circumstances except unlawful termination by [the employer]". It was argued on behalf of the employee that an unfair dismissal by the employer would fall within the expression "unlawful termination". At trial the judge ruled that "unlawful termination" meant unlawful termination at common law ie a wrongful dismissal not a mere unfair dismissal. The judge went on to hold the covenants enforceable.

42.12   Conflict of laws

Because the law of restraint of trade arises as a matter of public policy, foreign law, even if it is the proper law of the contract, cannot dictate the validity or invalidity of a provision in restraint of trade. Contracts of employment the proper law of which is a foreign law will not be enforced by an English court if the restraints in question are unenforceable under the public policy of England and Wales: see *Rousillon v Rousillon* (1880) 14 Ch D 351. A distinction must be made between principles relating to mandatory rules of English law and English public policy. The restraint of trade doctrine is not a mandatory rule for the purposes of Article 6(1) of the Rome Convention. Rather, it falls under Article 16 of that Convention: see *Duarte v Black and Decker Corpn* [2007] EWHC 2720 (QB), [2008] 1 All ER (Comm) 401 and *BGC Capital Markets (Switzerland) LLC v Rees* [2011] EWHC 2009 (QB). Accordingly, where covenants in restraint of trade are expressed to be governed by a proper law other than the law of England, and would be enforceable under that proper law, but not under the English doctrine of restraint of trade, then the result of the application of the specified foreign law would be 'manifestly incompatible with English public policy': *Duarte*, ibid. It follows that the approach that should be taken to covenants expressed to be governed by foreign law is for the English court first to determine whether those covenants would be valid under that foreign law. If not, then there is no need to apply the doctrine of restraint of trade to them. If, however, the court decides that the covenants would be valid under the chosen foreign law, then the English court must go on to apply its own doctrine of restraint of trade to those covenants. If invalid under the English doctrine of restraint of trade, then the English law 'trumps' the chosen foreign law.

42.13   TRADE SECRETS AND CONFIDENTIAL INFORMATION

The law in relation to trade secrets and confidential information is now not only found at common law / equity, but also has a statutory underpinning by reason of the *Trade Secrets (Enforcement etc.) Regulations 2018*. Those regulations are intended to implement *Council Directive (EU) 2016/943*. The regulations came into force on 9 June 2018.

The courts have long recognised that trade secrets are a legitimate interest which an employer may protect by imposing a covenant limiting the field of activity in which an ex employee may engage after leaving his employment (see, for example, Lord Parker in *Herbert Morris v Saxelby*, above, and *Printers and Finishers Ltd v Holloway* [1964] 3 All ER 54n, [1965] RPC 239, [1964] 3 All ER 731). In this respect, therefore, obligations of confidentiality that an employee owes his employer have an important role to play in the doctrine of restraint of trade. However, obligations of confidentiality, if breached by an employee either during or after the employment contract has ended, may give rise to claims for relief which lie outside any claim for breach of restrictive covenants in employment contracts, specifically the so-called 'springboard injunction'. In recent years, decisions of the court have led to much confusion in these areas, such that discussions of the principles of the law of confidentiality now resemble medieval theological debates about how many angels can dance on pinheads.

It is necessary, therefore, to identify certain basic principles relating to the obligations of confidence owed by employees to their employers. The obligation of good faith and fidelity (now transmuted into an obligation of trust and confidence: see generally **8.13** CONTRACT OF EMPLOYMENT) implied into all contracts of employment has as an incident of that larger duty a specific obligation that the employee shall not make use of, or disclose, for the benefit of a competing business information acquired by the employee about his employer's business in the course of his employment (see *Robb v Green* [1895] 2 QB 1). In that case an employee during his contract of employment made a list of the names and addresses of his employer's clients and, following the termination of his employment, used that list to canvas the clients of the former employer for a rival business established by the employee. The employee was held to have breached the implied duty of good faith and fidelity in so acting and was ordered by injunction to hand over the list he had made to his former employer and to pay damages. The decision was affirmed on appeal ([1895] 2 QB 315, [1895–9] All ER Rep 1053). It is of the greatest significance to observe that the defendant contended that the information contained on the list which he had made was information that could be obtained from sources within the public domain. The trial judge (Hawkins J) did not accept that all the information could have been so sourced, but added (p 18) that even were that true the employee had nonetheless acted in breach of his duty in creating a convenient compilation of material for the purpose of assisting an intended competitor. (For a more recent case on the scope of the employee's obligations of good faith and fidelity while in employment, see *Helmet Integrated Systems Ltd v Tunnard* [2006] EWCA Civ 1735, [2007] IRLR 126, in which the Court of Appeal accepted that the employee had not breached his obligations to his employer by taking, during his employment and unbeknownst to his employer, steps preparatory to competing with his employer; see also *Khan v Landskerr Childcare Ltd* UKEAT/0036/12/DM, *Imam-Sadeque v BlueBay Asset Management (Services) Ltd* [2012] EWHC 3511 (QB), [2013] IRLR 344 and **8.16 CONTRACT OF EMPLOYMENT**. Note, however, that the position is otherwise for company directors and very senior employees: see *Crowson Fabrics Ltd v Rider and ors* [2007] EWHC 2942 (Ch), [2008] IRLR 288; *Reuse Collections Ltd v Sendall* [2015] IRLR 226; and **10.16 DIRECTORS**.)

Some ninety years after *Robb v Green* [1895] 2 QB 1 the Court of Appeal embarked on an analysis of the duties of confidentiality owed by an employee: see *Faccenda Chicken Ltd v Fowler* [1986] ICR 297, [1986] IRLR 69, CA. At first instance in that case, Goulding J had analysed the position thus ([1984] ICR 589, [1984] IRLR 61 at 598–599):

'Let me now deal with the alleged abuse of confidential information. I must make it clear that anything I say about the law is intended to apply only to cases of master and servant. In my view information acquired by an employee in the course of his service, and not the subject of any relevant express agreement, may fall as regards confidence into any of three classes. First, there is information which, because of its trivial character or its easy accessibility from public sources of information, cannot be regarded by reasonable persons or by the law as confidential at all. The servant is at liberty to impart it during his service or afterwards to anyone he pleases, even his master's competitor. An example might be a published patent specification well known to people in the industry concerned . . . Secondly, there is information which the servant must treat as confidential (either because he is expressly told it is confidential, or because from its character it obviously is so) but which once learned necessarily remains in the servant's head and becomes part of his own skill and knowledge applied in the course of his master's business. So long as the employment continues, he cannot otherwise use or disclose such information without infidelity and therefore breach of contract. But when he is no longer in the same service, the law allows him to use his full skill and knowledge for his own benefit in competition with his former master; and . . . there seems to be no established distinction between the use of such information where its possessor trades as a principal, and where he enters the employment of a new master, even though the latter case involves disclosure and not mere personal use of the information. If an employer wants to protect information of this kind, he can do so by an express stipulation restraining the servant from competing with him (within reasonable limits of time and space after the termination of his employment). Thirdly, however, there are, to my mind, specific trade secrets so confidential that, even though they may necessarily have been learned by heart and even though the servant may have left the service, they cannot lawfully be used for anyone's benefit but the master's. An example is the secret process which was the subject matter of *Amber Size & Chemical Co Ltd v Menzel* [1913] 2 Ch 239.'

Goulding J went on to hold that the information that had been used by the defendants upon leaving the plaintiff company's employment and setting up a rival business fell into the second of the three categories and, accordingly, there was no breach of duty involved in its use by the defendants. This was not a case in which there were any post-termination restraints in the defendants' contract of employment with Faccenda limiting their business activities in any way. Goulding J, however, opined (above, 599E) that an employer can protect the use of information in the second category, even though it does not include any information in the third category (ie a trade secret or its equivalent) by means of a restrictive covenant. The Court of Appeal held:

(1)   That in contracts of employment confidentiality obligations of the employee are to be determined by that contract.

(2)   Absent any express term relating to confidential information in an employment contract, the obligations of the employee in respect of the use and disclosure of information are the subject of implied terms.

(3)   During the currency of the employment relationship the obligations in relation to the use and disclosure of information are included in the implied term imposing a duty of good faith and fidelity (or trust and confidence) on the employee. The Court of Appeal declined to consider the precise limits of the confidentiality obligation arising out of that implied term during the currency of the employment contract, but observed:

   (a)   that the extent of the duty of good faith will vary according to the nature of the contract; and

   (b)   that that duty would be broken if an employee makes a list of customers, or memorises such a list, for use after his employment ends, even though there is no legal impediment on the employee soliciting or doing business with those customers after he leaves his employment. For this proposition the Court of Appeal returned to and relied on *Robb v Green* (above).

(4)   The implied term imposing an obligation on the employee not to use or disclose information learnt during his employment after the determination of the same is more restricted in its scope than the obligation during the currency of the employment contract and arising from the general duty of good faith and fidelity. Specifically, the implied post-termination obligation does not extend to all information given to, or acquired by, the employee while in his employment, and may not cover information which is only 'confidential' in the sense that it falls within the broader category of information that is protected during the currency of the employment contract as an incident of the obligation of good faith and fidelity. For this proposition the Court of Appeal relied upon the judgment of Cross J in *Printers and Finishers Ltd v Holloway* [1965] RPC 239 at 253:

> 'In this connection one must bear in mind that not all information which is given to a servant in confidence and which it would be a breach of his duty for him to disclose to another person during his employment is a trade secret which he can be prevented from using for his own advantage after the employment is over, even though he has entered into no express covenant with regard to the matter in hand. For example, the printing instructions were handed to Holloway to be used by him during his employment exclusively for the plaintiffs' benefit. It would have been a breach of duty on his part to divulge any of the contents to a stranger while he was employed, but many of these instructions are not really 'trade secrets' at all. Holloway was not, indeed, entitled to take a copy of the instructions away with him; but in so far as the

instructions cannot be called 'trade secrets' and he carried them in his head, he is entitled to use them for his own benefit or the benefit of any future employer.'

(See also *E Worsley & Co Ltd v Cooper* [1939] 1 All ER 290.)

Accordingly, the Court of Appeal (*obiter*) disagreed with Goulding J's judgment where he stated that an employer can protect 'category 2' information (not also falling within 'category 3') by means of an express post-termination restraint. The Court said:

> 'In our view the circumstances in which a restrictive covenant would be appropriate and could be successfully invoked emerge very clearly from the words used by Cross J in *Printers & Finishers Ltd v Holloway* [ibid] . . . If the managing director is right in thinking that there are features in the plaintiffs' process which can fairly be regarded as trade secrets and which their employees will inevitably carry away with them in their heads, then the proper way for the plaintiffs to protect themselves would be by exacting covenants from their employees restricting their field of activity after they have left their employment, not by asking the court to extend the general equitable doctrine to prevent breaking confidence beyond all reasonable bounds.'

On this analysis, as the Court of Appeal pointed out, it is impossible to provide a comprehensive list of those things which constitute trade secrets, or equivalent confidential information, that will be protected by the implied obligation of confidence operating post-termination and which would therefore form a legitimate interest justifying an express post-termination restraint limiting the fields of activity in which the ex employee may work for a period of time. Secret processes of manufacture are an obvious example of such information but 'innumerable other pieces of information are capable of being trade secrets, though the secrecy of some information may be only short lived . . . the fact that the circulation of certain information is restricted to a limited number of individuals may throw light on the status of the information and its degree of confidentiality'.

(5) The Court of Appeal went on to hold that in order to determine whether any particular item of information falls to be protected under the implied obligation of confidentiality operative <u>after</u> the termination of the employment contract a court must consider all the circumstances of the case, including the following matters:-

(a) the nature of the employment (ie was the employee engaged in a capacity where confidential material was habitually handled by him and he might, accordingly, be expected to realise its sensitivity);

(b) the nature of the information itself (ie only information which is a 'trade secret' or the equivalent of a trade secret is protected by the post-termination implied obligation);

(c) whether the employer impressed on the employee the confidentiality of the information;

(d) whether the relevant information can be easily isolated from other information which the employee is free to use or disclose.

The decision by the Court of Appeal in *Faccenda Chicken* has been criticised by some judges and by some textbook writers. In *Balston Ltd v Headline Filters Ltd* [1987] FSR 330 Scott J doubted the Court of Appeal's opinion that information falling within Goulding J's second category which did not also fall within his third category (termed by some textbook writers as 'mere confidential information') could not be protected by an express post-termination restraint. Similarly, in *Systems Reliability Holdings plc v Smith* [1990] IRLR 377, Harman J refused to follow this part of the Court of Appeal's judgment in *Faccenda*. See also *Lancashire Fire Ltd v SA Lyons & Co Ltd* [1997] IRLR 113, CA, per Bingham LJ, para 16 and *A T Poeton (Gloucester Plating) Ltd v Horton* [2001] FSR 169, [2000] ICR 1208, [2000] All ER (D) 748, CA.

It is respectfully submitted that these doubts are erroneous. First, it is unquestionably a matter of principle that it is against public policy to restrain the use by an ex employee of knowledge and skills that he has acquired in the course of his employment: see *Herbert Morris v Saxelby*, above, per Lord Parker and *Commercial Plastics Ltd v Vincent* [1965] 1 QB 623, [1964] 3 All ER 546. If the employer is to have a legitimate interest to protect in confidential information that information must fall into a special category of sensitivity beyond the mass of more mundane information that an employee will necessarily accumulate during his employment. Second, the Court of Appeal's decision in *Faccenda* does not warrant the criticism that has been levelled against it that it constitutes an excessively narrow view of the obligations of confidentiality in employment contracts or the class of information that may legitimately be protected by an express post-termination restraint or by the implied obligation of confidence operating after the contract of employment has come to an end. As the Court of Appeal pointed out, innumerable other pieces of information besides secret processes of manufacturing may constitute trade secrets, or their equivalent, and thus fall within the protection of express or implied post-termination obligations. Thus in one industry the identity of clients or customers may constitute the equivalent of a trade secret, as will information about the prices charged to those customers by the employer. In other businesses (as in *Faccenda* itself) the same kind of information will constitute only information protectable during the currency of the employment contract, but not afterwards. To an extent, confusion that has arisen since *Faccenda* is the product of quibbles about vocabulary: the expression 'trade secrets' is no doubt more apt to describe information relating to secret processes of manufacture than it is to describe information such as the identity of customers, but there is no sensible reason why one should not describe the latter information as 'information the equivalent of a trade secret' where it is treated as so equivalent in certain industries or businesses. It would, perhaps, be better if the use of the expression 'trade secrets' was abandoned altogether and replaced with the expression 'protectable confidential information'. It was certainly the view of Staughton LJ in *Lansing Linde Ltd v Kerr* [1991] 1 WLR 251, 260B, [1991] IRLR 80 that the problem was one of vocabulary: 'It appears to me that the problem is one of definition: what are trade secrets, and how do they differ (if at all) from confidential information? [It has been] suggested that a trade secret is information which, if disclosed to a competitor, would be liable to cause real (or significant) harm to the owner of the secret. I would add, first, that it must be information used in a trade or business and, secondly, that the owner must limit the dissemination of it or at least not encourage or permit widespread publication.'

There are reasons to doubt the test there propounded by Staughton LJ for identifying protectable confidential information, not least because it appears to place too much emphasis on the subjective view of the employer as to the status of information as distinct from the correct test which must needs be based upon the objective view of the court, but Staughton LJ, nonetheless, correctly identified the confusion that can arise from the terminology that abounds in these cases.

A second area of confusion arises from the difference between the implied obligation of confidentiality which survives after the employment contract has come to an end and the protection that may be afforded by an express post-termination restraint. The implied obligation is limited to an obligation not to disclose or make use of 'protectable confidential information'. This obligation should not be extended to prohibit an employee who possesses such information from going to work for a competitor of his former employer: see *Caterpillar Logistics Services (UK) Ltd v Paula Huesca de Crean* [2012] EWCA Civ 156, [2012] ICR 981, [2012] IRLR 410 and *Generics (UK) Ltd v Yeda Research and Develop-*

ment Co Ltd [2012] EWCA Civ 726, [2012] C.P. Rep. 39, [2012] All ER (D) 01 (Jun). It merely restrains him, when working for that competitor, from disclosing or using, the protectable confidential information. (Note that the position is different for self-employed professionals such as lawyers, accountants and patent attorneys who may be made the subject of so-called 'barring-out' orders preventing them from acting in litigation against a former client where it is necessary in order to avoid a significant risk of disclosure of 'protectable confidential information': see *Bolkiah v KPMG* [1999] 2 AC 222, [1999] 1 All ER 517 and note the view of Sir Robin Jacobs in *Generics (UK)* ibid that the same principle might apply to in-house lawyers.)

As has been pointed out above (**42.8**), an obligation not to disclose or make use of confidential information in the course of new employment is virtually impossible to police. Accordingly, employers frequently resort to an express post-termination restraint limiting the fields of activity in which the former employee may be involved for a period following the termination of the employment (ie a non-compete provision or, at least, an obligation not to join that part of a competitor's business which competes with the former employer). It is respectfully submitted that Scott J's reservations in *Balston* about the Court of Appeal's decision in *Faccenda* were based on confusion between the scope of the implied obligation of confidentiality and the more practical protection that can be afforded by post-termination non-compete restraints. Equally, in the *Systems Reliability* case, it should be observed that the learned judge had characterised the restraints that he was dealing with as having arisen with respect to a business sale agreement, and not an employment contract. As has also been pointed out above (**42.8**), the court's approach to business sale agreements and the restraint of trade doctrine is very different to the approach adopted to restraints in employment contracts.

The Court of Appeal re-stated the *Faccenda* principle in *Thomas v Farr plc* [2007] EWCA Civ 118, [2007] IRLR 419 and held that only information the equivalent of a trade secret can be protected by a post-termination non-compete restraint.

In conclusion, it is submitted that the law on an employee's obligations of confidentiality may be stated as follows:

(a)   During the currency of the employment contract the employee is bound as an incident of his implied obligations of fidelity and trust and confidence not to disclose or make use of the mass of information he acquires about his employer's business. The information covered by that obligation is limited so as to exclude only information which is trivial or in the public domain. However, it should be noted that if the employee sources and removes lists of customers or other information from the records of his employer for use in a rival business it does not matter that that information may be available in the public domain or that that information was originally compiled by the employee in the service of the employer. That information belongs to the employer and the employee cannot use it without breaching the implied obligation of confidentiality that existed during the life of his employment contract: see *Crowson Fabrics Ltd v Rider* [2008] IRLR 288 and *Pennwell Publishing (UK) Ltd v Ornstien* [2007] EWHC 1570 (QB), [2007] IRLR 700 (and see outside the employment context *The Racing Partnership Ltd and others v Done Brothers (Cash Betting) Ltd and others* [2019] EWHC 1156 (Ch), [2019] 3 WLR 779 where information in the public domain was nonetheless confidential because its dissemination was controlled). NB many compilations of information contained within an employer's computer systems will independently attract protection as databases under the *Copyright, Designs and Patents Act 1988 (as amended)*, but this lies outside the scope of this chapter.

(b)   After the contract of employment comes to an end the employee is subject to an implied obligation not to disclose to, or make use for the benefit of, a competitor information which constitutes protectable confidential information, ie information which has the status of a trade secret or its equivalent. It is an issue of fact, in every case, depending on all the circumstances and applying the various guidelines, whether or not information falls into this category. Certain information, such as the identity of clients or customers is capable of falling into this category, but not necessarily in all businesses. The same is true of price information and many other kinds of information. No comprehensive list can therefore be drawn up of this kind of information. It is, however, clear that technical information regarding manufacturing processes and high level strategic business plans (for example, whether and, if so, when old models are to be replaced by new) will be likely to fall into this third category of protectable confidential information regardless of the nature of the business concerned.

(c)   The protection afforded by the implied confidentiality obligation operating after the employment contract has come to an end is limited to disclosing or making use of the information concerned. This implied obligation is therefore of limited practical use to an employer because it does not prevent the employee from going to work for a rival and, once within a rival's business, it is impossible for the employer to monitor whether or not the employee is disclosing or making use of the concerned information.

(d)   Accordingly, an employer who rightly considers that an employee may in the course of his employment acquire information falling within the class of protectable confidential information (ie a trade secret or equivalent confidential information) has a legitimate interest to protect under the doctrine of restraint of trade and may justify imposing a covenant restricting the field of activity of that employee when he leaves his employment. The covenant must, however, be reasonable as to its ambit and duration. Although 'category 3' confidential information can, in certain circumstances, justify worldwide restraints because confidentiality knows no territorial limitations (see *Scully v Lee*, above), in other cases, the evidence may show that a worldwide restraint will be held to be too wide to be enforceable (see *Lansing Linde Ltd v Kerr*, above and *Commercial Plastics Ltd v Vincent*, above). It may also be the case that a non-compete provision, ie one prohibiting an employee who possesses confidential information in the third category from working in any capacity for a competitor will also be held to be too wide in its ambit: see *Commercial Plastics v Vincent*. The contrary argument, however, is that it is legitimate to restrain an employee with 'category 3' confidential information from working in any capacity for a competitor because he is still in a position, at the very least, to reveal that information to the competitor that he joins even where he may be employed by that competitor in the part of its business which does not compete with the former employer or he joins it in a capacity in which he does not need to make use of or disclose that information in order to perform his new duties. These are difficult considerations which the court must weigh in considering the reasonableness of any post-termination restraint taken to protect 'category 3' confidential information.

(e)   An express restrictive covenant in an employment contract not to make use of the employer's confidential information during or after the employment will be construed so as to apply to 'Faccenda Category 2' information during the contract but only 'Faccenda Category 3' information after the contract has ended: see *SBJ Stephenson Ltd v Mandy* [2000] IRLR 233.

(f)   The duration of an express restrictive covenant is frequently unlimited in time, but this is not fatal to the validity of such an express covenant: *SBJ Stephenson v Mandy* (ibid) and *Caterpillar Logistics Services (UK) Ltd v Huesca de Crean* [2012] EWCA Civ 156, [2012] ICR 981, [2012] IRLR 410.

The action for breach of confidence in relation to trade secrets by employees will normally be based on breach of contract. A claim for breach of contract will not normally require any form of *mens rea* on the part of the employee. It is, however, clear that an employee cannot be in breach of an express or implied obligation not to make use of or disclose confidential information if:– (a) they had never acquired that information in the first place and/or (b) they had not themselves used or disclosed the information or (c) had cause to know that the information in question had been used or disclosed. So much, one might have thought, was axiomatic. However, in a recent case, *Vestergaard Frandsen A/S and ors v Bestnet Europe Ltd and ors* [2013] 1 WLR 1556, [2013] IRLR 654 an attempt was made to persuade the Supreme Court that a former employee who was not privy to confidential information of the former employer, nor had any knowledge that it was being used in a rival business which she had joined as a director was nonetheless liable for misuse of that information because she information because she had entered a common design, one element of which was the misuse of her former employers' confidential information. Unsurprisingly, the attempt failed. Some useful propositions about the *mens rea* required for primary and secondary liability for breach of confidence in relation to trade secrets may be extracted from the decision of the Supreme Court, viz:

(a) The classic case of breach of confidence involves the claimants' confidential information being used inconsistently with its confidential nature by a defendant who received it in circumstances where he/she had agreed or ought to have appreciated that it was confidential. Thus the *mens rea* for the classic case of breach is that the defendant must have agreed (expressly or impliedly) or must know that the information is confidential. Thus a defendant who receives information imparted in confidence who then goes on to use that information even unconsciously and under a mistake as to their legal obligations will be liable for breach of confidence (see *Seagar v Copydex Ltd* [1967] 1 WLR 923, [1967] 2 All ER 415) and a defendant who is found to have received information in confidence has no defence if he uses that information that he did not realise that he was breaching confidence or even using the information in question;

(b) A defendant who receives information not knowing that it is a trade secret and where there is no reasonable basis for suspecting that it is, he/she will nonetheless be liable to maintain confidentiality in that 'secret' from the moment he/she is told or otherwise becomes aware that it is in fact confidential;

(c) Secondary liability for breach of confidence can arise where a person assisting the recipient of confidential information to misuse it. However such secondary liability would 'normally' require the assistant either to know or to be reckless (by turning a 'blind eye') to the recipient's misuse of that information;

(d) A third party who does not know and does not turn a blind eye to a recipient's misuse of confidential information may nonetheless be liable for that misuse by virtue of vicarious liability (eg if the third party employs the recipient who then abuses confidentiality obligations);

(e) A person who has not received and has not used confidential information nor has assisted a breach of confidence by another knowing that it is a breach of confidence or being reckless as to whether it is cannot be liable for that breach either as a primary or a secondary party.

In *Brandeaux Advisers (UK) Ltd v Chadwick* [2010] EWHC 3241 (QB), [2011] IRLR 224, the defendant employee transferred by email from her work computer to her personal computer vast quantities of confidential materials concerning the claimants' investment funds. It appears that the employee was "storing" the materials for the purposes of using them in the event that litigation ensued between her and her employer and/or in case there was a dispute with Regulators (she had been chief compliance officer for the claimants' Group).

The claimant bought proceedings against the defendant for breach of express confidentiality terms in her contract and for breach of the implied duty of fidelity. The defendant contended that there were implied terms in her contract of employment which entitled her to use her employer's confidential information or disclose it to third parties where such use or disclosure was "fairly required for her legitimate interests or to protect her legal rights or to defend herself" and that she was so entitled where the use or disclosure was in the public interest including use or disclosure in relation to financial regulators.

The judge held that this was not a case involving legitimate whistleblowing (and even if it had been he doubted whether using confidential information in reporting matters to a regulator could ever justify the wholesale transfer of an employer's information onto an employee's personal computer). Moreover the judge doubted that the possibility of future litigation could ever justify an employee so transferring confidential information of their employer. An employee should, in the event of a dispute, rely upon the court's disclosure process to provide relevant documents. In the event, on the facts, the judge held that the employee was not entitled to transfer the information and in so doing was in repudiatory breach of her contract of employment. (Note that documents disclosed in the course of tribunal proceedings cannot be used in separate High Court proceedings without the permission of the Court: see *IG Index Ltd v Cloete* [2015] ICR 254.)

42.14   RESTRAINT OF TRADE AS A DISCRETIONARY ELEMENT IN GRANTING INJUNCTIVE RELIEF

Garden leave injunctions

It is now clear (see *Symbian v Christensen*, above) that considerations of restraint of trade play an important part in influencing the court's discretion to grant injunctive relief to enforce express or implied negative obligations of employees during notice periods. This is not the application of the 'classic' doctrine of restraint of trade. It differs in the following fundamental respects from the classic doctrine:

(a)   the court is enforcing contractual rights which at the time the contract is made would not be subject to the restraint of trade doctrine in its classic form because those rights of the employer (namely the right to exclusive service by the employee) would not, under the classic doctrine, be considered a restraint of trade;

(b)   the court looks to the position as at the date when garden leave is imposed rather than the position when the contract was first entered into;

(c)   the court is able to temper the relief granted, both as to the ambit of any injunction and as to its duration; the court is not obliged to impose injunctive relief which exactly mirrors the contractual provisions in question (see *GFI Group Inc v Eaglestone* [1994] IRLR 119);

(d)   it would seem that the court can take into account interests of the employer which go beyond the legitimate interests that the court would uphold in enforcing post-termination restraints under the restraint of trade doctrine. In *Provident Financial* Dillon LJ considered it legitimate, in principle, to grant garden leave injunctions not only when there was a risk to the employer's confidential information or client connection from the departing employee, but also where the employee would merely enhance a competitor's business if he joined it during his notice period. This appears to come perilously close to supporting covenants in gross (ie covenants against mere competition). (See also *Elsevier v Munro* [2014] IRLR 766, where the risk of unconscious use of confidential information by an employee provided additional justification for the grant of an injunction to support a prohibition on working for a competitor during the notice period.)

Thus, the court can impose injunctions restraining an employee on garden leave from joining or assisting a competitor of the employer for a period less than the notice period stipulated in the contract of employment (*GFI v Eaglestone*, above). Equally, the court may limit the injunctive relief granted – and will so limit it – to restrain the employee only from working for a competitor during the whole or part of the notice period, but will not restrain an employee during his notice period from working for a new employer not in competition with the existing employer: see *Provident Financial Group plc v Hayward* [1999] ICR 160, [1998] IRLR 399. There is no principle which requires a court to refuse to enforce a covenant in restraint of trade operating post termination of a contract of employment where a court has, during the notice period of the employee under that contract, granted a 'garden leave' injunction: see *Credit Suisse Asset Management Ltd v Armstrong* [1996] ICR 882, [1996] IRLR 450, CA. However, the Court of Appeal in that case opined that the position might be different, and the post-termination restraint not enforced, in circumstances where it was preceded by a very lengthy period of garden leave, ie of a year or more. It should also be observed that the decision in *Armstrong* does not prevent a court, when judging the reasonableness of a covenant operating post-termination, from taking into account a period of garden leave. Thus, if an employee is subject to a post-termination restraint prohibiting him from joining a competitor after termination of his employment and that employee is also subject to a garden leave provision during his notice period the court may conclude (looking at the contract from the date it was entered into) that the combination of the garden leave period and the non-compete period would involve too lengthy a 'sterilisation' of the employee in question. This is particularly so where the employee is subject to other post-termination restraints such as a non-solicitation or non-dealing covenant. Such an argument was considered and rejected on the facts in *Tradition Financial Services v Gamberoni* [2017] EWHC 768 (QB), [2017] IRLR 698. In that case, the combined period of garden leave and covenant was only 9 months, however. The court may strike down the non-competition covenant but uphold the non-solicitation and non-dealing provisions: see *Credit Suisse First Boston (Europe) Ltd v Padiachy* [1999] ICR 569, [1998] IRLR 504. Nevertheless, it should not be supposed that a period of garden leave is to be regarded as a desirable alternative to post-termination restraints: in *TFS Derivatives Ltd v Morgan* [2004] EWHC 3181 (QB), [2005] IRLR 246, counsel for the employee sought to argue that a three-month non-compete clause was unlawful because the interest to be protected (client connection) could more appropriately and reasonably have been protected by a 'garden leave' clause of six months. He invited Cox J to make general observations as to the reasonableness and greater attraction of garden leave clauses generally. Cox J declined, observing that a six-month garden leave clause could legitimately be regarded as more onerous for the employee than a three-month non-compete because it prevented the employee from working at all. She also noted that the employer may understandably not wish to pay the employee for six months of no work and, further, that such a clause may not, in any case, be adequate to protect the employer's interests because it would not operate on summary termination of the contract by either party. In *Elsevier Ltd v Munro* (ibid), it was held that the public policy underlying garden leave injunctions was not engaged in a case where the employer did not seek to place the employee on garden leave but the employee had instead sought to work for a competitor in breach of his contractual obligations. It was not open to an employee in those circumstances to complain that that the relief sought by the employer would compel the employee to a period of idleness.

In *Tullett Prebon plc v BGC Brokers LP* [2010] EWHC 484 (QB), [2010] IRLR 648 Jack J held that as a matter of discretion in imposing injunctive relief he could enforce fully by injunction for the full term of notice garden leave provisions and then enforce, but for a duration shorter than the contractual term, post-termination restraints. This is impermissible because it amounts to re-writing the post-termination restraints by reducing the duration thereof by means of an injunction. In so doing, he clearly overlooked *Mont v Mills* (supra) and *Provident Financial v Hayward* (supra). This point was not considered on appeal in *Tullett*: [2011] EWCA Civ 131, [2011] IRLR 420. However, in *QBE Management Services (UK) Ltd v Dymoke and ors* [2012] EWHC 80 (QB), [2012] IRLR 458 Haddon-Cave J confirmed the orthodox position.

42.15 Restraint of trade and springboard relief

Employees who commit breaches of duty to their employer whilst employees by copying or removing customer lists or other confidential information for use in a rival business either during or after the termination of their employment contracts may be restrained by 'springboard injunction' from dealing with the customers whose details they have filched from their employer (see *Roger Bullivant Ltd v Ellis* [1987] ICR 464, [1987] IRLR 491 and *PSM International plc v Whitehouse* [1992] IRLR 279, CA).

Recently the court has also shown itself to be willing to grant springboard relief to counteract the effect of breaches of duty other than the duty of confidentiality. Thus in *Midas IT Services Ltd v Opus Portfolios Ltd* (21 December 1999, unreported), Ch D, springboard relief injuncting a company which it was alleged had procured breaches of the duty of trust and confidence by a senior employee of the claimant for a period of six months from acquiring a licence to distribute software was granted. The breaches of duty allegedly induced by the enjoined company were not breaches of the obligations of confidentiality. This authority was followed in *UBS Wealth Management (UK) Ltd v Vestra Wealth LLP* [2008] EWHC 1974 (QB), [2008] IRLR 965, the court holding explicitly that springboard relief was not limited merely to breach of confidence cases. Where there has been mass poaching by illicit means of employees and/or clients, springboard injunctions may issue to restrain the poacher from employing employees illicitly poached or from dealing with clients illicitly solicited. The ambit and duration of such springboard injunctions are necessarily fact sensitive and it is not possible to formulate guidelines.

However, in all cases the ambit and duration of springboard injunctions will be influenced by considerations of restraint of trade. A springboard injunction necessarily interferes with the enjoined parties' right to do certain kinds of business with certain people and judges appreciate that the effect of imposing such injunction will be to impose restraints of trade in circumstances in which an employee may not have any express post-termination restraints in his contract of employment:

> 'I am acutely conscious of the fact that competition should be encouraged and I am acutely conscious of the fact that it must be quite wrong to impose a restraint which is effectively only going to operate to stop a man using his acquired skills rather than to stop him using confidential information which he ought never to have taken into use at all.'

Fisher-Karpark Industries Ltd v Nichols [1982] FSR 351.

Nonetheless, the judge granted the springboard injunction in that case against employees who it was alleged had misused confidential information of their employer in a rival business.

> 'Interim injunctions can be granted to prevent defendants . . . from obtaining an unjust headstart in, or a springboard for, activities detrimental to the person who provided them with confidential information. . . . However, in relation to that type of information, as distinct from that concerning real trade secrets, the court should be concerned that it does not, in granting such an injunction, give the injured party more protection than he realistically needs and, in particular, discourage or prohibit what in the course of time becomes legitimate competition.'

per May LJ in *Bullivant v Ellis*, above, at 481G-H.

> 'The [springboard] injunction is directed to fairness of competition. Because the policy of the law is to encourage and certainly not to restrain fair competition the injunction is limited in duration to that period in which, in the court's estimation, the person injuncted could reasonably be expected to have assembled the confidential information using lawful means if earlier the assembled information comes as such into the public domain'

per Blackburn J in *Midas IT Services Ltd v Opus Portfolios Ltd* (unreported, Ch D, 21 December 1999, pp 13–14)

In one springboard case at least (*Bullivant v Ellis*, above), the Court of Appeal considered that the appropriate duration of springboard relief in respect of an employee who had removed a card index of clients from his employer prior to the termination of his contract which he afterwards used in a rival business ought to be limited to the same period of a post-termination restraint in his contract of employment prohibiting dealing with his former employer's customers. It is submitted, however, that this direct correlation between springboard relief and the period of any post-termination restraint will not be invariably be adopted by the courts. Some forms of activity by employees in breach of their duties of trust and confidence whilst employed either in respect of the removal or misuse of confidential information or in respect of other wrongdoings, such as the canvassing or soliciting of the employer's customers during their employment for a rival business will cause serious harm requiring periods of restraint by springboard injunction of a longer duration than any post-termination restraint in the employment contract. After all, post-termination restraints are framed at the outset of a contract to protect a limited class of interests and in the expectation that the employee will abide by his contractual duties during his employment. The employer cannot, in framing covenants which are no more than adequate to protect his interests, anticipate and build into such covenants protection against any possible breach of trust and confidence which might be committed by the employee during his contract of employment.

In *Tullett Prebon plc v BGC Brokers LP* [2010] EWHC 484 (QB), [2010] IRLR 648 the court was invited to grant springboard relief against the defendant restraining it from recruiting any of the claimants' staff for a period of 18 months from the first grant of interim injunctive relief in the proceedings. The judge determined that an appropriate period for such form of relief would be approximately 12, not 18, months and that the basis on which it should be granted was not springboard relief, but as a *quia timet* injunction. The judge held that the recruitment of the claimant's staff had been achieved by illicit means and that the claimant was entitled to fear that such means might be deployed again. Since those means were difficult to detect it was necessary to injunct the defendants from any recruitment of the Claimant's staff. The difficulty with this approach is that the logic of it points not to a limited period of relief but, rather, to a permanent injunction. Moreover, there seems no principled basis upon which this form of *quia timet* relief can be subject to a limited duration. The judge appears to have held that he could limit the period of this form of relief to 14 days from the delivery of his judgment in this case. He stated "There is no justification for any further substantial extension of the relief. The court must assume that the exposure of BGC's conduct as set out in the judgment will curb unlawful recruitment in the future. BGC is a substantial and ostensibly responsible company. The relief against BGC will be continued for 14 days from the delivery of the judgment so the judgment may be absorbed. It will then end." The learned judge did not explain upon what basis it could be assumed that the defendant would, by reason of having absorbed his judgment, cease to pursue its illicit poaching operations. It is respectfully submitted that springboard relief is to be preferred in these kinds of case because it is relief which is intrinsically subject to limitations of duration. This point was not considered on appeal in *Tullett*: [2011] EWCA Civ 131; [2011] IRLR 420.

However, *QBE Management Services (UK) Ltd v Dymoke and ors* [2012] EWHC 80 (QB), [2012] IRLR 458 restores what it is submitted are the proper principles of springboard relief in this area, in particular, that the length of springboard relief must be a function of how long it would have taken the defendants to achieve the springboard advantage had they employed lawful means to do so. The analysis of Hadden-Cave J of the authorities in relation to springboard relief is now routinely referred to and applied by judges in dealing with such relief: see, for example *Aquinas Education Limited v Miller and others* [2018] EWHC 404 (QB), [2018] IRLR 518.

PROCEDURAL MATTERS

42.16 Pleading

Because the common law doctrine of restraint of trade requires contractual provisions falling within it to be justified before they are enforceable, employers seeking to enforce such provisions ought to plead in their particulars of claim the grounds justifying the restraint. Equally, a defendant who wishes to attack a covenant as unenforceable should raise in his defence the grounds upon which he claims the covenant is unenforceable. It would appear that a court cannot of its own motion raise issues of unenforceability of covenants under the restraint of trade doctrine: see *Petrofina (Great Britain) Ltd v Martin* [1966] Ch 146, [1966] 1 All ER 126. Accordingly, the parties must raise these issues themselves. It is to be observed, however, that there have been instances in which a court has, of its own volition, taken the point that a covenant is in unlawful restraint of trade: see *Marion White Ltd v Francis* [1972] 1 WLR 1423, [1972] 3 All ER 857.

In cases which raise issues of confidential information (whether as justifying a covenant in restraint of trade or otherwise) the information claimed to be confidential must be properly and fully particularised in any statement of case and as early as possible (see *Ocular Sciences Ltd v Aspect Vision Care Ltd* [1997] RPC 289). In particular, where injunctions restraining disclosure or use of confidential information are sought the confidential information to be protected must be fully particularised: see *Caterpillar Logistics Services (UK) Ltd v Huesca de Crean* [2012] EWCA Civ 156, [2012] ICR 981, [2012] IRLR 410. In order to protect highly confidential information from public disclosure in the course of proceedings orders should be sought from the court at the earliest possible stage that particulars of confidential information contained in any statement of case should not be available on the court file for public inspection. The best practice is to plead the details of any confidential information at issue between the parties in a confidential annexure to the statement of case.

42.17 Injunctions

It has long been recognised by the courts that the proof of loss and damage arising from a breach of a post-termination restraint in an employment contract is a difficult, if not impossible, matter. Accordingly, in the vast majority of cases, the covenantee will seek to enforce restraints by way of injunction. However, it must be remembered that an injunction is a discretionary remedy and, even where a court holds a restraint to be valid, it will retain a residual discretion as to whether to enforce that contractual restraint by injunction or not. Thus, if an employer delays before seeking an injunction, such that a substantial part of the period of the restraint sought to be enforced has elapsed before injunctive relief is sought, then the court may not grant an injunction at all: see *Wincanton Ltd v Cranny* [2000] IRLR 716, CA and *Legends Live Limited v Harrison* [2017] IRLR 59 (where an injunction was refused in the entertainment industry after some delay and where it appeared that the injunction was being sought as a weapon to cause disruption). That said, delay in and of itself, will be unlikely to result in a judge refusing injunctive relief: see *Law Society of*

England and Wales v Society for Lawyers [1996] FSR 739. The personal circumstances of the defendant in injunction cases may also be relevant in that the court will weigh any hardship that might be occasioned by the imposition of an injunction (see *Corporate Express Ltd v Day* [2004] EWHC 2943 (QB), [2004] All ER (D) 290 (Dec)). It is, however, submitted that injunctions should not be refused merely because the defendant is likely to be impoverished by them for that would create a licence to breach contractual duties based upon a means test. Some special or exceptional hardship would need to be shown for an injunction to be refused by a court: see the observations of Colman J in *Insurance Co v Lloyd's Syndicate* [1995] 1 Lloyd's Law Reports 272, 276-7 which were endorsed by the Court of Appeal (save that Rimer J did not think a test of exceptionality to be helpful) in *Dyson Technology Limited v Pellerey* [2016] IRLR 355 and applied by Freedman J in *Argus Media Ltd v Halim* [2019] EWHC 42 (QB), [2019] IRLR 442.

For the purposes of interim injunction, there is no special rule applicable to restrictive covenants in employment contracts. The principles in *American Cyanamid Co v Ethicon Ltd* [1975] AC 396, [1975] 1 All ER 504 will apply and if the covenantee raises serious issues to be tried as to the enforceability of that covenant an interim injunction will almost invariably be granted: see *Lawrence David Ltd v Ashton* [1991] 1 All ER 385, [1989] ICR 123, [1989] IRLR 22. The court will, if requested by the defendant against whom an interim injunction has been granted, generally order a 'speedy trial'. In the event that a 'speedy trial' is not possible before the period of the restraint in question elapses, however, a different approach might be taken by the court to the grant of an interim injunction. In such a case, the court might go beyond deciding whether there is a serious issue to be tried and attempt some assessment of the claimant's prospect of success at trial: see *Lansing Linde Ltd v Kerr* [1991] 1 WLR 251, [1991] IRLR 80, *per* Staughton LJ at 258. The court should not, however, allow the hearing of an application for interim injunctions in these circumstances to degenerate into a prolonged battle based upon evidence which cannot be tested at that stage by cross-examination. It is to be noted that issues as to the proper construction of a restrictive covenant (see above **42.6**) should normally be resolved at the interlocutory stage, unless the construction of the covenant depends on disputed facts that cannot properly be resolved without a trial: see *Arbuthnot Fund Managers Ltd v Rawlings* [2003] EWCA Civ 518, [2003] All ER (D) 181 (Mar). (See also *Le Puy v Potter* [2015] EWHC 193 (QB), [2015] IRLR 554, where the possibility of a speedy trial resulting in a judgment five or six months before the expiry of a 12-month restraint meant that the *American Cyanimid* approach was appropriate and *Allfiled UK Limited v Eltis* [2016] FSR 11 where Hildyard J suggested that the *American Cyanamid* test should only be "departed from in extreme circumstances where a trial is rendered plainly and obviously otiose".) The decision in *Landmark Brickwork Ltd v Sutcliffe and ors* [2011] IRLR 976 seems to be a departure from the *Arbuthnot* guidance. It is respectfully submitted that construction issues must be resolved by the Court on an interim application, unless (and this will be a rare case) there is a dispute as to the factual matrix from which the contract arose. It cannot be right for a Court to impose an injunction based on a contract in restraint of trade without the Court determining what the true ambit of the restraint may be. The approach in *Landmark*, it is respectfully submitted, cannot be correct.

For the procedure on obtaining interim injunctions see *Parts 23* and *25* of the *Civil Procedure Rules*. Injunctions can also be sought as final relief at trial.

When considering whether to make, and making, an application for an interim injunction without notice or on short notice, it is vital to take note of the guidance given by Silber J in *CEF Holdings Ltd v Mundey* [2012] EWHC 1524 (QB), [2012] IRLR 912. That case well illustrates the dangers of short notice and without notice applications. It should never be forgotten by practitioners that an action to restrain by injunction employees or former employees may have the effect of destroying a nascent business or otherwise seriously damaging a person's ability to earn a living in the manner of their choosing. To take such a step without affording the employee an opportunity properly to be represented and resist such an application should really only be contemplated in extreme cases, for example where there is clear evidence that a former employee has obtained and is misusing or proposing to misuse confidential information of his former employer or where there is clear evidence that former employees are engaged in surreptitious efforts to suborn the loyalty of other employees or surreptitious efforts illicitly to capture or divert work from former employer's customers. In any event, in all cases where an application for injunctive relief is made without notice or on short notice the applicant must have carried out as full an investigation as possible into the circumstances of alleged misconduct and relayed to the Court those circumstances together with any other factual or legal defence that may be available to the defendant to the Court asked to grant an injunction. Fundamental to the obligation to make full and frank legal disclosures as well as factual disclosures is the obligation to alert the Court to any matters which may go to whether or not the Court has a jurisdiction to grant the injunctive orders sought or any of them, as well as to alert the Court if the interim injunction may effectively dispose of the injunction part of the case such that the Court should consider whether to apply the principles in *Lansing Linde Ltd v Kerr* rather than the 'standard' *American Cyanamid* test.

Often where interim injunctions are sought, supporting orders are also sought such as interim delivery-up, disclosure and computer destruction orders (see *Warm Zones v Thurley* [2014] EWHC 988 (QB), [2014] IRLR 791 and *Arthur J Gallagher Services (UK) Ltd v Skriptchenkov* [2016] EWHC 603 (QB), *A v B* [2019] EWHC 2089 (Ch), [2019] 1 WLR 5832) or interim disclosure orders (see *Aon Limited v JLT Reinsurance Brokers* [2010] IRLR 600).

42.18 Declaration

It is, of course, open to a covenantor (employee) to challenge the enforceability of a covenant in restraint of trade by initiating legal proceedings seeking a declaration that the covenant in question is unenforceable. It is not clear, and must be open to doubt, whether a defendant could obtain an interim declaration to this effect pending trial, even a speedy trial. Alternatively, where a court refuses a claimant an injunction on the basis that there is only a very short period left for the restraint to run, it may nonetheless grant the claimant a declaration that the covenant in question is reasonable and enforceable (see *Corporate Express Ltd v Day* [2004] EWHC 2943 (QB), [2004] All ER (D) 290 (Dec); and see *Petter v EMC Europe Ltd* [2015] EWCA Civ 480, for a case where a speedy trial was considered appropriate in a claim brought by an employee for a declaration as to the enforceability of a restrictive covenant).

42.19 Damages where confidential information or trade secrets are involved

As for damages, there is a dearth of reported cases upon how damages for breach of a post-termination restraint are to be calculated. On ordinary principles, however, an employer can only recover for loss of any profit that he might have made had the covenant not been breached rather than his loss of revenue. In the event that customers have been filched by an ex employee in breach of a restraint against soliciting or dealing with them, the court may be able to assess at trial the loss of profits incurred by the employer up to the date of trial, but will be faced with the difficult task of assessing future loss which must be based on the employer's chance of retaining those customers: see *SBJ Stephenson Ltd v Mandy* [2000] IRLR 233. In *Merlin Financial Consultants Ltd v Cooper* [2014] IRLR 610 HHJ Peter Hughes QC was prepared to take a 'broad brush' approach as to the question of which clients the employer would have retained had the post-termination restraint been complied with. In that case, the judge held that the employer would have retained 70% of the clients in the first year, and 40% in the second year (see paragraph 83 of the judgment).

It was at one time thought that it may be possible to obtain damages for breach of a post-termination restraint on the basis set out in *Wrotham Park Estate Co Limited v Parkside Homes Limited* [1974] 1 WLR 798, [1974] 2 All ER 321 (that is, in the context of post-termination restraints, the notional fee that the parties would have agreed for the defendant to purchase his way out of the restraints). However, in *One Step (support) v Morris Garner* [2018] 2 WLR 1353, [2018] IRLR 661 the Supreme Court undertook a review of the availability of *Wrotham Park* damages and concluded that they were only available in cases '*where the breach of contract results in the loss of a valuable asset created or protected by the right which was infringed*' and where '*the claimant has in substance been deprived of a valuable asset, and his loss can therefore be measured by determining the economic value of the asset in question.*' Examples of such situation are '*a right to control the use of land, intellectual property or confidential information*'. It follows that *Wrotham Park* damages are very unlikely to be available for breaches of post-termination restraints found in employment contracts.

The position in relation to breach of confidence is more complicated. There are cases where the breach of confidence gives rise to a loss of profit which can be assessed on ordinary principles. However, in other cases, courts have awarded damages to compensate for the loss of a 'notional licence fee' which ought to have been paid for use of the confidential information (in place of or in addition to damages for loss of profit): see *Seager v Copydex Limited (No. 2)* [1969] 1 WLR 809, [1969] 2 All ER 718; *Force India Formula One Team Limited v 1 Malaysia Racing Team SDN BHD* [2013] EWCA Civ 780, [2013] All ER (D) 39 (Jul); *Vestergaard Frandsen A/S v Bestnet Europe Limited* [2014] EWHC 3159 (Ch), [2014] All ER (D) 279 (Oct). In addition, in *One Step* (see above) the Supreme Court accepted that *Wrotham Park* damages were available, in principle, in breach of confidence cases. The law as to the assessment of licence fee damages is developing. In *Marathon Asset Management LLP v Seddon* [2017] EWHC 300 (Comm), [2017] IRLR 503) it was suggested that the proper approach was to distinguish between cases where the claimant would or might have sold its confidential information to the defendant for a fee and such cases where it was unrealistic to suppose that any reasonable person in the position of the claimant might have licenced its confidential information. In the first type of case, the court should seek to estimate the 'licence fee'. In the second type of case, Leggatt J considered, "*Such a method makes no sense because in such a context the negotiation is not merely fictional in the sense that it did not actually happen but fictional in the stronger sense that it lacks any verisimilitude. The law ought not to employ fictions of the latter sought.*" In the latter case, the court should order an account of profits, or payment of a percentage of the defendant's profits as licence fee damages. In any event, in that case, no damages were ordered since it was held that there had been no use of the confidential information in question.

Licence fee damages will only be payable for such period as the confidential information is actually used. Where the use of confidential information has given rise to a 'derived product' which is subsequently sold in the marketplace resulting in increased competition for the claimant, then damages will be assessed to compensate the claimant for the fact that he will face such competition sooner than he otherwise would have done. Licence fee damages would only be appropriate, on this analysis, for the period of time in which the confidential information is used to derive the new product: *Vestergaard Frandsen A/S v Bestnet Europe Limited* [2017] FSR 5.

42.20   Accounts of profits

Where an employee has breached a post-termination restraint prohibiting him from joining a competitor and it can be demonstrated that he has revealed to that competitor confidential information or trade secrets of the employer, an account of profits may be ordered by the court. This will, however, be an account of profits for breach of confidence rather than for breach of the negative covenant not to join a competitor. Despite the House of Lords' decision in *A-G v Blake* [2001] 1 AC 268, [2001] IRLR 36 that accounts of profits can, in certain circumstances, be ordered against an employee for breach of a negative restraint, it is submitted that this principle cannot and should not be applied in the case of ordinary employees outside government security services.

The award of an account of profits for breaches of confidence is a discretionary one. Unlike in cases of breach of fiduciary duty, the claimant does not have an automatic entitlement to an account of profits for such breaches: *Vercoe v Rutland Fund Management Ltd* [2010] EWHC 424 (Ch), [2010] All ER (D) 79 (Jun), *Walsh v Shanahan, Leonard and SLH Properties Ltd* [2013] EWCA Civ 411, [2013] All ER (D) 221 (Apr).

43 Retirement

43.1 RETIREMENT AGE

The age of retirement was once a matter solely to be determined by the contract of employment. However, in recent years, "retirement" dismissals are unlawful unless they can be objectively justified.

The state pension age is not of itself a contractual retiring age. Indeed it would have been unlawful sex discrimination for an employer to require employees to retire at state pension age, since this disadvantaged women whilst pension age differed according to sex. However, as of November 2018, the state pension age has now been equalised. It will now increase to 66 for both men and women by October 2020. The government has also announced its intention to introduce further rises in the future and the *Pensions Act 2014* provides for a regular review of the state pension age, at least once every five years, to take account of changes to life expectancy.

Pensionable age under an occupational pension scheme is distinct from both the contractual retirement age and the state pension age (although each may be the same). It is unlawful to provide different pensionable ages for men and women in an occupational pension scheme following the decision of the ECJ in *Barber v Guardian Royal Exchange Assurance Group*: C-262/88 [1991] 1 QB 344, [1990] IRLR 240 that pension benefits were 'pay' within *art 141* of the *Treaty of Rome* (formerly *art 119*): see further Equal Pay **(23)** for the UK legislation giving effect to this decision; note that this does not affect pensions earned by service prior to 17 May 1990 (the date of the *Barber* decision). The courts have on occasion allowed rectification of pension schemes to equalise the retirement age for men and women where the trustees have intended but failed to amend the relevant scheme (see, for example, *Pioneer GB Ltd v Webb* [2011] EWHC 2683 (Ch) and *Industrial Accoustics Ltd v Crowhurst*, Ch (15 May 2011, unreported)). In *Safeway Ltd v Newton* (C-171/18) [2019] IRLR 1090, the Grand Chamber of the European Court of Justice held that EU law did not allow, in the absence of objective justification, a retrospective levelling down of a retirement age to equalise it between men and women, since the disadvantaged group were entitled to the more favourable treatment of the advantaged group while they were so advantaged.

The question as to whether an individual has retired (eg for the purposes of a pension scheme) is usually one of fact and degree; thus the House of Lords has held that a managing director who withdrew from active involvement in the running of a company but remained in office as an unpaid non-executive director had retired: *Venables v Hornby* [2003] UKHL 65, [2004] ICR 42, [2004] 1 All ER 627. The Court of Appeal has held that a provision in a pension scheme conferring enhanced benefits on employees who 'retire at the request of' the employer applies to those employees who take voluntary redundancy or early retirement, but not those who are made compulsorily redundant: *AGCO Ltd v Massey Ferguson Works Pension Trust Ltd* [2003] EWCA Civ 1044, [2004] ICR 15, [2003] IRLR 783.

43.2 EMPLOYMENT PROTECTION AND RETIRING AGE

The enforced retirement of an employee is often a source of resentment, and may provoke a claim for unfair dismissal and for age discrimination. (If there is no provision in the contract for retirement and contractual notice is not given, there could also be a claim for wrongful dismissal.)

There is no longer an "age ceiling" on the right to bring claims for unfair dismissal and "retirement" is no longer listed as a potentially fair reason for dismissal.

43.2 Retirement

This means that, unless the employer can prove that the retirement is "some other substantial reason" for the dismissal, the dismissal will be unfair within the meaning of *s 98* of the *Employment Rights Act 1996*. Unless the employer can objectively justify the dismissal, the dismissal will additionally constitute discrimination on the grounds of age.

An employee required to retire in breach (or in the absence) of a contractual retirement age will be able to make a claim for breach of contract. However, if the employer gives the notice required under the contract, the fact that the reason for giving notice is to enforce retirement will not render an otherwise lawful dismissal a breach of contract. This is so even where the employer has an equal opportunity policy which includes provisions excluding age discrimination: *Taylor v Secretary of State for Scotland* [2000] ICR 595, [2000] IRLR 502.

43.3 Retirement dismissals

The separate chapters on discrimination (DISCRIMINATION AND EQUAL OPPORTUNITIES I (12), II (13), and III (14)) set out further detail of the provisions of the *2006 Regulations* and the *Equality Act 2010*. In particular, those chapters address questions relating to matters such as objective justification.

In summary, the law on retirement dismissals can be summarised as follows:

(a)   A retirement dismissal at any age constitutes a potentially age discriminatory act unless it can be objectively justified by showing that the decision is a proportionate means of achieving a legitimate aim.

(b)   Retirement is not a potentially fair reason for dismissal (*s 98(2)(ba)* of the *Employment Rights Act 1996* was repealed). An employer has to show that such a dismissal is for "some other substantial reason" and fairness will be determined in accordance with the usual principles under *s 98(4)* (see UNFAIR DISMISSAL (53)).

43.4 JUSTIFYING RETIREMENT DISMISSALS

Employers can no longer rely simply on compulsory contractual retirement ages as a defence to claims for age discrimination or unfair dismissal. They are instead required objectively to justify any and all retirement dismissals. If a retirement dismissal cannot be justified, it will constitute discrimination on the grounds of age and would also be likely to be unfair.

Since the retirement exception never applied to contract-workers, office-holders, barristers, advocates and partners, there has always been a requirement to justify any "retirement" of those non-employees. A few domestic authorities addressed whether such retirements can be justified. In *Hampton v Lord Chancellor* [2008] IRLR 258, an employment tribunal held that the compulsory retirement of a part-time Recorder at the age of 65 could not be objectively justified.

In *Seldon v Clarkson Wright & Jakes* [2012] UKSC 16, [2012] ICR 716, [2012] IRLR 590, [2012] 3 All ER 1301 a firm of solicitors sought to justify the compulsory retirement of a partner at the age of 65. The tribunal at first instance accepted that the retirement was a proportionate means of achieving the legitimate aims of ensuring that associates were given a reasonable opportunity to become partners, facilitating the planning of the partnership and limiting the need to expel underperforming partners. The EAT held that, although the tribunal was entitled to find that having a compulsory retirement age was justified, there was no evidence to support the justification of fixing the retirement age at 65. The Court of Appeal disagreed. The Supreme Court dismissed a further appeal. In doing so, the following useful guidance was given as to how the courts will assess the justification of retirement dismissals (see paragraphs [50] to [58] per Lady Hale):

(1)   The justification of direct age discrimination is different from the justification of indirect discrimination. Only certain kinds of aim are capable of justifying direct age discrimination. The aims must be social policy objectives of a public interest nature rather than purely individual reasons particular to the employer's situation such as cost reduction or improving competitiveness.

(2)   A certain amount of flexibility is permitted to employers in the pursuit of legitimate social policy aims.

(3)   The ECJ has identified a number of different legitimate aims in the context of justifying direct age discrimination. The following are those most likely to be relevant in the context of justifying a retirement dismissal:

•   promoting access to employment for younger people,

•   the efficient planning of the departure and recruitment of staff,

•   sharing out employment opportunities fairly between the generations,

•   ensuring a mix of generations of staff so as to promote the exchange of experience and new ideas,

•   rewarding experience,

•   facilitating the participation of older workers in the workforce,

•   avoiding the need to dismiss employees on the ground that they are no longer capable of doing the job which may be humiliating to the employee concerned, and

•   avoiding disputes about the employee's fitness for work over a certain age.

(4)   These legitimate aims form two broad groups: inter-generational fairness and dignity.

(5)   It is necessary to ask whether an aim is legitimate in the particular circumstances of the employment concerned;

(6)   Even if there is a legitimate aim, it is still necessary to enquire whether that aim was in fact being pursued, although the aim need not have been articulated or even realised at the time when the measure was first adopted.

(7)   The means chosen must also be both appropriate and necessary to achieve the end.

(8)   The gravity of the effect upon the employees discriminated against has to be weighed against the importance of the legitimate aims in assessing the necessity of the particular measure.

(9)   Where a general rule was justified, the existence of that rule would usually justify the treatment which resulted from it.

(10)   In the context of intergenerational fairness, it is relevant that at an earlier stage of life, a partner or employee might have benefited from the rule.

On the facts of *Seldon*, the Supreme Court held that:

(1)   staff retention and workforce planning were both directly related to the legitimate social policy aim of sharing out professional employment opportunities fairly between generations;

(2)   limiting the need to expel partners by way of performance management was directly related to dignity aims;

(3)   the matter would be remitted to the employment tribunal because it was possible that the tribunal would have regarded the choice of a mandatory retirement age of 65 as a proportionate means of achieving the first two aims.

When *Seldon* was remitted back to the tribunal, it was found that the compulsory retirement age of 65 was justified on the facts. Upon a further appeal ([2014] ICR 1275, [2014] IRLR 748), it was held that the task for the tribunal was to determine the balance between the discriminatory effect of a particular retirement age and its success in achieving the legitimate aims. The fact that an employee could point to a different age which would also meet those aims does not mean that the age chosen could not be justified. Employers are entitled to select a "bright line" age. In addition, it was held that the agreement of the parties to a particular age can be a relevant consideration.

The Irish Equality Court ("IEC") considered the justification of compulsory retirement in two cases. In *Doyle v ESB International Ltd* [2013] 1 CMLR 48, the IEC held that the compulsory retirement of a graphic designer shortly after his 65th birthday was lawful. That Court held that the dismissal was justified by reason of the aims of avoiding the embarrassment of compulsory medical examinations, offering career pathways to new employees and having a consistent rule across the workplace. By contrast, in *Sweeny v Aer Lingus TEO* [2013] 1 CMLR 51, the IEC held that a compulsory retirement at age 65 was not justified. The only justification put forward by the employer was that it would be perverse for the complainant to receive a pension while still working. The IEC held that it was well established that receipt of a pension entitlement did not necessitate retirement and so no legitimate aim had been put forward.

The Court of Justice of the European Communities has also considered the justification of retirement dismissals in a number of cases.

In *Fuchs v Land Hessen* [2012] ICR 93, [2011] IRLR 1043, the CJEU held that a law providing for a compulsory retirement age was not precluded by the *Equal Treatment Directive* and that legitimate aims would include establishing an age structure that balances younger and older employees, encouraging the recruitment and promotion of young people and preventing disputes about employees' fitness to work beyond a certain age. By contrast, in *Prigge v Deutsche Lufthansa AG* [2011] IRLR 1052, the ECJ held that a compulsory retirement age of 60 for pilots set out in a collective agreement was unlawful. It was not "necessary for the protection of health" within the meaning of *Article 2(5)* and nor was it justified under *Article 6(1)* as an aim such as air traffic safety does not fall within the aims as it was not a "social policy objective" (but contrast *Sweeney v Aer Lingus TEO*, above). The CJEU has recognised that the automatic retirement of employees at an age when they are entitled to draw a pension has, for a long time, been a feature of employment law in many Member States and that it is widely used in employment relationships (see especially *Rosenbladt v Oellerking Gebaudereinigungsgesellschaft mbH*: C-45/09 [2011] 1 CMLR 32, [2011] IRLR 51; *Félix Palacios de la Villa v Cortefiel Servicios SA*: C-411/05 [2008] All ER (EC) 249, [2007] IRLR 989, and has noted that retirement issues require a balance to be struck between political, economic, social, demographic and/or budgetary considerations and the choice to be made between prolonging people's working lives or, conversely, providing for early retirement. It has repeatedly accepted that in such social policy matters the national authorities enjoy a wide margin of discretion (see also *Mangold v Helm*: C-144/04 [2005] ECR I-9981, [2006] 1 CMLR 43, [2006] IRLR 143). The CJEU has in these cases accepted that the aim of sharing employment between the generations, with its associated benefits, should, in principle, be regarded as objectively and reasonably justifying differences in treatment on grounds of age. However, the proportionality of the retirement or measure in question will be considered carefully, in particular whether it actually serves that legitimate aim, or whether the aim could be achieved in another way or without 'catching' the particular employee or employee group in issue.

In *Hörnfeldt v Posten Meddelande AB*: C-141/11 [2012] 3 CMLR 37, [2012] IRLR 785, [2012] Eq LR 892, the CJEU held that a Swedish law, under which compulsory retirement below 67 was prohibited but it was permissible above 67, was not precluded, despite not taking into account the amount of an employee's retirement pension. The CJEU reiterated the need for a balance to be struck and considered that promoting access of young people to a profession was a legitimate aim. The Court held that the measure was appropriate and necessary as it reduced obstacles for those who wished to work beyond 65, made it easier for young people to enter and/or remain in the labour market and made it possible to avoid situations in which elderly workers are terminated in humiliating circumstances. It was necessary, despite not taking into account the amount of retirement pension an individual would receive as it conferred an unconditional right to work until 67, did not provide a mandatory scheme of automatic retirement in that the contracting parties could agree to a fixed term contract beyond the age of 67 and took into account the availability (if not the amount) of a retirement pension. In *Fries v Lufthansa CityLine GmbH* Case C-190/16, [2017] IRLR 1003, the CJEU considered a provision by which those who had obtained the age of 65 years were not permitted to act as pilots of an aircraft engaged in commercial air transport. The court held that the provision had the objective of establishing a high uniform level of civil aviation safety in Europe which constituted an objective of general interest and did not go beyond what was necessary.

On references to the CJEU, the CJEU has in some cases ruled that the question of proportionality is one that must be addressed by the national court. Thus it was in the 'Heyday' challenge [2009] ICR 1080, [2009] IRLR 373, CJEU. On its return to the Administrative Court (*R (on the application of Age UK) v Secretary of State for Business, Innovation & Skills* [2010] ICR 260, [2009] IRLR 1017), Blake J held that the national default retirement age was based upon a social policy aim of certainty, clarity and maintaining confidence in the labour market and that it was proportionate for there to be such a blanket exception. The judge further held that the choice of age of 65 was within the margin of appreciation when it was adopted in 2006 but that the conclusion might have been different had there been no suggestion of an upcoming government review. Blake J also indicated that he did not see how 65 could remain as the appropriate age after that review. It was this decision that led to the removal of the *reg 30* exception to the *AR 2006* and the end of the national default retirement age.

In *Palacios* (above), however, the CJEU went so far as to find the measure in question actually justified and did not leave the matter to the national court. The significant difference between 'Heyday' and *Palacios* was that in *Palacios* the default retirement provision was contained in a collective agreement. The CJEU considered it important that it had specifically been considered and agreed by the social partners that a default retirement age (corresponding to the age at which individuals become entitled to a state pension) was appropriate and necessary in the context of the particular labour market at issue. In *Rosenbladt* (above), too, the CJEU held the compulsory retirement provision to be justified and did not leave the matter to the national court. Again, the provision in question was in a collective agreement which the CJEU considered enabled specific account to be taken of the nature of the labour market in question (cleaning in this case). The CJEU also considered it to be important that although there was a provision for automatic retirement at 65, German law also prohibited anyone over the age of 65 from being refused employment on grounds of age. This was thought important since it struck an appropriate balance between the aim of maintaining access to the labour market for younger people, whilst also permitting those who wished to work beyond 65 to do so. Similarly, in *Fuchs v Land Hessen*, Joined Cases C-159/10 and C-160/10: [2011] IRLR 1043 the CJEU found provisions of regional German law which required state prosecutors to retire at age 65 unless it was in the interests of the service for their employment to be extended by periods of up to one year, up to a maximum retirement age of 68, was justified. The factors that the CJEU held to be particularly important were: (i) that this was a profession in which the number of posts available was limited and accordingly there was a particular need to have a compulsory retirement age in order to allow the recruitment of younger workers; (ii) that the workers would not suffer financial hardship as they could continue working as independent legal advisers with no age limit, or they could draw a pension upon retirement; (iii) although budgetary considerations could not themselves provide justification, they could support the decision made about the age at which to draw the line; (iv) political considerations could also be taken into account; (v) the fact that the measure in question related only to one region of Germany was not significant; (vi) nor was the fact that there was (temporarily) a slight mismatch between the measure and the national retirement age (which had risen to 67 for workers other than civil servants). The CJEU emphasised the importance of the national authority adducing specific evidence of justification and not relying on assertions, as the CJEU considered had happened in the *Age UK* case (above).

Cases where compulsory retirement ages have been held not to be justified include:

Prigge v Deutsche Lufthansa AG: C-447/09 [2011] IRLR 1052 where the CJEU found that German legislation requiring pilots to retire at 60 was not justified in the interests of safety because, although the physical capabilities required of pilots did tend to become impaired in older age, there was no evidence that pilots ceased to possess the necessary physical capabilities at 60.

In *European Commission v Hungary*: C-286/12 [2013] CMLR 44, the CJEU held that a Hungarian law which created an abrupt change from a retirement age of 70 to one of 62 for judges, notaries and prosecutors was not justified and went beyond what was necessary. Although the aims (standardising age limits and facilitating access for young lawyers) were legitimate, the measure was not appropriate and necessary as there was no evidence that more lenient provisions could not have achieved the same ends.

Certain retirement-related measures have also been approached by the courts in the same way as retirement. See, eg *Georgiev v Tehnicheski universitet – Sofia, filial Plovdiv*: C-250/09 and C-268/09 [2011] 2 CMLR 179, [2012] All ER (EC) 840 (provision for university professors to have 12-month contracts only after 65 and to be compulsorily retired at 68 held by CJEU to be capable of justification, although it was for the national court to decide whether it was a proportionate means of pursuing the legitimate aim pursued), *Kraft Foods UK Ltd v Hastie* [2010] ICR 1355, [2011] 3 All ER 956 (provisions capping redundancy pay at the level that would have been received had employment ceased at 65 proportionate and justified) and compare *Ingeniorforeningen i Danmark v Region Syddanmark*: C-499/08 [2011] 1 CMLR 35 (measure providing severance payments for all long-serving employees but not those over 65 was disproportionate because it applied to all employees over 65 regardless of whether they were actually drawing a pension).

In *Chief Constable of West Midlands Police v Harrod* [2017] EWA Civ 191, [2017] IRLR 539, the Court of Appeal considered whether the compulsory retirement of all police officers who had become entitled to receive a pension of two thirds average pensionable pay constituted *indirect* age discrimination. It held it did not. The decision was justified as the only legal way in which force reduction could be achieved and it was not for the tribunal to consider whether the dismissals could be avoided.

For a detailed analysis of the law on objective justification outside the retirement context, see further Discrimination and Equal Opportunities II (13) at 13.9.

43.5 EARLY RETIREMENT

There is no legal impediment to employees voluntarily retiring early, subject only to the giving of any notice required under the contract of employment. Where there is a pension scheme, of which the employee is a member, the scheme may provide for the drawing of a pension on early retirement, generally with the consent of the employer. Occupational pension schemes which obey the tax rules, are precluded from paying a pension earlier than age 55 except where retirement is on grounds of ill-health. For employees over 55, early retirement may be used as an inducement to accept redundancy, and pension scheme rules typically offer one or more of the following benefits:

(a)   immediate payment of the pension that would have been payable at pensionable age, without reduction for early payment;

(b)   commutation of part of the pension to a lump sum;

(c)   conferment of additional years of service in computing the pension; and

(d)   permitting the employee to divert all or part of a severance payment into the pension scheme to purchase added years.

The position of individuals depends on the detail of usually complex scheme rules, operating within limits defined by Inland Revenue requirements. The European Court of Justice has ruled (*Beckmann v Dynamco Whicheloe Macfarlane Ltd:* C-164/00 [2002] All ER (EC) 865, [2002] IRLR 578) that benefits by way of payment of an immediate and/or augmented pension on termination of employment for redundancy are not 'old age, invalidity or survivors' benefits' within the meaning of the *Acquired Rights Directive 1977*, and accordingly the right to such benefits is preserved when an employee is transferred to a new employer as a result of a relevant transfer of the former employer's undertaking, or part thereof. The ECJ has reiterated these conclusions, in relation to voluntary early retirement, and confirmed their application to public sector pension schemes regulated by statutory provisions: *Martin v South Bank University:* C-4/01 [2004] 1 CMLR 472, [2004] IRLR 74. See also *reg 10* of the *Transfer of Undertakings (Protection of Employees) Regulations 2006* (see TRANSFER OF UNDERTAKINGS (53)). This has particular practical significance where employees transfer from public sector employers such as the NHS as a result of the contracting out of services, since the responsibility for funding often very expensive early retirement or redundancy terms will fall on the transferee employer. However, in *Procter & Gamble Co v Svenska Cellulosa Aktiebolaget SCA* [2012] EWHC 1257 (Ch), [2012] IRLR 733, it was held that benefits first triggered as early retirement benefits became "old age benefits" at normal retirement age. Accordingly, the transferee was liable to meet the cost of early retirement up to normal retirement age but not afterwards.

Where an employer offers employees the opportunity to take early retirement and receives too many applicants, it may be permissible to apply a "cheapness criteria" to select those whose applications would be successful, despite any indirect age discrimination: *HM Land Registry v Benson* [2012] IRLR 373.

Ill-health retirement is frequently provided for in pension scheme rules. There is no standard set of criteria or procedures. Rules typically require medical evidence sufficient to satisfy the employer, the trustees or both that the employee is incapacitated from either performing any work or from his usual occupation. The requirement may be that the incapacity is expected or likely to be permanent, and rules may provide for the suspension of the payment of a pension (during the period until the employee reaches pensionable age) on evidence that he or she is again capable of work. For guidance as to the interpretation and application of criteria in scheme rules determining eligibility for ill-health retirement, see *Derby Daily Telegraph Ltd v Pensions Ombudsman* [1999] IRLR 476.

The benefits provided under the rules of pension schemes vary considerably, but typically include immediate payment of an unreduced pension, sometimes with added years. The statutory pension schemes for police officers and firefighters provide for enhanced benefits, known as 'injury awards', where members retire on ill-health grounds as a result of an injury sustained in the course of duty. There are defined procedures for assessing the degree of incapacity (beyond incapacity for active police or fire service) and elaborate rights of appeal under each set of regulations.

43.5 Retirement

Despite the pension advantages of ill-health retirement, if the employee objects to retiring, and if he or she is disabled within the meaning of the *Equality Act 2010*, the possibility that enforced retirement constitutes disability discrimination needs to be considered. In *Williams v Trustees of Swansea University Pension & Assurance Scheme* [2018] UKSC 65, [2019] 1 WLR 93, [2019] IRLR 306, the Supreme Court held that ill-health retirement provisions did not discriminate on the grounds of disability when the amount paid out was dependent on a period of reduced income due to the employee's disability. There was nothing intrinsically unfavourable where the only reason that the employee received the pension at all was by reason of his disability.

See further DISCRIMINATION AND EQUAL OPPORTUNITIES II (13) at 13.9. Ill-health retirement may also constitute age discrimination, see further DISCRIMINATION AND EQUAL OPPORTUNITIES I (12) at 12.40.

In *Palmer v Royal Bank of Scotland* [2014] ICR 1288, [2014] All ER (D) 67 (Aug), an employer had permitted employees who were at risk of redundancy and over 50 to opt for early retirement. This was held not to constitute age discrimination against a 49 year old as there was no appropriate comparator.

Decisions whether to grant or refuse an ill-health pension are subject to limited control by the courts; good examples are *Harris v Shuttleworth (Lord)* [1994] ICR 991, [1994] IRLR 547, CA on the correct interpretation of the definition of incapacity and *Mihlenstedt v Barclays Bank International Ltd* [1989] IRLR 522 on the employer's duty to act in good faith in assessing medical evidence of incapacity (discussed further at **43.12** below) and the *Derby Daily Telegraph* case (above) on the duty to construe the rules in a purposive and practical way.

43.6 CHANGING THE RETIREMENT AGE

Where the contract provides for a particular retirement age, the legal principles governing changes in terms of the contract of employment apply equally to any attempt to change the retirement age. In the absence of consent by the employees, or incorporation of an agreement reached through collective bargaining, a change cannot be unilaterally imposed through the contract. The failure of an employee to object to a change notified to him, as by a new statement of particulars of terms, does not amount to acceptance of the change by silence. This is most clearly so where the change has no immediate practical effect on the employee: *Aparau v Iceland Frozen Foods plc (No 1)* [1996] IRLR 119.

This may have no practical consequences where the employer seeks to increase the retirement (as distinct from pension) age, since this would be no more than a promise to defer enforced retirement. Nor would a lowering of the age by unilateral notification, not accepted by the employee, prevent the employer from retiring an employee at the lower age by giving the contractual notice of termination (as a matter of contract). However, such a dismissal would in all probability be open to challenge as unfair and, might also amount to unlawful age discrimination (see above).

In *Air Products v Cockram* [2018] EWCA Civ 346, [2018] IRLR 755, the Court of Appeal upheld a tribunal's finding that an employer had objectively justified the less favourable treatment caused by an increase in its customary retirement age from 50 to 55.

A variation to a contractual retirement age agreed between an employee and the transferee following a TUPE transfer is enforceable by the employee against the transferee. However, the employee would also be able to hold the transferee to the pre-transfer contractual position. In effect, such an employee can choose which he prefers: *Regent Security Services Ltd v Power* [2007] EWCA Civ 1188, [2008] 2 All ER 977, [2008] IRLR 66.

A term of a contract is unenforceable against a person in so far as it constitutes, promotes, or provides for treatment of that or another person that constitutes discrimination contrary to the *Equality Act 2010*, including age discrimination (*s 142*).

Different considerations apply to changes in pensionable age under an occupational pension scheme. In relation to past service, such changes may be precluded by the rules of the scheme unless they are in all respects advantageous to the members affected. Changes designed to equalise pension ages between men and women following the ECJ's decision in *Barber v Guardian Royal Exchange Assurance Group:* C-262/88 [1991] 1 QB 344, [1990] IRLR 240 are, in addition, subject to restrictions arising from principles of EU law: *Smith v Avdel Systems Ltd:* C-408/92 [1995] All ER (EC) 132, [1994] IRLR 602; see further EQUAL PAY (23). Whilst these requirements do not prohibit a change that would have the effect, as regards future service, of 'levelling down' rights as a matter of European law, this is subject to the requirements of national law as to the validity of any change. The consent of individual employees would be required for a change in the pensionable age, even for benefits derived from future service, where that age is expressly or impliedly a term of the contract. Further, it should be noted, in *Safeway Ltd v Newton* (C-171/18) [2019] IRLR 1090, the Grand Chamber of the European Court of Justice held that EU law did not allow, in the absence of objective justification, a retrospective levelling down of a retirement age to equalise it between men and women, since the disadvantaged group were entitled to the more favourable treatment of the advantaged group while they were so advantaged.

43.7   BENEFITS AFTER RETIREMENT

Employers may provide certain benefits to employees which continue beyond retirement. Even if the benefits are expressly provided to be discretionary they will nevertheless almost certainly be 'pay' in EU law: *Garland v British Rail Engineering Ltd* [1983] 2 AC 751, ECJ (concessionary travel facilities for families of retired employees); such benefits must therefore be provided without discrimination on grounds of sex.

If a benefit is contractual it must be provided, even if it becomes unduly expensive to continue its provision: *Baynham v Philips Electronics (UK) Ltd* (1995) IDS Brief 551, [1995] OPLR 253 (private medical insurance during retirement). As there is no basis for compelling a former employee, who cannot be dismissed, to agree to abandon a continuing contractual right, the employer has no option but to 'buy out' the benefit or continue to provide it. The inclusion of such provisions in the contract of employment is therefore a matter requiring great caution.

43.8   PENSIONS

The law of pensions is outside the scope of this book. It is a large and complex area which it would not be practicable to cover in detail. Pensions law rests mainly on the principles of the law of trusts (most pension schemes are administered, and the funds held, by trustees) and increasingly detailed statutory regulation. The principal legislation governing pension schemes is the *Pension Schemes Act 1993*, a consolidating Act, together with the *Pensions Act 1995*, the *Pensions Act 2004*, the *Pensions Act 2011* and, most recently, the *Pensions Act 2014*. In addition, stakeholder pension schemes are the subject of *Part I* of the *Welfare Reform and Pensions Act 1999* and supporting Regulations: see **43.10** below for brief details.

The *Pensions Act 2004* was a major piece of legislation. Among other things, it established a new Pensions Regulator (replacing the Occupational Pensions Regulatory Authority) with a remit including the prevention of fraud and ensuring the proper funding of pension schemes as well as a Board of the Pension Protection Fund. The Board is responsible for administering a compensation scheme for employees in private sector pension schemes, who risk losing accrued pension rights if their employer becomes insolvent and the pension scheme is insufficiently funded. Other provisions include a requirement for the transferee employer following a transfer within the *Transfer of Undertakings (Protection of Employment) Regulations 2006* to provide those employees who have transferred with pension benefits for future service broadly comparable with those previously enjoyed.

Reform to the state pension was introduced in the *Pensions Act 2007* and to the private pension system in the *Pensions Act 2008*. The latter was aimed at enabling and encouraging more people to build up a private pension income to supplement the basic state pension. The *Pensions Act 2008* was followed by the *Workplace Pensions Reform Regulations 2010*. These reforms focused on the introduction of "automatic-enrolment" into workplace pensions schemes, from which an individual would need actively to opt-out, combined with a minimum employer contribution and the creation of a pension scheme, now known as the National Employment Savings Trust ("NEST") that could be used by any employer.

The *Pensions Act 2011* made a number of changes including:

(a)   increasing the state pension age to 66 between 2018 and 2020, to be applied to both men and women; and

(b)   an expansion of the requirement for automatic enrolment.

The *Pensions Act 2014* ("*2014 Act*") introduced a single-tier pension to replace the two-component State Pension with a single component flat-rate pension. This single-tier pension replaces the basic State Pension and additional State Pension with a flat-rate pension that is set above the basic level of means-tested support for people who reached State Pension Age on or after 6 April 2016. The act also provided for a new type of voluntary National Insurance contributions, Class 3A, to allow pensioners who reached State Pension Age before 6 April 2016 to top up their additional state pension. It also brought forward the increase in the State Pension age to 67 and set out a framework for a regular review of the State Pension age at least every five years. Such reviews are based around the principle that people should expect to spend a certain proportion of their adult life in retirement and are be informed by actuarial reports. The *2014 Act* also contains a number of mainly technical amendments to auto enrolment and contains powers to allow the government to introduce minimum governance and administration standards and restrict charges in workplace pensions. Finally, the *2014 Act* contains a number of other measures relating to private pensions which are outside the scope of this book.

Changes enacted in the *Taxation of Pensions Act 2014* permit much greater flexibility for pensioners. They allow, in principle, any person over the minimum pension age to access the funds in any money purchase scheme without constraint.

The *Pension Schemes Act 2015* received royal assent on 3 March 2015. It did two main things. First, it introduced a new category of pension scheme, "Defined Ambition", described further below. Second, it introduced further provisions supporting the increase in flexibility including rights to transfer pension funds between schemes.

Finally the *Pension Schemes Act 2017*, which received royal assent on 27 April 2017, introduced greater regulation for "master trusts". Master trusts operate on a large scale as a multi-employer occupational pension scheme. A number of them entered into the market after automatic enrolment. They are directed at employers who wish to have a trust based scheme but do not want to administer the fund themselves.

Areas of particular relevance to employment are dealt with below: stakeholder pensions; discrimination and pension rights and benefits; the rights of members to elect trustees under the *Pensions Act 1995* and the legal protection of employee trustees; employers' duties in respect of pension schemes; and the machinery available to resolve employees' disputes and grievances about pension rights. Brief notes about some of the principal features of pension schemes, and pension terminology are given first.

Pension schemes may be described as occupational or personal. *Personal pension schemes* are money purchase funds invested by the pension provider on behalf of the individual and used to purchase an annuity at retirement. Within statutory limits employee contributions are tax deductible. Employers may agree to make contributions, but are under no obligation to match contributions they would have made on the employee's behalf to the *occupational pension scheme*.

Occupational pension schemes may be *statutory* (the major public sector schemes covering a quarter of the employed workforce, principally the civil service and armed forces, local government and NHS workers, teachers and the police and fire service, under the *Superannuation Act 1972* and specific statutory regulations) or established by trust deed, to which the scheme rules are usually appended. They may be either *defined benefit*, also referred to as *final salary*, schemes, or *money purchase* schemes (sometimes referred to as *defined contribution* schemes). The former provide benefits based on pensionable salary and years of service, normally either 1/60 or 1/80 of pensionable salary for each year of pensionable service. A lump sum retirement benefit may be provided, in addition to pension based on 1/80 of salary, or by commuting the capital value of part of the pension in 1/60 schemes (subject to limits imposed by the Inland Revenue). All the principal statutory public sector schemes are final salary schemes. Following the *Pensions Schemes Act 2015*, there is also a third category of pension schemes, defined ambition schemes.

All major public sector schemes and most private sector schemes also provide for a (usually reduced) pension to be payable to a surviving spouse, often referred to as *survivor's benefit*. Some schemes extend the coverage of survivors' benefits to unmarried partners. In such cases, it would be unlawful to limit the benefit to partners of the opposite sex to the member concerned; but the restriction of benefits to the deceased member's spouse where the right to the benefit accrued or the benefit is payable in respect of periods of service prior to the coming into force of the *Civil Partnership Act 2004* is lawful, as is the conferring of a benefit on married persons and civil partners to the exclusion of other persons: see *Equality Act 2010, para 18* of Part 3 of Sch 9; or, prior to 1 October 2010, *reg 25* of the *2003 Regulations*. In *R (ota Cockburn) v Secretary of State for Health* [2011] EWHC 2095 (Admin), [2011] All ER (D) 18 (Aug), Supperstone J held that disregarding the period of pensionable service prior to a certain date when calculating widower's but not a widow's pension was lawful having regard to the cost of retrospective equalisation. However, in *Walker v Innospec Ltd* [2017] IRLR 928, the Supreme Court held that the provisions in the *Equality Act 2010* under which survivors' pensions for civil partners (or same sex married partners) do not have to take into account occupational pension benefits accrued before the introduction of civil partnerships was not compatible with the *Framework Directive 2000/78*. The case of *O'Brien v Ministry of Justice (No 2)* [2017] UKSC 46, [2017] 4 All ER 997, heard at the same time as *Walker*, was referred by the Supreme Court to the CJEU to consider the equivalent question with regard to part-time workers. In *R (on the application of Elmes) v Essex CC* [2018] EWHC 2055 (Admin), [2019] 1 WLR 1686, the court declared that it was unlawful to require unmarried partners to be nominated on a form as a condition of eligibility for receipt of survivor's benefits. In *Carter v Chief Constable of Essex* [2020] EWHC 77 (QB), the court confirmed that there was no discrimination in not paying a former police officer's second wife a survivor's pension when he was not married to her, but to his deceased first wife, throughout his police service.

Money purchase schemes (also referred to as *defined contribution* schemes) have fixed rates of contribution, and benefits are purchased according to market conditions from the investment yield of the contributions. Following *Bridge Trustees Ltd v Yates* [2011] UKSC 42, [2011] 1 WLR 1912, [2011] ICR 1069, [2012] 1 All ER 659, (in which the Supreme Court held that an equilibrium of assets and liabilities was not a requirement of a money purchase scheme), the government introduced a new clearer definition of a money purchase scheme (see *ss 181* and *181A* and *181B* of the *Pension Schemes Act 1993* as amended/inserted).

Defined benefit schemes are funded by employer and employee contributions. Employees contribute a fixed percentage of salary and other pensionable earnings. Some schemes are non–contributory. The employer contributes the balance required to fund the scheme sufficiently, in accordance with an actuarial review of the liabilities of the scheme conducted at regular intervals. If the scheme is in surplus, the employer's contributions may be temporarily suspended (a 'pensions holiday'). There are complex rules, largely outside the scope of this book, as to the permissible uses of pension fund surpluses; see **43.16** for the most important cases on this.

Defined ambition schemes are a more recent introduction in this country. In this new type of scheme, risks are shared between the employee and the employer, an insurance provider or the scheme itself. The aim is to provide greater certainty for members about the final value of their pension benefits than a defined contribution pension and to provide more cost predictability for employers than a defined benefit pension.

Pensionable salary is the reference point for the calculation both of benefits under a defined benefit scheme and employee contributions. What earnings fall to be treated as pensionable is primarily a matter for the rules of the particular scheme; normally this will cover basic salary, but the position may be more complex where total pay is made up of a number of additional components such as shift allowances, production bonuses and other allowances. In *Newham London Borough Council v Skingle* [2003] EWCA Civ 280, [2003] 2 All ER 761, [2003] IRLR 359, the Court of Appeal held that pensionable salary for the purpose of the *Local Government Pension Scheme Regulations 1997* included overtime payments, but only where, as in that case, the overtime was in effect obligatory on the employee, a school caretaker, who had been required to perform duties out of normal working hours by the nature of his job.

Schemes generally provide for employees to purchase additional years of pensionable service, up to the scheme maximum, by making *additional voluntary contributions* ('AVCs'). (These are distinct from *free-standing additional voluntary contributions* ('FSAVCs') which are either single payment or periodic contribution personal pension schemes marketed by pension companies and purchased direct by employees, using the balance of tax relief available to the employee and not used up by contributions to the employer's occupational scheme.)

Pension schemes may provide additional benefits, including (as well as survivors' benefits as described above) pensions for surviving children or other dependants. Death in service benefit, in effect life insurance, of up to a maximum of four times pensionable salary, is commonly provided. The availability of these benefits, and of increases in benefits provided, is a matter primarily for the rules of the particular scheme, but increasingly the statutory framework of approved pension schemes lays down not only maximum benefits permitted within the framework of a favourable tax regime, but minimum standards that must be met.

Contributions to personal pension schemes attract tax relief up to limits. The annual allowance is 100% of earnings capped at £40,000, subject to a lifetime limit of £1,030,000 (since April 2018).

The value of pension funds is necessarily dependent on the underlying value of investments in which the funds are held, and the amount of pension that can be bought from a fund of a given value depends on current annuity rates, which are lower for women than for men owing to differences in life expectancy. In a case relating to the *Goods and Services Directive*, the ECJ held, in *Association belge des Consommateurs Test-Achats ASBL v Conseil des ministres*: C-236/09 [2011] NLJR 363, [2011] Pens LR 145, [2012] All ER (EC) 441, that the use of gender based insurance premiums was contrary to the principle of equal treatment. In its decision, the ECJ did not refer to the *Equal Treatment Directive* (which prohibits occupational pension schemes from discriminating on the grounds of sex) or to its own previous case law such as *Coloroll Pension Trustees Ltd v Russell*: C-200/91 [1995] All ER (EC) 23, [1994] IRLR 586, in which it held that the use of gender based actuarial factors does not contravene *art 157* of the *Treaty on the Functioning of the EU* (formerly *art 141* and, prior to that, *art 119* of the *Treaty of Rome*). It is difficult to see why the use of gender-based actuarial factors would be contrary to the principle of equal treatment in relation to insurance premiums but not in relation to pensions.

Sharp falls in the values of equities, following a steady decline in the rate of annuities which can be purchased on the realisation of pension fund investments, led many major employer to conclude that the provision of defined benefit pension schemes had become too expensive. Accordingly employers, in significant numbers, adopted policies of closing their defined benefit schemes to new entrants, offering instead to contribute to new defined contribution schemes. Less commonly but more controversially, some employers sought to close their defined benefit schemes in relation to future service of current members. The legality of such a step may be open to challenge, but whether it is challengeable in any particular case will depend on the precise terms of the employees' contracts, and of the pension scheme rules. A further distinction is that the rights earned by past service are likely to be protected by the rules of the Scheme from any retrospective adverse change, whereas rights to be accrued by future service are likely only to be protected (if at all) as a matter of contract. There is a general consensus that the benefits available under a defined benefit scheme are of greater value to employees than the alternative of money purchase scheme membership.

In *R (ota Staff Side of the Police Negotiating Board) v Secretary of State for Work and Pensions* [2011] EWHC 3175 (Admin), [2012] 3 All ER 301, a judicial review of the Government's decision to alter the basis upon which public service pensions were adjusted to take account of inflation was unsuccessful. This change was likely to reduce the value of benefits to pension scheme members over time. In *R (ota Public and Commercial Services Union) v Minister for the Civil Service* [2011] EWHC 2041 (Admin), [2011] IRLR 903, McCombe J held that the rights of civil servants under the Civil Service Compensation Scheme which included redundancy and early retirement benefits, constituted possessions within the meaning of *Article 1* of the *First Protocol of the European Convention on Human Rights 1950*. However, the introduction of a new scheme that reduced those benefits was a lawful proportionate interference with those rights.

A different but related matter of concern has arisen in a number of cases where a pension scheme has been wound up following the insolvency of the employer. The rules of each scheme determine the order in which claims on the scheme must be met in such circumstances; typically these require that the claims of those already in receipt of a pension must be met first. If the scheme is in deficit (which is possible up to a permitted margin, and more likely at a time of declining share prices) this may leave a serious shortfall for employees who were active (ie contributing) members of the scheme at the date of its closure, whose pensions may be dramatically reduced as a result. The *Pensions Act 2004* addressed this problem in two ways, by changing the priorities required to be followed in distributing the scheme assets, and by creating a compensation scheme for employees who lose accrued pension rights.

The *members* of a pension scheme are those employees who, being eligible, have elected to join the scheme, retired employees in receipt of a pension, and those former employees who have retained the right to a deferred pension payable at pensionable age. Employees who leave the service of the employer may withdraw their contributions, but only if pensionable service is under two years, or transfer the value to another employer's scheme or a personal pension. In either case the employee ceases to be a member of the first scheme. *Transfer values* are calculated by reference to actuarial valuations, but actual criteria depend on the rules of each scheme. A lump-sum payment is made to the new scheme which gives credit for years of service depending on its own advisers' computations of the cost of purchasing service. *Transfer values* may not therefore fully reflect accrued service. Further, the actuarial factors used include mortality tables reflecting the different life expectancy of, and therefore different cost of providing pensions for, each sex, so that transfer values may differ according to sex. The ECJ has held that this does not contravene *art 157* (formerly *art 141* and before that *art 119*) of the *Treaty of Rome* (*Coloroll Pension Trustees Ltd v Russell*: C-200/91 [1995] All ER (EC) 23, [1994] IRLR 586). This exception is preserved by the UK legislation giving effect to EU law (see **23.19** EQUAL PAY for details) (but see above concerning the effect of the *Test-Achats* case). The same consequences, and legal exceptions, apply to the value attributed, in terms of additional years of service, to AVCs.

The *State Earnings Related Pension Scheme* ('SERPS'), established in 1975, was designed as a fallback for employees who do not benefit from occupational pensions. Pension schemes which met prescribed minimum standards could apply to be *contracted out* of SERPS. *Contracting out* was the norm for larger schemes, not least because both employer and employee paid lower rates of National Insurance if the employee was in a contracted-out scheme. In place of the SERPS pension the scheme was required to assure a *Guaranteed Minimum Pension*, protected by more stringent rules as to indexation and preservation where benefits are transferred or commuted. SERPS was replaced in April 2002, but for future earnings only, by the *State Second Pension*. Because the change is not retrospective, rights under SERPS will exist, in preserved form, for very many years. The State Second Pension accrues at different rates on banded earnings between the National Insurance lower earnings limit and the National Insurance upper earnings limit. Additionally, there are some credits for earnings for people with a long-term illness or disability.

The *Pensions Act 2007* provided for the abolition of contracting out on a money-purchase basis. Since 6 April 2012, it is no longer possible to contract out of the State Second Pension through a money-purchase scheme or a personal pension or stakeholder pension scheme. Those who already contract out will be able to continue to make their own contributions and benefit from any employer contributions but will not be able to benefit from any rebate of National Insurance contributions. It is, however, possible to contract out in a final salary or career average scheme.

The *Pensions Act 2014* has replaced the two-component state pension with a single component flat-rate pension that will be set above the basic level of means-tested report for those who reach State Pension age on or after 6 April 2016.

43.9 Stakeholder pensions

The legislation for this form of pension is *Part I* of the *Welfare Reform and Pensions Act 1999* (which is largely enabling) and the *Stakeholder Pensions Scheme Regulations 2000 (SI 2000/1403)* as amended. The intention behind these pensions was to encourage individuals, particularly those with modest earnings, and who are not members of occupational pension schemes, to make provision for their retirement. Stakeholder pensions are private sector schemes but subject to registration, minimum standards of performance and approved schemes of governance. Schemes are required to be flexible, so that contributions can be suspended or varied, and any individual who is not contributing to a contracted out occupational pension scheme, including minors and those not in employment, can contribute up to a fixed amount per year. Contributions are made net of standard rate income tax, which is made up by the State, even if the individual is not a taxpayer. If earnings are sufficient, contributions in excess of the fixed amount a year gross can be made, with corresponding tax relief.

In the past, employers could, but could not be obliged to, contribute to individual employees' pensions. However, employers are now required to enrol eligible workers into a qualifying workplace pension arrangement, see further below for details.

43.10 Automatic enrolment under the Pensions Act 2008

The *Pensions Act 2008* put into law a number of measures aimed at encouraging greater private pension saving.

The regime requires employers to enrol "eligible jobholders" automatically into an "automatic enrolment scheme" with effect from the date upon which such jobholders become eligible. Once an "eligible jobholder" is enrolled, the employer is under an obligation either to make minimum contributions (if it is a defined contribution scheme) or to offer a minimum level of benefits (if it is a defined benefit scheme). The minimum required contribution is 3% for employers and 5% for employees. Employers are also under an obligation to provide certain information to eligible jobholders including information about automatic enrolment, what it means and their right to opt out.

The key duties to be imposed are contained in *sections 2* to *8* of the *Pensions Act 2008*, as amended ("*2008 Act*"). They were imposed month by month over a multiple year "staging period" depending on the size of the employer. Employers with the most employees were required to comply with the duties first. The relevant date in relation to each employer is called the "staging date".

The first task is to identify who is an "eligible jobholder". A "jobholder" is defined in *section 1* of the *2008 Act* as a worker:

(a)   who is working or ordinarily works in Great Britain under the worker's contract;

(b)   who is aged at least 16 and under 75; and

(c)   to whom "qualifying earnings" are payable in the relevant pay reference period.

"Worker" is defined in *s 88(3)* as an individual who has entered into or works under a contract of employment or any other contract by which the individual undertakes to do work or perform services personally for another party to the contract. "Contract of employment" is defined as a contract of service or apprenticeship, whether express or implied and (if it is express) whether oral or in writing (*s 88(1)*). These definitions are very similar to those set out in *s 230* of the *Employment Rights Act* (see EMPLOYEE, SELF-EMPLOYED OR WORKER? **(16)**). However, contracts of a client or customer of a profession or business undertaking are excluded (*s 88(4)*).

In relation to agency workers, in the absence of a workers' contract between the worker and either the agent or the principal, then the regime applies as if there was a workers' contract and whichever of the agent or the principal is responsible for paying the agency worker in respect of the work (or which of them does actually pay (*s 89*). Further, that person is treated as the employer for the purposes of automatic enrolment.

"Qualifying earnings" are defined in *s 13(1)* as the part, if any, of the gross earnings payable to that person in that period that is within a range which has been amended by order annually. For the period from 6 April 2019, "qualifying earnings" were more than £6,136 but not more than £50,000. For period from 6 April 2020, they are between £6,240 and £50,000.

"Earnings" is defined to mean:

(a)   salary, wages, commission, bonuses and overtime;

(b)   statutory sick pay;

(c)   statutory maternity pay;

(d)   statutory paternity pay;

(e)   statutory adoption pay;

(f)   statutory shared parental pay;

(g)   statutory parental bereavement pay; and

(h)   sums prescribed for the purposes of the section.

(*2008 Act, s 13*, as amended)

Where the pay reference period is less than 12 months, the figures are adjusted proportionately (*s 13(2)*).

Workers who receive gross earnings of more than the maximum figure will still qualify as jobholders. However, contributions will only be payable on the qualifying earnings.

A "jobholder" is "eligible" for the purposes of automatic enrolment:

(a)   who is aged at least 22,

(b)   who has not reached pensionable age, and

(c)   to whom earnings of more than £10,000 are payable by the employer in the relevant pay reference period.

(*2008 Act, s 3*, as amended)

Further guidance has been published by the Pensions Regulator - see the Pensions Regulator's Guidance Note No. 1 "Employer duties and defining the workforce" as to who will count as a worker. The guidance states, for example, that office-holders such as non-executive directors, company secretaries, board members and trustees are not workers but that casual or zero hours workers are likely to be if the other conditions are satisfied.

Section 3 of the *Pensions Act* is the provision imposing the automatic enrolment duty. Employers must enrol eligible jobholders in an automatic enrolment scheme with effect from the "automatic enrolment date" (*s 3(2)*), all of which have now passed. New employers are required to comply immediately. There are, however, provisions for deferral for up to three months upon written notice in accordance with detailed rules set out in *section 4*.

In order to be a "qualifying automatic enrolment scheme", a pension scheme must be an "automatic enrolment scheme" which "qualifies" by meeting certain quality requirements. To be an "automatic enrolment scheme":

•   it must **not** prevent the employer from making the requirements for a jobholder automatically to become an active member of the scheme; or

•   require the jobholder to express a choice in relation to any matter or to provide any information, in order to remain an active member.

(*section 17*)

In order to be a "qualifying scheme" it must:

•   be an occupational pension scheme or a personal pension scheme;

•   be registered under *Chapter 2* of *Part 4* of the *Finance Act 2004* (ie be registered for tax purposes); and

•   satisfy the minimum "quality requirement" in relation to a particular jobholder whilst that jobholder is an active member.

(*section 16*)

The "quality requirement" is defined differently for different pension scheme types (money purchase, defined contribution etc) and for UK and non-UK schemes. The detailed provisions are set out in *sections 20 to 28* of the *2008 Act* with further guidance in the Pensions Regulator's detailed guidance Note No. 4 "Pension Schemes".

If an employer does not wish to use an existing pension scheme or set up a new pension scheme, then it may use the National Employment Savings Trust ("NEST"). NEST is a central pension scheme established by a corporation set up by the Government. NEST is an occupational direct contribution scheme. Employers who use it must meet the minimum contribution requirements for such schemes to satisfy the minimum "quality requirement". For more information, see the NEST website at www.nestpensions.org.uk.

In addition to the requirement of automatic enrolment, employers are also obliged not to take any action by which a jobholder would cease to be an active member of a qualifying scheme or by which the scheme would cease to be a qualifying scheme (*section 2(1)*, *2008 Act*). Employers are not in breach of the section if the jobholder remains an active member of another qualifying scheme or if he or she requests to leave the scheme (*section 2(2)*). Nor are they in breach if an eligible jobholder ceases to be a member of a scheme for a prescribed period before joining another scheme.

Employers are also required automatically to re-enrol jobholders who were but are no longer members of the scheme for particular reasons. For details, see *section 5* of the *2008 Act* and *Parts 2* and *3* of the *Occupational and Personal Pension Schemes (Automatic Enrolment) Regulations 2010, SI 2010/772* ("*2010 Regulations*").

Finally, the Secretary of State may make provisions to require employers to provide employees with prescribed information in relation to their rights under *sections 2 to 8* of the *2008 Act* (see *section 10* of the *2008 Act*). The details are clearly set out in the Pension Regulator's detailed guidance Note No. 10 "Information to workers: the new duties".

Opting out

Eligible jobholders are entitled to opt out of the scheme under *section 8* of the *2008 Act*. However, this is only possible during an "opt-out" period. This is a one month period following the later of the date on which the jobholder first became an active member of the pension scheme and the date upon which he or she was provided with written enrolment information (see *regulation 9* of the *2010 Regulations*). The notice is only valid if it also includes the following:

(a)   A statement in the terms set out in schedule 1 to the Regulations as follows:

"WHAT YOU NEED TO KNOW

Your employer cannot ask you or force you to opt out.

If you are asked or forced to opt out you can tell the Pensions Regulator – see www.thepensionsregulator.gov.uk/

If you change your mind you may be able to opt back in – write to your employer if you want to do this.

If you stay opted out your employer will normally put you back into pension saving in around 3 years.

If you change job your new employer will normally put you back into pension saving straight away.

If you have another job your other employer might also put you into pension saving, now or in the future. This notice only opts you out of pension saving with the employer you name above. A separate notice must be filled out and given to any other employer you work for if you wish to opt out of that pension saving as well."

(b)   statements from the jobholder to the effect that the jobholder wishes to opt out of pension saving and understands that, in so doing, he or she will lose the right to pension contributions from the employer and may have a lower income upon retirement;

(c)   the jobholder's name;

(d)   the jobholder's national insurance number or date of birth;

(e)   a signature by the jobholder or, if electronic, a statement confirming that the jobholder personally submitted the notice; and

(f)   the date.

(*reg 9(6)* of the *2010 Regulations*)

Jobholders who have opted out can choose to opt back in but they may only do so once in the 12 month period from when they first choose to opt back in (*2008 Act, section 7*).

There are also detailed obligations to keep records.

Enforcement

Employers who wilfully fail to comply with the automatic enrolment duty, the automatic re-enrolment duty or the duty to allow jobholders to opt in commit a criminal offence. The officers of a body corporate which commits such an offence may be liable to a fine or prison term of up to two years if the offence has been committed with the consent or connivance of an officer or is attributable to any neglect on the part of the officer (see *sections 45* to *47* of the *2008 Act*).

Employers are prohibited from making any statement or asking any question directly or by an agent for the purposes of recruitment which indicates (expressly or impliedly) that an application for employment may be determined by reference to whether or not an applicant might opt out of automatic enrolment (*s 50(1)*, *2008 Act*).

Pursuant to *section 55*, employees have a right not to be subjected to any detriment by an act, or a deliberate failure to act, by the worker's employer, done on the ground that:

(a)   any action was taken, or was proposed to be taken, with a view to enforcing in favour of a worker one of the specified employers' duties,

(b)   the employer was prosecuted under *s 45* as a result of action taken for the purpose of enforcing in favour of the worker one of the specified employers' duties, or

(c)   any of the specified employers' duties apply or will or might apply to the worker.

It is immaterial whether or not the requirement does apply or whether or not it has in fact been contravened but any claim that the requirement applies or has been contravened must be made in good faith (*s 55(2)*).

A dismissal cannot be a detriment within the meaning of *s 55*. However, a new *section 104D* has been inserted into the *Employment Rights Act 1996* ("*ERA*") (by *s 57* of the *2008 Act*) which provides that an employee is unfairly dismissed if the reason or principal reason for the dismissal is that:

(a)   any action was taken, or was proposed to be taken, with a view to enforcing in favour of a worker one of the specified employers' duties,

(b)   the employer was prosecuted under s 45 as a result of action taken for the purpose of enforcing in favour of the worker one of the specified employers' duties, or

(c)   any of the specified employers' duties apply or will or might apply to the worker.

Again, it is immaterial whether or not the requirement does apply or whether or not it has in fact been contravened but any claim that the requirement applies or has been contravened must be made in good faith (*s 104D(2)*, *ERA*).

A worker may present a complaint to an employment tribunal that he or she has been subjected to a detriment in contravention of *section 55*. Where the complaint is in relation to the termination of a contract which is not a contract of employment, the limits on compensation which apply to unfair dismissal compensation apply (see *ss 56(3)* and *(4)*).

There are restrictions on agreements to limit the operation of the scheme (*section 58, 2008 Act*) which are similar to those familiar from the *Equality Act 2010*.

43.11 Discrimination and occupational pension schemes

The *Equality Act 2010* ("*EA 2010*") contains provisions which prohibit discrimination in relation to pensions. Occupational pension schemes are deemed to include a "non-discrimination rule" (*s 61(1)*). A "non-discrimination rule" is a provision by virtue of which a responsible person (A) must not discriminate against another person (B) in carrying out any of A's functions in relation to the scheme, and must not, in relation to the scheme, harass or victimise B (*s 61(2)*).

The provisions of an occupational pension scheme have effect subject to the non-discrimination rule. A "responsible person" is a trustee or manager of the scheme, an employer whose employers are, or may be, members of the scheme and a person responsible for appointing a person to an office, where the office holder is or may be a member of the scheme (*s 61(4)*).

A discriminates against B for the purposes of *EA 2010* if A treats B less favourably than A treats or would treat others "because of a protected characteristic" (*s 13*). Disability, sex, and age are among the protected characteristics. A discriminates against B indirectly by applying a provision, criterion or practice which A applies or would apply to others with whom B does not share the characteristic, but puts those sharing the characteristic at a particular disadvantage, puts B to that disadvantage and which A cannot show to be a proportionate means of achieving a legitimate aim (*s 19*). A also discriminates against a disabled person, B, if A treats B unfavourably because of something arising in consequence of B's disability, and A cannot show that the treatment is a proportional means of achieving a legitimate aim (*s 15*). Harassment and victimisation are defined in *ss 26* and *27* respectively.

A duty to make reasonable adjustments also applies to a responsible person (*s 20*).

Section 62 provides trustees and managers of occupational pension schemes the power, by resolution, to alter their scheme's rules to conform to the non-discrimination rule.

Where there is a breach of a non-discrimination rule, it is possible to bring proceedings under *Part 9* of *EA 2010* in the employment tribunal. (This does not prevent the investigation or determination of any matter by the Pensions Ombudsman.) The tribunal, if it finds a complaint well-founded, may make an order declaring that the complainant has a right to be admitted to the scheme or to membership of the scheme without discrimination (*EA 2010, s 126(2)*). Such an order may have effect in relation to a period before the order was made (*s 126(4)*). In such cases, the tribunal may not make an order for compensation for age discrimination except for injury to feelings or where a respondent fails to comply with a recommendation (*s 126(3)*).

The particular position in relation to each of sex and age discrimination is addressed further below.

43.12 *Sex discrimination, maternity leave and pension benefits*

Pursuant to section 75 of *EA 2010*, a 'maternity equality rule' is deemed to be included in occupational pension schemes. This is the rule that any term of the scheme, or any discretion capable of being exercised under it, that purports to treat a woman differently in respect of time when she is on maternity leave compared to time when she is not, is modified so that both period fall to be treated in the same way (*s 75(3)* and *(4)*). Any term or discretion relating to membership of the scheme, accrual of rights or determination of benefits payable under the scheme falls within the scope of the rule.

The effect of this rule is that any period when a woman is on paid maternity leave must be treated as if she was not on leave. It must be treated as if it were a period during which she was attending work for the purposes of the occupational pension scheme.

The maternity equality rule does not require the woman's contributions to the scheme while she is on maternity leave to be determined other than by reference to the amount she is actually paid (ie statutory or contractual maternity pay). It is not clear from the statue whether or not the employer is required to pick up the shortfall. The Explanatory Notes to *EA 2010* state that 'a woman who is paid while on maternity leave will entitled to accrue rights in a scheme as though she were paid her usual salary but she will only be required to make contributions based on her actual pay'. The Guidance from the 'Pensions Trust" in its 'Pensions Bulletin – Fact Sheet 3' states that 'the employer is required to pay the shortfall in the member's contributions to ensure that the scheme receives the right amount of funding for the benefits being accrued

Section 75 of *EA 2010* applies to unpaid ordinary maternity leave as well as paid ordinary maternity leave. This means that employers should continue making contributions to any occupational pension scheme during unpaid ordinary maternity leave as if the employee was working normally and earning her normal remuneration.

This accords with the ECJ's ruling in *Boyle v Equal Opportunities Commission*: C-411/96 [1999] ICR 360, [1998] IRLR 717 that it is a breach of the *Pregnant Workers Directive (92/85)* to exclude from pensionable service any part of the core 14 weeks' maternity leave conferred by the *Directive*, whether it is paid or unpaid.

Section 75 of *EA 2010* provides that the maternity equality rule does not apply to the accrual of rights under an occupational pension scheme in respect of unpaid period of additional maternity leave (*s 75(9)(a)*). It is unclear whether or not this distinction in treatment between paid and unpaid additional maternity leave is sustainable in the light of the ECJ's decisions in *Boyle* and in *Lord Brandenburg v Sass* [2005] IRLR 147, ECJ. In *Sass*, the ECJ held that the fact that domestic law grants women maternity leave of more than 14 weeks does not preclude that leave from being considered to be maternity leave within the meaning of the Pregnant Workers Directive. That would suggest that there is no basis for differentiating the first 14 weeks from the remainder of the maternity leave period such that the Boyle ruling would apply in respect of the entirety of the period. The High Court in *R (Equal Opportunities Commission) v Secretary of State for Trade and Industry* [2007] ICR 1234, [2007] IRLR 327 held that Sass meant that there is no justification for giving employees on additional maternity leave any less protection from sex discrimination than those on ordinary maternity leave. However, the effect of the ECJ's decision in *Gillespie v Northern Health and Social Services Board*: C-342/93 [1996] All ER (EC) 284, [1996] IRLR 214 appears to be that exclusion of unpaid leave from service does not contravene either *art 157* or the *EU Equal Pay* or *Equal Treatment Directives*.

Section 75 of *EA 2010* provides that a woman's paid maternity leave (whether ordinary or additional) should be treated as if it were a period during which she was working normally for the purposes of occupational pension schemes. In other words, maternity leave is included within the period of pensionable service. The Maternity and Parental Leave Regulations make specific provision for an employee's seniority, pension rights and similar rights to be preserved during ordinary and additional maternity leave (*reg 18* and *18A(1)(a)*). However, since this is subject to what is now *s 75(7)* to *(9)* of *EA 2010*, a period of unpaid ordinary maternity leave does count as pensionable service but a period of unpaid additional maternity leave does not. In the case of unpaid additional maternity leave, even though the period is not counted as pensionable service, continuity is preserved. The employee is not treated as having left and rejoined the scheme.

Similar but not identical provisions with respect to paid paternity, adoption and shared parental leave are set out in *paras 5A, 5B* and *5C* of *Sch 5* to the *Social Security Act 1989* as inserted and amended.

The ECJ has also ruled that a reduction in the pension of civil servants who have worked part time contravened *art 157* since it affected a considerably higher proportion of women than men, if the reduction in the pension was greater than the proportion of the reduction of working hours: *Schönheit (Hilde) v Stadt Frankfurt am Main*: C-4/02 and C-5/02 [2003] ECR I-12575, [2004] IRLR 983.

However, where it is established that the denial of access to an employer's pension scheme indirectly discriminated against part-time workers on the grounds of sex, the part-time employees are not entitled to a declaration of entitlement if they would have opted out of the scheme even if they had been eligible to join: *Copple v Littlewoods Plc* [2011] EWCA Civ 1281, [2012] ICR 354, [2012] IRLR 121. In *Parker v MDU*, UKEAT/0113/17, the EAT upheld a tribunal's finding that a pension scheme did not discriminate against those with a mixture of full and part time service.

43.13 *Age discrimination and pension benefits*

EA 2010 does not itself contain exemptions specifically for age. However, there is a power for a Minister of the Crown to make exceptions in relation to rules, practices, actions or decisions relating to age. The relevant Order is the *Equality Act (Age Exceptions for Pension Schemes) Order 2010 (SI 2010/2133)*. That Order provides that it is not a breach of the non-discrimination rule:

(a)   for the employer, or trustees or managers of a scheme to maintain or use in relation to the scheme the rules, practices, actions or decisions:

        (i)   which are set out in *Schedule 1* to the *Order* (see the *Order* itself for the detail); or

        (ii)   as they relate to rights accrued or benefits payable in respect of periods of pensionable service prior to 1 December 2006;

(b)   for the employer to maintain or use practices, actions or decisions set out in *Schedule 2* to the *Order* in relation to the payment of contributions (see the *Order* itself for the detail);

(c)   for the trustees or managers to follow certain rules, practices, actions or decisions in relation to length of service (see *art 6*, as amended for the detail).

In *Lord Chancellor and Secretary of State for Justice v McCloud* [2018] EWCA Civ 2844, [2019] IRLR 477, [2019] ICR 1489, the CA held that transitional provisions which were part of the government reform of public sector pensions were indirectly discriminatory towards younger judges and firefighters on the grounds of age. The government's assertion that it "felt right" to protect those near to retirement could not justify the discriminatory effect, particularly since those near to retirement were in fact the least affected. In *Sargeant v London Fire and Emergency Planning Authority* [2018] 3 All ER 245, [2018] IRLR 302, the EAT held that a tribunal had failed properly to consider whether the government had justified transitional provisions protecting shortly retiring firefighters from the effect of pension reform. While the CJEU allows a margin of discretion, the tribunal was nevertheless required to scrutinise the means adopted to see whether they met legitimate aims. *Sargeant* is currently under appeal to the Court of Appeal.

43.14 *Part time workers*

Pursuant to the *Part-Time Workers (Prevention of Less Favourable Treatment) Regulations 2001, SI 2001/1107*, , a part-time worker has the right not to be treated less favourably than the employer treats a comparable full-time worker as regards contractual terms or being subjected to any other detriment, unless such treatment is justified on objective grounds. That protection extends to detriment by employers concerning pensions. In *O'Brien v Ministry of Justice (No. 2)* C-432/17 [2019] IRLR 185, [2018] All ER (D) 38 (Nov), the Court of Justice of the European Union held that a part-time judge's pension should be calculated taking into account the entirety of his service and not just that after the deadline for transposing the relevant EU Directive into UK law.

43.15   Employee pension trustees

Most pension schemes provide for the appointment by the employer of the trustees of the scheme. Many schemes provide for the appointment of a trustee company as sole trustee; its directors are in such cases usually nominated by the employer. Despite the stringent legal obligations of trustees to the members of the scheme, concern that in practice trustees are often vulnerable to pressure from the employer to take decisions in the employer's interest led to a significant change in the law.

Sections 241–242 of the *Pensions Act 2004* require at least one third of the trustees of a pension scheme established under a trust to be member-nominated, and the same minimum proportion of member-nominated directors where a trust company is the sole trustee. Further, the Secretary of State now has the power (by order) to increase the proportion to a half.

The *Occupational Pension Schemes (Member-nominated Trustees and Directors) Regulations 2006 (SI 2006/714)* set out detailed exceptions to the requirement for member-nominated trustees and member-nominated directors of corporate trustees for certain schemes, including small schemes and those that have few members.

The *Pensions Act 2004* also contains provisions requiring all individual trustees and corporate trustees to have knowledge and understanding of certain specified documents and legal principles.

Member-nominated trustees need not all be employees, but in practice most will be. Those who are employees have the right to be permitted to take reasonable time off for training in their duties and for the performance of those duties, and to be paid for such time off (*ERA 1996, ss 58–59*, consolidating provisions introduced by the *Pensions Act 1995*). They may bring a claim to the employment tribunal if the employer does not permit them to take the time off or pay them for it: *s 60, ERA 1996*. There is no equivalent right for candidates for election. Employee trustees are also protected from suffering detriment short of dismissal by reason of their performance or proposed performance of their functions as such (*ERA 1996, s 46*) and from dismissal for that reason (*ERA 1996, s 102*). The ambit of these provisions is similar to, but not identical to, the statutory rights and protection given to officials of an independent trade union and to statutory safety representatives and representatives of employee safety; see **50.2** and **50.9 TIME OFF WORK**.

Member-nominated trustees have the same duties in law to the beneficiaries of the trust funds as other trustees. Where (as will often be the case in practice) the nominated trustees have been put forward as candidates by trade unions there is a potential for conflict between their obligations as trustees and advocacy of union policy on such matters as ethical investment of funds or non-investment in competitor industries: see for a good practical example *Cowan v Scargill* [1985] Ch 270, [1984] IRLR 260 (resolving the conflict in favour of the trustee obligations).

43.16   Employers' duties in respect of pension schemes

The obligations of pension trustees in relation to the management of funds, the alteration of rules and decisions as to individual cases are outside the scope of this book. A helpful judicial discussion of the position is to be found in *Stannard v Fisons Pension Trust Ltd* [1992] IRLR 27 (and see *Hillsdown Holdings plc v Pensions Ombudsman* [1997] 1 All ER 862, where the employer was ordered to return to the pension fund a surplus improperly paid out by the trustees). Further, it was held in *Power v Trustees of the Open Text (UK) Ltd Group Life Assurance Scheme* [2009] EWHC 3064 (Ch), [2010] SWTI 567, [2009] All ER (D) 236 (Dec) that the obligation of pension trustees does not extend to proposing benefit improvements.

There have also been a number of important decisions dealing with the rights and obligations of employers as opposed to trustees.

In *Mihlenstedt v Barclays Bank International Ltd* [1989] IRLR 522, the Court of Appeal held that, where a contract of employment provides for membership of a pension scheme, there is an implied obligation upon the employer to discharge his functions under the scheme in good faith and, so far as lies within his power, to procure the scheme's benefits for the employee. However, as emphasised in *Prudential Staff Pensions Ltd v The Prudential Staff Assurance Co* [2011] EWHC 960 (Ch), [2011] All ER (D) 142 (Apr), this implied duty does not go so far as to require an employer to arrive at a decision which is substantially fair or reasonable, see discussion below.

In *Mettoy Pension Trustees Ltd v Evans* [1991] 2 All ER 513, (a case considered without adverse comment by the Supreme Court in *Pitt v Holt* [2013] 2 AC 108) it was held that, where an employer was given a discretion under the rules of the scheme as to how certain surplus funds were to be applied, that was to be treated as a fiduciary power: the employer was under a duty to the objects of the power (the beneficiaries under the scheme) to consider whether and how to exercise it, and (presumably) to do so fairly and in good faith. Similarly, it was held in *Imperial Group Pension Trust Ltd v Imperial Tobacco Ltd* [1991] 2 All ER 597, [1991] IRLR 66 that an employer's power under the rules of the scheme to give or withhold consent to an amendment of the rules had to be exercised in good faith, and the employer could only have regard to his own financial interests to the extent that to do so was consistent with that obligation of good faith. Thus the employer's rights had to be exercised with a view to the efficient running of the scheme, and not for the collateral purpose of forcing its members to give up their accrued rights. The Vice-Chancellor based this conclusion upon the employer's implied obligation to maintain the trust and confidence of its employees (see **8.15** CONTRACT OF EMPLOYMENT). However, in *British Coal Corpn v British Coal Staff Superannuation Scheme Trustees Ltd* [1995] 1 All ER 912, Vinelott J held that whilst the duty to act in good faith in relation to amendments was related to the duty applicable in cases of distribution of a surplus, it was not a fiduciary duty in the full sense. He found that it could not be said that *any* exercise of the relevant power of amendment had to be invalid if and insofar as the amendment might benefit the employer directly or indirectly. Further, in *Prudential Staff Pension Scheme, Re* (above), Newey J reiterated that the obligation of good faith was not to be taken as requiring an employer to arrive at a decision which was "fair" when exercising a power given to him in apparently unfettered terms by the scheme rules. In deciding to award pension increases on a less generous basis than previously, the employer was entitled to have regard to his own interests. In *IBM United Kingdom Pensions Trust Ltd v IBM United Kingdom Holdings Ltd* [2012] EWHC 3540 (Ch), [2013] Pens. L.R. 33, [2012] All ER (D) 118 (Dec), it was held that the scope of the duties set out in *Imperial* was controversial. Four principles could be confidently identified: (a) discretion had to be exercised in favour of consent to a change in rules if a refusal of consent would be irrational or perverse; (b) The correct test was not one of fairness - assessing whether a decision was irrational or perverse was not to be equated with the application of an objective standard of reasonableness; (c) the test was a "severe" one; (d) the test was an objective one (see [18]). In *Bradbury v BBC* [2015] EWHC 1368 (Ch), [2015] All ER (D) 153 (May), Warren J held that the pensions ombudsman was entitled to find that the BBC's decision to impose a 1% cap on increases to pensionable salary was not in breach of the implied term of trust and confidence. In *IBM United Kingdom Holdings v Dalgleish* [2018] IRLR 4, [2017] EWCA Civ 1212 the Court of Appeal held that an employer's previous indication that there would be no further changes to the pension scheme did not entail that a later change of heart could be challenged as a failure to honour reasonable expectations unless the decision was irrational.

43.16 Retirement

The question of recovery by the employer of surplus pension funds was considered in *National Grid Co plc v Mayes* [2001] UKHL 20, [2001] 2 All ER 417, [2001] IRLR 394, upholding the right of the employer to appropriate a substantial surplus in the pension fund to meet debts owed by it to the fund. This case turned principally on the construction of the particular rules, and does not lay down any new general principles.

Where the pension scheme rules afford a benefit to employee members which is only available subject to the employee making an application or taking steps which necessitate being aware of the availability of and conditions for the benefit, the employer is under an applied contractual duty to draw to employees' attention the benefit and the necessity to take action to obtain or preserve it: *Scally v Southern Health and Social Services Board* [1992] 1 AC 294, [1991] IRLR 522. An extension of this approach was shown in *Aspden v Webbs Poultry and Meat Group (Holdings) Ltd* [1996] IRLR 521, where the High Court held that an express term permitting dismissal on notice was subject to an implied term that it would not be used so as to defeat the employee's claim to disability benefits also provided for by the contract. This reasoning would apply equally to ill-health pension benefits. The implied term applied in *Aspden* received support, *obiter*, in the Court of Appeal in *Brompton v AOC International Ltd* [1997] IRLR 639 at 643, and was applied in the EAT in *Awan v ICTS UK Ltd* (2018) UKEAT/0087/18, [2019] IRLR 212 but was given a more limited construction in *Hill v General Accident Fire and Life Assurance Corpn plc* [1998] IRLR 641. See also *Villella v MFI Furniture Centres Ltd* [1999] IRLR 468.

The limits to the principle established by *Scally* are shown in *University of Nottingham v Eyett* [1999] 2 All ER 437, [1999] IRLR 87: where an employee is aware of his entitlement to a benefit and is taking a decision as to how to maximise it, the employer is not under a positive duty to warn him that he has not chosen the most advantageous way. *Eyett* was approved and applied in the Court of Appeal in *Outram v Academy Plastics* [2000] IRLR 499, where a claim that employers owed a duty of care to an employee who had resigned after 20 years' service and later re-joined the employer, to advise him to re-join the employer's pension scheme, was struck out as having no prospect of success. Two points were emphasised: the established law that trustees of a pension scheme do not owe a duty of care to advise scheme members faced with choices about pension matters; and the principle (confirmed in *Scally*) that there cannot be any wider duty owed by an employer to an employee in tort than that owed in contract.

An employer answering queries from pension scheme trustees about a former employee's work record owes no duty of care to that employee which could make him liable for damages in negligence (*Petch v Customs and Excise Comrs* [1993] ICR 789; but cf *Spring v Guardian Assurance plc* [1995] 2 AC 296, [1994] IRLR 460, referred to in **41.4 REFERENCES**).

43.17 Claims and disputes over pension rights

Some employees' claims in relation to pension rights may be taken to an employment tribunal. These include claims in respect of membership or benefits made under the *Equality Act 2010*. Such claims may be made in appropriate cases against the trustees as well as (or instead of) the employer.

In addition, employees' rights against employers in relation to pensions are in their nature contractual, and the Court of Appeal has held this to be so in principle also for the member's relationship to the trustees (*Harris v Shuttleworth (Lord)* [1994] ICR 991, [1994] IRLR 547, CA). Accordingly, pension disputes may be taken to an employment tribunal by an aggrieved employee, if they arise on or are outstanding at the termination of his employment, under the *Employment Tribunals Extension of Jurisdiction (England and Wales) Order 1994 (SI 1994/1623)* or the parallel Scottish Order. Claims against the trustees based on the contract of membership are permissible because the Order applies to claims under contracts connected with employment, and does not limit claims to those against the former employer. (This jurisdiction may not apply where the scheme is a statutory public sector scheme with the right to membership conferred, and benefits prescribed, by statute.)

However, there are important limitations to the tribunal's contractual jurisdiction. The only remedy it can award is damages, with a statutory maximum of £25,000. Claims can also be brought only following termination of employment, and within a three-month time limit. Claims must arise out of, or be outstanding on, the termination of the employment.

In pension claims, remedies such as a declaration of rights or a direction to the employer or trustees to determine a claim in accordance with law are often important. Further, claims frequently have values far in excess of £25,000, for example, where a pension payable for the rest of the claimant's life is in issue. For these reasons, such claims are typically brought in the ordinary courts.

However, there are other avenues to pursue claims and disputes, of increasing practical importance. The *Pensions Act 1995, s 50* created a statutory requirement for all occupational pension schemes (except those with only one member or where all the members are trustees) to establish a procedure for the internal resolution of all disputes raised by or on behalf of members or their dependents or prospective members. (This requirement applies equally to stakeholder pension schemes.) *Sections 50 to 50B of the Pensions Act 1995*, inserted by the *Pensions Act 2004*, set out requirements which these procedures must meet. Secondary legislation made under *s 50* sets out further detailed provisions.

A remedy of growing importance is a complaint to the Pensions Ombudsman (10 South Colonnade, Canary Wharf, London E14 4PU, tel: 0800 917 4487; www.pensions -ombudsman.org.uk). The Pensions Ombudsman is a statutory body constituted under *ss 145–151 of the Pension Schemes Act 1993* (as amended by the *Pensions Act 1995*), and his decisions are enforceable in law, subject to a right of any aggrieved party to appeal on a point of law to the High Court. For an example of a case exploring the extent of the right to appeal, see *Dolland v Trustees of BTG Pension Fund* [2011] All ER (D) 247 (Apr). The Pensions Ombudsman may determine any question of fact or law, or claim of maladministration raised by or on behalf of a scheme member, against either the employer or the scheme trustees, or the managers or administrators of a pension scheme. There are limited exceptions to this jurisdiction in relation to public sector schemes. The Ombudsman cannot normally act where the complainant has instituted court or tribunal proceedings (but the fact that such proceedings could be brought has no bearing on his jurisdiction). In a number of cases, the High Court has held that the Ombudsman may award damages for distress and inconvenience, including *Maclaine v Prudential Assurance Co Ltd* [2006] EWHC 2037 (Ch), [2006] All ER (D) 121 (Feb) and *Smith v Sheffield Teaching Hospitals NHS Foundation Trust* [2017] EWHC 2545 (Ch), [2018] Pens LR 5.

There is a time limit of three years for lodging complaints (extendable at his discretion in limited circumstances): *reg 5* of the *Personal and Occupational Pension Schemes (Pensions Ombudsman) Regulations 1996 (SI 1996/2475)*. Complaints should first be referred to The Pensions Advisory Service (TPAS) for possible informal resolution, and this step needs to have been completed, so that the complaint can be lodged before the expiry of the three-year time limit. TPAS can be contacted at 11 Belgrave Road, London SW1V 1RB, tel 0800 011 3797; further information is available on its website (www.opas.org.uk).There is a right of appeal to the High Court against final, but not preliminary, decisions of the Pensions Ombudsman. (However, in cases where there is no right of appeal an application for judicial review may be possible: see on both these points *Legal & General Assurance Society Ltd v Pensions Ombudsman* [2000] 2 All ER 577, [2000] 1 WLR 1524.) The Pensions Ombudsman is not automatically a party to an appeal, but may apply to appear in the appeal; in that event, if the decision is not upheld, the successful party may obtain an order for the Ombudsman to pay its costs on the appeal (*Moores (Wallisdown) Ltd v Pensions Ombudsman (Costs)* [2002] 1 All ER 737).

The Pensions Ombudsman has issued a number of determinations of far-reaching significance, particularly in relation to the use by employers of surpluses in pension funds; this has been accompanied by an increase in the number of appeals against his determinations, which have highlighted restrictions in the powers conferred on him by the *1993 Act*: see, eg *Westminster City Council v Haywood* (above) and *Edge v Pensions Ombudsman* [2000] Ch 602, [1999] 4 All ER 546, holding that the Pensions Ombudsman cannot entertain complaints which could only be remedied by steps which would adversely affect the interests of third parties not party to the determination. (See also on this point *Marsh & McLennan Companies UK Ltd v Pensions Ombudsman* [2001] IRLR 505.)

The Pensions Regulator is the principal regulatory body controlling the activities of pension funds and trustees. It was established under the *Pensions Act 2004*, replacing the Occupational Pensions Regulatory Authority. Individual complaints continue to be dealt with by The Pensions Advisory Service.

44   Service Lettings

44.1   Some employers provide residential accommodation for their employees. They may do so because the nature of the work is such that the job can be done more efficiently if the employee is close at hand. Another reason may be that the work is in a part of the country in which there is a shortage of accommodation, and the only way in which the employer can attract workers is to provide them with somewhere to live.

The provision of such accommodation poses a dilemma for both employee and employer when the employment relationship comes to an end. The interest of the employee in retaining security of tenure in his home conflicts with the interest of the employer in regaining the accommodation so that he can use it for the employee's replacement. Another question is the extent to which rent controls apply.

It is not possible to give more than a broad outline of this area of law in a book on employment law, and those wishing to find more detailed discussion should consult such works as *Woodfall's Landlord and Tenant* or *Hill and Redman's Law of Landlord and Tenant*. That is particularly true of some of the complex transitional provisions associated with the change from the regime of the *Rent Act 1977* ('*RA 1977*') to that of the *Housing Act 1988* ('*HA 1988*'). Nor have we sought to deal here with matters such as the scope of the landlord's and the tenant's respective repairing obligations. A summary of the law as it affects employees is set out below. It has been assumed that situations such as that of a resident landlord are unlikely to arise in the employment context.

44.2   NATURE OF THE OCCUPANCY

It is of the greatest importance to distinguish between a *service tenancy* and a *service licence*. The grounds on which possession may be recovered from a tenant as opposed to a licensee are limited by statute (see below).

The test for distinguishing between a tenancy and a licence has been re-stated by Lord Templeman, giving the decision of the House of Lords in *Street v Mountford* [1985] AC 809, [1985] 2 All ER 289 (see also *Bruton v London and Quadrant Housing Trust* [2000] 1 AC 406, [1999] 3 All ER 481, HL). In *Street v Mountford*, Lord Templeman also gave guidance about the position of service occupiers.

> 'To constitute a tenancy the occupier must be granted exclusive possession for a fixed or periodic term certain in consideration of a premium or periodical payments' (p 818E).

> 'A service occupier is a servant who occupies his master's premises in order to perform his duties as a servant. In those circumstances the possession and occupation of the servant is treated as the possession and occupation of the master and the relationship of landlord and tenant is not created; see *Mayhew v Suttle* (1854) 4 E & B 347. The test is whether the servant requires the premises he occupies in order the better to perform his duties as a servant:

>> "Where the occupation is necessary for the performance of services, and the occupier is required to reside in the house in order to perform those services, the occupation being strictly ancillary to the performance of the duties which the occupier has to perform, the occupation is that of a servant";

>> per Mellor J in *Smith v Seghill Overseers* (1875) LR 10 QB 422, 428'. (p 818G–H).

A requirement that the employee live in certain accommodation for the better performance of his duties (so that he is a licensee and not a tenant) may be expressed in his contract of employment or may be implied. A chauffeur who is given a flat above the garage, or a housekeeper who is given accommodation in the premises she is charged with looking after, would, save in exceptional circumstances, be considered to be occupying that accommodation for the better performance of his or her duties. So there will be a licence only, and no security of tenure, where a school caretaker is granted exclusive occupation of a bungalow in the school grounds but is required to occupy it in order better to perform his duties as an employee. In *Hertfordshire County Council v Davies* [2017] EWHC 1488 (QB), [2017] 1 WLR 4395 the Council succeeded in recovering possession even though it no longer ran the school, which had become an Academy, and so did not require the bungalow for a new caretaker, and even though the Council had no statutory housing functions. (Employers should be aware that certain duties associated with residency, e.g. sleep-in care duties at a residential care home, or a firefighter being on call, might attract employment protection legislation. Standby time at home is "working time", *Ville de Nivelle v Matzak* C-518/15. The Public Sector Equality Duty under *section 149* of the *Equality Act 2010* applies: *Forward v Aldwyck Housing Group Ltd* [2019] EWHC 24 (QB). However, the National Minimum Wage does not apply to sleep-in" workers for the time asleep: *Royal Mencap Society v Tomlinson-Blake* [2018] IRLR 932; but note that Judgment is awaited in the Supreme Court. Employers may consider it wise to state expressly in any contract of employment or letter of offer of employment (where it is the case) that the employee will be required to occupy certain premises for the better performance of his duties and that his occupation is to cease upon the termination of the employment. But such a statement will not avail the employer if it does not accurately reflect the reality of the situation: cf *Aslan v Murphy* [1989] 3 All ER 130; [1990] 1 WLR 766. An employee will be a licensee rather than a tenant where he exclusively occupies an employer's residential accommodation in anticipation that, at a reasonable time in the future, the employment will benefit from that occupation; this applies notwithstanding that at the time when the employee entered into occupation, the occupation was irrelevant to his existing duties (*Norris v Checksfield* [1991] ICR 63; [1991] 4 All ER 327).

If the employee is not a service licensee in this sense, he may still be a lodger and not a tenant if the employer provides attendance or services which require him or his servants to exercise unrestricted access to, and use of, the premises. Otherwise, however, the agreement to grant exclusive possession for a term at a rent points to the creation of a tenancy. Indeed, in *Ashburn Anstalt v Arnold* [1989] Ch 1, [1988] 2 All ER 147, the Court of Appeal held that even a rent was not an essential constituent of a lease (although this case was overruled by the House of Lords in *Prudential Assurance Co Ltd v London Residuary Body* [1992] 2 AC 386, [1992] 3 All ER 504; and cf *Bostock v Bryant* (1990) 61 P & CR 23, [1990] 2 EGLR 101). Two cases illustrate the application of these principles in employment cases.

In *Postcastle Properties Ltd v Perridge* [1985] 2 EGLR 107, the plaintiffs brought a possession action for an estate cottage. The occupant, a man of 80 years, had been employed by the plaintiffs' predecessor in title. He remained in occupation, and continued to work for and to pay £1.50 per week rent to the plaintiffs after they purchased the premises. He was held to have a tenancy. Strong evidence was needed to rebut the presumption of tenancy, which was not forthcoming in that case.

In *Royal Philanthropic Society v County* [1985] 2 EGLR 109, the defendant was employed as a houseparent at the plaintiff's school. Initially he was provided with furnished accommodation in the school building. He was a licensee of the room. On marrying, he was provided with a house some miles from the school. Approximately one year later his employment came to an end, whereupon a notice to quit was served. Possession was successfully claimed in the county court. This was overturned on appeal, the Court of Appeal holding that the defendant was a tenant. Fox LJ said:

> 'The overall effect of *Street v Mountford* as we understand it is that an occupier of residential accommodation at a rent for a term is either a lodger or a tenant . . . .' (p 1071).

> 'The employment, it seems to us, is material only if there is a true service occupancy, ie where the servant requires the premises for the better performance of his duties as a servant . . . ' (p 1072).

Referring to a variety of factors put forward by counsel for the plaintiffs in his attempt to show that no tenancy was created, such as the informality of the paperwork, the relationship of the parties, and the fact that the previous occupancy was that of lodger, Fox LJ said:

> ' . . . it seems to us that they amount really to an attempt to go back to the approach, disapproved by the House of Lords in *Street v Mountford*, of examining the circumstances with a view to ascertaining the intention of the parties. The only intention that is relevant under the law as it now stands "is the intention demonstrated by the agreement to grant exclusive possession for a term at a rent" (*Street v Mountford* at p 891).' (p 1072)

These decisions serve to demonstrate that, although the employment relationship continues as before, the nature of the employee's occupancy of premises may change.

Somewhat different considerations may apply in cases of joint occupation (see, eg *Mikeover Ltd v Brady* [1989] 3 All ER 618; *Stribling v Wickham* [1989] 2 EGLR 35).

44.3   RECOVERY OF POSSESSION

In order to recover possession from an occupying employee or ex-employee, the employer/landlord will first have to ensure that the employee's *contractual* right to occupy, whether under a licence or a tenancy, is brought to an end. If the employee does not leave voluntarily, it will then be necessary to obtain an order for possession, generally in the county court. In the case of a tenancy, the court's powers to make such an order are restricted by statute.

It is important that the employer does not seek to regain possession, whether by forcible eviction or by harassment without recourse to court proceedings. Such a course of action will contravene the *Protection from Eviction Act 1977* ('*PFEA 1977*').

Where premises are let as a dwelling under a tenancy or licence, even under a tenancy which is not statutorily protected, it is not lawful for the owner to exercise a right of re-entry or forfeiture under the lease, or to enforce his right to recover possession, otherwise than by court proceedings (*PFEA 1977, ss 2, 3(1), (2B)*). 'Let as a dwelling' means 'let wholly or partly as a dwelling', so *PFEA 1977, s 2* applies to premises which were let for mixed residential and business purposes (*Patel v Pirabakaran* [2006] EWCA Civ 685, [2006] 4 All ER 506). However, premises let for such mixed purposes are not 'let as a separate dwelling' within *Rent Act 1977, s 1* (*Tan v Sitkowski* [2007] EWCA Civ 30, [2007] 1 WLR 1628; [2007] All ER (D) 16 (Feb)). It has been held that *article 6* of the *European Convention on Human Rights* (ie. the right to a fair hearing before an independent and impartial tribunal for the determination of civil rights) was satisfied where *PFEA 1977, s 3* was invoked by a local authority (*R (on the application of Coombes) v Secretary of State for Communities and Local Government* [2010] 2 All ER 940).

There is a deemed tenancy for these purposes whenever a person has exclusive possession of any premises under the terms of his employment (*PFEA 1977, s 8(2)*).

It is a criminal offence unlawfully to deprive the employee of his occupation (*PFEA 1977, s 1(2)*). It is also an offence if a person, with the intention of causing the residential occupier to give up occupation or to refrain from exercising any rights or pursuing any remedy open to him, does acts which are likely to interfere with the peace and comfort of the occupier, or his family, or persistently withdraws or withholds services normally required for the occupation of the premises as a residence (*PFEA 1977, s 1(3)*, as amended by *HA 1988*, *s 29*). Where that intent cannot be shown, an offence is nonetheless committed if the employer or his agent, without reasonable grounds, does acts likely to interfere with the peace or comfort of the residential occupier or members of his household or persistently withdraws or withholds services reasonably required for the occupation of the premises as a residence, knowing or having reasonable cause to believe that that conduct is likely to cause the occupier to give up occupation or to refrain from exercising a right or remedy (*PFEA 1977, s 1(3A),(3B)*, as inserted by *HA 1988, s 29*). The offence of harassment under *PFEA 1977, s 1(3)* may be committed even if the actions complained of do not otherwise amount to a civil wrong (*R v Burke* [1991] 1 AC 135, [1990] 2 All ER 385). As to whether occupiers are 'residential occupiers' for the purposes of *PFEA 1977, s 1(3A)*, see *Prosecution Appeal (No 28 of 2007); R v Harris* [2008] All ER (D) 190 (Feb).

Further, a right to damages for unlawful eviction (in addition to any existing rights to claim in tort or for breach of contract) is created by *HA 1988, s 27* (see *Tagro v Cafane* [1991] 2 All ER 235, *Sampson v Wilson* [1996] Ch 39, *Osei-Bonsu v Wandsworth London Borough Council* [1999] 1 All ER 265 and *Lambeth London Borough Council v Loveridge* [2014] UKSC 65, [2014] 1 WLR 4516, [2015] 1 All ER 513). Where a landlord obtained an order for possession from the court and applied for a warrant for possession against a tenant, the tenant remained protected under *PFEA 1977, s 3(1)* (see above) until the warrant had been executed and was therefore entitled to damages. For a recent award of general, special aggravated and exemplary damages, see *Regency (UK) Ltd v Albu-Swalin* [2019] EWHC 3713 (QB).

Damages are payable until possession is restored, if a reinstatement order is sought and made, otherwise for the period of the right to possession, and include compensation for anxiety, inconvenience and stress involved in the loss of a home: *Smith v Khan* [2018] EWCA Civ 1137, [2019] 1 P & CR 71.

Once the licence or tenancy has been brought to an end and the employer is seeking to recover possession, the employer ought not to accept further payments of rent (at least without making clear in writing the basis on which he does so), because the acceptance of such payments may lead to the creation of a fresh tenancy. If the employee continues to occupy the premises after he should have left, compensation will eventually be recoverable by order of the court (called 'mesne profits'). As to the liability of a former secure tenant (who had become a 'tolerated trespasser') for mesne profits, see *Jones v Merton London Borough Council* [2008] EWCA Civ 660, [2008] 4 All ER 287. (However, note that provisions in *Schedule 11* to the *Housing and Regeneration Act 2008* (which, with some exceptions, came into force on 20 May 2009) in effect prevents the creation of 'tolerated trespassers' in future, by amending the *Housing Acts 1985, 1988* and *1996* so as to provide that a possession order made against (inter alia) a secure or assured tenant will not end the tenancy until the tenant is evicted.)

44.4   Service licence

A true *service licence* can be determined on termination of the relevant employment contract, with the notice period provided for in the contract. If the contract is silent on this point, then reasonable notice should be given. It is unlikely that a period of less than four weeks would be reasonable. If the licence is a *periodic licence* (ie one which continues from week to week or month to month, rather than for a fixed term), a minimum of four weeks' notice to terminate it must be given in the prescribed form (*PFEA 1977, s 5(1A)* as inserted by *HA 1988, s 32; Notices to Quit, etc (Prescribed Information) Regulations 1988 (SI 1988/2201)*). The termination of a licence which is expressed to come to an end with the termination of the employee's employment need not comply with the requirements of *PFEA 1977, s 5(1A)* as to notice, because such a licence is not a 'periodic licence' for the purposes of that provision (*Norris v Checksfield* [1991] ICR 632, [1991] 4 All ER 327).

On the termination of a *service licence* the employer can take proceedings for possession. He will have to show:

(a)   that the premises were occupied by the employee for the duration of his employment (or for some agreed lesser period), and for the better performance of his duties;

(b)   that the employment (or the lesser period) has ended, or that proper notice to determine the licence has been given;

(c)   that either the agreed notice has been given or the former employee has been given an adequate period in which to vacate the premises;

(d)   that no new arrangement has been created since the contract ended (therefore it is unwise to accept further payments of rent without specifying the basis on which this is done).

In *Whitbread West Pennines Ltd v Reedy* [1988] ICR 807, the former employee sought to argue that possession should not be ordered against him because there was pending an unfair dismissal claim in which he sought reinstatement (see **56.2** Unfair Dismissal – III). The argument failed. The Court of Appeal held that for the replacement employee to move into the accommodation would not make reinstatement any less practicable, and that in any event the employer could elect not to reinstate but to pay enhanced compensation instead. In a case where the licence to occupy terminates along with the employment, it does so notwithstanding that the dismissal is wrongful (*Ivory v Palmer* [1975] ICR 340) or contractually lawful but statutorily unfair (*Carroll v Manek*, (1999) 79 P & CR 173, [1999] All ER (D) 813).

44.5   Service tenancy

Tenancies in existence prior to 15 January 1989 continue to be governed by *RA 1977* or *Housing Act 1980* ('*HA 1980*'). Tenancies entered into on or after that date, however, are governed by *HA 1988*. Tenancies entered into on or after 28 February 1997 are affected by amendments made to *HA 1988* by the *Housing Act 1996* ('*HA 1996*'). Various kinds of tenancy therefore fall to be considered.

(i)   *Protected tenancies under RA 1977.* These are automatically converted into *statutory tenancies* when the original, contractual tenancy expires through effluxion of time or a notice to quit is served.

(ii)   *Protected shorthold tenancies under HA 1980.* These arose where, before the grant of the tenancy, the landlord served a prescribed notice indicating that this was the nature of the tenancy. The term must have been between one and five years, with the landlord having no right to end it sooner whilst the tenant complied with his obligations (*HA 1980, s 52*).

(iii)   *Assured tenancies under HA 1988.* This will now be the normal basic type of tenancy (but see (v) below). The tenant must be an individual who occupies the dwelling as his only or principal home, and the letting must not be one which is specifically excluded from protection (*HA 1988, s 1*). As to the meaning of 'dwelling' in *HA 1988, s 1*, see *Uratemp Ventures Ltd v Collins* [2001] UKHL 43, [2002] 1 AC 301.

(iv)   *Assured shorthold tenancies under HA 1988 (pre-HA 1996 tenancies).* These are similar in concept to the old protected shorthold tenancies, but their scope is less restricted. They must be for a fixed term of not less than six months, contain no landlord's right to terminate during the first six months if the tenant complies with his obligations, and the grant must be preceded by service of a notice in the prescribed form (*HA 1988, s 20*). The notice may be served on the tenant's authorised agent (*Yenula Properties Ltd v Naidu* [2002] EWCA Civ 719, [2003] HLR 229). A notice not in the prescribed form nor 'substantially to the same effect' is invalid (*Manel v Memon* (2000) 33 HLR 235 — applied in *Kahlon v Isherwood* [2011] EWCA Civ 602, [2011] All ER (D) 205 (May), a case on *HA 1988, s 19A* and

Sch 2A (see (v) below)). Also invalid is a notice which fails to state correctly the landlord's name (*Gill v Cremadez* [2000] CLY 3876); see also *Ravenseft Properties v Hall* [2001] EWCA Civ 2034, [2002] HLR 624 and *Osborn & Co Ltd v Dior* [2003] EWCA Civ 281, [2003] HLR 649.

(v)   *Assured shorthold tenancies under HA 1988 (post–HA 1996 tenancies).* Any assured tenancy which is entered into on or after 28 February 1997 (otherwise than pursuant to a contract entered into before that date) will be an assured shorthold tenancy, unless it falls within one of the exceptions set out in *HA 1988, Sch 2A* (as to which, see *Andrews v Cunningham* [2007] All ER (D) 343 (Jul)) (*HA 1988, s 19A*, inserted by *HA 1996, s 96*). Unlike pre–*HA 1996* assured shorthold tenancies, no notice need be served by the landlord on the tenant prior to the grant, and the tenancy need not be for a fixed term. However, if requested to do so in writing, a landlord under a post–*HA 1996* assured shorthold tenancy has a duty to provide a tenant with a written statement of the principal terms of the tenancy where these are not evidenced in writing (*HA 1988, s 20A*, inserted by *HA 1996, s 97*).

In order to recover possession from a service tenant, the contractual tenancy must be terminated. This will occur if (in the case of a fixed-term tenancy) the term of the tenancy expires without being renewed, if the landlord claims to forfeit the lease where the lease makes provision for forfeiture for breach of certain terms in it, or (in the case of a periodic tenancy) if the landlord serves a notice to quit.

Expiry of term. If the tenancy is for a fixed term of, for example, two years, the contractual tenancy will automatically terminate on the expiry of the two-year period and it is not necessary for a notice to quit to be served.

Forfeiture for breach of a term of the lease. Except in the case of forfeiture for the non-payment of rent, the landlord must serve a notice under the *Law of Property Act 1925, s 146* on the tenant, specifying the breaches complained of and requesting him to remedy the same within a reasonable period of time and to pay reasonable compensation.

Notice to quit. A notice to quit should be in writing and some acknowledgement of receipt should be asked for. If sent by post, it should be sent by recorded delivery. To be valid the notice to quit must expire on the proper day. The notice to quit must expire at the end of the period of the tenancy. Because specifying a wrong date is fatal to a notice to quit, landlords should add the following saving clause in the notice to quit after the specified date: 'or at the expiration of the (week/month) of your tenancy which shall expire next after the expiration of four weeks from the service upon you of this notice'. The notice to quit must be served not less than four weeks before the date on which it is to take effect (*Protection from Eviction Act 1977, s 5*). Information prescribed by the *Notices to Quit, etc (Prescribed Information) Regulations 1988 (SI 1988/2201)* must be included in the notice to quit; otherwise it will be invalid.

No rent must be accepted after discovery of a breach of a term in the lease which gives the landlord the right to forfeit, such as unlawful sub-letting. Accepting rent may be construed as waiving the breaches complained of or creating a new tenancy.

44.6   Situations in which possession may be claimed from tenant

Where a *protected shorthold tenancy* or an *assured shorthold tenancy* comes to an end, the court *must* grant the landlord possession if the proper procedure is followed. In the case of an assured shorthold tenancy, this involves giving the tenant not less than two months' notice in writing that possession is required. The notice must specify a date that is the last date of a period of the tenancy (*Fernandez v McDonald* [2003] EWCA Civ 1219, [2003] 4 All ER 1033; see also *Notting Hill Housing Trust v Roomus* [2006] EWCA Civ 407, [2006] 1 WLR

1375). In the case of a post-*HA 1996* assured shorthold tenancy (see category (v) in **44.5** above), a possession order may not be made so as to take effect earlier than six months after the beginning of the tenancy (where the tenancy is a replacement tenancy, the six-month period runs from the beginning of the *original* tenancy) (*HA 1988, s 21*, as amended by *HA 1996, ss 98, 99*). The procedural requirements in relation to the old protected shorthold tenancy were somewhat more complex: see *HA 1980, s 55; RA 1977, s 98(2), Sch 15 Case 19*. Possession of properties let on shorthold tenancies can also be recovered on the same grounds as are available in the case of ordinary tenancies. However, where a private registered provider of social housing had given two months' notice to recover possession during the starter or probationary period of a fixed term tenancy, the tenancy was no longer "a fixed term tenancy for a term certain of not less than two years" and the provisions of *HA 1988* requiring six months' notice no longer applied: *Livewest Homes Ltd (formerly known as Liverty Ltd) v Bamber* [2019] EWCA Civ 1174, [2020] 2 All ER 181.

In the case of a *protected tenancy* under *RA 1977*, the landlord must bring himself within one of a number of specified 'Cases' set out in *Sch 15*. Those Cases in *Sch 15 Part I* are 'discretionary' grounds, in that they require the court to be satisfied also that it is reasonable to grant possession; they include grounds such as arrears of rent or the causing of a nuisance. Those Cases in *Sch 15 Part II* constitute mandatory grounds for possession. In addition, the court may make an order, if it is reasonable to do so, where suitable alternative accommodation is or will be available for the tenant. See generally *RA 1977, s 98*.

The ground particularly relevant to pre-1989 service lettings is *Case 8* (a discretionary ground): this arises if the landlord requires the premises for a whole-time employee, the existing tenant was granted a tenancy in consequence of his employment, and he has ceased to be in that employment.

A similar approach governs recovery of possession under *assured tenancies* under *HA 1988*. Again, there are both mandatory and discretionary grounds, and where one of the latter is established the court will have to be persuaded that it is reasonable to order possession (*HA 1988, s 7, Sch 2*). *Ground 16* is a discretionary ground which applies where the dwelling-house was let to the tenant in consequence of his employment by the landlord or a previous landlord, and the tenant has ceased to be in that employment. It will be seen that this is less stringent, from the landlord's point of view, than *Case 8* under *RA 1977* (see above), because it is not necessary to show that the accommodation is required for another employee. However, to do so would obviously assist the argument that it was reasonable to order possession. The availability of suitable alternative accommodation is another discretionary ground (*Ground 9*).

As in the case of RA 1977 (see s 100), the court has a wide discretion under HA 1988, s 9 to adjourn possession proceedings and to suspend the execution of orders; see generally *White v Knowsley Housing Trust* [2008] UKHL 70, [2008] All ER (D) 115 (Dec) and *Armstrong v Ashfield District Council* [2018] EWCA Civ 873, [2018] HLR 474.

44.7   Tenants of public authorities

Under *HA 1985*, security of tenure was conferred upon tenants of local authorities and of certain other public bodies. However, various categories are excluded from security of tenure. Those which are pertinent to employment include:

(a)   Cases where the tenant is an employee of the landlord; or of:

   (i)   a local authority;

   (ii)   a development corporation;

   (iii)   the governors of an aided school;

   (iv)   an urban development corporation;

(v)   a housing action trust;

(vi)   a Mayoral Development Corporation;

and his contract of employment requires him to reside in the dwelling for the better performance of his duties.

In *Surrey County Council v Lamond* [1999] 1 EGLR 32, [1998] All ER (D) 745 (see also [1999] 2 CLY 3736), the Court of Appeal held that in deciding whether for this reason a tenancy was not a secure tenancy, the court needed to ascertain what duties the employee was to perform and then determine whether it was genuinely practicable for the employee to perform them if he did not occupy the dwelling concerned; see also *Hughes v Greenwich London Borough Council* [1994] 1 AC 170, [1993] 4 All ER 577, [1994] ICR 48, HL, *Elvidge v Coventry City Council* [1994] QB 241, [1993] 4 All ER 903, [1994] ICR 68 and *Brent London Borough Council v Charles* (1997) 29 HLR 876, CA. In *Wragg v Surrey County Council* [2008] EWCA Civ 19, [2008] All ER (D) 09 (Feb), the Court of Appeal construed this provision as laying down two distinct conditions: (i) that 'his contract of employment requires him to occupy the dwelling-house'; (ii) that the requirement was 'for the better performance of his duties'. Condition (i) looked only to the terms of the contract: did the contract contain such a requirement or not? However, condition (ii) raised an issue of fact outside the contract: 'the question was not whether the contract stated that the requirement was for the better performance of his duties, but whether the requirement was in fact for the better performance of his duties'.

(b)   Where the tenant is a member of the police force, and the dwelling is provided rent-free by regulations made under the *Police Act 1996*. (See *Holmes v South Yorkshire Police Authority* [2008] EWCA Civ 51, [2008] HLR 532, [2008] All ER (D) 93 (Feb).)

(c)   Where the tenant is employed by a fire and rescue authority; and

(i)   he is contractually bound to live close to a particular fire station; and

(ii)   the dwelling-house was let to him by the authority so that he could comply with the condition.

(d)   Cases where temporary accommodation is granted in order to assist employees who are new to an area to find permanent accommodation there, provided that it is linked to an offer of employment to a person who was not resident in the district immediately before the grant, that it does not exceed one year and that the tenant is informed, in writing, of the circumstances in which the exception applies and that the landlord is of the opinion that it falls within that exception.

(*Housing Act 1985, Sch 1 paras 2(1), (2), (3), 5(1)*, as amended.) (See also *Nicholas v Secretary of State for Defence* [2015] EWCA Civ 53, [2015] 1 WLR 2116, [2015] All ER (D) 53 (Feb) where it was held that there was no violation of *Art 8, ECHR* rights in seeking possession of Crown property from the former spouse of a member of the RAF who had a license to occupy the property for the better performance of his duties.)

44.8   RENT CONTROL

Occupation under a *licence* is not subject to rent control.

Where the employee went into occupation under a *RA 1977 protected tenancy* or a *protected shorthold tenancy*, he could apply under *Part IV* of that *Act* for a fair rent to be registered, and the landlord was not then entitled to charge a greater rent (*RA 1977, s 44*). Now that new protected tenancies cannot be created, that provision will be of diminishing importance, although the possibility of such an application remains.

A tenant under an *assured tenancy* under *HA 1988* has no right to challenge the contractual rent which he has agreed to pay, whether the rent demanded of him is that originally agreed upon, or has subsequently been varied pursuant to a rent review clause. However, if the contractual tenancy comes to an end and the landlord wishes to increase the rent, he must serve notice of the proposed increase upon the tenant in a prescribed form (*HA 1988, s 13*). The tenant may then go before the First-tier Tribunal and seek a determination that the proposed new rent exceeds that which might reasonably be expected to be obtained in the open market, by a willing landlord, on the same terms of letting (*HA 1988, s 14*). There are strict time limits within which any reference by the tenant to the Rent Assessment Committee or the First-tier Tribunal must be made: *Robertson v Webb* [2018] UKUT 235 (LC), (2018) L& TR 31.

A tenant under an *assured shorthold tenancy* may refer the rent charged to the FTT, during the initial fixed term of the tenancy (in the case of a pre-*HA 1996* assured shorthold tenancy) or during the first six months of the tenancy (in the case of a post-*HA 1996* assured shorthold tenancy). However, the Committee may reduce the rent only if:

(i)   there is a sufficient number of similar dwelling-houses in the locality let on assured tenancies (whether shorthold or not) for a proper determination to be possible; and

(ii)   the rent charged is *significantly* higher than the rent which the landlord might reasonably be expected to obtain having regard to the rents payable under other assured tenancies in the locality.

(*HA 1988, s 22*, as amended by *HA 1996, s 100*.)

44.9   AGRICULTURAL TIED HOUSES

Where the employee is or was engaged in agriculture or forestry, special rules may apply. A discussion of these rules is beyond the scope of this book. They are to be found in the *Rent (Agriculture) Act 1976* as amended by *HA 1988* and the *Civil Partnership Act 2004*, and in *HA 1988, ss 24, 25* (as amended by *HA 1996, s 103*).

44.10 MISCELLANEOUS

Accommodation provided by an employer can be taken into account when calculating the National Minimum Wage or National Living Wage. Accommodation offset rates are set in April each year.

Rent can be deducted from pay only when this is permitted by the rules in the *Employment Rights Act 1996* governing deductions, and in particular by the contract of employment or by an agreement in writing to the deduction.

An employer providing accommodation for employees has tax, national insurance and reporting obligations with respects to the costs of and associated with the provision.

45 Sickness and Sick Pay

Cross-references. See TERMINATION OF EMPLOYMENT **(49)** for sickness and frustration of contract of employment; for sickness and unfair dismissal, see **55.8** UNFAIR DISMISSAL – II.

45.1 In relation to pay for periods of sickness, the following may apply:

(a)   contractual provisions for sick pay (see **45.2** below);

(b)   the statutory right to a specified level of sick pay ('statutory sick pay', see **45.3** –**45.8** below).

As in many areas of employment law, statutory payments are offset against contractual payments and vice versa. This 'offsetting' of payments during sickness is considered in **45.9** –**45.11** below.

Employers may now opt out of the statutory sick pay scheme, so long as they provide the same minimum level of remuneration as an employee would be entitled to as a matter of statute. (See **45.3** below.)

Persistent illness may constitute such incapacity for work as to warrant dismissal (see **55.8** UNFAIR DISMISSAL – II).

In rare circumstances, sickness may render performance of the contract so radically different from that contemplated by the parties as to amount to a frustration of the contract (see **49.3** TERMINATION OF EMPLOYMENT).

45.2 CONTRACTUAL PROVISIONS FOR SICK PAY

An employer may agree to pay his employees while they are absent due to ill-health. Such payments commonly run for a specified period of time and are subject to conditions.

The written particulars given to an employee setting out the terms and conditions of his employment must state whether or not the employer makes payments for periods of absence due to sickness and, if so, upon what terms (see **8.4** CONTRACT OF EMPLOYMENT). In *Mears v Safecar Security Ltd* [1983] QB 54, [1982] 2 All ER 865, [1982] 3 WLR 366, [1982] ICR 626, [1982] IRLR 183, the Court of Appeal held that where such a term is not specified or agreed, the tribunal must consider all the facts and circumstances to ascertain the term to be implied. There is no presumption of a contractual right to sick pay. An employment tribunal must look to all the facts and circumstances, and to the conduct of the parties since the contract began.

Where there is a contractual right to sick pay, but no provision as to its duration, the court will imply a reasonable term (*Howman & Son v Blyth* [1983] ICR 416, [1983] IRLR 139).

For the failure to comply with the statutory duty to specify in the written particulars of terms of employment what provisions for sick pay apply, see **8.7** CONTRACT OF EMPLOYMENT.

45.3 STATUTORY SICK PAY

(For further details see HMRC's online guide at http://www.hmrc.gov.uk/courses/syob 4/ssp_guide.

Since 1983, all employees, subject to certain specified exceptions (see **45.4** below), have been entitled to receive statutory sick pay ('SSP') from their employers. The entitlement limit is, generally, 28 weeks in a three-year period. The basic provisions are now consolidated into the *Social Security Contributions and Benefits Act 1992* ('*SSCBA 1992*'). The main set of regulations is the *Statutory Sick Pay (General) Regulations 1982 (SI 1982/894)* as amended, principally by the *Statutory Sick Pay (General) Amendment Regulations 1986 (SI 1986/477)*, the *Statutory Sick Pay (General) Amendment (No 2) Regulations 1987 (SI 1987/868)* and the *Social Security Contributions, Statutory Maternity Pay and Statutory Sick Pay (Miscellaneous Amendments) Regulations 1996 (SI 1996/777)*.

The essential requirements for qualification are that an employee must:

(a)   have four or more consecutive days of sickness (including Sundays and holidays) during which he is too ill to be capable of doing his work (see further **45.5** below); and

(b)   notify his absence to his employer, subject to certain statutory requirements and any agreement between them; and

(c)   supply evidence of incapacity – this is also a matter for the employer: a common example of an employer's requirement would be:

  (i)   a 'self-certificate' for periods of four to seven days;

  (ii)   a doctor's certificate or other evidence of sickness for periods after the first seven days.

(*SSCBA 1992, ss 151, 152, 156; Statutory Sick Pay (General) Regulations 1982, reg 7.*) The medical evidence that can be required of an employee is prescribed by the *Statutory Sick Pay (Medical Evidence) Regulations 1985*, as amended in 2010 (*SI 2010/137*).

Employers cannot require employees to contribute towards payments (*SSCBA 1992, s 151(2)*).

Employees may still be entitled to SSP even if they are absent from Great Britain on holiday or for business purposes at any time during the incapacity (*SI 1996/777, reg 3*).

An employer may choose to opt out of the statutory sick pay scheme, provided that he continues to pay contractual remuneration to his employees at or above the SSP rate and does not make his employees contribute to the cost of their sick pay up to that rate. Such employers still have to comply with certain documentary and record keeping requirements (see **45.7** below).

45.4   Excluded employees

The following categories of employee are not entitled to receive SSP. These are an employee:

(a)   having average weekly earnings less than the weekly lower earnings limit for National Insurance ('NI') contribution liability (currently £118 per week);

(b)   going sick within 57 days of having previously been entitled to incapacity benefit;

(c)   going sick within 85 days of having previously been entitled to an employment and support allowance;

(d)   who has done no work for his employer under the contract of service;

(e)   going sick during a stoppage of work at his place of employment due to a trade dispute, unless he proves that at no time has he had a direct interest in that dispute;

(f)   who is pregnant and goes off sick during the maternity pay period (see **33.26** MATERNITY AND PARENTAL RIGHTS);

(g)   who has already been due 28 weeks' SSP from his employer in any one 'period of incapacity for work' (or any two or more 'linked' periods) (see **45.5** below);

(h)   who, subject to certain provisions, has already been due 28 weeks' SSP from his former employer, and the gap between the first day of incapacity with the new employer and the last day on which SSP was paid by the former employer is eight weeks or less;

(i)   who is in legal custody at any time on the first day of incapacity.

(*SSCBA 1992, Sch 11*, as amended by the *Statutory Sick Pay Act 1994, s 1*; *Social Security Act 1985, s 18(2)(d)*; *Statutory Sick Pay (General) Regulations 1982 (SI 1982/894)*; *Statutory Sick Pay (General) Amendment Regulations 1986 (SI 1986/477)*.)

Where the employer is notified that an excluded employee has been absent for four consecutive days or more, he is legally bound to send a form to the employee not later than seven days after being so notified (or, where this is impracticable, not later than the first pay day in the following tax month). This form provides the explanation to the employee and the DWP of why SSP is not being paid, and allows the employee to claim state sickness benefit instead (*Statutory Sick Pay (General) Regulations 1982 (SI 1982/894), reg 15*, as amended).

It should also be noted that agency workers on assignments of less than three months are not entitled to SSP. The repeal of the previous exclusion from SSP for those whose 'contract of service was entered into for a specified period of not more than three months' did not apply to agency workers: see *Revenue and Customs Comrs v Thorn Baker Ltd* [2007] EWCA Civ 626, [2008] ICR 46.

45.5   The payment period

The period of four or more days of sickness (see **45.3** above) is called a 'period of incapacity for work' ('PIW'). Two or more PIWs which are separated by eight weeks or less are said to be 'linked' and are counted as one PIW (*SSCBA, s 152; Statutory Sick Pay (General) Amendment Regulations 1986 (SI 1986/477)*).

During a PIW, SSP is payable *only*:

(a)   while there is a 'period of entitlement', as defined (eg payment will cease, in the normal case, if the employment ends); *and*

(b)   for days within the PIW which are 'qualifying days'.

The intention behind the idea of 'qualifying days' was that they would be the days on which the employee would normally be required to work, but it is open to employers in all cases to specify the pattern of qualifying days by agreement with the employees concerned. Each week must have at least one qualifying day, and qualifying days must not be defined by reference to the days of sickness (*Statutory Sick Pay (General) Regulations 1982 (SI 1982/894); Statutory Sick Pay (General) Amendment Regulations 1985 (SI 1985/126)*).

SSP is not payable for the first three qualifying days in a PIW (*SSCBA 1992, s 155(1)*). It is paid for the fourth qualifying day onwards until either the employee becomes well again or the maximum payment period is reached (*SSCBA 1992, s 155(2)*).

The maximum entitlement to SSP is now 28 weeks in any period of entitlement. A period of entitlement, as between an employee and his employer, is a period beginning with the commencement of a period of incapacity for work and ending with the earliest of:

(i)   the termination of that period of incapacity for work;

(ii)   the day on which the employee reaches, as against the employer concerned, his maximum entitlement to statutory sick pay;

(iii)   the day on which the employee's contract of service with the employer concerned expires or is brought to an end;

(iv)   in the case of an employee who is, or has been, pregnant, the day immediately preceding the beginning of the disqualifying period (as defined by *SSCBA 1992, s 153(12)*) (*SSCBA 1992, s 153(2)*).

A period of entitlement ends after three years if it has not otherwise ended (*Statutory Sick Pay (General) Regulations 1982 (SI 1982/894), reg 3(3)*, inserted by *SI 1986/477*).

Employees who are still sick when their entitlement to SSP terminates may be entitled to state benefits. Employers of such employees must inform them in a prescribed form of the reason for the termination of SSP (*Social Security Administration Act 1992, s 130; Statutory Sick Pay (General) Regulations 1982 (SI 1982/894), reg 15*, as amended by *Statutory Sick Pay (General) Amendment Regulations 1986 (SI 1986/477)*, and by *Statutory Sick Pay (General)(Amendment) Regulations 2008 (SI 2008/1735)*). *SSCBA 1992, Sch 12* deals with the relationship between statutory sick pay and other benefits and payments.

45.6   The amounts payable and recoverable

Employees who earn less than the lower weekly earnings limit for NI liability (£120) are excluded from SSP (*SSCBA 1992, Sch 11 para 2(c)*). In all other cases, the amount of SSP payable is £95.85. Thus, the maximum amount payable over 28 weeks is £2,683.80 (*SSCBA 1992, s 157(1)*, as amended by the *Social Security (Incapacity for Work) Act 1994, s 8(1)*).

SSP is considered as earnings for PAYE, income tax and NI contribution purposes (*SSCBA 1992, s 4(1); Income and Corporation Taxes Act 1988, s 150*).

Right of recovery. The right of employers to recover from their NI contributions amounts paid by way of SSP was abolished by the *Statutory Sick Pay Act 1994*. The right of employers to recover SSP paid above a certain threshold has also been abolished.

45.7   Records

Until recently, employers were statutorily obliged to keep records for SSP purposes, and to retain certain information for at least three years, stored in such a way that inspectors could have access to them. This requirement has now been abolished by the *Statutory Sick Pay (Maintenance of Records) Revocation Regulations 2014 (SI 2014/55)*.

It is still necessary, however, to keep accounting records, *inter alia*, details of all SSP payments made, along with those of pay, NIC and PAYE income tax. Revenue records must be retained for seven years.

Employers may also find it useful to keep fuller records, eg self-certification forms, medical certificates, dates of all absences and the reasons for them. Such records can be used for the purposes of audit, and may also help to identify personnel problems.

45.8   Disputes

If an employer does not pay an employee SSP, the employee may ask him to give written reasons for the decision, and the employer must comply within a reasonable time (*Social Security Administration Act 1992, s 14(3)*).

If the employee wishes to challenge the employer's decision as to whether he is entitled to sick pay, he may ask for a determination of the issue by Her Majesty's Revenue and Customs (*Statutory Sick Pay and Statutory Maternity Pay (Decisions) Regulations 1999 (SI 1999/776)*). A challenge to HMRC's decision can be made to the First-Tier Tax Tribunal (Tax). For a recent example of a dispute as to whether an employee was entitled to sick pay, see *Mitre Plastics v Revenue and Customs Comrs* (TC00720) [2010] UKFTT 455 (TC). An employment tribunal does not have jurisdiction to determine whether an employee is entitled to statutory sick pay, although it would have jurisdiction to determine a claim of unlawful deduction from wages if the employer admitted entitlement but withheld payment of SSP: *Taylor Gordon & Co Ltd (t/a Plan Personnel) v Timmons* [2004] IRLR 180, EAT; *Sarti (Sauchiehall St) Ltd v Polito* [2008] ICR 1279.

The First–Tier Tax Tribunal does not have power to order payment of any sick pay to which an employee is entitled. Payment must be enforced through the Courts: see *Cleaver (t/a B.R.E. Cleaver Fruit & Veg Wholesaler) v R&C Commrs* [2014] UKFTT 1075 (TC).

As far as evidence of incapacity is concerned, the employer cannot require the employee to produce a medical certificate from a doctor for the first seven days of sickness. With that qualification, he can request the employee to provide reasonable evidence of incapacity, such as a self-certificate for absences of up to seven days (*Social Security Administration Act 1992, s 14; Statutory Sick Pay (Medical Evidence) Regulations 1985 (SI 1985/1604)*).

45.9   OFFSETTING PAYMENTS MADE DURING SICKNESS AGAINST SSP

Any contractual remuneration paid to an employee for a day of sickness is to be offset against the SSP due for the *same day* (*SSCBA 1992, Sch 12 para 2*). An employer can never pay the employee an amount in total which is *less* than the SSP due.

In personal injury actions, any special damages claimed will be subject to a deduction for SSP paid (*Palfrey v Greater London Council* [1985] ICR 437). The same principle was applied to payments under a non-contributory permanent health insurance scheme in *Hussain v New Taplow Paper Mills Ltd* [1987] 1 All ER 417, [1987] 1 WLR 336, [1987] ICR 28.

45.10 Contributory sickness schemes

An employee must not contribute to his own SSP. Thus, in the case of a jointly funded, ie 'contributory', sickness scheme, the amount of sick pay which will be offset against SSP must be in the proportion that the employer's contribution bears to the joint contributions to the scheme.

45.11 Contributory pension schemes

In the case of contributory pension schemes, offsetting will depend on how the pension scheme defines salary for calculation purposes: if salary is defined as 'earnings subject to PAYE income tax', then any SSP paid should be included in earnings for pension purposes. In that case the employee's pension contribution would be deducted from his full gross sick pay, ie including the SSP element. (See, in particular, the *Occupational Pensions Board Announcement No 2 (March 1983)*.)

45.12 PERMANENT HEALTH AND SALARY CONTINUANCE BENEFITS

It is increasingly common for employers to provide their employees with permanent health or salary continuance benefits during periods of long-term sickness or incapacity, lasting usually more than six or twelve months. Employers will normally provide these benefits by taking out insurance coverage for the benefit of their employees.

The right of an employee to receive permanent health or salary continuance benefits will usually depend on the terms of the insurance policy entered into by the employer, as the contract of employment will probably state that the benefits payable to the employee in the event of long-term incapacity are 'subject to' or 'governed by' the rules of the insurance policy. However, where the employer makes no reference to its insurance policy in documents provided to an employee, then the employer cannot rely upon the terms of the policy as against the employee. The employer will be bound by the words of its own contractual documentation with the employee: see *Jowitt v Pioneer Technology (UK) Ltd* [2003] EWCA Civ 411, [2003] ICR 1120, [2003] IRLR 356; *Awan v ICTS UK Ltd* (2018) UKEAT/0087/18, [2019] ICR 696, [2019] IRLR 212. Also, where the insurance policy provides for significant exemptions to the payment of benefits (eg disentitling employees to benefits on leaving service), the employer will not be able to rely on these exemptions as against the employee if the employee was not shown the policy itself or was not told that he should read it (*Villella v MFI Furniture Centres Ltd* [1999] IRLR 468).

In *Briscoe v Lubrizol Ltd* [2002] EWCA Civ 508, [2002] IRLR 607, the Court of Appeal held that the claimant's entitlement to disability benefit depended upon his satisfying the definition of 'disablement' contained in the employer's insurance policy ('totally unable . . . to perform his normal occupation'), rather than the definition set out in the company information handbook ('unable to follow any occupation'). The court referred to the decision in *Villella*, and held that 'the court looks unfavourably upon an employer who seeks to restrict his contractual obligation as described in a handbook in reliance upon a policy which he has not brought to the attention of his employee; but that does not mean, by way of corollary, that where the handbook expressly or by implication refers to such a policy and purports to summarise its effect upon the employee's rights in a manner which is disadvantageous to the employee, the court will similarly regard the handbook as definitive of those rights'. The court looked at all the facts and determined that it was the clear contractual intention of the parties to bestow upon the employee the benefits provided for in the insurance policy, rather than the handbook.

As the employee will not be a party to the insurance policy, he will ordinarily not be entitled to enforce his rights to receive these benefits directly against the insurer. Rather, he will have to enforce those rights against the employer, who in turn will probably seek to join the insurer as a third party (*Rutherford v Radio Rentals Ltd* 1993 SLT 221). Where, under the contract of employment, the employer is obliged to pay over to the employee such sums as it receives from the insurer, then the employer will be under a duty to take all reasonable steps to secure that the insurance benefits are paid. This may include the pursuit of litigation against the insurer if necessary (*Marlow v East Thames Housing Group Ltd* [2002] IRLR 798).

An employee is not automatically deprived of his entitlement to receive salary continuance benefits from his employer merely because the employer ceases to pay his insurance premiums or terminates the policy (*Bainbridge v Circuit Foil UK Ltd* [1997] IRLR 305).

44.13   Effect on the right to terminate the contract of employment

The existence of these benefits may restrict the employer's ability to terminate the contract of employment. In circumstances where the insurance policy provides that benefits will only be paid in respect of employees who continue to be employed by the policy-holder (ie the employer), the courts may imply a term into the contract of employment to the effect that the employer cannot bring the contract to an end solely with a view to terminate those benefits, or for a specious or arbitrary reason or for no reason at all, while the employee was incapacitated for work (see *Hill v General Accident Fire and Life Assurance Corpn plc* [1998] IRLR 641 and *Awan v ICTS UK Ltd* (2018) UKEAT/0087/18, [2019] IRLR 212; compare *Aspden v Webbs Poultry and Meat Group (Holdings) Ltd* [1996] IRLR 521 and see *Lloyd v BCQ Ltd* [2013] 1 CMLR 1166, [2012] All ER (D) 343 (Nov)) (see **8.22B** CONTRACT OF EMPLOYMENT). In *Lloyd*, the EAT held that such a term would not be implied where the contract of employment made no reference to permanent health insurance benefits, and the contract expressly permitted termination for long-term absence. Relying on *Reda v Flag Ltd* [2002] UKPC 38, [2002] IRLR 747, the EAT held that an *Aspden*-type term could not be implied.

In *Briscoe v Lubrizol Ltd* [2002] EWCA Civ 508, [2002] IRLR 607, the Court of Appeal had to determine whether the employer was justified in terminating a contract of employment, the effect of which would be to deprive the employee of his entitlement to disability benefit. The Court of Appeal reviewed the case law and held that 'the employer ought not to terminate the employment as a means to remove the employee's entitlement to benefit but the employer can dismiss for good cause whether that be on the ground of gross misconduct or, more generally, for some repudiatory breach by the employee'. On the facts, the Court of Appeal held that the employer was entitled to treat the contract as having come to an end: the employee, who had been off work for a prolonged period of time, had disobeyed the employer's lawful instruction to attend so as to discuss his long-term absence; he was in breach of an instruction to return the employer's calls to re-arrange that appointment; and his continued absence from work was unexplained by any current medical report. In the circumstances, he was held to have been in breach of the duty of trust and confidence, which justified the employer in treating the contract of employment as having been terminated.

45.14 Effect of permanent health benefits on the calculation of damages

Payments made by an employer under a permanent health insurance plan are not treated as remuneration or earnings from employment within the meaning of the *Administration of Justice Act 1982, s 10(i)*. Rather, they are to be regarded as a 'contractual' pension or benefit and are therefore not taken into account so as to reduce damages to an employee suing in respect of injuries sustained as a result of an accident at work (*Lewicki v Brown and Root Wimpey Highland Fabricators Ltd* [1996] STC 145, [1996] IRLR 565).

45.15 'Unable to follow any occupation'

Permanent health insurance schemes often require the employee to show that he is unable to follow his own occupation for a period of time and thereafter that he is 'unable to follow any occupation' if he is to obtain long-term benefits. In *Walton v Airtours plc* [2002] EWCA Civ 1659, [2003] IRLR 161, the Court of Appeal held that the words 'unable to follow any occupation' had to be read in a common sense practical way and any inability must be assessed realistically. It was held that the phrase connoted being engaged in regular work for a substantial or indefinite period. It was enough that an employee could work on a temporary basis, or was able to start a new job for a few days but not continue thereafter to earn income. See also *Jowitt v Pioneer Technology (UK) Ltd* [2003] EWCA Civ 411, [2003] ICR 1120, [2003] IRLR 356.

46   Strikes and Industrial Action

Cross-references. See TRADE UNIONS – I (51) for the liability of unions for industrial action and HUMAN RIGHTS (31).

46.1   LIABILITY FOR INDUSTRIAL ACTION – BACKGROUND

The right to take industrial action takes the form, in this country, of statutory *immunity* for action which would otherwise attract legal liability at common law. The statutory immunity first appeared in something like its present form in the *Trade Disputes Act 1906, s 3*, and its scope has varied frequently since then.

This area of the law has been and is likely to continue to be influenced by the right to freedom of association embodied in *art 11* of the *ECHR*, which was incorporated into domestic law by the *Human Rights Act 1998*. In *Demir v Turkey* (App no 34503/97) (2008) 48 EHRR 1272, [2009] IRLR 766, the European Court of Human Rights held for the first time that the right to bargain collectively should in general form part of the right to freedom of association. In addition, the requirements of European law may impact on the ability of workers to take industrial action. In *International Transport Workers' Federation v Viking Line ABP*: C-438/05 [2008] All ER (EC) 127, [2008] ICR 741, [2008] IRLR 143 the European Court of Justice held that the right to freedom of establishment embodied in *art 43* of the EC Treaty could in principle be unlawfully restricted by industrial action aimed at preventing a ferry operator from registering one of its vessels in a different country in order to lower its labour costs. However, it was also held that such a restriction might be justified by an overriding public interest (such as the protection of workers) provided that it was proportionate to the objective in question. The ECJ adopted a similar approach to the potential impact of industrial action on the right of freedom to provide services under *art 49* of the EC Treaty in *Laval un Partneri Ltd v Svenska Byggnadsarbetareforbundet*: C-341/05 [2008] All ER (EC) 166, [2008] IRLR 160. The part-French owned claimant railway operating company in *Govia GTR Railway Ltd v ASLEF* [2017] ICR 497, [2017] IRLR 246 failed before the Court of Appeal in an argument that the union in calling strike action was acting in breach of its rights of establishment under *art 49* of the EC Treaty and its right to provide and receive services under *art 56*, even though the strike affected the rail link to Gatwick Airport.

The current basic immunity and the qualifications upon it are contained in the *Trade Union and Labour Relations (Consolidation) Act 1992* ('*TULR(C)A 1992*'), and were significantly amended with effect from 1 March 2017 when the *Trade Union Act 2016* came into force. In *Metrobus Ltd v Unite the Union* [2009] EWCA Civ 829, [2010] ICR 173, [2009] IRLR 851 the Court of Appeal rejected the argument that the notification provisions contained in *TULR(C)A 1992* were so difficult or onerous as to give rise to a breach of *art 11* of the *ECHR*. This approach was followed by the European Court of Human Rights in *National Union of Rail, Maritime and Transport Workers v United Kingdom* (App no 31045/10) [2014] IRLR 467, in which the applicant union's complaint that the strike-ballot notice requirements had violated *art 11* was held to be inadmissible. All that the union had been required to do was comply with the procedural requirements laid down by UK law. Moreover, it was significant that the union, having initially been restrained by injunction from calling a strike, subsequently was able to comply with the notice requirements and had successfully called a strike.

In deciding whether legal proceedings can be taken against individuals (or unions) carrying on industrial action, it first must be ascertained whether a tort is being committed, for example, inducing a breach of contract (see **46.2** below). Then it must be ascertained whether the act amounting to the commission of that tort attracts the immunity conferred by *TULR(C)A 1992*.

46.1   Strikes and Industrial Action

This will involve consideration of whether the act was done in contemplation or furtherance of a trade dispute, whether the industrial action has the support of a ballot, whether the industrial action has been properly initiated, and whether the immunity has been lost because the action is unlawful secondary action or for some other reason.

The law relating to trade disputes is extremely complex. What appears below is an outline of the principles involved.

46.2   LIABILITY AT COMMON LAW

The law relating to the so-called 'economic torts' has developed gradually over the years; it is a difficult area which in many respects is still unclear. The most frequently encountered of the torts relate, broadly, to interference with contractual relations (note that *TULR(C)A 1992, s 245* deems Crown servants to have contracts of employment for these purposes). They include:

(a)   direct inducement of a breach of contract. A union which calls a strike will almost always induce the relevant employees to breach their contracts of employment;

(b)   the indirect inducement or procurement of a breach of contract by unlawful means. For example, A may be able to sue the union if his contract to obtain goods from B is breached by B when the union induces B's employees to go on strike in breach of their contracts of employment;

(c)   interference with business by unlawful means. This may include the case where the performance of contracts is impeded but there is no actual breach;

(d)   intimidation. This is designed to deal with the situation where the harm results, directly or indirectly, not from the actual using of unlawful means, but from the threat of such use;

(e)   conspiracy, ie an agreement either to do an unlawful act or to do a lawful act by unlawful means. The effect of the second limb is that an act done by two or more people may be unlawful even though it would have been lawful if done by one person acting alone.

Apart from the usual requirements of causation and foreseeability, it will usually be necessary to show that the defendant knows of the relevant contract and intends to procure its breach or the interference with its performance. Conspiracy is made out only where the agreement is to do an unlawful act, or where the defendant's predominant purpose is to injure the plaintiff, and not to further his own legitimate interests (see *Lonrho plc v Fayed* [1992] 1 AC 448, [1991] 3 All ER 303).

Some of the most important of the many authorities on the economic torts are *D C Thomson & Co Ltd v Deakin* [1952] Ch 646, [1952] 2 All ER 361, *J T Stratford & Son Ltd v Lindley* [1965] AC 269, *Torquay Hotel Co Ltd v Cousins* [1969] 2 Ch 106, [1968] 3 All ER 43, *Merkur Island Shipping Corpn v Laughton* [1983] ICR 490, [1983] IRLR 218, *News Group Newspapers Ltd v SOGAT '82 (No 2)* [1987] ICR 181, [1986] IRLR 337, *Middlebrook Mushrooms Ltd v TGWU* [1993] ICR 612, [1993] IRLR 232; *Timeplan Education Group Ltd v National Union of Teachers* [1997] IRLR 457; *OBG Ltd v Allan* [2008] 1 AC 1, [2007] IRLR 608; and *Total Network SL v Revenue & Customs Comrs* [2008] UKHL 19, [2008] 1 AC 1174, [2008] 2 All ER 413.

Although it is usually a breach of contract which is ultimately at the root of liability, that is by no means necessarily the case. See, eg *Lonrho plc v Fayed*, above (allegation of intentional infliction of harm by unlawful means based upon fraudulent misrepresentation made to, but not causing loss to, a third party). Doubt surrounds the extent to which breach of a statutory duty or a penal statute may be relied upon as unlawful means if the breach is not itself actionable. See *Lonrho Ltd v Shell Petroleum Co Ltd (No 2)* [1982] AC 173, [1981] 2 All ER 456; *Barretts & Baird (Wholesale) Ltd v Institution of Professional Civil Servants* [1987] IRLR 3; *Associated British Ports v TGWU* [1989] 1 WLR 939, [1989] IRLR 399 (point not argued in the House of Lords); and *OBG Ltd v Allan* [2008] 1 AC 1, [2007] IRLR 608.

Any successful picket will almost certainly involve the *prima facie* commission of the tort of inducing a breach of contract or of interference with contract by unlawful means (see *Union Traffic Ltd v TGWU* [1989] ICR 98, [1989] IRLR 127). Picketing may also involve the torts of nuisance and intimidation (especially if it is mass picketing), or of trespass (see *Mersey Dock and Harbour Co v Verrinder* [1982] IRLR 152, *Thomas v National Union of Mineworkers (South Wales Area)* [1985] ICR 886, [1985] IRLR 136, *News Group Newspapers Ltd v SOGAT (1982)* [1987] ICR 181, [1986] IRLR 337) (see **46.9** below).

46.3   THE IMMUNITY FOR LIABILITY

TULR(C)A 1992, s 219 provides as follows:

'(1)   An act done by a person in contemplation or furtherance of a trade dispute shall not be actionable in tort on the ground only:

(*a*)   that it induces another person to break a contract or interferes or induces any other person to interfere with its performance; or

(*b*)   that it consists in his threatening that a contract (whether one to which he is a party or not) will be broken or its performance interfered with, or that he will induce another person to break a contract or to interfere with its performance.

(2)   An agreement or combination by two or more persons to do or procure the doing of any act in contemplation or furtherance of a trade dispute shall not be actionable in tort if the act is one which, if done without any such agreement or combination, would not be actionable in tort.'

This formula provides immunity from actions based upon the most common of the economic torts. However, it is possible to formulate a cause of action which falls outside *s 219* (see, eg *Prudential Assurance Co Ltd v Lorenz* (1971) 11 KIR 78 (inducing breach of fiduciary duty); *Associated British Ports v TGWU* [1989] 1 WLR 939, [1989] IRLR 399 (inducing breach of statutory duty; the point was not argued in the House of Lords)). In such cases it is probably irrelevant that the act complained of may also constitute an inducement to breach of contract which does fall within the immunity.

The statutory immunity does not protect employees from actions by their employers for breach of contract. However, in practice it is unlikely to be worthwhile for an employer to sue individual employees for losses arising from industrial action (see **46.16**(d) below).

46.4   'A TRADE DISPUTE'

'Trade dispute' is given a statutory definition for this purpose by *TULR(C)A 1992, s 244(1)*, namely:

' . . .   a dispute between workers and their employer which relates wholly or mainly to one or more of the following, that is to say:

(*a*)   terms and conditions of employment, or the physical conditions in which any workers are required to work;

(*b*)   engagement or non-engagement, or termination or suspension of employment or the duties of employment, of one or more workers;

(*c*)   allocation of work or the duties of employment as between workers or groups of workers;

(d)   matters of discipline;

(e)   a worker's membership or non-membership of a trade union;

(f)   facilities for officials of trade unions; and

(g)   machinery for negotiation or consultation, and other procedures, relating to any of the above matters, including the recognition by employers or employers' associations of the right of a trade union to represent workers in any such negotiation or consultation or in the carrying out of such procedures.'

In *s 244* 'employment' includes any relationship whereby one person personally does work or performs services for another (*TULR(C)A 1992, s 244(5)*).

'Worker', in relation to a dispute with an employer, means:

(a)   a worker employed by that employer; or

(b)   a person who has ceased to be employed by that employer where:

(i)   his employment was terminated in connection with the dispute; or

(ii)   the termination of his employment was one of the circumstances giving rise to the dispute.

(*TULR(C)A 1992, s 244(5)*.)

The test of whether there is a trade dispute is an *objective* test (*NWL Ltd v Woods* [1979] ICR 867, [1979] IRLR 478). A dispute for political reasons which is unconnected with terms and conditions of employment is not considered to be a trade dispute. One such case involved a refusal by broadcasting technicians to make a broadcast to South Africa during the apartheid era (*BBC v Hearn* [1977] IRLR 273). Similarly, a proposed strike intended as a protest against Government policies was held not to be in contemplation or furtherance of a trade dispute (*Express Newspapers v Keys* [1980] IRLR 247). However, in *Secretary of State for Education v NUT* [2016] IRLR 512, the High Court held that a dispute between a teaching union and the Secretary of State in relation to the funding of sixth form colleges did give rise to a trade dispute between the union and the Secretary of State, despite the fact that the sixth form colleges set teachers' pay on an individual basis.

In *Mercury Communications Ltd v Scott-Garner* [1984] ICR 74, an injunction was granted to restrain industrial action since the court held that the risk to jobs did not appear to be the major factor in the dispute. However, if the union genuinely wishes to achieve its demands relating to terms and conditions of employment (or any other matter falling within *TULR(C)A 1992, s 244(1)*), it is not relevant to establish whether those demands are realistic (*Associated British Ports v TGWU* [1989] 1 WLR 939, [1989] IRLR 399, a point not argued on appeal). See also *Newham London Borough Council v NALGO* [1993] ICR 189. In *ISS Mediclean Ltd v GMB* [2015] IRLR 96, the High Court rejected an application for an injunction based on the employer's contention that the matters in issue had essentially been resolved. It was clear that certain matters remained in dispute.

If workers take industrial action in this country in order to further a trade dispute abroad, then, provided that the outcome of the dispute relating to matters occurring outside the UK is likely to affect them in one or more of the aspects specified in *s 244(1)*, it will be considered to be a trade dispute for the purpose of the immunity conferred by *s 219* (*TULR(C)A 1992, s 244(3)*).

Although the dispute must be between workers (not merely the union) and their employer, it will be sufficient to show that it results from the breakdown of negotiations in which the union was acting on behalf of those workers; and in any event a 'Yes' vote in the strike ballot will amount to an adoption of the dispute by the workers (*Associated British Ports v TGWU* [1989] 1 WLR 939, [1989] IRLR 399, a point not argued on appeal).

Where a dispute relates to terms and conditions, a strike will be treated as 'in furtherance of a trade dispute' even if some of those balloted and who may be called out are not themselves affected by the terms and conditions in dispute: see *British Telecommunications plc v Communications Workers Union* [2003] EWHC 937 (QB), [2004] IRLR 58. However, in *University College London Hospitals NHS Trust v Unison* [1999] ICR 204, [1999] IRLR 31, the Court of Appeal upheld an injunction granted against the defendant union following a dispute relating to the future terms and conditions of the employees of a number of private companies which it was proposed should take over the activities of the claimant hospital trust. It was held that a dispute about the terms and conditions of employees of third party employers, who had never been employed by the subject of the proposed strike action, was not a trade dispute within the meaning of *TULR(C)A 1992, s 244(1)*. Nor was a dispute that was mainly concerned with the terms and conditions of existing employees with an unidentified future employer a trade dispute within the meaning of the section. This approach was held by the European Court of Human Rights to be in accordance with the right to freedom of association contained in *art 11(1)* of the European Convention of Human Rights in *Unison v United Kingdom* [2002] IRLR 497. The European court accepted in that case for the first time that the prohibition on the right to strike was an interference with the *art 11(1)* right which required justification under *art 11(2)*, albeit the restriction was justified in that case. However, in *Ognevenko v Russia* (App. No. 44873/09) [2019] IRLR 195, [2018] ECHR 44873/09 the Strasbourg Court held that a wide-ranging ban on strike action by railway operatives was not justified under *art 11(2)*, and the claim was upheld. A more limited limitation on strike action by (among others) health workers was held to be justified in *Association of Academics v Iceland* [2019] IRLR 189.

In contrast with the approach in the *University College London Hospitals NHS Trust* case, in *Westminster City Council v Unison* [2001] EWCA Civ 443, [2001] ICR 1046, [2001] IRLR 524, the Court of Appeal held that a dispute which was predominantly about the change in the identity of the employer consequent on the transfer of employees from a local authority to a private company did fall within the definition of trade dispute.

In *P (a minor) v National Association of School Masters/Union of Women Teachers* [2003] UKHL 8, [2003] ICR 386, [2003] IRLR 307, the House of Lords held that a dispute as to the reasonableness of an order by the head teacher of a school that the staff should teach an excluded pupil, who had subsequently been reinstated, did amount to a trade dispute as to the teachers' terms and conditions of employment. The dispute related to the teachers' terms and conditions in the sense that it concerned the nature and extent of their contractual obligation to teach the pupil.

Thus, subject to the limits outlined above and to the further restrictions considered below, a person or a trade union may take part in industrial action so long as it is in contemplation or furtherance of a trade dispute as defined.

46.5 **'In contemplation or furtherance . . . '**

If there is a trade dispute, the question whether a particular act is in contemplation or furtherance of it is to be judged *subjectively*. In *Express Newspapers Ltd v McShane* [1980] ICR 42, [1980] IRLR 35, the House of Lords held that 'If the party who does the act honestly thinks at the time he does it that it may help one of the parties to the trade dispute to achieve their objectives and does it for that reason, he is protected by the section' (*per* Lord Diplock at 57). The House of Lords reversed the decision of the Court of Appeal which had applied a more objective test. The subjective test was also applied by the House of Lords in *Duport Steels Ltd v Sirs* [1980] IRLR 116. It is sufficient if one purpose of the strike is the furtherance of the dispute, even though there may be other purposes not within the immunity (*Associated British Ports v TGWU* [1989] 1 WLR 939, [1989] IRLR 399, a point not argued on appeal).

46.6   LIMITS IMPOSED ON SECONDARY ACTION

In non-legal language, 'secondary action' is the term used to describe industrial action taken by workers where the real dispute is not between themselves and their own employer. The typical example is the 'sympathy strike'.

Nothing in *TULR(C)A 1992, s 219* prevents an act from being actionable in tort where one of the facts relied upon for the purpose of establishing liability is that there has been secondary action which is not lawful picketing (*TULR(C)A 1992, s 224(1)*). Lawful picketing means acts done in the course of such attendance as is declared lawful by *TULR(C)A 1992, s 220* by a worker employed or last employed by the employer who is party to the dispute, or by a trade union official whose attendance is lawful by virtue of *s 220(1)(b)*. There is secondary action in relation to a trade dispute when, and only when, a person:

(a)   induces another to break a contract of employment or interferes with or induces another to interfere with its performance, or

(b)   threatens that a contract of employment under which he or another is employed will be broken or its performance interfered with, or that he will induce another to break a contract of employment or to interfere with its performance,

and the employer under the contract of employment is not the employer party to the dispute (*TULR(C)A 1992, s 224(2)*). An employer cannot be party to a dispute between another employer and his workers, and if more than one employer is in dispute with his workers, each dispute is to be treated as separate (*TULR(C)A 1992, s 224(4)*). A contract of employment is defined to include any contract for personal service, and is thus not confined to the contracts of those who are employees in the strict sense (*TULR(C)A 1992, s 224(6)*; cf EMPLOYEE, SELF-EMPLOYED OR WORKER? **(16)**).

The effect of *TULR(C)A 1992, ss 220* and *224(1)* is that it will not be actionable if, for example, strikers in dispute with their own employer and picketing their workplace induce a lorry-driver not to cross the picket-line, and thus to breach his contract of employment with his own employer who is not a party to the dispute. Subject to this limited type of exception, however, it will be tortious to organise any form of secondary action, including secondary picketing. Unlike under earlier legislation, there is no exception where the aim of the secondary action is to disrupt the supply of goods and services to or from the employer who is party to the dispute or an associated employer of that party.

However, if a particular act constitutes primary action in relation to a trade dispute, the same act may not be relied upon as constituting secondary action so as to evade the immunity in tort. Primary action means the same as secondary action but where the employer under the contract of employment *is* party to the dispute (*TULR(C)A 1992, s 224(5)*).

In *National Union of Rail, Maritime and Transport Workers v United Kingdom* (App no 31045/10) [2014] IRLR 467 the RMT union argued before the European Court of Human Rights that the UK's blanket ban on secondary action amounted to an infringement of its rights under *art 11* of the ECHR. The court accepted that the ban on secondary action, as it applied in that case, constituted an interference with the RMT's rights under *art 11*. However, that interference was in pursuit of a legitimate aim. Secondary action may well have much broader ramifications than primary action. It may impinge on the rights of persons not party to the dispute, cause broad disruption to the economy and affect the delivery of services to the public. Further, the restriction was proportionate, particularly as a ban on secondary action did not strike at the very substance of the right of freedom of association. It is not wholly clear from the court's decision whether this is its final word on the point, or whether it considered the position might be different on different facts.

46.7   PRESSURE TO IMPOSE UNION MEMBERSHIP OR RECOGNITION

Under *TULR(C)A 1992, ss 222* and *225*, certain industrial action taken to impose union membership or recognition requirements does not have the protection of *s 219* and will therefore be unlawful. Specifically, there is no immunity from actions in tort for individuals who induce or attempt to induce another:

(a)   to incorporate in a contract to which that other person is a party, or proposed contract to which that other person intends to be a party, a term or conditions which would require that a party to the contract should recognise one or more trade unions for the purpose of negotiating on behalf of workers employed by him, or that he should negotiate with or consult with an official of one or more trade unions;

(b)   on grounds of union exclusion (that is, that the supplier or prospective supplier does not or is not likely to recognise, negotiate or consult as set out in (*a*) above), to:

    (i)   exclude a person from a list of approved suppliers of goods and services or persons from whom tenders for the supply of goods or services are invited;

    (ii)   exclude a person from the group of persons from whom tenders for the supply of goods or services are invited;

    (iii)   fail to permit a particular person to submit such a tender; or

    (iv)   terminate or determine not to enter into a contract with a particular person for the supply of goods or services.

(TULR(C)A 1992, ss 186, 187, 225.)

Nor is there any immunity where the act concerned is done because, or partly because, a particular employer is employing, has employed or might employ a person who is not a member of any, or any particular, trade union, or because a particular employer refrains from discriminating against such a person, or because it is believed that any of these things has occurred (*TULR(C)A 1992, s 222(1)*). In *Birmingham City Council v Unite the Union* [2019] EWHC 478 (QB), [2019] IRLR 423 Freedman J found that strike action taken with a view to obtaining settlement payments for members of one union where similar payments had been paid to members of another union did not fall within this exception. Far from seeking to force the employer to discriminate between members of different unions, the union was seeking to have its members to be treated in the same way.

Nor is there any immunity where the act concerned is, or is part of, an inducement or an attempted inducement of a person:

(a)   to incorporate in a contract to which that person is party or intends to be party a term or condition which would require that the whole, or some part, of the work done for the purposes of the contract be done only by persons who are or are not members of trade unions or a particular trade union; or

(b)   on union membership grounds (that is, that if the proposed contract were entered into with the person concerned, work for the purposes of the contract would be or would be likely to be done by persons who were or were not members of trade unions or a particular trade union; or in the case of the termination of a contract that such work has been or is likely to be done by such persons), to

    (i)   exclude a person from a list of approved suppliers of goods and services or persons from whom tenders for the supply of goods and services may be invited;

    (ii)   exclude a person from the group of persons from whom tenders for the supply of goods or services are invited;

(iii) fail to permit a particular person to submit such a tender;

(iv) determine not to enter into a contract with a particular person for the supply of goods or services; or

(v) terminate a contract with a particular person for the supply of goods or services.

(TULR(C)A 1992, ss 144, 145, 222(3).)

See also **52.19** Trade Unions – II.

46.8 Action in response to dismissal of unofficial strikers

The immunity under *TULR(C)A 1992, s 219* is lost where the reason, or one of the reasons, for doing the act in question (such as an inducing of breaches of contract by organising a strike) is the fact or belief that an employer has dismissed one or more employees in circumstances such that by virtue of *TULR(C)A 1992, s 237* they have no right to complain of unfair dismissal (*TULR(C)A 1992, s 223*).

TULR(C)A 1992, s 237, which is discussed in detail in **54.18** Unfair Dismissal – I, provides that an employee has no right to complain of unfair dismissal if at the time of dismissal he was taking part in an unofficial strike or other unofficial industrial action.

46.9 PICKETING

As noted above, any successful picket will be liable to involve the commission of a tort. The statutory immunity for picketing is contained in *TULR(C)A 1992, s 220*. A person acts lawfully if he attends:

(a) in contemplation or furtherance of a trade dispute; *and*

(b) at a specified place, namely:

 (i) at or near his own place of work; or

 (ii) if he is unemployed and either his last employment was terminated in connection with a trade dispute or if the termination was one of the circumstances giving rise to a trade dispute, at or near his former place of work; or

 (iii) if he does not work or normally work at any one place or if the place where he works or normally works is in a location such that attendance there for picketing is impracticable, at any premises of his employer from which he works or from which his work is administered; or

 (iv) if he is an official of a trade union, at or near the place of work or former place of work of a member of that union whom he is accompanying and whom he represents; and

(c) for the purpose only of peacefully obtaining or communicating information or peacefully persuading any person to work or abstain from working.

The requirements for a lawful picket have been expanded with effect from 1 March 2017 by *s 10* of the *Trade Union Act 2016*, which has inserted a new *s 220A* into *TULR(C)A 1992*, imposing additional duties on trade unions to supervise pickets. In particular, it is now a requirement of a lawful picket: that the union appoints someone to supervise the picketing, who is an official or other member of the union; that the supervisor must wear something that readily identifies him (such as an armband) and have a letter stating that the picketing is approved by the union, which he must show as soon as reasonably practicable if asked by a representative of the employer; that the union or supervisor must tell the police the supervisor's name and how to contact them, and where the picketing will be taking place; and that the supervisor must be present or readily contactable and able to attend at short notice while the picketing is taking place.

Any person who pickets outside these limits will lose the immunity from actions in tort. By reason of *TULR(C)A 1992, s 219(3)* he cannot rely upon the general immunity conferred by *s 219* upon acts done in contemplation or furtherance of a trade dispute unless *s 220* is also satisfied. Accordingly, he will be liable to a claim for an injunction and/or damages if, in the course of such picketing, he commits a tort.

The purpose of condition (*b*) above, relating to the specified place for a picket, is to remove the immunity from 'flying pickets'. The Court of Appeal considered its effects in *Union Traffic Ltd v Transport and General Workers Union* [1989] ICR 98, [1989] IRLR 127 in which it was held that lorry drivers were not entitled to picket depots at which they frequently called for deliveries, repairs and the like, because they were not the bases from which the drivers worked. In *Rayware Ltd v Transport and General Workers Union* [1989] ICR 457, [1989] IRLR 134 a gate leading to a private trading estate but some way from the employer's premises on that estate was held to be 'near' the place of work since it was the nearest the pickets could get to their place of work without committing a trespass.

Further, *s 220* only serves to give immunity from actions in tort where the tort arises out of the mere act of attendance at the place concerned. If the picket commits further torts, such as inducing breaches of the contracts of employment of those whom he seeks to dissuade from crossing the picket line, he will be liable unless he has the protection of *s 219*, which is discussed more fully elsewhere in this chapter. In *Thames Cleaning v United Voices of the World* [2016] IRLR 695 the High Court held that, when a union organised a protest, which did not amount to picketing in the sense of seeking to dissuade workers from entering their employer's premises, it was not appropriate to grant an injunction to prevent picketing. However, an injunction was granted imposing an exclusion zone around the entrance to the employer's premises, so as to prevent individuals with no connection to the employer harassing the employer through their protesting activities. The statutory immunity which applies to picketing does not extend to demonstrations which amount to harassment.

One of the circumstances in which the protection of *TULR(C)A 1992, s 219* is lost is where one of the facts relied on for the purpose of establishing liability is that there has been secondary action which is not lawful picketing (*TULR(C)A 1992, s 224(1)*) (see **46.6** above). Any picket is liable to involve secondary action, because the pickets will try to turn back the employees of third parties, hence the exception in *s 224(1)* for lawful picketing. Lawful picketing is defined in *TULR(C)A 1992, s 224(3)* as acts done, in the course of attendance declared lawful by *s 220*, by a worker employed (or, if not in employment, last employed) by the employer party to the dispute or by a trade union official whose attendance is lawful by virtue of *TULR(C)A 1992, s 220(1)(b)*. The effect of these provisions is to remove the immunity from secondary picketing whilst retaining it for direct picketing of the employer who is a party to the dispute, even if that involves pickets trying to turn back the employees of third parties.

46.10 Broome's case

In *Broome v DPP* [1974] ICR 84, [1974] IRLR 26, the defendant, a picket during an industrial dispute, stood holding a placard in front of a vehicle on a highway, urging the driver not to go to a nearby site and preventing him from so doing for some nine minutes. The Divisional Court reversed the decision of the Stockport magistrates acquitting the defendant and convicted him of obstructing the highway. The House of Lords affirmed the conviction. The law which their Lordships had to consider was *Industrial Relations Act 1971, s 134* (which was framed, for these purposes, in similar terms to the present *TULR(C)A 1992, s 220*). Lord Reid said of the defendant's conduct (at 89):

> '. . . his attendance there is only made lawful by subsection (2) if he attended only for the purpose of obtaining or communicating information or "peacefully persuading" the lorry driver. Attendance for that purpose must I think include the right to try to persuade anyone who chooses to stop and listen, at least in so far as this is done in a reasonable way with due consideration for the rights of others. A right to attend for the purpose of peaceful persuasion would be meaningless unless this were implied.

> But I see no ground for implying any right to require the person whom it is sought to persuade to submit to any kind of constraint or restriction of his personal freedom.'

Lord Salmon made similar observations.

Thus, police officers acted within their powers when they prevented pickets from approaching a lorry carrying 'strike breakers' during an industrial dispute because they feared an obstruction or a breach of the peace (*Kavanagh v Hiscock* [1974] ICR 282, [1974] IRLR 121).

46.11   Code of Practice

The Secretary of State for Employment has issued a Code of Practice on picketing under his statutory powers (see **5.4** CODES OF PRACTICE). The original Code was revised and reissued by virtue of the *Employment Code of Practice (Picketing) Order 1992 (SI 1992/476)*.

The most notable provisions of the *Code* include the recommendation that there should not generally be more than six pickets at any one entrance (*para 51*), recommendations as to the functions of the picket organiser (*paras 54* to *57*), and recommendations concerning avoiding impediments to the movement of essential supplies, services and operations (*paras 62* to *64*).

46.12   CRIMINAL LIABILITY

Action taken by pickets may give rise to criminal liability. For example, they may be prosecuted under *TULR(C)A 1992, s 241(1)(d)*, which provides that a person who:

> '. . . with a view to compelling another person to abstain from doing or to do any act which that person has a legal right to do or abstain from doing, wrongfully and without legal authority . . . watches or besets the house or other place where that person resides, or works, or carries on business, or happens to be, or the approach to such house or place',

shall, on summary conviction, be liable to a fine not exceeding level 5 on the Standard Scale, or up to six months' imprisonment, or both (*TULR(C)A 1992, s 241(2)*; see **1.10** INTRODUCTION).

However, compulsion of the other person, and not mere persuasion of him, must be the object of the watching and besetting (*DPP v Fidler* [1992] 1 WLR 91). The watching and besetting is not wrongful unless tortious (*Thomas v National Union of Mineworkers (South Wales Area)* [1985] ICR 886, [1985] IRLR 136), but it appears that it may be wrongful even if no action in tort could be brought because of the statutory immunity (*Galt v Philp* [1984] IRLR 156). Other criminal charges for assault, criminal damage and offences under the *Public Order Act 1986* (especially *ss 1–5*) may arise if the pickets behave unlawfully. In such cases *TULR(C)A 1992, s 220* cannot provide them with a defence. *Public Order Act 1986, Part II* gives the police certain powers to impose conditions upon public processions and assemblies, in addition to their common law powers to take such action as may be necessary to prevent a breach of the peace.

The House of Lords held in *DPP v Jones* [1999] 2 AC 240, [1999] 2 All ER 257 that the public have the right to use the highway for such reasonable and usual activities, including peaceful assembly, as are consistent with the primary right of passage. This important decision was plainly influenced by *art 11* of the European Convention on Human Rights (the right to freedom of peaceful assembly).

Any action which does not fall within the provisions of *TULR(C)A 1992, s 220* constitutes an offence if the obstruction takes place on the public highway, since the *Highways Act 1980, s 137(1)* provides:

> 'If a person, without lawful authority or excuse, in any way wilfully obstructs the free passage along a highway he is guilty of an offence . . . '.

For the definition of obstruction, see *Cooper v Metropolitan Police Comr* (1985) 82 Cr App Rep 238. However, picketing may take place outside factory gates which are on private property. In such a case, the pickets cannot be guilty of obstructing the highway but may be liable for a private trespass or nuisance.

46.13 THE LIABILITY OF TRADE UNIONS

Trade unions are no longer, as they once were, immune from all proceedings in tort arising from industrial action. They are now liable for tortious acts which they are taken to have authorised or endorsed (see **51.16 Trade Unions – I**). They enjoy the same statutory immunity as individuals, but only if they fulfil the ballot requirements of *TULR(C)A 1992*. The liability of trade unions in actions in tort is subject to statutory financial limits (see **51.17 Trade Unions – I**).

46.14 BALLOTS BEFORE INDUSTRIAL ACTION

In order to enjoy immunity from actions in tort for acts inducing persons to take part or continue to take part in industrial action, trade unions must be supported by a ballot (*TULR(C)A 1992, s 226(1)*). The ballot must comply with the complex procedural obligations contained in *Part V* of *TULR(C)A 1992*. The requirements of *Part V* have been substantially amended, and made more exacting, with effect from 1 March 2017, by the *Trade Union Act 2016*. Notwithstanding the onerous nature of these requirements, the Court of Appeal held in *Metrobus Ltd v Unite the Union* [2009] EWCA Civ 829, [2010] ICR 173, [2009] IRLR 851 that they were not incompatible with the right to freedom of association contained in *art 11* of the *European Convention on Human Rights*. A similar challenge raised in *National Union of Rail, Maritime and Transport Workers v United Kingdom* (App no 31045/10) [2014] IRLR 467 was ruled inadmissible by the European Court of Human Rights. The following are the prerequisites of a ballot before industrial action.

(a)   All of those members whom it is reasonable for the union to believe will be called upon to take part in the industrial action, and no others, must be balloted (*TULR(C)A 1992, s 227(1)*). Those "taking part" in the industrial action are not confined to members who will in fact be called upon to breach their contracts of employment; they may participate in other ways: see *London Underground Ltd v ASLEF* [2011] EWHC 3506, [2012] IRLR 196. The requirement in *s 227(1)* is mitigated by *TULR(C)A 1992, s 232B* which provides that a failure to comply which is accidental and on a scale which is unlikely to affect the result of the ballot will be disregarded. In *British Airways plc v Unite the Union* [2009] EWHC 3541, [2010] IRLR 423, the High Court held that the union had failed to comply with the requirement to ballot only those whom it reasonably believed would be called upon to take action, in circumstances where several hundred members had been balloted whom the union knew would no longer be employed by the employer at the time of the ballot. The union could gain no assistance from *TULR(C)A 1992, s 232B*, since the failure, though unintentional, could not properly be described as accidental. The Court of Appeal considered the requirement that a relevant failure must be "accidental" for *s 232B* to come into play in *London & Birmingham Railway Ltd v ASLEF; Serco Ltd v RMT* [2011] EWCA Civ 226, [2011] ICR 848, [2011] IRLR 399, and held that the union's actions in permitting two members to vote who should not have been should be disregarded. The mistake was due to human error, and it did not matter that it could have been avoided if reasonable steps had been taken to keep the union's records up to date. Moreover, the Court of Appeal went on to express the view that a general de minimis principle applies in the context of the balloting procedures. By virtue of *TULR(C)A 1992, s 232A*, industrial action will not be regarded as having the support of a ballot if any member whom it was reasonable at the time of the ballot for the union to believe would be induced to take part in the action is induced to take part. However, the union is not confined to balloting and inducing to take part in the action only those who will be directly affected by the subject matter of the trade dispute: see *United Closures and Plastics Ltd* [2012] IRLR 29. It was held by the Court of Appeal in *London Underground Ltd v National Union of Rail, Maritime and Transport Workers* [1996] ICR 170 that the defendant union could induce members who had not been balloted to take part in industrial action if those members had joined the union since the ballot. It was also recognised that a union may induce non-members to participate, even though they will not have been balloted. In *P (a minor) v National Association of School Masters/Union of Women Teachers* [2003] UKHL 8, [2003] ICR 386, [2003] IRLR 307 the House of Lords held that the union's failure to send ballot papers to two teachers who had recently joined the staff did not invalidate the ballot. In particular, the failure to send those teachers ballot papers did not necessarily mean that they had not been accorded entitlement to vote within the meaning of *TULR(C)A 1992, s 232A(c)*. The requirement to send out ballot papers to those defined as entitled to vote in *s 227(1)* is subject to the caveat 'so far as is reasonably practicable' in *s 230(2)*. Further, *s 232B* makes the requirement to send out ballot papers subject to the disregard of small accidental errors. Accordingly, the ballot was valid. By contrast, in *Midline Mainline Ltd v National Union of Rail, Maritime and Transport Workers* [2001] EWCA Civ 1206, [2001] IRLR 813 the failure to ballot 25 union members in a ballot of 91 members was held by the Court of Appeal to be too significant to be disregarded.

If the persons balloted have different places of work, *TULR(C)A 1992, s 228* requires a separate ballot for each workplace, unless those balloted share a common feature of terms and conditions of employment or occupational description which is not shared by other members with the same employer who are not balloted and, in a case where there are such other members, is not a factor which employees of that employer have in common by virtue of having the same place of work. A new *TULR(C)A 1992, ss 228* and *228A*, enable unions to hold a ballot across separate workplaces if the dispute affects at least one member of the union in each workplace, or if the ballot is limited to all members whom the union reasonably believes to have particular kinds of occupation and are employed by a particular employer or employers with whom the union is in dispute, or if entitlement to vote is given only to members of the union who are employed by an employer or employers with whom the union is in dispute. 'Workplace' is defined as the premises at which an employee works or, where an employee does not work at a particular premises, the premises with which his employment has the closest connection (*TULR(C)A 1992, s 228(4)*). Where separate workplace ballots are not required, the ballot may legitimately include employees of more than one employer, if a number of employers are party to the dispute (*University of Central England v NALGO* [1993] IRLR 81). Employees of different employers may be held to have the same place of work even if their respective employers each have only a licence over the premises at which they work (*Intercity West Coast Ltd v National Union of Rail, Maritime and Transport Workers* [1996] IRLR 583).

(b)   Every person who is entitled to vote in the ballot must be allowed to vote without interference from the union (*TULR(C)A 1992, 230(1)*). So far as is reasonably practicable, every person entitled to vote must have a voting paper sent to him by post at his home address (or other address which he has requested the union to treat as his postal address), and must be given a convenient opportunity to vote by post (*TULR(C)A 1992, s 230(2)*). In *Royal Mail Group Ltd v Communication Workers Union* [2019] EWCA Civ 2150, [2020] IRLR 213, the Court of Appeal held that this requirement had been breached when the union, which represented postal workers, had encouraged its members to intercept their ballot papers at their places of work, open them immediately and vote at the workplace, and to take part in filmed "mass posting" events. This subverted the legislative intention behind *s 230* and amounted to interference. Special provisions apply to merchant seamen. It was held in *British Railways Board v National Union of Railwaymen* [1989] ICR 678, [1989] IRLR 349 that the words 'reasonably practicable' mean that inadvertent errors such as missing some members off the list will not necessarily invalidate the ballot. This principle was given statutory force by *TULR(C)A 1992, s 232B* which provides for small-scale, accidental failures to be disregarded (see (*a*) above).

(c)   The voting paper must contain at least one of the following questions –

(i)   a question which requires the voter to say, by answering 'Yes' or 'No' whether he is prepared to take part, or to continue to take part, in a strike;

(ii)   a question which requires the voter to say, by answering 'Yes' or 'No', whether he is prepared to take part, or as the case may be to continue to take part, in industrial action falling short of a strike.

(*TULR(C)A 1992, s 229(2)*.)

This means that a strike and action short of a strike must be the subject of separate questions on the ballot paper (*Post Office v Union of Communications Workers* [1990] ICR 258, [1990] IRLR 143). The requirements for the voting paper will be augmented when *s 5* of the *Trade Union Act 2016* comes into force, at a date yet to be fixed, so as to require the inclusion of a summary of the matters in issue in the trade dispute, specifying the types of industrial action short of strike which are contemplated, and indicating the periods within which the industrial action of each type is expected to take place.

TULR(C)A 1992, s 229(2A) provides that an overtime ban and a call-out ban constitute action short of a strike for the purposes of the strike ballot provisions.

With effect from 1 March 2017, the voting paper must also include: a summary of the matters in issue in the relevant trade dispute; the types of any industrial action short of a strike proposed; and the period within which each relevant type of industrial action is expected to take place: *TULR(C)A 1992, ss 229(2B), (2C)* and *(2D)*. It was held in *Thomas Cook Airlines Ltd v British Airline Pilots Association* [2017] EWHC 2253 (QB), [2017] IRLR 1137 that when specifying the relevant period under *TULR(C)A 1992, s 229(2D)* it was sufficient to state the range of dates within which the industrial action would take place; it was not necessary to give specific dates.

(d)   The following statement must appear without comment on every voting paper:

'If you take part in a strike or other industrial action, you may be in breach of your contract of employment.

However, if you are dismissed for taking part in strike or other industrial action which is called officially and is otherwise lawful, the dismissal will be unfair if it takes place fewer than 12 weeks after you started taking part in the action, and depending on the circumstances may be unfair if it takes place later.'

(TULR(C)A 1992, s 229(4).)

(e)   The voting paper must clearly specify the address to which, and the date by which, it is to be returned, and must be numbered *(TULR(C)A 1992, s 229(1A))*.

(f)   The voting paper must specify who, in the event of a vote in favour of action, is authorised for the purposes of *TULR(C)A 1992, s 233* (see **46.15** below) to call upon members to take part or continue to take part in the industrial action *(TULR(C)A 1992, s 229(3))*. The specified person need not be authorised under the rules of the union, but must be within *TULR(C)A 1992, s 20(2)* (ie a person empowered by the rules to call for the action, or the principal executive committee, president or general secretary, or any other committee or official of the union; see also TRADE UNIONS – I (51)). It is thought that the voting paper may specify alternative persons as having the authority to call for action. Further, in a case where an independent scrutineer is required (see (*k*) below), the ballot paper must state his name *(TULR(C)A 1992, s 229(1A)(a))*.

(g)   So far as is reasonably practicable those voting must vote in secret *(TULR(C)A 1992, s 230(4)(a))*. They must be allowed to vote without interference from the union, and so far as reasonably practicable, without incurring direct costs to themselves (this presumably means that reply-paid envelopes must be used for the postal ballot) *(TULR(C)A 1992, s 230(1))*. For reasonable practicability, see (*b*) above.

(h)   The votes must be fairly and accurately counted, although an inaccuracy in counting is to be disregarded if it is accidental and on a scale which could not affect the result of the ballot *(TULR(C)A 1992, s 230(4))*.

(i)   The majority of those voting in the ballot must have answered 'Yes' to the appropriate question *(TULR(C)A 1992, s 226(2))*. Where a ballot poses two separate questions, one relating to strike action and the other to industrial action short of a strike, the relevant majority is a majority of those voting on the specific question. It is not necessary that the majority voting 'Yes' in response to the particular question also comprise a majority of those taking part in the ballot *(West Midlands Travel Ltd v Transport and General Workers' Union* [1994] ICR 978, [1994] IRLR 578). Further, with effect from 1 March 2017, at least 50% of those who were entitled to vote in the ballot must have done so.

(j)   Since 1 March 2017, an additional requirement has applied where the majority of those entitled to vote in the ballot are normally engaged in the provision of "important public services". In such cases, 40% of those entitled to vote in the ballot must have voted in favour of taking industrial action *(TULR(C)A 1992, s 226(2C))*. Services falling within health services, education of those aged under 17, fire services, transport services, decommissioning of nuclear installations and management of radioactive waste and border security may be specified by the Secretary of State by statutory instrument as falling within the definition of "important public services". The Secretary of State has issued regulations specifying such "important public services" in all these sectors (except decommissioning of nuclear installations and management of radioactive waste). The Department of Business, Energy and Industrial Strategy also issued non-statutory guidance on the application of this additional threshold in January 2017.

(k) In a case where the number of members entitled to vote in the ballot (the aggregated number is taken where there are separate workplace ballots in accordance with (*a*) above) exceeds 50, a qualified scrutineer must be appointed. The union must ensure that he duly carries out his functions without interference, and must comply with all his reasonable requests. The scrutineer will make a report as soon as reasonably practicable after the ballot, and in any event within four weeks, stating whether he is satisfied that there are no reasonable grounds for believing that there was any contravention of statutory requirements, that the ballot arrangements included all reasonably practicable security arrangements to minimise the risk of unfairness or malpractice, and that he has been able to carry out his functions without interference from the union. Any person entitled to vote in the ballot, and the employer of any such person, is entitled (upon request made within six months of the ballot and upon payment of any reasonable fee specified by the union) to be provided with a copy of the report (*TULR(C)A 1992, ss 226B, 226C, 231B*). The persons qualified to be scrutineers are those satisfying the requirements of the *Trade Union Ballots and Elections (Independent Scrutineer Qualifications) Order 1993 (SI 1993/1909)*.

(l) The union must take such steps as are reasonably necessary to secure that every person whom it is reasonable for the union to believe will be the employer of persons entitled to vote in the ballot receives both notice that the ballot will take place, and a sample voting paper. In *English, Welsh & Scottish Railway Ltd v National Union of Rail, Maritime and Transport Workers* [2004] EWCA Civ 1539, 148 Sol Jo LB 1246, [2004] All ER (D) 203 (Oct) the Court of Appeal held that, where a notice of intention to hold an industrial action ballot was addressed to only one of two very closely related employers involved in an industrial dispute with the union, the notice should be treated as having been given to both companies. The notice must be received not later than the seventh day before the opening of the ballot, and must specify the anticipated opening day and identify the categories of employees of that employer whom the union believes will be entitled to vote. The sample voting paper must be received not later than the third day before the opening day (*TULR(C)A 1992, s 226A*).

A valid notice must contain lists of the categories of employee whom the union reasonably believes will be entitled to vote in the ballot and the workplaces at which they work. The notice must also state the total number of employees to be balloted and the number in each category, together with an explanation of how those figures were arrived at (*TULR(C)A 1992, s 226A*). The Court of Appeal held in *National Union of Rail, Maritime & Transport Workers v Serco Ltd* [2011] EWCA Civ 226, [2011] IRLR 399, [2011] IRLR 399 that the duty to provide such an explanation is not an onerous one, usually requiring only an indication of the sources of the information and highlighting any major known deficiencies. Unions are expressed not to be under a duty to supply an employer with the names of the employees concerned. By *s 226(2D)*, the lists and figures supplied must be as accurate as is reasonably practicable in the light of the information in the possession of the union. In *London & Birmingham Railway Ltd v ASLEF; Serco Ltd v RMT* [2011] EWCA Civ 226, [2011] ICR 849 the Court of Appeal held that this obligation does not require unions to seek out additional information or set up systems to improve their record keeping. In *British Airways plc v British Airline Pilots' Association* [2019] EWCA Civ 1663, [2020] IRLR 43 the Court of Appeal rejected an argument from the employer that the union should have specified the numbers being balloted within each of the employer's fleets of aircraft. It was held that unions are not required to determine what information should be given by reference to what would help the employer make plans and bring information to those to be balloted. That would be too onerous an obligation and the legislation leaves it to the union to determine what categories should be specified.

In *British Airways plc v Unite the Union* [2009] EWHC 3541 (QB), [2010] IRLR 423, the High Court held that the union had failed to comply with the notice provisions in circumstances where it had included in the ballot notice a substantial number of employees whom it could not reasonably have believed would be entitled to vote in the ballot, since they would no longer be employed by the employer by the time the strike was called. In *Metrobus Ltd v Unite the Union* [2009] EWCA Civ 829, [2010] ICR 173, [2009] IRLR 851, a majority of the Court of Appeal held that, in respect of non-check off employees, the union is obliged to provide a list of the numbers of employees who will be entitled to vote, the numbers in each workplace, the numbers in each category of worker and an explanation of how the figures were worked out. However, a misstatement of the number of relevant check off employees (by 10 out of nearly 800) was held not to be sufficiently material to invalidate the ballot. As noted above, in *London & Birmingham Railway Ltd v ASLEF; Serco Ltd v RMT* [2011] EWCA Civ 226, [2011] ICR 849, [2011] IRLR 399, the Court of Appeal endorsed the view (obiter) that a general de minimis principle applies in the context of the balloting notification procedures, such that a very small error in the notice will not generally invalidate a ballot. By contrast, in *Metroline Travel Ltd v Unite the Union* [2012] EWHC 1778 (QB), [2012] IRLR 749 a notice was held to be invalid when it referred to balloting certain grades of employee working on the contract for a particular client "on a full time or part basis". This was too imprecise, as it was unclear whether this included employees who might be expected to work for the client, or who were associated with the client, and whether they had to be working for the client directly or indirectly. As noted above, the European Court of Human Rights held in *National Union of Rail, Maritime and Transport Workers v United Kingdom* (App no 31045/10) [2014] IRLR 467 that the notification requirements in relation to ballots were compatible with the right of freedom of association under *art 11* of the ECHR, notwithstanding their relatively onerous nature.

(m)   As soon as is reasonably practicable after the holding of the ballot, the union must take such steps as are reasonably necessary to ensure that all persons entitled to vote, and their employers, are informed of the number of votes cast, the number of 'Yes' and 'No' votes, and the number of spoiled voting papers (*TULR(C)A 1992, s 231, s 231A*). Since 1 March 2017, the information to be provided has been extended to include whether at least 50% of those entitled to vote have voted and, in cases relating to important public services, whether at least 40% have voted in favour of the industrial action. In *Metrobus Ltd v Unite the Union* [2009] EWCA Civ 829, [2010] ICR 173, [2009] IRLR 851 the Court of Appeal held that the union had acted in breach of *TULR(C)A 1992, s 231A(1)* by delaying just two days in notifying the employer of the result of a strike ballot. It further held that the duty to provide such information applies irrespective of whether the union proposes to initiate industrial action. However, not every technical challenge will succeed. In *British Airways plc v Unite the Union* [2010] EWCA Civ 669, [2010] ICR 1316, [2010] IRLR 809, a majority of the Court of Appeal held that the trade union had taken such steps as were reasonably necessary to comply with the duty to inform members of the results of the ballot by providing them on its website, on union notice boards and via news sheets, even though each member had not been sent an individual email or text message with the results.

Where there are separate ballots for different workplaces, paras (*b*) to (*l*) are to be tested in relation to the ballot for the workplace of the person whose inducement to take part in the action is relied upon to found the liability in tort (*TULR(C)A 1992, s 226(3)*). This means in particular that a 'Yes' vote is required at every workplace where the members are to be called upon to take action.

If there is a suspension of industrial action for negotiations, a further ballot need not be held before industrial action is resumed, provided that the terms of the original ballot cover the reason for the resumed action (*Monsanto plc v Transport and General Workers Union* [1987] ICR 269, [1986] IRLR 406). However, this will not apply where there is a substantial interruption of the action as opposed to a mere suspension; where the action is irregular and spasmodic, it is a question of fact and degree whether it is sufficiently continuous and self-contained to be covered by a single ballot (*Post Office v Union of Communications Workers* [1990] ICR 258, [1990] IRLR 143). In *London Underground Ltd v National Union of Railwaymen* [1989] IRLR 341 it was held that at the time of the ballot there must be a genuine, definite, substantial dispute (actual or reasonably foreseeable) between the parties, and that the ballot question must relate wholly to matters capable of constituting a trade dispute. However, in *Associated British Ports v TGWU* [1989] 1 WLR 939 it was held that there was no need for the ballot information to describe or define every issue with which the dispute was concerned, provided that it was possible to identify the strike which was called with the strike which was voted for (the point was not argued on appeal).

Special provisions apply to overseas members and to members in Northern Ireland (*TULR(C)A 1992, s 232*). A union which is a federation, and which does not have individual members whom it will call out on strike, cannot comply with the relevant provisions of *TULR(C)A 1992* and therefore will enjoy no immunity from action when calling a strike (*Shipping Co Uniform Inc v International Transport Workers Federation* [1985] ICR 245, [1985] IRLR 71).

The Secretary of State is empowered by *TULR(C)A 1992, ss 203, 204* to issue codes of practice relating to the conduct by trade unions of ballots and elections (see Codes of Practice (5)). The original *Code on Trade Union Ballots on Industrial Action* has been revised and reissued (*Employment Code of Practice (Industrial Action Ballots and Notice to Employers) Order 2005 (SI 2005/2420)*). The *Code* deals with, among other things, the situations in which an industrial action ballot is appropriate, establishment of the balloting 'constituency', preparation and distribution of voting papers, and the conduct and counting of the ballot.

46.15 CALLING FOR INDUSTRIAL ACTION

In order for the action to be treated as supported by the ballot, there must have been no call by the union to take part in or continue to take part in the action to which the ballot relates, or any authorisation or endorsement of such action (see 51.16 Trade Unions – I), *before* the date of the ballot (*TULR(C)A 1992, s 233(3)(a)*).

The call for industrial action must be made by the person specified on the ballot paper (see 46.14(*f*) above). It is permissible for the specified person to call for action subject to some condition whose fulfilment is a matter for the judgment of local officials, although he may not simply delegate his authority (*Tanks and Drums Ltd v TGWU* [1992] ICR 1, [1991] IRLR 372).

Industrial action which has the support of a ballot must take place within six months of the date of the ballot, or up to nine months thereafter with the agreement of the employer (*TULR(C)A 1992, 234(1)*).

The union must take such steps as are reasonably necessary to give notice to an employer whose employees it reasonably believes will be or have been induced to take part in the action, describing the categories of employees concerned and specifying whether the action is intended to be continuous (in which case it must state the intended commencement date for any of those employees) or discontinuous (in which case it must state the intended dates for any of them to take part). A valid notice must contain lists of the categories of employee whom the union reasonably believes will be induced to take part in industrial action. The notice must also state the total number of employees to be induced to participate and the number in each category. Unions are expressed not to be under a duty to supply an employer with the names of the employees concerned. The notice must be received within the period beginning with the day when the requirement to notify employers of the ballot result is satisfied (see **46.14**(*m*) above) and ending with (since the coming into force of *s 8* of the *Trade Unions Act 2016* on 1 March 2017) the fourteenth day before the first day specified in the notice, unless the union and employer agree that only seven days' notice need be given (*TULR(C)A 1992, s 234A*). Thus the union is effectively required to give an employer at least two weeks' notice of industrial action.

46.16   EMPLOYER'S RIGHTS AND REMEDIES

The withdrawal of labour will usually amount to a breach of the contracts of employment of the individuals concerned. A strike notice may, however, at least in theory, be construed as due notice to *terminate* the contracts of employment of the strikers. Whether this is so depends upon the words used and on the circumstances (*Boxfoldia Ltd v National Graphical Association* [1988] ICR 752, [1988] IRLR 383). Action taken in a go-slow or work-to-rule may also be considered a breach by each individual participant of his contract of employment. In *Secretary of State for Employment v Associated Society of Locomotive Engineers and Firemen* [1972] ICR 7, [1972] 2 All ER 853 at 56 Lord Denning MR said:

> 'If [an employee] with . . . others, takes steps wilfully to disrupt the undertaking, to produce chaos so that it will not run as it should, then each one who is a party to those steps is guilty of a breach of his contract. It is no answer for any one of them to say "I am only obeying the rule book", or "I am not bound to do more than a 40-hour week". That would be all very well if done in good faith without any wilful disruption of services; but what makes it wrong is the object with which it is done.'

See also *British Telecommunications plc v Ticehurst* [1992] ICR 383, [1992] IRLR 219. However, in *Burgess v Stevedoring Services Ltd* [2002] WLR 2838, [2002] IRLR 810 the Privy Council rejected an argument that a refusal to undertake non-contractual overtime gave rise to a breach of contract. Similarly, in *Ministry of Justice v Prison Officers Association* [2017] EWHC 1839 (QB), [2018] ICR 181, [2017] IRLR 1121 Jay J held that prison officers who ceased to perform only voluntary, non-contractual tasks were not thereby in breach of any implied term in their contracts of employment.

The courses of action open to an employer, and others affected by industrial action, include the following:

(a)   An employer may try to conciliate, if necessary with the assistance of the ADVISORY, CONCILIATION AND ARBITRATION SERVICE (2).

(b)   If employees are on strike or their work is disruptive within the meaning of Lord Denning's statement above, they do not have to be paid for the period during which industrial action persists. If employees are refusing to perform part of their contractual duties, employers may deduct an appropriate sum from their salaries (*Sim v Rotherham Metropolitan Borough Council* [1986] ICR 897, [1986] IRLR 391; *Miles v Wakefield Metropolitan District Council* [1987] ICR 368, [1987] IRLR 193; *Wiluszynski v Tower Hamlets London Borough Council* [1989] ICR 493, [1989] IRLR 259; and see PAY – I (35)). In *Spackman v London Metropolitan University* [2007] IRLR 744 the claimant complained at having been paid only 70% of her contractual salary in respect of a period during which she had been performing only some of her contractual duties as part of industrial action being taken against her employer. The county court rejected her argument that she was entitled to a *quantum meruit* payment for some or all of the balance of her salary. Such an approach was inappropriate in circumstances where the contract of employment continued to govern the relationship between the parties. Moreover, it was held that employees participating in this type of industrial action are taking the risk of recovering no pay at all when they carry out only some of their contractual duties.

(c)   If employees or unions are taking disruptive industrial action which is not in contemplation or furtherance of a trade dispute or is unprotected secondary action or action for a purpose not within the statutory immunities, or is action by trade unions taken without a ballot, an employer affected may apply to the High Court for an *injunction* to prevent them from continuing such action. He may sue either the individuals involved or the union responsible, or both. Note that *TULR(C)A 1992, s 221(1)* requires that any application for an injunction must be brought to the attention of the other party if it seems likely that he may claim that he is acting in contemplation or furtherance of a trade dispute. Unless the court is satisfied that all reasonable steps have been taken, an injunction will not be granted. However, it is important to apply to the court speedily.

In deciding whether or not to grant the injunction, a court must have regard to the likelihood of the defendant succeeding in establishing a defence under *TULR(C)A 1992, s 219* or *s 220 (TULR(C)A 1992, s 221(2))*. Although the likelihood of establishing the defence is only one factor to be considered in deciding where the 'balance of convenience' lies (that being the test of whether to grant an interim injunction if the plaintiff has an arguable case and an ultimate award of damages would not be an adequate remedy for either party), the injunction will normally be refused if it appears more likely than not that the statutory defence will be made out (*NWL Ltd v Woods* [1979] ICR 867, [1979] IRLR 478). Indeed, where it is more likely than not that a union will succeed at trial in establishing immunity, it is only in a 'very exceptional' case that an injunction should be granted: (*RMT v Serco Ltd* [2011] EWCA Civ 226, [2011] 3 All ER 913, [2011] ICR 848). The court will also have regard to whether it is likely that in practice the grant or refusal of the injunction will be decisive in determining the legal proceedings for an injunction (if so, it becomes more important to try to form a view of the ultimate chances of success); it will compare the disadvantage to the workers in being unable to strike while the iron is hot with the potential losses to the employer. In a proper case it may have regard to the public interest, and if all other considerations are evenly balanced it will usually attempt to preserve the status quo (see, eg *Dimbleby & Sons Ltd v NUJ* [1984] ICR 386, [1984] IRLR 67; *Union Traffic Ltd v TGWU* [1989] ICR 98, [1989] IRLR 127; *Associated British Ports v TGWU* [1989] 1 WLR 939 (point not argued in the House of Lords)). The court will, however, under no circumstances grant an injunction if its effect would be to compel the employees to work (*TULR(C)A 1992, s 236*).

In proceedings arising out of an act which is by virtue of *TULR(C)A 1992, s 20* is taken to have been one by a trade union (as to which see **51.16 TRADE UNIONS – I**), the court's power to grant an injunction includes power to require the union to take such steps as the court considers appropriate for ensuring that there is no, or no further, inducement of persons to take part in industrial action or to continue to do so, and that no person engages in any conduct after the granting of the injunction by virtue of such inducement prior to the injunction (*TULR(C)A 1992, s 20(6)*). This represents a statutory development of the decision in *Solihull Metropolitan Borough v National Union of Teachers* [1985] IRLR 211, that where industrial action was called without a ballot, union leaders could be required to rescind the instruction.

46.18 THIRD PARTIES' RIGHTS AND REMEDIES

At common law, parties whose contracts were interfered with by unlawful industrial action could apply to the High Court for an injunction and damages, provided that the loss caused was not too remote or unforeseeable. The holder of a train ticket was able to recover damages from the rail unions for wrongfully interfering with his contract with British Rail (*Falconer v ASLEF and NUR* [1986] IRLR 331).

There is a statutory right under *TULR(C)A 1992, s 235A*, for an individual to apply to the High Court where he claims that any trade union or other person has done or is likely to do an unlawful act to induce any person to take part or continue to take part in industrial action, if a likely effect of the industrial action is to prevent or delay the supply of goods or services to the applicant, or to reduce the quality of goods or services supplied to him (*TULR(C)A 1992, s 235A(1)*). For these purposes an act is unlawful if it is actionable in tort by any one or more persons (which need not include the applicant himself), or in the case of an act by a trade union, if it could form the basis of an application by a member under *TULR(C)A 1992, s 62* (see **46.17** above) (*TULR(C)A 1992, s 235A(2)*). It is immaterial whether the applicant has any entitlement to be supplied with the goods or services in question (*TULR(C)A 1992, s 235A(3)*).

If the court is satisfied that the claim is well-founded, it must make such order as it considers appropriate for requiring the person by whom the act of inducement has been or is likely to be done to take steps for ensuring that no or no further act of inducement is done by him, and that no person engages in further conduct by virtue of his prior inducement (cf **46.16**(*c*) above) (*TULR(C)A 1992, s 235A(4)*). The court also has power to grant interlocutory relief (*TULR(C)A 1992, s 235A(5)*).

46.19 CONSEQUENCES FOR EMPLOYEES

For any industrial action, whether or not in contemplation or furtherance of a trade dispute:

(a)   the employee loses his right to pay during the industrial action (see **46.16**(b) above and PAY – I (35));

(b)   he is not entitled to receive jobseeker's allowance or income support, although his family may in some circumstances receive income support (see *Cartlidge v Chief Adjudication Officer* [1986] ICR 256, [1986] IRLR 182) subject to the deduction of a prescribed sum in respect of notional strike pay (see *Tolley's Social Security and State Benefits Handbook* for further details);

(c)   he is not entitled to any guarantee payment in respect of the days on which he is engaged in industrial action;

(d)   if dismissed during a strike, a participant in that strike may not be able to claim compensation for unfair dismissal (although he will be treated as automatically unfairly dismissed in the circumstances outlined in **46.16**(e) above);

(e)   so far as the computation of periods of continuous employment is concerned (for example, for redundancy and unfair dismissal claims), absence due to participation in a strike will not break continuity, but the period of absence is not counted in the computation. The start of the period of employment will be deemed to be postponed by the appropriate number of days (see **7.11** CONTINUOUS EMPLOYMENT).

46.20 EMPLOYEES WHO MAY NOT STRIKE

Some employees are forbidden by law to strike. These include members of the armed services, prison officers and police officers. In *Ministry of Justice v Prison Officers Association* [2008] EWHC 239 (QB), [2008] ICR 702, [2008] IRLR 380 Wyn Williams J rejected an argument by the Prison Officers' Union that he should refuse to grant an injunction to restrain strike action on the basis of the right to freedom of association conferred by *art 11(1)* of the Convention. That article, as he found, does not confer any right to strike. Whilst that proposition must be regarded as requiring further analysis following the European Court of Human Rights' decision in *Demir v Turkey* (App no 34503/970) (2008) 48 EHRR 1272, [2009] IRLR 766, the European Court since held in *Professional Trades Union for Prison, Correctional and Secure Psychiatric Workers v United Kingdom* (App No 59253/11) (2013) 57 EHRR SE9 that the application challenging the UK's statutory ban on industrial action by prison officers was inadmissible, on the grounds that the matter had already been considered by the Committee on Freedom of Association of the International Labour Organisation.

In *Ministry of Justice v Prison Officers Association* [2017] EWHC 1839 (QB), [2018] ICR 181, [2017] IRLR 1121 Jay J held that the statutory prohibition on strike action by prison officers extended to industrial action short of a strike. Although the union contended that their instruction was merely to withdraw from voluntary duties, in practice the instruction would lead prison officers to withdraw their services, and would be likely to put at risk the safety of prisoners and staff, in breach of the prohibition, and so it was unlawful.

Attempts have been made to argue that, given that inducement of a breach of statutory duty does not fall within the *TULR(C)A 1992, s 219* immunity (see **46.3** above), such provisions effectively prohibit organised strike action. But the decisions of the House of Lords in *Associated British Ports v TGWU* [1989] 1 WLR 939 at 970 and of Mantell J in *Wandsworth London Borough Council v NASUWT* [1994] ICR 81, [1993] IRLR 344 (the point was not argued on appeal), suggest that the courts will be reluctant to construe the relevant statutes so as to reach such a result.

It is a criminal offence for a person 'wilfully and maliciously [to break] a contract of service or of hiring, knowing or having reasonable cause to believe that the probable consequences of his so doing, either alone or in combination with others, will be to endanger human life, or cause serious bodily injury, or to expose valuable property whether real or personal to destruction or serious injury' (*TULR(C)A 1992, s 240(1)*). The penalty is a fine not exceeding level 2 on the Standard Scale (see **1.10** INTRODUCTION) or imprisonment for not more than three months (*TULR(C)A 1992, s 240(3)*).

47 Taxation

OUTLINE OF TAXATION

47.1 ITEPA 2003

The employment tax legislation is contained in the main in the *Income Tax (Earnings and Pensions) Act 2003* which is referred to in this chapter as *ITEPA 2003*. This is supported by various regulations, including the *Income Tax (Pay As You Earn) Regulations 2003* (*SI 2003/2682*).

47.2 Employment income

For income tax purposes, income from employment includes 'general earnings' and 'specific employment income'.

(a)   General earnings include (in each case, excluding exempt amounts):

    (i)   earnings which are defined by *ITEPA 2003, s 62* as including any salary, wage or fee, gratuities or other profit or benefit obtained if it is money or money's worth, or anything else constituting an emolument of employment ('money's worth' means something of direct monetary value to the employee or capable of being converted into money or something of direct monetary value to the employee); and

    (ii)   amounts treated as earnings which include amounts paid to agency workers (*ss 44–47*), amounts paid through intermediaries (*ss 48–61*) and managed service companies (*s 61A*), benefits in kind (*ss 63–220*), sickness and disability pay (*s 221*), payments of tax by the employer (ss *222, 223*), payments to non-approved personal pension arrangements (*s 224*), payments or valuable consideration given for restrictive undertakings (*ss 225, 226*), shares of employee shareholders (*ss 226A–226D*) or balancing charges treated as earnings (*Capital Allowances Act 2001, s 262*).

(b)   Specific employment income includes (in each case, excluding exempt amounts):

    (i)   other non-share related income including benefits from employer-financed retirement benefit schemes (*ss 393–400*) and payments on termination of employment (*ss 401–416*);

    (ii)   share related payments and benefits (*ss 417–554*); and

    (iii)   payments which count as employment income under any other enactment.

(*ITEPA 2003, s 7*.)

General earnings include 'benefits in kind' as per (*a*)(ii) above (see **47.21** et seq below). From 6 April 2016 onwards, the tax treatment of expenses and benefits in kind is the same regardless of the earnings level of the employee and the benefits code in its entirety applies to all employee (subject to an exception for certain lower-paid ministers of religion). However, 2015/16 and earlier tax years, different rules applied depending on whether the employee was a director or earned at a rate of above £8,500 a year or whether the employee was a 'lower-paid employee' earning at a rate of less than £8,500 inclusive of any benefits in kind.

(*FA 2015, s 13(1)* (omitting *ITEPA 2003, Pt 3 Ch 11* with effect from 6 April 2016).)

47.2 Taxation

In general terms, the amount assessable to tax in respect of a benefit is its cash equivalent value. Unless specific rules apply to determine the calculation of the cash equivalent value of the benefit (as, for example in the case of company cars and fuel, living accommodation, employment-related loans etc) or the benefit is provided under an optional remuneration arrangement (such as a salary sacrifice arrangement) on or after 6 April 2017 and the alternative valuation rules apply, the cash equivalent value is simply the cost to the employer less any amount made good by the employee (*ITEPA 2003, ss 203–206*) The charging provisions also cover the provision of benefits to the family or household of the employee or director. The benefit is essentially taxed in the same way as if it were provided to the employee (see **47.28**).

PAY AS YOU EARN (PAYE)

47.4 Definition and earnings limits

PAYE is the statutory system of deducting income tax from the employment income (see **47.2** above) of an employee at the time that the employee is paid by the employer so as to secure, as far as possible, that the income tax liability in respect of the employment income is satisfied by the deductions made. The employer effectively acts as a tax collector for HM Revenue and Customs. In addition, the PAYE system collects National Insurance contributions of both employee and employer. It is also used for the operation of Statutory Sick Pay (SSP), Statutory Maternity Pay (SMP), Statutory Paternity Pay (SPP), Statutory Adoption Pay (SAP), Shared Parental Pay (ShPP), Statutory Parental Bereavement pay (SPBP), to collect student loan repayments and to collect charitable donations under Payroll Giving (see **47.33** below).

Under Real Time Information (RTI) employers are required to send details of pay and deductions to HM Revenue and Customs electronically each time that an employer is paid.

The PAYE system applies to all payments of employment income assessable to income tax in excess of certain defined limits. These limits (the 'PAYE thresholds') are as laid down from time to time by HM Revenue and Customs. For a person with one employment only, the PAYE threshold is broadly aligned with the weekly/monthly equivalent of the personal allowance for income tax.

For 2020/21 the PAYE thresholds are as follows:

Weekly	£240
Monthly	£1,042
Annual	£12,500

The regulations governing the operation of PAYE are the *Income Tax (Pay As You Earn) Regulations 2003 (SI 2003/2682)*.

47.5 Sources of information

Guidance on PAYE is available on the GOV.UK website (www.gov.uk). HMRC publish guidance for employers on PAYE, which can be found on the GOV.UK website (see www.gov.uk/topic/business-tax/paye). Detailed instructions on the operation of PAYE can also be found in the HM Revenue and Customs booklet 'Employer's Further Guide to PAYE and NICs' (CWG2). The 2020/21 edition is available to download from the GOV.UK website (see www.gov.uk/government/publications/cwg2-further-guide-to-paye-and-national-insurance-contributions).

Guidance on the operation of PAYE is also contained in the HM Revenue and Customs guidance manuals – PAYE Instructions (collection) manual and PAYE Online Manual. Guidance on employment income generally is found in the Employment Income Manual. The manuals are also available on the GOV.UK website (see www.gov.uk/government/collections/hmrc-manuals).

HMRC also publish an online magazine for employers, Employer Bulletin, which is available to download from the GOV.UK website (see www.gov.uk/government/collections/hm -revenue-and-customs-employer-bulletin). The bulletin is published bi-monthly and aims to provide employers and agents with the latest information on payroll topics and other issues that affect them.

To help small employers to work out their PAYE and NIC liabilities, HMRC also publish a free RTI-compatible software package, Basic PAYE Tools, which is available to download from the GOV.UK website (see www.gov.uk/basic-paye-tools). The product is designed for employers with nine or fewer employees and can be used to work out payroll deductions and to produce and send RTI submissions to HMRC.

See also the *Payroll Management Handbook 2008* (or later edition).

47.6 Method of deduction

Employers must maintain (among other documents) a deductions working sheet (P11 or equivalent) for each employee known to be earning amounts above the PAYE threshold. This will almost always be maintained electronically by means of a payroll software package as this is required under real time information (RTI. The employee's tax code determines the amount that the employee is able to earn before paying tax and is used to work out the appropriate amount of tax to be deducted from that employee's wages. The employee's tax code must be recorded on the P11 or equivalent. A tax code will vary to reflect the circumstances of the employee. The tax code number will be the appropriate amount of personal allowances less the final digit. For example, an employee who receives the basic personal allowance for of £12,500 for 2020/21 would have a code number of 1250. A suffix or prefix is then added to the code.

The suffix code letter indicates how the code should be updated to reflect changes announced in the Budget. The suffix code letters in use for 2020/21 for English and Northern Irish taxpayers are as follows:

L = Personal allowance

M = Individual has received the marriage allowance from their spouse or civil partner

N = Individual has transferred the marriage allowance to their spouse or civil partner

T = Specific notification required from HM Revenue and Customs.

Sometimes a code will have a prefix instead of a suffix:

D0 = Higher rate tax and no personal allowances)

D1 = Additional rate (and no personal allowances)

K = Where state pension or benefits in kind exceed personal allowances

BR = Basic rate tax and no personal allowances

0T = No personal allowances

NT = No tax to be deducted

C	BR cumulative
Starter declaration not completed	0T week 1/month 1

Under RTI, employers must supply details of new starters to HM Revenue and Customs electronically as part of the Full Payment Submission (FPS).

47.8 Employee leaving or dismissed

Form P45 must be issued to an employee who leaves the employer's employment. Form P45 is the mechanism by which details of the employee's pay to date and tax deducted are transferred from one employer to the next.

Under RTI the employer is not required to send form P45 to HM Revenue and Customs. Instead, leaver details notified to HM Revenue and Customs as part of the FPS.

Where payments are made to the former employee after the form P45 has been issued, tax must be deducted using the 0T code rather than by reference to the employee's normal tax code. Where payments are made after the P45 has been issued, under no circumstances should a further form P45 should be issued. Code 0T must also be used for share-based payments made after the issue of form P45.

If the amount of the payment made after the leaving date is known before the employee leaves, it must be entered on the deductions working sheet by reference to the date of the future payment. In this situation, the amount is therefore included within the amount shown on form P45.

Pay in lieu of notice. The tax treatment of termination payments was reformed with effect from 6 April 2018. Where the PILON is paid on or after 6 April 2018 and the employee's employment terminated on or after that date, the basic approach is to compare the relevant termination award (broadly payments received on the termination of the employment not already taxed as earnings (as for salary payments etc) but excluding statutory or contractual redundancy pay with the 'post-employment notice pay' (PENP). The PENP is broadly the basic pay that the employee would have received had he or she worked their notice period, and is found by applying a statutory formula (in *ITEPA 2003, s 402D(1)*). Basic pay in the normal salary or wages, but excludes one-off and unusual items, such as overtime, commission, bonuses etc (*ITEPA 2003, s 402D*). The calculation is adjusted for items that have been received in connection with the employment and have already been charged to tax, to avoid double taxation.

Statutory redundancy pay and that received under a contractual scheme is excluded from the termination award (pay received on termination falling within *ITEPA 2003, Pt 6, Ch 3*) to arrive at the relevant termination award. This is then compared to the PENP. If the relevant termination award is less than the PENP, the whole amount is taxed as earnings under *ITEPA 2003, s 402B*. If the relevant termination award is more than the PENP, the relevant termination award is taxed as earnings up to the level of the PENP, with the balance taxed under *ITEPA 2003, s 403* and benefitting from the £30,000 threshold, and taxable only to the extent that this is exceeded. Any statutory or contractual redundancy pay counts towards the £30,000 threshold. From 6 April 2020, any payments benefitting from the £30,000 threshold will attract an employer's Class 1A National Insurance liability to the extent that the £30,000 threshold is exceeded. Unlike Class 1A National Insurance contributions on benefits in kind, the Class 1A liability on taxable termination payments should be reported to HMRC under real time information for the pay period in which the termination occurred and the liability paid with the Class 1 National Insurance and PAYE for that period. It does not need to be included in the Class 1A figure on the P11D(b).

The effect of this approach is that all PILONs, regardless of whether they are contractual or expected or not, are taxed as earnings up to the level of the PENP. Where the contract does not provide for a notice period, the statutory minimum period is used to work out the PENP.

Where the termination occurred before 6 April 2018, the treatment of PILONs depended on the nature of the payment. The tax treatment of pay in lieu of notice under these rules was complex as the term is often used to describe payments with varying characteristics. Broadly, if the employee was contractually entitled to the payment or had an expectation that it would be paid, it was taxed as earning. However, if there was no contractual entitlement or expectation the payment was treated as damages for the failure to give proper notice and taxe das a termination payment benefitting from the £30,000 tax-free threshold.

A number of cases were decided in relation to the treatment of PILONs under the rules as they applied to termination payment received prior to 6 April 2018. In *Delaney v Staples* [1992] 1 All ER 944, [1992] IRLR 191 it was held that *non-contractual* payments in lieu of notice were not to be regarded as wages for the purposes of what is now *ERA 1996, s 27*. However, HM Revenue and Customs takes the view that 'what constitutes wages under employment law is not the same as what constitutes emoluments under tax law'.

In *Richardson v Delaney* [2001] STC 1328, [2001] IRLR 663 it was held that a discretionary PILON was taxable as earnings. The contract was brought to an end by mutual consent and a payment agreed in lieu of notice. The court found that there was no breach of earnings and consequently the payment was taxable as earnings.

In *EMI Group Electronics Ltd v Coldicott* [1999] STC 803, [1999] IRLR 630 the Court of Appeal confirmed the HM Revenue and Customs' long-standing practice that *contractual* payments in lieu of notice are assessable as employment income but it was accepted that payments made to junior employees were not taxable since those employees had no contractual right to them. See HM Revenue and Customs' Employment Income Manual EIM 12977.

The need to take care when drafting termination letters was illustrated in the decision in *Ibe v McNally (Inspector of Taxes)* [2005] EWHC 1551 (Ch), [2005] STC 1426, [2005] All ER (D) 389 (Mar).

47.9 Employee retiring on pension from employer

The employer must notify the tax office within 14 days and continue operating the code but on the non–cumulative basis until revised instructions are received from the tax office. However, if the pension is to be paid by the trustees of a pension scheme etc, the employee should be treated as leaving (see **47.8** above).

47.10 Death of employee

If an employee dies the employer must complete a form P45. Under RTI, the death of an employee is notified to HM Revenue and Customs electronically as for starters and leavers as part of the FPS. The same procedure applies if a pensioner dies.

The same rules apply in the case of payments made after the date of death as for payments made after the date an employee leaves (see **47.8** above).

47.11 Students employed during vacation

A student is treated in the same way as any other employee, even if the student only works during the holidays. However, where this is the case, the student may be entitled to a tax repayment at the end of the tax year, which if the student is not working (for example over the Easter holidays), may need to be reclaimed from HMRC.

The penalties are charged in-year and are issued quarterly (July, October, January and April). HM Revenue and Customs will issue electronic warnings where expected information has not been received. The FPS includes an RTI 'late reporting reason' data item to enable employers to tell HM Revenue and Customs why they are filing a submission late. HMRC allow a three-day period of grace before a submission is regarded as 'late'.

47.14 PAYE – PAYMENT OF TAX BY EMPLOYER

The employer must pay to the Collector of Taxes, within 17 days (ie by the 22nd of each month) where the payment is made by an approved electronic method or within 14 days of the end of every tax month (ie by the 19th of each month) where payment is made by post, all tax and National Insurance contributions deducted together with the employer's National Insurance contributions; plus any student loan deductions; less any recoveries of statutory maternity pay, statutory paternity pay, statutory adoption pay, shared parental pay or statutory parental bereavement pay (see **33.30** MATERNITY AND PARENTAL RIGHTS and **45.6** SICKNESS AND SICK PAY) (where applicable including an amount to compensate for employer's National Insurance contributions thereon). A single remittance is sufficient. Where the deadline falls on a non-banking day, such as weekend or bank holiday, postal payments must reach HM Revenue and Customs on the previous banking day and in the case of electronic payment, cleared funds must reach HM Revenue and Customs' bank account on the previous banking day. If these deadlines are missed the payment will be treated as being made late.

Employers with 250 or more employees are required to make their monthly payments of PAYE electronically. Penalties are charged where PAYE is paid late on more than one occasion during the tax year (see **47.14A**).

Employers who have reasonable grounds for believing that the average monthly total tax and National Insurance to be paid to the Collector will be less than £1,500 are able to make payments quarterly instead of monthly (*reg 70* (before 6 April 2004, *regs 41, 42*)). New employers must notify HM Revenue and Customs if they wish to make quarterly payments, but existing employers need not do so unless a demand is received from HMRC.

Under RTI, where an employer makes no payments to employees during a tax month, the employer must submit an employer payment summary (EPS) to HM Revenue and Customs to advise them of this. In this way, the EPS acts as a nil declaration telling HM Revenue and Customs that no PAYE or NIC is due for the tax month in question.

HM Revenue and Customs has the power under *reg 80* of the PAYE regulations to determine the amount of tax payable where it appears to it that tax may have been payable but has not been paid; and interest at the prescribed rate on unpaid tax in respect of *reg 80* determinations can be charged under *reg 82*.

Interest at the prescribed rate is charged automatically on late payments of PAYE. Interest is charged in-year once the outstanding payment has been made. Interest is charged from the due date to the date on which payment is made. A repayment supplement at the prescribed rate is also available where overpaid deductions are later refunded (*regs 82, 83*).

47.14A PENALTIES FOR LATE PAYMENT OF PAYE

Employers may suffer a penalty if they do not pay the PAYE they owe on time and in full on more than one occasion in the tax year. The penalty regime applies to all employers including large employers who are required to make payments of PAYE electronically. The penalty amount is a percentage of the amount of PAYE that is owed. No penalty is charged if payment is made late only on one occasion in the tax year and the first late payment is not counted as a default. Thereafter, the penalty rate depends on the number of occasions on which payment is made late. Each late payment after the first one is regarded as a default The penalty rate starts at 1% (2 to 4 defaults), rising to 2% (5 to 7 defaults) then to 3% (8 to 10 defaults) with a top penalty rate of 4% applying to 11 or more defaults. A further penalty of 5% will apply if the any of the PAYE remains unpaid after six months and again after 12 months.

Late payment penalties are levied in-year on a quarterly basis.

Penalties will not be charged if HMRC accept that the employer had a reasonable excuse for the late payment.

47.15 PAYE – END OF YEAR PROCEDURE

RTI end of year procedures

Under RTI employers supply pay and deductions information to HM Revenue and Customs progressively throughout the tax year. As a result there is no need to file annual returns at the year end. Instead, the employer must indicate on their final Full Payment Submission (FPS) for the tax year that it is the last FPS for the tax year. The final FPS must be submitted on or before the date on which the last payment in the tax year is made to an employee. The final submission can be made either as part of the last FPS, or by means of an EPS. Where an error comes to light on or before 19 April after the end of the tax year, an additional FPS should be submitted with corrected year-to-date figures as at 5 April 2020. Where the error is discovered after 19 April, an earlier year update (EYU) or, if the software allows it, a FPS, should be submitted to correct the error. An EYU or FPS can be submitted to correct original FPS information up to 6 years after the original FPS or EPS was filed. If the final submission is not made before 20 May, a late filing penalty may be charged. The penalty is charged at the rate of £100 for each group or part group of 50 employees for each month or part month that the final submission remains outstanding after 19 May.

Certificate of Pay and Tax Deducted (P60)

The employer is required to provide each employee employed on 5 April at the end of the tax year with a certificate of pay and tax deducted (form P60) by 31 May following the end of the tax year. The P60 (which is usually provided by the payroll software package) can be given to the employee in paper format or electronically.

Details of payrolled benefits

Where benefits in kind or expenses were payrolled in a tax year, the employer must provide the employee with details of their payrolled benefits by 31 May after the end of the tax year.

47.16 Forms P11D and P11D(b)

From 6 April 2016 onwards, the benefits code in its entirety applies to all employees regardless of their earnings rate (subject to a limited exception for certain lower paid ministers of religion).

Where non-cash benefits and expenses have been provided to employees or directors, a return of those benefits must be made to HM Revenue and Customs by 6 July after the end of the tax year unless those benefits have been taxed via the payroll in a process known as payrolling.

Benefits which have not been payrolled must be notified to HMRC on form P11D. The employer must also submit form P11D(b) by 6 July following the end of the tax year to which it relates. Form P11D is a return of 'Expenses and Benefits' and return P11D(b) is a 'Return of Class 1A National Insurance Contributions' which declares the total amount of Class 1A contributions due to be paid on P11D benefits (see **47.17** below) and includes a declaration that all the required forms P11D have been completed and submitted to HM Revenue and Customs. Form P11D(b) is required regardless of whether of benefits are payrolled.

For self-assessment purposes, employers must provide to each employee or director either a copy of the form P11D or a statement of their benefits by 6 July after the end of the tax year. Where benefits have been payrolled, the employee must be given details of payrolled benefits by 31 May after the end of the tax year.

Items covered included within a PAYE settlement agreement do not need to be returned on form P11D. Similarly, items covered by an exemption, including that for qualifying paid and reimbursed expenses. See **47.18** in relation to PAYE settlement agreements.

Forms P11D and P11D(b) can be submitted electronically using commercial software packages or via HM Revenue and Customs' Expenses and Benefits Online Service or PAYE Online service. Forms can also be submitted in paper format as electronic submission is not compulsory. They can also be filed using electronic data interchange (EDI).

47.16a Payrolling

Employers can choose to account for the tax on a most benefits in kind via the payroll (a process known as 'payrolling') rather than reporting them on form P11D. Employers wishing to payroll benefits must register to do so before the start of the tax year in question using HMRC's online Payrolling Benefits in Kind service (see https ://www.gov.uk/guidance/payrolling-tax-employees-benefits-and-expenses-through-your -payroll). Employers who wished to payroll benefits for 2020/21 needed to register before 6 April 2020. The deadline for registering to payroll 2021/22 benefits is 5 April 2021. Once a benefit has been registered for payrolling it remains registered unless deregistered – there is no need to register the benefits each year. Where the deadline is missed, HMRC may allow the employer to payroll informally but where this is the case, the employer will still need to report the benefit on form P11D after the year end. Employers choosing to payroll benefits must ensure that they have a payroll software package which is able to support payrolling. Employers who have previously registered benefits for payrolling must de-register those benefits if they wish to stop payrolling them. As for registration, this must be done before the start of the tax year for which it is to have effect.

Payrolling is voluntary and employers can choose what benefits are payrolled and for which employees. It is possible to payroll all benefits with the exception of employer-provided living accommodation and low interest and interest-free loans.

Once an employer has registered to payroll benefits for particular employees for a tax year, they must continue to do so throughout the tax year unless the employee has insufficient pay to cover the tax on the benefit or the employer stops providing that benefit to the employee.

The amount that is payrolled in respect of a non–cash benefit is the taxable amount of the benefit divided by the employee's pay frequency. Unless the benefit is provided through an optional remuneration arrangement, this will be the cash equivalent value. Where a benefit is provided through an optional remuneration arrangement and the alterative valuation rules apply, the taxable amount is the relevant amount. This is the higher of the salary foregone (or, where appropriate, the cash alternative offered) and the cash alternative. For example, if an employee was paid monthly and received private medical insurance with a cash equivalent value of £480, the employee would include £40 as 'pay' each month in respect of the benefit, being the annual cash equivalent value of £480 divided by the number of pay days in the year (12). The tax on the 'pay' of £40 in respect of the benefit is deducted from the employee's cash pay each month, along with tax due on the employee's salary for the month.

Employers who choose to payroll must provide employees with a letter explaining what payrolling is and what it means for them. Before 1 June following the end of the tax year, employers must also provide employees with a description of the benefits that have been payrolled and the associated cash equivalent value. Benefits that are taxable and which have not been payrolled must be notified to HMRC by 6 July following the end of the tax year on form P11D. Employers must also make a return of Class 1A National Insurance contributions due on form P11D(b) by the same date, regardless of whether the benefits have been payrolled or returned on form P11D.

Where employers have opted to payroll car and fuel benefits, changes to these benefits must be notified via the Full Payment Submission (FPS) rather than on form P46(Car).

Guidance on payrolling is available on the gov.uk website at www.gov.uk/government/publications/payrolling-benefits-in-kind-draft -guidance/payrolling-benefits-in-kind.

(*Income Tax (Pay As You Earn) Regulations 2003 (SI 2003/2682), Pt 3 Ch 3A* (as inserted by *SI 2015/1927, reg 6.*)

47.17   Class 1A National insurance contributions

Class 1A National Insurance contributions are employer-only contributions payable on most taxable benefits in kind. From 6 April 2020, a Class 1A liability also arises on taxable termination payments in excess of £30,000 and on sporting testimonial payments in excess of £100,000. The Class 1A rate is 13.8% for 2020/21.

As far as the Class 1a liability on benefits in kind is concerned, a Class 1A liability arises where a benefit is taxable regardless of the earnings level of the employee, unless that benefit is specifically exempt from the Class 1A charge or within the scope of Class 1.

Class 1A National Insurance contributions on benefits in kind must be paid by 22 July following the end of the tax year to which they relate if paid electrically (or by 19 July otherwise) and must be reported to HM Revenue and Customs on form P11D(b) (see **47.16** above) by 6 July following the end of the tax year. Employers are still required to submit form P11D(b) where they opt to payroll benefits in kind. Returns filed late may attract a penalty and interest is charged on Class 1A National Insurance contributions paid late. As with PAYE, if the deadline falls on a non-banking day, payment must reach HM Revenue and Customs by the previous banking day.

Where an item that would otherwise attract a Class 1A charge is included within a PAYE settlement agreement (see **47.18**), Class 1B contributions are payable instead.

From 6 April 2020, a liability to Class 1A National Insurance also arises on taxable termination payments in excess of £30,000 and on sporting testimonial payments in excess of £100,000.

As far as termination payments are concerned, payments made on a termination that are taxable as a termination payment rather than as earnings are taxable to the extent that the £30,000 tax-free threshold is exceeded. Where a tax liability arises and the termination award is made on or after 6 April 2020, there is also a Class 1A liability to the extent that the award exceeds £30,000. The liability is paid and reported by the employer through real time information for the pay period in which the termination award is made.

Non-contractual and non-customary sporting testimonial payments are taxable to the extent that they exceed £100,000. From 6 April 2020, a Class 1A National Insurance liability also arises to the extent that the sporting testimonial exceeds £100,000. The liability falls on the sporting testimonial committee and the testimonial committee controller is responsible for reporting and paying that liability to HMRC. The liability is reported and paid through real time information. However, there is no liability if the sporting testimonial was announced within the public domain before 6 April 2020.

(*Social Security Contributions and Benefits Act 1992, ss 10, 10ZA; Child Support, Pensions and Social Security Act 2000, ss 74, 75*); *National Insurance Contributions (Termination Award and Sporting Testimonial Act) 2019.* For further details of Class 1A contributions, see *Tolley's National Insurance Contributions 2006/07* (or later edition).

47.18 PAYE Settlement Agreements

A PAYE Settlement Agreement is an agreement with HM Revenue and Customs whereby the employer can settle, in a single payment, the income tax and National Insurance liability on certain expenses payments and benefits provided to employees. Such expenses payments and benefits do not then need to be processed through the PAYE system or recorded on forms P11D. A formal written agreement to make such a payment must be made with HM Revenue and Customs by 6 July following the end of the tax year.

The benefits which are covered by the agreement are subject to tax and Class 1B National Insurance contributions which must be paid by 22 October where payment is made electronically (or by 19 October otherwise). Class 1B National Insurance contributions are payable on the benefits that would otherwise be subject to Class 1 or Class 1A contributions if they were not included in the agreement. The rate of Class 1B contributions is 13.8% for 2020/21 and 2019/20. The tax payable must be 'grossed-up' at either appropriate of tax depending on the marginal rate of tax payable by the employees concerned since the payment of the tax liability is itself a benefit subject to tax. Where Scottish taxpayers are provided with benefits which are included within a PAYE Settlement Agreement, the tax calculation must be performed using the relevant Scottish rates of income tax. Likewise, where benefits are provided to Welsh taxpayers, the Welsh rates of income tax must be used in the calculating the tax payable. However, it should be noted that for 2020/21, the Welsh rates of income tax are the same as the rest of the UK, excluding Scotland.

Class 1B National Insurance contributions are payable on the aggregate of the total value of the benefits and the grossed-up amount of income tax due.

A PAYE Settlement Agreement is not suitable for all benefits in kind. The items which may be included within a PAYE Settlement Agreement are set out in HM Revenue and Customs Statement of Practice 5/96.

The procedures for setting up a PAYE Settlement Agreement simplified from 6 April 2018. From that date it will no longer be necessary to agree the PAYE Settlement Agreement with HMRC each year. Once a PSA has been agreed, it remains an enduring agreement unless circumstances change.

47.19 PAYE ONLINE

The PAYE online service was used to provide information to HMRC electronically prior to the introduction of RTI. It can also be used to send and receive payroll information and can be used by employers, agents and payroll bureaux alike. Since the introduction of RTI, PAYE Online can be used for P11Ds and P11D(b)s and for a range of other forms, notices and reminders. Expenses and benefits forms can also be submitted using the HM Revenue and Customs' Expenses and Benefits Online Service.

Before using the service, employers and agents must register on the HM Revenue and Customs' web page and then activate the service using the activation PIN that is sent through the post. Employers must be registered for PAYE Online in order to be able to send pay and deductions information to HMRC electronically under RTI.

47.19A SECURITY FOR PAYE

Since 6 April 2012, HM Revenue and Customs have had the power to ask employers to pay a security where there is a serious risk that the employer in question will not pay over PAYE and NIC to HMRC. The required security will usually take the form of a cash deposit from the business or director, which will be held in a joint taxpayer/HMRC bank account, or in the form of a bond from an approved financial institution which is payable on demand.

The power to require a security will only be exercised for employers who deliberately seek to defraud the Government. This includes employers who deliberately choose not to pay, who engage in pheonixism (whereby the business evades tax by becoming insolvent and then setting up a new company almost immediately to continue trading), companies that have no qualms about building up large PAYE and NIC debts and companies that do not respond to HMRC's attempts to contact them to address their tax issues.

The amount of security required will be calculated on a case-by-case basis depending on the amount of tax that is at risk and the previous behaviour of the employer. Employers who are asked for a security for PAYE can appeal against this decision. Employers who are asked for a security and who fail to provide it risk prosecution by HMRC and may be fined.

47.20 RECORDS

The PAYE regulations stipulate various records that employers must keep for PAYE purposes. The records that the employer is required to maintain, but which do not need to be sent to HM Revenue and Customs, must be retained for not less than three years after the end of the year to which they relate. Under self-assessment, regulations require employees to keep sufficient records to enable them to make a correct and complete return.

47.21 TAXABLE BENEFITS – GENERAL RULES

Detailed information on the tax treatment of benefits in kind is to be found in *Tolley's Income Tax 2019/20*. Concise factual information, in tabular form, is contained in *Tolley's Tax Data 2019/20*. A brief account of general principles in relation to those benefits most commonly derived from employment is given in this paragraph and in **47.22–47.28** below. Special rules applying to employee share schemes are outlined briefly in **47.29–47.33** below.

From 6 April 2016 onwards, the benefits code in its entirety applies to all employees irrespective of their earnings rate (subject to a limited exception for certain lower paid ministers of religion). For 2015/16 and earlier tax years, 'lower paid' employees (ie those earning at a rate of less than £8,500 inclusive of the cash equivalent of benefits in kind) were only taxed on a limited range of benefits, whereas the full benefits code applied to directors (irrespective of their earnings rate) and to employees earning at a rate of at least £8,500 a year. The £8,500 threshold and the concept of a 'lower paid' employee were abolished from 6 April 2016.

Where benefits are provided via an optional remuneration arrangement, such as a salary sacrifice arrangement, alternative valuation rules apply from 6 April 2017 (subject to transitional rules), unless the benefit is one of a limited range of protected benefits. Where the alternative valuation rules apply, the amount charged to tax is the relevant amount. This is the higher of the salary foregone (or cash alternative offered, as appropriate) and the cash equivalent value. The effect of these rules is that the benefit of most tax and National Insurance exemptions are lost where the benefit is provided under a salary sacrifice or other optional remuneration arrangement (see **47.27A**).

Some of the main taxable benefits are as follows.

(a)   Expense payments and allowances – taxable subject to exemption for actual expenses incurred in the performance of the duties; see **47.28** below (*ITEPA 2003, ss 70–72*).

(b)   Cash vouchers – taxed on their redemption value.

        Non-cash vouchers and transport vouchers – taxed on the cost to the employer of providing them less any contribution from employee (unless used to obtain certain non-taxable benefits).

        Credit tokens – taxed on the cost to the employer of the money, goods or services obtained less any contribution from employee (unless used to obtain certain non-taxable benefits).

        (*ITEPA 2003, ss 73–96.*)

(c)   'Living accommodation' – taxed on the annual value (as defined) or the actual rent paid by the employer if greater, subject to exemptions (eg where the employee is a representative occupier). For accommodation costing in excess of £75,000 an additional charge is made on the excess value over £75,000 (*ITEPA 2003, ss 97–113*).

(d)   Cars, vans and related expenses – taxed on the cash equivalent values, see **47.24** to **47.27** below (*ITEPA 2003, ss 114–172*) (unless the alternative valuation rules are in point). For cars the cash equivalent depends on the level of CO_2 emissions and the list price and, for 2020/21 and 2021/22, the date on which the car was registered. If the car's emissions fall in the 1–50g/km band, from 2020/21 onwards, the appropriate percentage also depends on the car's electric range. For car fuel, the cash equivalent value depends on the level of CO_2 emissions (which determines the appropriate percentage) and the multiplier set by HMRC. Vans are taxed by reference to a scale charge. A separate fuel charge also applies to vans.

(e)   Interest-free or reduced interest employment-related loans – the taxable benefit is the difference between the interest paid (if any) and the 'official rate' of interest at a rate prescribed by the Treasury. There are certain reliefs for loans made at fixed rates not below market value when made, and loans for some specified purposes. No tax charge arises on loans made to employees on commercial terms where the employer lends to the general public. Nor is there any charge where the aggregate value of beneficial loans does not exceed £10,000 at any time in the tax year.

        Loans written off are taxed on the amount written off.

        (*ITEPA 2003, ss 173–191.*)

(f)   Shares and securities – an employee who is given shares or securities or options over shares and securities, or is allowed to acquire them on terms more favourable than those available to the public, is taxed on the value of the benefit he receives. Tax and National Insurance advantages are available in relation to certain approved share option and share incentive schemes (*ITEPA 2003, ss 192–200*).

(g)   Assets gifted – if new, charged at cost to employer and if used, generally taxed at market value (*ITEPA 2003, ss 203, 204*).

(h)   Mileage allowances paid to employees using their own vehicles for business journeys– taxed on excess over approved amounts (*ITEPA 2003, ss 229–232, 235, 236*).

(i)   Medical treatment or insurance premiums, unless for treatment outside the UK while the employee is working abroad or the treatment is 'recommended medical treatment' the cost of which is no more than £500 a year (*ITEPA 2003, ss 320C, 325*).

(j)   Relocation expenses – non-qualifying expenses and benefits and qualifying expenses and benefits exceeding £8,000 per move (*ITEPA 2003, ss 271–289*).

(k)   Use of employer's assets – land taxable at annual value, other assets at 20% of market value when first lent or rental charge if higher (*ITEPA 2003, ss 203–205*). Exemptions are available for computers loaned prior to 6 April 2006 (costing up to £2,500) and bicycles. Special rules apply to company cars, company vans, and living accommodation. No charge arises in respect of employer-provided mobile phones (limited to one per employee).

(l)   Services supplied by employer, such as in-house goods or services provided at less than cost – taxed on the direct extra (marginal) cost the employer incurs, less any payments made by the employee or director. This was found to be the correct way of computing such benefits in *Pepper (Inspector of Taxes) v Hart* [1993] AC 593, [1993] ICR 291, [1993] IRLR 33, [1993] 1 All ER 42, HL.

47.23 Tax-free benefits

A number of exemptions exist which enable a benefit to be provided free of tax. However, in the majority of cases, the exemption is conditional on certain conditions being met. It should be noted that from 6 April 2017 onwards, the majority of exemptions do not apply where the benefit is made available under an optional remuneration scheme, such as a salary sacrifice or flexible remuneration scheme, or where a cash alternative is offered instead. See **47.27A** for the rules applying to salary sacrifice schemes.

(a)   Meals provided in a canteen – not assessable, but taxable if not provided for the staff generally *(ITEPA 2003, s 317)*. From 6 April 2011 the exemption does not apply if the meals are made available under salary sacrifice arrangements.

(b)   Contributions to registered pension schemes – contributions by an employer are not taxable.

(c)   Medical insurance premiums or medical treatment outside the UK where the employee performs duties abroad but not including the cost of an air ambulance back to or treatment in the UK (*ITEPA 2003, s 325*). Medical check-up, health screening, eye tests and corrective appliances (such as glasses) can also be provided tax-free as long as certain conditions are met. Since 1 January 2015, the provision medical treatment recommended to an employee as part of occupational health services designed to help the employee to return to work sooner is exempt, subject to a cap of £500 per employee per tax year (*ITEPA 2003, s 320C*).

(d)   Childcare facilities, such as workplace nurseries, for employees' children under 18 provided by the employer alone or with other employers, local authorities etc. Since 6 April 2005 the exemption has also applied (subject to qualifying conditions) to the provision of childcare at or away from the workplace at registered, non-residential facilities provided by the employer (either alone or in partnership with other parties but financed and managed wholly by the employer). Care provided by means of a workplace nurseries is tax-free without limit as long as the associated conditions are met. Employers can also provide childcare vouchers and/or employer supported childcare tax-free up to certain limits. Certain conditions must be met. The exemption is only available where the employee joined the employer's childcare voucher or supported childcare scheme by 4 October 2018. However, once in the scheme, the employee is able to benefit from the associated tax exemption as long as the employer continues to offer the scheme. The exemption applies (subject to the conditions) to the provision of childcare vouchers up to the weekly limit (plus the cost of supplying the vouchers) used to obtain qualifying childcare and to the provision of employer-supported childcare. (*ITEPA 2003, ss 84(2A), 270A, 318–318D; FA 2004, s 78, Sch 13*). The tax-free weekly limit depends on the date that the employee joined the childcare or voucher scheme and the employee's marginal rate of tax. The limit for employees who joined before 6 April 2011 is set at £55 per week, regardless of their marginal rate of tax. For 2020/21, where the employee joined the scheme on or after 6 April 2011 and on or before 4 October 2018, for 2020/21 the tax-free limit is £55 per week for a basic rate taxpayer, £28 per week for a higher rate taxpayer £25 per week for an additional rate taxpayer. The relief is worth £11 per week to all employees who join the scheme after 6 April 2011 regardless of their marginal rate of tax. The exemptions for employer supported childcare and childcare vouchers is being phased out as a result of the Government-supported childcare scheme which was introduced from 28 April 2017, and employees are not able to join an employer scheme after 4 October 2018. Under the Government scheme, parents are able to open an online account to cover the cost of childcare with a registered provider. The Government provide a 20p top-up for every 80p that the parents pay into the account. The top-up is capped at £2,000 per child per tax year (or £4,000 per year where the child is disabled) and is tax-free. Employees who joined an employer scheme on or before 4 October 2018 are able to remain in it as long as the employer continues to offer the scheme. Alternatively, the employee can opt to leave the scheme and join the Government top-up scheme instead. An employee cannot benefit from both the employer scheme and the Government scheme and will need to weigh up which scheme is best for their needs. Where provision is made under a salary sacrifice or other optional remuneration arrangement, the tax exemption for employer-supported childcare and childcare vouchers remains available; the alternative valuation rules for benefits provided under optional remuneration arrangements do not apply.

(e) Work-related training (*ITEPA 2003, ss 250–260*) and outplacement counselling services for employees who are or become redundant. Also welfare counselling (*SI 2000/2080*).

(f) For employees starting a new job or moving with their existing employer, qualifying relocation expenses and benefits up to the value of £8,000 per move (*ITEPA 2003, ss 271–289*).

(g) In-house workplace sports and recreational facilities provided by employers for use by the staff generally, provided overnight accommodation is not available and the facilities are not on domestic premises. The exemption does not cover the use of assets such as yachts, cars and aircraft for private use (*ITEPA 2003, ss 261–263*).

(h) The provision of living accommodation for employees (but not directors) in certain circumstances where it is necessary for their job. This exemption extends to the employer's payment of employees' council tax. Accommodation provided as a result of a security threat is also exempt (*ITEPA 2003, ss 99, 100*).

(i) The provision of accommodation, supplies or services used by the employee in performing the duties of the employment, provided that any private use is insignificant, and that the sole purpose of providing the benefit is to enable the employee to perform the duties (from 6 April 2000) (*ITEPA 2003, s 316*).

(j) Alterations and additions to premises of a structural nature or landlord's repairs to premises of living accommodation which is provided by reason of a person's employment (*ITEPA 2003, s 313*).

(k)   The provision of parking facilities at or near the workplace for a car, cycle or motorcycle (*ITEPA 2003, s 237*).

(l)   Provision of travel, accommodation and subsistence during public transport disruption caused by industrial action (*ITEPA 2003, s 245*).

(m)   Provision of transport between home and place of employment or the provision of cars for severely disabled employees (*ITEPA 2003, ss 246, 247*).

(n)   Provision of transport for occasional late night journeys from work to home (*ITEPA 2003, s 248*).

(o)   Private use of mobile phones provided by the employer (from 6 April 1999) – limited to one phone per employee from 6 April 2006 (*ITEPA 2003, s 319*). The exemption applies equally to smartphones (Business Brief 02/12).

(p)   The loan of certain computer equipment provided prior to 6 April 2006 with a value not exceeding £2,500 (equating to a cash equivalent of £500) by the employer to the employee (providing that loans are not restricted to senior employees) (from 6 April 1999). The exemption does not apply to computer equipment loaned to the employee after 5 April 2006.

(q)   Provision of works buses with a seating capacity of nine or more, provided for employees to travel to and from work. Additionally, (from 6 April 2002) where employees benefit from their employer's subsidy of a bus service by receiving free or reduced-price travel, there is no tax charge on this benefit (*ITEPA 2003, ss 242, 243*). Also (from 6 April 2002) there is an exemption for the provision of buses for local shopping services (*SI 2002/205*).

(r)   The loan of bicycles and cycling safety equipment provided for employees to travel from home to work (from 6 April 1999) (*ITEPA 2003, s 244*). This exemption remains available beyond April 2017 where provision is made under a salary sacrifice or other optional remuneration agreement.

(s)   The cost of an annual Christmas party or similar event, providing that it is open to all staff generally and the cost per person attending does not exceed £150. (*ITEPA 2003, s 264*).

(t)   Paid and qualifying reimbursed expenses which would be deductible if the employee met the expense him or herself (from 6 April 2016, replacing the dispensation regime that applied prior to that date) (*ITEPA 2003, s 289A–289E*);

(u)   Trivial benefits costing not more than £50 (subject to an annual cap of £300 where provided to directors of close companies and their families (from 6 April 2016) (*ITEPA 2003, s 323A to 323C*).

(v)   The provision, at or near the employee's place of work, of facilities for charging a battery of a vehicle used by an employee (including one in which the employee is a passenger (from 6 April 2018) (*ITEPA 2003, s 237A*).

47.24 COMPANY CARS, VANS AND FUEL

The provision of company cars, vans and fuel are taxable benefits when available for the private use of the employee.

For 2016/17 onwards the tax charge on company cars, van and fuel available for private arises whenever these are provided to an employee (subject to the availability of any specific exemptions), regardless of the employee's earnings rate.

Appropriate percentages – cars registered on or after 6 April 2020

CO2 emissions (g/km)	Electric range	Appropriate percentage (%)		
		2020/21	2021/22	2022/23
0		0	1	2
1–50	More than 130 miles	0	1	2
	70 to 129 miles	3	4	5
	40 to 69 miles	6	7	8
	30 to 69 miles	10	11	12
	Less than 30 miles	12	13	14
51–54		13	14	15
55–59		14	15	16
60–64		15	16	17
65–69		16	17	18
70–74		17	18	19
75–79		18	19	20
80–84		19	20	21
85–89		20	21	22
90–94		21	22	23
95–99		22	23	24
100–104		23	24	25
105–109		24	25	26
110–114		25	26	27
115–119		26	27	28
120–124		27	28	29
125–129		28	29	30
130–134		29	30	31
135–139		30	31	32
140–144		31	32	33
145–149		32	33	34
150–154		33	34	35
155–159		34	35	36
160–164		35	36	37
165–169		36	37	37
170 and over		37	37	37

Where a car does not have a CO_2 emissions figure, the appropriate percentage depends on the engine size and the date on which the car was registered as shown in the table below.

Engine size	Registration pre 1 January 1998	Registration 1 January 1998 to 30 September 1999
1400cc or less	16%	16%
1401cc to 2000cc	27%	27%
2001cc or more	37%	37%
No cylinder capacity	37% otherwise	37% otherwise

The 'list price' is the price published by the manufacturer, importer or distributor (inclusive of delivery charges and taxes) at the time of registration. It is important to note that this is unlikely to be the price actually paid by the employer for the car. The list price for the car includes any standard accessories provided with the car, but the price of any optional extras supplied with the car when first made available to the employee, together with any further accessory costing £100 or more must be added in. Where an employee makes a capital contribution to the initial cost of the car, the price of the car for the year of contribution and subsequent years is reduced by that contribution or £5,000 if less. The list price is always used in calculating the cash equivalent value, even if the car was purchased second-hand.

The value of the benefit is reduced proportionately if the car is 'unavailable' for part of the year. The benefit is further reduced (or extinguished) by the amount of contributions which an employee is required to make for private use. Cars more than 15 years old and worth over £15,000 are taxed by reference to their open market value in accordance with special rules for classic cars.

(*ITEPA 2003, ss 114–148.*)

47.26 Car fuel

The benefit on car fuel provided for private motoring in a company car is calculated by applying the car benefit appropriate percentage ascertained in **47.25** above to a multiplier. For 2020/21 the multiplier is set at £24, 500 (for 2019/20 the multiplier was set at £24,100. The multiplier is increased annually by inflation.

The value of the fuel benefit is proportionately reduced if the car is not available for part of the year. No charge applies if the employee is required to, and does, make good to the employer the cost of all fuel used for private purposes (including travel between home and work). The charge is proportionately reduced if the employee begins to meet the cost of the fuel provided for private use, or fuel ceases to be provided for private use, from a date part way through the year, provided this condition continues to be met for the rest of the year. However, if the provision of fuel is withdrawn and then reinstated before the end of the year, the charge applies in full.

Before providing fuel for private motoring in a company car, employers and employees should consider whether this is a worthwhile benefit. At current levels of taxation it is unlikely to be a tax-efficient benefit unless private mileage is very high, especially in a climate of falling fuel prices.

Where the employer does not provide a company car driver with fuel and the company car driver uses the company car for business purposes, the employer will usually reimburse the cost of that fuel. HM Revenue and Customs publish 'advisory' fuel rates for company cars which can be used to reimburse employees tax-free mileage payments for business motoring in company cars. The figures may also be used for reimbursement by employers of fuel used for private motoring. The advisory rates will not be binding where the employer can demonstrate that the cost of business motoring is higher than the advisory rates. With effect from 1 March 2020, the rates are as follows:

Engine size	Petrol	LPG
1,400cc or less	12p	0p
1,401 to 2,000cc	14p	10p
Over 2,000cc	20p	14p

Engine size	Diesel
1,600cc or less	9p
1601cc to 2000cc	11p
Over 2,000cc	13p

The rates are revised quarterly (*ITEPA 2003, ss 149–153.*)

47.27 Vans

The provision of a company van weighing no more than 3.5 tonnes for the private use of employees is taxed by reference to an annual scale charge. For 2020/21, it is set at £3,490. For 2019/20 the charge was £3,430 a year. It is increased annually in line with inflation. The charge is reduced proportionally if the van is not available for the whole year, or is unavailable for 30 consecutive days or more. Payments by an employee towards private use of the van will also reduce the tax charge. Special provisions apply where vans are shared between several employees. Since 6 April 2005, no charge has applied to employees who have to take their van home and are not allowed, and do not make, any private use of the van (insignificant use being disregarded).

The charge for zero–emission vans is being increased progressively, with the charge being set at 20% of the full van benefit charge for 2015/16, 2016/17 and 2017/18, 40% for 2018/19, 60% for 2019/20, 80% for 2020/21. Consequently, for 2020/21, the charge for a zero emission van is £2,792. However, legislation is to be introduced to reduce the charge for zero emission vans to 0% from 6 April 2021.

A separate fuel scale charge applies where fuel is provided for private mileage in the company van. For 2020/21 the charge is set at £666 (for 2019/20 the charge was set at £655) (*ITEPA 2003, s 248A*).

47.27A SALARY SACRIFICE ARRANGEMENTS

The attractiveness of salary sacrifice schemes was seriously curtailed following the introduction of the alternative valuation rules for benefits provided under optional remuneration arrangements, such as salary sacrifice schemes.

Under a salary sacrifice scheme, an employee gives up an amount of cash salary in return for a benefit in kind. Prior to 6 April 2017, where the benefit was exempt from tax and National Insurance, this allowed the employee to save tax and primary Class 1 National Insurance contributions and the employer to save secondary Class 1 National Insurance contributions. However, the introduction of the alternative valuation rules seriously reduced the advantages associated with salary sacrifice arrangements such that for all but a handful of protected benefits, the benefit of any associated tax exemption is lost where the benefit is provided through a salary sacrifice or other optional remuneration arrangement, or where a cash alternative to a benefit is offered instead.

Under the alternative valuation rules, the amount charged to tax where the benefit is provided under a salary sacrifice or other optional remuneration agreement or where a cash alternative is offered instead is the amount of salary foregone or the cash alternative offered where this is higher that the cash equivalent value computed in accordance with normal rules. As the cash alternative is nil where an exemption applies, under these valuation rules the amount charged to tax in respect of an exempt benefit will be the cash foregone or the cash alternative, as appropriate, unless the benefit is one of a limited range of benefits to which the alternative rules do not apply.

The new valuation rules do not apply to the following protected benefits:

- pension savings;

- employer-provided pension advice;

- childcare and childcare vouchers;

- cycles and cyclists' safety equipment under cycle to work schemes; and

- ultra-low emission cars.

As such, they continue to benefit from associated tax exemptions where provided via a salary sacrifice or other optional remuneration scheme or where a cash alternative is offered. In the case of a low emission car, the benefit is taxed according to the cash equivalent value calculated under the company car rules rather than by reference to any cash alternative offered where this is higher than the cash equivalent.

Where an arrangement is in place on 5 April 2017, the start date of the new rules is delayed until the earlier of the date on which the contract ends, is modified or renewed, and 6 April 2021 where the benefit taken in exchange is a car (other than an ultra-low emissions car) living accommodation or school fees, and 6 April 2018 in all other cases.

TAX RELIEF FOR EXPENSES AND EXEMPTION FOR QUALIFYING PAID AND REIMBURSED EXPENSES

47.28 Tax relief for expenses

Tax relief is available for expenses incurred wholly, exclusively and necessarily in the performance of the duties. This is an especially difficult test to satisfy and it must be shown that the employee is obliged to incur and pay the expense as the office holder. Similarly, reimbursements to employees (other than employees in an excluded employment, as defined in 47.3 above) in respect of expenses, or any sum put at their disposal to cover expenses (such as for business travel and subsistence), are treated as earnings and relief can be claimed for the allowable part (*ITEPA 2003, ss 333–336*, previously *ICTA 1988, s 198*).

For 2016/17 and later tax years, expenses that are fully deductible are exempt from tax if paid or reimbursed by the employer (see 47.28A). The exemption replaced the dispensation regime applying for 2015/16 and earlier tax years.

47.28a Exemption for qualifying paid and reimbursed expenses

An exemption, which applies for 2016/17 and later tax years, is available where the expense that is paid or reimbursed is fully deductible by the employee (*ITEPA 2003, s 289A*). The exemption is conditional on two conditions being met. Condition A is that the payer or another person operates a system for checking that the employee is incurring and paying amounts in respect of expenses of the same kind and a deduction would be allowed in respect of those expenses. Condition B is neither the payer nor any other person operating the system knows or suspects or could reasonably be expected to know or suspect that the employee had not incurred and paid an amount in respect of the expenses or that a deduction would not be allowed in respect of the amount. The exemption is not be available if the payment or reimbursement is provided pursuant to a salary sacrifice arrangement.

Also from 6 April 2016 the employer can instead apply to HMRC to pay expenses tax-free in accordance with an agreed flat rate (*ITEPA 2003, s 289B*).

47.29   EMPLOYEE SHARE SCHEMES

Tax advantages are available where employees are provided with shares or share options via an approved share or share option scheme.

Shares and share options can also be made available to employees by means of unapproved schemes. Although these lack the tax advantages available to approved schemes, they are not bound by the associated conditions and offer more flexibility.

47.29a Savings-related share option schemes

Savings-related share option schemes are tax-advantaged schemes established in accordance with *ITEPA 2003 ss 516–520, Sch 3* (amended by *FA 2003, Schs 21, 22*) whereby a company may establish a scheme for its employees to obtain options to acquire the company's shares without charge to income tax either on the value of the options or on any subsequent increase in the value of the shares before the options are exercised. The scheme must be linked to an approved savings scheme (subject to a monthly limit of £500 (£250 prior to 6 April 2014)) to provide the funds for the acquisition of the shares when the option is exercised. For capital gains tax purposes, the market value is not substituted for the consideration given so the base cost is the amount paid for both the shares and the option. For further details of the scheme rules, see *Tolley's Income Tax 2005/06* (or later edition).

47.30 Company share option schemes

A company share option plan (CSOP) is a tax-advantaged share option plan set up in accordance with *ITEPA 2003, ss 521–526, Sch 4* (as amended by *FA 2003, Sch 21 para 16*). The scheme applies to options granted from 17 July 1995 (before that date, options were granted under what was known as the 'executive share option scheme' which provided more generous tax relief). The aggregate market value of shares acquired under the option and any other approved options held by the employee (other than savings-related schemes) must not exceed £30,000. There is no tax charge when the options are granted, if all the conditions have been complied with. Options under the scheme have to be exercised between three and ten years after being granted but may be exercised within three years of the grant where the individual ceases to be an employee due to injury, disablement redundancy or retirement. Options granted before 9 April 2003 must be exercised between three and ten years after being granted (without exception), and not more frequently than once in every three years. For capital gains tax purposes, the base cost is the amount paid for both the shares and the option. For further details of the plan rules, see *Tolley's Income Tax 2005/06* (or later edition).

47.31 Share incentive plans

Share incentive plans were introduced by *FA 2000, s 47, Sch 8*, and were originally known as the all-employee share ownership plan. The legislation is now found in *ITEPA 2003, ss 418, 488–515, Sch 2* (amended by *FA 2003, Schs 21, 22*). Share Incentive Plans (SIPs) are intended to be available to all employees, and were designed to replace profit-sharing schemes. Employees can receive up to £3,600 (£3,000 prior to 6 April 2014) worth of free shares per year, with the option of purchasing shares up to £1,800 per year (£1,500 per year prior to 6 April 2014) by deductions from salary. For every share purchased, the employee can be given two free shares. To remain free of tax and National Insurance, all shares acquired must be held in the plan for a specified period of time, normally at least three years.

Dividends of up to £1,500 per employee per tax year can be reinvested tax-free in additional shares in the company. Withdrawals of shares from the plan are not subject to capital gains tax and they are treated as acquired by the employee at their market value at that time. For further details of the plan rules, see *Tolley's Income Tax 2005/06* (or later edition).

47.32 Enterprise management incentives

The 'enterprise management incentive scheme' was introduced by *FA 2000, s 62, Sch 14* and amended by *FA 2001, s 62, Sch 14*. The legislation is now contained within *ITEPA 2003, ss 527–541, Sch 5*. The scheme allows small independent trading companies to reward employees with tax-advantaged share options worth up to £120,000 per employee. Any gain on the sale of such shares is chargeable to capital gains tax. The company must be an independent UK company carrying on a qualifying trade, and its gross assets must not exceed £15,000,000. For further details *Tolley's Income Tax 2005/06* (or later edition).

The availability of enterprise management incentives is now limited to companies with fewer than 250 employees.

It should be noted that state aid for the EMI regime lapsed on 6 April 2018. Renewal was sought from the European Commission and was granted on 15 May 2018. The new approval will run until 6 April 2023, but will be subject to the condition of any Brexit withdrawal agreement.

EMI options may not be eligible for the associated tax advantages where granted between 6 April 2018 and the new approval date. HMRC have confirmed that EMI options granted before 6 April 2018 will benefit from the tax advantages; but those issued from 6 April 2018 until the date on which EU State Aid approval was received may not qualify. For a thorough discussion of the schemes outlined in **47.29–47.32**, see *Tolley's Tax Planning 2005/06* (or later edition).

47.32A EMPLOYEE SHAREHOLDER STATUS

Employee shareholder status is an employment status which has been available since 1 September 2013. Employee shareholders have fewer employment rights than employees, but enjoyed tax advantages as compensation for the lost employment rights. The income tax and capital gains tax advantages associated with employee shareholder status were abolished in relation to employee shareholder agreements made on or after 1 December 2016.

47.33 PAYROLL GIVING SCHEME

Employees can authorise their employers to deduct charitable donations from their earnings before tax, for passing on to nominated charities approved through agency charities with which the employer has made arrangements. Deductions must be made under a scheme authorised by HM Revenue and Customs and subject to regulations made by Statutory Instrument. National Insurance contributions remain payable on the gross earnings.

PROVISION OF SERVICES THROUGH AN INTERMEDIARY

IR35 rules

Provisions were introduced with effect from 6 April 2000 by *FA 2000, Sch 12* which are designed to counter what the Government considers to be tax avoidance where services are provided through an intermediary, ie typically single workers contracting out their services to a client via their own personal services company. The provisions are generally referred to as IR35 after the Budget Press Release in which they were announced. The legislation is now found within *ITEPA 2003, Pt 1 Ch 8 (ss 48–61)* (as amended by *FA 2003, s 136*).

The provisions were modified in their application where the end client is a public sector body with effect from 6 April 2017. See https://www.gov.uk/guidance/off-payroll-working -in the public sector reform-of intermediaries-legislation. These rules are to be extended to engagements where the end client is a medium or large private sector organisation from 6 April 2021. The reforms to the off-payroll working rules were due to take effect from 6 April 2020, but were delayed as a result of the Covid-19 pandemic.

Since 6 April 2017, the IR35 rules apply where a worker provides his or her services through an intermediary (such as a personal service company) to a private sector end client and, but for the intermediary, the worker would be an employee of the end client. Prior to 6 April 2017, the rules applied equally regardless of whether the end client was a private sector organisation or public sector body. From 6 April 2021 once the off-payroll working rules are extended, the original IR35 rules will only apply where the end client is a small private sector organisation.

The responsibility for determining whether the IR35 rules apply (i.e. whether ignoring the intermediary, the worker would be an employee of the end client) rests with the worker's intermediary. HMRC's Check Employment Status for Tax (CEST) tool can be used for this purpose. Where they do, the intermediary must calculate a deemed employment payment in accordance with *ITEPA 2003, s 54*. The deemed employment payments is deemed to be paid to the worker on 5 April at the end of the tax year. Tax and National Insurance (employer's and employee's) on the deemed payment must be paid over to HMRC.

The rules are designed to ensure that a comparable amount of PAYE and NIC is payable on contractors' income as would be the case if the service company did not exist and the contractor were employed directly by the client. There are corresponding NIC provisions, contained in the *Welfare Reform and Pensions Act 1999, s 75 (SI 1999/3420)* and the *Social Security Contributions (Intermediaries) Regulations 2000*.

For further details of the provisions, see *Tolley's Income Tax 2019/20*. A substantial library of information about these provisions is available on the GOV.UK website and a list of the available resources of relevance can be found at https://www.gov.uk/guidance/ir35-find-out -if-it-applies.

The Court of Appeal confirmed the legality of the provisions in the judicial review case of *R (on the application of Professional Contractors Group Ltd) v IRC* [2001] EWCA Civ 1945, [2002] STC 165, [2001] All ER (D) 356 (Dec) employee-like services will be taxed as if there was a real employment situation.

The corresponding NIC provisions (contained in the *Social Security Contributions (Intermediaries) Regulations 2000 (SI 2000/727)*) were held to apply in *Battersby v Campbell (Inspector of Taxes)* (Sp C 287) [2001] STC (SCD) 189 and *FS Consulting Ltd v McCaul* (Sp C 305) [2002] STC (SCD) 138.

Off-payroll working rules – services provided to public sector bodies

From 6 April 2017 the rules were reformed where the end client is a public sector body. The reformed 'off-payroll' public sector rules apply to contracts for work after 5 April 2017 and to payments made after 5 April 2017 in respect of work done before that date. The rules are contained in *ITEPA 2003, Pt. 2, Ch. 10 (ss. 61K to 61X)*.

Under these rules, where the services are provided to a public sector body, it is the public sector body rather than the intermediary who is responsible for deciding whether the off-rules apply. HMRC's Check Employment Status for Tax (CEST) tool can be used for this purpose. Where the off-payroll working rules are in point, the fee payer, which may be the public sector body or which may be an agency, is responsible for deducting payments of tax and primary Class 1 National Insurance contributions from payments made to the worker's intermediary. Guidance on the application of the rules can be found in a technical note available on the GOV.UK website at https://www.gov.uk/government/publications/off -payroll-working-in-the-public-sector-reform-of-the-intermediaries-legislation-technical -note.

Extension of the off-payroll working rules to the private sector

The off-payroll working rules as they apply where the end client is a public sector body are to be extended (with some modifications) to the private sector from 6 April 2021, the start date having been delayed by one year as a result of the Covid-19 pandemic. The rules, as extended, will apply where a worker provides services through an intermediary to an end client which is a medium or large private sector organisation (as defined for Companies Act 2006 purposes). Under the rules, the private sector engager must determine the status of the worker. HMRC's Check Employment Status for Tax (CEST) tool can be used for this purpose, and as long as the information provided is accurate, HMRC will stand by the result. The engager must provide a copy of the determination and the reasons for reaching it to the worker and to other parties in the chain. If the determination is that the off-payroll working rules apply, the fee payer (which may be the end client or a third party such as an agency) must deduct tax and National Insurance from the payment made to the worker's intermediary and pay it over to HMRC together with employer's National Insurance on the payment.

The extended rules will not apply where the end client is a small private sector organisation. From April 2021 onwards, small private sector organisations engaging workers who provide their services through an intermediary will continue to make payments to the intermediary gross without deducting tax and National Insurance. The worker's intermediary remains responsible for determining whether the IR35 rules apply, and operating them if they do.

47.35   MANAGED SERVICE COMPANIES

Managed service companies are intermediary companies through which the services of a worker are provided to an end client. They are not the same as personal service companies and in contrast to a personal service company the worker is not usually in business on his own account and does not exercise control over the business. The control is with the provider of the managed service company.

Legislation was introduced to counter the use of managed service companies to avoid tax and National Insurance contributions. The tax legislation, which is contained in *FA 2007*, *s 25* and *Sch 3*, applies from 6 April 2007. Corresponding National Insurance provisions, contained in the *Social Security Contributions (Managed Service Companies) Regulations 2007 (SI 2007/2070)*, apply from 6 August 2007.

Under the rules all payments made by a managed service company to a worker are treated as payments of employment income, regardless or the nature of the payment or how it is described. This means that PAYE and NIC must be applied, even if the payment is described as a dividend. The managed service company is responsible for the operation of PAYE and NIC.

The managed service company rules also reduced the scope for the worker to claim deductible travel expenses.

From 6 August 2007, where the PAYE and NIC debts of a managed service company cannot be recovered from the company, HMRC may transfer the debt personally to the company director or to the managed service company provider. Debts may be transferred to third parties from 6 January 2008.

47.36 DISGUISED REMUNERATION

Provisions were introduced from 6 April 2011 (*ITEPA 2003, Pt 7A*) to tackle arrangements that use trusts and other vehicles to reward employees in a way that is designed to avoid, defer or reduce tax and National Insurance liabilities by disguising what is in effect remuneration. The rules also target arrangements that are designed to be used as a tax-advantaged way to save for retirement by using an employer financed retirement benefit scheme as an alternative to, or a top up to, savings in a registered pension scheme.

The rules provide for an income tax charge to apply where trusts or other intermediate vehicles are used in arrangements aimed at providing value to an individual in what is in substance a reward or recognition in connection with the individual's employment. Although the rules are not limited to arrangements involving employee benefit trusts (EBTs), in practice many of the arrangements that fall within their scope will feature EBTs. A charge will also apply where a loan is provided in connection with the employee's arrangement. The tax charge will operate in the following ways.

- Sums or assets that are earmarked for employees by trusts or other intermediaries will be treated as if the amount of the sum or the value of the asset earmarked for the employee is a payment of PAYE income provided by the employer's employee to the employee.

- Loans provided to employees by trusts and other intermediaries will be treated as if the value of the loan is a payment of PAYE income provided by the employee's employer to the employee.

- Assets provided to employees by trusts or other intermediaries will be regarded for tax purposes as a payment of PAYE income by the employer where certain conditions (as specified in the legislation) are met.

- Sums or assets that are earmarked by the employer with a view to a trust to other intermediary providing retirement benefits to the employee are treated as if the amount of the sum or value of the asset earmarked for the employee is a payment of PAYE income provided by the employee's employer to the employee.

The disguised remuneration rules apply from 6 April 2011 in relation to rewards which are earmarked for an individual employee or otherwise made available on or after that date. Anti-forestalling rules applied in certain situations in relation to sums paid or assets provided between 9 December 2010 and 6 April 2011, where if provision had been made on or after 6 April 2011, the new rules would be in point.

Regulations impose a National Insurance charge on the amounts chargeable to tax from the same date.

A loan charge was levied on 5 April 2019 on outstanding loans from disguised remuneration arrangements. The loan charge initially applied to loans made under disguised remuneration arrangements since April 1999 which remain outstanding on 5 April 2019. The amount of the loan is taxed as if it were remuneration received on that date. HMRC offered settlement opportunity for users of disguised remuneration schemes with outstanding loans. The loan charge only applies where settlement has not been reached with HMRC.

Following an independent review of the loan charge chaired by Sir Amyas Morse, the Government announced a number of changes to the loan charge, accepting all but one of the recommendations of the review. As a result, the loan charge will now only apply to outstanding balances on loans made between 9 December 2010 and 5 April 2019 inclusive. However, it will not apply to loans made prior to 6 April 2016 where a reasonable disclosure of the use of a disguised remuneration scheme was made to HMRC within the relevant tax return or accompanying documents and HMRC failed to take an action. Those affected by the loan charge will be able to elect to split the loan balance over three consecutive years – 2018/19, 2019/20 and 2020/21. Late payment interest will not be charged for the period from 1 February 2020 to 30 September 2020 on any self-assessment liability for 2018/19, as long as the tax return is filed, or an arrangement with HMRC reached, by 30 September 2020. The date for online reporting of disguised remuneration loans to HMRC is also delayed by one year – from 1 October 2019 to 1 October 2020. HMRC will also repay certain voluntary payments made under qualifying agreements made on or after 16 March 2016 which cover periods which now fall outside the loan charge.

47.37 CORONAVIRUS JOB RETENTION SCHEME

The Coronavirus Job Retention Scheme provides help to businesses who are unable to maintain their workforce due the Covid-19 pandemic. Affected businesses can furlough their employees and apply for a grant from HMRC to cover 80% of their usual monthly wages, to a maximum of £2,500, plus the associated employer's National Insurance contributions (to the extent that these are not covered by the Employment Allowance) and the minimum employer pension contribution required under auto-enrolment on that wage. The scheme is a temporary scheme which, initially, was initially introduced for a period of three months from 1 March 2020. It was extended for additional month to run until the end of June, before being further extended to remain available until the end of October. Changes to the scheme are to apply from August 2020 to allow furloughed employees to return to work in a measured way.

To benefit from the scheme, the business must have a UK payroll on 28 February 2020. The business must also have a PAYE online account and a UK bank account. Claims can be made for furloughed employees who were on the payroll on 19 March 2020 and in respect of whom a RTI submission had been made by that date.. Employees who started work after 28 February 2020 cannot be furloughed under this scheme. However, employees who were made redundant before 28 February can be re-employed and paid through the scheme. They did not need to be re-employed by 19 March 2020.

The scheme applies to employees on any type of contract, including full-time, part-time, flexible and zero-hours contracts. It is also available to company directors operating through personal service companies in respect of their PAYE pay. While furloughed, under the scheme as it applies from 1 March 2020 to 31 July 2020, employees cannot undertake work for or on behalf of the organisation, but can take on alternative work for another employer. Company directors can meet their statutory obligations while furloughed, but cannot undertake fee generating work. From August 2020, furloughed employees will be able to work part time with employers contributing to their salary costs. Payments that an employee receives while furloughed are subject to tax and National Insurance in the usual way.

Employees who are ill or who are self-isolating are eligible for statutory sick pay.

Claims for the grant can be made online. A single claim only can be made for each pay period and must include all employees in respect of whom the grant is claimed. Grants paid to cover employees' wages must be paid over to the employees in full.

Detailed guidance on the scheme is available on the Gov.uk website at https ://www.gov.uk/guidance/claim-for-wage-costs-through-the-coronavirus-job-retention -scheme.

48 Temporary and Seasonal Employees

Cross-references. See 16.3 EMPLOYEE, SELF-EMPLOYED OR WORKER? for the distinction between a contract for services and a contract of service/employment. See TAXATION (47) for vacation employment of students. See also ENGAGEMENT OF EMPLOYEES (22) and PROBATIONARY EMPLOYEES (37).

48.1 An employer may sometimes engage workers on a temporary basis. This might be to take over work while a permanent employee is away or to cope with fluctuating workloads (eg due to seasonal work requirements). In this chapter, the description 'temporary' is applied to a worker who is referred to an employer by an employment agency (the kind of worker commonly referred to as a 'temp') and also to an employee who is employed for a limited period. 'Seasonal worker' is applied to a person who enters into the direct employment of the employer for a limited period at a busy time of the year. Employees who are engaged for a limited period (including seasonal workers) may be fixed-term employees and accordingly will qualify for protection under the provisions of the *Fixed-Term Employees (Prevention of Less Favourable Treatment) Regulations 2002 (SI 2002/2034)* (these *Regulations* are considered below at **48.13**).

As to employment of part-time workers or job-sharers, their employment rights are not dependent on their working a specified number of hours in a week: see CONTINUOUS EMPLOYMENT (7). See also the *Part-time Workers (Prevention of Less Favourable Treatment) Regulations 2000 (SI 2000/ 1551)* as amended by *SI 2002/2035* (see **23.12** EQUAL PAY).

48.2 TEMPORARY WORKERS

Employment agencies

Employment agencies fulfil two main functions: they effect introductions of permanent staff to employers and they supply temporary staff for a short period of time. So far as the first category is concerned, after the introduction has been made, the employment agency drops out of the picture, and the employer enters into a direct relationship with the employee with all the attendant duties and responsibilities of a normal employment contract. If, however, the worker is supplied on a temporary basis – the agency charging its client a weekly fee out of which it pays the worker – the client is more accurately to be regarded in most circumstances as a user of that worker's services and not his employer (here called the 'quasi employer'). Because the quasi employer controls not only what the agency worker does but how he does it, the quasi employer may be vicariously liable for any wrong done by the worker while working for him (see VICARIOUS LIABILITY (57)) and be liable to the worker for any claim by him for damages for personal injuries (*Mersey Docks and Harbour Board v Coggins and Griffiths (Liverpool) Ltd* [1947] AC 1, [1946] 2 All ER 345; *Denham v Midland Employers' Mutual Assurance Ltd* [1955] 2 QB 437, [1955] 2 All ER 561). However, it was for a considerable period doubtful whether the quasi employer would be liable to the worker for unfair dismissal or redundancy if the employment agency could be regarded as the primary employer who lends the worker's services to other employers (*Cross v Redpath Dorman Long (Contracting) Ltd* [1978] ICR 730, EAT). In *Ironmonger v Movefield Ltd* [1988] IRLR 461, it was held that the contract with the employment agency was one *sui generis*, somewhere between a contract of employment and a contract for services. A similar approach was taken in *Wickens v Champion Employment* [1984] ICR 365 where there was held to be no contract of employment between a worker and an employment agency.

In *McMeechan v Secretary of State for Employment* [1997] IRLR 353 the Court of Appeal held that an agency worker *may* have the status of an employee in relation to a *particular engagement* actually worked even if there is no such status as an employee under the *general terms of engagement* between the worker and the employment agency. In this case, the appellant's claim to employee status was limited to a specific contract in relation to which he was owed money. The Court of Appeal held, despite an express term describing the appellant as 'a self-employed worker' that he was in fact an employee in relation to the specific engagement under consideration. It was, accordingly, unnecessary for the Court of Appeal to determine whether the appellant was to be considered an employee under the general terms of the engagement with the employment agency.

The issue of the employment status of temporary and agency workers has been a difficult and ongoing problem with conflicting judicial decision and bursts of judicial activism and then retreat as the cases summarised below illustrate. What is clear is that it will be a matter for Parliament to address ultimately and not the courts – a point made with particular clarity by the Court of Appeal in *James v Greenwich London Borough Council* [2008] EWCA Civ 35, [2008] ICR 545, [2008] IRLR 302 (below).

48.3   *Similar facts different results*

In *Costain Building and Civil Engineering Ltd v Smith* [2000] ICR 215, the EAT had reversed a finding by an employment tribunal that a worker supplied by an agency and appointed by a trade union as a safety representative was an employee. The worker was paid without deduction of tax or National Insurance. The EAT held that the only contracts were between the employment agency and the worker and between the employment agency and the company. By way of contrast, in *Motorola Ltd v Davidson* [2001] IRLR 4, the EAT held that a worker supplied by an agency was an employee of the hiring company (Motorola) and could, accordingly, present a complaint of unfair dismissal. The EAT held that Motorola exercised sufficient control in reality over the worker to give rise to employee status, rejecting Motorola's argument that the worker was controlled by the agency. This was a significant decision in that there was no express contract between the worker and Motorola, a factor which had previously been fatal to the contention that the worker was an employee of the quasi employer. The facts of the case should also be noted in that the employee was specifically selected to work at Motorola and had done so permanently for over two years.

While each case may turn upon its own facts, in the area of employment status of agency workers even on similar facts, wholly different conclusions have been reached by different courts. This left agency workers in a very unsatisfactory and uncertain position with regard to employment protection rights. A clear illustration of the problem was provided by *Johnson Underwood Ltd v Montgomery* [2001] EWCA Civ 318, [2001] IRLR 269. In that case the claimant had worked for the client of the employment business for some two and a half years. Upon the termination of her 'employment' she presented a claim for unfair dismissal. The issue of who was the employer arose as a preliminary issue. The case eventually reached the Court of Appeal which concluded, applying the tests of control and mutuality of obligation, that, on the particular facts, the claimant was not an employee of the employment business. The unfortunate consequence of this decision was that the claimant was left without a remedy as the original employment tribunal decision (to the effect that she was not an employee of the client business at which she had worked for two and a half years) had not been appealed. A striking example of very long term agency workers being found not to have employment status was provided by *Esso Petroleum Co Ltd v Jarvis* [2002] All ER (D) 112 (Jan). In that case, agency workers who had worked for the same client for 9 and 11 years, respectively, were found not to be employees of the client on the basis of the absence of a contractual relationship between the workers and the client. This may be contrasted with the *Motorola* decision above. In *Hewlett Packard Ltd v O'Murphy* [2002] IRLR 4 it was held that there was no contractual nexus between the worker (who had worked for six years) and the appellant client. Accordingly, he was not an employee. *Motorola* was not, however, referred to in the *Hewlett Packard* case.

48.4 *Activism – the search for an implied contract of employment*

The lack of certainty in this area of the law and the apparently conflicting decisions at EAT level lead to a trilogy of decisions of the Court of Appeal which developed the concept of an *implied contract of employment* arising between the worker and the client using his services. In *Franks v Reuters Ltd* [2003] EWCA Civ 417, [2003] IRLR 423 the claimant entered into a temporary worker agreement with an employment agency and was supplied to Reuters where he worked for five years working hours fixed by Reuters but paid by the employment agency. The Court of Appeal held that the worker was an employee of Reuters. The question to be addressed by an employment tribunal was whether a contract of employment could be implied between the worker and Reuters from the circumstances of his work and what was said by the parties at the time work commenced and subsequently. The Court of Appeal explained that although a person cannot become an employee simply by reason of length of the time which they have worked, the length of 'service' was not irrelevant evidence in the context of a person who was allowed to stay working in the same place for the same client for over five years because dealings between parties over a period of years, as distinct from weeks or months, are capable of generating implied contractual relationships.

The principles in *Franks* were developed in *Dacas v Brook Street Bureau (UK) Ltd* [2004] EWCA Civ 217, [2004] IRLR 358. In *Dacas* the applicant had worked exclusively as a cleaner at a hostel run by Wandsworth Council for at least four years until the engagement was terminated. Mrs Dacas brought proceedings for unfair dismissal against the supplying agency and, alternatively, the Council. In a striking illustration of the unsatisfactory nature of the law in this area the employment tribunal concluded that she was employed by neither the agency nor the council. This result – that Mrs Dacas was employed by nobody – was described in the Court of Appeal (by Sedley LJ) as 'simply not credible'. The Court of Appeal concluded that the agency was not the employer of the claimant as the necessary mutuality of obligation or control was not present. As to the Council, Mummery LJ concluded that employment by that body would accord with 'practical reality and commonsense' and in Sedley LJ's view there was an inference to be drawn that the Council was the employer. The Court of Appeal in *Dacas* stressed that, in proceedings before an employment tribunal where the status of a claimant is in issue, the Tribunal is required as a matter of law to consider whether there is an *implied* contract between the parties who are not in an express contractual relationship with each other. (On the facts of *Dacas* there was a contract between Mrs Dacas and the agency and between the agency and the Council. The relationship between Mrs Dacas and the Council was considered by the majority (Munby J dissenting) to be an *implied* contract of employment.)

In *Cable and Wireless plc v Muscat* [2006] EWCA Civ 220, [2006] IRLR 354 the implied contract approach was again considered but on somewhat atypical facts. The Court of Appeal held for the first (and only) time that there was *in fact* an implied contract of employment between the worker and the client end-user (in *Franks* the issue had been remitted to the employment tribunal and the observations in *Dacas* as to implied contract status of the claimant were, on the particular facts of that appeal, *obiter*). The facts of *Muscat* were complicated and somewhat unusual. The worker had originally been an employee who was then required to go to agency provided services followed by a *TUPE* transfer. As such, the case did not illustrate the more common factual circumstances of a worker providing services to a client consistently through an agency for a period of time in excess of, say, one year. Further the Court held that the guidance of the majority in *Dacas* was to be applied and followed by employment tribunals in future cases. On the issue of the fact that payment of the worker was made by the agency rather than the client end user (which factor was one of the main reasons for Munby J's dissent in *Dacas*), the Court held that this is not a particularly strong factor against employee status if the other factors point to employment by the end user client.

48.5   Temporary and Seasonal Employees

In *Protectacoat Firthglow Ltd v Szilagyi* [2009] IRLR 365 and in *Autoclenz Ltd v Belcher & Others* [2010] IRLR 70 the Court of Appeal held that it was not necessary for a term to be properly characterised as a "sham" before it could be not applied. *Protectacoat* and *Autoclenz* established that where there is a dispute as to the genuineness of an express term there is no need to show a common intention to mislead. Instead it is enough if the written term did not represent the intentions or expectations of the parties. The court or tribunal was to consider whether or not the words of the written contract represented the true intentions or expectations of the parties (and therefore their implied agreement and contractual obligations) not only at the inception of the contract but at any later stage where the evidence shows that the parties have expressly or impliedly varied the agreement between them. The focus of the enquiry had to be to discover the actual legal obligations of the parties and to carry out that exercise the tribunal had to examine all the relevant evidence including the written term itself as read in the context of the whole agreement. It would include evidence of how the parties conducted themselves in practice and what their expectations of each other were. This approach gave rise to what was perceived to be a conflict with the earlier Court of Appeal decision in *Consistent Group Limited v Kalwak* [2008] IRLR 505 which had suggested that the term must be a "sham" before it could be disapplied.

The matter has now been resolved beyond doubt by the decision of the Supreme Court in *Autoclenz Ltd v Belcher* [2011] UKSC 41, [2011] IRLR 820. The Supreme Court approved the judgments of the Court of Appeal in *Autoclenz* and *Protectacoat* (as well as that of the EAT in *Kalwak* so that the decision of the Court of Appeal in *Kalwak* is, effectively, overruled). The real question for the court is what was the true agreement between the parties? The concept or requirement of "a sham" was unhelpful in the employment context where a broader enquiry was required into the true terms of the agreement as the agreements in issue were frequently drafted by the employer and where inequality of bargaining power was present. The enquiry permitted consideration to be given to the subsequent conduct of the parties as evidence of what was originally agreed between them. The court must consider the relative bargaining power of the parties in deciding whether the terms of any written agreement in truth represented what was agreed and this required a purposive approach to the problem.

48.6   *The Temporary Agency Work Directive (2008/104/EC) and the Agency Worker Regulations 2010 (SI 2010/93)*

In May 2008 the then Government announced that it had reached agreement with the TUC and the CBI on legislating to give agency workers the right to terms and conditions of employment comparable to those enjoyed by permanent employees.

Under the agreement, agency workers were to be entitled to equal treatment with comparable permanent workers after 12 weeks of employment. The agreement defines equal treatment as 'at least the basic working and employment conditions that would apply to the workers concerned if they had been recruited directly by that undertaking to occupy the same job'. The agreement does not cover occupational social security schemes. The agreement also requires that these arrangements be reviewed after a suitable period to establish how they are working in practice.

In June 2008 the Council of the European Union announced that a common position had been reached on the draft Directive on agency work resulting in the *Temporary Agency Work Directive (2008/104/EC)*. The *Directive* is limited to temporary *agency* workers and thus does not affect the employment status of temporary workers but permits the UK to implement the agreement between the Government, the CBI and the TUC.

The purpose of the *Directive* is to ensure the protection of temporary agency workers by applying the principle of equal treatment (*art 5*) so that, after 12 weeks in a given job, the basic working and employment conditions (duration of working time, overtime, breaks, rest periods, night work, holidays and public holidays and pay) of temporary agency workers shall be, for the duration of their assignment at a hirer, at least those that would apply if they had been recruited directly by that undertaking to occupy the same job. There are also other entitlements that aim to improve the situation for agency workers in other areas, for example, in terms of improved access to permanent employment and training. Member states had until 5 December 2011 to implement the *Directive*.

In the first case on the construction of the *Directive Auto- ja Kuljetusalan Työntekijäliitto AKT ry v Öljytuote ry* [2015] IRLR 502, the ECJ held that restrictions on the use of temporary agency workers imposed by a collective agreement were not contrary to the provisions of *art 4* of the *Directive*. In *Betriebsrat der Ruhrlandklinik gGmbH v Ruhrland-klinik gGmbH* [2017] IRLR 194 the ECJ held that the characterisation of the relationship under national law is not determinative of worker status and that a "worker" is not limited to persons with a contract of employment with the temporary work agency. The issue is whether there is an "employment relationship" which is determined by whether a person for a period of time "performs services for and under the direction of another person, in return for which he receives remuneration".

The Agency Worker Regulations 2010 (SI 2010/93)

Following consultation in relation to the implementation of the *Directive*, the *Agency Worker Regulations 2010 (SI 2010/93)* were passed by the previous Government and were due to come into force on 1 October 2011. The *Regulations* were, however, further amended prior to their coming into force by the *Agency Workers (Amendment) Regulations 2011 (SI 2011/1941)*. Accordingly, particular care should be taken to ensure that the most up to date version of the *Regulations* is consulted. References to the *Regulations* below are to the amended *Regulations*. In May 2011 the Government's 51 page guidance document on the *Regulations* and their effect was published. See the "Agency Workers Regulations Guidance" which may be obtained from https://www.gov.uk/government/publications/agency-workers-regulations-2010-guidance-for-recruiters. The Guidance is not a Code of Practice and does not, accordingly, have any specific legal status but it is likely that it will be used by the employment tribunals in interpreting and applying the Regulations as a body of relevant case law is developed.

In summary, the *Regulations* introduce, with effect from 1 October 2011, a right to equal treatment in relation to terms and conditions of employment for agency workers in comparison to the permanent employees and workers of the hirer.

Definitions

Under the *Regulations* (*reg 3*) an "agency worker" means an individual who is supplied by a "temporary work agency" to work temporarily for and under the supervision and direction of "a hirer" and who has a contract with the temporary work agency which is a contract of employment or any other contract to perform work and services personally for the agency. The meaning of "temporary" is not defined in the *Regulations* (or the *Directive*) but was considered by the EAT in *Moran v Ideal Cleaning Services Ltd* [2014] IRLR 172. In that case the claimants had worked as cleaners for between 6 and 25 years employed as agency workers on contracts of indefinite duration. On termination of their engagements they brought claims under the *Regulations*. The EAT held that the arrangements under which the claimants worked were indefinite in duration and permanent and that "temporary" meant not permanent. A purposive construction to the effect that all agency workers satisfying the *Regulations*' 12 week qualifying period were agency workers benefiting from the protection of the *Regulations* was rejected as giving no meaning or effect to the word "temporary" at all. Insofar as that construction left a lacuna of protection, that lacuna, the EAT held, was a deliberate consequence of the drafting of the *Directive* as limited to temporary workers. In contrast, in *Brooknight Guarding v Matei* (UKEAT/0309/17/LA) a security guard employed on a "zero hours" contract for 21 months prior to dismissal was held to be an

48.6 Temporary and Seasonal Employees

In contrast to the *Agency Worker Regulations reg 5* rights which are subject to the *reg 7* qualifying period, all agency worker during an assignment are entitled to immediate equal access to "collective facilities and amenities" provided by the hirer (*reg 12*) as are available to a comparable worker. The facilities include canteen, childcare and transport services (*reg 12(3)*) and a "comparable worker" is and employee or worker of the hirer engaged in broadly similar work for the hirer with (where relevant) a similar level of qualification and skills working at the same establishment (*reg 12(4)*). Agency workers also have the right to be informed by the hirer of any relevant vacant posts with the hirer, to give that agency worker the same opportunity as a comparable worker to find permanent employment with the hirer (*reg 13*). This does not amount to a right of preference in selection for the position - it is an obligation to provide information and no more. An argument that *reg 13* should be construed to give the relevant agency worker preference in the permanent appointment or, alternatively, a guaranteed interview was robustly rejected by the EAT in *Coles v Ministry of Defence* (2015) UKEAT/0403/14, [2015] IRLR 872.

Liability for Breach of the *Agency Workers Regulations*

Under *reg 14* breach of *reg 5* will lead to liability in the temporary work agency and/or the hirer to the extent each is liable for breach. Under *reg 16* an agency worker may make a written request to the temporary work agency for a written statement containing information relating to a suspected breach of *reg 5* and a similar right exists in relation to a hirer in suspected breach of *reg 12* or *reg 13*. Failure to provide the information will permit adverse inferences to be drawn by an employment tribunal (*reg 16(9)*). Where the agency worker is an employee the usual protection against detriment in employment is provided along with provision for automatically unfair dismissal if the reason for the detriment or dismissal was the doing of any of a number of protected acts (see *reg 17*). The rights under the *Regulations* may be enforced in the employment tribunal subject to the normal time limits (*reg 18*) and just and equitable extension (*regs 18(4)* and *(5)*). Compensation is assessed on the just and equitable basis and is not subject to a statutory limit but excludes an injury to feelings award (*reg 18(15)* but an additional sum of up to £5000 may be awarded for seeking to avoid the rights under the *Regulations* accruing (*reg 18(14)* and *reg 9(4)*). An award may be made against the temporary work agency and/or the hirer. The issue of assessment of compensation under *Reg 18* was considered by the EAT in *Amissah v Trainpeople.Co.UK Ltd* [2017] IRLR 318 which provides useful guidance on the approach to compensation, particularly in a case of joint liability of the temporary work agency and the hirer. The Regulations make provision for consequential amendment to the relevant primary (principally *TULR(C)A* and *ERA*) and secondary legislation as set out in *Sch 2* to the *Regulations*.

The issue of assessment of compensation under *Reg 18* was considered by the Court of Appeal in *London Underground Ltd v Amissah* [2019] EWCA Civ 125, [2019] IRLR 545. The claim was for back payments against both the agency which had become insolvent and the client (London Underground). The Court of Appeal held that *Reg 5* created a statutory right to be paid an equal salary and thus was recoverable under the *Regulations* themselves. LUL and the agency were held equally liable for the breach under *Reg 14*. However, London Underground had put the agency in funds to make the payment but it had not done so. Pursuant to *reg 18(9)* on just and equitable appointment the employment tribunal concluded that it was not just and equitable for London Underground to pay its 50% as it had already put the agency in funds for that amount. The Court of Appeal concluded this was wrong. The claimants should be paid by a respondent to the extent a respondent was found liable under *reg 14* in that amount without further just and equitable reduction unless there was serious fault on the claimant's own part.

48.7   Statutory control of employment agencies

Persons who carry on employment agencies or employment businesses had formerly to be licensed by the Secretary of State. The licensing provisions have now been replaced by a system under which the Secretary of State may apply to an employment tribunal for an order prohibiting a person from carrying on, or being concerned with the carrying on, of any employment agency or employment business or any specified description of such agency or business. The Tribunal may make the order if it is satisfied that the person concerned is unsuitable, on account of misconduct or for other sufficient reason, to do what the order prohibits; there are detailed provisions concerning the application of this test to companies and partnerships. There is an appeal on a question of law to the Employment Appeal Tribunal.

The prohibition, which may be for a maximum period of 10 years, may be absolute or it may be on carrying on the business otherwise than in accordance with specified conditions. Non-compliance with a prohibition order without reasonable excuse is an offence punishable by a fine. The person to whom the order applies may apply to the tribunal to have it varied or revoked where there has been a material change in circumstances.

(*Employment Agencies Act 1973, ss 3–3D*, as inserted by *Deregulation and Contracting Out Act 1994, Sch 10 para 1*.)

It is a criminal offence to charge a person a fee for finding or seeking to find him employment, save in such cases as the Secretary of State prescribes (*Employment Agencies Act 1973, s 6*). The classes which have been prescribed relate to occupations in the entertainment industry, to modelling and to *au pairs*.

The *Employment Act 2008* introduced with effect from 6 April 2009 a strengthening of the enforcement regime. Certain offences under the Act are now triable on indictment as well as summarily (*s 15* of the *Employment Act 2008*). The offences affected are those of: (i) failure to comply with a prohibition order, (ii) contravention of any regulations made under the *1973 Act* and (iii) requesting or receiving a fee for providing work-finding services (except in those sectors such as entertaining and modelling where agencies are entitled to charge for these services under certain circumstances). As a result of the option of trial on indictment the Employment Agency Standards Inspectorate ('EAS') will be able to prosecute for 'attempting' to commit offences under the 1973 Act (eg attempting to obtain money for providing work-finding services). The EAS will be able to bring a prosecution for attempting to commit one of these offences on the basis of evidence obtained from the agency's records, without the need for agency workers to give evidence as witnesses.

If tried on indictment the penalty is a fine but may exceed that which may be imposed on summary conviction (see **1.10** INTRODUCTION for the Standards Scale of fines applicable to summary offences). In addition, significant amendments are made to *s 9* of the *Employment Agencies Act 1973* in relation to rights of inspection and disclosure of documents to officers by *s 16* of the *Employment Act 2008*. The EAS is now able to require a person carrying on an agency to provide financial records and documents and information at such time and place as the inspector may specify. In addition, banks may be required to provide financial information regarding agencies (where the agency has been asked to provide the information specified and has not done so). The inspectors are also given powers to remove documents from an agency in order to take copies. By *s 18* of the *Employment Act 2008* enforcement of the National Minimum Wage and employment agency standards is enabled by allowing officers appointed under the relevant legislation to share information with each other for the purpose of their respective enforcement functions. *Section 18* now allows minimum wage and employment agency officers to pass information about an employer's compliance to each other for the purposes of their enforcement functions.

In *First Point International Ltd v Department of Trade and Industry* (1999) 164 JP 89 the Court of Appeal, considered the scope of the unamended *s 6*. The section provides that a person 'shall not demand or directly or indirectly receive from any person a fee for finding him employment or seeking to find him employment'. The facts of *First Point International* were as follows. A person interested in work in Thailand contacted First Point International which sent him promotional materials and details of a 'personal client appraisal service' which required payment of almost £100 for an 'appraisal pack' containing appraisal questionnaires to be completed by the potential employee. The potential employee duly paid the fee, completing the questionnaires. First Point International then offered to identify suitable employment for him, for which service they would charge £3,150. The potential employee did not avail himself of this opportunity but First Point International was convicted of two offences under *s* 6. The £100 payment was found to be a fee for seeking to find employment; the £3,150 was found to be a 'demand' for payment for seeking to find employment. On appeal, the Court of Appeal upheld the convictions concluding that the fee for the appraisal documents was, as a matter of law, part of the 'seeking of employment'. As to the invitation to pay £3,150, the Court of Appeal concluded that *s* 6 was not limited to cases where there was an enforceable legal right to payment but extended to invitations to make payments.

The *Employment Relations Act 1999* clarifies the application of *s* 6 by providing that the prohibition on the charging of fees will extend to 'requests' for payment or the provision of information. The relevant amendments came into force on 25 October 1999.

The conduct of employment agencies was further regulated by the *Conduct of Employment Agencies and Employment Businesses Regulations 1976 (SI 1976/715)*. These *Regulations* have now been replaced with the *Conduct of Employment Agencies and Employment Businesses Regulations 2003 (SI 2003/3319)* with effect from 6 April 2004 (as amended) (see below **48.9**).

48.8 Statutory control of employment agencies: the 2003 reforms

As far back as 1999, the Government published a consultation paper, 'Regulation of the Private Recruitment Industries', proposing the replacement of, *inter alia*, the *Conduct of Employment Agencies and Employment Businesses Regulations 1976 (SI 1976/715)*. The key proposals in that document sought to clarify the legal rights and obligations of agencies, their workers and clients, to require checks to be made upon the relevant qualifications of workers and, in certain cases, to require references and to prevent workers engaging in hazardous work for which they were not qualified. Consultation of the proposed changes had a lengthy history continuing into 2002–2003. From 6 April 2004 the *Conduct of Employment Agencies and Employment Business Regulations 2003 (SI 2003/3319)* ('the *2003 Regulations*') have been in force.

The Department for Trade and Industry (now BIS) consulted on new measures to protect vulnerable agency workers in 2007. As a consequence of the responses to that consultation the Government made amendments to the *Regulations* by the *Conduct of Employment Agencies and Employment Businesses (Amendment) Regulations 2007 (SI 2007/3575)* ('the *2007 Regulations*') which came into force on 6 April 2008.

The Government engaged in further consultation which closed in June 2009 in relation to the *Regulations* with particular regard to vulnerable categories of agency workers in the entertainment and modelling field and the use of upfront fees and umbrella companies in the employment of temporary workers. New regulations, the *Conduct of Employment Agencies and Employment Business Regulations (Amendment) Regulations 2010 (SI 2010/1782)*, came into force on 1 October 2010. The *2010 Regulations* take effect by amendment to the *2003 Regulations*. The amendments increase the protection of performers seeking work through employment agencies and employment businesses by limiting when upfront fees can be charged and by extending cooling off periods. In addition the changes made by the amendments in the *2010 Regulations* purport to reduce the administrative burden placed on employment agencies and business expect in situations where the person seeking work will be working with or caring for vulnerable groups. The *2003 Regulations* were most recently amended by the *Conduct of Employment Agencies and Employment Businesses (Amendment) Regulations (SI 2016/510)* with effect from 8 May 2016 which in summary matters removes *Regulations 9, 11* and *17*, amends *Regulations 23* and *27A*, amends *Schedules 4* and *5* (on various record keeping obligations) and removes altogether *Schedule 6*.

The *2003 Regulations* (as amended by the *2010 Regulations* and the *2016 Regulations*) are considered below.

48.9   **The Conduct of Employment Agencies and Employment Businesses Regulations 2003 (SI 2003/3319) (as amended)**

The majority of provisions of the *2003 Regulations* came into force with effect from 6 April 2004 Transitional provisions dealt with engagements which were in place prior to the coming into force of the *2003 Regulations*. At the outset it is important to identify the precise terminology used by the *Regulations*. Under the *2003 Regulations* a person seeking work through an agency or employment business is a 'work-seeker'. The client to whom the services are supplied is the 'hirer' (*reg 2*). As to the agencies, the relevant definitions are found in the *Employment Agencies Act 1973* as follows. An 'employment agency' finds work-seekers employment with hirers or supplies hirers with work-seekers for employment (*s 13(2)*). An 'employment business' engages work seekers directly and supplies them on a temporary basis to the hirer (*s 13(3)*). Thus in ordinary usage headhunters are employment *agencies* and temping agencies are employment *businesses*.

Under the *2003 Regulations*, an employment agency or business (as the case may be) must on the first occasion of offering to provide or arrange the provision of a service to a work-seeker provide certain notice to the work seeker in relation to the service and fee calculations (*reg 13(1)*). However, it is important to note that *reg 13(1)* only applies where one or more services or goods referred to in *reg 13(1)(b)* for which the work-seeker will or may be charged a fee may be provided to the work-seeker. By *reg 13(1)(b)* (as amended by the *2007 Regulations* and the *2010 Regulations*) where an employment agency or business offers to provide or arrange additional charged for services they are required to provide (i) the amount or method of calculation of the fee (ii) the identity of the person to whom the fee is or will be payable (iii) a description of the services or goods to which the fee relates and a statement of the work-seeker's right to cancel or withdraw from the service and the notice period required and (iv) the circumstances, if any, in which refunds or rebates are payable to the work-seeker, the scale of such refunds or rebates, and if no refunds or rebates are payable, a statement to that effect.

By *reg 12* there are prohibitions on employment businesses withholding payment to work-seekers on certain grounds. By *reg 14* employment businesses are required to obtain agreement to terms with work-seekers, which terms must be recorded in documentary form. In relation to a work-seeker, terms must be agreed in advance of provision of services in one document or a number of documents given at the same time (*reg 14(2)*). The terms of engagement can only be varied with the work-seeker's consent and the variation must be agreed in writing (*reg 14(4), (5)*). When terms have been agreed, the employment business cannot threaten to withdraw its services in order to induce the work-seeker to accept a variation to the terms of business (*reg 14(6)*). It should be noted that the obligations under *reg 14* no longer apply to employment agencies after 1 October 2010. This was one of the amendments to ease administrative burdens introduced by the *2010 Regulations*.

Also in the case of employment businesses, the written terms must state whether the work-seeker is to be an employee of the business (*reg 15*). The terms must also specify the terms of employment, including notice periods, holidays and holiday pay and remuneration intervals. There must be an undertaking from the employment business to pay the agreed rate of pay (even if the hirer does not pay) and the level of remuneration must be specified (or at least the minimum rate expected to be obtained) (*reg 15*).

By *reg 16* employment agencies are required to obtain agreement from the work-seeker as to the terms which will apply, including details of services to be provided, the agency's authority to act for the work-seeker and details of fees. It should be noted that this provision only applies to any work-finding services for which the employment agency is permitted by *reg 26(1)* to charge a fee.

The *2003 Regulations* (as amended) contain detailed provisions in relation to the charging for the services of an employment agency or employment business. In general, employment agencies and businesses are prohibited from charging a fee to work-seekers for finding a job. Under the *Employment Agencies Act 1973* it is not unlawful to charge for certain services such as training or assistance with CV drafting and the like. By *reg 5* it is, however, unlawful to insist that a work-seeker avails themselves of such additional services as a condition for the provision of employment business services. Where the worker uses such services as are not unlawful under the *Act* by *reg 5(2)* (added by the *2007 Regulations*), the agency or business must ensure that the work-seeker is able to cancel or withdraw from those services at any time without incurring any detriment or penalty, subject to the work-seeker giving to the provider of those services in paper form or by electronic means notice of five business days or, for services relating to the provision of living accommodation, notice of ten business days. In the case of employment as an actor, background artist, dancer, extra, musician, singer or other performer or as a photographic or fashion model, where that work-seeker uses a service for which the *Act* does not prohibit the charging of a fee, then *reg 5(3)* provides for a 30 day cooling off period during which the agency or the employment business shall not charge a fee to a work-seeker for that part of the service which consists of providing photographs, audio or video recording of the work-seeker. Further, the work-seeker shall be entitled without detriment or penalty to cancel or withdraw from any contract with the agency or employment business for such a service with immediate effect by informing the agency or employment business of cancellation or withdrawal. Where the work-seeker informs the agency or employment business of cancellation or withdrawal the work-seeker has no obligation to make any payment under the contract.

Reg 6 restricts an employment business or agency from taking detrimental action relating to work-seekers working elsewhere and *reg 7* restricts employment businesses from providing work-seekers in cases of industrial disputes. *Reg 8* restricts agencies and employment businesses from purporting to act on a different basis (eg purporting to be an agency when in fact acting as a business). *Reg 10* restricts the charging of certain fees to hirers and *reg 11* limits the entering into of contracts on behalf of clients.

Limited exceptions to the general principles apply in relation to employment agencies who deal with actors, musicians, models, sportspersons and those engaged in the creative arts, film or theatrical businesses such as composers, writers, artists, directors, production managers and the like (see *Sch 3* to the *Regulations* as amended). Even in these categories, the practice of demanding payment of fees in advance of securing an engagement is, in the main, prohibited (see *regs 26(3), (5)* and *(6)* as amended) along with the practice of charging both the work-seeker and the hirer a fee. The *2007 Regulations* add a seven day 'cooling off period' in which work seekers may cancel or withdraw from any contract to include their details in a publication without detriment or penalty. Agencies thus cannot take a fee for including a work seeker in a publication until after seven days from the work seeker entering into a contract with the agency (*reg 26(5)(d)*).

The *2003 Regulations* permit charges to be made to hirers on a broader basis. One important area of limitation is, however, in relation to 'transfer fees' (ie where a hirer wishes to permanently engage a temporary worker supplied by an employment business or where the hirer wishes to re-engage the worker through a different employment business). In the light of concerns about such fees being an unhelpful restriction on the provision of labour, the *Regulations* limit transfer fees as follows: in cases of workers becoming permanent employees, transfer fees may only be charged if the hirer employs the worker within eight weeks of the end of the engagement or within 14 weeks of the start of the assignment. Further, the contract between the employment business and the hirer must provide the option for the hirer to extend the period of the original hire on no less favourable terms (*reg 10*).

Part IV of the *2003 Regulations* makes provision for requirements to be satisfied in relation to the introduction or supply of a work-seeker to a hirer (see *regs 18–22*). The *Regulations* impose minimum obligations on the employment agency or employment business to take steps to ensure that the work-seeker is suitable and also that the hirer is suitable (see *reg 20*). In relation to the work-seeker the employment business or agency must obtain confirmation of identity and willingness to perform the role (*regs 19, 21(1)(a)(i)*). Where an employment business receives information relevant to the suitability of a worker supplied it must inform the hirer or terminate the engagement (*reg 20(2), (3), (4)*). Similar provisions apply in relation to an employment agency (*reg 20(5), (6)*). Further obligations arise in relation to checking professional qualifications (*reg 22*) and in relation to suitability for working with vulnerable persons (*reg 22*). Information about the post, health and safety risks, qualifications required and rates payable and other terms of engagement must be obtained by the agency or employment business from the hirer (*reg 18*) and the employment business or agency should ensure that the hirer has carried out an adequate risk assessment for health and safety purposes. In relation to assignments of five consecutive days or less the administrative burden in relation to provision of information is reduced (*regs 21(4)* and *(5)*). Written notifications must still however be provided to the hirer in relation to the name of the work-seeker and confirmation of identity and experience and to the work-seeker in relation to the identity of the hirer, the nature of the business and the duration or likely duration of the work.

Further, an employment business or agency must not withhold pay due to a work-seeker in a number of circumstances (including that the hirer has not paid the employment business) (see *reg 12*) and must not disclose information relating to the work-seeker without prior consent, save for the purposes of providing the job finding services or for legal proceedings or to professional bodies relevant to the work-seeker (*reg 28*). An employment agency or business may not subject a work-seeker to any detriment on the ground that the work-seeker has terminated the contract or given notice to terminate the contract and cannot require a work-seeker to provide information as to the identity of future employers (*reg 6*).

As to work-seekers who provide their services via limited companies, the provisions of the *Regulations* were, by *reg 32(1)*, extended to this category of work-seeker with effect from 6 July 2004. The work-seeker is the limited company providing the individual's services and the individual is termed the 'person supplied by the work-seeker to carry out the work'. In this category the worker with a service company may opt out of the application of the *Regulations*. Any such opt out must be signed by the individual and the company before any assignment starts (*reg 32(9)*). By an amendment made by the *2007 Regulations* the agency or employment business must inform the hirer that such an opt-out agreement exists so that the *Regulations* do not apply. The opt-out option does not apply to engagements which involve working with vulnerable groups such as children and the elderly (*reg 32(12)*).

Breach of the *Regulations* (or breach of the *Employment Agencies Act 1973*) resulting in damage is actionable in the civil courts (*reg 30(1)*) and an employment agency or employment business which breaches the *Regulations* may be liable to prosecution and a fine (*Employment Agencies Act 1973, s 5(2)*). By *reg 31(1), (2)* contractual terms in agreements with work-seekers or hirers which are prohibited by the *Regulations* are unenforceable and transfer fees which are in breach of the *Regulations* are liable to be repaid.

48.10 The application of the National Minimum Wage

The *National Minimum Wage Act 1998*, applies to all workers (as defined in *s 54(3)*). By *s 34* of the *National Minimum Wage Act 1998*, agency workers shall have the right to the National Minimum Wage in relation to whichever of the parties (agent or principal) is responsible for the employer college on a succession of fixed-term contracts since March 2005. He claimed that the terms of his employment were less favourable than those of a comparator employed on a permanent basis. The EAT held that an employment tribunal must first determine if the claimant and comparator were engaged in the same or broadly similar work. If so, it must then consider whether the less favourable treatment was on the ground that the claimant was a fixed term employee. Only if the second question is answered affirmatively is there a need to consider objective justification. In *Cocliff* the tribunal erred in considering the question of whether the less favourable treatment was justified before it had considered the reason for the treatment. Further the tribunal erred in rejecting justification based on differences in the jobs. The finding that the work was broadly similar does not preclude justification based upon such differences as do exist. The question is whether they are sufficient to justify the different treatment.

In relation to the opportunity to secure permanent positions, the fixed term employee has the right to be informed of available vacancies in the establishment by the employer *(reg 3(6), (7))*. An employer is not obliged in every case to positively look for alternative employment but the way in which an employer treats a fixed term employee can, in appropriate factual circumstances, give rise to a situation of unfair dismissal *(Royal Surrey County NHS Foundation Trust v Drzymala* UKEAT/0063/17 [2018] All ER (D) 65 (Jan). The protection against less favourable treatment applies only if the treatment in issue is on the grounds that the employee is a fixed term employee and the treatment is not justified on objective grounds *(reg 3(3))*. Thus, for example, if an employer pays a fixed term employee at a lower rate than comparable permanent employees by reason of the fixed term status, this may (but not must) be less favourable treatment which the employer may have to objectively justify. On the application of the *Fixed-Term Work Directive 99/70/EC* and, hence, the *Regulations* (as a matter of purposive construction) to issues of inequality of pay see the ECJ's decision in *Del Cerro Alonso v Osakidetza-Servicio Vasco de Salud*: C-307/05 [2007] 3 CMLR 1492, [2008] ICR 145, [2007] IRLR 911. In *Impact v Minister for Agriculture and Food*: C-268/06 [2008] IRLR 552 (ECJ) the principles in *Del Cerro* are developed, holding that *cl 4* of the Directive must be interpreted to cover not only pay but also pensions and thus exclusion from such rights will require objective justification. The ECJ in *Impact* (and in *Zentralbetriebsrat der Landeskrankenhäuser Tirols v Land Tirol*: C-486/08 [2010] IRLR 631) also held that *cl 4* was precise enough to be directly effective at national level but *cl 5* (on successive contracts) was not directly effective but nevertheless provided a guide to interpretation. Also, the ECJ held that employment adjudicating bodies (ie the employment tribunals in the UK) must have jurisdiction to hear directly arguments based on the Directive. See also *Gavieiro v Conselleria de Educacion e Ordinacion Universitaria del la Xunta de Galicia*: C-444/09 [2011] IRLR 504 (ECJ) in which an argument that the inevitably temporary nature of fixed term employment could itself objectively justify unequal treatment was (unsurprisingly) rejected but which also upheld the direct effect of *art 4* of the Framework Agreement on fixed term work so that it could be relied upon during a period of failure to implement the Directive.

Similarly, if, say, the employer limits certain facilities to permanent staff such as health care or other benefits, this may (but not must) be less favourable treatment of the fixed term employee which may require objective justification if it is to be permissible. It is not every difference in treatment, however, that will amount to less favourable treatment. *Regulation 3(5)* is an important provision which provides that, in order to determine whether a fixed term employee has been treated less favourably than a comparator, the 'pro rata' principle shall be applied unless it is inappropriate. The pro rata principle is defined in *reg 1* as follows:

"where a comparable permanent employee receives or is entitled to pay or any other benefit, a fixed term employee is to receive or be entitled to such proportion of that pay or other benefit as is reasonable in the circumstances having regard to the length of his contract of employment and to the terms on which the pay or other benefit is offered."

The less favourable treatment in issue under *reg 3* must, however, be the act of the employer (or his agent). Less favourable treatment of a fixed term worker by a third party (eg an insurer in relation to the provision of less favourable health care insurance in comparison to permanent employees) will not render the employer liable unless the relationship of principal and agent is established (*Hall v Xerox UK Ltd* UKEAT/0061/14).

Regulation 4 provides an important gloss on objective justification providing that, in the event of less favourable treatment of a fixed term employee as regards any term in his contract, that treatment is to be regarded as objectively justified if the terms of the fixed term employee's contract 'taken as a whole' are at least as favourable as the comparator's contract of employment. Thus it is appropriate to look at the whole employment package afforded to the fixed term employee and not to concentrate on any single term when considering objective justification of contractual differences.

By *reg 5* a fixed term employee has the right to request in writing a statement from the employer setting out the reasons for any treatment in issue. That statement is to be provided within 21 days of the request (*reg 5(1)*). The statement is admissible in evidence before an employment tribunal (*reg 5(2)*) and failure to provide a statement without reasonable excuse or provision of an evasive or equivocal statement permits the tribunal to draw such inferences as appear just and equitable including an inference that the right in question has been infringed (*reg 5(3)*).

By *reg 6* a fixed term employee who is dismissed by reason of (i) bringing proceedings or (ii) giving evidence in relation to proceedings under the *Regulations*, or (iii) requesting a statement of reasons or (iv) alleging that the employer had contravened the *Regulations* or (v) doing anything under the *Regulations* or (vi) refusing forego a right conferred by the *Regulations*, is to be regarded as having been unfairly dismissed for the purposes of *Part 10* of the *ERA*. (See *reg 6(3)*). If the fixed term employee is dismissed in contravention of *reg 6*, then no qualifying period of service applies for the purposes of the *ERA*: see *ERA s 108(3)(j)*. By *reg 6(2)* a fixed term worker has the right not to be subjected to any detriment for like reasons to those applying to dismissal (see *reg 6(3)*).

The right to present complaints to the employment tribunal is set out in *reg 7* and the normal three month time limit subject to just and equitable extension applies (*reg 7(2), (3)*). Time runs from the act of less favourable treatment but can also apply when the act in question is the last in a series of similar acts or failures. In *Ibarz v University of Sheffield* (UKEAT/0018/15) the series concept was found to be capable, in an appropriate case, of applying where a claimant had worked on a series of separate contracts for a period of years with gaps between the contracts. If, as a matter of fact, the less favourable treatment satisfied the test of a "series of acts similar to each other" then a claim of less favourable treatment over the whole period of the successive contracts could be advanced. By *reg 7(6)* it is for the employer to identify the ground for the less favourable treatment or detriment. If an employment tribunal finds a complaint well founded it may provide a declaration as to the claimant's right and may award compensation assessed on the just and equitable basis including compensation for any loss suffered by the claimant (*reg 7(8), (9)*). Infringement of *reg 3* (Less favourable treatment) shall not, however, include an injury to feelings award (*reg 7(10)*). The employment tribunal also has power to make recommendations for the purpose of obviating or reducing the adverse effect on the complainant (*reg 7(7)(c)*). Failure without reasonable justification to comply with such recommendations may lead to an increase in the award of compensation (*reg 7(13)*).

An important right arises under *reg 8* to deal with the situation of persons employed on a succession of purported fixed-term contracts or a lengthy fixed term contract which is renewed. *Regulation 8* provides that, where a fixed term employee has been continuously

49   Termination of Employment

49.1   A contract of employment may be terminated in several ways: by mutual agreement; by frustration; by expiry; by dismissal by the employer; by notice given by the employee; or by acceptance of a fundamental repudiatory breach of contract by the employer or the employee. The distinction between these different modes of termination may be of importance in determining whether the employee may bring a claim for UNFAIR DISMISSAL – I (54), WRONGFUL DISMISSAL (59) or REDUNDANCY – I (39).

The death of either party terminates the contract of employment, unless the contract expressly or impliedly provides otherwise. The bankruptcy of the employer does not operate as a dissolution of the contracts of employment between himself and his employees, but in general the winding-up of a company and the dissolution of a partnership do operate to terminate the contract (see, eg *Briggs v Oates* [1990] ICR 473, [1990] IRLR 472, [1991] 1 All ER 407, holding that the expiration of the partnership represented a breach of the employee's contract, but suggesting that mere departures from, and additions to, a body of partners would not have such an effect). This is subject to the effect of the *Transfer of Undertakings (Protection of Employment) Regulations 2006 (SI 2006/246)* (see TRANSFER OF UNDERTAKINGS (53)).

It may be held in a particular case that, where an employee starts to work for his old employer in a new capacity, then the old contract has come to an end and has been replaced by a new one. Whether or not this is so is a question of degree (*Hogg v Dover College* [1990] ICR 39; *Alcan Extrusions v Yates* [1996] IRLR 327; and, more recently, *Smith v Trafford Housing Trust* [2013] IRLR 86 where the demotion of an employee, and a reduction in his salary, as a disciplinary sanction for posting a comment about gay marriage on his Facebook wall was held to be a (wrongful) termination of the earlier contract).

49.2   MUTUAL AGREEMENT

Termination by agreement between employer and employee may be effected either orally or in writing. The agreement to terminate may take effect on any day in the month or year, and does not have to coincide with a pay-day.

The courts will scrutinise an apparent agreement to terminate if the employee alleges that he was given no choice but to consent to the ending of his employment. The general principle which the courts will apply is that if the cause of the employee's willingness to agree to the termination of his employment is the threat of dismissal, he will be held to have been dismissed. If, however, other additional factors, such as financial inducements, affected his decision he will be taken to have resigned by mutual agreement. He will then not be entitled to bring any claim for unfair or wrongful dismissal.

In *Sheffield v Oxford Controls Co Ltd* [1979] ICR 396, [1979] IRLR 133, the employee was told that if he did not resign he would be dismissed. He signed an agreement to resign in return for certain financial benefits. The Employment Appeal Tribunal found that he had resigned and had not been dismissed because his resignation had been brought about not by the threat of dismissal but by other factors such as the offer of financial benefits. See also *Birch v University of Liverpool* [1985] ICR 470, [1985] IRLR 165, *Scott v Coalite Fuels and Chemicals Ltd* [1988] ICR 355, [1988] IRLR 131, *Hellyer Bros Ltd v Atkinson and Dickinson* [1992] IRLR 540 and *Optare Group Ltd v Transport and General Workers' Union* [2007] IRLR 931.

The authorities were reviewed in *Sandhu v Jan de Rijk Transport Ltd* [2007] ICR 1137, [2007] IRLR 519. On the facts of that case, the Court of Appeal held that the employee had not resigned even though he had entered into a severance agreement. The employee had thereafter agree that the contract continues to subsist: see *G F Sharp & Co Ltd v McMillan* [1998] IRLR 632. In that case, a joiner lost the use of his left hand and could never work for his employer in that capacity again. Although the parties agreed to keep the employee 'on the books' so that he could gain access to greater pension benefits, the EAT held that this did not amount to a continuation of the contract of employment. The contract had been nullified by the employee's injury. As a consequence, the employee was not entitled to notice of termination of his employment or payment in lieu.

49.4 EXPIRY

If a contract is for a fixed period, it will automatically terminate at the end of that period. No notice need be given. It should be noted that, for the purposes of a claim for redundancy pay or in respect of unfair dismissal, the expiry of a fixed-term contract may nevertheless constitute a dismissal (see **39.7** REDUNDANCY – I and **54.4–54.6** UNFAIR DISMISSAL – I). If an employee remains in his employment after the expiry of the term, he will be considered to be working under the same terms and conditions as before, save only that his employment is subject to an implied term that it can be terminated by either party upon giving reasonable notice (see **49.6** below).

49.5 DISMISSAL BY THE EMPLOYER

'Dismissal' is here used in its popular sense, to mean termination of a contract of employment by the employer. For the purposes of the unfair dismissal and redundancy payments legislation, the concept of dismissal is given a special statutory meaning which includes both the expiry of a fixed-term contract without its renewal and 'constructive dismissal' (see **39.7** REDUNDANCY – I and **54.4** UNFAIR DISMISSAL – I).

Sometimes there may be a dispute as to whether the words used by the employer (or the employee in the case of a resignation) in fact amount to a dismissal. Where those words are ambiguous, the court or tribunal should ask how they would have been understood by a reasonable listener in the circumstances (*Sothern v Franks Charlesly & Co* [1981] IRLR 278).

A party who has used unambiguous words cannot normally be heard to say that he did not mean what he appeared to mean. There are 'special circumstances', however, in which the words used will not be treated as definitive. In those circumstances, the person purportedly giving notice should be given an opportunity to satisfy the recipient that he did not intend to bring the employment relationship to an end (*Willoughby v CF Capital Ltd* [2011] IRLR 985). See, for instance, *Barclay v City of Glasgow District Council* [1983] IRLR 313, where a mentally handicapped employee purported to resign and the EAT held that there are circumstances where words are spoken under emotional stress, which the other party ought to know are not meant to be taken seriously. Similarly, where words are spoken in the heat of the moment: see *Sovereign House Security Services Ltd v Savage* [1989] IRLR 115. See also *Kwik-Fit (GB) Ltd v Lineham* [1992] ICR 183, [1992] IRLR 156.

Termination of employment can be communicated by conduct as well as by words. Whether a termination has been communicated is to be judged by how the words or conduct would be understood by the objective observer. There can be no dismissal unless the reasonable observer would understand that the contract of employment had been unequivocally terminated. The mere fact that an employee was notified that his particular role was coming to an end did not mean that the objective observer would infer that the contract of employment was being terminated: see *East London NHS Foundation Trust v O'Connor* (2019) UKEAT/0113/19, [2020] IRLR 16.

Dismissal may be either *summary* or with *notice*. At common law, either party to the contract of employment is always free to terminate the relationship by giving the proper notice provided that the contract is one which, whether expressly or impliedly, is terminable upon giving notice. Thus, if such notice is given, there can be no claim for Wrongful Dismissal **(59)**. To be effective in law, the notice must expire on a certain specified day (*Morton Sundour Fabrics Ltd v Shaw* (1966) 2 ITR 84), or upon the occurrence of a specified event (*Burton Group Ltd v Smith* [1977] IRLR 351). There is no dismissal on notice where an employer informs an absent employee that if he does not return to work by a particular date he will be treated as having terminated his employment, even if the employee does not turn up on that date and the employer treats the employment as having been terminated (*Rai v Somerfield Stores Ltd* [2004] ICR 656, [2004] IRLR 124).

For the date at which termination takes effect, see **54.13** Unfair Dismissal – I. Where notice of termination is sent by post, unless the contract makes express provision for some other test, the notice period begins to run when the letter comes to the attention of the employee and he has either read it or had a reasonable opportunity of doing so (*Newcastle upon Tyne Hospitals NHS Foundation Trust v Haywood* [2018] UKSC 22, [2018] ICR 882, [2018] 4 All ER 467. The parties may by agreement either advance or postpone the date of termination (*Mowlem Northern Ltd v Watson* [1990] ICR 751, [1990] IRLR 500; and see also *Palfrey v Transco plc* [2004] IRLR 916).

The contract of employment may provide for summary termination in certain circumstances. Summary dismissal in other circumstances is *prima facie* a breach of contract, unless the employee is in fundamental breach of the contract (see **49.13** below). Whether the dismissal is or is not fair is an entirely separate question. A dismissal may be fair even though proper notice is not given, and a dismissal on notice may nonetheless be unfair (see *Treganowan v Robert Knee & Co Ltd* [1975] ICR 405, [1975] IRLR 247; *BSC Sports and Social Club v Morgan* [1987] IRLR 391; and Unfair Dismissal – II **(55)**).

Where an employer is expressly permitted to terminate the contract of employment by making a payment in lieu of notice, there is an implied obligation on the employer to notify the employee in clear and unambiguous terms that such payment has been made and that it is made in the exercise of the contractual right to terminate the employment with immediate effect (*Société Générale v Geys* [2013] ICR 117, [2013] IRLR 122).

Where an employer exercises the power to terminate the contract of employment by making a payment in lieu, a debt will accrue, and it will not be open to the employer to resile from making the necessary payment on discovering conduct which would otherwise have justified a wrongful dismissal. There has been no wrongful dismissal, but a termination in accordance with the contract's own terms: see *Cavenagh v William Evans Ltd* [2012] ICR 1231, [2012] IRLR 679. The principle set out in *Boston Deep Sea Fishing and Ice Co v Ansell* 39 Ch D 339 did not go as far as to say that after-discovered misconduct provided an employer with a defence to an action for payment of an accrued debt. Where an employer gives notice of termination, however, no debt for the notice monies accrues and, if the employer dismisses the employee summarily during the notice period, the principle in *Boston Deep Sea Fishing* can be relied upon by the employer to resist a claim for damages: see *Williams v Leeds United Football Club* [2015] IRLR 383.

A 'dismissal' by the employer can result from the termination of one contract and its replacement by another: see *Hogg v Dover College* [1990] ICR 39; and *Smith v Trafford Housing Trust* [2013] IRLR 86 (see **49.1**).

49.6   Termination on notice – the contractual notice period

The contract of employment will usually specify the period of notice to be given to terminate the contract; indeed, the written particulars given to the employee must include the length of notice which the employee is obliged to give or entitled to receive (see **8.7** Contract of Employment).

If the contract is not for a fixed term and the notice period has not been expressly agreed, there is an implied term that it may be terminated upon reasonable notice (see *Reda v Flag Ltd* [2002] UKPC 38, [2002] IRLR 747). The court will determine what amounts to reasonable notice. Factors taken into account include the seniority and remuneration of the employee, his age, his length of service and what is usual in the particular trade. As a very rough guide, a period of two weeks or one month might be appropriate in the case of a manual worker, three months in the case of senior skilled workers or middle management, and between three months and one year in the case of more senior managers. However, the period of notice must be determined on the particular facts of each case. (For a discussion of the factors, see *Clark v Fahrenheit 451 (Communications) Ltd* (EAT 591/99) (1999) IDS Brief 666, p 11, [2000] All ER (D) 849.)

49.7 Termination on notice – statutory minimum notice

Whatever may be the contractual provisions – whether express or implied – for termination of the contract, the notice actually given must not be less than the statutory minimum period of notice. The contractual notice must be given if that is longer. The statutory rules are as follows:

(a) an employee who has been continuously employed for one month or more but less than two years is entitled to not less than one week's notice;

(b) an employee who has been continuously employed for two years or more but less than 12 years is entitled to one week's notice for each year of continuous employment;

(c) any employee who has been employed for 12 years or more is entitled to not less than 12 weeks' notice.

  (ERA 1996, s 86(1).)

This results in the following:

Table of statutory minimum notice

Period of continuous employment (years)	Minimum period (weeks)
Less than 2 (but 1 month or more)	1
At least 2 but less than 3	2
At least 3 but less than 4	3
At least 4 but less than 5	4
At least 5 but less than 6	5
At least 6 but less than 7	6
At least 7 but less than 8	7
At least 8 but less than 9	8
At least 9 but less than 10	9
At least 10 but less than 11	10
At least 11 but less than 12	11
12 or more	12

For example, if a clerk has been employed for 12 years under a contract which does not specify the period of notice to which he is entitled, a term of reasonable notice would be implied which in his case may well be one month. However, his length of service entitled him to 12 weeks' notice and that is the minimum notice he must be given.

An employee cannot contract out of his right to the statutory minimum period of notice (*ERA 1996, s 203*). However, he may waive his right to notice on a particular occasion, or accept a payment in lieu of notice (*ERA 1996, s 86(3)*; *Trotter v Forth Ports Authority* [1991] IRLR 419).

49.8   Exceptions

Certain seamen do not have the right to be given the statutory minimum period of notice: (*ERA 1996, s 199*).

49.9   Pay in lieu of notice

An employer who intends to dismiss an employee may consider it desirable that the employee should cease work immediately and not work out his notice period. For example, some employers consider it unwise to let a sales representative, who knows that he is to be dismissed, have any further contact with the employer's customers, for fear of endangering their goodwill. If an employee is dismissed without notice or with short notice it is usual to give him pay in lieu of notice. It would be possible, although unusual, to give an employee notice to expire halfway through the contractual or statutory notice period and to make a payment in lieu of notice in respect of the remainder of the period. Another possibility is to continue to pay the employee as usual, but to ask him to remain at home. This will not normally represent a breach of contract by the employer (but see **8.13** CONTRACT OF EMPLOYMENT). Even if he makes a payment in lieu of notice, an employer will nevertheless in theory be guilty of a breach of contract (unless the contract provides for this possibility – as, for example, in *Cavenagh v William Evans Ltd* [2012] ICR 1231, [2012] IRLR 679). However, the employee will not normally have a right of action in damages unless, through the premature determination of his contract, he has been deprived of valuable statutory rights. (See observations in *Robert Cort & Son Ltd v Charman* [1981] ICR 816, [1981] IRLR 437; *Delaney v Staples* [1992] IRLR 191, [1992] 1 All ER 944; and *Abrahams v Performing Rights Society* [1995] IRLR 486, CA.) However, in certain circumstances, the employee may be able to obtain an injunction to restrain a termination before the expiry of the contractual notice period. Such relief may be obtained where, by the employer's breach, the employee will suffer loss for which he cannot be compensated in damages, as where during the notice period the employee would have been able to exercise a share option in respect of which a claim in damages has been excluded.

The practice of giving pay in lieu of notice is virtually universal, but it does not fit easily into the traditional legal framework. Two connected problem areas are:

(a)   whether pay in lieu of notice is taxable (see **49.10** below);

(b)   if tax-free, whether it should be paid gross or net (see **49.11** below).

49.10

Taxation of pay in lieu of notice. The contract of employment may expressly empower the employer to dismiss the employee summarily on making a payment in lieu of notice. If the contract does set out such a right then the payment in lieu constitutes an 'emolument' of the employment, and tax should be deducted under PAYE in the usual way (see *EMI Group Electronics Ltd v Coldicott (Inspector of Taxes)* [1999] IRLR 630). The employee is not entitled to the benefit of the £30,000 exemption referred to below. It is probable that any appropriate National Insurance contributions should be paid as well.

Normally, there is no express contractual term relating to the making of payments in lieu of notice, but the employer may have an almost invariable custom of giving pay in lieu of notice. The House of Lords has held that such a payment is a payment of compensation for the employer's breach of contract in not giving due notice (*Delaney v Staples* [1992] ICR 483, [1992] IRLR 191, [1992] 1 All ER 944). Accordingly, the payment escapes the general Schedule E charge. It follows that neither the frequency with which such payments are made nor any expectation on the part of the employee would affect this. Since a non-contractual payment in lieu of notice falls to be regarded as compensation, it will be tax-free under the general rules. It may nevertheless be taxable under the special rules on compensation payments for loss of office (eg 'golden handshakes'), but only if the *total* amount paid to the employee, including any redundancy payment and any other termination payments, exceeds £30,000 (*Income Tax (Earnings and Pensions) Act 2003, ss 401, 403*). A non-contractual payment in lieu of notice is not subject to National Insurance contributions.

Where the employer and employee genuinely negotiate an agreement to terminate the employment contract, and no question of breach of contract by the employer arises, then any lump sum payable as part of the agreement will be treated as an 'emolument' from employment and will be taxable under Schedule E. The £30,000 exemption will not apply: see *Richardson (HM Inspector of Taxes) v Delaney* [2001] IRLR 663.

49.11 *Payment gross or net?* Most employers who make a payment in lieu of notice which is tax-free, pay over to the employee his full gross wages or salary. Legally, however, if pay in lieu of notice is to be regarded as compensation for breach of contract (see above), it would follow that the employer is only liable to pay the net amount that the employee would have received after deduction of tax and National Insurance. This is because the measure of damages for breach of contract is calculated on the basis of *the amount lost* by the employee in not being allowed to work his notice. However, there is nothing to prevent an employer from paying the gross amount and there may be sound reasons for doing so, eg to maintain good industrial relations or public relations. It is also conceivable, although unlikely, that an employer who had a consistent practice of making payments gross might be held liable to pay the gross amount to an employee on the ground that the consistent practice had given rise to an implied contractual term (see, eg *Gothard v Mirror Group Newspapers Ltd* [1988] ICR 729, [1988] IRLR 396). (To avoid the tax charge it would be necessary to establish that this term related only to the manner of calculating pay in lieu and not to the employer's liability to make the payment.) Pay in lieu of notice does not amount to wages for the purposes of the provisions relating to protection of wages (*ERA 1996, ss 13–27*) (see **35.6** PAY – I).

49.12 Employee's rights during period of notice

Where an employee has been continuously employed for one month or more (see CONTINUOUS EMPLOYMENT (7)), and his employment is terminated either by the employer giving notice, or by notice given by himself, the employee is given certain rights during the statutory minimum notice period, ie the period shown in **49.7** above where the employer gives notice, and one week where the employee gives notice (*ERA 1996, s 87(1), (2)*). This does not apply, however, where notice is given by the employer and the contractual notice period exceeds the statutory minimum by at least one week (*ERA 1996, s 87(4)*), as illustrated in the case of *Budd v Scotts Co (UK) Ltd* [2004] ICR 299, [2003] IRLR 145, EAT.

The rights in question are set out in *ERA 1996, ss 87–91*. Although it will not be possible to rely upon them directly if the statutory minimum notice is not given by the employer, they are to be taken into account in assessing damages in a WRONGFUL DISMISSAL (59) action (*ERA 1996, s 91(5)*).

The principal right conferred is to be paid in cases where the employee is ready and willing to work, but no work is provided for him by his employer, or where the employee is incapable of work because of sickness or injury, or where the employee is absent from work wholly or partly because of pregnancy or childbirth, or is absent in accordance with the terms of his employment relating to holidays. Where there are normal working hours, the amount payable is arrived at by taking the number of hours covered by the above situations and applying to them the hourly rate of remuneration produced by dividing a week's pay by the number of normal working hours (*ERA 1996, s 88*). Where there are no normal working hours, the employer must pay a week's pay in each week of the notice period, provided that the employee is ready and willing to do work of a reasonable nature and amount to earn a week's pay (*ERA 1996, s 89*). In each case, any payments in fact made (including holiday pay and sick pay) go towards meeting the employer's liability.

Accordingly, an employee who has been dismissed on account of prolonged sickness absence is entitled to receive full salary during his notice period if his sickness continues during that period. This is the case even if the employee had by the time of his dismissal exhausted his rights to sick pay, and would have received no payment from his employer if his contract had not been terminated.

The employer is not liable to make payments in respect of a period during which the employee is on leave at his own request (*ERA 1996, s 91(1)*), nor where the employee has given notice and thereafter takes part in a strike (*ERA 1996, s 91(2)*).

Where the employer breaks the contract during the notice period, payments made under *ERA 1996, ss 87–91* go to mitigate the damage suffered (*ERA 1996, s 91(3)*). Where the employer terminates the contract during the notice period and is entitled to do so because of the employee's breach of contract (see **49.13** below), there is no liability under *ERA 1996, s 88 or s 89* in respect of the subsequent part of the full notice period (*ERA 1996, s 91(4)*).

49.13   Summary dismissal

If the employee acts in a way which is incompatible with the faithful discharge of his duty to his employer he may be dismissed instantly, without notice or wages in lieu of notice. Examples of misconduct which can in certain circumstances give rise to the right to dismiss summarily are wilful disobedience of a lawful order from the employer, theft of the employer's property, and drunkenness such as to impair the performance of his duties. The misconduct must be gross or grave, seen in the light of all the circumstances of the case. In general, employees should be given a clear indication of the type of conduct which the employer regards as warranting summary dismissal (*ACAS Code of Practice 1, para 23*).

Summary dismissal for misconduct which is not gross is a breach of contract rendering the employer liable in damages for WRONGFUL DISMISSAL **(59)**.

For a discussion of the exact moment when a dismissal without notice takes effect, see *Octavius Atkinson & Sons Ltd v Morris* [1989] ICR 431, [1989] IRLR 158.

49.14   Written statement of reasons for dismissal

An employee is entitled to be provided by his employer, on request, within 14 days of that request, with a written statement giving particulars of the reasons for his dismissal if:

(a)   he is given by his employer notice of termination of his contract of employment; or

(b)   his contract of employment is terminated by his employer without notice; or

(c)   where he is employed under a contract for a fixed term, that term expires without being renewed under the same contract.

(*ERA 1996, s 92(1)*.)

The reasons given by an employer are admissible in evidence in any proceedings. The employer's reply to a request may refer to full reasons given in an earlier written communication, a copy of which should be sent with the reply. Where a legal adviser is appointed by the employee, as a duly authorised agent to receive the information, it is sufficient to communicate the information to the legal adviser (*Kent County Council v Gilham* [1985] ICR 227, [1985] IRLR 16).

An employee is not normally entitled to written reasons unless he has been continuously employed for a period of two years ending with the effective date of termination (*Unfair Dismissal and Reasons for Dismissal (Variation of Qualifying Period) Order 2012 (SI 2012/989)*) (an exception is made for employees whose continuous period of employment commenced before 6th April 2012: for these employees, only one year's continuous employment is required).

Special rules apply if an employee is dismissed at any time while she is pregnant, or after childbirth in circumstances in which her maternity leave period ends by reason of her dismissal (for the maternity leave period, see **33.38** Maternity and Parental Rights). She is entitled to a written statement of reasons for the dismissal, irrespective of the length of her employment, and without having to make any request (*ERA 1996, s 92(4)*).

49.15   Remedy for failure to give reasons

A complaint may be made by the employee to an employment tribunal on the grounds:

(a)   that his employer unreasonably failed to provide a written statement under *ERA 1996, s 92* of the reason for dismissal; or

(b)   that the particulars given in purported compliance with that section are inadequate or untrue.

(*ERA 1996, s 93(1)*.)

The obligation is, of course, to give the actual reason for dismissal; the question is not whether that reason is in fact well-founded.

In *Daynecourt Insurance Brokers Ltd v Iles* [1978] IRLR 335, the company failed to answer an employee's request for written reasons for his dismissal. Its justification for doing so was a general request by the police officer who investigated the alleged theft of company funds by the employee, that the company should not answer any correspondence or deal with any matter that related to the police investigations of the company's records. The EAT held that the employment tribunal's finding, that the company should not have simply ignored the employee's statutory request but should have sought further advice of the police officer, was not wrong in law. A failure to provide written reasons may be unreasonable even if the employee knows perfectly well why he has been dismissed, since one purpose of the provision is that the employee should be able to show the reasons to third parties (*McBrearty v Thomson*, IDS Brief 450, p 15).

Except in maternity cases (see **49.14** above), there cannot be a complaint to the tribunal that the reasons given are inadequate if there has been no request for proper reasons by the employee pursuant to *ERA 1996, s 92(1)* (*Catherine Haigh Harlequin Hair Design v Seed* [1990] IRLR 175).

In *Banks v Lavin*, IDS Brief 410, p 6, the EAT held that the statement 'many jobs not being done' was an inadequate reason, because it was not sufficiently specific.

The time limit for presentation of the complaint is three months from the effective date of termination of employment. This period can be extended if the employment tribunal is satisfied that it was not reasonably practicable to present it within the three-month period (*ERA 1996, s 93(3)*; and see **19.20** Employment Tribunals – I).

If the tribunal finds the complaint well-founded, it will make an award that the employer pay to the employee a sum equal to the amount of two weeks' pay. It may also make a declaration as to what it finds that the employer's reasons were for dismissing the employee (*ERA 1996, s 93(2)*). A week's pay is calculated in accordance with the provisions of *ERA 1996, ss 221–229*, formerly *EPCA 1978, Sch 14* and the calculation date is:

(i)   where the dismissal was with notice, the date on which the employer's notice was given; or

(ii)   in any other case, the effective date of termination.

(*ERA 1996, s 226(2)*.)

(See further REDUNDANCY – I (39).)

The amount of a week's pay is not subject to a statutory maximum for this purpose.

49.16 RESIGNATION BY THE EMPLOYEE

As in the case of dismissal by the employer, the employee may resign with or without notice. For the question of whether the words used will amount to a resignation, see **49.5** above. No particular terms of art are required for resignations (*Walmsley v C&R Ferguson Ltd* [1989] IRLR 112).

In *East Kent Hospitals University NHS Foundation Trust v Levy* (UKEAT/0232/17/LA) it was held that a statement by an employee that she is giving 'notice' might not be found to an unambiguous resignation from employment. The particular context and circumstances must be taken into account. Where a statement is ambiguous, the question for the Court will be how the statement would have been understood by a reasonable recipient, taking into account the particular circumstances known to the recipient at the time. Light may be shed on those circumstances by events afterwards but only if they are genuinely explanatory of what had happened and do not reflect a change of mind by the employee.

A failure to give due notice is *prima facie* a breach of contract, but may be justified where the employee resigns in response to a repudiatory breach of contract by the employer (see **49.18** below).

The more difficult question will usually be what, if any, are the damages payable by the employee. In *Giraud UK Ltd v Smith* [2000] IRLR 763, the Employment Appeal Tribunal struck down a clause in an employment contract which provided that 'failure to give the proper notice and work it out will result in a reduction from your final payment equivalent to the number of days short'. This was held to be an unlawful penalty clause rather than a lawful liquidated damages clause. There was evidence to suggest that the employer could easily find replacements for the employee in question (he worked as a driver), so that it was not a genuine pre-estimate of loss. Furthermore, the clause was oppressive, as there was no limitation on the right of the employers to recover damages for actual loss if this was greater than that specified in the clause. Therefore, the employee was in a position where if the actual loss turned out to be nil, he would be liable for the sum set out in the clause, but if the actual loss was greater than the sum set out in the clause, he could face an unlimited claim for the balance. The clause enabled the employer to say, 'Heads I win, tails you lose'.

49.17 Termination by the employee giving notice

The statutory minimum period of notice to be given by an employee, who has been continuously employed for one month or more, is one week (*ERA 1996, s 86(2)*). However, the contractual period of notice to be given will, in many cases, be longer. The contractual notice may be either expressly agreed upon or implied. If it is implied, the notice to be given is that which is a reasonable period in all the circumstances (see **49.6** above).

49.18 Summary termination by the employee

If an employer is in breach of a fundamental term of the contract of employment, the employee is entitled to leave the employment forthwith. Leaving the employment in these circumstances is known as 'constructive dismissal' for redundancy payments and unfair dismissal purposes, since although the employee takes the initiative in leaving his employment he will be considered to have been dismissed within the meaning of *ERA 1996, s 136(1)* (see **39.6** REDUNDANCY – I) and *ERA 1996, s 95(1)* (see **54.4** UNFAIR DISMISSAL – I). In such circumstances, the employee would also be able to claim damages for WRONGFUL DISMISSAL **(59)**.

49.19 REPUDIATORY CONDUCT

It has already been seen (see **49.13** and **49.18** above) that a repudiatory breach of contract by either the employer or the employee entitles the other party to terminate the relationship without giving notice or by giving short notice. A dismissal in such circumstances is not necessarily fair, nor a constructive dismissal following the employer's breach necessarily unfair, although they often will be.

The courts have sometimes gone further, and suggested that a repudiatory breach *automatically* brings a contract of employment to an end (see, eg *Marriott v Oxford and District Co-operative Society Ltd (No 2)* [1970] 1 QB 186, [1969] 3 All ER 1126). The 'automatic' theory has now been rejected by the Supreme Court in *Société Générale v Geys* [2013] ICR 117, [2013] IRLR 122. This means that (leaving aside questions of frustration and expiry at a specified time or upon the occurrence of a specified event) there is no such thing as an automatic termination because of one party's conduct. There must always be an acceptance of the breach constituting a dismissal by the employer or a resignation by the employee.

However, it is of the nature of the employment relationship that, where one party is unwilling to perform the contract, it will be very difficult for the other party to say that the relationship remains alive. An acceptance of the breach by the innocent party will readily be inferred from his conduct. See also *Marsh v National Autistic Society* [1993] ICR 453.

The Court of Appeal in *Weathersfield Ltd (t/a Van & Truck Rentals) v Sargent* [1999] IRLR 94 overruled the decision of the EAT in *Holland v Glendale Industries Ltd* [1998] ICR 493 that an employee must make plain to his employer the reason for leaving if he is to rely upon his employer's repudiatory conduct as justifying his resignation and subsequent claim of constructive dismissal. The court held that whether there has been an 'acceptance' of the employer's repudiatory conduct is for the employment tribunal (or court) to determine on the facts and evidence in each case. On the facts of that case (where an employee had been instructed to discriminate against black and Asian customers), the employee had been put in 'an outrageous and embarrassing position', and so did not want to confront her employers with the reason for leaving. She just left the job a few days after being issued with the instruction. This did not prevent her from claiming successfully that she had been constructively dismissed on the grounds of the instruction.

It is always a question of fact for the court or tribunal as to whether the employee resigned in consequence of the employer's repudiatory breach of contract. In *TSB Bank plc v Harris* [2000] IRLR 157, the Employment Appeal Tribunal upheld a finding of constructive dismissal where the employee was considering leaving her job in any case before the repudiatory breach of contract occurred (the breach arose out of the contents of a reference supplied to a prospective employer). See also *White v Bristol Rugby Ltd* [2002] IRLR 204. In *Ishaq v Royal Mail Group Ltd* [2017] IRLR 208, on the other hand, the Employment Appeal Tribunal held that there was no constructive dismissal where the 'true' or 'real' reason for a postal worker's resignation was not a repudiatory breach (failure to make adjustments for his disability and putting him on unsuitable postal routes), even though that breach was referred to in his letter of resignation. Rather, the EAT found that the postal worker had really resigned to avoid a disciplinary hearing that was due to take place the day after he wrote his resignation letter.

In *Da'Bell v NSPCC* [2010] IRLR 19, the Employment Appeal Tribunal observed that where a person reacts to offensive conduct by writing a letter the next day, this will easily lead to a finding that he resigned in response to that conduct. If he leaves the matter for a year, however, and digs it up again, his resignation at that point is less likely to be treated as directly related to the breach.

49.20 RETRACTION OF RESIGNATION OR DISMISSAL

The general rule is that words of resignation or dismissal, once communicated to the other party and accepted by him, cannot unilaterally be withdrawn (*Riordan v War Office* [1959] 3 All ER 552, *Willoughby v CF Capital plc* [2011] IRLR 985). However, the EAT has suggested that good industrial relations practice requires that an employer should be able to withdraw words of dismissal provided that he does so almost immediately (*Martin v Yeoman Aggregates Ltd* [1983] ICR 314, [1983] IRLR 49). If this view is correct, it should apply equally to a case of resignation by the employee.

In *Wallace v Ladbrokes Betting and Gaming Ltd* (UKEAT/0168/15/JOJ) [2015] All ER (D) 308 (Nov), the EAT discussed the so-called 'cooling off period' following a resignation made in the 'heat of the moment'. This was regarded as a period during which the employer might be satisfied that its understanding that there has been an unequivocal resignation is correct. It was not a period in which the employee was given the opportunity to unilaterally withdraw her resignation.

49.21 REMEDIES FOR WRONGFUL TERMINATION

An employee who has been dismissed, or who has resigned in circumstances amounting to a constructive dismissal, may complain of UNFAIR DISMISSAL – I (54) to an employment tribunal, whether or not proper notice was given to him. If proper notice was not given, or if he resigned summarily in response to the employer's repudiatory breach, he may bring a claim for WRONGFUL DISMISSAL (59) in the ordinary courts. Where the employee fails to give proper notice, the employer may also in principle sue for damages. Also, either party may in certain, limited circumstances be able to obtain an injunction restraining an unlawful termination. See further 8.23 CONTRACT OF EMPLOYMENT.

50   Time Off Work

Cross references. See CHILDREN AND YOUNG PERSONS (4.8), EDUCATION AND TRAINING (15), HOLIDAYS (30), MATERNITY AND PARENTAL RIGHTS (33), SICKNESS AND SICK PAY (45) and STRIKES AND INDUSTRIAL ACTION (46).

50.1   In addition to the rights to take time off work covered elsewhere in this book, there are several distinct rights in exercise of which an employee may take time off work in specific circumstances.

—   Trade union officials and members may take time off work for certain duties and activities (see **50.2–50.5** below).

—   Employees have the right to take time off work to perform certain public duties (see **50.4–50.5** below).

—   An employee under notice of redundancy may take time off to look for work, etc (see **50.6–50.7** below).

—   Safety representatives, and elected representatives, must be given time off to perform their duties (see **50.8–50.9** below).

—   Employees who are trustees of occupational pension schemes have a right to time off for performing their duties (see **50.10–50.11** below).

—   Employee representatives must be given time off to perform their functions (see **50.12–50.13** below).

—   Employees have the right to time off for European Works Council duties (see **50.14** below).

—   Employees have the right to time off to care for dependants (see **50.15–50.16** below).

—   Employees have the right to request flexible working to care for children (see **50.17** below).

This chapter also considers the obligation to reinstate members of the reserve forces in employment after military service (see **50.18** below). For the question of whether such time off (at least in the trade union and health and safety representative context) amounts to "working time" for the purposes of the *Working Time Regulations* see *Edwards v Encirc Ltd* [2015] IRLR 528 and **58.5** WORKING TIME

50.2   TRADE UNION OFFICIALS

An employer is obliged to permit an employee, who is an official of an independent trade union recognised by the employer, to take time off during working hours to:

(a)   carry out duties, as such an official, which are concerned with:

(i)   negotiations with the employer that are related to or connected with any matters that fall within *TULR(C)A 1992, s 178(2)* (see **40.4** REDUNDANCY – II) and in relation to which the trade union is recognised by the employer, or

(ii)   the performance, on behalf of employees of the employer, of any functions that are related to or connected with any matters falling within *TULR(C)A 1992, s 178(2)* that the employer has agreed may be so performed by the trade union, or

     (iii)   receipt of information from the employer and consultation with the employer under *TULR(C)A 1992, s 188* or under the *Transfer of Undertakings (Protection of Employment) Regulations 2006 (SI 2006/246)* (see **Redundancy – II (40)** and **Transfer of Undertakings (53)**);

     (iv)   negotiations with a view to entering into an agreement under *regulation 9* of the *Transfer of Undertakings (Protection of Employment) Regulations 2006 (SI 2006/246)* that applies to employees of the employer, or the performance on behalf of employees of the employer of functions related to or connected with the making of an agreement under that regulation.

(b)   undergo training in aspects of industrial relations which is:

     (i)   relevant to the carrying out of any such duties as are mentioned in (*a*); and

     (ii)   approved by the Trades Union Congress or by the independent trade union of which he is an official.

(TULR(C)A 1992, s 168(1), (2).)

The Court of Appeal in *British Bakeries (Northern) Ltd v Adlington* [1989] ICR 438, [1989] IRLR 218 held that it was a question of fact, dependent on the particular circumstances of the case, whether a preparatory meeting was sufficiently proximate to carrying out duties concerned with (at that time) industrial relations to come within the statutory predecessor of *TULR(C)A 1992, s 168*. Although the section has been amended since *Adlington*, it is thought that the decision is equally applicable to whether attendance at a meeting is sufficiently proximate to carrying out the duties now specified in *s 168*. See also *London Ambulance Service v Charlton* [1992] ICR 773, [1992] IRLR 510.

It is to be noted that the right accrues only to officials of independent trade unions recognised by the employer (see **51.19 Trade Unions – I**). There is no right to time off if, for example, the purpose is to attend a demonstration in support of a dispute with another employer or to carry out internal union duties. Nor would *s 168* extend to, say, taking part in a course on pension schemes if the employer does not consult or bargain with the union about pensions and has not agreed to it performing any pension-related functions on behalf of his employees.

In *Ashley v Ministry of Defence* [1984] ICR 298, [1984] IRLR 57, the EAT held that unless it can be shown that the recognised union expressly or impliedly required the attendance of its official at a meeting, the attendance of the official at such a meeting cannot constitute the carrying out by the official of a duty within the meaning of *s 168*. The EAT further held that attendance at an advisory meeting could be a duty within the meaning of *s 168*; whether it is, is a question of fact.

The amount of time a trade union official is permitted to take off in the exercise of his statutory right, the purposes for which, the occasions on which, and any conditions subject to which, time off may be so taken are those that are reasonable in all the circumstances, having regard to any relevant provisions in the ACAS Code of Practice (*TULR(C)A 1992, s 168(3)*).

In considering whether the request for time off is reasonable in all the circumstances, tribunals will take into account such matters as the nature, extent and purpose of time off already being taken by that employee (*Wignall v British Gas Corpn* [1984] ICR 716, [1984] IRLR 493; *Borders Regional Council v Maule* [1993] IRLR 199). *Section 168(3)* assumes that a request for time off has been made and that such request has come to the notice of the employer. It is only if these two conditions are satisfied that the employee can have a remedy for an employer's failure to permit him to take time off (see *Ryford Ltd v Drinkwater* [1996] IRLR 16 and **50.5** below).

In deciding whether the right to time off is being exercised reasonably within the meaning of *s 168(3)*, the EAT in *Depledge v Pye Telecommunications Ltd* [1981] ICR 82, [1980] IRLR 390, considered that where comprehensive arrangements existed for the discussion of industrial relations matters it would be reasonable for trade union officials to use them.

An employee who is a member of an independent trade union recognised by the employer and who is a learning representative of the trade union is entitled to time off under *s 168A, TULR(C)A 1992*. An employee who is a learning representative is entitled to time off in order to undertake, in relation to qualifying members of the trade union, the analysis of learning and training needs, the provision of information and advice on learning and training matters, the promotion of the values of learning and training, the consultation of the employer on learning and training activities, and preparation for the learning representative's activities. The right to time off arises only where the trade union has provided the employer with written notice that the employee is a learning representative and that (a) he has undergone sufficient training for his learning representative activities within the last six months and the trade union has given the employer notice in writing of this fact; (b) the trade union has given the employer notice in the last six months that the employee will be undergoing such training; or (c) within six months of such notice, the employee has undergone the training and the trade union has given the employer notice of that fact. The employer is also required to permit the employee time off for training that is relevant to his functions as a learning representative. The employer's obligation to permit time off is subject to a reasonableness test.

The trade union official who is entitled to take time off work to perform his duties under *section 168* or *168A, TULR(C)A 1992* is entitled to be paid for the period of his absence. Where his pay does not vary with the amount of work done, he is paid as if he had worked during the period of absence. Where his pay does vary according to the amount of work done, the amount he is to be paid during his absence is calculated by reference to the average hourly earnings for that work. The average hourly earnings are those of the employee concerned unless they cannot fairly be estimated, in which case the tribunal will take the average earnings of persons in comparable employment with the same employer or (if there are no such persons) a reasonable figure (*TULR(C)A 1992, s 169*).

The employee is entitled to paid time off only at a time when he would otherwise be working, and not to paid time off in lieu if the trade union duties are performed at a time when he would not otherwise be working (*Hairsine v Kingston upon Hull City Council* [1992] ICR 212, [1992] IRLR 211 and *Diamond v Park Lane College* UKEAT/0249/05/LA). However, a part time worker is entitled to receive pay for the actual hours attended on a training course, rather than just for the part time hours that they normally worked; a failure to pay for the actual hours worked would be unjustifiable indirect sex discrimination: *Davies v Neath Port Talbot County Borough Council* [1999] ICR 1132, [1999] IRLR 769, EAT.

If an employer is obliged under a contract of employment to pay an employee for time off taken to perform trade union duties, then those payments will go to discharge any statutory liability he may have to make such payments, and vice versa (*TULR(C)A 1992, s 169(4)*).

Trade union officials are statutorily entitled to a reasonable amount of paid time off to accompany a worker at a disciplinary or grievance hearing, provided that they are certified by the union as being capable of acting as the worker's companion (*ERA 1999, s 10(6)*). This right applies whether or not the union is recognised by the employer, but the worker must be employed by the same employer as the union official.

See also the ACAS Code of Practice 3: Time off for trade union duties and activities which lays down guidelines. The Code is to be taken into account in determining what is reasonable and the current version came into force on 1 January 2010.

It should be noted that since October 2012, civil servants who are trade union representatives have been obliged to spend at least 50% of their working hours delivering their civil service role, with any exemptions requiring specific agreement. According to a Cabinet

Office report published on 29 September 2014, as a result of this the number of full-time union representatives in government departments has gone down from 200 in November 2011 to less than 10, and resulted in approximately £6m of savings per year.

50.3   TRADE UNION ACTIVITIES

An employer is obliged to permit an employee of his, who is a member of an independent trade union recognised by him, to take part in certain trade union activities during working hours. The activities are defined as:

(a)   any activities of the trade union of which the employee is a member; and

(b)   any activities in relation to which the employee is acting as a representative of such union;

(*TULR(C)A 1992, s 170(1)*). This excludes activities which themselves consist of industrial action whether or not in contemplation or furtherance of a trade dispute (*TULR(C)A 1992, s 170(2)*).

The right in *TULR(C)A 1992, s 170(1)* does not include a right to time off for the purpose of acting as, or having access to services provided by, a learning representative of a trade union (*TULR(C)A 1992, s 170(2A)*). However, where the trade union learning representative in question is carrying out activities for which he is entitled to time off under *TULR(C)A 1992, s 68A*, the employer is obliged to permit an employee to take time off in his working hours to access those services (*TULR(C)A 1992, s 170(2B)–(2C)*).

In *Luce v Bexley London Borough Council* [1990] ICR 591, [1990] IRLR 422, the EAT held that whether trade union activity fell within the definition was a matter of fact and degree, but that it must in a broad sense be linked to the employment relationship; the tribunal had been entitled to hold that teachers were not entitled to time off to lobby Parliament against the *Education Reform Bill*. See also **55.3**(a) Unfair Dismissal – II.

The amount of time that may be taken, and the purposes for which and the occasions on which it may be taken, are those that are reasonable in all the circumstances; the same test applies to the imposition of conditions by the employer (*TULR(C)A 1992, s 170(3)*). The employee is not entitled to be paid for time he takes off to participate in trade union activities unless he is a trade union official and the time is taken in accordance with **50.2** above.

Worth noting in this regard is the decision of the European Court of Human Rights in *Güler v Turkey* [2018] IRLR 880 where a civil servant received a formal warning for being absent without leave on 1 May when he had attended a demonstration organised by his trade union to celebrate Labour Day. The Court found that 1 May was a highly symbolic day for trade-union members, that the employer must have been well aware of the reason for the applicant's absence, and that the disciplinary sanction, although very light, was such as to dissuade trade union members from participation in trade union activities. As such it held that there had been a breach of the employee's right to freedom of assembly under *article 11*.

50.4   PUBLIC DUTIES

An employer is obliged to permit an employee of his who is:

(a)   a justice of the peace;

(b)   a member of a local authority (within the meaning of the *Local Government Act 1972*), the Common Council of the City of London, a National Park Authority or the Broads Authority;

(c)   a member of any statutory tribunal;

(d)   a member of an independent monitoring board for a prison;

(e)   a member of the NHS Commissioning Board, a clinical commissioning group, an NHS Trust, an NHS foundation trust, the National Institute for Health and Care Excellence, the Health and Social Care Information Centre, a Local Health Board, or a Special Health Authority;

(f)   a member of the managing or governing body of an educational establishment maintained by a local authority, a further education corporation, sixth form college corporation or higher education corporation, or the General Teaching Council for England or Wales;

(g)   a member of the Environment Agency;

(h)   a member of a panel of lay observers appointed in accordance with section 81(1)(b) of the Criminal Justice Act 1991, a Visiting Committee appointed in accordance with section 152(1) of the Immigration and Asylum Act 1999, or a Visiting Committee appointed by the Secretary of State for a short-term holding facility;

(i)   a member of various similar bodies in Scotland.

to take time off work during the employee's contractual working hours for certain specified purposes (*ERA 1996, s 50*). There is no right to be paid for this time off work.

The right does not extend to specified classes of employees (*ERA 1996, ss 191–195, 199* and *200*). Clergy of the Church of England also have a right to time off work for public duties by virtue of the *Ecclesiastical Offices (Terms of Service) Regulations 2009 (SI 2009/2108)*.

In deciding when and how much time is to be taken off, regard will be paid to:

(i)   how much time off is required for the performance of the duties of the office, or as a member of the body in question, and how much time off is required for the performance of the particular duty;

(ii)   how much time off has already been permitted for the performance of any relevant public duty, union duty or activity;

(iii)   the circumstances of the employer's business and the effect of the employee's absence on the running of that business;

and these considerations will be applied in deciding what is reasonable in the circumstances (*ERA 1996, s 50(4)*). (See *Borders Regional Council v Maule* [1993] IRLR 199 and *Riley-Williams v Argos Ltd* EAT/811/02, (2003) 147 SJLB 695.)

Local authorities may not allow their employees more than 208 hours' paid time off in any financial year for the purpose of performing duties as councillors (other than council chairmen) (*Local Government and Housing Act 1989, s 10*).

Although there is no statutory provision entitling an employee to time off for jury service, prevention of a person from attending as a juror is a contempt of court and employees are protected from being subjected to a detriment or dismissal as a result of jury service (*ERA 1996, ss 43M, 98B*).

50.5   EMPLOYEE'S REMEDIES IN RESPECT OF TIME OFF FOR TRADE UNION AND PUBLIC DUTIES

An employee may present a complaint to an employment tribunal that (*a*) he has not been allowed time off to carry out public duties or trade union duties or activities, or (*b*) in the case of a trade union official's duties that he has not been paid for time he has been permitted to take off (*ERA 1996, s 51(1); TULR(C)A 1992, ss 168(4), 168A(9), 169(5), 170(4)*). An employee can only bring a complaint under *TULR(C)A 1992, s 168(4)* that an employer has failed to permit him to take time off, in circumstances where a request for time off has been made by the employee and that request has come to the notice of the employer (see *Ryford Ltd v Drinkwater* [1996] IRLR 16).

If it finds such a complaint well-founded, the tribunal will make a declaration to that effect and may order the employer to pay the employee compensation for the default and for any loss caused thereby (*ERA 1996, s 51(3); TULR(C)A 1992, s 172(1), (2)*). In the case of a union official who has not been paid for time taken off, the tribunal will order the employer to make the appropriate payment (*TULR(C)A 1992, s 172(3);* see **50.2** above). In *Skiggs v South West Trains Ltd* [2005] IRLR 459 a union official was prevented by his employer from attending meetings in the capacity of union representative pending the outcome of a grievance investigation into his behaviour. The EAT held that although he had suffered no financial loss nor injury to feelings, he was entitled to recover compensation to reflect the fact that a wrong was done to him, because *TULR(C)A 1992, s 172(2)* makes reference to both the employer's default and any loss sustained by the employee.

An employment tribunal does not have the power to impose conditions upon the parties as to the way in which the time off shall be taken or to specify the amount of time off which should be allowed (*Corner v Buckinghamshire County Council* [1978] IRLR 320).

The time limit for presenting such complaints is three months from the date of the failure complained of, but pre-action conciliation (see **ACAS CONCILIATION (3)**) is compulsory and time spent on this does not count towards this period (*ERA 1996, s 51(2)–(2A); TULR(C)A 1992, s 171(1)–(2)*). If the tribunal is satisfied that it was not reasonably practicable for the complaint to be presented within the time limit (see **19.2 EMPLOYMENT TRIBUNALS – I**), then it may be extended (*ERA 1996, s 51(2); TULR(C)A 1992, s 171(2)*). Time may also be extended for claims under *ERA 1996* where there is mediation in certain cross-border disputes (*ERA 1996, s 51(2A)*).

In *Gayle v Sandwell and West Birmingham Hospitals NHS Trust* [2011] EWCA Civ 924, [2011] IRLR 810, [2012] ICR D3, the statutory rights to unpaid time off for trade union activities were not relied upon but the employer had a recognition agreement whereby it would permit accredited representatives such time off for trade union activities as was reasonable and subject to the needs of the service. The employee attended a trade union meeting without complying to a management instruction to resolve the issue of time off under the recognition agreement and was disciplined. The Court of Appeal upheld the tribunal's finding that this was on the basis of her failure to comply with the management request and not her trade union activities therefore there was no breach of *TULR(C)A 1992, s 146*.

50.6   TIME OFF TO LOOK FOR WORK OR MAKE ARRANGEMENTS FOR TRAINING

An employee who has been given notice of dismissal by reason of redundancy must be allowed reasonable time off by his employer, during his working hours before the end of his notice period, to look for new employment or to make arrangements for training for future employment (*ERA 1996, s 52(1)*). In order to qualify for this right, the employee must have been continuously employed for a period of at least two years, by the date on which (*a*) the notice is due to expire, or (*b*) the date on which it would expire had the statutory minimum period of notice been given, whichever is the longer (*ERA 1996, s 52(2)*). (See CONTINUOUS EMPLOYMENT (7).) For an employee's general rights relating to education and training, see EDUCATION AND TRAINING (15).)

An employee who is so allowed time off is entitled to be paid for the time taken off at the appropriate hourly rate, which is calculated by the amount of one week's pay divided by the number of normal working hours in a week or, where the number of those hours varies, by taking the average of the 12 weeks ending with the last complete week before the notice was given (*ERA 1996, s 53(1)–(3)*). The maximum amount payable cannot exceed 40% of a week's pay (*ERA 1996, s 53(5)*). The right to be paid is dependent upon the right to take time off. Thus, if an employee with less than two years' continuous service is given time off to seek other employment, there is no statutory obligation on the employer to pay him for time so taken.

An employee who is under notice of redundancy is entitled to time off to look for work irrespective of whether he has an appointment to attend a specific interview (*Dutton v Hawker Siddeley Aviation Ltd* [1978] ICR 1057, [1978] IRLR 390).

50.7 Remedy

If an employer has unreasonably refused the employee time off or has failed to pay him, the employee may present a complaint to an employment tribunal (*ERA 1996, s 54(1)*). The time limit for the presentation of such a complaint is three months beginning with the day on which it is alleged that time off should have been allowed, but pre-action conciliation is compulsory (see **50.17**) and time spent on this does not count towards this period (*ERA 1996, s 54(2)–(2A)*). If the tribunal is satisfied that it was not reasonably practicable for the complaint to be presented within the time limit (see **19.21** EMPLOYMENT TRIBUNALS – I), then it may be extended (*ERA 1996, s 54(2)*). Time may also be extended where there is mediation in certain cross-border disputes (*ERA 1996, s 54(2A)*).

The employer may be made liable to pay (i) remuneration for the period of absence or (ii) remuneration for the period during which he should have allowed time off, or both. The maximum amount, where both these provisions are applicable together, cannot exceed 40% of a week's pay (*ERA 1996, s 54(4)*).

If an employer unreasonably refuses to allow an employee time off work when statutorily obliged to do so, the employee is entitled to be paid the remuneration to which he would have been entitled if he had been allowed time off, in addition to his normal pay (*ERA 1996, s 53(4)–(6)*).

Any contractual remuneration paid to an employee for a period of time which he takes off to seek or train for new employment when he is under notice of dismissal for redundancy goes towards discharging the employer's statutory liability, and vice versa (*ERA 1996, s 53(7)*).

50.8 SAFETY REPRESENTATIVES AND ELECTED REPRESENTATIVES

The *Safety Representatives and Safety Committees Regulations 1977 (SI 1977/500)*, as amended, impose a duty upon employers to allow safety representatives time off with pay for the performance of their duties as safety representatives, and to undergo training in health and safety matters. Such persons are only entitled to be paid for time given off: in *Howlett v Royal Mail Group Ltd* (UKEAT/0368/13/DA) an engineer who had 60% release from a shift pattern that permitted (but did not require) one Sunday per month paid at overtime rates but then became a full-time safety representative working from Monday to Friday was only entitled to be paid as he would have been for working as an engineer from Monday to Friday. In relation to the right to time off for training, the 1978 Code of Practice approved by the Health and Safety Commission on time off for the training of safety representatives remains in force. The two questions are (1) whether the proposed training was reasonable in all the circumstances, and (2) whether it was necessary for the employee to take paid time off work: *Duthie v Bath and North East Somerset Council* [2003] ICR 1405, [2003] All ER (D) 358 (Apr) and *Walker v North Tees and Hartlepool NHS Trust* UKEAT/0563/07/RN [2008] All ER (D) 55 (Oct). Also see *Coats v Strathclyde Fire Board* UKEATS/0022/09/BI [2009] All ER (D) 106 (Aug), where an employee failed to establish

being elected, be such a member or representative, is entitled to take reasonable time off during working hours in order to perform the functions of member, representative or candidate (the *European Public Limited-Liability Company (Employee Involvement) (Great Britain) Regulations 2009 (SI 2009/2401), reg 26*). Where an employee takes time off in this way, he is entitled to be paid remuneration at the appropriate hourly rate (*reg 27*).

The *Occupational and Personal Pension Schemes (Consultation by Employers and Miscellaneous Amendment) Regulations 2006 (SI 2006/349)* provide that an employee who is a representative falling within *reg 12(2)(a)* or *(3)* or *13(2)*, and is consulted under the *Regulations* about a listed change by a relevant employer is entitled to be permitted by his employer to take reasonable time off during the employee's contractual working hours in order to perform his functions as such a representative (*para 2, Sch*). He is entitled to be paid for such time off at the appropriate hourly rate (*para 3, Sch*).

The *European Cooperative Society (Involvement of Employees) Regulations 2006 (SI 2006/2059)* give under *reg 28* a right to reasonable time off to an employee who is a member of a special negotiating body or representative body, an information and consultation representative, an employee member of a supervisory or administrative organ, an election candidate or meeting participant under *reg 17(2)(h)* or *para 11(2)(h)* of *Sch 1* or *para 7(4)* of *Sch 2*. *Regulation 29* entitles the employee to payment at the appropriate hourly rate and *reg 30* gives the employee the right to present an employment tribunal claim where time off or payment are denied.

The *Companies (Cross-Border Mergers) Regulations 2007 (SI 2007/2974)* give an employee who is a member of a special negotiating body, a director of a transferee company, or a candidate in an election for a director or member, a right to take reasonable time off during working hours in order to perform his functions as such a member, director or candidate (*reg 43*). The right to remuneration at the appropriate hourly rate is provided by *reg 44*. The right to present a claim to an employment tribunal where time off or payment are denied is provided by *reg 45*.

Note that some of the above rights only apply where there is a minimum number of employees.

50.13 Remedy

All of the above regulations enable an employee to complain to an employment tribunal that his employer has denied him the rights conferred thereunder. In all cases the claim must be presented within three months of the day on which time off was taken, or which it is alleged time off should have been allowed but pre-action conciliation (see **ACAS** CONCILIATION (3)) is compulsory and time spent on this does not count towards this period. The tribunal may extend time if it was not reasonably practicable to present the claim within this period. Where the complaint is that time off has unreasonably been denied, the tribunal may order payment at the appropriate rate for the period which should have been allowed.

50.14 TIME OFF FOR EUROPEAN WORKS COUNCIL DUTIES

An employee who is a member of a European Works Council, a member of a special negotiating body, an information and consultation representative, or a candidate for election to be such a representative, is entitled to paid time off in order to carry out his or her duties (*Transnational Information and Consultation of Employees Regulations 1999, regs 25* and *26 (SI 1999/3323)*). An employee who is a member of a special negotiating board or a European Works Council has the right to take reasonable time off during working hours to undertake training (*regs 19B* and *25*). An employee who is unreasonably refused such time off, or denied payment in accordance with the formula contained in *reg 26*, may bring a complaint to an employment tribunal under *reg 27*. The claim must be presented within three months of the day on which time off was taken, or which it is alleged time off should have been allowed but pre-action conciliation (see **ACAS** CONCILIATION **(3)**) is compulsory and time spent on this does not count towards this period (*regs 27* and *27A*). The tribunal may extend time if it was not reasonably practicable to present the claim within this period (*reg 27*). Where the complaint is that time off has unreasonably been denied, the tribunal may order payment at the appropriate rate for the period which should have been allowed (*reg 27*).

50.15 TIME OFF FOR DEPENDANTS

Under *ERA 1996, s 57A* employees are entitled to be permitted by their employer to take a reasonable amount of time off during working hours in order to take action which is necessary:

(a)   to provide assistance when a dependant falls ill, gives birth, is injured or assaulted;

(b)   to make arrangements for the provision of care for a dependant who is ill or injured;

(c)   in consequence of the death of a dependant;

(d)   because of the unexpected disruption or termination of arrangements for the care of a dependant; or

(e)   to deal with an incident which involves the employee's child which occurs unexpectedly in a period during which an educational establishment which the child attends is responsible for him.

(*ERA 1996, s 57A(1)*.) There is no right to be paid for this time off work. Any disruption caused to the employer is irrelevant in determining whether the employee's circumstances trigger the right: *Qua v John Ford Morrison Solicitors* [2003] ICR 482, [2003] IRLR 184.

An employee must inform his employer as soon as reasonably practicable of the reason for his absence, and, where he is able to inform his employer in advance of his absence, how long he expects to be absent (*ERA 1996, s 57A(2)*). In *Ellis v Ratcliff Palfinger Ltd* (UKEAT/0438/13/BA) [2014] All ER (D) 78 (Oct) the employee whose wife was taken into hospital to give birth on Tuesday but did not inform his employer of his absence or the reason until Wednesday evening was held not to have done so as soon as reasonably practicable.

'Dependant' is defined as a spouse or civil partner, child or parent of the employee, or a person who lives in the same household as the employee (excluding live-in employees, tenants, lodgers and boarders). In addition, for the purposes of (*a*), (*b*) and (*d*) above, a dependant includes any person who reasonably relies on the employee to assist him if ill or injured, or who reasonably relies on the employee to make arrangements to provide care for him (*ERA 1996, s 57A(3), (4)* and *(5)*). Illness and injury are defined to include mental illness and injury (*ERA 1996, s 57A(6)*).

In a case concerning a childminder's unavailability, of which the employee had 16 days' notice during which period she had tried and failed to make alternative childcare arrangements, the EAT considered whether, given the length of time, she had been entitled to take a day off and provide childcare herself (*Harrison v Royal Bank of Scotland plc* [2009] IRLR 28). The EAT held that the relevant question was whether the action taken by the employee was necessary because of the unexpected disruption or termination in the care of her dependant. The length of notice of the disruption was significant, because it enabled the employee to explore alternative arrangements, however, there were no hard and fast rules.

A period of a month or more for a parent to care for a child would almost never fall within *ERA 1996, s 57A*: *Cortest Ltd v O'Toole* UKEAT/0470/07/LA [2008] All ER (D) 220 (May).

Sick leave taken because of a bereavement reaction does not qualify as time off in consequence of the death of a dependant (*Forster v Cartwright Black* [2004] ICR 1728, [2004] IRLR 781).

50.16 Remedy

An employee who has unreasonably been refused permission to take time off in accordance with his right under *s 57A* may complain to an employment tribunal (*ERA 1996, s 57B(1)*). The time limit for such complaints is three months beginning with the date the refusal occurred, but pre-action conciliation is compulsory (see ACAS CONCILIATION (3)) and time spent on this does not count towards this period (*ERA 1996, s 57B(2)–(2A)*). The tribunal has a discretion to extend time where it was not reasonably practicable for the employee to present his claim in the three-month period (*ERA 1996, s 57B(2)*). Time may be extended where there is mediation in certain cross-border disputes (*ERA 1996, s 57B(2A)*). If a tribunal finds the complaint well-founded, it may make a declaration to that effect, and may award such compensation as it considers just and equitable, having regard to the employer's default in refusing to permit time off to be taken by the employee, and any loss sustained by the employee (*ERA 1996, s 57B(3)* and *(4)*).

50.17 TIME OFF TO CARE FOR CHILDREN

Maternity, paternity, adoption leave and leave for ante-natal care are covered in detail in MATERNITY AND PARENTAL RIGHTS (33).

FLEXIBLE WORKING

An employee who has been continuously employed for 26 weeks has the right to apply in writing to his or her employer to request a change in hours, times or location of work (*Employment Rights Act 1996, ss 80F–80I; Flexible Working Regulations 2014 (SI 2014/1398)*). Only one such statutory request can be made in any 12 month period (*ERA 1996, s 80F(4)*). The employer must deal with the application in a reasonable manner, notify the employee of the decision within 3 months (or such longer period as may be agreed) and may refuse such an application only on grounds of the burden of additional costs, detrimental effect on the ability to meet customer demand, inability to re-organise work among existing staff, inability to recruit additional staff, detrimental impact on quality, detrimental impact on performance, insufficiency of work during the periods during which the employee proposes to work, or planned structural changes (*ERA 1996, s 80G(1)*). An employer can notify the employee that the application is treated as withdrawn if the employee fails to attend meetings arranged to discuss the application (*ERA 1996, s 80G(1D)*). Guidance on the obligation to handle such requests in a reasonable manner is contained in "Code of Practice 5 – Handling in a reasonable manner requests to work flexibly", published by ACAS in June 2014.

An employee is protected against detriment (*ERA 1996, s 47E*) and dismissal (*ERA 1996, s 104C*) on the ground that he or she made (or proposed to make) an application under *section 80F* or brought proceedings under *section 80H* or alleged the existence of any circumstance which would constitute a ground for bringing such proceedings.

An employee may complain to an employment tribunal that an employer has failed to deal with his or her flexible working application as required by *section 80G* or has rejected the application on the basis of incorrect facts or has wrongly treated the application as having been withdrawn (*ERA 1996, s 80H*). It is not for the employment tribunal to judge the reasonableness of an employer's refusal to provide flexible working (*Commotion Ltd v Rutty* [2006] ICR 290). The time limit for such a complaint is three months but pre-action conciliation is compulsory (see ACAS CONCILIATION (3)) and time spent on this does not count towards this period (*ERA 1996, s 80H(5)–(7)*). The tribunal has a discretion to extend time where it was not reasonably practicable for the employee to present his claim within this period (*ERA 1996, s 80H(5)*). Time may be extended where there is mediation in certain cross-border disputes (*ERA 1996, s 80H(7)*).

If the complaint is upheld the employment tribunal may order the employer to reconsider the application and may award compensation of up to eight weeks' pay (*ERA 1996, s 80I*). The employment tribunal does not have the power to order the employer to implement the employee's request for flexible working.

50.18   REINSTATEMENT AFTER MILITARY SERVICE

The *Reserve Forces (Safeguard of Employment) Act 1985* provides two basic types of employment protection for reservists in the armed forces: (1) protection (on pain not just of liability to pay compensation but also of criminal prosecution) against dismissal on account of the reservist's liability to be mobilised, and (2) a right to reinstatement when the reservist returns to his civilian job after a period of mobilisation.

50.19   So far as the right of reinstatement is concerned, the following is a short summary of the main provisions in the *1985 Act*.

Where a person has entered upon a period of whole-time service in the armed forces of the Crown, and has done so in pursuance of a notice or directions for the calling out of reserve or auxiliary forces, or for the recall of service pensioners, or in pursuance of an obligation or undertaking to serve as a commissioned officer, then he has certain rights to be reinstated in employment by his former employer.

The former employee must apply in writing to his former employer after the period of military service ends and not later than the third Monday after the end of that period, or as soon afterwards as reasonably possible (*s 3*). He must also notify the employer of a date, not later than 21 days after the latest date allowed for the application, when he will be available for employment (*s 4*).

The employer must then reinstate the former employee in his old occupation on terms no less favourable than would have applied but for the military service, or (if that is not reasonable and practicable – as to which, see *s 5*), in the most favourable occupation and on the most favourable terms and conditions which are reasonable and practicable in his case (*s 1(2)*). The person concerned must then be employed for at least 13, 26 or 52 weeks, depending on the length of his continuous employment prior to the military service, or for so much of that time as is reasonable and practicable (*s 7*; see *Slaven v Thermo Engineers Ltd* [1992] ICR 295).

Complaints that a person's statutory rights have been infringed may be made to a Reinstatement Committee, which may order employment to be made available to the applicant, and order the payment of compensation to him (*s 8*). There are rights of appeal in certain circumstances to an umpire sitting with assessors (*s 9*). Non-compliance with an order is a criminal offence (*s 10*). The procedure upon applications and appeals is governed by the *Reinstatement in Civil Employment (Procedure) Regulations 1944 (SI 1944/880)*.

It should also be noted that there is no qualifying period of employment for the purposes of a claim for unfair dismissal where the reason for the dismissal is, or is connected with, the employee's membership of a reserve force (*Employment Rights Act 1996, s 108(5)*).

51   Trade Unions – I: Nature and Liabilities

Cross-references. See also Strikes and Industrial Action (**46**); Time off Work (**50**) for time off for trade union duties or activities; Trade Unions – **II** (**52**) for individual rights and union membership; 55.3 Unfair Dismissal – **II** for dismissal for participation in union activities.

51.1   THE STATUS OF A TRADE UNION

The present law on the status and liability of trade unions is governed by the *Trade Union and Labour Relations (Consolidation) Act 1992* ('*TULR(C)A 1992*'). 'Trade union' is statutorily defined in *TULR(C)A 1992, s 1* as an organisation (whether permanent or temporary) which either:

(a)   consists wholly or mainly of workers of one or more descriptions and is an organisation whose principal purposes include the regulation of relations between workers of that description or those descriptions and employers or employers' associations; or

(b)   consists wholly or mainly of:

   (i)   constituent or affiliated organisations which fulfil the conditions specified in para (*a*) above (or themselves consist wholly or mainly of constituent or affiliated organisations which fulfil those conditions), or

   (ii)   representatives of such constituent or affiliated organisations;

   and in either case is an organisation whose principal purposes include the regulation of relations between workers and employers or between workers and employers' associations, or include the regulation of relations between its constituent or affiliated organisations.

In *British Association of Advisers and Lecturers in Physical Education v National Union of Teachers* [1986] IRLR 497, the Court of Appeal construed this definition broadly so as to include an association 'concerned with the professional interests of its members'. In *National Union of Professional Carers v Certification Office* [2019] IRLR 860 the EAT rejected an appeal by a union of foster carers against the refusal of the Certification Officer to list it as a trade union. The EAT held that "workers" must work under a contract of some description. Foster carers were not workers for this purpose, as they worked under non-contractual arrangements with local authorities. Nor did the refusal to list the union breach their rights under *ECHR, Art 11*, as it did not prevent it from entering into voluntary collective bargaining on behalf of its members.

Several of the larger trade unions are made up of a number of constituent sections. The definition in *TULR(C)A 1992, s 1* ensures that both the conglomerate organisation and its constituent parts are considered to be trade unions. The National Union of Mineworkers is made up of a number of areas such as the National Union of Mineworkers (South Wales area), all of which are, under *TULR(C)A 1992*, to be considered trade unions. Similarly, a branch of a trade union may be held to be a trade union (see *News Group Newspapers Ltd v Society of Graphical and Allied Trades '82 (No 2)* [1987] ICR 181, [1986] IRLR 337).

51.2   Legal capacity

Unless a trade union is a special registered body as defined by *TULR(C)A 1992, s 117* (such bodies are mostly incorporated professional associations), it is not, nor to be treated as if it were, a corporate entity (*TULR(C)A 1992, s 10*). However, *TULR(C)A 1992, s 10(1)* gives a trade union a statutory legal personality which it would otherwise lack so that it can:

(a)   make contracts;

(b)   sue or be sued in its own name (see **51.16** and **51.17** below for certain immunities enjoyed by trade unions); and

(c)   be a defendant in criminal proceedings.

All property belonging to a trade union must be vested in trustees in trust for the union (*TULR(C)A 1992, s 12(1)*).

51.3 CERTIFICATION OFFICER

The Secretary of State appoints a Certification Officer in consultation with ACAS under *TULR(C)A 1992, s 254*. He makes an annual report to the Secretary of State, who presents it to Parliament and publishes it (*TULR(C)A 1992, s 258*). His functions include:

(a)   dealing with complaints relating to the keeping of the register of a union's members (see **51.13** below);

(b)   dealing with complaints relating to trade union internal elections (see **51.14** below);

(c)   dealing with complaints relating to political fund ballots (see **51.15** below);

(d)   maintaining a list of trade unions (see **51.21** below);

(e)   certifying whether trade unions are independent (see **51.22** below);

(f)   certain supervisory functions in relation to trade union amalgamations (see **51.39** below); and

(g)   administering the scheme for financial contributions towards trade union ballots.

The Certification Officer may at any time, if he thinks there is good reason to do so, require a trade union (or any person who appears to be in possession of the documents) to produce specified documents which are accounting documents or which may be relevant in considering the union's financial affairs (*TULR(C)A 1992, s 37A*). He may also appoint inspectors to investigate and report upon a union's financial affairs if there are circumstances suggesting fraud, misconduct or a breach of statutory obligations or union rules in relation to those affairs, and all past and present officials and agents of the union and other persons appearing to be in possession of relevant information must then co-operate with the investigation, including by producing documents and attending before the inspectors (*TULR(C)A 1992, s 37B*). Reports made will be published by the Certification Officer, and there are various other administrative provisions, as well as criminal sanctions for contravention of statutory requirements (*TULR(C)A 1992, ss 37C–37E; TULR(C)A 1992, ss 45, 45A*).

The Certification Officer has jurisdiction to consider applications by members or former members of a trade union claiming that there has been a breach or threatened breach of the union's rules, pursuant to a new *TULR(C)A 1992, s 108A*. The Certification Officer may consider such a claim only if it relates to:

(a)   the appointment or election of a person to, or their removal from, any office;

(b)   disciplinary proceedings (including expulsion);

(c)   the balloting of members on any issue other than industrial action;

(d)   the constitution or proceedings of any executive committee or of any decision-making meeting; and

(e)   such other matters as the Secretary of State may specify.

With effect from 1 March 2017, the Certification Officer gained a range of new and additional powers in relation to investigations and enforcement by virtue of *ss 17–21* of the *Trade Union Act 2016* coming into force.

In *UNISON v Gallagher* (2005) IDS Brief 791 the Employment Appeal Tribunal found that the Certification Officer had exceeded his jurisdiction in holding that the appellant union had breached its disciplinary rules by excluding a member, who had previously been disciplined and debarred from holding office for five years, from is annual delegate conference. The exclusion followed a decision by the union that all those who had been expelled or debarred from holding office should no longer be allowed to attend the conference. Although the exclusion was consequent upon the previous disciplinary determination, it was held to be administrative in nature, and therefore fell outside the Certification Officer's jurisdiction.

The limited nature of the Certification Officer's jurisdiction was again emphasised in *Irving v GMB* [2008] IRLR 202. In that case, the EAT upheld the decision of the Certification Officer that he had no jurisdiction to consider the applicant's complaint about the way in which a complaint against him had been handled. This was because the matter was dealt with by way of grievance proceedings rather than disciplinary proceedings, and so fell outside the Certification Officer's jurisdiction.

The complaint must be made within six months of either the alleged breach or threatened breach, the conclusion of an internal complaints procedure relating to the breach or the expiry of one year from such a complaints procedure being invoked. *TULR(C)A 1992, s 108B* provides that the Certification Officer must accept an application only if satisfied that the applicant has taken all reasonable steps to resolve the claim through internal complaints procedures. If he accepts an application, he may make a declaration and an enforcement order requiring steps to be taken to remedy the breach. By *TULR(C)A 1992, s 108C* an appeal lies to the Employment Appeal Tribunal. Since 1 March 2017, such an appeal has no longer been confined to appeal on a point of law.

51.4   CENTRAL ARBITRATION COMMITTEE

The Central Arbitration Committee ('CAC') was established pursuant to the *Employment Protection Act 1975* and continues by virtue of *s 259* of the *Trade Union and Labour Relations (Consolidation) Act 1992* ('*TULR(C)A 1992*').

51.5   Constitution

The Secretary of State for Trade and Industry is responsible for appointing members of the CAC whom he selects from persons nominated by ACAS as being experienced in industrial relations and who include both employers' and workers' representatives. In addition, the Secretary of State appoints a chairman and may appoint one or more deputy chairmen after consultation with ACAS (*TULR(C)A 1992, s 260*).

51.6   Functions

These are:

(a)   Arbitration in trade disputes (see **51.7** below).

(b)   Resolution of complaints that an employer has failed to disclose information which he was required to disclose by *TULR(C)A 1992, s 181* (*TULR(C)A 1992, s 183*) (see **51.8** below).

(c) ⸱ Determination of questions previously referred to the Industrial Arbitration Board (*TULR(C)A 1992, Sch 3 para 7*). (The Board was the successor of the Industrial Court created by the *Industrial Courts Act 1919*, to which trade disputes of various kinds could be referred.)

(d) Union recognition disputes (see **51.11** below).

(e) Resolution of complaints that an employer has failed to comply with its duty to provide data requested under the *Information and Consultation of Employees Regulations 2004 (SI 2004/3426)* (see EMPLOYEE PARTICIPATION (**17**)).

51.7 Arbitration

The CAC may arbitrate on trade disputes at the request of one or more parties to the dispute, provided that all parties consent to the arbitration. The request for arbitration is made to ACAS in the first instance, which may refer the matter to the CAC (*TULR(C)A 1992, s 212(1)(b)*; and see **2.6** ADVISORY, CONCILIATION AND ARBITRATION SERVICE).

51.8 Complaint of failure to disclose information

The CAC may hear and determine complaints made by an independent trade union recognised for collective bargaining purposes that the employer by whom it is recognised has not disclosed information to which the union is statutorily entitled (see **11.3** DISCLOSURE OF INFORMATION) (*TULR(C)A 1992, ss 181, 183*). The CAC is only empowered to make a declaration if the union is recognised by the employer for the particular purpose to which the information relates (*R v Central Arbitration Committee, ex p BTP Tioxide Ltd* [1981] ICR 843, [1982] IRLR 60). The CAC will refer the complaint for conciliation by ACAS if it considers that it is reasonably likely to be settled in that way (*TULR(C)A 1992, s 183(2)*). Any person with a proper interest in the complaint is entitled to be heard by the CAC (*TULR(C)A 1992, s 183(4)*). If the CAC finds the complaint well-founded, it will make a declaration specifying the information which must be disclosed, the date upon which the employer refused or failed to disclose it and the period within which it must be disclosed (*TULR(C)A 1992, s 183(3), (5)*).

If the employer fails to comply with the order of the CAC, the union may present a further complaint which may be coupled with, or followed by, a claim that certain terms and conditions should be included in the contracts of one or more descriptions of employees in respect of whom the union is recognised by the employer (*TULR(C)A 1992, ss 184, 185*).

If the CAC finds the further complaint wholly or partly well-founded, it may make an award that, in respect of any description of employees specified in a claim for the inclusion of terms and conditions, the employer shall from a certain date observe either the terms and conditions specified in the claim or other terms and conditions which the CAC considers appropriate (*TULR(C)A 1992, ss 184(2), (4), 185(3)*). These terms and conditions have effect as part of the contract of employment of any such employee, unless superseded or varied by a further award, a collective agreement, or an agreement with the employee which improves those terms (*TULR(C)A 1992, s 185(5)*).

An award may only be made in respect of a description of employees, and may only comprise terms and conditions relating to matters in respect of which the trade union making the claim is recognised by the employer (*TULR(C)A 1992, s 185(4)*). The right to present a claim for terms and conditions expires if the employer discloses, or confirms in writing, the information specified in the declaration, and a claim presented shall be treated as withdrawn if the employer does so before the CAC makes an award on the claim (*TULR(C)A 1992, s 185(2)*).

51.9   No contracting out

Any provision in an agreement is void insofar as it purports to prevent a person from bringing proceedings before the CAC, unless a conciliation officer has taken action pursuant to his statutory duties or unless the agreement varies or supersedes an award under *TULR(C)A 1992, s 185* (*TULR(C)A 1992, s 288*).

51.10   Appeal

There is no appeal against an award of the CAC, but its decision may be challenged by judicial review proceedings in the High Court (or, in Scotland, the Court of Session) and set aside if it can be shown that the CAC:

(a)   misdirected itself in law or exceeded its jurisdiction;

(b)   failed to take into account relevant considerations or took into account irrelevant ones; or

(c)   acted unreasonably or in breach of natural justice.

For an example of the very limited basis on which the Court of Session was prepared to intervene in a decision of the CAC, see *Fullarton Computer Industries Ltd v Central Arbitration Committee* [2001] IRLR 752.

51.11   Statutory trade union recognition

With the coming into force of *s 70A* and *Sch A1* of *TULR(C)A 1992*, introduced by the *Employment Relations Act 1999* ('*ERA 1999*'), the role of the CAC was considerably expanded and enhanced. With effect from 6 June 2000, trade unions gained a statutory right to be recognised by employers for collective bargaining purposes. See further **51.19–51.38**.

The CAC plays a central role in relation to the recognition procedures. Applications to the CAC in relation to recognition are heard by a panel of three members, including the chairman or a deputy chairman.

51.12   OBLIGATIONS OF TRADE UNIONS

Trade unions have statutory obligations to keep accounting records (for members' rights of inspection, see **52.2** Trade Unions – **II**), to make annual returns, to appoint auditors and to make arrangements for the inspection of their members' superannuation schemes (*TULR(C)A 1992, ss 28, 32, 32A, 32ZA, 33, 40*). Additional requirements in relation to the making of annual returns were introduced by *ss 7* and *12* of the *Trade Union Act 2016* which came into force on 1 March 2017. In particular, if industrial action has been taken during the return period details of that must be set out (*TULR(C)A 1992, s 32AZ*). Similarly, details for expenditure out of a union's political fund must be included if they exceed £2,000 for the year (*TULR(C)A 1992, s 32ZB*). Unions must keep an up-to-date register of members (see **51.13** below), hold periodic elections for membership of the principal executive committee and for certain other positions (see **51.14** below), and hold ballots on the continued application of trade union funds for political purposes (see **51.15** below) (*TULR(C)A 1992, ss 24, 46, 71*). In *Paul v NALGO* [1987] IRLR 43 the Certification Officer considered several of these obligations. A trade union must, at the request of any person, supply him with a copy of its rules either free or on payment of a reasonable charge (*TULR(C)A 1992, s 27*).

51.13   Register of members

Every trade union is obliged by *TULR(C)A 1992, s 24* to compile and keep up to date a register of members. A member has a right to a copy of any register entry relating to him (*TULR(C)A 1992, s 24(3)*).

A member of the union may apply to the Certification Officer, or to the High Court in England or the Court of Session in Scotland, for a declaration that these requirements have not been complied with (*TULR(C)A 1992, ss 25, 26*). The court or (since 25 October 1999) the Certification Officer may also make an enforcement order requiring the union to compile or update the register (*TULR(C)A 1992, ss 25(5A), 26(4)*). There is a right of appeal against this Certification Officer's decisions under this section to the Employment Appeal Tribunal pursuant to *TULR(C)A 1992, s 45D*. Since 1 March 2017, such an appeal has no longer been confined to appeal on a point of law.

51.14 Elections and disqualification from office

Trade unions are obliged to secure that, with certain exceptions, all members of its principal executive committee, and its president and general secretary, stand for election at least every five years (*TULR(C)A 1992, ss 46(1), 119*). Members of the principal executive committee are those who, under the rules or practice of the union, may attend at some or all of its meetings (other than merely to provide factual information or professional advice) (*TULR(C)A 1992, s 46(3)*). The position of president or general secretary is exempted from the election requirement if its holder is not an employee of the union, is not a voting member of the executive and holds the position for not more than 13 months (*TULR(C)A 1992, s 46(4)*). The position of president is also exempted if the incumbent was appointed or elected in accordance with the union's rules, at the time of such appointment or election he or she held a designated executive position by virtue of having been elected in accordance with the election requirements under the section and continues to hold such a designated position, and has held such a position for no more than five years (*TULR(C)A 1992, s 46(4A)*).

In *GMB Union v Corrigan* [2008] ICR 197, [2007] All ER (D) 288 (Oct) the claimant alleged that *TULR(C)A 1992, s 46* had been breached because, following the suspension of its general secretary, the union had appointed an acting general secretary but failed to hold an election for over a year, pending the completion of an internal investigation. The EAT held that there had been no breach of the statutory duty, since the acting general secretary continued to play an acting role only, and the investigation was a legitimate reason for postponing the election of a new general secretary.

The ballot must, as far as is reasonably practicable, be secret. An independent scrutineer must be appointed to oversee the ballot, and his name must appear on the voting paper. Among his other duties, the scrutineer is obliged to make a report on the ballot to the union which must send it or notify its contents to members. Handling of voting papers and counting of votes must also be independently undertaken. Candidates must, so far as reasonably practicable, be enabled to distribute election addresses without cost to themselves. The members entitled to vote must, so far as is reasonably practicable, be given a convenient opportunity to vote by post. Members may not be unreasonably excluded from standing as candidates, and may not be required, directly or indirectly, to belong to a political party. There are detailed provisions governing the circumstances in which particular classes of members may be excluded from voting (*TULR(C)A 1992, ss 47–52; Trade Union Ballots and Elections (Independent Scrutineer Qualifications) Order 1993 (SI 1993/1909)*). In *Thompson v NUM* (2015) IDS Brief No 1019 the EAT held that union rules which permitted only current members of the union's national executive committee to stand for national office did not unreasonably exclude other members from standing, even though this in practice reduced the number of potential candidates to a very small pool of 10 or 11.

Although *TULR(C)A 1992, s 51(6)* requires the election result to be determined solely by counting the number of votes cast, this did not invalidate a rule limiting the number of members of the National Executive Council ('NEC') who could be elected from any one geographical division (*R v Certification Officer for Trade Unions and Employers' Associations, ex p Electrical Power Engineers' Association* [1990] ICR 682, [1990] IRLR 398, HL). The House of Lords took the view that the statutory provision was intended only to exclude weighted or block votes and electoral colleges.

The Certification Officer has held that it is permissible for ballot papers to contain information, such as the names of nominating branches, other than that prescribed by the statute (*Decision D/3/89*).

A person who claims that his union is in breach of the election provisions may apply to the Certification Officer, or to the High Court in England or to the Court of Session in Scotland. He must have been a member of the union at the date of the election, and at the date of the application. The application must be made within one year of the date on which the result of the election was announced (*TULR(C)A 1992, s 54*). The Certification Officer or the court may make a declaration specifying the provisions with which the trade union has failed to comply (*TULR(C)A 1992, ss 55(2), (3), 56(3)*). If it makes a declaration, the court or the Certification Officer must also, unless it is considered that to do so would be inappropriate, make an enforcement order to secure the holding of an election specified in the order (*TULR(C)A 1992, ss 55(5A), 56(4)*). There is a right of appeal to the Employment Appeal Tribunal against a decision of the Certification Officer, or a question of law, under *TULR(C)A 1992, s 56A*.

The Secretary of State is empowered by *TULR(C)A 1992, ss 203* and *204* to issue a Code of Practice relating to the conduct by trade unions of ballots and elections (see CODES OF PRACTICE (5)). Codes of Practice have been issued, which deal with ballots on industrial action (see STRIKES AND INDUSTRIAL ACTION (46)) and access to workers during recognition and derecognition ballots.

In the event that the executive council of a union seeks to breach the union's election rules, individual members of the union have a contractual right by virtue of their contracts of membership to challenge the validity of the council's decision (*Wise v Union of Shop, Distributive and Allied Workers* [1996] ICR 691, [1996] IRLR 609). It was held by the High Court in *Ecclestone v National Union of Journalists* [1999] IRLR 166 that a union's exclusion of a candidate for election on the basis that he did not have the confidence of the NEC was both a breach of the union's rules and contrary to the prohibition on unreasonably excluding candidates within *TULR(C)A 1992, s 47*.

Persons who have previously been convicted of certain offences under *TULR(C)A 1992, s 45* as amended (which deals in particular with failure to comply with statutory obligations, and with dishonest falsification or destruction of documents) are disqualified from membership of the principal executive committee and from being president or general secretary (subject to the same exemptions as set out above). The disqualification is for five or ten years, depending upon the offence committed (*TULR(C)A 1992, s 45B*). If a union allows a disqualified person to hold office, a member of the union may apply to the Certification Officer or to the court for a declaration to that effect. They have the power to require the union to take steps to remedy the position (*TULR(C)A 1992, s 45C, 45C(5A)*). There is a right of appeal against the Certification Officer's decisions under this section to the Employment Appeal Tribunal on any question of law, under *TULR(C)A 1992, s 45D*.

In *AB v CD* [2001] IRLR 808, the Court of Appeal considered the appropriate mechanism for resolving a tied vote in the second round of the election, by single transferable vote, of a regional union representative. The rules of the union, the RMT, were silent as to how such a tie should be resolved. In the absence of any express rule, the candidate who had received the most votes in the first round was declared elected.

The Court of Appeal upheld this decision. A term was to be implied into the union rules that a tie would be resolved in this way, in order to give efficacy to the contract, as an obvious inference from the express terms of the rules and in order to complete the contract between the members. However, such a term was not to be implied from custom and practice. In order for custom and practice to warrant the implication of a contractual term in the rules of a trade union, the relevant custom must be known, or at least readily ascertainable, by all members.

51.15 Political levy

A trade union may not apply its ordinary funds in the furtherance of political objects as defined by *TULR(C)A 1992, s 72*, which deals mainly with support for political parties and with attempts to influence the outcome of elections. Payments for such purposes may only be made out of a separate political fund, and then only if there is a political resolution in force approving the furtherance of those objects (*TULR(C)A 1992, s 71*). Union members have a right to apply to the Certification Officer for a decision that funds have been applied in breach of *s 71* (*TULR(C)A 1992, s 72A*). Such a resolution must be passed at least every 10 years by a ballot held in accordance with union rules which have been approved by the Certification Officer as complying with the relevant statutory requirements (*TULR(C)A 1992, ss 73, 74*). Those requirements, found in *TULR(C)A 1992, ss 75–78* are very similar to those which apply to ballots for union elections (see **51.14** above). Complaints of non-compliance with the ballot requirements may be made either to the Certification Officer or to the court within a year after the announcement of the result (*TULR(C)A 1992, ss 79–81*).

A union member is entitled to give notice that he objects to contributing to the political fund, and he is then to be exempted from making such contributions, and must not be put at any disadvantage or excluded from the union as a result (*TULR(C)A 1992, s 82*). A member who complains of a breach of these requirements may complain to the Certification Officer, who may make such order for remedying the breach as he thinks just under the circumstances (*TULR(C)A 1992, s 82(2), (3)*). A notice of objection should be in the form set out in *TULR(C)A 1992, s 84(1)* or to like effect. When a political resolution is adopted, members must be notified of their right to object and be given the opportunity to obtain exemption notice forms from union offices or from the Certification Officer (*TULR(C)A 1992, s 84(2)*). *Section 11* of the *Trade Union Act 2016*, which came into force on 1 March 2017, imposes additional restrictions in relation to trade union political funds. By *s 84* of *TULR(C)A 1992*, as amended, a member must have been given an "opt in" notice before he can be required to contribute to a political fund. However, these amendments apply only from 1 March 2018, and then apply only to persons who join the union after that date or where the union establishes its political fund for the first time after that date.

If a union member certifies to his employer that he is exempt from making political contributions, the employer must ensure that they are not deducted from his wages (*TULR(C)A 1992, s 86*). There is a right to apply to an employment tribunal for a declaration that the employer has breached this obligation, and for an order that the employer repay sums deducted and, if considered appropriate, require the employer to take specified steps in relation to emoluments payable to the union member. If the member considers that the employer has failed to comply with an order to take such specified steps, he may present a further complaint to the tribunal (*TULR(C)A 1992, ss 86, 87*; and see Pay – I (35)).

51.16 LIABILITY IN TORT

The immunity of trade unions in proceedings in tort arising out of strikes or industrial action is now similar to that of individuals (see Strikes and Industrial Action (46)). Such immunity only applies to action taken in contemplation or furtherance of a trade dispute. With certain narrowly defined exceptions, it does not protect secondary action or action taken to enforce trade union membership. Further, a trade union does not enjoy immunity from liability in tort for inducing breaches of contracts of employment unless its action has the support of a ballot (see **46.14** Strikes and Industrial Action). However, where proceedings in tort are brought against a trade union:

(a)   for a reason specified in *TULR(C)A 1992, s 219* (inducing breach of, and interference with, contracts; see **46.2** Strikes and Industrial Action); or

(b)   in respect of an agreement or combination by two or more persons to induce or do an unlawful act;

then that act will only be taken to have been done by the union if it is taken to have been authorised or endorsed by the union (*TULR(C)A 1992, s 20(1)*). An act will only be taken to have been authorised or endorsed if it was done, authorised or endorsed by one of the following:

(i)   the principal executive committee; or

(ii)   any person who is empowered by the rules to do, authorise or endorse acts of the kind in question; or

(iii)   the president or general secretary as defined in *TULR(C)A 1992, s 119*; or

(iv)   any other official of the union (whether employed by it or not), or by any member of a group to which such an official belongs and whose purposes include organising or co-ordinating industrial action; or

(v)   any other committee of the union, by which is meant any group of persons constituted in accordance with the rules of the union.

(*TULR(C)A 1992, s 20(2), (3)*).

An act will not be taken to have been endorsed by a person in category (iv) or (v) above if it was repudiated by the principal executive committee or the president or general secretary as soon as reasonably practicable after coming to the knowledge of any of them (*TULR(C)A 1992, s 21(1)*).

In order to be effective, written notice of the repudiation must be given without delay to the committee or official in question, and the union must also do its best to give individual written notice without delay to every member who it has reason to believe is taking part in, or might otherwise take part in, industrial action as a result of the repudiated act, and to the employer of every such member. The written notice must contain a statement in statutorily prescribed form (*TULR(C)A 1992, s 21(2)–(4)*).

The union will not be able to rely upon such a repudiation if the principal executive committee, or president or general secretary, has subsequently behaved in a way which is inconsistent with the purported repudiation (*TULR(C)A 1992, s 21(5)*). They will be treated as so behaving if, upon a request made within three months of the purported repudiation by a party to a commercial contract whose performance has been or may have been interfered with by the repudiated act and to whom written notice of the repudiation has not been given, they do not forthwith confirm in writing that the act has been repudiated (*TULR(C)A 1992, s 21(6)*). (See also *Express and Star Ltd v National Graphical Association* [1985] IRLR 455; upheld on other grounds, [1986] ICR 589, [1986] IRLR 222.)

The liability of trade unions in such actions in tort is subject to financial limits, considered below.

51.17 Limits on damages awarded against a trade union, enforcement of judgments and protected property

With the exception of amounts awarded in actions for personal injury or for breach of duty in connection with the ownership, occupation, possession, control or use of property, the amount of damages awarded (not including interest; see *Boxfoldia Ltd v National Graphical Association* [1988] ICR 752, [1988] IRLR 383) in any proceedings in tort brought against a trade union must not exceed the following limits:

(i)   £10,000, if the union has fewer than 5,000 members;

(ii)   £50,000, if it has 5,000 or more members but fewer than 25,000 members;

(iii)   £125,000, if it has 25,000 or more members but fewer than 100,000 members;

(iv)   £250,000, if it has 100,000 or more members.

(*TULR(C)A 1992, s 22(2)*.)

The Secretary of State may by order vary any of these sums (*TULR(C)A 1992, s 22(3)*).

A judgment, order or award made in proceedings of any description brought against a trade union is enforceable against any property held in trust for the union (see **51.2** above) to the same extent and in the same manner as if it were a body corporate (*TULR(C)A 1992, s 12(2)*). However, no award of damages, costs or expenses is recoverable by enforcement against protected property (*TULR(C)A 1992, s 23(1)*). Protected property includes the property of individual members, officials and trustees, the contents of a political fund which cannot, under the rules, be used to finance industrial action (see **51.15** above), and the contents of separate provident benefit funds (*TULR(C)A 1992, s 23(2)*).

51.18 LIABILITY OF INDIVIDUAL MEMBERS

The individual participants in industrial action have the same immunity as trade unions. Such immunity only applies to action taken in contemplation or furtherance of a trade dispute. There is, however, no limit on the damages which may be awarded if an individual is found liable. With certain narrowly defined exceptions, secondary industrial action is not protected. (See **46.6** Strikes and Industrial Action.)

TULR(C)A 1992, s 15 renders unlawful the application of the property of a trade union towards the payment of any penalty imposed upon an individual for an offence or for contempt of court, or towards any indemnity in respect of such liabilities. This applies to all kinds of offences unless designated otherwise by order made by the Secretary of State (*TULR(C)A 1992, s 15(5)*). However, the prohibition does not extend to civil liabilities, provided that the indemnity or contribution is otherwise lawful and *intra vires* the union. The union is given the right to recover property or its value applied in contravention of these provisions from the individual concerned (*TULR(C)A 1992, s 15(2)*), and in the event of its unreasonable failure to take proceedings to this end, the court may order, upon application by a union member, that that member shall be authorised to do so in the union's name and at its expense (*TULR(C)A 1992, s 15(3)*).

51.19 RECOGNITION, INDEPENDENCE AND RIGHTS

The *Employment Relations Act 1999* introduced new recognition machinery for collective bargaining purposes contained in *Sch 1* to that *Act*. The relevant provisions, which are now contained in *Sch A1* to *TULR(C)A 1992*, confer a right upon trade unions to be recognised by employers for collective bargaining purposes, provided various (extremely complex) conditions are fulfilled. The principal features of the recognition machinery are summarised at **51.25–51.38** below.

The European Court of Human Rights held in *Wilson and National Union of Journalists v United Kingdom* (Applications 30668/96, 30679/61 and 30678/96) [2002] IRLR 568 that *art 11* of the European Convention of Human Rights did not impose a requirement for compulsory collective bargaining. However, in *Demir v Turkey* (Application No 34503/97) (2008) 48 EHRR 1272, [2009] IRLR 766, the European Court held that the right to bargain collectively is one of the essential elements of the right to form and join trade unions for the protection of workers' interests and so should in general (and subject to any lawful restrictions) be recognised as forming part of the right to freedom of association. In *Pharmacists' Defence Association Union v Boots Management Services Ltd* [2017] EWCA Civ 66, [2017] IRLR 355 the Court of Appeal confirmed that the right to bargain collectively with the employer is an essential element of the rights protected by *art 11*. However, it went on to observe that any such right will be qualified by the principles of domestic law providing for recognition, and that the state has a wide margin of appreciation in deciding how the right to recognition may be constrained.

Previous provisions in the *Employment Protection Act 1975* (*'EPA 1975'*), covering the statutory procedure by which independent trade unions could refer recognition issues to ACAS, were repealed in 1980. Although the previous statutory recognition machinery in the *EPA 1975* was repealed, the concepts of 'independence' and 'recognition' discussed below continue to be relevant for some purposes. One is the procedure for handling redundancies laid down in *TULR(C)A 1992, Part IV* (see **40.2** REDUNDANCY – II). Others are disclosure of information for collective bargaining purposes under *TULR(C)A 1992, s 181* (see **11.2** DISCLOSURE OF INFORMATION), the information and consultation requirements contained in the *Transfer of Undertakings (Protection of Employment Regulations 2006 (SI 2006/246)* (see **53.22** TRANSFER OF UNDERTAKINGS) and the right to time off for trade union duties and activities (see **50.2, 50.3** TIME OFF WORK). In addition, the concept of 'independence' is central to the new procedures for recognition for collective bargaining purposes (see below).

51.20 Voluntary recognition

The recognition provisions contained in *TULR(C)A 1992, Sch A1* provide specifically for voluntary recognition. Even before those provisions came into effect, however, an employer could voluntarily agree to recognise a trade union. Recognition can be express or implied. An employer need not have entered into a formal recognition agreement in order to be considered to have recognised a particular trade union. 'Recognition' is defined in *TULR(C)A 1992, s 178(3)* as 'the recognition of the union by an employer . . . to any extent, for the purpose of collective bargaining', and 'collective bargaining' means negotiations relating to or connected with: terms and conditions of employment; physical conditions of work; recruitment, dismissal and suspension; allocation of work; matters of discipline; union membership; facilities for officials of trade unions; and bargaining machinery and other procedures (*TULR(C)A 1992, s 178(1)(2)*). A different definition of collective bargaining applies under the new recognition machinery (see below).

If management in fact consult a trade union about some or all of these matters they may be taken to have recognised that trade union (*Joshua Wilson & Bros Ltd v Union of Shop, Distributive and Allied Workers* [1978] IRLR 120, [1978] 3 All ER 4). In *National Union of Gold, Silver and Allied Trades v Albury Bros Ltd* [1979] ICR 84, [1978] IRLR 504, the Court of Appeal held that an act of recognition is such an important matter that it should not be held to be established unless the evidence is clear, either by actual agreement for recognition or clear and distinct conduct showing an implied agreement to recognise the trade union for the purposes of collective bargaining. In that case, the Court of Appeal held that an attempt by the union to negotiate with the management increased wages for one man did not establish recognition by the employer. Recognition will not be inferred from the fact that a union has been given a right of representation in pay bargaining where that right is given by a third party over whom the employer has no control (*Cleveland County Council v Springett* [1985] IRLR 131).

51.21 Listing

A list of trade unions is maintained by the Certification Officer (*TULR(C)A 1992, s 2*). Any trade union whose name is entered on the list may apply to the Certification Officer for a certificate that it is independent (*TULR(C)A 1992, s 6(1)*). A union which is not on the list maintained by the Certification Officer will automatically be refused a certificate of independence (*TULR(C)A 1992, s 6(3)*).

51.22 Independence

If the union is listed, the Certification Officer will proceed to determine whether the applicant is an independent trade union. An independent trade union is defined in *TULR(C)A 1992, s 5* as:

' . . . a trade union which –

(*a*) is not under the domination or control of an employer or a group of employers or of one or more employers' associations; and

(*b*) is not liable to interference by an employer or any such group or association (arising out of the provision of financial or material support or by any other means whatsoever) tending towards such control.'

In *Squibb UK Staff Association v Certification Officer* [1979] ICR 235, [1979] IRLR 75, [1979] 2 All ER 452, CA, the Certification Officer refused to grant a certificate of independence to a staff association which relied to a considerable extent upon facilities provided by the employers. He considered that the association could not be said to be free from liability to interference by the employers. The Court of Appeal upheld the refusal of the grant of the certificate. For a more recent example, see *Government Communications Staff Federation v Certification Officer* [1993] ICR 163, [1993] IRLR 260.

In *Bone v North Essex Partnership NHS Foundation Trust* [2014] ICR 1053, [2014] IRLR 635, [2014] 3 All ER 964, the Court of Appeal held that a certificate of independence is retrospective for a reasonable period prior to the issue of the certificate. In those circumstances, a union representative's claim for detriment on grounds of trade union activities could be heard, even though the certificate of independence was not issued until after the events of which he complained.

51.23 Factors implying independence

In *Blue Circle Staff Association v Certification Officer* [1977] 1 WLR 239, [1977] IRLR 20, [1977] 2 All ER 145, some of the principles upon which the Certification Officer acts are set out (at 245–246):

'1 *Finance*: If there is any evidence that a union is getting a direct subsidy from an employer, it is immediately ruled out.

2 *Other assistance*: The Certification Officer's inspectors see what material support, such as free premises, time off work for officials, or office facilities a union is getting from an employer, and attempt to cost them out.

3 *Employer interference*: If a union is very small and weak and gets a good deal of help, then on the face of it its independence will be considered to be in danger and liable to employer interference.

4 *History*: The recent history of a union . . . is considered. It was not unusual for a staff association to start as a "creature of management and grow into something independent".

5 *Rules*: The applicant union's rule book is scrutinised to see if the employer can interfere with or control it, and if there are any restrictions on membership. If a union is run by people near the top of a company it could be detrimental to rank and file members.

6   *Single company unions*: While they are not debarred from getting certificates, because such a rule could exclude unions like those of miners and railwaymen, they are considered to be more liable to employer interference. Broadly based multi-company unions are considered more difficult to influence.

7   *Organisation*: The Certification Officer's inspectors then examine the applicant union in detail, its size and recruiting ability, whether it is run by competent and experienced officers, the state of its finance, and its branch and committee structure. Again, if the union was run by senior men in a company, employer interference was a greater risk.

8   *Attitude*: Once the other factors have been assessed, inspectors looked for a "robust attitude in negotiation" as a sign of genuine independence, backed up by a good negotiating record . . . '

Before making a determination on the question of independence, the Certification Officer makes such inquiries as he sees fit and takes into account any relevant information submitted to him (*TULR(C)A 1992, s 6(4)*). In general, he should not be cross-examined upon his reasons for his decision (*Squibb* at **51.22** above).

51.24 Withdrawal of certificate of independence and appeals against Certification Officer's decision

The Certification Officer may at any time withdraw a certificate, after giving notice to the trade union affected and determining the relevant questions, if he is of the opinion that the trade union in question is no longer independent (*TULR(C)A 1992, s 7(1)*).

A trade union aggrieved by the refusal of the Certification Officer to issue it with a certificate, or by a decision of his to withdraw its certificate, may appeal to the Employment Appeal Tribunal. If the appeal is successful the Employment Appeal Tribunal will give directions to the Certification Officer to act according to its findings (*TULR(C)A 1992, s 9*).

51.25 RECOGNITION FOR COLLECTIVE BARGAINING PURPOSES

The current procedure for the recognition of trade unions by employers for the purposes of collective bargaining was introduced by *ERA 1999, Sch 1*. This recognition machinery came into effect on 6 June 2000 and is contained in *TULR(C)A 1992, Sch A1*. This represented a fundamental change in industrial relations in the United Kingdom, since it conferred upon trade unions a right to be recognised by employers for collective bargaining purposes, provided various conditions are satisfied. The current regime does, however, seek to promote voluntary recognition wherever possible. Also significant is the enhanced role for the Central Arbitration Committee ('CAC') (see **51.4**) in determining a range of issues relating to recognition. In carrying out these functions, the CAC is under a duty to have regard to the object of encouraging and promoting fair and efficient practices in the workplace. The provisions relating to the membership of the CAC contained in *TULR(C)A 1992, s 260* were amended by *ERA 1999, s 24* so as to require the Secretary of State to appoint only persons experienced in industrial relations, having first consulted with ACAS and such other persons as he may choose to consult (*TULR(C)A 1992, Sch A1 para 171*) (see **51.11** above). The new recognition procedures are extremely complex. Below is set out a summary of the principal provisions.

51.26 The scope of the recognition procedure

The recognition procedures apply only to employers which, taken with any associated employers, employ either at least 21 workers on the day on which a request for recognition is received, or have employed an average of at least 21 workers in the 13 preceding weeks

(TULR(C)A 1992, Sch A1 para 7(1)). For this purpose, the definition of 'worker' contained in *TULR(C)A 1992, s 296(1)* applies. In *R (on the application of the BBC) v Central Arbitration Committee* [2003] EWHC 1375 (Admin), [2003] ICR 1542, [2003] IRLR 460 it was held that an application for recognition should not have been entertained by the CAC in respect of freelance cameramen and women working for the BBC, since they were excluded from the definition of 'workers' as 'professionals'. The CAC had erred in finding that the cameramen and women were not 'professionals' merely because they had no regulatory body. Similarly, in *R (on the application of Independent Workers Union of Great Britain) v Central Arbitration Committee* [2018] EWHC 3342 (Admin), [2019] IRLR 249 the High Court upheld the CAC's rejection of an application for recognition on the basis that Deliveroo's drivers were not 'workers' as there was a genuine right of substitution, albeit one that was rarely used in practice. The union's argument that this breached the right to freedom of association under *Art 11* was also rejected. In *R (on the application of Independent Workers' Union of Great Britain) v Central Arbitration Committee* [2019] EWHC 728 (Admin), [2019] IRLR 530 the High Court similarly rejected an argument that a union could apply for recognition by an end-user of contracted out workers, which the union sought to characterise as the workers' *de facto* employer, in circumstances where there was no direct employment relationship.

Only unions which have been certified as independent under *TULR(C)A 1992, s 6* may make a request for recognition.

The territorial reach of the CAC union recognition procedures was considered in *Netjets Management Ltd v CAC* [2012] EWHC 2685 (Admin), [2012] IRLR 986, [2013] 1 All ER 288. The employer, which ran private business flights throughout Europe, sought to argue that the union's application for recognition in respect of all pilots fell outside the CAC's remit because most of the pilots were based outside the United Kingdom. The High Court upheld the CAC's decision that it had jurisdiction. There were "sufficiently strong" connections with Great Britain. In particular, the pilots' contracts were governed by English law and subject to the exclusive jurisdiction of the English Courts. No other EU states have been put forward as a more appropriate forum for collective bargaining. Moreover, if there was no collective bargaining on pay, hours and holidays in Great Britain, the pilots would be prevented from exercising their right to collective bargaining under art 11 of the Convention.

51.27 Collective bargaining

The definition of collective bargaining contained in *TULR(C)A 1992, s 178* does not apply to the new recognition provisions. Instead, collective bargaining is defined as negotiations relating to pay, hours and holidays, subject to the parties agreeing that additional matters may also be the subject of collective bargaining *(Sch A1, paras 1–4)*. For the purposes of this provision, the CAC has held that pension benefits fall within the definition of pay (see *UNIFI v Union Bank of Nigeria* [2001] IRLR 712).

51.28 The request for recognition

A union or unions seeking recognition must apply first to the employer. The request must be made in writing, identify the relevant unions and bargaining unit and state that it is made under *TULR(C)A 1992, Sch A1 para 8*. If the parties agree within 10 working days on the appropriate bargaining unit and further agree that the union is (or unions are) to be recognised to conduct collective bargaining on behalf of that unit, then the union is (or unions are) deemed to be recognised, and no further steps need be taken. If the employer does not accept the request, but agrees to negotiate, then the union will be deemed to be recognised if the parties are able to agree within a further 20-day period. The parties may request ACAS to assist in conducting such negotiations *(Sch A1, para 10)*.

51.29 Reference to the CAC

If the employer either rejects or fails to respond to the request within 10 days, or if negotiations break down during the subsequent 20-day period, the union may apply to the CAC to decide on the appropriate bargaining unit and whether the union has the support of a majority of workers within that unit. The union may ask the CAC to determine the question of majority support if the parties have agreed on the appropriate bargaining unit, but have not agreed on whether the union should be entitled to conduct collective bargaining on its behalf. However, the union may not apply to the CAC if it has rejected or failed to respond to a proposal by the employer that ACAS be requested to assist in negotiations (*Sch A1, paras 11, 12*).

TULR(C)A 1992, Sch A1 sets out a detailed procedure for the various sequential steps that must be taken by the CAC once it has received an application for union recognition. This procedure is subject to a relatively strict timetable, with the CAC generally being given 10 days to reach a determination at each stage of the procedure. The time limits within the recognition procedure are subject to extension by the CAC in most cases, although in some circumstances the CAC is under a duty to give reasons for such an extension to the parties.

The CAC must decide whether any application for recognition is 'valid' within the meaning of *TULR(C)A 1992, Sch A1 paras 5–9* and 'admissible' within the meaning of *TULR(C)A 1992, Sch A1 paras 33–42*, having considered any evidence provided by the employer or the union (*Sch A1, para 15*). The criteria of 'validity' are essentially the requirements as to union independence and number of workers employed referred to above. On the literal wording of *Sch A1*, an application may be 'inadmissible' if there is already in force a collective agreement under which a union is recognised for collective bargaining purposes (*Sch A1, para 35*). This exclusion can have far-reaching consequences. In *R (on the application of National Union of Journalists) v Central Arbitration Committee* [2005] EWCA Civ 1309, [2006] ICR 1, [2006] IRLR 53 the Court of Appeal upheld the decision of the High Court that the NUJ's application to the CAC was inadmissible, because the employer already had a recognition agreement with another union. This was the case notwithstanding that that agreement had not been used to determine the terms and conditions of workers within the bargaining unit and the other union had at most one member working in the relevant division of the employer's business. Similarly, in *Transport and General Workers' Union v Asda* [2004] IRLR 836 the CAC held the union's application inadmissible because the employer had a 'partnership agreement' in place with another union. This was despite the fact that the 'partnership agreement' provided for only limited representational rights, and specifically excluded collective bargaining on terms and conditions of employment, including pay.

However, this approach was challenged by the CAC in *Pharmacists' Defence Association v Boots Management Services Ltd* [2013] IRLR 262. The employer had a long-standing relationship with a listed trade union, but the union was not recognised for the purposes of collective bargaining in relation to terms and conditions of employment. On the literal wording of *Sch A1, para 35*, the application by a rival union for recognition was precluded, because another union was already recognised for some collective bargaining purposes. The CAC held that a literal reading of the paragraph would be incompatible with *art 11* of the Convention. Accordingly, it re-wrote *Sch A1, para 35*, so that a recognition application by another union will be precluded only if another union is already recognised as entitled to conduct collective bargaining "*in respect of pay, hours and holidays*". The employer successfully applied for judicial review of the CAC's decision, on the basis that this interpretation of *Sch A1, para 35* was not properly open to the CAC, even applying the interpretive duty contained in *Human Rights Act 1998, s 3(1)*: see *R (Boots Management Services Ltd) v CAC* [2014] IRLR 278. However, in *R (Boots Management Services Ltd) v CAC* [2014] IRLR 887, following intervention by the Government, the High Court reversed its decision and held that the plain wording of *Sch A1, para 35* was compatible with the ECHR after all. This was because the derecognition procedures contained in *Part VI* of *Sch A1* permitted a union to apply for the incumbent union to be derecognised, even if the incumbent union had very limited collective bargaining rights. The Court of Appeal upheld the decision of the High Court: [2017] IRLR 355. An application for derecognition of the incumbent union was subsequently held to be admissible (*Parker v Boots Pharmacists Association* IDS Brief 1087). In *R (on the application of Independent Workers' Union of Great Britain) v Central Arbitration Committee* [2019] EWHC 728 (Admin), [2019] IRLR 530 the High Court similarly rejected a challenge to *Sch A1, para 35* based on the fact that it precludes an application for recognition when there is already a voluntary collective agreement in place in respect of the same bargaining unit with another independent union, even though in those circumstances there is no derecognition procedure available. The Government had been entitled to enact legislation which gave primary to voluntary arrangements with an independent trade union.

An application will be inadmissible unless members of the relevant union (or unions) constitute at least 10% of workers within the bargaining unit and a majority of the workers within that unit are likely to favour recognition (*Sch A1, para 36*). Further, where an application is made by more than one union, the application will be inadmissible unless they show that they will co-operate with each other so as to secure and maintain a stable and effective collective bargaining arrangement, and further that they will act together for collective bargaining purposes if the employer wishes (*Sch A1, para 37*). An application will also be inadmissible if brought within three years of a previous application by the same union or unions in respect of the same or substantially the same bargaining unit (*Sch A1, paras 39–40*). If the application does not fulfil the criteria of 'validity' and 'admissibility', it must not be accepted by the CAC.

If the CAC accepts an application, it must first try to assist the parties in seeking to agree on the appropriate bargaining unit within a period of 20 working days (which may be extended). In the absence of agreement, the CAC must decide on the appropriate bargaining unit (*Sch A1, paras 18, 19*).

In *Prison Officers' Association and Securicor Custodial Services Ltd*, Re (2000) IDS Brief 670, the CAC accepted that the employer's recognition of a non-independent staff association precluded the application by an independent trade union for recognition pursuant to *Sch A1, para 35*. Where such an association is recognised, therefore, the independent union may well have to seek to initiate derecognition proceedings.

51.30   The appropriate bargaining unit

In deciding on the appropriate bargaining unit, the CAC must take into account the need for the unit to be compatible with effective management and, in so far as they do not conflict with that primary need, the following additional factors:

(a)   the views of the parties;

(b)   existing national and local bargaining arrangements;

(c)   the desirability of avoiding small fragmented bargaining units within an undertaking;

(d)   the characteristics of the workforce falling within and outside of the unit; and

(e)   the location of workers (*Sch A1, para 19*).

In *R (on the application of Kwik-Fit (GB) Ltd) v Central Arbitration Committee* [2002] EWCA Civ 512, [2002] ICR 1212, [2002] IRLR 395, the Court of Appeal considered the approach to be adopted by the CAC when considering competing contentions by the union and employer as to the appropriate bargaining unit. Buxton LJ rejected the employer's contention that the CAC has a duty to treat on equal terms the unit proposed by the union and any alternative proposed by the employer. The recognition machinery is put in motion by a request from the union. Provided the CAC finds that the unit put forward by the union is 'appropriate', it need not go further and consider whether there is a more appropriate unit that might be identified. It must take into account the employer's views, but should not weigh up whether an alternative unit put forward by the employer might be better than that proposed by the union, provided that that proposed by the union meets the requirement of being 'appropriate'. The decision highlights the way in which the recognition process is essentially union-driven.

In *Re Benteler Automotive UK and ISTC* (Central Arbitration Committee, 17 October 2000) (IDS Brief 677), the CAC broadly accepted the union's argument that the relevant bargaining unit was shop-floor employees only. Although the employer argued that supervisory, technical and administrative staff should be included, so as to reflect their 'whole company' ethos, the CAC noted that this did not reflect the existing management organisation and practice at the company. Although the CAC did not wish to impede the employers in achieving a 'whole company' approach, existing economic realities determined the appropriate bargaining unit.

In *Graphical Paper and Media Union v Derry Print Ltd* [2002] IRLR 380, the CAC considered the proper approach to determining the appropriate bargaining unit where a single business was run through two separate companies, with members of the workforce being allocated to one business or the other. The CAC concluded that, under the recognition machinery in *TULR(C)A 1992, Sch A1*, a bargaining unit could not include the employees of more than one employer. The language and scheme of the recognition provisions envisaged the determination of a bargaining unit by reference to a single employer.

However, the CAC went on to hold that, on the facts of the case, it was permissible to treat the two companies in question as a single employer. A more liberal approach to lifting the corporate veil in this way was appropriate here than in some other legal contexts. The CAC accordingly determined that the appropriate bargaining unit comprised the production workers of both companies. The CAC thereby recognised the importance of determining the bargaining unit by reference to the economic realities on the shop floor.

In *R (on the application of Cable & Wireless Services UK Ltd) v Central Arbitration Committee* [2008] EWHC 115 (Admin), [2008] IRLR 425, [2008] ICR 693 Collins J upheld a decision of the CAC that the smallness of a bargaining unit would not in itself necessary lead to fragmentation. Whilst small fragmented bargaining units were undesirable, the mischief underlying this criterion was avoiding the proliferation of such units resulting from the creation of a unit lacking in any obviously identifiable boundary. In *R (Lidl) v Central Arbitration Committee* [2017] EWCA Civ 328, [2017] ICR 1145, [2017] IRLR 646 the Court of Appeal held that the specific criterion of the desirability of avoiding small fragmented bargaining units applies only where there is more than one potential bargaining unit in play.

If the parties have agreed, or the CAC has decided on, a bargaining unit which differs from that originally proposed, the CAC must consider whether the application is valid by reference to further criteria of 'validity' set out in *paras 43–50* (*Sch A1, para 20*). These further criteria of validity closely mirror those of 'admissibility' set out above (see *paras 33–42*). Where there is no such disparity, and where the CAC is satisfied that the criteria of validity are satisfied, the CAC must proceed with the application for union recognition.

51.31 Union recognition

The central provisions of the new recognition procedure are those which provide for the compulsory recognition of unions for collective bargaining purposes. Such recognition may or may not be preceded by a secret ballot of the workers within the relevant bargaining unit.

Where the CAC is satisfied that a majority of the workers within the bargaining unit are members of the union, it must issue a declaration that the union is recognised as entitled to conduct collective bargaining on behalf of the workers within the bargaining unit, unless:

(a)   it is satisfied that a ballot should be held in the interests of good industrial relations; or

(b)   there is credible evidence from a significant number of union members within the bargaining unit that they do not want the union to conduct collective bargaining on their behalf; or

(c)   evidence about the circumstances in which members joined the union or about the length of time they have been members is produced, which leads the CAC to conclude that there are doubts about whether a significant number of members wish the union to conduct collective bargaining on their behalf.

If any of those circumstances apply, the CAC must give notice that it intends to arrange for the holding of a secret ballot in which the workers will be asked whether they want the union to be recognised. Equally, the CAC must give notice of its intention to arrange for the holding of a secret ballot if it is not satisfied that a majority of workers within the bargaining unit are members of the union. The CAC must then arrange for the holding of a ballot unless it receives notification within 10 working days (or such longer period as the CAC specifies) from the union (or from the union and employer jointly) that they do not want a ballot to take place (*Sch A1, paras 20–24*).

In *Fullarton Computer Industries Ltd v Central Arbitration Committee* [2001] IRLR 752, the Court of Session upheld the CAC's decision that a trade union should be recognised without a ballot on the grounds that a ballot would not be in the interests of good industrial relations. The Court of Session approached the case on the basis that the CAC was under no obligation to give reasons for its decision. (The CAC is obliged by the statute to give reasons for some of its decisions, particularly those relating to the extension of time limits within the recognition procedure, but not, ironically, for those substantive decisions, such as this one, which are likely to be determinative of the outcome of the recognition application.) If reasons were given, the decision could be set aside only if they disclosed some manifest error or flaw on the face of the record. This case highlights the difficulty inherent in challenging the CAC's decision as to whether a ballot is likely to be in the interests of good industrial relations.

51.32 The recognition ballot

The recognition ballot, which must be conducted by a qualified independent person appointed by the CAC, may be conducted in the workplace, by post or, exceptionally, by some combination of the two. A 'qualified independent person' is defined for these purposes as someone who fulfils the conditions of either being a practicing solicitor or being eligible for appointment as a company auditor. In addition, a number of organisations providing electoral services are specified by name to be such persons (*Recognition and Derecognition Ballots (Qualified Persons) Order 2000 (SI 2000/1306)*). The costs of the ballot are divided equally between the employer on the one hand and the union (or unions) on the other. In deciding on the appropriate method, the CAC must take into account the risk of unfairness or malpractice if the ballot is conducted in the workplace, costs and practicality, and such other matters as it considers appropriate (*Sch A1, paras 25, 28*).

The employer is placed under five duties in relation to a recognition ballot:

(a)   it must co-operate generally with both the union and the person appointed to conduct the ballot;

(b)   it must give the union such reasonable access to the workers within the bargaining unit as will enable it to inform the workers of its object and seek their support and opinions;

(c)   it must give the CAC the names and home addresses of the workers within the bargaining unit, including any workers who join the unit after the initial list has been provided, and must further inform the CAC if any such workers have ceased to be within the unit. The CAC passes this information on to the person appointed to conduct the ballot;

(d)   it must refrain from unreasonably seeking to induce workers to refrain from attending meetings with a union regarding recognition;

(e)   it must refrain from taking or threatening action against a worker because he has attended or intends to attend a meeting with a union regarding recognition.

A new code of practice on access to workers during recognition and derecognition ballots came into effect on 1 October 2005 pursuant to *TULR(C)A 1992, ss 203–204* and the *Employment Code of Practice (Access to Workers during Recognition and Derecognition Ballots) Order 2005 (SI 2005/2421)*.

It the employer fails to comply with any of these duties, the CAC may order the employer to take remedial steps. If the employer fails to comply with such an order, the CAC may cancel the ballot (or ignore it if it has taken place) and make a declaration of recognition (*Sch A1, paras 26, 27*).

The person appointed to conduct the ballot must send all relevant workers any information supplied by the union, provided that the union bears the cost of sending such information.

The most important (and controversial) provision in the union recognition procedure is that which determines the effect of the outcome of the recognition ballot. If union recognition for collective bargaining purposes is supported by:

(a)   a majority of the workers voting, and

(b)   at least 40% of the workers within the bargaining unit,

then the CAC must issue a declaration that the union is recognised for collective bargaining purposes. If those conditions are not satisfied, then the CAC must declare that the union is not so recognised. The Secretary of State may by order amend this provision so as to specify a different degree of requisite support (*Sch A1, para 29*). It follows that, even if a majority of those voting support recognition, the union will not be recognised if a low turnout entails that those in favour constitute less than 40% of the workforce within the bargaining unit.

In *R (on the application of Ultraframe (UK) Ltd) v Central Arbitration Committee* [2005] EWCA Civ 560, [2005] ICR 1194, [2005] IRLR 641 the Court of Appeal upheld a decision of the CAC directing a re-run of a recognition ballot. Although a majority of those voting had supported recognition, the 40% requirement had not been achieved by four votes. The unions complained that a number of employees had not received ballot papers, and the CAC concluded that five employees, who would have voted in favour of recognition, had not been given a reasonable opportunity to vote. The Court of Appeal concluded that the CAC had jurisdiction to investigate and, if appropriate, to annul the ballot, and so had acted within its powers in ordering a re-run.

All parties informed by the CAC of a recognition ballot must refrain from using unfair practices in relation to such a ballot (*Sch A1, para 27A*). 'Unfair practices' are defined so as to include; making inducements to vote in a particular way; coercion; undue influence; and dismissal, disciplinary action or detriment, or threats of such actions, aimed at influencing the outcome of the ballot. A party may complain to the CAC if it believes that unfair practices have been used (*Sch A1, para 27C*). If the CAC finds a complaint well-founded, it must make a declaration to that effect, and may order the party concerned to take specified action, or give notice that it intends to arrange a secret ballot in which the workers are asked whether they want the union to conduct collective bargaining on their behalf (*Sch A1, para 27C*). The CAC's further powers upon such a finding also include a power in certain circumstances to cancel or annul a ballot.

51.33 The method of collective bargaining

Once a declaration of recognition has been made, the parties may seek to negotiate an agreement as to the method by which they will conduct collective bargaining during a 30-day period or such longer period as they agree. If no agreement is reached, the parties may apply to the CAC for assistance. The CAC must try to help the parties to reach an agreement. If after a further 20 days (or such further period as the CAC agrees with the parties) still no agreement has been reached, the CAC must specify the method by which the parties will conduct collective bargaining. A detailed 'specified method' is set out in the *Trade Union Recognition (Method of Collective Bargaining) Order 2000 (SI 2000/1300)*. This must be taken into account by the CAC when specifying a method of collective bargaining for the parties. In those circumstances, unless the parties agree otherwise, the specified method has effect as if made in a legally enforceable contract between parties. However, specific performance will be the only remedy available for any breach of the specified method. If the parties have agreed the method by which they will conduct collective bargaining, but one or more of the parties fails to carry it out, the parties may apply to the CAC for assistance (*Sch A1, paras 30–32*).

In *British Airline Pilots' Association v Jet2.com Ltd* [2017] ICR 457, [2017] IRLR 233 the Court of Appeal held that the specified method in that case, which provided for collective bargaining relating to 'pay, hours and holidays', included collective bargaining over rostering. The language of *Sch A1, para 3(3)* was not confined to collective bargaining over proposals which, if agreed, would give rise to individual contractual rights.

51.34 Voluntary recognition

TULR(C)A 1992, Sch A1 Part II contains additional provisions relating specifically to voluntary recognition. These provisions apply where the parties reach agreement that the union should be recognised as entitled to conduct collective bargaining at some point before the compulsory recognition procedure summarised above has been exhausted. Agreement may have been reached either before or after an application to the CAC has been made (*Sch A1, para 52*). Any party to such an agreement may apply to the CAC for a decision whether or not the agreement is indeed an 'agreement for recognition' as defined (*Sch A1, para 55*).

If the CAC decides that the agreement is an 'agreement for recognition', the employer may not terminate the agreement for a period of three years. The union, however, may terminate such an agreement at any time, with or without the consent of the employer. It follows that an employer, but not a union, who enters into a recognition agreement may be bound by that agreement for up to three years (but see below for the provisions relating to changes in the bargaining unit and derecognition) (*Sch A1, para 56*).

Where the parties have entered into a recognition agreement, but have failed to agree on a method for conducting collective bargaining, they may apply to the CAC for assistance. Equally, if the parties have agreed on a method, but one or more of the parties fails to carry it out, they may apply to the CAC for assistance. The CAC must not accept either type of application unless the requirements as to number of workers employed and union certification are satisfied. Once it has decided that an application is admissible, the CAC must try to help the parties to reach an agreement. If after a period of 20 days (or such further period as the parties agree) still no agreement has been reached, the CAC must specify the method by which the parties will conduct collective bargaining, taking into account the 'specified method' set out in the *Trade Union Recognition (Method of Collective Bargaining) Order 2000 (SI 2000/1300)*. As in the case of compulsory recognition, unless the parties agree otherwise, the specified method has effect as if made in a legally enforceable contract between parties. Again, however, specific performance is the only remedy available for any breach of the specified method (*Sch A1, paras 58–63*).

51.35 Changes in the bargaining unit

If either party believes that the original bargaining unit is no longer appropriate, it may apply to the CAC for a decision as to the appropriate bargaining unit. Such an application is admissible only if the CAC decides that the original unit is likely to be no longer appropriate, either because the organisation or structure of the employer's business or the employer's business activities have changed, or because there has been a substantial change in the number of workers employed in the original unit (*Sch A1, paras 64–68*). Once the CAC has accepted the application, the parties may agree on a new bargaining unit. If no such agreement is reached, the parties must decide whether the original unit is appropriate and, if not, decide on a new unit or units. Again, in deciding whether the original unit is appropriate, the CAC must take into account only changes in the organisation or structure of the employer's business or the employer's business activities, or any substantial change in the number of workers employed in the original unit. In deciding what new unit might be appropriate, the CAC must adopt similar criteria to those outlined above in respect of an initial application for recognition (*Sch A1, paras 69–73*).

If an employer believes that the original bargaining unit has ceased to exist and wishes the collective bargaining arrangements to cease to have effect, it must give notice to the union, copied to the CAC. Provided proper notice is given, the collective bargaining arrangements will cease to have effect unless the union applies to the CAC within 10 days for a decision on whether the original unit has ceased to exist and whether it is no longer appropriate in any event. If such an application is made, the CAC must determine these questions, having given the employer and the unions an opportunity to put forward their views on whether the unit has ceased to exist or is no longer appropriate. Again, in deciding whether the original unit is no longer appropriate, the CAC must take into account only any changes in the organisation or structure of the employer's business or the employer's business activities, or any substantial change in the number of workers employed in the original unit. If the CAC decides that the original unit has ceased to exist, the collective bargaining arrangements cease to have effect. If it decides that it has not ceased to exist and remains an appropriate bargaining unit, the collective bargaining arrangements remain in place. If, however, the CAC decides that the original unit has not ceased to exist, but that it is no longer an appropriate unit, it must decide what other bargaining unit is (or units are) appropriate by reference to the same criteria as apply when initially deciding on the appropriate bargaining unit (see above) (*Sch A1, paras 74–81*).

The CAC must further decide whether the difference between the original unit and the new unit is such that the level of support for the union within the new unit needs to be assessed. If not, then the CAC simply issues a declaration that the union is recognised as entitled to conduct collective bargaining on behalf of the new unit. If, however, the CAC decides that the level of support needs to be assessed, it must carry out a procedure similar to that in respect of an initial application for recognition before determining whether to make a recognition declaration. This procedure may require the holding of a secret ballot. The threshold for recognition is the same as in the case of an initial application for recognition (ie a majority of those voting and 40% of workers within the unit voting in favour of union recognition) (*Sch A1, paras 85–89*).

A trade union may complain to an employment tribunal if an employer fails to comply with the obligation to consult on training. Such a complaint must be presented within three months of the alleged failure complained of, or within such further period as the tribunal considers reasonable in a case where it is satisfied that it was not reasonably practicable for the complaint to be presented within three months. Where a complaint is upheld, the tribunal shall make a declaration to that effect and may award compensation to each person who was, at the time when the failure occurred, a member of the bargaining unit. The maximum amount of compensation is two weeks' pay per worker (subject to the limit on a week's pay set out in *ERA 1996, s 227(1)*, currently £538).

51.39 AMALGAMATIONS AND TRANSFERS OF ENGAGEMENTS

One trade union may amalgamate with or transfer its engagements to another trade union. However, it may not do so unless a resolution which approves the amalgamation or transfer, in a form approved by the Certification Officer, has been passed by a vote of members. The right to be balloted may not extend to members who are not full members of the union (see *National Union of Mineworkers (Yorkshire Area) v Millward* [1995] ICR 482, [1995] IRLR 411). *TULR(C)A 1992, ss 97–105* and the *Trade Unions and Employers' Associations (Amalgamations, etc) Regulations 1975 (SI 1975/536)*, as amended, regulate amalgamations and specify the information which must be given to union members and the manner in which the ballot must be taken. *TULR(C)A 1992, s 103* provides a remedy, by way of complaint to the Certification Officer, to a union member dissatisfied with the way in which the vote on the resolution was taken.

52   Trade Unions – II: Individual Rights and Union Membership

52.1   RIGHTS OF UNION MEMBERS IN RELATION TO EMPLOYER

An employee who is a member of a trade union has the following rights in relation to his employer.

(a)   He may not be refused employment because of his membership of a trade union (see **52.3** below).

(b)   Dismissal for membership of, or for taking part in the activities of, an independent trade union is automatically unfair, as is dismissal on union recognition-related grounds (see **55.3** Unfair Dismissal – II).

(c)   Subjection to detriment by his employer for membership of, or for taking part in the activities of, or using the services of, an independent trade union, or on union recognition-related grounds, gives the employee the right to complain to an employment tribunal which may award him compensation (see **52.18** below).

(d)   The right to time off from work to take part in trade union activities (see **50.3** Time off Work).

(e)   The right not to suffer the deduction of unauthorised or excessive union subscriptions from his wages (see **52.21** below).

(f)   Where a trade union is recognised for collective bargaining purposes within *TULR(C)A 1992, Sch A1, TULR(C)A 1992, s 70B* imposes upon the employer a duty to consult with trade union representatives on training for workers within the bargaining unit (see Trade Unions – I (**51**)).

(g)   A worker who is required or invited to attend a disciplinary or grievance hearing by his employer has the right to be accompanied by a trade union official (see **52.22** below).

In addition, a trade union *official* has the right to take time off with pay for his trade union duties (see **50.2** Time off Work).

52.2   RIGHTS OF UNION MEMBERS OR INTENDING MEMBERS IN RELATION TO UNION

A trade union member or would-be member has the following rights in relation to his union.

(a)   The right not to be excluded or expelled save on certain specified grounds and in accordance with the rules of the union (see **52.11** to **52.14** below).

(b)   The right under *TULR(C)A 1992, s 69* to terminate his membership with the union on giving reasonable notice and complying with any reasonable conditions.

(c)   The right not to have disciplinary action taken against him by the union save in accordance with the rules of the union and to be protected from disciplinary action taken on certain grounds (see **52.15** and **52.16** below).

(d)   The right under *TULR(C)A 1992, s 62* to apply to the High Court (or, in Scotland, the Court of Session) if members of his union, including himself, have been called on to take industrial action which has not received prior ballot approval (see **46.18** Strikes and Industrial Action).

compensation for injury to feelings (*TULR(C)A 1992, s 140(1), (2)*). The tribunal will presumably ask itself whether the applicant would have obtained the job had it not been for his membership or non-membership of a union, or the percentage chance of his doing so, and will compensate him for lost earnings if so. The maximum award of compensation is the same as for unfair dismissal, currently £88,519 (*ERA 1999, s 34; Employment Rights (Increase of Limits) Order 2020 (SI 2020/205)*).

The tribunal may also, or alternatively, make a recommendation that the respondent take within a specified period action appearing to the tribunal to be practicable for the purpose of obviating or reducing the adverse effect on the applicant of the conduct complained of, and may make or increase an award of compensation (up to the statutory maximum) if the respondent fails without reasonable justification to comply (*TULR(C)A 1992, s 140(1)(b), (3)*).

An appeal on a question of law lies from the decision of the tribunal to the Employment Appeal Tribunal (*TULR(C)A 1992, s 291(2)*).

Any agreement purporting to exclude the right to complain under these provisions is void, unless reached as part of a settlement after a conciliation officer has taken action, or where the statutory conditions governing compromise contracts have been satisfied, including that the complainant should have had advice from a relevant independent advisor (*TULR(C)A 1992, s 288*; and see **2.4** Advisory, Conciliation and Arbitration Service and **19.22** Employment Tribunals – I).

There are also provisions dealing similarly with cases where an employment agency acts on behalf of an employer, or where such an agency refuses its services on unlawful grounds (*TULR(C)A 1992, s 138*; see also *TULR(C)A 1992, ss 141* and *143(2)*).

52.5 Dismissal and the closed shop

The dismissal of an employee or his selection for redundancy will automatically be regarded as unfair if the principal reason for the dismissal or selection was that he was not a member of any trade union, or of a particular trade union, or of one of a number of particular trade unions, or had refused or proposed to refuse to become or remain a member (*TULR(C)A 1992, ss 152(1)(c), 153*) (see **55.3** Unfair Dismissal – II). References to trade union membership include membership of any trade union, or of a particular trade union or one of a number of particular trade unions, or of a particular branch or section of a trade union (*TULR(C)A 1992, s 152(4)*).

'Proposing to refuse to remain a member' covers the situation where the proposed refusal is contingent upon a particular event (*Crosville Motor Services Ltd v Ashfield* [1986] IRLR 475).

For the relevance of the employer's belief in the employee's membership or non-membership, see *Leyland Vehicles Ltd v Jones* [1981] ICR 428, [1981] IRLR 269.

Compensation for the dismissal is assessed as described in **52.7** below.

Note that there is no minimum qualifying period of employment before an employee is entitled to make such a complaint of unfair dismissal, nor is there any upper age limit (*TULR(C)A 1992, s 154*).

52.6 FAILURE TO MAKE PAYMENTS

Instead of being a member of a trade union, an employee may be subject to a requirement to make a payment, eg to a charity. If such an employee who is not or ceases to be a union member refuses, in breach of a requirement, to make such a payment and is dismissed for that reason, he will be treated as dismissed for failure to become or remain a member of a trade union. The same is true if he is dismissed for objecting to a provision which entitles his employer to deduct such a payment from his wages (*TULR(C)A 1992, s 152(3)*). A dismissal for failure to make such a payment or for objecting to such a provision will be regarded as automatically unfair, and will be compensated as described in **52.7** below.

An employer may only deduct a trade union subscription from an employee's pay if certain statutory requirements are complied with (see **52.21** below).

52.7   COMPENSATION FOR CLOSED SHOP DISMISSALS

For the detailed rules on compensation, see **56.6–56.19** Unfair Dismissal – **III**. Note in particular, however, that *in addition* to the general rules governing unfair dismissal awards, the following apply to 'automatically' unfair dismissals to enforce a closed shop.

(a)   There is a minimum basic award of £6,562, although the compensatory award is calculated in the normal way.

(b)   There is provision that conduct of the employee in refusing to join a union or to make payments in lieu of joining, or in objecting to such payments, should be disregarded in assessing contributory fault for possible reduction of any part of the award (*TULR(C)A 1992, s 155*). However, it seems that confrontational conduct by the employee could form the basis for a finding of contributory fault provided that the immediate circumstances constituting the principal reason for dismissal are excluded from consideration (*TGWU v Howard* [1992] ICR 106, [1992] IRLR 170).

(c)   The employee may request that a third party (eg a union) be joined in the unfair dismissal proceedings if pressure by it has induced the dismissal and the award may be made wholly or partly against that third party.

(*TULR(C)A 1992, ss 155–156, 160.*)

52.8   DETRIMENT

Every worker has the right not to be subjected to detriment by his employer for the purpose of compelling him to be or become a member of a trade union or a particular trade union, or for the purpose of enforcing a requirement that in the event of his failing to become or ceasing to be a member he must make one or more payments (*TULR(C)A 1992, s 146(1)(c), (3)*). Infringement of this right entitles the employee to complain to an employment tribunal and seek a declaration and compensation (*TULR(C)A 1992, s 146(5)*; and see **52.18**, **52.19** below).

52.9   INDUSTRIAL ACTION, TRADE UNION DISCIPLINE AND THE CLOSED SHOP

The statutory immunity for industrial action is inapplicable where the purpose of the action is to impose union membership requirements or to enforce a closed shop. For a more detailed account of the relevant provisions, see **46.7** Strikes and Industrial Action.

An individual member of a trade union may not be disciplined either for proposing to resign from the union, or for working with non-union members or for an employer who employs non-union labour (*TULR(C)A 1992, s 65(2)* as amended; for further details, see **52.16** below).

objective is reasonable ascertainable). However, exclusion or expulsion for membership of a political party will not be permissible if it was done contrary to the union's rules, if the decision was taken unfairly, or if the individual would lose his livelihood or suffer exceptional hardship by reason of not being, or ceasing to be, a member of the union.

(*TULR(C)A 1992, s 174(1)–(4)*.)

The earlier provision in *s 174* preventing a trade union from excluding or expelling a member for being or ceasing to be a member of a political party was held by the European Court of Human Rights in *Associated Society of Locomotive Engineers & Firemen v United Kingdom (Application No 11002/05)* [2007] IRLR 361, ECtHR to infringe the right to freedom of association under *art 11* of the European Convention. The Court found that the UK law did not strike the right balance between the member's rights and those of the union in so far as it prevented the union from expelling the member on grounds of his membership of the British National Party. As a result, with effect from 6 April 2009 *s 174* was amended by *EA 2008, s 19* so as to permit expulsion on grounds of membership of a political party in the circumstances set out in the legislation.

For these purposes, if an application for membership of a trade union is neither granted nor rejected, it will be treated as having been refused on the expiry of the period within which it might reasonably have been expected to have been granted or refused. In addition, if under the rules of a trade union any person ceases to be a member of the trade union on the happening of an event specified in the rules, he will be treated as having been expelled from the union (*TULR(C)A 1992, s 177(2)*).

An employee, who had voluntarily surrendered his membership of a union, could not make a complaint under the predecessor of *s 174* on the basis that his resignation had been forced on him by the conduct of union officials, although there might be cases where the resignation was not truly voluntary (*McGhee v Midlands British Road Services Ltd* [1985] ICR 503, [1985] IRLR 198). Furthermore, an employee who had been suspended from a union beyond the six-month period allowed in the union's rule book was held to have been neither excluded nor expelled within the meaning of *s 174* (*NACODS v Gluchowski* [1996] IRLR 252).

These rights are additional to common law rights in relation to expulsion or exemptions (see **52.12** above) (*TULR(C)A 1992, s 177(5)*).

52.14 The remedy

TULR(C)A 1992 provides for a two-stage remedy for an employee who complains that he has been expelled or excluded in breach of *s 174*. He must begin by presenting a complaint to an employment tribunal against the union in question, within the period of six months from the refusal or expulsion. Applications outside this time limit can only be heard if the tribunal is satisfied that it was not reasonably practicable to present the complaint in time and the complaint was presented within such further period as the tribunal considers reasonable (*TULR(C)A 1992, ss 174(4), 175*; and see **19.20** EMPLOYMENT TRIBUNALS – I).

At the first stage, the tribunal's function is limited to rejecting the application or finding that it is well-founded, and, if the latter, making a declaration to that effect (*TULR(C)A 1992, s 176(1)*).

Where the tribunal declares that the applicant has been wrongly refused or expelled from union membership, he will be entitled to compensation. However, he cannot apply for compensation until four weeks have elapsed after the declaration. This four-week period is designed to give the trade union an opportunity of admitting or readmitting the applicant to membership. The application must be made to an employment tribunal, however, within six months of the declaration. (*TULR(C)A 1992, s 176(2), (3)*).

Amount of compensation. Compensation will be of such amount as is considered just and equitable in all the circumstances, but the minimum award is £10,022. The maximum award of compensation is equal to the aggregate of:

(a)   30 times the current limit on the amount of a week's pay for the purposes of calculating the basic award in unfair dismissal cases, which is at present £538; and

(b)   the current maximum compensatory award in unfair dismissal cases, which is at present £88,519.

(See Unfair Dismissal – III (56).) Thus the present maximum award is £104,659. Since it will now be unusual, because the closed shop has been outlawed, for the inability to belong to a union to cause financial loss, it is unclear how the assessment of compensation should be approached. In *Bradley v NALGO* [1991] ICR 359, [1991] IRLR 159, the EAT indicated that, assuming compensation for injury to feelings to be available, it should be on a modest scale. However, in *Adams v Hackney London Borough Council* [2003] IRLR 402 the EAT held, in the context of action short of dismissal by an employer on trade union grounds, that in principle awards for injury to feelings should not be approached any differently whatever the ground of discrimination relied upon, although each case will depend on its own facts. (See also *Beaumont v Amicus MSF* (2004) 148 Sol Jo LB 1063, [2004] All ER (D) 34 (Aug) in which an award for injury to feelings was made in a claim for unjustifiable discipline by a trade union.)

Compensation may be reduced where the exclusion or expulsion was, to any extent, caused or contributed to by the action of the applicant (*TULR(C)A 1992, s 176(5)*). It appears that this step should precede the application of the statutory maximum or minimum.

Where a complaint of expulsion under *s 174* succeeds, the applicant cannot also complain of the expulsion under *TULR(C)A 1992, s 66* (unjustifiable disciplining; see **52.16** below).

52.15 DISCIPLINING BY A TRADE UNION – COMMON LAW

A member of a trade union has a right to be dealt with in accordance with the rules of his union and in accordance with natural justice (see also **52.12** above). If a union acts in breach of the rules or in breach of natural justice, the member affected may apply to the High Court for an injunction and a declaration of his rights. Members of the National Union of Mineworkers ('NUM'), disciplined for breach of a union instruction given in breach of the rules, were held to be entitled to a declaration of the invalidity of the instruction and the unlawfulness of the disciplinary action (*Taylor v National Union of Mineworkers (Derbyshire Area)* [1984] IRLR 440). Injunctions were granted to NUM members to restrain their union from instructing or seeking to persuade them or others not to work. The NUM had described the strike as official, where it had been called without a ballot as required by the rules, and had threatened disciplinary action. However, the courts will not review a decision of a trade union which is taken in accordance with the rules but which is attacked on the basis that it is one which no reasonable trade union could have reached in the circumstances (*Hamlet v General Municipal Boilermakers and Allied Trades Union* [1987] ICR 150, [1986] IRLR 293, [1987] 1 All ER 631). Nevertheless, the rules may be subject to an implied obligation not to act capriciously or arbitrarily (*Goring v British Actors Equity Association* [1987] IRLR 122). For examples of the courts intervening where there has been a breach of natural justice (ie the right to a fair hearing before an unbiased decision-maker), see *Roebuck v National Union of Mineworkers (Yorkshire Area)* [1977] ICR 573 and *Stevenson v United Road Transport Union* [1977] ICR 893, [1977] 2 All ER 941. However, the rules of natural justice are not generally applicable in the context of a union's contractual relations with its officials, in its capacity as an employer (*Meacham v Amalgamated Engineering and Electrical Union* [1994] IRLR 218). The court may imply into a union's rule-book a power to discipline its members where no express power exists (*McVitae v UNISON* [1996] IRLR 33).

The court will ignore any provision of the union's rules which purports to provide that his only remedy is by way of some form of determination or conciliation in accordance with the rules (*TULR(C)A 1992, s 63(1)*). It will also ignore any provision which requires or permits such determination or conciliation, provided that the member has made a valid application to the union for determination or conciliation more than six months before bringing court proceedings (*TULR(C)A 1992, s 63(2)*), unless the member has himself unreasonably delayed matters (*TULR(C)A 1992, s 63(4)*). Applications are deemed valid unless the union informs the member of invalidity within 28 days of receipt (*TULR(C)A 1992, s 63(3)*).

52.16   DISCIPLINING BY A TRADE UNION – STATUTORY PROVISIONS

TULR(C)A 1992, s 64(1) confers an important right 'not to be unjustifiably disciplined' by a union of which a person is or has at any time been a member. This right is conferred in addition to any existing rights and the only remedies for any infringement are those conferred by *ss 66* and *67 (TULR(C)A 1992, s 64(4), (5))*. In *Unison v Kelly* (UKEAT/0188/11/SM) [2012] IRLR 442 the EAT rejected an argument put forward by the union that the statutory right not to be unjustifiably disciplined amounted to an unlawful interference with *art 11* of the Convention. Union members have a right to hold their unions to account in this regard.

A person is unjustifiably disciplined if the conduct or supposed conduct for which he is disciplined falls within, or is believed by the union to amount to conduct which falls within, any of the 12 categories which may be summarised as follows:

(a)   failing to participate in or support, or opposing, any industrial action;

(b)   failing to break a contract of employment or other agreement with the employer for the purposes of industrial action;

(c)   asserting, including by bringing proceedings, that the union or any of its officials or representatives is in breach of its obligations under the general law, its rules or any agreement (although false assertions made in bad faith are excluded by *s 65(6)*);

(d)   encouraging or assisting another person to fulfil obligations to the employer or to make or to attempt to vindicate assertions of the kind described in para (*c*);

(e)   failing to comply with any requirement imposed as a result of unjustifiable disciplinary action taken against himself or another;

(f)   failing to agree to the deduction of union dues from his wages;

(g)   resigning or proposing to resign from the union or another union, or being or becoming, or proposing or refusing to become, a member of another union;

(h)   working or proposing to work with individuals who do not belong to the union, or who are or are not members of another union;

(i)   working or proposing to work for an employer of such individuals;

(j)   requiring the union to do an act which any provision of *TULR(C)A 1992* requires it to do on a member's requisition;

(k)   consulting or requesting assistance from the Certification Officer (see **51.3** Trade Unions – I), or from any other person in relation to assertions of the kind described in para (*c*);

(l)   proposing to do any of these things, or doing acts which are preparatory or incidental to them, unless that conduct would independently and justifiably lead to disciplinary action (*TULR(C)A 1992, s 65(2)–(5)*).

The disciplinary action against which members are protected includes expulsion, fines, deprivation of benefits or facilities, encouragement to another union not to accept him as a member, or subjection to any other detriment (*TULR(C)A 1992, s 64(2)*). This extends to suspension from membership, and to naming a strike-breaker in a branch circular with the intention of causing embarrassment (*NALGO v Killorn and Simm* [1991] ICR 1, [1990] IRLR 464).

Complaints of unjustifiable disciplinary action are to be made to an employment tribunal within three months of the determination complained of (*TULR(C)A 1992, s 66(1), (2)*). A mere recommendation is not a determination (*TGWU v Webber* [1990] ICR 711, [1990] IRLR 462). Time may be extended for such period as the tribunal considers reasonable, either where it was not reasonably practicable to present the complaint within three months (see **19.20** EMPLOYMENT TRIBUNALS **– I**), or where any delay is wholly or partly attributable to a reasonable attempt to pursue an appeal or otherwise to have the decision reconsidered (see *NALGO v Killorn and Simm*, above). If the complaint is well-founded, the tribunal will make a declaration to that effect (*TULR(C)A 1992, s 66(3)*). If such a declaration is made, the complainant may make an application to the employment tribunal to seek compensation and/or the repayment of any sums paid by him as the result of the disciplinary action (*TULR(C)A 1992, s 67(1)*). Applications for compensation are to be made not less than four weeks or more than six months after the disciplinary action is declared unjustifiable (*TULR(C)A 1992, s 67(3)*).

The compensation awarded will be that sum which is just and equitable in all the circumstances, taking account of the duty to mitigate loss and of any contributory fault (*TULR(C)A 1992, s 67(5)–(7)*). The Court of Appeal considered the principles to be applied in awarding compensation for unjustified discipline by a trade union in *Massey v Unifi* [2007] EWCA Civ 800, [2008] ICR 62, [2007] IRLR 902. Among other matters, the approach to injury to feelings in *Vento v Chief Constable of West Yorkshire Police* [2002] EWCA Civ 1871, [2003] ICR 318, [2003] IRLR 102 was applied and it was accepted in principle (although not on the facts of the case) that aggravated damages could be awarded. Before dealing with mitigation or contribution, however, the tribunal is required by *TULR(C)A 1992, s 67(9)* to apply the statutory maxima and minima contained in *s 67(8)*. The maximum is the aggregate of (*a*) 30 times the maximum week's pay for calculating the basic award in unfair dismissal cases (*ERA 1996, s 227*), and (*b*) the maximum compensatory award in such cases (*ERA 1996, s 124*). These figures are at present £538 and £88,519, respectively, giving a maximum award under *s 67(8)* of £104,659. If the determination has not been revoked, or the union has failed to take all reasonable steps to reverse the determination, the minimum award is the amount for the time being specified in *TULR(C)A 1992, s 176(6A)*, which is at present £10,022. (See also **56.14** UNFAIR DISMISSAL **– III**.)

52.17 DETRIMENT ON GROUNDS OF UNION MEMBERSHIP OR ACTIVITIES

TULR(C)A 1992, s 146 concerns detriment caused by an employer against a worker as an individual:

(a)   to prevent or deter him from, or to penalise him for, belonging to an independent trade union; or

(b)   to prevent him or deter him from taking part in the activities of an independent union at an appropriate time (ie a time outside working hours or a time when the employer has consented to him taking part in union activities), or to penalise him for doing so; or

(c)   to prevent him or deter him from making use of trade union services at an appropriate time, or to penalise him for doing so; or

(d)   to compel him to join any trade union.

The Court of Appeal held in *Bone v North Essex Partnership NHS Foundation Trust* [2014] ICR 1053, [2014] IRLR 635, [2014] 3 All ER 964 that it was not necessary in a claim under *s 146* for the independence of the trade union to be established in order for an employment tribunal to have jurisdiction. Having failed to dispute independence at the employment tribunal, it was too late for the employer to argue that the trade union was not independent at the EAT.

There was previously considerable doubt as to whether omissions could constitute 'action' for those purposes. In *Associated Newspapers Ltd v Wilson; Associated British Ports v Palmer* [1995] ICR 406, [1995] IRLR 258, [1995] 2 All ER 100, a majority of the House of Lords held that withholding a salary increase from employees who refused to sign personal contracts and give up collectively bargained terms and conditions did not amount to a breach of *s 146*.

However, the *ERA 1999, Sch 2* had the effect of reversing this aspect of the House of Lords' decision in *Wilson/Palmer* with effect from 25 October 1999. In particular, *TULR(C)A 1992, s 146(1)* now prohibits subjecting an individual to a detriment by any act, or any deliberate failure to act, by the employer on grounds of trade union membership or activities.

Wilson/Palmer subsequently went to the European Court of Human Rights in *Wilson and National Union of Journalists v United Kingdom* (Applications 30668/96, 30679/61 and 30678/96) [2002] IRLR 568. The Court held that, by permitting employers to use financial incentives to induce employees to surrender the right to union representation (as opposed to deterring union membership altogether), the United Kingdom had failed in its positive duty to secure the enjoyment of the right to freedom of association under *art 11* of the *European Convention on Human Rights*. In response to that decision, *s 29* of the *Employment Rights Act 2004* inserted new *ss 145A–145F* into *TULR(C)A 1992* which from 1 October 2004 conferred upon workers a right not to have an offer made to them by their employer for the sole or main purpose of inducing the worker:

(a)   not to be or seek to become a member of a trade union;

(b)   not to take part, at an appropriate time, in trade union activities;

(c)   not to make use, at an appropriate time, of trade union services; or

(d)   to be or become a member of a trade union (*s 145A*).

In addition, a worker who is a member of an independent trade union which is recognised, or is seeking to be recognised, by his employer, has the right not to have an offer made to him by his employer if:

(a)   acceptance of that offer, together with other workers' acceptance of similar offers, would result in the workers' terms and conditions no longer being determined by collective bargaining with the union; and

(b)   the employer's sole or main purpose in making the offers is to achieve that result (*s 145B*).

In *Davies v Asda Stores Ltd* (IDS Brief 801) an employment tribunal held that the employer had breached *s 145B* of *TULR(C)A 1992* by offering new terms and conditions to union members provided they relinquished collective bargaining. The 340 members were each awarded £2,500. In *Kostal UK Ltd v Dunkley* [2019] IRLR 817 the Court of Appeal held that *s 145B* did not apply where an employer made an offer which was only likely to be a "one off" exception to otherwise continuing collective bargaining arrangements.

In *Department of Transport v Gallacher* [1994] ICR 967, [1994] IRLR 231, the Court of Appeal held that an employer's advice that an employee's prospects of promotion would be improved if he returned to a line management position, instead of engaging in full-time trade union duties, was not given for the purpose of deterring the employee from taking part in union activities within the meaning of *TULR(C)A 1992, s 146*. The relevant purpose is the object which the employer desires or seeks to achieve – in *Gallacher*, his purpose was to assist the employee in obtaining promotion.

In *FW Farnsworth Ltd v McCoid* [1998] IRLR 362, it was held that the derecognition of a shop steward by an employer could amount to action taken against the shop steward as an individual for the purpose of preventing or deterring him from taking part in trade union activities or penalising him for doing so within the meaning of *TULR(C)A 1992, s 146*.

In *Morris v Metrolink Ratp Dev Ltd* [2019] ICR 90 the Court of Appeal held that the scope of "trade union activities" was wide enough to include conduct which was ill-judged or unreasonable. In that case, a union representative was given a copy of a diary belonging to a manager which made adverse comments on the performance of certain trade union members. He passed it on to HR. The fact that this might have been a departure from good industrial relations practice did not prevent it amounting to a protected trade union activity (in that case, for the purposes of a claim of automatically unfair dismissal).

A worker also has the right not to be subjected to a detriment in order to require him to make payments in lieu of union subscriptions when he is not (or is no longer) a union member (*TULR(C)A 1992, s 146(3)*). In addition, *ERA 1999, Sch 1* introduced a new right not to be subjected to a detriment on union recognition-related grounds (see **51.37 Trade Unions – I**).

See also **55.3 Unfair Dismissal – II**.

52.18   The remedy

The employee may make a complaint to an employment tribunal within three months of the action complained of, or within such further period as the tribunal considers reasonable in a case where it is satisfied that it was not reasonably practicable for the complaint to be presented within three months (see **19.20 Employment Tribunals – I**) (*TULR(C)A 1992, ss 146(5), 147*).

It is for the employer to show the purpose for which action was taken against the employee (*TULR(C)A 1992, s 148(1)*). However, notwithstanding this statutory language, the tribunal should not apply the approach to the burden of proof applicable in discrimination cases: see *Serco Ltd v Dahou* [2015] IRLR 30. If the tribunal finds the complaint well-founded, it will make a declaration to that effect and may order compensation to be paid. The compensation will be such amount as it considers just and equitable in all the circumstances, having regard to the right infringed and any loss sustained by the complainant. Compensation may be reduced on account of the applicant's contributory fault (*TULR(C)A 1992, s 149*). It would appear that compensation for an action short of dismissal may include an award in respect of injury to feelings (*Cleveland Ambulance NHS Trust v Blane* [1997] ICR 851, [1997] IRLR 332). In *Adams v Hackney London Borough Council* [2003] IRLR 402 the EAT held that in principle awards for injury to feelings should not be approached any differently in cases of discrimination on trade union grounds than in other cases of discrimination. However, the level of award will depend on the individual applicant. Some may feel deeply hurt by trade union discrimination, whilst other more robust characters may suffer little, if any, distress. Since the aim is to compensate and not to punish, the compensation ought not to be the same in each case.

Joinder of third parties. Where the employer was induced to take the action complained of by industrial action or threat of such action, although no account is to be taken by the tribunal of such pressure when deciding the complaint, the union (or unions) may be joined as a third party to the proceedings and may be ordered to pay all or part of the compensation as the tribunal considers just in the circumstances (*TULR(C)A 1992, ss 148(2), 150*).

52.19 PROHIBITION ON UNION MEMBERSHIP AND UNION RECOGNITION REQUIREMENTS IN CONTRACTS FOR GOODS OR SERVICES

Any term or condition of a contract for the supply of goods or services is void insofar as it purports:

(a)   to require that the whole, or some part, of the work done for the purposes of the contract is to be done only by persons who are or who are not members of trade unions or of a particular trade union (*TULR(C)A 1992, s 144*);

(b)   to require any party to the contract to recognise one or more trade unions (whether or not named in the contract) for the purpose of negotiating on behalf of workers, or any class of worker, employed by him or to negotiate or consult with, or with any official of, one or more trade unions (whether or not so named) (*TULR(C)A 1992, s 186*).

(For the prohibition of industrial action to impose union membership or recognition requirements, see **46.7 Strikes and Industrial Action.**)

Further, it is unlawful for a person to refuse to deal with a supplier or prospective supplier of goods or services on union membership grounds (*TULR(C)A 1992, s 145(1)*). Refusing to deal with a person means excluding that person's name from a list of approved suppliers or of persons from whom tenders may be or are invited, or if he fails to permit that person to submit a tender, decides not to enter into a contract with that person, or terminates an existing contract (*TULR(C)A 1992, s 145(2), (3), (4)*). Such a refusal is on union membership grounds if the ground or one of the grounds for it is that work done for the purposes of any contract would be done, or would be likely to be done, by persons who were or were not members of a trade union or of a particular union (*TULR(C)A 1992, s 145(2)*).

It is also unlawful to refuse to deal with such a person on the ground that he does not, or is not likely to, recognise one or more trade unions for negotiating purposes or negotiate or consult with one or more trade unions or their officials (*TULR(C)A 1992, s 187*).

In the case of an unlawful refusal to deal, an action for breach of statutory duty may be brought by the person with whom the defendant has refused to deal or by any other person adversely affected (*TULR(C)A 1992, ss 145(5), 187(3)*).

52.20 DEDUCTION OR SUBSCRIPTIONS: THE 'CHECK-OFF'

The following provisions are to be found in *TULR(C)A 1992, ss 68 and 68A* as amended by the *Deregulation (Deduction from Pay of Union Subscriptions) Order 1998 (SI 1998/1529)*.

Where arrangements exist between an employer and a union relating to the making of deductions from wages in respect of union subscriptions (commonly known as the 'check-off'), the employer must ensure that deductions are only made in accordance with an authorisation signed and dated by the worker concerned (*TULR(C)A 1992, s 68(1), (2)*). A worker has the same meaning as in *Part II* of the *Employment Rights Act 1996* (see Pay – I (35)), and is thus not confined to employees in the strict sense (*TULR(C)A 1992, s 68(4)*). If the worker subsequently withdraws the authorisation in writing, the employer must cease to make deductions as soon as is reasonably practicable (*TULR(C)A 1992, s 68(2)*).

In *Cavanagh v Secretary of State for Work & Pension* [2016] ICR 826, [2016] IRLR 591 the High Court held that employees within a government department had gained a contractual right to have their union subscriptions deducted through the 'check-off' by virtue of the clear and specific provisions to that effect in the civil service code.

The signing of an authorisation does not oblige the employer to maintain or continue to maintain the arrangements for making deductions (*TULR(C)A 1992, s 68(3)*).

If the employer makes a deduction in contravention of these provisions, the worker may present a complaint to an employment tribunal within the period of three months beginning with the date of payment of the wages from which the deduction (or the last deduction, if the complaint relates to more than one) was made (*TULR(C)A 1992, s 68A(1)*). If the tribunal is satisfied that it was not reasonably practicable for the complaint to be presented within that period, it may extend time for such further period as it considers reasonable.

Where the tribunal finds a complaint well-founded, it will make a declaration to that effect, and will order the employer to repay the amount improperly deducted and not already repaid (*TULR(C)A 1992, s 68A(2)*). Provision is made to avoid double recovery where the same deduction also contravenes other statutory provisions (*TULR(C)A 1992, s 68A(3)*). It is not clear whether, if the sums deducted had already been paid by the employer to the union, the employer would be able to recover them from the union in a common law claim for restitution.

Prior to 23 June 1998, the 'check-off' provisions further required that the worker's authorisations must have been signed within the last three years. They also required that an increased subscription could only be deducted if the employer had given the worker at least one month's written notice. These requirements were removed by the *Deregulation (Deduction from Pay of Union Subscriptions) Order 1998 (SI 1998/1529)* made under the *Deregulation and Contracting Out Act 1994*.

The repealed requirements continue to apply to authorisations given before 23 June 1998 (*reg 3(1)*). However, by *reg 3(2), (3)*, an employer may give a worker notice in a form prescribed in the *Schedule* to the *Regulations* that such an authorisation is to be treated as having been given under the new provisions (and so will be treated as of unlimited duration until withdrawal, and as not requiring advance notice of any increase in the amount deducted). Provided the worker does not object by written notice within 14 days, the new provisions will apply.

With effect from 1 March 2017, additional restrictions have been imposed on the use of the 'check-off' in the public sector, by virtue of *s 15* of the *Trade Union Act 2016*. In particular, deductions from a worker's wages in respect of union subscriptions may be made only if the workers have been given the option to pay by other means, and only if the arrangements have been made for the union to make reasonable payments to the employer in respect of making the deductions. An employer is a relevant public sector employer if specified as such in regulations made by a Minister of the Crown (*TULR(C)A 1992, s 116B*).

52.21 THE RIGHT TO BE ACCOMPANIED

A new right to be accompanied by a trade union official (or a fellow employee) was introduced by *s 10* of the *Employment Relations Act 1999*. Any worker who is required or invited to attend a disciplinary or grievance hearing by his employer is now entitled to be accompanied either by a trade union official (as defined in *TULR(C)A 1992, ss 1, 119*) or fellow worker of his choice. The employer must permit the companion to put the worker's case, respond to any views expressed and confer with the worker during the hearing. However, the employer is not required to permit the companion to answer questions on the worker's behalf (*ERA 1999, s 10(2B), (2C)*). If the worker's chosen companion is not available at the time of the hearing, and the worker proposes a reasonable alternative time within the subsequent period of five working days, the employer must postpone the hearing to the time proposed (*ERA 1999, s 10(4), (5)*). The employer must also give the worker's companion time off for the purpose of accompanying the worker to the meeting (*ERA 1999, s 10(6)*). Guidance on the application of this right is given in the ACAS Code of Practice on Disciplinary and Grievance Procedures (2009).

A 'disciplinary hearing' is defined for these purposes so as to include a hearing which could result in a formal warning (*ERA 1999, s 13(4)*). For these purposes, the test of whether a warning is 'formal' is one of substance. If the warning will become part of the worker's disciplinary record, then the right to be accompanied applies (*Ferenc-Batchelor v London Underground Ltd* [2003] ICR 656, [2003] IRLR 252). However, the right is confined to disciplinary or grievance matters. It therefore did not apply to a meeting which led to an employee's dismissal on grounds of redundancy: see *Heathmill Multimedia ASP Ltd v Jones* [2003] IRLR 856. The EAT held in *Skiggs v South West Trains Ltd* [2005] IRLR 459 that an investigative interview regarding a grievance raised by another employee against the claimant was not a disciplinary hearing at which the claimant had a right to be accompanied.

This statutory right does not require a union to provide representation to an employee. However, a member may have a contractual right to representation deriving from the union rule-book. In *English v UNISON* (2000) IDS Brief 668, the county court held that a qualified right to representation arose as a matter of contract from the union's guide to disciplinary hearings.

A worker denied the right to be accompanied may complain to the employment tribunal within three months of the employer's failure (or such further period as is considered reasonable where it was not reasonably practicable to present the complaint within three months) (*ERA 1999, s 11(1), (2)*). Where a complaint is upheld, the tribunal may make an award of up to two weeks' pay, subject to the statutory maximum contained in *ERA 1996, s 227(1)*, currently £538. In addition, a worker has a right not to be subjected to a detriment or dismissed for seeking to exercise the right to be accompanied. Dismissal on this ground will be automatically unfair (*ERA 1999, s 12*).

52.22   ADVICE BY TRADE UNIONS TO MEMBERS

The scope of a trade union's duty of care towards its members in giving advice was considered by the High Court in *Friend v Institution of Professional Managers and Specialists* [1999] IRLR 173. It was held that a trade union advising or acting for a member in an employment dispute owed the member a duty of care in tort to use ordinary skill and care. However, once solicitors had been engaged on the member's behalf, any duty there might previously have been on the union to advise on the dispute came to an end.

The Court of Appeal held in *Unite the Union v Nailard* [2018] EWCA Civ 1203, [2019] ICR 28 that a union could be liable as principal under the *Equality Act 2010* for acts of sexual harassment of a member carried out by two elected branch officials.

53 Transfer of Undertakings

53.1   Far-reaching rules for the protection of employees' rights on the transfer of an undertaking are contained in the *Transfer of Undertakings (Protection of Employment) Regulations 2006 (SI 2006/246)* ('the *Regulations*'). These came into force on 6 April 2006. They replace entirely the previous legislation, the *Transfer of Undertakings (Protection of Employment) Regulations 1981 (SI 1981/1794)* as amended by the *Transfer of Undertakings (Protection of Employment) (Amendment) Regulations 1987 (SI 1987/442)*, by the *Trade Union Reform and Employment Rights Act 1993*, by the *Collective Redundancies and Transfer of Undertakings (Protection of Employment) (Amendment) Regulations 1995 (SI 1995/2587)* and by the *Collective Redundancies and Transfer of Undertakings (Protection of Employment) (Amendment) Regulations 1999 (SI 1999/1925.)* With effect from 31 January 2014 the *Regulations* were amended by the *Collective Redundancies and Transfer of Undertakings (Protection of Employment) (Amendment) Regulations 2014 (SI 2014/16)*.

The purpose of the original 1981 Regulations was to fulfil the United Kingdom's obligations under European Community law to give effect to *EC Council Directive 77/187*, generally known as the *Acquired Rights Directive*. A new *Directive* was adopted on 29 June 1998 which amends *Directive 77/187* by wholly replacing the texts of *arts 1–7*. Member states had three years within which to bring into force measures which implement the amended *Directive*. See *Official Journal, 17 July 1998 (L201/88)*. The provisions of the original and the amending *Directive* have been consolidated in a further *Directive* adopted on 12 March 2001: *Directive 2001/23/EC*, Official Journal, 22 March 2001 (L82/16). It was the need to transpose the new provisions into UK law which prompted the introduction of the *Regulations*. However, the *Regulations* go further than is required by European law and introduce an additional concept, that of 'a service provision change'. That they go further than European law is emphasised by the fact that the *Regulations* are made not only under *s 2(2)* of the *European Communities Act 1972* but also under *s 38* of the *Employment Relations Act 1999*, which empowered the Secretary of State to make regulations in circumstances other than those to which the Community obligation applies. In addition, the *Regulations* seek to clarify the meaning of certain terms by incorporating concepts developed by the courts.

Historically, English courts and tribunals have so far as possible construed the *Regulations* consistently with the *Directive*, even to the extent of reading in additional words (see **53.10** below, and **24.2** EUROPEAN UNION LAW). However, when considering the meaning of a service provision change, they may not feel obliged so to do, although the concepts of 'service provision change' and 'transfer of an undertaking' are not mutually exclusive.

References below are to provisions of the *Regulations* unless stated otherwise.

53.2   Where there is a 'relevant transfer', that is either where there is a 'service provision change' (see **53.3** below) from person *A* to person *B*, or where an 'undertaking' (see **53.4** below) is 'transferred' (see **53.5** below) from person *A* to person *B*:

(a)   individuals who are employed by *A* 'immediately before the transfer' (see **53.14** and **53.12** below) automatically become the employees of *B* from the time of the transfer, on the terms and conditions they previously held with *A* (see **53.13** below);

(b)   *B* inherits *A's* rights and liabilities in relation to those individuals (see **53.18** below);

(c)   collective agreements, made by or on behalf of *A* with a trade union recognised by *A*, are inherited by *B* (see **53.20** below);

(d)   where *A* recognises a union in respect of employees in the undertaking to be transferred and, following the transfer, the undertaking transferred maintains an identity distinct from any other undertaking owned by *B*, *B* must recognise the union in respect of those employees (see **53.21** below);

(e)   *A* must inform recognised trade unions or employee representatives about the consequences of the transfer, and *B* must provide *A* with sufficient information in this regard (see **53.22** below);

(f)   in certain circumstances, it may be necessary for *A* or *B* to consult with recognised trade unions or elected employee representatives concerning the transfer (see **53.23** below); and

(g)   dismissal of any employee (whether before or after the transfer) where the reason for dismissal is the transfer is automatically unfair unless the reason is 'an economic, technical or organisational reason entailing changes in the workforce' in which case the dismissal is for a fair reason and the question is whether it is fair in all the circumstances, applying the normal principles of unfair dismissal (see **53.24** below).

53.3   WHAT IS A 'RELEVANT TRANSFER'?

Service provision change

There are three situations which may amount to a service provision change (*reg 3(1)(b)*):

(a)   Activities cease to be carried out by a person ('a client') on his own behalf and are carried out instead by another person on the client's behalf ('a contractor'). This situation is sometimes referred to as contracting out or outsourcing.

(b)   Activities cease to be carried out by a contractor on a client's behalf (whether or not those activities had previously been carried out by the client on his own behalf) and are carried out instead by another person ('a subsequent contractor') on the client's behalf. This situation is sometimes referred to as reassigning.

(c)   Activities cease to be carried out by a contractor or a subsequent contractor on a client's behalf (whether or not those activities had previously been carried out by the client on his own behalf) and are carried out instead by the client on his own behalf. This situation is sometimes referred to as contracting in or insourcing.

In any of these three situations there will be a relevant transfer if immediately before the service provision change:

(a)   There is an organised grouping of employees situated in Great Britain which has as its principal purpose the carrying out of the activities concerned on behalf of the client; and

(b)   The client intends that the activities will, following the service provision change, be carried out by the transferee other than in connection with a single specific event or task of short-term duration (*reg 3(3)(a)*). The focus here is on the intention of the client, rather than on that of the transferee: *SNR Denton UK LLP v Kirwan* [2013] ICR 101, [2012] IRLR 966. It is possible for "client" to refer to a group of clients, and for there to be more than one contract, provided that there is some common intent between the members of that group with regard to the provision of the service in question: *Ottimo Property Services Ltd v Duncan* [2015] ICR 859, [2015] IRLR 806. There are conflicting views on whether activities are excluded if they relate to either a single specific event or task of short-term duration or whether they must relate to both: see *SNR Denton* and *Liddell's Coaches v Cook* [2013] ICR 547. In *Swanbridge Hire & Sales Ltd v Butler* (UKEAT/0056/13) the EAT preferred the approach in *SNR Denton*. The event or task must be intended to be of short-term duration: it is not enough that this was the client's hope (*Robert Sage Ltd v O'Connell* [2014] IRLR 428). The question is one of fact almost invariably requiring the tribunal to draw an inference from all the relevant surrounding circumstances, including both contemporaneous events and subsequent matters which might throw light on the relevant party's intention at the relevant date: *ICTS UK Ltd v Mahdi* [2016] ICR 274, [2016] IRLR 113.

The activities before and after the transfer must be fundamentally the same (*reg 3(2A)* and see *QLog Ltd v O'Brien* UKEAT/0301/13 [2014] All ER (D) 303 (Mar)).

However, a service provision change will not be a relevant transfer if the activities concerned consist wholly or mainly of the supply of goods for the client's use (*reg 3(3)(b)*). The application of this exception is essentially one of fact: the supply of sandwiches and drinks to a client's canteen for sale to its staff would fall within the exception, but if the supplier also provided the canteen staff to dispense the goods, then this might not fall within the exception: *Pannu v Geo W King Ltd* [2012] IRLR 193.

There is no service provision change where there is a change of both contractor and of client; the activities carried out by different contractors before and after the transfer must be carried out for the same client: *Hunter v McCarrick* [2012] EWCA Civ 1399, [2013] ICR 235, [2013] IRLR 26. For these purposes, client means an organisation that is in a position to carry out activities either itself or by commissioning them from others to carry out those activities on its behalf: *CT Plus (Yorkshire) CIC v Black* UKEAT/0035/16 [2016] All ER (D) 35 (Sep). In deciding whether there is a single client for these purposes, it may be relevant that "contractor" is defined to include a "sub-contractor": see *Jinks v London Borough of Havering* UKEAT/0157/14 [2015] All ER (D) 352 (Feb); cf *Horizon Security Services Ltd v Ndeze* [2014] IRLR 854.

The requirement for an organised grouping of employees involves consideration of four steps. The first is to identify the service which the putative transferor was providing to the client. The next is to list the activities which the staff of that company performed in order to provide that service. The term "activities" should be given its ordinary, everyday meaning, defined in a common sense and pragmatic way without excess generality (*Arch Initiatives v Greater Manchester West Mental Health NHS Foundation Trust* [2016] ICR 607, [2016] IRLR 406 as approved in *Salvation Army Trustee Co v Bahi* [2017] IRLR 410). The third is to identify the employee or employees of that company who ordinarily carried on those activities. The fourth is to consider whether that company organised that employee or those employees into a 'grouping' for the principal purpose of carrying out the listed activities. See *Rynda (UK) Ltd v Rhijnsburger* [2015] EWCA Civ 75, [2015] ICR 1300, [2015] IRLR 394. These principles were drawn from the following earlier EAT authorities. The requirement for an organised grouping of employees connotes that the employees be organised in some sense by reference to the requirements of the client in question, a deliberate putting together of a group of employees for the purpose of the relevant client work: *Seawell Ltd v Ceva Freight (UK) Ltd* [2012] IRLR 802). The client work need not be the sole purpose, provided it is the principal purpose: *Argyll Coastal Services Ltd v Stirling* (UKEATS/0012/11, 15 February 2012). There is no such grouping where a group of employees happen to work mostly on tasks for a particular client only from a combination of circumstances such as shift patterns and working practices, where there was no deliberate planning or intent: *Eddie Stobart Ltd v Moreman* [2012] ICR 919, [2012] IRLR 356. A director involved in a mainly strategic role and spending little time on actual service delivery may not be part of an organised grouping: *Edinburgh Home-Link Partnership v The City of Edinburgh Council* (UKEATS/0061/11, 10 July 2012). Whilst there may be more than one purpose, the carrying out of the activities in question has to be the principal purpose of the grouping, whether or not it is in fact carrying them out at any particular time; on the other hand, the activities undertaken may change to such an extent that the principal purpose of the grouping has changed by the date of the transfer (*Tees, Esk & Wear Valleys NHS Foundation Trust v Harland* [2017] ICR 760).

The EAT has considered the question of service provision change in three cases in particular: *Kimberley Group Housing Ltd v Hambley* [2008] ICR 1030, [2008] IRLR 682; *Churchill Dulwich Ltd (in liq) v Metropolitan Resources Ltd* [2009] ICR 1380, [2009] IRLR 700; and *OCS Group Ltd v Jones* (UKEAT/0038/09) [2009] All ER (D) 138 (Sep). From these cases, the following principles can be drawn:

(a)   Service provision change is a wholly new statutory concept. The circumstances in which one is established are comprehensively and clearly set out in *reg 3(1)(b)* itself and *reg 3(3)*. The new provisions appear straightforward and their application to an individual case is essentially a question of fact.

(b)   There is no need to adopt a purposive construction as opposed to a straightforward and common sense application of the relevant statutory words. See also *Hunter v McCarrick* [2012] EWCA Civ 1399, [2013] ICR 235, [2013] IRLR 26.

(c)   Under *reg 3(1)(b)*, the first question for the Tribunal is to identify the relevant activity or activities, since only then can one consider whether those activities cease to be carried on by the contractor on a client's behalf and are carried out instead by another person on the client's behalf. See further *SNR Denton UK LLP v Kirwan* [2013] ICR 101, [2012] IRLR 966.

(d)   The conditions in *reg 3(3)* cannot be considered until a decision is made as to whether or not there is a service provision change falling within *reg 3(1)(b)*.

(e)   Whether the activities carried out by the putative transferee are fundamentally or essentially the same as those carried out by the putative transferor is a question of fact and degree. Some minor differences between the nature of the tasks carried on after what is said to have been a service provision change as compared with before it, or in the way in which they are performed as compared with the nature or mode of performance of those tasks in the hands of the alleged transferor, does not mean that there is no service provision change. Further, a substantial change in the amount of the particular activity required by the client could show that the post-transfer activity was not the same as it was pre-transfer: *Department for Education v Huke* (UKEAT/0080/12) [2012] All ER (D) 61 (Nov). The focus for this purpose is the work done on the ground, not the work which might be done under the contract (*Lorne Stewart plc v Hyde* (UKEAT/0408/12)).

(f)   It is possible for a transferor to transfer the provision of a service to more than one transferee. It is also possible for some activities carried out by the putative transferor to be transferred, whilst others are not: *Arch Initiatives v Greater Manchester West Mental Health NHS Foundation Trust* [2016] ICR 607, [2016] IRLR 406.

(g)   However, there may be some circumstances in which a service which is being provided by one contractor to a client is in the event so fragmented that nothing which one can properly determine as being a service provision change has taken place.

(h)   In considering whether an employee is assigned to the part of the provision of the service transferred to a particular transferee, the tribunal applies the same approach as to a transfer under *reg 3(1)(a)*.

In *Ankers v Clearsprings Management Ltd* [2009] All ER (D) 261 (Feb) the tribunal found that there was no discernible pattern in the transfer of accommodation services to asylum seekers from one service provider to another. The EAT determined that where the service provided is so fragmented, a tribunal may be entitled to find that no relevant transfer took place. The EAT subsequently rejected a tribunal's finding that there was no service provision change based upon a combination of 'fragmentation' and a finding that 15% of the work done by the original contractor would not be required by the new contractor and so the "activities" undertaken before and after the contract would not be essentially or fundamentally the same: *Enterprise Management Services Ltd v Connect–Up Ltd* [2012] IRLR 190.

In *Ward Hadaway Solicitors v Love* (UKEAT/0471/09) [2010] All ER (D) 250 (May) the EAT refused to interfere with a tribunal's judgment that there was no service provision change following a competitive tender for future solicitors' regulatory services in circumstances in which none of the work in progress was handed over and no employee transferred. Similarly, in *Johnson Controls Ltd v Campbell* (UKEAT/0041/12) [2012] All ER (D) 220 (May) the EAT refused to interfere with a tribunal's judgment that there was no service provision change where a client ceased to use a centralised taxi administration service, but instead arranged for its secretaries to book taxis with taxi firms directly, since the activity undertaken by the contractor was not continued by the client.

Where there is a service provision change which is a relevant transfer, 'the transferor' means the person who carried out the activities prior to the service provision change and 'the transferee' means the person who carries out the activities as a result of the service provision change (*reg 2(1)*).

53.4   Transfer of an undertaking or business

Undertaking or business

The *Regulations* apply to the transfer of an undertaking or of a business situated immediately before the transfer in the United Kingdom.

The *Regulations* also cover the transfer of part of an undertaking or business. A 'part' of an 'undertaking' means a unit which is to some extent separate and self-contained from the remainder of the enterprise such as an operating division which is autonomous from the remainder of the business by virtue, for example, of having its own accounts, management structure, and product specialisation. However, the *Regulations* may apply even where the part does not retain its organisational autonomy, provided that the functional link between the various elements of production transferred is preserved and that functional link enables the transferee to use those elements to pursue an identical or analogous economic activity: see *Klarenberg v Ferrotron Technologies GmbH*: C-466/07 [2009] ICR 1263, [2009] IRLR 301.

In *Fairhurst Ward Abbotts Ltd v Botes Building Ltd* [2004] EWCA Civ 83, [2004] ICR 919, [2004] IRLR 304 the Court of Appeal ruled that, provided that there is an identifiable stable economic entity before the transfer takes place, the law does not require that the particular part transferred should itself, before the date of the transfer, exist as a discrete and identifiable economic entity: it is sufficient if a part of the larger entity becomes identified for the first time as a separate economic entity on the occasion of the transfer separating a part from the whole. This approach was applied in *Transport & General Workers Union v Swissport (UK) Ltd (in administration)* [2007] ICR 1593, [2007] All ER (D) 329 (Jun).

'Undertaking' would appear to include a professional practice, such as that of an NHS doctor (see *Jeetle v Elster* [1985] ICR 389, [1985] IRLR 227), the activities of a charitable foundation (*Redmond (Dr Sophie) Stichting v Bartol*: C-29/91 [1992] ECR I-3189, [1992] IRLR 366), and the carrying out of an activity pursuant to a contract (see **53.5** below). An undertaking which is carried out on a non-profit making basis but is contracted out to be carried out on a commercial basis may still transfer where all the other characteristics of the activity remained the same before and after the alleged transfer: *Alderson v Secretary of State for Trade and Industry* [2003] EWCA Civ 1767, [2004] ICR 512, [2004] 1 All ER 1148.

However, an economic entity is not defined only by the employment status of a group of employees, but also by the function which that group undertakes: *Wynnwith Engineering Co Ltd v Bennett* [2002] IRLR 170. In *Wain v Guernsey Ship Management Ltd* [2007] EWCA Civ 294, [2007] ICR 1350, [2007] All ER (D) 35 (Apr) the Court of Appeal rejected the contention that a group of short-term contract employees comprised an economic entity.

53.5   *Transfer*

A relevant transfer occurs where there is a transfer of an economic identity which retains its identity (*reg 3(1)(a)*).

Thus, in deciding whether there has been a transfer of an undertaking, the critical question is whether the undertaking retains its identity and is carried on by the transferee. In answering that question, all the factual circumstances must be considered, but particular factors include: the type of undertaking or business concerned; whether tangible assets such as buildings and moveable property are transferred; the value of intangible assets at the time of the transfer; whether the majority of employees are taken over by the new employer; whether customers are transferred; the degree of similarity between the activities carried on before and after the alleged transfer; and the period, if any, for which those activities are suspended (*Spijkers v Gebroeders Benedik Abbatoir CV*: 24/85 [1986] 2 CMLR 296; *Redmond (Dr Sophie) Stichting v Bartol*: C-29/91 [1992] ECR I-3189, [1992] IRLR 366; *Rask and Christensen v ISS Kantineservice A/S*: C-209/91 [1993] IRLR 133, ECJ).

The ECJ has considered the application of this test in a number of cases involving the contracting out of services and changes of contractors. The importance within the UK of this line of authority is likely to be limited in the future since such cases are likely to constitute service provision changes, whether or not there is a transfer of an undertaking.

In *Schmidt v Spar und Leihkasse der Früheren Ämter Bordersholm, Kiel und Cronshagen*: C-392/92 [1995] ICR 237, [1994] IRLR 302 it was held that there could be a transfer of contracted-out cleaning services, even where the services are performed by a single employee and there is no transfer of tangible assets; and *Merckx v Ford Motors Co Belgium SA*: C-171/94 and C-172/94 [1996] IRLR 467. The ECJ held in *Ledernes Hovedorganisation (acting for Rygard) v Dansk Arbejdsgiverforening (acting for Sto Molle Akustik A/S)*: C-48/94 [1995] ECR I-2745, [1996] ICR 333, [1996] IRLR 51, however, that the transfer of an undertaking must involve the transfer of a 'stable economic entity' and went on to hold in *Süzen v Zehnacker Gebäudereingung GmbH Krankenhausservice*: C- 13/95 [1997] ICR 662, [1997] IRLR 255 that an activity does not, in itself, constitute such an entity. It follows, the ECJ stated, that the mere fact that a similar activity is carried on before and after a change of contractors does not mean there is a transfer of an undertaking. In the case of a labour-intensive undertaking with no significant assets (eg contract cleaning), there will generally be no transfer unless the new contractor takes on a majority of the old contractor's staff. This approach was reinforced in *Vidal (Francisco Hernandez) SA v Gomez Perez*: C-127/96, C-229/96 and C-74/97 [1999] IRLR 132, ECJ and in *Sánchez Hidalgo v Asociación de Servicios Aser*: C-173/96 [2002] ICR 73, [1999] IRLR 136. The ECJ again emphasised the requirement for a stable economic entity, adding that 'an organised group of wage earners who are specifically and permanently assigned to a common task may, in the absence of other factors of production, amount to an economic entity'. Examples of the application of this approach include *Oy Liikenne Ab v Liskojarvi*: C-172/99 [2002] ICR 155, [2001] IRLR 171 (the absence of a transfer of assets conclusive where the activity required substantial tangible assets) and *Jouini v Princess Personal Service GmbH*: C-458/05 [2008] ICR 128, [2007] IRLR 1005 (the possibility of a transfer of a part of a temporary employment agency). However, there was something of a gloss on the *Liskijarvi* approach in *Grafe and Pohle v Südbrandenburger Nahverkehrs GmbH*: C-298/18 [2020] IRLR 399, in which the Court ruled that the refusal of the new contractor to take on tangible assets does not automatically mean that there cannot be a transfer of assets. On the facts, it was relevant that the reason the buses were not transferred was that new environmental restrictions did not allow buses of a certain age to be used (and so it was relevant to take into account the fact that the service involved the same routes and the re-hiring of the majority of employees). The weight to be placed on each factual element would "vary according to the activity carried on and the production or operating methods employed in the undertaking".

Dodič v Banka Koper: C-194/18 [2019] ICR 1352, [2019] IRLR 938 concerned the alleged transfer of investment services. The transfer of the underlying securities was a question for each individual client. However, that fact did not preclude their being a transfer of part of an undertaking. Relevant questions included whether there was an effective choice, the extent of incentives offered, and whether there was a default transfer. Numbers alone might be indicative, but not determinative.

In order to be a 'stable economic entity', the economic entity must have a sufficient degree of functional autonomy, the concept of autonomy referring to the powers granted to those in charge of the group of workers concerned to organise, relatively freely and independently, the work within that group, including to give instructions and allocate tasks to subordinates within the group without direct intervention from other organisational structures of the employer; such autonomy must exist before the transfer (*Amatori v Telecom Italia SpA*: C-458/12 [2014] IRLR 400). The fact that there is a break in the provision of the services that are at the heart of the alleged undertaking is one relevant factor to be taken into account, but the fact that the undertaking was, at the time of the transfer, temporarily closed and as a result had no employees in its service does not preclude the possibility that there has been a transfer of an undertaking: *Sigüenza v Ayuntamiento de Vallodolid* C-472/16 [2018] IRLR 1056, [2018] All ER (D) 75 (Aug).

The importance of the distinction between a labour-intensive undertaking and an asset reliant undertaking was crucial in *Abler v Sodexho MM Catering Betriebsgesellschaft mbH*: C-340/01 [2004] IRLR 168, in which the ECJ found that the catering sector was based essentially on equipment. Thus, where a new contractor took over the use of that equipment then there was a transfer, even though the equipment was in fact owned by neither the transferor nor the transferee but by the party contracting out the activity. The ECJ specifically held that the degree of importance to be attached to each factor will vary according to the activity carried on. (See also *Guney-Gorres v Securicor Aviation (Germany) Ltd*: C-232/04 and C-233/04 [2006] IRLR 305, *ADIF v Aira Pascual*: C-509/14 [2016] IRLR 156 and *Securitas-Serviços e Tecnologia de Segurança SA v ICTS Portugal* C-200/16 [2018] ICR 525, [2017] All ER (D) 168 (Oct).) A further pronouncement, again in relation to the labour-intensive cleaning of premises, was in *CLECE SA v Valor*: C-463/09 [2011] ICR 1319, [2011] IRLR 251. In *Ferreira da Silva v Estado Portugues*: C-160/14 [2015] IRLR 1021 the CJEU emphasised the importance of "the functional link of interdependence and complementarity" of the various elements of production (eg staff and assets) rather than the retention of the specific organisation of those elements.

The Court of Appeal has emphasised that the correct approach is 'multi-factorial': *Balfour Beatty Power Networks Ltd v Wilcox* [2006] EWCA Civ 1240, [2007] IRLR 63. No single aspect need determine the question. All factors must be balanced before a decision is reached. The CA considered that there could be a relevant transfer even in an industry which was asset reliant and where there was no transfer of tangible assets: the ECJ had not, the CA considered, laid down any stark rule to the contrary in *Oy Liikenne*. On the facts, the assets were in any event leased and so they could be better characterised as tools and equipment. The CA also observed that an enterprise may be 'stable' as a matter of practical and industrial reality, even though its long-term future is not assured. A similar, multi-factorial approach had been followed by the EAT in *P & O Trans European Ltd v Initial Transport Service Ltd* [2003] IRLR 128 and in *NUMAST v P&O Scottish Ferries Ltd* [2005] ICR 1270, [2005] All ER (D) 27 (Apr).

A number of cases involving contracting out and changes of contractors have also come before the UK courts, many arising out of local government compulsory competitive tendering. The courts have held in this context that if similar activities are carried on before and after a change of service provider, there can be a transfer of an undertaking notwithstanding that no assets are transferred (*Dines v Initial Health Care Services Ltd* [1995] ICR 11, [1994] IRLR 336) or that neither assets nor staff are transferred (*BSG Property Services v Tuck* [1996] IRLR 134). See also *Kenny v South Manchester College* [1993] IRLR 265, *Isles of Scilly Council v Brintel Helicopters Ltd* [1995] ICR 249, [1995] IRLR 6 and *Kelman v Care Contract Services Ltd* [1995] ICR 260. The reasoning of these cases must now, however, be reconsidered in the light of *Betts v Brintel Helicopters Ltd* [1997] IRLR 361, [1997] 2 All ER 840, in which the Court of Appeal followed *Süzen* (see above) and held that there was no transfer on a change of contractor providing helicopter services to a company, where the new contractor took over no staff, and only a limited part of the old contractor's assets. The court distinguished labour intensive undertakings, where the key factor is whether the majority of employees are taken over by the new employer, and other types of undertaking, where a broader range of factors must be considered.

The Court of Appeal reconsidered the scope of *Süzen* (with express reference to *Sánchez Hidalgo*) in *ECM (Vehicle Delivery Service) v Cox* [1999] IRLR 559, [1999] 4 All ER 669. The court stated that the importance of *Süzen* had been overstated: the ECJ had not overruled its previous interpretive rulings. It is for the national court to make the necessary factual appraisal, considering in particular the factors identified in *Spijkers*. One relevant factor is whether the majority of employees are taken over by the new employer to enable it to carry on the activities of the undertaking on a regular basis. The mere loss of a service contract to a competitor does not of itself indicate the existence of a transfer. This appeal was followed by Lindsay J in *RCO Support Services Ltd v Unison* [2000] ICR 1502, [2000] IRLR 624 and in *Cheesman v R Brewer Contracts Ltd* [2001] IRLR 144.

The Court of Appeal's judgment in *RCO Support Services Ltd v Unison* [2002] EWCA Civ 464, [2002] ICR 751, [2002] IRLR 401 appeared to accept that *Süzen* represented a shift on the previous position, such that a mere similarity in the activities of the entity before and after the transfer cannot be enough to establish a transfer. However, the additional factors required need not amount to a transfer of a majority of the workforce (in terms of numbers and skills) as had been the case in *Süzen*. On the facts of *RCO* a similarity in operating methods and training within the activities was found to be enough, even where the location of the activity had moved.

As to the question of the relevance of an intention of the transferee to avoid the application of TUPE, the Court of Appeal in *RCO* stated that a subjective motive of the putative transferee to avoid the application of TUPE is not the real point. However, in deciding whether or not there is a transfer, it may be relevant to take into account the objective circumstances surrounding a decision not to take on the workforce. It is far from clear how that distinction will be drawn in practice. Some guidance is to be found in the decision in *Astle v Cheshire County Council* [2005] IRLR 12. The EAT held that if a tribunal finds that the reason or principal reason of the transferee was to avoid the application of TUPE then it is a relevant factor to take into account in the *Spijkers* exercise, and may be decisive.

In *RCO* the Court of Appeal made reference to its earlier decision in *ADI (UK) Ltd v Willer* [2001] EWCA Civ 971, [2001] IRLR 542 in which it had recognised that *Süzen* represented something of a retreat by the ECJ from its earlier decisions. In *ADI* it concluded that, in a labour-intensive operation, the absence of a transfer of staff from the outgoing contractor to the incoming contractor should lead to the conclusion that there is no transfer of an undertaking, even though the work, the equipment used, the location and the ultimate customers are the same. However, in such cases, the balance would be tipped the other way if the reason why there was no transfer of staff was that the parties wished to avoid the application of the *Regulations*. If such an intention is established, then there will be deemed to have been a transfer. This ruling substantially supersedes the decisions in *Whitewater Leisure Management Ltd v Barnes* [2000] ICR 1049, [2000] IRLR 456, EAT and *Lightways (Contractors) Ltd v Associated Holdings Ltd* [2000] IRLR 247, Ct of Sess.

In *Rygaard v Stro Molle Akustik* [1996] IRLR 51, the ECJ held that existing authorities presuppose that the transfer relates to a stable economic entity whose activity is not limited to one specific works contract. However, the scope of this ruling was restricted to its facts (ie single contracts for building works) by the EAT in *Argyll Training Ltd v Sinclair* [2000] IRLR 630, in which it stated that there is no basis for automatically excluding all single-contract undertakings from the possibility of being transferred. Indeed, it is possible (though not common) for a single employee to constitute a stable economic entity, provided that the entity can be said to be sufficiently structured and autonomous: *Dudley Bower Building Services Ltd v Lowe* [2003] ICR 843, [2003] IRLR 260.

53.6   Other concepts defining 'relevant transfer'

General

The *Regulations* apply to public and private undertakings engaged in economic activities, whether or not they are operating for gain (*reg 3(4)(a)*).

The *Regulations* apply even if the transfer is governed or effected by foreign law, or if the employees in the undertaking, business or activities work outside the UK or if their employment is governed by foreign law (*reg 3(4)(b)*). The *Regulations* have the potential to apply to a transfer from the UK to a non-EU entity in the event that on the transfer the undertaking did not remain within the jurisdiction: *Holis Metal Industries Ltd v GMB and Newell Ltd* [2008] ICR 464, [2008] IRLR 187, EAT.

In *Allen v Amalgamated Construction Co Ltd*: C-234/98 [1999] ECR I-8643, [2000] ICR 436, [2000] IRLR 119, the ECJ held that the *Acquired Rights Directive* can apply to a transfer between two subsidiary companies in the same group, provided that they are distinct legal persons each with specific employment relationships with their employees. This was so even though the two companies had the same management, were in the same premises, and were engaged in the same works. Where the putative transfer is to a number of group companies which includes the original employer, there is no relevant transfer: *Hyde Housing Association Ltd v Layton* [2016] ICR 261, [2016] IRLR 107.

On the other hand, where an individual is employed by one group company but works on a permanent basis in an undertaking run by another company within the group, the latter company may be the 'transferor' for the purposes of the *Directive*, even though there is no contractual relationship between that company and the individual: *Albron Catering BV v FNV Bondgenoten*: C-242/09 [2011] ICR 373, [2011] IRLR 76.

In *Foreningen af Arbejdsledere i Danmark v Daddy's Dance Hall A/S*: 324/86 [1988] IRLR 315 the European Court of Justice held that there was a relevant transfer where a lessee of restaurant premises gave notice to its employees upon the determination of the lease, and the lessor then granted a new lease to a third party which continued to run the business without any interruption. Where the identity of the economic unit was retained, it did not matter that the transfer took place in two phases. The same result was reached on similar facts in *Litster v Forth Dry Dock and Engineering Co Ltd* [1989] ICR 341, [1989] IRLR 161 and in *P Bork International A/S v Foreningen af Arbejdsledere i Danmark*: 101/87 [1989] IRLR 41 (owner of leased undertaking repossessed it after forfeiture of the lease and then sold it on to a third party who resumed operation of the business). These decisions will be important where businesses are operated on a franchise (see also *LMC Drains Ltd v Waugh* [1991] 3 CMLR 172).

If the agreement pursuant to which the transfer occurred is rescinded, there may be a relevant 'retransfer' back to the original transferor (*Berg and Busschers v Besselsen*: 144/87 and 145/87 [1990] ICR 396, [1989] IRLR 447).

53.7 *More than one transaction*

A relevant transfer may be affected by a series of two or more transactions (*reg 3(6)(a)*). In construing the *1981 Regulations* purposively, it has been held that the court will seek to identify whether there is in truth a single transfer and will look beyond an 'ingenious device' whereby an intermediary company is introduced for the sole purpose of achieving the contracting parties' mutual wish to transfer an undertaking between them which is stripped of liability to the employees (see *Re Maxwell Fleet and Facilities Management Ltd (No 2)* [2000] ICR 717, [2000] IRLR 368). In *Temco Service Industries SA v Imzilyen*: C-51/00 [2002] IRLR 214 the ECJ confirmed that the absence of a contractual link does not in itself prevent the application of the *Directive*; it was enough if the transferor and transferee were part of the web of contractual relations.

53.8 *Transfer of property*

A transfer may take place whether or not any property is transferred to the transferee by the transferor (*reg 3(6)(b)*).

53.9 *Administrative functions carried out by a public body*

'A relevant transfer' does not include an administrative reorganisation of public administrative authorities, or the transfer of administrative functions between public administrative authorities (*reg 3(5)*). This limited exclusion was originally explained by the European Court of Justice in *Henke v Gemeinde Schierke*: C-298/94 [1996] IRLR 701 and was then recognised in *art 1(1)(c)* of *Directive 2001/23*. It was further clarified in two subsequent decisions of the European Court of Justice: *Mayeur v Association Promotion de l'Information Messine*: C-175/99 [2002] ICR 1316, [2000] IRLR 783 (transfer where the work of a non-profit making tourist agency was taken over by the municipality); and *Collino v Telecom Italia SpA*: C-343/98 [2002] ICR 38, [2000] IRLR 788 (transfer on a reorganisation of telephone service providers). In *Viggosdottir v Islandspostur HF* [2002] IRLR 425, the EFTA Court held that the *Directive* could apply to the conversion of a state entity into a wholly state-owned limited liability company, and that it is for the national court to decide whether the individuals fall under the protection of national employment law in accordance with the principles set out by the ECJ in *Collino*. The *Henke* exception was applied by the High Court in *Law Society of England and Wales v Secretary of State for Justice* [2010] EWHC 352 (QB), [2010] IRLR 407, [2010] All ER (D) 10 (Mar) to extend to the Legal Complaints Service on the basis that it was a body which had exercised public authority in that it carried out regulatory and quasi-judicial functions which are subject to judicial review. However, the exception did not apply to auxiliary services within Italian State schools, such as cleaning, caretaking and administrative assistance: *Scattolon v Ministero dell'Istruzione, dell'Università e della Ricerca*: C-108/10 [2012] ICR 740, [2011] IRLR 1020. These cases were comprehensively reviewed by Lavender J in *Nicholls v London Borough of Croydon* UKEAT/0003/18, UKEAT/0004/18, [2018] IRLR 988, [2019] ICR 542, who identified 10 factors to be considered in determining whether the public body is engaged in the exercise of public authority (paragraph 55) and noted that in a 'mixed case', the mere fact that the body carries on some ancillary activities of an economic nature does not prevent it from being engaged in the exercise of public authority (paragraph 68).

53.10 *Share transfers*

The *Regulations* apply only to the transfer of an undertaking from one legal person to another. They do not apply, for example, to the transfer of shares in a company which carries on the undertaking (*Initial Supplies Ltd v McCall* 1992 SLT 67, 1990 SCLR 463). This is so even though this form of transaction was adopted with the purpose of avoiding the *Regulations* (*Brookes v Borough Care Services* [1998] IRLR 636).

In *Millam v Print Factory (London) 1991 Ltd* [2007] EWCA Civ 322, [2007] ICR 1331, [2007] IRLR 526 the Court of Appeal reiterated this principle, but went on to uphold a tribunal's conclusion that the business nevertheless transferred to the acquiring company. The CA also rejected the EAT's analysis that it could pierce the corporate veil. An issue of piercing the corporate veil arises only when it is established that activity X is carried on by company A, but for policy reasons it is sought to show that in reality the activity is the responsibility of the owner of company A, company B; to pierce the corporate veil it must generally be shown that the subsidiary company is a sham or façade. In the present case, the activity was in fact carried on by company B, and so there was a relevant transfer from A to B.

The position was reconsidered in *ICAP Management Services Ltd v Berry* [2017] IRLR 811. The crucial question is whether the "business" in which the individual was employed has been transferred from one company to another. On the facts, the sale by a holding company of shares in the employing business to another holding company had not affected the business within which the individual was employed.

53.11   *Insolvency*

The ECJ held in *Abels v Administrative Board of the Bedrijfsvereniging voor de Metaalindustrie en de Electrotechnische Industrie*: 135/83 [1985] ECR 469 that the *Directive* does not apply to the transfer of an undertaking, business or part of a business in the course of insolvency proceedings. In *Jules Dethier Equipment SA v Dassy*: C-319/94 [1998] ICR 541, [1998] IRLR 266, it ruled that it does apply in the event of the transfer of an undertaking which is being wound up by a court if the undertaking continues to trade. It also applies where the undertaking transferred is being wound up voluntarily (*Europièces SA (in liq) v Sanders*: C-399/96 [1998] ECR I-6965, [1999] All ER (EC) 831, ECJ). The distinction drawn in *Donaldson v Perth & Kinross Council* [2004] ICR 667, [2004] IRLR 121 was between an 'irretrievable insolvency and cessation of business' and 'the sale of the business as a going concern', but this was not followed in *Transport & General Workers Union v Swissport (UK) Ltd (in administration)* [2007] ICR 1593, [2007] All ER (D) 329 (Jun).

Clarification is now given in *reg 8(7)*, which provides that *reg 4* (effect of relevant transfer on contracts of employment) and *reg 7* (dismissal of employee because of relevant transfer) do not apply to any relevant transfer where the transferor is the subject of 'bankruptcy proceedings or any analogous insolvency proceedings which have been instituted with a view to the liquidation of the assets of the transferor and are under the supervision of an insolvency practitioner'. The underlying directive was found not to apply to a pre-pack procedure because it was aimed at ensuring the continuation of the undertaking in question, rather than with a view to the liquidation of assets: *Federatie Nederlandse Vakvereniging v Smallsteps BV* (C-126/16) [2017] ICR 1316, [2017] IRLR 852.

Furthermore, *regs 8(1)* to *(6)* apply to 'relevant insolvency proceedings', that is insolvency proceedings which have been opened in relation to the transferor not with a view to the liquidation of the assets of the transferor and which are under the supervision of an insolvency practitioner. They extend the statutory regimes for payments by the Secretary of State (under chapter VI of *Part XI* and *Part XII* of the *Employment Rights Act 1996*) to transfers in such cases. The relevant debts (those falling within *s 184* of the *Employment Rights Act 1996*) have to arise before the transfer in order to come within that state guarantee: *Pressure Coolers Ltd v Molloy* [2012] ICR 51, [2011] IRLR 630 (applied in *Secretary of State for BIS v Dobrucki* (UKEAT/0505/13)). Sums due as a result of a breach of an equality clause amounted to "arrears of pay" falling within *s 184* but where those sums exceeded the amount of the statutory regime, a transferee was liable for the excess: *Graysons Restaurants Ltd v Jones* [2019] EWCA Civ 725, [2019] ICR 1342, [2019] IRLR 649.

In order to determine whether 'insolvency proceedings' had commenced, it is necessary to identify the particular proceedings and then determine, in accordance with the statutory provisions relating to those proceedings, whether they had commenced or not at the time of the transfer: *Secretary of State for Trade and Industry v Slater* [2008] ICR 54, [2007] IRLR 928. The Court of Appeal has confirmed that the directive requires an 'absolute approach' such that administration proceedings under *Schedule B1* of the *Insolvency Act 1986* can never constitute "insolvency proceedings" within the meaning of *reg 8(7)*: *Key2Law (Surrey) LLP v De'Antiquis* [2011] EWCA Civ 1567, [2012] ICR 881, [2012] IRLR 212.

53.12 Time of the transfer

It may be important to identify the precise time of the transfer, because of the requirement (see **53.13** below) that the employee be employed by his old employer immediately before the transfer. However, following the decision of the House of Lords in *Litster v Forth Dry Dock and Engineering Co Ltd* [1989] ICR 341, [1989] IRLR 161, a gloss is effectively put on that requirement if the employee is dismissed for a because of the transfer, and some of the reported cases would now be decided differently as a result (a principle now enshrined in *reg 4(3);* see **53.14** below).

A number of cases have arisen where, for example, the employee has been dismissed between the exchange of contracts for the sale of the business and the completion date (*Wheeler v Patel* [1987] ICR 631, [1987] IRLR 211), or joined the new employers after they were let into possession under a deed of assignment but before completion (*Brook Lane Finance Co Ltd v Bradley* [1988] ICR 423, [1988] IRLR 283). In these cases it was held that the contract of employment was not automatically continued by virtue of the *Regulations*. In both *Wheeler* and *Brook Lane* the EAT considered that it was bound by the decision of the Court of Appeal in *Secretary of State for Employment v Spence* [1986] ICR 651, [1986] IRLR 248 to hold that a transfer was only capable of taking place at a particular moment, and not over a period of time. However, after the judgment of the House of Lords in *Litster*, the EAT in *Macer v Abafast Ltd* [1990] ICR 234, [1990] IRLR 137 did not follow the approach adopted in *Brook Lane*.

In *Celtec Ltd v Astley* C-478/03 [2005] ICR 1409, [2005] IRLR 647 the ECJ considered a reference from the House of Lords which raised this issue. It recognised that a transfer may take place over a period of time. However, there is a 'date of a transfer' and this must be understood a referring to the date on which responsibility as employer for carrying on the business of the unit in question moves from the transferor to the transferee. The ECJ was clear that the date of the transfer cannot be postponed to another date at the will of either party. This judgment was applied by the House of Lords at [2006] ICR 992, [2006] IRLR 635, [2006] 4 All ER 27. This was applied (and *Wheeler v Patel* distinguished) by the EAT in *Commercial Motors (Wales) Ltd v M Howley* (UKEAT/0491/11) and subsequently in *Housing Maintenance Solutions Ltd v McAteer* [2015] ICR 87, [2014] All ER (D) 02 (Sep).

53.13 THE AUTOMATIC ASSIGNMENT OF CONTRACTS OF EMPLOYMENT AND ASSOCIATED RIGHTS AND LIABILITIES

The most drastic consequences of a transfer of an undertaking are specified in *reg 4*. Those of the transferor's employees:

(i)   who were employed by the transferor immediately before the transfer; and

(ii)   who were assigned to the organised grouping of resources or employees that is subject to the relevant transfer; and

(iii)   whose contracts would otherwise have been terminated by the transfer,

automatically become, from the moment of the transfer, employed by the transferee on the terms and conditions which they enjoyed with the transferor. This is subject only to an employee's right of objection (see **53.16** below); it cannot be prevented by an intention on the part of the transferor and transferee, or agreement between them, to the contrary (*Hertaing v Benoidt*: C-305/94 [1997] IRLR 127), nor by ignorance on the part of the employee of the transfer or identity of the transferee (*Secretary of State for Trade and Industry v Cook* [1997] ICR 288, [1997] IRLR 150) disapproving the decision of the EAT to the contrary in *Photostatic Copiers (Southern) Ltd v Okuda* [1995] IRLR 11). A failure to comply with the duty to provide information (see **50.23** below) cannot of itself lead to the avoidance of a transfer: *Marcroft v Heartland (Midlands) Ltd* [2011] EWCA Civ 438, [2011] IRLR 599. With certain specified exceptions, all the transferor's rights and liabilities connected with their contracts of employment are likewise assigned to the transferee, and anything done by the transferor prior to the transfer in relation to those employees or their contracts is deemed to have been done by the transferee.

Under the *Regulations*, an 'employee' covers an individual who works for another person under a contract of employment or apprenticeship, or otherwise, but does not include an independent contractor (*reg 2(1)*). The words 'or otherwise' in the definition do not exclude the fact that there must be a contract between the individual and the transferor. Thus, the *Regulations* did not apply on the reorganisation of a school by its governing body since the teacher was employed by the local education authority and not the governing body (*Clifton Middle School Governing Body* [2000] ICR 286, [1999] IRLR 708, CA). In *Morris Angel & Son Ltd v Hollande* [1993] ICR 71, [1993] IRLR 169 Dillon LJ queried whether the unique nature of a managing director's position might mean that employment in that capacity was incapable of being transferred, but the correctness of this suggestion is doubted. Significantly, in *Dewhurst v Revisecatch Ltd* (30 October 2019, case number 2201909/2018) an employment tribunal determined that "employees" within the meaning of *reg 2(1)* extended to "workers" under the *Working Time Regulations 1998, reg 2(1)* and the *Employment Rights Act 1996, s 230(3)(b)*.

Reg 2(1) defines "assigned" as "assigned other than on a temporary basis". An individual is not assigned on a temporary basis simply because he is serving notice: *Marcroft v Heartland (Midlands) Ltd* [2011] EWCA Civ 438, [2011] IRLR 599. If an employee is permanently unable to return to work, then he is not assigned at the time of the transfer: *BT Managed Services Ltd v Edwards* [2015] ICR 733, [2015] All ER (D) 201 (Dec).

53.14 Immediately before the transfer

Regulation 4(1) applies to a person employed in an undertaking or part of one transferred, provided that he is so employed immediately before the transfer or would have been so employed if he had not been dismissed in the circumstances described in *reg 7*, that is for a reason which is the transfer itself (*reg 4(3)*). This enshrines the approach adopted by the House of Lords in *Litster v Forth Dry Dock and Engineering Co Ltd* [1989] ICR 341, [1989] IRLR 161, [1989] 1 All ER 1134: if the dismissal in fact took place solely or principally because of the prospective transfer, then the employee would be deemed to have been employed immediately before the transfer. Their Lordships accepted the reasoning of the European Court of Justice in *P Bork International A/S v Foreningen af Arbejdslederen i Danmark*: 101/87 [1989] IRLR 41, namely, that the fact that *Directive 77/187* prohibited dismissal because of a transfer (see **53.25** below) meant that a dismissal in breach of that prohibition could not effectively exclude the operation of the *Regulations*. See also *Macer v Abafast Ltd* [1990] ICR 234, [1990] IRLR 137, where the EAT warned in a similar context that the courts would lean against artificial attempts to break continuity; and *Harrison Bowden Ltd v Bowden* [1994] ICR 186 and *A & G Tuck Ltd v Bartlett* [1994] ICR 379, [1994] IRLR 162. However, contrast *Longden v Ferrari Ltd* [1994] ICR 443, [1994] IRLR 157, where the EAT held that a succession of events over a period of a few weeks, causally connected to one another, were not a series of transactions by which a transfer of the employers' undertaking was 'effected' and that the transfer was effected only by the final act, a single agreement for sale. As a consequence, the employees (dismissed nearly two weeks before the agreement) were not employed 'immediately before the transfer', even though they were dismissed after the agreement had been submitted in draft.

A temporary lay off of workers between contracts may not prevent them being an organised group of employees employed immediately before the transfer; this was a question of fact to be determined by reference to all the facts, including the length of and reason for the cessation: *Inex Home Improvements Ltd v Hodgkins* [2016] ICR 71, considered with approval in *Mustafa v Trek Highways Services Ltd* [2016] IRLR 326.

Regulation 4(3) also deals with cases where there is more than one transaction by which the transfer is effected, and provides that *reg 4* catches any person employed immediately before any of the transactions in question.

Where an employee has been dismissed at the time of the transfer but is subsequently reinstated on appeal, he is deemed to have been employed immediately before the transfer and so transfer to the transferee: *Anstey v G4S Justice Services (UK) Ltd* [2006] IRLR 588. This principle appears to extend to the case where the individual is not even told that her appeal has been successful and where there is no express decision to reinstate: see *Salmon v Castlebeck Care (Teesdale) Ltd* [2015] IRLR 189 (but see, to the contrary, *Bangura v Southern Cross Healthcare Group plc* (UKEAT/0432/12)). Where an individual's employment was suspended for a period of unpaid leave (but his employment status was protected under national law) the individual's employment transferred: *Piscarreta Ricardo v Portimão Urbis EM SA* C-416/16 [2017] ICR 1451.

53.15 'Would otherwise have been terminated'

Regulation 4 transfers the contracts of employment of those, and only those, whose contracts of employment would otherwise have been terminated by the transfer. The contracts of employment of individuals employed in a part of the undertaking which is not being transferred will not be assigned by the *Regulations* to the transferee. If the employee is employed at the time of the transfer in the business transferred then he will automatically transfer to the transferee. That is so even where the employer has the power to transfer the employee away from the business transferred so that he is not assigned to it at the point of transfer; if that is not in fact done, then the transfer takes effect: *Communication Workers Union v Royal Mail Group Ltd* [2009] ICR 357, [2009] IRLR 108 (this aspect of the judgment was not the subject of the appeal to the Court of Appeal reported at [2010] ICR 83, [2009] IRLR 1046, [2010] 2 All ER 823). Similarly, where a local authority directed that an employee be removed from working on a contract, but the contractor protested and the employee remained on the contract, she was assigned to the contract when it transferred to a different contractor: *Jakowlew v Nestor Primecare Services Ltd* [2015] ICR 1100.

A difficult question may arise if the employee divides his time between two or more parts of the undertaking, some but not all of which are transferred. In *Botzen v Rotterdamsche Droogdok Maatschappij BV*: 186/83 [1986] 2 CMLR 50 the Advocate General of the ECJ suggested that an employee could only be transferred if he worked wholly or almost wholly in the part transferred, but it is also possible that the court would apply a test of where the employee was predominantly employed. See also *Northern General Hospital NHS Trust Ltd v Gale* [1994] ICR 426; *Sunley Turriff Holdings Ltd v Thomson* [1995] IRLR 184; *Michael Peters Ltd v Farnfield* [1995] IRLR 190; *Duncan Web Offset (Maidstone) Ltd v Cooper* [1995] IRLR 633; and *Buchanan-Smith v Schleicher & Co International Ltd* [1996] ICR 613, [1996] IRLR 547. In *CPL Distribution Ltd v Todd* [2002] EWCA Civ 1481, [2003] IRLR 28, the Court of Appeal upheld a decision that a personal assistant was not assigned to the part of an undertaking transferred, even though the majority of her work related to the contract transferred. The employee was effectively assigned to a particular manager and there was no evidence that the manager was assigned to the undertaking transferred since a substantial part of his time was involved in other activities. The same approach is to be applied in cases of a service provision change, for example where overlapping activities were outsourced to two contractors: see *Kimberley Group Housing Ltd v Hambley* [2008] ICR 1030, [2008] IRLR 682, applying *Botzen* and *Duncan Webb Offset*.

53.16 The employee's right of objection

In *Katsikas v Konstantinidis* [1993] IRLR 179 the ECJ held that an employee could not be transferred to the employment of a new employer against his will. As a result, *reg 4(7)* provides that the transfer of the contract of employment and rights, powers, duties and liabilities under and in connection with it will not occur if the employee informs the transferor or the transferee that he objects to becoming employed by the transferee. In that event, the transfer will terminate the employee's contract of employment with the transferor, but he will not be treated for any purpose as having been dismissed by the transferor (*reg 4(8)*).

Indeed, where the employee is not told of the identity of the new employer until after the transfer, *reg 4(7)* must be purposively construed in order to allow the employee to object: *New ISG Ltd v Vernon* [2007] EWHC 2665 (Ch), [2008] ICR 319, [2008] IRLR 115.

The question of whether an employee has objected is an objective one. Thus, where an individual purported to object but then worked for the transferee for a period of six weeks after the transfer, she had not in fact objected. The parties cannot consistently with an objection agree that an individual's employment continues even for a limited period after the transfer: *Capita Health Solutions v McLean* [2008] IRLR 595.

The ECJ held, however, in *Merckx v Ford Motors Co Belgium* [1997] ICR 352, [1996] IRLR 467 that where an employee resigns prior to a transfer because the transferee refuses to guarantee his level of remuneration after the transfer, his 'employer' is to be treated, under *art 4(2)* of the *Directive*, as having dismissed him. In *P & O Property Ltd v Allen* [1997] ICR 436 the EAT held that the 'employer' responsible for the dismissal in these circumstances is the transferee. The EAT has held that an employee objects to his employment being transferred if he refuses to give his consent to the transfer, and that refusal is communicated to the transferor or transferee prior to the transfer (*Hay v George Hanson (Building Contractors) Ltd* [1996] IRLR 427).

In *Senior Heat Treatment Ltd v Bell* [1997] IRLR 614 an employee who 'opted out' of the transfer and accepted a severance payment from the transferor was found not to have objected within the meaning of the *Regulations*. He had accepted employment with the transferee from the date of transfer and so his contract of employment had not terminated.

Under the *Regulations*, where a relevant transfer involves or would involve a substantial change in the working conditions to the material detriment of a person whose employment contract is or would be transferred, such an employee may treat the contract as having been terminated. If he does so, the employee shall be treated for any purpose as having been dismissed by the employer, although no damages are payable by the employer in respect of wages otherwise payable in respect of a notice period which the employee has failed to work (*reg 4(9)* and *(10)*). The meaning of 'substantial change' was considered by the EAT in *Tapere v South London and Maudsley NHS Trust* [2009] ICR 1563, [2009] IRLR 972. It is a factual matter for the tribunal, focusing on the nature as well as the degree of the change and considering the impact of the proposed change from the employee's point of view. The requirement is for a substantial change in working conditions, a phrase which is wider than "contractual conditions" and so may apply to the physical conditions of work (such as the place from which the work is based): see *Abellio London Ltd v Musse* [2012] IRLR 360.

In any event, an employee retains the right to resign in response to a repudiatory breach of contract by his employer (*reg 4(11)*).

53.16 Transfer of Undertakings

Relying upon the decision in *Merckx*, the Court of Appeal in *University of Oxford (Chancellor, Master and Scholars) v Humphreys* [2000] ICR 405, [2000] IRLR 183, [2000] 1 All ER 996 emphasised that it is necessary to distinguish the case where an employee objects to his transfer under what is now *reg 4(7)* and will not then be able to claim that he has been dismissed, from the case where an employee treats his contract as terminated by the employer. In the latter case, the employee could seek compensation.

53.17 What the transferee acquires

As noted above, the transferee inherits those employees employed by the transferor immediately before the transfer on their existing terms and conditions, assuming that they do not object in accordance with **53.16** above. He has no power to impose, without the agreement of the individual employee (see **53.28** below), any different terms and conditions from those he has inherited from the transferor (see **53.26** below). Equally, the transferred employee has no right to insist that he be given the benefit of any superior terms and conditions enjoyed by the transferee's existing staff (see *Jackson v Computershare Investor Services plc* [2007] EWCA Civ 1065, [2008] ICR 341, [2008] IRLR 70) (except possibly by means of a claim for EQUAL PAY **(23)**). Nor can an employee insist that he move to a different place of work but on the same terms rather than local terms: *Xerox Business Services Philippines Inc Ltd v Zeb* (2017) UKEAT/0121/16, [2018] IRLR 495, [2018] ICR 419.

For the effect of a transfer upon restrictive covenants expressed in terms of the transferor's customers, see *Morris Angel & Son Ltd v Hollande* [1993] ICR 71, [1993] IRLR 169, [1993] 3 All ER 569; see also **53.29** below and RESTRAINT OF TRADE, CONFIDENTIALITY AND EMPLOYEE INTERVENTIONS **(42)**. For the effect of a transfer on the question whether employees are redundant, see *Chapman and Elkin v CPS Computer Group plc* [1987] IRLR 462. For the effect of a transfer on an employee's normal retiring age, see *Cross v British Airways* [2006] EWCA Civ 549, [2006] ICR 1239, [2006] IRLR 804.

53.18

The transferee inherits all accrued rights and liabilities connected with the contract of employment of the transferred employee. This includes liability for negligence and breach of statutory duty (*Taylor v Serviceteam Ltd* [1998] PIQR P201) and under the equal pay legislation (*Graysons Restaurants td v Jones* (2017) UKEAT/0277/16, [2018] IRLR 795, [2018] ICR 670). If, for example, the transferor was in arrears with wages at the time of the transfer, the employee can sue the transferee as if the original liability had been the transferee's. The transferor is relieved of his former obligations without any need for the employee's consent (*Berg and Busschers v Besselsen* [1990] ICR 396, [1989] IRLR 447). Equally, the transferee can sue an employee for a breach of contract committed against the transferor prior to transfer. The transferee will also inherit all the statutory rights and liabilities which are connected with the individual contract of employment. The transferred employee's period of continuous employment will date from the beginning of his period of employment with the transferor, and the statutory particulars of terms and conditions of employment, which every employer is obliged to issue, must take account of any continuity enjoyed by virtue of the *Regulations* (a proposition approved by the Court of Justice in *Unionen v Almega Tjänsteförbunden* C-336/15 [2017] ICR 909). (As to continuity of employment when a school transfers to grant-maintained status, see *Pickwell v Lincolnshire County Council* [1993] ICR 87.)

Liability for (for example) sex discrimination transfers to the transferee, even though the employee was employed part-time at the time of the transfer and the discrimination concerned the termination of a previous full-time contract (*DJM International Ltd v Nicholas* [1996] IRLR 76). In *Bernadone v Pall Mall Services Group* [2001] ICR 197, [2000] IRLR 487, [2000] 3 All ER 544, the Court of Appeal held that an employee's claim for personal injuries against his former employer was transferred to the new employer, together with the right of the former employer to an indemnity from its insurers: it was an implied term of the employee's contract of employment that he would be protected by insurance, as required by statute and that right to an indemnity fell within *reg 4(2)*. It did not matter whether the employee's claim was pleaded in contract, tort or breach of statutory duty.

The obligation to maintain employees' wage records under the *National Minimum Wage Act 1998, s 9* transfers to the transferee: *Mears Homecare Ltd v Bradburn* (2020) UKEAT/170/18, [2020] ICR 31, [2019] IRLR 882. Following the transfer, the transferor is no longer obliged to maintain those records or to comply with a production notice, but there is no reason why the transferee should not be in a position to insist that (as part of the transfer) all of the transferor's records are provided to the transferee.

Where a contract provides that nationally agreed pay rates will normally be paid by an employer, it is an implied term that the employer must give notice if it intends to depart from that normal situation. That implied term will transfer, so that if a transferee employer fails to give such notice it will be bound to pay a nationally agreed pay increase, even though it is not itself part of the transferor's bargaining structure: *Glendale Managed Services v Graham* [2003] EWCA Civ 773, [2003] IRLR 465.

However, in *French v MITIE Management Services Ltd* [2002] IRLR 512 the EAT accepted the transferee's argument that the employees' right to benefit from a profit sharing or share option scheme required only that the transferee provide the right to participate in a scheme of 'substantial equivalence, but one which is free from unjust, absurd or impossible features'. That concept cannot be applied to a mobility clause which operates within a defined geographic area: *Tapere v South London and Maudsley NHS Trust* [2009] ICR 1563, [2009] IRLR 972.

53.19   Rights and liabilities which are not assigned under the Regulations

The *Regulations* do not have the effect of assigning:

(a)   criminal liabilities (*reg 4(6)*); or

(b)   rights and liabilities relating to provisions of occupational pension schemes which relate to benefits for old age, invalidity or survivors (*reg 10*).

In *Walden Engineering Co Ltd v Warrener* [1993] ICR 967, [1993] IRLR 420, the EAT rejected arguments that employees should be entitled to equivalent pension benefits after the transfer. Moreover, it was held by the Court of Appeal in *Adams v Lancashire County Council* [1997] ICR 834, [1997] IRLR 436 that the *Regulations* and the *Directive* do not cover transfer of future pension rights, that the exclusion of pension rights from the *Regulations* is consistent with the *Directive*, and that therefore there was no duty on a private contractor to provide an occupational pension scheme for former local government catering workers; see *Eidesund v Stavanger Catering A/S*: C-2/95 [1996] IRLR 684. Since the term relating to pension does not transfer under the *Regulations*, time to bring a claim under the *Equal Pay Act 1970* starts to run from the time of the transfer: *Preston v Wolverhampton Healthcare NHS Trust (No 3); Powerhouse Retail Ltd v Burroughs* [2004] EWCA Civ 1281, [2005] ICR 222, [2004] IRLR 979 (applied to all pay terms in *Gutridge v Sodexo Ltd* [2009] EWCA Civ 729, [2009] ICR 1486, [2009] IRLR 721).

However, these exceptions are to be interpreted strictly: *Beckmann v Dynamco Whicheloe Macfarlane Ltd*: C-164/00 [2003] ICR 50, [2002] IRLR 578. The ECJ ruled that early retirement benefits and benefits intended to enhance the conditions of such retirement did not fall within the meaning of rights to old-age pension schemes and so the obligation to pay such benefits did transfer to the new employer. These principles were applied by the ECJ in *Martin v South Bank University*: C-4/01 [2004] IRLR 74.

Moreover, *ss 257* and *258* of the *Pensions Act 2004* (together with the *Transfer of Employment (Pension Protection) Regulations 2005 (SI 2005/649)*) require a transferee to provide certain pension benefits to employees for whom there was an occupational pension scheme with the transferor.

The application of the distinction as to what does and does not transfer is illustrated by *Procter & Gamble Co v Svenska Cellulosa Aktiebolaget SCA* [2012] IRLR 733: the High Court held that the employees' right to be considered for early retirement benefits transferred under TUPE, whereas benefits payable after normal retirement age (including those first triggered as early retirement benefits) do not transfer.

53.20   TRANSFER OF AN UNDERTAKING AND THE TRADE UNION

Collective agreements

Under *reg 5*, a collective agreement, which:

(a)   is made between the transferor and a union recognised by the transferor; and

(b)   applies to an employee whose contract has become automatically assigned to the transferee by virtue of the transfer,

is automatically transferred to the transferee in its application to that employee. Further, anything done by or under or in connection with that agreement by the transferor before the transfer is deemed to have been done by the transferee.

The practical effect of this provision is probably minimal, since collective agreements are in English law presumed to be unenforceable (see *TULRCA 1992, s 179* and **6.2 COLLECTIVE AGREEMENTS**) unless, which is rare, the contrary is stated in the agreement. It is only in this rare case where a binding agreement is entered into that *reg 5* will pass any legal obligation to the transferee. If the terms of a collective agreement are incorporated into the contract of employment of an individual, whose service is automatically assigned on the transfer, then its terms will bind the transferee simply by virtue of the general rule that the transferee inherits the rights and liabilities in the individual's contract: *Whent v T Cartledge Ltd* [1997] IRLR 153. However, a contract which incorporates a collective agreement will not transfer any rights or liabilities in relation to a provision of a collective agreement where that provision is agreed after the date of the transfer and the transferee is not a participant in the collective bargaining for that provision (*reg 4A*). This regulation (introduced in the 2014 amendments) effectively applies the judgment in *Alemo-Herron v Parkwood Leisure Ltd*: C-426/11 [2013] ICR 1116, [2013] IRLR 744 (see also *ÖGB v WKO*: C-328/13 [2014] ICR 1152, [2014] All ER (D) 110 (Sep)). That case was itself revisited in *Asklepios Kliniken Langen-Seligenstadt GmbH v Felja* C-680-15 [2017] IRLR 653. The Court of Justice took the approach that a dynamic clause may in fact have some effect where the transferee is able to asserts its interests effectively in a contractual process to which it is party and to negotiate the aspects determining chances in the working conditions of its employees with a view to its future economic activity. In other words, if the transferee can effectively participate in the bargaining process, that process may continue to apply post-transfer.

Regulation 5(b) provides that any order made in respect of a collective agreement transferred under *reg 5* takes effect as if the transferee were a party to the agreement. In effect, this means that awards of the Central Arbitration Committee ('CAC') made against the transferor are binding against the transferee to the extent that they previously bound the transferor.

53.21   Recognition

Where the transferor recognises a union in respect of employees in the undertaking or part of the undertaking to be transferred and, following the transfer, the undertaking or part of the undertaking transferred maintains an identity distinct from the rest of the transferee's business or businesses, the transferee must recognise the union in respect of those employees (*reg 6*). The underlying provision within the *Directive* was considered by the ECJ in *Federación de Servicios Públicos de la UGT (UGT-FSP) v Ayuntamiento de La Línea de la Concepción*: C-151/09 [2010] ICR 1248, [2010] All ER (D) 30 (Dec).

The general provisions applicable to recognition are to be found in *s 70A* of and *Schedule A1* to the *Trade Union and Labour Relations (Consolidation) Act 1992* (see **50.11** TIME OFF WORK).

53.22 Information and consultation

Employee Liability Information

Regulations 11 to 16 provide an important code for the provision of information by the transferor to the transferee, and by employers to affected employees.

Regulation 11 imposes a duty on the transferor to notify the transferee of certain information relating to any person employed by him who is assigned to the activity which is the subject of the relevant transfer. The information must be in writing or some other readily accessible form.

That information, defined as 'employee liability information' is:

(a)   the identity and age of the employee;

(b)   the information specified in *s 1* of the *Employment Rights Act 1996* (see **8.6** CONTRACT OF EMPLOYMENT); if further information is given than required (for example, whether a bonus is contractual or not, then the recipient has no claim if that additional information is wrong: see *Born London Ltd v Spire Production Services Ltd* [2017] ICR 998;

(c)   information of any disciplinary action taken against the employee and of any grievance raised by them within the previous two years to which a Code of Practice issued under *Part IV* of the *TULR(C)A 1992* applies;

(d)   information relating to actual or potential claims against the transferor;

(e)   information of any collective agreement which will apply to the employee pursuant to *reg 5*.

This information must also be provided in relation to an employee who has resigned because of the transfer: *reg 11(4)*.

This information must be provided not less than 28 days before the relevant transfer, unless there are special circumstances which mean that this is not reasonably practicable, in which case it must be given as soon as reasonably practicable thereafter: *reg 11(6)*.

If the transferor fails to comply with this obligation, the transferee may present a complaint to an employment tribunal. If successful, the tribunal may make an award of compensation to the transferee, such as is just and equitable in particular having regard to any loss sustained by the transferor which is attributable to the breach and the terms of any contract between transferor and transferee which provide for the payment of such a sum in any event. The minimum level of such an award is, however, fixed at £500 per employer (subject to a discretion to award a lower figure if the tribunal considers that just and equitable).

53.23 *Information and consultation of employees*

Under *reg 13*, the employer of employees affected by the transfer, whether he is the transferor or transferee, must inform all the appropriate representatives of any of the affected employees, long enough before the transfer to enable consultations to take place between the employer and those representatives, of the following:

(a)   the fact that a relevant transfer is to take place;

(b)   when it is to take place;

(c)   the reasons for it;

(d)   the legal, economic and social implications of the transfer for affected employees;

(e)   the measures which he envisages taking in relation to those employees (and if no measures are envisaged, that fact);

(f)   if the employer is the transferor, the measures which the transferee envisages that he will take in relation to those employees who are to be automatically assigned to him on the transfer (or if no measures are envisaged, that fact).

If a transfer does not in fact take place, then the duty to inform and consult will have not arisen: *I Lab Facilities Ltd v Metcalfe* [2013] IRLR 605.

Where such information is provided, the employer must also include specified information relating to the use of agency workers (if any) by that employer: *reg 13(2A)*.

The obligation under sub-para (*d*) is satisfied where the employer states a genuine belief, even if that belief is wrong in law: *Communication Workers Union v Royal Mail Group Ltd* [2010] ICR 83, [2009] IRLR 1046, [2010] 2 All ER 823.

Appropriate representatives are representatives of an independent trade union recognised by the employer for employees of that description. If there is no such union then the appropriate representatives are, at the employer's choice, either (i) employee representatives elected by the affected employees for this purpose in an election complying with the requirements of *reg 14*, or (ii) employee representatives appointed or elected by the affected employees for some other purpose but who have authority from those employees to receive information and to be consulted about the proposed dismissals on their behalf (*reg 13(3)(b)*). If there are no appropriate representatives at the relevant time, the employer is under a positive duty to invite the affected employees to elect employee representatives for this purpose: *Howard v Millrise Ltd* [2005] ICR 435, [2005] IRLR 84. However, where the employer employs fewer than 10 employees, then it may inform and consult directly with the workforce (*reg 13A*).

If a question arises as to whether or not any employee representative was an appropriate representative, it is for the employer to show that the employee representative had the necessary authority to represent the affected employees (*reg 15(3)*).

Regulation 14 sets out the requirements for the election of employee representatives under *reg 13(3)*. In particular, all affected employees on the date of the election are entitled to vote for employee representatives and so far as reasonably practicable the vote should be in secret. It is for the employer to show that the requirements of *reg 14* have been satisfied (*reg 15(4)*). If the employer has invited affected employees to elect representatives and they fail to do so within a reasonable time, then the employer must give the information required by *reg 13(2)* to each affected employee (*reg 13(11)*).

Employee representatives are afforded special protection in certain circumstances. They have the right not to be subjected to any detriment on the ground that they perform or propose to perform any function or activity as an employee representative (*ERA 1996, s 47*, as amended by *SI 1999/1925*) and any dismissal of an employee representative on that ground is automatically unfair (*ERA 1996, s 103*, as amended by *SI 1999/1925*). They have the right to take reasonable time off (which is paid) in order to perform their functions as an employee representative (*ERA 1996, ss 61–63*).

Where assurances are given by the transferee employer in the course of the consultation process and those assurances are accepted by employee representatives, that alone cannot constitute an independent contractual commitment. Thus, a non-contractual bonus scheme could not be elevated to a contractual entitlement simply because the transferee had given assurances about the continuation of the scheme: *Small v Boots Co plc* [2009] IRLR 328.

These provisions (as enacted in another context) were extensively discussed in *Institution of Professional Civil Servants v Secretary of State for Defence* [1987] IRLR 373, which is authority for several of the propositions referred to below, although not all of them were essential to the decision.

The transferee must give the transferor the information necessary to enable him to comply in time with sub-para (*f*) above (*reg 13(4)*). But the transferee is under no *obligation* to envisage any measures, and sometimes he may envisage them too late for there to be compliance with sub-para (*f*). Note that the duty to inform arises independently of the obligation to consult: even where there is no duty to consult, there will be a duty to inform under *reg 13(2)* since that duty is intended to anticipate both compulsory and voluntary consultation (*Cable Realisations Ltd v GMB Northern* [2010] IRLR 42 and *Todd v Strain* [2011] IRLR 11).

There is no obligation to consult post-transfer concerning measures in connection with the transfer: *Amicus v City Building (Glasgow) LLP* [2009] IRLR 253.

The information to be given to the representatives is to be delivered to them personally or (in the case of union representatives) sent by post to the union's head office or other address notified by the representatives (*reg 13(5)*).

If either the transferor or the transferee envisages that he will take measures in relation to any of the affected employees, he must enter into consultation with their appropriate representatives with a view to seeking their agreement to measures to be taken. (This is the only *obligation* to consult. Although, as stated above, there are other obligations to give information in time for consultation, consultation itself is voluntary in those cases.) The measures referred to must be definite plans or proposals, not mere hopes or possibilities, and must be such as would not have happened but for the transfer; they do not need to be disadvantageous in order to trigger the requirement to consult: *Todd v Strain* [2011] IRLR 11. The information to be disclosed does not include the calculations and assumptions underlying those plans. Consultation involves considering and replying to representations made by the representatives and, insofar as representations are rejected, stating the reasons for the rejection. Reasons need not be given in writing, though this may be advisable. It is as yet unclear how the content of the obligation has been affected by the addition of the stipulation that the consultation must be with a view to seeking agreement (*reg 13(6)*).

In *Unison v Somerset County Council* [2010] ICR 498, [2010] IRLR 207 the EAT considered that the category of 'affected employees' (identified in *reg 13(1)*) extends not only to those who are to transfer, but to those who will be or may be transferred or whose jobs are in jeopardy by reason of the proposed transfer, or who have job applications with the organisation pending at the time of the transfer.' It does not extend to employees of the transferor whose future career opportunities might be diminished by a change in the recruitment arrangements in the part transferred.

If an employer fails to inform or consult, then a complaint may be made to an employment tribunal by the trade union (where the failure relates to trade union representatives) or by the employee representatives or any of them (where the failure relates to employee representatives) or by any of his employees who are affected employees (where the failure relates to the election of employee representatives and in any other case) (*reg 15(1)*). If it is not reasonably practicable to bring the complaint within three months, it may be presented within a reasonable time thereafter (*reg 15(12)*; and see **19.20** EMPLOYMENT

TRIBUNALS – I). There is no need to wait for the transfer to take place before presenting the complaint (*South Durham Health Authority v Unison* [1995] ICR 495, [1995] IRLR 407), and it appears that the complaint may proceed even if in fact the transfer never takes place (*Banking Insurance and Finance Union v Barclays Bank plc* [1987] ICR 495).

Where a complaint succeeds, the tribunal must make a declaration to this effect and may order the employer to pay compensation to affected employees (*reg 15(7)*). The maximum payable is 13 weeks' pay for each employee affected (*reg 16(3)*). The amount of a week's pay is not capped: *Zaman v Kozee Sleep Products Ltd* [2011] IRLR 196. The transferee is jointly and severally liable with the transferor in respect of compensation payable (*reg 15(9)*). In determining the amount of an award, the tribunal must apply the same approach as it does to protective awards in redundancy cases and in particular follow the guidance of the Court of Appeal in *Susie Radin Ltd v GMB* [2004] IRLR 400, [2004] 2 All ER 279 (see *Sweetin v Coral Racing* [2006] IRLR 252; and see **40.6** REDUNDANCY – **II**). The approach in *Susie Radin* was applied in *Todd v Strain* [2011] IRLR 11. The purpose of the award is not to compensate the employee: in *Shields Automotive Ltd v Langdon* (UKEATS/0059/12) a tribunal's failure to have regard to this led the EAT to reduce the level of a protective award.

It is a defence for the employer to show that there were special circumstances which rendered it not reasonably practicable to perform the duty in question, provided that he took whatever steps to perform that duty as were reasonably practicable in the circumstances (*reg 13(9)*). By analogy with the case law on *TULRCA 1992, s 188* (see **40.5** REDUNDANCY – **II**), an employer is unlikely to show that a failure to inform or consult was due to 'special circumstances' unless the transfer has to be arranged or expedited because of a sudden and unforeseen emergency. However, the tribunal should look at the matter broadly, and ought not ordinarily to grant relief unless the employer has plainly been recalcitrant or neglectful of his obligations.

If a transferor wishes to allege that the reason for his default is the failure of the transferee to supply him with information, he must give the transferee notice of that fact and the transferee must be made a party to the proceedings (*reg 15(5)*). Employees who had been employed by the transferor cannot, post-transfer, bring claims against the transferee for its failure to provide information to the transferor; such a claim lay against the transferor: see *Allen v Morrisons Facilities Services Ltd* (UKEAT/0298/13) [2014] IRLR 514.

If an employer fails to pay compensation ordered to be paid by the tribunal, the employee concerned may present a complaint to an employment tribunal (*reg 15(10)*). This is subject to the same time limits as the original complaint under *reg 15(12)*.

In addition, where there is, or is likely to be, a relevant transfer and the transferee is proposing to dismiss as redundant 20 or more employees at one establishment within a period of 90 days or less, amongst whom are likely to be one or more of the transferring employees, then the transferee may engage in collective consultation prior to the transfer but only if the transferor agrees to this having received written notice (*Trade Union and Labour Relations (Consolidation) Act 1992, s 198A*). This effectively permits the early engagement of the provisions on collective consultation on redundancy (as to which see **40.2**).

53.24   DISMISSAL ON THE TRANSFER OF AN UNDERTAKING

If an individual employed in an undertaking is dismissed:

(a)   by the transferor in advance of the transfer of that undertaking; or

(b)   by the transferee after the transfer,

he may wish to bring a claim for unfair dismissal, a redundancy payment or wrongful dismissal.

53.25 Unfair dismissal and transfer of an undertaking

Dismissal

In order to complain of unfair dismissal the individual must first show that he has been dismissed within the statutory definition, that is to say:

(a)   that his contract of employment has been terminated by the employer (direct dismissal);

(b)   that he was employed for a fixed term which has expired and not been renewed; or

(c)   that he resigned in circumstances where he was entitled to do so without notice on account of his employer's conduct (constructive dismissal).

(*ERA 1996, s 95.*)

(For a discussion of the statutory definition of dismissal see **54.4–54.10** UNFAIR DISMISSAL – I.)

The *Regulations* affect the operation of this definition in a number of ways.

First, the transfer itself cannot be treated as a dismissal. As can be seen from **53.9** above, the transfer operates to assign to the transferee the contracts of employment of those who would otherwise have been dismissed upon the transfer. An employee who exercises his right of objection to the transfer (see **53.16** above) will not be treated as having been dismissed. Nor is a transfer a repudiatory breach of contract by the transferor which the employee can obtain an injunction to restrain, at least where the transferor is acting in good faith (*Newns v British Airways plc* [1992] IRLR 575); and see *Sita (GB) Ltd v Burton* [1998] ICR 17, [1997] IRLR 501.

Second, if the transferor refrains from dismissing employees before the transfer so that they are automatically assigned to the transferee, but the transferee indicates – before the transfer – that he is unwilling to employ them, it appears that the employees will be treated as dismissed by the transferee immediately after the transfer (see *Premier Motors (Medway) Ltd v Total Oil (Great Britain) Ltd* [1984] ICR 58, [1983] IRLR 471).

Third, if the transferee substantially changes the terms and conditions of employment previously enjoyed by the transferred staff to their detriment, the staff may resign and treat themselves as constructively dismissed. For this purpose, the change must amount to a repudiatory breach of contract (*reg 4(11)*).

Where an employee treats himself as constructively dismissed on the grounds that the transfer will involve a substantial and detrimental change in his terms and conditions of employment the employee's right lies against the transferor (*University of Oxford (Chancellor, Master and Scholars) v Humphreys* [2000] ICR 405, [2000] IRLR 183, [2000] 1 All ER 996). In that case, the Court of Appeal said that it would be inconsistent with the scheme of the *Directive* and the *1981 Regulations* for existing rights and liabilities to pass to the transferee when existing contracts of employment did not.

Fourth, where a relevant transfer involves or would involve a substantial change in working conditions to the material detriment of a person whose contract of employment is or would be transferred, such an employee may treat the contract as having been terminated and the employee shall be treated for any purpose as having been dismissed by the employer (*reg 4(9)*). "Working conditions" includes contractual terms and conditions, as well as physical conditions; whether or not there has been a "substantial change" is a factual matter for the tribunal focusing on the nature as well as the degree of the change; what has to be considered was the impact of the proposed change from the employee's point of view: *Tapere v South London and Maudsley NHS Trust* [2009] ICR 1563, [2009] IRLR 972; *Abelio*

London Ltd v Musse [2012] IRLR 360 and see **53.16** above. However, no damages are payable by the employer in respect of any failure by the employer to pay wages to an employee in respect of a notice period which the employee has failed to work.

53.26   *The fairness of the dismissal*

If an employee has been dismissed by either the transferee or the transferor and the reason for the dismissal is the transfer, the dismissal is automatically unfair (*reg 7(1)(a)*). (The normal conditions to bringing a claim for unfair dismissal, including the qualifying period of service, apply.)

Hare Wines Ltd v Kaur [2019] EWCA Civ 216, [2019] IRLR 555, [2019] All ER (D) 10 (Mar) is a useful case in delineating whether the reason for the dismissal is the transfer. The claimant was dismissed on the date of the transfer because of anticipated difficulties in her working relationship with an employee of the transferee. The Court of Appeal considered that the timing of the dismissal (whilst not determinative) was strong evidence in favour of a conclusion that the transfer was the reason for the transfer. This was reinforced by the fact that the two individuals had worked together prior to the transfer and the claimant had not been dismissed. Merely because there were reasons personal to the claimant did not preclude a finding that the transfer was the reason for the dismissal: the personal reasons had not changed; all that had changed was the transfer. The claimant's dismissal was automatically unfair.

However, where the reason for the dismissal is an 'economic, technical or organisational reason entailing changes in the workforce' of either the transferor or the transferee then the dismissal will not be automatically unfair (*reg 7(2), (3)(a)*). Changes in the workforce includes a change to the place where employees are employed (*reg 7(3A)*). If the reason falls within this category ('an ETO reason') it will be held to be for a fair reason, either by reason of redundancy or for some other substantial reason justifying dismissal (*reg 7(3)(b)* and see UNFAIR DISMISSAL – **II (55)**). The employee's remedy for a breach of *reg 7(1)* is to complain of unfair dismissal. Both transferee and transferor may dismiss employees for an economic, technical or organisational reason (*Jules Dethier Equipement v Dassy* [1998] ICR 541, [1998] IRLR 266).

In considering a claim for unfair dismissal, the burden of proof is applied in the same manner as where it is alleged that the reason or principal reason for the dismissal was that the employee had made a protected disclosure, as set out in *Kuzel v Roche Products Ltd* [2008] EWCA Civ 789, [2008] ICR 799, [2008] IRLR 530 (see para **55.2**): see *Marshall v Game Retail Ltd* (UKEAT/0276/13) [2015] All ER (D) 286 (Feb). Thus, the employee must produce some evidence in support of his case but, having done so, the burden lies on the employer to establish that the reason for the dismissal was not the automatically unfair reason.

The original version of *Regulation 7(1)* was to be read in sequence. Consider first whether the transfer was the reason for the dismissal. If so, the dismissal is unfair. Then consider whether the reason for the dismissal was connected with the transfer. If not, there is no need to enquire further; if so, it may be necessary to consider whether the reason for dismissal was an economic, technical or organisational reason. *Warner v Adnet Ltd* [1998] IRLR 394 and *Collins v John Ansell & Partners Ltd*, IDS Brief 659 [2000] All ER (D) 309. However, the concept of 'a reason connected with the transfer' no longer features in the amended provision.

In *Kerry Foods Ltd v Creber* [2000] ICR 556, [2000] IRLR 10, receivers dismissed all of the employees of an undertaking prior to its transfer. The employment tribunal found that the reason for this dismissal was the transfer. The EAT ruled that the tribunal should then have concluded that (by reason of the *Litster* principle – see **53.10** above) the employees were employed in the undertaking immediately before the transfer, that their employment was transferred and the transferee was then treated as having dismissed them. However, if the main reason for the dismissal is an ETO reason within *reg 7(1)(b)*, then the employee is not deemed to have been employed immediately before the transfer, his employment does not transfer and his only remedy for unfair dismissal is against the transferor. If the dismissal is in fact effected by the transferee, then the employee's remedy lies against the transferee, which may itself invoke an ETO reason.

In *Wilson v St Helens Borough Council* [1999] 2 AC 52, [1998] IRLR 706, [1998] 4 All ER 609 the House of Lords (reversing the decision of the Court of Appeal) held that an actual dismissal before, on or after the transfer is effective, even where the transfer was the reason for the dismissal. The dismissal is not a nullity and the employee cannot compel the transferee to employ him on the same terms and conditions as those on which the transferor employed him.

For the transfer to be the reason for dismissal within *reg 7(1)*, it is not necessary that the employer had in mind a specific transferee at the time of the dismissal (*Morris v John Grose Group Ltd* [1998] ICR 655, [1998] IRLR 499, an approach approved in *Spaceright Europe Ltd v Baillavoine* [2011] EWCA Civ 1656, [2012] ICR 520, [2012] IRLR 111, [2012] 2 All ER 812).

The passage of time may increase the chances that the chain of causation between the transfer and the reason for the dismissal has been broken; however, the mere passage of time without anything happening does not in itself constitute a weakening to the point of dissolution of the chain of causation: *Taylor v Connex South Eastern Ltd*, IDS Brief 670, p 10.

The reason for dismissal may be connected with the transfer, even though the employee dismissed was never employed in the undertaking or part transferred (*reg 7(4)*). If, for example, the transferee dismisses his existing staff to accommodate the employees he is to inherit from the transferor, or if the job of an existing employee disappears following a reorganisation consequent upon the transfer, the dismissal will nonetheless be connected with the transfer.

It appears that a transferor may not invoke the defence of an 'organisational' or 'economic' reason where a transferee is willing to acquire the undertaking only on terms that the transferor's staff are first dismissed, because the reason must relate to the conduct of the business for those words to apply (*Wheeler v Patel* [1987] ICR 631, [1987] IRLR 211 and *Gateway Hotels Ltd v Stewart* [1988] IRLR 287, not following *Anderson v Dalkeith Engineering Ltd* [1985] ICR 66, [1984] IRLR 429, EAT. See also *Ibex Trading Co Ltd v Walton* [1994] ICR 907, [1994] IRLR 564).

Whitehouse v Blatchford & Sons Ltd [2000] ICR 542, [1999] IRLR 492 concerned a transfer following the award of a new contract for the provision of services to a hospital. It was a stipulation of that contract that the number of employees be reduced. The applicant was dismissed following the transfer. The Court of Appeal held that the employment tribunal had been entitled to find that the applicant's dismissal was for an economic, technical or organisational reason. If the transferee had not complied with the stipulation then it would not have won the contract. The court followed *Wheeler v Patel*: the reason must be connected with the future conduct of the business as a going concern. See also *Thompson v SCS Consulting Ltd* [2001] IRLR 801. A transferor cannot dismiss and then rely upon the future conduct of the business by the transferee after the transfer in an attempt to establish an ETO reason; the transferor itself has no intention of continuing the business and so the reason for the dismissal does not relate to its future conduct of the business: *Hynd v Armstrong* [2007] CSIH 16, [2007] IRLR 338 (Court of Session, Inner House). Similarly, an administrator may not rely upon an ETO reason where it dismisses an employee to make the business of the company a more attractive proposition to prospective transferees as a going concern, since here the intention is not to continue to conduct the business but to sell it: *Spaceright Europe Ltd v Baillavoine* [2011] EWCA Civ 1656, [2012] ICR 520, [2012] IRLR 111, [2012] 2 All ER 812, applied in *Kavanagh v Crystal Palace FC (2000) Ltd* [2013] IRLR 291.

Where the sole or principal reason for a variation is the transfer itself, then the variation is void under *reg 4(4)*, even if the variation is such as to improve terms in the employee's employment contract: *Ferguson v Astrea Asset Management Ltd* (UKEAT/0139/19, 15 May 2020).

The ECJ has ruled that the *Directive* does not preclude a public body, as a transferee, from reducing the pay of its incoming staff where it is necessary to do so in order to comply with national rules in force for public employees. However, if the variation is sufficiently detrimental, then the employees will be entitled to resign and claim that the employer was responsible for their dismissal (under *art 4(2)*): *Delahaye (Boor) v Ministre de la Fonction Publique et de la Réforme Administrative* (Case C-425/02) [2005] IRLR 61.

In *Cornwall County Care Ltd v Brightman* [1998] ICR 529, [1998] IRLR 228, employees were dismissed by the transferee after the transfer and re-employed on less favourable terms and conditions. The EAT held that they had been unfairly dismissed since the reason for the dismissals had been the transfer. However, the employees had 'accepted' the new terms and conditions by continuing to work for the transferee. They were unable to continue to claim a right to their original terms and conditions – that claim was 'bought out' by the compensation for unfair dismissal. A change in terms and conditions brought about merely because of the expiry of employees' fixed-term contract may be effective: *Ralton v Havering College of Further and Higher Education* [2001] IRLR 738. The tribunal had been right to apply the test of whether the variation was solely by reason of the transfer. In *Enterprise Managed Services Ltd v Dance* (UKEAT/0200/11) a variation in terms was effective where it was introduced in order to achieve improved performance and efficiency, and so the harmonisation of terms amongst employees was simply a by-product of the variation, rather than the principal reason for it. In *Tabberer v Mears Ltd* (UKEAT/0064/17) a travel allowance was removed following a transfer, but the reason for the removal was that the allowance 'prehistoric with no resemblance to modern times', rather than the transfer itself. The question is not whether the variation would not have happened 'but for' the transfer, but what the operative reason in fact was and so where the reason was a mistaken view that the employee was being overpaid, then this was not a reason connected with the transfer: *Smith v Trustees of Brooklands College* (UKEAT/0128/11).

54   Unfair Dismissal – I: The Right to Make a Claim

Cross-references. See TERMINATION OF EMPLOYMENT **(49)** for the various ways of terminating the contract at common law; UNFAIR DISMISSAL – II **(55)** for whether the dismissal was fair; UNFAIR DISMISSAL – III **(56)** for remedies for unfair dismissal; WRONGFUL DISMISSAL **(59)** for dismissals in breach of contract.

54.1   The *Industrial Relations Act 1971* originally created the right not to be unfairly dismissed. The right was then re-enacted in the *Employment Protection (Consolidation) Act 1978* and then in the *Employment Rights Act 1996* ('*ERA 1996*'). *ERA 1996* is a consolidation Act, so the rights thereunder are exactly the same as those which previously existed under the earlier statutes and the old case law remains relevant.

An employer who dismisses an employee without good reason or without following a fair procedure lays itself open to a claim for unfair dismissal. When such a claim is brought, the employer bears the burden of proof in establishing the reason for the dismissal. The employment tribunal will then consider whether the dismissal was fair in all the circumstances, neither party having the evidential burden in this enquiry. If the dismissal is held to be unfair, the employer can be ordered to re-engage, reinstate or to pay compensation to the ex-employee. The parties to a claim for unfair dismissal are known as the *claimant* (employee) and the *respondent* (employer). The claimant was formerly called the applicant.

54.2   PRE-CONDITIONS OF A CLAIM

A complaint of unfair dismissal must be presented to an employment tribunal before the end of the period of three months beginning with the effective date of termination of the employment (or within such further period as the tribunal considers reasonable in a case where it is satisfied that it was not reasonably practicable for the complaint to be presented within the period of three months) (*ERA 1996, s 111(2)*).

Prior to 6 April 2009, an employee benefited from a limitation period of six months from the effective date of termination of the employment (*EmA 2002, s 32* and *Employment Act 2002 (Dispute Resolution) Regulations 2004, reg 15*) in certain circumstances. The provisions for the extension of time in this way were repealed by the *Employment Act 2008, s 1*. (See further **19.24–19.25** EMPLOYMENT TRIBUNALS-I and also **54.13** below for effective date of termination.) This chapter used to contain detailed reference to the statutory dispute resolution procedures. These references have now been removed on the assumption that no cases remain live where the trigger date was before 6 April 2009. Readers should consult earlier editions of this work if required.

Leaving aside the now almost universal requirement for an early conciliation certificate (dealt with elsewhere in this work at **3.1**) a claimant must also satisfy the conditions set out below if they wish to bring a claim for unfair dismissal. If these conditions are not disputed by the respondent, no evidence need be brought by the claimant to establish them. If, however, there are grounds for suspecting that any of those necessary prerequisites is absent, the employment tribunal will inquire into the matter, as it affects their jurisdiction to hear the case. The burden is on the claimant to show that they satisfy those conditions. The conditions are:

(a)   that the claimant was employed by the respondent under a contract of employment (see **54.3** below);

(b)   that the claimant was dismissed, as defined (see **54.4** below);

54.6 Expiry of a fixed-term contract

It used to be thought that a fixed-term contract was one which did not contain a provision for prior determination by notice. However, in *Dixon v BBC* [1979] ICR 281, [1979] IRLR 114, [1979] 2 All ER 112, the Court of Appeal held that the words 'a fixed term' include a specified stated term even though the contract is determinable by notice within its term. *Regulation 1* of the *Fixed-term Employees (Prevention of Less Favourable Treatment) Regulations 2002 (SI 2002/2034)* provides that a fixed-term contract is a contract of employment that, under its provisions determining how it will terminate in the normal course, will terminate – (a) on the expiry of a specific term, (b) on the completion of a particular task, or (c) on the occurrence or non-occurrence of any other specific event other than the attainment by the employee of any normal and *bona fide* retiring age in the establishment for an employee holding the position held by him. (see PART-TIME WORKERS (34)).

54.7 Constructive dismissal

In order to establish that they have been constructively dismissed, an employee must show the following:

(i)   His employer has committed a repudiatory breach of contract. A repudiatory breach is a significant breach going to the root of the contract (*Western Excavating (ECC) Ltd v Sharp* [1978] ICR 221, [1978] IRLR 27, [1978] 1 All ER 713). In *Tullett Prebon Plc v BGC Brokers LP* [2011] EWCA Civ 131, [2011] IRLR 420 the Court of Appeal applied the orthodox contractual test for a repudiatory breach in holding that it is one in which the contract-breaker has shown an intention, objectively judged, to abandon and altogether refuse to perform the contract. In *Leeds Dental Team Ltd v Rose* [2014] ICR 94, [2014] IRLR 8, the EAT rejected a submission to the effect that *Tullett* had changed the law. It follows that – at least in a case based on a breach of the implied term of mutual trust and confidence – it is not necessary for a tribunal to make a factual finding as to the employer's actual (subjective) intention with regards to the contract, simply a finding as to whether, objectively, the conduct complained of was likely to destroy or seriously damage the relationship of trust and confidence. It is not enough to show merely that the employer has behaved unreasonably although "*reasonableness is one of the tools in the employment tribunal's factual analysis kit for deciding whether there has been a fundamental breach*" (*Buckland v Bournemouth University Higher Education Corporation* [2010] EWCA Civ 121, [2010] IRLR 445, [2010] 4 All ER 186). The line between serious unreasonableness and a breach of the implied term of trust and confidence (see **8.13** CONTRACT OF EMPLOYMENT) is a fine one (see eg *Sheridan v Stanley Cole (Wainfleet) Ltd* [2003] ICR 297, [2003] IRLR 52). Likewise, there is no rule that an act of direct or indirect discrimination by an employer will constitute a repudiatory breach, but the line between repudiatory and non-repudiatory acts of discrimination is narrow (see eg *Shaw v CCL Ltd* [2008] IRLR 284). Every breach of the implied term of trust and confidence is a repudiatory breach of contract (*Morrow v Safeway Stores* [2002] IRLR 9, *Ahmed v Amnesty International* [2009] ICR 1450, [2009] IRLR 884). The breach of contract may be an *anticipatory* rather than an *actual* one, i.e. even though no breach has yet occurred, it is sufficient if the employer has indicated a clear intention not to fulfil the terms of the contract in the future, and the employee accepts that intention to commit a breach as bringing the contract to an end (*Norwest Holst Group Administration Ltd v Harrison* [1985] ICR 668, [1985] IRLR 240; *Greenaway Harrison Ltd v Wiles* [1994] IRLR 380). However, in *Kerry Foods Ltd v Lynch* [2005] IRLR 680 the EAT held that an employee had resigned prematurely in response to his employer's notice that it intended to terminate his employment and re-engage him on varied terms to which he had refused to agree. The EAT considered that the giving of lawful notice of termination could not by itself constitute a repudiatory breach of contract.

(ii)　They have left because of the breach (*Walker v Josiah Wedgwood & Sons Ltd* [1978] ICR 744, [1978] IRLR 105; *Holland v Glendale Industries Ltd* [1998] ICR 493). It was also suggested in *Walker* that the employee must make clear when he resigns that he regards himself as having been constructively dismissed. Note that it is an error of law for the tribunal to focus on the question of whether the repudiatory breach of contract was the main, predominant or 'effective' cause of the employee's resignation. The question is whether a repudiatory breach has played a part in the employee's resignation (*Wright v North Ayrshire Council* [2014] ICR 77, [2014] IRLR 4). In *United First Partners Research v Carreras* [2018] EWCA Civ 323 the Court of Appeal said that where an employee has mixed reasons for resigning, the resignation would constitute a constructive dismissal if the repudiatory breach relied on was at least a substantial part of those reasons.

(iii)　They have not waived the breach (also known as 'affirming' the contract). In other words, he must not delay his resignation too long, or do anything else which indicates acceptance of the changed basis of his employment. See the discussion in *WE Cox Toner (International) Ltd v Crook* [1981] ICR 823, [1981] IRLR 443. Merely to protest at the time will not prevent such acceptance being inferred. An express reservation of rights may in certain circumstances be effective (see *Bliss v South East Thames Regional Health Authority* [1987] ICR 700, [1985] IRLR 308; *Waltons & Morse v Dorrington* [1997] IRLR 488) but not in others (see *Robinson v Tescom Corp* [2008] IRLR 408). Where there has been a repudiatory breach of contract by a party to a contract of employment, the breach is not capable of remedy in such a way as to preclude acceptance by the other party (*Buckland v Bournemouth University Higher Education Corporation* [2010] EWCA Civ 121, [2010] IRLR 445, [2010] 4 All ER 186). The wronged party has an unfettered choice whether to accept the breach or not, whatever his motives. All the defaulting party can do is to invite affirmation of the contract by making amends.

Examples of breaches of contract upon which a complaint of constructive dismissal might be founded include: a reduction in pay (*Industrial Rubber Products v Gillon* [1977] IRLR 389) and, more recently, *Mostyn v S&P Casuals Ltd* UKEAT/0158/17); a complete change in the nature of the job (*Ford v Milthorn Toleman Ltd* [1980] IRLR 30; *Pedersen v Camden London Borough Council* [1981] ICR 674, [1981] IRLR 173; *Land Securities Trillium Ltd v Thornley* [2005] IRLR 765); a failure to follow the prescribed disciplinary procedure (*Post Office v Strange* [1981] IRLR 515); an act of sex discrimination (*Shaw v CCL Ltd* [2008] IRLR 284), giving a misleading reason for dismissal (*Rawlinson v Brightside Group Ltd* [2018] IRLR 180, [2018] ICR 621) and failure to pay the National Minimum Wage (*Mruke v Khan* [2018] EWCA Civ 280, in which it was also held that it was not necessary for an employee to be aware that she was not being paid in accordance with the legislation in order to resign because of such conduct). In *Crawford v Suffolk Mental Health Partnership* [2012] EWCA Civ 138, [2012] IRLR 402 Elias LJ observed, *obiter*, that suspending an employee as a 'knee-jerk' reaction would be a breach of the implied term of mutual trust and confidence. See also CONTRACT OF EMPLOYMENT (8).

A complaint of constructive dismissal may be based upon the conduct of a fellow employee even though that employee would not have had the authority to dismiss the complainant; the test is whether the employer is vicariously liable for the conduct complained of (*Hilton International Hotels (UK) Ltd v Protopapa* [1990] IRLR 316; see also *Warnes v Trustees of Cheriton Oddfellows Social Club* [1993] IRLR 58; and VICARIOUS LIABILITY (57)).

rather than to be dismissed (the alternative having been expressed to him by the employer in the terms of the threat that if he does not resign he will be dismissed), the mechanics of the resignation do not cause that to be other than a dismissal. The cases do not in terms go further than that. We find the principle to be one of causation."

Sheffield v Oxford Controls was endorsed by the Court of Appeal in *Jones v Mid-Glamorgan County Council* [1997] ICR 815, [1997] IRLR 685. Again, in *Sandhu v Jan de Rijk Transport Ltd* [2007] EWCA Civ 430, [2007] IRLR 519, the Court of Appeal construed a forced resignation during one meeting as a dismissal, holding that resignation implies some form of negotiation and discussion and must be a genuine choice on the part of the employee. The Court of Appeal observed that none of the authorities treated as a resignation a decision made during a single meeting, and placed weight on the facts that the employee had had no warning that the purpose of the meeting was to dismiss him, had had no advice, and had had no time to reflect.

In considering these authorities regard must now be had to the terms of *ERA 1996, s 111A*. That section (inserted by *Enterprise and Regulatory Reform Act 2013, s 14*) provides that pre-termination negotiations will not be admissible as evidence in a complaint of unfair dismissal unless the tribunal considers that there has been improper behaviour. The precise implications are yet to be fully worked out, but one potential effect of the section is that the circumstances of many 'forced resignations' which hitherto might have founded a complaint of constructive dismissal will not now be admissible before a tribunal at all. The leading case on *section 111A* is now *Faithorn Farell Timms v Bailey* [2016] ICR 1054, [2016] IRLR 839.

54.9   Repudiatory conduct by the employee

Employers sometimes consider that an employee has 'dismissed himself' by breaching some fundamental term of his contract of employment, such as failing to attend work. This approach is incorrect. In *Thomas Marshall (Exports) Ltd v Guinle* [1978] ICR 905, [1978] IRLR 174, [1978] 3 All ER 193, Megarry VC held that an employee's repudiation of his contract of employment had to be accepted by the employer to bring the contract to an end. This 'acceptance' view was approved by a majority of the Court of Appeal in *Gunton v Richmond-upon-Thames London Borough Council* [1980] ICR 755, [1980] IRLR 321, [1980] 3 All ER 577, and by a majority of the Court of Appeal in *London Transport Executive v Clarke* [1981] ICR 355, [1981] IRLR 166. Similarly, in *Boyo v Lambeth London Borough Council* [1994] ICR 727, [1995] IRLR 50, the Court of Appeal endorsed the 'acceptance' view of the termination of a contract of employment. The Court of Appeal took this approach in *Triggs v GAB Robins (UK) Ltd* [2008] EWCA Civ 17, [2008] IRLR 317 in respect of a requirement for an employee to accept an employer's repudiatory breach, making a conceptual distinction between the repudiatory breach and the acceptance which effects the dismissal (see TERMINATION OF EMPLOYMENT (49)).

There is now an authoritative exposition of the law in this area in the Supreme Court's decision in *Société Générale v Geys* [2012] UKSC 63, [2013] ICR 117, [2013] IRLR 122, [2013] 1 All ER 1061. By a majority, the Supreme Court approved the *Gunton/Boyo* 'acceptance' approach which it described as the 'elective theory' (as opposed to the 'automatic theory'). It remains the case, therefore, that an unaccepted repudiatory breach of contract by an employee is a 'thing writ in water'.

54.10   Situations of no dismissal

There is *no dismissal* in the following cases.

(a)   *Termination of the contract of employment by consent of both parties* (see *52.8* above).

(b)   *Termination by the employee whether with or without notice* in the absence of 'constructive dismissal' or forced resignation (see **54.7** and **54.8** above). A valid notice given by an employee cannot usually be withdrawn without the employer's consent (*Riordan v War Office* [1959] 3 All ER 552, [1960] 3 All ER 774; *Sothern v Franks Charlesly & Co* [1981] IRLR 278). However, it may be that words of resignation (or dismissal) spoken in the heat of the moment can be regarded as not being a true resignation, or else can be withdrawn if this is done very quickly (*Martin v Yeoman Aggregates Ltd* [1983] ICR 314, [1983] IRLR 49; *Barclay v City of Glasgow District Council* [1983] IRLR 313 and *Willoughby v CF Capital* [2011] EWCA Civ 1115, [2011] IRLR 985 (above **54.5**)).

(c)   *Termination of employment by 'frustration'*. If the contract of employment cannot be performed or if its performance becomes radically different from that contemplated when the contract was entered into, it may be considered to have been terminated by frustration. The doctrine of frustration continues to apply to contracts of employment, though the EAT has recently let it be known that that is only due to binding Court of Appeal authority and its application is "not beyond question" (*Warner v Armfield Retail & Leisure Ltd* [2014] ICR 239; see further **49.3** Termination of Employment).

(d)   *Termination on the occurrence of an external event*. A contract for a voyage may be terminated 'automatically' when the voyage is completed (*Ryan v Shipboard Maintenance Ltd* [1980] ICR 88, [1980] IRLR 16). An appointment for 'as long as sufficient funds are provided either by the Manpower Services Commission or by other firms/sponsors to fund it' was held to come to an end automatically when the specified event took place (*Brown v Knowsley Borough Council* [1986] IRLR 102). See also **54.6** above.

54.11 EMPLOYMENT FOR QUALIFYING PERIOD

From 1 June 1999, the qualifying period for claims of unfair dismissal was reduced from two years to one year (*ERA 1996, s 108(1)* and the *Unfair Dismissal and Statement of Reasons for Dismissal (Variation of Qualifying Period) Order 1999 (SI 1999/1436)*). For persons whose period of continuous employment begins on or after 6 April 2012, the qualifying period is once again two years (*Unfair Dismissal and Statement of Reasons for Dismissal (Variation of Qualifying Period) Order 2012 (SI 2012/989)* and *ERA 1996, s 108(1)* as amended).

The original two-year qualifying period was challenged in *R v Secretary of State for Employment, ex p Seymour-Smith (No 2)* [2000] IRLR 263, [2000] 1 All ER 857 on the basis that it had a disproportionately adverse effect on women and was inconsistent with the *EC Treaty, art 119*, now *TFEU, art 157* (equal pay). This battleground has not been re-entered following the recent reversion to a two-year qualifying period.

The qualifying period is calculated from the beginning of the employee's employment under the relevant contract of employment. This could be earlier than the date the employee starts performing duties under the contract (*General of the Salvation Army v Dewsbury* [1984] ICR 498, [1984] IRLR 222; but in *Wood v Cunard Line Ltd* [1991] ICR 13, [1990] IRLR 281 the Court of Appeal expressed some doubt as to whether *Dewsbury* was correctly decided. See also *Koenig v Mind Gym Ltd* (UKEAT/0201/12) [2013] All ER (D) 261 (May)). The first day on which the employee started work is included, so that an employee who has worked 365 days (and whose period of continuous employment commenced prior to 6 April 2012) is protected against unfair dismissal (*O'Brien v Pacitti Jones (a firm)* [2005] CSIH 56, [2005] IRLR 888).

If an employee is dismissed on medical grounds in compliance with any law, regulation or code of practice providing for health and safety at work, the qualifying period for a claim is only one month (*ERA 1996, s 108(2)*).

54.11   Unfair Dismissal – I: The Right to Make a Claim

An employee who is wrongfully dismissed in breach of the contractual notice entitlements and whose dismissal has the effect of preventing him or her from attaining the qualifying period for a complaint of unfair dismissal may not in an action for wrongful dismissal recover damages representing the loss of the chance to bring unfair dismissal proceedings (*Harper v Virgin Net Ltd* [2004] EWCA Civ 271, [2004] IRLR 390). Note also that in *Lancaster & Duke v Wileman* [2019] IRLR 112, [2019] ICR 125, the EAT held that an employee dismissed summarily shortly before the qualifying period for bringing an unfair dismissal was reached could not as of right rely on the statutory minimum notice period to extend the period of employment. *Section 86(6)* of *ERA 1996* preserves the right of the employer to terminate the contract of employment without notice for repudiatory breach, and in those circumstances the effective date of termination is not extended by the statutory minimum period of notice.

In certain other cases, no qualifying period is necessary. Generally speaking, the cases in which no qualifying period of employment is necessary in order to acquire the right to complain of unfair dismissal also involve reasons for dismissal which are automatically unfair (see UNFAIR DISMISSAL II, 55.3). These are where the reason or principal reason for the dismissal was:

(a)   that the employee was summoned for jury service or was absent from work because he attended at any place in pursuance of being summoned for jury service, unless the employee's absence was likely to cause substantial injury to the employer's undertaking, the employer brought those circumstances to the employee's attention, and the employee unreasonably refused or failed to apply to the appropriate officer for excusal from or deferral of the obligation to attend (*ERA 1996, s 108(3)(aa)*);

(b)   a prescribed reason in connection with leave for family reasons (*ERA 1996, s 108(3)(b)*);

(c)   a health and safety-related reason (*ERA 1996, s 108(3)(c)*);

(d)   a reason connected with the refusal of Sunday work by a shop worker or betting worker (*ERA 1996, s 108(3)(d)*);

(e)   a reason connected with the refusal of additional hours on Sunday by a shop worker (*ERA 1996, s 108(3)(da)*);

(f)   a reason related to working time (*ERA 1996, s 108(3)(dd)*);

(g)   a reason connected with the performance by an employee who is a pension scheme trustee of his functions as such a trustee (*ERA 1996, s 108(3)(e)*);

(h)   a reason connected with the performance by an employee representative (see **40.4** REDUNDANCY – II and **53.23** TRANSFER OF UNDERTAKINGS), or a candidate in an election for such an employee representative, or of his functions as such an employee representative or candidate in a redundancy or transfer of undertakings context (*ERA 1996, s 108(3)(f)*);

(i)   a reason connected with the making of a protected disclosure under *ERA 1996, ss 43A–43L* (*ERA 1996, s 108(3)(ff)*);

(j)   the assertion of a statutory right (*ERA 1996, s 108(3)(g)*);

(k)   a reason connected with the assertion of rights under the *National Minimum Wage Act 1998* (*ERA 1996, s 108(3)(gg)*);

(l)   that the worker took, or proposed to take, action with a view to enforcing or securing the benefit of a right under the *Tax Credits Act 2002*, or a penalty was imposed upon the employer as a result of action taken by, or on behalf of, the employee for the purpose of enforcing his or her rights under the *Act (ERA 1996, s 108(3)(gh))*;

(m)   a prescribed reason in connection with flexible working (*ERA 1996, s 108(3)(gi)*);

(n)   a prescribed reason in connection with pension enrolment (*ERA 1996, s 108(3)(gj)*);

(o)   a prescribed reason in connection with applications for study and training (*ERA 1996, s 108(3)(gk)*);

(p)   a prescribed reason in connection with blacklists (*ERA 1996, s 108(3)(gl)*);

(q)   that the employee had refused to accept an offer of employee shareholder status (*ERA 1996, s 108(3)(gm)*);

(r)   a selection for redundancy for a reason which would have been automatically unfair if it had been the reason for dismissal (*ERA 1996, s 108(3)(h)*);

(s)   that the worker had carried out activities as a member of a special negotiating body, a European Works Council, as an information and consultation representative, or as a candidate in an election for such a position, or that the employee exercised the specific rights relevant to the above bodies which are listed in the *Transnational Information and Consultation of Employees Regulations 1999, reg 28* (*ERA 1996, s 108(3)(hh)*);

(t)   that the worker has brought proceedings against his employer under the *Part-time Workers (Prevention of Less Favourable Treatment) Regulations 2000* or has otherwise done anything under the *Regulations* in relation to the employer or any other person (*ERA 1996, s 108(3)(i)*);

(u)   that the employee brought proceedings against his employer under the *Fixed-term Employees (Prevention of Less Favourable Treatment) Regulations 2002* or has otherwise done anything under the *Regulations* in relation to the employer or any other person (*ERA 1996, s 108(3)(j)*);

(v)   the performance or attempted performance by an employee representative or election candidate in the context of the *European Public Limited-Liability Company Regulations 2004* (*ERA 1996, s 108(3)(k)*);

(w)   the performance or attempted performance by an employee representative or election candidate in the context of the *Information and Consultation of Employees Regulations 2004* (*ERA 1996, s 108(3)(l)*);

(x)   the performance or attempted performance of functions or activities as a representative or candidate under the *Occupational and Personal Pension Schemes (Consultation by Employers and Miscellaneous Amendment) Regulations 2006* (*ERA 1996, s 108(3)(m)*);

(y)   that the employee performed or proposed to perform any functions or activities as a member, representative, candidate or participant under the *European Cooperative Society (Involvement of Employees) Regulations 2006 (SI 2006/2059)* or that the employee or a person on his behalf made or proposed to make a request for time off or remuneration for time off under the Regulations (*ERA 1996, s 108(3)(o)*);

(z)   that the employee took or proposed to take any proceedings to enforce a right conferred by the *Companies (Cross-Border Mergers) Regulations 2007*, exercised or proposed to exercise any entitlement to apply, complain or appeal to the CAC or Appeal Tribunal, acted with a view to securing that a special negotiating body did or did not come into existence, indicated whether he did or did not support the coming into existence of a special negotiating body, stood for election as a member of a special negotiating body or director of UK transferee company, canvassed lawfully before a ballot under the Regulations, voted, expressed doubts about the proper conduct of a ballot, or proposed to do, failed to do, or proposed to decline to do, various acts in relation to such a ballot; and in respect of an employee who is a member of a special negotiating body, a director of a transferee company or a candidate in an election to such a position, that the reason is: that the employee performed or proposed to perform any functions or activities as a member, director or candidate, or the employee or someone on his behalf made or proposed to make a request for time off work or remuneration for time off work (*ERA 1996, s 108(3)(p)*);

(A)   that the employee did a protected act pursuant to rights conferred by the *European Public Limited Liability Company (Employee Involvement) (Great Britain) Regulations 2009* (*ERA 1996, s 108(3)(q)*);

(B)   that the employee did a protected act under the *Agency Workers Regulations 2010, reg 17* (*ERA 1996, s 108(3)(r)*);

(C)   that the employee was dismissed for a reason relating to his political opinions or affiliation (*ERA 1996, s 108(4)*. This provision implements the decision of the European Court of Human Rights in *Redfearn v United Kingdom* [2013] IRLR 51);

(D)   a union-related reason (or where selection for redundancy was for a union-related reason) (*TULR(C)A 1992, s 154*);

(E)   a reason connected with trade union recognition or bargaining arrangements (*TULR(C)A 1992, Sch A1, para 162* inserted by *Employment Relations Act 1999, s 1(2) and Sch 1*);

(F)   that the employee exercised or sought to exercise the right, pursuant to *Employment Relations Act 1999, s 10*, to be accompanied to a disciplinary or grievance hearing or that the employee accompanied or sought to accompany another worker to such a hearing (*Employment Relations Act 1999, s 12(4)*);

(G)   that the employee was dismissed for taking part in protected industrial action in the circumstances set out in *TULR(C)A 1992, s 138A*, introduced by *Employment Relations Act 1999, s 16 and Sch 5*. See **54.17** below;

(H)   a reason connected with the employee's membership of a reserve force (as defined in *section 374* of the *Armed Forces Act 2006*).

54.12   Calculation of period of continuous employment

The detailed provisions relating to the calculation of a period of continuous employment are set out in *ERA 1996, ss 210–219*. They are considered fully in CONTINUOUS EMPLOYMENT (7). They provide, for example, that there is continuity of employment when the business in which an employee works is transferred from one owner to another (see *Oakland v Wellswood (Yorkshire) Ltd* [2009] EWCA Civ 1094, [2010] IRLR 82, in which the Court avoided deciding the question whether the situation involved "analogous insolvency proceedings" and the fact of the transfer was conceded), when the employee is incapable of work because of sickness or injury, or absent from work wholly or partly because of pregnancy or childbirth or family-related leave.

54.13   Effective date of termination

The qualifying period is calculated up to and including the effective date of termination. The effective date of termination is defined as:

(a)   in relation to an employee whose contract of employment is *terminated by notice*, whether given by his employer or by the employee, the date on which that notice expires;

(b)   in relation to an employee whose contract of employment is terminated *without notice*, the date on which the termination takes effect; and

(c)   in relation to an employee who is employed under a *contract for a fixed term*, where that term expires without being renewed under the same contract, the date on which that term expires.

(ERA 1996, s 97(1).)

The effective date of termination is an objectively determined statutory construct, which it is not open to the employer and employee to agree between themselves (*Fitzgerald v University of Kent at Canterbury* [2004] EWCA Civ 143, [2004] IRLR 300). It is possible therefore for the EDT not to coincide with when an employment contract terminates at common law (see for example *Geys v Société Générale* [2011] EWCA Civ 307, [2011] IRLR 482). In most cases, the effective date of termination is the date on which the employee ceases work. If an employer makes it clear to an employee that he is terminating his employment forthwith and pays him a sum of money in lieu of notice, the effective date of termination is the actual date of termination of the employment whether or not the employee was dismissed in breach of contract (*Dedman v British Building and Engineering Appliances Ltd* [1974] ICR 53, [1973] IRLR 379, [1974] 1 All ER 520; *Robert Cort and Son Ltd v Charman* [1981] ICR 816, [1981] IRLR 437; see also *Stapp v Shaftesbury Society* [1982] IRLR 326; *Leech v Preston Borough Council* [1985] ICR 192, [1985] IRLR 337; *Batchelor v British Railways Board* [1987] IRLR 136; *Octavius Atkinson & Sons Ltd v Morris* [1989] ICR 431, [1989] IRLR 158) and *Rabess v London Fire and Emergency Planning Authority* [2017] IRLR 147). If, however, the contract continues although the employee stays away from work, the effective date of termination will be the date upon which the contract comes to an end in accordance with the notice.

The Court of Appeal in *Kirklees Metropolitan Borough Council v Radecki* [2009] EWCA Civ 298, [2009] IRLR 555 held that the effective date of termination is the date of summary dismissal, as long as the summary dismissal is known to the employee. The question of the effective date of termination should, however, be freed from the niceties of contract law concerning acceptance of a repudiatory breach, so that ordinary employees are able to understand when employment has come to an end and time starts running for the purposes of presenting employment tribunal claims. Where, after protracted compromise discussions, the local authority had informed the employee that it would cease to pay him on a particular date, the cessation of payment unequivocally and unilaterally ended the employment. In *Gisda Cyf v Barratt*, [2010] UKSC 41, [2010] ICR 1475, however, the Supreme Court held that the effective date of termination was the date on which the employee actually read the letter of summary dismissal, or had had a reasonable opportunity to read it. The letter had been sent on 29 November, but the employee had left home before the post arrived on 30 November in order to visit her sister who had just had a baby in another city. The employee did not return home until late on 3 December, and she did not enquire about her post until 4 December, when she read the letter dismissing her. The 'general law of contract' the Court held, should not even provide a preliminary guide to the proper interpretation of *ERA 1996, s 97* as it is part of a charter protecting employee's rights, and an interpretation that promotes those rights is to be preferred. Note, however, that in *Newcastle Upon Tyne Hospitals NHS Foundation Trust v Haywood* [2018] UKSC 22, [2018] IRLR 644, the Supreme Court drew on the *Gisda Cyf* approach in order to find that at common law, save where express provision is made otherwise, a term was to be implied into an employment contract that a period of notice would begin to run from the date when the letter giving it was received by the employee and the employee had either read or had a reasonable opportunity to read it.

The question of the effective date of termination is a mixed question of fact and law, not a simple question of fact (*Robinson v Bowskill* [2014] ICR D7, [2013] All ER (D) 351 (Nov)).

In *West v Kneels Ltd* [1987] ICR 146, [1986] IRLR 430, the EAT held that 'seven days' notice', used on dismissal, meant seven *clear* days. The contract cannot be terminated until the employee receives notification of the dismissal (*Brown v Southall and Knight* [1980] IRLR 130, *McMaster v Manchester Airport plc* [1998] IRLR 112 and *Gisda Cyf v Barratt* [2010] ICR 1475, [2010] IRLR 1073, [2010] 4 All ER 851) (and note *Newcastle Upon Tyne v Haywood* (above), applying the same approach to the provision of notice at common law). Where an employee exercises a right of appeal against his dismissal but his appeal is not allowed, in the absence of any contrary contractual provision the effective date of termination will be the date of the original dismissal (*J Sainsbury Ltd v Savage* [1981] ICR 1, [1980] IRLR 109, approved in *West Midlands Co-operative Society Ltd v Tipton* [1986] ICR 192, [1986] IRLR 112, [1986] 1 All ER 513). For cases in which a successful contractual appeal has led to the contract being revived see *Roberts v West Coast Trains Ltd* [2005] ICR 254, [2004] IRLR 788, *Salmon v Castleback Care (Teesdale) Ltd* [2015] ICR 735, [2015] IRLR 189 and *Folkestone Nursing Home Ltd v Patel* [2018] EWCA Civ 1843, [2019] ICR 273.

For the purpose of deciding whether the employee had the necessary qualifying period of employment, if an employer dismisses an employee giving him no notice or less notice than that required by *ERA 1996, s 86*, the effective date will be the date on which the statutory minimum period of notice would have expired had it been given (*ERA 1996, s 97(2)*). Thus, if an employer dismisses an employee without notice after 51 weeks, the effective date of termination will be taken to be one week later, as the minimum period of notice after more than one month's employment is one week (see **49.7** TERMINATION OF EMPLOYMENT). The employee will thus be entitled to claim compensation for unfair dismissal (assuming the period of continuous employment commenced prior to 6 April 2012). However, the extra time will not be added where an employee is summarily dismissed in circumstances where the employer is entitled to dismiss summarily, eg for gross misconduct (see **49.13** TERMINATION OF EMPLOYMENT and *Lancaster & Duke Ltd v Wileman* [2019] IRLR 112, [2019] ICR 125). An employer is not entitled simply to define a dismissal as being for gross misconduct without the tribunal investigating whether that description is justified (*Lanton Leisure Ltd v White and Gibson* [1987] IRLR 119 and *Lancaster & Duke v Wileman* (2018) UKEAT/0256/17, [2019] IRLR 112, [2019] ICR 125). The statutory extension of the effective date of termination applies even where the employee waives his right to notice (*Secretary of State for Employment v Staffordshire County Council* [1989] IRLR 117, the Court of Appeal holding that the fact that an employee has waived his right to notice or has accepted a payment in lieu of notice under *ERA 1996, s 97(4)* is relevant only to his rights in contract).

For the purpose of calculating the qualifying period of employment where an employee terminates his contract of employment in circumstances in which he is entitled to do so by reason of his employer's conduct, the effective date of termination will be considered to be the date on which the statutory minimum notice required of the employer would have expired (*ERA 1996, s 97(4)*).

54.14 RETIRING AGE

The *Employment Equality (Age) Regulations 2006 (SI 2006/1031)* came into force on 1 October 2006 and were largely repealed with effect from 1st October 2010 by *Equality Act 2010, s 211(2), Schedule 27, Part 2*.

The upper age limit for complaining of unfair dismissal, contained in *ERA 1996, s 109*, was removed and was replaced by a byzantine statutory process contained in *ERA 1996, sections 98ZA–98ZH*. With effect from 6 April 2011 however, those provisions were repealed and the concept of default retirement age abolished by the *Employment Equality (Repeal of*

Retirement Age Provisions) Regulations 2011 (SI 2011/1069) (subject to savings in *regulation 5*). See **54.4** UNFAIR DISMISSAL **II (55)**, RETIREMENT **(43)**. Retirement is no longer a potentially fair reason for dismissal under *ERA 1996, section 98*.

54.15 EXCLUDED CLASSES OF EMPLOYEES

Certain classes of employment are excluded from the protection of the unfair dismissal provisions. If a respondent wishes to show that a claimant falls within an excluded class, the burden of proof is on him to do so (*Kapur v Shields* [1976] ICR 26). The excluded cases are defined by *ERA 1996, ss 199* and *200*.

(a)   Dismissal from any employment as a master or as a member of the crew of a *fishing vessel* where the employee is not remunerated otherwise than by a share in the profits or gross earnings of the vessel (*ERA 1996, s 199(2)*);

(b)   Dismissal from employment under a contract of employment in police service or to persons engaged in such employment (*ERA 1996, s 200* and see *Spence v British Railways Board* [2001] ICR 232, *Redbridge LBC v Dhinsa* [2014] EWCA Civ 178 and *Vining v Wandsworth LBC* [2018] ICR 499, except for unfair dismissals on health and safety grounds (contrary to *ERA 1996, s 100*), or because the employee has made a protected disclosure (contrary to *ERA 1996, s 103A*));

(c)   Dismissal from employment where the employee is an "employee shareholder" within the meaning of *ERA 1996, s 205A*. Such individuals (of whom there are thought to be very few) retain the protection of the automatically unfair dismissal provisions. For the circumstances in which an employee will be found to have given up the right not to be unfairly dismissed as an employee shareholder see *Barrasso v New Look Retailers Ltd* [2020] ICR 448.

Certain other employees may also, for a variety of reasons short of an absolute statutory bar be excluded from the right to complain of unfair dismissal:

(a)   Dismissal from employment in respect of which the employee has validly contracted out of his right to claim compensation for unfair dismissal (*ERA 1996, s 203(2)* and see **54.19**, **54.20** below);

(b)   Those whose employment lacks a sufficient connection with Great Britain. *Section 196 of the ERA 1996* was repealed in its entirety by *s 32(3)* of the *Employment Relations Act 1999* and so, with effect from 25 October 1999, the territorial limits were removed. For those dismissed before 25 October 1999, any employment where under his contract of employment the employee ordinarily worked outside Great Britain was an excluded case.

The position is now governed by a series of decisions of the appellate courts. In *Lawson v Serco Ltd* [2006] UKHL 3, [2006] IRLR 289, [2006] 1 All ER 823 the House of Lords gave guidance on the circumstances in which the right not to be unfairly dismissed applies. A claimant will generally be protected if they were working in Great Britain at the time of his dismissal and peripatetic employees are subject to a 'base' test. It is a question of law where an employee is based. The EAT applied the *Serco* test in *Williams v University of Nottingham* [2007] IRLR 660, *Bleuse v MBT Transport Ltd* [2008] IRLR 264, *Ministry of Defence v Wallis* [2010] ICR 1301, [2010] IRLR 1035 (and see [2011] EWCA Civ 231) and *Pervez v Macquarie* [2011] ICR 266, [2011] IRLR 284. The Supreme Court revisited the *Serco* test in *Duncombe v Secretary of State for Children, Schools and Families (No 2)* [2011] ICR 1312, [2011] IRLR 840, [2011] 4 All ER 1020 and *Ravat v Halliburton & Manufacturing & Services Ltd* [2012] ICR 389, [2012] IRLR 315, [2012] 2 All ER 905 and examples of the synthesis of these authorities and their application are to be found in the Court of

Appeal's decisions in *Bates van Winkelhof v Clyde & Co LLP* [2013] ICR 883, [2012] IRLR 992, [2013] 1 All ER 844 and *Dhunna v Creditsights Ltd* [2015] ICR 105, [2014] IRLR 953. In *Smania v Standard Chartered Bank* [2015] ICR 436, [2015] IRLR 271, the EAT held that the test was no different if the complaint was of automatically unfair dismissal on whistleblowing grounds. In *British Council v Jeffery* [2018] EWCA Civ 2253, [2019] IRLR 123 the Court of Appeal held that whilst there were certain inconsistencies between the judgments in *Lawson* and those in *Ravat*, the 'sufficient connection' test was a matter of evaluative judgment based on the facts, and as such would only be interfered with on appeal if the appellate court was satisfied that the assessment of the various factors was 'wrong'.

The factual examples within the case law on *ERA 1996, s 196* remain of relevance to cases where it is asserted that an employment tribunal has jurisdiction over certain employment, even though the legal test for jurisdiction over unfair dismissal claims changed with the repeal of *s 196*. Where an employee worked both inside and outside Great Britain, one would look at the terms of the contract, express or implied, and how the contract operated in practice, in order to ascertain where the employee's base was (cf *Wilson v Maynard Shipbuilding Consultants AB* [1978] ICR 376, [1977] IRLR 491, [1978] 2 All ER 78, and per Lord Denning MR and Sir David Cairns in *Todd v British Midland Airways Ltd* [1978] ICR 959, [1978] IRLR 370). See also *Jackson v Ghost Ltd* [2003] IRLR 824, *Crofts v Cathay Pacific Airways Ltd* [2005] EWCA Civ 599, [2005] IRLR 624, *Diggins v Condor Marine Crewing Services Ltd* [2009] EWCA Civ 1133, [2010] IRLR 119 and *Green v SIG Trading Ltd* [2017] ICR 1274. In *Windstar Management Services Ltd v Harris* [2016] ICR 847, [2016] IRLR 929 Elisabeth Laing J rejected the suggestion that she should follow the approach taken to place of work for a seafarer adopted by Leggatt J in *R (Fleet Maritime Services Bermuda Ltd) v Pensions Regulator* [2016] IRLR 199 (a case concerned with pension auto-enrolment under the *Pensions Act 2008*) and instead applied the approach in *Lawson, Duncombe* and *Ravat*.

The contract to be considered is that subsisting at the time of dismissal, and not any previous contract between the parties *(Weston v Vega Space Systems Engineering Ltd* [1989] IRLR 429). Where the contract of employment is of little assistance, the tribunal should go by the conduct of the parties and the way they have operated the contract (per Lord Denning MR in *Todd* at 964).

The relevant location used to be the employer's operational base, not the actual place of work (*Addison v Denholm Ship Management (UK) Ltd* [1997] IRLR 389).

A person employed to work on board a ship registered in the United Kingdom (not being a ship registered at a port outside Great Britain) used to be regarded as a person who under his contract ordinarily worked in Great Britain unless:

(i)   the employment was wholly outside Great Britain; or

(ii)   the employee was not ordinarily resident in Great Britain.

   (*ERA 1996, s 196(5)* now repealed); see, eg *Wood v Cunard Line Ltd* [1991] ICR 13, [1990] IRLR 281.)

Employees engaged upon certain activities connected with offshore drilling were given employment protection rights by the *Employment Protection (Offshore Employment) Order 1976 (SI 1976/766)*. See *Addison v Denholm Ship Management (UK) Ltd*, above, and *ERA 1996, s 201*.

54.16 EMPLOYEE CANNOT ENFORCE RIGHTS IF CONTRACT ILLEGAL

The courts will not enforce an illegal contract. Thus, if it appears to an employment tribunal that, for example, a contract of employment was entered into with an agreement that no tax be paid on some part or all of the remuneration, the tribunal may consider the agreement to be a fraud on the Revenue and may dismiss the claim. The position will normally be different if the employee was innocent of any wrongdoing, or if they merely performed some unlawful act in the course of an otherwise lawful employment. The leading case is *Colen v Cebrian (UK) Ltd* [2004] IRLR 210 and reference should also be made to *Enfield Technical Services v Payne* [2008] ICR 1423, [2008] IRLR 500, *ParkingEye Ltd v Somerfield Stores Ltd* [2013] QB 840 and *Patel v Mirza* [2017] 1 All ER 191, [2017] AC 467. For a fuller discussion, see **8.24** CONTRACT OF EMPLOYMENT.

54.17 DISMISSAL IN CONNECTION WITH A LOCK-OUT OR STRIKE

Official action

The law relating to unfair dismissals in the context of official industrial action was changed substantially by *Employment Relations Act 1999, s 16* and *Sch 5*, which introduced a new *TULCRA 1992, s 238A* from 24 April 2000. (See *Employment Relations Act 1999 (Commencement No 5 and Transitional Provision) Order 2000, art 3 (SI 2000/875)*) (*TULR(C)A 1992, s 238*, as amended by *TURERA 1993, Sch 8 para 77* and *ERA 1996, Sch 1 para 56*). *Section 238A* was amended further by the *Employment Relations Act 2004*.

Prior to the changes introduced by *Sch 5* and the *Employment Relations Act 2004*, employees who took part in lawful industrial action lost their right to claim unfair dismissal if they were dismissed whilst the industrial action was taking place and all other employees who were taking part in the industrial action were similarly dismissed. The main consequences of the changes were that:

(a)   the right to claim unfair dismissal is restored for many employees who are taking part in lawful, official, industrial action, provided that the reason for their dismissal is their participation in the industrial action; and

(b)   dismissal for such a reason will, in such cases, be automatically unfair.

TULR(C)A 1992, s 238, as amended by *Sch 5*, provides that the exclusion from the right to claim unfair dismissal if dismissal takes place during industrial action will not apply where the employee is regarded as unfairly dismissed by reason of *TULR(C)A 1992, s 238A*. An employee will be treated as being unfairly dismissed by reason of *s 238A* if the employee is taking part in protected industrial action and if certain other conditions (set out below) are satisfied.

Section 238A defines 'protected industrial action' as meaning action which was induced by an act protected by *TULR(C)A 1992, s 219* (see **46.3** STRIKES AND INDUSTRIAL ACTION). In effect, 'protected industrial action' is official industrial action in respect of which the trade union concerned and its officials enjoy immunity from suit.

An employee will be treated as having been automatically unfairly dismissed if the reason or principal reason for dismissal was that the employee has taken part in protected industrial action and:

(i)   the date of dismissal is within the protected period; or

(ii)   the date of dismissal is after the end of protected period and the employee had stopped taking protected industrial action before the end of that period; or

accordingly, it was void by reason of *EPCA 1978, s 140(1)* (the predecessor section of *ERA 1996, s 203(1)*). However, in *Scott v Coalite Fuels and Chemicals Ltd* [1988] ICR 355, [1988] IRLR 131, an employee who had agreed to accept voluntary retirement as an alternative to redundancy was not successful in putting forward a similar argument. In *Salton (Logan) v Durham County Council* [1989] IRLR 99, EAT, a case where an employee under threat of dismissal agreed terms for termination, *Igbo* was distinguished on the grounds that this was a separate contract from the contract of employment, entered into without duress, after proper advice and for good consideration, and that termination was not contingent upon the happening of future events in circumstances which the parties might not have envisaged. In *M&P Steelcraft Ltd v Ellis* [2008] ICR 578, [2008] IRLR 355 the EAT suggested that the conditions necessary for an infringement of *ERA 1996, s 203* were (i) that 'but for' the clause in question the employee would have enforceable statutory rights and (ii) that the only purpose of the clause must be to alter, or seek to alter, what would, absent the clause, be the legal effect of the contractual arrangements.

Similarly, any agreement to pay an ex-employee money in consideration for his refraining from presenting or pursuing a complaint in an employment tribunal is normally unenforceable, subject to the exceptions considered in **54.20** below.

54.20   Exceptions

An agreement restricting the right to claim for unfair dismissal is enforceable if it is contained in the following agreements:

(a)   a valid settlement agreement satisfying the statutory conditions, including that the employee should have taken independent legal advice (see **19.20** EMPLOYMENT TRIBUNALS – **I** and note *Hinton v University of East London* [2005] EWCA Civ 532, [2005] IRLR 552 and *Industrious Ltd v Horizon Recruitment Ltd (in liq)* [2010] IRLR 204) (*ERA 1996, s 203(2)*);

(b)   a dismissal procedure agreement reached between employers and one or more independent trade unions which has been approved by the Secretary of State;

(c)   any agreement to refrain from presenting a complaint that he was unfairly dismissed where the conciliation officer has taken action in accordance with his statutory duties (see **2.3** ADVISORY, CONCILIATION AND ARBITRATION SERVICE (ACAS));

(d)   any agreement to refrain from proceeding with a complaint where the conciliation officer has taken action in accordance with his statutory duties (see **2.3** ADVISORY, CONCILIATION AND ARBITRATION SERVICE (ACAS)). Where there has been a transfer of an undertaking for the purposes of the *Transfer of Undertakings (Protection of Employment) Regulations 2006 (SI 2006/246)*, such an agreement if made by the transferor and not finalised until after the transfer will not prevent an employee from claiming against the transferee (*Thompson v Walon Car Delivery* [1997] IRLR 343).

55   Unfair Dismissal – II: The Fairness of the Dismissal

Cross-references. See UNFAIR DISMISSAL – I (54) for the right to make a claim; UNFAIR DISMISSAL – III (56) for remedies for unfair dismissal.

55.1   REASONS FOR DISMISSAL

Once the fact of dismissal has been established, it is for the employer to show (*ERA 1996, s 98(1)*):

(a)   what was the reason (or, if there was more than one, the principal reason) for the dismissal; and

(b)   that it was one of the reasons set out in **55.2** below.

An employment tribunal will investigate the real reason for the employee's dismissal. The fact that an employer told an employee that the reason for his dismissal was, for example, redundancy will not preclude the tribunal from deciding that the real reason for dismissal was, say, lack of capability. If there is a dispute over the reason for the dismissal, the burden of proving which one of the competing reasons for the dismissal was the principal reason is on the employer (*Maund v Penwith District Council* [1984] ICR 143, [1984] IRLR 24).

The reason for dismissal is the set of facts known to the employer or of beliefs held by it, which cause it to dismiss the employee (*Abernethy v Mott, Hay and Anderson* [1974] ICR 323, [1974] IRLR 213). This can also be expressed as the factor or factors operating on the mind of the decision-maker which cause them to make the decision to dismiss, or alternatively as what motivates them to do so (*Jhuti v Royal Mail Ltd* [2018] ICR 982). The same approach will be adopted in a case in which the organisation did not believe at the time that it was in fact the employee's employer, though this may of course impact on the issue of fairness when the procedure followed comes to be assessed (*Dye v Royal Free London NHS Foundation Trust* (UKEAT/0350/15/DA) [2016] All ER (D) 99 (Sep)). Equally, the facts which cause the employer to act as it does are to be treated as the reason for the dismissal even if the employer does not realise that its actions amount to a dismissal as a matter of law (*Ely v YKK Fasteners (UK) Ltd* [1994] ICR 164). The tribunal should not find for the employer on a ground not argued before it if this would prejudice the employee who, for example, might have put his case differently if he was aware that the argument was being run (*Hannan v TNT-Ipec (UK) Ltd* [1986] IRLR 165). Whether or not it does so is a fact-sensitive question for the Tribunal (*Secretary of State for Justice v Norridge* (UKEAT/0443/13/LA) [2014] All ER (D) 85 (Aug) and see further the relevance of label attached to the reason at **55.2**).

What of a case in which one of the employer's employees, say the claimant's line manager, causes the claimant's dismissal, for example by giving a series of unfair performance appraisals, but does not himself take the decision to dismiss? Should his reason, or that of the dismissing officer, be treated as the reason for dismissal? This takes on particular significance if the reason for which the line manager so acted would render the dismissal automatically unfair (the reasons for dismissal falling within this category are set out further below). This issue has attracted a significant volume of appellate litigation in recent years. The general starting point is that when assessing the fairness of the dismissal, the circumstances known to the employer are those known to the dismissing officer, and those known to other senior officers not party to the decision to dismiss will not be attributed to that officer (*Orr v Milton Keynes Council* [2011] ICR 704, [2011] IRLR 317, [2011] 4 All ER 1256 (Sedley LJ dissenting)). In *Jhuti v Royal Mail Ltd* [2018] ICR 982 the Court of Appeal example is *Kelly v Royal Mail Group Ltd* (UKEAT/0262/18) (14 February 2019, unreported), in which the EAT again emphasised that how the reason for dismissal (in that case unsatisfactory performance) was labelled (in that case as capability or "some other substantial reason") was not determinative and, to that end, the pleaded label was of less significance. Of central importance is the operative, factual reason for dismissal. In *Secretary of State for Justice v Norridge* (UKEAT/0443/13/LA) [2014] All ER (D) 85 (Aug) detailed consideration was given to whether a dismissal can be fair where the reason relied upon is not the one pleaded or argued by the employer. The EAT was of the view that it could. The issue is whether or not the difference is one of substance, or is merely a matter of labelling. The question is a fact-sensitive one for the Tribunal to take in the circumstances of each case.

The tribunal should focus on the whole of the conduct which caused the employer to dismiss, not just part of it (*GM Packaging (UK) Ltd v Haslem* (UKEAT/0259/13/LA29) [2014] All ER (D) 209 (Feb) and *Marl International Ltd v Dickinson* (UKEAT/0447/12/KN) (22 February 2013, unreported)). However, it remains possible for a dismissal being found to be fair by reference to part of the reason for dismissal, even if the employer could not reasonably have dismissed in reliance upon some other part of the reason (*Robinson v Combat Stress* (UKEAT/0310/14/JOJ) [2014] All ER (D) 254 (Dec)). The EAT has confirmed that the same analysis applies in relation to reasons for dismissal other than misconduct, such as capability (*Devon & Cornwall Police and Crime Commissioner v Weavin* (UKEAT/0215/14/DA) (13 November 2014)).

In *Choksi v Royal Mail Group Ltd* (UKEAT/0280/15/LA) [2016] All ER (D) 261 (Jan), the EAT considered the following situation: (i) a dismissing officer dismisses for two instances of misconduct (A and B), but accepts that A, by itself, would not have justified the dismissal; (ii) an appeal officer upholds the dismissal, but also states that in his view, A by itself justified dismissal; (iii) the Employment Tribunal finds that the employer did not act reasonably in dismissing the employee for B, but acted reasonably in dismissing in relation to A. Is that approach permissible? As the EAT noted, if it is, it leads to an odd result. The employee would have been better placed having not appealed and gone straight to the Employment Tribunal, as the dismissal based on B would have been found to be unfair, and the dismissing officer would not have dismissed for A alone. That said, the reasonableness of a decision to dismiss will usually be scrutinised by reference to the process as a whole, including any appeal hearing (*West Midland Co-operative Society Ltd v Tipton* [1986] ICR 192, [1986] IRLR 112, [1986] 1 All ER 513). The EAT did not provide an absolute answer to this issue. Rather it found that the Employment Tribunal erred in law by failing to consider the differences in the reasoning of the dismissing and appeal officers on its decision, and remitted the matter for further consideration. As the EAT noted, the issue no doubt requires further analysis. In the meantime, it is submitted that the orthodox approach remains that the Employment Tribunal should examine the process as a whole, including the appeal, by reference to *ERA 1996, s 98(4)*. The view taken by the appeal officer remains relevant. That said, the fact that the dismissing officer did not consider dismissal justified for a certain act is likely to impact significantly upon the Employment Tribunal's analysis of whether or not the dismissal was ultimately within the range of reasonable responses or not.

If a claimant positively asserts a different and inadmissible reason for dismissal, he must produce some evidence to support his case (see *Kuzel v Roche Products Ltd* [2008] ICR 799, [2008] IRLR 530 where the claimant asserted that he had been dismissed because he made a protected disclosure (see **55.3** below)). The claimant does not bear the burden of proving that reason (unless he lacks the necessary qualifying service to bring a claim for "ordinary unfair dismissal", but some evidence must be put before the tribunal in support of his assertion. As the Court of Appeal stated in *Kuzel*, if the tribunal finds that the reason put forward by the employer was not, in fact, the reason for the dismissal, it is not correct to say, as a matter of law or logic, that it must find that the reason was that asserted by the employee (though as the court also noted, this will often be the case, and the conclusion that the reason advanced has not been proved may well support the employee's case as to the true reason). An illustration of that principle being applied in practice can be found in the EAT's decision in *Smith v Mid-Essex Hospital Services NHS Trust* (UKEAT/0239/17) (5 March 2018, unreported). The same analysis applies outside the context of whistleblowing to other automatically unfair reasons for dismissal (see, in the context of trade union activities, the decision in *Serco Ltd v Dahou* [2015] IRLR 30)).

So in cases where the employee asserts a different reason for dismissal, the tribunal should first consider the potentially fair reason advanced by the employer, since it bears the primary burden, before considering the alternative reasons for dismissal, including those advanced by the employee (*Whitelock and Storr v Khan* (UKEAT/0017/10/RN) (26 October 2010, unreported)), though note the view of the EAT in *Governing Body of John Loughborough School v Alexis* (UKEAT/0583/10/JOJ) (16 December 2011, unreported) to the effect that if an employer's reason is rejected, it has failed to discharge the burden placed upon it by *ERA, s 98(1)* and the dismissal must therefore be unfair (see also *Earl v Slater and Wheeler (Airlyne) Ltd* [1973] 1 WLR 51, [1972] IRLR 115, [1973] 1 All ER 145, observation of Sir John Donaldson *obiter* at 149)).

The fact that an employer has a prior reason for wishing to dismiss an employee (such as poor performance) does not by itself mean that, if a different ground for dismissal arises (such as the employee committing an act of gross misconduct), this cannot be the reason or principal reason for a subsequent dismissal. The fact that the employer welcomes the opportunity to dismiss does not mean that, in this example, misconduct was not the sole or principal reason for the dismissal having occurred (*Governing Body of John Loughborough School v Alexis* (UKEAT/0583/10/JOJ) (16 December 2011, unreported), following *ASLEF v Brady* [2006] IRLR 576). These principles have been confirmed by the Court of Appeal in *Co-operative Group Ltd v Baddeley* [2014] EWCA Civ 658 (and see *St Nicholas School (Fleet) Educational Trust Ltd v Sleet* (UKEAT/0118/17/0311) (3 November 2017, unreported) for an example of this principle being applied in practice). However, as the Court of Appeal emphasised in *Baddeley*, in such a case, determining the reason or principal reason will be a complex factual question for the tribunal and the employer's case is likely to be subject to a significant degree of scrutiny. The latter point is well illustrated by the facts in *Alexis*, in which the EAT upheld the tribunal's finding that the principal reason for the dismissal was not misconduct as alleged by the employer, but the employer's pre-existing views about the claimant's inadequate performance.

This chapter first considers the unacceptable reasons for dismissal (see **55.3** below), followed by the criteria for assessment of the fairness of a dismissal where the reason is acceptable (see **55.4** below). Finally, each of the acceptable reasons listed above are addressed in more detail in turn (see **55.5** and onwards below).

55.3   DISMISSALS WHICH ARE DEEMED UNFAIR

The *Employment Rights Act 1996* sets out a number of circumstances in which a dismissal will be deemed to be unfair automatically. Additionally, most of the following automatically unfair reasons for dismissal will render the dismissal unfair if they constitute the reason for which an employee was selected for redundancy (see **55.11**(a) below). In most cases, where an employee has been dismissed for an automatically unfair reason it will also be possible for the tribunal to hear the claim and pronounce the dismissal unfair when it would not normally have jurisdiction to do so because the employee lacked sufficient continuous service though significantly, this is not the case in relation to dismissals rendered unfair by the *Transfer of Undertakings (Protection of Employment) Regulations 2006 (SI 2006/246)* (see UNFAIR DISMISSAL – I (54)). However, in such cases the burden of proving that the reason for dismissal was the inadmissible reason rests on the employee (*Smith v Hayle Town Council* [1978] ICR 996, [1978] IRLR 413; *Maund v Penwith District Council* [1984] ICR 143, [1984] IRLR 24; *Ross v Eddie Stobart Ltd* (UKEAT/0068/13/RN) [2013] All ER (D) 209 (Aug).

55.3 Unfair Dismissal – II

(a) Employer's failure to follow statutory dismissal and disciplinary procedures

The *Employment Act 2002, s 34* inserted a new *s 98A* into the *Employment Rights Act 1996*, concerning statutory dismissal and disciplinary procedures. These procedures were repealed on 6 April 2009. They continued to apply, during a transitional period, to cases where the trigger event occurred prior to the date of repeal. These procedures will not be considered further in this chapter due to their diminishing significance in practice. Previous editions may be referred to for a detailed discussion of their operation.

(b) Union-membership, participation and non-membership dismissals

The dismissal of an employee will automatically be regarded as unfair if the reason or principal reason for it was that the employee (*TULR(C)A 1992, s 152*):

(i)   was, or proposed to become, a member of an independent trade union;

(ii)   had taken part, or proposed to take part, in the activities of an independent trade union at an appropriate time;

(iii)   had made use, or proposed to make use, of trade union services at an appropriate time;

(iv)   had failed to accept an inducement contrary to *TULR(C)A 1992, s 145A* or *145B*; or

(v)   was not a member of any trade union, or of a particular trade union, or of one of a number of particular trade unions, or had refused, or proposed to refuse, to become or remain a member.

An 'independent trade union' is defined as any union which is not under the control or domination of an employer (*TULR(C)A 1992, s 5*) (see **51.22 TRADE UNIONS – I**).

'Membership of a trade union' within the meaning of *TULR(C)A 1992, s 152* was construed broadly by the EAT in *Discount Tobacco and Confectionery Ltd v Armitage* [1995] ICR 431, [1990] IRLR 15 to include approaching a trade union officer to enlist his help in elucidating and attempting to negotiate terms and conditions of employment. *Discount Tobacco v Armitage* was followed by the EAT in *Speciality Care plc v Pachela* [1996] ICR 633, [1996] IRLR 248.

Such action may, alternatively, be considered to be taking part in the activities of a trade union (*Dixon and Shaw v West Ella Developments* [1978] ICR 856, [1978] IRLR 151; see also *British Airways Engine Overhaul Ltd v Francis* [1981] ICR 278, [1981] IRLR 9). For an employee to be taking part in the activities of a trade union, the activity must be that of the union and not merely that of an individual who happens to belong to a union (*Drew v St Edmundsbury Borough Council* [1980] ICR 513, [1980] IRLR 459, holding also that trade union activity within *s 152* did not include the taking of industrial action). The dismissal of an employee because of union activities with a previous employer can come within *s 152*, although dismissing an employee for failing to tell the truth about past activities would not (*Fitzpatrick v British Railways Board* [1992] ICR 221, [1991] IRLR 376).

'An appropriate time', in relation to an employee taking part in the activities of a trade union, means a time which either (*TULR(C)A 1992, s 152(2)*):

(A)   is outside his working hours; or

(B)   is a time within his working hours at which, in accordance with arrangements agreed with or consent given by his employers, it is permissible for him to take part in those activities or make use of trade union services.

'Working hours', in relation to an employee, means any time when, in accordance with his contract of employment, he is required to be at work (*TULR(C)A 1992, s 152(2)*). Consent for these purposes may be express or implied (*Marley Tile Co Ltd v Shaw* [1980] ICR 72, [1980] IRLR 25).

It is not necessary for the employee to show that the employer's actions were motivated by malice or anti-union hostility (*Dundon v GPT Ltd* [1995] IRLR 403).

Dismissal for conduct which on its own would justify dismissal, such as assault, may not become automatically unfair simply because it took place in the course of union activities, though in *Bass Taverns v Burgess* [1995] IRLR 596 the Court of Appeal held a dismissal to be automatically unfair under *s 152* even though the employee had gone 'over the top' in making critical remarks about the employer. A similar point was made in relation to the retention of information unlawfully retained by a trade union representative by the Court of Appeal in *Metrolink Ratpdev Ltd v Morris* [2018] EWCA Civ 1358, [2018] IRLR 853, [2019] ICR 90, in which *s 152* was given detailed consideration. Having analysed the authorities the court held that there will be cases in which it is right to treat a dismissal for things said or done by an employee in the course of trade union activities as falling outside the protection of *s 152* because what was said or done can fairly be regarded as a genuinely separable reason for dismissal. References in the earlier authorities to acts which were "wholly unreasonable, extraneous or malicious" were seen as a useful guide to capture the distinction, but the court emphasised that the phraseology should not be treated as definitive. That distinction should not be allowed, the court reiterated, to undermine the important protection that *s 152* is intended to confer.

Closed shop. Under the relevant provisions of *TULR(C)A 1992*, all dismissals to enforce a closed shop are now automatically unfair (see TRADE UNIONS – II (52) for more detail on the issue of closed shops).

(c) Health and safety-related dismissals

The dismissal of an employee will automatically be regarded as unfair if the reason or principal reason for it was that the employee (*ERA 1996, s 100(1)*, as amended):

(i)   having been designated by the employer to carry out activities in connection with preventing or reducing risks to health and safety at work, carried out, or proposed to carry out, any such activities;

(ii)   being a representative of workers on matters of health and safety at work, or member of a safety committee in accordance with arrangements established under or by virtue of any enactment, or by reason of being acknowledged as such by the employer, performed or proposed to perform any functions as such a representative or a member of such a committee;

(iii)   took part (or proposed to take part) in consultation with the employer pursuant to the *Health and Safety (Consultation with Employees) Regulations 1996 (SI 1996/1513)* (see **29.22** HEALTH AND SAFETY AT WORK – II) or in an election of representatives within the meaning of those *Regulations*, whether as a candidate or otherwise;

(iv)   being an employee at a place where there was no such representative or safety committee, or where it was not reasonably practicable for the employee to raise the matter by means of the representative or safety committee, brought to his employer's attention by reasonable means circumstances connected with his work which he reasonably believed were harmful or potentially harmful to health or safety;

(v)   in circumstances of danger which he reasonably believed to be serious and imminent and which he could not reasonably have been expected to avert, left or proposed to leave or (while the danger persisted) refused to return to his place of work or any dangerous part of his place of work; or

(vi)   in circumstances of danger which he reasonably believed to be serious and imminent, took or proposed to take appropriate steps to protect himself or other persons from the danger.

In the case of (vi) above, whether the steps in question were appropriate will be judged by reference to all the circumstances, including, in particular, the employee's knowledge and the facilities and advice available to him at the time. The dismissal will not be unfair if the employer shows that it was or would have been so negligent for the employee to take those steps that a reasonable employer might have dismissed him for taking or proposing to take them (*ERA 1996, s 100(2), (3)*).

In *Goodwin v Cabletel UK Ltd* [1998] ICR 112, the EAT applied by analogy the approach adopted by the Court of Appeal in *Bass Taverns Ltd v Burgess* [1995] IRLR 596 in holding that the manner in which an activity is carried out may be protected, as well as the actual doing of it. The protection afforded to the way in which a protected employee carries out his health and safety activities must not be diluted too easily by finding that acts done for that purpose in fact justify dismissal. On the other hand, not every act should be treated as a protected act, however malicious or irrelevant to the task in hand.

For a claim under (iv) above to succeed the tribunal must find that: (i) it was not reasonably practicable for the employee to raise the health and safety matters through a safety representative or committee; (ii) he brought to the employer's attention by reasonable means the circumstances that he reasonably believed were harmful or potentially harmful to health or safety; and (iii) the principal reason for his dismissal was the fact the employee was exercising his rights under *ERA 1996, s 100(1)(c)* (*Balfour Kilpatrick Ltd v Acheson & Ors* [2003] IRLR 683). As such, *ERA 1996, s 100(1)(c)* only applies if there is no safety representative/committee or it is not reasonably practicable for the employee to raise matters through those channels (*Balfour Kilpatrick*). Where the matters raised relate to a serious and imminent danger, however, the employee who does not go through those channels may be able to rely instead upon *ERA 1996, s 100(1)(e)*, following the construction of that subsection adopted by the EAT in *Balfour Kilpatrick* (above), which was approved in *Oudahar v Esporta Group Ltd* [2011] ICR 1406, [2011] IRLR 730.

In determining whether an employee's belief that circumstances connected with his work were harmful or potentially harmful to health or safety, the tribunal should focus upon what is in his mind and determine whether that constituted reasonable grounds for holding that belief. An employee might, for example, reasonably believe that his employer is acting in breach of a legislative provision designed to protect health and safety, even though there is in fact no such breach (*Joao v Jurys Hotel Management UK Ltd* (UKEAT/0210/11/SM) (11 October 2011, unreported)).

In *Harvest Press Ltd v McCaffrey* [1999] IRLR 778, a night-shift worker walked out because he was frightened of the abusive behaviour of his co-worker and was dismissed for leaving his post. The EAT upheld the finding of the tribunal that Mr McCaffrey was automatically unfairly dismissed because he was dismissed for leaving his post in circumstances of danger (*s 100(1)(d), ERA 1996*), even though the danger was caused by his co-worker and did not arise from the workplace itself.

ERA 1996, s 100(1)(e) should be applied in two stages. First, the tribunal should consider whether, as a matter of fact: (i) there were circumstances of danger which the employee reasonably believed to be serious and imminent and; (ii) the employee took or proposed to take appropriate steps to protect himself or others from danger. Secondly, if those criteria are met, the tribunal should consider whether the sole or principal reason for the dismissal was that the employee took or proposed to take such steps. If it was, the dismissal will be unfair. The fact that the employer disagreed with the employee's view as to whether there were circumstances of danger, or whether the steps taken were appropriate, is irrelevant. An employer who is indifferent to the reason for an employee's absence, or does not bother to ascertain that reason, is equally liable (*Oudahar v Esporta Group Ltd* [2011] ICR 1406, [2011] IRLR 730). In *Masiak v City Restaurants (UK) Ltd* [1999] IRLR 780, a chef left his employment after refusing to cook food which he considered to be a hazard to public health. The EAT held that Mr Masiak was automatically unfairly dismissed, under *s 100(1)(e)*, because he had been dismissed for 'taking steps to protect other persons from danger' and it was not necessary, for *s 100(1)(e)* to apply, that the 'other persons' were co-workers.

For safety representatives and safety committees, see **29.20** HEALTH AND SAFETY AT WORK – II. For the right not to suffer detriment short of dismissal on these grounds, see **29.9** HEALTH AND SAFETY AT WORK – II.

Since 25 October 1999, there has been no statutory maximum upon compensation in automatically unfair health and safety unfair dismissal cases (*ERA 1996, s 124(1A)*).

(d) Dismissals for asserting statutory rights

The dismissal of an employee will automatically be regarded as unfair if the reason or principal reason for it was that the employee brought proceedings against the employer to enforce a right of his which is a relevant statutory right, or alleged that the employer had infringed a right of his which is a relevant statutory right (*ERA 1996, s 104(1)*).

The relevant statutory rights are:

(i)   any right conferred by the *ERA 1996* for which the remedy for its infringement is by way of complaint or reference to an employment tribunal;

(ii)   the right to statutory minimum notice under *ERA 1996, s 86* (see **49.7** TERMINATION OF EMPLOYMENT);

(iii)   the rights conferred by *ss 68, 86, 145 A, 145B, 146, 168, 168A, 169* and *170* of *TULR(C)A 1992* (deductions from pay, union activities and time off);

(iv)   the rights conferred by the *Working Time Regulations 1998*, the *Merchant Shipping (Maritime Labour Convention) (Hours of Work) Regulations 2018*, the *Merchant Shipping (Working Time: Inland Waterways) Regulations 2003*, the *Fishing Vessels (Working Time: Sea-fishermen) Regulations 2004*, or the *Cross-border Railway Services (Working Time) Regulations 2008*; and

(v)   the rights conferred by the *Transfer of Undertakings (Protection of Employment) Regulations 2006*.

Provided that the employee's claim is made in good faith, it does not matter whether he in fact had the right or whether it was in fact infringed (*ERA 1996, s 104(2)*; and see *Mennell v Newell & Wright (Transport Contractors) Ltd* [1997] ICR 1039, [1997] IRLR 519). The employee need not have specified the right concerned if he made it reasonably clear to the employer what the right claimed to have been infringed was (*ERA 1996, s 104(3)*). However, the employee is protected only if he or she has alleged that the employer has already infringed his statutory right. An allegation that it will in future be infringed will not suffice (*Spaceman v ISS Mediclean Ltd* [2019] ICR 687).

The statutory rights whose assertion is protected under *ERA 1996, s 104* do not include the rights protecting against unlawful discrimination. The various anti-discrimination legislation contain their own anti-victimisation provisions (see DISCRIMINATION AND EQUAL OPPORTUNITIES – I (12)); in any event, the dismissal of an employee who had asserted such rights would probably be unfair on normal principles (see **55.4** below).

(e) Family-related dismissals

ERA 1996, s 99 provides that an employee's dismissal will automatically be unfair if the reason or principal reason for the dismissal was a reason relating to:

(i)   pregnancy, childbirth or maternity;

(ii)   ordinary, compulsory or additional maternity leave;

(iii)   ordinary or additional adoption leave;

(iv)   parental leave or shared parental leave;

(v)   paternity leave;

(vi)   parental bereavement leave;

(vii)   time off for dependants under *ERA 1996, s 57A*;

(viii) time off for ante-natal appointments under *ERA 1996, s 57ZE*; and

(ix)   time off for adoption appointments under *ERA 1996, s 57ZJ* or *s 57ZL*.

and which reason has been prescribed by the Secretary of State in regulations.

Given recent steps to provide parents with great flexibility in relation to time off, it is important that employers and practitioners give careful consideration to the various regulations which give effect to these rights. A full discussion of these complicated provisions is outside the scope of this chapter, which are instead considered in detail at **33.7** Maternity and Parental Rights.

(f) Pension scheme trustees

An employee's dismissal will automatically be regarded as unfair if the reason or principal reason for it is that, being a trustee of a trust scheme which relates to his employment, the employee performed (or proposed to perform) any functions as such a trustee (*ERA 1996, s 102*).

(g) Employee representatives

An employee's dismissal will automatically be regarded as unfair if the reason or principal reason for it is that the employee, being (*ERA 1996, s 103*):

(i)   an employee representative for the purposes of *TULR(C)A 1992, Part IV Chapter 2* (see **40.4** Redundancy – II) or *Transfer of Undertakings (Protection of Employment) Regulations 2006 (SI 2006/246)* (see **53.18** Transfer of Undertakings); or

(ii)   a candidate in an election for such an employee representative,

performed, or proposed to perform, any functions or activities as such an employee representative or candidate. A dismissal will also be automatically unfair if the reason or principal reason is the employee's participation in an election for employee representatives in a redundancy or transfer of undertakings context.

Similarly, dismissals of employee representatives contrary to the *Occupational and Personal Pension Schemes (Consultation by Employers and Miscellaneous Amendment) Regulations 2006 (SI 2006/349) (para 5, Sch)* are automatically unfair, as are dismissals contrary to the *European Cooperative Society (Involvement of Employees) Regulations 2006 (SI 2006/2059) (reg 31)*.

(h) Shop workers and betting workers who refuse Sunday work

These provisions were introduced by the *Sunday Trading Act 1994* (shop workers) and the *Deregulation and Contracting Out Act 1994* (betting workers) and are now contained in *ERA 1996, s 101* (see **8.7** CONTRACT OF EMPLOYMENT). The dismissal of an employee who is a shop worker or betting worker will automatically be regarded as unfair if the reason or principal reason for the dismissal is that the employee:

(i)　　being a protected shop worker or an opted-out shop worker, or a protected betting worker or an opted-out betting worker, refused (or proposed to refuse) to do shop work, or betting work, on Sunday or on a particular Sunday, except (in the case of an opted-out shop worker or an opted-out betting worker) in respect of any Sunday or Sundays falling before the opting-out notice expired; or

(ii)　　gave (or proposed to give) an opting-out notice to the employer.

ERA 1996, ss 36 to *43ZB* contain detailed provisions on the operation of the employee's right to opt out of Sunday work which should be considered in detail in any case to which these provisions are relevant.

(j) Working time cases

An employee's dismissal will automatically be regarded as unfair if the reason or principal reason for the dismissal is that the employee (*ERA 1996, s 101A*):

(i)　　refused (or proposed to refuse) to comply with a requirement which the employer imposed (or proposed to impose) in contravention of the *Working Time Regulations 1998* (or the *Merchant Shipping (Working Time: Inland Waterways) Regulations 2003*; the *Fishing Vessels (Working Time: Sea-fishermen) Regulations 2004*; the *Cross-border Railway Services (Working Time) Regulations 2008*; or the *Merchant Shipping (Maritime Labour Convention) (Hours of Work) Regulations 2018*);

(ii)　　refused (or proposed to refuse) to forgo a right conferred on him by those regulations;

(iii)　　failed to sign a workforce agreement for the purposes of those regulations, or to enter into, or agree to vary or extend, any other agreement with his employer which is provided for in those *Regulations*; or

(iv)　　being a representative of members of the workforce for the purposes of *Sch 1* to those regulations, or a candidate in an election for such a representative, performed (or proposed to perform) any functions or activities as such a representative or candidate.

Where these provisions refer to a refusal, there has to be something that signifies that the employee was refusing or proposing to refuse to comply with a requirement that would contravene the *WTR*. The communication of the refusal, or proposal to refuse, must be explicit; it is not enough that the employee simply does not comply with the requirement. However, it is not necessary that the refusal be by a specific means, or that the employee states precisely which provision is in issue (*Pazur v Lexington Catering Services Ltd* (UKEAT/0018/19) (20 August 2019, unreported), which contains a thorough and helpful analysis of the previous authorities considering these provisions).

(k) Unfair selection for redundancy

A dismissal for redundancy will be unfair if the circumstances constituting the redundancy applied equally to one or more other employees in similar positions and the sole or principal reason for dismissal was automatically unfair. These are set out in *ERA 1996, s 105* (see below) and are broadly aligned with the automatically unfair reasons for dismissal.

(l) Dismissals on a transfer of an undertaking

Where either before or after a relevant transfer, any employee of the transferor or transferee is dismissed, that employee is to be treated as unfairly dismissed if the sole or principle reason for the dismissal is the transfer (*Transfer of Undertakings (Protection of Employment) Regulations 2006 (SI 2006/246), reg 7(1)(a)*). However, the dismissal is not automatically unfair if the reason for it falls within *reg 7(2)*, that is, if it is for an economic, technical or organisational reason entailing changes in the workforce of either the transferor or the transferee before or after a relevant transfer. In that case, the reason for dismissal will be treated as redundancy or alternatively some other substantial reason of a kind such as to justify dismissal, and fairness will be assessed in accordance with *ERA 1996, s 98(4)*. This is a complicated area of law outside the scope of this Chapter. It is considered in detail in TRANSFER OF UNDERTAKINGS (53).

(m) Spent convictions

A spent conviction or a failure to disclose it is not a proper ground for dismissal (see **18.3** EMPLOYEE'S PAST CRIMINAL CONVICTIONS).

(n) National Minimum Wage cases

This provision was inserted into *ERA 1996* by the *National Minimum Wage Act 1998, s 25* (see **35.9** PAY – I). A dismissal will automatically be regarded as unfair if the reason or principal reason for the dismissal is that (*ERA 1996, s 104A*):

(i)   any action was taken, or was proposed to be taken, by or on behalf of the employee with a view to enforcing, or otherwise securing the benefit of, specified rights granted under the *National Minimum Wage Act 1998* (namely any right for which the remedy for its infringement is a complaint to the Employment Tribunal and any right conferred by *section 17*);

(ii)   the employer was prosecuted for any offence under the *National Minimum Wage Act 1998, s 31*, by reason of any action taken by or on behalf of the employee; or

(iii)   the employee qualifies, or will or might qualify, for the National Minimum Wage or for a particular rate of the National Minimum Wage.

It is immaterial whether the employee in fact has the right to the National Minimum Wage or that right has been infringed, provided that the claim made by or on behalf of the employee was made in good faith.

(o) Public interest disclosure cases

This provision was inserted into *ERA 1996, ss 103A and 105(6A)* by the *Public Interest Disclosure Act 1998, s 5* (see **11.14** DISCLOSURE OF INFORMATION for a detailed discussion of this complicated topic). An employee's dismissal will automatically be regarded as unfair if the reason or principal reason for the dismissal is that the employee made a protected disclosure as defined in *ERA 1996, ss 43A–43L (ERA 1996, s 103A)*. There is no statutory maximum cap upon compensation in public interest disclosure cases (*ERA 1996, s 124(1A)*). In *Stolt Offshore Ltd v Miklaszewicz* [2002] IRLR 344, the Scottish Court of Session upheld the EAT's ruling that it was possible to bring a claim under *ERA 1996, ss 103 and 105(6A)* even if the disclosure itself took place many years before the *Public Interest Disclosure Act 1998* came into force, provided that the dismissal itself took place after 2 July 1999.

(p) Dismissals connected with union recognition

Dismissals connected with union recognition are automatically unfair *(TULR(C)A 1992, Sch A1, para 161,* inserted by *Employment Relations Act 1999, s 1(2)* and *Sch 1).* This applies to dismissals where the reason or main reason is that the employee: (i) acted with a view to obtaining or preventing recognition; (ii) indicated that he supported or did not support recognition; (iii) acted with a view to securing or preventing the ending of bargaining arrangements; (iv) indicated that he supported or did not support the ending of bargaining arrangements; (v) influenced or sought to influence whether other employees voted or how they voted; (vi) voted in such a ballot; or (vii) proposed to do or failed to do or proposed to decline to do, any of the above acts. A dismissal for one of the above reasons will not be automatically unfair, however, if the reason was an unreasonable act or omission by the employee.

(q) Right to be accompanied at disciplinary and grievance hearings

This set of automatically unfair dismissals consists of dismissals of employees because they exercised or sought to exercise the right under *s 10* of the *ERA 1999* to be accompanied at disciplinary and grievance hearings, or because they accompanied a fellow worker to such a hearing *(Employment Relations Act 1999, s 12). Sections 10–12* do not apply only to employees in the normal sense used for the purposes of the *ERA 1996 (ERA 1996, s 230(3)),* but to a wider group of workers set out in *Employment Relations Act 1999, s 13* and include agency workers and home workers.

(r) Protected industrial action

Employment Relations Act 1999, s 16 and *Sch 5* provide that the dismissal of employees who are taking part in protected (ie official) industrial action will be automatically unfair if the conditions set out in the new *TULR(C)A 1992, s 238A* are satisfied.

(s) Dismissals for asserting the rights of part-time workers

Regulation 7 of the *Part-time Workers (Prevention of Less Favourable Treatment) Regulations 2000* provides that an employee who is dismissed for any of the following reasons will automatically be regarded as having been unfairly dismissed:

(i)   if the employee has brought proceedings against his employer under the *Regulations* or requested a written statement of reasons under the *Regulations;*

(ii)   if the employee has given evidence or information in connection with such proceedings brought by a worker or otherwise done anything under the *Regulations* in relation to the employer or any other person, or alleged that the employer had infringed the *Regulations;*

(iii)   if the employee refused (or proposed to refuse) to forgo a right conferred on him by the *Regulations;* or

(iv)   if the employer believes or suspects that the employee has done or intends to do any of the above things.

(See PART-TIME WORKERS (34))

(t) Action to enforce rights under the Tax Credits Act 1999

ERA 1996, s 104B provides that a dismissal will be automatically unfair if the reason, or principal reason, is that the employee took, or proposed to take, action with a view to enforcing or securing the benefit of a right under *section 25* of the *Tax Credits Act 1999,* or that a penalty was imposed upon the employer or proceedings for a penalty brought as a result of action taken by or on behalf of the employee for the purpose of enforcing that right, or that the employee is entitled, or will or may be entitled to working tax credit.

(u) Activities as a member of special negotiating body, European Works Council, etc

The *Transnational Information and Consultation of Employees Regulations 1999, reg 28* provides that a worker will be automatically unfairly dismissed if the reason or principal reason for the employee's dismissal was that:

(i)   the employee had performed any functions or activities as a member or representative of, or a candidate for, a special negotiating body, a European Works Council, or as an information and consultation representative or as a candidate for such a position; or

(ii)   the employee or a person acting on his behalf asked, or proposed to ask, for time off in relation to such activities; or

(iii)   the employee took specific steps in relation to such activities specified in *reg 28(6)*, including taking proceedings before the Employment Tribunal, the Employment Appeal Tribunal or the CAC, acting with a view to securing that a relevant body did or did not come into existence, voting in a ballot, or seeking to influence others' votes.

The *European Public Limited-Liability Company (Great Britain) Regulations 2009, reg 42* and the *Information and Consultation of Employees Regulations 2004, reg 30* create similar protections for employee representatives and candidates, as do the *Companies (Cross-Border) Mergers Regulations 2007*.

(v) Dismissals for asserting the rights of fixed-term employees

Regulation 6 of the *Fixed-term Employees (Prevention of Less Favourable Treatment) Regulations 2002* provides that a dismissal will be automatically unfair if the reason or principal reason was that:

(i)   the employee brought proceedings against his employer under the *Regulations* or requested a written statement of reasons under the *Regulations;*

(ii)   the employee gave evidence or information in connection with such proceedings brought by an employee or otherwise did anything under the *Regulations* in relation to the employer or any other person, or alleged that the employer had infringed the *Regulations*;

(iii)   the employee refused (or proposed to refuse) to forgo a right conferred on him by the *Regulations*;

(iv)   the employee declined to sign a workforce agreement for the purpose of the *Regulations;*

(v)   the employee, being a workforce representative or candidate for the purpose of the *Regulations*, performed (or proposed to perform) any functions or activities in that capacity; or

(vi)   the employer believes or suspects that the employee has done or intends to do any of the above things.

(w) Dismissals for asserting the right to request flexible working

Section 104C of the *ERA 1996* renders a dismissal automatically unfair where the reason (or if more than one, the principal reason) was that the employee:

(i)   made (or proposed to make) an application for a contract variation (see *ERA 1996, s 80F*);

(ii)   brought proceedings against his employer to enforce the right to request flexible working under *ERA 1996, s 80H*; or

(iii)   alleged the existence of any circumstance which would constitute a ground for bringing such proceedings against his employer.

(See **50.17 Time Off Work**)

(x) Jury service

ERA 1996, s 98B makes a dismissal automatically unfair where the reason or principal reason was that the employee was summoned to do jury service, or was absent from work because he attended at any place in pursuance of being called to perform jury service. The dismissal is not unfair if the employer shows that the circumstances were such that the employee's absence in pursuance of being summoned was likely to cause substantial injury to the employer's undertaking, that the employer brought those circumstances to the attention of the employee, and the employee unreasonably failed or refused to apply to the appropriate officer for excusal from or deferral of the obligation to attend in pursuance of being so summoned.

(y) Participation in Education or Training

ERA 1996, s 101B makes a dismissal automatically unfair where the reason or principal reason was that, being entitled to be permitted to participate in education or training by the *Education and Skills Act 2008, s 27* or *s 28*, the employees exercised or proposed to exercise that right. This provision is yet to be brought into force.

(z) Pension Enrolment

ERA 1996, s 104D makes a dismissal automatically unfair where the reason or principal reason was that:

(i)   any action was taken or was proposed to be taken with a view to enforcing in favour of the employee a requirement to which *ERA 1996, s 104D* applied;

(ii)   the employer was prosecuted for an offence under *Pensions Act 1998, s 45* as a result of action taken for the purpose of enforcing in favour of the employee a requirement to which *ERA 1996, s 104D* applied; or

(iii)   any provision of *Chapter 1* of *Part 1* of the *Pensions Act 1998* applied to the employee or would apply or might have applied.

It is immaterial whether or not the statutory requirement applied in the favour of the employee or whether or not the requirement had been contravened, but the claim that the requirement applied or had been contravened must have been made in good faith (*ERA 1996, s 104D(2)*).

(A) Study and Training

ERA 1996, s 104E makes a dismissal automatically unfair where the reason or principal reason was that the employee:

(i)   made (or proposed to make) an application for time off for study and training under *ERA 1996, s 63D,*

(ii)   exercised (or proposed to exercise) a right conferred on the employee under *ERA 1996, s 63F,*

(iii)   brought proceedings against the employer under *ERA 1996, s 63I,* or

(iv)   alleged the existence of any circumstance which would constitute a ground for bringing such proceedings.

(See Education And Training (15)). This does not apply to "small employers" as defined in *Schedule 3* of the *Apprenticeships, Skills, Children and Learning Act 2009 (Commencement No. 2 and Transitional and Saving Provisions) Order 2010.*

(B) Blacklists

ERA 1996, s 104F makes a dismissal automatically unfair where the reason or principal reason relates to a prohibited list and either:

(i)   the employer contravenes *Employment Relations Act 1999 (Blacklists) Regulations 2010, reg 3* in relation to that prohibited list, or

(ii)   the employer—

(a)   relies on information supplied by a person who contravenes that regulation in relation to that list, and

(b)   knows or ought reasonably to know that the information relied on is supplied in contravention of that regulation.

(See **52.10 Trade Unions II: Individual Rights And Union Membership**)

A reverse burden of proof, similar to that used in discrimination claims, applies, so that if there are facts from which the tribunal could conclude, in the absence of any other explanation, that the employer:

(i)   contravened *Employment Relations Act 1999 (Blacklists) Regulations 2010, reg 3,* or

(ii)   relied on information supplied in contravention of that *Regulation,*

the tribunal must find that such a contravention or reliance on information occurred, unless the employer shows that it did not (*ERA 1996 s 104F(2)*).

(C) Agency Workers

Under the *Agency Workers Regulations 2010, reg 17,* a dismissal will be unfair where the reason or principal reason is that:

(i)   the agency worker brought proceedings under the *Agency Workers Regulations 2010,*

(ii)   the agency worker gave evidence or information in connection with such proceedings brought by any agency worker,

(iii)   the agency worker made a request for a written statement under *Agency Workers Regulations, reg 16,*

(iv)   the agency worker otherwise did anything under the *Regulations* in relation to a temporary work agency, hirer or any other person,

(v)   the agency worker alleged that a temporary work agency or hirer had breached the *Regulations,* provided that the allegation is not false and is made in good faith; or

(vi)   the agency worker refused or proposed to refuse to forgo a right conferred by the *Regulations*,

(vii)   the hirer or temporary work agency believes or suspects that the agency worker has done or intends to do any of the above protected acts.

(See Temporary and Seasonal Employees (48))

(D) Employee Shareholder status

An employee will be regarded as being unfairly dismissed if the reason or principal reason for the dismissal is that the employee refused to accept an offer by the employer for the employee to become an employee shareholder within the meaning of *ERA, s 205A* (*ERA, s 104G*).

(E) Zero Hours Contracts

An employee who works under a zero hours contract will be regarded as having been unfairly dismissed if the reason or principal reason for the dismissal is that he breached a provision or purported provision to which *ERA 1996, s 27A(3)* applies (*Exclusivity in Zero Hours Contracts (Redress) Regulations 2015, reg 2*). This means, in effect, that if an employee is dismissed for breaching an unlawful exclusivity clause in a zero hours contract, his dismissal will be automatically unfair.

55.4   FAIRNESS IN THE CIRCUMSTANCES

If the employer establishes that the reason for the dismissal is an acceptable reason, the tribunal will proceed to determine whether the dismissal was fair or unfair in all the circumstances (which expressly include the size and administrative resources of the employer's undertaking), having regard to equity and the substantial merits of the case (*ERA 1996, s 98(4)*). Whereas the burden of establishing the reason for the dismissal rests on the employer, the burden in relation to this second limb of the tribunal's inquiry is neutral.

A number of principles apply to tribunals' assessment of whether an employer has acted reasonably in dismissing an employee, regardless of the reason for dismissal relied upon. These will be discussed in this section. The chapter will then go on to consider the issues which commonly arise when assessing reasonableness in relation to each of the acceptable reasons for dismissal. However, practitioners should have in mind, as the appellate courts frequently reiterate, that the overall question for the tribunal remains whether or not the employer has acted reasonably in dismissing the employee for the reason established in all the circumstances of the particular case, in accordance with *section 98(4)*.

Previously, where an employer could show that the reason for dismissal was retirement, the dismissal was presumed to be fair provided that the employer had followed the procedure set out in *Schedule 6* to the *Employment Equality (Age) Regulations 2006 (ERA 1996, s 98(3A)* and *98ZG*). These provisions have now been repealed by the *Employment Equality (Repeal of Retirement Age Provisions) Regulations 2011*. Employers continuing to operate a retirement age in their workplace will now need to objectively justify the policy, to avoid the dismissal being an act of age discrimination. Further, for the purposes of unfair dismissal, it seems likely that employers will rely upon the dismissal being for "some other substantial reason". If that dismissal is to be fair, it must be procedurally and substantively reasonable. In the absence of detailed authority on the question of what is required in such circumstances, the consultation provisions detailed in the now repealed *Schedule 6* to the *Employment Equality (Age) Regulations 2006* would seem to be a sensible place for an employer to start.

When addressing fairness in the circumstances, the tribunal will consider whether the employer acted reasonably or unreasonably in treating the reason for the dismissal as a sufficient reason for dismissing the employee. The EAT has reiterated that the tribunal must focus on whether the employer acted reasonably in dismissing for the reason(s) for which the tribunal has found that the employee has been dismissed (see for example *Beaumont v Costco Wholesale UK Limited* UKEAT/0080/15/DA) (7 July 2015, unreported)). The Tribunal should look at the totality of the reasons which caused the employer to dismiss (*Governing Body of Beardwood Humanities College v Ham* UKEAT/0379/13/MC [2014] All ER (D) 136 (Apr). The tribunal should not add or exclude certain reasons based upon its own view or findings when it comes to consider whether the employer acted reasonably in dismissing for those reasons for the purposes of *ERA 1996, s 98(4)* (*O'Hanlon v Post Office Ltd* UKEAT/0202/12/LA [2013] All ER (D) 50 (Mar) and *Nejjary v Aramark Ltd* UKEAT/0054/12/CEA [2012] All ER (D) 03 (Oct)). That said, a dismissal may be found to be fair by reference to part of the reason for dismissal, even if the employer could not reasonably have dismissed in reliance upon some other part of the reason (*Robinson v Combat Stress* UKEAT/0310/14/JOJ [2014] All ER (D) 254 (Dec)), though it is important in assessing this question to consider why the employer did in fact dismiss the employee (*Broecker v Metroline Travel Ltd* UKEAT/0124/16/DM [2016] All ER (D) 211 (Oct)).

The tribunal will take into account not only whether the employer had reasonable grounds for dismissing the employee, but also whether it adopted a fair procedure in dismissing him. The correct approach for a tribunal, when applying *ERA 1996, s 98(4)*, is to consider whether the employer's actions, including its decision to dismiss, fell within the band of responses which a reasonable employer could adopt (*Iceland Frozen Foods Ltd v Jones* [1983] ICR 17, [1982] IRLR 439; *British Leyland (UK) Ltd v Swift* [1981] IRLR 91, CA; *Gilham v Kent County Council (No 2)* [1985] ICR 233, [1985] IRLR 18; *Neale v Hereford and Worcester County Council* [1986] ICR 471, [1986] IRLR 168). The tribunal must not substitute its view for that of the employer and judge whether the employer has taken the "correct" approach. Rather it should recognise that different employers may reasonably react in different ways to a particular situation. A finding of unfair dismissal should only be made where an employer's conduct and decision making fell outside the range of reasonable responses. The question is not, therefore, whether a reasonable employer "would" have dismissed, but whether dismissal was within the range of reasonable responses taking into account that different employers might reach different decisions (see *Mundangepfupfu v Penning Care NHS Foundation Trust* UKEAT/0109/15/DA [2015] All ER (D) 265 (Dec)).

This approach is different to the approach taken by courts or tribunals in cases of wrongful dismissal (see for instance *Cossington v C2C Rail Ltd* UKEAT/0053/13/BA [2013] All ER (D) 304 (Nov)). With this in mind, tribunals have been encouraged by the EAT to make clear in their Reasons what findings of fact they have made about the employer's knowledge and view at the time of the decision to dismiss and what findings they have made for themselves having heard oral evidence. The EAT in *Corbin v Portsmouth Hospitals NHS Trust* UKEAT/0164/16/LA [2017] All ER (D) 131 (Jan) emphasised that the Employment Tribunal has to judge the Respondent's decision at the time it was taken in the light of the circumstances at that stage, not in the light of the claimant's admissions during cross examination before the Employment Tribunal. Likewise, unlike a claim for wrongful dismissal, the question of fairness for the purpose of *ERA 1996, s 98(4)* does not turn on whether the dismissal is summary or on notice, as affirmed in *Savigar v Stoke on Trent City Council* UKEAT/0228/14/BA [2015] All ER (D) 244 (May).

The 'band of reasonable responses' test does not apply solely to the decision to dismiss. It applies also to the procedure followed by the employer (*Whitbread plc v Hall* [2001] ICR 699, [2001] IRLR 275; *Sainsbury's Supermarkets Ltd v Hitt* [2003] ICR 111, [2003] IRLR 23). This includes, in a conduct case, the investigation and the employer's findings and conclusions (*Cossington v C2C Rail Ltd* (above)). Whether or not a procedural defect is sufficient to undermine the fairness of the dismissal as a whole, for the purposes of *ERA 1996, s 98(4)*, is a question for the Tribunal. Not every procedural error will do so. The fairness of the whole process should be looked at, alongside the other relevant factors (*Fuller v Lloyds Bank plc* [1991] IRLR 336); *South London and Maudsley NHS Foundation Trust v Balogun* UKEAT/0212/14/BA [2014] All ER (D) 116 (Dec)). It is crucial to assess the gravity of any procedural defect and consider its impact on the fairness of the decision as a whole (*Pillar v NHS 24* UKEAT/0005/16/JW [2017] All ER (D) 173 (Apr), (2018) 159 BMLR 183). In *Pillar* the EAT sounded a note of caution about the danger of treating procedural fairness separately in this regard, though it is likely that most Employment Tribunals will continue to do so in practice. The same approach applies where the procedure is underpinned by a statutory framework. Procedural defects, whether underpinned by reference to statutory powers or not, fall to be considered as part of the process as a whole (*D'Silva v Manchester Metropolitan University* (UKEAT/0328/16/RN) (7 June 2017, unreported)).

Doubt was cast upon the correctness of the band of reasonable responses test in *Haddon v Van den Bergh Foods Ltd* [1999] ICR 1150, [1999] IRLR 672. However, the matter was reconsidered by the Court of Appeal in *Foley v Post Office and HSBC Bank (formerly Midland Bank) v Madden* [2000] ICR 1283, [2000] IRLR 827 and the orthodox position was restored. The Court of Appeal held that tribunals were not to approach the issue of reasonableness by reference to their own judgment of what would have been done if they had been the employer. The test has been applied consistently since *Foley* (see, for example, *Sarkar v West London Mental Health NHS Trust* [2010] IRLR 508). In *Turner v East Midlands Trains Ltd* [2013] ICR 525, [2013] IRLR 107, [2013] 3 All ER 375 the Court of Appeal confirmed that the range of reasonable responses test is compatible with *ECHR, art 8* and reiterated that it should not be equated with the *Wednesbury* unreasonable test applied in administrative law. The Court of Appeal emphasised that the range of reasonable responses is not limitless in *Newbound v Thames Water Utilities Ltd* [2015] IRLR 734. In *O'Brien v Bolton St Catherine's Academy* [2017] EWCA Civ 145, [2017] ICR 737, [2017] IRLR 547 the Court of Appeal again reiterated that the range of reasonable responses test was different to that of *Wednesbury* unreasonableness.

Before deciding to dismiss, the employer must have investigated the relevant facts adequately. Whether seen as part of following a fair procedure, or as a stand-alone requirement, failing to conduct a reasonable investigation is highly likely to render the dismissal unfair. What is required will of course depend upon the context in each case, as considered in more detail in relation to the different reasons for dismissal below. Provided that requirement is met, however, the reason for, and the fairness of, the action taken by the employer is determined by examining the circumstances known to it at the time of the dismissal or when he maintains that decision at the conclusion of an internal appeal (*West Midlands Co-operative Society Ltd v Tipton* [1986] ICR 192, [1986] IRLR 112, [1986] 1 All ER 513). An employer cannot, therefore, be criticised for failing to have regard to material which came to light for the first time as evidence during the tribunal hearing (*Dick v Glasgow University* [1993] IRLR 581), unless, of course, a reasonable investigation ought to have uncovered it. In *Orr v Milton Keynes Council* [2011] ICR 704, [2011] IRLR 317, [2011] 4 All ER 1256, the Court of Appeal (Sedley LJ dissenting) held that the knowledge of an employee is not to be attributed to the dismissing officer for the purposes of deciding whether or not dismissal was fair in the circumstances (though the claimant employee is likely to argue that the employer would have uncovered that knowledge had it conducted a reasonable investigation) (see also **55.10, 55.15** below). However, in *Jhuti v Royal Mail Ltd* [2018] ICR 982 the Court of Appeal suggested, strictly obiter, that where a manager who is not the dismissing officer but has "some responsibility for the investigation" there is a "strong case" for attributing to the employer both the knowledge and motivation of that manager. It also commented that there may be a case for doing so where the process is manipulated by someone at or near the top of the management hierarchy. This line of authority was developed further by the Supreme Court in *Jhuti* ([2020] IRLR 129), discussed in detail above in relation to the determination of the reason for dismissal. The Supreme Court there held where someone above the employee in the managerial hierarchy acts to ensure that an employee is dismissed for a certain reason, but manipulates the process to ensure that some other manager acting in good faith dismisses him for another reason, the tribunal can look behind this and attribute the true reason for dismissal to the employer. The Supreme Court suggested that its reasoning applies equally to determining the employer's knowledge for the purpose of *ERA 1996, s 98(4)*, without exploring the full implications of that in detail. The application of *Jhuti* to a case in which the issue was whether the employer had acted reasonably in all the circumstances, rather than a case in which the reason for dismissal was to be determined, was considered recently by the EAT in *Uddin v London Borough of Ealing* (UKEAT/0165/19/RN) (9 December 2019, unreported). In *Uddin*, the investigating officer knew that a police complaint referred to in the investigation report had been withdrawn by the complainant, but did not draw this to the dismissing officer's attention. The EAT held that the effect of the Court of Appeal's and Supreme Court's judgments in *Jhuti* was that: (i) the question of whether the knowledge or conduct of a person other than the person who actually decided to dismiss could be relevant to the fairness of a dismissal could arise both in relation to the tribunal's consideration of the reason for dismissal and/or is consideration of *ERA 1996, s 98(4)*; and (ii) in a case where someone responsible for the conduct of a pre-investigation did not share a material fact with the decision-maker, that could be regarded as relevant to the tribunal's adjudication of the *ERA 1996, s 98(4)* question. On the facts of *Uddin* that meant, held the EAT, that the failure of the investigating officer to notify the decision maker that the complaint had been withdrawn was something that the tribunal ought to have considered in deciding if the dismissal was reasonable in all the circumstances. The reason that he did not do so did not matter. His role in the process meant that the information was to be attributed to the employer and it was at least potentially supportive of the claimant's position. It should be noted, however, that the EAT's decision in *Uddin* was influenced, at least in part, by the serious nature of the allegations (sexual misconduct) and the heightened procedural standards which applied accordingly. This is likely to continue to be a fruitful source of appellate litigation as the full implications of the Supreme Court's decision in *Jhuti* come to be applied in practice.

With regards procedural matters, even if the employer has complied with its own dismissal procedures, or the ACAS Code, the tribunal may nevertheless consider that the employer did not adopt a fair procedure in dismissing the employee. It is therefore important to consider in each case what procedural requirements fairness called for. In this context, the paragraphs in the *ACAS Code of Practice* relating to disciplinary practice and procedures provide useful guidelines but are not prescriptive or exhaustive (*Lock v Cardiff Rly Co* [1998] IRLR 358). The main point of these provisions is that there should be a known disciplinary procedure which should be followed. If there is a complaint against an employee, he should be informed in detail and preferably in writing of the complaint, and be given an opportunity to make representations, if necessary through, or in the presence of, an employee representative.

In *Clark v Civil Aviation Authority* [1991] IRLR 412 at para 20, the EAT gave guidance as to how a disciplinary hearing should be conducted. A failure to follow the ACAS Codes of Practice, or internal procedures, is not determinative of the fairness of a dismissal (see *UPS Ltd v Harrison* (UKEAT/0038/11/RN) (16 January 2012, unreported) emphasising that the tribunal must address whether the procedure followed, overall, was reasonable, it being insufficient to simply find that the employer did not follow its own policy). That said, it is important to bear in mind that such a failure can affect the outcome (and frequently does so in practice), and, with the shift of the burden of proof in discrimination cases, a failure to follow a relevant Code of Practice or internal procedure may lead an employment tribunal to infer unlawful discrimination **12.21 DISCRIMINATION AND EQUAL OPPORTUNITIES – I**). In that regard, as a general rule, whether a dismissal has been carried out in breach of contract is a relevant factor in assessing its fairness, but is not conclusive (*Hooper v British Railways Board* [1988] IRLR 517; *Post Office v Marney* [1990] IRLR 170; and see *Stoker v*

Lancashire County Council [1992] IRLR 75). *Johnston v Welsh National Opera Ltd* [2012] EWCA Civ 1046, [2012] All ER (D) 348 (Jul) provides an example of a case where a failure to follow a contractual disciplinary procedure played a very significant role in a finding of unfair dismissal which was upheld by the Court of Appeal. In *Shevlin v Innotech Advisers Ltd & Ors* UKEAT/0278/14/BA [2015] All ER (D) 401 (Jul), after a detailed analysis of the above authorities and others, the EAT held that the link between a contractual obligation and fairness arises where there can be said to be a coincidence between the right in question and the statutory right not to be dismissed unfairly. A similar approach to a university's statute was applied by the EAT in *Dronsfield v University of Reading* [2016] ICR 1107, [2016] All ER (D) 08 (Aug). This approach applies not only to a dismissal in breach of a contractual procedure, but also in breach of other contractual terms. So in *Awan v LCTS UK Ltd* (2018) UKEAT/0087/18, [2019] ICR 696, the EAT commented that breach of an implied term that there be no dismissal for incapacity when an employee is benefiting from permanent health insurance falls towards the "very relevant indeed" end of the spectrum when considering if the resulting dismissal is unfair. It is important to note that the construction of the contract is a question of law for the Employment Tribunal, rather than a matter for the employer to determine (*Idu v East Suffolk & Norfolk Essex NHS Foundation Trust* ([2019] ICR 623, a decision upheld by the Court of Appeal at [2019] EWCA Civ 1649).

The employee should also be given the opportunity, where practicable, to appeal to a level of management not previously involved (although cf *Robinson v Ulster Carpet Mills Ltd* [1991] IRLR 348). As a matter of law, the failure to offer an employee a chance to appeal will not automatically render a dismissal unfair; the question remains whether the procedural followed was within the range of reasonable responses in the circumstances of the case (*Hussain v Jurys Inn Group Ltd* (UKEAT/0283/15/JOJ) (3 February 2016, unreported) and *Herry v Dudley Metropolitan Borough Council* (UKEAT/0069/19) (7 June 2019, unreported)). In practice, however, an appeal is likely to be considered necessary in the vast majority of cases, and employers would be well advised to offer one unless the grounds for not doing so are particularly compelling.

The tribunal must have regard to the appeal process when considering the unfair dismissal claim before it. The Court of Appeal has emphasised that there is no rule of law that earlier unfairness can be cured only by an appeal by way of a rehearing and not by way of a review. The Tribunal should examine the fairness of the disciplinary process as a whole and each case will depend upon its own facts (*Taylor v OCS Group Ltd* [2006] ICR 1602, [2006] IRLR 613). It is therefore wrong in law to say that an appeal is relevant only if the original process is unfair and that an unfair appeal can never render an original fair decision unfair (*Mirab v Mentor Graphics (UK) Limited* (UKEAT/0172/17) (4 January 2018, unreported)). There are no limitations on the nature and extent of the deficiencies which a thorough and effective appeal can cure (*Khan v Stripestar Ltd* UKEAT/0022/15/SM [2016] All ER (D) 217 (May)). Two examples illustrate the important role which an appeal can play depending on those facts. In *Scott v Northumbria Probation Board* UKEAT/0451/11/RN (22 May 2012, unreported) a substantial aspect of the original decision to dismiss was overturned by an internal appeal board, but the dismissal was upheld. The EAT held that in such circumstances the individual hearing the appeal necessarily puts itself in the position of being the principal decision-maker and the tribunal must focus carefully upon its decision. The EAT reiterated that whether the appeal was classified as a review or a re-hearing was irrelevant in this regard. In *First Hampshire & Dorset Ltd v Parhar* UKEAT/0643/11/LA [2012] All ER (D) 202 (Jun), the EAT reminded tribunals to consider the whole process, including the appeal, when examining ill-health capability dismissals, particularly where new facts or evidence were available by the time of the appeal (see also *Fox v British Airways Plc* UKEAT/0315/14/RN [2015] All ER (D) 142 (Sep)). This applies whether the new facts or evidence assist the employee or, as they did on the facts of *Parhar* (above), the employer (see also *Holt v Res On Site Limited* (UKEAT/0410/13/BA) (27 February 2014, unreported) in which the EAT again emphasised the importance of assessing the process as whole). Where an employer uses an independent third party to conduct an appeal, its refusal to implement the third party's decision to uphold the appeal will not necessarily render the dismissal unfair (*Kisoka v Ratnpinyotip* (UKEAT/0311/13/LA) (11 December 2013, unreported)), though in practice it seems likely that that would often be the case.

In an appropriate case, it may fall to the Employment Tribunal to consider whether a human resources department had an improper degree of influence over the decisions made by the officers in question (see *Ramphal v Department for Transport* [2015] IRLR 985 where the Employment Tribunal erred in failing to consider adequately whether such influence had been exerted improperly over an investigating officer's report and see also *Dronsfield v University of Reading* [2016] ICR 1107).

Although notice once given cannot unilaterally be withdrawn, it may be withdrawn by agreement. The result is that the tribunal has regard, in appropriate cases, to what takes place between the giving of notice and the ultimate termination of employment in determining whether a dismissal was reasonable in all the circumstances. Dismissal is better analysed as a process than an event as highlighted, for example, by the fact that tribunals take internal appeals into account in assessing fairness (*South Tyneside Council v Ward* (UKEAT/0358/10/RN) (12 July 2011, unreported)).

The most common procedural failings in practice include: a failure to give warnings when shortcomings in an employee's performance first emerge, or to record them properly in writing; failure to give adequate advance notice of a disciplinary hearing, or to inform the employee before the hearing of the substance of the complaint to be considered or the fact that, if the complaint is found proved, the employee may be dismissed; failure to inform the employee of or to permit him to exercise the right to be accompanied to a disciplinary hearing; managers acting on evidence on which the employee has had no chance to comment; decisions being taken or influenced by persons other than those who have considered what the employee has to say; and appeals being determined by persons with a prior involvement in the matter. Procedural requirements in particular contexts are dealt with in more detail in **55.6–55.14** below.

It will be very difficult, though not impossible, to argue that a course of action agreed with an employee's representative fell outside the range of reasonable responses (*Olalekan v Serco Ltd* [2019] IRLR 314).

For several years it was thought that if an employer had adopted an unfair procedure in dismissing an employee, but established that if he had adopted a fair procedure the employee would still have been dismissed, the dismissal could be held to be fair. However, in *Polkey v A E Dauton (or Dayton) Services Ltd* [1988] ICR 142, [1987] IRLR 503, [1987] 3 All ER 974, the House of Lords confirmed that the sole question for the tribunal was whether the employer acted reasonably at the time. In the vast majority of cases, there was no scope to consider what might have happened if the employer had acted differently, except at the stage of assessing compensation (see **56.13** UNFAIR DISMISSAL – III). However, the House of Lords also stated that where the employer could reasonably have concluded in the light of circumstances known to him at the time of dismissal that it would have been utterly useless to follow the normal procedure, he might well have acted reasonably if he did not follow the procedure. In *Duffy v Yeomans & Partners Ltd* [1995] ICR 642, the Court of Appeal said that it was not necessary, in order to come within this exception, that the employer actually applied his mind to the question whether normal procedures would be utterly useless. It will, however, be an unusual case where following procedures would meet this high threshold (see *Nabili v Norfolk Community Health and Care NHS Trust* UKEAT/0039/16/RN [2016] All ER (D) 200 (Jun) and *Afzal v East London Pizza Ltd* [2018] ICR 652 for examples of cases which did not). The Employment Tribunal addressing such an argument must scrutinise whether and why the employer decided that the procedural step was not required and consider if that decision was within the range of reasonable responses (*Radia v Jefferies International Limited*

(UKEAT/0123/18) (30 November 2018, unreported)). For an example of a case where the significance of the procedural defect was relevant to the decision on liability see *London Central Bus Company Ltd v Manning* (UKEAT/0103/13/DM) (11 December 2013, unreported).

An employer acting on a mistaken view of the law will not necessarily render a dismissal unfair. Nor, however, will the employer necessarily be acting reasonably in all the circumstances if it acts upon a mistaken view of the law. The Employment Tribunal will need to consider the reasonableness of the ignorance or mistake, considering, for example, what the employer did to inform itself properly of the position (*Eversheds Legal Services Ltd v De Belin* [2011] ICR 1137, [2011] IRLR 448 and *Cooper v National Crime Agency* (UKEAT/0016/17/LA) (16 June 2017, unreported), upheld by the Court of Appeal at [2019] EWCA Civ 16)).

55.5   GROUNDS FOR DISMISSAL – LACK OF CAPABILITY OR QUALIFICATIONS

Capability means capability assessed by reference to skill, aptitude, health, or any other physical or mental quality. *Qualifications* means any degree, diploma or other academic, technical or professional qualification, *relevant to the position which the employee held* (*ERA 1996, s 98(3)*).

55.6   Capability

As with other reasons for dismissal, the employer is not required to prove that the employee was incapable of performing his job in order to defeat a claim for unfair dismissal. The employer need only establish an honest belief on reasonable grounds that the employee was incapable (*Taylor v Alidair Ltd* [1978] ICR 445, [1978] IRLR 82).

In cases of lack of capability, it has long been established that before dismissal an employer should inform the employee what is required, inform the employee of the ways in which he is failing to perform his job adequately, warn him of the possibility that he may be dismissed because of this, and provide him with an opportunity to improve (see, for example, *James v Waltham Holy Cross UDC* [1973] ICR 398, [1973] IRLR 202). Where warnings have been given, an employee will only be able to reopen them in exceptional circumstances. The approach applicable in the context of misconduct dismissals (see the detailed discussion of *Davies v Sandwell MBC* at **55.9** below) will apply equally to warnings issued in good faith on prima facie grounds for capability reasons (*General Dynamics Information Technology Limited v Carranza* [2015] ICR 169, [2015] IRLR 43).

There are some cases where a tribunal might be prepared to accept that a warning was not required. For example, in *James v Waltham Holy Cross UDC* itself, it was suggested that a capability defect may be so extreme that there is an irredeemable incapability, with the result that a warning would be of no benefit to the employee. Equally, in *Taylor v Alidair Ltd* (above), the Court of Appeal stated that the potential consequences of incompetence may be so serious that one failure to perform may justify dismiss for example, a failure committed by a passenger-carrying airline pilot. However, in practice such cases are likely to be very rare, and should be treated as exceptional departures from the general rule that a warning, and time for improvement, are likely to be seen as pre-requisites for a fair dismissal (though of course the extent of the procedural steps which are necessary will be very context dependent).

There is no general principle that an employer will be acting unreasonably if he does not give an underperforming employee an opportunity of alternative employment in a less demanding role, even where it was the employer that put the employee in the elevated role in the first place. Whether this is required will depend upon an assessment of what is reasonable in all the circumstances (*Awojobi v London Borough of Newham* (UKEAT/0243/16/LA) (20 April 2017, unreported)).

55.6A Procedure for capability dismissals

(See also **55.10** below.) In regard to capability and performance management, employers should follow procedures agreed with or notified to their employees. Such procedures may include the following steps.

(i)   If an employee falls short of the performance required of him, a meeting (of which the employee is given prior written notice containing an outline of the matters to be considered) should be arranged with him and his representative at which he is informed of:

    (a)   the respects (in detail) in which he falls short of the required standards;

    (b)   the time within which his performance must improve; and

    (c)   the fact that if he fails to improve he will receive a written warning and if he still fails to improve within a reasonable time he may be dismissed.

If possible, a note taker should attend this meeting and take a contemporaneous note of what is said. If this cannot be done, a written record of what was said should be made as soon as possible after the meeting. The employee and his representative/companion (if appropriate) should be sent a letter setting out a brief summary of the meeting and of the conclusions reached, including any warning given.

(ii)   If the employee's performance fails to improve, he should be sent a letter:

    (a)   setting out the respects in which he has failed to improve; and

    (b)   inviting him and his representative to another meeting to explain this failure.

(iii)   At the second meeting, at which again there should be a witness and a record kept:

    (a)   the complaints against the employee should be reiterated; and

    (b)   he should be given an opportunity to explain.

If he has no satisfactory explanation for his failure to improve, he should be informed that:

    (c)   he has a further time in which to improve; and

    (d)   failure to improve within this time will result in dismissal.

The employee and his representative should again be sent a summary of the meeting.

(iv)   If there is no improvement, repeat step (ii), warning him that his dismissal will be considered.

(v)   At the third meeting, repeat steps (iii)(*a*) and (*b*) and if no satisfactory explanation is given, give notice of dismissal if the circumstances warrant such a sanction.

(vi)   If practicable, and in any event if the contract or any disciplinary or grievance procedure requires it, if the employee wishes to challenge his dismissal, a manager or managers not involved in the original decision to dismiss should conduct an appeal hearing.

Other steps which may be taken are the offer of training to assist the employee's performance, and consultation with his union representative. Consideration should be given to whether the employer has other work available to which the employee would be better suited.

The importance of these steps will vary according to the circumstances. They should not be treated as a checklist of steps which must be taken in every case, but simply represent a suggested approach to managing performance issues. For example, it may be that a senior employee ought to be well aware of what is required of him and the consequences of failing to perform his duties adequately. It might be that the context of a particular case takes a less formal approach within the range of reasonable responses. However, where possible it is best to give formal warnings in cases of incapability, irrespective of the seniority of the employee.

55.7   Qualifications

Dismissal for lack of qualifications is not common since an employer will have difficulty in convincing a tribunal that an employee whom he engaged with full knowledge of his qualifications is not qualified for the job. If, however, the employee misled the employer into believing that he possessed certain qualifications which were essential for the performance of the task to which he was appointed, he may be dismissed for his lack of qualifications. Some of the cases on lack of qualifications have arisen where someone employed as a driver is disqualified from driving and is therefore no longer able to perform his duties (see, for example, *Appleyard v F M Smith (Hull) Ltd* [1972] IRLR 19). Consideration should be given to offering a disqualified employee suitable alternative employment.

55.8   Lack of capability due to ill-health

In cases of ill-health which make future performance of the contract of employment impossible, the contract may be considered to have been frustrated and the employee not to have been dismissed (see **49.3** TERMINATION OF EMPLOYMENT). However, instances of frustration of the contract of employment are extremely rare in practice.

Before dismissing an employee for reasons of ill-health, an employer should find out the current medical position. This will usually involve obtaining, with the employee's consent, a report from the employee's general practitioner and, if appropriate, his consultant (see **11.12** DISCLOSURE OF INFORMATION for the *Access to Medical Reports Act 1988* and the *Access to Health Records Act 1990*). In some cases, it may be thought necessary to have the employee examined, with his consent, by a doctor appointed by the employer (increasing numbers of employers have access to either internal or external occupational health advice for such purposes).

In *D B Schenker Rail (UK) Ltd v Doolan* (UKEATS/0053/09/BI) (13 April 2011, unreported), the Scottish EAT reiterated that whilst employers were obliged to take steps to inform themselves of the employee's medical position, this should be judged against a standard of reasonableness. The Scottish EAT, by analogy with the *Burchell* test applied to cases of misconduct, considered that a tribunal should ask whether a reasonable employer could find, from the material before it, that the employee was not capable of returning to his post (or could reasonably believe in whatever other reason for dismissal was proved). The tribunal was not to substitute its own answer to that question for that given by the employer. The Scottish EAT further emphasised that whilst medical and expert reports may assist the employer, the question is ultimately managerial, rather than medical.

Once the employer has properly informed himself of the employee's state of health and the prognosis, he should consider the requirements of his business, the employee's past sickness record and whether the employee could be offered an alternative position more suitable to his state of health (*Spencer v Paragon Wallpapers Ltd* [1977] ICR 301, [1976] IRLR 373). The employer should also consider whether the employee should be regarded as disabled and, if so, whether any reasonable adjustments should be made for the employee. The employer should consult the employee and any representative before dismissing him (*East Lindsay District Council v Daubney* [1977] ICR 566, [1977] IRLR 181; *Merseyside and North Wales Electricity Board v Taylor* [1975] ICR 185, [1975] IRLR 60).

Having properly informed itself of the position and consulted with the employee, the employer must decide what action to take. The central question is whether a reasonable employer would have waited longer to dismiss and, if so, how long (*Harris v Monmouthshire County Council* UKEAT/0332/14/DA [2015] All ER (D) 320 (Oct), *BS v Dundee City Council* [2014] IRLR 131 and *Spencer* (above)). The EAT in *Lynock v Cereal Packaging Ltd* [1988] ICR 670, [1988] IRLR 510 stated that whilst each case will turn on its facts, some factors which may be important include: (i) the nature of the illness; (ii) the likelihood of it recurring or some other illness arising; (iii) the length of the various absences and the spaces of good health between them; (iv) the need of the employer for the work done by the particular employee; (v) the impact of the absences on others who work with the employee; (vi) the adoption and the carrying out of the policy; (vii) the emphasis on a personal assessment in the ultimate decision and of course, (viii) the extent to which the difficulty of the situation and the position of the employer has been made clear to the employee so that the employee realises that the point of no return, the moment when the decision was ultimately being made may be approaching. The EAT also held that the mere fact that an employee is fit at the time of dismissal will not render the dismissal unfair, as the tribunal has to look at the history as a whole.

Whilst it is important to consider whether an employee can be offered an alternative position, an employer will not act unreasonably if he offers the employee alternative employment at a reduced rate of pay where this is the only suitable alternative employment which is available for him (*British Gas Services Ltd v McCaull* [2001] IRLR 60). Fairness requires the employer to consider eligibility under an ill-health early retirement scheme before dismissing an employee for long-term ill-health (*First West Yorkshire Ltd t/a First Leeds v Haigh* [2008] IRLR 182) and the employee's contractual entitlements are a relevant consideration in this regard (*Visram v ICTS (UK) Limited* UKEAT/0344/15/LA [2017] All ER (D) 229 (Jul)). The employee, on the other hand, has no duty to volunteer information about his prospects of recovery to his employer (*Mitchell v Arkwood Plastics (Engineering) Ltd* [1993] ICR 471), though if he elects not to do so this may reduce the information which the employer has to take into account if it is to have acted reasonably; it will be difficult for the employee to later criticise the employer for not discovering information that he could have provided if he takes this course of action.

Where the problem consists of persistent short absences caused by unconnected minor ailments, rather than a long absence for a common cause, a medical examination has little purpose. The employee should be told what level of attendance he is expected to attain, the period within which that is to be achieved and that dismissal may follow if there is no sufficient improvement. The situation should then be monitored to see whether absence is reduced below a reasonable level. A second warning would be appropriate in borderline cases (see *International Sports Co Ltd v Thomson* [1980] IRLR 340; *Rolls-Royce Ltd v Walpole* [1980] IRLR 343; *Lynock v Cereal Packaging Ltd* [1988] ICR 670, [1988] IRLR 510). In some cases, particularly where the employee's inability to attend work is not linked to ill-health, such a dismissal may be better analysed as dismissal for "some other substantial reason", as addressed at paragraph **55.14** below (see, for example, (*Wilson v Post Office* [2000] IRLR 834 and *Kelly v Royal Mail Group Ltd* (UKEAT/0262/18) (14 February 2019, unreported)).

Whether the ill health was caused by the employer's actions will not determine fairness. The issue of responsibility for the illness or injury is tangential to the question of fairness of the dismissal (*London Fire and Civil Defence Authority v Betty* [1994] IRLR 384; *Edwards v Governors of Hanson School* [2001] IRLR 733; *McAdie v Royal Bank of Scotland* [2008] ICR

1087, [2007] IRLR 895). The question can, however, arise where the employer is in some sense responsible for the incapacity, rather than merely where it can be found to have caused it (*L v M* (UKEAT/0382/13/DXA) (16 May 2014, unreported) and (*Iwuchukwu v City Hospitals Sunderland NHS Foundation Trust* [2019] EWCA Civ 498, [2019] IRLR 1022).

Equally, the fact that the employee is not at fault for his or her absence does not prevent the employer from being able to dismiss him or her as a result. Indeed, in the vast majority of cases the employee will not be at fault for his or her absence (*Kelly v Royal Mail Group Ltd* (UKEAT/0262/18) (14 February 2019, unreported), a case actually analysed under the some other substantial reason label, as set out further below)).

In *H J Heinz Co Ltd v Kenrick* [2000] IRLR 144, the EAT held that it would be an error of law for a tribunal to proceed on the basis that a disability-related dismissal which is not 'justified' under the *Disability Discrimination Act 1995* is, without more, automatically unfair under the *ERA 1996*. Separate consideration must be given to the question of unfairness (see confirmation of this in *Perratt v City of Cardiff Council* UKEAT/0079/16/RN [2016] All ER (D) 196 (Jun)). Observations of the Court of Appeal in *O'Brien v Bolton St Catherine's Academy* [2017] ICR 737, [2017] IRLR 547, emphasised the undesirability of the range of reasonable responses test and the proportionality test in *section 15* of the *Equality Act 2010* yielding different results. Those remarks in *O'Brien* were re-visited by the Court of Appeal in *Grosset v City of York Council* [2018] EWCA Civ 1105, [2018] ICR 1492. In Grosset, Sales LJ reiterated that the test under *section 15* of the *Equality Act 2010* is different to the test for unfair dismissal. Whilst in some factual situations they may have a similar effect (such as those in *O'Brien*), Sales LJ dismissed the argument that there was an inconsistency between the Tribunal in that case having upheld a claim under *section 15* but having dismissed a claim of unfair dismissal. The same point was made recently by the EAT in *Scott v Kenton Schools Academy Trust* (UKEAT/0031/19/DA) (30 September 2019, unreported). A related issue arose in *Rochford v WNS Global Services (UK) Limited* [2017] EWCA Civ 2205, [2018] All ER (D) 12 (Jan), in which the Court of Appeal held that in a case where an employee refuses to work because the employer's refusal to allow him to resume his full role immediately is held to have been discriminatory, whether it is reasonable for the employer to dismiss the employee for that refusal is a question of fact and degree.

The ACAS Code does not apply to ill health dismissals not involving allegations of culpable conduct (*Holmes v Qinetiq Ltd* [2016] ICR 1016, [2016] IRLR 664. The decision in *Holmes* leaves open precisely which cases involving culpable actions will and will not attract the application of the ACAS Code.

55.9 GROUNDS FOR DISMISSAL – CONDUCT

It is worth noting that in order to prove a potentially fair reason for dismissal, an employer need only show that the reason for the dismissal related to the employee's conduct. Tribunals should not be drawn into the trap of construing the concept of "conduct" too narrowly. This point has been reiterated by the Scottish EAT, which has held that the conduct need not be of any particular character, and found that the tribunal erred in that case by asking whether the conduct was "reprehensible" (*Royal Bank of Scotland v Donaghay* (UKEATS/0049/10/BI) (11 November 2011, unreported)). This was an impermissible gloss on the statutory language. Likewise, there is no need, at the stage of considering *ERA 1996, s 98(2)(b)*, to determine whether the conduct in question was "culpable" or whether the employee himself was aware that what he was doing would be subject to disapproval by his employer (*JP Morgan Securities Plc v Ktorza* (UKEAT/0311/16/JOJ) (11 May 2017, unreported)). There is also no requirement that the conduct in question be wilful on the part of the employee; serious neglect, an omission or carelessness can suffice (*Burdis v Dorset County Council* (UKEAT/0084/18) (3 August 2018, unreported)). More generally, in *Smo v Hywel DDA University Health Board* [2020] EWHC 727 (QB), Linden J emphasised that the statutory formulation *"relate[d] to the conduct"* does not necessarily require *"misconduct"*. There must, however, be some form of conduct personal to the employee in issue.

A particular instance of that general principle, it seems, is that the conduct need not amount to a breach of the contract of employment (*Redbridge London Borough Council v Fishman* [1978] ICR 569, [1978] IRLR 69, *Weston Recovery Services v Fisher* UKEAT/0062/10/ZT, and *Reilly v Sandwell Metropolitan Borough Council* [2018] UKSC 16, [2018] ICR 705). In a short concurring judgment in *Reilly*, however, Lady Hale made it clear that this question remains open for consideration, at least at the level of the Supreme Court.

The starting point in most cases where misconduct is found to have been the reason for dismissal is the approach formulated by Arnold J in *British Home Stores Ltd v Burchell* [1980] ICR 303n, [1978] IRLR 379. At 304 he stated:

> 'What the tribunal have to decide every time is, broadly expressed, whether the employer who discharged the employee on the grounds of misconduct in question (usually, though not necessarily, dishonest conduct) entertained a reasonable suspicion amounting to a belief in the guilt of the employee of that misconduct at that time. That is really stating shortly and compendiously what is in fact more than one element. First of all, there must be established by the employer the fact of that belief; that the employer did believe it. Secondly, that the employer had in his mind reasonable grounds upon which to sustain that belief. And thirdly, we think, that the employer, at the stage at which he formed that belief on those grounds, at any rate at the final stage at which he formed that belief on those grounds, had carried out as much investigation into the matter as was reasonable in all the circumstances of the case.'

In *Boys and Girls Welfare Society v McDonald* [1997] ICR 693, the EAT pointed out that *Burchell* had been decided when the burden of proving reasonableness rested with the employer, rather than neutrally as is the position today. The above passage must be read subject to this qualification to avoid the tribunal falling into error and requiring the employer to prove reasonableness (see also *Singh v DHL Services Ltd* (UKEAT/0462/12/LA) (4 September 2013, unreported)).

The EAT in *McDonald* added that (i) in any event, *Burchell* may not be appropriate where there is no real conflict on the facts; and (ii) *Burchell* does not mean that an employer who fails one or more of the three tests is, without more, guilty of unfair dismissal. The tribunal should focus upon the question whether the employer's action fell within the range of reasonable responses open to a reasonable employer. Notwithstanding the comments made by the EAT in *McDonald*, the *Burchell* test was approved by the *Court of Appeal in Foley v Post Office, HSBC Bank (formerly Midland Bank) v Madden* [2000] ICR 1283, [2000] IRLR 827, [2001] 1 All ER 550 (amongst other cases), and is applied almost as a matter of course by tribunals considering misconduct dismissals. In *Reilly v Sandwell Metropolitan Borough Council* [2018] UKSC 16, [2018] ICR 705 the Supreme Court noted that the *Burchell* test was better suited to identifying the reason for dismissal than it was to answering the question posed by *ERA 1996, s 98(4)*. However, the Supreme Court went on to note that the Court of Appeal had long applied the *Burchell* test when determining reasonableness in all the circumstances. In the absence of full argument, no harm appeared to have resulted, and so the test remains good law. In a short concurring judgment, however, Lady Hale indicated the subject of the correctness and application of the *Burchell* test remain open to argument, albeit only for parties willing to pursue their cases to the Supreme Court.

In addition to the test set out in *Burchell*, if the dismissal is to be fair it must have been reasonable for the employer to have dismissed the employee for the misconduct in question. In other words, dismissal must be a fair sanction. As with other aspects of the law on unfair dismissal, the tribunal will again focus on whether or not the sanction imposed fell within the band of responses which a reasonable employer might have adopted (see *Foley* above) (the same test will be applied when the tribunal assesses the reasonableness of the investigation undertaken by the employer (see *Sainsbury's Supermarkets Ltd v Hitt* [2003] ICR 111, [2003] IRLR 23, above)). The test should not be confused with the different question about whether or not the employer was contractually entitled to dismiss without notice for gross misconduct (a question determined by the tribunal making findings of its own on the balance of probabilities). The tribunal should focus upon the sufficiency of the conduct in which the employer found the employee to have engaged as a reason for dismissal (*Weston Recovery Services v Fisher* (UKEAT/0062/10) (7 October 2010, unreported); *Vodafone Ltd v Nicholson* (UKEAT/0605/12/SM) [2013] All ER (D) 139 (Sep)). Even in a case where the employer's decision is framed in terms of gross misconduct, and the Employment Tribunal concludes that there has been no gross misconduct, the Tribunal must still consider whether the substantive reason it found to be the reason for dismissal was reasonably treated by the employer as justifying the dismissal (*Uddin v Camden and Islington NHS Foundation Trust* (UKEAT/0151/18) (11 December 2018, unreported)).

The final point follows from the fact that the range of reasonable responses test is being applied. The consequence of this objective approach is that the tribunal should not substitute its own factual findings about events giving rise to the dismissal for those of the dismissing officer, nor should it impose its view of the appropriate sanction in exchange for that of the employer. Instead that tribunal should ask (i) whether there were reasonable grounds upon which the employer could believe that the employee had committed the misconduct in question; (ii) whether the employer completed a reasonable investigation prior to dismissal; and (iii) whether the decision to dismiss for the misconduct in question fell within the band of reasonable responses (*London Ambulance Service NHS Trust v Small* [2009] IRLR 563). The Court of Appeal emphasised this principle in *Boardman v Nugent Care Society* [2013] EWCA Civ 198, [2013] ICR 927, [2013] All ER (D) 146 (Mar). An example of this principle in practice is *Quadrant Catering Ltd v Smith* (UKEAT/0362/10/RN) (10 December 2010, unreported), in which the EAT held that the tribunal erred by suggesting that dismissal should have been used only as a last resort, and in substituting its view of the facts for those of the employer.

In *Tayeh v Barchester Healthcare Ltd* [2013] EWCA Civ 29, [2013] IRLR 387 the Court of Appeal emphasised that it is therefore for the employer to judge the severity of offence. In that case the tribunal's decision was overturned as it had substituted its own mistaken view of the severity of the offence for that of the employer. Equally, however, the EAT should not substitute its view for that of the employment tribunal, and should avoid an overly "pernickety" scrutiny of the tribunal's reasons (*Fuller v Brent London Borough Council* [2011] ICR 806, [2011] IRLR 414).

The ACAS Guidance on disciplinary proceedings suggests the following factors may be relevant when determining what, if any, disciplinary penalty to impose: whether the employer's rules indicate the likely penalty; the penalty imposed in similar cases in the past; the employee's disciplinary record, work record, experience and length of service; whether there are any special mitigating circumstances which might make it appropriate to adjust the severity of the penalty; and whether the proposed penalty is reasonable in all the circumstances. An employment tribunal is likely to have similar factors in mind when determining whether or not dismissal was a reasonable sanction in the circumstances of the case.

When deciding what sanction to impose, it is important to consider the circumstances of the individual case, and not simply to apply an inflexible policy (*Post Office v Marney* [1990] IRLR 170; *Rentokil Ltd v Mackin* [1989] IRLR 286, EAT). For example, even where an employee is dismissed for misconduct such as dishonesty which is referred to in the employer's disciplinary code as being misconduct which would normally lead to dismissal, the duty on an employer to act fairly and reasonably requires that they should investigate the seriousness of the offence in the particular case (*John Lewis plc v Coyne* [2001] IRLR 139). It cannot be assumed that an instance of what would usually be seen as serious misconduct will automatically result in a fair dismissal (*Centrewest London Buses Ltd v Spencer* (UKEAT/0481/12/DM) [2013] All ER (D) 199 (Aug)). Indeed, a finding of gross misconduct does not automatically justify dismissal as a matter of law (*Brito-Babapulle v Ealing Hospital NHS Trust* [2013] IRLR 854). Taking an example to illustrate the above point, it is important to consider any mitigating features which might justify a lesser sanction for reasons specific to the employee, or to the incident in question (see *Department for Work and Pensions v Coulson* (UKEAT/0572/12/LA) [2013] All ER (D) 31 (Sep) and *Corbin v Portsmouth Hospitals NHS Trust* (UKEAT/0163/16/LA) [2017] All ER (D) 131 (Jan) for examples of cases where the failure by the employer to give any weight to mitigating features rendered the dismissal unfair).

Conversely, whilst the employer's policy on conduct which will and will not be treated as gross misconduct is of course relevant to the reasonableness of the dismissal, the fact that the employee is dismissed for conduct not set out in a handbook or similar document will not inevitably lead to a finding that the dismissal is unfair. For example, the tribunal is entitled to take into account whether the employee should have been aware of the gravity of the misconduct in question in determining whether a reasonable employer would necessarily have warned the employee of the consequences of his actions (*Royal Bank of Scotland v Nwosuagwe-Ibe* (UKEAT/0594/10/ZT) (February 2010, unreported) provides an example of such reasoning).

Is a concession by the employee during cross examination that the sanction of dismissal was reasonable determinative of this issue? No, held the EAT in *Adama v Partnerships in Care Limited* UKEAT/0047/14/MC *[2011] All ER (D) 153 (Oct)*. The tribunal must consider for itself if the sanction is within the range of reasonable responses. The concession is clearly relevant to that decision, but it is not determinative.

An employer is entitled to take into account both the actual impact of the impugned conduct, and the potential impact of that conduct when determining whether dismissal was a reasonable sanction (*Wincanton Plc v Atkinson* (UKEAT/0040/11/DM) (19 July 2011, unreported)). In that case, two employees failed to renew their HGV licences with the effect that they had been driving the employer's vehicles in breach of regulations and without valid insurance. The tribunal took the view that as they had not caused an accident, and the employer had not been subject to regulatory sanctions, no harm had resulted and their dismissals were unfair. The EAT overturned the tribunal on the grounds that insufficient weight have been given to the very serious potential consequences of the misconduct.

If the employer reasonably believes that one of a number of employees is guilty of dishonesty and, despite proper investigation, cannot identify the culprit, it may be reasonable to dismiss all those who could have been responsible (*Monie v Coral Racing Ltd* [1981] ICR 109, [1980] IRLR 464; *Whitbread & Co plc v Thomas* [1988] ICR 135, [1988] IRLR 43; *Parr v Whitbread & Co plc* [1990] ICR 427, [1990] IRLR 39; *Frames Snooker Centre v Boyce* [1992] IRLR 472).

In *John Lewis plc v Coyne* [2001] IRLR 139, the EAT gave useful guidance on what type of misconduct can be said to amount to 'dishonesty', holding that the best working test is that set out in *R v Ghosh* [1982] QB 1053, [1982] 2 All ER 689. In summary, there are two aspects to dishonesty – the objective and the subjective – and judging whether or not there has been dishonesty involves going through a two-stage process. First, it must be decided whether according to the ordinary standards of reasonable and honest people, what was done was dishonest. If so, then second, consideration must be given to whether the person concerned must have realised that what he or she was doing was by those standards dishonest. The question, of course, remains whether or not the employer could reasonably have believed that the employee was guilty of fraud, by reference to that definition (*Brito-Babapulle v Ealing Hospital NHS Trust* [2013] IRLR 854). See also *Panama v*

Hackney London Borough Council [2003] IRLR 278 on proof of fraudulent conduct and *Centrewest London Buses Ltd v Spencer* UKEAT/0481/12/DM [2013] All ER (D) 199 (Aug) on the application of the *Theft Act 1968* in the employment context). Notwithstanding the above, doubt has been cast upon the appropriateness of referring to definitions from the field of criminal law in *Gondalia v Tesco Stores Ltd* UKEAT/0320/14/JOJ [2015] All ER (D) 270 (Jan). In that case the EAT emphasised that the employee's state of mind is important, but so are other factors. In the light of the above, and until there is clear guidance to the contrary, employers would be well advised to continue to exercise care when using the labels of dishonesty or theft as a justification for a dismissal. However, where they have done so *Gondalia* may allow room for argument that a more flexible approach should be taken by the tribunal.

Length of service is a factor which an employment tribunal may properly take into account in deciding whether the decision of an employer to dismiss in reaction to the employee's conduct was an appropriate one (*Strouthos v London Underground Ltd* [2004] IRLR 636).

Although employers should consider each disciplinary case on its individual merits, on occasion a dismissal may be held unfair on the ground that the dismissed employee has been treated inconsistently, in that the employer has on other occasions dealt more leniently with similar instances of misconduct (*Cain v Leeds Western Health Authority* [1990] ICR 585, [1990] IRLR 168, *Post Office v Fennell* [1981] IRLR 221). In *Hadjioannous v Coral Casinos Ltd* [1981] IRLR 352, the EAT held that evidence of inconsistency is relevant in a limited range of circumstances, namely: (i) it may be evidence as to how an employee has been led to believe that certain categories of conduct will be viewed by his employer; (ii) it may suggest that the purported reason for dismissal advanced by the employer is not real or genuine; and (iii) it may support an argument that the sanction of dismissal was unreasonable. However, this should only be the case if the two cases in question were, to adopt the language used by the EAT in *Hadjioannous*, "truly parallel" "similar or sufficiently similar", the emphasis should be on the individual employee's case. Tribunals should generally be cautious in finding a dismissal to have been unfair on grounds of inconsistent treatment (*Hadjioannous* (above); *Paul v East Surrey District Health Authority* [1995] IRLR 305; *Harrow London Borough Council v Cunningham* [1996] IRLR 256, EAT). The EAT generally continues to apply a test of strict parity in cases where comparators are relied upon (see *Honey v City and County of Swansea* UKEAT/0465/09/JOJ) (16 April 2010, unreported) where a difference in seniority and job description justified a difference in sanction). However, in *Doy v Clays Ltd* (UKEAT/0034/18) (3 August 2018, unreported), the EAT adopted what appears to be a slightly less strict approach. The EAT suggested that the correct test was whether the circumstances were "similar or sufficiently similar", not whether they were "truly parallel". That, it is suggested, goes somewhat against the trend of the authorities, and is a remark to be treated with a degree of caution. The EAT has emphasised that the appropriate question remains whether a reasonable employer could properly, within the bounds of a range of reasonable responses, have decided to deal with the two cases differently (an example being *Wilko Retail Limited v Gaskell* UKEAT/0191/18 (22 November 2018, unreported)). Where the tribunal accepts the employer's reason for having treated the two cases differently, the dismissal will only be unfair if that reason can be said to have been outside the range of responses open to the employer (*General Mills (Berwick) Ltd v Glowacki* UKEAT/0139/11/ZT (22 September 2011, unreported) and see also *SPS Technologies Ltd v Chughtai* UKEAT/0204/12/SM [2012] All ER (D) 254 (Dec) where the employer was held to have drawn a reasonable distinction between two cases because it reasonably found on the evidence that charges were made out against one employee but not another). It follows from the analysis above that it is in practice difficult (though by no means impossible) for an employee to succeed on a claim for unfair dismissal by reference to a comparator.

There remains a debate, noted implicitly in *Doy v Clays Ltd* (UKEAT/0034/18) (3 August 2018, unreported), about whether the consistency point needs to be raised before the employer if it is to be evaluated by the Employment Tribunal. Cases such as *General Mills (Berwick) Ltd v Glowacki* (UKEAT/0139/11) and *Cain v Leeds Western Health Authority* [1990] ICR 585 support the view that they need not be raised. Given, however, that as the EAT noted in *Doy*, knowledge of other managers is not generally to be attributed to the decision maker (*Orr v Milton Keynes Council* [2011] ICR 704), it is unclear on what basis it might be open to an Employment Tribunal to consider something about which the decision maker was (reasonably) unaware. It is likely that this issue will need to be considered further by the appellate courts accordingly. That is particularly so in light of *Jhuti v Royal Mail Ltd* [2020] IRLR 129 and *Uddin v London Borough of Ealing* (UKEAT/0165/19/RN) (9 December 2019, unreported), discussed at paragraph **55.4** above. In the light of those decisions, it is likely that there will, at least in some cases, be an argument for attributing to the dismissing officer the knowledge of others, likely at managerial level, about other instances in which employees have or have not been dismissed.

If an employee has recently been given a disciplinary warning (especially if it was for a similar offence), this may make it more reasonable to dismiss for the act of misconduct. The EAT in *Auguste Noel Ltd v Curtis* [1990] ICR 604, [1990] IRLR 326 confirmed that previous warnings for dissimilar conduct may also be relevant (though the converse, that summary dismissal without a prior warning will be outside the range of reasonable responses for anything less than gross misconduct, does not reflect the position (*Mbubaegbu v Homerton University Hospital NHS Foundation Trust* (UKEAT/0307/17) (18 May 2018, unreported) and *Barongo v Quintiles Commercial UK Ltd* UKEAT/0255/17) (16 March 2018, unreported)). In *Wincanton Group Plc v Stone & Ors* [2013] IRLR 178 the EAT emphasised that the misconduct for which the employee is dismissed need not necessarily be of the same nature as the conduct which led to the warning being imposed. The EAT further noted that a final written warning always implies, subject only to the individual terms of a contract, that any misconduct of whatever nature will often, and usually, be met with dismissal, and it is likely to be by way of exception that that will not occur. Where an appeal against a prior warning is pending, the employer should take into account both the warning and the fact that it is subject to an undetermined appeal in considering whether to dismiss, although he is not precluded from dismissing before the appeal is heard (*Tower Hamlets Health Authority v Anthony* [1989] ICR 656, [1989] IRLR 394, see also *Wincanton Group Plc v Stone & Ors* [2013] IRLR 178 in which the EAT further suggested that an employer ought to take account of any challenge to the warning being made in legal proceedings). Both of those authorities were applied by the EAT in *Rooney v Dundee City Council* UKEATS/0020/13/BI [2014] All ER (D) 230 (Jan). Nor is it necessarily unfair to take into account a warning which was not extant at the time of the misconduct in question; the question remains what is reasonable in all the circumstances (*John–Charles v NHS Business Services Authority* UKEAT/0105/15/BA [2015] All ER (D) 314 (Oct), though note the need, made clear by the EAT's judgment, for the employee to have an opportunity to make representations on the relevance of the warning). In *Davies v Sandwell Metropolitan Borough Council* [2013] EWCA Civ 135, [2013] IRLR 374 the Court of Appeal doubted, albeit *obiter*, whether the EAT had been correct in that case to suggest that it was unreasonable for the employer to take into account the fact that an appeal against historic disciplinary sanction had been abandoned.

In *Diosynth Ltd v Thomson* [2006] CSIH 5, [2006] IRLR 284 the Court of Session concluded that it had been unreasonable for an employer to dismiss an employee for breaches of safety procedures after a fatality, because the employer had treated an expired warning for breach of safety procedures as a determining factor in the decision to dismiss. In *Webb v Airbus UK Ltd* [2008] ICR 561, [2008] IRLR 309, however, the Court of Appeal held that it is open to an employment tribunal to find a dismissal fair even where an employer has taken into account a spent warning. *Diosynth* was distinguished on the basis that in that case the expired warning tipped the balance towards the decision to dismiss, but in *Airbus* the employer had shown that the reason for dismissal was the later misconduct, and the previous misconduct affected the decision as to what sanction to impose. The EAT has confirmed that the Court of Appeal's decision in *Webb* correctly articulates the legal position (*Stratford v Auto Trial VR Ltd* UKEAT/0116/16/JOJ [2016] All ER (D) 208 (Oct)).

In *Pillar v NHS 24* UKEAT/0005/16/JW [2017] All ER (D) 173 (Apr), (2018) 159 BMLR 183 the EAT considered a case in which reference had been made to earlier conduct on the part of the claimant that had not been dealt with as misconduct at all. The EAT overturned a finding of unfair dismissal, albeit on the narrow and rather technical ground that the claimant had only challenged the inclusion of the earlier conduct in the investigation report, rather than challenging the fairness of the disciplinary officer's reliance on that information. There is, at the very least, room for further argument on this issue in an appropriate case.

In the past few years there has been a great deal of litigation concerning the circumstances in which it will be appropriate for a tribunal to investigate and determine the reasonableness of an earlier written warning during an unfair dismissal hearing. In *Nunn v Royal Mail Group* [2011] ICR 162 the EAT considered a case where an employee was dismissed because he failed to accept a demotion sanction imposed on him following disciplinary proceedings. The EAT held that unless there is a glaringly obvious reason why the demotion (or, presumably, any other previous sanction) was unfair, the tribunal is not required to examine in detail the precise nature of the allegations and procedure involved. If the employee is dissatisfied with the demotion, his proper remedy is a claim for constructive unfair dismissal. In *Davies v Sandwell Metropolitan Borough Council* [2013] EWCA Civ 135, [2013] IRLR 374 the Court of Appeal considered in detail the approach employers and tribunals should take to previous warnings in unfair dismissal cases. The Court of Appeal approved the central principle laid down in earlier authorities to the effect that it is legitimate for an employer to rely on a final warning, provided that it was issued in good faith, that there were at least prima facie grounds for imposing it and that it was not manifestly inappropriate to issue it. The Court of Appeal added that in answering that question it is not for the tribunal to re-open the warning and consider the adequacy of the evidence in detail. There need to be exceptional circumstances before a tribunal goes behind an earlier disciplinary process (see also *Wincanton Group Plc v Stone & Ors* [2013] IRLR 178). Whilst the issue for the tribunal is therefore relatively narrow, it remains necessary for the tribunal to apply its mind to that question and consider and decide whether the warning given was manifestly inappropriate (*Simmonds v Milford Club* [2013] ICR D14, [2013] All ER (D) 182 (Mar)). In *Simmonds*, the EAT held that if an Employment Tribunal has cause on the facts to consider that a previous disciplinary sanction may have been manifestly inappropriate, it should hear evidence and decide on the relevant facts whether it was. Likewise, in *Way v Spectrum Property Care Ltd* [2015] EWCA Civ 381, [2015] IRLR 657, the Court of Appeal emphasised that a warning given in bad faith ought not to be taken into account in deciding if a dismissal was fair, even if an internal appeal against the warning had rejected the employee's assertion of bad faith. The Court of Appeal allowed the claimant's appeal following the Employment Tribunal's failure to consider if the warning had been issued in bad faith. However, even where the warning is manifestly inappropriate, the extent to which the employer relied upon it in reaching the decision to dismiss must be considered when deciding whether or not the ultimate dismissal if unfair (*Bandara v BBC* (UKEAT/0335/15/JOJ) (9 June 2015, unreported)).

Similarly, where, during a disciplinary process, the employee raises an issue of bad faith, lack of prima facie grounds, or manifest impropriety in relation to an earlier warning, the employer may be required to examine that issue, though that is unlikely to extend to an obligation to conduct a full reinvestigation (*Appiah v Compass Group UK & Ireland Ltd* UKEAT/0129/16/DM [2016] All ER (D) 98 (Sep)).

What of the different position where an employer conducts a second disciplinary process in relation to the same matter? Or, having addressed an issue first as a customer complaint (for example), then brings disciplinary proceedings in relation to the same issue? There is no absolute answer to this question. It is, in effect, a matter for the Employment Tribunal to consider in all the circumstances, by reference to *ERA 1996, s 98(4)* and the range of reasonable responses test. The civil law doctrines of res judicata and abuse of process should not be imported into this consideration, nor should an "exceptional circumstances" test be applied (see *Northamptonshire Healthcare NHS Foundation Trust v Chawla* UKEAT/0075/15/JOJ [2016] All ER (D) 253 (Jan), applying *Christou v London Borough of Haringey* [2013] IRLR 379, [2014] 1 All ER 135). The decision in *Chawla* contains useful practical guidance on the types of issues which will be relevant to the Employment Tribunal's consideration of fairness on this issue, such as whether the employee had been assured that no further action would be taken, or whether there was such a delay that the employee could reasonably have considered the matter resolved.

Where an employer relies upon the employee's conduct in refusing to obey an instruction, the lawfulness of that instruction was not decisive when considering the reasonableness of the dismissal under *ERA 1996, s 98(4)*, although it is a relevant factor (*Farrant v Woodroffe School* [1998] ICR 184, [1998] IRLR 176). The same principle applies where an employee is dismissed for breach of an absence policy (*Sakharkar v Northern Foods Grocery Group Ltd* UKEAT/0442/10/ZT [2011] All ER (D) 61 (Apr)) or for failing to comply with an instruction given pursuant to a contractual mobility clause (*Kellogg Brown & Root (UK) Ltd v Fitton* (UKEAT/0205/16/BA) (21 November 2016, unreported). Likewise, in a case where an employee refuses to work because the employer's refusal to allow him to resume his full role immediately is held to have been discriminatory, whether it is reasonable for the employer to dismiss the employee for that refusal is a question of fact and degree (*Rochford v WNS Global Services (UK) Limited* [2017] EWCA Civ 2205, [2018] All ER (D) 12 (Jan)). This, however, does not excuse the Employment Tribunal from considering whether the instruction was lawful, which will be relevant to the question of fairness and is a question with which it must engage (*Aziz v Freemantle Trust* (UKEAT/0027/17/LA) (25 July 2017, unreported)). In *Aziz*, the Claimant sought to argue that the instruction given to her pursuant to a mobility clause was an unlawful exercise of the employer's contractual discretion, pursuant to the decision in *Braganza v BP Shipping Ltd* [2015] 1 WLR 1661. On further appeal, the Court of Appeal ([2018] EWCA Civ 2605) held that as the *Braganza* point had not been raised before the Employment Tribunal it was too late for it to be considered, and ought to have been disregarded by the EAT. Whilst, therefore, the point did not receive final determination, this remains an open and interesting argument for an employee dismissed for refusing to obey an instruction which the employer contends was unlawful.

The conduct for which an employee is dismissed usually relates to behaviour during working hours, but in certain cases an employee may be dismissed fairly for other behaviour, if it is likely to affect the performance of his contract. If, for example, a playgroup leader is convicted of an indecent assault on a child outside his hours of work, his conviction for such an offence may make him unsuitable for carrying on his employment (eg *Nottinghamshire County Council v Bowly* [1978] IRLR 252, in which the EAT held to be fair the dismissal of a teacher after his conviction for an offence of gross indecency with a man and similarly the Court of Appeal in *X v Y* [2004] ICR 1634, [2004] IRLR 625 including consideration of *art 8* of the *ECHR*).

Article 8 arose again, in a slightly different way, in *Garamukanwa v Solent NHS Trust* [2016] IRLR 476. In that case the employer (which was a public authority for the purposes of the *HRA 1998*) used in its internal disciplinary process material seized from the employee's home by the police in the course of a criminal investigation which the police provided to the employer. The police had specifically informed the employer that it was entitled to use the information. This was argued by the claimant to have been contrary to *art 8*. The EAT reiterated that, following *X v Y*, the first question is whether the circumstances of the dismissal are such that they fall within the ambit of *art 8* (the Court of Appeal in *Vining v London Borough of Wandsworth* [2018] ICR 499, [2017] IRLR 1140 has again made it clear that *art 8* is not engaged by the mere fact of dismissal alone and the wider circumstances must be considered). The EAT held that the Employment Tribunal had been entitled to conclude that the claimant had no reasonable expectation of privacy in relation to the material and that *art 8* was not therefore engaged. It is clear from the EAT's judgment, however, that human rights questions of this nature require a careful analysis of the facts of the case, following the framework set out in *X v Y*. Whilst as a matter of legal principle the position differs between public and private employers, in practice the EAT has held that this distinction is unlikely to make a significant difference (*Q v Secretary of State for Justice* (UKEAT/0120/19/JOJ) (10 January 2019, unreported)

In *Cooper v National Crime Agency* (UKEAT/0016/17/LA) (16 June 2017, unreported) the claimant challenged the practice of information sharing between the police and his employer pursuant to the *Data Protection Act 1998*. The EAT emphasised that the Employment Tribunal's task is not to conduct a judicial review determination of the lawfulness of the employer's actions, but to assess whether the employer acted within the range of reasonable responses, having regard to the information before it and the arguments pursued during the disciplinary process. As set out above, for example, an employer's reasonable mistake as to the law will not necessarily render a dismissal unfair. The decision was upheld by the Court of Appeal ([2019] EWCA Civ 16).

The issue of employee's privacy away from the workplace has taken on renewed importance in the context of dismissals involving employee's use of social media, which frequently occurs after hours. This matter came before the EAT in *Game Retail Ltd v Laws* (UKEAT/0188/14/DA) (3 November 2014, unreported). The EAT refused to lay down general guidance for dismissals in such cases. The EAT agreed that the existence of a policy, the nature and seriousness of the misuse in question, any previous warning, and any actual or potential damage to the business were likely to be relevant. The EAT considered them to be so obvious that they did not constitute helpful points of guidance but they do, with respect, at least provide a starting point. On the issue of the use being in the employee's own time, the EAT also accepted that the extent to which the usage was "private" was a relevant question, owing to employees having the right to express themselves. Ultimately, however, the question is whether the decision to dismiss was reasonable. That will depend upon the particular employment and the circumstances. The EAT's view was that the range of reasonable responses test was sufficiently flexible to meet the challenge of social media dismissals. The EAT's judgment provides a reminder that in this context, as in any other, the Employment Tribunal must not substitute its own view, but must objectively scrutinise that of the employer.

What if the misconduct in question occurs during the course of an investigation into the employee's other misconduct? The EAT considered this in *Kids City Limited v Gayle* (UKEAT/0106/13/MC) (24 February 2014, unreported) and held that it is open to the employer to have regard to such matters, subject to the usual requirement of fairness that the employee has the opportunity to answer its concerns.

Even in a case of misconduct justifying dismissal from the employee's existing job, it may sometimes be necessary to consider whether the employee could still be employed in some other capacity. However, it may be reasonable to leave investigation of that possibility until after the time when notice is given (*P v Nottinghamshire County Council* [1992] ICR 706). The EAT gave further consideration to this point in *Wincanton Group Plc v Stone & Ors* [2013] IRLR 178. The EAT consider it "highly arguable" that when an employee is dismissed from a job he has been employed to do in circumstances in which he cannot be expected legally to continue doing it, the employer may owe no duty to seek alternative employment. However, as both sides accepted that was such a duty in that case, the EAT declined to resolve the point conclusively.

Cases in which an employee is arrested by the police and charged with theft of his employer's property pose particular difficulties. Even if the employee may be charged with a criminal offence, he must be given an opportunity by his employer to state his case (*Read v Phoenix Preservation Ltd* [1985] ICR 164, [1985] IRLR 93). In *Leach v Office of Communications* [2012] ICR 1269, [2012] IRLR 839 the Court of Appeal upheld the EAT's decision to the effect that an employer which receives information from a third party must, as far as practicable, assess for itself the reliability of the information. For example, it should check the integrity of the informant body and the safeguards within the body's internal processes to assess the accuracy of the information supplied. The employer should not simply take an uncritical view of the information provided. However, the Court acknowledged that there will be cases where an employer cannot be expected to carry out his own independent investigation in order to test the reliability of the information provided by a responsible public authority. The EAT has emphasised that a tribunal is not bound to hold that because the police have reported an allegation without endorsing it, a dismissal based on that report is fair (*Z v A* [2014] IRLR 244). The EAT went on to explain that the applicable principles are those set out in *Leach v Office of Communications*, but reiterated that those principles leave room for a tribunal to draw its own conclusions as to the reasonableness of the dismiss. The issues which arise in cases such as these are complex and those advising on such matters should consider the judgments of the EAT in *Z v A* and of the EAT and Court of Appeal in *Leach v Office of Communications* in full. Although strictly a case concerning dismissal for some other substantial reason, discussed further in the relevant section below, *Lafferty v Nuffield Health* (UKEATS/0006/19/SS) (15 August 2019, unreported) also contains useful guidance on this issue.

Is it proper for the employer to conduct his own investigation and question the employee whilst police investigations are proceeding? In *Harris v Courage (Eastern) Ltd* [1982] ICR 530, [1982] IRLR 509, the Court of Appeal approved the decision of the EAT that there is no absolute rule that once an employee had been charged with an offence and advised to say nothing until his criminal trial, an employer could not dismiss him for the alleged offence (see also *Secretary of State for Justice v Mansfield* UKEAT/0539/09 [2010] All ER (D) 144 (May) on the relevant factors to consider in cases of this type). Because of the long delay before a criminal prosecution is finally disposed of, it will often be necessary or desirable for the employer to act before its conclusion. Employers frequently carry out their own investigations and dismiss for dishonest conduct before a prosecution is concluded. If the employer awaits the outcome of a criminal trial and the employee is acquitted, he may find it harder to justify a subsequent dismissal, although the burden on the prosecution at the criminal trial is heavier than upon the employer in showing that he acted reasonably. The evidence which it is permissible for the employer to rely upon is less restricted than that which is admissible in the criminal trial, but how far it is reasonable for the employer to rely upon evidence which has been ruled inadmissible in a criminal trial depends on the facts in each case (*Dhaliwal v British Airways Board* [1985] ICR 513). In *Close v Rhondda Cynon Taff Borough Council* [2008] IRLR 868, the EAT held that it was not outside the range of reasonable responses for the employer to choose not to conduct its own independent questioning of witnesses during its disciplinary process but instead to rely on statements given by the witnesses to the police, even though the statements had been given in a police investigation into different allegations against the employee. According to the EAT, the focus of the police investigation was irrelevant and there was no duty on the employer to allow cross examination of the witnesses.

55.10 Procedure for misconduct dismissals

Employers are no longer under a legal obligation to follow the statutory dismissal procedures but they are advised to adopt and use rigorous internal procedures instead. It is important to have a known disciplinary procedure. Employers are also advised to consult the ACAS Code of Practice. The statutory dismissal and disciplinary procedures, although repealed from 6 April 2009, may still affect some ongoing cases.

If an employee is suspected of misconduct, the employer should investigate the matter fully and give the employee an opportunity to explain himself.

An employer will often wish to suspend an employee during the course of an investigation, for example where it suspects that an employee has engaged in dishonest or fraudulent conduct. However, as Elias LJ has pointed out in *obiter* (but nevertheless important) remarks, employers should not automatically suspend employees and assume that this action will be justified. A suspension which amounts to nothing more than a knee jerk reaction will be a breach of the implied term of mutual trust and confidence. Elias LJ further doubted the cogency of the widely expressed view that suspension is in the best interest of both the employer and the employee (*Crawford & Ors v Suffolk Mental Health Partnership NHR Trust* [2012] IRLR 402). However, in both *Graham v Secretary of State for Work and Pensions* [2012] IRLR 759 and *Tayeh v Barchester Healthcare Ltd* [2013] EWCA Civ 29, [2013] IRLR 387 the Court of Appeal was of the view that a tribunal could take into account the fact that an employee had not been suspended promptly when assessing the reasonableness of the employer's decision to dismiss for misconduct. This places employers in a difficult position where, on the one hand, any suspension should not be a knee jerk reaction on their part but, on the other, the decision not to suspend might later be taken to indicate that they did not regard the offence as serious.

An employer has no right to suspend an employee without pay unless this is expressly provided for in the contract of employment. A suspension without pay in the absence of a contractual right to do so may be a serious breach of contract enabling the employee to resign and claim constructive dismissal (*Morrison v Amalgamated Transport and General Workers Union* [1989] IRLR 361). It is also important to make sure that the employee understands that the suspension is not a disciplinary sanction, and that the employer has not yet decided whether he committed the alleged acts.

The extent of the investigation required will depend on the circumstances. There is no absolute requirement that there be a separate investigation stage before a disciplinary hearing. Whether that is required, and if so in what guise, will depend upon what is reasonable in all the circumstances of the case (*Radia v Jefferies International Limited* (UKEAT/0123/18) (unreported, 30 November 2018) and *Sattar v Citibank NA* [2020] IRLR 104). Employers should, it is suggested, exercise great caution before deciding that a separate investigation is not required.

In *Royal Society for the Protection of Birds v Croucher* [1984] ICR 604, [1984] IRLR 425, the EAT held that in a case in which an employee admitted offences of dishonesty there was very little scope for the kind of investigation referred to in *Burchell* (see **55.9** above) (see also *CRO Ports London Ltd v Wiltshire* UKEAT/0344/14/DM [2015] All ER (D) 261 (Jan) for an illustration of this principle). However, in certain cases, the admission itself will not be sufficient and the employer will need to investigate further. For instance, it might be necessary to make findings on the employee's culpability even where the fact that the conduct in question did occur is admitted (see *Burdett v Aviva Employment Service Ltd* UKEAT/0439/13/JOJ [2014] All ER (D) 27 (Dec) in which the misconduct had been admitted, but the employee said it was attributable to his mental illness).

Where the facts are disputed, it is of great importance that employers take seriously their responsibility to conduct a fair investigation, particularly where the employee's ability to work in his/her chosen career could be blighted by a finding of misconduct (*Salford Royal NHS Foundation Trust v Roldan* [2010] ICR 1457, [2010] IRLR 721 and see also *Tykocki v Royal Bournemouth and Christchurch Hospitals NHS Foundation Trust* (UKEAT/0081/16/JOJ) (17 October 2016, unreported)). Serious allegations of criminal misbehaviour should also be investigated very carefully and conscientiously, albeit tribunals should remember that the investigation is being conducted by an employer and it is inappropriate to require the safeguards found in a criminal trial (*A v B* [2003] IRLR 405). The Court of Appeal applied the decisions in *Roldan* and *A v B* in *Crawford v Suffolk Mental Health Partnership NHS Trust* [2012] IRLR 402. In *Turner v East Midlands Trains Ltd* [2013] ICR 525, [2013] IRLR 107, [2013] 3 All ER 375, the Court of Appeal again reiterated that when determining whether an employer has acted within the range of reasonable responses, it will be relevant to have regard to the nature and consequences of the allegations, as a reasonable employer should have regard to the gravity of those consequences when determining the nature and scope of the appropriate investigation. The Court of Appeal went on to hold that where an employee's rights under *ECHR, art 8* are engaged, matters bearing on the culpability of the employee must be investigated with a full appreciation of the potentially adverse consequences to the employee and that the band of reasonable responses test allows for a heightened standard to be adopted where those consequences are particularly grave (see also *Miller v William Hill Organisation Ltd* UKEAT/0336/12/SM [2013] All ER (D) 110 (Sep) in which the EAT overturned a finding of a fair dismissal because the employer had failed to check CCTV footage which would have exculpated the claimant, as well as that which incriminated her, before finding that the employee had committed a criminal offence, even though it could have done so at no additional cost). In *Stuart v London City Airport* UKEAT/0273/12/BA [2013] All ER (D) 33 (Jan) the EAT rejected an argument that the "heightened scrutiny" test set out in *A v B* did not apply to a case where an employee was alleged to have dishonestly taken goods from premises without paying for them and overturned the Tribunal's finding of a fair dismissal on the basis that the investigation had not been sufficiently thorough. However, the Court of Appeal ([2013] EWCA Civ 973, [2013] All ER (D) 406 (Jul)) in turn reversed the EAT's decision and reinstated that of the tribunal. This shows that the trend evident in *Roldan* and the cases following it should not be taken too far (see also in this regard *Moncrieffe v London Underground Limited* (UKEAT/0235/16/DA) (20 January 2017, unreported)). The Court of Appeal considered there to be no basis for finding that the tribunal overlooked the gravity of the allegation when assessing the extent of the investigation.

In *Stuart v London City Airport* (above), the Court of Appeal held that the reasonableness of the investigation can be assessed by reference to the way in which the employee put his/her case during the internal procedure. In particular, if it is debatable whether or not an investigatory step was required, whether or not the employee asked for it to be undertaken is an important consideration. The Court of Appeal provided a strong reminder that the question remains whether the investigation was a reasonable one in *Shrestha v Genesis Housing Association Limited* [2015] EWCA Civ 94, [2015] IRLR 399, in which it refused to hold that each line of an employee's defence must be investigated unless it is manifestly false or unarguable. That approach was said to be too narrow and, the Court of Appeal held, it is always necessary to have regard to the context when assessing the reasonableness or otherwise of the investigation.

For certain professions, where internal disciplinary procedures are likely to lead to external statutory procedures, the standards of procedural fairness required for the internal disciplinary process may be higher than in the general case, in order to ensure that the employee's rights under *ECHR, art 6* are respected. In *Kulkarni v Milton Keynes Hospital NHS Trust* [2010] ICR 101, [2009] IRLR 829 the Court of Appeal held that a doctor facing allegations of sexual misconduct was entitled to legal representation during his internal disciplinary hearing. Likewise, in *R(G) v Governors of X School* [2010] 1 WLR 2218, [2010] IRLR 222, [2010] 2 All ER 555, which involved a teaching assistant at a primary school who was accused of sexual misconduct, the Court of Appeal held that he was entitled to legal representation at the school's disciplinary hearing, because *ECHR, art 6* applied to an internal disciplinary process which was determinative of the employee's civil right to practise his profession. In *Mattu v University Hospitals of Coventry and Warwickshire NHS Trust* [2013] ICR 270, [2012] IRLR 661, [2012] 4 All ER 359 the Court of Appeal again considered the impact of *art 6* to disciplinary proceedings, concluding that the *NHS Trusts'* decision to dismiss an employee under his contract of employment did not determine his civil rights as defined in *art 6* (see HUMAN RIGHTS (31.7(a)) for a more detailed discussion of the authorities in this area).

It does not matter if the employer's view, if reasonable at the time, is subsequently found to be mistaken (*St Anne's Board Mill Co Ltd v Brien* [1973] ICR 444, [1973] IRLR 309; *British Home Stores Ltd v Burchell* [1980] ICR 303n, [1978] IRLR 379). Equally, if the employer did not have reasonable grounds to dismiss at the time, the dismissal will be considered to be unfair even if evidence subsequently comes to light which proves him right (*W Devis & Sons Ltd v Atkins* [1977] ICR 662, [1977] IRLR 314, [1977] 3 All ER 40). In such a case, however, the employee may be awarded little or no compensation (see UNFAIR DISMISSAL – III (56)). The reasonableness of the decision will be scrutinised at the time of the final decision to dismiss, namely, at the conclusion of any appeal hearing (*West Midland Co-operative Society Ltd v Tipton* [1986] ICR 192, [1986] IRLR 112, [1986] 1 All ER 513).

In *Salford Royal NHS Foundation Trust v Roldan* [2010] ICR 1457, [2010] IRLR 721, Elias LJ gave guidance, albeit *obiter*, about the approach an employer should take to allegations of misconduct where the evidence consists of diametrically conflicting accounts of an alleged incident with little other evidence to provide corroboration to either account. Employers are not obliged to believe one employee and disbelieve the other. It may be, for example, that the parties are both seeking to be truthful, but perceive events differently. Alternatively, in some cases the employer will be entitled to find that they are not satisfied that they can resolve the conflict of evidence and simply find the case not proved and give the employee the benefit of the doubt. This need not mean that they do not believe the complainant.

An employer's disciplinary procedures should follow the principles of natural justice, although a breach of the rules of these principles does not automatically make a dismissal unfair (*Slater v Leicestershire Health Authority* [1989] IRLR 16). Each case will turn on its facts and, as with the extent of the investigation, what is required will depend upon the relevant circumstances, such as the resources of the employer and the nature of the allegation.

It is important to frame the disciplinary charge carefully in order to ensure that a misconduct dismissal is for a matter charged, which has been fully investigated and to which the employee has had a proper opportunity to respond (*Strouthos v London Underground Ltd* [2004] IRLR 636). Whilst in some cases it might be arguable that the employee knows the essence of the case against him, and the dismissal is accordingly fair, an employee is entitled to know the specific charge against him. For example, where money has gone missing, an employee is entitled to know whether the employer is alleging fraud or mere incompetence, as these are likely to lead to different reactions from the employee (*Celebi v Scolarest Compass Group UK & Ireland Ltd* UKEAT/0032/10/LA [2010] All ER (D) 136 (Sep), where additional matters came to light during the process, and allegations were added to the charge with the employee's consent). A further example of this principle is found in *Royal Mail Group Ltd v Lall* UKEAT/0228/12/ZT [2013] All ER (D) 272 (Jan) in which the employee was disbelieved as to his integrity without being given the opportunity to address the allegation. Whilst thee framing of the charge is important, this issue should not be looked at over-technically by tribunals. The important point is that the employee knows the charge he is facing. The substance of the allegation is more important than the precise label that is attached to it (see, for instance, *Brito-Babapulle v Ealing Hospital NHS Trust* [2014] EWCA Civ 1626, [2014] All ER (D) 366 (Oct) and *Adeshina v St George's University Hospitals NHS Foundation Trust & Ors* [2017] EWCA Civ 257, [2017] All ER (D) 13 (May)). The central question for the Tribunal is whether the employee would understand from the way the case was put that the charges in issue were being made, though any doubt should be resolved in the employee's favour (*Sattar v Citibank NA* [2004] EWCA Civ 2000).

In *Khanum v Mid-Glamorgan Area Health Authority* [1979] ICR 40, [1978] IRLR 215, it was held that natural justice required that the employee should know the accusations made against her, that she should be given an opportunity to state her case and that the members of the management team and the appeals panel should act in good faith. Further, in *Bentley Engineering Co Ltd v Mistry* [1979] ICR 47, [1978] IRLR 436, the EAT held that natural justice required not merely that an employee should have a chance to state his own case but that he must know sufficiently what was being said against him so that he could put forward his own case properly. This principle was reaffirmed in *Louies v Coventry Hood and Seating Co Ltd* [1990] ICR 54, [1990] IRLR 324: if heavy reliance is placed upon the statements of witnesses, the dismissal is likely to be unfair unless the employee has sight of the statements or is told what is in them. However, in *Hussain v Elonex plc* [1999] IRLR 420, the Court of Appeal stressed that there is no hard and fast rule that in all cases an employee must be shown copies of witness statements obtained by an employer about the employee's conduct. Whether a failure to disclose information renders a dismissal unfair will be a fact-sensitive question (*Old v Palace Fields Primary Academy* UKEAT/0085/14/BA [2014] All ER (D) 358 (Oct)).

Nor is there a rule obliging an employer to make witnesses available for cross examination by the employee (*Santamera v Express Cargo Forwarding* [2003] IRLR 273). It is a matter of what is fair and reasonable in each case; the gravity of the allegation and the consequences for the employee might allow a tribunal to find that an employer's refusal to allow the employee to question a witness was unreasonable (*TDG Chemical Ltd v Benton* (UKEAT/0166/10/DM) (10 September 2010, (unreported). For guidance in cases where an informant does not wish to be identified, see *Linfood Cash and Carry Ltd v Thomson* [1989] ICR 518, [1989] IRLR 235 and *Asda Stores Ltd v Thompson (No 2)* [2004] IRLR 598.

The EAT has held that unjustifiable delay in carrying out disciplinary proceedings can render unfair a dismissal which would otherwise have been held fair (*Royal Society for the Prevention of Cruelty to Animals v Cruden* [1986] ICR 205, [1986] IRLR 83).

If possible, the employer should avoid a situation where the same members of management act as witnesses or complainants and as decision makers (*Slater v Leicestershire Health Authority* [1989] IRLR 16). In *Slater* the Court of Appeal recognised that avoidance of this might sometimes prove impracticable, especially where the employer is a very small organisation. The case of *St Nicholas School (Fleet) Educational Trust Ltd v Sleet* (UKEAT/0118/17) (3 November 2017, unreported) provides a cautionary reminder that Employment Tribunals should not carry this principle too far. The EAT there overturned a first instance decision that was overly critical of a Head Teacher's involvement in the decision to dismiss when she had also been involved in performance managing the claimant and in giving an earlier written warning. The focus in such cases is on the impartiality (or otherwise) of the decision maker. The tribunal needs to consider how the decision maker might have been influenced by the allegedly improper involvement of a given employee in some part of the process (*UCATT v Dooley* (UKEAT/0346/12/JOJ) (3 May 2013, unreported)).

Other points to bear in mind are: that the employee should be given reasonable advance warning of the hearing and that disciplinary action is under consideration; that the employee should be given the opportunity to call witnesses if appropriate; and that the decision to dismiss should be taken by those who conduct the hearing, and not by someone who had only received a report of the disciplinary hearing (this was held to be an essential requirement of fairness by the EAT in *Budgen & Co v Thomas* [1976] ICR 344, [1976] IRLR 174 though see *Parker v Clifford Dunn Ltd* [1979] ICR 463, [1979] IRLR 56 to the effect that that will not inevitably be the case). A failure to keep adequate notes of a disciplinary hearing may amount to a procedural defect (*Vauxhall Motors Ltd v Ghafoor* [1993] ICR 376). A clandestine recording of a disciplinary hearing may be admissible evidence during an unfair dismissal claim, as in *Chairman and Governors of Amwell View School v Dagherty* [2007] ICR 135, [2007] IRLR 198, although the EAT held that those parts of the secret recording which contained the disciplinary panel's private deliberations were not admissible. A finding that a member of a disciplinary panel fell asleep might justify a finding of procedural unfairness (*UCATT v Dooley* (UKEAT/0346/12/JOJ) (3 May 2013, unreported)).

It is often alleged that decision makers were biased against the employee. In *Adeshina v St George's University Hospitals NHS Foundation Trust* (2015) UKEAT/0293/14, [2015] IRLR 704, the EAT conducted a detailed review of the authorities in this area (the decision was upheld by the Court of Appeal [2017] EWCA Civ 257 without detailed consideration of this issue). In short, the strict rules of apparent bias do not apply, though the appearance of bias remains a relevant consideration for the purpose of *ERA 1996, s 98(4)*, whilst actual bias is more likely to give rise to a breach of natural justice fundamental to the question of fairness. Ultimately, the question remains one of fact for the Employment Tribunal, and it should not be approached as it would be in judicial proceedings.

If the decision is being taken by a panel, the employee is entitled to expect that the composition of the panel will remain the same from the start of the proceedings to the end. However, there may be circumstances where it is fair to proceed with reduced numbers. Where the expectation is not met, this may, though not inevitably, justify a finding of serious procedural unfairness sufficient to render the dismissal unfair. The reason for the change in the composition of the panel, and the prejudice to the employee of the change, are both relevant to the seriousness of the defect (*UCATT v Dooley* (UKEAT/0346/12/JOJ) (3 May 2013, unreported)).

The EAT considered the fairness of a dismissal founded in part upon covert surveillance conducted by an employer in *City and County of Swansea v Gayle* [2013] IRLR 768. There the employer used a private investigator who found the claimant at a sports centre during hours for which he was being paid. The tribunal found the dismissal unfair, on the basis that the employer should not have used covert surveillance in circumstances where the claimant's colleagues had already said that they had seen him at the centre. The EAT overturned the decision. It gave detailed consideration to *Article 8* of the *ECHR*, noting that in this case it was not breached because the photographs were taken in a public place during the employer's time whilst the claimant was engaged in wrongdoing. More generally, the EAT emphasised that in such cases the central question remains that posed by *s 98* of the *ERA*, and that only faults relevant to the dismissal were likely to render it unreasonable. The EAT went on to comment that the tribunal in this case had essentially found that the investigation was too thorough, which was unlikely to lead to the conclusion that the dismissal was unfair.

In *Bailey v BP Oil (Kent Refinery) Ltd* [1980] ICR 642, [1980] IRLR 287, the Court of Appeal held that the failure by employers to comply with a disciplinary procedure agreement was a factor to be taken into account, but that the weight to be given to it depended upon the circumstances; see also *Stoker v Lancashire County Council* [1992] IRLR 75. Similarly, in *Westminster City Council v Cabaj* [1996] ICR 960, [1996] IRLR 399, the Court of Appeal held that failure by an employer to follow its own contractually enforceable disciplinary procedure does not inevitably mean that the dismissal was unfair. In *Sarkar v West London Mental Health NHS Trust* [2010] IRLR 508 an employee's misconduct was initially dealt with under one procedure (under which an employee could receive, at most, a written warning) but it was later dealt with by a disciplinary panel when the more informal procedure broke down, and the employee was dismissed. The Court of Appeal held that the employer had not fettered its disciplinary options by using the first procedure, and was entitled to revise its approach to the misconduct following a detailed assessment of the evidence of the employee's conduct and its impact. However, the tribunal had been entitled to conclude that the use of the first procedure indicated a view on the employer's part that the misconduct alleged was relatively minor, and that it was inconsistent with this approach to later make a finding of gross misconduct based on the same matters.

As with other reasons for dismissal, defects in the original procedure may be capable of being cured by a fair appeal, depending upon the seriousness of any allegations made against the employee, how bad the initial unfairness was and the substance of the appeal process. The Court of Appeal has emphasised that there is no rule of law that earlier unfairness can

(xxv) the reason (or, if more than one, the principal reason) for which he or she was selected related to pregnancy, maternity leave etc within the meaning of *ERA 1996, s 99* and the *Maternity and Parental Leave etc Regulations 1999, reg 29*, the *Paternity and Adoption Leave Regulations 2002, reg 20*, and the *Shared Parental Leave Regulations 2014, reg 43.*;

(xxvi) the reason (or, if more than one, the principal reason) for which the employee was selected for dismissal related to trade union membership or activities under the *Trade Union and Labour Relations (Consolidation) Act 1992, s 153*;

(xxvii) the reason (or, if more than one, the principal reason) for which the employee was selected for dismissal was one of those specified in *ERA 1996, s 104D(1)* (pension enrolment).

An employer should not, however, give preferential consideration to an employee in a redundancy selection process on the ground that he or she is a health and safety representative (*Smiths Industries Aerospace and Defence Systems v Rawlings* [1996] IRLR 656).

A redundancy dismissal which is not automatically unfair may nevertheless be unfair 'in all the circumstances' within the meaning of *ERA 1996, s 98(4)*. Whilst a tribunal will not investigate the commercial merits of an employer's decision that redundancies were required (*James W Cook & Co (Wivenhoe) Ltd (in liq) v Tipper* [1990] ICR 716, [1990] IRLR 386, CA; *Campbell v Dunoon and Cowal Housing Association* [1993] IRLR 496), there are other ways in which a dismissal by reason of redundancy might be found to be unfair. The position was summarised by Lord Bridge in *Polkey v A E Dayton Services Ltd* [1988] ICR 142 at 162–163, [1987] IRLR 503, [1987] 3 All ER 974:

> " . . . in the case of redundancy, the employer will normally not act reasonably unless he warns and consults any employees affected or their representative, adopts a fair basis on which to select for redundancy and takes such steps as may be reasonable to avoid or minimise redundancy by redeployment within his own organisation . . . It is quite a different matter if the tribunal is able to conclude that the employer himself, at the time of dismissal, acted reasonably in taking the view that, in the exceptional circumstances of the particular case, the procedural steps normally appropriate would have been futile, could not have altered the decision to dismiss and therefore could be dispensed with."

TULR(C)A 1992, s 188 (as amended by *TURERA 1993, s 34* and *SI 1995/2587*) imposes a duty on employers to consult appropriate representatives of the employees concerned. A failure to comply with that requirement will probably – although not necessarily – render the dismissal unfair (*Hough v Leyland DAF Ltd* [1991] ICR 696, [1991] IRLR 194). In order to comply with the requirements of *s 188*, the employer must begin consultations before giving individual notices of dismissal (*National Union of Teachers v Avon County Council* [1978] ICR 626, [1978] IRLR 55). See **40.2–40.5 REDUNDANCY – II** for further details on this topic and the specific remedies for breach of the collective consultation provisions.

Even where no trade union is recognised for bargaining purposes, in respect of dismissals taking effect on or after 1 March 1996, employers must (by virtue of *SI 1995/2587*) consult with employee representatives before deciding which employees should be made redundant, where at least 20 or more employees are proposed to be made redundant at one establishment within 90 days or less (see **40.2** et seq REDUNDANCY – II).

The EAT in *Williams v Compair Maxam Ltd* [1982] ICR 156, [1982] IRLR 83 listed the principles which, in the experience of the two lay members, reasonable employers adopted when dismissing for redundancy employees who are represented by an independent trade union recognised by them. The EAT stressed that the principles would not stay unaltered forever, and that they are not principles of law, but standards of behaviour. However, the principles outlined in *Williams* have been adopted by employment tribunals and the EAT as standards by which to judge the fairness of dismissals for redundancy where a trade union is recognised by an employer.

(i)   The employer will seek to give as much warning as possible of impending redundancies so as to enable the union and the employees who may be affected to take early steps to inform themselves of the relevant facts, consider possible alternative solutions and, if necessary, find alternative employment in the undertaking or elsewhere.

(ii)   The employer will consult the union as to the best means by which the desired management result can be achieved fairly and with as little hardship to the employees as possible. In particular, the employer will seek to agree with the union the criteria to be applied in selecting the employees to be made redundant. When a selection has been made, the employer will consider with the union whether the selection has been made in accordance with those criteria.

(iii)   Whether or not an agreement as to the criteria to be adopted has been agreed with the union, the employer will seek to establish criteria for selection which so far as possible do not depend solely upon the opinion of the person making the selection but can be objectively checked against such things as attendance record, efficiency at the job, experience, or length of service.

(iv)   The employer will seek to ensure that the selection is made fairly in accordance with these criteria and will consider any representations the union may make as to such selection.

(v)   The employer will seek to see whether instead of dismissing an employee he could offer him alternative employment.

The extent to which any one or more of these principles apply depends on the circumstances of the particular case, and an employer's failure to adopt any one or more of these practices will not necessarily lead to a finding of unfair dismissal (*Grundy (Teddington) Ltd v Plummer* [1983] ICR 367, [1983] IRLR 98). Moreover, the principles set out in *Williams* should not be treated as if they were a statute or check list (*Rolls-Royce Motors Ltd v Dewhurst* [1985] ICR 869, [1985] IRLR 184). In particular, it is now a common and accepted practice for employers to adopt a system of selection for redundancy which relies upon managerial assessment of employees' abilities and performance as well as upon more purely objective criteria (see the EAT's summary of the authorities to this effect in *Mitchells of Lancaster v Tattersall* UKEAT/0605/11/SM [2012] All ER (D) 207 (Jun)). However, it remains the case that a simple subjective judgement by line managers about 'who should stay and who should go' is unlikely to be a fair method of selection (see, by way of example, the EAT's consideration of a "requirements of the business" criterion in *Watkins v Crouch (t/a Temple Bird Solicitors)* [2011] IRLR 382).

Where redundancy arises in consequence of a re-organisation and there are new roles to be filled, the employer's decision is likely to centre upon the assessment of the ability of the individual to perform in the new role. The *Williams* criteria are unlikely to be useful in such cases, as appointment to the new role is likely to involve something more akin to an interview than a traditional selection process. The tribunal remains entitled to consider how far the process was objective, but should recognise that the decision as to which candidate will perform best in the new role will involve a substantial element of judgment (*Morgan v Welsh Rugby Union* [2011] IRLR 376). Furthermore, the information which a reasonable employer must have provided an employee in advance of such an interview may differ from what an employee would need to be told about a traditional scoring exercise (*Samsung Electronics*

(*Taymech Limited v Ryan* (UKEAT/663/94) (15 November 1994, unreported), *Capita Hartshead Ltd v Byard* [2012] ICR 1256, [2012] IRLR 814) where the EAT emphasised the italicised words above and stated the tribunal is entitled, if not obliged, to consider with care and scrutinise carefully the reasoning of the employer to determine if he has genuinely applied his mind to the issue of who should be in the pool for consideration for redundancy). The question for the Tribunal is whether the pool adopted by the employer was one which a reasonable employer could have adopted. However, where the employer fails to consider the applicable pool the employee will be able to argue that his dismissal is unfair. This sometimes occurs in cases where one job is redundant and the employer simply assumes that it will make the current holder of that position redundant, without considering placing other employees into a pool. In *Fulcrum Pharma (Europe) Ltd v Bonassera* (UKEAT/0198/10/DM) (22 October 2010, unreported), the EAT approved the tribunal's finding that the employer erred in that case by automatically assuming that because an employee's role had to go, the pool should include that employee alone, without further consideration or consultation on the issue of the appropriate pool (see also *Mitchells of Lancaster v Tattersall* UKEAT/0605/11/SM [2012] All ER (D) 207 (Jun)). In *Fulcrum*, the EAT also approved guidance given earlier by another division of the EAT in *Lionel Leventhal Ltd v North* UKEAT/0265/04 [2005] All ER (D) 82 (Jan) on the factors which an employer should consider when deciding whether or not subordinate employees ought to be brought into the pool. These include: (i) whether or not there is a vacancy; (ii) how different the two jobs are; (iii) the difference in remuneration between them; (iv) the relative length of service of the two employees; and (v) the qualifications of the employee in danger of redundancy. However, the EAT in *Wrexham Golf Co Ltd v Ingham* UKEAT/0190/12/RN [2012] All ER (D) 209 (Oct) reiterated that there will be cases, of which that was one, where it was reasonable for the employer to focus upon a single employee without developing or even considering the development of a pool. Until case law provides further guidance on those circumstances in which that will be the case, however, it is suggested that it is sensible for the employer to give the pool careful consideration so that it can justify its position if challenged at a later date, particularly if it is considering placing an employee in a pool of one.

A dismissal of an employee may be considered unfair if no consideration is given to finding him another job within that company, or if the company is a member of a group, within that group (*Vokes Ltd v Bear* [1974] ICR 1, [1973] IRLR 363; *Euroguard Ltd v Rycroft*, IDS Brief 498, p 2). The redundant employee may need to be offered an available vacancy even if it is at a lower salary or is of lower status than the post from which he is being made redundant (*Avonmouth Construction Co Ltd v Shipway* [1979] IRLR 14). In some cases, the employer may consider dismissing some other (perhaps less long-serving) employee to make way for the employee whose job has disappeared (*Thomas and Betts Manufacturing Ltd v Harding* [1980] IRLR 255) and there is no rule of law that this is dependent upon it being raised by the claimant (*Mirab v Mentor Graphics (UK) Limited*) (UKEAT/0172/17) (4 January 2018, unreported). This is known as 'bumping'. However, the Court of Appeal in *Samels v University of Creative Arts* [2012] EWCA Civ 1152, [2012] All ER (D) 213 (Jun) suggested that it is not compulsory for an employer to consider whether he should "bump" another employee. It is permissible to take 'spent' convictions into account when considering whether a redundant employee is suitable for alternative positions (*Wood v Coverage Care Ltd* [1996] IRLR 264).

When an employee is interviewed for an alternative role, the tribunal remains entitled to consider how far the process was objective, but should recognise that the decision as to which candidate will perform best in the new role will involve a substantial element of judgment. There is no obligation to always use objective criteria (*Samsung Electronics (UK) Ltd v Mote-D'cruz* (UKEAT/0039/11/DM) (1 March 2012, unreported)). In the same case the EAT emphasised that terms used in such processes may appear to lawyers to be nebulous and vague, but might have a clearer meaning to managers who utilise them on a regular basis. The assessment tools used are, in the first instance, a matter for the employer. Nor, the EAT held, should a finding of unfair dismissal in such a case turn upon the minutiae of good interview practice.

The fairness of a dismissal for redundancy will be judged not simply at the date on which notice is given but also with regard to events up to the date on which it takes effect (*Stacey v Babcock Power Ltd* [1986] ICR 221, [1986] IRLR 3; see also *Dyke*, above, and *White v South London Transport Ltd* [1998] ICR 293). Hence, if a suitable vacancy arises during the notice period it should be offered to the otherwise redundant employee. The EAT considered the fairness of foreshortening a notice period in circumstances where there is a potential for alternative work to arise in *Missirlis v Queen Mary University of London* UKEAT/0038/15/LA [2016] All ER (D) 213 (May), though as the case was remitted to the Employment Tribunal, the guidance is not definitive, save for reiterating the importance of *section 98(4)* of the *ERA*.

In *Lloyd v Taylor Woodrow Construction* [1999] IRLR 782, the EAT held that, as with conduct and capability cases, a defect in a redundancy consultation process could be cured on appeal, provided that the appeal is a rehearing and not merely a review of the original decision. The Court of Appeal, however, has ruled that the appeal need not take the form of a rehearing (see *Taylor v OCS Group Ltd* above).

> 'If the employer can establish that had he taken reasonable steps to consult with the employee or find him other employment, he would still have been dismissed, an employment tribunal may find the dismissal to be unfair but award no compensation, or compensate only for the wages and benefits which would have been received while consultation was taking place. (See also **55.4** above; and **55.13**.) The question to be asked in the exceptional case contemplated by *Polkey* (above) where consultation would be pointless is not whether the employer in fact made a conscious decision not to consult, but whether a reasonable employer could have decided not to consult in the light of the facts that were known at the time (*Duffy v Yeomans & Partners Ltd* [1993] IRLR 368; cf *Dick v Boots the Chemists Ltd* IDS Brief 451, p 12; see also *Heron v Citylink – Nottingham* [1993] IRLR 372).'

55.12 Dismissal procedure

From decided cases (see **55.11** above) the following guidelines emerge:

(a)   consult with employee representatives;

(b)   consider possible alternatives to redundancies, eg short-time working, work sharing, other costs savings, etc;

(c)   if redundancy becomes necessary, in consultation with employee representatives, agree objective criteria for selection for redundancy;

(d)   apply the criteria objectively;

(e)   inform the employees affected at the earliest opportunity and give the employees an opportunity to contest the scores they are given;

(f)   investigate the possibilities of offering them alternative employment within the company or group, continuing the investigation until the employment has come to an end;

(g)   give them time off to seek employment;

(h)   pay all moneys due;

(i)   conduct an appeal; and

(j)   keep careful records and minutes of these steps.

Whilst the failure to follow the above will not necessarily render a dismissal unfair, they provide a useful starting point for an employer undertaking a redundancy exercise. As emphasised above, they should not be treated as a statutory checklist for achieving a fair dismissal.

55.13   GROUNDS FOR DISMISSAL – CONTRAVENTION OF ANY ENACTMENT

If an employer dismisses an employee because the employee could not continue to work in the position which he held without contravention (either on his part or on that of his employer) of a duty or restriction imposed by or under an enactment, the reason for the dismissal falls within *ERA 1996, s 98(2)(d)*.

The fact that an employer genuinely but erroneously believes that he would be breaking the law by continuing to employ an employee does not make the reason for the dismissal of that employee a reason falling within *ERA 1996, s 98(2)(d)*, but it could be 'some other substantial reason' justifying the dismissal within *ERA 1996, s 98(1)(b)* (see **55.14** below) (*Bouchaala v Trusthouse Forte Hotels Ltd* [1980] ICR 721, [1980] IRLR 382 and *Baker v Abellio London Limited* [2018] IRLR 186).

In these cases employers should:

(a)   arrange a formal meeting at which the employee (ideally with an accompanying person) should be informed of the situation and invited (himself or through a representative) to express his views; and

(b)   in appropriate cases, find out if the company or an associated company has a suitable vacancy which the employee can be offered instead.

55.14   GROUNDS FOR DISMISSAL – 'SOME OTHER SUBSTANTIAL REASON'

These reasons need not be of the same type as those that are specified in the *Act*. If the reason for dismissal is not one of those set out in *ERA 1996, s 98(2)* (see **55.2** above), it may nevertheless be an acceptable reason if the employer can show that it was 'some other substantial reason of a kind such as to justify the dismissal of an employee holding the position which that employee held' (*ERA 1996, s 98(1)(b)*). Examples of such reasons are the following.

(a)   *Necessary re-organisation of the business* (*Hollister v National Farmers' Union* [1979] ICR 542, [1979] IRLR 238; *Richmond Precision Engineering Ltd v Pearce* [1985] IRLR 179; *Catamaran Cruisers Ltd v Williams* [1994] IRLR 386; *Cobley v Forward Technology Industries plc* [2003] ICR 1050, [2003] IRLR 706). This may also apply in cases where changes in terms and conditions have led the employee to claim constructive dismissal (*Genower v Ealing, Hammersmith and Hounslow Area Health Authority* [1980] IRLR 297). But note that the employee must be fairly considered for any new job created by the reorganisation (*Oakley v Labour Party* [1988] ICR 403, [1988] IRLR 34). An employer does not need to establish that the change in terms of employment in such cases is essential in order to show that the reason falls within *ERA, s 98(1)(b)*. There is no principle of law that the survival of the business must depend upon the adoption of the terms (*Garside and Laycock Ltd v Booth* [2011] IRLR 735). If ostensibly the reason could justify the dismissal, it is a substantial reason and the enquiry moves to the fairness of the dismissal. It is at this later stage when the balancing exercise between the needs of the employer and the detriment to the employee falls to be considered (*Roberts v Acumed Ltd* (UKEAT/0466/09/DA) (25 November 2010, unreported). This balancing exercise requires a focus on the words "in accordance with equity" in *ERA 1996, s 98(4)*, as well as a careful scrutiny of the procedure followed (*Garside and Laycock v Booth* (above)). For an example of a successful dismissal followed by re-engagement on new terms, see *Slade & Ors v TNT (UK) Ltd* (UKEAT/0113/11/DA) (13 September 2011, unreported). See also *Taylor v Crockford* (UKEAT/0370/13/SM) (28 February 2014, unreported) for an example of a case involving a failure to agree upon a change of hours.

(b)   *Economic, technical or organisational reasons entailing changes in the workforce* of the transferor or the transferee before or after a relevant transfer within the meaning of the *Transfer of Undertakings (Protection of Employment) Regulations 2006 (SI 2006/246), reg 7(3)(b)* (see **53.26** TRANSFER OF UNDERTAKINGS).

(c)   Reasons of *necessary economies* such as in *Durrant and Cheshire v Clariston Clothing Co Ltd* [1974] IRLR 360 in which a tribunal held that it was reasonable for a company to dismiss two employees who were earning £25.87 per week each but for whom they had to provide transport costing the company £24 per week each. See also *Buckland v Bournemouth University Higher Education Corporation* [2010] IRLR 445, [2010] 4 All ER 186, in which the Court of Appeal speculated about a case of constructive dismissal which could be characterised as a fair dismissal for some other substantial reason, where a major customer of the employer had defaulted on a payment with the consequence that the employer had an unexpected lack of funds and had, in repudiatory breach of contract, failed to pay the employee.

(d)   *Protection of the interest of the business* such as in *RS Components Ltd v Irwin* [1974] 1 All ER 41, [1973] IRLR 239 in which the company was held to have fairly dismissed an employee for refusing to sign a reasonable restrictive covenant which was considered necessary. In considering the fairness of a dismissal for a refusal to accept new terms and conditions, it is material to consider what proportion of the workforce had accepted the change when the decision to dismiss was taken (*St John of God (Care Services) Ltd v Brooks* [1992] ICR 715, [1992] IRLR 546). The Court of Appeal has now gone further in *Willow Oak Developments Ltd (t/a Windsor Recruitment) v Silverwood* [2006] EWCA Civ 660, [2007] IRLR 607 and held a dismissal lawful for refusal to sign restrictive covenants, where the new covenants were provided to the employee earlier on the same day and were unreasonably wide, on the basis that the employer's reliance on the refusal to sign was lawful because the reliance was on a reason of the 'kind' capable of justifying dismissal.

(e)   *An employee's personality* cannot, by itself, be a fair reason for dismissal, however, in certain circumstances the manifestations of that personality can give rise to 'some other substantial reason' for dismissal (*Perkin v St George's Healthcare NHS Trust* [2005] EWCA Civ 1174, [2005] IRLR 934, though note the comments of Linden J in *Smo v Hywel DDA University Health Board* [2020] EWHC 727 (QB) as to the possibility that this could be analysed also as a conduct case, given that the statutory formulation "*relate[d] to the conduct*" does not necessarily require "*misconduct*".)

(f)   *Expiry of a fixed-term contract* when it is shown that the contract was adopted for a genuine purpose and that fact was known to the employee, and it is also shown that the specific purpose for which the contract was adopted has ceased to be applicable (*North Yorkshire County Council v Fay* [1986] ICR 133, [1985] IRLR 247. See also *Terry v East Sussex County Council* [1976] ICR 536, [1976] IRLR 332, [1977] 1 All ER 567 and *Tasneem v Dudley Group of Hospitals NHS Trust* UKEAT/0232/10/CEA [2011] All ER (D) 35 (Sep)). Note, in this regard the *Fixed-term Employees (Prevention of Less Favourable Treatment) Regulations 2002*. The EAT has made it clear that compliance with those regulations will not necessarily render a dismissal upon the expiry of a fixed-term contract fair (*Drzymala v Royal Surrey County NHS Foundation Trust* UKEAT/0063/17 [2018] All ER (D) 65 (Jan)). The fairness of the dismissal, unsurprisingly, turns on an assessment of what was reasonable in all the circumstances pursuant to *ERA 1996, s 98(4)*, assessed against the range of reasonable responses. For instance, a failure to consider the employee for an alternative position might, depending on the facts (such as in *Drzymala* where the employer itself raised the issue), render the dismissal unfair.

(g)   The imposition of a *sentence of imprisonment* (*Kingston v British Railways Board* [1984] ICR 781, [1984] IRLR 146). In some cases, this may have the effect of *frustrating* the contract, thus bringing it to an end without a dismissal (see **49.3** TERMINATION OF EMPLOYMENT). A perhaps more difficult case is one an employee has been charged, but not yet convicted, of a serious offence, and the employer considers that it will suffer significant reputational harm if the employee is not dismissed. A dismissal in such circumstances is potentially fair, but the circumstances of the individual case will need to be analysed carefully (*Lafferty v Nuffield Health* (UKEATS/0006/19/SS) (15 August 2019, unreported), applying *Leach v Office of Communications* [2012] ICR 1269 and *Z v A* [2014] IRLR 244, addressed above in respect of conduct dismissals).

(h)   *Dismissal of the replacement of an employee suspended on medical or maternity grounds (ERA 1996, s 106(3))*. Where an employer suspends an employee on medical grounds in compliance with a statutory requirement and engages another in his place, he should inform the replacement employee in writing when engaging him that his employment will be terminated at the end of the suspension of the original employee. If he dismisses the replacement employee in order to allow the original employee to resume work, the dismissal will be regarded as having been for a reason falling within *ERA 1996, s 98(1)(b)*.

(i)   *Dismissal of the replacement of an employee absent due to pregnancy or childbirth (ERA 1996, s 106(2))*. Where an employer engages an employee to replace another employee who is absent due to pregnancy and on engaging the replacement employee the employer informs him in writing that his employment will be terminated on the return to work of the pregnant employee, a dismissal of the replacement employee to give work to the original employee will be considered as a dismissal for a reason falling within *ERA 1996, s 98(1)(b)*.

(j)   *Relationship breakdown*. In *Ezsias v North Glamorgan NHS Trust* [2011] IRLR 550 the EAT accepted the employment tribunal's finding that the employer had dismissed the employee because of a breakdown in relationship, rather than the employee's conduct which led to that breakdown. The result was that the employer was not required to follow a contractual disciplinary hearing. However, the EAT noted that tribunals would be on the lookout for an employer using the rubric of "some other substantial reason" as a pretext to conceal the real reason for dismissal. This was reiterated by the Court of Appeal in *Leach v Office of Communications* [2012] ICR 1269, [2012] IRLR 839 which stated that "breakdown of trust" is not a mantra that can be mouthed by an employer faced with difficulties in establishing a more conventional conduct reason for dismissal. The seniority of the individual and the size of the employer are both likely to be relevant to the question of whether or not the breakdown justifies dismissal (*Phoenix House Ltd v Stockman & Ors* [2017] ICR 84, [2016] IRLR 848).

(k)   A mistaken belief that continued employment would contravene an enactment. Whilst the fact that an employer genuinely but erroneously believes that he would be breaking the law by continuing to employ an employee does not bring the reason for dismissal within *ERA 1996, s 98(2)(d)*, this can still be some other substantial reason (*Bouchaala v Trusthouse Forte Hotels Ltd* [1980] ICR 721, [1980] IRLR 382 and *Baker v Abellio London Limited* [2018] IRLR 186). Relevant factors to the fairness of such a dismissal include the reasonableness of the employer's belief and the steps the employer took to inform itself of the proper position. In *Baker* the Employment Tribunal erred by failing to consider whether the employer had given the relevant authorities facts and information relevant to the claimant's right to work.

(l)   Unsatisfactory attendance will in some cases be better analysed under this label than under capability, particularly where inability to attend work due to ill health is not in issue (see, for example, *Wilson v Post Office* [2000] IRLR 834 and *Kelly v Royal Mail Group Ltd* (UKEAT/0262/18) (14 February 2019, unreported)).

As usual, dismissal for such a reason will be fair if it was within the 'range of reasonable responses' (see **55.4** above) and a fair procedure was followed. In *Alboni v Ind Coope Retail Ltd* [1998] IRLR 131, the Court of Appeal held that an employment tribunal is bound to have regard to events between notice of dismissal and the date that dismissal took effect, both in determining the reason for dismissal and whether the employers acted reasonably in the circumstances in treating it as a sufficient reason for dismissal.

Clearly the factors relevant to assessing whether an 'SOSR' dismissal was within the range of reasonable responses will vary depending on the nature of the reason. The EAT's decision in *Ssekisonge v Barts Health NHS Trust* (UKEAT/0133/16/LA) (2 March 2017, unreported) contains an interesting discussion of this issue, in the context of an employee dismissed after doubts arose as to her true identity.

When breakdown of trust and confidence is given as the reason for the dismissal, what is the scope of the tribunal's examination of the facts which resulted in that position having been reached? This was considered by the EAT in *Governing Body of Tubbenden Primary School v Sylvester* UKEAT/0527/11/RN [2012] ICR D29. The EAT held that where, as in that case, the reason was essentially a consequence of conduct, it made sense for the tribunal to have regard to the immediate history leading up to the dismissal when assessing reasonableness. The EAT made it clear that it was not holding that in every case in which there is a dismissal because of a breakdown of trust and confidence the tribunal must have regard to how that situation came about. Tribunals are, however, entitled to do so in an appropriate case, of which that was an example.

The fact that a client which procures the dismissal of an employee may have acted unfairly does not mean the dismissal is unfair (*Henderson v Connect (South Tyneside) Ltd* [2010] IRLR 468). If the employer has done everything he reasonably can to avoid or mitigate the injustice brought about by the stance of the client, most obviously by trying to get the client to change his mind and, if that is impossible, by trying to find alternative work for the employee, but has failed, the eventual dismissal is likely to be fair. The employer does, however, need to take into account the injustice and take the steps which it can to remedy it. See *Dobie v Burns International Security Services (UK) Ltd* [1984] ICR 812, [1984] IRLR 329, [1984] 3 All ER 333 for a discussion of factors to be considered when assessing the question of injustice for these purposes. *Bancroft v Interserve (Facilities Management) Ltd* (UKEAT/0329/12/KN) [2013] All ER (D) 183 (Mar) is an example of such a case. The employee in that case was dismissed because of third party pressure from a client. The EAT applied *Henderson* and found that the tribunal had failed to grapple properly with the question of whether or not the employer had done everything it could to mitigate the injustice caused by the third party's request. The EAT also raised an interesting question as to whether the employer was required to have taken steps earlier in the employment history to seek to remedy a problem before it became an insuperable problem leading to dismissal at the behest of the client, but did not find it necessary to resolve the issue in its decision.

In *Jefferson (Commercial) LLP v Westgate* (UKEAT/0128/12/SM) [2013] All ER (D) 303 (Feb) the EAT considered the question of procedural fairness in the context of an SOSR dismissal. Westgate was applied by the EAT in *Express Medicals Ltd v O'Donnell* (UKEAT/0263/15/DA) (9 February 2016, unreported). In *Westgate* both the employer and

However, a trade union or an individual who induced the employer to dismiss an employee may, in certain circumstances, be joined in the proceedings and be ordered to pay all or part of any compensation awarded for unfair dismissal (TULRCA s 160). (See 56.17.)

Unfair Dismissal—III ...

... the EAT reiterated that in every case it is necessary for the tribunal to consider ERA 1996 s 98(4) and apply it sensibly to the facts of the case. The EAT in *Cheema Bham v Hackney & Co* [2017] ICR ... [2016] IRLR 545 came to the same conclusion in relation to the application of the ACAS Code in the context of a dismissal following a breakdown in trust and confidence. The EAT held that what is required in such a case is that the employer considers whether or not the relationship has deteriorated to such an extent that the employee cannot be reinstated ... to the position without unacceptable ... The aims of the ACAS Code incorporate basic common sense principles of fairness which are capable of being and should be applied to such a decision, such as giving the employee the chance to show that he can return to work. The EAT emphasised, however, that this does not mean that the ACAS Code applies in terms. More generally, putting the ACAS Code to one side, many SOSR cases will require a degree of consultation or discussion with the employee, but the content of the employer's procedural duty is fact sensitive (*Drysdale v Royal Surrey County NHS Foundation Trust* (UKEAT/0/09 ... 17) [2018] All ER (D) 65 (Jun)).

In certain circumstances, it may be necessary to consider suitable alternative employment before dismissing for "some other substantial reason", though it is ... not automatic requirement of a fair dismissal (see *OSD/H ... v Barry* (UKEAT/ ... ... April 2014, unreported)).

55.15 DISMISSAL FOLLOWING AN INTERNAL APPEAL

If an employee uses an internal appeal procedure to challenge a decision to dismiss him, and his appeal is rejected, he will be regarded as having been dismissed from the date of his original dismissal, unless his contract provides otherwise (see, eg *J Sainsbury Ltd v Savage* [1981] ICR 1, [1980] IRLR 109, approved in *West Midlands Co-operative Society Ltd v Tipton* [1986] ICR 192, [1986] IRLR 112, ... SC, [1986] 1 All ER 513).

In *Tipton*, the House of Lords held that the facts and matters as they exist ... existed at the time of the final decision to dismiss which, if there is an internal appeal, will be at the conclusion of such an appeal. Lord Bridge said at 200D:

A dismissal is unfair if the employer, ... unless he can treat as sufficient reason to dismiss the employee, either when he makes his original decision to dismiss or when he maintains that decision at the ... to dismiss, or when he maintains that decision at the conclusion of an internal appeal.

In other words, facts and matters that come to light on ... an appeal, whether in favour of the employer or against him, must be taken into account (see 55.4 above ... ... further discussion about the role of the appeal).

55.16 PRESSURE ON AN EMPLOYER TO DISMISS

In determining the reason for a dismissal, or whether ... the reason ... no account is taken of any pressure which by way of organising, promising or threatening ... ... or threatening to organise industrial action, or threatening to dismiss exercised on the employer to dismiss the employee. Any question relating to dismissal is to be determined as if no such pressure had been exercised (ERA 1996 s 107).

56   Unfair Dismissal – III: Remedies

56.1   When an employment tribunal finds that a complaint of unfair dismissal is well-founded, it may make an order for the reinstatement or re-engagement of the complainant, or an order for compensation. This chapter deals with the remedies for unfair dismissal and the settlement of claims, as follows.

—   Reinstatement (see **56.2** below) and re-engagement (see **56.3** below) and related rules (see **56.4**, **56.5** below).

—   Awards of compensation (see **56.6–56.16** below), comprising the following:

•   Basic award (see **56.7–56.9** below).

•   Compensatory award (see **56.10–56.13** below).

•   Additional award in case of non-compliance with order for reinstatement or re-engagement (except union-related, health and safety, pension scheme trustee and employee representative cases) (see **56.14** below).

•   Maximum awards (see **56.16** below).

•   Union-related, health and safety, pension scheme trustees and employee representative dismissals – special award (see **56.16–56.18** below) and reduction of total award (see **56.19** below).

—   Joinder of parties (see **56.17** below).

—   Interim relief (see **56.18** below).

—   Settlement (see **56.19** below).

For the enforcement of, and interest upon, tribunal awards, see **20.121** and **20.122** EMPLOYMENT TRIBUNALS – II.

In practice, a successful complainant will in most cases receive an award of compensation which is made up of a basic award and a compensatory award. Orders for reinstatement and re-engagement are rare. Other payments are restricted to special circumstances as indicated in the relevant paragraphs.

The tribunal's first step on finding a dismissal to be unfair should be to explain to the employee the possibility of an order for reinstatement or re-engagement, and to ask him whether he wishes such an order to be made (*ERA 1996, s 112(1)*). This question should be asked even if the employee has indicated his preferred remedy in his ET1. Although the tribunal's failure to ask the claimant whether he wishes to be reinstated or re-engaged does not render its decision on remedies a nullity, at least where the claimant was legally represented (*Cowley v Manson Timber Ltd* [1995] ICR 367, [1995] IRLR 153), an appeal tribunal should be very ready to remit a case for further consideration of remedy in these circumstances (*Constantine v McGregor Cory Ltd* [2000] ICR 938).

Even where an employer has offered to pay the maximum possible award of compensation, but has not admitted that the dismissal was unfair, the employee is entitled to proceed with his complaint (*Telephone Information Services Ltd v Wilkinson* [1991] IRLR 148; see also *NRG Victory Reinsurance Ltd v Alexander* [1992] ICR 675).

56.2   **REINSTATEMENT**

An order for reinstatement is defined as *an order that the employer shall treat the complainant in all respects as if he had not been dismissed.* In deciding whether to make such an order, the tribunal must consider:

engagement was broadly endorsed by the Supreme Court in *McBride v Scottish Police Authority* [2016] ICR 788, [2016] IRLR 633, [2017] 2 All ER 875, but the Supreme Court there emphasised that what was important in reinstatement was the contractual terms and conditions, not every factual detail of the employment situation.

In *Manchester College v Hazel* [2014] ICR 989, [2014] IRLR 392 the Court of Appeal pointed out that it is entirely in accordance with the policy of the legislation that employees who are unfairly dismissed for a refusal to accept less favourable terms and conditions after a *TUPE* transfer be reinstated or re-engaged on their pre-transfer terms.

For the purpose of deciding whether it is practicable to make an order for reinstatement or re-engagement, the tribunal will not take into account the fact that the employer has engaged a permanent replacement for the dismissed employee unless he can show *either* that it was not practicable for him to arrange for the dismissed employee's work to be done without engaging a permanent replacement, *or* that he engaged the replacement after the lapse of a reasonable period of time, without having heard from the dismissed employee that he wished to be reinstated or re-engaged, and that when the employer engaged the replacement it was no longer reasonable for him to arrange for the dismissed employee's work to be done except by a permanent replacement (*ERA 1996, s 116(5), (6)*).

In *Dafiaghor-Olomu v Community Integrated Care and another* [2018] ICR 585 the EAT held that it was incumbent upon the tribunal to explore the issue of practicability of employment in another geographic location when considering the practicability of an order for re-engagement under *section 116(3)(b)*, even though the parties had not expressly raised it. The same approach no doubt applies equally to an order for reinstatement.

Where the employee has indicated at least seven days before the hearing of his complaint of unfair dismissal that he will seek such an order, the employer must come ready with evidence as to the availability of the old job or comparable or suitable employment, or else bear the costs of any adjournment in the absence of a special reason for the failure (*Employment Tribunals (Constitution and Rules of Procedure) Regulations 2013 (SI 2013/1237), rule 76*).

The continuity of employment of the employee is preserved, and any week falling between the effective date of termination and his re-employment counts towards his period of continuous employment (*ERA 1996, s 219; Employment Protection (Continuity of Employment) Regulations 1996 (SI 1996/3147)*). The *Regulations* deal not only with cases where the tribunal orders reinstatement or re-engagement, but also where that is part of an agreed settlement (see **19.21** EMPLOYMENT TRIBUNALS – I).

In calculating the amount payable on account of arrears of pay and benefits, the tribunal will take into account, so as to reduce the employer's liability, any sums received by the complainant in respect of the period between the date of termination of employment and the date of reinstatement or re-engagement by way of:

(a) wages in lieu of notice or *ex gratia* payments paid by the employer;

(b) remuneration paid in respect of employment with another employer;

and such other benefits as the tribunal thinks appropriate in the circumstances (*ERA 1996, ss 114(4), 115(3)*). It is not permissible to reduce the award of arrears on the ground of delay in asserting the employee's rights in relation to re-engagement (*City and Hackney Health Authority v Crisp* [1990] ICR 95, [1990] IRLR 47).

If an order for reinstatement or re-engagement is made but the terms of the order are not fully complied with, the tribunal will make an award of compensation of such an amount as it thinks fit having regard to the loss sustained by the complainant as a result of the employer's failure to comply with the particular terms in question (*ERA 1996, s 117(1)*,

(2)). This is subject to the same statutory maximum as the compensatory award, save that the usual maximum may be exceeded to the extent necessary to enable the award fully to reflect any sums which ought to have been paid pursuant to the original order (*ERA 1996, s 124(3)*; and see **56.10** below). A purported reinstatement which is on much inferior terms will be treated as a refusal to reinstate at all, so that additional compensation may be awarded in accordance with *ERA 1996, s 117(3), (4)* (see **56.5** below) (*Artisan Press Ltd v Srawley and Parker* [1986] IRLR 126).

56.5 REFUSAL TO REINSTATE OR RE-ENGAGE

If an order for reinstatement or re-engagement is made but the employer refuses to comply with it, the tribunal will award the complainant additional compensation over and above the basic and compensatory awards (see **56.15** below), unless the employer can satisfy the tribunal that it was not practicable to comply with the order (*ERA 1996, s 117(3), (4)*). Although the tribunal should carefully scrutinise the reasons advanced by the employer, it should give due weight to the commercial judgment of the employer unless the employer was to be disbelieved. The tribunal should not set the standard of proof too high, since the test is practicability, not possibility (*Port of London Authority v Payne* [1994] ICR 555, [1994] IRLR 9).

For the purpose of deciding whether it was practicable for the employer to comply with the order, the tribunal will not take into account the fact that he has engaged a permanent replacement unless the employer can show that it was not practicable for the dismissed employee's work to be done without engaging a permanent replacement (*ERA 1996, s 117(7)*).

The employee's only remedy for the employer's failure to reinstate or to re-engage in breach of an order to do so is to obtain compensation under *s 117(3)*, comprising a compensatory, basic and additional award (see **56.7–56.15** below). The calculation under *s 117(3)* must have regard to the loss sustained by the employee and the tribunal can have regard to the amount of lost benefit even in the period between dismissal and the date set for reinstatement (*Awotona v South Tyneside Healthcare NHS Trust* [2005] EWCA Civ 217, [2005] ICR 958, [2005] All ER (D) 221 (Feb)). The employee cannot ask for a renewed order that he be reinstated or re-engaged (*Mabirizi v National Hospital for Nervous Diseases* [1990] ICR 281, [1990] IRLR 133, EAT). However, in awarding the additional compensation, the tribunal will be able to reflect any amounts which should have been paid to the employee under the reinstatement or re-engagement order (see *Selfridges Ltd v Malik* [1998] ICR 268, [1997] IRLR 577 and **56.10** below). The employer will not be permitted to obtain a financial advantage through non-compliance with an order for reinstatement. The statutory cap on compensation for unfair dismissal may be disapplied, if the amount of back pay due to an employee exceeds that cap and the employer has refused to comply with an order for reinstatement (*Parry v National Westminster Bank plc* [2004] EWCA Civ 1563, [2005] IRLR 193). There is no incompatibility with rights derived from the European Convention on Human Rights by an employer refusing to reinstate or re-engage and simply paying the additional compensation due under *ERA 1996, s 117(3)*: see *R (Mackenzie) v Chancellor, Masters and Scholars of the University of Cambridge* [2019] EWCA Civ 1060, [2019] 4 All ER 289.

If the employer reinstates or re-engages an employee following an order, but the terms of the order are not fully complied with, then, subject to the upper limit on compensatory awards (see **56.14** below), the employee will be awarded compensation of such amount as the tribunal thinks fit having regard to the loss sustained by the complainant in consequence of the failure to comply fully with the terms of the order (*ERA 1996, s 117(2)*).

In practice, the employee rarely desires reinstatement or re-engagement and, even if he does, it is rarely ordered. If no such order is made, the amount of compensation will be calculated as set out below.

56.9 Reduction of basic award

Where the tribunal considers that any conduct of the complainant before the dismissal (or, where the dismissal was with notice, before the notice was given) was such that it would be just and equitable to reduce or further reduce the amount of the basic award to any extent, the tribunal will so reduce the award (*ERA 1996, s 122(2); TULR(C)A 1992, s 156(2)*). The exercise required by *s 122(2)* is to be undertaken by the tribunal in three stages: (i) identification of the conduct said to give rise to contributory fault (ii) assessment of whether that conduct was blameworthy (iii) decision on whether it is just and equitable to reduce the award. In making the assessment at stages (i) and (ii) the tribunal's focus should be on what the employee has done, not the employer's assessment of how wrongful the conduct is (*Steen v ASP Packaging Ltd* [2014] ICR 56 and *Singh v Glass Express Midlands Ltd* [2018] ICR D15). See also **56.13** below. However, a basic award can never be reduced on the basis of a failure to mitigate (*Lock v Connell Estate Agents* [1994] IRLR 444).

The amount of the basic award will not be reduced by virtue of the above provisions where the reason or principal reason for the dismissal was that the employee was redundant, unless the dismissal is to be regarded as unfair (*a*) by virtue of *TULR(C)A 1992, s 153* (selection for redundancy for a 'union-related' reason), or (*b*) because the reason for selecting the employee for dismissal was one of those specified in *ERA 1996, s 100(1)(a)* or *(b)*, *101A(1)(d)*, *102(1)* or *103* (see (ii)–(v) in **56.8** above). In that event, the reduction will apply only to so much of the basic award as is payable because of *TULR(C)A 1992, s 156(1)* or *ERA 1996, s 120* (see **56.8** above) (*ERA 1996, s 122(3); TULR(C)A 1992, s 156(2)*).

Where the tribunal finds that the complainant has unreasonably refused an offer by the employer which, if accepted, would have the effect of reinstating the complainant in his employment in all respects as if he had not been dismissed, the tribunal will reduce or further reduce the amount of the basic award to such extent as it considers just and equitable having regard to that finding (*ERA 1996, s 122(1)*).

The basic award may also be reduced where the employee has been awarded any amount in respect of the dismissal under a designated dismissal procedures agreement, to such extent as the tribunal considers it just and equitable having regard to that award (*ERA 1996, s 122(3A)* inserted by the *Employment Rights (Dispute Resolution) Act 1998, s 15, Sch 1, para 22*).

The amount of the basic award will be reduced or, as the case may be, further reduced, by the amount of any redundancy payment awarded by the tribunal in respect of the same dismissal or of any payment made by the employer to the employee on the ground that the dismissal was by reason of redundancy, whether in pursuance of statutory provisions or otherwise (*ERA 1996, s 122(4)*). No reduction of the basic award will be made, however, when the employer makes a payment in respect of redundancy but, objectively viewed, the employee was not redundant (*Boorman v Allmakes Ltd* [1995] IRLR 553).

Note that, where an employee had received an *ex gratia* payment from his former employers which included his statutory entitlement and which was sufficient to cover any basic or compensatory award, the EAT held that an employment tribunal was not obliged to make a basic award (*Chelsea Football Club and Athletic Co Ltd v Heath* [1981] ICR 323, [1981] IRLR 73; cf *Barnsley Metropolitan Borough Council v Prest* [1996] ICR 85).

See also **56.14** below for reduction in union-related cases.

56.10 COMPENSATORY AWARD

The compensation recoverable on a complaint of unfair dismissal increased dramatically in 1999, but, in the current job market, the maximum award is often criticised as being unrealistically low. There are some calls substantially to increase or even remove the cap, though such calls are very unlikely to be heeded in the present political climate.

The statutory maxima notwithstanding, most awards of compensation in unfair dismissal cases are of comparatively modest amounts. Statistics on awards made by Employment Tribunals are published quarterly by the Ministry of Justice. In 2018/2019 the median award of compensation in unfair dismissal cases was £6,243 and the mean was £13,704. Only 16% of awards exceeded £20,000.

For dismissals before 25 October 1999, the maximum amount of the compensatory award was £12,000. With effect from 25 October 1999, the maximum amount of the compensatory award was increased to £50,000, and was abolished altogether in a small number of cases (*Employment Relations Act 1999, ss 34(4)* and *37(1)*; *SI 1999/2830*). For dismissals on or after 6 April 2020, the maximum compensatory award has again increased from £86,444 to £88,519 (*SI 2019/324*). Note, however, that pursuant to *ERA 1996, s 124(1ZA)* the maximum compensatory award is the lower of £88,519 and "52 multiplied by a week's pay" of the individual employee. For these purposes, a 'week's pay' is to be calculated in accordance with the provisions of *ERA 1996, ss 221–229* (*s 227* is of course not applicable). Note that in *University of Sunderland v Drossou* [2017] ICR D23, [2017] IRLR 1087 the EAT held that a week's pay for these purposes includes pension contributions.

There is no maximum compensatory award in health and safety cases (*ERA 1996, s 100*), protected disclosure cases (*ERA 1996, s 103A*), selection for redundancy on health and safety grounds (*ERA 1996, s 105(3)*), and selection for redundancy on protected disclosure grounds (*ERA 1996, s 105(6A)*): *ERA 1996, s 124(1A)*. In the case of a refusal to reinstate or re-engage (see **56.5** above), the tribunal may exceed the normal maximum to the extent necessary fully to reflect the sums which would have been payable under its original order (*ERA 1996, s 124(4)*).

The application of the statutory limit is the last step in the calculation, applied after assessing the amount of loss and after taking into account any payments made by the respondent to the claimant and after any increase or reduction required by any statute or rule of law (*ERA 1996, s 124(5)*). For example, if a claimant's loss was assessed at £90,000 and the tribunal found that he was 50% to blame for the dismissal, he would be awarded £45,000 and not 50% of the statutory maximum (*Walter Braund (London) Ltd v Murray* [1991] ICR 327, [1991] IRLR 100). Similarly, an employment tribunal must first deduct an *ex gratia* payment and then apply the statutory maximum (*McCarthy v British Insulated Callenders Cables plc* [1985] IRLR 94).

The order in which deductions should be made is further considered at **56.13** below.

For the relationship between compensation for unfair and wrongful dismissal, see **59.33** Wrongful Dismissal.

56.11 Amount

The amount of compensation is such amount as the tribunal considers just and equitable in all the circumstances, having regard to the loss sustained by the complainant in consequence of the dismissal insofar as that loss is attributable to action taken by the employer (*ERA 1996, s 123(1)*).

The loss shall be taken to include:

(a)   any expenses reasonably incurred by the complainant in consequence of the dismissal; and

(b)   loss of any benefit save for the contingent right to a redundancy payment which he might reasonably be expected to have had but for the dismissal.

(*ERA 1996, s 123(2), (3)*.)

Loss of reputation. It had long been believed that the claimant is not entitled to damages for the loss to his reputation which has resulted from the dismissal (*Addis v Gramophone Co Ltd* [1909] AC 488). However in *Malik v BCCI* [1997] ICR 606, [1997] IRLR 462, [1997] 3 All ER 1, the House of Lords held that the claimant will be entitled to 'stigma damages' to compensate for difficulties in finding work which may result from the poor reputation of the employer at the time of dismissal, on the basis that the employer breached its duty of trust and confidence to the employee by acting in a manner which gave rise to its poor reputation. A claimant may not receive damages for the stress or injury to feelings resulting from the manner of dismissal (*Bliss v South-East Thames Regional Health Authority* [1987] ICR 700, [1985] IRLR 308, *French v Barclays Bank plc* [1998] IRLR 646, CA and *Dunnachie v Kingston-Upon-Hull City Council* [2004] UKHL 36, [2004] IRLR 727, [2004] 3 All ER 1011 in which the HL ended the uncertainty created by Lord Hoffman's comments in *Johnson v Unisys Ltd* [2001] UKHL 13, [2001] IRLR 279, [2001] 2 All ER 801 and the CA's decision [2004] EWCA Civ 84, [2004] IRLR 287). If an employee suffers from a reactive depression following a dismissal, which renders him unfit for employment between the date of dismissal and the date on which compensation is determined, the employment tribunal must ask what caused his loss. It may be just and equitable to compensate him for all or part of his loss of earnings, despite his unfitness for work, depending on the degree to which the dismissal caused his loss (*Dignity Funerals v Bruce* [2005] IRLR 189).

Pension rights. If, prior to his dismissal, the complainant was a member of a company pension scheme, and fails to obtain new employment, or obtains new employment where there is no company pension scheme, he will almost certainly suffer financial loss because any deferred pension payable will be based on the employee's salary at the date of dismissal (subject to statutory uplifting) instead of on the salary he would have received at normal retiring age. Even if he has obtained employment in another company which operates such a scheme, so that he is able to transfer his accrued rights under the previous scheme to the new scheme, it is likely that this will still involve a degree of loss because the transfer value will only reflect the value of those accrued rights at the date of leaving rather than reflecting the enhanced value which would have been added to those accrued rights, had the complainant remained with the previous company until retirement age instead of being dismissed. In any of these circumstances, the task of assessing compensation for loss of pension rights is a hard one. Some guidance was previously provided by a booklet prepared by a committee of employment tribunal judges in consultation with the Government Actuary's Department ('Employment Tribunals – Compensation for Loss of Pension Rights', 3rd ed. TSO, 2003). That booklet was not binding upon tribunals (*Bingham v Hobourn Engineering Ltd* [1992] IRLR 298; see also *Manpower Ltd v Hearne* [1983] ICR 567, [1983] IRLR 281; *Tradewinds Airways Ltd v Fletcher* [1981] IRLR 272; *Willment Bros Ltd v Oliver* [1979] ICR 378, [1979] IRLR 393; *Mono Pumps Ltd v Froggatt and Radford* [1987] IRLR 368 and has now been overtaken by the guidance referred to below. In *Griffin v Plymouth Hospital NHS Trust* [2015] ICR 347, [2014] IRLR 962 Underhill LJ recognised the value of the booklet but cautioned that it is not to be regarded as gospel and observed that it will not yield the appropriate approach in every case.

Following the decision in *Griffin*, in March 2016 a working group of Employment Judges published a consultation paper which recommended that the booklet be replaced by Presidential Guidance in a similar form. The long awaited outcome of the consultation process was the publication, on 10 August 2017, of new Presidential Guidance and new 'Principles for Compensating Pension Loss', both of which are available on the judiciary-.gov.uk website. The Guidance and Principles speak for themselves, but it remains to be seen how they will be interpreted by the courts.

On the assumption that the Guidance and the Principles are not binding on Tribunals (even though in practice they are expected to be, and likely will be, followed), it may be that a permissible alternative approach remains for the tribunal to assess the period for which the employee should be compensated for loss of pension rights (which may be longer than the period for which the compensation for loss of salary is awarded: see, for example, *Dumfries and Galloway Council v Carroll* (2019) UKEATS/0001/19/AT), and to make an award based upon the cost of purchasing a policy to make up the difference between the pension which he will receive and the amount he would have received had he remained in employment until the end of the period. An award for loss of pension rights which is based solely on the value of the employer's contributions is not appropriate in assessing loss of pension rights under a scheme which yields not only an income benefit but also a lump sum arising as of right rather than by commutation (see for example *Lund v St Edmund's School* [2013] ICR D26, [2013] All ER (D) 365 (May)). In *Bentwood Bros (Manchester) Ltd v Shepherd* [2003] EWCA Civ 380, [2003] IRLR 364 the Court of Appeal held that an employment tribunal had erred in applying only a 5% discount for accelerated receipt, even though the sum represented two and a half years' future earnings and ten years' pension payments. In some cases it may be appropriate to use the Ogden tables to calculate pension loss and is not an error of law for a tribunal so to do: *Chief Constable of West Midlands Police v Gardner* [2012] Eq LR 20, [2012] All ER (D) 39 (Mar).

Payments received by an employee under an occupational or private pension scheme, whether contributory or not, should not be offset against compensation awarded for unfair dismissal. This is because pensions are deferred pay and a decision by an employee to take an early pension after unfair dismissal is a personal decision about money management, rather than a factor which reduces the loss suffered in consequence of the unfair dismissal (*Knapton v ECC Card Clothing Ltd* [2006] IRLR 756).

Loss of statutory rights. The tribunal will assess a nominal figure for loss of protection from unfair dismissal for the first two years (the period for acquiring unfair dismissal protection) of any new employment.

It will also award compensation for loss of the accrued right to the statutory minimum period of notice. The loss was assessed in *Daley v AE Dorsett (Almar Dolls) Ltd* [1982] ICR 1, [1981] IRLR 385 as half the wages due during that period, but it is thought that this may be too high in the ordinary case. See also *Arthur Guinness Son & Co (Great Britain) Ltd v Green* [1989] ICR 241, [1989] IRLR 288.

Frequently, employment tribunals will award just one sum for loss of statutory rights, commonly in the region of £300–£350, to cover loss of protection from unfair dismissal and loss of accrued right to statutory notice.

56.13 FACTORS REDUCING OR INCREASING THE COMPENSATORY AWARD

Just and equitable. The tribunal has a discretion to make an award which is less than the full amount of the claimant's loss if the tribunal considers it just and equitable to do so (*ERA 1996, s 123(1)*). Thus, if the employee has been guilty of misconduct which was only discovered after the dismissal, and therefore could not be relied upon to establish contributory fault (see below), a reduced award or no award may be made (*W Devis & Sons Ltd v Atkins* [1977] ICR 662, [1977] IRLR 314, [1977] 3 All ER 40; *Tele-Trading Ltd v Jenkins* [1990] IRLR 430; *Chaplin v H J Rawlinson Ltd* [1991] ICR 553). See *Slaughter v C Brewer & Sons Ltd* [1990] ICR 730, [1990] IRLR 426 for reductions under *s 123(1)* in cases of ill-health.

The fact that an employer could have dismissed an employee fairly for poor attendance when he dismissed her unfairly for ill-health was held by the Court of Appeal not to justify a reduction in the compensatory award on just and equitable grounds where the employer, in full knowledge of the facts, chose not to dismiss her on grounds of poor attendance (*Devonshire v Trico-Folberth Ltd* [1989] ICR 747, [1989] IRLR 396).

It is only events which took place before dismissal which can render it just and equitable to reduce the compensatory award. A tribunal may not, for example, take account of a breach of a duty of confidentiality which took place after dismissal (*Soros v Davison* [1994] ICR 590, [1994] IRLR 264).

Whether the unfairness made any difference. It was initially thought that, if the employee would have been dismissed even if the employer had done all that he ought to have done, the dismissal ought not to be regarded as unfair. That approach was held to be wrong in *Polkey v AE Dayton Services Ltd* [1988] ICR 142, [1987] IRLR 503, [1987] 3 All ER 974 (see **55.4** UNFAIR DISMISSAL – II) which introduced an approach requiring the tribunal to reduce compensation by a percentage to take account of the possibility that the employee would have been dismissed even if a fair procedure had been followed.

The Scottish Court of Session in *King v Eaton (No 2)* [1998] IRLR 686 said that it was open to a tribunal to decline to permit an employer at a remedies hearing to lead additional evidence to show that the result would have been the same even if fair procedures had been followed. If it is not realistic or practicable to embark upon such an exercise or the exercise would be highly speculative, the tribunal should not do so. To ask what would have happened if the employer had acted fairly is still relevant to compensation. For example, if the company shut down and all the employees were made redundant a few weeks after the claimant was unfairly dismissed, his compensatory award ought not to run beyond that date (see *James W Cook & Co (Wivenhoe) Ltd v Tipper* [1990] ICR 716, [1990] IRLR 386, holding also that the tribunal cannot investigate the commercial and economic reasons behind the closure). The tribunal may take account of the fact that an employee with a short period of service is more at risk of being selected for redundancy if job losses occur (*Morris v Acco Ltd* [1985] ICR 306). Again, it may be that the tribunal considers that an employee dismissed for misconduct without a hearing could not, in fact, have said anything effective in his own defence, or that an employee dismissed without warning for lack of capability was not capable of improvement in any event. In a different context, it has been suggested that it ought not to be assumed too readily that a failure to observe the principles of natural justice made no difference to the result (*John v Rees* [1970] Ch 345, at 402, [1969] 2 All ER 274).

The tribunal ought also to consider *when* that dismissal would have taken place, eg even if it is certain that a fair procedure would have led to the same result, it may be that its adoption would have prolonged the period of earning for a number of weeks (see *Mining Supplies (Longwall) Ltd v Baker* [1988] ICR 676, [1988] IRLR 417) or perhaps not at all (*Robertson v Magnet Ltd (Retail Division)* [1993] IRLR 512). If the employee could only have hoped for continued employment in a different and less well-paid job, the calculation of his loss ought to be based upon those lower earnings (*Red Bank*, above).

In *O'Donoghue v Redcar and Cleveland Borough Council* [2001] EWCA Civ 701, [2001] IRLR 615, the Court of Appeal made it clear that it was not always necessary or appropriate to make a percentage assessment as to whether the claimant would have been dismissed fairly if there had been no unfair dismissal. This was especially the case if the tribunal was assessing the likelihood that the claimant might have been fairly dismissed, not at the time of dismissal, but at some time in the future. In such circumstances, it may not be possible to identify an overall percentage risk, because there may be, say, a 20% chance of dismissal in six months but a 30% chance in a year. In Miss O'Donoghue's case the tribunal concluded that her divisive and antagonistic approach was such that she would have been bound to be dismissed fairly within six months, and so the tribunal limited compensation for future loss to the six-month period. The Court of Appeal held that the tribunal had approached the matter correctly and that it had been appropriate to assess a safe date by which the tribunal was certain that that dismissal would take place and then to make an award of full compensation in respect of the period prior thereto. See also *Scope v Thornett* [2006] EWCA Civ 1600, [2007] IRLR 155.

The EAT in *Chagger v Abbey National plc* [2009] IRLR 86 advised tribunals that even where the dismissal was unfair because of discriminatory grounds, it is necessary to conduct a *Polkey* exercise, to consider what would have happened if the claimant had not been dismissed for discriminatory reasons and whether there would have been a lawful dismissal for a fair reason. The Court of Appeal [2009] EWCA Civ 1202, [2010] IRLR 47, however, held that the EAT had erred in limiting the future loss to that period during which the claimant would have been employed by the respondent, observing that an employee's success in finding new employment is influenced by the particular job market at the time when he finds himself seeking work and that it is generally easier for someone who is still working to find a new job than someone who has been unemployed or out of the industry. Most notably, the Court held that a discriminatory dismissal can alter someone's career path, by necessitating his bringing an employment tribunal claim against the employer, which can create a stigma making him unattractive to future employers, for which the original employer must remain liable. Such future loss flowing from stigma would be equally recoverable in a general unfair dismissal claim as in a claim of a discriminatory dismissal. For a recent application of the *Chagger* principle see *Small v Shrewsbury & Telford Hospitals NHS Trust* [2017] IRLR 889.

In *Andrews v Software 2000 Ltd* [2007] IRLR 568 the EAT said that the following principles as to the *Polkey* exercise emerged from the relevant case law:

(a) In assessing compensation the task of the tribunal is to assess the loss flowing from the dismissal, using its common sense, experience and sense of justice. In the normal case, that requires it to assess for how long the employee would have been employed but for the dismissal.

(b) If the employer seeks to contend that the employee would or might have ceased to be employed in any event had fair procedures been followed, or alternatively would not have continued in employment indefinitely, it is for him to adduce any relevant evidence on which he wishes to rely. However, the tribunal must have regard to all the evidence when making that assessment, including any evidence from the employee himself.

(c) There will, however, be circumstances where the nature of the evidence which the employer wishes to adduce, or on which he seeks to rely, is so unreliable that the tribunal may take the view that the whole exercise of seeking to reconstruct what might have been is so riddled with uncertainty that no sensible prediction based on that evidence can properly be made.

(d) Whether that is the position is a matter of impression and judgment for the tribunal; but in reaching that decision the tribunal must direct itself properly. It must recognise that it should have regard to any material and reliable evidence which might assist it in fixing just compensation, even if there are limits to the extent to which it can confidently predict what might have been; and it must appreciate that a degree of uncertainty is an inevitable feature of the exercise. The mere fact that an element of speculation is involved is not a reason for refusing to have regard to the evidence.

(e) An appellate court must be wary about interfering with the tribunal's assessment that the exercise is too speculative. However, it must interfere if the tribunal has not directed itself properly and has taken too narrow a view of its role.

(f) Even if a tribunal considers some of the evidence or potential evidence to be too speculative to form any sensible view as to whether dismissal would have occurred on the balance of probabilities, it must nevertheless take into account any evidence on which it considers it can properly rely and from which it could in principle conclude that the employment may have come to an end when it did, or alternatively would not have continued indefinitely.

(g) Having considered the evidence, the tribunal may determine:

Payments made by the employer. Payments made by the claimant's former employer, whether under a contractual liability or *ex gratia*, will generally be taken into account (*Rushton v Harcros Timber and Building Supplies Ltd* [1993] ICR 230, [1993] IRLR 254). In *Simrad Ltd v Scott* [1997] IRLR 147, however, the EAT held that a loan which was to be repaid by way of work need not be taken into account for these purposes as it would not be just and equitable to do so since the employee had been deprived of the opportunity to carry on working.

It was formerly understood that the employee must give credit for pay in lieu of notice and other benefits received from the old employer during the notice period (*Addison v Babcock FATA Ltd* [1987] ICR 805, [1987] IRLR 173, [1987] 2 All ER 784) and for earnings from any new employment during the notice period, because the contractual right to notice pay does not create a debt owed by the employer which must be paid irrespective of the employee's real loss, but gives rise merely to a claim in damages or compensation where the employer breaches his contractual or statutory notice obligations (*Rowley v Cerberus Software Ltd* [2001] EWCA Civ 78, [2001] IRLR 160). Similarly, neither pension payments (*Hopkins v Norcros plc* [1994] ICR 11, [1994] IRLR 18), nor an educational grant received in connection with a course embarked upon after dismissal (*Justfern Ltd v D'Ingerthorpe* [1994] ICR 286, [1994] IRLR 164) were taken into account. The full amount of invalidity benefit was deducted in *Puglia v James & Sons* ([1996] IRLR 70), which did not follow *Hilton International Hotels (UK) Ltd v Faraji* ([1994] ICR 259, [1994] IRLR 267). *Puglia v James* was itself not followed in *Rubenstein and Roskin (t/a McGuffies Dispensing Chemists) v McGloughlin* [1996] IRLR 557, in which the EAT deducted only half the amount of invalidity benefit. In a further variation, the EAT in *Sheffield Forgemasters International Ltd v Fox* [2009] ICR 333, [2009] IRLR 192 held that receipt of incapacity benefit did not preclude a claimant from obtaining compensation for loss of earnings during such a period, because some people can lawfully claim incapacity benefit while performing light work.

There were subsequently conflicting decisions at EAT level concerning the deductibility from the compensatory award of monies which the employee earns or receives during the notice period. In *Hardy v Polk (Leeds) Ltd* [2004] IRLR 420 the EAT held that the same duty to mitigate arises as there is at common law and account should be taken of earnings from new employment. A differently-constituted EAT in *Voith Turbo Ltd v Stowe* [2005] IRLR 228 held that it was open to an employment tribunal not to deduct earnings from new employment from the pay in lieu of notice, in accordance with good industrial practice. A more recent EAT decision, however, in *Morgans v Alpha Plus Security* [2005] IRLR 234, [2005] 4 All ER 655, held that incapacity benefit received following a dismissal was properly deducted from the compensatory award, in order to ensure that the employee was compensated for his actual loss only. The Court of Appeal has now concluded that an employee is not required to give credit against his unfair dismissal compensatory award for earnings from another employer during the notice period, when unfairly dismissed without pay in lieu of notice, but that his entitlement for compensation in respect of the notice period is limited to his actual loss (see *Burlo v Langley* above [2006] EWCA Civ 1178, [2007] IRLR 145, [2007] 2 All ER 462).

Jobseeker's allowance received will not be taken into account (but see **56.6** above for the rules on recoupment).

The payments made by the employer are deducted by the employment tribunal from the gross sum after compensation has been reduced to take account of contributory fault and/or the fact that dismissal might have taken place anyway: *Digital Equipment Co Ltd v Clements (No 2)* [1998] IRLR 134.

Delayed Payment. In *Melia v Magna Kansei Ltd* [2005] EWCA Civ 1547, [2006] IRLR 117, the Court of Appeal held that when assessing a claimant's loss, an employment tribunal may make an allowance for delayed payment. According to the Court, this is distinct from a tribunal awarding interest, which it may not do.

The order in which deductions should be made. The Court of Appeal in *Digital Equipment v Clements (No 2)* [1998] IRLR 134 and the Scottish Court of Session in *Leonard v Strathclyde Buses Ltd* [1998] IRLR 693 have considered the order in which deductions should be made from the compensatory award. The position is now clear, except where non-statutory redundancy payments are concerned. The order of deduction is as follows:

(a)   calculate the total loss actually suffered by the claimant;

(b)   deduct amounts received in mitigation and any payment made by the former employer (other than a non-statutory redundancy payment);

(c)   make any adjustment for failure on the part of the employee or employer to follow statutory procedures;

(d)   make any reduction for contributory fault;

(e)   apply the statutory maximum.

The controversy as regards non-statutory redundancy payments is as to whether the effect of *ERA 1996, s 123(7)* is that such payments should be deducted after the reduction for contributory fault but before the statutory maximum is applied, or whether they should only be deducted after the statutory maximum is applied. It is not clear from the judgments in *Digital Equipment v Clements (No 2)* which of the two alternative approaches should be followed. In *Leonard v Strathclyde Buses*, however, the Court of Session held that non-statutory redundancy payments should be deducted before the statutory maximum is applied and said that there was nothing in *Digital Equipment v Clements (No 2)* which points to any different view.

The approach taken by the Court of Appeal in *Digital Equipment v Clements (No 2)* was adopted once again by the Scottish Court of Session in *Heggie v Uniroyal Englebert Tyres Ltd* [1999] IRLR 802.

56.14 ADDITIONAL AWARD – NON-COMPLIANCE WITH AN ORDER

Additional compensation is payable in cases where an order for reinstatement or re-engagement is made but not complied with (see **56.5** above) consisting of not less than 26 weeks' and not more than 52 weeks' pay (except union-related, health and safety, pension scheme trustee and employee representative cases where a special award may be made, see **56.16** below) (*ERA 1996, s 117*).

The tribunal may not simply make the maximum award in order to force compliance with its order. It must consider factors such as the employer's conduct and the extent to which the compensatory award has met the actual loss suffered (*Morganite Electrical Carbon Ltd v Donne* [1988] ICR 18, [1987] IRLR 363).

Where the employer has made an *ex gratia* payment which exceeds the amount of any loss suffered, it may be possible to set off the surplus against any additional award (*Darr v LRC Products Ltd* [1993] IRLR 257).

56.15 REDUCTION OF AWARD – 'UNION-RELATED' CASES

Where an award of compensation is made in respect of a dismissal which is to be regarded as unfair by virtue of *TULR(C)A 1992, s 152* or *s 153*, a tribunal, in considering whether it would be just and equitable to reduce or further reduce the amount of *any part* of the award, will disregard any conduct or action which constitutes:

(a)   a breach or proposed breach of a requirement that the complainant should:

may apply to an employment tribunal for an order for interim relief (*TULR(C)A 1992, s 161(1)*; *ERA 1996, s 128*; and see **55.3** UNFAIR DISMISSAL – **II**). Note that this does not apply to all the cases where a health and safety dismissal or 'working time' dismissal is automatically unfair. In *Bombardier Aerospace/Short Brothers Plc v McConnell* [2007] NICA 27, [2008] IRLR 51, the Northern Ireland Court of Appeal held that interim relief was not available where the true reason for dismissal was redundancy, but there was an unlawful union-related reason for the selection. This is because interim relief in the form of reinstatement or re-engagement would be of no value where the employer had ceased to carry on business due to redundancy. If an employer dismissed the employee for a reason in respect of which interim relief was available and then created a spurious redundancy in order to mask the real reason for dismissal, then interim relief would be available. The case returned to the tribunal, at which the claimants conceded that there was a genuine redundancy situation, although arguing that the principal reason for their own dismissals was their trade union and health and safety activities. The tribunal denied them interim relief, and the case again returned to the NICA ([2008] NICA 50; [2009] IRLR 201). The NICA agreed with the tribunal that interim relief was not available, because there was a true redundancy situation, which made it unlikely that the tribunal would conclude that the sole or principal reason for the dismissals was trade union or health and safety activities. On the other hand, the tribunal might find that there had been unfair selection for redundancy, but interim relief was not available for such a claim.

An order for interim relief may be made pending a substantive hearing where the tribunal considers that the complainant is likely to succeed. The order is either for reinstatement or re-engagement, or for continuation of the terms of the contract.

An application for interim relief will only be entertained if it is presented to the tribunal within seven days following the effective date of termination and (where the complainant relies on (*a*) or (*b*) above) if there is also presented within that time a certificate from an authorised official of the union that the complainant was, or proposed to become, a member of the union and that there are good grounds for supposing that the reason or principal reason for the dismissal was one alleged in the complaint (*TULR(C)A 1992, s 161(2),(3)*; *ERA 1996, s 128(2)*). The tribunal should deal with the interim application as soon as possible (*TULR(C)A 1992, s 162(1)*; *ERA 1996, s 128(3)*). Both parties may be present at the hearing, the employer having had at least seven days' notice of the application (*TULR(C)A 1992, s 162(2)*; *ERA 1996, s 128(4)*). A party who has been joined to the proceedings in accordance with a request made under *TULR(C)A 1992, s 160* made at least three days before the hearing (see **55.20** above), must have as much notice as is reasonably practicable (*TULR(C)A 1992, s 162(3)*). The hearing may only be postponed in special circumstances (*TULR(C)A 1992, s 162(4)*; *ERA 1996, s 128(5)*). Guidance as to the procedure to be followed in interim relief cases was given by the EAT in *Derby Daily Telegraph Ltd v Foss*, IDS Brief 471, p 15.

The tribunal should consider whether the complaint is well-founded by applying a test of whether or not the complainant has 'a pretty good chance' of success, which is the proper meaning of 'likely to succeed' in ERA 1996, s 129: see *Taplin v C Shippam Ltd* [1978] ICR 1068, [1978] IRLR 450, *Dandpat v University of Bath* UKEAT/0408/09 and *London City Airport v Chacko* [2013] IRLR 610. The tribunal is quite entitled to take a summary approach and not delve too deeply into the underlying merits of the claim: *Parsons v Airplus Intl Ltd* UKEAT/0023/16 [2016] All ER (D) 217 (Mar). The 'likely to succeed' or 'pretty good chance' test applies to the question of employment status where that is also in issue: see *Hancock v Ter-Berg* [2020] IRLR 97. Where the test is fulfilled the tribunal will ask the employer, if he is present, whether he is willing to reinstate or re-engage the complainant pending the full hearing or settlement of the matter. If the employer states that he is willing to reinstate the employee, the tribunal will make an order to that effect.

If the employer states that he is willing to re-engage the employee in another job and specifies the terms and conditions on which he is willing to do so, the tribunal will ask the employee whether he is willing to accept the job on those terms and conditions, and:

(i)   if he is willing, make an order to that effect; and

(ii)   if he is unwilling to accept the job on those terms and conditions, then if the tribunal is of the opinion that the refusal is reasonable, it will make an order for the *continuation* of his contract of employment (a 'continuation order').

If the employer has failed to attend the hearing before the tribunal or states that he is unwilling either to reinstate the employee or re-engage him, the tribunal will make a continuation order.

(TULR(C)A 1992, s 163; ERA 1996, s 129.)

A continuation order is an order that, until the complaint has been dealt with, the employee's contract will be treated as continuing for the purposes of his entitlement to benefits, including pay, and for the purposes of determining the length and continuity of his employment. If an employer fails to comply with a continuation order, compensation for such non-compliance may also be awarded if the complainant has thereby suffered loss, and the employer will be ordered to pay any amount of wages due under the continuation order *(TULR(C)A 1992, ss 164, 166; ERA 1996, ss 130, 132).*

At any time between the making of an order by an employment tribunal under these interim provisions and the determination or settlement of the complaint to which it relates, the employer or the employee may apply to the tribunal for the revocation of the order on the ground of a relevant change of circumstances which has occurred since the making of the order *(TULR(C)A 1992, s 165; ERA 1996, s 131).*

56.19 SETTLEMENT

Employers may wish to settle a claim or a potential claim for unfair dismissal rather than proceed to a hearing. The process of ACAS early conciliation increases the incentive on parties to settle their differences before proceedings are even commenced. The tribunals have a duty to encourage settlement and may do so at the hearing. If settlement is reached, one of two courses must be followed for any agreement reached with the employee to be binding. Either a conciliation officer must be involved (see **2.4** ADVISORY, CONCILIATION AND ARBITRATION SERVICE and note *BNP Paribas v Mezzotero* [2004] IRLR 508, EAT and *Hinton v University of East London* [2005] EWCA Civ 532, [2005] IRLR 552) or the conditions of a statutorily valid settlement agreement must be fulfilled, including that the employee has had independent advice *(ERA 1996, s 203).* In *Industrious Ltd v Horizon Recruitment Ltd* [2010] IRLR 204, the EAT held that an employment tribunal was empowered to decide whether a settlement agreement ought to be set aside for misrepresentation.

If this is not done, an employee will be free to bring a claim notwithstanding that he has received a sum in settlement. Although this amount may be taken into account in assessing compensation (as in the example at **56.10** above), nevertheless it may not be sufficient to extinguish the employer's liability. If a compromise is reached after a tribunal has held a dismissal to be unfair but before making an award of compensation, the same is required in order for the agreement to be binding (see *Courage Take Home Trade Ltd v Keys* [1986] ICR 874). It was also held in *Courage* that where a settlement was fairly reached, but was not binding because of what is now *ERA 1996, s 203*, it might well not be 'just and equitable' to award any further compensation.

In the light of the increasing exercise of the employment tribunal's power to award costs, note *Kopel v Safeway Stores plc* [2003] IRLR 753 with regard to 'Calderbank' letters in the tribunal context, and see further **20.22** EMPLOYMENT TRIBUNALS – II.

56.19   Unfair Dismissal – III: Remedies

Sums paid by an employer to an employee under a settlement of tribunal proceedings may be subject to different tax liabilities and recoupment rules from sums payable by order of a tribunal or sums payable under the contract of employment itself, therefore care is needed in negotiating and concluding settlements (see eg *Wilson (HM Inspector of Taxes) v Clayton* [2004] EWHC 898 (Ch), [2004] IRLR 611).

57   Vicarious Liability

57.1   'Vicarious liability' describes the principle of law which allows an employer to be held liable for the unlawful acts of its employees committed in the course of their employment. Such liability would extend, for example, to the case of a van driver who drives negligently in the normal course of his duties and causes an accident; the driver's employer will be held vicariously liable for any resulting injury. The employer may also be held vicariously liable where one employee injures another at work, or where an employee steals from a customer, again providing that the act is done in the course of employment.

Importantly, the doctrine of vicarious liability does not rest on the employer itself having committed an actionable wrong, for which it can be held directly liable; rather it is a doctrine which fixes an innocent employer with a form of *secondary* liability on the basis that this is what is required by the principle of social justice. The employer, despite itself being innocent of any wrongdoing, must pay the price for the wrongs of its employees, provided that those wrongs occur in the course of the employee's employment. Compare the situation where an employer can be held *directly* liable for the wrongs of the employee because it authorised the particular wrongful act or, alternatively, because the wrongful act was itself the product of the employer breaching a relevant legal duty. The latter situation might arise, for example, where an injury occurs at work and that injury would not have come about had the employer complied with its obligation to ensure that employees had received health and safety training or where an employee is able to misuse personal data to which he or she has had access because the employer failed to put in place appropriate data security measures.

This chapter discusses: (a) the operation of the common law doctrine of vicarious liability; (b) the relationship between statutory employment rights and vicarious liability principles and (c) how vicarious liability principles apply in a *pro hac vice* scenario, where the wrong is committed by a worker lent to the employer by a third party.

57.2   VICARIOUS LIABILITY AT COMMON LAW

The common law doctrine of vicarious liability has its roots in the principle that where an employer puts an enterprise into the community it should bear the legal responsibility for wrongful acts done by its employee in the course of their employment. In effect, the doctrine amounts to a form of distributive justice in that it enables a claimant who may well be unable to recover damages from the wrongdoer (because of the latter's lack of means) to obtain justice for the wrongs they have suffered by recovering damages from the employer, who is likely to have deeper pockets. However, as with all social justice doctrines, it is important that it is kept within proper limits, and in particular that innocent employers are not excessively burdened with liability. The courts have sought to ensure that the vicarious liability doctrine does not overreach itself so as to achieve outcomes that are unjust by proceeding on the basis that vicarious liability will be established only where the wrong occurred 'in the course of the employee's employment'. Whilst the test sounds straightforward, its practical application has often proved to be rather challenging, particularly where the employee's wrongful act appears in some respects to be wholly remote from what he or she was employed to do.

Following *Lister v Helsley Hall Ltd* [2001] UKHL 22, [2002] 1 AC 215, [2001] IRLR 472, [2001] 2 All ER 769 and the more recent judgments of the Supreme Court in *Mohamud v WM Morrison Supermarkets plc* [2016] UKSC 11, [2016] 2 WLR 821, [2016] IRLR 362, [2017] 1 All ER 15 and *Various Claimants v WM Morrison Supermarkets plc* [2020] UKSC 12, it is clear that when seeking to determine whether vicarious liability is established, the courts will focus heavily on two questions: (1) what was the field of the employee's activities in his or her employed role (essentially what did the job comprise) and (2) what was the degree of connection between the employee's wrongful act and those activities? It is only if the wrongful act was sufficiently connected with the employee's employed activities that vicarious liability will be established, consistent with the principle of social justice. However, where that sufficient connection is present, vicarious liability will be established irrespective of whether the relevant wrongful act was ostensibly inconsistent with the employee's employed activities or otherwise conflicted with specific instructions given by the employer.

The following cases give a flavour of how the courts have been applying these principles in recent years:

—   In *Mohamud* the Supreme Court held that the employer was vicariously liable for the employee's assault on a customer essentially because the field of activity which had been entrusted to the employee included dealing with customers, and the assault came about in the context of the employee dealing with a particular customer on behalf of the employer. Importantly, the Supreme Court reached this conclusion even though the manner in which the employee dealt with the customer was an abuse of his position and positively conflicted with his employer's instructions to its employees as to how they should behave in the workplace. In the court's eyes, the wrong occurred in the midst of the employee doing the job he was employed to do, and in those circumstances vicarious liability was established.

—   In *Bellman v Northampton Recruitment Ltd* [2018] EWCA Civ 2214, the Court of Appeal, overturning the judgment of the High Court, held that a company could be held vicariously liable in circumstances where the managing director of the company violently assaulted the employee during a drinking session at a hotel which followed on from a work drinks event. It is clear from the judgment that the facts that the managing director was the directing mind of the company, that he was always effectively on the job and that the assault took place whilst the managing director was discussing work related matters with the employee were central to the Court of Appeal's conclusions on vicarious liability. The outcome in *Bellman* was effectively approved by the Supreme Court in *Various Claimants v Morrisons* (supra).

—   Compare the even more recent case of *Various Claimants v Morrisons*, where the Supreme Court, overturning the judgments of the High Court and the Court of Appeal, held that no vicarious liability could be imposed in a case where an employee, acting so as to damage his employer, secretly copied employee payroll data concerning 100,0000 fellow employees (to which he had been given access in his employed role), and then disclosed that data online; the disclosure was effected by the rogue employee when he was at home, not working, using his own personal devices and in circumstances where he had attempted to frame another employee. In essence, the Supreme Court held that Morrisons could not be held liable for the employee's unlawful online disclosure because the disclosure was not undertaken by the rogue in his employed role (he was not employed to disclose data online to the world at large); instead the disclosure was effected in the context of the rogue's own entirely personal enterprise, which enterprise was itself undertaken not on behalf of his employer but rather with a view to damaging the employer.

—   Note also the recent Supreme Court judgment in *Various Claimants v Barclays Bank*, where the Supreme Court, overturning the Court of Appeal's judgment, held that an employer could in principle be held vicariously liable for the actions of an independent medical practitioner whom the Bank had appointed to medically examine its employees and who had, it was alleged, assaulted a number of employees in the course of their being examined. The Supreme Court concluded that this case was wrongly decided because the Court of Appeal had not properly analysed the relevant question which was whether the Bank could in principle be held vicariously liable for the actions of a person who was not an employee at all but an independent contractor. The Supreme Court held that the doctrine of vicarious liability could not be applied on the facts of the case, because the doctor was not "anything close to an employee" but was instead *in business on his own account as a medical practitioner with a portfolio of patients and clients. One of those clients was the Bank.*" (paragraph 29). Compare the earlier case of *Cox v Ministry of Justice* [2016] UKSC 10, [2017] 1 All ER 1, [2016] 2 WLR 806, [2016] IRLR 370, where the Supreme Court held that the Ministry of Justice was vicariously liable for injuries sustained by a catering manager employed in one of Her Majesty's prisons, where the injuries were inflicted by a prisoner working in the prison kitchens. Key factual considerations here included that the prisoner had been integrated into the operation of the kitchen; the prisoner's activities were of benefit to the prison; the prisoner had been bound to engage in the work and received a nominal wage for that work and the prisoner had been placed by the Ministry in a position where he could commit negligent acts within the fields of activities assigned to him. The facts that the Ministry did not profit from the arrangement and that the Ministry was under a statutory duty to provide the prisoner with useful work did not militate against the doctrine of vicarious liability being applicable in principle.

As will be apparent from the analysis of the relevant jurisprudence in this area (as set out above and below), the question of whether an employee can be taken to be acting in the course of their employment turns fundamentally on the facts of the particular case. However, it is important to bear in mind that the courts will generally also be heavily influenced by the approach taken by the courts in previous cases, particularly where the earlier cases are similar on their facts to the case before the court. Indeed, it will be an error of law for the court to fail to take into account the existing jurisprudence, which jurisprudence ought to shape the court's approach to the case before it (*Various Claimants v Morrisons*).

A number of the cases in this area have focussed on the issue of the employer's liability where an employee assaults a colleague or a third party – see *Mohamud* and *Bellman* supra. In *Mohamud*, the violent assault, for which the employer was held vicariously liable, came about in circumstances where the employee was responding to a customer query. The employee was certainly not employed to assault customers and in fact his actions directly conflicted with his employer's instructions as to how he should behave when at work. However, the Supreme Court took the view that the assault occurred in the course of the employee's conduct because it occurred in the context of him doing something he was employed to do, namely dealing with customers who attended the petrol station where the employee worked, and at a time when he was in effect wearing his 'metaphorical uniform'. Compare the case of *Bellman* where the employer was held liable for a violent assault by the managing director of a company on a subordinate which took place outside of the workplace at an informal drinks which ran on from a work Christmas party. It is clear from the judgment that the Court of Appeal took the view that liability should be imposed notwithstanding that the assault occurred outside the work place because the managing director was effectively always on the job and was effectively engaging with the employee on work-related matters when the assault took place (an outcome that was approved of by the Supreme Court in *Various Claimants v Morrisons*). Compare *Gravil v Carroll* [2008] EWCA Civ 689, [2008] ICR 1222, [2008] IRLR 829, where the Court of Appeal concluded that a rugby club was vicariously liable when one of its players assaulted another player in the course of a game.

In the case of *Various Claimants v Morrisons*, the High Court and the Court of Appeal both took the view that, particularly in light of the judgment in *Mohammud*, the employer could be held liable in a case where an employee had deliberately effected a large scale data breach affecting some 100,000 individuals. The facts of the case were stark: the employee was a senior internal IT auditor; he harboured a secret grudge against his employer in connection with an earlier disciplinary process to which he had been subject; having been given access to a spreadsheet containing payroll data relating to the employer's entire workforce (some 120,000 people) for the purposes of a statutory audit process; the employee, acting for his own criminal purposes, secretly copied the spreadsheet from his work laptop onto a personal USB; some months later, after the employee's role in the internal audit process had concluded, and whilst he was at home, not working, and using his own personal devices, the employee published a significant proportion of the data online – altogether some 100,000 individuals were affected; the employee had taken various steps designed to conceal his role in the publication of the data, and indeed he had sought to 'frame' an entirely innocent fellow employee; it was established in his criminal trial that the employee's actions were undertaken specifically for the purposes of damaging his employer; it was also established that, from a data protection perspective, it was the employee and not the employer who had controlling powers over the data that was published. The High Court and thereafter the Court of Appeal held that the employee's act of publishing the data online was sufficiently connected with his employment to render the employer liable. This was essentially because there was a causal connection between the employee's wrongful disclosure and his employment: he was given access to the relevant data in the course of his employed role and that in turn is what enabled his wrongful disclosure. In reaching the conclusion that vicarious liability should be imposed, both courts took the view that they should ignore the fact that the employee's wrongful acts were intended and designed to damage his employer. They did so on the basis that such an approach was consistent with certain comments made by Lord Toulson in the course of his judgment in *Mohamud*, which both the High Court and the Court of appeal construed as meaning that the wrongdoer's motive was irrelevant to the analysis.

In an important judgment which is bound to cast a long shadow over this area for years to come, the Supreme Court overturned the Court of Appeal's judgment. The Supreme Court identified four errors in the Court of Appeal's approach to the case, which are summarised below:

(1)   In essence, the Court of Appeal had found that vicarious liability could be imposed because of the causal connection between the wrongful disclosure and the rogue employee's employment. However, vicarious liability could not be established merely because there was a temporal or causal connection with the employment. Such an approach would result in an extravagant application of the doctrine.

(2)   The Court of Appeal had also erred in its approach to the question of what fell within the employee's field of activities. The fact that the wrongful act had certain similarities to what the employee was required to do in his employed role (i.e. because it entailed the processing/disclosure of data, which was something the employee also had to do in his employed role) did not mean that that act could be treated as being within the employee's field of activities. The point was illustrated by the moonlighting case of *Koorgang Investments Pty Ltd v Richardson & Wrench Ltd* [1982] AC 462. In that case, a surveyor had provided negligent surveying services to a third party whilst moonlighting. The court held that the employer of the surveyor could not be held vicariously liable in respect of those negligent services. This was because the services in question were not provided whilst the surveyor was going about his employer's business but whilst he was providing services on his own behalf as part of an independent enterprise. In *Morrisons*, the rogue employee was not going about his employer's business, acting in the capacity of employee when he effected his wrongdoing. Instead, he was instead acting in a purely personal capacity in the context of his purely personal enterprise, i.e. on a personal frolic of his own. (See further below the discussion of cases where the wrongful act occurs in circumstances where the employee is exploiting the authority conferred by his employer, where different considerations will come into play).

(3)   The Court of Appeal had also erred by relying heavily on the five factors identified by the Supreme Court in *Various Claimants v Catholic Child Welfare Society* [2012] UKSC 56, [2013] 2 AC 1. Those factors, which required the court to consider amongst other things the employer's means and whether they had relevant insurance, were relevant when the court was seeking to determine whether the acts of a person who was not an employee could attract the application of the vicarious liability doctrine. They did not assist in a case involving wrongful acts by an employee.

(4)   Finally, the Court of Appeal's conclusion that the rogue employee's motive was irrelevant to the analysis was erroneous. The Court of Appeal had misunderstood the point being made by Lord Toulson in *Mohamud*. Far from being irrelevant, the question of whether the employee was acting on his employer's business or for purely personal reasons was highly material to the analysis.

The Supreme Court went on to conclude that having regard to the facts of the case, Morrisons could not be held vicariously liable for the actions of the rogue employee. Notably, the Supreme Court used its judgment not only to identify errors in the Court of Appeal's judgment but also, more widely, to address certain 'misunderstandings' which had arisen following the judgment in *Mohamud*, which misunderstandings had inclined the lower courts to assume that the law on vicarious liability had a wider reach than was in fact the case (see paragraph 1). The Supreme Court made a point of emphasising that the question of whether an employer could be held vicariously liable for the wrongs of its employee did not turn on what the judges felt was the just result but rather on a scrupulous analysis of the field of activities question and the sufficiency of connection question.

It is also worth noting that the Supreme Court in *Various Claimants v Morrisons* specifically commented on cases involving child sexual abuse (including the *Lister* case referred to supra), finding that they required a focus on the criteria that are particularly relevant in those cases, including in particular the conferral of authority on the employee in question, which authority the wrongdoer then sought to exploit in the context of the abuse (per Lord Reed, paragraph 23). It must be assumed that the Supreme Court made these comments because it did not want its judgment to create a situation in which it was assumed in every case that vicarious liability could only be imposed where the employee was doing their job in the moment when the relevant wrong occurs. Obviously such a narrow approach to the vicarious liability doctrine might operate so as to prevent an employer being held vicariously liable for an employee who sexually abuses a child in their care but does so, for example, out of working hours. Importantly, the notion that the employer's conferral of authority can be relevant to the assessment of whether vicarious liability can be imposed is a notion that potentially applies beyond the child sexual abuse cases. It was a key consideration, for example, in *Lloyd v Grace* [1912] AC 716 (where a managing clerk in a law firm exploited the authority given to him by the firm to defraud one of the firm's clients for his own benefit) and also in *Bernard v Attorney General of Jamaica* [2004] UKPC 46, [2005] IRLR 398 (where an off-duty police officer engaged in an assault at the same time as he was asserting his authority as an officer for his own personal purposes).

Separately, the Supreme Court has given permission to appeal in the case of *Frederick v Positive Solutions (Financial Services) Limited* [2018] EWCA Civ 431, [2018] All ER (D) 99 (Mar) where the Court of Appeal held that a company was not vicariously liable for the acts of its agent where the agent had effectively misused his position as agent for the company so as to effect a fraud on a third party. The Court of Appeal concluded that the first instance judge had been right to hold that the company was not vicariously liable for the fraud, particularly given that the fraud had been effected by the agent for the purposes of his own independent business. The Court of Appeal otherwise upheld the judge's conclusion that there could be no vicarious liability because not all of the wrongful acts necessary to make the agent liable were undertaken by him in the course of his discharging his role as agent. It remains to be seen whether, in light of the judgment in *Various Claimants v Morrisons*, that case will now proceed to a hearing before the Supreme Court.

Other types of case in which the courts have considered the application of the doctrine of vicarious liability include: cases involving negligent driving; cases involving a theft by the employee and cases involving employee 'horseplay'. Consider the following:

–   negligent driving – In *Fletcher v Chancery Lane* [2016] EWCA Civ 1112, [2016] All ER (D) 205 (Oct), the Court of Appeal held that the first instance judge had erred when he concluded that an employer was vicariously liable in negligence in circumstances where its employee had crossed the road and collided with a cyclist. The evidence was such that it was impossible to conclude that the employee's act of crossing the road was sufficiently connected with his employment so as to render the employer vicariously liable. See further *Smith v Stages* [1989] ICR 272, [1989] IRLR 177, [1989] 1 All ER 833: the House of Lords held an employer vicariously liable for injuries sustained in a crash caused by the negligent driving of an employee driving his workmate (the injured claimant) home to Staffordshire after completing a job in Pembroke

–   employee theft – In *Brink's Global Services Inc v Igrox Ltd* [2010] EWCA Civ 1207, [2011] IRLR 343, the Court of Appeal held that an employer who had employed an individual to fumigate the vaults of a third party was vicariously liable when the employee stole a number of silver bars from the vaults in question. The Court held that the theft from the very vault which he had been instructed to fumigate was reasonably incidental to the purpose for which the employee was employed and it was otherwise fair and just to hold the employer liable. Similarly, in *Morris v C W Martin & Sons Ltd* [1966] 1 QB 716, [1965] 2 All ER 725, the House of Lords held that the employer was vicariously liable in circumstances where its employee had stolen a fur coat which had been entrusted to the employer by a third party.

–   employee 'horseplay' – In *Paul Graham v Commercial Bodyworks Ltd* [2015] EWCA Civ 47, [2015] All ER (D) 72 (Feb), the employee had been engaging in horseplay with his colleague whilst both were working with highly flammable thinning agents in the employer's repair shop. In the course of their interaction, the employee accidentally set his colleague alight, causing terrible burns. The facts that the incident occurred whilst both employees were at work and the employees had been required to work with highly flammable substances were not sufficient to render the employer vicariously liable for the employee's acts.

It is possible to analyse all of these cases on the basis that, consistent with the principles approved in *Various Claimants v Morrisons*, the question of whether liability was imposed turned substantially on the question of whether the employee was going about his employer's business in the moment when the wrongful act occurred.

Both *Igrox* and *Morris* concerned cases where the third party affected by the criminal conduct had a direct commercial relationship with the employer. Different considerations may arise where no such relationship exists between the wronged party and the employer, as was the case in *Dubai Aluminium Co Ltd v Salaam* [2002] UKHL 48, [2003] 2 AC 366, [2003] IRLR 608, [2003] 1 All ER 97. In *Dubai Aluminium*, the question was whether a law firm was vicariously liable in a case where a partner of the firm was alleged to have knowingly drafted various legal agreements in support of a fraudulent enterprise. The persons who were the target of that enterprise had themselves had no dealings with the firm in question. The House of Lords held that vicarious liability was established. This was particularly on the basis that, although the partner was alleged to have drafted the agreements for dishonest purposes, his acts of drafting the agreements were so closely connected with the acts that he was authorised to undertake by the firm in his own role as partner that it was fair and just to treat the firm as being vicariously liable for those acts. The approach adopted in *Dubai Aluminium* was approved by the Supreme Court in *Mohamud*, and was also discussed approvingly in *Various Claimants v Morrisons*. A question arises as to how the outcome in *Dubai Aluminium* can be reconciled with the approach taken by the Supreme Court in *Morrisons* to the concept of the employee's field of activities, where the Supreme Court appeared anxious to distinguish between those cases where the employee committed the wrong when acting about his employer's business and those cases where the employee was acting in the context of a purely personal enterprise. Arguably the wrongdoer in *Dubai Aluminium* fell into the latter category, and yet vicarious liability was nonetheless established. The answer to the question is likely to be that vicarious liability was properly established because the acts were done by an individual acting in his capacity as partner of the firm, albeit that the work he was doing was being done other than on behalf of and for the benefit of his employer (i.e. this was not a pure moonlighting case).

An important and controversial question which arises in connection with vicarious liability is the question of whether churches which are caught up in child sex abuse cases can be held vicariously liable for abuses committed by their priests. In *Maga v Birmingham Roman Catholic Archdiocese Trustees* [2010] EWCA Civ 256, [2010] 1 WLR 1441, [2010] All ER (D) 141 (Mar), the Court Appeal held that church trustees were vicariously liable for the sexual abuse of a minor by an assistant priest (overturning the judgment of the High Court ([2009] EWHC 780 (QB), [2009] All ER (D) 176 (Apr)). In *Maga*, the Court of Appeal concluded it was fair and just to impose vicarious liability for the sexual abuse on the trustees because there were a number of factors which, when taken together, showed that there was a sufficiently close connection between the employment at the church of the assistant priest (C) and the abuse which C had inflicted on M. The factors relied upon by the Court of Appeal included in particular that: through being employed by the church as a priest, C had been able to hold himself out to M as being particularly trustworthy and authoritative; C had also used his functions as a priest, including his duty to evangelise, to get to know M; the church had given C particular responsibilities for youth work and C had been able to 'groom' M through that work; moreover, C had developed his relationship with M in the course of a disco which had been organised by the church, took place on church premises and which C attended as a priest. It is clear that central to the Court of Appeal's analysis was the fact that it was C's role as a priest in the archdiocese which gave him the status, authority and opportunity to draw M into his sexually abusive orbit (compare *JGE v Trustees of the Portsmouth Roman Catholic Diocesan Trust* [2012] EWCA Civ 938, [2012] IRLR 846, [2012] 4 All ER 1152 where the Court of Appeal held that the fact that the relationship between the Trust and the priest was not an employment relationship per se did not prevent the Trust being vicariously liable for the priest's conduct). The Supreme Court has since taken a similar approach in *Catholic Child Welfare Society & Ors v Institute of the Brothers of Christian Schools* [2012] UKSC 56, [2013] 1 All ER 670, [2012] 3 WLR 1319, [2013] IRLR 219. In that case, a lay Roman Catholic order provided education to children. The diocesan bodies responsible for the Institute and the Institute itself were found vicariously liable for sexual abuse by the teachers. Having reviewed the cases on vicarious liability, the Court took the view that establishing vicarious liability required the application of a two stage test. At the first stage, the question was whether the relationship between the defendant and the tortfeasor was one which was capable of giving rise to vicarious liability, for example was it akin to an employer/employee relationship. At the second stage, the question was whether the defendant had not only used the tortfeasor to carry on its own business but had done so in a manner which created or significantly increased the risk that the victims would be subject to the relevant unlawful act. In other words, there had to be a strong causal link between the relationship between the defendant and the tortfeasor on the one hand and the unlawful act on the other. It was this 'close connection' which was required between the relationship and the unlawful act which established the defen-

57.2 Vicarious Liability

An employer which is liable to a third party for damages resulting from the negligence of its employee may seek to recover those damages from the negligent employee. See for example: *Lister v Romford Ice and Cold Storage Co Ltd* [1957] AC 555, [1957] 1 All ER 125, HL.

57.3 STATUTORY VICARIOUS LIABILITY

In the field of statutory employment rights, vicarious liability is very often imposed by statute, see e.g. the *Equality Act 2010, s 109(1)* (see **13.26** Discrimination and Equal Opportunities – II). Where the legislation contains express vicarious liability provisions, the common law cannot be relied upon to supplement those provisions and effectively increase the scope of the employer's vicarious liability (*Jones v Tower Boot Co Ltd* [1997] IRLR 168, [1997] 2 All ER 406). This principle finds illustration in the case of *Mahood v Irish Centre Housing* (2011) (UKEAT/0228/10/ZT). In *Mahood*, the Employment Appeal held that an employer was not vicariously liable for the alleged harassment of an employee by a temporary agency worker under the *RRA 1976*. Even if the employer exerted a sufficient degree of control over the agency worker to render the employer tortiously liable at common law for his actions, that did not impact on the question of whether the employer was vicariously liable under statutory provisions contained in the *RRA 1976*. The relevant provisions on vicarious liability did not create liability for third parties. If, however, the tribunal found that the agency worker, as a matter of implication, could be deemed to be an employee of the employer or alternatively, if the harassment occurred in circumstances where the agency worker was exercising authority conferred on him by the employer, and therefore was acting as the employer's agent, then the employer may yet be vicariously liable for the agency worker's actions. Compare *Timis & Sage v Osipov* [2018] EWCA Civ 2321: a company which employed a worker was held to be vicariously liable where two of its directors decided to dismiss the worker in response to the worker making protected disclosures; the directors were directly liable for the dismissal in their position as co-workers, pursuant to *section 47B(1A)* of the *Employment Rights Act 1996*; the company was vicariously liable for the directors' unlawful act pursuant to the express vicarious liability provision embodied in *ERA 1996, s 47B(1B)*.

Mahood and *Osipov* were both cases where the legislation contained express vicarious liability provisions. However, the common law tests of vicarious liability may yet be relevant even where the statute that renders the employee's conduct wrongful does not itself make any express provision as to vicarious liability: *Majrowski v Guys and St Thomas' NHS Hospital Trust* [2006] UKHL 34, [2006] 3 WLR 125, [2006] ICR 1199, [2006] IRLR 695, [2006] 4 All ER 395. In *Majrowski*, the House of Lords held that an employer may be vicariously liable at common law for an act of harassment committed by its employee where that act was itself unlawful pursuant to *s 3* of the *Protection from Harassment Act 1997* (a provision that on its face only applies to individuals). Importantly, the House of Lords did not posit any general rule to the effect that in principle there could always be common law vicarious liability for a statutory wrong committed by an employee, provided that the statutory wrong was effected in the course of the employee's employment. Instead, the ratio of the judgment makes clear that the question of whether an employer can in principle be held vicariously liable for the statutory wrongs of their employees committed in the course of their employment turns on whether the statute in question either expressly or impliedly excludes such liability. This has the result that an employer will not be vicariously liable for the statutory wrongs of its employee where either (a) the legislation expressly or impliedly excludes the imposition of such liability or (b) the legislation does not per se exclude the imposition of common law vicarious liability but there is no vicarious liability on the facts because the relevant wrong was not committed in the course of the employee's employment.

The latter principles were considered in *Various Claimants v Morrisons*, discussed further *supra*, where the Supreme Court held that the *Data Protection Act 1998* did not expressly or impliedly exclude the application of common law vicarious liability in circumstances where an employee, acting in his own capacity as data controller, unlawfully misused extensive third party personal data. The Supreme Court held that the *1998 Act* simply did not speak to the question of whether the employer could be held vicariously liable for the acts of a third party data controller and so there was no question of the Act impliedly seeking to exclude the application of the vicarious liability doctrine.

The judgments in *Majrowski* and *Morrisons* should be compared with the judgment of the Court of Appeal in *NHS Manchester v Fecitt & Ors* [2011] EWCA Civ 1190, [2012] IRLR 64. In *Fecitt*, an employee had been subject to victimising behaviour on the part of her colleagues in response to the fact she had made a protected disclosure. The Court of Appeal held that the employer was not vicariously liable for the acts of victimisation. This was because the *Employment Rights Act 1996*, which affords protection to employees who have made protected disclosures, does not prohibit victimisation of a whistle-blower by co-workers. In the circumstances, the co-workers victimisation of the employee, whilst being morally repugnant, was not unlawful per se. It followed that there was no unlawful act in respect of which the employer could be held vicariously liable (*Cumbria CC v Carlisle-Morgan* [2007] IRLR 314 overruled). It should be noted that the *Employment Rights Act 1996* was in fact amended following *Fecitt* so as to enable co-workers who engaged in victimising behaviour towards whistleblowers to be subject to primary liability under the *Act* – see further *sections 47B(1A)* and *47B(1B)* of the *Act* and the case of *Osipov*, discussed supra. Perhaps unsurprisingly, the *Equality Act 2010* adopts a similarly expansive approach to vicarious liability. *Section 109* of that *Act* renders the employer vicariously liable in circumstances where the employer's employee or agent engages in acts of discrimination or victimisation in the course of their employment, subject to the defence provided for in *s 109(4)*, namely that the employer has taken all reasonable steps to avoid the unlawful conduct. *Section 110* of that *Act* operates to render employees and agents of the employer personally liable for any act of discrimination or victimisation undertaken in the course of their employment. Importantly, these provisions make clear that there will be no liability either for the employer or for the employee where the unlawful discrimination or victimisation occurs outside the course of the employee's employment.

57.4 'PRO HAC VICE' EMPLOYMENT

Sometimes an employer (the general employer) may lend or hire his employee to another employer (the special employer) for a particular task or transaction. Although the employee continues to be employed by the general employer under his contract of employment, he may in certain circumstances be treated as the employee of the special and not of the general employer for the purposes of establishing vicarious liability. One term for this situation is *pro hac vice* ('for this occasion') employment.

Whether the potential liability has in fact been transferred from the general to the special employer must depend upon the arrangements that exist between them, and in particular upon which of them has the right to control the way in which the work is done. It will not be easy to show such a transfer (see, eg *Mersey Docks and Harbour Board v Coggins and Griffith (Liverpool) Ltd* [1947] AC 1, [1946] 2 All ER 345), but it was established in the case of *Sime v Sutcliffe Catering Scotland Ltd* [1990] IRLR 228 where the special employer had complete control over day-to-day management and the way the work was carried out. The question of whether potential liability has transferred from the general employer to the special employer was considered by the Court of Appeal in *Hawley v Luminar Leisure Ltd* [2006] EWCA Civ 18, [2006] IRLR 817. In that case, a company which owned a nightclub ('L') contracted with a third party supplier of personnel ('S') for the supply of a doorman. The doorman went on to assault a member of the public whilst working at the nightclub. The Court of Appeal found that the doorman should be deemed to be a temporary employee of L for the purposes of determining vicarious liability. The Court of Appeal went on to find that vicarious liability should be attributed to L rather than S even though S employed the

58 Working Time

58.1 THE WORKING TIME DIRECTIVE

Until shortly before the turn of the century, working hours were not regulated by statute for the vast majority of workers in the UK. Special provisions have applied to specific groups in the past but most were swept away in the 1980s and 1990s. For example, restrictions on the employment of retail workers contained in the *Shops Act 1950* were repealed by the *Deregulation and Contracting Out Act 1994*, although some protection against enforced Sunday working has remained (now contained in *ss 36–43 Employment Rights Act 1996*).

This situation changed in 1998 as a result of European legislation, but only after a protracted battle. In November 1993 *EC Directive 93/104* 'concerning certain aspects of the organisation of working time' ('the *Working Time Directive*') was adopted; it came into force in Member States on 23 November 1996. The legal basis for the *Directive* was as a health and safety measure under *art 118A* of the *Treaty of Rome* (the current equivalent is *art 154* of the *Treaty on the Functioning of the European Union*), which requires only qualified majority voting. Hence it could be, and was, adopted without the assent of the UK Government. However, the Conservative Government of the day refused to accept the legitimacy of the *Directive* on the grounds that it could not be categorised as health and safety legislation. No attempt was made by the UK to comply with the 1996 deadline for implementation, pending the outcome of a challenge to the *Directive* in the ECJ.

In the event the Court ruled, in *United Kingdom v EU Council*: C-84/94 [1997] ICR 443, [1997] IRLR 30, that (with one minor exception) the UK's objections should be rejected. Following a change of government, implementation of the *Directive* eventually took place on 1 October 1998, by means of the *Working Time Regulations 1998 (SI 1998/1833)*. The *1998 Regulations* have been supplemented by guidance published by the Department of Trade and Industry (now the Department for Business, Energy and Industrial Strategy (BEIS)), in accordance with a duty imposed on the Secretary of State by *reg 35A* (a provision added in 1999). It should, however, be noted that this guidance has no formal legal status as an interpretation of the *Regulations*. For further details see **58.26**.

The *Directive*, which covers working hours, rest breaks and holidays, initially did not apply to a number of sectors of activity. The exceptions were: air, rail, road, sea, inland waterway and lake transport, sea fishing, other work at sea and the activities of doctors in training. (For the scope of these exceptions see further **58.3** below.)

However, agreement was reached in 2000 on the extension of the *Directive* to excluded sectors and activities. The *Working Time Directive* was amended by *Directive 2000/34* to cover all non-mobile workers in the excluded sectors, doctors in training, and offshore and railway workers (including mobile railway workers). The *Directive* was implemented domestically by amendments to the *Working Time Regulations* with effect from 1 August 2003, with implementation for doctors in training phased over several years but finally completed from 1 August 2011. The *Directive*, as amended by the *2000 Directive*, was in turn replaced by *Directive 2003/88/EC*, a purely consolidating measure, which came into force on 2 August 2004. References in this chapter to the *Directive* apply equally to the 2003 version.

In addition to this general extension of the original *Directive*, further *Directives* have been adopted for those specific categories of workers still not covered by the principal provisions. The working time of seafarers engaged on merchant ships was covered in *Directive 99/63*, which was given effect in the UK by the *Merchant Shipping (Hours of Work) Regulations* safety'. The Court added that 'Member States are under an obligation to guarantee that each of the minimum requirements laid down by the directive is observed'. The DTI amended the passage in the Guidance criticised by the Court, by deleting the second half of the quoted passage.

58.3   Coverage

Workers covered by the *1998 Regulations* include employees working under a contract of employment and other individuals who work under a contract personally to perform work or provide services for the 'employer' (except for people genuinely in business on their own account who are in a client or customer relationship with the 'employer') (*reg 2(1)*). *Regulation 36* provides that an agency worker who would not otherwise fall within the definition of a worker under these provisions will be treated as being employed by whichever of the agent or principal is responsible for paying him or her or, if that is not ascertainable, by whichever in fact pays the worker (see further for the position of agency workers generally 58.37 below). The extended definition of 'worker' has been held to include self–employed building subcontractors who in practice worked exclusively for one employer: *Byrne Bros (Formwork) Ltd v Baird* [2002] IRLR 96. (See further on this *Wright v Redrow Homes (Yorkshire) Ltd* [2004] EWCA Civ 469, [2004] IRLR 720, [2004] 3 All ER 98, *Uber N V v Aslam* [2018] EWCA Civ 2748, [2019] IRLR 257, and *Pimlico Plumbers Ltd v Smith* [2018] UKSC 29, [2018] IRLR 872, [2018] ICR 1511. For a fuller discussion of these and the authorities on this much–litigated issue, see EMPLOYEE, SELF–EMPLOYED OR WORKER? 16.9.)

In *Sindicatul Familia ConstanÈ›a and others v DirecÈ›ia Generală de AsistenÈ›ă Socială È™i ProtecÈ›ia Copilului ConstanÈ›a* C-147-17; [2019] IRLR 167, [2019] ICR 211, the CJEU determined that foster parents were "workers" but fell outside of the scope of the *Directive* because they fell within *Art 2(2)* of the *Framework Health and Safety Directive 89/391/EC* which excludes certain specific service activities (such as the armed forces, police and civil protection services) whose peculiar characteristics inevitably conflict with the Directive. The CJEU considered that the armed forces, police and civil protection services were simply examples of a more general principle and that the expression "public service" applied to sectors in which workers carried out their work for a private person who performed, under the control of the public authorities, a task in the public interest which formed part of the essential functions of the state. The work of a foster parent was not compatible with the rights conferred by the *Working Time Directive*. Leave was, for instance, an opportunity to develop family life. It would make no sense to allow foster parents time off from their foster family.

Notwithstanding the exclusions arising from the *Art 2(2)* of the *Framework Health and Safety Directive*, *Regulations* also apply, by express provision, to those in Crown service and the armed forces, and to police officers (who would otherwise fall outside the definition of 'workers'): *regs 37–41*. Certain non–employed trainees are also covered by the *Regulations* (*reg 42*). The breadth of the application of the *Regulations* reflects the point that the ECJ has repeatedly held that the term 'worker' 'has an autonomous meaning specific to European Union Law' applicable to the scope of the *Working Time Directive*, which 'may not be interpreted differently according to the law of member States': see most recently *Union syndicale Solidaires Isère v Premier Ministre*: C-428/09 [2011] 1 CMLR 1206, [2011] IRLR 84, para 28 and *Fenoll v Centre d'Aide par le Travail "la Jouvenne"*: C-316/13 [2016] IRLR 67, para 29, where the Court stated that 'The essential feature of an employment relationship is that for a certain period of time a person performs services for and under the direction of another person in return for which he receives remuneration'. The court in these cases held in turn that casual or seasonal workers working no more than 80 days a year, and disabled individuals attending rehabilitation centres performing work for modest pay as part of a rehabilitation programme, could potentially fall within the terms of this definition.

The *Regulations* also apply, with separate provisions in relation to several important points, to young workers. Those requirements of the *Young Workers' Directive* which were not implemented by the *1998 Regulations* were implemented by amendments to the *1998 Regulations* introduced by the *Working Time (Amendment) Regulations 2002*. The principal changes are the imposition of a maximum working day of 8 hours, and a maximum working week of 40 hours (neither of which is subject to averaging over a longer period) for workers below the age of 18 (but above compulsory school age: see below). See further **58.6**.

In addition, the *2002 Regulations* restrict the employment of a young worker during the 'restricted period', which is normally 10 pm to 6 am, but 11 pm to 7 am if the worker is contractually required to work later than 10 pm: for details of these restrictions see **58.10** below.

There are separate provisions in the *Children and Young Persons Act 1933, s 18(1)*, as amended in compliance with *Directive 94/33*, which regulate the working hours and holiday entitlements of children below the maximum compulsory school age. (For Scotland, the equivalent provisions are in the *Children and Young Persons (Scotland) Act 1937*.) The EAT has held, by reference to these provisions, that such children are not 'workers' for the purposes of the *1998 Regulations*, and accordingly not covered by them: *Ashby v Addison (t/a Brayton News)* [2003] ICR 667, [2003] IRLR 211, a case involving a claim for holiday pay by a 15 year old paper boy.

Following amendments made by the *Working Time (Amendment) Regulations 2003*, the *1998 Regulations* now apply to all workers (with the exclusion of school age children) other than those mobile workers in certain transport sectors, who are now all covered by separate legislation. Doctors in training were brought fully within the scope of the *Regulations* with effect from August 2009, subject to limited and specific exemptions from the 48 hour working week the last of which expired on 31 July 2011.

The *Regulations* do not apply to 'certain activities of the armed forces, police or other civil protection services', but only to the extent that certain characteristics of the particular service concerned 'inevitably conflict' with the *Regulations: reg 18*. This exception mirrors a provision in *art 1(3)* of the *Directive*, which was narrowly construed by the ECJ in *Pfeiffer v Deutsches Rotes Kreuz, Kreisverband Waldshut eV*: C-397/01 to C-403/01 [2005] IRLR 137 as applying to the emergency services only in the context of the provision of services essential for the protection of public health, safety or order in situations of exceptional gravity, and thus not excluding from the *Directive* the routine operation of a public ambulance service. The same conclusion was reached in relation to a public fire service in *Personalrat der Feuerwehr Hamburg v Leiter der Feuerwehr Hamburg*: C-52/04, unreported, with the proviso that the 48 hour limit on weekly working time could be exceeded 'in exceptional circumstances of such gravity and scale that the aim of ensuring the proper functioning of services essential for the protection of public interests, such as public order, health and safety, must temporarily prevail over the aim of guaranteeing the health and safety of workers assigned to intervention and rescue teams'. This interpretation is very likely to be followed in the construction of the exception in the *1998 Regulations*.

With regard to the former exclusion of transport workers, the position initially was that all workers, whether mobile or non-mobile, within undertakings in the excluded sectors, were excluded from the *Directive*: *Bowden v Tuffnells Parcels Express Ltd*: C-133/00 [2001] IRLR 838, [2001] All ER (EC) 865. This is still relevant to the exclusion of mobile workers in the civil aviation and road transport sectors referred to at (i) and (iii) below, but non-mobile workers in these sectors were brought within the scope of the *Regulations* by the amendments made in 2003. The Court in *Pfeiffer*, above, held that emergency ambulance services were outside the road transport sector. It was accepted that bus drivers engaged in the provision of scheduled services fall within the provisions of the *1998 Regulations*, rather than the *Road Transport (Working Time) Regulations 2005*, in *Feist v First Hampshire & Dorset Ltd* [2007] All ER (D) 180 (Feb), EAT.

(e) before the agreement was signed, the employer provided all workers to whom the agreement applies with copies and such guidance as is reasonable to understand it fully.

Requirements concerning the election of representatives are set out at *Sch 1 para 3*.

A *relevant agreement* includes both collective and workforce agreements and, in addition, any other agreement in writing which is legally enforceable as between worker and employer. This definition may therefore include the written terms of a contract of employment.

Where a provision of the *Regulations* is modified or excluded by a workforce or collective agreement and a worker is thereby required to work during what would be a rest period or break, the employer must allow, where possible, an equivalent period of compensatory rest. In exceptional cases where it is not possible for objective reasons to grant compensatory rest, the employer must provide appropriate protection to safeguard the worker's health and safety (*reg 24*). The scope of the concept of compensatory rest is considered more fully at **58.29** below.

58.5 WORKING TIME

In relation to a worker, 'working time' is defined in *reg 2(1)* as:

(a) any period during which the individual is working, at the employer's disposal and carrying out his or her activity or duties;

(b) any period during which he or she is receiving 'relevant training'; and

(c) any additional period which is to be treated as working time for the purpose of the *Regulations* under a relevant agreement.

'Relevant training' means work experience or training provided on a training course or programme of training for employment, other than courses run by educational institutions or organisations whose main business is the provision of training (see further as to the position under the *Directive* of training provided by third parties *European Commission v Ireland*: C-87/14 [2016] IRLR 77).

According to the BEIS Guidance (now provided on the www.gov.uk website: https ://www.gov.uk/maximum-weekly-working-hours), the definition of working time includes: working lunches, business travel time, and 'in some [unspecified] cases' time spent working abroad. It does not include: home-to-work travel, rest breaks when no work is done, time spent travelling outside normal working time or non-job-related training.

The position in relation to travelling time has been clarified by a decision of the ECJ, *Federacion de Servicios Privados del Sindicato Comisiones Obreras v Tyco Integrated Security SL*: C-266/14 [2015] IRLR 935 ('*Tyco*'). The case concerned security equipment engineers who had formerly worked from a depot at which they collected instructions and a company vehicle, which they used to visit customers' premises, returning to the depot at the end of the working day. The employer closed the depots and the employees thereafter worked from home, receiving daily schedules by mobile phone and travelling from home to the first customer of the day, and returning from the last, in company provided transport. On these facts the ECJ held that the time spent travelling to the first customer, and home from the last, met all three elements of the definition of working time. It is not yet clear whether there are any particular features of this work pattern the absence of which would affect the position, but it is likely to be the case that time spent travelling between the worker's home and customers' premises, as well as between customers, where the worker performs work at the premises of different customers during the working day or from day to day, will always be working time for the purposes of the *reg 2(1)(a)* of the *Regulations*, which reproduce verbatim the wording in the *Directive*. The position for travel between customers' premises is a fortiori: see *Kennedy v Cordia (Services) LLP* [2016] UKSC 6, [2016] 1 WLR 597, [2016] ICR 325, [2016] All ER (D) 99 (Feb) (a health and safety case).

The EAT has held that time spent by workers who are also trade union representatives or health and safety representatives, attending meetings at the request of the employer but outside their normal working hours, is working time for the purposes of the *Regulations*: *Edwards v Encirc Ltd* [2015] IRLR 528. The principal practical consequence of this in the particular case was that the claimants were entitled to the minimum daily rest period of 11 hours between the conclusion of the meeting and the start of the following working day.

There is no corresponding definition of 'rest', and a rest period is defined in such a way as to exclude any period of working time from being treated as a rest period, but not otherwise more specifically. In effect the two concepts are mutually exclusive, and any time that is not working time or annual leave can be attributed as part of an entitlement to a rest period, including (subject to the *Tyco* case) time spent on such activities as travel between the workplace and the worker's home. See further **58.14–58.17**, below.

One important issue as to the ambit of the definition of working time is the status of time 'on call'. This has been the subject of four decisions of the ECJ, to the effect that 'on-call' time constitutes working time where the worker is required to be at, or in close proximity to, his or her place of work during this period. If the worker is away from the workplace when on call and can pursue leisure activities, on-call time is not working time (*Sindicato de Médicos de Asistencia Pública (Simap) v Conselleria de Sanidad y Consumo de la Generalidad Valenciana*: C-303/98 [2000] IRLR 845, [2001] All ER (EC) 609). The Court has subsequently confirmed that time spent on call and at the workplace, but not actually performing the worker's duties, was to be regarded as working time in circumstances where the worker (a hospital doctor) was permitted to rest when his services were not required, and rest facilities were provided for this purpose by the employer: *Landeshauptstadt Kiel v Jaeger*, above: C-151/02 [2003] IRLR 804, [2004] All ER (EC) 604. In *Ville de Nivelles v Matzak*: C-518/15 [2018] IRLR 457, the ECJ held that time spent by retained firefighters on standby, who were required to be at their homes, which were required to be within eight minutes' travelling distance from the fire station, was working time.

A similar conclusion had earlier been reiterated in *Vorel v Nemocnice Český Krumlov*: C-437/05 [2007] ECR-I 331, but with the important additional qualification that this did not prevent national law from providing for a lower rate of pay for the inactive parts of periods on-call (as the Czech law under reference did).

However, in *Dellas v Premier Ministre*: C-14/04 [2006] IRLR 225 the ECJ held to be incompatible with the *Directive* a French law which provided for time spent on call and at the employer's premises, but not actually working, to count at the rate of only a half or a third of actual time; the principal objection of the Court was that it was (at least theoretically) possible for workers subject to this law to work in excess of the 48 hour week, although France has adopted a lower maximum of 44 hours. Thus whilst the rate of pay for time on call may be lower (subject, in the UK context, to the application of the National Minimum Wage, the rules in relation to which differ from the definition of working time), in most situations, time on call itself must be taken into account fully.

These decisions of the ECJ have been controversial for their implications for the staffing of hospital medical services in particular, and would have been affected by the implementation of the Commission's proposals for revision of the *Directive*, referred to at **58.1** above. The failure of negotiations between the Social Partners on amendments to the *Directive* however precludes any immediate change in the position.

The EAT has held that the effect of the decision in *Jaeger* is that a warden employed at a sheltered housing complex on 24 hour call is to be regarded as working throughout the period on call although she was provided with a flat to occupy at the premises, and was free employers to limit the aggregate working hours of those workers who work for more than one employer, and no mechanism for enabling employers to police such arrangements. The statement to the contrary in the Guidance issued by BEIS on www.gov.uk is simply wrong. The sole exceptions to this are the provisions relating to young workers: see *reg 5A(2)*, which specifically limits the total working time which may be undertaken for *all* employers; and *reg 12(5)*, which requires the aggregation of working time for different employers in calculating young workers' rest break entitlements. Whilst the absence of any equivalent provisions for adult workers is a significant weakness in the protection of workers from excessive hours, it is not considered to be contrary to the *Working Time Directive*. One of the amendments to the *Directive* proposed by the Parliament would have applied the 48 hour maximum to the aggregate time worked for all employers, but this proposal fell with the breakdown of negotiations over the proposed amended *Directive* in April 2009, and is unlikely to feature in any future amendment to the *Directive*.

58.7   Opt-out agreements

It is permissible to disapply the 48-hour weekly maximum if the employer obtains the worker's written agreement to exceed these hours (*reg 4(1)* implementing a facility provided by *art 6* of the *Directive*). Any such opt-out agreement may relate to a specified period or apply indefinitely. Agreements are to be terminable by the worker giving not less than seven days' notice in writing. The employer may not require more than three months' notice (*reg 5(2), (3)*). Employers are required to maintain up-to-date records of all workers who have signed an opt-out agreement (*reg 4(2)*). Opt-outs must be made voluntarily. It is unlawful to victimise or dismiss a worker for refusing to sign an opt-out.

In addition to recording the names of workers who have opted out, employers are required to keep records for two years to show that they have complied with the provisions on maximum weekly working time (*reg 9*). However, following amendment of the *1998 Regulations* in 1999 it is no longer necessary to maintain records of hours actually worked by a worker who has opted out.

The consent of each individual worker to an opt-out agreement is required. Consent given by trade union representatives in the context of a collective agreement is not equivalent to that given by the worker (*SIMAP* [2000] IRLR 845, [2001] All ER (EC) 609 and *M'Bye v Stiftelsen Fossumkollektivet*: E-5/15 [2016] IRLR 227, EFTA Court). There is no specific provision in either the *1998 Regulations* or the *Directive* restricting the way in which consent may be recorded, provided it is in writing, and in practice it is not uncommon for employers to incorporate a requirement for consent in the offer of employment, so that agreement to opt out is tied in to the acceptance of the job offered. The validity of such agreements may be open to challenge on the basis that, giving effect to the approach of the ECJ to construe exemptions from the *Directive* narrowly, such an arrangement does not ensure that genuine consent is freely given. However, there is no reported authority on this point.

The facility to opt out is only available to adult workers, and there is no equivalent in the regulations governing specific sectors of employment. Nor is there any right to opt out of the limits on night work, considered at 58.9 below.

58.8   Enforcement

The right not to have to work more than a 48 hour week is not one of the rights in respect of which the *Regulations* confer a right for individual workers to complain to an employment tribunal; the *Regulations* instead provide for enforcement by the authorities responsible for enforcing health and safety legislation for whichever sector of employment is involved. However the High Court has held that *reg 4(1)* creates contractual rights not to have to work in excess of the limits on working time: *Barber v RJB Mining (UK) Ltd* [1999] IRLR 308; and the corresponding provision in the *Working Time Directive, art 6(2)*, has been held by the CJEU to be directly enforceable against employers which are state authorities (*Pfeiffer v Deutsches Rotes Kreuz, Kreisverband Waldshut eV*: C-397/01 to 401/01 [2005] IRLR 137). The CJEU has subsequently held that Member States must provide a means for individual workers to obtain reparation for breaches of the right conferred by *art 6(2)*: *Fuß v Stadt Halle (No 2)*: C-429/09 [2011] IRLR 176. Whether this entails that such claims may be considered by employment tribunals despite the absence of any provision in the *Working Time Regulations* conferring jurisdiction is a matter which will require to be determined by further case law; the point is discussed more fully (together with the rights, which are enforceable by way of individual complaint to a tribunal, not to be dismissed or suffer detriment for insisting on the right not to work more than 48 hours a week) at **58.20–58.22** below. Steps reasonably taken by an employer to ensure that a worker who has not opted out does not exceed the 48 hour working week will not normally constitute detriments to that worker: *Arriva London South Ltd v Nicolaou (No 2)* [2012] ICR 510, discussed at **58.23** below.

58.9   NIGHT WORK

In the *1998 Regulations* 'night time' means a period of not less than seven hours which includes the period between midnight and 5 am (*reg 2(1)*). The precise period may be determined by a relevant agreement (see **58.4** above). Where it has not been so agreed, the period will be 11 pm to 6 am. A 'night worker' is an individual who, as a normal course, works at least three hours of daily working time during night time or who is likely during night time to work at least such proportion of annual working time as may be specified for these purposes in a collective or workforce agreement. The definition provides that someone works hours 'as a normal course' if he or she works those hours on the majority of his or her working days, but this does not mean that other patterns of work do not qualify as being 'in the normal course'. In *R v A-G for Northern Ireland, ex p Burns* [1999] IRLR 315, the Northern Ireland High Court held that 'as a normal course' means simply that night work should be a regular feature of employment. Therefore, a worker who spent one week in three of a rotating shift working at least three hours during the night was a night worker for the purposes of the *Directive*.

58.10   Length of night work

Employers are required to take all reasonable steps, in keeping with the need to protect workers' health and safety, to ensure that night workers' normal hours of work do not exceed an average of eight in each 24 hours during a 17-week reference period (*reg 6(1), (2)*). This will be a rolling 17-week period unless a relevant agreement specifies successive periods (*reg 6(3)*). For individuals who have worked for less than 17 weeks, the average is calculated over the period since they started work for the employer (*reg 6(4)*).

Regulation 6(5) provides that average normal hours of work for a night worker are calculated according to the formula:

$$\frac{A}{B-C}$$

where:

'A' is the number of normal working hours during the reference period;

'B' is the number of days during the reference period; and

'C' is the total number of hours during the reference period spent by the worker in statutory weekly rest periods (see **58.17** below) divided by 24. The effect of the formula is to create a maximum of 48 hours a week (8 hours in each of the 6 days a week, excluding one weekly rest day).

periods onshore, notwithstanding that these were periods during which they would not otherwise be required to work, and provided that there was also sufficient time during onshore 'field breaks' for rest periods and any compensatory rest.

58.15 Daily rest periods

Adult workers are entitled to a rest period of at least 11 consecutive hours in each 24-hour working period (*reg 10(1)*). See *R (on the application of the Fire Brigades Union) v South Yorkshire Fire and Rescue Authority* [2018] IRLR 717, EWHC where a shift pattern that involved continuous duty over a working week of 96 hours was declared to be a breach of *Reg 10*. It is not necessary for the 11 hours to fall within the same calendar day provided they are consecutive.

The 11-hour rule does not apply to shift workers when they change shifts and cannot take a daily rest period between the end of one shift and the start of the next (*reg 22(1)(a)*). Similarly, it does not apply to workers whose activities involve periods of work split up over the day, such as cleaning or catering staff working split shifts (*reg 22(1)(c)*). 'Shift work' means 'any method of organising work in shifts whereby workers succeed each other at the same workstations according to a certain pattern, including a rotating pattern, and which may be continuous or discontinuous, entailing the need for workers to work at different times over a given period of days or weeks'.

Compensatory rest must normally be offered to shift workers who have to work during what would otherwise be a rest period. If this is not possible, 'appropriate protection' is required to safeguard health and safety (*reg 24*). The ECJ has held (*Landeshauptstadt Kiel v Jaeger*: C-151/02 [2003] IRLR 804, [2004] All ER (EC) 604; *Union syndicale Solidaires Isère v Premier Ministre*: C-428/09 [2011] 1 CMLR 1206, [2011] IRLR 84) that compensatory rest must be provided immediately following the period of work without a rest period or rest break for which it compensates. See further the discussion of compensatory rest in relation to rest breaks at 58.17 below.

There is a separate provision in *reg 24A* for those mobile workers not excluded from the right to rest periods generally (see as to this 58.33–58.36 below), excluding the right to rest periods provided that 'adequate rest' is afforded, the requirements of which are defined in *reg 24A(3)*. The right to adequate rest in such cases is in substitution for, not cumulative with, the right to compensatory rest under *Reg 24*: *Feist v First Hampshire & Dorset Ltd* [2007] All ER (D) 180 (Feb), EAT.

Adult workers whose time is 'unmeasured' (see 58.28 below) and those who are considered 'special case' exceptions under *reg 21* (subject to certain conditions, see 58.29 below) are not covered by the entitlement to daily rest. The entitlement may also be modified or excluded by collective or workforce agreement under *reg 23*. The second and third of these exceptions are subject to the provision of compensatory rest, or 'appropriate protection' in default.

Subject to these exceptions, where a daily rest period is interrupted, for instance by an out-of-hours call-out, or a requirement to attend a health and safety meeting with the employer (as in *Edwards v Encirc Ltd* [2015] IRLR 528, EAT; see 58.5 above) there is an entitlement to a full 11 hour rest period before the individual resumes work.

For young workers (ie those over compulsory school age but under 18) the requirement is to provide not less than 12 consecutive hours' rest in any 24-hour period (*reg 10(2)*). Where activities involve periods of work that are split up over the day or are of short duration, the 12-hour rest period may be interrupted (*reg 10(3)*). In addition a *force majeure* clause applies, which gives the employer leeway to require a young worker to work during the 12-hour minimum where work has to be done which no adult worker is available to do and the requirement:

(a)   is due to unusual and unforeseeable circumstances beyond the employer's control or exceptional events which could not have been avoided despite all due care by the employer;

(b)   is of a temporary nature; and

(c)   must be carried out straight away.

An equivalent period of compensatory rest must be allowed within the following three weeks (*reg 27*). This concession is designed to cope with exceptional circumstances which cannot be handled in any other way.

Entitlement to rest periods entails at the least that the employer must *allow* employees who wish to do so to take their rest period. The extent to which it also entails an obligation on the employer to *ensure* that rest periods are *taken* is more contentious. The DTI (as BEIS then was) view, as expressed in the original Guidance on the *Regulations*, was that it does not. This view was, however, successfully challenged by the Commission in proceedings before the European Court (*European Commission v United Kingdom*: C-484/04 [2006] IRLR 888). (For further details see **58.2** above.)

Despite this, the EAT initially held that there is no breach of *reg 10* until the worker requests that he or she be allowed rest periods and the employer refuses: *Miles v Linkage Community Trust Ltd* [2008] IRLR 602 and *Carter v Prestige Nursing Ltd* (UKEAT/0014/12) (11 May 2012, unreported). However this gives little weight to the obligation to afford rest periods and rest breaks set out in the *Working Time Directive*. A different approach appeared to be taken in *Scottish Ambulance Service v Truslove* UKEATS/0028/11 (12 January 2012, unreported), a case on time limits. The authorities were thoroughly reviewed by the EAT in *Grange v Abellio London Ltd* [2017] IRLR 108, [2017] ICR 287, a case on the identically worded provisions of *reg 12* on rest breaks. The EAT declined to follow *Miles* and *Carter*, and held that *reg 12* must be read as imposing an obligation on employers to ensure proactively that workers are in fact able to take the required rest breaks, although a worker could not be forced to take a break. 'Refusal to permit' the taking of a rest break, the statutory condition for a remedy for an infringement of the right to take rest breaks, must be read as covering denial of the right by the practical effect of the way that the worker's work is organised, without the need for a positive request. This position applies equally to rest breaks under *reg 12* and to rest periods under *regs 10* and *11* (as to which see below). *Miles* and *Carter* should not now be regarded as correctly stating the law.

58.16 Weekly rest periods

Adult workers are normally entitled (as to the meaning of this see the final paragraph of **58.15**) to an uninterrupted rest period of at least 24 hours in each seven-day period of working. The UK took advantage of a provision in the *Directive* which allows the weekly rest period to be averaged over a 14 day period, so that the rest periods may be arranged as two uninterrupted rest periods of not less than 24 hours in each 14-day period, or one uninterrupted period of not less than 48 hours in each 14-day period (*reg 11(1), (2)*). The minimum weekly rest period must not run concurrently with any part of a daily rest period (see **58.15** above) except where this is justified by objective or technical reasons, or reasons 'concerning the organisation of work' (*reg 11(7)*). Thus the combined effect of the daily and weekly rest entitlements is to create a minimum entitlement of 35 consecutive hours each week, or 59 hours in each 14-day period. See **58.15** for the correct approach to when the right to weekly rest periods is infringed.

For young workers the minimum weekly rest period is 48 hours. This may be interrupted where activities involve periods of work that are split up over the day or are of short duration, and may be reduced where this is justified by technical or organisational reasons. However the period may not be reduced to less than 36 consecutive hours (*reg 11(3), (8)*).

EAT's decision. An equivalent period of compensatory rest had to have the characteristics of rest, in the sense of being a break from work, and as far as possible must ensure that the period free from work was at least the 20 minutes required for a rest break; however on the facts these requirements had been met.

In *Network Rail Infrastructure Ltd v Crawford* [2019] EWCA Civ 269, [2019] ICR 1206, [2019] IRLR 538 the claimant was a relief railway signalman. The nature of his duties meant that he had opportunities to take short breaks during each shift amounting in total to more than 20 minutes per shift, but with no single 20 minute period free from duties. The Court of Appeal found that the aggregate periods of inactivity and rest met the requirement of being equivalent compensatory rest.

The issue of compensatory rest did not fall directly for decision in *Martin*, above, but it is implicit in the decision in that case that a right to claim time off in lieu (it appears without loss of pay) for any break which in the event was interrupted did satisfy the requirements for compensatory rest. The judgment does not indicate when time off in lieu was in practice taken. As noted above, the ECJ has twice held that compensatory rest must be afforded immediately following the period of work without the required rest break for which it is compensation; however as the point did not arise directly in the light of its decision on what constitutes a rest break, the Court in *Martin* did not have to consider whether the requirements of timing of the compensatory rest were met by these arrangements.

If in exceptional cases it is not possible 'for objective reasons' to afford compensatory rest, 'appropriate protection' must if possible be offered instead (*reg 24(b)*; the phrase is taken directly from the wording of the *Directive*). This provision was considered, obiter, in *Hughes (No 2)*; the EAT suggested that it could include a range of measures other than the provision of rest such as the way that work is organised or health checks for affected workers. The ECJ subsequently expressed the view in *Union syndicale*, above, that 'only in absolutely exceptional circumstances' could resort be had to 'appropriate protection', and that limiting the number of days in a year that seasonal workers could work to a maximum of 80 was not a permissible means of affording 'appropriate protection' for the denial of daily rest periods. This judgment was not cited to the Court of Appeal when the appeal in *Hughes (No 2)* reached the Court, which rejected the argument that there must be 'exceptional circumstances' in addition to objective reasons for not providing compensatory rest: it would be exceptional that there were objective reasons, and that was sufficient. Whether the Court would have reached this conclusion if it had been aware of the decision in *Union syndicale* is unclear. The Court of Appeal did not consider in any detail the range of what could constitute protection under *reg 24(b)*, as it was satisfied that the arrangements for a deferred break were sufficient; but it did reject, as had the EAT, a submission that the employer would have to conduct a risk assessment to assess the sufficiency of the protection afforded.

An example of a situation where objective reasons might make it impossible to afford compensatory rest, given in an Advisory Opinion by the EFTA Court in *M'Bye v Stiftelsen Fossumkollektivet*: E-5/15 [2016] IRLR 227, is where therapists were providing treatment for young people with drug or alcohol problems which entailed the therapists living together with their patients, to the extent that continuity of service by the same therapists was regarded as beneficial for the patients.

In the case of young workers, there is an entitlement to a break of at least 30 minutes, consecutive if possible, if the individual's daily working time exceeds four and a half hours. The worker is entitled to take the break away from the workstation if applicable. When a young worker has more than one employment, the daily working time must be calculated by aggregating the number of hours worked for each employer (*reg 12(4), (5)*). There is an exception to the entitlements of young workers under a *force majeure* clause (*reg 27*). This specifies that *reg 12(4)* does not apply where work has to be done which no adult worker is available to do and:

(a)   the requirement is due to unusual and unforeseeable circumstances beyond the employer's control or exceptional events which could not have been avoided despite all due care by the employer;

(b)   is of a temporary nature; and

(c)   must be carried out straight away.

An equivalent period of compensatory rest must be allowed within the following three weeks.

Agricultural workers in Wales are entitled to more generous daily rest breaks under the *Agricultural Wages (Wales) Order 2018*; see **58.39** for details.

58.18 Monotonous work

Apart from the specific obligations to provide rest breaks described in **58.17**, an employer is required to ensure that workers are given adequate rest breaks where the work pattern puts workers' health and safety at risk, in particular because the work is monotonous or the work rate pre-determined (*reg 8*). This appears to be a requirement which is additional to the basic entitlement to rest breaks set out in *reg 12*. The wording of the regulation is a paraphrase of *art 13* of the *Directive*, and it has not to date been the subject of judicial interpretation. Apart from those in excluded sectors to whom the *Regulations* do not apply at all, there are no exceptions to the application of *reg 8*.

58.19 ANNUAL LEAVE

Workers within the *1998 Regulations* are entitled to a total of 5.6 weeks' statutory holiday in respect of each leave year (subject to a maximum entitlement of 28 working days (*regs 13* and *13A*). This entitlement was increased from the original three weeks to four weeks in 1999, to 4.8 weeks from 1 October 2007, and to 5.6 weeks from 1 April 2009; the latter increases were made by the *Working Time (Amendment) Regulations 2007, SI 2007/2079*, which give workers a separate right to the additional annual leave under slightly different conditions, rather than simply increasing the basic entitlement. The *Regulations* also cover statutory holiday pay, notice requirements in respect of taking annual leave, and pay in lieu on termination. Full details of the annual leave provisions in the *1998 Regulations*, including accrual of leave during sick leave and how holiday pay is to be calculated, are set out in **30 - HOLIDAYS**.

Special rules as to the timing of the holiday year apply to agricultural workers in Wales and Scotland, and those in England first employed before 1 October 2013 (*reg 43, Sch 2*). The equivalent Regulations for workers in civil aviation also have different provisions as to the computation of holiday pay: see *British Airways plc v Williams* [2012] UKSC 43, [2012] IRLR 1014, [2012] ICR 1375, [2013] 1 All ER 443.

58.20 ENFORCEMENT AND REMEDIES

Different enforcement arrangements operate according to the nature of the breach of the *1998 Regulations*. Working time limits are enforced by the Health and Safety Executive ('HSE') and local authorities, and within their areas of responsibility the Civil Aviation Authority ('CAA') and the Driver and Vehicle Standards Agency ('DVSA', the successor to the Vehicle and Operator Services Agency) and the Office of Rail and Road ('ORR', formerly the Office of Rail Regulation). The HSE enforces the limits in factories, building sites, mines, farms, fairgrounds, quarries, chemical plants, nuclear installations, schools and hospitals. Local authority officers have the same role in respect of shops and retailing,

IRLR 29 (a case where a claim for damages for personal injury failed on the facts) the High Court held that a breach of *reg 4* by the employer does not as such confer a right for the worker to sue for damages for breach of statutory duty.

58.22 Individual remedies

Under *reg 30(1)(a)* a complaint may be made to an employment tribunal that the employer has refused to permit a worker to exercise his or her rights in connection with: daily rest (*reg 10(1), (2)*); weekly rest (*reg 11(1), (2), (3)*); rest breaks (*reg 12(1), (4)*); entitlement to annual leave (*reg 13(1)*); entitlement to compensatory rest (except in relation to night work) (*regs 24, 25, 27*) or to adequate rest (*reg 24A*).

Reg 30(1)(b) makes similar provision for complaints of failure to pay any sums due as payments in respect of annual leave entitlement or accrued holiday pay on termination under *reg 16(1)* or *14(2)* respectively. The House of Lords has ruled that claims for holiday pay can in the alternative be brought as claims for unlawful deductions from wages under *Part II* of the *Employment Rights Act 1996*, which are subject to somewhat less strict time limits (*Stringer v HM Revenue and Customs* [2009] UKHL 31, [2009] IRLR 677, [2009] 4 All ER 1205, reversing the decision of the Court of Appeal (*IRC v Ainsworth* [2005] EWCA Civ 441, [2005] IRLR 465). However this is only possible for claims for unpaid holiday pay or pay in lieu; other claims can in their nature only be brought under *reg 30*.

It should be noted that (apart from complaints of failure to pay sums due), the basis for complaints is of a refusal to permit the worker to exercise a relevant right. It is not enough that the right was not in fact exercised, unless this was attributable to the employer.

Tribunals have no express jurisdiction to hear claims by individuals for breach of the 48-hour limit on weekly working time. (See **58.20** above as to possible claims under the *Directive* itself for infringement of a worker's right not to work more than 48 hours a week). Following the lead given by the High Court in *Barber v RJB Mining (UK) Ltd* [1999] IRLR 308 (see **58.21**), tribunals may accept that a term is implied into a contract of employment that the employer must not require the employee to work more than 48 hours a week in the reference period. The effect of this is, however, limited. An employee complaining of constructive dismissal could rely on being required to work excessive hours as a breach of contract, but the tribunal has no power to award compensation for excessive hours as such, unless overtime is required under the terms of the employee's contract to be paid, in which case a claim for unlawful deductions could be made (*Forbouys Ltd v Rich* [2002] All ER (D) 156 (Apr), EAT), or there is a claim under the *National Minimum Wage Act 1998*.

Claims brought under *reg 30* must normally be presented within three months of the date on which the right should have been permitted or the payment should have been made. This period is extended to six months for complaints by members of the armed forces (who are required to utilise internal redress procedures before commencing tribunal proceedings). Where a tribunal is satisfied that it was not reasonably practicable to present a claim within the time limit, it may extend the period to a date it considers reasonable. In relation to claims for refusal to permit the claimant to take rest breaks or rest periods, the time limit for making a complaint runs from the date of each refusal: *Scottish Ambulance Service v Truslove* (UKEATS/0028/11), 12 January 2012, unreported. The EAT in that case rejected an argument that where the employee had raised a grievance, time ran from the date on which the grievance was rejected, or on the date (if later, of the first refusal of a rest period, holding that each refusal was a fresh cause of action with its own time limit (and thus the claims were in time so far as relating to refusals occurring within three months prior to the claims being presented). It follows that claims presented more than three months after any particular refusal of rest will be out of time (subject to any extension of time); there is no provision in *reg 30* for time not to run during a series of refusals.

Claims under *reg 30* (and under *Part II* of the *Employment Rights Act 1996*) are subject to the Early Conciliation procedure, so that a reference to ACAS, and the issuing of an Early Conciliation Certificate is required before a claim can be presented; consequential extensions to the time limit for presenting claims in certain circumstances are provided for by *reg 30B*, or as the case may be *section 207B* of the *1996 Act*.

Following an amendment to the *Employment Tribunals Act 1996, s 4*, claims for holiday pay, and for pay in lieu of holiday not taken prior to the termination of employment, may be heard by an employment judge sitting alone: see *SI 2009/789*. This amendment is intended to facilitate tribunals dealing with claims for holiday pay speedily together with claims for unpaid wages, as the two are often brought together, and frequently not defended (usually because the employer is insolvent). Other claims made under *reg 30* of the *Working Time Regulations* require to be heard by a full tribunal of three.

Where a complaint is considered to be well-founded, the tribunal will make a declaration to that effect and may make an award of such compensation (if any) as it considers to be just and equitable in all the circumstances, having regard to the employer's default and any loss sustained by the worker. It should be emphasised that the award of compensation is discretionary, and a nil award is permissible; such an award was upheld by the EAT in *Miles v Linkage Community Trust Ltd* [2008] IRLR 602, and the fact that the reasoning in this case as to what constitutes a refusal by an employer to afford a rest period or rest break has since been disapproved (see *Grange v Abellio London Ltd* [2017] IRLR 108, [2017] ICR 287, and **58.15** above) the possibility of no compensation being awarded remains open. However, insofar as the reasoning in that case is based on the claimant's failure to complain for some time about the denial of his rights, it is of doubtful authority following the subsequent decision of the CJEU in *Fuß v Stadt Halle (No 2)*: C-429/09 [2011] IRLR 176 that a right to reparation for an infringement of rights under the *Directive* (in that case by a requirement to work more than 48 hours a week) could not be made conditional on the worker having first complained about the continuing infringement of rights.

The heads of loss for which compensation can be awarded on a successful complaint under *reg 30* do not include injury to feelings; this was finally confirmed by the Court of Appeal in *Santos Gomes v Higher Level Care Ltd* [2018] EWCA Civ 418 [2018] IRLR 440, [2018] 2 All ER 740. However in *Grange v Abellio London Ltd (No. 2)* [2019] ICR D2, the EAT held that, while compensation for refusal to permit a worker to take rest breaks under *reg 12* could not include an award for injury to feelings, it could include an award of damages for personal injury.

Where the complaint involves failure to pay holiday pay or pay in lieu of holiday not taken prior to termination of employment (the issues arising in the vast majority of claims under the *1998 Regulations*), the tribunal will order the employer to pay the amount owed.

58.23 Victimisation

ERA 1996, s 45A (as inserted by *reg 31* of the *1998 Regulations*) provides that a worker has the right not to be subjected to any detriment by any act, or any deliberate failure to act, by his or her employer on the ground that the worker:

(a)   refused (or proposed to refuse) to comply with a requirement of the employer imposed in contravention of the *Regulations*;

(b)   refused (or proposed to refuse) to forgo a right conferred by the *Regulations*;

(c)   failed to sign a workforce agreement, or to enter into or agree to vary or extend any other agreement provided for in the *Regulations*;

(d)   being a representative of members of the workforce for the purposes of *Sch 1* or a candidate in an election for such a representative, performed (or proposed to perform) any functions or activities as such a representative or candidate;

58.25 Restrictions on contracting out

A provision in an agreement which purports to exclude or limit the operation of any part of the *1998 Regulations* or to prevent a person from making a tribunal claim connected with the *Regulations* will be void, except, of course, where the *Regulations* themselves permit exclusion or modification (*reg 35*). The general rule does not apply where worker and employer have entered into an ACAS-conciliated settlement or a settlement agreement. For comments on the potential breadth of the restrictions on contracting out, see the contrasting reasoning of the Court of Session in *MPB Structure Ltd v Munro* [2003] IRLR 350 and the Court of Appeal in *Caulfield v Marshalls Clay Products Ltd* [2004] EWCA Civ 422, [2004] IRLR 564, and the views of the ECJ in *Robinson-Steele v RD Retail Services Ltd*: C-131/04 [2006] IRLR 386, [2006] All ER (EC) 749, broadly endorsing the approach of the Court of Session.

58.26 GUIDANCE

The Secretary of State for Business, Energy and Industrial Strategy is responsible for arranging publication of information and advice on the *1998 Regulations* after consultation with both sides of industry (*reg 35A*). The Guidance was updated in August 2003 to reflect the changes made in the *Regulations* by the *2003 Amendment Regulations*, and was further amended following the decision of the ECJ in *European Commission v United Kingdom*: C-484/04 [2006] IRLR 888 that the guidance on workers' rights to rest periods and rest breaks put the UK in breach of its obligations to implement the *Directive* (see **58.2**). For a time, separate guidance for employers and employees was given via separate websites, but these have been replaced by (much less detailed) guidance on the website www.gov.uk. It should be noted that the Guidance does not have the force of law, and is not necessarily entirely accurate (both because of brevity and specific inaccuracies, such as that the 48 hour limit on the working week applies to the total working time of those who work for more than one employer). Useful additional guidance for enforcing authorities has been issued by the Health and Safety Executive: see www.hse.gov.uk/lau/lacs/95-1.htm.

58.27 EXCEPTIONS

In addition to sectors of activity wholly excluded from the ambit of the *1998 Regulations* (see **58.3** above) various categories of worker are excepted from the full scope of the *Regulations*.

58.28 Unmeasured working time

The limit on the average working week, requirements as to daily and weekly rest periods and breaks for adults, and restrictions on hours of work for night workers are disapplied for workers whose working time is not measured or pre-determined or can be determined by the workers themselves, on account of the specific characteristics of their job (*reg 20(1)*). *Regulation 20* suggests that this may be the case for:

(a)   managing executives or other persons with autonomous decision-taking powers;

(b)   family workers; or

(c)   workers officiating at religious ceremonies in churches and religious communities.

(Annual leave entitlements nevertheless apply to workers within the exemptions created by *reg 20*.)

Following the enforcement proceedings by the Commission described in **56.2** above, the partial exemption from *reg 20* for those whose working time is partially unmeasured (*reg 20(2)*) was revoked by the *Working Time (Amendment) Regulations 2006 (SI 2006/99)* with effect from 6 April 2006.

There have as yet been no reported cases in the UK courts on the scope of the exception. The scope of the exception was briefly considered by the ECJ in *Union syndicale Solidaires Isère v Premier Ministre*: C-428/09 [2011] 1 CMLR 1206, [2011] IRLR 84, but the Court went no further than concluding that as there was no indication in the papers before it that the workers concerned could decide the number of hours they worked, they did not fall within the exception. The issue arose more directly in *Hannele Halva v SOS Lapsikyla ry*: C-175/16, [2017] IRLR 942, [2017] ICR 1408, a case concerning 'relief parents' who provided cover for foster parents at residential care facilities for children. The relief parents were responsible for the children for 24 hours a day but given a degree of autonomy as to when they undertook particular tasks; they only had limited opportunities to leave the care home when the children themselves were absent. The ECJ ruled that their work was not 'unmeasured' within the *Directive*, because the nature of their work was such that mere presence was work.

In some other EU Member States the domestic legislation specifies particular categories or levels of management as being within the exemption, but in the UK the approach has been simply to reproduce the rather imprecise wording of the *Directive* itself. In consequence the contractual arrangements in each case, and not just the individual's job title, would need to be considered to determine whether the individual falls within the exemption.

58.29 Special cases

Regulation 21 provides that in relation to certain specified situations or types of activity, the *Regulations* relating to daily and weekly rest periods and breaks (in respect of adults only) and hours of work for night workers are disapplied. This is subject to workers being permitted to take compensatory rest or, if that is not possible, being provided with appropriate protection; see for a discussion of this **58.17** above. The following groups fall within the *reg 21* exception:

(a) where the worker's activities are such that the place of work and home are distant from one another or different places of work are distant from one another, including cases where the worker is involved in offshore work;

(b) where the worker is engaged in security and surveillance activities requiring a permanent presence in order to protect property and persons, as may be the case for security guards and caretakers or security firms;

(c) where the worker's activities involve the need for continuity of service or production, as may be the case in relation to:

(i) services relating to the reception, treatment or care provided by hospitals or similar establishments (including the activities of doctors in training), residential institutions and prisons;

(ii) work at docks or airports;

(iii) press, radio, television, cinematographic production, postal and telecommunications services and civil protection services;

(iv) gas, water and electricity production, transmission and distribution, household refuse collection and incineration;

(v) industries in which work cannot be interrupted on technical grounds;

(vi) research and development activities;

(vii) agriculture;

(viii) the carriage of passengers on regular urban passenger services;

as those based in the UK and working on non–MLC flagged vessels operating from British ports: see by way of analogy *Diggins v Condor Marine Crewing Services Ltd* [2009] EWCA Civ 1133, [2010] IRLR 119 and *Harris v Windstar Management Services Ltd* UKEAT/0001/16, [2016] IRLR 929, [2016] All ER (D) 189 (May), EAT.

Separate regulations, the *Fishing Vessels (Working Time: Sea-fishermen) Regulations 2004 (SI 2004/1713)* apply to the crews of UK registered fishing vessels. The *1998 Regulations* do not apply at all to those workers covered by the *2004 Regulations: 1998 Regulations, reg 18(1)(b)*. The *2004 Regulations* apply to those employed on sea fishing vessels registered in the UK, wherever the vessel may be, and also (but in relation only to rights to rest periods and certain enforcement provisions) to those working on vessels registered in an EU Member State whilst in UK waters. They apply only to those employed under a contract of employment, not to workers in the wider sense; that point apart, the definitions used are essentially the same as those used in the *1998 Regulations*. The principal rights conferred are:

(a)   a maximum 48 hour working week (averaged over 52 weeks, but with no facility for individual opt-outs);

(b)   adequate rest (with minimum entitlements of 10 hours in 24, in no more than two separate periods, and 77 hours in any week);

(c)   health assessments, and transfer from night work if the health assessment discloses health problems associated with night work;

(d)   paid annual leave; and

(e)   to make a complaint to an employment tribunal if denied adequate rest or paid leave.

The rights not to be subjected to detriment, or dismissed, for asserting rights under the *Regulations*, are conferred by amendments to the *ERA 1996*. Other enforcement provisions include powers for the Maritime and Coastguard Agency to inspect records and detain vessels. The Secretary of State has a limited power to grant exemptions from the limits on working time and the minimum required periods of rest, and there is a general exemption for emergencies.

A further *Directive, No 2017/159*, was adopted by the EU in April 2017; this will give effect to a framework agreement between representatives of employers and unions to implement the International Labour Organisation *Convention on Work in Fishing*. Parts of the Convention were given effect in UK Law by the *Merchant Shipping (Work in Fishing Convention) Regulations 2018, (SI 2018/1106)* the provisions of which (with a single exception) came into force on 31 December 2018. The *Regulations* apply to UK fishing vessels wherever they may be and other fishing vessels in UK waters (*Reg 3*). *Reg 8* imposes an obligation to enter into a "fisherman's work agreement". One of the matters that the work agreement must deal with is "minimum periods of rest" (*Para 16* of the *Schedule*).

58.32   Workers employed on UK vessels operating under certificates limiting the vessel to inland waterways and lakes, or not requiring to be certificated, or on non-UK registered vessels operating solely within such waters, are covered by the *Merchant Shipping (Hours of Work: Inland Waterways) Regulations 2003 (SI 2003/3049)* as amended by the *Merchant Shipping (Working Time: Inland Waterways)(Amendment) Regulations 2017 (SI 2017/1149)*, made under *s 85* of the *Merchant Shipping Act 1995*. The amendments, in force since 5 January 2018, give effect to *Directive 2014/112* which itself implements a European sectoral partners' agreement on working time for mobile workers in inland waterways transport.

In summary, these *Regulations* provide for: a maximum daily working time of 14 hours in any 24 hour period (*Reg 6*); an absolute maximum weekly working time of 84 hours in any seven day period (*Reg 6A*) (or 42 hours in the case of night work (*Reg 7B*)), with a maximum weekly average of 48 hours assessed over a reference period (*Reg 6C*), and a maximum weekly average of 72 hours assessed over a four month period (*Reg 6D*); a maximum annual working time of 2,304 hours within 12 months (*Reg 6B*); rights for workers to free health assessments (*Reg 7*) and for night workers to be transferred to other work if possible if a worker's health suffers as a result of by night working (*Reg 7b*), rights to adequate rest (*Reg 9*), which must be of at least 10 hours in any 24 hour period (of which at least six must be uninterrupted) and 84 hours in total in any week (*Reg 10*); rest breaks (*Reg 10A*); a prohibition on working moire than 31 consecutive days (*Reg 10B*) and to four weeks' paid annual leave in each leave year (*Reg 11*) and 1.6 weeks of additional leave (*Reg 11A*). There are limited exceptions for workers whose working time is unmeasured (*Reg 13*) Employers are under a duty to maintain records (*Reg 9*). Breach of the provisions relating to maximum working time, health assessments and record keeping are offences, whilst the remedy for breaches of the provisions on rest periods and annual leave is by way of complaint to an employment tribunal. The *2003 Regulations* contain the usual prohibition on contracting out, except by way of a settlement agreement (*Reg 19*).

58.33 AVIATION SECTOR

In November 2000 the Social Affairs Council formally adopted a *Directive* implementing the social partners' agreement on working time in the aviation sector, *Directive 2000/79* on the organisation of working time of mobile workers in civil aviation. The domestic implementation of this *Directive* has been effected by the *Civil Aviation (Working Time) Regulations 2004 (SI 2004/756)*. The *2004 Regulations* apply to crew members of civil aircraft flying for the purposes of public transport, and confer the following rights:

(a)   paid annual leave of at least four weeks, as to which see *British Airways plc v Williams* [2012] UKSC 43, [2012] IRLR 1014, [2012] ICR 1375, [2013] 1 All ER 443;

(b)   free health assessments;

(c)   right of transfer from night work to day work where possible if health problems are caused by night work;

(d)   appropriate health and safety protection;

(e)   maximum working time of 2,000 hours a year, calculated on a rolling basis;

(f)   a maximum of 900 hours block flying time in any one (rolling) year;

(g)   at least seven local days (ie days at the crew member's home base) each month and at least 96 local days each year free of all duty and standby.

Infringements of the rights at (a), (b) and (c) may be made the subject of a complaint to an employment tribunal; however there is no equivalent to the protection from detriment or dismissal for asserting rights under the *1998 Regulations* for workers covered by the *Civil Aviation Regulations*; the reason for this omission is unclear. In other respects the *Regulations* are enforceable by the Civil Aviation Authority, following the model of the *1998 Regulations*.

Workers covered by *Directive 2000/79* are excluded from the operative provisions of the *1998 Regulations* governing adult workers: *reg 18(2)(b)*. However, unlike those in the sectors discussed in **58.31** and **58.32** above, this is not an exclusion of the *Regulations* in their entirety; the principal practical difference appears to be that specific provisions on young workers' hours in the *1998 Regulations* and the provisions for their enforcement by the CAA, do apply to the civil aviation sector. One issue which has arisen under the *2004 Regulations* is the treatment in calculating an individual's total annual working time (see (e) above) of standby duty. The *Regulations* were amended, following consultations by the Department for Transport, by the *Civil Aviation (Working Time) (Amendment) Regulations 2010, SI 2010/1226*, to provide that standby time counts in full towards the permitted annual working hours, subject to certain exceptions the effect of which is that time counts at half the rate of actual time.

58.38   CHURCH OF ENGLAND CLERGY

By virtue of the *Ecclesiastical Offices (Terms of Service) Regulations 2009*, which came into force on 1 January 2010, the holders of certain ecclesiastical offices in the Church of England (who are neither employees nor workers for the purposes of the *1998 Regulations*) are given rights to a weekly rest day (but it may be stipulated by the relevant Church authorities that this must not be taken on a Sunday or any of the principal feast days of the Church of England) and to annual leave without loss of stipend. Enforcement of these rights is a matter of internal Church procedures: there is no right of recourse to an employment tribunal. The rights conferred by the *2009 Regulations* do not apply to ministers of any church other than the Church of England; the position in other cases will therefore depend on whether the individual is held to be a worker within the *1998 Regulations*.

58.39   AGRICULTURAL WORKERS IN WALES

Following the abolition of Wages Councils in England and Wales by the *Enterprise and Regulatory Reform Act 2013, s 72*, the National Assembly for Wales passed legislation, the *Agricultural Sector (Wales) Act 2014*, giving power to make Agricultural Wages Orders for agricultural workers in Wales. The current Order, the *Agricultural Wages (Wales) Order 2018*, in addition to setting out minimum rates of pay and sick pay for workers within the scope of its provisions, also makes provisions on a more generous basis than the *Working Time Regulations* covering not only paid annual leave but also rest breaks. *Regulation 28* in particular provides that any adult agricultural worker who has a daily working time of more than 5 ½ hours is entitled to a rest break of 30 minutes. There are a number of exceptions which largely mirror those in *reg 21* of the *1998 Regulations*. Where any of these apply, an equivalent period of compensatory rest must be provided.

The rights conferred in relation to rest breaks are in addition to, rather than in substitution for, those conferred on workers generally by the *1998 Regulations*. This does not mean that a worker meeting the relevant conditions is entitled to two separate breaks; the entitlement is to the more favourable provision, but as noted below, the range of enforcement actions available is wider for the less generous entitlement under the *1998 Regulations*.

The *2014 Act* provides for enforcement of the agricultural minimum wage and holiday pay provisions by application of the provisions for the enforcement by HMRC of the National Minimum Wage under the *National Minimum Wage Act 1998*. In addition it is a criminal offence for employers not to permit the taking of holidays. However the offence does not appear to cover failure to permit the taking of rest breaks, and there is no provision in either the *Act* or the *Order* for claims to be presented by workers to an employment tribunal, other than a provision in the *Act* extending the scope of the automatically unfair dismissal provisions of the *Employment Rights Act 1996* to cover dismissals for asserting rights under an Order made under the *2014 Act*. In addition, failure to afford rest breaks in accordance with the *Order* necessarily also entails failure to afford the minimum entitlement under the *1998 Regulations*, in respect of which a claim may be made to an employment tribunal; so too can a claim of detriment for having asserted the right: see **58.22** and **58.23** above.

59 Wrongful Dismissal

59.1 INTRODUCTION TO WRONGFUL DISMISSAL

A wrongful dismissal occurs when an employer dismisses an employee in a way which is in breach of the employee's contract of employment. Most commonly, this arises when the employer dismisses the employee summarily (ie without any notice at all) or with short notice, and has no sufficient justification for doing so. However, there may also be a wrongful dismissal in other situations: for example, if the employer terminates the employment without following some procedure prescribed by the contract. Further, if the employee resigns in response to some repudiatory breach of contract by the employer, that will give rise to a claim which is in effect for wrongful dismissal.

Thus, wrongful dismissal is a common law cause of action based upon a breach of contract. The right not to be wrongfully dismissed, unlike the right not to be unfairly dismissed, is not one which depends upon statute. A dismissal which is wrongful need not necessarily be unfair, and vice versa. This is because an employer may behave unreasonably in dismissing an employee even though he has observed the letter of their contract, whilst a decision to dismiss may be reasonable even if it involves a breach of contract (although failure to comply with contractual procedures is one factor to be taken into account in deciding whether a dismissal is unfair). See *Treganowan v Robert Knee & Co Ltd* [1975] ICR 405, [1975] IRLR 247; *BSC Sports and Social Club v Morgan* [1987] IRLR 391 and *Westminster City Council v Cabaj* [1996] ICR 960, [1996] IRLR 399.

The primary remedy for an employee who is wrongfully dismissed is an action for damages for breach of contract. In certain circumstances, however, the employee may seek the assistance of the court in keeping the contract of employment alive.

59.2 Contracts whose breach may give rise to wrongful dismissal claims

The wrongful termination of any normal contract of employment will give rise to an action for wrongful dismissal. Certain special categories of employment are dealt with below (see **59.43** and **59.44**). Where the contract pursuant to which a self-employed person provides services is wrongfully terminated, the action for breach of contract is not strictly speaking one for wrongful dismissal but similar principles will apply.

59.3 WHAT CONSTITUTES A DISMISSAL

The fundamental precondition for a wrongful dismissal claim is that the employee should have been dismissed. This will usually occur in one of the following ways:

(a)   dismissal upon notice by the employer (see **59.5** below), although there will normally be no wrongful dismissal if full notice has been given;

(b)   summary dismissal by the employer; and

(c)   constructive dismissal (see **59.6** below).

However, there may also be a deemed dismissal in certain other circumstances (see **59.8–59.10** below).

59.7 Wrongful Dismissal

Nonetheless, it is clear that in the employment context such acceptance will be readily inferred from the employee's words or conduct. For instance, an employee who seeks other work, or signs on for jobseeker's allowance, or even one who simply does not return to work and says nothing, will very probably be held to have ceased to be employed. (However, see *Brompton v AOC International Ltd* (above) where, on the facts of that case, the employee's request for his P45 did not amount to acceptance of the repudiatory breach; and see *Geys v Société Générale, London Branch* [2010] EWHC 648 (Ch), [2010] IRLR 950, where a request by an employee's solicitors for delivery of 'termination documentation' was treated by the Court as the employee keeping his options open, rather than affirmation of the breach.) To be on the safe side, an employee who wishes to argue that his employment continues should assert clearly and quickly that he regards himself as still employed, and that he is available for work if required.

59.8 Employer changing identity or ceasing to exist

If the employer is an individual, the death of that individual will bring the contract to an end. However, it appears that this will be regarded as a case of termination pursuant to an implied term of the contract, and not of wrongful dismissal (see *Farrow v Wilson* (1869) LR 4 CP 744).

If the employer is a partnership, then the dissolution of that partnership or a major change in its composition amounts to a dismissal of the employee (*Tunstall v Condon* [1980] ICR 786; *Briggs v Oates* [1990] ICR 473, [1990] IRLR 472, [1991] 1 All ER 407). It was held in *Brace v Calder* [1895] 2 QB 253 that the same applied when there was any change in the identity of the partners. However, it is not thought that this approach would be taken by the courts in modern cases of large partnerships whose membership frequently fluctuates. Firms should insert appropriate express terms into their contracts of employment to deal with this situation.

The permanent closure of the workplace amounts to a termination of the contracts of those employed there (*Glenboig Union Fireclay Co Ltd v Stewart* (1971) 6 ITR 14). This is not true of a temporary shutdown, although that might, depending upon the circumstances, amount to a repudiatory breach of contract.

59.9 Insolvency

Where the employer is a company, then an order for the compulsory winding up of that company has the immediate effect of terminating the contracts of employment of the company's employees (*Re General Rolling Stock Co* (1866) LR 1 Eq 346; *Measures Bros Ltd v Measures* [1910] 2 Ch 248, CA). However, contracts of employment continue during a voluntary winding up (*Midland Counties District Bank Ltd v Attwood* [1905] 1 Ch 357).

Again, contracts of employment are treated as coming immediately to an end if the employing company is put into receivership by an order of the court (*Reid v Explosives Co Ltd* (1887) 19 QBD 264; *Re Foster Clark Ltd's Indenture Trusts* [1966] 1 WLR 125, [1966] 1 All ER 43). By contrast, the employment continues if the receiver is appointed otherwise by the court and as agent for the company, as typically occurs under, say, a creditor bank's debenture (*Hopley-Dodd v Highfield Motors (Derby) Ltd* (1969) 4 ITR 289; *Griffiths v Secretary of State for Social Services* [1974] QB 468, [1973] 3 All ER 1184). However, even a receivership of this latter kind may have the effect of terminating the contract of employment of a senior manager, if there is a fundamental inconsistency between the continuation of that individual's employment and the receiver's power and duty to conduct the business of the company (*Re Mack Trucks (Britain) Ltd* [1967] 1 WLR 780, [1967] 1 All ER 977).

(See INSOLVENCY OF EMPLOYER (32).)

59.10 Removal from board of directors

In principle, a person's status as a director of the company and his status as an employee of that company are separate and distinct. Accordingly, the employee may cease to be a director without any impact upon his contract of employment.

Sometimes, however, it may be an express or implied term of the contract of employment that the employee is to be a director, either of the employing company itself, or of some associated company. In such a case, removal from the board will amount to a repudiation of the contract of employment, allowing the employee to sue for wrongful dismissal (*Shindler*, below).

However, even in a case where removal from the board brings the employment to an end, it may be contended that the company's articles of association were incorporated into the contract of employment when it was made, and have the effect of ending the employment without any breach on the company's part (see eg *Read v Astoria Garage (Streatham) Ltd* [1952] Ch 637, [1952] 2 All ER 292; cf *Southern Foundries (1926) Ltd v Shirlaw* [1940] AC 701, [1940] 2 All ER 445; *Shindler v Northern Raincoat Co Ltd* [1960] 1 WLR 1038, [1960] 2 All ER 239).

(See DIRECTORS (10).)

59.11 DISMISSAL WITHOUT DUE NOTICE

Express notice periods

There will usually be a written contract of employment which stipulates expressly the period of notice to which the employee is entitled. Indeed, in most cases, the employer will be under a statutory obligation to provide this information as part of the written particulars of employment (see CONTRACT OF EMPLOYMENT (8)).

59.12 Fixed term contracts

Where the contract is for a fixed term, rather than one which contains a provision for the employer to give notice, damages for early termination will be awarded so as to put the employee in the same position as if the contract had continued until the end of that term. There is no need for the employer to give any advance notice that the contract will terminate at the end of the fixed term (although it may be sensible to do so), because it will do so automatically.

A contract which is for a fixed term, in that it will expire automatically on a given date, may also include provisions enabling either party to give notice to take effect at some earlier date.

Analogous to the fixed term contract is the contract which is expressed to terminate upon the occurrence of a specified event, such as the completion of a particular task.

59.13 Rolling contracts

A 'rolling contract' is not a precisely defined legal concept. However, the term is in general used to describe a contract which is of a length (say, two years) generally associated with a fixed term contract, but where the unexpired term always remains the same unless notice has been given. There is no difference in substance between a two-year rolling contract and a contract incorporating a two-year notice period.

59.14 Directors' notice periods

A restriction upon the length of notice periods in directors' contracts of employment is contained in *s 188* of the *Companies Act 2006*. Save with the approval by resolution of the members of the company, a company cannot validly enter into contracts with its directors

59.17 Wrongful Dismissal

All-out strike action will almost certainly amount to a repudiatory breach of contract entitling the employer to dismiss summarily (see *Simmons v Hoover Ltd* [1977] ICR 61, [1976] IRLR 266, [1977] 1 All ER 775), although it is possible that a very short walk-out might be considered insufficiently serious to have this consequence. Lesser forms of industrial action may or may not amount to a breach of contract at all (for example, an overtime ban is only a breach of contract if the contract provides for compulsory overtime) and may or may not be fundamental enough to be considered repudiatory.

59.18 DISMISSAL IN BREACH OF OTHER CONTRACTUAL REQUIREMENTS

Dismissal procedures

If the contract of employment stipulates that a particular procedure must be followed before an employee is dismissed, then a dismissal which is carried out without that procedure having been followed is necessarily wrongful (see, eg *Gunton v Richmond-upon-Thames London Borough Council* [1980] ICR 755, [1980] IRLR 321, [1980] 3 All ER 577; *R v BBC, ex p Lavelle* [1983] ICR 99, [1982] IRLR 404, [1983] 1 All ER 241; and *Dietman v Brent London Borough Council* [1988] ICR 842, [1988] IRLR 299; but cf *Boyo v Lambeth London Borough Council* [1994] ICR 727, [1995] IRLR 50).

However, it will be a question of fact in every case as to whether any disciplinary or similar procedure has in fact been incorporated into the contract of employment, or whether it merely represents a statement of the employer's current policy. If it is the latter, then breach of the procedure may well have the effect of making the dismissal unfair but it will not render it wrongful so far as the law of contract is concerned.

In *Johnson v Unisys Ltd* [2001] UKHL 13, [2001] ICR 480, [2001] IRLR 279, [2001] 2 All ER 801, the House of Lords rejected the contention that there could be implied into a contract of employment a provision that the employer would not dismiss save for good cause, and after giving the employee a reasonable opportunity to demonstrate that no such cause existed, in circumstances where there was an express term entitling the employer to dismiss on notice without any cause. In other words, the courts will not readily imply any procedural safeguards against dismissal into a contract of employment.

59.19 Other requirements

A dismissal might also be wrongful because, for example, it was carried out in contravention of a contractual term concerning the manner in which employees would be selected for redundancy. Such an argument was rejected on the facts in *Alexander v Standard Telephones and Cables Ltd (No 2)* [1991] IRLR 286.

Also, where the contract of employment contains the right to receive benefits under a permanent health insurance scheme, the court may imply a term preventing an employer from dismissing the employee (in the absence of conduct amounting to a repudiatory breach or for other cause, such as redundancy) during the period in which that employee is incapacitated from work. Dismissal in breach of this implied term would be wrongful, and may entitle the employee to recover damages reflecting the loss of permanent health benefits to which he would otherwise have been entitled (compare *Aspden v Webbs Poultry and Meat Group (Holdings) Ltd* [1996] IRLR 521 and *Hill v General Accident Fire and Life Assurance Corpn plc* [1998] IRLR 641; see also *Villella v MFI Furniture Centres Ltd* [1999] IRLR 468).

Similarly, if an employer decides to make an employee redundant, it cannot subsequently deny the employee of the benefits of the contractual redundancy scheme by dismissing him for another reason where it had no cause to do so. This would be a breach of an implied term of the employee's contract of employment, allowing the employee to claim damages to be assessed on the basis of the contractual redundancy scheme: see *Jenvey v Australian Broadcasting Corp* [2003] ICR 79, [2002] IRLR 520.

59.20 RELEVANCE OF ACTUAL REASON FOR DISMISSAL

In a complaint of unfair dismissal, the reason for which the employer actually chose to dismiss the employee is of central importance. But in an action for wrongful dismissal, it is possible to justify the dismissal by reference to conduct of the employee of which the employer was unaware at the time of the dismissal, and which may have happened a considerable time prior to the dismissal (*Boston Deep Sea Fishing and Ice Co v Ansell* (1888) 39 Ch D 339; *Cyril Leonard & Co v Simo Securities Trust Ltd* [1972] 1 WLR 80, [1971] 3 All ER 1313; *Item Software (UK) Ltd v Fassihi* [2003] IRLR 769).

In principle, it should also be possible for the employer to rely upon conduct of which he was aware at the time of the dismissal, but was not in fact his reason for dismissing the employee. However, unless that conduct occurred or was discovered only a short time prior to the dismissal, the employer is likely to be held to have waived his right to terminate the contract on account of it.

Where an employee's misconduct was well known to the employer and it was not treated by them as justifying his dismissal, it will not be open to new owners or managers to seek to rely on that earlier misconduct on the grounds that they were not aware of it themselves. The issue is tested by reference to the legal personality of the employer, and by its actions and knowledge from time to time (*Welsh v Cowdenbeath Football Club Ltd* [2009] IRLR 362).

59.21 WAIVER OF NOTICE, PAY IN LIEU OF NOTICE AND GARDEN LEAVE

Frequently, an employer who has resolved to dismiss an employee will not wish that employee to continue working for him until the notice period has expired. It may, for example, be thought that the disgruntled employee's presence will be disruptive or bad for morale, or that there is a threat to confidential information, or simply that the employee will be unproductive and that a replacement should start work at the earliest opportunity.

In this situation, there are three principal options open to the employer (assuming that there are no grounds for a summary dismissal). The first is to negotiate an early termination with the employee. Some financial incentive may be offered, or the employee may simply be happy to be released from his obligations sooner rather than later. There is no legal obstacle to this course, because *s 86(3)* of the *ERA 1996* permits the employee to waive his right even to the statutory minimum period of notice (or to accept a payment in lieu of notice).

The second option is for the employer to pay the employee wages in lieu of notice. This course is frequently adopted. However, it should be borne in mind that to dismiss an employee with pay in lieu rather than to give due notice is in fact to dismiss wrongfully. The true legal analysis of this situation is that there is a summary dismissal carried out in breach of contract, and the wages paid in lieu in fact represent a payment of damages for that breach of contract (see *Gothard v Mirror Group Newspapers Ltd* [1988] IRLR 396). In some cases, the fact that the dismissal is theoretically wrongful may be of no practical significance. But that will not always be so. For instance, the dismissed employee may have a residual claim for the value of lost benefits in kind during the notice period. (See, for example, *Silvey v Pendragon plc* [2001] IRLR 685, where the early termination deprived an employee of enhanced pension rights. Even though the employee had accepted pay in lieu of notice, the Court of Appeal held that the loss of these pension rights was recoverable as damages for wrongful dismissal). The wrongful dismissal may also prevent the employer from relying upon restrictive covenants in the contract of employment (see **59.34** below).

An employee has no statutory or common law right to be paid in lieu of notice (*Rowley v Cerberus Software Ltd* [2001] EWCA Civ 78, [2001] ICR 376, [2001] IRLR 160; *Hardy v Polk (Leeds) Ltd* [2004] IRLR 420. However, provision may be made by contract. In order to avoid the problems of the 'theoretically wrongful' dismissal described above, many service agreements now incorporate a clause which gives the employer the option of terminating the contract lawfully by making a payment in lieu of notice instead of actually giving notice. Such a clause ought to define clearly whether the payment is to be based upon basic pay only, or whether the calculation is also to have regard to other elements of the remuneration package, and whether the payment is to be made gross or net of tax. Where the contract of employment does not expressly define the payment that will be made in lieu of notice the court will interpret the contract 'holistically', without any preconception that it necessarily seeks to give the employee what he would have earned had he remained in employment during the notice period (*Locke v Candy & Candy Ltd* [2010] EWCA Civ 1350, [2011] IRLR 163).

Summary termination pursuant to a payment in lieu (PILON) provision does not constitute a breach of contract (*Rex Stewart Jeffries Parker Ginsberg Ltd v Parker* [1988] IRLR 483). Where payment in lieu has been made in accordance with a PILON provision, this will bring the contract of employment to an end, so long as the employer notifies the employee in clear and unambiguous terms that such payment has been made and that it is made in the exercise of the contractual right to terminate the employment with immediate effect (*Société Générale v Geys* [2013] ICR 117, [2013] IRLR 122, [2013] 1 All ER 1061).

Where the employer exercises the right to terminate the contract with a payment in lieu of notice, the employee is under no obligation to give credit for actual or imputed earnings during what would have been the notice period. In other words, there is no duty on the employee to mitigate loss (as to which, see **59.30** below). He is entitled to claim for the full sum due to him under the contract as a debt (*Abrahams v Performing Rights Society* [1995] ICR 1028, [1995] IRLR 486).

The sum paid to the employee in lieu of notice will be taxable in his hands under Schedule E (*EMI Group Electronics Ltd v Coldicott (Inspector of Taxes)* [1999] IRLR 630).

Merely because a contract of employment contains a payment in lieu clause, however, does not mean that every termination will be treated as if the employer exercised the right to dismiss and then make the payment in lieu without any deduction for mitigation. Much will depend on the precise wording of the contract. In *Gregory v Wallace* [1998] IRLR 387, the Court of Appeal held that, on the facts, the employer did not exercise the right to make a payment in lieu, where notice of termination had to be in writing and termination had been oral. Instead, the employer was treated as having dismissed the employee wrongfully and in breach of contract.

In *Cerberus Software Ltd v Rowley* [2001] ICR 376, [2001] IRLR 160, on the other hand, where the contract stated that the employer 'may' make a payment in lieu of notice to the employee, the Court of Appeal held that this gave the employer the choice whether or not to make the payment.

There is no breach of contract even if it is the employee who has originally given notice, and the employer who then brings the employment to an immediate end with a payment in lieu (*Marshall (Cambridge) Ltd v Hamblin* [1994] IRLR 260). In *Hamblin* it was also held that the employment could be lawfully terminated with a payment in lieu of salary only, notwithstanding that the employee typically received a high proportion of his remuneration from commission; however, the EAT's reasoning is hard to follow and may depend upon the fact that the payment of commission was held to be discretionary and not a contractual right.

The third option is for the employee to be put on so-called 'garden leave'. This means that notice is duly given and the employee continues to be paid and to receive his full contractual benefits but he is not required or permitted to attend for work. This may be achieved by an express garden leave clause or, in certain circumstances, by 'implying' such a clause into the contract.

The power to place an employee on garden leave will not be implied if the refusal to provide work would constitute a repudiatory breach of contract. There will be a repudiatory breach if the contractual consideration moving from the employer includes an obligation to permit the employee to perform work but not if the contractual consideration is confined to payment of remuneration only (*Collier v Sunday Referee Publishing Co Ltd* [1940] 2 KB 647, [1940] 4 All ER 234).

The Court of Appeal has acknowledged that employees increasingly regard work itself as important to them, and not just remuneration (*William Hill Organisation Ltd v Tucker* [1999] ICR 291, [1998] IRLR 313). Moreover, it held that whether there is an obligation to provide work, rather than merely pay, will depend on a careful construction of the contractual arrangements. Of particular importance will be whether the position of the employee was 'specific and unique'; and whether the employee has some skill which will be lost if not practised. Other factors may be whether the contractual remuneration consists in part of a commission which depends upon work actually done (see eg *Devonald v Rosser & Sons* [1906] 2 KB 728, [1904–7] All ER Rep 988). See also *Langston v Amalgamated Union of Engineering Workers* [1974] ICR 180, 510, [1974] IRLR 15, [1974] 1 All ER 980, CA; *Breach v Epsylon Industries Ltd* [1976] ICR 316, [1976] IRLR 180; *Spencer v Marchington* [1988] IRLR 392; *SBJ Stephenson Ltd v Mandy* [2000] IRLR 233 (no obligation to provide work to a divisional director of an insurance brokerage).

In *SG&R Valuation Service Co LLC v Boudrais* [2008] IRLR 770, the court held that the defendant employees had a right to work, based on the *Tucker* analysis. However, this right was qualified, and was subject to the employees being ready and willing to work. The employees' wrongdoing (removal of confidential information, solicitation of staff and diversion of business opportunities) demonstrated that they were not ready and willing to work, and so the employer was entitled to withhold work from them during their notice period.

It should be borne in mind, however, that the existence of an express garden leave clause may be taken into account by a court in determining the validity of any post-termination restraints on the employee (*Credit Suisse Asset Management Ltd v Armstrong* [1996] ICR 882, [1996] IRLR 450; see further RESTRAINT OF TRADE (42)).

59.22 ANTICIPATORY BREACHES OF CONTRACT

It is important to remember that a breach of contract, in this as in other contexts, may be either *actual* or *anticipatory*. An anticipatory breach of contract occurs where there has not yet been any actual breach, because the time for performance of the relevant obligation has not yet arrived, but one party has indicated a clear refusal to perform the contract, or has made it impossible for himself to fulfil his obligations when the time comes. In the case of an employment contract, this might occur, for example, if the employer announced that the employee's salary would be unilaterally reduced by a significant amount the following month.

Where an anticipatory breach of contract occurs, and it is sufficiently serious to be repudiatory, the innocent party is faced with a choice. First, he may immediately accept the breach as bringing the contract to an end, and sue for damages. Secondly, he may keep the contract alive, and continue to call for performance by the other party. Thus, in the example above, the employee could immediately resign and sue for damages for wrongful dismissal.

Alternatively, he could continue to assert his right to be paid a full salary the following month, which would give the employer an opportunity to change his mind; if the salary was indeed reduced, then the employee would at that point have to choose between resigning and affirming the contract, as discussed in **59.6** above. In the latter event, he might also be able to sue in debt for arrears of salary, as discussed in **59.24** below.

It has been suggested that an anticipatory breach, as opposed to an actual breach of contract, will not be repudiatory if it stems from an innocent mistake on the part of the party in breach as to what the contract requires of him (see *Frank Wright & Co (Holdings) Ltd v Punch* [1980] IRLR 217, EAT; *United Bank Ltd v Akhtar* [1989] IRLR 507; and *Brown v JBD Engineering Ltd* [1993] IRLR 568).

59.23 REMEDIES FOR WRONGFUL DISMISSAL

Remedies other than claims for damages

Injunctions

If the employee moves swiftly, he may be able to obtain an injunction restraining the employer from dismissing him wrongfully. However, it is unusual for the court to agree to insist upon performance of a contract of employment, because of the personal relationship between employer and employee without which the contract cannot properly function. Nevertheless, the breakdown of the relationship of trust and confidence will not automatically prevent an employee from obtaining injunctive relief (see *Gryf-Lowczowski (Jan) v Hinchingbrooke Healthcare NHS Trust* [2005] EWHC 2407 (QB), [2006] IRLR 100 (see further CONTRACT OF EMPLOYMENT (8)).

59.24 *Claims in debt*

If the employer's breach of contract consists of the failure to pay a sum of money that is due, for example by imposing a reduction in salary, the employee's sole choice is not between resigning and claiming to have been wrongfully dismissed on the one hand, and accepting the reduced salary on the other. Rather, he may choose to affirm the contract of employment despite the employer's breach, yet continue to assert his entitlement to the unpaid moneys, and sue in debt for those moneys if they remain unpaid. For examples, see the decisions of the House of Lords in *Rigby v Ferodo Ltd* [1988] ICR 29, [1987] IRLR 516 and the EAT in *Bruce v Wiggins Teape (Stationery) Ltd* [1994] IRLR 536.

59.25   Actions for damages for wrongful dismissal

General approach to assessment of damages

The basic principle in assessing the damages payable for wrongful dismissal is that the employee must be put into the same position as if the employer had properly performed the contract. However, it is to be assumed for these purposes that the employer would have performed the contract in the way least burdensome to himself, and would have minimised his obligations to the employee by giving due notice to terminate the contract at the earliest opportunity (see *Lavarack v Woods of Colchester Ltd* [1967] 1 QB 278, [1966] 3 All ER 683 and *Clark v BET plc* [1997] IRLR 348, though see *Horkulak v Cantor Fitzgerald International* [2004] EWCA Civ 1287, [2005] ICR 402, [2004] IRLR 942. In that case, the Court of Appeal held that the rule did not apply to the failure to make discretionary bonus payments where the employer is contractually obliged to exercise his discretion rationally and in good faith. In those circumstances, the court will look to see what bonus the employee probably would have received if he had continued in employment, rather than the minimum sum that his employer might have awarded him consistent with his contractual obligation to act rationally and in good faith).

Two main consequences follow from this basic principle. First, the court will have to ask itself how much better off the employee would have been if he had been given proper notice on the date when he was wrongfully dismissed (or if notice which had already been given had been allowed to run its course). This will normally mean that the *prima facie* measure of the damages is the net amount of the employee's salary and benefits for the notice period. In the case of a fixed term contract, the equivalent period is of course the unexpired portion of the term remaining as at the date of dismissal.

Second, the court (unlike an employment tribunal assessing compensation for unfair dismissal) will only compensate the employee for the loss of benefits to which he was contractually entitled, and not for those which he would probably have received in practice but to which he had no legal right (*Laverack*, above). It may also be necessary to consider questions of causation arising upon the particular facts of a given case. For example, the employer may be able to prove upon a balance of probabilities that the employee would have left his job voluntarily within the notice period in any event, or that an employee dismissed because of long-term absence through sickness would have remained off work throughout the notice period and would therefore have earned nothing during that period.

Where the wrongfulness of the dismissal stems from a failure to follow a proper procedure (see **59.18** above), the traditional view has been that damages should be awarded on the basis that notice could lawfully have been given on the day when the necessary procedures, if followed, could have been concluded (*Gunton v Richmond-upon-Thames London Borough Council* [1980] ICR 755, [1980] IRLR 321, [1980] 3 All ER 577; see also *Alexander v Standard Telephones and Cables Ltd (No 2)* [1991] IRLR 286 and *Boyo v Lambeth London Borough Council* [1994] ICR 727, [1995] IRLR 50). The court will not speculate as to whether or not the employee would have remained in employment if the disciplinary procedure had been followed (*Focsa Services (UK) Ltd v Birkett* [1996] IRLR 325; *Janciuk v Winerite Ltd* [1998] IRLR 63; *Wise Group v Mitchell* [2005] ICR 896). The Supreme Court in *Edwards v Chesterfield Royal Hospital NHS Foundation Trust* [2012] ICR 201, [2012] IRLR 129, [2012] 2 All ER 278 declined to consider whether *Gunton* was properly decided.

59.26 *'Liquidated damages' clauses and other provisions for termination payments*

Sometimes a service agreement may contain a provision that the employer is to pay a specified sum, or a sum calculated in a specified way, to the employee if the employment comes to an end in particular circumstances.

If the employee seeks to enforce such a provision, a basic question which may arise is whether the clause is a penalty clause. If so, the court will not give effect to it, and the employee will simply have to sue for damages in the normal way (assuming that he has been wrongfully dismissed). In order to decide whether a particular provision is indeed a penalty clause, it is necessary to apply a two-stage test.

First, does the clause apply where there has been a breach of contract? A provision which provides for a particular sum to be payable upon an occurrence which does *not* amount to a breach of contract cannot be a penalty clause. If the triggering event may or may not amount to a breach of contract depending upon the circumstances, the court will ask whether there was a breach of contract in the case in question. Thus, a provision in a contract of employment that, if the employer gave due notice to terminate the contract, he would pay £1,000 to the employee could not be a penalty clause, because there would be no breach of contract in circumstances to which it applied. If the contract provided for the employer to pay £1,000 if he dismissed *without* due notice, then that could be a penalty clause, depending upon the application of the second stage of the test (see below). If the provision was for £1,000 to be paid in any case in which the employee was dismissed, then that might amount to a penalty clause, but only in a case in which the dismissal was in fact wrongful. For these somewhat anomalous distinctions, see *Export Credit Guarantee Department v Universal Oil Products Co* [1983] 1 WLR 399, [1983] 2 All ER 205.

Assuming that the provision operates upon a breach of contract (as will be the case if one is dealing with a wrongful dismissal), the second stage of the test is to ask whether it represents a genuine pre-estimate of the loss suffered (in which case it is a valid liquidated damages clause, and will be enforced), or whether it is in effect designed to terrorise the other party into performing the contract (see *Dunlop Pneumatic Tyre Co Ltd v New Garage and Motor Co Ltd* [1915] AC 79, [1914–15] All ER Rep 739). In *Imam-Sadeque v Bluebay Asset Management (Services) Ltd* [2013] IRLR 344, the court explained that a penalty clause is one which is 'without commercial justification', and is designed to secure performance of the contract rather than to compensate for the loss occasioned by the breach.

A comparison between the amount that would be payable on breach with the loss which might be sustained is, therefore, a 'guide' as to whether the clause is penal. Thus, in *Murray v Leisureplay plc* [2005] EWCA Civ 963, [2005] IRLR 946, the Court of Appeal overturned the trial judge's finding that a clause requiring the payment of one year's gross salary in the event of wrongful termination was a 'penalty', emphasising Lord Dunedin's approach in *Dunlop* that a clause 'will be held to be a penalty if the sum stipulated for is extravagant and unconscionable in amount in comparison with the greatest loss that could conceivably be provided to have followed from the breach.' On the facts of the case, the court held that the clause was 'generous' but 'not unconscionable', and did not meet the test of 'extravagance'. The court held that it was appropriate for the remuneration package to provide 'generous reassurance against the consequences of dismissal'.

The difference between a liquidated damages clause and a penalty clause was considered in *Giraud UK Ltd v Smith* [2000] IRLR 763, a case that illustrates that an employee may be liable for damages if he gives short notice. In that case, the contract of employment provided that if an employee failed to give his contractual notice when resigning, it would result in a deduction from his wages equivalent to the number of days short. The EAT upheld the decision of the employment tribunal that this was a penalty clause (and thus invalid). It was not a liquidated damages clause because it was not a genuine pre-estimate of the loss to the employer if the employee failed to give proper notice. Further, it did not prohibit the employer from seeking further damages through the courts greater than that specified in the clause. There was evidence to suggest that the employer could easily find replacements for the employee in question (he was a lorry driver). In the circumstances, therefore, the clause enabled the employer to say 'Heads I win, tails you lose!'

The advantage of a valid liquidated damages clause is that, in a case where liability for wrongful dismissal is accepted, it may enable the parties to avoid costly and lengthy litigation involving disputes about the precise valuation of benefits and the adequacy of attempts at mitigation (cf *Abrahams* above).

59.27   *Rights of employee in period of notice*

As set out in **59.16** above, s *86* of the *ERA 1996* provides for statutory minimum notice periods. *ERA 1996, s 87(1)* provides that, if an employer gives notice of dismissal to an employee who has been continuously employed for at least one month, then during the statutory minimum period, the employee will enjoy the rights conferred by *ss 88* to *91, ERA 1996*.

The importance for present purposes of the rights conferred by these provisions is that they are to be taken into account in assessing any claim for damages for wrongful dismissal (*ERA 1996, s 91(5)*). In other words, when assessing what the employee would have received if the employer had performed his minimum obligations, it is necessary to take account not only of his contractual obligations, but of these statutory obligations as well.

The principal right conferred by these statutory provisions is for the employee to be paid in cases where he is ready and willing to work, but no work is provided for him by his employer, or where the employee is absent from work through sickness, pregnancy or being on holiday. This would include employees absent on long-term ill-health grounds. The precise qualifications for payment, and the amount to which the employee is entitled, are the subject of detailed provisions.

Where sums which should have been payable pursuant to these provisions fall to be taken into account in assessing damages, they are subject to reduction for mitigation in the usual way (*Westwood v Secretary of State for Employment* [1985] ICR 209, [1984] IRLR 209, [1984] 1 All ER 874).

It is significant to note that these rights do not apply where the contractual period of notice exceeds the statutory minimum period by at least one week (*ERA 1996, s 87(4)*). This point was highlighted in *Budd v Scotts Co (UK) Ltd* [2003] IRLR 145, where the employee's contractual notice period exceeded the statutory period. The EAT held that the employee was not entitled to be paid for his contractual notice period as he was sick throughout and was not capable of working. By contrast, he would have been paid for the entire period if the contractual notice period had been the same or less than the statutory period.

59.28 *Valuation of particular benefits*

Salary. This will normally be straightforward to calculate, since it will simply be a question of applying the rate of pay enjoyed by the claimant at the date of dismissal to the length of the notice period. Sometimes the employee is entitled to an annual increase either of a set amount, or related to the prevailing rate of inflation, and such an entitlement must of course be built into the calculation if the notice period extends beyond the date upon which the next increase was due (*Re Crowther & Nicholson Ltd* (1981) Times, 10 June).

Where the contract provides for an annual increase but the amount of the increase is in the absolute discretion of the employer, the employer will be obliged to exercise that discretion in good faith and not capriciously (*Clark*, above). Perhaps more commonly, the contract may stipulate that salary will be reviewed on an annual basis. However, in *Runciman v Walter Runciman plc* [1992] BCLC 1084 the court refused to award any damages to represent the loss of a chance that such a review would have led to a salary increase.

Bonuses and commission. Where the employee was entitled to receive a bonus or commission as part of his remuneration, the court will have to assess what the value of that entitlement would have been if the employee had remained employed through the notice period. Sometimes an exact figure will be readily ascertainable, as where the bonus depends upon the pre-tax profits of a large company, whose profits for the relevant period have already been declared and cannot have been significantly affected by the absence of the claimant. In other cases, such as where the employee was entitled to a percentage of the value of sales which he himself achieved, the court will have to make the best estimate possible of what would have happened if due notice had been given. It will consider, for example, evidence of past performance by that employee, and performance by other employees during the relevant period as compared with their own past performance. In yet other cases, the court may be required to assess the employer's likely profits in years which are yet to come, in which case expert evidence is likely to be required if the claim is of any size. Where an employer operates a discretionary bonus scheme an employee who has a contractual entitlement to participate in that scheme is entitled to a bona fide and rational exercise of discretion by his employer as to whether or not he receives his bonus and in what sum (*Clark v Nomura International plc* [2000] IRLR 766, EAT; *Horkulak v Cantor Fitzgerald International* [2004] EWCA Civ 1287, [2005] ICR 402, [2004] IRLR 942). In deciding how much compensation to award an employee where his employer has failed to exercise its discretion rationally and in good faith, the court may take into account the range of bonus payments made to other employees. The court is not obliged to award the employee the minimum bonus that the employer could lawfully have paid if it is not fair and reasonable to do so (see *Horkulak*).

Share options. The effect of dismissal may be that the employee loses the right to exercise share options which he holds, or that he is compelled to exercise them within a shorter timescale than would otherwise have been the case, with adverse implications for the differential between the exercise price and the market price of the shares. Where this is so, and where there is no valid exclusion clause in respect of liability for such loss (see **59.37** below), the court will have to assess the value of the shares which the employee could otherwise have obtained, less what it would have cost him to acquire them.

Cars. Company cars often represent a substantial head of loss, although for any damages to be recoverable it is obviously essential that the claimant should have been permitted to make some personal use of the car.

There are a number of possible ways in which the loss may be assessed. If the employee has actually had to hire a replacement car, and has acted reasonably in doing so, then the hire charges should be recoverable. Alternatively, a fairly rough and ready lump sum may be awarded.

More commonly, however, the court will be invited to have regard either to the value which the HMRC places upon the car for tax purposes, or to the AA's estimated running costs. The HMRC scales, which are based on size or value, age and mileage, were formerly not much relied upon by employees, because the tax treatment of such benefits was generous, and did not reflect their true value. More recently, changes in policy have made the Revenue scales a better and fairer guide.

The AA estimates provided the basis of valuation adopted by the court in *Shove v Downs Surgical plc* [1984] ICR 532, [1984] IRLR 17. They are annual figures comprising standing charges and running costs per mile for various sizes of car and a given annual mileage.

Clearly, whatever basis of valuation is adopted, it is necessary to examine the terms of the contract (either express, or implied through practice) as to what costs associated with running the car were to be met by the employer, and which by the employee. In particular, it is necessary to know which party was responsible for meeting the cost of petrol for private use.

Pensions. The loss of pension contributions, or pension rights, is also in many cases an extremely important head of damages.

Insurance cover. It is commonplace for employees to be contractually entitled to the benefit of free medical insurance, permanent health insurance and the like, both for themselves and for their families.

The value of such benefits is frequently assessed as if it could be equated with the cost to the employer of providing the insurance cover, and this may be convenient when the sums at stake are small. However, it is not a strictly accurate approach. If the employee has in fact obtained replacement cover, then the loss suffered is the reasonable cost to him of doing so (and an individual may have to pay more than a company purchasing the same cover on a group basis). However, if the employee has chosen not to take out such insurance himself, then he suffers no loss (save, perhaps for the 'peace of mind' which the employee previously enjoyed, knowing that insurance coverage was in place) unless during the relevant period some event occurs which would have led to the making of a payment under the policy, had it still been in force. In that event, there may be arguments as to whether the whole amount of the lost payment is recoverable, or whether the employee should have mitigated his loss by obtaining replacement cover.

It is also necessary to bear in mind that, depending upon the basis on which the insurance is arranged and paid for, the period for which cover is lost through the wrongful dismissal (or replacement cover has to be purchased) may not exactly correspond to the period between the dismissal and the date when due notice would have expired.

Holidays. The conventional view is that the right to paid holiday is not a separate compensatable head of loss, since the pay which would have been received is covered by the claim for lost salary. However, it is at least arguable that the opportunity to receive that salary, without having to work for it, is itself a valuable benefit, and that the salary payable in respect of the relevant period is the appropriate measure of that value. The counter-argument is that the wrongfully dismissed employee in effect finds himself enjoying a good deal of holiday time, whether he likes it or not. On the other hand, he is not truly on holiday (because he has a continuing duty to look for ways of mitigating his loss), and he may find other employment which offers the same pay but less generous holiday arrangements.

Accommodation. If it was a contractual benefit that the employee should be provided with free or cheap accommodation, and the employee has had to vacate that accommodation as a result of the dismissal, then the cost of finding alternative accommodation for the duration of the notice period is a recoverable head of loss.

Sometimes employees who have lost accommodation seek to claim for their removal expenses. However, it is unlikely that such expenses are properly recoverable in most cases, since the employee would have had to leave the accommodation in due course even if proper notice had been given.

Miscellaneous. In advising employees with wrongful dismissal claims, it is important to ensure that all contractual benefits have been identified and claims made for their value. Other than the common and valuable benefits discussed above, benefits in kind may include, for example, meals, payment of telephone bills and the use of a mobile phone, discounts on particular products (such as mortgages for bank employees), and personal use of credit cards offering preferential interest rates. See also **59.33** below for loss of the right to complain of unfair dismissal.

However, a right to reimbursement of expenses only represents a head of loss if the expenses in question were not confined to expenditure incurred for the purposes of the job (the point being that such expenditure will cease to be incurred once the job is lost).

In all cases, it is wise to be sure that benefits have been properly declared to tax before they are introduced into the calculation of loss, lest an argument be put forward that the contract is void for illegality (see **59.35** below).

A claim for damages for wrongful dismissal will often be combined with a claim in debt for wages accrued to the date of dismissal, and for accrued holiday pay if that is a contractual right. Claims in debt are not subject to the obligation to mitigate. Nor can the employer avoid paying accrued wages even if there was misconduct prior to the dismissal which justified summary termination (*Healey v Française Rubastic SA* [1917] 1 KB 946). Wages accrue on a daily basis and an employee will normally be entitled to claim an apportionment of wages for a period worked even where he has been summarily dismissed before his salary became due under the terms of his contract: *Item Software (UK) Ltd v Fassihi* [2004] EWCA Civ 1244, [2005] ICR 450, [2004] IRLR 928.

59.29 *Compensation for distress and other intangible loss*

The normal rule is that in an action for breach of contract, including an action for wrongful dismissal, it is not possible to recover damages for distress or injured feelings for the manner of the breach (*Addis v Gramophone Co Ltd* [1909] AC 488, [1908–10] All ER Rep 1; *Johnson v Unisys Ltd* [2001] UKHL 13, [2001] ICR 480, [2001] IRLR 279, [2001] 2 All ER 801).

Further, while an employee may recover damages at common law for a breach of the implied term of trust and confidence occurring prior to a dismissal, the House of Lords has held that such a claim cannot be made in respect of the dismissal itself, for this would impinge on the statutory right not to be unfairly dismissed, the jurisdictional and compensatory limits for which have been determined by Parliament (*Johnson*, ibid). Their Lordships considered this

59.31 *Interest and accelerated receipt*

Depending upon the length of the notice period or fixed term contract, and how long it takes for the wrongful dismissal claim to be brought to trial, the claimant may find either that he has suffered a loss through being deprived of the use and benefit of his salary for the period between the dismissal and the trial, or that he gains because the award of damages is in his pocket much sooner than the salary which it represents would have been paid.

Accordingly, that part of the award of damages which represents salary which ought to have been paid in the past will normally carry an award of interest. The discretionary power of the High Court to award interest is found in *s 35A* of the *Supreme Court Act 1981*, and that of the county court in *s 69* of the *County Courts Act 1984*. The rate and period of interest, as well as whether to award it at all, are in the court's discretion. However, the award will always be of simple interest; it will generally run from the date when payment should have been made until the date of judgment, unless the claimant has been culpably slow in prosecuting the proceedings; and it will frequently reflect the judgment rate of interest over the relevant period (currently 8%).

Where damages are being received earlier than the payments for whose loss they compensate were due, it is normal for a percentage discount to be applied on account of accelerated receipt, generally reflecting the anticipated rate of inflation over the relevant period.

Sometimes, where the award of damages covers a very long period, the percentage discount may be increased (or a further discount applied) to take account of the so-called 'vicissitudes of life' – in other words, the intangible chance that the claimant might never have served the full notice period because he fell ill, chose to depart, or encountered the proverbial number 57 bus. It is not thought that any very large discount is generally appropriate on this score.

59.32 *Taxation of damages*

The ultimate objective of the award of damages, as explained above, is to put the claimant into exactly the same position as if the contract had been duly performed. In that event, he would of course have been paid his salary net of tax and National Insurance contributions, and would have had to pay tax upon most benefits in kind. However, simply to deduct tax and National Insurance from the gross loss would be too simplistic an approach, because the award of damages will itself be subject to tax in the hands of the employee. A further complication is that the damages will only be taxed insofar as they exceed the tax-free allowance of £30,000 which applies to compensation payments for loss of office. The principal relevant taxing provisions are contained in *Part 6* of the *Income tax (Earnings and Pensions) Act 2003*. Employers are required to report to HMRC details of any award of payment and/or benefits upon termination of an employment contract where the total amount of the award exceeds £30,000 (*Income Tax (Pay as You Earn) Regulations 2003 (SI 2003/2682), regs 91 to 93*).

The correct approach is therefore for the court to ascertain the net sum which the employee ought ultimately to receive, and to gross that amount up until it has arrived at a grossed-up sum which, when the damages are taxed, will reduce again to the correct net sum. Authority for this grossing-up procedure is to be found in *Stewart v Glentaggart* 1963 SLT 119 and *Shove v Downs Surgical plc* [1984] ICR 532, [1984] IRLR 17, [1984] 1 All ER 7. In order to ensure the correct application of tax rates, bands and allowances, it may be necessary to have details of the employee's income from all sources.

Similar principles should apply where one is calculating a settlement figure rather than an award of damages. It will be necessary to look at each element that makes up the overall settlement sum.

An employer who pays a grossed-up sum by way of settlement should first ensure either that HMRC is content for moneys to be paid gross and taxed in the employee's hands, or that the employee has agreed as part of the settlement to reimburse the employer for any demand for tax upon the sums paid which may subsequently be made.

59.33 *Relationship with compensation for unfair dismissal*

An employee who has been both wrongfully and unfairly dismissed cannot be compensated twice for the same loss. However, there are a number of important respects in which the rules governing the compensatory award for unfair dismissal differ from those governing damages for wrongful dismissal. In particular: damages for wrongful dismissal are essentially limited to the notice period, whereas compensation for unfair dismissal may in principle extend indefinitely; in wrongful dismissal only strict contractual rights are taken into account, whereas the employment tribunal may allow for other benefits and heads of loss (eg likely future pay increases, discretionary bonuses, loss of statutory rights); and the compensatory award in unfair dismissal may not exceed a statutory maximum.

Therefore, if an employee who has already received damages for wrongful dismissal goes on to obtain a ruling from an employment tribunal that he has been unfairly dismissed, he may ask for compensation (up to the statutory maximum) representing his loss beyond the notice period and his non-contractual benefits within the notice period.

If an employee who has already been compensated for unfair dismissal brings an action for wrongful dismissal, the court must examine the way in which that compensation has been calculated, and deduct from the wrongful dismissal damages those elements already covered by the tribunal award. The same will apply where the unfair dismissal claim has been settled by payment of a sum to the former employee (*Aspden* — see **59.19** above). However, if the sum actually awarded by the tribunal has been capped at the statutory maximum, it will frequently not be possible to say whether the award actually received represents one sort of loss rather than another. In that situation, the court will therefore not make any deduction from the damages which it awards (*O'Laoire v Jackel International Ltd (No 2)* [1991] ICR 718, [1991] IRLR 170).

A summary dismissal, albeit wrongful, is nonetheless effective to terminate the employment at once (subject to the question of acceptance of the breach, as to which see **59.7** above). It is not generally possible for an employee to complain of unfair dismissal unless he has been continuously employed for two years prior to the effective date of termination (see UNFAIR DISMISSAL – I (54)). Hence it is possible that the effect of a wrongful dismissal may be to deprive the employee of an unfair dismissal claim, if the absence of due notice or proper application of contractual disciplinary procedures makes the difference to whether there is the necessary period of service prior to termination. However, an employee cannot claim that lost right of complaint as a head of damages in the wrongful dismissal proceedings (*Harper v Virgin Net Ltd* [2004] EWCA Civ 271, [2005] ICR 921, [2004] IRLR 390; applied in *Wise Group v Mitchell* [2005] ICR 896, [2005] All ER (D) 168 (Feb)).

59.34 EFFECT OF A WRONGFUL DISMISSAL UPON OTHER CONTRACTUAL OBLIGATIONS

If the employee is wrongfully dismissed, the effect will normally be to release him from any further performance of his own contractual obligations, even those which are expressed to continue after the termination of the employment. In particular, this means that the employer will be unable to enforce any restrictive covenants contained in the contract of employment (*General Billposting Co Ltd v Atkinson* [1909] AC 118, [1908–10] All ER Rep 619; *Rock Refrigeration Ltd v Jones* [1996] IRLR 675, [1997] 1 All ER 1).

However, an arbitration clause will normally remain enforceable even after a wrongful dismissal.

59.40 Wrongful Dismissal

59.40 Limitation periods

A wrongful dismissal action in the High Court or county court is a claim for breach of contract, and as such is subject to a limitation period of six years from the accrual of the cause of action (*Limitation Act 1980, s 5*). Hence, proceedings must be commenced before the sixth anniversary of the dismissal.

In the employment tribunal, the complaint will have to be presented within the period of three months beginning with the effective date of termination of the contract of employment, or (where the tribunal is satisfied that it was not reasonably practicable for the complaint to be presented within that period) within such further period as the tribunal considers reasonable (*Employment Tribunals Extension of Jurisdiction (England and Wales) Order 1994 (SI 1994/1623), art 7* – see *art 7* of *SI 1994/1624* in relation to Scotland).

59.41 Summary judgment, interim payments, payments into court, and hearings on liability and quantum

In the High Court and county court, although not the employment tribunal, the claimant employee who considers that the defendant employer has no real prospect of successfully defending the claim may apply for summary judgment on written evidence alone (*Civil Procedure Rules 1998, Part 24*). This is particularly important in wrongful dismissal claims, where the true issue between the parties is often not whether the employer was entitled to dismiss without due notice, but what loss the employee has suffered, and in particular the extent to which that loss could or should have been mitigated. In such a case the court may be persuaded to enter judgment for damages to be assessed, or at least to make the granting of leave to defend the action conditional upon the defendant making a payment into court (which will act as an incentive to settlement of the claim, and should ensure that the claimant is able to enforce any judgment ultimately obtained).

The application for summary judgment will often be combined with an application for an interim payment (*CPR 1998, rule 25.6*), which will also be appropriate in a case where the employer has admitted liability but contests the amount of damages.

If the defendant employer believes that the claimant is likely to succeed on the issue of whether he was wrongfully dismissed, but that he is claiming damages substantially in excess of those to which he is truly entitled, then it may be appropriate for that defendant to make a payment into court in satisfaction of the claimant's cause of action (*CPR 1998, Part 36*). If the claimant accepts the payment in within a specified period, the proceedings will come to an end, and the claimant will automatically be entitled to his costs up until the date of payment in. If the claimant does not do so, and ultimately recovers less at trial than the sum paid in, then he will have to pay the defendant's costs since payment in.

Where both liability and quantum are in dispute, the parties will wish to consider (especially where the calculation of loss raises complex points of detail) whether liability should be tried as a preliminary issue, with a hearing on quantum to follow only if the claimant establishes that he has been wrongfully dismissed and the parties are still unable to compromise their differences at that point.

Save for the possibility of separate hearings on liability and quantum, none of these procedural opportunities will be available if the claim is brought in the employment tribunal.

59.42 Compromise of claims

The various statutory restrictions, which prescribe that an employee may compromise claims based upon his statutory rights only in certain specified ways, do not apply to wrongful dismissal claims (*Sutherland v Network Appliance Ltd* [2001] IRLR 12). Any